CRIMINAL PROCEDURE AND THE CONSTITUTION

LEADING SUPREME COURT CASES AND INTRODUCTORY TEXT

2021 Edition

Jerold H. Israel
Alene and Allan F. Smith Professor Emeritus of Law,
University of Michigan
Emeritus Ed Rood Eminent Scholar in Trial Advocacy and Procedure,
University of Florida, Fredric G. Levin College of Law

Yale Kamisar
Clarence Darrow Distinguished University Professor Emeritus of Law,
University of Michigan
Distinguished Professor Emeritus of Law, University of San Diego

Wayne R. LaFave
David C. Baum Professor Emeritus of Law
and Center for Advanced Study Professor Emeritus,
University of Illinois

Nancy J. King
Lee S. & Charles A. Speir Professor of Law,
Vanderbilt University Law School

Eve Brensike Primus
Yale Kamisar Collegiate Professor of Law,
University of Michigan

Orin S. Kerr
Professor
University of California, Berkeley
School of Law

AMERICAN CASEBOOK SERIES®

American Casebook Series is a trademark registered in the U.S. Patent and Trademark Office.

COPYRIGHT © 1989–1997 WEST PUBLISHING CO.
© West, a Thomson business, 1998–2008
© 2009–2012 Thomson Reuters
© 2013 LEG, Inc. d/b/a West Academic Publishing
© 2014–2020 LEG, Inc. d/b/a West Academic
© 2021 LEG, Inc. d/b/a West Academic
    444 Cedar Street, Suite 700
    St. Paul, MN 55101
    1-877-888-1330

West, West Academic Publishing, and West Academic are trademarks of West Publishing Corporation, used under license.

Printed in the United States of America

ISBN: 978-1-64708-894-1

PREFACE

This collection of leading Supreme Court cases is designed for instructors who want to cover a wide range of criminal procedure topics but have available only a limited amount of time. In the main, the cases in this book were selected because of their substantial contemporary significance; they reflect the Supreme Court's current position on issues of major importance regarding the operation of our federal and state criminal justice systems. But we have also included some venerable cases that contribute significantly to an understanding of current trends and developments.

These materials differ in important ways from our three other sets of teaching materials in this field, *Modern Criminal Procedure (Modern)*, *Basic Criminal Procedure (Basic)* and *Advanced Criminal Procedure (Advanced)*. Those materials also include a goodly number of lower court cases, many of which focus on state law developments, and contain many authors' Notes and Questions and extracts from books, reports, articles, model codes, and proposed standards. By contrast, the present book is limited to the Supreme Court decisions themselves.

The editorial commentary in this book also is significantly different from that in our other books. We have, of course, relied on and profited by the rich literature in this field in the course of preparing the introductory comments that appear at the outset of each chapter and at the beginning of most sections of each chapter. But this introductory text does not explore any particular issue in depth. Nor is it contentious, as are many of the law review articles extracted in our other books. The brief introductory comments, rather, are designed only to place the selected cases that follow in general historical and doctrinal perspective. The same is true of occasional Notes describing the post-decision treatment of the principal case.

The coverage of this book also differs from that in our other books. Our focus here is entirely on constitutional regulation, and it extends to the entirety of the criminal justice process. *Basic*'s major emphasis is on police practices, e.g., arrest, search and seizure, police interrogation and confessions, and pre-trial identification procedures; no attention is given to the more formal phases of the criminal process (which are treated separately in *Advanced*). The present volume, on the other hand, not only gives issues involving the police considerable attention but covers a number of other aspects of the criminal process, e.g., criminal discovery, double jeopardy, fair trial/free press, plea bargaining, and the trial. Our "big book," *Modern*, also covers a wide range of topics, but because it explores these topics in much greater depth (including non-constitutional regulation), it is about twice the size of this book. (There is, of course, no law prohibiting an instructor from dipping into *Modern* in order to enrich class discussion of one or more of the issues raised by the materials in this book.)

As is apparent from these comparisons, we envision this collection of leading cases as being used in a course of a distinctly different character than the various possibilities we contemplated with respect to either *Modern, Advanced* or *Basic*. This book is especially suited to a survey course having as its purpose a critical examination of how the United States Supreme Court has grappled with a range of basic and highly controversial issues that arise at various stages of the criminal process— issues as diverse as when the police should be permitted to "search" or "seize" without prior judicial approval or traditional "probable cause," what police interrogation techniques will render inadmissible any resulting confession, when a defense lawyer's performance is so "ineffective" as to vitiate a conviction, when a prosecutor must disclose information in his files, and when a defendant must endure a second trial for the same or a related offense.

In *Modern, Advanced,* and *Basic*, our hope and expectation has been that a student working with those materials descry not only the forest (or in the case of *Advanced* and *Basic*, at least a good-sized grove), but also the trees. Here, by contrast, the emphasis is decidedly sylvan.

It is possible, of course, to produce a thin volume of teaching materials by collecting snippets of many opinions. This approach has been emphatically rejected. The modest size of this volume has been attained, rather, by the judicious selection of leading cases. Those cases that have been selected are set forth at considerable length.

Moreover, because the use of these materials will mark many students' first real exposure to the U.S. Supreme Court as an institution, we have resisted the temptation to delete, or even to summarize, concurring and dissenting opinions. Instead, we have taken pains to set forth the views of *all* members of the Court at considerable length, particularly in seminal cases.

In the main, we have followed a chronological approach in ordering the cases which appear in this book. Following the introductory materials, which include an overview of the criminal justice system and a general consideration of due process, the criminal justice system is examined from arrest and search and "on the street" questioning all the way through to the decision on guilt and imposition of sentence.

We have occasionally departed from the chronological scheme when it seemed appropriate to do so.[a] For example, the right to counsel, "the most pervasive right" of an accused, is first considered in advance of the confession and lineup chapters so that the Court's reliance on the right to counsel in those contexts may be better understood. (Other aspects of the right to counsel, such as the necessary character and quality of representation at trial and in preparing for trial, are considered later in the book.) So too, post-conviction review is considered in the context of the review of particular claims rather than in a separate chapter on habeas corpus.

The cases in this book have been edited with the above-stated purposes in mind. We have tried hard—indeed, it would not be an exaggeration to say that we have made heroic efforts—to keep these materials lean and manageable. Still, we recognize that complete coverage may not be feasible (depending upon the course's credit-hours) or desirable (depending upon the instructor's goals). Deletions can be geared to whole chapters, sections within chapters, or cases within sections (as the sections in Chapters 3, 6, and 15, in particular, include collections of more than 5 cases). The case selection has focused on including in each section at least one case that directs the student's attention to the broader themes and issues presented by the particular subject matter.

Case citations and footnotes have been eliminated from the judicial opinions without so specifying. When three asterisks appear, this designates omission of a portion of the opinion deemed inessential to an understanding and appraisal of the issues and holding in that case.

Numbered footnotes are from the original materials; lettered footnotes are ours. We would call particular attention to those lettered footnotes which contain summaries of Supreme Court decisions related to the major cases presented in this book. These footnotes often indicate how the Court later dealt with a problem alluded to in the principal case, or how a comment in the principal case later came to have importance regarding a related issue.

To make our sentence structure as short and direct as possible, we often have not used the phrases "he or she" or "his or her." Where we have used the masculine or feminine pronoun alone, consistent with the traditional rules of construction in legal texts, the pronoun should be read

---

[a] Within each chapter, the organization of the materials rests, in large part, on the experience of a particular coauthor in teaching these materials. Some instructors will undoubtedly want to depart from that organization. Thus, many instructors prefer to treat the exclusionary rule at the end, rather than the start, of Chapter 3. So too, in Chapter 6, *Dickerson v. United States*, the case that reaffirms *Miranda*, is placed in § 5 (where it comes after key pre-*Dickerson* rulings), but in the past, we placed it immediately after *Miranda*. Similarly, because the *Pantane* and *Seibert* cases in § 4 shed light on the meaning of *Dickerson* and *Chavez v. Martinez* (in § 6), the instructor may want to postpone treatment of (or return to) those cases after assigning § 6.

to encompass both male and female actors unless the context clearly indicates otherwise.

Our collection of cases is updated annually to include decisions from the latest Supreme Court term. The annual editions typically add at least a few decisions from the last term as principal cases and often refer to several other cases from that term in the introductory notes, post-decision Notes, or footnotes. At the same time, various deletions are made to ensure that the size of the volume remains roughly the same.

The cut-off point for inclusion of cases in this volume was the end of the Court's 2020–2021 term. Citations are to the United States Reports, unless the case had not yet appeared in those reports. In that event, we have used the Supreme Court Reporter citation (if available).

Experience has taught us that there will undoubtedly be some typographical errors in a publication of this length. We would appreciate your calling such errors to our attention, so they can be corrected in the next printing. We would, of course, also appreciate hearing from readers who have criticisms or suggestions regarding the substantive content of the volume. Please send your comments and corrections to israelj@umich.edu.

We are most appreciative of the able secretarial assistance provided, too often under great stress, by Cheri Fidh in the preparation of the current edition of this volume.

Yale Kamisar & Wayne LaFave, two of the originators of this publication, have now retired. They continue to be listed as authors, however, as their contributions remain intact in numerous chapters, and their influence continues to shape the efforts of the current authors.

JEROLD H. ISRAEL
NANCY J. KING
EVE BRENSIKE PRIMUS
ORIN S. KERR

July 2021

SUMMARY OF CONTENTS

PREFACE III

TABLE OF CASES XIX

Chapter 1. A Criminal Justice Process Overview 1
1. The Lawmaking Structure.. 1
2. The Administrative Structure 4
3. The Steps in the Process 12

Chapter 2. The Nature and Scope of Due Process; the Applicability of the Bill of Rights to the States 31
1. "Fundamental Rights" and "Incorporation"........................... 31
2. The Shift to "Selective Incorporation"................................. 33
3. "Free Standing" Due Process 46

Chapter 3. Arrest, Search and Seizure 59
1. The Exclusionary Rule 59
2. Protected Areas and Interests 94
3. Probable Cause 141
4. Search Warrants 164
5. Arrest and Search of Persons 175
6. Seizure and Search of Premises 222
7. Seizure and Search of Vehicles and Effects......................... 239
8. Stop and Frisk 283
9. Consent Searches 324

Chapter 4. The Scope of the Exclusionary Rule 343
1. Introduction 344
2. Proximate Cause: Attenuation Doctrine............................... 346
3. Cause in Fact: Independent Source 361
4. Cause in Fact: Inevitable Discovery.................................... 364

Chapter 5. The Right to Counsel... 373
1. The Right to Appointed Counsel 373
2. The "Beginnings" of the Right to Counsel 389
3. The *Griffin-Douglas* "Equality" Principle............................. 396

Chapter 6. Police Interrogation and Confessions 409
1. The "Voluntariness" Test.. 409
2. *Massiah* and *Escobedo* 420
3. *Miranda* 431
4. Applying and Explaining *Miranda* 454
5. The Court Reaffirms *Miranda*.. 536

6.   When Is *Miranda* Violated?.. 550
7.   *Massiah* Revisited 557

Chapter 7. Pre-Trial Identification Procedures 573
1.   *Wade* and *Gilbert*: Reliability Concerns................................ 574
2.   The Court Retreats: *Kirby* and *Ash*...................................... 580
3.   Due Process Limitations 583

Chapter 8. Investigation by Subpoena 597
1.   Introduction 597
2.   Fourth Amendment Limitations 600
3.   The Privilege Against Self-Incrimination............................ 623

Chapter 9. Pretrial Release 659

Chapter 10. The Decision Whether to Prosecute 673
1.   The Decision to Prosecute 673
2.   Selection of the Charge 682

Chapter 11. Screening the Prosecutor's Charging Decision 693

Chapter 12. Speedy Trial and Other Speedy Disposition 713

Chapter 13. The Duty to Disclose 733

Chapter 14. Guilty Pleas 757
1.   Plea Bargaining.. 757
2.   Requisites of a Valid Plea 776
3.   The Effect of a Guilty Plea.. 787

Chapter 15. Trial by Jury; Judicial Impartiality 795
1.   Right to Jury Trial 795
2.   Jury Selection 813
3.   Right to Impartial Judge 855

Chapter 16. Fair Trial/Free Press 865

Chapter 17. The Role of Counsel 923
1.   Introduction 923
2.   Ineffective Assistance of Counsel 924
3.   Counsel Conflicts of Interests... 969
4.   Counsel Control vs. Client Control 992
5.   The Right of Self-Representation 1004

Chapter 18. The Trial 1015
1.   Presence of the Defendant 1015
2.   Confrontation and Compulsory Process................................ 1019
3.   The Right to Remain Silent—or Testify 1050
4.   Due Process Requirements 1061

Chapter 19. Retrials 1079
1. The "Same Offense" Limitation... 1079
2. Aborted Proceedings.. 1128
3. Reprosecution Post-Acquittal/Conviction 1139

Chapter 20. Sentencing Procedures 1151

**Appendix A. Selected Provisions of the United States
     Constitution** 1253

Appendix B. Justices of the Supreme Court................................... 1257

TABLE OF CONTENTS

PREFACE III

TABLE OF CASES XIX

Chapter 1. A Criminal Justice Process Overview 1
1. The Lawmaking Structure 1
2. The Administrative Structure 4
3. The Steps in the Process 12

Chapter 2. The Nature and Scope of Due Process; the Applicability of the Bill of Rights to the States 31
1. "Fundamental Rights" and "Incorporation" 31
2. The Shift to "Selective Incorporation" 33
   Duncan v. Louisiana 35
3. "Free Standing" Due Process 46
   District Attorney's Office v. Osborne 46

Chapter 3. Arrest, Search and Seizure 59
1. The Exclusionary Rule 59
   Wolf v. Colorado 59
   Mapp v. Ohio 62
   United States v. Leon 68
   Hudson v. Michigan 80
   Herring v. United States 88
2. Protected Areas and Interests 94
   Katz v. United States 95
   California v. Greenwood 99
   Florida v. Riley 104
   United States v. Jones 107
   Carpenter v. United States 114
   Florida v. Jardines 121
   United States v. White 126
   Torres v. Madrid 130
   Zurcher v. Stanford Daily 136
3. Probable Cause 141
   Spinelli v. United States 142
   Illinois v. Gates 145
   Maryland v. Pringle 162
4. Search Warrants 164
   Maryland v. Garrison 165
   Richards v. Wisconsin 172
5. Arrest and Search of Persons 175
   United States v. Watson 176

United States v. Robinson 182
Whren v. United States 191
Atwater v. City of Lago Vista 197
Maryland v. King.. 205
Mitchell v. Wisconsin 214
6. Seizure and Search of Premises 222
Payton v. New York.. 222
Chimel v. California 228
Kentucky v. King.. 233
7. Seizure and Search of Vehicles and Effects........................... 239
California v. Carney 240
Arizona v. Gant.. 244
California v. Acevedo... 253
Wyoming v. Houghton.. 263
Colorado v. Bertine.. 270
Riley v. California.. 275
8. Stop and Frisk 283
Terry v. Ohio.. 283
Kansas v. Glover.. 294
Florida v. J. L. 299
Florida v. Royer 303
United States v. Drayton 311
Brendlin v. California 318
Rodriguez v. United States 321
9. Consent Searches 324
Schneckloth v. Bustamonte 325
Georgia v. Randolph.. 332

Chapter 4. The Scope of the Exclusionary Rule 343
1. Introduction 344
Wong Sun v. United States... 344
2. Proximate Cause: Attenuation Doctrine................................. 346
Brown v. Illinois 346
New York v. Harris 351
Utah v. Strieff.. 355
3. Cause in Fact: Independent Source 361
Murray v. United States 361
4. Cause in Fact: Inevitable Discovery....................................... 364
Nix v. Williams 364
Hudson v. Michigan 366

Chapter 5. The Right to Counsel... 373
1. The Right to Appointed Counsel 373
Betts v. Brady 376
Gideon v. Wainwright 380
Alabama v. Shelton 383

2. The "Beginnings" of the Right to Counsel 389
   Rothgery v. Gillespie County 389
3. The *Griffin-Douglas* "Equality" Principle 396
   Douglas v. California 397
   Ross v. Moffitt 401

Chapter 6. Police Interrogation and Confessions 409
1. The "Voluntariness" Test 409
   Ashcraft v. Tennessee 412
   Spano v. New York 418
2. *Massiah* and *Escobedo* 420
   Massiah v. United States 422
   Escobedo v. Illinois 426
3. *Miranda* 431
   Miranda v. Arizona (No. 759) 433
4. Applying and Explaining *Miranda* 454
   1. What constitutes "custody" or "custodial interrogation?" 458
      J.D.B. v. North Carolina 458
      Howes v. Fields 464
   2. What constitutes "interrogation" within the meaning of
      Miranda? 468
      Rhode Island v. Innis 468
      Illinois v. Perkins 474
   3. What constitutes a waiver of the right to remain silent? If, after
      being advised of his *Miranda* rights, a custodial suspect remains
      silent, can the police interrogate him? At some point, does a
      suspect's silence in the face of police questions amount to an
      assertion of his right to remain silent? Or must the suspect
      explicitly invoke the right to remain silent? Does the case set
      forth below demonstrate that there is a significant difference
      between (a) the right to remain silent and (b) the right not to
      be interrogated? 477
      Berghuis v. Thompkins 477
   4. When suspects are not in custody, and therefore not given any
      Miranda warnings, do they have a "right to remain silent"? If
      they do, must they expressly invoke this right? 488
      Salinas v. Texas 488
   5. If a suspect invokes his right to counsel and there is a break in
      Miranda custody, at what point, if at all, can the police try to
      interrogate the suspect again? If a suspect is serving a prison
      sentence (for an unrelated crime) at the time the police try to
      question him, does his release back into the general prison
      population constitute a break in custody? 495
      Maryland v. Shatzer 495

6. May a police officer initiate counselless questioning of a formally charged defendant who has accepted the appointment of an attorney? 506

Montejo v. Louisiana 506

7. Questioning prompted by concern for "public safety" 515

New York v. Quarles 515

8. Must physical evidence derived from a failure to give the *Miranda* warnings be excluded? Does an initial failure to advise a suspect of her rights bar subsequent admissions by the suspect after she has been fully advised of her rights? Does the "fruit of the poisonous tree" doctrine apply to violations of the *Miranda* rules? 520

United States v. Patane 520

Missouri v. Seibert 523

9. If a suspect does not request a lawyer but, unbeknownst to him, a relative or friend retains a lawyer for him, does the failure of the police to allow the lawyer to see the suspect or the failure to inform the suspect that an attorney is trying to reach him vitiate an otherwise valid waiver of *Miranda* rights? 531

Moran v. Burbine 531

5. The Court Reaffirms *Miranda* 536

Dickerson v. United States 541

6. When Is *Miranda* Violated? 550

Chavez v. Martinez 550

7. *Massiah* Revisited 557

Brewer v. Williams (Williams I) 559

Kuhlmann v. Wilson 568

Chapter 7. Pre-Trial Identification Procedures 573

1. *Wade* and *Gilbert*: Reliability Concerns 574

United States v. Wade 574

2. The Court Retreats: *Kirby* and *Ash* 580

Kirby v. Illinois 580

3. Due Process Limitations 583

Manson v. Brathwaite 584

Perry v. New Hampshire 589

Chapter 8. Investigation by Subpoena 597

1. Introduction 597

2. Fourth Amendment Limitations 600

Boyd v. United States 601

Note: The post-Boyd substitution of a Fourth Amendment prohibition of overbreadth/ unreasonableness in subpoenas ducas tecum 605

United States v. Dionisio 609

Carpenter v. United States 615

3. The Privilege Against Self-Incrimination 623

United States v. Mandujano 626

Kastigar v. United States 633
Fisher v. United States 642
United States v. Hubbell... 650

Chapter 9. Pretrial Release... **659**
Stack v. Boyle 660
United States v. Salerno... 661

Chapter 10. The Decision Whether to Prosecute.............................. **673**
1.   The Decision to Prosecute... 673
     United States v. Armstrong.. 673
2.   Selection of the Charge 682
     United States v. Batchelder.. 683
     United States v. Goodwin 685

Chapter 11. Screening the Prosecutor's Charging Decision **693**
Coleman v. Alabama 696
Vasquez v. Hillery 702
Costello v. United States 710

Chapter 12. Speedy Trial and Other Speedy Disposition.................. **713**
Barker v. Wingo 713
Doggett v. United States... 720
United States v. Lovasco 727

Chapter 13. The Duty to Disclose **733**
Williams v. Florida.. 734
United States v. Bagley 739
Pennsylvania v. Ritchie 748

Chapter 14. Guilty Pleas... **757**
1.   Plea Bargaining... 757
     Bordenkircher v. Hayes 758
     Santobello v. New York.. 764
     Missouri v. Frye... 766
     United States v. Ruiz 773
2.   Requisites of a Valid Plea 776
     Boykin v. Alabama 778
     Henderson v. Morgan... 780
     North Carolina v. Alford 783
3.   The Effect of a Guilty Plea... 787
     Class v. United States.. 787

Chapter 15. Trial by Jury; Judicial Impartiality............................... **795**
1.   Right to Jury Trial 795
     Duncan v. Louisiana 795
     Blanton v. City of North Las Vegas 795
     Ramos v. Louisiana 798

Singer v. United States 810
2.   Jury Selection 813
Taylor v. Louisiana 814
Turner v. Murray 817
Lockhart v. McCree 821
Batson v. Kentucky 828
Note: Post-Batson Developments 837
Peña-Rodriguez v. Colorado 839
3.   Right to Impartial Judge 855
Williams v. Pennsylvania 856

Chapter 16. Fair Trial/Free Press **865**
Skilling v. United States 869
Gentile v. State Bar of Nevada 890
Press-Enterprise Co. v. Superior Court [Press-Enterprise II] 907
Chandler v. Florida 914

Chapter 17. The Role of Counsel **923**
1.   Introduction 923
2.   Ineffective Assistance of Counsel 924
Strickland v. Washington 928
Harrington v. Richter 941
Lafler v. Cooper 951
Weaver v. Massachusetts 960
3.   Counsel Conflicts of Interests 969
Mickens v. Taylor 971
Wheat v. United States 986
4.   Counsel Control vs. Client Control 992
McCoy v. Louisiana 994
5.   The Right of Self-Representation 1004
Faretta v. California 1007

Chapter 18. The Trial **1015**
1.   Presence of the Defendant 1015
Illinois v. Allen 1016
2.   Confrontation and Compulsory Process 1019
Michigan v. Bryant 1020
Richardson v. Marsh 1038
Davis v. Alaska 1045
3.   The Right to Remain Silent—or Testify 1050
Griffin v. California 1051
Rock v. Arkansas 1055
4.   Due Process Requirements 1061
Holmes v. South Carolina 1061
Taylor v. Kentucky 1066
Darden v. Wainwright 1070

Chapter 19. Retrials 1079
1. The "Same Offense" Limitation 1079
    Ashe v. Swenson 1080
    United States v. Dixon 1086
    Gamble v. United States 1102
    Hudson v. United States 1122
2. Aborted Proceedings 1128
    Arizona v. Washington 1128
    Oregon v. Kennedy 1134
3. Reprosecution Post-Acquittal/Conviction 1139
    United States v. Scott 1140
    Burks v. United States 1145

Chapter 20. Sentencing Procedures 1151
United States v. Grayson 1153
Mitchell v. United States 1159
Blakely v. Washington 1169
McCleskey v. Kemp 1188
Graham v. Florida 1206
Glossip et al. v. Gross et al. 1236

Appendix A. Selected Provisions of the United States Constitution 1253

Appendix B. Justices of the Supreme Court 1257

TABLE OF CASES

The principal cases are in bold type.
For United States v. _____, see the name of the other party.

Abbate v. United States, 1106
Abel v. United States, 195
Adams v. Texas, 825
Adamson v. California, 38
Aetna Life Ins. Co. v. Lavoie, 860
Agnello v. United States, 228
Aguilar v. Texas, 142, 151, 158
Agurs, United States v., 740, 741, 742, 774, 936
Ah Sin v. Wittman, 677
Ake v. Oklahoma, 405, 775
Alabama v. Shelton, 376, **383**
Alabama v. White, 299
Alderman v. United States, 108, 112
Alleyne v. United States, 1173
Almendarez-Torres v. United States, 1171
American Tobacco Co. v. United States, 1148
Andresen v. Maryland, 94, 601
Apodaca v. Oregon, 800
Apprendi v. New Jersey, 1171, 1180, 1186
Argersinger v. Hamlin, 376, **383**, 931, 1010
Arizona v. Evans, 85, 89
Arizona v. Fulminante, 962, 985, 999
Arizona v. Gant, 203, 239, **244**, 256, 262, 275, 511, 513, 515
Arizona v. Johnson, 319
Arizona v. Mauro, 471
Arizona v. Roberson, 456, 496
Arizona v. Rumsey, 1102
Arizona v. Washington, **1128**, 1145
Arizona v. Youngblood, 51, 755
Arkansas v. Sanders, 254, 271, 275
Arkansas v. Sullivan, 197
Arlington Heights v. Metropolitan Housing Dev. Corp., 1193
Armstrong, United States v., 673
Ash, United States v., 573, 582
Ashcraft v. Tennessee, 409, **412**
Ashcroft v. al-Kidd, 193
Ashe v. Swenson, **1080**, 1091, 1093
Atkins v. Virginia, 1211
Atwater v. City of Lago Vista, 176, 197, 360
Bagley, United States v., 733, **739**, 751, 1061
Baldwin v. New York, 795

Ball v. United States, 1141, 1146
Ballard v. United States, 815
Balsys, United States v., 637
Banks, United States v., 80, 172
Barker v. Wingo, 713
Bartkus v. Illinois, 1106
Batchelder, United States v., 683, 704
Batson v. Kentucky, 678, 810, 814, **828**, 964, 1192, 1195, 1203, 1205
Baxter v. Palmigiano, 1163, 1165
Baze v. Rees, 1236, 1238
Bearden v. Georgia, 405
Beets v. Scott, 975
Bell v. Cone, 970
Bellis v. United States, 644
Benton v. Maryland, 1114
Berger v. New York, 97
Berger v. United States, 741, 1061, 1075
Berghuis v. Thompkins, 456, **477**, 490
Berkemer v. McCarty, 455, 465
Betterman v. Montana, 729
Betts v. Brady, 32, 374, **376**, 380, 381, 397, 440, 1013
Birchfield v. North Dakota, 216
Bivens v. Six Unknown Fed. Narcotics Agents, 83
Blackledge v. Perry, 686, 688, 758, 759, 761, 787, 928
Blair v. United States, 605, 610
Blakely v. Washington, 1152, **1169**
Blanton v. City of North Las Vegas, 795
Blockburger v. United States, 1085, 1088, 1103
Bloom v. Illinois, 1088, 1090, 1096
Bobby v. Van Hook, 946
Boerne v. Flores, 542
Bond v. United States, 104
Booker, United States v., 1181, 1188
Bordenkircher v. Hayes, 688, **758**
Bose Corp. v. Consumers Union of United States, Inc., 893
Boyd v. United States, 600, **601**, 610, 618, 644, 647, 650, 658
Boykin v. Alabama, 774, **778**
Bradshaw v. Stumpf, 1082

Brady v. Maryland, 55, 733, 739, 740, 746, 751, 755, 760, 774
Brady v. United States, 760, 764, 765, 774, 783
Branzburg v. Hayes, 610, 611
Braswell v. United States, 646
Brecht v. Abrahamson, 743
Brendlin v. California, 283, **318**
Brewer v. Marshall, 851
Brewer v. Williams (Williams I), 364, 390, 392, 395, 470, 557, **559**
Bridges v. California, 902
Brigham City v. Stuart, 234
Brignoni-Ponce, United States v., 360
Broce, United States v., 775, 788, 791
Brookhart v. Janis, 997, 1002
Brooks v. Tennessee, 932
Brower v. County of Inyo, 134, 318
Brown v. Illinois, 64, 343, **346**, 352, 355
Brown v. Mississippi, 409, 432, 541
Brown v. Ohio, 1088, 1091, 1100
Brown v. Walker, 634, 635
Bruton v. United States, 1038, 1043
Bryan v. United States, 1146
Bryson v. United States, 628, 630
Bullcoming v. New Mexico, 1037
Burks v. United States, 1139, 1141, **1145**
Burnet v. Coronado Oil & Gas Co., 705, 706
Burr, United States v., 640
Burton v. United States, 1092, 1102
Calandra, United States v., 85, 89, 566, 696, 712
California Bankers Assn. v. Shultz, 618, 621
California v. Acevedo, 239, **253**
California v. Beheler, 455
California v. Carney, 123, 239, **240**, 258
California v. Ciraolo, 104, 107
California v. Greenwood, 94, **99**
California v. Hodari D., 131, 313
California v. Stewart, 433, 436, 446
Camara v. Municipal Court, 283
Caperton v. A. T. Massey Coal Co., 856, 861
Carlson v. Landon, 667, 668
Carnley v. Cochran, 442
Carpenter v. United States, 94, 114, **615**
Carroll v. United States, 228, 240, 264
Carter v. Kentucky, 1054, 1164, 1165, 1169
Carter, State v., 996
Catena, United States ex rel. v. Elias, 639

Chadwick, United States v., 243, 254, 271, 275
Chaffin v. Stynchcombe, 1156
Chalmers v. H.M. Advocate, 444
Chambers v. Florida, 409
Chambers v. Mississippi, 1057, 1063
Chandler v. Florida, 869, **914**
Chapman v. California, 578, 695, 698, 706, 747, 748, 961, 992
Chapman v. United States, 103
Chavez v. Martinez, 521, **550**, 554, 557
Chewning v. Cunningham, 375
Chicago Council of Lawyers v. Bauer, 899
Chimel v. California, 222, **228**, 244, 249, 259, 275, 335
Ciambrone, United States v., 704
Class v. United States, **787**
Codispoti v. Pennsylvania, 797
Coffin v. United States, 1067, 1069
Coker v. Georgia, 1200, 1211
Coleman v. Alabama, 694, 695, **696**
Coleman v. Thompson, 925
Collins v. Virginia, 123
Colorado v. Bertine, 193, **270**
Colorado v. Connelly, 411, 479
Colorado v. Spring, 532, 774
Cooke v. State, 996
Cooke v. United States, 1088
Coolidge v. New Hampshire, 221, 341
Costello v. United States, 696, **710**
Couch v. United States, 642, 643, 648
Counselman v. Hitchcock, 623, 635, 639
Countess of Rutland's Case, 133, 135
Crane v. Kentucky, 1063
Crawford v. Washington, 810, 1020, 1022, 1032
Crews, United States v., 64, 352
Crist v. Bretz, 1079
Cronic, United States v., 935, 957, 969, 972, 978, 998
Crooker v. California, 421, 440
Cupp v. Murphy, 186
Cuyler v. Sullivan, 925, 932, 935, 972, 973
Darden v. Wainwright, 1061, **1070**
Davila, United States v., 778
Davis v. Alaska, 750, 1020, **1045**
Davis v. Georgia, 821
Davis v. Mississippi, 304, 609, 610
Davis v. United States (1994), 478, 540
Davis v. United States (2011), 74
Davis v. Washington, 1020, 1023
Davis, United States v., 340
Debs, In re, 1099
Deck v. Missouri, 1017

Defore, People v., 63, 65

Delaware v. Fensterer, 750

Department of Revenue of Mont. v. Kurth Ranch, 1124, 1126

Desist v. United States, 128

Devenpeck v. Alford, 360

Di Re, United States v., 163, 266, 268, 269

Dickerson v. United States, v, 457, 479, 494, 520, **541**

Dickerson, United States v., 540

DiFrancesco, United States v., 1079

Dinitz, United States v., 1131, 1135, 1136

Dionisio, United States v., **609**, 617, 618, 621

District Attorney's Office v. Osborne, 46

District of Columbia v. Heller, 31

District of Columbia v. Wesby, 163

Dixon, United States v., 1080, **1086**, 1104

Doe v. United States (Doe II), 653

Doe, United States v. (Doe I), 650, 656

Doggett v. United States, **720**

Donnelly v. DeChristoforo, 1073

Donovan v. Lone Steer, Inc., 618, 621

Donovan, People v., 438

Dorman v. United States, 223

Douglas v. Alabama, 1048, 1049

Douglas v. California, 374, 396, **397**, 441, 925

Dowling v. United States, 46

Doyle v. Ohio, 455, 490

Draper v. United States, 144, 152, 153, 156, 158, 159

Drayton, United States v., 283, **311**

Dred Scott v. Sandford, 1119

Dunaway v. New York, 304, 310, 350, 352

Duncan v. Louisiana, 32, **35**, **795**, 800, 810, 839

Dunnigan, United States v., 1159

Eddings v. Oklahoma, 1225

Edmonson v. Leesville Concrete Co., 838

Edwards v. Arizona, 456, 495, 501, 507

Edwards v. Indiana, 1005, 1012

Edwards v. Vannoy, 34, 810

Elkins v. United States, 63, 84

Enmund v. Florida, 1211, 1247

Entick v. Carrington and Three Other King's Messengers, 246, 602

Escobedo v. Illinois, 421, 426, 541, 631

Estelle v. Gamble, 1210

Estelle v. Smith, 1162

Estelle v. Williams, 1066

Estes v. Texas, 869, 873, 916, 920, 922

Evitts v. Lucey, 405

Faretta v. California, 566, 962, 992, 996, 1004, **1007**, 1056, 1057

Felix, United States v., 1092

Ferguson v. Georgia, 932, 1056, 1060

Fernandez v. California, 337

Fisher v. United States, 600, **642**, 650, 653, 656, 658

Fletcher v. Weir, 455

Florence v. Board of Chosen Freeholders of County of Burlington, 203, 210, 360

Florida v. Bostick, 312, 318, 319, 360

Florida v. Harris, 148

Florida v. J. L., 283, **299**

Florida v. Jardines, 94, **121**

Florida v. Jimeno, 330

Florida v. Nixon, 994, 997

Florida v. Riley, 94, **104**

Florida v. Rodriguez, 314

Florida v. Royer, 283, **303**

Florida v. Wells, 193, 273

Florida v. White, 242

Flowers v. Mississippi, 837

Foster v. Chatman, 837

Fox v. Ohio, 1105

Franks v. Delaware, 70, 90

Frisbie v. Collins, 64

Fry v. Pliler, 1063

Furman v. Georgia, 921, 1193, 1198, 1210, 1243

G.M. Leasing Corp. v. United States, 242

Gagnon v. Scarpelli, 384

Gagnon, United States v., 1015

Gamble v. United States, 1080, **1102**, 1103

Gannett Co., Inc. v. DePasquale, 911

Garner v. United States, 492

Garrity v. New Jersey, 493

Garza v. Idaho, 1004

Gavieres v. United States, 1088, 1092, 1102

Geders v. United States, 932, 969

Genner v. Sparks, 132

Gentile v. State Bar of Nevada, 867, **890**

Georgia v. McCollum, 838

Georgia v. Randolph, 325, **332**

Gerstein v. Pugh, 21, 177, 393, 498, 663, 665, 667, 671, 695, 707

Gideon v. Wainwright, 32, 33, 42, 56, 373, 374, **380**, 707, 931, 1010

Giglio v. United States, 774

Gilbert v. California, 328, 573, 576

Giles v. Maryland, 741

Glasser v. United States, 988

Globe Newspaper Co. v. Superior Court, 909
Glossip et al. v. Gross et al., 1236
Glover v. United States, 952
Go-Bart Importing Co. v. United States, 187, 228
Godinez v. Moran, 997, 1006
Gompers v. Buck's Stove & Range Co., 1088
Gonzales v. Raich, 1110
Gonzalez v. United States, 993, 996
Gonzalez-Lopez, United States v., 936, 956, 962, 992, 999, 1001
Goodwin, United States v., 548, 683, **685**
Gore, State v., 1170, 1173
Gouveia, United States v., 390, 391
Grady v. Corbin, 1080, 1087, 1091, 1099, 1102, 1104
Graham v. Florida, 1153, **1206**
Gray v. Maryland, 1043
Gray v. Mississippi, 821
Grayned v. City of Rockford, 896
Grayson, United States v., 1152, **1153**
Green v. United States, 1083, 1084, 1142
Greene v. McElroy, 1048
Gregg v. Georgia, 1193, 1194, 1196, 1198, 1215, 1243
Gregory, State v., 1062
Griffin v. California, 439, 489, 491, **1051**, 1163, 1165, 1169
Griffin v. Illinois, 396, 632
Griffith v. Kentucky, 34
Groban, In re, 427, 629, 631
Groh v. Ramirez, 166
Grubbs, United States v., 141
Gustafson v. Florida, 191
Halbert v. Michigan, 407
Hale v. Henkel, 605, 610, 612, 621, 640, 644
Hall v. Florida, 1236, 1245
Halliday v. United States, 780
Halper, United States v., 1096, 1123, 1126, 1127
Ham v. South Carolina, 818
Hamdi v. Rumsfeld, 54
Hamilton v. Alabama, 697
Hammon v. Indiana, 1023
Haring v. Prosise, 788
Harlan, People v., 851
Harmelin v. Michigan, 1210
Harrington v. California, 707
Harrington v. Richter, 924, **941**, 965
Harris v. Alabama, 1245
Harris v. New York, 454, 1002, 1041, 1057

Harris v. Oklahoma, 1089, 1094, 1099
Harris v. United States, 228, 251, 1173
Harris, United States v., 155
Hayes v. Florida, 306
Haynes v. United States, 787
Heien v. North Carolina, 287, 360
Henderson v. Kibbe, 1069
Henderson v. Morgan, 778, **780**
Henry, United States v., 475, 558, 569
Hensley, United States v., 288, 305
Hernandez v. New York, 838
Herrera v. Collins, 49, 50, 863, 927
Herring v. New York, 932
Herring v. United States, 59, 88
Hiibel v. Sixth Judicial District, 293
Hill v. California, 168
Hill v. Lockhart, 766, 777, 952
Hinds, In re, 903
Hobby v. United States, 707
Hoffa v. United States, 126, 475
Hoffman v. United States, 624
Holland v. Illinois, 829
Holloway v. Arkansas, 972, 980
Holmes v. South Carolina, 1020, **1061**
Holt v. United States, 711
Holt, United States v., 322
Horton v. California, 235
House v. Bell, 50
Howes v. Fields, 455, **464**
Hoyt v. Florida, 816
Hubbell, United States v., 521, 522, 523, 622, **650**
Hudson v. Michigan, 59, 80, 344, **366**
Hudson v. United States, 785, 1080, **1122**
Humes v. United States, 1156
Hurtado v. California, 694
Hutto v. Davis, 1211
Illinois v. Allen, 1011, 1015, **1016**
Illinois v. Caballes, 123, 124, 125, 306
Illinois v. Gates, 69, 142, **145**
Illinois v. Krull, 74, 89
Illinois v. Lafayette, 259, 271, 273, 274
Illinois v. McArthur, 217, 238
Illinois v. Perkins, 456, **474**
Illinois v. Rodriguez, 333
Illinois v. Vitale, 1089, 1092, 1099
Illinois v. Wardlow, 360
Indianapolis, City of v. Edmond, 211
INS v. Delgado, 314, 315, 317
INS v. Lopez-Mendoza, 85
Iowa v. Tovar, 1005
Irvin v. Dowd, 867, 873
J. E. B. v. Alabama ex rel. T. B., 838
J.D.B. v. North Carolina, 455, **458**
Jackson, Ex parte, 622

Jacobsen, United States v., 123
James v. Illinois, 455
Janis, United States v., 85, 566
Jencks v. United States, 754
Jenkins v. Anderson, 454, 492
Jenkins, United States v., 1140
Johns, United States v., 255
Johnson v. Commonwealth, 1084
Johnson v. Louisiana, 800
Johnson v. Texas, 1217
Johnson v. United States, 259, 335
Johnson v. Zerbst, 327, 329, 374, 377,
   382, 442, 449, 482, 563, 1010
Jones v. Barnes, 992, 996
Jones v. United States, 149, 153
Jones, United States v., 94, **107**
Jorn, United States v., 1144
Kaley v. United States, 712
Kansas v. Glover, 283, **294**
Kansas v. Marsh, 1243
Kansas v. Ventris, 454
Karo, United States v., 109
Kastigar v. United States, 523, **633**,
   643, 654
Katz v. United States, 94, **95**, 101,
   112, 121, 128, 611, 643
Kaupp v. Texas, 350, 357
Kelly, United States v., 209
Kennedy v. Louisiana, 1210
Kennedy v. Mendoza-Martinez, 1123,
   1127
Kentucky v. King, 222, **233**
Kentucky v. Stincer, 1015, 1019
Kentucky v. Whorton, 1070
Ker v. California, 149, 153
Kimmelman v. Morrison, 954, 957
Kirby v. Illinois, 390, 393, 394, 534,
   562, 573, **580**, 629, 631
Knotts, United States v., 109, 111
Korematsu v. United States, 1119
Krivda, People v., 100
Kuhlmann v. Wilson, 559, **568**
Kyles v. Whitley, 743, 774
Kyllo v. United States, 124, 125
Lafler v. Cooper, 771, 924, **951**
Lakeside v. Oregon, 1054
Landmark Communications, Inc. v.
   Virginia, 892, 893
Lange, Ex parte, 1079
Lanza, United States v., 1106
Lee v. United States, 777, 1128
Lefkowitz v. Cunningham, 493
Lefkowitz v. Turley, 493
Lefkowitz, United States v., 228
Lem Woon v. Oregon, 695
Leon, United States v., 59, **68**, 81,
   89, 707, 975
Lewis v. United States, 796
Lockhart v. Fretwell, 926, 953, 957

Lockhart v. McCree, 821
Lockhart v. Nelson, 1149
Lockyer v. Andrade, 1210
Lo-Ji Sales, Inc. v. New York, 72
Loud Hawk, United States v., 723, 725
Lovasco, United States v., 713, **727**
Loving v. Virginia, 1191
Lynch v. Overholser, 785
MacCollom, United States v., 405
MacDonald, United States v., 723, 725
Mackey v. Montrym, 216
Mackey v. United States, 630
Maine v. Moulton, 475, 570
Mallory v. United States, 438
Malloy v. Hogan, 32, 43, 433, 437, 438,
   800
Mandujano, United States v., **626**
Manson v. Brathwaite, 573, **584**
Mapp v. Ohio, 33, 59, **62**, 90, 232,
   396
Marbury v. Madison, 544
Marigold, United States v., 1105
Marion, United States v., 723, 725,
   728
Marks v. United States, 807
Marron v. United States, 228
Martin Linen Supply Company,
   United States v., 1143
Martinez v. Court of Appeal of
   California, 1005, 1009, 1010
Martinez v. Ryan, 925, 927
Martinez-Salazar, United States v.,
   879
Maryland v. Buie, 174, 230, 248
Maryland v. Dyson, 242
Maryland v. Garrison, 165
Maryland v. King, 176, **205**, 360
Maryland v. Pringle, 142, **162**
Maryland v. Shatzer, 456, 465, **495**
Maryland v. Wilson, 320
Massachusetts v. Sheppard, 73, 89
Massiah v. United States, 421, **422**,
   475, 557
Matlock, United States v., 333
Maxwell v. Dow, 35, 36
Mayberry v. Pennsylvania, 861
Mayer v. Chicago, 396, 400
McCarthy v. Arndstein, 635
McCarthy v. United States, 775
McCleskey v. Kemp, 845, 1153, **1188**
McCoy v. Louisiana, 993, **994**
McDonald v. City of Chicago, 31
McDonald v. Pless, 842
McGowan v. Maryland, 1191
McKane v. Durston, 400, 403
McKaskle v. Wiggins, 962, 1005, 1014
McLaughlin v. Florida, 844
McMann v. Richardson, 775, 928, 932

McMillan v. Pennsylvania, 1167, 1173, 1175
McNabb v. United States, 438
McPhail v. United States, 621
McPhaul v. United States, 619
Medina v. California, 46, 49
Melendez-Diaz v. Massachusetts, 1037
Mendenhall, United States v., 318
Menna v. New York, 788, 928
Michigan v. Bryant, 1020
Michigan v. Fisher, 234
Michigan v. Jackson, 390, 392, 395, 506
Michigan v. Long, 248, 291
Michigan v. Mosley, 455, 486, 501, 535
Michigan v. Tucker, 86, 456, 457, 516, 538, 546
Michigan v. Tyler, 335
Mickens v. Taylor, 970, **971**
Miller v. Alabama, 1236
Miller v. Fenton, 420
Miller, United States v., 114, 618, 622
Miller-El v. Dretke, 837
Milligan, Ex parte, 1195
Milton v. Wainwright, 707
Mincey v. Arizona, 263, 454, 553, 554
Minnesota v. Murphy, 489
Minnick v. Mississippi, 456, 496
Miranda v. Arizona, 327, 328, 347, 351, 432, **433**, 436, 445, 524, 624, 626, 631, 697, 700, 707, 1041
Miranda, State v., 445
Missouri v. Frye, **766**, 926, 951, 953, 954
Missouri v. Hunter, 1096, 1100
Missouri v. McNeely, 185, 216
Missouri v. Seibert, 457, 458, **523**
Mistretta v. United States, 1182
Mitchell v. United States, 779, 1054, 1152, **1159**
Mitchell v. Wisconsin, 214
Monell v. New York City Dept. of Social Servs., 83
Monia, United States v., 627, 630
Monroe v. Pape, 83
Montejo v. Louisiana, 456, 505, **506**
Montgomery v. Louisiana, 34
Mooney v. Holohan, 742
Moore v. Illinois, 393, 1105
Moran v. Burbine, 458, **531**
Morgan v. Illinois, 821
Morton Salt Co., United States v., 619, 621, 622
Mu'Min v. Virgina, 876
Muckenstrum, United States v., 1068
Muehler v. Mena, 306
Murchison, In re, 857
Murphy v. Florida, 873, 887, 906

Murphy v. Waterfront Comm'n, 623, 633, 636, 639, 643
Murray v. Carrier, 949
Murray v. United States, 344, **361**, 369
Naovarath v. State, 1216
Napue v. Illinois, 741, 742
Nardone v. United States, 343, 345
Nathanson v. United States, 143, 151
National Dairy Products Corp., United States v., 906
Navarette v. California, 301
Nebraska Press Association v. Stuart, 865, 876, 892, 898, 901, 903, 918
Neder v. United States, 963, 968
Neil v. Biggers, 585
New State Ice Co. v. Liebmann, 45, 920
New York v. Belton, 203, 244, 262, 511
New York v. Burger, 193
New York v. Harris, 344, **351**, 367
New York v. Hill, 1003
New York v. Quarles, 456, **515**, 539, 546
Nicholl v. Darley, 132
Nichols, United States v., 384
Nielsen, In re, 1091, 1101, 1102
Nix v. Whiteside, 953, 976, 998, 1074
Nix v. Williams (Williams II), 344, 361, **364**, 369, 518, 564
Nixon v. Warner Communications, Inc., 916
Nobles, United States v., 644
North Carolina v. Alford, 778, **783**
North Carolina v. Butler, 479
North Carolina v. Pearce, 548, 686, 687, 761
O'Connor v. Ortega, 103, 258
Obergefell v. Hodges, 1110
Offutt v. United States, 980
Ohio Adult Parole Authority v. Woodard, 1163
Ohio v. Clark, 1031
Ohio v. Roberts, 1021, 1022, 1168
Oklahoma Press Publishing Co. v. Walling, 119, 607, 619, 621
Oliver v. United States, 106
Oliver, In re, 865, 892, 1088
Olmstead v. United States, 65, 96, 117, 600, 617
Oppenheimer, United States v., 1082
Oregon v. Elstad, 457, 520, 539, 546
Oregon v. Hass, 454
Oregon v. Ice, 1172
Oregon v. Kennedy, 1128, **1134**
Oregon v. Mathiason, 455
Oyler v. Boles, 677, 1191
Padilla v. Kentucky, 766, 777, 926, 956

Palermo v. United States, 754

Palko v. Connecticut, 1121

Patane, United States v., 457, 518, **520**

Patterson v. Colorado ex rel. Attorney General of Colo., 882

Patterson v. Illinois, 511

Patton v. United States, 800, 811

Patton v. Yount, 873, 874, 894

Payne v. Tennessee, 1093

Payton v. New York, **222**, 351

Peña-Rodriguez v. Colorado, 807, 814, **839**

Pennsylvania Bd. of Probation and Parole v. Scott, 81, 89

Pennsylvania v. Finley, 862, 925

Pennsylvania v. Mimms, 292

Pennsylvania v. Ritchie, 734, **748**, 1020

Penry v. Lynaugh, 34

Perez, United States v., 1134

Perry v. New Hampshire, 574, 584, **589**

Petite v. United States, 1115

Place, United States v., 96, 123, 288

Plessy v. Ferguson, 1119

Poe v. Ullman, 57

Pointer v. Texas, 697

Portuondo v. Agard, 1054, 1060

Potter, Commonwealth v., 1138

Powell v. Alabama, 56, 373, 379, 423, 574, 577, 581, 696, 698, 970, 1010

Powell v. Nevada, 177

Powell, United States v., 618, 621

Powers v. Ohio, 838, 845

Premo v. Moore, 768

Presley v. Georgia, 960, 966

Press-Enterprise Co. v. Superior Court [Press-Enterprise I], 868

Press-Enterprise Co. v. Superior Court [Press-Enterprise II], 868, **907**, 963

Procter & Gamble Co., United States v., 733

Puckett v. United States, 860

Puerto Rico v. Sánchez Valle, 1106, 1110, 1112

Pulley v. Harris, 1194, 1196

Rabinowitz, United States v., 229, 246, 251

Rachmiel, In re, 904

Rakas v. Illinois, 97

Ramos v. Louisiana, 33, 40, 795, **798**

Rawlings v. Kentucky, 186

Rea v. United States, 63

Reed, United States v., 711

Regents of the University of California v. Bakke, 1197

Reina v. United States, 1162

Rhode Island v. Innis, 456, **468**, 558

Richards v. Wisconsin, 80, 165, **172**

Richardson v. Marsh, 1020, 1038

Richmond Newspapers, Inc. v. Virginia, 868, 869, 892, 912

Rideau v. Louisiana, 872

Riley v. California, **275**

Ring v. Arizona, 1172

Ristaino v. Ross, 818, 820

Rita v. United States, 1188

Riverside, County of v. McLaughlin, 177, 203, 498

Robbins v. California, 249

Roberts v. LaVallee, 396

Roberts v. United States, 1168

Robinson, United States v., 175, **182**, 193, 195, 200, 202, 203, 210, 275, 292, 1054

Rochin v. California, 31, 39, 410

Rock v. Arkansas, 1051, 1054, **1055**, 1064

Rodriguez v. United States, 283, **321**

Roe v. Flores Ortega, 1004

Rogers v. Richmond, 410

Rogers v. United States, 624, 1161

Roper v. Simmons, 1211, 1243

Rosales-Lopez v. United States, 846

Rose v. Mitchell, 703, 707, 709, 845

Ross v. Moffitt, **401**, 405

Ross, United States v., 248, 253, 268, 269

Rothgery v. Gillespie County, **389**, 512

Rugendorf v. United States, 149

Ruiz, United States v., 734, **773**

Rummel v. Estelle, 1211

Russell, United States v., 1143

Sacramento, County of v. Lewis, 133, 313

Salerno, United States v., 660, **661**, 1097

Salinas v. Texas, **488**

Samson v. California, 211

Sanabria v. United States, 1140, 1142

Santobello v. New York, 764, 1013

Sawyer, In re, 898, 903

Schall v. Martin, 663, 664

Scheffer, United States v., 1063, 1064

Schmerber v. California, 215, 220, 626

Schneckloth v. Bustamonte, 315, **325**

Schriro v. Summerlin, 1181

Scott v. Illinois, 376, **383**, 400

Scott v. United States, 194, 1156

Scott, United States v., **1136**, **1140**

Sealfon v. United States, 1082

Seattle Times Co. v. Rhinehart, 897, 903

See v. Seattle, 618
Segura v. United States, 238, 359, 362, 367
Serfass v. United States, 1141
Sharpe, United States v., 305
Sheppard v. Maxwell, 867, 868, 873, 902, 903
Silverman v. United States, 121
Silverthorne Lumber Co. v. United States, 344, 368
Singer v. United States, 795, **810**, 1009
Skilling v. United States, 867, **869**
Smith v. Illinois, 1049
Smith v. Maryland, 101, 115, 280, 620
Snyder v. Louisiana, 837
Snyder v. Massachusetts, 36, 1016
Sokolow, United States v., 360
Soldal v. Cook County, 109, 112
Solem v. Helm, 1210
Solorio v. United States, 1093
South Dakota v. Neville, 215
South Dakota v. Opperman, 271, 274
Spano v. New York, 410, **418**, 421, 422
Spinelli v. United States, 142, 147, 158
Stack v. Boyle, 659, **660**, 667, 672
Steagald v. United States, 225
Stone v. Powell, 86, 89, 566
Stoner v. California, 103
Stovall v. Denno, 575, 583
Strauder v. West Virginia, 703, 798
Strickland v. Washington, 707, 743, 777, 924, **928**, 951, 956, 967, 972, 977, 998
Sullivan v. Florida, 1219
Sullivan v. Louisiana, 964
Swain v. Alabama, 828, 829, 1205
Swidler & Berlin v. United States, 979
Tanner v. United States, 843
Tateo, United States v., 1147
Taylor v. Alabama, 350, 352
Taylor v. Illinois, 738
Taylor v. Kentucky, 1051, 1061, **1066**
Taylor v. Louisiana, 809, 813, 814
Taylor v. United States, 1015
Teague v. Lane, 34, 805
Tennessee v. Garner, 196
Terry v. Ohio, 174, 184, 188, 266, **283**, 303, 307, 360
Texas v. Cobb, 560
Texas v. McCullough, 687
Thompson v. Oklahoma, 1213
Thompson v. Utah, 800
Thornton v. United States, 245
Timbs v. Indiana, 33, 801
Tollett v. Henderson, 775, 787, 789

Torres v. Madrid, 130
Trop v. Dulles, 1210, 1240
Trupiano v. United States, 228
Tucker, United States v., 1155
Tumey v. Ohio, 696, 704, 855, 861, 863, 964
Turner v. Murray, 814, **817**, 1195, 1206
Ullmann v. United States, 623, 634, 1164
Ungar v. Sarafite, 924
Ursery, United States v., 1124
Utah v. Strieff, 344, **355**
Uttecht v. Brown, 825
Vaise v. Delaval, 841
Vale v. Louisiana, 237
Valenzuela-Bernal, United States v., 743, 936, 1056
Vandercomb, King v., 1084, 1092
Vasquez v. Hillery, 695, **702**, 964
Vermont v. Brillon, 718
Vignera v. New York, 433
Villamonte-Marquez, United States v., 193
Virginia v. Moore, 202
Virginia, Ex parte, 1205
Von Moltke v. Gillies, 979
Wade v. Hunter, 1139
Wade, United States v., 328, 573, **574**, 590, 697, 700
Wainwright v. Torna, 925
Walder v. United States, 85
Waller v. Georgia, 865, 908, 962, 968, 999
Ward v. Texas, 409
Ward, United States v., 1123, 1127
Warden v. Hayden, 335, 601, 644
Wardius v. Oregon, 735
Warger v. Shauers, 844, 850
Warshak, United States v., 622
Washington v. Texas, 1020, 1063
Washington, United States v., 516, 631
Watson, United States v., 175, **176**, 227, 259, 352
Watts v. Indiana, 410, 447
Watts, United States v., 1157
Wayte v. United States, 677, 1205
Weatherford v. Bursey, 733, 767
Weaver v. Massachusetts, 696, 865, 924, **960**, 999
Weeks v. United States, 60, 76, 90, 184, 228, 258, 281
Weems v. United States, 1210
Welch v. United States, 34
Welsh v. Wisconsin, 196, 199, 203, 221, 239
Westover v. United States, 433, 436
Wheat v. United States, 936, **986**

Wheat, United States v., 970
White v. Woodall, 1164
White, United States v., 94, **126**, 625
Whorton v. Bockting, 34
Whren v. United States, 176, **191**,
    201, 205, 234, 359
Wiggins v. Smith, 948
Wilkerson v. Utah, 1210
Williams v. Florida, 733, **734**
Williams v. Illinois, 1037
Williams v. New York, 1154, 1155,
    1173
Williams v. Pennsylvania, **856**
Williams v. Taylor, 953
Williams, United States v., 712
Wilson v. Arkansas, 80, 172, 196
Wilson v. Layne, 168
Wilson v. United States, 646, 1052
Wilson, United States v., 1140, 1144
Winship, In re, 1061
Winston v. Lee, 196
Witherspoon v. Illinois, 821
Withrow v. Larkin, 856
Withrow v. Williams, 521, 552
Witte v. United States, 1157
Wolf v. Colorado, 32, **59**, 62, 329
Wong Sun v. United States, 64, 141,
    343, **344**, 347, 367, 370, 578
Wood v. Georgia, 693, 902, 903, 972,
    973, 979
Woodson v. North Carolina, 1245
Woodward v. Alabama, 1244
Workman v. Commonwealth, 1217
Wyoming v. Houghton, 164, 239,
    247, **263**
Yarborough v. Alvarado, 459
Yarborough v. Gentry, 948
Yates v. Evatt, 999
Ybarra v. Illinois, 163, 266
Yick Wo v. Hopkins, 677
Young, United States v., 1074
Zurcher v. Stanford Daily, 95, **136**,
    599

CRIMINAL PROCEDURE AND THE CONSTITUTION

LEADING SUPREME COURT CASES AND INTRODUCTORY TEXT

2021 Edition

CHAPTER 1

A CRIMINAL JUSTICE
PROCESS OVERVIEW

■ ■ ■

This book presents a collection of leading Supreme Court decisions in the field of "constitutional criminal procedure"—that is, decisions dealing with application of the United States Constitution to what is commonly described as the "criminal justice process". That process consists of a variety of different procedures, some applied by enforcement officials (police and prosecutor) and some applied by courts, through which the substantive criminal law is enforced. The Court's opinions commonly focus on the application of a single procedure in the context of the individual case before the Court. The Court tends to refer only briefly (if at all) to other procedures that are part of the process, and only occasionally describes the overall legal and institutional structure that provides a frame of reference for its criminal procedure rulings. That backdrop is assumed to be familiar territory for the lower court judges who will have the responsibility of interpreting and applying the Court's opinions, and the prosecutors and defense counsel who will advance legal arguments based on those opinions. We assume that it is not familiar territory for the students using this casebook, and therefore seek in this chapter to briefly describe the three key components of that backdrop—the division of lawmaking authority in the legal regulation of the criminal justice process (§ 1); the division of responsibility for the administration of the process and the range of diversity within each administrative grouping (§ 2); and the basic steps that carry the administration of the process from its starting point to its conclusion (§ 3).

1. THE LAWMAKING STRUCTURE

1. *Fifty-two lawmaking jurisdictions.* Under the United States' version of federalism, each of the fifty state governments retains the authority to enact its own criminal code. Each state also retains the power to provide for the enforcement of that criminal code through agencies and procedures that it creates. That authority has been used in each state to establish what is basically a single, general criminal justice process applicable throughout the state.[1] Congress has added to these fifty state criminal justice processes its two distinct federal criminal justice processes. First, it has created a separate criminal justice process for the District of Columbia, used to enforce a separate criminal code that applies only in the

---

[1]   While the same criminal justice process applies throughout the state, as discussed at p. 12 infra, that process may vary with the level of the crime. Also, as to certain matters, state law may allow the local government or courts to formulate additional procedural requirements that apply only to the particular county, municipality, or judicial district, thereby creating further variation.

..trict. Second, it has created a criminal justice process for the enforcement of the general federal criminal code, which applies throughout the country.[2] This process utilizes national federal law enforcement agencies and relies on prosecutions brought in the federal district courts.

While the federal criminal justice system has expanded greatly over the last half of the twentieth century, the state criminal justice systems remain the source of the vast majority of criminal prosecutions. The state systems account for almost 99% of the nation's total criminal docket (i.e., all prosecutions of felonies, misdemeanors, and those local ordinance violations that carry a potential sentence of an incarceration), and roughly 96% of all prosecutions charging "major" offenses (i.e., felonies).[3] Thus, not surprisingly, a substantial majority of the Supreme Court decisions contained in this volume review state prosecutions.

2.   *Diversity in state law.* The presence of fifty-two lawmaking jurisdictions does not invariably produce substantial diversity in the laws of those jurisdictions. In other fields of law, the individual states have almost uniformly adhered to a single model, so that the governing law is quite similar in almost every state. That has not been the case, however, for criminal procedure. The English common law provided a common starting point for the criminal justice systems of the original states and the federal system, and continues to provide an element of commonality even to this day. However, as the common law concepts have been adjusted to accommodate new developments in the administrative structure of the process (such as the creation of police departments), and as the process has been reshaped to accommodate new concerns, various factors have led the states to take

---

[2]   The criminal laws of a state are limited in application to offenses that occurred in their entirety or in part within that state. The federal criminal law, in contrast, has a territorial reach that extends throughout the United States and its territories. However, the federal government, unlike the state governments, cannot declare an action to be criminal simply because it is contrary to the public welfare. The federal government's regulatory authority in the criminal field, as in other fields, is limited to those subjects as to which the federal constitution grants Congress legislative authority, such as interstate and foreign commerce and the maintenance of national services (e.g., the postal service and the armed forces). As to District of Columbia, Congress' authority is more extensive, and basically is similar to that of a state.

[3]   See LaFave, Israel, King, & Kerr, 1 *Criminal Procedure Treatise* § 1.2(e) (4th ed. 2015) (also estimating the nation's annual criminal caseload as at least 12 million—and likely somewhat higher—and the nation's annual felony caseload as falling in the range of 2.6–2.9 million).

At various points in this chapter distinctions will be drawn between felony offenses and misdemeanor offenses. All but a handful of jurisdictions utilize one of two seemingly distinct standards to distinguish between felonies and misdemeanors. The federal system and roughly half of the states classify as felonies all crimes punishable by a term of incarceration of more than one year; crimes not punishable by incarceration, or punishable by incarceration for a maximum term of one year or less, are misdemeanors. Most of the remaining states look to the location of the possible sentence of incarceration. If the offense is punishable by incarceration in a penitentiary, it is a felony; offenses punishable by incarceration only in a jail are misdemeanors. States using this distinction, however, commonly also provide for possible incarceration in a penitentiary only if the offense of conviction carries a maximum term of incarceration exceeding one year. Thus, both standards, in practice, will classify as felonies all offenses punishable by a term of imprisonment of more than one year.

In many states, municipal ordinances may duplicate lower-level state misdemeanors, prohibiting the same conduct and carrying the same potential penalties (including possible incarceration) as the state-law misdemeanors, but typically providing also that fines go to the municipality. These offenses generally are treated procedurally in much the same fashion as misdemeanors. See LaFave et al., supra, § 1.7(k).

diverse approaches on common issues. Four factors, in particular, point toward different states adopting somewhat different legal regulations: (1) criminal procedure is not one of those areas of lawmaking in which a need for reciprocity or the interaction of transactions forces the states to seek uniformity; a lack of uniformity in the criminal justice processes of adjoining states is not likely to be a deterrent to the free flow of goods, services, or persons between the states or to restrain economic development within the state; (2) the criminal justice process must be shaped in light of the state's administrative environment, including the demography of the population, the resources available to the process, and the structure of the institutions responsible for the administration of the process (particularly police and prosecutor agencies), and states vary considerably as to that administrative environment; (3) criminal process issues tend to be issues of high visibility and, often, high emotional content, leading to lawmaking decisions (at least legislative lawmaking decisions[4]) that are influenced more by symbolic politics (which tend to vary with the ideological assumptions of the local constituency) than the views of those with presumed technical expertise; and (4) the integrated character of the criminal justice means that a divergence between states in their law governing one part of the process most likely will necessitate further differences at other stages of the process.

3. ***The unifying role of federal constitutional regulation.*** The Bill of Rights of the Federal Constitution includes a large number of guarantees dealing specifically with the criminal justice process—all the guarantees of the Fourth, Sixth, and Eighth Amendments, and with the inclusion of the Fifth Amendment's due process clause (which clearly applies to criminal proceedings, although extending also to certain non-criminal proceedings), all but one of the guarantees (the "just compensation" guarantee) of the Fifth Amendment. As discussed in chapter two, these provisions originally applied only to the federal criminal justice process (and the District of Columbia process). However, as a result of a series of decisions described in chapter two, almost all of these provisions now apply as well to the states. Moreover, in its reading of the due process clauses of the Fifth and Fourteenth Amendment, the Court has carried constitutional regulation far beyond the subjects regulated by the more specific guarantees (recognizing that, as it applies to the states, due process also has a content independent of the selective incorporation of the specific guarantees noted in Ch. 2, § 3). The equal protection clause of the Fourteenth Amendment, in its prohibition against discrimination, provides still another layer of constitutional regulation of the criminal justice process.

Federal constitutional law regulating criminal procedure, as interpreted by the Supreme Court, is commonly described as "our most important source of

---

[4] Legislative lawmaking plays a critical role in the field of criminal procedure as every state has an extensive group of statutes regulating the criminal justice process (commonly described as a "code of criminal procedure"). Judicial lawmaking through common law rulings, once the most common form of criminal process lawmaking, today plays a very limited role. Judicial lawmaking more commonly occurs in the adoption of court rules, with roughly two-thirds of the states having a comprehensive set of court rules of criminal procedure. Of course, courts also may be viewed as engaged in judicial lawmaking in their interpretation of state constitutions, statutes, and court rules.

_riminal procedure law". LaFave et al., fn. 3 supra, § 1.3(b). This characterization stems in part from the fundamental character of the issues considered in the Court's constitutional decisions and the symbolic significance of the principles announced in its rulings. The characterization also is based, in part, on the practical bearing of the Court's constitutional rulings. Federal constitutional law is the only source of substantial legal regulation applicable to all fifty-two jurisdictions. As such it provides a common foundation that significantly shapes major portions of the process in all fifty-two jurisdictions.

It should be kept in mind, however, that constitutional regulation is subject to two significant limitations insofar as it relates to achieving uniformity among the fifty-two jurisdictions. Initially, the Constitution imposes no more than a baseline standard. It prescribes procedural prerequisites that each jurisdiction must meet as a minimum, but the jurisdictions remain free to prescribe additional procedural protections if they so desire. As to almost every area of constitutional regulation, at least one jurisdiction has imposed a limitation upon governmental action more restrictive than that imposed by the federal constitution. Very often, where the Court majority has rejected an expansive view of a particular guarantee and dissenting Justices have favored that interpretation, at least a few states have adopted the expansive view under state law (in some cases, in the interpretation of state constitutional guarantees almost identical to the federal guarantee). In many areas, a substantial majority of the states have adopted standards that go beyond the constitutional minimum. Thus, while the constitutional right to jury trial allows for six person jury for the trial of non-capital felonies (see Ch. 24, § 1), all but six states require twelve person juries in such cases.

Second, constitutional regulation is far from comprehensive across the totality of the criminal justice process. As to some procedures, such as searches and seizures, federal constitutional regulation is quite detailed (indeed, some would argue that it rivals the Internal Revenue Code in its complexity). However, as to many other aspects of the process (e.g., the negotiation of guilty plea agreements), constitutional regulation will reach only a few major features of the particular procedure. The remaining aspects of the procedure will be regulated by state law (if regulated at all).

Thus, the cases presented in this volume, which do not cover even the totality of constitutional regulation, should not be viewed presenting anything close to a complete picture of the legal regulation of the criminal justice processes in all fifty-two jurisdictions. What those cases do illustrate are the fundamental, over-arching principles that largely shape the legal regulation of this nation's criminal justice processes and the complexities that arise in applying those principles to specific cases.

2. THE ADMINISTRATIVE STRUCTURE

1. *Administrative diversity.* Throughout the Supreme Court opinions reprinted in this volume, you will find references of a generic nature to "police," "prosecutors," "defense counsel," and "courts". These are the four groups primarily responsible for the administration of the criminal justice process. Police officers,

prosecutors, and judges all hold official positions within governmental units, and in describing the procedural history of the case, the Court will often refer to the position held by a particular actor in a particular governmental unit (e.g., that the arresting officer was a detective in a municipal police department). Rarely, however, will the Court go beyond that brief designation. Opinions presume familiarity with the institutional structures of the wide variety of governmental agencies that have the responsibility for performing the administrative functions of police, prosecutor, and courts.[5] So too, as to defense counsel, the opinions assume a familiarity with the institutional arrangements that provide counsel for defendants. This section briefly describes those institutional structures. It concentrates largely on the state systems, although significant distinctions in the administrative structure of the federal system are briefly described in the accompanying footnotes.

2. *Police agencies.* Of the four major groups involved in the administration of the state criminal justice systems, the police group is the largest and has the most diverse range of functions and most complex organizational structure.

Fragmentation. A key feature of the organizational structure of police agencies is the fragmentation in the allocation of policing authority. Indeed, the fifty state criminal justice systems together have almost 18,000 different agencies that can be classified as "police agencies," in that (1) they have among their primary responsibilities the enforcement of the state criminal law, and (2) at least some of their employees have been given the special criminal justice enforcement powers that distinguish "police officers" from other personnel involved in enforcement (typically full arrest powers and weapon-carrying authority). The vast majority of these governmental agencies are units of local governments (e.g., municipal police departments or county sheriff's offices), although there are over 1,000 agencies that are part of special geographical units (e.g., a park police department or a college campus department) or the state government. Apart from Hawaii, no state has less than 40 different police agencies and most have at least 250 different agencies.

The fragmentation of police authority invariably produces substantial variation in the exercise of that authority from one community to another within a single state. A dominant characteristic of state law regulating police conduct is its recognition of broad areas of police discretion.[6] Typically, where the law allows the

---

[5] As discussed below, there is considerable diversity in the institutional structures of these governmental agencies. However, with rare exceptions, constitutional regulation is geared to the function being performed without regard to differences in the structure of the governmental units assigned to the performance of that role. Indeed, to a large extend, the same is true of state law (or in the federal system, federal law). Thus, a state's law governing police actions typically will apply to all government employees who fall within a broad definition of "peace officers," including, for example, officers in specialized agencies that have authority in special geographical enclaves (e.g., park police), officers in general purpose municipal police departments, officers in a sheriff's department, officers in a state highway patrol agency, and officers in a state administrative agency enforcing a limited class of offenses (e.g., liquor laws). See LaFave et al., fn. 3 supra, § 1.8(f).

[6] Discretionary authority is not always the product of a grant of authority accompanied by a completely normless framework for its exercise. Discretion more often exists where the law impose only a very limited restriction on the administrator's choice of action (e.g., where it states

police to take a particular action only if certain prerequisites are met, it does not mandate that such action be taken simply because those prerequisites exist. An arresting officer, for example, has the authority to search the pockets of the arrested person, but also has the discretion to choose not to do so. In many instances, the law gives the officer the discretion to either act or take no action, but in others it also grants discretion to choose between two alternative paths of action (e.g., where probable cause exists, either taking the person into custody via an arrest or simply issuing a summons directing the person to appear in court at some later date).

Where state law allows for such discretionary decisionmaking, police agencies often seek to fill that regulatory void. In one fashion or another, they seek to channel the exercise of discretion by their individual officers. Many do so informally, through an organizational ethos that utilizes a variety of devices (e.g., training programs, socialization, and incentives) to influence the exercise of authority by individual officers. Others adopt written guidelines that are enforced internally through employment sanctions. In some instances, municipal governments have adopted ordinances that require officers in municipal police departments to exercise or not exercise discretionary authority in a particular way. The end result is that policies on the exercise of discretion differ from one community to another (and sometimes within a community when more than one agency is exercising police authority in that community).[7] The differences are often so substantial that commentators will describe a particular state as having many different criminal justice systems "in practice" although the "law on the books" seemingly creates a single system.

Agency responsibilities. Police agencies within the state criminal justice systems vary in their responsibilities. Some agencies, primarily at the state level, are largely limited in their responsibilities to the enforcement of the state's entire criminal code or a portion of that code. Their agents are involved almost exclusively in investigating possible violations, collecting evidence, and apprehending offenders, often acting in conjunction with other police agencies. However, the vast majority of police agencies in the state systems are "general purpose" agencies, which gives them numerous additional responsibilities. Municipal police departments for example, also are responsible for providing basic social services

---

that the administrator ordinarily can take action one way or another as he or she chooses, but cannot base his or her decision on a bribe). Thus, discretion has been described as analogous to a large hole in a legal-regulation doughnut.

[7] In the federal system, there is far less fragmentation, but some diversity in policies does exist among the much smaller group of key police agencies. While over 60 federal agencies employ agents with the authority of sworn police officers, a group of eight agencies account for all but a small portion of the federal criminal docket. See LaFave et al., fn. 3 supra, § 1.4(c). Most of these agencies are responsible for the enforcement of a specific group of offenses (as in the case of the Drug Enforcement Agency and the Bureau of Alcohol, Tobacco, Firearms, and Explosives). The prominent exception is the Federal Bureau of Investigation. Although the agencies promulgate separately internal standards governing the exercise of discretionary authority by their respective agents, seven of the eight key agencies are subject to the executive authority of either the Attorney General or the Secretary of the Department of Homeland Security, and all federal police agencies ultimately are subject to the executive authority of the President of the United States. Differences in enforcement responsibilities and other institutional characteristics have led these officials to accept some diversity among federal police agencies in their approach to similar problems.

(e.g., providing emergency aid), maintenance of public order (e.g., traffic control), and efforts directed at the prevention of crime (e.g., providing a physical presence through patrol activities). Sheriffs' departments commonly add two other functions—a corrections function in the administration of jails, and a court operations function that includes serving civil process and providing court security.

The more diverse responsibilities of general purpose agencies may impact in various ways the agency's approach to its law enforcement function. Initially, the general purpose agency must take account of the fact that, with its resources spread over a broad range of responsibilities, a large proportion of it personnel—including, in particular, its largest segment, patrol officers (who spend the bulk of their time on order maintenance and service functions)—will be relatively inexperienced in the investigation of serious crime. Second, the diverse responsibilities of the agency may lead it to adopt a somewhat different focus in its selection of officers, as the qualities needed in criminal investigation are often viewed as quite different from the qualities that lead officers to excel in performing other police roles. Third, the diverse responsibilities may lead the general purpose agency to adopt a flexible and informal style in community interactions that will work well in performing other functions, but make officers less likely to adhere closely to the formal, legalistic requirements that apply to police investigations.

Agency size. Another important variable among police agencies is the agency size. Sharp differences in agency size exist in almost every state. While a substantial majority of all local agencies have fewer than 25 officers, over one-third of all officers of local agencies are employed by the 50 departments with 1,000 or more officers.

Agency size, particularly as to small agencies, bears a substantial correlation to differences in the organizational structure, resources, and patrol and enforcement policies of police agencies (although the community served, e.g., whether rural or suburban, adds an important further layer of distinction for small agencies). Smaller departments do not have the specialized units commonly found in the larger departments (e.g., vice, burglary), although many do utilize the oldest of all specialized groupings—a separate detective unit. Smaller departments also are far less likely to utilize proactive investigative procedures (e.g., undercover agents, decoys), or tactical patrol techniques (e.g., the aggressive pattern of stopping and incidental frisks and searches that are associated with police "crackdowns"). Because small police agencies are more likely to rely on the assistance of a centralized state agency for forensic investigations, they similarly tend to make less use of forensics than larger agencies with internal forensic units. Having less financial support, smaller agencies also are less likely to take advantage of advanced technology (e.g., in-field computers).

3. Prosecutors. All state systems separate prosecution agencies from police agencies. None simulate the federal structure, which places several of the major federal police agencies and all federal prosecutors in the same government department (Justice), under the executive authority of a single official (the

Attorney General).[8] Thus, county prosecutors, although commonly described as the "chief law enforcement officer" of the county, actually have no direct regulatory authority over the various police agencies operating in the county. Of course, the prosecutor does have the authority to refuse to proceed in a case presented by the police, and that power-base may be utilized to convince the police to discontinue practices that the prosecutor views as contrary to the public interest. That authority, however, hardly puts the prosecutor in a position comparable to a supervisory official; police are not always interested in obtaining a prosecution, and they are aware that, if they produce evidence adequate to gain a trial conviction or plea bargain as to a serious offender, the prosecutor will be under considerable pressure to go forward with the prosecution even though the police did not proceed as the prosecutor would have preferred.

In many respects, the same factors that produce organizational diversity among police agencies also produce organizational diversity among prosecution agencies. Here, differences in agency responsibility are not quite so significant, although the distinction between agencies that have responsibility only for criminal law enforcement and agencies that also have civil litigation responsibilities can occasionally contribute to the adoption of different positions on a limited range of criminal enforcement issues. On the other hand, the fragmentation of authority and differences in agency size, as in the case of police agencies, contribute substantially to diversity in the exercise of prosecutorial functions.

Fragmentation. In three states (Alaska, Delaware, and Rhode Island), the Attorney General's office is the sole prosecution agency (although the staff may be assigned, in part, to local offices). In the remaining states, the primary responsibility for prosecutions is vested in local prosecutors, who are local government officials (typically for individual counties or multiple-county judicial districts). These prosecutors (having a variety of titles, including "District Attorney," "State's Attorney," and "County Prosecutor") generally are elected officials, who ran for office as political party nominees. In some states, they are the only prosecuting officials. In others, the Attorney General also has separate prosecutorial authority, but that authority either will be limited to a narrow band of offenses or will be exercised only under special circumstances (e.g., where the crime has a statewide impact). In some states also, the city or county attorney has the authority to prosecute ordinance violations that carry criminal penalties (see fn. 3 supra).

---

[8]   As to the federal police agencies within the Department of Justice, see fn. 7 supra. Federal prosecutorial authority is exercised primarily by the offices of the United States Attorney, each of which represents the United States in criminal and civil matters in a particular federal judicial district. Although these offices are given considerable discretion, they remain subject to the final prosecutorial authority of the Attorney General (which includes the authority to overturn the decision of a United States Attorney to prosecute in a particular case). Also, the Attorney General, acting through the Criminal Division of the Justice Department, will establish prosecutorial priorities and guidelines for specific decisions (set forth largely in the *United States Attorneys Manual*) that bind local U.S. Attorney offices as to various prosecutorial practices. In addition, prosecutions in selected fields are brought directly by the Criminal Division or other divisions (e.g., Antitrust) of the Department of Justice, rather than by U.S. Attorneys.

The forty-seven states relying on local prosecutors have over 2,300 prosecutorial districts. Several states have over 100 districts and even smaller states are likely to have a dozen or more. As in the case of police, prosecutors are granted broad discretion in exercising their authority (particularly as to the decision to prosecute, see step 4 at p. 19 infra, and in plea negotiations, see step 14 at p. 25 infra). Not surprisingly, different prosecutor offices in the same state often will adopt quite different policies in exercising that discretion. Indeed, the fragmentation of the responsibility for prosecution is designed to produce such variations, as its purpose, in large part, is to ensure responsiveness to the particular values of the local community that elected the prosecutor.

Size. Prosecutors' offices do not vary in size quite so dramatically as police departments, but differences are substantial and do have a bearing on organizational policies. While offices in large urban districts commonly have over a hundred assistant prosecutors, over half of all prosecutors' offices have no more than three assistant prosecutors. Prosecutors in smaller offices have limited resources and a limited range of experience, which impacts their approach to prosecuting such offenses as multiparty conspiracies or complex white collar crimes. These offices typically do not have access to the array of non-lawyer support personnel common in large offices (e.g., victim advocates), and that may produce a difference in their approach as to still other aspects of the docket. Small offices also tend to adopt a more flexible decisionmaking process, allowing for ad hoc variations. Large offices, in contrast, often adopt fairly specific internal standards governing such basic decisions as the use of diversion (see fn. 14 infra), and often create special programs for specific offenses (e.g., sex offenses) or offenders (e.g., recidivists) that seek to ensure uniform prosecutorial implementation of a clearly defined mission (e.g., obtaining the longest possible incarceration).

4.   *Defense counsel.* Defense counsel in criminal cases may be privately retained counsel or counsel provided by the state for indigent defendants. A study of prosecutions in the 75 largest counties determined that 82 percent of state felony defendants were found indigent and received counsel provided by the state. While the percentage may be somewhat lower in some states, state-funded counsel clearly dominate representation in felony cases in all jurisdictions. In misdemeanor cases, the percentage of retained counsel probably is higher, because counsel is more readily afforded, but state-funded counsel also will represent a substantial portion of all misdemeanor defendants.

Retained counsel. Retained counsel in felony cases represent various segments of the private bar. They include general practitioners (particularly in small communities) who handle all types of litigation, big city "courthouse regulars" (primarily solo practitioners who handle heavy criminal caseloads, basically involving garden-variety charges against clients of lower economic status), corporate lawyers who handle white collar cases, and the highly publicized litigators who represent affluent defendants in drug cases, conspiracy cases, and occasional homicide cases.

Appointment systems. Where the state provides counsel, various different delivery systems are used. The most common are: (1) appointment of an individual assigned counsel; (2) appointment of an entity that has contracted to represent indigent defendants on a bulk basis (known as a "contract-attorney" system); and (3) automatic representation by a public defender agency. Many states utilize local government funding and therefore allow the local government to select the appointment system it prefers. Where a contract-attorney or public defender system is used, it will be supplemented by individual appointments where the contract or defender office's representation of one defendant creates a potential conflict of interest in the representation of other defendants.

The appointment process in systems relying on individual assigned counsel will vary. In some judicial districts, the appointment will be made by the court, with the judge either exercising discretion in choice or automatically rotating appointments among a panel of approved attorneys seeking appointments. In others, the court is removed from the appointment process, with a rotation system administered by an independent authority or agency that approves the panel. Contract systems may utilize a variety of different contract agencies, but such agencies most often will be a private law firm or a non-profit entity sponsored by the local bar association or the legal aid society. The contract may cover all cases or a specific number of cases, and may be based on a flat fee or an hourly fee with caps (the typical fee system for appointed counsel). Public defender agencies will be either statewide agencies (with local offices) or local government agencies. Their attorneys are government employees, engaged full time in representing indigent criminal defendants. In larger offices, other personnel include investigators and social workers.[9]

5.   *Judges*. Basically three levels of judges are involved in the administration of the criminal justice process. At the first level are the courts of limited jurisdiction. These courts are known by a variety of different titles, including "Justice of the Peace Courts," "Police Courts" and "County Courts." Because they perform many of the same functions that were assigned to "magistrates" in the English common law system, these courts often are described as "magistrate courts." The second level consists of trial courts of general jurisdiction. These courts have a variety of different titles, including "District Court," "Court of Common Pleas," "Superior Court," and "Circuit Court," but often are described as a group as "felony trial courts" or "general trial courts." Finally, the third tier consists of the state appellate courts. Since these courts basically have a single function, appellate review, which is discussed in section three (see step 17, p. 28 infra), and a fairly standard structure (also discussed there), our discussion here will focus on the "magistrate courts" and the "felony trial courts".

Magistrate courts. The trial jurisdiction of magistrate courts will not extend beyond misdemeanors, and some states will exclude from that jurisdiction more serious misdemeanors. These courts, however, also have considerable additional

---

[9]   All but a handful of the 94 federal districts now have either a Federal Public Defender or a Community Defender Organization (similar, but not a government entity). Those organizations are supplemented by private attorneys, as each district assigns only a predetermined portion of its docket to the FPD or CDO. The private attorneys are commonly known as "panel attorneys" because they are selected from a court-approved panel of "qualified" attorneys (typically attorneys who meet certain experience requirements that evidence a defense expertise).

authority that extends to offenses (e.g., felonies) that are not within their trial jurisdiction. That authority begins with matters that can occur even before the defendant is arrested, such as the issuance of arrest warrants and search warrants.

Once arrested, the defendant must be brought to court for a first appearance, which also is known as an "initial presentment," "arraignment on the complaint," or "preliminary arraignment" (see step 7, p. 21 infra). Although this proceeding can occur before any judge, it traditionally is the magistrate's responsibility. The magistrate's functions here include determining the conditions for pretrial release and if the person is eligible for court-appointed counsel, ensuring that steps have been taken to provide appointed counsel. If the charge is a felony, and a preliminary hearing is held (see step 8, p. 23 infra), the magistrate also will conduct that proceeding.

In most states, the magistrate judge sits on a court that is separate from the trial court, but in some states, the magistrate court is part of a consolidated trial court (i.e., the magistrate court is, in effect, a division of the trial court).[10] In states where the magistrate court is separate, there may be several different types of magistrate courts, including some designated as courts "not-of-record". Such courts are designed to provide a swift, inexpensive, and convenient mode of disposition of minor criminal charges, with a more formal "backup" adjudication available to the defendant through a *trial de novo* (i.e., a new trial on both facts and law) before the trial court of general jurisdiction. Judges of magistrate courts not-of-record frequently are part-time, lay judges. In contrast to their exercise of trial jurisdiction, magistrates in a court not-of-record will have the same authority with respect to preliminary proceedings in both misdemeanor and felony cases (e.g., on the issuance of arrest warrants) as magistrates in courts of record.

Felony trial courts. These courts will be part of a statewide system, but they will be divided into judicial districts that consist of a single county or several contiguous counties. In most respects, felony trial courts are similar in their authority from one state to another. The primary distinction is that in some states their trial authority will include a portion of the misdemeanor docket (e.g., all misdemeanors punishable by incarceration of more than six months). The primary organizational distinction relates to the size of the court. Even where multi-county districts are utilized, there is likely to be a number of courts that have three or fewer judges. On the other side, roughly half of all state felony trial judges sit in districts with fifteen or more judges. Larger districts often use a structure that emphasizes specialization. Many utilize separate criminal and civil divisions. The criminal division may be further divided to create a special court for particular types of cases (e.g., narcotics). Some multi-judge courts assign judges to specialized calendars, dealing with such matters as pretrial motions, grand jury items, and the acceptance of pleas negotiated prior to placing a case on the trial calendar. Very

---

[10] In the federal system, magistrate judges are part of the federal district court. Like state magistrates, they are judges with limited trial jurisdiction, and conduct various proceedings relating to felonies as well as misdemeanors. However, with the approval of the federal trial court (the United States District Court), their authority can be extended beyond preliminary proceedings (e.g., setting bail and issuing warrants) and also include duties that relate directly to the adjudication of felonies (e.g., ruling on pretrial motions, and presiding over jury selection with the consent of defense counsel).

often, judges are assigned to particular divisions in anticipation that they will exercise their discretion in a particular fashion that is deemed in the best interests of the court as whole (typically reflecting an interest in "moving the docket" and maintaining a degree of uniformity in the treatment of similar administrative decisions).

3. THE STEPS IN THE PROCESS

Supreme Court opinions almost always will describe in detail the particular procedural application that is being challenged as unconstitutional. Other procedures that were applied in the particular case commonly will be summarized briefly, so as to place the challenged procedure in context, but that summary will assume familiarity with the general procedural structure of the process (e.g., the Court will simply note that the defendant was "indicted" or "arrested," without explaining what those steps entail). A similar approach often is taken when the Court refers to a procedure that typically would follow the contested procedure and discusses how it would be impacted by the Court's ruling on the contested procedure. Some commentators argue that even where the Court's opinion fails to specifically refers to other procedural steps, its ruling is likely to have taken into account the general character of at least some of those steps. They maintain that constitutional regulation, like all regulation of the criminal justice process, builds upon an understanding of the likely interplay of the procedures applied at different stages of the process. This section seeks to provide a "big picture" understanding of that interplay through an overview of the basic steps that typically carry the process from its initiation to its completion.

The specific objectives of this overview are to position each of the basic steps within the "typical" progression of the process, to introduce the relevant terminology, and to briefly describe the character of the individual procedures that may be part of the particular step. As a result of the diversity in legal regulation described in section one, there is no "standard" set of procedures that are potentially applicable to all cases in all jurisdictions. What the overview describes is the "typical" steps in the progression of a "typical felony case" in a "typical" jurisdiction. That objective incorporates several important limitations, which should be kept in mind.

Initially, the overview concentrates on procedures adopted in a substantial majority of our fifty-two lawmaking jurisdictions. Where the jurisdictions are fairly evenly divided, that division will be noted, but where only a small group of states depart from the majority position, that minority position will not be noted. In addition, the overview describes the majority position by reference only to the basic character of a procedure; it ignores variations in other aspects of the procedure. Thus, it lumps together all states requiring grand jury issuance of a charging instrument, ignoring state variations in such matters as the composition of the grand jury and the evidentiary standard applied by the grand jury in deciding to charge.

Jurisdictions often draw substantial distinctions in the procedures applied to "minor" and "major" offenses, with the critical line of distinction commonly drawn between misdemeanors and felonies (see fn. 3 supra). Our overview is limited to the processes applied to non-capital felony cases. A substantial majority of the Court's leading criminal justice opinions have involved felony offenses (although, nationally, there are roughly 5 or 6 times as many misdemeanor prosecutions as felony prosecutions).

The exercise of discretion will determine, in part, which procedures are applied in a particular case. A procedure may be authorized under the law of a particular jurisdiction, but not required, making its use dependent upon the discretionary choice of an enforcement official (police or prosecutor), a judicial official (magistrate or trial judge), or a defendant. Our overview, in large part, looks only to whether a procedure is authorized. Where available statistics indicate that a widely authorized procedure is rarely utilized in practice in a substantial group of states, the overview will take note of that pattern of discretionary choice. In general, however, the overview does not seek to access how often an authorized procedure actually is used in practice.

Finally, our overview will not take account of variations in chronology. It will assume the chronology that occurs in the majority of felony cases, although many felony cases do not follow that chronology. Similarly, the overview discusses each step as occupying a specific place in the progression of a case, but that is not true of all procedures. While some steps have a definite starting and ending point, others are continuing and overlap other steps in the process. Investigatory procedures, for example, do not always stop with the filing of charges, but may continue through to the initiation (and sometimes the end) of the trial. So too, the decision on pretrial release, though it comes initially at the first appearance, is subject to possible reconsideration as the case progresses.

Step 1: Pre-arrest investigation. The first step in the processing of what eventually may become a felony prosecution most often is a pre-arrest investigation by the police. Criminal justice analysts commonly divide pre-arrest police investigative procedures by reference to the general focus of the investigation—distinguishing between investigations aimed at solving specific past crimes which police believe to have been committed (commonly described as "reactive" investigations), and investigations aimed at unknown but anticipated ongoing or future criminal activity (commonly described as "proactive" investigations). A less common, third category of pre-arrest investigation is the investigation conducted primarily through the use of the subpoena authority of the grand jury. Each of these three categories of pre-arrest investigative activities is briefly discussed below.

Reactive investigations. General purpose police agencies (e.g., local police departments), traditionally have devoted the vast majority of their investigative efforts to reactive investigations. This is an "incident driven" or "complaint-responsive" style of policing, flowing from various aspects of local policing, including the neighborhood patrol and the 911 emergency telephone link. The police receive a citizen report of a crime (typically from the victim or an eyewitness), or they discover through personal observations indicators of a committed crime, and they then proceed to initiate an investigation responsive to that "known crime." Depending upon the type of information that initially identifies the crime, the pre-arrest investigative activity will have one or more of the following objectives: (1) determining that the crime actually was committed; (2) determining who committed the crime; (3) collecting sufficient reliable information to support the level of probability needed to arrest that person ("probable cause")[11]; and (4) locating the offender so that he may be arrested. Not all cases involve significant pre-arrest investigation. In cases involving "on-scene arrests," where, for example, a patrol officer comes across an individual who is in the process of a crime and immediately arrests that person, the observation which establishes the "known offense" often is the totality of the pre-arrest investigation. At the other extreme are the very small percentage of cases in which police detectives engage in weeks or months of pre-arrest investigation.

An immense range of pre-arrest investigative procedures may be utilized by the police in reactive investigations. A variety of factors—including the character of the crime, the "traces" of the offense immediately available to the investigators, police agency resources, police agency policies, and the strictness of any legal prerequisites—will determine which investigative practices will be used in a particular case. The most common pre-arrest investigative practices include: (1) interviewing of victims; (2) interviewing witnesses present when the investigating officer arrives at the scene of the crime; (3) canvassing the neighborhood for (and interviewing) still other persons with relevant information; (4) interviewing persons who are viewed as having possibly committed the crime (e.g., persons matching the reported description of the offender, persons observed acting suspiciously, or persons fitting a general profile of the likely offender), which sometimes will involve the exercise of police authority to temporarily detain the suspect ("a stop") and pat-down the suspect's outer-clothing for weapons (a "frisk"); (5) the examination of the crime scene and the collection of physical evidence found there (including matter that can be used in forensic comparisons, such as fingerprints); and (6) examining criminal history and other computer files for information that might be helpful in interviewing witnesses and identifying and locating suspects.

Most of the above procedures, though fairly common, are not the subject of Supreme Court opinions (or any other judicial opinions) as they are not subject to constitutional regulation (or regulation under state law). The "stop" and the "frisk" are the two notable exceptions. Various far less common pre-arrest investigative procedures are subject to constitutional regulation, and those are the procedures

---

[11] An investigative procedure that promises to provide information establishing probable cause most often also will provide evidence that can be used at trial to establish guilt (or, at the least, leads to such evidence). Thus, most of the investigative procedures discussed in this section serve the objectives of both pre-arrest and post-arrest investigation. Whether a particular procedure is employed before or after arrest often depends on whether (1) probable cause as to a suspect can more conveniently be obtained through another procedure, and (2) whether the police perceive a need to take the suspect into custody promptly after establishing probable cause. Police typically look first to the procedure that is most promising and most convenient in establishing probable cause. Once probable cause is established, where a prompt arrest is desirable, police ordinarily will make the arrest and then look to other investigative procedures that appear likely to produce incriminating evidence. Where a prompt arrest is not needed (or cannot be achieved due to flight of the suspect), police may turn to those other procedures prior to the arrest.

that have been treated in Supreme Court caselaw. Such procedures include the pre-arrest search for evidence of a crime in the dwelling or office of a suspect (typically requiring a court order authorizing the search, described as a "search warrant"), electronic surveillance aimed at intercepting incriminating conversations (also typically requiring a court order, and used in only a small fraction of 1% of all felony investigations), and providing various incentives to persons to become informants (a practice that tends to be useful only as to limited classes of offenses and offenders).

Proactive investigations. Although general purpose police agencies traditionally have concentrated their investigative efforts on solving known crimes, those agencies also have regularly used, in a limited fashion, proactive investigations. Indeed, in recent years, many local police departments in large communities have sharply increased their utilization of proactive investigative procedures. Also, many special-function police agencies (such as the federal Drug Enforcement Administration) traditionally have devoted a quite substantial portion of their resources to proactive investigations.

Proactive investigations are aimed at uncovering criminal activity that is not specifically known to the police. The investigation may be aimed at placing the police in a position where they can observe ongoing criminal activity that otherwise would both be hidden from public view and not reported (as typically is the case with offenses that prohibit the possession of contraband or proscribe transactions between willing participants). It may be aimed at inducing persons who have committed crimes of a certain type, including many unknown to the police, to reveal themselves (as in a "fencing sting"). Proactive investigations also often are aimed at anticipating future criminality and placing police in a position to intercept when the crime is attempted. Here, the investigative technique may be designed simply to gain information that will permit the police to predict when and where a crime is likely to be committed, or it may be designed to "induce" the criminal attempt at a particular time and place by creating a setting likely to spur into action those prone to criminality.

A variety of different procedures may be used in a proactive investigation, with the choice of procedure largely tied to the specific objective of the investigation. Deception is a common element of many proactive procedures. In traditional undercover operations, the police assume a false identity and present themselves as willing to participate in criminal activities (as where undercover agents "set-up" fencing operations or narcotics transactions). So too, deception is the key to a "decoy tactic" of providing what appears to be an easy target for victimization (e.g., a drunk with an exposed wallet or a business of the type that is readily subject to extortion). Surveillance through stakeouts, covert patrols, and electronic monitoring also rests on deception by hiding the surveillance.

Other proactive techniques rely on intrusive confrontations designed to place police in a position where they can observe what otherwise would be hidden or to elicit nervous or unthinking incriminatory responses that will provide a legal grounding for taking further investigative action (e.g., an arrest or stop). Thus, police following an aggressive motorized patrol strategy will fully utilize traffic laws to maximize stops of motorists, thereby gaining greater opportunity to peer into car windows, to ask questions, and to request consent to a search of the vehicle. Similarly, under a practice of heavy field interrogation, police will frequently approach pedestrians and initiate questions to determine who they are and what they are doing. Such intrusive confrontations are most often used on a selective basis, with police concentrating their efforts on those characteristics of the social environment that suggest to them possible criminality (e.g., high-crime neighborhood, suspicious class of persons, unusual behavior). In general, proactive investigative procedures are more resource intensive, more intrusive, arguably more likely to foster community opposition, and clearly pose more legal problems than typical reactive investigative procedures. Not surprisingly, they have received considerable attention in judicial rulings (including Supreme Court rulings), disproportionate to their limited portion of the total sum of police investigative activities.

Prosecutorial investigations. Not all prearrest investigations are conducted by police. For certain types of crimes, the best investigatory tool is the subpoena—a court order directing a person to appear in a particular proceeding for the purpose of testifying and presenting specified physical evidence (e.g., documents) within his possession. The subpoena authority generally is available for the investigation of crime only through the grand jury, although many jurisdictions also grant a limited subpoena authority to enforcement agencies charged with regulating particular types of potentially criminal activities. The grand jury, although it tends to be known more for its screening function in reviewing the prosecution's decision to charge (see step 10), also has authority to conduct investigations into the possible commission of crimes within the judicial district in which it sits. In carrying out this function, the grand jurors, being a group of laypersons with no special expertise in investigation, quite naturally rely heavily on the direction provided by their legal advisor, who is the prosecutor. Thus, grand jury investigations become, for all practical purposes, investigations by the prosecutor.

Grand jury investigations tend to be used where (1) witnesses will not cooperate with the police (they can be compelled by subpoena to testify before the grand jury and given immunity to replace their self-incrimination privilege should they refuse to testify on that ground); (2) the critical evidence of the crime is likely to be a "paper trail" buried in voluminous records of business dealings (as the subpoena can be used to require production of such records where the police lack the necessary probable cause predicate for obtaining those documents through a search); and (3) the area of investigation is especially sensitive, reflecting a strong need to keep the ongoing investigation from the public gaze (an objective facilitated by grand jury secrecy requirements) or to ensure public confidence in the integrity of the investigation (an objective facilitated by the participation of the lay grand jurors). Criminal investigations presenting such special needs tend to deal with crimes of public corruption (e.g., bribery), misuse of economic power (e.g., price-fixing), or widespread distribution of illegal services or goods (e.g., organized crime operations). The investigation of such offenses through the grand jury often has both reactive and proactive qualities. The investigation starts with some information (typically coming from informants or investigators) suggesting that a specific offense has been committed, but once that offense is established, the investigation often will branch out to determine whether there also exists similar or related criminal activity, not previously identified, by the same or other parties (a portion of the grand jury investigation often characterized as a "fishing expedition").

Step 2: Arrest. Once a police officer has obtained sufficient information to justify arresting a suspect (i.e., "probable cause" to believe the person has committed a crime), the arrest ordinarily becomes the next step in the criminal justice process. While the definition of an arrest may vary with the context in which that term is used, police agencies traditionally describe an arrest as the taking of a suspect into custody for the purpose of charging him with a crime. While this definition makes the arrest the first step in the charging process, and the first step in ensuring the person's presence at any prospective trial, it also plays an important role in the continuation of the investigation of the crime. The arrest allows for a search of arrestee's person, which can disclose incriminating evidence, and as discussed in step 3 infra, it facilitates investigative procedures that require the participation of the suspect.

Police may have various options in dealing with a situation in which an arrest is authorized. Initially, as an alternative to a "full custody" arrest, many jurisdictions authorize a police officer to briefly detain the suspect and then release him upon issuance of an official document (commonly titled a "citation," "summons" or "appearance ticket") which directs the suspect to appear in court on a set date to respond to the charge specified in the document. In most communities, this release-on-citation alternative is only infrequently used (if at all) for felonies (in contrast to misdemeanors, where its use is fairly common).

Secondly, the police may have the option of making the arrest with or without an "arrest warrant" (a court order authorizing the police to arrest a particular person). In some circumstances, the law may require that the police obtain a warrant unless there is not ample time to do so. The warrant is obtained by making a showing before a judge (typically a magistrate) that there exists probable cause to believe that the prospective arrestee committed the crime for which he will be arrested. In most circumstances, the police also have the option of making an arrest without a court authorization in advance (a "warrantless arrest"), although a showing of probable cause then will have to be made subsequently to the magistrate court (see step 6 infra). When the choice is available, the clearly dominant practice in all jurisdictions is to proceed without first obtaining a warrant.

In making an arrest, the officer's first task is to secure the arrestee, using force if necessary. The officer usually then will search the arrestee's person and remove any weapons, contraband, or evidence relating to a crime (although some agencies encourage use of only a frisk, for weapons, rather than a full search, in certain situations). Under the appropriate circumstances, this "search incident to an arrest" may be extended beyond the person of the arrestee to include a contemporaneous search of: containers being carried by the arrestee (e.g. a purse or package); the passenger compartment of a vehicle and containers therein, in the case of a roadside arrest of the driver or passenger; and that portion of a room that is within the reaching distance of the arrestee where the arrest is made within a structure (e.g. a residence or office).

Once the search incident to the arrest is completed, the arrestee will be transported, by the arresting officer or other officers called to the scene, to a police station or similar "holding" facility. It is at this facility that the arrestee will be taken through a process known as "booking." Initially, the arrestee's name, the time of his arrival, and the offense for which he was arrested are noted in the police "blotter" or "log."[12] The arrestee then will be photographed and fingerprinted. After that, the arrestee ordinarily will be allowed one telephone call.

Once the booking process is complete, the arrestee will be placed in a "lockup" (usually some kind of cell) pending his subsequent presentation at a first appearance (step 7 infra). Before entering the lockup, the arrestee will be subjected to another search, often more thorough than that conducted incident to the arrest, with his personal belongings removed and inventoried. In some jurisdictions, persons arrested on lower-level felonies can gain release from the lockup by meeting the prerequisites of a "stationhouse bail program" (i.e., making a cash deposit, in an amount specified by a judicially approved "bail schedule," and agreeing to certain conduct-restrictions, including appearance in court on a specified date).

Step 3: Post-arrest investigation. Not all of the post-arrest investigative procedures that may produce further evidence of criminal activity will necessarily have been designed for that purpose. Concerns such as guaranteeing officer safety and the protection of valuables play a role in several standard post-arrest investigative practices, such as the search of arrestee's person incident to both the arrest and the placement of the arrestee in a lockup, and the search of the arrestee's automobile where it is impounded. Most post-arrest investigative procedures, however, are aimed solely at gaining further evidence that the defendant committed the identified crime, and whether they are used depends in large part on the strength of the evidence obtained prior to the arrest. Many of these procedures could have been utilized prior to the arrest, but were postponed until after the arrest as they were not needed to establish probable cause (see fn. 11 supra). Others, however, will be procedures that build upon information and evidence that has been obtained as a result of the arrest (e.g., a forensic examination of a weapon seized in a search incident to an arrest).

One critical source made available by the arrest itself is the person of the arrestee. That source allows police, for example, to obtain eyewitness identification by placing the arrestee in a grouping of physically similar persons shown to the witness (a "lineup"), having a witness view the arrestee individually (a "showup"), or taking the arrestee's picture and showing it to witnesses (usually with photographs of other persons in a "photographic lineup"). Similarly, the police may

---

[12] The arrestee's age also will be noted, and if the arrestee is subject to juvenile court jurisdiction, the arrestee will be separated from the adult arrestees, and separately processed through the juvenile justice process. The discussion that follows assumes the arrestee is subject to the criminal justice process.

obtain from the arrestee identification exemplars, such as handwriting or hair samples, that can be compared with evidence found at the scene of the crime. As the arrestee is now in police custody, police questioning of the arrestee also is greatly facilitated (although custodial interrogation does require that the arrestee be advised of certain rights, including the right not to respond, and that he agree to forego those rights).

Step 4: The decision to charge. For the vast majority of felony cases, the initial decision to charge a suspect with a crime is made when a police officer makes a warrantless arrest of the suspect. That decision may be reversed on internal review within the police department, typically by the "booking officer." Police departments vary in their willingness to utilize that authority. Some will decide against charging (and immediately release the arrestee) only where the arrest is clearly in error, while others will more fully evaluate the available evidence, and reject proceeding where probable cause may exist but the case clearly is "weak". As to lower-level felonies, some will decide against charging where the evidence is promising but the reviewing officer concludes that the offense can more appropriately be handled by a "stationhouse adjustment" (e.g., reconciliation with a family-member victim, or the arrestee's willingness to become an informant). Even where the police agency provides an in-depth internal review, only a very small percentage of felony arrests will be rejected within the police department (although a somewhat larger percentage of felony arrestees are likely to have their booking charge reduced to a misdemeanor).

The ultimate authority over charging rests with the prosecutor, rather than the police. The prosecutor is engaged in an ongoing evaluation of the charge throughout the post-arrest criminal justice process, but a prosecutor's decision not to go forward on a charge requires a different processing action depending upon whether that decision is made: (1) prior to the filing of complaint (step 5 infra); (2) after the complaint is filed, and prior to the filing of an indictment or information (step 10 infra); or (3) after the filing of the indictment or information. A decision not to proceed at the first stage simply results in the complaint not being filed (leading to the common description of that decision as a "no-paper decision"), and the release of the arrestee from police custody without any involvement of the judiciary. A decision not to proceed at the second stage commonly occurs in connection with the prosecutor's review of the case against the defendant prior to presenting it to a magistrate at a preliminary hearing (step 8 infra) or to a grand jury (step 9 infra). This decision commonly is formalized in a prosecution motion before the magistrate to withdraw the complaint (although, where grand jury review is being used, the prosecutor can ask the grand jury to vote against indicting, which similarly terminates the prosecution). A decision not to proceed further at the third stage (i.e., following the filing of an indictment or information) requires a prosecutor's *nolle prosequi* ("no wish to prosecute") motion, which must be approved by the trial court. The combination of all three non-prosecution decisions typically accounts for the disposition of a significant portion of all felony arrests.[13]

Prosecutorial review of the police charging decision prior to the filing of the complaint must occur in a short time span, as the arrested defendant must be brought before the magistrate within 24 or 48 hours (see step 7 infra), and the complaint must have been filed at that point. Not surprisingly, there is considerable variation among prosecutors' offices as to the scope of their review at this stage, with some largely leaving the decision to file the complaint to the police, and delaying their initial review of the charge in most felony cases until the second stage noted above.

Where a prosecutor decides against proceeding in the prosecutor's initial screening of the police department's charging decision (whether before or after the filing of the complaint), that conclusion most often will have been based upon anticipated difficulties of proof (e.g., the evidence is insufficient to convict, the victim is reluctant to testify, or key evidence was obtained illegally and therefore will not be admissible). However, the prosecutor also may decide against prosecution, even though the evidence clearly is sufficient, because there exists an adequate alternative to prosecution (e.g., the arrestee is willing to participate in a diversion program,[14] or the arrestee is on probation and can be proceeded against more expeditiously by revoking his probation), or special circumstances render prosecution not "in the interest of justice". A decision not to proceed made on reexamination of an earlier decision to prosecute (the typical situation where the prosecutor decides to drop charges at the third stage) is most likely to be the product of a change in circumstances that has either eliminated the need for prosecution (e.g., the defendant has been convicted on other charges) or substantially reduced the likelihood of success (e.g., a critical witness is no longer available).

Where the prosecutor in the initial screening process decides in favor of criminal prosecution, other decisions also must be made. Initially, the prosecutor must determine whether the proposed charge is set at the correct level, or whether there is a need to reduce or raise the offense-level recommended by the police. In many instances, the prosecutor must also consider the potential for charging

---

[13] Complete statistics on prosecutor screening are available only for a comparatively small group of states. These statistics show considerable variation among prosecutors' offices as to the frequency of their decisions not to prosecute at any one stage of the process. At the same time, however, the statistics present a fairly consistent picture of the significance of the totality of the non-prosecution decisions made by prosecutors through the process as a whole. For states providing statistics on the disposition of felony arrests, prosecutorial non-prosecution decisions invariably account for the second highest percentage of dispositions, trailing only guilty pleas (albeit, trailing by a wide margin. e.g., 25% non-prosecutions to 70% guilty pleas).

[14] A diversion program offers the arrestee the opportunity to avoid conviction if he or she is willing to perform prescribed "rehabilitative steps" (e.g., making restitution to the victim, undertaking a treatment program). The diversion agreement operates, in effect, to place the arrestee on a probationary status without conviction. In many jurisdictions, this is achieved by the prosecutor promising not to file charges if the arrestee complies with the prescribed conditions. In others, charges initially are filed with the court, then held in abeyance for the period during which the arrestee is to meet the prescribed conditions, and dismissed with prejudice once the arrestee meets those conditions. If the arrestee fails to meet the prescribed conditions, the prosecution against the arrestee proceeds (with the charges then filed, if that had not been done previously).

multiple separate offenses (as where the arrested person allegedly committed several separate crimes in a single criminal transaction or engaged in more than one criminal transaction). Here the prosecutor must determine whether the charging instrument should allege all offenses or simply some of the offenses (e.g., only the most serious, or only those easiest to prove). Where the prosecutor chooses to proceed on more than one charge, the law may give to the prosecutor another choice—whether to bring the charges in a single prosecution or in multiple, separate prosecutions. A similar choice must be made where several people have been arrested for their participation in same crime, as each can be proceeded against separately or the group can be prosecuted jointly through a single charging instrument naming multiple defendants.

Step 5: Filing the complaint. Assuming that the police decide to charge and that decision is not overturned in a pre-filing prosecutorial review, the next step is the filing of charges with the magistrate court, which must be done prior to the arrestee's scheduled first appearance (see step 7 infra). The initial charging instrument commonly is called a "complaint". For most offenses, the complaint will be a fairly brief document. Its basic function is to set forth concisely the allegation that the accused, at a particular time and place, committed specified acts constituting a violation of a particular criminal statute. The complaint will be signed by a "complainant," a person who swears under oath that he or she believes the factual allegations of the complaint to be true. The complainant usually will be either the victim or the investigating officer. When an officer-complainant did not observe the offense being committed, but relies on information received from the victim or other witnesses, the officer ordinarily will note that the allegations in the complaint are based on "information and belief." With the filing of the complaint, the arrestee officially becomes a "defendant" in a criminal prosecution.[15]

Step 6: Magistrate review of the arrest. Following the filing of the complaint and prior to or at the start of the first appearance (see step 7 infra), the magistrate must undertake what is often described as the "*Gerstein* review." As prescribed by the Supreme Court's decision in *Gerstein v. Pugh*, [fn. a, p. 177] if the accused was arrested without a warrant and remains in custody (or is subject to restraints on his liberty as a condition of stationhouse bail), the magistrate must determine that there exists probable cause for the offense charged in the complaint. This ordinarily is an *ex parte* determination, similar to that made in the issuance of an arrest warrant. If the magistrate finds that probable cause has not been established, she will direct the prosecution to promptly produce more information or release the arrested person. Such instances are exceedingly rare, however. Since a judicial probable cause determination already has been made where an arrest warrant was issued, a *Gerstein* review is not required in such cases (or in case in which the arrestee was indicted by a grand jury prior to his arrest).

Step 7: The first appearance. An arrestee who is held in custody, or who otherwise remains subject to custodial restraints (as where released on

---

[15] Where the pre-arrest investigation was conducted through the grand jury (see step 1 supra), the grand jury is likely to have issued an indictment even before the person charged in the indictment is arrestee. Here, an arrestee became a "defendant" (through the charge of the indictment) even before he was arrested.

stationhouse bail), must be presented before the magistrate court within a time period typically specified as either 24 or 48 hours. Since the arrestee is now a defendant (the complaint having been filed), and this is his initial appearance in that capacity, this proceeding before the magistrate is described in many jurisdictions as the "first appearance," (although other jurisdictions use "initial presentment," "preliminary arraignment," or "arraignment on the complaint"). Where the accused person was not arrested by the police, but issued a citation (see step 2 supra), the 24 or 48 hour timing requirement does not apply and the first appearance may be scheduled a week or more after the issuance of the citation.

The first appearance in a felony case commonly is a quite brief proceeding. Initially, the magistrate will inform the defendant of the charge in the complaint, of various rights possessed by the defendant, and of the nature of further proceedings. The range of rights and proceedings mentioned will vary from one jurisdiction to another. Commonly, the magistrate will inform the defendant of his right to remain silent, and warn him that anything he says to the court or the police may be used against him at trial. The defendant always will be informed of at least the very next proceeding in the process, which usually will be a preliminary hearing. The magistrate also will set a date for the preliminary hearing unless the defendant at that point waives his right to that hearing.

Where the felony defendant is not represented by counsel at the first appearance, the magistrate's responsibilities include making certain that the defendant is aware of his right to be represented by counsel, including the right to counsel funded by the state if the defendant is indigent. In some jurisdictions the indigency determination is made at the first appearance, and the magistrate initiates the appointment of state-funded counsel on a finding of indigency. In others, the indigency determination will be made prior to the first appearance, by a court administrator or public defender, and the assignment of counsel will have occurred prior to the first appearance.

One of the most important first-appearance functions of the magistrate is to fix the terms under which the defendant can obtain his release from custody pending the disposition of the charges against him. This process is still described as "setting bail," although release today often is conditioned on non-financial requirements (e.g., curfew and a restriction on travel) rather than traditional "bail" (i.e., the posting of a security, such as cash or a bond). A person released on no more than a promise to appear at trial is said to be "released on his own recognizance." Setting bail requires consideration of various information relating to the alleged offense (e.g., aggravating circumstances) and the offender (e.g., prior criminal history and community ties). This information may be collected prior to the first appearance (typically by a pretrial services agency) or at the first appearance itself. In many jurisdictions, various classes of arrestees are drug-tested (typically using a urine sample) as part of the pre-appearance information gathering process. Drug-testing may also be imposed as a condition of release.

Where the magistrate imposes a financial condition (e.g., requires a bailbond), and the defendant is not prepared to meet that condition, the defendant will be held in custody in a jail and will remain there until the financial condition is met or there is a final disposition of the charges. Available statistics indicate that, in metropolitan judicial districts, a substantial portion of felony defendants (e.g., 30–40%) fail to gain their release prior to the final disposition of the charges. Many jurisdictions also have a "preventive detention" exception to the setting of bail. Here, upon a necessary finding of danger or likely flight, the magistrate does not set release terms, but instead orders that the defendant continue to be held in custody pending final disposition of the charges.

Step 8: Preliminary hearing. Following the first appearance, the next scheduled step in a felony case ordinarily is the preliminary hearing (sometimes called a preliminary "examination"). All but a handful of our fifty-two jurisdictions grant the felony defendant a right to a preliminary hearing, to be held within a specified period (typically, within a week or two if the defendant does not gain pretrial release and within a few weeks if released). Actual use of the preliminary hearing varies considerably from one jurisdiction to another (and sometimes from one judicial district to another in the same jurisdiction). In many jurisdictions, the prosecution, if it so chooses, can preclude a preliminary hearing by obtaining a grand jury indictment prior to the scheduled date of the hearing. Also, in some jurisdictions, defendants who intend to plead guilty commonly waive the hearing and move directly to the trial court. The end result is that preliminary hearings are held in almost all felony prosecutions in some jurisdictions, in a substantial majority in others, in a significant minority in still others, and almost never in several jurisdictions.

Where the preliminary hearing is held, it will provide, like grand jury review (see step 9 infra), a screening of the decision to charge by a neutral body. In the preliminary hearing, that neutral body is the magistrate, who must determine whether, on the evidence presented, there is sufficient evidence to send the case forward. Ordinarily, the magistrate will already have determined that probable cause exists as part of the *ex parte* screening of the complaint (see step 6 supra). The preliminary hearing, however, provides screening in an adversary proceeding in which both sides are represented by counsel. Typically, the prosecution will present its key witnesses and the defense will limit its response to the cross-examination of those witnesses (although the defense has the right to present its own witnesses and may occasionally do so).

If the magistrate concludes that the evidence presented is sufficient for the prosecution to move forward (usually that it establishes probable cause), she will "bind the case over" to the next stage in the proceedings. In an indictment jurisdiction (see step 9 infra), the case is bound over to the grand jury, and in a jurisdiction that permits the direct filing of an information (see step 10 infra), the case is bound over directly to the general trial court. If the magistrate finds that the evidence supports only a lesser charge (e.g., a misdemeanor), the charge will be reduced. If the magistrate finds that the evidence is insufficient to support any charge, the prosecution will be terminated.

Step 9: Grand jury review. Although almost all American jurisdictions still have provisions authorizing grand jury screening of felony charges, such screening is mandatory only in those jurisdictions requiring felony prosecutions to be instituted by an "indictment," a charging instrument issued by the grand jury. In a majority of the states, the prosecution is now allowed to proceed either by grand jury indictment or by information at its option. Because prosecutors in these states most often choose to prosecute by information, the states providing this option commonly are referred to as "information" states. Eighteen states, the federal system, and the District of Columbia currently require grand jury indictments for all felony prosecutions. These jurisdictions commonly are described as "indictment" jurisdictions. Four additional states are "limited indictment" jurisdictions, requiring prosecution by indictment only for their most severely punished offenses (capital, life imprisonment, or both).

The grand jury typically is selected randomly from the same pool of prospective jurors (the "venire") as the trial jury. Unlike the trial jury, however, it sits not for a single case, but for a term that may range from one to several months. As in the case of the magistrate at the preliminary hearing, the primary function of the grand jury is to determine whether there is sufficient evidence to justify a trial on the charge sought by the prosecution. The grand jury, however, participates in a screening process quite different from the preliminary hearing. It meets in a closed session and hears only the evidence presented by the prosecution. The defendant has no right to offer his own evidence or to be present during grand jury proceedings.

If a majority of the grand jurors conclude that the prosecution's evidence is sufficient, the grand jury will issue the indictment requested by the prosecutor. The indictment will set forth a brief description of the offense charged, and the grand jury's approval of that charge will be indicated by its designation of the indictment as a "true bill." If the grand jury majority refuses to approve the proposed indictment, the charges against the defendant will be dismissed.

Step 10: The filing of the indictment or information. If an indictment is issued, it will be filed with the general trial court and will replace the complaint as the accusatory instrument in the case. Where grand jury review either is not required or has been waived, an information will be filed with the trial court. Like the indictment, the information is a charging instrument which replaces the complaint, but it is issued by the prosecutor rather than the grand jury.

Step 11: Arraignment on the information or indictment. After the indictment or information has been filed, the felony defendant is "arraigned"—i.e., he is brought before the felony trial court, informed of the charges against him, and asked to enter a plea of guilty, not guilty, or, as is permitted under some circumstances, *nolo contendere* (a plea in which the defendant accepts a judgment of conviction, but does not admit guilt). In the end, most of those felony defendants whose cases reach the trial court will plead guilty. At the arraignment, however, they are likely to enter a plea of not guilty. Where there has not been a preliminary hearing, defense counsel probably will not be fully apprised of the strength of the prosecution's case at this point in the proceedings. Also, in the vast majority of jurisdictions, guilty pleas in felony cases are the product of plea negotiations with the prosecution, and in many places, that process does not start until after the arraignment. When the defendant enters a plea of not guilty at the arraignment, the judge will set a trial date, but the expectation generally is that the trial will not be held.

Step 12: *Pretrial motions.* In most jurisdictions, a broad range of objections must be raised by a pretrial motion. Those motions commonly present challenges to the institution of the prosecution (e.g., claims regarding the grand jury indictment process), attacks upon the sufficiency of the charging instrument, challenges to the scope, location, and timing of the prosecution (claiming improper joinder of charges or parties, improper "venue"—i.e., the case is being prosecuted in the wrong judicial district, or violation of speedy trial requirements), requests for discovery (see step 13 infra) when there is a dispute over what is discoverable, and requests for the suppression of evidence allegedly obtained through a constitutional violation. While some pretrial motions are made only by defendants who intend to go to trial, other motions (e.g., for discovery) may benefit as well defendants who expect in the end to plead guilty. Nevertheless, pretrial motions are likely to be made in only a small portion of the felony cases that reach the trial court. Their use does vary considerably, however, with the nature of the case. In narcotics cases, for example, motions to suppress are quite common. In the typical forgery case, on the other, pretrial motions of any type are quite rare.

Step 13: *Pretrial discovery.* Pretrial discovery is the process by which the prosecution and defense mutually disclose to each other some aspects of the evidence that they probably would present at trial. Discovery is aimed not only at avoiding "trial by surprise," but also at facilitating pretrial settlement of the case through a negotiated plea. States vary in the scope of the disclosure they require, although the prosecution universally is required to disclose substantially more than the defense. The prosecution, for example, is required to disclose certain relevant information in its possession that it does not intend to use at trial (e.g., all forensic testing, whether or not the results will be used). In jurisdictions with the narrowest discovery requirements, neither side is required to disclose the names of the witnesses it might call at trial.

Step 14: *Guilty plea negotiation and acceptance.* Guilty pleas in felony cases most often are the product of a plea agreement under which the prosecution offers certain concessions in return for the defendant's plea. The offering of concessions lies in the discretion of the prosecutor, and there is considerable variation among prosecutors' offices as to what types of concessions will be offered to defendants charged with particular offenses. There also is considerable variation as to the negotiation process (e.g., whether the prosecutor will actually "bargain," or simply present a "take-it-or leave-it offer"). Where a plea is entered as result of an agreement with the prosecutor, that agreement must be set forth on the record before the trial court. The trial judge will review the agreement to ensure that its terms are within the law, but cannot second-guess its soundness as a smaller of criminal justice policy.

The trial judge's primary responsibility in accepting a guilty plea is to ensure that the defendant understands the legal consequences of entering a guilty plea and the terms of the plea agreement. If that understanding is present, and there exists a factual basis for the plea (typically provided by the defendant admitting in court the acts constituting the offense), the plea will be accepted and a date set for sentencing.

Step 15: The trial. Assuming that there has not been a dismissal and the defendant has not entered a guilty plea (or a *nolo contendere* plea), the next step in the criminal process is the trial. In most respects, the criminal trial resembles the civil trial. There are, however, several distinguishing features that are either unique to criminal trials or of special importance in such trials. These include (1) the presumption of defendant's innocence, (2) the requirement of proof beyond a reasonable doubt, (3) the right of the defendant not to take the stand, (4) the exclusion of evidence obtained by the state in an illegal manner, and (5) the more frequent use (by the prosecution) of incriminating statements previously made by the defendant (often to police).

As noted previously, most felony cases are likely to be disposed of either by a guilty plea or a dismissal. In the vast majority of jurisdictions, of those felony prosecutions reaching the trial court, no more than 10% will be resolved by trial. Setting aside dismissals, and looking only to guilty pleas and trials, the ratio of guilty pleas to trial quite often will be 12 to 1 or higher.

In felony cases, the defendant is entitled to a jury trial, but in many jurisdictions, for certain types of offenses, defendants commonly will waive the jury, in favor of a bench trial. Where the trial is to a jury, the verdict, whether for acquittal or conviction, in all but six states, must be unanimous. Where the jury cannot reach agreement, it is commonly described as a "hung jury". Such a jury is discharged without reaching a verdict, and the case may be retried.

The median time frame from the arrest of the defendant to the start of the felony trial can exceed a year in judicial districts with slow moving dockets, but for most judicial districts, it is likely to fall within the range of 5–8 months. The median will be influenced, in particular, by the mix of jury and bench trials, as the time frame tends to be considerably longer for jury trials. While most jurisdictions have speedy trial requirements that impose time limits of 6 months or less, there are various excludable time periods (for factors such as witness unavailability and the processing of motions) which commonly extend the time limit by at least a few months.

In state courts, most jury trials will be completed within 2–3 days. A key variable affecting the length of the trial is the character of the crime charged, as certain types of crimes (e.g., white collar offenses and capital homicides) produce trials substantially longer than the typical felony. The prevalence of complex charges explains, in large part, why trials lasting a week or more are so common in the federal courts. In general, trials to the bench are considerably shorter, and in state courts, unlikely to last more than a day.

Whether a criminal case is tried to the bench or the jury, the odds favor conviction over acquittal. A fairly typical ratio for felony charges will be three convictions for every acquittal. That ratio may vary significantly, however, with the nature of the offense. In some jurisdictions, the rate of conviction at trial tends

to be substantially lower (though still above 50%) for some crimes (e.g., rape) than for others (e.g., drug trafficking).

Step 16: Sentencing. Following conviction, the next step in the process is the determination of the sentence. In all but a handful of jurisdictions (those allowing for jury sentencing, even apart from capital punishment), the sentence determination is the exclusive function of the court. Basically three different types of sentences may be used: financial sanctions (e.g., fines, restitution orders); some form of release into the community (e.g., probation, unsupervised release, house arrest); and incarceration in a jail (for lesser sentences) or prison (for longer sentences). The process applied in determining the sentence is shaped in considerable part by the sentencing options made available to the court by the legislature. For a particular offense, the court may have no choice. The legislature may have prescribed that conviction automatically carries with it a certain sentence and there is nothing left for the court to do except impose that sentence. Most frequently, however, legislative narrowing of options on a particular offense does not go beyond eliminating the community release option (by requiring incarceration) and setting maximums (and sometimes mandatory minimums) for incarceration and fines. However, states vary considerably in shaping the court's authority to choose within available options, particularly as to the length of incarceration. Their approaches include: allowing the sentencing judge considerable discretion within a broad range set by the legislature; narrowing the range and the discretion by imposing certain mandated minimums based on specified factual findings, and channeling discretion through the use of sentencing guidelines that also depend upon factual determinations.

The process utilized in felony sentencing varies to some extent according to whether judicial discretion is broad or is channeled or limited by guideline or legislative reference to specific sentencing circumstances. In all jurisdictions, the process is designed to obtain for the court information beyond that which will have come to its attention in the course of trial or in the acceptance of a guilty plea. The primary vehicle here is the presentence report prepared by the probation department, although the prosecution and defense commonly will be allowed to present additional information and to challenge the information contained in the presentence report. The presentation of this information is not subject to the rules governing the presentation of information at trial. The rules of evidence do not apply, and neither the prosecution nor the defense has a right to call witnesses or to cross-examine the sources of adverse information presented in the presentence report or in any additional documentation presented by the opposing side. However, where the sentencing authority of the judge is restricted or channeled by the reference to specific factors, a judge commonly is required to make findings of fact as to those factors. Here, if relevant facts are in dispute, the court commonly will find it necessary to hold an evidentiary hearing and to utilize trial-type procedures to resolve that dispute.

Step 17: Appeals.[16] For criminal convictions imposed by the general trial court, the initial appeal is to the intermediate appellate court. That appeal ordinarily is guaranteed as a matter of right. The defendant may seek further appellate review from the state's appellate court of last resort (usually, but not always, titled the "Supreme Court"), but review there lies in the discretion of the court. In the handful of states that have no intermediate appellate court, the initial and final appeal within the state system is to the state's court of last resort. All states allow the convicted defendant to appeal his conviction, and many allow an appeal as to sentence as well.

The vast majority of appeals in felony cases are taken by convicted defendants who were sentenced to imprisonment. Imprisoned defendants convicted on a guilty plea are a part of this group, but their portion of the appeals is likely to be small where the appeal is limited to the conviction (the potential grounds for challenging a guilty plea conviction being considerably narrower than the potential grounds for challenging a trial conviction). Reversals of conviction on appeals as of right vary with the state, but a reversal rate in the 5–10% range is fairly typical (with the rate somewhat higher where reversals in part—not overturning the entire conviction—are included). Where the state defendant raised a constitutional issue in his state appeal, he may seek further review on that issue in the Supreme Court of the United States, but the Supreme Court grants review (by granting a petition for a "writ of certiorari") to only a very small percentage of the defendants seeking review.

Step 18: Collateral remedies. After the appellate process is exhausted, imprisoned defendants may be able to use postconviction procedures to challenge their conviction, although the grounds for challenge tend to be limited (e.g., to constitutional violations). Since these procedures are separate from the basic criminal justice process (indeed, some are viewed as civil in nature), they are described as "collateral remedies." The primary common law collateral remedy is the writ of habeas corpus. That writ allows a convicted defendant to bring an action against the person holding him in custody (typically the prison warden), challenging that custody as based on a constitutionally invalid conviction.

Congress by statute has made the habeas writ available to state prisoners to bring habeas actions in federal courts challenging the constitutionality of their state convictions. Many of the Supreme Court opinions included in this volume review state convictions that were challenged through habeas actions filed in a federal district court, with that court's ruling subsequently appealed (by the losing party, defendant or state) to the federal Court of Appeals, and the Supreme Court than granting review of the Court of Appeals' ruling. Prior to a change in the federal habeas statute in 1996, federal courts on habeas review applied their own independent interpretation of the Constitution in determining whether the state court correctly resolved the defendant's constitutional claim. Since 1996, the

---

[16] The focus here is on defense appeals from a conviction. The prosecution may appeal from certain types of dismissals, but may not appeal from an acquittal. Since the percentage of dismissals over the objection of the prosecution is low, and prosecutors do not regularly appeal such rulings (even when they could do so), prosecution appeals are infrequent as compared to defense appeals.

review standard is whether the state court ruling "was contrary to, or involved an unreasonable application of, clearly established Federal law, as determined by the supreme court of the United States; or (2) resulted in a decision that was based on an unreasonable determination of the facts in light of the evidence presented in the state court proceeding." 28 U.S.C.A. § 2254(d).

CHAPTER 2

THE NATURE AND SCOPE OF DUE PROCESS; THE APPLICABILITY OF THE BILL OF RIGHTS TO THE STATES

■ ■ ■

1. "FUNDAMENTAL RIGHTS" AND "INCORPORATION"

The first eight amendments were enacted as limitations solely upon the federal government. But some argued that the Fourteenth Amendment had "totally incorporated" all the provisions of the Bill of Rights, i.e., made them fully applicable to the states. A series of rulings, spread over several decades, rejected this "total incorporation" interpretation of the Fourteenth Amendment (although the Court was often divided, including one 5–4 ruling). Instead, the Court adopted what has been called the "fundamental rights" or "ordered liberty" interpretation of the Fourteenth Amendment's due process clause, an approach that prevailed until the early 1960s. This approach finds no necessary relationship between the content of the Fourteenth Amendment and the guarantees of the Bill of Rights. It regards the due process clause as simply incorporating all principles of justice "implicit in the concept of ordered liberty" or "so rooted in the traditions and conscience of our people as to be ranked as fundamental." As applied to criminal procedure, this approach requires only that the state afford a defendant "that fundamental fairness essential to the very concept of justice." This standard could encompass all, some, or none of the protection that a Bill of Rights guarantee provided against federal governmental action. As Justice Harlan observed [p. 42], the key was not that the particular protection "had been found in the Bill of Rights," but that it was "deemed * * * fundamental."

While the presence of a Bill of Rights guarantee is not decisive under this approach, neither is its absence. A particular practice may violate "fundamental fairness" even though it is not specifically prohibited by the Bill of Rights. As recognized in rulings applying the Fifth Amendment's due process clause, the due process clause of the Fourteenth Amendment "has an independent potency." See Frankfurter, J., explaining the ruling in *Rochin v. California* [fn. a, p. 39].

In *McDonald v. City of Chicago*, 561 U.S. 742 (2010), the Supreme Court offered a brief review of both the period in which this "fundamental fairness" approach prevailed and the eventual displacement of that approach with the "selective incorporation" doctrine. *McDonald* followed *District of Columbia v. Heller*, 554 U.S. 570 (2008), where the Court had held that the Second Amendment protects the individual's right to keep and bear arms for the purpose of self-defense.

31

The *Heller* Court had struck down a District of Columbia law that banned the possession of handguns in the home. After *Heller* was decided, petitioners filed a federal suit against the City of Chicago, maintaining that Chicago's handgun ban violated the Fourteenth Amendment. In *McDonald*, a 5–4 majority agreed.

Justice Alito (joined by Roberts C.J., and Scalia and Kennedy, J.J.) reached this conclusion via Fourteenth Amendment incorporation of the Second Amendment under the Fourteenth Amendment's due process clause. Justice Thomas agreed that the Second Amendment is "fully applicable to the States," "fundamental" to the American "scheme of ordered liberty" and "deeply rooted in the Nation's history and tradition." However, he could not agree that the Second Amendment is enforceable against the States through a clause that speaks only "to process." Instead, he viewed the right to keep and bear arms as a privilege of American citizenship applicable to the States through the Fourteenth Amendment's privileges or immunities clause.

In Part ID of his opinion, speaking for a majority of the Court at this point, Justice Alito looked back on various cases dealing with the relationship between the Bill of Rights and Fourteenth Amendment Due Process:

"[During an earlier era], even when a right set out in the Bill of Rights was held to fall within the conception of due process, the protection or remedies afforded against state infringement sometimes differed from the protection or remedies provided against abridgement by the Federal Government. To give an example, in *Betts v. Brady* [p. 376] the Court held that, although the Sixth Amendment required the appointment of counsel in all federal criminal cases in which the defendant was unable to retain an attorney, the Due Process Clause required appointment of counsel in state criminal proceedings only where 'want of counsel in [the] particular [case] resulted in a conviction lacking [in] fundamental fairness.' Similarly, in *Wolf v. Colorado* [p. 59], the Court held that the 'core of the Fourth Amendment' was implicit in the concept of ordered liberty and thus 'enforceable against the States through the Due Process Clause,' but that the exclusionary rule, which applied in federal cases, did not apply to the States.

"An alternative theory regarding the relationship between the Bill of Rights and § 1 of the Fourteenth Amendment was championed by Justice Black. This theory held that § 1 of the Fourteenth Amendment totally incorporated all of the provisions of the Bill of Rights. [As] Justice Black noted, the chief congressional proponents of the Fourteenth Amendment espoused the view that the Amendment made the Bill of Rights applicable to the States * * *. Nonetheless, the Court never has embraced Justice Black's 'total incorporation' theory.

"While Justice Black's theory was never adopted, the Court eventually moved in that direction by initiating what has been called a process of 'selective incorporation,' i.e., the Court began to hold that the Due Process Clause fully incorporates particular rights contained in the first eight Amendments. See, e.g., *Gideon v. Wainwright* (1963) [p. 380]; *Malloy v. Hogan* (1964) [fn. a, p. 33]; *Duncan v. Louisiana* (1968) [p. 35].

"The decisions during this time abandoned three of the previously noted characteristics of the earlier period. The Court made it clear that the governing standard is not whether *any* 'civilized system [can] be imagined that would not accord the particular protection.' *Duncan*. Instead, the Court inquired whether a particular Bill of Rights guarantee is fundamental to *our* scheme of ordered liberty and system of justice. * * *

"The Court also shed any reluctance to hold that rights guaranteed by the Bill of Rights met the requirements for protection under the Due Process Clause. The Court eventually incorporated almost all of the provisions of the Bill of Rights. Only a handful of the Bill of Rights protections remain unincorporated.[13]

"Finally, the Court abandoned the 'notion that the Fourteenth Amendment applies to the States only a watered-down, subjective version of the individual guarantees of the Bill of Rights', stating that it would be 'incongruous' to apply different standards 'depending on whether the claim was asserted in a state or federal court.' *Malloy*.[a] Instead, the court decisively held that incorporated Bill of Rights protections 'are all to be enforced against the States under the Fourteenth Amendment according to the same standards that protect those personal rights against federal encroachment.' Id. See also *Mapp v. Ohio* [p. 62].

"Employing this approach, the Court overruled earlier decisions in which it had held that particular Bill of Rights guarantees or remedies did not apply to the States. See, e.g., *Mapp*; *Gideon*; and *Malloy*."

2. THE SHIFT TO "SELECTIVE INCORPORATION"

As noted in *McDonald*, in the 1960s, the Warren Court "selectively incorporated" or "absorbed" more and more of the specific provisions of the Bill of Rights under the Fourteen Amendment due process. Although strongly criticized as an artificial compromise between the fundamental rights and total incorporation approaches, and lacking even the "internal consistency" of the total incorporation view of the Fourteenth Amendment (Harlan, J., dissenting in *Duncan*), selective incorporation was firmly established in the *Duncan* ruling. The

---

[13] [T]he only [other] rights not fully incorporated are (1) the Third Amendment's protection against quartering of soldiers; (2) the Fifth Amendment's grand jury indictment requirement; [and] (3) the Seventh Amendment right to a jury trial in civil cases. * * *

We never have decided whether the Third Amendment * * * applies to the States through the Due Process Clause. * * * Our governing decisions regarding the Grand Jury Clause of the Fifth Amendment and the Seventh Amendment's civil jury requirement long predate the era of selective incorporation.

[The Supreme Court recently incorporated the Eighth Amendment's prohibition on excessive fines in *Timbs v. Indiana*, 139 S.Ct. 682 (2019), and the Sixth Amendment right to a unanimous jury verdict in *Ramos v. Louisiana*, 140 S.Ct. 1390 (2020). For a more extended discussion of *Ramos*, see infra p. 798.]

[a] In *Malloy*, the Court applied the Fifth Amendment's privilege against self-incrimination to the states to the same extent it applied to the federal government. Justice Brennan observed for a majority of the Court that recently various provisions of the Bill of Rights had been applied to the states according to the same standards protecting these rights against federal encroachment. He mentioned "the guarantees of the First Amendment, the prohibition of unreasonable searches and seizures of the Fourth Amendment [*Mapp v. Ohio*, p. 62], and the right to counsel guaranteed by the Sixth Amendment, *Gideon v. Wainwright* [p. 380]."

adoption of this position was accompanied by a movement towards a broader view of the nature of "fundamental procedural rights," as described in *McDonald* (see p. 33). The end result was the incorporation of all Bill of Rights' guarantees bearing on the criminal justice process, except for the Fifth Amendment's grand jury clause. See fn. 13 of *McDonald* [p. 33].

"Selective incorporation" combines aspects of both the "fundamental rights" and "total incorporation" approaches. It accepts the basic premise of the fundamental rights proponents that the Fourteenth Amendment encompasses only rights that are "of the very essence of the scheme of ordered liberty." It also recognizes that not all rights enumerated in the Bill of Rights are necessarily fundamental and that other rights may be fundamental even though not found in the first eight Amendments. But the "selective incorporation" approach rejects the fundamental rights interpretation insofar as that view emphasizes the "totality of the circumstances" in the particular case.

In determining whether an enumerated right is "fundamental," therefore, the selective incorporation doctrine requires that the Court look at the total right guaranteed by the particular Bill of Rights provision, not merely at a single aspect of that right nor the application of that aspect in the case before it. If a particular guarantee is determined to be "fundamental," that provision is incorporated into the Fourteenth Amendment and applied to the states *to the same extent* that it applies to the federal government—or, as critics of this approach expressed it, applied "jot-for-jot and case-for-case" (Harlan, J., joined by Stewart, J., concurring in *Duncan v. Louisiana,* infra); "bag and baggage, however securely or insecurely affixed they may be by law and precedent to federal proceedings" (Fortas, J., concurring in *Duncan*).[a]

---

[a]   To say that a right has been incorporated against the States is different from saying that the right should be retroactively applied to cases involving criminal defendants who were convicted at trials that took place *before* the Supreme Court recognized and incorporated the right in question. The Supreme Court has decided that newly-recognized constitutional rights are retroactively applicable to individuals whose convictions are not yet final, meaning that they have not completed the direct appellate review process. *See Griffith v. Kentucky,* 479 U.S. 314 (1987). At the same time, the Supreme Court has held that there is a presumption that new constitutional rules will not be retroactively applied to defendants whose convictions are final, meaning that they have completed their direct appeals and are at the state or federal postconviction stages. *See Teague v. Lane,* 489 U.S. 288 (1989).

In *Teague,* the Court articulated two exceptions—situations where a new rule of criminal procedure would be applied retroactively even to defendants whose convictions were already final. First, a new substantive constitutional rule applies retroactively if it either (a) provides that the conduct for which the defendant was prosecuted is constitutionally protected or (b) prohibits a certain category of punishment for a class of defendants based on their status or offense. *See, e.g., Montgomery v. Louisiana,* 577 U.S. 190 (2016); *Welch v. United States,* 136 S.Ct. 1257 (2016); *Penry v. Lynaugh,* 492 U.S. 302 (1989).

Second, a new procedural constitutional rule applies retroactively if it is deemed to be a watershed rule of criminal procedure that is necessary to prevent "an impermissibly large risk of an inaccurate conviction" and "alter[s] our understanding of the bedrock procedural elements essential to the fairness of a proceeding." *Whorton v. Bockting,* 549 U.S. 406, 418 (2007). In *Bockting,* the Supreme Court described this second exception as "extremely narrow," noted that *Gideon v. Wainwright* is the only case that it has identified as qualifying under this exception, and emphasized that "it is 'unlikely' that any such rules 'ha[ve] yet to emerge.' " *Id.* at 417. In *Edwards v. Vannoy,* 141 S.Ct. 1547 (2021), the Supreme Court eliminated this second exception noting that "[c]ontinuing to articulate a theoretical exception that never actually applies in practice offers false

DUNCAN V. LOUISIANA

391 U.S. 145, 88 S.Ct. 1444, 20 L.Ed.2d 491 (1968).

JUSTICE WHITE delivered the opinion of the Court.

[Appellant] was convicted of simple battery [which under Louisiana law] is a misdemeanor, punishable by two years' imprisonment and a $300 fine. Appellant sought trial by jury, but because the Louisiana Constitution grants jury trials only in cases in which capital punishment or imprisonment at hard labor may be imposed, the trial judge denied the request. Appellant was convicted and sentenced to serve 60 days in the parish prison and pay a fine of $150.

* * * Because we believe that trial by jury in criminal cases is fundamental to the American scheme of justice, we hold that the Fourteenth Amendment guarantees a right of jury trial in all criminal cases which—were they to be tried in a federal court—would come within the Sixth Amendment's guarantee.[14] Since we consider the appeal before us to be such a case, we hold that the Constitution was violated when appellant's demand for jury trial was refused.

[B]y the time our Constitution was written, jury trial in criminal cases had been in existence in England for several centuries and carried impressive credentials traced by many to Magna Carta. Its preservation and proper operation as a protection against arbitrary rule were among the major objectives of the revolutionary settlement which was expressed in the Declaration and Bill of Rights of 1689. * * *

---

hope to defendants, distorts the law, misleads judges, and wastes the resources of defense counsel, prosecutors, and courts." *Id.* at 1560.

[14] In one sense recent cases applying provisions of the first eight amendments to the States represent a new approach to the "incorporation" debate. Earlier the Court can be seen as having asked, when inquiring into whether some particular procedural safeguard was required of a State, if a civilized system could be imagined that would not accord the particular protection. [The] recent cases, on the other hand, have proceeded upon the valid assumption that state criminal processes are not imaginary and theoretical schemes but actual systems bearing virtually every characteristic of the common-law system that has been developing contemporaneously in England and in this country. The question thus is whether given this kind of system a particular procedure is fundamental—whether, that is, a procedure is necessary to an Anglo-American regime of ordered liberty. [Of] immediate relevance for this case are the Court's holdings that the States must comply with certain provisions of the Sixth Amendment, specifically that the States may not refuse a speedy trial, confrontation of witnesses, and the assistance, at state expense if necessary, of counsel. Of each of these determinations that a constitutional provision originally written to bind the Federal Government should bind the States as well it might be said that the limitation in question is not necessarily fundamental to fairness in every criminal system that might be imagined but is fundamental in the context of the criminal processes maintained by the American States.

When the inquiry is approached in this way the question whether the States can impose criminal punishment without granting a jury trial appears quite different from the way it appeared in the older cases opining that States might abolish jury trial. See, e.g., *Maxwell v. Dow*, 176 U.S. 581 (1900). A criminal process which was fair and equitable but used no juries is easy to imagine. It would make use of alternative guarantees and protections which would serve the purposes that the jury serves in the English and American systems. Yet no American State has undertaken to construct such a system. Instead, every American State, including Louisiana, uses the jury extensively, and imposes very serious punishments only after a trial at which the defendant has a right to a jury's verdict. In every State, including Louisiana, the structure and style of the criminal process—the supporting framework and the subsidiary procedures—are of the sort that naturally complement jury trial, and have developed in connection with and in reliance upon jury trial.

Jury trial came to America with English colonists, and received strong support from them. Royal interference with the jury trial was deeply resented. Among the resolutions adopted by the First Congress of the American Colonies (the Stamp Act Congress) on October 19, 1765—resolutions deemed by their authors to state "the most essential rights and liberties of the colonists"—was the declaration: "That trial by jury is the inherent and invaluable right of every British subject in these colonies."

[The] constitutions adopted by the original States guaranteed jury trial. Also, the constitution of every State entering the Union thereafter in one form or another protected the right to jury trial in criminal cases. * * *

Jury trial continues to receive strong support. The laws of every State guarantee a right to jury trial in serious criminal cases; no State has dispensed with it; nor are there significant movements underway to do so. * * *

We are aware of prior cases in this Court in which the prevailing opinion contains statements contrary to our holding today that the right to jury trial in serious criminal cases is a fundamental right and hence must be recognized by the States as part of their obligation to extend due process of law to all persons within their jurisdiction. Louisiana relies especially on *Maxwell v. Dow; Palko;* and *Snyder v. Massachusetts,* 291 U.S. 97 (1934). None of these cases, however, dealt with a State which had purported to dispense entirely with a jury trial in serious criminal cases. * * *

The guarantees of jury trial in the Federal and State Constitutions reflect a profound judgment about the way in which law should be enforced and justice administered. A right to jury trial is granted to criminal defendants in order to prevent oppression by the Government. Those who wrote our constitutions knew from history and experience that it was necessary to protect against unfounded criminal charges brought to eliminate enemies and against judges too responsive to the voice of higher authority. The framers of the constitutions strove to create an independent judiciary but insisted upon further protection against arbitrary action. Providing an accused with the right to be tried by a jury of his peers gave him an inestimable safeguard against the corrupt or overzealous prosecutor and against the compliant, biased, or eccentric judge. If the defendant preferred the commonsense judgment of a jury to the more tutored but perhaps less sympathetic reaction of the single judge, he was to have it. Beyond this, the jury trial provisions in the Federal and State Constitutions reflect a fundamental decision about the exercise of official power—a reluctance to entrust plenary powers over the life and liberty of the citizen to one judge or to a group of judges. Fear of unchecked power, so typical of our State and Federal Governments in other respects, found expression in the criminal law in this insistence upon community participation in the determination of guilt or innocence. The deep commitment of the Nation to the right of jury trial in serious criminal cases as a defense against arbitrary law enforcement qualifies for protection under the Due Process Clause of the Fourteenth Amendment, and must therefore be respected by the States.

Of course jury trial has "its weaknesses and the potential for misuse." We are aware of the long debate, especially in this century, among those who write about the administration of justice, as to the wisdom of permitting untrained laymen to determine the facts in civil and criminal proceedings. Although the debate has been intense, with powerful voices on either side, most of the controversy has centered on the jury in civil cases. Indeed, some of the severest critics of civil juries acknowledge that the arguments for criminal juries are much stronger. In addition, at the heart of the dispute have been express or implicit assertions that juries are incapable of adequately understanding evidence or determining issues of fact, and that they are unpredictable, quixotic, and little better than a roll of dice. Yet, the most recent and exhaustive study of the jury in criminal cases concluded that juries do understand the evidence and come to sound conclusions in most of the cases presented to them and that when juries differ with the result at which the judge would have arrived, it is usually because they are serving some of the very purposes for which they were created and for which they are now employed.

The State of Louisiana urges that holding that the Fourteenth Amendment assures a right to jury trial will cast doubt on the integrity of every trial conducted without a jury. Plainly, this is not the import of our holding. * * *

We would not assert [that] every criminal trial—or any particular trial—held before a judge alone is unfair or that a defendant may never be as fairly treated by a judge as he would be by a jury. Thus we hold no constitutional doubts about the practices, common in both federal and state courts, of accepting waivers of jury trial and prosecuting petty crimes without extending a right to jury trial. However, the fact is that in most places more trials for serious crimes are to juries than to a court alone; a great many defendants prefer the judgment of a jury to that of a court. Even where defendants are satisfied with bench trials, the right to a jury trial very likely serves its intended purpose of making judicial or prosecutorial unfairness less likely.

Louisiana's final contention is that even if it must grant jury trials in serious criminal cases, the conviction before us is valid and constitutional because here the petitioner was tried for simple battery and was sentenced to only 60 days in the parish prison. We are not persuaded. It is doubtless true that there is a category of petty crimes or offenses which is not subject to the Sixth Amendment jury trial provision and should not be subject to the Fourteenth Amendment jury trial requirement here applied to the States. [But] the penalty authorized for a particular crime is of major relevance in determining whether it is serious or not and may in itself, if severe enough, subject the trial to the mandates of the Sixth Amendment. [In] the case before us the Legislature of Louisiana has made simple battery a criminal offense punishable by imprisonment for two years and a fine. The question, then is whether a crime carrying such a penalty is an offense which Louisiana may insist on trying without a jury. * * *

In determining whether the length of the authorized prison term or the seriousness of other punishment is enough in itself to require a jury trial, we are counseled [by precedent] to refer to objective criteria, chiefly the existing laws and practices in the Nation. In the federal system, petty offenses are defined as those punishable by no more than six months in prison and a $500 fine. In 49 of the 50 States crimes subject to trial without a jury, which occasionally include simple battery, are punishable by no more than one year in jail. Moreover, in the late 18th century in America crimes triable without a jury were for the most part punishable by no more than a six-month prison term * * *. We need not, however, settle in this case the exact location of the line between petty offenses and serious crimes. It is sufficient for our purposes to hold that a crime punishable by two years in prison is, based on past and contemporary standards in this country, a serious crime and not a petty offense. Consequently, appellant was entitled to a jury trial and it was error to deny it. * * *

JUSTICE BLACK, with whom JUSTICE DOUGLAS joins, concurring.

* * * I said in *Adamson v. California*, 332 U.S. 46 (1947) (dissent), that while I would "extend to all the people of the nation the complete protection of the Bill of Rights," that "[i]f the choice must be between the selective process of the *Palko* decision applying some of the Bill of Rights to the States, or the *Twining* rule applying none of them, I would choose the *Palko* selective process." And I am very happy to support this selective process through which our Court has since the *Adamson* case held most of the specific Bill of Rights' protections applicable to the States to the same extent they are applicable to the Federal Government. * * *

All of these holdings making Bill of Rights' provisions applicable as such to the States mark, of course, a departure from the *Twining* doctrine holding that none of those provisions were enforceable as such against the States. The dissent in this case, however, makes a spirited and forceful defense of that now discredited doctrine.

[In] addition to the adoption of Professor Fairman's "history," the dissent states that "the great words of the four clauses of the first section of the Fourteenth Amendment would have been an exceedingly peculiar way to say that 'The rights heretofore guaranteed against federal intrusion by the first eight amendments are henceforth guaranteed against State intrusion as well.' " In response to this I can say only that the words "No State shall make or enforce any law which shall abridge the privileges or immunities of citizens of the United States" seems to me an eminently reasonable way of expressing the idea that henceforth the Bill of Rights shall apply to the States.[1] What more precious "privilege" of American citizenship could there be than that privilege to claim the protections of our great Bill of Rights? * * *

While I do not wish at this time to discuss at length my disagreement with Brother Harlan's forthright and frank restatement of the now discredited *Twining* doctrine, I do want to point out what appears to me to be the basic difference between us. His view, as was indeed the view of *Twining*, is that "due process is an evolving concept" and therefore that it entails a "gradual process of judicial inclusion and exclusion" to ascertain those "immutable principles [of] free government which no member of the Union may disregard." Thus the Due Process Clause is treated as prescribing no specific and clearly ascertainable constitutional command that judges must obey in interpreting the Constitution, but rather as

---

[1]   My view has been and is that the Fourteenth Amendment, *as a whole,* makes the Bill of Rights applicable to the States. This would certainly include the language of the Privileges and Immunities Clause, as well as the Due Process Clause.

leaving judges free to decide at any particular time whether a particular rule or judicial formulation embodies an "immutable principl[e] of free government" or is "implicit in the concept of ordered liberty," or whether certain conduct "shocks the judge's conscience" or runs counter to some other similar, undefined and undefinable standard.[b] Thus due process, according to my Brother Harlan, is to be a phrase with no permanent meaning, but one which is found to shift from time to time in accordance with judges' predilections and understandings of what is best for the country. If due process means this, the Fourteenth Amendment, in my opinion, might as well have been written that "no person shall be deprived of life, liberty or property except by laws that the judges of the United States Supreme Court shall find to be consistent with the immutable principles of free government." It is impossible for me to believe that such unconfined power is given to judges in our Constitution that is a written one in order to limit governmental power.

Another tenet of the *Twining* doctrine as restated by my Brother Harlan is that "due process of law requires only fundamental fairness." But the "fundamental fairness" test is one on a par with that of shocking the conscience of the Court. Each of such tests depends entirely on the particular judge's idea of ethics and morals instead of requiring him to depend on the boundaries fixed by the written words of the Constitution. Nothing in the history of the phrase "due process of law" suggests that constitutional controls are to depend on any particular judge's sense of values. * * *

Finally I want to add that I am not bothered by the argument that applying the Bill of Rights to the States "according to the same standards that protect those rights against federal encroachment," interferes with our concept of federalism in that it may prevent States from trying novel social and economic experiments. I have never believed that under the guise of federalism the States should be able to experiment with the protections afforded our citizens through the Bill of Rights. [It] seems to me totally inconsistent to advocate on the one hand, the power of this Court to strike down any state law or practice which it finds "unreasonable" or "unfair," and on the other hand urge that the States be given maximum power to develop their own laws and procedures. Yet the due process approach of my Brothers Harlan and Fortas (see other concurring opinion) does just that since in effect it restricts the States to practices which a majority of this Court is willing to approve on a case-by-case basis. No one is more concerned than I that the States be allowed to use the full scope of their powers as their citizens see fit. And that is why I have continually fought against the expansion of this Court's authority over

---

[b]   Although Justice Black cites no case at this point, this appears to be a reference to the famous "stomach-pumping" case of *Rochin v. California*, 342 U.S. 165 (1952). When Rochin swallowed two capsules in the presence of the police he was handcuffed and taken to a hospital. There, at the direction of the police, a doctor forced an emetic solution into Rochin's stomach. This "stomach pumping" produced vomiting—and two morphine capsules.

The Court, per Frankfurter, Jr., held that the morphine should have been excluded from evidence because the methods used to obtain it violated Fourteenth Amendment Due Process: "This is conduct that shocks the conscience. [The police behavior] is bound to offend even hardened sensibilities . . . [It is] too close to the rack and screw . . . "

Justice Black concurred in the result, but criticized the "nebulous" and "accordion-like" quality of Justice Frankfurter's approach. According to Justice Black, "faithful adherence to the specific guarantees in the Bill of Rights ensures a more permanent protection of individual liberty."

the States through the use of a broad, general interpretation of due process that permits judges to strike down state laws they do not like.

In closing I want to emphasize that I believe as strongly as ever that the Fourteenth Amendment was intended to make the Bill of Rights applicable to the States. I have been willing to support the selective incorporation doctrine, however, as an alternative, although perhaps less historically supportable than complete incorporation. The selective incorporation process, if used properly, does limit the Supreme Court in the Fourteenth Amendment field to specific Bill of Rights' protections only and keeps judges from roaming at will in their own notions of what policies outside the Bill of Rights are desirable and what are not. And, most importantly for me, the selective incorporation process has the virtue of having already worked to make most of the Bill of Rights' protections applicable to the States.

JUSTICE FORTAS, concurring * * *

[A]lthough I agree with the decision of the Court, I cannot agree [that] the tail must go with the hide: that when we hold, influenced by the Sixth Amendment, that "due process" requires that the States accord the right of jury trial for all but petty offenses, we automatically import all of the ancillary rules which have been or may hereafter be developed incidental to the right to jury trial in the federal courts. I see no reason whatever, for example, to assume that our decision today should require us to impose federal requirements such as unanimous verdicts or a jury of 12 upon the States. We may well conclude that these and other features of federal jury practice are by no means fundamental—that they are not essential to due process of law—and that they are not obligatory on the States.[c]

I would make these points clear today. Neither logic nor history nor the intent of the draftsmen of the Fourteenth Amendment can possibly be said to require that the Sixth Amendment or its jury trial provision be applied to the States together with the total gloss that this Court's decisions have supplied. The draftsmen of the Fourteenth Amendment intended what they said, not more or less: that no State shall deprive any person of life, liberty, or property without due process of law. It is ultimately the duty of this Court to interpret, to ascribe specific meaning to this phrase. There is no reason whatever for us to conclude that, in so doing, we are bound slavishly to follow not only the Sixth Amendment but all of its bag and baggage, however securely or insecurely affixed they may be by law and precedent to federal proceedings. To take this course, in my judgment, would be not only unnecessary but mischievous because it would inflict a serious blow upon the principle of federalism. The Due Process Clause commands us to apply its great standard to state court proceedings to assure basic fairness. It does not command us rigidly and arbitrarily to impose the exact pattern of federal proceedings upon

---

[c]   Justice Fortas's predictions turned out to be half true. In *Williams v. Florida*, 399 U.S. 78 (1970), the Supreme Court addressed the issue of jury size, concluding that the Sixth Amendment permits six-person juries in state *or federal* non-capital felony cases. In so holding, the Court noted that the fact "that [the] jury at common law was composed of precisely 12 is an historical accident, unnecessary to effect the purposes of the jury system." But in *Ramos v. Louisiana*, 140 S.Ct. 1390 (2020), the Court deemed the unanimous jury requirement fundamental and incorporated the unanimity requirement against the states.

the 50 States. On the contrary, the Constitution's command, in my view, is that in our insistence upon state observance of due process, we should, so far as possible, allow the greatest latitude for state differences. It requires, within the limits of the lofty basic standards that it prescribes for the States as well as the Federal Government, maximum opportunity for diversity and minimal imposition of uniformity of method and detail upon the States. Our Constitution sets up a federal union, not a monolith.

This Court has heretofore held that various provisions of the Bill of Rights such as the freedom of speech and religion guarantees of the First Amendment, the prohibition of unreasonable searches and seizures in the Fourth Amendment, the privilege against self-incrimination of the Fifth Amendment, and the right to counsel and to confrontation under the Sixth Amendment "are all to be enforced against the States under the Fourteenth Amendment according to the same standards that protect those rights against federal encroachment." I need not quarrel with the specific conclusion in those specific instances. But unless one adheres slavishly to the incorporation theory, body and substance, the same conclusion need not be superimposed upon the jury trial right. I respectfully but urgently suggest that it should not be. Jury trial is more than a principle of justice applicable to individual cases. It is a system of administration of the business of the State. * * * We should be ready to welcome state variations which do not impair—indeed, which may advance—the theory and purpose of trial by jury.

JUSTICE HARLAN, whom JUSTICE STEWART joins, dissenting.

Every American jurisdiction provides for trial by jury in criminal cases. The question before us is not whether jury trial is an ancient institution, which it is; nor whether it plays a significant role in the administration of criminal justice, which it does; nor whether it will endure, which it shall. The question in this case is whether the State of Louisiana, which provides trial by jury for all felonies, is prohibited by the Constitution from trying charges of simple battery to the court alone. In my view, the answer to that question, mandated alike by our constitutional history and by the longer history of trial by jury, is clearly "no." * * *

The Court's approach to this case is an uneasy and illogical compromise among the views of various Justices on how the Due Process Clause should be interpreted. The Court does not say that those who framed the Fourteenth Amendment intended to make the Sixth Amendment applicable to the States. And the Court concedes that it finds nothing unfair about the procedure by which the present appellant was tried. Nevertheless, the Court reverses his conviction: it holds, for some reason not apparent to me, that the Due Process Clause incorporates the particular clause of the Sixth Amendment that requires trial by jury in federal criminal cases—including, as I read its opinion, the sometimes trivial accompanying baggage of judicial interpretation in federal contexts. * * *

A few members of the Court have taken the position that the intention of those who drafted the first section of the Fourteenth Amendment was simply, and exclusively, to make the provisions of the first eight amendments applicable to state action. This view has never been accepted by this Court. In my view [the] first section of the Fourteenth Amendment was meant neither to incorporate, nor to be limited to, the specific guarantees of the first eight amendments. The overwhelming historical evidence marshalled by Professor Fairman demonstrates, to me conclusively, that the Congressmen and state legislators who wrote, debated, and ratified the Fourteenth Amendment did not think they were "incorporating" the Bill of Rights and the very breadth and generality of the Amendment's provisions suggests that its authors did not suppose that the Nation would always be limited to mid19th century conceptions of "liberty" and "due process of law" but that the increasing experience and evolving conscience of the American people would add new "intermediate premises." In short, neither history, nor sense, supports using the Fourteenth Amendment to put the States in a constitutional straitjacket with respect to their own development in the administration of criminal or civil law.

Although I therefore fundamentally disagree with the total incorporation view of the Fourteenth Amendment, it seems to me that such a position does at least have the virtue, lacking in the Court's selective incorporation approach, of internal consistency: we look to the Bill of Rights, word for word, clause for clause, precedent for precedent because, it is said, the men who wrote the Amendment wanted it that way. For those who do not accept this "history," a different source of "intermediate premises" must be found. The Bill of Rights is not necessarily irrelevant to the search for guidance in interpreting the Fourteenth Amendment, but the reason for and the nature of its relevance must be articulated.

Apart from the approach taken by the absolute incorporationists, I can see only one method of analysis that has any internal logic. That is to start with the words "liberty" and "due process of law" and attempt to define them in a way that accords with American traditions and our system of government. This approach, involving a much more discriminating process of adjudication than does "incorporation," is, albeit difficult, the one that was followed throughout the Nineteenth and most of the present century. It entails a "gradual process of judicial inclusion and exclusion," seeking, with due recognition of constitutional tolerance for state experimentation and disparity, to ascertain those "immutable principles of justice which inhere in the very idea of free government which no member of the Union may disregard." * * *

The relationship of the Bill of Rights to this "gradual process" seems to me to be twofold. In the first place it has long been clear that the Due Process Clause imposes some restrictions on state action that parallel Bill of Rights restrictions on federal action. Second, and more important than this accidental overlap, is the fact that the Bill of Rights is evidence, at various points, of the content Americans find in the term "liberty" and of American standards of fundamental fairness.

[In *Gideon v. Wainwright* (1963), set forth at p. 380, and other cases], the right guaranteed against the States by the Fourteenth Amendment was one that had also been guaranteed against the Federal Government by one of the first eight amendments. The logically critical thing, however, was not that the rights had been found in the Bill of Rights, but that they were deemed, in the context of American legal history, to be fundamental. * * *

Today's Court still remains unwilling to accept the total incorporationists' view of the history of the Fourteenth Amendment. This, if accepted, would afford a cogent reason for applying the Sixth Amendment to the States. The Court is also, apparently, unwilling to face the task of determining whether denial of trial by jury in the situation before us, or in other situations, is fundamentally unfair. Consequently, the Court has compromised on the ease of the incorporationist position, without its internal logic. It has simply assumed that the question before us is whether the Jury Trial Clause of the Sixth Amendment should be incorporated into the Fourteenth, jot-for-jot and case-for-case, or ignored. Then the Court merely declares that the clause in question is "in" rather than "out."

The Court has justified neither its starting place nor its conclusion. If the problem is to discover and articulate the rules of fundamental fairness in criminal proceedings, there is no reason to assume that the whole body of rules developed in this Court constituting Sixth Amendment jury trial must be regarded as a unit. The requirement of trial by jury in federal criminal cases has given rise to numerous subsidiary questions respecting the exact scope and content of the right. It surely cannot be that every answer the Court has given, or will give, to such a question is attributable to the Founders; or even that every rule announced carries equal conviction of this Court; still less can it be that every such subprinciple is equally fundamental to ordered liberty.[18]

Examples abound. I should suppose it obviously fundamental to fairness that a "jury" means an "impartial jury." I should think it equally obvious that the rule, imposed long ago in the federal courts, that "jury" means "jury of exactly twelve," is not fundamental to anything: there is no significance except to mystics in the number 12. Again, trial by jury has been held to require a unanimous verdict of jurors in the federal courts, although unanimity has not been found essential to liberty in Britain, where the requirement has been abandoned. * * *

Even if I could agree that the question before us is whether Sixth Amendment jury trial is totally "in" or totally "out," I can find in the Court's opinion no real reasons for concluding that it should be "in." The basis for differentiating among clauses in the Bill of Rights cannot be that only some clauses are in the Bill of Rights, or that only some are old and much praised, or that only some have played an important role in the development of federal law. These things are true of all. The Court says that some clauses are more "fundamental" than others, but it turns out to be using this word in a sense that would have astonished Mr. Justice Cardozo and which, in addition, is of no help. The word does not mean "analytically critical to procedural fairness" for no real analysis of the role of the jury in making procedures fair is even attempted. Instead, the word turns out to mean "old," "much

---

[18] The same illogical way of dealing with a Fourteenth Amendment problem was employed in *Malloy v. Hogan* [discussed in fn. a, p. 33, which held that the Due Process Clause guaranteed the protection of the Self-Incrimination Clause of the Fifth Amendment against state action]. I disagreed at that time both with the way the question was framed and with the result the Court reached. I consider myself bound by the Court's holding in *Malloy* with respect to self-incrimination. I do not think that *Malloy* held, nor would I consider myself bound by a holding, that every question arising under the Due Process Clause shall be settled by an arbitrary decision whether a clause in the Bill of Rights is "in" or "out."

praised," and "found in the Bill of Rights." The definition of "fundamental" thus turns out to be circular.

Since, as I see it, the Court has not even come to grips with the issues in this case, it is necessary to start from the beginning. When a criminal defendant contends that his state conviction lacked "due process of law," the question before this Court, in my view, is whether he was denied any element of fundamental procedural fairness. Believing, as I do, that due process is an evolving concept and that old principles are subject to re-evaluation in light of later experience, I think it appropriate to deal on its merits with the question whether Louisiana denied appellant due process of law when it tried him for simple assault without a jury. * * *

The argument that jury trial is not a requisite of due process is quite simple. The central proposition of *Palko,* a proposition to which I would adhere, is that "due process of law" requires only that criminal trials be fundamentally fair. [A]part from the theory that it was historically intended as a mere shorthand for the Bill of Rights, I do not see what else "due process of law" can intelligibly be thought to mean. If due process of law requires only fundamental fairness, then the inquiry in each case must be whether a state trial process was a fair one. The Court has held, properly I think, that in an adversary process it is a requisite of fairness, for which there is no adequate substitute, that a criminal defendant be afforded a right to counsel and to cross-examine opposing witnesses. But it simply has not been demonstrated, nor, I think, can it be demonstrated, that trial by jury is the only fair means of resolving issues of fact.

The jury is of course not without virtues. It affords ordinary citizens a valuable opportunity to participate in a process of government, an experience fostering, one hopes, a respect for law. It eases the burden on judges by enabling them to share a part of their sometimes awesome responsibility. A jury may, at times, afford a higher justice by refusing to enforce harsh laws (although it necessarily does so haphazardly, raising the questions whether arbitrary enforcement of harsh laws is better than total enforcement, and whether the jury system is to be defended on the ground that jurors sometimes disobey their oaths). And the jury may, or may not, contribute desirably to the willingness of the general public to accept criminal judgments as just.

It can hardly be gainsaid, however, that the principal original virtue of the jury trial—the limitations a jury imposes on a tyrannous judiciary—has largely disappeared. We no longer live in a medieval or colonial society. Judges enforce laws enacted by democratic decision, not by regal fiat. They are elected by the people or appointed by the people's elected officials, and are responsible not to a distant monarch alone but to reviewing courts, including this one.

The jury system can also be said to have some inherent defects, which are multiplied by the emergence of the criminal law from the relative simplicity that existed when the jury system was devised. It is a cumbersome process, not only imposing great cost in time and money on both the State and the jurors themselves, but also contributing to delay in the machinery of justice. Untrained jurors are presumably less adept at reaching accurate conclusions of fact than judges, particularly if the issues are many or complex. And it is argued by some that trial by jury, far from increasing public respect for law, impairs it: the average man, it is said, reacts favorably neither to the notion that matters he knows to be complex are being decided by other average men, nor to the way the jury system distorts the process of adjudication.

That trial by jury is not the only fair way of adjudicating criminal guilt is well attested by the fact that it is not the prevailing way, either in England or in this country. * * *

In the United States, where it has not been as generally assumed that jury waiver is permissible, the statistics are only slightly less revealing. Two experts have estimated that, of all prosecutions for crimes triable to a jury, 75% are settled by guilty plea and 40% of the remainder are tried to the court. In one State, Maryland, which has always provided for waiver, the rate of court trial appears in some years to have reached 90%. The Court recognizes the force of these statistics in stating, "We would not assert, however, that every criminal trial—or any particular trial—held before a judge alone is unfair or that a defendant may never be as fairly treated by a judge as he would be by a jury." I agree. I therefore see no reason why this Court should reverse the conviction of appellant, absent any suggestion that his particular trial was in fact unfair, or compel the State of Louisiana to afford jury trial in an as yet unbounded category of cases that can, without unfairness, be tried to a court.

Indeed, even if I were persuaded that trial by jury is a fundamental right in some criminal cases, I could see nothing fundamental in the rule, not yet formulated by the Court, that places the prosecution of appellant for simple battery within the category of "jury crimes" rather than "petty crimes."

[The] point is not that many offenses that English-speaking communities have, at one time or another, regarded as triable without a jury are more serious, and carry more serious penalties, than the one involved here. The point is rather that until today few people would have thought the exact location of the line mattered very much. There is no obvious reason why a jury trial is a requisite of fundamental fairness when the charge is robbery, and not a requisite of fairness when the same defendant, for the same actions, is charged with assault and petit theft. The reason for the historic exception for relatively minor crimes is the obvious one: the burden of jury trial was thought to outweigh its marginal advantages. Exactly why the States should not be allowed to make continuing adjustments, based on the state of their criminal dockets and the difficulty of summoning jurors, simply escapes me.

In sum, there is a wide range of views on the desirability of trial by jury, and on the ways to make it most effective when it is used; there is also considerable variation from State to State in local conditions such as the size of the criminal caseload, the ease or difficulty of summoning jurors, and other trial conditions bearing on fairness. We have before us, therefore, an almost perfect example of a situation in which the celebrated dictum of Mr. Justice Brandeis should be invoked. It is, he said, "one of the happy incidents of the federal system that a single courageous state may, if its citizens choose, serve as a laboratory * * *." *New State*

Ice Co. v. Liebmann, 285 U.S. 262 (1932) (dissenting opinion). This Court, other courts, and the political process are available to correct any experiments in criminal procedure that prove fundamentally unfair to defendants. That is not what is being done today: instead, and quite without reason, the Court has chosen to impose upon every State one means of trying criminal cases; it is a good means, but it is not the only fair means, and it is not demonstrably better than the alternatives States might devise. * * *

3. "FREE STANDING" DUE PROCESS

The Supreme Court in the "post-selective-incorporation-era" has continued to apply due process as a guarantee that has "independent content," standing apart from the selectively incorporated guarantees. At times, the Court has suggested that this "free-standing" element of due process should be approached with caution. Thus, *Dowling v. United States*, 493 U.S. 342 (1990), noted that "beyond the specific guarantees enumerated in the Bill of Rights, the Due Process Clause has 'limited operation' and will be 'construed very narrowly.'" This position rests on the ground that, since the "Bill of Rights speaks in explicit terms to many aspects of criminal procedure, * * * the expansion of constitutional regulation under the open-ended rubric of the Due Process Clause invites undue interference with both considered legislative judgments and the careful balance that the Constitution strikes between liberty and order." *Medina v. California*, 505 U.S. 437 (1992). Notwithstanding such statements, freestanding due process has emerged as: (1) the dominant source of constitutional regulation of the pre-trial and post-trial stages of the process (most notable as to guilty pleas and sentencing); (2) a major source of constitutional regulation of the trial; (3) a lesser, but still significant source of regulation of police practices. Thus, rulings relying on the independent content of due process are scattered throughout this volume. *District Attorney's Office v. Osborne*, set forth below, reflects the differing perspectives that have often divided the Court in its determination of the independent content of due process.

DISTRICT ATTORNEY'S OFFICE V. OSBORNE
557 U.S. 52, 129 S.Ct. 2308, 174 L.Ed.2d 38 (2009).

CHIEF JUSTICE ROBERTS delivered the opinion of the Court.

[In 1993, respondent Osborne was convicted of kidnapping and sexual assault. He claimed that at trial he had asked his attorney to seek DNA testing of biological evidence on a condom found at the scene of the crime, but she refused. His lawyer testified that she refused for various reasons, including her belief her client was guilty. This led her to conclude that further testing would do more harm than good. There was considerable evidence of Osborne's guilt. Moreover, he confessed to the parole board, which released him after 14 years. Osborne subsequently claimed he lied to the parole board because he hoped his lie would lead to a quicker release. Osborne was recently rearrested for another crime and the state has petitioned to revoke his parole.

[Osborne asked the Alaska Court of Appeals to provide the DNA testing that his trial lawyer had failed to request. But that court denied relief, relying heavily on the fact that Osborne had confessed to some of his crimes in an application for parole. Osborne also brought a federal action under § 1983 claiming that the Due Process Clause entitled him to a form of DNA testing more discriminating than the methods available at the time of his trial. A federal district court concluded that Osborne had a right, but a very limited one, to the testing sought. The U.S. Court of Appeals for the Ninth Circuit affirmed, concluding that the prosecutorial duty to disclose exculpatory evidence extends the government's duty (or the defendant's right of access) to post-conviction proceedings. Although it acknowledged that Osborne's prior admissions of guilt were certainly relevant, the Ninth Circuit concluded that they did not "necessarily trump" the right to obtain post-conviction relief, considering the "emerging reality of wrongful convictions based on false confessions."]

DNA testing has an unparalleled ability to exonerate the wrongly convicted and to identify the guilty.[a] It has the potential to significantly improve both the criminal justice system and police investigative practices. The Federal Government and the States have recognized this, and have developed special approaches to ensure that this evidentiary tool can be effectively incorporated into established criminal procedure—usually but not always through legislation.

Against this prompt and considered response, the [respondent,] William Osborne, proposes a different approach. [His] approach would take the development [in] this area out of the hands of legislatures and state courts shaping policy in a focused manner and turn it over to federal courts applying the broad parameters of the Due Process Clause. There is no reason to constitutionalize the issue in this way. * * *

DNA testing alone does not always resolve a case. Where there is enough other incriminating evidence and an explanation for the DNA result, science alone cannot prove a prisoner innocent. The availability of technologies not available at trial cannot mean that every criminal conviction, or even every criminal conviction involving biological evidence, is suddenly in doubt. The dilemma is how to harness DNA's power to prove innocence without necessarily overthrowing the established system of criminal justice.

That task belongs primarily to the legislature. * * * Forty-six States have already enacted statutes dealing specifically with access to DNA evidence. [The] Federal Government has also passed the Innocence Protection Act of 2004, which allows federal prisoners to move for court-ordered DNA testing under certain specified conditions. That Act also grants money to States that enact comparable statutes.

[These] laws recognize the value of DNA evidence but also the need for certain conditions on access to the State's evidence. A requirement of demonstrating

---

[a] According to the Innocence Project at Cardozo Law School, which represented respondent Osborne, DNA testing has played a role in 240 exonerations and in 103 of those cases the testing also identified the actual perpetrator. Adam Liptak, *Court Rejects Inmate Rights to DNA Tests*, New York Times, June 19, 2009, p. 1.

materiality is common, but is not the only one. The federal statute, for example, requires a sworn statement that the applicant is innocent. States also impose a range of diligence requirements. Several require the requested testing to "have been technologically impossible at trial." Others deny testing to those who declined testing at trial for tactical reasons.

Alaska is one of a handful of States yet to enact legislation specifically addressing the issue of evidence requested for DNA testing. But that does not mean that such evidence is unavailable for those seeking to prove their innocence. Instead, Alaska courts are addressing how to apply existing laws for discovery and postconviction relief to this novel technology. * * *

First, access to evidence is available under Alaska law for those who seek to subject it to newly available DNA testing that will prove them to be actually innocent. Under the State's general postconviction relief statute, a prisoner may challenge his conviction when "there exists evidence of material facts, not previously presented and heard by the court, that requires vacation of the conviction or sentence in the interest of justice." Such a claim is exempt from otherwise applicable time limits if "newly discovered evidence," pursued with due diligence, "establishes by clear and convincing evidence that the applicant is innocent."

Both parties agree that under these provisions "a defendant is entitled to post-conviction relief if the defendant presents newly discovered evidence that establishes by clear and convincing evidence that the defendant is innocent." If such a claim is brought, state law permits general discovery. Alaska courts have explained that these procedures are available to request DNA evidence for newly available testing to establish actual innocence.

In addition to this statutory procedure, the Alaska Court of Appeals has invoked a widely accepted three-part test to govern additional rights to DNA access under the State Constitution. Drawing on the experience with DNA evidence of State Supreme Courts around the country, the Court of Appeals explained that it was "reluctant to hold that Alaska law offers no remedy to defendants who could prove their factual innocence." It was "prepared to hold, however, that a defendant who seeks post-conviction DNA testing . . . must show (1) that the conviction rested primarily on eyewitness identification evidence, (2) that there was a demonstrable doubt concerning the defendant's identification as the perpetrator, and (3) that scientific testing would likely be conclusive on this issue." Thus, the Alaska's courts have suggested that even those who do not get discovery under the State's criminal rules have available to them a safety valve under the State Constitution.

This is the background against which the Federal Court of Appeals ordered the State to turn over the DNA evidence in its possession, and it is our starting point in analyzing Osborne's constitutional claims.

[The Due Process Clause] imposes procedural limitations on a State's power to take away protected entitlements. Osborne argues that access to the State's evidence is a "process" needed to vindicate his right to prove himself innocent and get out of jail. Process is not an end in itself, so a necessary premise of this argument is that he has an entitlement (what our precedents call a "liberty interest") to prove his innocence even after a fair trial has proved otherwise. We must first examine this asserted liberty interest to determine what process (if any) is due.

Osborne [does] have a liberty interest in demonstrating his innocence with new evidence under state law. As explained, Alaska law provides that those who use "newly discovered evidence" to "establis[h] by clear and convincing evidence that [they are] innocent" may obtain "vacation of [their] conviction or sentence in the interest of justice." This "state-created right can, in some circumstances, beget yet other rights to procedures essential to the realization of the parent right."

The Court of Appeals went too far, however, in concluding that the Due Process Clause requires that certain familiar preconviction trial rights be extended to protect Osborne's postconviction liberty interest. * * *

A criminal defendant proved guilty after a fair trial does not have the same liberty interests as a free man. At trial, the defendant is presumed innocent and may demand that the government prove its case beyond reasonable doubt. But "[o]nce a defendant has been afforded a fair trial and convicted of the offense for which he was charged, the presumption of innocence disappears." *Herrera v. Collins* [fn. b infra]. The State accordingly has more flexibility in deciding what procedures are needed in the context of postconviction relief. * * * Osborne's right to due process is not parallel to a trial right, but rather must be analyzed in light of the fact that he has already been found guilty at a fair trial, and has only a limited interest in postconviction relief. * * * The question is whether consideration of Osborne's claim within the framework of the State's procedures for postconviction relief "offends some principle of justice so rooted in the traditions and conscience of our people as to be ranked as fundamental," or "transgresses any recognized principle of fundamental fairness in operation." *Medina v. California* [p. 46]. Federal courts may upset a State's postconviction relief procedures only if they are fundamentally inadequate to vindicate the substantive rights provided.

[We] see nothing inadequate about the procedures Alaska has provided to vindicate its state right to postconviction relief in general, and nothing inadequate about how those procedures apply to those who seek access to DNA evidence. Alaska provides a substantive right to be released on a sufficiently compelling showing of new evidence that establishes innocence. It exempts such claims from otherwise applicable time limits. The State provides for discovery in postconviction proceedings, and has—through judicial decision—specified that this discovery procedure is available to those seeking access to DNA evidence. These procedures are not without limits. The evidence must indeed be newly available to qualify under Alaska's statute, must have been diligently pursued, and must also be sufficiently material. These procedures are similar to those provided for DNA evidence by federal law and the law of other States. * * *

His attempt to sidestep state process through a new federal lawsuit puts Osborne in a very awkward position. If he simply seeks the DNA through the State's discovery procedures, he might well get it. If he does not, it may be for a perfectly adequate reason, just as the federal statute and all state statutes impose conditions and limits on access to DNA evidence. It is difficult to criticize the State's procedures when Osborne has not invoked them. [These] procedures are adequate on their face, and without trying them. Osborne can hardly complain that they do not work in practice.

As a fallback, Osborne also obliquely relies on an asserted federal constitutional right to be released upon proof of "actual innocence." Whether such a federal right exists is an open question. We have struggled with it over the years, in some cases assuming, arguendo, that it exists while also noting the difficult questions such a right would pose and the high standards any claimant would have to meet. *House v. Bell*; *Herrera v. Collins*.[b] In this case too we can assume without deciding that such a claim exists, because even if so there is no due process problem. Osborne does not dispute that a federal actual innocence claim (as opposed to a DNA access claim) would be brought in habeas. If such a habeas claim is viable, federal procedural rules permit discovery "for good cause." Just as with state law, Osborne cannot show that available discovery is facially inadequate, and cannot show that it would be arbitrarily denied to him.

The Court of Appeals below relied only on procedural due process, but Osborne seeks to defend the judgment on the basis of substantive due process as well. He asks that we recognize a freestanding right to DNA evidence untethered from the liberty interests he hopes to vindicate with it. We reject the invitation and conclude, in the circumstances of this case, that there is no such substantive due process right. "As a general matter, the Court has always been reluctant to expand the concept of substantive due process because guideposts for responsible decisionmaking in this unchartered area are scarce and open-ended." Osborne seeks access to state evidence so that he can apply new DNA-testing technology

---

b   In *Herrera v. Collins*, 506 U.S. 390 (1993), the Court considered whether federal habeas relief was available for claims of "bare innocence," and if so, when such claims required relief. Herrera had been convicted of murder and sentenced to death, but claimed that several new affidavits demonstrated that his brother had committed the crime. State law required defendants to bring motions for new trial based on newly discovered evidence within a short time after trial. Herrera had missed this deadline having raised this evidence eight years after trial, so a state challenge to his conviction and sentence was unavailable. He argued in federal court that the execution of an innocent man would violate the Eighth and Fourteenth Amendments, although he alleged no constitutional violation during the state prosecution. A majority of the justices seemed to agree that in extremely unusual circumstances, a claim of innocence, even one unaccompanied by a separate constitutional claim, could compel relief. Justice Rehnquist wrote: "We may assume, for the sake of argument in deciding this case, that in a capital case a truly persuasive demonstration of 'actual innocence' made after trial would render the execution of a defendant unconstitutional, and warrants federal habeas relief if there were no state avenue open to process such a claim." The "threshold showing for such an assumed right would necessarily be extraordinarily high," and Herrera's showing fell "far short of any such threshold."

In *House v. Bell*, 547 U.S. 518 (2006), the Court again declined to decide whether federal habeas courts have authority to review a freestanding claim of actual innocence as a basis for invalidating a state conviction or death sentence. Although House had managed to gather new witnesses, as well as DNA and other forensic evidence that "cast considerable doubt on his guilt," so much so that the Court found that it was "more likely than not that no reasonable juror would have convicted him in the light of the new evidence," his was "not a case of conclusive exoneration," and fell "short of the threshold implied in *Herrera*." The Court did remand the case for consideration of House's other constitutional claims (failure to disclose exculpatory evidence and ineffective assistance of counsel). A federal court subsequently found in Herrera's favor on those claims and ordered him released or retried. In May of 2009, after House had spent more than twenty years on death row, the state prosecutor dropped all charges.

that might prove him innocent. There is no long history of such a right, and "[t]he mere novelty of such a claim is reason enough to doubt that 'substantive due process' sustains it."

And there are further reasons to doubt. The elected governments of the States are actively confronting the challenges DNA technology poses to our criminal justice systems and our traditional notions of finality, as well as the opportunities it affords. To suddenly constitutionalize this area would short-circuit what looks to be a prompt and considered legislative response. * * * "By extending constitutional protection to an asserted right or liberty interest, we, to a great extent, place the matter outside the arena of public debate and legislative action. We must therefore exercise the utmost care whenever we are asked to break new ground in this field." * * * We are reluctant to enlist the Federal Judiciary in creating a new constitutional code of rules for handling DNA. * * *

Establishing a freestanding right to access DNA evidence for testing would force us to act as policymakers, and our substantive-due-process rulemaking authority would not only have to cover the right of access but a myriad of other issues. We would soon have to decide if there is a constitutional obligation to preserve forensic evidence that might later be tested. Cf. *Arizona v. Youngblood,* [fn. b, p. 755]. If so, for how long? Would it be different for different types of evidence? Would the State also have some obligation to gather such evidence in the first place? How much and when? No doubt there would be a miscellany of other minor directives.

DNA evidence will undoubtedly lead to changes in the criminal justice system. It has done so already. The question is whether further change will primarily be made by legislative revision and judicial interpretation of the existing system, or whether the Federal Judiciary must leap ahead—revising (or even discarding) the system by creating a new constitutional right and taking over responsibility for refining it. * * * Federal courts should not presume that state criminal procedure will be inadequate to deal with technological change. * * *

JUSTICE ALITO, with whom JUSTICE KENNEDY joins, and with whom JUSTICE THOMAS joins as to Part II, concurring.

* * * I agree with the Court's resolution of respondent's constitutional claim, [but also believe that the] claim also fails for two independent reasons beyond those given by the majority. First, a state prisoner asserting a federal constitutional right to perform [DNA] testing must file a petition for a writ of habeas corpus, not [a § 1983 action], as respondent did here, and thus must exhaust state remedies. Second, [his] claim may be rejected on the merits because a defendant who declines the opportunity to perform DNA testing at trial for tactical reasons has no constitutional right to perform such testing after conviction. * * *

II

[DNA] evidence creates special opportunities, risks, and burdens that implicate important state interests. Given those interests—and especially in light of the rapidly evolving nature of DNA testing technology—this is an area that should be (and is being) explored "through the workings of normal democratic processes in the laboratories of the States." Justice Stevens argues that the State should welcome respondent's offer to perform modern DNA testing (at his own expense) on the State's DNA evidence; the test will either confirm respondent's guilt (in which case the State has lost nothing) or exonerate him (in which case the State has no valid interest in detaining him). Alas, it is far from that simple. First, DNA testing—even when performed with modern STR technology and even when performed in perfect accordance with protocols—often fails to provide "absolute proof" of anything. * * * [That limitation applies] with particular force where, as here, the sample is minuscule, it may contain three or more persons' DNA, and it may have degraded significantly during the 24 or more hours it took police to recover it. Second, the State has important interests in maintaining the integrity of its evidence, and the risks associated with evidence contamination increase every time someone attempts to extract new DNA from a sample. * * * Indeed, modern DNA testing technology is so powerful that it actually increases the risks associated with mishandling evidence. * * * Third, even if every test was guaranteed to provide a conclusive answer, and even if no one ever contaminated a DNA sample, that still would not justify disregarding the other costs associated with the DNA-access regime proposed by respondent. * * * Even without our creation and imposition of a mandatory-DNA-access regime, state crime labs are already responsible for maintaining and controlling hundreds of thousands of new DNA samples every year. * * * The resources required to process and analyze these hundreds of thousands of samples have created severe backlogs in state crime labs across the country. * * *

My point in recounting the burdens that postconviction DNA testing imposes on the Federal Government and the States is not to denigrate the importance of such testing. Instead, my point is that requests for postconviction DNA testing are not cost free. The Federal Government and the States have a substantial interest in the implementation of rules that regulate such testing in a way that harnesses the unique power of DNA testing while also respecting the important governmental interests noted above. * * * When a criminal defendant, for tactical purposes, passes up the opportunity for DNA testing at trial, that defendant, in my judgment, has no constitutional right to demand to perform DNA testing after conviction. Recognition of such a right would allow defendants to play games with the criminal justice system. A guilty defendant could forgo DNA testing at trial for fear that the results would confirm his guilt, and in the hope that the other evidence would be insufficient to persuade the jury to find him guilty. Then, after conviction, with nothing to lose, the defendant could demand DNA testing in the hope that some happy accident—for example, degradation or contamination of the evidence—would provide the basis for seeking postconviction relief. Denying the opportunity for such an attempt to game the criminal justice system should not shock the conscience of the Court. There is ample evidence in this case that respondent attempted to game the system. * * *

Justice Stevens contends that respondent should not be bound by his attorney's tactical decision and notes that respondent testified in the state postconviction proceeding that he strongly objected to his attorney's strategy. His attorney, however, had no memory of that objection, and the state court did not find that respondent's testimony was truthful.

[In] any event, even assuming for the sake of argument that respondent did object at trial to his attorney's strategy, it is a well-accepted principle that, except in a few carefully defined circumstances, a criminal defendant is bound by his attorney's tactical decisions unless the attorney provided constitutionally ineffective assistance. Here, the state postconviction court rejected respondent's ineffective-assistance claim; respondent does not challenge that holding; and we must therefore proceed on the assumption that his attorney's decision was reasonable and binding.

If a state prisoner wants to challenge the State's refusal to permit postconviction DNA testing, the prisoner should proceed under the habeas statute, which duly accounts for the interests of federalism, comity, and finality. And in considering the merits of such a claim, the State's weighty interests cannot be summarily dismissed as " 'arbitrary, or conscience shocking' " [referring to language in Justice Stevens' dissenting opinion].

JUSTICE STEVENS, with whom JUSTICE GINSBURG and JUSTICE BREYER join, and with whom JUSTICE SOUTER joins as to Part I, dissenting.

The State of Alaska possesses physical evidence that, if tested, will conclusively establish whether [respondent] committed rape and [other crimes]. If he did, justice has been served. [If] not, Osborne has needlessly spent decades behind bars while the true culprit has not been brought to justice. [Yet] for reasons the State has been unable or unwilling to articulate, it refuses to allow Osborne to test the evidence at his own expense and to thereby ascertain the truth once and for all.

I

[Osborne] first anchors his due process right in [Alaska's postconviction statute]. Although States are under no obligation to provide mechanisms for postconviction relief, when they choose to do so, the procedures they employ must comport with the demands of the Due Process Clause by providing litigants with fair opportunity to assert their state-created rights.

[In] determining that Osborne was not entitled to relief under [Alaska's] postconviction statute, the Alaska Court of Appeals concluded that the DNA testing Osborne wished to obtain could not qualify as "newly discovered" because it was available at the time of trial. [However, as Osborne has made plain, he had requested] a form of DNA testing not yet in use at the time of his trial. [The state appellate court's conclusion to the contrary] was therefore clearly erroneous.

[The] same holds true with respect to the majority's suggestion that the Alaska Constitution might provide additional protections to Osborne above and beyond those afforded under [the state's postconviction statute]. In Osborne's state postconviction proceedings, the Alaska Court of Appeals held out the possibility that even when evidence does not meet the requirements of [the state postconviction statute], the State Constitution might offer relief to a defendant [able] to make certain threshold showings. On remand from that decision, however, the state trial court denied Osborne relief on the ground that he failed to show that (1) his conviction rested primarily on eyewitness identification; (2) there was a demonstrable doubt concerning his identity as the perpetrator; and (3) scientific testing would likely be conclusive on this issue.

[The] first two reasons reduce to an evaluation of the strength of the prosecution's original case—a consideration that carries little weight when balanced against evidence as powerfully dispositive as an exculpatory DNA test. [As for the final reason offered by the state court, the] conclusion that such testing would not be conclusive in this case is indefensible, as evidenced by the State's recent concession on that point.

[Osborne] made full use of available state procedures in his efforts to secure access to evidence for DNA testing so that he might avail himself of the postconviction relief afforded by the State of Alaska. He was rebuffed at every turn. The manner in which the Alaska courts applied state law in this case leaves me in grave doubt about the adequacy of the procedural protections afforded to litigants under [the state's postconviction statute].

II

Wholly apart from his state-created interest in obtaining postconviction relief under [state law], Osborne asserts a right to access the State's evidence that derives from the Due Process Clause itself. Whether framed as a "substantive liberty interest [protected] through a procedural due process right" to have evidence made available for testing, or as a substantive due process right to be free of arbitrary government action, the result is the same: On the record now before us, Osborne has established his entitlement to test the State's evidence.

The liberty protected by the Due Process Clause is not a creation of the Bill of Rights. Indeed, our Nation has long recognized that the liberty safeguarded by the Constitution has far deeper roots. [The] "most elemental" of the liberties protected by the Due Process Clause is "the interest in being free from physical detention by one's own government." *Hamdi v. Rumsfeld*, 542 U.S. 507 (2004) (plurality opinion).

Although a valid criminal conviction justifies punitive detention, it does not entirely eliminate the liberty interests of convicted persons. * * * Our cases have recognized protected interests in a variety of postconviction contexts, extending substantive constitutional protections to state prisoners on the premise that the Due Process Clause of the Fourteenth Amendment requires States to respect certain fundamental liberties in the postconviction context. [It] is therefore far too late in the day to question the basic proposition that convicted persons such as Osborne retain a constitutionally protected measure of interest in liberty, including the fundamental liberty of freedom from physical restraint.

Recognition of this right draws strength from the fact that 46 States and the Federal Government have passed statutes providing access to evidence for DNA testing, and 3 additional states (including Alaska) provide similar access through court-made rules alone. These legislative developments are consistent with recent trends in legal ethics recognizing that prosecutors are obliged to disclose all forms

of exculpatory evidence that come into their possession following conviction. [The] fact that nearly all the States have now recognized some post-conviction right to DNA evidence makes it more, not less, appropriate to recognize a limited federal right to such evidence in cases where litigants are unfairly barred from obtaining relief in state court. * * * Recent scientific advances in DNA analysis have made "it literally possible to confirm guilt or innocence beyond any question whatsoever, at least in some categories of cases." As the Court recognizes today, the powerful new evidence that modern DNA testing can provide is "unlike anything known before."
* * *

Observing that the DNA evidence in this case would be so probative of Osborne's guilt or innocence that it exceeds the materiality standard that governs the disclosure of evidence under *Brady v. Maryland* [p. 740], the Ninth Circuit granted Osborne's request for access to the State's evidence. In doing so, [it] recognized that Osborne possesses a narrow right of postconviction access to biological evidence for DNA testing "where [such] evidence was used to secure his conviction, the DNA testing is to be conducted using methods that were unavailable at the time of trial and are far more precise than the methods that were then available, such methods are capable of conclusively determining whether Osborne is the source of the genetic material, the testing can be conducted without cost or prejudice to the State, and the evidence is material to available forms of post-conviction relief." That conclusion does not merit reversal.

If the right Osborne seeks to vindicate is framed as purely substantive, the proper result is no less clear. "The touchstone of due process is protection of the individual against arbitrary action of government." When government action is so lacking in justification that it "can properly be characterized as arbitrary, or conscience shocking, in a constitutional sense," it violates the Due Process Clause. In my view, the State's refusal to provide Osborne with access to evidence for DNA testing qualifies as arbitrary.

Throughout the course of state and federal litigation, the State has failed to provide any concrete reason for denying Osborne the DNA testing he seeks, and none is apparent. Because Osborne has offered to pay for the tests, cost is not a factor. And as the State now concedes, there is no reason to doubt that such testing would provide conclusive confirmation of Osborne's guilt or revelation of his innocence. [Insofar] as the State has articulated any reason at all, it appears to be a generalized interest in protecting the finality of the judgment of conviction from any possible future attacks. While we have long recognized that States have an interest in securing the finality of their judgments, finality is not a stand-alone value that trumps a State's overriding interest in ensuring that justice is done in its courts and secured to its citizens. * * * DNA evidence has led to an extraordinary series of exonerations, not only in cases where the trial evidence was weak, but also in cases where the convicted parties confessed their guilt and where the trial evidence against them appeared overwhelming.

[The] arbitrariness of the State's conduct is highlighted by comparison to the private interests it denies. It seems to me obvious that if a wrongly convicted person were to produce proof of his actual innocence, no state interest would be sufficient to justify his continued punitive detention. If such proof can be readily obtained without imposing a significant burden on the State, a refusal to provide access to such evidence is wholly unjustified.

[In] this case, the State has suggested no countervailing interest that justifies its refusal to allow Osborne to test the evidence in its possession and has not provided any other nonarbitrary explanation for its conduct. Consequently, I am left to conclude that the State's failure to provide Osborne access to the evidence constitutes arbitrary action that offends basic principles of due process.

III

[The] majority [asserts] that this Court's recognition of a limited federal right of access to DNA evidence would be ill advised because it would "short circuit what looks to be a prompt and considered legislative response" by the States and Federal Government to the issue of access to DNA evidence. [The] majority's arguments in this respect bear close resemblance to the manner in which the Court once approached the now-venerable right to counsel for indigent defendants. Before our decision in *Powell v. Alabama* (1932) [p. 373], state law alone governed the manner in which counsel was appointed for indigent defendants. [When] at last this Court recognized the Sixth Amendment right to counsel for all indigent criminal defendants in *Gideon v. Wainwright* (1963) [p. 380], our decision did not impede the ability of States to tailor their appointment processes to local needs, nor did it unnecessarily interfere with their sovereignty. It did, however, ensure that criminal defendants were provided with the counsel to which they were constitutionally entitled. In the same way, a decision to recognize a limited right of postconviction access to DNA testing would not prevent the States from creating procedures by which litigants request and obtain such access; it would merely ensure that States do so in a manner that is nonarbitrary. * * *

IV

Osborne has demonstrated a constitutionally protected right to due process which the State of Alaska thus far has not vindicated and which this Court is both empowered and obliged to safeguard. On the record before us, there is no reason to deny access to the evidence and there are many reasons to provide it, not least of which is a fundamental concern in ensuring that justice has been done in this case. * * *

JUSTICE SOUTER, dissenting.

I respectfully dissent on the ground that Alaska has failed to provide the effective procedure required by the Fourteenth Amendment for vindicating the liberty interest in demonstrating innocence that the state law recognizes. I therefore join Part I of Justice Steven's dissenting opinion.

I would not decide Osborne's broad claim that the Fourteenth Amendment's guarantee of due process requires our recognition at this time of a substantive right of access to biological evidence for DNA analysis and comparison. I would reserve judgment on the issue simply because there is no need to reach it; at a general level Alaska does not deny a right to postconviction testing to prove innocence, and in any event, Osborne's claim can be resolved by resort to the procedural due process requirement of an effective way to vindicate a liberty interest already recognized in state law. My choice to decide this case on that procedural ground should not, therefore, be taken either as expressing skepticism that a new substantive right to test should be cognizable in some circumstances, or as implying agreement with the Court that it would necessarily be premature for the Judicial Branch to decide whether such a general right should be recognized.

There is no denying that the Court is correct when it notes that a claim of right to DNA testing, post-trial at that, is a novel one, but that only reflects the relative novelty of testing DNA, and in any event is not a sufficient reason alone to reject the right asserted. Tradition is of course one serious consideration in judging whether a challenged rule or practice, or the failure to provide a new one, should be seen as violating the guarantee of substantive due process as being arbitrary, or as falling wholly outside the realm of reasonable governmental action. See *Poe v. Ullman*, 367 U.S. 497, 542 (1961) (Harlan, J., dissenting). We recognize the value and lessons of continuity with the past, but as Justice Harlan pointed out, society finds reasons to modify some of its traditional practices and the accumulation of new empirical knowledge can turn yesterday's reasonable range of the government's options into a due process anomaly over time. * * *

Changes in societal understanding of the fundamental reasonableness of government actions work out in much the same way that individuals reconsider issues of fundamental belief. We can change our own inherited views just so fast, and a person is not labeled a stick-in-the-mud for refusing to endorse a new moral claim without having some time to work through it intellectually and emotionally. Just as attachment to the familiar and the limits of experience affect the capacity of an individual to see the potential legitimacy of a moral position, the broader society needs the chance to take part in the dialectic of public and political back and forth about a new liberty claim before it makes sense to declare unsympathetic state or national laws arbitrary to the point of being unconstitutional. The time required is a matter for judgment depending on the issue involved, but the need for some time to pass before a court entertains a substantive due process claim on the subject is not merely the requirement of judicial restraint as a general approach, but a doctrinal demand to be satisfied before an allegedly lagging legal regime can be held to lie beyond the discretion of reason able political judgment.

Despite my agreement with the Court on this importance of timing, though, I do not think that the doctrinal requirement necessarily stands in the way of any substantive due process consideration of a postconviction right to DNA testing, even as a right that is freestanding. Given the pace at which DNA testing has come to be recognized as potentially dispositive in many cases with biological evidence, there is no obvious argument that considering DNA testing at a general level would subject wholly intransigent legal systems to substantive due process review prematurely. But, as I said, there is no such issue before us, for Alaska does not flatly deny access to evidence for DNA testing in postconviction cases. * * *

Standing alone, the inadequacy of each of the State's reasons for denying Osborne access to the DNA evidence he seeks would not make out a due process violation.[4] But taken as a whole the record convinces me that, while Alaska has created an entitlement of access to DNA evidence under conditions that are facially reasonable, the State has demonstrated a combination of inattentiveness and intransigence in applying those conditions that add up to procedural unfairness that violates the Due Process Clause.

---

[4]   [This Court is not in a position to correct individual errors of the Alaska Court of Appeals or Alaska officials, as § 1983 does not serve as a mechanism to review specific, unfavorable state-law determinations.]

CHAPTER 3

ARREST, SEARCH AND SEIZURE

■ ■ ■

1. THE EXCLUSIONARY RULE

The Fourth Amendment to the United States Constitution reads: "The right of the people to be secure in their persons, houses, papers, and effects, against unreasonable searches and seizures, shall not be violated, and no Warrants shall issue, but upon probable cause, supported by Oath or affirmation, and particularly describing the place to be searched, and the persons or things to be seized." The Amendment says nothing about how it is to be enforced, a matter which has been the subject of vigorous debate for a good many years. Most of this debate has focused upon the wisdom of and constitutional necessity for the so-called exclusionary rule, whereunder evidence obtained in violation of the Fourth Amendment is ordinarily inadmissible in a criminal trial. This exclusionary rule has existed in the federal criminal justice system for nearly 75 years, but has been mandated at the state level not nearly as long. In the first two cases in this section, *Wolf v. Colorado* and *Mapp v. Ohio,* we see the Court first rejecting and then accepting the notion that this exclusionary rule is constitutionally required in the state courts.

Mapp by no means ended the argument, though in more recent years much of the debate has centered upon the proper scope of the exclusionary rule. If, as the Supreme Court often indicated, a primary purpose of the rule is deterrence of the police, then precisely when is exclusion appropriate in the sense that it will likely have such a deterrent effect? The Court gives some answers to this question in *United States v. Leon, Hudson v. Michigan*, and *Herring v. United States*, the final three cases in this section.

WOLF v. COLORADO
338 U.S. 25, 69 S.Ct. 1359, 93 L.Ed. 1782 (1949).

JUSTICE FRANKFURTER delivered the opinion of the Court.

The precise question for consideration is this: Does a conviction by a State court for a State offense deny the "due process of law" required by the Fourteenth Amendment, solely because evidence that was admitted at the trial was obtained under circumstances which would have rendered it inadmissible in a prosecution for violation of a federal law in a court of the United States because there deemed to be an infraction of the Fourth Amendment? * * *

The security of one's privacy against arbitrary intrusion by the police—which is at the core of the Fourth Amendment—is basic to a free society. It is therefore implicit in "the concept of ordered liberty" and as such enforceable against the States through the Due Process Clause. * * *

Accordingly, we have no hesitation in saying that were a State affirmatively to sanction such police incursion into privacy it would run counter to the guaranty of the Fourteenth Amendment. But the ways of enforcing such a basic right raise questions of a different order. How such arbitrary conduct should be checked, what remedies against it should be afforded, the means by which the right should be made effective, are all questions that are not to be so dogmatically answered as to preclude the varying solutions which spring from an allowable range of judgment on issues not susceptible of quantitative solution.

In *Weeks v. United States,* 232 U.S. 383 (1914), this Court held that in a federal prosecution the Fourth Amendment barred the use of evidence secured through an illegal search and seizure. This ruling * * * was not derived from the explicit requirements of the Fourth Amendment; it was not based on legislation expressing Congressional policy in the enforcement of the Constitution. The decision was a matter of judicial implication. Since then it has been frequently applied and we stoutly adhere to it. But the immediate question is whether the basic right to protection against arbitrary intrusion by the police demands the exclusion of logically relevant evidence obtained by an unreasonable search and seizure because, in a federal prosecution for a federal crime, it would be excluded. As a matter of inherent reason, one would suppose this to be an issue as to which men with complete devotion to the protection of the right of privacy might give different answers. When we find that in fact most of the English-speaking world does not regard as vital to such protection the exclusion of evidence thus obtained, we must hesitate to treat this remedy as an essential ingredient of the right. The contrariety of views of the States is particularly impressive in view of the careful reconsideration which they have given the problem in the light of the *Weeks* decision.

* * * As of today 30 States reject the *Weeks* doctrine, 17 States are in agreement with it. * * * Of 10 jurisdictions within the United Kingdom and the British Commonwealth of Nations which have passed on the question, none has held evidence obtained by illegal search and seizure inadmissible. * * *

The jurisdictions which have rejected the *Weeks* doctrine have not left the right to privacy without other means of protection. Indeed, the exclusion of evidence is a remedy which directly serves only to protect those upon whose person or premises something incriminating has been found. We cannot, therefore, regard it as a departure from basic standards to remand such persons, together with those who emerge scatheless from a search, to the remedies of private action and such protection as the internal discipline of the police, under the eyes of an alert public opinion, may afford. Granting that in practice the exclusion of evidence may be an effective way of deterring unreasonable searches, it is not for this Court to condemn as falling below the minimal standards assured by the Due Process Clause a State's reliance upon other methods which, if consistently enforced, would be equally effective. * * * There are, moreover, reasons for excluding evidence unreasonably obtained by the federal police which are less compelling in the case of police under

State or local authority. The public opinion of a community can far more effectively be exerted against oppressive conduct on the part of police directly responsible to the community itself than can local opinion, sporadically aroused, be brought to bear upon remote authority pervasively exerted throughout the country.

We hold, therefore, that in a prosecution in a State court for a State crime the Fourteenth Amendment does not forbid the admission of evidence obtained by an unreasonable search and seizure. * * *

JUSTICE BLACK, concurring.

* * * I agree with what appears to be a plain implication of the Court's opinion that the federal exclusionary rule is not a command of the Fourth Amendment but is a judicially created rule of evidence which Congress might negate. * * *

JUSTICE MURPHY, with whom JUSTICE RUTLEDGE joins, dissenting.

[T]here is but one alternative to the rule of exclusion. That is no sanction at all.

* * * Little need be said concerning the possibilities of criminal prosecution. Self-scrutiny is a lofty ideal, but its exaltation reaches new heights if we expect a District Attorney to prosecute himself or his associates for well-meaning violations of the search and seizure clause during a raid the District Attorney or his associates have ordered. But there is an appealing ring in another alternative. A trespass action for damages is a venerable means of securing reparation for unauthorized invasion of the home. Why not put the old writ to a new use? When the Court cites cases permitting the action, the remedy seems complete.

But what an illusory remedy this is, if by "remedy" we mean a positive deterrent to police and prosecutors tempted to violate the Fourth Amendment. The appealing ring softens when we recall that in a trespass action the measure of damages is simply the extent of the injury to physical property. If the officer searches with care, he can avoid all but nominal damages—a penny, or a dollar. Are punitive damages possible? Perhaps. But a few states permit none, whatever the circumstances. In those that do, the plaintiff must show the real ill will or malice of the defendant, and surely it is not unreasonable to assume that one in honest pursuit of crime bears no malice toward the search victim. If that burden is carried, recovery may yet be defeated by the rule that there must be physical damages before punitive damages may be awarded. In addition, some states limit punitive damages to the actual expenses of litigation. * * * Even assuming the ill will of the officer, his reasonable grounds for belief that the home he searched harbored evidence of crime is admissible in mitigation of punitive damages. * * * The bad reputation of the plaintiff is likewise admissible. * * * If the evidence seized was actually used at a trial, that fact has been held a complete justification of the search, and a defense against the trespass action. * * * And even if the plaintiff hurdles all these obstacles, and gains a substantial verdict, the individual officer's finances may well make the judgment useless—for the municipality, of course, is not liable without its consent. Is it surprising that there is so little in the books concerning trespass actions for violation of the search and seizure clause? * * *

JUSTICE DOUGLAS, dissenting.

* * * I agree with Justice Murphy that * * * in absence of [an exclusionary] rule of evidence the Amendment would have no effective sanction. * * *

MAPP V. OHIO
367 U.S. 643, 81 S.Ct. 1684, 6 L.Ed.2d 1081 (1961).

JUSTICE CLARK delivered the opinion of the Court. * * *

On May 23, 1957, three Cleveland police officers arrived at appellant's residence in that city pursuant to information that "a person [was] hiding out in the home who was wanted for questioning in connection with a recent bombing, and that there was a large amount of policy paraphernalia being hidden in the home." Miss Mapp and her daughter by a former marriage lived on the top floor of the two-family dwelling. Upon their arrival at that house, the officers knocked on the door and demanded entrance but appellant, after telephoning her attorney, refused to admit them without a search warrant. * * *

The officers again sought entrance some three hours later when four or more additional officers arrived on the scene. When Miss Mapp did not come to the door immediately, at least one of the several doors to the house was forcibly opened and the policemen gained admittance. Meanwhile Miss Mapp's attorney arrived, but the officers, having secured their own entry, and continuing in their defiance of the law, would permit him neither to see Miss Mapp nor to enter the house. [When the officers broke into the hall, Miss Mapp] demanded to see the search warrant. A paper, claimed to be a warrant, was held up by one of the officers. She grabbed the "warrant" and placed it in her bosom. A struggle ensued in which the officers recovered the piece of paper and as a result of which they handcuffed appellant because she had been "belligerent" in resisting their official rescue of the "warrant" from her person. * * * Appellant, in handcuffs, was then forcibly taken upstairs to her bedroom where the officers searched a dresser, a chest of drawers, a closet and some suitcases. * * * The search spread to the rest of the second floor * * *. The basement of the building and a trunk found therein were also searched. The obscene materials for possession of which she was ultimately convicted were discovered in the course of that widespread search.

At the trial no search warrant was produced by the prosecution, nor was the failure to produce one explained or accounted for. At best [as the Ohio Supreme Court, which affirmed the conviction, expressed it], "there is, in the record, considerable doubt as to whether there ever was any warrant for the search of defendant's home." * * *

The State says that even if the search were made without authority, or otherwise unreasonably, it is not prevented from using the unconstitutionally seized evidence at trial, citing *Wolf v. Colorado,* * * *. On this appeal, * * * it is urged once again that we review that holding. * * *

The Court in *Wolf* first stated that "[t]he contrariety of views of the States" on the adoption of the exclusionary rule of *Weeks* was "particularly impressive" * * *.

While in 1949, prior to the *Wolf* case, almost two-thirds of the States were opposed to the use of the exclusionary rule, now, despite the *Wolf* case, more than half of those since passing upon it, by their own legislative or judicial decision, have wholly or partly adopted or adhered to the *Weeks* rule. * * * Significantly, among those now following the rule is California which, according to its highest court, was "compelled to reach that conclusion because other remedies have completely failed to secure compliance with the constitutional provisions * * *." In connection with this California case, we note that the second basis elaborated in *Wolf* in support of its failure to enforce the exclusionary doctrine against the States was that "other means of protection" have been afforded "the right to privacy." The experience of California that such other remedies have been worthless and futile is buttressed by the experience of other States.

Likewise, time has set its face against what *Wolf* called the "weighty testimony" of *People v. Defore,* 1926, 242 N.Y. 13, 150 N.E. 585. There Justice (then Judge) Cardozo, rejecting adoption of the *Weeks* exclusionary rule in New York, had said that "[t]he Federal rule as it stands is either too strict or too lax." However the force of that reasoning has been largely vitiated by later decisions of this Court. These include the recent discarding of the "silver platter" doctrine, *Elkins v. United States;*[a] the relaxation of the formerly strict requirements as to standing to challenge the use of evidence thus seized, * * * and finally, the formulation of a method to prevent state use of evidence unconstitutionally seized by federal agents, *Rea v. United States.*[b] * * *

It, therefore, plainly appears that the factual considerations supporting the failure of the *Wolf* Court to include the *Weeks* exclusionary rule when it recognized the enforceability of the right to privacy against the States in 1949, while not basically relevant to the constitutional consideration, could not, in any analysis, now be deemed controlling.

* * * Today we once again examine *Wolf's* constitutional documentation of the right to privacy free from unreasonable state intrusion, and, after its dozen years on our books, are led by it to close the only courtroom door remaining open to evidence secured by official lawlessness in flagrant abuse of that basic right, reserved to all persons as a specific guarantee against that very same unlawful

---

[a] 364 U.S. 206 (1960). Under the "silver platter" doctrine, evidence of a federal crime seized by state police in the course of an illegal search while investigating a state crime could be turned over to federal authorities and used in a federal prosecution so long as federal agents had not participated in the illegal search but had simply received the evidence on a "silver platter." In rejecting the doctrine, the Court pointed out that the determination in *Wolf* that Fourteenth Amendment Due Process prohibited illegal searches and seizures by state officers, marked the "removal of the doctrinal underpinning" for the admissibility of state-seized evidence in federal prosecutions.

[b] 350 U.S. 214 (1956), where the Court held that a federal law enforcement agent who seized evidence on the basis of an invalid search warrant should be enjoined from turning over such evidence to state authorities for use in a state prosecution and from giving testimony concerning the evidence: "The District Court is not asked to enjoin state officials nor in any way to interfere with state agencies in enforcement of state law. * * * The only relief asked is against a federal agent, who obtained the property as a result of the abuse of process issued by a United States Commissioner. * * * In this posture we have then a case that raises not a constitutional question but one concerning our supervisory powers over federal law enforcement agencies."

conduct. We hold that all evidence obtained by searches and seizures in violation of the Constitution is, by that same authority, inadmissible in a state court.[c]

Since the Fourth Amendment's right of privacy has been declared enforceable against the States through the Due Process Clause of the Fourteenth, it is enforceable against them by the same sanction of exclusion as is used against the Federal Government. Were it otherwise then just as without the *Weeks* rule the assurance against unreasonable federal searches and seizures would be "a form of words," valueless and undeserving of mention in a perpetual charter of inestimable human liberties, so too, without that rule the freedom from state invasions of privacy would be so ephemeral and so neatly severed from its conceptual nexus with the freedom from all brutish means of coercing evidence as not to merit this Court's high regard as a freedom "implicit in 'the concept of ordered liberty.' "

* * * [I]n extending the substantive protections of due process to all constitutionally unreasonable searches—state or federal—it was logically and constitutionally necessary that the exclusion doctrine—an essential part of the right to privacy—be also insisted upon as an essential ingredient of the right newly recognized by the *Wolf* case. In short, the admission of the new constitutional right by *Wolf* could not consistently tolerate denial of its most important constitutional privilege, namely, the exclusion of the evidence which an accused had been forced to give by reason of the unlawful seizure. To hold otherwise is to grant the right but in reality to withhold its privilege and enjoyment. Only last year the Court itself recognized that the purpose of the exclusionary rule "is to deter—to compel

---

[c]   Although an illegal arrest or other unreasonable seizure of the person is itself a violation of the Fourth and Fourteenth Amendments, the *Mapp* exclusionary sanction comes into play only when the police have obtained evidence as a result of the unconstitutional seizure. Such is the case when, for example, the police make an illegal arrest and then conduct a fruitful search which is "incident to" that arrest and thus dependent upon the lawfulness of the arrest for its legality. Such may also be the case when the connection between the illegality and the evidence is less apparent, and even when the evidence is verbal, such as a confession obtained from a defendant some time after his illegal arrest. As explained in *Wong Sun v. United States*, 371 U.S. 471 (1963), not "all evidence is 'fruit of the poisonous tree' simply because it would not have come to light but for the illegal actions of the police. Rather, the more apt question in such a case is 'whether, granting establishment of the primary illegality [the evidence] has been come at by exploitation of that illegality or instead by means sufficiently distinguishable to be purged of the primary taint.' " In making that judgment, the "temporal proximity of the arrest and the confession, the presence of intervening circumstances and, particularly, the purpose and flagrancy of the official misconduct, are all relevant. The voluntariness of the statement is a threshold requirement." *Brown v. Illinois*, 422 U.S. 590 (1975).

In *United States v. Crews*, 445 U.S. 463 (1980), the Court held that an illegally arrested defendant "is not himself a suppressible 'fruit' and the illegality of his detention cannot deprive the Government of the opportunity to prove his guilt through the introduction of evidence wholly untainted by the police misconduct." Moreover, it is no defense to a state or federal criminal prosecution that the defendant was illegally arrested or forcibly brought within the jurisdiction of the court. The trial of such a defendant violates neither Fifth nor Fourteenth Amendment due process. As explained in *Frisbie v. Collins*, 342 U.S. 519 (1952), this rule rests "on the sound basis that due process of law is satisfied when one present in court is convicted of crime after having been fairly apprized of the charges against him and after a fair trial in accordance with constitutional procedural safeguards. There is nothing in the Constitution that requires a court to permit a guilty person rightfully convicted to escape justice because he was brought to trial against his will." The Court added that even if the conduct in obtaining defendant's presence violated the federal kidnapping statute the result would be the same, for Congress had not included a bar to prosecution as an available sanction under that law.

respect for the constitutional guaranty in the only effectively available way—by removing the incentive to disregard it."

Indeed, we are aware of no restraint, similar to that rejected today, conditioning the enforcement of any other basic constitutional right. The right to privacy, no less important than any other right carefully and particularly reserved to the people, would stand in marked contrast to all other rights declared as "basic to a free society." * * * [N]othing could be more certain than that when a coerced confession is involved, "the relevant rules of evidence" are overridden without regard to "the incidence of such conduct by the police," slight or frequent. Why should not the same rule apply to what is tantamount to coerced testimony by way of unconstitutional seizure of goods, papers, effects, documents, etc.? We find that, as to the Federal Government the Fourth and Fifth Amendments and, as to the States, the freedom from unconscionable invasions of privacy and the freedom from convictions based upon coerced confessions do enjoy an "intimate relation" in their perpetuation of "principles of humanity and civil liberty * * *." They express "supplementing phases of the same constitutional purpose—to maintain inviolate large areas of personal privacy." The philosophy of each Amendment and of each freedom is complementary to, although not dependent upon, that of the other in its sphere of influence—the very least that together they assure in either sphere is that no man is to be convicted on unconstitutional evidence.

Moreover, our holding * * * is not only the logical dictate of prior cases, but it also makes very good sense. There is no war between the Constitution and common sense. Presently, a federal prosecutor may make no use of evidence illegally seized, but a State's attorney across the street may, although he supposedly is operating under the enforceable prohibitions of the same Amendment. Thus the State, by admitting evidence unlawfully seized, serves to encourage disobedience to the Federal Constitution which it is bound to uphold. * * *

There are those who say, as did Justice (then Judge) Cardozo, that under our constitutional exclusionary doctrine "[t]he criminal is to go free because the constable has blundered." *People v. Defore.* In some cases this will undoubtedly be the result. But, as was said in *Elkins,* "there is another consideration—the imperative of judicial integrity." The criminal goes free, if he must, but it is the law that sets him free. Nothing can destroy a government more quickly than its failure to observe its own laws, or worse, its disregard of the charter of its own existence. As Mr. Justice Brandeis, dissenting, said in *Olmstead v. United States,* 277 U.S. 438 (1928): "Our government is the potent, the omnipresent teacher. For good or for ill, it teaches the whole people by its example. * * * If the government becomes a lawbreaker, it breeds contempt for law; it invites every man to become a law unto himself; it invites anarchy." Nor can it lightly be assumed that, as a practical matter, adoption of the exclusionary rule fetters law enforcement. Only last year this Court expressly considered that contention and found that "pragmatic evidence of a sort" to the contrary was not wanting. * * *. The Court noted that:

> "The federal courts themselves have operated under the exclusionary rule of *Weeks* for almost half a century; yet it has not been suggested either that the Federal Bureau of Investigation has thereby

been rendered ineffective, or that the administration of criminal justice in the federal courts has thereby been disrupted. Moreover, the experience of the states is impressive * * *. The movement toward the rule of exclusion has been halting but seemingly inexorable."

The ignoble shortcut to conviction left open to the State tends to destroy the entire system of constitutional restraints on which the liberties of the people rest. Having once recognized that the right to privacy embodied in the Fourth Amendment is enforceable against the States, and that the right to be secure against rude invasions of privacy by state officers is, therefore, constitutional in origin, we can no longer permit that right to remain an empty promise. Because it is enforceable in the same manner and to like effect as other basic rights secured by the Due Process Clause, we can no longer permit it to be revocable at the whim of any police officer who, in the name of law enforcement itself, chooses to suspend its enjoyment. Our decision, founded on reason and truth, gives to the individual no more than that which the Constitution guarantees him, to the police officer no less than that to which honest law enforcement is entitled, and, to the courts, that judicial integrity so necessary in the true administration of justice. * * *

Reversed and remanded.

JUSTICE BLACK, concurring. * * *

I am still not persuaded that the Fourth Amendment, standing alone, would be enough to bar the introduction into evidence against an accused of papers and effects seized from him in violation of its commands. For the Fourth Amendment does not itself contain any provision expressly precluding the use of such evidence, and I am extremely doubtful that such a provision could properly be inferred from nothing more than the basic command against unreasonable searches and seizures. Reflection on the problem, however, in the light of cases coming before the Court since *Wolf,* has led me to conclude that when the Fourth Amendment's ban against unreasonable searches and seizures is considered together with the Fifth Amendment's ban against compelled self-incrimination, a constitutional basis emerges which not only justifies but actually requires the exclusionary rule. * * *

JUSTICE DOUGLAS, concurring.

* * * I believe that this is an appropriate case in which to put an end to the asymmetry which *Wolf* imported into the law. * * *

Memorandum of JUSTICE STEWART.

* * * I express no view as to the merits of the constitutional issue which the Court today decides. * * *

JUSTICE HARLAN, whom JUSTICE FRANKFURTER and JUSTICE WHITTAKER join, dissenting.

* * * I would not impose upon the States this federal exclusionary remedy. The reasons given by the majority for now suddenly turning its back on *Wolf* seem to me notably unconvincing.

First, it is said that "the factual grounds upon which *Wolf* was based" have since changed, in that more States now follow the *Weeks* exclusionary rule than was so at the time *Wolf* was decided. While that is true, a recent survey indicates that at present one half of the States still adhere to the common-law non-exclusionary rule, and one, Maryland, retains the rule as to felonies. * * * But in any case surely all this is beside the point, as the majority itself indeed seems to recognize. Our concern here, as it was in *Wolf,* is not with the desirability of that rule but only with the question whether the States are Constitutionally free to follow it or not as they may themselves determine, and the relevance of the disparity of views among the States on this point lies simply in the fact that the judgment involved is a debatable one. Moreover, the very fact on which the majority relies, instead of lending support to what is now being done, points away from the need of replacing voluntary state action with federal compulsion.

The preservation of a proper balance between state and federal responsibility in the administration of criminal justice demands patience on the part of those who might like to see things move faster among the States in this respect. Problems of criminal law enforcement vary widely from State to State. One State, in considering the totality of its legal picture, may conclude that the need for embracing the *Weeks* rule is pressing because other remedies are unavailable or inadequate to secure compliance with the substantive Constitutional principle involved. Another, though equally solicitous of Constitutional rights, may choose to pursue one purpose at a time, allowing all evidence relevant to guilt to be brought into a criminal trial, and dealing with Constitutional infractions by other means. Still another may consider the exclusionary rule too rough and ready a remedy, in that it reaches only unconstitutional intrusions which eventuate in criminal prosecution of the victims. Further, a State after experimenting with the *Weeks* rule for a time may, because of unsatisfactory experience with it, decide to revert to a non-exclusionary rule. And so on. * * * For us the question remains, as it has always been, one of state power, not one of passing judgment on the wisdom of one state course or another. In my view this Court should continue to forbear from fettering the States with an adamant rule which may embarrass them in coping with their own peculiar problems in criminal law enforcement. * * *

* * * Our role in promulgating the *Weeks* rule and its extensions * * * was quite a different one than it is here. There, in implementing the Fourth Amendment, we occupied the position of a tribunal having the ultimate responsibility for developing the standards and procedures of judicial administration within the judicial system over which it presides. Here we review State procedures whose measure is to be taken not against the specific substantive commands of the Fourth Amendment but under the flexible contours of the Due Process Clause. I do not believe that the Fourteenth Amendment empowers this Court to mould state remedies effectuating the right to freedom from "arbitrary intrusion by the police" to suit its own notions of how things should be done * * *.

Finally, it is said that the overruling of *Wolf* is supported by the established doctrine that the admission in evidence of an involuntary confession renders a state conviction constitutionally invalid. Since such a confession may often be entirely reliable, and therefore of the greatest relevance to the issue of the trial, the argument continues, this doctrine is ample warrant in precedent that the way evidence was obtained and not just its relevance, is constitutionally significant to the fairness of a trial. I believe this analogy is not a true one. The "coerced confession" rule is certainly not a rule that any illegally obtained statements may not be used in evidence. I would suppose that a statement which is procured during a period of illegal detention is, as much as unlawfully seized evidence, illegally obtained, but this Court has consistently refused to reverse state convictions resting on the use of such statements. * * *

The point, then, must be that in requiring exclusion of an involuntary statement of an accused, we are concerned not with an appropriate remedy for what the police have done, but with something which is regarded as going to the heart of our concepts of fairness in judicial procedure. The operative assumption of our procedural system is that "ours is the accusatorial as opposed to the inquisitorial system. * * *." * * * The pressures brought to bear against an accused leading to a confession, unlike an unconstitutional violation of privacy, do not, apart from the use of the confession at trial, necessarily involve independent Constitutional violations. What is crucial is that the trial defense to which an accused is entitled should not be rendered an empty formality by reason of statements wrung from him, for then "a prisoner * * * [has been] made the deluded instrument of his own conviction." That this is a *procedural right,* and that its violation occurs at the time his improperly obtained statement is admitted at trial, is manifest. * * *

This, and not the disciplining of the police, as with illegally seized evidence, is surely the true basis for excluding a statement of the accused which was unconstitutionally obtained. In sum, I think the coerced confession analogy works strongly *against* what the Court does today. * * *

UNITED STATES V. LEON
468 U.S. 897, 104 S.Ct. 3405, 82 L.Ed.2d 677 (1984).

JUSTICE WHITE delivered the opinion of the Court. * * *

This case presents the question whether the Fourth Amendment exclusionary rule should be modified so as not to bar the use in the prosecution's case-in-chief of evidence obtained by officers acting in reasonable reliance on a search warrant issued by a detached and neutral magistrate but ultimately found to be unsupported by probable cause. * * *

The Fourth Amendment contains no provision expressly precluding the use of evidence obtained in violation of its commands, and an examination of its origin and purposes makes clear that the use of fruits of a past unlawful search or seizure "work[s] no new Fourth Amendment wrong." The wrong condemned by the Amendment is "fully accomplished" by the unlawful search or seizure itself, and the exclusionary rule is neither intended nor able to "cure the invasion of the defendant's rights which he has already suffered." The rule thus operates as "a judicially created remedy designed to safeguard Fourth Amendment rights generally through its deterrent effect, rather than a personal constitutional right of the person aggrieved."

Whether the exclusionary sanction is appropriately imposed in a particular case, our decisions make clear, is "an issue separate from the question whether the Fourth Amendment rights of the party seeking to invoke the rule were violated by police conduct." Only the former question is currently before us,[a] and it must be resolved by weighing the costs and benefits of preventing the use in the prosecution's case-in-chief of inherently trustworthy tangible evidence obtained in reliance on a search warrant issued by a detached and neutral magistrate that ultimately is found to be defective.

The substantial social costs exacted by the exclusionary rule for the vindication of Fourth Amendment rights have long been a source of concern. "Our cases have consistently recognized that unbending application of the exclusionary sanction to enforce ideals of governmental rectitude would impede unacceptably the truth-finding functions of judge and jury." An objectionable collateral consequence of this interference with the criminal justice system's truth-finding function is that some guilty defendants may go free or receive reduced sentences as a result of favorable plea bargains.[6] Particularly when law enforcement officers have acted in objective good faith or their transgressions have been minor, the magnitude of the benefit conferred on such guilty defendants offends basic concepts of the criminal justice system. Indiscriminate application of the exclusionary rule, therefore, may well "generat[e] disrespect for the law and the administration of justice." Accordingly, "[a]s with any remedial device, the application of the rule has been restricted to those areas where its remedial objectives are thought most efficaciously served."

---

[a] A large quantity of drugs were suppressed on the ground the warrant had not issued on probable cause, in that the affidavit reported only the allegations of an untested informant and limited corroboration by police surveillance of events themselves "as consistent with innocence as * * * with guilt." The Court earlier noted that whether this warrant would pass muster under the intervening and less demanding test of *Illinois v. Gates*, § 3 infra, "has not been briefed or argued," and thus chose "to take the case as it comes to us."

[6] Researchers have only recently begun to study extensively the effects of the exclusionary rule on the disposition of felony arrests. One study suggests that the rule results in the non-prosecution or nonconviction of between 0.6% and 2.35% of individuals arrested for felonies. Davies, *A Hard Look at What We Know (and Still Need to Learn) About the "Costs" of the Exclusionary Rule: The NIJ Study and Other Studies of "Lost" Arrests*, 1983 A.B.F.Res.J. 611, 621. The estimates are higher for particular crimes the prosecution of which depends heavily on physical evidence. Thus, the cumulative loss due to nonprosecution or nonconviction of individuals arrested on felony drug charges is probably in the range of 2.8% to 7.1%. Davies' analysis of California data suggests that screening by police and prosecutors results in the release because of illegal searches or seizures of as many as 1.4% of all felony arrestees, id., at 650, that 0.9% of felony arrestees are released because of illegal searches or seizures at the preliminary hearing or after trial, id., at 653, and that roughly 0.5% of all felony arrestees benefit from reversals on appeal because of illegal searches. * * *

Many of these researchers have concluded that the impact of the exclusionary rule is insubstantial, but the small percentages with which they deal mask a large absolute number of felons who are released because the cases against them were based in part on illegal searches or seizures. * * * Because we find that the rule can have no substantial deterrent effect in the sorts of situations under consideration in this case, we conclude that it cannot pay its way in those situations.

Close attention to those remedial objectives has characterized our recent decisions concerning the scope of the Fourth Amendment exclusionary rule. The Court has, to be sure, not seriously questioned, "in the absence of a more efficacious sanction, the continued application of the rule to suppress evidence from the [prosecution's] case where a Fourth Amendment violation has been substantial and deliberate * * *." Nevertheless, the balancing approach that has evolved in various contexts—including criminal trials—"forcefully suggest[s] that the exclusionary rule be more generally modified to permit the introduction of evidence obtained in the reasonable good-faith belief that a search or seizure was in accord with the Fourth Amendment." * * *

Only [when a warrant is grounded upon an affidavit knowingly or recklessly false] has the Court set forth a rationale for suppressing evidence obtained pursuant to a search warrant;[b] in the other areas, it has simply excluded such evidence without considering whether Fourth Amendment interests will be advanced. To the extent that proponents of exclusion rely on its behavioral effects on judges and magistrates in these areas, their reliance is misplaced. First, the exclusionary rule is designed to deter police misconduct rather than to punish the errors of judges and magistrates. Second, there exists no evidence suggesting that judges and magistrates are inclined to ignore or subvert the Fourth Amendment or that lawlessness among these actors requires application of the extreme sanction of exclusion.[14]

Third, and most important, we discern no basis, and are offered none, for believing that exclusion of evidence seized pursuant to a warrant will have a significant deterrent effect on the issuing judge or magistrate. Many of the factors that indicate that the exclusionary rule cannot provide an effective "special" or "general" deterrent for individual offending law enforcement officers apply as well to judges or magistrates. And, to the extent that the rule is thought to operate as a "systemic" deterrent on a wider audience, it clearly can have no such effect on individuals empowered to issue warrants. Judges and magistrates are not adjuncts to the law enforcement team; as neutral judicial officers, they have no stake in the outcome of particular criminal prosecutions. The threat of exclusion thus cannot be expected significantly to deter them. Imposition of the exclusionary sanction is not necessary meaningfully to inform judicial officers of their errors, and we cannot conclude that admitting evidence obtained pursuant to a warrant while at the same time declaring that the warrant was somehow defective will in any way reduce judicial officers' professional incentives to comply with the Fourth Amendment, encourage them to repeat their mistakes, or lead to the granting of all colorable warrant requests.[18]

---

b   The reference is to *Franks v. Delaware,* 438 U.S. 154 (1978), where the Court declared "it would be an unthinkable imposition upon [the magistrate's] authority if a warrant affidavit, revealed after the fact to contain a deliberately or recklessly false statement, were to stand beyond impeachment."

14   Although there are assertions that some magistrates become rubber stamps for the police and others may be unable effectively to screen police conduct, we are not convinced that this is a problem of major proportions.

18   Limiting the application of the exclusionary sanction may well increase the care with which magistrates scrutinize warrant applications. We doubt that magistrates are more desirous

If exclusion of evidence obtained pursuant to a subsequently invalidated warrant is to have any deterrent effect, therefore, it must alter the behavior of individual law enforcement officers or the policies of their departments. One could argue that applying the exclusionary rule in cases where the police failed to demonstrate probable cause in the warrant application deters future inadequate presentations or "magistrate shopping" and thus promotes the ends of the Fourth Amendment. Suppressing evidence obtained pursuant to a technically defective warrant supported by probable cause also might encourage officers to scrutinize more closely the form of the warrant and to point out suspected judicial errors. We find such arguments speculative and conclude that suppression of evidence obtained pursuant to a warrant should be ordered only on a case-by-case basis and only in those unusual cases in which exclusion will further the purposes of the exclusionary rule.[19]

We have frequently questioned whether the exclusionary rule can have any deterrent effect when the offending officers acted in the objectively reasonable belief that their conduct did not violate the Fourth Amendment. "No empirical researcher, proponent or opponent of the rule, has yet been able to establish with any assurance whether the rule has a deterrent effect * * *." But even assuming that the rule effectively deters some police misconduct and provides incentives for the law enforcement profession as a whole to conduct itself in accord with the Fourth Amendment, it cannot be expected, and should not be applied, to deter objectively reasonable law enforcement activity. * * * [20]

---

of avoiding the exclusion of evidence obtained pursuant to warrants they have issued than of avoiding invasions of privacy.

Federal magistrates, moreover, are subject to the direct supervision of district courts. They may be removed for "incompetency, misconduct, neglect of duty, or physical or mental disability." 28 U.S.C. § 631(i). If a magistrate serves merely as a "rubber stamp" for the police or is unable to exercise mature judgment, closer supervision or removal provides a more effective remedy than the exclusionary rule.

[19] Our discussion of the deterrent effect of excluding evidence obtained in reasonable reliance on a subsequently invalidated warrant assumes, of course, that the officers properly executed the warrant and searched only those places and for those objects that it was reasonable to believe were covered by the warrant. * * *

[20] We emphasize that the standard of reasonableness we adopt is an objective one. Many objections to a good-faith exception assume that the exception will turn on the subjective good faith of individual officers. "Grounding the modification in objective reasonableness, however, retains the value of the exclusionary rule as an incentive for the law enforcement profession as a whole to conduct themselves in accord with the Fourth Amendment." The objective standard we adopt, moreover, requires officers to have a reasonable knowledge of what the law prohibits. As Professor Jerold Israel has observed:

"The key to the [exclusionary] rule's effectiveness as a deterrent lies, I believe, in the impetus it has provided to police training programs that make officers aware of the limits imposed by the fourth amendment and emphasize the need to operate within those limits. [An objective good-faith exception] * * * is not likely to result in the elimination of such programs, which are now viewed as an important aspect of police professionalism. Neither is it likely to alter the tenor of those programs; the possibility that illegally obtained evidence may be admitted in borderline cases is unlikely to encourage police instructors to pay less attention to fourth amendment limitations. Finally, [it] * * * should not encourage officers to pay less attention to what they are taught, as the requirement that the officer act in 'good faith' is inconsistent with closing one's mind to the possibility of illegality."

This is particularly true, we believe, when an officer acting with objective good faith has obtained a search warrant from a judge or magistrate and acted within its scope. In most such cases, there is no police illegality and thus nothing to deter. It is the magistrate's responsibility to determine whether the officer's allegations establish probable cause and, if so, to issue a warrant comporting in form with the requirements of the Fourth Amendment. In the ordinary case, an officer cannot be expected to question the magistrate's probable-cause determination or his judgment that the form of the warrant is technically sufficient. "[O]nce the warrant issues, there is literally nothing more the policeman can do in seeking to comply with the law." Penalizing the officer for the magistrate's error, rather than his own, cannot logically contribute to the deterrence of Fourth Amendment violations.[22]

We conclude that the marginal or nonexistent benefits produced by suppressing evidence obtained in objectively reasonable reliance on a subsequently invalidated search warrant cannot justify the substantial costs of exclusion. We do not suggest, however, that exclusion is always inappropriate in cases where an officer has obtained a warrant and abided by its terms. [T]he officer's reliance on the magistrate's probable-cause determination and on the technical sufficiency of the warrant he issues must be objectively reasonable,[23] and it is clear that in some circumstances the officer[24] will have no reasonable grounds for believing that the warrant was properly issued.

Suppression therefore remains an appropriate remedy if the magistrate or judge in issuing a warrant was misled by information in an affidavit that the affiant knew was false or would have known was false except for his reckless disregard of the truth. The exception we recognize today will also not apply in cases where the issuing magistrate wholly abandoned his judicial role in the manner condemned in *Lo-Ji Sales, Inc. v. New York*, 442 U.S. 319 (1979);[c] in such circumstances, no reasonably well-trained officer should rely on the warrant. Nor would an officer manifest objective good faith in relying on a warrant based on an

---

[22] * * * Our cases establish that the question whether the use of illegally obtained evidence in judicial proceedings represents judicial participation in a Fourth Amendment violation and offends the integrity of the courts "is essentially the same as the inquiry into whether exclusion would serve a deterrent purpose." * * * Absent unusual circumstances, when a Fourth Amendment violation has occurred because the police have reasonably relied on a warrant issued by a detached and neutral magistrate but ultimately found to be defective, "the integrity of the courts is not implicated."

[23] [O]ur good-faith inquiry is confined to the objectively ascertainable question whether a reasonably well-trained officer would have known that the search was illegal despite the magistrate's authorization. In making this determination, all of the circumstances—including whether the warrant application had previously been rejected by a different magistrate—may be considered.

[24] References to "officer" throughout this opinion should not be read too narrowly. It is necessary to consider the objective reasonableness, not only of the officers who eventually executed a warrant, but also of the officers who originally obtained it or who provided information material to the probable-cause determination. Nothing in our opinion suggests, for example, that an officer could obtain a warrant on the basis of a "bare bones" affidavit and then rely on colleagues who are ignorant of the circumstances under which the warrant was obtained to conduct the search.

[c] There the magistrate was held not to have "manifest[ed] that neutrality and detachment demanded of a judicial officer when presented with a warrant application," where he went to the scene and made judgments there about what should be seized as obscene, as he "allowed himself to become a member, if not the leader of the search party which was essentially a police operation."

affidavit "so lacking in indicia of probable cause as to render official belief in its existence entirely unreasonable." Finally, depending on the circumstances of the particular case, a warrant may be so facially deficient—i.e., in failing to particularize the place to be searched or the things to be seized—that the executing officers cannot reasonably presume it to be valid.[d]

* * * The good-faith exception for searches conducted pursuant to warrants is not intended to signal our unwillingness strictly to enforce the requirements of the Fourth Amendment, and we do not believe that it will have this effect. As we have already suggested, the good-faith exception, turning as it does on objective reasonableness, should not be difficult to apply in practice. When officers have acted pursuant to a warrant, the prosecution should ordinarily be able to establish objective good faith without a substantial expenditure of judicial time.

Nor are we persuaded that application of a good-faith exception to searches conducted pursuant to warrants will preclude review of the constitutionality of the search or seizure, deny needed guidance from the courts, or freeze Fourth Amendment law in its present state.[25] There is no need for courts to adopt the inflexible practice of always deciding whether the officers' conduct manifested objective good faith before turning to the question whether the Fourth Amendment has been violated. * * *

If the resolution of a particular Fourth Amendment question is necessary to guide future action by law enforcement officers and magistrates, nothing will prevent reviewing courts from deciding that question before turning to the good-faith issue.[26] Indeed, it frequently will be difficult to determine whether the officers acted reasonably without resolving the Fourth Amendment issue. Even if the

---

[d] Compare the companion case of *Massachusetts v. Sheppard*, 468 U.S. 981 (1984), where a detective prepared an affidavit for a search warrant to search for various specified items of evidence of a homicide but, because it was Sunday, could only find a warrant form for controlled substances. He presented his affidavit and that form to a judge at his home and pointed out the problem to him, and the judge, unable to locate a more suitable form, told the detective that he would make the necessary changes to make it a proper warrant. He made some changes, but failed to change that part of the warrant which authorized a search only for controlled substances and related paraphernalia. The detective took the two documents and he and other officers then executed the warrant, seizing evidence of the homicide. That evidence was suppressed in the state court because the warrant failed to particularly describe the items to be seized, as required by the Fourth Amendment. The Supreme Court, per White, J., held this situation fell within *Leon* because "there was an objectively reasonable basis for the officers' mistaken belief" that "the warrant authorized the search that they conducted." As for defendant's objection that the detective knew when he went to the judge that the warrant was defective, the Court stated: "Whatever an officer may be required to do when he executes a warrant without knowing beforehand what items are to be seized, we refuse to rule that an officer is required to disbelieve a judge who has just advised him, by word and by action, that the warrant he possesses authorizes him to conduct the search he has requested."

[25] The argument that defendants will lose their incentive to litigate meritorious Fourth Amendment claims as a result of the good-faith exception we adopt today is unpersuasive. Although the exception might discourage presentation of insubstantial suppression motions, the magnitude of the benefit conferred on defendants by a successful motion makes it unlikely that litigation of colorable claims will be substantially diminished.

[26] It has been suggested, in fact, that "the recognition of a 'penumbral zone,' within which an inadvertent mistake would not call for exclusion, * * * will make it less tempting for judges to bend fourth amendment standards to avoid releasing a possibly dangerous criminal because of a minor and unintentional miscalculation by the police."

Fourth Amendment question is not one of broad import, reviewing courts could decide in particular cases that magistrates under their supervision need to be informed of their errors and so evaluate the officers' good faith only after finding a violation. In other circumstances, those courts could reject suppression motions posing no important Fourth Amendment questions by turning immediately to a consideration of the officers' good faith. We have no reason to believe that our Fourth Amendment jurisprudence would suffer by allowing reviewing courts to exercise an informed discretion in making this choice. * * *

In the absence of an allegation that the magistrate abandoned his detached and neutral role, suppression is appropriate only if the officers were dishonest or reckless in preparing their affidavit or could not have harbored an objectively reasonable belief in the existence of probable cause. Only respondent Leon has contended that no reasonably well-trained police officer could have believed that there existed probable cause to search his house; significantly, the other respondents advance no comparable argument. Officer Rombach's application for a warrant clearly was supported by much more than a "bare bones" affidavit. The affidavit related the results of an extensive investigation and, as the opinions of the divided panel of the Court of Appeals make clear, provided evidence sufficient to create disagreement among thoughtful and competent judges as to the existence of probable cause. Under these circumstances, the officers' reliance on the magistrate's determination of probable cause was objectively reasonable, and application of the extreme sanction of exclusion is inappropriate.[e]

_____

[e] Prior to *Leon*, the Supreme Court had often applied the exclusionary rule even when the police acted in reliance upon a subsequently invalidated statute conferring authority to search. But when confronted with such a situation once again in *Illinois v. Krull*, 480 U.S. 340 (1987), the Court, 5–4, ruled otherwise. Blackmun, J., reasoned for the majority: "The approach used in *Leon* is equally applicable to the present case. The application of the exclusionary rule to suppress evidence obtained by an officer acting in objectively reasonable reliance on a statute would have as little deterrent effect on the officer's actions as would the exclusion of evidence when an officer acts in objectively reasonable reliance on a warrant. Unless a statute is clearly unconstitutional, an officer cannot be expected to question the judgment of the legislature that passed the law." The Court in *Krull* further reasoned that there was no "evidence to suggest that legislators 'are inclined to ignore or subvert the Fourth Amendment' " or "to indicate that applying the exclusionary rule to evidence seized pursuant to the statute prior to the declaration of its invalidity will act as a significant additional deterrent" of legislators.

O'Connor, J., for the dissenters, emphasized: (1) "The distinction drawn between the legislator and the judicial officer is sound" because "a legislature's unreasonable authorization of searches may affect thousands or millions" and thus "poses a greater threat to liberty." (2) "[L]egislators by virtue of their political role are more often subjected to the political pressures that may threaten Fourth Amendment values than are judicial officers." (3) "Providing legislatures a grace period during which the police may freely perform unreasonable searches in order to convict those who might have otherwise escaped creates a positive incentive to promulgate unconstitutional laws."

Analogizing to *Leon* and *Krull*, the Court in *Davis v. United States*, 564 U.S. 229 (2011), concluded that since the exclusionary rule does not apply when the police reasonably relied on a search warrant or statute later determined to violate the Fourth Amendment, the same should be true with respect to "searches conducted in objectively reasonable reliance on binding appellate precedent" that is later overruled. Sotomayor, J., concurring, stressed that the instant case "does not present the markedly different question whether the exclusionary rule applies when the law governing the constitutionality of a particular search is unsettled," where the fact "that the officer's conduct could be characterized as nonculpable" would not necessarily foreclose the conclusion that "exclusion would result in appreciable deterrence." Breyer and Ginsburg, JJ., dissenting, read the majority opinion as "plac[ing] determinative weight upon the culpability of an individual officer's conduct," which would mean "the 'good faith' exception will swallow the exclusionary rule."

Accordingly, the judgment of the Court of Appeals is reversed.

JUSTICE BLACKMUN, concurring.

[A]ny empirical judgment about the effect of the exclusionary rule in a particular class of cases necessarily is a provisional one. * * * If it should emerge from experience that, contrary to our expectations, the good faith exception to the exclusionary rule results in a material change in police compliance with the Fourth Amendment, we shall have to reconsider what we have undertaken here. The logic of a decision that rests on untested predictions about police conduct demands no less. * * *

JUSTICE BRENNAN, with whom JUSTICE MARSHALL joins, dissenting. * * *

[The majority's reading of the Fourth Amendment] appears plausible, because, as critics of the exclusionary rule never tire of repeating, the Fourth Amendment makes no express provision for the exclusion of evidence secured in violation of its commands. A short answer to this claim, of course, is that many of the Constitution's most vital imperatives are stated in general terms and the task of giving meaning to these precepts is therefore left to subsequent judicial decision-making in the context of concrete cases. The nature of our Constitution, as Chief Justice Marshall long ago explained, "requires that only its great outlines should be marked, its important objects designated, and the minor ingredients which compose those objects be deduced from the nature of the objects themselves."

A more direct answer may be supplied by recognizing that the Amendment, like other provisions of the Bill of Rights, restrains the power of the government as a whole; it does not specify only a particular agency and exempt all others. The judiciary is responsible, no less than the executive, for ensuring that constitutional rights are respected.

When that fact is kept in mind, the role of the courts and their possible involvement in the concerns of the Fourth Amendment comes into sharper focus. Because seizures are executed principally to secure evidence, and because such evidence generally has utility in our legal system only in the context of a trial supervised by a judge, it is apparent that the admission of illegally obtained evidence implicates the same constitutional concerns as the initial seizure of that evidence. Indeed, by admitting unlawfully seized evidence, the judiciary becomes a part of what is in fact a single governmental action prohibited by the terms of the Amendment. Once that connection between the evidence-gathering role of the police and the evidence-admitting function of the courts is acknowledged, the plausibility of the Court's interpretation becomes more suspect. Certainly nothing in the language or history of the Fourth Amendment suggests that a recognition of this evidentiary link between the police and the courts was meant to be foreclosed. It is difficult to give any meaning at all to the limitations imposed by the Amendment if they are read to proscribe only certain conduct by the police but to allow other agents of the same government to take advantage of evidence secured by the police in violation of its requirements. The Amendment therefore must be read to condemn not only the initial unconstitutional invasion of privacy—which is done, after all, for the purpose of securing evidence—but also the subsequent use of any evidence so obtained. * * *

Such a conception of the rights secured by the Fourth Amendment was unquestionably the original basis of what has come to be called the exclusionary rule when it was first formulated in *Weeks v. United States.* * * *

[T]he question whether the exclusion of evidence would deter future police misconduct was never considered a relevant concern in the early cases * * *. In those formative decisions, the Court plainly understood that the exclusion of illegally obtained evidence was compelled not by judicially fashioned remedial purposes, but rather by a direct constitutional command. * * *

* * * Indeed, no other explanation suffices to account for the Court's holding in *Mapp,* since the only possible predicate for the Court's conclusion that the States were bound by the Fourteenth Amendment to honor the *Weeks* doctrine is that the exclusionary rule was "part and parcel of the Fourth Amendment's limitation upon [governmental] encroachment of individual privacy."

Despite this clear pronouncement, however, the Court * * * has gradually pressed the deterrence rationale for the rule back to center stage. The various arguments advanced by the Court in this campaign have only strengthened my conviction that the deterrence theory is both misguided and unworkable. First, the Court has frequently bewailed the "cost" of excluding reliable evidence. In large part, this criticism rests upon a refusal to acknowledge the function of the Fourth Amendment itself. If nothing else, the Amendment plainly operates to disable the government from gathering information and securing evidence in certain ways. In practical terms, of course, this restriction of official power means that some incriminating evidence inevitably will go undetected if the government obeys these constitutional restraints. It is the loss of that evidence that is the "price" our society pays for enjoying the freedom and privacy safeguarded by the Fourth Amendment. Thus, some criminals will go free *not,* in Justice (then Judge) Cardozo's misleading epigram, "because the constable has blundered," but rather because official compliance with Fourth Amendment requirements makes it more difficult to catch criminals. Understood in this way, the Amendment directly contemplates that some reliable and incriminating evidence will be lost to the government; therefore, it is not the exclusionary rule, but the Amendment itself that has imposed this cost.

In addition, the Court's decisions over the past decade have made plain that the entire enterprise of attempting to assess the benefits and costs of the exclusionary rule in various contexts is a virtually impossible task for the judiciary to perform honestly or accurately. Although the Court's language in those cases suggests that some specific empirical basis may support its analyses, the reality is that the Court's opinions represent inherently unstable compounds of intuition, hunches, and occasional pieces of partial and often inconclusive data. * * * To the extent empirical data is available regarding the general costs and benefits of the exclusionary rule, it has shown, on the one hand, as the Court acknowledges today, that the costs are not as substantial as critics have asserted in the past, and, on the other hand, that while the exclusionary rule may well have certain deterrent effects, it is extremely difficult to determine with any degree of precision whether the incidence of unlawful conduct by police is now lower than it was prior to *Mapp*. The Court has sought to turn this uncertainty to its advantage by casting the burden of proof upon proponents of the rule. "Obviously," however, "the assignment of the burden of proof on an issue where evidence does not exist and cannot be obtained is outcome determinative. [The] assignment of the burden is merely a way of announcing a predetermined conclusion."

By remaining within its redoubt of empiricism and by basing the rule solely on the deterrence rationale, the Court has robbed the rule of legitimacy. A doctrine that is explained as if it were an empirical proposition but for which there is only limited empirical support is both inherently unstable and an easy mark for critics. The extent of this Court's fidelity to Fourth Amendment requirements, however, should not turn on such statistical uncertainties. * * *

Even if I were to accept the Court's general approach to the exclusionary rule, I could not agree with today's result. * * *

At the outset, the Court suggests that society has been asked to pay a high price—in terms either of setting guilty persons free or of impeding the proper functioning of trials—as a result of excluding relevant physical evidence in cases where the police, in conducting searches and seizing evidence, have made only an "objectively reasonable" mistake concerning the constitutionality of their actions. But what evidence is there to support such a claim?

Significantly, the Court points to none, and, indeed, as the Court acknowledges, recent studies have demonstrated that the "costs" of the exclusionary rule—calculated in terms of dropped prosecutions and lost convictions—are quite low. Contrary to the claims of the rule's critics that exclusion leads to "the release of countless guilty criminals," these studies have demonstrated that federal and state prosecutors very rarely drop cases because of potential search and seizure problems. For example, a 1979 study prepared at the request of Congress by the General Accounting Office reported that only 0.4% of all cases actually declined for prosecution by federal prosecutors were declined primarily because of illegal search problems. If the GAO data are restated as a percentage of *all* arrests, the study shows that only 0.2% of all felony arrests are declined for prosecution because of potential exclusionary rule problems.[11] Of

---

[11] In a series of recent studies, researchers have attempted to quantify the actual costs of the rule. A recent National Institute of Justice study based on data for the four year period 1976–1979 gathered by the California Bureau of Criminal Statistics showed that 4.8% of all cases that were declined for prosecution by California prosecutors were rejected because of illegally seized evidence. However, if these data are calculated as a percentage of all arrests that were declined for prosecution, they show that only 0.8% of all arrests were rejected for prosecution because of illegally seized evidence.

In another measure of the rule's impact—the number of prosecutions that are dismissed or result in acquittals in cases where evidence has been excluded—the available data again show that the Court's past assessment of the rule's costs has generally been exaggerated. For example, a study based on data from 9 mid-sized counties in Illinois, Michigan and Pennsylvania reveals that motions to suppress physical evidence were filed in approximately 5% of the 7,500 cases studied, but that such motions were successful in only 0.7% of all these cases. The study also shows that only 0.6% of all cases resulted in acquittals because evidence had been excluded. In the GAO study, suppression motions were filed in 10.5% of all federal criminal cases surveyed, but of the motions filed, approximately 80–90% were denied. Evidence was actually excluded in only 1.3% of the cases studied, and only 0.7% of all cases resulted in acquittals or dismissals after evidence was

course, these data describe only the costs attributable to the exclusion of evidence in all cases; the costs due to the exclusion of evidence in the narrower category of cases where police have made objectively reasonable mistakes must necessarily be even smaller. The Court, however, ignores this distinction and mistakenly weighs the aggregated costs of exclusion in *all* cases, irrespective of the circumstances that led to exclusion, against the potential benefits associated with only those cases in which evidence is excluded because police reasonably but mistakenly believe that their conduct does not violate the Fourth Amendment. When such faulty scales are used, it is little wonder that the balance tips in favor of restricting the application of the rule.

What then supports the Court's insistence that this evidence be admitted? Apparently, the Court's only answer is that even though the costs of exclusion are not very substantial, the potential deterrent effect in these circumstances is so marginal that exclusion cannot be justified. The key to the Court's conclusion in this respect is its belief that the prospective deterrent effect of the exclusionary rule operates only in those situations in which police officers, when deciding whether to go forward with some particular search, have reason to know that their planned conduct will violate the requirements of the Fourth Amendment.

* * * But what the Court overlooks is that the deterrence rationale for the rule is not designed to be, nor should it be thought of as, a form of "punishment" of individual police officers for their failures to obey the restraints imposed by the Fourth Amendment. Instead, the chief deterrent function of the rule is its tendency to promote institutional compliance with Fourth Amendment requirements on the part of law enforcement agencies generally. Thus, as the Court has previously recognized, "over the long term, [the] demonstration [provided by the exclusionary rule] that our society attaches serious consequences to violation of constitutional rights is thought to encourage those who formulate law enforcement policies, and the officers who implement them, to incorporate Fourth Amendment ideals into their value system." It is only through such an institution-wide mechanism that information concerning Fourth Amendment standards can be effectively communicated to rank and file officers.[13]

If the overall educational effect of the exclusionary rule is considered, application of the rule to even those situations in which individual police officers have acted on the basis of a reasonable but mistaken belief that their conduct was authorized can still be expected to have a considerable long-term deterrent effect. If evidence is consistently excluded in these circumstances, police departments will surely be prompted to instruct their officers to devote greater care and attention to providing sufficient information to establish probable cause when applying for a

---

excluded. And in another study based on data from cases during 1978 and 1979 in San Diego and Jacksonville, it was shown that only 1% of all cases resulting in nonconviction were caused by illegal searches.

　[13] * * * A former United States Attorney and now Attorney General of Maryland, Stephen Sachs, has described the impact of the rule on police practices in similar terms: "I have watched the rule deter, routinely, throughout my years as a prosecutor * * *. [P]olice-prosecutor consultation is customary in all our cases when Fourth Amendment concerns arise * * *. In at least three Maryland jurisdictions, for example, prosecutors are on twenty-four hour call to field search and seizure questions presented by police officers."

warrant, and to review with some attention the form of the warrant that they have been issued, rather than automatically assuming that whatever document the magistrate has signed will necessarily comport with Fourth Amendment requirements.

After today's decision, however, that institutional incentive will be lost. Indeed, the Court's "reasonable mistake" exception to the exclusionary rule will tend to put a premium on police ignorance of the law. Armed with the assurance provided by today's decision that evidence will always be admissible whenever an officer has "reasonably" relied upon a warrant, police departments will be encouraged to train officers that if a warrant has simply been signed, it is reasonable, without more, to rely on it. Since in close cases there will no longer be any incentive to err on the side of constitutional behavior, police would have every reason to adopt a "let's-wait-until-its-decided" approach in situations in which there is a question about a warrant's validity or the basis for its issuance.[14]

Although the Court brushes these concerns aside, a host of grave consequences can be expected to result from its decision to carve this new exception out of the exclusionary rule. A chief consequence of today's decision will be to convey a clear and unambiguous message to magistrates that their decisions to issue warrants are now insulated from subsequent judicial review. Creation of this new exception for good faith reliance upon a warrant implicitly tells magistrates that they need not take much care in reviewing warrant applications, since their mistakes will from now on have virtually no consequence: If their decision to issue a warrant was correct, the evidence will be admitted; if their decision was incorrect but the police relied in good faith on the warrant, the evidence will also be admitted. Inevitably, the care and attention devoted to such an inconsequential chore will dwindle. Although the Court is correct to note that magistrates do not share the same stake in the outcome of a criminal case as the police, they nevertheless need to appreciate that their role is of some moment in order to continue performing the important task of carefully reviewing warrant applications. Today's decision effectively removes that incentive.

Moreover, the good faith exception will encourage police to provide only the bare minimum of information in future warrant applications. The police will now know that if they can secure a warrant, so long as the circumstances of its issuance are not "entirely unreasonable," all police conduct pursuant to that warrant will be protected from further judicial review. The clear incentive that operated in the past to establish probable cause adequately because reviewing courts would examine the magistrate's judgment carefully, has now been so completely vitiated that the police need only show that it was not "entirely unreasonable" under the circumstances of a particular case for them to believe that the warrant they were issued was valid. The long-run effect unquestionably will be to undermine the integrity of the warrant process. * * *

---

[14] The authors of a recent study of the warrant process in seven cities concluded that application of a good faith exception where an officer relies upon a warrant "would further encourage police officers to seek out the less inquisitive magistrates and to rely on boilerplate formulae, thereby lessening the value of search warrants overall." * * *

JUSTICE STEVENS, * * * dissenting * * *.

* * * It is probable, though admittedly not certain, that the Court of Appeals would now conclude that the warrant in *Leon* satisfied the Fourth Amendment if it were given the opportunity to reconsider the issue in the light of *Gates*. Adherence to our normal practice following the announcement of a new rule would therefore postpone, and probably obviate, the need for the promulgation of the broad new rule the Court announces today.

[W]hen the Court goes beyond what is necessary to decide the case before it, it can only encourage the perception that it is pursuing its own notions of wise social policy, rather than adhering to its judicial role. I do not believe the Court should reach out to decide what is undoubtedly a profound question concerning the administration of criminal justice before assuring itself that this question is actually and of necessity presented by the concrete facts before the Court. * * *

HUDSON V. MICHIGAN
547 U.S. 586, 126 S.Ct. 2159, 165 L.Ed.2d 56 (2006).

JUSTICE SCALIA delivered the opinion of the Court * * *.

[Police executing a warrant authorizing search for drugs and firearms at Hudson's home announced their presence, but waited only a short time, perhaps "three to five seconds," before entering. Hudson moved to suppress the drugs and weapon found, arguing that the premature entry violated his Fourth Amendment rights. The trial court granted his motion, but the appellate court reversed on the ground that suppression is inappropriate when entry is made pursuant to warrant but without proper "knock and announce."]

The common-law principle that law enforcement officers must announce their presence and provide residents an opportunity to open the door is an ancient one. See *Wilson v. Arkansas*, 514 U.S. 927 (1995). * * * Finally, in *Wilson*, we were asked whether the rule was also a command of the Fourth Amendment. Tracing its origins in our English legal heritage, we concluded that it was.

We recognized that the new constitutional rule we had announced is not easily applied. *Wilson* and cases following it have noted the many situations in which it is not necessary to knock and announce. It is not necessary when "circumstances presen[t] a threat of physical violence," or if there is "reason to believe that evidence would likely be destroyed if advance notice were given," or if knocking and announcing would be "futile." *Richards v. Wisconsin*, 520 U.S. 385 (1997). We require only that police "have a reasonable suspicion . . . under the particular circumstances" that one of these grounds for failing to knock and announce exists, and we have acknowledged that "[t]his showing is not high."

When the knock-and-announce rule does apply, it is not easy to determine precisely what officers must do. How many seconds' wait are too few? Our "reasonable wait time" standard, see *United States v. Banks*, 540 U.S. 31 (2003), is necessarily vague. *Banks* (a drug case, like this one) held that the proper measure was not how long it would take the resident to reach the door, but how long it would take to dispose of the suspected drugs—but that such a time (15 to 20 seconds in that case) would necessarily be extended when, for instance, the suspected contraband was not easily concealed. If our ex post evaluation is subject to such calculations, it is unsurprising that, ex ante, police officers about to encounter someone who may try to harm them will be uncertain how long to wait.

Happily, these issues do not confront us here. From the trial level onward, Michigan has conceded that the entry was a knock-and-announce violation. The issue here is remedy. *Wilson* specifically declined to decide whether the exclusionary rule is appropriate for violation of the knock-and-announce requirement. That question is squarely before us now.

* * * Suppression of evidence * * * has always been our last resort, not our first impulse. The exclusionary rule generates "substantial social costs," *United States v. Leon*, 468 U.S. 897 (1984), which sometimes include setting the guilty free and the dangerous at large. We have therefore been "cautio[us] against expanding" it, and "have repeatedly emphasized that the rule's 'costly toll' upon truth-seeking and law enforcement objectives presents a high obstacle for those urging [its] application," *Pennsylvania Bd. of Probation and Parole v. Scott*, 524 U.S. 357 (1998). We have rejected "[i]ndiscriminate application" of the rule, *Leon*, and have held it to be applicable only "where its remedial objectives are thought most efficaciously served"—that is, "where its deterrence benefits outweigh its 'substantial social costs,'" *Scott* (quoting *Leon*).

We did not always speak so guardedly. Expansive dicta in *Mapp*, for example, suggested wide scope for the exclusionary rule. ("[A]ll evidence obtained by searches and seizures in violation of the Constitution is, by that same authority, inadmissible in a state court"). * * * But we have long since rejected that approach. [I]n *Leon*, * * * we explained that "[w]hether the exclusionary sanction is appropriately imposed in a particular case, . . . is 'an issue separate from the question whether the Fourth Amendment rights of the party seeking to invoke the rule were violated by police conduct.'"

Quite apart from the requirement of unattenuated causation,[a] the exclusionary rule has never been applied except "where its deterrence benefits outweigh its 'substantial social costs,'" *Scott*. The costs here are considerable. In addition to the grave adverse consequence that exclusion of relevant incriminating evidence always entails (viz., the risk of releasing dangerous criminals into society), imposing that massive remedy for a knock-and-announce violation would generate a constant flood of alleged failures to observe the rule, and claims that any asserted *Richards* justification for a no-knock entry, had inadequate support. The cost of entering this lottery would be small, but the jackpot enormous: suppression of all evidence, amounting in many cases to a get-out-of-jail-free card. Courts would experience as never before the reality that "[t]he exclusionary rule frequently requires extensive litigation to determine whether particular evidence must be excluded." *Scott*. Unlike the warrant or *Miranda* requirements,

---

[a]   This is a reference to the fact that in an omitted part of the majority opinion the Court has another reason for nonexclusion, namely, that the drugs and weapon seized were not a fruit of the Fourth Amendment violation. That branch of the case appears at p. 366.

compliance with which is readily determined (either there was or was not a warrant; either the *Miranda* warning was given, or it was not), what constituted a "reasonable wait time" in a particular case (or, for that matter, how many seconds the police in fact waited), or whether there was "reasonable suspicion" of the sort that would invoke the *Richards* exceptions, is difficult for the trial court to determine and even more difficult for an appellate court to review.

Another consequence of the incongruent remedy Hudson proposes would be police officers' refraining from timely entry after knocking and announcing. As we have observed, the amount of time they must wait is necessarily uncertain. If the consequences of running afoul of the rule were so massive, officers would be inclined to wait longer than the law requires—producing preventable violence against officers in some cases, and the destruction of evidence in many others. We deemed these consequences severe enough to produce our unanimous agreement that a mere "reasonable suspicion" that knocking and announcing "under the particular circumstances, would be dangerous or futile, or that it would inhibit the effective investigation of the crime," will cause the requirement to yield. *Richards.*

Next to these "substantial social costs" we must consider the deterrence benefits, existence of which is a necessary condition for exclusion. * * * To begin with, the value of deterrence depends upon the strength of the incentive to commit the forbidden act. Viewed from this perspective, deterrence of knock-and-announce violations is not worth a lot. Violation of the warrant requirement sometimes produces incriminating evidence that could not otherwise be obtained. But ignoring knock-and-announce can realistically be expected to achieve absolutely nothing except the prevention of destruction of evidence and the avoidance of life-threatening resistance by occupants of the premises—dangers which, if there is even "reasonable suspicion" of their existence, suspend the knock-and-announce requirement anyway. Massive deterrence is hardly required.

It seems to us not even true, as Hudson contends, that without suppression there will be no deterrence of knock-and-announce violations at all. Of course even if this assertion were accurate, it would not necessarily justify suppression. Assuming (as the assertion must) that civil suit is not an effective deterrent, one can think of many forms of police misconduct that are similarly "undeterred." When, for example, a confessed suspect in the killing of a police officer, arrested (along with incriminating evidence) in a lawful warranted search, is subjected to physical abuse at the station house, would it seriously be suggested that the evidence must be excluded, since that is the only "effective deterrent"? And what, other than civil suit, is the "effective deterrent" of police violation of an already-confessed suspect's Sixth Amendment rights by denying him prompt access to counsel? Many would regard these violated rights as more significant than the right not to be intruded upon in one's nightclothes—and yet nothing but "ineffective" civil suit is available as a deterrent. And the police incentive for those violations is arguably greater than the incentive for disregarding the knock-and-announce rule.

We cannot assume that exclusion in this context is necessary deterrence simply because we found that it was necessary deterrence in different contexts and long ago. That would be forcing the public today to pay for the sins and inadequacies of a legal regime that existed almost half a century ago. Dollree Mapp could not turn to 42 U.S.C. § 1983 for meaningful relief; *Monroe v. Pape*, 365 U.S. 167 (1961), which began the slow but steady expansion of that remedy, was decided the same Term as *Mapp*. It would be another 17 years before the § 1983 remedy was extended to reach the deep pocket of municipalities, *Monell v. New York City Dept. of Social Servs.*, 436 U.S. 658 (1978). Citizens whose Fourth Amendment rights were violated by federal officers could not bring suit until 10 years after *Mapp*, with this Court's decision in *Bivens v. Six Unknown Fed. Narcotics Agents*, 403 U.S. 388 (1971).

Hudson complains that "it would be very hard to find a lawyer to take a case such as this," but 42 U.S.C. § 1988(b) answers this objection. Since some civil-rights violations would yield damages too small to justify the expense of litigation, Congress has authorized attorney's fees for civil-rights plaintiffs. This remedy was unavailable in the heydays of our exclusionary-rule jurisprudence, because it is tied to the availability of a cause of action. For years after *Mapp*, "very few lawyers would even consider representation of persons who had civil rights claims against the police," but now "much has changed. Citizens and lawyers are much more willing to seek relief in the courts for police misconduct." The number of public-interest law firms and lawyers who specialize in civil-rights grievances has greatly expanded.

Hudson points out that few published decisions to date announce huge awards for knock-and-announce violations. But this is an unhelpful statistic. Even if we thought that only large damages would deter police misconduct (and that police somehow are deterred by "damages" but indifferent to the prospect of large § 1988 attorney's fees), we do not know how many claims have been settled, or indeed how many violations have occurred that produced anything more than nominal injury. It is clear, at least, that the lower courts are allowing colorable knock-and-announce suits to go forward, unimpeded by assertions of qualified immunity. As far as we know, civil liability is an effective deterrent here, as we have assumed it is in other contexts.

Another development over the past half-century that deters civil-rights violations is the increasing professionalism of police forces, including a new emphasis on internal police discipline. Even as long ago as 1980 we felt it proper to "assume" that unlawful police behavior would "be dealt with appropriately" by the authorities, but we now have increasing evidence that police forces across the United States take the constitutional rights of citizens seriously. There have been "wide-ranging reforms in the education, training, and supervision of police officers." Numerous sources are now available to teach officers and their supervisors what is required of them under this Court's cases, how to respect constitutional guarantees in various situations, and how to craft an effective regime for internal discipline. Failure to teach and enforce constitutional requirements exposes municipalities to financial liability. Moreover, modern police forces are staffed with professionals; it is not credible to assert that internal discipline, which can limit successful careers, will not have a deterrent effect.

There is also evidence that the increasing use of various forms of citizen review can enhance police accountability.

In sum, the social costs of applying the exclusionary rule to knock-and-announce violations are considerable; the incentive to such violations is minimal to begin with, and the extant deterrences against them are substantial—incomparably greater than the factors deterring warrantless entries when *Mapp* was decided. Resort to the massive remedy of suppressing evidence of guilt is unjustified. * * *

JUSTICE KENNEDY, concurring in part and concurring in the judgment.

Two points should be underscored with respect to today's decision. First, the knock-and-announce requirement protects rights and expectations linked to ancient principles in our constitutional order. The Court's decision should not be interpreted as suggesting that violations of the requirement are trivial or beyond the law's concern. Second, the continued operation of the exclusionary rule, as settled and defined by our precedents, is not in doubt. Today's decision determines only that in the specific context of the knock-and-announce requirement, a violation is not sufficiently related to the later discovery of evidence to justify suppression. * * *

JUSTICE BREYER, with whom JUSTICE STEVENS, JUSTICE SOUTER, and JUSTICE GINSBURG join, dissenting. * * *

[T]he driving legal purpose underlying the exclusionary rule, namely, the deterrence of unlawful government behavior, argues strongly for suppression. See *Elkins v. United States*, 364 U.S. 206 (1960) (purpose of the exclusionary rule is "to deter—to compel respect for the constitutional guaranty . . . by removing the incentive to disregard it"). * * * Indeed, this Court in *Mapp* held that the exclusionary rule applies to the States in large part due to its belief that alternative state mechanisms for enforcing the Fourth Amendment's guarantees had proved "worthless and futile."

Why is application of the exclusionary rule any the less necessary here? Without such a rule, as in *Mapp*, police know that they can ignore the Constitution's requirements without risking suppression of evidence discovered after an unreasonable entry. As in *Mapp*, some government officers will find it easier, or believe it less risky, to proceed with what they consider a necessary search immediately and without the requisite constitutional (say, warrant or knock-and-announce) compliance.

Of course, the State or the Federal Government may provide alternative remedies for knock-and-announce violations. But that circumstance was true of *Mapp* as well. What reason is there to believe that those remedies (such as private damages actions under 42 U.S.C. § 1983), which the Court found inadequate in *Mapp*, can adequately deter unconstitutional police behavior here? See Kamisar, In Defense of the Search and Seizure Exclusionary Rule, 26 Harv. J.L. & Pub. Pol'y 119, 126–129 (2003) (arguing that "five decades of post-*Weeks* 'freedom' from the inhibiting effect of the federal exclusionary rule failed to produce any meaningful alternative to the exclusionary rule in any jurisdiction" and that there is no evidence that "times have changed" post-*Mapp*).

The cases reporting knock-and-announce violations are legion. Indeed, these cases of reported violations seem sufficiently frequent and serious as to indicate "a widespread pattern." Yet the majority, like Michigan and the United States, has failed to cite a single reported case in which a plaintiff has collected more than nominal damages solely as a result of a knock-and-announce violation. Even Michigan concedes that, "in cases like the present one . . . , damages may be virtually non-existent." And Michigan's amici further concede that civil immunities prevent tort law from being an effective substitute for the exclusionary rule at this time.

As Justice Stewart, the author of a number of significant Fourth Amendment opinions, explained, the deterrent effect of damage actions "can hardly be said to be great," as such actions are "expensive, time-consuming, not readily available, and rarely successful." The upshot is that the need for deterrence—the critical factor driving this Court's Fourth Amendment cases for close to a century—argues with at least comparable strength for evidentiary exclusion here.

To argue, as the majority does, that new remedies, such as 42 U.S.C. § 1983 actions or better trained police, make suppression unnecessary is to argue that *Wolf*, not *Mapp*, is now the law. * * * To argue that there may be few civil suits because violations may produce nothing "more than nominal injury" is to confirm, not to deny, the inability of civil suits to deter violations. And to argue without evidence (and despite myriad reported cases of violations, no reported case of civil damages, and Michigan's concession of their nonexistence) that civil suits may provide deterrence because claims may "have been settled" is, perhaps, to search in desperation for an argument. Rather, the majority, as it candidly admits, has simply "assumed" that, "[a]s far as [it] know[s], civil liability is an effective deterrent," a support-free assumption that *Mapp* and subsequent cases make clear does not embody the Court's normal approach to difficult questions of Fourth Amendment law. * * *

The Court has declined to apply the exclusionary rule only:

(1)   where there is a specific reason to believe that application of the rule would "not result in appreciable deterrence," *United States v. Janis*, 428 U.S. 433 (1976); see, e.g., *United States v. Leon* (exception where searching officer executes defective search warrant in "good faith"); *Arizona v. Evans*, 514 U.S. 1, 14 (1995) (exception for clerical errors by court employees); *Walder v. United States*, 347 U.S. 62 (1954) (exception for impeachment purposes), or

(2)   where admissibility in proceedings other than criminal trials was at issue, see, e.g., *Pennsylvania Bd. of Probation and Parole v. Scott* (exception for parole revocation proceedings); *INS v. Lopez-Mendoza*, 468 U.S. 1032 (1984) (plurality opinion) (exception for deportation proceedings); *Janis* (exception for civil tax proceedings); *United States v. Calandra*, 414 U.S. 338 (1974) (exception for grand jury proceedings);

Stone v. Powell, 428 U.S. 465 (1976) (exception for federal habeas proceedings).

Neither of these two exceptions applies here. The second does not apply because this case is an ordinary criminal trial. The first does not apply because (1) officers who violate the rule are not acting "as a reasonable officer would and should act in similar circumstances," *Leon,* (2) this case does not involve government employees other than police, *Evans,* and (3), most importantly, the key rationale for any exception, "lack of deterrence," is missing, see *Pennsylvania Bd. of Probation* (noting that the rationale for not applying the rule in noncriminal cases has been that the deterrence achieved by having the rule apply in those contexts is "minimal" because "application of the rule in the criminal trial context already provides significant deterrence of unconstitutional searches"); *Michigan v. Tucker,* 417 U.S. 433 (1974) (noting that deterrence rationale would not be served if rule applied to police officers acting in good faith, as the "deterrent purpose of the exclusionary rule necessarily assumes that the police have engaged in willful, or at the very least negligent, conduct"). That critical latter rationale, which underlies every exception, does not apply here, as there is no reason to think that, in the case of knock-and-announce violations by the police, "the exclusion of evidence at trial would not sufficiently deter future errors," *Evans,* or " 'further the ends of the exclusionary rule in any appreciable way,' " *Leon.*

I am aware of no other basis for an exception. * * *

Neither can the majority justify its failure to respect the need for deterrence, as set forth consistently in the Court's prior case law, through its claim of "substantial social costs"—at least if it means that those "social costs" are somehow special here. The only costs it mentions are those that typically accompany any use of the Fourth Amendment's exclusionary principle: (1) that where the constable blunders, a guilty defendant may be set free (consider *Mapp* itself); (2) that defendants may assert claims where Fourth Amendment rights are uncertain (consider the Court's qualified immunity jurisprudence), and (3) that sometimes it is difficult to decide the merits of those uncertain claims. In fact, the "no-knock" warrants that are provided by many States, by diminishing uncertainty, may make application of the knock-and-announce principle less "cost[ly]" on the whole than application of comparable Fourth Amendment principles, such as determining whether a particular warrantless search was justified by exigency. The majority's "substantial social costs" argument is an argument against the Fourth Amendment's exclusionary principle itself. And it is an argument that this Court, until now, has consistently rejected.

The United States, in its brief and at oral argument, has argued that suppression is "an especially harsh remedy given the nature of the violation in this case." This argument focuses upon the fact that entering a house after knocking and announcing can, in some cases, prove dangerous to a police officer. Perhaps someone inside has a gun, as turned out to be the case here. The majority adds that police officers about to encounter someone who may try to harm them will be "uncertain" as to how long to wait. It says that, "[i]f the consequences of running afoul" of the knock-and-announce "rule were so massive," i.e., would lead to the exclusion of evidence, then "officers would be inclined to wait longer than the law requires—producing preventable violence against officers in some cases."

To argue that police efforts to assure compliance with the rule may prove dangerous, however, is not to argue against evidence suppression. It is to argue against the validity of the rule itself. Similarly, to argue that enforcement means uncertainty, which in turn means the potential for dangerous and longer-than-necessary delay, is (if true) to argue against meaningful compliance with the rule.

The answer to the first argument is that the rule itself does not require police to knock or to announce their presence where police have a "reasonable suspicion" that doing so "would be dangerous or futile" or "would inhibit the effective investigation of the crime by, for example, allowing the destruction of evidence."

The answer to the second argument is that States can, and many do, reduce police uncertainty while assuring a neutral evaluation of concerns about risks to officers or the destruction of evidence by permitting police to obtain a "no-knock" search warrant from a magistrate judge, thereby assuring police that a prior announcement is not necessary. While such a procedure cannot remove all uncertainty, it does provide an easy way for officers to comply with the knock-and-announce rule.

Of course, even without such a warrant, police maintain the backup "authority to exercise independent judgment concerning the wisdom of a no-knock entry at the time the warrant is being executed." "[I]f circumstances support a reasonable suspicion of exigency when the officers arrive at the door, they may go straight in." And "[r]easonable suspicion is a less demanding standard than probable cause. . . ."

There is perhaps one additional argument implicit in the majority's approach. The majority says, for example, that the "cost" to a defendant of "entering this lottery," i.e., of claiming a "knock-and-announce" violation, "would be small, but the jackpot enormous"—namely, a potential "get-out-of-jail-free card." It adds that the "social costs" of applying the exclusionary rule here are not worth the deterrence benefits. Leaving aside what I believe are invalid arguments based on precedent or the majority's own estimate that suppression is not necessary to deter constitutional violations, one is left with a simple unvarnished conclusion, namely, that in this kind of case, a knock-and-announce case, "[r]esort to the massive remedy of suppressing evidence of guilt is unjustified." Why is that judicial judgment, taken on its own, inappropriate? Could it not be argued that the knock-and-announce rule, a subsidiary Fourth Amendment rule, is simply not important enough to warrant a suppression remedy? Could the majority not simply claim that the suppression game is not worth the candle?

The answer, I believe, is "no." That "no" reflects history, a history that shows the knock-and-announce rule is important. That "no" reflects precedent, precedent that shows there is no pre-existing legal category of exceptions to the exclusionary rule into which the knock-and-announce cases might fit. That "no" reflects empirical fact, experience that provides confirmation of what common sense suggests: without suppression there is little to deter knock-and-announce violations. * * *

HERRING V. UNITED STATES

555 U.S. 135, 129 S.Ct. 695, 172 L.Ed.2d 496 (2009).

CHIEF JUSTICE ROBERTS delivered the opinion of the Court.

The Fourth Amendment forbids "unreasonable searches and seizures," and this usually requires the police to have probable cause or a warrant before making an arrest. What if an officer reasonably believes there is an outstanding arrest warrant, but that belief turns out to be wrong because of a negligent bookkeeping error by another police employee? The parties here agree that the ensuing arrest is still a violation of the Fourth Amendment, but dispute whether contraband found during a search incident to that arrest must be excluded in a later prosecution.

Our cases establish that such suppression is not an automatic consequence of a Fourth Amendment violation. Instead, the question turns on the culpability of the police and the potential of exclusion to deter wrongful police conduct. Here the error was the result of isolated negligence attenuated from the arrest. We hold that in these circumstances the jury should not be barred from considering all the evidence.

On July 7, 2004, Investigator Mark Anderson learned that Bennie Dean Herring had driven to the Coffee County Sheriff's Department to retrieve something from his impounded truck. Herring was no stranger to law enforcement, and Anderson asked the county's warrant clerk, Sandy Pope, to check for any outstanding warrants for Herring's arrest. When she found none, Anderson asked Pope to check with Sharon Morgan, her counterpart in neighboring Dale County. After checking Dale County's computer database, Morgan replied that there was an active arrest warrant for Herring's failure to appear on a felony charge. Pope relayed the information to Anderson and asked Morgan to fax over a copy of the warrant as confirmation. Anderson and a deputy followed Herring as he left the impound lot, pulled him over, and arrested him. A search incident to the arrest revealed methamphetamine in Herring's pocket, and a pistol (which as a felon he could not possess) in his vehicle.

There had, however, been a mistake about the warrant. The Dale County sheriff's computer records are supposed to correspond to actual arrest warrants, which the office also maintains. But when Morgan went to the files to retrieve the actual warrant to fax to Pope, Morgan was unable to find it. She called a court clerk and learned that the warrant had been recalled five months earlier. Normally when a warrant is recalled the court clerk's office or a judge's chambers calls Morgan, who enters the information in the sheriff's computer database and disposes of the physical copy. For whatever reason, the information about the recall of the warrant for Herring did not appear in the database. Morgan immediately called Pope to alert her to the mixup, and Pope contacted Anderson over a secure radio. This all unfolded in 10 to 15 minutes, but Herring had already been arrested and found with the gun and drugs, just a few hundred yards from the sheriff's office.

Herring was indicted in the District Court for the Middle District of Alabama for illegally possessing the gun and drugs * * *. He moved to suppress the evidence on the ground that his initial arrest had been illegal because the warrant had been rescinded. The Magistrate Judge recommended denying the motion because the arresting officers had acted in a good-faith belief that the warrant was still outstanding. * * * The District Court adopted the Magistrate Judge's recommendation, and the Court of Appeals for the Eleventh Circuit affirmed.

The Eleventh Circuit found that the arresting officers in Coffee County "were entirely innocent of any wrongdoing or carelessness." The court assumed that whoever failed to update the Dale County sheriff's records was also a law enforcement official, but noted that "the conduct in question [wa]s a negligent failure to act, not a deliberate or tactical choice to act." Because the error was merely negligent and attenuated from the arrest, the Eleventh Circuit concluded that the benefit of suppressing the evidence "would be marginal or nonexistent," and the evidence was therefore admissible under the good-faith rule of *United States v. Leon*, [p. 68]. * * *

The fact that a Fourth Amendment violation occurred—*i.e.*, that a search or arrest was unreasonable—does not necessarily mean that the exclusionary rule applies. * * *

First, the exclusionary rule is not an individual right and applies only where it " 'result[s] in appreciable deterrence.' " *Leon*. We have repeatedly rejected the argument that exclusion is a necessary consequence of a Fourth Amendment violation. *Leon*; [*Arizona v.*] *Evans*, [p. 85]; *Pennsylvania Bd. of Probation and Parole v. Scott*, [p. 81]. Instead we have focused on the efficacy of the rule in deterring Fourth Amendment violations in the future. See *Calandra*, [p. 85]; *Stone v. Powell*, [p. 86].[2]

In addition, the benefits of deterrence must outweigh the costs. *Leon*, supra. "We have never suggested that the exclusionary rule must apply in every circumstance in which it might provide marginal deterrence." *Scott*. "[T]o the extent that application of the exclusionary rule could provide some incremental deterrent, that possible benefit must be weighed against [its] substantial social costs." *Illinois v. Krull*, [fn. e, p. 74]. The principal cost of applying the rule is, of course, letting guilty and possibly dangerous defendants go free—something that "offends basic concepts of the criminal justice system." *Leon*. * * *

These principles are reflected in the holding of *Leon*: When police act under a warrant that is invalid for lack of probable cause, the exclusionary rule does not apply if the police acted "in objectively reasonable reliance" on the subsequently invalidated search warrant. We (perhaps confusingly) called this objectively reasonable reliance "good faith." In a companion case, *Massachusetts v. Sheppard*, [fn. d, p. 73], we held that the exclusionary rule did not apply when a warrant was invalid because a judge forgot to make "clerical corrections" to it.

Shortly thereafter we extended these holdings to warrantless administrative searches performed in good-faith reliance on a statute later declared unconstitutional. *Krull*. Finally, in *Evans*, we applied this good-faith rule to police

---

[2] Justice Ginsburg's dissent champions what she describes as " 'a more majestic conception' of . . . the exclusionary rule," which would exclude evidence even where deterrence does not justify doing so. Majestic or not, our cases reject this conception, see, *e.g.*, *United States v. Leon* * * *.

who reasonably relied on mistaken information in a court's database that an arrest warrant was outstanding. * * *

The extent to which the exclusionary rule is justified by these deterrence principles varies with the culpability of the law enforcement conduct. As we said in *Leon,* "an assessment of the flagrancy of the police misconduct constitutes an important step in the calculus" of applying the exclusionary rule. Similarly, in *Krull* we elaborated that "evidence should be suppressed 'only if it can be said that the law enforcement officer had knowledge, or may properly be charged with knowledge, that the search was unconstitutional under the Fourth Amendment.'"

Anticipating the good-faith exception to the exclusionary rule, Judge Friendly wrote that "[t]he beneficent aim of the exclusionary rule to deter police misconduct can be sufficiently accomplished by a practice . . . outlawing evidence obtained by flagrant or deliberate violation of rights." The Bill of Rights as a Code of Criminal Procedure, 53 Calif. L.Rev. 929, 953 (1965).

Indeed, the abuses that gave rise to the exclusionary rule featured intentional conduct that was patently unconstitutional. In *Weeks,* [*v. United States*, 232 U.S. 383 (1914)], a foundational exclusionary rule case, the officers had broken into the defendant's home (using a key shown to them by a neighbor), confiscated incriminating papers, then returned again with a U.S. Marshal to confiscate even more. Not only did they have no search warrant, which the Court held was required, but they could not have gotten one had they tried. * * *

Equally flagrant conduct was at issue in *Mapp v. Ohio,* [p. 62], which * * * extended the exclusionary rule to the States. Officers forced open a door to Ms. Mapp's house, kept her lawyer from entering, brandished what the court concluded was a false warrant, then forced her into handcuffs and canvassed the house for obscenity. An error that arises from nonrecurring and attenuated negligence is thus far removed from the core concerns that led us to adopt the rule in the first place. And in fact since *Leon,* we have never applied the rule to exclude evidence obtained in violation of the Fourth Amendment, where the police conduct was no more intentional or culpable than this.

To trigger the exclusionary rule, police conduct must be sufficiently deliberate that exclusion can meaningfully deter it, and sufficiently culpable that such deterrence is worth the price paid by the justice system. As laid out in our cases, the exclusionary rule serves to deter deliberate, reckless, or grossly negligent conduct, or in some circumstances recurring or systemic negligence. The error in this case does not rise to that level.[4]

Our decision in *Franks v. Delaware,* [fn. b, p. 70], provides an analogy. In *Franks,* we held that police negligence in obtaining a warrant did not even rise to the level of a Fourth Amendment violation, let alone meet the more stringent test for triggering the exclusionary rule. We held that the Constitution allowed

---

4 We do not quarrel with Justice Ginsburg's claim that "liability for negligence . . . creates an incentive to act with greater care," and we do not suggest that the exclusion of this evidence could have *no* deterrent effect. But our cases require any deterrence to "be weighed against the 'substantial social costs exacted by the exclusionary rule,'" *Illinois v. Krull,* and here exclusion is not worth the cost.

defendants, in some circumstances, "to challenge the truthfulness of factual statements made in an affidavit supporting the warrant," even after the warrant had issued. If those false statements were necessary to the Magistrate Judge's probable-cause determination, the warrant would be "voided." But we did not find all false statements relevant: "There must be allegations of deliberate falsehood or of reckless disregard for the truth," and "[a]llegations of negligence or innocent mistake are insufficient."

Both this case and *Franks* concern false information provided by police. Under *Franks,* negligent police miscommunications in the course of acquiring a warrant do not provide a basis to rescind a warrant and render a search or arrest invalid. Here, the miscommunications occurred in a different context—after the warrant had been issued and recalled—but that fact should not require excluding the evidence obtained.

The pertinent analysis of deterrence and culpability is objective, not an "inquiry into the subjective awareness of arresting officers." We have already held that "our good-faith inquiry is confined to the objectively ascertainable question whether a reasonably well trained officer would have known that the search was illegal" in light of "all of the circumstances." *Leon.* These circumstances frequently include a particular officer's knowledge and experience, but that does not make the test any more subjective than the one for probable cause, which looks to an officer's knowledge and experience, but not his subjective intent.

We do not suggest that all recordkeeping errors by the police are immune from the exclusionary rule. In this case, however, the conduct at issue was not so objectively culpable as to require exclusion. In *Leon* we held that "the marginal or nonexistent benefits produced by suppressing evidence obtained in objectively reasonable reliance on a subsequently invalidated search warrant cannot justify the substantial costs of exclusion." The same is true when evidence is obtained in objectively reasonable reliance on a subsequently recalled warrant.

If the police have been shown to be reckless in maintaining a warrant system, or to have knowingly made false entries to lay the groundwork for future false arrests, exclusion would certainly be justified under our cases should such misconduct cause a Fourth Amendment violation. * * *

The dissent also adverts to the possible unreliability of a number of databases not relevant to this case. In a case where systemic errors were demonstrated, it might be reckless for officers to rely on an unreliable warrant system. * * * But there is no evidence that errors in Dale County's system are routine or widespread. * * *

The judgment of the Court of Appeals for the Eleventh Circuit is affirmed. * * *

JUSTICE GINSBURG, with whom JUSTICE STEVENS, JUSTICE SOUTER, and JUSTICE BREYER join, dissenting. * * *

Beyond doubt, a main objective of the rule "is to deter—to compel respect for the constitutional guaranty in the only effectively available way—by removing the incentive to disregard it." But the rule also serves other important purposes: It "enabl[es] the judiciary to avoid the taint of partnership in official lawlessness," and it "assur[es] the people—all potential victims of unlawful government conduct—that the government would not profit from its lawless behavior, thus minimizing the risk of seriously undermining popular trust in government."

The exclusionary rule, the Court suggests, is capable of only marginal deterrence when the misconduct at issue is merely careless, not intentional or reckless. The suggestion runs counter to a foundational premise of tort law—that liability for negligence, *i.e.*, lack of due care, creates an incentive to act with greater care. The Government so acknowledges.

That the mistake here involved the failure to make a computer entry hardly means that application of the exclusionary rule would have minimal value. "Just as the risk of *respondeat superior* liability encourages employers to supervise . . . their employees' conduct [more carefully], so the risk of exclusion of evidence encourages policymakers and systems managers to monitor the performance of the systems they install and the personnel employed to operate those systems."

Consider the potential impact of a decision applying the exclusionary rule in this case. As earlier observed, the record indicates that there is no electronic connection between the warrant database of the Dale County Sheriff's Department and that of the County Circuit Clerk's office, which is located in the basement of the same building. When a warrant is recalled, one of the "many different people that have access to th[e] warrants," must find the hard copy of the warrant in the "two or three different places" where the department houses warrants, return it to the Clerk's office, and manually update the Department's database. The record reflects no routine practice of checking the database for accuracy, and the failure to remove the entry for Herring's warrant was not discovered until Investigator Anderson sought to pursue Herring five months later. Is it not altogether obvious that the Department could take further precautions to ensure the integrity of its database? The Sheriff's Department "is in a position to remedy the situation and might well do so if the exclusionary rule is there to remove the incentive to do otherwise." 1 W. LaFave, Search and Seizure § 1.8(e), p. 313 (4th ed.2004).

Is the potential deterrence here worth the costs it imposes? In light of the paramount importance of accurate recordkeeping in law enforcement, I would answer yes, and next explain why, as I see it, Herring's motion presents a particularly strong case for suppression.

Electronic databases form the nervous system of contemporary criminal justice operations. In recent years, their breadth and influence have dramatically expanded. Police today can access databases that include not only the updated National Crime Information Center (NCIC), but also terrorist watchlists, the Federal Government's employee eligibility system, and various commercial databases. Moreover, States are actively expanding information sharing between jurisdictions. As a result, law enforcement has an increasing supply of information within its easy electronic reach.

The risk of error stemming from these databases is not slim. Herring's *amici* warn that law enforcement databases are insufficiently monitored and often out of date. Government reports describe, for example, flaws in NCIC databases, terrorist watchlist databases, and databases associated with the Federal Government's employment eligibility verification system.

Inaccuracies in expansive, interconnected collections of electronic information raise grave concerns for individual liberty. "The offense to the dignity of the citizen who is arrested, handcuffed, and searched on a public street simply because some bureaucrat has failed to maintain an accurate computer data base" is evocative of the use of general warrants that so outraged the authors of our Bill of Rights.

The Court assures that "exclusion would certainly be justified" if "the police have been shown to be reckless in maintaining a warrant system, or to have knowingly made false entries to lay the groundwork for future false arrests." This concession provides little comfort.

First, by restricting suppression to bookkeeping errors that are deliberate or reckless, the majority leaves Herring, and others like him, with no remedy for violations of their constitutional rights. There can be no serious assertion that relief is available under 42 U.S.C. § 1983. The arresting officer would be sheltered by qualified immunity, and the police department itself is not liable for the negligent acts of its employees. Moreover, identifying the department employee who committed the error may be impossible.

Second, I doubt that police forces already possess sufficient incentives to maintain up-to-date records. The Government argues that police have no desire to send officers out on arrests unnecessarily, because arrests consume resources and place officers in danger. The facts of this case do not fit that description of police motivation. Here the officer wanted to arrest Herring and consulted the Department's records to legitimate his predisposition.[6]

Third, even when deliberate or reckless conduct is afoot, the Court's assurance will often be an empty promise: How is an impecunious defendant to make the required showing? If the answer is that a defendant is entitled to discovery (and if necessary, an audit of police databases), then the Court has imposed a considerable administrative burden on courts and law enforcement.[7]

JUSTICE BREYER, with whom JUSTICE SOUTER joins, dissenting. * * *

Distinguishing between police recordkeeping errors and judicial ones not only is consistent with our precedent [in *Evans*], but also is far easier for courts to administer than The Chief Justice's case-by-case, multifactored inquiry into the degree of police culpability. I therefore would apply the exclusionary rule when police personnel are responsible for a recordkeeping error that results in a Fourth Amendment violation. * * *

---

[6] It has been asserted that police departments have become sufficiently "professional" that they do not need external deterrence to avoid Fourth Amendment violations. But professionalism is a sign of the exclusionary rule's efficacy—not of its superfluity.

[7] It is not clear how the Court squares its focus on deliberate conduct with its recognition that application of the exclusionary rule does not require inquiry into the mental state of the police.

2. PROTECTED AREAS AND INTERESTS

If certain police activity is neither a "search" nor a "seizure" in the Fourth Amendment sense, then the protections of the Amendment are inapplicable. Deciding just what constitutes a "search" has been especially troublesome. In the leading case (and the first case in this section) of *Katz v. United States,* holding electronic eavesdropping is governed by the Fourth Amendment, the Court decided a search could occur without a physical intrusion into a constitutionally protected area. By requiring instead an infringement upon a justified expectation of privacy, *Katz* unquestionably broadened the scope of the Fourth Amendment. But the Court has since taken a rather narrow view of what privacy expectations are in fact "justified," as is illustrated by the next two cases, *California v. Greenwood* and *Florida v. Riley,* dealing, respectively, with examination of garbage and aerial surveillance.

Two other cases in this section, *United States v. Jones* and *Florida v. Jardines,* dealing respectively with use of GPS tracking devices and on-curtilage drug-sniffing dogs, both use a property-interest (rather than privacy) approach in determining when those activities constitute a search. *Carpenter v. United States,* relying upon the locational-privacy aspect of *Jones,* held it is a search for police to keep track of a suspect's extended movements via cell-phone tracking records of a service provider, and in the process placed limits upon the so-called "third-party doctrine," generally deeming a lack of privacy in records held by a third party.[a] The meaning of *Katz* is also explored in *United States v. White,* concerning the troublesome question of whether it is a search or seizure for an undercover agent secretly to record or transmit the conversations he has with others.

The materials then turn to what is a seizure, as opposed to a search, focusing on the recent case of *Torres v. Madrid.* The government can seize a person or property, and *Torres* considers the Fourth Amendment standards for seizing a person.

Those objecting to police search activity have sometimes relied upon constitutional protections in addition to those in the Fourth Amendment. The claim that the Fifth Amendment privilege against self-incrimination bars a search for or seizure of private papers was rejected in *Andresen v. Maryland,* 427 U.S. 463 (1976). Distinguishing the situation discussed in Chapter Eight (§ 2), the Court in *Andresen* concluded that "although the Fifth Amendment may protect an individual from complying with a subpoena for the production of his personal records in his possession because the very act of production may constitute a compulsory authentication of incriminating information, a seizure of the same materials by law enforcement officers differs in a crucial respect—the individual against whom the search is directed is not required to aid in the discovery, production, or authentication of incriminating evidence." The claim that the First Amendment freedom of the press is violated by the search of the office of a

---

[a] The opinions in *Carpenter* also addressed Fourth Amendment limitations upon subpoena authority, as described in Ch. 8, § 2.

newsgathering organization is considered in *Zurcher v. Stanford Daily,* the final case in this section.

KATZ V. UNITED STATES
389 U.S. 347, 88 S.Ct. 507, 19 L.Ed.2d 576 (1967).

JUSTICE STEWART delivered the opinion of the Court.

The petitioner was convicted [of] transmitting wagering information by telephone from Los Angeles to Miami and Boston in violation of a federal statute. At trial the Government was permitted, over the petitioner's objection, to introduce evidence of the petitioner's end of telephone conversations, overheard by FBI agents who had attached an electronic listening and recording device to the outside of the public telephone booth from which he had placed his calls. In affirming his conviction, the Court of Appeals rejected the contention that the recordings had been obtained in violation of the Fourth Amendment, because "[t]here was no physical entrance into the area occupied by [the petitioner]." We granted certiorari in order to consider the constitutional questions thus presented.

The petitioner has phrased those questions as follows:

"A. Whether a public telephone booth is a constitutionally protected area so that evidence obtained by attaching an electronic listening recording device to the top of such a booth is obtained in violation of the right to privacy of the user of the booth.

"B. Whether physical penetration of a constitutionally protected area is necessary before a search and seizure can be said to be violative of the Fourth Amendment to the United States Constitution."

We decline to adopt this formulation of the issues. In the first place the correct solution of Fourth Amendment problems is not necessarily promoted by incantation of the phrase "constitutionally protected area." Secondly, the Fourth Amendment cannot be translated into a general constitutional "right to privacy." That Amendment protects individual privacy against certain kinds of governmental intrusion, but its protections go further, and often have nothing to do with privacy at all. Other provisions of the Constitution protect personal privacy from other forms of governmental invasion. But the protection of a person's *general* right to privacy—his right to be let alone by other people—is, like the protection of his property and of his very life, left largely to the law of the individual States.

Because of the misleading way the issues have been formulated, the parties have attached great significance to the characterization of the telephone booth from which the petitioner placed his calls. The petitioner has strenuously argued that the booth was a "constitutionally protected area." The Government has maintained with equal vigor that it was not. But this effort to decide whether or not a given "area," viewed in the abstract, is "constitutionally protected" deflects attention from the problem presented by this case. For the Fourth Amendment protects people, not places. What a person knowingly exposes to the public, even in his own home or office, is not a subject of Fourth Amendment protection. * * * But what he seeks to preserve as private, even in an area accessible to the public, may be constitutionally protected. * * *

The Government stresses the fact that the telephone booth from which the petitioner made his calls was constructed partly of glass, so that he was as visible after he entered it as he would have been if he had remained outside. But what he sought to exclude when he entered the booth was not the intruding eye—it was the uninvited ear. He did not shed his right to do so simply because he made his calls from a place where he might be seen. No less than an individual in a business office, in a friend's apartment, or in a taxicab, a person in a telephone booth may rely upon the protection of the Fourth Amendment. One who occupies it, shuts the door behind him, and pays the toll that permits him to place a call, is surely entitled to assume that the words he utters into the mouthpiece will not be broadcast to the world. To read the Constitution more narrowly is to ignore the vital role that the public telephone has come to play in private communication.

The Government contends, however, that the activities of its agents in this case should not be tested by Fourth Amendment requirements, for the surveillance technique they employed involved no physical penetration of the telephone booth from which the petitioner placed his calls.

* * * [A]lthough a closely divided Court supposed in *Olmstead* [*v. United States,* 277 U.S. 438 (1928),] that surveillance without any trespass and without the seizure of any material object fell outside the ambit of the Constitution, we have since departed from the narrow view on which that decision rested. Indeed, we have expressly held that the Fourth Amendment governs not only the seizure of tangible items, but extends as well to the recording of oral statements overheard without any "technical trespass under * * * local property law." Once this much is acknowledged, and once it is recognized that the Fourth Amendment protects people—and not simply "areas"—against unreasonable searches and seizures it becomes clear that the reach of that Amendment cannot turn upon the presence or absence of a physical intrusion into any given enclosure.

We conclude that the underpinnings of *Olmstead* have been so eroded by our subsequent decisions that the "trespass" doctrine there enunciated can no longer be regarded as controlling. The Government's activities in electronically listening to and recording the petitioner's words violated the privacy upon which he justifiably relied while using the telephone booth and thus constituted a "search and seizure"[a] within the meaning of the Fourth Amendment.[b] The fact that the

---

[a]   This does not mean that privacy is the *only* interest protected by the Fourth Amendment, or that the Amendment comes into play *only* if there is both a "search" and a "seizure." The Fourth Amendment also protects the interests in possession of property and liberty of person, as in *United States v. Place,* fn. a, p. 288 (detention of traveler's luggage 90 minutes was an unreasonable seizure in two respects, as it constituted a deprivation of defendant's "possessory interest in his luggage" and his "liberty interest in proceeding with his itinerary"). In *Soldal v. Cook County,* 506 U.S. 56 (1992), where sheriff's deputies knowingly participated in an unlawful eviction which involved hauling the plaintiff's trailer home off the landlord's property, the court of appeals ruled that the Fourth Amendment offers no protection where, as here, the intrusion upon a possessory interest was unaccompanied by an intrusion upon a privacy interest. A unanimous Supreme Court reversed, holding "that seizures of property are subject to Fourth Amendment scrutiny even though no search within the meaning of the Amendment has taken place."

[b]   More precisely, it could be said that if the government's activities have violated *anyone's* justified expectation of privacy, then that activity constitutes a Fourth Amendment search. However, it has long been established that a defendant in a criminal case who is seeking the suppression of evidence on Fourth Amendment grounds may invoke the violation of his own rights

electronic device employed to achieve that end did not happen to penetrate the wall of the booth can have no constitutional significance.

The question remaining for decision, then, is whether the search and seizure conducted in this case complied with constitutional standards. In that regard, the Government's position is that its agents acted in an entirely defensible manner: They did not begin their electronic surveillance until investigation of the petitioner's activities had established a strong probability that he was using the telephone in question to transmit gambling information to persons in other States, in violation of federal law. Moreover, the surveillance was limited, both in scope and in duration to the specific purpose of establishing the contents of the petitioner's unlawful telephonic communications. The agents confined their surveillance to the brief periods during which he used the telephone booth, and they took great care to overhear only the conversations of the petitioner himself.

Accepting this account of the Government's actions as accurate, it is clear that this surveillance was so narrowly circumscribed that a duly authorized magistrate, properly notified of the need for such investigation, specifically informed of the basis on which it was to proceed, and clearly apprised of the precise intrusion it would entail, could constitutionally have authorized, with appropriate safeguards, the very limited search and seizure that the Government asserts in fact took place. * * *c

---

but not the rights of third parties; this concept has traditionally been referred to as "standing." In more recent years the *Katz* analysis has been utilized on that issue: a defendant has standing only if the government violated the privacy on which *he* (as opposed to some other person) justifiably relied. Illustrative is *Rakas v. Illinois*, 439 U.S. 128 (1978), holding that passengers in a car who did not challenge the stopping of the vehicle in which they were riding but only the subsequent search under the seat and in the glove compartment lacked standing to challenge that search; because they asserted no property or possessory interest in the automobile searched or in the property seized, they had not shown they had a legitimate expectation of privacy in the places searched.

Indeed, the Court in *Rakas* suggested that separate treatment of standing was no longer necessary. The Court saw no "useful analytical purpose" in considering the defendant's victim-status as a matter "apart from the merits of the defendant's Fourth Amendment claim." The appropriate question, the Court noted, is whether the "disputed search infringed an interest of the defendant which the Fourth Amendment was designed to protect." This was more direct, it reasoned, than asking whether the defendant's alleged standing is based on his own rights or those of a third party. The Court acknowledged, however, that looking directly at the merits would not alter the results in past cases or make the issue any easier to resolve. Perhaps because the Court foresaw some confusion between the question asked in determining whether there was a search (did the police intrude upon *anyone's* justified expectation of privacy) and the question traditionally labeled as one of standing (did the police intrude upon *this defendant's* expectation of privacy), the Court's subsequent opinions have not totally discarded the practice of referring to the latter issue as one of standing.

c   The Court went on to distinguish the present situation from the kind of electronic surveillance possible under a New York statute which was invalidated in *Berger v. New York*, 388 U.S. 41 (1967), as a "blanket grant of permission to eavesdrop * * * without adequate supervision or protective procedures." That statute, the Court explained in *Berger*, (1) permitted a court order to issue merely on reasonable grounds to believe that evidence of crime may be obtained, without specifying what crime has been or is being committed and without describing what conversations are to be overheard, thus failing to "particularly [describe] the place to be searched, and the person or things to be seized," as required by the Fourth Amendment; (2) permitted installation and operation of surveillance equipment for 60 days, "the equivalent of a series of intrusions, searches and seizures pursuant to a single showing of probable cause"; (3) permitted renewal of the order on the basis of the original grounds on which the initial order was issued, deemed "insufficient

The Government * * * urges the creation of a new exception to cover this case. It argues that surveillance of a telephone booth should be exempted from the usual requirement of advance authorization by a magistrate upon a showing of probable cause. We cannot agree. Omission of such authorization "bypasses the safeguards provided by an objective predetermination of probable cause, and substitutes instead the far less reliable procedure of an after-the-event justification for the * * * search, too likely to be subtly influenced by the familiar shortcomings of hindsight judgment." And bypassing a neutral predetermination of the *scope* of a search leaves individuals secure from Fourth Amendment violations "only in the discretion of the police."

These considerations do not vanish when the search in question is transferred from the setting of a home, an office, or a hotel room, to that of a telephone booth. Wherever a man may be, he is entitled to know that he will remain free from unreasonable searches and seizures. The government agents here ignored "the procedure of antecedent justification * * * that is central to the Fourth Amendment," procedure that we hold to be a constitutional precondition of the kind of electronic surveillance involved in this case. * * *

Judgment reversed.[d]

JUSTICE HARLAN, concurring.

* * * As the Court's opinion states, "The Fourth Amendment protects people, not places." The question, however, is what protection it affords to those people. Generally, as here, the answer to that question requires reference to a "place." My understanding of the rule that has emerged from prior decisions is that there is a twofold requirement, first that a person have exhibited an actual (subjective) expectation of privacy and, second, that the expectation be one that society is prepared to recognize as "reasonable." Thus a man's home is, for most purposes, a place where he expects privacy, but objects, activities, or statements that he exposes to the "plain view" of outsiders are not "protected" because no intention to keep them to himself has been exhibited. On the other hand, conversations in the open would not be protected against being overheard, for the expectation of privacy under the circumstances would be unreasonable. * * *

The critical fact in this case is that "[o]ne who occupies it, [a telephone booth] shuts the door behind him, and pays the toll that permits him to place a call, is surely entitled to assume" that his conversation is not being intercepted. The point is not that the booth is "accessible to the public" at other times, but that it is a

---

without a showing of present probable cause for continuance of the eavesdrop"; (4) placed no termination on the eavesdrop once the conversation sought is seized, as "this is left entirely to the discretion of the officer"; and (5) did not provide for a return on the warrant, "thereby leaving full discretion in the officer as to the use of seized conversations of innocent as well as guilty parties."

Nonconsensual electronic surveillance is authorized in limited circumstances by Title III of the Omnibus Crime Control and Safe Streets Act of 1968, 18 U.S.C.A. §§ 2510–2520. Although the Supreme Court has never passed upon the Act, it has been consistently upheld by the lower courts. Consequently, the focus of litigation in recent years has been upon whether particular wiretapping and electronic eavesdropping activities conform to the requirements of the Act.

    [d] The concurring opinions of Justice Douglas and Justice White are omitted. Justice Marshall did not participate.

temporarily private place whose momentary occupants' expectations of freedom from intrusion are recognized as reasonable. * * *

JUSTICE BLACK, dissenting.

* * * Tapping telephone wires, of course, was an unknown possibility at the time the Fourth Amendment was adopted. But eavesdropping (and wiretapping is nothing more than eavesdropping by telephone) was "an ancient practice which at common law was condemned as a nuisance. In those days the eavesdropper listened by naked ear under the eaves of houses or their windows, or beyond their walls seeking out private discourse." There can be no doubt that the Framers were aware of this practice, and if they had desired to outlaw or restrict the use of evidence obtained by eavesdropping, I believe that they would have used the appropriate language to do so in the Fourth Amendment. They certainly would not have left such a task to the ingenuity of language-stretching judges. * * *

* * * By clever word juggling the Court finds it plausible to argue that language aimed specifically at searches and seizures of things that can be searched and seized may, to protect privacy, be applied to eavesdropped evidence of conversations that can neither be searched nor seized. Few things happen to an individual that do not affect his privacy in one way or another. Thus, by arbitrarily substituting the Court's language, designed to protect privacy, for the Constitution's language, designed to protect against unreasonable searches and seizures, the Court has made the Fourth Amendment its vehicle for holding all laws violative of the Constitution which offend the Court's broadest concept of privacy. * * *

The Fourth Amendment protects privacy only to the extent that it prohibits unreasonable searches and seizures of "persons, houses, papers and effects." No general right is created by the Amendment so as to give this Court the unlimited power to hold unconstitutional everything which affects privacy. Certainly the Framers, well acquainted as they were with the excesses of governmental power, did not intend to grant this Court such omnipotent lawmaking authority as that. The history of governments proves that it is dangerous to freedom to repose such powers in courts. * * *

CALIFORNIA V. GREENWOOD
486 U.S. 35, 108 S.Ct. 1625, 100 L.Ed.2d 30 (1988).

JUSTICE WHITE delivered the opinion of the Court. * * *

In early 1984, Investigator Jenny Stracner of the Laguna Beach Police Department received information indicating that respondent Greenwood might be engaged in narcotics trafficking. * * *

On April 6, 1984, Stracner asked the neighborhood's regular trash collector to pick up the plastic garbage bags that Greenwood had left on the curb in front of his house and to turn the bags over to her without mixing their contents with garbage from other houses. The trash collector cleaned his truck bin of other refuse, collected the garbage bags from the street in front of Greenwood's house, and turned the bags over to Stracner. The officer searched through the rubbish and found items indicative of narcotics use. She recited the information that she had gleaned from the trash search in an affidavit in support of a warrant to search Greenwood's home.

Police officers encountered both respondents at the house later that day when they arrived to execute the warrant. The police discovered quantities of cocaine and hashish during their search of the house. Respondents were arrested on felony narcotics charges. They subsequently posted bail.

The police continued to receive reports of many late-night visitors to the Greenwood house. On May 4, Investigator Robert Rahaeuser obtained Greenwood's garbage from the regular trash collector in the same manner as had Stracner. The garbage again contained evidence of narcotics use.

Rahaeuser secured another search warrant for Greenwood's home based on the information from the second trash search. The police found more narcotics and evidence of narcotics trafficking when they executed the warrant. Greenwood was again arrested.

The Superior Court dismissed the charges against respondents on the authority of *People v. Krivda,* 5 Cal.3d 357, 96 Cal.Rptr. 62, 486 P.2d 1262 (1971), which held that warrantless trash searches violate the Fourth Amendment and the California Constitution. The court found that the police would not have had probable cause to search the Greenwood home without the evidence obtained from the trash searches.

The Court of Appeal affirmed. * * *

The California Supreme Court denied the State's petition for review of the Court of Appeal's decision. We granted certiorari, and now reverse.

The warrantless search and seizure of the garbage bags left at the curb outside the Greenwood house would violate the Fourth Amendment only if respondents manifested a subjective expectation of privacy in their garbage that society accepts as objectively reasonable. Respondents do not disagree with this standard.

They assert, however, that they had, and exhibited, an expectation of privacy with respect to the trash that was searched by the police: The trash, which was placed on the street for collection at a fixed time, was contained in opaque plastic bags, which the garbage collector was expected to pick up, mingle with the trash of others, and deposit at the garbage dump. The trash was only temporarily on the street, and there was little likelihood that it would be inspected by anyone.

It may well be that respondents did not expect that the contents of their garbage bags would become known to the police or other members of the public. An expectation of privacy does not give rise to Fourth Amendment protection, however, unless society is prepared to accept that expectation as objectively reasonable.

Here, we conclude that respondents exposed their garbage to the public sufficiently to defeat their claim to Fourth Amendment protection. It is common knowledge that plastic garbage bags left on or at the side of a public street are readily accessible to animals, children, scavengers, snoops,[4] and other members of the public. Moreover, respondents placed their refuse at the curb for the express purpose of conveying it to a third party, the trash collector, who might himself have sorted through respondents' trash or permitted others, such as the police, to do so. Accordingly, having deposited their garbage "in an area particularly suited for public inspection and, in a manner of speaking, public consumption, for the express purpose of having strangers take it," respondents could have had no reasonable expectation of privacy in the inculpatory items that they discarded.

Furthermore, as we have held, the police cannot reasonably be expected to avert their eyes from evidence of criminal activity that could have been observed by any member of the public. Hence, "[w]hat a person knowingly exposes to the public, even in his own home or office, is not a subject of Fourth Amendment protection." *Katz v. United States.* We held in *Smith v. Maryland,* 442 U.S. 735 (1979), for example, that the police did not violate the Fourth Amendment by causing a pen register to be installed at the telephone company's offices to record the telephone numbers dialed by a criminal suspect. An individual has no legitimate expectation of privacy in the numbers dialed on his telephone, we reasoned, because he voluntarily conveys those numbers to the telephone company when he uses the telephone. Again, we observed that "a person has no legitimate expectation of privacy in information he voluntarily turns over to third parties." * * *

Our conclusion that society would not accept as reasonable respondents' claim to an expectation of privacy in trash left for collection in an area accessible to the public is reinforced by the unanimous rejection of similar claims by the Federal Courts of Appeals. In addition, of those state appellate courts that have considered the issue, the vast majority have held that the police may conduct warrantless searches and seizures of garbage discarded in public areas.

* * * a

JUSTICE BRENNAN, with whom JUSTICE MARSHALL joins, dissenting. * * *

The Framers of the Fourth Amendment understood that "unreasonable searches" of "paper[s] and effects"—no less than "unreasonable searches" of "person[s] and houses"—infringe privacy. * * * In short, so long as a package is "closed against inspection," the Fourth Amendment protects its contents, "wherever they may be," and the police must obtain a warrant to search it just "as is required when papers are subjected to search in one's own household." * * *

Our precedent, therefore, leaves no room to doubt that had respondents been carrying their personal effects in opaque, sealed plastic bags—identical to the ones

---

[4]   Even the refuse of prominent Americans has not been invulnerable. In 1975, for example, a reporter for a weekly tabloid seized five bags of garbage from the sidewalk outside the home of Secretary of State Henry Kissinger. Washington Post, July 9, 1975, p. A1, col. 8. A newspaper editorial criticizing this journalistic "trashpicking" observed that "[e]vidently . . . 'everybody does it.' " Washington Post, July 10, 1975, p. A18, col. 1. We of course do not, as the dissent implies, "bas[e] [our] conclusion" that individuals have no reasonable expectation of privacy in their garbage on this "sole incident."

a   Justice Kennedy took no part in the consideration or decision of this case.

they placed on the curb—their privacy would have been protected from warrantless police intrusion. * * *

Respondents deserve no less protection just because Greenwood used the bags to discard rather than to transport his personal effects. Their contents are not inherently any less private, and Greenwood's decision to discard them, at least in the manner in which he did, does not diminish his expectation of privacy.[2]

A trash bag, like any of the above-mentioned containers, "is a common repository for one's personal effects" and, even more than many of them, is "therefore * * * inevitably associated with the expectation of privacy." * * * A single bag of trash testifies eloquently to the eating, reading, and recreational habits of the person who produced it. A search of trash, like a search of the bedroom, can relate intimate details about sexual practices, health, and personal hygiene. Like rifling through desk drawers or intercepting phone calls, rummaging through trash can divulge the target's financial and professional status, political affiliations and inclinations, private thoughts, personal relationships, and romantic interests. It cannot be doubted that a sealed trash bag harbors telling evidence of the "intimate activity associated with the 'sanctity of a man's home and the privacies of life,' " which the Fourth Amendment is designed to protect.

The Court properly rejects the State's attempt to distinguish trash searches from other searches on the theory that trash is abandoned and therefore not entitled to an expectation of privacy. As the author of the Court's opinion observed last Term, a defendant's "property interest [in trash] does not settle the matter for Fourth Amendment purposes, for the reach of the Fourth Amendment is not determined by state property law." In evaluating the reasonableness of Greenwood's expectation that his sealed trash bags would not be invaded, the Court has held that we must look to "understandings that are recognized and permitted by society." Most of us, I believe, would be incensed to discover a meddler—whether a neighbor, a reporter, or a detective—scrutinizing our sealed trash containers to discover some detail of our personal lives. That was, quite naturally, the reaction to the sole incident on which the Court bases its conclusion that "snoops" and the like defeat the expectation of privacy in trash. When a tabloid reporter examined then-Secretary of State Henry Kissinger's trash and published his findings, Kissinger was "really revolted" by the intrusion and his wife suffered "grave anguish." N.Y. Times, July 9, 1975, p. A1, col. 8. The public response roundly condemning the reporter demonstrates that society not only recognized those reactions as reasonable, but shared them as well. Commentators variously characterized his conduct as "a disgusting invasion of personal privacy," Flieger, Investigative Trash, U.S. News & World Report, July 28, 1975, p. A18 (editor's page); "indefensible * * * as civilized behavior," Washington Post, July 10, 1975, p.

---

[2] Both to support its position that society recognizes no reasonable privacy interest in sealed, opaque trash bags and to refute the prediction that "society will be shocked to learn" of that conclusion, the Court relies heavily upon a collection of lower court cases finding no Fourth Amendment bar to trash searches. But the authority that leads the Court to be "distinctively unimpressed" with our position, is itself impressively undistinguished. Of 11 Federal Court of Appeals cases cited by the Court, at least two are factually or legally distinguishable, and seven rely entirely or almost entirely on an abandonment theory that the Court has discredited. A reading of the Court's collection of state-court cases reveals an equally unimpressive pattern.

A18, col. 1 (editorial); and contrary to "the way decent people behave in relation to each other," ibid. * * *

That is not to deny that isolated intrusions into opaque, sealed trash containers occur. When, acting on their own, "animals, children, scavengers, snoops, [or] other members of the general public," *actually* rummage through a bag of trash and expose its contents to plain view, "police cannot reasonably be expected to avert their eyes from evidence of criminal activity that could have been observed by any member of the public."

Had Greenwood flaunted his intimate activity by strewing his trash all over the curb for all to see, or had some nongovernmental intruder invaded his privacy and done the same, I could accept the Court's conclusion that an expectation of privacy would have been unreasonable. Similarly, had police searching the city dump run across incriminating evidence that, despite commingling with the trash of others, still retained its identity as Greenwood's, we would have a different case. But all that Greenwood "exposed * * * to the public" were the exteriors of several opaque, sealed containers. * * *

The mere *possibility* that unwelcome meddlers *might* open and rummage through the containers does not negate the expectation of privacy in its contents any more than the possibility of a burglary negates an expectation of privacy in the home; or the possibility of a private intrusion negates an expectation of privacy in an unopened package; or the possibility that an operator will listen in on a telephone conversation negates an expectation of privacy in the words spoken on the telephone. "What a person * * * seeks to preserve as private, *even in an area accessible to the public,* may be constitutionally protected." *Katz.* We have therefore repeatedly rejected attempts to justify a State's invasion of privacy on the ground that the privacy is not absolute. See *Chapman v. United States,* 365 U.S. 610 (1961) (search of a house invaded tenant's Fourth Amendment rights even though landlord had authority to enter house for some purposes); *Stoner v. California,* 376 U.S. 483 (1964) (implicit consent to janitorial personnel to enter motel room does not amount to consent to police search of room); *O'Connor v. Ortega,* 480 U.S. 709 (1987) (a government employee has a reasonable expectation of privacy in his office, even though "it is the nature of government offices that others—such as fellow employees, supervisors, consensual visitors, and the general public—may have frequent access to an individual's office"). * * *

Nor is it dispositive that "respondents placed their refuse at the curb for the express purpose of conveying it to a third party, * * * who might himself have sorted through respondents' trash or permitted others, such as police, to do so." In the first place, Greenwood can hardly be faulted for leaving trash on his curb when a county ordinance commanded him to do so and prohibited him from disposing of it in any other way. * * * More importantly, even the voluntary relinquishment of possession or control over an effect does not necessarily amount to a relinquishment of a privacy expectation in it. Were it otherwise, a letter or package would lose all Fourth Amendment protection when placed in a mail box or other depository with the "express purpose" of entrusting it to the postal officer or a private carrier; those bailees are just as likely as trash collectors (and certainly have greater incentive) to "sor[t] through" the personal effects entrusted to them, "or permi[t] others, such as police to do so." Yet, it has been clear for at least 110 years that the possibility of such an intrusion does not justify a warrantless search by police in the first instance. * * *

FLORIDA V. RILEY

488 U.S. 445, 109 S.Ct. 693, 102 L.Ed.2d 835 (1989).

JUSTICE WHITE announced the judgment of the Court and delivered an opinion, in which THE CHIEF JUSTICE, JUSTICE SCALIA and JUSTICE KENNEDY join.

On certification to it by a lower state court, the Florida Supreme Court addressed the following question: "Whether surveillance of the interior of a partially covered greenhouse in a residential backyard from the vantage point of a helicopter located 400 feet above the greenhouse constitutes a 'search' for which a warrant is required under the Fourth Amendment and Article I, Section 12 of the Florida Constitution." The court answered the question in the affirmative, and we granted the State's petition for certiorari challenging that conclusion. * * *

We agree with the State's submission that our decision in *California v. Ciraolo*, 476 U.S. 207 (1986), controls this case. There, acting on a tip, the police inspected the back yard of a particular house while flying in a fixed-wing aircraft at 1,000 feet. With the naked-eye the officers saw what they concluded was marijuana growing in the yard. A search warrant was obtained on the strength of this airborne inspection, and marijuana plants were found. The trial court refused to suppress this evidence, but a state appellate court held that the inspection violated the Fourth and Fourteenth Amendments of the United States Constitution and that the warrant was therefore invalid. We in turn reversed, holding that the inspection was not a search subject to the Fourth Amendment. We recognized that the yard was within the curtilage of the house, that a fence shielded the yard from observation from the street and that the occupant had a subjective expectation of privacy. We held, however, that such an expectation was not reasonable and not one "that society is prepared to honor." * * * "In an age where private and commercial flight in the public airways is routine, it is unreasonable for respondent to expect that his marijuana plants were constitutionally protected from being observed with the naked eye from an altitude of 1,000 feet. The Fourth Amendment simply does not require the police traveling in the public airways at this altitude to obtain a warrant in order to observe what is visible to the naked eye."

We arrive at the same conclusion in the present case.[a] * * *

---

[a] In *Bond v. United States*, 529 U.S. 334 (2000), involving the question of whether the squeezing of soft luggage passengers had placed in the overhead rack of a bus was a search, the Court rejected the government's reliance upon *Ciraolo* and *Riley*, stating that "[p]hysical invasive inspection is simply more intrusive than purely visual inspection." The Court then concluded: "When a bus passenger places a bag in an overhead bin, he expects that other passengers or bus employees may move it for one reason or another. Thus, a bus passenger clearly expects that his bag may be handled. He does not expect that other passengers or bus employees will, as a matter of course, feel the bag in an exploratory manner. But this is exactly what the agent did here. We therefore hold that the agent's physical manipulation of petitioner's bag violated the Fourth Amendment." Two dissenters in *Bond* objected that the squeezing did not "differ from the

Nor on the facts before us, does it make a difference for Fourth Amendment purposes that the helicopter was flying at 400 feet when the officer saw what was growing in the greenhouse through the partially open roof and sides of the structure. We would have a different case if flying at that altitude had been contrary to law or regulation. But helicopters are not bound by the lower limits of the navigable airspace allowed to other aircraft. Any member of the public could legally have been flying over Riley's property in a helicopter at the altitude of 400 feet and could have observed Riley's greenhouse. The police officer did no more. This is not to say that an inspection of the curtilage of a house from an aircraft will always pass muster under the Fourth Amendment simply because the plane is within the navigable airspace specified by law. But it is of obvious importance that the helicopter in this case was *not* violating the law, and there is nothing in the record or before us to suggest that helicopters flying at 400 feet are sufficiently rare in this country to lend substance to respondent's claim that he reasonably anticipated that his greenhouse would not be subject to observation from that altitude. Neither is there any intimation here that the helicopter interfered with respondent's normal use of the greenhouse or of other parts of the curtilage. As far as this record reveals, no intimate details connected with the use of the home or curtilage were observed, and there was no undue noise, no wind, dust, or threat of injury. In these circumstances, there was no violation of the Fourth Amendment. * * *

JUSTICE O'CONNOR, concurring in the judgment. * * *

In determining whether Riley had a reasonable expectation of privacy from aerial observation, the relevant inquiry after *Ciraolo* is not whether the helicopter was where it had a right to be under FAA regulations. Rather, consistent with *Katz*, we must ask whether the helicopter was in the public airways at an altitude at which members of the public travel with sufficient regularity that Riley's expectation of privacy from aerial observation was not "one that society is prepared to recognize as 'reasonable.'" * * *

Because there is reason to believe that there is considerable public use of airspace at altitudes of 400 feet and above, and because Riley introduced no evidence to the contrary before the Florida courts, I conclude that Riley's expectation that his curtilage was protected from naked-eye aerial observation from that altitude was not a reasonable one. However, public use of altitudes lower than that—particularly public observations from helicopters circling over the curtilage of a home—may be sufficiently rare that police surveillance from such altitudes would violate reasonable expectations of privacy, despite compliance with FAA air safety regulations.

---

treatment that overhead luggage is likely to receive from strangers in a world of travel that is somewhat less gentle than it used to be," and that whether "tactile manipulation * * * is more intrusive or less intrusive than visual observation * * * necessarily depends on the particular circumstances."

JUSTICE BRENNAN, with whom JUSTICE MARSHALL and JUSTICE STEVENS, join, dissenting.

* * * Under the plurality's exceedingly grudging Fourth Amendment theory, the expectation of privacy is defeated if a single member of the public could conceivably position herself to see into the area in question without doing anything illegal. It is defeated whatever the difficulty a person would have in so positioning herself, and however infrequently anyone would in fact do so. In taking this view the plurality ignores the very essence of *Katz*. * * *

It is a curious notion that the reach of the Fourth Amendment can be so largely defined by administrative regulations issued for purposes of flight safety. It is more curious still that the plurality relies to such an extent on the legality of the officer's act, when we have consistently refused to equate police violation of the law with infringement of the Fourth Amendment.[3] But the plurality's willingness to end its inquiry when it finds that the officer was in a position he had a right to be in is misguided for an even more fundamental reason. Finding determinative the fact that the officer was where he had a right to be is, at bottom, an attempt to analogize surveillance from a helicopter to surveillance by a police officer standing on a public road and viewing evidence of crime through an open window or a gap in a fence. In such a situation, the occupant of the home may be said to lack any reasonable expectation of privacy in what can be seen from that road—even if, in fact, people rarely pass that way.

The police officer positioned 400 feet above Riley's backyard was not, however, standing on a public road. The vantage point he enjoyed was not one any citizen could readily share. His ability to see over Riley's fence depended on his use of a very expensive and sophisticated piece of machinery to which few ordinary citizens have access. In such circumstances it makes no more sense to rely on the legality of the officer's position in the skies than it would to judge the constitutionality of the wiretap in *Katz* by the legality of the officer's position outside the telephone booth. The simply inquiry whether the police officer had the legal right to be in the position from which he made his observations cannot suffice, for we cannot assume that Riley's curtilage was so open to the observations of passersby in the skies that he retained little privacy or personal security to be lost to police surveillance. The question before us must be not whether the police were where they had a right to be, but whether public observation of Riley's curtilage was so commonplace that Riley's expectation of privacy in his backyard could not be considered reasonable. * * *

What separates me from Justice O'Connor is essentially an empirical matter concerning the extent of public use of the airspace at that altitude, together with the question of how to resolve that issue. I do not think the constitutional claims should fail simply because "there is reason to believe" that there is "considerable" public flying this close to earth or because Riley "introduced no evidence to the

---

[3] In *Oliver v. United States*, 466 U.S. 170 (1984), for example, we held that police officers who trespassed upon posted and fenced private land did not violate the Fourth Amendment, despite the fact that their action was subject to criminal sanctions. We noted that the interests vindicated by the Fourth Amendment were not identical with those served by the common law of trespass.

contrary before the Florida courts." * * * I think we could take judicial notice that, while there may be an occasional privately owned helicopter that flies over populated areas at an altitude of 400 feet, such flights are a rarity and are almost entirely limited to approaching or leaving airports or to reporting traffic congestion near major roadways. And, as the concurring opinion agrees, the extent of police surveillance traffic cannot serve as a bootstrap to demonstrate public use of the airspace.

If, however, we are to resolve the issue by considering whether the appropriate party carried its burden of proof, I again think that Riley must prevail. Because the State has greater access to information concerning customary flight patterns and because the coercive power of the State ought not be brought to bear in cases in which it is unclear whether the prosecution is a product of an unconstitutional, warrantless search, the burden of proof properly rests with the State and not with the individual defendant. The State quite clearly has not carried this burden. * * *

JUSTICE BLACKMUN, dissenting.

[B]ecause I believe that private helicopters rarely fly over curtilages at an altitude of 400 feet, I would impose upon the prosecution the burden of proving contrary facts necessary to show that Riley lacked a reasonable expectation of privacy. Indeed, I would establish this burden of proof for any helicopter surveillance case in which the flight occurred below 1000 feet—in other words, for any aerial surveillance case not governed by the Court's decision in *California v. Ciraolo.*

In this case, the prosecution did not meet this burden of proof, as Justice Brennan notes. This failure should compel a finding that a Fourth Amendment search occurred. But because our prior cases gave the parties little guidance on the burden of proof issue, I would remand this case to allow the prosecution an opportunity to meet this burden. * * *

UNITED STATES V. JONES
565 U.S. 400, 132 S.Ct. 945, 181 L.Ed.2d 911 (2012).

JUSTICE SCALIA delivered the opinion of the Court.

[Government agents installed a GPS tracking device on the undercarriage of a Jeep used by Jones, suspected of trafficking in narcotics, while it was parked in a public parking lot. Over the next 28 days the government used the device to track the vehicle's movements; the device established the vehicle's location within 50 to 100 feet and communicated its location by cell phone to a government computer. It relayed more than 2,000 pages of data over a 4-week period. The court of appeals reversed Jones' conviction on the ground that the evidence obtained by warrantless use of the GPS device violated the Fourth Amendment.]

* * * We hold that the Government's installation of a GPS device on a target's vehicle, and its use of that device to monitor the vehicle's movements, constitutes a "search."

It is important to be clear about what occurred in this case: The Government physically occupied private property for the purpose of obtaining information. We have no doubt that such a physical intrusion would have been considered a "search" within the meaning of the Fourth Amendment when it was adopted. * * *

The text of the Fourth Amendment reflects its close connection to property, since otherwise it would have referred simply to "the right of the people to be secure against unreasonable searches and seizures"; the phrase "in their persons, houses, papers, and effects" would have been superfluous.

Consistent with this understanding, our Fourth Amendment jurisprudence was tied to common-law trespass, at least until the latter half of the 20th century. * * *

Our later cases, of course, [as in *Katz*,] have deviated from that exclusively property-based approach. * * *

The Government contends that the Harlan standard [in *Katz*] shows that no search occurred here, since Jones had no "reasonable expectation of privacy" in the area of the Jeep accessed by Government agents (its underbody) and in the locations of the Jeep on the public roads, which were visible to all. But we need not address the Government's contentions, because Jones's Fourth Amendment rights do not rise or fall with the *Katz* formulation. At bottom, we must "assur[e] preservation of that degree of privacy against government that existed when the Fourth Amendment was adopted." As explained, for most of our history the Fourth Amendment was understood to embody a particular concern for government trespass upon the areas ("persons, houses, papers, and effects") it enumerates.[3] *Katz* did not repudiate that understanding. Less than two years later the Court upheld defendants' contention that the Government could not introduce against them conversations between *other* people obtained by warrantless placement of electronic surveillance devices in their homes. The opinion rejected the dissent's contention that there was no Fourth Amendment violation "unless the conversational privacy of the homeowner himself is invaded."[4] *Alderman v. United States*, 394 U.S. 165 (1969). "[W]e [do not] believe that *Katz,* by holding that the Fourth Amendment protects persons and their private conversations, was intended to withdraw any of the protection which the Amendment extends to the home. . . ."

---

[3]   Justice Alito's concurrence (hereinafter concurrence) doubts the wisdom of our approach because "it is almost impossible to think of late-18th-century situations that are analogous to what took place in this case." But in fact it posits a situation that is not far afield—a constable's concealing himself in the target's coach in order to track its movements. There is no doubt that the information gained by that trespassory activity would be the product of an unlawful search— whether that information consisted of the conversations occurring in the coach, or of the destinations to which the coach traveled.

In any case, it is quite irrelevant whether there was an 18th-century analog. Whatever new methods of investigation may be devised, our task, *at a minimum,* is to decide whether the action in question would have constituted a "search" within the original meaning of the Fourth Amendment. Where, as here, the Government obtains information by physically intruding on a constitutionally protected area, such a search has undoubtedly occurred.

[4]   Thus, the concurrence's attempt to recast *Alderman* as meaning that individuals have a "legitimate expectation of privacy in all conversations that [take] place under their roof" is foreclosed by the Court's opinion. The Court took as a given that the homeowner's "conversational privacy" had not been violated.

More recently, in *Soldal v. Cook County,* 506 U.S. 56 (1992), the Court unanimously rejected the argument that although a "seizure" had occurred "in a 'technical' sense" when a trailer home was forcibly removed, no Fourth Amendment violation occurred because law enforcement had not "invade[d] the [individuals'] privacy." *Katz,* the Court explained, established that "property rights are not the sole measure of Fourth Amendment violations," but did not "snuf[f] out the previously recognized protection for property." * * * *Katz* did not narrow the Fourth Amendment's scope.[5]

The Government contends that several of our post-*Katz* cases foreclose the conclusion that what occurred here constituted a search. It relies principally on two cases in which we rejected Fourth Amendment challenges to "beepers," electronic tracking devices that represent another form of electronic monitoring. The first case, [*United States v.*] *Knotts,* [460 U.S. 276 (1983),] upheld against Fourth Amendment challenge the use of a "beeper" that had been placed in a container of chloroform, allowing law enforcement to monitor the location of the container. We said that there had been no infringement of Knotts' reasonable expectation of privacy since the information obtained—the location of the automobile carrying the container on public roads, and the location of the off-loaded container in open fields near Knotts' cabin—had been voluntarily conveyed to the public.[6] But as we have discussed, the *Katz* reasonable-expectation-of-privacy test has been *added to,* not *substituted for,* the common-law trespassory test. The holding in *Knotts* addressed only the former, since the latter was not at issue. The beeper had been placed in the container before it came into Knotts' possession, with the consent of the then-owner. Knotts did not challenge that installation, and we specifically declined to consider its effect on the Fourth Amendment analysis. * * *

The second "beeper" case, *United States v. Karo,* 468 U.S. 705 (1984), does not suggest a different conclusion. There we addressed the question left open by *Knotts,* whether the installation of a beeper in a container amounted to a search or seizure. As in *Knotts,* at the time the beeper was installed the container belonged to a third party, and it did not come into possession of the defendant until later. Thus, the specific question we considered was whether the installation "*with the consent of the original owner* constitute[d] a search or seizure . . . when the container is

---

[5] The concurrence notes that post-*Katz* we have explained that " 'an actual trespass is neither necessary *nor sufficient* to establish a constitutional violation.' " (quoting *United States v. Karo,* infra). That is undoubtedly true, and undoubtedly irrelevant. *Karo* was considering whether a seizure occurred, and as the concurrence explains, a seizure of property occurs, not when there is a trespass, but "when there is some meaningful interference with an individual's possessory interests in that property." Likewise with a search. Trespass alone does not qualify, but there must be conjoined with that what was present here: an attempt to find something or to obtain information.

Related to this, and similarly irrelevant, is the concurrence's point that, if analyzed separately, neither the installation of the device nor its use would constitute a Fourth Amendment search. Of course not. A trespass on "houses" or "effects," or a *Katz* invasion of privacy, is not alone a search unless it is done to obtain information; and the obtaining of information is not alone a search unless it is achieved by such a trespass or invasion of privacy.

[6] *Knotts* noted the "limited use which the government made of the signals from this particular beeper," and reserved the question whether "different constitutional principles may be applicable" to "dragnet-type law enforcement practices" of the type that GPS tracking made possible here.

delivered to a buyer having no knowledge of the presence of the beeper" (emphasis added). We held not. The Government, we said, came into physical contact with the container only before it belonged to the defendant Karo; and the transfer of the container with the unmonitored beeper inside did not convey any information and thus did not invade Karo's privacy.[a] That conclusion is perfectly consistent with the one we reach here. Karo accepted the container as it came to him, beeper and all, and was therefore not entitled to object to the beeper's presence, even though it was used to monitor the container's location. Jones, who possessed the Jeep at the time the Government trespassorily inserted the information-gathering device, is on much different footing. * * *

* * * The concurrence posits that "relatively short-term monitoring of a person's movements on public streets" is okay, but that "the use of longer term GPS monitoring in investigations *of most offenses*" is no good (emphasis added). That introduces yet another novelty into our jurisprudence. There is no precedent for the proposition that whether a search has occurred depends on the nature of the crime being investigated. And even accepting that novelty, it remains unexplained why a 4-week investigation is "surely" too long and why a drug-trafficking conspiracy involving substantial amounts of cash and narcotics is not an "extraordinary offens[e]" which may permit longer observation. What of a 2-day monitoring of a suspected purveyor of stolen electronics? Or of a 6-month monitoring of a suspected terrorist? We may have to grapple with these "vexing problems" in some future case where a classic trespassory search is not involved and resort must be had to *Katz* analysis; but there is no reason for rushing forward to resolve them here. * * *

JUSTICE SOTOMAYOR, concurring.

* * * When the Government physically invades personal property to gather information, a search occurs. The reaffirmation of that principle suffices to decide this case.

Nonetheless, as Justice Alito notes, physical intrusion is now unnecessary to many forms of surveillance. * * *

In cases involving even short-term monitoring, some unique attributes of GPS surveillance relevant to the *Katz* analysis will require particular attention. GPS monitoring generates a precise, comprehensive record of a person's public

---

a   The Court in *Karo* went on to hold, however, with respect to use of the "beeper" to determine the location of the container within particular premises, that this would be a search, an invasion of the rights of those having a privacy expectation in that place, if such monitoring "reveals information that could not have been obtained through visual surveillance," which is the case even "if visual surveillance has revealed that the article to which the beeper is attached has entered the house" where "the later monitoring not only verifies the officers' observations but also establishes that the article remains on the premises." Absent "truly exigent circumstances," the Court added, such use of the beeper would require resort to a search warrant.

In response to the government's claim that a warrant should not be required because of the difficulty in satisfying the particularity requirement of the Fourth Amendment, in that it is usually not known in advance to what place the container with the beeper in it will be taken, the Court concluded that it would suffice if the warrant were to describe the object into which the beeper is to be placed, the circumstances that led the agents to wish to install the beeper, and the length of time for which beeper surveillance is requested."

movements that reflects a wealth of detail about her familial, political, professional, religious, and sexual associations. The Government can store such records and efficiently mine them for information years into the future. And because GPS monitoring is cheap in comparison to conventional surveillance techniques and, by design, proceeds surreptitiously, it evades the ordinary checks that constrain abusive law enforcement practices: "limited police resources and community hostility." * * *

I would take these attributes of GPS monitoring into account when considering the existence of a reasonable societal expectation of privacy in the sum of one's public movements. * * *

JUSTICE ALITO, with whom JUSTICE GINSBURG, JUSTICE BREYER, and JUSTICE KAGAN join, concurring in the judgment. * * *

This holding, in my judgment, is unwise. It strains the language of the Fourth Amendment; it has little if any support in current Fourth Amendment case law; and it is highly artificial. * * *

The Fourth Amendment prohibits "unreasonable searches and seizures," and the Court makes very little effort to explain how the attachment or use of the GPS device fits within these terms. The Court does not contend that there was a seizure. * * *

The Court does claim that the installation and use of the GPS constituted a search, but this conclusion is dependent on the questionable proposition that these two procedures cannot be separated for purposes of Fourth Amendment analysis. If these two procedures are analyzed separately, it is not at all clear from the Court's opinion why either should be regarded as a search. It is clear that the attachment of the GPS device was not itself a search; if the device had not functioned or if the officers had not used it, no information would have been obtained. And the Court does not contend that the use of the device constituted a search either. On the contrary, the Court accepts the holding in *United States v. Knotts* that the use of a surreptitiously planted electronic device to monitor a vehicle's movements on public roads did not amount to a search.

The Court argues—and I agree—that "we must 'assur[e] preservation of that degree of privacy against government that existed when the Fourth Amendment was adopted.'" But it is almost impossible to think of late 18th-century situations that are analogous to what took place in this case. (Is it possible to imagine a case in which a constable secreted himself somewhere in a coach and remained there for a period of time in order to monitor the movements of the coach's owner?[3]) The Court's theory seems to be that the concept of a search, as originally understood, comprehended any technical trespass that led to the gathering of evidence, but we know that this is incorrect. At common law, any unauthorized intrusion on private property was actionable, but a trespass on open fields, as opposed to the "curtilage' of a home, does not fall within the scope of the Fourth Amendment because private

---

[3] The Court suggests that something like this might have occurred in 1791, but this would have required either a gigantic coach, a very tiny constable, or both—not to mention a constable with incredible fortitude and patience.

property outside the curtilage is not part of a 'hous[e]' " within the meaning of the Fourth Amendment.

The Court's reasoning in this case is very similar to that in the Court's early decisions involving wiretapping and electronic eavesdropping, namely, that a technical trespass followed by the gathering of evidence constitutes a search. * * *

Katz v. United States finally did away with the old approach, holding that a trespass was not required for a Fourth Amendment violation. * * *

The majority suggests that two post-*Katz* decisions' *Soldal v. Cook County* and *Alderman v. United States*—show that a technical trespass is sufficient to establish the existence of a search, but they provide little support.

In *Soldal,* the Court held that towing away a trailer home without the owner's consent constituted a seizure even if this did not invade the occupants' personal privacy. But in the present case, the Court does not find that there was a seizure, and it is clear that none occurred.

In *Alderman,* the Court held that the Fourth Amendment rights of homeowners were implicated by the use of a surreptitiously planted listening device to monitor third-party conversations that occurred within their home. *Alderman* is best understood to mean that the homeowners had a legitimate expectation of privacy in all conversations that took place under their roof.

In sum, the majority is hard pressed to find support in post-*Katz* cases for its trespass-based theory.

Disharmony with a substantial body of existing case law is only one of the problems with the Court's approach in this case.

I will briefly note [some] others. First, the Court's reasoning largely disregards what is really important (the *use* of a GPS for the purpose of long-term tracking) and instead attaches great significance to something that most would view as relatively minor (attaching to the bottom of a car a small, light object that does not interfere in any way with the car's operation). Attaching such an object is generally regarded as so trivial that it does not provide a basis for recovery under modern tort law. * * *

Second, the Court's approach leads to incongruous results. If the police attach a GPS device to a car and use the device to follow the car for even a brief time, under the Court's theory, the Fourth Amendment applies. But if the police follow the same car for a much longer period using unmarked cars and aerial assistance, this tracking is not subject to any Fourth Amendment constraints.

[Also], the Court's reliance on the law of trespass will present particularly vexing problems in cases involving surveillance that is carried out by making electronic, as opposed to physical, contact with the item to be tracked. For example, suppose that the officers in the present case had followed respondent by surreptitiously activating a stolen vehicle detection system that came with the car when it was purchased. Would the sending of a radio signal to activate this system constitute a trespass to chattels? Trespass to chattels has traditionally required a physical touching of the property. * * *

The *Katz* expectation-of-privacy test avoids the problems and complications noted above, but it is not without its own difficulties. [T]he *Katz* test rests on the assumption that this hypothetical reasonable person has a well-developed and stable set of privacy expectations. But technology can change those expectations. * * *

Recent years have seen the emergence of many new devices that permit the monitoring of a person's movements. In some locales, closed-circuit television video monitoring is becoming ubiquitous. On toll roads, automatic toll collection systems create a precise record of the movements of motorists who choose to make use of that convenience. Many motorists purchase cars that are equipped with devices that permit a central station to ascertain the car's location at any time so that roadside assistance may be provided if needed and the car may be found if it is stolen.

Perhaps most significant, cell phones and other wireless devices now permit wireless carriers to track and record the location of users—and as of June 2011, it has been reported, there were more than 322 million wireless devices in use in the United States. For older phones, the accuracy of the location information depends on the density of the tower network, but new "smart phones," which are equipped with a GPS device, permit more precise tracking. * * * The availability and use of these and other new devices will continue to shape the average person's expectations about the privacy of his or her daily movements.

* * * A legislative body is well situated to gauge changing public attitudes, to draw detailed lines, and to balance privacy and public safety in a comprehensive way.

To date, however, Congress and most States have not enacted statutes regulating the use of GPS tracking technology for law enforcement purposes. The best that we can do in this case is to apply existing Fourth Amendment doctrine and to ask whether the use of GPS tracking in a particular case involved a degree of intrusion that a reasonable person would not have anticipated.

Under this approach, relatively short-term monitoring of a person's movements on public streets accords with expectations of privacy that our society has recognized as reasonable. But the use of longer term GPS monitoring in investigations of most offenses impinges on expectations of privacy. For such offenses, society's expectation has been that law enforcement agents and others would not—and indeed, in the main, simply could not—secretly monitor and catalogue every single movement of an individual's car for a very long period. In this case, for four weeks, law enforcement agents tracked every movement that respondent made in the vehicle he was driving. We need not identify with precision the point at which the tracking of this vehicle became a search, for the line was surely crossed before the 4-week mark. Other cases may present more difficult questions. But where uncertainty exists with respect to whether a certain period of GPS surveillance is long enough to constitute a Fourth Amendment search, the police may always seek a warrant. We also need not consider whether prolonged GPS monitoring in the context of investigations involving extraordinary offenses would similarly intrude on a constitutionally protected sphere of privacy. In such cases, long-term tracking might have been mounted using previously available techniques. * * *

CARPENTER V. UNITED STATES

585 U.S. ___, 138 S.Ct. 2206, 201 L.Ed.2d 507 (2018).

CHIEF JUSTICE ROBERTS delivered the opinion of the Court.

[After the FBI identified the cell phone numbers of several robbery suspects, prosecutors obtained the suspects' cell phone records via court order under the Stored Communications Act, which requires information short of probable cause. 18 U.S.C.A. § 2703(d). Whenever a person places a cell phone call, the call is routed through local cell sites that are needed to transmit the call. Cell phone providers keep records for their own business purposes of which cell sites were used by particular phones to route particular calls, which enable them to know the rough location of the phone when a call was placed (called cell-cite location information, or CSLI).ᵃ In Carpenter's case, the FBI obtained 12,898 locations points cataloging Carpenter's movements over 127 days—an average of 101 data points per day. Carpenter unsuccessfully sought to suppress that data, which showed he was near four robbery locations at the time those robberies occurred, and the Sixth Circuit affirmed on the ground that Carpenter lacked a reasonable expectation of privacy in the information he shared with his wireless carriers.]

[R]equests for cell-site records lie at the intersection of two lines of cases, both of which inform our understanding of the privacy interests at stake.

The first set of cases addresses a person's expectation of privacy in his physical location and movements[, as in *Jones*].

In a second set of decisions, the Court has drawn a line between what a person keeps to himself and what he shares with others. We have previously held that "a person has no legitimate expectation of privacy in information he voluntarily turns over to third parties." * * *

This third-party doctrine largely traces its roots to *United States v. Miller*, 425 U.S. 435 (1976). While investigating Miller for tax evasion, the Government subpoenaed his banks, seeking several months of canceled checks, deposit slips, and monthly statements. The Court rejected a Fourth Amendment challenge to the records collection. For one, Miller could "assert neither ownership nor possession" of the documents; they were "business records of the banks." For another, the nature of those records confirmed Miller's limited expectation of privacy, because the checks were "not confidential communications but negotiable instruments to be used in commercial transactions," and the bank statements contained information "exposed to [bank] employees in the ordinary course of business." The Court thus concluded that Miller had "take[n] the risk, in revealing his affairs to

---

ᵃ   While, as the Court noted, "modern devices, such as smartphones, tap into the wireless network several times a minute whenever their signal is on," the court orders obtained only required the two carriers to disclose information for Carpenter's phone "at call origination and at call termination for incoming and outgoing calls" for the specified time periods.

another, that the information [would] be conveyed by that person to the Government."

Three years later, *Smith* [*v. Maryland*, 442 U.S. 735 (1979),] applied the same principles in the context of information conveyed to a telephone company. The Court ruled that the Government's use of a pen register—a device that recorded the outgoing phone numbers dialed on a landline telephone—was not a search. Noting the pen register's "limited capabilities," the Court "doubt[ed] that people in general entertain any actual expectation of privacy in the numbers they dial." Telephone subscribers know, after all, that the numbers are used by the telephone company "for a variety of legitimate business purposes," including routing calls. And at any rate, the Court explained, such an expectation "is not one that society is prepared to recognize as reasonable." When Smith placed a call, he "voluntarily conveyed" the dialed numbers to the phone company by "expos[ing] that information to its equipment in the ordinary course of business." Once again, we held that the defendant "assumed the risk" that the company's records "would be divulged to police." * * *

* * * The location information obtained from Carpenter's wireless carriers was the product of a search.[3] A person does not surrender all Fourth Amendment protection by venturing into the public sphere. To the contrary, "what [one] seeks to preserve as private, even in an area accessible to the public, may be constitutionally protected." *Katz*. A majority of this Court has already recognized that individuals have a reasonable expectation of privacy in the whole of their physical movements. *Jones*. Prior to the digital age, law enforcement might have pursued a suspect for a brief stretch, but doing so "for any extended period of time was difficult and costly and therefore rarely undertaken." For that reason, "society's expectation has been that law enforcement agents and others would not—and indeed, in the main, simply could not—secretly monitor and catalogue every single movement of an individual's car for a very long period."

Allowing government access to cell-site records contravenes that expectation. Although such records are generated for commercial purposes, that distinction does not negate Carpenter's anticipation of privacy in his physical location. Mapping a cell phone's location over the course of 127 days provides an all-encompassing record of the holder's whereabouts. As with GPS information, the time-stamped data provides an intimate window into a person's life, revealing not only his particular movements, but through them his "familial, political, professional, religious, and sexual associations." These location records "hold for many Americans the 'privacies of life.'" And like GPS monitoring, cell phone tracking is remarkably easy, cheap, and efficient compared to traditional investigative tools.

---

[3] The parties suggest as an alternative to their primary submissions that the acquisition of CSLI becomes a search only if it extends beyond a limited period. See Reply Brief 12 (proposing a 24-hour cutoff); Brief for United States 55–56 (suggesting a seven-day cutoff). As part of its argument, the Government treats the seven days of CSLI requested from Sprint as the pertinent period, even though Sprint produced only two days of records. Brief for United States 56. Contrary to JUSTICE KENNEDY's assertion, we need not decide whether there is a limited period for which the Government may obtain an individual's historical CSLI free from Fourth Amendment scrutiny, and if so, how long that period might be. It is sufficient for our purposes today to hold that accessing seven days of CSLI constitutes a Fourth Amendment search.

With just the click of a button, the Government can access each carrier's deep repository of historical location information at practically no expense.

In fact, historical cell-site records present even greater privacy concerns than the GPS monitoring of a vehicle we considered in *Jones*. Unlike the bugged container in *Knotts* or the car in *Jones*, a cell phone—almost a "feature of human anatomy"—tracks nearly exactly the movements of its owner. While individuals regularly leave their vehicles, they compulsively carry cell phones with them all the time. A cell phone faithfully follows its owner beyond public thoroughfares and into private residences, doctor's offices, political headquarters, and other potentially revealing locales. * * * Accordingly, when the Government tracks the location of a cell phone it achieves near perfect surveillance, as if it had attached an ankle monitor to the phone's user.

Moreover, the retrospective quality of the data here gives police access to a category of information otherwise unknowable. In the past, attempts to reconstruct a person's movements were limited by a dearth of records and the frailties of recollection. With access to CSLI, the Government can now travel back in time to retrace a person's whereabouts, subject only to the retention policies of the wireless carriers, which currently maintain records for up to five years. Critically, because location information is continually logged for all of the 400 million devices in the United States—not just those belonging to persons who might happen to come under investigation—this newfound tracking capacity runs against everyone. Unlike with the GPS device in *Jones*, police need not even know in advance whether they want to follow a particular individual, or when.

Whoever the suspect turns out to be, he has effectively been tailed every moment of every day for five years, and the police may—in the Government's view—call upon the results of that surveillance without regard to the constraints of the Fourth Amendment. Only the few without cell phones could escape this tireless and absolute surveillance.

The Government and Justice Kennedy contend, however, that the collection of CSLI should be permitted because the data is less precise than GPS information. Not to worry, they maintain, because the location records did "not on their own suffice to place [Carpenter] at the crime scene"; they placed him within a wedge-shaped sector ranging from one-eighth to four square miles. From the 127 days of location data it received, the Government could, in combination with other information, deduce a detailed log of Carpenter's movements, including when he was at the site of the robberies. And the Government thought the CSLI accurate enough to highlight it during the closing argument of his trial.

At any rate, the rule the Court adopts "must take account of more sophisticated systems that are already in use or in development." While the records in this case reflect the state of technology at the start of the decade, the accuracy of CSLI is rapidly approaching GPS-level precision. As the number of cell sites has proliferated, the geographic area covered by each cell sector has shrunk, particularly in urban areas. In addition, with new technology measuring the time and angle of signals hitting their towers, wireless carriers already have the capability to pinpoint a phone's location within 50 meters. * * *

Accordingly, when the Government accessed CSLI from the wireless carriers, it invaded Carpenter's reasonable expectation of privacy in the whole of his physical movements.

The Government's primary contention to the contrary is that the third-party doctrine governs this case. In its view, cell-site records are fair game because they are "business records" created and maintained by the wireless carriers. The Government (along with Justice Kennedy) recognizes that this case features new technology, but asserts that the legal question nonetheless turns on a garden-variety request for information from a third-party witness.

The Government's position fails to contend with the seismic shifts in digital technology that made possible the tracking of not only Carpenter's location but also everyone else's, not for a short period but for years and years. Sprint Corporation and its competitors are not your typical witnesses. Unlike the nosy neighbor who keeps an eye on comings and goings, they are ever alert, and their memory is nearly infallible. There is a world of difference between the limited types of personal information addressed in *Smith* and *Miller* and the exhaustive chronicle of location information casually collected by wireless carriers today. The Government thus is not asking for a straightforward application of the third-party doctrine, but instead a significant extension of it to a distinct category of information. * * *

Our decision today is a narrow one. We do not express a view on matters not before us: real-time CSLI or "tower dumps" (a download of information on all the devices that connected to a particular cell site during a particular interval). * * *

Having found that the acquisition of Carpenter's CSLI was a search, we also conclude that the Government must generally obtain a warrant supported by probable cause before acquiring such records. * * *

Further, even though the Government will generally need a warrant to access CSLI, case-specific exceptions may support a warrantless search of an individual's cellsite records under certain circumstances. "One well recognized exception applies when ' "the exigencies of the situation" make the needs of law enforcement so compelling that [a] warrantless search is objectively reasonable under the Fourth Amendment.' " Such exigencies include the need to pursue a fleeing suspect, protect individuals who are threatened with imminent harm, or prevent the imminent destruction of evidence.

As a result, if law enforcement is confronted with an urgent situation, such fact-specific threats will likely justify the warrantless collection of CSLI. Lower courts, for instance, have approved warrantless searches related to bomb threats, active shootings, and child abductions. Our decision today does not call into doubt warrantless access to CSLI in such circumstances. While police must get a warrant when collecting CSLI to assist in the minerun criminal investigation, the rule we set forth does not limit their ability to respond to an ongoing emergency.

As Justice Brandeis explained in his famous dissent, the Court is obligated— as "[s]ubtler and more far-reaching means of invading privacy have become available to the Government"—to ensure that the "progress of science" does not erode Fourth Amendment protections. *Olmstead v. United States,* 277 U.S. 438,

473–74 (1928). Here the progress of science has afforded law enforcement a powerful new tool to carry out its important responsibilities. At the same time, this tool risks Government encroachment of the sort the Framers, "after consulting the lessons of history," drafted the Fourth Amendment to prevent.

We decline to grant the state unrestricted access to a wireless carrier's database of physical location information. In light of the deeply revealing nature of CSLI, its depth, breadth, and comprehensive reach, and the inescapable and automatic nature of its collection, the fact that such information is gathered by a third party does not make it any less deserving of Fourth Amendment protection. The Government's acquisition of the cell-site records here was a search under that Amendment.

JUSTICE KENNEDY, with whom JUSTICE THOMAS and JUSTICE ALITO join, dissenting. * * *

The location information revealed by cell-site records is imprecise, because an individual cell-site sector usually covers a large geographic area. The FBI agent who offered expert testimony about the cell-site records at issue here testified that a cell site in a city reaches between a half mile and two miles in all directions. That means a 60-degree sector covers between approximately one-eighth and two square miles (and a 120-degree sector twice that area). To put that in perspective, in urban areas cell-site records often would reveal the location of a cell phone user within an area covering between around a dozen and several hundred city blocks. In rural areas cell-site records can be up to 40 times more imprecise. By contrast, a Global Positioning System (GPS) can reveal an individual's location within around 15 feet. * * *

Here the only question necessary to decide is whether the Government searched anything of Carpenter's when it used compulsory process to obtain cell-site records from Carpenter's cell phone service providers. This Court's decisions in *Miller* and *Smith* dictate that the answer is no, as every Court of Appeals to have considered the question has recognized.

Miller and *Smith* hold that individuals lack any protected Fourth Amendment interests in records that are possessed, owned, and controlled only by a third party. In *Miller* federal law enforcement officers obtained four months of the defendant's banking records. And in *Smith* state police obtained records of the phone numbers dialed from the defendant's home phone. The Court held in both cases that the officers did not search anything belonging to the defendants within the meaning of the Fourth Amendment. The defendants could "assert neither ownership nor possession" of the records because the records were created, owned, and controlled by the companies. And the defendants had no reasonable expectation of privacy in information they "voluntarily conveyed to the [companies] and exposed to their employees in the ordinary course of business." Rather, the defendants "assumed the risk that the information would be divulged to police." * * *

The second principle supporting *Miller* and *Smith* is the longstanding rule that the Government may use compulsory process to compel persons to disclose documents and other evidence within their possession and control. A subpoena is different from a warrant in its force and intrusive power. While a warrant allows the Government to enter and seize and make the examination itself, a subpoena simply requires the person to whom it is directed to make the disclosure. A subpoena, moreover, provides the recipient the "opportunity to present objections" before complying, which further mitigates the intrusion. *Oklahoma Press Publishing Co. v. Walling,* 327 U.S. 186 (1946). * * *

Carpenter argues that he has Fourth Amendment interests in the cell-site records because they are in essence his personal papers by operation of 47 U.S.C. § 222. * * *

Carpenter's argument is unpersuasive, however, for § 222 does not grant cell phone customers any meaningful interest in cell-site records. The statute's confidentiality protections may be overridden by the interests of the providers or the Government. The providers may disclose the records "to protect the[ir] rights or property" or to "initiate, render, bill, and collect for telecommunications services." They also may disclose the records "as required by law"—which, of course, is how they were disclosed in this case.

In fact, Carpenter's Fourth Amendment objection is even weaker than those of the defendants in *Miller* and *Smith.* Here the Government did not use a mere subpoena to obtain the cell-site records. It acquired the records only after it proved to a Magistrate Judge reasonable grounds to believe that the records were relevant and material to an ongoing criminal investigation. So even if § 222 gave Carpenter some attenuated interest in the records, the Government's conduct here would be reasonable under the standards governing subpoenas.

The Court's reliance on *Jones* fares no better. In *Jones* the Government installed a GPS tracking device on the defendant's automobile. The Court held the Government searched the automobile because it "physically occupied private property [of the defendant] for the purpose of obtaining information." So in *Jones* it was "not necessary to inquire about the target's expectation of privacy in his vehicle's movements."

Despite that clear delineation of the Court's holding in *Jones,* the Court today declares that *Jones* applied the " 'different constitutional principles' " alluded to in *Knotts* to establish that an individual has an expectation of privacy in the sum of his whereabouts. For that proposition the majority relies on the two concurring opinions in *Jones,* one of which stated that "longer term GPS monitoring in investigations of most offenses impinges on expectations of privacy." But *Jones* involved direct governmental surveillance of a defendant's automobile without judicial authorization—specifically, GPS surveillance accurate within 50 to 100 feet. Even assuming that the different constitutional principles mentioned in *Knotts* would apply in a case like *Jones*—a proposition the Court was careful not to announce in *Jones*—those principles are inapplicable here[,] where the Government uses court-approved compulsory process to obtain records owned and controlled by a third party * * *.

* * * Still the Court errs, in my submission, when it concludes that cellsite records implicate greater privacy interests—and thus deserve greater Fourth Amendment protection—than financial records and telephone records.

Indeed, the opposite is true. A person's movements are not particularly private. As the Court recognized in *Knotts*, when the defendant there "traveled over the public streets he voluntarily conveyed to anyone who wanted to look the fact that he was traveling over particular roads in a particular direction, the fact of whatever stops he made, and the fact of his final destination." Today expectations of privacy in one's location are, if anything, even less reasonable than when the Court decided *Knotts* over 30 years ago. Millions of Americans choose to share their location on a daily basis, whether by using a variety of location-based services on their phones, or by sharing their location with friends and the public at large via social media.

And cell-site records, as already discussed, disclose a person's location only in a general area. The records at issue here, for example, revealed Carpenter's location within an area covering between around a dozen and several hundred city blocks. * * *

JUSTICE THOMAS, dissenting. * * *

The more fundamental problem with the Court's opinion, however, is its use of the "reasonable expectation of privacy" test * * *. The *Katz* test has no basis in the text or history of the Fourth Amendment. And, it invites courts to make judgments about policy, not law. * * *

JUSTICE ALITO, with whom JUSTICE THOMAS joins, dissenting. [This dissent and the majority's response appear in Ch. 8, section 2.]

JUSTICE GORSUCH, dissenting.

* * * Instead, I would look to a more traditional Fourth Amendment approach. Even if *Katz* may still supply one way to prove a Fourth Amendment interest, it has never been the only way. Neglecting more traditional approaches may mean failing to vindicate the full protections of the Fourth Amendment.

Our case offers a cautionary example. It seems to me entirely possible a person's cell-site data could qualify as his papers or effects under existing law. Yes, the telephone carrier holds the information. But 47 U.S.C. § 222 designates a customer's cell-site location information as "customer proprietary network information" (CPNI), § 222(h)(1)(A), and gives customers certain rights to control use of and access to CPNI about themselves. The statute generally forbids a carrier to "use, disclose, or permit access to individually identifiable" CPNI without the customer's consent, except as needed to provide the customer's telecommunications services. § 222(c)(1). It also requires the carrier to disclose CPNI "upon affirmative written request by the customer, to any person designated by the customer." § 222(c)(2). Congress even afforded customers a private cause of action for damages against carriers who violate the Act's terms. § 207. Plainly, customers have substantial legal interests in this information, including at least some right to include, exclude, and control its use. Those interests might even rise to the level of a property right.

The problem is that we do not know anything more. Before the district court and court of appeals, Mr. Carpenter pursued only a *Katz* "reasonable expectations" argument. He did not invoke the law of property or any analogies to the common law, either there or in his petition for certiorari. * * * In these circumstances, I cannot help but conclude—reluctantly—that Mr. Carpenter forfeited perhaps his most promising line of argument. * * *

FLORIDA V. JARDINES
569 U.S. 1, 133 S.Ct. 1409, 185 L.Ed.2d 495 (2013).

JUSTICE SCALIA delivered the opinion of the Court. * * *

[After police received an unverified tip that Jardines was growing marijuana in his home, they took a drug-detection dog onto Jardine's front porch, where the dog "alerted" at the front door. On this basis, police obtained and executed a search warrant at Jardines' residence and seized marijuana plants, but the evidence was excluded below as the fruit of an unreasonable search.]

* * * By reason of our decision in *Katz v. United States*, [p. 95], property rights "are not the sole measure of Fourth Amendment violations," but though *Katz* may add to the baseline, it does not subtract anything from the Amendment's protections "when the Government does engage in [a] physical intrusion of a constitutionally protected area."

That principle renders this case a straightforward one. The officers were gathering information in an area belonging to Jardines and immediately surrounding his house—in the curtilage of the house, which we have held enjoys protection as part of the home itself. And they gathered that information by physically entering and occupying the area to engage in conduct not explicitly or implicitly permitted by the homeowner.

The Fourth Amendment "indicates with some precision the places and things encompassed by its protections": persons, houses, papers, and effects. The Fourth Amendment does not, therefore, prevent all investigations conducted on private property; for example, an officer may (subject to *Katz*) gather information in what we have called "open fields"—even if those fields are privately owned—because such fields are not enumerated in the Amendment's text.

But when it comes to the Fourth Amendment, the home is first among equals. At the Amendment's "very core" stands "the right of a man to retreat into his own home and there be free from unreasonable governmental intrusion." *Silverman v. United States*, 365 U.S. 505, 511 (1961). This right would be of little practical value if the State's agents could stand in a home's porch or side garden and trawl for evidence with impunity; the right to retreat would be significantly diminished if the police could enter a man's property to observe his repose from just outside the front window.

We therefore regard the area "immediately surrounding and associated with the home"—what our cases call the curtilage—as "part of the home itself for Fourth Amendment purposes." That principle has ancient and durable roots. Just as the distinction between the home and the open fields is "as old as the common law," so too is the identity of home and what Blackstone called the "curtilage or homestall," for the "house protects and privileges all its branches and appurtenants." This area around the home is "intimately linked to the home, both physically and psychologically," and is where "privacy expectations are most heightened."

While the boundaries of the curtilage are generally "clearly marked," the "conception defining the curtilage" is at any rate familiar enough that it is "easily understood from our daily experience." Here there is no doubt that the officers entered it: The front porch is the classic exemplar of an area adjacent to the home and "to which the activity of home life extends."

Since the officers' investigation took place in a constitutionally protected area, we turn to the question of whether it was accomplished through an unlicensed physical intrusion. While law enforcement officers need not "shield their eyes" when passing by the home "on public thoroughfares," an officer's leave to gather information is sharply circumscribed when he steps off those thoroughfares and enters the Fourth Amendment's protected areas. * * * As it is undisputed that the detectives had all four of their feet and all four of their companion's firmly planted on the constitutionally protected extension of Jardines' home, the only question is whether he had given his leave (even implicitly) for them to do so. He had not.

"A license may be implied from the habits of the country," notwithstanding the "strict rule of the English common law as to entry upon a close." * * * This implicit license typically permits the visitor to approach the home by the front path, knock promptly, wait briefly to be received, and then (absent invitation to linger longer) leave. Complying with the terms of that traditional invitation does not require fine-grained legal knowledge; it is generally managed without incident by the Nation's Girl Scouts and trick-or-treaters. Thus, a police officer not armed with a warrant may approach a home and knock, precisely because that is "no more than any private citizen might do."

But introducing a trained police dog to explore the area around the home in hopes of discovering incriminating evidence is something else. There is no customary invitation to do that. An invitation to engage in canine forensic investigation assuredly does not inhere in the very act of hanging a knocker.[3] To find a visitor knocking on the door is routine (even if sometimes unwelcome); to spot that same visitor exploring the front path with a metal detector, or marching his bloodhound into the garden before saying hello and asking permission, would inspire most of us to—well, call the police. The scope of a license—express or implied—is limited not only to a particular area but also to a specific purpose. * * *

---

[3] The dissent insists that our argument must rest upon "the particular instrument that Detective Bartelt used to detect the odor of marijuana"—the dog. It is not the dog that is the problem, but the behavior that here involved use of the dog. We think a typical person would find it " 'a cause for great alarm' " * * * to find a stranger snooping about his front porch with or without a dog. The dissent would let the police do whatever they want by way of gathering evidence so long as they stay on the base-path, to use a baseball analogy—so long as they "stick to the path that is typically used to approach a front door, such as a paved walkway." From that vantage point they can presumably peer into the house through binoculars with impunity. That is not the law, as even the State concedes.

Here, the background social norms that invite a visitor to the front door do not invite him there to conduct a search.

The State points to our decisions holding that the subjective intent of the officer is irrelevant. But those cases merely hold that a stop or search that is objectively reasonable is not vitiated by the fact that the officer's real reason for making the stop or search has nothing to do with the validating reason. * * * Here, however, the question before the court is precisely whether the officer's conduct was an objectively reasonable search. As we have described, that depends upon whether the officers had an implied license to enter the porch, which in turn depends upon the purpose for which they entered. Here, their behavior objectively reveals a purpose to conduct a search, which is not what anyone would think he had license to do.

The State argues that investigation by a forensic narcotics dog by definition cannot implicate any legitimate privacy interest. The State cites for authority our decisions in *United States v. Place*, [fn. a, p. 288], *United States v. Jacobsen*, 466 U.S. 109 (1984), and *Illinois v. Caballes*, [fn. c, p. 306] * * *.

[But], we need not decide whether the officers' investigation of Jardines' home violated his expectation of privacy under *Katz*. One virtue of the Fourth Amendment's property-rights baseline is that it keeps easy cases easy. That the officers learned what they learned only by physically intruding on Jardines' property to gather evidence is enough to establish that a search occurred. * * *[a]

JUSTICE KAGAN, with whom JUSTICE GINSBURG and JUSTICE SOTOMAYOR join, concurring. * * *

The Court today treats this case under a property rubric; I write separately to note that I could just as happily have decided it by looking to Jardines' privacy interests. A decision along those lines would have looked . . . well, much like this one. * * *

It is not surprising that in a case involving a search of a home, property concepts and privacy concepts should so align. The law of property "naturally enough influence[s]" our "shared social expectations" of what places should be free from governmental incursions. And so the sentiment "my home is my own," while originating in property law, now also denotes a common understanding—extending even beyond that law's formal protections—about an especially private sphere. Jardines' home was his property; it was also his most intimate and familiar space.

---

[a] In *Collins v. Virginia*, 138 S.Ct. 1663 (2018), involving a warrantless search of a vehicle parked within a dwelling's adjacent curtilage, the Court emphasized that the automobile exception recognized in *California v. Carney*, p. 240 infra, extends no further than the vehicle itself, and thus did not justify physical entry of the curtilage in order to conduct a search under a tarp covering a motorcycle, in light of *Jardines*. Because both *Jardines* and *Collins* were search cases and not seizure cases, query what the result would be if the cycle had not been covered, so that the officer had probable cause to seize it before entering the curtilage for the sole purpose of making a seizure. Consider that the Court in *Collins* said that the reasoning underlying existing limits on "warrantless entry into the home," such as that "under the plain-view doctrine, 'any valid warrantless seizure of incriminating evidence' requires that the officer 'have a lawful right of access to the object itself,' applies equally well in this context."

The analysis proceeding from each of those facts, as today's decision reveals, runs mostly along the same path.

I can think of only one divergence: If we had decided this case on privacy grounds, we would have realized that *Kyllo v. United States*, 533 U.S. 27 (2001), already resolved it.[1] The *Kyllo* Court held that police officers conducted a search when they used a thermal-imaging device to detect heat emanating from a private home, even though they committed no trespass. Highlighting our intention to draw both a "firm" and a "bright" line at "the entrance to the house," we announced the following rule:

"Where, as here, the Government uses a device that is not in general public use, to explore details of the home that would previously have been unknowable without physical intrusion, the surveillance is a 'search' and is presumptively unreasonable without a warrant."

That "firm" and "bright" rule governs this case: The police officers here conducted a search because they used a "device . . . not in general public use" (a trained drug-detection dog) to "explore details of the home" (the presence of certain substances) that they would not otherwise have discovered without entering the premises.

And again, the dissent's argument that the device is just a dog cannot change the equation. As *Kyllo* made clear, the "sense-enhancing" tool at issue may be "crude" or "sophisticated," may be old or new (drug-detection dogs actually go back not "12,000 years" or "centuries," but only a few decades), may be either smaller or bigger than a breadbox; still, "at least where (as here)" the device is not "in general public use," training it on a home violates our "minimal expectation of privacy"—an expectation "that exists, and that is acknowledged to be *reasonable*." * * *

With these further thoughts, suggesting that a focus on Jardines' privacy interests would make an "easy cas[e] easy" twice over, I join the Court's opinion in full.

JUSTICE ALITO, with whom THE CHIEF JUSTICE, JUSTICE KENNEDY, and JUSTICE BREYER join, dissenting. * * *

The Court concludes that the conduct in this case was a search because Detective Bartelt exceeded the boundaries of the license to approach the house that is recognized by the law of trespass, but the Court's interpretation of the scope of that license is unfounded.

It is said that members of the public may lawfully proceed along a walkway leading to the front door of a house because custom grants them a license to do so. This rule encompasses categories of visitors whom most homeowners almost certainly wish to allow to approach their front doors—friends, relatives, mail

---

[1] The dissent claims, alternatively, that *Illinois v. Caballes*, [fn. c, p. 306], controls this case (or nearly does). But *Caballes* concerned a drug-detection dog's sniff of an automobile during a traffic stop. And we have held, over and over again, that people's expectations of privacy are much lower in their cars than in their homes.

carriers, persons making deliveries. But it also reaches categories of visitors who are less universally welcome—"solicitors," "hawkers," "peddlers," and the like. * * *

Of course, this license has certain spatial and temporal limits. A visitor must stick to the path that is typically used to approach a front door, such as a paved walkway. * * *

Nor, as a general matter, may a visitor come to the front door in the middle of the night without an express invitation. * * *

Similarly, a visitor may not linger at the front door for an extended period. * * * The license is limited to the amount of time it would customarily take to approach the door, pause long enough to see if someone is home, and (if not expressly invited to stay longer), leave.

As I understand the law of trespass and the scope of the implied license, a visitor who adheres to these limitations is not necessarily required to ring the doorbell, knock on the door, or attempt to speak with an occupant. For example, mail carriers, persons making deliveries, and individuals distributing flyers may leave the items they are carrying and depart without making any attempt to converse. * * *

As the majority acknowledges, this implied license to approach the front door extends to the police. * * * Even when the objective of a "knock and talk" is to obtain evidence that will lead to the homeowner's arrest and prosecution, the license to approach still applies. In other words, gathering evidence—even damning evidence—is a lawful activity that falls within the scope of the license to approach. * * *

Detective Bartelt did not exceed the scope of the license to approach respondent's front door. He adhered to the customary path; he did not approach in the middle of the night; and he remained at the front door for only a very short period (less than a minute or two). * * *

What the Court must fall back on, then, is the particular instrument that Detective Bartelt used to detect the odor of marijuana, namely, his dog. But in the entire body of common-law decisions, the Court has not found a single case holding that a visitor to the front door of a home commits a trespass if the visitor is accompanied by a dog on a leash. On the contrary, the common law allowed even unleashed dogs to wander on private property without committing a trespass. * * *

The concurring opinion attempts to provide an alternative ground for today's decision, namely, that Detective Bartelt's conduct violated respondent's reasonable expectations of privacy. But we have already rejected a very similar, if not identical argument, see *Illinois v. Caballes*, and in any event I see no basis for concluding that the occupants of a dwelling have a reasonable expectation of privacy in odors that emanate from the dwelling and reach spots where members of the public may lawfully stand. * * *

In an attempt to show that respondent had a reasonable expectation of privacy in the odor of marijuana wafting from his house, the concurrence argues that this case is just like *Kyllo v. United States*, which held that police officers conducted a search when they used a thermal imaging device to detect heat emanating from a house. This Court, however, has already rejected the argument that the use of a drug-sniffing dog is the same as the use of a thermal imaging device. See *Caballes*. * * *

Contrary to the interpretation propounded by the concurrence, *Kyllo* is best understood as a decision about the use of new technology. * * * A dog, however, is not a new form of "technology" or a "device." And, as noted, the use of dogs' acute sense of smell in law enforcement dates back many centuries.

The concurrence suggests that a *Kyllo*-based decision would be "much like" the actual decision of the Court, but that is simply not so. * * *

The concurrence's *Kyllo*-based approach would have a much wider reach. When the police used the thermal imaging device in *Kyllo*, they were on a public street, and "committed no trespass." Therefore, if a dog's nose is just like a thermal imaging device for Fourth Amendment purposes, a search would occur if a dog alerted while on a public sidewalk or in the corridor of an apartment building. * * *

UNITED STATES v. WHITE
401 U.S. 745, 91 S.Ct. 1122, 28 L.Ed.2d 453 (1971).

[On numerous occasions a government informer, carrying a concealed radio transmitter, engaged defendant in conversations which were electronically overheard by federal narcotics agents. The conversations in a restaurant, defendant's home and in the informer's car were overheard by the use of radio equipment. A number of conversations in the informer's home were not only electronically overheard by an agent stationed outside the house but by another agent who, with the informer's consent, concealed himself in the latter's kitchen closet. At no time did the agents obtain a warrant or court order. The informer was not produced at the trial, but the testimony of the "eavesdropping" agents was admitted and led to defendant's conviction of narcotics violations. The Court of Appeals Circuit read *Katz* as prohibiting testimony about the electronically overheard statements.]

JUSTICE WHITE announced the judgment of the Court and an opinion in which THE CHIEF JUSTICE, JUSTICE STEWART, and JUSTICE BLACKMUN join. * * *

Hoffa v. United States, 385 U.S. 293 (1966), which was left undisturbed by *Katz,* held that however strongly a defendant may trust an apparent colleague, his expectations in this respect are not protected by the Fourth Amendment when it turns out that the colleague is a government agent regularly communicating with the authorities. In these circumstances, "no interest legitimately protected by the Fourth Amendment is involved," for that amendment affords no protection to "a wrongdoer's misplaced belief that a person to whom he voluntarily confides his wrongdoing will not reveal it." * * *

Concededly a police agent who conceals his police connections may write down for official use his conversations with a defendant and testify concerning them, without a warrant authorizing his encounters with the defendant and without otherwise violating the latter's Fourth Amendment rights. For constitutional purposes, no different result is required if the agent instead of immediately reporting and transcribing his conversations with defendant, either (1) simultaneously records them with electronic equipment which he is carrying on his person, (2) or carries radio equipment which simultaneously transmits the conversations either to recording equipment located elsewhere or to other agents monitoring the transmitting frequency. If the conduct and revelations of an agent operating without electronic equipment do not invade the defendant's constitutionally justifiable expectations of privacy, neither does a simultaneous recording of the same conversations made by the agent or by others from transmissions received from the agent to whom the defendant is talking and whose trustworthiness the defendant necessarily risks.

Our problem is not what the privacy expectations of particular defendants in particular situations may be or the extent to which they may in fact have relied on the discretion of their companions. Very probably, individual defendants neither know nor suspect that their colleagues have gone or will go to the police or are carrying recorders or transmitters. Otherwise, conversation would cease and our problem with these encounters would be nonexistent or far different from those now before us. Our problem, in terms of the principles announced in *Katz*, is what expectations of privacy are constitutionally "justifiable"—what expectations the Fourth Amendment will protect in the absence of a warrant. * * * If the law gives no protection to the wrongdoer whose trusted accomplice is or becomes a police agent, neither should it protect him when that same agent has recorded or transmitted the conversations which are later offered in evidence to prove the State's case.

Inescapably, one contemplating illegal activities must realize and risk that his companions may be reporting to the police. If he sufficiently doubts their trustworthiness, the association will very probably end or never materialize. But if he has no doubts, or allays them, or risks what doubt he has, the risk is his. In terms of what his course will be, what he will or will not do or say, we are unpersuaded that he would distinguish between probable informers on the one hand and probable informers with transmitters on the other. Given the possibility or probability that one of his colleagues is cooperating with the police, it is only speculation to assert that the defendant's utterances would be substantially different or his sense of security any less if he also thought it possible that the suspected colleague is wired for sound. At least there is no persuasive evidence that the difference in this respect between the electronically equipped and the unequipped agent is substantial enough to require discrete constitutional recognition, particularly under the Fourth Amendment which is ruled by fluid concepts of "reasonableness."

Nor should we be too ready to erect constitutional barriers to relevant and probative evidence which is also accurate and reliable. An electronic recording will many times produce a more reliable rendition of what a defendant has said than will the unaided memory of a police agent. It may also be that with the recording in existence it is less likely that the informant will change his mind, less chance that threat or injury will suppress unfavorable evidence and less chance that cross-examination will confound the testimony. Considerations like these obviously do not favor the defendant, but we are not prepared to hold that a defendant who has no constitutional right to exclude the informer's unaided testimony nevertheless has a Fourth Amendment privilege against a more accurate version of the events in question.

It is thus untenable to consider the activities and reports of the police agent himself, though acting without a warrant, to be a "reasonable" investigative effort and lawful under the Fourth Amendment but to view the same agent with a recorder or transmitter as conducting an "unreasonable" and unconstitutional search and seizure. * * *

No different result should obtain where, as in the instant case, the informer disappears and is unavailable at trial; for the issue of whether specified events on a certain day violate the Fourth Amendment should not be determined by what later happens to the informer. His unavailability at trial and proffering the testimony of other agents may raise evidentiary problems or pose issues of prosecutorial misconduct with respect to the informer's disappearance, but they do not appear critical to deciding whether prior events invaded the defendant's Fourth Amendment rights.

The Court of Appeals was in error for another reason. In *Desist v. United States,* 394 U.S. 244 (1969), we held that our decision in *Katz v. United States* applied only to those electronic surveillances that occurred subsequent to the date of that decision. Here the events in question took place in late 1965 and early 1966, long prior to *Katz.* * * *

The judgment of the Court of Appeals is reversed.

JUSTICE BLACK * * * concurs in the judgment of the Court for the reasons set forth in his dissent in Katz v. United States.

JUSTICE BRENNAN, concurring in the result.

I agree that Desist requires reversal of the judgment of the Court of Appeals. * * * [I]t is my view that current Fourth Amendment jurisprudence interposes a warrant requirement not only in cases of third-party electronic monitoring (the situation in this case) but also in cases of electronic recording by a government agent of a face-to-face conversation with a criminal suspect. * * *

JUSTICE DOUGLAS, dissenting.

* * * Monitoring, if prevalent, certainly kills free discourse and spontaneous utterances. Free discourse—a First Amendment value—may be frivolous or serious, humble or defiant, reactionary or revolutionary, profane or in good taste; but it is not free if there is surveillance. Free discourse liberates the spirit, though it may produce only froth. The individual must keep some facts concerning his thoughts within a small zone of people. At the same time he must be free to pour out his woes or inspirations or dreams to others. He remains the sole judge as to what must be said and what must remain unspoken. This is the essence of the idea of privacy implicit in the First and Fifth Amendments as well as in the Fourth. * * *

JUSTICE HARLAN, dissenting.

* * * Since it is the task of the law to form and project, as well as mirror and reflect, we should not, as judges, merely recite the expectations and risks without examining the desirability of saddling them upon society. The critical question, therefore, is whether under our system of government, as reflected in the Constitution, we should impose on our citizens the risks of the electronic listener or observer without at least the protection of a warrant requirement.

This question must, in my view, be answered by assessing the nature of a particular practice and the likely extent of its impact on the individual's sense of security balanced against the utility of the conduct as a technique of law enforcement. For those more extensive intrusions that significantly jeopardize the sense of security which is the paramount concern of Fourth Amendment liberties, I am of the view that more than self-restraint by law enforcement officials is required and at the least warrants should be necessary.

The impact of the practice of third-party bugging, must, I think, be considered such as to undermine that confidence and sense of security in dealing with one another that is characteristic of individual relationships between citizens in a free society. * * * The argument of the plurality opinion, to the effect that it is irrelevant whether secrets are revealed by the mere tattletale or the transistor, ignores the differences occasioned by third-party monitoring and recording which insures full and accurate disclosure of all that is said, free of the possibility of error and oversight that inheres in human reporting.

Authority is hardly required to support the proposition that words would be measured a good deal more carefully and communication inhibited if one suspected his conversations were being transmitted and transcribed. Were third-party bugging a prevalent practice, it might well smother that spontaneity—reflected in frivolous, impetuous, sacrilegious, and defiant discourse—that liberates daily life. Much offhand exchange is easily forgotten and one may count on the obscurity of his remarks, protected by the very fact of a limited audience, and the likelihood that the listener will either overlook or forget what is said, as well as the listener's inability to reformulate a conversation without having to contend with a documented record. All these values are sacrificed by a rule of law that permits official monitoring of private discourse limited only by the need to locate a willing assistant.

* * * The interest [the plurality] fails to protect is the expectation of the ordinary citizen, who has never engaged in illegal conduct in his life, that he may carry on his private discourse freely, openly, and spontaneously without measuring his every word against the connotations it might carry when instantaneously heard by others unknown to him and unfamiliar with his situation or analyzed in a cold, formal record played days, months, or years after the conversation. Interposition of a warrant requirement is designed not to shield "wrongdoers," but to secure a measure of privacy and a sense of personal security throughout our society. * * *

JUSTICE MARSHALL, dissenting.

I am convinced that the correct view of the Fourth Amendment in the area of electronic surveillance is one that brings the safeguards of the warrant requirement to bear on the investigatory activity involved in this case. In this regard I agree with the dissents of Justice Douglas and Justice Harlan.

* * *

In addition to limiting "searches," the Fourth Amendment also limits "seizures." As explained in *Soldal v. Cook County*, 506 U.S. 56 (1992), the two concepts are distinct: "seizures of property are subject to Fourth Amendment scrutiny even though no search within the meaning of the Amendment has taken place." Seizures can be broken down into two basic types: (1) seizures of persons, such as arrests or temporary detentions, and (2) seizures of inanimate objects, such as when the government takes property into police custody. The following case considers the Fourth Amendment standards for seizures of a person.

TORRES V. MADRID

141 S.Ct. 989, 209 L.Ed.2d 190 (2021).

CHIEF JUSTICE ROBERTS delivered the opinion of the Court.

The Fourth Amendment prohibits unreasonable "seizures" to safeguard "the right of the people to be secure in their persons." Under our cases, an officer seizes a person when he uses force to apprehend her. The question in this case is whether a seizure occurs when an officer shoots someone who temporarily eludes capture after the shooting. The answer is yes: The application of physical force to the body of a person with intent to restrain is a seizure, even if the force does not succeed in subduing the person.

I

At dawn on July 15, 2014, four New Mexico State Police officers arrived at an apartment complex in Albuquerque to execute an arrest warrant for a woman accused of white collar crimes, but also suspected of having been involved in drug trafficking, murder, and other violent crimes. What happened next is hotly contested. We recount the facts in the light most favorable to petitioner Roxanne Torres because the court below granted summary judgment to Officers Janice Madrid and Richard Williamson, the two respondents here.

The officers observed Torres standing with another person near a Toyota FJ Cruiser in the parking lot of the complex. Officer Williamson concluded that neither Torres nor her companion was the target of the warrant. As the officers approached the vehicle, the companion departed, and Torres—at the time experiencing methamphetamine withdrawal—got into the driver's seat. The officers attempted to speak with her, but she did not notice their presence until one of them tried to open the door of her car.

Although the officers wore tactical vests marked with police identification, Torres saw only that they had guns. She thought the officers were carjackers trying to steal her car, and she hit the gas to escape them. Neither Officer Madrid nor Officer Williamson, according to Torres, stood in the path of the vehicle, but both fired their service pistols to stop her. All told, the two officers fired 13 shots at Torres, striking her twice in the back and temporarily paralyzing her left arm.

Steering with her right arm, Torres accelerated through the fusillade of bullets, exited the apartment complex, drove a short distance, and stopped in a parking lot. After asking a bystander to report an attempted carjacking, Torres stole a Kia Soul that happened to be idling nearby and drove 75 miles to Grants, New Mexico. The good news for Torres was that the hospital in Grants was able to airlift her to another hospital where she could receive appropriate care. The bad news was that the hospital was back in Albuquerque, where the police arrested her the next day. She pleaded no contest to aggravated fleeing from a law enforcement officer, assault on a peace officer, and unlawfully taking a motor vehicle.

Torres later sought damages from Officers Madrid and Williamson under 42 U.S.C. § 1983, which provides a cause of action for the deprivation of constitutional rights by persons acting under color of state law. She claimed that the officers applied excessive force, making the shooting an unreasonable seizure under the Fourth Amendment. The District Court granted summary judgment to the officers, and the Court of Appeals for the Tenth Circuit affirmed on the ground that a suspect's continued flight after being shot by police negates a Fourth Amendment excessive-force claim. The court relied on Circuit precedent providing that no seizure can occur unless there is physical touch or a show of authority, and that such physical touch (or force) must terminate the suspect's movement or otherwise give rise to physical control over the suspect.

II

This case concerns the "seizure" of a "person," which can take the form of physical force or a show of authority that in some way restrains the liberty of the person. The question before us is whether the application of physical force is a seizure if the force, despite hitting its target, fails to stop the person.

We largely covered this ground in *California v. Hodari D.*, 499 U.S. 621 (1991). There we interpreted the term "seizure" by consulting the common law of arrest, the quintessential seizure of the person under our Fourth Amendment jurisprudence. As Justice Scalia explained for himself and six other Members of the Court, the common law treated "the mere grasping or application of physical force with lawful authority" as an arrest, "whether or not it succeeded in subduing the arrestee." Put another way, an officer's application of physical force to the body of a person "for the purpose of arresting him" was itself an arrest—not an *attempted* arrest—even if the person did not yield.

The common law distinguished the application of force from a show of authority, such as an order for a suspect to halt. The latter does not become an arrest unless and until the arrestee complies with the demand. As the Court explained in *Hodari D.*, an arrest requires *either* physical force *or*, where that is absent, *submission* to the assertion of authority.

Hodari D. articulates two pertinent principles. First, common law arrests are Fourth Amendment seizures. And second, the common law considered the application of force to the body of a person with intent to restrain to be an arrest, no matter whether the arrestee escaped. We need not decide whether *Hodari D.*, which principally concerned a show of authority, controls the outcome of this case as a matter of *stare decisis*, because we independently reach the same conclusions.

At the adoption of the Fourth Amendment, a "seizure" was the act of taking by warrant. A seizure did not necessarily result in actual control or detention. It is true that, when speaking of property, from the time of the founding to the present, the word 'seizure' has meant a 'taking possession. But the Framers selected a term—seizure—broad enough to apply to all the concerns of the Fourth Amendment: "persons," as well as "houses, papers, and effects." As applied to a person, the word 'seizure' readily bears the meaning of a laying on of hands or application of physical force to restrain movement, even when it is ultimately unsuccessful. Then, as now, an ordinary user of the English language could remark: "She seized the purse-snatcher, but he broke out of her grasp."

The "seizure" of a "person" plainly refers to an arrest. That linkage existed at the founding. Samuel Johnson, for example, defined an "arrest" as "any seizure of the person." 1 A Dictionary of the English Language 108 (1773).

The common law rule identified in *Hodari D.*—that the application of force gives rise to an arrest, even if the officer does not secure control over the arrestee— achieved recognition to such an extent that English lawyers could confidently (and accurately) proclaim that "all the authorities, from the earliest time to the present, establish that a corporal touch is sufficient to constitute an arrest, even though the defendant do not submit." *Nicholl* v. *Darley*, 148 Eng. Rep. 974 (Exch. 1828).

The slightest application of force could satisfy this rule. In *Genner* v. *Sparks*, 87 Eng. Rep. 928 (Q. B. 1704), the defendant did not submit to the authority of an arrest warrant, but the court explained that the bailiff would have made an arrest if he "had but touched the defendant even with the end of his finger." The touching of the person—frequently called a laying of hands—was enough. Only later did English law grow to recognize arrest without touching through a submission to a show of authority. Even so, the traditional rule persisted that all an arrest required was "corporal seising or touching the defendant's body." 3 W. Blackstone, Commentaries on the Laws of England 288 (1768).

Early American courts adopted this mere-touch rule from England, just as they embraced other common law principles of search and seizure. Justice Baldwin, instructing a jury in his capacity as Circuit Justice, defined an arrest to include touching or putting hands upon the arrestee in the execution of process. State courts agreed that any touching, however slight, is enough, provided the officer made his intent to arrest clear. Courts continued to hold that an arrest required only the application of force—not control or custody—through the framing of the Fourteenth Amendment, which incorporated the protections of the Fourth Amendment against the States.

This case, of course, does not involve laying hands, but instead a shooting. Neither the parties nor the United States as *amicus curiae* suggests that the officers' use of bullets to restrain Torres alters the analysis in any way. And we are aware of no common law authority addressing an arrest under such circumstances, or indeed any case involving an application of force from a distance.

The closest decision seems to be *Countess of Rutland's Case*, 77 Eng. Rep. 332 (Star Chamber 1605). In that case, serjeants-at-mace tracked down Isabel Holcroft, Countess of Rutland, to execute a writ for a judgment of debt. They "shewed her their mace, and touching her body with it, said to her, we arrest you, madam." We think the case is best understood as an example of an arrest made by touching with an object, for the serjeants-at-mace announced the arrest at the time they touched the countess with the mace. However one reads *Countess of Rutland*, we see no basis for drawing an artificial line between grasping with a hand and other means of applying physical force to effect an arrest.

We will not carve out this greater intrusion on personal security from the mere-touch rule just because founding-era courts did not confront apprehension by firearm. While firearms have existed for a millennium and were certainly familiar at the founding, we have observed that law enforcement did not carry handguns until the latter half of the 19th century, at which point it became possible to use deadly force from a distance as a means of apprehension. So it should come as no surprise that neither we nor the dissent has located a common law case in which an officer used a gun to apprehend a suspect. But the focus of the Fourth Amendment is the privacy and security of individuals, not the particular manner of arbitrary invasion by governmental officials. There is nothing subtle about a bullet, but the Fourth Amendment preserves personal security with respect to methods of apprehension old and new.

We stress, however, that the application of the common law rule does not transform every physical contact between a government employee and a member of the public into a Fourth Amendment seizure. A seizure requires the use of force *with intent to restrain*. Accidental force will not qualify. See *County of Sacramento v. Lewis*, 523 U.S. 833 (1998). Nor will force intentionally applied for some other purpose satisfy this rule. In this opinion, we consider only force used to apprehend. We do not accept the dissent's invitation to opine on matters not presented here— pepper spray, flash-bang grenades, lasers, and more.

Moreover, the appropriate inquiry is whether the challenged conduct *objectively* manifests an intent to restrain, for we rarely probe the subjective motivations of police officers in the Fourth Amendment context. Only an objective test allows the police to determine in advance whether the conduct contemplated will implicate the Fourth Amendment. While a mere touch can be enough for a seizure, the amount of force remains pertinent in assessing the objective intent to restrain. A tap on the shoulder to get one's attention will rarely exhibit such an intent.

Nor does the seizure depend on the subjective perceptions of the seized person. Here, for example, Torres claims to have perceived the officers' actions as an attempted carjacking. But the conduct of the officers—ordering Torres to stop and then shooting to restrain her movement—satisfies the objective test for a seizure, regardless whether Torres comprehended the governmental character of their actions.

The rule we announce today is narrow. In addition to the requirement of intent to restrain, a seizure by force—absent submission—lasts only as long as the application of force. That is to say that the Fourth Amendment does not recognize any *continuing* arrest during the period of fugitivity. The fleeting nature of some seizures by force undoubtedly may inform what damages a civil plaintiff may recover, and what evidence a criminal defendant may exclude from trial. But brief seizures are seizures all the same.

Applying these principles to the facts viewed in the light most favorable to Torres, the officers' shooting applied physical force to her body and objectively manifested an intent to restrain her from driving away. We therefore conclude that the officers seized Torres for the instant that the bullets struck her.

The officers and the dissent derive from our cases a different touchstone for the seizure of a person: "an intentional acquisition of physical control." *Brower v. County of Inyo*, 489 U.S. 593, 596 (1989). Under their alternative rule, the use of force becomes a seizure only when there is a governmental termination of freedom of movement through means intentionally applied. This approach improperly erases the distinction between seizures by *control* and seizures by *force*. In all fairness, we too have not always been attentive to this distinction when a case did not implicate the issue. But each type of seizure enjoys a separate common law pedigree that gives rise to a separate rule.

Unlike a seizure by force, a seizure by acquisition of control involves either voluntary submission to a show of authority or the termination of freedom of movement. A prime example of the latter comes from *Brower*, where the police seized a driver when he crashed into their roadblock. Under the common law rules of arrest, actual control is a necessary element for this type of seizure. Such a seizure requires that a person be stopped by the very instrumentality set in motion or put in place in order to achieve that result. But that requirement of control or submission never extended to seizures by force.

We hold that the application of physical force to the body of a person with intent to restrain is a seizure even if the person does not submit and is not subdued. Of course, a seizure is just the first step in the analysis. The Fourth Amendment does not forbid all or even most seizures—only unreasonable ones. All we decide today is that the officers seized Torres by shooting her with intent to restrain her movement.

JUSTICE GORSUCH, with whom JUSTICE THOMAS and JUSTICE ALITO join, dissenting.

The majority holds that a criminal suspect can be simultaneously seized and roaming at large. On the majority's account, a Fourth Amendment "seizure" takes place whenever an officer "merely touches" a suspect. It's a seizure even if the suspect refuses to stop, evades capture, and rides off into the sunset never to be seen again. That view is as mistaken as it is novel.

Today's majority . . . accepts that a seizure of the inanimate objects mentioned in the Fourth Amendment (houses, papers, and effects) requires possession. And when it comes to persons, the majority agrees (as *Hodari D.* held) that a seizure in response to a "show of authority" takes place if and when the suspect submits to an officer's possession. The majority insists that a different rule should apply *only* in cases where an officer "touches" the suspect. Here—and here alone—possession is not required. So, under the majority's logic, we are quite literally asked to believe the officers in this case "seized" Ms. Torres's person, but *not* her car, when they shot both and both continued speeding down the highway.

The majority's need to resort to such a schizophrenic reading of the word "seizure" should be a signal that something has gone seriously wrong.

[The majority] scrambles to locate a case—any case—suggesting that common law courts considered "touchings" by weapon enough to effect an arrest in the debt-collection context. Ultimately, the majority asks us to dwell at length on the Countess of Rutland's case. In at least that lone instance, the majority promises, we will find bailiffs who arrested a debtor by touching her with an object (a mace) rather than a laying on of hands. See *ante* (citing *Countess of Rutland's Case*, 77 Eng. Rep. 332 (Star Chamber 1605)). But it turns out the dispute concerned whether a countess could be civilly arrested *at all*, not when or how the arrest was completed. The court had no reason to (and did not) decide whether the bailiffs accomplished their arrest when they "shewed her their mace," "touched" her with the mace, or "compelled the coachman to carry" her to jail. And no one questions that these things together—a show of authority followed by compelled detention—have always been enough to complete an arrest.

The common law offers a vast legal library. Like any other, it must be used thoughtfully. We have no business wandering about and randomly grabbing volumes off the shelf, plucking out passages we like, scratching out bits we don't, all before pasting our own new pastiche into the U. S. Reports. That does not respect legal history; it rewrites it.

If text, history, and precedent cannot explain today's result, what can? The majority seems to offer a clue when it promises its new rule will help us avoid line-drawing problems. Any different standard, the majority worries, would be difficult to apply.

Even within its field of operation, the majority's rule seems destined to underdeliver on its predicted efficiencies. The majority tells us that its new test requires an "objective intent to restrain." But what qualifies is far from clear. The majority assures us that a "tap on the shoulder to get one's attention will rarely exhibit such an intent." Suppose, though, the circumstances "objectively" indicate that the tap was "intended" to secure a person's attention for a minute, a quarter hour, or longer. Would that be enough?

Then there's the question what kind of "touching" will suffice. Imagine that, with an objective intent to detain a suspect, officers deploy pepper spray that enters a suspect's lungs as he sprints away. Does the application of the pepper spray count? Suppose that, intending to capture a fleeing suspect, officers detonate flash-bang grenades that are so loud they damage the suspect's eardrum, even though he manages to run off. Or imagine an officer shines a laser into a suspect's eyes to get him to stop, but the suspect is able to drive away with now-damaged retinas. Are these "touchings"? What about an officer's bullet that shatters the driver's windshield, a piece of which cuts her as she speeds away? Maybe the officer didn't touch the suspect, but he set in motion a series of events that yielded a touching. Does that count? While assuring us that its new rule will prove easy to administer, the majority refuses to confront its certain complications. Lower courts and law enforcement won't have that luxury.

If efficiency cannot explain today's decision, what's left? Maybe it is an impulse that individuals like Ms. Torres *should* be able to sue for damages. Sometimes police shootings are justified, but other times they cry out for a remedy. The majority seems to give voice to this sentiment when it disparages the traditional possession rule as "artificial" and promotes its alternative as more sensitive to "personal security" and "new" policing realities. It takes pains to explain, too, that its new rule will provide greater protection for personal "privacy" interests, which we're told make up the "essence" of the Fourth Amendment.

But tasked only with applying the Constitution's terms, we have no authority to posit penumbras of "privacy" and "personal security" and devise whatever rules we think might best serve the Amendment's "essence." The Fourth Amendment allows this Court to protect against specific governmental actions—unreasonable searches and seizures of persons, houses, papers, and effects—and that is the limit of our license.

ZURCHER V. STANFORD DAILY

436 U.S. 547, 98 S.Ct. 1970, 56 L.Ed.2d 525 (1978).

JUSTICE WHITE delivered the opinion of the Court.

[Nine policemen were injured by demonstrators at Stanford University Hospital. Two days later the Stanford Daily carried articles and photos devoted to the demonstration and attack; the photos by a staff member indicated he had been located where he could have photographed the assailants. A warrant was obtained to search the Daily's offices for negatives, film and pictures relevant to identification of the assailants. Executing officers searched photo labs, filing cabinets and desks, but found no evidence. The Daily later brought a civil action in district court, where declaratory relief was granted. That court held (i) that the Fourth Amendment forbade the issuance of a warrant to search for materials in the possession of one not suspected of crime except upon a showing of probable cause a subpoena *duces tecum* would be impracticable; and (ii) that the First Amendment bars search of newspaper offices except upon a clear showing that important materials would otherwise be destroyed or removed and that a restraining order would be futile.]

It is an understatement to say that there is no direct authority in this or any other federal court for the District Court's sweeping revision of the Fourth Amendment. Under existing law, valid warrants may be issued to search *any* property, whether or not occupied by a third party, at which there is probable cause to believe that fruits, instrumentalities, or evidence of a crime will be found. Nothing on the face of the Amendment suggests that a third-party search warrant should not normally issue. * * *

Against this background, it is untenable to conclude that property may not be searched unless its occupant is reasonably suspected of crime and is subject to arrest. * * * The Fourth Amendment has itself struck the balance between privacy and public need, and there is no occasion or justification for a court to revise the Amendment and strike a new balance by denying the search warrant in the circumstances present here and by insisting that the investigation proceed by subpoena *duces tecum,* whether on the theory that the latter is a less intrusive alternative, or otherwise. * * *

In any event, the reasons presented by the District Court and adopted by the Court of Appeals for arriving at its remarkable conclusion do not withstand analysis. First, as we have said, it is apparent that whether the third-party occupant is suspect or not, the State's interest in enforcing the criminal law and recovering the evidence remains the same; and it is the seeming innocence of the property owner that the District Court relied on to foreclose the warrant to search. But as respondents themselves now concede, if the third party knows that contraband or other illegal materials are on his property, he is sufficiently culpable to justify the issuance of a search warrant. Similarly, if his ethical stance is the determining factor, it seems to us that whether or not he knows that the sought-after articles are secreted on his property and whether or not he knows that the articles are in fact the fruits, instrumentalities, or evidence of crime, he will be so informed when the search warrant is served, and it is doubtful that he should then be permitted to object to the search, to withhold, if it is there, the evidence of crime reasonably believed to be possessed by him or secreted on his property, and to forbid the search and insist that the officers serve him with a subpoena *duces tecum.*

Second, we are unpersuaded that the District Court's new rule denying search warrants against third parties and insisting on subpoenas would substantially further privacy interests without seriously undermining law enforcement efforts. As the District Court understands it, denying third-party search warrants would not have substantial adverse effects on criminal investigations because the nonsuspect third party, once served with a subpoena, will preserve the evidence and ultimately, lawfully respond. The difficulty with this assumption is that search warrants are often employed early in an investigation, perhaps before the identity of any likely criminal and certainly before all the perpetrators are or could be known. The seemingly blameless third party in possession of the fruits or evidence may not be innocent at all; and if he is, he may nevertheless be so related to or so sympathetic with the culpable that he cannot be relied upon to retain and preserve the articles that may implicate his friends, or at least not to notify those who would be damaged by the evidence that the authorities are aware of its location. In any event, it is likely that the real culprits will have access to the property, and the delay involved in employing the subpoena *duces tecum,* offering as it does the opportunity to litigate its validity, could easily result in the disappearance of the evidence, whatever the good faith of the third party. * * * [8]

We are also not convinced that the net gain to privacy interests by the District Court's new rule would be worth the candle.[9] In the normal course of events, search warrants are more difficult to obtain than subpoenas, since the latter do not involve the judiciary and do not require proof of probable cause. Where, in the real world, subpoenas would suffice, it can be expected that they will be employed by the rational prosecutor. On the other hand, when choice is available under local law and the prosecutor chooses to use the search warrant, it is unlikely that he has needlessly selected the more difficult course. His choice is more likely to be based on the solid belief, arrived at through experience but difficult, if not impossible, to sustain a specific case, that the warranted search is necessary to secure and to avoid the destruction of evidence.

[The Framers] did not forbid warrants where the press was involved, did not require special showings that subpoenas would be impractical, and did not insist that the owner of the place to be searched, if connected with the press, must be shown to be implicated in the offense being investigated. Further, the prior cases do no more than insist that the courts apply the warrant requirements with particular exactitude when First Amendment interests would be endangered by the search. As we see it, no more than this is required where the warrant requested is for the seizure of criminal evidence reasonably believed to be on the premises occupied by a newspaper. Properly administered, the pre-conditions for a warrant—probable cause, specificity with respect to the place to be searched and the things to be seized, and overall reasonableness—should afford sufficient protection against the harms that are assertedly threatened by warrants for searching newspaper offices.

There is no reason to believe, for example, that magistrates cannot guard against searches of the type, scope, and intrusiveness that would actually interfere with the timely publication of a newspaper. Nor, if the requirements of specificity and reasonableness are properly applied, policed, and observed, will there be any

---

[8]   It is also far from clear, even apart from the dangers of destruction and removal, whether the use of the subpoena *duces tecum* under circumstances where there is probable cause to believe that a crime has been committed and that the materials sought constitute evidence of its commission will result in the production of evidence with sufficient regularity to satisfy the public interest in law enforcement. Unlike the individual whose privacy is invaded by a search, the recipient of a subpoena may assert the Fifth Amendment privilege against self-incrimination in response to a summons to produce evidence or give testimony. This privilege is not restricted to suspects. We have construed it broadly as covering any individual who might be incriminated by the evidence in connection with which the privilege is asserted. The burden of overcoming an assertion of the Fifth Amendment privilege, even if prompted by a desire not to cooperate rather than any real fear of self-incrimination, is one which prosecutors would rarely be able to meet in the early stages of an investigation despite the fact they did not regard the witness as a suspect. Even time spent litigating such matters could seriously impede criminal investigations.

[9]   We reject totally the reasoning of the District Court that additional protections are required to assure that the Fourth Amendment rights of third parties are not violated because of the unavailability of the exclusionary rule as a deterrent to improper searches of premises in the control of nonsuspects. * * * It is probably seldom that police during the investigatory stage when most searches occur will be so convinced that no potential defendant will have standing to exclude evidence on Fourth Amendment grounds that they will feel free to ignore constitutional restraints. * * *

occasion or opportunity for officers to rummage at large in newspaper files or to intrude into or to deter normal editorial and publication decisions. The warrant issued in this case authorized nothing of this sort. Nor are we convinced, * * * that confidential sources will disappear and that the press will suppress news because of fears of warranted searches. Whatever incremental effect there may be in this regard if search warrants, as well as subpoenas, are permissible in proper circumstances, it does not make a constitutional difference in our judgment.

The fact is that respondents and *amici* have pointed to only a very few instances in the entire United States since 1971 involving the issuance of warrants for searching newspaper premises. This reality hardly suggests abuse; and if abuse occurs, there will be time enough to deal with it. Furthermore, the press is not only an important, critical, and valuable asset to society, but it is not easily intimidated—nor should it be. * * *

JUSTICE BRENNAN took no part in the consideration or decision of this case.

JUSTICE POWELL, concurring.

* * * Even aside from the difficulties involved in deciding on a case-by-case basis whether a subpoena can serve as an adequate substitute,[1] I agree with the Court that there is no constitutional basis for such a reading. * * *

JUSTICE STEWART, with whom JUSTICE MARSHALL joins, dissenting.

* * * It seems to me self-evident that police searches of newspaper offices burden the freedom of the press. The most immediate and obvious First Amendment injury caused by such a visitation by the police is physical disruption of the operation of the newspaper. Policemen occupying a newsroom and searching it thoroughly for what may be an extended period of time will inevitably interrupt its normal operations, and thus impair or even temporarily prevent the processes of newsgathering, writing, editing, and publishing. By contrast, a subpoena would afford the newspaper itself an opportunity to locate whatever material might be requested and produce it.

But there is another and more serious burden on a free press imposed by an unannounced police search of a newspaper office: the possibility of disclosure of information received from confidential sources, or of the identity of the sources themselves. Protection of those sources is necessary to ensure that the press can fulfill its constitutionally designated function of informing the public, because important information can often be obtained only by an assurance that the source will not be revealed. * * *

Today the Court does not question the existence of this constitutional protection, but says only that it is not "convinced . . . that confidential sources will

---

[1] For example, respondents had announced a policy of destroying any photographs that might aid prosecution of protestors. While this policy probably reflected the deep feelings of the Vietnam era, and one may assume that under normal circumstances few, if any, press entities would adopt a policy so hostile to law enforcement, respondent's policy at least illustrates the possibility of such hostility. Use of a subpoena, as proposed by the dissent would be of no utility in face of a policy of destroying evidence. And unless the policy were publicly announced, it probably would be difficult to show the impracticality of a subpoena as opposed to a search warrant.

disappear and that the press will suppress news because of fears of warranted searches." This facile conclusion seems to me to ignore common experience. It requires no blind leap of faith to understand that a person who gives information to a journalist only on condition that his identity will not be revealed will be less likely to give that information if he knows that, despite the journalist's assurance his identity may in fact be disclosed. And it cannot be denied that confidential information may be exposed to the eyes of police officers who execute a search warrant by rummaging through the files, cabinets, desks and wastebaskets of a newsroom. Since the indisputable effect of such searches will thus be to prevent a newsman from being able to promise confidentiality to his potential sources, it seems obvious to me that a journalist's access to information, and thus the public's will thereby be impaired.

A search warrant allows police officers to ransack the files of a newspaper, reading each and every document until they have found the one named in the warrant,[7] while a subpoena would permit the newspaper itself to produce only the specific documents requested. A search, unlike a subpoena, will therefore lead to the needless exposure of confidential information completely unrelated to the purpose of the investigation. The knowledge that police officers can make an unannounced raid on a newsroom is thus bound to have a deterrent effect on the availability of confidential news sources. The end result, wholly inimical to the First Amendment, will be a diminishing flow of potentially important information to the public. * * *

JUSTICE STEVENS, dissenting.

* * * [Before 1967] warrants were used to search for contraband, weapons and plunder, but not for "mere evidence." The practical effect of the rule prohibiting the issuance of warrants to search for mere evidence was to narrowly limit not only the category of objects, but also the category of persons and the character of the privacy interests that might be affected by an unannounced police search.

Just as the witnesses who participate in an investigation or a trial far outnumber the defendants, the persons who possess evidence that may help to identify an offender, or explain an aspect of a criminal transaction, far outnumber those who have custody of weapons or plunder. Countless law abiding citizens— doctors, lawyers, merchants, customers, bystanders—may have documents in their possession that relate to an ongoing criminal investigation. The consequences of subjecting this large category of persons to unannounced police searches are extremely serious. The *ex parte* warrant procedure enables the prosecutor to obtain access to privileged documents that could not be examined if advance notice gave the custodian an opportunity to object. The search for the documents described in a warrant may involve the inspection of files containing other private matter. The

---

[7] The Court says that "if the requirements of specificity and reasonableness are properly applied, policed, and observed" there will be no opportunity for the police to "rummage at large in newspaper files." But in order to find a particular document, no matter how specifically it is identified in the warrant, the police will have to search every place where it might be—including, presumably, every file in the office—and to examine each document they find to see if it is the correct one. I thus fail to see how the Fourth Amendment would provide an effective limit to these searches.

dramatic character of a sudden search may cause an entirely unjustified injury to the reputation of the persons searched. * * *

A showing of probable cause that was adequate to justify the issuance of a warrant to search for stolen goods in the 18th century does not automatically satisfy the new dimensions of the Fourth Amendment [whereunder a warrant may issue for "mere evidence"]. The only conceivable justification for an unannounced search of an innocent citizen is the fear that, if notice were given, he would conceal or destroy the object of the search. Probable cause to believe that the custodian is a criminal, or that he holds a criminal's weapons, spoils, or the like, justifies that fear, and therefore such a showing complies with the Clause. But if nothing said under oath in the warrant application demonstrates the need for an unannounced search by force, the probable cause requirement is not satisfied. In the absence of some other showing of reasonableness, the ensuing search violates the Fourth Amendment. * * *

3. PROBABLE CAUSE

Because the warrant clause of the Fourth Amendment provides that "no Warrants shall issue, but upon probable cause," it is apparent that a valid arrest warrant or search warrant may issue only upon a showing of probable cause to the issuing authority.[a] In the many instances in which police may arrest and search without first obtaining a warrant, their conduct is governed by the other half of the Amendment, which declares the right of the people to be secure "against unreasonable searches and seizures." But such an arrest or search is unreasonable unless based upon probable cause; as stated in *Wong Sun v. United States*, 371 U.S. 471 (1963), were the requirements less stringent than when a warrant is obtained, then "a principal incentive now existing for the procurement of * * * warrants would be destroyed."

When the police arrest or search without a warrant, they initially make the probable cause decision themselves. But upon a motion to suppress evidence found

---

[a]   As explained in *United States v. Grubbs*, 547 U.S. 90 (2006), this requirement can be met even in the case of an "anticipatory" search warrant, e.g., one issued upon an affidavit indicating that a controlled delivery of a package containing a videotape of child pornography would later be made to defendant's residence and that the warrant would thereafter be executed there. The Court reasoned that anticipatory warrants are "no different in principle from ordinary warrants. They require the magistrate to determine (1) that it is *now probable* that (2) contraband, evidence of a crime, or a fugitive *will be* on the described premises (3) when the warrant is executed. It should be noted, however, that where the anticipatory warrant places a condition (other than the mere passage of time) upon its execution, the first of these determinations goes not merely to what will probably be found *if* the condition is met. (If that were the extent of the probability determination, an anticipatory warrant could be issued for every house in the country, authorizing search and seizure *if* contraband should be delivered—though for any single location there is no likelihood that contraband will be delivered.) Rather, the probability determination for a conditioned anticipatory warrant looks also to the likelihood that the condition will occur, and thus that a proper object of seizure will be on the described premises. In other words, for a conditioned anticipatory warrant to comply with the Fourth Amendment's requirement of probable cause, two prerequisites of probability must be satisfied. It must be true not only that *if* the triggering condition occurs 'there is a fair probability that contraband or evidence of a crime will be found in a particular place,' but also that there is probable cause to believe the triggering condition *will occur*. The supporting affidavit must provide the magistrate with sufficient information to evaluate both aspects of the probable-cause determination."

in the arrest or search (or, sometimes, pursuant to efforts to justify continued custody of the arrestee) there will occur a subsequent judicial determination of the probable cause issue. When the police arrest or search with a warrant, the probable cause determination is made by a magistrate in the first instance. But his decision is not final; subject to the *Leon* "good faith" limitation, the defendant on a motion to suppress may still seek exclusion of evidence on the ground that the warrant was not in fact issued upon probable cause.

The first two cases in this section, *Spinelli v. United States* and *Illinois v. Gates*, reflect how the Supreme Court's approach to the probable cause issue has changed in recent years as the Court shifted to a less structured "totality of the circumstances" test. The third, *Maryland v. Pringle*, raises a classic probable issue.

SPINELLI V. UNITED STATES
393 U.S. 410, 89 S.Ct. 584, 21 L.Ed.2d 637 (1969).

JUSTICE HARLAN delivered the opinion of the Court.

William Spinelli was convicted * * * of traveling to St. Louis, Missouri, from a nearby Illinois suburb with the intention of conducting gambling activities proscribed by Missouri law. At every appropriate stage in the proceedings in the lower courts, the petitioner challenged the constitutionality of the warrant which authorized the FBI search that uncovered the evidence necessary for his conviction. * * * Believing it desirable that the principles of [*Aguilar v. Texas*, 378 U.S. 108 (1964)] should be further explicated, we granted certiorari * * *.

In *Aguilar*, a search warrant had issued upon an affidavit of police officers who swore only that they had "received reliable information from a credible person and do believe" that narcotics were being illegally stored on the described premises. While recognizing that the constitutional requirement of probable cause can be satisfied by hearsay information, this Court held the affidavit inadequate for two reasons. First, the application failed to set forth any of the "underlying circumstances" necessary to enable the magistrate independently to judge of the validity of the informant's conclusion that the narcotics were where he said they were. Second, the affiant-officers did not attempt to support their claim that their informant was "'credible' or his information 'reliable.'" The Government is, however, quite right in saying that the FBI affidavit in the present case is more ample than that in *Aguilar*. Not only does it contain a report from an anonymous informant, but it also contains a report of an independent FBI investigation which is said to corroborate the informant's tip. We are, then, required to delineate the manner in which *Aguilar's* two-pronged test should be applied in these circumstances.

In essence, the affidavit * * * contained the following allegations:

1.   The FBI had kept track of Spinelli's movements on five days during the month of August 1965. On four of these occasions, Spinelli was seen crossing one of two bridges leading from Illinois into St. Louis, Missouri, between 11 a.m. and 12:15 p.m. On four of the five days, Spinelli was also seen parking his car in a lot used by residents of an

apartment house at 1108 Indian Circle Drive in St. Louis, between 3:30 p.m. and 4:45 p.m. On one day, Spinelli was followed further and seen to enter a particular apartment in the building.

    2.   An FBI check with the telephone company revealed that this apartment contained two telephones listed under the name of Grace P. Hagen, and carrying the numbers WYdown 4–0029 and WYdown 4–0136.

    3.   The application stated that "William Spinelli is known to this affiant and to federal law enforcement agents and local law enforcement agents as a bookmaker, an associate of bookmakers, a gambler, and an associate of gamblers."

    4.   Finally, it was stated that the FBI "has been informed by a confidential reliable informant that William Spinelli is operating a handbook and accepting wagers and disseminating wagering information by means of the telephones which have been assigned the numbers WYdown 4–0029 and WYdown 4–0136."

There can be no question that the last item mentioned, detailing the informant's tip, has a fundamental place in this warrant application. Without it, probable cause could not be established. The first two items reflect only innocent-seeming activity and data. Spinelli's travels to and from the apartment building and his entry into a particular apartment on one occasion could hardly be taken as bespeaking gambling activity; and there is surely nothing unusual about an apartment containing two separate telephones. Many a householder indulges himself in this petty luxury. Finally, the allegation that Spinelli was "known" to the affiant and to other federal and local law enforcement officers as a gambler and an associate of gamblers is but a bald and unilluminating assertion of suspicion that is entitled to no weight in appraising the magistrate's decision. *Nathanson v. United States*, 290 U.S. 41 (1933).

So much indeed the Government does not deny. Rather, following the reasoning of the Court of Appeals, the Government claims that the informant's tip gives a suspicious color to the FBI's reports detailing Spinelli's innocent-seeming conduct and that, conversely, the FBI's surveillance corroborates the informant's tip, thereby entitling it to more weight. * * * We believe, however, that the "totality of circumstances" approach taken by the Court of Appeals paints with too broad a brush. Where, as here, the informer's tip is a necessary element in a finding of probable cause, its proper weight must be determined by a more precise analysis.

The informer's report must first be measured against *Aguilar's* standards so that its probative value can be assessed. If the tip is found inadequate under *Aguilar*, the other allegations which corroborate the information contained in the hearsay report should then be considered. At this stage as well, however, the standards enunciated in *Aguilar* must inform the magistrate's decision. He must ask: Can it fairly be said that the tip, even when certain parts of it have been corroborated by independent sources, is as trustworthy as a tip which would pass *Aguilar's* tests without independent corroboration? * * *

Applying these principles to the present case, we first consider the weight to be given the informer's tip when it is considered apart from the rest of the affidavit. It is clear that a Commissioner could not credit it without abdicating his constitutional function. Though the affiant swore that his confidant was "reliable," he offered the magistrate no reason in support of this conclusion. Perhaps even more important is the fact that *Aguilar's* other test has not been satisfied. The tip does not contain a sufficient statement of the underlying circumstances from which the informer concluded that Spinelli was running a bookmaking operation. We are not told how the FBI's source received his information—it is not alleged that the informant personally observed Spinelli at work or that he had ever placed a bet with him. Moreover, if the informant came by the information indirectly, he did not explain why his sources were reliable. In the absence of a statement detailing the manner in which the information was gathered, it is especially important that the tip describe the accused's criminal activity in sufficient detail so that the magistrate may know that he is relying on something more substantial than a casual rumor circulating in the underworld or an accusation based merely on an individual's general reputation.

The detail provided by the informant in *Draper v. United States*, 358 U.S. 307 (1959), provides a suitable benchmark. While Hereford, the FBI's informer in that case, did not state the way in which he had obtained his information, he reported that Draper had gone to Chicago the day before by train and that he would return to Denver by train with three ounces of heroin on one of two specified mornings. Moreover, Hereford went on to describe, with minute particularity, the clothes that Draper would be wearing upon his arrival at the Denver station. A magistrate, when confronted with such detail, could reasonably infer that the informant had gained his information in a reliable way. Such an inference cannot be made in the present case. Here, the only facts supplied were that Spinelli was using two specified telephones and that these phones were being used in gambling operations. This meager report could easily have been obtained from an off-hand remark heard at a neighborhood bar.

Nor do we believe that the patent doubts *Aguilar* raises as to the report's reliability are adequately resolved by a consideration of the allegations detailing the FBI's independent investigative efforts. At most, these allegations indicated that Spinelli could have used the telephones specified by the informant for some purpose. This cannot by itself be said to support both the inference that the informer was generally trustworthy and that he had made his charge against Spinelli on the basis of information obtained in a reliable way. Once again, *Draper* provides a relevant comparison. Independent police work in that case corroborated much more than one small detail that had been provided by the informant. There, the police, upon greeting the inbound Denver train on the second morning specified by informer Hereford, saw a man whose dress corresponded precisely to Hereford's detailed description. It was then apparent that the informant had not been fabricating his report out of whole cloth; since the report was of the sort which in common experience may be recognized as having been obtained in a reliable way, it was perfectly clear that probable cause had been established.

We conclude, then, that in the present case the informant's tip—even when corroborated to the extent indicated—was not sufficient to provide the basis for a finding of probable cause. * * * The judgment of the Court of Appeals is reversed * * *.

JUSTICE WHITE, concurring.

* * * The tension between *Draper* and the *Nathanson-Aguilar* line of cases is evident from the course followed by the majority opinion. * * * Since [the informant's] specific information about Spinelli using two phones with particular numbers had been verified, did not his allegation about gambling thereby become sufficiently more believable if the *Draper* principle is to be given any scope at all? I would think so, particularly since the information from the informant which was verified was not neutral, irrelevant information but was material to proving the gambling allegation: two phones with different numbers in an apartment used away from home indicates a business use in an operation, like bookmaking, where multiple phones are needed. The *Draper* approach would reasonably justify the issuance of a warrant in this case, particularly since the police had some awareness of Spinelli's past activities. The majority, however, while seemingly embracing *Draper*, confines that case to its own facts. Pending full scale reconsideration of that case, on the one hand, or of the *Nathanson-Aguilar* cases on the other, I join the opinion of the Court and the judgment of reversal especially since a vote to affirm would produce an equally divided Court.[a]

ILLINOIS V. GATES
462 U.S. 213, 103 S.Ct. 2317, 76 L.Ed.2d 527 (1983).

JUSTICE REHNQUIST delivered the opinion of the Court.

* * * A chronological statement of events usefully introduces the issues at stake. Bloomingdale, Ill., is a suburb of Chicago located in DuPage County. On May 3, 1978, the Bloomingdale Police Department received by mail an anonymous handwritten letter which read as follows:

> "This letter is to inform you that you have a couple in your town who strictly make their living on selling drugs. They are Sue and Lance Gates, they live on Greenway, off Bloomingdale Rd. in the condominiums. Most of their buys are done in Florida. Sue his wife drives their car to Florida, where she leaves it to be loaded up with drugs, then Lance flys down and drives it back. Sue flys back after she drops the car off in Florida. May 3 she is driving down there again and Lance will be flying down in a few days to drive it back. At the time Lance drives the car back he has the trunk loaded with over $100,000.00 in drugs. Presently they have over $100,000.00 worth of drugs in their basement.

> They brag about the fact they never have to work, and make their entire living on pushers.

---

a   The separate dissents of Black, Fortas, and Stewart, JJ., are omitted. Marshall, J., did not participate.

I guarantee if you watch them carefully you will make a big catch. They
are friends with some big drugs dealers, who visit their house often.

Lance & Susan Gates

Greenway

in Condominiums"

The letter was referred by the Chief of Police of the Bloomingdale Police
Department to Detective Mader, who decided to pursue the tip. Mader learned,
from the office of the Illinois Secretary of State, that an Illinois driver's license had
been issued to one Lance Gates, residing at a stated address in Bloomingdale. He
contacted a confidential informant, whose examination of certain financial records
revealed a more recent address for the Gates, and he also learned from a police
officer assigned to O'Hare Airport that "L. Gates" had made a reservation on
Eastern Airlines flight 245 to West Palm Beach, Fla., scheduled to depart from
Chicago on May 5 at 4:15 p.m.

Mader then made arrangements with an agent of the Drug Enforcement
Administration for surveillance of the May 5 Eastern Airlines flight. The agent
later reported to Mader that Gates had boarded the flight, and that federal agents
in Florida had observed him arrive in West Palm Beach and take a taxi to the
nearby Holiday Inn. They also reported that Gates went to a room registered to
one Susan Gates and that, at 7:00 a.m. the next morning, Gates and an
unidentified woman left the motel in a Mercury bearing Illinois license plates and
drove northbound on an interstate frequently used by travelers to the Chicago area.
In addition, the DEA agent informed Mader that the license plate number on the
Mercury registered to a Hornet station wagon owned by Gates. The agent also
advised Mader that the driving time between West Palm Beach and Bloomingdale
was approximately 22 to 24 hours.

Mader signed an affidavit setting forth the foregoing facts, and submitted it
to a judge of the Circuit Court of DuPage County, together with a copy of the
anonymous letter. The judge of that court thereupon issued a search warrant for
the Gates' residence and for their automobile. The judge, in deciding to issue the
warrant, could have determined that the *modus operandi* of the Gates had been
substantially corroborated. As the anonymous letter predicted, Lance Gates had
flown from Chicago to West Palm Beach late in the afternoon of May 5th, had
checked into a hotel room registered in the name of his wife, and, at 7:00 a.m. the
following morning, had headed north, accompanied by an unidentified woman, out
of West Palm Beach on an interstate highway used by travelers from South Florida
to Chicago in an automobile bearing a license plate issued to him.

At 5:15 a.m. on May 7th, only 36 hours after he had flown out of Chicago,
Lance Gates, and his wife, returned to their home in Bloomingdale, driving the car
in which they had left West Palm Beach some 22 hours earlier. The Bloomingdale
police were awaiting them, searched the trunk of the Mercury, and uncovered
approximately 350 pounds of marijuana. A search of the Gates' home revealed
marijuana, weapons, and other contraband. The Illinois Circuit Court ordered
suppression of all these items, on the ground that the affidavit submitted to the

Circuit Judge failed to support the necessary determination of probable cause to believe that the Gates' automobile and home contained the contraband in question. This decision was affirmed in turn by the Illinois Appellate Court and by a divided vote of the Supreme Court of Illinois.

The Illinois Supreme Court concluded—and we are inclined to agree—that, standing alone, the anonymous letter sent to the Bloomingdale Police Department would not provide the basis for a magistrate's determination that there was probable cause to believe contraband would be found in the Gates' car and home. The letter provides virtually nothing from which one might conclude that its author is either honest or his information reliable; likewise, the letter gives absolutely no indication of the basis for the writer's predictions regarding the Gates' criminal activities. Something more was required, then, before a magistrate could conclude that there was probable cause to believe that contraband would be found in the Gates' home and car.

The Illinois Supreme Court also properly recognized that Detective Mader's affidavit might be capable of supplementing the anonymous letter with information sufficient to permit a determination of probable cause. In holding that the affidavit in fact did not contain sufficient additional information to sustain a determination of probable cause, the Illinois court applied a "two-pronged test," derived from our decision in *Spinelli v. United States.* The Illinois Supreme Court, like some others, apparently understood *Spinelli* as requiring that the anonymous letter satisfy each of two independent requirements before it could be relied on. According to this view, the letter, as supplemented by Mader's affidavit, first had to adequately reveal the "basis of knowledge" of the letter writer—the particular means by which he came by the information given in his report. Second, it had to provide facts sufficiently establishing either the "veracity" of the affiant's informant, or, alternatively, the "reliability" of the informant's report in this particular case.

The Illinois court, alluding to an elaborate set of legal rules that have developed among various lower courts to enforce the "two-pronged test,"[4] found that the test had not been satisfied. First, the "veracity" prong was not satisfied because, "there was simply no basis [for] * * * conclud[ing] that the anonymous person [who wrote the letter to the Bloomingdale Police Department] was credible." The court indicated that corroboration by police of details contained in the letter might never satisfy the "veracity" prong, and in any event, could not do so if, as in the present case, only "innocent" details are corroborated. In addition, the letter gave no indication of the basis of its writer's knowledge of the Gates' activities. The Illinois court understood *Spinelli* as permitting the detail contained in a tip to be

---

[4] In summary, these rules posit that the "veracity" prong of the *Spinelli* test has two "spurs"—the informant's "credibility" and the "reliability" of his information. Various interpretations are advanced for the meaning of the "reliability" spur of the "veracity" prong. Both the "basis of knowledge" prong and the "veracity" prong are treated as entirely separate requirements, which must be independently satisfied in every case in order to sustain a determination of probable cause. Some ancillary doctrines are relied on to satisfy certain of the foregoing requirements. For example, the "self-verifying detail" of a tip may satisfy the "basis of knowledge" requirement, although not the "credibility" spur of the "veracity" prong. Conversely, corroboration would seem not capable of supporting the "basis of knowledge" prong, but only the "veracity" prong. * * *

used to infer that the informant had a reliable basis for his statements, but it thought that the anonymous letter failed to provide sufficient detail to permit such an inference. Thus, it concluded that no showing of probable cause had been made.

We agree with the Illinois Supreme Court that an informant's "veracity," "reliability" and "basis of knowledge" are all highly relevant in determining the value of his report. We do not agree, however, that these elements should be understood as entirely separate and independent requirements to be rigidly exacted in every case, which the opinion of the Supreme Court of Illinois would imply. Rather, as detailed below, they should be understood simply as closely intertwined issues that may usefully illuminate the common sense, practical question whether there is "probable cause" to believe that contraband or evidence is located in a particular place.

This totality of the circumstances approach is far more consistent with our prior treatment of probable cause than is any rigid demand that specific "tests" be satisfied by every informant's tip.[b] Perhaps the central teaching of our decisions bearing on the probable cause standard is that it is a "practical, nontechnical conception." "In dealing with probable cause, * * * as the very name implies, we deal with probabilities. These are not technical; they are the factual and practical considerations of everyday life on which reasonable and prudent men, not legal technicians, act." Our observation regarding "particularized suspicion," is also applicable to the probable cause standard:

> The process does not deal with hard certainties, but with probabilities. Long before the law of probabilities was articulated as such, practical people formulated certain common-sense conclusions about human behavior; jurors as factfinders are permitted to do the same—and so are law enforcement officers. Finally, the evidence thus collected must be seen and weighed not in terms of library analysis by scholars, but as understood by those versed in the field of law enforcement.

As these comments illustrate, probable cause is a fluid concept—turning on the assessment of probabilities in particular factual contexts—not readily, or even usefully, reduced to a neat set of legal rules. Informants' tips doubtless come in many shapes and sizes from many different types of persons. * * * Rigid legal rules

---

[b] "No more for dogs than for human informants" is a rigid approach to determining reliability called for, the Court stated in *Florida v. Harris*, 568 U.S. 237 (2013), unanimously rejecting a state court's holding "that the State must in every case present an exhaustive set of records" showing a drug-detection dog's reliability. Rather, under *Gates'* "flexible, common-sense standard" an "all-things-considered approach" is needed: "The court should allow the parties to make their best case, consistent with the usual rules of criminal procedure. And the court should then evaluate the proffered evidence to decide what all the circumstances demonstrate. If the State has produced proof from controlled settings that a dog performs reliably in detecting drugs, and the defendant has not contested that showing, then the court should find probable cause. If, in contrast, the defendant has challenged the State's case (by disputing the reliability of the dog overall or of a particular alert), then the court should weigh the competing evidence." The Court then concluded probable cause existed in the instant case, as the state showed the dog "had successfully completed two drug-detection courses and maintained his proficiency through weekly training exercises," while defendant's evidence purporting to show two false alerts to his vehicle might be attributable to defendant, a regular meth user, transferring the odor to the door handle.

are ill-suited to an area of such diversity. "One simple rule will not cover every situation."[7]

Moreover, the "two-pronged test" directs analysis into two largely independent channels—the informant's "veracity" or "reliability" and his "basis of knowledge." There are persuasive arguments against according these two elements such independent status. Instead, they are better understood as relevant considerations in the totality of circumstances analysis that traditionally has guided probable cause determinations: a deficiency in one may be compensated for, in determining the overall reliability of a tip, by a strong showing as to the other, or by some other indicia of reliability.

If, for example, a particular informant is known for the unusual reliability of his predictions of certain types of criminal activities in a locality, his failure, in a particular case, to thoroughly set forth the basis of his knowledge surely should not serve as an absolute bar to a finding of probable cause based on his tip. Likewise, if an unquestionably honest citizen comes forward with a report of criminal activity—which if fabricated would subject him to criminal liability—we have found rigorous scrutiny of the basis of his knowledge unnecessary. Conversely, even if we entertain some doubt as to an informant's motives, his explicit and detailed description of alleged wrongdoing, along with a statement that the event was observed firsthand, entitles his tip to greater weight than might otherwise be the case. Unlike a totality of circumstances analysis, which permits a balanced assessment of the relative weights of all the various indicia of reliability (and unreliability) attending an informant's tip, the "two-pronged test" has encouraged

---

[7] The diversity of informants' tips, as well as the usefulness of the totality of the circumstances approach to probable cause, is reflected in our prior decisions on the subject. In *Jones v. United States*, 362 U.S. 257 (1960), we held that probable cause to search petitioners' apartment was established by an affidavit based principally on an informant's tip. The unnamed informant claimed to have purchased narcotics from petitioners at their apartment; the affiant stated that he had been given correct information from the informant on a prior occasion. This, and the fact that petitioners had admitted to police officers on another occasion that they were narcotics users, sufficed to support the magistrate's determination of probable cause.

Likewise, in *Rugendorf v. United States*, 376 U.S. 528 (1964), the Court upheld a magistrate's determination that there was probable cause to believe that certain stolen property would be found in petitioner's apartment. The affidavit submitted to the magistrate stated that certain furs had been stolen, and that a confidential informant, who previously had furnished confidential information, said that he saw the furs in petitioner's home. Moreover, another confidential informant, also claimed to be reliable, stated that one Schweihs had stolen the furs. Police reports indicated that petitioner had been seen in Schweihs' company and a third informant stated that petitioner was a fence for Schweihs.

Finally, in *Ker v. California*, 374 U.S. 23 (1963), we held that information within the knowledge of officers who searched the Ker's apartment provided them with probable cause to believe drugs would be found there. The officers were aware that one Murphy had previously sold marijuana to a police officer; the transaction had occurred in an isolated area, to which Murphy had led the police. The night after this transaction, police observed Ker and Murphy meet in the same location. Murphy approached Ker's car, and, although police could see nothing change hands, Murphy's *modus operandi* was identical to what it had been the night before. Moreover, when police followed Ker from the scene of the meeting with Murphy he managed to lose them after performing an abrupt U-turn. Finally, the police had a statement from an informant who had provided reliable information previously, that Ker was engaged in selling marijuana, and that his source was Murphy. We concluded that "To say that this coincidence of information was sufficient to support a reasonable belief of the officers that Ker was illegally in possession of marijuana is to indulge in understatement."

an excessively technical dissection of informants' tips, with undue attention being focused on isolated issues that cannot sensibly be divorced from the other facts presented to the magistrate. * * *

We also have recognized that affidavits "are normally drafted by non-lawyers in the midst and haste of a criminal investigation. Technical requirements of elaborate specificity once exacted under common law pleading have no proper place in this area." Likewise, search and arrest warrants long have been issued by persons who are neither lawyers nor judges, and who certainly do not remain abreast of each judicial refinement of the nature of "probable cause." The rigorous inquiry into the *Spinelli* prongs and the complex superstructure of evidentiary and analytical rules that some have seen implicit in our *Spinelli* decision, cannot be reconciled with the fact that many warrants are—quite properly—issued on the basis of nontechnical, common-sense judgments of laymen applying a standard less demanding than those used in more formal legal proceedings. Likewise, given the informal, often hurried context in which it must be applied, the "built-in subtleties" of the "two-pronged test" are particularly unlikely to assist magistrates in determining probable cause.

Similarly, we have repeatedly said that after-the-fact scrutiny by courts of the sufficiency of an affidavit should not take the form of *de novo* review. A magistrate's "determination of probable cause should be paid great deference by reviewing courts." "A grudging or negative attitude by reviewing courts toward warrants" is inconsistent with the Fourth Amendment's strong preference for searches conducted pursuant to a warrant [and] "courts should not invalidate * * * warrant[s] by interpreting affidavit[s] in a hypertechnical, rather than a common-sense, manner."

If the affidavits submitted by police officers are subjected to the type of scrutiny some courts have deemed appropriate, police might well resort to warrantless searches, with the hope of relying on consent or some other exception to the warrant clause that might develop at the time of the search. In addition, the possession of a warrant by officers conducting an arrest or search greatly reduces the perception of unlawful or intrusive police conduct, by assuring "the individual whose property is searched or seized of the lawful authority of the executing officer, his need to search, and the limits of his power to search." Reflecting this preference for the warrant process, the traditional standard for review of an issuing magistrate's probable cause determination has been that so long as the magistrate had a "substantial basis for * * * conclud[ing]" that a search would uncover evidence of wrongdoing, the Fourth Amendment requires no more. We think reaffirmation of this standard better serves the purpose of encouraging recourse to the warrant procedure and is more consistent with our traditional deference to the probable cause determinations of magistrates than is the "two-pronged test."

Finally, the direction taken by decisions following *Spinelli* poorly serves "the most basic function of any government": "to provide for the security of the individual and of his property." The strictures that inevitably accompany the "two-pronged test" cannot avoid seriously impeding the task of law enforcement. If, as the Illinois Supreme Court apparently thought, that test must be rigorously applied in every case, [anonymous tips would be] of greatly diminished value in police work. Ordinary citizens, like ordinary witnesses, generally do not provide extensive recitations of the basis of their everyday observations. Likewise, as the Illinois Supreme Court observed in this case, the veracity of persons supplying anonymous tips is by hypothesis largely unknown, and unknowable. As a result, anonymous tips seldom could survive a rigorous application of either of the *Spinelli* prongs. Yet, such tips, particularly when supplemented by independent police investigation, frequently contribute to the solution of otherwise "perfect crimes." While a conscientious assessment of the basis for crediting such tips is required by the Fourth Amendment, a standard that leaves virtually no place for anonymous citizen informants is not.

For all these reasons, we conclude that it is wiser to abandon the "two-pronged test" established by our decisions in *Aguilar* and *Spinelli*.[11] In its place we reaffirm the totality of the circumstances analysis that traditionally has informed probable cause determinations. The task of the issuing magistrate is simply to make a practical, common-sense decision whether, given all the circumstances set forth in the affidavit before him, including the "veracity" and "basis of knowledge" of persons supplying hearsay information, there is a fair probability that contraband or evidence of a crime will be found in a particular place. And the duty of a reviewing court is simply to ensure that the magistrate had a "substantial basis for * * * conclud[ing]" that probable cause existed. We are convinced that this flexible, easily applied standard will better achieve the accommodation of public and private interests that the Fourth Amendment requires than does the approach that has developed from *Aguilar* and *Spinelli*.

Our earlier cases illustrate the limits beyond which a magistrate may not venture in issuing a warrant. A sworn statement of an affiant that "he has cause to suspect and does believe that" liquor illegally brought into the United States is located on certain premises will not do. *Nathanson v. United States*. An affidavit must provide the magistrate with a substantial basis for determining the existence of probable cause, and the wholly conclusory statement at issue in *Nathanson* failed to meet this requirement. An officer's statement that "affiants have received reliable information from a credible person and believe" that heroin is stored in a home, is likewise inadequate. *Aguilar v. Texas*. As in *Nathanson*, this is a mere conclusory statement that gives the magistrate virtually no basis at all for making a judgment regarding probable cause. Sufficient information must be presented to the magistrate to allow that official to determine probable cause; his action cannot be a mere ratification of the bare conclusions of others. In order to ensure that such an abdication of the magistrate's duty does not occur, courts must continue to conscientiously review the sufficiency of affidavits on which warrants are issued. But when we move beyond the "bare bones" affidavits present in cases such as

---

[11] * * * Whether the allegations submitted to the magistrate in *Spinelli* would, under the view we now take, have supported a finding of probable cause, we think it would not be profitable to decide. There are so many variables in the probable cause equation that one determination will seldom be a useful "precedent" for another. Suffice it to say that while we in no way abandon *Spinelli's* concern for the trustworthiness of informers and for the principle that it is the magistrate who must ultimately make a finding of probable cause, we reject the rigid categorization suggested by some of its language.

Nathanson and *Aguilar*, this area simply does not lend itself to a prescribed set of rules, like that which had developed from *Spinelli*. Instead, the flexible, common-sense standard articulated in *Jones* [and other cases] better served the purposes of the Fourth Amendment's probable cause requirement.

Justice Brennan's dissent suggests in several places that the approach we take today somehow downgrades the role of the neutral magistrate, because *Aguilar* and *Spinelli* "preserve the role of magistrates as independent arbiters of probable cause * * *." Quite the contrary, we believe, is the case. Nothing in our opinion in any way lessens the authority of the magistrate to draw such reasonable inferences as he will from the material supplied to him by applicants for a warrant; indeed, he is freer than under the regime of *Aguilar* and *Spinelli* to draw such inferences, or to refuse to draw them if he is so minded.

The real gist of Justice Brennan's criticism seems to be a second argument, somewhat at odds with the first, that magistrates should be restricted in their authority to make probable cause determinations by the standards laid down in *Aguilar* and *Spinelli* and that such findings "should not be authorized unless there is some assurance that the information on which they are based has been obtained in a reliable way by an honest or credible person." However, under our opinion magistrates remain perfectly free to exact such assurances as they deem necessary, as well as those required by this opinion, in making probable cause determinations. Justice Brennan would apparently prefer that magistrates be restricted in their findings of probable cause by the development of an elaborate body of case law dealing with the "veracity" prong of the *Spinelli* test, which in turn is broken down into two "spurs"—the informant's "credibility" and the "reliability" of his information, together with the "basis of knowledge" prong of the *Spinelli* test. That such a labyrinthine body of judicial refinement bears any relationship to familiar definitions of probable cause is hard to imagine. * * *

Justice Brennan's dissent also suggests that "words such as 'practical,' 'nontechnical,' and 'common sense,' as used in the Court's opinion, are but code words for an overly permissive attitude towards police practices in derogation of the rights secured by the Fourth Amendment." * * * "Fidelity" to the commands of the Constitution suggests balanced judgment rather than exhortation. The highest "fidelity" is achieved neither by the judge who instinctively goes furthest in upholding even the most bizarre claim of individual constitutional rights, any more than it is achieved by a judge who instinctively goes furthest in accepting the most restrictive claims of governmental authorities. The task of this Court, as of other courts, is to "hold the balance true," and we think we have done that in this case.

Our decisions applying the totality of circumstances analysis outlined above have consistently recognized the value of corroboration of details of an informant's tip by independent police work.

Our decision in *Draper v. United States,* however, is the classic case on the value of corroborative efforts of police officials. There, an informant named Hereford reported that Draper would arrive in Denver on a train from Chicago on one of two days, and that he would be carrying a quantity of heroin. The informant also supplied a fairly detailed physical description of Draper, and predicted that he would be wearing a light colored raincoat, brown slacks and black shoes, and would be walking "real fast." Hereford gave no indication of the basis for his information.[12]

On one of the stated dates police officers observed a man matching this description exit a train arriving from Chicago; his attire and luggage matched Hereford's report and he was walking rapidly. We explained in *Draper* that, by this point in his investigation, the arresting officer "had personally verified every facet of the information given him by Hereford except whether petitioner had accomplished his mission and had the three ounces of heroin on his person or in his bag. And surely with every other bit of Hereford's information being thus personally verified, [the officer] had 'reasonable grounds' to believe that the remaining unverified bit of Hereford's information—that Draper would have the heroin with him—was likewise true."

The showing of probable cause in the present case was fully as compelling as that in *Draper*. Even standing alone, the facts obtained through the independent investigation of Mader and the DEA at least suggested that the Gates were involved in drug trafficking. In addition to being a popular vacation site, Florida is well-known as a source of narcotics and other illegal drugs. Lance Gates' flight to Palm Beach, his brief, overnight stay in a motel, and apparent immediate return north to Chicago in the family car, conveniently awaiting him in West Palm Beach, is as suggestive of a prearranged drug run, as it is of an ordinary vacation trip.

In addition, the magistrate could rely on the anonymous letter, which had been corroborated in major part by Mader's efforts—just as had occurred in *Draper*.[13] The Supreme Court of Illinois reasoned that *Draper* involved an informant who had given reliable information on previous occasions, while the honesty and reliability of the anonymous informant in this case were unknown to

---

[12] The tip in *Draper* might well not have survived the rigid application of the "two-pronged test" that developed following *Spinelli*. The only reference to Hereford's reliability was that he had "been engaged as a 'special employee' of the Bureau of Narcotics at Denver for about six months, and from time to time gave information to [the police] for small sums of money, and that [the officer] had always found the information given by Hereford to be accurate and reliable." Likewise, the tip gave no indication of how Hereford came by his information. At most, the detailed and accurate predictions in the tip indicated that, however Hereford obtained his information, it was reliable.

[13] The Illinois Supreme Court thought that the verification of details contained in the anonymous letter in this case amounted only to "the corroboration of innocent activity," and that this was insufficient to support a finding of probable cause. We are inclined to agree, however, with the observation of Justice Moran in his dissenting opinion that "In this case, just as in *Draper*, seemingly innocent activity became suspicious in the light of the initial tip." And it bears noting that *all* of the corroborating detail established in *Draper*, supra, was of entirely innocent activity— a fact later pointed out by the Court in both *Jones v. United States*, and *Ker v. California*.

This is perfectly reasonable. As discussed previously, probable cause requires only a probability or substantial chance of criminal activity, not an actual showing of such activity. By hypothesis, therefore, innocent behavior frequently will provide the basis for a showing of probable cause; to require otherwise would be to *sub silentio* impose a drastically more rigorous definition of probable cause than the security of our citizens demands. We think the Illinois court attempted a too rigid classification of the types of conduct that may be relied upon in seeking to demonstrate probable cause. In making a determination of probable cause the relevant inquiry is not whether particular conduct is "innocent" or "guilty," but the degree of suspicion that attaches to particular types of non-criminal acts.

the Bloomingdale police. While this distinction might be an apt one at the time the police department received the anonymous letter, it became far less significant after Mader's independent investigative work occurred. The corroboration of the letter's predictions that the Gates' car would be in Florida, that Lance Gates would fly to Florida in the next day or so, and that he would drive the car north toward Bloomingdale all indicated, albeit not with certainty, that the informant's other assertions also were true. "Because an informant is right about some things, he is more probably right about other facts," *Spinelli*, supra (White, J., concurring)—including the claim regarding the Gates' illegal activity. This may well not be the type of "reliability" or "veracity" necessary to satisfy some view of the "veracity prong" of *Spinelli*, but we think it suffices for the practical, common-sense judgment called for in making a probable cause determination. It is enough, for purposes of assessing probable cause, that "corroboration through other sources of information reduced the chances of a reckless or prevaricating tale," thus providing "a substantial basis for crediting the hearsay."

Finally, the anonymous letter contained a range of details relating not just to easily obtained facts and conditions existing at the time of the tip, but to future actions of third parties ordinarily not easily predicted. The letter writer's accurate information as to the travel plans of each of the Gates was of a character likely obtained only from the Gates themselves, or from someone familiar with their not entirely ordinary travel plans. If the informant had access to accurate information of this type a magistrate could properly conclude that it was not unlikely that he also had access to reliable information of the Gates' alleged illegal activities.[14] Of course, the Gates' travel plans might have been learned from a talkative neighbor or travel agent; under the "two-pronged test" developed from *Spinelli*, the character of the details in the anonymous letter might well not permit a sufficiently clear inference regarding the letter writer's "basis of knowledge." But, as discussed previously, probable cause does not demand the certainty we associate with formal trials. It is enough that there was a fair probability that the writer of the

---

[14] The dissent seizes on one inaccuracy in the anonymous informant's letter—its statement that Sue Gates would fly from Florida to Illinois, when in fact she drove—and argues that the probative value of the entire tip was undermined by this allegedly "material mistake." We have never required that informants used by the police be infallible, and can see no reason to impose such a requirement in this case. Probable cause, particularly when police have obtained a warrant, simply does not require the perfection the dissent finds necessary.

Likewise, there is no force to the dissent's argument that the Gates' action in leaving their home unguarded undercut the informant's claim that drugs were hidden there. Indeed, the line-by-line scrutiny that the dissent applies to the anonymous letter is akin to that we find inappropriate in reviewing magistrate's decisions. The dissent apparently attributes to the magistrate who issued the warrant in this case the rather implausible notion that persons dealing in drugs always stay at home, apparently out of fear that to leave might risk intrusion by criminals. If accurate, one could not help sympathizing with the self-imposed isolation of people so situated. In reality, however, it is scarcely likely that the magistrate ever thought that the anonymous tip "kept one spouse" at home, much less that he relied on the theory advanced by the dissent. The letter simply says that Sue would fly from Florida to Illinois, without indicating whether the Gates' made the bitter choice of leaving the drugs in their house, or those in their car, unguarded. The magistrate's determination that there might be drugs or evidence of criminal activity in the Gates' home was well-supported by the less speculative theory, noted in text, that if the informant could predict with considerable accuracy the somewhat unusual travel plans of the Gates, he probably also had a reliable basis for his statements that the Gates' kept a large quantity of drugs in their home and frequently were visited by other drug traffickers there.

anonymous letter had obtained his entire story either from the Gates or someone they trusted. And corroboration of major portions of the letter's predictions provides just this probability. It is apparent, therefore, that the judge issuing the warrant had a "substantial basis for * * * conclud[ing]" that probable cause to search the Gates' home and car existed. The judgment of the Supreme Court of Illinois therefore must be reversed.

JUSTICE WHITE, concurring in the judgment.[a]

* * * Although I agree that the warrant should be upheld, I reach this conclusion in accordance with the *Aguilar-Spinelli* framework.

For present purposes, the *Aguilar-Spinelli* rules can be summed up as follows. First, an affidavit based on an informer's tip, standing alone, cannot provide probable cause for issuance of a warrant unless the tip includes information that apprises the magistrate of the informant's basis for concluding that the contraband is where he claims it is (the "basis of knowledge" prong), *and* the affiant informs the magistrate of his basis for believing that the informant is credible (the "veracity" prong).[20] Second, if a tip fails under either or both of the two prongs, probable cause may yet be established by independent police investigatory work that corroborates the tip to such an extent that it supports "both the inference that the informer was generally trustworthy and that he made his charge on the basis of information obtained in a reliable way." In instances where the officers rely on corroboration, the ultimate question is whether the corroborated tip "is as trustworthy as a tip which would pass *Aguilar's* tests without independent corroboration."

In the present case, it is undisputed that the anonymous tip, by itself, did not furnish probable cause. The question is whether those portions of the affidavit describing the results of the police investigation of the respondents, when considered in light of the tip, "would permit the suspicions engendered by the

---

[a]   In an omitted portion of his opinion, Justice White argued for adoption of a "good-faith" exception to the exclusionary rule.

[20] The "veracity" prong is satisfied by a recitation in the affidavit that the informant previously supplied accurate information to the police, or by proof that the informant gave his information against his penal interest, see *United States v. Harris*, 403 U.S. 573 (1971) (plurality opinion). [**Editors' note:** In *Harris*, the informant said that he had purchased illicit whiskey from defendant for two years, most recently within the past two weeks, and had often seen defendant get the whiskey for him and others from a certain building. The plurality opinion concluded that because "people do not lightly admit a crime and place critical evidence in the hands of the police in the form of their own admissions," such admissions "carry their own indicia of credibility—sufficient at least to support finding of probable cause to search" when, as here, the basis of knowledge is also indicated (as almost inevitably will be the case when there is such an admission). The four dissenters objected that "the effect of adopting such a rule would be to encourage the Government to prefer as informants participants in criminal enterprises rather than ordinary citizens, a goal the Government specifically eschews in its brief in this case upon the explicit premise that such persons are often less reliable than those who obey the law."] The "basis of knowledge" prong is satisfied by a statement from the informant that he personally observed the criminal activity, or, if he came by the information indirectly, by a satisfactory explanation of why his sources were reliable, or, in the absence of a statement detailing the manner in which the information was gathered, by a description of the accused's criminal activity in sufficient detail that the magistrate may infer that the informant is relying on something more substantial than casual rumor or an individual's general reputation.

informant's report to ripen into a judgment that a crime was probably being committed." * * *

In my view, the lower court's characterization of the Gates' activity here as totally "innocent" is dubious. In fact, the behavior was quite suspicious. I agree with the Court that Lance Gates' flight to Palm Beach, an area known to be a source of narcotics, the brief overnight stay in a motel, and apparent immediate return North, suggest a pattern that trained law-enforcement officers have recognized as indicative of illicit drug-dealing activity.

Even, however, had the corroboration related only to completely innocuous activities, this fact alone would not preclude the issuance of a valid warrant. The critical issue is not whether the activities observed by the police are innocent or suspicious. Instead, the proper focus should be on whether the actions of the suspects, whatever their nature, give rise to an inference that the informant is credible and that he obtained his information in a reliable manner.

Thus, in *Draper v. United States* an informant stated on Sept. 7 that Draper would be carrying narcotics when he arrived by train in Denver on the morning of Sept. 8 or Sept. 9. The informant also provided the police with a detailed physical description of the clothes Draper would be wearing when he alighted from the train. The police observed Draper leaving a train on the morning of Sept. 9, and he was wearing the precise clothing described by the informant. The Court held that the police had probable cause to arrest Draper at this point, even though the police had seen nothing more than the totally innocent act of a man getting off a train carrying a briefcase. As we later explained in *Spinelli*, the important point was that the corroboration showed both that the informant was credible, i.e. that he "had not been fabricating his report out of whole cloth," and that he had an adequate basis of knowledge for his allegations, "since the report was of the sort which in common experience may be recognized as having been obtained in a reliable way." The fact that the informer was able to predict, two days in advance, the exact clothing Draper would be wearing dispelled the possibility that his tip was just based on rumor or "an off-hand remark heard at a neighborhood bar." Probably Draper had planned in advance to wear these specific clothes so that an accomplice could identify him. A clear inference could therefore be drawn that the informant was either involved in the criminal scheme himself or that he otherwise had access to reliable, inside information.[22]

---

[22] Thus, as interpreted in *Spinelli*, the Court in *Draper* held that there was probable cause because "the kind of information related by the informant [was] not generally sent ahead of a person's arrival in a city except to those who are intimately connected with making careful arrangements for meeting him." *Spinelli* (White, J., concurring). As I said in *Spinelli*, the conclusion that *Draper* itself was based on this fact is far from inescapable. Prior to *Spinelli*, *Draper* was susceptible to the interpretation that it stood for the proposition that "the existence of the tenth and critical fact is made sufficiently probable to justify the issuance of a warrant by verifying nine other facts coming from the same source." *Spinelli* (White, J., concurring). But it now seems clear that the Court in *Spinelli* rejected this reading of *Draper*.

Justice Brennan erroneously interprets my *Spinelli* concurrence as espousing the view that "corroboration of certain details in a tip may be sufficient to satisfy the veracity, but not the basis of knowledge, prong of *Aguilar*." I did not say that corroboration could *never* satisfy the basis of knowledge prong. My concern was, and still is, that the prong might be deemed satisfied on the basis of corroboration of information that does not in any way suggest that the informant had an

As in *Draper*, the police investigation in the present case satisfactorily demonstrated that the informant's tip was as trustworthy as one that would alone satisfy the *Aguilar* tests. The tip predicted that Sue Gates would drive to Florida, that Lance Gates would fly there a few days after May 3, and that Lance would then drive the car back. After the police corroborated these facts, the magistrate could reasonably have inferred, as he apparently did, that the informant, who had specific knowledge of these unusual travel plans, did not make up his story and that he obtained his information in a reliable way. It is theoretically possible, as respondents insist, that the tip could have been supplied by a "vindictive travel agent" and that the Gates' activities, although unusual, might not have been unlawful. But *Aguilar* and *Spinelli*, like our other cases, do not require that certain guilt be established before a warrant may properly be issued. "[O]nly the probability, and not a prima facie showing, of criminal activity is the standard of probable cause." I therefore conclude that the judgment of the Illinois Supreme Court invalidating the warrant must be reversed.

The Court agrees that the warrant was valid, but, in the process of reaching this conclusion, it overrules the *Aguilar-Spinelli* tests and replaces them with a "totality of the circumstances" standard. As shown above, it is not at all necessary to overrule *Aguilar-Spinelli* in order to reverse the judgment below. Therefore, because I am inclined to believe that, when applied properly, the *Aguilar-Spinelli* rules play an appropriate role in probable cause determinations, and because the Court's holding may foretell an evisceration of the probable cause standard, I do not join the Court's holding.

The Court reasons that the "veracity" and "basis of knowledge" tests are not independent, and that a deficiency as to one can be compensated for by a strong showing as to the other. Thus, a finding of probable cause may be based on a tip from an informant "known for the unusual reliability of his predictions" or from "an unquestionably honest citizen," even if the report fails thoroughly to set forth the basis upon which the information was obtained. If this is so, then it must follow *a fortiori* that "the affidavit of an officer, known by the magistrate to be honest and experienced, stating that [contraband] is located in a certain building" must be acceptable. It would be "quixotic" if a similar statement from an honest informant, but not one from an honest officer, could furnish probable cause. But we have repeatedly held that the unsupported assertion or belief of an officer does not satisfy the probable cause requirement. Thus, this portion of today's holding can be read as implicitly rejecting the teachings of these prior holdings.

The Court may not intend so drastic a result. Indeed, the Court expressly reaffirms the validity of cases such as *Nathanson* that have held that, no matter how reliable the affiant-officer may be, a warrant should not be issued unless the affidavit discloses supporting facts and circumstances. The Court limits these cases

---

adequate basis of knowledge for his report. If, however, as in *Draper*, the police corroborate information from which it can be inferred that the informant's tip was grounded on inside information, this corroboration is sufficient to satisfy the basis of knowledge prong. *Spinelli* (White, J., concurring). The rules would indeed be strange if, as Justice Brennan suggests, the basis of knowledge prong could be satisfied by detail in the tip alone, but not by independent police work.

to situations involving affidavits containing only "bare conclusions" and holds that, if an affidavit contains anything more, it should be left to the issuing magistrate to decide, based solely on "practical[ity]" and "common-sense," whether there is a fair probability that contraband will be found in a particular place.

Thus, as I read the majority opinion, it appears that the question whether the probable cause standard is to be diluted is left to the common-sense judgments of issuing magistrates. I am reluctant to approve any standard that does not expressly require, as a prerequisite to issuance of a warrant, some showing of facts from which an inference may be drawn that the informant is credible and that his information was obtained in a reliable way. The Court is correctly concerned with the fact that some lower courts have been applying *Aguilar-Spinelli* in an unduly rigid manner. I believe, however, that with clarification of the rule of corroborating information, the lower courts are fully able to properly interpret *Aguilar-Spinelli* and avoid such unduly-rigid applications. I may be wrong; it ultimately may prove to be the case that the only profitable instruction we can provide to magistrates is to rely on common sense. But the question whether a particular anonymous tip provides the basis for issuance of a warrant will often be a difficult one, and I would at least attempt to provide more precise guidance by clarifying *Aguilar-Spinelli* and the relationship of those cases with *Draper* before totally abdicating our responsibility in this area. Hence, I do not join the Court's opinion rejecting the *Aguilar-Spinelli* rules.

JUSTICE BRENNAN, with whom JUSTICE MARSHALL joins, dissenting.

Although I join Justice Stevens' dissenting opinion and agree with him that the warrant is invalid even under the Court's newly announced "totality of the circumstances" test, I write separately to dissent from the Court's unjustified and ill-advised rejection of the two-prong test for evaluating the validity of a warrant based on hearsay announced in *Aguilar v. Texas*, and refined in *Spinelli v. United States*.

* * * In *Spinelli*, the Court reviewed a search warrant based on an affidavit that was "more ample" than the one in *Aguilar*. The affidavit in *Spinelli* contained not only a tip from an informant, but also a report of an independent police investigation that allegedly corroborated the informant's tip. Under these circumstances, the Court stated that it was "required to delineate the manner in which *Aguilar's* two-pronged test should be applied * * *."

The Court held that the *Aguilar* test should be applied to the tip, and approved two additional ways of satisfying that test. First, the Court suggested that if the tip contained sufficient detail describing the accused's criminal activity it might satisfy *Aguilar's* basis of knowledge prong. Such detail might assure the magistrate that he is "relying on something more substantial than a casual rumor circulating in the underworld or an accusation based merely on an individual's general reputation." Although the tip in the case before it did not meet this standard, "[t]he detail provided by the informant in *Draper v. United States* provide[d] a suitable benchmark" because "[a] magistrate, when confronted with such detail, could reasonably infer that the informant had gained his information in a reliable way."

Second, the Court stated that police corroboration of the details of a tip could provide a basis for satisfying *Aguilar.* The Court's opinion is not a model of clarity on this issue since it appears to suggest that corroboration can satisfy both the basis of knowledge and veracity prongs of *Aguilar.* Justice White's concurring opinion, however, points the way to a proper reading of the Court's opinion. After reviewing the Court's decision in *Draper v. United States,* Justice White concluded that "[t]he thrust of *Draper* is not that the verified facts have independent significance with respect to proof of [another unverified fact]." In his view, "[t]he argument instead relates to the reliability of the source: because an informant is right about some things, he is more probably right about other facts, usually the critical, unverified facts." Justice White then pointed out that prior cases had rejected "the notion that the past reliability of an officer is sufficient reason for believing his current assertions." Justice White went on to state:

> "Nor would it suffice, I suppose, if a reliable informant states there is gambling equipment in Apartment 607 and then proceeds to describe in detail Apartment 201, a description which is verified before applying for the warrant. He was right about 201, but that hardly makes him more believable about the equipment in 607. But what if he states that there are narcotics locked in a safe in Apartment 300, which is described in detail, and the apartment manager verifies everything but the contents of the safe? I doubt that the report about the narcotics is made appreciably more believable by the verification. The informant could still have gotten his information concerning the safe from others about whom nothing is known or could have inferred the presence of narcotics from circumstances which a magistrate would find unacceptable."

I find this reasoning persuasive. Properly understood, therefore, *Spinelli* stands for the proposition that corroboration of certain details in a tip may be sufficient to satisfy the veracity, but not the basis of knowledge, prong of *Aguilar.* As noted, *Spinelli* also suggests that in some limited circumstances considerable detail in an informant's tip may be adequate to satisfy the basis of knowledge prong of *Aguilar.* * * *

In rejecting the Aguilar-Spinelli standards, the Court * * * relies on * * * the "practical, nontechnical" nature of probable cause.

[O]ne can concede that probable cause is a "practical, nontechnical" concept without betraying the values that Aguilar and Spinelli reflect. As noted, Aguilar and Spinelli require the police to provide magistrates with certain crucial information. They also provide structure for magistrates' probable cause inquiries. In so doing, Aguilar and Spinelli preserve the role of magistrates as independent arbiters of probable cause, insure greater accuracy in probable cause determinations, and advance the substantive value of precluding findings of probable cause, and attendant intrusions, based on anything less than information from an honest or credible person who has acquired his information in a reliable way. Neither the standards nor their effects are inconsistent with a "practical, nontechnical" conception of probable cause. Once a magistrate has determined that he has information before him that he can reasonably say has been obtained in a reliable way by a credible person, he has ample room to use his common sense and to apply a practical, nontechnical conception of probable cause. * * *

The Court also insists that the Aguilar-Spinelli standards must be abandoned because they are inconsistent with the fact that non-lawyers frequently serve as magistrates. To the contrary, the standards help to structure probable cause inquiries and, properly interpreted, may actually help a non-lawyer magistrate in making a probable cause determination. * * *

At the heart of the Court's decision to abandon Aguilar and Spinelli appears to be its belief that "the direction taken by decisions following Spinelli poorly serves 'the most basic function of any government: to provide for the security of the individual and of his property.' " This conclusion rests on the judgment that Aguilar and Spinelli "seriously imped[e] the task of law enforcement," and render anonymous tips valueless in police work. Surely, the Court overstates its case. But of particular concern to all Americans must be that the Court gives virtually no consideration to the value of insuring that findings of probable cause are based on information that a magistrate can reasonably say has been obtained in a reliable way by an honest or credible person. * * *

The Court's complete failure to provide any persuasive reason for rejecting Aguilar and Spinelli doubtlessly reflects impatience with what it perceives to be "overly technical" rules governing searches and seizures under the Fourth Amendment. Words such as "practical," "nontechnical," and "commonsense," as used in the Court's opinion, are but code words for an overly permissive attitude towards police practices in derogation of the rights secured by the Fourth Amendment. Everyone shares the Court's concern over the horrors of drug trafficking, but under our Constitution only measures consistent with the Fourth Amendment may be employed by government to cure this evil. We must be ever mindful of Justice Stewart's admonition that "[i]n times of unrest, whether caused by crime or racial conflict or fear of internal subversion, this basic law and the values that it represents may appear unrealistic or 'extravagant' to some. But the values were those of the authors of our fundamental constitutional concepts." * * *

Rights secured by the Fourth Amendment are particularly difficult to protect because their "advocates are usually criminals." But the rules "we fashion [are] for the innocent and guilty alike." By replacing Aguilar and Spinelli with a test that provides no assurance that magistrates, rather than the police, or informants, will make determinations of probable cause; imposes no structure on magistrates' probable cause inquiries; and invites the possibility that intrusions may be justified on less than reliable information from an honest or credible person, today's decision threatens to "obliterate one of the most fundamental distinctions between our form of government, where officers are under the law, and the police-state where they are the law."

JUSTICE STEVENS, with whom JUSTICE BRENNAN joins, dissenting.

* * * The informant had indicated that "Sue drives their car to Florida where she leaves it to be loaded up with drugs * * *. Sue flies back after she drops the car

off in Florida." (emphasis added). Yet Detective Mader's affidavit reported that she "left the West Palm Beach area driving the Mercury northbound."

The discrepancy between the informant's predictions and the facts known to Detective Mader is significant for three reasons. First, it cast doubt on the informant's hypothesis that the Gates already had "over $100,000 worth of drugs in their basement." The informant had predicted an itinerary that always kept one spouse in Bloomingdale, suggesting that the Gates did not want to leave their home unguarded because something valuable was hidden within. That inference obviously could not be drawn when it was known that the pair was actually together over a thousand miles from home.

Second, the discrepancy made the Gates' conduct seem substantially less unusual than the informant had predicted it would be. It would have been odd if, as predicted, Sue had driven down to Florida on Wednesday, left the car, and flown right back to Illinois. But the mere facts that Sue was in West Palm Beach with the car,[1] that she was joined by her husband at the Holiday Inn on Friday,[2] and that the couple drove north together the next morning[3] are neither unusual nor probative of criminal activity.

Third, the fact that the anonymous letter contained a material mistake undermines the reasonableness of relying on it as a basis for making a forcible entry into a private home.

Of course, the activities in this case did not stop when the magistrate issued the warrant. The Gates drove all night to Bloomingdale, the officers searched the car and found 400 pounds of marijuana, and then they searched the house. However, none of these subsequent events may be considered in evaluating the warrant, and the search of the house was legal only if the warrant was valid. I cannot accept the Court's casual conclusion that, before the Gates arrived in Bloomingdale, there was probable cause to justify a valid entry and search of a private home. No one knows who the informant in this case was, or what motivated him or her to write the note. Given that the note's predictions were faulty in one significant respect, and were corroborated by nothing except ordinary innocent activity, I must surmise that the Court's evaluation of the warrant's validity has been colored by subsequent events. * * *

---

[1] The anonymous note suggested that she was going down on Wednesday, but for all the officers knew she had been in Florida for a month.

[2] Lance does not appear to have behaved suspiciously in flying down to Florida. He made a reservation in his own name and gave an accurate home phone number to the airlines. And Detective Mader's affidavit does not report that he did any of the other things drug couriers are notorious for doing, such as paying for the ticket in cash, dressing casually, looking pale and nervous, improperly filling out baggage tags, carrying American Tourister luggage, not carrying any luggage, or changing airlines en route.

[3] Detective Mader's affidavit hinted darkly that the couple had set out upon "that interstate highway commonly used by travelers to the Chicago area." But the same highway is also commonly used by travelers to Disney World, Sea World, and Ringling Brothers and Barnum and Bailey Circus World. It is also the road to Cocoa Beach, Cape Canaveral, and Washington, D.C. I would venture that each year dozens of perfectly innocent people fly to Florida, meet a waiting spouse, and drive off together in the family car.

MARYLAND V. PRINGLE

540 U.S. 366, 124 S.Ct. 795, 157 L.Ed.2d 769 (2003).

CHIEF JUSTICE REHNQUIST delivered the opinion of the Court. * * *

At 3:16 a.m. on August 7, 1999, a Baltimore County Police officer stopped a Nissan Maxima for speeding. There were three occupants in the car: Donte Partlow, the driver and owner, respondent Pringle, the front-seat passenger, and Otis Smith, the back-seat passenger. The officer asked Partlow for his license and registration. When Partlow opened the glove compartment to retrieve the vehicle registration, the officer observed a large amount of rolled-up money in the glove compartment. The officer returned to his patrol car with Partlow's license and registration to check the computer system for outstanding violations. The computer check did not reveal any violations. The officer returned to the stopped car, had Partlow get out, and issued him an oral warning.

After a second patrol car arrived, the officer asked Partlow if he had any weapons or narcotics in the vehicle. Partlow indicated that he did not. Partlow then consented to a search of the vehicle. The search yielded $763 from the glove compartment and five plastic glassine baggies containing cocaine from behind the back-seat armrest. When the officer began the search the armrest was in the upright position flat against the rear seat. The officer pulled down the armrest and found the drugs, which had been placed between the armrest and the back seat of the car.

The officer questioned all three men about the ownership of the drugs and money, and told them that if no one admitted to ownership of the drugs he was going to arrest them all. The men offered no information regarding the ownership of the drugs or money. All three were placed under arrest and transported to the police station.

Later that morning, Pringle * * * gave an oral and written confession in which he acknowledged that the cocaine belonged to him, that he and his friends were going to a party, and that he intended to sell the cocaine or "[u]se it for sex." Pringle maintained that the other occupants of the car did not know about the drugs, and they were released.

The trial court denied Pringle's motion to suppress his confession as the fruit of an illegal arrest, holding that the officer had probable cause to arrest Pringle. A jury convicted Pringle of possession with intent to distribute cocaine and possession of cocaine. He was sentenced to 10 years' incarceration without the possibility of parole. * * *

The Court of Appeals of Maryland, by divided vote, reversed, holding that, absent specific facts tending to show Pringle's knowledge and dominion or control over the drugs, "the mere finding of cocaine in the back armrest when [Pringle] was a front seat passenger in a car being driven by its owner is insufficient to establish probable cause for an arrest for possession." * * *

It is uncontested in the present case that the officer, upon recovering the five plastic glassine baggies containing suspected cocaine, had probable cause to believe a felony had been committed. The sole question is whether the officer had probable cause to believe that Pringle committed that crime.[1] * * *

The probable-cause standard is incapable of precise definition or quantification into percentages because it deals with probabilities and depends on the totality of the circumstances. We have stated, however, that "[t]he substance of all the definitions of probable cause is a reasonable ground for belief of guilt," and that the belief of guilt must be particularized with respect to the person to be searched or seized. * * *

In this case, Pringle was one of three men riding in a Nissan Maxima at 3:16 a.m. There was $763 of rolled-up cash in the glove compartment directly in front of Pringle.[2] Five plastic glassine baggies of cocaine were behind the back-seat armrest and accessible to all three men. Upon questioning, the three men failed to offer any information with respect to the ownership of the cocaine or the money.

We think it an entirely reasonable inference from these facts that any or all three of the occupants had knowledge of, and exercised dominion and control over, the cocaine. Thus a reasonable officer could conclude that there was probable cause to believe Pringle committed the crime of possession of cocaine, either solely or jointly.

Pringle's attempt to characterize this case as a guilt-by-association case is unavailing. His reliance on *Ybarra v. Illinois*, [444 U.S. 85 (1979)], and *United States v. Di Re*, 332 U.S. 581 (1948), is misplaced. In *Ybarra*, police officers obtained a warrant to search a tavern and its bartender for evidence of possession of a controlled substance. Upon entering the tavern, the officers conducted patdown searches of the customers present in the tavern, including Ybarra. Inside a cigarette pack retrieved from Ybarra's pocket, an officer found six tinfoil packets containing heroin. We stated:

> "[A] person's mere propinquity to others independently suspected of criminal activity does not, without more, give rise to probable cause to search that person. Where the standard is probable cause, a search or

---

[1]   Maryland law defines "possession" as "the exercise of actual or constructive dominion or control over a thing by one or more persons."

[2]   The Court of Appeals of Maryland dismissed the $763 seized from the glove compartment as a factor in the probable-cause determination, stating that "[m]oney, without more, is innocuous." The court's consideration of the money in isolation, rather than as a factor in the totality of the circumstances, is mistaken in light of our precedents. * * * We think it is abundantly clear from the facts that this case involves more than money alone.

[Editors' note: This footnote was relied upon in *District of Columbia v. Wesby*, 138 S.Ct. 577 (2018), where police called to a loud, late-night party at a home with no owner in attendance were deemed to have probable cause of unlawful entry (a crime only if the partygoers knew or should have known they were present without an owner's permission), despite the fact that each of the partygoers had theretofore "claimed that someone * * * invited them to the house." The lower court erred in concluding otherwise because it improperly "viewed each fact in isolation, rather than as a factor in the totality of the circumstances." Assessing "the plausibility of the explanation itself" in light of "all the surrounding circumstances," the Court concluded the officers had probable cause, given (i) "the condition of the house" (vacant for months and without any signs of inhabitance), (ii) "the partygoers' conduct" (strip club in the living room, sex in the bedroom), and (iii) "the partygoers' reaction to the officers" ("scattering and hiding" and giving "vague and implausible responses").]

seizure of a person must be supported by probable cause particularized with respect to that person. This requirement cannot be undercut or avoided by simply pointing to the fact that coincidentally there exists probable cause to search or seize another or to search the premises where the person may happen to be."

We held that the search warrant did not permit body searches of all of the tavern's patrons and that the police could not pat down the patrons for weapons, absent individualized suspicion.

This case is quite different from *Ybarra*. Pringle and his two companions were in a relatively small automobile, not a public tavern. In *Wyoming v. Houghton*, [Ch. 3, § 7], we noted that "a car passenger—unlike the unwitting tavern patron in *Ybarra*—will often be engaged in a common enterprise with the driver, and have the same interest in concealing the fruits or the evidence of their wrongdoing." Here we think it was reasonable for the officer to infer a common enterprise among the three men. The quantity of drugs and cash in the car indicated the likelihood of drug dealing, an enterprise to which a dealer would be unlikely to admit an innocent person with the potential to furnish evidence against him.

In *Di Re*, a federal investigator had been told by an informant, Reed, that he was to receive counterfeit gasoline ration coupons from a certain Buttitta at a particular place. The investigator went to the appointed place and saw Reed, the sole occupant of the rear seat of the car, holding gasoline ration coupons. There were two other occupants in the car: Buttitta in the driver's seat and Di Re in the front passenger's seat. Reed informed the investigator that Buttitta had given him counterfeit coupons. Thereupon, all three men were arrested and searched. After noting that the officers had no information implicating Di Re and no information pointing to Di Re's possession of coupons, unless presence in the car warranted that inference, we concluded that the officer lacked probable cause to believe that Di Re was involved in the crime. We said "[a]ny inference that everyone on the scene of a crime is a party to it must disappear if the Government informer singles out the guilty person." No such singling out occurred in this case; none of the three men provided information with respect to the ownership of the cocaine or money.

We hold that the officer had probable cause to believe that Pringle had committed the crime of possession of a controlled substance. Pringle's arrest therefore did not contravene the Fourth and Fourteenth Amendments. Accordingly, the judgment of the Court of Appeals of Maryland is reversed, and the case is remanded for further proceedings not inconsistent with this opinion. * * *

4. SEARCH WARRANTS

As the cases in the three sections following this one illustrate, there are many instances in which the police may seize or search on probable cause without first obtaining a warrant. However, the obtaining and executing of search warrants is nonetheless a common means for obtaining evidence of crime, for with rare exceptions extended searches of premises may be conducted only pursuant to a warrant. The Fourth Amendment sets out several requirements for warrants, stating that "no Warrants shall issue, but upon probable cause, supported by Oath or affirmation, and particularly describing the place to be searched, and the persons or things to be seized."

The first case in this section, *Maryland v. Garrison,* considers the meaning and significance of the particular description requirement. *Garrison,* together with the other case included here, *Richards v. Wisconsin,* also explores what it takes for the execution of a valid search warrant to be reasonable, still another requirement under the Fourth Amendment.

MARYLAND V. GARRISON

480 U.S. 79, 107 S.Ct. 1013, 94 L.Ed.2d 72 (1987).

JUSTICE STEVENS delivered the opinion of the Court.

Baltimore police officers obtained and executed a warrant to search the person of Lawrence McWebb and "the premises known as 2036 Park Avenue third floor apartment." When the police applied for the warrant and when they conducted the search pursuant to the warrant, they reasonably believed that there was only one apartment on the premises described in the warrant. In fact, the third floor was divided into two apartments, one occupied by McWebb and one by respondent Garrison. Before the officers executing the warrant became aware that they were in a separate apartment occupied by respondent, they had discovered the contraband that provided the basis for respondent's conviction for violating Maryland's Controlled Substances Act. The question presented is whether the seizure of that contraband was prohibited by the Fourth Amendment.

The trial court denied respondent's motion to suppress the evidence seized from his apartment, and the Maryland Court of Special Appeals affirmed. The Court of Appeals of Maryland reversed and remanded with instructions to remand the case for a new trial.

There is no question that the warrant was valid and was supported by probable cause. The trial court found, and the two appellate courts did not dispute, that after making a reasonable investigation, including a verification of information obtained from a reliable informant, an exterior examination of the three-story building at 2036 Park Avenue, and an inquiry of the utility company, the officer who obtained the warrant reasonably concluded that there was only one apartment on the third floor and that it was occupied by McWebb. When six Baltimore police officers executed the warrant, they fortuitously encountered McWebb in front of the building and used his key to gain admittance to the first-floor hallway and to the locked door at the top of the stairs to the third floor. As they entered the vestibule on the third floor, they encountered respondent, who was standing in the hallway area. The police could see into the interior of both McWebb's apartment to the left and respondent's to the right, for the doors to both were open. Only after respondent's apartment had been entered and heroin, cash, and drug paraphernalia had been found did any of the officers realize that the third floor contained two apartments. As soon as they became aware of that fact, the search was discontinued. All of the officers reasonably believed that they were searching McWebb's apartment. No further search of respondent's apartment was made.

The matter on which there is a difference of opinion concerns the proper interpretation of the warrant. A literal reading of its plain language, as well as the language used in the application for the warrant, indicates that it was intended to authorize a search of the entire third floor. This is the construction adopted by the intermediate appellate court, and it also appears to be the construction adopted by the trial judge. One sentence in the trial judge's oral opinion, however, lends support to the construction adopted by the Court of Appeals, namely, that the warrant authorized a search of McWebb's apartment only. Under that interpretation, the Court of Appeals concluded that the warrant did not authorize the search of respondent's apartment and the police had no justification for making a warrantless entry into his premises. * * *

In our view, the case presents two separate constitutional issues, one concerning the validity of the warrant and the other concerning the reasonableness of the manner in which it was executed. We shall discuss the questions separately.

I

The Warrant Clause of the Fourth Amendment categorically prohibits the issuance of any warrant except one "particularly describing the place to be searched and the persons or things to be seized." The manifest purpose of this particularity requirement was to prevent general searches. By limiting the authorization to search to the specific areas and things for which there is probable cause to search, the requirement ensures that the search will be carefully tailored to its justifications, and will not take on the character of the wide-ranging exploratory searches the Framers intended to prohibit. Thus, the scope of a lawful search is "defined by the object of the search and the places in which there is probable cause to believe that it may be found. Just as probable cause to believe that a stolen lawnmower may be found in a garage will not support a warrant to search an upstairs bedroom, probable cause to believe that undocumented aliens are being transported in a van will not justify a warrantless search of a suitcase."

In this case there is no claim that the "persons or things to be seized" were inadequately described[a] or that there was no probable cause to believe that those

---

[a]   Courts have frequently been confronted with the question of whether a particularity defect in a warrant can be overcome by an sufficient description in the supporting affidavit, and the Supreme Court had occasion to deal with a rather unusual fact situation in this regard in *Groh v. Ramirez*, 540 U.S. 551 (2004). The affiant, who was also the executing officer, correctly stated the items to be seized in the search warrant application and the supporting affidavit, but in the search warrant itself mistakenly entered in the space for that specification a description of the place to be searched. That error was not noticed by the magistrate who issued the warrant, and was not noticed by the affiant/executing officer until after the warrant was executed, and he instructed his search team on the basis of the items listed in the application and affidavit. On whether there had been a valid with-warrant search, the Court concluded:

"The fact that the *application* adequately described the 'things to be seized' does not save the *warrant* from its facial invalidity. The Fourth Amendment by its terms requires particularity in the warrant, not in the supporting documents. * * * And for good reason: 'The presence of a search warrant served a high function,' * * * and that high function is not necessarily vindicated when some other document, somewhere, says something about the objects of the search, but the contents of that document are neither known to the person whose home is being searched nor available for

things might be found in "the place to be searched" as it was described in the warrant. With the benefit of hindsight, however, we now know that the description of that place was broader than appropriate because it was based on the mistaken belief that there was only one apartment on the third floor of the building at 2036 Park Avenue. The question is whether that factual mistake invalidated a warrant that undoubtedly would have been valid if it had reflected a completely accurate understanding of the building's floor plan.

Plainly, if the officers had known, or even if they should have known, that there were two separate dwelling units on the third floor of 2036 Park Avenue, they would have been obligated to exclude respondent's apartment from the scope of the requested warrant. But we must judge the constitutionality of their conduct in light of the information available to them at the time they acted. Those items of evidence that emerge after the warrant is issued have no bearing on whether or not a warrant was validly issued. Just as the discovery of contraband cannot validate a warrant invalid when issued, so is it equally clear that the discovery of facts demonstrating that a valid warrant was unnecessarily broad does not retroactively invalidate the warrant. The validity of the warrant must be assessed on the basis of the information that the officers disclosed, or had a duty to discover and to disclose, to the issuing Magistrate.[10] On the basis of that information, we agree

---

her inspection. We do not say that the Fourth Amendment forbids a warrant from cross-referencing other documents. Indeed, most Courts of Appeals have held that a court may construe a warrant with reference to a supporting application or affidavit if the warrant uses appropriate words of incorporation, and if the supporting document accompanies the warrant. * * * But in this case the warrant did not incorporate other documents by reference, nor did either the affidavit or the application * * * accompany the warrant. Hence, we need not further explore the matter of incorporation."

The Court in *Groh* then turned to the question of whether the case was one in which it could be concluded a reasonable warrantless search was made because the search "was functionally equivalent to a search authorized by a valid warrant," in that "the goals served by the particularity requirement are otherwise satisfied." In examining that premise, the Court first considered the assertion that because the executing officers acted upon the basis of the sufficient description in the supporting documents, "the scope of the search did not exceed the limits set forth in the application." As to this, the Court concluded: "But unless the particular items described in the affidavit are also set forth in the warrant itself (or at least incorporated by reference, and the affidavit present at the search), there can be no written assurance that the Magistrate actually found probable cause to search for, and to seize, every item mentioned in the affidavit. * * * In this case, for example, it is at least theoretically possible that the Magistrate was satisfied that the search for weapons and explosives was justified by the showing in the affidavit, but not convinced that any evidentiary basis existed for rummaging through respondents' files and papers for receipts pertaining to the purchase or manufacture of such items. * * * Or, conceivably, the Magistrate might have believed that some of the weapons mentioned in the affidavit could have been lawfully possessed and therefore should not be seized. * * * The mere fact that the Magistrate issued a warrant does not necessarily establish that he agreed that the scope of the search should be as broad as the affiant's request." (Two Justices disagreed on this branch of the case because "the more reasonable inference is that the Magistrate intended to authorize everything in the warrant application, as he signed the application and did not make any written adjustments to the application or the warrant itself.") The Court then went on to hold, 5–4, that the "good faith" exception under *Leon*, p. 68, did not apply "because [the affiant] himself prepared the invalid warrant."

[10] Arguments can certainly be made that the police in this case should have been able to ascertain that there was more than one apartment on the third floor of this building. It contained seven separate dwelling units and it was surely possible that two of them might be on the third floor. But the record also establishes that Officer Marcus made specific inquiries to determine the identity of the occupants of the third-floor premises. The officer went to 2036 Park Avenue and

with the conclusion of all three Maryland courts that the warrant, insofar as it authorized a search that turned out to be ambiguous in scope, was valid when it issued.

II

The question whether the execution of the warrant violated respondent's constitutional right to be secure in his home is somewhat less clear. We have no difficulty concluding that the officers' entry into the third-floor common area was legal; they carried a warrant for those premises, and they were accompanied by McWebb, who provided the key that they used to open the door giving access to the third-floor common area. If the officers had known, or should have known, that the third floor contained two apartments before they entered the living quarters on the third floor, and thus had been aware of the error of the warrant, they would have been obligated to limit their search to McWebb's apartment. Moreover, as the officers recognized, they were required to discontinue the search of respondent's apartment as soon as they discovered that there were two separate units on the third floor and therefore were put on notice of the risk that they might be in a unit erroneously included within the terms of the warrant. The officers' conduct and the limits of the search were based on the information available as the search proceeded. While the purposes justifying a police search strictly limit the permissible extent of the search,[b] the Court has also recognized the need to allow some latitude for honest mistakes that are made by officers in the dangerous and difficult process of making arrests and executing search warrants.

In *Hill v. California*, 401 U.S. 797 (1971), we considered the validity of the arrest of a man named Miller based on the mistaken belief that he was Hill. The police had probable cause to arrest Hill and they in good faith believed that Miller

---

found that it matched the description given by the informant: a three-story brick dwelling with the numerals 2–0–3–6 affixed to the front of the premises. The officer "made a check with the Baltimore Gas and Electric Company and discovered that the premises of 2036 Park Ave. third floor was in the name of Lawrence McWebb." Ibid. Officer Marcus testified at the suppression hearing that he inquired of the Baltimore Gas and Electric Company in whose name the third floor apartment was listed: "I asked if there is a front or rear or middle room. They told me, one third floor was only listed to Lawrence McWebb." The officer also discovered from a check with the Baltimore Police Department that the police records of Lawrence McWebb matched the address and physical description given by the informant. The Maryland courts that are presumptively familiar with local conditions were unanimous in concluding that the officer reasonably believed McWebb was the only tenant on that floor. Because the evidence supports their conclusion, we accept that conclusion for the purpose of our decision.

   [b] Relying upon this principle from *Garrison*, the Court in *Wilson v. Layne*, 526 U.S. 603 (1999), involving police execution of an *arrest* warrant while accompanied by a newspaper reporter and photographer, held that "it is a violation of the Fourth Amendment for police to bring members of the media or other third parties into a home during the execution of a warrant when the presence of the third parties in the home was not in aid of the execution of the warrant." To emphasize that the presence of a third party is not always improper, the Court commented: "Where the police enter a home under the authority of a warrant to search for stolen property, the presence of third parties for the purpose of identifying the stolen property has long been approved by this Court and our common-law tradition." *Wilson* was a § 1983 case and thus involved no exclusionary rule issue, and the Court dropped this footnote: "Even though such actions might violate the Fourth Amendment, if the police are lawfully present, the violation of the Fourth Amendment is the presence of the media and not the presence of the police in the home. We have no occasion here to decide whether the exclusionary rule would apply to any evidence discovered or developed by the media representatives."

was Hill when they found him in Hill's apartment. As we explained: "The upshot was that the officers in good faith believed Miller was Hill and arrested him. They were quite wrong as it turned out, and subjective good-faith belief would not in itself justify either the arrest or the subsequent search. But sufficient probability, not certainty, is the touchstone of reasonableness under the Fourth Amendment and on the record before us the officers' mistake was understandable and the arrest a reasonable response to the situation facing them at the time."

While *Hill* involved an arrest without a warrant, its underlying rationale that an officer's reasonable misidentification of a person does not invalidate a valid arrest is equally applicable to an officer's reasonable failure to appreciate that a valid warrant describes too broadly the premises to be searched. Under the reasoning in *Hill,* the validity of the search of respondent's apartment pursuant to a warrant authorizing the search of the entire third floor depends on whether the officers' failure to realize the overbreadth of the warrant was objectively understandable and reasonable. Here it unquestionably was. The objective facts available to the officers at the time suggested no distinction between McWebb's apartment and the third-floor premises.[12]

For that reason, the officers properly responded to the command contained in a valid warrant even if the warrant is interpreted as authorizing a search limited to McWebb's apartment rather than the entire third floor. Prior to the officers' discovery of the factual mistake, they perceived McWebb's apartment and the third-floor premises as one and the same; therefore their execution of the warrant reasonably included the entire third floor.[13] Under either interpretation of the warrant, the officers' conduct was consistent with a reasonable effort to ascertain and identify the place intended to be searched within the meaning of the Fourth Amendment.

The judgment of the Court of Appeals is reversed, and the case is remanded for further proceedings not inconsistent with this opinion.

It is so ordered.

JUSTICE BLACKMUN, with whom JUSTICE BRENNAN and JUSTICE MARSHALL join, dissenting. * * *

I

* * * I conclude that the search of respondent's apartment was improper. The words of the warrant were plain and distinctive: the warrant directed the officers

---

[12] Nothing McWebb did or said after he was detained outside 2036 Park Avenue would have suggested to the police that there were two apartments on the third floor. McWebb provided the key that opened the doors on the first floor and on the third floor. The police could reasonably have believed that McWebb was admitting them to an undivided apartment on the third floor. When the officers entered the foyer on the third floor, neither McWebb nor Garrison informed them that they lived in separate apartments.

[13] We expressly distinguish the facts of this case from a situation in which the police know there are two apartments on a certain floor of a building, and have probable cause to believe that drugs are being sold out of that floor, but do not know in which of the two apartments the illegal transactions are taking place. A search pursuant to a warrant authorizing a search of the entire floor under those circumstances would present quite different issues from the ones before us in this case.

to seize marijuana and drug paraphernalia on the person of McWebb and in McWebb's apartment, i.e., "on the premises known as 2036 Park Avenue third floor apartment." As the Court of Appeals observed, this warrant specifically authorized a search only of McWebb's—not respondent's—residence. In its interpretation of the warrant, the majority suggests that the language of this document, as well as that in the supporting affidavit, permitted a search of the entire third floor. It escapes me why the language in question, "third floor apartment," when used with reference to a single unit in a multiple-occupancy building and in the context of one person's residence, plainly has the meaning the majority discerns, rather than its apparent and, indeed, obvious signification—one apartment located on the third floor. Accordingly, if, as appears to be the case, the warrant was limited in its description to the third floor apartment of McWebb, then the search of an additional apartment—respondent's—was warrantless and is presumed unreasonable "in the absence of some one of a number of well defined 'exigent circumstances.' " Because the State has not advanced any such exception to the warrant requirement, the evidence obtained as a result of this search should have been excluded.

II

* * * Even if one accepts the majority's view that there is no Fourth Amendment violation where the officers' mistake is reasonable, it is questionable whether that standard was met in this case. * * *

The efforts of Detective Marcus, the officer who procured the search warrant, do not meet a standard of reasonableness, particularly considering that the detective knew the search concerned a unit in a multiple-occupancy building. Upon learning from his informant that McWebb was selling marijuana in his third-floor apartment, Marcus inspected the outside of the building. He did not approach it, however, to gather information about the configuration of the apartments. Had he done so, he would have discovered, as did another officer on the day of executing the warrant, that there were seven separate mailboxes and bells on the porch outside the main entrance to the house. Although there is some dispute over whether names were affixed near these boxes and bells, their existence alone puts a reasonable observer on notice that the three-story structure (with, possibly, a basement) had seven individual units. The detective, therefore, should have been aware that further investigation was necessary to eliminate the possibility of more than one unit's being located on the third floor. Moreover, when Detective Marcus' informant told him that he had purchased drugs in McWebb's apartment, it appears that the detective never thought to ask the informant whether McWebb's apartment was the only one on the third floor. These efforts, which would have placed a slight burden upon the detective, are necessary in order to render reasonable the officer's behavior in seeking the warrant.

Moreover, even if one believed that Marcus' efforts in providing information for issuance of the warrant were reasonable, I doubt whether the officers' execution of the warrant could meet such a standard. In the Court's view, the "objective facts" did not put the officers on notice that they were dealing with two separate apartments on the third floor until the moment, considerably into the search after they had rummaged through a dresser and a closet in respondent's apartment and had discovered evidence incriminating him, when they realized their "mistake." The Court appears to base its conclusion that the officers' error here was reasonable on the fact that neither McWebb nor respondent ever told the officers during the search that they lived in separate apartments.

In my view, however, the "objective facts" should have made the officers aware that there were two different apartments on the third floor well before they discovered the incriminating evidence in respondent's apartment. Before McWebb happened to drive up while the search party was preparing to execute the warrant, one of the officers, Detective Shea, somewhat disguised as a construction worker, was already on the porch of the row house and was seeking to gain access to the locked first-floor door that permitted entrance into the building. From this vantage point he had time to observe the seven mailboxes and bells; indeed, he rang all seven bells, apparently in an effort to summon some resident to open the front door to the search party. A reasonable officer in Detective Shea's position, already aware that this was a multiunit building and now armed with further knowledge of the number of units in the structure, would have conducted at that time more investigation to specify the exact location of McWebb's apartment before proceeding further. For example, he might have questioned another resident of the building. * * *

Moreover, a reasonable officer would have realized the mistake in the warrant during the moments following the officers' entrance to the third floor. The officers gained access to the vestibule separating McWebb's and respondent's apartments through a locked door for which McWebb supplied the key. There, in the open doorway to his apartment, they encountered respondent, clad in pajamas and wearing a half-body cast as a result of a recent spinal operation. Although the facts concerning what next occurred are somewhat in dispute, it appears that respondent, together with McWebb and the passenger from McWebb's car, were shepherded into McWebb's apartment across the vestibule from his own. Once again, the officers were curiously silent. The informant had not led the officers to believe that anyone other than McWebb lived in the third-floor apartment; the search party had McWebb, the person targeted by the search warrant, in custody when it gained access to the vestibule; yet when they met respondent on the third floor, they simply asked him who he was but never where he lived. Had they done so, it is likely that they would have discovered the mistake in the warrant before they began their search.

Finally and most importantly, even if the officers had learned nothing from respondent, they should have realized the error in the warrant from their initial security sweep. Once on the third floor, the officers first fanned out through the rooms to conduct a preliminary check for other occupants who might pose a danger to them. As the map of the third floor demonstrates, the two apartments were almost a mirror image of each other—each had a bathroom, a kitchen, a living room, and a bedroom. Given the somewhat symmetrical layout of the apartments, it is difficult to imagine that, in the initial security sweep, a reasonable officer would not have discerned that two apartments were on the third floor, realized his mistake, and then confined the ensuing search to McWebb's residence.

Accordingly, even if a reasonable error on the part of police officers prevents a Fourth Amendment violation, the mistakes here, both with respect to obtaining and executing the warrant, are not reasonable and could easily have been avoided.

I respectfully dissent.

RICHARDS V. WISCONSIN
520 U.S. 385, 117 S.Ct. 1416, 137 L.Ed.2d 615 (1997).

JUSTICE STEVENS delivered the opinion of the Court.

In *Wilson v. Arkansas*, 514 U.S. 927 (1995), we held that the Fourth Amendment incorporates the common-law requirement that police officers entering a dwelling must knock on the door and announce their identity and purpose before attempting forcible entry.[a] At the same time, we recognized that the "flexible requirement of reasonableness should not be read to mandate a rigid rule of announcement that ignores countervailing law enforcement interests," and left "to the lower courts the task of determining the circumstances under which an unannounced entry is reasonable under the Fourth Amendment."

In this case, the Wisconsin Supreme Court concluded that police officers are never required to knock and announce their presence when executing a search warrant in a felony drug investigation. * * * We disagree * * *.

On December 31, 1991, police officers in Madison, Wisconsin obtained a warrant to search Steiney Richards' hotel room for drugs and related paraphernalia. The search warrant was the culmination of an investigation that had uncovered substantial evidence that Richards was one of several individuals dealing drugs out of hotel rooms in Madison. The police requested a warrant that would have given advance authorization for a "no-knock" entry into the hotel room, but the magistrate explicitly deleted those portions of the warrant.

The officers arrived at the hotel room at 3:40 a.m. Officer Pharo, dressed as a maintenance man, led the team. With him were several plainclothes officers and at least one man in uniform. Officer Pharo knocked on Richards' door and, responding to the query from inside the room, stated that he was a maintenance man. With the chain still on the door, Richards cracked it open. Although there is some dispute as to what occurred next, Richards acknowledges that when he opened the door he saw the man in uniform standing behind Officer Pharo. He

---

[a]   In *United States v. Banks*, 540 U.S. 31 (2003), a unanimous Court decided how long a wait is necessary before the police may reasonably conclude they have been refused admittance, concluding that in the absence of exigent circumstances, the issue is simply whether the occupant's "failure to admit [the police] fairly suggested a refusal to let them in," which means the question would be whether it reasonably appeared to the police that "an occupant has had time to get to the door." This judgment, the Court emphasized, is to be made upon the facts known by the police at the time (so that it would not be relevant that, as in *Banks*, the occupant "was actually in the shower and did not hear the officers"). The amount of time needed would vary, the Court added, depending on "the size of the establishment," as it would take "perhaps five seconds to open a motel room door, or several minutes to move through a townhouse." But, the Court cautioned, "in the case with no reason to suspect an immediate risk of frustration or futility in waiting at all, the reasonable wait time may well be longer when police make a forced entry, since they ought to be more certain the occupant has had time to answer the door."

quickly slammed the door closed and, after waiting two or three seconds, the officers began kicking and ramming the door to gain entry to the locked room. At trial, the officers testified that they identified themselves as police while they were kicking the door in. When they finally did break into the room, the officers caught Richards trying to escape through the window. They also found cash and cocaine hidden in plastic bags above the bathroom ceiling tiles.

Richards sought to have the evidence from his hotel room suppressed on the ground that the officers had failed to knock and announce their presence prior to forcing entry into the room. The trial court denied the motion, concluding that the officers could gather from Richards' strange behavior when they first sought entry that he knew they were police officers and that he might try to destroy evidence or to escape. * * * Richards appealed the decision to the Wisconsin Supreme Court and that court affirmed.

The Wisconsin Supreme Court did not delve into the events underlying Richards' arrest in any detail, but [instead] found it reasonable—after considering criminal conduct surveys, newspaper articles, and other judicial opinions—to assume that all felony drug crimes will involve "an extremely high risk of serious if not deadly injury to the police as well as the potential for the disposal of drugs by the occupants prior to entry by the police." Notwithstanding its acknowledgment that in "some cases, police officers will undoubtedly decide that their safety, the safety of others, and the effective execution of the warrant dictate that they knock and announce," the court concluded that exigent circumstances justifying a no-knock entry are always present in felony drug cases. * * * Accordingly, the court determined that police in Wisconsin do not need specific information about dangerousness, or the possible destruction of drugs in a particular case, in order to dispense with the knock-and-announce requirement in felony drug cases. * * *

We recognized in *Wilson* that the knock-and-announce requirement could give way "under circumstances presenting a threat of physical violence," or "where police officers have reason to believe that evidence would likely be destroyed if advance notice were given." It is indisputable that felony drug investigations may frequently involve both of these circumstances. The question we must resolve is whether this fact justifies dispensing with case-by-case evaluation of the manner in which a search was executed.

The Wisconsin court explained its blanket exception as necessitated by the special circumstances of today's drug culture, and the State asserted at oral argument that the blanket exception was reasonable in "felony drug cases because of the convergence in a violent and dangerous form of commerce of weapons and the destruction of drugs." But creating exceptions to the knock-and-announce rule based on the "culture" surrounding a general category of criminal behavior presents at least two serious concerns.

First, the exception contains considerable overgeneralization. For example, while drug investigation frequently does pose special risks to officer safety and the preservation of evidence, not every drug investigation will pose these risks to a substantial degree. For example, a search could be conducted at a time when the only individuals present in a residence have no connection with the drug activity and thus will be unlikely to threaten officers or destroy evidence. Or the police could know that the drugs being searched for were of a type or in a location that made them impossible to destroy quickly. In those situations, the asserted governmental interests in preserving evidence and maintaining safety may not outweigh the individual privacy interests intruded upon by a no-knock entry. Wisconsin's blanket rule impermissibly insulates these cases from judicial review.

A second difficulty with permitting a criminal-category exception to the knock-and-announce requirement is that the reasons for creating an exception in one category can, relatively easily, be applied to others. Armed bank robbers, for example, are, by definition, likely to have weapons, and the fruits of their crime may be destroyed without too much difficulty. If a per se exception were allowed for each category of criminal investigation that included a considerable—albeit hypothetical—risk of danger to officers or destruction of evidence, the knock-and-announce element of the Fourth Amendment's reasonableness requirement would be meaningless.

Thus, the fact that felony drug investigations may frequently present circumstances warranting a no-knock entry cannot remove from the neutral scrutiny of a reviewing court the reasonableness of the police decision not to knock and announce in a particular case. Instead, in each case, it is the duty of a court confronted with the question to determine whether the facts and circumstances of the particular entry justified dispensing with the knock-and-announce requirement.

In order to justify a "no-knock" entry, the police must have a reasonable suspicion that knocking and announcing their presence, under the particular circumstances, would be dangerous or futile, or that it would inhibit the effective investigation of the crime by, for example, allowing the destruction of evidence. This standard—as opposed to a probable cause requirement—strikes the appropriate balance between the legitimate law enforcement concerns at issue in the execution of search warrants and the individual privacy interests affected by no-knock entries. Cf. *Maryland v. Buie* [fn. b, p. 230]; *Terry v. Ohio* [p. 283]. This showing is not high, but the police should be required to make it whenever the reasonableness of a no-knock entry is challenged.[b]

---

    b   In *United States v. Ramirez*, 523 U.S. 65 (1998), the Court held that whether this reasonable suspicion test has been met "depends in no way on whether police must destroy property in order to enter," and then concluded no Fourth Amendment violation had occurred in the instant case, where police executing a search warrant authorizing entry to seize a wanted person broke a garage window in order to deter the occupants of the premises (who thereafter exited and surrendered) from entering the garage to obtain weapons: "A reliable confidential informant had notified the police that Alan Shelby might be inside respondent's home, and an officer had confirmed this possibility. Shelby was a prison escapee with a violent past who reportedly had access to a large supply of weapons. He had vowed that he would 'not do federal time.' The police certainly had a 'reasonable suspicion' that knocking and announcing their presence might be dangerous to themselves or to others."

    In *Banks*, note a supra, the Court went on to consider the question of what shorter wait will suffice because of what kind of exigent circumstances, deciding that where "the police claim exigent need to enter" and such claim is deemed legitimate under "the same criteria" stated in *Richards*, then the "crucial fact" is "not time to reach the door but the particularly exigency claimed." The risk in *Banks*, re execution of a search warrant at Banks's apartment for cocaine, was that once the police announced their authority and purpose, the defendant would attempt to "flush away the

Although we reject the Wisconsin court's blanket exception to the knock-and-announce requirement, we conclude that the officers' no-knock entry into Richards' hotel room did not violate the Fourth Amendment. We agree with the trial court, and with Justice Abrahamson, that the circumstances in this case show that the officers had a reasonable suspicion that Richards might destroy evidence if given further opportunity to do so.

The judge who heard testimony at Richards' suppression hearing concluded that it was reasonable for the officers executing the warrant to believe that Richards knew, after opening the door to his hotel room the first time, that the men seeking entry to his room were the police. Once the officers reasonably believed that Richards knew who they were, the court concluded, it was reasonable for them to force entry immediately given the disposable nature of the drugs.

In arguing that the officers' entry was unreasonable, Richards places great emphasis on the fact that the magistrate who signed the search warrant for his hotel room deleted the portions of the proposed warrant that would have given the officers permission to execute a no-knock entry. But this fact does not alter the reasonableness of the officers' decision, which must be evaluated as of the time they entered the hotel room. * * *

5. ARREST AND SEARCH OF PERSONS

The Supreme Court has long expressed a strong preference for the use of arrest warrants and search warrants. As the Court has indicated in a host of cases, resort to the warrant process is preferred because it "interposes an orderly procedure" involving "judicial impartiality" whereby "a neutral and detached magistrate" can make "informed and deliberate determinations" on the issue of probable cause. To leave such decisions to the police would allow "hurried actions" by those "engaged in the often competitive enterprise of ferreting out crime." Yet, as the cases in this section and the two following—dealing, respectively, with search of premises and search of vehicles—clearly demonstrate, there are a great many exceptions to the warrant requirement. When the Court approves warrantless activity, it is typically because of a view that the police (1) were acting in exigent circumstances, (2) were intruding upon lesser Fourth Amendment interests, or (3) were otherwise not involved in activity as to which before-the-fact judicial scrutiny would be useful.

The first case in this section, *United States v. Watson*, explains why it is that no warrant is required to make an arrest. The next case, *United States v. Robinson*,

---

easily disposable cocaine," which the Court concluded made it "reasonable to suspect imminent loss of evidence" after the 15–20 second wait. This was because such a lapse of time would suffice "for getting to the bathroom or the kitchen to start flushing cocaine down the drain," considering that "a prudent dealer will keep [the drugs] near a commode or kitchen sink," and also that the warrant was being executed "during the day, when anyone inside would probably have been up and around." The Court added that "since the bathroom and kitchen are usually in the interior of a dwelling, not the front hall, there is no reason generally to peg the travel time to the location of the door, and no reliable basis for giving the proprietor of a mansion a longer wait than the resident of a bungalow, or an apartment like Banks's." Moreover, once "the exigency had matured, * * * the officers were not bound to learn anything more or wait any longer before going in, even though their entry entailed some harm to the building."

addresses warrantless search of the person incident to arrest. *Robinson* gave rise to two significant issues, later addressed in the next two cases, *Whren v. United States* and *Atwater v. City of Lago Vista*, respectively: whether an arrest or other Fourth Amendment seizure made on probable cause may nonetheless be "unreasonable" because of the officer's ulterior motives or his departure from usual practice (e.g., as set out in police regulations); and whether an arrest on probable cause may nonetheless be "unreasonable" because releasing the offender on a citation would have sufficed. *Maryland v. King*, concerns whether taking and analyzing a cheek swab of the arrestee's DNA is a permissible aspect of police booking procedure. The final case in this section, *Mitchell v. Wisconsin*, considers whether blood and breath testing to determine intoxication qualify as searches incident to arrest and, if not, whether they are properly mandated by "implied consent" laws.

UNITED STATES V. WATSON
423 U.S. 411, 96 S.Ct. 820, 46 L.Ed.2d 598 (1976).

JUSTICE WHITE delivered the opinion of the Court.

[Reliable informant Khoury told a federal postal inspector that Watson had supplied him with a stolen credit card and had agreed to furnish additional cards at their next meeting, scheduled for a few days later. At that meeting, which occurred in a restaurant, Khoury signaled the inspector that Watson had the cards, at which point the inspector arrested Watson without a warrant, as he was authorized to do under 18 U.S.C. § 3061 and applicable postal regulations. The court of appeals held the arrest unconstitutional because the inspector had failed to secure an arrest warrant although he concededly had time to do so, and this was a significant factor in the court's additional holding that Watson's consent to a search of his car was not voluntary.]

* * * Section 3061 represents a judgment by Congress that it is not unreasonable under the Fourth Amendment for postal inspectors to arrest without a warrant provided they have probable cause to do so. This was not an isolated or quixotic judgment of the legislative branch. Other federal law enforcement officers have been expressly authorized by statute for many years to make felony arrests on probable cause but without a warrant. * * *

Because there is a "strong presumption of constitutionality due to an Act of Congress, especially when it turns on what is 'reasonable,' * * * [o]bviously the Court should be reluctant to decide that a search thus authorized by Congress was unreasonable and that the Act was therefore unconstitutional." Moreover, there is nothing in the Court's prior cases indicating that under the Fourth Amendment a warrant is required to make a valid arrest for a felony. Indeed, the relevant prior decisions are uniformly to the contrary. * * *

* * * Just last Term, while recognizing that maximum protection of individual rights could be assured by requiring a magistrate's review of the factual justification prior to any arrest, we stated that "such a requirement would constitute an intolerable handicap for legitimate law enforcement" and noted that

the Court "has never invalidated an arrest supported by probable cause solely because the officers failed to secure a warrant." *Gerstein v. Pugh*, 420 U.S. 103 (1975).[a]

The cases construing the Fourth Amendment thus reflect the ancient common-law rule that a peace officer was permitted to arrest without a warrant for a misdemeanor or felony committed in his presence as well as for a felony not

---

[a]   The Supreme Court in *Gerstein* went on to say:

"Under this practical compromise, a policeman's on-the-scene assessment of probable cause provides legal justification for arresting a person suspected of crime, and for a brief period of detention to take the administrative steps incident to arrest. Once the suspect is in custody, however, the reasons that justify dispensing with the magistrate's neutral judgment evaporate. There no longer is any danger that the suspect will escape or commit further crimes while the police submit their evidence to a magistrate. And, while the State's reasons for taking summary action subside, the suspect's need for a neutral determination of probable cause increases significantly. The consequences of prolonged detention may be more serious than the interference occasioned by arrest. Pretrial confinement may imperil the suspect's job, interrupt his source of income, and impair his family relationships. Even pretrial release may be accompanied by burdensome conditions that effect a significant restraint of liberty. When the stakes are this high, the detached judgment of a neutral magistrate is essential if the Fourth Amendment is to furnish meaningful protection from unfounded interference with liberty. Accordingly, we hold that the Fourth Amendment requires a judicial determination of probable cause as a prerequisite to extended restraint of liberty following arrest."

In *County of Riverside v. McLaughlin*, 500 U.S. 44 (1991), the Court, 5–4, concluded "that a jurisdiction that provides judicial determinations of probable cause within 48 hours of arrest will, as a general matter, comply with the promptness requirement of *Gerstein*. For this reason, such jurisdictions will be immune from systematic challenges."

"This is not to say that the probable cause determination in a particular case passes constitutional muster simply because it is provided within 48 hours. Such a hearing may nonetheless violate *Gerstein* if the arrested individual can prove that his or her probable cause determination was delayed unreasonably. Examples of unreasonable delay are delays for the purpose of gathering additional evidence to justify the arrest, a delay motivated by ill will against the arrested individual, or delay for delay's sake. In evaluating whether the delay in a particular case is unreasonable, however, courts must allow a substantial degree of flexibility. Courts cannot ignore the often unavoidable delays in transporting arrested persons from one facility to another, handling late-night bookings where no magistrate is readily available, obtaining the presence of an arresting officer who may be busy processing other suspects or securing the premises of an arrest, and other practical realities.

"Where an arrested individual does not receive a probable cause determination within 48 hours, the calculus changes. In such a case, the arrested individual does not bear the burden of proving an unreasonable delay. Rather, the burden shifts to the government to demonstrate the existence of a bona fide emergency or other extraordinary circumstance. The fact that in a particular case it may take longer than 48 hours to consolidate pretrial proceedings does not qualify as an extraordinary circumstance. Nor, for that matter, do intervening weekends. A jurisdiction that chooses to offer combined proceedings [e.g., incorporating the probable cause determination with arraignment] must do so as soon as is reasonably feasible, but in no event later than 48 hours after arrest."

In *Powell v. Nevada*, 511 U.S. 79 (1994), holding *McLaughlin* retroactive to that case, the Court noted: "It does not necessarily follow, however, that Powell must 'be set free' or gain other relief, for several questions remain open for decision on remand," including "the appropriate remedy for a delay in determining probable cause (an issue not resolved by *McLaughlin*)." In *Powell*, an untimely probable cause determination was made four days after defendant's arrest, shortly after he gave the police an incriminating statement. The Court declared that "whether a suppression remedy applies in that setting remains an unresolved question."

committed in his presence if there was reasonable grounds for making the arrest. This has also been the prevailing rule under state constitutions and statutes. * * *

Because the common-law rule authorizing arrests without warrant generally prevailed in the States, it is important for present purposes to note that in 1792 Congress invested United States Marshals and their deputies with "the same powers in executing the laws of the United States, as sheriffs and their deputies in their several states have by law, in executing the laws of their respective states." The Second Congress thus saw no inconsistency between the Fourth Amendment and giving United States Marshals the same power as local peace officers to arrest for a felony without a warrant. * * *

The balance struck by the common law in generally authorizing felony arrests on probable cause, but without a warrant, has survived substantially intact. It appears in almost all of the States in the form of express statutory authorization. * * *

This is the rule Congress has long directed its principal law enforcement officers to follow. Congress has plainly decided against conditioning warrantless arrest power on proof of exigent circumstances. Law enforcement officers may find it wise to seek arrest warrants where practicable to do so, and their judgments about probable cause may be more readily accepted where backed by a warrant issued by a magistrate. But we decline to transform this judicial preference into a constitutional rule when the judgment of the Nation and Congress has for so long been to authorize warrantless public arrests on probable cause rather than to encumber criminal prosecutions with endless litigation with respect to the existence of exigent circumstances, whether it was practicable to get a warrant, whether the suspect was about to flee, and the like. * * *

Reversed.

JUSTICE STEVENS took no part in the consideration or decision of this case.

JUSTICE POWELL, concurring.

* * * On its face, our decision today creates a certain anomaly. There is no more basic constitutional rule in the Fourth Amendment area than that which makes a warrantless search unreasonable except in a few "jealously and carefully drawn" exceptional circumstances. * * * In short, the course of judicial development of the Fourth Amendment with respect to searches has remained true to the principles so well expressed by Mr. Justice Jackson:

> "Any assumption that evidence sufficient to support a magistrate's disinterested determination to issue a search warrant will justify the officers in making a search without a warrant would reduce the Amendment to a nullity and leave the people's homes secure only in the discretion of police officers. * * * When the right of privacy must reasonably yield to the right of search is, as a rule, to be decided by a judicial officer, not by a policeman or Government enforcement agent."

Since the Fourth Amendment speaks equally to both searches and seizures, and since an arrest, the taking hold of one's person, is quintessentially a seizure, it would seem that the constitutional provision should impose the same limitations upon arrests that it does upon searches. Indeed, as an abstract matter an argument can be made that the restrictions upon arrest perhaps should be greater. A search may cause only annoyance and temporary inconvenience to the law-abiding citizen, assuming more serious dimension only when it turns up evidence of criminality. An arrest, however, is a serious personal intrusion regardless of whether the person seized is guilty or innocent. Although an arrestee cannot be held for a significant period without some neutral determination that there are grounds to do so, no decision that he should go free can come quickly enough to erase the invasion of his privacy that already will have occurred. Logic therefore would seem to dictate that arrests be subject to the warrant requirement at least to the same extent as searches.

But logic sometimes must defer to history and experience. The Court's opinion emphasizes the historical sanction accorded warrantless felony arrests. * * *

The historical momentum for acceptance of warrantless arrests, already strong at the adoption of the Fourth Amendment, has gained strength during the ensuing two centuries. * * * Given the revolutionary implications of such a holding, a declaration at this late date that warrantless felony arrests are constitutionally infirm would have to rest upon reasons more substantial than a desire to harmonize the rules for arrest with those governing searches.

Moreover, a constitutional rule permitting felony arrests only with a warrant or in exigent circumstances could severely hamper effective law enforcement. Good police practice often requires postponing an arrest, even after probable cause has been established, in order to place the suspect under surveillance or otherwise develop further evidence necessary to prove guilt to a jury. Under the holding of the Court of Appeals such additional investigative work could imperil the entire prosecution. Should the officers fail to obtain a warrant initially, and later be required by unforeseen circumstances to arrest immediately with no chance to procure a last-minute warrant, they would risk a court decision that the subsequent exigency did not excuse their failure to get a warrant in the interim since they first developed probable cause. If the officers attempted to meet such a contingency by procuring a warrant as soon as they had probable cause and then merely held it during their subsequent investigation, they would risk a court decision that the warrant had grown stale by the time it was used.[5] Law enforcement personnel caught in this squeeze could ensure validity of their arrests only by obtaining a warrant and arresting as soon as probable cause existed, thereby foreclosing the possibility of gathering vital additional evidence from the suspect's continued actions. * * * [6]

---

[5] The probable cause to support issuance of an arrest warrant normally would not grow stale as easily as that which supports a warrant to search a particular place for particular objects. This is true because once there is probable cause to believe that someone is a felon the passage of time often will bring new supporting evidence. But in some cases the original grounds supporting the warrant could be disproved by subsequent investigation that at the same time turns up wholly new evidence supporting probable cause on a different theory. In those cases the warrant could be stale because based upon discredited information.

[6] Justice Stewart's opinion concurring in the result is omitted.

JUSTICE MARSHALL, with whom JUSTICE BRENNAN joins, dissenting. * * *

The signal of the reliable informant that Watson was in possession of stolen credit cards gave the postal inspectors probable cause to make the arrest. This probable cause was separate and distinct from the probable cause relating to the offense six days earlier, and provided an adequate independent basis for the arrest. Whether or not a warrant ordinarily is required prior to making an arrest, no warrant is required when exigent circumstances are present. When law enforcement officers have probable cause to believe that an offense is taking place in their presence and that the suspect is at that moment in possession of the evidence, exigent circumstances exist. Delay could cause the escape of the suspect or the destruction of the evidence. Accordingly, Watson's warrantless arrest was valid under the recognized exigent circumstances exception to the warrant requirement, and the Court has no occasion to consider whether a warrant would otherwise be necessary. * * *

Since, for reasons it leaves unexpressed, the Court does not take this traditional course, I am constrained to express my views on the issues it unnecessarily decides. The Court reaches its conclusion that a warrant is not necessary for a police officer to make an arrest in a public place, so long as he has probable cause to believe a felony has been committed, on the basis of its views of precedent and history. As my Brother Powell correctly observes, the precedent is spurious. None of the cases cited by the Court squarely confronted the issue decided today. * * *

The Court next turns to history. It relies on the English common-law rule of arrest and the many state and federal statutes following it. There are two serious flaws in this approach. First, as a matter of factual analysis, the substance of the ancient common-law rule provides no support for the far-reaching modern rule that the Court fashions on its model. Second, as a matter of doctrine, the longstanding existence of a Government practice does not immunize the practice from scrutiny under the mandate of our Constitution.

* * * Only the most serious crimes were felonies at common law, and many crimes now classified as felonies under federal or state law were treated as misdemeanors. * * * To make an arrest for any of these crimes at common law, the police officer was required to obtain a warrant, unless the crime was committed in his presence. Since many of these same crimes are commonly classified as felonies today however, under the Court's holding a warrant is no longer needed to make such arrests, a result in contravention of the common law.

* * * As a matter of substance, the balance struck by the common law in accommodating the public need for the most certain and immediate arrest of criminal suspects with the requirement of magisterial oversight to protect against mistaken insults to privacy decreed that only in the most serious of cases could the warrant be dispensed with. This balance is not recognized when the common-law rule is unthinkingly transposed to our present classifications of criminal offenses. Indeed, the only clear lesson of history is contrary to the one the Court draws: the common law considered the arrest warrant far more important than today's decision leaves it.

I do not mean by this that a modern warrant requirement should apply only to arrests precisely analogous to common-law misdemeanors, and be inapplicable to analogues of common-law felonies. Rather, the point is simply that the Court's unblinking literalism cannot replace analysis of the constitutional interests involved. * * *

Lastly, the Court relies on the numerous state and federal statutes codifying the common-law rule. But this, too, is no substitute for reasoned analysis. * * *

The Court has typically engaged in a two-part analysis in deciding whether the presumption favoring a warrant should be given effect in situations where a warrant has not previously been clearly required. Utilizing that approach we must now consider (1) whether the privacy of our citizens will be better protected by ordinarily requiring a warrant to be issued before they may be arrested; and (2) whether a warrant requirement would unduly burden legitimate governmental interests.

The first question is easily answered. Of course the privacy of our citizens will be better protected by a warrant requirement. We have recognized that "the Fourth Amendment protects people, not places." Indeed, the privacy guaranteed by the Fourth Amendment is quintessentially personal. Thus a warrant is required in search situations not because of some high regard for property, but because of our regard for the individual, and *his* interest in his possessions and person. * * *

The Government's assertion that a warrant requirement would impose an intolerable burden stems, in large part, from the specious supposition that procurement of an arrest warrant would be necessary as soon as probable cause ripens. There is no requirement that a search warrant be obtained the moment police have probable cause to search. The rule is only that present probable cause be shown and a warrant obtained before a search is undertaken. The same rule should obtain for arrest warrants, where it may even make more sense. Certainly, there is less need for prompt procurement of a warrant in the arrest situation. Unlike probable cause to search, probable cause to arrest, once formed will continue to exist for the indefinite future, at least if no intervening exculpatory facts come to light.

This sensible approach obviates most of the difficulties that have been suggested with an arrest warrant rule. Police would not have to cut their investigation short the moment they obtain probable cause to arrest, nor would undercover agents be forced suddenly to terminate their work and forfeit their covers. Moreover, if in the course of the continued police investigation exigent circumstances develop that demand an immediate arrest, the arrest may be made without fear of unconstitutionality, so long as the exigency was unanticipated and not used to avoid the arrest warrant requirement. Likewise, if in the course of the continued investigation police uncover evidence tying the suspect to another crime, they may immediately arrest him for that crime if exigency demands it, and still be in full conformity with the warrant rule. This is why the arrest in this case was not improper.[15] Other than where police attempt to evade the warrant requirement, the rule would invalidate an arrest only in the obvious situation: where police, with probable cause but without exigent circumstances, set out to arrest a suspect. Such an arrest must be void, even if exigency develops in the course of the arrest that would ordinarily validate it; otherwise the warrant requirement would be reduced to a toothless prescription. * * *

It is suggested, however, that even if application of this rule does not require police to secure a warrant as soon as they obtain probable cause, the confused officer would nonetheless be prone to do so. If so, police "would risk a court decision that the warrant had grown stale by the time it was used." (Powell, J., concurring). This fear is groundless. First, as suggested above, the requirement that police procure a warrant before an arrest is made is rather simple of application. Thus, there is no need for the police to find themselves in this "squeeze." Second, the "squeeze" is nonexistent. Just as it is virtually impossible for probable cause for an arrest to grow stale between the time of formation and the time a warrant is procured, it is virtually impossible for probable cause to become stale between procurement and arrest. Delay by law enforcement officers in executing an arrest warrant does not ordinarily affect the legality of the arrest. * * *

UNITED STATES V. ROBINSON
414 U.S. 218, 94 S.Ct. 467, 38 L.Ed.2d 427 (1973).

JUSTICE REHNQUIST delivered the opinion of the Court.

Respondent Robinson was convicted in United States District Court for the District of Columbia of the possession and facilitation of concealment of heroin. * * * [T]he Court of Appeals *en banc* reversed the judgment of conviction, holding that the heroin introduced in evidence against respondent had been obtained as a result of a search which violated the Fourth Amendment to the United States Constitution.

On April 23, 1968, at approximately 11 o'clock p.m., Officer Richard Jenks, a 15-year veteran of the District of Columbia Metropolitan Police Department, observed the respondent driving a 1965 Cadillac near the intersection of 8th and C Streets, Southeast, in the District of Columbia. Jenks, as a result of previous investigation following a check of respondent's operator's permit four days earlier, determined there was reason to believe that respondent was operating a motor vehicle after the revocation of his operator's permit. This is an offense defined by statute in the District of Columbia which carries a mandatory minimum jail term, a mandatory minimum fine, or both.

Jenks signaled respondent to stop the automobile, which respondent did, and all three of the occupants emerged from the car. At that point Jenks informed respondent that he was under arrest for "operating after revocation and obtaining a permit by misrepresentation." It was assumed by the majority of the Court of

---

[15] Although the postal inspectors here anticipated the occurrence of the second crime, they could not have obtained a warrant for Watson's arrest for that crime until probable cause formed, just moments before the arrest. A warrant based on anticipated facts is premature and void.

Appeals, and is conceded by the respondent here, that Jenks had probable cause to arrest respondent, and that he effected a full custody arrest.

In accordance with procedures prescribed in Police Department instructions,[2] Jenks then began to search respondent. He explained at a subsequent hearing that he was "face to face" with the respondent, and "placed [his] hands on [the respondent], my right hand to his left breast like this (demonstrating) and proceeded to pat him down thus (with the right hand)." During this patdown, Jenks felt an object in the left breast pocket of the heavy coat respondent was wearing, but testified that he "couldn't tell what it was" and also that he "couldn't actually tell the size of it." Jenks then reached into the pocket and pulled out the object, which turned out to be a "crumpled up cigarette package." Jenks testified that at this point he still did not know what was in the package:

> "As I felt the package I could feel objects in the package but I couldn't tell what they were. * * * I knew they weren't cigarettes."

The officer then opened the cigarette pack and found 14 gelatin capsules of white powder which he thought to be, and which later analysis proved to be, heroin. Jenks then continued his search of respondent to completion, feeling around his waist and trouser legs, and examining the remaining pockets. The heroin seized from the respondent was admitted into evidence at the trial which resulted in his conviction in the District Court. * * *

It is well settled that a search incident to a lawful arrest is a traditional exception to the warrant requirement of the Fourth Amendment. This general exception has historically been formulated into two distinct propositions. The first is that a search may be made of the *person* of the arrestee by virtue of the lawful arrest. The second is that a search may be made of the area within the control of the arrestee.

Examination of this Court's decisions in the area show that these two propositions have been treated quite differently. The validity of the search of a person incident to a lawful arrest has been regarded as settled from its first enunciation, and has remained virtually unchallenged until the present case. The validity of the second proposition, while likewise conceded in principle, has been subject to differing interpretations as to the extent of the area which may be searched. * * *

---

[2] The government introduced testimony at the evidentiary hearing upon the original remand by the Court of Appeals as to certain standard operating procedures of the Metropolitan Police Department. Sergeant Dennis C. Donaldson, a Training Division Instructor, testified that when a police officer makes "a full custody arrest" which he defined as where an officer "would arrest a subject and subsequently transport him to a police facility for booking," the officer is trained to make a full "field type search" * * *. Sergeant Donaldson testified that officers are instructed to examine the "contents of all of the pockets" of the arrestee in the course of the field search. * * * Those regulations also provide that in the case of some traffic offenses, including the crime of operating a motor vehicle after revocation of an operator's permit, the officer shall make a summary arrest of the violator and take the violator, in custody, to the stationhouse for booking. D.C. Metropolitan Police Department General Order No. 3, series 1959 (April 24, 1959). Such operating procedures are not, of course, determinative of the constitutional issues presented by this case.

Throughout the series of cases in which the Court has addressed the second proposition relating to a search incident to a lawful arrest—the permissible area beyond the person of the arrestee which such a search may cover—no doubt has been expressed as to the unqualified authority of the arresting authority to search the person of the arrestee. * * *

Thus the broadly stated rule, and the reasons for it, have been repeatedly affirmed in the decisions of this Court since *Weeks v. United States* nearly 60 years ago. Since the statements in the cases speak not simply in terms of an exception to the warrant requirement, but in terms of an affirmative authority to search, they clearly imply that such searches also meet the Fourth Amendment's requirement of reasonableness. * * *

Virtually all of the statements of this Court affirming the existence of an unqualified authority to search incident to a lawful arrest are dicta. We would not therefore be foreclosed by principles of *stare decisis* from further examination into history and practice in order to see whether the sort of qualifications imposed by the Court of Appeals in this case were in fact intended by the Framers of the Fourth Amendment or recognized in cases decided prior to *Weeks*. Unfortunately such authorities as exist are sparse. * * *

While these earlier authorities are sketchy, they tend to support the broad statement of the authority to search incident to arrest found in the successive decisions of this Court, rather than the restrictive one which was applied by the Court of Appeals in this case. * * *

The justification or reason for the authority to search incident to a lawful arrest rests quite as much on the need to disarm the suspect in order to take him into custody as it does on the need to preserve evidence on his person for later use at trial. The standards traditionally governing a search incident to lawful arrest are not, therefore, commuted to the stricter *Terry* standards[a] by the absence of probable fruits or further evidence of the particular crime for which the arrest is made.

Nor are we inclined, on the basis of what seems to us to be a rather speculative judgment, to qualify the breadth of the general authority to search incident to a lawful custodial arrest on an assumption that persons arrested for the offense of driving while their license has been revoked are less likely to be possessed of dangerous weapons than are those arrested for other crimes.[5] It is scarcely open to

---

[a]   The reference is to *Terry v. Ohio* [p. 283], relied upon here by the Court of Appeals, where the Supreme Court held that on reasonable suspicion (that is, individualized suspicion short of the probable cause needed for arrest) the police may stop a person for investigation. The Court also held that incident to such a stop the police may take limited steps for their own protection: a full incident-to-arrest type search of the person is not permitted, but upon reasonable suspicion that the person is "armed and dangerous" the officer may pat him down and then reach into pockets upon feeling an object which might be a weapon.

[5]   Such an assumption appears at least questionable in light of the available statistical data concerning assaults on police officers who are in the course of making arrests. The danger to the police officer flows from the fact of the arrest, and its attendant proximity, stress and uncertainty, and not from the grounds for arrest. One study concludes that approximately 30% of the shootings of police officers occur when the officer approaches a person seated in a car. Bristow, *Police Officer Shootings—A Tactical Evaluation,* 54 J.Crim.L.C. & P.S. 93 (1963). The Government in its brief

doubt that the danger to an officer is far greater in the case of the extended exposure which follows the taking of a suspect into custody and transporting him to the police station than in the case of the relatively fleeting contact resulting from the typical *Terry*-type stop. This is an adequate basis for treating all custodial arrests alike for purposes of search justification.

But quite apart from these distinctions, our more fundamental disagreement with the Court of Appeals arises from its suggestion that there must be litigated in each case the issue of whether or not there was present one of the reasons supporting the authority for a search of the person incident to a lawful arrest. We do not think the long line of authorities of this Court dating back to *Weeks,* nor what we can glean from the history of practice in this country and in England, requires such a case by case adjudication. A police officer's determination as to how and where to search the person of a suspect whom he has arrested is necessarily a quick *ad hoc* judgment which the Fourth Amendment does not require to be broken down in each instance into an analysis of each step in the search. The authority to search the person incident to a lawful custodial arrest, while based upon the need to disarm and to discover evidence, does not depend on what a court may later decide was the probability in a particular arrest situation that weapons or evidence would in fact be found upon the person of the suspect. A custodial arrest of a suspect based on probable cause is a reasonable intrusion under the Fourth Amendment; that intrusion being lawful, a search incident to the arrest requires no additional justification. It is the fact of the lawful arrest which establishes the authority to search, and we hold that in the case of a lawful custodial arrest a full search[b] of the person is not only an exception to the warrant requirement of the

---

notes that the Uniform Crime Reports, prepared by the Federal Bureau of Investigation, indicate that a significant percentage of police officers murders occur when the officers are making traffic stops. Those reports indicate that during January–March, 1973, 35 police officers were murdered; 11 of those officers were killed while engaged in traffic stops.

[b]   This is not to suggest that any warrantless search of an arrested person may be justified under *Robinson.* In *Schmerber v. California,* 384 U.S. 757 (1966), the Court held that "intrusions into the human body" ordinarily require a warrant, but acknowledged that often exigent circumstances would excuse a warrant before taking a blood sample to determine a DUI suspect's blood-alcohol content.

In *Missouri v. McNeely,* 569 U.S. 141 (2013), the Court "granted certiorari to resolve a split of authority on the question whether the natural dissipation of alcohol in the bloodstream establishes a per se exigency that suffices on its own to justify an exception to the warrant requirement for nonconsensual blood testing in drunk-driving investigations." The majority, per Sotomayor, J., acknowledged "that because an individual's alcohol level gradually declines soon after he stops drinking, a significant delay in testing will negatively affect the probative value of the results," but asserted "it does not follow that we should depart from careful case-by-case assessment of exigency and adopt the categorical rule proposed by the State and its amici. In those drunk-driving investigations where police officers can reasonably obtain a warrant before a blood sample can be drawn without significantly undermining the efficacy of the search, the Fourth Amendment mandates that they do so." Blood testing, the majority asserted, "is different in critical respects from other destruction-of-evidence cases," as the evidence "naturally dissipates over time in a gradual and relatively predictable manner," and "some delay" is "inevitable" in any event because "a police officer must typically transport a drunk-driving suspect to a medical facility and obtain the assistance of someone with appropriate medical training before conducting a blood test." Moreover, there have been "advances in the 47 years since *Schmerber* was decided," as the "Federal Rules of Criminal Procedure [and] well over a majority of States allow police officers or prosecutors to apply for search warrants remotely through various means, including telephonic or radio communication, electronic communication such as e-mail, and video conferencing."

Fourth Amendment, but is also a "reasonable" search under that Amendment.[c]

The search of respondent's person conducted by Officer Jenks in this case and the seizure from him of the heroin, were permissible under established Fourth Amendment law. * * * Since it is the fact of custodial arrest which gives rise to the authority to search, it is of no moment that Jenks did not indicate any subjective fear of the respondent or that he did not himself suspect that respondent was armed.[7] Having in the course of a lawful search come upon the crumpled package of cigarettes, he was entitled to inspect it; and when his inspection revealed the heroin capsules, he was entitled to seize them as "fruits, instrumentalities, or

---

Roberts, C.J., for three Justices, dissenting in part in *McNeely*, objected that a police officer reading the majority opinion "would have no idea—no idea—what the Fourth Amendment requires of him," and then concluded that "the proper rule is straightforward": "The natural dissipation of alcohol in the bloodstream constitutes not only the imminent but ongoing destruction of critical evidence. That would qualify as an exigent circumstance, except that there may be time to secure a warrant before blood can be drawn. If there is, an officer must seek a warrant. If an officer could reasonably conclude that there is not, the exigent circumstances exception applies by its terms, and the blood may be drawn without a warrant." (One member of the majority, Kennedy, J., concurring in part, emphasized that the posture of the case—the state had raised *only* the per se exigency claim—meant the Court had only decided that "always dispensing with a warrant" in these kinds of cases "is inconsistent with the Fourth Amendment," apparently meaning he neither embraced nor rejected the Roberts approach.) Thomas, J., dissenting, who "would hold that a warrantless blood draw does not violate the Fourth Amendment," objected that the majority had adopted "a rule that requires police to guess whether they will be able to obtain a warrant before 'too much' evidence is destroyed, for the police lack reliable information concerning the relevant variables," i.e., "how intoxicated a suspect is at the time of arrest" and "how long it will take to roust a magistrate from his bed, reach the hospital, or obtain a blood sample once there."

[c] Compare the situation where there is a warrantless search of a person without any contemporaneous arrest, confronted by the Court in the pre-*Robinson* case of *Cupp v. Murphy*, 412 U.S. 291 (1973). The Court, per Stewart, J., held that where Murphy voluntarily appeared at the station for questioning concerning the strangulation of his wife, at which time the police noticed what appeared to be blood on his finger, and the police had probable cause to arrest him but did not formally place him under arrest, the warrantless taking of scrapings from his fingernails "was constitutionally permissible." Noting that Murphy was aware of the police suspicion and tried to wipe his fingers clean, the Court concluded that the rationale underlying the search-incident-to-arrest doctrine "justified the police in subjecting him to the very limited search necessary to preserve the highly evanescent evidence they found under his fingernails." But, because a person not under formal arrest "might well be less hostile to the police and less likely to take conspicuous, immediate steps to destroy incriminating evidence on his person," the Court emphasized it was *not* holding "that a full * * * search would have been justified in this case without a formal arrest and without a warrant." Marshall, J., concurring, noted that the police could not have preserved the evidence by "close surveillance" and that detaining Murphy while a warrant was sought "would have been as much a seizure as detaining him while his fingernails were scraped." Douglas, J., dissenting, argued: "There was time to get a warrant; Murphy could have been detained while one was sought; and that detention would have preserved the perishable evidence the police sought."

Murphy was not arrested until over a month later, and thus the case is unlike those in which the arrest followed the search by a matter of minutes. The prevailing view is that a search "incident" to arrest may actually come before the formal making of an arrest if the police had grounds to arrest at the time the search was made. As stated in *Rawlings v. Kentucky,* 448 U.S. 98 (1980): "Where the formal arrest followed quickly on the heels of the challenged search of petitioner's person, we do not believe it particularly important that the search preceded the arrest rather than vice versa."

[7] The United States concedes that "in searching respondent, [Officer Jenks] was not motivated by a feeling of imminent danger and was not specifically looking for weapons." Brief for the United States. Officer Jenks testified, "I just searched him [Robinson]. I didn't think about what I was looking for. I just searched him." Officer Jenks also testified that upon removing the cigarette package from the respondent's custody, he was still unsure what was in the package, but that he knew it was not cigarettes.

contraband" probative of criminal conduct. The judgment of the Court of Appeals holding otherwise is reversed.[d]

Reversed.

JUSTICE MARSHALL, with whom JUSTICE DOUGLAS and JUSTICE BRENNAN join, dissenting.

Certain fundamental principles have characterized this Court's Fourth Amendment jurisprudence over the years. Perhaps the most basic of these was expressed by Justice Butler, speaking for a unanimous Court in *Go-Bart Importing Co. v. United States,* 282 U.S. 344 (1931): "There is no formula for the determination of reasonableness. Each case is to be decided on its own facts and circumstances." * * *

The majority's attempt to avoid case-by-case adjudication of Fourth Amendment issues is not only misguided as a matter of principle, but is also doomed to fail as a matter of practical application. As the majority itself is well aware, the powers granted the police in this case are strong ones, subject to potential abuse. Although, in this particular case, Officer Jenks was required by Police Department regulation to make an in-custody arrest rather than to issue a citation, in most jurisdictions and for most traffic offenses the determination of whether to issue a citation or effect a full arrest is discretionary with the officer. There is always the possibility that a police officer, lacking probable cause to obtain a search warrant, will use a traffic arrest as a pretext to conduct a search. I suggest

---

[d]　Consider also *Illinois v. Lafayette,* 462 U.S. 640 (1983), concerning the basis for search upon the arrestee's arrival at the place of detention:

"The governmental interests underlying a stationhouse search of the arrestee's person and possessions may in some circumstances be even greater than those supporting a search immediately following arrest. Consequently, the scope of a stationhouse search will often vary from that made at the time of arrest. Police conduct that would be impractical or unreasonable—or embarrassingly intrusive—on the street can more readily—and privately—be performed at the station. For example, the interests supporting a search incident to arrest would hardly justify disrobing an arrestee on the street, but the practical necessities of routine jail administration may even justify taking a prisoner's clothes before confining him, although that step would be rare. * * *.

"At the stationhouse, it is entirely proper for police to remove and list or inventory property found on the person or in the possession of an arrested person who is to be jailed. A range of governmental interests support an inventory process. It is not unheard of for persons employed in police activities to steal property taken from arrested persons; similarly, arrested persons have been known to make false claims regarding what was taken from their possession at the stationhouse. A standardized procedure for making a list or inventory as soon as reasonable after reaching the stationhouse not only deters false claims but also inhibits theft or careless handling of articles taken from the arrested person. Arrested persons have also been known to injure themselves—or others—with belts, knives, drugs or other items on their person while being detained. Dangerous instrumentalities—such as razor blades, bombs, or weapons—can be concealed in innocent-looking articles taken from the arrestee's possession. The bare recital of these mundane realities justifies reasonable measures by police to limit these risks—either while the items are in the police possession or at the time they are returned to the arrestee upon his release. Examining all the items removed from the arrestee's person or possession and listing or inventorying them is an entirely reasonable administrative procedure. It is immaterial whether the police actually fear any particular package or container; the need to protect against such risks arises independent of a particular officer's subjective concerns. Finally, inspection of an arrestee's personal property may assist the police in ascertaining or verifying his identity."

this possibility not to impugn the integrity of our police, but merely to point out that case-by-case adjudication will always be necessary to determine whether a full arrest was effected for purely legitimate reasons or, rather, as a pretext for searching the arrestee.

The majority states that "A police officer's determination as to how and where to search the person of a suspect whom he has arrested is necessarily a quick *ad hoc* judgment which the Fourth Amendment does not require to be broken down in each instance into an analysis of each step in the search." No precedent is cited for this broad assertion—not surprisingly, since there is none. Indeed, we only recently rejected such "a rigid all-or-nothing model of justification and regulation under the Amendment, [for] it obscures the utility of limitations upon the scope, as well as the initiation, of police action as a means of constitutional regulation. This Court has held in the past that a search which is reasonable at its inception may violate the Fourth Amendment by virtue of its intolerable intensity and scope." *Terry v. Ohio.* As we there concluded, "in determining whether the seizure and search were 'unreasonable' our inquiry is a dual one—whether the officer's action was justified at its inception, and whether it was reasonably related in scope to the circumstances which justified the interference in the first place."

As I view the matter, the search in this case divides into three distinct phases: the patdown of respondent's coat pocket; the removal of the unknown object from the pocket; and the opening of the crumpled up cigarette package.

No question is raised here concerning the lawfulness of the patdown of respondent's coat pocket. The Court of Appeals unanimously affirmed the right of a police officer to conduct a limited frisk for weapons when making an in-custody arrest, regardless of the nature of the crime for which the arrest was made. As it said,

> "it would seem clearly unreasonable to expect a police officer to place a suspect in his squad car for transportation to the station house without first taking reasonable measures to insure that the suspect is unarmed. We therefore conclude that whenever a police officer, acting within the bounds of his authority, makes an in-custody arrest, he may also conduct a limited *frisk* of the suspect's outer clothing in order to remove any weapons the suspect may have in his possession."

With respect to the removal of the unknown object from the coat pocket, * * * Officer Jenks had no reason to believe and did not in fact believe that the object in respondent's coat pocket was a weapon. He admitted later that the object did not feel like a gun. * * *

Since the removal of the object from the pocket cannot be justified as part of a limited *Terry* weapons frisk, the question arises whether it is reasonable for a police officer, when effecting an in-custody arrest of a traffic offender, to make a fuller search of the person than is permitted pursuant to *Terry.* * * *

The Government does not now contend that the search of respondent's pocket can be justified by any need to find and seize evidence in order to prevent its concealment or destruction, for as the Court of Appeals found, there are no evidence or fruits of the offense with which respondent was charged. The only rationale for a search in this case, then, is the removal of weapons which the arrestee might use to harm the officer and attempt an escape. This rationale, of course, is identical to the rationale of the search permitted in *Terry.* * * *

Since the underlying rationale of a *Terry* search and the search of a traffic violator are identical, the Court of Appeals held that the scope of the searches must be the same. * * *

The problem with this approach, however, is that it ignores several significant differences between the context in which a search incident to arrest for a traffic violation is made, and the situation presented in *Terry.* Some of these differences would appear to suggest permitting a more thorough search in this case than was permitted in *Terry;* other differences suggest a narrower, more limited right to search than was there recognized.

The most obvious difference between the two contexts relates to whether the officer has cause to believe that the individual he is dealing with possesses weapons which might be used against him. *Terry* did not permit an officer to conduct a weapons frisk of anyone he lawfully stopped on the street, but rather, only where "he has reason to believe that he is dealing with an armed and dangerous individual. * * *" While the policeman who arrests a suspected rapist or robber may well have reason to believe he is dealing with an armed and dangerous person, certainly this does not hold true with equal force with respect to persons arrested for motor vehicle violations of the sort involved in this case.

Nor was there any particular reason in this case to believe that respondent was dangerous. He had not attempted to evade arrest, but had quickly complied with the police both in bringing his car to a stop after being signalled to do so and in producing the documents Officer Jenks requested. In fact, Jenks admitted that he searched respondent face-to-face rather than in spread-eagle fashion because he had no reason to believe respondent would be violent.

While this difference between the situation presented in *Terry* and the context presented in this case would tend to suggest a lesser authority to search here than was permitted in *Terry,* other distinctions between the two contexts suggest just the opposite. As the Court of Appeals noted, a crucial feature distinguishing the in-custody arrest from the *Terry* context "is not the greater likelihood that a person taken into custody is armed, but rather the increased likelihood of danger to the officer *if* in fact the person is armed." A *Terry* stop involves a momentary encounter between officer and suspect, while an in-custody arrest places the two in close proximity for a much longer period of time. If the individual happens to have a weapon on his person, he will certainly have much more opportunity to use it against the officer in the in-custody situation. The prolonged proximity also makes it more likely that the individual will be able to extricate any small hidden weapon which might go undetected in a weapons frisk, such as a safety pin or razor blade. In addition, a suspect taken into custody may feel more threatened by the serious restraint on his liberty than a person who is simply stopped by an officer for questioning, and may therefore be more likely to resort to force.

Thus, in some senses there is less need for a weapons search in the in-custody traffic arrest situation than in a *Terry* context, while in other ways, there is a greater need. Balancing these competing considerations in order to determine what is a reasonable warrantless search in the traffic arrest context is a difficult process, one for which there may be no easy analytical guideposts. We are dealing in factors not easily quantified and, therefore, not easily weighed one against the other. And the competing interests we are protecting—the individual's interest in remaining free from unnecessarily intrusive invasions of privacy and society's interest that police officers not take unnecessary risks in the performance of their duties—are each deserving of our most serious attention and do not themselves tip the balance in any particular direction. * * *

The majority relies on statistics indicating that a significant percentage of police officer murders occur when the officers are making traffic stops. But these statistics only confirm what we recognized in *Terry*—that "American criminals have a long tradition of armed violence, and every year in this country many law enforcement officers are killed in the line of duty, and thousands more are wounded." As the very next sentence in *Terry* recognized, however, "Virtually all of these deaths and a substantial portion of the injuries are inflicted with guns and knives." The statistics relied on by the Government in this case support this observation. Virtually all of the killings are caused by guns and knives, the very type of weapons which will not go undetected in a properly conducted weapons frisk.[5] * * *

The majority opinion fails to recognize that the search conducted by Officer Jenks did not merely involve a search of respondent's person. It also included a separate search of effects found on his person. And even were we to assume, *arguendo,* that it was reasonable for Jenks to remove the object he felt in respondent's pocket, clearly there was no justification consistent with the Fourth Amendment which would authorize his opening the package and looking inside.

To begin with, after Jenks had the cigarette package in his hands, there is no indication that he had reason to believe or did in fact believe that the package contained a weapon. More importantly, even if the crumpled up cigarette package had in fact contained some sort of small weapon, it would have been impossible for respondent to have used it once the package was in the officer's hands. Opening the package therefore did not further the protective purpose of the search. * * *

The Government argues that it is difficult to see what constitutionally protected "expectation of privacy" a prisoner has in the interior of a cigarette pack. One wonders if the result in this case would have been the same were respondent a businessman who was lawfully taken into custody for driving without a license and whose wallet was taken from him by the police. Would it be reasonable for the police officer, because of the possibility that a razor blade was hidden somewhere in the wallet, to open it, remove all the contents, and examine each item carefully?

---

[5]   The Uniform Crime Reports prepared by the Federal Bureau of Investigation which are relied on by the majority, see n. 5, indicate that 112 police officers were killed nationwide in 1972. Of these, 108 were killed by firearms. Two of the remaining four were killed with knives, and the last two cases involved a bomb and an automobile.

Or suppose a lawyer lawfully arrested for a traffic offense is found to have a sealed envelope on his person. Would it be permissible for the arresting officer to tear open the envelope in order to make sure that it did not contain a clandestine weapon—perhaps a pin or a razor blade? Would it not be more consonant with the purpose of the Fourth Amendment and the legitimate needs of the police to require the officer, if he has any question whatsoever about what the wallet or letter contains, to hold onto it until the arrestee is brought to the precinct station?

I, for one, cannot characterize any of these intrusions into the privacy of an individual's papers and effects as being negligible incidents to the more serious intrusion into the individual's privacy stemming from the arrest itself. Nor can any principled distinction be drawn between the hypothetical searches I have posed and the search of the cigarette package in this case. The only reasoned distinction is between warrantless searches which serve legitimate protective and evidentiary functions and those that do not.[e]

WHREN V. UNITED STATES
517 U.S. 806, 116 S.Ct. 1769, 135 L.Ed.2d 89 (1996).

JUSTICE SCALIA delivered the opinion of the Court. * * *

On the evening of June 10, 1993, plainclothes vice-squad officers of the District of Columbia Metropolitan Police Department were patrolling a "high drug area" of the city in an unmarked car. Their suspicions were aroused when they passed a dark Pathfinder truck with temporary license plates and youthful occupants waiting at a stop sign, the driver looking down into the lap of the passenger at his right. The truck remained stopped at the intersection for what seemed an unusually long time—more than 20 seconds. When the police car executed a U-turn in order to head back toward the truck, the Pathfinder turned suddenly to its right, without signalling, and sped off at an "unreasonable" speed. The policemen followed, and in a short while overtook the Pathfinder when it stopped behind other traffic at a red light. They pulled up alongside, and Officer Ephraim Soto stepped out and approached the driver's door, identifying himself as

---

e   In the companion case of *Gustafson v. Florida,* 414 U.S. 260 (1973), petitioner was arrested for failure to have an operator's license after the car he was driving was observed weaving across the center line several times, and was then searched, resulting in the discovery of a cigarette box within which the arresting officer found marijuana cigarettes. Petitioner contended his case was different from *Robinson* in that (a) he had experienced no previous encounters with the officer; (b) the offense for which he was arrested was "benign or trivial in nature," carrying with it no mandatory minimum sentence; and (c) there were no police regulations which required the officer to take petitioner into custody or which required full scale body searches upon arrest in the field. The Court, per Rehnquist, J., did "not find these differences determinative of the constitutional issue," and thus upheld the search on the basis of *Robinson.*

Marshall, Douglas, and Brennan, JJ., dissented for the reasons stated in *Robinson.* Stewart, J., concurring, noted "that a persuasive claim might have been made in this case that the custodial arrest of the petitioner for a minor traffic offense violated his rights under the Fourth and Fourteenth Amendments," but since petitioner had "fully conceded the constitutional validity of his custodial arrest," the search of his person should be accepted as incidental to that arrest. Powell, J., concurring in both cases, emphasized that for him the "essential premise" of both decisions was "that an individual lawfully subjected to a custodial arrest retains no significant Fourth Amendment interest in the privacy of his person."

a police officer and directing the driver, petitioner Brown, to put the vehicle in park. When Soto drew up to the driver's window, he immediately observed two large plastic bags of what appeared to be crack cocaine in petitioner Whren's hands. Petitioners were arrested, and quantities of several types of illegal drugs were retrieved from the vehicle.

Petitioners were charged in a four-count indictment with violating various federal drug laws. At a pretrial suppression hearing, they challenged the legality of the stop and the resulting seizure of the drugs. They argued that the stop had not been justified by probable cause to believe, or even reasonable suspicion, that petitioners were engaged in illegal drug-dealing activity; and that Officer Soto's asserted ground for approaching the vehicle—to give the driver a warning concerning traffic violations—was pretextual. The District Court denied the suppression motion * * *.

Petitioners were convicted of the counts at issue here. The Court of Appeals affirmed the convictions, holding with respect to the suppression issue that, "regardless of whether a police officer subjectively believes that the occupants of an automobile may be engaging in some other illegal behavior, a traffic stop is permissible as long as a reasonable officer in the same circumstances could have stopped the car for the suspected traffic violation."

The Fourth Amendment guarantees "[t]he right of the people to be secure in their persons, houses, papers, and effects, against unreasonable searches and seizures." Temporary detention of individuals during the stop of an automobile by the police, even if only for a brief period and for a limited purpose, constitutes a "seizure" of "persons" within the meaning of this provision. An automobile stop is thus subject to the constitutional imperative that it not be "unreasonable" under the circumstances. As a general matter, the decision to stop an automobile is reasonable where the police have probable cause to believe that a traffic violation has occurred.

Petitioners accept that Officer Soto had probable cause to believe that various provisions of the District of Columbia traffic code [regarding inattentive driving, speeding, and turning without signalling] had been violated. They argue, however, that "in the unique context of civil traffic regulations" probable cause is not enough. Since, they contend, the use of automobiles is so heavily and minutely regulated that total compliance with traffic and safety rules is nearly impossible, a police officer will almost invariably be able to catch any given motorist in a technical violation. This creates the temptation to use traffic stops as a means of investigating other law violations, as to which no probable cause or even articulable suspicion exists. Petitioners, who are both black, further contend that police officers might decide which motorists to stop based on decidedly impermissible factors, such as the race of the car's occupants. To avoid this danger, they say, the Fourth Amendment test for traffic stops should be, not the normal one (applied by the Court of Appeals) of whether probable cause existed to justify the stop; but rather, whether a police officer, acting reasonably, would have made the stop for the reason given.

Petitioners contend that the standard they propose is consistent with our past cases' disapproval of police attempts to use valid bases of action against citizens as pretexts for pursuing other investigatory agendas. We are reminded that in *Florida v. Wells*, [fn. a, p. 273], we stated that "an inventory search must not be used as a ruse for a general rummaging in order to discover incriminating evidence"; that in *Colorado v. Bertine*, [p. 270], in approving an inventory search, we apparently thought it significant that there had been "no showing that the police, who were following standard procedures, acted in bad faith or for the sole purpose of investigation"; and that in *New York v. Burger*, 482 U.S. 691 (1987), we observed, in upholding the constitutionality of a warrantless administrative inspection, that the search did not appear to be "a 'pretext' for obtaining evidence of . . . violation of . . . penal laws." But only an undiscerning reader would regard these cases as endorsing the principle that ulterior motives can invalidate police conduct that is justifiable on the basis of probable cause to believe that a violation of law has occurred. In each case we were addressing the validity of a search conducted in the absence of probable cause. Our quoted statements simply explain that the exemption from the need for probable cause (and warrant), which is accorded to searches made for the purpose of inventory or administrative regulation, is not accorded to searches that are not made for those purposes.[a]

* * * Not only have we never held, outside the context of inventory search or administrative inspection (discussed above), that an officer's motive invalidates objectively justifiable behavior under the Fourth Amendment; but we have repeatedly held and asserted the contrary. In *United States v. Villamonte-Marquez*, 462 U.S. 579 (1983), we held that an otherwise valid warrantless boarding of a vessel by customs officials was not rendered invalid "because the customs officers were accompanied by a Louisiana state policeman, and were following an informant's tip that a vessel in the ship channel was thought to be carrying marihuana." We flatly dismissed the idea that an ulterior motive might serve to strip the agents of their legal justification. In *United States v. Robinson*, [p. 182],

---

[a]   This paragraph in *Whren* was the focus of attention when that case was revisited in *Ashcroft v. al-Kidd*, 563 U.S. 731 (2011), involving a *Bivens* action brought by al-Kidd alleging his Fourth Amendment rights were violated by a pretextual detention policy whereby, after 9/11, then Attorney General Ashcroft authorized federal officials to use the federal material witness law, 18 U.S.C.A. § 3144, to detain terrorist suspects. While all eight participating Justices agreed that Ashcroft was entitled to qualified immunity because the purported right to nonpretextual application of the statute was not "clearly established" at the time of the challenged conduct, the 5-Justice majority then appeared to address the merits of the Fourth Amendment claim. As for al-Kidd's claim "that *Whren* establishes that we ignore subjective intent only when there exists 'probable cause to believe that a violation of law has occurred,' " the Court responded that the reference to probable cause in *Whren* merely reflected "that was the legitimating factor in the case at hand," and that "the opinion swept broadly to reject inquiries into motive generally." Characterizing the instant case as one involving "a validly obtained warrant" which was "based on individualized suspicion" (purportedly conceded by al-Kidd), it was thus deemed to be outside the "two limited exception[s]" to *Whren*, i.e., "special-needs and administrative-search cases"; that is, "subjective intent" can come into play only in the case of warrantless action not based upon individualized suspicion.

The other three Justices, concurring in the judgment, objected (1) "to the Court's disposition of al-Kidd's Fourth Amendment claim on the merits"; and (2) that *Whren* did not settle "whether an official's subjective intent matters" in the "novel context" of the instant case, involving "prolonged detention of an individual without probable cause to believe he had committed any criminal offense."

we held that a traffic-violation arrest (of the sort here) would not be rendered invalid by the fact that it was "a mere pretext for a narcotics search," and that a lawful postarrest search of the person would not be rendered invalid by the fact that it was not motivated by the officer-safety concern that justifies such searches. And in *Scott v. United States*, 436 U.S. 128 (1978), in rejecting the contention that wiretap evidence was subject to exclusion because the agents conducting the tap had failed to make any effort to comply with the statutory requirement that unauthorized acquisitions be minimized, we said that "[s]ubjective intent alone . . . does not make otherwise lawful conduct illegal or unconstitutional." We described *Robinson* as having established that "the fact that the officer does not have the state of mind which is hypothecated by the reasons which provide the legal justification for the officer's action does not invalidate the action taken as long as the circumstances, viewed objectively, justify that action."

We think these cases foreclose any argument that the constitutional reasonableness of traffic stops depends on the actual motivations of the individual officers involved. We of course agree with petitioners that the Constitution prohibits selective enforcement of the law based on considerations such as race. But the constitutional basis for objecting to intentionally discriminatory application of laws is the Equal Protection Clause, not the Fourth Amendment. Subjective intentions play no role in ordinary, probable-cause Fourth Amendment analysis.

Recognizing that we have been unwilling to entertain Fourth Amendment challenges based on the actual motivations of individual officers, petitioners disavow any intention to make the individual officer's subjective good faith the touchstone of "reasonableness." They insist that the standard they have put forward—whether the officer's conduct deviated materially from usual police practices, so that a reasonable officer in the same circumstances would not have made the stop for the reasons given—is an "objective" one.

But although framed in empirical terms, this approach is plainly and indisputably driven by subjective considerations. Its whole purpose is to prevent the police from doing under the guise of enforcing the traffic code what they would like to do for different reasons. Petitioners' proposed standard may not use the word "pretext," but it is designed to combat nothing other than the perceived "danger" of the pretextual stop, albeit only indirectly and over the run of cases. Instead of asking whether the individual officer had the proper state of mind, the petitioners would have us ask, in effect, whether (based on general police practices) it is plausible to believe that the officer had the proper state of mind.

Why one would frame a test designed to combat pretext in such fashion that the court cannot take into account actual and admitted pretext is a curiosity that can only be explained by the fact that our cases have foreclosed the more sensible option. If those cases were based only upon the evidentiary difficulty of establishing subjective intent, petitioners' attempt to root out subjective vices through objective means might make sense. But they were not based only upon that, or indeed even principally upon that. Their principal basis—which applies equally to attempts to reach subjective intent through ostensibly objective means—is simply that the

Fourth Amendment's concern with "reasonableness" allows certain actions to be taken in certain circumstances, whatever the subjective intent. See, e.g., *Robinson*, supra ("Since it is the fact of custodial arrest which gives rise to the authority to search, it is of no moment that [the officer] did not indicate any subjective fear of the [arrestee] or that he did not himself suspect that [the arrestee] was armed"). But even if our concern had been only an evidentiary one, petitioners' proposal would by no means assuage it. Indeed, it seems to us somewhat easier to figure out the intent of an individual officer than to plumb the collective consciousness of law enforcement in order to determine whether a "reasonable officer" would have been moved to act upon the traffic violation. While police manuals and standard procedures may sometimes provide objective assistance, ordinarily one would be reduced to speculating about the hypothetical reaction of a hypothetical constable—an exercise that might be called virtual subjectivity.

Moreover, police enforcement practices, even if they could be practicably assessed by a judge, vary from place to place and from time to time. We cannot accept that the search and seizure protections of the Fourth Amendment are so variable, and can be made to turn upon such trivialities. The difficulty is illustrated by petitioners' arguments in this case. Their claim that a reasonable officer would not have made this stop is based largely on District of Columbia police regulations which permit plainclothes officers in unmarked vehicles to enforce traffic laws "only in the case of a violation that is so grave as to pose an immediate threat to the safety of others." This basis of invalidation would not apply in jurisdictions that had a different practice. And it would not have applied even in the District of Columbia, if Officer Soto had been wearing a uniform or patrolling in a marked police cruiser.

Petitioners argue that our cases support insistence upon police adherence to standard practices as an objective means of rooting out pretext. They cite no holding to that effect, and dicta in only two cases. In *Abel v. United States*, 362 U.S. 217 (1960), the petitioner had been arrested by the Immigration and Naturalization Service (INS), on the basis of an administrative warrant that, he claimed, had been issued on pretextual grounds in order to enable the Federal Bureau of Investigation (FBI) to search his room after his arrest. We regarded this as an allegation of "serious misconduct," but rejected Abel's claims on the ground that "[a] finding of bad faith is . . . not open to us on th[e] record" in light of the findings below, including the finding that " 'the proceedings taken by the [INS] differed in no respect from what would have been done in the case of an individual concerning whom [there was no pending FBI investigation].' " But it is a long leap from the proposition that following regular procedures is some evidence of lack of pretext to the proposition that failure to follow regular procedures proves (or is an operational substitute for) pretext. *Abel*, moreover, did not involve the assertion that pretext could invalidate a search or seizure for which there was probable cause—and even what it said about pretext in other contexts is plainly inconsistent with the views we later stated in [the cases summarized above]. In the other case claimed to contain supportive dicta, *United States v. Robinson*, in approving a search incident to an arrest for driving without a license, we noted that the arrest was "not a departure from established police department practice." That was followed, however, by the statement that "[w]e leave for another day questions which would arise on facts different from these." This is not even a dictum that purports to provide an answer, but merely one that leaves the question open.

In what would appear to be an elaboration on the "reasonable officer" test, petitioners argue that the balancing inherent in any Fourth Amendment inquiry requires us to weigh the governmental and individual interests implicated in a traffic stop such as we have here. That balancing, petitioners claim, does not support investigation of minor traffic infractions by plainclothes police in unmarked vehicles; such investigation only minimally advances the government's interest in traffic safety, and may indeed retard it by producing motorist confusion and alarm—a view said to be supported by the Metropolitan Police Department's own regulations generally prohibiting this practice. And as for the Fourth Amendment interests of the individuals concerned, petitioners point out that our cases acknowledge that even ordinary traffic stops entail "a possibly unsettling show of authority"; that they at best "interfere with freedom of movement, are inconvenient, and consume time" and at worst "may create substantial anxiety." That anxiety is likely to be even more pronounced when the stop is conducted by plainclothes officers in unmarked cars.

It is of course true that in principle every Fourth Amendment case, since it turns upon a "reasonableness" determination, involves a balancing of all relevant factors. With rare exceptions not applicable here, however, the result of that balancing is not in doubt where the search or seizure is based upon probable cause. That is why petitioners must rely upon cases like *Prouse* to provide examples of actual "balancing" analysis. There, the police action in question was a random traffic stop for the purpose of checking a motorist's license and vehicle registration, a practice that—like the practices at issue in the inventory search and administrative inspection cases upon which petitioners rely in making their "pretext" claim—involves police intrusion without the probable cause that is its traditional justification. Our opinion in *Prouse* expressly distinguished the case from a stop based on precisely what is at issue here: "probable cause to believe that a driver is violating any one of the multitude of applicable traffic and equipment regulations." It noted approvingly that "[t]he foremost method of enforcing traffic and vehicle safety regulations . . . is acting upon observed violations," which afford the " 'quantum of individualized suspicion' " necessary to ensure that police discretion is sufficiently constrained. What is true of *Prouse* is also true of other cases that engaged in detailed "balancing" to decide the constitutionality of automobile stops: the detailed "balancing" analysis was necessary because they involved seizures without probable cause.

Where probable cause has existed, the only cases in which we have found it necessary actually to perform the "balancing" analysis involved searches or seizures conducted in an extraordinary manner, unusually harmful to an individual's privacy or even physical interests—such as, for example, seizure by means of deadly force, see *Tennessee v. Garner*, 475 U.S. 1 (1985), unannounced entry into a home, see *Wilson v. Arkansas*, [p. 172], entry into a home without a warrant, see *Welsh v. Wisconsin*, 466 U.S. 740 (1984), or physical penetration of the body, see *Winston v. Lee*, 470 U.S. 753 (1985). The making of a traffic stop out-of-uniform does not remotely qualify as such an extreme practice, and so is governed by the usual rule that probable cause to believe the law has been broken "outbalances" private interest in avoiding police contact.

Petitioners urge as an extraordinary factor in this case that the "multitude of applicable traffic and equipment regulations" is so large and so difficult to obey perfectly that virtually everyone is guilty of violation, permitting the police to single out almost whomever they wish for a stop. But we are aware of no principle that would allow us to decide at what point a code of law becomes so expansive and so commonly violated that infraction itself can no longer be the ordinary measure of the lawfulness of enforcement. And even if we could identify such exorbitant codes, we do not know by what standard (or what right) we would decide, as petitioners would have us do, which particular provisions are sufficiently important to merit enforcement.

For the run-of-the-mine case, which this surely is, we think there is no realistic alternative to the traditional common-law rule that probable cause justifies a search and seizure.

* * *

Here the District Court found that the officers had probable cause to believe that petitioners had violated the traffic code. That rendered the stop reasonable under the Fourth Amendment, the evidence thereby discovered admissible, and the upholding of the convictions by the Court of Appeals for the District of Columbia Circuit correct.

Judgment affirmed.[b]

ATWATER V. CITY OF LAGO VISTA
532 U.S. 318, 121 S.Ct. 1536, 149 L.Ed.2d 549 (2001).

JUSTICE SOUTER delivered the opinion of the Court.

The question is whether the Fourth Amendment forbids a warrantless arrest for a minor criminal offense, such as a misdemeanor seatbelt violation punishable only by a fine. We hold that it does not.

In Texas, if a car is equipped with safety belts, a front-seat passenger must wear one, and the driver must secure any small child riding in front. Violation of either provision is "a misdemeanor punishable by a fine not less than $25 or more than $50." Texas law expressly authorizes "[a]ny peace officer [to] arrest without warrant a person found committing a violation" of these seatbelt laws, although it permits police to issue citations in lieu of arrest.

In March 1997, Petitioner Gail Atwater was driving her pickup truck in Lago Vista, Texas, with her 3-year-old son and 5-year-old daughter in the front seat. None of them was wearing a seatbelt. Respondent Bart Turek, a Lago Vista police officer at the time, observed the seatbelt violations and pulled Atwater over.

---

b   Although *Whren* involved a traffic stop, it was assumed to apply to custodial arrests as well, as the Court later confirmed in *Arkansas v. Sullivan*, 532 U.S. 769 (2001).

According to Atwater's complaint (the allegations of which we assume to be true for present purposes), Turek approached the truck and "yell[ed]" something to the effect of "[w]e've met before" and "[y]ou're going to jail."[1] He then called for backup and asked to see Atwater's driver's license and insurance documentation, which state law required her to carry. When Atwater told Turek that she did not have the papers because her purse had been stolen the day before, Turek said that he had "heard that story two-hundred times."

Atwater asked to take her "frightened, upset, and crying" children to a friend's house nearby, but Turek told her, "[y]ou're not going anywhere." As it turned out, Atwater's friend learned what was going on and soon arrived to take charge of the children. Turek then handcuffed Atwater, placed her in his squad car, and drove her to the local police station, where booking officers had her remove her shoes, jewelry, and eyeglasses, and empty her pockets. Officers took Atwater's "mug shot" and placed her, alone, in a jail cell for about one hour, after which she was taken before a magistrate and released on $310 bond.

Atwater was charged with driving without her seatbelt fastened, failing to secure her children in seatbelts, driving without a license, and failing to provide proof of insurance. She ultimately pleaded no contest to the misdemeanor seatbelt offenses and paid a $50 fine; the other charges were dismissed.

[Atwater filed suit in a Texas state court under 42 U.S.C. § 1983 against Turek, the police chief and the city; the city removed to federal district court, which granted the city's summary judgment motion. A panel of the court of appeals reversed, but the court of appeals sitting en banc vacated the panel's decision and affirmed the district court.]

We granted certiorari to consider whether the Fourth Amendment, either by incorporating common-law restrictions on misdemeanor arrests or otherwise, limits police officers' authority to arrest without warrant for minor criminal offenses. We now affirm.

The Fourth Amendment safeguards "[t]he right of the people to be secure in their persons, houses, papers, and effects, against unreasonable searches and seizures." In reading the Amendment, we are guided by "the traditional protections against unreasonable searches and seizures afforded by the common law at the time of the framing," since "[a]n examination of the common-law understanding of an officer's authority to arrest sheds light on the obviously relevant, if not entirely dispositive, consideration of what the Framers of the Amendment might have thought to be reasonable." Thus, the first step here is to assess Atwater's claim that peace officers' authority to make warrantless arrests for misdemeanors was restricted at common law ("common law" is understood strictly as law judicially derived or, instead, as the whole body of law extant at the time of the framing). Atwater's specific contention is that "founding-era common-law rules" forbade peace officers to make warrantless misdemeanor arrests except in cases of "breach

---

[1]   Turek had previously stopped Atwater for what he had thought was a seatbelt violation, but had realized that Atwater's son, although seated on the vehicle's armrest, was in fact belted in. Atwater acknowledged that her son's seating position was unsafe, and Turek issued a verbal warning.

of the peace," a category she claims was then understood narrowly as covering only those nonfelony offenses "involving or tending toward violence." Although her historical argument is by no means insubstantial, it ultimately fails.

We begin with the state of pre-founding English common law and find that, even after making some allowance for variations in the common-law usage of the term "breach of the peace," the "founding-era common-law" were not nearly as clear as Atwater claims; on the contrary, the common-law commentators (as well as the sparsely reported cases) reached divergent conclusions with respect to officer' warrantless misdemeanor arrest power. Moreover, in the years leading up to American independence, Parliament repeatedly extended express warrantless arrest authority to cover misdemeanor-level offenses not amounting to or involving any violent breach of the peace. * * *

Nor does Atwater's argument from tradition pick up any steam from the historical record as it has unfolded since the framing, there being no indication that her claimed rule has ever become "woven . . . into the fabric" of American law. The story, on the contrary, is of two centuries of uninterrupted (and largely unchallenged) state and federal practice permitting warrantless arrests for misdemeanors not amounting to or involving breach of the peace.

* * * Although the Court has not had much to say about warrantless misdemeanor arrest authority, what little we have said tends to cut against Atwater's argument. In discussing this authority, we have focused on the circumstance that an offense was committed in an officer's presence, to the omission of any reference to a breach-of-the-peace limitation.[11] * * *

While it is true here that history, if not unequivocal, has expressed a decided, majority view that the police need not obtain an arrest warrant merely because a misdemeanor stopped short of violence or a threat of it, Atwater does not wager all on history. Instead, she asks us to mint a new rule of constitutional law on the understanding that when historical practice fails to speak conclusively to a claim grounded on the Fourth Amendment, courts are left to strike a current balance between individual and societal interests by subjecting particular contemporary circumstances to traditional standards of reasonableness. Atwater accordingly argues for a modern arrest rule, one not necessarily requiring violent breach of the peace, but nonetheless forbidding custodial arrest, even upon probable cause, when conviction could not ultimately carry any jail time and when the government shows no compelling need for immediate detention.

If we were to derive a rule exclusively to address the uncontested facts of this case, Atwater might well prevail. She was a known and established resident of Lago Vista with no place to hide and no incentive to flee, and common sense says she would almost certainly have buckled up as a condition of driving off with a citation. In her case, the physical incidents of arrest were merely gratuitous humiliations imposed by a police officer who was (at best) exercising extremely poor

---

[11] We need not, and thus do not, speculate whether the Fourth Amendment entails an "in the presence" requirement for purposes of misdemeanor arrests. Cf. *Welsh v. Wisconsin*, 466 U.S. 740 (1984) (White, J., dissenting) ("[T]he requirement that a misdemeanor must have occurred in the officer's presence to justify a warrantless arrest is not grounded in the Fourth Amendment").

judgment. Atwater's claim to live free of pointless indignity and confinement clearly outweighs anything the City can raise against it specific to her case.

But we have traditionally recognized that a responsible Fourth Amendment balance is not well served by standards requiring sensitive, case-by-case determinations of government need, lest every discretionary judgment in the field be converted into an occasion for constitutional review. See, e.g., *United States v. Robinson*, [Ch. 3, § 5]. Often enough, the Fourth Amendment has to be applied on the spur (and in the heat) of the moment, and the object in implementing its command of reasonableness is to draw standards sufficiently clear and simple to be applied with a fair prospect of surviving judicial second-guessing months and years after an arrest or search is made. Courts attempting to strike a reasonable Fourth Amendment balance thus credit the government's side with an essential interest in readily administrable rules.

At first glance, Atwater's argument may seem to respect the values of clarity and simplicity, so far as she claims that the Fourth Amendment generally forbids warrantless arrests for minor crimes not accompanied by violence or some demonstrable threat of it (whether "minor crime" be defined as a fine-only traffic offense, a fine-only offense more generally, or a misdemeanor). But the claim is not ultimately so simple, nor could it be, for complications arise the moment we begin to think about the possible applications of the several criteria Atwater proposes for drawing a line between minor crimes with limited arrest authority and others not so restricted.

One line, she suggests, might be between "jailable" and "fine-only" offenses, between those for which conviction could result in commitment and those for which it could not. The trouble with this distinction, of course, is that an officer on the street might not be able to tell. It is not merely that we cannot expect every police officer to know the details of frequently complex penalty schemes, but that penalties for ostensibly identical conduct can vary on account of facts difficult (if not impossible) to know at the scene of an arrest. Is this the first offense or is the suspect a repeat offender? Is the weight of the marijuana a gram above or a gram below the fine-only line? Where conduct could implicate more than one criminal prohibition, which one will the district attorney ultimately decide to charge? And so on.

But Atwater's refinements would not end there. She represents that if the line were drawn at nonjailable traffic offenses, her proposed limitation should be qualified by a proviso authorizing warrantless arrests where "necessary for enforcement of the traffic laws or when [an] offense would otherwise continue and pose a danger to others on the road." (Were the line drawn at misdemeanors generally, a comparable qualification would presumably apply.) The proviso only compounds the difficulties. Would, for instance, either exception apply to speeding? * * *

There is no need for more examples to show that Atwater's general rule and limiting proviso promise very little in the way of administrability. It is no answer that the police routinely make judgments on grounds like risk of immediate repetition; they surely do and should. But there is a world of difference between making that judgment in choosing between the discretionary leniency of a summons in place of a clearly lawful arrest, and making the same judgment when the question is the lawfulness of the warrantless arrest itself. It is the difference between no basis for legal action challenging the discretionary judgment, on the one hand, and the prospect of evidentiary exclusion or (as here) personal § 1983 liability for the misapplication of a constitutional standard, on the other. Atwater's rule therefore would not only place police in an almost impossible spot but would guarantee increased litigation over many of the arrests that would occur. * * *

One may ask, of course, why these difficulties may not be answered by a simple tie breaker for the police to follow in the field: if in doubt, do not arrest. The first answer is that in practice the tie breaker would boil down to something akin to a least-restrictive-alternative limitation, which is itself one of those "ifs, ands, and buts" rules, generally thought inappropriate in working out Fourth Amendment protection. Beyond that, whatever help the tie breaker might give would come at the price of a systematic disincentive to arrest in situations where even Atwater concedes that arresting would serve an important societal interest. An officer not quite sure that the drugs weighed enough to warrant jail time or not quite certain about a suspect's risk of flight would not arrest, even though it could perfectly well turn out that, in fact, the offense called for incarceration and the defendant was long gone on the day of trial. Multiplied many times over, the costs to society of such underenforcement could easily outweigh the costs to defendants of being needlessly arrested and booked, as Atwater herself acknowledges.

Just how easily the costs could outweigh the benefits may be shown by asking, as one Member of this Court did at oral argument, "how bad the problem is out there." The very fact that the law has never jelled the way Atwater would have it leads one to wonder whether warrantless misdemeanor arrests need constitutional attention, and there is cause to think the answer is no. So far as such arrests might be thought to pose a threat to the probable-cause requirement, anyone arrested for a crime without formal process, whether for felony or misdemeanor, is entitled to a magistrate's review of probable cause within 48 hours, and there is no reason to think the procedure in this case atypical in giving the suspect a prompt opportunity to request release. Many jurisdictions, moreover, have chosen to impose more restrictive safeguards through statutes limiting warrantless arrests for minor offenses. It is of course easier to devise a minor-offense limitation by statute than to derive one through the Constitution, simply because the statute can let the arrest power turn on any sort of practical consideration without having to subsume it under a broader principle. It is, in fact, only natural that States should resort to this sort of legislative regulation, for * * * it is in the interest of the police to limit petty-offense arrests, which carry costs that are simply too great to incur without good reason. Finally, and significantly, under current doctrine the preference for categorical treatment of Fourth Amendment claims gives way to individualized review when a defendant makes a colorable argument that an arrest, with or without a warrant, was "conducted in an extraordinary manner, unusually harmful to [his] privacy or even physical interests." *Whren v. United States*, [p. 191].

The upshot of all these influences, combined with the good sense (and, failing that, the political accountability) of most local lawmakers and law-enforcement officials, is a dearth of horribles demanding redress. Indeed, when Atwater's counsel was asked at oral argument for any indications of comparably foolish, warrantless misdemeanor arrests, he could offer only one. We are sure that there are others, but just as surely the country is not confronting anything like an epidemic of unnecessary minor-offense arrests. That fact caps the reasons for rejecting Atwater's request for the development of a new and distinct body of constitutional law.

Accordingly, we confirm today what our prior cases have intimated: the standard of probable cause "applie[s] to all arrests, without the need to 'balance' the interests and circumstances involved in particular situations." If an officer has probable cause to believe that an individual has committed even a very minor criminal offense in his presence, he may, without violating the Fourth Amendment, arrest the offender.[a]

Atwater's arrest satisfied constitutional requirements. There is no dispute that Officer Turek had probable cause * * *.

Nor was the arrest made in an "extraordinary manner, unusually harmful to [her] privacy or . . . physical interests." As our citations in *Whren* make clear, the question whether a search or seizure is "extraordinary" turns, above all else, on the manner in which the search or seizure is executed. Atwater's arrest was surely "humiliating," as she says in her brief, but it was no more "harmful to . . . privacy or . . . physical interests" than the normal custodial arrest. * * *

JUSTICE O'CONNOR, with whom JUSTICE STEVENS, JUSTICE GINSBURG, and JUSTICE BREYER join, dissenting.

* * * The Court's thorough exegesis makes it abundantly clear that warrantless misdemeanor arrests were not the subject of a clear and consistently

---

[a] Would the result in *Atwater* have been different had there been a state law proscribing custodial arrest in the case of a seat belt violation? No, the Court answered in *Virginia v. Moore*, 553 U.S. 164 (2008), where defendant was arrested for driving on a suspended license although state law mandated that a summons be utilized, and the state court held evidence found in a search incident to that arrest had to be suppressed on Fourth Amendment grounds. A unanimous Supreme Court, per Scalia, J., concluded that neither the arrest nor the search was unconstitutional. After finding "no historical indication that those who ratified the Fourth Amendment understood it as a redundant guarantee of whatever limits on search and seizure legislatures might have enacted," the Court turned to an examination of "traditional standards of reasonableness," whereby "[i]n a long line of cases, we have said that when an officer has probable cause to believe a person committed even a minor crime in his presence, the balancing of private and public interests is not in doubt." The Court could see no reason for "changing this calculus when a State chooses to protect privacy beyond the level that the Fourth Amendment requires," and several reasons for not doing so. A contrary result "would often frustrate rather than further state policy" (as illustrated by the instant case, where state law mandated use of a summons in minor cases but did not attach a state-law exclusionary sanction to violation of that mandate), "would produce a constitutional regime no less vague and unpredictable than the one we rejected in *Atwater*," and "would cause [Fourth Amendment protections] to 'vary from place to place and from time to time.'" (As for Moore's separate argument that the search was unconstitutional even if the arrest was not because of the "lawful custodial arrest" requirement in *United States v. Robinson*, p. 182, the Court responded that this term in was used *Robinson* "as shorthand for compliance with constitutional constraints.")

applied rule at common law. We therefore must engage in the balancing test required by the Fourth Amendment. While probable cause is surely a necessary condition for warrantless arrests for fine-only offenses, any realistic assessment of the interests implicated by such arrests demonstrates that probable cause alone is not a sufficient condition.

A custodial arrest exacts an obvious toll on an individual's liberty and privacy, even when the period of custody is relatively brief. The arrestee is subject to a full search of her person and confiscation of her possessions.[b] *United States v. Robinson*, supra. If the arrestee is the occupant of a car, the entire passenger compartment of the car, including packages therein, is subject to search as well. See *New York v. Belton*, 453 U.S. 454 (1981) [modified in *Arizona v. Gant*, p. 244]. The arrestee may be detained for up to 48 hours without having a magistrate determine whether there in fact was probable cause for the arrest. See *County of Riverside v. McLaughlin*, [fn. a, p. 177]. Because people arrested for all types of violent and nonviolent offenses may be housed together awaiting such review, this detention period is potentially dangerous. And once the period of custody is over, the fact of the arrest is a permanent part of the public record.

We have said that "the penalty that may attach to any particular offense seems to provide the clearest and most consistent indication of the State's interest in arresting individuals suspected of committing that offense." *Welsh v. Wisconsin*, [supra]. If the State has decided that a fine, and not imprisonment, is the appropriate punishment for an offense, the State's interest in taking a person suspected of committing that offense into custody is surely limited, at best. This is not to say that the State will never have such an interest. A full custodial arrest may on occasion vindicate legitimate state interests, even if the crime is punishable only by fine. Arrest is the surest way to abate criminal conduct. It may also allow

---

    [b] Consider in this regard *Florence v. Board of Chosen Freeholders*, 566 U.S. 318 (2012). The plaintiff in that § 1983 action, following his arrest for failure to appear at a court hearing, was subjected to a strip search in which "he was required to lift his genitals, turn around, and cough in a squatting position." Stating the question as being "whether undoubted security imperatives involved in jail supervision override the assertion that some detainees must be exempt from the more invasive search procedures at issue absent reasonable suspicion of a concealed weapon or other contraband," the majority concluded plaintiff had not met the applicable standard under prior case law: "that deference must be given to the officials in charge of the jail unless there is 'substantial evidence' demonstrating their response to the situation is exaggerated." While plaintiff maintained such procedures were unnecessary regarding "a new detainee who has not been arrested for a serious crime or for any offense involving a weapon or drugs," the Court responded that it was reasonable "for correctional officials to conclude this standard would be unworkable," as (i) "the seriousness of an offense is a poor predictor of who has contraband," and (ii) "it would be difficult in practice to determine whether individual detainees fall within the proposed exemption." The majority in *Florence* concluded: "One of the central principles in *Atwater* applies with equal force here. Officers who interact with those suspected of violating the law have an 'essential interest in readily administrable rules.'" (The four dissenters objected that a reasonable suspicion standard had been endorsed by many "professional bodies," was applied by "many correctional facilities," was required by law "in at least 10 States" and by "at least seven Courts of Appeals," but yet "neither the majority's opinion nor the briefs set forth any clear example of an instance in which contraband was smuggled into the general jail population during intake that could not have been discovered if the jail was employing a reasonable suspicion standard.") Four of the majority's Justices cautioned that there remained open the question "whether an arrestee whose detention has not yet been reviewed by a magistrate or other judicial officer, and who can be held in available facilities removed from the general population, may be subjected to the types of searches at issue here."

the police to verify the offender's identity and, if the offender poses a flight risk, to ensure her appearance at trial. But when such considerations are not present, a citation or summons may serve the State's remaining law enforcement interests every bit as effectively as an arrest.

Because a full custodial arrest is such a severe intrusion on an individual's liberty, its reasonableness hinges on "the degree to which it is needed for the promotion of legitimate governmental interests." In light of the availability of citations to promote a State's interests when a fine-only offense has been committed, I cannot concur in a rule which deems a full custodial arrest to be reasonable in every circumstance. Giving police officers constitutional carte blanche to effect an arrest whenever there is probable cause to believe a fine-only misdemeanor has been committed is irreconcilable with the Fourth Amendment's command that seizures be reasonable. Instead, I would require that when there is probable cause to believe that a fine-only offense has been committed, the police officer should issue a citation unless the officer is "able to point to specific and articulable facts which, taken together with rational inferences from those facts, reasonably warrant [the additional] intrusion" of a full custodial arrest.

The majority insists that a bright-line rule focused on probable cause is necessary to vindicate the State's interest in easily administrable law enforcement rules. Probable cause itself, however, is not a model of precision. * * * The rule I propose—which merely requires a legitimate reason for the decision to escalate the seizure into a full custodial arrest—thus does not undermine an otherwise "clear and simple" rule.

While clarity is certainly a value worthy of consideration in our Fourth Amendment jurisprudence, it by no means trumps the values of liberty and privacy at the heart of the Amendment's protections. * * *

The Court's error, however, does not merely affect the disposition of this case. The per se rule that the Court creates has potentially serious consequences for the everyday lives of Americans. A broad range of conduct falls into the category of fine-only misdemeanors. * * *

To be sure, such laws are valid and wise exercises of the States' power to protect the public health and welfare. My concern lies not with the decision to enact or enforce these laws, but rather with the manner in which they may be enforced. Under today's holding, when a police officer has probable cause to believe that a fine-only misdemeanor offense has occurred, that officer may stop the suspect, issue a citation, and let the person continue on her way. Or, if a traffic violation, the officer may stop the car, arrest the driver, search the driver, search the entire passenger compartment of the car including any purse or package inside, and impound the car and inventory all of its contents. Although the Fourth Amendment expressly requires that the latter course be a reasonable and proportional response to the circumstances of the offense, the majority gives officers unfettered discretion to choose that course without articulating a single reason why such action is appropriate.

Such unbounded discretion carries with it grave potential for abuse. The majority takes comfort in the lack of evidence of "an epidemic of unnecessary minor-offense arrests." But the relatively small number of published cases dealing with such arrests proves little and should provide little solace. Indeed, as the recent debate over racial profiling demonstrates all too clearly, a relatively minor traffic infraction may often serve as an excuse for stopping and harassing an individual. After today, the arsenal available to any officer extends to a full arrest and the searches permissible concomitant to that arrest. An officer's subjective motivations for making a traffic stop are not relevant considerations in determining the reasonableness of the stop. See *Whren v. United States*, supra. But it is precisely because these motivations are beyond our purview that we must vigilantly ensure that officers' poststop actions—which are properly within our reach—comport with the Fourth Amendment's guarantee of reasonableness. * * *

MARYLAND V. KING
569 U.S. 435, 133 S.Ct. 1958, 186 L.Ed.2d 1 (2013).

JUSTICE KENNEDY delivered the opinion of the Court. * * *

In 2009 Alonzo King was arrested in Wicomico County, Maryland, and charged with first-and second-degree assault for menacing a group of people with a shotgun. As part of a routine booking procedure for serious offenses [pursuant to the Md. DNA Collection Act], his DNA sample was taken by applying a cotton swab or filter paper—known as a buccal swab—to the inside of his cheeks. The DNA was found to match the DNA taken from [a 2003] rape victim. King was tried and convicted for the rape. * * *

The Court of Appeals of Maryland, on review of King's rape conviction, ruled that the DNA taken when King was booked for the 2009 charge was an unlawful seizure because obtaining and using the cheek swab was an unreasonable search of the person. It set the rape conviction aside. This Court granted certiorari and now reverses the judgment of the Maryland court. * * *

The advent of DNA technology is one of the most significant scientific advancements of our era. * * * Since the first use of forensic DNA analysis to catch a rapist and murderer in England in 1986, law enforcement, the defense bar, and the courts have acknowledged DNA testing's "unparalleled ability both to exonerate the wrongly convicted and to identify the guilty. It has the potential to significantly improve both the criminal justice system and police investigative practices." * * *

The Act authorizes Maryland law enforcement authorities to collect DNA samples from "an individual who is charged with . . . a crime of violence or an attempt to commit a crime of violence; or . . . burglary or an attempt to commit burglary." Maryland law defines a crime of violence to include murder, rape, first-degree assault, kidnaping, arson, sexual assault, and a variety of other serious crimes. Once taken, a DNA sample may not be processed or placed in a database before the individual is arraigned (unless the individual consents). It is at this point that a judicial officer ensures that there is probable cause to detain the arrestee on a qualifying serious offense. If "all qualifying criminal charges are determined to be unsupported by probable cause . . . the DNA sample shall be immediately destroyed." DNA samples are also destroyed if "a criminal action begun against the individual . . . does not result in a conviction," "the conviction is finally reversed or vacated and no new trial is permitted," or "the individual is granted an unconditional pardon."

The Act also limits the information added to a DNA database and how it may be used. * * * No purpose other than identification is permissible * * *. Tests for familial matches are also prohibited. * * * The officers involved in taking and analyzing respondent's DNA sample complied with the Act in all respects. * * *

Respondent's identification as the rapist resulted in part through the operation of a national project to standardize collection and storage of DNA profiles. Authorized by Congress and supervised by the Federal Bureau of Investigation, the Combined DNA Index System (CODIS) connects DNA laboratories at the local, state, and national level. Since its authorization in 1994, the CODIS system has grown to include all 50 States and a number of federal agencies. * * *

All 50 States require the collection of DNA from felony convicts, and respondent does not dispute the validity of that practice. Twenty-eight States and the Federal Government have adopted laws similar to the Maryland Act authorizing the collection of DNA from some or all arrestees. Although those statutes vary in their particulars, such as what charges require a DNA sample, their similarity means that this case implicates more than the specific Maryland law. At issue is a standard, expanding technology already in widespread use throughout the Nation. * * *

A buccal swab is a far more gentle process than a venipuncture to draw blood. It involves but a light touch on the inside of the cheek; and although it can be deemed a search within the body of the arrestee, it requires no "surgical intrusions beneath the skin." The fact than an intrusion is negligible is of central relevance to determining reasonableness, although it is still a search as the law defines that term.

* * * In giving content to the inquiry whether an intrusion is reasonable, the Court has preferred "some quantum of individualized suspicion . . . [as] a prerequisite to a constitutional search or seizure. But the Fourth Amendment imposes no irreducible requirement of such suspicion."

In some circumstances, such as "[w]hen faced with special law enforcement needs, diminished expectations of privacy, minimal intrusions, or the like, the Court has found that certain general, or individual, circumstances may render a warrantless search or seizure reasonable." * * * The need for a warrant is perhaps least when the search involves no discretion that could properly be limited by the "interpo[lation of] a neutral magistrate between the citizen and the law enforcement officer."

The instant case can be addressed with this background. * * * The arrestee is already in valid police custody for a serious offense supported by probable cause.

The DNA collection is not subject to the judgment of officers whose perspective might be "colored by their primary involvement in 'the often competitive enterprise of ferreting out crime.' " * * * Here, the search effected by the buccal swab of respondent falls within the category of cases this Court has analyzed by reference to the proposition that the "touchstone of the Fourth Amendment is reasonableness, not individualized suspicion."

Even if a warrant is not required, a search is not beyond Fourth Amendment scrutiny; for it must be reasonable in its scope and manner of execution. * * * This application of "traditional standards of reasonableness" requires a court to weigh "the promotion of legitimate governmental interests" against "the degree to which [the search] intrudes upon an individual's privacy." An assessment of reasonableness to determine the lawfulness of requiring this class of arrestees to provide a DNA sample is central to the instant case.

The legitimate government interest served by the Maryland DNA Collection Act is one that is well established: the need for law enforcement officers in a safe and accurate way to process and identify the persons and possessions they must take into custody. It is beyond dispute that "probable cause provides legal justification for arresting a person suspected of crime, and for a brief period of detention to take the administrative steps incident to arrest." Also uncontested is the "right on the part of the Government, always recognized under English and American law, to search the person of the accused when legally arrested." * * * Even in that context, the Court has been clear that individual suspicion is not necessary, because "[t]he constitutionality of a search incident to an arrest does not depend on whether there is any indication that the person arrested possesses weapons or evidence. The fact of a lawful arrest, standing alone, authorizes a search."

The "routine administrative procedure[s] at a police station house incident to booking and jailing the suspect" derive from different origins and have different constitutional justifications than, say, the search of a place * * *. The interests are further different when an individual is formally processed into police custody. * * * When probable cause exists to remove an individual from the normal channels of society and hold him in legal custody, DNA identification plays a critical role in serving those interests.

First, "[i]n every criminal case, it is known and must be known who has been arrested and who is being tried." An individual's identity is more than just his name or Social Security number, and the government's interest in identification goes beyond ensuring that the proper name is typed on the indictment. Identity has never been considered limited to the name on the arrestee's birth certificate. In fact, a name is of little value compared to the real interest in identification at stake when an individual is brought into custody. "It is a well recognized aspect of criminal conduct that the perpetrator will take unusual steps to conceal not only his conduct, but also his identity. * * * An "arrestee may be carrying a false ID or lie about his identity," and "criminal history records . . . can be inaccurate or incomplete."

A suspect's criminal history is a critical part of his identity that officers should know when processing him for detention. It is a common occurrence that "[p]eople detained for minor offenses can turn out to be the most devious and dangerous criminals. * * * Police already seek this crucial identifying information. They use routine and accepted means as varied as comparing the suspect's booking photograph to sketch artists' depictions of persons of interest, showing his mugshot to potential witnesses, and of course making a computerized comparison of the arrestee's fingerprints against electronic databases of known criminals and unsolved crimes. In this respect the only difference between DNA analysis and the accepted use of fingerprint databases is the unparalleled accuracy DNA provides.

* * * A DNA profile is useful to the police because it gives them a form of identification to search the records already in their valid possession. In this respect the use of DNA for identification is no different than matching an arrestee's face to a wanted poster of a previously unidentified suspect; or matching tattoos to known gang symbols to reveal a criminal affiliation; or matching the arrestee's fingerprints to those recovered from a crime scene. * * *

Second, law enforcement officers bear a responsibility for ensuring that the custody of an arrestee does not create inordinate "risks for facility staff, for the existing detainee population, and for a new detainee." DNA identification can provide untainted information to those charged with detaining suspects and detaining the property of any felon. For these purposes officers must know the type of person whom they are detaining, and DNA allows them to make critical choices about how to proceed. * * *

Third, looking forward to future stages of criminal prosecution, "the Government has a substantial interest in ensuring that persons accused of crimes are available for trials." A person who is arrested for one offense but knows that he has yet to answer for some past crime may be more inclined to flee the instant charges, lest continued contact with the criminal justice system expose one or more other serious offenses. * * *

Fourth, an arrestee's past conduct is essential to an assessment of the danger he poses to the public, and this will inform a court's determination whether the individual should be released on bail. * * * Knowing that the defendant is wanted for a previous violent crime based on DNA identification is especially probative of the court's consideration of "the danger of the defendant to the alleged victim, another person, or the community."

This interest is not speculative. In considering laws to require collecting DNA from arrestees, government agencies around the Nation found evidence of numerous cases in which felony arrestees would have been identified as violent through DNA identification matching them to previous crimes but who later committed additional crimes because such identification was not used to detain them.

Present capabilities make it possible to complete a DNA identification that provides information essential to determining whether a detained suspect can be released pending trial. See, e.g., States Brief 18, n. 10 ("DNA identification database samples have been processed in as few as two days in California, although around 30 days has been average"). Regardless of when the initial bail decision is made, release is not appropriate until a further determination is made as to the person's identity in the sense not only of what his birth certificate states but also what other records and data disclose to give that identity more meaning in the whole context of who the person really is. * * * During this entire period, additional and supplemental data establishing more about the person's identity and background can provide critical information relevant to the conditions of release and whether to revisit an initial release determination. * * *

Even if an arrestee is released on bail, development of DNA identification revealing the defendant's unknown violent past can and should lead to the revocation of his conditional release. * * *

Finally, in the interests of justice, the identification of an arrestee as the perpetrator of some heinous crime may have the salutary effect of freeing a person wrongfully imprisoned for the same offense. "[P]rompt [DNA] testing . . . would speed up apprehension of criminals before they commit additional crimes, and prevent the grotesque detention of . . . innocent people." * * *

Perhaps the most direct historical analogue to the DNA technology used to identify respondent is the familiar practice of fingerprinting arrestees. From the advent of this technique, courts had no trouble determining that fingerprinting was a natural part of "the administrative steps incident to arrest." In the seminal case of *United States v. Kelly*, 55 F.2d 67 (C.A.2 1932), Judge Augustus Hand wrote that routine fingerprinting did not violate the Fourth Amendment precisely because it fit within the accepted means of processing an arrestee into custody:

> "Finger printing seems to be no more than an extension of methods of identification long used in dealing with persons under arrest for real or supposed violations of the criminal laws. It is known to be a very certain means devised by modern science to reach the desired end, and has become especially important in a time when increased population and vast aggregations of people in urban centers have rendered the notoriety of the individual in the community no longer a ready means of identification.

* * *

> "We find no ground in reason or authority for interfering with a method of identifying persons charged with crime which has now become widely known and frequently practiced."

By the middle of the 20th century, it was considered "elementary that a person in lawful custody may be required to submit to photographing and fingerprinting as part of routine identification processes."

DNA identification is an advanced technique superior to fingerprinting in many ways, so much so that to insist on fingerprints as the norm would make little sense to either the forensic expert or a layperson. The additional intrusion upon the arrestee's privacy beyond that associated with fingerprinting is not significant, and DNA is a markedly more accurate form of identifying arrestees. A suspect who has changed his facial features to evade photographic identification or even one who has undertaken the more arduous task of altering his fingerprints cannot escape the revealing power of his DNA.

The respondent's primary objection to this analogy is that DNA identification is not as fast as fingerprinting, and so it should not be considered to be the 21st-century equivalent. But rapid analysis of fingerprints is itself of recent vintage. * * * The question of how long it takes to process identifying information obtained from a valid search goes only to the efficacy of the search for its purpose of prompt identification, not the constitutionality of the search. And the FBI has already begun testing devices that will enable police to process the DNA of arrestees within 90 minutes. * * *

By comparison to this substantial government interest and the unique effectiveness of DNA identification, the intrusion of a cheek swab to obtain a DNA sample is a minimal one. * * *

The reasonableness of any search must be considered in the context of the person's legitimate expectations of privacy. * * *

The expectations of privacy of an individual taken into police custody "necessarily [are] of a diminished scope." "[B]oth the person and the property in his immediate possession may be searched at the station house." A search of the detainee's person when he is booked into custody may " 'involve a relatively extensive exploration,' " [*United States v.*] *Robinson*, [p. 182], including "requir[ing] at least some detainees to lift their genitals or cough in a squatting position," *Florence* [*v. Board of Chosen Freeholders*], [p. 203 fn. b]. * * *

The reasonableness inquiry here considers two other circumstances in which the Court has held that particularized suspicion is not categorically required: "diminished expectations of privacy [and] minimal intrusions." * * *

Here, by contrast to the approved standard procedures incident to any arrest detailed above, a buccal swab involves an even more brief and still minimal intrusion. * * * A brief intrusion of an arrestee's person is subject to the Fourth Amendment, but a swab of this nature does not increase the indignity already attendant to normal incidents of arrest. * * *

Finally, the Act provides statutory protections that guard against further invasion of privacy. As noted above, the Act requires that "[o]nly DNA records that directly relate to the identification of individuals shall be collected and stored." No purpose other than identification is permissible * * *.

In light of the context of a valid arrest supported by probable cause respondent's expectations of privacy were not offended by the minor intrusion of a brief swab of his cheeks. By contrast, that same context of arrest gives rise to significant state interests in identifying respondent not only so that the proper name can be attached to his charges but also so that the criminal justice system can make informed decisions concerning pretrial custody. Upon these considerations the Court concludes that DNA identification of arrestees is a reasonable search that can be considered part of a routine booking procedure. When officers make an arrest supported by probable cause to hold for a serious offense and they bring the suspect to the station to be detained in custody, taking and analyzing a cheek swab of the arrestee's DNA is, like fingerprinting and photographing, a legitimate police booking procedure that is reasonable under the Fourth Amendment. * * *

JUSTICE SCALIA, with whom JUSTICE GINSBURG, JUSTICE SOTOMAYOR, and JUSTICE KAGAN join, dissenting. * * *

Although there is a "closely guarded category of constitutionally permissible suspicionless searches," that has never included searches designed to serve "the normal need for law enforcement." Even the common name for suspicionless searches—"special needs" searches—itself reflects that they must be justified, always, by concerns "other than crime detection." * * *

So while the Court is correct to note that there are instances in which we have permitted searches without individualized suspicion, "[i]n none of these cases . . . did we indicate approval of a [search] whose primary purpose was to detect evidence of ordinary criminal wrongdoing."[a] That limitation is crucial. It is only when a governmental purpose aside from crime-solving is at stake that we engage in the free-form "reasonableness" inquiry that the Court indulges at length today. To put it another way, both the legitimacy of the Court's method and the correctness of its outcome hinge entirely on the truth of a single proposition: that the primary purpose of these DNA searches is something other than simply discovering evidence of criminal wrongdoing. As I detail below, that proposition is wrong.

The Court alludes at several points to the fact that King was an arrestee, and arrestees may be validly searched incident to their arrest. But the Court does not really *rest* on this principle, and for good reason: The objects of a search incident to arrest must be either (1) weapons or evidence that might easily be destroyed, or (2) evidence relevant to the crime of arrest. Neither is the object of the search at issue here. * * *

Sensing (correctly) that it needs more, the Court elaborates at length the ways that the search here served the special purpose of "identifying" King. But that seems to me quite wrong—unless what one means by "identifying" someone is "searching for evidence that he has committed crimes unrelated to the crime of his arrest." At points the Court does appear to use "identifying" in that peculiar sense—claiming, for example, that knowing "an arrestee's past conduct is essential to an assessment of the danger he poses." If identifying someone means finding out what unsolved crimes he has committed, then identification is indistinguishable from the ordinary law-enforcement aims that have never been thought to justify a suspicionless search. Searching every lawfully stopped car, for example, might turn up information about unsolved crimes the driver had committed, but no one would

---

[a] If this quotation from *City of Indianapolis v. Edmond*, 531 U.S. 32 (2000), is no longer literally correct in view of the intervening decision in *Samson v. California*, 547 U.S. 843 (2006) (holding a parole release condition "can so diminish or eliminate a released prisoner's reasonable expectation of privacy that a suspicionless search by a law enforcement officer would not offend the Fourth Amendment"), but the dissent in *King* is correct in asserting that the majority has misrepresented the main purpose of pre-conviction DNA testing, and appropriate weight is given to the real purpose, then what would be the correct result on the facts of *King*?

say that such a search was aimed at "identifying" him, and no court would hold such a search lawful. I will therefore assume that the Court means that the DNA search at issue here was useful to "identify" King in the normal sense of that word * * *.

The portion of the Court's opinion that explains the identification rationale is strangely silent on the actual workings of the DNA search at issue here. To know those facts is to be instantly disabused of the notion that what happened had anything to do with identifying King.

[The dissent here notes a swab was taken from King on April 10 following his arrest on that day, but that King's DNA sample was not received by the State Police Forensic Services Division until April 23, where it sat until mailed to a testing lab on June 25, and the lab tests were not available until July 13, when they were entered into the state's DNA database, but it was not until August 4, nearly four months after King's arrest, that the sample forwarded to the FBI national database connected King with the rape.]

This places in a rather different light the Court's solemn declaration that the search here was necessary so that King could be identified at "every stage of the criminal process." * * *

In fact, if anything was "identified" at the moment that the DNA database returned a match, it was not King—his identity was already known. (The docket for the original criminal charges lists his full name, his race, his sex, his height, his weight, his date of birth, and his address.) Rather, what the August 4 match "identified" was *the previously-taken sample from the earlier crime*. That sample was genuinely mysterious to Maryland; the State knew that it had probably been left by the victim's attacker, but nothing else. King was not identified by his association with the sample; rather, the sample was identified by its association with King. The Court effectively destroys its own "identification" theory when it acknowledges that the object of this search was "to see what [was] already known about [King]." King was who he was, and volumes of his biography could not make him any more or any less King. No minimally competent speaker of English would say, upon noticing a known arrestee's similarity "to a wanted poster of a previously unidentified suspect," that the *arrestee* had thereby been identified. It was the previously unidentified suspect who had been identified—just as, here, it was the previously unidentified rapist. * * *

So, to review: DNA testing does not even begin until after arraignment and bail decisions are already made. The samples sit in storage for months, and take weeks to test. When they are tested, they are checked against the Unsolved Crimes Collection—rather than the Convict and Arrestee Collection, which could be used to identify them. The Act forbids the Court's purpose (identification), but prescribes as its purpose what our suspicionless-search cases forbid ("official investigation into a crime"). Against all of that, it is safe to say that if the Court's identification theory is not wrong, there is no such thing as error.

The Court also attempts to bolster its identification theory with a series of inapposite analogies. * * *

It is on the fingerprinting of arrestees, however, that the Court relies most heavily. The Court does not actually say whether it believes that taking a person's fingerprints is a Fourth Amendment search, and our cases provide no ready answer to that question. Even assuming so, however, law enforcement's post-arrest use of fingerprints could not be more different from its post-arrest use of DNA. Fingerprints of arrestees are taken primarily to identify them (though that process sometimes solves crimes); the DNA of arrestees is taken to solve crimes (and nothing else). * * *

The Court also accepts uncritically the Government's representation at oral argument that it is developing devices that will be able to test DNA in mere minutes. [But the] issue before us is not whether DNA can some day be used for identification; nor even whether it can today be used for identification; but whether it *was used for identification here.*

* * * I cannot imagine what principle could possibly justify [the majority's "serious offense"] limitation, and the Court does not attempt to suggest any. If one believes that DNA will "identify" someone arrested for assault, he must believe that it will "identify" someone arrested for a traffic offense. This Court does not base its judgments on senseless distinctions. At the end of the day, *logic will out.* When there comes before us the taking of DNA from an arrestee for a traffic violation, the Court will predictably (and quite rightly) say, "We can find no significant difference between this case and *King.*" Make no mistake about it: As an entirely predictable consequence of today's decision, your DNA can be taken and entered into a national DNA database if you are ever arrested, rightly or wrongly, and for whatever reason.

The most regrettable aspect of the suspicionless search that occurred here is that it proved to be quite unnecessary. All parties concede that it would have been entirely permissible, as far as the Fourth Amendment is concerned, for Maryland to take a sample of King's DNA as a consequence of his conviction for second-degree assault. So the ironic result of the Court's error is this: The only arrestees to whom the outcome here will ever make a difference are those who *have been acquitted* of the crime of arrest (so that their DNA could not have been taken upon conviction). In other words, this Act manages to burden uniquely the sole group for whom the Fourth Amendment's protections ought to be most jealously guarded: people who are innocent of the State's accusations.

Today's judgment will, to be sure, have the beneficial effect of solving more crimes; then again, so would the taking of DNA samples from anyone who flies on an airplane (surely the Transportation Security Administration needs to know the "identity" of the flying public), applies for a driver's license, or attends a public school. Perhaps the construction of such a genetic panopticon is wise. But I doubt that the proud men who wrote the charter of our liberties would have been so eager to open their mouths for royal inspection. * * *

MITCHELL V. WISCONSIN

588 U.S. ___, 139 S.Ct. 2525, 204 L.Ed.2d 1040 (2019).

JUSTICE ALITO announced the judgment of the Court and delivered an opinion, in which THE CHIEF JUSTICE, JUSTICE BREYER, and JUSTICE KAVANAUGH join.

In this case, we return to a topic that we have addressed twice in recent years: the circumstances under which a police officer may administer a warrantless blood alcohol concentration (BAC) test to a motorist who appears to have been driving under the influence of alcohol. We have previously addressed what officers may do in two broad categories of cases. First, an officer may conduct a BAC test if the facts of a particular case bring it within the exigent-circumstances exception to the Fourth Amendment's general requirement of a warrant. Second, if an officer has probable cause to arrest a motorist for drunk driving, the officer may conduct a breath test (but not a blood test) under the rule allowing warrantless searches of a person incident to arrest.

Today, we consider what police officers may do in a narrow but important category of cases: those in which the driver is unconscious and therefore cannot be given a breath test. In such cases, we hold, the exigent-circumstances rule almost always permits a blood test without a warrant. When a breath test is impossible, enforcement of the drunk-driving laws depends upon the administration of a blood test. And when a police officer encounters an unconscious driver, it is very likely that the driver would be taken to an emergency room and that his blood would be drawn for diagnostic purposes even if the police were not seeking BAC information. In addition, police officers most frequently come upon unconscious drivers when they report to the scene of an accident, and under those circumstances, the officers' many responsibilities—such as attending to other injured drivers or passengers and preventing further accidents—may be incompatible with the procedures that would be required to obtain a warrant. Thus, when a driver is unconscious, the general rule is that a warrant is not needed. * * *

Wisconsin's implied-consent law is much like those of the other 49 States and the District of Columbia. It deems drivers to have consented to breath or blood tests if an officer has reason to believe they have committed one of several drug- or alcohol-related offenses. Officers seeking to conduct a BAC test must read aloud a statement declaring their intent to administer the test and advising drivers of their options and the implications of their choice. If a driver's BAC level proves too high, his license will be suspended; but if he refuses testing, his license will be revoked and his refusal may be used against him in court. No test will be administered if a driver refuses—or, as the State would put it, "withdraws" his statutorily presumed consent. But "[a] person who is unconscious or otherwise not capable of withdrawing consent is presumed not to have" withdrawn it. More than half the States have provisions like this one regarding unconscious drivers.

The sequence of events that gave rise to this case began when Officer Alexander Jaeger of the Sheboygan Police Department received a report that petitioner Gerald Mitchell, appearing to be very drunk, had climbed into a van and driven off. Jaeger soon found Mitchell wandering near a lake. Stumbling and slurring his words, Mitchell could hardly stand without the support of two officers.

Jaeger judged a field sobriety test hopeless, if not dangerous, and gave Mitchell a preliminary breath test. It registered a BAC level of 0.24%, triple the legal limit for driving in Wisconsin. Jaeger arrested Mitchell for operating a vehicle while intoxicated and, as is standard practice, drove him to a police station for a more reliable breath test using better equipment.

On the way, Mitchell's condition continued to deteriorate—so much so that by the time the squad car had reached the station, he was too lethargic even for a breath test. Jaeger therefore drove Mitchell to a nearby hospital for a blood test; Mitchell lost consciousness on the ride over and had to be wheeled in. Even so, Jaeger read aloud to a slumped Mitchell the standard statement giving drivers a chance to refuse BAC testing. Hearing no response, Jaeger asked hospital staff to draw a blood sample. Mitchell remained unconscious while the sample was taken, and analysis of his blood showed that his BAC, about 90 minutes after his arrest, was 0.222%.

Mitchell was charged with violating two related drunk-driving provisions. He moved to suppress the results of the blood test on the ground that it violated his Fourth Amendment right against "unreasonable searches" because it was conducted without a warrant. Wisconsin chose to rest its response on the notion that its implied-consent law (together with Mitchell's free choice to drive on its highways) rendered the blood test a consensual one, thus curing any Fourth Amendment problem. In the end, the trial court denied Mitchell's motion to suppress, and a jury found him guilty of the charged offenses. The intermediate appellate court certified two questions to the Wisconsin Supreme Court: first, whether compliance with the State's implied-consent law was sufficient to show that Mitchell's test was consistent with the Fourth Amendment and, second, whether a warrantless blood draw from an unconscious person violates the Fourth Amendment. The Wisconsin Supreme Court affirmed Mitchell's convictions, and we granted certiorari to decide "[w]hether a statute authorizing a blood draw from an unconscious motorist provides an exception to the Fourth Amendment warrant requirement.

In considering Wisconsin's implied-consent law, we do not write on a blank slate. "Our prior opinions have referred approvingly to the general concept of implied-consent laws that impose civil penalties and evidentiary consequences on motorists who refuse to comply." But our decisions have not rested on the idea that these laws do what their popular name might seem to suggest—that is, create actual consent to all the searches they authorize. Instead, we have based our decisions on the precedent regarding the specific constitutional claims in each case, while keeping in mind the wider regulatory scheme developed over the years to combat drunk driving. That scheme is centered on legally specified BAC limits for drivers—limits enforced by the BAC tests promoted by implied-consent laws.

Over the last 50 years, we have approved many of the defining elements of this scheme. We have held that forcing drunk-driving suspects to undergo a blood test does not violate their constitutional right against self-incrimination. See *Schmerber v. California*, 384 U.S. 757, 765 (1966). Nor does using their refusal against them in court. See *South Dakota v. Neville*, 459 U.S. 553, 563 (1983). And punishing that refusal with automatic license revocation does not violate drivers' due process rights if they have been arrested upon probable cause, *Mackey v. Montrym*, 443 U.S. 1 (1979); on the contrary, this kind of summary penalty is "unquestionably legitimate." *Neville*, supra.

These cases generally concerned the Fifth and Fourteenth Amendments, but motorists charged with drunk driving have also invoked the Fourth Amendment's ban on "unreasonable searches" since BAC tests are "searches." See *Birchfield* [*v. North Dakota*, 136 S.Ct. 2160 (2016). Though our precedent normally requires a warrant for a lawful search, there are well-defined exceptions to this rule. In *Birchfield*, we applied precedent on the "search-incident-to-arrest" exception to BAC testing of conscious drunk-driving suspects. We held that their drunk-driving arrests, taken alone, justify warrantless breath tests but not blood tests, since breath tests are less intrusive, just as informative, and (in the case of conscious suspects) readily available.

We have also reviewed BAC tests under the "exigent circumstances" exception—which, as noted, allows warrantless searches "to prevent the imminent destruction of evidence." *Missouri v. McNeely*, 569 U.S. 141, 149 (2013). In *McNeely*, we were asked if this exception covers BAC testing of drunk-driving suspects in light of the fact that blood-alcohol evidence is always dissipating due to "natural metabolic processes." We answered that the fleeting quality of BAC evidence alone is not enough. But in *Schmerber* it did justify a blood test of a drunk driver who had gotten into a car accident that gave police other pressing duties, for then the "further delay" caused by a warrant application really "would have threatened the destruction of evidence." *McNeely*, supra (emphasis added).

Like *Schmerber*, this case sits much higher than *McNeely* on the exigency spectrum. *McNeely* was about the minimum degree of urgency common to all drunk-driving cases. In *Schmerber*, a car accident heightened that urgency. And here Mitchell's medical condition did just the same.

Mitchell's stupor and eventual unconsciousness also deprived officials of a reasonable opportunity to administer a breath test. To be sure, Officer Jaeger managed to conduct "a preliminary breath test" using a portable machine when he first encountered Mitchell at the lake. But he had no reasonable opportunity to give Mitchell a breath test using "evidence-grade breath testing machinery." As a result, it was reasonable for Jaeger to seek a better breath test at the station; he acted with reasonable dispatch to procure one; and when Mitchell's condition got in the way, it was reasonable for Jaeger to pursue a blood test. * * * Because the "standard evidentiary breath test is conducted after a motorist is arrested and transported to a police station" or another appropriate facility, ibid., the important question here is what officers may do when a driver's unconsciousness (or stupor) eliminates any reasonable opportunity for that kind of breath test.

The Fourth Amendment guards the "right of the people to be secure in their persons . . . against unreasonable searches" and provides that "no Warrants shall issue, but upon probable cause." A blood draw is a search of the person, so we must determine if its administration here without a warrant was reasonable. Though we have held that a warrant is normally required, we have also "made it clear that there are exceptions to the warrant requirement." *Illinois v. McArthur*, 531 U.S. 326, 330 (2001). And under the exception for exigent circumstances, a warrantless search is allowed when " 'there is compelling need for official action and no time to secure a warrant.' " In *McNeely*, we considered how the exigent-circumstances exception applies to the broad category of cases in which a police officer has probable cause to believe that a motorist was driving under the influence of alcohol, and we do not revisit that question. Nor do we settle whether the exigent-circumstances exception covers the specific facts of this case. Instead, we address how the exception bears on the category of cases encompassed by the question on which we granted certiorari—those involving unconscious drivers. In those cases, the need for a blood test is compelling, and an officer's duty to attend to more pressing needs may leave no time to seek a warrant.

The importance of the needs served by BAC testing is hard to overstate. The bottom line is that BAC tests are needed for enforcing laws that save lives. The specifics, in short, are these: Highway safety is critical; it is served by laws that criminalize driving with a certain BAC level; and enforcing these legal BAC limits requires efficient testing to obtain BAC evidence, which naturally dissipates. So BAC tests are crucial links in a chain on which vital interests hang. And when a breath test is unavailable to advance those aims, a blood test becomes essential. * * *

Enforcement of BAC limits also requires prompt testing because it is "a biological certainty" that "[a]lcohol dissipates from the bloodstream at a rate of 0.01 percent to 0.025 percent per hour. . . . Evidence is literally disappearing by the minute." * * *

Finally, when a breath test is unavailable to promote those interests, "a blood draw becomes necessary." Thus, in the case of unconscious drivers, who cannot blow into a breathalyzer, blood tests are essential for achieving the compelling interests described above.

Indeed, not only is the link to pressing interests here tighter; the interests themselves are greater: Drivers who are drunk enough to pass out at the wheel or soon afterward pose a much greater risk. It would be perverse if the more wanton behavior were rewarded—if the more harrowing threat were harder to punish.

For these reasons, there clearly is a "compelling need" for a blood test of drunk-driving suspects whose condition deprives officials of a reasonable opportunity to conduct a breath test. The only question left, under our exigency doctrine, is whether this compelling need justifies a warrantless search because there is, furthermore, " 'no time to secure a warrant.' "

We held that there was no time to secure a warrant before a blood test of a drunk-driving suspect in *Schmerber* because the officer there could "reasonably have believed that he was confronted with an emergency, in which the delay necessary to obtain a warrant, under the circumstances, threatened the destruction of evidence." So even if the constant dissipation of BAC evidence alone does not create an exigency, *Schmerber* shows that it does so when combined with other pressing needs. * * * Thus, exigency exists when (1) BAC evidence is dissipating and (2) some other factor creates pressing health, safety, or law enforcement needs that would take priority over a warrant application. Both conditions are met when a drunk-driving suspect is unconscious, so *Schmerber* controls: With such suspects, too, a warrantless blood draw is lawful.

In *Schmerber*, the extra factor giving rise to urgent needs that would only add to the delay caused by a warrant application was a car accident; here it is the driver's unconsciousness. Indeed, unconsciousness does not just create pressing needs; it is itself a medical emergency. It means that the suspect will have to be rushed to the hospital or similar facility not just for the blood test itself but for urgent medical care. Police can reasonably anticipate that such a driver might require monitoring, positioning, and support on the way to the hospital; that his blood may be drawn anyway, for diagnostic purposes, immediately on arrival;8 and that immediate medical treatment could delay (or otherwise distort the results of) a blood draw conducted later, upon receipt of a warrant, thus reducing its evidentiary value. All of that sets this case apart from the uncomplicated drunk-driving scenarios addressed in *McNeely*. Just as the ramifications of a car accident pushed *Schmerber* over the line into exigency, so does the condition of an unconscious driver bring his blood draw under the exception. In such a case, as in *Schmerber*, an officer could "reasonably have believed that he was confronted with an emergency."

Indeed, in many unconscious-driver cases, the exigency will be more acute, as elaborated in the briefing and argument in this case. A driver so drunk as to lose consciousness is quite likely to crash, especially if he passes out before managing to park. And then the accident might give officers a slew of urgent tasks beyond that of securing (and working around) medical care for the suspect. Police may have to ensure that others who are injured receive prompt medical attention; they may have to provide first aid themselves until medical personnel arrive at the scene. In some cases, they may have to deal with fatalities. They may have to preserve evidence at the scene and block or redirect traffic to prevent further accidents. These pressing matters, too, would require responsible officers to put off applying for a warrant, and that would only exacerbate the delay—and imprecision—of any subsequent BAC test.

In sum, all these rival priorities would put officers, who must often engage in a form of triage, to a dilemma. It would force them to choose between prioritizing a warrant application, to the detriment of critical health and safety needs, and delaying the warrant application, and thus the BAC test, to the detriment of its evidentiary value and all the compelling interests served by BAC limits. This is just the kind of scenario for which the exigency rule was born—just the kind of grim dilemma it lives to dissolve.

Mitchell objects that a warrantless search is unnecessary in cases involving unconscious drivers because warrants these days can be obtained faster and more easily. But even * * * with better technology, the time required has shrunk, but it has not disappeared. In the emergency scenarios created by unconscious drivers, forcing police to put off other tasks for even a relatively short period of time may have terrible collateral costs. That is just what it means for these situations to be emergencies.

When police have probable cause to believe a person has committed a drunk-driving offense and the driver's unconsciousness or stupor requires him to be taken to the hospital or similar facility before police have a reasonable opportunity to administer a standard evidentiary breath test, they may almost always order a warrantless blood test to measure the driver's BAC without offending the Fourth Amendment. We do not rule out the possibility that in an unusual case a defendant would be able to show that his blood would not have been drawn if police had not been seeking BAC information, and that police could not have reasonably judged that a warrant application would interfere with other pressing needs or duties. Because Mitchell did not have a chance to attempt to make that showing, a remand for that purpose is necessary. * * *

JUSTICE THOMAS, concurring in the judgment.

Today, the plurality adopts a difficult-to-administer rule: Exigent circumstances are generally present when police encounter a person suspected of drunk driving—except when they aren't. The plurality's presumption will rarely be rebutted, but it will nevertheless burden both officers and courts who must attempt to apply it. "The better (and far simpler) way to resolve" this case is to apply "the per se rule" I proposed [in *McNeely* and *Birchfield*, under which the natural metabolization of alcohol in the blood stream " 'creates an exigency once police have probable cause to believe the driver is drunk,' " regardless of whether the driver is conscious. Because I am of the view that the Wisconsin Supreme Court should apply that rule on remand, I concur only in the judgment. * * *

As I have explained before, "the imminent destruction of evidence" is a risk in every drunk-driving arrest and thus "implicates the exigent-circumstances doctrine." *McNeely*. * * *

JUSTICE SOTOMAYOR, with whom JUSTICE GINSBURG and JUSTICE KAGAN join, dissenting.

The plurality's decision rests on the false premise that today's holding is necessary to spare law enforcement from a choice between attending to emergency situations and securing evidence used to enforce state drunk-driving laws. Not so. To be sure, drunk driving poses significant dangers that Wisconsin and other States must be able to curb. But the question here is narrow: What must police do before ordering a blood draw of a person suspected of drunk driving who has become unconscious? Under the Fourth Amendment, the answer is clear: If there is time, get a warrant.

The State of Wisconsin conceded in the state courts that it had time to get a warrant to draw Gerald Mitchell's blood, and that should be the end of the matter. Because the plurality needlessly casts aside the established protections of the warrant requirement in favor of a brand new presumption of exigent circumstances that Wisconsin does not urge, that the state courts did not consider, and that contravenes this Court's precedent, I respectfully dissent.* * *

The Fourth Amendment guarantees "[t]he right of the people to be secure in their persons . . . against unreasonable searches and seizures." When the aim of a search is to uncover evidence of a crime, the Fourth Amendment generally requires police to obtain a warrant.

The warrant requirement is not a mere formality; it ensures that necessary judgment calls are made " 'by a neutral and detached magistrate,' " not " 'by the officer engaged in the often competitive enterprise of ferreting out crime.' " *Schmerber v. California*, 384 U.S. 757, 770 (1966). A warrant thus serves as a check against searches that violate the Fourth Amendment by ensuring that a police officer is not made the sole interpreter of the Constitution's protections. * * *

For decades, this Court has stayed true to the Fourth Amendment's warrant requirement and the narrowness of its exceptions, even in the face of attempts categorically to exempt blood testing from its protections. In *Schmerber*, a man was hospitalized following a car accident. At the scene of the accident and later at the hospital, a police officer noticed signs of intoxication, and he arrested Schmerber for drunk driving. Without obtaining a warrant, the officer ordered a blood draw to measure Schmerber's BAC, and Schmerber later challenged the blood test as an unreasonable search under the Fourth Amendment. The Court reinforced that search warrants are "ordinarily required . . . where intrusions into the human body are concerned," but it ultimately held that exigent circumstances justified the particular search at issue because certain "special facts"—namely, an unusual delay caused by the investigation at the scene and the subsequent hospital trip— left the police with "no time to seek out a magistrate and secure a warrant" before losing the evidence.

More recently, in *McNeely*, the Court held that blood tests are not categorically exempt from the warrant requirement, explaining that exigency "must be determined case by case based on the totality of the circumstances." "[T]he natural dissipation of alcohol in the blood may support a finding of exigency in a specific case," but "it does not do so categorically." If officers "can reasonably obtain a warrant before a blood sample can be drawn without significantly undermining the efficacy of the search," the Court made clear, "the Fourth Amendment mandates that they do so." * * *

In *Birchfield*, the Court rejected another attempt categorically to exempt blood draws from the warrant requirement. The Court considered whether warrantless breath and blood tests to determine a person's BAC level were permissible as searches incident to arrest. The Court held that warrantless breath tests were permitted because they are insufficiently intrusive to outweigh the State's need for BAC testing. As to blood tests, however, the Court held the opposite: Because they are significantly more intrusive than breath tests, the warrant requirement applies unless particular exigent circumstances prevent officers from obtaining a warrant. * * *

Those cases resolve this one. * * *

Against this precedential backdrop, Wisconsin's primary argument has always been that Mitchell consented to the blood draw through the State's "implied-consent law." Under that statute, a motorist who drives on the State's roads is "deemed" to have consented to a blood draw, breath test, and urine test, and that supposed consent allows a warrantless blood draw from an unconscious motorist as long as the police have probable cause to believe that the motorist has violated one of the State's impaired driving statutes.

The plurality does not rely on the consent exception here. With that sliver of the plurality's reasoning I agree. I would go further and hold that the state statute, however phrased, cannot itself create the actual and informed consent that the Fourth Amendment requires. * * *

Rather than simply applying this Court's precedents to address—and reject—Wisconsin's implied-consent theory, the plurality today takes the extraordinary step of relying on an issue, exigency, that Wisconsin has affirmatively waived. Wisconsin has not once, in any of its briefing before this Court or the state courts, argued that exigent circumstances were present here. * * *

Rather than hold Wisconsin to a concession from which it has never wavered, the plurality takes on the waived theory. As " 'a court of review, not of first view,' " however, this Court is not in the business of volunteering new rationales neither raised nor addressed below, and even less ones that no party has raised here. * * *

There are good reasons why Wisconsin never asked any court to consider applying any version of the exigency exception here: This Court's precedents foreclose it. According to the plurality, when the police attempt to obtain a blood sample from a person suspected of drunk driving, there will "almost always" be exigent circumstances if the person falls unconscious. As this case demonstrates, however, the fact that a suspect fell unconscious at some point before the blood draw does not mean that there was insufficient time to get a warrant. * * *

[A]s the Court has observed, significant technological advances have allowed for "more expeditious processing of warrant applications." In the federal system, magistrate judges can issue warrants based on sworn testimony communicated over the phone or through " 'other reliable electronic means.' " In a sizable majority of States, police officers can apply for warrants "remotely through various means, including telephonic or radio communication, electronic communication such as e-mail, and video conferencing." And the use of "standard-form warrant applications" has streamlined the warrant process in many States as well, especially in this context. As a result, judges can often issue warrants in 5 to 15 minutes. * * *

* * * The plurality instead bases its de facto categorical exigency exception on nothing more than a " 'considerable overgeneralization,' " as well as empirical assumptions that the parties not only lacked a chance to address, but that are also belied by Wisconsin's concession in this case.[7] * * *

---

    [7] In addition to offering a justification for Wisconsin's warrantless search that the State itself has disavowed, the plurality also relieves all States of their burden to justify similar warrantless searches. Until now, the Court has said that "the police bear a heavy burden when attempting to demonstrate an urgent need that might justify warrantless searches." *Welsh v. Wisconsin*, 466 U.S. 740 (1984); see *Coolidge v. New Hampshire*, 403 U.S. 443 (1971). Today, the plurality turns that presumption on its head in favor of a new one that "almost always" authorizes the police to conduct warrantless blood draws even in the absence of an actual emergency.

The Fourth Amendment, as interpreted by our precedents, requires police officers seeking to draw blood from a person suspected of drunk driving to get a warrant if possible. That rule should resolve this case.

JUSTICE GORSUCH, dissenting.

[T]he application of the exigent circumstances doctrine in this area poses complex and difficult questions that neither the parties nor the courts below discussed. Rather than proceeding solely by self-direction, I would have dismissed this case as improvidently granted and waited for a case presenting the exigent circumstances question.

6. SEIZURE AND SEARCH OF PREMISES

The cases in this section reflect the basic notion that in the hierarchy of Fourth Amendment values, the privacy and sanctity of the home rank very high. Thus *Payton v. New York,* in contrast to the *Watson* case in the last section, holds that a warrant usually is required for an in-premises arrest. *Chimel v. California* permits only a limited search of the premises incident to an arrest therein, and *Kentucky v. King* illustrates that a search warrant is excused only in the event of exigent circumstances.

PAYTON V. NEW YORK
445 U.S. 573, 100 S.Ct. 1371, 63 L.Ed.2d 639 (1980).

JUSTICE STEVENS delivered the opinion of the Court. * * *

On January 14, 1970, after two days of intensive investigation, New York detectives had assembled evidence sufficient to establish probable cause to believe that Theodore Payton had murdered the manager of a gas station two days earlier. At about 7:30 a.m. on January 15, six officers went to Payton's apartment in the Bronx, intending to arrest him. They had not obtained a warrant. Although light and music emanated from the apartment, there was no response to their knock on the metal door. They summoned emergency assistance and, about 30 minutes later, used crowbars to break open the door and enter the apartment. No one was there. In plain view, however, was a 30-caliber shell casing that was seized and later admitted into evidence at Payton's murder trial. * * *

On March 14, 1974, Obie Riddick was arrested for the commission of two armed robberies that had occurred in 1971. He had been identified by the victims in June of 1973 and in January 1974 the police had learned his address. They did not obtain a warrant for his arrest. At about noon on March 14, a detective, accompanied by three other officers, knocked on the door of the Queens house where Riddick was living. When his young son opened the door, they could see Riddick sitting in bed covered by a sheet. They entered the house and placed him under arrest. Before permitting him to dress, they opened a chest of drawers two feet from the bed in search of weapons and found narcotics and related paraphernalia. Riddick was subsequently indicted on narcotics charges. * * *

The New York Court of Appeals, in a single opinion, affirmed the convictions of both Payton and Riddick. * * *

Before addressing the narrow question presented by these appeals, we put to one side other related problems that are *not* presented today. Although it is arguable that the warrantless entry to effect Payton's arrest might have been justified by exigent circumstances, none of the New York courts relied on any such justification. The Court of Appeals majority treated both *Payton's* and *Riddick's* cases as involving routine arrests in which there was ample time to obtain a warrant, and we will do the same. Accordingly, we have no occasion to consider the sort of emergency or dangerous situation, described in our cases as "exigent circumstances," that would justify a warrantless entry into a home for the purpose of either arrest or search.

Nor do these cases raise any question concerning the authority of the police, without either a search or arrest warrant, to enter a third party's home to arrest a suspect. The police broke into Payton's apartment intending to arrest Payton and they arrested Riddick in his own dwelling. We also note that in neither case is it argued that the police lacked probable cause to believe that the suspect was at home when they entered. Finally, in both cases we are dealing with entries into homes made without the consent of any occupant. In *Payton,* the police used crowbars to break down the door and in *Riddick,* although his three-year-old son answered the door, the police entered before Riddick had an opportunity either to object or to consent. * * *

It is a "basic principle of Fourth Amendment law" that searches and seizures inside a home without a warrant are presumptively unreasonable. Yet it is also well-settled that objects such as weapons or contraband found in a public place may be seized by the police without a warrant. The seizure of property in plain view involves no invasion of privacy and is presumptively reasonable, assuming that there is probable cause to associate the property with criminal activity. * * *

As the late Judge Leventhal recognized, this distinction has equal force when the seizure of a person is involved. Writing on the constitutional issue now before us for the United States Court of Appeals for the District of Columbia Circuit sitting en banc, *Dorman v. United States,* 435 F.2d 385 (D.C.Cir.1970), Judge Leventhal first noted the settled rule that warrantless arrests in public places are valid. He immediately recognized, however, that

> "[a] greater burden is placed [ ] on officials who enter a home or dwelling without consent. Freedom from intrusion into the home or dwelling is the archetype of the privacy protection secured by the Fourth Amendment."

His analysis of this question then focused on the long-settled premise that, absent exigent circumstances, a warrantless entry to search for weapons or contraband is unconstitutional even when a felony has been committed and there is probable cause to believe that incriminating evidence will be found within. He reasoned that the constitutional protection afforded to the individual's interest in the privacy of his own home is equally applicable to a warrantless entry for the purpose of arresting a resident of the house; for it is inherent in such an entry that a search for the suspect may be required before he can be apprehended. Judge Leventhal concluded that an entry to arrest and an entry to search for and to seize property implicate the same interest in preserving the privacy and the sanctity of the home, and justify the same level of constitutional protection. * * * We find this reasoning to be persuasive and in accord with this Court's Fourth Amendment decisions.

The majority of the New York Court of Appeals, however, suggested that there is a substantial difference in the relative intrusiveness of an entry to search for property and an entry to search for a person. It is true that the area that may legally be searched is broader when executing a search warrant than when executing an arrest warrant in the home. This difference may be more theoretical than real, however, because the police may need to check the entire premises for safety reasons, and sometimes they ignore the restrictions on searches incident to arrest.

But the critical point is that any differences in the intrusiveness of entries to search and entries to arrest are merely ones of degree rather than kind. The two intrusions share this fundamental characteristic: the breach of the entrance to an individual's home. * * * In terms that apply equally to seizures of property and to seizures of persons, the Fourth Amendment has drawn a firm line at the entrance to the house. Absent exigent circumstances, that threshold may not reasonably be crossed without a warrant. * * * a

The parties have argued at some length about the practical consequences of a warrant requirement as a precondition to a felony arrest in the home. In the absence of any evidence that effective law enforcement has suffered in those States that already have such a requirement, we are inclined to view such arguments with skepticism. More fundamentally, however, such arguments of policy must give way to a constitutional command that we consider to be unequivocal.

Finally, we note the State's suggestion that only a search warrant based on probable cause to believe the suspect is at home at a given time can adequately protect the privacy interests at stake, and since such a warrant requirement is manifestly impractical, there need be no warrant of any kind. We find this

---

a   At this point, Stevens, J., observed that New York argued that "the reasons supporting the *Watson* holding require a similar result here. In *Watson* the Court relied on (a) the well-settled common-law rule that a warrantless arrest in a public place is valid if the arresting officer had probable cause to believe the suspect is a felon; (b) the clear consensus among the States adhering to that well-settled common-law rule; and (c) the expression of the judgment of Congress that such an arrest is 'reasonable.' We consider each of these reasons as it applies to a warrantless entry into a home for the purpose of making a routine felony arrest."

In an extended analysis, the *Payton* majority concluded (a) that "the relevant common law does not provide the same guidance that was present in *Watson*," as there is "no direct authority supporting forcible entries into a home to make a routine arrest and the weight of the scholarly opinion is somewhat to the contrary"; (b) that presently 24 states permit such warrantless entries, 15 prohibit them, and 11 have taken no position, with "a significant decline during the last decade in the number of States permitting warrantless entries for arrest"; and (c) that "no congressional determination that warrantless entries into the home are 'reasonable' has been called to our attention." While the majority then concluded from this that "neither history nor this Nation's experience" lent support to the New York position, the *Payton* dissenters read essentially the same data as supporting their position.

ingenious argument unpersuasive. It is true that an arrest warrant requirement may afford less protection than a search warrant requirement, but it will suffice to interpose the magistrate's determination of probable cause between the zealous officer and the citizen. If there is sufficient evidence of a citizen's participation in a felony to persuade a judicial officer that his arrest is justified, it is constitutionally reasonable to require him to open his doors to the officers of the law. Thus, for Fourth Amendment purposes, an arrest warrant founded on probable cause implicitly carries with it the limited authority to enter a dwelling in which the suspect lives[b] when there is reason to believe the suspect is within.

Because no arrest warrant was obtained in either of these cases, the judgments must be reversed * * *.[c]

JUSTICE WHITE, with whom THE CHIEF JUSTICE and JUSTICE REHNQUIST join, dissenting. * * *

Today's decision ignores the carefully crafted restrictions on the common-law power of arrest entry and thereby overestimates the dangers inherent in that practice. At common law, absent exigent circumstances, entries to arrest could be made only for felony. Even in cases of felony, the officers were required to announce their presence, demand admission, and be refused entry before they were entitled to break doors. Further, it seems generally accepted that entries could be made only during daylight hours. And, in my view, the officer entering to arrest must have reasonable grounds to believe, not only that the arrestee has committed a crime, but also that the person suspected is present in the house at the time of the entry.[13]

---

[b]   In *Steagald v. United States*, 451 U.S. 204 (1981), police entered Steagald's home in an effort to find one Lyons, for whom they had an arrest warrant; they did not find Lyons but did find drugs in plain view, resulting in Steagald's prosecution and conviction. In reversing the conviction, the Court, per Marshall, J., reasoned that "whether the arrest warrant issued in this case adequately safeguarded the interests protected by the Fourth Amendment depends upon what the warrant authorized the agents to do. To be sure, the warrant embodied a judicial finding that there was probable cause to believe that Ricky Lyons had committed a felony, and the warrant therefore authorized the officers to seize Lyons. However, the agents sought to do more than use the warrant to arrest Lyons in a public place or in his home; instead, they relied on the warrant as legal authority to enter the home of a third person based on their belief that Ricky Lyons might be a guest there. Regardless of how reasonable this belief might have been, it was never subjected to the detached scrutiny of a judicial officer. Thus, while the warrant in this case may have protected Lyons from an unreasonable seizure, it did absolutely nothing to protect petitioner's privacy interest in being free from an unreasonable invasion and search of his home. Instead, petitioner's only protection from an illegal entry and search was the agent's personal determination of probable cause. In the absence of exigent circumstances, we have consistently held that such judicially untested determinations are not reliable enough to justify an entry into a person's home to arrest him without a warrant, or a search of a home for objects in the absence of a search warrant. We see no reason to depart from this settled course when the search of a home is for a person rather than an object."

[c]   Justice Blackmun's concurring opinion is omitted.

[13]   I do not necessarily disagree with the Court's discussion of the quantum of probable cause necessary to make a valid home arrest. The Court indicates that only an arrest warrant, and not a search warrant, is required. To obtain the warrant, therefore, the officers need only show probable cause that a crime has been committed and that the suspect committed it. However, under today's decision, the officers apparently need an extra increment of probable cause when executing the arrest warrant, namely grounds to believe that the suspect is within the dwelling.

These four restrictions on home arrests—felony, knock and announce, daytime, and stringent probable cause—constitute powerful and complementary protections for the privacy interests associated with the home. The felony requirement guards against abusive or arbitrary enforcement and ensures that invasions of the home occur only in case of the most serious crimes. The knock and announce and daytime requirement protect individuals against the fear, humiliation and embarrassment of being aroused from the beds in states of partial or complete undress. And these requirements allow the arrestee to surrender at his front door, thereby maintaining his dignity and preventing the officers from entering other rooms of the dwelling. The stringent probable cause requirement would help ensure against the possibility that the police would enter when the suspect was not home, and, in searching for him, frighten members of the family or ransack parts of the house, seizing items in plain view. In short, these requirements, taken together, permit an individual suspected of a serious crime to surrender at the front door of his dwelling and thereby avoid most of the humiliation and indignity that the Court seems to believe necessarily accompany a house arrest entry. Such a front door arrest, in my view, is no more intrusive on personal privacy than the public warrantless arrests which we found to pass constitutional muster in *Watson*.[14]

All of these limitations on warrantless arrest entries are satisfied on the facts of the present cases. The arrests here were for serious felonies—murder and armed robbery—and both occurred during daylight hours. The authorizing statutes required that the police announce their business and demand entry; neither Payton nor Riddick makes any contention that these statutory requirements were not fulfilled. And it is not argued that the police had no probable cause to believe that both Payton and Riddick were in their dwellings at the time of the entries. Today's decision, therefore, sweeps away any possibility that warrantless home entries might be permitted in some limited situations other than those in which exigent circumstances are present. The Court substitutes, in one sweeping decision, a rigid constitutional rule in place of the common-law approach, evolved over hundreds of years, which achieved a flexible accommodation between the demands of personal privacy and the legitimate needs of law enforcement.

A rule permitting warrantless arrest entries would not pose a danger that officers would use their entry power as a pretext to justify an otherwise invalid warrantless search. A search pursuant to a warrantless arrest entry will rarely, if ever, be as complete as one under authority of a search warrant. If the suspect surrenders at the door, the officers may not enter other rooms. Of course, the suspect may flee or hide, or may not be at home, but the officers cannot anticipate the first two of these possibilities and the last is unlikely given the requirement of probable cause to believe that the suspect is at home. Even when officers are justified in searching other rooms, they may seize only items within the arrestee's position [sic] or immediate control or items in plain view discovered during the course of a search reasonably directed at discovering a hiding suspect. Hence a

---

[14] If the suspect flees or hides, of course, the intrusiveness of the entry will be somewhat greater; but the policeman's hands should not be tied merely because of the possibility that the suspect will fail to cooperate with legitimate actions by law enforcement personnel.

warrantless home entry is likely to uncover far less evidence than a search conducted under authority of a search warrant. Furthermore, an arrest entry will inevitably tip off the suspects and likely result in destruction or removal of evidence not uncovered during the arrest. I therefore cannot believe that the police would take the risk of losing valuable evidence through a pretextual arrest entry rather than applying to a magistrate for a search warrant.

While exaggerating the invasion of personal privacy involved in home arrests, the Court fails to account for the danger that its rule will "severely hamper effective law enforcement." The policeman on his beat must now make subtle discriminations that perplex even judges in their chambers. As Justice Powell noted, concurring in *United States v. Watson,* police will sometimes delay making an arrest, even after probable cause is established, in order to be sure that they have enough evidence to convict. Then, if they suddenly have to arrest, they run the risk that the subsequent exigency will not excuse their prior failure to obtain a warrant. This problem cannot effectively be cured by obtaining a warrant as soon as probable cause is established because of the chance that the warrant will go stale before the arrest is made.

Further, police officers will often face the difficult task of deciding whether the circumstances are sufficiently exigent to justify their entry to arrest without a warrant. This is a decision that must be made quickly in the most trying of circumstances. If the officers mistakenly decide that the circumstances are exigent, the arrest will be invalid and any evidence seized incident to the arrest or in plain view will be excluded at trial. On the other hand, if the officers mistakenly determine that exigent circumstances are lacking, they may refrain from making the arrest, thus creating the possibility that a dangerous criminal will escape into the community. The police could reduce the likelihood of escape by staking out all possible exits until the circumstances become clearly exigent or a warrant is obtained. But the costs of such a stakeout seem excessive in an era of rising crime and scarce police resources.

The uncertainty inherent in the exigent circumstances determination burdens the judicial system as well. In the case of searches, exigent circumstances are sufficiently unusual that this Court has determined that the benefits of a warrant outweigh the burdens imposed, including the burdens on the judicial system. In contrast, arrests recurringly involve exigent circumstances, and this Court has heretofore held that a warrant can be dispensed with without undue sacrifice in Fourth Amendment values. The situation should be no different with respect to arrests in the home. Under today's decision, whenever the police have made a warrantless home arrest there will be the possibility of "endless litigation with respect to the existence of exigent circumstances, whether it was practicable to get a warrant, whether the suspect was about to flee, and the like."

* * * It would be far preferable to adopt a clear and simple rule: after knocking and announcing their presence, police may enter the home to make a daytime arrest without a warrant when there is probable cause to believe that the person to be arrested committed a felony and is present in the house. * * *

CHIMEL V. CALIFORNIA

395 U.S. 752, 89 S.Ct. 2034, 23 L.Ed.2d 685 (1969).

JUSTICE STEWART delivered the opinion of the Court. * * *

The relevant facts are essentially undisputed. Late in the afternoon of September 13, 1965, three police officers arrived at the Santa Ana, California, home of the petitioner with a warrant authorizing his arrest for the burglary of a coin shop. The officers knocked on the door, identified themselves to the petitioner's wife, and asked if they might come inside. She ushered them into the house, where they waited 10 or 15 minutes until the petitioner returned home from work. When the petitioner entered the house, one of the officers handed him the arrest warrant and asked for permission to "look around." The petitioner objected, but was advised that "on the basis of the lawful arrest," the officers would nonetheless conduct a search. No search warrant had been issued.

Accompanied by the petitioner's wife, the officers then looked through the entire three-bedroom house, including the attic, the garage, and a small workshop. In some rooms the search was relatively cursory. In the master bedroom and sewing room, however the officers directed the petitioner's wife to open drawers and "to physically move contents of the drawers from side to side so that [they] might view any items that would have come from [the] burglary." After completing the search, they seized numerous items—primarily coins, but also several medals, tokens, and a few other objects. The entire search took between 45 minutes and an hour.

At the petitioner's subsequent state trial on two charges of burglary, the items taken from his house were admitted into evidence against him, over his objection that they had been unconstitutionally seized. He was convicted, and the judgments * * * affirmed * * *.

Without deciding the question, we proceed on the hypothesis that the California courts were correct in holding that the arrest of the petitioner was valid under the Constitution. This brings us directly to the question whether the warrantless search of the petitioner's entire house can be constitutionally justified as incident to that arrest. The decisions of this Court bearing upon that question have been far from consistent, as even the most cursory review makes evident.[a]

---

[a]　In an omitted portion of the opinion, the Court described how dictum on search incident to arrest broadened from search of the "person," *Weeks v. United States*, 232 U.S. 383 (1914), to search for what is "upon his person or in his control," *Carroll v. United States*, 267 U.S. 132 (1925), to search of "persons lawfully arrested" and "the place where the arrest is made," *Agnello v. United States*, 269 U.S. 20 (1925). Then, in *Marron v. United States*, 275 U.S. 192 (1927), concerning seizure of evidence at a place where illegal liquor sales were occurring, the Court held that because the police had made an arrest on the premises they "had a right without a warrant contemporaneously to search the place in order to find and seize the things used to carry on the criminal enterprise." But in *Go-Bart Importing Co. v. United States*, 282 U.S. 344 (1931), *Marron* was limited to where the items seized "were visible and accessible and in the offender's immediate custody" and there "was no threat of force or general search or rummaging of the place." This limitation was reiterated in *United States v. Lefkowitz*, 285 U.S. 452 (1932), which, like *Go-Bart*, held unlawful a search of a desk despite the fact the search had accompanied a lawful arrest, but was abandoned in *Harris v. United States*, 331 U.S. 145 (1947), upholding the search of a four-room apartment as "incident to arrest." But *Harris* was not followed in *Trupiano v. United States*,

In 1950 * * * came *United States v. Rabinowitz,* 339 U.S. 56 (1950), the decision upon which California primarily relies in the case now before us. In *Rabinowitz,* federal authorities had been informed that the defendant was dealing in stamps bearing forged overprints. On the basis of that information they secured a warrant for his arrest, which they executed at his one-room business office. At the time of the arrest, the officers "searched the desk, safe, and file cabinets in the office for about an hour and a half," and seized 573 stamps with forged overprints. The stamps were admitted into evidence at the defendant's trial, and this Court affirmed his conviction, rejecting the contention that the warrantless search had been unlawful. The Court held that the search in its entirety fell within the principle giving law enforcement authorities "[t]he right 'to search the place where the arrest is made in order to find and seize things connected with the crime * * *.' " * * * The test, said the Court, "is not whether it is reasonable to procure a search warrant, but whether the search was reasonable."

Rabinowitz has come to stand for the proposition, inter alia, that a warrantless search "incident to a lawful arrest" may generally extend to the area that is considered to be in the "possession" or under the "control" of the person arrested. And it was on the basis of that proposition that the California courts upheld the search of the petitioner's entire house in this case. That doctrine, however, at least in the broad sense in which it was applied by the California courts in this case, can withstand neither historical nor rational analysis.

Even limited to its own facts, the *Rabinowitz* decision was, as we have seen, hardly founded on an unimpeachable line of authority. * * *

Nor is the rationale by which the State seeks here to sustain the search of the petitioner's house supported by a reasoned view of the background and purpose of the Fourth Amendment. Mr. Justice Frankfurter wisely pointed out in his *Rabinowitz* dissent that the Amendment's proscription of "unreasonable searches and seizures" must be read in light of "the history that gave rise to the words"—a history of "abuses so deeply felt by the Colonies as to be one of the potent causes of the Revolution * * *." The Amendment was in large part a reaction to the general warrants and warrantless searches that had so alienated the colonists and had helped speed the movement for independence. In the scheme of the Amendment, therefore, the requirement that "no Warrants shall issue, but upon probable cause," plays a crucial part. * * * Even in the *Agnello* case the Court relied upon the rule that "[b]elief, however well founded, that an article sought is concealed in a dwelling house furnishes no justification for a search of that place without a warrant. And such searches are held unlawful notwithstanding facts unquestionably showing probable cause." Clearly, the general requirement that a search warrant be obtained is not lightly to be dispensed with, and "the burden is on those seeking [an] exemption [from the requirement] to show the need for it * * *."

* * * When an arrest is made, it is reasonable for the arresting officer to search the person arrested in order to remove any weapons that the latter might seek to

---

334 U.S. 699 (1948), declaring that "law enforcement agents must secure and use search warrants wherever reasonably practicable."

use in order to resist arrest or effect his escape. Otherwise, the officer's safety might well be endangered, and the arrest itself frustrated. In addition, it is entirely reasonable for the arresting officer to search for and seize any evidence on the arrestee's person in order to prevent its concealment or destruction. And the area into which an arrestee might reach in order to grab a weapon or evidentiary items must, of course, be governed by a like rule. A gun on a table or in a drawer in front of one who is arrested can be as dangerous to the arresting officer as one concealed in the clothing of the person arrested. There is ample justification, therefore, for a search of the arrestee's person and the area "within his immediate control"— construing that phrase to mean the area from within which he might gain possession of a weapon or destructible evidence.

There is no comparable justification, however, for routinely searching rooms other than that in which an arrest occurs—or, for that matter, for searching through all the desk drawers or other closed or concealed areas in that room itself.[b] Such searches, in the absence of well-recognized exceptions, may be made only under the authority of a search warrant. The "adherence to judicial processes" mandated by the Fourth Amendment requires no less. * * *

It is argued in the present case that it is "reasonable" to search a man's house when he is arrested in it. But that argument is founded on little more than a subjective view regarding the acceptability of certain sorts of police conduct, and not on considerations relevant to Fourth Amendment interests. Under such an unconfined analysis, Fourth Amendment protection in this area would approach the evaporation point. It is not easy to explain why, for instance, it is less subjectively "reasonable" to search a man's house when he is arrested on his front lawn—or just down the street—than it is when he happens to be in the house at the time of arrest. * * *

It would be possible, of course, to draw a line between *Rabinowitz* and *Harris* on the one hand, and this case on the other. For *Rabinowitz* involved a single room, and *Harris* a four-room apartment, while in the case before us an entire house was searched. But such a distinction would be highly artificial. The rationale that allowed the searches and seizures in *Rabinowitz* and *Harris* would allow the searches and seizures in this case. No consideration relevant to the Fourth Amendment suggests any point of rational limitation, once the search is allowed to

---

b   But the Court later held 7–2, in *Maryland v. Buie*, 494 U.S. 325 (1990), that police lawfully inside premises for the purpose of making an arrest may make a "protective sweep" for their own protection:

"We agree with the State, as did the court below, that a warrant was not required. We also hold that as an incident to the arrest the officers could, as a precautionary matter and without probable cause or reasonable suspicion, look in closets and other spaces immediately adjoining the place of arrest from which an attack could be immediately launched. Beyond that, however, we hold that there must be articulable facts which, taken together with the rational inferences from those facts, would warrant a reasonable prudent officer in believing that the area to be swept harbors an individual posing a danger to those on the arrest scene. * * *

"We should emphasize that such a protective sweep, aimed at protecting the arresting officers, if justified by the circumstances, is nevertheless not a full search of the premises, but may extend only to a cursory inspection of those spaces where a person may be found. The sweep lasts no longer than is necessary to dispel the reasonable suspicion of danger and in any event no longer than it takes to complete the arrest and depart the premises."

go beyond the area from which the person arrested might obtain weapons or evidentiary items. The only reasoned distinction is one between a search of the person arrested and the area within his reach on the one hand, and more extensive searches on the other.[12]

The petitioner correctly points out that one result of decisions such as *Rabinowitz* and *Harris* is to give law enforcement officials the opportunity to engage in searches not justified by probable cause, by the simple expedient of arranging to arrest suspects at home rather than elsewhere. We do not suggest that the petitioner is necessarily correct in his assertion that such a strategy was utilized here, but the fact remains that had he been arrested earlier in the day, at his place of employment rather than at home, no search of his house could have been made without a search warrant. In any event, even apart from the possibility of such police tactics, the general point so forcefully made by Judge Learned Hand remains:

> "After arresting a man in his house, to rummage at will among his papers in search of whatever will convict him, appears to us to be indistinguishable from what might be done under a general warrant; indeed, the warrant would give more protection, for presumably it must be issued by a magistrate. True, by hypothesis the power would not exist, if the supposed offender were not found on the premises; but it is small consolation to know that one's papers are safe only so long as one is not at home."

Rabinowitz and *Harris* have been the subject of critical commentary for many years, and have been relied upon less and less in our own decisions. It is time, for the reasons we have stated, to hold that on their own facts, and insofar as the principles they stand for are inconsistent with those that we have endorsed today, they are no longer to be followed.

Application of sound Fourth Amendment principles to the facts of this case produces a clear result. The search here went far beyond the petitioner's person and the area from within which he might have obtained either a weapon or something that could have been used as evidence against him. There was no constitutional justification, in the absence of a search warrant, for extending the

---

[12] It is argued in dissent that so long as there is probable cause to search the place where an arrest occurs, a search of that place would be permitted even though no search warrant has been obtained. This position seems to be based principally on two premises: first, that once an arrest has been made, the additional invasion of privacy stemming from the accompanying search is "relatively minor"; and second, that the victim of the search may "shortly thereafter" obtain a judicial determination of whether the search was justified by probable cause. With respect to the second premise, one may initially question whether all of the States in fact provide the speedy suppression procedures the dissent assumes. More fundamentally, however, we cannot accept the view that Fourth Amendment interests are vindicated so long as "the rights of the criminal" are "protect[ed] * * * against introduction of evidence seized without probable cause." The Amendment is designed to prevent, not simply to redress, unlawful police action. In any event, we cannot join in characterizing the invasion of privacy that results from a top-to-bottom search of a man's house as "minor." And we can see no reason why, simply because some interference with an individual's privacy and freedom of movement has lawfully taken place, further intrusions should automatically be allowed despite the absence of a warrant that the Fourth Amendment would otherwise require.

search beyond that area. The scope of the search was, therefore, "unreasonable" under the Fourth and Fourteenth Amendments, and the petitioner's conviction cannot stand.

Reversed.

JUSTICE HARLAN, concurring.

* * * The only thing that has given me pause in voting to overrule *Harris* and *Rabinowitz* is that as a result of *Mapp v. Ohio,* every change in Fourth Amendment law must now be obeyed by state officials facing widely different problems of local law enforcement. We simply do not know the extent to which cities and towns across the Nation are prepared to administer the greatly expanded warrant system which will be required by today's decision; nor can we say with assurance that in each and every local situation, the warrant requirement plays an essential role in the protection of those fundamental liberties protected against state infringement by the Fourteenth Amendment. * * *

JUSTICE WHITE, with whom JUSTICE BLACK joins, dissenting.

* * * The Court has always held, and does not today deny, that when there is probable cause to search and it is "impracticable" for one reason or another to get a search warrant, then a warrantless search may be reasonable. This is the case whether an arrest was made at the time of the search or not. * * *

This case provides a good illustration of my point that it is unreasonable to require police to leave the scene of an arrest in order to obtain a search warrant when they already have probable cause to search and there is a clear danger that the items for which they may reasonably search will be removed before they return with a warrant. Petitioner was arrested in his home after an arrest whose validity will be explored below, but which I will now assume was valid. There was doubtless probable cause not only to arrest petitioner, but to search his house. He had obliquely admitted both to a neighbor, and to the owner of the burglarized store, that he had committed the burglary. In light of this, and the fact that the neighbor had seen other admittedly stolen property in petitioner's house, there was surely probable cause on which a warrant could have issued to search the house for the stolen coins. Moreover, had the police simply arrested petitioner, taken him off to the station house, and later returned with a warrant,[5] it seems very likely that petitioner's wife, who in view of petitioner's generally garrulous nature must have known of the robbery, would have removed the coins. For the police to search the house while the evidence they had probable cause to search out and seize was still there cannot be considered unreasonable.

---

[5] There were three officers at the scene of the arrest, one from the city where the coin burglary had occurred, and two from the city where the arrest was made. Assuming that one policeman from each city would be needed to bring the petitioner in and obtain a search warrant, one policeman could have been left to guard the house. However, if he not only could have remained in the house against petitioner's wife's will, but followed her about to assure that no evidence was being tampered with, the invasion of her privacy would be almost as great as that accompanying an actual search. Moreover, had the wife summoned an accomplice, one officer could not have watched them both.

This line of analysis, supported by the precedents of this Court, hinges on two assumptions. One is that the arrest of petitioner without a valid warrant[7] was constitutional as the majority assumes; the other is that the police were not required to obtain a search warrant in advance, even though they knew that the effect of the arrest might well be to alert petitioner's wife that the coins had better be removed soon. * * * It must very often be the case that by the time probable cause to arrest a man is accumulated, the man is aware of police interest in him or for other good reasons is on the verge of flight. Moreover, it will likely be very difficult to determine the probability of his flight. Given this situation, it may be best in all cases simply to allow the arrest if there is probable cause, especially since that issue can be determined very shortly after the arrest. * * *

If circumstances so often require the warrantless arrest that the law generally permits it, the typical situation will find the arresting officers lawfully on the premises without arrest or search warrant. * * * [W]here as here the existence of probable cause is independently established and would justify a warrant for a broader search for evidence, I would follow past cases and permit such a search to be carried out without a warrant, since the fact of arrest supplies an exigent circumstance justifying police action before the evidence can be removed, and also alerts the suspect to the fact of the search so that he can immediately seek judicial determination of probable cause in an adversary proceeding, and appropriate redress. * * *

KENTUCKY V. KING

563 U.S. 452, 131 S.Ct. 1849, 179 L.Ed.2d 865 (2011).

JUSTICE ALITO delivered the opinion of the Court.

[An undercover officer watching a controlled buy of crack cocaine radioed nearby uniformed officers to apprehend the suspect, who was moving quickly toward the breezeway of a nearby apartment building. As officers entered the breezeway they heard a door shut and detected a strong odor of burnt marijuana. The officers did not know which of the two apartments at the end of the breezeway the suspect had entered, but because they smelled marijuana smoke emanating from the apartment on the left they knocked on that door and announced their presence. They immediately "could hear people inside moving," as well as sounds as though "things were being moved inside the apartment," which, one officer later testified, "led the officers to believe that drug-related evidence was about to be destroyed." The officers then entered that apartment, occupied by King and others, and in a subsequent search found drugs, cash, and drug paraphernalia. (The original suspect was later found in the apartment to the right!) King was convicted on drug charges after the court denied his motion to suppress, ruling the search was (i) based on probable cause, and (ii) properly made without a search warrant given an important variety of exigent circumstances—as the Supreme Court has put it, the need "to prevent the imminent destruction of evidence." The Kentucky

---

[7] An arrest warrant was in fact issued, but it was issued on an inadequate supporting affidavit and was therefore invalid, so that the case must be considered as though no warrant had issued.

supreme court reversed, concluding police may not rely on exigent circumstances if "it was reasonably foreseeable that the investigative tactics employed by the police would create the exigent circumstances."]

Over the years, lower courts have developed an exception to the exigent circumstances rule, the so-called "police-created exigency" doctrine. Under this doctrine, police may not rely on the need to prevent destruction of evidence[a] when that exigency was "created" or "manufactured" by the conduct of the police. * * *

[T]he lower courts have held that the police-created exigency doctrine requires more than simple causation, but the lower courts have not agreed on the test to be applied. * * *

Some lower courts have adopted a rule that is similar to the one that we recognize today. * * * But others, including the Kentucky Supreme Court, have imposed additional requirements that are unsound and that we now reject.

Bad faith. Some courts, including the Kentucky Supreme Court, ask whether law enforcement officers " 'deliberately created the exigent circumstances with the bad faith intent to avoid the warrant requirement.' "

This approach is fundamentally inconsistent with our Fourth Amendment jurisprudence. "Our cases have repeatedly rejected" a subjective approach, asking only whether "the circumstances, viewed *objectively,* justify the action." Indeed, we have never held, outside limited contexts such as an "inventory search or administrative inspection . . . , that an officer's motive invalidates objectively justifiable behavior under the Fourth Amendment." *Whren v. United States,* [p. 191].

The reasons for looking to objective factors, rather than subjective intent, are clear. Legal tests based on reasonableness are generally objective, and this Court

---

[a]   Another type of exigency was addressed in *Brigham City v. Stuart,* 547 U.S. 398 (2006), where a unanimous Court declared: "One exigency obviating the requirement of a warrant is the need to assist persons who are seriously injured or threatened with such injury. * * * Accordingly, law enforcement officers may enter a home without a warrant to render emergency assistance to an injured occupant or to protect an occupant from imminent injury." The officers' entry in the instant case was lawful, for they had seen through a screen door and window that a juvenile being held back by several adults had broken loose and struck one of them sufficiently hard that the victim was spitting blood, and thus "had an objectively reasonable basis for believing both that the injured adult might need help and that the violence in the kitchen was just beginning." While the state court had suggested the "emergency aid doctrine" was inapplicable because the officer had entered not to assist the injured adult, but instead had acted "exclusively in their law enforcement capacity," the Supreme Court, citing *Whren* [p. 191], responded: "An action is 'reasonable' under the Fourth Amendment, regardless of the individual officer's state of mind, 'as long as the circumstances, viewed *objectively,* justify [the] action.' * * *It therefore does not matter here—even if their subjective motives could be so neatly unraveled—whether the officers entered the kitchen to arrest respondents and gather evidence against them or to assist the injured and prevent further violence."

Similarly, in *Michigan v. Fisher,* 558 U.S. 45 (2009), the Court rejected Fisher's argument "that the officers here could not have been motivated by a perceived need to provide medical assistance, since they never summoned emergency medical personnel," responding that "even if the failure to summon medical personnel conclusively established that [the officer] did not subjectively believe * * * that Fisher or someone else was seriously injured * * *, the test, as we have said, is not what [the officer] believed, but whether there was 'an objectively reasonable basis for believing' that medical assistance was needed, or persons were in danger."

has long taken the view that "evenhanded law enforcement is best achieved by the application of objective standards of conduct, rather than standards that depend upon the subjective state of mind of the officer."

Reasonable foreseeability. Some courts, again including the Kentucky Supreme Court, hold that police may not rely on an exigency if " 'it was reasonably foreseeable that the investigative tactics employed by the police would create the exigent circumstances.' " Courts applying this test have invalidated warrantless home searches on the ground that it was reasonably foreseeable that police officers, by knocking on the door and announcing their presence, would lead a drug suspect to destroy evidence.

Contrary to this reasoning, however, we have rejected the notion that police may seize evidence without a warrant only when they come across the evidence by happenstance. In *Horton* [*v. California*, 496 U.S. 128 (1990)], we held that the police may seize evidence in plain view even though the officers may be "interested in an item of evidence and fully expec[t] to find it in the course of a search."

Adoption of a reasonable foreseeability test would also introduce an unacceptable degree of unpredictability. For example, whenever law enforcement officers knock on the door of premises occupied by a person who may be involved in the drug trade, there is *some* possibility that the occupants may possess drugs and may seek to destroy them. Under a reasonable foreseeability test, it would be necessary to quantify the degree of predictability that must be reached before the police-created exigency doctrine comes into play.

A simple example illustrates the difficulties that such an approach would produce. Suppose that the officers in the present case did not smell marijuana smoke and thus knew only that there was a 50% chance that the fleeing suspect had entered the apartment on the left rather than the apartment on the right. Under those circumstances, would it have been reasonably foreseeable that the occupants of the apartment on the left would seek to destroy evidence upon learning that the police were at the door? Or suppose that the officers knew only that the suspect had disappeared into one of the apartments on a floor with 3, 5, 10, or even 20 units? If the police chose a door at random and knocked for the purpose of asking the occupants if they knew a person who fit the description of the suspect, would it have been reasonably foreseeable that the occupants would seek to destroy evidence?

We have noted that "[t]he calculus of reasonableness must embody allowance for the fact that police officers are often forced to make split-second judgments—in circumstances that are tense, uncertain, and rapidly evolving." The reasonable foreseeability test would create unacceptable and unwarranted difficulties for law enforcement officers who must make quick decisions in the field, as well as for judges who would be required to determine after the fact whether the destruction of evidence in response to a knock on the door was reasonably foreseeable based on what the officers knew at the time.

Probable cause and time to secure a warrant. Some courts, in applying the police-created exigency doctrine, fault law enforcement officers if, after acquiring evidence that is sufficient to establish probable cause to search particular premises, the officers do not seek a warrant but instead knock on the door and seek either to speak with an occupant or to obtain consent to search.

This approach unjustifiably interferes with legitimate law enforcement strategies. There are many entirely proper reasons why police may not want to seek a search warrant as soon as the bare minimum of evidence needed to establish probable cause is acquired. Without attempting to provide a comprehensive list of these reasons, we note a few.

First, the police may wish to speak with the occupants of a dwelling before deciding whether it is worthwhile to seek authorization for a search. They may think that a short and simple conversation may obviate the need to apply for and execute a warrant. Second, the police may want to ask an occupant of the premises for consent to search because doing so is simpler, faster, and less burdensome than applying for a warrant. A consensual search also "may result in considerably less inconvenience" and embarrassment to the occupants than a search conducted pursuant to a warrant. Third, law enforcement officers may wish to obtain more evidence before submitting what might otherwise be considered a marginal warrant application. Fourth, prosecutors may wish to wait until they acquire evidence that can justify a search that is broader in scope than the search that a judicial officer is likely to authorize based on the evidence then available. And finally, in many cases, law enforcement may not want to execute a search that will disclose the existence of an investigation because doing so may interfere with the acquisition of additional evidence against those already under suspicion or evidence about additional but as yet unknown participants in a criminal scheme.

We have said that "[l]aw enforcement officers are under no constitutional duty to call a halt to criminal investigation the moment they have the minimum evidence to establish probable cause." Faulting the police for failing to apply for a search warrant at the earliest possible time after obtaining probable cause imposes a duty that is nowhere to be found in the Constitution.

Standard or good investigative tactics. Finally, some lower court cases suggest that law enforcement officers may be found to have created or manufactured an exigency if the court concludes that the course of their investigation was "contrary to standard or good law enforcement practices (or to the policies or practices of their jurisdictions)." This approach fails to provide clear guidance for law enforcement officers and authorizes courts to make judgments on matters that are the province of those who are responsible for federal and state law enforcement agencies.

Respondent argues for a rule that differs from those discussed above, but his rule is also flawed. Respondent contends that law enforcement officers impermissibly create an exigency when they "engage in conduct that would cause a reasonable person to believe that entry is imminent and inevitable." In respondent's view, relevant factors include the officers' tone of voice in announcing their presence and the forcefulness of their knocks. But the ability of law enforcement officers to respond to an exigency cannot turn on such subtleties. * * *

If respondent's test were adopted, it would be extremely difficult for police officers to know how loudly they may announce their presence or how forcefully they may knock on a door without running afoul of the police-created exigency rule. And in most cases, it would be nearly impossible for a court to determine whether that threshold had been passed. The Fourth Amendment does not require the nebulous and impractical test that respondent proposes.

For these reasons, we conclude that the exigent circumstances rule applies when the police do not gain entry to premises by means of an actual or threatened violation of the Fourth Amendment. This holding provides ample protection for the privacy rights that the Amendment protects.

When law enforcement officers who are not armed with a warrant knock on a door, they do no more than any private citizen might do. And whether the person who knocks on the door and requests the opportunity to speak is a police officer or a private citizen, the occupant has no obligation to open the door or to speak. When the police knock on a door but the occupants choose not to respond or to speak, "the investigation will have reached a conspicuously low point," and the occupants "will have the kind of warning that even the most elaborate security system cannot provide." And even if an occupant chooses to open the door and speak with the officers, the occupant need not allow the officers to enter the premises and may refuse to answer any questions at any time.

Occupants who choose not to stand on their constitutional rights but instead elect to attempt to destroy evidence have only themselves to blame for the warrantless exigent-circumstances search that may ensue. * * *

We need not decide whether exigent circumstances existed in this case. * * * The Kentucky Supreme Court "assum[ed] for the purpose of argument that exigent circumstances existed," and it held that the police had impermissibly manufactured the exigency.

We, too, assume for purposes of argument that an exigency existed.[b] * * * Any question about whether an exigency actually existed is better addressed by the Kentucky Supreme Court on remand.

In this case, we see no evidence that the officers either violated the Fourth Amendment or threatened to do so prior to the point when they entered the apartment. Officer Cobb testified without contradiction that the officers "banged on the door as loud as [they] could" and announced either " 'Police, police, police' " or " 'This is the police.' " This conduct was entirely consistent with the Fourth Amendment, and we are aware of no other evidence that might show that the officers either violated the Fourth Amendment or threatened to do so (for example,

---

[b] Consider *Vale v. Louisiana*, 399 U.S. 30 (1970), where police arrested Vale in front of his house after observing him make a drug sale there, then made a cursory inspection of the house to see if anyone else was present, when his mother and brother entered the premises, prompting the police to conduct a warrantless search of the premises uncovering narcotics. In holding that search to be unconstitutional, the majority asserted the "officers were not responding to an emergency," as the "goods ultimately seized were not in the process of destruction" or "about to be removed from the jurisdiction." The two dissenters claimed that the Court's earlier cases indicated that exigent circumstances exist when "evidence or contraband was *threatened* with removal of destruction," which was so on the facts of the instant case.

by announcing that they would break down the door if the occupants did not open the door voluntarily). * * *

JUSTICE GINSBURG, dissenting.

The Court today arms the police with a way routinely to dishonor the Fourth Amendment's warrant requirement in drug cases. In lieu of presenting their evidence to a neutral magistrate, police officers may now knock, listen, then break the door down, nevermind that they had ample time to obtain a warrant. I dissent from the Court's reduction of the Fourth Amendment's force. * * *

Under an appropriately reined-in "emergency" or "exigent circumstances" exception, the result in this case should not be in doubt. The target of the investigation's entry into the building, and the smell of marijuana seeping under the apartment door into the hallway, the Kentucky Supreme Court rightly determined, gave the police "probable cause . . . sufficient . . . to obtain a warrant to search the . . . apartment." As that court observed, nothing made it impracticable for the police to post officers on the premises[c] while proceeding to obtain a warrant authorizing their entry. Before this Court, Kentucky does not urge otherwise. * * *

---

[c]   While Justice Ginsburg is apparently referring to posting of police in the apartment building but outside the apartment, could the supposed exigency have been dealt with by the police entering as they did and then simply detaining the three people found within while a search warrant was obtained? Consider the following two Supreme Court decisions addressing similar but not identical situations.

(1) In *Segura v. United States*, 468 U.S. 796 (1984), the police, upon confirming that they had observed a drug sale by Colon and Segura, went to their apartment building, arrested Segura in the lobby, and then arrested Colon when she answered a knock on the door of their apartment. Police then made a warrantless entry of the apartment and remained there until a search warrant was issued, which occurred some 19 hours later. The Court held "that where officers, having probable cause, enter premises, and with probable cause, arrest the occupants who have legitimate possessory interests in its contents and take them into custody and, for no more than the period here involved, secure the premises from within to preserve the status quo while others, in good faith, are in the process of obtaining a warrant, they do not violate the Fourth Amendment's proscription against unreasonable seizures." That holding was explicated in an opinion by two Justices stating: "Securing of the premises from within * * * was no more an interference with the petitioners' possessory interests in the contents of the apartment than a perimeter 'stakeout.' In other words, the initial entry—legal or not—does not affect the reasonableness of the seizure. Under either method—entry and securing from within or a perimeter stakeout—agents control the apartment pending arrival of the warrant; both an internal securing and a perimeter stakeout interfere to the same extent with the possessory interests of the owners. * * *

"* * * Here, of course, Segura and Colon, whose possessory interests were interfered with by the occupation, were under arrest and in the custody of the police throughout the entire period the agents occupied the apartment. The actual interference with their possessory interests in the apartment and its contents was, thus, virtually nonexistent."

The four dissenters argued that the occupation was an unreasonable search, infringing upon a reasonable expectation of privacy, and an unreasonable seizure, involving exercise of "complete dominion and control over the apartment and its contents"; and that the Fourth Amendment protects possessory interests in a residence even when the occupants are in custody.

(2) In *Illinois v. McArthur*, 531 U.S. 326 (2001), two police officers stood by outside to keep the peace while defendant's wife removed her effects from the family residence, a trailer. Upon exiting, she told the officers her husband had hidden marijuana under the couch, so the officers sought his permission to search the premises. When he refused, one officer left to obtain a search warrant, while another officer remained on the porch with defendant, who was told he could not reenter unless he was accompanied by the officer. A warrant was obtained an executed two hours later, but in the interim defendant entered the trailer two or three times, and on each occasion the officer stood just inside the door and observe his actions.

7. SEIZURE AND SEARCH OF VEHICLES AND EFFECTS

Several of the cases in this section clearly illustrate that motor vehicles receive substantially less Fourth Amendment protection than premises. *California v. Carney* (in contradistinction to *Vale*) permits probable cause searches of vehicles without a warrant; *Arizona v. Gant* (in contradistinction to *Chimel*) sometimes allows a broad search of vehicles incident to arrest of an "occupant" or "recent occupant"; and *Colorado v. Bertine* authorizes a warrantless inventory of lawfully seized vehicles.

Personal effects, such as luggage, rank somewhere between premises and vehicles in the Fourth Amendment hierarchy of values. Another case in this section, *California v. Acevedo*, explores why this is so and addresses the eventuating issue of what rules should control when personal effects are located inside a vehicle. But when a search is directed at an apparently nonimplicated passengers, as in *Wyoming v. Houghton*, the critical distinction becomes the differing privacy expectations as to a passenger's effects as compared to his or her person.

The final case in this section, *Riley v. California*, has to do with search of a cell phone found on the person of an arrestee. While search of containers taken from an arrestee's person has traditionally been dealt with as an aspect of search of the person, *Riley* has been reserved until this point because the Court's analysis makes use of a wider array of search-incident-to-arrest jurisprudence covering also search of premises and search of vehicles.

By a process of "balanc[ing] the privacy-related and law enforcement-related concerns," the Court concluded "that the restriction at issue was reasonable, and hence lawful, in light of" four enumerated circumstances: (i) "the police had probable cause to believe that McArthur's trailer home contained evidence of a crime and contraband, namely, unlawful drugs"; (ii) "the police had good reason to fear that, unless restrained, McArthur would destroy the drugs before they could return with a warrant," as they reasonably concluded that even before the requested consent to search he realized his angry wife had informed the police about the drugs; (iii) "the police made reasonable efforts to reconcile their law enforcement needs with the demands of personal privacy" by imposing "a significantly less restrictive restraint" than a warrantless search of the premises; and (iv) "the police imposed the restraint for a limited period of time, namely, two hours."

As for defendant's reliance upon *Welsh v. Wisconsin*, 466 U.S. 740 (1984), holding that police could not enter a home without a warrant in order to prevent the loss of evidence (namely, the defendant's blood alcohol level) of the "nonjailable traffic offense" of driving while intoxicated, the *McArthur* majority distinguished *Welsh* because (a) the offense involved here was punishable by up to 30 days in jail, and (b) "the restriction at issue here is less serious." (Only Justice Stevens concluded otherwise as to the *Welsh* doctrine.)

Justice Souter, concurring in *McArthur*, reasoned that had defendant remained inside the trailer then the "probability of destruction" of the marijuana "in anticipation of a warrant * * * would have justified the police in entering McArthur's trailer promptly to make a lawful, warrantless search," that this risk "abated and so did the reasonableness of entry by the police" once he came outside, but that once he came outside it was reasonable for the police to keep him from reentering not because "the law officiously insists on safeguarding a suspect's privacy from search," but rather because of "the law's strong preference for warrants, which underlies the rule that a search with a warrant has a stronger claim to justification on later, judicial review than a search without one. * * * The law can hardly raise incentives to obtain a warrant without giving the police a fair chance to take their probable cause to a magistrate and get one."

CALIFORNIA V. CARNEY

471 U.S. 386, 105 S.Ct. 2066, 85 L.Ed.2d 406 (1985).

CHIEF JUSTICE BURGER delivered the opinion of the Court. * * *

On May 31, 1979, Drug Enforcement Agency Agent Robert Williams watched respondent, Charles Carney, approach a youth in downtown San Diego. The youth accompanied Carney to a Dodge Mini Motor Home parked in a nearby lot. Carney and the youth closed the window shades in the motor home, including one across the front window. Agent Williams had previously received uncorroborated information that the same motor home was used by another person who was exchanging marihuana for sex. Williams, with assistance from other agents, kept the motor home under surveillance for the entire one and one-quarter hours that Carney and the youth remained inside. When the youth left the motor home, the agents followed and stopped him. The youth told the agents that he had received marijuana in return for allowing Carney sexual contacts.

At the officers' request, the youth returned to the motor home and knocked on its door; Carney stepped out. The agents identified themselves as law enforcement officers. Without a warrant or consent, one agent entered the motor home and observed marihuana, plastic bags, and a scale of the kind used in weighing drugs on a table. Agent Williams took Carney into custody and took possession of the motor home. A subsequent search of the motor home at the police station revealed additional marihuana in the cupboards and refrigerator.

Respondent was charged with possession of marihuana for sale. At a preliminary hearing, he moved to suppress the evidence discovered in the motor home. The Magistrate denied the motion, [but later the state supreme court reversed the conviction, holding the search was unreasonable because no warrant was obtained.]

* * * There are, of course, exceptions to the general rule that a warrant must be secured before a search is undertaken; one is the so-called "automobile exception" at issue in this case. This exception to the warrant requirement was first set forth by the Court 60 years ago in *Carroll v. United States*, 267 U.S. 132 (1925). There, the Court recognized that the privacy interests in an automobile are constitutionally protected; however, it held that the ready mobility of the automobile justifies a lesser degree of protection of those interests. The Court rested this exception on a long-recognized distinction between stationary structures and vehicles:

> "[T]he guaranty of freedom from unreasonable searches and seizures by the Fourth Amendment has been construed, practically since the beginning of Government, as recognizing a necessary difference between a search of a store, dwelling house or other structure in respect of which a proper official warrant readily may be obtained, and a search of a ship, motor boat, wagon or automobile, for contraband goods, where it is not practicable to secure a warrant because the vehicle can be *quickly moved* out of the locality or jurisdiction in which the warrant must be sought."

The capacity to be "quickly moved" was clearly the basis of the holding in *Carroll*, and our cases have consistently recognized ready mobility as one of the principal bases of the automobile exception. * * *

However, although ready mobility alone was perhaps the original justification for the vehicle exception, our later cases have made clear that ready mobility is not the only basis for the exception. The reasons for the vehicle exception, we have said, are twofold. "Besides the element of mobility, less rigorous warrant requirements govern because the expectation of privacy with respect to one's automobile is significantly less than that relating to one's home or office."

Even in cases where an automobile was not immediately mobile, the lesser expectation of privacy resulting from its use as a readily mobile vehicle justified application of the vehicular exception. In some cases, the configuration of the vehicle contributed to the lower expectations of privacy; for example, we held that, because the passenger compartment of a standard automobile is relatively open to plain view, there are lesser expectations of privacy. But even when enclosed "repository" areas have been involved, we have concluded that the lesser expectations of privacy warrant application of the exception. We have applied the exception in the context of a locked car trunk, a sealed package in a car trunk, a closed compartment under the dashboard, the interior of a vehicle's upholstery, or sealed packages inside a covered pickup truck.

These reduced expectations of privacy derive not from the fact that the area to be searched is in plain view, but from the pervasive regulation of vehicles capable of traveling on the public highways. As we explained in [an earlier] case:

> "Automobiles, unlike homes, are subjected to pervasive and continuing governmental regulation and controls, including periodic inspection and licensing requirements. As an everyday occurrence, police stop and examine vehicles when license plates or inspection stickers have expired, or if other violations, such as exhaust fumes or excessive noise, are noted, or if headlights or other safety equipment are not in proper working order."

The public is fully aware that it is accorded less privacy in its automobiles because of this compelling governmental need for regulation. Historically, "individuals always [have] been on notice that movable vessels may be stopped and searched on facts giving rise to probable cause that the vehicle contains contraband, without the protection afforded by a magistrate's prior evaluation of those facts." In short, the pervasive schemes of regulation, which necessarily lead to reduced expectations of privacy, and the exigencies attendant to ready mobility justify searches without prior recourse to the authority of a magistrate so long as the overriding standard of probable cause is met.

When a vehicle is being used on the highways, or if it is readily capable of such use and is found stationary in a place not regularly used for residential purposes—temporary or otherwise—the two justifications for the vehicle exception come into play. First, the vehicle is obviously readily mobile by the turn of a switch key, if not actually moving. Second, there is a reduced expectation of privacy stemming from its use as a licensed motor vehicle subject to a range of police regulation inapplicable to a fixed dwelling. At least in these circumstances, the overriding societal interests in effective law enforcement justify an immediate search before the vehicle and its occupants become unavailable.[a]

While it is true that respondent's vehicle possessed some, if not many of the attributes of a home, it is equally clear that the vehicle falls clearly within the scope of the exception laid down in *Carroll* and applied in succeeding cases. Like the automobile in *Carroll*, respondent's motor home was readily mobile. Absent the prompt search and seizure, it could readily have been moved beyond the reach of the police. Furthermore, the vehicle was licensed to "operate on public streets; [was] serviced in public places; * * * and [was] subject to extensive regulation and inspection." And the vehicle was so situated that an objective observer would conclude that it was being used not as a residence, but as a vehicle.

Respondent urges us to distinguish his vehicle from other vehicles within the exception because it was *capable of functioning as a home*. In our increasingly mobile society, many vehicles used for transportation can be and are being used not only for transportation but for shelter, i.e., as a "home" or "residence." To distinguish between respondent's motor home and an ordinary sedan for purposes of the vehicle exception would require that we apply the exception depending upon the size of the vehicle and the quality of its appointments. Moreover, to fail to apply the exception to vehicles such as a motor home ignores the fact that a motor home lends itself easily to use as an instrument of illicit drug traffic and other illegal activity. * * *

Our application of the vehicle exception has never turned on the other uses to which a vehicle might be put. The exception has historically turned on the ready mobility of the vehicle, and on the presence of the vehicle in a setting that objectively indicates that the vehicle is being used for transportation.[3] These two

---

a In *Maryland v. Dyson*, 527 U.S. 465 (1999), the Court, per curiam, summarily reversed a state court decision holding "that in order for the automobile exception to the warrant requirement to apply, there must not only be probable cause to believe that evidence of a crime is contained in the automobile, but also a separate finding of exigency precluding the police from obtaining a warrant." That holding, the Court declared, "rests upon an incorrect interpretation of the automobile exception to the Fourth Amendment's warrant requirement," which "does not have a separate exigency requirement."

In *Florida v. White*, 526 U.S. 559 (1999), upholding the warrantless *seizure* of a car on probable cause that the vehicle was contraband under the state forfeiture law, the Court took note of "the special considerations recognized in the context of movable items" in the *Carroll-Carney* line of cases, and then concluded the need was "equally weighty when the *automobile*, as opposed to its contents, is the contraband that the police seek to secure." The Court also observed that "our Fourth Amendment jurisprudence has consistently accorded law enforcement officials greater latitude in exercising their duties in public places," and deemed the instant case "nearly indistinguishable" from *G.M. Leasing Corp. v. United States*, 429 U.S. 338 (1977), upholding the warrantless seizure from a public area of automobiles in partial satisfaction of income tax assessments. Two dissenters in *White* objected (i) that an exigent circumstances rationale had no application "when the seizure is based upon a belief that the automobile may have been used at some time in the past to assist in illegal activity and the owner is already in custody," and (ii) that a warrant requirement "is bolstered by the inherent risks of hindsight at post-seizure hearings and law enforcement agencies' pecuniary interest in the seizure of such property."

3 We need not pass on the application of the vehicle exception to a motor home that is situated in a way or place that objectively indicates that it is being used as a residence. Among the factors that might be relevant in determining whether a warrant would be required in such a

requirements for application of the exception ensure that law enforcement officials are not unnecessarily hamstrung in their efforts to detect and prosecute criminal activity, and that the legitimate privacy interests of the public are protected. Applying the vehicle exception in these circumstances allows the essential purposes served by the exception to be fulfilled, while assuring that the exception will acknowledge legitimate privacy interests. * * *

This search was not unreasonable; it was plainly one that the magistrate could authorize if presented with these facts. * * *

The judgment of the California Supreme Court is reversed * * *.

JUSTICE STEVENS, with whom JUSTICE BRENNAN and JUSTICE MARSHALL join, dissenting. * * *

In this case, the motor home was parked in an off-the-street lot only a few blocks from the courthouse in downtown San Diego where dozens of magistrates were available to entertain a warrant application. The officers clearly had the element of surprise with them, and with curtains covering the windshield, the motor home offered no indication of any imminent departure. The officers plainly had probable cause to arrest the petitioner and search the motor home, and on this record, it is inexplicable why they eschewed the safe harbor of a warrant.

In the absence of any evidence of exigency in the circumstances of this case, the Court relies on the inherent mobility of the motor home to create a conclusive presumption of exigency. This Court, however, has squarely held that mobility of the place to be searched is not a sufficient justification for abandoning the warrant requirement. In *United States v. Chadwick*, 433 U.S. 1 (1977), the Court held that a warrantless search of a footlocker violated the Fourth Amendment even though there was ample probable cause to believe it contained contraband. The Government had argued that the rationale of the automobile exception applied to movable containers in general, and that the warrant requirement should be limited to searches of homes and other "core" areas of privacy. We categorically rejected the Government's argument observing that there are greater privacy interests associated with containers than with automobiles, and that there are less practical problems associated with the temporary detention of a container than with the detention of an automobile.

* * * It is perfectly obvious that the citizen has a much greater expectation of privacy concerning the interior of a mobile home than of a piece of luggage such as a footlocker. If "inherent mobility" does not justify warrantless searches of containers, it cannot rationally provide a sufficient justification for the search of a person's dwelling place.

Unlike a brick bungalow or a frame Victorian, a motor home seldom serves as a permanent lifetime abode. The motor home in this case, however, was designed to accommodate a breadth of ordinary everyday living. Photographs in the record indicate that its height, length and beam provided substantial living space inside:

---

circumstance is its location, whether the vehicle is readily mobile or instead, for instance, elevated on blocks, whether the vehicle is licensed, whether it is connected to utilities, and whether it has convenient access to a public road.

stuffed chairs surround a table; cupboards provide room for storage of personal effects; bunk-beds provide sleeping space; and a refrigerator provides ample space for food and beverages. Moreover, curtains and large opaque walls inhibit viewing the activities inside from the exterior of the vehicle. The interior configuration of the motor home establishes that the vehicle's size, shape, and mode of construction should have indicated to the officers that it was a vehicle containing mobile living quarters.

The State contends that officers in the field will have an impossible task determining whether or not other vehicles contain mobile living quarters. It is not necessary for the Court to resolve every unanswered question in this area in a single case, but common English usage suggests that we already distinguish between a "motor home" which is "equipped as a self-contained traveling home," a "camper" which is only equipped for "casual travel and camping," and an automobile which is "designed for passenger transportation." Surely the exteriors of these vehicles contain clues about their different functions which could alert officers in the field to the necessity of a warrant. * * *

In my opinion, searches of places that regularly accommodate a wide range of private human activity are fundamentally different from searches of automobiles which primarily serve a public transportation function. Although it may not be a castle, a motor home is usually the functional equivalent of a hotel room, a vacation and retirement home, or a hunting and fishing cabin. These places may be as spartan as a humble cottage when compared to the most majestic mansion, but the highest and most legitimate expectations of privacy associated with these temporary abodes should command the respect of this Court. In my opinion, a warrantless search of living quarters in a motor home is "presumptively unreasonable absent exigent circumstances."

I respectfully dissent.

ARIZONA V. GANT

556 U.S. 332, 129 S.Ct. 1710, 173 L.Ed.2d 485 (2009).

JUSTICE STEVENS delivered the opinion of the Court.

After Rodney Gant was arrested for driving with a suspended license, handcuffed, and locked in the back of a patrol car, police officers searched his car and discovered cocaine in the pocket of a jacket on the backseat. Because Gant could not have accessed his car to retrieve weapons or evidence at the time of the search, the Arizona Supreme Court held that the search-incident-to-arrest exception to the Fourth Amendment's warrant requirement, as defined in *Chimel v. California,* [p. 228], and applied to vehicle searches in *New York v. Belton,* 453 U.S. 454 (1981), did not justify the search in this case. We agree with that conclusion. * * *

In *Chimel,* we held that a search incident to arrest may only include "the arrestee's person and the area 'within his immediate control'—construing that phrase to mean the area from within which he might gain possession of a weapon or destructible evidence." That limitation, which continues to define the boundaries of the exception, ensures that the scope of a search incident to arrest is commensurate with its purposes of protecting arresting officers and safeguarding any evidence of the offense of arrest that an arrestee might conceal or destroy. * * *

In *Belton,* we considered *Chimel's* application to the automobile context. A lone police officer in that case stopped a speeding car in which Belton was one of four occupants. While asking for the driver's license and registration, the officer smelled burnt marijuana and observed an envelope on the car floor marked "Supergold"—a name he associated with marijuana. Thus having probable cause to believe the occupants had committed a drug offense, the officer ordered them out of the vehicle, placed them under arrest, and patted them down. Without handcuffing the arrestees, the officer " 'split them up into four separate areas of the Thruway . . . so they would not be in physical touching area of each other' " and searched the vehicle, including the pocket of a jacket on the backseat, in which he found cocaine.

The New York Court of Appeals found the search unconstitutional, concluding that after the occupants were arrested the vehicle and its contents were "safely within the exclusive custody and control of the police." [But] we held that when an officer lawfully arrests "the occupant of an automobile, he may, as a contemporaneous incident of that arrest, search the passenger compartment of the automobile" and any containers therein. That holding was based in large part on our assumption "that articles inside the relatively narrow compass of the passenger compartment of an automobile are in fact generally, even if not inevitably, within 'the area into which an arrestee might reach.' " * * *

Despite the textual and evidentiary support for the Arizona Supreme Court's reading of *Belton,* our opinion has been widely understood to allow a vehicle search incident to the arrest of a recent occupant even if there is no possibility the arrestee could gain access to the vehicle at the time of the search. This reading may be attributable to Justice Brennan's dissent in *Belton,* in which he characterized the Court's holding as resting on the "fiction . . . that the interior of a car is *always* within the immediate control of an arrestee who has recently been in the car." Under the majority's approach, he argued, "the result would presumably be the same even if [the officer] had handcuffed Belton and his companions in the patrol car" before conducting the search.

Since we decided *Belton,* Courts of Appeals have given different answers to the question whether a vehicle must be within an arrestee's reach to justify a vehicle search incident to arrest, but Justice Brennan's reading of the Court's opinion has predominated. * * *

Under this broad reading of *Belton,* a vehicle search would be authorized incident to every arrest of a recent occupant[a] notwithstanding that in most cases

---

a   While the rule in *Belton* was stated in terms of "a lawful custodial arrest of the occupant of an automobile," in *Thornton v. United States,* 541 U.S. 615 (2004), it was applied as well to a "recent occupant" of the vehicle because "the arrest of a suspect who is next to a vehicle presents identical concerns regarding officer safety and the destruction of evidence as the arrest of one who is inside the vehicle." After Thornton parked his vehicle without any prior officer contact, the officer approached him about a license tag violation and then asked if he had any illegal narcotics

the vehicle's passenger compartment will not be within the arrestee's reach at the time of the search. To read *Belton* as authorizing a vehicle search incident to every recent occupant's arrest would thus untether the rule from the justifications underlying the *Chimel* exception—a result clearly incompatible with our statement in *Belton* that it "in no way alters the fundamental principles established in the *Chimel* case regarding the basic scope of searches incident to lawful custodial arrests." Accordingly, we reject this reading of *Belton* and hold that the *Chimel* rationale authorizes police to search a vehicle incident to a recent occupant's arrest only when the arrestee is unsecured and within reaching distance of the passenger compartment at the time of the search.[4]

Although it does not follow from *Chimel,* we also conclude that circumstances unique to the vehicle context justify a search incident to a lawful arrest when it is "reasonable to believe evidence relevant to the crime of arrest might be found in the vehicle." *Thornton* (Scalia, J., concurring in judgment).[b] In many cases, as when

---

on him; Thornton produced "three bags of marijuana" plus "a large amount of crack cocaine," resulting in his arrest.

[4]　Because officers have many means of ensuring the safe arrest of vehicle occupants, it will be the rare case in which an officer is unable to fully effectuate an arrest so that a real possibility of access to the arrestee's vehicle remains. Cf. 3 W. LaFave, Search and Seizure § 7.1(c), p. 525 (4th ed. 2004) (hereinafter LaFave) (noting that the availability of protective measures "ensur[es] the nonexistence of circumstances in which the arrestee's 'control' of the car is in doubt"). But in such a case a search incident to arrest is reasonable under the Fourth Amendment.

[b]　The relevant portion of the Scalia concurrence in *Thornton* is as follows:

"If *Belton* searches are justifiable, it is not because the arrestee might grab a weapon or evidentiary item from his car, but simply because the car might contain evidence relevant to the crime for which he was arrested. This more general sort of evidence-gathering search is not without antecedent. For example, in *United States v. Rabinowitz*, 339 U.S. 56 (1950), we upheld a search of the suspect's place of business after he was arrested there. We did not restrict the officers' search authority to 'the area into which [the] arrestee might reach in order to grab a weapon or evidentiary ite[m],' and we did not justify the search as a means to prevent concealment or destruction of evidence. Rather, we relied on a more general interest in gathering evidence relevant to the crime for which the suspect had been arrested.

"Numerous earlier authorities support this approach, referring to the general interest in gathering evidence related to the crime of arrest with no mention of the more specific interest in preventing its concealment or destruction. * * * Only in the years leading up to *Chimel* did we start consistently referring to the narrower interest in frustrating concealment or destruction of evidence.

"There is nothing irrational about broader police authority to search for evidence when and where the perpetrator of a crime is lawfully arrested. The fact of prior lawful arrest distinguishes the arrestee from society at large, and distinguishes a search for evidence of *his* crime from general rummaging. Moreover, it is not illogical to assume that evidence of a crime is most likely to be found where the suspect was apprehended.

"Nevertheless, *Chimel's* narrower focus on concealment or destruction of evidence also has historical support. And some of the authorities supporting the broader rule address only searches of the arrestee's *person*, as to which *Chimel's* limitation might fairly be implicit. Moreover, carried to its logical end, the broader rule is hard to reconcile with the influential case of *Entick v. Carrington*, 19 How. St. Tr. 1029, 1031, 1063–1074 (C.P. 1765) (disapproving search of plaintiff's private papers under general warrant, despite arrest).

"In short, both *Rabinowitz* and *Chimel* are plausible accounts of what the Constitution requires, and neither is so persuasive as to justify departing from settled law. But if we are going to continue to allow *Belton* searches on *stare decisis* grounds, we should at least be honest about why we are doing so. *Belton* cannot reasonably be explained as a mere application of *Chimel.* Rather, it is a return to the broader sort of search incident to arrest that we allowed before *Chimel*—limited, of course, to searches of motor vehicles, a category of 'effects' which give rise to

a recent occupant is arrested for a traffic violation, there will be no reasonable basis to believe the vehicle contains relevant evidence. But in others, including *Belton* and *Thornton,* the offense of arrest will supply a basis for searching the passenger compartment of an arrestee's vehicle and any containers therein.

Neither the possibility of access nor the likelihood of discovering offense-related evidence authorized the search in this case. Unlike in *Belton,* which involved a single officer confronted with four unsecured arrestees, the five officers in this case outnumbered the three arrestees,[c] all of whom had been handcuffed and secured in separate patrol cars before the officers searched Gant's car. Under those circumstances, Gant clearly was not within reaching distance of his car at the time of the search. An evidentiary basis for the search was also lacking in this case. Whereas Belton and Thornton were arrested for drug offenses, Gant was arrested for driving with a suspended license—an offense for which police could not expect to find evidence in the passenger compartment of Gant's car. Because police could not reasonably have believed either that Gant could have accessed his car at the time of the search or that evidence of the offense for which he was arrested might have been found therein, the search in this case was unreasonable.

The State does not seriously disagree with the Arizona Supreme Court's conclusion that Gant could not have accessed his vehicle at the time of the search, but it nevertheless asks us to uphold the search of his vehicle under the broad reading of *Belton* discussed above. The State argues that *Belton* searches are reasonable regardless of the possibility of access in a given case because that expansive rule correctly balances law enforcement interests, including the interest in a bright-line rule, with an arrestee's limited privacy interest in his vehicle.

For several reasons, we reject the State's argument. First, the State seriously undervalues the privacy interests at stake. Although we have recognized that a motorist's privacy interest in his vehicle is less substantial than in his home, the former interest is nevertheless important and deserving of constitutional protection. It is particularly significant that *Belton* searches authorize police officers to search not just the passenger compartment but every purse, briefcase, or other container within that space. A rule that gives police the power to conduct such a search whenever an individual is caught committing a traffic offense, when there is no basis for believing evidence of the offense might be found in the vehicle, creates a serious and recurring threat to the privacy of countless individuals. Indeed, the character of that threat implicates the central concern underlying the Fourth Amendment—the concern about giving police officers unbridled discretion to rummage at will among a person's private effects.[5]

---

a reduced expectation of privacy, see *Wyoming v. Houghton* [p. 263], and heightened law enforcement needs."

  c Prior to Gant's arrest when he drove up to premises suspected as the locale of drug distribution, a man and a woman outside those premises had already been arrested for providing a false name and possession of drug paraphernalia, respectively.

  5 Many have observed that a broad reading of *Belton* gives police limitless discretion to conduct exploratory searches. See 3 LaFave § 7.1(c), at 527 (observing that *Belton* creates the risk "that police will make custodial arrests which they otherwise would not make as a cover for a search which the Fourth Amendment otherwise prohibits") * * *.

At the same time as it undervalues these privacy concerns, the State exaggerates the clarity that its reading of *Belton* provides. Courts that have read *Belton* expansively are at odds regarding how close in time to the arrest and how proximate to the arrestee's vehicle an officer's first contact with the arrestee must be to bring the encounter within *Belton*'s purview and whether a search is reasonable when it commences or continues after the arrestee has been removed from the scene. The rule has thus generated a great deal of uncertainty, particularly for a rule touted as providing a "bright line."

Contrary to the State's suggestion, a broad reading of *Belton* is also unnecessary to protect law enforcement safety and evidentiary interests. Under our view, *Belton* and *Thornton* permit an officer to conduct a vehicle search when an arrestee is within reaching distance of the vehicle or it is reasonable to believe the vehicle contains evidence of the offense of arrest. Other established exceptions to the warrant requirement authorize a vehicle search under additional circumstances when safety or evidentiary concerns demand. For instance, *Michigan v. Long,* [fn. b, p. 291], permits an officer to search a vehicle's passenger compartment when he has reasonable suspicion that an individual, whether or not the arrestee, is "dangerous" and might access the vehicle to "gain immediate control of weapons." If there is probable cause to believe a vehicle contains evidence of criminal activity, *United States v. Ross,* [p. 253], authorizes a search of any area of the vehicle in which the evidence might be found. Unlike the searches permitted by Justice Scalia's opinion concurring in the judgment in *Thornton,* which we conclude today are reasonable for purposes of the Fourth Amendment, *Ross* allows searches for evidence relevant to offenses other than the offense of arrest, and the scope of the search authorized is broader. Finally, there may be still other circumstances in which safety or evidentiary interests would justify a search. Cf. *Maryland v. Buie,* [fn. b, p. 230] (holding that, incident to arrest, an officer may conduct a limited protective sweep of those areas of a house in which he reasonably suspects a dangerous person may be hiding).

These exceptions together ensure that officers may search a vehicle when genuine safety or evidentiary concerns encountered during the arrest of a vehicle's recent occupant justify a search. Construing *Belton* broadly to allow vehicle searches incident to any arrest would serve no purpose except to provide a police entitlement, and it is anathema to the Fourth Amendment to permit a warrantless search on that basis. For these reasons, we are unpersuaded by the State's arguments that a broad reading of *Belton* would meaningfully further law enforcement interests and justify a substantial intrusion on individuals' privacy.

Our dissenting colleagues argue that the doctrine of *stare decisis* requires adherence to a broad reading of *Belton* even though the justifications for searching a vehicle incident to arrest are in most cases absent. The doctrine of *stare decisis* is of course "essential to the respect accorded to the judgments of the Court and to the stability of the law," but it does not compel us to follow a past decision when its rationale no longer withstands "careful analysis." * * *

We have never relied on *stare decisis* to justify the continuance of an unconstitutional police practice. And we would be particularly loath to uphold an unconstitutional result in a case that is so easily distinguished from the decisions that arguably compel it. The safety and evidentiary interests that supported the search in *Belton* simply are not present in this case. Indeed, it is hard to imagine two cases that are factually more distinct, as *Belton* involved one officer confronted by four unsecured arrestees suspected of committing a drug offense and this case involves several officers confronted with a securely detained arrestee apprehended for driving with a suspended license. This case is also distinguishable from *Thornton,* in which the petitioner was arrested for a drug offense. It is thus unsurprising that Members of this Court who concurred in the judgments in *Belton* and *Thornton* also concur in the decision in this case.[10]

Police may search a vehicle incident to a recent occupant's arrest only if the arrestee is within reaching distance of the passenger compartment at the time of the search or it is reasonable to believe the vehicle contains evidence of the offense of arrest. When these justifications are absent, a search of an arrestee's vehicle will be unreasonable unless police obtain a warrant or show that another exception to the warrant requirement applies. The Arizona Supreme Court correctly held that this case involved an unreasonable search. Accordingly, the judgment of the State Supreme Court is affirmed. * * *

JUSTICE SCALIA, concurring. * * *

Justice Stevens acknowledges that an officer-safety rationale cannot justify all vehicle searches incident to arrest, but asserts that that is not the rule *Belton* and *Thornton* adopted. * * * Justice Stevens would therefore retain the application of *Chimel v. California* in the car-search context but would apply in the future what he believes our cases held in the past: that officers making a roadside stop may search the vehicle so long as the "arrestee is within reaching distance of the passenger compartment at the time of the search." I believe that this standard fails to provide the needed guidance to arresting officers and also leaves much room for manipulation, inviting officers to leave the scene unsecured (at least where dangerous suspects are not involved) in order to conduct a vehicle search. In my view we should simply abandon the *Belton-Thornton* charade of officer safety and overrule those cases. I would hold that a vehicle search incident to arrest is *ipso facto* "reasonable" only when the object of the search is evidence of the crime for which the arrest was made, or of another crime that the officer has probable cause to believe occurred. Because respondent was arrested for driving without a license (a crime for which no evidence could be expected to be found in the vehicle), I would hold in the present case that the search was unlawful. * * *

No other Justice, however, shares my view that application of *Chimel* in this context should be entirely abandoned. It seems to me unacceptable for the Court to come forth with a 4-to-1-to-4 opinion that leaves the governing rule uncertain. I am therefore confronted with the choice of either leaving the current understanding of *Belton* and *Thornton* in effect, or acceding to what seems to me

---

[10] Justice Stevens concurred in the judgment in *Belton* for the reasons stated in his dissenting opinion in *Robbins v. California*, 453 U.S. 420 (1981)[, namely, that the search was made on "probable cause to believe that the vehicle contained contraband"], Justice Thomas joined the Court's opinion in *Thornton,* and Justice Scalia and Justice Ginsburg concurred in the judgment in that case.

the artificial narrowing of those cases adopted by Justice Stevens. The latter, as I have said, does not provide the degree of certainty I think desirable in this field; but the former opens the field to what I think are plainly unconstitutional searches—which is the greater evil. I therefore join the opinion of the Court. * * *

JUSTICE ALITO, with whom THE CHIEF JUSTICE and JUSTICE KENNEDY join, and with whom JUSTICE BREYER joins[c] except as to Part IE, dissenting. * * *

I

Although the Court refuses to acknowledge that it is overruling *Belton* and *Thornton,* there can be no doubt that it does so.

The precise holding in *Belton* could not be clearer. The Court stated unequivocally: "[W]e hold that when a policeman has made a lawful custodial arrest of the occupant of an automobile, he may, as a contemporaneous incident of that arrest, search the passenger compartment of that automobile."

Despite this explicit statement, the opinion of the Court in the present case curiously suggests that *Belton* may reasonably be read as adopting a holding that is narrower than the one explicitly set out in the *Belton* opinion, namely, that an officer arresting a vehicle occupant may search the passenger compartment "*when* the passenger compartment is within an arrestee's reaching distance." According to the Court, the broader reading of *Belton* that has gained wide acceptance "may be attributable to Justice Brennan's dissent."

Contrary to the Court's suggestion, however, Justice Brennan's *Belton* dissent did not mischaracterize the Court's holding in that case or cause that holding to be misinterpreted. As noted, the *Belton* Court explicitly stated precisely what it held. * * *.

II

Because the Court has substantially overruled *Belton* and *Thornton,* the Court must explain why its departure from the usual rule of *stare decisis* is justified. I recognize that stare decisis is not an "inexorable command," and applies less rigidly in constitutional cases. But the Court has said that a constitutional precedent should be followed unless there is a " 'special justification' " for its abandonment. Relevant factors identified in prior cases include whether the precedent has engendered reliance, whether there has been an important change in circumstances in the outside world, whether the precedent has proved to be unworkable, whether the precedent has been undermined by later decisions, and whether the decision was badly reasoned. These factors weigh in favor of retaining the rule established in *Belton.* * * *

C

Workability. The *Belton* rule has not proved to be unworkable. On the contrary, the rule was adopted for the express purpose of providing a test that

---

c   A separate dissent by Justice Breyer is omitted. Relying on stare decisis, he declared that "those who wish this Court to change a well established precedent—where as here there has been considerable reliance on the rule in question—bear a heavy burden," and concluded that burden had not been met.

would be relatively easy for police officers and judges to apply. The Court correctly notes that even the *Belton* rule is not perfectly clear in all situations. Specifically, it is sometimes debatable whether a search is or is not contemporaneous with an arrest, but that problem is small in comparison with the problems that the Court's new two-part rule will produce.

The first part of the Court's new rule—which permits the search of a vehicle's passenger compartment if it is within an arrestee's reach at the time of the search—reintroduces the same sort of case-by-case, fact-specific decisionmaking that the *Belton* rule was adopted to avoid. As the situation in *Belton* illustrated, there are cases in which it is unclear whether an arrestee could retrieve a weapon or evidence in the passenger compartment of a car.

Even more serious problems will also result from the second part of the Court's new rule, which requires officers making roadside arrests to determine whether there is reason to believe that the vehicle contains evidence of the crime of arrest. What this rule permits in a variety of situations is entirely unclear. * * *

E

Bad reasoning. The Court is harshly critical of *Belton*'s reasoning, but the problem that the Court perceives cannot be remedied simply by overruling *Belton*. *Belton* represented only a modest—and quite defensible—extension of *Chimel*, as I understand that decision.

Prior to *Chimel*, the Court's precedents permitted an arresting officer to search the area within an arrestee's "possession" and "control" for the purpose of gathering evidence. Based on this "abstract doctrine," the Court had sustained searches that extended far beyond an arrestee's grabbing area. See *United States v. Rabinowitz*, 339 U.S. 56 (1950) (search of entire office); *Harris v. United States*, 331 U.S. 145 (1947) (search of entire apartment).

The *Chimel* Court, in an opinion written by Justice Stewart, overruled these cases. Concluding that there are only two justifications for a warrantless search incident to arrest—officer safety and the preservation of evidence—the Court stated that such a search must be confined to "the arrestee's person" and "the area from within which he might gain possession of a weapon or destructible evidence."

Unfortunately, *Chimel* did not say whether "the area from within which [an arrestee] might gain possession of a weapon or destructible evidence" is to be measured at the time of the arrest or at the time of the search, but unless the *Chimel* rule was meant to be a specialty rule, applicable to only a few unusual cases, the Court must have intended for this area to be measured at the time of arrest.

This is so because the Court can hardly have failed to appreciate the following two facts. First, in the great majority of cases, an officer making an arrest is able to handcuff the arrestee and remove him to a secure place before conducting a search incident to the arrest. Second, because it is safer for an arresting officer to secure an arrestee before searching, it is likely that this is what arresting officers do in the great majority of cases. (And it appears, not surprisingly, that this is in fact the prevailing practice.) Thus, if the area within an arrestee's reach were assessed, not at the time of arrest, but at the time of the search, the *Chimel* rule would rarely come into play.

Moreover, if the applicability of the *Chimel* rule turned on whether an arresting officer chooses to secure an arrestee prior to conducting a search, rather than searching first and securing the arrestee later, the rule would "create a perverse incentive for an arresting officer to prolong the period during which the arrestee is kept in an area where he could pose a danger to the officer." If this is the law, the D.C. Circuit observed, "the law would truly be, as Mr. Bumble said, 'a ass.'" * * *

I do not think that this is what the *Chimel* Court intended. Handcuffs were in use in 1969. The ability of arresting officers to secure arrestees before conducting a search—and their incentive to do so—are facts that can hardly have escaped the Court's attention. I therefore believe that the *Chimel* Court intended that its new rule apply in cases in which the arrestee is handcuffed before the search is conducted.

The *Belton* Court, in my view, proceeded on the basis of this interpretation of *Chimel*. Again speaking through Justice Stewart, the *Belton* Court reasoned that articles in the passenger compartment of a car are "generally, even if not inevitably" within an arrestee's reach. This is undoubtedly true at the time of the arrest of a person who is seated in a car but plainly not true when the person has been removed from the car and placed in handcuffs. Accordingly, the *Belton* Court must have proceeded on the assumption that the *Chimel* rule was to be applied at the time of arrest. And that is why the *Belton* Court was able to say that its decision "in no way alter[ed] the fundamental principles established in the *Chimel* case regarding the basic scope of searches incident to lawful custodial arrests." Viewing *Chimel* as having focused on the time of arrest, *Belton*'s only new step was to eliminate the need to decide on a case-by-case basis whether a particular person seated in a car actually could have reached the part of the passenger compartment where a weapon or evidence was hidden. For this reason, if we are going to reexamine *Belton,* we should also reexamine the reasoning in *Chimel* on which *Belton* rests.

F

The Court, however, does not reexamine *Chimel* and thus leaves the law relating to searches incident to arrest in a confused and unstable state. The first part of the Court's new two-part rule—which permits an arresting officer to search the area within an arrestee's reach at the time of the search—applies, at least for now, only to vehicle occupants and recent occupants, but there is no logical reason why the same rule should not apply to all arrestees.

The second part of the Court's new rule, which the Court takes uncritically from Justice Scalia's separate opinion in *Thornton,* raises doctrinal and practical problems that the Court makes no effort to address. Why, for example, is the standard for this type of evidence-gathering search "reason to believe" rather than probable cause? And why is this type of search restricted to evidence of the offense of arrest? It is true that an arrestee's vehicle is probably more likely to contain evidence of the crime of arrest than of some other crime, but if reason-to-believe is the governing standard for an evidence-gathering search incident to arrest, it is not easy to see why an officer should not be able to search when the officer has reason to believe that the vehicle in question possesses evidence of a crime other than the crime of arrest.

Nor is it easy to see why an evidence-gathering search incident to arrest should be restricted to the passenger compartment. The *Belton* rule was limited in this way because the passenger compartment was considered to be the area that vehicle occupants can generally reach, but since the second part of the new rule is not based on officer safety or the preservation of evidence, the ground for this limitation is obscure.[2] * * *

CALIFORNIA V. ACEVEDO
500 U.S. 565, 111 S.Ct. 1982, 114 L.Ed.2d 619 (1991).

JUSTICE BLACKMUN delivered the opinion of the Court.

[One Daza picked up a package the police knew contained marijuana from a Federal Express office and took it to his apartment. About two hours later, Acevedo entered that apartment and shortly thereafter left carrying a brown paper bag the size of one of the wrapped marijuana packages. He placed the bag in the trunk of his car and drove off; the police then stopped him, opened the trunk and bag, and found marijuana. The California Court of Appeals held the marijuana should have been suppressed, the state supreme court denied review, and the Supreme Court then granted certiorari.]

In *United States v. Ross*, 456 U.S. 798, decided in 1982, we held that a warrantless search of an automobile under the *Carroll* doctrine could include a search of a container or package found inside the car when such a search was supported by probable cause. The warrantless search of Ross' car occurred after an informant told the police that he had seen Ross complete a drug transaction using drugs stored in the trunk of his car. The police stopped the car, searched it, and discovered in the trunk a brown paper bag containing drugs. We decided that the search of Ross' car was not unreasonable under the Fourth Amendment: "The scope of a warrantless search based on probable cause is no narrower—and no broader—than the scope of a search authorized by a warrant supported by probable cause." Thus, "[i]f probable cause justifies the search of a lawfully stopped vehicle, it justifies the search of every part of the vehicle and its contents that may conceal the object of the search." In *Ross*, therefore, we clarified the scope of the *Carroll*

---

[2]   I do not understand the Court's decision to reach the following situations. First, it is not uncommon for an officer to arrest some but not all of the occupants of a vehicle. The Court's decision in this case does not address the question whether in such a situation a search of the passenger compartment may be justified on the ground that the occupants who are not arrested could gain access to the car and retrieve a weapon or destroy evidence. Second, there may be situations in which an arresting officer has cause to fear that persons who were not passengers in the car might attempt to retrieve a weapon or evidence from the car while the officer is still on the scene. The decision in this case, as I understand it, does not address that situation either.

doctrine as properly including a "probing search" of compartments and containers within the automobile so long as the search is supported by probable cause.

In addition to this clarification, *Ross* distinguished the *Carroll* doctrine from the separate rule that governed the search of closed containers. The Court had announced this separate rule, unique to luggage and other closed packages, bags, and containers, in *United States v. Chadwick*, 433 U.S. 1 (1977). In *Chadwick*, federal narcotics agents had probable cause to believe that a 200-pound double-locked footlocker contained marijuana. The agents tracked the locker as the defendants removed it from a train and carried it through the station to a waiting car. As soon as the defendants lifted the locker into the trunk of the car, the agents arrested them, seized the locker, and searched it. In this Court, the United States did not contend that the locker's brief contact with the automobile's trunk sufficed to make the *Carroll* doctrine applicable. Rather, the United States urged that the search of movable luggage could be considered analogous to the search of an automobile.

The Court rejected this argument because, it reasoned, a person expects more privacy in his luggage and personal effects than he does in his automobile. Moreover, it concluded that as "may often not be the case when automobiles are seized," secure storage facilities are usually available when the police seize luggage.

In *Arkansas v. Sanders*, 442 U.S. 753 (1979), the Court extended *Chadwick's* rule to apply to a suitcase actually being transported in the trunk of a car. In *Sanders*, the police had probable cause to believe a suitcase contained marijuana. They watched as the defendant placed the suitcase in the trunk of a taxi and was driven away. The police pursued the taxi for several blocks, stopped it, found the suitcase in the trunk, and searched it. Although the Court had applied the *Carroll* doctrine to searches of integral parts of the automobile itself (indeed, in *Carroll*, contraband whiskey was in the upholstery of the seats), it did not extend the doctrine to the warrantless search of personal luggage "merely because it was located in an automobile lawfully stopped by the police." Again, the *Sanders* majority stressed the heightened privacy expectation in personal luggage and concluded that the presence of luggage in an automobile did not diminish the owner's expectation of privacy in his personal items.

In *Ross*, the Court endeavored to distinguish between *Carroll*, which governed the *Ross* automobile search, and *Chadwick*, which governed the *Sanders* automobile search. It held that the *Carroll* doctrine covered searches of automobiles when the police had probable cause to search an entire vehicle but that the *Chadwick* doctrine governed searches of luggage when the officers had probable cause to search only a container within the vehicle. Thus, in a *Ross* situation, the police could conduct a reasonable search under the Fourth Amendment without obtaining a warrant, whereas in a *Sanders* situation, the police had to obtain a warrant before they searched.

The dissent is correct, of course, that *Ross* involved the scope of an automobile search. *Ross* held that closed containers encountered by the police during a warrantless search of a car pursuant to the automobile exception could also be searched. Thus, this Court in *Ross* took the critical step of saying that closed containers in cars could be searched without a warrant because of their presence within the automobile. Despite the protection that *Sanders* purported to extend to closed containers, the privacy interest in those closed containers yielded to the broad scope of an automobile search. * * *

This Court in *Ross* rejected *Chadwick's* distinction between containers and cars. It concluded that the expectation of privacy in one's vehicle is equal to one's expectation of privacy in the container, and noted that "the privacy interests in a car's trunk or glove compartment may be no less than those in a movable container." It also recognized that it was arguable that the same exigent circumstances that permit a warrantless search of an automobile would justify the warrantless search of a movable container. In deference to the rule of *Chadwick* and *Sanders,* however, the Court put that question to one side. It concluded that the time and expense of the warrant process would be misdirected if the police could search every cubic inch of an automobile until they discovered a paper sack, at which point the Fourth Amendment required them to take the sack to a magistrate for permission to look inside. We now must decide the question deferred in *Ross:* whether the Fourth Amendment requires the police to obtain a warrant to open the sack in a movable vehicle simply because they lack probable cause to search the entire car. We conclude that it does not.

Dissenters in *Ross* asked why the suitcase in *Sanders* was "more private, less difficult for police to seize and store, or in any other relevant respect more properly subject to the warrant requirement, than a container that police discover in a probable-cause search of an entire automobile?" We now agree that a container found after a general search of the automobile and a container found in a car after a limited search for the container are equally easy for the police to store and for the suspect to hide or destroy. In fact, we see no principled distinction in terms of either the privacy expectation or the exigent circumstances between the paper bag found by the police in *Ross* and the paper bag found by the police here. Furthermore, by attempting to distinguish between a container for which the police are specifically searching and a container which they come across in a car, we have provided only minimal protection for privacy and have impeded effective law enforcement.

The line between probable cause to search a vehicle and probable cause to search a package in that vehicle is not always clear, and separate rules that govern the two objects to be searched may enable the police to broaden their power to make warrantless searches and disserve privacy interests. * * * At the moment when officers stop an automobile, it may be less than clear whether they suspect with a high degree of certainty that the vehicle contains drugs in a bag or simply contains drugs. If the police know that they may open a bag only if they are actually searching the entire car, they may search more extensively than they otherwise would in order to establish the general probable cause required by *Ross*.

Such a situation is not far fetched. In *United States v. Johns*, 469 U.S. 478 (1985), customs agents saw two trucks drive to a private airstrip and approach two small planes. The agents drew near the trucks, smelled marijuana, and then saw in the backs of the trucks packages wrapped in a manner that marijuana smugglers customarily employed. The agents took the trucks to headquarters and searched the packages without a warrant. Relying on *Chadwick,* the defendants argued that the search was unlawful. The defendants contended that *Ross* was inapplicable because the agents lacked probable cause to search anything but the packages themselves and supported this contention by noting that a search of the entire vehicle never occurred. We rejected that argument and found *Chadwick* and *Sanders* inapposite because the agents had probable cause to search the entire body of each truck, although they had chosen not to do so. We cannot see the benefit of a rule that requires law enforcement officers to conduct a more intrusive search in order to justify a less intrusive one.

To the extent that the *Chadwick-Sanders* rule protects privacy, its protection is minimal. Law enforcement officers may seize a container and hold it until they obtain a search warrant. "Since the police, by hypothesis, have probable cause to seize the property, we can assume that a warrant will be routinely forthcoming in the overwhelming majority of cases." And the police often will be able to search containers without a warrant, despite the *Chadwick-Sanders* rule, as a search incident to a lawful arrest [under] *Belton* [modified in *Arizona v. Gant,* p. 244]. * * *

Finally, the search of a paper bag intrudes far less on individual privacy than does the incursion sanctioned long ago in *Carroll.* In that case, prohibition agents slashed the upholstery of the automobile. This Court nonetheless found their search to be reasonable under the Fourth Amendment. If destroying the interior of an automobile is not unreasonable, we cannot conclude that looking inside a closed container is. In light of the minimal protection to privacy afforded by the *Chadwick-Sanders* rule, and our serious doubt whether that rule substantially serves privacy interests, we now hold that the Fourth Amendment does not compel separate treatment for an automobile search that extends only to a container within the vehicle.

The *Chadwick-Sanders* rule not only has failed to protect privacy but it has also confused courts and police officers and impeded effective law enforcement. * * *

The discrepancy between the two rules has led to confusion for law enforcement officers. For example, when an officer, who has developed probable cause to believe that a vehicle contains drugs, begins to search the vehicle and immediately discovers a closed container, which rule applies? The defendant will argue that the fact that the officer first chose to search the container indicates that his probable cause extended only to the container and that *Chadwick* and *Sanders* therefore require a warrant. On the other hand, the fact that the officer first chose to search in the most obvious location should not restrict the propriety of the search. The *Chadwick* rule, as applied in *Sanders,* has devolved into an anomaly such that the more likely the police are to discover drugs in a container, the less authority they have to search it. * * *

Although we have recognized firmly that the doctrine of *stare decisis* serves profoundly important purposes in our legal system, this Court has overruled a prior case on the comparatively rare occasion when it has bred confusion or been derelict or led to anomalous results. *Sanders* was explicitly undermined in *Ross,* and the existence of the dual regimes for automobile searches that uncover containers has proved as confusing as the *Chadwick* and *Sanders* dissenters predicted. We conclude that it is better to adopt one clear-cut rule to govern automobile searches and eliminate the warrant requirement for closed containers set forth in *Sanders.*

The interpretation of the *Carroll* doctrine set forth in *Ross* now applies to all searches of containers found in an automobile. In other words, the police may search without a warrant if their search is supported by probable cause. The Court in *Ross* put it this way:

> "The scope of a warrantless search of an automobile * * * is not defined by the nature of the container in which the contraband is secreted. Rather, it is defined by the object of the search and the places in which there is probable cause to believe that it may be found."

It went on to note: "Probable cause to believe that a container placed in the trunk of a taxi contains contraband or evidence does not justify a search of the entire cab." We reaffirm that principle. In the case before us, the police had probable cause to believe that the paper bag in the automobile's trunk contained marijuana. That probable cause now allows a warrantless search of the paper bag. The facts in the record reveal that the police did not have probable cause to believe that contraband was hidden in any other part of the automobile and a search of the entire vehicle would have been without probable cause and unreasonable under the Fourth Amendment.

Our holding today neither extends the *Carroll* doctrine nor broadens the scope of the permissible automobile search delineated in *Carroll, Chambers,* and *Ross.* It remains a "cardinal principle that 'searches conducted outside the judicial process, without prior approval by judge or magistrate, are *per se* unreasonable under the Fourth Amendment—subject only to a few specifically established and well-delineated exceptions.' " We held in *Ross:* "The exception recognized in *Carroll* is unquestionably one that is 'specifically established and well delineated.' "

Until today, this Court has drawn a curious line between the search of an automobile that coincidentally turns up a container and the search of a container that coincidentally turns up in an automobile. The protections of the Fourth Amendment must not turn on such coincidences. We therefore interpret *Carroll* as providing one rule to govern all automobile searches. The police may search an automobile and the containers within it where they have probable cause to believe contraband or evidence is contained. * * *

JUSTICE SCALIA, concurring in the judgment.

I agree with the dissent that it is anomalous for a briefcase to be protected by the "general requirement" of a prior warrant when it is being carried along the street, but for that same briefcase to become unprotected as soon as it is carried into an automobile. On the other hand, I agree with the Court that it would be anomalous for a locked compartment in an automobile to be unprotected by the "general requirement" of a prior warrant, but for an unlocked briefcase within the automobile to be protected. I join in the judgment of the Court because I think its holding is more faithful to the text and tradition of the Fourth Amendment, and if these anomalies in our jurisprudence are ever to be eliminated that is the direction in which we should travel. * * *

Although the Fourth Amendment does not explicitly impose the requirement of a warrant, it is of course textually possible to consider that implicit within the requirement of reasonableness. For some years after the (still continuing) explosion in Fourth Amendment litigation that followed our announcement of the exclusionary rule in *Weeks v. United States,* 232 U.S. 383 (1914), our jurisprudence lurched back and forth between imposing a categorical warrant requirement and looking to reasonableness alone. * * *

The victory was illusory. Even before today's decision, the "warrant requirement" had become so riddled with exceptions that it was basically unrecognizable. In 1985, one commentator cataloged nearly 20 such exceptions, including "searches incident to arrest * * * automobile searches * * * border searches * * * administrative searches of regulated businesses * * * exigent circumstances * * * search[es] incident to nonarrest when there is probable cause to arrest * * * boat boarding for document checks * * * welfare searches * * * inventory searches * * * airport searches * * * school search[es] * * *." *Bradley, Two Models of the Fourth Amendment,* 83 Mich.L.Rev. 1468, 1473–1474 (1985) (footnotes omitted). Since then, we have added at least two more. *California v. Carney,* 471 U.S. 386 (1985) (searches of mobile homes); *O'Connor v. Ortega,* 480 U.S. 709 (1987) (searches of offices of government employees). Our intricate body of law regarding "reasonable expectation of privacy" has been developed largely as a means of creating these exceptions, enabling a search to be denominated not a Fourth Amendment "search" and therefore not subject to the general warrant requirement.

Unlike the dissent, therefore, I do not regard today's holding as some momentous departure, but rather as merely the continuation of an inconsistent jurisprudence that has been with us for years. There can be no clarity in this area unless we make up our minds, and unless the principles we express comport with the actions we take.

In my view, the path out of this confusion should be sought by returning to the first principle that the "reasonableness" requirement of the Fourth Amendment affords the protection that the common law afforded. I have no difficulty with the proposition that that includes the requirement of a warrant, where the common law required a warrant; and it may even be that changes in the surrounding legal rules (for example, elimination of the common-law rule that reasonable, good-faith belief was no defense to absolute liability for trespass), may make a warrant indispensable to reasonableness where it once was not. But the supposed "general rule" that a warrant is always required does not appear to have any basis in the common law, and confuses rather than facilitates any attempt to develop rules of reasonableness in light of changed legal circumstances, as the anomaly eliminated and the anomaly created by today's holding both demonstrate.

And there are more anomalies still. Under our precedents (as at common law), a person may be arrested outside the home on the basis of probable cause, without an arrest warrant. *United States v. Watson.* Upon arrest, the person, as well as the area within his grasp, may be searched for evidence related to the crime. *Chimel v. California.* Under these principles, if a known drug dealer is carrying a briefcase reasonably believed to contain marijuana (the unauthorized possession of which is a crime), the police may arrest him and search his person on the basis of probable cause alone. And, under our precedents, upon arrival at the station house, the police may inventory his possessions, including the briefcase, even if there is no reason to suspect that they contain contraband. *Illinois v. Lafayette,* 462 U.S. 640 (1983). According to our current law, however, the police may not, on the basis of the same probable cause, take the less intrusive step of stopping the individual on the street and demanding to see the contents of his briefcase. That makes no sense *a priori,* and in the absence of any common-law tradition supporting such a distinction, I see no reason to continue it.

I would reverse the judgment in the present case, not because a closed container carried inside a car becomes subject to the "automobile" exception to the general warrant requirement, but because the search of a closed container, outside a privately owned building, with probable cause to believe that the container contains contraband, and when it in fact does contain contraband, is not one of those searches whose Fourth Amendment reasonableness depends upon a warrant. For that reason I concur in the judgment of the Court.

JUSTICE WHITE, dissenting.

Agreeing as I do with most of Justice Stevens' opinion and with the result he reaches, I dissent and would affirm the judgment below.

JUSTICE STEVENS, with whom JUSTICE MARSHALL joins, dissenting.

At the end of its opinion, the Court pays lip service to the proposition that should provide the basis for a correct analysis of the legal question presented by this case: It is " 'a cardinal principle that "searches conducted outside the judicial process, without prior approval by judge or magistrate, are *per se* unreasonable under the Fourth Amendment—subject only to a few specifically established and well-delineated exceptions." ' " * * *

The Fourth Amendment is a restraint on Executive power. The Amendment constitutes the Framers' direct constitutional response to the unreasonable law enforcement practices employed by agents of the British Crown. Over the years— particularly in the period immediately after World War II and particularly in opinions authored by Justice Jackson after his service as a special prosecutor at the Nuremburg trials—the Court has recognized the importance of this restraint as a bulwark against police practices that prevail in totalitarian regimes.

This history is, however, only part of the explanation for the warrant requirement. The requirement also reflects the sound policy judgment that, absent exceptional circumstances, the decision to invade the privacy of an individual's personal effects should be made by a neutral magistrate rather than an agent of the Executive. In his opinion for the Court in *Johnson v. United States,* [333 U.S. 10 (1948)], Justice Jackson explained:

"The point of the Fourth Amendment, which often is not grasped by zealous officers, is not that it denies law enforcement the support of the usual inferences which reasonable men draw from evidence. Its protection consists in requiring that those inferences be drawn by a neutral and detached magistrate instead of being judged by the officer engaged in the often competitive enterprise of ferreting out crime."

Our decisions have always acknowledged that the warrant requirement imposes a burden on law enforcement. And our cases have not questioned that trained professionals normally make reliable assessments of the existence of probable cause to conduct a search. We have repeatedly held, however, that these factors are outweighed by the individual interest in privacy that is protected by advance judicial approval. The Fourth Amendment dictates that the privacy interest is paramount, no matter how marginal the risk of error might be if the legality of warrantless searches were judged only after the fact. * * *

In *Chadwick,* the Department of Justice had mounted a frontal attack on the warrant requirement. The Government's principal contention was that "the Fourth Amendment Warrant Clause protects only interests traditionally identified with the home." We categorically rejected that contention, relying on the history and text of the amendment, the policy underlying the warrant requirement, and a line of cases spanning over a century of our jurisprudence. We also rejected the Government's alternative argument that the rationale of our automobile search cases demonstrated the reasonableness of permitting warrantless searches of luggage.

We concluded that neither of the justifications for the automobile exception could support a similar exception for luggage. We first held that the privacy interest in luggage is "substantially greater than in an automobile." Unlike automobiles and their contents, we reasoned, "[l]uggage contents are not open to public view, except as a condition to a border entry or common carrier travel; nor is luggage subject to regular inspections and official scrutiny on a continuing basis." Indeed, luggage is specifically intended to safeguard the privacy of personal effects, unlike an automobile, "whose primary function is transportation."

We then held that the mobility of luggage did not justify creating an additional exception to the Warrant Clause. Unlike an automobile, luggage can easily be seized and detained pending judicial approval of a search. Once the police have luggage "under their exclusive control, there [i]s not the slightest danger that the [luggage] or its contents could [be] removed before a valid search warrant could be obtained. * * * With the [luggage] safely immobilized, it [i]s unreasonable to undertake the additional and greater intrusion of a search without a warrant" (footnote omitted). * * *

[W]e recognized in *Ross* that *Chadwick* and *Sanders* had not created a special rule for container searches, but rather had merely applied the cardinal principle that warrantless searches are *per se* unreasonable unless justified by an exception to the general rule. *Ross* dealt with the scope of the automobile exception; *Chadwick* and *Sanders* were cases in which the exception simply did not apply.

In its opinion today, the Court recognizes that the police did not have probable cause to search respondent's vehicle and that a search of anything but the paper bag that respondent had carried from Daza's apartment and placed in the trunk of his car would have been unconstitutional. Moreover, as I read the opinion, the Court assumes that the police could not have made a warrantless inspection of the bag before it was placed in the car. Finally, the Court also does not question the fact that, under our prior cases, it would have been lawful for the police to seize the container and detain it (and respondent) until they obtained a search warrant. Thus, all of the relevant facts that governed our decisions in *Chadwick* and *Sanders* are present here whereas the relevant fact that justified the vehicle search in *Ross* is not present.

The Court does not attempt to identify any exigent circumstances that would justify its refusal to apply the general rule against warrantless searches. Instead, it advances these three arguments: First, the rules identified in the foregoing cases are confusing and anomalous. Second, the rules do not protect any significant interest in privacy. And, third, the rules impede effective law enforcement. None of these arguments withstands scrutiny. * * *

The Court summarizes the alleged "anomaly" created by the coexistence of *Ross, Chadwick,* and *Sanders* with the statement that "the more likely the police are to discover drugs in a container, the less authority they have to search it." This juxtaposition is only anomalous, however, if one accepts the flawed premise that the degree to which the police are likely to discover contraband is correlated with their authority to search *without a warrant*. Yet, even proof beyond a reasonable doubt will not justify a warrantless search that is not supported by one of the exceptions to the warrant requirement. And, even when the police have a warrant or an exception applies, once the police possess probable cause, the extent to which they are more or less certain of the contents of a container has no bearing on their authority to search it.

To the extent there was any "anomaly" in our prior jurisprudence, the Court has "cured" it at the expense of creating a more serious paradox. For, surely it is anomalous to prohibit a search of a briefcase while the owner is carrying it exposed on a public street yet to permit a search once the owner has placed the briefcase in the locked trunk of his car. One's privacy interest in one's luggage can certainly not be diminished by one's removing it from a public thoroughfare and placing it—out of sight—in a privately owned vehicle. Nor is the danger that evidence will escape increased if the luggage is in a car rather than on the street. In either location, if the police have probable cause, they are authorized to seize the luggage and to detain it until they obtain judicial approval for a search. Any line demarking an exception to the warrant requirement will appear blurred at the edges, but the Court has certainly erred if it believes that, by erasing one line and drawing another, it has drawn a clearer boundary.

The Court's statement that *Chadwick* and *Sanders* provide only "minimal protection to privacy" is also unpersuasive. Every citizen clearly has an interest in the privacy of the contents of his or her luggage, briefcase, handbag or any other container that conceals private papers and effects from public scrutiny. That privacy interest has been recognized repeatedly in cases spanning more than a century.

Under the Court's holding today, the privacy interest that protects the contents of a suitcase or a briefcase from a warrantless search when it is in public view simply vanishes when its owner climbs into a taxicab. Unquestionably the rejection of the *Sanders* line of cases by today's decision will result in a significant loss of individual privacy.

To support its argument that today's holding works only a minimal intrusion on privacy, the Court suggests that "[i]f the police know that they may open a bag only if they are actually searching the entire car, they may search more extensively than they otherwise would in order to establish the general probable cause required by *Ross*." As I have already noted, this fear is unexplained and inexplicable. Neither evidence uncovered in the course of a search nor the scope of the search conducted can be used to provide *post hoc* justification for a search unsupported by probable cause at its inception.

The Court also justifies its claim that its holding inflicts only minor damage by suggesting that, under *New York v. Belton,* [modified in *Arizona v. Gant*, p. 244] the police could have arrested respondent and searched his bag if respondent had placed the bag in the passenger compartment of the automobile instead of the trunk. In *Belton,* however, the justification for stopping the car and arresting the driver had nothing to do with the subsequent search, which was based on the potential danger to the arresting officer. The holding in *Belton* was supportable under a straightforward application of the automobile exception. I would not extend *Belton*'s holding to this case, in which the container—which was protected from a warrantless search before it was placed in the car—provided the only justification for the arrest. Even accepting *Belton*'s application to a case like this one, however, the Court's logic extends its holding to a container placed in the *trunk* of a vehicle, rather than in the passenger compartment. And the Court makes this extension without any justification whatsoever other than convenience to law enforcement.

The Court's suggestion that *Chadwick* and *Sanders* have created a significant burden on effective law enforcement is unsupported, inaccurate, and, in any event, an insufficient reason for creating a new exception to the warrant requirement.

Despite repeated claims that *Chadwick* and *Sanders* have "impeded effective law enforcement," the Court cites no authority for its contentions. * * *

Even if the warrant requirement does inconvenience the police to some extent, that fact does not distinguish this constitutional requirement from any other procedural protection secured by the Bill of Rights. It is merely a part of the price that our society must pay in order to preserve its freedom. Thus, in a unanimous opinion that relied on both *Johnson* and *Chadwick,* Justice Stewart wrote:

> "Moreover, the mere fact that law enforcement may be made more efficient can never by itself justify disregard of the Fourth Amendment. The investigation of crime would always be simplified if warrants were unnecessary. But the Fourth Amendment reflects the view of those who

wrote the Bill of Rights that the privacy of a person's home and property may not be totally sacrificed in the name of maximum simplicity in enforcement of the criminal law." *Mincey v. Arizona,* 437 U.S. 385, 393 (1978).

It is too early to know how much freedom America has lost today. The magnitude of the loss is, however, not nearly as significant as the Court's willingness to inflict it without even a colorable basis for its rejection of prior law.

I respectfully dissent.

WYOMING V. HOUGHTON
526 U.S. 295, 119 S.Ct. 1297, 143 L.Ed.2d 408 (1999).

JUSTICE SCALIA delivered the opinion of the Court. * * *

In the early morning hours of July 23, 1995, a Wyoming Highway Patrol officer stopped an automobile for speeding and driving with a faulty brake light. There were three passengers in the front seat of the car: David Young (the driver), his girlfriend, and respondent. While questioning Young, the officer noticed a hypodermic syringe in Young's shirt pocket. He left the occupants under the supervision of two backup officers as he went to get gloves from his patrol car. Upon his return, he instructed Young to step out of the car and place the syringe on the hood. The officer then asked Young why he had a syringe; with refreshing candor, Young replied that he used it to take drugs.

At this point, the backup officers ordered the two female passengers out of the car and asked them for identification. Respondent falsely identified herself as "Sandra James" and stated that she did not have any identification. Meanwhile, in light of Young's admission, the officer searched the passenger compartment of the car for contraband. On the back seat, he found a purse, which respondent claimed as hers. He removed from the purse a wallet containing respondent's driver's license, identifying her properly as Sandra K. Houghton. When the officer asked her why she had lied about her name, she replied: "In case things went bad."

Continuing his search of the purse, the officer found a brown pouch and a black wallet-type container. Respondent denied that the former was hers, and claimed ignorance of how it came to be there; it was found to contain drug paraphernalia and a syringe with 60 ccs of methamphetamine. Respondent admitted ownership of the black container, which was also found to contain drug paraphernalia, and a syringe (which respondent acknowledged was hers) with 10 ccs of methamphetamine—an amount insufficient to support the felony conviction at issue in this case. The officer also found fresh needle-track marks on respondent's arms. He placed her under arrest.

The State of Wyoming charged respondent with felony possession of methamphetamine in a liquid amount greater than three-tenths of a gram. After a hearing, the trial court denied her motion to suppress all evidence obtained from the purse as the fruit of a violation of the Fourth and Fourteenth Amendments. The court held that the officer had probable cause to search the car for contraband,

and, by extension, any containers therein that could hold such contraband. A jury convicted respondent as charged.

The Wyoming Supreme Court, by divided vote, reversed the conviction and * * * held that the search of respondent's purse violated the Fourth and Fourteenth Amendments because the officer "knew or should have known that the purse did not belong to the driver, but to one of the passengers," and because "here was no probable cause to search the passengers' personal effects and no reason to believe that contraband had been placed within the purse."

The Fourth Amendment protects "[t]he right of the people to be secure in their persons, houses, papers, and effects, against unreasonable searches and seizures." In determining whether a particular governmental action violates this provision, we inquire first whether the action was regarded as an unlawful search or seizure under the common law when the Amendment was framed. Where that inquiry yields no answer, we must evaluate the search or seizure under traditional standards of reasonableness by assessing, on the one hand, the degree to which it intrudes upon an individual's privacy and, on the other, the degree to which it is needed for the promotion of legitimate governmental interests.

It is uncontested in the present case that the police officers had probable cause to believe there were illegal drugs in the car. *Carroll v. United States*, 267 U.S. 132 (1925), similarly involved the warrantless search of a car that law enforcement officials had probable cause to believe contained contraband—in that case, bootleg liquor. The Court concluded that the Framers would have regarded such a search as reasonable in light of legislation enacted by Congress from 1789 through 1799— as well as subsequent legislation from the Founding era and beyond—that empowered customs officials to search any ship or vessel without a warrant if they had probable cause to believe that it contained goods subject to a duty. Thus, the Court held that "contraband goods concealed and illegally transported in an automobile or other vehicle may be searched for without a warrant" where probable cause exists.

We have furthermore read the historical evidence to show that the Framers would have regarded as reasonable (if there was probable cause) the warrantless search of containers within an automobile. In [*United States v.*] *Ross*, [456 U.S. 798 (1982)], we upheld as reasonable the warrantless search of a paper bag and leather pouch found in the trunk of the defendant's car by officers who had probable cause to believe that the trunk contained drugs. JUSTICE STEVENS, writing for the Court, observed:

> "It is noteworthy that the early legislation on which the Court relied in *Carroll* concerned the enforcement of laws imposing duties on imported merchandise. . . . Presumably such merchandise was shipped then in containers of various kinds, just as it is today. Since Congress had authorized warrantless searches of vessels and beasts for imported merchandise, it is inconceivable that it intended a customs officer to obtain a warrant for every package discovered during the search; certainly Congress intended customs officers to open shipping containers when necessary and not merely to examine the exterior of cartons or

boxes in which smuggled goods might be concealed. During virtually the entire history of our country—whether contraband was transported in a horse-drawn carriage, a 1921 roadster, or a modern automobile—it has been assumed that a lawful search of a vehicle would include a search of any container that might conceal the object of the search."

Ross summarized its holding as follows: "If probable cause justifies the search of a lawfully stopped vehicle, it justifies the search of *every part of the vehicle and its contents* that may conceal the object of the search" (emphasis added). And our later cases describing *Ross* have characterized it as applying broadly to all containers within a car, without qualification as to ownership. * * *

To be sure, there was no passenger in *Ross*, and it was not claimed that the package in the trunk belonged to anyone other than the driver. Even so, if the rule of law that *Ross* announced were limited to contents belonging to the driver, or contents other than those belonging to passengers, one would have expected that substantial limitation to be expressed. And, more importantly, one would have expected that limitation to be apparent in the historical evidence that formed the basis for *Ross*'s holding. In fact, however, nothing in the statutes *Ross* relied upon, or in the practice under those statutes, would except from authorized warrantless search packages belonging to passengers on the suspect ship, horse-drawn carriage, or automobile.

Finally, we must observe that the analytical principle underlying the rule announced in *Ross* is fully consistent—as respondent's proposal is not—with the balance of our Fourth Amendment jurisprudence. *Ross* concluded from the historical evidence that the permissible scope of a warrantless car search "is defined by the object of the search and the places in which there is probable cause to believe that it may be found." The same principle is reflected in an earlier case involving the constitutionality of a search warrant directed at premises belonging to one who is not suspected of any crime: "The critical element in a reasonable search is not that the owner of the property is suspected of crime but that there is reasonable cause to believe that the specific 'things' to be searched for and seized are located on the property to which entry is sought." *Zurcher v. Stanford Daily*, 436 U.S. 547 (1978). * * *

In sum, neither *Ross* itself nor the historical evidence it relied upon admits of a distinction among packages or containers based on ownership. When there is probable cause to search for contraband in a car, it is reasonable for police officers—like customs officials in the Founding era—to examine packages and containers without a showing of individualized probable cause for each one. A passenger's personal belongings, just like the driver's belongings or containers attached to the car like a glove compartment, are "in" the car, and the officer has probable cause to search for contraband in the car.

Even if the historical evidence, as described by *Ross*, were thought to be equivocal, we would find that the balancing of the relative interests weighs decidedly in favor of allowing searches of a passenger's belongings. Passengers, no less than drivers, possess a reduced expectation of privacy with regard to the property that they transport in cars, which "trave[l] public thoroughfares," "seldom serv[e] as . . . the repository of personal effects," are subjected to police stop and examination to enforce "pervasive" governmental controls "[a]s an everyday occurrence," and, finally, are exposed to traffic accidents that may render all their contents open to public scrutiny.

In this regard—the degree of intrusiveness upon personal privacy and indeed even personal dignity—the two cases the Wyoming Supreme Court found dispositive differ substantially from the package search at issue here. *United States v. Di Re*, 332 U.S. 581 (1948), held that probable cause to search a car did not justify a body search of a passenger. And *Ybarra v. Illinois*, 444 U.S. 85 (1979), held that a search warrant for a tavern and its bartender did not permit body searches of all the bar's patrons. These cases turned on the unique, significantly heightened protection afforded against searches of one's person. "Even a limited search of the outer clothing . . . constitutes a severe, though brief, intrusion upon cherished personal security, and it must surely be an annoying, frightening, and perhaps humiliating experience." *Terry v. Ohio*, 392 U.S. 1 (1968). Such traumatic consequences are not to be expected when the police examine an item of personal property found in a car.[1]

Whereas the passenger's privacy expectations are, as we have described, considerably diminished, the governmental interests at stake are substantial. Effective law enforcement would be appreciably impaired without the ability to search a passenger's personal belongings when there is reason to believe contraband or evidence of criminal wrongdoing is hidden in the car. As in all car-search cases, the "ready mobility" of an automobile creates a risk that the evidence or contraband will be permanently lost while a warrant is obtained. In addition, a car passenger—unlike the unwitting tavern patron in Ybarra—will often be engaged in a common enterprise with the driver, and have the same interest in concealing the fruits or the evidence of their wrongdoing. A criminal might be able to hide contraband in a passenger's belongings as readily as in other containers in the car—perhaps even surreptitiously, without the passenger's knowledge or

---

[1] The dissent begins its analysis with an assertion that this case is governed by our decision in *United States v. Di Re*, which held, as the dissent describes it, that the automobile exception to the warrant requirement did not justify "searches of the passenger's pockets and the space between his shirt and underwear." It attributes that holding to "the settled distinction between drivers and passengers," rather than to a distinction between search of the person and search of property, which the dissent claims is "newly minted" by today's opinion—a "new rule that is based on a distinction between property contained in clothing worn by a passenger and property contained in a passenger's briefcase or purse."

In its peroration, however, the dissent quotes extensively from Justice Jackson's opinion in *Di Re*, which makes it very clear that it is precisely this distinction between search of the person and search of property that the case relied upon: "The Government says it would not contend that, armed 'with a search warrant for a residence only, it could search all persons found in it. But an occupant of a house could be used to conceal this contraband on his person quite as readily as can an occupant of a car.'" Does the dissent really believe that Justice Jackson was saying that a house-search could not inspect property belonging to persons found in the house—say a large standing safe or violin case belonging to the owner's visiting godfather? Of course that is not what Justice Jackson meant at all. He was referring precisely to that "distinction between property contained in clothing worn by a passenger and property contained in a passenger's briefcase or purse" that the dissent disparages. This distinction between searches of the person and searches of property is assuredly not "newly minted." And if the dissent thinks "pockets" and "clothing" do not count as part of the person, it must believe that the only searches of the person are strip searches.

permission. (This last possibility provided the basis for respondent's defense at trial; she testified that most of the seized contraband must have been placed in her purse by her traveling companions at one or another of various times, including the time she was "half asleep" in the car.)

To be sure, these factors favoring a search will not always be present, but the balancing of interests must be conducted with an eye to the generality of cases. To require that the investigating officer have positive reason to believe that the passenger and driver were engaged in a common enterprise, or positive reason to believe that the driver had time and occasion to conceal the item in the passenger's belongings, surreptitiously or with friendly permission, is to impose requirements so seldom met that a "passenger's property" rule would dramatically reduce the ability to find and seize contraband and evidence of crime. Of course these requirements would not attach (under the Wyoming Supreme Court's rule) until the police officer knows or has reason to know that the container belongs to a passenger. But once a "passenger's property" exception to car searches became widely known, one would expect passenger-confederates to claim everything as their own. And one would anticipate a bog of litigation—in the form of both civil lawsuits and motions to suppress in criminal trials—involving such questions as whether the officer should have believed a passenger's claim of ownership, whether he should have inferred ownership from various objective factors, whether he had probable cause to believe that the passenger was a confederate, or to believe that the driver might have introduced the contraband into the package with or without the passenger's knowledge.[2] When balancing the competing interests, our determinations of "reasonableness" under the Fourth Amendment must take account of these practical realities. We think they militate in favor of the needs of law enforcement, and against a personal-privacy interest that is ordinarily weak.

Finally, if we were to invent an exception from the historical practice that *Ross* accurately described and summarized, it is perplexing why that exception should protect only property belonging to a passenger, rather than (what seems much more logical) property belonging to anyone other than the driver. Surely Houghton's privacy would have been invaded to the same degree whether she was present or absent when her purse was searched. And surely her presence in the car with the driver provided more, rather than less, reason to believe that the two were in league. It may ordinarily be easier to identify the property as belonging to someone other than the driver when the purported owner is present to identify it—

---

[2]   The dissent is "confident in a police officer's ability to apply a rule requiring a warrant or individualized probable cause to search belongings that are . . . obviously owned by and in the custody of a passenger." If this is the dissent's strange criterion for warrant protection ("obviously owned by and in the custody of") its preceding paean to the importance of preserving passengers' privacy rings a little hollow on rehearing. Should it not be enough if the passenger says he owns the briefcase, and the officer has no concrete reason to believe otherwise? Or would the dissent consider that an example of "obvious" ownership? On reflection, it seems not at all obvious precisely what constitutes obviousness—and so even the dissent's on-the-cheap protection of passengers' privacy interest in their property turns out to be unclear, and hence unadministrable. But maybe the dissent does not mean to propose an obviously-owned-by-and-in-the-custody-of test after all, since a few sentences later it endorses, simpliciter, "a rule requiring a warrant or individualized probable cause to search passenger belongings." For the reasons described in text, that will not work.

but in the many cases (like *Ross* itself) where the car is seized, that identification may occur later, at the station-house; and even at the site of the stop one can readily imagine a package clearly marked with the owner's name and phone number, by which the officer can confirm the driver's denial of ownership. The sensible rule (and the one supported by history and caselaw) is that such a package may be searched, whether or not its owner is present as a passenger or otherwise, because it may contain the contraband that the officer has reason to believe is in the car.

We hold that police officers with probable cause to search a car may inspect passengers' belongings found in the car that are capable of concealing the object of the search. The judgment of the Wyoming Supreme Court is reversed.

It is so ordered.

JUSTICE BREYER, concurring.

I join the Court's opinion with the understanding that history is meant to inform, but not automatically to determine, the answer to a Fourth Amendment question. I also agree with the Court that when a police officer has probable cause to search a car, say, for drugs, it is reasonable for that officer also to search containers within the car. If the police must establish a container's ownership prior to the search of that container (whenever, for example, a passenger says "that's mine"), the resulting uncertainty will destroy the workability of the bright-line rule set forth in *United States v. Ross*. At the same time, police officers with probable cause to search a car for drugs would often have probable cause to search containers regardless. Hence a bright-line rule will authorize only a limited number of searches that the law would not otherwise justify.

At the same time, I would point out certain limitations upon the scope of the bright-line rule that the Court describes. Obviously, the rule applies only to automobile searches. Equally obviously, the rule applies only to containers found within automobiles. And it does not extend to the search of a person found in that automobile. As the Court notes, and as *United States v. Di Re*, relied on heavily by Justice Stevens' dissent, makes clear, the search of a person, including even " 'a limited search of the outer clothing,' " is a very different matter in respect to which the law provides "significantly heightened protection."

Less obviously, but in my view also important, is the fact that the container here at issue, a woman's purse, was found at a considerable distance from its owner, who did not claim ownership until the officer discovered her identification while looking through it. Purses are special containers. They are repositories of especially personal items that people generally like to keep with them at all times. So I am tempted to say that a search of a purse involves an intrusion so similar to a search of one's person that the same rule should govern both. However, given this Court's prior cases, I cannot argue that the fact that the container was a purse automatically makes a legal difference, for the Court has warned against trying to make that kind of distinction. But I say that it would matter if a woman's purse, like a man's billfold, were attached to her person. It might then amount to a kind of "outer clothing" which under the Court's cases would properly receive increased protection. In this case, the purse was separate from the person, and no one has claimed that, under those circumstances, the type of container makes a difference. For that reason, I join the Court's opinion.

JUSTICE STEVENS, with whom JUSTICE SOUTER and JUSTICE GINSBURG join, dissenting. * * *

In all of our prior cases applying the automobile exception to the Fourth Amendment's warrant requirement, either the defendant was the operator of the vehicle and in custody of the object of the search, or no question was raised as to the defendant's ownership or custody. In the only automobile case confronting the search of a passenger defendant—*United States v. Di Re*—the Court held that the exception to the warrant requirement did not apply. In *Di Re*, as here, the information prompting the search directly implicated the driver, not the passenger. Today, instead of adhering to the settled distinction between drivers and passengers, the Court fashions a new rule that is based on a distinction between property contained in clothing worn by a passenger and property contained in a passenger's briefcase or purse. In cases on both sides of the Court's newly minted test, the property is in a "container" (whether a pocket or a pouch) located in the vehicle. Moreover, unlike the Court, I think it quite plain that the search of a passenger's purse or briefcase involves an intrusion on privacy that may be just as serious as was the intrusion in *Di Re*.

Even apart from *Di Re*, the Court's rights-restrictive approach is not dictated by precedent. For example, in *United States v. Ross* we were concerned with the interest of the driver in the integrity of "his automobile," and we categorically rejected the notion that the scope of a warrantless search of a vehicle might be "defined by the nature of the container in which the contraband is secreted." "Rather, it is defined by the object of the search and the places in which there is probable cause to believe that it may be found." We thus disapproved of a possible container-based distinction between a man's pocket and a woman's pocketbook. Ironically, while we concluded in *Ross* that "[p]robable cause to believe that a container placed in the trunk of a taxi contains contraband or evidence does not justify a search of the entire cab," the rule the Court fashions would apparently permit a warrantless search of a passenger's briefcase if there is probable cause to believe the taxidriver had a syringe somewhere in his vehicle.

Nor am I persuaded that the mere spatial association between a passenger and a driver provides an acceptable basis for presuming that they are partners in crime or for ignoring privacy interests in a purse. Whether or not the Fourth Amendment required a warrant to search Houghton's purse, at the very least the trooper in this case had to have probable cause to believe that her purse contained contraband. The Wyoming Supreme Court concluded that he did not.

Finally, in my view, the State's legitimate interest in effective law enforcement does not outweigh the privacy concerns at issue. I am as confident in a police officer's ability to apply a rule requiring a warrant or individualized probable cause to search belongings that are—as in this case—obviously owned by and in the custody of a passenger as is the Court in a "passenger-confederate[']s" ability to circumvent the rule. Certainly the ostensible clarity of the Court's rule is attractive. But that virtue is insufficient justification for its adoption. Moreover, a rule requiring a warrant or individualized probable cause to search passenger belongings is every bit as simple as the Court's rule; it simply protects more privacy.

I would decide this case in accord with what we have said about passengers and privacy, rather than what we might have said in cases where the issue was not squarely presented. What Justice Jackson wrote for the Court fifty years ago is just as sound today:

> "The Government says it would not contend that, armed with a search warrant for a residence only, it could search all persons found in it. But an occupant of a house could be used to conceal this contraband on his person quite as readily as can an occupant of a car. Necessity, an argument advanced in support of this search, would seem as strong a reason for searching guests of a house for which a search warrant had issued as for search of guests in a car for which none had been issued. By a parity of reasoning with that on which the Government disclaims the right to search occupants of a house, we suppose the Government would not contend that if it had a valid search warrant for the car only it could search the occupants as an incident to its execution. How then could we say that the right to search a car without a warrant confers greater latitude to search occupants than a search by warrant would permit?

> "We see no ground for expanding the ruling in the *Carroll* case to justify this arrest and search as incident to the search of a car. We are not convinced that a person, by mere presence in a suspected car, loses immunities from search of his person to which he would otherwise be entitled." *Di Re.*[4]

Instead of applying ordinary Fourth Amendment principles to this case, the majority extends the automobile warrant exception to allow searches of passenger belongings based on the driver's misconduct. Thankfully, the Court's automobile-centered analysis limits the scope of its holding. But it does not justify the outcome in this case.

I respectfully dissent.

COLORADO V. BERTINE
479 U.S. 367, 107 S.Ct. 738, 93 L.Ed.2d 739 (1987).

CHIEF JUSTICE REHNQUIST delivered the opinion of the Court.

[A Boulder, Colorado, police officer arrested respondent for driving his van while under the influence of alcohol. After respondent was taken into custody and

---

[4] In response to this dissent the Court has crafted an imaginative footnote suggesting that the *Di Re* decision rested, not on Di Re's status as a mere occupant of the vehicle and the importance of individualized suspicion, but rather on the intrusive character of the search. That the search of a safe or violin case would be less intrusive than a strip search does not, however, persuade me that the *Di Re* case would have been decided differently if Di Re had been a woman and the gas coupons had been found in her purse. * * *

before a tow truck arrived to take the van to an impoundment lot, another officer, acting in accordance with local police procedures, inventoried the van's contents, opening a closed backpack in which he found various containers holding controlled substances, cocaine paraphernalia, and a large amount of cash. Prior to his trial on charges including drug offenses, the state trial court granted respondent's motion to suppress the evidence found during the inventory search. Although the court determined that the search did not violate respondent's rights under the Fourth Amendment of the Federal Constitution, it held that the search violated the Colorado Constitution. The Colorado Supreme Court affirmed, but premised its ruling on the Federal Constitution.]

We granted certiorari to consider the important and recurring question of federal law decided by the Colorado Supreme Court. As that court recognized, inventory searches are now a well-defined exception to the warrant requirement of the Fourth Amendment. The policies behind the warrant requirement are not implicated in an inventory search, nor is the related concept of probable cause:

> "The standard of probable cause is peculiarly related to criminal investigations, not routine, noncriminal procedures * * *. The probable-cause approach is unhelpful when analysis centers upon the reasonableness of routine administrative caretaking functions, particularly when no claim is made that the protective procedures are a subterfuge for criminal investigations."

For these reasons, the Colorado Supreme Court's reliance on *Arkansas v. Sanders, supra,* and *United States v. Chadwick, supra,* was incorrect. Both of these cases concerned searches solely for the purpose of investigating criminal conduct, with the validity of the searches therefore dependent on the application of the probable cause and warrant requirements of the Fourth Amendment.

By contrast, an inventory search may be "reasonable" under the Fourth Amendment even though it is not conducted pursuant to warrant based upon probable cause. In [*South Dakota v.*] *Opperman* [428 U.S. 364 (1976),] this Court assessed the reasonableness of an inventory search of the glove compartment in an abandoned automobile impounded by the police. We found that inventory procedures serve to protect an owner's property while it is in the custody of the police, to insure against claims of lost, stolen, or vandalized property, and to guard the police from danger. In light of these strong governmental interests and the diminished expectation of privacy in an automobile, we upheld the search. In reaching this decision, we observed that our cases accorded deference to police caretaking procedures designed to secure and protect vehicles and their contents within police custody.

In our more recent decision, [*Illinois v.*] *Lafayette* [462 U.S. 640 (1983),] a police officer conducted an inventory search of the contents of a shoulder bag in the possession of an individual being taken into custody. In deciding whether this search was reasonable, we recognized that the search served legitimate governmental interests similar to those identified in *Opperman.* We determined that those interests outweighed the individual's Fourth Amendment interests and upheld the search.

In the present case, as in *Opperman* and *Lafayette,* there was no showing that the police, who were following standardized procedures, acted in bad faith or for the sole purpose of investigation. In addition, the governmental interests justifying the inventory searches in *Opperman* and *Lafayette* are nearly the same as those which obtain here. In each case, the police were potentially responsible for the property taken into their custody. By securing the property, the police protected the property from unauthorized interference. Knowledge of the precise nature of the property helped guard against claims of theft, vandalism, or negligence. Such knowledge also helped to avert any danger to police or others that may have been posed by the property.[5]

The Supreme Court of Colorado opined that *Lafayette* was not controlling here because there was no danger of introducing contraband or weapons into a jail facility. Our opinion in *Lafayette,* however, did not suggest that the station-house setting of the inventory search was critical to our holding in that case. Both in the present case and in *Lafayette,* the common governmental interests described above were served by the inventory searches.

The Supreme Court of Colorado also expressed the view that the search in this case was unreasonable because Bertine's van was towed to a secure, lighted facility and because Bertine himself could have been offered the opportunity to make other arrangements for the safekeeping of his property. But the security of the storage facility does not completely eliminate the need for inventorying; the police may still wish to protect themselves or the owners of the lot against false claims of theft or dangerous instrumentalities. And while giving Bertine an opportunity to make alternate arrangements would undoubtedly have been possible, we said in *Lafayette:*

> "[t]he real question is not what 'could have been achieved,' but whether the Fourth Amendment *requires* such steps * * * The reasonableness of any particular governmental activity does not necessarily or invariably turn on the existence of alternative 'less intrusive' means."

We conclude that here, as in *Lafayette,* reasonable police regulations relating to inventory procedures administered in good faith satisfy the Fourth Amendment, even though courts might as a matter of hindsight be able to devise equally reasonable rules requiring a different procedure.[6]

The Supreme Court of Colorado also thought it necessary to require that police, before inventorying a container, weigh the strength of the individual's

---

[5] In arguing that the latter two interests are not implicated here, the dissent overlooks the testimony of the back-up officer who conducted the inventory of Bertine's van. According to the officer, the vehicle inventory procedures of the Boulder Police Department are designed for the "[p]rotection of the police department" in the event that an individual later claims that "there was something of value taken from within the vehicle." The officer added that inventories are also conducted in order to check "[f]or any dangerous items such as explosives [or] weapons." The officer testified that he had found such items in vehicles.

[6] We emphasize that, in this case, the trial court found that the police department's procedures mandated the opening of closed containers and the listing of their contents. Our decisions have always adhered to the requirement that inventories be conducted according to standardized criteria.

privacy interest in the container against the possibility that the container might serve as a repository for dangerous or valuable items. We think that such a requirement is contrary to our decisions in *Opperman* and *Lafayette*:

> "Even if less intrusive means existed of protecting some particular types of property, it would be unreasonable to expect police officers in the everyday course of business to make fine and subtle distinctions in deciding which containers or items may be searched and which must be sealed as a unit." *Lafayette,* supra. * * *

Bertine finally argues that the inventory search of his van was unconstitutional because departmental regulations gave the police officers discretion to choose between impounding his van and parking and locking it in a public parking place. The Supreme Court of Colorado did not rely on this argument in reaching its conclusion, and we reject it. Nothing in *Opperman* or *Lafayette* prohibits the exercise of police discretion so long as that discretion is exercised according to standard criteria and on the basis of something other than suspicion of evidence of criminal activity. Here, the discretion afforded the Boulder police was exercised in light of standardized criteria, related to the feasibility and appropriateness of parking and locking a vehicle rather than impounding it. There was no showing that the police chose to impound Bertine's van in order to investigate suspected criminal activity. * * * The judgment of the Supreme Court of Colorado is therefore reversed.

JUSTICE BLACKMUN, with whom JUSTICE POWELL and JUSTICE O'CONNOR join, concurring.

* * * I join the Court's opinion, but write separately to underscore the importance of having such inventories conducted only pursuant to standardized police procedures * * * that mandate the opening of such containers in every impounded vehicle. * * *a

---

a In *Florida v. Wells*, 495 U.S. 1 (1990), where all members of the Court agreed that the inventory of a locked suitcase found in an impounded vehicle was unlawful under *Bertine* because "the Florida Highway Patrol had no policy whatever with respect to the opening of closed containers encountered during an inventory search," five members of the Court went on to say that the state court erred in saying *Bertine* requires a policy either mandating or barring inventory of all containers: "A police officer may be allowed sufficient latitude to determine whether a particular container should or should not be opened in light of the nature of the search and characteristics of the container itself. Thus, while policies of opening all containers or opening no containers are unquestionably permissible, it would be equally permissible, for example, to allow the opening of closed containers whose contents officers determine they are unable to ascertain from examining the containers' exteriors."

Brennan and Marshall, JJ., concurring, disagreed with that assertion, which they characterized as "pure dictum given the disposition of the case." Blackmun, J. concurring, agreed that the Fourth Amendment did not impose an "all or nothing" requirement, so that a state "probably could adopt a policy which requires the opening of all containers that are not locked, or a policy which requires the opening of all containers over or under a certain size," but objected it was "an entirely different matter * * * to say, as this majority does, that an individual policeman may be afforded discretion in conducting an inventory search." Stevens, J., concurring separately, agreed with Blackmun.

JUSTICE MARSHALL, with whom JUSTICE BRENNAN joins, dissenting.

* * * [T]he record indicates that *no* standardized criteria limit a Boulder police officer's discretion. According to a departmental directive, after placing a driver under arrest, an officer has three options for disposing of the vehicle. First, he can allow a third party to take custody. Second, the officer or the driver (depending on the nature of the arrest) may take the car to the nearest public parking facility, lock it, and take the keys. Finally, the officer can do what was done in this case: impound the vehicle, and search and inventory its contents, including closed containers.

Under the first option, the police have no occasion to search the automobile. Under the "park and lock" option, "[c]losed containers that give no indication of containing either valuables or a weapon *may not be opened and the contents searched* (i.e., inventoried)." (emphasis added). Only if the police choose the third option are they entitled to search closed containers in the vehicle. Where the vehicle is not itself evidence of a crime, as in this case, the police apparently have totally unbridled discretion as to which procedure to use. Consistent with this conclusion, Officer Reichenbach testified that such decisions were left to the discretion of the officer on the scene.

Once a Boulder police officer has made this initial completely discretionary decision to impound a vehicle, he is given little guidance as to which areas to search and what sort of items to inventory. The arresting officer, Officer Toporek, testified at the suppression hearing as to what items would be inventoried: "That would I think be very individualistic as far as what an officer may or may not go into. I think whatever arouses his suspicious [*sic*] as far as what may be contained in any type of article in the car." * * *

Inventory searches are not subject to the warrant requirement because they are conducted by the government as part of "community caretaking" function, "totally divorced from the detection, investigation, or acquisition of evidence relating to the violation of a criminal statute." Standardized procedures are necessary to ensure that this narrow exception is not improperly used to justify, after the fact, a warrantless investigative foray. Accordingly, to invalidate a search that is conducted without established procedures, it is not necessary to establish that the police actually acted in bad faith, or that the inventory was in fact a "pretext." By allowing the police unfettered discretion, Boulder's discretionary scheme is unreasonable because of the " 'grave danger' of abuse of discretion."

In *South Dakota v. Opperman,* and *Illinois v. Lafayette,* both of which involved inventories conducted pursuant to standardized procedures, we balanced the individual's expectation of privacy against the government's interests to determine whether the search was reasonable. Even if the search in this case did constitute a legitimate inventory, it would nonetheless be unreasonable under this analysis. * * *

Not only are the government's interests weaker here than in *Opperman* and *Lafayette,* but respondent's privacy interest is greater. In upholding the search in *Opperman,* the Court emphasized the fact that the defendant had a diminished expectation of privacy in his automobile, due to "pervasive and continuing governmental regulation and controls, including periodic inspection and licensing requirements" and "the obviously public nature of automobile travel." Similarly, in *Lafayette,* the Court emphasized the fact that the defendant was in custody at the time the inventory took place.

Here the Court completely ignores respondent's expectation of privacy in his backpack. Whatever his expectation of privacy in his automobile generally, our prior decisions clearly establish that he retained a reasonable expectation of privacy in the backpack and its contents. See *Arkansas v. Sanders* ("[L]uggage is a common repository for one's personal effects, and therefore is inevitably associated with the expectation of privacy"); *United States v. Chadwick* ("[A] person's expectations of privacy in personal luggage are substantially greater than in an automobile"). Indeed, the Boulder police officer who conducted the inventory acknowledged that backpacks commonly serve as repositories for personal effects. Thus, even if the governmental interests in this case were the same as those in *Opperman,* they would nonetheless be outweighed by respondent's comparatively greater expectation of privacy in his luggage. * * *

RILEY V. CALIFORNIA
573 U.S. 373, 134 S.Ct. 2473, 189 L.Ed.2d 430 (2014).

CHIEF JUSTICE ROBERTS delivered the opinion of the Court.

These two cases raise a common question: whether the police may, without a warrant, search digital information on a cell phone seized from an individual who has been arrested. [In the first case, police searched Riley's person incident to his arrest on a weapons charge and seized a sophisticated cell phone of the "smart phone" variety found in his pocket. That officer found some evidence of gang activity, and a detective at the station later examined the phone more thoroughly and found photos and videos that were introduced into evidence at Riley's trial for a recent shooting. On appeal, that evidence was deemed to have been lawfully obtained in a valid search incident to arrest. In the second case, Wurie was arrested for a drug sale, and at the station a less sophisticated phone of the "flip phone" variety was found on his person. It was receiving multiple calls from a source identified as "my house," so the officer accessed the call log to determine the number, which led to issuance of a search warrant for Wurie's apartment. Evidence found therein was admitted at his trial, but on appeal that evidence was held to constitute the fruits of an illegal search of the phone.]

The two cases before us concern the reasonableness of a warrantless search incident to a lawful arrest. * * * Three related precedents set forth the rules governing such searches: [The Court here summarized the search-incident-to-arrest holdings research of the person, premises and a vehicle in *United States v. Robinson* [p. 182], *Chimel v. California* [p. 228], and *Arizona v. Gant* [p. 244], respectively.]

Absent more precise guidance from the founding era, we generally determine whether to exempt a given type of search from the warrant requirement "by assessing, on the one hand, the degree to which it intrudes upon an individual's privacy and, on the other, the degree to which it is needed for the promotion of legitimate governmental interests." Such a balancing of interests supported the search incident to arrest exception in *Robinson*, and a mechanical application of *Robinson* might well support the warrantless searches at issue here.

But while *Robinson*'s categorical rule strikes the appropriate balance in the context of physical objects, neither of its rationales has much force with respect to digital content on cell phones. On the government interest side, *Robinson* concluded that the two risks identified in *Chimel*—harm to officers and destruction of evidence—are present in all custodial arrests. There are no comparable risks when the search is of digital data. In addition, *Robinson* regarded any privacy interests retained by an individual after arrest as significantly diminished by the fact of the arrest itself. Cell phones, however, place vast quantities of personal information literally in the hands of individuals. A search of the information on a cell phone bears little resemblance to the type of brief physical search considered in *Robinson*.

We therefore decline to extend *Robinson* to searches of data on cell phones, and hold instead that officers must generally secure a warrant before conducting such a search.

We first consider each *Chimel* concern in turn. In doing so, we do not overlook *Robinson*'s admonition that searches of a person incident to arrest, "while based upon the need to disarm and to discover evidence," are reasonable regardless of "the probability in a particular arrest situation that weapons or evidence would in fact be found." Rather than requiring the "case-by-case adjudication" that *Robinson* rejected, we ask instead whether application of the search incident to arrest doctrine to this particular category of effects would "untether the rule from the justifications underlying the *Chimel* exception," *Gant*.

Digital data stored on a cell phone cannot itself be used as a weapon to harm an arresting officer or to effectuate the arrestee's escape. Law enforcement officers remain free to examine the physical aspects of a phone to ensure that it will not be used as a weapon—say, to determine whether there is a razor blade hidden between the phone and its case. Once an officer has secured a phone and eliminated any potential physical threats, however, data on the phone can endanger no one.

Perhaps the same might have been said of the cigarette pack seized from Robinson's pocket. Once an officer gained control of the pack, it was unlikely that Robinson could have accessed the pack's contents. But unknown physical objects may always pose risks, no matter how slight, during the tense atmosphere of a custodial arrest. The officer in *Robinson* testified that he could not identify the objects in the cigarette pack but knew they were not cigarettes. Given that, a further search was a reasonable protective measure. No such unknowns exist with respect to digital data. * * *

The United States and California both suggest that a search of cell phone data might help ensure officer safety in more indirect ways, for example by alerting officers that confederates of the arrestee are headed to the scene. There is undoubtedly a strong government interest in warning officers about such possibilities, but neither the United States nor California offers evidence to suggest that their concerns are based on actual experience. * * * To the extent dangers to arresting officers may be implicated in a particular way in a particular case, they are better addressed through consideration of case-specific exceptions to the warrant requirement, such as the one for exigent circumstances.

The United States and California focus primarily on the second *Chimel* rationale: preventing the destruction of evidence.

Both Riley and Wurie concede that officers could have seized and secured their cell phones to prevent destruction of evidence while seeking a warrant. And once law enforcement officers have secured a cell phone, there is no longer any risk that the arrestee himself will be able to delete incriminating data from the phone.

The United States and California argue that information on a cell phone may nevertheless be vulnerable to two types of evidence destruction unique to digital data—remote wiping and data encryption. Remote wiping occurs when a phone, connected to a wireless network, receives a signal that erases stored data. This can happen when a third party sends a remote signal or when a phone is preprogrammed to delete data upon entering or leaving certain geographic areas (so-called "geofencing"). Encryption is a security feature that some modern cell phones use in addition to password protection. When such phones lock, data becomes protected by sophisticated encryption that renders a phone all but "unbreakable" unless police know the password.

As an initial matter, these broader concerns about the loss of evidence are distinct from *Chimel*'s focus on a defendant who responds to arrest by trying to conceal or destroy evidence within his reach. * * *

We have also been given little reason to believe that either problem is prevalent. * * *

In any event, as to remote wiping, law enforcement is not without specific means to address the threat. Remote wiping can be fully prevented by disconnecting a phone from the network. There are at least two simple ways to do this: First, law enforcement officers can turn the phone off or remove its battery. Second, if they are concerned about encryption or other potential problems, they can leave a phone powered on and place it in an enclosure that isolates the phone from radio waves. * * *

To the extent that law enforcement still has specific concerns about the potential loss of evidence in a particular case, there remain more targeted ways to address those concerns. If "the police are truly confronted with a 'now or never' situation,"—for example, circumstances suggesting that a defendant's phone will be the target of an imminent remote-wipe attempt—they may be able to rely on exigent circumstances to search the phone immediately. * * *

The search incident to arrest exception rests not only on the heightened government interests at stake in a volatile arrest situation, but also on an arrestee's reduced privacy interests upon being taken into police custody. *Robinson* focused primarily on the first of those rationales. But it also quoted with approval then-Judge Cardozo's account of the historical basis for the search incident to arrest exception: "Search of the person becomes lawful when grounds for arrest and accusation have been discovered, and the law is in the act of subjecting the body of the accused to its physical dominion." Put simply, a patdown of Robinson's clothing and an inspection of the cigarette pack found in his pocket constituted only minor additional intrusions compared to the substantial government authority exercised in taking Robinson into custody.

The fact that an arrestee has diminished privacy interests does not mean that the Fourth Amendment falls out of the picture entirely. * * * One such example, of course, is *Chimel*. *Chimel* refused to "characteriz[e] the invasion of privacy that results from a top-to-bottom search of a man's house as 'minor.'" * * *

Robinson is the only decision from this Court applying *Chimel* to a search of the contents of an item found on an arrestee's person. * * * Lower courts applying *Robinson* and *Chimel*, however, have approved searches of a variety of personal items carried by an arrestee.

The United States asserts that a search of all data stored on a cell phone is "materially indistinguishable" from searches of these sorts of physical items. That is like saying a ride on horseback is materially indistinguishable from a flight to the moon. Both are ways of getting from point A to point B, but little else justifies lumping them together. Modern cell phones, as a category, implicate privacy concerns far beyond those implicated by the search of a cigarette pack, a wallet, or a purse. A conclusion that inspecting the contents of an arrestee's pockets works no substantial additional intrusion on privacy beyond the arrest itself may make sense as applied to physical items, but any extension of that reasoning to digital data has to rest on its own bottom.

One of the most notable distinguishing features of modern cell phones is their immense storage capacity. Before cell phones, a search of a person was limited by physical realities and tended as a general matter to constitute only a narrow intrusion on privacy. * * *

But the possible intrusion on privacy is not physically limited in the same way when it comes to cell phones. The current top-selling smart phone has a standard capacity of 16 gigabytes (and is available with up to 64 gigabytes). Sixteen gigabytes translates to millions of pages of text, thousands of pictures, or hundreds of videos. * * * Even the most basic phones that sell for less than $20 might hold photographs, picture messages, text messages, Internet browsing history, a calendar, a thousand-entry phone book, and so on. * * *

The storage capacity of cell phones has several interrelated consequences for privacy. First, a cell phone collects in one place many distinct types of information—an address, a note, a prescription, a bank statement, a video—that reveal much more in combination than any isolated record. Second, a cell phone's capacity allows even just one type of information to convey far more than previously possible. The sum of an individual's private life can be reconstructed through a thousand photographs labeled with dates, locations, and descriptions; the same cannot be said of a photograph or two of loved ones tucked into a wallet.

Third, the data on a phone can date back to the purchase of the phone, or even earlier. A person might carry in his pocket a slip of paper reminding him to call Mr. Jones; he would not carry a record of all his communications with Mr. Jones for the past several months, as would routinely be kept on a phone.[1]

Finally, there is an element of pervasiveness that characterizes cell phones but not physical records. Prior to the digital age, people did not typically carry a cache of sensitive personal information with them as they went about their day. Now it is the person who is not carrying a cell phone, with all that it contains, who is the exception. * * *

Although the data stored on a cell phone is distinguished from physical records by quantity alone, certain types of data are also qualitatively different. An Internet search and browsing history, for example, can be found on an Internet-enabled phone and could reveal an individual's private interests or concerns—perhaps a search for certain symptoms of disease, coupled with frequent visits to WebMD. Data on a cell phone can also reveal where a person has been. Historic location information is a standard feature on many smart phones and can reconstruct someone's specific movements down to the minute, not only around town but also within a particular building.

Mobile application software on a cell phone, or "apps," offer a range of tools for managing detailed information about all aspects of a person's life. * * * The average smart phone user has installed 33 apps, which together can form a revealing montage of the user's life.

In 1926, Learned Hand observed (in an opinion later quoted in *Chimel*) that it is "a totally different thing to search a man's pockets and use against him what they contain, from ransacking his house for everything which may incriminate him." If his pockets contain a cell phone, however, that is no longer true. Indeed, a cell phone search would typically expose to the government far more than the most exhaustive search of a house: A phone not only contains in digital form many sensitive records previously found in the home; it also contains a broad array of private information never found in a home in any form—unless the phone is.

To further complicate the scope of the privacy interests at stake, the data a user views on many modern cell phones may not in fact be stored on the device itself. * * *

The United States concedes that the search incident to arrest exception may not be stretched to cover a search of files accessed remotely—that is, a search of files stored in the cloud. Such a search would be like finding a key in a suspect's pocket and arguing that it allowed law enforcement to unlock and search a house. But officers searching a phone's data would not typically know whether the information they are viewing was stored locally at the time of the arrest or has been pulled from the cloud.

---

[1] Because the United States and California agree that these cases involve searches incident to arrest, these cases do not implicate the question whether the collection or inspection of aggregated digital information amounts to a search under other circumstances.

Apart from their arguments for a direct extension of *Robinson*, the United States and California offer various fallback options for permitting warrantless cell phone searches under certain circumstances. * * *

The United States first proposes that the *Gant* standard be imported from the vehicle context, allowing a warrantless search of an arrestee's cell phone whenever it is reasonable to believe that the phone contains evidence of the crime of arrest. But *Gant* relied on "circumstances unique to the vehicle context" to endorse a search solely for the purpose of gathering evidence.

At any rate, a *Gant* standard would prove no practical limit at all when it comes to cell phone searches. In the vehicle context, *Gant* generally protects against searches for evidence of past crimes. In the cell phone context, however, it is reasonable to expect that incriminating information will be found on a phone regardless of when the crime occurred. Similarly, in the vehicle context *Gant* restricts broad searches resulting from minor crimes such as traffic violations. That would not necessarily be true for cell phones. * * *

The United States also proposes a rule that would restrict the scope of a cell phone search to those areas of the phone where an officer reasonably believes that information relevant to the crime, the arrestee's identity, or officer safety will be discovered. This approach would again impose few meaningful constraints on officers. The proposed categories would sweep in a great deal of information, and officers would not always be able to discern in advance what information would be found where.

We also reject the United States' final suggestion that officers should always be able to search a phone's call log, as they did in Wurie's case. The Government relies on *Smith v. Maryland* [p. 101],which held that no warrant was required to use a pen register at telephone company premises to identify numbers dialed by a particular caller. The Court in that case, however, concluded that the use of a pen register was not a "search" at all under the Fourth Amendment. There is no dispute here that the officers engaged in a search of Wurie's cell phone. Moreover, call logs typically contain more than just phone numbers; they include any identifying information that an individual might add, such as the label "my house" in Wurie's case.

Finally, at oral argument California suggested a different limiting principle, under which officers could search cell phone data if they could have obtained the same information from a pre-digital counterpart. But the fact that a search in the pre-digital era could have turned up a photograph or two in a wallet does not justify a search of thousands of photos in a digital gallery. The fact that someone could have tucked a paper bank statement in a pocket does not justify a search of every bank statement from the last five years. And to make matters worse, such an analogue test would allow law enforcement to search a range of items contained on a phone, even though people would be unlikely to carry such a variety of information in physical form. * * *

In addition, an analogue test would launch courts on a difficult line-drawing expedition to determine which digital files are comparable to physical records. Is an e-mail equivalent to a letter? Is a voicemail equivalent to a phone message slip? It is not clear how officers could make these kinds of decisions before conducting a search, or how courts would apply the proposed rule after the fact. * * *

Our holding, of course, is not that the information on a cell phone is immune from search; it is instead that a warrant is generally required before such a search, even when a cell phone is seized incident to arrest. * * *

Moreover, even though the search incident to arrest exception does not apply to cell phones, other case-specific exceptions may still justify a warrantless search of a particular phone. "One well-recognized exception applies when ' "the exigencies of the situation" make the needs of law enforcement so compelling that [a] warrantless search is objectively reasonable under the Fourth Amendment.' " Such exigencies could include the need to prevent the imminent destruction of evidence in individual cases, to pursue a fleeing suspect, and to assist persons who are seriously injured or are threatened with imminent injury. * * *

In light of the availability of the exigent circumstances exception, there is no reason to believe that law enforcement officers will not be able to address some of the more extreme hypotheticals that have been suggested: a suspect texting an accomplice who, it is feared, is preparing to detonate a bomb, or a child abductor who may have information about the child's location on his cell phone. * * *[2]

JUSTICE ALITO, concurring in part and concurring in the judgment.

I agree with the Court that law enforcement officers, in conducting a lawful search incident to arrest, must generally obtain a warrant before searching information stored or accessible on a cell phone. I write separately to address two points.

First, I am not convinced at this time that the ancient rule on searches incident to arrest is based exclusively (or even primarily) on the need to protect the safety of arresting officers and the need to prevent the destruction of evidence. This rule antedates the adoption of the Fourth Amendment by at least a century. In *Weeks v. United States*, 232 U.S. 383 (1914), we held that the Fourth Amendment did not disturb this rule. * * *

[W]hen pre-*Weeks* authorities discussed the basis for the rule, what was mentioned was the need to obtain probative evidence. For example, an 1839 case stated that "it is clear, and beyond doubt, that . . . constables . . . are entitled, upon a lawful arrest by them of one charged with treason or felony, to take and detain property found in his possession which will form material evidence in his prosecution for that crime."

What ultimately convinces me that the rule is not closely linked to the need for officer safety and evidence preservation is that these rationales fail to explain the rule's well-recognized scope. It has long been accepted that written items found

---

[2] In Wurie's case, for example, the dissenting First Circuit judge argued that exigent circumstances could have justified a search of Wurie's phone (discussing the repeated unanswered calls from "my house," the suspected location of a drug stash). But the majority concluded that the Government had not made an exigent circumstances argument. The Government acknowledges the same in this Court.

on the person of an arrestee may be examined and used at trial. But once these items are taken away from an arrestee (something that obviously must be done before the items are read), there is no risk that the arrestee will destroy them. Nor is there any risk that leaving these items unread will endanger the arresting officers. * * *

Despite my view on the point discussed above, I agree that we should not mechanically apply the rule used in the predigital era to the search of a cell phone. Many cell phones now in use are capable of storing and accessing a quantity of information, some highly personal, that no person would ever have had on his person in hard-copy form. This calls for a new balancing of law enforcement and privacy interests.

The Court strikes this balance in favor of privacy interests with respect to all cell phones and all information found in them, and this approach leads to anomalies. For example, the Court's broad holding favors information in digital form over information in hard-copy form. Suppose that two suspects are arrested. Suspect number one has in his pocket a monthly bill for his land-line phone, and the bill lists an incriminating call to a long-distance number. He also has in his a wallet a few snapshots, and one of these is incriminating. Suspect number two has in his pocket a cell phone, the call log of which shows a call to the same incriminating number. In addition, a number of photos are stored in the memory of the cell phone, and one of these is incriminating. Under established law, the police may seize and examine the phone bill and the snapshots in the wallet without obtaining a warrant, but under the Court's holding today, the information stored in the cell phone is out.

While the Court's approach leads to anomalies, I do not see a workable alternative. Law enforcement officers need clear rules regarding searches incident to arrest, and it would take many cases and many years for the courts to develop more nuanced rules. And during that time, the nature of the electronic devices that ordinary Americans carry on their persons would continue to change.

This brings me to my second point. While I agree with the holding of the Court, I would reconsider the question presented here if either Congress or state legislatures, after assessing the legitimate needs of law enforcement and the privacy interests of cell phone owners, enact legislation that draws reasonable distinctions based on categories of information or perhaps other variables.

The regulation of electronic surveillance provides an instructive example. After this Court held that electronic surveillance constitutes a search even when no property interest is invaded, Congress responded by enacting Title III of the Omnibus Crime Control and Safe Streets Act of 1968. Since that time, electronic surveillance has been governed primarily, not by decisions of this Court, but by the statute, which authorizes but imposes detailed restrictions on electronic surveillance.

* * * Many forms of modern technology are making it easier and easier for both government and private entities to amass a wealth of information about the lives of ordinary Americans, and at the same time, many ordinary Americans are

choosing to make public much information that was seldom revealed to outsiders just a few decades ago.

In light of these developments, it would be very unfortunate if privacy protection in the 21st century were left primarily to the federal courts using the blunt instrument of the Fourth Amendment. Legislatures, elected by the people, are in a better position than we are to assess and respond to the changes that have already occurred and those that almost certainly will take place in the future.

8. STOP AND FRISK

Under the monolithic approach to the Fourth Amendment which once obtained, the assumption was that every form of activity which constituted either a search or a seizure had to be grounded in the same quantum of evidence suggested by the Amendment's "probable cause" requirement. But this changed when the Supreme Court recognized in *Camara v. Municipal Court,* 387 U.S. 523 (1967), that at least some Fourth Amendment activity should be judged under a balancing test, that is, by "balancing the need to search against the invasion which the search entails." Doubtless the most significant application of this new balancing test came a year later when, in *Terry v. Ohio,* the first case in this section, the Court applied it to the common police practice of detaining suspicious persons briefly on the street for purposes of investigation. The next two cases, *Kansas v. Glover* and *Florida v. J. L.,* are two recent efforts by the Court to elaborate what constitutes sufficient grounds for a *Terry* stop.

If there is to be a discrete form of police activity, typically called stop-and-frisk, which is subject to a lesser evidentiary standard, then it is necessary to distinguish such activity from full-fledged arrests requiring probable cause on the one hand and no-seizure police encounters requiring no justification whatsoever on the other. The problems attendant the drawing of such lines are seen in *Florida v. Royer, United States v. Drayton, Brendlin v. California,* and *Rodriguez v. United States.*

TERRY V. OHIO
392 U.S. 1, 88 S.Ct. 1868, 20 L.Ed.2d 889 (1968).

CHIEF JUSTICE WARREN delivered the opinion of the Court.

[Officer McFadden, a Cleveland plainclothes detective, became suspicious of two men standing on a street corner in the downtown area at about 2:30 in the afternoon. One of the suspects walked up the street, peered into a store, walked on, started back, looked into the same store, and then joined and conferred with his companion. The other suspect repeated this ritual, and between them the two men went through this performance about a dozen times. They also talked with a third man, and then followed him up the street about ten minutes after his departure. The officer, thinking that the suspects were "casing" a stickup and might be armed, followed and confronted the three men as they were again conversing. He identified himself and asked the suspects for their names. The men only mumbled something, and the officer spun Terry around and patted his breast pocket. He felt a pistol, which he removed. A frisk of Terry's companion also uncovered a pistol; a frisk of the third man did not disclose that he was armed, and he was not searched further. Terry was charged with carrying a concealed weapon, and he moved to suppress the weapon as evidence. The motion was denied by the trial judge, who upheld the officer's actions on a stop-and-frisk theory. The Ohio court of appeals affirmed, and the state supreme court dismissed Terry's appeal.]

* * * The question is whether in all the circumstances of this on-the-street encounter, [Terry's] right to personal security was violated by an unreasonable search and seizure.

We would be less than candid if we did not acknowledge that this question thrusts to the fore difficult and troublesome issues regarding a sensitive area of police activity—issues which have never before been squarely presented to this Court. * * *

On the one hand, it is frequently argued that in dealing with the rapidly unfolding and often dangerous situations on city streets the police are in need of an escalating set of flexible responses, graduated in relation to the amount of information they possess. For this purpose it is urged that distinctions should be made between a "stop" and an "arrest" (or a "seizure" of a person), and between a "frisk" and a "search." Thus, it is argued, the police should be allowed to "stop" a person and detain him briefly for questioning upon suspicion that he may be connected with criminal activity. Upon suspicion that the person may be armed, the police should have the power to "frisk" him for weapons. If the "stop" and the "frisk" give rise to probable cause to believe that the suspect has committed a crime, then the police should be empowered to make a formal "arrest," and a full incident "search" of the person. This scheme is justified in part upon the notion that a "stop" and a "frisk" amount to a mere "minor inconvenience and petty indignity," which can properly be imposed upon the citizen in the interest of effective law enforcement on the basis of a police officer's suspicion.

On the other side the argument is made that the authority of the police must be strictly circumscribed by the law of arrest and search as it has developed to date in the traditional jurisprudence of the Fourth Amendment. It is contended with some force that there is not—and cannot be—a variety of police activity which does not depend solely upon the voluntary cooperation of the citizen and yet which stops short of an arrest based upon probable cause to make such an arrest. The heart of the Fourth Amendment, the argument runs, is a severe requirement of specific justification for any intrusion upon protected personal security, coupled with a highly developed system of judicial controls to enforce upon the agents of the State the commands of the Constitution. * * *

* * * The State has characterized the issue here as "the right of a police officer * * * to make an on-the-street stop, interrogate and pat down for weapons (known in the street vernacular as 'stop and frisk')." But this is only partly accurate. For the issue is not the abstract propriety of the police conduct, but the admissibility against petitioner of the evidence uncovered by the search and seizure. * * * [I]n our system evidentiary rulings provide the context in which the judicial process of inclusion and exclusion approves some conduct as comporting with constitutional guarantees and disapproves other actions by state agents. A ruling admitting evidence in a criminal trial, we recognize, has the necessary effect of legitimizing the conduct which produced the evidence, while an application of the exclusionary rule withholds the constitutional imprimatur.

The exclusionary rule has its limitations, however, as a tool of judicial control. It cannot properly be invoked to exclude the products of legitimate police investigative techniques on the ground that much conduct which is closely similar involves unwarranted intrusions upon constitutional protections. Moreover, in some contexts the rule is ineffective as a deterrent. Street encounters between citizens and police officers are incredibly rich in diversity. They range from wholly friendly exchanges of pleasantries or mutually useful information to hostile confrontations of armed men involving arrests, or injuries, or loss of life. Moreover, hostile confrontations are not all of a piece. Some of them begin in a friendly enough manner, only to take a different turn upon the injection of some unexpected element into the conversation. Encounters are initiated by the police for a wide variety of purposes, some of which are wholly unrelated to a desire to prosecute for crime. Doubtless some police "field interrogation" conduct violates the Fourth Amendment. But a stern refusal by this Court to condone such activity does not necessarily render it responsive to the exclusionary rule. Regardless of how effective the rule may be where obtaining convictions is an important objective of the police, it is powerless to deter invasions of constitutionally guaranteed rights where the police either have no interest in prosecuting or are willing to forego successful prosecution in the interest of serving some other goal.

Proper adjudication of cases in which the exclusionary rule is invoked demands a constant awareness of these limitations. The wholesale harassment by certain elements of the police community, of which minority groups, particularly Negroes, frequently complain, will not be stopped by the exclusion of any evidence from any criminal trial. Yet a rigid and unthinking application of the exclusionary rule, in futile protest against practices which it can never be used effectively to control, may exact a high toll in human injury and frustration of efforts to prevent crime. No judicial opinion can comprehend the protean variety of the street encounter, and we can only judge the facts of the case before us. * * *

[W]e turn our attention to the quite narrow question posed by the facts before us: whether it is always unreasonable for a policeman to seize a person and subject him to a limited search for weapons unless there is probable cause for an arrest.

* * * It is quite plain that the Fourth Amendment governs "seizures" of the person which do not eventuate in a trip to the station house and prosecution for crime—"arrests" in traditional terminology. It must be recognized that whenever a police officer accosts an individual and restrains his freedom to walk away, he has "seized" that person. And it is nothing less than sheer torture of the English language to suggest that a careful exploration of the outer surfaces of a person's clothing all over his or her body in an attempt to find weapons is not a "search." Moreover, it is simply fantastic to urge that such a procedure performed in public by a policeman while the citizen stands helpless, perhaps facing a wall with his

hands raised, is a "petty indignity."[13] It is a serious intrusion upon the sanctity of the person, which may inflict great indignity and arouse strong resentment, and it is not to be undertaken lightly.

* * * We therefore reject the notions that the Fourth Amendment does not come into play at all as a limitation upon police conduct if the officers stop short of something called a "technical arrest" or a "full-blown search."

In this case there can be no question, then, that Officer McFadden "seized" petitioner and subjected him to a "search" when he took hold of him and patted down the outer surfaces of his clothing. We must decide whether at that point it was reasonable for Officer McFadden to have interfered with petitioner's personal security as he did.[16] And in determining whether the seizure and search were "unreasonable" our inquiry is a dual one—whether the officer's action was justified at its inception, and whether it was reasonably related in scope to the circumstances which justified the interference in the first place.

If this case involved police conduct subject to the Warrant Clause of the Fourth Amendment, we would have to ascertain whether "probable cause" existed to justify the search and seizure which took place. However, that is not the case. We do not retreat from our holdings that the police must, whenever practicable, obtain advance judicial approval of searches and seizures through the warrant procedure, * * * or that in most instances failure to comply with the warrant requirement can only be excused by exigent circumstances. * * * But we deal here with an entire rubric of police conduct—necessarily swift action predicated upon the on-the-spot observations of the officer on the beat—which historically has not been, and as a practical matter could not be, subjected to the warrant procedure. Instead, the conduct involved in this case must be tested by the Fourth Amendment's general proscription against unreasonable searches and seizures.

Nonetheless, the notions which underlie both the warrant procedure and the requirement of probable cause remain fully relevant in this context. In order to assess the reasonableness of Officer McFadden's conduct as a general proposition, it is necessary "first to focus upon the governmental interest which allegedly justifies official intrusion upon the constitutionally protected interests of the private citizen," for there is "no ready test for determining reasonableness other than by balancing the need to search [or seize] against the invasion which the search [or seizure] entails." And in justifying the particular intrusion the police

---

[13] Consider the following apt description:

"[T]he officer must feel with sensitive fingers every portion of the prisoner's body. A thorough search must be made of the prisoner's arms and armpits, waistline and back, the groin and area about the testicles, and entire surface of the legs down to the feet." Priar & Martin, *Searching and Disarming Criminals,* 45 J.Crim.L.C. & P.S. 481 (1954).

[16] We thus decide nothing today concerning the constitutional propriety of an investigative "seizure" upon less than probable cause for purposes of "detention" and/or interrogation. Obviously, not all personal intercourse between policemen and citizens involves "seizures" of persons. Only when the officer, by means of physical force or show of authority, has in some way restrained the liberty of a citizen may we conclude that a "seizure" has occurred. We cannot tell with any certainty upon this record whether any such "seizure" took place here prior to Officer McFadden's initiation of physical contact for purposes of searching Terry for weapons, and we thus may assume that up to that point no intrusion upon constitutionally protected rights had occurred.

officer must be able to point to specific and articulable facts which, taken together with rational inferences from those facts, reasonably warrant that intrusion. The scheme of the Fourth Amendment becomes meaningful only when it is assured that at some point the conduct of those charged with enforcing the laws can be subjected to the more detached, neutral scrutiny of a judge who must evaluate the reasonableness of a particular search or seizure in light of the particular circumstances. And in making that assessment it is imperative that the facts be judged against an objective standard: would the facts available to the officer at the moment of the seizure or the search "warrant a man of reasonable caution in the belief" that the action taken was appropriate?[a] * * * Anything less would invite intrusions upon constitutionally guaranteed rights based on nothing more substantial than inarticulate hunches, a result this Court has consistently refused to sanction. * * *

Applying these principles to this case, we consider first the nature and extent of the governmental interests involved. One general interest is of course that of effective crime prevention and detection; it is this interest which underlies the recognition that a police officer may in appropriate circumstances and in an appropriate manner approach a person for purposes of investigating possibly criminal behavior even though there is no probable cause to make an arrest. It was this legitimate investigative function Officer McFadden was discharging when he decided to approach petitioner and his companions. He had observed Terry, Chilton, and Katz go through a series of acts, each of them perhaps innocent in itself, but which taken together warranted further investigation. There is nothing unusual in two men standing together on a street corner, perhaps waiting for someone. Nor is there anything suspicious about people in such circumstances strolling up and down the street, singly or in pairs. Store windows, moreover, are made to be looked in. But the story is quite different where, as here, two men hover

---

[a]   This is not to suggest that the purported "facts" must, with the benefit of hindsight, turn out to have actually existed. As emphasized in *Heien v. North Carolina*, 574 U.S. 54 (2015), the Court has long "recognized that searches and seizures based on mistakes of fact can be reasonable." The Court in *Heien* went on to hold: "But reasonable men make mistakes of law, too, and such mistakes are no less compatible with the concept of reasonable suspicion. Reasonable suspicion arises from the combination of an officer's understanding of the facts and his understanding of the relevant law. The officer may be reasonably mistaken on either ground. Whether the facts turn out to be not what was thought, or the law turns out to be not what was thought, the result is the same: the facts are outside the scope of the law. There is no reason, under the text of the Fourth Amendment or our precedents, why this same result should be acceptable when reached by way of a reasonable mistake of fact, but not when reached by way of a similarly reasonable mistake of law."

The *Heien* majority did not elaborate upon its holding other than to say (i) that its ruling extended only to mistakes of law that were "objectively reasonable," meaning "the subjective understanding of the particular officer involved" is not controlling; and (ii) that "the inquiry is not as forgiving as the one employed in the distinct context of deciding whether an officer is entitled to qualified immunity for a constitutional or statutory violation," meaning "an officer can gain no Fourth Amendment advantage through a sloppy study of the laws he is duty-bound to enforce. Two concurring Justices, whose votes were *not* essential to create a majority, apparently seeking nonetheless to confine the holding, asserted (a) that the government "cannot defend an officer's mistaken legal interpretation on the ground that the officer was unaware of or untrained in the law," (b) that "an officer's reliance on 'an incorrect memo or training program from the police department' makes no difference to the analysis," and (c) that the test is satisfied only when the law at issue is 'so doubtful in construction' that a reasonable judge could agree with the officer's view."

about a street corner for an extended period of time, at the end of which it becomes apparent that they are not waiting for anyone or anything; where these men pace alternately along an identical route, pausing to stare in the same store window roughly 24 times; where each completion of this route is followed immediately by a conference between the two men on the corner; where they are joined in one of these conferences by a third man who leaves swiftly; and where the two men finally follow the third and rejoin him a couple of blocks away. It would have been poor police work indeed for an officer of 30 years' experience in the detection of thievery from stores in this same neighborhood to have failed to investigate this behavior further.[a]

The crux of this case, however, is not the propriety of Officer McFadden's taking steps to investigate petitioner's suspicious behavior, but rather, whether there was justification for McFadden's invasion of Terry's personal security by searching him for weapons in the course of that investigation. We are now

---

[a] This does not mean that a *Terry* stop is never permissible upon suspicion of *past* criminal activity. In *United States v. Hensley*, 469 U.S. 221 (1985), rejecting the lower court's position that *Terry* is limited to ongoing criminal activity, the Court explained:

"The factors in the balance may be somewhat different when a stop to investigate past criminal activity is involved rather than a stop to investigate ongoing criminal conduct. This is because the governmental interest and the nature of the intrusions involved in the two situations may differ. As we noted in *Terry*, one general interest present in the context of ongoing or imminent criminal activity is 'that of effective crime prevention and detection.' A stop to investigate an already completed crime does not necessarily promote the interest of crime prevention as directly as a stop to investigate suspected ongoing criminal activity. Similarly, the exigent circumstances which require a police officer to step in before a crime is committed or completed are not necessarily as pressing long afterwards. Public safety may be less threatened by a suspect in a past crime who now appears to be going about his lawful business than it is by a suspect who is currently in the process of violating the law. Finally, officers making a stop to investigate past crimes may have a wider range of opportunity to choose the time and circumstances of the stop.

"Despite these differences, where police have been unable to locate a person suspected of involvement in a past crime, the ability to briefly stop that person, ask questions, or check identification in the absence of probable cause promotes the strong government interest in solving crimes and bringing offenders to justice. Restraining police action until after probable cause is obtained would not only hinder the investigation, but might also enable the suspect to flee in the interim and to remain at large. Particularly in the context of felonies or crimes involving a threat to public safety, it is in the public interest that the crime be solved and the suspect detained as promptly as possible. The law enforcement interests at stake in these circumstances outweigh the individual's interest to be free of a stop and detention that is no more extensive than permissible in the investigation of imminent or ongoing crimes.

"We need not and do not decide today whether *Terry* stops to investigate all past crimes, however serious, are permitted. It is enough to say that, if police have a reasonable suspicion, grounded in specific and articulable facts, that a person they encounter was involved in or is wanted in connection with a completed felony, then a *Terry* stop may be made to investigate that suspicion."

Terry has also been relied upon as a basis for police briefly to seize personal effects upon reasonable suspicion. In *United States v. Place*, 462 U.S. 696 (1983), the Court concluded "that when an officer's observations lead him reasonably to believe that a traveler is carrying luggage that contains narcotics, the principles of *Terry* and its progeny would permit the officer to detain the luggage briefly to investigate the circumstances that aroused his suspicion, provided that the investigative detention is properly limited in scope." But the Court then concluded the seizure in *Place* was unreasonable, given that "we have never approved a seizure of the person for the prolonged 90-minute period involved here," especially since "the violation was exacerbated by the failure of the agents to accurately inform respondent of the place to which they were transporting his luggage, of the length of time he might be dispossessed, and of what arrangements would be made for return of the luggage if the investigation dispelled the suspicion."

concerned with more than the governmental interest in investigating crime; in addition, there is the more immediate interest of the police officer in taking steps to assure himself that the person with whom he is dealing is not armed with a weapon that could unexpectedly and fatally be used against him. Certainly it would be unreasonable to require that police officers take unnecessary risks in the performance of their duties. American criminals have a long tradition of armed violence, and every year in this country many law enforcement officers are killed in the line of duty, and thousands more are wounded. Virtually all of these deaths and a substantial portion of the injuries are inflicted with guns and knives.

In view of these facts, we cannot blind ourselves to the need for law enforcement officers to protect themselves and other prospective victims of violence in situations where they may lack probable cause for an arrest. When an officer is justified in believing that the individual whose suspicious behavior he is investigating at close range is armed and presently dangerous to the officer or to others, it would appear to be clearly unreasonable to deny the officer the power to take necessary measures to determine whether the person is in fact carrying a weapon and to neutralize the threat of physical harm. * * *

Petitioner * * * does not say that an officer is always unjustified in searching a suspect to discover weapons. Rather, he says it is unreasonable for the policeman to take that step until such time as the situation evolves to a point where there is probable cause to make an arrest. * * *

There are two weaknesses in this line of reasoning however. First, it fails to take account of traditional limitations upon the scope of searches, and thus recognizes no distinction in purpose, character, and extent between a search incident to an arrest and a limited search for weapons. The former, although justified in part by the acknowledged necessity to protect the arresting officer from assault with a concealed weapon, is also justified on other grounds, and can therefore involve a relatively extensive exploration of the person. A search for weapons in the absence of probable cause to arrest, however, must, like any other search, be strictly circumscribed by the exigencies which justify its initiation. Thus it must be limited to that which is necessary for the discovery of weapons which might be used to harm the officer or others nearby, and may realistically be characterized as something less than a "full" search, even though it remains a serious intrusion.

A second, and related, objection to petitioner's argument is that it assumes that the law of arrest has already worked out the balance between the particular interests involved here—the neutralization of danger to the policeman in the investigative circumstance and the sanctity of the individual. But this is not so. An arrest is a wholly different kind of intrusion upon individual freedom from a limited search for weapons, and the interests each is designed to serve are likewise quite different. An arrest is the initial stage of a criminal prosecution. It is intended to vindicate society's interest in having its laws obeyed, and it is inevitably accompanied by future interference with the individual's freedom of movement, whether or not trial or conviction ultimately follows. The protective search for weapons, on the other hand, constitutes a brief, though far from inconsiderable intrusion upon the sanctity of the person. It does not follow that because an officer may lawfully arrest a person only when he is apprised of facts sufficient to warrant a belief that the person has committed or is committing a crime, the officer is equally unjustified, absent that kind of evidence, in making any intrusions short of an arrest. Moreover, a perfectly reasonable apprehension of danger may arise long before the officer is possessed of adequate information to justify taking a person into custody for the purpose of prosecuting him for a crime. * * *

Our evaluation of the proper balance that has to be struck in this type of case leads us to conclude that there must be a narrowly drawn authority to permit a reasonable search for weapons for the protection of the police officer, where he has reason to believe that he is dealing with an armed and dangerous individual, regardless of whether he has probable cause to arrest the individual for a crime. The officer need not be absolutely certain that the individual is armed; the issue is whether a reasonably prudent man in the circumstances would be warranted in the belief that his safety or that of others was in danger. * * * And in determining whether the officer acted reasonably in such circumstances, due weight must be given, not to his inchoate and unparticularized suspicion or "hunch", but to the specific reasonable inferences which he is entitled to draw from the facts in light of his experience.

We must now examine the conduct of Officer McFadden in this case to determine whether his search and seizure of petitioner were reasonable, both at their inception and as conducted. He had observed Terry, together with Chilton and another man, acting in a manner he took to be preface to a "stick-up." We think on the facts and circumstances Officer McFadden detailed before the trial judge a reasonably prudent man would have been warranted in believing petitioner was armed and thus presented a threat to the officer's safety while he was investigating his suspicious behavior. The actions of Terry and Chilton were consistent with McFadden's hypothesis that these men were contemplating a daylight robbery—which, it is reasonable to assume, would be likely to involve the use of weapons—and nothing in their conduct from the time he first noticed them until the time he confronted them and identified himself as a police officer gave him sufficient reason to negate that hypothesis. Although the trio had departed the original scene, there was nothing to indicate abandonment of an intent to commit a robbery at some point. Thus, when Officer McFadden approached the three men gathered before the display window at Zucker's store he had observed enough to make it quite reasonable to fear that they were armed; and nothing in their response to his hailing them, identifying himself as a police officer, and asking their names served to dispel that reasonable belief. We cannot say his decision at that point to seize Terry and pat his clothing for weapons was the product of a volatile or inventive imagination, or was undertaken simply as an act of harassment; the record evidences the tempered act of a policeman who in the course of an investigation had to make a quick decision as to how to protect himself and others from possible danger, and took limited steps to do so.

The manner in which the seizure and search were conducted is, of course, as vital a part of the inquiry as whether they were warranted at all. The Fourth Amendment proceeds as much by limitations upon the scope of governmental action as by imposing preconditions upon its initiation. The entire deterrent purpose of the rule excluding evidence seized in violation of the Fourth Amendment rests on the assumption that "limitations upon the fruit to be gathered tend to limit the quest itself." * * * Thus, evidence may not be introduced if it was discovered by means of a seizure and search which were not reasonably related in scope to the justification for their initiation.

[A protective search for weapons,] unlike a search without a warrant incident to a lawful arrest, is not justified by any need to prevent the disappearance or destruction of evidence of crime. The sole justification of the search in the present situation is the protection of the police officer and others nearby, and it must therefore be confined in scope to an intrusion reasonably designed to discover guns, knives, clubs, or other hidden instruments for the assault of the police officer.

The scope of the search in this case presents no serious problem in light of these standards. Officer McFadden patted down the outer clothing of petitioner and his two companions. He did not place his hands in their pockets or under the outer surface of their garments until he had felt weapons, and then he merely reached for and removed the guns. He never did invade Katz's person beyond the outer surfaces of his clothes, since he discovered nothing in his pat down which might have been a weapon. Officer McFadden confined his search strictly to what was minimally necessary to learn whether the men were armed and to disarm them once he discovered the weapons. He did not conduct a general exploratory search for whatever evidence of criminal activity he might find.

We conclude that the revolver seized from Terry was properly admitted in evidence against him. At the time he seized petitioner and searched him for weapons, Officer McFadden had reasonable grounds to believe that petitioner was armed and dangerous, and it was necessary for the protection of himself and others to take swift measures to discover the true facts and neutralize the threat of harm if it materialized. The policeman carefully restricted his search to what was appropriate to the discovery of the particular items which he sought. Each case of this sort will, of course, have to be decided on its own facts. We merely hold today that where a police officer observes unusual conduct which leads him reasonably to conclude in light of his experience that criminal activity may be afoot and that the persons with whom he is dealing may be armed and presently dangerous; where in the course of investigating this behavior he identifies himself as a policeman and makes reasonable inquiries; and where nothing in the initial stages of the encounter serves to dispel his reasonable fear for his own or others' safety, he is entitled for the protection of himself and others in the area to conduct a carefully limited search of the outer clothing of such persons[b] in an attempt to

---

[b] *Michigan v. Long*, 463 U.S. 1032 (1983), extended the self-protective search principle of *Terry* to search of a vehicle. Two deputies saw a car swerve into a ditch and stopped to investigate. Long, the only occupant of the car, met the deputies at the rear of the car, supplied his driver's license upon demand, and started back toward the open door when asked for his vehicle registration. The officers saw a large hunting knife on the floorboard, so Long was frisked and one officer then entered the vehicle and found an open pouch of marijuana under an armrest. The Court concluded "that the search of the passenger compartment of an automobile, limited to those areas in which a weapon may be placed or hidden, is permissible if the police officer possesses a reasonable belief based on 'specific and articulable facts which, taken together with the rational

discover weapons which might be used to assault him. Such a search is a reasonable search under the Fourth Amendment, and any weapons seized may properly be introduced in evidence against the person from whom they were taken.

Affirmed.

JUSTICE HARLAN, concurring.

* * * The holding has * * * two logical corollaries that I do not think the Court has fully expressed.

In the first place, if the frisk is justified in order to protect the officer during an encounter with a citizen, the officer must first have constitutional grounds to insist on an encounter, to make a *forcible* stop. Any person, including a policeman, is at liberty to avoid a person he considers dangerous. If and when a policeman has a right instead to disarm such a person for his own protection, he must first have a right not to avoid him but to be in his presence. That right must be more than the liberty (again, possessed by every citizen) to address questions to other persons,

---

inferences from those facts, reasonably warrant' the officers in believing that the suspect is dangerous and the suspect may gain immediate control of weapons." In explaining why this was such a case, the Court stated:

"The Michigan Supreme Court appeared to believe that it was not reasonable for the officers to fear that Long could injure them, because he was effectively under their control during the investigative stop and could not get access to any weapons that might have been located in the automobile. This reasoning is mistaken in several respects. During any investigative detention, the suspect is 'in the control' of the officers in the sense that he 'may be briefly detained against his will * * *.' Just as a *Terry* suspect on the street may, despite being under the brief control of a police officer, reach into his clothing and retrieve a weapon, so might a *Terry* suspect in Long's position break away from police control and retrieve a weapon from his automobile. In addition, if the suspect is not placed under arrest, he will be permitted to reenter his automobile, and he will then have access to any weapons inside. Or, as here, the suspect may be permitted to reenter the vehicle before the *Terry* investigation is over, and again, may have access to weapons. In any event, we stress that a *Terry* investigation, such as the one that occurred here, involves a police investigation 'at close range,' when the officer remains particularly vulnerable in part *because* a full custodial arrest has not been effected, and the officer must make a 'quick decision as to how to protect himself and others from possible danger * * *.' In such circumstances, we have not required that officers adopt alternative means to ensure their safety in order to avoid the intrusion involved in a *Terry* encounter."

Brennan and Marshall, JJ., dissenting, objected: "Putting aside the fact that the search at issue here involved a far more serious intrusion than that 'involved in a *Terry* encounter,' and as such might suggest the need for resort to 'alternate means,' the Court's reasoning is perverse. The Court's argument in essence is that the *absence* of probable cause to arrest compels the conclusion that a broad search, traditionally associated in scope with a search incident to arrest, must be permitted based on reasonable suspicion. But *United States v. Robinson* stated: 'It is scarcely open to doubt that the danger to an officer is far greater in the case of the extended exposure which follows the taking of a suspect into custody and transporting him to the police station than in the case of the relatively fleeting contact resulting from the typical *Terry*-type stop.' In light of *Robinson*'s observation, today's holding leaves in grave doubt the question of whether the Court's assessment of the relative dangers posed by given confrontations is based on any principled standard."

Even if the *Long* test for a vehicle search cannot be met, the officer may take other steps in the interest of self-protection. In *Pennsylvania v. Mimms*, 434 U.S. 106 (1977), the Court held that without any showing the particular suspect may be armed, an officer may require a person lawfully stopped to alight from his car in order to diminish "the possibility, otherwise, substantial, that the driver can make unobserved movements." In *Maryland v. Wilson*, 519 U.S. 408 (1997), the *Mimms* rule was held to be equally applicable to passengers; though there has been no reason to detain the passenger, such detention occurs as a practical matter when the vehicle is stopped, and so the minimal added intrusion is justified in the interest of the officer's safety.

for ordinarily the person addressed has an equal right to ignore his interrogator and walk away; he certainly need not submit to a frisk for the questioner's protection. I would make it perfectly clear that the right to frisk in this case depends upon the reasonableness of a forcible stop to investigate a suspected crime.

Where such a stop is reasonable, however, the right to frisk must be immediate and automatic if the reason for the stop is, as here, an articulable suspicion of a crime of violence. Just as a full search incident to a lawful arrest requires no additional justification, a limited frisk incident to a lawful stop must often be rapid and routine. There is no reason why an officer, rightfully but forcibly confronting a person suspected of a serious crime, should have to ask one question and take the risk that the answer might be a bullet. * * *

JUSTICE WHITE, concurring.

* * * I think an additional word is in order concerning the matter of interrogation during an investigative stop. There is nothing in the Constitution which prevents a policeman from addressing questions to anyone on the streets. Absent special circumstances, the person approached may not be detained or frisked but may refuse to cooperate and go on his way. However, given the proper circumstances, such as those in this case, it seems to me the person may be briefly detained against his will while pertinent questions are directed to him. Of course, the person stopped is not obliged to answer, answers may not be compelled, and refusal to answer furnishes no basis for an arrest, although it may alert the officer to the need for continued observation. * * *c

---

c   But in *Hiibel v. Sixth Judicial District*, 542 U.S. 177 (2004), where defendant was convicted of obstructing justice for failing to comply with a statutory requirement that he identify himself during a lawful *Terry* stop, the Court held, 5–4, that defendant's conviction did not violate either the Fourth Amendment or the Fifth Amendment's privilege against self-incrimination. On the Fourth Amendment issue, the majority declared Justice White's statement meant only that "the Fourth Amendment itself cannot require a suspect to answer questions," while the instant case posed the "different issue" of whether state law could impose such a requirement without violating the Fourth Amendment. Using a *Terry*-style balancing of interests, the Court answered the latter question in the affirmative, reasoning that the "request for identity has an immediate relation to the purpose, rationale, and practical demands of a *Terry* stop," that the "threat of criminal sanction helps ensure that the request for identity does not become a legal nullity," and that such threat "does not alter the nature of the stop itself," provided "the request for identification was 'reasonably related in scope to the circumstances which justified' the stop." On the Fifth Amendment issue, the majority held the conviction did not violate the privilege against self-incrimination because "petitioner's refusal to disclose his name was not based on any articulable real and appreciable fear that his name would be used to incriminate him, or that it 'would furnish a link in the chain of evidence needed to prosecute' him." (Both the Fourth and Fifth Amendment holdings in *Hiibel* are limited to the question of "whether a State can compel a suspect to disclose his name during a *Terry* stop," which the state court indicated was the extent of the statutory obligation, although the facts of the case indicate that Hiibel was repeatedly asked "to produce a driver's license or some other form of written identification" but apparently was never asked merely to state his name.) The dissenters concluded there was "no good reason now to reject" a "generation-old statement of law," the "strong dicta" in *Berkemer v. McCarty*, 468 U.S. 420 (1984), that a *Terry* detainee "is not obliged to respond" to questions about identity, especially in light of the Fifth Amendment problem, i.e., that it would not be possible for "a police officer in the midst of a *Terry* stop to distinguish between the majority's ordinary case and the special case" where providing the name would provide the police with "a link in the chain of evidence needed to convict the individual of a separate offense."

JUSTICE DOUGLAS, dissenting.

* * * Had a warrant been sought, a magistrate would, therefore, have been unauthorized to issue one, for he can act only if there is a showing of "probable cause." We hold today that the police have greater authority to make a "seizure" and conduct a "search" than a judge has to authorize such action. We have said precisely the opposite over and over again. * * *

The infringement on personal liberty of any "seizure" of a person can only be "reasonable" under the Fourth Amendment if we require the police to possess "probable cause" before they seize him. Only that line draws a meaningful distinction between an officer's mere inkling and the presence of facts within the officer's personal knowledge which would convince a reasonable man that the person seized has committed, is committing, or is about to commit a particular crime. * * *

KANSAS V. GLOVER
589 U.S. ___, 140 S.Ct. 1183, 206 L.Ed.2d 412 (2020).

JUSTICE THOMAS delivered the opinion of the Court.

This case presents the question whether a police officer violates the Fourth Amendment by initiating an investigative traffic stop after running a vehicle's license plate and learning that the registered owner has a revoked driver's license. We hold that when the officer lacks information negating an inference that the owner is the driver of the vehicle, the stop is reasonable. * * *

Under this Court's precedents, the Fourth Amendment permits an officer to initiate a brief investigative traffic stop when he has "a particularized and objective basis for suspecting the particular person stopped of criminal activity." "Although a mere 'hunch' does not create reasonable suspicion, the level of suspicion the standard requires is considerably less than proof of wrongdoing by a preponderance of the evidence, and obviously less than is necessary for probable cause."

Because it is a "less demanding" standard, "reasonable suspicion can be established with information that is different in quantity or content than that required to establish probable cause." The standard "depends on the factual and practical considerations of everyday life on which reasonable and prudent men, not legal technicians, act." Courts "cannot reasonably demand scientific certainty . . . where none exists." Rather, they must permit officers to make "commonsense judgments and inferences about human behavior." * * *

Before initiating the stop, Deputy Mehrer observed an individual operating a 1995 Chevrolet 1500 pickup truck with Kansas plate 295ATJ. He also knew that the registered owner of the truck had a revoked license and that the model of the truck matched the observed vehicle. From these three facts, Deputy Mehrer drew the commonsense inference that Glover was likely the driver of the vehicle, which provided more than reasonable suspicion to initiate the stop.

The fact that the registered owner of a vehicle is not always the driver of the vehicle does not negate the reasonableness of Deputy Mehrer's inference. Such is the case with all reasonable inferences. The reasonable suspicion inquiry "falls considerably short" of 51% accuracy.

Glover's revoked license does not render Deputy Mehrer's inference unreasonable either. Empirical studies demonstrate what common experience readily reveals: Drivers with revoked licenses frequently continue to drive and therefore to pose safety risks to other motorists and pedestrians. * * *

Glover and the dissent respond with two arguments as to why Deputy Mehrer lacked reasonable suspicion. Neither is persuasive.

First, Glover and the dissent argue that Deputy Mehrer's inference was unreasonable because it was not grounded in his law enforcement training or experience. Nothing in our Fourth Amendment precedent supports the notion that, in determining whether reasonable suspicion exists, an officer can draw inferences based on knowledge gained only through law enforcement training and experience. We have repeatedly recognized the opposite. * * * The inference that the driver of a car is its registered owner does not require any specialized training; rather, it is a reasonable inference made by ordinary people on a daily basis. * * *

The dissent's rule would also impose on police the burden of pointing to specific training materials or field experiences justifying reasonable suspicion for the myriad infractions in municipal criminal codes. And by removing common sense as a source of evidence, the dissent would considerably narrow the daylight between the showing required for probable cause and the "less stringent" showing required for reasonable suspicion. Finally, it would impermissibly tie a traffic stop's validity to the officer's length of service. * * *

In reaching this conclusion, we in no way minimize the significant role that specialized training and experience routinely play in law enforcement investigations. We simply hold that such experience is not required in every instance.

Glover and the dissent also contend that adopting Kansas' view would eviscerate the need for officers to base reasonable suspicion on "specific and articulable facts" particularized to the individual, because police could instead rely exclusively on probabilities. Their argument carries little force.

As an initial matter, we have previously stated that officers, like jurors, may rely on probabilities in the reasonable suspicion context. Moreover, as explained above, Deputy Mehrer did not rely exclusively on probabilities. He knew that the license plate was linked to a truck matching the observed vehicle and that the registered owner of the vehicle had a revoked license. Based on these minimal facts, he used common sense to form a reasonable suspicion that a specific individual was potentially engaged in specific criminal activity—driving with a revoked license. * * * "The standard takes into account the totality of the circumstances—the whole picture." As a result, the presence of additional facts might dispel reasonable suspicion. For example, if an officer knows that the registered owner of the vehicle is in his mid-sixties but observes that the driver is in her mid-twenties, then the totality of the circumstances would not "raise a suspicion that the particular individual being stopped is engaged in wrongdoing." Here, Deputy Mehrer possessed no exculpatory information—let alone sufficient information to rebut the reasonable inference that Glover was driving his own truck—and thus the stop was justified.[2] * * *

    JUSTICE KAGAN, with whom JUSTICE GINSBURG joins, concurring.

    When you see a car coming down the street, your common sense tells you that the registered owner may well be behind the wheel. Not always, of course. Families share cars; friends borrow them. Still, a person often buys a vehicle to drive it himself. So your suspicion that the owner is driving would be perfectly reasonable.

    Now, though, consider a wrinkle: Suppose you knew that the registered owner of the vehicle no longer had a valid driver's license. That added fact raises a new question. What are the odds that someone who has lost his license would continue to drive? The answer is by no means obvious. You might think that a person told not to drive on pain of criminal penalty would obey the order—so that if his car was on the road, someone else (a family member, a friend) must be doing the driving. Or you might have the opposite intuition—that a person's reasons for driving would overcome his worries about violating the law, no matter the possible punishment. But most likely (let's be honest), you just wouldn't know. Especially if you've not had your own license taken away, your everyday experience has given you little basis to assess the probabilities. Your common sense can therefore no longer guide you.

    Even so, Deputy Mark Mehrer had reasonable suspicion to stop the truck in this case, and I join the Court's opinion holding as much. Crucially for me, Mehrer knew yet one more thing about the vehicle's registered owner, and it related to his proclivity for breaking driving laws. As the Court recounts, Mehrer learned from a state database that Charles Glover, the truck's owner, had had his license revoked under Kansas law. And Kansas almost never revokes a license except for serious or repeated driving offenses. Crimes like vehicular homicide and manslaughter, or vehicular flight from a police officer, provoke a license revocation; so too do multiple convictions for moving traffic violations within a short time. In other words, a person with a revoked license has already shown a willingness to flout driving restrictions. That fact, as the Court states, provides a "reason[ ] to infer" that such a person will drive without a license—at least often enough to warrant an investigatory stop. And there is nothing else here to call that inference into question. That is because the parties' unusually austere stipulation confined the case to the facts stated above—i.e., that Mehrer stopped Glover's truck because he knew that Kansas had revoked Glover's license.

    But as already suggested, I would find this a different case if Kansas had barred Glover from driving on a ground that provided no similar evidence of his penchant for ignoring driving laws. Consider, for example, if Kansas had suspended rather than revoked Glover's license. Along with many other States,

---

    [2] The dissent argues that this approach impermissibly places the burden of proof on the individual to negate the inference of reasonable suspicion. Not so. As the above analysis makes clear, it is the information possessed by *the officer* at the time of the stop, not any information offered by the individual after the fact, that can negate the inference.

Kansas suspends licenses for matters having nothing to do with road safety, such as failing to pay parking tickets, court fees, or child support. * * *

JUSTICE SOTOMAYOR, dissenting.

In upholding routine stops of vehicles whose owners have revoked licenses, the Court ignores key foundations of our reasonable-suspicion jurisprudence and impermissibly and unnecessarily reduces the State's burden of proof. I therefore dissent.

* * * To assess whether an officer had the requisite suspicion to seize a driver, past cases have considered the "totality of the circumstances—the whole picture," and analyzed whether the officer assembled "fact on fact and clue on clue."

The stop at issue here, however, rests on just one key fact: that the vehicle was owned by someone with a revoked license. The majority concludes—erroneously, in my view—that seizing this vehicle was constitutional on the record below because drivers with revoked licenses (as opposed to suspended licenses) in Kansas "have already demonstrated a disregard for the law or are categorically unfit to drive." This analysis breaks from settled doctrine and dramatically alters both the quantum and nature of evidence a State may rely on to prove suspicion.

The State bears the burden of justifying a seizure. This requires the government to articulate factors supporting its reasonable suspicion, usually through a trained agent. While the Court has not dictated precisely what evidence a government must produce, it has stressed that an officer must at least "articulate more than an 'inchoate and unparticularized suspicion or "hunch" ' of criminal activity." That articulation must include both facts and an officer's "rational inferences from those facts." * * *

Additionally, reasonable suspicion eschews judicial common sense, in favor of the perspectives and inferences of a reasonable officer viewing "the facts through the lens of his police experience and expertise." It is the reasonable officer's assessment, not the ordinary person's—or judge's—judgment, that matters.[1]

Finally, a stop must be individualized—that is, based on "a suspicion that the particular [subject] being stopped is engaged in wrongdoing." * * * The inquiry ordinarily involves some observation or report about the target's behavior—not merely the class to which he belongs. * * *

Faithful adherence to these precepts would yield a significantly different analysis and outcome than that offered by the majority. For starters, the majority flips the burden of proof. It permits Kansas police officers to effectuate roadside stops whenever they lack "information negating an inference" that a vehicle's unlicensed owner is its driver.

This has it backwards: The State shoulders the burden to supply the key inference that tethers observation to suspicion. The majority repeatedly attributes

---

1   * * *. Law enforcement officers, behaving akin to "jurors as factfinders," have "formulated certain commonsense conclusions about human behavior" as it relates to "the field of law enforcement." A trained officer thus "draws inferences and makes deductions—inferences and deductions that might well elude an untrained person."

such an inference to Deputy Mehrer. But that is an after-the-fact gloss on a seven-paragraph stipulation. Nowhere in his terse submission did Deputy Mehrer indicate that he had any informed belief about the propensity of unlicensed drivers to operate motor vehicles in the area—let alone that he relied on such a belief in seizing Glover.

The consequence of the majority's approach is to absolve officers from any responsibility to investigate the identity of a driver where feasible. But that is precisely what officers ought to do—and are more than capable of doing. Of course, some circumstances may not warrant an officer approaching a car to take a closer look at its occupants. But there are countless other instances where officers have been able to ascertain the identity of a driver from a distance and make out their approximate age and gender. Indeed, our cases are rife with examples of officers who have perceived more than just basic driver demographics. The majority underestimates officers' capabilities and instead gives them free rein to stop a vehicle involved in no suspicious activity simply because it is registered to an unlicensed person. That stop is based merely on a guess or a "hunch" about the driver's identity.

With no basis in the record to presume that unlicensed drivers routinely continue driving, the majority endeavors to fill the gap with its own "common sense." But simply labeling an inference "common sense" does not make it so, no matter how many times the majority repeats it. Whether the driver of a vehicle is likely to be its unlicensed owner is "by no means obvious." And like the concurrence, I "doubt" that our collective judicial common sense could answer that question, even if our Fourth Amendment jurisprudence allowed us to do so.

Contrary to the majority's claims, the reasonable-suspicion inquiry does not accommodate the average person's intuition. Rather, it permits reliance on a particular type of common sense—that of the reasonable officer, developed through her experiences in law enforcement. This approach acknowledges that what may be "common sense" to a layperson may not be relevant (or correct) in a law enforcement context. Indeed, this case presents the type of geographically localized inquiry where an officer's "inferences and deductions that might well elude an untrained person" would come in handy. By relying on judicial inferences instead, the majority promotes broad, inflexible rules that overlook regional differences.

Allowing judges to offer their own brand of common sense where the State's proffered justifications for a search come up short also shifts police work to the judiciary. Our cases—including those the majority cites—have looked to officer sensibility to establish inferences about human behavior, even though they just as easily could have relied on the inferences "made by ordinary people on a daily basis." There is no reason to depart from that practice here. * * *

The majority today has paved the road to finding reasonable suspicion based on nothing more than a demographic profile. Its logic has thus made the State's task all but automatic. That has never been the law, and it never should be.

The majority's justifications for this new approach have no foundation in fact or logic. It supposes that requiring officers to point to "training materials or field experiences" would demand " 'scientific certainty.' " But that is no truer in this case than in other circumstances where the reasonable-suspicion inquiry applies. * * *

* * * The State below left unexplained key components of the reasonable-suspicion inquiry. In an effort to uphold the conviction, the Court destroys Fourth Amendment jurisprudence that requires individualized suspicion. I respectfully dissent

FLORIDA V. J. L.

529 U.S. 266, 120 S.Ct. 1375, 146 L.Ed.2d 254 (2000).

JUSTICE GINSBURG delivered the opinion of the Court.

The question presented in this case is whether an anonymous tip that a person is carrying a gun is, without more, sufficient to justify a police officer's stop and frisk of that person. We hold that it is not.

On October 13, 1995, an anonymous caller reported to the Miami-Dade Police that a young black male standing at a particular bus stop and wearing a plaid shirt was carrying a gun. So far as the record reveals, there is no audio recording of the tip, and nothing is known about the informant. Sometime after the police received the tip—the record does not say how long—two officers were instructed to respond. They arrived at the bus stop about six minutes later and saw three black males "just hanging out [there]." One of the three, respondent J.L., was wearing a plaid shirt. Apart from the tip, the officers had no reason to suspect any of the three of illegal conduct. The officers did not see a firearm, and J.L. made no threatening or otherwise unusual movements. One of the officers approached J.L., told him to put his hands up on the bus stop, frisked him, and seized a gun from J.L.'s pocket. The second officer frisked the other two individuals, against whom no allegations had been made, and found nothing.

J.L., who was at the time of the frisk "10 days shy of his 16th birth[day]," was charged under state law with carrying a concealed firearm without a license and possessing a firearm while under the age of 18. He moved to suppress the gun as the fruit of an unlawful search, and the trial court granted his motion. The intermediate appellate court reversed, but the Supreme Court of Florida quashed that decision and held the search invalid under the Fourth Amendment. * * *

In the instant case, the officers' suspicion that J.L. was carrying a weapon arose not from any observations of their own but solely from a call made from an unknown location by an unknown caller. Unlike a tip from a known informant whose reputation can be assessed and who can be held responsible if her allegations turn out to be fabricated, "an anonymous tip alone seldom demonstrates the informant's basis of knowledge or veracity," *Alabama v. White*, [496 U.S. 325 (1990)]. As we have recognized, however, there are situations in which an anonymous tip, suitably corroborated, exhibits "sufficient indicia of reliability to provide reasonable suspicion to make the investigatory stop." The question we here confront is whether the tip pointing to J.L. had those indicia of reliability.

In *White*, the police received an anonymous tip asserting that a woman was carrying cocaine and predicting that she would leave an apartment building at a specified time, get into a car matching a particular description, and drive to a named motel. Standing alone, the tip would not have justified a *Terry* stop. Only after police observation showed that the informant had accurately predicted the woman's movements, we explained, did it become reasonable to think the tipster had inside knowledge about the suspect and therefore to credit his assertion about the cocaine. Although the Court held that the suspicion in *White* became reasonable after police surveillance, we regarded the case as borderline. Knowledge about a person's future movements indicates some familiarity with that person's affairs, but having such knowledge does not necessarily imply that the informant knows, in particular, whether that person is carrying hidden contraband. We accordingly classified *White* as a "close case."

The tip in the instant case lacked the moderate indicia of reliability present in *White* and essential to the Court's decision in that case. The anonymous call concerning J.L. provided no predictive information and therefore left the police without means to test the informant's knowledge or credibility. That the allegation about the gun turned out to be correct does not suggest that the officers, prior to the frisks, had a reasonable basis for suspecting J.L. of engaging in unlawful conduct: The reasonableness of official suspicion must be measured by what the officers knew before they conducted their search. All the police had to go on in this case was the bare report of an unknown, unaccountable informant who neither explained how he knew about the gun nor supplied any basis for believing he had inside information about J.L. If *White* was a close case on the reliability of anonymous tips, this one surely falls on the other side of the line. * * *

An accurate description of a subject's readily observable location and appearance is of course reliable in this limited sense: It will help the police correctly identify the person whom the tipster means to accuse. Such a tip, however, does not show that the tipster has knowledge of concealed criminal activity. The reasonable suspicion here at issue requires that a tip be reliable in its assertion of illegality, not just in its tendency to identify a determinate person. * * *

Firearms are dangerous, and extraordinary dangers sometimes justify unusual precautions. Our decisions recognize the serious threat that armed criminals pose to public safety; *Terry*'s rule, which permits protective police searches on the basis of reasonable suspicion rather than demanding that officers meet the higher standard of probable cause, responds to this very concern. But an automatic firearm exception to our established reliability analysis [advanced by Florida and the United States as *amicus*] would rove too far. Such an exception would enable any person seeking to harass another to set in motion an intrusive, embarrassing police search of the targeted person simply by placing an anonymous call falsely reporting the target's unlawful carriage of a gun. Nor could one securely confine such an exception to allegations involving firearms. Several Courts of Appeals have held it per se foreseeable for people carrying significant amounts of illegal drugs to be carrying guns as well. If police officers may properly conduct Terry frisks on the basis of bare-boned tips about guns, it would be reasonable to maintain under the above-cited decisions that the police should similarly have discretion to frisk based on bare-boned tips about narcotics. * * *

The facts of this case do not require us to speculate about the circumstances under which the danger alleged in an anonymous tip might be so great as to justify a search even without a showing of reliability.[a] We do not say, for example, that a report of a person carrying a bomb need bear the indicia of reliability we demand for a report of a person carrying a firearm before the police can constitutionally

---

[a] In *Navarette v. California*, 572 U.S. 393 (2014), police stopped a pickup truck because it matched the description of a vehicle an anonymous 911 caller recently reported had run her off the road; officers approaching the stopped vehicle smelled marijuana, searched the truck's bed, and found 30 pounds of marijuana. The lower court ruling upholding the stop was grounded in the proposition "that the danger exception postulated in *J.L.* applies when an anonymous tipster contemporaneously reports drunken or erratic driving on a public roadway and officers are able to corroborate significant innocent details of the tip, such as detailed descriptions of the vehicle and its location." The Supreme Court affirmed, 5–4, in an opinion (as the dissent put it) that "does not explicitly adopt such a departure from our normal Fourth Amendment requirement that anonymous tips must be corroborated" and "purports to adhere to our prior cases," such as *White* and *J.L.*

As for the "initial question" in the instant case, "whether the 911 call was sufficiently reliable to credit the allegation" therein, the majority relied upon two propositions: (1) the anonymous caller, who "claimed eyewitness knowledge," "reported the incident soon after she was run off the road" (as indicated by the fact the police located the vehicle 19 miles away from the reported location roughly 18 minutes after the 911 call), and such a "contemporaneous report has long been treated as especially reliable," as is indicated by the "present sense impression" and "excited utterance" exceptions to the hearsay rule; and (2) "the caller's use of the 911 emergency system" is relevant, as such calls "can be recorded" and permit police "to verify important information about the caller," i.e., the caller's phone number and approximate location, and thus "a reasonable officer could conclude that a false tipster would think twice before using such a system." The dissenters, per Scalia, J., responded: (1) that for the majority's hearsay exceptions, it "is the immediacy that gives the statement some credibility," as "the declarant has not had time to dissemble or embellish," but there "is no such immediacy here," as between the purported event and the 911 call shortly thereafter there would have been "[p]lenty of time to dissemble or embellish," and also it is "unsettled" whether those exceptions apply absent other evidence of the alleged event or when the declarant's identity is unknown; and (2) "the ease of identifying 911 callers * * * proves absolutely nothing * * * unless the anonymous caller was *aware* of that fact," for it "is the tipster's *belief* in anonymity, not its *reality*, that will control his behavior."

The second issue in the case, as stated by the majority, was "whether the 911 caller's report of being run off the roadway created reasonable suspicion of an ongoing crime such as drunk driving as opposed to an isolated episode of past recklessness." As to this, the majority asserted: (3) that the alleged conduct, "running another car off the highway," "bears too great a resemblance to paradigmatic manifestations of drunk driving to be dismissed as the isolated example of recklessness," as such conduct "suggests lane-positioning problems, decreased vigilance, impaired judgment, or some combination of those recognized drunk driving cues"; (4) that petitioners' claim that the reported behavior could also be explained by, e.g., "an unruly child or other distraction," ignores the Court's consistent recognition that reasonable suspicion "need not rule out the possibility of innocent conduct," and (5) that the absence of "additional suspicious conduct" when the officers spotted the vehicle did not "dispel the reasonable suspicion of drunk driving," as it "is hardly surprising that the appearance of a marked police car would inspire more careful driving for a time." The dissenters responded: (3) that even assuming "a careless, reckless, or even intentional maneuver" by the driver of the truck, there is no basis for concluding that "reasonable suspicion of a *discrete instance* of irregular or hazardous driving generates a reasonable suspicion of *ongoing intoxicated driving*"; (4) that the caller's statement at most "conveys * * * that the truck did some apparently nontypical thing that forced the tipster off the roadway," so it may be that the truck "swerved to avoid an animal, a pothole, or a jaywalking pedestrian"; and (5) that while the police wisely "followed the truck for five minutes, presumably to see if it was being operated recklessly," during that interval the driver's conduct "was irreproachable," for which the majority's explanation is inadequate under the "traditional view that the dangers of intoxicated driving are the intoxicant's impairing effects on the body—effects that no mere act of the will can resist."

conduct a frisk. Nor do we hold that public safety officials in quarters where the reasonable expectation of Fourth Amendment privacy is diminished, such as airports and schools, cannot conduct protective searches on the basis of information insufficient to justify searches elsewhere.

Finally, the requirement that an anonymous tip bear standard indicia of reliability in order to justify a stop in no way diminishes a police officer's prerogative, in accord with *Terry*, to conduct a protective search of a person who has already been legitimately stopped. We speak in today's decision only of cases in which the officer's authority to make the initial stop is at issue. In that context, we hold that an anonymous tip lacking indicia of reliability of the kind contemplated in *Adams* and *White* does not justify a stop and frisk whenever and however it alleges the illegal possession of a firearm. * * *

JUSTICE KENNEDY, with whom THE CHIEF JUSTICE joins, concurring. * * *

It seems appropriate to observe that a tip might be anonymous in some sense yet have certain other features, either supporting reliability or narrowing the likely class of informants, so that the tip does provide the lawful basis for some police action. One such feature, as the Court recognizes, is that the tip predicts future conduct of the alleged criminal. There may be others. For example, if an unnamed caller with a voice which sounds the same each time tells police on two successive nights about criminal activity which in fact occurs each night, a similar call on the third night ought not be treated automatically like the tip in the case now before us. In the instance supposed, there would be a plausible argument that experience cures some of the uncertainty surrounding the anonymity, justifying a proportionate police response. In today's case, however, the State provides us with no data about the reliability of anonymous tips. Nor do we know whether the dispatcher or arresting officer had any objective reason to believe that this tip had some particular indicia of reliability.

If an informant places his anonymity at risk, a court can consider this factor in weighing the reliability of the tip. An instance where a tip might be considered anonymous but nevertheless sufficiently reliable to justify a proportionate police response may be when an unnamed person driving a car the police officer later describes stops for a moment and, face to face, informs the police that criminal activity is occurring. This too seems to be different from the tip in the present case.

Instant caller identification is widely available to police, and, if anonymous tips are proving unreliable and distracting to police, squad cars can be sent within seconds to the location of the telephone used by the informant. Voice recording of telephone tips might, in appropriate cases, be used by police to locate the caller. It is unlawful to make false reports to the police, and the ability of the police to trace the identity of anonymous telephone informants may be a factor which lends reliability to what, years earlier, might have been considered unreliable anonymous tips.

These matters, of course, must await discussion in other cases, where the issues are presented by the record.

FLORIDA V. ROYER

460 U.S. 491, 103 S.Ct. 1319, 75 L.Ed.2d 229 (1983).

JUSTICE WHITE announced the judgment of the Court and delivered an opinion, in which JUSTICE MARSHALL, JUSTICE POWELL, and JUSTICE STEVENS joined.

[After purchasing a one-way airline ticket to New York City at Miami International Airport under an assumed name and checking his two suitcases bearing identification tags with the same assumed name, respondent went to the concourse leading to the airline boarding area, where he was approached by two detectives, who previously had observed him and believed that his characteristics fit the so-called "drug courier profile." Upon request, but without oral consent, respondent produced his airline ticket and driver's license, which carried his correct name. When the detectives asked about the discrepancy in names, respondent explained that a friend had made the ticket reservation in the assumed name. The detectives then informed respondent that they were narcotics investigators and that they had reason to suspect him of transporting narcotics, and, without returning his airline ticket or driver's license, asked him to accompany them to a small room adjacent to the concourse. Without respondent's consent, one of the detectives retrieved respondent's luggage from the airline and brought it to the room. While he did not respond to the detectives' request that he consent to a search of the luggage, respondent produced a key and unlocked one of the suitcases in which marihuana was found. When respondent said he did not know the combination to the lock on the second suitcase but did not object to its being opened, the officers pried it open and found more marihuana. Respondent was then told he was under arrest. Following the Florida trial court's denial of his pretrial motion to suppress the evidence obtained in the search of the suitcases, respondent was convicted of felony possession of marihuana. The Florida District Court of Appeal reversed, holding that respondent had been involuntarily confined within the small room without probable cause, that at the time his consent to search was obtained, the involuntary detention had exceeded the limited restraint permitted by *Terry v. Ohio,* and that such consent was therefore invalid because tainted by the unlawful confinement.]

Some preliminary observations are in order. First, it is unquestioned that without a warrant to search Royer's luggage and in the absence of probable cause and exigent circumstances, the validity of the search depended on Royer's purported consent. Neither is it disputed that where the validity of a search rests on consent, the State has the burden of proving that the necessary consent was obtained and that it was freely and voluntarily given, a burden that is not satisfied by showing a mere submission to a claim of lawful authority.

Second, law enforcement officers do not violate the Fourth Amendment by merely approaching an individual on the street or in another public place, by asking him if he is willing to answer some questions, by putting questions to him if the person is willing to listen, or by offering in evidence in a criminal prosecution his voluntary answers to such questions. Nor would the fact that the officer identifies himself as a police officer, without more, convert the encounter into a seizure requiring some level of objective justification. The person approached, however, need not answer any question put to him; indeed, he may decline to listen to the questions at all and may go on his way. He may not be detained even momentarily without reasonable, objective grounds for doing so; and his refusal to listen or answer does not, without more, furnish those grounds. If there is no detention—no seizure within the meaning of the Fourth Amendment—then no constitutional rights have been infringed.

Third, it is also clear that not all seizures of the person must be justified by probable cause to arrest for a crime. * * * *Terry* created a limited exception to this general rule: certain seizures are justifiable under the Fourth Amendment if there is articulable suspicion that a person has committed or is about to commit a crime. * * * Royer does not suggest, nor do we, that a similar rationale would not warrant temporary detention for questioning on less than probable cause where the public interest involved is the suppression of illegal transactions in drugs or of any other serious crime. * * *

Fourth, *Terry* and its progeny nevertheless created only limited exceptions to the general rule that seizures of the person require probable cause to arrest. Detentions may be "investigative" yet violative of the Fourth Amendment absent probable cause. In the name of investigating a person who is no more than suspected of criminal activity, the police may not carry out a full search of the person or of his automobile or other effects. Nor may the police seek to verify their suspicions by means that approach the conditions of arrest. *Dunaway v. New York*, [442 U.S. 200 (1979)], made this clear. There, the suspect was taken to the police station from his home and, without being formally arrested, interrogated for an hour. The resulting incriminating statements were held inadmissible: reasonable suspicion of crime is insufficient to justify custodial interrogation even though the interrogation is investigative.[a]

---

[a]   This is not to suggest that all at-the-station investigation must be on full probable cause. In *Davis v. Mississippi*, 394 U.S. 721 (1969), petitioner and 24 other black youths were detained for questioning and fingerprinting in connection with a rape for which the only leads were a general description given by the victim and a set of fingerprints around the window through which the assailant entered. Petitioner's prints were found to match those at the scene of the crime, and this evidence was admitted at his trial. The Court, per Brennan, J., held that the prints should have been excluded as the fruits of a seizure of petitioner in violation of the Fourth Amendment, but intimated that a detention for such a purpose might sometimes be permissible on evidence insufficient for arrest:

"Detentions for the sole purpose of obtaining fingerprints are no less subject to the constraints of the Fourth Amendment. It is arguable, however, that because of the unique nature of the fingerprinting process, such detentions might, under narrowly defined circumstances, be found to comply with the Fourth Amendment even though there is no probable cause in the traditional sense. Detention for fingerprinting may constitute a much less serious intrusion upon personal security than other types of police searches and detentions. Fingerprinting involves none of the probing into an individual's private life and thoughts which marks an interrogation or search. Nor can fingerprint detention be employed repeatedly to harass any individual, since the police need only one set of each person's prints. Furthermore, fingerprinting is an inherently more reliable and effective crime-solving tool than eyewitness identifications or confessions and is not subject to such abuses as the improper line-up and the 'third degree.' Finally, because there is no danger of destruction of fingerprints, the limited detention need not come unexpectedly or at an inconvenient time. For this same reason, the general requirement that the authorization of a judicial officer be obtained in advance of detention would seem not to admit of any exception in the fingerprinting context.

The Fourth Amendment's prohibition against unreasonable searches and seizures has always been interpreted to prevent a search that is not limited to the particularly described "place to be searched, and the persons or things to be seized," even if the search is made pursuant to a warrant and based upon probable cause. The Amendment's protection is not diluted in those situations where it has been determined that legitimate law enforcement interests justify a warrantless search: the search must be limited in scope to that which is justified by the particular purposes served by the exception. * * * The reasonableness requirement of the Fourth Amendment requires no less when the police action is a seizure permitted on less than probable cause because of legitimate law enforcement interests. The scope of the detention must be carefully tailored to its underlying justification.

The predicate permitting seizures on suspicion short of probable cause is that law enforcement interests warrant a limited intrusion on the personal security of the suspect. The scope of the intrusion permitted will vary to some extent with the particular facts and circumstances of each case. This much, however, is clear: an investigative detention must be temporary and last no longer than is necessary to effectuate the purpose of the stop. Similarly, the investigative methods employed should be the least intrusive means reasonably available to verify or dispel the officer's suspicion in a short period of time.[b] It is the State's burden to demonstrate that the seizure it seeks to justify on the basis of a reasonable suspicion was sufficiently limited in scope and duration[c] to satisfy the conditions of an investigative seizure.

"We have no occasion in this case, however, to determine whether the requirements of the Fourth Amendment could be met by narrowly circumscribed procedures for obtaining, during the course of a criminal investigation, the fingerprints of individuals for whom there is no probable cause to arrest. For it is clear that no attempt was made here to employ procedures which might comply with the requirements of the Fourth Amendment: the detention at police headquarters of petitioner and the other young Negroes was not authorized by a judicial officer; petitioner was unnecessarily required to undergo two fingerprinting sessions; and petitioner was not merely fingerprinted during the December 3 detention but also subjected to interrogation."

b But in *United States v. Sharpe*, 470 U.S. 675 (1985), the Court cautioned:

"In assessing whether a detention is too long in duration to be justified as an investigative stop, we consider it appropriate to examine whether the police diligently pursued a means of investigation that was likely to confirm or dispel their suspicions quickly, during which time it was necessary to detain the defendant. A court making this assessment should take care to consider whether the police are acting in a swiftly developing situation, and in such cases the court should not indulge in unrealistic second-guessing. A creative judge engaged in *post hoc* evaluation of police conduct can almost always imagine some alternative means by which the objectives of the police might have been accomplished. But '[t]he fact that the protection of the public might, in the abstract, have been accomplished by "less intrusive" means does not, in itself, render the search unreasonable.' The question is not simply whether some other alternative was available, but whether the police acted unreasonably in failing to recognize or to pursue it."

c In *Terry*, the reasonableness of a stop was said to depend upon "whether the officer's action * * * was reasonably related in scope to the circumstances which justified the interference in the first place," thus raising but not resolving the question of whether "scope" concerns only the length of the detention or also the kind and direction of the questioning and investigating that occurs during the stop. Some lower courts concluded the latter, holding, e.g., that any interrogation during a *Terry* stop kept within proper time limits must also be limited to offenses as to which there was then reasonable suspicion. Such a conclusion appeared to draw support from the language the Supreme Court subsequently used regarding *Terry* stops, such as the above language in *Royer* and the assertion in *United States v. Hensley*, 469 U.S. 221 (1985), that the circumstances must have "justified the length *and* intrusiveness of the stop." Particularly significant in this regard was the *Hiibel* case, fn. c, p. 293, where, after noting the *Terry* scope limitation and the

Fifth, statements given during a period of illegal detention are inadmissible even though voluntarily given if they are the product of the illegal detention and not the result of an independent act of free will. * * *

Sixth, if the events in this case amounted to no more than a permissible police encounter in a public place or a justifiable *Terry*-type detention, Royer's consent, if voluntary, would have been effective to legalize the search of his two suitcases. * * *

The State proffers three reasons for holding that when Royer consented to the search of his luggage, he was not being illegally detained. First, it is submitted that the entire encounter was consensual and hence Royer was not being held against his will at all. We find this submission untenable. Asking for and examining Royer's ticket and his driver's license were no doubt permissible in themselves, but when the officers identified themselves as narcotics agents, told Royer that he was suspected of transporting narcotics, and asked him to accompany them to the police room, while retaining his ticket and driver's license and without indicating in any way that he was free to depart, Royer was effectively seized for the purposes of the Fourth Amendment. These circumstances surely amount to a show of official authority such that "a reasonable person would have believed that he was not free to leave."

Second, the State submits that if Royer was seized, there existed reasonable, articulable suspicion to justify a temporary detention and that the limits of a *Terry*-type stop were never exceeded. We agree with the State that when the officers discovered that Royer was traveling under an assumed name, this fact, and the facts already known to the officers—paying cash for a one-way ticket, the mode of

---

"similar limitation" in *Hayes v. Florida*, 470 U.S. 811 (1985) (i.e., that detention for fingerprinting would be permissible only if there were "a reasonable basis for believing that fingerprinting will establish or negate the suspect's connection with" the crime justifying the stop), the Court concluded that refusal to state one's name during a *Terry* stop could be criminalized *only* if "the request for identification was 'reasonably related in scope to the circumstances which justified' the stop."

But then came *Illinois v. Caballes*, 543 U.S. 405 (2005), where, after defendant had been stopped for a minor traffic violation, another trooper without request appeared with a drug dog and led the dog around the stopped car while the driver was being ticketed in the patrol car; the dog then alerted, resulting in a full search of the vehicle and discovery of marijuana in the trunk. While the state supreme court overturned defendant's conviction on the ground that use of the dog "unjustifiably enlarge[d] the scope of a routine traffic stop into a drug investigation," the Supreme Court concluded otherwise. In a very brief opinion which cited none of the foregoing cases (or, for that matter, any prior decisions of the Court), the Court in *Caballes* (1) reaffirmed *Terry*'s "duration"/"length" limitation, declaring that a seizure "can become unlawful if it is prolonged beyond the time reasonably required" to serve its lawful purpose, but (2) severely weakened the "scope"/"intrusiveness" limitation by holding that an investigative technique, even when directed toward criminality not reasonably suspected, does not violate that limitation unless the particular tactic employed "itself infringed [the detainee's] constitutionally protected interest in privacy," i.e., was *itself* a search. Because use of the drug dog was not a search and "the duration of the stop in this case was entirely justified by the traffic offense and the ordinary inquiries incident to such a stop," the defendant's Fourth Amendment rights had therefore not been violated. While *Caballes* involved a traffic stop on probable cause rather than a *Terry* investigative stop on reasonable suspicion, there is no suggestion in the case that the ruling extends only to the former and not the latter. Indeed, soon after *Caballes* was decided, it was relied upon the Court in another case, *Muehler v. Mena*, 544 U.S. 93 (2005), which did not involve a traffic stop or other seizure on full probable cause.

checking the two bags, and Royer's appearance and conduct in general—were adequate grounds for suspecting Royer of carrying drugs and for temporarily detaining him and his luggage while they attempted to verify or dispel their suspicions in a manner that did not exceed the limits of an investigative detention. We also agree that had Royer voluntarily consented to the search of his luggage while he was justifiably being detained on reasonable suspicion, the products of the search would be admissible against him. We have concluded, however, that at the time Royer produced the key to his suitcase, the detention to which he was then subjected was a more serious intrusion on his personal liberty than is allowable on mere suspicion of criminal activity.

By the time Royer was informed that the officers wished to examine his luggage, he had identified himself when approached by the officers and had attempted to explain the discrepancy between the name shown on his identification and the name under which he had purchased his ticket and identified his luggage. The officers were not satisfied, for they informed him they were narcotics agents and had reason to believe that he was carrying illegal drugs. They requested him to accompany them to the police room. Royer went with them. He found himself in a small room—a large closet—equipped with a desk and two chairs. He was alone with two police officers who again told him that they thought he was carrying narcotics. He also found that the officers, without his consent, had retrieved his checked luggage from the airline. What had begun as a consensual inquiry in a public place had escalated into an investigatory procedure in a police interrogation room, where the police, unsatisfied with previous explanations, sought to confirm their suspicions. The officers had Royer's ticket, they had his identification, and they had seized his luggage. Royer was never informed that he was free to board his plane if he so chose, and he reasonably believed that he was being detained. At least as of that moment, any consensual aspects of the encounter had evaporated, and we cannot fault the Florida District Court of Appeal for concluding that *Terry v. Ohio* and the cases following it did not justify the restraint to which Royer was then subjected. As a practical matter, Royer was under arrest. Consistent with this conclusion, the State conceded in the Florida courts that Royer would not have been free to leave the interrogation room had he asked to do so. Furthermore, the State's brief in this Court interprets the testimony of the officers at the suppression hearing as indicating that had Royer refused to consent to a search of his luggage, the officers would have held the luggage and sought a warrant to authorize the search.

We also think that the officers' conduct was more intrusive than necessary to effectuate an investigative detention otherwise authorized by the *Terry* line of cases. First, by returning his ticket and driver's license, and informing him that he was free to go if he so desired, the officers might have obviated any claim that the encounter was anything but a consensual matter from start to finish. Second, there are undoubtedly reasons of safety and security that would justify moving a suspect from one location to another during an investigatory detention, such as from an airport concourse to a more private area. There is no indication in this case that such reasons prompted the officers to transfer the site of the encounter from the concourse to the interrogation room. It appears, rather, that the primary interest of the officers was not in having an extended conversation with Royer but in the contents of his luggage, a matter which the officers did not pursue orally with Royer until after the encounter was relocated to the police room. The record does not reflect any facts which would support a finding that the legitimate law enforcement purposes which justified the detention in the first instance were furthered by removing Royer to the police room prior to the officer's attempt to gain his consent to a search of his luggage. As we have noted, had Royer consented to a search on the spot, the search could have been conducted with Royer present in the area where the bags were retrieved by Detective Johnson and any evidence recovered would have been admissible against him. If the search proved negative, Royer would have been free to go much earlier and with less likelihood of missing his flight, which in itself can be a very serious matter in a variety of circumstances.

Third, the State has not touched on the question whether it would have been feasible to investigate the contents of Royer's bags in a more expeditious way. The courts are not strangers to the use of trained dogs to detect the presence of controlled substances in luggage. There is no indication here that this means was not feasible and available. If it had been used, Royer and his luggage could have been momentarily detained while this investigative procedure was carried out. Indeed, it may be that no detention at all would have been necessary. A negative result would have freed Royer in short order; a positive result would have resulted in his justifiable arrest on probable cause.

We do not suggest that there is a litmus-paper test for distinguishing a consensual encounter from a seizure or for determining when a seizure exceeds the bounds of an investigative stop. Even in the discrete category of airport encounters, there will be endless variations in the facts and circumstances, so much variation that it is unlikely that the courts can reduce to a sentence or a paragraph a rule that will provide unarguable answers to the question whether there has been an unreasonable search or seizure in violation of the Fourth Amendment. Nevertheless, we must render judgment, and we think that the Florida District Court of Appeal cannot be faulted in concluding that the limits of a *Terry*-stop had been exceeded.

The State's third and final argument is that Royer was not being illegally held when he gave his consent because there was probable cause to arrest him at that time. Detective Johnson testified at the suppression hearing and the Florida District Court of Appeal held that there was no probable cause to arrest until Royer's bags were opened, but the fact that the officers did not believe there was probable cause and proceeded on a consensual or *Terry*-stop rationale would not foreclose the State from justifying Royer's custody by proving probable cause and hence removing any barrier to relying on Royer's consent to search. We agree with the Florida District Court of Appeal, however, that probable cause to arrest Royer did not exist at the time he consented to the search of his luggage. The facts are that a nervous young man with two American Tourister bags paid cash for an airline ticket to a "target city". These facts led to inquiry, which in turn revealed that the ticket had been bought under an assumed name. The proffered explanation did not satisfy the officers. We cannot agree with the State, if this is its position, that every nervous young man paying cash for a ticket to New York

City under an assumed name and carrying two heavy American Tourister bags may be arrested and held to answer for a serious felony charge.

Because we affirm the Florida District Court of Appeal's conclusion that Royer was being illegally detained when he consented to the search of his luggage, we agree that the consent was tainted by the illegality and was ineffective to justify the search. The judgment of the Florida District Court of Appeal is accordingly affirmed.[d]

JUSTICE BRENNAN, concurring in the result. * * *

To the extent that the plurality endorses the legality of the officers' initial stop of Royer, it was wholly unnecessary to reach that question. For even assuming the legality of the initial stop, the plurality correctly holds, and I agree, that the officers' subsequent actions clearly exceeded the permissible bounds of a *Terry* "investigative" stop. * * *

The scope of a *Terry*-type "investigative" stop and any attendant search must be extremely limited or the *Terry* exception would "swallow the general rule that Fourth Amendment seizures [and searches] are 'reasonable' only if based on probable cause." In my view, any suggestion that the *Terry* reasonable-suspicion standard justifies anything but the briefest of detentions or the most limited of searches finds no support in the *Terry* line of cases.[*]

In any event, I dissent from the plurality's view that the initial stop of Royer was legal. For plainly Royer was "seized" for purposes of the Fourth Amendment when the officers asked him to produce his driver's license and airline ticket. * * * By identifying themselves and asking for Royer's airline ticket and driver's license the officers, as a practical matter, engaged in a "show of authority" and "restrained [Royer's] liberty." It is simply wrong to suggest that a traveler feels free to walk away when he has been approached by individuals who have identified themselves as police officers and asked for, and received, his airline ticket and driver's license. * * *

JUSTICE BLACKMUN, dissenting.

* * * In my view, the police conduct in this case was minimally intrusive. Given the strength of society's interest in overcoming the extraordinary obstacles to the detection of drug traffickers, such conduct should not be subjected to a requirement of probable cause. Because the Court holds otherwise, I dissent. * * *

At the suppression hearing in this case, Royer agreed that he was not formally arrested until after his suitcases were opened. In my view, it cannot fairly be said that, prior to the formal arrest, the functional equivalent of an arrest had taken place. The encounter had far more in common with automobile stops justifiable on

---

[d]　Justice Powell's concurring opinion (in which he noted that he "join[ed] the plurality opinion") is omitted.

[*]　I interpret the plurality's requirement that the investigative methods employed pursuant to a *Terry* stop be "the least intrusive means reasonably available to verify or dispel the officer's suspicion in a short period of time," to mean that the availability of a less intrusive means may make an otherwise reasonable stop unreasonable. I do not interpret it to mean that the absence of a less intrusive means can make an otherwise unreasonable stop reasonable. * * *

reasonable suspicion, than with the detention deemed the functional equivalent of a formal arrest in *Dunaway v. New York*. In *Dunaway*, the suspect was taken from his neighbor's home and involuntarily transported to the police station in a squad car. At the precinct house, he was placed in an interrogation room and subjected to extended custodial interrogation. Here, Royer was not taken from a private residence, where reasonable expectations of privacy perhaps are at their greatest. Instead, he was approached in a major international airport where, due in part to extensive antihijacking surveillance and equipment, reasonable privacy expectations are of significantly lesser magnitude, certainly no greater than the reasonable privacy expectations of travelers in automobiles. * * *

What followed was within the scope of the lesser intrusions approved on less than probable cause in our prior cases, and was far removed from the circumstances of *Dunaway*. * * * Like Justice Rehnquist, I do not understand the plurality to dispute that Royer consented to go to the police room. Because the detention up to this point was not unlawful, the voluntariness of Royer's consent is to be judged on the totality of the circumstances.

JUSTICE REHNQUIST, with whom THE CHIEF JUSTICE and JUSTICE O'CONNOR join, dissenting. * * *

The point at which I part company with the plurality's opinion is in the assessment of the reasonableness of the officers' conduct following their initial conversation with Royer. The plurality focuses on the transfer of the place of the interview from the main concourse of the airport to the room off the concourse and observes that Royer "found himself in a small room—a large closet—equipped with a desk and two chairs. He was alone with two police officers who again told him that they thought he was carrying narcotics. He also found that the officers, without his consent, had retrieved his checked luggage from the airlines."

Obviously, this quoted language is intended to convey stern disapproval of the described conduct of the officers. To my mind, it merits no such disapproval and was eminently reasonable. Would it have been preferable for the officers to have detained Royer for further questioning, as they concededly had a right to do, without paying any attention to the fact that his luggage had already been checked on the flight to New York, and might be put aboard the flight even though Royer himself was not on the plane? Would it have been more "reasonable" to interrogate Royer about the contents of his suitcases, and to seek his permission to open the suitcases when they were retrieved, in the busy main concourse of the Miami Airport, rather than to find a room off the concourse where the confrontation would surely be less embarrassing to Royer? If the room had been large and spacious, rather than small, if it had possessed three chairs rather than two, would the officers' conduct have been made reasonable by these facts?

The plurality's answers to these questions, to the extent that it attempts any, are scarcely satisfying. It commences with the observation that "the officers' conduct was more intrusive than necessary to effectuate an investigative detention otherwise authorized by the *Terry* line of cases." * * *

All of this to my mind adds up to little more than saying that if my aunt were a man, she would be my uncle. The officers might have taken different steps than they did to investigate Royer, but the same may be said of virtually every investigative encounter that has more than one step to it. The question we must decide is what was *unreasonable* about the steps which *these officers* took with respect to *this* suspect in the Miami Airport on this particular day. * * * But since even the plurality concedes that there was articulable suspicion warranting an investigatory detention, the fact that the inquiry had become an "investigatory procedure in a police interrogation room" would seem to have little bearing on the proper disposition of a claim that the officers violated the Fourth Amendment. * * *

The reasonableness of the officers' activity in this case did not depend on Royer's consent to the investigation. Nevertheless, the presence of consent further justifies the action taken. The plurality does not seem to dispute that Royer consented to go to the room in the first instance. Certainly that conclusion is warranted by the totality of the circumstances. * * *

[I]f Royer was legally approached in the first instance and consented to accompany the detectives to the room, it does not follow that his consent went up in smoke and he was "arrested" upon entering the room. As we made clear in *Mendenhall*, logical analysis would focus on whether the environment in the room rendered the subsequent consent to a search of the luggage involuntary. * * *

UNITED STATES V. DRAYTON

536 U.S. 194, 122 S.Ct. 2105, 153 L.Ed.2d 242 (2002).

JUSTICE KENNEDY delivered the opinion of the Court. * * *

On February 4, 1999, respondents Christopher Drayton and Clifton Brown, Jr., were traveling on a Greyhound bus en route from Ft. Lauderdale, Florida, to Detroit, Michigan. The bus made a scheduled stop in Tallahassee, Florida. The passengers were required to disembark so the bus could be refueled and cleaned. As the passengers reboarded, the driver checked their tickets and then left to complete paperwork inside the terminal. As he left, the driver allowed three members of the Tallahassee Police Department to board the bus as part of a routine drug and weapons interdiction effort. The officers were dressed in plain clothes and carried concealed weapons and visible badges.

Once onboard Officer Hoover knelt on the driver's seat and faced the rear of the bus. He could observe the passengers and ensure the safety of the two other officers without blocking the aisle or otherwise obstructing the bus exit. Officers Lang and Blackburn went to the rear of the bus. Blackburn remained stationed there, facing forward. Lang worked his way toward the front of the bus, speaking with individual passengers as he went. He asked the passengers about their travel plans and sought to match passengers with luggage in the overhead racks. To avoid blocking the aisle, Lang stood next to or just behind each passenger with whom he spoke.

According to Lang's testimony, passengers who declined to cooperate with him or who chose to exit the bus at any time would have been allowed to do so without argument. In Lang's experience, however, most people are willing to cooperate. Some passengers go so far as to commend the police for their efforts to ensure the safety of their travel. Lang could recall five to six instances in the previous year in which passengers had declined to have their luggage searched. It also was common for passengers to leave the bus for a cigarette or a snack while the officers were on board. Lang sometimes informed passengers of their right to refuse to cooperate. On the day in question, however, he did not.

Respondents were seated next to each other on the bus. Drayton was in the aisle seat, Brown in the seat next to the window. Lang approached respondents from the rear and leaned over Drayton's shoulder. He held up his badge long enough for respondents to identify him as a police officer. With his face 12 to18 inches away from Drayton's, Lang spoke in a voice just loud enough for respondents to hear:

> "I'm Investigator Lang with the Tallahassee Police Department. We're conducting bus interdiction [sic], attempting to deter drugs and illegal weapons being transported on the bus. Do you have any bags on the bus?"

Both respondents pointed to a single green bag in the overhead luggage rack. Lang asked, "Do you mind if I check it?," and Brown responded, "Go ahead." Lang handed the bag to Officer Blackburn to check. The bag contained no contraband.

Officer Lang noticed that both respondents were wearing heavy jackets and baggy pants despite the warm weather. In Lang's experience drug traffickers often use baggy clothing to conceal weapons or narcotics. The officer thus asked Brown if he had any weapons or drugs in his possession. And he asked Brown: "Do you mind if I check your person?" Brown answered, "Sure," and cooperated by leaning up in his seat, pulling a cell phone out of his pocket, and opening up his jacket. Lang reached across Drayton and patted down Brown's jacket and pockets, including his waist area, sides, and upper thighs. In both thigh areas, Lang detected hard objects similar to drug packages detected on other occasions. Lang arrested and handcuffed Brown. Officer Hoover escorted Brown from the bus.

Lang then asked Drayton, "Mind if I check you?" Drayton responded by lifting his hands about eight inches from his legs. Lang conducted a pat-down of Drayton's thighs and detected hard objects similar to those found on Brown. He arrested Drayton and escorted him from the bus. A further search revealed that respondents had duct-taped plastic bundles of powder cocaine between several pairs of their boxer shorts. Brown possessed three bundles containing 483 grams of cocaine. Drayton possessed two bundles containing 295 grams of cocaine.

Respondents were charged with conspiring to distribute cocaine, and with possessing cocaine with intent to distribute it. They moved to suppress the cocaine, [but the motion was denied, although respondents prevailed on appeal.]

The Court has addressed on a previous occasion the specific question of drug interdiction efforts on buses. In [*Florida v. Bostick*, 501 U.S. 429 (1991),] two police officers requested a bus passenger's consent to a search of his luggage. The passenger agreed, and the resulting search revealed cocaine in his suitcase. The Florida Supreme Court suppressed the cocaine. In doing so it adopted a per se rule that due to the cramped confines onboard a bus the act of questioning would deprive a person of his or her freedom of movement and so constitute a seizure under the Fourth Amendment.

This Court reversed. *Bostick* first made it clear that for the most part per se rules are inappropriate in the Fourth Amendment context. The proper inquiry necessitates a consideration of "all the circumstances surrounding the encounter." The Court noted next that the traditional rule, which states that a seizure does not occur so long as a reasonable person would feel free "to disregard the police and go about his business,"[a] is not an accurate measure of the coercive effect of a bus encounter. A passenger may not want to get off a bus if there is a risk it will depart before the opportunity to reboard. A bus rider's movements are confined in this sense, but this is the natural result of choosing to take the bus; it says nothing about whether the police conduct is coercive. The proper inquiry "is whether a reasonable person would feel free to decline the officers' requests or otherwise terminate the encounter." Finally, the Court rejected Bostick's argument that he must have been seized because no reasonable person would consent to a search of luggage containing drugs. The reasonable person test, the Court explained, is objective and "presupposes an innocent person."

---

[a]   But, in the case cited by the Court as supporting this "test," *California v. Hodari D.*, 499 U.S. 621 (1991), the Court concluded that a person is not free to "go about his business" does not inevitably constitute a seizure. The defendant ran upon seeing a police car, only to be pursued on foot by police, after which the defendant threw away cocaine and the police retrieved it. The state court suppressed the cocaine as the fruit of a seizure made without reasonable suspicion. The Supreme Court, 7–2, stated:

"The narrow question before us is whether, with respect to a show of authority as with respect to application of physical force, a seizure occurs even though the subject does not yield. We hold that it does not.

"The language of the Fourth Amendment, of course, cannot sustain respondent's contention. The word 'seizure' readily bears the meaning of a laying on of hands or application of physical force to restrain movement, even when it is ultimately unsuccessful. ('She seized the purse-snatcher, but he broke out of her grasp.') It does not remotely apply, however, to the prospect of a policeman yelling 'Stop, in the name of the law!' at a fleeing form that continues to flee. That is no seizure. Nor can the result respondent wishes to achieve be produced—indirectly, as it were—by suggesting that Pertoso's uncomplied-with show of authority was a common-law arrest, and then appealing to the principle that all common-law arrests are seizures. An arrest requires *either* physical force (as described above) *or*, where that is absent, *submission* to the assertion of authority. * * *

"We do not think it desirable, even as a policy matter, to stretch the Fourth Amendment beyond its words and beyond the meaning of arrest, as respondent urges. Street pursuits always place the public at some risk, and compliance with police orders to stop should therefore be encouraged. Only a few of those orders, we must presume, will be without adequate basis, and since the addressee has no ready means of identifying the deficient ones it almost invariably is the responsible course to comply. Unlawful orders will not be deterred, moreover, by sanctioning through the exclusionary rule those of them are *not* obeyed. Since policemen do not command 'Stop!' expecting to be ignored, or give chase hoping to be outrun, it fully suffices to apply the deterrent to their genuine, successful seizures."

Citing *Hodari D.* for the proposition "that a police pursuit in attempting to seize a person does not amount to a 'seizure' within the meaning of the Fourth Amendment," the Court in *County of Sacramento v. Lewis*, 523 U.S. 833 (1998), also concluded "that no Fourth Amendment seizure would take place where a 'pursuing police car sought to stop the suspect only by the show of authority represented by flashing lights and continuing pursuit,' but accidentally stopped the suspect by crashing into him." This is because for a seizure there must be "a governmental termination of freedom of movement *through means intentionally applied.*"

In light of the limited record, *Bostick* refrained from deciding whether a seizure occurred. The Court, however, identified two factors "particularly worth noting" on remand. First, although it was obvious that an officer was armed, he did not remove the gun from its pouch or use it in a threatening way. Second, the officer advised the passenger that he could refuse consent to the search.

Relying upon this latter factor, the Eleventh Circuit has adopted what is in effect a per se rule that evidence obtained during suspicionless drug interdiction efforts aboard buses must be suppressed unless the officers have advised passengers of their right not to cooperate and to refuse consent to a search. * * *

Although the Court of Appeals has disavowed a per se requirement, the lack of an explicit warning to passengers is the only element common to all its cases. * * * Under these cases, it appears that the Court of Appeals would suppress any evidence obtained during suspicionless drug interdiction efforts aboard buses in the absence of a warning that passengers may refuse to cooperate. The Court of Appeals erred in adopting this approach.

Applying the *Bostick* framework to the facts of this particular case, we conclude that the police did not seize respondents when they boarded the bus and began questioning passengers. The officers gave the passengers no reason to believe that they were required to answer the officers' questions. When Officer Lang approached respondents, he did not brandish a weapon or make any intimidating movements. He left the aisle free so that respondents could exit. He spoke to passengers one by one and in a polite, quiet voice. Nothing he said would suggest to a reasonable person that he or she was barred from leaving the bus or otherwise terminating the encounter.

There were ample grounds for the District Court to conclude that "everything that took place between Officer Lang and [respondents] suggests that it was cooperative" and that there "was nothing coercive [or] confrontational" about the encounter. There was no application of force, no intimidating movement, no overwhelming show of force, no brandishing of weapons, no blocking of exits, no threat, no command, not even an authoritative tone of voice. It is beyond question that had this encounter occurred on the street, it would be constitutional. The fact that an encounter takes place on a bus does not on its own transform standard police questioning of citizens into an illegal seizure. Indeed, because many fellow passengers are present to witness officers' conduct, a reasonable person may feel even more secure in his or her decision not to cooperate with police on a bus than in other circumstances.

Respondents make much of the fact that Officer Lang displayed his badge. In *Florida v. Rodriguez*, 469 U.S. 1 (1984), however, the Court rejected the claim that the defendant was seized when an officer approached him in an airport, showed him his badge, and asked him to answer some questions. Likewise, in *INS v. Delgado*, 466 U.S. 210 (1984), the Court held that INS agents' wearing badges and questioning workers in a factory did not constitute a seizure. And while neither Lang nor his colleagues were in uniform or visibly armed, those factors should have little weight in the analysis. Officers are often required to wear uniforms and in many circumstances this is cause for assurance, not discomfort. Much the same can be said for wearing sidearms. That most law enforcement officers are armed is a fact well known to the public. The presence of a holstered firearm thus is unlikely to contribute to the coerciveness of the encounter absent active brandishing of the weapon.

Officer Hoover's position at the front of the bus also does not tip the scale in respondents' favor. Hoover did nothing to intimidate passengers, and he said nothing to suggest that people could not exit and indeed he left the aisle clear. In *Delgado*, the Court determined there was no seizure even though several uniformed INS officers were stationed near the exits of the factory. The Court noted: "The presence of agents by the exits posed no reasonable threat of detention to these workers, . . . the mere possibility that they would be questioned if they sought to leave the buildings should not have resulted in any reasonable apprehension by any of them that they would be seized or detained in any meaningful way."

Finally, the fact that in Officer Lang's experience only a few passengers have refused to cooperate does not suggest that a reasonable person would not feel free to terminate the bus encounter. In Lang's experience it was common for passengers to leave the bus for a cigarette or a snack while the officers were questioning passengers. And of more importance, bus passengers answer officers' questions and otherwise cooperate not because of coercion but because the passengers know that their participation enhances their own safety and the safety of those around them. "While most citizens will respond to a police request, the fact that people do so, and do so without being told they are free not to respond, hardly eliminates the consensual nature of the response." *Delgado*, supra.

Drayton contends that even if Brown's cooperation with the officers was consensual, Drayton was seized because no reasonable person would feel free to terminate the encounter with the officers after Brown had been arrested. The Court of Appeals did not address this claim; and in any event the argument fails. The arrest of one person does not mean that everyone around him has been seized by police. If anything, Brown's arrest should have put Drayton on notice of the consequences of continuing the encounter by answering the officers' questions. Even after arresting Brown, Lang addressed Drayton in a polite manner and provided him with no indication that he was required to answer Lang's questions. * * *b

JUSTICE SOUTER, with whom JUSTICE STEVENS and JUSTICE GINSBURG join, dissenting.

Anyone who travels by air today submits to searches of the person and luggage as a condition of boarding the aircraft. It is universally accepted that such intrusions are necessary to hedge against risks that, nowadays, even small children understand. The commonplace precautions of air travel have not, thus far, been justified for ground transportation, however, and no such conditions have

---

b The majority then went on to hold, on the authority of *Schneckloth v. Bustamonte*, § 10, that the consents to search by Brown and Drayton were voluntary even though the police did not advise them of their right to refuse. The dissenters believed the consents were tainted by prior illegal seizures, and thus did not discuss the voluntariness issue.

been placed on passengers getting on trains or buses. There is therefore an air of unreality about the Court's explanation that bus passengers consent to searches of their luggage to "enhanc[e] their own safety and the safety of those around them." Nor are the other factual assessments underlying the Court's conclusion in favor of the Government more convincing. * * *

Before applying the [*Bostick*] standard in this case, it may be worth getting some perspective from different sets of facts. A perfect example of police conduct that supports no colorable claim of seizure is the act of an officer who simply goes up to a pedestrian on the street and asks him a question. A pair of officers questioning a pedestrian, without more, would presumably support the same conclusion. Now consider three officers, one of whom stands behind the pedestrian, another at his side toward the open sidewalk, with the third addressing questions to the pedestrian a foot or two from his face. Finally, consider the same scene in a narrow alley. On such barebones facts, one may not be able to say a seizure occurred, even in the last case, but one can say without qualification that the atmosphere of the encounters differed significantly from the first to the last examples. In the final instance there is every reason to believe that the pedestrian would have understood, to his considerable discomfort, what Justice Stewart described as the "threatening presence of several officers." The police not only carry legitimate authority but also exercise power free from immediate check, and when the attention of several officers is brought to bear on one civilian the imbalance of immediate power is unmistakable. We all understand this, as well as we understand that a display of power rising to Justice Stewart's "threatening" level may overbear a normal person's ability to act freely, even in the absence of explicit commands or the formalities of detention. As common as this understanding is, however, there is little sign of it in the Court's opinion. My own understanding of the relevant facts and their significance follows.

When the bus in question made its scheduled stop in Tallahassee, the passengers were required to disembark while the vehicle was cleaned and refueled. When the passengers returned, they gave their tickets to the driver, who kept them and then left himself, after giving three police officers permission to board the bus in his absence. Although they were not in uniform, the officers displayed badges and identified themselves as police. One stationed himself in the driver's seat by the door at the front, facing back to observe the passengers. The two others went to the rear, from which they worked their way forward, with one of them speaking to passengers, the other backing him up. They necessarily addressed the passengers at very close range; the aisle was only fifteen inches wide, and each seat only eighteen. The quarters were cramped further by the overhead rack, nineteen inches above the top of the passenger seats. The passenger by the window could not have stood up straight, and the face of the nearest officer was only a foot or eighteen inches from the face of the nearest passenger being addressed. During the exchanges, the officers looked down, and the passengers had to look up if they were to face the police. The officer asking the questions spoke quietly. He prefaced his requests for permission to search luggage and do a body patdown by identifying himself by name as a police investigator "conducting bus interdiction" and saying, " 'We would like for your cooperation. Do you have any luggage on the bus?' "

Thus, for reasons unexplained, the driver with the tickets entitling the passengers to travel had yielded his custody of the bus and its seated travelers to three police officers, whose authority apparently superseded the driver's own. The officers took control of the entire passenger compartment, one stationed at the door keeping surveillance of all the occupants, the others working forward from the back. With one officer right behind him and the other one forward, a third officer accosted each passenger at quarters extremely close and so cramped that as many as half the passengers could not even have stood to face the speaker. None was asked whether he was willing to converse with the police or to take part in the enquiry. Instead the officer said the police were "conducting bus interdiction," in the course of which they "would like . . . cooperation." The reasonable inference was that the "interdiction" was not a consensual exercise, but one the police would carry out whatever the circumstances; that they would prefer "cooperation" but would not let the lack of it stand in their way. There was no contrary indication that day, since no passenger had refused the cooperation requested, and there was no reason for any passenger to believe that the driver would return and the trip resume until the police were satisfied. The scene was set and an atmosphere of obligatory participation was established by this introduction. Later requests to search prefaced with "Do you mind . . ." would naturally have been understood in the terms with which the encounter began.

It is very hard to imagine that either Brown or Drayton would have believed that he stood to lose nothing if he refused to cooperate with the police, or that he had any free choice to ignore the police altogether. No reasonable passenger could have believed that, only an uncomprehending one. It is neither here nor there that the interdiction was conducted by three officers, not one, as a safety precaution. The fact was that there were three, and when Brown and Drayton were called upon to respond, each one was presumably conscious of an officer in front watching, one at his side questioning him, and one behind for cover, in case he became unruly, perhaps, or "cooperation" was not forthcoming. The situation is much like the one in the alley, with civilians in close quarters, unable to move effectively, being told their cooperation is expected. While I am not prepared to say that no bus interrogation and search can pass the Bostick test without a warning that passengers are free to say no, the facts here surely required more from the officers than a quiet tone of voice. A police officer who is certain to get his way has no need to shout.

It is true of course that the police testified that a bus passenger sometimes says no, but that evidence does nothing to cast the facts here in a different light. We have no way of knowing the circumstances in which a passenger elsewhere refused a request; maybe that has happened only when the police have told passengers they had a right to refuse (as the officers sometimes advised them). Nor is it fairly possible to see the facts of this case differently by recalling *INS v. Delgado* as precedent. In that case, a majority of this Court found no seizure when a factory force was questioned by immigration officers, with an officer posted at every door leading from the workplace. Whether that opinion was well reasoned or not, the facts as the Court viewed them differed from the case here. *Delgado* considered an order granting summary judgment in favor of respondents, with the consequence that the Court was required to construe the record and all issues of fact favorably to the Immigration and Naturalization Service. The Court therefore emphasized that even after "th[e] surveys were initiated, the employees were about their ordinary business, operating machinery and performing other job assignments." In this case, however, Brown and Drayton were seemingly pinned-in by the officers and the customary course of events was stopped flat. The bus was going nowhere, and with one officer in the driver's seat, it was reasonable to suppose no passenger would tend to his own business until the officers were ready to let him.

In any event, I am less concerned to parse this case against *Delgado* than to apply *Bostick*'s totality of circumstances test, and to ask whether a passenger would reasonably have felt free to end his encounter with the three officers by saying no and ignoring them thereafter. In my view the answer is clear. The Court's contrary conclusion tells me that the majority cannot see what Justice Stewart saw, and I respectfully dissent.

BRENDLIN V. CALIFORNIA
551 U.S. 249, 127 S.Ct. 2400, 168 L.Ed.2d 132 (2007).

JUSTICE SOUTER delivered the opinion of the Court.

[Following a traffic stop conceded to be illegal for lack of reasonable suspicion, passenger Brendlin was found to have an outstanding arrest warrant; he was arrested, and drugs and drug paraphernalia were found on his person and in the car in searches incident to his arrest. Brendlin's claim that evidence was the fruit of his illegal seizure by stopping the car was rejected by the California supreme court on the ground that Brendlin, as a mere passenger, had not been seized by virtue of the vehicle being stopped.]

A person is seized by the police and thus entitled to challenge the government's action under the Fourth Amendment when the officer, " 'by means of physical force or show of authority,' " terminates or restrains his freedom of movement, *Florida v. Bostick*, 501 U.S. 429, 434 (1991), "through means intentionally applied," *Brower v. County of Inyo*, 489 U.S. 593, 597 (1989). Thus, an "unintended person . . . [may be] the object of the detention," so long as the detention is "willful" and not merely the consequence of "an unknowing act." A police officer may make a seizure by a show of authority and without the use of physical force, but there is no seizure without actual submission; otherwise, there is at most an attempted seizure, so far as the Fourth Amendment is concerned.

When the actions of the police do not show an unambiguous intent to restrain or when an individual's submission to a show of governmental authority takes the form of passive acquiescence, there needs to be some test for telling when a seizure occurs in response to authority, and when it does not. The test was devised by Justice Stewart in *United States v. Mendenhall*, 446 U.S. 544 (1980), who wrote that a seizure occurs if "in view of all of the circumstances surrounding the incident, a reasonable person would have believed that he was not free to leave." Later on, the Court * * * added that when a person "has no desire to leave" for reasons unrelated to the police presence, the "coercive effect of the encounter" can be measured better by asking whether "a reasonable person would feel free to decline the officers' requests or otherwise terminate the encounter," *Bostick*, supra.

The law is settled that in Fourth Amendment terms a traffic stop entails a seizure of the driver "even though the purpose of the stop is limited and the resulting detention quite brief." And although we have not, until today, squarely answered the question whether a passenger is also seized, we have said over and over in dicta that during a traffic stop an officer seizes everyone in the vehicle, not just the driver. * * *

The State concedes that the police had no adequate justification to pull the car over, but argues that the passenger was not seized and thus cannot claim that the evidence was tainted by an unconstitutional stop. We resolve this question by asking whether a reasonable person in Brendlin's position when the car stopped would have believed himself free to "terminate the encounter" between the police and himself. We think that in these circumstances any reasonable passenger would have understood the police officers to be exercising control to the point that no one in the car was free to depart without police permission.

A traffic stop necessarily curtails the travel a passenger has chosen just as much as it halts the driver, diverting both from the stream of traffic to the side of the road, and the police activity that normally amounts to intrusion on "privacy and personal security" does not normally (and did not here) distinguish between passenger and driver. An officer who orders one particular car to pull over acts with an implicit claim of right based on fault of some sort, and a sensible person would not expect a police officer to allow people to come and go freely from the physical focal point of an investigation into faulty behavior or wrongdoing. If the likely wrongdoing is not the driving, the passenger will reasonably feel subject to suspicion owing to close association; but even when the wrongdoing is only bad driving, the passenger will expect to be subject to some scrutiny, and his attempt to leave the scene would be so obviously likely to prompt an objection from the officer that no passenger would feel free to leave in the first place.[a]

---

[a]   In *Arizona v. Johnson*, 555 U.S. 323 (2009), three officers stopped a vehicle with three occupants after a license plate check revealed the vehicle's registration had been suspended, a civil infraction warranting a citation. One officer "attended to" back-seat passenger Johnson, who watched the police closely as they approached, was wearing gang clothing, was carrying a scanner, had no identification, and admitted serving time in prison for burglary. She asked him to get out of the car and then, suspecting he "might have a weapon on him," frisked Johnson and found a gun at his waist. The state court concluded that absent "reason to believe Johnson was involved in criminal activity," the officer "had no right to pat him down for weapons, even if she had reason to suspect he was armed and dangerous." A unanimous Supreme Court reversed. Noting that the *Terry* prerequisites for a frisk were (i) a lawful stop, there present because of reasonable suspicion of criminal activity, and (ii) grounds for a frisk, and that per *Brendlin* a traffic stop seized "everyone in the vehicle," the Court held that "in a traffic-stop setting, the first *Terry* condition—a lawful investigatory stop—is met whenever it is lawful for police to detain an automobile and its occupants pending inquiry into a vehicular violation. The police need not have, in addition, cause to believe any occupant of the vehicle is involved in criminal activity. To justify a patdown of the driver or a passenger during a traffic stop, however, just as in the case of a pedestrian reasonably suspected of criminal activity, the police must harbor reasonable suspicion that the person subjected to the frisk is armed and dangerous." In concluding that the stop of Johnson had not terminated before the frisk, the Court stated: "Nothing occurred in this case that would have conveyed to Johnson that, prior to the frisk, the traffic stop had ended or that he was otherwise

It is also reasonable for passengers to expect that a police officer at the scene of a crime, arrest, or investigation will not let people move around in ways that could jeopardize his safety. In *Maryland v. Wilson*, 519 U.S. 408 (1997), we held that during a lawful traffic stop an officer may order a passenger out of the car as a precautionary measure, without reasonable suspicion that the passenger poses a safety risk. In fashioning this rule, we invoked our earlier statement that " '[t]he risk of harm to both the police and the occupants is minimized if the officers routinely exercise unquestioned command of the situation.' " What we have said in these opinions probably reflects a societal expectation of " 'unquestioned [police] command' " at odds with any notion that a passenger would feel free to leave, or to terminate the personal encounter any other way, without advance permission.

Our conclusion comports with the views of all nine Federal Courts of Appeals, and nearly every state court, to have ruled on the question. And the treatise writers share this prevailing judicial view that a passenger may bring a Fourth Amendment challenge to the legality of a traffic stop.

The contrary conclusion drawn by the Supreme Court of California, that seizure came only with formal arrest, reflects three premises as to which we respectfully disagree. First, the State Supreme Court reasoned that Brendlin was not seized by the stop because Deputy Sheriff Brokenbrough only intended to investigate [driver] Simeroth and did not direct a show of authority toward Brendlin. The court saw Brokenbrough's "flashing lights [as] directed at the driver," and pointed to the lack of record evidence that Brokenbrough "was even aware [Brendlin] was in the car prior to the vehicle stop." But that view of the facts ignores the objective *Mendenhall* test of what a reasonable passenger would understand. To the extent that there is anything ambiguous in the show of force (was it fairly seen as directed only at the driver or at the car and its occupants?), the test resolves the ambiguity, and here it leads to the intuitive conclusion that all the occupants were subject to like control by the successful display of authority. * * *

California defends the State Supreme Court's ruling on this point by citing our cases holding that seizure requires a purposeful, deliberate act of detention. But [t]he intent that counts under the Fourth Amendment is the "intent [that] has been conveyed to the person confronted," and the criterion of willful restriction on freedom of movement is no invitation to look to subjective intent when determining who is seized. [T]he issue is whether a reasonable passenger would have perceived that the show of authority was at least partly directed at him, and that he was thus not free to ignore the police presence and go about his business.

Second, the Supreme Court of California assumed that Brendlin, "as the passenger, had no ability to submit to the deputy's show of authority" because only the driver was in control of the moving vehicle. But what may amount to submission depends on what a person was doing before the show of authority: a fleeing man is not seized until he is physically overpowered, but one sitting in a

_____

free 'to depart without police permission.' [The officer] surely was not constitutionally required to give Johnson an opportunity to depart the scene after he exited the vehicle without first ensuring that, in so doing, she was not permitting a dangerous person to get behind her."

chair may submit to authority by not getting up to run away. Here, Brendlin had no effective way to signal submission while the car was still moving on the roadway, but once it came to a stop he could, and apparently did, submit by staying inside.

Third, the State Supreme Court shied away from the rule we apply today for fear that it "would encompass even those motorists following the vehicle subject to the traffic stop who, by virtue of the original detention, are forced to slow down and perhaps even come to a halt in order to accommodate that vehicle's submission to police authority." But an occupant of a car who knows that he is stuck in traffic because another car has been pulled over (like the motorist who can't even make out why the road is suddenly clogged) would not perceive a show of authority as directed at him or his car. Such incidental restrictions on freedom of movement would not tend to affect an individual's "sense of security and privacy in traveling in an automobile." * * *[6]

Indeed, the consequence to worry about would not flow from our conclusion, but from the rule that almost all courts have rejected. Holding that the passenger in a private car is not (without more) seized in a traffic stop would invite police officers to stop cars with passengers regardless of probable cause or reasonable suspicion of anything illegal. The fact that evidence uncovered as a result of an arbitrary traffic stop would still be admissible against any passengers would be a powerful incentive to run the kind of "roving patrols" that would still violate the driver's Fourth Amendment right. * * *

RODRIGUEZ V. UNITED STATES
575 U.S. 348, 135 S.Ct. 1609, 191 L.Ed.2d 492 (2015).

JUSTICE GINSBURG delivered the opinion of the Court.

[A Nebraska K-9 police officer saw a vehicle drive onto a highway shoulder, a violation of state law, so he pulled the vehicle over at 12:06 a.m. The officer questioned driver Rodriguez about his conduct; obtained Rodriguez's license, registration and proof of insurance; ran a records check on Rodriguez; asked passenger Pollman for his driver's license and questioned him about the nature and purpose of their travels; ran a records check on Pollman; prepared a written warning for Rodriguez; called for a second officer; explained the warning to Rodriguez and returned the documents to the two men; asked for but was refused permission to walk his dog around the vehicle; and, 7 or 8 minutes after the written warning was issued, at 12:33 a.m. (when the other officer arrived) led his dog around the vehicle. The dog alerted, the vehicle was searched, and a bag of methamphetamine was discovered. In the subsequent federal prosecution, resulting in a conviction upheld on appeal, Rodriguez' suppression motion was

---

[6] California claims that, under today's rule, "all taxi cab and bus passengers would be 'seized' under the Fourth Amendment when the cab or bus driver is pulled over by the police for running a red light." But the relationship between driver and passenger is not the same in a common carrier as it is in a private vehicle, and the expectations of police officers and passengers differ accordingly. In those cases, as here, the crucial question would be whether a reasonable person in the passenger's position would feel free to take steps to terminate the encounter.

denied by reliance upon Eighth Circuit precedent that "dog sniffs that occur within a short time following the completion of a traffic stop are not constitutionally prohibited if they constitute only *de minimis* intrusions."]

A seizure for a traffic violation justifies a police investigation of that violation. "[A] relatively brief encounter," a routine traffic stop is "more analogous to a so-called '*Terry* stop' . . . than to a formal arrest." Like a *Terry* stop, the tolerable duration of police inquiries in the traffic-stop context is determined by the seizure's "mission"—to address the traffic violation that warranted the stop, and attend to related safety concerns. Because addressing the infraction is the purpose of the stop, it may "last no longer than is necessary to effectuate th[at] purpose." Authority for the seizure thus ends when tasks tied to the traffic infraction are— or reasonably should have been—completed.

Our decisions in *Caballes* [p. 306, fn. c] and *Johnson* [p. 319, fn. a] heed these constraints. In both cases, we concluded that the Fourth Amendment tolerated certain unrelated investigations that did not lengthen the roadside detention. * * * An officer, in other words, may conduct certain unrelated checks during an otherwise lawful traffic stop. But * * * he may not do so in a way that prolongs the stop, absent the reasonable suspicion ordinarily demanded to justify detaining an individual.

Beyond determining whether to issue a traffic ticket, an officer's mission includes "ordinary inquiries incident to [the traffic] stop." Typically such inquiries involve checking the driver's license, determining whether there are outstanding warrants against the driver, and inspecting the automobile's registration and proof of insurance. These checks serve the same objective as enforcement of the traffic code: ensuring that vehicles on the road are operated safely and responsibly.

* * * Lacking the same close connection to roadway safety as the ordinary inquiries, a dog sniff is not fairly characterized as part of the officer's traffic mission.

In advancing its de minimis rule, the Eighth Circuit relied heavily on our decision in *Pennsylvania v. Mimms*, [p. 291, fn. b]. In *Mimms*, we reasoned that the government's "legitimate and weighty" interest in officer safety outweighs the "de minimis" additional intrusion of requiring a driver, already lawfully stopped, to exit the vehicle. * * *

Unlike a general interest in criminal enforcement, however, the government's officer safety interest stems from the mission of the stop itself. Traffic stops are "especially fraught with danger to police officers," so an officer may need to take certain negligibly burdensome precautions in order to complete his mission safely. Cf. *United States v. Holt*, 264 F.3d 1215, 1221–1222 (C.A.10 2001) (en banc) (recognizing officer safety justification for criminal record and outstanding warrant checks). On-scene investigation into other crimes, however, detours from that mission. So too do safety precautions taken in order to facilitate such detours. Thus, even assuming that the imposition here was no more intrusive than the exit order in *Mimms*, the dog sniff could not be justified on the same basis. * * *

The Government argues that an officer may "incremental[ly]" prolong a stop to conduct a dog sniff so long as the officer is reasonably diligent in pursuing the traffic-related purpose of the stop, and the overall duration of the stop remains reasonable in relation to the duration of other traffic stops involving similar circumstances. The Government's argument, in effect, is that by completing all traffic-related tasks expeditiously, an officer can earn bonus time to pursue an unrelated criminal investigation. The reasonableness of a seizure, however, depends on what the police in fact do. In this regard, the Government acknowledges that "an officer always has to be reasonably diligent." How could diligence be gauged other than by noting what the officer actually did and how he did it? If an officer can complete traffic-based inquiries expeditiously, then that is the amount of "time reasonably required to complete [the stop's] mission." As we said in *Caballes* and reiterate today, a traffic stop "prolonged beyond" that point is "unlawful." The critical question, then, is not whether the dog sniff occurs before or after the officer issues a ticket, as JUSTICE ALITO supposes, but whether conducting the sniff "prolongs"—i.e., adds time to—"the stop."

* * * The question whether reasonable suspicion of criminal activity justified detaining Rodriguez beyond completion of the traffic infraction investigation, [not heretofore addressed by the court of appeals,] therefore, remains open for Eighth Circuit consideration on remand.

JUSTICE THOMAS, with whom JUSTICE ALITO joins, and with whom JUSTICE KENNEDY joins [in part].

[T]he only question is whether the stop was otherwise executed in a reasonable manner. I easily conclude that it was. Approximately 29 minutes passed from the time Officer Struble stopped Rodriguez until his narcotics-detection dog alerted to the presence of drugs. That amount of time is hardly out of the ordinary for a traffic stop by a single officer of a vehicle containing multiple occupant even when no dog sniff is involved. * * *

The majority's rule * * * imposes a one-way ratchet for constitutional protection linked to the characteristics of the individual officer conducting the stop: If a driver is stopped by a particularly efficient officer, then he will be entitled to be released from the traffic stop after a shorter period of time than a driver stopped by a less efficient officer. Similarly, if a driver is stopped by an officer with access to technology that can shorten a records check, then he will be entitled to be released from the stop after a shorter period of time than an individual stopped by an officer without access to such technology. * * * [This is contrary to our prior cases, where we] have repeatedly explained that the reasonableness inquiry must not hinge on the characteristics of the individual officer conducting the seizure. * * *

The majority's logic would produce * * * arbitrary results. Under its reasoning, a traffic stop made by a rookie could be executed in a reasonable manner, whereas the same traffic stop made by a knowledgeable, veteran officer in precisely the same circumstances might not, if in fact his knowledge and experience made him capable of completing the stop faster. We have long rejected interpretations of the Fourth Amendment that would produce such haphazard results, and I see no reason to depart from our consistent practice today. * * *

The majority's approach draws an artificial line between dog sniffs and other common police practices. The lower courts have routinely confirmed that warrant checks are a constitutionally permissible part of a traffic stop, and the majority confirms that it finds no fault in these measures. Yet its reasoning suggests the opposite. Such warrant checks look more like they are directed to " 'detecting evidence of ordinary criminal wrongdoing" than to "ensuring that vehicles on the road are operated safely and responsibly." Perhaps one could argue that the existence of an outstanding warrant might make a driver less likely to operate his vehicle safely and responsibly on the road, but the same could be said about a driver in possession of contraband. * * *

Traffic stops can be initiated based on probable cause or reasonable suspicion. * * *

Although all traffic stops must be executed reasonably, our precedents make clear that traffic stops justified by reasonable suspicion are subject to additional limitations that those justified by probable cause are not. A * * * stop based on probable cause affords an officer considerably more leeway. In such seizures, an officer may engage in a warrantless arrest of the driver, a warrantless search incident to arrest of the driver, and a warrantless search incident to arrest of the vehicle if it is reasonable to believe evidence relevant to the crime of arrest might be found there.

The majority casually tosses this distinction aside. It asserts that the traffic stop in this case, which was undisputedly initiated on the basis of probable cause, can last no longer than is in fact necessary to effectuate the mission of the stop. And, it assumes that the mission of the stop was merely to write a traffic ticket, rather than to consider making a custodial arrest. * * *

Today's revision of our Fourth Amendment jurisprudence was also entirely unnecessary. Rodriguez suffered no Fourth Amendment violation here for an entirely independent reason: Officer Struble had reasonable suspicion to continue to hold him for investigative purposes. * * *

JUSTICE ALITO, dissenting. * * *

The rule that the Court adopts will do little good going forward. It is unlikely to have any appreciable effect on the length of future traffic stops. Most officers will learn the prescribed sequence of events even if they cannot fathom the reason for that requirement. * * *

9. CONSENT SEARCHES

So-called consent searches are frequently relied upon by police as a means of investigating suspected criminal conduct. Sometimes probable cause is present but the police feel either that they do not have time to get a warrant or that they would simply like to avoid that time-consuming process, but more often an effort is made to obtain consent where probable cause is lacking and no warrant could be obtained. The exact meaning of "consent" in this context, the question explored in *Schneckloth v. Bustamonte,* is thus a matter of some importance.

In *Schneckloth,* by way of showing that the protections of the Fourth Amendment "are of a wholly different order" than various other constitutional rights, the Court noted that a person's privacy may sometimes be lawfully invaded by virtue of consent obtained by police from a third party. This raises the question of whether, at least in some circumstances, that third party consent can even "trump" a refusal to consent by a co-occupant of the place to be searched, considered in *Georgia v. Randolph.*

SCHNECKLOTH V. BUSTAMONTE
412 U.S. 218, 93 S.Ct. 2041, 36 L.Ed.2d 854 (1973).

JUSTICE STEWART delivered the opinion of the Court. * * *

[While on routine patrol at 2:40 a.m., a police officer stopped an automobile when he observed that one headlight and its license plate light were burned out. Six men were in the vehicle. When the driver could not produce a driver's license, the officer asked if any of the other five had any evidence of identification. Only Alcala produced a license, and he explained that the car was his brother's. The officer asked Alcala if he could search the car. Alcala replied, "Sure, go ahead," and actually helped in the search of the car, by opening the trunk and glove compartment. Three checks that had previously been stolen from a car wash were found wadded up under the left rear seat. The checks in question were admitted in evidence at Bustamonte's trial. He was convicted, and the California Court of Appeal affirmed the conviction. Thereafter, the respondent sought a writ of habeas corpus in a federal district court. It was denied. On appeal, the Court of Appeals for the Ninth Circuit set aside the District Court's order.]

The precise question in this case is what must the state prove to demonstrate that a consent was "voluntarily" given. * * *

The most extensive judicial exposition of the meaning of "voluntariness" has been developed in those cases in which the Court has had to determine the "voluntariness" of a defendant's confession for purposes of the Fourteenth Amendment. * * * It is to that body of case law to which we turn for initial guidance on the meaning of "voluntariness" in the present context. * * *

The significant fact about all of these decisions is that none of them turned on the presence or absence of a single controlling criterion; each reflected a careful scrutiny of all the surrounding circumstances. In none of them did the Court rule that the Due Process Clause required the prosecution to prove as part of its initial burden that the defendant knew he had a right to refuse to answer the questions that were put. While the state of the accused's mind, and the failure of the police to advise the accused of his rights, were certainly factors to be evaluated in assessing the "voluntariness" of an accused's responses, they were not in and of themselves determinative.

Similar considerations lead us to agree with the courts of California that the question whether a consent to a search was in fact "voluntary" or was the product of duress or coercion, express or implied, is a question of fact to be determined from the totality of all the circumstances. While knowledge of the right to refuse consent is one factor to be taken into account, the government need not establish such knowledge as the *sine qua non* of an effective consent. As with police questioning, two competing concerns must be accommodated in determining the meaning of a "voluntary" consent—the legitimate need for such searches and the equally important requirement of assuring the absence of coercion.

In situations where the police have some evidence of illicit activity, but lack probable cause to arrest or search, a search authorized by a valid consent may be the only means of obtaining important and reliable evidence. In the present case for example, while the police had reason to stop the car for traffic violations, the State does not contend that there was probable cause to search the vehicle or that the search was incident to a valid arrest of any of the occupants. Yet, the search yielded tangible evidence that served as a basis for a prosecution, and provided some assurance that others, wholly innocent of the crime, were not mistakenly brought to trial. And in those cases where there is probable cause to arrest or search, but where the police lack a warrant, a consent search may still be valuable. If the search is conducted and proves fruitless, that in itself may convince the police that an arrest with its possible stigma and embarrassment is unnecessary, or that a far more extensive search pursuant to a warrant is not justified. In short a search pursuant to consent may result in considerably less inconvenience for the subject of the search, and, properly conducted, is a constitutionally permissible and wholly legitimate aspect of effective police activity.

But the Fourth and Fourteenth Amendments require that a consent not be coerced, by explicit or implicit means, by implied threat or covert force. For, no matter how subtly the coercion were applied, the resulting "consent" would be no more than a pretext for the unjustified police intrusion against which the Fourth Amendment is directed. * * *

The problem of reconciling the recognized legitimacy of consent searches with the requirement that they be free from any aspect of official coercion cannot be resolved by an infallible touchstone. To approve such searches without the most careful scrutiny would sanction the possibility of official coercion; to place artificial restrictions upon such searches would jeopardize their basic validity. Just as was true with confessions, the requirement of a "voluntary" consent reflects a fair accommodation of the constitutional requirements involved. In examining all the surrounding circumstances to determine if in fact the consent to search was coerced, account must be taken of subtly coercive police questions, as well as the possibly vulnerable subjective state of the person who consents. Those searches that are the product of police coercion can thus be filtered out without undermining the continuing validity of consent searches. In sum, there is no reason for us to depart in the area of consent searches, from the traditional definition of "voluntariness."

The approach of the Court of Appeals for the Ninth Circuit finds no support in any of our decisions that have attempted to define the meaning of "voluntariness." Its ruling, that the State must affirmatively prove that the subject of the search knew that he had a right to refuse consent, would, in practice, create serious doubt whether consent searches could continue to be conducted. There might be rare cases where it could be proved from the record that a person in fact affirmatively knew of his right to refuse—such as a case where he announced to the police that if he didn't sign the consent form, "you [police] are going to get a search warrant;" or a case where by prior experience and training a person had clearly and convincingly demonstrated such knowledge. But more commonly where there was no evidence of any coercion, explicit or implicit, the prosecution would nevertheless be unable to demonstrate that the subject of the search in fact had known of his right to refuse consent.

The very object of the inquiry—the nature of a person's subjective understanding—underlines the difficulty of the prosecution's burden under the rule applied by the Court of Appeals in this case. Any defendant who was the subject of a search authorized solely by his consent could effectively frustrate the introduction into evidence of the fruits of that search by simply failing to testify that he in fact knew he could refuse to consent. And the near impossibility of meeting this prosecutorial burden suggests why this Court has never accepted any such litmus-paper test of voluntariness. * * *

One alternative that would go far towards proving that the subject of a search did know he had a right to refuse consent would be to advise him of that right before eliciting his consent. That, however, is a suggestion that has been almost universally repudiated by both federal and state courts, and, we think, rightly so. For it would be thoroughly impractical to impose on the normal consent search the detailed requirements of an effective warning. Consent searches are part of the standard investigatory techniques of law enforcement agencies. They normally occur on the highway, or in a person's home or office, and under informal and unstructured conditions. The circumstances that prompt the initial request to search may develop quickly or be a logical extension of investigative police questioning. The police may seek to investigate further suspicious circumstances or to follow up leads developed in questioning persons at the scene of a crime. These situations are a far cry from the structured atmosphere of a trial where, assisted by counsel if he chooses, a defendant is informed of his trial rights. And, while surely a closer question, these situations are still immeasurably far removed from "custodial interrogation" where, in *Miranda v. Arizona* [Ch. 6, § 3] we found that the Constitution required certain now familiar warnings as a prerequisite to police interrogation. * * *

It is said, however, that a "consent" is a "waiver" of a person's rights under the Fourth and Fourteenth Amendments. The argument is that by allowing the police to conduct a search, a person "waives" whatever right he had to prevent the police from searching. It is argued that under the doctrine of *Johnson v. Zerbst*, 304 U.S. 458 (1938), to establish such a "waiver" the state must demonstrate "an intentional relinquishment or abandonment of a known right or privilege." * * *

Almost without exception the requirement of a knowing and intelligent waiver has been applied only to those rights which the Constitution guarantees to a criminal defendant in order to preserve a fair trial. Hence, and hardly surprisingly in view of the facts of *Johnson* itself, the standard of a knowing and intelligent waiver has most often been applied to test the validity of a waiver of counsel, either at trial, or upon a guilty plea. And the Court has also applied the *Johnson* criteria to assess the effectiveness of a waiver of other trial rights such as the right to confrontation, to a jury trial, and to a speedy trial, and the right to be free from twice being placed in jeopardy. Guilty pleas have been carefully scrutinized to determine whether the accused knew and understood all the rights to which he would be entitled at trial, and that he had intentionally chosen to forgo them. And the Court has evaluated the knowing and intelligent nature of the waiver of trial rights in trial-type situations, such as the waiver of the privilege against compulsory self-incrimination before an administrative agency or a congressional committee, or the waiver of counsel in a juvenile proceeding.

The guarantees afforded a criminal defendant at trial also protect him at certain stages before the actual trial, and any alleged waiver must meet the strict standard of an intentional relinquishment of a "known" right. But the "trial" guarantees that have been applied to the "pretrial" stage of the criminal process are similarly designed to protect the fairness of the trial itself. * * *a

The standards of *Johnson* were, therefore, found to be a necessary prerequisite to a finding of a valid waiver.[29] * * *

A strict standard of waiver has been applied to those rights guaranteed to a criminal defendant to insure that he will be accorded the greatest possible opportunity to utilize every facet of the constitutional model of a fair criminal trial. Any trial conducted in derogation of that model leaves open the possibility that the trial reached an unfair result precisely because all the protections specified in the Constitution were not provided. A prime example is the right to counsel. For without that right, a wholly innocent accused faces the real and substantial danger that simply because of his lack of legal expertise he may be convicted. * * *

The protections of the Fourth Amendment are of a wholly different order, and have nothing whatever to do with promoting the fair ascertainment of truth at a criminal trial. Rather, as Mr. Justice Frankfurter's opinion for the Court put it in

---

a At this point, the Court noted that "the standard of a knowing and intelligent waiver" applies to waiver of counsel at a lineup under *United States v. Wade,* [p. 574], and *Gilbert v. California,* [fn. b, p. 578] because counsel is provided to protect the right of cross-examination at trial; and that the same standard applies to waiver of counsel at custodial interrogation under *Miranda v. Arizona* because counsel is provided to ensure that the safeguards concerning the giving of testimony at trial do not "become empty formalities."

29 As we have already noted, *Miranda* itself involved interrogation of a suspect detained in custody and did not concern the investigatory procedures of the police in general on-the-scene questioning. By the same token, the present case does not require a determination of the proper standard to be applied in assessing the validity of a search authorized solely by an alleged consent that is obtained from a person after he has been placed in custody. We do note, however, that other courts have been particularly sensitive to the heightened possibilities for coercion when the "consent" to a search was given by a person in custody.

Wolf v. Colorado [p. 60] the Fourth Amendment protects the "security of one's privacy against arbitrary intrusion by the police. * * *". * * *

Nor can it even be said that a search, as opposed to an eventual trial, is somehow "unfair" if a person consents to a search. While the Fourth and Fourteenth Amendments limit the circumstances under which the police can conduct a search, there is nothing constitutionally suspect in a person voluntarily allowing a search. The actual conduct of the search may be precisely the same as if the police had obtained a warrant. And, unlike those constitutional guarantees that protect a defendant at trial, it cannot be said every reasonable presumption ought to be indulged against voluntary relinquishment. We have only recently stated: "[I]t is no part of the policy underlying the Fourth and Fourteenth Amendments to discourage citizens from aiding to the utmost of their ability in the apprehension of criminals." Rather the community has a real interest in encouraging consent, for the resulting search may yield necessary evidence for the solution and prosecution of crime, evidence that may insure that a wholly innocent person is not wrongly charged with a criminal offense.

Those cases that have dealt with the application of the *Johnson v. Zerbst* rule make clear that it would be next to impossible to apply to a consent search the standard of "an intentional relinquishment or abandonment of a known right or privilege." To be true to *Johnson* and its progeny, there must be examination into the knowing and understanding nature of the waiver, an examination that was designed for a trial judge in the structured atmosphere of a courtroom. * * * It would be unrealistic to expect that in the informal, unstructured context of a consent search, a policeman, upon pain of tainting the evidence obtained, could make the detailed type of examination demanded by *Johnson*. And, if for this reason a diluted form of "waiver" were found acceptable, that would itself be ample recognition of the fact that there is no universal standard that must be applied in every situation where a person forgoes a constitutional right.[33]

Similarly, a "waiver" approach to consent searches would be thoroughly inconsistent with our decisions that have approved "third party consents." [I]t is inconceivable that the Constitution could countenance the waiver of a defendant's right to counsel by a third party, or that a waiver could be found because a trial judge reasonably though mistakenly believed a defendant had waived his right to plead not guilty. * * *

Much of what has already been said disposes of the argument that the Court's decision in the *Miranda* case requires the conclusion that knowledge of a right to refuse is an indispensable element of a valid consent. The considerations that informed the Court's holding in *Miranda* are simply inapplicable in the present

---

[33] It seems clear that even a limited view of the demands of "an intentional relinquishment or abandonment of a known right or privilege" standard would inevitably lead to a requirement of detailed warnings before any consent search—a requirement all but universally rejected to date. As the Court stated in *Miranda* with respect to the privilege against compulsory self-incrimination: "[W]e will not pause to inquire in individual cases whether the defendant was aware of his rights without a warning being given. Assessments of the knowledge the defendant possessed, based on information as to his age, education, intelligence, or prior contact with authorities, can never be more than speculation; a warning is a clearcut fact."

case. In *Miranda* the Court found that the techniques of police questioning and the nature of custodial surroundings produce an inherently coercive situation. The Court concluded that "[u]nless adequate protective devices are employed to dispel the compulsion inherent in custodial surroundings, no statement obtained from the defendant can truly be the product of his free choice." And at another point the Court noted that "without proper safeguards the process of in-custody interrogation of persons suspected or accused of crime contains inherently compelling pressures which work to undermine the individual's will to resist and to compel him to speak where he would not otherwise do so freely."

In this case there is no evidence of any inherently coercive tactics—either from the nature of the police questioning or the environment in which it took place. Indeed, since consent searches will normally occur on a person's own familiar territory, the spectre of incommunicado police interrogation in some remote station house is simply inapposite. There is no reason to believe, under circumstances such as are present here, that the response to a policeman's question is presumptively coerced; and there is, therefore, no reason to reject the traditional test for determining the voluntariness of a person's response. *Miranda,* of course, did not reach investigative questioning of a person not in custody, which is most directly analogous to the situation of a consent search, and it assuredly did not indicate that such questioning ought to be deemed inherently coercive.

It is also argued that the failure to require the Government to establish knowledge as a prerequisite to a valid consent, will relegate the Fourth Amendment to the special province of "the sophisticated, the knowledgeable, and the privileged." We cannot agree. The traditional definition of voluntariness we accept today has always taken into account evidence of minimal schooling, low intelligence, and the lack of any effective warnings to a person of his rights; and the voluntariness of any statement taken under those conditions has been carefully scrutinized to determine whether it was in fact voluntarily given.

Our decision today is a narrow one. We hold only that when the subject of a search is not in custody and the State attempts to justify a search on the basis of his consent, the Fourth and Fourteenth Amendments require that it demonstrate that the consent was in fact voluntarily given, and not the result of duress or coercion, express or implied.[b] Voluntariness is a question of fact to be determined from all the circumstances, and while the subject's knowledge of a right to refuse

---

[b] The standard for measuring the scope of a suspect's consent, the Court concluded in *Florida v. Jimeno,* 500 U.S. 248 (1991), is neither the suspect's intent nor the officer's perception thereof but rather "that of 'objective' reasonableness—what would the typical reasonable person have understood by the exchange between the officer and the suspect?" Given the officer's statement in *Jimeno* that he would be looking for narcotics, "it was objectively reasonable for the police to conclude that the general consent to search respondent's car included consent to search containers within that car which might bear drugs." But, the nature of the container is also relevant. "It is very likely unreasonable to think that a suspect, by consenting to the search of his trunk, has agreed to the breaking open of a locked briefcase within the trunk, but it is otherwise with respect to a closed paper bag."

is a factor to be taken into account, the prosecution is not required to demonstrate such knowledge as a prerequisite to establishing a voluntary consent.[c]

JUSTICE MARSHALL, dissenting.

* * * The Court assumes that the issue in this case is, what are the standards by which courts are to determine that consent is voluntarily given? It then imports into the law of search and seizure standards developed to decide entirely different questions about coerced confessions.

The Fifth Amendment, in terms, provides that no person "shall be compelled in any criminal case to be a witness against himself." Nor is the interest protected by the Due Process Clause of the Fourteenth Amendment any different. The inquiry in a case where a confession is challenged as having been elicited in an unconstitutional manner is, therefore, whether the behavior of the police amounted to compulsion of the defendant. * * *

In contrast, this case deals not with "coercion," but with "consent," a subtly different concept to which different standards have been applied in the past. Freedom from coercion is a substantive right, guaranteed by the Fifth and Fourteenth Amendments. Consent, however, is a mechanism by which substantive requirements, otherwise applicable, are avoided. * * * Thus, consent searches are permitted not because such an exception to the requirements of probable cause and warrant is essential to proper law enforcement, but because we permit our citizens to choose whether or not they wish to exercise their constitutional rights. Our prior decisions simply do not support the view that a meaningful choice has been made solely because no coercion was brought to bear on the subject. * * *

If consent to search means that a person has chosen to forego his right to exclude the police from the place they seek to search, it follows that his consent cannot be considered a meaningful choice unless he knew that he could in fact exclude the police. * * * I would therefore hold, at a minimum, that the prosecution may not rely on a purported consent to search if the subject of the search did not know that he could refuse to give consent. Where the police claim authority to search yet in fact lack such authority, the subject does not know that he may permissibly refuse them entry, and it is this lack of knowledge that invalidates the consent. * * *

The burden on the prosecutor would disappear, of course, if the police, at the time they requested consent to search, also told the subject that he had a right to refuse consent and thus his decision to refuse would be respected. The Court's

---

c Powell, J., joined by the Chief Justice and Rehnquist, J., concurred on the ground "that federal collateral review of a state prisoner's Fourth Amendment claims—claims which rarely bear on innocence—should be confined solely to the question of whether the petitioner was provided a fair opportunity to raise and have adjudicated the question in state courts." Blackmun, J., concurred to express substantial agreement with the Powell opinion. Douglas, J., dissenting, would have remanded for a determination of whether Alcala knew he had the right to refuse. Brennan, J., dissenting, declared: "It wholly escapes me how our citizens can meaningfully be said to have waived something as precious as a constitutional guarantee without ever being aware of its existence."

assertions to the contrary notwithstanding, there is nothing impractical about this method of satisfying the prosecution's burden of proof. * * *

The Court contends that if an officer paused to inform the subject of his rights, the informality of the exchange would be destroyed. I doubt that a simple statement by an officer of an individual's right to refuse consent would do much to alter the informality of the exchange, except to alert the subject to a fact that he surely is entitled to know. It is not without significance that for many years the agents of the Federal Bureau of Investigation have routinely informed subjects of their right to refuse consent, when they request consent to search. The reported cases in which the police have informed subject of their right to refuse consent show, also, that the information can be given without disrupting the casual flow of events. What evidence there is, then, rather strongly suggests that nothing disastrous would happen if the police, before requesting consent, informed the subject that he had a right to refuse consent and that his refusal would be respected.[12]

I must conclude, with some reluctance, that when the Court speaks of practicality, what it really is talking of is the continued ability of the police to capitalize on the ignorance of citizens so as to accomplish by subterfuge what they could not achieve by relying only on the knowing relinquishment of constitutional rights. Of course it would be "practical" for the police to ignore the commands of the Fourth Amendment, if by practicality we mean that more criminals will be apprehended, even though the constitutional rights of innocent people also go by the boards. But such a practical advantage is achieved only at the cost of permitting the police to disregard the limitations that the Constitution places on their behavior, a cost that a constitutional democracy cannot long absorb. * * *

GEORGIA v. RANDOLPH
547 U.S. 103, 126 S.Ct. 1515, 164 L.Ed.2d 208 (2006).

JUSTICE SOUTER delivered the opinion of the Court.

[When police responded to a domestic dispute,] Janet Randolph * * * complain[ed] about her husband's drug use, but also volunteered that there were " 'items of drug evidence' " in the house. Sergeant Murray asked Scott Randolph for permission to search the house, which he unequivocally refused.

The sergeant turned to Janet Randolph for consent to search, which she readily gave. She led the officer upstairs to a bedroom that she identified as Scott's, where the sergeant noticed a section of a drinking straw with a powdery residue he suspected was cocaine. He then left the house to get an evidence bag from his

---

[12] The Court's suggestion that it would be "unrealistic" to require the officers to make "the detailed type of examination" involved when a court considers whether a defendant has waived a trial right, deserves little comment. The question before us relates to the inquiry to be made in court when the prosecution seeks to establish that consent was given. I therefore do not address the Court's strained argument that one may waive constitutional rights without making a knowing and intentional choice so long as the rights do not relate to the fairness of a criminal trial. I would suggest, however, that that argument is fundamentally inconsistent with the law of unconstitutional conditions.

car and to call the district attorney's office, which instructed him to stop the search and apply for a warrant. When Sergeant Murray returned to the house, Janet Randolph withdrew her consent. The police took the straw to the police station, along with the Randolphs. After getting a search warrant, they returned to the house and seized further evidence of drug use, on the basis of which Scott Randolph was indicted for possession of cocaine.

He moved to suppress the evidence, as products of a warrantless search of his house unauthorized by his wife's consent over his express refusal. The trial court denied the motion, ruling that Janet Randolph had common authority to consent to the search.

The Court of Appeals of Georgia reversed. * * * It held that an individual who chooses to live with another assumes a risk no greater than " 'an inability to control access to the premises during [his] absence,' " (quoting 3 W. LaFave, *Search and Seizure* § 8.3(d), p. 731 (3d ed.1996)), and does not contemplate that his objection to a request to search commonly shared premises, if made, will be overlooked.

We granted certiorari to resolve a split of authority on whether one occupant may give law enforcement effective consent to search shared premises, as against a co-tenant who is present and states a refusal to permit the search. We now affirm.

To the Fourth Amendment rule ordinarily prohibiting the warrantless entry of a person's house as unreasonable *per se,* one "jealously and carefully drawn" exception recognizes the validity of searches with the voluntary consent of an individual possessing authority. That person might be the householder against whom evidence is sought, or a fellow occupant who shares common authority over property, when the suspect is absent, [*United States] v. Matlock,* 415 U.S. 164 (1974), and the exception for consent extends even to entries and searches with the permission of a co-occupant whom the police reasonably, but erroneously, believe to possess shared authority as an occupant, *Illinois v. Rodriguez,* [497 U.S. 177 (1990)].[c] None of our co-occupant consent-to-search cases, however, has presented the further fact of a second occupant physically present and refusing permission to search, and later moving to suppress evidence so obtained. The significance of such a refusal turns on the underpinnings of the co-occupant consent rule, as recognized since *Matlock.*

The defendant in that case was arrested in the yard of a house where he lived with a Mrs. Graff and several of her relatives, and was detained in a squad car parked nearby. When the police went to the door, Mrs. Graff admitted them and consented to a search of the house. In resolving the defendant's objection to use of the evidence taken in the warrantless search, we said that "the consent of one who possesses common authority over premises or effects is valid as against the absent, nonconsenting person with whom that authority is shared." Consistent with our prior understanding that Fourth Amendment rights are not limited by the law of

---

[c] As the Court explained in *Rodriguez*: "The Constitution is no more violated when officers enter without a warrant because they reasonably (though erroneously) believe that the person who has consented to their entry is a resident of the premises, than it is violated when they enter without a warrant because they reasonably (though erroneously) believed they are in pursuit of a violent felon who is about to escape."

property, we explained that the third party's "common authority" is not synonymous with a technical property interest:

> "The authority which justified the third-party consent does not rest upon the law of property, with its attendant historical and legal refinement, but rests rather on mutual use of the property by persons generally having joint access or control for most purposes, so that it is reasonable to recognize that any of the co-inhabitants has the right to permit the inspection in his own right and that the others have assumed the risk that one of their number might permit the common area to be searched."
> * * *

The constant element in assessing Fourth Amendment reasonableness in the consent cases, then, is the great significance given to widely shared social expectations, which are naturally enough influenced by the law of property, but not controlled by its rules. * * *

Matlock's example of common understanding is readily apparent. When someone comes to the door of a domestic dwelling with a baby at her hip, as Mrs. Graff did, she shows that she belongs there, and that fact standing alone is enough to tell a law enforcement officer or any other visitor that if she occupies the place along with others, she probably lives there subject to the assumption tenants usually make about their common authority when they share quarters. They understand that any one of them may admit visitors, with the consequence that a guest obnoxious to one may nevertheless be admitted in his absence by another. As *Matlock* put it, shared tenancy is understood to include an "assumption of risk," on which police officers are entitled to rely, and although some group living together might make an exceptional arrangement that no one could admit a guest without the agreement of all, the chance of such an eccentric scheme is too remote to expect visitors to investigate a particular household's rules before accepting an invitation to come in. So, *Matlock* relied on what was usual and placed no burden on the police to eliminate the possibility of atypical arrangements, in the absence of reason to doubt that the regular scheme was in place.

It is also easy to imagine different facts on which, if known, no common authority could sensibly be suspected. A person on the scene who identifies himself, say, as a landlord or a hotel manager calls up no customary understanding of authority to admit guests without the consent of the current occupant. * * * And when it comes to searching through bureau drawers, there will be instances in which even a person clearly belonging on premises as an occupant may lack any perceived authority to consent; "a child of eight might well be considered to have the power to consent to the police crossing the threshold into that part of the house where any caller, such as a pollster or salesman, might well be admitted," 4 LaFave § 8.4(c), at 207 (4th ed.2004), but no one would reasonably expect such a child to be in a position to authorize anyone to rummage through his parents' bedroom. * * *

[I]t is fair to say that a caller standing at the door of shared premises would have no confidence that one occupant's invitation was a sufficiently good reason to enter when a fellow tenant stood there saying, "stay out." Without some very good reason, no sensible person would go inside under those conditions. Fear for the safety of the occupant issuing the invitation, or of someone else inside, would be thought to justify entry, but the justification then would be the personal risk, the threats to life or limb, not the disputed invitation.

The visitor's reticence without some such good reason would show not timidity but a realization that when people living together disagree over the use of their common quarters, a resolution must come through voluntary accommodation, not by appeals to authority. Unless the people living together fall within some recognized hierarchy, like a household of parent and child or barracks housing military personnel of different grades, there is no societal understanding of superior and inferior, a fact reflected in a standard formulation of domestic property law, that "[e]ach cotenant . . . has the right to use and enjoy the entire property as if he or she were the sole owner, limited only by the same right in the other cotenants." * * * In sum, there is no common understanding that one co-tenant generally has a right or authority to prevail over the express wishes of another, whether the issue is the color of the curtains or invitations to outsiders.

Since the co-tenant wishing to open the door to a third party has no recognized authority in law or social practice to prevail over a present and objecting co-tenant, his disputed invitation, without more, gives a police officer no better claim to reasonableness in entering than the officer would have in the absence of any consent at all. Accordingly, in the balancing of competing individual and governmental interests entailed by the bar to unreasonable searches, the cooperative occupant's invitation adds nothing to the government's side to counter the force of an objecting individual's claim to security against the government's intrusion into his dwelling place.

Disputed permission is thus no match for this central value of the Fourth Amendment, and the State's other countervailing claims do not add up to outweigh it. Yes, we recognize the consenting tenant's interest as a citizen in bringing criminal activity to light * * *. And we understand a co-tenant's legitimate self-interest in siding with the police to deflect suspicion raised by sharing quarters with a criminal * * *.

But society can often have the benefit of these interests without relying on a theory of consent that ignores an inhabitant's refusal to allow a warrantless search. The co-tenant acting on his own initiative may be able to deliver evidence to the police, and can tell the police what he knows, for use before a magistrate in getting a warrant.[6] The reliance on a co-tenant's information instead of disputed consent

---

[6] Sometimes, of course, the very exchange of information like this in front of the objecting inhabitant may render consent irrelevant by creating an exigency that justifies immediate action on the police's part; if the objecting tenant cannot be incapacitated from destroying easily disposable evidence during the time required to get a warrant, a fairly perceived need to act on the spot to preserve evidence may justify entry and search under the exigent circumstances exception to the warrant requirement.

Additional exigent circumstances might justify warrantless searches. See, *e.g.*, *Warden, Md. Penitentiary v. Hayden*, 387 U.S. 294 (1967) (hot pursuit); *Chimel v. California*, 395 U.S. 752 (1969) (protecting the safety of the police officers); *Michigan v. Tyler*, 436 U.S. 499 (1978) (imminent destruction to building); *Johnson v. United States*, 333 U.S. 10 (1948) (likelihood that suspect will imminently flee).

accords with the law's general partiality toward "police action taken under a warrant [as against] searches and seizures without one."

Nor should this established policy of Fourth Amendment law be undermined by the principal dissent's claim that it shields spousal abusers and other violent co-tenants who will refuse to allow the police to enter a dwelling when their victims ask the police for help, [as] this case has no bearing on the capacity of the police to protect domestic victims. The dissent's argument rests on the failure to distinguish two different issues: when the police may enter without committing a trespass, and when the police may enter to search for evidence. No question has been raised, or reasonably could be, about the authority of the police to enter a dwelling to protect a resident from domestic violence; so long as they have good reason to believe such a threat exists, it would be silly to suggest that the police would commit a tort by entering, say, to give a complaining tenant the opportunity to collect belongings and get out safely, or to determine whether violence (or threat of violence) has just occurred or is about to (or soon will) occur, however much a spouse or other co-tenant objected. * * * Thus, the question whether the police might lawfully enter over objection in order to provide any protection that might be reasonable is easily answered yes. See 4 LaFave § 8.3(d), at 161 ("[E]ven when . . . two persons quite clearly have equal rights in the place, as where two individuals are sharing an apartment on an equal basis, there may nonetheless sometimes exist a basis for giving greater recognition to the interests of one over the other. . . . [W]here the defendant has victimized the third-party . . . the emergency nature of the situation is such that the third-party consent should validate a warrantless search despite defendant's objections"). The undoubted right of the police to enter in order to protect a victim, however, has nothing to do with the question in this case, whether a search with the consent of one co-tenant is good against another, standing at the door and expressly refusing consent. * * *

The dissent's red herring aside, we know, of course, that alternatives to disputed consent will not always open the door to search for evidence that the police suspect is inside. The consenting tenant may simply not disclose enough information, or information factual enough, to add up to a showing of probable cause, and there may be no exigency to justify fast action. But nothing in social custom or its reflection in private law argues for placing a higher value on delving into private premises to search for evidence in the face of disputed consent, than on requiring clear justification before the government searches private living quarters over a resident's objection. We therefore hold that a warrantless search of a shared dwelling for evidence over the express refusal of consent by a physically present resident cannot be justified as reasonable as to him on the basis of consent given to the police by another resident.

There are two loose ends, the first being the explanation given in *Matlock* for the constitutional sufficiency of a co-tenant's consent to enter and search: it "rests . . . on mutual use of the property by persons generally having joint access or control for most purposes, so that it is reasonable to recognize that any of the co-inhabitants has the right to permit the inspection in his own right. . . ." If *Matlock*'s co-tenant is giving permission "in his own right," how can his "own right" be eliminated by another tenant's objection? The answer appears in the very footnote from which the quoted statement is taken: the "right" to admit the police to which *Matlock* refers is not an enduring and enforceable ownership right as understood by the private law of property, but is instead the authority recognized by customary social usage as having a substantial bearing on Fourth Amendment reasonableness in specific circumstances. Thus, to ask whether the consenting tenant has the right to admit the police when a physically present fellow tenant objects is not to question whether some property right may be divested by the mere objection of another. It is, rather, the question whether customary social understanding accords the consenting tenant authority powerful enough to prevail over the co-tenant's objection. The *Matlock* Court did not purport to answer this question, a point made clear by another statement (which the dissent does not quote): the Court described the co-tenant's consent as good against "the absent, nonconsenting resident."

The second loose end is the significance of *Matlock* and *Rodriguez* after today's decision. Although the *Matlock* defendant was not present with the opportunity to object, he was in a squad car not far away; the *Rodriguez* defendant was actually asleep in the apartment, and the police might have roused him with a knock on the door before they entered with only the consent of an apparent co-tenant. If those cases are not to be undercut by today's holding, we have to admit that we are drawing a fine line; if a potential defendant with self-interest in objecting is in fact at the door and objects, the co-tenant's permission does not suffice for a reasonable search, whereas the potential objector, nearby but not invited to take part in the threshold colloquy, loses out.

This is the line we draw, and we think the formalism is justified. So long as there is no evidence that the police have removed the potentially objecting tenant from the entrance for the sake of avoiding a possible objection,[d] there is practical

---

d   Consider *Fernandez v. California*, 571 U.S. 292 (2014), where police saw a robbery suspect run into a building and then heard screams coming from one of the apartments therein. Roxanne Rojas, who appeared to be battered and bleeding, answered the door, and when officers indicated they wanted to conduct a protective sweep Fernandez came to the door and objected. Officers removed him from the apartment and placed him under arrest; he was then identified as the robber and taken to the station. About an hour later police returned to the apartment and obtained Rojas' consent to search, and items linking Fernandez to the robbery were found within; they were admitted at a trial resulting in his conviction, which was affirmed on an appeal subsequently affirmed by the Supreme Court (6–3) per Alito, J.

In responding to Fernandez's reliance upon the above language in *Randolph*, the Court stated: "The *Randolph* dictum is best understood not to require an inquiry into the subjective intent of officers who detain or arrest a potential objector but instead to refer to situations in which the removal of the potential objector is not objectively reasonable," as "our Fourth Amendment cases 'have repeatedly rejected' a subjective approach. [O]nce it is recognized that the test is one of objective reasonableness, petitioner's argument collapses. He does not contest the fact that the police had reasonable grounds for removing him from the apartment so that they could speak with Rojas, an apparent victim of domestic violence, outside of petitioner's potentially intimidating presence. In fact, he does not even contest the existence of probable cause to place him under arrest. We therefore hold that an occupant who is absent due to a lawful detention or arrest stands in the same shoes as an occupant who is absent for any other reason."

Fernandez next argued "that his objection, made at the threshold of the premises that the police wanted to search, remained effective until he changed his mind and withdrew his objection," to which the Court first responded that this position could not be squared with the analysis in *Randolph*, as the "calculus of the hypothetical caller" discussed there "would likely be quite different if the objecting tenant was not standing at the door." Moreover, such an approach "would produce a plethora of practical problems" (e.g., as to how long the objection could reasonably

value in the simple clarity of complementary rules, one recognizing the co-tenant's permission when there is no fellow occupant on hand, the other according dispositive weight to the fellow occupant's contrary indication when he expresses it. For the very reason that *Rodriguez* held it would be unjustifiably impractical to require the police to take affirmative steps to confirm the actual authority of a consenting individual whose authority was apparent, we think it would needlessly limit the capacity of the police to respond to ostensibly legitimate opportunities in the field if we were to hold that reasonableness required the police to take affirmative steps to find a potentially objecting co-tenant before acting on the permission they had already received. There is no ready reason to believe that efforts to invite a refusal would make a difference in many cases, whereas every co-tenant consent case would turn into a test about the adequacy of the police's efforts to consult with a potential objector. Better to accept the formalism of distinguishing *Matlock* from this case than to impose a requirement, time-consuming in the field and in the courtroom, with no apparent systemic justification. The pragmatic decision to accept the simplicity of this line is, moreover, supported by the substantial number of instances in which suspects who are asked for permission to search actually consent, albeit imprudently, a fact that undercuts any argument that the police should try to locate a suspected inhabitant because his denial of consent would be a foregone conclusion. * * *

JUSTICE ALITO took no part in the consideration or decision of this case.

JUSTICE STEVENS, concurring. * * * This case illustrates why even the most dedicated adherent to an approach to constitutional interpretation that places primary reliance on the search for original understanding would recognize the relevance of changes in our society. * * *

JUSTICE BREYER, concurring. * * *

If a possible abuse victim invites a responding officer to enter a home or consents to the officer's entry request, that invitation (or consent) itself could reflect the victim's fear about being left alone with an abuser. It could also indicate the availability of evidence, in the form of an immediate willingness to speak, that might not otherwise exist. In that context, an invitation (or consent) would provide

---

remain effective, how the objector's continuing "common authority" would be determined, and whether an effective objection could be made by one not present). The *Fernandez* majority thus concluded that *Randolph* "applies only where the objector is standing in the door saying 'stay out' when the officers propose to make a consent search."

Ginsburg, J., for the dissenters, objected: "The circumstances triggering 'the Fourth Amendment's traditional hostility to police entry into a home without a warrant' are at least as salient here as they were in *Randolph*. In both case, '[t]he search at issue was a search solely for evidence'; '[t]he objecting party,' while on the premises, 'made his objection [to police entry] known clearly and directly to the officers seeking to enter the [residence]'; and 'the officers might easily have secured the premises and sought a warrant permitting them to enter.' Here, moreover, with the objector in custody, there was scant danger to persons on the premises, or risk that evidence might be destroyed or concealed, pending request for, and receipt of, a warrant." As for the majority's "practical problems" argument, the dissenters noted that "reading *Randolph* to require continuous physical presence poses administrative difficulties of its own. Does an occupant's refusal to consent lose force as soon as she absents herself from the doorstep, even if only for a moment? Are the police free to enter the instant after the objector leaves the door to retire for a nap, answer the phone, use the bathroom, or speak to another officer outside?"

a special reason for immediate, rather than later, police entry. And, entry following invitation or consent by one party ordinarily would be reasonable even in the face of direct objection by the other. That being so, contrary to THE CHIEF JUSTICE's suggestion, today's decision will not adversely affect ordinary law enforcement practices. * * *

CHIEF JUSTICE ROBERTS, with whom JUSTICE SCALIA joins, dissenting. * * *

[T]he majority is confident in assuming—confident enough to incorporate its assumption into the Constitution—that an invited social guest who arrives at the door of a shared residence, and is greeted by a disagreeable co-occupant shouting " 'stay out,' " would simply go away. The Court observes that "no sensible person would go inside under those conditions," and concludes from this that the inviting co-occupant has no "authority" to insist on getting her way over the wishes of her co-occupant. But it seems equally accurate to say—based on the majority's conclusion that one does not have a right to prevail over the express wishes of his co-occupant—that the objector has no "authority" to insist on getting *his* way over his co-occupant's wish that her guest be admitted.

The fact is that a wide variety of differing social situations can readily be imagined, giving rise to quite different social expectations. A relative or good friend of one of two feuding roommates might well enter the apartment over the objection of the other roommate. The reason the invitee appeared at the door also affects expectations: A guest who came to celebrate an occupant's birthday, or one who had traveled some distance for a particular reason, might not readily turn away simply because of a roommate's objection. The nature of the place itself is also pertinent: Invitees may react one way if the feuding roommates share one room, differently if there are common areas from which the objecting roommate could readily be expected to absent himself. Altering the numbers might well change the social expectations: Invitees might enter if two of three co-occupants encourage them to do so, over one dissenter.

The possible scenarios are limitless, and slight variations in the fact pattern yield vastly different expectations about whether the invitee might be expected to enter or to go away. Such shifting expectations are not a promising foundation on which to ground a constitutional rule, particularly because the majority has no support for its basic assumption—that an invited guest encountering two disagreeing co-occupants would flee—beyond a hunch about how people would typically act in an atypical situation. * * *

A wide variety of often subtle social conventions may shape expectations about how we act when another shares with us what is otherwise private, and those conventions go by a variety of labels—courtesy, good manners, custom, protocol, even honor among thieves. The Constitution, however, protects not these but privacy, and once privacy has been shared, the shared information, documents, or places remain private only at the discretion of the confidant. * * *

Just as the source of the majority's rule is not privacy, so too the interest it protects cannot reasonably be described as such. That interest is not protected if a co-owner happens to be absent when the police arrive, in the backyard gardening, asleep in the next room, or listening to music through earphones so that only his co-occupant hears the knock on the door. That the rule is so random in its application confirms that it bears no real relation to the privacy protected by the Fourth Amendment. What the majority's rule protects is not so much privacy as the good luck of a co-owner who just happens to be present at the door when the police arrive. Usually when the development of Fourth Amendment jurisprudence leads to such arbitrary lines, we take it as a signal that the rules need to be rethought. We should not embrace a rule at the outset that its *sponsors* appreciate will result in drawing fine, formalistic lines. * * *

While the majority's rule protects something random, its consequences are particularly severe. The question presented often arises when innocent cotenants seek to disassociate or protect themselves from ongoing criminal activity. Under the majority's rule, there will be many cases in which a consenting co-occupant's wish to have the police enter is overridden by an objection from another present co-occupant. What does the majority imagine will happen, in a case in which the consenting co-occupant is concerned about the other's criminal activity, once the door clicks shut? The objecting co-occupant may pause briefly to decide whether to destroy any evidence of wrongdoing or to inflict retribution on the consenting co-occupant first, but there can be little doubt that he will attend to both in short order. It is no answer to say that the consenting co-occupant can depart with the police; remember that it is her home, too, and the other co-occupant's very presence, which allowed him to object, may also prevent the consenting co-occupant from doing more than urging the police to enter.

Perhaps the most serious consequence of the majority's rule is its operation in domestic abuse situations, a context in which the present question often arises. While people living together might typically be accommodating to the wishes of their cotenants, requests for police assistance may well come from coinhabitants who are having a disagreement. The Court concludes that because "no sensible person would go inside" in the face of disputed consent, and the consenting cotenant thus has "no recognized authority" to insist on the guest's admission, a "police officer [has] no better claim to reasonableness in entering than the officer would have in the absence of any consent at all." But the police officer's superior claim to enter is obvious: Mrs. Randolph did not invite the police to join her for dessert and coffee; the officer's precise purpose in knocking on the door was to assist with a dispute between the Randolphs—one in which Mrs. Randolph felt the need for the protective presence of the police. The majority's rule apparently forbids police from entering to assist with a domestic dispute if the abuser whose behavior prompted the request for police assistance objects.

The majority acknowledges these concerns, but dismisses them on the ground that its rule can be expected to give rise to exigent situations, and police can then rely on an exigent circumstances exception to justify entry. This is a strange way to justify a rule, and the fact that alternative justifications for entry might arise does not show that entry pursuant to consent is unreasonable. In addition, it is far from clear that an exception for emergency entries suffices to protect the safety of occupants in domestic disputes. See, *e.g.*, *United States v. Davis*, 290 F.3d 1239 (10th Cir.2002) (finding no exigent circumstances justifying entry when police responded to a report of domestic abuse, officers heard no noise upon arrival, defendant told officers that his wife was out of town, and wife then appeared at the door seemingly unharmed but resisted husband's efforts to close the door). * * *

JUSTICE SCALIA, dissenting.

I * * * add these few words in response to JUSTICE STEVENS' concurrence.

It is not as clear to me as it is to Justice STEVENS that, at the time the Fourth Amendment was adopted, a police officer could enter a married woman's home over her objection, and could not enter with only her consent. Nor is it clear to me that the answers to these questions depended solely on who owned the house. It is entirely clear, however, that *if* the matter *did* depend solely on property rights, a latter-day alteration of property rights would also produce a latter-day alteration of the Fourth Amendment outcome—without altering the Fourth Amendment itself. * * *

JUSTICE THOMAS, dissenting.

The Court has long recognized that "[i]t is an act of responsible citizenship for individuals to give whatever information they may have to aid in law enforcement." Consistent with this principle, the Court held in *Coolidge v. New Hampshire,* 403 U.S. 443 (1971), that no Fourth Amendment search occurs where, as here, the spouse of an accused voluntarily leads the police to potential evidence of wrongdoing by the accused. Because *Coolidge* squarely controls this case, the Court need not address whether police could permissibly have conducted a general search of the Randolph home, based on Mrs. Randolph's consent. I respectfully dissent. * * *

Review of the facts in *Coolidge* clearly demonstrates that it governs this case. While the police interrogated Coolidge as part of their investigation into a murder, two other officers were sent to his house to speak with his wife. During the course of questioning Mrs. Coolidge, the police asked whether her husband owned any guns. Mrs. Coolidge replied in the affirmative, and offered to retrieve the weapons for the police, apparently operating under the assumption that doing so would help to exonerate her husband. The police accompanied Mrs. Coolidge to the bedroom to collect the guns, as well as clothing that Mrs. Coolidge told them her husband had been wearing the night of the murder. * * *

CHAPTER 4

THE SCOPE OF THE EXCLUSIONARY RULE

■ ■ ■

In many cases, the police obtain evidence as a direct or primary result of an illegal arrest, search, or seizure. For example, the police find drugs as a result of an illegal search, and those drugs are suppressed pursuant to the exclusionary rule. *See supra* Chapter 3. Often, however, the police will also obtain evidence that is secondary or derivative in character. For example, the police may illegally arrest someone and then later obtain a confession from the suspect at the stationhouse. That confession, in turn, may direct them to important physical evidence. When is that secondary or derivative evidence "tainted" by the prior constitutional violation? Or, to use the phrase coined by Justice Frankfurter in *Nardone v. United States*, 308 U.S. 338 (1939), when is the secondary or derivative evidence a "fruit of the poisonous tree"? The first case in this section, *Wong Sun v. United States*, answers this question by explaining that much of the "fruit of the poisonous tree" analysis can be likened to causation inquiries. First, there is the question whether "but for" the illegal action in question the government would have discovered the evidence? The exclusionary rule has no application when the Government learned of the evidence from an independent source. This means that if the Fourth Amendment violation is not the "cause in fact" of the police discovering the challenged evidence, that evidence is not a fruit of the prior violation. A violation of a person's rights does not put him beyond the law's reach if his guilt can be established by evidence unconnected with or "untainted" by the violation.

A variation of the "independent source" exception is the "inevitable discovery" or "hypothetical independent source" rule. This doctrine differs from the independent source exception in that the question is not whether the police *actually* acquired certain evidence by reliance upon an untainted source, but whether evidence in fact obtained illegally would inevitably or eventually or probably have been discovered lawfully. If so, then it is not the police illegality in question that, in fact, caused the police to discover the evidence. They would have discovered it anyway.

In addition to these two "but for" causation inquiries, there is also a proximate causation analysis under the fruit of the poisonous tree doctrine. The discovery of evidence can become so attenuated in time, place, and circumstances from the initial Fourth Amendment violation as to dissipate the taint and result in the admission of the evidence.

After the *Wong Sun* case lays out this basic framework for analyzing the admissibility of derivative fruits, the subsequent cases further explain the proximate and but for causation inquiries. The *Brown v. Illinois, New York v.*

Harris, and *Utah v. Strieff* cases examine how the Supreme Court has developed the proximate cause part of the fruits inquiry. *Murray v. United States, Nix v. Williams,* and *Hudson v. Michigan* then explore the cause in fact or but for prong of the analysis and focus on the independent source and inevitable discovery doctrines.

1. INTRODUCTION

WONG SUN V. UNITED STATES
371 U.S. 471, 83 S.Ct. 407, 9 L.E.2d 441 (1963).

JUSTICE BRENNAN delivered the opinion of the Court.

[Six federal narcotics agents illegally broke into Toy's laundry and arrested him for violating federal narcotics laws. Toy then told the agents that Yee had been selling narcotics and that he and Yee had smoked some the night before. The agents immediately went to Yee's house, entered, and found Yee, who surrendered heroin to them and gave a statement implicating Toy and a third party, Wong Sun, in narcotics trafficking. Agents entered Wong Sun's home and arrested him. Toy, Yee, and Wong Sun were all arraigned before a commissioner on narcotics charges and released on their own recognizance. A few days later, they came to the office of the Narcotics Bureau where agents interrogated them after informing them of their right to withhold inculpatory information and to seek the advice of counsel. All three of them gave incriminating statements.]

[At Toy and Wong Sun's later trial, Yee was called as the Government's principal witness but he was excused after he invoked his privilege against self-incrimination and repudiated the statement that he had given. Instead the government relied on the statements Toy made in his home at the time of his arrest, the narcotics surrendered by Yee, Toy's later statement at the office of the Narcotics Bureau, and Wong Sun's statement at the office of the Narcotics Bureau. Toy and Wong Sun objected that all four pieces of evidence were inadmissible fruits of unlawful arrests and searches. The trial court denied their suppression motion and they were both convicted of violating federal narcotics laws. The Ninth Circuit, although recognizing that both petitioners' arrests were illegal because not based on probable cause, affirmed.]

[We agree with the Ninth Circuit that there was not probable cause to support Toy's arrest.] The exclusionary [rule] extends as well to the indirect as the direct products of [Fourth Amendment violations]. Mr. Justice Holmes, speaking for the Court in [*Silverthorne Lumber Co. v. United States,* 251 U.S. 385 (1920)], in holding that the Government might not make use of information obtained during an unlawful search to subpoena from the victims the very documents illegally viewed, expressed succinctly the policy of the broad exclusionary rule:

"The essence of a provision forbidding the acquisition of evidence in a certain way is that not merely evidence so acquired shall not be used before the Court but that it shall not be used at all. Of course this does not mean that the facts thus obtained become sacred and inaccessible. If knowledge of them is gained from an independent source they may be proved like any others, but the knowledge gained by the Government's own wrong cannot be used by it in the way proposed."

The exclusionary rule has traditionally barred from trial physical, tangible materials obtained either during or as a direct result of an unlawful invasion. [The] policies underlying the exclusionary rule [do not] invite any logical distinction between physical and verbal evidence. Either in terms of deterring lawless conduct by federal officers, or of closing the doors of the federal courts to any use of evidence unconstitutionally obtained, the danger in relaxing the exclusionary rules in the case of verbal evidence would seem too great to warrant introducing such a distinction.

The Government argues that Toy's statements to the officers in his bedroom [were] admissible because they resulted from "an intervening independent act of a free will." This contention, however, takes insufficient account of the circumstances. Six or seven officers had broken the door and followed on Toy's heels into the bedroom where his wife and child were sleeping. He had been almost immediately handcuffed and arrested. Under such circumstances it is unreasonable to infer that Toy's response was sufficiently an act of free will to purge the primary taint of the unlawful invasion.

[With respect to the drugs found at Yee's house, the Government] candidly told the trial court that "we wouldn't have found those drugs except that Mr. Toy helped us to." Hence this is not the case envisioned by this Court [in *Silverthorne Lumber Co.*] where the exclusionary rule has no application because the Government learned of the evidence "from an independent source." [Nor] is this a case in which the connection between the lawless conduct of the police and the discovery of the challenged evidence has "become so attenuated as to dissipate the taint." *Nardone v. United States*, 308 U.S. 338, 341 (1939). We need not hold that all evidence is "fruit of the poisonous tree" simply because it would not have come to light but for the illegal actions of the police. Rather, the more apt question in such a case is "whether, granting establishment of the primary illegality, the evidence to which instant objection is made has been come at by exploitation of that illegality or instead by means sufficiently distinguishable, to be purged of the primary taint." Maguire, *Evidence of Guilt,* 221 (1959). We think it clear that the narcotics were "come at by the exploitation of that illegality" and hence that they may not be used against Toy.

[Having determined that Toy's statement in his home and the narcotics found in Yee's house were inadmissible against Toy, the Court found it unnecessary to determine whether Toy's later statement at the Narcotics Bureau was a fruit of his illegal arrest because it held, based on evidentiary principles, that (a) Wong Sun's statement was inadmissible against Toy and (b) Toy's statement, standing alone, was not sufficient evidence to support his conviction.]

[With respect to Wong Sun, the Court also agreed with the Ninth Circuit that his arrest was illegally made without probable cause, but it held that] no evidentiary consequences turn upon that question. For Wong Sun's [confession] was not the fruit of that arrest, and was therefore properly admitted at trial. On the evidence that Wong Sun had been released on his own recognizance after a lawful arraignment, and had returned voluntarily several days later to make the statement, we hold that the connection between the arrest and the statement had "become so attenuated as to dissipate the taint."

[As for the narcotics surrendered by Yee,] that this ounce of heroin was inadmissible against Toy does not compel a like result with respect to Wong Sun. The exclusion of the narcotics as to Toy was required solely by their tainted relationship to information unlawfully obtained from Toy, and not by any official impropriety connected with their surrender by Yee. The seizure of this heroin invaded no right of privacy of person or premises which would entitle Wong Sun to object to its use at his trial.

[Even though Wong Sun's statement at the Narcotics Bureau and the narcotics found at Yee's house were admissible against Wong Sun, the Supreme Court reversed his conviction because it could not be sure that the trial court had not improperly considered Toy's statements, which were inadmissible against Wong Sun based on evidentiary rules, when determining Wong Sun's guilt.][a]

2. PROXIMATE CAUSE: ATTENUATION DOCTRINE

BROWN V. ILLINOIS
422 U.S. 590, 95 S.Ct. 2254, 45 L.E.2d 416 (1975).

JUSTICE BLACKMUN delivered the opinion of the Court.

[Roger Corpus was murdered and Corpus's brother told police that Richard Brown was one of Corpus's acquaintances. Police then broke into Brown's apartment and searched it without a warrant. When Brown arrived home during their search, they arrested him at gunpoint. They later testified that they made the arrest for the purpose of questioning Brown about the Corpus murder. Detectives took Brown to the police station, placed him in an interrogation room, and read him his *Miranda* rights. They informed him that they knew of an incident in a poolroom when Brown, angry at having been cheated at dice, fired a shot from a revolver into the ceiling. Brown answered: "Oh, you know about that." Police then informed him that a bullet had been obtained from the ceiling of the poolroom and had been taken to the crime laboratory to be compared with bullets taken from Corpus's body. Brown responded: "Oh, you know that, too."

At this point—it was about 8:45 p.m.—police asked Brown if he wanted to talk about the Corpus homicide. Petitioner answered that he did. For the next 20 to 25 minutes Brown answered questions implicating himself in the homicide. This questioning produced a two-page, inculpatory statement, which Brown signed. At about 2:00 a.m., the Assistant State's Attorney arrived, read Brown his *Miranda* rights, and obtained another incriminating statement from him. Brown was

---

[a] Justice Clark, joined by Justices Harlan, Stewart, and White dissented. With respect to Toy, they did not challenge the manner in which the Court applied the "fruits" doctrine, but maintained that Toy's arrest was lawful and thus provided "no 'poisonous tree' whose fruits we must evaluate." With respect to Wong Sun, they argued that there was sufficient evidence to affirm the conviction.

charged with murder and unsuccessfully moved to suppress both statements. He was convicted and sentenced to imprisonment for not less than 15 years nor more than 30 years. On appeal, the Supreme Court of Illinois affirmed the judgment of conviction, believing that the *Miranda* warnings had purged the taint of any earlier Fourth Amendment violation.]

Petitioner was arrested without probable cause and without a warrant. He was given, in full, the warnings prescribed by *Miranda v. Arizona*, 384 U.S. 436 (1966). Thereafter, while in custody, he made two inculpatory statements. The issue is whether evidence of those statements was properly admitted, or should have been excluded, in petitioner's subsequent trial for murder in state court. Expressed another way, the issue is whether the statements were to be excluded as the fruit of the illegal arrest, or were admissible because the giving of the *Miranda* warnings sufficiently attenuated the taint of the arrest. See *Wong Sun v. United States*, 371 U.S. 471 (1963). * * *

In order for the causal chain, between the illegal arrest and the statements made subsequent thereto, to be broken, *Wong Sun* requires . . . an act of free will to purge the primary taint. * * *

If *Miranda* warnings, by themselves, were held to attenuate the taint of an unconstitutional arrest, regardless of how wanton and purposeful the Fourth Amendment violation, the effect of the exclusionary rule would be substantially diluted. Arrests made without warrant or without probable cause, for questioning or "investigation," would be encouraged by the knowledge that evidence derived therefrom could well be made admissible at trial by the simple expendent of giving *Miranda* warnings. Any incentive to avoid Fourth Amendment violations would be eviscerated by making the warnings, in effect, a "cure-all," and the constitutional guarantee against unlawful searches and seizures could be said to be reduced to "a form of words."

It is entirely possible, of course, as the State here argues, that persons arrested illegally frequently may decide to confess, as an act of free will unaffected by the initial illegality. But the *Miranda* warnings, alone and per se, cannot always make the act sufficiently a product of free will be break, for Fourth Amendment purposes, the causal connection between the illegality and the confession. They cannot assure in every case that the Fourth Amendment violation has not been unduly exploited.

While we therefore reject the per se rule which the Illinois courts appear to have accepted, we also decline to adopt any alternative per se or "but for" rule. The petitioner himself professes not to demand so much. The question whether a confession is the product of a free will under *Wong Sun* must be answered on the facts of each case. No single fact is dispositive. The workings of the human mind are too complex, and the possibilities of misconduct too diverse, to permit protection of the Fourth Amendment to turn on such a talismanic test. The *Miranda* warnings are an important factor, to be sure, in determining whether the confession is obtained by exploitation of an illegal arrest. But they are not the only factor to be considered. The temporal proximity of the arrest and the confession, the presence of intervening circumstances, and, particularly, the purpose and flagrancy of the official misconduct are all relevant. . . . And the burden of showing admissibility rests, of course, on the prosecution.

[On the facts of the instant case, w]e conclude that the State failed to sustain the burden of showing that the evidence in question was admissible under *Wong Sun*.

Brown's first statement was separated from his illegal arrest by less than two hours, and there was no intervening event of significance whatsoever. In its essentials, his situation is remarkably like that of James Wah Toy in Wong Sun. We could hold Brown's first statement admissible only if we overrule *Wong Sun*. We decline to do so. And the second statement was clearly the result and the fruit of the first.

The illegality here, moreover, had a quality of purposefulness. The impropriety of the arrest was obvious; awareness of that fact was virtually conceded by the two detectives when they repeatedly acknowledged, in their testimony, that the purpose of their action was "for investigation" or for "questioning." The arrest, both in design and in execution, was investigatory. The detectives embarked upon this expedition for evidence in the hope that something might turn up. The manner in which Brown's arrest was affected gives the appearance of having been calculated to cause surprise, fright, and confusion.

We emphasize that our holding is a limited one. We decide only that the Illinois courts were in error in assuming that the *Miranda* warnings, by themselves, under *Wong Sun* always purge the taint of an illegal arrest.

The judgment of the Supreme Court of Illinois is reversed and the case is remanded for further proceedings not inconsistent with this opinion.

JUSTICE WHITE, concurring in the judgment.

Insofar as the Court holds (1) that despite *Miranda* warnings the Fourth and Fourteenth Amendments require the exclusion from evidence of statements obtained as the fruit of an arrest which the arresting officers knew or should have known was without probable cause and unconstitutional, and (2) that the statements obtained in this case were in this category, I am in agreement and therefore concur in the judgment.

JUSTICE POWELL, with whom JUSTICE REHNQUIST joins, concurring in part.

The Court's rejection in *Wong Sun* of a "but for" test, reaffirmed today, recognizes that in some circumstances strict adherence to the Fourth Amendment exclusionary rule imposes greater cost on the legitimate demands of law enforcement than can be justified by the rule's deterrent purposes. The notion of the "dissipation of the taint" attempts to mark the point at which the detrimental consequences of illegal police action become so attenuated that the deterrent effect of the exclusionary rule no longer justifies its cost. Application of the *Wong Sun* doctrine will generate fact-specific cases bearing distinct differences as well as similarities, and the question of attenuation inevitably is largely a matter of degree. The Court today identifies the general factors that the trial court must consider in making this determination. I think it appropriate, however, to attempt to articulate the possible relationships to those factors in particular, broad categories of cases.

All Fourth Amendment violations are, by constitutional definition, "unreasonable." There are, however, significant practical differences that distinguish among violations, differences that measurably assist in identifying the kinds of cases in which disqualifying the evidence is likely to serve the deterrent purposes of the exclusionary rule. In my view, the point at which the taint can be said to have dissipated should be related, in the absence of other controlling circumstances, to the nature of that taint.

That police have not succeeded in coercing the accused's confession through willful or negligent misuse of the power of arrest does not remove the fact that they may have tried. The impermissibility of the attempt, and the extent to which such attempts can be deterred by the use of the exclusionary rule, are of primary relevance in determining whether exclusion is an appropriate remedy. The basic purpose of the rule, briefly stated, is to remove possible motivations for illegal arrests. Given this purpose the notion of voluntariness has practical value in deciding whether the rule should apply to statements removed from the immediate circumstances of the illegal arrest. If an illegal arrest merely provides the occasion of initial contact between the police and the accused, and because of time or other intervening factors the accused's eventual statement is the product of his own reflection and free will, application of the exclusionary rule can serve little purpose: the police normally will not make an illegal arrest in the hope of eventually obtaining such a truly volunteered statement. In a similar manner, the role of the *Miranda* warnings in the *Wong Sun* inquiry is indirect. To the extent that they dissipate the psychological pressures of custodial interrogation, *Miranda* warnings serve to assure that the accused's decision to make a statement has been relatively unaffected by the preceding illegal arrest. Correspondingly, to the extent that the police perceive *Miranda* warnings to have this equalizing potential, their motivation to abuse the power of arrest is diminished. Bearing these considerations in mind, and recognizing that the deterrent value of the Fourth Amendment exclusionary rule is limited to certain kinds of police conduct, the following general categories can be identified.

Those most readily identifiable are on the extremes: the flagrantly abusive violation of Fourth Amendment rights, on the one hand, and "technical" Fourth Amendment violations, on the other. In my view, these extremes call for significantly different judicial responses.

I would require the clearest indication of attenuation in cases in which official conduct was flagrantly abusive of Fourth Amendment rights. If, for example, the factors relied on by the police in determining to make the arrest were so lacking in indicia of probable cause as to render official belief in its existence entirely unreasonable, or if the evidence clearly suggested that the arrest was effectuated as a pretext for collateral objectives, or the physical circumstances of the arrest unnecessarily intrusive on personal privacy, I would consider the equalizing potential of *Miranda* warnings rarely sufficient to dissipate the taint. In such cases the deterrent value of the exclusionary rule is most likely to be effective, and the corresponding mandate to preserve judicial integrity, most clearly demands that the fruits of official misconduct be denied. I thus would require some demonstrably effective break in the chain of events leading from the illegal arrest to the statement, such as actual consultation with counsel or the accused's presentation before a magistrate for a determination of probable cause, before the taint can be deemed removed.

At the opposite end of the spectrum lie "technical" violations of Fourth Amendment rights * * *. "The deterrent purpose of the exclusionary rule necessarily assumes that the police have engaged in willful, or at the very least negligent, conduct which has deprived the defendant of some right." In cases in which this underlying premise is lacking, the deterrence rationale of the exclusionary rule does not obtain, and I can see no legitimate justification for depriving the prosecution of reliable and probative evidence. Thus, with the exception of statements given in the immediate circumstances of the illegal arrest—a constraint I think is imposed by existing exclusionary-rule law—I would not require more than proof that effective *Miranda* warnings were given and that the ensuing statement was voluntary in the Fifth Amendment sense. Absent aggravating circumstances, I would consider a statement given at the station house after one has been advised of *Miranda* rights to be sufficiently removed from the immediate circumstances of the illegal arrest to justify its admission at trial.

Between these extremes lies a wide range of situations that defy ready categorization, and I will not attempt to embellish on the factors set forth in the Court's opinion other than to emphasize that the *Wong Sun* inquiry always should be conducted with the deterrent purpose of the Fourth Amendment exclusionary rule sharply in focus. And, in view of the inevitably fact-specific nature of the inquiry, we must place primary reliance on the "learning, good sense, fairness and courage" of judges who must make the determination in the first instance.

On the facts of record as I view them, it is possible that the police may have believed reasonably that there was probable cause for petitioner's arrest. * * * The trial court made no determination as to whether probable cause existed for petitioner's arrest. I therefore would remand for reconsideration with directions to conduct such further factual inquiries as may be necessary to resolve the admissibility issue.[a]

---

[a] The Supreme Court has reaffirmed its view that the *Miranda* warnings, by themselves are not necessarily sufficient to attenuate the taint of an unconstitutional arrest. *See Kaupp v. Texas*, 538 U.S. 626 (2003); *Taylor v. Alabama*, 457 U.S. 687 (1982); *Dunaway v. New York*, 442 U.S. 200 (1979). In *Taylor*, a 5–4 majority held that petitioner's confession was the impermissible fruit of his illegal arrest even though (a) six hours had elapsed between the illegal arrest and the time petitioner confessed; (b) petitioner was advised of his rights three times; and (c) he was allowed to visit briefly with his girlfriend and his neighbor shortly before he confessed.

NEW YORK V. HARRIS

495 U.S. 14, 110 S.Ct. 1640, 109 L.E.2d 13 (1990).

JUSTICE WHITE delivered the opinion of the Court.

On January 11, 1984, New York City police found the body of Ms. Thelma Staton murdered in her apartment. Various facts gave the officers probable cause to believe that the respondent in this case, Bernard Harris, had killed Ms. Staton. As a result, on January 16, 1984, three police officers went to Harris' apartment to take him into custody. They did not first obtain an arrest warrant.

When the police arrived, they knocked on the door, displaying their guns and badges. Harris let them enter. Once inside, the officers read Harris his rights under *Miranda v. Arizona.* Harris acknowledged that he understood the warnings, and agreed to answer the officers' questions. At that point, he reportedly admitted that he had killed Ms. Staton.

Harris was arrested, taken to the station house, and again informed of his *Miranda* rights. He then signed a written inculpatory statement. The police subsequently read Harris the *Miranda* warnings a third time and videotaped an incriminating interview between Harris and a district attorney, even though Harris had indicated that he wanted to end the interrogation.

The trial court suppressed Harris' first and third statements; the State does not challenge those rulings. The sole issue in this case is whether Harris' second statement—the written statement made at the station house—should have been suppressed because the police, by entering Harris' home without a warrant and without his consent, violated *Payton v. New York,* 445 U.S. 573 (1980) [discussed *supra* p. 222], which held that the Fourth Amendment prohibits the police from effecting a warrantless and nonconsensual entry into a suspect's home in order to make a routine felony arrest.

For present purposes, we accept the finding below that Harris did not consent to the police officers' entry into his home and the conclusion that the police had probable cause to arrest him. It is also evident, in light of *Payton,* that arresting Harris in his home without an arrest warrant violated the Fourth Amendment. But, as emphasized in earlier cases, "we have declined to adopt a '*per se* or "but for" rule' that would make inadmissible any evidence, whether tangible or live-witness testimony, which somehow came to light through a chain of causation that began with an illegal arrest." Rather, in this context, we have stated that "[t]he penalties visited upon the Government, and in turn upon the public, because its officers have violated the law must bear some relation to the purposes which the law is to serve." In light of these principles, we decline to apply the exclusionary rule in this context because the rule in *Payton* was designed to protect the physical integrity of the home; it was not intended to grant criminal suspects, like Harris, protection for statements made outside their premises where the police have probable cause to arrest the suspect for committing a crime.

Payton itself emphasized that our holding in that case stemmed from the "overriding respect for the sanctity of the home that has been embedded in our traditions since the origins of the Republic." Although it had long been settled that a warrantless arrest in a public place was permissible as long as the arresting officer had probable cause, see *United States v. Watson,* 423 U.S. 411 (1976) [discussed *supra* p. 176], *Payton* nevertheless drew a line at the entrance to the home. This special solicitude was necessary because " 'physical entry of the home is the chief evil against which the wording of the Fourth Amendment is directed.' " The arrest warrant was required to "interpose the magistrate's determination of probable cause" to arrest before the officers could enter a house to effect an arrest.

Nothing in the reasoning of that case suggests that an arrest in a home without a warrant but with probable cause somehow renders unlawful continued custody of the suspect once he is removed from the house. There could be no valid claim here that Harris was immune from prosecution because his person was the fruit of an illegal arrest. *United States v. Crews,* 445 U.S. 463 (1980).[a] Nor is there any claim that the warrantless arrest required the police to release Harris or that Harris could not be immediately rearrested if momentarily released. Because the officers had probable cause to arrest Harris for a crime, Harris was not unlawfully in custody when he was removed to the station house, given *Miranda* warnings, and allowed to talk. For Fourth Amendment purposes, the legal issue is the same as it would be had the police arrested Harris on his doorstep, illegally entered his home to search for evidence, and later interrogated Harris at the station house. Similarly, if the police had made a warrantless entry into Harris' home, not found him there, but arrested him on the street when he returned, a later statement made by him after proper warnings would no doubt be admissible.

This case is therefore different from *Brown v. Illinois, Dunaway v. New York,* and *Taylor v. Alabama.* In each of those cases, evidence obtained from a criminal defendant following arrest was suppressed because the police lacked probable cause. The three cases stand for the familiar proposition that the indirect fruits of an illegal search or arrest should be suppressed when they bear a sufficiently close relationship to the underlying illegality. We have emphasized, however, that attenuation analysis is only appropriate where, as a threshold matter, courts determine that "the challenged evidence is in some sense the product of illegal governmental activity." *United States v. Crews.* * * *

Harris' statement taken at the police station was not the product of being in unlawful custody. Neither was it the fruit of having been arrested in the home rather than someplace else. The case is analogous to *United States v. Crews, supra.* In that case, we refused to suppress a victim's in-court identification despite the defendant's illegal arrest. The Court found that the evidence was not " 'come at by exploitation' of . . . the defendant's Fourth Amendment rights," and that it was not necessary to inquire whether the "taint" of the Fourth Amendment violation was sufficiently attenuated to permit the introduction of the evidence. Here, likewise, the police had a justification to question Harris prior to his arrest; therefore, his subsequent statement was not an exploitation of the illegal entry into Harris' home. * * *

The warrant requirement for an arrest in the home is imposed to protect the home, and anything incriminating the police gathered from arresting Harris in his

---

[a] In *Crews,* the Court held that a defendant is not a suppressible fruit.

home, rather than elsewhere, has been excluded, as it should have been; the purpose of the rule has thereby been vindicated. * * * Even though we decline to suppress statements made outside the home following a *Payton* violation, the principal incentive to obey *Payton* still obtains: the police know that a warrantless entry will lead to the suppression of any evidence found, or statements taken, inside the home. If we did suppress statements like Harris', moreover, the incremental deterrent value would be minimal. Given that the police have probable cause to arrest a suspect in Harris' position, they need not violate *Payton* in order to interrogate the suspect. It is doubtful therefore that the desire to secure a statement from a criminal suspect would motivate the police to violate *Payton*. As a result, suppressing a station house statement obtained after a *Payton* violation will have little effect on the officers' actions, one way or another.

We hold that, where the police have probable cause to arrest a suspect, the exclusionary rule does not bar the State's use of a statement made by the defendant outside of his home, even though the statement is taken after an arrest made in the home in violation of *Payton*.

JUSTICE MARSHALL, with whom JUSTICE BRENNAN, JUSTICE BLACKMUN, and JUSTICE STEVENS join, dissenting.

[W]e have identified several factors as relevant to the issue of attenuation: the length of time between the arrest and the statement, the presence of intervening circumstances, and the "purpose and flagrancy" of the violation. See, *e.g., Brown.* * * *

An application of the *Brown* factors to this case compels the conclusion that Harris' statement at the station house must be suppressed. About an hour elapsed between the illegal arrest and Harris' confession, without any intervening factor other than the warnings required by *Miranda.* This Court has held, however, that "*Miranda* warnings, *alone* and *per se,* . . . cannot assure in every case that the Fourth Amendment violation has not been unduly exploited." *Brown.* Indeed, in *Brown,* we held that a statement made almost *two* hours after an illegal arrest, and after *Miranda* warnings had been given, was not sufficiently removed from the violation so as to dissipate the taint.

As to the flagrancy of the violation, petitioner does not dispute that the officers were aware that the Fourth Amendment prohibited them from arresting Harris in his home without a warrant. Notwithstanding the officers' knowledge that a warrant is required for a routine arrest in the home, "the police went to defendant's apartment to arrest him and, as the police conceded, if defendant refused to talk to them there they intended to take him into custody for questioning. Nevertheless, they made no attempt to obtain a warrant although five days had elapsed between the killing and the arrest and they had developed evidence of probable cause early in their investigation. Indeed, one of the officers testified that it was departmental policy not to get warrants before making arrests in the home. From this statement a reasonable inference can be drawn . . . that the department's policy was a device used to avoid restrictions on questioning a suspect until after the police had strengthened their case with a confession. Thus, the police illegality was knowing and intentional, in the language of *Brown,* it 'had a quality of purposefulness,' and the linkage between the illegality and the confession is clearly established."

In short, the officers decided, apparently consistent with a "departmental policy," to violate Harris' Fourth Amendment rights so they could get evidence that they could not otherwise obtain. As the trial court held, "No more clear violation of [*Payton*], in my view, could be established." Where, as here, there is a particularly flagrant constitutional violation and little in the way of elapsed time or intervening circumstances, the statement in the police station must be suppressed.

[But the majority does not apply the *Brown* factors in this case.] In the majority's view, when police officers make a warrantless home arrest in violation of *Payton,* their physical exit from the suspect's home *necessarily* breaks the causal chain between the illegality and any subsequent statement by the suspect, such that the statement is admissible regardless of the *Brown* factors. * * *

The majority's *per se* rule in this case fails to take account of our repeated holdings that violations of privacy in the home are especially invasive. Rather, its rule is necessarily premised on the proposition that the effect of a *Payton* violation magically vanishes once the suspect is dragged from his home. But the concerns that make a warrantless home arrest a violation of the Fourth Amendment are nothing so evanescent. A person who is forcibly separated from his family and home in the dark of night after uniformed officers have broken down his door, handcuffed him, and forced him at gunpoint to accompany them to a police station does not suddenly breathe a sigh of relief at the moment he is dragged across his doorstep. Rather, the suspect is likely to be so frightened and rattled that he will say something incriminating. These effects, of course, extend far beyond the moment the physical occupation of the home ends. The entire focus of the *Brown* factors is to fix the point at which those effects are sufficiently dissipated that deterrence is not meaningfully advanced by suppression. The majority's assertion, as though the proposition were axiomatic, that the effects of such an intrusion *must* end when the violation ends is both undefended and indefensible. * * *

Perhaps the most alarming aspect of the Court's ruling is its practical consequences for the deterrence of *Payton* violations. Imagine a police officer who has probable cause to arrest a suspect but lacks a warrant. The officer knows if he were to break into the home to make the arrest without first securing a warrant, he would violate the Fourth Amendment and any evidence he finds in the house would be suppressed. Of course, if he does not enter the house, he will not be able to use any evidence inside the house either, for the simple reason that he will never see it. The officer also knows, though, that waiting for the suspect to leave his house before arresting him could entail a lot of waiting, and the time he would spend getting a warrant would be better spent arresting criminals. The officer could leave the scene to obtain a warrant, thus avoiding some of the delay, but that would entail giving the suspect an opportunity to flee.

More important, the officer knows that if he breaks into the house without a warrant and drags the suspect outside, the suspect, shaken by the enormous invasion of privacy he has just undergone, may say something incriminating. Before today's decision, the government would only be able to use that evidence if the Court found that the taint of the arrest had been attenuated; after the decision, the evidence will be admissible regardless of whether it was the product of the unconstitutional arrest. Thus, the officer envisions the following best-case scenario if he chooses to violate the Constitution: He avoids a major expenditure of time and effort, ensures that the suspect will not escape, and procures the most damaging evidence of all, a confession. His worst-case scenario is that he will avoid a major expenditure of effort, ensure that the suspect will not escape, and will see evidence in the house (which would have remained unknown absent the constitutional violation) that cannot be used in the prosecution's case in chief. The Court thus creates powerful incentives for police officers to violate the Fourth Amendment. In the context of our constitutional rights and the sanctity of our homes, we cannot afford to presume that officers will be entirely impervious to those incentives.

UTAH V. STRIEFF
579 U.S. ___, 136 S.Ct. 2056, 195 L.E.2d 400 (2016).

JUSTICE THOMAS delivered the opinion of the Court.

[Utah police had received an anonymous tip reporting "narcotics activity" at a particular residence. Officer Fackrell saw Strieff leaving that home. Without any reasonable suspicion that Strieff had been engaged in criminal activity, Fackrell stopped him, asked him what he was doing at the house, requested his identification, and detained him while he relayed Strieff's information to a police dispatcher. Upon learning that Strieff had an outstanding arrest warrant for a traffic violation, Fackrell arrested him and found methamphetamine during a search incident to arrest.]

To enforce the Fourth Amendment's prohibition against "unreasonable searches and seizures," this Court has at times required courts to exclude evidence obtained by unconstitutional police conduct. But the Court has also held that, even when there is a Fourth Amendment violation, this exclusionary rule does not apply when the costs of exclusion outweigh its deterrent benefits. In some cases, for example, the link between the unconstitutional conduct and the discovery of the evidence is too attenuated to justify suppression. The question in this case is whether this attenuation doctrine applies when an officer makes an unconstitutional investigatory stop; learns during that stop that the suspect is subject to a valid arrest warrant; and proceeds to arrest the suspect and seize incriminating evidence during a search incident to that arrest. We hold that the evidence the officer seized as part of the search incident to arrest is admissible because the officer's discovery of the arrest warrant attenuated the connection between the unlawful stop and the evidence seized incident to arrest. * * *

The three factors articulated in *Brown v. Illinois* guide our analysis. First, we look to the "temporal proximity" between the unconstitutional conduct and the discovery of evidence to determine how closely the discovery of evidence followed the unconstitutional search. Second, we consider "the presence of intervening circumstances." Third, and "particularly" significant, we examine "the purpose and flagrancy of the official misconduct." * * *

The first factor, temporal proximity between the initially unlawful stop and the search, favors suppressing the evidence. Our precedents have declined to find that this factor favors attenuation unless "substantial time" elapses between an unlawful act and when the evidence is obtained. Here, however, Officer Fackrell discovered drug contraband on Strieff's person only minutes after the illegal stop. As the Court explained in *Brown,* such a short time interval counsels in favor of suppression; there, we found that the confession should be suppressed, relying in part on the "less than two hours" that separated the unconstitutional arrest and the confession.

In contrast, the second factor, the presence of intervening circumstances, strongly favors the State. In *Segura* [*v. United States,* 468 U.S. 796 (1984)], the Court addressed similar facts to those here and found sufficient intervening circumstances to allow the admission of evidence. There, agents had probable cause to believe that apartment occupants were dealing cocaine. They sought a warrant. In the meantime, they entered the apartment, arrested an occupant, and discovered evidence of drug activity during a limited search for security reasons. The next evening, the Magistrate Judge issued the search warrant. This Court deemed the evidence admissible notwithstanding the illegal search because the information supporting the warrant was "wholly unconnected with the [arguably illegal] entry and was known to the agents well before the initial entry."

Segura, of course, applied the independent source doctrine because the unlawful entry "did not contribute in any way to discovery of the evidence seized under the warrant." But the *Segura* Court suggested that the existence of a valid warrant favors finding that the connection between unlawful conduct and the discovery of evidence is "sufficiently attenuated to dissipate the taint." That principle applies here.

In this case, the warrant was valid, it predated Officer Fackrell's investigation, and it was entirely unconnected with the stop. And once Officer Fackrell discovered the warrant, he had an obligation to arrest Strieff. "A warrant is a judicial mandate to an officer to conduct a search or make an arrest, and the officer has a sworn duty to carry out its provisions." Officer Fackrell's arrest of Strieff thus was a ministerial act that was independently compelled by the pre-existing warrant. And once Officer Fackrell was authorized to arrest Strieff, it was undisputedly lawful to search Strieff as an incident of his arrest to protect Officer Fackrell's safety.

Finally, the third factor, "the purpose and flagrancy of the official misconduct," also strongly favors the State. The exclusionary rule exists to deter police misconduct. The third factor of the attenuation doctrine reflects that rationale by favoring exclusion only when the police misconduct is most in need of deterrence—that is, when it is purposeful or flagrant.

Officer Fackrell was at most negligent. In stopping Strieff, Officer Fackrell made two good-faith mistakes. First, he had not observed what time Strieff entered the suspected drug house, so he did not know how long Strieff had been there. Officer Fackrell thus lacked a sufficient basis to conclude that Strieff was a short-term visitor who may have been consummating a drug transaction. Second, because he lacked confirmation that Strieff was a short-term visitor, Officer Fackrell should have asked Strieff whether he would speak with him, instead of demanding that Strieff do so. Officer Fackrell's stated purpose was to "find out what was going on [in] the house." Nothing prevented him from approaching Strieff simply to ask. But these errors in judgment hardly rise to a purposeful or flagrant violation of Strieff's Fourth Amendment rights.

While Officer Fackrell's decision to initiate the stop was mistaken, his conduct thereafter was lawful. The officer's decision to run the warrant check was a "negligibly burdensome precautio[n]" for officer safety. And Officer Fackrell's actual search of Strieff was a lawful search incident to arrest.

Moreover, there is no indication that this unlawful stop was part of any systemic or recurrent police misconduct. To the contrary, all the evidence suggests that the stop was an isolated instance of negligence that occurred in connection with a bona fide investigation of a suspected drug house. Officer Fackrell saw Strieff leave a suspected drug house. And his suspicion about the house was based on an anonymous tip and his personal observations.

Applying these factors, we hold that the evidence discovered on Strieff's person was admissible because the unlawful stop was sufficiently attenuated by the pre-existing arrest warrant. Although the illegal stop was close in time to Strieff's arrest, that consideration is outweighed by two factors supporting the State. The outstanding arrest warrant for Strieff's arrest is a critical intervening circumstance that is wholly independent of the illegal stop. The discovery of that warrant broke the causal chain between the unconstitutional stop and the discovery of evidence by compelling Officer Fackrell to arrest Strieff. And, it is especially significant that there is no evidence that Officer Fackrell's illegal stop reflected flagrantly unlawful police misconduct. * * *

Strieff argues * * * that Officer Fackrell's conduct was flagrant because he detained Strieff without the necessary level of cause (here, reasonable suspicion). But that conflates the standard for an illegal stop with the standard for flagrancy. For the violation to be flagrant, more severe police misconduct is required than the mere absence of proper cause for the seizure. See, *e.g., Kaupp* [*v. Texas*, 538 U.S. 626 (2003)] (finding flagrant violation where a warrantless arrest was made in the arrestee's home after police were denied a warrant and at least some officers knew they lacked probable cause). Neither the officer's alleged purpose nor the flagrancy of the violation rise to a level of misconduct to warrant suppression.

Second, Strieff argues that, because of the prevalence of outstanding arrest warrants in many jurisdictions, police will engage in dragnet searches if the exclusionary rule is not applied. We think that this outcome is unlikely. Such wanton conduct would expose police to civil liability. And in any event, the *Brown* factors take account of the purpose and flagrancy of police misconduct. Were evidence of a dragnet search presented here, the application of the *Brown* factors could be different. But there is no evidence that the concerns that Strieff raises with the criminal justice system are present in South Salt Lake City, Utah.

JUSTICE KAGAN, with whom JUSTICE GINSBURG joins, dissenting.

[Each of the three *Brown* attenuation factors points toward suppression.] Start where the majority does: The temporal proximity factor, it forthrightly admits, "favors suppressing the evidence." After all, Fackrell's discovery of drugs came just minutes after the unconstitutional stop. And in prior decisions, this Court has made clear that only the lapse of "substantial time" between the two could favor admission. So the State, by all accounts, takes strike one.

Move on to the purposefulness of Fackrell's conduct, where the majority is less willing to see a problem for what it is. The majority chalks up Fackrell's Fourth Amendment violation to a couple of innocent "mistakes." But far from a Barney Fife-type mishap, Fackrell's seizure of Strieff was a calculated decision, taken with so little justification that the State has never tried to defend its legality. At the suppression hearing, Fackrell acknowledged that the stop was designed for investigatory purposes—*i.e.,* to "find out what was going on [in] the house" he had been watching, and to figure out "what [Strieff] was doing there." And Fackrell frankly admitted that he had no basis for his action except that Strieff "was coming out of the house." Plug in Fackrell's and Strieff's names, substitute "stop" for "arrest" and "reasonable suspicion" for "probable cause," and this Court's decision in *Brown* perfectly describes this case:

"[I]t is not disputed that [Fackrell stopped Strieff] without [reasonable suspicion]. [He] later testified that [he] made the [stop] for the purpose of questioning [Strieff] as part of [his] investigation. . . . The illegality here . . . had a quality of purposefulness. The impropriety of the [stop] was obvious. [A]wareness of that fact was virtually conceded by [Fackrell] when [he] repeatedly acknowledged, in [his] testimony, that the purpose of [his] action was 'for investigation': [Fackrell] embarked upon this expedition for evidence in the hope that something might turn up."

In *Brown,* the Court held those facts to support suppression—and they do here as well. Swing and a miss for strike two.

Finally, consider whether any intervening circumstance "br[oke] the causal chain" between the stop and the evidence. The notion of such a disrupting event comes from the tort law doctrine of proximate causation. And as in the tort context, a circumstance counts as intervening only when it is unforeseeable—not when it can be seen coming from miles away. For rather than breaking the causal chain, predictable effects (*e.g.,* X leads naturally to Y leads naturally to Z) are its very links.

And Fackrell's discovery of an arrest warrant—the only event the majority thinks intervened—was an eminently foreseeable consequence of stopping Strieff. As Fackrell testified, checking for outstanding warrants during a stop is the "normal" practice of South Salt Lake City police. In other words, the department's standard detention procedures—stop, ask for identification, run a check—are partly designed to find outstanding warrants. And find them they will, given the staggering number of such warrants on the books. To take just a few examples: The State of California has 2.5 million outstanding arrest warrants (a number corresponding to about 9% of its adult population); Pennsylvania (with a population of about 12.8 million) contributes 1.4 million more; and New York City (population 8.4 million) adds another 1.2 million.[1] So outstanding warrants do not appear as bolts from the blue. They are the run-of-the-mill results of police stops—what officers look for when they run a routine check of a person's identification and what they know will turn up with fair regularity. In short, they are nothing like what intervening circumstances are supposed to be.[2] Strike three.

The majority's misapplication of *Brown's* three-part inquiry creates unfortunate incentives for the police—indeed, practically invites them to do what Fackrell did here. Consider an officer who, like Fackrell, wishes to stop someone for investigative reasons, but does not have what a court would view as reasonable suspicion. If the officer believes that any evidence he discovers will be inadmissible, he is likely to think the unlawful stop not worth making—precisely the deterrence the exclusionary rule is meant to achieve. But when he is told of today's decision? Now the officer knows that the stop may well yield admissible evidence: So long as the target is one of the many millions of people in this country with an outstanding arrest warrant, anything the officer finds in a search is fair game for use in a criminal prosecution. The officer's incentive to violate the Constitution thus increases: From here on, he sees potential advantage in stopping individuals without reasonable suspicion—exactly the temptation the exclusionary rule is supposed to remove. Because the majority thus places Fourth Amendment protections at risk, I respectfully dissent.

JUSTICE SOTOMAYOR, dissenting.[a]

Writing only for myself, and drawing on my professional experiences, I would add that unlawful "stops" have severe consequences much greater than the inconvenience suggested by the name. This Court has given officers an array of instruments to probe and examine you. When we condone officers' use of these devices without adequate cause, we give them reason to target pedestrians in an arbitrary manner. We also risk treating members of our communities as second-class citizens.

Although many Americans have been stopped for speeding or jaywalking, few may realize how degrading a stop can be when the officer is looking for more. This Court has allowed an officer to stop you for whatever reason he wants—so long as he can point to a pretextual justification after the fact. *Whren v. United States*, 517

---

[1]   What is more, outstanding arrest warrants are not distributed evenly across the population. To the contrary, they are concentrated in cities, towns, and neighborhoods where stops are most likely to occur—and so the odds of any given stop revealing a warrant are even higher than the above numbers indicate. One study found, for example, that Cincinnati, Ohio had over 100,000 outstanding warrants with only 300,000 residents. And as Justice Sotomayor notes, 16,000 of the 21,000 people residing in the town of Ferguson, Missouri have outstanding warrants.

[2]   The majority relies on *Segura v. United States* to reach the opposite conclusion, but that decision lacks any relevance to this case. The Court there held that the Fourth Amendment violation at issue "did not contribute in any way" to the police's subsequent procurement of a warrant and discovery of contraband. So the Court had no occasion to consider the question here: What happens when an unconstitutional act in fact leads to a warrant which then leads to evidence?

[a]   Justice Sotomayor wrote a longer dissent, parts of which were joined by Justice Ginsburg. This excerpted portion comes from the part of the dissent she wrote for herself only.

U.S. 806 (1996). That justification must provide specific reasons why the officer suspected you were breaking the law, but it may factor in your ethnicity, *United States v. Brignoni-Ponce,* 422 U.S. 873 (1975), where you live, *Adams v. Williams,* 407 U.S. 143 (1972), what you were wearing, *United States v. Sokolow,* 490 U.S. 1 (1989), and how you behaved, *Illinois v. Wardlow,* 528 U.S. 119 (2000). The officer does not even need to know which law you might have broken so long as he can later point to any possible infraction—even one that is minor, unrelated, or ambiguous. *Devenpeck v. Alford,* 543 U.S. 146 (2004); *Heien v. North Carolina,* 135 S.Ct. 530 (2014).

The indignity of the stop is not limited to an officer telling you that you look like a criminal. The officer may next ask for your "consent" to inspect your bag or purse without telling you that you can decline. See *Florida v. Bostick,* 501 U.S. 429 (1991). Regardless of your answer, he may order you to stand "helpless, perhaps facing a wall with [your] hands raised." *Terry,* 392 U.S., at 17. If the officer thinks you might be dangerous, he may then "frisk" you for weapons. This involves more than just a pat down. As onlookers pass by, the officer may " 'feel with sensitive fingers every portion of [your] body. A thorough search [may] be made of [your] arms and armpits, waistline and back, the groin and area about the testicles, and entire surface of the legs down to the feet.' " *Id.,* at 17, n. 13.

The officer's control over you does not end with the stop. If the officer chooses, he may handcuff you and take you to jail for doing nothing more than speeding, jaywalking, or "driving [your] pickup truck . . . with [your] 3-year-old son and 5-year-old daughter . . . without [your] seatbelt fastened." *Atwater v. Lago Vista,* 532 U.S. 318 (2001). At the jail, he can fingerprint you, swab DNA from the inside of your mouth, and force you to "shower with a delousing agent" while you "lift [your] tongue, hold out [your] arms, turn around, and lift [your] genitals." *Florence v. Board of Chosen Freeholders of County of Burlington,* 132 S.Ct. 1510 (2012); *Maryland v. King,* 133 S.Ct. 1958 (2013). Even if you are innocent, you will now join the 65 million Americans with an arrest record and experience the "civil death" of discrimination by employers, landlords, and whoever else conducts a background check. And, of course, if you fail to pay bail or appear for court, a judge will issue a warrant to render you "arrestable on sight" in the future.

This case involves a *suspicionless* stop, one in which the officer initiated this chain of events without justification. As the Justice Department notes, many innocent people are subjected to the humiliations of these unconstitutional searches. The white defendant in this case shows that anyone's dignity can be violated in this manner. But it is no secret that people of color are disproportionate victims of this type of scrutiny. See M. Alexander, The New Jim Crow 95–136 (2010). For generations, black and brown parents have given their children "the talk"—instructing them never to run down the street; always keep your hands where they can be seen; do not even think of talking back to a stranger—all out of fear of how an officer with a gun will react to them. See, *e.g.,* W.E.B. Du Bois, The Souls of Black Folk (1903); J. Baldwin, The Fire Next Time (1963); T. Coates, Between the World and Me (2015).

By legitimizing the conduct that produces this double consciousness, this case tells everyone, white and black, guilty and innocent, that an officer can verify your legal status at any time. It says that your body is subject to invasion while courts excuse the violation of your rights. It implies that you are not a citizen of a democracy but the subject of a carceral state, just waiting to be cataloged.

We must not pretend that the countless people who are routinely targeted by police are "isolated." They are the canaries in the coal mine whose deaths, civil and literal, warn us that no one can breathe in this atmosphere. See L. Guinier & G. Torres, The Miner's Canary 274–283 (2002). They are the ones who recognize that unlawful police stops corrode all our civil liberties and threaten all our lives. Until their voices matter too, our justice system will continue to be anything but.

3. CAUSE IN FACT: INDEPENDENT SOURCE

MURRAY v. UNITED STATES
487 U.S. 533, 108 S.Ct. 2529, 101 L.E.2d 472 (1988).

JUSTICE SCALIA delivered the opinion of the Court.[a]

[After receiving information that a warehouse was being used for illegal drug activities, federal agents forced their way into the warehouse and observed in plain view bales of marijuana. The agents then left without disturbing the bales and applied for a search warrant. In their application, they did not mention the prior entry or include any recitations of their observations during that entry. Upon issuance of the warrant, the agents reentered the warehouse and seized the bales and notebooks listing customers for whom the bales were destined. Petitioners unsuccessfully moved to suppress the evidence and were convicted for conspiracy to possess and distribute illegal drugs.]

The exclusionary rule prohibits introduction into evidence of tangible materials seized during an unlawful search, and of testimony concerning knowledge acquired during an unlawful search. Beyond that, the exclusionary rule also prohibits the introduction of derivative evidence, both tangible and testimonial, that is the product of the primary evidence. * * *

Almost simultaneously with our development of the exclusionary rule, [we] also announced what has come to be known as the "independent source doctrine." See *Silverthorne Lumber Co.* That doctrine [has] recently been described as follows:

"[T]he interest of society in deterring unlawful police conduct and the public interest in having juries receive all probative evidence of a crime are properly balanced by putting the police in the same, not a *worse*, position that they would have been in if no police error or misconduct had occurred. . . . When the challenged evidence has an independent source, exclusion of such evidence would put the police in a worse position than they would have been in absent any error or violation." *Nix v. Williams.* * * *

---

[a]   The case was decided by a 4–3 vote with Justices Brennan and Kennedy not participating.

Our cases have used the concept of "independent source" in a more general and a more specific sense. The more general sense identifies *all* evidence acquired in a fashion untainted by the illegal evidence-gathering activity. Thus, where an unlawful entry has given investigators knowledge of facts x and y, but fact z has been learned by other means, fact z can be said to be admissible because derived from an "independent source." This is how we used the term in *Segura v. United States,* 468 U.S. 796 (1984). In that case, agents unlawfully entered the defendant's apartment and remained there until a search warrant was obtained. The admissibility of what they discovered while waiting in the apartment was not before us, but we held that the evidence found for the first time during the execution of the valid and untainted search warrant was admissible because it was discovered pursuant to an "independent source."

The original use of the term, however, and it's more important use for purposes of [this] case, was more specific. It was originally applied [with] reference to that particular category of evidence acquired by an untainted search *which is identical to the evidence unlawfully acquired*—that is, in the example just given, to knowledge of facts x and y derived from an independent source. * * *

Petitioners' asserted policy basis for excluding evidence which is initially discovered during an illegal search, but is subsequently acquired through an independent and lawful source, is that a contrary rule will remove all deterrence to, and indeed positively encourage, unlawful police searches. As petitioners see the incentives, law enforcement officers will routinely enter without a warrant to make sure that what they expect to be on the premises is in fact there. If it is not, they will have spared themselves the time and trouble of getting a warrant; if it is, they can get the warrant and use the evidence despite the unlawful entry. We see the incentives differently. An officer with probable cause sufficient to obtain a search warrant would be foolish to enter the premises first in an unlawful manner. By doing so, he would risk suppression of all evidence on the premises, both seen and unseen, since his action would add to the normal burden of convincing a magistrate that there is probable cause the much more onerous burden of convincing a trial court that no information gained from the illegal entry affected either the law enforcement officers' decision to seek a warrant or the magistrate's decision to grant it. Nor would the officer *without* sufficient probable cause to obtain a search warrant have any added incentive to conduct an unlawful entry, since whatever he finds cannot be used to establish probable cause before a magistrate.[2] * * *

Knowledge that the marijuana was in the warehouse was assuredly acquired at the time of the unlawful entry. But it was also acquired at the time of entry pursuant to the warrant, and if that later acquisition was not the result of the earlier entry there is no reason why the independent source doctrine should not apply. * * *

---

[2]   [The] District Court found that the agents entered the warehouse "in an effort to apprehend any participants who might have remained inside and to guard against the destruction of possibly critical evidence." While they may have misjudged the existence of sufficient exigent circumstances to justify the warrantless entry[,] there is nothing to suggest that they went in merely to see if there was anything worth getting a warrant for.

The ultimate question, therefore, is whether the search pursuant to warrant was in fact a genuinely independent source of the information and tangible evidence at issue here. This would not have been the case if the agents' decision to seek the warrant was prompted by what they had seen during the initial entry,[3] or if information obtained during that entry was presented to the Magistrate and affected her decision to issue the warrant. * * *

The District Court found that the agents did not reveal their warrantless entry to the Magistrate, and that they did not include in their application for a warrant any recitation of their observations in the warehouse. It did not, however, explicitly find that the agents would have sought a warrant if they had not earlier entered the warehouse. * * *

Accordingly, we vacate the judgment and remand [for] determination whether the warrant-authorized search of the warehouse was an independent source of the challenged evidence in the sense we have described.

JUSTICE MARSHALL, with whom JUSTICE STEVENS and JUSTICE O'CONNOR join, dissenting.

[T]he Court's decision, by failing to provide sufficient guarantees that the subsequent search was, in fact, independent of the illegal search, emasculates the Warrant Clause and undermines the deterrence function of the exclusionary rule. * * *

[A]dmission in these cases affirmatively encourages illegal searches. The incentives for such illegal conduct are clear. Obtaining a warrant is inconvenient and time consuming. Even when officers have probable cause to support a warrant application, therefore, they have an incentive first to determine whether it worthwhile to obtain a warrant. * * *

[I]t is a simple matter [to] exclude from the warrant application any information gained from the initial entry * * *. [T]oday's decision makes the application of the independent source exception turn entirely on an evaluation of the officer's intent. It normally will be difficult for the trial court to verify, or the defendant to rebut, an assertion by officers that they always intended to obtain a warrant, regardless of the results of the illegal search. * * *

When, as here, the same team of investigators is involved in both the first and second search, there is a significant danger that the "independence" of the source will in fact be illusory, and that the initial search will have affected the decision to obtain a warrant notwithstanding the officers' subsequent assertions to the contrary. It is therefore crucial that the factual premise of the exception—complete independence—be clearly established before the exception can [apply]. I believe the Court's reliance on the intent of the law enforcement officers who conducted the

---

[3] [To] determine whether the warrant was independent of the illegal entry, one must ask whether it would have been sought even if what actually happened had not occurred—not whether it would have been sought if something else had happened. That is to say, what counts is whether the actual illegal search had any effect in producing the warrant, not whether some hypothetical illegal search would have aborted the warrant. * * *

warrantless search provides insufficient guarantees that the subsequent legal search was unaffected by the prior illegal search. * * *

Segura is readily distinguished from the present cases. The admission of evidence first discovered during a legal search does not significantly lessen the deterrence facing the law enforcement officers contemplating an illegal entry *so long as* the evidence that is seen is excluded. This was clearly the view of [the *Segura* majority]. [E]xtending *Segura* to cover evidence discovered during an initial illegal search will eradicate this remaining deterrence to illegal entry. Moreover, there is less reason to believe that an initial illegal entry was prompted by a desire to determine whether to bother to get a warrant in the first place, and thus was not wholly independent of the second search, if officers understand that evidence they discover during the illegal search will be excluded even if they subsequently return with a warrant."[b]

4. CAUSE IN FACT: INEVITABLE DISCOVERY

NIX V. WILLIAMS
467 U.S. 431, 104 S.Ct. 2501, 81 L.E.2d 377 (1984).

CHIEF JUSTICE BURGER delivered the opinion of the Court.

[Police suspected that Williams was involved in the kidnaping and murder of a ten-year-old girl. The police questioned him in violation of his Sixth Amendment right to counsel. In response to the questioning, Williams led the police to the girl's body. At his second murder trial,[a] the prosecution did not offer Williams's statements into evidence. Nor did it seek to show that Williams had directed the police to the child's body. The only evidence admitted was the condition of the victim's body as it was found, articles of the victim's clothing, and the results of post mortem medical and chemical tests on her body. The trial court concluded that the State had proved by a preponderance of the evidence that, even if the search had not been suspended and Williams had not led the police to the victim, the searching party would still have discovered the body in essentially the same condition as it was actually found. The trial court also ruled that if the police had not located the body, "the search would clearly have been taken up again where it left off, given the extreme circumstances of this case, and the body would [have] been found *in short order*" (emphasis added). Thus, the trial court determined that the evidence about the condition of the body was admissible. The U.S. Court of Appeals for the Eighth Circuit, addressing the case on federal habeas review, disagreed maintaining that an "inevitable discovery" exception requires proof that the police did not act in "bad faith," and noting that the state trial record could not support such a finding.]

---

[b] While Justice Stevens joined Justice Marshall's dissent, he noted in a separate dissent that he "remain[ed] convinced that the *Segura* decision itself was unacceptable" because it provided government agents with an "affirmative incentive" to conduct illegal searches.

[a] Williams's first conviction was vacated because the statements he made had been admitted into evidence in violation of his Sixth Amendment rights. *See Brewer v. Williams, infra* p. 559.

The core rationale consistently advanced by this Court for extending the exclusionary rule to evidence that is the fruit of unlawful police conduct has been that this admittedly drastic and socially costly course is needed to deter police from violations of constitutional and statutory protections. This Court has accepted the argument that the way to ensure such protections is to exclude evidence seized as a result of such violations notwithstanding the high social cost of letting persons obviously guilty go unpunished for their crimes. On this rationale, the prosecution is not to be put in a better position than it would have been in if no illegality had transpired.

By contrast, the derivative evidence analysis ensures that the prosecution is not put in a worse position simply because of some earlier police error or misconduct. The independent source doctrine allows admission of evidence that has been discovered by means wholly independent of any constitutional violation. That doctrine, although closely related to the inevitable discovery doctrine, does not apply here; Williams' statements to [the Detective] indeed led police to the child's body, but that is not the whole story. The independent source doctrine teaches us that the interest of society in deterring unlawful police conduct and the public interest in having juries receive all probative evidence of a crime are properly balanced by putting the police in the same, not a worse, position that they would have been in if no police error or misconduct had occurred. When the challenged evidence has an independent source, exclusion of such evidence would put the police in a worse position than they would have been in absent any error or violation. There is a functional similarity between these two doctrines in that exclusion of evidence that would inevitably have been discovered would also put the government in a worse position, because the police would have obtained that evidence if no misconduct had taken place. Thus, while the independent source exception would not justify admission of evidence in this case, its rationale is wholly consistent with and justifies our adoption of the ultimate or inevitable discovery exception to the exclusionary rule.

It is clear that the cases implementing the exclusionary rule "begin with the premise that the challenged evidence is in some sense the product of illegal governmental activity." Of course, this does not end the inquiry. If the prosecution can establish by a preponderance of the evidence that the information ultimately or inevitably would have been discovered by lawful means—here the volunteers' search—then the deterrence rationale has so little basis that the evidence should be received. Anything less would reject logic, experience, and common sense.

The requirement that the prosecution must prove the absence of bad faith, imposed here by the Court of Appeals, would place courts in the position of withholding from juries relevant and undoubted truth that would have been available to police absent any unlawful police activity. Of course, that view would put the police in a worse position than they would have been in if no unlawful conduct had transpired. And, of equal importance, it wholly fails to take into account the enormous societal cost of excluding truth in the search for truth in the administration of justice. Nothing in this Court's prior holdings supports any such formalistic, pointless, and punitive approach.

The Court of Appeals concluded, without analysis, that if an absence-of-bad-faith requirement were not imposed, "the temptation to risk deliberate violations of the Sixth Amendment would be too great, and the deterrent effect of the Exclusionary Rule reduced too far." We reject that view. A police officer who is faced with the opportunity to obtain evidence illegally will rarely, if ever, be in a position to calculate whether the evidence sought would inevitably be discovered. * * *

On the other hand, when an officer is aware that the evidence will inevitably be discovered, he will try to avoid engaging in any questionable practice. In that situation, there will be little to gain from taking any dubious "shortcuts" to obtain the evidence. Significant disincentives to obtaining evidence illegally—including the possibility of departmental discipline and civil liability—also lessen the likelihood that the ultimate or inevitable discovery exception will promote police misconduct. In these circumstances, the societal costs of the exclusionary rule far outweigh any possible benefits to deterrence that a good-faith requirement might produce. * * *

[T]hree courts independently reviewing the evidence have found that the body of the child inevitably would have been found by the searchers. Williams challenges these findings, asserting that the record contains only the "post hoc rationalization" that the search efforts would have proceeded two and one-half miles into Polk County where Williams had led police to the body. * * *

On this record it is clear that the search parties were approaching the actual location of the body, and we are satisfied, along with three courts earlier, that the volunteer search teams would have resumed the search had Williams not earlier led the police to the body and the body inevitably would have been found.[b]

HUDSON V. MICHIGAN
547 U.S. 586, 126 S.Ct. 2159, 165 L.E.2d 56 (2006).

JUSTICE SCALIA delivered the opinion of the Court.[a]

* * *

[E]xclusion may not be premised on the mere fact that a constitutional violation was a "but-for" cause of obtaining evidence. Our cases show that but-for causality is only a necessary, not a sufficient, condition for suppression. In this case, of course, the constitutional violation of an illegal manner of entry was not a but-for cause of obtaining the evidence. Whether that preliminary misstep had

---

[b] Concurring opinions by Justices White and Stevens, both of which focus on the nature of the underlying Sixth Amendment violation, have been omitted. A separate dissent by Justice Brennan (joined by Justice Marshall) is also omitted. In that dissent, Justice Brennan agreed with the majority that evidence that would have been inevitably discovered despite the constitutional violation should be admissible at a later trial, but he would have required the government to satisfy a heightened burden of proof—clear and convincing evidence—before it would be allowed to use such evidence. Because the lower courts did not impose such a requirement, he would have remanded the case.

[a] See supra p. 80 for the facts of this case and excerpts from the Court's alternative holding that the exclusionary rule does not apply to knock and announce violations.

occurred or not, the police would have executed the warrant they had obtained, and would have discovered the gun and drugs inside the house. But even if the illegal entry here could be characterized as a but-for cause of discovering what was inside, we have "never held that evidence is 'fruit of the poisonous tree' simply because 'it would not have come to light but for the illegal actions of the police.' " *Segura v. United States*, 468 U.S. 796, 815 (1984). Rather, but-for cause, or "causation in the logical sense alone," can be too attenuated to justify exclusion. Even in the early days of the exclusionary rule, we declined to

> "hold that all evidence is 'fruit of the poisonous tree' simply because it would not have come to light *but for* the illegal actions of the police. Rather, the more apt question in such a case is 'whether, granting establishment of the primary illegality, the evidence to which instant objection is made has been come at by exploitation of that illegality or instead by means sufficiently distinguishable to be purged of the primary taint.' " *Wong Sun v. United States*, 371 U.S. 471 (1963) (emphasis added).

Attenuation can occur, of course, when the causal connection is remote. Attenuation also occurs when, even given a direct causal connection, the interest protected by the constitutional guarantee that has been violated would not be served by suppression of the evidence obtained. "The penalties visited upon the Government, and in turn upon the public, because its officers have violated the law must bear some relation to the purposes which the law is to serve." Thus, in *New York v. Harris*, 495 U.S. 14 (1990), where an illegal warrantless arrest was made in Harris' house, we held that

> "suppressing [Harris'] statement taken outside the house would not serve the purpose of the rule that made Harris' in-house arrest illegal. The warrant requirement for an arrest in the home is imposed to protect the home, and anything incriminating the police gathered from arresting Harris in his home, rather than elsewhere, has been excluded, as it should have been; the purpose of the rule has thereby been vindicated."

For this reason, cases excluding the fruits of unlawful warrantless searches say nothing about the appropriateness of exclusion to vindicate the interests protected by the knock-and-announce requirement. Until a valid warrant has issued, citizens are entitled to shield "their persons, houses, papers, and effects," U.S. Const., Amdt. 4, from the government's scrutiny. Exclusion of the evidence obtained by a warrantless search vindicates that entitlement. The interests protected by the knock-and-announce requirement are quite different—and do not include the shielding of potential evidence from the government's eyes.

One of those interests is the protection of human life and limb, because an unannounced entry may provoke violence in supposed self-defense by the surprised resident. Another interest is the protection of property. * * * The knock-and-announce rule gives individuals "the opportunity to comply with the law and to avoid the destruction of property occasioned by a forcible entry." And thirdly, the knock-and-announce rule protects those elements of privacy and dignity that can be destroyed by a sudden entrance. It gives residents the "opportunity to prepare themselves for" the entry of the police. "The brief interlude between announcement and entry with a warrant may be the opportunity that an individual has to pull on clothes or get out of bed." In other words, it assures the opportunity to collect oneself before answering the door.

What the knock-and-announce rule has never protected, however, is one's interest in preventing the government from seeing or taking evidence described in a warrant. Since the interests that were violated in this case have nothing to do with the seizure of the evidence, the exclusionary rule is inapplicable. * * *

JUSTICE BREYER, with whom JUSTICE STEVENS, JUSTICE SOUTER, and JUSTICE GINSBURG join, dissenting. * * *

The majority first argues that "the constitutional violation of an illegal manner of entry was not a but-for cause of obtaining the evidence." But taking causation as it is commonly understood in the law, I do not see how that can be so. Although the police might have entered Hudson's home lawfully, they did not in fact do so. Their unlawful behavior inseparably characterizes their actual entry; that entry was a necessary condition of their presence in Hudson's home; and their presence in Hudson's home was a necessary condition of their finding and seizing the evidence. At the same time, their discovery of evidence in Hudson's home was a readily foreseeable consequence of their entry and their unlawful presence within the home.

Moreover, separating the "manner of entry" from the related search slices the violation too finely. [W]e have described a failure to comply with the knock-and-announce rule, not as an independently unlawful event, but as a factor that renders the *search* "constitutionally defective." *Wilson* (emphasis added).

The Court nonetheless accepts Michigan's argument that the requisite but-for-causation is not satisfied in this case because, whether or not the constitutional violation occurred (what the Court refers to as a "preliminary misstep"), "the police would have executed the warrant they had obtained, and would have discovered the gun and drugs inside the house." As support for this proposition, Michigan rests on this Court's inevitable discovery cases.

This claim, however, misunderstands the inevitable discovery doctrine. Justice Holmes in *Silverthorne* [*Lumber Co. v. United States,* 251 U.S. 385 (1920)], in discussing an "independent source" exception, set forth the principles underlying the inevitable discovery rule. That rule does not refer to discovery that would have taken place if the police behavior in question had (contrary to fact) been lawful. The doctrine does not treat as critical what hypothetically could have happened had the police acted lawfully in the first place. Rather, "independent" or "inevitable" discovery refers to discovery that did occur or that would have occurred (1) despite (not simply in the absence of) the unlawful behavior and (2) independently of that unlawful behavior. The government cannot, for example, avoid suppression of evidence seized without a warrant (or pursuant to a defective warrant) simply by showing that it could have obtained a valid warrant had it sought one. Instead, it must show that the same evidence "inevitably would have been discovered by *lawful means.*" *Nix v. Williams,* 467 U.S. [431 (1984)] (emphasis added). "What a man could do is not at all the same as what he would do."

The inevitable discovery exception rests upon the principle that the remedial purposes of the exclusionary rule are not served by suppressing evidence discovered through a "later, lawful seizure" that is "genuinely independent of an earlier, tainted one." *Murray v. United States,* 487 U.S. 533 (1988).

Case law well illustrates the meaning of this principle. In *Nix,* police officers violated a defendant's Sixth Amendment right by eliciting incriminating statements from him after he invoked his right to counsel. Those statements led to the discovery of the victim's body. The Court concluded that evidence obtained from the victim's body was admissible because it would ultimately or inevitably have been discovered by a volunteer search party effort that was ongoing—whether or not the Sixth Amendment violation had taken place. In other words, the evidence would have been found *despite,* and *independent of,* the Sixth Amendment violation.

In *Segura v. United States,* [a case upon which the majority relies,] the Court held that an earlier illegal entry into an apartment did not require suppression of evidence that police later seized when executing a search warrant obtained on the basis of information unconnected to the initial entry. The Court reasoned that the "evidence was discovered the day following the entry, *during the search conducted under a valid warrant*"—i.e., a warrant obtained independently without use of any information found during the illegal entry—and that "it was the product of that search, wholly unrelated to the prior [unlawful] entry" (emphasis added).

In *Murray,* the Court upheld the admissibility of seized evidence where agents entered a warehouse without a warrant, and then later returned with a valid warrant that was not obtained on the basis of evidence observed during the first (illegal) entry. The Court reasoned that while the agents' "[k]nowledge that the marijuana was in the warehouse was assuredly acquired at the time of the unlawful entry . . . it was also acquired at the time of entry pursuant to the warrant, and *if that later acquisition was not the result of the earlier entry* there is no reason why the independent source doctrine should not apply" (emphasis added).

Thus, the Court's opinion reflects a misunderstanding of what "inevitable discovery" means when it says, "[i]n this case, of course, the constitutional violation of an illegal manner of entry was not a but-for cause of obtaining the evidence." The majority rests this conclusion on its next statement: "Whether that preliminary misstep has occurred or not, the police . . . would have discovered the gun and the drugs inside the house." Despite the phrase "of course," neither of these statements is correct. It is not true that, had the illegal entry not occurred, "police would have discovered the guns and drugs inside the house." Without that unlawful entry they would not have been inside the house; so there would have been no discovery.

Of course, had the police entered the house lawfully, they would have found the gun and drugs. But that fact is beside the point. The question is not what police might have done had they not behaved unlawfully. The question is what they did do. Was there set in motion an independent chain of events that would have inevitably led to the discovery and seizure of the evidence despite, and independent of, that behavior? The answer here is "no." * * *

The majority, Michigan, and the United States point out that the officers here possessed a warrant authorizing a search. That fact, they argue, means that the evidence would have been discovered independently or somehow diminishes the need to suppress the evidence. But I do not see why that is so. The warrant in question was not a "no-knock" warrant, which many States (but not Michigan) issue to assure police that a prior knock is not necessary. It did not authorize a search that fails to comply with knock-and-announce requirements. Rather, it was an ordinary search warrant. It authorized a search that complied with, not a search that disregarded, the Constitution's knock-and-announce rule.

Would a warrant that authorizes entry into a home on Tuesday permit the police to enter on Monday? Would a warrant that authorizes entry during the day authorize the police to enter during the middle of the night? It is difficult for me to see how the presence of a warrant that does not authorize the entry in question has anything to do with the "inevitable discovery" exception or otherwise diminishes the need to enforce the knock-and-announce requirement through suppression. * * *

The majority and the United States set forth a policy-related variant of the causal connection theme: The United States argues that the law should suppress evidence only insofar as a Fourth Amendment violation causes the kind of harm that the particular Fourth Amendment rule seeks to protect against. It adds that the constitutional purpose of the knock-and-announce rule is to prevent needless destruction of property (such as breaking down a door) and to avoid unpleasant surprise. And it concludes that the exclusionary rule should suppress evidence of, say, damage to property, the discovery of a defendant in an "intimate or compromising moment," or an excited utterance from the occupant caught by surprise, but nothing more.

The majority makes a similar argument. It says that evidence should not be suppressed once the causal connection between unlawful behavior and discovery of the evidence becomes too "attenuated." But the majority then makes clear that it is not using the word "attenuated" to mean what this Court's precedents have typically used that word to mean, namely, that the discovery of the evidence has come about long after the unlawful behavior took place or in an independent way, i.e., through " 'means sufficiently distinguishable to be purged of the primary taint.' " *Wong Sun v. United States.*

Rather, the majority gives the word "attenuation" a new meaning (thereby, in effect, making the same argument as the United States). "Attenuation," it says, "also occurs when, even given a direct causal connection, the interest protected by the constitutional guarantee that has been violated would not be served by suppression of the evidence obtained." The interests the knock-and-announce rule seeks to protect, the Court adds, are "human life" (at stake when a householder is "surprised"), "property" (such as the front door), and "those elements of privacy and dignity that can be destroyed by a sudden entrance," namely, "the opportunity to collect oneself before answering the door." Since none of those interests led to the discovery of the evidence seized here, there is no reason to suppress it.

There are three serious problems with this argument. First, it does not fully describe the constitutional values, purposes, and objectives underlying the knock-and-announce requirement. That rule does help to protect homeowners from damaged doors; it does help to protect occupants from surprise. But it does more than that. It protects the occupants' privacy by assuring them that government agents will not enter their home without complying with those requirements (among others) that diminish the offensive nature of any such intrusion. Many years ago, Justice Frankfurter wrote for the Court that the "knock at the door, . . . as a prelude to a search, without authority of law . . . [is] inconsistent with the conception of human rights enshrined in [our] history" and Constitution. How much the more offensive when the search takes place without any knock at all.

* * * The knock-and-announce requirement is no less a part of the "centuries-old principle" of special protection for the privacy of the home than the warrant requirement. The Court is therefore wrong to reduce the essence of its protection to "the right not to be intruded upon in one's nightclothes."

Second, whether the interests underlying the knock-and-announce rule are implicated in any given case is, in a sense, beside the point. As we have explained, failure to comply with the knock-and-announce rule renders the related search unlawful. And where a search is unlawful, the law insists upon suppression of the evidence consequently discovered, even if that evidence or its possession has little or nothing to do with the reasons underlying the unconstitutionality of a search. The Fourth Amendment does not seek to protect contraband, yet we have required suppression of contraband seized in an unlawful search. That is because the exclusionary rule protects more general "privacy values through deterrence of future police misconduct." The same is true here.

Third, the majority's interest-based approach departs from prior law. Ordinarily a court will simply look to see if the unconstitutional search produced the evidence. The majority does not refer to any relevant case in which, beyond that, suppression turned on the far more detailed relation between, say, (1) a particular materially false statement made to the magistrate who issued a (consequently) invalid warrant and (2) evidence found after a search with that warrant. And the majority's failure does not surprise me, for such efforts to trace causal connections at retail could well complicate Fourth Amendment suppression law, threatening its workability. * * *

CHAPTER 5

THE RIGHT TO COUNSEL[a]

■ ■ ■

1. THE RIGHT TO APPOINTED COUNSEL

When the Court, per Sutherland, J., spoke eloquently of the importance of the right to counsel and the essential relationship between "the right to be heard" and "the right to be heard by counsel" in the landmark case of *Powell v. Alabama,* 287 U.S. 45 (1932), which has been called the first "modern" procedural due process case, it was talking about a person's right to be heard by counsel "employed by and appearing for him." Although Justice Black's analysis for the Court thirty years later in *Gideon v. Wainwright* appears to ignore this fact, *Powell* dealt primarily not with the right to appointed counsel, but the historically separate right of the individual to employ her own counsel.

The *Powell* opinion spelled out at some length why the defendants were not afforded "a fair opportunity to secure counsel of [their] own choice" and why, under the circumstances, this constituted a denial of due process. The *Powell* Court went on to say however, and it did this only in the last few pages of a lengthy opinion, that "assuming the inability, even if opportunity had been given, to employ counsel," the failure of the trial court "to make an effective appointment of counsel was likewise a denial of due process." Continued the Court, using very measured language:

> "Whether this would be so in other criminal prosecutions, or under other circumstances, we need not determine. All that is necessary now to decide, as we do decide, is that in a capital case, where the defendant is unable to employ counsel, and is incapable adequately of making his own defense because of ignorance, feeble-mindedness, illiteracy, or the like, it is the duty of the court, whether requested or not, to assign counsel for him as a necessary requisite of due process of law; and that duty is not discharged by an assignment at such a time or under such circumstances as to preclude the giving of effective aid in the preparation and trial of the case."

Despite the *Powell* Court's carefully limited statement about the right to appointed counsel in state criminal cases, when the Court held, six years later, in

---

[a] The right to counsel is treated in Chapter 17 as well as in this chapter. Because the right to appointed counsel and the *Griffin-Douglas* "equality" principle provide important background for the confessions cases (Ch. 6) and the lineup cases (Ch. 7), these aspects of the right to counsel are treated at this point. Because other aspects of the right to counsel, such as the right to "effective" assistance of counsel, relate to later stages in the process, these aspects of the right are treated in Chapter 17.

Johnson v. Zerbst, 304 U.S. 458 (1938), that the Sixth Amendment required *federal* courts to provide indigent defendants with appointed counsel in all serious criminal cases (at least all felony cases), many thought the same rule would soon be applied to state prosecutions. For Justice Black, who wrote the opinion for the *Johnson* Court, painted with a broad brush, giving the impression that the Court was prepared to say that the right to counsel, appointed or retained, was a "fundamental" right made obligatory upon the states by the Fourteenth Amendment.

Thus, Justice Black called the right to counsel "one of the safeguards * * * deemed necessary to insure fundamental human rights of life and liberty" and the Sixth Amendment "a constant admonition that if the constitutional safeguards it provides be lost, justice will not 'still be done.'" Relying heavily on *Powell's* discussion of the general need for, and importance of, the right to counsel, *Johnson* concluded that the Sixth Amendment embodies "the obvious truth that the average defendant does not have the professional legal skill to protect himself when brought before a tribunal" and that the Amendment "withholds from federal courts, in all criminal proceedings, the power and authority to deprive an accused of his life or liberty unless he has or waives the assistance of counsel."

However, in *Betts v. Brady*, the first case set forth in this section, the Court refused to read *Powell* broadly or to apply *Johnson* to the states via the Fourteenth Amendment's due process clause. Instead, the Court formulated a "prejudice" or "special circumstances" rule: an indigent defendant in a non-capital case[b] had to show specifically that he had been "prejudiced" by the absence of a lawyer or that "special circumstances" (e.g., the defendant's lack of education or intelligence or the gravity and complexity of the offense charged) rendered criminal proceedings without the assistance of defense counsel "fundamentally unfair."[c]

One of the troubles with the *Betts v. Brady* doctrine was that its application was inherently speculative and problematic. A record produced by a layperson defending himself often makes the person *look* overwhelmingly guilty and the case *look* exceedingly simple. Such a record does not reflect what defenses or mitigating circumstances a trained advocate would have seen or what lines of inquiry she would have pursued. This point was made very forcefully by Justice Black (joined by Douglas and Murphy, JJ.), dissenting in *Betts*. Twenty-one years later, Justice Black wrote the opinion for the Court in *Gideon v. Wainwright,* overruling *Betts*.

The opinion in *Gideon,* the second case set forth in this section[d], might have been written differently. It might, to use concurring Justice Harlan's phrase, have

---

[b] Soon after *Betts,* the Court indicated that an indigent person had a "flat" or unqualified right to appointed counsel when (but only when) charged with a crime punishable by death.

[c] When the Court reviewed Betts' case, he had appellate counsel, but his lawyer was confident—too confident—that the Court would apply the full measure of the Sixth Amendment right to counsel to the states. Thus, he did not make any analysis of the trial and present any specific examples of how Betts was, or might have been, prejudiced by the absence of counsel. Commentators, upon review of the *Betts* record, have maintained that a number of such examples could have been shown.

[d] *Douglas v. California*, decided the same day as *Gideon,* also deals with the right to appointed counsel—on the first appeal, granted as a matter of right—but because it is based primarily on the Equal Protection Clause it is set forth in the next section.

accorded *Betts* "a more respectful burial." For example, Justice Black might have pointed out that in the two decades since *Betts* the assumption that a lawyerless defendant would usually be able to defend himself had fared poorly as the Court repeatedly found "special circumstances" requiring the services of counsel and constantly expanded the concept of "special circumstances."[e] Justice Black might also have noted that the assumption that a "special circumstances" test was more consistent with the "obligations of federalism" than an "absolute rule" had collapsed in the face of the proliferation of federal habeas corpus cases produced by the *Betts* rule and the resulting friction between state and federal courts.

But Justice Black made no attempt to show that developments in the two decades since *Betts* militated in favor of its demise. Perhaps he was reluctant to admit even the *original validity* of a decision that exemplified the evils (to him) of the "fundamental rights" interpretation of Fourteenth Amendment Due Process.[f] Perhaps he was determined to vindicate his own dissenting opinion in *Betts*.

Although *Gideon* was one of the most popular cases ever decided by the Supreme Court, it came fairly late in the day. Indeed, it is quite surprising that the Court did not establish the constitutional right to appointed counsel in all serious criminal cases until *two years after* it imposed the Fourth Amendment exclusionary rule on state courts as a matter of due process.

It is helpful to view criminal procedural due process as containing two major values or objectives. The first and the more obvious one is insuring the reliability of the guilt-determining process. The second and more elusive one is insuring respect for the dignity or liberty of the individual without regard to the reliability of the criminal process. The exclusionary rule (Ch. 3, § 1) implements the second goal; the right to counsel (sometimes called "the most pervasive right" of the accused or "the master key" to all rights) effectuates the first—and the most basic goal. Yet the Court moved ahead on the search and seizure front before it overruled the *Betts* rule.

Moreover, a major criticism of *Weeks* and *Mapp* (Ch. 3, § 1) was that because they addressed problems beyond the direct control of the courts these cases could not accomplish their goal—deterring illegal searches and seizures. But this criticism was not applicable to enlargement of the indigent defendant's right to counsel. For the *Betts-Gideon* line of cases dealt with the right to appointed counsel at arraignment, trial and sentencing, matters within the immediate and continuing control of the courts. Assuming arguendo that police officers and sheriffs are insensitive to acquittals and reversals, trial judges and prosecutors are not—and they would be entrusted with the task of carrying out the requirements of an enlarged right to appointed counsel.

---

[e] In *Chewning v. Cunningham*, 368 U.S. 443 (1962), the last of the *Betts* rule cases, the Court not only found "special circumstances" requiring the services of counsel, as it had in every case after 1950, but indicated that these circumstances would be made out whenever issues existed that "may well be considered by an *imaginative lawyer*" (emphasis added) without regard to "whether *any would have merit*" (emphasis added). As concurring Justice Harlan protested on that occasion, "the bare possibility that any of these improbable claims could have been asserted does not amount [to] 'exceptional circumstances' " as the *Betts* rule had long been understood.

[f] He had previously rejected that interpretation in *Adamson*. See pp. 38–40.

Note, too, that when the Court in *Mapp* imposed the exclusionary rule on the states in 1961, the states were evenly split on the question. But when the Court in *Gideon* reconsidered the *Betts* doctrine in 1963, some thirty-seven states—about a three to one margin—provided counsel for all indigent felony defendants regardless of special circumstances. Moreover, as Mr. Gideon's lawyers pointed out to the Supreme Court, of the thirteen states whose laws or rules did not require the appointment of counsel in all felony cases, eight usually did so as a matter of practice. Only five southern states made no regular provision for counsel in noncapital cases.

Of course, three years after *Gideon,* when the Court applied the right to assigned counsel to the proceedings in the police station (see *Miranda,* p. 433), *no* state had chosen to go nearly that far on its own and, unlike *Gideon* (when twenty-two states asked the Court to overrule *Betts*), no state urged the Court to go that far. That is one reason (but hardly the only reason) that *Miranda* had a much colder reception than *Gideon*.

How early in the criminal process the right to counsel should "begin" was not the only question left open by *Gideon*. Another was: At what stage in the criminal process does the right to counsel "end"? The first appeal as of right? Discretionary review in the state supreme court? Discretionary review in the U.S. Supreme Court? (See the next section, infra.) Still another question left open by *Gideon* was: What *kinds* of criminal cases are covered by *Gideon*?

Some thought *Gideon* should be limited to felony cases. Others thought it should include any crime *punishable* by a term of imprisonment. Still others thought a line should be drawn, as it had been in cases dealing with the right to jury, between serious misdemeanors and "petty offenses" (those punishable by six months imprisonment or less). As demonstrated by two cases discussed in this section, *Argersinger v. Hamlin* and *Scott v. Illinois,* the Court chose none of the aforementioned approaches. Instead, it adopted an "actual imprisonment" test: counsel must be appointed for an indigent defendant in any criminal case that actually leads to incarceration, even for a very brief period.

However, *Argersinger* and *Scott* left open another question: Does the *Gideon* right to appointed counsel apply to a situation where an unrepresented indigent defendant convicted of a misdemeanor is given a suspended jail sentence and placed on probation? This issue is addressed in *Alabama v. Shelton,* the last case set forth in this section.

BETTS V. BRADY
316 U.S. 455, 62 S.Ct. 1252, 86 L.Ed. 1595 (1942).

JUSTICE ROBERTS delivered the opinion of the Court.

Petitioner, an indigent, was indicted for robbery. His request for counsel was denied because local practice permitted appointment only in rape and murder prosecutions. Petitioner then pled not guilty and elected to be tried without a jury. At the trial he chose not to take the stand. He was convicted and sentenced to eight years imprisonment.

[The] due process clause of the Fourteenth Amendment does not incorporate, as such, the specific guarantees found in the Sixth Amendment although a denial by a state of rights or privileges specifically embodied in that and others of the first eight amendments may, in certain circumstances, or in connection with other elements, operate, in a given case, to deprive a litigant of due process of law in violation of the Fourteenth. [Due process] formulates a concept less rigid and more fluid than those envisaged in other specific and particular provisions of the Bill of Rights. Its application is less a matter of rule. Asserted denial is to be tested by an appraisal of the totality of facts in a given case.

[Petitioner] says the rule to be deduced from our former decisions is that, in every case, whatever the circumstances, one charged with crime, who is unable to obtain counsel, must be furnished counsel by the state. Expressions in the opinions of this court lend color to the argument, but, as the petitioner admits, none of our decisions squarely adjudicates the question now presented.

In *Powell v. Alabama,* 287 U.S. 45 (1932), ignorant and friendless negro youths, strangers in the community, without friends or means to obtain counsel, were hurried to trial for a capital offense without effective appointment of counsel [and] without adequate opportunity to consult even the counsel casually appointed to represent them. This occurred in a State whose statute law required the appointment of counsel for indigent defendants prosecuted for the offense charged. Thus the trial was conducted in disregard of every principle of fairness and in disregard of that which was declared by the law of the State a requisite of a fair trial. This court [stated] further that "under the circumstances [the] necessity of counsel was so vital and imperative that the failure of the trial court to make an effective appointment of counsel was likewise a denial of due process," but added: "whether this would be so in other criminal prosecutions, or under other circumstances, we need not determine. All that it is necessary now to decide, as we do decide, is that in a capital case, where the defendant is unable to employ counsel, and is incapable adequately of making his own defense because of ignorance, feeble-mindedness, illiteracy, or the like, it is the duty of the court, whether requested or not, to assign counsel for him as a necessary requisite of due process of law * * *"

* * * We have construed the [Sixth Amendment] to require appointment of counsel in all [federal] cases where a defendant is unable to procure the services of an attorney, and where the right has not been intentionally and competently waived. [*Johnson v. Zerbst,* 304 U.S. 458 (1938)]. Though [the] amendment lays down no rule for the conduct of the states, the question recurs whether the constraint laid by the amendment upon the national courts expresses a rule so fundamental and essential to a fair trial, and so, to due process of law, that it is made obligatory upon the states by the Fourteenth Amendment. Relevant data on the subject are afforded by constitutional and statutory provisions subsisting in the colonies and the states prior to the inclusion of the Bill of Rights in the national Constitution, and in the constitutional, legislative, and judicial history of the states to the present date.

[I]n the great majority of the states, it has been the considered judgment of the people, their representatives and their courts that appointment of counsel is not a fundamental right, essential to a fair trial. On the contrary, the matter has generally been deemed one of legislative policy. In the light of this evidence we are unable to say that the concept of due process incorporated in the Fourteenth Amendment obligates the states, whatever may be their own views, to furnish counsel in every such case. Every court has power, if it deems proper, to appoint counsel where that course seems to be required in the interest of fairness.

The practice of the courts of Maryland gives point to the principle that the states should not be straight-jacketed in this respect, by a construction of the Fourteenth Amendment. Judge Bond's opinion states, and counsel at the bar confirmed the fact, that in Maryland the usual practice is for the defendant to waive a trial by jury. This the petitioner did in the present case. Such trials, as Judge Bond remarks, are much more informal than jury trials and it is obvious that the judge can much better control the course of the trial and is in a better position to see impartial justice done than when the formalities of a jury trial are involved.

In this case there was no question of the commission of a robbery. The State's case consisted of evidence identifying the petitioner as the perpetrator. The defense was an alibi. Petitioner called and examined witnesses to prove that he was at another place at the time of the commission of the offense. The simple issue was the veracity of the testimony for the State and that for the defendant. As Judge Bond says, the accused was not helpless, but was a man forty-three years old, of ordinary intelligence and ability to take care of his own interests on the trial of that narrow issue. He had once before been in a criminal court, pleaded guilty to larceny and served a sentence and was not wholly unfamiliar with criminal procedure. It is quite clear that in Maryland, if the situation had been otherwise and it had appeared that the petitioner was, for any reason, at a serious disadvantage by reason of the lack of counsel, a refusal to appoint would have resulted in the reversal of a judgment of conviction.

[To] deduce from the due process clause a rule binding upon the states in this matter would be to impose upon them, as Judge Bond points out, a requirement without distinction between criminal charges of different magnitude or in respect of courts of varying jurisdiction. As he says: "Charges of small crimes tried before justices of the peace and capital charges tried in the higher courts would equally require the appointment of counsel. Presumably it would be argued that trials in the Traffic Court would require it." * * *

As we have said, the Fourteenth Amendment prohibits the conviction and incarceration of one whose trial is offensive to the common and fundamental ideas of fairness and right, and while want of counsel in a particular case may result in a conviction lacking in such fundamental fairness, we cannot say that the amendment embodies an inexorable command that no trial for any offense, or in any court, can be fairly conducted and justice accorded a defendant who is not represented by counsel.

The judgment is affirmed.

JUSTICE BLACK, dissenting, with whom JUSTICE DOUGLAS and JUSTICE MURPHY concur.

To hold that the petitioner had a constitutional right to counsel in this case does not require us to say that "no trial for any offense, or in any court, can be fairly conducted and justice accorded a defendant who is not represented by counsel." This case can be determined by resolution of a narrower question: whether in view of the nature of the offense and the circumstances of his trial and conviction, this petitioner was denied the procedural protection which is his right under the federal constitution. I think he was.

The petitioner [was] a farm hand, out of a job and on relief. [The] court below found that [he] had "at least an ordinary amount of intelligence." It is clear from his examination of witnesses that he was a man of little education.

If this case had come to us from a federal court, it is clear we should have to reverse it, because the Sixth Amendment makes the right to counsel in criminal cases inviolable by the federal government. I believe that the Fourteenth Amendment made the sixth applicable to the states. But this view [has] never been accepted by a majority of this Court and is not accepted today. * * * I believe, however, that under the prevailing view of due process, as reflected in the opinion just announced, a view which gives this Court such vast supervisory powers that I am not prepared to accept it without grave doubts, the judgment below should be reversed.

[The] right to counsel in a criminal proceeding is "fundamental." *Powell v. Alabama.* [A] practice cannot be reconciled with "common and fundamental ideas of fairness and right" which subjects innocent men to increased dangers of conviction merely because of their poverty. Whether a man is innocent cannot be determined from a trial in which as here, denial of counsel has made it impossible to conclude, with any satisfactory degree of certainty, that the defendant's case was adequately presented. * * *

Denial to the poor of the request for counsel in proceedings based on charges of serious crime has long been regarded as shocking to the "universal sense of justice" throughout this country. In 1854, for example, the Supreme Court of Indiana said: "It is not to be thought of, in a civilized community, for a moment, that any citizen put in jeopardy of life or liberty should be debarred of counsel because he was too poor to employ such aid. No Court could be respected, or respect itself, to sit and hear such a trial. The defence of the poor, in such cases, is a duty resting somewhere, which will be at once conceded as essential to the accused, to the Court, and to the public." And most of the other states have shown their agreement by constitutional provisions, statutes, or established practice judicially approved which assure that no man shall be deprived of counsel merely because of his poverty. Any other practice seems to me to defeat the promise of our democratic society to provide equal justice under the law.

GIDEON V. WAINWRIGHT

372 U.S. 335, 83 S.Ct. 792, 9 L.Ed.2d 799 (1963).

JUSTICE BLACK delivered the opinion of the Court.

Petitioner was charged in a Florida state court with having broken and entered a poolroom with intent to commit a misdemeanor. This offense is a felony under Florida law. Appearing in court without funds and without a lawyer, petitioner asked the court to appoint counsel for him, whereupon the following colloquy took place:

"The Court: Mr. Gideon, I am sorry, but I cannot appoint Counsel to represent you in this case. Under the laws of the State of Florida, the only time the Court can appoint Counsel to represent a Defendant is when that person is charged with a capital offense. * * *

"The Defendant: The United States Supreme Court says I am entitled to be represented by Counsel."

Put to trial before a jury, Gideon conducted his defense about as well as could be expected from a layman. He made an opening statement to the jury, cross-examined the State's witnesses, presented witnesses in his own defense, declined to testify himself, and made a short argument "emphasizing his innocence to the charge contained in the Information filed in this case." The jury returned a verdict of guilty, and petitioner was sentenced to serve five years in the state prison. Later, petitioner [unsuccessfully attacked his conviction and sentence in the state supreme court on the ground that the trial court's refusal to appoint counsel for him violated his constitutional rights]. Since 1942, when *Betts v. Brady* was decided by a divided Court, the problem of a defendant's federal constitutional right to counsel in a state court has been a continuing source of controversy and litigation in both state and federal courts. To give this problem another review here, we granted certiorari [and] appointed counsel to represent [petitioner].

We accept *Betts*'s assumption, based as it was on our prior cases, that a provision of the Bill of Rights which is "fundamental and essential to a fair trial" is made obligatory upon the States by the Fourteenth Amendment. We think the Court in *Betts* was wrong, however, in concluding that the Sixth Amendment's guarantee of counsel is not one of these fundamental rights. Ten years before *Betts*, this Court, after full consideration of all the historical data examined in *Betts*, had unequivocally declared that "the right to the aid of counsel is of this fundamental character." *Powell*. While the Court at the close of its *Powell* opinion did by its language, as this Court frequently does, limit its holding to the particular facts and circumstances of that case, its conclusions about the fundamental nature of the right to counsel are unmistakable. [The] fact is that in deciding as it did—that "appointment of counsel is not a fundamental right, essential to a fair trial"—the [*Betts* Court] made an abrupt break with its own well-considered precedents. In returning to these old precedents, sounder we believe than the new, we but restore constitutional principles established to achieve a fair system of justice. Not only these precedents but also reason and reflection require us to recognize that in our adversary system of criminal justice, any person haled into court, who is too poor to hire a lawyer, cannot be assured a fair trial unless counsel is provided for him. This seems to us to be an obvious truth. Governments, both state and federal, quite properly spend vast sums of money to establish machinery to try defendants accused of crime. Lawyers to prosecute are everywhere deemed essential to protect the public's interest in an orderly society. Similarly, there are few defendants charged with crime, few indeed, who fail to hire the best lawyers they can get to prepare and present their defenses. That government hires lawyers to prosecute and defendants who have the money hire lawyers to defend are the strongest indications of the widespread belief that lawyers in criminal courts are necessities, not luxuries. The right of one charged with crime to counsel may not be deemed fundamental and essential to fair trials in some countries, but it is in ours. From the very beginning, our state and national constitutions and laws have laid great emphasis on procedural and substantive safeguards designed to assure fair trials before impartial tribunals in which every defendant stands equal before the law. This noble ideal cannot be realized if the poor man charged with crime has to face his accusers without a lawyer to assist him. * * *

The Court in *Betts* departed from the sound wisdom upon which the Court's holding in *Powell* rested. Florida, supported by two other States, has asked that *Betts v. Brady* be left intact. Twenty-two States, as friends of the Court, argue that *Betts* was "an anachronism when handed down" and that it should now be overruled. We agree. * * * Reversed.[a]

JUSTICE CLARK, concurring in the result. * * *

[T]he Constitution makes no distinction between capital and noncapital cases. The Fourteenth Amendment requires due process of law for the deprival of "liberty" just as for deprival of "life," and there cannot constitutionally be a difference in the quality of the process based merely upon a supposed difference in the sanction involved. How can the Fourteenth Amendment tolerate a procedure which it condemns in capital cases on the ground that deprival of liberty may be less onerous than deprival of life—a value judgment not universally accepted—or that only the latter deprival is irrevocable? * * *

JUSTICE HARLAN, concurring.

I agree that *Betts* should be overruled, but consider it entitled to a more respectful burial than has been accorded, at least on the part of those of us who were not on the Court when that case was decided.

I cannot subscribe to the view that *Betts* represented "an abrupt break with its own well-considered precedents." [In *Powell*] this Court declared that under the particular facts there presented—"the ignorance and illiteracy of the defendants, their youth, the circumstances of public hostility [and] above all that they stood in deadly peril of their lives"—the state court had a duty to assign counsel for the trial as a necessary requisite of due process of law. It is evident that these limiting facts were not added to the opinion as an afterthought; they were repeatedly emphasized [and] were clearly regarded as important to the result.

---

[a] Gideon was retried, this time with appointed counsel, and acquitted. See Lewis, *Gideon's Trumpet* 223–38 (1964).

Thus when this Court, a decade later, decided *Betts,* it did no more than to admit of the possible existence of special circumstances in noncapital as well as capital trials, while at the same time to insist that such circumstances be shown in order to establish a denial of due process. The right to appointed counsel had been recognized as being considerably broader in federal prosecutions, see *Johnson v. Zerbst,* but to have imposed these requirements on the States would indeed have been "an abrupt break" with the almost immediate past. The declaration that the right to appointed counsel in state prosecutions, as established in *Powell,* was not limited to capital cases was in truth not a departure from, but an extension of, existing precedent.

The principles declared in *Powell* and in *Betts,* however, had a troubled journey throughout the years that have followed first the one case and then the other. Even by the time of the *Betts* decision, dictum in at least one of the Court's opinions had indicated that there was an absolute right to the services of counsel in the trial of state capital cases. * * *

In noncapital cases, the "special circumstances" rule has continued to exist in form while its substance has been substantially and steadily eroded. In the first decade after *Betts,* there were cases in which the Court found special circumstances to be lacking, but usually by a sharply divided vote. However, no such decision has been cited to us, and I have found none, [after] 1950. At the same time, there have been not a few cases in which special circumstances were found in little or nothing more than the "complexity" of the legal questions presented, although those questions were often of only routine difficulty. The Court has come to recognize, in other words, that the mere existence of a serious criminal charge constituted in itself special circumstances requiring the services of counsel at trial. In truth the *Betts* rule is no longer a reality.

This evolution, however, appears not to have been fully recognized by many state courts, in this instance charged with the front-line responsibility for the enforcement of constitutional rights. To continue a rule which is honored by this Court only with lip service is not a healthy thing and in the long run will do disservice to the federal system.

The special circumstances rule has been formally abandoned in capital cases, and the time has now come when it should be similarly abandoned in noncapital cases, at least as to offenses which, as the one involved here, carry the possibility of a substantial prison sentence. (Whether the rule should extend to *all* criminal cases need not now be decided.)

* * * In what is done today I do not understand the Court to depart from the principles laid down in *Palko* [or] to embrace the concept that the Fourteenth Amendment "incorporates" the Sixth Amendment as such. On these premises I join in the judgment of the Court.

ALABAMA V. SHELTON
535 U.S. 654, 122 S.Ct. 1764, 152 L.Ed.2d 888 (2002).

JUSTICE GINSBURG delivered the opinion of the Court. * * *

[*Gideon* left open the question whether, and to what extent, the right to appointed counsel in state criminal prosecutions applied to misdemeanor cases. *Argersinger v. Hamlin,* 407 U.S. 25 (1972) and *Scott v. Illinois,* 440 U.S. 367 (1979) addressed this issue.

[Argersinger, an indigent unrepresented by counsel, was convicted of carrying a concealed weapon, an offense punishable by imprisonment up to six months, and sentenced to 90 days in jail. The Florida Supreme Court took the position that the right to court-appointed counsel applied only to trials "for non-petty offenses punishable by more than six months imprisonment." But the Court, per DOUGLAS, J., disagreed: "While there is historical support for limiting the [right] to trial by jury [to] 'serious criminal cases,' there is no support for a similar limitation on the right to assistance of counsel. [Thus,] we reject [the] premise that since prosecutions for crimes punishable by imprisonment for less than six months may be tried without a jury, they may also be tried without a lawyer. [The] requirement for counsel may well be necessary for a fair trial even in a petty offense prosecution."

[Concurring JUSTICE POWELL, joined by Rehnquist, J., "would hold that the right to counsel in petty offenses is not absolute but is one to be determined by the trial courts expressing a judicial discretion on a case-by-case basis." Justice Powell believed that the majority opinion "foreshadows the adoption of a broad prophylactic rule applicable to all petty offenses [whether or not the defendant is actually incarcerated]. No one can foresee the consequences of such a drastic enlargement of the constitutional right to free counsel." However, as *Scott* made plain seven years later, Justice Powell's prediction turned out to be wrong.

[Scott, an indigent, was charged with shoplifting, punishable by as much as one year in jail. He was not provided counsel. After a bench trial he was convicted and fined $50. Writing for a 5–4 majority, REHNQUIST, J., saw no constitutional error: "[W]e believe that the central premise of *Argersinger*—that actual imprisonment is a penalty different in kind from fines or the mere threat of imprisonment—is essentially sound and warrants adoption of actual imprisonment as the line defining the constitutional right to appointment of counsel."

[JUSTICE BRENNAN, joined by Marshall and Stewart, JJ., dissented, emphasizing that the " 'theft' with which Scott was charged is certainly not a 'petty' one. It is punishable by a sentence of up to one year in jail. Unlike many traffic or other 'regulatory' offenses, it carries the moral stigma associated with common-law crimes traditionally recognized as indicative of moral depravity." The Court's opinion, mentioned Justice Brennan, "turns the reasoning of *Argersinger* on its head. It restricts the right to counsel, perhaps the most fundamental Sixth

Amendment right, more narrowly than the admittedly less fundamental right to jury trial * * *."[a]

[However, neither *Argersinger* nor *Scott* dealt with the question presented in *Shelton*: May a trial court impose a suspended or probationary prison sentence upon an indigent misdemeanor defendant who has not been provided counsel? After being convicted of a misdemeanor, third-degree assault, Shelton, an indigent defendant who had not been afforded counsel, was sentenced to a jail term of 30 days, which the trial court immediately suspended. Shelton was then placed on two years unsupervised probation.]

The Supreme Court of Alabama [took the position that] a suspended sentence constitutes a "term of imprisonment" within the meaning of *Argersinger* and *Scott* even though incarceration is not immediate or inevitable. [Accordingly,] the court affirmed Shelton's conviction and the monetary portion of his punishment, but invalidated "that aspect of his sentence imposing 30 days of suspended jail time." By reversing Shelton's suspended sentence, [the] court also vacated the two-year term of probation. * * *

Three positions are before us in this case. In line with the decision of the Supreme Court of Alabama, Shelton argues that an indigent defendant may not receive a suspended sentence unless he is offered or waives the assistance of state-appointed counsel. Alabama now concedes that the Sixth Amendment bars *activation* of a suspended sentence for an uncounseled conviction, but maintains that the Constitution does not prohibit *imposition* of such a sentence as a method of effectuating probationary punishment. [*Amicus* argues] in support of a third position, one Alabama has abandoned: Failure to appoint counsel to an indigent defendant "does not bar the imposition of a suspended or probationary sentence upon conviction of a misdemeanor, even though the defendant might be incarcerated in the event probation is revoked."

[Where] the State provides no counsel to an indigent defendant, does the Sixth Amendment permit activation of a suspended sentence upon the defendant's violation of the terms of probation? We conclude that it does not. A suspended sentence is a prison term imposed for the offense of conviction. Once the prison term is triggered, the defendant is incarcerated not for the probation violation, but for the underlying offense. The uncounseled conviction at that point "result[s] in imprisonment"; it "ends up in the actual deprivation of a person's liberty." This is precisely what the Sixth Amendment as interpreted in *Argersinger* and *Scott*, does not allow.

Amicus resists this reasoning primarily on two grounds. First, he attempts to align this case with our decisions in *Nichols*, 511 U.S. 738 (1994), and *Gagnon* v. *Scarpelli*, 411 U.S. 778 (1973). We conclude that Shelton's case is not properly bracketed with those dispositions.

---

[a] In a separate dissent, Blackmun, J., maintained that the right to appointed counsel "extends at least as far as the right to jury trial" and thus that "an indigent defendant in a state criminal case must be afforded appointed counsel whenever [he] is prosecuted for a nonpetty criminal offense, that is, one punishable by more than six months' imprisonment *or* whenever the defendant is actually subjected to a term of imprisonment."

Nichols presented the question whether the Sixth Amendment barred consideration of a defendant's prior uncounseled misdemeanor conviction in determining his sentence for a subsequent felony offense. [We ruled] that "an uncounseled misdemeanor conviction, valid under *Scott* because no prison term was imposed, is also valid when used to enhance punishment at a subsequent conviction." In *Gagnon*, the question was whether the defendant, who was placed on probation pursuant to a suspended sentence for armed robbery, had a due process right to representation by appointed counsel at a probation revocation hearing. We held that counsel was not invariably required in parole or probation revocation proceedings; we directed, instead, a "case-by-case approach" turning on the character of the issues involved.

[The] dispositive factor in [both *Gagnon* and *Nichols*] was not whether incarceration occurred immediately or only after some delay. Rather, the critical point was that the defendant had a recognized right to counsel when adjudicated guilty of the felony offense for which he was imprisoned. Unlike this case, in which revocation of probation would trigger a prison term imposed for a misdemeanor of which Shelton was found guilty without the aid of counsel, the sentences imposed in *Nichols* and *Gagnon* were for felony convictions—a federal drug conviction in *Nichols*, and a state armed robbery conviction in *Gagnon*—for which the right to counsel is unquestioned.

[Thus,] neither *Nichols* nor *Gagnon* altered or diminished *Argersinger's* command that "no person may be imprisoned *for any offense* [unless] he was represented by counsel at his trial" (emphasis added). Far from supporting *amicus'* position, *Gagnon* and *Nichols* simply highlight that the Sixth Amendment inquiry trains on the stage of the proceedings corresponding to [Shelton's] trial where his guilt was adjudicated, eligibility for imprisonment established, and prison sentence determined.

[*Amicus*] also contends that "practical considerations clearly weigh against" the extension of the Sixth Amendment appointed-counsel right to a defendant in Shelton's situation. [On the basis of figures suggesting that conditional sentences are commonly imposed but rarely activated,] *amicus* argues that a rule requiring appointed counsel in every case involving a suspended sentence would unduly hamper the States' attempts to impose effective probationary punishment. A more "workable solution," he contends, would permit imposition of a suspended sentence on an uncounseled defendant and require appointment of counsel, if at all, only at the probation revocation stage, when incarceration is imminent.

[*Amicus*] does not describe the contours of the hearing, that, he suggests, might precede revocation of a term of probation imposed on an uncounseled defendant. [In] Alabama, however, the character of the probation revocation hearing currently afforded is not in doubt. The proceeding is an "informal" one at which the defendant has no right to counsel, and the court no obligation to observe customary rules of evidence.

More significant, the sole issue at the hearing—apart from determinations about the necessity of confinement—is whether the defendant breached the terms of probation. [The] validity or reliability of the underlying conviction is beyond attack. * * *

We think it plain that a hearing so timed and structured cannot compensate for the absence of trial counsel, for it does not even address the key Sixth Amendment inquiry: whether the adjudication of guilt corresponding to the prison sentence is sufficiently reliable to permit incarceration. Deprived of counsel when tried, convicted, and sentenced, and unable to challenge the original judgment at a subsequent probation revocation hearing, a defendant in Shelton's circumstances faces incarceration on a conviction that has never been subjected to "the crucible of meaningful adversarial testing."

[The] dissent imagines a set of safeguards Alabama might provide at the probation revocation stage sufficient to cure its failure to appoint counsel prior to sentencing, including, perhaps, "complete retrial of the misdemeanor violation with assistance of counsel." But there is no cause for speculation about Alabama's procedures; they are established by Alabama statute and decisional law, and they bear no resemblance to those the dissent invents in its effort to sanction the prospect of Shelton's imprisonment on an uncounseled conviction.[5] Assessing the issue before us in light of actual circumstances, we do not comprehend how the procedures Alabama in fact provides at the probation revocation hearing could bring Shelton's sentence within constitutional bounds.

Nor do we agree with *amicus* or the dissent that our holding will "substantially limit the states' ability" to impose probation or encumber them with a "large, new burden." Most jurisdictions already provide a state-law right to appointed counsel more generous than that afforded by the Federal Constitution. All but 16 States, for example, would provide counsel to a defendant in Shelton's circumstances, either because he received a substantial fine or because state law authorized incarceration for the charged offense or provided for a maximum prison term of one year. There is thus scant reason to believe that a rule conditioning imposition of a suspended sentence on provision of appointed counsel would affect existing practice in the large majority of the States. And given the current commitment of most jurisdictions to affording court-appointed counsel to indigent misdemeanants while simultaneously preserving the option of probationary punishment, we do not share *amicus*' concern that other States may lack the capacity and resources to do the same.

Moreover, even if *amicus* is correct that "some courts and jurisdictions at least [can] not bear" the costs of the rule we confirm today, those States need not abandon probation or equivalent measures as viable forms of punishment. Although they may not attach probation to an imposed and suspended prison sentence, States unable or unwilling routinely to provide appointed counsel to misdemeanants in Shelton's situation are not without recourse to another option capable of yielding a similar result.

---

[5] In any event, the dissent is simply incorrect that our decision today effectively "deprive[s] the State of th[e] option" of placing an uncounseled defendant on probation, with incarceration conditioned on a guilty verdict following a trial *de novo*. That option is the functional equivalent of pretrial probation, as to which we entertain no constitutional doubt. * * *

That option is pretrial probation, employed in some form by at least 23 States. Under such an arrangement, the prosecutor and defendant agree to the defendant's participation in a pretrial rehabilitation program, which includes conditions typical of post-trial probation. The adjudication of guilt and imposition of sentence for the underlying offense then occur only if and when the defendant breaches those conditions.

[This] system reserves the appointed-counsel requirement for the "small percentage" of cases in which incarceration proves necessary, thus allowing a State to "supervise a course of rehabilitation" without providing a lawyer every time it wishes to pursue such a course. Unlike *amicus'* position, however, pretrial probation also respects the constitutional imperative that "no person may be imprisoned for any offense [unless] he was represented by counsel at his trial."

[Although Alabama concedes that *activation* of a suspended sentence in a case like *Shelton* is unconstitutional, it maintains] that there is no constitutional barrier to *imposition* of a suspended sentence that can never be enforced. [In] effect, Alabama invites us to regard two years' probation for Shelton as a separate and independent sentence, which "the State would have the same power to enforce [as] a judgment of a mere fine." [Similarly,] Alabama maintains, probation uncoupled from a prison sentence should trigger no immediate right to appointed counsel. Seen as a freestanding sentence, Alabama further asserts, probation could be enforced, as a criminal fine or restitution order could, in a contempt proceeding.

Alabama describes the contempt proceeding it envisions as one in which Shelton would receive "the full panoply of due process," including the assistance of counsel. Any sanction imposed would be for "post-conviction wrongdoing," not for the offense of conviction. "The maximum penalty faced would be a $100 fine and five days' imprisonment," not the 30 days ordered and suspended by the Alabama Circuit Court.

There is not so much as a hint, however, in the decision of the Supreme Court of Alabama, that Shelton's probation term is separable from the prison term to which it was tethered. Absent any prior presentation of the position the State now takes, we resist passing on it in the first instance. Our resistance to acting as a court of first view instead of one of review is heightened by the Alabama Attorney General's acknowledgment at oral argument that he did not know of any State that imposes, postconviction, on a par with a fine, a term of probation unattached to a suspended sentence.

[In] short, Alabama has developed its position late in this litigation and before the wrong forum. It is for the Alabama Supreme Court to consider before this Court does whether the suspended sentence alone is invalid, leaving Shelton's probation term freestanding and independently effective. * * * We confine our review to the ruling that the Alabama Supreme Court made in the case as presented to it: "[A] defendant who receives a suspended or probated sentence *to imprisonment* has a constitutional right to counsel" (emphasis added). We find no infirmity in that holding.

    * * *

Satisfied that Shelton is entitled to appointed counsel at the critical stage when his guilt or innocence of the charged crime is decided and his vulnerability to imprisonment is determined, we affirm the judgment of the Supreme Court of Alabama.

JUSTICE SCALIA, with whom THE CHIEF JUSTICE, JUSTICE KENNEDY, and JUSTICE THOMAS join, dissenting. * * *

[Respondent's] 30-day suspended sentence, and the accompanying 2-year term of probation, are invalidated for lack of appointed counsel even though respondent has not suffered, and may never suffer, a deprivation of liberty. The Court holds that the suspended sentence violates respondent's Sixth Amendment right to counsel because it "*may* 'end up in the actual deprivation of [respondent's] liberty' " (emphasis added), *if* he someday violates the terms of probation, *if* the court determines that no other punishment will "adequately protect the community from further criminal activity" or "avoid depreciating the seriousness of the violation." And to all of these contingencies there must yet be added, before the Court's decision makes sense, an element of rank speculation. Should all these contingencies occur, the Court speculates, the Alabama Supreme Court would mechanically apply its decisional law applicable to routine probation revocation (which establishes procedures that the Court finds inadequate) rather than adopt special procedures for situations that raise constitutional questions in light of *Argersinger* and *Scott*. The Court has miraculously divined how the Alabama justices would resolve a constitutional question.

But that question is not the one before us, and the Court has no business offering an advisory opinion on its answer. We are asked to decide whether "imposition of a suspended or conditional sentence in a misdemeanor case invoke[s] a defendant's Sixth Amendment right to counsel." Since *imposition* of a suspended sentence does not deprive a defendant of his personal liberty, the answer to *that* question is plainly no. In the future, *if and when* the State of Alabama seeks to imprison respondent on the previously suspended sentence, we can ask whether the procedural safeguards attending the imposition of that sentence comply with the Constitution. But that question is *not* before us now. * * *

Although the Court at one point purports to limit its decision to suspended sentences imposed on uncounseled misdemeanants in States, like Alabama, that offer only "minimal procedures" during probation revocation hearings, the text of today's opinion repudiates that limitation. In answering the question we asked *amicus* to address—whether "the Sixth Amendment permit[s] activation of a suspended sentence upon the defendant's violation of the terms of probation"—the Court states without qualification that "it does not." Thus, when the Court says it "doubt[s]" that any procedures attending the reimposition of the suspended sentence "could satisfy the Sixth Amendment," it must be using doubt as a euphemism for certitude.

The Court has no basis, moreover, for its "doubt." Surely the procedures attending reimposition of a suspended sentence would be adequate if they required, upon the defendant's request, complete retrial of the misdemeanor violation with assistance of counsel. By what right does the Court deprive the State of that option?[2] It may well be a sensible option, since most defendants will be induced to comply with the terms of their probation by the mere threat of a retrial that could send them to jail, and since the expense of those rare, counseled retrials may be much less than the expense of providing counsel initially in all misdemeanor cases that bear a possible sentence of imprisonment. And it may well be that, in some cases, even procedures short of complete retrial will suffice.

Our prior opinions placed considerable weight on the practical consequences of expanding the right to appointed counsel beyond cases of actual imprisonment. * * * Today, the Court gives this consideration the back of its hand. Its observation that "[a]ll but 16 States" already appoint counsel for defendants like respondent is interesting but quite irrelevant, since today's holding is not confined to *defendants like respondent*. Appointed counsel must henceforth be offered before *any* defendant can be awarded a suspended sentence, no matter how short. Only 24 States have announced a rule of this scope. Thus, the Court's decision imposes a large, new burden on a majority of the States, including some of the poorest. [Nor] should we discount the burden placed on the minority 24 States that currently provide counsel: that they keep their current disposition forever in place, however imprudent experience proves it to be.

Today's imposition upon the States finds justification neither in the text of the Constitution, nor in the settled practices of our people, nor in the prior jurisprudence of this Court. I respectfully dissent.

2. THE "BEGINNINGS" OF THE RIGHT TO COUNSEL

ROTHGERY V. GILLESPIE COUNTY
554 U.S. 191, 128 S.Ct. 2578, 171 L.Ed.2d 366 (2008).

JUSTICE SOUTER delivered the opinion of the Court.

[Relying on erroneous information that petitioner Rothgery had a previous felony conviction, Texas police made a warrantless arrest and promptly brought Rothgery before a magistrate judge for what is sometimes called an "article 15.17 hearing." At this hearing, a probable-cause determination is made (based on a police affidavit), bail is set and the defendant is apprised of the accusation against him. In Rothgery's case the magistrate judge concluded that probable cause existed and bail was set at $5,000. Rothgery was committed to jail, from which he was released after posting a security bond. Rothgery had no money for a lawyer and made several unheeded requests for appointed counsel.

---

[2] The Court asserts that pretrial probation, which its opinion permits, is the "functional equivalent" of post-trial probation with later retrial if the suspended sentence is to be activated. Even if that were so, I see no basis for forcing the State to employ one "functional equivalent" rather than the other. But in fact there is nothing but the Court's implausible speculation to support the proposition that pretrial probation will "yiel[d] a similar result." That would certainly be a curious coincidence, inasmuch as pretrial probation has the quite different purpose of conserving prosecutorial and judicial resources by forgoing trial. * * *

[Approximately six months later, Rothgery was indicted by a Texas grand jury for unlawful possession of a firearm by a felon, resulting in his rearrest the next day. When bail was increased to $15,000, Rothgery could not post it. As a result, he was placed in jail and remained there for three weeks.

[Shortly thereafter, Rothgery was finally assigned a lawyer. The lawyer's work led to the dismissal of the indictment. Rothgery then brought this 42 U.S.C. § 1983 action, claiming that if the county had provided him a lawyer within a reasonable time after the hearing, he would not have been indicted, rearrested, or jailed. He maintained that the county's unwritten policy of denying appointed counsel to indigent defendants out on bail until an indictment is entered violated his Sixth Amendment right to counsel. The Court of Appeal concluded, however, that the Sixth Amendment right to counsel had not attached at the article 15.17 hearing since there was "no indication that the officer who filed the probable cause affidavit * * * had any power to commit the state to prosecute," as there was "no knowledge or involvement of the prosecutor."]

The Sixth Amendment right of the "accused" to assistance of counsel in "all criminal prosecutions" is limited by its terms: "it does not attach until a prosecution is commenced." We have, for purposes of the right to counsel, pegged commencement to "the initiation of adversary judicial criminal proceedings—whether by way of formal charge, preliminary hearing, indictment, information, or arraignment," *United States v. Gouveia*, 467 U.S. 180 (1984). [The] rule is [a] recognition of the point at which "the government has committed itself to prosecute" [and] the accused "finds himself faced with the prosecutorial forces of organized society, and immersed in the intricacies of substantive and procedural criminal law." *Kirby v. Illinois* (1972) [p. 580]. The issue is whether Texas's article 15.17 hearing marks that point, with the consequent state obligation to appoint counsel within a reasonable time once a request for assistance is made.

[We] have twice held that the right to counsel attaches at the initial appearance before a judicial officer, see *Michigan v. Jackson,* 475 U.S. 625 (1986); *Brewer v. Williams* (1977) [p. 559]. This first time before a court, also known as a "preliminary arraignment" or "arraignment on the complaint," is generally the hearing at which "the magistrate informs the defendant of the charge in the complaint and of various rights in further proceedings," and "determine[s] the conditions for pretrial release." Texas's article 15.17 hearing is an initial appearance. * * * *Brewer* and *Jackson* control. * * *

[The *Jackson* case] flatly rejected the distinction [advanced by the State] between initial arraignment and arraignment on the indictment. [Our] conclusion was driven by the same considerations the Court has endorsed in *Brewer*: by the time a defendant is brought before a judicial officer, is informed of a formally lodged accusation, and has restrictions imposed on his liberty in aid of the prosecution, the State's relationship with the defendant has become solidly adversarial. And that is just as true when the proceeding comes before the indictment (in the case of the initial arraignment on a formal complaint) as when it comes after it (at an arraignment on an indictment).

[The] overwhelming consensus practice conforms to the rule that the first formal proceedings is the point of attachment. We are advised without contradiction that not only the Federal Government, including the District of Columbia, but 43 States take the first step toward appointing counsel "before, at, or just after initial appearance." [To] the extent [that 7 States] have been denying appointed counsel on the heels of the first appearance, they are a distinct minority. * * * Neither *Brewer* nor *Jackson* said a word about the prosecutor's involvement as a relevant fact, much less a controlling one. [An] attachment rule that turned on determining the moment of a prosecutor's first involvement would be "wholly unworkable and impossible to administer." [And] it would have the practical effect of resting attachment on such absurd distinctions as the day of the month an arrest is made [or] "the sophistication or lack thereof, of a jurisdiction's computer intake system."

[What] counts as a commitment to prosecute is an issue of federal law unaffected by allocations of power among state officials under a State's law [and] under the federal standard, an accusation filed with a judicial officer is sufficiently formal, and the government's commitment to prosecute it sufficiently concrete, when the accusation prompts arraignment and restrictions on the accused's liberty to facilitate the prosecution.

The County [argues] that in considering the significance of the initial appearance, we must ignore prejudice to a defendant's pretrial liberty, reasoning that it is the concern, not of the right to counsel, but of the speedy-trial right and the Fourth Amendment. * * * We think the County's reliance on *United States v. Gouveia* is misplaced, and its argument mistaken. The defendants in *Gouveia* were prison inmates, suspected of murder, who had been placed in an administrative detention unit and denied counsel up until an indictment was filed. [They] argued that their administrative detention should be treated as an accusation for purposes of the right to counsel because the government was actively investigating the crimes. * * * We [saw] no basis for "depart[ing] from our traditional interpretation of the Sixth Amendment right to counsel in order to provide additional protections for [the inmates]." *Gouveia*'s holding that the Sixth Amendment right to counsel had not attached has no application here. [Since] we are not asked to extend the right to counsel to a point earlier than formal judicial proceedings (as in *Gouveia*), but to defer it to those proceedings in which a prosecutor is involved, *Gouveia* does not speak to the question before us. * * *

[According] to the County, our cases (*Brewer* and *Jackson* aside) actually establish a "general rule that the right to counsel attaches at the point that [what the County calls] formal charges are filed," with exceptions allowed only in the case of "a very limited set of specific preindictment situations." The County suggests that the latter category should be limited to those appearances at which the aid of counsel is urgent and "the dangers to the accused of proceeding without counsel" are great. Texas's article 15.17 hearing should not count as one of those situations, the County says, because it is not of critical significance, since it "allows no presentation of witness testimony and provides no opportunity to expose weaknesses in the government's evidence, create a basis for later impeachment, or even engage in basic discovery."

We think the County is wrong. * * * Attachment occurs when the government has used the judicial machinery to signal a commitment to prosecute as spelled out in *Brewer* and *Jackson*. Once attachment occurs, the accused at least is entitled to the presence of appointed counsel during any "critical stage" of the postattachment proceedings; what makes a stage critical is what shows the need for counsel's presence. Thus, counsel must be appointed within a reasonable time after attachment to allow for adequate representation at any critical stage before trial, as well as trial itself.

[The County] makes an analytical mistake in its assumption that attachment necessarily requires the occurrence or imminence of a critical stage. On the contrary, it is irrelevant to attachment that the presence of counsel at an article 15.17 hearing, say, may not be critical, just as it is irrelevant that counsel's presence may not be critical when a prosecutor walks over to the trial court to file an information. * * *

Our holding is narrow. We do not decide whether the 6-month delay in appointment of counsel resulted in prejudice to Rothgery's Sixth Amendment rights, and have no occasion to consider what standards should apply in deciding this. We merely affirm what we have held before and what an overwhelming majority of American jurisdictions understand in practice: a criminal defendant's initial appearance before a judicial officer, where he learns the charge against him and his liberty is subject to restriction, marks the start of adversary judicial proceedings that trigger attachment of the Sixth Amendment right to counsel. * * *

CHIEF JUSTICE ROBERTS, with whom JUSTICE SCALIA joins, concurring.

Justice Thomas's analysis of the present issue is compelling, but I believe the result here is controlled by *Brewer v. Williams* (1977) and *Michigan v. Jackson* (1986). A sufficient case has not been made for revisiting those precedents, and accordingly I join the Court's opinion.

I also join Justice Alito's concurrence, which correctly distinguishes between the time the right to counsel attaches and the circumstances under which counsel must be provided.

JUSTICE ALITO, with whom the CHIEF JUSTICE and JUSTICE SCALIA join, concurring.

I join the Court's opinion because I do not understand it to hold that a defendant is entitled to the assistance of appointed counsel as soon as his Sixth Amendment right attaches. As I interpret our precedents, the term "attachment" signifies nothing more than the beginning of the defendant's prosecution. It does not mark the beginning of a substantive entitlement to the assistance of counsel.

[The] Sixth Amendment provides [that] "[i]n all criminal prosecutions, the accused shall enjoy the right [to] have the Assistance of Counsel for his defence." The Amendment thus defines the scope of the right to counsel in three ways: It provides *who* may assert the right ("the accused"); *when* the right may be asserted ("[i]n all criminal prosecutions"); and *what* the right guarantees ("the right [to] have the Assistance of Counsel for his defence").

It is in the context of interpreting the Amendment's answer to the second of these questions—when the right may be asserted—that we have spoken of the right "attaching." In *Kirby v. Illinois* (1972) [p. 580], a plurality of the Court explained that "a person's Sixth and Fourteenth Amendment right to counsel attaches only at or after the time that adversary judicial proceedings have been initiated against him." A majority of the Court elaborated on that explanation in *Moore v. Illinois*, 434 U.S. 220 (1977).

[When] we wrote in *Kirby* and *Moore* that the Sixth Amendment right had "attached," we evidently meant nothing more than that a "criminal prosecutio[n]" had begun. Our cases have generally used the term in that narrow fashion.

[As] the Court, notes, however, we have previously held that "arraignments" that were functionally indistinguishable from the Texas magistration marked the point at which the Sixth Amendment right to counsel "attached." It does not follow, however, and I do not understand the Court to hold, that the county had an obligation to appoint an attorney to represent petitioner within some specified period after his magistration. To so hold, the Court would need to do more than conclude that petitioner's criminal prosecution had begun. It would also need to conclude that the assistance of counsel in the wake of a Texas magistration is part of the substantive guarantee of the Sixth Amendment. That question lies beyond our reach, petitioner having never sought our review of it. [To] recall the framework laid out earlier, we have been asked to address only the *when* question, not the *what* question. Whereas the temporal scope of the right is defined by the words "[i]n all criminal prosecutions," the right's substantive guarantee flows from a different textual font: the words "Assistance of Counsel for his defence." * * *

We have thus rejected the argument that the Sixth Amendment entitles the criminal defendant to the assistance of appointed counsel at a probable cause hearing. See *Gerstein v. Pugh* (1975) [fn. a, p. 177]. [At] the same time, we have recognized that certain pretrial events may so prejudice the outcome of the defendant's prosecution that, as a practical matter, the defendant must be represented at those events in order to enjoy genuinely effective assistance at trial [referring to the lineup cases at Ch. 7, § 1]. [We] have also held that the assistance of counsel is guaranteed at a pretrial lineup, since "the confrontation compelled by the State between the accused and the victim or witnesses to a crime to elicit identification evidence is peculiarly riddled with innumerable dangers and variable factors which might seriously, even crucially, derogate from a fair trial." Other "critical stages" of the prosecution include pretrial interrogation, a pretrial psychiatric exam, and certain kinds of arraignments.

* * * I interpret the Sixth Amendment to require the appointment of counsel only after the defendant's prosecution has begun, and then only as necessary to guarantee the defendant effective assistance at trial. * * * Texas counties need only appoint counsel as far in advance of trial, and as far in advance of any pretrial "critical stage," as necessary to guarantee effective assistance at trial.

[The] Court expresses no opinion on whether Gillespie County satisfied that obligation in this case. Petitioner has asked us to decide only the limited question whether his magistration marked the beginning of his "criminal prosecutio[n]" within the meaning of the Sixth Amendment. Because I agree with the Court's resolution of that limited question, I join its opinion in full.

JUSTICE THOMAS, dissenting.

* * * Because the Court's holding is not supported by the original meaning of the Sixth Amendment or any reasonable interpretation of our precedents, I respectfully dissent.

[Neither] today's decision nor any of the other numerous decisions in which the Court has construed the right to counsel has attempted to discern the original meaning of "criminal prosecutio[n]" I think it appropriate to examine what a criminal prosecutio[n] would have been understood to entail by those who adopted the Sixth Amendment. * * *

"Prosecution," as Blackstone used the term, referred to "instituting a criminal suit" by filing a formal charging document—an indictment, presentment, or information—upon which the defendant was to be tried in a court with power to punish the alleged offense. And, significantly, Blackstone's usage appears to have accorded with the ordinary meaning of the term. * * *

[After examining the historical background of the term, Justice Thomas concludes that history furnishes] strong evidence that the term "criminal prosecutio[n]" in the Sixth Amendment refers to the commencement of a criminal suit by filing formal charges in a court with jurisdiction to try and punish the defendant. And on this understanding of the Sixth Amendment, it is clear that petitioner's initial appearance before the magistrate did not commence a "criminal prosecutio[n]." No formal charges had been filed. The only document submitted to the magistrate was the arresting officer's affidavit of probable cause. [As] the Court notes, our cases have "pegged commencement" of a criminal prosecution to "the initiation of adversary judicial criminal proceedings—whether by way of formal charge, preliminary hearing, indictment, information, or arraignment," *Kirby v. Illinois* (plurality opinion). The Court has repeated this formulation in virtually every right-to-counsel case decided since *Kirby*. * * *

It is noteworthy that *Kirby* did not purport to announce anything new; rather, it simply catalogued what the Court had previously held. And the point of the plurality's discussion was that the criminal process contains stages *prior* to commencement of a criminal prosecution. The holding of the case was that the right to counsel did not apply at a station house lineup that took place "*before* the defendant had been indicted or otherwise formally charged with any criminal offense."

[Rothgery's] initial appearance was not what *Kirby* described as an "arraignment." An arraignment, in its traditional and usual sense, is a postindictment proceeding at which the defendant enters a plea. Although the word "arraignment" is sometimes used to describe an initial appearance before a magistrate, that is not what *Kirby* meant when it said that the right to counsel attaches at an "arraignment." Rather, it meant the traditional, postindictment arraignment where the defendant enters a plea. This would be the most reasonable assumption even if there were nothing else to go on, since that is the primary meaning of the word, especially when used unmodified.

But there is no need to assume. *Kirby* purported to describe only what the Court had already held, and none of the cases *Kirby* cited involved an initial appearance.

[It] is clear that when *Kirby* was decided in 1972 there was no precedent in this Court for the conclusion that a criminal prosecution begins, and the right to counsel therefore attaches, at an initial appearance before a magistrate. The Court concludes, however, that two subsequent decisions—*Brewer v. Williams* and *Michigan v. Jackson*—stand for that proposition. Those decisions, which relied almost exclusively on *Kirby*, cannot bear the weight the Court puts on them. * * *

Even assuming, that the arraignment in *Brewer* was functionally identical to the initial appearance here, *Brewer* offered no reasoning for its conclusion that the right to counsel attached at such a proceeding. [There] is no indication that *Brewer* considered the difference between an arraignment on a warrant and an arraignment at which the defendant pleads to the indictment.

[The] only rule that can be derived from the face of the opinion in *Jackson* is that if a proceeding is called an "arraignment," the right to counsel attaches. That rule would not govern this case because petitioner's initial appearance was not called an "arraignment" (the parties refer to it as a "magistration"). And that would, in any case, be a silly rule. The Sixth Amendment consequences of a proceeding should turn on the substance of what happens there, not on what the State chooses to call it. But the Court in *Jackson* did not focus on the substantive distinction between an initial arraignment and an arraignment on the indictment. Instead, the Court simply cited *Kirby* and left it at that. In these circumstances, I would recognize *Jackson* for what it is—a cursory treatment of an issue that was not the primary focus of the Court's opinion. Surely *Jackson*'s footnote must yield to our reasoned precedents. * * * And our reasoned precedents provide no support for the conclusion that the right to counsel attaches on an initial appearance before a magistrate.

[Neither] petitioner nor the Court identifies any way in which petitioner's ability to receive a fair trial was undermined by the absence of counsel during the period between his initial appearance and his indictment. Nothing during that period exposed petitioner to the risk that he would be convicted as the result of ignorance of his rights. Instead, the gravamen of petitioner's complaint is that if counsel had been appointed earlier, he would have been able to stave off indictment by convincing the prosecutor that petitioner was not guilty of the crime alleged. But the Sixth Amendment protects against the risk of erroneous *conviction*, not the risk of unwarranted *prosecution*. See *Gouveia* (rejecting the notion that the "purpose of the right to counsel is to provide a defendant with a preindictment private investigator").

Petitioner argues that the right to counsel is implicated here because restrictions were imposed on his liberty when he was required to post bail. But we have never suggested that the accused's right to the assistance of counsel "for his defence" entails a right to use counsel as a sword to contest pretrial detention. To the contrary, we have flatly rejected that notion, reasoning that a defendant's liberty interests are protected by other constitutional guarantees.

[In] sum, neither the original meaning of the Sixth Amendment right to counsel nor our precedents interpreting the scope of that right supports the Court's holding that the right attaches at an initial appearance before a magistrate. * * *

3. THE *GRIFFIN-DOUGLAS* "EQUALITY" PRINCIPLE

Many commentators believe that the Warren Court's "revolution" in criminal procedure got underway when it handed down *Mapp v. Ohio* [p. 62] in 1961. But arguably the revolution began five years earlier, with *Griffin v. Illinois,* 351 U.S. 12 (1956).

In holding that indigent defendants must be furnished trial transcripts at state expense if such transcripts were necessary to effectuate appellate review, *Griffin* departed from then traditional equal protection doctrine. It viewed the "equality" principle as not only prohibiting the creation of inequalities by a state but imposing an "affirmative duty" to eliminate at least some inequalities not of the state's own doing. Illinois had simply ignored private inequalities of wealth and offered trial transcripts to every appellant on "equal terms," i.e., at a price which amounted to the cost of preparing them. But this was not enough.

There was no opinion of the Court in *Griffin*. Justice Black announced the judgment in a forceful and oft-quoted four-Justice opinion. He called the denial of a transcript for those who need but are unable to pay for one "a misfit in a country dedicated to affording equal justice to all and special privileges to none in the administration of its criminal law." Continued Black: "There can be no equal justice where the kind of trial a man gets depends on the amount of money he has. Destitute defendants must be afforded as adequate appellate review as defendants who have money enough to buy transcripts."

Dissenting Justice Harlan voiced sharp disagreement with Justice Black's approach. Harlan maintained that the Court's resolution of the equal protection claim in effect *required state discrimination*—in favor of indigents. It forced Illinois to give free to indigents "what it requires others to pay for."

But for *Douglas v. California,* the first case set forth in this section, *Griffin* and its early progeny,[a] could be narrowly interpreted as not affecting the right to

---

[a]   In the decade and a half following *Griffin,* its underlying principle was broadly applied. *Mayer v. Chicago,* 404 U.S. 189 (1971) carried the *Griffin* principle further than the Court ever carried the *Gideon* principle by holding that an indigent appellant cannot be denied a record of sufficient completeness to permit proper consideration of his claims even though he was convicted of ordinary violations punishable by fine only. More generally, a number of cases seemed to read *Griffin* for the proposition that an indigent defendant must be furnished any valuable or useful "tool" or instrument available for a price to others. See, e.g., *Roberts v. LaVallee,* 389 U.S. 40 (1967) (indigent defendant entitled to free transcript of preliminary hearing for use at trial, even though both defendant and his lawyer attended preliminary hearing and no indication of use to which preliminary hearing transcript could be put—points stressed by dissenting Justice Harlan).

counsel at all. Rather, the *Griffin* principle could be viewed as concerned merely with the *availability* of direct and collateral review, not the *quality* of such review. But for the *Douglas* case, *Griffin* could be read as requiring only that an indigent be allowed *access* to the courts, not that he be furnished with counsel as well. For the presence of counsel is not a *sine qua non* to access to the courts, as was the availability of the transcript in *Griffin* or the payment of filing fees in other cases applying *Griffin.*

Under this analysis, *Griffin* and the pre-*Gideon* doctrine of *Betts v. Brady* were reconcilable: The state need only provide a road, not guarantee that every person have equally as good a car to drive down it. After *Douglas,* however, the "access to the courts" interpretation of *Griffin* seemed untenable. For the *Douglas* Court considered denying counsel to an indigent appellant "a discrimination at least as invidious as that condemned in *Griffin.*"

Although it was careful to note that it was "dealing only with the *first appeal* granted as a matter of right to [all]" (emphasis in the original), the *Douglas* opinion contains language suggesting that *whenever* an indigent is permitted access to the courts he is *entitled to counsel* as well—that the state must do more than simply place a defendant "on the road," it must see that he has some vehicle—counsel—to use in travelling that "road." Nor is that all. *Griffin* and *Douglas,* at least if read generously, also suggest that the government must furnish an indigent defendant with *any* and *every* legal tool or legal service that a wealthy defendant is able to purchase.

In short, more than a few people thought that the *Griffin-Douglas* "equality" principle—the view that the administration of criminal justice cannot turn on the amount of money a defendant has—had no "stopping point," at least no obvious one. But the Court found a stopping point in *Ross v. Moffitt,* the second case set forth in this section.

DOUGLAS V. CALIFORNIA
372 U.S. 353, 83 S.Ct. 814, 9 L.Ed.2d 811 (1963).

JUSTICE DOUGLAS delivered the opinion of the Court. * * *

[The] record shows that petitioners requested, and were denied, the assistance of counsel on appeal, even though it plainly appeared they were indigents. In denying petitioners' requests, the California District Court of Appeal stated that it had "gone through" the record and had come to the conclusion that "no good whatever could be served by appointment of counsel." [The court] was acting in accordance with a California rule of criminal procedure which provides that state appellate courts, upon the request of an indigent for counsel, may make "an independent investigation of the record and determine whether it would be of advantage to the defendant or helpful to the appellate court to have counsel appointed. [After] such investigation, appellate courts should appoint counsel if in their opinion it would be helpful to the defendant or the court, and should deny the appointment of counsel only if in their judgment such appointment would be of no value to either the defendant or the court." * * *

We agree, however, with Justice Traynor of the California Supreme Court, who said that the "[d]enial of counsel on appeal [to an indigent] would seem to be a discrimination at least as invidious as that condemned in [*Griffin*," where] we held that a State may not grant appellate review in such a way as to discriminate against some convicted defendants on account of their poverty. [Whether the issue is a transcript on appeal or the assistance of counsel on appeal] the evil is the same: discrimination against the indigent. For there can be no equal justice where the kind of an appeal a man enjoys "depends on the amount of money he has." * * *

[Under California's] present practice the type of an appeal [one is afforded] hinges upon whether or not he can pay for the assistance of counsel. If he can the appellate court passes on the merits of his case only after having the full benefit of written briefs and oral argument by counsel. If he cannot the appellate court is forced to prejudge the merits before it can even determine whether counsel should be provided. At this stage in the proceedings only the barren record speaks for the indigent, and, unless the printed pages show that an injustice has been committed, he is forced to go without a champion on appeal. Any real chance he may have had of showing that his appeal has hidden merit is deprived him when the court decides on an *ex parte* examination of the record that the assistance of counsel is not required.

* * * We are dealing only with the first appeal, granted as a matter of right to rich and poor alike, from a criminal conviction. We need not now decide whether California would have to provide counsel for an indigent seeking [discretionary review or] whether counsel must be appointed for an indigent seeking review of an appellate affirmance of his conviction in this Court. [But] it is appropriate to observe that a State can, consistently with the Fourteenth Amendment, provide for differences so long as the result does not amount to a denial of due process or an "invidious discrimination." Absolute equality is not required; lines can be and are drawn and we often sustain them. [But] where the merits of the one and only appeal an indigent has as of right are decided without benefit of counsel, we think an unconstitutional line has been drawn between rich and poor.

When an indigent is forced to run this gantlet of a preliminary showing of merit, the right to appeal does not comport with fair procedure. [T]he discrimination is not between "possibly good and obviously bad cases," but between cases where the rich man can require the court to listen to argument of counsel before deciding on the merits, but a poor man cannot. There is lacking that equality demanded by the Fourteenth Amendment where the rich man, who appeals as of right, enjoys the benefit of counsel's examination into the record, research of the law, and marshalling of arguments on his behalf, while the indigent, already burdened by a preliminary determination that his case is without merit, is forced to shift for himself. The indigent, where the record is unclear or the errors are hidden, has only the right to a meaningless ritual, while the rich man has a meaningful appeal. * * *

Judgment of the District Court of Appeals vacated and case remanded.

JUSTICE CLARK, dissenting.

* * * We all know that the overwhelming percentage of *in forma pauperis* appeals are frivolous. Statistics of this Court show that over 96% of the petitions filed here are of this variety. [California's courts] after examining the record certified that [an] appointment [of counsel] would be neither advantageous to the petitioners nor helpful to the court. It, therefore, refused to go through the useless gesture of appointing an attorney. In my view neither the Equal Protection Clause nor the Due Process Clause requires more. I cannot understand why the Court says that this procedure afforded petitioners "a meaningless ritual." To appoint an attorney would not only have been utter extravagance and a waste of the State's funds but as surely "meaningless" to petitioners.

JUSTICE HARLAN, whom JUSTICE STEWART joins, dissenting.

[T]he Court appears to rely both on the Equal Protection Clause and on the guarantees of fair procedure inherent in the Due Process Clause of the Fourteenth Amendment, with obvious emphasis on "equal protection." In my view the Equal Protection Clause is not apposite, and its application to cases like the present one can lead only to mischievous results. This case should be judged solely under the Due Process Clause, and I do not believe that the California procedure violates that provision.

EQUAL PROTECTION

To approach the present problem in terms of the Equal Protection Clause is, I submit, but to substitute resounding phrases for analysis. I dissented from this approach in [*Griffin*] and I am constrained to dissent from the implicit extension of the equal protection approach here—to a case in which the State denies no one an appeal, but seeks only to keep within reasonable bounds the instances in which appellate counsel will be assigned to indigents.

The States, of course, are prohibited by the Equal Protection Clause from discriminating between "rich" and "poor" *as such* in the formulation and application of their laws. But it is a far different thing to suggest that this provision prevents the State from adopting a law of general applicability that may affect the poor more harshly than it does the rich, or, on the other hand, from making some effort to redress economic imbalances while not eliminating them entirely.

Every financial exaction which the State imposes on a uniform basis is more easily satisfied by the well-to-do than by the indigent. Yet I take it that no one would dispute the constitutional power of the State to levy a uniform sales tax, to charge tuition at a state university, to fix rates for the purchase of water from a municipal corporation, to impose a standard fine for criminal violations, or to establish minimum bail for various categories of offenses. Nor could it be contended that the State may not classify as crimes acts which the poor are more likely to commit than are the rich. And surely, there would be no basis for attacking a state law which provided benefits for the needy simply because those benefits fell short of the goods or services that others could purchase for themselves.

Laws such as these do not deny equal protection to the less fortunate for one essential reason: the Equal Protection Clause does not impose on the States "an affirmative duty to lift the handicaps flowing from differences in economic circumstances." To so construe it would be to read into the Constitution a philosophy of leveling that would be foreign to many of our basic concepts of the proper relations between government and society. The State may have a moral obligation to eliminate the evils of poverty, but it is not required by the Equal Protection Clause to give to some whatever others can afford.

* * * [I]t should be noted that if the present problem may be viewed as one of equal protection, so may the question of the right to appointed counsel at trial, and the Court's analysis of that right in *Gideon* [is] wholly unnecessary. The short way to dispose of *Gideon,* in other words, would be simply to say that the State deprives the indigent of equal protection whenever it fails to furnish him with legal services, and perhaps with other services as well, equivalent to those that the affluent defendant can obtain.[a]

The real question in this case, I submit, and the only one that permits of satisfactory analysis, is whether or not the state rule, as applied in this case, is consistent with the requirements of fair procedure guaranteed by the Due Process Clause. Of course, in considering this question, it must not be lost sight of that the State's responsibility under the Due Process Clause is to provide justice for all. Refusal to furnish criminal indigents with some things that others can afford may fall short of constitutional standards of fairness. The problem before us is whether this is such a case.

DUE PROCESS * * *

We have today held that in a case such as the one before us, there is an absolute right to the services of counsel at trial. *Gideon.* [But] the appellate procedures involved here stand on an entirely different constitutional footing. *First,* appellate review is in itself not required by the Fourteenth Amendment, *McKane v. Durston,* 153 U.S. 684 (1894); see *Griffin,* and thus the question presented is the narrow one whether the State's rules with respect to the appointment of counsel are so arbitrary or unreasonable, *in the context of the particular appellate procedure that it has established,* as to require their invalidation. *Second,* the kinds of questions that may arise on appeal are circumscribed by the record of the proceedings that led to the conviction; they do not encompass the large variety of tactical and strategic problems that must be resolved at the trial. *Third,* as California applies its rule, the indigent appellant receives the benefit of expert and conscientious legal appraisal of the merits of his case on the basis of the trial record, and whether or not he is assigned counsel, is guaranteed full consideration of his appeal. It would be painting with too broad a brush to conclude that under these circumstances an appeal is just like a trial.

---

[a] One may ask, too, why the Court failed even to discuss the applicability of the *Griffin-Douglas* "equality" principle to the issue raised in *Scott v. Illinois* [p. 383]. Since it is plain that one charged with an offense *punishable* by incarceration may *retain* counsel for his defense, does not the "equality" principle—especially in light of its application in *Mayer v. Chicago,* fn. a, p. 396—suggest that the "actual imprisonment" standard, even if it defensibly defines the Sixth Amendment right to appointed counsel, is unsatisfactory under the equal protection clause?

What the Court finds constitutionally offensive in California's procedure bears a striking resemblance to the rules of this Court and many state courts of last resort on petitions for certiorari or for leave to appeal filed by indigent defendants *pro se*. Under the practice of this Court, only if it appears from the petition for certiorari that a case merits review is leave to proceed *in forma pauperis* granted, the case transferred to the Appellate Docket, and counsel appointed. Since our review is generally discretionary, and since we are often not even given the benefit of a record in the proceedings below, the disadvantages to the indigent petitioner might be regarded as more substantial than in California. But as conscientiously committed as this Court is to the great principle of "Equal Justice Under Law," it has never deemed itself constitutionally required to appoint counsel to assist in the preparation of each of the more than 1,000 *pro se* petitions for certiorari currently being filed each Term. We should know from our own experience that appellate courts generally go out of their way to give fair consideration to those who are unrepresented.

The Court distinguishes our review from the present case on the grounds that the California rule relates to "the first appeal, granted as a matter of right." [But] I fail to see the significance of this difference. Surely, it cannot be contended that the requirements of fair procedure are exhausted once an indigent has been given one appellate review. Nor can it well be suggested that having appointed counsel is more necessary to the fair administration of justice in an initial appeal taken as a matter of right, which the reviewing court on the full record has already determined to be frivolous, than in a petition asking a higher appellate court to exercise its discretion to consider what may be a substantial constitutional claim.

I cannot agree that the Constitution prohibits a State in seeking to redress economic imbalances at its bar of justice and to provide indigents with full review, from taking reasonable steps to guard against needless expense. This is all that California has done. * * *

ROSS V. MOFFITT
417 U.S. 600, 94 S.Ct. 2437, 41 L.Ed.2d 341 (1974).

[Like many other states, the North Carolina appellate system is multitiered, providing for both an intermediate Court of Appeals and a Supreme Court. North Carolina authorizes appointment of counsel for a convicted defendant appealing to the intermediate court of appeals, but not for a defendant who seeks either discretionary review in the state supreme court or a writ of certiorari in the U.S. Supreme Court. In one case, the Mecklenburg County forgery conviction, respondent sought appointed counsel for discretionary review in the state supreme court. In another case, the Guilford County forgery conviction, respondent was represented by the public defender in the state supreme court, but sought court-appointed counsel to prepare a writ of certiorari to the U.S. Supreme Court. On federal habeas corpus, a unanimous panel of the U.S. Court of Appeals for the Fourth Circuit, per Haynsworth, C.J., held that the *Douglas* rationale required appointment of counsel in both instances.]

JUSTICE REHNQUIST delivered the opinion of the Court.

[In *Griffin*, the Court struck down] an Illinois rule allowing a convicted criminal defendant to present claims of trial error to the [state supreme court] only if he procured a transcript of the testimony adduced at his trial. No exception was made for the indigent defendant, and thus one who was unable to pay the cost of obtaining such a transcript was precluded from obtaining appellate review of asserted trial error * * *.

[*Griffin* and succeeding cases] stand for the proposition that a State cannot arbitrarily cut off appeal rights for indigents while leaving open avenues of appeal for more affluent persons. In *Douglas*, however, [the] Court departed somewhat from the limited doctrine of [these] cases and undertook an examination of whether an indigent's access to the appellate system was adequate. [The *Douglas* Court] concluded that a State does not fulfill its responsibility toward indigent defendants merely by waiving its own requirements that a convicted defendant procure a transcript or pay a fee in order to appeal, and held that the State must go further and provide counsel for the indigent on his first appeal as of right. It is this decision we are asked to extend today. * * *

The precise rationale for the *Griffin* and *Douglas* lines of cases has never been explicitly stated, some support being derived from the Equal Protection Clause of the Fourteenth Amendment, and some from the Due Process Clause of that Amendment. Neither clause by itself provides an entirely satisfactory basis for the result reached, each depending on a different inquiry which emphasizes different factors. "Due process" emphasizes fairness between the State and the individual dealing with the State, regardless of how other individuals in the same situation may be treated. "Equal protection," on the other hand, emphasizes disparity in treatment by a State between classes of individuals whose situations are arguably indistinguishable. We will address these issues separately in the succeeding sections.

Recognition of the due process rationale in *Douglas* is found both in the Court's opinion and in the dissenting opinion of Mr. Justice Harlan. The Court in *Douglas* stated that "[w]hen an individual is forced to run this gantlet of a preliminary showing of merit, the right to appeal does not comport with fair procedure." Mr. Justice Harlan thought that the due process issue in *Douglas* was the only one worthy of extended consideration. * * *

We do not believe that the Due Process Clause requires North Carolina to provide respondent with counsel on his discretionary appeal to the State Supreme Court. At the trial stage of a criminal proceeding, the right of an indigent defendant to counsel [is] fundamental and binding upon the States by virtue of the Sixth and Fourteenth Amendments. But there are significant differences between the trial and appellate stages of a criminal proceeding. The purpose of the trial stage from the State's point of view is to convert a criminal defendant from a person presumed innocent to one found guilty beyond a reasonable doubt. To accomplish this purpose, the State employs a prosecuting attorney who presents evidence to the court, challenges any witnesses offered by the defendant, argues rulings of the court, and makes direct arguments to the court or jury seeking to persuade them of the defendant's guilt. Under these circumstances " * * * reason and reflection require us to recognize that in our adversary system of criminal justice, any person haled into court, who is too poor to hire a lawyer, cannot be assured a fair trial unless counsel is provided for him." *Gideon.*

By contrast, it is ordinarily the defendant, rather than the State, who initiates the appellate process, seeking not to fend off the efforts of the State's prosecutor but rather to overturn a finding of guilt made by a judge or jury below. The defendant needs an attorney on appeal not as a shield to protect him against being "haled into court" by the State and stripped of his presumption of innocence, but rather as a sword to upset the prior determination of guilt. This difference is significant for, while no one would agree that the State may simply dispense with the trial stage of proceedings without a criminal defendant's consent, it is clear that the State need not provide any appeal at all. *McKane v. Durston.* The fact that an appeal *has* been provided does not automatically mean that a State then acts unfairly by refusing to provide counsel to indigent defendants at every stage of the way. Unfairness results only if indigents are singled out by the State and denied meaningful access to that system because of their poverty. That question is more profitably considered under an equal protection analysis.

Language invoking equal protection notions is prominent both in *Douglas* and in other cases treating the rights of indigents on appeal. * * * Despite the tendency of all rights "to declare themselves absolute to their logical extreme," there are obviously limits beyond which the equal protection analysis may not be pressed without doing violence to principles recognized in other decisions of this Court. The Fourteenth Amendment "does not require absolute equality or precisely equal advantages," nor does it require the State to "equalize economic conditions." *Griffin* (Frankfurter, J., concurring). It does require [that] indigents have an adequate opportunity to present their claims fairly within the adversarial system. The State cannot adopt procedures which leave an indigent defendant "entirely cut off from any appeal at all," by virtue of his indigency, *Lane,* or extend to such indigent defendants merely a "meaningless ritual" while others in better economic circumstances have a "meaningful appeal." *Douglas.* The question is not one of absolutes, but one of degrees. In this case we do not believe that the Equal Protection Clause when interpreted in the context of these cases, requires North Carolina to provide free counsel for indigent defendants seeking to take discretionary appeals to the North Carolina Supreme Court, or to file petitions for certiorari in this Court.

[The] facts show that respondent, in connection with his Mecklenburg County conviction, received the benefit of counsel in examining the record of his trial and in preparing an appellate brief on his behalf for the state Court of Appeals. Thus, prior to his seeking discretionary review in the State Supreme Court, his claims "had once been presented by a lawyer and passed upon by an appellate court." *Douglas.* We do not believe that it can be said, therefore, that a defendant in respondent's circumstances is denied meaningful access to the North Carolina Supreme Court simply because the State does not appoint counsel to aid him in seeking review in that court. At that stage he will have, at the very least, a transcript or other record of trial proceedings, a brief on his behalf in the Court of

Appeals setting forth his claims of error, and in many cases an opinion by the Court of Appeals disposing of his case. These materials, supplemented by whatever submission respondent may make *pro se,* would appear to provide the Supreme Court of North Carolina with an adequate basis on which to base its decision to grant or deny review.

We are fortified in this conclusion by our understanding of the function served by discretionary review in the North Carolina Supreme Court. The critical issue in that court, as we perceive it, is not whether there has been "a correct adjudication of guilt" in every individual case, but rather whether "the subject matter of the appeal has significant public interest," whether "the cause involves legal principles of major significance to the jurisprudence of the state," or whether the decision below is in probable conflict with a decision of the Supreme Court. The Supreme Court may deny certiorari even though it believes that the decision of the Court of Appeals was incorrect, since a decision which appears incorrect may nevertheless fail to satisfy any of the criteria discussed above. Once a defendant's claims of error are organized and presented in a lawyer-like fashion to the Court of Appeals, the justices of the Supreme Court of North Carolina who make the decision to grant or deny discretionary review should be able to ascertain whether his case satisfies the standards established by the legislature for such review.

This is not to say, of course, that a skilled lawyer, particularly one trained in the somewhat arcane art of preparing petitions for discretionary review, would not prove helpful to any litigant able to employ him. An indigent defendant seeking review in the Supreme Court of North Carolina is therefore somewhat handicapped in comparison with a wealthy defendant who has counsel assisting him in every conceivable manner at every stage in the proceeding. But both the opportunity to have counsel prepare an initial brief in the Court of Appeals and the nature of discretionary review in the Supreme Court of North Carolina make this relative handicap far less than the handicap borne by the indigent defendant denied counsel on his initial appeal as of right in *Douglas.* And the fact that a particular service might be of benefit to an indigent defendant does not mean that the service is constitutionally required. The duty of the State under our cases is not to duplicate the legal arsenal that may be privately retained by a criminal defendant in a continuing effort to reverse his conviction, but only to assure the indigent defendant an adequate opportunity to present his claims fairly in the context of the State's appellate process. We think respondent was given that opportunity under the existing North Carolina system.

Much of the discussion in the preceding section is equally relevant to the question of whether a State must provide counsel for a defendant seeking review of his conviction in this Court. North Carolina will have provided counsel for a convicted defendant's only appeal as of right, and the brief prepared by that counsel together with one and perhaps two North Carolina appellate opinions will be available to this Court in order that it may decide whether or not to grant certiorari. This Court's review, much like that of the Supreme Court of North Carolina, is discretionary and depends on numerous factors other than the perceived correctness of the judgment we are asked to review.

There is also a significant difference between the source of the right to seek discretionary review in the Supreme Court of North Carolina and the source of the right to seek discretionary review in this Court. The former is conferred by the statutes of the State of North Carolina, but the latter is granted by statutes enacted by Congress. Thus the argument relied upon in the *Griffin* and *Douglas* cases, that the State having once created a right of appeal must give all persons an equal opportunity to enjoy the right, is by its terms inapplicable. The right to seek certiorari in this Court is not granted by any State, and exists by virtue of federal statute with or without the consent of the State whose judgment is sought to be reviewed.

The suggestion that a State is responsible for providing counsel to one petitioning this Court simply because it initiated the prosecution which led to the judgment sought to be reviewed is unsupported by either reason or authority. It would be quite as logical under the rationale of *Douglas* and *Griffin,* and indeed perhaps more so, to require that the Federal Government or this Court furnish and compensate counsel for petitioners who seek certiorari here to review state judgments of conviction. Yet this Court has followed a consistent policy of denying applications for appointment of counsel by persons seeking to file jurisdictional statements or petitions for certiorari in this Court. In the light of these authorities, it would be odd, indeed, to read the Fourteenth Amendment to impose such a requirement on the States, and we decline to do so.

We do not mean by this opinion to in any way discourage those States which have, as a matter of legislative choice, made counsel available to convicted defendants at all stages of judicial review. Some States which might well choose to do so as a matter of legislative policy may conceivably find that other claims for public funds within or without the criminal justice system preclude the implementation of such a policy at the present time. [T]he Fourteenth Amendment leaves these choices to the State * * *.[a]

JUSTICE DOUGLAS, with whom JUSTICE BRENNAN and JUSTICE MARSHALL concur, dissenting.

[In his opinion below] Chief Judge Haynsworth could find "no logical basis for differentiation between appeals of right and permissive review procedures in the context of the Constitution and the right to counsel." More familiar with the functioning of the North Carolina criminal justice system than are we, he

---

[a]   A decade after *Ross v. Moffitt,* the Court broke its many years of silence on the issue of an indigent defendant's right to a psychiatrist and other expert assistance and held that, at least when an indigent defendant has made a preliminary showing that his sanity at the time of the offense is likely to be a significant factor at the trial, the state must provide the assistance of a psychiatrist for his defense. *Ake v. Oklahoma,* 470 U.S. 68 (1985).

Ake confirms the tendency of the post-*Ross* cases to rely on due process rather than equal protection analysis in determining the constitutional rights of indigent criminal defendants. Thus the *Ake* Court reaffirmed the need for the state to take steps to assure that an indigent defendant had "a fair opportunity" or "an adequate opportunity" to present his defense. The Court also noted that in implementing the *Griffin* "equality" principle it had "focused on identifying the 'basic tools of an adequate defense or appeal' [and] required that such tools be provided to [those] who cannot afford to pay for them." See also *Evitts v. Lucey,* 469 U.S. 387, 403 (1985); *Bearden v. Georgia,* 461 U.S. 660, 665 (1983); *United States v. MacCollom,* 426 U.S. 317, 324 (1976).

concluded that "in the context of constitutional questions arising in criminal prosecutions, permissive review in the state's highest court may be predictably the most meaningful review the conviction will receive." The North Carolina Court of Appeals, for example, will be constrained in diverging from an earlier opinion of the State Supreme Court, even if subsequent developments have rendered the earlier Supreme Court decision suspect. "[T]he state's highest court remains the ultimate arbiter of the rights of its citizens."

Chief Judge Haynsworth also correctly observed that the indigent defendant proceeding without counsel is at a substantial disadvantage relative to wealthy defendants represented by counsel when he is forced to fend for himself in seeking discretionary review from the State Supreme Court or from this Court. It may well not be enough to allege error in the courts below in layman's terms; a more sophisticated approach may be demanded:

"An indigent defendant is as much in need of the assistance of a lawyer in preparing and filing a petition for certiorari as he is in the handling of an appeal as of right. In many appeals, an articulate defendant could file an effective brief by telling his story in simple language without legalisms, but the technical requirement for applications for writs of certiorari are hazards which one untrained in the law could hardly be expected to negotiate.

" 'Certiorari proceedings constitute a highly specialized aspect of appellate work. The factors which [a court] deems important in connection with deciding whether to grant certiorari are certainly not within the normal knowledge of an indigent appellant.' Boskey, *The Right to Counsel in Appellate Proceedings*, 45 Minn.L.Rev. 783, 797 (1961)."

* * * The right to discretionary review is a substantial one, and one where a lawyer can be of significant assistance to an indigent defendant. It was correctly perceived below that the "same concepts of fairness and equality which require counsel in a first appeal of right, require counsel in other and subsequent discretionary appeals."[b]

---

[b] Must counsel be appointed for indigent defendants seeking first-tier discretionary appellate review of guilty pleas or *nolo contendere* pleas? Yes, answered a 6–3 majority, per Ginsberg J., in *Halbert v. Michigan* 545 U.S. 605 (2005); the Due Process and Equal Protection Clauses require the appointment of counsel in such instances.

Michigan has a two-tier appellate system. The State Supreme Court hears appeals by leave only. The intermediate Court of Appeals hears appeals from criminal convictions as of right, *except* that one convicted on a guilty or *nolo contendere* plea who seeks intermediate appellate review must apply for leave to appeal. Under Michigan law, most indigent defendants convicted on a plea had to proceed *pro se* in seeking leave to appeal to the Court of Appeals.

The *Halbert* majority recalled that two considerations were key in *Douglas*: (1) an appeal "of right" yields an adjudication on the merits; (2) first-tier appellate review differs from subsequent appellate stages because at the later stages of review the defendant's claims "have once been presented by a lawyer and passed upon by an appellate court." *Ross* declined to extend the *Douglas* rationale to *second-tier* discretionary review, explained the Court, because (1) at that stage, error correction is not the reviewing court's primary function and (2) a defendant who has received counsel's assistance in a first-tier appeal as of right would be armed with a record of the trial proceedings, a brief in the appellate court and, often, an opinion by the appellate court resolving the case.

Two aspects of Michigan's appellate review system led the Court to conclude that the instant case should be aligned with *Douglas*, not *Ross*: "First in determining how to dispose of an application for leave to appeal, Michigan's intermediate appellate court looks to the merits of the claims made in the application. Second, indigent defendants pursuing first-tier review in the Court of Appeals are generally ill-equipped to represent themselves."

Dissenting Justice Thomas, joined by Rehnquist, C.J., and Scalia, J., protested:

"[*Douglas*] does not support extending the right to counsel to any form of discretionary review, as *Ross* and later cases make clear. Moreover, Michigan has not engaged in the sort of invidious discrimination against indigent defendants that *Douglas* condemns. Michigan has done no more than recognize the undeniable difference between defendants who plead guilty and those who maintain their innocence, in an effort to divert resources from largely frivolous appeals to more meritorious ones.

" * * * Like the defendant in *Douglas*, Halbert requests appointment counsel for an initial appeal before an intermediate appellate court. But like the defendant in *Ross*, Halbert requests appointed counsel for an appeal that is discretionary, not as of right. Crucially, however, *Douglas* noted that its decision extended only to initial appeals *as of right*—and later cases have reaffirmed that understanding. This Court has never required States to appoint counsel for discretionary review. * * *

"Just as important, the rationale of *Douglas* does not support extending the right to counsel to this particular form of discretionary review. [The *Griffin/Douglas* cases] have a common theme. States may not impose financial barriers that preclude indigent defendants from securing appellate review altogether."

CHAPTER 6

POLICE INTERROGATION
AND CONFESSIONS

■ ■ ■

1. THE "VOLUNTARINESS" TEST

Whatever the meaning of the elusive terms "involuntary" and "coerced" confessions in the 1950s and 1960s, for centuries the rule that a confession was admissible so long as it was "voluntary" was more or less an alternative statement of the rule that a confession was admissible so long as it was free of influences which made it "untrustworthy" or "probably untrue." Thus, Wigmore, the leading authority on evidence, reflected the law prevailing at the time when in 1940 he pointed out that a confession was not inadmissible because of "any *illegality* in the method of obtaining it" or "because of any connection with the *privilege against self-incrimination.*" (The Court did not apply the privilege against compulsory self-incrimination to the proceedings in the police station and other "in-custody questioning" until its 1966 decision in *Miranda.*)

The "untrustworthiness" rationale, the view that the rules governing the admissibility of confessions were merely a system of safeguards against false confessions, could explain the exclusion of the confession in *Brown v. Mississippi,* 297 U.S. 278 (1936), the first Fourteenth Amendment Due Process confession case, where the deputy sheriff who had presided over the beatings of the defendants conceded that one had been whipped, "but not too much for a Negro." And the same rationale was also adequate to explain the exclusion of confessions in the cases that immediately followed the *Brown* case, such as *Chambers v. Florida,* 309 U.S. 227 (1940) and *Ward v. Texas,* 316 U.S. 547 (1942), for they too, involved actual or threatened physical violence. But as the crude practices of the early cases grew outmoded and cases involving more subtle pressures began to appear, it became more difficult to assume that the resulting confessions were untrustworthy.

The first case in this section, *Ashcraft v. Tennessee,* illustrates how the rationale for excluding confessions was changing. There was good reason to think that Ashcraft had indeed been involved in his wife's murder. Nevertheless, calling the extended police questioning to which Ashcraft had been subjected "inherently coercive," the Court ruled that the defendant's confession should not have been allowed into evidence. Under the circumstances, *Ashcraft* seems to reflect less concern with the reliability of the confession than disapproval of police methods which the Court considered to be dangerous and subject to abuse.

Although he joined Justice Jackson's dissent in *Ashcraft,* Justice Frankfurter soon became the leading exponent of the "police misconduct" or "police methods" rationale for barring the use of confessions. According to this rationale, in order to condemn, and deter, offensive or otherwise objectionable police interrogation methods, it was necessary to exclude confessions produced by such methods regardless of how trustworthy they might be.

Thus in *Watts v. Indiana,* 338 U.S. 49 (1949), and two companion cases, the Court reversed three convictions resting on coerced confessions without disputing the accuracy of Justice Jackson's observation (concurring in *Watts* and dissenting in the other cases) that "checked with external evidence [the confessions in each case] are inherently believable and were not shaken as to truth by anything that occurred at the trial." Justice Frankfurter, who wrote the principal opinion in *Watts,* commented: "In holding that the Due Process Clause *bars police procedure* which violates the basic notions of our accusatorial mode of prosecuting crime and vitiates a conviction based on the fruits of such procedure, we apply the Due Process Clause to its historic function of *assuring appropriate procedure* before liberty is curtailed or life is taken." (Emphasis added.)

Three years later, speaking for the Court in the famous "stomach-pumping" case of *Rochin v. California,* discussed fn. a, p. 39, Justice Frankfurter viewed the coerced confession cases as "only instances of the general requirement that states in their prosecution respect certain decencies of civilized conduct." Involuntary confessions, he pointed out, "are inadmissible under the Due Process Clause even though statements contained in them may be independently established as true" because they "offend the community's sense of fair play and decency."

The second case in this section demonstrates how the totality of the circumstances voluntariness test was applied in a world where the Court was more focused on police methods than reliability. Whereas the Court in *Ashcraft* adopted a *per se* prohibition on thirty-six hours of continuous questioning as inherently compulsive, the Court in *Spano v. New York,* 360 U.S. 315 (1959), relied on the more traditional totality of the circumstances approach to conclude that the methods used by the police to obtain a confession were sufficient to overbear the suspect's will.

Perhaps the most emphatic statement of the "police methods" rationale appears in *Rogers v. Richmond,* 365 U.S. 534 (1961), one of Justice Frankfurter's last opinions on confessions. After more conventional methods had failed to produce any incriminating statements, a police chief pretended to order petitioner's ailing wife brought down to headquarters for questioning. Petitioner promptly confessed to the murder for which he was later convicted. The trial judge found that the police chief's pretense had "no tendency to produce a confession that was not in accord with the truth" and in his charge to the jury he indicated that the admissibility of the confession should turn on its probable reliability. But the Court, speaking through Justice Frankfurter, disagreed:

> "[Convictions based on involuntary confessions must fall] not so much because such confessions are unlikely to be true but because the methods used to extract them offend an underlying principle in the enforcement of our criminal law; that ours is an accusatorial and not an inquisitional system. * * * Indeed, in many of the cases [reversing] state

convictions involving the use of confessions obtained by impermissible methods, independent corroborating evidence left little doubt of the truth of what the defendant had confessed. * * * The attention of the trial judge should have been focused [on] whether the [police behavior] was such as to overbear petitioner's will to resist and bring about confessions not freely self determined—a question to be answered with complete disregard of whether or not petitioner in fact spoke the truth."[a]

Justice Jackson strongly resisted the expansion of the grounds for excluding confessions. *Ashcraft* is a great case only because Jackson's dissent made it so. No piece of writing better illustrates his famed powers of advocacy and extraordinary directness of approach. The crucial question, maintained Jackson, was not whether other suspects might have been overcome by the prolonged questioning, but whether *this particular defendant* had been. Jackson insisted that he had not; Ashcraft "was in possession of his own will and self-control at the time of confession." Ashcraft had decided to match wits with the police and after accusing another who in turn accused him "he knew he had lost the battle of wits." What was wrong with that? If the state is denied the right to apply any pressure to get someone to confess which is "inherently coercive," what pressure *could* it apply? And if it could not apply any "pressure," how could it be expected to get any suspect to confess?

Concurring in *Watts* and dissenting in the two companion cases, Justice Jackson again manifested his resistance to the expansion of the rights of suspects. He articulated concerns that many critics of the Warren Court's "revolution" in criminal procedure would repeat decades later. He underscored the "dilemma" facing a free society: To subject one without counsel to police interrogation "is a real peril to individual freedom," but bringing in a lawyer "means a real peril to solution of the crime."

---

[a]   At least in its advanced stage (the early 1960s), some commentators thought that the "due process" or "voluntariness" test had *three* underlying values or goals, barring the use of confessions (a) which were of doubtful reliability because of the police methods used to obtain them; (b) which were produced by offensive police methods even though the reliability of the confession was not in question; and (c) which were obtained from a person whose volitional power was seriously impaired (e.g., a drugged, extremely intoxicated or "insane" person), even though the confession was neither untrustworthy (because impressively corroborated) nor the product of any conscious police wrongdoing. However, in *Colorado v. Connelly*, 479 U.S. 157 (1986), upholding the confession of a mentally ill person (according to expert testimony, "God's voice" told defendant he had only two options: confess his murder or commit suicide), the Court, per Rehnquist, C.J., rejected the third value or goal:

"[All the 'involuntary' confession cases] have contained a substantial element of coercive police conduct. Absent police conduct causally related to the confession, there is simply no basis for concluding that any state action has deprived a criminal defendant of due process of law.

" * * * The flaw in respondent's argument is that it would expand our previous line of 'voluntariness' cases into a far-ranging requirement that courts must divine a defendant's motivation for speaking or acting as he did even though there be no claim that governmental conduct coerced his decision.

" * * * We think the Constitution rightly leaves [inquiries into the state of mind of one who has confessed quite apart from any state coercion] to be resolved by state laws governing the admission of evidence and erects no standard of its own in this area. A statement rendered by one in the condition of respondent might be proved to be quite unreliable, but this is a matter to be governed by the evidentiary laws of the forum and not by the Due Process Clause * * *."

Jackson voiced strong doubts that prohibiting the police from taking a suspect into custody and questioning him about an unwitnessed murder without advising him of his rights was "a necessary price to pay for the fairness which we know as 'due process of law.'" He recognized that the Bill of Rights, "even if construed as these provisions traditionally have been, * * * contain an aggregate of restrictions which seriously limit the power of society to solve such crimes as confront us in these cases," but he considered that "good reason for indulging in no unnecessary expansion of them."

A majority of the Court, however, was unpersuaded. As perhaps he knew, Jackson was swimming against the tide.

ASHCRAFT V. TENNESSEE
322 U.S. 143, 64 S.Ct. 921, 88 L.Ed. 1192 (1944).

JUSTICE BLACK delivered the opinion of the Court. * * *

[Early in the evening of Saturday, June 14, nine days after Ashcraft's wife had been murdered,] the officers came to Ashcraft's home and "took him into custody." In the words of the Tennessee Supreme Court,

"They took him to an office or room on the northwest corner of the fifth floor of the Shelby County jail. This office is equipped with all sorts of crime and detective devices such as a fingerprint outfit, cameras, high-powered lights, and such other devices as might be found in a homicide investigating office. * * * It appears that the officers placed Ashcraft at a table in this room on the fifth floor of the county jail with a light over his head and began to quiz him. They questioned him in relays until the following Monday morning, June 16, 1941, around nine-thirty or ten o'clock. It appears that Ashcraft from Saturday evening at seven o'clock until Monday morning at approximately nine-thirty never left this homicide room on the fifth floor."

Testimony of the officers shows that the reason they questioned Ashcraft "in relays" was that they became so tired they were compelled to rest. But from 7:00 Saturday evening until 9:30 Monday morning Ashcraft had no rest. One officer did say that he gave the suspect a single five minutes' respite, but except for this five minutes the procedure consisted of one continuous stream of questions.

As to what happened in the fifth-floor jail room during this thirty-six hour secret examination the testimony follows the usual pattern and is in hopeless conflict. Ashcraft swears that the first thing said to him when he was taken into custody was, "Why in hell did you kill your wife?"; that during the course of the examination he was threatened and abused in various ways; and that as the hours passed his eyes became blinded by a powerful electric light, his body became weary, and the strain on his nerves became unbearable. The officers, on the other hand, swear that throughout the questioning they were kind and considerate. They say that they did not accuse Ashcraft of the murder until four hours after he was brought to the jail building, though they freely admit that from that time on their barrage of questions was constantly directed at him on the assumption that he was the murderer. Together with other persons whom they brought in on Monday morning to witness the culmination of the thirty-six hour ordeal the officers declare that at that time Ashcraft was "cool," "calm," "collected," "normal;" that his vision was unimpaired and his eyes not bloodshot; and that he showed no outward signs of being tired or sleepy.

As to whether Ashcraft actually confessed there is a similar conflict of testimony. Ashcraft maintains that although the officers incessantly attempted by various tactics of intimidation to entrap him into a confession, not once did he admit knowledge concerning or participation in the crime. [The] officers' version of what happened, however, is that about 11 P.M. on Sunday night, after twenty-eight hours' constant questioning, Ashcraft made a statement that Ware had overpowered him at his home and abducted the deceased, and was probably the killer. About midnight the officers found Ware and took him into custody, and, according to their testimony, Ware made a self-incriminating statement as of early Monday morning, and at 5:40 A.M. signed by mark a written confession in which appeared the statement that Ashcraft had hired him to commit the murder. This alleged confession of Ware was read to Ashcraft about six o'clock Monday morning, whereupon Ashcraft is said substantially to have admitted its truth in a detailed statement taken down by a reporter. About 9:30 Monday morning a transcript of Ashcraft's purported statement was read to him. The State's position is that he affirmed its truth but refused to sign the transcript, saying that he first wanted to consult his lawyer. As to this latter 9:30 episode the officers' testimony is reinforced by testimony of the several persons whom they brought in to witness the end of the examination.

In reaching our conclusion as to the validity of Ashcraft's confession we do not resolve any of the disputed questions of fact relating to the details of what transpired within the confession chamber of the jail or whether Ashcraft actually did confess.[7] Such disputes, we may say, are an inescapable consequence of secret inquisitorial practices. And always evidence concerning the inner details of secret inquisitions[8] is weighted against an accused, particularly where, as here, he is charged with a brutal crime, or where, as in many other cases, his supposed offense bears relation to an unpopular economic, political, or religious cause.

Our conclusion is that if Ashcraft made a confession it was not voluntary but compelled. We reach this conclusion from facts which are not in dispute at all. * * *

We think a situation such as that here shown by uncontradicted evidence is so inherently coercive that its very existence is irreconcilable with the possession of mental freedom by a lone suspect against whom its full coercive force is brought to bear. It is inconceivable that any court of justice in the land, conducted as our courts are, open to the public, would permit prosecutors serving in relays to keep a defendant witness under continuous cross examination for thirty-six hours without

---

[7] The use in evidence of a defendant's coerced confession cannot be justified on the ground that the defendant has denied he ever gave the confession.

[8] State and federal courts, textbook writers, legal commentators, and governmental commissions consistently have applied the name of "inquisition" to prolonged examination of suspects conducted as was the examination of Ashcraft. * * *

rest or sleep in an effort to extract a "voluntary" confession. Nor can we, consistently with Constitutional due process of law, hold voluntary a confession where prosecutors do the same thing away from the restraining influences of a public trial in an open court room.

The Constitution of the United States stands as a bar against the conviction of any individual in an American court by means of a coerced confession. There have been, and are now, certain foreign nations with governments dedicated to an opposite policy: governments which convict individuals with testimony obtained by police organizations possessed of an unrestrained power to seize persons suspected of crimes against the state, hold them in secret custody, and wring from them confessions by physical or mental torture. So long as the Constitution remains the basic law of our Republic, America will not have that kind of government. * * *

JUSTICE JACKSON, with whom JUSTICE ROBERTS and JUSTICE FRANKFURTER join, dissenting. * * *

As we read the present decision the Court in effect [departs from] well-established principles. Instead, it: (1) substitutes for determination on conflicting evidence the question whether the confession was actually produced by coercion, a presumption that it was, on a new doctrine that examination in custody of this duration is "inherently coercive;" (2) it makes that presumption irrebuttable—i.e., a rule of law—because, while it goes back of the State decisions to find certain facts, it refuses to resolve conflicts in evidence to determine whether other of the State's proof is sufficient to overcome such presumption; and, in so doing, (3) it sets aside the findings by the courts of Tennessee that on all the facts this confession did not result from coercion, either giving those findings no weight or regarding them as immaterial. * * *

The burden of protecting society from most crimes against persons and property falls upon the state. Different states have different crime problems and some freedom to vary procedures according to their own ideas. Here, a state was forced by an unwitnessed and baffling murder to vindicate its law and protect its society. To nullify its conviction in this particular case upon a consideration of all the facts would be a delicate exercise of federal judicial power. But to go beyond this, as the Court does today, and divine in the due process clause of the Fourteenth Amendment an exclusion of confessions on an irrebuttable presumption that custody and examination are "inherently coercive" if of some unspecified duration within thirty-six hours, requires us to make more than a passing expression of our doubts and disagreements. * * *

This Court never yet has held that the Constitution denies a State the right to use a confession just because the confessor was questioned in custody where it did not also find other circumstances that deprived him of a "free choice to admit, to deny, or to refuse to answer." The Constitution requires that a conviction rest on a fair trial. Forced confessions are ruled out of a fair trial. They are ruled out because they have been wrung from a prisoner by measures which are offensive to concepts of fundamental fairness. Different courts have used different terms to express the test by which to judge the inadmissibility of a confession, such as "forced," "coerced," "involuntary," "extorted," "loss of freedom of will." But always where we have professed to speak with the voice of the due process clause, the test, in whatever words stated, has been applied to the particular confessor at the time of confession.

* * * Interrogation per se is not, while violence per se is, an outlaw. Questioning is an indispensable instrumentality of justice. It may be abused, of course, as cross-examination in court may be abused, but the principles by which we may adjudge when it passes constitutional limits are quite different from those that condemn police brutality, and are far more difficult to apply. And they call for a more responsible and cautious exercise of our office. For we may err on the side of hostility to violence without doing injury to legitimate prosecution of crime; we cannot read an undiscriminating hostility to mere interrogation into the Constitution without unduly fettering the States in protecting society from the criminal.

It probably is the normal instinct to deny and conceal any shameful or guilty act. [The] term "voluntary" confession does not mean voluntary in the sense of a confession to a priest merely to rid one's soul of a sense of guilt. "Voluntary confessions" in criminal law are the product of calculations of a different order, and usually proceed from a belief that further denial is useless and perhaps prejudicial. To speak of any confessions of crime made after arrest as being "voluntary" or "uncoerced" is somewhat inaccurate, although traditional.

A confession is wholly and incontestably voluntary only if a guilty person gives himself up to the law and becomes his own accuser. The Court bases its decision on the premise that custody and examination of a prisoner for thirty-six hours is "inherently coercive." Of course it is. And so is custody and examination for one hour. Arrest itself is inherently coercive, and so is detention. When not justified, infliction of such indignities upon the person is actionable as a tort. Of course such acts put pressure upon the prisoner to answer questions, to answer them truthfully, and to confess if guilty.

But does the Constitution prohibit use of all confessions made after arrest because questioning, while one is deprived of freedom, is "inherently coercive?" The Court does not quite say so, but it is moving far and fast in that direction. The step it now takes is to hold this confession inadmissible because of the time taken in getting it.

[Some] men would withstand for days pressures that would destroy the will of another in hours. Always heretofore the ultimate question has been whether the confessor was in possession of his own will and self-control at the time of confession. For its bearing on this question the Court always has considered the confessor's strength or weakness, whether he was educated or illiterate, intelligent or moronic, well or ill, Negro or white. * * *

If the constitutional admissibility of a confession is no longer to be measured by the mental state of the individual confessor but by a general doctrine dependent on the clock, it should be capable of statement in definite terms. If thirty-six hours is more than is permissible, what about 24? or 12? or 6? or 1? All are "inherently coercive." Of course questions of law like this often turn on matters of degree. But are not the states entitled to know, if this Court is able to state, what the considerations are which make any particular degree decisive? How else may state courts apply our tests? * * *

Apart from Ashcraft's uncorroborated testimony, which the Tennessee courts refused to believe, there is much evidence in this record from persons whom they did believe and were justified in believing. This evidence shows that despite the "inherent coerciveness" of the circumstances of his examination, the confession when made was deliberate, free, and voluntary in the sense in which that term is used in criminal law. This Court could not, in our opinion, hold this confession an involuntary one except by substituting its presumption in place of analysis of the evidence and refusing to weigh the evidence even in rebuttal of its presumption. * * *

This Court rejects the testimony of the officers and disinterested witnesses in this case that the confession was voluntary not because it lacked probative value in itself nor because the witnesses were self-contradictory or were impeached. On the contrary, it is impugned only on grounds such as that such disputes "are an inescapable consequence of secret inquisitorial practices." We infer from this that since a prisoner's unsupported word often conflicts with that of the officers, the officer's testimony for constitutional purposes is always prima facie false. We know that police standards often leave much to be desired, but we are not ready to believe that the democratic process brings to office men generally less believable than the average of those accused of crime. * * *

This questioning is characterized as a "secret inquisition," invoking all of the horrendous historical associations of those words. Certainly the inquiry was participated in by a good many persons, and we do not see how it could have been much less "secret" unless the press should have been called in. Of course, any questioning may be characterized as an "inquisition," but the use of such characterizations is no substitute for the detached and judicial consideration that the court below gave to the case.

We conclude that even going behind the state court decisions into the facts, no independent judgment on the whole evidence that Ashcraft's confession was in fact coerced is possible. And against this background of facts the extreme character of the Court's ruling becomes apparent.

I am not sure whether the Court denies the State all right to arrest and question the husband of the slain woman. No investigation worthy of the name could fail to examine him. Of all persons he was most likely to know whether she had enemies or rivals. Would not the State have a constitutional right, whether he was accused or not, to arrest and detain him as a material witness? If it has the right to detain one as a witness, presumably it has the right to examine him.

Could the State not confront Ashcraft with his false statements and ask his explanation? He did not throw himself at any time on his rights, refuse to answer, and demand counsel, even according to his own testimony. The strategy of the officers evidently was to keep him talking, to give him plenty of rope and see if he would not hang himself. He does not claim to have made objection to this. Instead he relied on his wits. The time came when it dawned on him that his own story brought him under suspicion, and that he could not meet it. Must the officers stop at this point because he was coming to appreciate the uselessness of deception?

Then he became desperate and accused [Ware]. Certainly from this point the State was justified in holding and questioning him as a witness, for he claimed to know the killer. That accusation backfired and only turned up a witness against him. He had run out of expedients and inventions; he knew he had lost the battle of wits. After all honesty seemed to be the best, even if the last, policy. He confessed in detail.

At what point in all this investigation does the Court hold that the Constitution commands these officers to send Ashcraft on his way and give up the murder as insoluble? If the state is denied the right to apply any pressure to him which is "inherently coercive" it could hardly deprive him of his freedom at all. I, too, dislike to think of any man, under the disadvantages and indignities of detention being questioned about his personal life for thirty-six hours or for one hour. In fact, there is much in our whole system of penology that seems archaic and vindictive and badly managed. Every person in the community, no matter how inconvenient or embarrassing, no matter what retaliation it exposes him to, may be called upon to take the witness stand and tell all he knows about a crime— except the person who knows most about it. * * *

No conclusion that this confession was actually coerced can be reached on this record except by reliance upon the utterly uncorroborated statements of defendant Ashcraft. His testimony does not carry even ordinary guaranties of truthfulness, and the courts and jury were not bound to accept it. Perjury is a light offense compared to murder and they may well have believed that Ashcraft was ready to resort to a lesser crime to avoid conviction of a greater one. Furthermore, the very grounds on which this Court now upsets his conviction Ashcraft repudiated at the trial. He asserts that he was abused, but he does not testify as this Court holds that it had the effect of forcing an involuntary confession from him. On the contrary, he flatly insists that it had no such effect and that he never did confess at all.

Against Ashcraft's word the state courts and jury accepted the testimony of several apparently disinterested witnesses of high standing in their communities, in addition to that of the accused officers. One of the witnesses to Ashcraft's admission of guilt was his own family physician, two were disinterested business men of substance and standing, another was an experienced court reporter who had long held this position of considerable trust. Another was a member of the bar. Certainly, the state courts were not committing an offense against the Constitution of the United States in refusing to believe that this whole group of apparently reputable citizens entered into a conspiracy to swear a murder onto an innocent man, against whom not one of them is shown to have had a grievance or a grudge.

This is not the case of an ignorant and unrepresented defendant who has been the victim of prejudice. Ashcraft was a white man of good reputation, good position, and substantial property. For a week after this crime was discovered he was not detained, although his stories to the officers did not hang together, but was at large, free to consult his friends and counsel. There was no indecent haste, but on the contrary evident deliberation, in suspecting and accusing him. * * *

The use of the due process clause to disable the states in protection of society from crime is quite as dangerous and delicate a use of federal judicial power as to use it to disable them from social or economic experimentation.

SPANO V. NEW YORK
360 U.S. 315, 79 S.Ct. 1202, 3 L.Ed. 1265 (1959).

CHIEF JUSTICE WARREN delivered the opinion of the Court.

This is another in the long line of cases presenting the question whether a confession was properly admitted into evidence under the Fourteenth Amendment. As in all such cases, we are forced to resolve a conflict between two fundamental interests of society; its interest in prompt and efficient law enforcement, and its interest in preventing the rights of its individual members from being abridged by unconstitutional methods of law enforcement. * * *

[Spano was drinking in a bar when he got into an altercation with another patron. Spano then went home, got a gun, found the patron, and shot him. Spano was charged with first-degree murder. After retaining an attorney, Spano turned himself in. Officers took him to the district attorney's office where questioning began at 7:15 p.m.] The record reveals that the questioning was both persistent and continuous. [Spano,] in accordance with his attorney's instructions, steadfastly refused to answer. [Spano asked one officer if he could speak to his attorney, but that request was denied.]

[A]fter five hours of questioning in which it became evident that [Spano] was following his attorney's instructions, * * * [he] was transferred to the * * * Police Station [where] questioning was resumed at 12:40 [a.m.] [Spano] persisted in his refusal to answer, and again requested permission to see his attorney * * *. His request was again denied.

[Spano had a close friend named Gaspar Bruno who worked for the police department. Spano had gone to school with Bruno and had been close friends with him for 8–10 years. Spano had called Bruno before turning himself in to tell him what had happened. When Spano continued to refuse to answer questions,] those in charge of the investigation decided that [his] close friend, Bruno, could be of use. * * * Although, in fact, his job was in no way threatened, Bruno was told to tell [Spano] that [Spano's earlier] telephone call had gotten him "in a lot of trouble," and that he should seek to extract sympathy from [Spano] for Bruno's pregnant wife and three children.

[Bruno tried on three different occasions to develop this theme with Spano to no avail. Spano continued to refuse to answer questions and ask for his attorney.] Inevitably, in the fourth such session directed by the Lieutenant, lasting a full hour, [Spano] succumbed to his friend's prevarications and agreed to make a statement. * * * The statement was completed at 4:05 a.m.

[Detectives then took Spano to try and locate the murder weapon and did not return with him until well after 6 a.m. Spano made other incriminating statements in response to questions during that trip.]

The abhorrence of society to the use of involuntary confessions does not turn alone on their inherent untrustworthiness. It also turns on the deep-rooted feeling that police must obey the law while enforcing the law; that in the end life and liberty can be as much endangered from illegal methods used to convict those thought to be criminals as from the actual criminals themselves. Accordingly, the actions of police in obtaining confessions have come under scrutiny in a long series of cases. Those cases suggest that in recent years law enforcement officials have become increasingly aware of the burden which they share, along with our courts, in protecting fundamental rights of our citizenry, including that portion of our citizenry suspected of crime. The facts of no case recently in this Court have quite approached the brutal beatings in *Brown v. Mississippi* or the 36 consecutive hours of questioning present in *Ashcraft*. But as law enforcement officers become more responsible, and the methods used to extract confessions more sophisticated, our duty to enforce federal constitutional protections does not cease. It only becomes more difficult because of the more delicate judgments to be made. Our judgment here is that, on all the facts, this conviction cannot stand.

[Spano] was a foreign-born young man of 25 with no past history of law violation or of subjection to official interrogation, at least insofar as the record shows. He had progressed only one-half year into high school and the record indicates that he had a history of emotional instability. He did not make a narrative statement, but was subject to the leading questions of a skillful prosecutor in a question and answer confession. He was subjected to questioning not by a few men, but by many. * * * All played some part, and the effect of such massive official interrogation must have been felt. [Spano] was questioned for virtually eight straight hours before he confessed, with his only respite being a transfer to an arena presumably considered more appropriate by the police for the task at hand. Nor was the questioning conducted during normal business hours, but began in early evening, continued into the night, and did not bear fruition until the not-too-early morning. The drama was not played out, with the final admissions obtained, until almost sunrise. In such circumstances slowly mounting fatigue does, and is calculated to, play its part. The questioners persisted in the face of his repeated refusals to answer on the advice of his attorney, and they ignored his reasonable requests to contact the local attorney whom he had already retained and who had personally delivered him into the custody of these officers in obedience to the bench warrant.

The use of Bruno * * * is another factor which deserves mention in the totality of the situation. Bruno's was the one face visible to [Spano] in which he could put some trust. There was a bond of friendship between them going back a decade into adolescence. It was with this material that the officers felt that they could overcome [Spano]'s will. They instructed Bruno falsely to state that [Spano]'s telephone call had gotten him into trouble, that his job was in jeopardy, and that loss of his job would be disastrous to his three children, his wife and his unborn child. And Bruno played this part of a worried father, harried by his superiors, in not one, but four different acts, the final one lasting an hour. * * *

We conclude that [Spano]'s will was overborne by official pressure, fatigue and sympathy falsely aroused after considering all the facts in their post-indictment setting. Here a grand jury had already found sufficient cause to require [Spano] to face trial on a charge of first-degree murder, and the police had an eyewitness to the shooting. The police were not therefore merely trying to solve a crime, or even to absolve a suspect. They were rather concerned primarily with securing a statement from defendant on which they could convict him. The undeviating intent of the officers to extract a confession * * * is therefore patent. When such an intent is shown, this Court has held that the confession obtained must be examined with the most careful scrutiny * * *. Accordingly, we hold that [Spano]'s conviction cannot stand under the Fourteenth Amendment.[a]

2. *MASSIAH* AND *ESCOBEDO*

As the rationales for the Court's coerced confession cases evolved, it became increasingly doubtful that terms such as "voluntariness," "coercion" and "breaking the will" were very helpful in deciding the admissibility of confessions. It appeared that such terms were not being used as tools of analysis, but as mere conclusions. When a court concluded that the police had resorted to unacceptable interrogation techniques, it called the resulting confession "involuntary." On the other hand, it seemed, when a court decided the methods the police had employed were permissible or tolerable, it called the resulting confession "voluntary." Moreover, such terms as "voluntariness," "coercion" and "overbearing the will" focused directly on neither of the two underlying reasons that led the courts to bar the use of confessions—the offensiveness of police interrogation methods or the risk that these methods had produced an untrue confession. Thus, as the Court, per O'Connor, J., recently noted in *Miller v. Fenton,* 474 U.S. 104 (1985), "[t]he voluntariness rubric has been variously condemned as 'useless,' 'perplexing,' and 'legal "doubletalk." ' "

Almost everything was relevant under the due process "totality of the circumstances"—"voluntariness" test, e.g., the suspect's age, intelligence, education and prior criminal record; whether he was advised of his rights, held incommunicado or given meals at regular intervals. But with a very few exceptions, e.g. the use or threatened use of physical violence, no single factor was decisive. Because there were so many variables in the voluntariness equation that one determination seldom served as a useful precedent for another, the test offered neither the police nor the courts much guidance. Trial courts were almost invited to give weight to their subjective preferences and appellate courts were discouraged from active review.

Understandably, some members of the Court looked for an alternative approach. In the 1959 *Crooker* case, discussed below, the four dissenters turned to the right to counsel. Five years later, as illustrated by the two cases in this section,

---

[a] Four Justices (Black, Douglas, Brennan, and Stewart) concurred, noting that, once a person was formally charged by indictment or information, his right to counsel has begun.

Massiah v. United States and *Escobedo v. Illinois,* the right to counsel approach to confessions had gained ascendancy.

Crooker v. California, 357 U.S. 433 (1958), involved a petitioner who had attended one year of law school, during which time he studied criminal law, and who indicated that he was fully aware of his right to remain silent. On the basis of a challenged confession, he was convicted of the murder of his paramour and sentenced to death. A 5–4 majority rejected his argument that by persisting in interrogating him after denying his specific request to contact his lawyer the police had violated his due process right to legal representation and advice and that therefore the use of any confession obtained from him under these circumstances should be barred, even though "voluntarily" made under traditional standards. Such a rule, retorted the Court, per Clark, J., "would have [a] devastating effect on enforcement of criminal law, for it would effectively preclude police questioning— fair as well as unfair—until the accused was afforded opportunity to call his lawyer. Due process * * * demands no such rule." But four dissenting Justices, Douglas, J., joined by Warren, C.J., and Black and Brennan, JJ., maintained that "[t]he demands of our civilization, expressed in the Due Process Clause require that the accused who wants a counsel should have one at any time after the moment of arrest."

The following year, by virtue of *Spano v. New York,* 360 U.S. 315 (1959), it appeared that a majority of the Court may have arrived at the view that once a person is *formally charged* by indictment or information her constitutional right to counsel has "begun"—at least the right to the assistance of counsel she herself has retained. Four concurring Justices took this position in *Spano*: Justices Black, Douglas and Brennan, all of whom had dissented in *Crooker,* and newly appointed Justice Stewart, who had replaced Justice Burton. In two separate opinions, the concurring Justices emphasized that *Spano* was not a case where the police were questioning a suspect in the course of investigating an unsolved crime, but one where the person interrogated was already under indictment for murder when he surrendered to the authorities.

A majority of the *Spano* Court did not decide the case on the grounds suggested by the concurring Justices because it found the confession inadmissible under the traditional due process "voluntariness" test. But Chief Justice Warren, who wrote the majority opinion, had taken the position a year earlier in *Crooker* that the right to counsel should "begin" even earlier than at the point of indictment. Thus, counting heads, it appeared that by 1959 the views of the concurring Justices in *Spano* commanded a majority of the Court. Any doubts were dispelled by *Massiah v. United States,* the first case in this section.

When, a short five weeks after it had decided *Massiah,* the Court threw out the confession in *Escobedo v. Illinois,* the second case in this section, even though Escobedo had been interrogated *before* "judicial" or "adversary" proceedings had commenced against him, many members of the bench and bar grew alarmed. As they saw it, the "right to counsel" approach to the confession problem threatened the admissibility of even *"volunteered"* statements. They feared that the Court might be in the process of shaping a novel right not to confess except knowingly and with the tactical assistance of counsel.

Perhaps the enthusiastic public reaction to the *Gideon* decision a year earlier had led some members of the Court to believe that *Massiah* and *Escobedo* would also be well-received. But many members of the bench and bar, and the general public as well, soon left little doubt that they were much more enthusiastic about a lawyer for a defendant in the courtroom than they were about a lawyer for a suspect in the police station.

MASSIAH V. UNITED STATES
377 U.S. 201, 84 S.Ct. 1199, 12 L.Ed.2d 246 (1964).

JUSTICE STEWART delivered the opinion of the Court. * * *

[After he had been indicted for conspiracy to possess narcotics aboard a United States vessel and other federal narcotics violations, Massiah retained a lawyer, pled not guilty, and was released on bail. Colson, a codefendant, also retained a lawyer, pled not guilty, and was released on bail. Colson then invited Massiah to discuss the pending case in Colson's car, parked on a city street. Unknown to Massiah, Colson had decided to cooperate with federal agents in their continuing investigation of the case. A radio transmitter was installed under the front seat of Colson's car, enabling a nearby federal agent (Murphy), who was equipped with a recording device, to overhear the Massiah-Colson conversation. As expected, Massiah made several damaging admissions. On the basis of these admissions, Massiah was convicted of several narcotics offenses. The convictions were affirmed by the U.S. Court of Appeals for the Second Circuit.]

In *Spano v. New York*, this Court reversed a state criminal conviction because a confession had been wrongly admitted into evidence against the defendant at his trial. In that case the defendant had already been indicted for first-degree murder at the time he confessed. The Court held that the defendant's conviction could not stand under the Fourteenth Amendment. While the Court's opinion relied upon the totality of the circumstances under which the confession had been obtained, four concurring Justices pointed out that the Constitution required reversal of the conviction upon the sole and specific ground that the confession had been deliberately elicited by the police after the defendant had been indicted, and therefore at a time when he was clearly entitled to a lawyer's help. It was pointed out that under our system of justice the most elemental concepts of due process of law contemplate that an indictment be followed by a trial, "in an orderly courtroom, presided over by a judge, open to the public, and protected by all the procedural safeguards of the law." (Stewart, J., concurring). It was said that a Constitution which guarantees a defendant the aid of counsel at such a trial could surely vouchsafe no less to an indicted defendant under interrogation by the police in a completely extrajudicial proceeding. Anything less, it was said, might deny a defendant "effective representation by counsel at the only stage when legal aid and advice would help him." (Douglas, J., concurring).

[The view taken by the *Spano* concurring Justices] no more than reflects a constitutional principle established as long ago as *Powell v. Alabama,* where the Court noted that "during perhaps the most critical period of the proceedings, [that] is to say, from the time of their arraignment until the beginning of their trial, when consultation, thoroughgoing investigation and preparation [are] vitally important, the defendants [are] as much entitled to such aid [of counsel] during that period as at the trial itself." * * *

Here we deal not with a state court conviction, but with a federal case, where the specific guarantee of the Sixth Amendment directly applies. We hold that the petitioner was denied the basic protections of that guarantee when there was used against him at his trial evidence of his own incriminating words, which federal agents had deliberately elicited from him after he had been indicted and in the absence of his counsel. It is true that in the Spano case the defendant was interrogated in a police station, while here the damaging testimony was elicited from the defendant without his knowledge while he was free on bail. But, as Judge Hays pointed out in his dissent in the Court of Appeals, "if such a rule is to have any efficacy it must apply to indirect and surreptitious interrogations as well as those conducted in the jailhouse. In this case, Massiah was more seriously imposed upon * * * because he did not even know that he was under interrogation by a government agent."

The Solicitor General [has] strenuously contended that the federal law enforcement agents had the right, if not indeed the duty, to continue their investigation of the petitioner and his alleged criminal associates even though the petitioner had been indicted. [He] says that the quantity of narcotics involved was such as to suggest that the petitioner was part of a large and well-organized ring, and indeed that the continuing investigation confirmed this suspicion, since it resulted in criminal charges against many defendants. Under these circumstances the Solicitor General concludes that the government agents were completely "justified in making use of Colson's cooperation by having Colson continue his normal associations and by surveilling them."

* * * We do not question that in this case, as in many cases, it was entirely proper to continue an investigation of the suspected criminal activities of the defendant and his alleged confederates, even though the defendant had already been indicted. All that we hold is that the defendant's own incriminating statements, obtained by federal agents under the circumstances here disclosed, could not constitutionally be used by the prosecution as evidence against *him* at his trial. * * *

JUSTICE WHITE, with whom JUSTICE CLARK and JUSTICE HARLAN join, dissenting.

* * * [It is] a rather portentous occasion when a constitutional rule is established barring the use of evidence which is relevant, reliable and highly probative of the issue which the trial court has before it—whether the accused committed the act with which he is charged. Without the evidence, the quest for truth may be seriously impeded and in many cases the trial court, although aware of proof showing defendant's guilt, must nevertheless release him because the

crucial evidence is deemed inadmissible. This result is entirely justified in some circumstances because exclusion serves other policies of overriding importance, as where evidence seized in an illegal search is excluded, not because of the quality of the proof, but to secure meaningful enforcement of the Fourth Amendment. But this only emphasizes that the soundest of reasons is necessary to warrant the exclusion of evidence otherwise admissible and the creation of another area of privileged testimony. With all due deference, I am not at all convinced that the additional barriers to the pursuit of truth which the Court today erects rest on anything like the solid foundations which decisions of this gravity should require.

The importance of the matter should not be underestimated, for today's rule promises to have wide application well beyond the facts of this case. The reason given for the result here—the admissions were obtained in the absence of counsel— would seem equally pertinent to statements obtained at any time after the right to counsel attaches, whether there has been an indictment or not; to admissions made prior to arraignment, at least where the defendant has counsel or asks for it; to the fruits of admissions improperly obtained under the new rule; to criminal proceedings in state courts; and to defendants long since convicted upon evidence including such admissions. The new rule will immediately do service in a great many cases.

Whatever the content or scope of the rule may prove to be, I am unable to see how this case presents an unconstitutional interference with Massiah's right to counsel. Massiah was not prevented from consulting with counsel as often as he wished. No meetings with counsel were disturbed or spied upon. Preparation for trial was in no way obstructed. It is only a sterile syllogism—an unsound one, besides—to say that because Massiah had a right to counsel's aid before and during the trial, his out-of-court conversations and admissions must be excluded if obtained without counsel's consent or presence. The right to counsel has never meant as much before and its extension in this case requires some further explanation, so far unarticulated by the Court.

Since the new rule would exclude all admissions made to the police, no matter how voluntary and reliable, the requirement of counsel's presence or approval would seem to rest upon the probability that counsel would foreclose any admissions at all. This is nothing more than a thinly disguised constitutional policy of minimizing or entirely prohibiting the use in evidence of voluntary out-of-court admissions and confessions made by the accused. Carried as far as blind logic may compel some to go, the notion that statements from the mouth of the defendant should not be used in evidence would have a severe and unfortunate impact upon the great bulk of criminal cases.

Viewed in this light, the Court's newly fashioned exclusionary principle goes far beyond the constitutional privilege against self-incrimination, which neither requires nor suggests the barring of voluntary pretrial admissions.

* * * Whether as a matter of self-incrimination or of due process, the proscription is against compulsion—coerced incrimination. Under the prior law, announced in countless cases in this Court, the defendant's pretrial statements were admissible evidence if voluntarily made; inadmissible if not the product of his

free will. Hardly any constitutional area has been more carefully patrolled by this Court, and until now the Court has expressly rejected the argument that admissions are to be deemed involuntary if made outside the presence of counsel.

The Court presents no facts, no objective evidence, no reasons to warrant scrapping the voluntary-involuntary test for admissibility in this area. Without such evidence I would retain it in its present form.

This case cannot be analogized to the American Bar Association's rule forbidding an attorney to talk to the opposing party litigant outside the presence of his counsel. Aside from the fact that the Association's canons are not of constitutional dimensions, the specific canon argued is inapposite because it deals with the conduct of lawyers and not with the conduct of investigators. Lawyers are forbidden to interview the opposing party because of the supposed imbalance of legal skill and acumen between the lawyer and the party litigant; the reason for the rule does not apply to nonlawyers and certainly not to Colson, Massiah's codefendant.

Applying the new exclusionary rule is peculiarly inappropriate in this case. At the time of the conversation in question, petitioner was not in custody but free on bail. He was not questioned in what anyone could call an atmosphere of official coercion. What he said was said to his partner in crime who had also been indicted. There was no suggestion or any possibility of coercion. What petitioner did not know was that Colson had decided to report the conversation to the police. Had there been no prior arrangements between Colson and the police, had Colson simply gone to the police after the conversation had occurred, his testimony relating Massiah's statements would be readily admissible at the trial, as would a recording which he might have made of the conversation. In such event, it would simply be said that Massiah risked talking to a friend who decided to disclose what he knew of Massiah's criminal activities. But if, as occurred here, Colson had been cooperating with the police prior to his meeting with Massiah, both his evidence and the recorded conversation are somehow transformed into inadmissible evidence despite the fact that the hazard to Massiah remains precisely the same— the defection of a confederate in crime. * * *

[The question presented] is this: when the police have arrested and released on bail one member of a criminal ring and another member, a confederate, is cooperating with the police, can the confederate be allowed to continue his association with the ring or must he somehow be withdrawn to avoid challenge to trial evidence on the ground that it was acquired after rather than before the arrest, after rather than before the indictment?

Defendants who are out on bail have been known to continue their illicit operations. That an attorney is advising them should not constitutionally immunize their statements made in furtherance of these operations and relevant to the question of their guilt at the pending prosecution. * * * Undoubtedly, the evidence excluded in this case would not have been available but for the conduct of Colson in cooperation with Agent Murphy, but is it this kind of conduct which should be forbidden to those charged with law enforcement? It is one thing to establish safeguards against procedures fraught with the potentiality of coercion and to outlaw "easy but self-defeating ways in which brutality is substituted for brains as an instrument of crime detection." But here there was no substitution of brutality for brains, no inherent danger of police coercion justifying the prophylactic effect of another exclusionary rule. Massiah was not being interrogated in a police station, was not surrounded by numerous officers or questioned in relays, and was not forbidden access to others. Law enforcement may have the elements of a contest about it, but it is not a game. Massiah and those like him receive ample protection from the long line of precedents in this Court holding that confessions may not be introduced unless they are voluntary. In making these determinations the courts must consider the absence of counsel as one of several factors by which voluntariness is to be judged. This is a wiser rule than the automatic rule announced by the Court, which requires courts and juries to disregard voluntary admissions which they might well find to be the best possible evidence in discharging their responsibility for ascertaining truth.

ESCOBEDO V. ILLINOIS
378 U.S. 478, 84 S.Ct. 1758, 12 L.Ed.2d 977 (1964).

JUSTICE GOLDBERG delivered the opinion of the Court.

[On the night of January 19, petitioner's brother-in-law was fatally shot. A few hours later petitioner was taken into custody for questioning, but he made no statement and was released the following afternoon pursuant to a writ of habeas corpus obtained by his retained counsel. On January 30, one DiGerlando, who was then in police custody and who was later indicted for the murder along with petitioner, stated that petitioner had fired the shots which killed his brother-in-law. That evening petitioner was again arrested and taken to police headquarters. En route to the police station he was told that DiGerlando had named him as the one who fired the fatal shots and that he might as well admit it, but petitioner replied (probably because his attorney had obtained his release from police custody only 11 days earlier or because he had consulted with his attorney in the meantime): "I am sorry but I would like to have advice from my lawyer."

[Shortly after petitioner reached police headquarters, his retained lawyer arrived and spent the next three or four hours trying unsuccessfully to speak to his client. He talked to every officer he could find, but was repeatedly told that he could not see his client and that he would have to get a writ of habeas corpus. In the meantime, petitioner repeatedly but unsuccessfully asked to speak to his lawyer. At one point, petitioner and his attorney came into each other's view for a few moments, but the attorney was quickly ushered away. Petitioner testified that he heard a detective tell his attorney that the latter could not see him until the police "were done."

[Instead of allowing petitioner to meet with his lawyer, the police arranged a confrontation between petitioner and DiGerlando. Petitioner denied that he had fired the fatal shots. He maintained that DiGerlando was lying and, in the presence of the police, told him: "I didn't shoot Manuel, you did it." In this way, petitioner admitted to some knowledge of the crime. After that, he made other statements further implicating himself in the murder plot. At this point, an assistant prosecutor arrived "to take" a statement. The statement, made in response to carefully framed questions, was admitted into evidence. Petitioner was convicted of murder. The Supreme Court of Illinois affirmed.]

The critical question in this case is whether, under the circumstances, the refusal by the police to honor petitioner's request to consult with his lawyer during the course of an interrogation constitutes a denial of "the Assistance of Counsel" in violation of the Sixth Amendment to the Constitution as "made obligatory upon the States by the Fourteenth Amendment," *Gideon,* and thereby renders inadmissible in a state criminal trial any incriminating statement elicited by the police during the interrogation. * * *

In *Massiah* this Court observed that "a Constitution which guarantees a defendant the aid of counsel [at] trial could surely vouchsafe no less to an indicted defendant under interrogation by the police in a completely extrajudicial proceeding. Anything less [might] deny a defendant 'effective representation by counsel at the only stage when legal aid and advice would help him.'"

The interrogation here was conducted before petitioner was formally indicted. But in the context of this case, that fact should make no difference. When petitioner requested, and was denied, an opportunity to consult with his lawyer, the investigation had ceased to be a general investigation of "an unsolved crime." Petitioner had become the accused, and the purpose of the interrogation was to "get him" to confess his guilt despite his constitutional right not to do so. At the time of his arrest and throughout the course of the interrogation, the police told petitioner that they had convincing evidence that he had fired the fatal shots. Without informing him of his absolute right to remain silent in the face of this accusation, the police urged him to make a statement.[5] * * *

Petitioner, a layman, was undoubtedly unaware that under Illinois law an admission of "mere" complicity in the murder plot was legally as damaging as an admission of firing of the fatal shots. The "guiding hand of counsel" was essential to advise petitioner of his rights in this delicate situation. This was the "stage when legal aid and advice" were most critical to petitioner. *Massiah.* * * * It would exalt form over substance to make the right to counsel, under these circumstances, depend on whether at the time of the interrogation, the authorities had secured a formal indictment. Petitioner had, for all practical purposes, already been charged with murder. * * *

In *Gideon* we held that every person accused of a crime, whether state or federal, is entitled to a lawyer at trial. The rule sought by the State here, however, would make the trial no more than an appeal from the interrogation; and the "right to use counsel at the formal trial [would be] a very hollow thing [if], for all practical purposes, the conviction is already assured by pretrial examination." *In re Groban,* 352 U.S. 330 (1957) (Black, J., dissenting). "One can imagine a cynical prosecutor

---

[5] Although there is testimony in the record that petitioner and his lawyer had previously discussed what petitioner should do in the event of interrogation, there is no evidence that they discussed what petitioner should, or could, do in the face of a false accusation that he had fired the fatal bullets.

saying: 'Let them have the most illustrious counsel, now. They can't escape the noose. There is nothing that counsel can do for them at the trial.'"

It is argued that if the right to counsel is afforded prior to indictment, the number of confessions obtained by the police will diminish significantly, because most confessions are obtained during the period between arrest and indictment, and "any lawyer worth his salt will tell the suspect in no uncertain terms to make no statement to police under any circumstances." This argument, of course, cuts two ways. The fact that many confessions are obtained during this period points up its critical nature as a "stage when legal aid and advice" are surely needed. *Massiah.* The right to counsel would indeed be hollow if it began at a period when few confessions were obtained. There is necessarily a direct relationship between the importance of a stage to the police in their quest for a confession and the criticalness of that stage to the accused in his need for legal advice. Our Constitution, unlike some others, strikes the balance in favor of the right of the accused to be advised by his lawyer of his privilege against self-incrimination.

We have learned the lesson of history, ancient and modern, that a system of criminal law enforcement which comes to depend on the "confession" will, in the long run, be less reliable and more subject to abuses than a system which depends on extrinsic evidence independently secured through skillful investigation. * * *

We have also learned the companion lesson of history that no system of criminal justice can, or should, survive if it comes to depend for its continued effectiveness on the citizens' abdication through unawareness of their constitutional rights. No system worth preserving should have to *fear* that if an accused is permitted to consult with a lawyer, he will become aware of, and exercise, these rights. If the exercise of constitutional rights will thwart the effectiveness of a system of law enforcement, then there is something very wrong with that system.[14]

We hold, therefore, that where, as here, the investigation is no longer a general inquiry into an unsolved crime but has begun to focus on a particular suspect, the suspect has been taken into police custody, the police carry out a process of interrogations that lends itself to eliciting incriminating statements, the suspect has requested and been denied an opportunity to consult with his lawyer, and the police have not effectively warned him of his absolute constitutional right to remain silent, the accused has been denied "the Assistance of Counsel" in violation of the Sixth Amendment to the Constitution as "made obligatory upon the States by the Fourteenth Amendment," *Gideon,* and that no statement elicited by the police during the interrogation may be used against him at a criminal trial. * * *

Nothing we have said today affects the powers of the police to investigate "an unsolved crime" by gathering information from witnesses and by other "proper investigative efforts." We hold only that when the process shifts from investigatory

---

[14] The accused may, of course, intelligently and knowingly waive his privilege against self-incrimination and his right to counsel either at a pretrial stage or at the trial. But no knowing and intelligent waiver of any constitutional right can be said to have occurred under the circumstances of this case.

to accusatory—when its focus is on the accused and its purpose is to elicit a confession—our adversary system begins to operate, and, under the circumstances here, the accused must be permitted to consult with his lawyer.

The judgment of the Illinois Supreme Court is reversed and the case remanded for proceedings not inconsistent with this opinion. * * *

JUSTICE HARLAN, dissenting.

* * * Like my Brother White, I think the rule announced today is most ill-conceived and that it seriously and unjustifiably fetters perfectly legitimate methods of criminal law enforcement.

JUSTICE STEWART, dissenting. * * *

Massiah is not in point here. * * * Putting to one side the fact that the case now before us is not a federal case, the vital fact remains that this case does not involve the deliberate interrogation of a defendant after the initiation of judicial proceedings against him. The Court disregards this basic difference between the present case and Massiah's, with the bland assertion that "that fact should make no difference."

It is "that fact," I submit, which makes all the difference. Under our system of criminal justice the institution of formal, meaningful judicial proceedings, by way of indictment, information, or arraignment, marks the point at which a criminal investigation has ended and adversary proceedings have commenced. It is at this point that the constitutional guarantees attach which pertain to a criminal trial. Among those guarantees are the right to a speedy trial, the right of confrontation, and the right to trial by jury. Another is the guarantee of the assistance of counsel.

The confession which the Court today holds inadmissible was a voluntary one. It was given during the course of a perfectly legitimate police investigation of an unsolved murder. The Court says that what happened during this investigation "affected" the trial. I had always supposed that the whole purpose of a police investigation of a murder was to "affect" the trial of the murderer, and that it would be only an incompetent, unsuccessful, or corrupt investigation which would not do so. The Court further says that the Illinois police officers did not advise the petitioner of his "constitutional rights" before he confessed to the murder. This Court has never held that the Constitution requires the police to give any "advice" under circumstances such as these.

Supported by no stronger authority than its own rhetoric, the Court today converts a routine police investigation of an unsolved murder into a distorted analogue of a judicial trial. It imports into this investigation constitutional concepts historically applicable only after the onset of formal prosecutorial proceedings. By doing so, I think the Court perverts those precious constitutional guarantees, and frustrates the vital interests of society in preserving the legitimate and proper function of honest and purposeful police investigation. * * *

JUSTICE WHITE, whom JUSTICE CLARK and JUSTICE STEWART join, dissenting.

In *Massiah* the Court held that as of the date of the indictment the prosecution is disentitled to secure admissions from the accused. The Court now moves that date back to the time when the prosecution begins to "focus" on the accused. Although the opinion purports to be limited to the facts of this case, it would be naive to think that the new constitutional right announced will depend upon whether the accused has retained his own counsel, or has asked to consult with counsel in the course of interrogation. At the very least the Court holds that once the accused becomes a suspect and, presumably, is arrested, any admission made to the police thereafter is inadmissible in evidence unless the accused has waived his right to counsel. The decision is thus another major step in the direction of the goal which the Court seemingly has in mind—to bar from evidence all admissions obtained from an individual suspected of crime, whether involuntarily made or not. It does of course put us one step "ahead" of the English judges who have had the good sense to leave the matter a discretionary one with the trial court. I reject this step and the invitation to go farther which the court has now issued.

By abandoning the voluntary-involuntary test for admissibility of confessions, the Court seems driven by the notion that it is uncivilized law enforcement to use an accused's own admissions against him at his trial. It attempts to find a home for this new and nebulous rule of due process by attaching it to the right to counsel guaranteed in the federal system by the Sixth Amendment and binding upon the States by virtue of the due process guarantee of the Fourteenth Amendment. The right to counsel now not only entitles the accused to counsel's advice and aid in preparing for trial but stands as an impenetrable barrier to any interrogation once the accused has become a suspect. From that very moment apparently his right to counsel attaches, a rule wholly unworkable and impossible to administer unless police cars are equipped with public defenders and undercover agents and police informants have defense counsel at their side. I would not abandon the Court's prior cases defining with some care and analysis the circumstances requiring the presence or aid of counsel and substitute the amorphous and wholly unworkable principle that counsel is constitutionally required whenever he would or could be helpful. [Under the Court's] new approach one might just as well argue that a potential defendant is constitutionally entitled to a lawyer before, not after, he commits a crime, since it is then that crucial incriminating evidence is put within the reach of the Government by the would-be accused. Until now there simply has been no right guaranteed by the Federal Constitution to be free from the use at trial of a voluntary admission made prior to indictment.

It is incongruous to assume that the provision for counsel in the Sixth Amendment was meant to amend or supersede the self-incrimination provision of the Fifth Amendment, which is now applicable to the States. That amendment addresses itself to the very issue of incriminating admissions of an accused and resolves it by proscribing only compelled statements. Neither the Framers, the constitutional language, a century of decisions of this Court nor Professor Wigmore provides an iota of support for the idea that an accused has an absolute constitutional right not to answer even in the absence of compulsion—the constitutional right not to incriminate himself by making voluntary disclosures. * * *

The Court chooses [to] rely on the virtues and morality of a system of criminal law enforcement which does not depend on the "confession." No such judgment is to be found in the Constitution. It might be appropriate for a legislature to provide that a suspect should not be consulted during a criminal investigation; that an accused should never be called before a grand jury to answer, even if he wants to, what may well be incriminating questions; and that no person, whether he be a suspect, guilty criminal or innocent bystander, should be put to the ordeal of responding to orderly noncompulsory inquiry by the State. But this is not the system our Constitution requires. The only "inquisitions" the Constitution forbids are those which compel incrimination. Escobedo's statements were not compelled and the Court does not hold that they were.

This new American judges' rule, which is to be applied in both federal and state courts, is perhaps thought to be a necessary safeguard against the possibility of extorted confessions. To this extent it reflects a deep-seated distrust of law enforcement officers everywhere, unsupported by relevant data or current material based upon our own experience. Obviously law enforcement officers can make mistakes and exceed their authority, as today's decision shows that even judges can do, but I have somewhat more faith than the Court evidently has in the ability and desire of prosecutors and of the power of the appellate courts to discern and correct such violations of the law.

The Court may be concerned with a narrower matter: the unknowing defendant who responds to police questioning because he mistakenly believes that he must and that his admissions will not be used against him. But this worry hardly calls for the broadside the Court has now fired. The failure to inform an accused that he need not answer and that his answers may be used against him is very relevant indeed to whether the disclosures are compelled. Cases in this Court, to say the least, have never placed a premium on ignorance of constitutional rights. If an accused is told he must answer and does not know better, it would be very doubtful that the resulting admissions could be used against him. When the accused has not been informed of his rights at all the Court characteristically and properly looks very closely at the surrounding circumstances. I would continue to do so. But in this case Danny Escobedo knew full well that he did not have to answer and knew full well that his lawyer had advised him not to answer.

I do not suggest for a moment that law enforcement will be destroyed by the rule announced today. The need for peace and order is too insistent for that. But it will be crippled and its task made a great deal more difficult, all in my opinion, for unsound, unstated reasons, which can find no home in any of the provisions of the Constitution.

3. *MIRANDA*

Recall that dissenting in the 1944 *Ashcraft* case, Justice Jackson agreed that the detention and questioning of a suspect for thirty-six hours is "inherently coercive," but quickly added: "[S]o is custody and examination for one hour. Arrest itself is inherently coercive and so is detention. * * * But does the Constitution prohibit use of all confessions made after arrest because questioning, while one is deprived of freedom, is 'inherently coercive'?" Both Jackson and Justice Black, who wrote the majority opinion in *Ashcraft*, knew that in 1944 the Court was not ready for an affirmative answer to Jackson's question. But by 1966 the Court had grown ready.

Yes, answered a 5–4 majority in *Miranda v. Arizona*, the Constitution does prohibit use of all confessions obtained by "in-custody questioning" unless "adequate protective devices" are used to dispel the coercion inherent in such questioning. The protective devices deemed necessary to neutralize the compulsion inherent in the interrogation environment (unless the government adopts other equally effective means, and what they may be remains unclear) are the now familiar "*Miranda* warnings."

The *Miranda* Court's reasoning, if not its result, surprised the late John J. Flynn, Miranda's lawyer in the U.S. Supreme Court. As Flynn later recalled, he and others working on the case had "agreed that the briefs should be written with the entire focus on the Sixth Amendment [right to counsel] because that is where the Court was headed after *Escobedo*," but "in the very first paragraph [of the *Miranda* opinion] Chief Justice Warren said [in effect], 'It is the Fifth Amendment [privilege against compulsory self-incrimination] that is at issue today.' That was Miranda's effective use of counsel."

Although not happy with the continued momentum of the Warren Court in favor of the rights of suspects, those alarmed by *Massiah* and *Escobedo* must have found some comfort in the *Miranda* Court's switch in emphasis from the right to counsel to the privilege against compelled self-incrimination. Recall that the *Escobedo* dissenters expressed a preference for a self-incrimination approach, rather than a right to counsel approach, because the self-incrimination clause proscribes only *compelled* statements. Of course, the four *Escobedo* dissenters (all of whom also dissented in *Miranda*) were not pleased with the way the *Miranda* majority defined "compulsion" within the meaning of the privilege.

Why, in the thirty years between *Brown v. Mississippi* (1936), the first Fourteenth Amendment Due Process case, and *Miranda*, had the Fifth Amendment's ban against compelling a person in any criminal case "to be a witness against himself" been so neglected in the confession cases? For one thing, this prohibition had not been deemed applicable to the states until 1964, and by that time a large body of law pertaining to "involuntary" or "coerced" confessions had developed. Moreover, and more important, the prevailing pre-*Miranda* view was that compulsion to testify meant *legal* compulsion.

Since a suspect is threatened neither with perjury for testifying falsely nor contempt for refusing to testify at all, it cannot be said, ran the argument, that a person undergoing police interrogation is being "compelled" to be "a witness against himself" within the meaning of the privilege—even though under such circumstances a person may assume or be led to believe that there *are* legal (or extralegal) sanctions for "refusing to cooperate." Since the police have no *legal right* to make a suspect answer (although, prior to *Miranda*, the police did not have to *tell* a person that), there was no legal obligation to answer, ran the argument, to which a privilege in the technical sense could apply.

Although the right to counsel had dominated the confessions scene in the years immediately preceding *Miranda,* there was some reason to think that, at long last, the self-incrimination clause might move to centerstage. In *Malloy v. Hogan,* 378 U.S. 1 (1964) (which did not involve a confession), the Court, per Brennan, J., performed what some called a "shotgun wedding" of the privilege against self-incrimination to the confession rule. *Malloy* not only held the self-incrimination clause applicable to the states, but declared that whenever a question arises in a state *or* federal court "whether a confession is incompetent because not voluntary, the issue is controlled by [the self-incrimination] portion of the Fifth Amendment."

Whether or not this view made good sense, it constituted very questionable recent history. In none of the dozens of state *or* federal confession cases decided in the 1930s, 40s or 50s had the self-incrimination clause been the basis for judgment (although it had occasionally been mentioned in an opinion). But how the *Malloy* opinion looked back was not as important as how it looked forward. The confession rules and the privilege against self-incrimination had become intertwined in *Malloy*—and they would be fused in *Miranda.*

MIRANDA V. ARIZONA (No. 759)[*]
384 U.S. 436, 86 S.Ct. 1602, 16 L.Ed.2d 694 (1966).

Chief Justice Warren delivered the opinion of the Court.

The cases before us raise questions which go to the roots of American criminal jurisprudence: the restraints society must observe consistent with the Federal Constitution in prosecuting individuals for crime. More specifically, we deal with the admissibility of statements obtained from an individual who is subjected to custodial police interrogation and the necessity for procedures which assure that the individual is accorded his privilege under the Fifth Amendment to the Constitution not to be compelled to incriminate himself. * * *

We start here, as we did in *Escobedo* with the premise that our holding is not an innovation in our jurisprudence, but is an application of principles long recognized and applied in other settings. We have undertaken a thorough re-examination of the *Escobedo* decision and the principles it announced, and we reaffirm it. That case was but an explication of basic rights that are enshrined in our Constitution—that "No person * * * shall be compelled in any criminal case to be a witness against himself," and that "the accused [shall] have the Assistance of Counsel"—rights which were put in jeopardy in that case through official overbearing. * * *

Our holding will be spelled out with some specificity in the pages which follow but briefly stated it is this: the prosecution may not use statements, whether exculpatory or inculpatory, stemming from custodial interrogation of the defendant unless it demonstrates the use of procedural safeguards effective to secure the privilege against self-incrimination. By custodial interrogation, we mean

---

[*]   Together with No. 760, *Vignera v. New York* [and] No. 761, *Westover v. United States* [and] No. 584, *California v. Stewart* * * *.

questioning initiated by law enforcement officers after a person has been taken into custody or otherwise deprived of his freedom of action in any significant way.[4] As for the procedural safeguards to be employed, unless other fully effective means are devised to inform accused persons of their right of silence and to assure a continuous opportunity to exercise it, the following measures are required. Prior to any questioning, the person must be warned that he has a right to remain silent, that any statement he does make may be used as evidence against him, and that he has a right to the presence of an attorney, either retained or appointed. The defendant may waive effectuation of these rights, provided the waiver is made voluntarily, knowingly and intelligently. If, however, he indicates in any manner and at any stage of the process that he wishes to consult with an attorney before speaking there can be no questioning. Likewise, if the individual is alone and indicates in any manner that he does not wish to be interrogated, the police may not question him. The mere fact that he may have answered some questions or volunteered some statements on his own does not deprive him of the right to refrain from answering any further inquiries until he has consulted with an attorney and thereafter consents to be questioned.

The constitutional issue we decide in each of these cases is the admissibility of statements obtained from a defendant questioned while in custody and deprived of his freedom of action in any significant way. In each, the defendant was questioned by police officers, detectives, or a prosecuting attorney in a room in which he was cut off from the outside world. In none of these cases was the defendant given a full and effective warning of his rights at the outset of the interrogation process. In all the cases, the questioning elicited oral admissions, and in three of them, signed statements as well which were admitted at their trials. They all thus share silent features—incommunicado interrogation of individuals in a police-dominated atmosphere, resulting in self-incriminating statements without full warnings of constitutional rights. * * *

Again we stress that the modern practice of in-custody interrogation is psychologically rather than physically oriented. * * * Interrogation still takes place in privacy. Privacy results in secrecy and this in turn results in a gap in our knowledge as to what in fact goes on in the interrogation rooms. A valuable source of information about present police practices, however, may be found in various police manuals and texts which document procedures employed with success in the past, and which recommend various other effective tactics. These texts are used by law enforcement agencies themselves as guides.[9] It should be noted that these texts

---

[4]   This is what we meant in *Escobedo* when we spoke of an investigation which had focused on an accused.

[9]   The methods described in Inbau and Reid, *Criminal Interrogation and Confessions* (1962), are a revision and enlargement of material presented in three prior editions of a predecessor text, *Lie Detection and Criminal Interrogation* (3d ed. 1953). The authors and their associates are officers of the Chicago Police Scientific Crime-Detection Laboratory and have had extensive experience in writing, lecturing and speaking to law enforcement authorities over a 20-year period. They say that the techniques portrayed in their manuals reflect their experiences and are the most effective psychological strategems to employ during interrogations. Similarly, the techniques described in O'Hara, *Fundamentals of Criminal Investigation* (1959), were gleaned from long service as observer, lecturer in police science, and work as a federal criminal investigator. All these

professedly present the most enlightened and effective means presently used to obtain statements through custodial interrogation. By considering these texts and other data, it is possible to describe procedures observed and noted around the country. * * *

To highlight the isolation and unfamiliar surroundings, the manuals instruct the police to display an air of confidence in the suspect's guilt and from outward appearance to maintain only an interest in confirming certain details. The guilt of the subject is to be posited as a fact. The interrogator should direct his comments toward the reasons why the subject committed the act, rather than court failure by asking the subject whether he did it. Like other men, perhaps the subject has had a bad family life, had an unhappy childhood, had too much to drink, had an unrequited desire for women. The officers are instructed to minimize the moral seriousness of the offense, to cast blame on the victim or on society. These tactics are designed to put the subject in a psychological state where his story is but an elaboration of what the police purport to know already—that he is guilty. Explanations to the contrary are dismissed and discouraged.

The texts thus stress that the major qualities an interrogator should possess are patience and perseverance. * * *

[When other techniques] prove unavailing, the texts recommend they be alternated with a show of some hostility. One ploy often used has been termed the "friendly-unfriendly" or the "Mutt and Jeff" act:

> "[In] this technique, two agents are employed. Mutt, the relentless investigator, who knows the subject is guilty and is not going to waste any time. He's sent a dozen men away for this crime and he's going to send the subject away for the full term. Jeff, on the other hand, is obviously a kindhearted man. He has a family himself. He has a brother who was involved in a little scrape like this. He disapproves of Mutt and his tactics and will arrange to get him off the case if the subject will cooperate. He can't hold Mutt off for very long. The subject would be wise to make a quick decision. The technique is applied by having both investigators present while Mutt acts out his role. Jeff may stand by quietly and demur at some of Mutt's tactics. When Jeff makes his plea for cooperation, Mutt is not present in the room."

The interrogators sometimes are instructed to induce a confession out of trickery. The technique here is quite effective in crimes which require identification or which run in series. In the identification situation, the interrogator may take a break in his questioning to place the subject among a group of men in a line-up. "The witness or complainant (previously coached, if necessary) studies the line-up and confidently points out the subject as the guilty party." Then the questioning resumes "as though there were now no doubt about the guilt of the subject." A variation on this technique is called the "reverse line-up":

---

texts have had rather extensive use among law enforcement agencies and among students of police science, with total sales and circulation of over 44,000.

"The accused is placed in a line-up, but this time he is identified by several fictitious witnesses or victims who associated him with different offenses. It is expected that the subject will become desperate and confess to the offense under investigation in order to escape from the false accusations."

The manuals also contain instructions for police on how to handle the individual who refuses to discuss the matter entirely, or who asks for an attorney or relatives. The examiner is to concede him the right to remain silent. "This usually has a very undermining effect. First of all, he is disappointed in his expectation of an unfavorable reaction on the part of the interrogator. Secondly, a concession of this right to remain silent impresses the subject with the apparent fairness of his interrogator." After this psychological conditioning, however, the officer is told to point out the incriminating significance of the suspect's refusal to talk * * *.

From these representative samples of interrogation techniques, the setting prescribed by the manuals and observed in practice becomes clear. In essence, it is this: To be alone with the subject is essential to prevent distraction and to deprive him of any outside support. The aura of confidence in his guilt undermines his will to resist. He merely confirms the preconceived story the police seek to have him describe. Patience and persistence, at times relentless questioning, are employed. To obtain a confession, the interrogator must "patiently maneuver himself or his quarry into a position from which the desired object may be obtained." When normal procedures fail to produce the needed result, the police may resort to deceptive stratagems such as giving false legal advice. It is important to keep the subject off balance, for example, by trading on his insecurity about himself or his surroundings. The police then persuade, trick, or cajole him out of exercising his constitutional rights.

Even without employing brutality, the "third degree" or the specific stratagems described above, the very fact of custodial interrogation exacts a heavy toll on individual liberty and trades on the weakness of individuals. * * *

In the cases before us today, given this background, we concern ourselves primarily with this interrogation atmosphere and the evils it can bring. In *Miranda v. Arizona*, the police arrested the defendant and took him to a special interrogation room where they secured a confession. In *Vignera v. New York*, the defendant made oral admissions to the police after interrogation in the afternoon, and then signed an inculpatory statement upon being questioned by an assistant district attorney later the same evening. In *Westover v. United States*, the defendant was handed over to the Federal Bureau of Investigation by local authorities after they had detained and interrogated him for a lengthy period, both at night and the following morning. After some two hours of questioning, the federal officers had obtained signed statements from the defendant. Lastly, in *California v. Stewart*, the local police held the defendant five days in the station and interrogated him on nine separate occasions before they secured his inculpatory statement.

In these cases, we might not find the defendants' statements to have been involuntary in traditional terms. Our concern for adequate safeguards to protect precious Fifth Amendment rights is, of course, not lessened in the slightest. In each of the cases, the defendant was thrust into an unfamiliar atmosphere and run through menacing police interrogation procedures. The potentiality for compulsion is forcefully apparent, for example, in *Miranda,* where the indigent Mexican defendant was a seriously disturbed individual with pronounced sexual fantasies, and in *Stewart,* in which the defendant was an indigent Los Angeles Negro who had dropped out of school in the sixth grade. To be sure, the records do not evince overt physical coercion or patented psychological ploys. The fact remains that in none of these cases did the officers undertake to afford appropriate safeguards at the outset of the interrogation to insure that the statements were truly the product of free choice.

It is obvious that such an interrogation environment is created for no purpose other than to subjugate the individual to the will of his examiner. This atmosphere carries its own badge of intimidation. To be sure, this is not physical intimidation, but it is equally destructive of human dignity. The current practice of incommunicado interrogation is at odds with one of our Nation's most cherished principles—that the individual may not be compelled to incriminate himself. Unless adequate protective devices are employed to dispel the compulsion inherent in custodial surroundings, no statement obtained from the defendant can truly be the product of his free choice.

From the foregoing, we can readily perceive an intimate connection between the privilege against self-incrimination and police custodial questioning. It is fitting to turn to history and precedent underlying the Self-Incrimination Clause to determine its applicability in this situation.

[W]e may view the historical development of the privilege as one which groped for the proper scope of governmental power over the citizen. As a "noble principle often transcends its origins," the privilege has come rightfully to be recognized in part as an individual's substantive right, a "right to a private enclave where he may lead a private life. That right is the hallmark of our democracy." We have recently noted that the privilege against self-incrimination—the essential mainstay of our adversary system—is founded on a complex of values. All these policies point to one overriding thought: the constitutional foundation underlying the privilege is the respect a government—state or federal—must accord to the dignity and integrity of its citizens. To maintain a "fair state-individual balance," to require the government "to shoulder the entire load," 8 Wigmore, *Evidence* (McNaughton rev., 1961), 317, to respect the inviolability of the human personality, our accusatory system of criminal justice demands that the government seeking to punish an individual produce the evidence against him by its own independent labors, rather than by the cruel, simple expedient of compelling it from his own mouth. In sum, the privilege is fulfilled only when the person is guaranteed the right "to remain silent unless he chooses to speak in the unfettered exercise of his own will." *Malloy v. Hogan.*

* * * We are satisfied that all the principles embodied in the privilege apply to informal compulsion exerted by law-enforcement officers during in-custody questioning. An individual swept from familiar surroundings into police custody,

surrounded by antagonistic forces, and subjected to the techniques of persuasion described above cannot be otherwise than under compulsion to speak. As a practical matter, the compulsion to speak in the isolated setting of the police station may well be greater than in courts or other official investigations, where there are often impartial observers to guard against intimidation or trickery. * * *

Because of the adoption by Congress of Rule 5(a) of the Federal Rules of Criminal Procedure, and this Court's effectuation of that Rule in *McNabb v. United States*, 318 U.S. 332 (1943) and *Mallory v. United States*, 354 U.S. 449 (1957), we have had little occasion in the past quarter century to reach the constitutional issues in dealing with federal interrogations. These supervisory rules, requiring production of an arrested person before a commissioner "without unnecessary delay" and excluding evidence obtained in default of that statutory obligation, were nonetheless responsive to the same considerations of Fifth Amendment policy that unavoidably face us now as to the States. In [the *McNabb* and *Mallory* cases] we recognized both the dangers of interrogation and the appropriateness of prophylaxis stemming from the very fact of interrogation itself.[32]

Our decision in *Malloy v. Hogan* necessitates an examination of the scope of the privilege in state cases as well. In *Malloy,* we squarely held the privilege applicable to the States, and held that the substantive standards underlying the privilege applied with full force to state court proceedings. [T]he reasoning in *Malloy* made clear what had already become apparent—that the substantive and procedural safeguards surrounding admissibility of confessions in state cases had become exceedingly exacting, reflecting all the policies embedded in the privilege. The voluntariness doctrine in the state cases, as *Malloy* indicates, encompasses all interrogation practices which are likely to exert such pressure upon an individual as to disable him from making a free and rational choice. The implications of this proposition were elaborated in our decision in *Escobedo,* decided one week after *Malloy* applied the privilege to the States. * * *

[In *Escobedo*], as in the cases today, we sought a protective device to dispel the compelling atmosphere of the interrogation. In *Escobedo,* however, the police did not relieve the defendant of the anxieties which they had created in the interrogation rooms. Rather, they denied his request for the assistance of counsel.[35] This heightened his dilemma, and made his later statements the product of this compulsion. * * * The denial of the defendant's request for his attorney thus undermined his ability to exercise the privilege—to remain silent if he chose or to speak without any intimidation, blatant or subtle. The presence of counsel, in all the cases before us today, would be the adequate protective device necessary to make the process of police interrogation conform to the dictates of the privilege.

---

[32] Our decision today does not indicate in any manner, of course, that these rules can be disregarded. When federal officials arrest an individual, they must as always comply with the dictates of the congressional legislation and cases thereunder. * * *

[35] The police also prevented the attorney from consulting with his client. Independent of any other constitutional proscription, this action constitutes a violation of the Sixth Amendment right to the assistance of counsel and excludes any statement obtained in its wake. See *People v. Donovan,* 193 N.E.2d 628 (N.Y.1963) (Fuld, J.).

His presence would insure that statements made in the government-established atmosphere are not the product of compulsion. * * *

Today, then, there can be no doubt that the Fifth Amendment privilege is available outside of criminal court proceedings and serves to protect persons in all settings in which their freedom of action is curtailed from being compelled to incriminate themselves. We have concluded that without proper safeguards the process of in-custody interrogation of persons suspected or accused of crime contains inherently compelling pressures which work to undermine the individual's will to resist and to compel him to speak where he would not otherwise do so freely. In order to combat these pressures and to permit a full opportunity to exercise the privilege against self-incrimination, the accused must be adequately and effectively apprised of his rights and the exercise of those rights must be fully honored.

It is impossible for us to foresee the potential alternatives for protecting the privilege which might be devised by Congress or the States in the exercise of their creative rule-making capacities. Therefore we cannot say that the Constitution necessarily requires adherence to any particular solution for the inherent compulsions of the interrogation process as it is presently conducted. Our decision in no way creates a constitutional straitjacket which will handicap sound efforts at reform, nor is it intended to have this effect. We encourage Congress and the States to continue their laudable search for increasingly effective ways of protecting the rights of the individual while promoting efficient enforcement of our criminal laws. However, unless we are shown other procedures which are at least as effective in apprising accused persons of their right of silence and in assuring a continuous opportunity to exercise it, the following safeguards must be observed.

At the outset, if a person in custody is to be subjected to interrogation, he must first be informed in clear and unequivocal terms that he has the right to remain silent. For those unaware of the privilege, the warning is needed simply to make them aware of it—the threshold requirement for an intelligent decision as to its exercise. More important, such a warning is an absolute prerequisite in overcoming the inherent pressures of the interrogation atmosphere. It is not just the subnormal or woefully ignorant who succumb to an interrogator's imprecations, whether implied or expressly stated, that the interrogation will continue until a confession is obtained or that silence in the face of accusation is itself damning and will bode ill when presented to a jury.[37] Further, the warning will show the individual that his interrogators are prepared to recognize his privilege should he choose to exercise it.

The Fifth Amendment privilege is so fundamental to our system of constitutional rule and the expedient of giving an adequate warning as to the availability of the privilege so simple, we will not pause to inquire in individual cases whether the defendant was aware of his rights without a warning being

---

[37] * * * In accord with this decision, it is impermissible to penalize an individual for exercising his Fifth Amendment privilege when he is under police custodial interrogation. The prosecution may not, therefore, use at trial the fact that he stood mute or claimed his privilege in the face of accusation. Cf. *Griffin v. California* [p. 1051].

given. Assessments of the knowledge the defendant possessed, based on information as to his age, education, intelligence, or prior contact with authorities, can never be more than speculation;[38] a warning is a clearcut fact. More important, whatever the background of the person interrogated, a warning at the time of the interrogation is indispensable to overcome its pressures and to insure that the individual knows he is free to exercise the privilege at that point in time.

The warning of the right to remain silent must be accompanied by the explanation that anything said can and will be used against the individual in court. This warning is needed in order to make him aware not only of the privilege, but also of the consequences of forgoing it. It is only through an awareness of these consequences that there can be any assurance of real understanding and intelligent exercise of the privilege. Moreover, this warning may serve to make the individual more acutely aware that he is faced with a phase of the adversary system—that he is not in the presence of persons acting solely in his interest.

The circumstances surrounding in-custody interrogation can operate very quickly to overbear the will of one merely made aware of his privilege by his interrogators. Therefore, the right to have counsel present at the interrogation is indispensable to the protection of the Fifth Amendment privilege under the system we delineate today. Our aim is to assure that the individual's right to choose between silence and speech remains unfettered throughout the interrogation process. A once-stated warning, delivered by those who will conduct the interrogation, cannot itself suffice to that end among those who must require knowledge of their rights. A mere warning given by the interrogators is not alone sufficient to accomplish that end. Prosecutors themselves claim that the admonishment of the right to remain silent without more "will benefit only the recidivist and the professional." Brief for the National District Attorneys Association as *amicus curiae*. Even preliminary advice given to the accused by his own attorney can be swiftly overcome by the secret interrogation process. Thus, the need for counsel to protect the Fifth Amendment privilege comprehends not merely a right to consult with counsel prior to questioning but also to have counsel present during any questioning if the defendant so desires.

The presence of counsel at the interrogation may serve several significant subsidiary functions as well. If the accused decides to talk to his interrogators, the assistance of counsel can mitigate the dangers of untrustworthiness. With a lawyer present the likelihood that the police will practice coercion is reduced, and if coercion is nevertheless exercised the lawyer can testify to it in court. The presence of a lawyer can also help to guarantee that the accused gives a fully accurate statement to the police and that the statement is rightly reported by the prosecution at trial. See *Crooker v. California* (Douglas, J., dissenting).

An individual need not make a preinterrogation request for a lawyer. While such request affirmatively secures his right to have one, his failure to ask for a lawyer does not constitute a waiver. No effective waiver of the right to counsel during interrogation can be recognized unless specifically made after the warnings

---

[38] Cf. *Betts v. Brady* [p. 376], and the recurrent inquiry into special circumstances it necessitated. * * *

we here delineate have been given. The accused who does not know his rights and therefore does not make a request may be the person who most needs counsel. * * *

Accordingly we hold that an individual held for interrogation must be clearly informed that he has the right to consult with a lawyer and to have the lawyer with him during interrogation under the system for protecting the privilege we delineate today. As with the warnings of the right to remain silent and that anything stated can be used in evidence against him, this warning is an absolute prerequisite to interrogation. No amount of circumstantial evidence that the person may have been aware of this right will suffice to stand in its stead. Only through such a warning is there ascertainable assurance that the accused was aware of this right.

If an individual indicates that he wishes the assistance of counsel before any interrogation occurs, the authorities cannot rationally ignore or deny his request on the basis that the individual does not have or cannot afford a retained attorney. The financial ability of the individual has no relationship to the scope of the rights involved here. The privilege against self-incrimination secured by the Constitution applies to all individuals. The need for counsel in order to protect the privilege exists for the indigent as well as the affluent. In fact, were we to limit these constitutional rights to those who can retain an attorney, our decisions today would be of little significance. The cases before us as well as the vast majority of confession cases with which we have dealt in the past involve those unable to retain counsel. While authorities are not required to relieve the accused of his poverty, they have the obligation not to take advantage of indigence in the administration of justice.[41] Denial of counsel to the indigent at the time of interrogation while allowing an attorney to those who can afford one would be no more supportable by reason or logic than the similar situation at trial and on appeal struck down in *Gideon* and *Douglas v. California*.

In order fully to apprise a person interrogated of the extent of his rights under this system then, it is necessary to warn him not only that he has the right to consult with an attorney, but also that if he is indigent a lawyer will be appointed to represent him. Without this additional warning, the admonition of the right to consult with counsel would often be understood as meaning only that he can consult with a lawyer if he has one or has the funds to obtain one. The warning of a right to counsel would be hollow if not couched in terms that would convey to the indigent—the person most often subjected to interrogation—the knowledge that he too has a right to have counsel present. As with the warnings of the right to remain silent and of the general right to counsel, only by effective and express explanation to the indigent of this right can there be assurance that he was truly in a position to exercise it.[43]

---

[41] See Kamisar, *Equal Justice in the Gatehouses and Mansions of American Criminal Procedure,* in Criminal Justice in Our Time (1965), 64–81; * * * Report of the Attorney General's Committee on *Poverty and the Administration of Federal Criminal Justice* (1963), p. 9 * * *.

[43] While a warning that the indigent may have counsel appointed need not be given to the person who is known to have an attorney or is known to have ample funds to secure one, the expedient of giving a warning is too simple and the rights involved too important to engage in *ex post facto* inquiries into financial ability when there is any doubt at all on that score.

Once warnings have been given, the subsequent procedure is clear. If the individual indicates in any manner, at any time prior to or during questioning, that he wishes to remain silent, the interrogation must cease.[44] At this point he has shown that he intends to exercise his Fifth Amendment privilege; any statement taken after the person invokes his privilege cannot be other than the product of compulsion, subtle or otherwise. Without the right to cut off questioning, the setting of in-custody interrogation operates on the individual to overcome free choice in producing a statement after the privilege has been once invoked. If the individual states that he wants an attorney, the interrogation must cease until an attorney is present. At that time, the individual must have an opportunity to confer with the attorney and to have him present during any subsequent questioning. If the individual cannot obtain an attorney and he indicates that he wants one before speaking to police, they must respect his decision to remain silent.

This does not mean, as some have suggested, that each police station must have a "station house lawyer" present at all times to advise prisoners. It does mean, however, that if police propose to interrogate a person they must make known to him that he is entitled to a lawyer and that if he cannot afford one, a lawyer will be provided for him prior to any interrogation. If authorities conclude that they will not provide counsel during a reasonable period of time in which investigation in the field is carried out, they may do so without violating the person's Fifth Amendment privilege so long as they do not question him during that time.

If the interrogation continues without the presence of an attorney and a statement is taken, a heavy burden rests on the Government to demonstrate that the defendant knowingly and intelligently waived his privilege against self-incrimination and his right to retained or appointed counsel. This Court has always set high standards of proof for the waiver of constitutional rights, *Johnson v. Zerbst,* and we reassert these standards as applied to in-custody interrogation. Since the State is responsible for establishing the isolated circumstances under which the interrogation takes place and has the only means of making available corroborated evidence of warnings given during incommunicado interrogation, the burden is rightly on its shoulders.

An express statement that the individual is willing to make a statement and does not want an attorney followed closely by a statement could constitute a waiver. But a valid waiver will not be presumed simply from the silence of the accused after warnings are given or simply from the fact that a confession was in fact eventually obtained. A statement we made in *Carnley v. Cochran,* 369 U.S. 506 (1962), is applicable here:

"Presuming waiver from a silent record is impermissible. The record must show, or there must be an allegation and evidence which show, that

---

[44] If an individual indicates his desire to remain silent, but has an attorney present, there may be some circumstances in which further questioning would be permissible. In the absence of evidence of overbearing, statements then made in the presence of counsel might be free of the compelling influence of the interrogation process and might fairly be construed as a waiver of the privilege for purposes of these statements.

an accused was offered counsel but intelligently and understandably rejected the offer. Anything less is not waiver."

* * * Moreover, where in-custody interrogation is involved, there is no room for the contention that the privilege is waived if the individual answers some questions or gives some information on his own prior to invoking his right to remain silent when interrogated.[45]

Whatever the testimony of the authorities as to waiver of rights by an accused, the fact of lengthy interrogation or incommunicado incarceration before a statement is made is strong evidence that the accused did not validly waive his rights. In these circumstances the fact that the individual eventually made a statement is consistent with the conclusion that the compelling influence of the interrogation finally forced him to do so. It is inconsistent with any notion of a voluntary relinquishment of the privilege. Moreover, any evidence that the accused was threatened, tricked, or cajoled into a waiver will, of course, show that the defendant did not voluntarily waive his privilege. The requirement of warnings and waiver of rights is a fundamental with respect to the Fifth Amendment privilege and not simply a preliminary ritual to existing methods of interrogation.

The warnings required and the waiver necessary in accordance with our opinion today are, in the absence of a fully effective equivalent, prerequisites to the admissibility of any statement made by a defendant. No distinction can be drawn between statements which are direct confessions and statements which amount to "admissions" of part or all of an offense. The privilege against self-incrimination protects the individual from being compelled to incriminate himself in any manner; it does not distinguish degrees of incrimination. Similarly, for precisely the same reason, no distinction may be drawn between inculpatory statements and statements alleged to be merely "exculpatory." If a statement made were in fact truly exculpatory it would, of course, never be used by the prosecution. In fact, statements merely intended to be exculpatory by the defendant are often used to impeach his testimony at trial or to demonstrate untruths in the statement given under interrogation and thus to prove guilt by implication. These statements are incriminating in any meaningful sense of the word and may not be used without the full warnings and effective waiver required for any other statement. In *Escobedo* itself, the defendant fully intended his accusation of another as the slayer to be exculpatory as to himself.

The principles announced today deal with the protection which must be given to the privilege against self-incrimination when the individual is first subjected to police interrogation while in custody at the station or otherwise deprived of his freedom of action in any significant way. It is at this point that our adversary system of criminal proceedings commences, distinguishing itself at the outset from the inquisitorial system recognized in some countries. Under the system of

---

[45] Although this Court held in *Rogers v. United States,* 340 U.S. 367 (1951), over strong dissent, that a witness before a grand jury may not in certain circumstances decide to answer some questions and then refuse to answer others that decision has no application to the interrogation situation we deal with today. No legislative or judicial fact-finding authority is involved here, nor is there a possibility that the individual might make self-serving statements of which he could make use at trial while refusing to answer incriminating statements.

warnings we delineate today or under any other system which may be devised and found effective, the safeguards to be erected about the privilege must come into play at this point.

Our decision is not intended to hamper the traditional function of police officers in investigating crime. When an individual is in custody on probable cause, the police may, of course, seek out evidence in the field to be used at trial against him. Such investigation may include inquiry of persons not under restraint. General on-the-scene questioning as to facts surrounding a crime or other general questioning of citizens in the fact-finding process is not affected by our holding. It is an act of responsible citizenship for individuals to give whatever information they may have to aid in law enforcement. In such situations the compelling atmosphere inherent in the process of in-custody interrogation is not necessarily present.[46]

[To] summarize, we hold that when an individual is taken into custody or otherwise deprived of his freedom by the authorities in any significant way and is subjected to questioning, the privilege against self-incrimination is jeopardized. Procedural safeguards must be employed to protect the privilege, and unless other fully effective means are adopted to notify the person of his right of silence and to assure that the exercise of the right will be scrupulously honored, the following measures are required. He must be warned prior to any questioning that he has the right to remain silent, that anything he says can be used against him in a court of law, that he has the right to the presence of an attorney, and that if he cannot afford an attorney one will be appointed for him prior to any questioning if he so desires. Opportunity to exercise these rights must be afforded to him throughout the interrogation. After such warnings have been given, and such opportunity afforded him, the individual may knowingly and intelligently waive these rights and agree to answer questions or make a statement. But unless and until such warnings and waiver are demonstrated by the prosecution at trial, no evidence obtained as a result of interrogation can be used against him. * * *

If the individual desires to exercise his privilege, he has the right to do so. This is not for the authorities to decide. An attorney may advise his client not to talk to police until he has had an opportunity to investigate the case, or he may wish to be present with his client during any police questioning. In doing so an attorney is merely exercising the good professional judgment he has been taught. This is not cause for considering the attorney a menace to law enforcement. He is merely carrying out what he is sworn to do under his oath—to protect to the extent of his ability the rights of his client. In fulfilling this responsibility the attorney plays a vital role in the administration of criminal justice under our Constitution.

---

[46] The distinction and its significance has been aptly described in the opinion of a Scottish court:

"In former times such questioning, if undertaken, would be conducted by police officers visiting the house or place of business of the suspect and there questioning him, probably in the presence of a relation or friend. However convenient the modern practice may be, it must normally create a situation very unfavorable to the suspect." *Chalmers v. H.M. Advocate,* [1954] Sess.Cas. 66, 78 (J.C.).

[The] experience in some other countries * * * suggests that the danger to law enforcement in curbs on interrogation is overplayed. The English procedure since 1912 under the Judge's Rules is significant. As recently strengthened, the Rules require that a cautionary warning be given an accused by a police officer as soon as he has evidence that affords reasonable grounds for suspicion; they also require that any statement made be given by the accused without questioning by police. The right of the individual to consult with an attorney during this period is expressly recognized. * * *

Because of the nature of the problem and because of its recurrent significance in numerous cases, we have to this point discussed the relationship of the Fifth Amendment privilege to police interrogation without specific concentration on the facts of the cases before us. We turn now to these facts to consider the application to these cases of the constitutional principles discussed above. In each instance, we have concluded that statements were obtained from the defendant under circumstances that did not meet constitutional standards for protection of the privilege.

No. 759. *Miranda v. Arizona.*

On March 13, 1963, petitioner, Ernesto Miranda, was arrested at his home and taken in custody to a Phoenix police station. He was there identified by the complaining witness. The police then took him to "Interrogation Room No. 2" of the detective bureau. There he was questioned by two police officers. The officers admitted at trial that Miranda was not advised that he had a right to have an attorney present. Two hours later, the officers emerged from the interrogation room with a written confession signed by Miranda. At the top of the statement was a typed paragraph stating that the confession was made voluntarily, without threats or promises of immunity and "with full knowledge of my legal rights, understanding any statement I make may be used against me."[67]

[Miranda] was found guilty of kidnapping and rape. [On] appeal, the Supreme Court of Arizona held that Miranda's constitutional rights were not violated in obtaining the confession and affirmed the conviction. In reaching its decision, the court emphasized heavily the fact that Miranda did not specifically request counsel.

We reverse. From the testimony of the officers and by the admission of respondent, it is clear that Miranda was not in any way apprised of his right to consult with an attorney and to have one present during the interrogation, nor was his right not to be compelled to incriminate himself effectively protected in any other manner. Without these warnings the statements were inadmissible. The mere fact that he signed a statement which contained a typed-in clause stating that he had "full knowledge" of his legal rights does not approach the knowing and intelligent waiver required to relinquish constitutional rights. * * *[a]

---

[67] One of the officers testified that he read this paragraph to Miranda. Apparently, however, he did not do so until after Miranda had confessed orally.

[a] On retrial, Miranda was again convicted of kidnapping and rape. The conviction was affirmed in *State v. Miranda*, 450 P.2d 364 (Ariz. 1969). For a rich narrative of *Miranda* from arrest to reconviction, see Liva Baker, *Miranda: Crime, Law & Politics* (1983).

[The Court also reversed the convictions in two companion cases, *Vignera* and *Westover*, and affirmed the reversal of the conviction in the third companion case, *California v. Stewart*.[b]]

JUSTICE CLARK, dissenting in [*Miranda*, *Vignera*, and *Westover*, and concurring in the result in *Stewart*.]

[I cannot] agree with the Court's characterization of the present practices of police and investigatory agencies as to custodial interrogation. The materials referred to as "police manuals" are not shown by the record here to be the official manuals of any police department, much less in universal use in crime detection. Moreover, the examples of police brutality mentioned by the Court are rare exceptions to the thousands of cases that appear every year in the law reports. * * *

[The Court's] strict constitutional specific inserted at the nerve center of crime detection may well kill the patient. Since there is at this time a paucity of information and an almost total lack of empirical knowledge on the practical operation of requirements truly comparable to those announced by the majority, I would be more restrained lest we go too far too fast. * * *

Rather than employing the arbitrary Fifth Amendment rule which the Court lays down I would follow the more pliable dictates of Due Process Clauses of the Fifth and Fourteenth Amendments which we are accustomed to administering and which we know from our cases are effective instruments in protecting persons in police custody. In this way we would not be acting in the dark nor in one full sweep changing the traditional rules of custodial interrogation which this Court has for so long recognized as a justifiable and proper tool in balancing individual rights against the rights of society. It will be soon enough to go further when we are able to appraise with somewhat better accuracy the effect of such a holding. * * *

JUSTICE HARLAN, whom JUSTICE STEWART and JUSTICE WHITE join, dissenting. * * *

While the fine points of [the Court's new constitutional code of rules for confessions] are far less clear than the Court admits, the tenor is quite apparent. The new rules are not designed to guard against police brutality or other unmistakably banned forms of coercion. Those who use third-degree tactics and deny them in court are equally able and destined to lie as skillfully about warnings and waivers. Rather, the thrust of the new rules is to negate all pressures, to reinforce the nervous or ignorant suspect, and ultimately to discourage any confession at all. The aim in short is toward "voluntariness" in a utopian sense, or to view it from a different angle, voluntariness with a vengeance.

[The] Court's asserted reliance on the Fifth Amendment [is] an approach which I frankly regard as a *trompe l'oeil*. The Court's opinion in my view reveals no adequate basis for extending the Fifth Amendment's privilege against self-incrimination to the police station. Far more important, it fails to show that the Court's new rules are well supported, let alone compelled, by Fifth Amendment precedents. Instead, the new rules actually derive from quotation and analogy

---

b   A week later, the Court ruled that *Escobedo* and *Miranda* applied only to trials begun after the decisions were announced.

drawn from precedents under the Sixth Amendment, which should properly have no bearing on police interrogation. * * *

Having decided that the Fifth Amendment privilege does apply in the police station, the Court reveals that the privilege imposes more exacting restrictions than does the Fourteenth Amendment's voluntariness test. It then emerges from a discussion of *Escobedo* that the Fifth Amendment requires for an admissible confession that it be given by one distinctly aware of his right not to speak and shielded from "the compelling atmosphere" of interrogation. From these key premises, the Court finally develops the safeguards of warning, counsel, and so forth. I do not believe these premises are sustained by precedents under the Fifth Amendment.[9]

The more important premise is that pressure on the suspect must be eliminated though it be only the subtle influence of the atmosphere and surroundings. The Fifth Amendment, however, has never been thought to forbid *all* pressure to incriminate one's self in the situations covered by it. * * *

A closing word must be said about the Assistance of Counsel Clause of the Sixth Amendment, which is never expressly relied on by the Court but whose judicial precedents turn out to be linchpins of the confession rules announced today. * * *

The only attempt in this Court to carry the right to counsel into the station house occurred in *Escobedo,* the Court repeating several times that that stage was no less "critical" than trial itself. * * * This is hardly persuasive when we consider that a grand jury inquiry, the filing of a certiorari petition, and certainly the purchase of narcotics by an undercover agent from a prospective defendant may all be equally "critical" yet provision of counsel and advice on that score have never been thought compelled by the Constitution in such cases. The sound reason why this right is so freely extended for a criminal trial is the severe injustice risked by confronting an untrained defendant with a range of technical points of law, evidence, and tactics familiar to the prosecutor but not to himself. This danger shrinks markedly in the police station where indeed the lawyer in fulfilling his professional responsibilities of necessity may become an obstacle to truthfinding. See infra, n. 12. * * *

The Court's new rules aim to offset [the] minor pressures and disadvantages intrinsic to any kind of police interrogation. The rules do not serve due process interests in preventing blatant coercion since, as I noted earlier, they do nothing to contain the policeman who is prepared to lie from the start. The rules work for reliability in confessions almost only in the Pickwickian sense that they can prevent some from being given at all.[12] * * *

---

[9] I lay aside *Escobedo* itself; it contains no reasoning or even general conclusions addressed to the Fifth Amendment and indeed its citation in this regard seems surprising in view of *Escobedo's* primary reliance on the Sixth Amendment.

[12] The Court's vision of a lawyer "mitigat[ing] the dangers of untrustworthiness" by witnessing coercion and assisting accuracy in the confession is largely a fancy; for if counsel arrives, there is rarely going to be a police station confession. *Watts v. Indiana* (separate opinion

What the Court largely ignores is that its rules impair, if they will not eventually serve wholly to frustrate, an instrument of law enforcement that has long and quite reasonably been thought worth the price paid for it. There can be little doubt that the Court's new code would markedly decrease the number of confessions. To warn the suspect that he may remain silent and remind him that his confession may be used in court are minor obstructions. To require also an express waiver by the suspect and an end to questioning whenever he demurs must heavily handicap questioning. And to suggest or provide counsel for the suspect simply invites the end of the interrogation. See supra, n. 12. * * *

While passing over the costs and risks of its experiment, the Court portrays the evils of normal police questioning in terms which I think are exaggerated. Albeit stringently confined by the due process standards interrogation is no doubt often inconvenient and unpleasant for the suspect. However, it is no less so for a man to be arrested and jailed, to have his house searched, or to stand trial in court, yet all this may properly happen to the most innocent given probable cause, a warrant, or an indictment. Society has always paid a stiff price for law and order, and peaceful interrogation is not one of the dark moments of the law.

This brief statement of the competing considerations seems to me ample proof that the Court's preference is highly debatable at best and therefore not to be read into the Constitution. However, it may make the analysis more graphic to consider the actual facts of one of the four cases reversed by the Court. *Miranda* serves best, being neither the hardest nor easiest of the four under the Court's standards.[15]

On March 3, 1963, an 18-year-old girl was kidnapped and forcibly raped near Phoenix, Arizona. Ten days later, on the morning of March 13, petitioner Miranda was arrested and taken to the police station. At this time Miranda was 23 years old, indigent, and educated to the extent of completing half the ninth grade. He had "an emotional illness" of the schizophrenic type, according to the doctor who eventually examined him; the doctor's report also stated that Miranda was "alert and oriented as to time, place, and person", intelligent within normal limits, competent to stand trial, and sane within the legal definition. At the police station, the victim picked Miranda out of a lineup, and two officers then took him into a separate room to interrogate him, starting about 11:30 a.m. Though at first denying his guilt, within a short time Miranda gave a detailed oral confession and then wrote out in his own hand and signed a brief statement admitting and describing the crime. All this was accomplished in two hours or less without any force, threats or promises and—I will assume this though the record is uncertain * * *—without any effective warnings at all.

Miranda's oral and written confessions are now held inadmissible under the Court's new rules. One is entitled to feel astonished that the Constitution can be read to produce this result. These confessions were obtained during brief, daytime

---

of Jackson, J.): "[A]ny lawyer worth his salt will tell the suspect in no uncertain terms to make no statement to police under any circumstances."

[15] In *Westover,* a seasoned criminal was practically given the Court's full complement of warnings and did not heed them. The *Stewart* case, on the other hand, involves long detention and successive questioning. In *Vignera,* the facts are complicated and the record somewhat incomplete.

questioning conducted by two officers and unmarked by any of the traditional indicia of coercion. They assured a conviction for a brutal and unsettling crime, for which the police had and quite possibly could obtain little evidence other than the victim's identifications, evidence which is frequently unreliable. There was, in sum, a legitimate purpose, no perceptible unfairness, and certainly little risk of injustice in the interrogation. Yet the resulting confessions, and the responsible course of police practice they represent, are to be sacrificed to the Court's own finespun conception of fairness which I seriously doubt is shared by many thinking citizens in this country. * * *

[It is] instructive to compare the attitude in this case of those responsible for law enforcement with the official views that existed when the Court undertook three major revisions of prosecutorial practice prior to this case, *Johnson v. Zerbst, Mapp,* and *Gideon.* In *Johnson,* which established that appointed counsel must be offered the indigent in federal criminal trials, the Federal Government all but conceded the basic issue, which had in fact been recently fixed as Department of Justice policy. In *Mapp,* which imposed the exclusionary rule on the States for Fourth Amendment violations, more than half of the States had themselves already adopted some such rule. In *Gideon,* which extended *Johnson v. Zerbst* to the States, an *amicus* brief was filed by 22 States and Commonwealths urging that course; only two States beside the respondent came forward to protest. By contrast, in this case new restrictions on police questioning have been opposed by the United States and in an *amicus* brief signed by 27 States and Commonwealths, not including the three other States who are parties. No State in the country has urged this Court to impose the newly announced rules, nor has any State chosen to go nearly so far on its own. * * *

The law of the foreign countries described by the Court * * * reflects a more moderate conception of the rights of the accused as against those of society when other data is considered. Concededly, the English experience is most relevant. In that country, a caution as to silence but not counsel has long been mandated by the "Judges' Rules," which also place other somewhat imprecise limits on police cross-examination of suspects. However, in the court's discretion confessions can be and apparently quite frequently are admitted in evidence despite disregard of the Judges' Rules, so long as they are found voluntary under the common-law test. Moreover, the check that exists on the use of pretrial statements is counter-balanced by the evident admissibility of fruits of an illegal confession and by the judge's often-used authority to comment adversely on the defendant's failure to testify. * * *

[S]ome reference must be made to [the] ironic untimeliness [of these confession rules]. There is now in progress in this country a massive re-examination of criminal law enforcement procedures on a scale never before witnessed. Participants in this undertaking include a Special Committee of the American Bar Association, under the chairmanship of Chief Judge Lumbard of the Court of Appeals for the Second Circuit; a distinguished study group of the American Law Institute, headed by Professor Vorenberg of the Harvard Law School; and the President's Commission on Law Enforcement and Administration of Justice, under the leadership of the Attorney General of the United States.

Studies are also being conducted by [other groups] equipped to do practical research. * * *

It is no secret that concern has been expressed lest long-range and lasting reforms be frustrated by this Court's too rapid departure from existing constitutional standards. Despite the Court's disclaimer, the practical effect of the decision made today must inevitably be to handicap seriously sound efforts at reform, not least by removing options necessary to a just compromise of competing interests. [T]he legislative reforms when they came would have the vast advantage of empirical data and comprehensive study, they would allow experimentation and use of solutions not open to the courts, and they would restore the initiative in criminal law reform to those forums where it truly belongs. * * *

JUSTICE WHITE, with whom JUSTICE HARLAN and JUSTICE STEWART join, dissenting.

The proposition that the privilege against self-incrimination forbids in-custody interrogation without the warnings specified in the majority opinion and without a clear waiver of counsel has no significant support in the history of the privilege or in the language of the Fifth Amendment. As for the English authorities and the common-law history, the privilege, firmly established in the second half of the seventeenth century, was never applied except to prohibit compelled judicial interrogations. The rule excluding coerced confessions matured about 100 years later, "[b]ut there is nothing in the reports to suggest that the theory has its roots in the privilege against self-incrimination. And so far as the cases reveal, the privilege, as such, seems to have been given effect only in judicial proceedings, including the preliminary examinations by authorized magistrates." Morgan, *The Privilege Against Self-Incrimination,* 34 Minn.L.Rev. 1, 18 (1949). * * *

That the Court's holding today is neither compelled nor even strongly suggested by the language of the Fifth Amendment, is at odds with American and English legal history, and involves a departure from a long line of precedent does not prove either that the Court has exceeded its powers or that the Court is wrong or unwise in its present reinterpretation of the Fifth Amendment. It does, however, underscore the obvious—that the Court has not discovered or found the law in making today's decision, nor has it derived it from some irrefutable sources; what it has done is to make new law and new public policy in much the same way that it has in the course of interpreting other great clauses of the Constitution. This is what the Court historically has done. Indeed, it is what it must do and will continue to do until and unless there is some fundamental change in the constitutional distribution of governmental powers.

But if the Court is here and now to announce new and fundamental policy to govern certain aspects of our affairs, it is wholly legitimate to examine the mode of this or any other constitutional decision in this Court and to inquire into the advisability of its end product in terms of the long-range interest of the country. At the very least the Court's text and reasoning should withstand analysis and be a fair exposition of the constitutional provision which its opinion interprets. Decisions like these cannot rest alone on syllogism, metaphysics or some ill-defined notions of natural justice, although each will perhaps play its part. * * *

[The Court] extrapolates a picture of what it conceives to be the norm from police investigatorial manuals, published in 1959 and 1962 or earlier, without any attempt to allow for adjustments in police practices that may have occurred in the wake of more recent decisions of state appellate tribunals or this Court. But even if the relentless application of the described procedures could lead to involuntary confessions, it most assuredly does not follow that each and every case will disclose this kind of interrogation or this kind of consequence.[2] Insofar as it appears from the Court's opinion, it has not examined a single transcript of any police interrogation, let alone the interrogation that took place in any one of these cases which it decides today. Judged by any of the standards for empirical investigation utilized in the social sciences the factual basis for the Court's premises is patently inadequate.

Although in the Court's view in-custody interrogation is inherently coercive, it says that the spontaneous product of the coercion of arrest and detention is still to be deemed voluntary. An accused, arrested on probable cause, may blurt out a confession which will be admissible despite the fact that he is alone and in custody, without any showing that he had any notion of his right to remain silent or of the consequences of his admission. Yet, under the Court's rule, if the police ask him a single question such as "Do you have anything to say?" or "Did you kill your wife?" his response, if there is one, has somehow been compelled, even if the accused has been clearly warned of his right to remain silent. Common sense informs us to the contrary. While one may say that the response was "involuntary" in the sense the question provoked or was the occasion for the response and thus the defendant was induced to speak out when he might have remained silent if not arrested and not questioned, it is patently unsound to say the response is compelled. * * *

If the rule announced today were truly based on a conclusion that all confessions resulting from custodial interrogation are coerced, then it would simply have no rational foundation. * * * Even if one were to postulate that the Court's concern is not that all confessions induced by police interrogation are coerced but rather that some such confessions are coerced and present judicial procedures are believed to be inadequate to identify the confessions that are coerced and those that are not, it would still not be essential to impose the rule that the Court has now fashioned. Transcripts or observers could be required, specific time limits, tailored to fit the cause, could be imposed, or other devices could be utilized to reduce the chances that otherwise indiscernible coercion will produce an inadmissible confession.

On the other hand, even if one assumed that there was an adequate factual basis for the conclusion that all confessions obtained during in-custody interrogation are the product of compulsion, the rule propounded by the Court

---

[2] In fact, the type of sustained interrogation described by the Court appears to be the exception rather than the rule. A survey of 399 cases in one city found that in almost half of the cases the interrogation lasted less than 30 minutes. Barrett, *Police Practices and the Law—From Arrest to Release or Charge,* 50 Calif.L.Rev. 11, 41–45 (1962). Questioning tends to be confused and sporadic and is usually concentrated on confrontations with witnesses or new items of evidence, as these are obtained by officers conducting the investigation. See generally LaFave, *Arrest: The Decision to Take a Suspect into Custody* 386 (1965); ALI, *Model Pre-Arraignment Procedure Code,* Commentary § 5.01, at 170, n. 4 (Tent.Draft No. 1, 1966).

would still be irrational, for, apparently, it is only if the accused is also warned of his right to counsel and waives both that right and the right against self-incrimination that the inherent compulsiveness of interrogation disappears. But if the defendant may not answer without a warning a question such as "Where were you last night?" without having his answer be a compelled one, how can the court ever accept his negative answer to the question of whether he wants to consult his retained counsel or counsel whom the court will appoint? And why if counsel is present and the accused nevertheless confesses, or counsel tells the accused to tell the truth, and that is what the accused does, is the situation any less coercive insofar as the accused is concerned? The court apparently realizes its dilemma of foreclosing questioning without the necessary warnings but at the same time permitting the accused, sitting in the same chair in front of the same policemen, to waive his right to consult an attorney. It expects, however, that not too many will waive the right; and if it is claimed that he has, the State faces a severe, if not impossible burden of proof.

All of this makes very little sense in terms of the compulsion which the Fifth Amendment proscribes. That amendment deals with compelling the accused himself. It is his free will that is involved. Confessions and incriminating admissions, as such, are not forbidden evidence; only those which are compelled are banned. I doubt that the Court observes these distinctions today. By considering any answers to any interrogation to be compelled regardless of the content and course of examination and by escalating the requirements to prove waiver, the Court not only prevents the use of compelled confessions but for all practical purposes forbids interrogation except in the presence of counsel. That is, instead of confining itself to protection of the right against compelled self-incrimination the Court has created a limited Fifth Amendment right to counsel—or, as the Court expresses it, a "right to counsel to protect the Fifth Amendment privilege * * *." The focus then is not on the will of the accused but on the will of counsel and how much influence he can have on the accused. Obviously there is no warrant in the Fifth Amendment for thus installing counsel as the arbiter of the privilege.

In sum, for all the Court's expounding on the menacing atmosphere of police interrogation procedures it has failed to supply any foundation for the conclusions it draws or the measures it adopts.

Criticism of the Court's opinion, however, cannot stop at a demonstration that the factual and textual bases for the rule it propounds are, at best, less than compelling. Equally relevant is an assessment of the rule's consequences measured against community values. The Court's duty to assess the consequences of its action is not satisfied by the utterance of the truth that a value of our system of criminal justice is "to respect the inviolability of the human personality" and to require government to produce the evidence against the accused by its own independent labors. More than the human dignity of the accused is involved; the human personality of others in the society must also be preserved. Thus the values reflected by the privilege are not the sole desideratum; society's interest in the general security is of equal weight.

The obvious underpinning of the Court's decision is a deep-seated distrust of all confessions. As the Court declares that the accused may not be interrogated without counsel present, absent a waiver of the right to counsel, and as the Court all but admonishes the lawyer to advise the accused to remain silent, the result adds up to a judicial judgment that evidence from the accused should not be used against him in any way, whether compelled or not. This is the not so subtle overtone of the opinion—that it is inherently wrong for the police to gather evidence from the accused himself. And this is precisely the nub of this dissent. I see nothing wrong or immoral, and certainly nothing unconstitutional, with the police asking a suspect whom they have reasonable cause to arrest whether or not he killed his wife or with confronting him with the evidence on which the arrest was based, at least where he has been plainly advised that he may remain completely silent. * * * Particularly when corroborated, as where the police have confirmed the accused's disclosure of the hiding place of implements or fruits of the crime, such confessions have the highest reliability and significantly contribute to the certitude with which we may believe the accused is guilty. * * *

The rule announced today [is] a deliberate calculus to prevent interrogations, to reduce the incidence of confessions and pleas of guilty and to increase the number of trials. [Under] the present law, the prosecution fails to prove its case in about 30% of the criminal cases actually tried in the federal courts. But it is something else again to remove from the ordinary criminal case all those confessions which heretofore have been held to be free and voluntary acts of the accused and to thus establish a new constitutional barrier to the ascertainment of truth by the judicial process. There is, in my view, every reason to believe that a good many criminal defendants, who otherwise would have been convicted on what this Court has previously thought to be the most satisfactory kind of evidence, will now, under this new version of the Fifth Amendment, either not be tried at all or acquitted if the State's evidence, minus the confession, is put to the test of litigation.

I have no desire whatsoever to share the responsibility for any such impact on the present criminal process. * * *

Much of the trouble with the Court's new rule is that it will operate indiscriminately in all criminal cases, regardless of the severity of the crime or the circumstances involved. It applies to every defendant whether the professional criminal or one committing a crime of momentary passion who is not part and parcel of organized crime. It will slow down the investigation and the apprehension of confederates in those cases where time is of the essence, such as kidnapping, [those] involving the national security, [and] some organized crime situations. In the latter context the lawyer who arrives may also be the lawyer for the defendants' colleagues and can be relied upon to insure that no breach of the organization's security takes place even though the accused may feel that the best thing he can do is to cooperate.

At the same time, the Court's *per se* approach may not be justified on the ground that it provides a "bright line" permitting the authorities to judge in advance whether interrogation may safely be pursued without jeopardizing the admissibility of any information obtained as a consequence. Nor can it be claimed that judicial time and effort, assuming that is a relevant consideration, will be conserved because of the ease of application of the new rule. Today's decision leaves open such questions as whether the accused was in custody, whether his statements were spontaneous or the product of interrogation, whether the accused has effectively waived his rights, and whether nontestimonial evidence introduced at trial is the fruit of statements made during a prohibited interrogation, all of which are certain to prove productive of uncertainty during investigation and litigation during prosecution. For all these reasons, if further restrictions on police interrogation are desirable at this time, a more flexible approach makes much more sense than the Court's constitutional strait-jacket which forecloses more discriminating treatment by legislative or rule-making pronouncements. * * *

4. APPLYING AND EXPLAINING *MIRANDA*

Because *Miranda* was the centerpiece of the Warren Court's "revolution in American criminal procedure" and the prime target of those who thought the courts were "soft" on criminals, almost everyone expected the so-called Burger Court to treat *Miranda* unkindly. And it did—at first. But it must also be said that the Burger Court interpreted *Miranda* fairly generously in some important respects.

The first blows the Burger Court dealt *Miranda* were the impeachment cases, *Harris v. New York,* 401 U.S. 222 (1971) and *Oregon v. Hass,* 420 U.S. 714 (1975). *Harris* held that statements preceded by defective warnings, and thus inadmissible to establish the prosecution's case-in-chief, could nevertheless be used to impeach the defendant's credibility if he chose to take the stand in his own defense.[a] The Court noted, but seemed unperturbed by the fact, that some language in the *Miranda* opinion could be read as barring the use of statements obtained in violation of *Miranda* for *any* purpose.

The Court went a step beyond *Harris* in the *Hass* case. In this case, after being advised of his rights, the defendant *asserted* them. Nevertheless, the police refused to honor the defendant's request for a lawyer and continued to question him. The Court ruled that here, too, the resulting incriminating statements could be used for impeachment purposes. Since many suspects make incriminating statements even after the receipt of complete *Miranda* warnings, *Harris* might have been explained—and contained—on the ground that permitting impeachment use of statements acquired without complete warnings would not greatly encourage the police to violate *Miranda*. But in light of the *Hass* ruling, when a suspect asserts his rights, the police arguably have very little to lose and everything to gain by continuing to question him.[b]

---

[a] Four decades later, in *Kansas v. Ventris,* 556 U.S. 586 (2009), the Court made clear that incriminating statements obtained in violation of the *Massiah* doctrine (often called the Sixth Amendment right to counsel) could also be used to impeach the defendant's trial testimony. However, as the Court indicated in *Harris* and subsequently held in *Mincey v. Arizona,* 437 U.S. 385 (1978), "involuntary" or "coerced" confessions—as opposed to those obtained only in violation of *Massiah* and *Miranda*—cannot be used for impeachment purposes.

[b] The Court subsequently held that a defendant's prior silence could be used to impeach him when he testified in his own defense, *Jenkins v. Anderson* (described at p. 492), and that even a

Although language in *Miranda* could be read as establishing a *per se* rule against any further questioning of one who has asserted his "right to silence" (as opposed to his *right to counsel,* discussed below), *Michigan v. Mosley,* 423 U.S. 96 (1975) held that under certain circumstances (and what they are is unclear), if they cease questioning on the spot, the police may "try again," and succeed at a later interrogation session. At the very least, it seems, the police must promptly terminate the original interrogation, resume questioning after the passage of a significant period of time, and give the suspect a fresh set of warnings at the outset of the second session. Whether *Mosley* requires more is a matter of dispute.

Perhaps the most frequently litigated *Miranda* question is what constitutes "custody" or "custodial interrogation"? In *Berkemer v. McCarty,* 468 U.S. 420 (1984), the Court, per Marshall, J., one of *Miranda*'s strongest defenders, held (without a dissent) that the "roadside questioning" of a motorist detained pursuant to a traffic stop is quite different from stationhouse investigation and thus should not be considered "custodial interrogation." *Oregon v. Mathiason,* 429 U.S. 492 (1977) and *California v. Beheler,* 463 U.S. 1121 (1983) demonstrate that if the suspect goes to the stationhouse on his own or "voluntarily" agrees to accompany the police to that site, even *police station* questioning designed to produce incriminating statements may not be "custodial interrogation."

The Court has often said that "custody" for *Miranda* purposes is an objective test—how would reasonable people in the suspect's situation have perceived their circumstances? But it is not always easy to apply this principle to the particular facts. The first case in this section, *J.D.B. v. North Carolina,* involved a 13-year-old, seventh-grade student questioned by a police officer in a closed-door conference room. The 13-year-old was not given the *Miranda* warnings until after he had confessed. A 5–4 majority held that police officers should take into account the suspect's age in determining whether a suspect is in custody and that the police can do so without damaging the objective nature of the custody analysis. (Should the police also take into account the suspect's intelligence or cultural background?) The second case in this section, *Howes v. Fields,* asks whether a prisoner who is taken from his prison cell to a conference room and questioned by armed deputies about an unrelated, uncharged offense is in custody. A 6–3 majority held that imprisonment alone is not enough to create a custodial environment under *Miranda.*

Another frequently litigated question is what constitutes "interrogation" or "questioning" within the meaning of *Miranda*? This question is addressed by the

---

defendant's *post*arrest silence (so long as he was not given the *Miranda* warnings) could be used for impeachment purposes, *Fletcher v. Weir,* 455 U.S. 603 (1982). Both *Jenkins* and *Weir* distinguished *Doyle v. Ohio,* 426 U.S. 610 (1976), which deemed it a violation of due process to use a defendant's silence for impeachment purposes when the defendant remained silent *after* being given *Miranda* warnings.

But the Court balked at further expansion of the "impeachment exception" to the ban against illegally seized evidence in *James v. Illinois,* 493 U.S. 307 (1990). *James* refused to expand the class of impeachable witnesses from the defendant alone to *all* defense witnesses, maintaining such an expansion "would not promote the truthseeking function to the same extent as did creation of the original exception, and yet it would significantly undermine the deterrent effect of the general exclusionary rule."

next two cases in the section: *Rhode Island v. Innis* (1980) and *Illinois v. Perkins* (1990). Considering the alternatives (e.g., limiting "interrogation" to instances where the police directly address a suspect or to situations where the record establishes that the police *intended* to elicit a response), *Innis* gave the key term "interrogation" a fairly generous reading. *Perkins* holds that the coercive atmosphere calling for the *Miranda* warnings is not present when a suspect is *unaware* that he is speaking to a law enforcement officer (in this instance an undercover agent posing as a fellow-prisoner).

Still another important issue is: what constitutes a waiver of the right to remain silent? After advising a suspect of his *Miranda* rights, must the police specifically ask a suspect whether he is willing to talk to them or wishes to remain silent? At what point, if any, does a suspect's silence in the face of police questions constitute an assertion of her right to remain silent? These questions are addressed by *Berghuis v. Thompkins* (2010), the next case in this section.

In *Edwards v. Arizona*, 451 U.S. 477 (1981), the Court gladdened the hearts of *Miranda* supporters by invigorating that case in an important respect. Sharply distinguishing the *Mosley* case, supra, the *Edwards* Court held that when a suspect asserts his right to counsel (as opposed to his right to remain silent), the police *cannot* "try again"—unless (the Court told us 29 years later in *Maryland v. Shatzer* (2010), the next case set forth in this section), the custodial suspect has experienced a 14-day break in *Miranda* custody between the first and second attempts at interrogation. Once a suspect "expresse[s] his desire to deal with the police only through counsel," *Edwards* instructs us, the suspect may not be subjected to further interrogation by the authorities "until counsel has been made available to him unless [he] himself initiates further communication, exchanges, or conversations with the police."

Prior to *Shatzer*, the Court had construed the *Edwards* rule quite broadly. It told us in *Arizona v. Roberson*, 486 U.S. 675 (1988), that the rule applies even when the police want to question a suspect about an offense *unrelated* to the subject of their initial interrogation. And it ruled in *Minnick v. Mississippi*, 498 U.S. 146 (1990)—over a strongly worded dissent by Justice Scalia, joined by Chief Justice Rehnquist—that once a suspect invokes the right to counsel, the police may not reinitiate interrogation in the absence of counsel *even if* the suspect has consulted with an attorney in the interim.

Once a person asks for counsel, or is appointed counsel, at a pre-trial appearance, can she ever be approached by a law enforcement official and asked to consent to interrogation? This question and related ones are addressed by *Montejo v. Louisiana*, 556 U.S. 778 (2009), the next case in this section.

As discussed in Note, *Can (Did) Congress "Overrule" Miranda?*, § 5 infra, Justice Rehnquist's view that the *Miranda* warnings were only second-class prophylactic safeguards, a view that had first surfaced in *Michigan v. Tucker* (1974) (discussed in § 5 infra), reappeared in *New York v. Quarles*, set forth in this section. *Quarles* recognized a "public safety" exception to *Miranda*, observing that "the prophylactic *Miranda* warnings [are] 'not themselves rights protected by the

Constitution,' but only measures designed 'to insure that the right against compulsory self-incrimination is protected.' *Michigan v. Tucker*."

The next two cases, *United States v. Patane* and *Missouri v. Seibert* deal with the important question whether physical evidence or other evidence derived from a failure to give the *Miranda* warnings, when the warnings are called for, must be excluded. To put it another way, does the "fruit of the poisonous tree" doctrine, which applies in Fourth Amendment cases, apply to a failure to administer the *Miranda* warnings as well?

The Supreme Court first addressed this question in *Oregon v. Elstad*, 470 U.S. 298 (1985). Two police officers had gone to Mr. Elstad's house and, without administering *Miranda* warnings, asked him about his involvement in a burglary. Elstad made an incriminating statement. About an hour later, after being taken to the sheriff's office, Elstad was first advised of his rights. He waived his rights and then gave the police a statement detailing his participation in the burglary. The state conceded that the statement made in his house had to be excluded, but argued that the statement Elstad made after being advised of, and waiving, his rights should be admissible. A 6–3 majority, per O'Connor, J., agreed.

The *Elstad* majority emphasized that a failure to administer the *Miranda* warnings does not "breed the same consequences as the violation of a constitutional right," pointing out that "a procedural *Miranda* violation" * * * may be triggered even in the absence of a Fifth Amendment violation. The *Elstad* Court seemed to say—it certainly could plausibly be read as saying—that because a violation of *Miranda* is not a violation of a true constitutional right, it is not entitled to the "fruit of the poisonous tree" doctrine. Thus, unlike evidence obtained as the result of an unreasonable search or a coerced confession (which are true constitutional violations), secondary evidence derived from a violation of the *Miranda* rules should not be suppressed as the tainted fruit.

Elstad was one of the post-Warren Court cases that encouraged critics of *Miranda* to believe that some day the Court would overrule that much-maligned case. Instead, fifteen years after *Elstad* was decided, in *Dickerson v. United States* (§ 5, infra) the Court struck down a federal statute purporting to abolish *Miranda* because "Congress may not legislatively supersede our decisions interpreting and applying the Constitution."

Although *Elstad* seemed to rest largely on the premise that *Miranda* is not a constitutional decision, the *Dickerson* Court had nothing negative to say about *Elstad*. Chief Justice Rehnquist commented only that *Elstad* "simply recognizes the fact that unreasonable searches under the Fourth Amendment are different from interrogations under the Fifth Amendment."

Did *Dickerson* undermine the logic underlying cases like *Elstad*? Or does *Elstad* survive *Dickerson*? The *Patane* and *Seibert* cases provide the answer—the *Dickerson* Court's discussion of *Elstad* and other *Miranda*-debilitating decisions demonstrated the continued validity of those cases.

The derivative evidence in *Elstad* was a "second confession" and at one point the *Elstad* majority seemed to cast its holding in terms of a suspect's freedom to decide his own course of action. Thus, one could plausibly argue that the *Elstad* Court relied to some degree on "individual volition" as an insulating factor in successive confession cases—a factor altogether missing in the context of inanimate evidence such as a Glock pistol (the derivative evidence at issue in *Patane*). But a majority of the *Patane* Court rejected this argument.

In *Elstad*, the failure of the police to give the *Miranda* warnings the first time they talked to the suspect seems to have been quite inadvertent. On the other hand, in *Missouri v. Seibert*, the second derivative evidence case in this section, the failure to advise the suspect of her rights was admittedly deliberate. Indeed, the officer who withheld the *Miranda* warnings the first time he questioned the suspect admitted that he had been *trained* to utilize such a tactic in order to obtain an initial admission of guilt. Moreover, the officer also conceded that the statement ultimately obtained and admitted into evidence had been "largely a repeat" of the statement the police had elicited from Ms. Seibert prior to giving any warning. All this was too much for the Supreme Court to tolerate—but only by a 5–4 vote.

Some of *Miranda*'s defenders found cause for concern in *Moran v. Burbine*, the last case in this section. That case held that a confession preceded by an otherwise valid waiver of *Miranda* rights should not be excluded either because the police misled an inquiring attorney (asked by defendant's sister to represent him) or because the police failed to inform the defendant that an attorney was trying to reach him. But other commentators noted that the *Burbine* Court had viewed *Miranda* as a serious effort to strike a "proper balance" between, or to "reconcile," law enforcement needs and a suspect's rights and pointed out that this is the way many of *Miranda*'s defenders—not its critics—have talked about the case for the past twenty years.

1. What constitutes "custody" or "custodial interrogation?"

J.D.B. v. NORTH CAROLINA
564 U.S. 261, 131 S.Ct. 2394, 180 L.Ed.2d 310 (2011).

JUSTICE SOTOMAYOR delivered the opinion of the Court.

This case presents the question whether the age of a child subjected to a police questioning is relevant to the custody analysis of *Miranda*. It is beyond dispute that children will often feel bound to submit to police questioning when an adult in the same circumstances would feel free to leave. Seeing no reason for police officers or courts to blind themselves to that commonsense reality, we hold that a child's age properly informs the *Miranda* custody analysis. * * *

[Petitioner J.D.B., a 13-year-old, seventh grade student, was suspected of being involved in two home break-ins. He was taken out of his classroom by a uniformed police officer and brought to a closed-door conference room. There, he was met by two school administrators and a second police officer, a juvenile investigator with the local police force who had been assigned to this case.

[The juvenile investigator informed J.D.B. he was there to question him about the break-ins. In the presence of the others, J.D.B. was then questioned for the next 30 to 45 minutes. Prior to the questioning, J.D.B. was given neither *Miranda* warnings nor the opportunity to speak to his grandmother, his legal guardian. Nor was he told he was free to leave the room. Only after he confessed to his involvement in the break-ins was he told he could refuse to answer the investigator's questions and that he was free to leave the room. The trial court adjudicated J.D.B. delinquent and the North Carolina Supreme Court affirmed, ruling that J.D.B. was not in custody when he confessed and declining to "extend the test for custody" to include the age of the individual questioned by the police.]

[W]hether a suspect is "in custody" is an objective inquiry. [The] "subjective views harbored by either the interrogating officers or the person being questioned" are irrelevant. The test, in other words, involves no consideration of the "actual mindset" of the particular suspect subjected to police questioning. *Yarborough v. Alvarado*, 541 U.S. 652, 662 (2004). [By] limiting analysis to the objective circumstances of the interrogation, and asking how a reasonable person in the suspect's position would understand his freedom to terminate questioning and leave, the objective test avoids burdening police with the task of anticipating the idiosyncrasies of every individual suspect and divining how these particular traits affect each person's subjective state of mind.

[The] State [contends] that a child's age has no place in the custody analysis, no matter how young the child subjected to police questioning. We cannot agree. [A] reasonable child subjected to police questioning will sometimes feel pressured to submit when a reasonable adult will feel free to go. We think it clear that courts can account for that reality without doing any damage to the objective nature of the custody analysis.

[Even] where a "reasonable person" standard otherwise applies, the common law has reflected the reality that children are not adults. In negligence suits, for instance, where liability turns on what an objectively reasonable person would do in the circumstances, "[a]ll American jurisdictions accept the idea that a person's childhood is a relevant circumstance" to be considered. "[O]ur history is replete with laws and judicial recognition" that children cannot be viewed simply as miniature adults. We see no justification for taking a different course here. So long as the child's age was known to the officer at the time of the interview, or would have been objectively apparent to any reasonable officer, including age as part of the custody analysis requires officers neither to consider circumstances "unknowable" to them, nor to "anticipate the frailties or idiosyncrasies" of the particular suspect whom they question.

[In] many cases involving juvenile suspects, the custody analysis would be nonsensical absent some consideration of the suspect's age. This case is a prime example. Were the court precluded from taking J.D.B.'s youth into account, it would be forced to evaluate the circumstances present here through the eyes of a reasonable person of average years. In other words, how would a reasonable adult understand his situation, after being removed from a seventh-grade social studies class by a uniformed school resource officer; being encouraged by his assistant principal to "do the right thing"; and being warned by a police investigator of the prospect of juvenile detention and separation from his guardian and primary caretaker? To describe such an inquiry is to demonstrate its absurdity.

[A] student—whose presence at school is compulsory and whose disobedience at school is cause for disciplinary action—is in a far different position than, say, a parent volunteer on school grounds to chaperone an event, or an adult from the community on school grounds to attend a basketball game. Without asking whether the person "questioned in school" is a "minor," the coercive effect of the schoolhouse setting is unknowable. * * *

Relying on our statements that the objective custody test is "designed to give clear guidance to the police," *Alvarado*, [the State] argues that a child's age must be excluded from the analysis in order to preserve clarity. Similarly, the dissent insists that the clarity of the custody analysis will be destroyed unless a "one-size-fits-all reasonable-person test" applies. In reality, however, ignoring a juvenile defendant's age will often make the inquiry more artificial, and thus only add confusion. And in any event, a child's age, when known or apparent, is hardly an obscure factor to assess. Though the State and the dissent worry about gradations among children of different ages, that concern cannot justify ignoring a child's age altogether. Just as police officers are competent to account for other objective circumstances that are a matter of degree such as the length of questioning or the number of officers present, so too are they competent to evaluate the effect of relative age. [T]he same is true of judges, including those whose childhoods have long since passed. In short, officers and judges need no imaginative powers, knowledge of developmental psychology, training in cognitive science, or expertise in social and cultural anthropology to account for a child's age. They simply need the common sense to know that a 7-year-old is not a 13-year-old and neither is an adult. * * *

Finally, the State and the dissent suggest that excluding age from the custody analysis comes at no cost to juveniles' constitutional rights because the due process voluntariness test independently accounts for a child's youth. [But] *Miranda*'s procedural safeguards exist precisely because the voluntariness test is an inadequate barrier when custodial interrogation is at stake. [To] hold, as the State requests, that a child's age is never relevant to whether a suspect has been taken into custody—and thus to ignore the very real differences between children and adults—would be to deny children the full scope of the procedural safeguards that *Miranda* guarantees to adults.

* * *

The question remains whether J.D.B. was in custody when police interrogated him. We remand for the state courts to address that question, this time taking account of all of the relevant circumstances of the interrogation, including J.D.B.'s age at the time. * * *

JUSTICE ALITO, with whom THE CHIEF JUSTICE, JUSTICE SCALIA, and JUSTICE THOMAS join, dissenting.

The Court's decision in this case may seem on first consideration to be modest and sensible, but in truth it is neither. It is fundamentally inconsistent with one of the main justifications for the *Miranda* rule: the perceived need for a clear rule that can be easily applied in all cases. And today's holding is not needed to protect the constitutional rights of minors who are questioned by the police.

* * * Dissatisfied with the highly fact specific constitutional rule against the admission of in-voluntary confessions, the *Miranda* Court set down rigid standards that often require courts to ignore personal characteristics that may be highly relevant to a particular suspect's actual susceptibility to police pressure. This rigidity, however, has brought with it one of *Miranda*'s principal strengths—"the ease and clarity of its application" by law enforcement officials and courts. A key contributor to this clarity, at least up until now, has been *Miranda*'s objective reasonable-person test for determining custody. * * *

Many suspects, of course, will differ from this hypothetical reasonable person. Some, including those who have been hardened by past interrogations, may have no need for *Miranda* warnings at all. And for other suspects—those who are unusually sensitive to the pressures of police questioning—*Miranda* warnings may come too late to be of any use. That is a necessary consequence of *Miranda*'s rigid standards, but it does not mean that the constitutional rights of these especially sensitive suspects are left unprotected. A vulnerable defendant can still turn to the constitutional rule against *actual* coercion and contend that that his confession was extracted against his will.

Today's decision shifts the *Miranda* custody determination from a one-size-fits-all reasonable-person test into an inquiry that must account for at least one individualized characteristic—age—that is thought to correlate with susceptibility to coercive pressures. Age, however, is in no way the only personal characteristic that may correlate with pliability, and in future cases the Court will be forced to choose between two unpalatable alternatives. It may choose to limit today's decision by arbitrarily distinguishing a suspect's age from other personal characteristics—such as intelligence, education, occupation, or prior experience with law enforcement—that may also correlate with susceptibility to coercive pressures. Or, if the Court is unwilling to draw these arbitrary lines, it will be forced to effect a fundamental transformation of the *Miranda* custody test—from a clear, easily applied prophylactic rule into a highly fact-intensive standard resembling the voluntariness test that the *Miranda* Court found to be unsatisfactory.

For at least three reasons, there is no need to go down this road. First, many minors subjected to police interrogation are near the age of majority, and for these suspects the one-size-fits-all *Miranda* custody rule may not be a bad fit. Second, many of the difficulties in applying the *Miranda* custody rule to minors arise because of the unique circumstances present when the police conduct interrogations at school. The *Miranda* custody rule has always taken into account the setting in which questioning occurs, and accounting for the school setting in such cases will address many of these problems. Third, in cases like the one now before us, where the suspect is especially young, courts applying the constitutional voluntariness standard can take special care to ensure that incriminating statements were not obtained through coercion.

Safeguarding the constitutional rights of minors does not require the extreme makeover of *Miranda* that today's decision may portend.

[The] Court's rationale for importing age into the custody standard is that minors tend to lack adults' "capacity to exercise mature judgment" and that failing to account for that "reality" will leave some minors unprotected under *Miranda* in situations where they perceive themselves to be confined. I do not dispute that many suspects who are under 18 will be more susceptible to police pressure than the average adult. [It] is no less a "reality," however, that many persons *over* the age of 18 are also more susceptible to police pressure than the hypothetical reasonable person. Yet the *Miranda* custody standard has never accounted for the personal characteristics of these or any other individual defendants.

Indeed, it has always been the case under *Miranda* that the unusually meek or compliant are subject to the same fixed rules, including the same custody requirement, as those who are unusually resistant to police pressure. *Miranda's* rigid standards are both overinclusive and underinclusive. They are overinclusive to the extent that they provide a windfall to the most hardened and savvy of suspects, who often have no need for *Miranda's* protections. [And] *Miranda's* requirements are underinclusive to the extent that they fail to account for "frailties," "idiosyncrasies," and other individualized considerations that might cause a person to bend more easily during a confrontation with the police.

[That] is undoubtedly why this Court's *Miranda* cases have never before mentioned "the suspect's age" or any other individualized consideration in applying the custody standard. And unless the *Miranda* custody rule is now to be radically transformed into one that takes into account the wide range of individual characteristics that are relevant in determining whether a confession is voluntary, the Court must shoulder the burden of explaining why age is different from these other personal characteristics.

Why, for example, is age different from intelligence?

[How] about the suspect's cultural background? Suppose the police learn (or should have learned) that a suspect they wish to question is a recent immigrant from a country in which dire consequences often befall any person who dares to attempt to cut short any meeting with the police. Is this really less relevant than the fact that a suspect is a month or so away from his 18th birthday?

The defendant's education is another personal characteristic that may generate "conclusions about behavior and perception." Under today's decision, why should police officers and courts "blind themselves" to the fact that a suspect has "only a fifth-grade education"? Alternatively, what if the police know or should know that the suspect is "a college-educated man with law school training"?

[In] time, the Court will have to confront these issues, and it will be faced with a difficult choice. It may choose to distinguish today's decision and adhere to the arbitrary proclamation that "age [is] different." Or it may choose to extend today's holding and, in doing so, further undermine the very rationale for the *Miranda* regime.

[The] Court holds that age must be taken into account when it "was known to the officer at the time of the interview," or when it "would have been objectively apparent" to a reasonable officer. The first half of this test overturns the rule that the "initial determination of custody" does not depend on the "subjective views harbored [by] interrogating officers." The second half will generate time-consuming satellite litigation over a reasonable officer's perceptions. When, as here, the interrogation takes place in school, the inquiry may be relatively simple. But not all police questioning of minors takes place in schools. In many cases, courts will presumably have to make findings as to whether a particular suspect had a sufficiently youthful look to alert a reasonable officer to the possibility that the suspect was under 18, or whether a reasonable officer would have recognized that a suspect's I.D. was a fake. The inquiry will be both "time-consuming and disruptive" for the police and the courts. * * *

Take a fairly typical case in which today's holding may make a difference. A 16½-year-old moves to suppress incriminating statements made prior to the administration of *Miranda* warnings. [The] judge will not have the luxury of merely saying: "It is common sense that a 16½-year-old is not an 18-year-old. Motion granted." Rather, the judge will be required to determine whether the differences between a typical 16½-year-old and a typical 18-year-old with respect to susceptibility to the pressures of interrogation are sufficient to change the outcome of the custody determination. Today's opinion contains not a word of actual guidance as to how judges are supposed to go about making that determination.

Petitioner and the Court attempt to show that this task is not unmanageable by pointing out that age is taken into account in other legal contexts. In particular, the Court relies on the fact that the age of a defendant is a relevant factor under the reasonable-person standard applicable in negligence suits. But negligence is generally a question for the jury, the members of which can draw on their varied experiences with persons of different ages. It also involves a *post hoc* determination, in the reflective atmosphere of a deliberation room, about whether the defendant conformed to a standard of care. The *Miranda* custody determination, by contrast, must be made in the first instance by police officers in the course of an investigation that may require quick decisionmaking.

[The] Court's decision greatly diminishes the clarity and administrability that have long been recognized as "principal advantages" of *Miranda*'s prophylactic requirements. But what is worse, the Court takes this step unnecessarily, as there are other, less disruptive tools available to ensure that minors are not coerced into confessing.

As an initial matter, the difficulties that the Court's standard introduces will likely yield little added protection for most juvenile defendants. Most juveniles who are subjected to police interrogation are teenagers nearing the age of majority. These defendants' reactions to police pressure are unlikely to be much different from the reaction of a typical 18-year-old in similar circumstances. A one-size-fits-all *Miranda* custody rule thus provides a roughly reasonable fit for these defendants.

In addition, many of the concerns that petitioner raises regarding the application of the *Miranda* custody rule to minors can be accommodated by considering the unique circumstances present when minors are questioned in school. * * *

Finally, in cases like the one now before us, where the suspect is much younger than the typical juvenile defendant, courts should be instructed to take particular care to ensure that incriminating statements were not obtained involuntarily. The voluntariness inquiry is flexible and accommodating by nature, and the Court's precedents already make clear that "special care" must be exercised in applying the voluntariness test where the confession of a "mere child" is at issue. If *Miranda*'s rigid, one-size-fits-all standards fail to account for the unique needs of juveniles, the response should be to rigorously apply the constitutional rule against coercion to ensure that the rights of minors are protected. There is no need to run *Miranda* off the rails. * * *

HOWES V. FIELDS

565 U.S. 499, 132 S.Ct. 1181, 182 L.E.2d 17 (2012).

JUSTICE ALITO delivered the opinion of the Court.

[Fields, a Michigan state prisoner, was taken from his prison cell by a corrections officer to a conference room, where he was questioned by two sheriff's deputies about criminal activity he may have engaged in before being sent to prison. He was questioned for between five and seven hours. At no time was he given *Miranda* warnings or told that he did not have to speak with the deputies. However, he was told more than once that he was free to leave and return to his cell. Although the deputies were armed, Fields remained free of restraints. The conference room was sometimes open and other time shut. Several times, Fields told the deputies he no longer wanted to talk to them, but he never asked to go back to his cell. Fields eventually confessed to engaging in sex acts with a 12-year-old boy. After he confessed, and the questioning concluded, he had to wait an additional 20 minutes for an escort back to his cell. He returned to his cell well after the hour he usually retired. After his conviction, Fields sought federal habeas relief under the Antiterrorism and Effective Death Penalty Act of 1996 (AEDPA). The Sixth Circuit granted such relief, maintaining, as the Supreme Court described it, that the questioning of Fields in the conference room was "a 'custodial interrogation' within the meaning of Miranda because isolation from the general prison population combined with questioning about conduct occurring outside the prison makes any such interrogation custodial per se."]

[I]t is abundantly clear that our precedents do not clearly establish the categorical rule on which the Court of Appeals relied, *i.e.*, that the questioning of a prisoner is always custodial when the prisoner is removed from the general prison population and questioned about events outside the prison. * * *

Not only does the categorical rule applied below go well beyond anything that is clearly established in our prior decisions, it is simply wrong. The three elements of that rule—(1) imprisonment, (2) questioning in private, and (3) questioning about events in the outside world—are not necessarily enough to create a custodial situation for *Miranda* purposes.

As used in our *Miranda* case law, "custody" is a term of art that specifies circumstances that are thought generally to present a serious danger of coercion. In determining whether a person is in custody in this sense, the initial step is to ascertain whether, in light of "the objective circumstances of the interrogation," a "reasonable person [would] have felt he or she was not at liberty to terminate the interrogation and leave." And in order to determine how a suspect would have "gauge[d]" his "freedom of movement," courts must examine "all of the circumstances surrounding the interrogation." Relevant factors include the location of the questioning, its duration, statements made during the interview, the presence or absence of physical restraints during the questioning, and the release of the interviewee at the end of the questioning.

Determining whether an individual's freedom of movement was curtailed, however, is simply the first step in the analysis, not the last. Not all restraints on freedom of movement amount to custody for purposes of *Miranda*. We have "decline[d] to accord talismanic power" to the freedom-of-movement inquiry, and have instead asked the additional question whether the relevant environment presents the same inherently coercive pressures as the type of station house questioning at issue in *Miranda*. * * *

This important point is illustrated by our decision in *Berkemer v. McCarty*, [468 U.S. 420 (1984)]. In that case, we held that the roadside questioning of a motorist who was pulled over in a routine traffic stop did not constitute custodial interrogation. We acknowledged that "a traffic stop significantly curtails the 'freedom of action' of the driver and the passengers," and that it is generally "a crime either to ignore a policeman's signal to stop one's car or, once having stopped, to drive away without permission." "[F]ew motorists," we noted, "would feel free either to disobey a directive to pull over or to leave the scene of a traffic stop without being told they might do so." Nevertheless, we held that a person detained as a result of a traffic stop is not in *Miranda* custody because such detention does not "sufficiently impair [the detained person's] free exercise of his privilege against self-incrimination to require that he be warned of his constitutional rights." * * *

It may be thought that the situation in *Berkemer*—the questioning of a motorist subjected to a brief traffic stop—is worlds away from those present when an inmate is questioned in a prison, but the same cannot be said of [*Maryland v.*] *Shatzer*, [559 U.S. 98 (2010),] where we again distinguished between restraints on freedom of movement and *Miranda* custody. *Shatzer*, as noted, concerned the *Edwards* prophylactic rule, which limits the ability of the police to initiate further questioning of a suspect in *Miranda* custody once the suspect invokes the right to counsel.

We held in *Shatzer* that [the *Edwards* rule] does not apply when there is a sufficient break in custody between the suspect's invocation of the right to counsel and the initiation of subsequent questioning. And, what is significant for present purposes, we further held that a break in custody may occur while a suspect is serving a term in prison. If a break in custody can occur while a prisoner is serving an uninterrupted term of imprisonment, it must follow that imprisonment alone is not enough to create a custodial situation within the meaning of *Miranda*.

There are at least three strong grounds for this conclusion. First, questioning a person who is already serving a prison term does not generally involve the shock that very often accompanies arrest. In the paradigmatic *Miranda* situation—a person is arrested in his home or on the street and whisked to a police station for questioning—detention represents a sharp and ominous change, and the shock may give rise to coercive pressures. A person who is "cut off from his normal life and companions," and abruptly transported from the street into a "police-dominated atmosphere" may feel coerced into answering questions.

By contrast, when a person who is already serving a term of imprisonment is questioned, there is usually no such change. "Interrogated suspects who have previously been convicted of crime live in prison." For a person serving a term of incarceration, we reasoned in *Shatzer*, the ordinary restrictions of prison life, while no doubt unpleasant, are expected and familiar and thus do not involve the same "inherently compelling pressures" that are often present when a suspect is yanked from familiar surroundings in the outside world and subjected to interrogation in a police station.

Second, a prisoner, unlike a person who has not been sentenced to a term of incarceration, is unlikely to be lured into speaking by a longing for prompt release. When a person is arrested and taken to a station house for interrogation, the person who is questioned may be pressured to speak by the hope that, after doing so, he will be allowed to leave and go home. On the other hand, when a prisoner is questioned, he knows that when the questioning ceases, he will remain under confinement.

Third, a prisoner, unlike a person who has not been convicted and sentenced, knows that the law enforcement officers who question him probably lack the authority to affect the duration of his sentence. And "where the possibility of parole exists," the interrogating officers probably also lack the power to bring about an early release. "When the suspect has no reason to think that the listeners have official power over him, it should not be assumed that his words are motivated by the reaction he expects from his listeners." Under such circumstances, there is little "basis for the assumption that a suspect . . . will feel compelled to speak by the fear of reprisal for remaining silent or in the hope of [a] more lenient treatment should he confess." * * *

The two other elements included in the Court of Appeals' rule—questioning in private and questioning about events that took place outside the prison—are likewise insufficient.

Taking a prisoner aside for questioning—as opposed to questioning the prisoner in the presence of fellow inmates—does not necessarily convert a "noncustodial situation . . . to one in which *Miranda* applies." When a person who is not serving a prison term is questioned, isolation may contribute to a coercive atmosphere by preventing family members, friends, and others who may be sympathetic from providing either advice or emotional support. And without any such assistance, the person who is questioned may feel overwhelming pressure to speak and to refrain from asking that the interview be terminated.

By contrast, questioning a prisoner in private does not generally remove the prisoner from a supportive atmosphere. Fellow inmates are by no means necessarily friends. On the contrary, they may be hostile and, for a variety of reasons, may react negatively to what the questioning reveals. In the present case, for example, would respondent have felt more at ease if he had been questioned in the presence of other inmates about the sexual abuse of an adolescent boy? Isolation from the general prison population is often in the best interest of the interviewee and, in any event, does not suggest on its own the atmosphere of coercion that concerned the Court in *Miranda*.

It is true that taking a prisoner aside for questioning may necessitate some additional limitations on his freedom of movement. A prisoner may, for example, be removed from an exercise yard and taken, under close guard, to the room where the interview is to be held. But such procedures are an ordinary and familiar attribute of life behind bars. Escorts and special security precautions may be standard procedures regardless of the purpose for which an inmate is removed from his regular routine and taken to a special location. For example, ordinary prison procedure may require such measures when a prisoner is led to a meeting with an attorney.

Finally, we fail to see why questioning about criminal activity outside the prison should be regarded as having a significantly greater potential for coercion than questioning under otherwise identical circumstances about criminal activity within the prison walls. In both instances, there is the potential for additional criminal liability and punishment. If anything, the distinction would seem to cut the other way, as an inmate who confesses to misconduct that occurred within the prison may also incur administrative penalties, but even this is not enough to tip the scale in the direction of custody. "The threat to a citizen's Fifth Amendment rights that *Miranda* was designed to neutralize" is neither mitigated nor magnified by the location of the conduct about which questions are asked. * * *

Because he was in prison, [respondent Fields] was not free to leave the conference room by himself and to make his own way through the facility to his cell. Instead, he was escorted to the conference room and, when he ultimately decided to end the interview, he had to wait about 20 minutes for a corrections officer to arrive and escort him to his cell. But he would have been subject to this same restraint even if he had been taken to the conference room for some reason other than police questioning; under no circumstances could he have reasonably expected to be able to roam free. And while respondent testified that he "was told . . . if I did not want to cooperate, I needed to go back to my cell," these words did not coerce cooperation by threatening harsher conditions. Returning to his cell would merely have returned him to his usual environment. See *Shatzer*, supra.

Taking into account all of the circumstances of the questioning—including especially the undisputed fact that respondent was told that he was free to end the questioning and to return to his cell—we hold that respondent was not in custody within the meaning of *Miranda*.

JUSTICE GINSBURG, with whom JUSTICES BREYER and SOTOMAYOR join, concurring in part and dissenting in part. * * *

I agree that the law is not "clearly established" in respondent Field's favor. But I disagree with the Court's further determination that Fields was not in custody under *Miranda*. Were the case here on direct review, I would vote to hold that *Miranda* precludes the State's introduction of Fields's confession as evidence against him. * * *

Fields, serving time for disorderly conduct, was of course "i[n] custody," but not "for purposes of *Miranda*," the Court concludes. I would not train, as the Court does, on the question whether there can be custody within custody. Instead, I would ask, as *Miranda* put it, whether Fields was subjected to "incommunicado interrogation . . . in a police-dominated atmosphere," whether his "freedom of action [was] curtailed in any significant way." Those should be the key questions, and to each I would answer "yes." * * *

Critical to the Court's judgment is "the undisputed fact that [Fields] was told that he was free to end the questioning and return to his cell." Never mind the facts suggesting that Fields's submission to the overnight interview was anything but voluntary. Was Fields "held for interrogation"? Brought to, and left alone with, the gun-bearing deputies, he surely was in my judgment. * * *

Today, for people already in prison, the Court finds it adequate for the police to say: "You are free to terminate this interrogation and return to your cell." Such a statement is no substitute for one ensuring that an individual is aware of his rights.

2. What constitutes "interrogation" within the meaning of Miranda?

RHODE ISLAND V. INNIS
446 U.S. 291, 100 S.Ct. 1682, 64 L.Ed.2d 297 (1980).

JUSTICE STEWART delivered the opinion of the Court.

[*Miranda*] held that, once a defendant in custody asks to speak with a lawyer, all interrogation must cease until a lawyer is present. The issue in this case is whether the respondent was "interrogated" in violation [of *Miranda*].

[At approximately 4:30 a.m., a patrolman arrested respondent, suspected of robbing a taxicab driver and murdering him with a shotgun blast to the back of the head. Respondent was unarmed. He was advised of his rights. Within minutes a sergeant (who advised respondent of his rights) and then a captain arrived at the scene of the arrest. The captain also gave respondent the *Miranda* warnings, whereupon respondent asked to speak with a lawyer. The captain then directed that respondent be placed in a police vehicle with a wire screen mesh between the front and rear seats and be driven to the police station. Three officers were assigned to accompany the arrestee. Although the record is somewhat unclear, it appears that Patrolman Williams was in the back seat with respondent and that Patrolmen Gleckman and McKenna were in front.]

While enroute to the central station, Patrolman Gleckman initiated a conversation with Patrolman McKenna concerning the missing shotgun.[1] As Patrolman Gleckman later testified:

> "A. At this point, I was talking back and forth with Patrolman McKenna stating that I frequent this area while on patrol and [that because a school for handicapped children is located nearby,] there's a lot of handicapped children running around in this area, and God forbid one of them might find a weapon with shells and they might hurt themselves."

Patrolman McKenna apparently shared his fellow officer's concern:

> "A. I more or less concurred with him [Gleckman] that it was a safety factor and that we should, you know, continue to search for the weapon and try to find it."

* * *

[Respondent then interrupted the conversation, stating that he would show the officers where the gun was located. The police vehicle then returned to the scene of the arrest where a search for the shotgun was in progress. There, the captain again advised respondent of his rights. He replied that he understood his rights, but "wanted to get the gun out of the way because of the kids in the area in the school." He then led the police to a nearby field, where he pointed out the shotgun under some rocks.

[Respondent was convicted of murder. The trial judge admitted the shotgun and testimony related to its discovery. On appeal, the Rhode Island Supreme Court concluded that the police had "interrogated" respondent without a valid waiver of his right to counsel; the conversation in the police vehicle had constituted "subtle coercion" that was the equivalent of *Miranda* "interrogation."]

[Since the parties agree that respondent was fully informed of his *Miranda* rights, that he asserted his right to counsel, and that he was "in custody" while being driven to the police station, the issue is whether he was "interrogated" in violation of *Miranda*.] In resolving this issue, we first define the term "interrogation" under *Miranda* before turning to a consideration of the facts of this case.

[Various references throughout the *Miranda* opinion] to "questioning" might suggest that the *Miranda* rules were to apply only to those police interrogation practices that involve express questioning of a defendant while in custody.

We do not, however, construe the *Miranda* opinion so narrowly. The concern of the Court in *Miranda* was that the "interrogation environment" created by the interplay of interrogation and custody would "subjugate the individual to the will of his examiner" and thereby undermine the privilege against compulsory self-incrimination. The police practices that evoked this concern included several that did not involve express questioning [such as] the so-called "reverse lineup" in which

---

[1] Although there was conflicting testimony about the exact seating arrangements, it is clear that everyone in the vehicle heard the conversation.

a defendant would be identified by coached witnesses as the perpetrator of a fictitious crime, [to induce] him to confess to the actual crime of which he was suspected in order to escape the false prosecution. The Court in *Miranda* also included in its survey of interrogation practices the use of psychological ploys, such as to "posi[t]" "the guilt of the subject," to "minimize the moral seriousness of the offense," and "to cast blame on the victim or on society." It is clear that these techniques of persuasion, no less than express questioning, were thought, in a custodial setting, to amount to interrogation.

This is not to say, however, that all statements obtained by the police after a person has been taken into custody are to be considered the product of interrogation. * * * It is clear [that the *Miranda* warnings] are required not where a suspect is simply taken into custody, but rather where a suspect in custody is subjected to interrogation. "Interrogation," as conceptualized [in *Miranda*], must reflect a measure of compulsion above and beyond that inherent in custody itself.[4]

We conclude that the *Miranda* safeguards come into play whenever a person in custody is subjected to either express questioning or its functional equivalent. That is to say, the term "interrogation" under *Miranda* refers not only to express questioning, but also to any words or actions on the part of the police (other than those normally attendant to arrest and custody) that the police should know are reasonably likely to elicit an incriminating response from the suspect. The latter portion of this definition focuses primarily upon the perceptions of the suspect, rather than the intent of the police. This focus reflects the fact that the *Miranda* safeguards were designed to vest a suspect in custody with an added measure of protection against coercive police practices, without regard to objective proof of the underlying intent of the police. A practice that the police should know is reasonably likely to evoke an incriminating response from a suspect thus amounts to interrogation.[7] But, since the police surely cannot be held accountable for the unforeseeable results of their words or actions, the definition of interrogation can extend only to words or actions on the part of police officers that they *should have known* were reasonably likely to elicit an incriminating response.[8]

---

[4] There is language in the opinion of the Rhode Island Supreme Court in this case suggesting that the definition of "interrogation" under *Miranda* is informed by this Court's decision in *Brewer v. Williams*, [p. 559, reaffirming and expansively interpreting the *Massiah* doctrine]. This suggestion is erroneous. Our decision in *Brewer* rested solely on the Sixth and Fourteenth Amendment right to counsel. That right, as we held in *Massiah*, prohibits law enforcement officers from "deliberately elicit[ing]" incriminating information from a defendant in the absence of counsel after a formal charge against the defendant has been filed. Custody in such a case is not controlling; indeed, the petitioner in *Massiah* was not in custody. By contrast, the right to counsel at issue in the present case is based not on the Sixth and Fourteenth Amendments, but rather on the Fifth and Fourteenth Amendments as interpreted in the *Miranda* opinion. The definitions of "interrogation" under the Fifth and Sixth Amendments, if indeed the term "interrogation" is even apt in the Sixth Amendment context, are not necessarily interchangeable, since the policies underlying the two constitutional protections are quite distinct.

[7] This is not to say that the intent of the police is irrelevant, for it may well have a bearing on whether the police should have known that their words or actions were reasonably likely to evoke an incriminating response. In particular, where a police practice is designed to elicit an incriminating response from the accused, it is unlikely that the practice will not also be one which the police should have known was reasonably likely to have that effect.

[8] Any knowledge the police may have had concerning the unusual susceptibility of a defendant to a particular form of persuasion might be an important factor in determining whether

Turning to the facts of the present case, we conclude that the respondent was not "interrogated" within the meaning of *Miranda*. It is undisputed that the first prong of the definition of "interrogation" was not satisfied, for the [Gleckman-McKenna conversation] included no express questioning of the respondent. Rather, that conversation was, at least in form, nothing more than a dialogue between the two officers to which no response from the respondent was invited.

Moreover, it cannot be fairly concluded that the respondent was subjected to the "functional equivalent" of questioning. It cannot be said, in short, that [the officers] should have known that their conversation was reasonably likely to elicit an incriminating response from the respondent. There is nothing in the record to suggest that the officers were aware that the respondent was peculiarly susceptible to an appeal to his conscience concerning the safety of handicapped children [or that] the police knew that the respondent was unusually disoriented or upset at the time of his arrest.[9]

[The] Rhode Island Supreme Court erred, in short, in equating "subtle compulsion" with interrogation. That the officers' comments struck a responsive cord is readily apparent. Thus, it may be said, as the Rhode Island Supreme Court did say, that one respondent was subjected to "subtle compulsion." But that is not the end of the inquiry. It must also be established that a suspect's incriminating response was the product of words or actions on the part of the police that they should have known were reasonably likely to elicit an incriminating response.[10] This was not established in the present case. * * *a

---

the police should have known that their words or actions were reasonably likely to elicit an incriminating response from the suspect.

[9] The record in no way suggests that the officers' remarks were *designed* to elicit a response. It is significant that the trial judge, after hearing the officers' testimony, concluded that it was "entirely understandable that [the officers] would voice their concern [for the safety of the handicapped children] to each other."

[10] By way of example, if the police had done no more than to drive past the site of the concealed weapon while taking the most direct route to the police station, and if the respondent, upon noticing for the first time the proximity of the school for handicapped children, had blurted out that he would show the officers where the gun was located, it could not seriously be argued that this "subtle compulsion" would have constituted "interrogation" within the meaning of the *Miranda* opinion.

a Notwithstanding language in *Innis*, as *Arizona v. Mauro*, 481 U.S. 520 (1987) illustrates, it is not inevitably "interrogation" within the meaning of *Miranda* for the police to allow a scenario to occur which they know may prompt the defendant to incriminate himself. In *Mauro*, a 5–4 majority, per Powell, J., held that it was not interrogation for the police to accede to the request of defendant's wife, also a suspect in the murder of their son, to speak with defendant (who had been given the *Miranda* warnings and had asserted his right to counsel) in the presence of a police officer, who placed a tape recorder in plain sight on a desk. Observed the Court:

"The tape recording of the conversation between Mauro and his wife shows that [the detective who attended their meeting] asked Mauro no questions about the crime or his conduct. Nor is it suggested [that the police decision] to allow Mauro's wife to see him was the kind of psychological ploy that properly could be treated as the functional equivalent of interrogation.

" * * * Mauro was not subjected to compelling influences, psychological ploys, or direct questioning. Thus, his volunteered statements cannot properly be considered the result of police interrogation.

"In deciding whether particular police conduct is interrogation, we must remember the purpose behind [*Miranda*]: preventing government officials from using the coercive nature of confinement to extract confessions that would not be given in an unrestrained environment. The

CHIEF JUSTICE BURGER, concurring in the judgment. * * *

The meaning of *Miranda* has become reasonably clear and law enforcement practices have adjusted to its strictures; I would neither overrule *Miranda,* disparage it, nor extend it at this late date. I fear, however, that [the Court's opinion] may introduce new elements of uncertainty; under the Court's test, a police officer, in the brief time available, apparently must evaluate the suggestibility and susceptibility of an accused. Few, if any, police officers are competent to make the kind of evaluation seemingly contemplated; even a psychiatrist asked to express an expert opinion on these aspects of a suspect in custody would very likely employ extensive questioning and observation to make the judgment now charged to police officers. * * *

JUSTICE MARSHALL, with whom JUSTICE BRENNAN joins, dissenting.

I am substantially in agreement with the Court's definition of "interrogation" within the meaning of *Miranda.* In my view, the *Miranda* safeguards apply whenever police conduct is intended or likely to produce a response from a suspect in custody. As I read the Court's opinion, its definition of "interrogation" for *Miranda* purposes is equivalent, for practical purposes, to my formulation, since it contemplates that "where a police practice is designed to elicit an incriminating response from the accused, it is unlikely that the practice will not also be one which the police should have known was reasonably likely to have that effect" [fn. 7]. Thus, the Court requires an objective inquiry into the likely effect of police conduct on a typical individual, taking into account any special susceptibility of the suspect to certain kinds of pressure of which the police know or have reason to know.

I am utterly at a loss, however, to understand how this objective standard as applied to the facts before us can rationally lead to the conclusion that there was no interrogation. * * *

One can scarcely imagine a stronger appeal to the conscience of a suspect— *any* suspect—than the assertion that if the weapon is not found an innocent person will be hurt or killed. And not just any innocent person, but an innocent child—a little girl—a helpless, handicapped little girl on her way to school. The notion that such an appeal could not be expected to have any effect unless the suspect were known to have some special interest in handicapped children verges on the ludicrous. As a matter of fact, the appeal to a suspect to confess for the sake of others, to "display some evidence of decency and honor," is a classic interrogation technique.

Gleckman's remarks would obviously have constituted interrogation if they had been explicitly directed to petitioner, and the result should not be different because they were nominally addressed to McKenna. This is not a case where police officers speaking among themselves are accidentally overheard by a suspect. [The officers] knew petitioner would hear and attend to their conversation, and they are

---

government actions in this case do not implicate this purpose in any way. Police departments need not adopt inflexible rules barring suspects from speaking with their spouses, nor must they ignore legitimate security concerns by allowing spouses to meet in private. In short, the officers in this case acted reasonably and lawfully by allowing Mrs. Mauro to speak with her husband."

chargeable with knowledge of and responsibility for the pressures to speak which they created.

I firmly believe that this case is simply an aberration, and that in future cases the Court will apply the standard adopted today in accordance with its plain meaning.

JUSTICE STEVENS, dissenting.

* * * In my view any statement that would normally be understood by the average listener as calling for a response is the functional equivalent of a direct question, whether or not it is punctuated by a question mark. The Court, however, takes a much narrower view. It holds that police conduct is not the "functional equivalent" of direct questioning unless the police should have known that what they were saying or doing was likely to elicit an incriminating response from the suspect. This holding represents a plain departure from the principles set forth in *Miranda*.

[In] order to give full protection to a suspect's right to be free from any interrogation at all, the definition of "interrogation" must include any police statement or conduct that has the same purpose or effect as a direct question. Statements that appear to call for a response from the suspect, as well as those that are designed to do so, should be considered interrogation. By prohibiting only those relatively few statements or actions that a police officer should know are likely to elicit an incriminating response, the Court today accords a suspect considerably less protection. Indeed, since I suppose most suspects are unlikely to incriminate themselves even when questioned directly, this new definition will almost certainly exclude every statement that is not punctuated with a question mark from the concept of "interrogation."

The difference between the approach required by a faithful adherence to *Miranda* and the stinted test applied by the Court today can be illustrated by comparing three different ways in which Officer Gleckman could have communicated his fears about the possible dangers posed by the shotgun to handicapped children. He could have:

(1) directly asked Innis:

Will you please tell me where the shotgun is so we can protect handicapped schoolchildren from danger?

(2) announced to the other officers in the wagon:

If the man sitting in the back seat with me should decide to tell us where the gun is, we can protect handicapped children from danger.

or (3) stated to the other officers:

It would be too bad if a little handicapped girl would pick up the gun that this man left in the area and maybe kill herself.

In my opinion, all three of these statements should be considered interrogation because all three appear to be designed to elicit a response from anyone who in fact knew where the gun was located. Under the Court's test, on the other hand, the form of the statements would be critical. Statement # 3 would not be interrogation because in the Court's view there was no reason for Officer Gleckman to believe that Innis was susceptible to this type of an implied appeal; therefore, the statement would not be reasonably likely to elicit an incriminating response. Assuming that this is true, then it seems to me that the first two statements, which would be just as unlikely to elicit such a response, should also not be considered interrogation. But, because the first statement is clearly an express question, it *would* be considered interrogation under the Court's test. The second statement, although just as clearly a deliberate appeal to Innis to reveal the location of the gun, would presumably not be interrogation because (a) it was not in form a direct question and (b) it does not fit within the "reasonably likely to elicit an incriminating response" category that applies to indirect interrogation.

As this example illustrates, the Court's test creates an incentive for police to ignore a suspect's invocation of his rights in order to make continued attempts to extract information from him. If a suspect does not appear to be susceptible to a particular type of psychological pressure, the police are apparently free to exert that pressure on him despite his request for counsel, so long as they are careful not to punctuate their statements with question marks. And if, contrary to all reasonable expectations, the suspect makes an incriminating statement, that statement can be used against him at trial. The Court thus turns *Miranda's* unequivocal rule against any interrogation at all into a trap in which unwary suspects may be caught by police deception. * * *

ILLINOIS V. PERKINS
496 U.S. 292, 110 S.Ct. 2394, 110 L.Ed.2d 243 (1990).

JUSTICE KENNEDY delivered the opinion of the Court.

* * * We hold [that] *Miranda* warnings are not required when the suspect is unaware that he is speaking to a law enforcement officer and gives a voluntary statement.

[When Charlton, who had been a fellow inmate of respondent Perkins in another prison, told police that Perkins had implicated himself in the Stephenson murder, the police placed Charlton and Parisi, an undercover agent, in the same cellblock with Perkins, who was incarcerated on charges unrelated to the Stephenson murder. Parisi and Charlton posed as escapees from a work release program who had been arrested in the course of a burglary. They were instructed to engage Perkins in casual conversation and to report anything he said about the Stephenson murder.

[The cellblock consisted of 12 separate cells that opened onto a common room. Perkins greeted Charlton, who introduced Parisi by his alias. Parisi suggested that the three of them escape. There was further conversation. After telling Charlton that he would be responsible for any killing that might occur during a prison break, Parisi asked Perkins if he had ever "done" anybody. Perkins replied that he had, and proceeded to describe the Stephenson murder in detail.

[The trial court suppressed the statements made to Parisi in the jail. The Appellate Court of Illinois affirmed, reading *Miranda* as prohibiting all undercover contacts with incarcerated suspects which are reasonably likely to elicit an incriminating response.]

Conversations between suspects and undercover agents do not implicate the concerns underlying *Miranda*. The essential ingredients of a "police-dominated atmosphere" and compulsion are not present when an incarcerated person speaks freely to someone that he believes to be a fellow inmate. Coercion is determined from the perspective of the suspect. When a suspect considers himself in the company of cellmates and not officers, the coercive atmosphere is lacking. * * * There is no empirical basis for the assumption that a suspect speaking to those whom he assumes are not officers will feel compelled to speak by the fear of reprisal for remaining silent or in the hope of more lenient treatment should he confess.

It is the premise of *Miranda* that the danger of coercion results from the interaction of custody and official interrogation. We reject the argument that *Miranda* warnings are required whenever a suspect is in custody in a technical sense and converses with someone who happens to be a government agent. Questioning by captors, who appear to control the suspect's fate, may create mutually reinforcing pressures that the Court has assumed will weaken the suspect's will, but where a suspect does not know that he is conversing with a government agent, these pressures do not exist. The State Court here mistakenly assumed that because the suspect was in custody, no undercover questioning could take place. When the suspect has no reason to think that the listeners have official power over him, it should not be assumed that his words are motivated by the reaction he expects from his listeners. "[W]hen the agent carries neither badge nor gun and wears not 'police blue,' but the same prison gray" as the suspect, there is no "*interplay* between police interrogation and police custody." Kamisar, *Brewer v. Williams, Massiah and Miranda: What is "Interrogation"? When Does it Matter?*, 67 Geo.L.J. 1, 67, 63 (1978). * * *

The tactic employed here to elicit a voluntary confession from a suspect does not violate the Self-Incrimination Clause. We held in *Hoffa v. United States*, 385 U.S. 293 (1966), that placing an undercover agent near a suspect in order to gather incriminating information was permissible under the Fifth Amendment. In *Hoffa*, while petitioner Hoffa was on trial, he met often with one Partin, who, unbeknownst to Hoffa, was cooperating with law enforcement officials. Partin reported to officials that Hoffa had divulged his attempts to bribe jury members. We approved using Hoffa's statements at his subsequent trial for jury tampering, on the rationale that "no claim ha[d] been or could [have been] made that [Hoffa's] incriminating statements were the product of any sort of coercion, legal or factual." [The] only difference between this case and *Hoffa* is that the suspect here was incarcerated, but detention, whether or not for the crime in question, does not warrant a presumption that the use of an undercover agent to speak with an incarcerated suspect makes any confession thus obtained involuntary. * * *

This Court's Sixth Amendment decisions in *Massiah v. United States, United States v. Henry, and Maine v. Moulton* [all discussed in Section 5 of this Chapter], also do not avail respondent. We held in those cases that the government may not use an undercover agent to circumvent the Sixth Amendment right to counsel once a suspect has been charged with the crime. After charges have been filed, the Sixth Amendment prevents the government from interfering with the accused's right to counsel. In the instant case no charges had been filed on the subject of the interrogation, and our Sixth Amendment precedents are not applicable. * * *

JUSTICE BRENNAN, concurring in the judgment.

Although I do not subscribe to the majority's characterization of *Miranda* in its entirety, I do agree that when a suspect does not know that his questioner is a police agent, such questioning does not amount to "interrogation" in an "inherently coercive" environment so as to require application of *Miranda*. Since the only issue raised at this stage of the litigation is the applicability of *Miranda*, I concur in the judgment of the Court.

This is not to say that I believe the Constitution condones the method by which the police extracted the confession in this case. To the contrary, the deception and manipulation practiced on respondent raise a substantial claim that the confession was obtained in violation of the Due Process Clause.

[The] method used to elicit the confession in this case deserves close scrutiny. [As] Justice Marshall points out, the pressures of custody make a suspect more likely to confide in others and to engage in "jailhouse bravado." The State is in a unique position to exploit this vulnerability because it has virtually complete control over the suspect's environment. Thus, the State can ensure that a suspect is barraged with questions from an undercover agent until the suspect confesses. The testimony in this case suggests the State did just that.

The deliberate use of deception and manipulation by the police appears to be incompatible "with a system that presumes innocence and assures that a conviction will not be secured by inquisitorial means," *Miller*, and raises serious concerns that respondent's will was overborne. It is open to the lower court on remand to determine whether, under the totality of the circumstances, respondent's confession was elicited in a manner that violated the Due Process Clause. * * *

JUSTICE MARSHALL, dissenting.

The conditions that require the police to apprise a defendant of his constitutional rights—custodial interrogation conducted by an agent of the police— were present in this case. [Because] Perkins received no *Miranda* warnings before he was subjected to custodial interrogation, his confession was not admissible. * * *

Because Perkins was interrogated by police while he was in custody, *Miranda* required that the officer inform him of his rights. In rejecting that conclusion, the Court finds that "conversations" between undercover agents and suspects are devoid of the coercion inherent in stationhouse interrogations conducted by law enforcement officials who openly represent the State. *Miranda* was not, however, concerned solely with police *coercion*. It dealt with *any* police tactics that may operate to compel a suspect in custody to make incriminating statements without full awareness of his constitutional rights. [Thus,] when a law enforcement agent structures a custodial interrogation so that a suspect feels compelled to reveal incriminating information, he must inform the suspect of his constitutional rights and give him an opportunity to decide whether or not to talk. * * *

Custody works to the State's advantage in obtaining incriminating information. The psychological pressures inherent in confinement increase the suspect's anxiety, making him likely to seek relief by talking with others. Dix, *Undercover Investigations and Police Rulemaking*, 53 Texas L.Rev. 203, 230 (1975). The inmate is thus more susceptible to efforts by undercover agents to elicit information from him. Similarly, where the suspect is incarcerated, the constant threat of physical danger peculiar to the prison environment may make him demonstrate his toughness to other inmates by recounting or inventing past violent acts. [In] this case, the police deceptively took advantage of Perkins' psychological vulnerability by including him in a sham escape plot, a situation in which he would feel compelled to demonstrate his willingness to shoot a prison guard by revealing his past involvement in a murder. ([The] agent stressed that a killing might be necessary in the escape and then asked Perkins if he had ever murdered someone).

Thus, the pressures unique to custody allow the police to use deceptive interrogation tactics to compel a suspect to make an incriminating statement. The compulsion is not eliminated by the suspect's ignorance of his interrogator's true identity. The Court therefore need not inquire past the bare facts of custody and interrogation to determine whether *Miranda* warnings are required. * * *

3. What constitutes a waiver of the right to remain silent? If, after being advised of his Miranda rights, a custodial suspect remains silent, can the police interrogate him? At some point, does a suspect's silence in the face of police questions amount to an assertion of his right to remain silent? Or must the suspect explicitly invoke the right to remain silent? Does the case set forth below demonstrate that there is a significant difference between (a) the right to remain silent and (b) the right not to be interrogated?

BERGHUIS V. THOMPKINS
560 U.S. 370, 130 S.Ct. 2250, 176 L.Ed.2d 1098 (2010).

JUSTICE KENNEDY delivered the opinion of the Court.

[Detective Helgert and another police officer questioned defendant Thompkins about a shooting in which one person died. The interrogation was conducted in the early afternoon in a room 8 by 10 feet. Thompkins sat in a chair resembling a desk.

[At the outset of the interrogation, Detective Helgert presented Thompkins with a form containing the four standard *Miranda* warnings and a fifth warning which read: "You have the right to decide at any time before or during questioning to use your right to remain silent and your right to talk with a lawyer while you are being questioned." At Helgert's request, Thompkins read the fifth warning out loud. The detective himself then read the four *Miranda* warnings out loud.

[The Michigan trial court refused to suppress Thompkin's statements under *Miranda*. The defendant was found guilty of murder and sentenced to life in prison without parole. The Michigan Court of Appeals affirmed. On habeas corpus, the federal district court denied relief. But a unanimous three-judge panel of the U.S. Court of Appeals for the Sixth Circuit reversed, concluding that the state courts had unreasonably applied clearly established law and based its decision on an unreasonable determination of the facts. Under the Antiterrorism and Effective Death Penalty Act of 1966 (AEDPA), a federal court cannot grant a petition for a writ of habeas corpus unless the state court's adjudication of the merits was "contrary to, or involved an unreasonable application of, clearly established Federal law."

[The Sixth Circuit found that the state court unreasonably determined the facts because "the evidence demonstrates that Thompkins was silent for two hours and forty-five minutes." Moreover, concluded the Sixth Circuit, the defendant's "persistent silence for nearly three hours in response to questioning and repeated invitations to tell his side of the story offered a clear and unequivocal message to the officers: Thompkins did not wish to waive his rights."]

Thompkins [first] contends that he "invoke[d] his privilege" to remain silent by not saying anything for a sufficient period of time, so the interrogation should have "cease[d]" before he made his inculpatory statements.

[This] argument is unpersuasive. In the context of invoking the *Miranda* right to counsel, the Court in *Davis v. United States,* 512 U.S. 452 (1994), held that a suspect must do so "unambiguously." If an accused makes a statement concerning the right to counsel "that is ambiguous or equivocal" or makes no statement, the police are not required to end the interrogation or ask questions to clarify whether the accused wants to invoke his or her *Miranda* rights.

The Court has not yet stated whether an invocation of the right to remain silent can be ambiguous or equivocal, but there is no principled reason to adopt different standards for determining when an accused has invoked the *Miranda* right to remain silent and the *Miranda* right to counsel at issue in *Davis*. [There] is good reason to require an accused who wants to invoke his or her right to remain silent to do so unambiguously. A requirement of an unambiguous invocation of *Miranda* rights results in an objective inquiry that "avoid[s] difficulties of proof [and] provide[s] guidance to officers" on how to proceed in the face of ambiguity. *Davis*. [If] an ambiguous act, omission, or statement could require police to end the interrogation, police would be required to make difficult decisions about an accused's unclear intent and face the consequence of suppression "if they guess wrong." Suppression of a voluntary confession in these circumstances would place a significant burden on society's interest in prosecuting criminal activity. * * *

Thompkins did not say that he wanted to remain silent or that he did not want to talk with the police. Had he made either of these simple, unambiguous statements, he would have invoked his " 'right to cut off questioning.' " Here he did neither, so he did not invoke his right to remain silent.

We next consider whether Thompkins waived his right to remain silent. Even absent the accused's invocation of the right to remain silent, the accused's statement during a custodial interrogation is inadmissible at trial unless the prosecution can establish that the accused "in fact knowingly and voluntarily waived *[Miranda]* rights" when making the statement. The waiver inquiry "has two distinct dimensions": waiver must be "voluntary in the sense that it was the product of a free and deliberate choice rather than intimidation, coercion, or deception," and "made with a full awareness of both the nature of the right being abandoned and the consequences of the decision to abandon it."

Some language in *Miranda* could be read to indicate that waivers are difficult to establish absent an explicit written waiver or a formal, express oral statement. [But the] course of decisions since *Miranda*, informed by the application of *Miranda* warnings in the whole course of law enforcement, demonstrates that waivers can be established even absent formal or express statements of waiver that would be expected in, say, a judicial hearing to determine if a guilty plea has been properly entered. The main purpose of *Miranda* is to ensure that an accused is advised of and understands the right to remain silent and the right to counsel. Thus, "[i]f anything, our subsequent cases have reduced the impact of the *Miranda* rule on legitimate law enforcement while reaffirming the decision's core ruling that unwarned statements may not be used as evidence in the prosecution's case in chief." *Dickerson v. United States* [p. 541].

One of the first cases to decide the meaning and import of *Miranda* with respect to the question of waiver was *North Carolina v. Butler*, 441 U.S. 369 (1979). [This case] interpreted the *Miranda* language concerning the "heavy burden" to show waiver in accord with usual principles of determining waiver, which can include waiver implied from all the circumstances. And in a later case, the Court stated that this "heavy burden" is not more than the burden to establish waiver by a preponderance of the evidence. *Colorado v. Connelly* [p. 411, fn. a].

The prosecution therefore does not need to show that a waiver of *Miranda* rights was express. An "implicit waiver" of the "right to remain silent" is sufficient to admit a suspect's statement into evidence. [*Butler*] made clear that a waiver of *Miranda* rights may be implied through "the defendant's silence, coupled with an understanding of his rights and a course of conduct indicating waiver." [*Butler*] therefore "retreated" from the "language and tenor of the *Miranda* opinion," which "suggested that the Court would require that a waiver [be] 'specifically made.' "

If the State establishes that a *Miranda* warning was given and the accused made an uncoerced statement, this showing, standing alone, is insufficient to demonstrate "a valid waiver" of *Miranda* rights. The prosecution must make the additional showing that the accused understood these rights. [Where] the prosecution shows that a *Miranda* warning was given and that it was understood by the accused, an accused's uncoerced statement establishes an implied waiver of the right to remain silent.

Although *Miranda* imposes on the police a rule that is both formalistic and practical when it prevents them from interrogating suspects without first providing them with a *Miranda* warning, it does not impose a formalistic waiver procedure that a suspect must follow to relinquish those rights. As a general proposition, the law can presume that an individual who, with a full understanding of his or her rights, acts in a manner inconsistent with their exercise has made a deliberate choice to relinquish the protection those rights afford. [As] *Butler* recognized, *Miranda* rights can therefore be waived through means less formal than a typical waiver on the record in a courtroom, given the practical constraints and necessities of interrogation and the fact that *Miranda*'s main protection lies in advising defendants of their rights.

The record in this case shows that Thompkins waived his right to remain silent. There is no basis in this case to conclude that he did not understand his rights; and on these facts it follows that he chose not to invoke or rely on those rights when he did speak. First, there is no contention that Thompkins did not understand his rights; and from this it follows that he knew what he gave up when he spoke. There was more than enough evidence in the record to conclude that Thompkins understood his *Miranda* rights. Thompkins received a written copy of the *Miranda* warnings; Detective Helgert determined that Thompkins could read and understand English; and Thompkins was given time to read the warnings. Thompkins, furthermore, read aloud the fifth warning, which stated that "you have the right to decide at any time before or during questioning to use your right to remain silent and your right to talk with a lawyer while you are being questioned." He was thus aware that his right to remain silent would not dissipate after a certain amount of time and that police would have to honor his right to be silent and his right to counsel during the whole course of interrogation. Those rights, the warning made clear, could be asserted at any time. Helgert, moreover, read the warnings aloud.

Second, Thompkins's answer to Detective Helgert's question about whether Thompkins prayed to God for forgiveness for shooting the victim is a "course of conduct indicating waiver" of the right to remain silent. If Thompkins wanted to remain silent, he could have said nothing in response to Helgert's questions, or he could have unambiguously invoked his *Miranda* rights and ended the interrogation. The fact that Thompkins made a statement about three hours after receiving a *Miranda* warning does not overcome the fact that he engaged in a course of conduct indicating waiver. Police are not required to rewarn suspects from time to time. Thompkins's answer to Helgert's question about praying to God for forgiveness for shooting the victim was sufficient to show a course of conduct indicating waiver. This is confirmed by the fact that before then Thompkins had given sporadic answers to questions throughout the interrogation.

Third, there is no evidence that Thompkins's statement was coerced. Thompkins does not claim that police threatened or injured him during the interrogation or that he was in any way fearful. [The] fact that Helgert's question referred to Thompkins's religious beliefs also did not render Thompkins's statement involuntary. [In] these circumstances, Thompkins knowingly and voluntarily made a statement to police, so he waived his right to remain silent.

Thompkins next argues that, even if his answer to Detective Helgert could constitute a waiver of his right to remain silent, the police were not allowed to question him until they obtained a waiver first. *Butler* forecloses this argument. The *Butler* Court held that courts can infer a waiver of *Miranda* rights "from the actions and words of the person interrogated." This principle would be inconsistent with a rule that requires a waiver at the outset. The *Butler* Court thus rejected the rule proposed by the *Butler* dissent, which would have "requir[ed] the police to obtain an express waiver of [*Miranda* rights] before proceeding with interrogation." This holding also makes sense given that "the primary protection afforded suspects subject[ed] to custodial interrogation is the *Miranda* warnings themselves." The *Miranda* rule and its requirements are met if a suspect receives adequate *Miranda* warnings, understands them, and has an opportunity to invoke the rights before giving any answers or admissions. Any waiver, express or implied, may be contradicted by an invocation at any time. If the right to counsel or the right to remain silent is invoked at any point during questioning, further interrogation must cease.

Interrogation provides the suspect with additional information that can put his or her decision to waive, or not to invoke, into perspective. As questioning commences and then continues, the suspect has the opportunity to consider the choices he or she faces and to make a more informed decision, either to insist on silence or to cooperate. When the suspect knows that *Miranda* rights can be invoked at any time, he or she has the opportunity to reassess his or her immediate and long-term interests. Cooperation with the police may result in more favorable treatment for the suspect; the apprehension of accomplices; the prevention of continuing injury and fear; beginning steps towards relief or solace for the victims; and the beginning of the suspect's own return to the law and the social order it seeks to protect.

[In] sum, a suspect who has received and understood the *Miranda* warnings, and has not invoked his *Miranda* rights, waives the right to remain silent by making an uncoerced statement to the police. Thompkins did not invoke his right to remain silent and stop the questioning. Understanding his rights in full, he waived his right to remain silent by making a voluntary statement to the police. The police, moreover, were not required to obtain a waiver of Thompkins's right to remain silent before interrogating him. The state court's decision rejecting Thompkins's *Miranda* claim was thus correct under *de novo* review and therefore necessarily reasonable under the more deferential AEDPA standard of review. * * *

JUSTICE SOTOMAYOR, with whom JUSTICE STEVENS, JUSTICE GINSBURG, and JUSTICE BREYER join, dissenting.

The Court concludes today that a criminal suspect waives his right to remain silent if, after sitting tacit and uncommunicative through nearly three hours of police interrogation, he utters a few one-word responses. The Court also concludes that a suspect who wishes to guard his right to remain silent against such a finding of "waiver" must, counterintuitively, speak—and must do so with sufficient precision to satisfy a clear-statement rule that construes ambiguity in favor of the police. Both propositions mark a substantial retreat from the protection against compelled self-incrimination that *Miranda* has long provided during custodial interrogation. The broad rules the Court announces today are also troubling because they are unnecessary to decide this case, which is governed by the deferential standard of review set forth in the AEDPA. Because I believe Thompkins is entitled to relief [on] the ground that his statements were admitted at trial without the prosecution having carried its burden to show that he waived his right to remain silent; because longstanding principles of judicial restraint counsel leaving for another day the questions of law the Court reaches out to decide; and because the Court's answers to those questions do not result from a faithful application of our prior decisions, I respectfully dissent.

[The] strength of Thompkins' *Miranda* claims depends in large part on the circumstances of the 3-hour interrogation, at the end of which he made inculpatory statements later introduced at trial. The Court's opinion downplays record evidence that Thompkins remained almost completely silent and unresponsive throughout that session. One of the interrogating officers, Detective Helgert, testified that although Thompkins was administered *Miranda* warnings, the last of which he read aloud, Thompkins expressly declined to sign a written acknowledgment that he had been advised of and understood his rights. There is conflicting evidence in the record about whether Thompkins ever verbally confirmed understanding his rights. The record contains no indication that the officers sought or obtained an express waiver.

As to the interrogation itself, Helgert candidly characterized it as "very, very one-sided" and "nearly a monologue." Thompkins was "[p]eculiar," "[s]ullen," and "[g]enerally quiet." Helgert and his partner "did most of the talking," as Thompkins was "not verbally communicative" and "[l]argely" remained silent. [After] proceeding in this fashion for approximately 2 hours and 45 minutes, Helgert asked Thompkins three questions relating to his faith in God. The prosecution relied at trial on Thompkins' one-word answers of "yes."

Thompkins' nonresponsiveness is particularly striking in the context of the officers' interview strategy, later explained as conveying to Thompkins that "this was his opportunity to explain his side [of the story]" because "[e]verybody else, including [his] co-[d]efendants, had given their version," and asking him "[w]ho is going to speak up for you if you don't speak up for yourself?" Yet, Helgert confirmed that the "*only* thing [Thompkins said] relative to his involvement [in the shooting]" occurred near the end of the interview—i.e., in response to the questions about God (emphasis added).

[Even] when warnings have been administered and a suspect has not affirmatively invoked his rights, statements made in custodial interrogation may not be admitted as part of the prosecution's case in chief "unless and until" the prosecution demonstrates that an individual "knowingly and intelligently waive[d] [his] rights." *Miranda*. "[A] heavy burden rests on the government to demonstrate that the defendant knowingly and intelligently waived his privilege against self-incrimination and his right to retained or appointed counsel." Id. The government must satisfy the "high standar[d] of proof for the waiver of constitutional rights [set forth in] *Johnson v. Zerbst*," [discussed at pp. 327, 329].

The question whether a suspect has validly waived his right is "entirely distinct" as a matter of law from whether he invoked that right. The questions are related, however, in terms of the practical effect on the exercise of a suspect's rights. A suspect may at any time revoke his prior waiver of rights—or, closer to the facts of this case, guard against the possibility of a future finding that he implicitly waived his rights—by invoking the rights and thereby requiring the police to cease questioning.

[This] Court's decisions subsequent to *Miranda* have emphasized the prosecution's "heavy burden" in proving waiver. We have also reaffirmed that a court may not presume waiver from a suspect's silence or from the mere fact that a confession was eventually obtained. See *Butler.*

Even in concluding that *Miranda* does not invariably require an express waiver of the right to silence or the right to counsel, *Butler* made clear that the prosecution bears a substantial burden in establishing an implied waiver. The FBI had obtained statements after advising Butler of his rights and confirming that he understood them. When presented with a written waiver-of-rights form, Butler told the agents, " 'I will talk to you but I am not signing any form.' " He then made inculpatory statements, which he later sought to suppress on the ground that he had not expressly waived his right to counsel.

Although this Court reversed the state-court judgment concluding that the statements were inadmissible, we quoted at length portions of the *Miranda* opinion reproduced above. We cautioned that even an "express written or oral statement of waiver of the right to remain silent or of the right to counsel" is not "inevitably * * * sufficient to establish waiver," emphasizing that "[t]he question [is] whether the defendant in fact knowingly and voluntarily waived the rights delineated in the *Miranda* case." *Miranda,* we observed, "unequivocally [said] mere silence is not enough." While we stopped short in *Butler* of announcing a *per se* rule that "the defendant's silence, coupled with an understanding of his rights and a course of conduct indicating waiver, may never support a conclusion that a defendant has waived his rights," we reiterated that "courts must presume that a defendant did not waive his rights; the prosecution's burden is great."

Rarely do this Court's precedents provide clearly established law so closely on point with the facts of a particular case. Together, *Miranda* and *Butler* establish that a court "must presume that a defendant did not waive his right[s]"; the prosecution bears a "heavy burden" in attempting to demonstrate waiver; the fact of a "lengthy interrogation" prior to obtaining statements is "strong evidence" against a finding of valid waiver; "mere silence" in response to questioning is "not enough"; and waiver may not be presumed "simply from the fact that a confession was in fact eventually obtained."[3]

---

[3]   Likely reflecting the great weight of the prosecution's burden in proving implied waiver, many contemporary police training resources instruct officers to obtain a waiver of rights prior to proceeding at all with an interrogation. See, e.g., F. Inbau, J. Reid, J. Buckley, & B. Jayne, Criminal Interrogation and Confessions 491 (4th ed. 2004) (hereinafter Inbau) ("Once [a] waiver is given, the police may proceed with the interrogation"). * * *

It is undisputed here that Thompkins never expressly waived his right to remain silent. His refusal to sign even an acknowledgment that he understood his *Miranda* rights evinces, if anything, an intent not to waive those rights. [That] Thompkins did not make the inculpatory statements at issue until after approximately 2 hours and 45 minutes of interrogation serves as "strong evidence" against waiver. *Miranda* and *Butler* expressly preclude the possibility that the inculpatory statements themselves are sufficient to establish waiver. * * *

Michigan and the United States concede that no waiver occurred in this case until Thompkins responded "yes" to the questions about God. I believe it is objectively unreasonable under our clearly established precedents to conclude the prosecution met its "heavy burden" of proof on a record consisting of three one-word answers, following 2 hours and 45 minutes of silence punctuated by a few largely nonverbal responses to unidentified questions.

Perhaps because our prior *Miranda* precedents so clearly favor Thompkins, the Court today goes beyond AEDPA's deferential standard of review and announces a new general principle of law. Any new rule, it must be emphasized, is unnecessary to the disposition of this case. If, in the Court's view, the Michigan court did not unreasonably apply our *Miranda* precedents in denying Thompkins relief, it should simply say so and reverse the Sixth Circuit's judgment on that ground.

[The] Court concludes that when *Miranda* warnings have been given and understood, "an accused's uncoerced statement establishes an implied waiver of the right to remain silent." More broadly still, the Court states that, "[a]s a general proposition, the law can presume that an individual who, with a full understanding of his or her rights, acts in a manner inconsistent with their exercise has made a deliberate choice to relinquish the protection those rights afford."

These principles flatly contradict our longstanding views that "a valid waiver will not be presumed * * * simply from the fact that a confession was in fact eventually obtained," *Miranda*, and that "[t]he courts must presume that a defendant did not waive his rights," *Butler*. [At] best, the Court today creates an unworkable and conflicting set of presumptions that will undermine *Miranda*'s goal of providing "concrete constitutional guidelines for law enforcement agencies and courts to follow." At worst, it overrules *sub silentio* an essential aspect of the protections *Miranda* has long provided for the constitutional guarantee against self-incrimination.

The Court's conclusion that Thompkins' inculpatory statements were sufficient to establish an implied waiver, finds no support in *Butler*. *Butler* itself distinguished between a sufficient "course of conduct" and inculpatory statements, reiterating *Miranda*'s admonition that " 'a valid waiver will not be presumed simply [from] the fact that a confession was in fact eventually obtained.' " [The] evidence of implied waiver in *Butler* was worlds apart from the evidence in this case, because Butler unequivocally said "I will talk to you" after having been read *Miranda* warnings. Thompkins, of course, made no such statement. * * *

Today's dilution of the prosecution's burden of proof to the bare fact that a suspect made inculpatory statements after *Miranda* warnings were given and understood takes an unprecedented step away from the "high standards of proof for the waiver of constitutional rights" this Court has long demanded. [When] waiver is to be inferred during a custodial interrogation, there are sound reasons to require evidence beyond inculpatory statements themselves. *Miranda* and our subsequent cases are premised on the idea that custodial interrogation is inherently coercive. * * *

Thompkins separately argues that his conduct during the interrogation invoked his right to remain silent, requiring police to terminate questioning. Like the Sixth Circuit, I would not reach this question because Thompkins is in any case entitled to relief as to waiver. But even if Thompkins would not prevail on his invocation claim under AEDPA's deferential standard of review, I cannot agree with the Court's much broader ruling that a suspect must clearly invoke his right to silence by speaking. Taken together with the Court's reformulation of the prosecution's burden of proof as to waiver, today's novel clear-statement rule for invocation invites police to question a suspect at length—notwithstanding his persistent refusal to answer questions—in the hope of eventually obtaining a single inculpatory response which will suffice to prove waiver of rights. Such a result bears little semblance to the "fully effective" prophylaxis [that] *Miranda* requires. * * *

Thompkins contends that in refusing to respond to questions he effectively invoked his right to remain silent, such that police were required to terminate the interrogation prior to his inculpatory statements. * * * Notwithstanding *Miranda's* statement that "there can be no questioning" if a suspect "indicates in any manner [that] he wishes to consult with an attorney," the Court in *Davis* established a clear-statement rule for invoking the right to counsel. After a suspect has knowingly and voluntarily waived his *Miranda* rights, *Davis* held, police may continue questioning "until and unless the suspect *clearly* requests an attorney" (emphasis added).

Because this Court has never decided whether *Davis'* clear-statement rule applies to an invocation of the right to silence, Michigan contends, there was no clearly established federal law prohibiting the state court from requiring an unambiguous invocation. That the state court's decision was not objectively unreasonable is confirmed, in Michigan's view, by the number of federal Courts of Appeals to have applied *Davis* to invocation of the right to silence.

Under AEDPA's deferential standard of review, it is indeed difficult to conclude that the state court's application of our precedents was objectively unreasonable. Although the duration and consistency of Thompkins' refusal to answer questions throughout the 3-hour interrogation provide substantial evidence in support of his claim, Thompkins did not remain absolutely silent, and this Court has not previously addressed whether a suspect can invoke the right to silence by remaining uncooperative and nearly silent for 2 hours and 45 minutes.

The Court, however, eschews this narrow ground of decision, instead extending *Davis* to hold that police may continue questioning a suspect until he unambiguously invokes his right to remain silent. Because Thompkins neither said "he wanted to remain silent" nor said "he did not want to talk with the police," the Court concludes, he did not clearly invoke his right to silence.

I disagree with this novel application of *Davis*. Neither the rationale nor holding of that case compels today's result. *Davis* involved the right to counsel, not the right to silence. * * * *Michigan v. Mosley* [p. 455] upheld the admission of statements when police immediately stopped interrogating a suspect who invoked his right to silence, but reapproached him after a 2-hour delay and obtained inculpatory responses relating to a different crime after administering fresh *Miranda* warnings. The different effects of invoking the rights are consistent with distinct standards for invocation. To the extent *Mosley* contemplates a more flexible form of prophylaxis than *Edwards*—and, in particular, does not categorically bar police from reapproaching a suspect who has invoked his right to remain silent—*Davis*' concern about " 'wholly irrational obstacles' " to police investigation applies with less force.

In addition, the suspect's equivocal reference to a lawyer in *Davis* occurred only *after* he had given express oral and written waivers of his rights. *Davis*' holding is explicitly predicated on that fact. [The] Court ignores this aspect of *Davis*, as well as the decisions of numerous federal and state courts declining to apply a clear-statement rule when a suspect has not previously given an express waiver of rights.

In my mind, a more appropriate standard for addressing a suspect's ambiguous invocation of the right to remain silent is the constraint *Mosley* places on questioning a suspect who has invoked that right: The suspect's " 'right to cut off questioning' " must be " 'scrupulously honored.' " Such a standard is necessarily precautionary and fact specific. The rule would acknowledge that some statements or conduct are so equivocal that police may scrupulously honor a suspect's rights without terminating questioning—for instance, if a suspect's actions are reasonably understood to indicate a willingness to listen before deciding whether to respond. But other statements or actions—in particular, when a suspect sits silent throughout prolonged interrogation, long past the point when he could be deciding whether to respond—cannot reasonably be understood other than as an invocation of the right to remain silent. Under such circumstances, "scrupulous" respect for the suspect's rights will require police to terminate questioning under *Mosley*.[8]

To be sure, such a standard does not provide police with a bright-line rule. But, as we have previously recognized, *Mosley* itself does not offer clear guidance to police about when and how interrogation may continue after a suspect invokes his rights. * * * Given that police have for nearly 35 years applied *Mosley*'s fact-specific standard in questioning suspects who have invoked their right to remain

---

[8] Indeed, this rule appears to reflect widespread contemporary police practice. Thompkins' *amici* collect a range of training materials that instruct police not to engage in prolonged interrogation after a suspect has failed to respond to initial questioning. One widely used police manual, for example, teaches that a suspect who "indicates," "even by silence itself," his unwillingness to answer questions "has obviously exercised his constitutional privilege against self-incrimination."

silent; that our cases did not during that time resolve what statements or actions suffice to invoke that right; and that neither Michigan nor the Solicitor General have provided evidence in this case that the status quo has proved unworkable, I see little reason to believe today's clear-statement rule is necessary to ensure effective law enforcement.

Davis' clear-statement rule is also a poor fit for the right to silence. Advising a suspect that he has a "right to remain silent" is unlikely to convey that he must speak (and must do so in some particular fashion) to ensure the right will be protected. [By] contrast, telling a suspect "he has the right to the presence of an attorney, and that if he cannot afford an attorney one will be appointed for him prior to any questioning if he so desires," *Miranda*, implies the need for speech to exercise that right. *Davis'* requirement that a suspect must "clearly reques[t] an attorney" to terminate questioning thus aligns with a suspect's likely understanding of the *Miranda* warnings in a way today's rule does not. The Court suggests Thompkins could have employed the "simple, unambiguous" means of saying "he wanted to remain silent" or "did not want to talk with the police." But the *Miranda* warnings give no hint that a suspect should use those magic words, and there is little reason to believe police—who have ample incentives to avoid invocation—will provide such guidance.

Conversely, the Court's concern that police will face "difficult decisions about an accused's unclear intent" and suffer the consequences of " 'guess[ing] wrong,' " [is] misplaced. If a suspect makes an ambiguous statement or engages in conduct that creates uncertainty about his intent to invoke his right, police can simply ask for clarification. It is hardly an unreasonable burden for police to ask a suspect, for instance, "Do you want to talk to us?" The majority in *Davis* itself approved of this approach as protecting suspects' rights while "minimiz[ing] the chance of a confession [later] being suppressed." Given this straightforward mechanism by which police can "scrupulously hono[r]" a suspect's right to silence, today's clear-statement rule can only be seen as accepting "as tolerable the certainty that some poorly expressed requests [to remain silent] will be disregarded" without any countervailing benefit. Police may well prefer not to seek clarification of an ambiguous statement out of fear that a suspect will invoke his rights. But "our system of justice is not founded on a fear that a suspect will exercise his rights."

In the 16 years since *Davis* was decided, ample evidence has accrued that criminal suspects often use equivocal or colloquial language in attempting to invoke their right to silence. A number of lower courts that have (erroneously, in my view) imposed a clear-statement requirement for invocation of the right to silence have rejected as ambiguous an array of statements whose meaning might otherwise be thought plain. At a minimum, these decisions suggest that differentiating "clear" from "ambiguous" statements is often a subjective inquiry. Even if some of the cited decisions are themselves in tension with *Davis'* admonition that a suspect need not " 'speak with the discrimination of an Oxford don' " to invoke his rights, they demonstrate that today's decision will significantly burden the exercise of the right to silence.

[For] these reasons, I believe a precautionary requirement that police "scrupulously hono[r]" a suspect's right to cut off questioning is a more faithful application of our precedents than the Court's awkward and needless extension of *Davis*.

* * *

Today's decision turns *Miranda* upside down. Criminal suspects must now unambiguously invoke their right to remain silent—which, counterintuitively, requires them to speak. At the same time, suspects will be legally presumed to have waived their rights even if they have given no clear expression of their intent to do so. Those results, in my view, find no basis in *Miranda* or our subsequent cases and are inconsistent with the fair-trial principles on which those precedents are grounded. Today's broad new rules are all the more unfortunate because they are unnecessary to the disposition of the case before us. I respectfully dissent.

4. When suspects are not in custody, and therefore not given any Miranda warnings, do they have a "right to remain silent"? If they do, must they expressly invoke this right?

SALINAS V. TEXAS
570 U.S. 178, 133 S.Ct. 2174, 186 L.Ed.2d 376 (2013).

JUSTICE ALITO announced the judgment of the Court and delivered an opinion in which THE CHIEF JUSTICE and JUSTICE KENNEDY join.

[The police asked defendant to come to the police station to clear himself as a suspect in a murder case. When the defendant arrived at the station, he was not in custody; he was free to leave at that time. As a result, he was not given any *Miranda* warnings.

[Defendant was asked a number of questions and answered them. Then he was asked whether the shotgun from his home would match the shells recovered at the scene of the murder. At this point, defendant declined to answer. Instead, he looked down at the floor, shuffled his feet, bit his bottom lip, and clenched his hands in his lap. After a few moments of silence, the defendant answered other questions.

[During the prosecutor's closing argument, he used the defendant's reaction when questioned earlier as evidence of his guilt. He pointed out to the jury that the defendant had remained silent when asked about the shotgun. The prosecutor told the jury that an innocent person would not have reacted the same way. Instead, an innocent person would have denied that he was involved. He would have said: "I wasn't there." But Salinas "didn't respond that way."

[The Court noted that it granted certiorari to resolve a division of authority in the lower courts over whether the prosecution may use a defendant's assertion of the privilege against self-incrimination during noncustodial police questioning of a suspect as part of its case in chief. However, because the defendant never did invoke the privilege during the police questioning of him, the Court found it "unnecessary to reach that question."]

The privilege against self-incrimination "is an exception to the general rule that the Government has the right to everyone's testimony." To prevent the privilege from shielding information not properly within its scope, we have long held that a witness who "desires the protection of the privilege * * * must claim it" at the time relies on it. *Minnesota v. Murphy*, 465 U.S. 420, 427 (1984).[1]

That requirement ensures that the Government is put on notice when a witness intends to rely on the privilege so that it may either argue that the testimony sought could not be self-incriminating or cure any potential self-incrimination through a grant of immunity. * * *

We have previously recognized two exceptions to the requirement that witnesses invoke the privilege, but neither applies here. First, we held in *Griffin v. California*, 380 U.S. 609 (1965) [set forth at p. 1051], that a criminal defendant need not take the stand and assert the privilege at his own trial. That exception reflects the fact that a criminal defendant has an "absolute right not to testify." [Because the defendant] had no comparable unqualified right during his interview with the police, his silence falls outside the *Griffin* exception.

Second, we have held that a witness' failure to invoke the privilege must be excused where governmental coercion makes his forfeiture of the privilege involuntary. Thus, in *Miranda*, we said that a suspect who is subjected to the "inherently compelling pressures" of an unwarned custodial interrogation need not invoke the privilege.

[However, as the defendant] himself acknowledges, he agreed to accompany the officers to the station and "was free to leave at any time during the interview." * * * We have before us no allegation that [the defendant's] failure to assert the privilege was involuntary, and it would have been a simple matter for him to say that he was not answering the officer's question on Fifth Amendment grounds. Because he failed to do so, the prosecution's use of his noncustodial silence did not violate the Fifth Amendment. * * *

Our cases establish that a defendant normally does not invoke the privilege by remaining silent. * * * We have also repeatedly held that the express invocation requirement applies when an official has reason to suspect that the answer to his question would incriminate the witness. Thus, in *Murphy*, supra, we held that the defendant's self-incriminating answers to his probation officer were properly admitted at trial because he failed to invoke the privilege. In reaching that conclusion, we rejected the notion "that a witness must 'put the Government on notice' by formally availing himself of the privilege only when he alone 'is reasonably aware of the incriminating tendency of the questions.' "

---

[1]   Murphy, a probationer, arranged to meet with his probation officer as she had requested. He then admitted he had committed serious crimes a number of years earlier. A 6–3 majority, per White, J., concluded that Murphy could not claim the "in custody" exception to the general rule that the privilege against self-incrimination is not self-executing: "[A]ny compulsion [Murphy] might have felt from the possibility that terminating the meeting would have led to revocation of probation was not comparable to the pressure on a suspect who is painfully aware that he literally cannot escape a persistent custodial interrogation."

[The defendant] does not dispute the vitality of either of those lines of precedent but instead argues that we should adopt an exception for cases at their intersection. [Defendant] would have us hold that although neither a witness' silence nor official suspicions are enough to excuse the express invocation requirement, the invocation requirement does not apply where a witness is silent in the face of official suspicions. [Such a view] would do little to protect those genuinely relying on the Fifth Amendment privilege while placing a needless new burden on society's interest in the admission of evidence that is protective of a defendant's guilt.

[The defendant's] proposed exception would also be very difficult to reconcile with *Berghuis v. Thompkins*. There, we held in the closely related context of post-*Miranda* silence that a defendant failed to invoke the privilege when he refused to respond to police questioning for 2 hours and 45 minutes. If the extended custodial silence in that case did not invoke the privilege, then surely the momentary silence in this case did not do so either.

[The dissent attempts] to distinguish *Berghuis* by observing that it did not concern the admissibility of the defendant's silence but instead involved the admissibility of his subsequent statements. But regardless of whether prosecutors seek to use silence or a confession that follows, the logic of *Berghuis* applies with equal force: A suspect who stands mute has not done enough to put police on notice that he is relying on his Fifth Amendment privilege.

[Defendant and the dissent also maintain that] release on the Fifth Amendment privilege is the most likely explanation for silence in a case such as this one. But whatever the most probable explanation, such silence is "insolubly ambiguous." See *Doyle v. Ohio* [p. 454, fn. b] * * *. [Defendant] alone knew why he did not answer the officer's question, and it was therefore his "burden [to] make a timely assertion of the privilege."

[Defendant suggests] that it would be unfair to require a suspect unschooled in the particulars of legal doctrine to do anything more than remain silent in order to invoke his "right to remain silent." [But] popular misconceptions notwithstanding, the Fifth Amendment guarantees that no one may be "compelled in any criminal case to be a witness against himself"; it does not establish an unqualified "right to remain silent." A witness' constitutional right to refuse to answer questions depends on his reason for doing so, and courts need to know those reasons to evaluate the merits of a Fifth Amendment claim. * * *

Finally, we are not persuaded by [defendant's] arguments that applying the usual express invocation requirement where a witness is silent during a noncustodial police interview will prove unworkable in practice. * * * Notably, [defendant's] approach would produce its own line-drawing problems, as this case vividly illustrates. When the interviewing officer asked [the defendant] if his shotgun would match the shell casings found at the crime scene, [the defendant] made movements that suggested surprise and anxiety. At precisely what point such reactions transform "silence" into expressive conduct would be a difficult and recurring question that our decision allows us to avoid.

[Defendant] worries that officers could unduly pressure suspects into talking by telling them that their silence could be used in a future prosecution. But as [defendant] himself concedes, police officers "have done nothing wrong" when they "accurately state the law." We found no constitutional infirmity in government officials telling the defendant in *Murphy* that he was required to speak truthfully to his parole officer, and we see no greater danger in the interview tactics [the defendant] identifies."

JUSTICE THOMAS, with whom JUSTICE SCALIA joins, concurring in the judgment.

* * * In my view, Salinas' claim would fail even if he had invoked the privilege because the prosecutor's comments regarding his precustodial silence did not compel him to give self-incriminating testimony.

In *Griffin v. California* [p. 1051], this Court held that the Fifth Amendment prohibits a prosecutor or judge from commenting on a defendant's failure to testify. * * * Salinas argues that we should extend *Griffin*'s no-adverse inference rule to a defendant's silence during a precustodial interview. I have previously explained that [*Griffin*] "lacks foundation in the Constitution's text, history, or logic" and should not be extended. I adhere to that view today. * * *

At the time of the founding, English and American courts strongly encouraged defendants to give unsworn statements and drew adverse inference when they failed to do so. Given *Griffin*'s indefensible foundation, I would not extend it to a defendant's silence during a precustodial interview. * * *

JUSTICE BREYER, with whom JUSTICE GINSBURG, JUSTICE SOTOMAYOR, and JUSTICE KAGAN join, dissenting.

In my view the Fifth Amendment here prohibits the prosecution from commenting on the petitioner's silence in response to police questioning. And I dissent from the Court's contrary conclusion. * * *

* * * To permit a prosecutor to comment on a defendant's constitutionally protected silence would put that defendant in an impossible predicament. He must either answer the question or remain silent. If he answers the question, he may well reveal, for example, prejudicial facts, disreputable associates, or suspicious circumstances—even if he is innocent. * * * If he remains silent, the prosecutor may well use that silence to suggest a consciousness of guilt. And if the defendant then takes the witness stand in order to explain either his speech or his silence, the prosecution may introduce, say for impeachment purposes, a prior conviction that the law would otherwise make inadmissible. Thus, where the Fifth Amendment is at issue, to allow comment on silence directly or indirectly can compel an individual to act as "a witness against himself "—very much what the Fifth Amendment forbids. * * * And that is similarly so whether the questioned individual, as part of his decision to remain silent, invokes the Fifth Amendment explicitly or implicitly, through words, through deeds, or through reference to surrounding circumstances.

It is consequently not surprising that this Court, more than half a century ago, explained that "no ritualistic formula is necessary in order to invoke the privilege." Thus, a prosecutor may not comment on a defendant's failure to testify at trial—even if neither the defendant nor anyone else ever mentions a Fifth Amendment right not to do so. Circumstances, not a defendant's statement, tie the defendant's silence to the right. Similarly, a prosecutor may not comment on the fact that a defendant in custody, *after* receiving *Miranda* warnings, "stood mute"— regardless of whether he "claimed his privilege" in so many words. Again, it is not any explicit statement but, instead, the defendant's deeds (silence) and circumstances (receipt of the warnings) that tie together silence and constitutional right. Most lower courts have so construed the law, even where the defendant, having received *Miranda* warnings, answers some questions while remaining silent as to others.

The cases in which this Court has insisted that a defendant expressly mention the Fifth Amendment by name in order to rely on its privilege to protect silence are cases where (1) the circumstances surrounding the silence (unlike the present case) did not give rise to an inference that the defendant intended, by his silence, to exercise his Fifth Amendment rights; *and* (2) the questioner greeted by the silence (again unlike the present case) had a special need to know whether the defendant sought to rely on the protections of the Fifth Amendment. [In] such cases, the government needs to know the basis for refusing to answer "so that it may either argue that the testimony sought could not be self-incriminating or cure any potential self-incrimination through a grant of immunity." * * *

Perhaps most illustrative is *Jenkins v. Anderson*, 447 U.S. 231 (1980), a case upon which the plurality relies, and upon which the Texas Court of Criminal Appeals relied almost exclusively. Jenkins killed someone, and was not arrested until he turned himself in two weeks later. On cross-examination at his trial, Jenkins claimed that his killing was in self-defense after being attacked. The prosecutor then asked why he did not report the alleged attack, and in closing argument suggested that Jenkins' failure to do so cast doubt on his claim to have acted in self-defense. We explained that this unusual form of "prearrest silence" was not constitutionally protected from use at trial. Perhaps even more aptly, Justice Stevens' concurrence noted that "the privilege against compulsory self-incrimination is simply irrelevant" in such circumstances." How would anyone have known that Jenkins, while failing to report an attack, was relying on the Fifth Amendment? And how would the government have had any way of determining whether his claim was valid? In *Jenkins*, no one had any reason to connect silence to the Fifth Amendment; and the government had no opportunity to contest any alleged connection.

Still further afield from today's case are *Murphy* and *Garner*, neither of which involved silence at all. Rather, in both cases, a defendant had earlier *answered* questions posed by the government—in *Murphy*, by speaking with a probation officer, and in *Garner*, by completing a tax return. [See] *Garner v. United States*, 424 U.S. 648 (1976). At the time of providing answers, neither circumstances nor deeds nor words suggested reliance on the Fifth Amendment: Murphy simply answered questions posed by his probation officer; Garner simply filled out a tax return. They did not argue that their self incriminating statements had been "compelled" in violation of the Fifth Amendment until later, at trial. The Court held that those statements were *not* compelled. The circumstances indicated that the defendants had affirmatively chosen to speak and to write.

Thus, we have two sets of cases: One where express invocation of the Fifth Amendment was not required to tie one's silence to its protections, and another where something like express invocation was required, because circumstances demanded some explanation for the silence (or the statements) in order to indicate that the Fifth Amendment was at issue.

There is also a third set of cases, cases that may well fit into the second category but where the Court has held that the Fifth Amendment both applies and does not require express invocation *despite* ambiguous circumstances. The Court in those cases has made clear that an individual, when silent, need not expressly invoke the Fifth Amendment if there are "inherently compelling pressures" not to do so. *Miranda.* Thus, in *Garrity* v. *New Jersey,* 385 U.S. 493, 497 (1967), the Court held that no explicit assertion of the Fifth Amendment was required where, in the course of an investigation, such assertion would, by law, have cost police officers their jobs. Similarly, this Court did not require explicit assertion in response to a grand jury subpoena where that assertion would have cost two architects their public contracts or a political official his job. *Lefkowitz* v. *Turley,* 414 U.S. 70, 75–76 (1973); *Lefkowitz* v. *Cunningham,* 431 U.S. 801, 802–804 (1977). * * *

The plurality refers to one additional case, namely *Berghuis* v. *Thompkins.* But that case is here beside the point. In *Berghuis,* the defendant was in custody, he had been informed of his *Miranda* rights, and he was subsequently silent in the face of 2 hours and 45 minutes of questioning before he offered any substantive answers. The Court held that he had waived his Fifth Amendment rights in respect to his *later speech.* The Court said nothing at all about a prosecutor's right to comment on his preceding silence and no prosecutor sought to do so. Indeed, how could a prosecutor lawfully have tried to do so, given this Court's statement in *Miranda* itself that a prosecutor cannot comment on the fact that, after receiving *Miranda* warnings, the suspect "stood mute"?

We end where we began. "[N]o ritualistic formula is necessary in order to invoke the privilege." Much depends on the circumstances of the particular case, the most important circumstances being: (1) whether one can fairly infer that the individual being questioned is invoking the Amendment's protection; (2) if that is unclear, whether it is particularly important for the questioner to know whether the individual is doing so; and (3) even if it is, whether, in any event, there is a good reason for excusing the individual from referring to the Fifth Amendment, such as inherent penalization simply by answering.

Applying these principles to the present case, I would hold that Salinas need not have expressly invoked the Fifth Amendment. The context was that of a criminal investigation. Police told Salinas that and made clear that he was a suspect. His interrogation took place at the police station. Salinas was not represented by counsel. The relevant question—about whether the shotgun from Salinas' home would incriminate him—amounted to a switch in subject matter. And it was obvious that the new question sought to ferret out whether Salinas was guilty of murder.

These circumstances give rise to a reasonable inference that Salinas' silence derived from an exercise of his Fifth Amendment rights. This Court has recognized repeatedly that many, indeed most, Americans are aware that they have a constitutional right not to incriminate themselves by answering questions posed by the police during an interrogation conducted in order to figure out the perpetrator of a crime. See *Dickerson* v. *United States* [p. 541]. The nature of the surroundings, the switch of topic, the particular question—all suggested that the right we have and generally *know* we have was at issue at the critical moment here. Salinas, not being represented by counsel, would not likely have used the precise words "Fifth Amendment" to invoke his rights because he would not likely have been aware of technical legal requirements, such as a need to identify the Fifth Amendment by name.

At the same time, the need to categorize Salinas' silence as based on the Fifth Amendment is supported here by the presence, in full force, of the predicament I discussed earlier, namely that of not forcing Salinas to choose between incrimination through speech and incrimination through silence. That need is also supported by the absence of any special reason that the police had to know, with certainty, whether Salinas was, in fact, relying on the Fifth Amendment—such as whether to doubt that there really was a risk of self-incrimination, or whether to grant immunity. Given these circumstances, Salinas' silence was "sufficient to put the [government] on notice of an apparent claim of the privilege." That being so, for reasons similar to those given in *Griffin*, the Fifth Amendment bars the evidence of silence admitted against Salinas and mentioned by the prosecutor.

I recognize that other cases may arise where facts and circumstances surrounding an individual's silence present a closer question. The critical question—whether those circumstances give rise to a fair inference that the silence rests on the Fifth Amendment—will not always prove easy to administer. But that consideration does not support the plurality's rule-based approach here, for the administrative problems accompanying the plurality's approach are even worse.

The plurality says that a suspect must "expressly invoke the privilege against self-incrimination." But does it really mean that the suspect must use the exact words "Fifth Amendment"? How can an individual who is not a lawyer know that these particular words are legally magic? Nor does the Solicitor General help when he adds that the suspect may "mak[e] the claim 'in any language that [the questioner] may reasonably be expected to understand as an attempt to invoke the privilege.' " What counts as "making the claim"? Suppose the individual says, "Let's discuss something else," or "I'm not sure I want to answer that"; or suppose he just gets up and leaves the room. * * * How is simple silence in the present context any different?

The basic problem for the plurality is that an effort to have a simple, clear "explicit statement" rule poses a serious obstacle to those who, like Salinas, seek to assert their basic Fifth Amendment right to remain silent, for they are likely unaware of any such linguistic detail. At the same time, acknowledging that our case law does not require use of specific words leaves the plurality without the administrative benefits it might hope to find in requiring that detail.

Far better, in my view, to pose the relevant question directly: Can one fairly infer from an individual's silence and surrounding circumstances an exercise of the Fifth Amendment's privilege? The need for simplicity, the constitutional importance of applying the Fifth Amendment to those who seek its protection, and this Court's case law all suggest that this is the right question to ask here. And the answer to that question in the circumstances of today's case is clearly: yes.

For these reasons, I believe that the Fifth Amendment prohibits a prosecutor from commenting on Salinas's silence. I respectfully dissent from the Court's contrary conclusion.

5.   If a suspect invokes his right to counsel and there is a break in Miranda custody, at what point, if at all, can the police try to interrogate the suspect again? If a suspect is serving a prison sentence (for an unrelated crime) at the time the police try to question him, does his release back into the general prison population constitute a break in custody?

MARYLAND V. SHATZER
559 U.S. 98, 130 S.Ct. 1213, 175 L.Ed.2d 1045 (2010).

JUSTICE SCALIA delivered the opinion of the Court.

[In August 2003, when defendant Shatzer was serving a sentence in a state correctional facility for an unrelated crime, a detective tried to question him about allegations that he had sexually assaulted his own son. However, when Shatzer invoked his right to counsel, the detective ended the meeting and Shatzer was then released back into the general prison population.

[Two and a half years later, on March 2, 2006, another detective obtained more information about the incident and decided to discuss the matter once more. (Shatzer was still serving time in a correctional facility and his meeting with the detectives took place in a small room, apart from the general prison population.) At this meeting Shatzer signed a written waiver of his *Miranda* rights. After 30 minutes of questioning, during which time Shatzer made an incriminating statement, he agreed to take a polygraph examination.

[Five days later, after again being advised of his rights and after again waiving his rights in writing, Shatzer took the polygraph examination. He was informed that he had failed the exam. He then made another incriminating statement.

[The trial court ruled that the *Edwards* protections did not apply because Shatzer had experienced a "break in custody" for *Miranda* purposes between the 2003 and 2006 interrogations. However, the Maryland Court of Appeals reversed, holding that the passing of time *alone* is insufficient to end the *Edwards* protections and that, even if a "break-in-custody" exception did exist, Shatzer's release into the general prison population did not constitute such an exception.]

We consider whether a break in custody ends the presumption of involuntariness established in *Edwards v. Arizona*, 451 U.S. 477 (1981). * * *

[The *Edwards* Court] determined that [the] traditional standard for waiver was not sufficient to protect a suspect's right to have counsel present at a subsequent interrogation if he had previously requested counsel; "additional safeguards" were necessary. The Court therefore superimposed a "second layer of prophylaxis" [describing *Edwards*].

The rationale of *Edwards* is that once a suspect indicates that "he is not capable of undergoing [custodial] questioning without advice of counsel," "any subsequent waiver that has come at the authorities' behest, and not at the suspect's own instigation, is itself the product of the 'inherently compelling pressures' and not the purely voluntary choice of the suspect." Under this rule, a voluntary *Miranda* waiver is sufficient at the time of an initial attempted interrogation to protect a suspect's right to have counsel present, but it is not sufficient at the time of subsequent attempts if the suspect initially requested the presence of counsel. The implicit assumption, of course, is that the subsequent requests for interrogation pose a significantly greater risk of coercion. That increased risk results not only from the police's persistence in trying to get the suspect to talk, but also from the continued pressure that begins when the individual is taken into custody as a suspect and sought to be interrogated—pressure likely to "increase as custody is prolonged," *Minnick v. Mississippi,* 498 U.S. 146 (1990). The *Edwards* presumption of involuntariness ensures that police will not take advantage of the mounting coercive pressures of "prolonged police custody" by repeatedly attempting to question a suspect who previously requested counsel until the suspect is "badgered into submission."

We have frequently emphasized that the *Edwards* rule is not a constitutional mandate, but judicially prescribed prophylaxis. Because *Edwards* is "our rule, not a constitutional command," "it is our obligation to justify its expansion." *Arizona v. Roberson,* 486 U.S. 675 (1988) (Kennedy, J., dissenting). Lower courts have uniformly held that a break in custody ends the *Edwards* presumption, but we have previously addressed the issue only in dicta.

A judicially crafted rule is "justified only by reference to its prophylactic purpose" and applies only where its benefits outweigh its costs. [*Edwards'*] fundamental purpose [is] to "[p]reserv[e] the integrity of an accused's choice to communicate with police only through counsel" by "prevent[ing] police from badgering a defendant into waiving his previously asserted *Miranda* rights." Thus, the benefits of the rule are measured by the number of coerced confessions it suppresses that otherwise would have been admitted.

It is easy to believe that a suspect may be coerced or badgered into abandoning his earlier refusal to be questioned without counsel in the paradigm *Edwards* case. That is a case in which the suspect has been arrested for a particular crime and is held in uninterrupted pretrial custody while that crime is being actively investigated. After the initial interrogation, and up to and including the second one, he remains cut off from his normal life and companions, "thrust into" and isolated in an "unfamiliar," "police-dominated atmosphere," *Miranda,* where his captors "appear to control [his] fate." That was the situation confronted by the suspects in *Edwards, Roberson,* and *Minnick,* the three cases in which we have held the *Edwards* rule applicable.

[When,] unlike what happened in these three cases, a suspect has been released from his pretrial custody and has returned to his normal life for some time before the later attempted interrogation, there is little reason to think that his change of heart regarding interrogation without counsel has been coerced. He has no longer been isolated. He has likely been able to seek advice from an attorney, family members, and friends.[3] And he knows from his earlier experience that he need only demand counsel to bring the interrogation to a halt; and that investigative custody does not last indefinitely. In these circumstances, it is far fetched to think that a police officer's asking the suspect whether he would like to waive his *Miranda* rights will any more "wear down the accused" than did the first such request at the original attempted interrogation—which is of course not deemed coercive. His change of heart is less likely attributable to "badgering" than it is to the fact that further deliberation in familiar surroundings has caused him to believe (rightly or wrongly) that cooperating with the investigation is in his interest. Uncritical extension of *Edwards* to this situation would not significantly increase the number of genuinely coerced confessions excluded. The "justification for a conclusive presumption disappears when application of the presumption will not reach the correct result most of the time."

At the same time that extending the *Edwards* rule yields diminished benefits, extending the rule also increases its costs: the in-fact voluntary confessions it excludes from trial, and the voluntary confessions it deters law enforcement officers from even trying to obtain. Voluntary confessions are not merely "a proper element in law enforcement," they are an "unmitigated good." * * *

The only logical endpoint of *Edwards* disability is termination of *Miranda* custody and any of its lingering effects. Without that limitation—and barring some purely arbitrary time-limit—every *Edwards* prohibition of custodial interrogation of a particular suspect would be eternal. The prohibition applies, of course, when the subsequent interrogation pertains to a different crime, when it is conducted by a different law enforcement authority, and even when the suspect has met with an attorney after the first interrogation. And it not only prevents questioning *ex ante;* it would render invalid *ex post,* confessions invited and obtained from suspects who (unbeknownst to the interrogators) have acquired *Edwards* immunity previously in connection with any offense in any jurisdiction. In a country that harbors a large number of repeat offenders, this consequence is disastrous.

We conclude that such an extension of *Edwards* is not justified; we have opened its "protective umbrella" far enough. The protections offered by *Miranda,* which we have deemed sufficient to ensure that the police respect the suspect's desire to have an attorney present the first time police interrogate him, adequately

---

[3]   Justice Stevens points out (opinion concurring in judgment), that in *Minnick,* actual pre-reinterrogation consultation with an attorney during *continued* custody did not suffice to avoid application of *Edwards.* That does not mean that the ability to consult freely with attorneys and others does not reduce the level of coercion at all, or that it is "only questionably relevant" to whether termination of custody reduces the coercive pressure that is the basis for *Edwards'* super-prophylactic rule.

ensure that result when a suspect who initially requested counsel is reinterrogated after a break in custody that is of sufficient duration to dissipate its coercive effects.

If Shatzer's return to the general prison population qualified as a break in custody (a question we address *infra*), there is no doubt that it lasted long enough (2½ years) to meet that durational requirement. But what about a break that has lasted only one year? Or only one week? It is impractical to leave the answer to that question for clarification in future case-by-case adjudication; law enforcement officers need to know, with certainty and beforehand, when renewed interrogation is lawful. And while it is certainly unusual for this Court to set forth precise time limits governing police action, it is not unheard-of. In *County of Riverside v. McLaughlin* [fn. a, p. 177], we specified 48 hours as the time within which the police must comply with the requirement of *Gerstein v. Pugh* [fn. a, p. 177], that a person arrested without a warrant be brought before a magistrate to establish probable cause for continued detention.

Like *McLaughlin*, this is a case in which the requisite police action (there, presentation to a magistrate; here, abstention from further interrogation) has not been prescribed by statute but has been established by opinion of this Court. We think it appropriate to specify a period of time to avoid the consequence that continuation of the *Edwards* presumption "will not reach the correct result most of the time." It seems to us that period is 14 days. That provides plenty of time for the suspect to get reacclimated to his normal life, to consult with friends and counsel, and to shake off any residual coercive effects of his prior custody.

The 14-day limitation meets Shatzer's concern that a break-in-custody rule lends itself to police abuse. He envisions that once a suspect invokes his *Miranda* right to counsel, the police will release the suspect briefly (to end the *Edwards* presumption) and then promptly bring him back into custody for reinterrogation. But once the suspect has been out of custody long enough (14 days) to eliminate its coercive effect, there will be nothing to gain by such gamesmanship—nothing, that is, except the entirely appropriate gain of being able to interrogate a suspect who has made a valid waiver of his *Miranda* rights.[7]

Shatzer argues that ending the *Edwards* protections at a break in custody will undermine *Edwards'* purpose to conserve judicial resources. To be sure, we have said that "[t]he merit of the *Edwards* decision lies in the clarity of its command and the certainty of its application." *Minnick.* But clarity and certainty are not goals in themselves. They are valuable only when they reasonably further the achievement of some substantive end—here, the exclusion of compelled confessions. Confessions obtained after a 2-week break in custody and a waiver of *Miranda* rights are most unlikely to be compelled, and hence are unreasonably excluded. In any case, a break-in-custody exception will dim only marginally, if at all, the bright-line nature of *Edwards.* * * *

---

[7] A defendant who experiences a 14-day break in custody after invoking the *Miranda* right to counsel is not left without protection. *Edwards* establishes a *presumption* that a suspect's waiver of *Miranda* rights is involuntary. Even without this "second layer of prophylaxis," a defendant is still free to claim the prophylactic protection of *Miranda*—arguing that his waiver of *Miranda* rights was in fact involuntary. * * *

[After] the 2003 interview, Shatzer was released back into the general prison population where he was serving an unrelated sentence. The issue is whether that constitutes a break in *Miranda* custody. * * *

Here, we are addressing the interim period during which a suspect was not interrogated, but was subject to a baseline set of restraints imposed pursuant to a prior conviction. Without minimizing the harsh realities of incarceration, we think lawful imprisonment imposed upon conviction of a crime does not create the coercive pressures identified in *Miranda*.

Interrogated suspects who have previously been convicted of crime live in prison. When they are released back into the general prison population, they return to their accustomed surroundings and daily routine—they regain the degree of control they had over their lives prior to the interrogation. Sentenced prisoners, in contrast to the *Miranda* paradigm, are not isolated with their accusers. They live among other inmates, guards, and workers, and often can receive visitors and communicate with people on the outside by mail or telephone.

Their detention, moreover, is relatively disconnected from their prior unwillingness to cooperate in an investigation. The former interrogator has no power to increase the duration of incarceration, which was determined at sentencing.[8] And even where the possibility of parole exists, the former interrogator has no apparent power to decrease the time served. This is in stark contrast to the circumstances faced by the defendants in *Edwards*, *Roberson*, and *Minnick*, whose continued detention as suspects rested with those controlling their interrogation, and who confronted the uncertainties of what final charges they would face, whether they would be convicted, and what sentence they would receive. * * *

A few words in response to Justice Stevens' concurrence: It claims we ignore that "[w]hen police tell an indigent suspect that he has the right to an attorney" and then "reinterrogate" him without providing a lawyer, "the suspect is likely to feel that the police lied to him and that he really does not have any right to a lawyer." The fallacy here is that we are not talking about "reinterrogating" the suspect; we are talking about *asking his permission* to be interrogated. An officer has in no sense lied to a suspect when, after advising, as *Miranda* requires, * * * he promptly ends the attempted interrogation because the suspect declines to speak without counsel present, and then, two weeks later, reapproaches the suspect and asks, "Are you now willing to speak without a lawyer present?" * * *

Contrary to the concurrence's conclusion, there is no reason to believe a suspect will view confession as " 'the only way to end his interrogation' " when, before the interrogation begins, he is told that he can avoid it by simply requesting

---

8   We distinguish the duration of incarceration from the duration of what might be termed interrogative custody. When a prisoner is removed from the general prison population and taken to a separate location for questioning, the duration of *that separation* is assuredly dependent upon his interrogators. For which reason once he has asserted a refusal to speak without assistance of counsel *Edwards* prevents any efforts to get him to change his mind during that interrogative custody.

that he not be interrogated without counsel present—an option that worked before. * * *

The concurrence also accuses the Court of "ignor[ing] that when a suspect asks for counsel, until his request is answered, there are still the same 'inherently compelling' pressures of custodial interrogation on which the *Miranda* line of cases is based." We do not ignore these pressures; nor do we suggest that they disappear when custody is recommenced after a break. But if those pressures are merely "the same" as before, then *Miranda* provides sufficient protection—as it did before. The *Edwards* presumption of involuntariness is justified only in circumstances where the coercive pressures have increased so much that suspects' waivers of *Miranda* rights are likely to be involuntary most of the time. Contrary to the concurrence's suggestion, it is only in those narrow circumstances—when custody is unbroken— that the Court has concluded a "fresh se[t] of *Miranda* warnings" is not sufficient.

In the last analysis, it turns out that the concurrence accepts our principal points. It agrees that *Edwards* prophylaxis is not perpetual; it agrees that a break in custody reduces the inherently compelling pressure upon which *Edwards* was based; it agrees that Shatzer's release back into the general prison population constituted a break in custody; and it agrees that in this case the break was long enough to render *Edwards* inapplicable. We differ in two respects: Instead of terminating *Edwards* protection when the custodial pressures that were the basis for that protection dissipate, the concurrence would terminate it when the suspect would no longer "feel that he has 'been denied the counsel he has clearly requested.'" This is entirely unrelated to the rationale of *Edwards*. If confidence in the police's promise to provide counsel were the touchstone, *Edwards* would not have applied in *Minnick*, where the suspect in continuing custody actually met with appointed counsel. The concurrence's rule is also entirely unrelated to the existence of a break in custody. While that may relieve the accumulated coercive pressures of custody that are the foundation for *Edwards*, it is hard to see how it bolsters the suspect's confidence that if he asks for counsel he will get one.

And secondly, the concurrence differs from us in declining to say *how long* after a break in custody the termination of *Edwards* protection occurs. Two and one-half years, it says, is clearly enough—but it gives law enforcement authorities no further guidance. The concurrence criticizes our use of 14 days as arbitrary and unexplained. But in fact that rests upon the same basis as the concurrence's own approval of a 2½-year break in custody: how much time will justify "treating the second interrogation as no more coercive than the first." Failure to say where the line falls short of 2½ years, and leaving that for future case-by-case determination, is certainly less helpful, but not at all less arbitrary.

* * *

Because Shatzer experienced a break in *Miranda* custody lasting more than two weeks between the first and second attempts at interrogation, *Edwards* does not mandate suppression of his March 2006 statements. * * *

JUSTICE THOMAS, concurring in part and concurring in the judgment.

I join [the part] of the Court's opinion, [holding] that release into the general prison population constitutes a break in custody. I do not join the Court's decision to extend the presumption of involuntariness established in *Edwards v. Arizona*, [for] 14 days after custody ends.

It is not apparent to me that the presumption of involuntariness the Court recognized in *Edwards* is justifiable even in the custodial setting to which *Edwards* applies it. Accordingly, I would not extend the *Edwards* rule "beyond the circumstances present in *Edwards* itself." But even if one believes that the Court is obliged to apply *Edwards* to any case involving continuing custody, the Court's opinion today goes well beyond that. It extends the presumption of involuntariness *Edwards* applies in custodial settings to interrogations that occur after custody ends.

The Court concedes that this extension, like the *Edwards* presumption itself, is not constitutionally required. The Court nevertheless defends the extension as a judicially created prophylaxis against compelled confessions. Even if one accepts that such prophylaxis is both permissible generally and advisable for some period following a break in custody,[1] the Court's 14-day rule fails to satisfy the criteria our precedents establish for the judicial creation of such a safeguard.

Our precedents insist that judicially created prophylactic rules like those in *Edwards* and *Miranda* maintain "the closest possible fit" between the rule and the Fifth Amendment interests they seek to protect. *United States v. Patane* [p. 520] (plurality opinion). The Court's 14-day rule does not satisfy this test. The Court relates its 14-day rule to the Fifth Amendment simply by asserting that 14 days between release and recapture should provide "plenty of time for the suspect [to] shake off any residual coercive effects of his prior custody."

This *ipse dixit* does not explain why extending the *Edwards* presumption for 14 days following a break in custody—as opposed to 0, 10, or 100 days—provides the "closest possible fit" with the Self-Incrimination Clause * * *. Nor does it explain how the benefits of a prophylactic 14-day rule (either on its own terms or compared with other possible rules) "outweigh its costs" (which would include the loss of law enforcement information as well as the exclusion of confessions that are in fact voluntary).

To be sure, the Court's rule has the benefit of providing a bright line. But bright-line rules are not necessary to prevent Fifth Amendment violations, as the Court has made clear when refusing to adopt such rules in cases involving other *Miranda* rights. See, *e.g.*, *Michigan v. Mosley* [p. 455]. And an otherwise arbitrary

---

[1] At a minimum the latter proposition is questionable. I concede that some police officers might badger a suspect during a subsequent interrogation after a break in custody, or might use catch-and-release tactics to suggest they will not take no for an answer. But if a suspect reenters custody after being questioned and released, he need only invoke his right to counsel to ensure *Edwards'* protection for the duration of the subsequent detention. And, if law enforcement officers repeatedly release and recapture a suspect to wear down his will—such that his participation in a subsequent interrogation is no longer truly voluntary—the "high standar[d] of proof for the waiver of constitutional rights * * *" will protect against the admission of the suspect's statement in court. * * *

rule is not justifiable merely because it gives clear instruction to law enforcement officers.

As the Court concedes, "clarity and certainty are not goals in themselves. They are valuable only when they reasonably further the achievement of some substantive end—here, the exclusion of compelled confessions" that the Fifth Amendment prohibits. The Court's arbitrary 14-day rule fails this test, even under the relatively permissive criteria set forth in our precedents. Accordingly, I do not join that portion of the Court's opinion.

JUSTICE STEVENS, concurring in the judgment.

While I agree that the presumption from *Edwards* is not "eternal" and does not mandate suppression of Shatzer's statement made after a 2½-year break in custody, I do not agree with the Court's newly announced rule: that *Edwards always* ceases to apply when there is a 14-day break in custody.

In conducting its "cost-benefit" analysis, the Court demeans *Edwards* as a " 'second layer' " of "judicially prescribed prophylaxis." [The] source of the holdings in the long line of cases that include both *Edwards* and *Miranda*, however, is the Fifth Amendment protection against compelled self-incrimination applied to the "compulsion inherent in custodial" interrogation, *Miranda* and the "significan[ce]" of "the assertion of the right to counsel," *Edwards*. The Court's analysis today is insufficiently sensitive to the concerns that motivated the *Edwards* line of cases.

The most troubling aspect of the Court's time-based rule is that it disregards the compulsion caused by a second (or third, or fourth) interrogation of an indigent suspect who was told that if he requests a lawyer, one will be provided for him. When police tell an indigent suspect that he has the right to an attorney, that he is not required to speak without an attorney present, and that an attorney will be provided to him at no cost before questioning, the police have made a significant promise. If they cease questioning and then reinterrogate the suspect 14 days later without providing him with a lawyer, the suspect is likely to feel that the police lied to him and that he really does not have any right to a lawyer.[2]

When officers informed Shatzer of his rights during the first interrogation, they presumably informed him that if he requested an attorney, one would be appointed for him before he was asked any further questions. But if an indigent suspect requests a lawyer, "any further interrogation" (even 14 days later) "without counsel having been provided will surely exacerbate whatever compulsion to speak the suspect may be feeling," *Roberson*. When police have not honored an earlier commitment to provide a detainee with a lawyer, the detainee likely will

---

[2]   The Court states that this argument rests on a "fallacy" because "we are not talking about 'reinterrogating' the suspect; we are talking about asking his permission to be interrogated." Because, however, a suspect always has the right to remain silent, this is a distinction without a difference: Any time that the police interrogate or reinterrogate, and read a suspect his *Miranda* rights, the suspect may decline to speak. And if this is a "fallacy," it is the same "fallacy" upon which this Court has relied in the *Edwards* line of cases that held that police may not continue to interrogate a suspect who has requested a lawyer: Police may not continue to ask such a suspect whether they may interrogate him until that suspect has a lawyer present. The Court's apparent belief that this is a "fallacy" only underscores my concern that its analysis is insufficiently sensitive to the concerns that motivated the *Edwards* line of cases.

"understan[d] his (expressed) wishes to have been ignored" and "may well see further objection as futile and confession (true or not) as the only way to end his interrogation." * * * Simply giving a "fresh se[t] of *Miranda* warnings" will not " 'reassure' a suspect who has been denied the counsel he has clearly requested that his rights have remained untrammeled."

The Court never explains why its rule cannot depend on, in addition to a break in custody and passage of time, a concrete event or state of affairs, such as the police having honored their commitment to provide counsel. Instead, the Court simply decides to create a time-based rule, and in so doing, disregards much of the analysis upon which *Edwards* and subsequent decisions were based. [The Court] ignores that when a suspect asks for counsel, until his request is answered, there are still the same "inherently compelling" pressures of custodial interrogation on which the *Miranda* line of cases is based and that the concern about compulsion is especially serious for a detainee who has requested a lawyer, an act that signals his "inability to cope with the pressures of custodial interrogation."

Instead of deferring to these well-settled understandings of the *Edwards* rule, the Court engages in its own speculation that a 14-day break in custody eliminates the compulsion that animated *Edwards*. But its opinion gives no strong basis for believing that this is the case.[7] A 14-day break in custody does not eliminate the rationale for the initial *Edwards* rule: The detainee has been told that he may remain silent and speak only through a lawyer and that if he cannot afford an attorney, one will be provided for him. He has asked for a lawyer. He does not have one. He is in custody. And police are still questioning him. A 14-day break in custody does not change the fact that custodial interrogation is inherently compelling. It is unlikely to change the fact that a detainee "considers himself unable to deal with the pressures of custodial interrogation without legal assistance." And in some instances, a 14-day break in custody may make matters worse[9] "[w]hen a suspect understands his (expressed) wishes to have been ignored" and thus "may well see further objection as futile and confession (true or not) as the only way to end his interrogation."

The Court ignores these understandings from the *Edwards* line of cases and instead speculates that if a suspect is reinterrogated and eventually talks, it must be that "further deliberation in familiar surroundings has caused him to believe (rightly or wrongly) that cooperating with the investigation is in his interest." But it is not apparent why that is the case. The answer, we are told, is that once a suspect has been out of *Miranda* custody for 14 days, "[h]e has likely been able to

---

[7]   Today's decision, moreover, offers no reason for its 14-day time period. To be sure, it may be difficult to marshal conclusive evidence when setting an arbitrary time period. But in light of the basis for *Edwards*, we should tread carefully. [Instead,] the only reason for choosing a 14-day time period, the Court tells us, is that "[i]t seems to us that period is 14 days." *Ante*, at 11 [p. 498]. That time period is "plenty of time for the suspect to get reacclimated to his normal life, to consult with friends and counsel, and to shake off any residual coercive effects of his prior custody." But the Court gives no reason for that speculation, which may well prove inaccurate in many circumstances.

[9]   The compulsion is heightened by the fact that "[t]he uncertainty of fate that being released from custody and then reapprehended entails is, in some circumstances, more coercive than continual custody." Strauss, *Reinterrogation*, 22 Hastings Const. L. Q. 359, 390 (1995).

seek advice from an attorney, family members, and friends." This speculation, however, is overconfident and only questionably relevant. As a factual matter, we do not know whether the defendant has been able to seek advice: First of all, suspects are told that if they cannot afford a lawyer, one will be provided for them. Yet under the majority's rule, an indigent suspect who took the police at their word when he asked for a lawyer will nonetheless be assumed to have "been able to seek advice from an attorney." Second, even suspects who are not indigent cannot necessarily access legal advice (or social advice as the Court presumes) within 14 days. Third, suspects may not realize that they *need* to seek advice from an attorney. Unless police warn suspects that the interrogation will resume in 14 days, why contact a lawyer? When a suspect is let go, he may assume that the police were satisfied. In any event, it is not apparent why interim advice matters.[11] In *Minnick* we held that it is not sufficient that a detainee happened to speak at some point with a lawyer. [If] the actual interim advice of an attorney is not sufficient, the hypothetical, interim advice of "an attorney, family members, and friends," is not enough.

The many problems with the Court's new rule are exacerbated in the very situation in this case: a suspect who is in prison. Even if, as the Court assumes, a trip to one's home significantly changes the *Edwards* calculus, a trip to one's prison cell is not the same. A prisoner's freedom is severely limited, and his entire life remains subject to government control. Such an environment is not conducive to "shak[ing] off any residual coercive effects of his prior custody." Nor can a prisoner easily "seek advice from an attorney, family members, and friends," especially not within 14 days; prisoners are frequently subject to restrictions on communications. Nor, in most cases, can he live comfortably knowing that he cannot be badgered by police; prison is not like a normal situation in which a suspect "is in control, and need only shut his door or walk away to avoid police badgering." Indeed, for a person whose every move is controlled by the State, it is likely that "his sense of dependence on, and trust in, counsel as the guardian of his interests in dealing with government officials intensified."[13] * * * The Court ignores these realities of prison, and instead rests its argument on the supposition that a prisoner's "detention [is] relatively disconnected from their prior unwillingness to cooperate in an investigation." But that is not necessarily the case. Prisoners are uniquely vulnerable to the officials who control every aspect of their lives; prison guards may not look kindly upon a prisoner who refuses to cooperate with police. And cooperation frequently is relevant to whether the prisoner can obtain parole. Moreover, even if it is true as a factual matter that a prisoner's fate is not controlled by the police who come to interrogate him, how is the prisoner supposed to know that? As the Court itself admits, compulsion is likely when a suspect's "captors appear to control [his] fate." [But] when a guard informs a suspect that he must go

---

[11] It is important to distinguish this from the point that I make above about indigent suspects. If the police promise to provide a lawyer and never do so, it sends a message to the suspect that the police have lied and that the rights read to him are hollow. But the mere fact that a suspect consulted a lawyer does not itself reduce the compulsion when police reinterrogate him.

[13] Prison also presents a troubling set of incentives for police. First, because investigators know that their suspect is also a prisoner, there is no need formally to place him under arrest. Thus, police generally can interview prisoners even without probable cause to hold them.

speak with police, it will "appear" to the prisoner that the guard and police are not independent. "Questioning by captors, who *appear* to control the suspect's fate, may create mutually reinforcing pressures that the Court has assumed will weaken the suspect's will."[14]

Because, at the very least, we do not know whether Shatzer could obtain a lawyer, and thus would have felt that police had lied about providing one, I cannot join the Court's opinion. I concur in today's judgment, however, on another ground: Even if Shatzer could not consult a lawyer and the police never provided him one, the 2½-year break in custody is a basis for treating the second interrogation as no more coercive than the first. Neither a break in custody nor the passage of time has an inherent, curative power. But certain things change over time. An indigent suspect who took police at their word that they would provide an attorney probably will feel that he has "been denied the counsel he has clearly requested" when police begin to question him, without a lawyer, only 14 days later. But, when a suspect has been left alone for a significant period of time, he is not as likely to draw such conclusions when the police interrogate him again. [In] the case before us [the] suspect was returned to the general prison population for 2½ years. I am convinced that this period of time is sufficient. I therefore concur in the judgment.

---

[14] The Court attempts to distinguish detention in prison from the "paradigm *Edwards* case," but it is not clear why that is so. The difference cannot be simply that convicted prisoners' "detention [is] relatively disconnected from their prior unwillingness to cooperate in an investigation," because in many instances of pretrial custody, the custody will continue regardless of whether a detainee answers questions. Take *Roberson* for example. Roberson was arrested and being held for one crime when, days later, a different officer interrogated him about a different crime. Regardless of whether he cooperated with the second investigation, he was still being held for the first crime. Yet under the Court's analysis, had Roberson been held long enough that he had become "accustomed" to the detention facility, there would have been a break in custody between each interrogation. Thus, despite the fact that coercive pressures "may increase as custody is prolonged," the real problem in *Roberson* may have been that the police did not leave him sitting in jail for long enough.

This problem of pretrial custody also highlights a tension with the Court's decision last Term in *Montejo v. Louisiana*. [p. 506]. In *Montejo*, the Court overturned *Michigan v. Jackson*, which had protected an accused's Sixth Amendment right to counsel by "forbidding police to initiate interrogation of a criminal defendant once he has requested counsel at an arraignment or similar proceeding." In so doing, the Court emphasized that because the *Edwards* "regime suffices to protect the integrity of 'a suspect's voluntary choice not to speak outside his lawyer's presence,' before his arraignment, it is hard to see why it would not also suffice to protect that same choice after arraignment." But typically, after arraignment, defendants are released on bail or placed in detention facilities, both of which, according to the majority's logic, sometimes constitute breaks in custody. How then, under the Court's decision today, will *Edwards* serve the role that the Court placed on it in *Montejo*?

6. *May a police officer initiate counselless questioning of a formally charged defendant who has accepted the appointment of an attorney?*

MONTEJO V. LOUISIANA

556 U.S. 778, 129 S.Ct. 2079, 173 L.Ed.2d 955 (2009).

JUSTICE SCALIA delivered the opinion of the Court.

We consider in this case the scope and continued viability of the rule announced by this Court in *Michigan v. Jackson*, 475 U.S. 625 (1986), forbidding police to initiate interrogation of a criminal defendant once he has requested counsel at an arraignment or similar proceeding.

[Petitioner Montejo, a murder suspect, waived his *Miranda* rights and was interrogated at the sheriff's office on September 6 and the morning of September 7. Three days later he was brought before a judge for what is known as a "72-hour hearing"—what the Supreme Court described as a "preliminary hearing required under state law." At this hearing the judge ordered that the Office of Indigent Defender be appointed to represent the defendant.

[Later that same day, two police detectives visited petitioner back at the prison and requested that he accompany them on an excursion to locate the murder weapon (which Montejo had earlier indicated he had thrown into a lake). He was again read his *Miranda* rights and agreed to accompany the detectives. During the trip, he wrote an inculpatory letter of apology to the victim's widow. Montejo did not meet his court-appointed attorney until his return.]

[At trial, the letter of apology was admitted over defense objection. Montejo was convicted of first-degree murder and sentenced to death. The Louisiana Supreme Court affirmed the conviction, rejecting petitioner's *Jackson* arguments on the ground that *Jackson*'s protection is not triggered unless and until the defendant has actually requested a lawyer or otherwise asserted his right to counsel. In the *Jackson* case, when brought before a magistrate during a pretrial appearance, the defendants had requested that counsel be appointed for them because they were indigent. In *Montejo*, however, petitioner had made no such request or assertion. He had simply stood mute. As the state supreme court saw it, therefore, the only issue presented in *Montejo* was whether petitioner had validly waived his right to have counsel present during the interaction with the police. Since Montejo had been read his *Miranda* rights and waived them, he had.]

[The rule adopted by the Louisiana Supreme Court] would apply well enough in States [such as Michigan, where the *Jackson* case arose,] that require indigent defendant formally to request counsel before any appointment is made, which usually occurs after the court has informed him that he will receive counsel if he asks for it. [But in] many States [the] appointment of counsel is automatic upon a finding of indigency, and in a number of others, appointment can be made either upon the defendant's request or *sua sponte* by the court. * * * Nothing in our *Jackson* opinion indicates whether we were then aware that not all States require that a defendant affirmatively request counsel before one is appointed; and of course we had no occasion there to decide how the rule we announced would apply to these other States.

[The] central distinction [the Louisiana Supreme Court] draws—between defendants who "assert" their right to counsel and those who do not—is exceedingly hazy when applied to States that appoint counsel absent request from the defendant. [To] the extent that the Louisiana Supreme Court's rule also permits a defendant to trigger *Jackson* through the "acceptance" of counsel, that notion is even more mysterious: How does one affirmatively accept counsel appointed by court order?

[In] practice, judicial application of the Louisiana rule in States that do not require a defendant to make a request for counsel could take either of two paths. Courts might ask on a case-by-case basis whether a defendant has somehow invoked his right to counsel, looking to his conduct at the preliminary hearing— his statements and gestures—and the totality of the circumstances. Or, courts might simply determine as a categorical matter that defendants in these States— over half of those in the Union—simply have no opportunity to assert their right to counsel at the hearing and are therefore out of luck.

Neither approach is desirable. The former would be particularly impractical in light of the fact [that] preliminary hearings are often rushed, and are frequently not recorded or transcribed. [The] second possible course fares no better, for it would achieve clarity and certainty only at the expense of introducing arbitrary distinctions: Defendants in States that automatically appoint counsel would have no opportunity to invoke their rights and trigger *Jackson*, while those in other States, effectively instructed by the court to request counsel, would be lucky winners. That sort of hollow formalism is out of place in a doctrine that purports to serve as a practical safeguard for defendants' rights.

But if the Louisiana Supreme Court's application of *Jackson* is unsound as a practical matter, then Montejo's solution is untenable as a theoretical and doctrinal matter. Under his approach, once a defendant is *represented* by counsel, police may not initiate any further interrogation. Such a rule would be entirely untethered from the original rationale of *Jackson*.

[The] *only* question raised by this case, and the only one addressed by the *Jackson* rule, is whether courts must *presume* that [a waiver of the Sixth Amendment right to counsel] is invalid under certain circumstances. We created such a presumption in *Jackson* by analogy to a similar prophylactic rule established to protect the Fifth Amendment based *Miranda* right to have counsel present at any custodial interrogation. *Edwards v. Arizona* [p. 495] decided that once "an accused has invoked his right to have counsel present during custodial interrogation [he] is not subject to further interrogation by the authorities until counsel has been made available," unless he initiates the contact.

The *Edwards* rule is "designed to prevent police from badgering a defendant into waiving his previously asserted *Miranda* rights." It does this by presuming his postassertion statements to be involuntary, "even where the suspect executes a waiver and his statements would be considered voluntary under traditional standards." This prophylactic rule thus "protect[s] a suspect's voluntary choice not to speak outside his lawyer's presence."

Jackson represented a "wholesale importation of the *Edwards* rule into the Sixth Amendment." [The] dissent presents us with a revisionist view of *Jackson*. The defendants' *request* for counsel, it contends, was important only because it proved that counsel *had been appointed*. Such a non sequitur (nowhere alluded to in the case) hardly needs rebuttal. Proceeding from this fanciful premise, the dissent claims that the decision actually established "a rule designed to safeguard a defendant's right to rely on the assistance of counsel," not one "designed to prevent police badgering." To safeguard the right to assistance of counsel from *what*? From a knowing and voluntary waiver by the defendant himself? [The] antibadgering rationale is the only way to make sense of *Jackson*'s repeated citations of *Edwards*, and the only way to reconcile the opinion with our waiver jurisprudence.

With this understanding of what *Jackson* stands for and whence it came, it should be clear that Montejo's interpretation of that decision—that no *represented* defendant can ever be approached by the State and asked to consent to interrogation—is off the mark. When a court appoints counsel for an indigent defendant in the absence of any request on his part, there is no basis for a presumption that any subsequent waiver of the right to counsel will be involuntary. * * * *Edwards* and *Jackson* are meant to prevent police from badgering defendants into changing their minds about their rights, but a defendant who never asked for counsel has not yet made up his mind in the first instance. * * *

[The] question in *Jackson* [was] not whether respondents were entitled to counsel (they unquestionably were), but "whether respondents validly waived their right to counsel," and even if it is reasonable to presume from a defendant's *request* for counsel that any subsequent waiver of the right was coerced, no such presumption can seriously be entertained when a lawyer was merely "secured" on the defendant's behalf, by the State itself, as a matter of course. Of course, reading the dissent's analysis, one would have no idea that Montejo executed any waiver at all.

In practice, Montejo's rule would prevent police-initiated interrogation entirely once the Sixth Amendment right attaches, at least in those States that appoint counsel promptly without request from the defendant. * * *

Montejo's rule appears to have its theoretical roots in codes of legal ethics, not the Sixth Amendment. The American Bar Association's Model Rules of Professional Conduct (which nearly all States have adopted into law in whole or in part) mandate that "a lawyer shall not communicate about the subject of [a] representation with a party the lawyer knows to be represented by another lawyer in the matter, unless the lawyer has the consent of the other lawyer or is authorized to do so by law or a court order." Model Rule 4.2 (2008). But the Constitution does not codify the ABA's Model Rules, and does not make investigating police officers lawyers. Montejo's proposed rule is both broader and narrower than the Model Rule. Broader, because Montejo would apply it to all agents of the State, including the detectives who interrogated him, while the ethical rule governs only lawyers.

And narrower, because he agrees that if a defendant initiates contact with the police, they may talk freely—whereas a lawyer could be sanctioned for interviewing a represented party even if that party "initiates" the communication and consents to the interview. Model Rule 4.2, Comment 3.

[On] the one hand, requiring an initial "invocation" of the right to counsel in order to trigger the *Jackson* presumption is consistent with the theory of that decision, but [would] be unworkable in more than half the States of the Union. On the other hand, eliminating the invocation requirement would render the rule easy to apply but depart fundamentally from the *Jackson* rationale.

We do not think that *stare decisis* requires us to expand significantly the holding of a prior decision—fundamentally revising its theoretical basis in the process—in order to cure its practical deficiencies. To the contrary, the fact that a decision has proved "unworkable" is a traditional ground for overruling it. * * *

When this Court creates a prophylactic rule in order to protect a constitutional right, the relevant "reasoning" is the weighing of the rule's benefits against its costs. * * * We think that the marginal benefits of *Jackson* (viz., the number of confessions obtained coercively that are suppressed by its bright-line rule and would otherwise have been admitted) are dwarfed by its substantial costs (viz., hindering "society's compelling interest in finding, convicting, and punishing those who violate the law").

What does the *Jackson* rule actually achieve by way of preventing unconstitutional conduct? Recall that the purpose of the rule is to preclude the State from badgering defendants into waiving their previously asserted rights. The effect of this badgering might be to coerce a waiver, which would render the subsequent interrogation a violation of the Sixth Amendment. Even though involuntary waivers are invalid even apart from *Jackson*, mistakes are of course possible when courts conduct case-by-case voluntariness review. A bright-line rule like that adopted in *Jackson* ensures that no fruits of interrogations made possible by badgering-induced involuntary waivers are ever erroneously admitted at trial.

But without *Jackson*, how many would be? The answer is few if any. The principal reason is that the Court has already taken substantial other, overlapping measures toward the same end. Under *Miranda*'s prophylactic protection of the right against compelled self-incrimination, any suspect subject to custodial interrogation has the right to have a lawyer present if he so requests, and to be advised of that right. Under *Edwards'* prophylactic protection of the *Miranda* right, once such a defendant "has invoked his right to have counsel present," interrogation must stop. And under *Minnick*'s prophylactic protection of the *Edwards* right, no subsequent interrogation may take place until counsel is present, "whether or not the accused has consulted with his attorney."

These three layers of prophylaxis are sufficient. * * * It is true [that] the doctrine established by *Miranda* and *Edwards* is designed to protect Fifth Amendment, not Sixth Amendment, rights. But that is irrelevant. What matters is that these cases, like *Jackson*, protect the right to have counsel during custodial interrogation—which right happens to be guaranteed (once the adversary judicial process has begun) by *two* sources of law. Since the right under both sources is waived using the same procedure, doctrines ensuring voluntariness of the Fifth Amendment waiver simultaneously ensure the voluntariness of the Sixth Amendment waiver.

Montejo also correctly observes that the *Miranda-Edwards* regime is narrower than *Jackson* in one respect: The former applies only in the context of custodial interrogation. If the defendant is not in custody then those decisions do not apply; nor do they govern other, noninterrogative types of interactions between the defendant and the State (like pretrial lineups). However, those uncovered situations are the *least* likely to pose a risk of coerced waivers. When a defendant is not in custody, he is in control, and need only shut his door or walk away to avoid police badgering. And noninterrogative interactions with the State do not involve the "inherently compelling pressures," *Miranda*, that one might reasonably fear could lead to involuntary waivers.

Jackson was policy driven, and if that policy is being adequately served through other means, there is no reason to retain its rule. *Miranda* and the cases that elaborate upon it already guarantee not simply noncoercion in the traditional sense, but what Justice Harlan referred to as "voluntariness with a vengeance." There is no need to take *Jackson*'s further step of requiring voluntariness on stilts.

On the other side of the equation are the costs of adding the bright-line *Jackson* rule on top of *Edwards* and other extant protections. * * * *Jackson* not only "operates to invalidate a confession given by the free choice of suspects who have received proper advice of their *Miranda* rights but waived them nonetheless," but also deters law enforcement officers from even trying to obtain voluntary confessions. The "ready ability to obtain uncoerced confessions is not an evil but an unmitigated good." Without these confessions, crimes go unsolved and criminals unpunished. These are not negligible costs, and in our view the *Jackson* Court gave them too short shrift.

[Montejo's] principal objection to [*Jackson*'s] elimination is that the *Edwards* regime which remains will not provide an administrable rule. But this Court has praised *Edwards* precisely because it provides " 'clear and unequivocal' guidelines to the law enforcement profession." * * * Montejo expresses concern that courts will have to determine whether statements made at preliminary hearings constitute *Edwards* invocations—thus implicating all the practical problems of the Louisiana rule we discussed above. That concern is misguided. "We have in fact never held that a person can invoke his *Miranda* rights anticipatorily, in a context other than 'custodial interrogation' * * *" What matters for *Miranda* and *Edwards* is what happens when the defendant is approached for interrogation, and (if he consents) what happens during the interrogation—not what happened at any preliminary hearing.

In sum, when the marginal benefits of the *Jackson* rule are weighed against its substantial costs to the truth-seeking process and the criminal justice system, we readily conclude that the rule does not "pay its way," *United States v. Leon*. *Michigan v. Jackson* should be and now is overruled.

Although our holding means that the Louisiana Supreme Court correctly rejected Montejo's claim under *Jackson*, we think that Montejo should be given an opportunity to contend that his letter of apology should still have been suppressed under the rule of *Edwards*. If Montejo made a clear assertion of the right to counsel when the officers approached him about accompanying them on the excursion for the murder weapon, then no interrogation should have taken place unless Montejo initiated it.

[Montejo] understandably did not pursue an *Edwards* objection, because *Jackson* served as the Sixth Amendment analogy to *Edwards* and offered broader protections. Our decision today, overruling *Jackson*, changes the legal landscape and does so in part based on the protections already provided by *Edwards*. Thus we think that a remand is appropriate so that Montejo can pursue this alternative avenue for relief. * * *

We [reject] the dissent's revisionist legal analysis of the "knowing and voluntary" issue. In determining whether a Sixth Amendment waiver was knowing and voluntary, there is no reason categorically to distinguish an unrepresented defendant from a represented one. It is equally true for each that, as we held in *Patterson v. Illinois*, 487 U.S. 285 (1988) [ruling that, as a general matter, the *Miranda* warnings adequately advise an indicted, but counselless, defendant of his right to counsel, so that his waiver of this right will be considered a valid one], the *Miranda* warnings adequately inform him "of his right to have counsel present during the questioning," and make him "aware of the consequences of a decision by him to waive his Sixth Amendment rights." Somewhat surprisingly for an opinion that extols the virtues of *stare decisis*, the dissent complains that our "treatment of the waiver question rests entirely on the dubious decision in *Patterson*." The Court in *Patterson* did not consider the result dubious, nor does the Court today. * * *

JUSTICE ALITO, with whom JUSTICE KENNEDY joins, concurring. * * *

In light of [the overruling of *New York v. Belton* in *Arizona v. Gant*, p. 244], the discussion of *stare decisis* in today's dissent is surprising. The dissent in the case at hand criticizes the Court for "[a]cting on its own" in reconsidering *Jackson*. But the same was true in *Gant*, and in this case, the Court gave the parties and interested amici the opportunity to submit supplemental briefs on the issue, a step not taken in *Gant*.

JUSTICE STEVENS, with whom JUSTICE SOUTER and JUSTICE GINSBURG join, and with whom Justice BREYER joins, except for footnote 5, dissenting.

[On] its own initiative and without any evidence that the longstanding Sixth Amendment protections established in *Jackson* have caused any harm to the workings of the criminal justice system, the Court rejects *Jackson* outright on the ground that it is "untenable as a theoretical and doctrinal matter." That conclusion rests on a misinterpretation of *Jackson*'s rationale and a gross undervaluation of the rule of *stare decisis*. The police interrogation in this case clearly violated petitioner's Sixth Amendment right to counsel.

The Sixth Amendment provides that "[i]n all criminal prosecutions, the accused shall enjoy the right [to] have the Assistance of Counsel for his defence." The right to counsel attaches during the initiation of adversary judicial criminal proceedings, *Rothgery v. Gillespie County* [p. 389] (internal quotation marks omitted), and it guarantees the assistance of counsel not only during in-court proceedings but during all critical stages, including postarraignment interviews with law enforcement officers, see *Patterson*.

In *Jackson*, this Court considered whether the Sixth Amendment bars police from interrogating defendants who have requested the appointment of counsel at arraignment. Applying the presumption that such a request constitutes an invocation of the right to counsel "at every critical stage of the prosecution," we held that "a defendant who has been formally charged with a crime and who has requested appointment of counsel at his arraignment" cannot be subject to uncounseled interrogation unless he initiates "exchanges or conversations with the police."

In this case, [relying] on the fact that the defendants in *Jackson* had "requested" counsel at arraignment, the state court held that *Jackson*'s protections did not apply to Montejo because his counsel was appointed automatically; Montejo had not explicitly requested counsel or affirmatively accepted the counsel appointed to represent him before he submitted to police interrogation.

I agree with the majority's conclusion that the Louisiana Supreme Court's decision, if allowed to stand, "would lead either to an unworkable standard, or to arbitrary and anomalous distinctions between defendants in different States." Neither option is tolerable, and neither is compelled by *Jackson* itself.

[The] majority's decision to overrule *Jackson* rests on its assumption that *Jackson*'s protective rule was intended to "prevent police from badgering defendants into changing their minds about their rights," just as the rule adopted in *Edwards* was designed to prevent police from coercing unindicted suspects into revoking their requests for counsel at interrogation. Operating on that limited understanding of the purpose behind *Jackson*'s protective rule, the Court concludes that *Jackson* provides no safeguard not already secured by this Court's Fifth Amendment jurisprudence.

[The] majority's analysis flagrantly misrepresents *Jackson*'s underlying rationale and the constitutional interests the decision sought to protect. While it is true that the rule adopted in *Jackson* was patterned after the rule in *Edwards*, the *Jackson* opinion does not even mention the anti-badgering considerations that provide the basis for the Court's decision today. Instead, *Jackson* relied primarily on cases discussing the broad protections guaranteed by the Sixth Amendment right to counsel—not its Fifth Amendment counterpart. * * * Underscoring that the commencement of criminal proceedings is a decisive event that transforms a suspect into an accused within the meaning of the Sixth Amendment, we concluded that arraigned defendants are entitled to "at least as much protection" during interrogation as the Fifth Amendment affords unindicted suspects. ("[T]he *difference* between the legal basis for the rule applied in *Edwards* and the Sixth Amendment claim asserted in these cases actually provides additional support for the application of the rule in these circumstances" (emphasis added)). Thus, although the rules adopted in *Edwards* and *Jackson* are similar, *Jackson* did not rely on the reasoning of *Edwards* but remained firmly rooted in the unique protections afforded to the attorney-client relationship by the Sixth Amendment.[2]

Once *Jackson* is placed in its proper Sixth Amendment context, the majority's justifications for overruling the decision crumble. * * *

[The] Court rejects the interests of criminal defendants with the flippant observation that any who are knowledgeable enough to rely on *Jackson* are too savvy to need its protections, and casts aside the reliance interests of law enforcement on the ground that police and prosecutors remain free to employ the *Jackson* rule if it suits them. Again as a result of its mistaken understanding of the purpose behind *Jackson*'s protective rule, the Court fails to identify the real reliance interest at issue in this case: the public's interest in knowing that counsel, once secured, may be reasonably relied upon as a medium between the accused and the power of the State. That interest lies at the heart of the Sixth Amendment's guarantee, and is surely worthy of greater consideration than it is given by today's decision. * * *

Despite the fact that the rule established in *Jackson* remains relevant, well grounded in constitutional precedent, and easily administrable, the Court today rejects it sua sponte. Such a decision can only diminish the public's confidence in the reliability and fairness of our system of justice.[5] * * *

[The] Court avoids confronting the serious Sixth Amendment concerns raised by the police interrogation in this case by assuming that Montejo validly waived his Sixth Amendment rights before submitting to interrogation.[6] It does so by

---

[2]   The majority insists that protection from police badgering is the only purpose the *Jackson* rule can plausibly serve. After all, it asks, from what other evil would the rule guard? There are two obvious answers. First, most narrowly, it protects the defendant from any police-initiated interrogation without notice to his counsel, not just from "badgering" which is not necessarily a part of police questioning. Second, and of prime importance, it assures that any waiver of counsel will be valid. The assistance offered by counsel protects a defendant from surrendering his rights with an insufficient appreciation of what those rights are and how the decision to respond to interrogation might advance or compromise his exercise of those rights throughout the course of criminal proceedings. A lawyer can provide her client with advice regarding the legal and practical options available to him; the potential consequences, both good and bad, of choosing to discuss his case with police; the likely effect of such a conversation on the resolution of the charges against him; and an informed assessment of the best course of action under the circumstances. Such assistance goes far beyond mere protection against police badgering.

[5]   In his concurrence, Justice Alito assumes that my consideration of the rule of *stare decisis* in this case is at odds with the Court's recent rejection of his reliance on that doctrine in his dissent in *Arizona v. Gant*. While I agree that the reasoning in his dissent supports my position in this case, I do not agree with his characterization of our opinion in *Gant*. Contrary to his representation, the Court did not overrule our precedent in *Belton*. Rather, we affirmed the narrow interpretation of *Belton*'s holding adopted by the Arizona Supreme Court, rejecting the broader interpretation adopted by other lower courts that had been roundly criticized by judges and scholars alike. By contrast, in this case the Court flatly overrules *Jackson*—a rule that has drawn virtually no criticism—on its own initiative. The two cases are hardly comparable. If they were, and if Justice Alito meant what he said in *Gant*, I would expect him to join this opinion.

[6]   The majority leaves open the possibility that, on remand, Montejo may argue that his waiver was invalid because police falsely told him he had not been appointed counsel. While such police deception would obviously invalidate any otherwise valid waiver of Montejo's Sixth Amendment rights, Montejo has a strong argument that, given his status as a *represented* criminal

summarily concluding that "doctrines ensuring voluntariness of the Fifth Amendment waiver simultaneously ensure the voluntariness of the Sixth Amendment waiver"; thus, because Montejo was given *Miranda* warnings prior to interrogation, his waiver was presumptively valid. Ironically, while the Court faults *Jackson* for blurring the line between this Court's Fifth and Sixth Amendment jurisprudence, it commits the same error by assuming that the *Miranda* warnings given in this case, designed purely to safeguard the Fifth Amendment right against self-incrimination, were somehow adequate to protect Montejo's more robust Sixth Amendment right to counsel.

The majority's cursory treatment of the waiver question rests entirely on the dubious decision in *Patterson*, in which we addressed whether, by providing *Miranda* warnings, police had adequately advised an indicted but unrepresented defendant of his Sixth Amendment right to counsel. The majority held that "[a]s a general matter [an] accused who is admonished with the warnings prescribed [in] *Miranda*, [has] been sufficiently apprised of the nature of his Sixth Amendment rights, and of the consequences of abandoning those rights." The Court recognized, however, that "because the Sixth Amendment's protection of the attorney-client relationship [extends] beyond *Miranda*'s protection of the Fifth Amendment right to counsel, [there] will be cases where a waiver which would be valid under *Miranda* will not suffice for Sixth Amendment purposes." This is such a case.

As I observed in *Patterson*, the conclusion that *Miranda* warnings ordinarily provide a sufficient basis for a knowing waiver of the right to counsel rests on the questionable assumption that those warnings make clear to defendants the assistance a lawyer can render during post-indictment interrogation. Because *Miranda* warnings do not hint at the ways in which a lawyer might assist her client during conversations with the police, I remain convinced that the warnings prescribed in *Miranda*, while sufficient to apprise a defendant of his Fifth Amendment right to remain silent, are inadequate to inform an unrepresented, indicted defendant of his Sixth Amendment right to have a lawyer present at all critical stages of a criminal prosecution. The inadequacy of those warnings is even more obvious in the case of a *represented* defendant. By glibly assuming that that the warnings given in this case were sufficient to ensure Montejo's waiver was both knowing and voluntary, the Court conveniently avoids any comment on the actual advice Montejo received, which did not adequately inform him of his relevant Sixth Amendment rights or alert him to the possible consequences of waiving those rights.

A defendant's decision to forgo counsel's assistance and speak openly with police is a momentous one. Given the high stakes of making such a choice and the potential value of counsel's advice and mediation at that critical stage of the criminal proceedings, it is imperative that a defendant possess "a full awareness of both the nature of the right being abandoned and the consequences of the decision to abandon it." Because the administration of *Miranda* warnings was insufficient to ensure Montejo understood the Sixth Amendment right he was being asked to

---

defendant, the *Miranda* warnings given to him by police were insufficient to permit him to make a knowing waiver of his Sixth Amendment rights even absent police deception.

surrender, the record in this case provides no basis for concluding that Montejo validly waived his right to counsel, even in the absence of *Jackson*'s enhanced protections.

The Court's decision to overrule *Jackson* is unwarranted. Not only does it rest on a flawed doctrinal premise, but the dubious benefits it hopes to achieve are far outweighed by the damage it does to the rule of law and the integrity of the Sixth Amendment right to counsel. Moreover, even apart from the protections afforded by *Jackson*, the police interrogation in this case violated [petitioner's] Sixth Amendment right to counsel. * * *a

7. Questioning prompted by concern for "public safety"

NEW YORK V. QUARLES
467 U.S. 649, 104 S.Ct. 2626, 81 L.Ed.2d 550 (1984).

JUSTICE REHNQUIST delivered the opinion of the Court.

[At approximately 12:30 a.m., police apprehended respondent in the rear of a supermarket. He matched the description of the man who had just raped a woman. The woman had told the police that the rapist had just entered the supermarket and that he was carrying a gun. Apparently upon seeing Officer Kraft enter the store, respondent turned and ran toward the rear. Officer Kraft pursued him with a drawn gun and, upon regaining sight of him, ordered him to stop and put his hands over his head. Although several other officers had arrived at the scene by then, Kraft was the first to reach respondent. He frisked him and discovered he was wearing an empty shoulder holster. After handcuffing him, the officer asked where the gun was. Respondent nodded in the direction of some empty cartons and responded, "the gun is over there." At that time, emphasized the New York Court of Appeals, respondent was surrounded by four officers whose guns had been returned to their holsters because, as one testified, the situation was under control.

[The gun was not visible, but Officer Kraft reached into one of the cartons and retrieved a loaded revolver. Respondent was then formally placed under arrest and advised of his *Miranda* rights. Respondent waived his rights. In response to questions, he then stated that he owned the revolver and had purchased it in Miami.

[In the subsequent prosecution of respondent for criminal possession of a weapon (the record does not reveal why the state failed to pursue the rape charge), the New York courts suppressed the statement "the gun is over there" as well as the gun itself because they had been obtained in violation of respondent's *Miranda* rights. Respondent's statements about his ownership of the gun and the place of purchase were also excluded as having been fatally tainted by the seizure of the gun and the prewarning response as to its location.]

---

a In a short separate dissenting opinion, Justice Breyer joined Justice Stevens' dissent "except for footnote 5." Justice Breyer believed that "the principles of *stare decisis* * * * bind the Court here." He noted that he had "reached a similar conclusion in *Arizona v. Gant*," fn. c, p. 250, and in several other recent cases.

* * * We conclude that under the circumstances involved in this case, overriding considerations of public safety justify the officer's failure to provide *Miranda* warnings before he asked questions devoted to locating the abandoned weapon. * * *

The Fifth Amendment itself does not prohibit all incriminating admissions; "[a]bsent some officially *coerced* self-accusation, the Fifth Amendment privilege is not violated by even the most damning admissions." *United States v. Washington*, 431 U.S. 181 (1977) (emphasis added).[a]

The *Miranda* Court, however, presumed that interrogation in certain custodial circumstances is inherently coercive and held that statements made under those circumstances are inadmissible unless the suspect is specifically informed of his *Miranda* rights and freely decides to forgo those rights. The prophylactic *Miranda* warnings therefore are "not themselves rights protected by the Constitution but [are] instead measures to insure that the right against compulsory self-incrimination [is] protected." *Michigan v. Tucker*. * * *

In this case we have before us no claim that respondent's statements were actually compelled by police conduct which overcame his will to resist. Thus the only issue before us is whether Officer Kraft was justified in failing to make available to respondent the procedural safeguards associated with the privilege against compulsory self-incrimination since *Miranda*.

The New York Court of Appeals was undoubtedly correct in deciding that the facts of this case come within the ambit of the *Miranda* decision as we have subsequently interpreted it. [As] the New York Court of Appeals observed, [when the questioning at issue took place] there was nothing to suggest that any of the officers were any longer concerned for their own physical safety. The New York Court of Appeals' majority declined to express an opinion as to whether there might be an exception to the *Miranda* rule if the police had been acting to protect the public, because the lower courts in New York had made no factual determination that the police had acted with that motive.

We hold that on these facts there is a "public safety" exception to the requirement that *Miranda* warnings be given before a suspect's answers may be admitted into evidence, and that the availability of that exception does not depend upon the motivation of the individual officers involved. In a kaleidoscopic situation such as the one confronting these officers, where spontaneity rather than adherence to a police manual is necessarily the order of the day, the application of the exception which we recognize today should not be made to depend on *post hoc* findings at a suppression hearing concerning the subjective motivation of the

---

[a] *Washington* held that a person appearing before a grand jury need not be warned that he is a target of the grand jury investigation. Defendant had been given *Miranda* warnings prior to any questioning. He replied that he understood these rights and was prepared to answer questions relating to the crime being investigated. He contended, however that his grand jury testimony should be suppressed on the ground that his privilege against self-incrimination had been violated by the prosecutor's failure to advise him that he was a potential defendant. In rejecting this argument the Court noted that because a witness' target status "neither enlarges nor diminishes the constitutional protection against compelled self-incrimination, potential defendant warnings add nothing of value to protection of Fifth Amendment rights." See also fn. c, p. 631.

arresting officer. Undoubtedly most police officers, if placed in Officer Kraft's position, would act out of a host of different, instinctive, and largely unverifiable motives—their own safety, the safety of others, and perhaps as well the desire to obtain incriminating evidence from the suspect.

Whatever the motivation of individual officers in such a situation, we do not believe that the doctrinal underpinnings of *Miranda* require that it be applied in all its rigor to a situation in which police officers ask questions reasonably prompted by a concern for the public safety.

[The] police in this case, in the very act of apprehending a suspect, were confronted with the immediate necessity of ascertaining the whereabouts of a gun which they had every reason to believe the suspect had just removed from his empty holster and discarded in the supermarket. So long as the gun was concealed somewhere in the supermarket, with its actual whereabouts unknown, it obviously posed more than one danger to the public safety: an accomplice might make use of it, a customer or employee might later come upon it.

In such a situation, if the police are required to recite the familiar *Miranda* warnings before asking the whereabouts of the gun, suspects in Quarles' position might well be deterred from responding. Procedural safeguards which deter a suspect from responding were deemed acceptable in *Miranda* in order to protect the Fifth Amendment privilege; when the primary social cost of those added protections is the possibility of fewer convictions, the *Miranda* majority was willing to bear that cost. Here, had *Miranda* warnings deterred Quarles from responding to Officer Kraft's question about the whereabouts of the gun, the cost would have been something more than merely the failure to obtain evidence useful in convicting Quarles. Officer Kraft needed an answer to his question not simply to make his case against Quarles but to insure that further danger to the public did not result from the concealment of the gun in a public area.

We conclude that the need for answers to questions in a situation posing a threat to the public safety outweighs the need for the prophylactic rule protecting the Fifth Amendment's privilege against self-incrimination. We decline to place officers such as Officer Kraft in the untenable position of having to consider, often in a matter of seconds, whether it best serves society for them to ask the necessary questions without the *Miranda* warnings and render whatever probative evidence they uncover inadmissible, or for them to give the warnings in order to preserve the admissibility of evidence they might uncover but possibly damage or destroy their ability to obtain that evidence and neutralize the volatile situation confronting them.[7] * * *

---

[7] The dissent argues that a public safety exception to *Miranda* is unnecessary because in every case an officer can simply ask the necessary questions to protect himself or the public, and then the prosecution can decline to introduce any incriminating responses at a subsequent trial. But absent actual coercion by the officer, there is no constitutional imperative requiring the exclusion of the evidence that results from police inquiry of this kind; and we do not believe that the doctrinal underpinnings of *Miranda* require us to exclude the evidence, thus penalizing officers for asking the very questions which are the most crucial to their efforts to protect themselves and the public.

We hold that the Court of Appeals in this case erred in excluding the statement, "the gun is over there," and the gun because of the officer's failure to read respondent his *Miranda* rights before attempting to locate the weapon. Accordingly we hold that it also erred in excluding the subsequent statements as illegal fruits of a *Miranda* violation.[9] * * *

JUSTICE O'CONNOR, concurring in part in the judgment and dissenting in part. * * *

In my view, a "public safety" exception unnecessarily blurs the edges of the clear line heretofore established and makes *Miranda's* requirements more difficult to understand. In some cases, police will benefit because a reviewing court will find that an exigency excused their failure to administer the required warnings. But in other cases, police will suffer because, though they thought an exigency excused their noncompliance, a reviewing court will view the "objective" circumstances differently and require exclusion of admissions thereby obtained. The end result will be a finespun new doctrine on public safety exigencies incident to custodial interrogation, complete with the hair-splitting distinctions that currently plague our Fourth Amendment jurisprudence. * * *

The justification the Court provides for upsetting the equilibrium that has finally been achieved—that police cannot and should not balance considerations of public safety against the individual's interest in avoiding compulsory testimonial self-incrimination—really misses the critical question to be decided. *Miranda* has never been read to prohibit the police from asking questions to secure the public safety. Rather, the critical question *Miranda* addresses is who shall bear the cost of securing the public safety when such questions are asked and answered: the defendant or the State. *Miranda,* for better or worse, found the resolution of that question implicit in the prohibition against compulsory self-incrimination and placed the burden on the State. When police ask custodial questions without administering the required warnings, *Miranda* quite clearly requires that the answers received be presumed compelled and that they be excluded from evidence at trial. * * *[c]

---

[9]   Because we hold that there is no violation of *Miranda* in this case, we have no occasion to [decide whether] the gun is admissible either because it is nontestimonial or because the police would inevitably have discovered it absent their questioning.

[In *Nix v. Williams* (Williams II), 467 U.S. 431 (1984), the Court ruled that the "fruit of the poisonous tree" doctrine did not bar the use of evidence derived from a constitutional violation if such evidence would "ultimately" or "inevitably" have been discovered as a result of lawful police investigatory work without regard to that violation. For more discussion of that case, *see supra* Chapter 4, p. 364.]

[c]   Although Justice O'Connor would suppress Quarles' initial statement, "the gun is over there," she would not exclude the gun itself because "nothing in *Miranda* or the privilege [against compelled self-incrimination] itself requires exclusion of nontestimonial evidence derived from informal custodial interrogation." "Only the introduction of a defendant's own *testimony*," maintained Justice O'Connor, "is proscribed by the Fifth Amendment's mandate that no person 'shall be compelled in any criminal case to be a witness against himself.' That mandate does not protect an accused from being compelled to surrender *nontestimonial* evidence against himself."

For further discussion of the application (or nonapplication) of the "fruit of the poisonous tree" doctrine to *Miranda* violations, see *United States v. Patane*, and *Missouri v. Seibert*, the next two cases set forth in this section.

JUSTICE MARSHALL, with whom JUSTICE BRENNAN and JUSTICE STEVENS join, dissenting * * *.

The majority's entire analysis rests on the factual assumption that the public was at risk during Quarles' interrogation. This assumption is completely in conflict with the facts as found by New York's highest court. Before the interrogation began, Quarles had been "reduced to a condition of physical powerlessness." Contrary to the majority's speculations, Quarles was not believed to have, nor did he in fact have, an accomplice to come to his rescue. When the questioning began, the arresting officers were sufficiently confident of their safety to put away their guns.

[The] New York court's conclusion that neither Quarles nor his missing gun posed a threat to the public's safety is amply supported by the evidence presented at the suppression hearing. * * * Although the supermarket was open to the public, Quarles' arrest took place during the middle of the night when the store was apparently deserted except for the clerks at the checkout counter. The police could easily have cordoned off the store and searched for the missing gun. Had they done so, they would have found the gun forthwith. [As] the State acknowledged before the New York Court of Appeals: "After Officer Kraft had handcuffed and frisked the defendant in the supermarket, *he knew with a high degree of certainty that the defendant's gun was within the immediate vicinity of the encounter.* He undoubtedly would have searched for it in the carton a few feet away without the defendant having looked in that direction and saying that it was there." (Emphasis added.) * * *

Whether society would be better off if the police warned suspects of their rights before beginning an interrogation or whether the advantages of giving such warnings would outweigh their costs did not inform the *Miranda* decision. On the contrary, the *Miranda* Court was concerned with the proscriptions of the Fifth Amendment, and, in particular, whether the Self-Incrimination Clause permits the government to prosecute individuals based on statements made in the course of custodial interrogations.

[In] fashioning its "public-safety" exception to *Miranda,* the majority makes no attempt to deal with the constitutional presumption established by that case. The majority does not argue that police questioning about issues of public safety is any less coercive than custodial interrogations into other matters. The majority's only contention is that police officers could more easily protect the public if *Miranda* did not apply to custodial interrogations concerning the public's safety. But *Miranda* was not a decision about public safety; it was a decision about coerced confessions. Without establishing that interrogations concerning the public's safety are less likely to be coercive than other interrogations, the majority cannot endorse the "public-safety" exception and remain faithful to the logic of *Miranda.*

[The] irony of the majority's decision is that the public's safety can be perfectly well protected without abridging the Fifth Amendment. If a bomb is about to explode or the public is otherwise imminently imperiled, the police are free to interrogate suspects without advising them of their constitutional rights. * * * If trickery is necessary to protect the public, then the police may trick a suspect into confessing. While the Fourteenth Amendment sets limits on such behavior, nothing in the Fifth Amendment or our decision in *Miranda* proscribes this sort of emergency questioning. All the Fifth Amendment forbids is the introduction of coerced statements at trial.

* * * [The] policies underlying the Fifth Amendment's privilege against self-incrimination are not diminished simply because testimony is compelled to protect the public's safety. The majority should not be permitted to elude the Amendment's absolute prohibition simply by calculating special costs that arise when the public's safety is at issue. Indeed, were constitutional adjudication always conducted in such an *ad hoc* manner, the Bill of Rights would be a most unreliable protector of individual liberties.

   8.   Must physical evidence derived from a failure to give the Miranda warnings be excluded? Does an initial failure to advise a suspect of her rights bar subsequent admissions by the suspect after she has been fully advised of her rights? Does the "fruit of the poisonous tree" doctrine apply to violations of the Miranda rules?

UNITED STATES V. PATANE
542 U.S. 630, 124 S.Ct. 2620, 159 L.Ed.2d 667 (2004).

JUSTICE THOMAS announced the judgment of the Court and delivered an opinion, in which THE CHIEF JUSTICE and JUSTICE SCALIA join.

[Defendant Patane was arrested outside his home and handcuffed. A federal agent, who had been told that defendant, a convicted felon, illegally possessed a Glock pistol, began giving him the *Miranda* warnings, but defendant interrupted the agent, stating that he knew his rights. No further *Miranda* warnings were given (which the government conceded on appeal resulted in a violation of the *Miranda* rules).

[When the federal agent told defendant he wanted to know about a Glock pistol he possessed, defendant replied: "The Glock is in my bedroom on a shelf * * *." The agent found the pistol where defendant said it would be and seized it. Defendant was indicted for being a convicted felon in possession of a firearm in violation of federal law.

[The Tenth Circuit held that the pistol itself, as well as the statement disclosing its location, was inadmissible. According to the Tenth Circuit, a 1985 case, *Oregon v. Elstad*, [discussed at p. 457], which indicated that the "fruit of the poisonous tree doctrine" did not apply to violations of the *Miranda* rules, was incompatible with the more recent case of *Dickerson v. United States* (2000) [p. 541]. *Dickerson* had made it clear that *Miranda* had announced a constitutional rule; *Elstad* had suggested otherwise. The Tenth Circuit equated *Dickerson's* holding with the proposition that a violation of one's *Miranda* rights is itself a violation of one's Fifth Amendment rights.]

As we explain below, the *Miranda* rule is a prophylactic employed to protect against violations of the Self-Incrimination Clause. [That clause], however, is not implicated by the admission into evidence of the physical fruit of a voluntary statement. Accordingly, there is no justification for extending the *Miranda* rule to this context. [The] *Miranda* rule is not a code of police conduct, and police do not violate the Constitution (or even the *Miranda* rules for that matter) by mere failures to warn. For this reason, the exclusionary rule articulated in various [Fourth Amendment cases] does not apply.

[The] core protection afforded by the Self-Incrimination Clause is a prohibition on compelling a criminal defendant to testify against himself at trial. See, e.g., *Chavez v. Martinez* (plurality opinion) [p. 550]. [The] Clause cannot be violated by the introduction of nontestimonial evidence obtained as a result of voluntary statements. See, e.g., *United States v. Hubbell* [p. 650] (noting that the word "witness" in the Self-Incrimination Clause "limits the relevant category of compelled incriminating statements to those that are 'testimonial' in character)."

[Because such] prophylactic rules [as the *Miranda* rule] necessarily sweep beyond the actual protections of the Self-Incrimination Clause, any further extension of these rules must be justified by its necessity for the protection of the actual right against compelled self-incrimination, *Chavez* (opinion of Souter, J.). [Furthermore,] the Self-Incrimination Clause contains its own exclusionary rule. It provides that "[n]o person [shall] be compelled in any criminal case to be a witness against himself." [We] have repeatedly explained "that those subjected to coercive interrogations have an *automatic* protection from the use of their involuntary statements (or evidence derived from their statements) in any subsequent criminal trial," *Chavez* (plurality opinion). This explicit textual protection supports a strong presumption against expanding the *Miranda* rule any further.

Finally, nothing in *Dickerson*, including its characterization of *Miranda* as announcing a constitutional rule, changes any of these observations. Indeed, [*Dickerson*] specifically noted that the Court's "subsequent cases have reduced the impact of the *Miranda* rule on legitimate law enforcement while reaffirming [*Miranda*'s] core ruling that unwarned statements may not be used as evidence in the prosecution's case in chief." [The *Dickerson* Court's] reliance on our *Miranda* precedents [including *Elstad*, which read *Miranda* narrowly] further demonstrates the continuing validity of those decisions. In short, nothing in *Dickerson* calls into question our continued insistence that the closest possible fit be maintained between the Self-Incrimination Clause and any rule designed to protect it.

Our cases also make clear the related point that a mere failure to give *Miranda* warnings does not, by itself, violate a suspect's constitutional rights or even the *Miranda* rule. See *Chavez*. [This], of course, follows from the nature of the right protected by the Self-Incrimination Clause, which the *Miranda* rule, in turn protects. "It is a fundamental *trial* right." *Withrow v. Williams*, 507 U.S. 680 (1993).

[It] follows that police do not violate a suspect's constitutional rights (or the *Miranda* rule) by negligent or even deliberate failures to provide the suspect with the full panoply of warnings prescribed by *Miranda*. Potential violations occur, if at all, only upon the admission of unwarned statements into evidence at trial. And, at that point, "the exclusion of unwarned statements [is] a complete and sufficient remedy" for any perceived *Miranda* violations. *Chavez.*

Thus, unlike unreasonable searches under the Fourth Amendment or actual violations of the Due Process Clause or the Self-Incrimination Clause, there is, with respect to mere failures to warn, nothing to deter. There is therefore no reason to apply the "fruit of the poisonous tree" doctrine [utilized in Fourth Amendment cases]. It is not for this Court to impose its preferred police practices on either federal law enforcement officials or their state counterparts.

[*Dickerson's*] characterization of *Miranda* as a constitutional rule does not lessen the need to maintain the closest possible fit between the Self-Incrimination Clause and any judge-made rule designed to protect it. And there is no such fit here. Introduction of the nontestimonial fruit of a voluntary statement, such as respondent's Glock, does not implicate the Self-Incrimination Clause. The admission of such fruit presents no risk that a defendant's coerced statements (however defined) will be used against him at a criminal trial. In any case, "[t]he exclusion of unwarned statements [is] a complete and sufficient remedy" for any perceived *Miranda* violation. *Chavez.* [There] is simply no need to extend (and therefore no justification for extending) the prophylactic rule of *Miranda* to this context.

[The Tenth Circuit] ascribed significance to the fact that, in this case, there might be "little [practical] difference between [respondent's] confessional statement" and the actual physical evidence. The distinction, the court said, "appears to make little sense as a matter of policy." But, putting policy aside, we have held that "[t]he word 'witness' in the constitutional text limits the" scope of the Self-Incrimination Clause to testimonial evidence. *United States v. Hubbell*, supra. The Constitution itself makes the distinction.[6] And although it is true that the Court requires the exclusion of the physical fruit of actually coerced confessions, it must be remembered that statements taken without sufficient *Miranda* warnings are presumed to have been coerced only for certain purposes and then only when necessary to protect the privilege against self-incrimination. [We] decline to extend that presumption further. * * *

JUSTICE KENNEDY, with whom JUSTICE O'CONNOR joins, concurring in the judgment.

[In such cases as *Elstad* and *Quarles*], evidence obtained following an unwarned interrogation was held admissible. The result was based in large part on our recognition that the concerns underlying the [*Miranda* rule] must be accommodated to other objectives of the criminal justice system. I agree with the plurality that *Dickerson* did not undermine these precedents and, in fact, cited them in support. [Unlike] the plurality, however, I find it unnecessary to decide whether the [federal agent's] failure to give Patane the full *Miranda* warnings should be characterized as a violation of the *Miranda* rule itself, or whether there

---

[6]   While Fourth Amendment protections extend to "persons, houses, papers, and effects," the Self-Incrimination Clause prohibits only compelling a defendant to be a "witness against himself."

is "[any]thing to deter" so long as the unwarned statements are not later introduced at trial.

JUSTICE SOUTER, with whom JUSTICE STEVENS and JUSTICE GINSBURG join, dissenting.

The majority repeatedly says that the Fifth Amendment does not address the admissibility of nontestimonial evidence, an overstatement that is beside the point. The issue actually presented today is whether courts should apply the fruit of the poisonous tree doctrine lest we create an incentive for the police to omit *Miranda* warnings before custodial interrogation. In closing their eyes to the consequences of giving an evidentiary advantage to those who ignore *Miranda*, the majority adds an important inducement for interrogators to ignore the rule in that case.

[There] is, of course, a price for excluding evidence, but the Fifth Amendment is worth a price, and in the absence of a very good reason, the logic of *Miranda* should be followed: a *Miranda* violation raises a presumption of coercion, and the Fifth Amendment privilege against compelled self-incrimination extends to the exclusion of derivative evidence, see *United States v. Hubbell* (recognizing "the Fifth Amendment's protection against the prosecutor's use of incriminating information derived directly or indirectly [from] [actually] compelled testimony"); *Kastigar v. United States* [p. 633]. That should be the end of this case.

[Of] course the premise of *Elstad* is not on point; although a failure to give *Miranda* warnings before one individual statement does not necessarily bar the admission of a subsequent statement given after adequate warnings, that rule obviously does not apply to physical evidence seized once and for all.

There is no way to read this case except as an unjustifiable invitation to law enforcement to flaunt *Miranda* when there may be physical evidence to be gained. The incentive is an odd one, coming from the Court on the same day it decides *Missouri v. Seibert* [the next main case].

JUSTICE BREYER, dissenting.

For reasons similar to those set forth in Justice Souter's dissent and in my concurring opinion in *Seibert*, I would extend to this context the "fruit of the poisonous tree" approach, which I believe the Court has come close to adopting in *Seibert*. Under that approach, courts would exclude physical evidence derived from unwarned questioning unless the failure to provide *Miranda* warnings was in good faith. Because the courts below made no explicit finding as to good or bad faith, I would remand for such a determination.

MISSOURI V. SEIBERT

542 U.S. 600, 124 S.Ct. 2601, 159 L.Ed.2d 643 (2004).

JUSTICE SOUTER announced the judgment of the Court and delivered an opinion, in which JUSTICE STEVENS, JUSTICE GINSBURG, and JUSTICE BREYER join.

This case tests a police protocol for custodial interrogation that calls for giving no warnings of the rights to silence and counsel until interrogation has produced a confession. Although such a statement is generally inadmissible, since taken in violation of *Miranda v. Arizona*, the interrogating officer follows it with *Miranda* warnings and then leads the suspect to cover the same ground a second time. The question here is the admissibility of the repeated statement. Because this midstream recitation of warnings after interrogation and unwarned confession could not effectively comply with *Miranda*'s constitutional requirement, we hold that a statement repeated after a warning in such circumstances is inadmissible.

[Officer Hanrahan arranged for another officer to arrest Ms. Seibert, a murder suspect, specifically instructing the officer not to advise Seibert of her *Miranda* rights. After Seibert had been taken to the police station and left alone in an "interview room" for 15 to 20 minutes, Hanrahan questioned her for 30 to 40 minutes. After she made an incriminating statement, she was given a 20-minute break. Hanrahan then resumed questioning, this time advising Seibert of her *Miranda* rights. After she waived her rights, Hanrahan confronted Seibert with the incriminating statement she had made at the prewarning questioning session. As Hanrahan acknowledged, Seibert's ultimate statement was "largely a repeat of information * * * obtained" prior to the *Miranda* warnings. The trial court excluded only the statement obtained during the first questioning session. A 4–3 majority of the state supreme court reversed, holding that the statement the defendant made after she had been given the *Miranda* warnings and waived her rights had to be suppressed as well.]

* * * *Miranda* conditioned the admissibility at trial of any custodial confession on warning a suspect of his rights: failure to give the prescribed warnings and obtain a waiver of rights before custodial questioning generally requires exclusion of any statements obtained. Conversely, giving the warnings and getting a waiver has generally produced a virtual ticket of admissibility; maintaining that a statement is involuntary even though given after warnings and voluntary waiver of rights requires unusual stamina, and litigation over voluntariness tends to end with the finding of a valid waiver. * * *

[The] technique of interrogating in successive, unwarned and warned phases raises a new challenge to *Miranda*. Although we have no statistics on the frequency of this practice, it is not confined to Rolla, Missouri. An officer of that police department testified that the strategy of withholding *Miranda* warnings until after interrogating and drawing out a confession was promoted not only by his own department, but by a national police training organization and other departments in which he had worked. [The] upshot of [various training programs'] advice is a question-first practice of some popularity, as one can see from the reported cases describing its use, sometimes in obedience to departmental policy.

[*Miranda*] addressed "interrogation practices [likely] to disable [an individual] from making a free and rational choice" about speaking and held that a suspect must be "adequately and effectively" advised of the choice the Constitution guarantees. The object of question-first is to render *Miranda* warnings ineffective by waiting for a particularly opportune time to give them, after the suspect has already confessed.

[The] threshold issue when interrogators question first and warn later is thus whether it would be reasonable to find that in these circumstances the warnings could function "effectively" as *Miranda* requires. Could the warnings effectively advise the suspect that he had a real choice about giving an admissible statement at that juncture? Could they reasonably convey that he could choose to stop talking even if he had talked earlier? For unless the warnings could place a suspect who has just been interrogated in a position to make such an informed choice, there is no practical justification for accepting the formal warnings as compliance with *Miranda,* or for treating the second stage of interrogation as distinct from the first, unwarned and inadmissible segment.[1]

There is no doubt about the answer that proponents of question-first give to this question about the effectiveness of warnings given only after successful interrogation, and we think their answer is correct. By any objective measure, applied to circumstances exemplified here, it is likely that if the interrogators employ the technique of withholding warnings until after interrogation succeeds in eliciting a confession, the warnings will be ineffective in preparing the suspect for successive interrogation, close in time and similar in content. After all, the reason that question-first is catching on is as obvious as its manifest purpose, which is to get a confession the suspect would not make if he understood his rights at the outset; the sensible underlying assumption is that with one confession in hand before the warnings, the interrogator can count on getting its duplicate, with trifling additional trouble. Upon hearing warnings only in the aftermath of interrogation and just after making a confession, a suspect would hardly think he had a genuine right to remain silent, let alone persist in so believing once the police began to lead him over the same ground again.[2] A more likely reaction on a suspect's part would be perplexity about the reason for discussing rights at that point, bewilderment being an unpromising frame of mind for knowledgeable decision. What is worse, telling a suspect that "anything you say can and will be used against you," without expressly excepting the statement just given, could lead to an entirely reasonable inference that what he has just said will be used, with subsequent silence being of no avail. * * *

---

[1]   Respondent Seibert argues that her second confession should be excluded from evidence under the doctrine known by the metaphor of the "fruit of the poisonous tree," developed [in] Fourth Amendment [cases]; evidence otherwise admissible but discovered as a result of an earlier violation is excluded as tainted, lest the law encourage future violations. But the Court in *Elstad* rejected the [Fourth Amendment] fruits doctrine for analyzing the admissibility of a subsequent warned confession following "an initial failure [to] administer the warnings required by *Miranda.*" * * * *Elstad* held that "a suspect who has once responded to unwarned yet uncoercive questioning is not thereby disabled from waiving his rights and confessing after he has been given the requisite *Miranda* warnings." In a sequential confession case, clarity is served if the later confession is approached by asking whether in the circumstances the *Miranda* warnings given could reasonably be found effective. If yes, a court can take up the standard issues of voluntary waiver and voluntary statement; if no, the subsequent statement is inadmissible for want of adequate *Miranda* warnings, because the earlier and later statements are realistically seen as parts of a single, unwarned sequence of questioning.

[2]   It bears emphasizing that the effectiveness *Miranda* assumes the warnings can have must potentially extend through the repeated interrogation, since a suspect has a right to stop at any time. It seems highly unlikely that a suspect could retain any such understanding when the interrogator leads him a second time through a line of questioning the suspect has already answered fully. The point is not that a later unknowing or involuntary confession cancels out an earlier, adequate warning; the point is that the warning is unlikely to be effective in the question-first sequence we have described.

Missouri argues that a confession repeated at the end of an interrogation sequence envisioned in a question-first strategy is admissible on the authority of *Elstad*, but the argument disfigures that case. In *Elstad*, the police went to the young suspect's house to take him into custody on a charge of burglary. Before the arrest, one officer spoke with the suspect's mother, while the other one joined the suspect in a "brief stop in the living room," where the officer said he "felt" the young man was involved in a burglary. The suspect acknowledged he had been at the scene. [The Court] took care to mention that the officer's initial failure to warn was an "oversight" that "may have been the result of confusion as to whether the brief exchange qualified as 'custodial interrogation' * * *. [At] the outset of a later and systematic station house interrogation going well beyond the scope of the laconic prior admission, the suspect was given *Miranda* warnings and made a full confession. [On] the facts of [the] case, the Court thought any causal connection between the first and second responses to the police was 'speculative and attenuated.' [It] is fair to read *Elstad* as treating the living room conversation as a good-faith *Miranda* mistake, not only open to correction by careful warnings before systematic questioning in that particular case, but posing no threat to warn-first practice generally."

[The] contrast between *Elstad* and this case reveals a series of relevant facts that bear on whether *Miranda* warnings delivered midstream could be effective enough to accomplish their object: the completeness and detail of the questions and answers in the first round of interrogation, the overlapping content of the two statements, the timing and setting of the first and the second, the continuity of police personnel, and the degree to which the interrogator's questions treated the second round as continuous with the first. In *Elstad*, it was not unreasonable to see the occasion for questioning at the station house as presenting a markedly different experience from the short conversation at home; since a reasonable person in the suspect's shoes could have seen the station house questioning as a new and distinct experience, the *Miranda* warnings could have made sense as presenting a genuine choice whether to follow up on the earlier admission.

At the opposite extreme are the facts here, which by any objective measure reveal a police strategy adapted to undermine the *Miranda* warnings.[6] The unwarned interrogation was conducted in the station house, and the questioning was systematic, exhaustive, and managed with psychological skill. When the police were finished there was little, if anything, of incriminating potential left unsaid. The warned phase of questioning proceeded after a pause of only 15 to 20 minutes, in the same place as the unwarned segment. [In] particular, the police did not advise that her prior statement could not be used.[7] Nothing was said or done to dispel the oddity of warning about legal rights to silence and counsel right after the police had led her through a systematic interrogation * * *. [The] impression

---

[6] Because the intent of the officer will rarely be as candidly admitted as it was here (even as it is likely to determine the conduct of the interrogation), the focus is on facts apart from intent that show the question-first tactic at work.

[7] We do not hold that a formal addendum warning that a previous statement could not be used would be sufficient to change the character of the question-first procedure to the point of rendering an ensuing statement admissible, but its absence is clearly a factor that blunts the efficacy of the warnings and points to a continuing, not a new, interrogation.

that the further questioning was a mere continuation of the earlier questions and responses was fostered by references back to the confession already given. It would have been reasonable to regard the two sessions as parts of a continuum, in which it would have been unnatural to refuse to repeat at the second stage what had been said before. These circumstances must be seen as challenging the comprehensibility and efficacy of the *Miranda* warnings to the point that a reasonable person in the suspect's shoes would not have understood them to convey a message that she retained a choice about continuing to talk.

Strategists dedicated to draining the substance out of *Miranda* cannot accomplish by training instructions what *Dickerson* held Congress could not do by statute. Because the question-first tactic effectively threatens to thwart *Miranda*'s purpose of reducing the risk that a coerced confession would be admitted, and because the facts here do not reasonably support a conclusion that the warnings given could have served their purpose, Seibert's postwarning statements are inadmissible.

JUSTICE BREYER, concurring.

In my view, the following simple rule should apply to the two-stage interrogation technique: Courts should exclude the "fruits" of the initial unwarned questioning unless the failure to warn was in good faith. I believe this is a sound and workable approach to the problem this case presents. Prosecutors and judges have long understood how to apply the "fruits" approach, which they use in other areas of law. And in the workaday world of criminal law enforcement the administrative simplicity of the familiar has significant advantages over a more complex exclusionary rule.

I believe the plurality's approach in practice will function as a "fruits" test. The truly "effective" *Miranda* warnings on which the plurality insists, will occur only when certain circumstances—a lapse in time, a change in location or interrogating officer, or a shift in the focus of the questioning—intervene between the unwarned questioning and any postwarning statement.

I consequently join the plurality's opinion in full. I also agree with Justice Kennedy's opinion insofar as it is consistent with this approach and makes clear that a good-faith exception applies.

JUSTICE KENNEDY, concurring in the judgment.

The interrogation technique used in this case is designed to circumvent *Miranda*. It undermines the *Miranda* warning and obscures its meaning. The plurality opinion is correct to conclude that statements obtained through the use of this technique are inadmissible. Although I agree with much in the careful and convincing opinion for the plurality, my approach does differ in some respects, requiring this separate statement.

The *Miranda* rule has become an important and accepted element of the criminal justice system. At the same time, not every violation of the rule requires suppression of the evidence obtained. Evidence is admissible when the central concerns of *Miranda* are not likely to be implicated and when other objectives of the criminal justice system are best served by its introduction. Thus, we have held that statements obtained in violation of the rule can be used for impeachment; [that] there is an exception to protect countervailing concerns of public safety; and that physical evidence obtained in reliance on statements taken in violation of the rule is admissible, see *Patane*. These cases, in my view, are correct. They recognize that admission of evidence is proper when it would further important objectives without compromising *Miranda*'s central concerns. Under these precedents, the scope of the *Miranda* suppression remedy depends on a consideration of those legitimate interests and on whether admission of the evidence under the circumstances would frustrate *Miranda*'s central concerns and objectives. *Elstad* reflects this approach.

[In] my view, *Elstad* was correct in its reasoning and its result. *Elstad* reflects a balanced and pragmatic approach to enforcement of the *Miranda* warning. An officer may not realize that a suspect is in custody and warnings are required. The officer may not plan to question the suspect or may be waiting for a more appropriate time. [In] light of these realities it would be extravagant to treat the presence of one statement that cannot be admitted under *Miranda* as sufficient reason to prohibit subsequent statements preceded by a proper warning.

[This] case presents different considerations. The police used a two-step questioning technique based on a deliberate violation of *Miranda*. [Further,] the interrogating officer here relied on the defendant's prewarning statement to obtain the postwarning statement used against her at trial. The postwarning interview resembled a cross-examination. The officer confronted the defendant with her inadmissible prewarning statements and pushed her to acknowledge them.

The technique used in this case distorts the meaning of *Miranda* and furthers no legitimate countervailing interest. The *Miranda* rule would be frustrated were we to allow police to undermine its meaning and effect. [When] an interrogator uses this deliberate, two-step strategy, predicated upon violating *Miranda* during an extended interview, postwarning statements that are related to the substance of prewarning statements must be excluded absent specific, curative steps.

The plurality concludes that whenever a two-stage interview occurs, admissibility of the postwarning statement should depend on "whether the *Miranda* warnings delivered midstream could have been effective enough to accomplish their object" given the specific facts of the case. This test envisions an objective inquiry from the perspective of the suspect, and applies in the case of both intentional and unintentional two-stage interrogations. In my view, this test cuts too broadly. *Miranda*'s clarity is one of its strengths, and a multifactor test that applies to every two-stage interrogation may serve to undermine that clarity. I would apply a narrower test applicable only in the infrequent case, such as we have here, in which the two-step interrogation technique was used in a calculated way to undermine the *Miranda* warning.

The admissibility of postwarning statements should continue to be governed by the principles of *Elstad* unless the deliberate two-step strategy was employed. If the deliberate two-step strategy has been used, postwarning statements that are related to the substance of prewarning statements must be excluded unless curative measures are taken before the postwarning statement is made. Curative measures should be designed to ensure that a reasonable person in the suspect's situation would understand the import and effect of the *Miranda* warning and of the *Miranda* waiver. For example, a substantial break in time and circumstances between the prewarning statement and the *Miranda* warning may suffice in most circumstances, as it allows the accused to distinguish the two contexts and appreciate that the interrogation has taken a new turn. Alternatively, an additional warning that explains the likely inadmissibility of the prewarning custodial statement may be sufficient. No curative steps were taken in this case, however, so the postwarning statements are inadmissible and the conviction cannot stand. * * *

JUSTICE O'CONNOR, with whom THE CHIEF JUSTICE, JUSTICE SCALIA, and JUSTICE THOMAS join, dissenting.

The plurality devours *Elstad* even as it accuses petitioner's argument of "disfigur[ing]" that decision. I believe that we are bound by *Elstad* to reach a different result, and I would vacate the judgment of the Supreme Court of Missouri.

On two preliminary questions I am in full agreement with the plurality. First, the plurality appropriately follows *Elstad* in concluding that Seibert's statement cannot be held inadmissible under a "fruit of the poisonous tree" theory. Second, the plurality correctly declines to focus its analysis on the subjective intent of the interrogating officer.

This Court has made clear that there simply is no place for a robust deterrence doctrine with regard to violations of *Miranda*. * * * Consistent with that view, the Court today refuses to apply the traditional "fruits" analysis to the physical fruit of a claimed *Miranda* violation. *Patane*. The plurality correctly refuses to apply a similar analysis to testimonial fruits.

Although the analysis the plurality ultimately espouses examines the same facts and circumstances that a "fruits" analysis would consider (such as the lapse of time between the two interrogations and change of questioner or location), it does so for entirely different reasons. The fruits analysis would examine those factors because they are relevant to the balance of deterrence value versus the "drastic and socially costly course" of excluding reliable evidence. The plurality, by contrast, looks to those factors to inform the *psychological* judgment regarding whether the suspect has been informed effectively of her right to remain silent. The analytical underpinnings of the two approaches are thus entirely distinct, and they should not be conflated just because they function similarly in practice.

The plurality's rejection of an intent-based test is also, in my view, correct. Freedom from compulsion lies at the heart of the Fifth Amendment, and requires us to assess whether a suspect's decision to speak truly was voluntary. Because voluntariness is a matter of the suspect's state of mind, we focus our analysis on the way in which suspects experience interrogation. * * *

Thoughts kept inside a police officer's head cannot affect that experience. [A] suspect who experienced the exact same interrogation as Seibert, save for a difference in the undivulged, subjective intent of the interrogating officer when he failed to give *Miranda* warnings, would not experience the interrogation any differently.

[Because] the isolated fact of Officer Hanrahan's intent could not have had any bearing on Seibert's "capacity to comprehend and knowingly relinquish" her right to remain silent, it could not by itself affect the voluntariness of her confession. Moreover, recognizing an exception to *Elstad* for intentional violations would require focusing constitutional analysis on a police officer's subjective intent, an unattractive proposition that we all but uniformly avoid. [This] case presents the uncommonly straightforward circumstance of an officer openly admitting that the violation was intentional. But the inquiry will be complicated in other situations probably more likely to occur. For example, different officers involved in an interrogation might claim different states of mind regarding the failure to give *Miranda* warnings. Even in the simple case of a single officer who claims that a failure to give *Miranda* warnings was inadvertent, the likelihood of error will be high. [These] evidentiary difficulties have led us to reject an intent-based test in several criminal procedure contexts.

[For] these reasons, I believe that the approach espoused by Justice Kennedy is ill advised. Justice Kennedy would extend *Miranda's* exclusionary rule to any case in which the use of the "two-step interrogation technique" was "deliberate" or "calculated." This approach untethers the analysis from facts knowable to, and therefore having any potential directly to affect, the suspect. Far from promoting "clarity," the approach will add a third step to the suppression inquiry. In virtually every two-stage interrogation case, in addition to addressing the standard *Miranda* and voluntariness questions, courts will be forced to conduct the kind of difficult, state-of-mind inquiry that we normally take pains to avoid.

The plurality's adherence to *Elstad,* and mine to the plurality, end there. Our decision in *Elstad* rejected two lines of argument advanced in favor of suppression. The first was based on the "fruit of the poisonous tree" doctrine. [The] second was the argument that the "lingering compulsion" inherent in a defendant's having let the "cat out of the bag" required suppression.

We rejected [the second] theory outright. We did so not because we refused to recognize the "psychological impact of the suspect's conviction that he has let the cat out of the bag," but because we refused to "endo[w]" those "psychological effects" with "constitutional implications." To do so, we said, would "effectively immuniz[e] a suspect who responds to pre-*Miranda* warning questions from the consequences of his subsequent informed waiver," an immunity that "comes at a high cost to legitimate law enforcement activity, while adding little desirable protection to the individual's interest in not being *compelled* to testify against himself."

I would analyze the two-step interrogation procedure under the voluntariness standards central to the Fifth Amendment and reiterated in *Elstad*. *Elstad* commands that if Seibert's first statement is shown to have been involuntary, the court must examine whether the taint dissipated through the passing of time or a change in circumstances. [In] addition, Seibert's second statement should be suppressed if she showed that it was involuntary despite the *Miranda* warnings. * * *

Because I believe that the plurality gives insufficient deference to *Elstad* and that Justice Kennedy places improper weight on subjective intent, I respectfully dissent.

9.   If a suspect does not request a lawyer but, unbeknownst to him, a relative or friend retains a lawyer for him, does the failure of the police to allow the lawyer to see the suspect or the failure to inform the suspect that an attorney is trying to reach him vitiate an otherwise valid waiver of Miranda rights?

MORAN V. BURBINE

475 U.S. 412, 106 S.Ct. 1135, 89 L.Ed.2d 410 (1986).

JUSTICE O'CONNOR delivered the opinion of the Court.

After being informed of his rights pursuant to *Miranda* and after executing a series of written waivers, respondent confessed to the murder of a young woman. At no point during the course of the interrogation, which occurred prior to arraignment, did he request an attorney. While he was in police custody, his sister attempted to retain a lawyer to represent him. The attorney telephoned the police station and received assurances that respondent would not be questioned further until the next day. In fact, the interrogation session that yielded the inculpatory statements began later that evening. The question presented is whether either the conduct of the police or respondent's ignorance of the attorney's efforts to reach him taints the validity of the waivers and therefore requires exclusion of the confessions.

[Several months after Mary Jo Hickey was beaten to death in Providence, Rhode Island, respondent Burbine and two others were arrested by Cranston, Rhode Island police for a local burglary. When the other burglary suspects implicated Burbine in the Hickey murder, a Cranston detective notified the Providence police. An hour later, in the early evening, three Providence officers arrived at Cranston police headquarters to question Burbine about the Providence murder.]

That same evening, at about 7:45 p.m., respondent's sister telephoned the Public Defender's Office to obtain legal assistance for her brother. Her sole concern was the breaking and entering charge, as she was unaware that respondent was then under suspicion for murder.

[At] 8:15 p.m., [Assistant Public Defender Allegra Munson] telephoned the Cranston police station and asked that her call be transferred to the detective division. [When a male voice responded with the word "Detective," Ms. Munson stated that she would act as Burbine's counsel in the event that the police would place him in a lineup or question him. An unidentified person told her that neither act would occur and that the police were "through" with Burbine "for the night." Ms. Munson was told neither that the Providence police were at the stationhouse nor that Burbine was a suspect in Ms. Hickey's murder.] At all relevant times, respondent was unaware of his sister's efforts to retain counsel and of the fact and contents of Ms. Munson's telephone conversation.

Less than an hour later, the police brought respondent to an interrogation room and conducted the first of a series of interviews concerning the murder. Prior to each session, respondent was informed of his *Miranda* rights, and on three separate occasions he signed a written form acknowledging that he understood his right to the presence of an attorney and explicitly indicating that he "[did] not want an attorney called or appointed for [him]" before he gave a statement. Uncontradicted evidence at the suppression hearing indicated that at least twice during the course of the evening, respondent was left in a room where he had access to a telephone, which he apparently declined to use. Eventually, respondent signed three written statements fully admitting to the murder. * * *

[The trial judge denied respondent's motion to suppress the statements. The jury found respondent guilty of first degree murder. On federal habeas, the First Circuit held that the police conduct had fatally tainted respondent's "otherwise valid" waiver. The U.S. Supreme Court reversed.] * * *

Events occurring outside of the presence of the suspect and entirely unknown to him surely can have no bearing on the capacity to comprehend and knowingly relinquish a constitutional right. Under the analysis of the Court of Appeals, the same defendant, armed with the same information and confronted with precisely the same police conduct, would have knowingly waived his *Miranda* rights had a lawyer not telephoned the police station to inquire about his status. Nothing in any of our waiver decisions or in our understanding of the essential components of a valid waiver requires so incongruous a result. No doubt the additional information would have been useful to respondent; perhaps even it might have affected his decision to confess. But we have never read the Constitution to require that the police supply a suspect with a flow of information to help him calibrate his self interest in deciding whether to speak or stand by his rights.[a] Once it is determined that a suspect's decision not to rely on his rights was uncoerced, that he at all times knew he could stand mute and request a lawyer, and that he was aware of the state's intention to use his statements to secure a conviction, the analysis is complete and the waiver is valid as a matter of law.[1] The Court of Appeals' conclusion to the contrary was in error.

Nor do we believe that the level of the police's culpability in failing to inform respondent of the telephone call has any bearing on the validity of the waiver. [Although] highly inappropriate, even deliberate deception of an attorney could not possibly affect a suspect's decision to waive his *Miranda* rights unless he were at least aware of the incident. [Because] respondent's voluntary decision to speak was

---

[a] A year later, this language was quoted with approval in *Colorado v. Spring,* 479 U.S. 564 (1987), holding that the police need not advise a suspect of the crimes they wish to question him about even though the subject matter of the interrogation is likely to be quite different from what the suspect expects.

[1] The dissent incorrectly reads our analysis of the components of a valid waiver to be inconsistent [with] *Edwards.* [But] the dissent never comes to grips with the crucial distinguishing feature of this case—that Burbine at no point requested the presence of counsel, as was his right under *Miranda* to do. [We reject] the dissent's entirely undefended suggestion that the Fifth Amendment "right to counsel" requires anything more than that the police inform the suspect of his right to representation and honor his request that the interrogation cease until his attorney is present.

made with full awareness and comprehension of all the information *Miranda* requires the police to convey, the waivers were valid.

* * * Regardless of any issue of waiver, [contends respondent], the Fifth Amendment requires the reversal of a conviction if the police are less than forthright in their dealings with an attorney or if they fail to tell a suspect of a lawyer's unilateral efforts to contact him. Because the proposed modification ignores the underlying purposes of the *Miranda* rules and because we think that the decision as written strikes the proper balance between society's legitimate law enforcement interests and the protection of the defendant's Fifth Amendment rights, we decline the invitation to further extend *Miranda's* reach.

At the outset, while we share respondent's distaste for the deliberate misleading of an officer of the court, reading *Miranda* to forbid police deception of an *attorney* "would cut [the decision] completely loose from its own explicitly stated rationale." [The] purpose of the *Miranda* warnings * * * is to dissipate the compulsion inherent in custodial interrogation and, in so doing, guard against abridgement of the suspect's Fifth Amendment rights. Clearly, a rule that focuses on how the police treat an attorney—conduct that has no relevance at all to the degree of compulsion experienced by the defendant during interrogation—would ignore both *Miranda's* mission and its only source of legitimacy.

Nor are we prepared to adopt a rule requiring that the police inform a suspect of an attorney's efforts to reach him. While such a rule might add marginally to *Miranda's* goal of dispelling the compulsion inherent in custodial interrogation, overriding practical considerations counsel against its adoption. [We] have little doubt that the approach urged by respondent and endorsed by the Court of Appeals would have the inevitable consequence of muddying *Miranda's* otherwise relatively clear waters. The legal questions it would spawn are legion: To what extent should the police be held accountable for knowing that the accused has counsel? Is it enough that someone in the station house knows, or must the interrogating officer himself know of counsel's efforts to contact the suspect? Do counsel's efforts to talk to the suspect concerning one criminal investigation trigger the obligation to inform the defendant before interrogation may proceed on a wholly separate matter?

[Moreover,] reading *Miranda* to require the police in each instance to inform a suspect of an attorney's efforts to reach him would work a substantial and, we think, inappropriate shift in the subtle balance struck in that decision. Custodial interrogations implicate two competing concerns. On the one hand, "the need for police questioning as a tool for effective enforcement of criminal laws" cannot be doubted. [On] the other hand, the Court has recognized that the interrogation process is "inherently coercive" and that, as a consequence, there exists a substantial risk that the police will inadvertently traverse the fine line between legitimate efforts to elicit admissions and constitutionally impermissible compulsion. *Miranda* attempted to reconcile these opposing concerns by giving the *defendant* the power to exert some control over the course of the interrogation. Declining to adopt the more extreme position that the actual presence of a lawyer was necessary to dispel the coercion inherent in custodial interrogation, the Court found that the suspect's Fifth Amendment rights could be adequately protected by less intrusive means. Police questioning, often an essential part of the investigatory process, could continue in its traditional form, the Court held, but only if the suspect clearly understood that, at any time, he could bring the proceeding to a halt or, short of that, call in an attorney to give advice and monitor the conduct of his interrogators.

The position urged by respondent would upset this carefully drawn approach in a manner that is both unnecessary for the protection of the Fifth Amendment privilege and injurious to legitimate law enforcement. Because, as *Miranda* holds, full comprehension of the rights to remain silent and request an attorney are sufficient to dispel whatever coercion is inherent in the interrogation process, a rule requiring the police to inform the suspect of an attorney's efforts to contact him would contribute to the protection of the Fifth Amendment privilege only incidentally, if at all. This minimal benefit, however, would come at a substantial cost to society's legitimate and substantial interest in securing admissions of guilt.

[Respondent] also contends that the Sixth Amendment requires exclusion of his three confessions. [The] difficulty for respondent is that the interrogation sessions that yielded the inculpatory statements took place *before* the initiation of "adversary judicial proceedings." * * * Placing principal reliance on a footnote in *Miranda* [n. 35] and on *Escobedo,* he maintains that [the] right to non-interference with an attorney's dealings with a [suspect] arises the moment that the relationship is formed, or, at the very least, once the defendant is placed in custodial interrogation.

We are not persuaded. At the outset, subsequent decisions foreclose any reliance on *Escobedo* and *Miranda* for the proposition that the Sixth Amendment right, in any of its manifestations, applies prior to the initiation of adversary judicial proceedings. Although *Escobedo* was originally decided as a Sixth Amendment case, "the Court in retrospect perceived that the 'prime purpose' of *Escobedo* was not to vindicate the constitutional right to counsel as such, but, like *Miranda,* 'to guarantee full effectuation of the privilege against self-incrimination. * * *'" *Kirby v. Illinois* [p. 580 holding that the right to counsel at pretrial identifications attaches "only at or after the time that adversary judicial proceedings have been initiated."] Clearly then, *Escobedo* provides no support for respondent's argument. Nor, of course, does *Miranda,* the holding of which rested exclusively on the Fifth Amendment. * * *

Questions of precedent to one side, we find respondent's understanding of the Sixth Amendment both practically and theoretically unsound. As a practical matter, it makes little sense to say that the Sixth Amendment right to counsel attaches at different times depending on the fortuity of whether the suspect or his family happens to have retained counsel prior to interrogation. More importantly, the suggestion that the existence of an attorney-client relationship itself triggers the protections of the Sixth Amendment misconceives the underlying purposes of the right to counsel. The Sixth Amendment's intended function is not to wrap a protective cloak around the attorney-client relationship for its own sake any more than it is to protect a suspect from the consequences of his own candor. [By] its very terms, [the Sixth Amendment] becomes applicable only when the government's role shifts from investigation to accusation. * * *[4]

JUSTICE STEVENS, with whom JUSTICE BRENNAN and JUSTICE MARSHALL join, dissenting.

[Until] today, incommunicado questioning has been viewed with the strictest scrutiny by this Court; today, incommunicado questioning is embraced as a societal goal of the highest order that justifies police deception of the shabbiest kind. * * * Police interference with communications between an attorney and his client is a recurrent problem. [The] near-consensus of state courts and the legal profession's Standards about this recurrent problem lends powerful support to the conclusion that police may not interfere with communications between an attorney and the client whom they are questioning. Indeed, at least two opinions from this Court seemed to express precisely that view.[20] The Court today flatly rejects that widely held view and responds to this recurrent problem by adopting the most restrictive interpretation of the federal constitutional restraints on police deception, misinformation, and interference in attorney-client communications. * * *

[Miranda] clearly condemns threats or trickery that cause a suspect to make an unwise waiver of his rights even though he fully understands those rights. In my opinion there can be no constitutional distinction—as the Court appears to draw—between a deceptive misstatement and the concealment by the police of the critical fact that an attorney retained by the accused or his family has offered assistance, either by telephone or in person.

[If,] as the Court asserts, "the analysis is at an end" as soon as the suspect is provided with enough information to have the *capacity* to understand and exercise his rights, I see no reason why the police should not be permitted to make the same kind of misstatements to the suspect that they are apparently allowed to make to

---

[4]   [The] dissent's misreading of *Miranda* itself is breathtaking in its scope. For example, it reads *Miranda* as creating an undifferentiated right to the presence of an attorney that is triggered automatically by the initiation of the interrogation itself. Yet, as both *Miranda* and subsequent decisions construing *Miranda* make clear beyond refute, " 'the interrogation must cease until an attorney is present' *only* '[i]f the individual states that he wants an attorney.' " *Michigan v. Mosley* (emphasis added). The dissent condemns us for embracing "incommunicado questioning [as] a societal goal of the highest order that justifies police deception of the shabbiest kind." We, of course, do nothing of the kind. As any reading of *Miranda* reveals, the decision, rather than proceeding from the premise that the rights and needs of the defendant are paramount to all others, embodies a carefully crafted balance designed to fully protect *both* the defendant's and society's interests. The dissent may not share our view that the Fifth Amendment rights of the defendant are amply protected by application of *Miranda as written*. But the dissent is "simply wrong" in suggesting that exclusion of Burbine's three confessions follows perfunctorily from *Miranda's* mandate. Y. Kamisar, *Police Interrogation and Confessions* 217–218, n. 94 (1980).

Quite understandably, the dissent is outraged by the very idea of police deception of a lawyer. Significantly less understandable is its willingness to misconstrue this Court's constitutional holdings in order to implement its subjective notions of sound policy.

[20]   See *Miranda* n. 35 (in *Escobedo*, "[t]he police also prevented the attorney from consulting with his client. Independent of any other constitutional proscription, this action constitutes a violation of the Sixth Amendment right to the assistance of counsel and excludes any statement obtained in its wake"); *Escobedo* ("[I]t 'would be highly incongruous if our system of justice permitted the district attorney, the lawyer representing the State, to extract a confession from the accused while his own lawyer, seeking to speak with him, was kept from him by the police' ").

his lawyer. *Miranda,* however, clearly establishes that both kinds of deception vitiate the suspect's waiver of his right to counsel. * * *

[In] short, settled principles about construing waivers of constitutional rights and about the need for strict presumptions in custodial interrogations, as well as a plain reading of the *Miranda* opinion itself, overwhelmingly support the conclusion reached by almost every state court that has considered the matter—a suspect's waiver of his right to counsel is invalid if police refuse to inform the suspect of his counsel's communications. * * *

What is the cost of requiring the police to inform a suspect of his attorney's call? It would decrease the likelihood that custodial interrogation will enable the police to obtain a confession. This is certainly a real cost, but it is the same cost that this Court has repeatedly found necessary to preserve the character of our free society and our rejection of an inquisitorial system.

[In] my view, as a matter of law, the police deception of Munson was tantamount to deception of Burbine himself. It constituted a violation of Burbine's right to have an attorney present during the questioning that began shortly thereafter. * * *

The possible reach of the Court's opinion is stunning. For the majority seems to suggest that police may deny counsel all access to a client who is being held. At least since *Escobedo,* it has been widely accepted that police may not simply deny attorneys access to their clients who are in custody. This view has survived the recasting of *Escobedo* from a Sixth Amendment to a Fifth Amendment case that the majority finds so critically important. That this prevailing view is shared *by the police* can be seen in the state court opinions detailing various forms of police deception of attorneys. For, if there were no obligation to give attorneys access, there would be no need to take elaborate steps to avoid access, such as shuttling the suspect to a different location, or taking the lawyer to different locations; police could simply refuse to allow the attorneys to see the suspects. But the law enforcement profession has apparently believed, quite rightly in my view, that denying lawyers access to their clients is impermissible.

[This] case turns on a proper appraisal of the role of the lawyer in our society. If a lawyer is seen as a nettlesome obstacle to the pursuit of wrongdoers—as in an inquisitorial society—then the Court's decision today makes a good deal of sense. If a lawyer is seen as an aid to the understanding and protection of constitutional rights—as in an accusatorial society—then today's decision makes no sense at all. * * *

5. THE COURT REAFFIRMS *MIRANDA*

Can (Did) Congress "Overrule" Miranda?

Title II of the Crime Control Act of 1968, which purports to repeal *Miranda* in federal prosecutions, amends Chapter 223, title 18, United States Code, by adding the following new sections:

"§ 3501. Admissibility of confessions

"(a) In any criminal prosecution brought by the United States or by the District of Columbia, a confession, as defined in subsection (e) hereof, shall be admissible in evidence if it is voluntarily given. Before such confession is received in evidence, the trial judge shall, out of the presence of the jury, determine any issue as to voluntariness. If the trial judge determines that the confession was voluntarily made it shall be admitted in evidence and the trial judge shall permit the jury to hear relevant evidence on the issue of voluntariness and shall instruct the jury to give such weight to the confession as the jury feels it deserves under all the circumstances.

"(b) The trial judge in determining the issue of voluntariness shall take into consideration all the circumstances surrounding the giving of the confession, including (1) the time elapsing between arrest and arraignment of the defendant making the confession, if it was made after arrest and before arraignment, (2) whether such defendant knew the nature of the offense with which he was charged or of which he was suspected at the time of making the confession, (3) whether or not such defendant was advised or knew that he was not required to make any statement and that any such statement could be used against him, (4) whether or not such defendant had been advised prior to questioning of his right to the assistance of counsel; and (5) whether or not such defendant was without the assistance of counsel when questioned and when giving such confession.

"The presence or absence of any of the above-mentioned factors to be taken into consideration by the judge need not be conclusive on the issue of voluntariness of the confession.

"(c) In any criminal prosecution by the United States or by the District of Columbia, a confession made or given by a person who is a defendant therein, while such person was under arrest or other detention in the custody of any law-enforcement officer or law-enforcement agency, shall not be inadmissible solely because of delay in bringing such person before a commissioner or other officer empowered to commit persons charged with offenses against the laws of the United States or of the District of Columbia if such confession is found by the trial judge to have been made voluntarily and if the weight to be given the confession is left to the jury and if such confession was made or given by such person within six hours immediately following his arrest or other detention: *Provided,* That the time limitation contained in this subsection shall not apply in any case in which the delay in bringing such person before such commissioner or other officer beyond such six-hour period is found by the trial judge to be reasonable considering the means of transportation and the distance to be traveled to the nearest available such commissioner or other officer.

"(d) Nothing contained in this section shall bar the admission in evidence of any confession made or given voluntarily by any person to any other person without interrogation by anyone, or at any time at which the person who made or gave such confession was not under arrest or other detention.

"(e) As used in this section, the term 'confession' means any confession of guilt of any criminal offense or any self-incriminating statement made or given orally or in writing."

Although § 3501 purported to overrule *Miranda,* for many years this federal statute did not provoke the head-on collision that might have been predicted. The Attorney General in office when the statute was passed instructed his subordinates not to rely on it where it differed from *Miranda,* and, although a later Attorney General changed this as official policy, most U.S. Attorneys appear to have continued to adhere to the restrained position initially taken. According to a 1986 report to the Attorney General by Assistant Attorney General Stephen Markman, head of the Office of Legal Policy (the "Markman report"), at some point the Department of Justice "attempted to establish the validity of [§ 3501] in litigation for several years with inconclusive results," but then "terminated this litigative effort." However, the Markman report urged the Department of Justice "to persuade the Supreme Court to abrogate or overrule the decision in *Miranda* " and viewed "reliance on [the 1968 statute] designed to achieve that end" as "the most promising line of attack."

When § 3501 was first enacted, most commentators thought it was invalid. Even those who conceded that *Miranda* was subject to congressional revision, i.e., could be displaced by a statute that provides an adequate alternative to the now-familiar warnings, maintained that Title II still fell short because it did little more than "turn the clock back" to the "voluntariness" test espoused by the *Miranda* dissents.

But the case for upholding § 3501 grew stronger with the passage of years. The Supreme Court repeatedly called the *Miranda* rules "not themselves rights protected by the Constitution" but only "procedural safeguards" or "prophylactic rules" designed to "provide practical reinforcement" for the privilege against compelled self-incrimination.

This language first appeared in *Michigan v. Tucker,* 417 U.S. 433 (1974). *Tucker* allowed the testimony of a prosecution witness whose identity had been discovered by questioning defendant in violation of *Miranda.* Although the case involved various factors that arguably limited its implications (e.g., the deviation between the warnings given and the *Miranda* requirements was not substantial and, although the defendant's trial took place after *Miranda,* the police questioning occurred before that case was decided), the *Tucker* Court, per Rehnquist, J., spoke in general terms of the difference between a *Miranda* violation and a constitutional violation:

"[T]he Court in *Miranda,* for the first time, expressly declared that the Self-Incrimination Clause was applicable to state interrogations at a police station, and that a defendant's statements might be excluded at trial despite their voluntary character under traditional principles.

"To supplement this new doctrine, and to help police officers conduct interrogations without facing a continued risk that valuable evidence would be lost, the [*Miranda* Court] established a set of specific guidelines, now commonly known as the *Miranda* rules. * * *

"The [*Miranda* Court] recognized that these procedural safeguards were not themselves rights protected by the Constitution but were instead measures to insure that the right against compulsory self-incrimination was protected. As [it] remarked: '[W]e cannot say that the Constitution necessarily requires adherence to any particular solution for the inherent compulsions of the interrogation process as it is presently conducted.' The suggested safeguards were not intended to 'create a constitutional straitjacket,' *Miranda,* but rather to provide practical reinforcement for the right against compulsory self-incrimination.[a]

"A comparison of the facts in this case with the historical circumstances underlying the privilege against compulsory self-incrimination strongly indicates that the police conduct here did not deprive [Tucker] of his privilege against self-incrimination as such, but rather failed to make available to him the full measure of procedural safeguards associated with that right since *Miranda.* Certainly no one could contend that the interrogation faced by [Tucker] bore any resemblance to the historical practices at which the right against compulsory self-incrimination was aimed. [H]is statements could hardly be termed involuntary as that term has been defined in the decisions of this Court. * * *

"Our determination that the interrogation in this case involved no compulsion sufficient to breach the right against compulsory self-incrimination does not mean there was not a disregard, albeit an inadvertent disregard, of the procedural rules later established in *Miranda.* The question for decision is how sweeping the judicially imposed consequences of this disregard shall be."

A decade later, first in *New York v. Quarles* (1984) [p. 515], and then in *Oregon v. Elstad* (1985) [p. 457], the Court reiterated *Tucker*'s way of looking at, and thinking about, *Miranda.* In both *Quarles* and *Elstad* the Court underscored the distinction between incriminating statements that are *actually* "coerced" or

---

[a] But as Justice Douglas observed in his *Tucker* dissent, the Court, per Rehnquist, J., overlooked other language in the *Miranda* opinion. For example, in the same paragraph from *Miranda* quoted by Justice Rehnquist in *Tucker,* the *Miranda* Court added: "However, unless we are shown other procedures which are at least as effective in apprising accused persons of their right of silence and in assuring a continuous opportunity to exercise it, the following safeguards [the *Miranda* warnings] must be observed." Moreover, later in the opinion, the *Miranda* Court reiterated: "The warnings required and the waiver necessary in accordance with our opinion today are, in the absence of a fully effective equivalent, prerequisites to the admissibility of any statements made by a defendant. * * * Procedural safeguards must be employed to protect the privilege, and unless other fully effective means are adopted to notify the person of his right of silence and to assure that the exercise of the right will be scrupulously honored, the following measures [the *Miranda* warnings] are required."

"compelled" and those obtained *merely* in violation of *Miranda*'s "procedural safeguards" or "prophylactic rules."

Did the language in *Tucker, Quarles* and *Elstad* imply that the Court would now uphold the validity of § 3501, which purports to "overrule" *Miranda?* Since the Court has no "supervisory power" over *state* criminal justice, if the *Miranda* rules are not constitutional requirements (but only "second-class" prophylactic safeguards) and *Miranda* violations not constitutional violations (but only "second-class" wrongs), where did the Court get the authority to impose *Miranda* on the states in the first place?

Concurring in *Davis v. United States* (1994) (discussed in *Berghuis*, at p. 478), Justice Scalia sharply criticized the Justice Department's "repeated refusal to invoke § 3501," a refusal that has "caused the federal judiciary to confront a host of '*Miranda*' issues that might be entirely irrelevant under federal law." Justice Scalia also maintained that because § 3501 "is a provision of law directed *to the courts,* reflecting the people's assessment of the proper balance to be struck [in this area], we shirk our duty if we systematically disregard that statutory command simply because the Justice Department declines to remind us of it."

Justice Scalia's comments probably encouraged two conservative legal groups, the Washington Legal Foundation and the Safe Streets Coalition. Led by then Utah Law School Professor Paul Cassell (now a federal district judge), who had become the nation's leading critic of *Miranda*, these groups repeatedly urged the federal courts to inject § 3501 into their cases.

In *United States v. Dickerson*, 166 F.3d 667 (4th Cir. 1999), the Washington Legal Foundation and the Safe Streets Coalition finally achieved some success. Although the dissenting judge protested that the ruling was made "without the benefit of any briefing in opposition" and "against the express wishes of the Department of Justice," a 2–1 majority of a panel of the U.S. Court of Appeals ruled that the pre-*Miranda* voluntariness test set forth in § 3501, rather than the famous *Miranda* case, governed the admissibility of confessions in the federal courts. Therefore, the district court had erred when it had suppressed a voluntary confession simply because it was obtained in violation of *Miranda*.

The reasoning of the Fourth Circuit may be summarized quite briefly: Congress has the power to "overrule" rules of evidence and procedure that are not required by the Constitution. The *Miranda* rules are not constitutionally required; they are only "prophylactic" rules designed to implement or reinforce the underlying constitutional right. Therefore, § 3501 is a valid exercise of Congressional authority to override judicially created rules not part of the Constitution. But the Supreme Court was to see matters quite differently:

DICKERSON V. UNITED STATES
530 U.S. 428, 120 S.Ct. 2326, 147 L.Ed.2d 405 (2000).

CHIEF JUSTICE REHNQUIST delivered the opinion of the Court.

In the wake of [*Miranda*], Congress enacted 18 U.S.C. § 3501, which in essence laid down a rule that the admissibility of [a custodial suspect's] statements should turn only on whether or not they were voluntarily made. We hold that *Miranda*, being a constitutional decision of this Court, may not be in effect overruled by an Act of Congress, and we decline to overrule *Miranda* ourselves. We therefore hold that *Miranda* and its progeny in this Court govern the admissibility of statements made during custodial interrogation in both state and federal courts.

* * * Prior to *Miranda*, we evaluated the admissibility of a suspect's confession under a voluntariness test. [Over] time, our cases recognized two constitutional bases for the requirement that a confession be voluntary to be admitted into evidence: the Fifth Amendment right against self-incrimination and the Due Process Clause of the Fourteenth Amendment. See, *e.g.*, Bram v. United States (1897) (stating that the voluntariness test "is controlled by that portion of the Fifth Amendment . . . commanding that no person 'shall be compelled in any criminal case to be a witness against himself'"); *Brown v. Mississippi* (1936) (reversing a criminal conviction under the Due Process Clause because it was based on a confession obtained by physical coercion).

While *Bram* was decided before *Brown* and its progeny, for the middle third of the 20th century our cases based the rule against admitting coerced confessions primarily, if not exclusively, on notions of due process. We applied the due process voluntariness test in "some 30 different cases decided during the era that intervened between *Brown* and *Escobedo v. Illinois*." Those cases refined the test into an inquiry that examines "whether a defendant's will was overborne" by the circumstances surrounding the giving of a confession. The due process test takes into consideration "the totality of all the surrounding circumstances—both the characteristics of the accused and the details of the interrogation." * * *

We have never abandoned this due process jurisprudence, and thus continue to exclude confessions that were obtained involuntarily. But our decisions in *Malloy* and *Miranda* changed the focus of much of the inquiry in determining the admissibility of suspects' incriminating statements. In *Malloy*, we held that the Fifth Amendment's Self-Incrimination Clause is incorporated in the Due Process Clause of the Fourteenth Amendment and thus applies to the States. We decided *Miranda* on the heels of *Malloy*.

In *Miranda*, we noted that the advent of modern custodial police interrogation brought with it an increased concern about confessions obtained by coercion. Because custodial police interrogation, by its very nature, isolates and pressures the individual, we stated that "even without employing brutality, the 'third degree' or [other] specific stratagems, . . . custodial interrogation exacts a heavy toll on individual liberty and trades on the weakness of individuals." We concluded that the coercion inherent in custodial interrogation blurs the line between voluntary and involuntary statements, and thus heightens the risk that an individual will not be "accorded his privilege under the Fifth Amendment . . . not to be compelled to incriminate himself." Accordingly, we laid down "concrete constitutional guidelines for law enforcement agencies and courts to follow."

Two years after *Miranda* was decided, Congress enacted § 3501. * * *

Given § 3501's express designation of voluntariness as the touchstone of admissibility, its omission of any warning requirement, and the instruction for trial courts to consider a nonexclusive list of factors relevant to the circumstances of a confession, we agree with the Court of Appeals that Congress intended by its enactment to overrule *Miranda*. Because of the obvious conflict between our decision in *Miranda* and § 3501, we must address whether Congress has constitutional authority to thus supersede *Miranda*.

[The] law in this area is clear. This Court has supervisory authority over the federal courts, and we may use that authority to prescribe rules of evidence and procedure that are binding in those tribunals. However, the power to judicially create and enforce nonconstitutional "rules of procedure and evidence for the federal courts exists only in the absence of a relevant Act of Congress." Congress retains the ultimate authority to modify or set aside any judicially created rules of evidence and procedure that are not required by the Constitution.

But Congress may not legislatively supersede our decisions interpreting and applying the Constitution. See, *e.g., Boerne v. Flores,* 521 U.S. 507 (1997). This case therefore turns on whether the *Miranda* Court announced a constitutional rule or merely exercised its supervisory authority to regulate evidence in the absence of congressional direction. [Relying] on the fact that we have created several exceptions to *Miranda*'s warnings requirement and that we have repeatedly referred to the *Miranda* warnings as "prophylactic," *Quarles,* and "not themselves rights protected by the Constitution," *Tucker,* the Court of Appeals concluded that the protections announced in *Miranda* are not constitutionally required.

We disagree * * *, although we concede that there is language in some of our opinions that supports the view taken by that court. But first and foremost of the factors on the other side—that *Miranda* is a constitutional decision—is that both *Miranda* and two of its companion cases applied the rule to proceedings in state courts—to wit, Arizona, California, and New York. Since that time, we have consistently applied *Miranda*'s rule to prosecutions arising in state courts. It is beyond dispute that we do not hold a supervisory power over the courts of the several States. With respect to proceedings in state courts, our "authority is limited to enforcing the commands of the United States Constitution."[1]

The *Miranda* opinion itself begins by stating that the Court granted certiorari "to explore some facets of the problems [of] applying the privilege against self-

---

[1] Our conclusion regarding *Miranda*'s constitutional basis is further buttressed by the fact that we have allowed prisoners to bring alleged *Miranda* violations before the federal courts in habeas corpus proceedings. * * * Habeas corpus proceedings are available only for claims that a person "is in custody in violation of the Constitution or laws or treaties of the United States." 28 U.S.C. § 2254(a). Since the *Miranda* rule is clearly not based on federal laws or treaties, our decision allowing habeas review for *Miranda* claims obviously assumes that *Miranda* is of constitutional origin.

incrimination to in-custody interrogation, *and to give concrete constitutional guidelines for law enforcement agencies and courts to follow*." (emphasis added). In fact, the majority opinion is replete with statements indicating that the majority thought it was announcing a constitutional rule. Indeed, the Court's ultimate conclusion was that the unwarned confessions obtained in the four cases before the Court in *Miranda* "were obtained from the defendant under circumstances that did not meet constitutional standards for protection of the privilege."

Additional support for our conclusion that *Miranda* is constitutionally based is found in the *Miranda* Court's invitation for legislative action to protect the constitutional right against coerced self-incrimination. [The Court] opined that the Constitution would not preclude legislative solutions that differed from the prescribed *Miranda* warnings but which were "at least as effective in apprising accused persons of their right of silence and in assuring a continuous opportunity to exercise it."

[Various decisions carving out exceptions to *Miranda*] illustrate the principle—not that *Miranda* is not a constitutional rule—but that no constitutional rule is immutable. No court laying down a general rule can possibly foresee the various circumstances in which counsel will seek to apply it, and the sort of modifications represented by these cases are as much a normal part of constitutional law as the original decision.

The Court of Appeals also noted that in *Elstad*, we stated that " 'the *Miranda* exclusionary rule . . . serves the Fifth Amendment and sweeps more broadly than the Fifth Amendment itself.' " Our decision in that case—refusing to apply the traditional "fruits" doctrine developed in Fourth Amendment cases—does not prove that *Miranda* is a nonconstitutional decision, but simply recognizes the fact that unreasonable searches under the Fourth Amendment are different from unwarned interrogation under the Fifth Amendment.

As an alternative argument for sustaining the Court of Appeals' decision, the court-invited *amicus curiae* contends that the section complies with the requirement that a legislative alternative to *Miranda* be equally as effective in preventing coerced confessions. We agree with the *amicus'* contention that there are more remedies available for abusive police conduct than there were at the time *Miranda* was decided. But we do not agree that these additional measures supplement § 3501's protections sufficiently to meet the constitutional minimum. *Miranda* requires procedures that will warn a suspect in custody of his right to remain silent and which will assure the suspect that the exercise of that right will be honored. As discussed above, § 3501 explicitly eschews a requirement of pre-interrogation warnings in favor of an approach that looks to the administration of such warnings as only one factor in determining the voluntariness of a suspect's confession. The additional remedies cited by *amicus* do not, in our view, render them, together with § 3501 an adequate substitute for the warnings required by *Miranda*.

[In] *Miranda*, the Court noted that reliance on the traditional totality-of-the-circumstances test raised a risk of overlooking an involuntary custodial confession, a risk that the Court found unacceptably great when the confession is offered in the case in chief to prove guilt. The Court therefore concluded that something more than the totality test was necessary. Section 3501 reinstates the totality test as sufficient. [The statute] therefore cannot be sustained if *Miranda* is to remain the law.

Whether or not we would agree with *Miranda*'s reasoning and its resulting rule, were we addressing the issue in the first instance, the principles of *stare decisis* weigh heavily against overruling it now.

* * * *Miranda* has become embedded in routine police practice to the point where the warnings have become part of our national culture. [While] we have overruled our precedents when subsequent cases have undermined their doctrinal underpinnings, we do not believe that this has happened to the *Miranda* decision. If anything, our subsequent cases have reduced the impact of the *Miranda* rule on legitimate law enforcement while reaffirming the decision's core ruling that unwarned statements may not be used as evidence in the prosecution's case in chief.

The disadvantage of the *Miranda* rule is that statements which may be by no means involuntary, made by a defendant who is aware of his "rights," may nonetheless be excluded and a guilty defendant go free as a result. But experience suggests that the totality-of-the-circumstances test which § 3501 seeks to revive is more difficult than *Miranda* for law enforcement officers to conform to, and for courts to apply in a consistent manner. The requirement that *Miranda* warnings be given does not, of course, dispense with the voluntariness inquiry. [But] "[c]ases in which a defendant can make a colorable argument that a self-incriminating statement was 'compelled' despite the fact that the law enforcement authorities adhered to the dictates of *Miranda* are rare."

In sum, we conclude that *Miranda* announced a constitutional rule that Congress may not supersede legislatively. Following the rule of *stare decisis*, we decline to overrule *Miranda* ourselves. * * *

JUSTICE SCALIA, with whom JUSTICE THOMAS joins, dissenting.

Those to whom judicial decisions are an unconnected series of judgments that produce either favored or disfavored results will doubtless greet today's decision as a paragon of moderation, since it declines to overrule *Miranda*. Those who understand the judicial process will appreciate that today's decision is not a reaffirmation of *Miranda*, but a radical revision of the most significant element of *Miranda* (as of all cases): the rationale that gives it a permanent place in our jurisprudence.

Marbury v. Madison, held that an Act of Congress will not be enforced by the courts if what it prescribes violates the Constitution of the United States. That was the basis on which *Miranda* was decided. One will search today's opinion in vain, however, for a statement (surely simple enough to make) that what § 3501 prescribes—the use at trial of a voluntary confession, even when a *Miranda* warning or its equivalent has failed to be given—violates the Constitution. The reason the statement does not appear is not only (and perhaps not so much) that it would be absurd, inasmuch as § 3501 excludes from trial precisely what the

Constitution excludes from trial, viz., compelled confessions; but also that Justices whose votes are needed to compose today's majority are on record as believing that a violation of *Miranda* is *not* a violation of the Constitution. And so, to justify today's agreed-upon result, the Court must adopt a significant *new*, if not entirely comprehensible, principle of constitutional law. As the Court chooses to describe that principle, statutes of Congress can be disregarded, not only when what they prescribe violates the Constitution, but when what they prescribe contradicts a decision of this Court that "announced a constitutional rule." As I shall discuss in some detail, the only thing that can possibly mean in the context of this case is that this Court has the power, not merely to apply the Constitution but to expand it, imposing what it regards as useful "prophylactic" restrictions upon Congress and the States. That is an immense and frightening antidemocratic power, and it does not exist.

It takes only a small step to bring today's opinion out of the realm of power-judging and into the mainstream of legal reasoning: The Court need only go beyond its carefully couched iterations that "*Miranda* is a constitutional decision," that "*Miranda* is constitutionally based," that *Miranda* has "constitutional underpinnings," and come out and say quite clearly: "We reaffirm today that custodial interrogation that is not preceded by *Miranda* warnings or their equivalent violates the Constitution of the United States." It cannot say that, because a majority of the Court does not believe it. The Court therefore acts in plain violation of the Constitution when it denies effect to this Act of Congress.

It was once possible to characterize the so-called *Miranda* rule as resting (however implausibly) upon the proposition that what the statute here before us permits—the admission at trial of un-*Mirandized* confessions—violates the Constitution. That is the fairest reading of the *Miranda* case itself. [Having] extended the privilege into the confines of the station house, the Court liberally sprinkled throughout its sprawling 60-page opinion suggestions that, because of the compulsion inherent in custodial interrogation, the privilege was violated by any statement thus obtained that did not conform to the rules set forth in *Miranda*, or some functional equivalent. * * *

So understood, *Miranda* was objectionable for innumerable reasons, not least the fact that cases spanning more than 70 years had rejected its core premise that, absent the warnings and an effective waiver of the right to remain silent and of the (thitherto unknown) right to have an attorney present, a statement obtained pursuant to custodial interrogation was necessarily the product of compulsion. [Moreover,] history and precedent aside, the decision in *Miranda*, if read as an explication of what the Constitution *requires*, is preposterous. There is, for example, simply no basis in reason for concluding that a response to the very first question asked, by a suspect who already *knows* all of the rights described in the *Miranda* warning, is anything other than a volitional act. And even if one assumes that the elimination of compulsion absolutely requires informing even the most knowledgeable suspect of his right to remain silent, it cannot conceivably require the right to have *counsel* present. There is a world of difference, which the Court recognized under the traditional voluntariness test but ignored in *Miranda*, between compelling a suspect to incriminate himself and preventing him from foolishly doing so of his own accord. Only the latter (which is *not* required by the Constitution) could explain the Court's inclusion of a right to counsel and the requirement that it, too, be knowingly and intelligently waived. Counsel's presence is not required to tell the suspect that he *need* not speak; the interrogators can do that. The only good reason for having counsel there is that he can be counted on to advise the suspect that he *should* not speak.

Preventing foolish (rather than compelled) confessions is likewise the only conceivable basis for the rules that courts must exclude any confession elicited by questioning conducted, without interruption, after the suspect has indicated a desire to stand on his right to remain silent or initiated by police after the suspect has expressed a desire to have counsel present. Nonthreatening attempts to persuade the suspect to reconsider that initial decision are not, without more, enough to render a change of heart the product of anything other than the suspect's free will. Thus, what is most remarkable about the *Miranda* decision—and what made it unacceptable as a matter of straightforward constitutional interpretation in the *Marbury* tradition—is its palpable hostility toward the act of confession *per se*, rather than toward what the Constitution abhors, *compelled* confession.

[For] these reasons, and others more than adequately developed in the *Miranda* dissents and in the subsequent works of the decision's many critics, any conclusion that a violation of the *Miranda* rules *necessarily* amounts to a violation of the privilege against compelled self-incrimination can claim no support in history, precedent, or common sense, and as a result would at least presumptively be worth reconsidering even at this late date. But that is unnecessary, since the Court has (thankfully) long since abandoned the notion that failure to comply with *Miranda*'s rules is itself a violation of the Constitution.

As the Court today acknowledges, since *Miranda* we have explicitly, and repeatedly, interpreted that decision as having announced, not the circumstances in which custodial interrogation runs afoul of the Fifth or Fourteenth Amendment, but rather only "prophylactic" rules that go beyond the right against compelled self-incrimination. Of course the seeds of this "prophylactic" interpretation of *Miranda* were present in the decision itself. [In] subsequent cases, the seeds have sprouted and borne fruit: The Court has squarely concluded that it is possible—indeed not uncommon—for the police to violate *Miranda* without also violating the Constitution.

Michigan v. Tucker, an opinion for the Court written by then-Justice Rehnquist, rejected the true-to-*Marbury*, failure-to-warn-as-constitutional-violation interpretation of *Miranda*. It held that exclusion of the "fruits" of a *Miranda* violation—the statement of a witness whose identity the defendant had revealed while in custody—was not required. [The] "procedural safeguards" adopted in *Miranda*, the Court said, "were not themselves rights protected by the Constitution but were instead measures to insure that the right against compulsory self-incrimination was protected," and to "provide practical reinforcement for the right."

[The dissent then discussed *New York v. Quarles*, *Oregon v. Elstad* and other cases applying and interpreting *Miranda*.]

In light of these cases, and our statements to the same effect in others, it is simply no longer possible for the Court to conclude, even if it wanted to, that a violation of *Miranda*'s rules is a violation of the Constitution. But as I explained at the outset, that is what is required before the Court may disregard a law of Congress governing the admissibility of evidence in federal court. The Court today insists that the *decision* in *Miranda* is a "constitutional" one, that it has "constitutional underpinnings," a "constitutional basis" and a "constitutional origin," that it was "constitutionally based," and that it announced a "constitutional rule." It is fine to play these word games; but what makes a decision "constitutional" in the only sense relevant here—in the sense that renders it impervious to supersession by congressional legislation such as § 3501—is the determination that the Constitution *requires* the result that the decision announces and the statute ignores. By disregarding congressional action that concededly does not violate the Constitution, the Court flagrantly offends fundamental principles of separation of powers, and arrogates to itself prerogatives reserved to the representatives of the people.

The Court seeks to avoid this conclusion in two ways: First, by misdescribing these post-*Miranda* cases as mere dicta. The Court concedes only "that there is language in some of our opinions that supports the view" that *Miranda*'s protections are not "constitutionally required." It is not a matter of *language*; it is a matter of *holdings*. The proposition that failure to comply with *Miranda*'s rules does not establish a constitutional violation was central to the *holdings* of *Tucker*, * * * *Quarles*, and *Elstad*.

The second way the Court seeks to avoid the impact of these cases is simply to disclaim responsibility for reasoned decisionmaking. It says: "These decisions illustrate the principle—not that *Miranda* is not a constitutional rule—but that no constitutional rule is immutable. * * *" The issue, however, is not whether court rules are "mutable"; they assuredly are. It is not whether, in the light of "various circumstances," they can be "modified"; they assuredly can. The issue is whether, *as mutated and modified*, they must *make sense*. The requirement that they do so is the only thing that prevents this Court from being some sort of nine-headed Caesar, giving thumbs-up or thumbs-down to whatever outcome, case by case, suits or offends its collective fancy. And if confessions procured in violation of *Miranda* are confessions "compelled" in violation of the Constitution, the post-*Miranda* decisions I have discussed do not make sense. The only reasoned basis for their outcome was that a violation of *Miranda* is *not* a violation of the Constitution. * * *

Finally, the Court asserts that *Miranda* must be a "constitutional decision" announcing a "constitutional rule," and thus immune to congressional modification, because we have since its inception applied it to the States. If this argument is meant as an invocation of *stare decisis*, it fails because, though it is true that our cases applying *Miranda* against the States must be reconsidered if *Miranda* is not required by the Constitution, it is likewise true that our cases [based] on the principle that *Miranda* is *not* required by the Constitution will have to be reconsidered if it *is*. So the *stare decisis* argument is a wash.

[There] was available to the Court a means of reconciling the established proposition that a violation of *Miranda* does not itself offend the Fifth Amendment with the Court's assertion of a right to ignore the present statute. That means of reconciliation was argued strenuously by both petitioner and the United States, who were evidently more concerned than the Court is with maintaining the coherence of our jurisprudence. It is not mentioned in the Court's opinion because, I assume, a majority of the Justices intent on reversing believes that incoherence is the lesser evil. They may be right.

Petitioner and the United States contend that there is nothing at all exceptional, much less unconstitutional, about the Court's adopting prophylactic rules to buttress constitutional rights, and enforcing them against Congress and the States. Indeed, the United States argues that "prophylactic rules are now and have been for many years a feature of this Court's constitutional adjudication." That statement is not wholly inaccurate, if by "many years" one means since the mid-1960s. However, in their zeal to validate what is in my view a lawless practice, the United States and petitioner greatly overstate the frequency with which we have engaged in it. * * *

Petitioner and the United States are right on target, [in] characterizing the Court's actions in a case decided within a few years of *Miranda, North Carolina v. Pearce* [discussed in *U.S. v. Goodwin*, at p. 686]. There, the Court concluded that due process would be offended were a judge vindictively to resentence with added severity a defendant who had successfully appealed his original conviction. Rather than simply announce that vindictive sentencing violates the Due Process Clause, the Court went on to hold that "in order to assure the absence of such a [vindictive] motivation, [the] reasons for [imposing the increased sentence] must affirmatively appear" and must "be based upon objective information concerning identifiable conduct on the part of the defendant occurring after the time of the original sentencing proceeding." The Court later explicitly acknowledged *Pearce*'s prophylactic character. It is true, therefore, that the case exhibits the same fundamental flaw as does *Miranda* when deprived (as it has been) of its original (implausible) pretension to announcement of what the Constitution itself required. That is, although the Due Process Clause may well prohibit punishment based on judicial vindictiveness, the Constitution by no means vests in the courts "any general power to prescribe particular devices 'in order to assure the absence of such a motivation'" (Black, J., dissenting). Justice Black surely had the right idea when he derided the Court's requirement as "pure legislation if there ever was legislation," although in truth *Pearce*'s rule pales as a legislative achievement when compared to the detailed code promulgated in *Miranda*.

The foregoing demonstrates that, petitioner's and the United States' suggestions to the contrary notwithstanding, what the Court did in *Miranda* (assuming, as later cases hold, that *Miranda* went beyond what the Constitution actually requires) is in fact extraordinary. [The] power with which the Court would endow itself under a "prophylactic" justification for *Miranda* goes far beyond what it has permitted Congress to do under authority of [U.S. Const., Amdt. 14, § 5].

I applaud [the] refusal of the Justices in the majority to enunciate this boundless doctrine of judicial empowerment as a means of rendering today's decision rational. In nonetheless joining the Court's judgment, however, they overlook two truisms: that actions speak louder than silence, and that (in judge-made law at least) logic will out. Since there is in fact no other principle that can reconcile today's judgment with the post-*Miranda* cases that the Court refuses to abandon, what today's decision will stand for, whether the Justices can bring themselves to say it or not, is the power of the Supreme Court to write a prophylactic, extraconstitutional Constitution, binding on Congress and the States.

[I am not] persuaded by the argument for retaining *Miranda* that touts its supposed workability as compared with the totality-of-the-circumstances test it purported to replace. *Miranda*'s proponents cite *ad nauseam* the fact that the Court was called upon to make difficult and subtle distinctions in applying the "voluntariness" test in some 30-odd due process "coerced confessions" cases in the 30 years between *Brown* and *Miranda*. It is not immediately apparent, however, that the judicial burden has been eased by the "bright-line" rules adopted in *Miranda*. In fact, in the 34 years since *Miranda* was decided, this Court has been called upon to decide nearly *60* cases involving a host of *Miranda* issues.

[But] even were I to agree that the old totality-of-the-circumstances test was more cumbersome, it is simply not true that *Miranda* has banished it from the law and replaced it with a new test. Under the current regime, which the Court today retains in its entirety, courts are frequently called upon to undertake *both* inquiries. That is because, as explained earlier, voluntariness remains the *constitutional* standard, and as such continues to govern the admissibility for impeachment purposes of statements taken in violation of *Miranda*, the admissibility of the "fruits" of such statements, and the admissibility of statements challenged as unconstitutionally obtained *despite* the interrogator's compliance with *Miranda*.

Finally, I am not convinced by petitioner's argument that *Miranda* should be preserved because the decision occupies a special place in the "public's consciousness." As far as I am aware, the public is not under the illusion that we are infallible. I see little harm in admitting that we made a mistake in taking away from the people the ability to decide for themselves what protections (beyond those required by the Constitution) are reasonably affordable in the criminal investigatory process. * * *.

Today's judgment converts *Miranda* from a milestone of judicial overreaching into the very Cheops' Pyramid (or perhaps the Sphinx would be a better analogue) of judicial arrogance. In imposing its Court-made code upon the States, the original opinion at least *asserted* that it was demanded by the Constitution. Today's decision does not pretend that it is—and yet *still* asserts the right to impose it against the will of the people's representatives in Congress. Far from believing that *stare decisis* compels this result, I believe we cannot allow to remain on the books even a celebrated decision—*especially* a celebrated decision—that has come to stand for the proposition that the Supreme Court has power to impose extraconstitutional constraints upon Congress and the States. * * *

I dissent from today's decision, and, until § 3501 is repealed, will continue to apply it in all cases where there has been a sustainable finding that the defendant's confession was voluntary.[a]

6. WHEN IS *MIRANDA* VIOLATED?

CHAVEZ V. MARTINEZ
538 U.S. 760, 123 S.Ct. 1994, 155 L.Ed.2d 984 (2003).

JUSTICE THOMAS announced the judgment of the Court and delivered an opinion [joined by the Chief Justice in its entirety, by JUSTICE O'CONNOR with respect to Parts I and II-A, and by JUSTICE SCALIA with respect to Parts I and II].

[This case involves a § 1983 suit arising out of petitioner Ben Chavez's allegedly coercive interrogation of respondent Oliverio Martinez. The [Ninth Circuit] held that Chavez was not entitled to a defense of qualified immunity because he violated Martinez's clearly established constitutional rights. We conclude that Chavez did not deprive Martinez of a constitutional right.

I

[During an altercation with the police, an officer shot Martinez five times, causing severe injuries that left him partially blinded and paralyzed from the waist down. Chavez, a patrol supervisor who had arrived on the scene a few minutes after the shooting, accompanied Martinez to the hospital where he questioned him while he was receiving treatment from medical personnel. The questioning lasted a total of about 10 minutes over a 45-minute period, with Chavez leaving the emergency room from time to time to permit medical personnel to treat Martinez. At no point during the exchange between Martinez and Chavez was Martinez given the *Miranda* warnings.

[At first Martinez's responses to Chavez's questions about what had happened between him and the police were simply "I don't know," "I am choking" or "My leg hurts." Later, however, Martinez admitted that he had taken a pistol from an officer's holster and pointed the weapon at him. On seven different occasions, Martinez told the officer: "I am dying," "I am dying, please," or "I don't want to die, I don't want to die," but the questioning continued. At one point, Martinez told the officer: "I am not telling you anything until they [the doctors] treat me." But he continued to answer questions. According to a tape recording, toward the end of questioning, the following exchange between Chavez and Martinez occurred:

Chavez: [Do] you think you are going to die?

Martinez: Aren't you going to treat me or what?

---

[a] In *United States v. Patane*, p. 520, upholding the admissibility of a pistol found as the result of a failure to administer the *Miranda* warnings fully, the plurality (Thomas, J., joined by Rehnquist, C.J., and Scalia, J.) observed: "[The *Dickerson* Court's] reliance on our *Miranda* precedents [including such cases as *Elstad* and *Quarles*, which read *Miranda* narrowly] further demonstrates the continuing validity of these decisions." Justice Kennedy, joined by O'Connor, J., who concurred in the judgment, "agree[d] with the plurality that *Dickerson* did not undermine [such precedents as *Elstad* and *Quarles*] and, in fact, cited them in support."

Chavez: [That's all] I want to know, if you think you're going to die?

Martinez: My belly hurts, please treat me.

Chavez: Sir?

Martinez: If you treat me I tell you everything, if not, no.

Chavez: Sir, I want to know if you think you are going to die right now?

Martinez: I think so.

Chavez: You think so? Ok, look, the doctors are going to help you with all they can do, Ok? . . .

Martinez: Get moving, I am dying, can't you see me? Come on.

Chavez: Ah, huh, right now they are giving you medication.

[Although Martinez was never charged with a crime and his answers were never used against him in any criminal prosecution, he brought a § 1983 action, claiming that Chavez had violated both his Fifth Amendment right not to be "compelled in any criminal case to a be a witness against himself" and his Fourteenth Amendment due process right to be free from coercive questioning. The Ninth Circuit agreed with Martinez. It viewed the Fifth and Fourteenth Amendment rights asserted by Martinez clearly established by federal law, explaining that a reasonable police officer "would have known that persistent interrogation of the suspect despite repeated requests to stop violated the suspect's Fifth and Fourteenth Amendment right to be free from coercive interrogation."]

II

In deciding whether an officer is entitled to qualified immunity, we must first determine whether the officer's alleged conduct violated a constitutional right. If not, the officer is entitled to qualified immunity, and we need not consider whether the asserted right was "clearly established." We conclude that Martinez's allegations fail to state a violation of his constitutional rights.

A

The Fifth Amendment, made applicable to the States by the Fourteenth Amendment, requires that "[n]o person . . . shall be compelled *in any criminal case* to be a *witness* against himself" (emphases added). We fail to see how, based on the text of the Fifth Amendment, Martinez can allege a violation of this right, since Martinez was never prosecuted for a crime, let alone compelled to be a witness against himself in a criminal case.

Although Martinez contends that the meaning of "criminal case" should encompass the entire criminal investigatory process, including police interrogations, we disagree. In our view, a "criminal case" at the very least requires the initiation of legal proceedings. * * * Statements compelled by police interrogations of course may not be used against a defendant at trial, but it is not until their use in a criminal case that a violation of the Self-Incrimination Clause occurs. [Although] conduct by law enforcement officials prior to trial may ultimately impair that right, *a constitutional violation occurs only at "trial"* (emphases added); *Withrow v. Williams* (describing the Fifth Amendment as a "trial right"); id. (O'Connor, J., concurring in part and dissenting in part) (describing "true Fifth Amendment claims" as "the extraction and use of compelled testimony" (emphasis altered)).

Here, Martinez was never made to be a "witness" against himself in violation of the Fifth Amendment's Self-Incrimination Clause because his statements were never admitted as testimony against him in a criminal case. Nor was he ever placed under oath and exposed to " 'the cruel trilemma of self-accusation, perjury or contempt.' " The text of the Self-Incrimination Clause simply cannot support the Ninth Circuit's view that the mere use of compulsive questioning, without more, violates the Constitution. * * *

We fail to see how Martinez was any more "compelled in any criminal case to be a witness against himself" than an immunized witness forced to testify on pain of contempt. One difference, perhaps, is that the immunized witness *knows* that his statements will not, and may not, be used against him, whereas Martinez likely did not. But this does not make the statements of the immunized witness any less "compelled" and lends no support to the Ninth Circuit's conclusion that coercive police interrogations, absent the use of the involuntary statements in a criminal case, violate the Fifth Amendment's Self-Incrimination Clause.

[Although] our cases have permitted the Fifth Amendment's self-incrimination privilege to be asserted in non-criminal cases, [that] does not alter our conclusion that a violation of the constitutional right against self-incrimination occurs only if one has been compelled to be a witness against himself in a criminal case.

In the Fifth Amendment context, we have created prophylactic rules designed to safeguard the core constitutional right protected by the Self-Incrimination Clause. [Among] these rules is an evidentiary privilege that protects witnesses from being forced to give incriminating testimony, even in noncriminal cases, unless that testimony has been immunized from use and derivative use in a future criminal proceeding before it is compelled. [By] allowing a witness to insist on an immunity agreement *before* being compelled to give incriminating testimony in a noncriminal case, the privilege preserves the core Fifth Amendment right from invasion by the use of that compelled testimony in a subsequent criminal case. * * * Because the failure to assert the privilege will often forfeit the right to exclude the evidence in a subsequent "criminal case," [it] is necessary to allow assertion of the privilege prior to the commencement of a "criminal case" to safeguard the core Fifth Amendment trial right. If the privilege could not be asserted in such situations, testimony given in those judicial proceedings would be deemed "voluntary"; hence, insistence on a prior grant of immunity is essential to memorialize the fact that the testimony had indeed been compelled and therefore protected from use against the speaker in any "criminal case."

Rules designed to safeguard a constitutional right, however, do not extend the scope of the constitutional right itself, just as violations of judicially crafted prophylactic rules do not violate the constitutional rights of any person. * * *[3] We have likewise established the *Miranda* exclusionary rule as a prophylactic measure to prevent violations of the right protected by the text of the Self-Incrimination Clause—the admission into evidence in criminal case of confessions obtained through coercive custodial questioning. [Accordingly,] Chavez's failure to read Miranda warnings to Martinez did not violate Martinez's constitutional rights and cannot be grounds for a § 1983 action. [The] Ninth Circuit's view that mere compulsion violates the Self-Incrimination Clause finds no support in the text of the Fifth Amendment and is irreconcilable with our case law.[4] Because we find that Chavez's alleged conduct did not violate the Self-Incrimination Clause, we reverse the Ninth Circuit's denial of qualified immunity as to Martinez's Fifth Amendment claim. * * *

We are satisfied that Chavez's questioning did not violate Martinez's due process rights. Even assuming, *arguendo*, that the persistent questioning of Martinez somehow deprived him of a liberty interest, we cannot agree with Martinez's characterization of Chavez's behavior as "egregious" or "conscience shocking." As we noted in *Lewis*, the official conduct "most likely to rise to the conscience-shocking level," is the "conduct intended to injure in some way unjustifiable by any government interest." Here, there is no evidence that Chavez acted with a purpose to harm Martinez by intentionally interfering with his medical treatment. Medical personnel were able to treat Martinez throughout the interview and Chavez ceased his questioning to allow tests and other procedures to be performed. Nor is there evidence that Chavez's conduct exacerbated Martinez's injuries or prolonged his stay in the hospital. Moreover, the need to investigate whether there had been police misconduct constituted a justifiable government interest given the risk that key evidence would have been lost if Martinez had died without the authorities ever hearing his side of the story. * * *

III

Because Chavez did not violate Martinez's Fifth and Fourteenth Amendment rights, he was entitled to qualified immunity. The judgment of the Court of Appeals for the Ninth Circuit is therefore reversed and the case is remanded for further proceedings. * * *

JUSTICE SOUTER, delivered an opinion, Part II of which is the opinion of the Court, and Part I of which is an opinion concurring in the judgment. [Justice Breyer

---

[3] That the privilege is a prophylactic one does not alter our penalty cases jurisprudence, which allows such privilege to be asserted prior to, and outside of, criminal proceedings.

[4] It is Justice Kennedy's indifference to the text of the Self-Incrimination Clause, as well as a conspicuous absence of a single citation to the actual text of the Fifth Amendment, that permits him to adopt the Ninth Circuit's interpretation.

Mincey v. Arizona 437 U.S. 385 (1978), on which Justice Kennedy and Justice Ginsburg rely in support of their reading of the Fifth Amendment, was a case addressing the admissibility of a coerced confession under the Due Process Clause. *Mincey* did not even mention the Fifth Amendment or the Self-Incrimination Clause, and refutes Justice Kennedy's and Justice Ginsburg's assertions that their interpretation of that Clause would have been known to any reasonable officer at the time Chavez conducted his interrogation.

joined the opinion in its entirety and Justices Stevens, Kennedy and Ginsburg joined Part II of the opinion.]

I

Respondent Martinez's claim [under] § 1983 for violation of his privilege against compelled self-incrimination should be rejected and his case remanded for further proceedings. I write separately because I believe that our decision requires a degree of discretionary judgment greater than Justice Thomas acknowledges. As he points out, the text of the Fifth Amendment * * * focuses on courtroom use of a criminal defendant's compelled, self-incriminating testimony, and the core of the guarantee against compelled self-incrimination is the exclusion of any such evidence. Justice Ginsburg makes it clear that the present case is very close to *Mincey v. Arizona*, and Martinez's testimony would clearly be inadmissible if offered in evidence against him. But Martinez claims more than evidentiary protection in asking this Court to hold that the questioning alone was a completed violation of the Fifth and Fourteenth Amendments subject to redress by an action for damages under § 1983. * * *

I do not [believe] that Martinez can make the "powerful showing," subject to a realistic assessment of costs and risks, necessary to expand protection of the privilege against compelled self-incrimination to the point of the civil liability he asks us to recognize here. The most obvious drawback inherent in Martinez's purely Fifth Amendment claim to damages is its risk of global application in every instance of interrogation producing a statement inadmissible under Fifth and Fourteenth Amendment principles, or violating one of the complementary rules we have accepted in aid of the privilege against evidentiary use. If obtaining Martinez's statement is to be treated as a stand-alone violation of the privilege subject to compensation, why should the same not be true whenever the police obtain any involuntary self-incriminating statement, or whenever the government so much as threatens a penalty in derogation of the right to immunity, or whenever the police fail to honor *Miranda*?[1] Martinez offers no limiting principle or reason to foresee a stopping place short of liability in all such cases. * * *

II

Whether Martinez may pursue a claim of liability for a substantive due process violation is thus an issue that should be addressed on remand, along with the scope and merits of any such action that may be found open to him.[a]

JUSTICE SCALIA, concurring in part in the judgment.

I agree with the Court's rejection of Martinez's Fifth Amendment claim, that is, his claim that Chavez violated his right not to be compelled in any criminal case to be a witness against himself. And without a violation of the right protected by the text of the Self-Incrimination Clause (what the plurality and Justice Souter call the Fifth Amendment's "core"), Martinez's § 1983 action is doomed. Section

---

[1] The question whether the absence of *Miranda* warnings may be a basis for a § 1983 action under any circumstance is not before the Court.

[a] Of the six opinions produced by *Chavez v. Martinez*, the only text that commanded a majority was Part II of Justice Souter's opinion.

1983 does not provide remedies for violations of judicially created prophylactic rules, such as the rule of *Miranda*, as the Court today holds [referring to Justice Thomas's and Justice Kennedy's opinions]; nor is it concerned with "extensions" of constitutional provisions designed to safeguard actual constitutional rights [referring to Justice Souter's opinion]. Rather, a plaintiff seeking redress through § 1983 must establish the violation of a federal constitutional or statutory right. * * *

JUSTICE STEVENS, concurring in part and dissenting in part.

As a matter of fact, the interrogation of respondent was the functional equivalent of an attempt to obtain an involuntary confession from a prisoner by torturous methods. As a matter of law, that type of brutal police conduct constitutes an immediate deprivation of the prisoner's constitutionally protected interest in liberty. Because these propositions are so clear, the [courts below] correctly held that petitioner is not entitled to qualified immunity.

I

[Most of this part of Justice Steven's opinion consists of an English translation of substantial portions of the tape-recorded questioning of Martinez in Spanish that occurred in the emergency room. This part of his opinion is omitted. However, portions of the recorded questioning are set forth at p. 550]

The sound recording of this interrogation, which has been lodged with the Court, vividly demonstrates that respondent was suffering severe pain and mental anguish throughout petitioner's persistent questioning.

II

* * *

I respectfully dissent, but for the reasons articulated by Justice Kennedy, concur in Part II of Justice Souter's opinion.

JUSTICE KENNEDY, with whom JUSTICE STEVENS joins, and with whom JUSTICE GINSBURG joins as to Parts II and III, concurring in part and dissenting in part.

A single police interrogation now presents us with two issues: first, whether failure to give a required warning under *Miranda* was itself a completed constitutional violation actionable § 1983; and second, whether an actionable violation arose at once under the Self-Incrimination Clause [when] the police, after failing to warn, used severe compulsion or extraordinary pressure in an attempt to elicit a statement or confession.

I agree with Justice Thomas that failure to give a *Miranda* warning does not, without more, establish a completed violation when the unwarned interrogation ensues. As to the second aspect of the case, which does not involve the simple failure to give a *Miranda* warning, it is my respectful submission that Justice Souter and Justice Thomas are incorrect. They conclude that a violation of the Self-Incrimination Clause does not arise until a privileged statement is introduced at some later criminal proceeding.

A constitutional right is traduced the moment torture or its close equivalents are brought to bear. Constitutional protection for a tortured suspect is not held in abeyance until some later criminal proceeding takes place. These are the premises of this separate opinion. * * *

II

Justice Souter and Justice Thomas are wrong, in my view, to maintain that in all instances a violation of the Self-Incrimination Clause simply does not occur unless and until a statement is introduced at trial, no matter how severe the pain or how direct and commanding the official compulsion used to extract it. * * *

The conclusion that the Self-Incrimination Clause is not violated until the government seeks to use a statement in some later criminal proceeding strips the Clause of an essential part of its force and meaning. This is no small matter. It should come as an unwelcome surprise to judges, attorneys, and the citizenry as a whole that if a legislative committee or a judge in a civil case demands incriminating testimony without offering immunity, and even imposes sanctions for failure to comply, that the witness and counsel cannot insist the right against compelled self-incrimination is applicable then and there. * * *

III

* * * Had the officer inflicted the initial injuries sustained by Martinez (the gunshot wounds) for purposes of extracting a statement, there would be a clear and immediate violation of the Constitution, and no further inquiry would be needed. That is not what happened, however. The initial injuries and anguish suffered by the suspect were not inflicted to aid the interrogation.

[There] is no rule against interrogating suspects who are in anguish and pain. The police may have legitimate reasons, borne of exigency, to question a person who is suffering or in distress. Locating the victim of a kidnaping, ascertaining the whereabouts of a dangerous assailant or accomplice, or determining whether there is a rogue police officer at large are some examples. That a suspect is in fear of dying, furthermore, may not show compulsion but just the opposite. The fear may be a motivating factor to volunteer information. The words of a declarant who believes his death is imminent have a special status in the law of evidence.

[There] are, however, actions police may not take if the prohibition against the use of coercion to elicit a statement is to be respected. The police may not prolong or increase a suspect's suffering against the suspect's will. That conduct would render government officials accountable for the increased pain. The officers must not give the impression that severe pain will be alleviated only if the declarant cooperates, for that, too, uses pain to extract a statement. In a case like this one, recovery should be available under § 1983 if a complainant can demonstrate that an officer exploited his pain and suffering with the purpose and intent of securing an incriminating statement. That showing has been made here.

The transcript of the interrogation set out by Justice Stevens, and other evidence considered by the District Court demonstrate that the suspect thought his treatment would be delayed, and thus his pain and condition worsened, by refusal to answer questions.

* * * I would affirm the decision of the Court of Appeals that a cause of action under § 1983 has been stated. The other opinions filed today, however, reach different conclusions as to the correct disposition of the case. Were Justice Stevens, Justice Ginsburg, and I to adhere to our position, there would be no controlling judgment of the Court. In these circumstances, and because a ruling on substantive due process in this case could provide much of the essential protection the Self-Incrimination Clause secures, I join Part II of Justice Souter's opinion and would remand the case for further consideration.

JUSTICE GINSBURG, concurring in part and dissenting in part.

I join Parts II and III of Justice Kennedy's opinion. For reasons well stated therein, I would hold that the Self-Incrimination Clause applies at the time and place police use severe compulsion to extract a statement from a suspect. * * * I write separately to state my view that, even if no finding were made concerning Martinez's belief that refusal to answer would delay his treatment, or Chavez's intent to create such an impression, the interrogation in this case would remain a clear instance of the kind of compulsion no reasonable officer would have thought constitutionally permissible. * * *

Martinez's interrogation strikingly resembles the hospital-bed questioning in *Mincey*. Like the suspect in *Mincey*, Martinez was "at the complete mercy of [his interrogator], unable to escape or resist the thrust of [the] interrogation." * * *

Convinced that Chavez's conduct violated Martinez's right to be spared from self-incriminating interrogation, I would affirm the judgment of the Court of Appeals. To assure a controlling judgment of the Court, however, * * * I join Part II of Justice Souter's opinion.[b]

7. *MASSIAH* REVISITED

Until the Court handed down the first case in this section, *Brewer v. Williams,* often called the "Christian burial speech" case, lasting fame had eluded *Massiah v. United States* [§ 2 supra]. Many thought that *Massiah* had been only a steppingstone to *Escobedo*, decided a scant five weeks later, and that both cases had been largely displaced by *Miranda.* But *Williams* made plain that despite the Court's shift from a "right to counsel" base in *Escobedo* to a "compelled self-incrimination base" in *Miranda,* the *Massiah* doctrine was still alive and well. Indeed, although few, if any, would have predicted it in the early 1970s, the *Massiah* doctrine has emerged as a much more potent force than it had ever been in the Warren Court era.

In the process of revivifying *Massiah,* however, the *Williams* Court blurred the *Massiah* and *Miranda* rationales. Although this is not clear from the *Williams* opinion, application of *Massiah* turns on neither "custody" nor "interrogation," the

---

    [b] In *United States v. Patane,* p. 520, upholding the admissibility of a pistol found as the result of a failure to administer the *Miranda* warnings fully, the plurality (Thomas, J., joined by Rehnquist, C.J., and Scalia, J.) relied heavily on *Chavez v. Martinez,* observing inter alia: "The *Miranda* rule is not a code of police conduct, and police do not violate the Constitution (or even the *Miranda* rule, for that matter) by mere failures to warn. For this reason the exclusionary rule articulated in [Fourth Amendment cases] does not apply."

key *Miranda* concepts. Rather, the *Massiah* doctrine represents a pure right to counsel approach.

Once adversary proceedings have commenced against an individual (e.g., he has been indicted or arraigned) he is entitled to the assistance of counsel and the government may not "deliberately elicit" incriminating statements from him, neither openly by uniformed police officers nor surreptitiously by "secret agents." This prohibition applies regardless of whether the individual is in "custody" or being subjected to "interrogation" in the *Miranda* sense. There need not be any compelling influences at work, inherent, informal or otherwise. (There certainly were not any in the *Massiah* case itself.)

Nevertheless, perhaps because the lower courts had treated *Williams* as a *Miranda* case, a majority of the *Williams* Court thought it important, if not crucial, to establish that the "Christian burial speech" delivered by Captain Leaming did constitute "interrogation"—and all four dissenters insisted it was not. Considering the Court's subsequent discussion of "interrogation" in *Rhode Island v. Innis* [§ 4 supra], the captain's "speech" does appear to have been a form of "*Miranda* interrogation," but *it did not have to be,* in order for the *Massiah* doctrine to have protected Williams.

United States v. Henry, 447 U.S. 264 (1980), not only reaffirmed the *Massiah-Williams* doctrine, but expanded it by applying it to a situation where the FBI had instructed its paid government informant, ostensibly defendant's "cellmate," not to question defendant about the crime, and there was no showing that he had. Nevertheless, the Court, per Burger, C.J., rejected the government's argument that the incriminating statements were not the result of any "affirmative conduct" on the part of government agents to elicit evidence. The informant "was not a passive listener; rather he had 'some conversations with Mr. Henry' while he was in jail and Henry's incriminatory statements were 'the product of this conversation.' "

Moreover, and more generally, observed the Court: Even if the FBI agent's statement is accepted that "he did not intend that [the informant] would take affirmative steps to secure incriminating information, he must have known that such propinquity likely would lead to that result. * * * By intentionally creating a situation likely to induce Henry to make incriminating statements without the assistance of counsel [after Henry had been indicted and counsel had been appointed for him], the government violated Henry's Sixth Amendment right to counsel."

This broad—some would say, loose—language would seem to prohibit the government from "planting" even a completely "passive" secret agent in a person's cell once adversary proceedings have commenced against him. But the *Henry* Court cautioned that it was not "called upon to pass on the situation where an informant is placed in [close] proximity [to a prisoner] but makes no effort to stimulate conversations about the crime charged." Moreover, concurring Justice Powell made it plain that he could not join the majority opinion if it held that "the mere presence or incidental conversation of an informant in a jail cell would violate *Massiah*." The *Massiah* doctrine, emphasized Powell, "does not prohibit the introduction of spontaneous conversations that are not elicited by governmental action."

May the government employ a "passive informant" without violating the *Massiah* doctrine? Must the informant be—is it possible for him to be—completely "passive"? These questions are addressed in the second case in this section, *Kuhlmann v. Wilson,* the most recent "jail plant" case. As is graphically illustrated by *Kuhlmann,* the line between "active" and "passive" secret agents—between "*stimulating*" conversations with a defendant in order to "elicit" incriminating statements from him and taking no action "beyond *merely listening*"—is an exceedingly difficult one to draw.

BREWER V. WILLIAMS (WILLIAMS I)
430 U.S. 387, 97 S.Ct. 1232, 51 L.Ed.2d 424 (1977).

JUSTICE STEWART delivered the opinion of the Court. * * *

On the afternoon of December 24, 1968, a 10-year-old girl named Pamela Powers went with her family to the YMCA in Des Moines, Iowa. [When] she failed to return from a trip to the washroom, a search for her began. The search was unsuccessful.

Robert Williams, who had recently escaped from a mental hospital, was a resident of the YMCA. Soon after the girl's disappearance Williams was seen in the YMCA lobby carrying some clothing and a large bundle wrapped in a blanket. He obtained help from a 14-year-old boy in opening the street door of the YMCA and the door to his automobile parked outside. When Williams placed the bundle in the front seat of his car the boy "saw two legs in it and they were skinny and white." Before anyone could see what was in the bundle Williams drove away. His abandoned car was found the following day in Davenport, Iowa, roughly 160 miles east of Des Moines. A warrant was then issued in Des Moines for his arrest on a charge of abduction.

On the morning of December 26, a Des Moines lawyer named Henry McKnight went to the Des Moines police station and informed the officers present that he had just received a long distance call from Williams, and that he had advised Williams to turn himself in to the Davenport police. Williams did surrender that morning to the police in Davenport, and they booked him on the charge specified in the arrest warrant and gave him the [*Miranda* warnings]. The Davenport police then telephoned their counterparts in Des Moines to inform them that Williams had surrendered. McKnight, the lawyer, was still at the Des Moines police headquarters, and Williams conversed with McKnight on the telephone. In the presence of the Des Moines Chief of Police and a Police Detective named Leaming [a captain and 20-year veteran of the Des Moines police department], McKnight advised Williams that Des Moines police officers would be driving to Davenport to pick him up, that the officers would not interrogate him or mistreat him, and that Williams was not to talk to the officers about Pamela Powers until after consulting with McKnight upon his return to Des Moines. As a result of these conversations, it was agreed between McKnight and the Des Moines police officials that Detective Leaming and a fellow officer would drive to Davenport to pick up Williams, that they would bring him directly back to Des Moines, and that they would not question him during the trip.

In the meantime Williams was arraigned before a judge in Davenport on the outstanding arrest warrant.[a] The judge advised him of his *Miranda* rights and committed him to jail. Before leaving the courtroom, Williams conferred with a lawyer named Kelly, who advised him not to make any statements until consulting with McKnight back in Des Moines.

Detective Leaming and his fellow officer arrived in Davenport about noon to pick up Williams and return him to Des Moines. Soon after their arrival they met with Williams and Kelly, who, they understood, was acting as Williams' lawyer. Detective Leaming repeated the *Miranda* warnings, and told Williams:

> " * * * we both know that you're being represented here by Mr. Kelly and you're being represented by Mr. McKnight in Des Moines, and * * * I want you to remember this because we'll be visiting between here and Des Moines."

Williams then conferred again with Kelly alone, and after this conference Kelly reiterated to Detective Leaming that Williams was not to be questioned about the disappearance of Pamela Powers until after he had consulted with McKnight back in Des Moines. When Leaming expressed some reservations, Kelly firmly stated that the agreement with McKnight was to be carried out—that there was to be no interrogation of Williams during the automobile journey to Des Moines. Kelly was denied permission to ride in the police car back to Des Moines with Williams and the two officers.

The two Detectives, with Williams in their charge, then set out on the 160-mile drive. At no time during the trip did Williams express a willingness to be interrogated in the absence of an attorney. Instead, he stated several times that "[w]hen I get to Des Moines and see Mr. McKnight, I am going to tell you the whole story." Detective Leaming knew that Williams was a former mental patient, and knew also that he was deeply religious.

The Detective and his prisoner soon embarked on a wide-ranging conversation covering a variety of topics, including the subject of religion. Then, not long after leaving Davenport and reaching the interstate highway, Detective Leaming delivered what has been referred to [as] the "Christian burial speech." Addressing Williams as "Reverend," the Detective said:

> "I want to give you something to think about while we're traveling down the road. * * * Number one, I want you to observe the weather conditions, it's raining, it's sleeting, it's freezing, driving is very treacherous, visibility is poor, it's going to be dark early this evening. They are

---

[a] At the time *Williams* was decided, it did not seem to matter that the defendant was arraigned on the charge of abduction, not the charge of murder that grew out of the abduction. Evidently the Court assumed that when the Sixth Amendment right to counsel attached to the abduction charge it attached to the factually related crime of murder as well. But consider *Texas v. Cobb*, 532 U.S. 162 (2001). Defendant had been indicted for the burglary of a home. While in police custody he confessed to the murder of a woman and child which had grown out of the burglary. Emphasizing that the Sixth Amendment right to counsel is "offense specific," and pointing out that, under Texas law, burglary and murder were not the same offense, a 5–4 majority held that the Sixth Amendment right to counsel did not prevent the police from questioning defendant about the murders.

predicting several inches of snow for tonight, and I feel that you yourself are the only person that knows where this little girl's body is, that you yourself have only been there once, and if you get a snow on top of it you yourself may be unable to find it. And, since we will be going right past the area on the way into Des Moines, I feel that we could stop and locate the body, that the parents of this little girl should be entitled to a Christian burial for the little girl who was snatched away from them on Christmas Eve and murdered. And I feel we should stop and locate it on the way in rather than waiting until morning and trying to come back out after a snow storm and possibly not being able to find it at all."

Williams asked Detective Leaming why he thought their route to Des Moines would be taking them past the girl's body, and Leaming responded that he knew the body was in the area of Mitchellville—a town they would be passing on the way to Des Moines.[1] Leaming then stated: "I do not want you to answer me. I don't want to discuss it further. Just think about it as we're riding down the road."

As the car approached Grinell, a town approximately 100 miles west of Davenport, Williams asked whether the police had found the victim's shoes. When Detective Leaming replied that he was unsure, Williams directed the officers to a service station where he said he had left the shoes; a search for them proved unsuccessful. As they continued towards Des Moines, Williams asked whether the police had found the blanket, and directed the officers to a rest area where he said he had disposed of the blanket. Nothing was found. The car continued towards Des Moines, and as it approached Mitchellville, Williams said that he would show the officers where the body was. He then directed the police to the body of Pamela Powers.

[The trial judge admitted all evidence relating to or resulting from statements Williams made in the car ride. He found that "an agreement" had been made between defense counsel and the police that Williams would not be questioned on the return trip to Des Moines, but ruled that Williams had waived his rights before giving such information.]

[On federal habeas corpus, the] District Court made findings of fact as summarized above, and concluded as a matter of law that the evidence in question had been wrongly admitted at Williams' trial. This conclusion was based on three alternative and independent grounds: (1) that Williams had been denied his constitutional right to the assistance of counsel; (2) that he had been denied [his *Miranda* rights]; and (3) that in any event, [his] statements [had] been involuntarily made.

[The] Court of Appeals appears to have affirmed the judgment on [the first two] grounds. We have concluded that only one of them need be considered here.

Specifically, there is no need to review the [*Miranda* doctrine] [or the] the ruling of the District Court that Williams' self-incriminating statements were, indeed, involuntarily made. For it is clear that the judgment before us must in any

---

[1]   The fact of the matter, of course, was that Detective Leaming possessed no such knowledge.

event be affirmed upon the ground that Williams was deprived of a different constitutional right—the right to the assistance of counsel.

* * * Whatever else it may mean, the right to counsel * * * means at least that a person is entitled to the help of a lawyer at or after the time that judicial proceedings have been initiated against him—"whether by way of formal charge, preliminary hearing, indictment, information, or arraignment." *Kirby v. Illinois* [p. 580].

There can be no doubt in the present case that judicial proceedings had been initiated against Williams before the start of the automobile ride from Davenport to Des Moines. A warrant had been issued for his arrest, he had been arraigned on that warrant before a judge in a Davenport courtroom, and he had been committed by the court to confinement in jail. The State does not contend otherwise.

There can be no serious doubt, either, that Detective Leaming deliberately and designedly set out to elicit information from Williams just as surely as—and perhaps more effectively than—if he had formally interrogated him. Detective Leaming was fully aware before departing for Des Moines that Williams was being represented in Davenport by Kelly and in Des Moines by McKnight. Yet he purposely sought during Williams' isolation from his lawyers to obtain as much incriminating information as possible. Indeed, Detective Leaming conceded as much when he testified at Williams' trial:

> "Q. In fact, Captain, whether he was a mental patient or not, you were trying to get all the information you could before he got to his lawyer, weren't you?
>
> "A. I was sure hoping to find out where that little girl was, yes, sir.
>
> * * *
>
> "Q. Well, I'll put it this way: You [were] hoping to get all the information you could before Williams got back to McKnight, weren't you?
>
> "A. Yes, sir."[6]

The state courts clearly proceeded upon the hypothesis that Detective Leaming's "Christian burial speech" had been tantamount to interrogation. Both courts recognized that Williams had been entitled to the assistance of counsel at the time he made the incriminating statements. Yet no such constitutional protection would have come into play if there had been no interrogation.

The circumstances of this case are thus constitutionally indistinguishable from those presented in *Massiah.* [That] the incriminating statements were elicited surreptitiously in [*Massiah*], and otherwise here, is constitutionally irrelevant. Rather, the clear rule of *Massiah* is that once adversary proceedings have commenced against an individual, he has a right to legal representation when the government interrogates him. It thus requires no wooden or technical application

---

[6]   Counsel for the State, in the course of oral argument in this Court, acknowledged that the "Christian burial speech" was tantamount to interrogation * * *.

of the *Massiah* doctrine to conclude that Williams was entitled to the assistance of counsel guaranteed to him by the Sixth and Fourteenth Amendments.

The Iowa courts recognized that Williams had been denied the constitutional right to the assistance of counsel. They held, however, that he had waived that right during the course of the automobile trip from Davenport to Des Moines. The state trial court explained its determination of waiver as follows:

> "The time element involved on the trip, the general circumstances of it, and more importantly the absence on the Defendant's part of any assertion of his right or desire not to give information absent the presence of his attorney, are the main foundations for the Court's conclusion that he voluntarily waived such right."

[The] District Court and the Court of Appeals were correct in the view that the question of waiver was not a question of historical fact, but one [that], requires "application of constitutional principles to the facts as found."

The [lower federal courts] were also correct in their understanding of the proper standard to be applied in determining the question of waiver as a matter of federal constitutional law—that it was incumbent upon the State to prove "an intentional relinquishment or abandonment of a known right or privilege." *Johnson v. Zerbst.* [That] strict standard applies equally to an alleged waiver of the right to counsel whether at trial or at a critical stage of pretrial proceedings.

We conclude, finally that the Court of Appeals was correct in holding that, judged by these standards, the record in this case falls far short of sustaining the State's burden. It is true that Williams had been informed of and appeared to understand his right to counsel. But waiver requires not merely comprehension but relinquishment, and Williams' consistent reliance upon the advice of counsel in dealing with the authorities refutes any suggestion that he waived that right. * * * His statements while in the car that he would tell the whole story *after* seeing McKnight in Des Moines were the clearest expressions by Williams himself that he desired the presence of an attorney before any interrogation took place. But even before making these statements, Williams had effectively asserted his right to counsel by having secured attorneys at both ends of the automobile trip, both of whom, acting as his agents, had made clear to the police that no interrogation was to occur during the journey. Williams knew of that agreement and, particularly in view of his consistent reliance on counsel, there is no basis for concluding that he disavowed it.

Despite Williams' express and implicit assertions of his right to counsel, Detective Leaming proceeded to elicit incriminating statements from Williams. Leaming did not preface this effort by telling Williams that he had a right to the presence of a lawyer, and made no effort at all to ascertain whether Williams wished to relinquish that right. The circumstances of record in this case thus provide no reasonable basis for finding that Williams waived his right to the assistance of counsel.

The Court of Appeals did not hold, nor do we, that under the circumstances of this case Williams *could not,* without notice to counsel, have waived his rights under the Sixth and Fourteenth Amendments. It only held, as do we, that he did not.

* * * Although we do not lightly affirm the issuance of a writ of habeas corpus in this case, so clear a violation of the Sixth and Fourteenth Amendments as here occurred cannot be condoned. * * * The judgment of the Court of Appeals is affirmed.[12]

JUSTICE MARSHALL, concurring.

I concur wholeheartedly in my Brother Stewart's opinion for the Court, but add these words in light of the dissenting opinions filed today. The dissenters have, I believe, lost sight of the fundamental constitutional backbone of our criminal law. They seem to think that Detective Leaming's actions were perfectly proper, indeed laudable, examples of "good police work." In my view, good police work is something far different from catching the criminal at any price. It is equally important that the police, as guardians of the law, fulfill their responsibility to obey its commands scrupulously.

[In] this case, there can be no doubt that Detective Leaming consciously and knowingly set out to violate Williams' Sixth Amendment right to counsel and his Fifth Amendment privilege against self-incrimination, as Leaming himself understood those rights. * * * Leaming surely understood, because he had overheard McKnight tell Williams as much, that the location of the body would be revealed to police. Undoubtedly Leaming realized the way in which that information would be conveyed to the police: McKnight would learn it from his client and then he would lead police to the body. Williams would thereby be protected by the attorney-client privilege from incriminating himself by directly demonstrating his knowledge of the body's location, and the unfortunate Powers child could be given a "Christian burial."

* * * If Williams is to go free—and given the ingenuity of Iowa prosecutors on retrial or in a civil commitment proceeding, I doubt very much that there is any chance a dangerous criminal will be loosed on the streets, the blood-curdling cries of the dissents notwithstanding—it will hardly be because he deserves it. It will be

---

[12] The District Court stated that its decision "does not touch upon the issue of what evidence, if any, beyond the incriminating statements themselves must be excluded as 'fruit of the poisonous tree.'" We too have no occasion to address this issue, and in the present posture of the case there is no basis for the view of our dissenting Brethren [that] any attempt to retry the respondent would probably be futile. While neither Williams' incriminating statements themselves nor any testimony describing his having led the police to the victim's body can constitutionally be admitted into evidence, evidence of where the body was found and of its condition might well be admissible on the theory that the body would have been discovered in any event, even had incriminating statements not been elicited from Williams. In the event that a retrial is instituted, it will be for the state courts in the first instance to determine whether particular items of evidence may be admitted.

[On retrial, the state court admitted evidence of the condition of the body of Pamela Powers and the results of post mortem tests on the body because the body "would have been found in any event"—if Williams had not led the police to the victim the search would have been taken up again where it left off and the body would have been discovered within a short time in essentially the same condition as it was actually found. Williams was again convicted of murder. The case came to the U.S. Supreme Court a second time in *Nix v. Williams* (*Williams II*), 467 U.S. 431 (1984), discussed *supra* Chapter 4, p. 364.]

because Detective Leaming, knowing full well that he risked reversal of Williams' conviction, intentionally denied Williams the right of *every* American under the Sixth Amendment to have the protective shield of a lawyer between himself and the awesome power of the State.

* * *

JUSTICE POWELL, concurring. * * *

The critical factual issue is whether there had been a voluntary waiver, and this turns in large part upon whether there was interrogation. * * *

Prior to the automobile trip from Davenport to Des Moines, Williams had been arrested, booked, and carefully given *Miranda* warnings. It is settled constitutional doctrine that he then had the right to the assistance of counsel. His exercise of this right was evidenced uniquely in this case. * * * Significantly, the recognition by the police of the status of counsel was evidenced by the *express agreement* between McKnight and the appropriate police officials that the officers who would drive Williams to Des Moines would not interrogate him in the absence of counsel.

The incriminating statements were made by Williams during the long ride while in the custody of two police officers, and in the absence of his retained counsel. The dissent of the Chief Justice concludes that prior to these statements, Williams had "made a valid waiver" of his right to have counsel present. This view disregards the record evidence clearly indicating that the police engaged in interrogation of Williams.

[The] dissenting opinion of the Chief Justice states that the Court's holding today "conclusively presumes a suspect is legally incompetent to change his mind and tell the truth until an attorney is present." I find no justification for this view. On the contrary, the opinion of the Court is explicitly clear that the right to assistance of counsel may be waived, after it has attached, without notice to or consultation with counsel. We would have such a case here if [the State] had proved that the police officers refrained from coercion and interrogation, as they had agreed, and that Williams freely on his own initiative had confessed the crime. * * * ᵃ

CHIEF JUSTICE BURGER, dissenting.

The result in this case ought to be intolerable in any society which purports to call itself an organized society. It continues the Court—by the narrowest margin—on the much-criticized course of punishing the public for the mistakes and misdeeds of law enforcement officers, instead of punishing the officer directly, if in fact he is guilty of wrongdoing. It mechanically and blindly keeps reliable evidence from juries whether the claimed constitutional violation involves gross police misconduct or honest human error.

Williams is guilty of the savage murder of a small child; no member of the Court contends he is not. While in custody, and after no fewer than *five* warnings

---

ᵃ   Stevens, J., joined the opinion of the Court, but also added a brief comment concluding: "If, in the long run, we are seriously concerned about the individual's effective representation by counsel, the State cannot be permitted to dishonor its promise to this lawyer."

of his rights to silence and to counsel, he led police to the concealed body of his victim. The Court concedes Williams was not threatened or coerced and that he spoke and acted voluntarily and with full awareness of his constitutional rights. In the face of all this, the Court now holds that because Williams was prompted by the detective's statement—not interrogation but a statement—the jury must not be told how the police found the body. * * *

The evidence is uncontradicted that Williams had abundant knowledge of his right to have counsel present and of his right to silence. Since the Court does not question his mental competence, it boggles the mind to suggest that Williams could not understand that leading police to the child's body would have other than the most serious consequences. * * *

One plausible but unarticulated basis for the result reached is that once a suspect has asserted his right not to talk without the presence of an attorney, it becomes legally impossible for him to waive that right until he has seen an attorney. But constitutional rights are *personal,* and an otherwise valid waiver should not be brushed aside by judges simply because an attorney was not present. * * * [2]

[Even] if there was no waiver, and assuming a technical violation occurred, the Court errs gravely in mechanically applying the exclusionary rule without considering whether that draconian judicial doctrine should be invoked in these circumstances, or indeed whether any of its conceivable goals will be furthered by its application here.

* * * Today's holding interrupts what has been a more rational perception of the constitutional and social utility of excluding reliable evidence from the truthseeking process. In its Fourth Amendment context, we have now recognized that the exclusionary rule is in no sense a *personal* constitutional right, but a judicially conceived remedial device designed to safeguard and effectuate guaranteed legal rights generally [referring to *Stone v. Powell,* 428 U.S. 465 (1976), holding the exclusionary rule inapplicable to habeas review, *United States v. Janis,* 428 U.S. 433 (1976), holding the exclusionary rule inapplicable in a civil tax proceeding, *United States v. Calandra,* holding the exclusionary rule inapplicable in a grand jury proceeding]. We have repeatedly emphasized that deterrence of unconstitutional or otherwise unlawful police conduct is the only valid justification for excluding reliable and probative evidence from the criminal factfinding process.

Accordingly, unlawfully obtained evidence is not automatically excluded from the factfinding process in all circumstances. In a variety of contexts we inquire whether application of the rule will promote its objectives sufficiently to justify the enormous cost it imposes on society. * * *

Against this background, it is striking that the Court fails even to consider whether the benefits secured by application of the exclusionary rule in this case outweigh its obvious social costs. Perhaps the failure is due to the fact that this

---

[2]   [A] paternalistic rule is particularly anomalous in the Sixth Amendment context, where this Court has only recently discovered an independent constitutional right of self-representation, allowing an accused the absolute right to proceed without a lawyer at trial, once he is aware of the consequences. *Faretta v. California* [p. 1007].

case arises not under the Fourth Amendment, but under *Miranda,* and the Sixth Amendment right to counsel. The Court apparently perceives the function of the exclusionary rule to be so different in these varying contexts that it must be mechanically and uncritically applied in all cases arising outside the Fourth Amendment. * * *

JUSTICE WHITE, with whom JUSTICE BLACKMUN and JUSTICE REHNQUIST join, dissenting.

* * * The issue in this case is whether respondent—who was entitled not to make any statements to the police without consultation with and/or presence of counsel[1]—validly waived those rights. * * *

[I disagree with the majority's finding that no waiver was proved in this case.] That respondent knew of his right not to say anything to the officers without advice and presence of counsel is established on this record to a moral certainty. He was advised of the right by three officials of the State—telling at least one that he understood the right—and by two lawyers.[4] Finally, he further demonstrated his knowledge of the right by informing the police that he would tell them the story in the presence of McKnight when they arrived in Des Moines. The issue in this case, then, is whether respondent relinquished that right intentionally.

Respondent relinquished his right not to talk to the police about his crime when the car approached the place where he had hidden the victim's clothes. Men usually intend to do what they do and there is nothing in the record to support the proposition that respondent's decision to talk was anything but an exercise of his own free will. Apparently, without any prodding from the officers, respondent—who had earlier said that he would tell the whole story when he arrived in Des Moines—spontaneously changed his mind about the timing of his disclosures when the car approached the places where he had hidden the evidence. However, even if his statements were influenced by Detective Leaming's above-quoted statement, respondent's decision to talk in the absence of counsel can hardly be viewed as the product of an overborn will. The statement by Leaming was not coercive; it was accompanied by a request that respondent not respond to it; and it was delivered hours before respondent decided to make any statement. Respondent's waiver was thus knowing and intentional.

[A] conceivable basis for the majority's holding is the implicit suggestion that the right involved in *Massiah,* as distinguished from the right involved in *Miranda,* is a right not to be *asked* any questions in counsel's absence rather than a right not to *answer* any questions in counsel's absence, and that the right not to be *asked* questions must be waived *before* the questions are asked. Such wafer thin distinctions cannot determine whether a guilty murderer should go free. The only conceivable purpose for the presence of counsel during questioning is to protect an

---

[1] It does not matter whether the right not to make statements in the absence of counsel stems from *Massiah* or *Miranda.* In either case the question is one of waiver. Waiver was not addressed in *Massiah* because there the statements were being made to an informant and the defendant had no way of knowing that he had a right not to talk to him without counsel.

[4] Moreover, he in fact received advice of counsel on at least two occasions on the question whether he should talk to the police on the trip to Des Moines.

accused from making incriminating *answers*. Questions, unanswered, have no significance at all. Absent coercion—no matter how the right involved is defined—an accused is amply protected by a rule requiring waiver before or simultaneously with the giving by him of an answer or the making by him of a statement.

* * *

MR. JUSTICE BLACKMUN, with whom MR. JUSTICE WHITE and MR. JUSTICE REHNQUIST join, dissenting. * * *

[The] Court rules that the Sixth Amendment was violated because Detective Leaming "purposely sought during Williams' isolation from his lawyers to obtain as much incriminating information as possible." I cannot regard that as unconstitutional *per se*.

First, the police did not deliberately seek to isolate Williams from his lawyers so as to deprive him of the assistance of counsel. Cf. *Escobedo*. The isolation in this case was a necessary incident of transporting Williams to the county where the crime was committed.

Second, Leaming's purpose was not solely to obtain incriminating evidence. The victim had been missing for only two days, and the police could not be certain that she was dead. Leaming, of course, and in accord with his duty, was "hoping to find out where that little girl was," but such motivation does not equate with an intention to evade the Sixth Amendment. * * *

Third, not every attempt to elicit information should be regarded as "tantamount to interrogation." I am not persuaded that Leaming's observations and comments, made as the police car traversed the snowy and slippery miles between Davenport and Des Moines that winter afternoon, were an interrogation, direct or subtle, of Williams. Williams, after all, was counseled by lawyers, and warned by the arraigning judge in Davenport and by the police, and yet it was he who started the travel conversations and brought up the subject of the criminal investigation.

[In] summary, it seems to me that the Court is holding that *Massiah* is violated whenever police engage in any conduct, in the absence of counsel, with the subjective desire to obtain information from a suspect after arraignment. Such a rule is far too broad. Persons in custody frequently volunteer statements in response to stimuli other than interrogation. * * *

KUHLMANN V. WILSON
477 U.S. 436, 106 S.Ct. 2616, 91 L.Ed.2d 364 (1986).

JUSTICE POWELL delivered the opinion of the Court.

[Respondent Wilson and two confederates robbed a garage and fatally shot the night dispatcher. Four days later, respondent turned himself in. He admitted that he had witnessed the robbery and murder, but denied any involvement in them, claiming that he had fled because he was afraid of being blamed for the crimes. He gave the police a description of the robbers, but denied knowing them.

[After his arraignment, Wilson was placed in a cell with a prisoner named Benny Lee. Unknown to Wilson, Lee had agreed to act as a police informant. Since the police had positive evidence of Wilson's involvement, the purpose of placing Lee in the cell was to determine the identities of the other perpetrators. According to his arrangement with Detective Cullen, Lee was not to ask Wilson any questions, but simply to "keep his ears open" for the names of Wilson's confederates. Wilson first spoke to Lee about the crimes after looking out the cellblock window at the garage, where the crime had occurred. He told Lee the same story he had given the police. Lee advised Wilson that his story "didn't sound too good" and that "things didn't look too good for him," but Wilson did not alter his story at that time. However, several days later, after a visit from his brother, who mentioned that members of the family were upset because they believed he had killed the dispatcher, Wilson changed his story. He admitted to Lee that he and two other men had planned and carried out the robbery and killed the dispatcher. Lee reported these incriminating statements to Detective Cullen.

[The trial court denied Wilson's motion to suppress the incriminating statements, finding that Lee had obeyed police instructions only to listen to Wilson for the purpose of identifying his confederates, but not to question him about the crime. The trial court also found that Wilson's statements were "spontaneous" and "unsolicited." After he was convicted of murder and the conviction was affirmed, Wilson sought federal habeas corpus relief. After considering *Massiah*, the district court denied relief, finding "no interrogation whatsoever" by Lee and "only spontaneous statements" from Wilson. A divided U.S. Court of Appeals affirmed.

[Following the decision in *Henry,* Wilson decided to relitigate his Sixth Amendment claim. After his motion to vacate his conviction was denied, Wilson again sought federal habeas corpus relief. The district court concluded that the trial court's findings were "fatal" to Wilson's claim under *Henry* since they showed that the informant made "no affirmative effort" of any kind to elicit information from him. A divided Court of Appeals reversed, finding the circumstances indistinguishable from the facts of *Henry.*]

* * *

In *United States v. Henry,* the Court applied the *Massiah* test to incriminating statements made to a jailhouse informant. The Court of Appeals in that case found a violation of *Massiah* because the informant had engaged the defendant in conversations and "had developed a relationship of trust and confidence with [the defendant] such that [the defendant] revealed incriminating information." This Court affirmed, holding that the Court of Appeals reasonably concluded that the government informant "deliberately used his position to secure incriminating information from [the defendant] when counsel was not present." Although the informant had not questioned the defendant, the informant had "stimulated" conversations with the defendant in order to "elicit" incriminating information. The Court emphasized that those facts, like the facts of *Massiah,* amounted to " 'indirect and surreptitious interrogatio[n]' " of the defendant. * * *

[As] *Maine v. Moulton,* 474 U.S. 159 (1985),[a] makes clear, the primary concern of the *Massiah* line of decisions is secret interrogation by investigatory techniques that are the equivalent of direct police interrogation. Since "the Sixth Amendment is not violated whenever—by luck or happenstance—the State obtains incriminating statements from the accused after the right to counsel has attached," a defendant does not make out a violation of that right simply by showing that an informant, either through prior arrangement or voluntarily, reported his incriminating statements to the police. Rather, the defendant must demonstrate that the police and their informant took some action, beyond merely listening, that was designed deliberately to elicit incriminating remarks.

It is thus apparent that the Court of Appeals erred in concluding that respondent's right to counsel was violated under the circumstances of this case. [It failed] to accord to the state trial court's factual findings the presumption of correctness expressly required by 28 U.S.C. § 2254(d).

The state court found that Officer Cullen had instructed Lee only to listen to respondent for the purpose of determining the identities of the other participants in the robbery and murder. The police already had solid evidence of respondent's participation. The court further found that Lee followed those instructions, that he "at no time asked any questions" of respondent concerning the pending charges, and that he "only listened" to respondent's "spontaneous" and "unsolicited" statements. The only remark made by Lee that has any support in this record was his comment that respondent's initial version of his participation in the crimes "didn't sound too good." Without holding that any of the state court's findings were not entitled to the presumption of correctness under § 2254(d), the Court of Appeals focused on that one remark and gave a description of Lee's interaction with respondent that is completely at odds with the facts found by the trial court. In the Court of Appeals' view, "Subtly and slowly, but surely, Lee's ongoing verbal intercourse with [respondent] served to exacerbate [respondent's] already troubled state of mind."[24] After thus revising some of the trial court's findings, and ignoring other more relevant findings, the Court of Appeals concluded that the police "deliberately elicited" respondent's incriminating statements. This conclusion

---

[a] *Moulton* holds that the *Massiah* doctrine applies to a crime for which the defendant has already been indicted even though the government had other, legitimate reasons for intercepting defendant's conversations—to insure the safety of its secret agent and to gather information concerning a report that defendant was planning to kill a witness. The Court, per Brennan, J., agreed that it was "entirely proper" for the government to conduct an investigation of defendant's activities, even though he had already been indicted, and statements obtained from him would be admissible at a subsequent trial for crimes *apart* from those for which defendant had already been indicted. But statement pertaining to *pending charges* had to be excluded at the trial of those charges despite the fact the government was also investigating other crimes. For to allow incriminating statements pertaining to pending charges to be used "whenever the police assert an alternative, legitimate reason for their surveillance invites abuse by law enforcement personnel in the form of fabricated investigations and risks the evisceration of the Sixth Amendment right recognized in *Massiah*."

[24] Curiously, the Court of Appeals expressed concern that respondent was placed in a cell that overlooked the scene of his crimes. For all the record shows, however, that fact was sheer coincidence. Nor do we perceive any reason to require police to isolate one charged with crime so that he cannot view the scene, whatever it may be, from his cell window.

conflicts with the decision of every other state and federal judge who reviewed this record, and is clear error in light of the provisions and intent of § 2254(d).[b]

JUSTICE BRENNAN, with whom JUSTICE MARSHALL joins, dissenting. * * *

The Court of Appeals did not disregard the state court's finding that Lee asked respondent no direct questions regarding the crime. Rather, the Court of Appeals *expressly accepted* that finding, but concluded that, as a matter of law, the deliberate elicitation standard of *Henry* and *Massiah,* encompasses other, more subtle forms of stimulating incriminating admissions than overt questioning. The court suggested that the police deliberately placed respondent in a cell that overlooked the scene of the crime, hoping that the view would trigger an inculpatory comment to respondent's cellmate.[8] The court also observed that, while Lee asked respondent no questions, Lee nonetheless stimulated conversation concerning respondents' role in [the] robbery and murder by remarking that respondent's exculpatory story did not " 'sound too good' " and that he had better come up with a better one. Thus, the Court of Appeals concluded that the respondent's case did not present the situation reserved in *Henry,* [but was] virtually indistinguishable from *Henry.* * * *

In Henry, [we] rejected the Government's argument that because Henry initiated the discussion of his crime, no Sixth Amendment violation had occurred. We pointed out that under Massiah, it is irrelevant whether the informant asks pointed questions about the crime or "merely engage[s] in general conversation about it." * * *

In the instant case, as in Henry, the accused was incarcerated and therefore was "susceptible to the ploys of undercover Government agents." Like Nichols, Lee was a secret informant, usually received consideration for the services he rendered the police, and therefore had an incentive to produce the information which he knew the police hoped to obtain. Just as Nichols had done, Lee obeyed instructions not to question respondent and to report to the police any statements made by the respondent in Lee's presence about the crime in question. And, like Nichols, Lee encouraged respondent to talk about his crime by conversing with him on the subject over the course of several days and by telling respondent that his exculpatory story would not convince anyone without more work. However, unlike the situation in Henry, a disturbing visit from respondent's brother, rather than a conversation with the informant, seems to have been the immediate catalyst for respondent's confession to Lee. While it might appear from this sequence of events that Lee's comment regarding respondent's story and his general willingness to converse with respondent about the crime were not the immediate causes of respondent's admission, I think that the deliberate elicitation standard requires consideration of the entire course of government behavior.

---

[b]   Chief Justice Burger, the author of *Henry,* joined the opinion of the Court, but also wrote a brief concurring opinion noting "a vast difference between placing an 'ear' in the suspect's cell and placing a voice in the cell to encourage conversation for the 'ear' to record."

[8]   The Court of Appeals noted that "[a]s soon as Wilson arrived and viewed the garage, he became upset and stated that 'someone's messing with me.' "

The State intentionally created a situation in which it was foreseeable that respondent would make incriminating statements without the assistance of counsel, Henry, it assigned respondent to a cell overlooking the scene of the crime and designated a secret informant to be respondent's cellmate. The informant, while avoiding direct questions, nonetheless developed a relationship of cellmate camaraderie with respondent and encouraged him to talk about his crime. While the coup de grace was delivered by respondent's brother, the groundwork for respondent's confession was laid by the State. Clearly the State's actions had a sufficient nexus with respondent's admission of guilt to constitute deliberate elicitation within the meaning of Henry.[c]

---

[c] Stevens, J., filed a separate dissent, agreeing with Justice Brennan's analysis of the merits of respondent's habeas petition.

CHAPTER 7

PRE-TRIAL IDENTIFICATION PROCEDURES

■ ■ ■

Although mistaken identifications are probably the single greatest cause of wrongful convictions, the Supreme Court did not come to grips with this problem until surprisingly late. When it finally did, in 1967, the Court seemed bent on making up for lost time. Although it might have undertaken a case-by-case analysis of various identification situations, as had been done in the confession area in the thirty years prior to *Escobedo* and *Miranda,* only throwing out convictions based on unreliable identifications, the Court leapfrogged the fairness stage and applied the right to counsel to pretrial identifications in one swoop.

United States v. Wade, the first case set forth in this chapter, seemed to require the presence of counsel at *all* pretrial identifications. Although the pretrial identifications in *Wade* and its companion case (*Gilbert v. California*) took place after the defendants had been indicted, the Court's reasoning did not seem premised on that fact. Rather, the Court emphasized that pre-trial identification procedures are riddled with innumerable dangers that might crucially derogate from a fair trial and held that counsel should be appointed to protect against possible unfairness.

Nevertheless, in *Kirby v. Illinois* (1972), the second case in this chapter, the Court did announce a "post-indictment" rule. Following *Kirby* it became the common practice of law enforcement agencies to avoid the applicability of the right to counsel by conducting identification proceedings before the filing of formal charges. A year after *Kirby,* the Burger Court struck the *Wade-Gilbert* rule another blow when it ruled in *United States v. Ash* (discussed infra in a footnote to *Kirby*) that photographic identification may take place without defense counsel's participation, whether conducted before or after the filing of formal charges.

Although *Kirby* and *Ash* severely restricted the potential reach of the original lineup decisions, abuses in photographic displays and in preindictment lineups are not, in theory at least, thereby placed beyond the reach of the Constitution: a defendant may still convince a court that the circumstances surrounding his identification present so "substantial" a "likelihood of misidentification" as to violate due process. But, as illustrated by the last two cases in this chapter, this is a difficult task. First, under *Manson v. Brathwaite,* an "unnecessarily suggestive" identification is not enough to require suppression of identification evidence; the "totality of the circumstances" may still allow identification evidence if, despite the unnecessary "suggestiveness," the out-of-court identification "possesses certain features of reliability." Recently, the Supreme Court further limited the applicability of the due process test in *Perry v. New Hampshire* when it held that only identification procedures that are police-orchestrated will trigger application of the *Brathwaite* test. A privately-arranged identification procedure, no matter how suggestive or unreliable, will never violate due process.

1. *WADE* AND *GILBERT*: RELIABILITY CONCERNS

UNITED STATES V. WADE
388 U.S. 218, 87 S.Ct. 1926, 18 L.Ed.2d 1149 (1967).

JUSTICE BRENNAN delivered the opinion of the Court.

The question here is whether courtroom identifications of an accused at trial are to be excluded from evidence because the accused was exhibited to the witnesses before trial at a post-indictment lineup conducted for identification purposes without notice to and in the absence of the accused's appointed counsel.

The federally insured bank in Eustace, Texas, was robbed on September 21, 1964. A man with a small strip of tape on each side of his face entered the bank, pointed a pistol at the female cashier and the vice president [and] forced them to fill a pillowcase with the bank's money. The man then drove away with an accomplice who had been waiting in a stolen car outside the bank. [On April 2, 1965, Wade and two others were arrested for the robbery. Counsel was appointed to represent Wade on April 26.] Fifteen days [after counsel's appointment], an FBI agent, without notice to Wade's lawyer, arranged to have the two bank employees observe a lineup made up of Wade and five or six other prisoners and conducted in a courtroom of the local county courthouse. [Both] bank employees identified Wade in the lineup as the bank robber.

At trial the two employees, when asked on direct examination if the robber was in the courtroom, pointed to Wade. The prior lineup identification was then elicited from both employees on cross-examination. At the close of testimony, Wade's counsel moved [to] strike the bank officials' courtroom identifications on [self-incrimination and right to counsel grounds]. The motion was denied, and Wade was convicted. The Court of Appeals for the Fifth Circuit reversed the conviction and ordered a new trial at which the in-court identification evidence was to be excluded, holding that [conducting the lineup in the absence of Wade's appointed counsel violated his Sixth Amendment rights]. * * *

[T]he principle of *Powell v. Alabama* and succeeding cases requires that we scrutinize *any* pretrial confrontation of the accused to determine whether the presence of his counsel is necessary to preserve the defendant's basic right to a fair trial as affected by his right meaningfully to cross-examine the witnesses against him and to have effective assistance of counsel at the trial itself. It calls upon us to analyze whether potential substantial prejudice to defendant's rights inheres in the particular confrontation and the ability of counsel to help avoid that prejudice.

The Government characterizes the lineup as a mere preparatory step in the gathering of the prosecution's evidence, not different—for Sixth Amendment purposes—from various other preparatory steps, such as systematized or scientific analyzing of the accused's fingerprints, blood sample, clothing, hair, and the like. We think there are differences which preclude such stages being characterized as critical stages at which the accused has the right to the presence of his counsel. Knowledge of the techniques of science and technology is sufficiently available, and the variables in techniques few enough, that the accused has the opportunity for a meaningful confrontation of the Government's case at trial through the ordinary processes of cross-examination of the Government's expert witnesses and the presentation of the evidence of his own experts. The denial of a right to have his counsel present at such analyses does not therefore violate the Sixth Amendment; they are not critical stages since there is minimal risk that his counsel's absence at such stages might derogate from his right to a fair trial.

But the confrontation compelled by the State between the accused and the victim or witnesses to a crime to elicit identification evidence is peculiarly riddled with innumerable dangers and variable factors which might seriously, even crucially, derogate from a fair trial. The vagaries of eyewitness identification are well-known; the annals of criminal law are rife with instances of mistaken identification. * * * A major factor contributing to the high incidence of miscarriage of justice from mistaken identification has been the degree of suggestion inherent in the manner in which the prosecution presents the suspect to witnesses for pretrial identification. A commentator has observed that "[t]he influence of improper suggestion upon identifying witnesses probably accounts for more miscarriages of justice than any other single factor—perhaps it is responsible for more such errors than all other factors combined." Suggestion can be created intentionally or unintentionally in many subtle ways. And the dangers for the suspect are particularly grave when the witness' opportunity for observation was insubstantial, and thus his susceptibility to suggestion the greatest.

Moreover, "[i]t is a matter of common experience that, once a witness has picked out the accused at the line-up, he is not likely to go back on his word later on, so that in practice the issue of identity may (in the absence of other relevant evidence) for all practical purposes be determined there and then, before the trial."

The pretrial confrontation for purpose of identification may take the form of a lineup, also known as an "identification parade" or "showup," as in the present case, or presentation of the suspect alone to the witness, as in *Stovall v. Denno.*[a] It is obvious that risks of suggestion attend either form of confrontation and increase the dangers inhering in eyewitness identification. But as is the case with secret interrogations, there is serious difficulty in depicting what transpires at lineups and other forms of identification confrontations. [For] the same reasons, the defense can seldom reconstruct the manner and mode of lineup identification for judge or jury at trial. [The] impediments to an objective observation are increased when the victim is the witness. Lineups are prevalent in rape and robbery prosecutions and present a particular hazard that a victim's understandable outrage may excite vengeful or spiteful motives. In any event, neither witnesses nor lineup participants are apt to be alert for conditions prejudicial to the suspect. And if they were, it would likely be of scant benefit to the suspect since neither

---

[a]   *Stovall* is discussed in § 3 infra, p. 583.

witnesses nor lineup participants are likely to be schooled in the detection of suggestive influences.[13] Improper influences may go undetected by a suspect, guilty or not, who experiences the emotional tension which we might expect in one being confronted with potential accusers. Even when he does observe abuse, if he has a criminal record he may be reluctant to take the stand and open up the admission of prior convictions. Moreover any protestations by the suspect of the fairness of the lineup made at trial are likely to be in vain; the jury's choice is between the accused's unsupported version and that of the police officers present. In short, the accused's inability effectively to reconstruct at trial any unfairness that occurred at the lineup may deprive him of his only opportunity meaningfully to attack the credibility of the witness' courtroom identification. * * *

The potential for improper influence is illustrated by the circumstances, insofar as they appear, surrounding the prior identifications in the three cases we decide today. In the present case, [the] witnesses were taken to the courthouse and seated in the courtroom to await assembly of the lineup. The courtroom faced on a hallway observable to the witnesses through an open door. The cashier testified that she saw Wade "standing in the hall" within sight of an FBI agent. Five or six other prisoners later appeared in the hall. The vice president testified that he saw a person in the hall in the custody of the agent who "resembled the person that we identified as the one that had entered the bank."

The lineup in *Gilbert* [*v. California*, 388 U.S. 263 (1967)], was conducted in an auditorium in which some 100 witnesses to several alleged state and federal robberies charged to Gilbert made wholesale identifications of Gilbert as the robber in each other's presence, a procedure said to be fraught with dangers of suggestion. And the vice of suggestion created by the identification in *Stovall* was the presentation to the witness of the suspect alone handcuffed to police officers. It is hard to imagine a situation more clearly conveying the suggestion to the witness that the one presented is believed guilty by the police.

The few cases that have surfaced therefore reveal the existence of a process attended with hazards of serious unfairness to the criminal accused and strongly suggest the plight of the more numerous defendants who are unable to ferret out suggestive influences in the secrecy of the confrontation. We do not assume that these risks are the result of police procedures intentionally designed to prejudice an accused. Rather we assume they derive from the dangers inherent in eyewitness identification and the suggestibility inherent in the context of the pretrial identification. * * *

Insofar as the accused's conviction may rest on a courtroom identification in fact the fruit of a suspect pretrial identification which the accused is helpless to subject to effective scrutiny at trial, the accused is deprived of that right of cross-examination which is an essential safeguard to his right to confront the witnesses against him. And even though cross-examination is a precious safeguard to a fair

---

[13] An additional impediment to the detection of such influences by participants, including the suspect, is the physical conditions often surrounding the conduct of the lineup. In many, lights shine on the stage in such a way that the suspect cannot see the witness. [In] some a one-way mirror is used and what is said on the witness' side cannot be heard. * * *

trial, it cannot be viewed as an absolute assurance of accuracy and reliability. Thus in the present context, where so many variables and pitfalls exist, the first line of defense must be the prevention of unfairness and the lessening of the hazards of eyewitness identification at the lineup itself. The trial which might determine the accused's fate may well not be that in the courtroom but that at the pretrial confrontation, with the State aligned against the accused, the witness the sole jury, and the accused unprotected against the overreaching, intentional or unintentional, and with little or no effective appeal from the judgment there rendered by the witness—"that's the man."

Since it appears that there is grave potential for prejudice, intentional or not, in the pretrial lineup, which may not be capable of reconstruction at trial, and since presence of counsel itself can often avert prejudice and assure a meaningful confrontation at trial, there can be little doubt that for Wade the post-indictment lineup was a critical stage of the prosecution at which he was "as much entitled to such aid [of counsel as] at the trial itself." *Powell v. Alabama.* Thus both Wade and his counsel should have been notified of the impending lineup, and counsel's presence should have been a requisite to conduct of the lineup, absent an "intelligent waiver." No substantial countervailing policy considerations have been advanced against the requirement of the presence of counsel. Concern is expressed that the requirement will forestall prompt identifications and result in obstruction of the confrontations. As for the first, we note that in the two cases in which the right to counsel is today held to apply, counsel had already been appointed and no argument is made in either case that notice to counsel would have prejudicially delayed the confrontations. Moreover, we leave open the question whether the presence of substitute counsel might not suffice where notification and presence of the suspect's own counsel would result in prejudicial delay. And to refuse to recognize the right to counsel for fear that counsel will obstruct the course of justice is contrary to the basic assumptions upon which this Court has operated in Sixth Amendment cases. [In] our view counsel can hardly impede legitimate law enforcement; on the contrary, for the reasons expressed, law enforcement may be assisted by preventing the infiltration of taint in the prosecution's identification evidence. That result cannot help the guilty avoid conviction but can only help assure that the right man has been brought to justice.

Legislative or other regulations, such as those of local police departments, which eliminate the risks of abuse and unintentional suggestion at lineup proceedings and the impediments to meaningful confrontation at trial may also remove the basis for regarding the stage as "critical." But neither Congress nor the federal authorities have seen fit to provide a solution.

We come now to the question whether the denial of Wade's motion to strike the courtroom identification by the bank witnesses at trial because of the absence of his counsel at the lineup required, as the Court of Appeals held, the grant of a new trial at which such evidence is to be excluded. We do not think this disposition can be justified without first giving the Government the opportunity to establish by clear and convincing evidence that the in-court identifications were based upon observations of the suspect other than the lineup identification. * * * Where, as here, the admissibility of evidence of the lineup identification itself is not involved, a *per se* rule of exclusion of courtroom identification would be unjustified. [A] rule limited solely to the exclusion of testimony concerning identification at the lineup itself, without regard to admissibility of the courtroom identification, would render the right to counsel an empty one. The lineup is most often used, as in the present case, to crystallize the witnesses' identification of the defendant for future reference. We have already noted that the lineup identification will have that effect. The State may then rest upon the witnesses' unequivocal courtroom identification, and not mention the pretrial identification as part of the State's case at trial. Counsel is then in the predicament in which Wade's counsel found himself—realizing that possible unfairness at the lineup may be the sole means of attack upon the unequivocal courtroom identification, and having to probe in the dark in an attempt to discover and reveal unfairness, while bolstering the government witness' courtroom identification by bringing out and dwelling upon his prior identification. Since counsel's presence at the lineup would equip him to attack not only the lineup identification but the courtroom identification as well, limiting the impact of violation of the right to counsel to exclusion of evidence only of identification at the lineup itself disregards a critical element of that right.

We think it follows that the proper test to be applied in these situations is that quoted in *Wong Sun v. United States,* 371 U.S. 471 (1963), " '[W]hether, granting establishment of the primary illegality the evidence to which instant objection is made has been come at by exploitation of that illegality or instead by means sufficiently distinguishable to be purged of the primary taint.' " Application of this test in the present context requires consideration of various factors; for example, the prior opportunity to observe the alleged criminal act, the existence of any discrepancy between any pre-lineup description and the defendant's actual description, any identification prior to lineup of another person, the identification by picture of the defendant prior to the lineup, failure to identify the defendant on a prior occasion, and the lapse of time between the alleged act and the lineup identification. It is also relevant to consider those facts which, despite the absence of counsel, are disclosed concerning the conduct of the lineup. * * *

On the record now before us we cannot make the determination whether the in-court identifications had an independent origin. [T]he appropriate procedure to be followed is to vacate the conviction pending a hearing to determine whether the in-court identifications had an independent source, or whether, in any event, the introduction of the evidence was harmless error, *Chapman v. California,* 386 U.S. 18 (1967), and for the District Court to reinstate the conviction or order a new trial, as may be proper.[b] * * *

---

[b]   Compare *Gilbert* [p. 576], where various witnesses who identified petitioner in the courtroom also testified, on direct examination by the prosecution, that they had identified petitioner at a prior lineup. "That [pretrial lineup] testimony," ruled the Court, "is the direct result of the illegal lineup 'come at by exploitation of [the primary] illegality.' *Wong Sun.* The State is therefore not entitled to an opportunity to show that that testimony had an independent source. Only a *per se* exclusionary rule as to such testimony can be an effective sanction to assure that law enforcement authorities will respect the accused's constitutional right to the presence of his counsel at the critical lineup. [That] conclusion is buttressed by the consideration that the witness' testimony of his lineup identification will enhance the impact of his in-court identification on the jury and seriously aggravate whatever derogation exists of the accused's right to a fair trial.

Judgment of Court of Appeals vacated and case remanded with direction.[c]

JUSTICE WHITE whom JUSTICE HARLAN and JUSTICE STEWART join, dissenting in part and concurring in part.

[The] Court's opinion is far-reaching. It proceeds first by creating a new *per se* rule of constitutional law: a criminal suspect cannot be subjected to a pretrial identification process in the absence of his counsel without violating the Sixth Amendment. If he is, the State may not buttress a later courtroom identification of the witness by any reference to the previous identification. Furthermore, the courtroom identification is not admissible at all unless the State can establish by clear and convincing proof that the testimony is not the fruit of the earlier identification made in the absence of defendant's counsel—admittedly a heavy burden for the State and probably an impossible one. To all intents and purposes, courtroom identifications are barred if pretrial identifications have occurred without counsel being present.

The rule applies to any lineup, to any other techniques employed to produce an identification and *a fortiori* to a face-to-face encounter between the witness and the suspect alone, regardless of when the identification occurs, in time or place, and whether before or after indictment or information.

[The] premise for the Court's rule is not the general unreliability of eyewitness identifications nor the difficulties inherent in observation, recall, and recognition. The Court assumes a narrower evil as the basis for its rule—improper police suggestion which contributes to erroneous identifications. The Court apparently believes that improper police procedures are so widespread that a broad prophylactic rule must be laid down, requiring the presence of counsel at all pretrial identifications, in order to detect recurring instances of police misconduct. I do not share this pervasive distrust of all official investigations. * * *

There are several striking aspects to the Court's holding. First, the rule does not bar courtroom identifications where there have been no previous identifications in the presence of the police, although when identified in the courtroom, the defendant is known to be in custody and charged with the commission of a crime. Second, the Court seems to say that if suitable legislative standards were adopted for the conduct of pretrial identifications, thereby lessening the hazards in such confrontations, it would not insist on the presence of counsel. But if this is true, why does not the Court simply fashion what it deems to be constitutionally acceptable procedures for the authorities to follow?

Third, courtroom identification may be barred, absent counsel at a prior identification, regardless of the extent of counsel's information concerning the circumstances of the previous confrontation between witness and defendant—apparently even if there were recordings or sound-movies of the events as they occurred. But if the rule is premised on the defendant's right to have his counsel know, there seems little basis for not accepting other means to inform. * * *

Therefore, unless the [state supreme court] is 'able to declare a belief that it was harmless beyond a reasonable doubt,' *Chapman,* Gilbert will be entitled on remand to a new trial * * *."

   [c] Justice Black's opinion, dissenting in part and concurring in part, is omitted.

Finally, I think the Court's new rule is vulnerable in terms of its own unimpeachable purpose of increasing the reliability of identification testimony. * * * [Defense c]ounsel's interest is in not having his client placed at the scene of the crime, regardless of his whereabouts. Some counsel may advise their clients to refuse to make any movements or to speak any words in a lineup or even to appear in one.[d] [Others] will hover over witnesses and begin their cross-examination then, menacing truthful factfinding as thoroughly as the Court fears the police now do. Certainly there is an implicit invitation to counsel to suggest rules for the lineup and to manage and produce it as best he can.[e] I therefore doubt that the Court's new rule, at least absent some clearly defined limits on counsel's role, will measurably contribute to more reliable pretrial identifications. My fears are that it will have precisely the opposite result. * * *

2. THE COURT RETREATS: *KIRBY* AND *ASH*

KIRBY V. ILLINOIS
406 U.S. 682, 92 S.Ct. 1877, 32 L.Ed.2d 411 (1972).

JUSTICE STEWART announced the judgment of the Court in an opinion in which THE CHIEF JUSTICE, JUSTICE BLACKMUN, and JUSTICE REHNQUIST join.

* * * In the present case we are asked to extend the *Wade-Gilbert* per se exclusionary rule to identification testimony based upon a police station show-up that took place *before* the defendant had been indicted or otherwise formally charged with any criminal offense.

On February 21, 1968, [Willie] Shard reported to the Chicago police that the previous day two men had robbed him on a Chicago street of a wallet containing, among other things, traveler's checks and a Social Security card. On February 22, two police officers [investigating an unrelated crime] stopped petitioner and a companion, [Bean], [on a Chicago street]. When asked for identification, the petitioner produced a wallet that contained three traveler's checks and a Social Security card, all bearing the name of Willie Shard. * * *

Only after arriving at the police station, and checking the records there, did the arresting officers learn of the Shard robbery. [A police car] picked up Shard and brought him to the police station. Immediately upon entering the room [where petitioner and Bean were seated], Shard positively identified them as [his robbers].

---

[d] Since requiring a person to appear in a lineup or to use his voice as an identifying physical characteristic or to provide handwriting exemplars is not prohibited by the privilege against self-incrimination, the prosecution may comment on the suspect's refusal to cooperate. On occasion, courts have utilized civil or criminal contempt to coerce or punish the suspect who refuses to comply with a court order to participate in some identification proceeding.

[e] The prevailing practice has been for counsel to attend the lineup merely as an observer to assure against abuse and bad faith by law enforcement officers, and to provide the basis for any attack she might wish to make on the identification at trial. Any attempt to give counsel at identification a more active role is fraught with difficulties not only for the police but for counsel herself. If she is entitled to make objections at the lineup procedure, she would be held to have waived these objections if she does not make them at the procedure. If such a possibility of waiver exists, will counsel be under an obligation to raise every conceivable objection?

No lawyer was present [and neither suspect had asked for] or been advised of any right to the presence of counsel. [At the trial, Shard] described his identification of the two men at the police station [and] identified them again in the courtroom as the men who had robbed him.

[In] a line of constitutional cases in this Court stemming back to the Court's landmark opinion in *Powell v. Alabama,* it has been firmly established that a person's Sixth and Fourteenth Amendment right to counsel attaches only at or after the time that adversary judicial proceedings have been initiated against him.

This is not to say that a defendant in a criminal case has a constitutional right to counsel only at the trial itself. [But] the point is [that] *all* of [the right to counsel cases] have involved points of time at or after the initiation of adversary judicial criminal proceedings—whether by way of formal charge, preliminary hearing, indictment, information, or arraignment.

The only seeming deviation from this long line of constitutional decisions was *Escobedo* [which] is not apposite here for two distinct reasons. First, the Court in retrospect perceived that the "prime purpose" of *Escobedo* was not to vindicate the constitutional right to counsel as such, but, like *Miranda,* "to guarantee full effectuation of the privilege against self-incrimination. * * *" Secondly, and perhaps even more important for purely practical purposes, the Court has limited the holding of *Escobedo* to its own facts, and those facts are not remotely akin to the facts of the case before us.

The initiation of judicial criminal proceedings is far from a mere formalism. It is the starting point of our whole system of adversary criminal justice. For it is only then that the Government has committed itself to prosecute, and only then that the adverse positions of Government and defendant have solidified. It is then that a defendant finds himself faced with the prosecutorial forces of organized society, and immersed in the intricacies of substantive and procedural criminal law. It is this point, therefore, that marks the commencement of the "criminal prosecutions" to which alone the explicit guarantees of the Sixth Amendment are applicable.

What has been said is not to suggest that there may not be occasions during the course of a criminal investigation when the police do abuse identification procedures. Such abuses are not beyond the reach of the Constitution. [The] Due Process Clause of the Fifth and Fourteenth Amendments forbids a lineup that is unnecessarily suggestive and conducive to irreparable mistaken identification. When a person has not been formally charged with a criminal offense, *Stovall* strikes the appropriate constitutional balance between the right of a suspect to be protected from prejudicial procedures and the interest of society in the prompt and purposeful investigation of an unsolved crime.

The judgment is affirmed.[a]

---

[a] As he "would not extend the *Wade-Gilbert* exclusionary rule," Justice Powell concurred in the result.

JUSTICE BRENNAN, with whom JUSTICE DOUGLAS and JUSTICE MARSHALL join, dissenting. * * *

In view of *Wade,* it is plain, and the plurality today does not attempt to dispute it, that there inhere in a confrontation for identification conducted after arrest the identical hazards to a fair trial that inhere in such a confrontation conducted "after the onset of formal prosecutorial proceedings." The plurality apparently considers an arrest, which for present purposes we must assume to be based upon probable cause, to be nothing more than part of "a routine police investigation," and thus not "the starting point of our whole system of adversary criminal justice." [The] plurality offers no reason, and I can think of none, for concluding that a post-arrest confrontation for identification, unlike a post-charge confrontation, is not among those "critical confrontations of the accused by the prosecution at pretrial proceedings where the results might well settle the accused's fate and reduce the trial itself to a mere formality."

The highly suggestive form of confrontation employed in this case underscores the point. This showup was particularly fraught with the peril of mistaken identification. In the setting of a police station squad room where all present except petitioner and Bean were police officers, the danger was quite real that Shard's understandable resentment might lead him too readily to agree with the police that the pair under arrest, and the only persons exhibited to him, were indeed the robbers. [On] direct examination, Shard identified petitioner and Bean not as the alleged robbers on trial in the courtroom, but as the pair he saw at the police station. * * *

Wade and *Gilbert,* of course, happened to involve post-indictment confrontations. Yet even a cursory perusal of the opinions in those cases reveals that nothing at all turned upon that particular circumstance. In short, it is fair to conclude that rather than "declin[ing] to depart from [the] rationale" of *Wade* and *Gilbert,* the plurality today, albeit purporting to be engaged in "principled constitutional adjudication," refuses even to recognize that "rationale." * * * Because Shard testified at trial about his identification of petitioner at the police station showup, the exclusionary rule of *Gilbert* requires reversal.

JUSTICE WHITE, dissenting.

Wade and *Gilbert* govern this case and compel reversal of the judgment below.[b]

---

[b] A year later, in a decision the dissenters there maintained "mark[ed] simply another step towards the complete evisceration of the fundamental constitutional principles" established in the 1967 identification cases, the Court held that a defendant has no right to have his counsel present while witnesses view pictures of him for identification purposes at a post-indictment photographic display. *United States v. Ash,* 413 U.S. 300 (1973). Shortly before trial, almost three years after the crime, and long after defendant had been incarcerated and appointed counsel, the prosecutor showed five color photographs to a number of witnesses who previously had tentatively identified the black-and-white photograph of defendant. Three witnesses selected defendant's photo. In holding that the right to counsel did not extend to post-indictment photo-identifications, the Court, per Blackmun, J., observed:

"[Although the right to counsel guarantee has been expanded beyond the formal trial itself], the function of the lawyer has remained essentially the same as his function at trial. In all cases

3. DUE PROCESS LIMITATIONS

As pointed out in *Stovall v. Denno*, 388 U.S. 293 (1967), one unable to make a *Wade-Gilbert* right to counsel argument may still establish that the identification procedure conducted in his case "was so unnecessarily suggestive and conducive to irreparable mistaken identification that he was denied due process of law." In *Stovall,* the stabbing victim (Mrs. Behrendt), was hospitalized for major surgery. Without affording petitioner time to retain counsel (an arraignment had been promptly held but then postponed until petitioner could retain counsel), the police, with the cooperation of the victim's surgeon, arranged a confrontation between petitioner and the victim in her hospital room. Petitioner was handcuffed to one of the seven law enforcement officials who brought him to the hospital room. He was the only black person in the room. After being asked by an officer whether petitioner "was the man," the victim identified him from her hospital bed. Both Mrs. Behrendt and the police then testified at the trial to her identification in the hospital. Despite the suggestiveness of the confrontation, the Court, per Brennan,

---

considered by the Court, counsel has continued to act as a spokesman for, or advisor to, the accused. * * *

"The function of counsel in rendering 'assistance' continued at the lineup under consideration in *Wade* and its companion cases. Although the accused was not confronted there with legal questions, the lineup offered opportunities for prosecuting authorities to take advantage of the accused. * * *

"Even if we were willing to view the counsel guarantee in broad terms as a generalized protection of the adversary process, we would be unwilling to go so far as to extend the right to a portion of the prosecutor's trial-preparation interviews with witnesses. [The] traditional counterbalance in the American adversary system for these interviews arises from the equal ability of defense counsel to seek and interview witnesses himself.

"That adversary mechanism remains as effective for a photographic display as for other parts of pretrial interviews. No greater limitations are placed on defense counsel in constructing displays, seeking witnesses, and conducting photographic identifications than those applicable to the prosecution. * * *

"Pretrial [photo-identifications] are hardly unique in offering possibilities for the actions of the prosecutor unfairly to prejudice the accused. [In] many ways the prosecutor, by accident or by design, may improperly subvert the trial. The primary safeguard against abuses of this kind is the ethical responsibility of the prosecutor. * * * If that safeguard fails, review remains available under due process standards. These same safeguards apply to misuse of photographs."

Dissenting Justice Brennan, joined by Douglas and Marshall, JJ., observed:

"[A]lthough retention of the photographs may mitigate the dangers of misidentification due to the suggestiveness of the photographs themselves, it cannot in any sense reveal to defense counsel the more subtle, and therefore more dangerous, suggestiveness that might derive from the manner in which the photographs were displayed or any accompanying comments or gestures.

"[Moreover] and unlike the lineup situation, the accused himself is not even present at the photographic identification, thereby reducing the likelihood that irregularities in the procedures will ever come to light. * * *

"[A]lthough apparently conceding that the right to counsel attached, not only at the trial itself, but at all 'critical stages' of the prosecution, the Court holds today that, in order to be deemed 'critical,' the particular 'stage of the prosecution' under consideration must, at the very least, involve the physical 'presence of the accused,' at a 'trial-like confrontation' with the Government, at which the accused requires the 'guiding hand of counsel.' A pretrial photographic identification does not, of course, meet these criteria. * * *

"[But the] fundamental premise underlying *all* of this Court's decisions holding the right to counsel applicable at 'critical' pretrial proceedings, is that a 'stage' of the prosecution must be deemed 'critical' for the purposes of the Sixth Amendment if it is one at which the presence of counsel is necessary 'to protect the fairness of *trial itself.*' "

J., affirmed the Second Circuit's denial of federal habeas corpus relief, observing that "a claimed violation of due process of law in the conduct of a confrontation depends on the totality of the circumstances surrounding it, and the record in the present case reveals that the showing of Stovall to Mrs. Behrendt in an immediate hospital confrontation was imperative." The Court then quoted with approval from the court below: "Here was the only person in the world who could possibly exonerate Stovall. * * * No one knew how long Mrs. Behrendt might live. [Under the circumstances] and with the knowledge that Mrs. Behrendt could not visit the jail, the police followed the only feasible procedure and took Stovall to the hospital."

The Court elaborated on its due process test for determining the admissibility of identification testimony in *Manson v. Brathwaite* and *Perry v. New Hampshire*, discussed below.

MANSON V. BRATHWAITE
432 U.S. 98, 97 S.Ct. 2243, 53 L.Ed.2d 140 (1977).

JUSTICE BLACKMUN delivered the opinion of the Court.

[Several minutes before sunset, Glover, a black undercover police officer, purchased heroin from a seller through the open doorway of an apartment while standing for two or three minutes within two feet of the seller in a hallway illuminated by natural light. A few minutes later, Glover described the seller to a back-up officer, D'Onofrio, as being "a colored man, approximately five feet eleven inches tall, dark complexion, black hair, short Afro style, and having high cheekbones, and of heavy build. He was wearing at the time blue pants and a plaid shirt."

[On the basis of the description, D'Onofrio thought that respondent might be the heroin seller. He obtained a single photograph of respondent from police files and left it at Glover's office. Two days later, while alone, Glover viewed the photograph and identified it as that of the seller. At respondent's trial, Glover testified that there was "no doubt whatsoever" that the person shown in the photograph was respondent. Glover also made a positive in-court identification. No explanation was offered by the prosecution for the failure to utilize a photographic array or to conduct a lineup.

[After the Connecticut Supreme Court affirmed respondent's conviction, he sought federal habeas corpus relief. The Second Circuit, per Friendly, J., held that because the showing of the single photograph was "suggestive" and concededly "unnecessarily so," evidence pertaining to it was subject to a *per se* rule of exclusion.]

Petitioner at the outset acknowledges that "the procedure in the instant case was suggestive [because only one photograph was used] and unnecessary" [because there was no emergency or exigent circumstance]. The respondent, in agreement with the Court of Appeals, proposes a *per se* rule of exclusion that he claims is dictated by the demands of the Fourteenth Amendment's guarantee of due process. He rightly observes that this is the first case in which this Court has had occasion to rule upon strictly post-*Stovall* out-of-court identification evidence of the challenged kind.[a]

[The] Courts of Appeals appear to have developed at least two approaches to such evidence. The first, or *per se* approach, employed by the Second Circuit in the present case, focuses on the procedures employed and requires exclusion of the out-of-court identification evidence, without regard to reliability, whenever it has been obtained through unnecessarily suggest[ive] confrontation procedures.[b] The justifications advanced are the elimination of evidence of uncertain reliability, deterrence of the police and prosecutors, and the stated "fair assurance against the awful risks of misidentification."

The second, or more lenient, approach is one that continues to rely on the totality of the circumstances. It permits the admission of the confrontation evidence if, despite the suggestive aspect, the out-of-court identification possesses certain features of reliability. This second approach, in contrast to the other, is ad hoc and serves to limit the societal costs imposed by a sanction that excludes relevant evidence from consideration and evaluation by the trier of fact. * * *

The driving force behind [*Wade, Gilbert* and *Stovall*] was the Court's concern with the problems of eyewitness identification. Usually the witness must testify about an encounter with a total stranger under circumstances of emergency or emotional stress. The witness' recollection of the stranger can be distorted easily by the circumstances or by later actions of the police. Thus, *Wade* and its companion cases reflect the concern that the jury not hear eyewitness testimony unless that evidence has aspects of reliability. It must be observed that both approaches before us are responsive to this concern. The *per se* rule, however, goes too far since its application automatically and peremptorily, and without consideration of alleviating factors, keeps evidence from the jury that is reliable and relevant.

The second factor is deterrence. Although the *per se* approach has the more significant deterrent effect, the totality approach also has an influence on police behavior. The police will guard against unnecessarily suggestive procedures under the totality rule, as well as the *per se* one, for fear that their actions will lead to the exclusion of identifications as unreliable.

The third factor is the effect on the administration of justice. Here the *per se* approach suffers serious drawbacks. Since it denies the trier reliable evidence, it may result, on occasion, in the guilty going free. Also, because of its rigidity, the *per se* approach may make error by the trial judge more likely than the totality approach. And in those cases in which the admission of identification evidence is error under the *per se* approach but not under the totality approach—cases in

---

a   In *Neil v. Biggers*, 409 U.S. 188 (1972), the Supreme Court admitted into evidence a pre-*Stovall* out-of-court identification made under suggestive circumstances, because, under the "totality of the circumstances," there was "no substantial likelihood of misidentification."

b   Although the *per se* approach demands the exclusion of testimony concerning unnecessarily suggestive identifications, it does permit the admission of testimony concerning a subsequent identification, including an in-court identification, if the subsequent identification is determined to be reliable.

which the identification is reliable despite an unnecessarily suggestive identification procedure—reversal is a Draconian sanction. * * *

We therefore conclude that reliability is the linchpin in determining the admissibility of identification testimony for both pre- and post-*Stovall* confrontations. The factors to be considered include the opportunity of the witness to view the criminal at the time of the crime, the witness' degree of attention, the accuracy of his prior description of the criminal, the level of certainty demonstrated at the confrontation, and the time between the crime and the confrontation. Against these factors is to be weighed the corrupting effect of the suggestive identification itself.

We turn, then, to the facts of this case and apply the analysis:

1. The opportunity to view. Glover testified that for two to three minutes he stood at the apartment door, within two feet of the respondent. The door opened twice, and each time the man stood at the door. * * * Natural light from outside entered the hallway through a window. There was natural light, as well, from inside the apartment.

2. The degree of attention. Glover was not a casual or passing observer, [but] a trained police officer on duty—and specialized and dangerous duty—when he [made the heroin purchase]. Glover himself was a Negro and unlikely to perceive only general features of [black males].

3. The accuracy of the description. Glover's description was given to D'Onofrio within minutes after the transaction. It included the vendor's race, his height, his build, the color and style of his hair, and the high cheekbone facial feature. It also included clothing the vendor wore. No claim has been made that respondent did not possess the physical characteristics so described. * * *

4. The witness' level of certainty. There is no dispute that the photograph in question was that of respondent. Glover, in response to a question whether the photograph was that of the person from whom he made the purchase, testified: "There is no question whatsoever." This positive assurance was repeated.

5. The time between the crime and the confrontation. Glover's description of his vendor was given to D'Onofrio within minutes of the crime. The photographic identification took place only two days later. We do not have here the passage of weeks or months between the crime and the viewing of the photograph.

These indicators of Glover's ability to make an accurate identification are hardly outweighed by the corrupting effect of the challenged identification itself. Although identifications arising from single-photograph displays may be viewed in general with suspicion, we find in the instant case little pressure on the witness to acquiesce in the suggestion that such a display entails. [Because] Glover examined the photograph alone, there was no coercive pressure to make an identification arising from the presence of another. The identification was made in circumstances allowing care and reflection. * * *

Surely, we cannot say that under all the circumstances of this case there is "a very substantial likelihood of irreparable misidentification." Short of that point, such evidence is for the jury to weigh. * * *

[Reversed].[c]

JUSTICE MARSHALL, with whom JUSTICE BRENNAN joins, dissenting.

Today's decision can come as no surprise to those who have been watching the Court dismantle the protections against mistaken eyewitness testimony erected a decade ago in [*Wade, Gilbert* and *Stovall*]. But it is still distressing to see the Court virtually ignore the teaching of experience embodied in those decisions and blindly uphold the conviction of a defendant who may well be innocent.

The Court weighs three factors in deciding that the totality approach should be applied [rather than a *per se* exclusionary rule]. In my view, the Court wrongly evaluates the impact of these factors.

First, the Court acknowledges that one of the factors, deterrence of police use of unnecessarily suggestive identification procedures, favors the *per se* rule. Indeed, it does so heavily, for such a rule would make it unquestionably clear to the police they must never use a suggestive procedure when a fairer alternative is available. I have no doubt that conduct would quickly conform to the rule.

Second, the Court gives passing consideration to the dangers of eyewitness identification recognized in the *Wade* trilogy. It concludes, however, that the grave risk of error does not justify adoption of the *per se* approach because that would too often result in exclusion of relevant evidence. In my view, this conclusion totally ignores the lessons of *Wade*. The dangers of mistaken identification are, as *Stovall* held, simply too great to permit unnecessarily suggestive identifications. * * *

Finally, the Court errs in its assessment of the relative impact of the two approaches on the administration of justice. * * * Relying on little more than a strong distaste for "inflexible rules of exclusion," the Court rejects the *per se* test. In so doing, the Court disregards two significant distinctions between the *per se* rule advocated in this case and the exclusionary remedies for certain other constitutional violations.

First, the *per se* rule here is not "inflexible." Where evidence is suppressed, for example, as the fruit of an unlawful search, it may well be forever lost to the prosecution. Identification evidence, however, can by its very nature be readily and effectively reproduced. The in-court identification, permitted under *Wade* [if] it has a source independent of an uncounseled or suggestive procedure, is one example. Similarly, when a prosecuting attorney learns that there has been a suggestive confrontation, he can easily arrange another lineup conducted under scrupulously fair conditions. * * *

---

[c] Justice Stevens concurred, but emphasized that although "the arguments in favor of fashioning new rules to minimize the danger of convicting the innocent on the basis of unreliable eyewitness testimony carry substantial force [this] rulemaking function can be performed 'more effectively by the legislative process than by somewhat clumsy judicial fiat,' and that the Federal Constitution does not foreclose experimentation by the States in the development of such rules."

Second, other exclusionary rules have been criticized for preventing jury consideration of relevant and usually reliable evidence in order to serve interest unrelated to guilt or innocence, such as discouraging illegal searches or denial of counsel. Suggestively obtained eyewitness testimony is excluded, in contrast, precisely because of its unreliability and concomitant irrelevance. Its exclusion both protects the integrity of the truth-seeking function of the trial and discourages police use of needlessly inaccurate and ineffective investigatory methods.

[For] these reasons, I conclude that adoption of the *per se* rule would enhance, rather than detract from, the effective administration of justice. In my view, the Court's totality test will allow seriously unreliable and misleading evidence to be put before juries. * * *

[Even under the Court's totality test, the Court reached the wrong conclusion on the facts.] I consider first the opportunity that Officer Glover had to view the suspect. Careful review of the record shows that he could see the heroin seller only for the time it took to speak three sentences of four or five short words, to hand over some money, and later after the door reopened, to receive the drugs in return. The entire face-to-face transaction could have taken as little as 15 or 20 seconds. But during this time, Glover's attention was not focused exclusively on the seller's face. He observed that the door was opened 12 to 18 inches, that there was a window in the room behind the door, and, most importantly, that there was a woman standing behind the man. Glover was, of course, also concentrating on the details of the transaction—he must have looked away from the seller's face to hand him the money and receive the drugs. The observation during the conversation thus may have been as brief as 5 or 10 seconds.

As the Court notes, Glover was a police officer trained in and attentive to the need for making accurate identifications. [But] the mere fact that he has been so trained is no guarantee that he is correct in a specific case. * * * Moreover, "identifications made by policemen in highly competitive activities, such as undercover narcotic [work], should be scrutinized with special care." Yet it is just such a searching inquiry that the Court fails to make here.

Another factor on which the Court relies—the witness' degree of certainty in making the identification—is worthless as an indicator that he is correct. Even if Glover had been unsure initially about his identification of respondent's picture, by the time he was called at trial to present a key piece of evidence for the State that paid his salary, it is impossible to imagine his responding negatively to such questions as "is there any doubt in your mind whatsoever" that the identification was correct. * * *

Next, the Court finds that because the identification procedure took place two days after the crime, its reliability is enhanced. While such temporal proximity makes the identification more reliable than one occurring months later, the fact is that the greatest memory loss occurs within hours after an event. After that, the drop-off continues much more slowly. * * *

Finally, the Court makes much of the fact that Glover gave a description of the seller to D'Onofrio shortly after the incident. [But the description] was actually no more than a general summary of the seller's appearance. * * * Conspicuously absent is any indication that the seller was a native of the West Indies, certainly something which a member of the black community could immediately recognize from both appearance and accent.

From all of this, I must conclude that the evidence of Glover's ability to make an accurate identification is far weaker than the Court finds it. In contrast, the procedure used to identify respondent was both extraordinarily suggestive and strongly conducive to error. * * *

[The] use of a single picture (or the display of a single live suspect, for that matter) is a grave error, of course, because it dramatically suggests to the witness that the person shown must be the culprit. Why else would the police choose the person? And it is deeply ingrained in human nature to agree with the expressed opinions of others—particularly others who should be more knowledgeable—when making a difficult decision. In this case, moreover, the pressure was not limited to that inherent in the display of a single photograph. Glover, the identifying witness, was a state police officer on special assignment. He knew that D'Onofrio, an [experienced] narcotics detective, presumably familiar with local drug operations, believed respondent to be the seller. There was at work, then, both loyalty to another police officer and deference to a better-informed colleague. Finally, of course, there was Glover's knowledge that without an identification and arrest, government funds used to buy heroin had been wasted. * * *

I must conclude that this record presents compelling evidence that there was "a very substantial likelihood of misidentification" of respondent Brathwaite. * * *

PERRY V. NEW HAMPSHIRE
565 U.S. 228, 132 S.Ct. 716, 181 L.Ed.2d 694 (2012).

JUSTICE GINSBURG delivered the opinion of the Court.

[Around 3:00 a.m., police responded to a call that an African-American male was trying to break into cars in an apartment parking lot. They found Perry in the parking lot standing near a metal bat and holding two car-stereo amplifiers in his hands. When asked where the amplifiers came from, Perry said that he found them on the ground. The owner of the amplifiers then appeared in the parking lot indicating that his neighbor had just told him that she saw someone break into his car. One police officer stayed in the parking lot with Perry while another went to speak to the neighbor. When the officer asked the neighbor to describe the man she saw break into her neighbor's car, she pointed to her kitchen window and said that the person she saw was standing in the parking lot next to the police officer. Perry was arrested after this identification. About a month later, the police showed the neighbor a photographic array that included a picture of Perry, but she was unable to identify him.

[Perry moved to suppress the neighbor's out-of-court identification on due process grounds. The New Hampshire courts denied his motion, holding that the Due Process Clause only required a trial court to assess the reliability of an out-of-court identification when the police employed suggestive identification techniques. Here, the courts held, the identification was not police-orchestrated.]

[Perry] contends [that] it was mere happenstance that each of the *Stovall* cases involved improper police action. The rationale underlying our decisions, Perry asserts, supports a rule requiring trial judges to prescreen eyewitness evidence for reliability any time an identification is made under suggestive circumstances. We disagree.

Perry's argument depends, in large part, on the Court's statement in *Brathwaite* that "reliability is the linchpin in determining the admissibility of identification testimony." * * * Perry has removed our statement in *Brathwaite* from its mooring, and thereby attributes to the statement a meaning a fair reading of our opinion does not bear. [The] *Brathwaite* Court's reference to reliability appears in a portion of the opinion concerning the appropriate remedy *when the police use an unnecessarily suggestive identification procedure.* The Court adopted a judicial screen for reliability as a course preferable to a *per se* rule requiring exclusion of identification evidence whenever law enforcement officers employ an improper procedure. The due process check for reliability, *Brathwaite* made plain, comes into play only after the defendant establishes improper police conduct. The very purpose of the check, the Court noted, was to avoid depriving the jury of identification evidence that is reliable, *notwithstanding* improper police conduct. * * *

[Perry] ignore[s] a key premise of the *Brathwaite* decision: A primary aim of excluding identification evidence obtained under unnecessarily suggestive circumstances, the Court said, is to deter law enforcement use of improper lineups, showups, and photo arrays in the first place. Alerted to the prospect that identification evidence improperly obtained may be excluded, the Court reasoned, police officers will "guard against unnecessarily suggestive procedures." This deterrence rationale is inapposite in cases, like Perry's, in which the police engaged in no improper conduct.

[Perry] place[s] significant weight on *United States v. Wade*, describing it as a decision not anchored to improper police conduct. In fact, the risk of police rigging was the very danger to which the Court responded in *Wade* when it recognized a defendant's right to counsel at postindictment, police-organized identification procedures. "[T]he confrontation *compelled by the State* between the accused and the victim or witnesses," the Court began, "is peculiarly riddled with innumerable dangers and variable factors which might seriously, even crucially, derogate from a fair trial." "A major factor contributing to the high incidence of miscarriage of justice from mistaken identification," the Court continued, "has been the degree of suggestion inherent in the manner in which *the prosecution* presents the suspect to witnesses for pretrial identification." To illustrate the improper suggestion it was concerned about, the Court pointed to police-designed lineups where "all in the lineup but the suspect were known to the identifying witness, . . . the other participants in [the] lineup were grossly dissimilar in appearance to the suspect, . . . only the suspect was required to wear distinctive clothing which the culprit allegedly wore, . . . the witness is told by the police that they have caught the culprit after which the defendant is brought before the witness alone or is viewed in jail, . . . the suspect is pointed out before or during a lineup, . . . the participants in the lineup are asked to try on an article of clothing which fits only the suspect." Beyond genuine debate, then, prevention of unfair police practices prompted the Court to extend a defendant's right to counsel to cover postindictment lineups and showups.

Perry's [argument] thus lacks support in the case law he cites. Moreover, his position would open the door to judicial preview, under the banner of due process, of most, if not all, eyewitness identifications. External suggestion is hardly the only factor that casts doubt on the trustworthiness of an eyewitness' testimony. [Many] other factors bear on "the likelihood of misidentification"—for example, the passage of time between exposure to and identification of the defendant, whether the witness was under stress when he first encountered the suspect, how much time the witness had to observe the suspect, how far the witness was from the suspect, whether the suspect carried a weapon, and the race of the suspect and witness. There is no reason why an identification made by an eyewitness with poor vision, for example, or one who harbors a grudge against the defendant, should be regarded as inherently more reliable, less a "threat to the fairness of trial," than the identification [in] this case. To embrace Perry's view would thus entail a vast enlargement of the reach of due process as a constraint on the admission of evidence.

Perry maintains that the Court can limit the due process check he proposes to identifications made under "suggestive circumstances." Even if we could rationally distinguish suggestiveness from other factors bearing on the reliability of eyewitness evidence, Perry's limitation would still involve trial courts, routinely, in preliminary examinations. Most eyewitness identifications involve some element of suggestion. Indeed, all in-court identifications do. Out-of-court identifications volunteered by witnesses are also likely to involve suggestive circumstances. For example, suppose a witness identifies the defendant to police officers after seeing a photograph of the defendant in the press captioned "theft suspect," or hearing a radio report implicating the defendant in the crime. Or suppose the witness knew that the defendant ran with the wrong crowd and saw him on the day and in the vicinity of the crime. Any of these circumstances might have "suggested" to the witness that the defendant was the person the witness observed committing the crime.

[In] urging a broadly applicable due process check on eyewitness identifications, Perry maintains that eyewitness identifications are a uniquely unreliable form of evidence. We do not doubt either the importance or the fallibility of eyewitness identifications. * * *

[However,] the potential unreliability of a type of evidence does not alone render its introduction at the defendant's trial fundamentally unfair. [The] fallibility of eyewitness evidence does not, without the taint of improper state conduct, warrant a due process rule requiring a trial court to screen such evidence for reliability before allowing the jury to assess its creditworthiness.

Our unwillingness to enlarge the domain of due process [rests,] in large part, on our recognition that the jury, not the judge traditionally determines the reliability of evidence. We also take account of other safeguards built into our adversary system that caution juries against placing undue weight on eyewitness testimony of questionable reliability. These protections include the defendant's Sixth Amendment right to confront the eyewitness. Another is the defendant's right to the effective assistance of an attorney, who can expose the flaws in the eyewitness' testimony during cross-examination and focus the jury's attention on the fallibility of such testimony during opening and closing arguments. Eyewitness-specific jury instructions, which many federal and state courts have adopted, likewise warn the jury to take care in appraising identification evidence. The constitutional requirement that the government prove the defendant's guilt beyond a reasonable doubt also impedes convictions based on dubious identification evidence.

State and federal rules of evidence, moreover, permit trial judges to exclude relevant evidence if its probative value is substantially outweighed by its prejudicial impact or potential for misleading the jury. In appropriate cases, some States also permit defendants to present expert testimony on the hazards of eyewitness identification evidence. * * *

Given the safeguards generally applicable in criminal trials, protections availed by the defense in Perry's case, we hold that the introduction of [the neighbor's] eyewitness testimony, without a preliminary judicial assessment of its reliability, did not render Perry's trial fundamentally unfair. * * * [The] Due Process Clause does not require a preliminary judicial inquiry into the reliability of an eyewitness identification when the identification was not procured under unnecessarily suggestive circumstances arranged by law enforcement.[a]

JUSTICE SOTOMAYOR dissenting:

This Court has long recognized that eyewitness identifications' unique confluence of features—their unreliability, susceptibility to suggestion, powerful impact on the jury, and resistance to the ordinary tests of the adversarial process—can undermine the fairness of a trial. Our cases thus establish a clear rule: The admission at trial of out-of-court eyewitness identifications derived from impermissibly suggestive circumstances that pose a very substantial likelihood of misidentification violates due process. The Court today announces that that rule does not even "com[e] into play" unless the suggestive circumstances are improperly "police-arranged."

Our due process concern, however, arises not from the act of suggestion, but rather from the corrosive effects of suggestion on the reliability of the resulting identification. By rendering protection contingent on improper police arrangement

---

a   Justice Thomas filed a concurring opinion in which he criticized the entire *Stovall* line of cases noting that the cases are all "premised on a 'substantive due process' right to 'fundamental fairness'" and arguing that "those cases are wrongly decided because the Fourteenth Amendment's Due Process Clause is not a 'secret repository of substantive guarantees against "unfairness."'" As a result, he indicated that he would "limit the Court's suggestive eyewitness identification cases to the precise circumstances that they involved."

of the suggestive circumstances, the Court effectively grafts a *mens rea* inquiry onto our rule. The Court's holding enshrines a murky distinction—between suggestive confrontations intentionally orchestrated by the police and, as here, those inadvertently caused by police actions—that will sow confusion. It ignores our precedents' acute sensitivity to the hazards of intentional and unintentional suggestion alike and unmoors our rule from the very interest it protects, inviting arbitrary results. And it recasts the driving force of our decisions as an interest in police deterrence, rather than reliability. Because I see no warrant for declining to assess the circumstances of this case under our ordinary approach, I respectfully dissent.

[The] majority maintains that the suggestive circumstances giving rise to the identification must be "police-arranged," "police rigg[ed]," "police-designed," or "police-organized." Those terms connote a degree of intentional orchestration or manipulation. The majority categorically exempts all eyewitness identifications derived from suggestive circumstances that were not police-manipulated—however, suggestive, and however unreliable—from our due process check. The majority thus appears to graft a *mens rea* requirement onto our existing rule.[4]

As this case illustrates, police intent is now paramount. [Perry] was the only African-American at the scene of the crime standing next to a police officer. For the majority, the fact that the police did not intend that showup, even if they inadvertently caused it in the course of a police procedure, ends the inquiry. The police were questioning the eyewitness [about] the perpetrator's identity, and were intentionally detaining Perry in the parking lot—but had not intended for [the eyewitness] to identify the perpetrator from her window. Presumably, in the majority's view, had the police asked [the eyewitness] to move to the window to identify the perpetrator, that could have made all the difference.

I note, however, that the majority leaves what is required by its arrangement-focused inquiry less than clear. In parts, the opinion suggests that the police must arrange an identification "procedure," regardless of whether they "inten[d] the arranged procedure to be suggestive." Elsewhere, it indicates that the police must arrange the "suggestive circumstances" that lead the witness to identify the accused. Still elsewhere it refers to "improper" police conduct, connoting bad faith. Does police "arrangement" relate to the procedure, the suggestiveness, or both? If it relates to the procedure, do suggestive preprocedure encounters no longer raise the same concerns? If the police need not "inten[d] the arranged procedure to be suggestive," what makes the police action "improper"? And does that mean that good-faith, unintentional police suggestiveness in a police-arranged lineup can be "impermissibly suggestive"? If no, the majority runs headlong into *Wade*. If yes, on what basis—if not deterrence—does it distinguish unintentional police suggestiveness in an accidental confrontation?

---

[4] The majority denies that it has imposed a *mens rea* requirement, but by confining our due process concerns to police-arranged identification procedures, that is just what it has done. The majority acknowledges that "whether or not [the police] intended the arranged procedure to be suggestive" is irrelevant under our precedents, but still places dispositive weight on whether or not the police intended the procedure itself.

The arrangement-focused inquiry will sow needless confusion. If the police had called Perry and [the eyewitness] to the police station for interviews, and [the eyewitness] saw Perry being questioned, would that be sufficiently "improper police arrangement"? If Perry had voluntarily come to the police station, would that change the result?

[The] majority regards its limitation on our two-step rule as compelled by precedent. Its chief rationale is that none of our prior cases involved situations where the police "did not arrange the suggestive circumstances." That is not necessarily true.[b] But even if it were true, it is unsurprising. The vast majority of eyewitness identifications that the State uses in criminal prosecutions are obtained in lineup, showup, and photograph displays arranged by the police. Our precedents reflect that practical reality.

[Indeed,] it is the majority's approach that lies in tension with our precedents. [We] once described the "primary evil to be avoided" as the likelihood of misidentification. Today's decision, however, means that even if that primary evil is at its apex, we need not avoid it at all so long as the suggestive circumstances do not stem from improper police arrangement.

The majority gives several additional reasons for why applying our due process rule beyond improperly police-arranged circumstances is unwarranted. In my view, none withstands close scrutiny.

[The majority's reading of our precedent as focusing on deterrence] mischaracterizes our cases. We discussed deterrence in *Brathwaite* because Brathwaite challenged our two-step inquiry as *lacking* deterrence value. [Our discussion of deterrence in that case was not a] list of "primary aim[s]." Nor was it a ringing endorsement of the primacy of deterrence. [To] the contrary, we clarified that deterrence was a subsidiary concern to reliability, the "driving force" of our doctrine.

[The] majority emphasizes that we should rely on the jury to determine the reliability of evidence. But our cases are rooted in the assumption that eyewitness identifications upend the ordinary expectation that it is "the province of the jury to weigh the credibility of competing witnesses." [Jurors] find eyewitness evidence unusually powerful and their ability to assess credibility is hindered by a witness' false confidence in the accuracy of his or her identification.

[The majority also] suggests that applying our rule beyond police-arranged suggestive circumstances would entail a heavy practical burden, requiring courts to engage in "preliminary judicial inquiry" into "most, if not all, eyewitness identifications." But that is inaccurate. [As] is implicit in the majority's reassurance that Perry may resort to the rules of evidence in lieu of our due process

---

[b] Justice Sotomayor had earlier suggested that *Wade* might not have involved police-orchestrated suggestiveness: "The two witnesses who later identified Wade in the lineup had seen Wade outside while 'await[ing] assembly of the lineup.' Wade had been standing in the hallway, which happened to be 'observable to the witnesses through an open door.' One witness saw Wade 'within sight of an FBI agent'; the other saw him 'in the custody of the agent.' In underscoring the hazards of these circumstances, we made no mention of whether the encounter had been arranged; indeed, the facts suggest that it was not."

precedents, trial courts will be entertaining defendants' objections, pretrial or at trial, to unreliable eyewitness evidence in any event. The relevant question, then, is what the standard of admissibility governing such objections should be.

[Finally,] the majority questions how to "rationally distinguish suggestiveness from other factors bearing on the reliability of eyewitness evidence," [and] more broadly, how to distinguish eyewitness evidence from other kinds of arguably unreliable evidence. Our precedents, however, did just that. We emphasized the "formidable number of instances in the records of English and American trials" of "miscarriage[s] of justice from mistaken identification." *Wade.* We then observed that "the influence of improper suggestion upon identifying witnesses probably accounts for more miscarriages of justice than any other single factor." *Id.* [The] majority points to no other type of evidence that shares the rare confluence of characteristics that makes eyewitness evidence a unique threat to the fairness of trial.

[It] would be one thing if the passage of time had cast doubt on the empirical premises of our precedents. But just the opposite has happened. A vast body of scientific literature has reinforced every concern our precedents articulated nearly a half-century ago. [Over] the past three decades, more than two thousand studies related to eyewitness identification have been published.

[The] empirical evidence demonstrates that eyewitness misidentification is "the single greatest cause of wrongful convictions in this country." Researchers have found that a staggering 76% of the first 250 convictions overturned due to DNA evidence since 1989 involved eyewitness misidentification. Study after study demonstrates that eyewitness recollections are highly susceptible to distortion by postevent information or social cues; that jurors routinely overestimate the accuracy of eyewitness identifications; that jurors place the greatest weight on eyewitness confidence in assessing identifications even though confidence is a poor gauge of accuracy; and that suggestiveness can stem from sources beyond police-orchestrated procedures. The majority today nevertheless adopts an artificially narrow conception of the dangers of suggestive identifications at a time when our concerns should have deepened. * * *

The Court's opinion today [lies] in tension with our precedents' more holistic conception of the dangers of suggestion and is untethered from the evidentiary interest the due process right protects. In my view, the ordinary two-step inquiry should apply, whether the police created the suggestive circumstances intentionally or inadvertently.

CHAPTER 8

INVESTIGATION BY SUBPOENA

■ ■ ■

1. INTRODUCTION

To understand the criminal investigation conducted by subpoena, one must understand the grand jury.[a] For the grand jury historically was the primary agency conducting investigations through the use of subpoenas, and the vast majority of investigations by subpoena today, though directed by prosecutors, continue to be conducted through the grand jury.

Few elements of our criminal justice process have more ancient roots than the grand jury, which was introduced into the English criminal process in the twelfth century. By the time the United States Constitution was adopted, the grand jury was well established in this country as both a screening and investigatory body. The grand jury performed its screening function in determining whether the government had developed sufficient evidence to bring criminal charges through an indictment. Under the federal constitution's Fifth Amendment and similar provisions in state constitutions, felony charges could be brought only on a grand jury's decision to indict. The grand jury performed its investigatory function through its own resources and its capacity to require potential witnesses to come before it and testify as to suspected crimes. As a result of its dual functions, the grand jury came to be known as the "shield and sword" of the criminal justice process. In its role as a screening agency, the grand jury provided a shield against mistaken or vindictive prosecution of the innocent by refusing to indict. In its role as an investigative agency, it provided the state with a sword to combat crime that could not be reached through other investigative processes.

The shielding or screening function of the grand jury will be discussed in Chapter Eleven. In this Chapter, we will look only at the investigative authority of the grand jury. While the grand jury remains an important investigative agency, its significance in this regard is less than it once was. With the development of professional police departments, the major share of the responsibility for investigation today falls on the police. Compared to police investigations, grand jury investigations are expensive, time-consuming, and logistically cumbersome. The grand jury is a group of lay persons (as large as 23, its traditional size, in some jurisdictions), who commonly are selected in much the same manner as the trial jury. The jurors meet as a body, hearing witnesses and examining physical evidence. While early grand juries, operating in small communities, often could bring to an investigation relevant information gathered through the jurors' own

---

[a] The organization and operation of the grand jury are briefly described in Chapter 1, particularly in the description of step 11 (grand jury review).

efforts, the grand jury today must rely primarily on the lead of the prosecutor, who serves as its legal advisor and sets the direction, scope, and pace of its investigation. It is the prosecutor who determines which witnesses will be presented before the grand jury, and the prosecutor who examines those witnesses, although the grand jury has the power to ask its own questions and to insist that the prosecutor present such additional witnesses as it specifies. Those rare grand juries that have made extensive use of such powers and have taken investigations in new directions (commonly assisted by special prosecutors, appointed by the court at the grand jury's request) have come to be known as "runaway grand juries."

The extra burdens of the grand jury investigation lead prosecutors today to turn to the grand jury process only where it offers a distinct investigative advantage over the police. That advantage is most likely to be present where investigators must unravel a complex criminal structure, deal with victims reluctant to cooperate, obtain information contained in extensive business records, or keep a continuing investigative effort from the public gaze. Criminal activities presenting such investigative problems include public corruption (e.g., bribery), misuse of economic power (e.g., price-fixing), and widespread distribution of illegal services and goods (e.g., gambling or narcotics distribution), and most grand jury investigations are directed at such activities. The grand jury's advantages in investigating this type of criminal activity stem primarily from its use of subpoena authority to compel the production of testimony and physical evidence, although certain other aspects of the grand jury investigation—most notably secrecy requirements[b] and lay participation[c]—may also contribute to its effectiveness.

The subpoena authority utilized in a grand jury investigation comes from the courts. Although described as an independent body, the grand jury exists as an arm of the court. The court calls the grand jury into being and grants to it the power of the court to compel persons to appear and testify or produce physical evidence. A subpoena is a court order directing a person to appear to testify (the subpoena "ad testificandum") or to present to it physical evidence (the subpoena "duces tecum").

---

[b] Grand jury secrecy requirements vary in scope from one jurisdiction to another, but all jurisdictions prohibit the prosecution's staff, the grand jurors, and court personnel from disclosing what occurred before the grand jury (absent a court order allowing such disclosure). In several jurisdictions the witness himself is also subject to a secrecy requirement (being allowed to discuss his testimony only with his lawyer), but most do not restrict disclosure by the witness. The end result is that the witness who wants his testimony to be kept secret knows that those who have heard his testimony have been sworn to secrecy; disclosure lies in his own hands—at least until charges are brought (when the witness' testimony will most likely be made public if he is to testify at trial).

[c] Lay participation is said to add primarily two elements to the effectiveness of grand jury investigations. First, witnesses are said to feel a "moral compulsion to be honest and forthright" in their testimony before a group of peers, who have themselves accepted the inconvenience of becoming involved. Second, particularly where the subject under investigation has political overtones that might produce claims of prosecutorial political partisanship, the participation of the lay jurors is said to help maintain public confidence in the integrity of the investigatory process. Critics discount both of these contentions. They suggest that the psychological pressures felt by the witness are more likely to come from the fact that the witness knows that he "stands alone"—that he must "appear before an often hostile prosecutor and a group of strangers, with no judge present to guard his rights, no counsel present to counsel him, and sometimes no indication of why he is being questioned." As for public confidence, critics suggest that the public recognizes that the key figure in a grand jury investigation is an elected official, the prosecutor, not the grand jury.

Both forms of subpoena may present significant investigative advantages over procedures available to the police.

The subpoena duces tecum offers various advantages over the primary device available to the police for obtaining physical evidence—the search pursuant to a warrant. Initially, as will be seen, the subpoena duces tecum can issue without the showing of probable cause required for a search warrant. In the grand jury setting the subpoena duces tecum usually seeks documents, and it also has the advantage of requiring the party subpoenaed to sort through what may be a vast quantity of records in order to find the document subpoenaed (a sorting task that might often be so burdensome for police to undertake that a search would be impracticable). Finally, where records are to be obtained from an uninvolved third party (e.g., a bank), a subpoena may be preferred because it will be far less disruptive than a police search of the files of that party.[d]

The subpoena to testify similarly offers several advantages over police questioning. Initially, as will be seen in section one, there is no need for a showing of probable cause or even reasonable suspicion to require a person to come before the grand jury and testify. Second, whereas a person may simply refuse to answer police questions (having no duty to cooperate), a subpoenaed person must give testimony as requested (absent the exercise of some valid privilege)—or be held in contempt by the court. Moreover, when that person does testify, a failure to tell the truth will subject him to criminal liability for perjury, for the testimony is given under oath. Lying to police officers generally is not a crime under state law (although the federal system makes it criminal as to federal officers).

The power of the subpoena to compel testimony commonly is supplemented by legislation authorizing the prosecutor to obtain a court order granting a form of "immunity" to the grand jury witness. The primary limit upon the witness' legal duty to testify, as well as be seen, is the privilege against self-incrimination. The witness' self-incrimination privilege may be supplanted, however, through the grant of immunity, as discussed in the *Kastigar* case (see § 2). The immunity grant gives the prosecution an opportunity to "break" a case by forcing critical testimony from a lower-level participant in a criminal enterprise who otherwise would rely on his self-incrimination privilege. Of course, the price for such testimony ordinarily will be foregoing the prosecution of that person, but that may be a worthwhile cost for gaining from the immunized witness evidence that will permit prosecution of the high-level participants. Also, immunity may be used for prospective witnesses who have only an incidental relationship to the enterprise which probably would not justify their prosecution but would allow them to refuse to testify on the basis of the privilege if not given immunity.

---

[d] But consider *Zurcher v. Stanford Daily*, p. 136 (concluding that the Fourth Amendment does not require use of a subpoena, rather than a search warrant, to obtain the property of a third-party "not suspected of crime"). Where a search warrant is obtained, the enforcement agency may opt for execution in much the same manner as a subpoena. Particularly where seeking electronically stored information, the agency may serve the search warrant on the third-party with the third-party then collecting the information through use of its data retrieval program, and delivering it to the enforcement agent by a designated date.

Desiring to keep the advantages of investigation by subpoena, but to eliminate the logistical limitations of grand jury use, a small group of states have created investigative alternatives to the grand jury that can make similar use of the court's subpoena authority and the grant of immunity. Several of these states allow the prosecutor to petition for a judicial inquiry into possible criminal activity. The judge so designated may then conduct an investigation (commonly assisted by the local prosecutor or a specially appointed prosecutor) through the use of the subpoena power. Such judicial investigations are known in different parts of the country as "one-man grand juries" or "John Doe" proceedings. Still other states authorize the prosecutor, acting alone, to conduct investigations upon application to the court for use of its subpoena power. This authority is commonly used for investigations less extensive than those submitted to the grand jury. The witnesses in these prosecutorial "investigatory deposition" proceedings are subpoenaed to appear at the prosecutor's office (with counsel, if they so choose), where they will be required to testify under oath or to present documents as specified in a subpoena duces tecum. Finally, most jurisdictions have allowed the subpoena authority to be used by administrative agencies or other bodies that have the responsibility for investigating possible infractions of civil laws, including those that may overlap with criminal offenses. Thus, one of the main cases in section three, *Fisher v. United States,* involves an Internal Revenue Service summons that is basically a subpoena duces tecum. So too, many of the cases discussed in the *Carpenter* opinions (§ 2) involved subpoenas issued by administrative agencies.

The investigation by subpoena, whether conducted through a grand jury or an alternative agency, is not without constitutional limitations. The cases presented in this chapter deal with the most significant of those limitations.

2. FOURTH AMENDMENT LIMITATIONS

The first case in this section, *Boyd v. United States,* is a widely celebrated case, once described by Justice Brandeis as a case "that will be remembered as long as civil liberty lives in the United States." *Olmstead v. United States,* 277 U.S. 438 (1928) (dissent). Although *Boyd* involved an order to produce documents at trial, its reasoning clearly encompassed as well a subpoena issued in the course of an investigatory setting. From one perspective, *Boyd* today constitutes no more than a "historic relic," a false start in the application to subpoenas of both the Fourth Amendment and the Fifth Amendment's self-incrimination clause, From another, *Boyd* remains a case of lasting influence, as: (1) critical cases in establishing the current law are shaped as responses to *Boyd*; (2) *Boyd* remains responsible for the application of the Fourth Amendment to the documentary subpoena; and (3) for some justices, certain other aspects of *Boyd* should (or might) have continuing vitality.

The demise of *Boyd*'s analysis of the application of the self-incrimination clause is discussed in the section three cases of *Fisher* and *Doe.* The rejection of *Boyd*'s absolute prohibition of the documentary subpoena under the Fourth

Amendment is discussed in this section.[a] That rejection, as discussed in the Note following *Boyd*, came in *Hale v. Henkel*, a case decided only two decades after *Boyd*. *Hale* agreed with *Boyd* as to the application of the Fourth Amendment, but applied a much more limited Fourth Amendment restriction. The *Hale* standard did not include the probable cause prerequisite commonly associated with searches or even some lesser prerequisite, such as "reasonable suspicion" that the subpoenaed party engaged in a criminal activity possibly revealed by the subpoenaed documents. The second principal case in this section, *United States v. Dionisio*, addresses the question of whether such a showing should be required where the subpoena is not seeking documents, but the individual's participation in the production of an identification exemplar (with the subpoena thereby performing a function that might be compared to a police action that would be subject to some probability showing). The last case in the section, *Carpenter v. United States*, also considers whether more than the *Hale* standard is required in a special subpoena setting— requiring a third-party to produce records relating to a customer with a content compared to the surveillance of the customer's movements over a full week.

BOYD V. UNITED STATES

116 U.S. 616, 6 S.Ct. 524, 29 L.Ed. 746 (1886).

[Customs officials seized 35 cases of glass, imported by the partnership of Boyd and Sons, and instituted a forfeiture proceeding. That proceeding was brought under a statute providing that any importer who defrauded the government and thereby avoided payment of customs revenue was subject to fine, incarceration, and forfeiture of the imported merchandise. Utilizing an 1874 statute, the government's attorney obtained a court "notice" directing Boyd to produce an invoice covering 29 of the cases of glass. That statute authorized the trial judge, on motion of the prosecutor describing a particular document and indicating what it might prove, to issue a notice directing the importer to produce the document. The importer could refuse to produce without being held in contempt (which distinguished the notice from a subpoena) but the consequence of a failure to produce was that the allegation of the prosecution as to what the document stated was "taken as confessed."]

[The defendants produced the invoice in compliance with the notice, but objected to the validity of the court's action, and objected again when the invoice was offered as evidence. The jury subsequently found for the United States, and a judgment of forfeiture against the 35 cases was granted.]

JUSTICE BRADLEY delivered the opinion of the Court.

* * * [I]n regard to Fourth Amendment, it is contended that * * * [the Act of 1874], under which the order in the present case was made, is free from

---

[a]   *Boyd* was initially seen as having a potential impact beyond the documentary subpoena. The reading of *Boyd* as prohibiting any kind of search for property the individual was entitled to possess (i.e., not contraband or the fruits or instrumentality of the crime) was finally rejected by the ruling in *Warden v. Hayden*, 387 U.S. 294 (1967) (allowing searches for "mere evidence") and the reading of *Boyd* as prohibiting a search for documents was rejected in *Andresen v. Maryland*, 427 U.S. 463 (1976) (p. 94).

constitutional objection, because it does not authorize the search and seizure of books and papers, but only requires the defendant or claimant to produce them. That is so; but it declares that if he does not produce them, the allegations which it is affirmed they will prove shall be taken as confessed. This is tantamount to compelling their production; for the prosecuting attorney will always be sure to state the evidence expected to be derived from them as strongly as the case will admit of. It is true that certain aggravating incidents of actual search and seizure, such as forcible entry into a man's house and searching amongst his papers, are wanting, and to this extent the proceeding under the act of 1874 is a mitigation of that which was authorized by the former acts; but it accomplishes the substantial object of those acts in forcing from a party evidence against himself. It is our opinion, therefore, that a compulsory production of a man's private papers to establish a criminal charge against him, or to forfeit his property, is within the scope of the Fourth Amendment to the Constitution, in all cases in which a search and seizure would be; because it is a material ingredient, and effects the sole object and purpose of search and seizure.

The principal question, however, remains to be considered. Is a search and seizure, or, what is equivalent thereto, a compulsory production of a man's private papers, to be used in evidence against him in a proceeding to forfeit his property for alleged fraud against the revenue laws—is such a proceeding for such a purpose an "*unreasonable* search and seizure" within the meaning of the Fourth Amendment of the Constitution? or, is it a legitimate proceeding? * * *

In order to ascertain the nature of the proceedings intended by the Fourth Amendment to the Constitution under the terms "unreasonable searches and seizures," it is only necessary to recall the contemporary or then recent history of the controversies on the subject, both in this country and in England. * * * Prominent and principal among these was the practice of issuing general warrants by the Secretary of State, for searching private houses for the discovery and seizure of books and papers that might be used to convict their owner of the charge of libel. * * * The case, * * * which will always be celebrated as being the occasion of Lord Camden's memorable discussion of the subject, was that of *Entick v. Carrington and Three Other King's Messengers* * * *. The action was trespass for entering the plaintiff's dwelling-house in November, 1762, and breaking open his desks, boxes, etc., and searching and examining his papers. The jury rendered a special verdict, and the case was twice solemnly argued at the bar. Lord Camden pronounced the judgment of the court in Michaelmas Term, 1765, and the law as expounded by him has been regarded as settled from that time to this, and his great judgment on that occasion is considered as one of the landmarks of English liberty. It was welcomed and applauded by the lovers of liberty in the colonies as well as in the mother country. It is regarded as one of the permanent monuments of the British Constitution, and is quoted as such by the English authorities on that subject down to the present time. As every American statesmen, during our revolutionary and formative period as a nation, was undoubtedly familiar with this monument of English freedom, and considered it as the true and ultimate expression of constitutional law, it may be confidently asserted that its propositions were in the minds of those who framed the Fourth Amendment to the Constitution, and were considered as sufficiently explanatory of what was meant by unreasonable searches and seizures. * * *

After describing the power claimed by the Secretary of State for issuing general search warrants, and the manner in which they were executed, Lord Camden says [in *Entick*]:

> * * * Papers are the owner's goods and chattels; they are his dearest property; and are so far from enduring a seizure, that they will hardly bear an inspection; and though the eye cannot by the laws of England be guilty of a trespass, yet where private papers are removed and carried away the secret nature of those goods will be an aggravation of the trespass, and demand more considerable damages in that respect. Where is the written law that gives any magistrate such a power? I can safely answer, there is none; and therefore, it is too much for us, without such authority, to pronounce a practice legal which would be subversive of all the comforts of society. * * *
>
> Lastly, it is urged as an argument of utility, that such a search is a means of detecting offenders by discovering evidence. I wish some cases had been shown, where the law forceth evidence out of the owner's custody by process. There is no process against papers in civil causes. It has been often tried, but never prevailed. Nay, where the adversary has by force or fraud got possession of your own proper evidence, there is no way to get it back but by action. In the criminal law such a proceeding was never heard of; and yet there are some crimes, such, for instance, as murder, rape, robbery, and house-breaking, to say nothing of forgery and perjury, that are more atrocious than libelling. But our law has provided no paper-search in these cases to help forward the conviction. Whether this proceedeth from the gentleness of the law towards criminals, or from a consideration that such a power would be more pernicious to the innocent than useful to the public, I will not say. It is very certain that the law obligeth no man to accuse himself; because the necessary means of compelling self-accusation, falling upon the innocent as well as the guilty, would be both cruel and unjust; and it would seem, that search for evidence is disallowed upon the same principle. Then, too, the innocent would be confounded with the guilty.

* * * The principles laid down in this opinion affect the very essence of constitutional liberty and security. They reach farther than the concrete form of the case then before the court, with its adventitious circumstances; they apply to all invasions on the part of the government and its employees of the sanctity of a man's home and the privacies of life. It is not the breaking of his doors, and the rummaging of his drawers, that constitutes the essence of the offence; but it is the invasion of his indefeasible right of personal security, personal liberty and private property, where that right has never been forfeited by his conviction of some public offence,—it is the invasion of this sacred right which underlies and constitutes the essence of Lord Camden's judgment. Breaking into a house and opening boxes and drawers are circumstances of aggravation; but any forcible and compulsory

extortion of a man's own testimony or of his private papers to be used as evidence to convict him of crime or to forfeit his goods, is within the condemnation of that judgment. In this regard the Fourth and Fifth Amendments run almost into each other. * * *

We have already noticed the intimate relation between the two amendments. They throw great light on each other. For the "unreasonable searches and seizures" condemned in the Fourth Amendment are almost always made for the purpose of compelling a man to give evidence against himself, which in criminal cases is condemned in the Fifth Amendment; and compelling a man "in a criminal case to be a witness against himself," which is condemned in the Fifth Amendment, throws light on the question as to what is an "unreasonable search and seizure" within the meaning of the Fourth Amendment. And we have been unable to perceive that the seizure of a man's private books and papers to be used in evidence against him is substantially different from compelling him to be a witness against himself. * * * We are also clearly of opinion that proceedings instituted for the purpose of declaring the forfeiture of a man's property by reason of offences committed by him, though they may be civil in form, are in their nature criminal. In this very case, the ground of forfeiture * * * consists of certain acts of fraud committed against the public revenue in relation to imported merchandise, which are made criminal by the statute * * *. As, therefore, suits for penalties and forfeitures incurred by the commission of offences against the law, are of this quasi-criminal nature, we think that they are within the reason of criminal proceedings for all the purposes of the Fourth Amendment of the Constitution, and of that portion of the Fifth Amendment which declares that no person shall be compelled in any criminal case to be a witness against himself; and we are further of opinion that a compulsory production of the private books and papers of the owner of goods sought to be forfeited in such a suit is compelling him to be a witness against himself, within the meaning of the Fifth Amendment to the Constitution, and is the equivalent of a search and seizure—and an unreasonable search and seizure—within the meaning of the Fourth Amendment.

Though the proceeding in question is divested of many of the aggravating incidents of actual search and seizure, yet, as before said, it contains their substance and essence, and effects their substantial purpose. It may be that it is the obnoxious thing in its mildest and least repulsive form; but illegitimate and unconstitutional practices get their first footing in that way, namely, by silent approaches and slight deviations from legal modes of procedure. This can only be obviated by adhering to the rule that constitutional provisions for the security of person and property should be liberally construed. A close and literal construction deprives them of half their efficacy, and leads to gradual depreciation of the right, as if it consisted more in sound than in substance. It is the duty of courts to be watchful for the constitutional rights of the citizen, and against any stealthy encroachments thereon. Their motto should be *obsta principiis*. * * *

JUSTICE MILLER, with whom was THE CHIEF JUSTICE concurring:

I concur in the judgment of the court * * * and in so much of the opinion of this court as holds the 5th section of the act of 1874 void as applicable to the present case. * * * The order of the court under the statute is in effect a subpoena duces tecum, and, though the penalty for the witness's failure to appear in court with the criminating papers is not fine and imprisonment, it is one which may be made more severe, namely, to have charges against him of a criminal nature, taken for confessed, and made the foundation of the judgment of the court. That this is within the protection which the Constitution intended against compelling a person to be a witness against himself, is, I think, quite clear.

But this being so, there is no reason why this court should assume that the action of the court below, in requiring a party to produce certain papers as evidence on the trial, authorizes an unreasonable search or seizure of the house, papers, or effects of that party. There is in fact no search and no seizure authorized by the statute. No order can be made by the court under it which requires or permits anything more than service of notice on a party to the suit. * * *

Note: The post-Boyd substitution of a Fourth Amendment prohibition of overbreadth/ unreasonableness in subpoenas ducas tecum

Hale v. Henkel, 201 U.S. 43 (1906), presented a grand jury subpoena directing the petitioner Hale, the secretary of McAndrews & Forbes Company, to both testify and produce a variety of company documents. The Court was unanimous in rejecting petitioner's contention that he could not be compelled to testify because (1) "there was no specific charge pending before the grand jury," and (2) "the answers would tend to incriminate him." The first contention was contrary to the "plenary inquisitorial power" of the grand jury,[b] which "assigns no limits, except those marked by diligence itself," to the course of [the juror's] inquiries. "The Court found unpersuasive the several state courts that had restricted that inquisitorial power, including "cases that lay down the principle that it must appear to the grand jury that there is reason to believe that a crime has been committed and that they have not the power to institute or prosecute an inquiry on the chance that some crime may be discovered." As for the petitioner's self-incrimination objection, he had been granted immunity under a federal statute and that served to render the privilege inapplicable. While that immunity extended only to the individual, McAndrews & Forbes Company was a corporation, and the privilege did not protect corporations (see fn. c, p. 625).

---

[b] Speaking to this authority, and relying in part on *Hale*, *Blair v. United States*, 250 U.S. 273 (1919) later noted: "At the foundation of our Federal Government, the inquisitorial function of the grand jury and the compulsion of witnesses were recognized as incidents of the judicial power. * * * The personal sacrifice * * * [of the witness] is a part of the necessary contribution of the individual to the welfare of the public. * * * [A]side from exceptions and qualifications—and none such is asserted in the present case—the witness is bound not only to attend but to tell what he knows in answer to questions framed for the purpose of bringing out the truth of the matter under inquiry. He is not entitled to urge objections of incompetency or irrelevancy, such as a party might raise, for this is no concern of his. On familiar principles, he is not entitled to challenge the authority of the court or of the grand jury, provided they have a *de facto* existence and organization. * * * It is a grand inquest, a body with powers of investigation and inquisition, the scope of whose inquiries is not to be limited narrowly by questions of propriety or forecasts of the probable result of the investigation, or by doubts whether any particular individual will be found properly subject to an accusation of crime."

Turning to petitioner's challenge to the subpoena duces tecum, a divided Court sustained the challenge. In doing so, it rejected: (1) the petitioner's argument that *Boyd* established an absolute prohibition under the combined impact of the Fourth and Fifth Amendments; (2) Justice Harlan's argument that the protection of the Fourth Amendment did not extend to corporations; and (3) Justice McKenna's questioning of the application of the Fourth Amendment to a subpoena duces tecum.[c]

In response to petitioner's *Boyd* argument, the Court noted that cases subsequent to *Boyd* had "treated the Fourth and Fifth Amendments as quite distinct, having different histories, and performing separate functions." Those cases and others had established that an absolute prohibition against the compelled production of records rested only on the self-incrimination clause. Thus, a post-*Boyd* ruling had sustained the authority of courts to issue subpoenas directing the production of documents to implement inquiries before the Interstate Commerce Commission, after concluding that a grant of immunity responded adequately to the subpoenaed person's self-incrimination claim. So too, it was "quite clear that the search and seizure clause of the Fourth Amendment was not intended to interfere with the power of courts to compel through a subpoena duces tecum the production upon trial in court of documentary evidence. As remarked in [an 1834 English civil case] * * * it would be 'utterly impossible to carry on the administration of justice' without this writ."

Having separated the two constitutional claims, the Fifth Amendment claim was easily rejected. The required production of documents did not present a self-incrimination issue for the same reasons that the required giving of testimony did not present a valid self-incrimination claim: The petitioner had been granted immunity and the self-incrimination privilege did not apply to the corporation. On the other hand, the Fourth Amendment objection to the subpoena duces tecum did have merit, although not on the Fifth Amendment-influenced concept of reasonableness that *Boyd* had imposed.

Responding to Justices Harlan and McKenna, Justice Brown initially reasoned: "Although * * * we are of the opinion that an officer of a corporation * * * cannot refuse to produce the books and papers of such a corporation, we do not wish to be understood as holding that a corporation is not entitled to immunity, under the Fourth Amendment, against *unreasonable* searches and seizures. A corporation is, after all, but an association of individuals under an assumed name and with a distinct legal entity. In organizing itself as a collective body, it waives

---

c   Justice McKenna noted: "It is said 'a search implies a quest by an officer of the law; a seizure contemplates a forcible dispossession of the owner.' Nothing can be more direct and plain; nothing more expressive to distinguish a subpoena from a search warrant. Can a subpoena lose this essential distinction from a search warrant by the generality or specialty of its terms? I think not. The distinction is based upon what is authorized or directed to be done—not upon the form of words by which the authority or command is given. The quest of an officer acts upon the things themselves—may be secret, intrusive, accompanied by force. The service of a subpoena is but the delivery of a paper to a party—is open and aboveboard. There is no element of trespass or force in it. It does not disturb the possession of property. It cannot be finally enforced except after challenge, and a judgment of the court upon the challenge. This is a safeguard against abuse the same as it is of other processes of the law, and it is all that can be allowed without serious embarrassment to the administration of justice."

no constitutional immunities appropriate to such a body. * * * We are also of opinion that an order for the production of books and papers may constitute an unreasonable search and seizure with the Fourth Amendment. While a search ordinarily implies a quest by an officer of the law, and a seizure contemplates a forcible dispossession of the owner, still, as was held in the *Boyd* case, the substance of the offense is the compulsory production of private papers, whether under a search warrant or a subpoena duces tecum, against which the person, be he individual or corporation, is entitled to protection."

Justice Brown then turned to the application of the Fourth Amendment to the *Hale* subpoena: "Applying the test of reasonableness to the present case, we think the subpoena duces tecum is far too sweeping in its terms to be regarded as reasonable. It does not require the production of a single contract, or of contracts with a particular corporation, or a limited number of documents, but all understandings, contracts, or correspondence between the MacAndrews & Forbes Company, and no less than six different companies, as well as all reports made, and accounts rendered by such companies from the date of the organization of the MacAndrews & Forbes Company, as well as all letters received by that company since its organization from more than a dozen different companies, situated in seven different States of the Union.

"If the writ had required the production of all the books, papers and documents found in the office of the MacAndrews & Forbes Company, it would scarcely be more universal in its operation, or more completely put a stop to the business of that company. Indeed, it is difficult to say how its business could be carried on after it had been denuded of this mass of material, which is not shown to be necessary in the prosecution of this case, and is clearly in violation of the general principle of law with regard to the particularity required in the description of documents necessary to a search warrant or subpoena. Doubtless many, if not all, of these documents may ultimately be required, but some necessity should be shown, either from an examination of the witnesses orally, or from the known transactions of these companies with the other companies implicated, or some evidence of their materiality produced, to justify an order for the production of such a mass of papers. A general subpoena of this description is equally indefensible as a search warrant would be if couched in similar terms."

Although *Hale*'s opinion referred to the burden imposed upon MacAndrews & Forbes, subsequent cases discussing the Fourth Amendment's application to documentary subpoenas spoke of a general prohibition against overbreadth that could be violated without the business impact cited in *Hale*. Moreover, the essence of that prohibition was extended beyond the grand jury context to subpoenas duces tecum issued by administrative agencies. One of those administrative agency cases *(Oklahoma Press Publishing Co. v. Walling)*, 327 U.S. 186 (1948), presented an extensive analysis of the character of the Fourth Amendment limitation in this context. The Court there considered challenges to subpoenas duces tecum, issued by the Wage and Hour Administrator of the Department of Labor, seeking records for the purpose of "determining questions of coverage and violation of the Fair Labor Standards Act." Responding to the petitioner's claim that the Fourth

Amendment prohibited the Administrator's "fishing expedition," Justice Rutledge's opinion for the Court noted:

"While we think [petitioners' Fourth Amendment arguments] reflect a confusion not justified by the actual state of the decisions, the confusion has acquired some currency, * * * [and] in order to remove any possible basis for like misunderstanding in the future, we give more detailed consideration to the views advanced and to the authorities than would otherwise be necessary. * * * The primary source of misconception concerning the Fourth Amendment's function lies perhaps in the identification of cases involving so-called 'figurative' or 'constructive' searches with cases of actual search and seizure. Only in this analogical sense can any questions related to search and seizure be thought to arise in situations which, like the present ones, involve only the validity of authorized judicial orders." * * *

"Without attempt[ing] to summarize or accurately distinguish all of the cases, the fair distillation, insofar as they apply merely to the production of corporate records and papers in response to a subpoena or order authorized by law and safeguarded by judicial sanction, seems to be that the Fifth Amendment affords no protection by virtue of the self-incrimination provision, whether for the corporation or for its officers; and the Fourth, if applicable, at the most guards against abuse only by way of too much indefiniteness or breadth in the things required to be 'particularly described,' if also the inquiry is one the demanding agency is authorized by law to make and the materials specified are relevant. The gist of the protection is in the requirement, expressed in terms, that the disclosure sought shall not be 'unreasonable.' "

"As this has taken form in the decisions, the following specific results have been worked out. It is not necessary, as in the case of a warrant, that a specific charge or complaint of violation of law be pending or that the order be made pursuant to one. It is enough that the investigation be for a lawfully authorized purpose, within the power of Congress to command. This has been ruled most often perhaps in relation to grand jury investigations, *Hale v. Henkel*, but also frequently in respect to general or statistical investigations authorized by Congress. The requirement of 'probable cause, supported by oath or affirmation,' literally applicable in the case of a warrant is satisfied, in that of an order for production, by the court's determination that the investigation is authorized by Congress, is for a purpose Congress can order, and the documents sought are relevant to the inquiry. Beyond this, the requirement of reasonableness, including particularity in 'describing the place to be searched, and the persons or things to be seized,' also literally applicable to warrants, comes down to specification of the documents to be produced adequate, but not excessive, for the purposes of the relevant inquiry. Necessarily, as has been said, this cannot be reduced to formula; for relevancy and adequacy or excess in the breadth of the subpoena are matters variable in relation to the nature, purposes and scope of the inquiry."

UNITED STATES V. DIONISIO

410 U.S. 1, 93 S.Ct. 764, 35 L.Ed.2d 67 (1973).

JUSTICE STEWART delivered the opinion of the Court.

A special grand jury was convened * * * to investigate possible violations of federal criminal statutes relating to gambling. In the course of its investigation the grand jury received in evidence certain voice recordings that had been obtained pursuant to court orders. The grand jury subpoenaed approximately 20 persons, including the respondent Dionisio, seeking to obtain from them voice exemplars for comparison with the recorded conversations that had been received in evidence. Each witness was advised that he was a potential defendant in a criminal prosecution. Each was asked to examine a transcript of an intercepted conversation, and to go to a nearby office of the United States Attorney to read the transcript into a recording device. The witnesses were advised that they would be allowed to have their attorneys present when they read the transcripts. Dionisio and other witnesses refused to furnish the voice exemplars, asserting that these disclosures would violate their rights under the Fourth and Fifth Amendments. The Government then filed separate petitions in the District Court to compel Dionisio and the other witnesses to furnish the voice exemplars to the grand jury. * * * Following a hearing, the district judge rejected the witnesses' constitutional arguments and ordered them to comply with the grand jury's request. * * * When Dionisio persisted in his refusal to respond to the grand jury's directive, the District Court adjudged him in civil contempt and ordered him committed to custody. * * *

The Court of Appeals for the Seventh Circuit reversed. * * * The court found that the Fourth Amendment applied to the grand jury process * * *. Equating the procedures followed by the grand jury in the present case to the fingerprint detentions in *Davis v. Mississippi* [fn. a, p. 304], the Court of Appeals reasoned that "[t]he dragnet effect here, where approximately 30 persons were subpoenaed for purposes of identification, has the same invidious effect on fourth amendment rights as the practice condemned in *Davis*." The Court of Appeals held that the Fourth Amendment required a preliminary showing of reasonableness before a grand jury witness could be compelled to furnish a voice exemplar, and that in this case the proposed "seizures" of the voice exemplars would be unreasonable because of the large number of witnesses summoned by the grand jury and directed to produce such exemplars. We disagree. * * *

[T]he obtaining of physical evidence from a person involves a potential Fourth Amendment violation at two different levels—the "seizure" of the "person" necessary to bring him into contact with government agents, see *Davis v. Mississippi,* and the subsequent search for and seizure of the evidence. * * * The constitutionality of the compulsory production of exemplars from a grand jury witness necessarily turns on the same dual inquiry—whether either the initial compulsion of the person to appear before the grand jury, or the subsequent directive to make a voice recording is an unreasonable "seizure" within the meaning of the Fourth Amendment.

It is clear that a subpoena to appear before a grand jury is not a "seizure" in the Fourth Amendment sense, even though that summons may be inconvenient or burdensome. Last Term we again acknowledged what has long been recognized, that "[c]itizens generally are not constitutionally immune from grand jury subpoenas. * * *" *Branzburg v. Hayes* [408 U.S. 665 (1972)].[a] * * * [*Branzburg* and other decisions] are recent reaffirmations of the historically grounded obligations of every person to appear and give his evidence before the grand jury. "The personal sacrifice involved is a part of the necessary contribution of the individual to the welfare of the public." *Blair v. United States,* [fn. b, p. 605].

The compulsion exerted by a grand jury subpoena differs from the seizure effected by an arrest or even an investigative "stop" in more than civic obligation. For, as Judge Friendly wrote for the Court of Appeals for the Second Circuit:

> "The latter is abrupt, is effected with force or the threat of it and often in demeaning circumstances, and, in the case of arrest, results in a record involving social stigma. A subpoena is served in the same manner as other legal process; it involves no stigma whatever; if the time for appearance is inconvenient, this can generally be altered; and it remains at all times under the control and supervision of a court."

Thus, the Court of Appeals for the Seventh Circuit correctly recognized in a case subsequent to the one now before us, that a "grand jury subpoena to testify is not that kind of governmental intrusion on privacy against which the Fourth Amendment affords protection, once the Fifth Amendment is satisfied."

This case is thus quite different from *Davis v. Mississippi,* on which the Court of Appeals primarily relied. For in *Davis* it was the initial seizure—the lawless dragnet detention—that violated the Fourth and Fourteenth Amendments—not the taking of the fingerprints. * * * *Davis* is plainly inapposite to a case where the initial restraint does not itself infringe the Fourth Amendment.

This is not to say that a grand jury subpoena is some talisman that dissolves all constitutional protections. The grand jury cannot require a witness to testify against himself. It cannot require the production by a person of private books and records that would incriminate him. See *Boyd v. United States.* The Fourth Amendment provides protection against a grand jury subpoena *duces tecum* too sweeping in its terms "to be regarded as reasonable." *Hale v. Henkel.* And last Term, in the context of a First Amendment claim, we indicated that the Constitution could not tolerate the transformation of the grand jury into an instrument of oppression: "Official harassment of the press undertaken not for purposes of law enforcement but to disrupt a reporter's relationship with his news sources would have no justification. Grand juries are subject to judicial control and subpoenas to motions to quash. We do not expect courts will forget that grand juries

---

[a] The Court in *Branzburg* rejected a First Amendment claim raised by reporters who had been subpoenaed to testify before grand juries. The reporters had argued that they should not be compelled to reveal the identity of confidential sources or relevant facts obtained from those sources, at least absent an initial showing by the grand jury of a "compelling need" to obtain such information. The Court majority responded that it was "unclear" whether requiring the reporters to testify before the grand jury might have a negative impact on their future newsgathering capacity, but, in any event, that impact did not outweigh the interest of the public in the grand jury's unencumbered investigation of crime.

must operate within the limits of the First Amendment as well as the Fifth." *Branzburg v. Hayes.*

But we are here faced with no such constitutional infirmities in the subpoena to appear before the grand jury or in the order to make the voice recordings. There is * * * no valid Fifth Amendment claim. There was no order to produce private books and papers, and no sweeping subpoena *duces tecum.* And even if *Branzburg* be extended beyond its First Amendment moorings and tied to a more generalized due process concept, there is still no indication in this case of the kind of harassment that was of concern there.

The Court of Appeals found critical significance in the fact that the grand jury had summoned approximately 20 witnesses to furnish voice exemplars. We think that fact is basically irrelevant to the constitutional issues here. The grand jury may have been attempting to identify a number of voices on the tapes in evidence, or it might have summoned the 20 witnesses in an effort to identify one voice. But whatever the case, "[a] grand jury's investigation is not fully carried out until every available clue has been run down and all witnesses examined in every proper way to find if a crime has been committed." * * * The grand jury may well find it desirable to call numerous witnesses in the course of an investigation. It does not follow that each witness may resist a subpoena on the ground that too many witnesses have been called. Neither the order to Dionisio to appear, nor the order to make a voice recording was rendered unreasonable by the fact that many others were subjected to the same compulsion.

But the conclusion that Dionisio's compulsory appearance before the grand jury was not an unreasonable "seizure" is the answer to only the first part of the Fourth Amendment inquiry here. Dionisio argues that the grand jury's subsequent directive to make the voice recording was itself an infringement of his rights under the Fourth Amendment. We cannot accept that argument. In *Katz v. United States* [p. 95], we said that the Fourth Amendment provides no protection for what "a person knowingly exposes to the public, even in his home or office * * *." The physical characteristics of a person's voice, its tone and manner, as opposed to the content of a specific conversation, are constantly exposed to the public. Like a man's facial characteristics, or handwriting, his voice is repeatedly produced for others to hear. No person can have a reasonable expectation that others will not know the sound of his voice, any more than he can reasonably expect that his face will be a mystery to the world. * * *

Since neither the summons to appear before the grand jury, nor its directive to make a voice recording infringed upon any interest protected by the Fourth Amendment, there was no justification for requiring the grand jury to satisfy even the minimal requirement of "reasonableness" imposed by the Court of Appeals. A grand jury has broad investigative powers to determine whether a crime has been committed and who has committed it. The jurors may act on tips, rumors, evidence offered by the prosecutor, or their own personal knowledge. *Branzburg v. Hayes.* No grand jury witness is "entitled to set limits to the investigation that the grand jury may conduct." And a sufficient basis for an indictment may only emerge at the end of the investigation when all the evidence has been received. * * * Since

Dionisio raised no valid Fourth Amendment claim, there is no more reason to require a preliminary showing of reasonableness here than there would be in the case of any witness who, despite the lack of any constitutional or statutory privilege, declined to answer a question or comply with a grand jury request. Neither the Constitution nor our prior cases justify any such interference with grand jury proceedings.[14]

The Fifth Amendment guarantees that no civilian may be brought to trial for an infamous crime "unless on a presentment or indictment of a Grand Jury." This constitutional guarantee presupposes an investigative body "acting independently of either prosecuting attorney or judge," whose mission is to clear the innocent, no less than to bring to trial those who may be guilty. Any holding that would saddle a grand jury with minitrials and preliminary showing would assuredly impede its investigation and frustrate the public's interest in the fair and expeditious administration of the criminal laws. The grand jury may not always serve its historic role as a protective bulwark standing solidly between the ordinary citizen and an overzealous prosecutor, but if it is even to approach the proper performance of its constitutional mission, it must be free to pursue its investigations unhindered by external influence or supervision so long as it does not trench upon the legitimate rights of any witness called before it. * * *

JUSTICE MARSHALL, dissenting.[b]

* * * There can be no question that investigatory seizures effected by the police are subject to the constraints of the Fourth and Fourteenth Amendments. *Davis v. Mississippi.* * * * Like *Davis,* the present cases involve official investigatory seizures which interfere with personal liberty. The Court considers dispositive, however, the fact that the seizures were effected by the grand jury, rather than the police. I cannot agree. * * * [I]n *Hale v. Henkel,* the Court held that a subpoena *duces tecum* ordering "the production of books and papers [before a grand jury] may constitute an unreasonable search and seizure within the Fourth Amendment," and on the particular facts of the case, it concluded that the subpoena was "far too sweeping in its terms to be regarded as reasonable." Considered alone, *Hale* would certainly seem to carry a strong implication that a subpoena compelling an individual's personal appearance before a grand jury, like a subpoena ordering the production of private papers, is subject to the Fourth Amendment standard of reasonableness. The protection of the Fourth Amendment is not, after all, limited to personal "papers," but extends also to "persons," "houses," and "effects." It would seem a strange hierarchy of constitutional values

---

[14] Mr. Justice Marshall in dissent suggests that a preliminary showing of "reasonableness" is required where the grand jury subpoenas a witness to appear and produce handwriting or voice exemplars, but not when it subpoenas him to appear and testify. Such a distinction finds no support in the Constitution. The dissent argues that there is a potential Fourth Amendment violation in the case of a subpoenaed grand jury witness because of the asserted intrusiveness of the initial subpoena to appear—the possible stigma from a grand jury appearance and the inconvenience of the official restraint. But the initial directive to appear is as intrusive if the witness is called simply to testify as it is if he is summoned to produce physical evidence.

[b] The separate dissents of Justices Douglas and Brennan are omitted.

that would afford papers more protection from arbitrary governmental intrusion than people.

The Court, however, offers two interrelated justifications for excepting grand jury subpoenas directed at "persons," rather than "papers," from the constraints of the Fourth Amendment. These are an "historically grounded obligation of every person to appear and give his evidence before the grand jury," and the relative unintrusiveness of the grand jury subpoena on an individual's liberty.

In my view, the Court makes more of history than is justified. The Court treats the "historically grounded obligation" which it now discerns as extending to all "evidence," whatever its character. Yet, so far as I am aware, the obligation "to appear and give evidence" has heretofore been applied by this Court only in the context of testimonial evidence, either oral or documentary. * * * In the present case, * * * it was not testimony that the grand jury sought from respondents, but physical evidence. * * *

The Court seems to reason that the exception to the Fourth Amendment for grand jury subpoenas directed at persons is justified by the relative unintrusiveness of the grand jury process on an individual's liberty. * * * It may be that service of a grand jury subpoena does not involve the same potential for momentary embarrassment as does an arrest or investigatory "stop." But this difference seems inconsequential in comparison to the substantial stigma which— contrary to the Court's assertion—may result from a grand jury appearance as well as from an arrest or investigatory seizure. Public knowledge that a man has been summoned by a federal grand jury investigating, for instance, organized criminal activity can mean loss of friends, irreparable injury to business, and tremendous pressures on one's family life. Whatever nice legal distinctions may be drawn between police and prosecutor, on the one hand, and the grand jury, on the other, the public often treats an appearance before a grand jury as tantamount to a visit to the station house. Indeed, the former is frequently more damaging than the latter, for a grand jury appearance has an air of far greater gravity than a brief visit "downtown" for a "talk." The Fourth Amendment was placed in our Bill of Rights to protect the individual citizen from such potentially disruptive governmental intrusion into his private life unless conducted reasonably and with sufficient cause.

Nor do I believe that the constitutional problems inherent in such governmental interference with an individual's person are substantially alleviated because one may seek to appear at a "convenient time." In *Davis v. Mississippi*, it was recognized that an investigatory detention effected by the police "need not come unexpectedly or at an inconvenient time." But this fact did not suggest to the Court that the Fourth Amendment was inapplicable * * *. No matter how considerate a grand jury may be in arranging for an individual's appearance, the basic fact remains that his liberty has been officially restrained for some period of time. In terms of its effect on the individual, this restraint does not differ meaningfully from the restraint imposed on a suspect compelled to visit the police station house. Thus, the nature of the intrusion on personal liberty caused by a grand jury subpoena cannot, without more, be considered sufficient basis for denying respondents the protection of the Fourth Amendment.

Of course, the Fourth Amendment does not bar all official seizures of the person, but only those that are unreasonable and are without sufficient cause. With this in mind, it is possible at least to explain, if not justify, the failure to apply the protection of the Fourth Amendment to grand jury subpoenas requiring individuals to appear and *testify*. Thus, while it is true that we have traditionally given the grand jury broad investigatory powers, particularly in terms of compelling the appearance of persons before it, it must be understood that we have done so in heavy reliance on certain essential assumptions.

Certainly the most celebrated function of the grand jury is to stand between the Government and the citizen and thus to protect the latter from harassment and unfounded prosecution. The grand jury does not shed those characteristics which give it insulating qualities when it acts in its investigative capacity. Properly functioning, the grand jury is to be the servant of neither the Government nor the courts, but of the people. As such, we assume that it comes to its task without bias or self-interest. Unlike the prosecutor or policeman, it has no election to win or executive appointment to keep. The anticipated neutrality of the grand jury, even when acting in its investigative capacity, may perhaps be relied upon to prevent unwarranted interference with the lives of private citizens and to ensure that the grand jury's subpoena powers over the person are exercised in only a reasonable fashion. Under such circumstances, it may be justifiable to give the grand jury broad personal subpoena powers that are outside the purview of the Fourth Amendment, for—in contrast to the police—it is not likely that it will abuse those powers.

Whatever the present day validity of the historical assumption of neutrality which underlies the grand jury process, it must at least be recognized that if a grand jury is deprived of the independence essential to the assumption of neutrality—if it effectively surrenders that independence to a prosecutor—the dangers of excessive and unreasonable official interference with personal liberty are exactly those which the Fourth Amendment was intended to prevent. So long as the grand jury carries on its investigatory activities only through the mechanism of testimonial inquiries, the danger of such official usurpation of the grand jury process may not be unreasonably great. Individuals called to testify before the grand jury will have available their Fifth Amendment privilege against self-incrimination. Thus, at least insofar as incriminating information is sought directly from a particular criminal suspect, the grand jury process would not appear to offer law enforcement officials a substantial advantage over ordinary investigative techniques.

But when we move beyond the realm of grand jury investigations limited to testimonial inquiries, as the Court does today, the danger increases that law enforcement officials may seek to usurp the grand jury process for the purpose of securing incriminating evidence from a particular suspect through the simple expedient of a subpoena. * * * Thus, if the grand jury may summon criminal suspects [to obtain handwriting and voice exemplars] without complying with the

Fourth Amendment, it will obviously present an attractive investigative tool to prosecutor and police. For what law enforcement officers could not accomplish directly themselves after our decision in *Davis v. Mississippi*, they may now accomplish indirectly through the grand jury process.

Thus, the Court's decisions today can serve only to encourage prosecutorial exploitation of the grand jury process, at the expense of both individual liberty and the traditional neutrality of the grand jury. * * * [B]y holding that the grand jury's power to subpoena these respondents for the purpose of obtaining exemplars is completely outside the purview of the Fourth Amendment, the Court fails to appreciate the essential difference between real and testimonial evidence in the context of these cases, and thereby hastens the reduction of the grand jury into simply another investigative device of law enforcement officials. By contrast, the Court of Appeals, in proper recognition of these dangers, imposed narrow limitations on the subpoena power of the grand jury which are necessary to guard against unreasonable official interference with individual liberty but which would not impair significantly the traditional investigatory powers of that body. * * *

CARPENTER V. UNITED STATES
585 U.S. ___, 138 S.Ct. 2206, 201 L.Ed.2d 507 (2018).

[The government had utilized a court order to obtain from wireless service providers the historic cell site location records (CSLI) for Carpenter's cell phones. Under the Stored Communication Act, grand jury subpoenas may be used to obtain certain customer information from a service provider, but obtaining CSLI requires a court order based on a finding that the government's allegation of "specific and articulable facts sho[w] * * * that there are reasonable grounds to believe that the * * * records sought are relevant and material to the ongoing criminal investigation." Carpenter subsequently objected to the admission of the CSLI records at his trial, claiming a Fourth Amendment violation. The Supreme Court (5–4) sustained that claim. The majority (per Roberts, CJ) held that: (1) a customer had a reasonable expectation of privacy where, as here, the CSLI covered at least seven days, and the government therefore engaged in a search in obtaining those records; and (2) that search was subject to the Fourth Amendment's traditional requirements of probable cause and a prior magistrate determination through the issuance of a search warrant.

The majority opinion's primary discussion of those rulings, the responses in the primary dissent (by Justice Kennedy, joined by Justices Thomas and Alito, and the separate dissents of Justices Thomas and Gorsuch), are set forth in § 2 of Chapter 3. Justice Alito, joined by Justice Thomas, questioned the impact of the Court's reasoning on the long line of precedent upholding the use of subpoenas duces tecum to compel the production of documents. That dissent and the majority's response to that dissent are set forth here.]

Justice Alito's Dissent in *Carpenter*

[T]he Court ignores the basic distinction between an actual search (dispatching law enforcement officers to enter private premises and root through private papers and effects) and an order merely requiring a party to look through its own records and produce specified documents. The former, which intrudes on personal privacy far more deeply, requires probable cause; the latter does not. Treating an order to produce like an actual search, as today's decision does, is revolutionary. It violates both the original understanding of the Fourth Amendment and more than a century of Supreme Court precedent. Unless it is somehow restricted to the particular situation in the present case, the Court's move will cause upheaval. Must every grand jury subpoena *duces tecum* be supported by probable cause? If so, investigations of terrorism, political corruption, white-collar crime, and many other offenses will be stymied. And what about subpoenas and other document-production orders issued by administrative agencies? * * * a

The order in this case was the functional equivalent of a subpoena for documents, and there is no evidence that these writs were regarded as "searches" at the time of the founding. Subpoenas duces tecum and other forms of compulsory document production were well known to the founding generation. Blackstone dated the first writ of subpoena to the reign of King Richard II in the late 14th century, and by the end of the 15th century, the use of such writs had "become the daily practice of the [Chancery] court." [The dissent here traced the development of the subpoena in English practice. The Court of Chancery extended the subpoena from the subpoena ad testificandum to also include the subpoena duces tecum. That practice was then extended to the common law courts, although it was "not complete there" when Blackstone published his commentaries, as it was an open issue whether parties could use the subpoena duces tecum "not only with respect to third parties but also with respect to each other"].

That question soon found an affirmative answer on both sides of the Atlantic. In the United States, the First Congress established the federal court system in the Judiciary Act of 1789. As part of that Act, Congress authorized "all the said courts of the United States . . . in the trial of actions at law, on motion and due notice thereof being given, to require the parties to produce books or writings in their possession or power, which contain evidence pertinent to the issue, in cases and under circumstances where they might be compelled to produce the same by the ordinary rules of proceeding in chancery." § 15, 1 Stat. 82. From that point forward, federal courts in the United States could compel the production of documents regardless of whether those documents were held by parties to the case or by third parties. * * *

The prevalence of subpoenas *duces tecum* at the time of the founding was not limited to the civil context. In criminal cases, courts and prosecutors were also

---

a   Justice Kennedy's dissent relied upon the third-party doctrine, also discussed in the majority opinion, rather than the Fourth Amendment standard previously applied to documentary subpoenas (typically to subpoenas addressed to entities or individuals who were the subject of the investigations, rather than neutral third-parties, such as a wireless service provider). However, as set forth at p. 118, Justice Kennedy described the third-party doctrine as supported not only by the customer's lack of a protected interest in the third-party's records, but also by the "longstanding rule that the Government may use compulsory process to compel persons to disclose documents and other evidence within their possession and control." Although not joining Justice Alito's dissent, Justice Kennedy also criticized the majority's opinion "for calling into question the subpoena practices of federal and state grand juries, legislatures, and other investigative bodies, as Justice Alito's opinion explains."

using the writ to compel the production of necessary documents. * * * [S]ubpoenas duces tecum were routine in part because of their close association with grand juries. Early American colonists imported the grand jury, like so many other common-law traditions, and they quickly flourished. See *United States v. Calandra*, 414 U.S. 338 (1974). Grand juries were empaneled by the federal courts almost as soon as the latter were established, and both they and their state counterparts actively exercised their wide-ranging common-law authority. See R. Younger, The People's Panel 47–55 (1963). Indeed, "the Founders thought the grand jury so essential . . . that they provided in the Fifth Amendment that federal prosecution of serious crimes can only be instituted by 'a presentment or indictment of a Grand Jury.'" *Calandra.*

Given the popularity and prevalence of grand juries at the time, the Founders must have been intimately familiar with the tools they used—including compulsory process—to accomplish their work. As a matter of tradition, grand juries were "accorded wide latitude to inquire into violations of criminal law," including the power to "compel the production of evidence or the testimony of witnesses as [they] conside[r] appropriate." *Ibid.* Long before national independence was achieved, grand juries were already using their broad inquisitorial powers not only to present and indict criminal suspects but also to inspect public buildings, to levy taxes, to supervise the administration of the laws, to advance municipal reforms such as street repair and bridge maintenance, and in some cases even to propose legislation. Of course, such work depended entirely on grand juries' ability to access any relevant documents. * * *

Talk of kings and common-law writs may seem out of place in a case about cell-site records and the protections afforded by the Fourth Amendment in the modern age. But this history matters, not least because it tells us what was on the minds of those who ratified the Fourth Amendment and how they understood its scope. That history makes it abundantly clear that the Fourth Amendment, as originally understood, did not apply to the compulsory production of documents at all. * * * Even Justice Brandeis—a stalwart proponent of construing the Fourth Amendment liberally—acknowledged that "under any ordinary construction of language," "there is no 'search' or 'seizure' when a defendant is required to produce a document in the orderly process of a court's procedure." *Olmstead v. United States*, 277 U.S. 438, 476 (1928) (dissenting opinion).[1]

Of course, our jurisprudence has not stood still since 1791. We now evaluate subpoenas duces tecum and other forms of compulsory document production under the Fourth Amendment, although we employ a reasonableness standard that is less demanding than the requirements for a warrant. But the road to that doctrinal destination was anything but smooth, and our initial missteps—and the

---

[1]   Any other interpretation of the Fourth Amendment's text would run into insuperable problems because it would apply not only to subpoenas duces tecum but to all other forms of compulsory process as well. If the Fourth Amendment applies to the compelled production of documents, then it must also apply to the compelled production of testimony—an outcome that we have repeatedly rejected and which, if accepted, would send much of the field of criminal procedure into a tailspin. See, e.g., *United States v. Dionisio.* * * * As a matter of original understanding, a subpoena duces tecum no more effects a "search" or "seizure" of papers within the meaning of the Fourth Amendment than a subpoena ad testificandum effects a "search" or "seizure" of a person.

subsequent struggle to extricate ourselves from their consequences—should provide an object lesson for today's majority about the dangers of holding compulsory process to the same standard as actual searches and seizures.

For almost a century after the Fourth Amendment was enacted, this Court said and did nothing to indicate that it might regulate the compulsory production of documents. But that changed temporarily when the Court decided *Boyd v. United States*, the first—and, until today, the only—case in which this Court has ever held the compulsory production of documents to the same standard as actual searches and seizures. * * * Although *Boyd* was replete with stirring rhetoric, its reasoning was confused from start to finish in a way that ultimately made the decision unworkable. See 3 W. LaFave, J. Israel, N. King & O. Kerr, Criminal Procedure § 8.7(a) (4th ed. 2015). Over the next 50 years, the Court would gradually roll back *Boyd*'s erroneous conflation of compulsory process with actual searches and seizures. [The dissent here discusses *Hale,* p. 605, which "did not entirely liberate subpoenas duces tecum from Fourth Amendment constraints," and *Oklahoma Press*, p. 607, described as having distinguished between "figurative or constructive searches" and "actual searches" and having applied to the former a "different standard," regulating production "less stringently".]

Having reversed *Boyd*'s conflation of the compelled production of documents with actual searches and seizures, the [*Oklahoma Press*] Court then set forth the relevant Fourth Amendment standard for the former. When it comes to "the production of corporate or other business records," the Court held that the Fourth Amendment "at the most guards against abuse only by way of too much indefiniteness or breadth in the things required to be 'particularly described,' if also the inquiry is one the demanding agency is authorized by law to make and the materials specified are relevant." *Oklahoma Press*. Notably, the Court held that a showing of probable cause was not necessary so long as "the investigation is authorized by Congress, is for a purpose Congress can order, and the documents sought are relevant to the inquiry." Id., at 209. Since *Oklahoma Press*, we have consistently hewed to that standard. See, e.g., *Donovan v. Lone Steer, Inc.*, 464 U.S. 408, 414–415 (1984); *United States v. Miller*, 425 U.S. 435 (1976)[b]; *California Bankers Assn. v. Shultz*, 416 U.S. 21, 67 (1974); *United States v. Dionisio*, [p. 609]; *See v. Seattle*, 387 U.S. 541, 544 (1967); *United States v. Powell*, 379 U.S. 48, 57–

---

[b]   *Miller* is one of the key third-party doctrine rulings discussed by the majority, and Justice Kennedy's dissent. The Court there held that Miller, a bank customer, lacked a protected Fourth Amendment interest that would allow his challenge to a subpoena directing the bank to produce records relating to his banking activities. The Court also commented on Miller's argument that the Fourth Amendment review here required "greater judicial scrutiny, equivalent to that required for a search warrant." It noted that *Oklahoma Press* had rejected requiring such review, and that "there was no indication [in *California Bankers Assn. v. Shultz*, discussing the Bank Secrecy Act's access provisions] that a new rule was to be devised or that the traditional distinction between a search warrant and a subpoena would not be recognized." The Court then added, "In any event, * * * we hold that the respondent [Miller] lacks the requisite Fourth Amendment interest to challenge the validity of the subpoena."

58 (1964)[c]; *McPhaul v. United States*, 364 U.S. 372, 382–383 (1960)[d]; *United States v. Morton Salt Co.*, 338 U.S. 632, 652–653 (1950); * * *. By applying *Oklahoma Press* and thereby respecting "the traditional distinction between a search warrant and a subpoena," *Miller*, supra, this Court has reinforced "the basic compromise" between "the public interest" in every man's evidence and the private interest "of men to be free from officious meddling." *Oklahoma Press*, supra.

Today, however, the majority inexplicably ignores the settled rule of *Oklahoma Press* in favor of a resurrected version of *Boyd*. That is mystifying. This should have been an easy case regardless of whether the Court looked to the original understanding of the Fourth Amendment or to our modern doctrine. * * * [T]here is no doubt that the Government met the *Oklahoma Press* standard here. Under *Oklahoma Press*, a court order must " 'be sufficiently limited in scope, relevant in purpose, and specific in directive so that compliance will not be unreasonably burdensome.' " *Lone Steer, Inc.* Here, the type of order obtained by the Government almost necessarily satisfies that standard. The Stored Communications Act allows a court to issue the relevant type of order "only if the governmental entity offers specific and articulable facts showing that there are reasonable grounds to believe that . . . the records . . . sough[t] are relevant and material to an ongoing criminal investigation." 18 U.S.C. § 2703(d). And the court "may quash or modify such order" if the provider objects that the "records requested are unusually voluminous in nature or compliance with such order otherwise would cause an undue burden on such provider." *Ibid.* No such objection was made in this case, and Carpenter does not suggest that the orders contravened the *Oklahoma Press* standard in any other way. * * *

Against centuries of precedent and practice, all that the Court can muster is the observation that "this Court has never held that the Government may subpoena third parties for records in which the suspect has a reasonable expectation of privacy." [p. 621]. Frankly, I cannot imagine a concession more damning to the Court's argument than that. As the Court well knows, the reason that we have never seen such a case is because—until today—defendants categorically had no "reasonable expectation of privacy" and no property interest in records belonging to third parties. * * * Not only that, but even if the Fourth

---

[c] *Powell* addressed the government showing needed to obtain judicial enforcement (via contempt sanction) of an IRS summons. The summons is used to obtain documents from both entities and individuals in both civil and criminal investigations relating to taxpayer compliance. Looking to *Oklahoma Press*, the *Powell* Court rejected the contention that the showing meet a probable cause prerequisite. In light of both *Oklahoma Press* and the text and function of the relevant statute, the Court adopted a four-part standard: (1) the investigation must be conducted for a "legitimate purpose"; (2) the documents demanded must be relevant to that purpose; (3) the IRS must be seeking information it does not already possess; and (4) the IRS must have followed the administrative steps prescribed by the statute and its own internal regulations.

[d] *McPhail* extended the *Oklahoma Press* standard to legislative investigations. The House of Representatives Un-American Activities committee subpoenaed a public organization (the Civil Rights Congress) to produce "all records, correspondence and memorandum pertaining to the organization of, and affiliation with, other organizations and all moneys received or expended." McPhail, the executive secretary, relied initially on the self-incrimination privilege, but also added a Fourth Amendment challenge based on the excessive breadth of the subpoena. The Court concluded that the subpoena met the prerequisites established in *Oklahoma Press*, in part because the documents sought were relevant to determining whether the Civil Rights Congress was in actuality an affiliate of "the Communist Party and international communist movement."

Amendment permitted someone to object to the subpoena of a third party's records, the Court cannot explain why that individual should be entitled to greater Fourth Amendment protection than the party actually being subpoenaed. When parties are subpoenaed to turn over their records, after all, they will at most receive the protection afforded by *Oklahoma Press* even though they will own and have a reasonable expectation of privacy in the records at issue. Under the Court's decision, however, the Fourth Amendment will extend greater protections to someone else who is not being subpoenaed and does not own the records. That outcome makes no sense, and the Court does not even attempt to defend it.

We have set forth the relevant Fourth Amendment standard for subpoenaing business records many times over. Out of those dozens of cases, the majority cannot find even one that so much as suggests an exception to the *Oklahoma Press* standard for sufficiently personal information. Instead, we have always "described the constitutional requirements" for compulsory process as being " 'settled' " and as applying categorically to all " 'subpoenas [of] corporate books or records.' " *Lone Steer, Inc.* That standard, we have held, is "the most" protection the Fourth Amendment gives "to the production of corporate records and papers." *Oklahoma Press* (emphasis added).

Although the majority announces its holding in the context of the Stored Communications Act, nothing stops its logic from sweeping much further. The Court has offered no meaningful limiting principle, and none is apparent. Cf. Tr. of Oral Arg. 31 (Carpenter's counsel admitting that "a grand jury subpoena . . . would be held to the same standard as any other subpoena or subpoena-like request for [cell-site] records"). * * * Holding that subpoenas must meet the same standard as conventional searches will seriously damage, if not destroy, their utility. Even more so than at the founding, today the Government regularly uses subpoenas *duces tecum* and other forms of compulsory process to carry out its essential functions. * * *

[The dissent then turned to a second point—that the Court "compounds its initial error" by holding that a defendant has a Fourth Amendment right to "object to the search of a third party's property." The dissent's conclusion, set forth below, refers to both criticisms.]

Although the majority professes a desire not to " 'embarrass the future,' " we can guess where today's decision will lead. One possibility is that the broad principles that the Court seems to embrace will be applied across the board. All subpoenas *duces tecum* and all other orders compelling the production of documents will require a demonstration of probable cause, and individuals will be able to claim a protected Fourth Amendment interest in any sensitive personal information about them that is collected and owned by third parties. Those would be revolutionary developments indeed. The other possibility is that this Court will face the embarrassment of explaining in case after case that the principles on which today's decision rests are subject to all sorts of qualifications and limitations that have not yet been discovered. If we take this latter course, we will inevitably end up "mak[ing] a crazy quilt of the Fourth Amendment." *Smith v. Maryland*, 442 U.S. 735, 745 (1979).

All of this is unnecessary. In the Stored Communications Act, Congress addressed the specific problem at issue in this case. The Act restricts the misuse of cell-site records by cell service providers, something that the Fourth Amendment cannot do. The Act also goes beyond current Fourth Amendment case law in restricting access by law enforcement. It permits law enforcement officers to acquire cell-site records only if they meet a heightened standard and obtain a court order. If the American people now think that the Act is inadequate or needs updating, they can turn to their elected representatives to adopt more protective provisions. Because the collection and storage of cell-site records affects nearly every American, it is unlikely that the question whether the current law requires strengthening will escape Congress's notice.

Legislation is much preferable to the development of an entirely new body of Fourth Amendment caselaw for many reasons, including the enormous complexity of the subject, the need to respond to rapidly changing technology, and the Fourth Amendment's limited scope. The Fourth Amendment restricts the conduct of the Federal Government and the States; it does not apply to private actors. But today, some of the greatest threats to individual privacy may come from powerful private companies that collect and sometimes misuse vast quantities of data about the lives of ordinary Americans. If today's decision encourages the public to think that this Court can protect them from this looming threat to their privacy, the decision will mislead as well as disrupt. And if holding a provision of the Stored Communications Act to be unconstitutional dissuades Congress from further legislation in this field, the goal of protecting privacy will be greatly disserved. * * *

The *Carpenter* Majority's Response to Justice Alito's Dissent

Justice Alito contends that the warrant requirement simply does not apply when the Government acquires records using compulsory process. Unlike an actual search, he says, subpoenas for documents do not involve the direct taking of evidence; they are at most a "constructive search" conducted by the target of the subpoena. Given this lesser intrusion on personal privacy, Justice Alito argues that the compulsory production of records is not held to the same probable cause standard. In his view, this Court's precedents set forth a categorical rule—separate and distinct from the third-party doctrine—subjecting subpoenas to lenient scrutiny without regard to the suspect's expectation of privacy in the records.

But this Court has never held that the Government may subpoena third parties for records in which the suspect has a reasonable expectation of privacy. Almost all of the examples Justice Alito cites contemplated requests for evidence implicating diminished privacy interests or for a corporation's own books.[5] The lone

---

[5]   See *United States v. Dionisio*, 410 U.S. 1, 14 (1973) ("No person can have a reasonable expectation that others will not know the sound of his voice"); *Donovan v. Lone Steer, Inc.*, 464 U.S. 408, 411, 415 (1984) (payroll and sales records); *California Bankers Assn. v. Shultz*, 416 U.S. 21, 67 (1974) (Bank Secrecy Act reporting requirements); *See v. Seattle*, 387 U.S. 541, 544 (1967) (financial books and records); *United States v. Powell*, 379 U.S. 48, 49, 57 (1964) (corporate tax records); *McPhail v. United States*, 364 U.S. 372, 374, 382 (1960) (books and records of an organization); *United States v. Morton Salt Co.*, 338 U.S. 632, 634, 651–653 (1950) (Federal Trade Commission reporting requirement); *Oklahoma Press Publishing Co. v. Walling*, 327 U.S. 186, 189, 204–208 (1946) (payroll records); *Hale v. Henkel*, 201 U.S. 43, 45, 75 (1906) (corporate books and papers).

exception, of course, is *United States v. Miller*, where the Court's analysis of the third-party subpoena [for the customer's banking records] merged with the application of the third-party doctrine. 425 U.S., at 444 (concluding that *Miller* lacked the necessary privacy interest to contest the issuance of a subpoena to his bank).

Justice Alito overlooks the critical issue. At some point, the dissent should recognize that CSLI is an entirely different species of business record—something that implicates basic Fourth Amendment concerns about arbitrary government power much more directly than corporate tax or payroll ledgers. When confronting new concerns wrought by digital technology, this Court has been careful not to uncritically extend existing precedents. * * * If the choice to proceed by subpoena provided a categorical limitation on Fourth Amendment protection, no type of record would ever be protected by the warrant requirement. Under Justice Alito's view, private letters, digital contents of a cell phone—any personal information reduced to document form, in fact—may be collected by subpoena for no reason other than "official curiosity." *United States v. Morton Salt Co.*, 338 U.S. 632, 652 (1950). Justice Kennedy declines to adopt the radical implications of this theory, leaving open the question whether the warrant requirement applies "when the Government obtains the modern-day equivalents of an individual's own 'papers' or 'effects,' even when those papers or effects are held by a third party." *Post*, at 13 (citing *United States v. Warshak*, 631 F. 3d 266, 283–288 (CA6 2010)).[e] That would be a sensible exception, because it would prevent the subpoena doctrine from overcoming any reasonable expectation of privacy. If the third-party doctrine does not apply to the "modern-day equivalents of an individual's own 'papers' or

---

[e]   *Warshak* held that a search warrant was required to obtain a target's e-mails from a remote computing service. The government had utilized a court order authorized under the Stored Communications Act, obtaining 27,000 e-mails. Justice Kennedy's *Carpenter* dissent, as previously noted, relied upon the third-party doctrine, but it also noted that the doctrine might not govern all third-party subpoenas. The dissent stated: "This is not to say that *Miller* and *Smith* are not without limits. They may not apply when the Government obtains the modern-day equivalents of an individual's own papers or effects, even when those papers or effects are held by a third party." It then cited both *Warshak* and *Ex parte Jackson*, 96 U.S. 727 (1878), which held that "letters and sealed packages subject to letter postage in the mail can be opened and examined only under a warrant."

Justice Gorsuch's dissent lent stronger support to *Warshak*. It noted: "Whatever may be left of *Smith* and *Miller*, few doubt that e-mail should be treated much like traditional mail it has largely supplanted—as a bailment in which the owner retains a vital and protected legal interest." The dissent cited *Warshak* in this connection, describing that ruling as "relying on an analogy to *Jackson* to extend Fourth Amendment protection to e-mail held by a third-party service provider."

Justice Gorsuch also addressed the bearing of the original understanding. He noted, "It may be that, as an original matter, a subpoena requiring the recipient to produce records wasn't thought of as a 'search or seizure' by the government implicating the Fourth Amendment, see ante, (opinion of Alito, J.), but instead as an act of compelled self-incrimination implicating the Fifth Amendment, see United States v. Hubbell. (Thomas, J., dissenting) [see p. 657]; Nagareda, Compulsion "To Be A Witness" and the Resurrection of Boyd [fn. d, p. 658]. But the common law of searches and seizures does not appear to have confronted a case where private documents equivalent to a mailed letter were entrusted to a bailee and then subpoenaed. As a result, '[t]he common-law rule regarding subpoenas for documents held by third parties entrusted with information from the target is . . . unknown and perhaps unknowable.' * * * Given that (perhaps insoluble) uncertainty, I am content to adhere to Jackson and its implications for now." * * * "[I]f we were to overthrow Jackson * * *, we would do well to reconsider the scope of the Fifth Amendment, * * * [while being] wary of returning to the doctrine of Boyd," * * * [which precluded the] "use of subpoenas even for ordinary business records."

'effects,'" then the clear implication is that the documents should receive full Fourth Amendment protection. We simply think that such protection should extend as well to a detailed log of a person's movements over several years.

This is certainly not to say that all orders compelling the production of documents will require a showing of probable cause. The Government will be able to use subpoenas to acquire records in the overwhelming majority of investigations. We hold only that a warrant is required in the rare case where the suspect has a legitimate privacy interest in records held by a third party.

3.   THE PRIVILEGE AGAINST SELF-INCRIMINATION

A person subpoenaed in connection with a grand jury or any other criminal investigation has available all of the evidentiary privileges available to witnesses in general (i.e., the right, at the witness' option, to refuse to provide information where the law designates that information as "privileged" and therefore free from compelled disclosure). In this context, clearly the most significant privilege is that guaranteed by the Fifth Amendment of the Constitution—the privilege against compulsory self-incrimination.[a] The Fifth Amendment states that no person "shall be compelled in any criminal case to be a witness against himself." The self-incrimination clause has an extensive common law background, and it was with respect to the interpretation of this clause that Justice Frankfurter once noted that "a page of history is worth a volume of logic." *Ullmann v. United States*, 350 U.S. 422 (1956) (concurring). Yet the Court also has frequently cited the important and diverse values underlying the privilege[b] and noted the need to give the privilege a construction "as broad as the mischief against which it seeks to guard." *Counselman v. Hitchcock*, 142 U.S. 547 (1892).

The Fifth Amendment prohibits compelling a person to be a witness against himself "in any criminal case." In *Counselman v. Hitchcock*, supra, the Court not

---

[a]   The other privileges that witnesses may raise as a grounding for refusing to disclose information ordinarily flow from the law of the particular jurisdiction, and therefore will vary in scope from one state to another. These include such privileges as the marital privilege (protecting at least the confidential communications between spouses), the doctor/patient privilege (protecting information passed between doctor and patient that is germane to treatment or consultation), and the lawyer/client privilege (protecting, with some exceptions, communications of clients to lawyers for the purpose of legal consultation). While all of these may arise in the grand jury context, none rivals the self-incrimination privilege either as to the frequency with which it arises or its practical significance.

[b]   The most frequently cited statement of those values comes from Justice Goldberg's opinion for the Court in *Murphy v. Waterfront Commission*, 378 U.S. 52 (1964), a case discussed infra in the *Kastigar* opinion. That opinion stated: "The privilege against self-incrimination * * * reflects many of our fundamental values and most noble aspirations: our unwillingness to subject those suspected of crime to the cruel trilemma of self-accusation, perjury or contempt; our preference for an accusatorial rather than an inquisitorial system of criminal justice; our fear that self-incriminating statements will be elicited by inhumane treatment and abuses; our sense of fair play which dictates 'a fair state-individual balance by requiring the government to leave the individual alone until good cause is shown for disturbing him and by requiring the government in its contest with the individual to shoulder the entire load'; our respect for the inviolability of the human personality and the right of each individual 'to a private enclave where he may lead a private life'; our distrust of self-deprecatory statements; and our realization that the privilege, while sometimes 'a shelter to the guilty,' is often 'a protection to the innocent.'"

only held the privilege available to a grand jury witness, but established its availability to witnesses in proceedings totally unrelated to the criminal process. The Fifth Amendment, it concluded, applies to a witness "in any proceeding" who is compelled to give testimony of potential use against him in a subsequent criminal prosecution. The key is not where the compulsion of testimony occurs, but where the compelled testimony might be used.

Of course, the compelled testimony must have an incriminating potential and the concept of potential incrimination is not without limits. The Court has noted that the threat of subsequent incriminatory use of compelled testimony must be "real and appreciable," not "imaginary and unsubstantial." Moreover, the witness' assertion of the privilege is not conclusive on this issue. Following the witness' assertion of the privilege, "it is for the court to say whether his silence is justified and to require him to answer 'if it clearly appears to the court that he is mistaken.' " *Hoffman v. United States*, 341 U.S. 479 (1951). However, since the witness asserting the privilege cannot be required to explain what his testimony would be, and why it might be incriminatory, the court must sustain the claim of privilege if it is evident "from the implications of the question, in the setting in which it is asked," that a responsive answer could possibly be incriminating. Moreover, incrimination does not require "answers that would in themselves support a conviction"; it is sufficient that the answers could "furnish a link in the chain of evidence needed to prosecute the claimant for a * * * crime." *Hoffman* supra.

A witness asserts the privilege as to the particular question (unlike the criminal defendant, who may simply refuse to testify), considering the incriminatory potential of a truthful response to that question. *Rogers v. United States*, 340 U.S. 367 (1951), concluded that once the witness answers and provides incriminating information regarding a particular offense, the witness cannot resort to the privilege to refuse to answer additional questions where the responses would be incriminating only in providing further incriminating details concerning that offense. To uphold such a claim of the privilege, the Court noted, would "open the way to distortion of facts by permitting a witness to select any stopping point in her testimony."

Of course, before a witness can decide whether to exercise the privilege, the witness must be aware of the availability of the privilege. Traditionally, witnesses in civil, criminal, and administrative proceedings are not informed upon taking the oath that they have a right to exercise the privilege. In *Miranda v. Arizona* [p. 433], the Supreme Court extended the privilege to the person subjected to custodial interrogation and insisted that such a person be informed of his right to remain silent through the *Miranda* warnings. Not surprisingly, the argument was then advanced that similar "self-incrimination warnings" must be provided the grand jury witness, at least where the witness is a person who may be viewed as the "target" of the grand jury investigation. A related contention was that such a target witness must be informed of his right to the assistance of counsel, and must be provided appointed counsel if indigent. The first case in this section, *Mandujano*, considered both of these issues but provided no majority resolution. Although *Mandujano* was decided in 1976, the Court has not returned to either issue. Following *Mandujano*, the Justice Department issued an internal guideline on federal grand jury practice which requires prosecutors to give the following notification to any grand jury witness "whose conduct is within the scope of the grand jury investigation": (1) "that the witness may refuse to answer any question if a truthful answer to the question would tend to incriminate him," (2) "that anything that the witness does say may be used against him," and (3) "that the grand jury will permit the witness the reasonable opportunity to step outside the grand jury room to consult with counsel if he desires." Warnings relating to the self-incrimination privilege are commonly used in state grand jury proceedings as well. As to consulting with counsel, most states follow the federal practice, but a fair number of states allow the witness to be assisted by counsel located within the grand jury room and several of these provide for appointment of counsel at the state's expense where the witness is indigent.

The second case, *Kastigar*, considers the important practice of providing to the witness a grant of immunity that precludes reliance upon the privilege. The federal immunity provision upheld in *Kastigar* became the model for many state immunity provisions, although a substantial minority continue to provide the transactional immunity that prevailed prior to the adoption of that statute.

The last two cases, *Fisher* and *Hubbell*, return to the issue first raised in *Boyd* (§ 2 supra)—the availability of the self-incrimination privilege in responding to a subpoena duces tecum requiring the production of documents. *Boyd* here had a longer lasting influence than it did in the application of the Fourth Amendment to prohibit the documentary subpoena (see *Hale*, p. 605). Yet, here as well, a series of cases, even prior to *Fisher*, had limited its impact. In particular, one line of cases had held that the privilege against self-incrimination did not apply to the compelled production of documents belonging to a corporation or similar entity, such as a partnership.[c] Thus, as the Court notes in *Fisher*, A.E. Boyd and Sons, a partnership, would no longer have the privilege available to it to contest the compelled production of a document.

Another line of post-*Boyd* rulings had held that the compelled production of identification evidence (e.g., blood samples or handwriting exemplars), whether compelled by subpoena duces tecum or otherwise, was not subject to the self-incrimination privilege. The privilege, the Court noted, applies only to the compelled production of "testimony," i.e., "communications." Though its protection extended beyond compelling words from a "person's own lips," reaching

---

[c]   The cases establishing this "entity" exception relied primarily upon two grounds. First, they characterized the self-incrimination privilege as designed in large part to protect interests unique to the individual (e.g., ensuring "respect for the inviolability of the human personality," and maintaining "the right of each individual to a private enclave")—interests that were inapplicable to a "fictional entity." See e.g., *United States v. White*, 322 U.S. 694 (1944). Second, the Court stressed that the practical impact of applying the privilege to the compelled production of entity documents. See e.g., *United States v. White*, supra. ("The greater portion of evidence of wrongdoing by an organization or its representatives is usually to be found in the official records and documents of that organization. Were the cloak of the privilege to be thrown around these impersonal records and documents, effective enforcement of many federal and state laws would be impossible. The framers of the constitutional guarantee against compulsory self-disclosure, who were interested primarily in protecting individual civil liberties, cannot be said to have intended the privilege to be available to protect economic or other interests of such organizations so as to nullify appropriate governmental regulations.")

"communications * * * in whatever form they may take," it did not encompass compulsion which makes a person the source of "real or physical evidence." See e.g., *Schmerber v. California*, 384 U.S. 757 (1966).

Fisher considers the extent to which the privilege applies to the compelled production of documents in light of these post-*Boyd* developments. *Hubbell* applies the *Fisher* analysis and considers its bearing on the grant of immunity as to the compelled production of documents.

UNITED STATES V. MANDUJANO

425 U.S. 564, 96 S.Ct. 1768, 48 L.Ed.2d 212 (1976).

CHIEF JUSTICE BURGER announced the judgment of the Court in an opinion in which JUSTICE WHITE, JUSTICE POWELL, and JUSTICE REHNQUIST join.

This case presents the question whether the warnings called for by *Miranda v. Arizona* [p. 433], must be given to a grand jury witness who is called to testify about criminal activities in which he may have been personally involved; and, whether absent such warnings, false statements made to the grand jury must be suppressed in a prosecution for perjury based on those statements.

[In March 1973, an undercover agent received information that Mandujano was dealing in narcotics. Keeping his identity secret, the agent met Mandujano and arranged for the purchase of heroin. Mandujano received $650.00 for the purchase, but returned the same night without the heroin and refunded the money. After Mandujano failed to keep a subsequent appointment, the agent closed the investigative file and reported his contact with Mandujano to federal prosecutors. Six weeks later Mandujano was subpoenaed to testify before a special grand jury investigating the drug traffic in the local area. Before testifying, the prosecutor informed Mandujano of his general duty to answer, his right not to answer incriminatory questions, and of possible perjury liability for false answers. Mandujano was also told that he could have a lawyer outside the room with whom he could consult. When asked if he had a lawyer, Mandujano responded: "I don't have one. I don't have the money to get one."]

[During the grand jury questioning, Mandujano admitted that he had purchased heroin as recently as five months ago, but denied knowledge of the identity of any dealers, except for one street-corner source. He maintained this position notwithstanding the prosecutor's suggestion that "our information is that you can tell us more * * * than you have today." Mandujano "steadfastly denied either selling or attempting to sell heroin since the time of his conviction 15 years before." He "specifically disclaimed having discussed the sale of heroin with anyone during the preceding year and stated that he would not even try to purchase an ounce of heroin for $650.00."]

[Mandujano subsequently was indicted for attempting to distribute heroin and for willfully and knowingly making a false material declaration to the grand jury. The prosecution sought to introduce the grand jury testimony as the basis for the false declaration charge. Mandujano argued that his grand jury testimony should be suppressed since he was not given full *Miranda* warnings prior to his testimony. The District Court sustained the motion on the ground that a "putative" or "virtual" defendant was entitled to *Miranda* warnings. The Court of Appeals affirmed.]

* * * The very availability of the Fifth Amendment privilege to grand jury witnesses suggests that occasions will often arise when potentially incriminating questions will be asked in the ordinary course of the jury's investigation. * * * It is in keeping with the grand jury's historic function as a shield against arbitrary accusations to call before it persons suspected of criminal activity, so that the investigation can be complete. This is true whether the grand jury embarks upon an inquiry focused upon individuals suspected of wrongdoing, or is directed at persons suspected of no misconduct but who may be able to provide links in a chain of evidence relating to criminal conduct of others, or is centered upon broader problems of concern to society. It is entirely appropriate—indeed imperative—to summon individuals who may be able to illuminate the shadowy precincts of corruption and crime. Since the subject matter of the inquiry is crime, and often organized, systematic crime—as is true with drug traffic—it is unrealistic to assume that all of the witnesses capable of providing useful information will be pristine pillars of the community untainted by criminality. * * *

Accordingly, the witness, though possibly engaged in some criminal enterprise, can be required to answer before a grand jury, so long as there is no compulsion to answer questions that are self-incriminating * * *. The witness must invoke the privilege, however, as the "Constitution does not forbid the asking of criminative questions." *United States v. Monia*, 317 U.S., at 433 (1943) (Frankfurter, J., dissenting).

> "The [Fifth] Amendment speaks of compulsion. It does not preclude a witness from testifying voluntarily in matters which may incriminate him. If, therefore, he desires the protection of the privilege, he must claim it or he will not be considered to have been 'compelled' within the meaning of the Amendment." Id.

Absent a claim of the privilege, the duty to give testimony remains absolute.

The stage is therefore set when the question is asked. If the witness interposes his privilege, the grand jury has two choices. If the desired testimony is of marginal value, the grand jury can pursue other avenues of inquiry; if the testimony is thought sufficiently important, the grand jury can seek a judicial determination as to the bona fides of the witness' Fifth Amendment claim, in which case the witness must satisfy the presiding judge that the claim of privilege is not a subterfuge. If in fact "there is reasonable ground to apprehend danger to the witness from his being compelled to answer," the prosecutor must then determine whether the answer is of such overriding importance as to justify a grant of immunity to the witness. If immunity is sought by the prosecutor and granted by the presiding judge, the witness can then be compelled to answer, on pain of contempt, even though the testimony would implicate the witness in criminal activity. * * *

In this constitutional process of securing a witness' testimony, perjury simply has no place whatever. Perjured testimony is an obvious and flagrant affront to the basic concepts of judicial proceedings. Effective restraints against this type of egregious offense are therefore imperative. The power of subpoena, broad as it is, and the power of contempt for refusing to answer, drastic as that is—and even the solemnity of the oath—cannot insure truthful answers. Hence, Congress has made the giving of false answers a criminal act punishable by severe penalties; in no other way can criminal conduct be flushed into the open where the law can deal with it.

Similarly, our cases have consistently—indeed without exception—allowed sanctions for false statements or perjury; they have done so even in instances where the perjurer complained that the Government exceeded its constitutional powers in making the inquiry. See, e.g., *Bryson v. United States*, 396 U.S. 64 (1969). In *Bryson*, a union officer was required by federal labor law to file an affidavit averring that he was not a Communist. The affidavit was false in material statements. In a collateral attack on his conviction, Bryson argued that since the statute required him either to incriminate himself or lie, he could not lawfully be imprisoned for failure to comply. This Court rejected the contention:

> "[I]t cannot be thought that as a general principle of our law a citizen has a privilege to answer fraudulently a question that the Government should not have asked. Our legal system provides methods for challenging the Government's right to ask questions—lying is not one of them."

* * * In this case, the Court of Appeals required the suppression of perjured testimony given by respondent, as a witness under oath, lawfully summoned before an investigative grand jury and questioned about matters directly related to the grand jury's inquiry. The court reached this result because the prosecutor failed to give *Miranda* warnings at the outset of Mandujano's interrogation. Those warnings were required, in the Court of Appeals' view, because Mandujano was a "virtual" or "putative" defendant—that is, the prosecutor had specific information concerning Mandujano's participation in an attempted sale of heroin and the focus of the grand jury interrogation, as evidenced by the prosecutor's questions, centered on Mandujano's involvement in narcotics traffic. * * *

The court's analysis, premised upon the prosecutor's failure to give *Miranda* warnings, erroneously applied the standards fashioned by this Court in *Miranda*. Those warnings were aimed at the evils seen by the Court as endemic to police interrogation of a person in custody. *Miranda* addressed extra-judicial confessions or admissions procured in a hostile, unfamiliar environment which lacked procedural safeguards. The decision expressly rested on the privilege against compulsory self-incrimination; the prescribed warnings sought to negate the "compulsion" thought to be inherent in police station interrogation. But the *Miranda* Court simply did not perceive judicial inquiries and custodial interrogation as equivalents: " * * * the compulsion to speak in the isolated setting of the police station may well be greater than in courts or other official investigations, where there are often impartial observers to guard against intimidation or trickery."

The Court thus recognized that many official investigations, such as grand jury questioning, take place in a setting wholly different from custodial police interrogation. Indeed, the Court's opinion in *Miranda* reveals a focus on what was seen by the Court as police "coercion" derived from "factual studies [relating to] police violence and the 'third degree' * * * physical brutality—beating, hanging, whipping—and to sustained and protracted questioning incommunicado in order to extort confessions. * * *" To extend these concepts to questioning before a grand jury inquiring into criminal activity under the guidance of a judge is an extravagant expansion never remotely contemplated by this Court in *Miranda*; the dynamics of constitutional interpretation do not compel constant extension of every doctrine announced by the Court. * * *

The warnings volunteered by the prosecutor to respondent in this case were more than sufficient to inform him of his rights—and his responsibilities—and particularly of the consequences of perjury.[a] To extend the concepts of *Miranda*, as contemplated by the Court of Appeals, would require that the witness be told that there was an absolute right to silence, and obviously any such warning would be incorrect, for there is no such right before a grand jury. Under *Miranda*, a person in police custody has, of course, an absolute right to decline to answer any question, incriminating or innocuous, whereas a grand jury witness, on the contrary, has an absolute duty to answer all questions, subject only to a valid Fifth Amendment claim. And even when the grand jury witness asserts the privilege, questioning need not cease, except as to the particular subject to which the privilege has been addressed. Other lines of inquiry may properly be pursued.

Respondent was also informed that if he desired he could have the assistance of counsel, but that counsel could not be inside the grand jury room. That statement was plainly a correct recital of the law. No criminal proceedings had been instituted against respondent, hence the Sixth Amendment right to counsel had not come into play. *Kirby v. Illinois* [p. 580].[6] A witness "before a grand jury cannot insist, as a matter of constitutional right, on being represented by his counsel * * *." *In re Groban*, 352 U.S. 330 (1957).[b] Under settled principles the witness may not insist upon the presence of his attorney in the grand jury room. Fed.Rule Crim.Proc. 6(d).

---

[a]   At a subsequent point in the opinion, Chief Justice Burger added in a footnote [n.7] the following: "The fact that warnings were provided in this case to advise respondent of his Fifth Amendment privilege makes it unnecessary to consider whether any warning is required, as the Government asks us to determine. In addition to the warning implicit in the oath, federal prosecutors apparently make it a practice to inform a witness of the privilege before questioning begins."

[6]   The right to counsel mandated by *Miranda* was fashioned to secure the suspect's Fifth Amendment privilege in a setting thought inherently coercive. The Sixth Amendment was not implicated.

[b]   In *Groban*, a witness was not allowed to have counsel present during his examination by a state fire marshal in a proceeding designed to determine the cause of a fire. In finding that the denial of counsel did not violate due process, the majority cited as analogous the grand jury proceeding, where "a witness [also] * * * cannot insist as a matter of constitutional right, on being represented by his counsel." The dissent, by Justice Black, argued that the fire marshal's investigation was not analogous, but agreed as to the lack of a constitutional right to counsel before the grand jury. The dissent noted: "They [the grand jurors] bring into the grand jury room the experience, knowledge and viewpoint of all sections of the community. They have no axes to grind and are not charged personally with the administration of the law. No one of them is a prosecuting

* * * Respondent was free at every stage to interpose his constitutional privilege against self-incrimination, but perjury was not a permissible option. * * * The judgment of the Court of Appeals is therefore reversed.

JUSTICE STEVENS took no part in the consideration or decision of this case.

JUSTICE BRENNAN, with whom JUSTICE MARSHALL joins, concurring in the judgment.

I concur in the result reached by the Court, for "even when the privilege against self-incrimination permits an individual to refuse to answer questions asked by the Government, if false answers are given the individual may be prosecuted for making false statements." *Mackey v. United States*, 401 U.S. 667 (1971) (Brennan, J., concurring). * * * "Our legal system provides methods for challenging the Government's right to ask questions—lying is not one of them." *Bryson v. United States*. Further, the record satisfies me that the respondent's false answers were not induced by governmental tactics or procedures so inherently unfair under all the circumstances as to constitute a prosecution for perjury a violation of the Due Process Clause of the Fifth Amendment.

However, two aspects of the plurality opinion for the Court suggests a denigration of the privilege against self-incrimination and the right to the assistance of counsel with which I do not agree.

The plurality opinion mechanically quotes *United States v. Monia*, for the proposition that

> "[t]he [Fifth] Amendment speaks of compulsion. It does not preclude a witness from testifying voluntarily in matters which may incriminate him. If, therefore, he desires the protection of the privilege, he must claim it or he will not be considered to have been 'compelled' within the meaning of the Amendment." * * *

In my view, the conception of the Fifth Amendment privilege expressed in the *Monia* dictum is explainable only by reference to the facts and circumstances of the only case cited in support by *Monia*—[a case, Justice Brennan explained, in which the potential for incrimination could not be evaluated without a claim by the witness because that potential was not readily apparent from the context of the question]. * * * It is only in a context where this "lack of notice on the part of the government" rationale has significance that we can possibly justify the *Monia* dictum that a witness testifying under judicial compulsion—that classic form of compulsion to which the Fifth Amendment is centrally addressed—must claim the privilege or else, without any further analysis, "he will not be considered to have been 'compelled' within the meaning of the Amendment." * * *

* * * [T]he use by prosecutors of the tactic of calling a putative defendant before a grand jury and interrogating him regarding the transactions and events for which he is about to be indicted is, in the absence of an "intentional

---

attorney or law-enforcement officer ferreting out crime. It would be very difficult for officers of the state seriously to abuse or deceive a witness in the presence of the grand jury. Similarly the presence of the jurors offers a substantial safeguard against the officers' misrepresentation, unintentional or otherwise, of the witness' statements and conduct before the grand jury."

relinquishment or abandonment" of his "known" privilege against compulsory self-incrimination, a blatant subversion of the fundamental adversary principle—that the State "establish its case, not by interrogation of the accused even under judicial safeguards, but by evidence independently secured through skillful investigation." * * * Such tactics by prosecutors are exemplars of the very evils sought to be prevented by the enshrinement of the Fifth Amendment privilege in the Constitution. * * *

Thus, I would hold that, in the absence of an intentional and intelligent waiver by the individual of his known right to be free from compulsory self-incrimination, the Government may not call before a grand jury one whom it has probable cause—as measured by an objective standard—to suspect committed a crime, and by use of judicial compulsion compel him to testify with regard to that crime. In the absence of such a waiver, the Fifth Amendment requires that any testimony obtained in this fashion be unavailable to the Government for use at trial. Such a waiver could readily be demonstrated by proof that the individual was warned prior to questioning that he is currently subject to possible criminal prosecution for the commission of a stated crime,[c] that he has a constitutional right to refuse to answer any and all questions that may tend to incriminate him, and by record evidence that the individual understood the nature of his situation and privilege prior to giving testimony. * * *

A second and also disturbing facet of the plurality opinion today is its statement that "[n]o criminal proceedings had been instituted against respondent, hence, the Sixth Amendment right to counsel had not come into play." It will not do simply to cite, as does the plurality opinion, *Kirby v. Illinois*, for this proposition. *Kirby's* premise, so fundamental that it was "note[d] at the outset," was that "the constitutional privilege against compulsory self-incrimination is in no way implicated here." In sharp contrast, the privilege against compulsory self-incrimination is inextricably involved in this case since a putative defendant is called and interrogated before a grand jury. Clearly in such a case a defendant is "faced with the prosecutorial forces of organized society, and immersed in the intricacies of substantive and procedural criminal law."

It is true that dictum in *In re Groban* [fn. b supra] denied there is any constitutional right of a witness to be represented by counsel when testifying before a grand jury. But neither *Groban* nor any other case in this Court has squarely presented the question. Moreover, more recent decisions, e.g., *Miranda v. Arizona*, and *Escobedo v. Illinois*, recognizing the "substantive affinity" and therefore the "coextensive[ness]" in certain circumstances of the right to counsel and the privilege against compulsory self-incrimination, have led many to question the continuing vitality of such older dicta.

---

[c] In *United States v. Washington*, 431 U.S. 181 (1977), the Court held that a witness need not be warned that he is a target of a grand jury investigation. The Court majority, per Burger, C.J., noted that "even in the presumed psychologically coercive atmosphere of police custodial interrogation, *Miranda* does not require that any additional warnings be given simply because the suspect is a potential defendant." Justice Brennan, joined by Justice Marshall, dissented, relying on Justice Brennan's opinion in *Mandujano*. See also fn. a, p. 516.

* * * Given the inherent danger of subversion of the adversary system in the case of a putative defendant called to testify before a grand jury, and the peculiarly critical role of the Fifth Amendment privilege as the bulwark against such abuse, it is plainly obvious that some guidance by counsel is required. * * * It may be that a putative defendant's Fifth Amendment privilege will be adequately preserved by a procedure whereby, in addition to warnings, he is told that he has a right to consult with an attorney prior to questioning, that if he cannot afford an attorney one will be appointed for him, that during the questioning he may have that attorney wait outside the grand jury room, and that he may at any and all times during questioning consult with the attorney prior to answering any question posed.[22] At least if such minimal protections were present, a putative defendant would be able to consult with counsel prior to answering any question that he might in any way suspect may incriminate him. * * *

It is of course unnecessary in this case to define the exact dimensions of the right to counsel since the testimony obtained by the grand jury interrogation was not introduced as evidence at respondent's trial on the charge concerning which he was questioned. I write only to make plain my disagreement with the implication in the plurality opinion that constitutional rights to counsel are not involved in a grand jury proceeding, and my disagreement with the further implication that there is a right to have counsel present for consultation outside the grand jury room but that it is not constitutionally derived and therefore may be enjoyed only by those wealthy enough to hire a lawyer. I cannot accede to a return to the regime of "squalid discrimination," where the justice "a man gets depends on the amount of money he has." *Griffin v. Illinois* [p. 396]. * * * If indeed there is, as the plurality opinion says, a right to have counsel present outside the door to the grand jury room, it is most assuredly in my view everyone's right, regardless of economic circumstance. * * *

JUSTICE STEWART, with whom JUSTICE BLACKMUN joins, concurring in the judgment.

The Fifth Amendment privilege against compulsory self-incrimination provides no protection for the commission of perjury. * * * *Bryson v. United States.* The respondent's grand jury testimony is relevant only to his prosecution for perjury and was not introduced in the prosecution for attempting to distribute heroin. Since this is not a case where it could plausibly be argued that the perjury prosecution must be barred because of prosecutorial conduct amounting to a denial of due process, I would reverse the judgment without reaching the other issues explored in The Chief Justice's opinion and by Mr. Justice Brennan in his separate opinion.

---

[22] [Justice Brennan here noted that several commentators had argued that more was needed, "that the presence of counsel inside the grand jury room is required." He then added: "Certainly there is no viable argument that allowing counsel to be present in the grand jury room for purposes of consultation regarding testimonial privileges would subvert the nature or functioning of the grand jury proceeding. Such a procedure is sanctioned by statute in several states."]

KASTIGAR V. UNITED STATES

406 U.S. 441, 92 S.Ct. 1653, 32 L.Ed.2d 212 (1972).

JUSTICE POWELL delivered the opinion of the Court.

This case presents the question whether the United States Government may compel testimony from an unwilling witness, who invokes the Fifth Amendment privilege against compulsory self-incrimination, by conferring on the witness immunity from use of the compelled testimony in subsequent criminal proceedings, as well as immunity from use of evidence derived from the testimony.

Petitioners were subpoenaed to appear before a United States grand jury * * *. The Government believed that petitioners were likely to assert their Fifth Amendment privilege. Prior to the scheduled appearances, the Government applied to the District Court for an order directing petitioners to answer questions and produce evidence before the grand jury under a grant of immunity conferred pursuant to 18 U.S.C. §§ 6002–6003. Petitioners opposed issuance of the order, contending primarily that the scope of the immunity provided by the statute was not coextensive with the scope of the privilege against self-incrimination, and therefore was not sufficient to supplant the privilege and compel their testimony. The District Court rejected this contention, and ordered petitioners to appear before the grand jury and answer its questions under the grant of immunity. * * *

The power of government to compel persons to testify in court or before grand juries and other governmental agencies is firmly established in Anglo-American jurisprudence. * * * While it is not clear when grand juries first resorted to compulsory process to secure the attendance and testimony of witnesses, the general common-law principle that "the public has a right to every man's evidence" was considered an "indubitable certainty" that "cannot be denied" by 1742. * * * Mr. Justice White noted the importance of this essential power of government in his concurring opinion in *Murphy v. Waterfront Comm'n*, 378 U.S. 52 (1964):

> "Among the necessary and most important of the powers of the States as well as the Federal Government to assure the effective functioning of government in an ordered society is the broad power to compel residents to testify in court or before grand juries or agencies. * * * Such testimony constitutes one of the Government's primary sources of information."

But the power to compel testimony is not absolute. There are a number of exemptions from the testimonial duty, the most important of which is the Fifth Amendment privilege against compulsory self-incrimination. The privilege reflects a complex of our fundamental values and aspirations, *Murphy*, supra, and marks an important advance in the development of our liberty. * * * This Court has been zealous to safeguard the values that underlie the privilege.

Immunity statutes, which have historical roots deep in Anglo-American jurisprudence, are not incompatible with these values. Rather, they seek a rational accommodation between the imperatives of the privilege and the legitimate demands of government to compel citizens to testify. The existence of these statutes reflects the importance of testimony, and the fact that many offenses are of such a character that the only persons capable of giving useful testimony are those implicated in the crime. Indeed, their origins were in the context of such offenses, and their primary use has been to investigate such offenses. Congress included immunity statutes in many of the regulatory measures adopted in the first half of this century. Indeed, prior to the enactment of the statute under consideration in this case, there were in force over 50 federal immunity statutes. In addition, every State in the Union, as well as the District of Columbia and Puerto Rico, has one or more such statutes. The commentators, and this Court on several occasions, have characterized immunity statutes as essential to the effective enforcement of various criminal statutes. As Mr. Justice Frankfurter observed, speaking for the Court in *Ullmann v. United States*, 350 U.S. 422 (1956), such statutes have "become part of our constitutional fabric."

Petitioners contend, first, that the Fifth Amendment's privilege against compulsory self-incrimination, which is that "[n]o person * * * shall be compelled in any criminal case to be a witness against himself," deprives Congress of power to enact laws that compel self-incrimination, even if complete immunity from prosecution is granted prior to the compulsion of the incriminatory testimony. In other words, petitioners assert that no immunity statute, however drawn, can afford a lawful basis for compelling incriminatory testimony. They ask us to reconsider and overrule *Brown v. Walker*, 161 U.S. 591 (1896), and *Ullmann v. United States*, decisions that uphold the constitutionality of immunity statutes. We find no merit to this contention and reaffirm the decisions in *Brown* and *Ullmann*.[a]

Petitioners' second contention is that the scope of immunity provided by the federal witness immunity statute, 18 U.S.C. § 6002, is not coextensive with the scope of the Fifth Amendment privilege against compulsory self-incrimination, and therefore is not sufficient to supplant the privilege and compel testimony over a claim of the privilege. The statute provides that when a witness is compelled by district court order to testify over a claim of the privilege:

> "the witness may not refuse to comply with the order on the basis of his privilege against self-incrimination; but no testimony or other information compelled under the order (or any information directly or indirectly derived from such testimony or other information) may be used against the witness in any criminal case, except a prosecution for perjury,

---

[a] In *Brown*, the Court reasoned that the Fifth Amendment could not be "construed literally as authorizing the witness to refuse to disclose any fact which might tend to incriminate, disgrace, or expose him to unfavorable comments." The history of the privilege clearly indicated that its objective was solely to "secure the witness against criminal prosecution." Thus the privilege had been held inapplicable where the witness' compelled testimony would relate only to an offense for which he had received a pardon or would tend to "disgrace him or bring him into disrepute" but would furnish no information relating to a criminal offense. In *Ullmann*, a witness who had received complete immunity from prosecution argued that the rationale of *Brown* should not apply where the compelled testimony (relating to alleged spying activities by certain members of the Communist Party) could subject him to a wide range of disabilities, such as "loss of job, expulsion from labor union, state registration and investigation statutes, passport eligibility, and general public opprobrium." Rejecting that contention, the Court majority concluded that *Brown* had correctly defined the total purpose of the privilege, and that purpose was fully met by granting the witness immunity from prosecution.

giving a false statement, or otherwise failing to comply with the order." 18 U.S.C. § 6002.

The constitutional inquiry, rooted in logic and history, as well as in the decisions of this Court, is whether the immunity granted under this statute is coextensive with the scope of the privilege. If so, petitioners' refusals to answer based on the privilege were unjustified, and the judgments of contempt were proper, for the grant of immunity has removed the dangers against which the privilege protects. *Brown v. Walker*. If, on the other hand, the immunity granted is not as comprehensive as the protection afforded by the privilege, petitioners were justified in refusing to answer, and the judgments of contempt must be vacated. *McCarthy v. Arndstein*, 266 U.S. 34 (1924).

Petitioners draw a distinction between statutes that provide transactional immunity and those that provide, as does the statute before us, immunity from use and derivative use. They contend that a statute must at a minimum grant full transactional immunity in order to be coextensive with the scope of the privilege. In support of this contention, they rely on *Counselman v. Hitchcock*, 142 U.S. 547 (1892), the first case in which this Court considered a constitutional challenge to an immunity statute. The statute, [there] * * * provided that no "evidence obtained from a party or witness by means of a judicial proceeding . . . shall be given in evidence, or in any manner used against him . . . in any court of the United States. . . ." * * * [T]his Court construed the statute as affording a witness protection only against the use of the specific testimony compelled from him under the grant of immunity. This construction meant that the statute "could not, and would not, prevent the use of his testimony to search out other testimony to be used in evidence against him." Since the [statute] * * * would permit the use against the immunized witness of evidence derived from his compelled testimony, it did not protect the witness to the same extent that a claim of the privilege would protect him. Accordingly, under the principle that a grant of immunity cannot supplant the privilege, and is not sufficient to compel testimony over a claim of the privilege, unless the scope of the grant of immunity is coextensive with the scope of the privilege, the witness' refusal to testify was held proper. In the course of its opinion, the Court made the following statement, on which petitioners heavily rely:

> "We are clearly of opinion that no statute which leaves the party or witness subject to prosecution after he answers the criminating question put to him, can have the effect of supplanting the privilege conferred by the Constitution of the United States. [The immunity statute under consideration] does not supply a complete protection from all the perils against which the constitutional prohibition was designed to guard, and is not a full substitute for that prohibition. In view of the constitutional provision, a statutory enactment, to be valid, must afford absolute immunity against future prosecution for the offence to which the question relates."

Sixteen days after the *Counselman* decision, a new immunity bill * * * was drafted specifically to meet the broad language in *Counselman* set forth above. The new Act removed the privilege against self-incrimination in [specified] hearings * * * and provided that:

> "no person shall be prosecuted or subjected to any penalty or forfeiture for or on account of any transaction, matter or thing, concerning which he may testify, or produce evidence, documentary or otherwise * * *." Act of Feb. 11, 1893.

This transactional immunity statute became the basic form for the numerous federal immunity statutes until 1970, when, after re-examining applicable constitutional principles and the adequacy of existing law, Congress enacted the statute here under consideration. The new statute, which does not "afford [the] absolute immunity against future prosecution" referred to in *Counselman*, was drafted to meet what Congress judged to be the conceptual basis of *Counselman*, as elaborated in subsequent decisions of the Court, namely, that immunity from the use of compelled testimony and evidence derived therefrom is coextensive with the scope of the privilege.

The statute's explicit proscription of the use in any criminal case of "testimony or other information compelled under the order (or any information directly or indirectly derived from such testimony or other information)" is consonant with Fifth Amendment standards. We hold that such immunity from use and derivative use is coextensive with the scope of the privilege against self-incrimination, and therefore is sufficient to compel testimony over a claim of the privilege. While a grant of immunity must afford protection commensurate with that afforded by the privilege, it need not be broader. Transactional immunity, which accords full immunity from prosecution for the offense to which the compelled testimony relates, affords the witness considerably broader protection than does the Fifth Amendment privilege. The privilege has never been construed to mean that one who invokes it cannot subsequently be prosecuted. Its sole concern is to afford protection against being "forced to give testimony leading to the infliction of 'penalties affixed to * * * criminal acts.'" Immunity from the use of compelled testimony, as well as evidence derived directly and indirectly therefrom, affords this protection. It prohibits the prosecutorial authorities from using the compelled testimony in *any* respect, and it therefore insures that the testimony cannot lead to the infliction of criminal penalties on the witness.

Our holding is consistent with the conceptual basis of *Counselman*. The *Counselman* statute, as construed by the Court, was plainly deficient in its failure to prohibit the use against the immunized witness of evidence derived from his compelled testimony. The Court repeatedly emphasized this deficiency * * *. The broad language in *Counselman* relied upon by petitioners was unnecessary to the Court's decision, and cannot be considered binding authority.

In *Murphy v. Waterfront Comm'n*, 378 U.S. 52 (1964), the Court carefully considered immunity from use of compelled testimony and evidence derived therefrom. The *Murphy* petitioners were subpoenaed to testify at a hearing conducted by the Waterfront Commission of New York Harbor. After refusing to answer certain questions on the ground that the answers might tend to incriminate them, petitioners were granted immunity from prosecution under the laws of New

Jersey and New York. They continued to refuse to testify, however, on the ground that their answers might tend to incriminate them under federal law, to which the immunity did not purport to extend. * * *

The issue before the Court in *Murphy* was whether New Jersey and New York could compel the witnesses, whom these States had immunized from prosecution under their laws, to give testimony that might then be used to convict them of a federal crime. Since New Jersey and New York had not purported to confer immunity from federal prosecution, the Court was faced with the question what limitations the Fifth Amendment privilege imposed on the prosecutorial powers of the Federal Government, a nonimmunizing sovereign. After undertaking an examination of the policies and purposes of the privilege, the Court overturned the rule that one jurisdiction within our federal structure may compel a witness to give testimony which could be used to convict him of a crime in another jurisdiction. The Court held that the privilege protects state witnesses against incrimination under federal as well as state law, and federal witnesses against incrimination under state as well as federal law.[b] Applying this principle to the state immunity legislation before it, the Court held the constitutional rule to be that:

> "[A] state witness may not be compelled to give testimony which may be incriminating under federal law unless the compelled testimony and its fruits cannot be used in any manner by federal officials in connection with a criminal prosecution against him. We conclude, moreover, that in order to implement this constitutional rule and accommodate the interests of the State and Federal Governments in investigating and prosecuting crime, the Federal Government must be prohibited from making any such use of compelled testimony and its fruits."

The Court emphasized that this rule left the state witness and the Federal Government, against which the witness had immunity only from the *use* of the compelled testimony and evidence derived therefrom, "in substantially the same position as if the witness had claimed his privilege in the absence of a state grant of immunity."

It is true that in *Murphy* the Court was not presented with the precise question presented by this case, whether a jurisdiction seeking to compel testimony may do so by granting only use and derivative-use immunity, for New Jersey and New York had granted petitioners transactional immunity. * * * But both the reasoning of the Court in *Murphy* and the result reached compel the conclusion that use and derivative-use immunity is constitutionally sufficient to compel testimony over a claim of the privilege. Since the privilege is fully applicable and its scope is the same whether invoked in a state or in a federal jurisdiction, the *Murphy* conclusion that a prohibition on use and derivative use secures a witness'

---

b   *United States v. Balsys,* 524 U.S. 666 (1998), held that the privilege does not protect against incrimination under the laws of a foreign government, as the Fifth Amendment applies only to "action of the government it binds." *Murphy* was grounded on the dual applicability of the self-incrimination clause to the federal government and to the states (via the due process clause of the Fourteenth Amendment) and the need to ensure that the witness not be "whipsawed into incriminating himself under both state and federal law even though the constitutional privilege against self-incrimination is applicable to each."

Fifth Amendment privilege against infringement by the Federal Government demonstrates that immunity from use and derivative use is coextensive with the scope of the privilege. As the *Murphy* Court noted, immunity from use and derivative use "leaves the witness and the Federal Government in substantially the same position as if the witness had claimed his privilege" in the absence of a grant of immunity. * * *

Although an analysis of prior decisions and the purpose of the Fifth Amendment privilege indicates that use and derivative-use immunity is coextensive with the privilege, we must consider additional arguments advanced by petitioners against the sufficiency of such immunity. * * * Petitioners argue that use and derivative-use immunity will not adequately protect a witness from various possible incriminating uses of the compelled testimony: for example, the prosecutor or other law enforcement officials may obtain leads, names of witnesses, or other information not otherwise available that might result in a prosecution. It will be difficult and perhaps impossible, the argument goes, to identify, by testimony or cross-examination, the subtle ways in which the compelled testimony may disadvantage a witness, especially in the jurisdiction granting the immunity.

This argument presupposes that the statute's prohibition will prove impossible to enforce. The statute provides a sweeping proscription of any use, direct or indirect, of the compelled testimony and any information derived therefrom:

> "[N]o testimony or other information compelled under the order (or any information directly or indirectly derived from such testimony or other information) may be used against the witness in any criminal case * * *."
> 18 U.S.C. § 6002.

This total prohibition on use provides a comprehensive safeguard, barring the use of compelled testimony as an "investigatory lead," and also barring the use of any evidence obtained by focusing investigation on a witness as a result of his compelled disclosures.

A person accorded this immunity under 18 U.S.C. § 6002, and subsequently prosecuted, is not dependent for the preservation of his rights upon the integrity and good faith of the prosecuting authorities. As stated in *Murphy*:

> "Once a defendant demonstrates that he has testified, under a state grant of immunity, to matters related to the federal prosecution, the federal authorities have the burden of showing that their evidence is not tainted by establishing that they had an independent, legitimate source for the disputed evidence."

This burden of proof, which we reaffirm as appropriate, is not limited to a negation of taint; rather, it imposes on the prosecution the affirmative duty to prove that the evidence it proposes to use is derived from a legitimate source wholly independent of the compelled testimony.

This is very substantial protection, commensurate with that resulting from invoking the privilege itself. The privilege assures that a citizen is not compelled to incriminate himself by his own testimony. It usually operates to allow a citizen to remain silent when asked a question requiring an incriminatory answer. This statute, which operates after a witness has given incriminatory testimony, affords the same protection by assuring that the compelled testimony can in no way lead to the infliction of criminal penalties. The statute, like the Fifth Amendment, grants neither pardon nor amnesty. Both the statute and the Fifth Amendment allow the government to prosecute using evidence from legitimate independent sources.

The statutory proscription is analogous to the Fifth Amendment requirement in cases of coerced confessions. A coerced confession, as revealing of leads as testimony given in exchange for immunity, is inadmissible in a criminal trial, but it does not bar prosecution. Moreover, a defendant against whom incriminating evidence has been obtained through a grant of immunity may be in a stronger position at trial than a defendant who asserts a Fifth Amendment coerced-confession claim. One raising a claim under this statute need only show that he testified under a grant of immunity in order to shift to the government the heavy burden of proving that all of the evidence it proposes to use was derived from legitimate independent sources. On the other hand, a defendant raising a coerced-confession claim under the Fifth Amendment must first prevail in a voluntariness hearing before his confession and evidence derived from it become inadmissible.

There can be no justification in reason or policy for holding that the Constitution requires an amnesty grant where, acting pursuant to statute and accompanying safeguards, testimony is compelled in exchange for immunity from use and derivative use when no such amnesty is required where the government, acting without colorable right, coerces a defendant into incriminating himself.

JUSTICE BRENNAN and JUSTICE REHNQUIST took no part in the consideration or decision of this case.

JUSTICE DOUGLAS, dissenting.

* * * In *Counselman v. Hitchcock*, the Court adopted the transactional immunity test. * * * This Court, however, apparently believes that *Counselman* and its progeny were overruled *sub silentio* in *Murphy v. Waterfront Comm'n*. *Murphy* involved state witnesses, granted transactional immunity under state law, who refused to testify for fear of subsequent federal prosecution. We held that the testimony in question could be compelled, but that the Federal Government would be barred from using any of the testimony, or its fruits, in a subsequent federal prosecution. * * *

* * * *Counselman*, as the *Murphy* Court recognized, "said nothing about the problem of incrimination under the law of another sovereign." That problem is one of federalism, as to require transactional immunity between jurisdictions might

> "deprive a state of the right to prosecute a violation of its criminal law on the basis of another state's grant of immunity [a result which] would be gravely in derogation of its sovereignty and obstructive of its administration of justice." *United States ex rel. Catena v. Elias*, 449 F.2d 40, 44 (C.A.3 1971).

* * * If, as some have thought, the Bill of Rights contained only "counsels of moderation" from which courts and legislatures could deviate according to their conscience or discretion, then today's contraction of the Self-Incrimination Clause of the Fifth Amendment would be understandable. But that has not been true, starting with Chief Justice Marshall's opinion in *United States v. Burr,* 25 F.Cas. 30 (C.C.D.Va. 1807) where he ruled that the reach of the Fifth Amendment was so broad as to make the privilege applicable when there was a mere possibility of a criminal charge being made. * * *

The Court said in *Hale v. Henkel,* 201 U.S. 43 (1906), that "if the criminality has already been taken away, the Amendment ceases to apply." In other words, the immunity granted is adequate if it operates as a complete pardon for the offense. *Brown v. Walker.* That is the true measure of the Self-Incrimination Clause. * * *

JUSTICE MARSHALL, dissenting.

* * * The Court recognizes that an immunity statute must be tested by * * * whether it "leaves the witness and the prosecutorial authorities in substantially the same position as if the witness had claimed the Fifth Amendment privilege." I assume, moreover, that in theory that test would be met by a complete ban on the use of the compelled testimony, including all derivative use, however remote and indirect. But I cannot agree that a ban on use will in practice be total, if it remains open for the government to convict the witness on the basis of evidence derived from a legitimate independent source. The Court asserts that the witness is adequately protected by a rule imposing on the government a heavy burden of proof if it would establish the independent character of evidence to be used against the witness. But in light of the inevitable uncertainties of the factfinding process, a greater margin of protection is required in order to provide a reliable guarantee that the witness is in exactly the same position as if he had not testified. That margin can be provided only by immunity from prosecution for the offenses to which the testimony relates, i.e., transactional immunity.

I do not see how it can suffice merely to put the burden of proof on the government. First, contrary to the Court's assertion, the Court's rule does leave the witness "dependent for the preservation of his rights upon the integrity and good faith of the prosecuting authorities." For the information relevant to the question of taint is uniquely within the knowledge of the prosecuting authorities. They alone are in a position to trace the chains of information and investigation that lead to the evidence to be used in a criminal prosecution. A witness who suspects that his compelled testimony was used to develop a lead will be hard pressed indeed to ferret out the evidence necessary to prove it. And of course it is no answer to say he need not prove it, for though the Court puts the burden of proof on the government, the government will have no difficulty in meeting its burden by mere assertion if the witness produces no contrary evidence. The good faith of the prosecuting authorities is thus the sole safeguard of the witness' rights. Second, even their good faith is not a sufficient safeguard. For the paths of information through the investigative bureaucracy may well be long and winding, and even a prosecutor acting in the best of faith cannot be certain that somewhere in the depths of his investigative apparatus, often including hundreds of employees, there was not some prohibited use of the compelled testimony. * * * The Court today sets out a loose net to trap tainted evidence and prevent its use against the witness, but it accepts an intolerably great risk that tainted evidence will in fact slip through that net.

In my view the Court turns reason on its head when it compares a statutory grant of immunity to the "immunity" that is inadvertently conferred by an unconstitutional interrogation. The exclusionary rule of evidence that applies in that situation has nothing whatever to do with this case. Evidence obtained through a coercive interrogation, like evidence obtained through an illegal search, is excluded at trial because the Constitution prohibits such methods of gathering evidence. The exclusionary rules provide a partial and inadequate remedy to some victims of illegal police conduct, and a similarly partial and inadequate deterrent to police officers. An immunity statute, on the other hand, is much more ambitious than any exclusionary rule. It does not merely attempt to provide a remedy for past police misconduct, which never should have occurred. An immunity statute operates in advance of the event, and it authorizes—even encourages—interrogation that would otherwise be prohibited by the Fifth Amendment. An immunity statute thus differs from an exclusionary rule of evidence in at least two critical respects.

First, because an immunity statute gives constitutional approval to the resulting interrogation, the government is under an obligation here to remove the danger of incrimination completely and absolutely, whereas in the case of the exclusionary rules it may be sufficient to shield the witness from the fruits of the illegal search or interrogation in a partial and reasonably adequate manner. * * * The Constitution does not authorize police officers to coerce confessions or to invade privacy without cause, so long as no use is made of the evidence they obtain. But this Court has held that the Constitution does authorize the government to compel a witness to give potentially incriminating testimony, so long as no incriminating use is made of the resulting evidence. Before the government puts its seal of approval on such an interrogation, it must provide an absolutely reliable guarantee that it will not use the testimony in any way at all in aid of prosecution of the witness. The only way to provide that guarantee is to give the witness immunity from prosecution for crimes to which his testimony relates.

Second, because an immunity statute operates in advance of the interrogation, there is room to require a broad grant of transactional immunity without imperiling large numbers of otherwise valid convictions. An exclusionary rule comes into play after the interrogation or search has occurred; and the decision to question or to search is often made in haste, under pressure, by an officer who is not a lawyer. If an unconstitutional interrogation or search were held to create transactional immunity, that might well be regarded as an excessively high price to pay for the "constable's blunder." An immunity statute, on the other hand, creates a framework in which the prosecuting attorney can make a calm and reasoned decision whether to compel testimony and suffer the resulting ban on prosecution, or to forgo the testimony.

For both these reasons it is clear to me that an immunity statute must be tested by a standard far more demanding than that appropriate for an exclusionary rule fashioned to deal with past constitutional violations. Measured by that standard, the statute approved today by the Court fails miserably. I respectfully dissent.

FISHER V. UNITED STATES
425 U.S. 391, 96 S.Ct. 1569, 48 L.Ed.2d 39 (1976).

JUSTICE WHITE delivered the opinion of the Court.

In these two cases we are called upon to decide whether a summons directing an attorney to produce documents delivered to him by his client in connection with the attorney-client relationship is enforceable over claims that the documents were constitutionally immune from summons in the hands of the client and retained that immunity in the hands of the attorney. In each case, an Internal Revenue agent visited the taxpayer or taxpayers and interviewed them in connection with an investigation of possible civil or criminal liability under the federal income tax laws. Shortly after the interviews * * *, the taxpayers obtained from their respective accountants certain documents relating to the preparation by the accountant of their tax returns. Shortly after obtaining the documents * * *, the taxpayers transferred the documents to their lawyers—each of whom was retained to assist the taxpayer in connection with the investigation. Upon learning of the whereabouts of the documents, the Internal Revenue Service served summonses on the attorneys directing them to produce documents listed therein. [Those documents were accountants' work sheets, retained copies of income tax returns, and the accountants' copies of correspondence between the accounting firm and the taxpayer]. * * * In each case, the lawyer declined to comply with the summons directing production of the documents, and enforcement actions were commenced by the Government. * * *

All of the parties in these cases and the Court of Appeals have concurred in the proposition that if the Fifth Amendment would have excused a *taxpayer* from turning over the accountant's papers had he possessed them, the *attorney* to whom they are delivered for the purpose of obtaining legal advice should also be immune from subpoena. Although we agree with this proposition for the reasons set forth infra, we are convinced that, under our decision in *Couch v. United States,* 409 U.S. 322 (1973), it is not the taxpayer's Fifth Amendment privilege that would excuse the *attorney* from production.

The relevant part of that Amendment provides:

> "No person * * * shall be *compelled* in any criminal case to be a *witness against himself.*" (Emphasis added.)

The taxpayer's privilege under this Amendment is not violated by enforcement of the summonses involved in these cases because enforcement against a taxpayer's lawyer would not "compel" the taxpayer to do anything—and certainly would not compel him to be a "witness" against himself. The Court has held repeatedly that the Fifth Amendment is limited to prohibiting the use of "physical or moral compulsion" exerted on the person asserting the privilege. In *Couch v. United States,* we recently ruled that the Fifth Amendment rights of a taxpayer were not violated by the enforcement of a documentary summons directed to her accountant and requiring production of the taxpayer's own records in the possession of the accountant. We did so on the ground that in such a case "the ingredient of personal compulsion against an accused is lacking." Here, the taxpayers are compelled to do no more than was the taxpayer in *Couch.* The taxpayers' Fifth Amendment privilege is therefore not violated by enforcement of the summonses directed toward their attorneys. This is true whether or not the Amendment would have barred a subpoena directing the taxpayer to produce the documents while they were in his hands.

The fact that the attorneys are agents of the taxpayers does not change this result. *Couch* held as much, since the accountant there was also the taxpayer's agent, and in this respect reflected a longstanding view. * * * "It is extortion of information from the accused which offends our sense of justice." *Couch v. United States.* Agent or no, the lawyer is not the taxpayer. The taxpayer is the "accused," and nothing is being extorted from him. Nor is this one of those situations, which *Couch* suggested might exist, where constructive possession is so clear or relinquishment of possession so temporary and insignificant as to leave the personal compulsion upon the taxpayer substantially intact. * * *

The Court of Appeals suggested that because legally and ethically the attorney was required to respect the confidences of his client, the latter had a reasonable expectation of privacy for the records in the hands of the attorney and therefore did not forfeit his Fifth Amendment privilege with respect to the records by transferring them in order to obtain legal advice. It is true that the Court has often stated that one of the several purposes served by the constitutional privilege against compelled testimonial self-incrimination is that of protecting personal privacy. See, e.g., *Murphy v. Waterfront Comm'n.* But the Court has never suggested that every invasion of privacy violates the privilege. Within the limits imposed by the language of the Fifth Amendment, which we necessarily observe, the privilege truly serves privacy interests; but the Court has never on any ground, personal privacy included, applied the Fifth Amendment to prevent the otherwise proper acquisition or use of evidence which, in the Court's view, did not involve compelled testimonial self-incrimination of some sort.

The proposition that the Fifth Amendment protects private information obtained without compelling self-incriminating testimony is contrary to the clear statements of this Court that under appropriate safeguards private incriminating statements of an accused may be overheard and used in evidence, if they are not compelled at the time they were uttered, *Katz v. United States* [p. 95], and that disclosure of private information may be compelled if immunity removes the risk of incrimination. *Kastigar v. United States.* If the Fifth Amendment protected generally against the obtaining of private information from a man's mouth or pen or house, its protections would presumably not be lifted by probable cause and a warrant or by immunity. * * * We cannot cut the Fifth Amendment completely loose from the moorings of its language, and make it serve as a general protector of privacy—a word not mentioned in its text and a concept directly addressed in the Fourth Amendment. We adhere to the view that the Fifth Amendment protects against "compelled self-incrimination, not [the disclosure of] private information." *United States v. Nobles,* 422 U.S. 225 (1975). * * *

* * * [While the] taxpayers have erroneously relied on the Fifth Amendment without urging the attorney-client privilege in so many words, they have nevertheless invoked the relevant body of law and policies that govern the attorney-client privilege. * * * This Court and the lower courts have * * * uniformly held that pre-existing documents which could have been obtained by court process from the client when he was in possession may also be obtained from the attorney by similar process following transfer by the client in order to obtain more informed legal advice. * * * It is otherwise if the documents are not obtainable by subpoena duces tecum or summons while in the exclusive possession of the client, for the client will then be reluctant to transfer possession to the lawyer unless the documents are also privileged in the latter's hands. Where the transfer is made for the purpose of obtaining legal advice, the purposes of the attorney-client privilege would be defeated unless the privilege is applicable. * * *

Since each taxpayer [here] transferred possession of the documents in question from himself to his attorney in order to obtain legal assistance in the tax investigations in question, the papers, if unobtainable by summons from the client, are unobtainable by summons directed to the attorney by reason of the attorney-client privilege. We accordingly proceed to the question whether the documents could have been obtained by summons addressed to the taxpayer while the documents were in his possession. The only bar to enforcement of such summons asserted by the parties or the courts below is the Fifth Amendment's privilege against self-incrimination. * * *

The proposition that the Fifth Amendment prevents compelled production of documents over objection that such production might incriminate stems from *Boyd v. United States* * * *.

Several of *Boyd's* express or implicit declarations have not stood the test of time. The application of the Fourth Amendment to subpoenas was limited by *Hale v. Henkel,* and more recent cases. Purely evidentiary (but "nontestimonial") materials, as well as contraband and fruits and instrumentalities of crime, may now be searched for and seized under proper circumstances, *Warden v. Hayden* [see fn. a following *Boyd,* § 1 supra]. Also, any notion that "testimonial" evidence may never be seized and used in evidence is inconsistent with [various cases] approving the seizure under appropriate circumstances of conversations of a person suspected of crime. It is also clear that the Fifth Amendment does not independently proscribe the compelled production of every sort of incriminating evidence but applies only when the accused is compelled to make a *testimonial* communication that is incriminating. * * * Furthermore, despite *Boyd,* neither a partnership nor the individual partners are shielded from compelled production of partnership records on self-incrimination grounds. *Bellis v. United States,* 417 U.S. 85 (1974). It would appear that under that case the precise claim sustained in *Boyd* would now be rejected for reasons not there considered.

The pronouncement in *Boyd* that a person may not be forced to produce his private papers has nonetheless often appeared as dictum in later opinions of this Court. * * * To the extent, however, that the rule against compelling production of private papers rested on the proposition that seizures of or subpoenas for "mere evidence," including documents, violated the Fourth Amendment and therefore also transgressed the Fifth, the foundations for the rule have been washed away. In consequence, the prohibition against forcing the production of private papers has long been a rule searching for a rationale consistent with the proscriptions of the Fifth Amendment against compelling a person to give "testimony" that incriminates him. Accordingly, we turn to the question of what, if any, incriminating testimony within the Fifth Amendment's protection, is compelled by a documentary summons.

A subpoena served on a taxpayer requiring him to produce an accountant's workpapers in his possession without doubt involves substantial compulsion. But it does not compel oral testimony; nor would it ordinarily compel the taxpayer to restate, repeat, or affirm the truth of the contents of the documents sought. Therefore, the Fifth Amendment would not be violated by the fact alone that the papers on their face might incriminate the taxpayer, for the privilege protects a person only against being incriminated by his own compelled testimonial communications. The accountant's workpapers are not the taxpayer's. They were not prepared by the taxpayer, and they contain no testimonial declarations by him. Furthermore, as far as this record demonstrates, the preparation of all of the papers sought in these cases was wholly voluntary, and they cannot be said to contain compelled testimonial evidence, either of the taxpayers or of anyone else. The taxpayer cannot avoid compliance with the subpoena merely by asserting that the item of evidence which he is required to produce contains incriminating writing, whether his own or that of someone else.

The act of producing evidence in response to a subpoena nevertheless has communicative aspects of its own, wholly aside from the contents of the papers produced. Compliance with the subpoena tacitly concedes the existence of the papers demanded and their possession or control by the taxpayer. It also would indicate the taxpayer's belief that the papers are those described in the subpoena. The elements of compulsion are clearly present, but the more difficult issues are whether the tacit averments of the taxpayer are both "testimonial" and "incriminating" for purposes of applying the Fifth Amendment. These questions perhaps do not lend themselves to categorical answers; their resolution may instead depend on the facts and circumstances of particular cases or classes thereof. In light of the records now before us, we are confident that however incriminating the contents of the accountant's workpapers might be, the act of producing them—the only thing which the taxpayer is compelled to do—would not itself involve testimonial self-incrimination.

It is doubtful that implicitly admitting the existence and possession of the papers rises to the level of testimony within the protection of the Fifth Amendment. The papers belong to the accountant, were prepared by him, and are the kind usually prepared by an accountant working on the tax returns of his client. Surely the Government is in no way relying on the "truthtelling" of the taxpayer to prove the existence of or his access to the documents. The existence and location of the papers are a foregone conclusion and the taxpayer adds little or nothing to the sum total of the Government's information by conceding that he in fact has the papers. Under these circumstances by enforcement of the summons "no constitutional rights are touched. The question is not one of testimony but of surrender."

When an accused is required to submit a handwriting exemplar he admits his ability to write and impliedly asserts that the exemplar is his writing. But in common experience, the first would be a near truism and the latter self-evident. In any event, although the exemplar may be incriminating to the accused and although he is compelled to furnish it, his Fifth Amendment privilege is not violated because nothing he has said or done is deemed to be sufficiently testimonial for purposes of the privilege. This Court has also time and again allowed subpoenas against the custodian of corporate documents or those belonging to other collective entities such as unions and partnerships and those of bankrupt businesses over claims that the documents will incriminate the custodian despite the fact that producing the documents tacitly admits their existence and their location in the hands of their possessor.[a] The existence and possession or

---

[a]   These rulings were based on the entity doctrine, described in fn. c, p. 625. The Court held that just as the entity could not assert the privilege against a subpoena compelling it to produce entity documents, neither could the entity custodian assert the privilege as to his or her production of entity documents. To allow the custodian to assert the privilege, based upon the potential incrimination personal to the custodian, would undermine the entity exception. See *Wilson v. United States*, 221 U.S. 361 (1911). Following *Fisher*, in *Braswell v. United States*, 487 U.S. 99 (1988), a divided Court held that *Fisher*'s adoption of an act-of-production analysis did not require the overturning of these "entity-custodian" rulings. While the earlier rulings had relied on the entity distinction as it related to *Boyd*'s Fifth Amendment analysis, they also had advanced a rationale that distinguished custodian production under *Fisher*'s act-of-production rationale. The individual called upon to produce entity records does so in a representative rather than an individual capacity. Also, by voluntarily accepting the custodianship of records, that individual assumes the entity responsibility for making the records available to a government agency, thereby waiving the right to assert the privilege.

While reaffirming the entity-custodian rulings, *Braswell* added an evidentiary limit that had not been mentioned in the earlier cases; since the custodian's action of production is an act of the entity and not the individual, the government "may make no evidentiary use of the 'individual act' against the individual." Illustrating this limitation, the Court noted that, "in a criminal prosecution against the custodian, the Government may not introduce into evidence before the jury the fact that the subpoena was served upon, and the corporation's documents were delivered by the particular individual, the custodian." The *Braswell* dissent responded that the majority's analysis rested on the "fiction that personal incrimination of the employee [i.e., custodian] is neither sought by the Government nor cognizable by the law," with the Court giving that "corporate agent fiction a weight it simply cannot bear," as implicitly recognized in the shaping of the above limitation. For if the government cannot subsequently use against the individual his act of production, it is "because the Fifth Amendment protects the person without regard to his status as a corporate employee."

The *Braswell* majority, in line with the entity cases generally (see fn. c, p. 625), emphasized the practical impact of what was at stake. The Court stated: "We note further that recognizing a Fifth Amendment privilege on behalf of the records custodian of collective entities would have a detrimental impact on the Government's effort to prosecute 'white collar crime,' one of the most serious problems confronting law enforcement." The dissent responded that the practical difficulties could be minimized by granting the custodian act-of-production immunity (a contention rejected by the majority, in light of "the burden of proving an independent source that a grant of immunity places on the Government"), but more importantly, the dissent noted, "the text of the Fifth Amendment does not authorize exceptions premised on such [impact-upon-enforcement] rationales."

control of the subpoenaed documents being no more in issue here than in the above cases, the summons is equally enforceable.

Moreover, assuming that these aspects of producing the accountant's papers have some minimal testimonial significance, surely it is not illegal to seek accounting help in connection with one's tax returns or for the accountant to prepare workpapers and deliver them to the taxpayer. At this juncture, we are quite unprepared to hold that either the fact of existence of the papers or of their possession by the taxpayer poses any realistic threat of incrimination to the taxpayer.

As for the possibility that responding to the subpoena would authenticate the workpapers, production would express nothing more than the taxpayer's belief that the papers are those described in the subpoena. The taxpayer would be no more competent to authenticate the accountant's workpapers or reports by producing them than he would be to authenticate them if testifying orally. The taxpayer did not prepare the papers and could not vouch for their accuracy. The documents would not be admissible in evidence against the taxpayer without authenticating testimony. Without more, responding to the subpoena in the circumstances before us would not appear to represent a substantial threat of self-incrimination. * * *

Whether the Fifth Amendment would shield the taxpayer from producing his own tax records in his possession is a question not involved here; for the papers demanded here are not his "private papers," see *Boyd v. United States,* supra. We do hold that compliance with a summons directing the taxpayer to produce the accountant's documents involved in this case would involve no incriminating testimony within the protection of the Fifth Amendment.

JUSTICE STEVENS took no part in the consideration or disposition of these cases.

JUSTICE BRENNAN, concurring in the judgment.

Given the prior access by accountants retained by the taxpayers to the papers involved in these cases and the wholly business rather than personal nature of the papers, I agree that the privilege against compelled self-incrimination did not in either of these cases protect the papers from production in response to the summonses. I do not join the Court's opinion, however, because of the portent of much of what is said of a serious crippling of the protection secured by the privilege against compelled production of one's private books and papers. * * * [I]t is but another step in the denigration of privacy principles settled nearly 100 years ago in *Boyd v. United States.* * * *

Expressions are legion in opinions of this Court that the protection of personal privacy is a central purpose of the privilege against compelled self-incrimination. * * * The Court pays lip-service to this bedrock premise of privacy in the statement that "[w]ithin the limits imposed by the language of the Fifth Amendment, which we necessarily observe, the privilege truly serves privacy interests." But this only makes explicit what elsewhere highlights the opinion, namely, the view that protection of personal privacy is merely a byproduct and not, as our precedents and history teach, a factor controlling in part the determination of the scope of the privilege. This cart-before-the-horse approach is fundamentally at odds with the settled principle that the scope of the privilege is not constrained by the limits of the wording of the Fifth Amendment but has the reach necessary to protect the cherished value of privacy which it safeguards. * * * History and principle, not the mechanical application of its wording, have been the life of the amendment. * * *

History and principle teach that the privacy protected by the Fifth Amendment extends not just to the individual's immediate declarations, oral or written, but also to his testimonial materials in the form of books and papers. * * * An individual's books and papers are generally little more than an extension of his person. They reveal no less than he could reveal upon being questioned directly. Many of the matters within an individual's knowledge may as easily be retained within his head as set down on a scrap of paper. I perceive no principle which does not permit compelling one to disclose the contents of one's mind but does permit compelling the disclosure of the contents of that scrap of paper by compelling its production. Under a contrary view, the constitutional protection would turn on fortuity, and persons would, at their peril, record their thoughts and the events of their lives. The ability to think private thoughts, facilitated as it is by pen and paper, and the ability to preserve intimate memories would be curtailed through fear that those thoughts or the events of those memories would become the subjects of criminal sanctions however invalidly imposed. Indeed, it was the very reality of those fears that helped provide the historical impetus for the privilege. * * *

The Court's treatment of the privilege falls far short of giving it the scope required by history and our precedents. * * * [The Court's] analysis is patently incomplete: the threshold inquiry is whether the taxpayer is compelled to produce incriminating papers. That inquiry is not answered in favor of production merely because the subpoena requires neither oral testimony from nor affirmation of the papers' contents by the taxpayer. To be sure, the Court correctly observes that "[t]he taxpayer cannot avoid compliance with the subpoena *merely* by asserting that the item of evidence which he is required to produce contains incriminating writing, whether his own or that of someone else." For it is not enough that the production of a writing, or books and papers, is compelled. Unless those materials are such as to come within the zone of privacy recognized by the Amendment, the privilege against compulsory self-incrimination does not protect against their production.

We are not without guideposts for determining what books, papers, and writings come within the zone of privacy recognized by the Amendment. * * * *Couch v. United States* expressly held that the Fifth Amendment protected against the compelled production of testimonial evidence only if the individual resisting production had a reasonable expectation of privacy with respect to the evidence. * * * Under *Couch,* therefore, one criterion is whether or not the information sought to be produced has been disclosed to or was within the knowledge of a third party. That is to say, one relevant consideration is the degree to which the paper holder has sought to keep private the contents of the papers he desires not to produce. * * *

A precise cataloguing of private papers within the ambit of the privacy protected by the privilege is probably impossible. Some papers, however, do lend themselves to classification. Production of documentary materials created or authenticated by a State or the Federal Government, such as automobile registrations or property deeds, would seem ordinarily to fall outside the protection of the privilege. They hardly reflect an extension of the person. Economic and business records may present difficulty in particular cases. The records of business entities generally fall without the scope of the privilege. But, as noted, the Court has recognized that the privilege extends to the business records of the sole proprietor or practitioner. Such records are at least an extension of an aspect of a person's activities, though concededly not the more intimate aspects of one's life. Where the privilege would have protected one's mental notes of his business affairs in a less complicated day and age, it would seem that that protection should not fall away because the complexities of another time compel one to keep business records.

Nonbusiness economic records in the possession of an individual, such as canceled checks or tax records, would also seem to be protected. They may provide clear insights into a person's total lifestyle. They are, however, like business records and the papers involved in these cases, frequently, though not always, disclosed to other parties; and disclosure, in proper cases, may foreclose reliance upon the privilege. Personal letters constitute an integral aspect of a person's private enclave. And while letters, being necessarily interpersonal, are not wholly private, their peculiarly private nature and the generally narrow extent of their disclosure would seem to render them within the scope of the privilege. Papers in the nature of a personal diary are *a fortiori* protected under the privilege.

The Court's treatment in the instant cases of the question whether the evidence involved here is within the protection of the privilege is, with all respect, most inadequate. The gaping hole is in the omission of any reference to the taxpayer's privacy interests and to whether the subpoenas impermissibly invade those interests. * * * For the reasons I have stated at the outset, however, I do not believe that the evidence involved in these cases falls within the scope of privacy protected by the Fifth Amendment. * * *

JUSTICE MARSHALL, concurring in the judgment.

* * * I would have preferred it had the Court found some room in its theory for recognition of the import of the contents of the documents themselves. * * * Nonetheless, I am hopeful that the Court's new theory, properly understood and applied, will provide substantially the same protection as our prior focus on the contents of the documents. * * * Indeed, there would appear to be a precise inverse relationship between the private nature of the document and the permissibility of assuming its existence. Therefore, under the Court's theory, the admission through production that one's diary, letters, prior tax returns, personally maintained financial records, or canceled checks exist would ordinarily provide substantial testimony. The incriminating nature of such an admission is clear, for while it may not be criminal to keep a diary, or write letters or checks, the admission that one does and that those documents are still available may quickly—or

simultaneously—lead to incriminating evidence. If there is a "real danger" of such a result, that is enough under our cases to make such testimony subject to the claim of privilege. Thus, in practice, the Court's approach should still focus upon the private nature of the papers subpoenaed and protect those about which *Boyd* and its progeny were most concerned. * * * For the reasons stated by Mr. Justice Brennan, I concur in the judgment of the Court.[b]

UNITED STATES V. HUBBELL

530 U.S. 27, 120 S.Ct. 2037, 147 L.Ed.2d 24 (2000).

JUSTICE STEVENS delivered the opinion of the Court.

The two questions presented concern the scope of a witness' protection against compelled self-incrimination: (1) whether the Fifth Amendment privilege protects a witness from being compelled to disclose the existence of incriminating documents that the Government is unable to describe with reasonable particularity; and (2) if the witness produces such documents pursuant to a grant of immunity, whether 18 U.S.C. § 6002 prevents the Government from using them to prepare criminal charges against him.

This proceeding arises out of the second prosecution of respondent, Webster Hubbell, commenced by the Independent Counsel appointed in August 1994 to investigate possible violations of federal law relating to the Whitewater Development Corporation. The first prosecution was terminated pursuant to a plea bargain. In December 1994, respondent pleaded guilty to charges of mail fraud and tax evasion arising out of his billing practices as a member of an Arkansas law firm from 1989 to 1992, and was sentenced to 21 months in prison. In the plea agreement, respondent promised to provide the Independent Counsel with "full, complete, accurate, and truthful information" about matters relating to the Whitewater investigation.

The second prosecution resulted from the Independent Counsel's attempt to determine whether respondent had violated that promise. In October 1996, while respondent was incarcerated, the Independent Counsel served him with a

---

[b] In *United States v. Doe*, 465 U.S. 605 (1984), the lower court had concluded that, notwithstanding *Fisher*, the reasoning of *Boyd* continued to hold privileged under the self-incrimination clause a sole proprietor's business records, so long as the content of those records was potentially incriminatory. Rejecting that ruling, the Supreme Court in *Doe* held that the rationale of *Fisher had* established that, where "the preparation of business records is voluntary," the "contents of those records are not privileged." A self-incrimination claim could be based only on the act of production, not the contents of the subpoenaed records. Justice O'Connor, wrote separately "to make explicit what is implicit in the analysis of [the Court's] opinion: that the Fifth Amendment provides absolutely no protection for the contents of private papers of any kind. The notion that the Fifth Amendment protects the privacy of papers originated in *Boyd v. United States,* but our decision in *Fisher v. United States,* sounded the death-knell for *Boyd.*" Justice Marshall, joined by Justice Brennan, responded to Justice O'Connor, noting: "Contrary to what Justice O'Connor contends, I do not view the Court's opinion in this case as having reconsidered whether the Fifth Amendment provides protection for the contents of 'private papers of any kind.' * * * [T]he documents at stake here are business records which implicate a lesser degree of concern for privacy interests than, for example, personal diaries. * * * I continue to believe that under the Fifth Amendment 'there are certain documents no person ought to be compelled to produce at the Government's request.' "

subpoena duces tecum calling for the production of 11 categories of documents before a grand jury sitting in Little Rock, Arkansas. See Appendix, infra.ᵃ On November 19, he appeared before the grand jury and invoked his Fifth Amendment privilege against self-incrimination. In response to questioning by the prosecutor, respondent initially refused "to state whether there are documents within my possession, custody, or control responsive to the Subpoena." Thereafter, the prosecutor produced an order, which had previously been obtained from the District Court pursuant to 18 U.S.C. § 6003(a), directing him to respond to the subpoena and granting him immunity "to the extent allowed by law." Respondent then produced 13,120 pages of documents and records and responded to a series of questions that established that those were all of the documents in his custody or control that were responsive to the commands in the subpoena, with the exception of a few documents he claimed were shielded by the attorney-client and attorney work-product privileges.

The contents of the documents produced by respondent provided the Independent Counsel with the information that led to this second prosecution. On April 30, 1998, a grand jury in the District of Columbia returned a 10-count indictment charging respondent with various tax-related crimes and mail and wire fraud. The District Court dismissed the indictment relying, in part, on the ground that the Independent Counsel's use of the subpoenaed documents violated § 6002 because all of the evidence he would offer against respondent at trial derived either directly or indirectly from the testimonial aspects of respondent's immunized act

---

ᵃ The Appendix to Justice Stevens' opinion set forth verbatim the "subpoena rider," which identified the 11 categories of documents in paragraphs (A)–(K). In essence, the 11 categories (each subject to a time frame limit of "January 1, 1993 to the present") were: (1) all documents "reflecting, referring, or relating to any direct or indirect sources of money or other things of value received by Webster Hubbell, his wife or children [collectively, the 'Hubbell family'] * * *, 'including but not limited to the identity of employers or clients of legal or any other type of work'; (2) all documents 'reflecting, referring, or related to' any 'direct or indirect sources of money or other things of value' received by the Hubbell family, including 'billing memoranda, draft statements, bills, final statements and/or bills for work performed or time billed'; (3) copies of all bank records of the Hubbell family, including 'statements, registers, ledgers, canceled checks, deposit items and wire transfers'; (4) all documents reflecting, referring, or related to 'time worked or billed by Webster Hubbell,' including 'original time sheets, books, notes, papers, and/or computer records'; (5) all documents reflecting 'expenses incurred by and/or disbursements of money by Webster Hubbell for work performed or to be performed'; (6) all documents 'reflecting, referring, or relating to Webster Hubbell's schedule of activities,' including 'all calendars, daytimers, time books, appointment books, diaries, records of reverse telephone toll charges, credit card calls, telephone message slips, logs, other telephone records, minutes databases, electronic mail messages, travel records, itineraries, tickets for transportation of any kind, payments, bills, expense backup documentation, schedules, and/or any other document or database that would disclose Webster Hubbell's activities'; (7) all documents 'reflecting, referring, or relating to any retainer agreements or contracts for employment' of the Hubbell family; (8) all 'tax returns, tax return information, including but not limited to all 2s, form 1099s, schedules, draft returns, work papers, and backup documents filed, created or held by or on behalf of [the Hubbell family], and/or any business in which [the Hubbell family] holds or has held an interest'; (9) all documents 'reflecting, referring, or relating to work performed or to be performed for the City of Los Angeles, the Los Angeles Department of Airports or any other Los Angeles municipal or governmental entity, Mary Leslie, and/or Alan Arkatov'; (10) all documents 'reflecting, referring, or related to work performed by [the Hubbell family] on the recommendation, counsel, or other influence of Mary Leslie and/or Alan Arkatov'; and (11) all documents related to work performed for or on behalf of specified entities (e.g., Lippo Ltd.) and specified individuals (e.g., James Riady) 'or any affiliate, subsidiary, or corporation owned or controlled by or related to the aforementioned entities or individuals.' "

of producing those documents. Noting that the Independent Counsel had admitted that he was not investigating tax-related issues when he issued the subpoena, and that he had "learned about the unreported income and other crimes from studying the records' contents," the District Court characterized the subpoena as "the quintessential fishing expedition." * * *

The Court of Appeals vacated the judgment and remanded for further proceedings. The majority concluded that the District Court had incorrectly relied on the fact that the Independent Counsel did not have prior knowledge of the contents of the subpoenaed documents. The question the District Court should have addressed was the extent of the Government's independent knowledge of the documents' existence and authenticity, and of respondent's possession or control of them. It explained: "On remand, the district court should hold a hearing in which it seeks to establish the extent and detail of the [G]overnment's knowledge of Hubbell's financial affairs (or of the paperwork documenting it) on the day the subpoena issued. It is only then that the court will be in a position to assess the testimonial value of Hubbell's response to the subpoena. Should the Independent Counsel prove capable of demonstrating with reasonable particularity a prior awareness that the exhaustive litany of documents sought in the subpoena existed and were in Hubbell's possession, then the wide distance evidently traveled from the subpoena to the substantive allegations contained in the indictment would be based upon legitimate intermediate steps. To the extent that the information conveyed through Hubbell's compelled act of production provides the necessary linkage, however, the indictment deriving therefrom is tainted."

In the opinion of the dissenting judge, the majority failed to give full effect to the distinction between the contents of the documents and the limited testimonial significance of the act of producing them. In his view, as long as the prosecutor could make use of information contained in the documents or derived therefrom without any reference to the fact that respondent had produced them in response to a subpoena, there would be no improper use of the testimonial aspect of the immunized act of production. In other words, the constitutional privilege and the statute conferring use immunity would only shield the witness from the use of any information resulting from his subpoena response "beyond what the prosecutor would receive if the documents appeared in the grand jury room or in his office unsolicited and unmarked, like manna from heaven."

On remand, the Independent Counsel acknowledged that he could not satisfy the "reasonable particularity" standard prescribed by the Court of Appeals and entered into a conditional plea agreement with respondent. In essence, the agreement provides for the dismissal of the charges unless this Court's disposition of the case makes it reasonably likely that respondent's "act of production immunity" would not pose a significant bar to his prosecution. The case is not moot, however, because the agreement also provides for the entry of a guilty plea and a sentence that will not include incarceration if we should reverse and issue an opinion that is sufficiently favorable to the Government to satisfy that condition. Despite that agreement, we granted the Independent Counsel's petition for a writ of certiorari in order to determine the precise scope of a grant of immunity with respect to the production of documents in response to a subpoena. We now affirm.

It is useful to preface our analysis of the constitutional issue with a restatement of certain propositions that are not in dispute. The term "privilege against self-incrimination" is not an entirely accurate description of a person's constitutional protection against being "compelled in any criminal case to be a witness against himself." The word "witness" in the constitutional text limits the relevant category of compelled incriminating communications to those that are "testimonial" in character.[8] As Justice Holmes observed, there is a significant difference between the use of compulsion to extort communications from a defendant and compelling a person to engage in conduct that may be incriminating. Thus, even though the act may provide incriminating evidence, a criminal suspect may be compelled to put on a shirt, to provide a blood sample or handwriting exemplar, or to make a recording of his voice. The act of exhibiting such physical characteristics is not the same as a sworn communication by a witness that relates either express or implied assertions of fact or belief. * * *

More relevant to this case is the settled proposition that a person may be required to produce specific documents even though they contain incriminating assertions of fact or belief because the creation of those documents was not "compelled" within the meaning of the privilege. [*Fisher v. United States*]. * * * It is clear, therefore, that respondent Hubbell could not avoid compliance with the subpoena served on him merely because the demanded documents contained incriminating evidence, whether written by others or voluntarily prepared by himself. * * * On the other hand, we have also made it clear that the act of producing documents in response to a subpoena may have a compelled testimonial aspect. We have held that "the act of production" itself may implicitly communicate "statements of fact" * * *. By "producing documents in compliance with a subpoena, the witness would admit that the papers existed, were in his possession or control, and were authentic." Moreover, as was true in this case, when the custodian of documents responds to a subpoena, he may be compelled to take the witness stand and answer questions designed to determine whether he has produced everything demanded by the subpoena. The answers to those questions, as well as the act of production itself, may certainly communicate information about the existence, custody, and authenticity of the documents. Whether the constitutional privilege protects the answers to such questions, or protects the act of production itself, is a question that is distinct from the question whether the unprotected contents of the documents themselves are incriminating.

Finally, the phrase "in any criminal case" in the text of the Fifth Amendment might have been read to limit its coverage to compelled testimony that is used against the defendant in the trial itself. It has, however, long been settled that its protection encompasses compelled statements that lead to the discovery of

---

[8] "It is consistent with the history of and the policies underlying the Self-Incrimination Clause to hold that the privilege may be asserted only to resist compelled explicit or implicit disclosures of incriminating information. Historically, the privilege was intended to prevent the use of legal compulsion to extract from the accused a sworn communication of facts which would incriminate him. Such was the process of the ecclesiastical courts and the Star Chamber—the inquisitorial method of putting the accused upon his oath and compelling him to answer questions designed to uncover uncharged offenses, without evidence from another source. * * *" *Doe v. United States* (cited as *Doe II*), 487 U.S. 201 (1988).

incriminating evidence even though the statements themselves are not incriminating and are not introduced into evidence. * * * Compelled testimony that communicates information that may "lead to incriminating evidence" is privileged even if the information itself is not inculpatory. * * * It is the Fifth Amendment's protection against the prosecutor's use of incriminating information derived directly or indirectly from the compelled testimony of the respondent that is of primary relevance in this case.

Acting pursuant to 18 U.S.C. § 6002, the District Court entered an order compelling respondent to produce "any and all documents" described in the grand jury subpoena and granting him "immunity to the extent allowed by law." In *Kastigar v. United States*, we upheld the constitutionality of § 6002 because the scope of the "use and derivative-use" immunity that it provides is coextensive with the scope of the constitutional privilege against self-incrimination. * * * We particularly emphasized the critical importance of protection against a future prosecution " 'based on knowledge and sources of information obtained from the compelled testimony.' " * * * [W]e held that the statute imposes an affirmative duty on the prosecution, not merely to show that its evidence is not tainted by the prior testimony, but "to prove that the evidence it proposes to use is derived from a legitimate source wholly independent of the compelled testimony." * * * The "compelled testimony" that is relevant in this case is not to be found in the contents of the documents produced in response to the subpoena. It is, rather, the testimony inherent in the act of producing those documents. The disagreement between the parties focuses entirely on the significance of that testimonial aspect.

The Government correctly emphasizes that the testimonial aspect of a response to a subpoena duces tecum does nothing more than establish the existence, authenticity, and custody of items that are produced. We assume that the Government is also entirely correct in its submission that it would not have to advert to respondent's act of production in order to prove the existence, authenticity, or custody of any documents that it might offer in evidence at a criminal trial; indeed, the Government disclaims any need to introduce any of the documents produced by respondent into evidence in order to prove the charges against him. It follows, according to the Government, that it has no intention of making improper "use" of respondent's compelled testimony. The question, however, is not whether the response to the subpoena may be introduced into evidence at his criminal trial. That would surely be a prohibited "use" of the immunized act of production. But the fact that the Government intends no such use of the act of production leaves open the separate question whether it has already made "derivative use" of the testimonial aspect of that act in obtaining the indictment against respondent and in preparing its case for trial. It clearly has.

It is apparent from the text of the subpoena itself that the prosecutor needed respondent's assistance both to identify potential sources of information and to produce those sources. See Appendix [fn. a supra]. Given the breadth of the description of the 11 categories of documents called for by the subpoena, the collection and production of the materials demanded was tantamount to answering a series of interrogatories asking a witness to disclose the existence and location of particular documents fitting certain broad descriptions. The assembly of literally hundreds of pages of material in response to a request for "any and all documents reflecting, referring, or relating to any direct or indirect sources of money or other things of value received by or provided to" an individual or members of his family during a 3-year period, is the functional equivalent of the preparation of an answer to either a detailed written interrogatory or a series of oral questions at a discovery deposition. Entirely apart from the contents of the 13,120 pages of materials that respondent produced in this case, it is undeniable that providing a catalog of existing documents fitting within any of the 11 broadly worded subpoena categories could provide a prosecutor with a "lead to incriminating evidence," or "a link in the chain of evidence needed to prosecute."

Indeed, the record makes it clear that that is what happened in this case. The documents were produced before a grand jury sitting in the Eastern District of Arkansas in aid of the Independent Counsel's attempt to determine whether respondent had violated a commitment in his first plea agreement. The use of those sources of information eventually led to the return of an indictment by a grand jury sitting in the District of Columbia for offenses that apparently are unrelated to that plea agreement. What the District Court characterized as a "fishing expedition" did produce a fish, but not the one that the Independent Counsel expected to hook. It is abundantly clear that the testimonial aspect of respondent's act of producing subpoenaed documents was the first step in a chain of evidence that led to this prosecution. The documents did not magically appear in the prosecutor's office like "manna from heaven." They arrived there only after respondent asserted his constitutional privilege, received a grant of immunity, and—under the compulsion of the District Court's order—took the mental and physical steps necessary to provide the prosecutor with an accurate inventory of the many sources of potentially incriminating evidence sought by the subpoena. It was only through respondent's truthful reply to the subpoena that the Government received the incriminating documents of which it made "substantial use . . . in the investigation that led to the indictment." Brief for United States 3.

For these reasons, we cannot accept the Government's submission that respondent's immunity did not preclude its derivative use of the produced documents because its "possession of the documents [was] the fruit only of a simple physical act—the act of producing the documents." Brief, at 29. It was unquestionably necessary for respondent to make extensive use of "the contents of his own mind" in identifying the hundreds of documents responsive to the requests in the subpoena. The assembly of those documents was like telling an inquisitor the combination to a wall safe, not like being forced to surrender the key to a strongbox. *Doe II*, at n.9.[b] The Government's anemic view of respondent's act of

---

b   *Doe II*, supra note 8, presented a self-incrimination challenge to a court order compelling a target of a grand jury investigation to sign a document authorizing foreign banks to disclose records of any accounts he might have, specifically noting that this directive had been signed pursuant to court order. The Court noted that the signed directive did not acknowledge the existence of the accounts or records regarding any accounts. Thus, as it did not require the individual to "relate a factual assertion or disclose information," it was not "testimonial." Responding to an analogy offered in dissent, the majority noted: "We simply disagree with the dissent's conclusion that the execution of the consent directive at issue here forced petitioner to express the contents of his mind. In our view, such compulsion is more like 'be[ing] forced to

production as a mere physical act that is principally non-testimonial in character and can be entirely divorced from its "implicit" testimonial aspect so as to constitute a "legitimate, wholly independent source" (as required by *Kastigar*) for the documents produced simply fails to account for these realities.

In sum, we have no doubt that the constitutional privilege against self-incrimination protects the target of a grand jury investigation from being compelled to answer questions designed to elicit information about the existence of sources of potentially incriminating evidence. That constitutional privilege has the same application to the testimonial aspect of a response to a subpoena seeking discovery of those sources. Before the District Court, the Government arguably conceded that respondent's act of production in this case had a testimonial aspect that entitled him to respond to the subpoena by asserting his privilege against self-incrimination. * * * On appeal and again before this Court, however, the Government has argued that the communicative aspect of respondent's act of producing ordinary business records is insufficiently "testimonial" to support a claim of privilege because the existence and possession of such records by any businessman is a "foregone conclusion" under our decision in *Fisher v. United States*. This argument both misreads *Fisher* and ignores our subsequent decision in *Doe I*.ᶜ * * * Whatever the scope of this "foregone conclusion" rationale, the facts of this case plainly fall outside of it. While in *Fisher* the Government already knew that the documents were in the attorneys' possession and could independently confirm their existence and authenticity through the accountants who created them, here the Government has not shown that it had any prior knowledge of either the existence or the whereabouts of the 13,120 pages of documents ultimately produced by respondent. The Government cannot cure this deficiency through the overbroad argument that a businessman such as respondent will always possess general business and tax records that fall within the broad categories described in

---

surrender a key to a strong box containing incriminating documents,' than it is like 'be[ing] compelled to reveal the combination to [petitioner's] wall safe.' "

   ᶜ   *United States v. Doe*, 465 U.S. 605 (1984) (cited as *Doe I*), presented a self-incrimination challenge to a grand jury that compelled a sole proprietor to produce a variety of business records. That challenge was sustained by both the District court and the Court of Appeals on an application of *Fisher*'s act-of-production analysis (although the Court of Appeals also relied on a privacy analysis rejected by the Supreme Court, see note b, p. 650). The Supreme Court also sustained the challenge, pointing to the factual determinations of the District Court and the Court of Appeals, and noting its "traditiona[l] reluctanc[e] to disturb findings of fact in which two courts below have concurred." Setting forth the reasoning of the two lower courts, the Supreme Court in *Doe* noted that the District Court had concluded that " 'enforcement of the subpoenas would compel [respondent] to admit that the records exist, that they are in his possession, and that they are authentic.' " The District Court had taken note of the government's contention that the " 'existence, possession, and authenticity of the documents can be proved without [respondent's] testimonial communication,' " but had responded that it was not satisfied " 'as to how that representation can be implemented.' " The Court of Appeals had stated that the record failed to indicate that the government knew that "each of the myriad documents demanded * * * in fact is in the appellee's possession," and that the " 'most plausible inference to be drawn from the broad-sweeping subpoenas is that the Government, unable to prove that the subpoenaed documents exist—or that the appellee even is somehow connected to the business entities under investigation—is attempting to compensate for its lack of knowledge by requiring the appellant to become in effect the primary informant against himself.' " The Supreme Court further noted that the Government was not foreclosed "from rebutting respondent's claim by producing evidence that possession, existence, and authentication were a 'foregone conclusion' [citing *Fisher*]," but "in this case * * * the Government failed to make such a showing."

this subpoena. The *Doe I* subpoenas also sought several broad categories of general business records, yet we upheld the District Court's finding that the act of producing those records would involve testimonial self-incrimination.

Given our conclusion that respondent's act of production had a testimonial aspect, at least with respect to the existence and location of the documents sought by the Government's subpoena, respondent could not be compelled to produce those documents without first receiving a grant of immunity under § 6003. As we construed § 6002 in *Kastigar*, such immunity is co-extensive with the constitutional privilege. *Kastigar* requires that respondent's motion to dismiss the indictment on immunity grounds be granted unless the Government proves that the evidence it used in obtaining the indictment and proposed to use at trial was derived from legitimate sources "wholly independent" of the testimonial aspect of respondent's immunized conduct in assembling and producing the documents described in the subpoena. The Government, however, does not claim that it could make such a showing. Rather, it contends that its prosecution of respondent must be considered proper unless someone—presumably respondent—shows that "there is some substantial relation between the compelled testimonial communications implicit in the act of production (as opposed to the act of production standing alone) and some aspect of the information used in the investigation or the evidence presented at trial." Brief for United States 9. We could not accept this submission without repudiating the basis for our conclusion in *Kastigar* that the statutory guarantee of use and derivative-use immunity is as broad as the constitutional privilege itself. This we are not prepared to do. Accordingly, the indictment against respondent must be dismissed. The judgment of the Court of Appeals is affirmed. * * *

CHIEF JUSTICE REHNQUIST dissents and would reverse the judgment of the Court of Appeals in part, for the reasons given by Judge Williams in his dissenting opinion in that court, 167 F.3d 552, 597 (C.A.D.C.1999).

JUSTICE THOMAS, with whom JUSTICE SCALIA joins, concurring.

Our decision today involves the application of the act-of-production doctrine, which provides that persons compelled to turn over incriminating papers or other physical evidence pursuant to a subpoena duces tecum or a summons may invoke the Fifth Amendment privilege against self-incrimination as a bar to production only where the act of producing the evidence would contain "testimonial" features. I join the opinion of the Court because it properly applies this doctrine, but I write separately to note that this doctrine may be inconsistent with the original meaning of the Fifth Amendment's Self-Incrimination Clause. A substantial body of evidence suggests that the Fifth Amendment privilege protects against the compelled production not just of incriminating testimony, but of any incriminating evidence. In a future case, I would be willing to reconsider the scope and meaning of the Self-Incrimination Clause.

The Fifth Amendment provides that "[n]o person . . . shall be compelled in any criminal case to be a witness against himself." The key word at issue in this case is "witness." The Court's opinion, relying on prior cases, essentially defines "witness" as a person who provides testimony, and thus restricts the Fifth

Amendment's ban to only those communications "that are 'testimonial' in character." None of this Court's cases, however, has undertaken an analysis of the meaning of the term at the time of the founding. A review of that period reveals substantial support for the view that the term "witness" meant a person who gives or furnishes evidence, a broader meaning than that which our case law currently ascribes to the term.[d] If this is so, a person who responds to a subpoena duces tecum would be just as much a "witness" as a person who responds to a subpoena ad testificandum[1] * * *

This Court has not always taken the approach to the Fifth Amendment that we follow today. The first case interpreting the Self-Incrimination Clause—*Boyd v. United States*—was decided, though not explicitly, in accordance with the understanding that "witness" means one who gives evidence. * * * But this Court's decision in *Fisher v. United States*, rejected this understanding, permitting the Government to force a person to furnish incriminating physical evidence and protecting only the "testimonial" aspects of that transfer. In so doing, *Fisher* not only failed to examine the historical backdrop to the Fifth Amendment, it also required—as illustrated by extended discussion in the opinions below in this case— a difficult parsing of the act of responding to a subpoena duces tecum. None of the parties in this case has asked us to depart from *Fisher*, but in light of the historical evidence that the Self-Incrimination Clause may have a broader reach than *Fisher* holds, I remain open to a reconsideration of that decision and its progeny in a proper case.

---

[d] Justice Thomas cited the following sources from that period: (1) dictionary definitions of the term "witness"; (2) state constitutional provisions that granted a right against compulsion "to give evidence" or to "furnish evidence"; (3) the use of similar wording by the four states that proposed inclusion of a self-incrimination provision in the Bill of Rights, and the lack of any indication that Madison's "unique phrasing" in the proposal he offered to Congress was designed to narrow those state proposals; and (4) the Sixth Amendment's compulsory process clause, which the Court had long held to encompass the right to secure papers as well as testimony. He also noted the more extensive discussion of those sources in Nagareda, "Compulsion to be a Witness" and the Resurrection of Boyd, 74 N.Y.U. L.Rev. 1575 (1999).

[1] Even if the term "witness" in the Fifth Amendment referred to someone who provides testimony, as this Court's recent cases suggest without historical analysis, it may well be that at the time of the founding a person who turned over documents would be described as providing testimony. See *Amey v. Long*, 9 East. 472, 484, 103 Eng. Rep. 653, 658 (K.B.1808) (referring to documents requested by subpoenas duces tecum as "written . . . testimony"). * * *

CHAPTER 9

PRETRIAL RELEASE

■ ■ ■

Persons apprehended by the police in the expectation that they will be prosecuted are usually provided an opportunity for pretrial release by one of a variety of means, depending upon the circumstances. If the offense is a very minor one, then release may occur in the field or at the stationhouse upon acceptance of a citation from the officer. In the case of more serious misdemeanors, the arrestee will be given the opportunity to obtain his release once at the police station by posting cash as a security payment in an amount set in a bail schedule, which simply lists bail amounts for various offenses. Those who cannot afford the bail amount and other arrestees must await their first appearance, when the magistrate will determine if the defendant can obtain his release from custody pending the final disposition of the case, and the conditions of that release if granted.

Though bail was once limited almost entirely to the posting of cash or a secured bond, purchased from a professional bondsman, many jurisdictions now permit the defendant to obtain his release by depositing cash amounting to 10% of the amount of bond set by the magistrate. Sometimes the judge will instead release the defendant on his unsecured promise to appear, or, in addition, impose such nonfinancial conditions as a curfew or reporting periodically to a designated agency. Because of the continued reliance on financial conditions for release, the burdens of pretrial detention are borne disproportionately by the poor. A growing body of research has found that reducing the use of money bail saves taxpayer dollars otherwise spent on incarceration and decreases financial, physical, and psychological harms to defendants and their families, all without significant increases in crime rates or the rates of non-appearance. Some jurisdictions are shifting away from money bail as a result. In the many cases in which a magistrate continues to set financial conditions upon release, the magistrate is subject to the Eighth Amendment command: "Excessive bail shall not be required." Just what this means is considered in the first case in this chapter, *Stack v. Boyle*.

The term "preventive detention" is usually used to describe the pretrial detention of a defendant to protect society from the risk of criminal conduct by him pending disposition of the outstanding charges. For many years this was accomplished sub rosa; the magistrate would set money bail purportedly for the purpose of ensuring defendant's appearance at trial, but the amount would be high enough to prevent defendant's release. But because of reform in bail laws along with more attention to whether such pretrial detention is justified, the process of preventive detention is today a much more open one. In the federal criminal justice system, for example, the Bail Reform Act of 1984 on the one hand provides that a judicial officer "may not impose a financial condition that results in the pretrial detention of the person," but on the other expressly authorizes judicially-ordered pretrial detention of defendants in some circumstances to ensure "the safety of any other person or the community." Whether such preventive detention can be squared with the Eighth Amendment provision quoted above is the issue addressed in the other case in this chapter, *United States v. Salerno.*

STACK V. BOYLE
342 U.S. 1, 72 S.Ct. 1, 96 L.Ed. 3 (1951).

CHIEF JUSTICE VINSON delivered the opinion of the Court.

Indictments have been returned in the Southern District of California charging the twelve petitioners with conspiring to violate the Smith Act, [proscribing advocacy of the overthrow of the government by force or violence]. Upon their arrest, bail was fixed for each petitioner in the widely varying amounts of $2,500, $7,500, $75,000 and $100,000. On motion of petitioner Schneiderman following arrest in the Southern District of New York, his bail was reduced to $50,000 before his removal to California. On motion of the Government to increase bail in the case of other petitioners, and after several intermediate procedural steps not material to the issues presented here, bail was fixed in the District Court for the Southern District of California in the uniform amount of $50,000 for each petitioner.

Petitioners moved to reduce bail on the ground that bail as fixed was excessive under the Eighth Amendment. In support of their motion, petitioners submitted statements as to their financial resources, family relationships, health, prior criminal records, and other information. The only evidence offered by the Government was a certified record showing that four persons previously convicted under the Smith Act in the Southern District of New York had forfeited bail. No evidence was produced relating those four persons to the petitioners in this case. At a hearing on the motion, petitioners were examined by the District Judge and cross-examined by an attorney for the Government. Petitioners' factual statements stand uncontroverted.

After their motion to reduce bail was denied, petitioners filed applications for habeas corpus in the same District Court. Upon consideration of the record on the motion to reduce bail, the writs were denied. The Court of Appeals for the Ninth Circuit affirmed.

* * * From the passage of the Judiciary Act of 1789 to the present Federal Rules of Criminal Procedure, Rule 46(a)(1), federal law has unequivocally provided that a person arrested for a non-capital offense *shall* be admitted to bail. This traditional right to freedom before conviction permits the unhampered preparation of a defense, and serves to prevent the infliction of punishment prior to conviction. Unless this right to bail before trial is preserved, the presumption of innocence, secured only after centuries of struggle, would lose its meaning.

The right to release before trial is conditioned upon the accused's giving adequate assurance that he will stand trial and submit to sentence if found guilty.

Like the ancient practice of securing the oaths of responsible persons to stand as sureties for the accused, the modern practice of requiring a bail bond or the deposit of a sum of money subject to forfeiture serves as additional assurance of the presence of an accused. Bail set at a figure higher than an amount reasonably calculated to fulfill this purpose is "excessive" under the Eighth Amendment.

Since the function of bail is limited, the fixing of bail for any individual defendant must be based upon standards relevant to the purpose of assuring the presence of that defendant. The traditional standards as expressed in the Federal Rules of Criminal Procedure[3] are to be applied in each case to each defendant. * * * Upon final judgment of conviction, petitioners face imprisonment of not more than five years and a fine of not more than $10,000. It is not denied that bail for each petitioner has been fixed in a sum much higher than that usually imposed for offenses with like penalties and yet there has been no factual showing to justify such action in this case. The Government asks the courts to depart from the norm by assuming, without the introduction of evidence, that each petitioner is a pawn in a conspiracy and will, in obedience to a superior, flee the jurisdiction. To infer from the fact of indictment alone a need for bail in an unusually high amount is an arbitrary act. Such conduct would inject into our own system of government the very principles of totalitarianism which Congress was seeking to guard against in passing the statute under which petitioners have been indicted.

If bail in an amount greater than that usually fixed for serious charges of crimes is required in the case of any of the petitioners, that is a matter to which evidence should be directed in a hearing so that the constitutional rights of each petitioner may be preserved. In the absence of such a showing, we are of the opinion that the fixing of bail before trial in these cases cannot be squared with the statutory and constitutional standards for admission to bail.

* * * Accordingly, [p]etitioners may move for reduction of bail in the criminal proceeding so that a hearing may be held for the purpose of fixing reasonable bail for each petitioner. * * *[a]

UNITED STATES V. SALERNO

481 U.S. 739, 107 S.Ct. 2095, 95 L.Ed.2d 697 (1987).

CHIEF JUSTICE REHNQUIST delivered the opinion of the Court. * * *

I

Responding to "the alarming problem of crimes committed by persons on release," Congress formulated the Bail Reform Act of 1984, 18 U.S.C. § 3141 et seq., as the solution to a bail crisis in the federal courts. The Act represents the National

---

[3] Rule 46(c). "AMOUNT. If the defendant is admitted to bail, the amount thereof shall be such as in the judgment of the commissioner or court or judge or justice will insure the presence of the defendant, having regard to the nature and circumstances of the offense charged, the weight of the evidence against him, the financial ability of the defendant to give bail and the character of the defendant."

[a] The separate opinion of Justice Jackson, joined by Justice Frankfurter, is omitted. Justice Minton did not participate.

Legislature's considered response to numerous perceived deficiencies in the federal bail process. By providing for sweeping changes in both the way federal courts consider bail applications and the circumstances under which bail is granted, Congress hoped to "give the courts adequate authority to make release decisions that give appropriate recognition to the danger a person may pose to others if released."

To this end, § 3141(a) of the Act requires a judicial officer to determine whether an arrestee shall be detained. Section 3142(e) provides that "[i]f, after a hearing pursuant to the provisions of subsection (f), the judicial officer finds that no condition or combination of conditions will reasonably assure the appearance of the person as required and the safety of any other person and the community, he shall order the detention of the person prior to trial." Section 3142(f) provides the arrestee with a number of procedural safeguards. He may request the presence of counsel at the detention hearing, he may testify and present witnesses in his behalf, as well as proffer evidence, and he may cross-examine other witnesses appearing at the hearing. If the judicial officer finds that no conditions of pretrial release can reasonably assure the safety of other persons and the community, he must state his findings of fact in writing, and support his conclusion with "clear and convincing evidence."

The judicial officer is not given unbridled discretion in making the detention determination. Congress has specified the considerations relevant to that decision. These factors include the nature and seriousness of the charges, the substantiality of the government's evidence against the arrestee, the arrestee's background and characteristics, and the nature and seriousness of the danger posed by the suspect's release. Should a judicial officer order detention, the detainee is entitled to expedited appellate review of the detention order.

Respondents Anthony Salerno and Vincent Cafaro were arrested on March 21, 1986, after being charged in a 29-count indictment alleging various Racketeer Influenced and Corrupt Organizations Act (RICO) violations, mail and wire fraud offenses, extortion, and various criminal gambling violations. The RICO counts alleged 35 acts of racketeering activity, including fraud, extortion, gambling, and conspiracy to commit murder. At respondents' arraignment, the Government moved to have Salerno and Cafaro detained pursuant to § 3142(e), on the ground that no condition of release would assure the safety of the community or any person. The District Court held a hearing at which the Government made a detailed proffer of evidence. The Government's case showed that Salerno was the "boss" of the Genovese Crime Family of La Cosa Nostra and that Cafaro was a "captain" in the Genovese Family. According to the Government's proffer, based in large part on conversations intercepted by a court-ordered wiretap, the two respondents had participated in wide-ranging conspiracies to aid their illegitimate enterprises through violent means. The Government also offered the testimony of two of its trial witnesses, who would assert that Salerno personally participated in two murder conspiracies. Salerno opposed the motion for detention, challenging the credibility of the Government's witnesses. He offered the testimony of several character witnesses as well as a letter from his doctor stating that he was suffering from a serious medical condition. Cafaro presented no evidence at the hearing, but instead characterized the wiretap conversations as merely "tough talk."

The District Court granted the Government's detention motion, concluding that the Government had established by clear and convincing evidence that no condition or combination of conditions of release would ensure the safety of the community or any person. * * *

Respondents appealed, contending that to the extent that the Bail Reform Act permits pretrial detention on the ground that the arrestee is likely to commit future crimes, it is unconstitutional on its face. Over a dissent, the United States Court of Appeals for the Second Circuit agreed. Although the court agreed that pretrial detention could be imposed if the defendants were likely to intimidate witnesses or otherwise jeopardize the trial process, it found "§ 3142(e)'s authorization of pretrial detention [on the ground of future dangerousness] repugnant to the concept of substantive due process, which we believe prohibits the total deprivation of liberty simply as a means of preventing future crimes." The court concluded that the Government could not, consistent with due process, detain persons who had not been accused of any crime merely because they were thought to present a danger to the community. It reasoned that our criminal law system holds persons accountable for past actions, not anticipated future actions. Although a court could detain an arrestee who threatened to flee before trial, such detention would be permissible because it would serve the basic objective of a criminal system— bringing the accused to trial. The court distinguished our decision in *Gerstein v. Pugh* [fn. a, p. 177], in which we upheld police detention pursuant to arrest. The court construed *Gerstein* as limiting such detention to the " 'administrative steps incident to arrest.' " The Court of Appeals also found our decision in *Schall v. Martin,* 467 U.S. 253 (1984), upholding postarrest pretrial detention of juveniles, inapposite because juveniles have a lesser interest in liberty than do adults. * * *

II

A facial challenge to a legislative Act is, of course, the most difficult challenge to mount successfully, since the challenger must establish that no set of circumstances exists under which the Act would be valid. The fact that the Bail Reform Act might operate unconstitutionally under some conceivable set of circumstances is insufficient to render it wholly invalid, since we have not recognized an "overbreadth" doctrine outside the limited context of the First Amendment. We think respondents have failed to shoulder their heavy burden to demonstrate that the Act is "facially" unconstitutional.[3]

Respondents present two grounds for invalidating the Bail Reform Act's provisions permitting pretrial detention on the basis of future dangerousness. First, they rely upon the Court of Appeals' conclusion that the Act exceeds the limitations placed upon the Federal Government by the Due Process Clause of the Fifth Amendment. Second, they contend that the Act contravenes the Eighth

---

[3] We intimate no view on the validity of any aspects of the Act that are not relevant to respondents' case. Nor have respondents claimed that the Act is unconstitutional because of the way it was applied to the particular facts of their case.

Amendment's proscription against excessive bail. We treat these contentions in turn.

A

The Due Process Clause of the Fifth Amendment provides that "No person shall * * * be deprived of life, liberty, or property, without due process of law * * *." This Court has held that the Due Process Clause protects individuals against two types of government action. So-called "substantive due process" prevents the government from engaging in conduct that "shocks the conscience," or interferes with rights "implicit in the concept of ordered liberty." When government action depriving a person of life, liberty, or property survives substantive due process scrutiny, it must still be implemented in a fair manner. This requirement has traditionally been referred to as "procedural" due process.

Respondents first argue that the Act violates substantive due process because the pretrial detention it authorizes constitutes impermissible punishment before trial. The Government, however, has never argued that pretrial detention could be upheld if it were "punishment." The Court of Appeals assumed that pretrial detention under the Bail Reform Act is regulatory, not penal, and we agree that it is.

As an initial matter, the mere fact that a person is detained does not inexorably lead to the conclusion that the government has imposed punishment. To determine whether a restriction on liberty constitutes impermissible punishment or permissible regulation, we first look to legislative intent. Unless Congress expressly intended to impose punitive restrictions, the punitive/regulatory distinction turns on " 'whether an alternative purpose to which [the restriction] may rationally be connected is assignable for it, and whether it appears excessive in relation to the alternative purpose assigned [to it].' "

We conclude that the detention imposed by the Act falls on the regulatory side of the dichotomy. The legislative history of the Bail Reform Act clearly indicates that Congress did not formulate the pretrial detention provisions as punishment for dangerous individuals. Congress instead perceived pretrial detention as a potential solution to a pressing societal problem. There is no doubt that preventing danger to the community is a legitimate regulatory goal.

Nor are the incidents of pretrial detention excessive in relation to the regulatory goal Congress sought to achieve. The Bail Reform Act carefully limits the circumstances under which detention may be sought to the most serious of crimes. See 18 U.S.C. § 3142(f) (detention hearings available if case involves crimes of violence, offenses for which the sentence is life imprisonment or death, serious drug offenses, or certain repeat offenders). The arrestee is entitled to a prompt detention hearing, and the maximum length of pretrial detention is limited by the stringent time limitations of the Speedy Trial Act.[4] Moreover, as in *Schall v. Martin,* the conditions of confinement envisioned by the Act "appear to reflect the regulatory purposes relied upon by the" government. As in *Schall,* the statute at

---

[4]   We intimate no view as to the point at which detention in a particular case might become excessively prolonged, and therefore punitive, in relation to Congress' regulatory goal.

issue here requires that detainees be housed in a "facility separate, to the extent practicable, from persons awaiting or serving sentences or being held in custody pending appeal." We conclude, therefore, that the pretrial detention contemplated by the Bail Reform Act is regulatory in nature, and does not constitute punishment before trial in violation of the Due Process Clause.

The Court of Appeals nevertheless concluded that "the Due Process Clause prohibits pretrial detention on the ground of danger to the community as a regulatory measure, without regard to the duration of the detention." Respondents characterize the Due Process Clause as erecting an impenetrable "wall" in this area that "no governmental interest—rational, important, compelling or otherwise— may surmount."

We do not think the Clause lays down any such categorical imperative. We have repeatedly held that the government's regulatory interest in community safety can, in appropriate circumstances, outweigh an individual's liberty interest. For example, in times of war or insurrection, when society's interest is at its peak, the government may detain individuals whom the government believes to be dangerous. Even outside the exigencies of war, we have found that sufficiently compelling governmental interests can justify detention of dangerous persons. Thus, we have found no absolute constitutional barrier to detention of potentially dangerous resident aliens pending deportation proceedings. We have also held that the government may detain mentally unstable individuals who present a danger to the public, and dangerous defendants who become incompetent to stand trial. We have approved of postarrest regulatory detention of juveniles when they present a continuing danger to the community. *Schall v. Martin.* Even competent adults may face substantial liberty restrictions as a result of the operation of our criminal justice system. If the police suspect an individual of a crime, they may arrest and hold him until a neutral magistrate determines whether probable cause exists. *Gerstein v. Pugh.* Finally, respondents concede and the Court of Appeals noted that an arrestee may be incarcerated until trial if he presents a risk of flight or a danger to witnesses.

Respondents characterize all of these cases as exceptions to the "general rule" of substantive due process that the government may not detain a person prior to a judgment of guilt in a criminal trial. Such a "general rule" may freely be conceded, but we think that these cases show a sufficient number of exceptions to the rule that the congressional action challenged here can hardly be characterized as totally novel. Given the well-established authority of the government, in special circumstances, to restrain individuals' liberty prior to or even without criminal trial and conviction, we think that the present statute providing for pretrial detention on the basis of dangerousness must be evaluated in precisely the same manner that we evaluated the laws in the cases discussed above.

The government's interest in preventing crime by arrestees is both legitimate and compelling. In *Schall,* we recognized the strength of the State's interest in preventing juvenile crime. This general concern with crime prevention is no less compelling when the suspects are adults. Indeed, "[t]he harm suffered by the victim of a crime is not dependent upon the age of the perpetrator." The Bail Reform Act of 1984 responds to an even more particularized governmental interest than the interest we sustained in *Schall*. The statute we upheld in *Schall* permitted pretrial detention of any juvenile arrested on any charge after a showing that the individual might commit some undefined further crimes. The Bail Reform Act, in contrast, narrowly focuses on a particularly acute problem in which the government interests are overwhelming. The Act operates only on individuals who have been arrested for a specific category of extremely serious offenses. Congress specifically found that these individuals are far more likely to be responsible for dangerous acts in the community after arrest. Nor is the Act by any means a scattershot attempt to incapacitate those who are merely suspected of these serious crimes. The government must first of all demonstrate probable cause to believe that the charged crime has been committed by the arrestee, but that is not enough. In a full-blown adversary hearing, the government must convince a neutral decisionmaker by clear and convincing evidence that no conditions of release can reasonably assure the safety of the community or any person. While the government's general interest in preventing crime is compelling, even this interest is heightened when the government musters convincing proof that the arrestee, already indicted or held to answer for a serious crime, presents a demonstrable danger to the community. Under these narrow circumstances, society's interest in crime prevention is at its greatest.

On the other side of the scale, of course, is the individual's strong interest in liberty. We do not minimize the importance and fundamental nature of this right. But, as our cases hold, this right may, in circumstances where the government's interest is sufficiently weighty, be subordinated to the greater needs of society. We think that Congress' careful delineation of the circumstances under which detention will be permitted satisfies this standard. When the government proves by clear and convincing evidence that an arrestee presents an identified and articulable threat to an individual or the community, we believe that, consistent with the Due Process Clause, a court may disable the arrestee from executing that threat. Under these circumstances, we cannot categorically state that pretrial detention "offends some principle of justice so rooted in the traditions and conscience of our people as to be ranked as fundamental."

Finally, we may dispose briefly of respondents' facial challenge to the procedures of the Bail Reform Act. To sustain them against such a challenge, we need only find them "adequate to authorize the pretrial detention of at least some [persons] charged with crimes," whether or not they might be insufficient in some particular circumstances. We think they pass that test. As we stated in *Schall*, "there is nothing inherently unattainable about a prediction of future criminal conduct."

Under the Bail Reform Act, the procedures by which a judicial officer evaluates the likelihood of future dangerousness are specifically designed to further the accuracy of that determination. Detainees have a right to counsel at the detention hearing. They may testify in their own behalf, present information by proffer or otherwise, and cross-examine witnesses who appear at the hearing. Ibid. The judicial officer charged with the responsibility of determining the appropriateness of detention is guided by statutorily enumerated factors, which include the nature and the circumstances of the charges, the weight of the evidence, the history and characteristics of the putative offender, and the danger to the community. The government must prove its case by clear and convincing evidence. Finally, the judicial officer must include written findings of fact and a written statement of reasons for a decision to detain. The Act's review provisions provide for immediate appellate review of the detention decision.

We think these extensive safeguards suffice to repel a facial challenge. The protections are more exacting than those we found sufficient in the juvenile context, see *Schall*, and they far exceed what we found necessary to effect limited postarrest detention in *Gerstein v. Pugh*. Given the legitimate and compelling regulatory purpose of the Act and the procedural protections it offers, we conclude that the Act is not facially invalid under the Due Process Clause of the Fifth Amendment.

B

Respondents also contend that the Bail Reform Act violates the Excessive Bail Clause of the Eighth Amendment. * * *

The Eighth Amendment addresses pretrial release by providing merely that "Excessive bail shall not be required." This Clause, of course, says nothing about whether bail shall be available at all. Respondents nevertheless contend that this Clause grants them a right to bail calculated solely upon considerations of flight. They rely on *Stack v. Boyle* in which the Court stated that "Bail set at a figure higher than an amount reasonably calculated [to ensure the defendant's presence at trial] is 'excessive' under the Eighth Amendment." In respondents' view, since the Bail Reform Act allows a court essentially to set bail at an infinite amount for reasons not related to the risk of flight, it violates the Excessive Bail Clause. Respondents concede that the right to bail they have discovered in the Eighth Amendment is not absolute. A court may, for example, refuse bail in capital cases. And, as the Court of Appeals noted and respondents admit, a court may refuse bail when the defendant presents a threat to the judicial process by intimidating witnesses. Respondents characterize these exceptions as consistent with what they claim to be the sole purpose of bail—to ensure integrity of the judicial process.

While we agree that a primary function of bail is to safeguard the courts' role in adjudicating the guilt or innocence of defendants, we reject the proposition that the Eighth Amendment categorically prohibits the government from pursuing other admittedly compelling interests through regulation of pretrial release. The above-quoted *dicta* in *Stack v. Boyle* is far too slender a reed on which to rest this argument. The Court in *Stack* had no occasion to consider whether the Excessive Bail Clause requires courts to admit all defendants to bail, because the statute before the Court in that case in fact allowed the defendants to be bailed. * * *

The holding of *Stack* is illuminated by the Court's holding just four months later in *Carlson v. Landon*, 342 U.S. 524 (1952). In that case, remarkably similar to the present action, the detainees had been arrested and held without bail pending a determination of deportability. The Attorney General refused to release the individuals, "on the ground that there was reasonable cause to believe that [their] release would be prejudicial to the public interest and *would endanger the welfare and safety of the United States.*" (emphasis added). The detainees brought the same challenge that respondents bring to us today: the Eighth Amendment required them to be admitted to bail. The Court squarely rejected this proposition:

> "The bail clause was lifted with slight changes from the English Bill of Rights Act. In England that clause has never been thought to accord a right to bail in all cases, but merely to provide that bail shall not be excessive in those cases where it is proper to grant bail. When this clause was carried over into our Bill of Rights, nothing was said that indicated any different concept. The Eighth Amendment has not prevented Congress from defining the classes of cases in which bail shall be allowed in this country. Thus, in criminal cases bail is not compulsory where the punishment may be death. Indeed, the very language of the Amendment fails to say all arrests must be bailable."

Carlson v. Landon was a civil case, and we need not decide today whether the Excessive Bail Clause speaks at all to Congress' power to define the classes of criminal arrestees who shall be admitted to bail. For even if we were to conclude that the Eighth Amendment imposes some substantive limitations on the National Legislature's powers in this area, we would still hold that the Bail Reform Act is valid. Nothing in the text of the Bail Clause limits permissible government considerations solely to questions of flight. The only arguable substantive limitation of the Bail Clause is that the government's proposed conditions of release or detention not be "excessive" in light of the perceived evil. Of course, to determine whether the government's response is excessive, we must compare that response against the interest the government seeks to protect by means of that response. Thus, when the government has admitted that its only interest is in preventing flight, bail must be set by a court at a sum designed to ensure that goal, and no more. We believe that when Congress has mandated detention on the basis of a compelling interest other than prevention of flight, as it has here, the Eighth Amendment does not require release on bail.

III

In our society liberty is the norm, and detention prior to trial or without trial is the carefully limited exception. We hold that the provisions for pretrial detention in the Bail Reform Act of 1984 fall within that carefully limited exception. * * * We are unwilling to say that this congressional determination, based as it is upon that primary concern of every government—a concern for the safety and indeed the lives of its citizens—on its face violates either the Due Process Clause of the Fifth Amendment or the Excessive Bail Clause of the Eighth Amendment.

JUSTICE MARSHALL, with whom JUSTICE BRENNAN joins, dissenting. * * *

II

The majority approaches respondents' challenge to the Act by dividing the discussion into two sections, one concerned with the substantive guarantees implicit in the Due Process Clause, and the other concerned with the protection afforded by the Excessive Bail Clause of the Eighth Amendment. This is a sterile formalism, which divides a unitary argument into two independent parts and then professes to demonstrate that the parts are individually inadequate.

On the due process side of this false dichotomy appears an argument concerning the distinction between regulatory and punitive legislation. The majority concludes that the Act is a regulatory rather than a punitive measure. The ease with which the conclusion is reached suggests the worthlessness of the achievement. The major premise is that "[u]nless Congress expressly intended to impose punitive restrictions, the punitive/regulatory distinction turns on ' "whether an alternative purpose to which [the restriction] may rationally be connected is assignable for it, and whether it appears excessive in relation to the alternative purpose assigned [to it]." ' " The majority finds that "Congress did not formulate the pretrial detention provisions as punishment for dangerous individuals," but instead was pursuing the "legitimate regulatory goal" of "preventing danger to the community." Concluding that pretrial detention is not an excessive solution to the problem of preventing danger to the community, the majority thus finds that no substantive element of the guarantee of due process invalidates the statute.

This argument does not demonstrate the conclusion it purports to justify. Let us apply the majority's reasoning to a similar, hypothetical case. After investigation, Congress determines (not unrealistically) that a large proportion of violent crime is perpetrated by persons who are unemployed. It also determines, equally reasonably, that much violent crime is committed at night. From amongst the panoply of "potential solutions," Congress chooses a statute which permits, after judicial proceedings, the imposition of a dusk-to-dawn curfew on anyone who is unemployed. Since this is not a measure enacted for the purpose of punishing the unemployed, and since the majority finds that preventing danger to the community is a legitimate regulatory goal, the curfew statute would, according to the majority's analysis, be a mere "regulatory" detention statute, entirely compatible with the substantive components of the Due Process Clause.

The absurdity of this conclusion arises, of course, from the majority's cramped concept of substantive due process. The majority proceeds as though the only substantive right protected by the Due Process Clause is a right to be free from punishment before conviction. The majority's technique for infringing this right is simple: merely redefine any measure which is claimed to be punishment as "regulation," and, magically, the Constitution no longer prohibits its imposition. Because, as I discuss in Part III, infra, the Due Process Clause protects other substantive rights which are infringed by this legislation, the majority's argument is merely an exercise in obfuscation.

The logic of the majority's Eighth Amendment analysis is equally unsatisfactory. The Eighth Amendment, as the majority notes, states that "[e]xcessive bail shall not be required." The majority then declares, as if it were undeniable, that: "[t]his Clause, of course, says nothing about whether bail shall be available at all." If excessive bail is imposed the defendant stays in jail. The same result is achieved if bail is denied altogether. Whether the magistrate sets bail at $1 billion or refuses to set bail at all, the consequences are indistinguishable.

It would be mere sophistry to suggest that the Eighth Amendment protects against the former decision, and not the latter. Indeed, such a result would lead to the conclusion that there was no need for Congress to pass a preventive detention measure of any kind; every federal magistrate and district judge could simply refuse, despite the absence of any evidence of risk of flight or danger to the community, to set bail. This would be entirely constitutional, since, according to the majority, the Eighth Amendment "says nothing about whether bail shall be available at all."

But perhaps, the majority says, this manifest absurdity can be avoided. Perhaps the Bail Clause is addressed only to the judiciary. "[W]e need not decide today," the majority says, "whether the Excessive Bail Clause speaks at all to Congress' power to define the classes of criminal arrestees who shall be admitted to bail." The majority is correct that this question need not be decided today; it was decided long ago. Federal and state statutes which purport to accomplish what the Eighth Amendment forbids, such as imposing cruel and unusual punishments, may not stand. The text of the Amendment, which provides simply that "[e]xcessive bail shall not be required, nor excessive fines imposed, nor cruel and unusual punishments inflicted," provides absolutely no support for the majority's speculation that both courts and Congress are forbidden to inflict cruel and unusual punishments, while only the courts are forbidden to require excessive bail.[5]

* * * The majority concedes, as it must, that "when the government has admitted that its only interest is in preventing flight, bail must be set by a court at a sum designed to ensure that goal, and no more." But, the majority says, "when Congress has mandated detention on the basis of a compelling interest other than prevention of flight, as it has here, the Eighth Amendment does not require release on bail." This conclusion follows only if the "compelling" interest upon which Congress acted is an interest which the Constitution permits Congress to further through the denial of bail. The majority does not ask, as a result of its disingenuous division of the analysis, if there are any substantive limits contained in both the Eighth Amendment and the Due Process Clause which render this system of preventive detention unconstitutional. The majority does not ask because the answer is apparent and, to the majority, inconvenient.

III

The essence of this case may be found, ironically enough, in a provision of the Act to which the majority does not refer. Title 18 U.S.C. § 3142(j) provides that "[n]othing in this section shall be construed as modifying or limiting the

---

[5] The majority refers to the statement in *Carlson v. Landon* that the Bail Clause was adopted by Congress from the English Bill of Rights Act of 1689, and that "[i]n England that clause has never been thought to accord a right to bail in all cases, but merely to provide that bail shall not be excessive in those cases where it is proper to grant bail." A sufficient answer to this meagre argument was made at the time by Justice Black:

"The Eighth Amendment is in the American Bill of Rights of 1789, not the English Bill of Rights of 1689." *Carlson v. Landon* (dissenting opinion). Our Bill of Rights is contained in a written Constitution one of whose purposes is to protect the rights of the people against infringement by the Legislature, and its provisions, whatever their origins, are interpreted in relation to those purposes.

presumption of innocence." But the very pith and purpose of this statute is an abhorrent limitation of the presumption of innocence. The majority's untenable conclusion that the present Act is constitutional arises from a specious denial of the role of the Bail Clause and the Due Process Clause in protecting the invaluable guarantee afforded by the presumption of innocence.

"The principle that there is a presumption of innocence in favor of the accused is the undoubted law, axiomatic and elementary, and its enforcement lies at the foundation of the administration of our criminal law." Our society's belief, reinforced over the centuries, that all are innocent until the state has proven them to be guilty, like the companion principle that guilt must be proved beyond a reasonable doubt, is "implicit in the concept of ordered liberty," and is established beyond legislative contravention in the Due Process Clause.

The statute now before us declares that persons who have been indicted may be detained if a judicial officer finds clear and convincing evidence that they pose a danger to individuals or to the community. The statute does not authorize the government to imprison anyone it has evidence is dangerous; indictment is necessary. But let us suppose that a defendant is indicted and the government shows by clear and convincing evidence that he is dangerous and should be detained pending a trial, at which trial the defendant is acquitted. May the government continue to hold the defendant in detention based upon its showing that he is dangerous? The answer cannot be yes, for that would allow the government to imprison someone for uncommitted crimes based upon "proof" not beyond a reasonable doubt. The result must therefore be that once the indictment has failed, detention cannot continue. But our fundamental principles of justice declare that the defendant is as innocent on the day before his trial as he is on the morning after his acquittal. Under this statute an untried indictment somehow acts to permit a detention, based on other charges, which after an acquittal would be unconstitutional. The conclusion is inescapable that the indictment has been turned into evidence, if not that the defendant is guilty of the crime charged, then that left to his own devices he will soon be guilty of something else.

To be sure, an indictment is not without legal consequences. It establishes that there is probable cause to believe that an offense was committed, and that the defendant committed it. Upon probable cause a warrant for the defendant's arrest may issue; a period of administrative detention may occur before the evidence of probable cause is presented to a neutral magistrate. See *Gerstein v. Pugh*. Once a defendant has been committed for trial he may be detained in custody if the magistrate finds that no conditions of release will prevent him from becoming a fugitive. But in this connection the charging instrument is evidence of nothing more than the fact that there will be a trial, and

> "release before trial is conditioned upon the accused's giving adequate assurance that he will stand trial and submit to sentence if found guilty. Like the ancient practice of securing the oaths of responsible persons to stand as sureties for the accused, the modern practice of requiring a bail

bond or the deposit of a sum of money subject to forfeiture serves as additional assurance of the presence of an accused." *Stack v. Boyle.*[6]

The finding of probable cause conveys power to try, and the power to try imports of necessity the power to assure that the processes of justice will not be evaded or obstructed. "Pretrial detention to prevent future crimes against society at large, however, is not justified by any concern for holding a trial on the charges for which a defendant has been arrested." The detention purportedly authorized by this statute bears no relation to the government's power to try charges supported by a finding of probable cause, and thus the interests it serves are outside the scope of interests which may be considered in weighing the excessiveness of bail under the Eighth Amendment. * * *

IV

* * * Honoring the presumption of innocence is often difficult; sometimes we must pay substantial social costs as a result of our commitment to the values we espouse. But at the end of the day the presumption of innocence protects the innocent; the shortcuts we take with those whom we believe to be guilty injure only those wrongfully accused and, ultimately, ourselves. * * *

I dissent.

JUSTICE STEVENS, dissenting.

There may be times when the government's interest in protecting the safety of the community will justify the brief detention of a person who has not committed any crime. * * * [But] it is clear to me that a pending indictment may not be given any weight in evaluating an individual's risk to the community or the need for immediate detention.

If the evidence of imminent danger is strong enough to warrant emergency detention, it should support that preventive measure regardless of whether the person has been charged, convicted, or acquitted of some other offense. In this case, for example, it is unrealistic to assume that the danger to the community that was present when respondents were at large did not justify their detention before they were indicted, but did require that measure the moment that the grand jury found probable cause to believe they had committed crimes in the past. It is equally unrealistic to assume that the danger will vanish if a jury happens to acquit them. Justice Marshall has demonstrated that the fact of indictment cannot, consistent with the presumption of innocence and the Eighth Amendment's Excessive Bail Clause, be used to create a special class the members of which are, alone, eligible for detention because of future dangerousness.

* * *

---

[6] The majority states that denial of bail in capital cases has traditionally been the rule rather than the exception. And this of course is so, for it has been the considered presumption of generations of judges that a defendant in danger of execution has an extremely strong incentive to flee. If in any particular case the presumed likelihood of flight should be made irrebuttable, it would in all probability violate the Due Process Clause. Thus what the majority perceives as an exception is nothing more than an example of the traditional operation of our system of bail.

CHAPTER 10

THE DECISION WHETHER TO PROSECUTE

■ ■ ■

1. THE DECISION TO PROSECUTE

The charging decision, made by the prosecutor except in minor cases, involves a determination of whether a person should be formally accused of a crime and thus subjected to trial if he does not first plead guilty. Although the charging decision is not inevitably so complex, it often involves these determinations: (i) whether there is sufficient evidence to support a prosecution (which, as a practical matter, the prosecutor will determine by assessing whether the likelihood of conviction is sufficiently strong to justify use of his resources to that end); (ii) if so, whether there are nonetheless reasons for not subjecting the defendant to the criminal process; and (iii) if so, whether nonprosecution should be conditioned upon the defendant's participation in a pretrial diversion program (much like probation, but without an antecedent conviction).

The American prosecutor has traditionally exercised considerable discretion in deciding whether or not to prosecute, that is, in determining whether prosecution is called for in a given case as a matter of enforcement policy. The explanations for this phenomenon most often given are (a) because of legislative "overcriminalization," (b) because of limitations in available enforcement resources; and (c) because of a need to individualize justice beyond that possible under existing crime definitions and sentencing options. This discretion is largely uncontrolled; especially when the prosecutor elects in a particular case *not* to proceed with prosecution, there is seldom available any mechanism by which any dissatisfied person may challenge that decision. When the prosecutor instead decides *in favor* of prosecution, the defendant is obviously motivated to challenge this exercise of discretion and at least sometimes may have a potential legal basis for doing so—such as that his selection for prosecution is a denial of equal protection of the laws or constitutes an impermissible "chilling" of some constitutional right (e.g., freedom of speech). But, as *United States v. Armstrong* teaches, it is very difficult for a defendant to prevail in such a challenge.

UNITED STATES V. ARMSTRONG
517 U.S. 456, 116 S.Ct. 1480, 134 L.Ed.2d 687 (1996).

CHIEF JUSTICE REHNQUIST delivered the opinion of the Court. * * *

In April 1992, respondents were indicted in the United States District Court for the Central District of California on charges of conspiring to possess with intent to distribute more than 50 grams of cocaine base (crack) and conspiring to distribute the same, in violation of 21 U.S.C. §§ 841 and 846, and federal firearms offenses. For three months prior to the indictment, agents of the Federal Bureau of Alcohol, Tobacco, and Firearms and the Narcotics Division of the Inglewood, California, Police Department had infiltrated a suspected crack distribution ring by using three confidential informants. On seven separate occasions during this period, the informants had bought a total of 124.3 grams of crack from respondents and witnessed respondents carrying firearms during the sales. The agents searched the hotel room in which the sales were transacted, arrested respondents Armstrong and Hampton in the room, and found more crack and a loaded gun. The agents later arrested the other respondents as part of the ring.

In response to the indictment, respondents filed a motion for discovery or for dismissal of the indictment, alleging that they were selected for federal prosecution because they are black. In support of their motion, they offered only an affidavit by a "Paralegal Specialist," employed by the Office of the Federal Public Defender representing one of the respondents. The only allegation in the affidavit was that, in every one of the 24 §§ 841 or 846 cases closed by the office during 1991, the defendant was black. Accompanying the affidavit was a "study" listing the 24 defendants, their race, whether they were prosecuted for dealing cocaine as well as crack, and the status of each case.

The Government opposed the discovery motion, arguing, among other things, that there was no evidence or allegation "that the Government has acted unfairly or has prosecuted non-black defendants or failed to prosecute them." The District Court granted the motion. It ordered the Government (1) to provide a list of all cases from the last three years in which the Government charged both cocaine and firearms offenses, (2) to identify the race of the defendants in those cases, (3) to identify what levels of law enforcement were involved in the investigations of those cases, and (4) to explain its criteria for deciding to prosecute those defendants for federal cocaine offenses.

The Government moved for reconsideration of the District Court's discovery order. With this motion it submitted affidavits and other evidence to explain why it had chosen to prosecute respondents and why respondents' study did not support the inference that the Government was singling out blacks for cocaine prosecution. The federal and local agents participating in the case alleged in affidavits that race played no role in their investigation. An Assistant United States Attorney explained in an affidavit that the decision to prosecute met the general criteria for prosecution, because "there was over 100 grams of cocaine base involved, over twice the threshold necessary for a ten year mandatory minimum sentence; there were multiple sales involving multiple defendants, thereby indicating a fairly substantial crack cocaine ring; . . . there were multiple federal firearms violations intertwined with the narcotics trafficking; the overall evidence in the case was extremely strong, including audio and videotapes of defendants; . . . and several of the defendants had criminal histories including narcotics and firearms violations." The Government also submitted sections of a published 1989 Drug Enforcement Administration report which concluded that "[l]arge-scale, interstate trafficking networks controlled by Jamaicans, Haitians and Black street gangs dominate the manufacture and distribution of crack."

In response, one of respondents' attorneys submitted an affidavit alleging that an intake coordinator at a drug treatment center had told her that there are "an equal number of caucasian users and dealers to minority users and dealers." Respondents also submitted an affidavit from a criminal defense attorney alleging that in his experience many nonblacks are prosecuted in state court for crack offenses, and a newspaper article reporting that Federal "crack criminals . . . are being punished far more severely than if they had been caught with powder cocaine, and almost every single one of them is black."

The District Court denied the motion for reconsideration. When the Government indicated it would not comply with the court's discovery order, the court dismissed the case.[2]

A divided three-judge panel of the Court of Appeals for the Ninth Circuit reversed, holding that, because of the proof requirements for a selective-prosecution claim, defendants must "provide a colorable basis for believing that 'others similarly situated have not been prosecuted' " to obtain discovery. The Court of Appeals voted to rehear the case en banc, and the en banc panel affirmed the District Court's order of dismissal, holding that "a defendant is not required to demonstrate that the government has failed to prosecute others who are similarly situated." We granted certiorari to determine the appropriate standard for discovery for a selective-prosecution claim.

Neither the District Court nor the Court of Appeals mentioned Federal Rule of Criminal Procedure 16, which by its terms governs discovery in criminal cases. Both parties now discuss the Rule in their briefs, and respondents contend that it supports the result reached by the Court of Appeals. Rule 16 provides, in pertinent part: "Upon request of the defendant the government shall permit the defendant to inspect and copy or photograph books, papers, documents, photographs, tangible objects, buildings or places, or copies or portions thereof, which are within the possession, custody or control of the government, and which are material to the preparation of the defendant's defense or are intended for use by the government as evidence in chief at the trial, or were obtained from or belong to the defendant." Fed.R.Crim.P. 16(a)(1)(C). Respondents argue that documents "within the possession . . . of the government" that discuss the government's prosecution strategy for cocaine cases are "material" to respondents' selective-prosecution claim. Respondents argue that the Rule applies because any claim that "results in nonconviction" if successful is a "defense" for the Rule's purposes, and a successful selective-prosecution claim has that effect.

We reject this argument, because we conclude that in the context of Rule 16 "the defendant's defense" means the defendant's response to the Government's case-in-chief. While it might be argued that as a general matter, the concept of a "defense" includes any claim that is a "sword," challenging the prosecution's conduct of the case, the term may encompass only the narrower class of "shield"

---

[2]   We have never determined whether dismissal of the indictment, or some other sanction, is the proper remedy if a court determines that a defendant has been the victim of prosecution on the basis of his race. Here, "it was the government itself that suggested dismissal of the indictments to the district court so that an appeal might lie."

claims, which refute the Government's arguments that the defendant committed the crime charged. Rule 16(a)(1)(C) tends to support the "shield-only" reading. If "defense" means an argument in response to the prosecution's case-in-chief, there is a perceptible symmetry between documents "material to the preparation of the defendant's defense," and, in the very next phrase, documents "intended for use by the government as evidence in chief at the trial."

If this symmetry were not persuasive enough, paragraph (a)(2) of Rule 16 establishes beyond peradventure that "defense" in section (a)(1)(C) can refer only to defenses in response to the Government's case-in-chief. Rule 16(a)(2), as relevant here, exempts from defense inspection "reports, memoranda, or other internal government documents made by the attorney for the government or other government agents in connection with the investigation or prosecution of the case."

Under Rule 16(a)(1)(C), a defendant may examine documents material to his defense, but, under Rule 16(a)(2), he may not examine Government work product in connection with his case. If a selective-prosecution claim is a "defense," Rule 16(a)(1)(C) gives the defendant the right to examine Government work product in every prosecution except his own. Because respondents' construction of "defense" creates the anomaly of a defendant's being able to examine all Government work product except the most pertinent, we find their construction implausible. We hold that Rule 16(a)(1)(C) authorizes defendants to examine Government documents material to the preparation of their defense against the Government's case-in-chief, but not to the preparation of selective-prosecution claims. * * *

A selective-prosecution claim is not a defense on the merits to the criminal charge itself, but an independent assertion that the prosecutor has brought the charge for reasons forbidden by the Constitution. Our cases delineating the necessary elements to prove a claim of selective prosecution have taken great pains to explain that the standard is a demanding one. These cases afford a "background presumption" that the showing necessary to obtain discovery should itself be a significant barrier to the litigation of insubstantial claims.

A selective-prosecution claim asks a court to exercise judicial power over a "special province" of the Executive. The Attorney General and United States Attorneys retain " 'broad discretion' " to enforce the Nation's criminal laws. They have this latitude because they are designated by statute as the President's delegates to help him discharge his constitutional responsibility to "take Care that the Laws be faithfully executed." U.S. Const., Art. II, § 3. As a result, "[t]he presumption of regularity supports" their prosecutorial decisions and "in the absence of clear evidence to the contrary, courts presume that they have properly discharged their official duties." In the ordinary case, "so long as the prosecutor has probable cause to believe that the accused committed an offense defined by statute, the decision whether or not to prosecute, and what charge to file or bring before a grand jury, generally rests entirely in his discretion."

Of course, a prosecutor's discretion is "subject to constitutional constraints." One of these constraints, imposed by the equal protection component of the Due Process Clause of the Fifth Amendment, is that the decision whether to prosecute may not be based on "an unjustifiable standard such as race, religion, or other arbitrary classification," *Oyler v. Boles*, 368 U.S. 448, 82 S.Ct. 501, 7 L.Ed.2d 446 (1962). A defendant may demonstrate that the administration of a criminal law is "directed so exclusively against a particular class of persons . . . with a mind so unequal and oppressive" that the system of prosecution amounts to "a practical denial" of equal protection of the law. *Yick Wo v. Hopkins*, 118 U.S. 356 (1886).

In order to dispel the presumption that a prosecutor has not violated equal protection, a criminal defendant must present "clear evidence to the contrary." We explained in *Wayte* [*v. United States*, 470 U.S. 598 (1985)], why courts are "properly hesitant to examine the decision whether to prosecute." Judicial deference to the decisions of these executive officers rests in part on an assessment of the relative competence of prosecutors and courts. "Such factors as the strength of the case, the prosecution's general deterrence value, the Government's enforcement priorities, and the case's relationship to the Government's overall enforcement plan are not readily susceptible to the kind of analysis the courts are competent to undertake." It also stems from a concern not to unnecessarily impair the performance of a core executive constitutional function. "Examining the basis of a prosecution delays the criminal proceeding, threatens to chill law enforcement by subjecting the prosecutor's motives and decisionmaking to outside inquiry, and may undermine prosecutorial effectiveness by revealing the Government's enforcement policy."

The requirements for a selective-prosecution claim draw on "ordinary equal protection standards." The claimant must demonstrate that the federal prosecutorial policy "had a discriminatory effect and that it was motivated by a discriminatory purpose." To establish a discriminatory effect in a race case, the claimant must show that similarly situated individuals of a different race were not prosecuted. This requirement has been established in our case law since *Ah Sin v. Wittman*, 198 U.S. 500 (1905). Ah Sin, a subject of China, petitioned a California state court for a writ of habeas corpus, seeking discharge from imprisonment under a San Francisco county ordinance prohibiting persons from setting up gambling tables in rooms barricaded to stop police from entering. He alleged in his habeas petition "that the ordinance is enforced 'solely and exclusively against persons of the Chinese race and not otherwise.'" We rejected his contention that this averment made out a claim under the Equal Protection Clause, because it did not allege "that the conditions and practices to which the ordinance was directed did not exist exclusively among the Chinese, or that there were other offenders against the ordinance than the Chinese as to whom it was not enforced."

The similarly situated requirement does not make a selective-prosecution claim impossible to prove. Twenty years before *Ah Sin*, we invalidated an ordinance, also adopted by San Francisco, that prohibited the operation of laundries in wooden buildings. *Yick Wo*, supra. The plaintiff in error successfully demonstrated that the ordinance was applied against Chinese nationals but not against other laundry-shop operators. The authorities had denied the applications of 200 Chinese subjects for permits to operate shops in wooden buildings, but granted the applications of 80 individuals who were not Chinese subjects to operate laundries in wooden buildings "under similar conditions." We explained in *Ah Sin* why the similarly situated requirement is necessary: "No latitude of intention should be indulged in a case like this. There should be certainty to every intent.

Plaintiff in error seeks to set aside a criminal law of the State, not on the ground that it is unconstitutional on its face, not that it is discriminatory in tendency and ultimate actual operation as the ordinance was which was passed on in the *Yick Wo* case, but that it was made so by the manner of its administration. This is a matter of proof, and no fact should be omitted to make it out completely, when the power of a Federal court is invoked to interfere with the course of criminal justice of a State." Although *Ah Sin* involved federal review of a state conviction, we think a similar rule applies where the power of a federal court is invoked to challenge an exercise of one of the core powers of the Executive Branch of the Federal Government, the power to prosecute.[a] * * *

Having reviewed the requirements to prove a selective-prosecution claim, we turn to the showing necessary to obtain discovery in support of such a claim. If discovery is ordered, the Government must assemble from its own files documents which might corroborate or refute the defendant's claim. Discovery thus imposes many of the costs present when the Government must respond to a prima facie case of selective prosecution. It will divert prosecutors' resources and may disclose the Government's prosecutorial strategy. The justifications for a rigorous standard for the elements of a selective-prosecution claim thus require a correspondingly rigorous standard for discovery in aid of such a claim.

The parties, and the Courts of Appeals which have considered the requisite showing to establish entitlement to discovery, describe this showing with a variety of phrases, like "colorable basis," "substantial threshold showing," "substantial and concrete basis," or "reasonable likelihood." However, the many labels for this showing conceal the degree of consensus about the evidence necessary to meet it. The Courts of Appeals "require some evidence tending to show the existence of the essential elements of the defense," discriminatory effect and discriminatory intent.

In this case we consider what evidence constitutes "some evidence tending to show the existence" of the discriminatory effect element. The Court of Appeals held that a defendant may establish a colorable basis for discriminatory effect without evidence that the Government has failed to prosecute others who are similarly situated to the defendant. We think it was mistaken in this view. The vast majority of the Courts of Appeals require the defendant to produce some evidence that similarly situated defendants of other races could have been prosecuted, but were not, and this requirement is consistent with our equal protection case law. * * *[3]

---

[a]   At this juncture, respondents urged that *Batson v. Kentucky* [p. 828] "cut against any absolute requirement that there be a showing of failure to prosecute similarly situated individuals", but the Court responded that *Batson* was different: "During jury selection, the entire res gestae take place in front of the trial judge. Because the judge has before him the entire venire, he is well situated to detect whether a challenge to the seating of one juror is part of a 'pattern' of singling out members of a single race for peremptory challenges. He is in a position to discern whether a challenge to a black juror has evidentiary significance; the significance may differ if the venire consists mostly of blacks or of whites. Similarly, if the defendant makes out a prima facie case, the prosecutor is called upon to justify only decisions made in the very case then before the court. The trial judge need not review prosecutorial conduct in relation to other venires in other cases."

[3]   We reserve the question whether a defendant must satisfy the similarly situated requirement in a case "involving direct admissions by [prosecutors] of discriminatory purpose."

The Court of Appeals reached its decision in part because it started "with the presumption that people of all races commit all types of crimes—not with the premise that any type of crime is the exclusive province of any particular racial or ethnic group." It cited no authority for this proposition, which seems contradicted by the most recent statistics of the United States Sentencing Commission. Those statistics show that: More than 90% of the persons sentenced in 1994 for crack cocaine trafficking were black; 93.4% of convicted LSD dealers were white; and 91% of those convicted for pornography or prostitution were white. Presumptions at war with presumably reliable statistics have no proper place in the analysis of this issue.

The Court of Appeals also expressed concern about the "evidentiary obstacles defendants face." But all of its sister Circuits that have confronted the issue have required that defendants produce some evidence of differential treatment of similarly situated members of other races or protected classes. In the present case, if the claim of selective prosecution were well founded, it should not have been an insuperable task to prove that persons of other races were being treated differently than respondents. For instance, respondents could have investigated whether similarly situated persons of other races were prosecuted by the State of California, were known to federal law enforcement officers, but were not prosecuted in federal court. We think the required threshold—a credible showing of different treatment of similarly situated persons—adequately balances the Government's interest in vigorous prosecution and the defendant's interest in avoiding selective prosecution.

In the case before us, respondents' "study" did not constitute "some evidence tending to show the existence of the essential elements of" a selective-prosecution claim. The study failed to identify individuals who were not black, could have been prosecuted for the offenses for which respondents were charged, but were not so prosecuted. This omission was not remedied by respondents' evidence in opposition to the Government's motion for reconsideration. The newspaper article, which discussed the discriminatory effect of federal drug sentencing laws, was not relevant to an allegation of discrimination in decisions to prosecute. Respondents' affidavits, which recounted one attorney's conversation with a drug treatment center employee and the experience of another attorney defending drug prosecutions in state court, recounted hearsay and reported personal conclusions based on anecdotal evidence. The judgment of the Court of Appeals is therefore reversed, and the case is remanded for proceedings consistent with this opinion.

It is so ordered.[b]

---

[b] Justice Souter, concurring, joined the Court's discussion of Rule 16 "only to the extent of its application to the issue in this case." Justice Ginsburg, concurring, emphasized that the "Court was not called upon to decide here whether Rule 16(a)(1)(C) applies in any other context, for example, to affirmative defenses unrelated to the merits." Justice Breyer, concurring in part and concurring in the judgment, though concluding that "neither the alleged 'symmetry' in the structure of Rule 16(a)(1)(C), nor the work product exception of Rule 16(a)(2), supports the majority's limitation of discovery under Rule 16(a)(1)(C) to documents related to the government's 'case-in-chief,'" concluded that the defendants' discovery request failed to satisfy the Rule's requirement that the discovery be "material to the preparation of the defendant's defense."

JUSTICE STEVENS, dissenting. * * *

The Court correctly concludes that in this case the facts presented to the District Court in support of respondents' claim that they had been singled out for prosecution because of their race were not sufficient to prove that defense. Moreover, I agree with the Court that their showing was not strong enough to give them a right to discovery, either under Rule 16 or under the District Court's inherent power to order discovery in appropriate circumstances. Like Chief Judge Wallace of the Court of Appeals, however, I am persuaded that the District Judge did not abuse her discretion when she concluded that the factual showing was sufficiently disturbing to require some response from the United States Attorney's Office. Perhaps the discovery order was broader than necessary, but I cannot agree with the Court's apparent conclusion that no inquiry was permissible.

The District Judge's order should be evaluated in light of three circumstances that underscore the need for judicial vigilance over certain types of drug prosecutions. First, the Anti-Drug Abuse Act of 1986 and subsequent legislation established a regime of extremely high penalties for the possession and distribution of so-called "crack" cocaine. Those provisions treat one gram of crack as the equivalent of 100 grams of powder cocaine. The distribution of 50 grams of crack is thus punishable by the same mandatory minimum sentence of 10 years in prison that applies to the distribution of 5,000 grams of powder cocaine. The Sentencing Guidelines extend this ratio to penalty levels above the mandatory minimums: for any given quantity of crack, the guideline range is the same as if the offense had involved 100 times that amount in powder cocaine. These penalties result in sentences for crack offenders that average three to eight times longer than sentences for comparable powder offenders.

Second, the disparity between the treatment of crack cocaine and powder cocaine is matched by the disparity between the severity of the punishment imposed by federal law and that imposed by state law for the same conduct. For a variety of reasons, often including the absence of mandatory minimums, the existence of parole, and lower baseline penalties, terms of imprisonment for drug offenses tend to be substantially lower in state systems than in the federal system. The difference is especially marked in the case of crack offenses. The majority of States draw no distinction between types of cocaine in their penalty schemes; of those that do, none has established as stark a differential as the Federal Government. For example, if respondent Hampton is found guilty, his federal sentence might be as long as a mandatory life term. Had he been tried in state court, his sentence could have been as short as 12 years, less worktime credits of half that amount.

Finally, it is undisputed that the brunt of the elevated federal penalties falls heavily on blacks. While 65% of the persons who have used crack are white, in 1993 they represented only 4% of the federal offenders convicted of trafficking in crack. Eighty-eight percent of such defendants were black. During the first 18 months of full guideline implementation, the sentencing disparity between black and white defendants grew from preguideline levels: blacks on average received sentences over 40% longer than whites. Those figures represent a major threat to the integrity of federal sentencing reform, whose main purpose was the elimination of disparity (especially racial) in sentencing. The Sentencing Commission acknowledges that the heightened crack penalties are a "primary cause of the growing disparity between sentences for Black and White federal defendants."

The extraordinary severity of the imposed penalties and the troubling racial patterns of enforcement give rise to a special concern about the fairness of charging practices for crack offenses. Evidence tending to prove that black defendants charged with distribution of crack in the Central District of California are prosecuted in federal court, whereas members of other races charged with similar offenses are prosecuted in state court, warrants close scrutiny by the federal judges in that District. In my view, the District Judge, who has sat on both the federal and the state benches in Los Angeles, acted well within her discretion to call for the development of facts that would demonstrate what standards, if any, governed the choice of forum where similarly situated offenders are prosecuted.

Respondents submitted a study showing that of all cases involving crack offenses that were closed by the Federal Public Defender's Office in 1991, 24 out of 24 involved black defendants. To supplement this evidence, they submitted affidavits from two of the attorneys in the defense team. The first reported a statement from an intake coordinator at a local drug treatment center that, in his experience, an equal number of crack users and dealers were caucasian as belonged to minorities. The second was from David R. Reed, counsel for respondent Armstrong. Reed was both an active court-appointed attorney in the Central District of California and one of the directors of the leading association of criminal defense lawyers who practice before the Los Angeles County courts. Reed stated that he did not recall "ever handling a [crack] cocaine case involving non-black defendants" in federal court, nor had he even heard of one. He further stated that "[t]here are many crack cocaine sales cases prosecuted in state court that do involve racial groups other than blacks."

The majority discounts the probative value of the affidavits, claiming that they recounted "hearsay" and reported "personal conclusions based on anecdotal evidence." But the Reed affidavit plainly contained more than mere hearsay; Reed offered information based on his own extensive experience in both federal and state courts. Given the breadth of his background, he was well qualified to compare the practices of federal and state prosecutors. In any event, the Government never objected to the admission of either affidavit on hearsay or any other grounds. It was certainly within the District Court's discretion to credit the affidavits of two members of the bar of that Court, at least one of whom had presumably acquired a reputation by his frequent appearances there, and both of whose statements were made on pains of perjury.

The criticism that the affidavits were based on "anecdotal evidence" is also unpersuasive. I thought it was agreed that defendants do not need to prepare sophisticated statistical studies in order to receive mere discovery in cases like this one. Certainly evidence based on a drug counselor's personal observations or on an attorney's practice in two sets of courts, state and federal, can "ten[d] to show the existence" of a selective prosecution.

Even if respondents failed to carry their burden of showing that there were individuals who were not black but who could have been prosecuted in federal court for the same offenses, it does not follow that the District Court abused its discretion in ordering discovery. There can be no doubt that such individuals exist, and indeed the Government has never denied the same. In those circumstances, I fail to see why the District Court was unable to take judicial notice of this obvious fact and demand information from the Government's files to support or refute respondents' evidence. The presumption that some whites are prosecuted in state court is not "contradicted" by the statistics the majority cites, which show only that high percentages of blacks are convicted of certain federal crimes, while high percentages of whites are convicted of other federal crimes. Those figures are entirely consistent with the allegation of selective prosecution. The relevant comparison, rather, would be with the percentages of blacks and whites who commit those crimes. But, as discussed above, in the case of crack far greater numbers of whites are believed guilty of using the substance. The District Court, therefore, was entitled to find the evidence before her significant and to require some explanation from the Government.[6]

In sum, I agree with the Sentencing Commission that "[w]hile the exercise of discretion by prosecutors and investigators has an impact on sentences in almost all cases to some extent, because of the 100-to-1 quantity ratio and federal mandatory minimum penalties, discretionary decisions in cocaine cases often have dramatic effects."[7] The severity of the penalty heightens both the danger of arbitrary enforcement and the need for careful scrutiny of any colorable claim of discriminatory enforcement. In this case, the evidence was sufficiently disturbing to persuade the District Judge to order discovery that might help explain the conspicuous racial pattern of cases before her Court. I cannot accept the majority's conclusion that the District Judge either exceeded her power or abused her discretion when she did so. I therefore respectfully dissent.

2. SELECTION OF THE CHARGE

If the prosecutor has decided upon prosecution, there often remains the question of what the charge should be. Sometimes this is simply a matter of

---

[6]   Also telling was the Government's response to respondents' evidentiary showing. It submitted a list of more than 3,500 defendants who had been charged with federal narcotics violations over the previous 3 years. It also offered the names of 11 nonblack defendants whom it had prosecuted for crack offenses. All 11, however, were members of other racial or ethnic minorities. The District Court was authorized to draw adverse inferences from the Government's inability to produce a single example of a white defendant, especially when the very purpose of its exercise was to allay the Court's concerns about the evidence of racially selective prosecutions. As another court has said: "Statistics are not, of course, the whole answer, but nothing is as emphatic as zero. . . ."

[7]   For this and other reasons, the Sentencing Commission in its Special Report to Congress "strongly recommend[ed] against a 100 to 1 quantity ratio." The Commission shortly thereafter, by a 4 to 3 vote, amended the guidelines so as to equalize the treatment of crack and other forms of cocaine, and proposed modification of the statutory mandatory minimum penalties for crack offenses. In October 1995, Congress overrode the Sentencing Commission's guideline amendments. Nevertheless, Congress at the same time directed the Commission to submit recommendations regarding changes to the statutory and guideline penalties for cocaine distribution, including specifically "revision of the drug quantity ratio of crack cocaine to powder cocaine."

whether the charge should be of a greater or lesser crime—for example, felony burglary versus misdemeanor breaking and entering. On other occasions, the prosecutor must determine whether to charge the defendant with more than one offense, either because the defendant has committed a series of offenses (e.g., a number of burglaries) over time or because the defendant violated more than one statute during a single course of conduct. In this third situation, the defendant's challenge, as in *United States v. Batchelder,* may be grounded primarily in the contention that the applicable statutes improperly overlap. More generally, as in the second case in this section, *United States v. Goodwin,* a defendant might challenge the prosecutor's charge selection decision on the ground of actual or apparent vindictiveness.

UNITED STATES V. BATCHELDER

442 U.S. 114, 99 S.Ct. 2198, 60 L.Ed.2d 755 (1979).

JUSTICE MARSHALL delivered the opinion of the Court.

At issue in this case are two overlapping provisions of the Omnibus Crime Control and Safe Streets Act of 1968 (the Omnibus Act). Both prohibit convicted felons from receiving firearms, but each authorizes different maximum penalties. We must determine whether a defendant convicted of the offense carrying the greater penalty may be sentenced only under the more lenient provision when his conduct violates both statutes.

Respondent, a previously convicted felon, was found guilty of receiving a firearm that had traveled in interstate commerce, in violation of 18 U.S.C. § 922(h).[2] The District Court sentenced him under 18 U.S.C. § 924(a) to five years' imprisonment, the maximum term authorized for violation of § 922(h).

The Court of Appeals affirmed the conviction but, by a divided vote, remanded for resentencing. The majority recognized that respondent had been indicted and convicted under § 922(h) and that § 924(a) permits five years' imprisonment for such violations. However, noting that the substantive elements of § 922(h) and 18 U.S.C.App. § 1202(a) are identical as applied to a convicted felon who unlawfully receives a firearm, the court interpreted the Omnibus Act to allow no more than the two-year maximum sentence provided by § 1202(a).[4] * * *

---

[2]   In pertinent part, 18 U.S.C. § 922(h) provides:

"It shall be unlawful for any person—

"(1) who is under indictment for, or who has been convicted in any court of, a crime punishable by imprisonment for a term exceeding one year;

"(2) who is a fugitive from justice;

"(3) who is an unlawful user of or addicted to marihuana or any depressant or stimulant drug * * * or narcotic drug * * *; or

"(4) who has been adjudicated as a mental defective or who has been committed to any mental institution;

"to receive any firearm or ammunition which has been shipped or transported in interstate or foreign commerce."

[4]   Section 1202(a) states:

"Any person who—

This Court has previously noted the partial redundancy of §§ 922(h) and 1202(a), both as to the conduct they proscribe and the individuals they reach. However, we find nothing in the language structure or legislative history of the Omnibus Act to suggest that because of this overlap, a defendant convicted under § 922(h) may be imprisoned for no more than the maximum term specified in § 1202(a). As we read the Act, each substantive statute, in conjunction with its own sentencing provision, operates independently of the other. * * *

In resolving the statutory question, the majority below expressed "serious doubts about the constitutionality of two statutes that provide different penalties for identical conduct." Specifically, the court suggested that the statutes might (1) be void for vagueness, (2) implicate "due process and equal protection interest[s] in avoiding excessive prosecutorial discretion and in obtaining equal justice," and (3) constitute an impermissible delegation of congressional authority. We find no constitutional infirmities.

It is a fundamental tenet of due process that "[n]o one may be required at peril of life, liberty or property to speculate as to the meaning of penal statutes." A criminal statute is therefore invalid if it "fails to give a person of ordinary intelligence fair notice that his contemplated conduct is forbidden." So too, vague sentencing provisions may pose constitutional questions if they do not state with sufficient clarity the consequences of violating a given criminal statute.

The provisions in issue here, however, unambiguously specify the activity proscribed and the penalties available upon conviction. That this particular conduct may violate both Titles does not detract from the notice afforded by each. Although the statutes create uncertainty as to which crime may be charged and therefore what penalties may be imposed, they do so to no greater extent than would a single statute authorizing various alternative punishments. So long as overlapping criminal provisions clearly define the conduct prohibited and the punishment authorized, the notice requirements of the Due Process Clause are satisfied.

This Court has long recognized that when an act violates more than one criminal statute, the Government may prosecute under either so long as it does not discriminate against any class of defendants. Whether to prosecute and what charge to file or bring before a grand jury are decisions that generally rest in the prosecutor's discretion.

The Court of Appeals acknowledged this "settled rule" allowing prosecutorial choice. Nevertheless, the court distinguished overlapping statutes with identical

---

"(1) has been convicted by a court of the United States or of a State or any political subdivision thereof of a felony, or

"(2) has been discharged from the Armed Forces under dishonorable conditions, or

"(3) has been adjudged by a court of the United States or of a State or any political subdivision thereof of being mentally incompetent, or

"(4) having been a citizen of the United States has renounced his citizenship, or

"(5) being an alien is illegally or unlawfully in the United States,

"and who receives, possesses, or transports in commerce or affecting commerce, after the date of enactment of this Act, any firearm shall be fined not more than $10,000 or imprisoned for not more than two years, or both." 18 U.S.C.App. § 1202(a).

standards of proof from provisions that vary in some particular. In the court's view, when two statutes prohibit "exactly the same conduct," the prosecutor's "selection of which of two penalties to apply" would be "unfettered." Because such prosecutorial discretion could produce "unequal justice," the court expressed doubt that this form of legislative redundancy was constitutional. We find this analysis factually and legally unsound.

Contrary to the Court of Appeals' assertions, a prosecutor's discretion to choose between §§ 922(h) and 1202(a) is not "unfettered." Selectivity in the enforcement of criminal laws is, of course, subject to constitutional constraints.[9] And a decision to proceed under § 922(h) does not empower the Government to predetermine ultimate criminal sanctions. Rather, it merely enables the sentencing judge to impose a longer prison sentence than § 1202(a) would permit and precludes him from imposing the greater fine authorized by § 1202(a). More importantly, there is no appreciable difference between the discretion a prosecutor exercises when deciding whether to charge under one of two statutes with different elements and the discretion he exercises when choosing one of two statutes with identical elements. In the former situation, once he determines that the proof will support conviction under either statute, his decision is indistinguishable from the one he faces in the latter context. The prosecutor may be influenced by the penalties available upon conviction, but this fact standing alone does not give rise to a violation of the Equal Protection or Due Process Clauses. Just as a defendant has no constitutional right to elect which of two applicable federal statutes shall be the basis of his indictment and prosecution neither is he entitled to choose the penalty scheme under which he will be sentenced.

Approaching the problem of prosecutorial discretion from a slightly different perspective, the Court of Appeals postulated that the statutes might impermissibly delegate to the Executive Branch the legislature's responsibility to fix criminal penalties. We do not agree. The provisions at issue plainly demarcate the range of penalties that prosecutors and judges may seek and impose. In light of that specificity, the power that Congress has delegated to those officials is no broader than the authority they routinely exercise in enforcing the criminal laws. Having informed the courts, prosecutors and defendants of the permissible punishment alternatives available under each Title, Congress has fulfilled its duty.

Accordingly, the judgment of the Court of Appeals is reversed.

UNITED STATES v. GOODWIN
457 U.S. 368, 102 S.Ct. 2485, 73 L.Ed.2d 74 (1982).

JUSTICE STEVENS delivered the opinion of the Court. * * *

Respondent Goodwin was stopped for speeding by a United States Park Policeman on the Baltimore-Washington Parkway. Goodwin emerged from his car to talk to the policeman. After a brief discussion, the officer noticed a clear plastic

---

9   The Equal Protection Clause prohibits selective enforcement "based upon an unjustifiable standard such as race, religion, or other arbitrary classification." Respondent does not allege that his prosecution was motivated by improper considerations.

bag underneath the armrest next to the driver's seat of Goodwin's car. The officer asked Goodwin to return to his car and to raise the armrest. Respondent did so, but as he raised the armrest he placed the car into gear and accelerated rapidly. The car struck the officer, knocking him first onto the back of the car and then onto the highway. The policeman returned to his car, but Goodwin eluded him in a highspeed chase.

The following day, the officer filed a complaint in the District Court charging respondent with several misdemeanor and petty offenses, including assault. Goodwin was arrested and arraigned before a United States Magistrate. The Magistrate set a date for trial, but respondent fled the jurisdiction. Three years later Goodwin was found in custody in Virginia and was returned to Maryland.

Upon his return, respondent's case was assigned to an attorney from the Department of Justice, who was detailed temporarily to try petty crime and misdemeanor cases before the Magistrate. The attorney did not have authority to try felony cases or to seek indictments from the grand jury. Respondent initiated plea negotiations with the prosecutor, but later advised the Government that he did not wish to plead guilty and desired a trial by jury in the District Court.[1]

The case was transferred to the District Court and responsibility for the prosecution was assumed by an Assistant United States Attorney. Approximately six weeks later, after reviewing the case and discussing it with several parties, the prosecutor obtained a four-count indictment charging respondent with one felony count of forcibly assaulting a federal officer and three related counts arising from the same incident.[2] A jury convicted respondent on the felony count and on one misdemeanor count.

Respondent moved to set aside the verdict on the ground of prosecutorial vindictiveness, contending that the indictment on the felony charge gave rise to an impermissible appearance of retaliation. The District Court denied the motion, finding that "the prosecutor in this case has adequately dispelled any appearance of retaliatory intent."

Although the Court of Appeals readily concluded that "the prosecutor did not act with actual vindictiveness in seeking a felony indictment," it nevertheless reversed. Relying on our decisions in *North Carolina v. Pearce*, [395 U.S. 711 (1969)], and *Blackledge v. Perry*, [417 U.S. 21 (1974)], the court held that the Due Process Clause of the Fifth Amendment prohibits the Government from bringing more serious charges against a defendant after he has invoked his right to a jury trial, unless the prosecutor comes forward with objective evidence to show that the increased charges could not have been brought before the defendant exercised his

---

[1] At that time, there was no statutory provision allowing a trial by jury before a magistrate.

[2] By affidavit, the Assistant United States Attorney later set forth his reasons for this action:

(1) he considered respondent's conduct on the date in question to be a serious violation of law, (2) respondent had a lengthy history of violent crime, (3) the prosecutor considered respondent's conduct to be related to major narcotics transactions, (4) the prosecutor believed that respondent had committed perjury at his preliminary hearing, and (5) respondent had failed to appear for trial as originally scheduled. The Government attorney stated that his decision to seek a felony indictment was not motivated in any way by Goodwin's request for a jury trial in District Court.

rights. Because the court believed that the circumstances surrounding the felony indictment gave rise to a genuine risk of retaliation, it adopted a legal presumption designed to spare courts the "unseemly task" of probing the actual motives of the prosecutor. * * *

In *North Carolina v. Pearce,* the Court held that neither the Double Jeopardy Clause nor the Equal Protection Clause prohibits a trial judge from imposing a harsher sentence on retrial after a criminal defendant successfully attacks an initial conviction on appeal. The Court stated, however, that "[i]t can hardly be doubted that it would be a flagrant violation [of the Due Process Clause] of the Fourteenth Amendment for a state trial court to follow an announced practice of imposing a heavier sentence upon every reconvicted defendant for the explicit purpose of punishing the defendant for his having succeeded in getting his original conviction set aside." The Court continued:

> "Due process of law, then, requires that vindictiveness against a defendant for having successfully attacked his first conviction must play no part in the sentence he receives after a new trial. And since the fear of such vindictiveness may unconstitutionally deter a defendant's exercise of the right to appeal or collaterally attack his first conviction, due process also requires that a defendant be freed of apprehension of such a retaliatory motivation on the part of the sentencing judge."

In order to assure the absence of such a motivation, the Court concluded:

> "[W]henever a judge imposes a more severe sentence upon a defendant after a new trial, the reasons for his doing so must affirmatively appear. Those reasons must be based upon objective information concerning identifiable conduct on the part of the defendant occurring after the time of the original sentencing proceeding. And the factual data upon which the increased sentence is based must be made part of the record, so that the constitutional legitimacy of the increased sentence may be fully reviewed on appeal."

In sum, the Court applied a presumption of vindictiveness, which may be overcome only by objective information in the record justifying the increased sentence.[a]

---

[a]   Stating that "the reach of *Pearce* is best captured" by this sentence, the Court in *Texas v. McCullough,* 475 U.S. 134 (1986), said of the above quotation from *Pearce:* "This language, however, was never intended to describe exhaustively all of the possible circumstances in which a sentence increase could be justified. Restricting justifications for a sentence increase to *only* 'events that occurred subsequent to the original sentencing proceedings' could in some circumstances lead to absurd results. The Solicitor General provides the following hypothetical example:

'Suppose * * * that a defendant is convicted of burglary, a non-violent, and apparently first, offense. He is sentenced to a short prison term or perhaps placed on probation. Following a successful appeal and a conviction on retrial, it is learned that the defendant has been using an alias and in fact has a long criminal record that includes other burglaries, several armed robbery convictions, and a conviction for murder committed in the course of a burglary. None of the reasons underlying *Pearce* in any way justifies the perverse result that the defendant receive no greater sentence in light of this information than he originally received when he was thought to be a first offender.'

We agree with the Solicitor General and find nothing in *Pearce* that would require such a bizarre conclusion."

In *Blackledge v. Perry,* the Court confronted the problem of increased punishment upon retrial after appeal in a setting different from that considered in *Pearce.* Perry was convicted of assault in an inferior court having exclusive jurisdiction for the trial of misdemeanors. The court imposed a 6-month sentence. Under North Carolina law, Perry had an absolute right to a trial *de novo* in the Superior Court, which possessed felony jurisdiction. After Perry filed his notice of appeal, the prosecutor obtained a felony indictment charging him with assault with a deadly weapon. Perry pleaded guilty to the felony and was sentenced to a term of five to seven years in prison.

In reviewing Perry's felony conviction and increased sentence, this Court first stated the essence of the holdings in *Pearce* and the cases that had followed it:

> "The lesson that emerges from *Pearce* is that the Due Process Clause is not offended by all possibilities of increased punishment upon retrial after appeal, but only by those that pose a realistic likelihood of 'vindictiveness.' "

The Court held that the opportunities for vindictiveness in the situation before it were such "as to impel the conclusion that due process of law requires a rule analogous to that of the *Pearce* case." It explained:

> "A prosecutor clearly has a considerable stake in discouraging convicted misdemeanants from appealing and thus obtaining a trial *de novo* in the Superior Court, since such an appeal will clearly require increased expenditures of prosecutorial resources before the defendant's conviction becomes final, and may even result in a formerly convicted defendant's going free. And, if the prosecutor has the means readily at hand to discourage such appeals—by 'upping the ante' through a felony indictment whenever a convicted misdemeanant pursues his statutory appellate remedy—the State can insure that only the most hardy defendants will brave the hazards of a *de novo* trial."

The Court emphasized in *Blackledge* that it did not matter that no evidence was present that the prosecutor had acted in bad faith or with malice in seeking the felony indictment. As in *Pearce,* the Court held that the likelihood of vindictiveness justified a presumption that would free defendants of apprehension of such a retaliatory motivation on the part of the prosecutor.[8] * * *

In *Bordenkircher v. Hayes* [p. 758], the Court for the first time considered an allegation of vindictiveness that arose in a pretrial setting. In that case the Court held that the Due Process Clause of the Fourteenth Amendment did not prohibit a

---

Marshall, J., joined by Blackmun and Stevens, JJ., dissenting, objected: "There is neither any reason nor any need for us to believe that dishonest and unconstitutionally vindictive judges actually hold sway in American courtrooms * * *. The message of *Pearce* is that the fear of such vindictiveness is real enough. And a defendant plagued by such an apprehension is likely to take small comfort in any presumption of vindictiveness established for his benefit if the means of rebutting that presumption will always be within the easy reach of the judge who will sentence him should the challenge to his conviction prove unsuccessful."

[8]   The presumption again could be overcome by objective evidence justifying the prosecutor's action. The Court noted: "This would clearly be a different case if the State had shown that it was impossible to proceed on the more serious charge at the outset."

prosecutor from carrying out a threat, made during plea negotiations, to bring additional charges against an accused who refused to plead guilty to the offense with which he was originally charged. * * *

The outcome in *Bordenkircher* was mandated by this Court's acceptance of plea negotiation as a legitimate process. In declining to apply a presumption of vindictiveness, the Court recognized that "additional" charges obtained by a prosecutor could not necessarily be characterized as an impermissible "penalty." Since charges brought in an original indictment may be abandoned by the prosecutor in the course of plea negotiation—in often what is clearly a "benefit" to the defendant—changes in the charging decision that occur in the context of plea negotiation are an inaccurate measure of improper prosecutorial "vindictiveness." An initial indictment—from which the prosecutor embarks on a course of plea negotiation—does not necessarily define the extent of the legitimate interest in prosecution. For just as a prosecutor may forgo legitimate charges already brought in an effort to save the time and expense of trial, a prosecutor may file additional charges if an initial expectation that a defendant would plead guilty to lesser charges proves unfounded.

This case, like *Bordenkircher,* arises from a pretrial decision to modify the charges against the defendant. Unlike *Bordenkircher,* however, there is no evidence in this case that could give rise to a claim of *actual* vindictiveness; the prosecutor never suggested that the charge was brought to influence the respondent's conduct. The conviction in this case may be reversed only if a *presumption* of vindictiveness—applicable in all cases—is warranted.

There is good reason to be cautious before adopting an inflexible presumption of prosecutorial vindictiveness in a pretrial setting. In the course of preparing a case for trial, the prosecutor may uncover additional information that suggests a basis for further prosecution or he simply may come to realize that information possessed by the State has a broader significance. At this stage of the proceedings, the prosecutor's assessment of the proper extent of prosecution may not have crystallized. In contrast, once a trial begins—and certainly by the time a conviction has been obtained—it is much more likely that the State has discovered and assessed all of the information against an accused and has made a determination, on the basis of that information, of the extent to which he should be prosecuted. Thus, a change in the charging decision made after an initial trial is completed is much more likely to be improperly motivated than is a pretrial decision.

In addition, a defendant before trial is expected to invoke procedural rights that inevitably impose some "burden" on the prosecutor. Defense counsel routinely file pretrial motions to suppress evidence; to challenge the sufficiency and form of an indictment; to plead an affirmative defense; to request psychiatric services; to obtain access to government files; to be tried by jury. It is unrealistic to assume that a prosecutor's probable response to such motions is to seek to penalize and to deter. The invocation of procedural rights is an integral part of the adversary process in which our criminal justice system operates.

Thus, the timing of the prosecutor's action in this case suggests that a presumption of vindictiveness is not warranted. A prosecutor should remain free before trial to exercise the broad discretion entrusted to him to determine the extent of the societal interest in prosecution. An initial decision should not freeze future conduct. As we made clear in *Bordenkircher,* the initial charges filed by a prosecutor may not reflect the extent to which an individual is legitimately subject to prosecution.

The nature of the right asserted by the respondent confirms that a presumption of vindictiveness is not warranted in this case. After initially expressing an interest in plea negotiation, respondent decided not to plead guilty and requested a trial by jury in District Court. In doing so, he forced the Government to bear the burdens and uncertainty of a trial. This Court in *Bordenkircher* made clear that the mere fact that a defendant refuses to plead guilty and forces the government to prove its case is insufficient to warrant a presumption that subsequent changes in the charging decision are unjustified. Respondent argues that such a presumption is warranted in this case, however, because he not only requested a trial—he requested a trial by jury.

We cannot agree. The distinction between a bench trial and a jury trial does not compel a special presumption of prosecutorial vindictiveness whenever additional charges are brought after a jury is demanded. To be sure, a jury trial is more burdensome than a bench trial. The defendant may challenge the selection of the venire; the jury itself must be impaneled; witnesses and arguments must be prepared more carefully to avoid the danger of a mistrial. These matters are much less significant, however, than the facts that before either a jury or a judge the State must present its full case against the accused and the defendant is entitled to offer a full defense. As compared to the complete trial *de novo* at issue in *Blackledge,* a jury trial—as opposed to a bench trial—does not require duplicative expenditures of prosecutorial resources before a final judgment may be obtained. Moreover, unlike the trial judge in *Pearce,* no party is asked "to do over what it thought it had already done correctly." A prosecutor has no "personal stake" in a bench trial and thus no reason to engage in "self-vindication" upon a defendant's request for a jury trial. Perhaps most importantly, the institutional bias against the retrial of a decided question that supported the decisions in *Pearce* and *Blackledge* simply has no counterpart in this case.

There is an opportunity for vindictiveness, [but] a mere opportunity for vindictiveness is insufficient to justify the imposition of a prophylactic rule. As *Blackledge* makes clear, "the Due Process Clause is not offended by all possibilities of increased punishment * * * but only by those that pose a realistic likelihood of 'vindictiveness.'" The possibility that a prosecutor would respond to a defendant's pretrial demand for a jury trial by bringing charges not in the public interest that could be explained only as a penalty imposed on the defendant is so *unlikely* that a presumption of vindictiveness certainly is not warranted.

In declining to apply a presumption of vindictiveness, we of course do not foreclose the possibility that a defendant in an appropriate case might prove objectively that the prosecutor's charging decision was motivated by a desire to punish him for doing something that the law plainly allowed him to do. * * *

JUSTICE BLACKMUN, concurring in the judgment.

* * * I find no support in our prior cases for any distinction between pretrial and post-trial vindictiveness. * * *

[T]he Due Process Clause does not deprive a prosecutor of the flexibility to add charges after a defendant has decided not to plead guilty and has elected a jury trial in District Court—so long as the adjustment is based on "objective information concerning identifiable conduct on the part of the defendant occurring after the time of the original" charging decision. In addition, I believe that the prosecutor adequately explains an increased charge by pointing to objective information that he could not reasonably have been aware of at the time charges were initially filed.

Because I find that the Assistant United States Attorney's explanation for seeking a felony indictment satisfies these standards, I conclude that the Government has dispelled the appearance of vindictiveness and, therefore, that the imposition of additional charges did not violate respondent's due process rights. Accordingly, I concur in the judgment.

JUSTICE BRENNAN, with whom JUSTICE MARSHALL joins, dissenting. * * *

The Court suggests that the distinction between a bench trial and a jury trial is unimportant in this context. Such a suggestion is demonstrably fallacious. Experienced criminal practitioners, for both prosecution and defense, know that a jury trial entails far more prosecutorial work than a bench trial. Defense challenges to the potential-juror array, *voir dire* examination of potential jurors, and suppression hearings all take up a prosecutor's time before a jury trial, adding to his scheduling difficulties and caseload. More care in the preparation of his requested instructions, of his witnesses, and of his own remarks is necessary in order to avoid mistrial or reversible error. And there is always the specter of the "irrational" acquittal by a jury that is unreviewable on appeal. Thus it is simply inconceivable that a criminal defendant's election to be tried by jury would be a matter of indifference to his prosecutor. On the contrary, the prosecutor would almost always prefer that the defendant waive such a "troublesome" right. And if the defendant refuses to do so, the prosecutor's subsequent elevation of the charges against the defendant manifestly poses a realistic likelihood of vindictiveness. * * *

CHAPTER 11

SCREENING THE PROSECUTOR'S CHARGING DECISION

■ ■ ■

An innocent individual subjected to a trial pays a substantial price even though acquitted. Being accused of a serious crime creates a blot on one's reputation that may not be fully erased by an acquittal. Even where the acquittal does provide full vindication, it does not remedy other burdens borne in the course of gaining that vindication. Once accused, a defendant must await trial, a process that brings with it a degree of anxiety and insecurity that often disrupts the flow of daily life. The trial itself is even more of an ordeal and carries with it a significant expense. In light of these burdens, it is not surprising that a criminal justice process concerned with the protection of the innocent will incorporate safeguards that go beyond ensuring against erroneous convictions and seek also to ensure that unfounded charges are not brought against the innocent. A major element of such protection comes from the requirement that the prosecution's decision to charge be reviewed by some neutral agency. That agency generally is either the grand jury that "screens" the prosecution's case in deciding whether to indict or the magistrate who must determine at a preliminary hearing whether a charge has sufficient support to be sent forward to the next step in the process.[a]

The Fifth Amendment provides that, except in certain military cases, "no person shall be held to answer for a capital, or otherwise infamous offense, unless on presentment or indictment of a Grand Jury." It thus guarantees to any potential defendant in a federal criminal case involving an "infamous offense" (held to encompass all felony offenses) that no charge will be brought against him without the concurrence of a group of his peers, as expressed in the decision of the grand jury to issue an indictment. (The alternative form of accusation, the presentment, which was issued at the grand jury's own initiative, is no longer used). In requiring prosecution by indictment, the Fifth Amendment interposes the grand jury between the prosecutor and the prospective defendant and casts upon it a "shielding" function. The classic description of that function is found in *Wood v. Georgia,* 370 U.S. 375 (1962):

> "Historically, this body [the grand jury] has been regarded as a primary security to the innocent against hasty, malicious and oppressive prosecution; it serves the invaluable function in our society of standing between the accuser and the accused, whether the latter be an

---

[a] These screening procedures are briefly described at pp. 23–24 (steps 8 and 9). As noted there, they are utilized in most jurisdictions only for felony charges. Neither is required for misdemeanors.

individual, minority group, or other, to determine whether a charge is founded upon reason or was dictated by an intimidating power or by malice and personal ill will."

At the time of the adoption of the Fifth Amendment, all of the states also required that felony prosecutions be brought by indictment. In the mid-1800s, however, several of the newer states shifted from prosecution by grand jury indictment to prosecution by an information (an accusation issued by the prosecutor, rather than the grand jury). To ensure independent screening, those states restricted use of the information to cases in which the magistrate made a finding of probable cause in support of the information at a preliminary hearing. In *Hurtado v. California,* 110 U.S. 516 (1884), that procedure was sustained against constitutional challenge. The Supreme Court there held that the guarantee of prosecution by grand jury indictment, though found in the Fifth Amendment, did not reflect a "fundamental principle of liberty and justice" and therefore was not applicable to the states under the due process clause of the Fourteenth Amendment. Although the Supreme Court, with the adoption in the 1960s of a different view of the Fourteenth Amendment generally overruled its earlier decisions that had refused to find in due process a right specified in the Bill of Rights (see Ch. 2, § 1), the *Hurtado* ruling provided the one major exception to that pattern. The Court has continued to hold that the states need not prosecute by indictment, and today only about twenty states still require grand jury review.[b] In the remaining states, the prosecution may proceed by indictment or information, and most prosecutors in those states proceed by information in most cases.

In the vast majority of the states allowing prosecution by information at the prosecutor's discretion, the information can be filed only if there has been a determination of probable cause by a magistrate at a preliminary hearing.[c] Defense counsel generally view this requirement as providing a more favorable screening process than the grand jury because the preliminary hearing is an adversary proceeding at which the defense may cross-examine the prosecution's witnesses and present its own evidence. This stands in contrast to the secret and non-adversary grand jury proceeding, in which only the prosecution participates, presenting its side of the case and serving as the legal advisor to the lay jurors. The

---

[b]   These jurisdictions commonly allow for defense waiver of the indictment, so a felony prosecution can be brought by information in such states when the defendant makes a proper waiver of his right to grand jury review.

[c]   These jurisdictions also allow for defense waiver of the preliminary hearing, so a felony information can be filed without a magistrate's probable cause determination when there has been a waiver.

Jurisdictions requiring prosecution by indictment also provide for a preliminary hearing in felony cases within a specified period after arrest, but that hearing will not be held if an indictment is obtained prior to the scheduled date of hearing. The indictment establishes probable cause as found by the grand jury, and since the grand jury finding prevails over any determination to the contrary that the magistrate might make, there is no need for the preliminary hearing. In some indictment jurisdictions, it is common for prosecutors to "bypass" the preliminary hearing by first obtaining an indictment, while the practice in other indictment jurisdictions is to have a prompt preliminary hearing followed by the taking of the case to the grand jury. The latter practice was followed in *Coleman v. Alabama,* infra.

preliminary hearing also may provide the defense with other procedural advantages, as noted in *Coleman v. Alabama,* infra.

In a few of the states allowing prosecution by information, the prosecution has available the option of direct filing of the information without a preliminary hearing. Because the practice upheld in *Hurtado* required a preliminary hearing, it was not clear from that case whether due process permitted a state to utilize an accusatory process in a felony case that dispensed with any form of screening procedure by a neutral agency. That issue was presented in *Lem Woon v. Oregon,* 229 U.S. 586 (1913), which presented a challenge to the direct filing of an information without "any examination, or commitment by a magistrate * * * or any verification other than [the prosecutor's] official oath." Relying on the fundamental fairness analysis of *Hurtado,* the Court in *Lem Woon* sustained the state's direct filing procedure. It noted:

> "[T]his court has * * * held [that] the 'due process of law' clause does not require the State to adopt the institution and procedure of a grand jury, [and] we are unable to see upon what theory it can be held that an examination or the opportunity for one, prior to the formal accusation by the district attorney, is obligatory upon the States."

Although the Supreme Court subsequently held in *Gerstein v. Pugh,* 420 U.S. 103 (1975), that the Fourth Amendment requires a magistrate's ex parte determination of probable cause (as in the issuance of an arrest warrant) where there is "extended restraint of liberty following arrest" (see fn. a, p. 177), the opinion there reaffirmed the holding in *Lem Woon* "that a judicial hearing is not a prerequisite to prosecution by information." The Constitution does not require the state to provide "judicial oversight or review [as in a preliminary hearing] of the decision to prosecute." *Gerstein.*

While states are not constitutionally required to provide for screening by either the grand jury or the preliminary hearing, once they do afford such screening, constitutional limitations may apply. The first two cases in this chapter, *Coleman v. Alabama* and *Vasquez v. Hillery,* treat the two major constitutional limitations applicable to the preliminary hearing (*Coleman*) and the grand jury (*Hillery*). Those cases also raise the question of whether a conviction should be reversed where there was constitutional error in the screening process but the defendant was then found guilty after a trial that complied in all respects with constitutional requirements.[d]

---

[d]   The issue posed in this regard relates to applicability of the constitutional "harmless error" doctrine set forth in *Chapman v. California,* 386 U.S. 18 (1967). Prior to *Chapman,* it frequently had been assumed that all constitutional errors automatically required reversal of a conviction on appeal because such errors were "per se injurious." *Chapman* held, however, that constitutional errors were not exempted from the usual rule of appellate review that requires affirmance where the error in prior proceedings is deemed "harmless". The Court reasoned that this "harmless error" principle served a "very useful purpose insofar as * * * [it] block[s] setting aside convictions for small errors or defects that have little, if any likelihood of having changed the result of the trial." Accordingly, as to most constitutional errors, reversal of a conviction would not be required where the state could establish that that error was in fact harmless. This required the state to "prove beyond a reasonable doubt that the error * * * did not contribute to the verdict obtained." The Court added, however, that "there are some constitutional rights so basic to a fair trial that their

In federal prosecutions, of course, the Fifth Amendment requires prosecution by grand jury indictment. The third case in the chapter, *Costello v. United States,* raises the question of whether the Fifth Amendment requires that the grand jury's decision to indict be based on evidence that would be admissible at trial. Following *Costello,* the Supreme Court indicated in a series of cases that the rationale of *Costello* was also applicable to grand jury consideration of evidence that would be inadmissible at trial because obtained in violation of the federal constitution. In the latest of those Supreme Court rulings, *United States v. Calandra,* 414 U.S. 338 (1974), holding that a grand jury witness could not refuse to answer questions based on information obtained through an unconstitutional search, the Court noted:

"The grand jury's sources of information are widely drawn and the validity of an indictment is not affected by the character of the evidence considered. Thus, an indictment valid on its face is not subject to challenge on the ground that the grand jury acted on the basis of inadequate or incompetent evidence, *Costello v. United States;* or even on the basis of information obtained in violation of a defendant's Fifth Amendment privilege against self-incrimination."

COLEMAN V. ALABAMA
399 U.S. 1, 90 S.Ct. 1999, 26 L.Ed.2d 387 (1970).

JUSTICE BRENNAN announced the judgment of the Court and delivered the following opinion.

Petitioners were convicted in an Alabama Circuit Court of assault with intent to murder in the shooting of one Reynolds after he and his wife parked their car on an Alabama highway to change a flat tire. The Alabama Court of Appeals affirmed, and the Alabama Supreme Court denied review. We vacate and remand.

Petitioners * * * argue that the preliminary hearing prior to their indictment was a "critical stage" of the prosecution and that Alabama's failure to provide them with appointed counsel at the hearing therefore unconstitutionally denied them the assistance of counsel. * * *

II[2]

This Court has held that a person accused of crime "requires the guiding hand of counsel at every step in the proceedings against him," *Powell v. Alabama* [p. 373], and that that constitutional principle is not limited to the presence of counsel at trial. "It is central to that principle that in addition to counsel's presence at trial, the accused is guaranteed that he need not stand alone against the State at any stage of the prosecution, formal or informal, in court or out, where counsel's

---

infraction can never be treated as harmless error." Cited as illustrations of such errors (calling for automatic reversal) were a state's failure to provide appointed counsel at trial as required under the Sixth Amendment (see Ch. 5, § 1), and a due process violation resulting from the possible bias of a trial judge whose fees were derived from the fines he imposed (see *Tumey v. Ohio,* described in the *Hillery* opinion). These errors came to be known as "structural errors." The grounding of the structural characterization is discussed in *Weaver v. Massachusetts,* pp. 961–963. See also fn. d, p. 747.

[2]   Justice Douglas, Justice White, and Justice Marshall join this Part II.

absence might derogate from the accused's right to a fair trial." *United States v. Wade* [p. 574]. Accordingly, "the principle of *Powell v. Alabama* and succeeding cases requires that we scrutinize *any* pretrial confrontation of the accused to determine whether the presence of his counsel is necessary to preserve the defendant's basic right to a fair trial as affected by his right meaningfully to cross-examine the witnesses against him and to have effective assistance of counsel at the trial itself. It calls upon us to analyze whether potential substantial prejudice to defendant's rights inheres in the particular confrontation and the ability of counsel to help avoid that prejudice."

Applying this test, the Court has held that "critical stages" include the pretrial type of arraignment where certain rights may be sacrificed or lost, *Hamilton v. Alabama,* 368 U.S. 52 (1961), and the pretrial lineup, *United States v. Wade.* Cf. *Miranda v. Arizona,* where the Court held that the privilege against compulsory self-incrimination includes a right to counsel at a pretrial custodial interrogation.

The preliminary hearing is not a required step in an Alabama prosecution. The prosecutor may seek an indictment directly from the grand jury without a preliminary hearing. The opinion of the Alabama Court of Appeals in this case instructs us that under Alabama law the sole purposes of a preliminary hearing are to determine whether there is sufficient evidence against the accused to warrant presenting his case to the grand jury, and if so to fix bail if the offense is bailable. See Code of Alabama, Tit. 15, §§ 139, 140, 151. The court continued:

> "At the preliminary hearing * * * the accused is not required to advance any defenses, and failure to do so does not preclude him from availing himself of every defense he may have upon the trial of the case. Also *Pointer v. Texas,* 380 U.S. 400 (1965), bars the admission of testimony given at a pre-trial proceeding where the accused did not have the benefit of cross-examination by and through counsel. Thus, nothing occurring at the preliminary hearing in the absence of counsel can substantially prejudice the rights of the accused on trial."

This Court is of course bound by this construction of the governing Alabama law. However, from the fact that in cases where the accused has no lawyer at the hearing the Alabama courts prohibit the State's use at trial of anything that occurred at the hearing, it does not follow that the Alabama preliminary hearing is not a "critical stage" of the State's criminal process. The determination whether the hearing is a "critical stage" requiring the provision of counsel depends, as noted, upon an analysis "whether potential substantial prejudice to defendant's rights inheres in the * * * confrontation and the ability of counsel to help avoid that prejudice." *United States v. Wade.* Plainly the guiding hand of counsel at the preliminary hearing is essential to protect the indigent accused against an erroneous or improper prosecution. First, the lawyer's skilled examination and cross-examination of witnesses may expose fatal weaknesses in the State's case, that may lead the magistrate to refuse to bind the accused over. Second, in any event, the skilled interrogation of witnesses by an experienced lawyer can fashion a vital impeachment tool for use in cross-examination of the State's witnesses at the trial, or preserve testimony favorable to the accused of a witness who does not appear at the trial. Third, trained counsel can more effectively discover the case the State has against his client and make possible the preparation of a proper defense to meet that case at the trial. Fourth, counsel can also be influential at the preliminary hearing in making effective arguments for the accused on such matters as the necessity for an early psychiatric examination or bail. The inability of the indigent accused on his own to realize these advantages of a lawyer's assistance compels the conclusion that the Alabama preliminary hearing is a "critical stage" of the State's criminal process at which the accused is "as much entitled to such aid [of counsel] * * * as at the trial itself." *Powell v. Alabama.*

III[4]

There remains, then, the question of the relief to which petitioners are entitled. The trial transcript indicates that the prohibition against use by the State at trial of anything that occurred at the preliminary hearing was scrupulously observed. But on the record it cannot be said whether or not petitioners were otherwise prejudiced by the absence of counsel at the preliminary hearing. That inquiry in the first instance should more properly be made by the Alabama courts. The test to be applied is whether the denial of counsel at the preliminary hearing was harmless error under *Chapman v. California* [fn. d, p. 695]. We accordingly vacate the petitioners' convictions and remand the case to the Alabama courts for such proceedings not inconsistent with this opinion as they may deem appropriate to determine whether such denial of counsel was harmless error, and therefore whether the convictions should be reinstated or a new trial ordered.

JUSTICE BLACK, concurring.

I wholeheartedly agree with the Court's holding in Part II of its opinion that an accused has a constitutional right to the assistance of counsel at the preliminary hearing which Alabama grants criminal defendants. * * * The preliminary hearing is * * * a definite part or stage of a criminal prosecution in Alabama, and the plain language of the Sixth Amendment requires that "[i]n all criminal prosecutions, the accused shall enjoy the right * * * to have the Assistance of Counsel for his defence." * * * I fear that the Court's opinion seems at times to proceed on the premise that the constitutional principle ultimately at stake here is not the defendant's right to counsel as guaranteed by the Sixth and Fourteenth Amendments but rather a right to a "fair trial" as conceived by judges. While that phrase is an appealing one, neither the Bill of Rights nor any other part of the Constitution contains it. * * *

JUSTICE DOUGLAS.

While I have joined Mr. Justice Brennan's opinion, I add a word as to why I think that a strict construction of the Constitution requires the result reached.

The critical words are "In all criminal prosecutions, the accused shall enjoy the right * * * to have the assistance of Counsel for his defence." As Mr. Justice Black states, a preliminary hearing is "a definite part or stage of a criminal prosecution in Alabama." A "criminal prosecution" certainly does not start only

---

[4]   Justice Black, Justice Douglas, Justice White, and Justice Marshall join this Part III.

when the trial starts. If the commencement of the trial were the start of the "criminal prosecution" in the constitutional sense, then indigents would likely go to trial without effective representation by counsel. Lawyers for the defense need time to prepare a defense. The prosecution needs time for investigations and procedures to make that investigation timely and telling. As a shorthand expression we have used the words "critical stage" to describe whether the preliminary phase of a criminal trial was part of the "criminal prosecution" as used in the Sixth Amendment. But it is the Sixth Amendment that controls, not our own ideas as to what an efficient criminal code should provide. It did not take nearly 200 years of doubt to decide whether Alabama's preliminary hearing is a part of the "criminal prosecution" within the meaning of the Sixth Amendment. The question has never been reached prior to this case. * * * If we are to adhere to the mandate of the Constitution and not give it merely that meaning which appeals to the personal tastes of those who from time to time sit here, we should read its terms in light of the realities of what "criminal prosecutions" truly mean. * * *

JUSTICE WHITE, concurring.

I agree with Mr. Justice Harlan that recent cases furnish ample ground for holding the preliminary hearing a critical event in the progress of a criminal case. I therefore join the opinion of the Court, but with some hesitation since requiring the appointment of counsel may result in fewer preliminary hearings in jurisdictions where the prosecutor is free to avoid them by taking a case directly to a grand jury. Our ruling may also invite eliminating the preliminary hearing system entirely.

I would expect the application of the harmless-error standard on remand to produce results approximating those contemplated by Mr. Justice Harlan's separately stated views. Whether denying petitioner counsel at the preliminary hearing was harmless beyond a reasonable doubt depends upon an assessment of those factors which made the denial error. But that assessment cannot ignore the fact that petitioner has been tried and found guilty by a jury.

The possibility that counsel would have detected preclusive flaws in the State's probable cause showing is for all practical purposes mooted by the trial where the State produced evidence satisfying the jury of the petitioner's guilt beyond a reasonable doubt. Also, it would be wholly speculative in this case to assume either (1) that the State's witnesses at the trial testified inconsistently with what their testimony would have been if petitioner had had counsel to cross-examine them at the preliminary hearing, or (2) that counsel, had he been present at the hearing, would have known so much more about the State's case than he actually did when he went to trial that the result of the trial might have been different. So too it seems extremely unlikely that matters related to bail or early psychiatric examination would ever raise reasonable doubts about the integrity of the trial. There remains the possibility, as Mr. Justice Harlan suggests, that important testimony of witnesses unavailable at the trial could have been preserved had counsel been present to cross-examine opposing witnesses or to examine witnesses for the defense. If such was the case, petitioner would be entitled to a new trial.

JUSTICE HARLAN, concurring in part and dissenting in part.

If I felt free to consider this case upon a clean slate I would have voted to affirm these convictions. But in light of the lengths to which the right to appointed counsel has been carried in recent decisions of this Court, see *Miranda v. Arizona, United States v. Wade,* * * *—I consider that course is not open to me with due regard for the way in which the adjudicatory process of this Court, as I conceive it, should work. * * *

While, given the cases referred to, I cannot escape the conclusion that petitioners' constitutional rights must be held to have been violated by denying them appointed counsel at the preliminary hearing, I consider the scope of the Court's remand too broad and amorphous. I do not think that reversal of these convictions, for lack of counsel at the preliminary hearing, should follow unless petitioners are able to show on remand that they have been prejudiced in their defense at trial, in that favorable testimony that might otherwise have been preserved was irretrievably lost by virtue of not having counsel to help present an affirmative case at the preliminary hearing. * * * In my opinion mere speculation that defense counsel might have been able to do better at trial had he been present at the preliminary hearing should not suffice to vitiate a conviction. The Court's remand under the *Chapman* harmless-error rule seems to me to leave the way open for that sort of speculation. * * *

JUSTICE STEWART, with whom THE CHIEF JUSTICE joins, dissenting.

* * * If at the trial the prosecution had used any incriminating statements made by the petitioners at the preliminary hearing, the convictions before us would quite properly have to be set aside. But that did not happen in this case. Or if the prosecution had used the statement of any other witness at the preliminary hearing against the petitioners at their trial, we would likewise quite properly have to set aside these convictions. But that did not happen in this case either. For as the Court today perforce concedes, "the prohibition against use by the State at trial of anything that occurred at the preliminary hearing was scrupulously observed." * * *

But the Court holds today that the Constitution required Alabama to provide a lawyer for the petitioners at their preliminary hearing, not so much, it seems, to assure a fair trial as to assure a fair preliminary hearing. A lawyer at the preliminary hearing, the Court says, might have led the magistrate to "refuse to bind the accused over." Or a lawyer might have made "effective arguments for the accused on such matters as bail or the necessity for an early psychiatric examination." If *those* are the reasons a lawyer must be provided, then the most elementary logic requires that a new preliminary hearing must now be held, with counsel made available to the petitioners. In order to provide such relief, it would, of course, be necessary not only to set aside these convictions, but also to set aside the grand jury indictments, and the magistrate's orders fixing bail and binding over the petitioners. Since the petitioners have now been found by a jury in a constitutional trial to be guilty beyond a reasonable doubt, the Court understandably boggles at these logical consequences of its own reasoning. It refrains, in short, from now turning back the clock by ordering a new preliminary hearing to determine all over again whether there is sufficient evidence against the accused to present their case to a grand jury. Instead, the Court sets aside these convictions and remands the case for determination "whether the convictions should be reinstated or a new trial ordered," and this action seems to me even more quixotic. * * *

No record or transcript of any kind was made of the preliminary hearing. Therefore, if the burden on remand is on the petitioners to show that they were prejudiced, it is clear that that burden cannot be met, and the remand is a futile gesture. If, on the other hand, the burden is on the State to disprove beyond a reasonable doubt any and all speculative advantages that the petitioners might conceivably have enjoyed if counsel had been present at their preliminary hearing, then obviously that burden cannot be met either, and the Court should simply reverse these convictions. All I can say is that if the Alabama courts can figure out what they are supposed to do with this case now that it has been remanded to them, their perceptiveness will far exceed mine.

The record before us makes clear that no evidence of what occurred at the preliminary hearing was used against the petitioners at their now completed trial. I would hold, therefore, that the absence of counsel at the preliminary hearing deprived the petitioners of no constitutional rights. Accordingly, I would affirm these convictions.

CHIEF JUSTICE BURGER, [dissenting].

I agree that as a matter of *sound policy* counsel should be made available to all persons subjected to a preliminary hearing and that this should be provided either by statute or by the rulemaking process. However, I cannot accept the notion that the Constitution commands it because it is a "criminal prosecution." * * * Certainly, as Mr. Justice Harlan and Mr. Justice White suggest, not a word in the Constitution itself either requires or contemplates the result reached; unlike them, however, I do not acquiesce in prior holdings which purportedly, but nonetheless erroneously, are based on the Constitution. That approach simply is an acknowledgment that the Court having previously amended the Sixth Amendment now feels bound by its action. While I do not rely solely on 183 years of contrary constitutional interpretation, it is indeed an odd business that it has taken this Court nearly two centuries to "discover" a constitutional mandate to have counsel at a preliminary hearing. Here there is not even the excuse that conditions have changed; the preliminary hearing is an ancient institution.

* * * If the Constitution provided that counsel be furnished for every "critical event in the progress of a criminal case," that would be another story, but it does not. In contrast to the variety of verbal combinations employed by the majority to justify today's disposition, the Sixth Amendment states with laudable precision that "In all *criminal prosecutions,* the accused shall * * * have the Assistance of Counsel." (Emphasis added.) The only relevant determination is whether a preliminary hearing is a "criminal prosecution," *not* whether it is a *"critical event* in the progress of a criminal case." By inventing its own verbal formula the Court simply seeks to reshape the Constitution in accordance with its own predilections of what is desirable. Constitutional interpretation is not an easy matter, but we

should be especially cautious of substituting our own notions for those of the Framers. * * *

Under today's holding we * * * have something of an anomaly under the new "discovery" of the Court that counsel is *constitutionally* required at the preliminary hearing since counsel cannot attend a subsequent grand jury inquiry, even though witnesses, including the person eventually charged, may be interrogated in secret session. If the current mode of constitutional analysis subscribed to by this Court in recent cases requires that counsel be present at preliminary hearings, how can this be reconciled with the fact that the Constitution itself does not permit the assistance of counsel at the decidedly more "critical" grand jury inquiry.

Finally, as pointed out, the Court has already protected an accused from absence of counsel at the preliminary hearing by providing that statements of an uncounseled person are inadmissible at trial. The Court fails to explain why that salutary—indeed drastic—remedy is no longer sufficient protection for the preliminary hearing stage, unless what the Court is doing—surreptitiously—is to convert the preliminary hearing into a discovery device. * * *

VASQUEZ V. HILLERY
474 U.S. 254, 106 S.Ct. 617, 88 L.Ed.2d 598 (1986).

JUSTICE MARSHALL delivered the opinion of the Court.

The Warden of San Quentin State Prison asks this Court to retire a doctrine of equal protection jurisprudence first announced in 1880. The time has come, he urges, for us to abandon the rule requiring reversal of the conviction of any defendant indicted by a grand jury from which members of his own race were systematically excluded.

In 1962, the grand jury of Kings County, California, indicted respondent, Booker T. Hillery, for a brutal murder. Before trial in Superior Court, respondent moved to quash the indictment on the ground that it had been issued by a grand jury from which blacks had been systematically excluded. A hearing on respondent's motion was held by Judge Meredith Wingrove, who was the sole Superior Court Judge in the county and had personally selected all grand juries, including the one that indicted respondent, for the previous seven years. Absolving himself of any discriminatory intent, Judge Wingrove refused to quash the indictment. Respondent was subsequently convicted of first-degree murder.

For the next 16 years, respondent pursued appeals and collateral relief in the state courts, raising at every opportunity his equal protection challenge to the grand jury that indicted him. Less than one month after the California Supreme Court foreclosed his final avenue of state relief in 1978, respondent filed a petition for a writ of habeas corpus in federal court, raising that same challenge. The District Court concluded that respondent had established discrimination in the grand jury, and granted the writ.[a] The Court of Appeals affirmed, and we granted certiorari.

* * * [P]etitioner urges this Court to find that discrimination in the grand jury amounted to harmless error in this case, claiming that the evidence against respondent was overwhelming and that discrimination no longer infects the selection of grand juries in Kings County. Respondent's conviction after a fair trial, we are told, purged any taint attributable to the indictment process. Our acceptance of this theory would require abandonment of more than a century of consistent precedent.

In 1880, this Court reversed a state conviction on the ground that the indictment charging the offense had been issued by a grand jury from which blacks had been excluded. We reasoned that deliberate exclusion of blacks "is practically a brand upon them, affixed by the law, an assertion of their inferiority, and a stimulant to that race prejudice which is an impediment to securing to individuals of the race that equal justice which the law aims to secure to all others." *Strauder v. West Virginia,* 100 U.S. 303 (1880).

Thereafter, the Court has repeatedly rejected all arguments that a conviction may stand despite racial discrimination in the selection of the grand jury.[b] Only six years ago, the Court explicitly addressed the question whether this unbroken line of case law should be reconsidered in favor of a harmless-error standard, and determined that it should not. *Rose v. Mitchell,* 443 U.S. 545 (1979). We reaffirmed our conviction that discrimination on the basis of race in the selection of grand jurors "strikes at the fundamental values of our judicial system and our society as a whole," and that the criminal defendant's right to equal protection of the laws has been denied when he is indicted by a grand jury from which members of a racial group purposefully have been excluded.

Petitioner argues here that requiring a State to retry a defendant, sometimes years later, imposes on it an unduly harsh penalty for a constitutional defect bearing no relation to the fundamental fairness of the trial. Yet intentional discrimination in the selection of grand jurors is a grave constitutional trespass, possible only under color of state authority, and wholly within the power of the State to prevent. Thus, the remedy we have embraced for over a century—the only effective remedy for this violation[5]—is not disproportionate to the evil that it seeks

---

[a]   In a portion of its opinion that has been deleted, the Court sustained the district court's consideration of a computer analysis that had not been submitted before the state courts. That analysis assessed the "mathematical probability that chance or accident could have accounted for the exclusion of blacks from the Kings County grand jury over the years at issue." The district court "accepted the experts conclusion that had the grand jurors been selected by chance, the probability that no black would have been selected over the 17 year period of Judge Wingrove's tenure was 2 in 1,000."

[b]   The Court here cited 13 Supreme Court opinion, decided between 1881 and 1972, in which convictions had been reversed on direct appeal based on racial discrimination in the selection of the grand jury.

[5]   As we pointed out in *Rose v. Mitchell,* alternative remedies are ineffectual. Federal law provides a criminal prohibition against discrimination in the selection of grand jurors, 18 U.S.C. § 243, but according to statistics compiled by the Administrative Office of the United States Courts, that section has not been the basis for a single prosecution in the past nine years. With respect to prior years, for which precise information is not available, we have been unable to find evidence of

to deter. If grand jury discrimination becomes a thing of the past, no conviction will ever again be lost on account of it.

Nor are we persuaded that discrimination in the grand jury has no effect on the fairness of the criminal trials that result from that grand jury's actions. The grand jury does not determine only that probable cause exists to believe that a defendant committed a crime, or that it does not. In the hands of the grand jury lies the power to charge a greater offense or a lesser offense; numerous counts or a single count; and perhaps most significant of all, a capital offense or a noncapital offense—all on the basis of the same facts. Moreover, "[t]he grand jury is not bound to indict in every case where a conviction can be obtained." *United States v. Ciambrone,* 601 F.2d 616, 629 (C.A.2 1979) (Friendly, J., dissenting). Thus, even if a grand jury's determination of probable cause is confirmed in hindsight by a conviction on the indicted offense, that confirmation in no way suggests that the discrimination did not impermissibly infect the framing of the indictment and, consequently, the nature or very existence of the proceedings to come.

When constitutional error calls into question the objectivity of those charged with bringing a defendant to judgment, a reviewing court can neither indulge a presumption of regularity nor evaluate the resulting harm. Accordingly, when the trial judge is discovered to have had some basis for rendering a biased judgment, his actual motivations are hidden from review, and we must presume that the process was impaired. See *Tumey v. Ohio,* 273 U.S. 510, 535 (1927) (reversal required when judge has financial interest in conviction, despite lack of indication that bias influenced decisions). Similarly, when a petit jury has been selected upon improper criteria or has been exposed to prejudicial publicity, we have required reversal of the conviction because the effect of the violation cannot be ascertained. Like these fundamental flaws, which never have been thought harmless, discrimination in the grand jury undermines the structural integrity of the criminal tribunal itself, and is not amenable to harmless-error review.[6]

Just as a conviction is void under the Equal Protection Clause if the prosecutor deliberately charged the defendant on account of his race, see *United States v. Batchelder* [p. 683], a conviction cannot be understood to cure the taint attributable to a charging body selected on the basis of race. Once having found discrimination in the selection of a grand jury, we simply cannot know that the need to indict would have been assessed in the same way by a grand jury properly constituted. The overriding imperative to eliminate this systemic flaw in the charging process, as well as the difficulty of assessing its effect on any given defendant, requires our continued adherence to a rule of mandatory reversal.

The opinion of the Court in *Mitchell* ably presented other justifications, based on the necessity for vindicating Fourteenth Amendment rights, supporting a policy

---

any prosecution or conviction under the statute in the last century. The other putative remedy for grand jury discrimination is 42 U.S.C. § 1983, which, in theory, allows redress for blacks who have been excluded from grand jury service. These suits are also extremely rare, undoubtedly because the potential plaintiffs, eligible blacks not called for grand jury service, are often without knowledge of the discriminatory practices and without incentive to launch costly legal battles to stop them.

6   Justice White does not join in the foregoing paragraph.

of automatic reversal in cases of grand jury discrimination. That analysis persuasively demonstrated that the justifications retain their validity in modern times, for "114 years after the close of the War Between the States and nearly 100 years after *Strauder,* racial and other forms of discrimination still remain a fact of life, in the administration of justice as in our society as a whole." The six years since *Mitchell* have given us no reason to doubt the continuing truth of that observation.

The dissent propounds a theory, not advanced by any party, which would condition the grant of relief upon the passage of time between a conviction and the filing of a petition for federal habeas corpus, depending upon the ability of a State to obtain a second conviction. Sound jurisprudence counsels against our adoption of that approach to habeas corpus claims.

The Habeas Corpus Rules permit a State to move for dismissal of a habeas petition when it "has been prejudiced in its ability to respond to the petition by delay in its filing." Indeed, petitioner filed such a motion in this case, and it was denied because the District Court found that no prejudicial delay had been caused by respondent. Congress has not seen fit, however, to provide the State with an additional defense to habeas corpus petitions based on the difficulties that it will face if forced to retry the defendant. * * *

Today's decision is supported, though not compelled, by the important doctrine of *stare decisis,* the means by which we ensure that the law will not merely change erratically, but will develop in a principled and intelligible fashion. That doctrine permits society to presume that bedrock principles are founded in the law rather than in the proclivities of individuals, and thereby contributes to the integrity of our constitutional system of government, both in appearance and in fact. While *stare decisis* is not an inexorable command, the careful observer will discern that any detours from the straight path of *stare decisis* in our past have occurred for articulable reasons, and only when the Court has felt obliged "to bring its opinions into agreement with experience and with facts newly ascertained." *Burnet v. Coronado Oil & Gas Co.,* 285 U.S. 393 (1932) (Brandeis, J., dissenting). * * * [E]very successful proponent of overruling precedent has borne the heavy burden of persuading the Court that changes in society or in the law dictate that the values served by *stare decisis* yield in favor of a greater objective. In the case of grand jury discrimination, we have been offered no reason to believe that any such metamorphosis has rendered the Court's long commitment to a rule of reversal outdated, ill-founded, unworkable, or otherwise legitimately vulnerable to serious reconsideration. On the contrary, the need for such a rule is as compelling today as it was at its inception.[c]

---

[c]   Justice O'Connor's opinion, concurring in the judgment, is omitted. Justice O'Connor noted that she shared the "view expressed by Justice Powell in *Rose* [that] a petitioner who has been afforded by the state courts a full and fair opportunity to litigate the claims that blacks were discriminatorily excluded from the grand jury * * * should be foreclosed from relitigating that claim on federal habeas." The district court here, however, had held that respondent Hillery "was not given a full and fair hearing on his discrimination claim in state court." Nor had a "sufficiently compelling case been made for reversing this Court's precedents with respect to the remedy applicable to properly cognizable claims of discriminatory exclusion of grand jurors."

JUSTICE POWELL, with whom THE CHIEF JUSTICE and JUSTICE REHNQUIST join, dissenting.

Respondent, a black man, was indicted by a grand jury having no black members for the stabbing murder of a 15-year-old girl. A petit jury found respondent guilty of that charge beyond a reasonable doubt, in a trial the fairness of which is unchallenged here. Twenty-three years later, we are asked to grant respondent's petition for a writ of habeas corpus—and thereby require a new trial if that is still feasible—on the ground that blacks were purposefully excluded from the grand jury that indicted him. It is undisputed that race discrimination has long since disappeared from the grand jury selection process in Kings County, California. It is undisputed that a grand jury that perfectly represented Kings County's population at the time of respondent's indictment would have contained only one black member. Yet the Court holds that respondent's petition must be granted, and that respondent must be freed unless the State is able to reconvict, more than two decades after the murder that led to his incarceration.

It is difficult to reconcile this result with a rational system of justice. The Court nevertheless finds its decision compelled by a century of precedent and by the interests of respondent and of society in ending race discrimination in the selection of grand juries. I dissent for two reasons. First, in my view, any error in the selection of the grand jury that indicted respondent is constitutionally harmless. Second, even assuming that the harmless-error rule does not apply, reversal of respondent's conviction is an inappropriate remedy for the wrong that prompts this case.

The Court concludes that the harmless-error rule does not apply to claims of grand jury discrimination. This conclusion is said to follow from a line of cases going back over 100 years. In my view, it follows from a misapplication of the doctrine of *stare decisis*. Adhering to precedent "is usually the wise policy, because in most matters it is more important that the applicable rule of law be settled than that it be settled right." *Burnet v. Coronado Oil & Gas Co.,* 285 U.S. 393 (1932) (Brandeis, J., dissenting). Accordingly, "any departure from the doctrine of *stare decisis* demands special justification." Nevertheless, when governing decisions are badly reasoned, or conflict with other, more recent authority, the Court "has never felt constrained to follow precedent." Instead, particularly where constitutional issues are involved, "[t]his Court has shown a readiness to correct its errors even though of long standing." In this case, the Court misapplies *stare decisis* because it relies only on decisions concerning grand jury discrimination. There is other precedent, including important cases of more recent vintage than those cited by the Court, that should control this case. Those cases hold, or clearly imply, that a conviction should not be reversed for constitutional error where the error did not affect the outcome of the prosecution.

In *Chapman v. California,* 386 U.S. 18 (1967), the Court held that a trial judge's improper comment on the defendant's failure to testify—a clear violation of the Fifth and Fourteenth Amendments—was not a proper basis for reversal if harmless. Since *Chapman,* "the Court has consistently made clear that it is the duty of a reviewing court to consider the trial record as a whole and to ignore errors that are harmless, including most constitutional violations." This rule has been applied to a variety of constitutional violations. See *Harrington v. California,* 395 U.S. 250 (1969) (use of co-conspirator confession in violation of Confrontation Clause); *Coleman v. Alabama,* 399 U.S. 1 (1970) (denial of counsel at preliminary hearing); *Milton v. Wainwright,* 407 U.S. 371 (1972) (use of confession obtained in violation of right to counsel); *Gerstein v. Pugh,* 420 U.S. 103 (1975) (illegal arrest). * * *

In *Rose v. Mitchell,* 443 U.S. 545 (1979), the Court contended that the principle of these cases is inapplicable to grand jury discrimination claims, because grand jury discrimination "destroys the appearance of justice and thereby casts doubt on the integrity of the judicial process." But *every* constitutional error may be said to raise questions as to the "appearance of justice" and the "integrity of the judicial process." Nevertheless, as the cases cited above show, the Court has required some showing of actual prejudice to the defendant as a prerequisite to reversal, even when the constitutional error directly affects the fairness of the defendant's trial. Compare *Strickland v. Washington* [p. 928] (requiring prejudice in ineffective assistance of counsel claims), with *Gideon v. Wainwright* [p. 380] (emphasizing importance of right to counsel to ensure fair trial). Grand jury discrimination is a serious violation of our constitutional order, but so also are the deprivations of rights guaranteed by the Fourth, Fifth, Sixth, and Fourteenth Amendments to which we have applied harmless-error analysis or an analogous prejudice requirement. Moreover, grand jury discrimination occurs *prior* to trial, while the asserted constitutional violations in most of the above-cited cases occurred *during* trial. The Court does not adequately explain why grand jury discrimination affects the "integrity of the judicial process" to a greater extent than the deprivation of equally vital constitutional rights, nor why it is exempt from a prejudice requirement while other constitutional errors are not. * * *

Even assuming that now-established harmless-error principles are inapplicable, this case unjustifiably extends the "century of precedent" on which the Court relies. * * * No one questions that race discrimination in grand jury selection violates the Equal Protection Clause of the Fourteenth Amendment. The issue in this case is not whether the State erred, but what should be done about it. The question is whether reversal of respondent's conviction either is compelled by the Constitution or is an appropriate, but not constitutionally required, remedy for racial discrimination in the selection of grand jurors.

The Constitution does not compel the rule of automatic reversal that the Court applies today. In *Hobby v. United States,* 468 U.S. 339 (1984), we acknowledged that discriminatory selection of grand jury foremen violated the Constitution, but we concluded that reversing the petitioner's conviction was an inappropriate remedy for the violation since grand jury foremen play a minor part in federal prosecutions. See also *Oregon v. Elstad* [p. 457] (suppression of evidence obtained in violation of *Miranda v. Arizona,* is not constitutionally compelled); *United States v. Leon* [p. 68] (suppression of evidence obtained in violation of the Fourth Amendment is not constitutionally compelled). * * * The rationale of *Hobby* cannot be squared with the claim that discriminatory selection of the body that charged the defendant *compels* reversal of the defendant's conviction. Rather, it is necessary to determine whether reversal of respondent's conviction is an "appropriate remedy" for the exclusion of blacks from grand juries in Kings County, California, in 1962. * * * That determination depends on (i) the utility of the remedy in either correcting any injustice to respondent or deterring unconstitutional conduct by state officials, and (ii) the remedy's costs to society. *United States v. Leon.*

The scope of the remedy depends in part on the nature and degree of the harm caused by the wrong. The Court perceives two kinds of harm flowing from grand jury discrimination: harm to the respondent's interest in not being charged and convicted because of his race, and harm to society's interest in deterring racial discrimination. I consider in turn these asserted interests and the degree to which they are served in this case by the Court's automatic reversal rule.

The Court does not contend that the discriminatory selection of the grand jury that indicted respondent calls into question the correctness of the decision to indict. Such a contention could not withstand analysis. Following his indictment for murder, respondent was convicted of that charge in a trial and by a jury whose fairness is not now challenged. The conviction, affirmed on direct appeal in 1965, establishes that the grand jury's decision to indict was indisputably correct. * * *

The Court nevertheless decides that discrimination in the selection of the grand jury potentially harmed respondent, because the grand jury is vested with broad discretion in deciding whether to indict and in framing the charges, and because it is impossible to know whether this discretion would have been exercised differently by a properly selected grand jury. The point appears to be that an all-white grand jury from which blacks are systematically excluded might be influenced by race in determining whether to indict and for what charge. Since the State may not imprison respondent for a crime if one of its elements is his race, the argument goes, his conviction must be set aside.

This reasoning ignores established principles of equal protection jurisprudence. We have consistently declined to find a violation of the Equal Protection Clause absent a finding of intentional discrimination. There has been no showing in this case—indeed, respondent does not even allege—that the Kings County grand jury indicted respondent because of his race, or that the grand jury declined to indict white suspects in the face of similarly strong evidence. Nor is it sensible to assume that impermissible discrimination might have occurred simply because the grand jury had no black members. This Court has never suggested that the racial composition of a grand jury gives rise to the inference that indictments are racially motivated, any more than it has suggested that a suspect arrested by a policeman of a different race may challenge his subsequent conviction on that basis. * * *

Once the inference of racial bias in the decision to indict is placed to one side, as it must be under our precedents, it is impossible to conclude that the discriminatory selection of Kings County's grand jurors caused respondent to suffer any cognizable injury. There may be a theoretical possibility that a different grand jury might have decided not to indict or to indict for a less serious charge. The fact remains, however, that the grand jury's decision to indict was *correct as a matter* *of law,* given respondent's subsequent, unchallenged conviction. A defendant has no right to a grand jury that errs in his favor. * * *

As respondent suffered no prejudice from the grand jury discrimination that prompted his claim, the Court's remedy must stand or fall on its utility as a deterrent to government officials who seek to exclude particular groups from grand juries, weighed against the cost that the remedy imposes on society. The Court properly emphasizes that grand jury discrimination is "a grave constitutional trespass," but it leaps from that observation to the conclusion that *no matter when the claim is raised* the appropriate response is to reverse the conviction of one indicted by a discriminatorily selected body. That conclusion is not, as the Court erroneously suggests, compelled by precedent; equally important, it seriously disserves the public interest.

The cases on which the Court relies involved relatively brief lapses of time between the defendant's trial and the granting of relief. This fact is unsurprising, since the Court only recently determined that claims of grand jury discrimination may be raised in federal habeas corpus proceedings. See *Rose v. Mitchell.* * * * In all of * * * [prior] cases, the time between the defendant's indictment and this Court's decision was six years or less. * * * This case raises the open question whether relief should be denied where the discrimination claim is pressed many years after conviction, and where the State can show that the delay prejudiced its ability to retry the defendant. * * * It is now almost a quarter-century since respondent was tried for murder and since the discrimination occurred. The Court finds this time lapse irrelevant. In my view, it is critically important, because it both increases the societal cost of the Court's chosen remedy and lessens any deterrent force the remedy may otherwise have.

In *Rose v. Mitchell,* supra, the Court reasoned that the rule of automatic reversal imposes limited costs on society, since the State is able to retry successful petitioners, and since "the State remains free to use all the proof it introduced to obtain the conviction in the first trial." This is not the case when relief is granted many years after the original conviction. In those circumstances, the State may find itself severely handicapped in its ability to carry its heavy burden of proving guilt beyond a reasonable doubt. * * * Witnesses die or move away; physical evidence is lost; memories fade. * * *

Long delays also dilute the effectiveness of the reversal rule as a deterrent. This case is illustrative. The architect of the discriminatory selection system that led to respondent's claim, Judge Wingrove, died 19 years ago. Respondent does not allege that the discriminatory practices survived Judge Wingrove, nor is there any evidence in the record to support such an allegation. It is hard to believe that Judge Wingrove might have behaved differently had he known that a convicted defendant might be freed 19 years after his death. Yet that is exactly the proposition that must justify the remedy imposed in this case: that people in positions similar to Judge Wingrove's will change their behavior out of the fear of successful habeas petitions long after they have left office or otherwise passed from the scene. * * *

Twenty-three years ago, respondent was fairly convicted of the most serious of crimes. Respondent's grand jury discrimination claim casts no doubt on the adequacy of the procedures used to convict him or on the sufficiency of the evidence of his guilt. For that reason alone, the Court should reverse the Court of Appeals' decision.[16] Even assuming the harmlessness of the error is irrelevant, however, reversal is still required. The Court inappropriately applies a deterrence rule in a context where it is unlikely to deter, and where its costs to society are likely to be especially high. These considerations should at least lead the Court to remand for a determination of whether the long lapse of time since respondent's conviction would prejudice the State's ability to retry respondent.

COSTELLO v. UNITED STATES
350 U.S. 359, 76 S.Ct. 406, 100 L.Ed. 397 (1956).

JUSTICE BLACK delivered the opinion of the Court.

We granted certiorari in this case to consider a single question: "May a defendant be required to stand trial and a conviction be sustained where only hearsay evidence was presented to the grand jury which indicted him?"

Petitioner, Frank Costello, was indicted for wilfully attempting to evade payment of income taxes due the United States for the years 1947, 1948 and 1949. The charge was that petitioner falsely and fraudulently reported less income than he and his wife actually received during the taxable years in question. Petitioner promptly filed a motion for inspection of the minutes of the grand jury and for a dismissal of the indictment. His motion was based on an affidavit stating that he was firmly convinced there could have been no legal or competent evidence before the grand jury which indicted him since he had reported all his income and paid all taxes due. The motion was denied. At the trial which followed the Government offered evidence designed to show increases in Costello's net worth in an attempt to prove that he had received more income during the years in question than he had reported. To establish its case the Government called and examined 144 witnesses and introduced 368 exhibits. All of the testimony and documents related to business transactions and expenditures by petitioner and his wife. The prosecution concluded its case by calling three government agents. Their investigations had produced the evidence used against petitioner at the trial. They were allowed to summarize the vast amount of evidence already heard and to introduce computations showing, if correct, that petitioner and his wife had received far greater income than they had reported. We have held such summarizations admissible in a "net worth" case like this.

Counsel for petitioner asked each government witness at the trial whether he had appeared before the grand jury which returned the indictment. This cross-examination developed the fact that the three investigating officers had been the only witnesses before the grand jury. After the Government concluded its case,

---

[16] Confidence in our system of justice is eroded when one found guilty of murder, in a trial conceded to be fair, is set free. It is important to remember that the criminal law's aim is twofold: "that guilt shall not escape or innocence suffer." The Court's decision in this case plainly undermines the State's interest in punishing the guilty, without either protecting the innocent or ensuring the fundamental fairness of the procedures pursuant to which one such as respondent is tried and convicted.

petitioner again moved to dismiss the indictment on the ground that the only evidence before the grand jury was "hearsay," since the three officers had no first-hand knowledge of the transactions upon which their computations were based. Nevertheless the trial court again refused to dismiss the indictment, and petitioner was convicted. The Court of Appeals affirmed. * * * Petitioner here urges: (1) that an indictment based solely on hearsay evidence violates that part of the Fifth Amendment providing that "No person shall be held to answer for a capital, or otherwise infamous crime, unless on a presentment or indictment of a Grand Jury * * *." and (2) that if the Fifth Amendment does not invalidate an indictment based solely on hearsay we should now lay down such a rule for the guidance of federal courts. * * * [N]either the Fifth Amendment nor any other constitutional provision prescribes the kind of evidence upon which grand juries must act. The grand jury is an English institution, brought to this country by the early colonists and incorporated in the Constitution by the Founders. There is every reason to believe that our constitutional grand jury was intended to operate substantially like its English progenitor. The basic purpose of the English grand jury was to provide a fair method for instituting criminal proceedings against persons believed to have committed crimes. Grand jurors were selected from the body of the people and their work was not hampered by rigid procedural or evidential rules. In fact, grand jurors could act on their own knowledge and were free to make their presentments or indictments on such information as they deemed satisfactory. Despite its broad power to institute criminal proceedings the grand jury grew in popular favor with the years. It acquired an independence in England free from control by the Crown or judges. Its adoption in our Constitution as the sole method for preferring charges in serious criminal cases shows the high place it held as an instrument of justice. And in this country as in England of old the grand jury has convened as a body of laymen, free from technical rules, acting in secret, pledged to indict no one because of prejudice and to free no one because of special favor. As late as 1927 an English historian could say that English grand juries were still free to act on their own knowledge if they pleased to do so. And in 1852 Mr. Justice Nelson on circuit could say "No case has been cited, nor have we been able to find any, furnishing an authority for looking into and revising the judgment of the grand jury upon the evidence, for the purpose of determining whether or not the finding was founded upon sufficient proof * * *." *United States v. Reed*, 27 Fed.Cas. 727, 738 (1852).

In *Holt v. United States*, 218 U.S. 245 (1910), this Court had to decide whether an indictment should be quashed because supported in part by incompetent evidence. Aside from the incompetent evidence "there was very little evidence against the accused." The Court refused to hold that such an indictment should be quashed, pointing out that "The abuses of criminal practice would be enhanced if indictments could be upset on such a ground." The same thing is true where as here all the evidence before the grand jury was in the nature of "hearsay." If indictments were to be held open to challenge on the ground that there was inadequate or incompetent evidence before the grand jury, the resulting delay would be great indeed. The result of such a rule would be that before trial on the merits a defendant could always insist on a kind of preliminary trial to determine the competency and adequacy of the evidence before the grand jury. This is not required by the Fifth Amendment. An indictment returned by a legally constituted and unbiased grand jury, like an information drawn by the prosecutor, if valid on its face, is enough to call for trial of the charge on the merits. The Fifth Amendment requires nothing more.

Petitioner urges that this Court should exercise its power to supervise the administration of justice in federal courts and establish a rule permitting defendants to challenge indictments on the ground that they are not supported by adequate or competent evidence. No persuasive reasons are advanced for establishing such a rule. It would run counter to the whole history of the grand jury institution, in which laymen conduct their inquiries unfettered by technical rules. Neither justice nor the concept of a fair trial requires such a change. In a trial on the merits, defendants are entitled to a strict observance of all the rules designed to bring about a fair verdict. Defendants are not entitled, however, to a rule which would result in interminable delay but add nothing to the assurance of a fair trial. Affirmed.[a]

JUSTICE CLARK and JUSTICE HARLAN took no part in the consideration or decision of this case.

JUSTICE BURTON, concurring.

I agree with the denial of the motion to quash the indictment. In my view, however, this case does not justify the breadth of the declarations made by the Court. I assume that this Court would not preclude an examination of grand jury action to ascertain the existence of bias or prejudice in an indictment. Likewise, it seems to me that if it is shown that the grand jury had before it no substantial or rationally persuasive evidence upon which to base its indictment, that indictment should be quashed. To hold a person to answer to such an empty indictment for a capital or otherwise infamous federal crime robs the Fifth Amendment of much of its protective value to the private citizen. * * *

---

[a]   Relying in part on *Costello*, the Supreme Court has concluded that an indicted federal defendant may not challenge an indictment on the grounds that: (1) the grand jury considered evidence obtained unconstitutionally by the police (e.g., the fruits of an illegal search), *United States v. Calandra*, p. 85; (2) the prosecutor failed to present known exculpatory evidence to the grand jury, *United States v. Williams*, 504 U.S. 36 (1992). So too, in light of "the grand jury's singular role in finding probable cause," an indictment "conclusively determines the existence" of probable cause for Fourth Amendment purposes, providing the grounding for the "issuance of an arrest warrant without further inquiry [by the magistrate] into the case's strength," and dispensing with the need for a *Gerstein* review (see fn. a., p. 177) where the individual was arrested without a warrant. *Kaley v. United States*, 571 U.S. 320 (2013) (insofar as due process might entitle a defendant to a hearing challenging the grounding of a pre-trial asset restraint order as to potentially forfeitable assets, the indictment also establishes "conclusively" the existence of probable cause in that hearing; the "grand jury gets to say—without any review oversight or second-guessing whether probable cause exists").

CHAPTER 12

SPEEDY TRIAL AND OTHER SPEEDY DISPOSITION

• • •

The matter of the time within which a trial must be commenced is often treated in statutes and court rules. Some of these provisions are rather general in nature, meaning courts have considerable discretion in determining how long a delay is excessive and what intervals in the pretrial stages are to be discounted in ascertaining what the period of delay has actually been. Some other provisions, as illustrated by the federal Speedy Trial Act of 1974, go into considerable detail by setting specific time limits and enumerating what events toll the running of the specified time.

But speedy trial is not simply a matter of local law. The Sixth Amendment declares: "In all criminal prosecutions, the accused shall enjoy the right to a speedy * * * trial." Just what this means is explored in the first case, *Barker v. Wingo*. Certain periods of delay (e.g., prior to arrest or charge) are not encompassed by the Sixth Amendment, so that a defendant's constitutional challenge to them will likely be grounded in the due process clause, as in *United States v. Lovasco*.

BARKER v. WINGO

407 U.S. 514, 92 S.Ct. 2182, 33 L.Ed.2d 101 (1972).

JUSTICE POWELL delivered the opinion of the Court.

[A] speedy trial is guaranteed the accused by the Sixth Amendment to the Constitution. [T]he right to speedy trial is "fundamental" and is imposed by the Due Process Clause of the Fourteenth Amendment on the States. [I]n none of [our prior] cases have we attempted to set out the criteria by which the speedy trial right is to be judged. This case compels us to make such an attempt.

On July 20, 1958, in Christian County, Kentucky, an elderly couple was beaten to death by intruders wielding an iron tire tool. Two suspects, Silas Manning and Willie Barker, the petitioner, were arrested shortly thereafter. The grand jury indicted them on September 15. Counsel was appointed on September 17, and Barker's trial was set for October 21. The Commonwealth had a stronger case against Manning, and it believed that Barker could not be convicted unless Manning testified against him. Manning was naturally unwilling to incriminate himself. Accordingly, on October 23, the day Silas Manning was brought to trial, the Commonwealth sought and obtained the first of what was to be a series of 16 continuances of Barker's trial. Barker made no objection. By first convicting

Manning, the Commonwealth would remove possible problems of self-incrimination and would be able to assure his testimony against Barker.

The Commonwealth encountered more than a few difficulties in its prosecution of Manning. The first trial ended in a hung jury. A second trial resulted in a conviction, but the Kentucky Court of Appeals reversed because of the admission of evidence obtained by an illegal search. At his third trial, Manning was again convicted, and the Court of Appeals again reversed because the trial court had not granted a change of venue. A fourth trial resulted in a hung jury. Finally, after five trials, Manning was convicted, in March 1962, of murdering one victim, and after a sixth trial, in December 1962, he was convicted of murdering the other.

The Christian County Circuit Court holds three terms each year—in February, June, and September. Barker's initial trial was to take place in the September term of 1958. The first continuance postponed it until the February 1959 term. The second continuance was granted for one month only. Every term thereafter for as long as the Manning prosecutions were in process, the Commonwealth routinely moved to continue Barker's case to the next term. When the case was continued from the June 1959 term until the following September, Barker, having spent 10 months in jail, obtained his release by posting a $5,000 bond. He thereafter remained free in the community until his trial. Barker made no objection, through his counsel, to the first 11 continuances.

When on February 12, 1962, the Commonwealth moved for the twelfth time to continue the case until the following term, Barker's counsel filed a motion to dismiss the indictment. The motion to dismiss was denied two weeks later, and the State's motion for a continuance was granted. The State was granted further continuances in June 1962 and September 1962, to which Barker did not object.

In February 1963, the first term of court following Manning's final conviction, the Commonwealth moved to set Barker's trial for March 19. But on the day scheduled for trial, it again moved for a continuance until the June term. It gave as its reason the illness of the ex-sheriff who was the chief investigating officer in the case. To this continuance, Barker objected unsuccessfully.

The witness was still unable to testify in June, and the trial, which had been set for June 19, was continued again until the September term over Barker's objection. This time the court announced that the case would be dismissed for lack of prosecution if it were not tried during the next term. The final trial date was set for October 9, 1963. On that date, Barker again moved to dismiss the indictment, and this time specified that his right to a speedy trial had been violated. The motion was denied; the trial commenced with Manning as the chief prosecution witness; Barker was convicted and given a life sentence. * * *

The right to a speedy trial is generically different from any of the other rights enshrined in the Constitution for the protection of the accused. In addition to the general concern that all accused persons be treated according to decent and fair procedures, there is a societal interest in providing a speedy trial which exists separate from and at times in opposition to the interests of the accused. The inability of courts to provide a prompt trial has contributed to a large backlog of cases in urban courts which, among other things, enables defendants to negotiate more effectively for pleas of guilty to lesser offenses and otherwise manipulate the system. In addition, persons released on bond for lengthy periods awaiting trial have an opportunity to commit other crimes. It must be of little comfort to the residents of Christian County, Kentucky, to know that Barker was at large on bail for over four years while accused of a vicious and brutal murder of which he was ultimately convicted. Moreover, the longer an accused is free awaiting trial, the more tempting becomes his opportunity to jump bail and escape. Finally, delay between arrest and punishment may have a detrimental effect on rehabilitation.

If an accused cannot make bail, he is generally confined, as was Barker for 10 months, in a local jail. This contributes to the overcrowding and generally deplorable state of those institutions. Lengthy exposure to these conditions "has a destructive effect on human character and makes the rehabilitation of the individual offender much more difficult." At times the result may even be violent rioting. Finally, lengthy pretrial detention is costly. The cost of maintaining a prisoner in jail varies from $3 to $9 per day, and this amounts to millions across the Nation. In addition, society loses wages which might have been earned, and it must often support families of incarcerated breadwinners.

A second difference between the right to speedy trial and the accused's other constitutional rights is that deprivation of the right may work to the accused's advantage. Delay is not an uncommon defense tactic. As the time between the commission of the crime and trial lengthens, witnesses may become unavailable or their memories may fade. If the witnesses support the prosecution, its case will be weakened, sometimes seriously so. And it is the prosecution which carries the burden of proof. Thus, unlike the right to counsel or the right to be free from compelled self-incrimination, deprivation of the right to speedy trial does not *per se* prejudice the accused's ability to defend himself.

Finally, and perhaps most importantly, the right to speedy trial is a more vague concept than other procedural rights. It is, for example, impossible to determine with precision when the right has been denied. * * * There is nothing comparable to the point in the process when a defendant exercises or waives his right to counsel or his right to a jury trial. * * *

The amorphous quality of the right also leads to the unsatisfactorily severe remedy of dismissal of the indictment when the right has been deprived. This is indeed a serious consequence because it means that a defendant who may be guilty of a serious crime will go free, without having been tried. Such a remedy is more serious than an exclusionary rule or a reversal for a new trial, but it is the only possible remedy.

Perhaps because the speedy trial right is so slippery, two rigid approaches are urged upon us as ways of eliminating some of the uncertainty which courts experience in protecting the right. The first suggestion is that we hold that the Constitution requires a criminal defendant to be offered a trial within a specified time period. The result of such a ruling would have the virtue of clarifying when the right is infringed and of simplifying courts' application of it. Recognizing this, some legislatures have enacted laws, and some courts have adopted procedural rules which more narrowly define the right. * * *

But such a result would require this Court to engage in legislative or rulemaking activity, rather than in the adjudicative process to which we should confine our efforts. We do not establish procedural rules for the States, except when mandated by the Constitution. We find no constitutional basis for holding that the speedy trial right can be quantified into a specified number of days or months. The States, of course, are free to prescribe a reasonable period consistent with constitutional standards, but our approach must be less precise.

The second suggested alternative would restrict consideration of the right to those cases in which the accused has demanded a speedy trial. * * * Under this rigid approach, a prior demand is a necessary condition to the consideration of the speedy trial right. This essentially was the approach the Sixth Circuit took below.

Such an approach, by presuming waiver of a fundamental right from inaction, is inconsistent with this Court's pronouncements on waiver of constitutional rights. The Court has defined waiver as "an intentional relinquishment or abandonment of a known right or privilege." Courts should "indulge every reasonable presumption against waiver," and they should "not presume acquiescence in the loss of fundamental rights." * * *

In excepting the right to speedy trial from the rule of waiver we have applied to other fundamental rights, courts * * * have relied on the assumption that delay usually works for the benefit of the accused and on the absence of any readily ascertainable time in the criminal process for a defendant to be given the choice of exercising or waiving his right. But it is not necessarily true that delay benefits the defendant. There are cases in which delay appreciably harms the defendant's ability to defend himself. Moreover, a defendant confined to jail prior to trial is obviously disadvantaged by delay as is a defendant released on bail but unable to lead a normal life because of community suspicion and his own anxiety.

The nature of the speedy-trial right does make it impossible to pinpoint a precise time in the process when the right must be asserted or waived, but that fact does not argue for placing the burden of protecting the right solely on defendants. A defendant has no duty to bring himself to trial; the State has that duty as well as the duty of insuring that the trial is consistent with due process. Moreover, for the reasons earlier expressed, society has a particular interest in bringing swift prosecutions, and society's representatives are the ones who should protect that interest.

It is also noteworthy that such a rigid view of the demand rule places defense counsel in an awkward position. Unless he demands a trial early and often, he is in danger of frustrating his client's right. If counsel is willing to tolerate some delay because he finds it reasonable and helpful in preparing his own case, he may be unable to obtain a speedy trial for his client at the end of that time. * * *

We reject, therefore, the rule that a defendant who fails to demand a speedy trial forever waives his right. This does not mean, however, that the defendant has no responsibility to assert his right. We think the better rule is that the defendant's assertion of or failure to assert his right to a speedy trial is one of the factors to be considered in an inquiry into the deprivation of the right. Such a formulation * * * allows the trial court to exercise a judicial discretion based on the circumstances, including due consideration of any applicable formal procedural rule. It would permit, for example, a court to attach a different weight to a situation in which the defendant knowingly fails to object from a situation in which his attorney acquiesces in long delay without adequately informing his client or from a situation in which no counsel is appointed. It would also allow a court to weigh the frequency and force of the objections as opposed to attaching significant weight to a purely *pro forma* objection.

In ruling that a defendant has some responsibility to assert a speedy-trial claim, we do not depart from our holdings in other cases concerning the waiver of fundamental rights, in which we have placed the entire responsibility on the prosecution to show that the claimed waiver was knowingly and voluntarily made. Such cases have involved rights which must be exercised or waived at a specific time or under clearly identifiable circumstances, such as the rights to plead not guilty, to demand a jury trial, to exercise the privilege against self-incrimination, and to have the assistance of counsel. We have shown above that the right to a speedy trial is unique in its uncertainty as to when and under what circumstances it must be asserted or may be deemed waived. But the rule we announce today, which comports with constitutional principles, places the primary burden on the courts and the prosecutors to assure that cases are brought to trial. We hardly need add that if delay is attributable to the defendant, then his waiver may be given effect under standard waiver doctrine, the demand rule aside.

* * * The approach we accept is a balancing test, in which the conduct of both the prosecution and the defendant are weighed.

A balancing test necessarily compels courts to approach speedy-trial cases on an *ad hoc* basis. We can do little more than identify some of the factors which courts should assess in determining whether a particular defendant has been deprived of his right. Though some might express them in different ways, we identify four such factors: Length of delay, the reason for the delay, the defendant's assertion of his right, and prejudice to the defendant.

The length of the delay is to some extent a triggering mechanism. Until there is some delay which is presumptively prejudicial, there is no necessity for inquiry into the other factors that go into the balance. Nevertheless, because of the imprecision of the right to speedy trial, the length of delay that will provoke such an inquiry is necessarily dependent upon the peculiar circumstances of the case. To take but one example, the delay that can be tolerated for an ordinary street crime is considerably less than for a serious, complex conspiracy charge.

Closely related to length of delay is the reason the government assigns to justify the delay. Here, too, different weights should be assigned to different reasons. A deliberate attempt to delay the trial in order to hamper the defense should be weighed heavily against the government. A more neutral reason such as negligence or overcrowded courts should be weighed less heavily but nevertheless should be considered since the ultimate responsibility for such circumstances must rest with the government rather than with the defendant. Finally, a valid reason, such as a missing witness, should serve to justify appropriate delay.[a]

We have already discussed the third factor, the defendant's responsibility to assert his right. Whether and how a defendant asserts his right is closely related to the other factors we have mentioned. The strength of his efforts will be affected by the length of the delay, to some extent by the reason for the delay, and most particularly by the personal prejudice, which is not always readily identifiable, that he experiences. The more serious the deprivation, the more likely a defendant is to complain. The defendant's assertion of his speedy trial right, then, is entitled to strong evidentiary weight in determining whether the right is being deprived. We emphasize that failure to assert the right will make it difficult for a defendant to prove that he was denied a speedy trial.

A fourth factor is prejudice to the defendant. Prejudice, of course, should be assessed in the light of the interests of defendants which the speedy trial right was designed to protect. This Court has identified three such interests: (i) to prevent oppressive pretrial incarceration; (ii) to minimize anxiety and concern of the accused; and (iii) to limit the possibility that the defense will be impaired. Of these, the most serious is the last, because the inability of a defendant adequately to prepare his case skews the fairness of the entire system. If witnesses die or disappear during a delay, the prejudice is obvious. There is also prejudice if defense witnesses are unable to recall accurately events of the distant past. Loss of memory, however, is not always reflected in the record because what has been forgotten can rarely be shown.

We have discussed previously the societal disadvantages of lengthy pretrial incarceration, but obviously the disadvantages for the accused who cannot obtain his release are even more serious. The time spent in jail awaiting trial has a detrimental impact on the individual. It often means loss of a job; it disrupts family life; and it enforces idleness. Most jails offer little or no recreational or rehabilitative programs. The time spent in jail is simply dead time. Moreover, if a defendant is locked up, he is hindered in his ability to gather evidence, contact witnesses, or otherwise prepare his defense. Imposing those consequences on anyone who has not yet been convicted is serious. It is especially unfortunate to impose them on those persons who are ultimately found to be innocent. Finally, even if an accused is not incarcerated prior to trial, he is still disadvantaged by restraints on his liberty and by living under a cloud of anxiety, suspicion, and often hostility.

---

[a] In *Vermont v. Brillon*, 556 U.S. 81 (2009), the Court concluded that "delay caused by the defense weighs against the defendant," that "delay caused by the defendant's counsel is also charged against the defendant," and that this is so "whether counsel is privately retained or publicly assigned," for "[u]nlike a prosecutor or the court, assigned counsel ordinarily is not considered a state actor." This means, the Court added, that an "assigned counsel's failure 'to move the case forward' does not warrant attribution of delay to the State," a sensible conclusion, for a contrary rule "could encourage appointed counsel to delay proceedings by seeking unreasonable continuances, hoping thereby to obtain a dismissal of the indictment on speedy-trial grounds." But the Court cautioned that the above-stated general rule "is not absolute," for "[d]elay resulting from a systemic 'breakdown in the public defender system' * * * could be charged to the State."

We regard none of the four factors identified above as either a necessary or sufficient condition to the finding of a deprivation of the right of speedy trial. Rather, they are related factors and must be considered together with such other circumstances as may be relevant. In sum, these factors have no talismanic qualities; courts must still engage in a difficult and sensitive balancing process. But, because we are dealing with a fundamental right of the accused, this process must be carried out with full recognition that the accused's interest in a speedy trial is specifically affirmed in the Constitution.

The difficulty of the task of balancing these factors is illustrated by this case, which we consider to be close. It is clear that the length of delay between arrest and trial—well over five years—was extraordinary. Only seven months of that period can be attributed to a strong excuse, the illness of the ex-sheriff who was in charge of the investigation. Perhaps some delay would have been permissible under ordinary circumstances, so that Manning could be utilized as a witness in Barker's trial, but more than four years was too long a period, particularly since a good part of that period was attributable to the Commonwealth's failure or inability to try Manning under circumstances that comported with due process.

Two counter-balancing factors, however, outweigh these deficiencies. The first is that prejudice was minimal. Of course, Barker was prejudiced to some extent by living for over four years under a cloud of suspicion and anxiety. Moreover, although he was released on bond for most of the period, he did spend 10 months in jail before trial. But there is no claim that any of Barker's witnesses died or otherwise became unavailable owing to the delay. The trial transcript indicates only two very minor lapses of memory—one on the part of a prosecution witness— which were in no way significant to the outcome.

More important than the absence of serious prejudice, is the fact that Barker did not want a speedy trial. Counsel was appointed for Barker immediately after his indictment and represented him throughout the period. No question is raised as to the competency of such counsel. Despite the fact that counsel had notice of the motions for continuances, the record shows no action whatever taken between October 21, 1958, and February 12, 1962, that could be construed as the assertion of the speedy-trial right. On the latter date, in response to another motion for continuance, Barker moved to dismiss the indictment. The record does not show on what ground this motion was based, although it is clear that no alternative motion was made for an immediate trial. Instead the record strongly suggests that while he hoped to take advantage of the delay in which he had acquiesced, and thereby obtain a dismissal of the charges, he definitely did not want to be tried. Counsel conceded as much at oral argument:

> "Your honor, I would concede that Willie Mae Barker—probably—I don't know this for a fact—probably did not want to be tried. I don't think any man wants to be tried. And I don't consider this a liability on his behalf. I don't blame him."

The probable reason for Barker's attitude was that he was gambling on Manning's acquittal. The evidence was not terribly strong against Manning, as the reversals and hung juries suggest, and Barker undoubtedly thought that if Manning were acquitted, he would never be tried. Counsel also conceded this:

> "Now, it's true that the reason for this delay was the Commonwealth of Kentucky's desire to secure the testimony of the accomplice, Silas Manning. And it's true that if Silas Manning were never convicted, Willie Mae Barker would never have been convicted. We concede this."

That Barker was gambling on Manning's acquittal is also suggested by his failure, following the *pro forma* motion to dismiss filed in February 1962, to object to the Commonwealth's next two motions for continuances. Indeed, it was not until March 1963, after Manning's convictions were final, that Barker, having lost his gamble, began to object to further continuances. At that time, the Commonwealth's excuse was the illness of the ex-sheriff, which Barker has conceded justified the further delay.

We do not hold that there may never be a situation in which an indictment may be dismissed on speedy-trial grounds where the defendant has failed to object to continuances. There may be a situation in which the defendant was represented by incompetent counsel, was severely prejudiced, or even cases in which the continuances were granted *ex parte*. But barring extraordinary circumstances, we would be reluctant indeed to rule that a defendant was denied this constitutional right on a record that strongly indicates, as does this one, that the defendant did not want a speedy trial. We hold, therefore, that Barker was not deprived of his due process right to a speedy trial. * * * b

DOGGETT V. UNITED STATES
505 U.S. 647, 112 S.Ct. 2686, 120 L.Ed.2d 520 (1992).

JUSTICE SOUTER delivered the opinion of the Court. * * *

On February 22, 1980, petitioner Marc Doggett was indicted for conspiring with several others to import and distribute cocaine. Douglas Driver, the Drug Enforcement Administration's principal agent investigating the conspiracy, told the United States Marshal's Service that the DEA would oversee the apprehension of Doggett and his confederates. On March 18, 1980, two police officers set out under Driver's orders to arrest Doggett at his parents' house in Raleigh, North Carolina, only to find that he was not there. His mother told the officers that he had left for Colombia four days earlier.

To catch Doggett on his return to the United States, Driver sent word of his outstanding arrest warrant to all United States Customs stations and to a number of law enforcement organizations. He also placed Doggett's name in the Treasury Enforcement Communication System (TECS), a computer network that helps Customs agents screen people entering the country, and in the National Crime Information Center computer system, which serves similar ends. The TECS entry expired that September, however, and Doggett's name vanished from the system.

---

b The concurring opinion of Justice White, joined by Justice Brennan, is omitted.

In September 1981, Driver found out that Doggett was under arrest on drug charges in Panama and, thinking that a formal extradition request would be futile, simply asked Panama to "expel" Doggett to the United States. Although the Panamanian authorities promised to comply when their own proceedings had run their course, they freed Doggett the following July and let him go to Colombia, where he stayed with an aunt for several months. On September 25, 1982, he passed unhindered through Customs in New York City and settled down in Virginia. Since his return to the United States, he has married, earned a college degree, found a steady job as a computer operations manager, lived openly under his own name, and stayed within the law.

Doggett's travels abroad had not wholly escaped the Government's notice, however. In 1982, the American Embassy in Panama told the State Department of his departure to Colombia, but that information, for whatever reason, eluded the DEA, and Agent Driver assumed for several years that his quarry was still serving time in a Panamanian prison. Driver never asked DEA officials in Panama to check into Doggett's status, and only after his own fortuitous assignment to that country in 1985 did he discover Doggett's departure for Colombia. Driver then simply assumed Doggett had settled there, and he made no effort to find out for sure or to track Doggett down, either abroad or in the United States. Thus Doggett remained lost to the American criminal justice system until September 1988, when the Marshal's Service ran a simple credit check on several thousand people subject to outstanding arrest warrants and, within minutes, found out where Doggett lived and worked. On September 5, 1988, nearly 6 years after his return to the United States and 8½ years after his indictment Doggett was arrested.

He naturally moved to dismiss the indictment, arguing that the Government's failure to prosecute him earlier violated his Sixth Amendment right to a speedy trial. The Federal Magistrate hearing his motion * * * found, however, that Doggett had made no affirmative showing that the delay had impaired his ability to mount a successful defense or had otherwise prejudiced him. In his recommendation to the District Court, the Magistrate contended that this failure to demonstrate particular prejudice sufficed to defeat Doggett's speedy trial claim.

The District Court took the recommendation and denied Doggett's motion. * * *

A split panel of the Court of Appeals affirmed. * * *

The Sixth Amendment guarantees that, "[i]n all criminal prosecutions, the accused shall enjoy the right to a speedy * * * trial * * *." On its face, the Speedy Trial Clause is written with such breadth that, taken literally, it would forbid the government to delay the trial of an "accused" for any reason at all. Our cases, however, have qualified the literal sweep of the provision by specifically recognizing the relevance of four separate enquiries: whether delay before trial was uncommonly long, whether the government or the criminal defendant is more to blame for that delay, whether, in due course, the defendant asserted his right to a speedy trial, and whether he suffered prejudice as the delay's result.

The first of these is actually a double enquiry. Simply to trigger a speedy trial analysis, an accused must allege that the interval between accusation and trial has crossed the threshold dividing ordinary from "presumptively prejudicial" delay, since, by definition, he cannot complain that the government has denied him a "speedy" trial if it has, in fact, prosecuted his case with customary promptness. If the accused makes this showing, the court must then consider, as one factor among several, the extent to which the delay stretches beyond the bare minimum needed to trigger judicial examination of the claim. This latter enquiry is significant to the speedy trial analysis because, as we discuss below, the presumption that pretrial delay has prejudiced the accused intensifies over time. In this case, the extraordinary 8½ year lag between Doggett's indictment and arrest clearly suffices to trigger the speedy trial enquiry; its further significance within that enquiry will be dealt with later.

As for *Barker's* second criterion, the Government claims to have sought Doggett with diligence. The findings of the courts below are to the contrary, however, and we review trial court determinations of negligence with considerable deference. The Government gives us nothing to gainsay the findings that have come up to us, and we see nothing fatal to them in the record. For six years, the Government's investigators made no serious effort to test their progressively more questionable assumption that Doggett was living abroad, and, had they done so, they could have found him within minutes. While the Government's lethargy may have reflected no more than Doggett's relative unimportance in the world of drug trafficking, it was still findable negligence, and the finding stands.

The Government goes against the record again in suggesting that Doggett knew of his indictment years before he was arrested. Were this true, *Barker's* third factor, concerning invocation of the right to a speedy trial, would be weighed heavily against him. But here again, the Government is trying to revisit the facts. At the hearing on Doggett's speedy trial motion, it introduced no evidence challenging the testimony of Doggett's wife, who said that she did not know of the charges until his arrest, and of his mother, who claimed not to have told him or anyone else that the police had come looking for him. * * *

The Government is left, then, with its principal contention: that Doggett fails to make out a successful speedy trial claim because he has not shown precisely how he was prejudiced by the delay between his indictment and trial.

We have observed in prior cases that unreasonable delay between formal accusation and trial threatens to produce more than one sort of harm, including "oppressive pretrial incarceration," "anxiety and concern of the accused," and "the possibility that the [accused's] defense will be impaired" by dimming memories and loss of exculpatory evidence. Of these forms of prejudice, "the most serious is the last, because the inability of a defendant adequately to prepare his case skews the fairness of the entire system." Doggett claims this kind of prejudice, and there is probably no other kind that he can claim, since he was subjected neither to pretrial detention nor, he has successfully contended, to awareness of unresolved charges against him.

The Government answers Doggett's claim by citing language in three cases, *United States v. Marion*, 404 U.S. 307 (1971), *United States v. MacDonald*, 456 U.S. 1 (1982), and *United States v. Loud Hawk*, 474 U.S. 302 (1986), for the proposition that the Speedy Trial Clause does not significantly protect a criminal defendant's interest in fair adjudication. In so arguing, the Government asks us, in effect, to read part of *Barker* right out of the law, and that we will not do. In context, the cited passages support nothing beyond the principle, which we have independently based on textual and historical grounds, that the Sixth Amendment right of the accused to a speedy trial has no application beyond the confines of a formal criminal prosecution. Once triggered by arrest, indictment, or other official accusation, however, the speedy trial enquiry must weigh the effect of delay on the accused's defense just as it has to weigh any other form of prejudice that *Barker* recognized.

As an alternative to limiting *Barker*, the Government claims Doggett has failed to make any affirmative showing that the delay weakened his ability to raise specific defenses, elicit specific testimony, or produce specific items of evidence. Though Doggett did indeed come up short in this respect, the Government's argument takes it only so far: consideration of prejudice is not limited to the specifically demonstrable, and, as it concedes, affirmative proof of particularized prejudice is not essential to every speedy trial claim. *Barker* explicitly recognized that impairment of one's defense is the most difficult form of speedy trial prejudice to prove because time's erosion of exculpatory evidence and testimony "can rarely be shown." And though time can tilt the case against either side, one cannot generally be sure which of them it has prejudiced more severely. Thus, we generally have to recognize that excessive delay presumptively compromises the reliability of a trial in ways that neither party can prove or, for that matter, identify. While such presumptive prejudice cannot alone carry a Sixth Amendment claim without regard to the other *Barker* criteria, it is part of the mix of relevant facts, and its importance increases with the length of delay.

This brings us to an enquiry into the role that presumptive prejudice should play in the disposition of Doggett's speedy trial claim. We begin with hypothetical and somewhat easier cases and work our way to this one.

Our speedy trial standards recognize that pretrial delay is often both inevitable and wholly justifiable. The government may need time to collect witnesses against the accused, oppose his pretrial motions, or, if he goes into hiding, track him down. We attach great weight to such considerations when balancing them against the costs of going forward with a trial whose probative accuracy the passage of time has begun by degrees to throw into question. Thus, in this case, if the Government had pursued Doggett with reasonable diligence from his indictment to his arrest, his speedy trial claim would fail. Indeed, that conclusion would generally follow as a matter of course however great the delay, so long as Doggett could not show specific prejudice to his defense.

The Government concedes, on the other hand that Doggett would prevail if he could show that the Government had intentionally held back in its prosecution of him to gain some impermissible advantage at trial. That we cannot doubt. *Barker* stressed that official bad faith in causing delay will be weighed heavily against the government, and a bad-faith delay the length of this negligent one would present an overwhelming case for dismissal.

Between diligent prosecution and bad-faith delay, official negligence in bringing an accused to trial occupies the middle ground. While not compelling relief in every case where bad-faith delay would make relief virtually automatic, neither is negligence automatically tolerable simply because the accused cannot demonstrate exactly how it has prejudiced him. It was on this point that the Court of Appeals erred, and on the facts before us, it was reversible error.

Barker made it clear that "different weights [are to be] assigned to different reasons" for delay. Although negligence is obviously to be weighed more lightly than a deliberate intent to harm the accused's defense, it still falls on the wrong side of the divide between acceptable and unacceptable reasons for delaying a criminal prosecution once it has begun. And such is the nature of the prejudice presumed that the weight we assign to official negligence compounds over time as the presumption of evidentiary prejudice grows. Thus, our toleration of such negligence varies inversely with its protractedness, and its consequent threat to the fairness of the accused's trial. Condoning prolonged and unjustifiable delays in prosecution would both penalize many defendants for the state's fault and simply encourage the government to gamble with the interests of criminal suspects assigned a low prosecutorial priority. The Government, indeed, can hardly complain too loudly, for persistent neglect in concluding a criminal prosecution indicates an uncommonly feeble interest in bringing an accused to justice; the more weight the Government attaches to securing a conviction, the harder it will try to get it.

To be sure, to warrant granting relief, negligence unaccompanied by particularized trial prejudice must have lasted longer than negligence demonstrably causing such prejudice. But even so, the Government's egregious persistence in failing to prosecute Doggett is clearly sufficient. The lag between Doggett's indictment and arrest was 8½ years, and he would have faced trial 6 years earlier than he did but for the Government's inexcusable oversights. The portion of the delay attributable to the Government's negligence far exceeds the threshold needed to state a speedy trial claim; indeed, we have called shorter delays "extraordinary." When the Government's negligence thus causes delay six times as long as that generally sufficient to trigger judicial review, and when the presumption of prejudice, albeit unspecified, is neither extenuated, as by the defendant's acquiescence, nor persuasively rebutted, the defendant is entitled to relief.

JUSTICE THOMAS, with whom THE CHIEF JUSTICE and JUSTICE SCALIA join, dissenting. * * * a

We have long identified the "major evils" against which the Speedy Trial Clause is directed as "undue and oppressive incarceration" and the "anxiety and concern accompanying public accusation." * * *

---

a   O'Connor, J., dissented separately on the ground that "a showing of actual prejudice to the defense" is required.

Thus, this unusual case presents the question whether, independent of these core concerns, the Speedy Trial Clause protects an accused from two additional harms: (1) prejudice to his ability to defend himself caused by the passage of time; and (2) disruption of his life years after the alleged commission of his crime. The Court today proclaims that the first of these additional harms is indeed an independent concern of the Clause, and on that basis compels reversal of Doggett's conviction and outright dismissal of the indictment against him. As to the second of these harms, the Court remains mum—despite the fact that we requested supplemental briefing on this very point.

I disagree with the Court's analysis. In my view, the Sixth Amendment's speedy trial guarantee does not provide independent protection against either prejudice to an accused's defense or the disruption of his life. I shall consider each in turn. * * *

We are * * * confronted with two conflicting lines of authority, the one declaring that "limit[ing] the possibility that the defense will be impaired" is an independent and fundamental objective of the Speedy Trial Clause, e.g., *Barker*, supra, and the other declaring that it is not, e.g., *Marion*, supra; *MacDonald*, supra; *Loud Hawk*, supra. The Court refuses to acknowledge this conflict. Instead, it simply reiterates the relevant language from *Barker* and asserts that *Marion*, *MacDonald*, and *Loud Hawk* "support nothing beyond the principle . . . that the Sixth Amendment right of the accused to a speedy trial has no application beyond the confines of a formal criminal prosecution." That attempt at reconciliation is eminently unpersuasive.

It is true, of course, that the Speedy Trial Clause by its terms applies only to an "accused"; the right does not attach before indictment or arrest. But that limitation on the Clause's protection only confirms that preventing prejudice to the defense is not one of its independent and fundamental objectives. For prejudice to the defense stems from the interval between crime and trial, which is quite distinct from the interval between accusation and trial. If the Clause were indeed aimed at safeguarding against prejudice to the defense, then it would presumably limit all prosecutions that occur long after the criminal events at issue. A defendant prosecuted 10 years after a crime is just as hampered in his ability to defend himself whether he was indicted the week after the crime or the week before the trial—but no one would suggest that the Clause protects him in the latter situation, where the delay did not substantially impair his liberty, either through oppressive incarceration or the anxiety of known criminal charges. * * *

It is misleading, then, for the Court to accuse the Government of "ask[ing] us, in effect, to read part of *Barker* right out of the law," a course the Court resolutely rejects. For the issue here is not simply whether the relevant language from *Barker* should be read out of the law, but whether that language trumps the contrary logic of *Marion*, *MacDonald*, and *Loud Hawk*. The Court's protestations notwithstanding, the two lines of authority cannot be reconciled; to reaffirm the one is to undercut the other.

In my view, the choice presented is not a hard one. *Barker*'s suggestion that preventing prejudice to the defense is a fundamental and independent objective of the Clause is plainly dictum. Never, until today, have we confronted a case where a defendant subjected to a lengthy delay after indictment nonetheless failed to suffer any substantial impairment of his liberty. I think it fair to say that *Barker* simply did not contemplate such an unusual situation. Moreover, to the extent that the *Barker* dictum purports to elevate considerations of prejudice to the defense to fundamental and independent status under the Clause, it cannot be deemed to have survived our subsequent decisions in *MacDonald* and *Loud Hawk.* * * *

Therefore, I see no basis for the Court's conclusion that Doggett is entitled to relief under the Speedy Trial Clause simply because the Government was negligent in prosecuting him and because the resulting delay may have prejudiced his defense.

It remains to be considered, however, whether Doggett is entitled to relief under the Speedy Trial Clause because of the disruption of his life years after the criminal events at issue. In other words, does the Clause protect a right to repose, free from secret or unknown indictments? In my view, it does not, for much the same reasons set forth above.

The common law recognized no right of criminals to repose. * * *

That is not to deny that our legal system has long recognized the value of repose, both to the individual and to society. But that recognition finds expression not in the sweeping commands of the Constitution, or in the common law, but in any number of specific statutes of limitations enacted by the federal and state legislatures. * * *

Doggett, however, asks us to hold that a defendant's interest in repose is a value independently protected by the Speedy Trial Clause. He emphasizes that at the time of his arrest he was "leading a normal, productive and law-abiding life," and that his "arrest and prosecution at this late date interrupted his life as a productive member of society and forced him to answer for actions taken in the distant past." However uplifting this tale of personal redemption, our task is to illuminate the protections of the Speedy Trial Clause, not to take the measure of one man's life.

There is no basis for concluding that the disruption of an accused's life years after the commission of his alleged crime is an evil independently protected by the Speedy Trial Clause. Such disruption occurs regardless of whether the individual is under indictment during the period of delay. Thus, had Doggett been indicted shortly before his 1988 arrest rather than shortly after his 1980 crime, his repose would have been equally shattered—but he would not have even a colorable speedy-trial claim. To recognize a constitutional right to repose is to recognize a right to be tried speedily after the offense. That would, of course, convert the Speedy Trial Clause into a constitutional statute of limitations—a result with no basis in the text or history of the Clause or in our precedents. * * *

Today's opinion, I fear, will transform the courts of the land into boards of law-enforcement supervision. For the Court compels dismissal of the charges against Doggett not because he was harmed in any way by the delay between his indictment and arrest,[6] but simply because the Government's efforts to catch him are found wanting. * * * Our Constitution neither contemplates nor tolerates such a role. I respectfully dissent.

UNITED STATES V. LOVASCO

431 U.S. 783, 97 S.Ct. 2044, 52 L.Ed.2d 752 (1977).

JUSTICE MARSHALL delivered the opinion of the Court. * * *

On March 6, 1975, respondent was indicted for possessing eight firearms stolen from the United States mail, and for dealing in firearms without a license. The offenses were alleged to have occurred between July 25 and August 31, 1973, more than 18 months before the indictment was filed. Respondent moved to dismiss the indictment due to the delay.

The District Court conducted a hearing on respondent's motion at which the respondent sought to prove that the delay was unnecessary and that it had prejudiced his defense. In an effort to establish the former proposition, respondent presented a Postal Inspector's report on his investigation that was prepared one month after the crimes were committed, and a stipulation concerning the post-report progress of the probe. The report stated, in brief, that within the first month of the investigation respondent had admitted to Government agents that he had possessed and then sold five of the stolen guns, and that the agents had developed strong evidence linking respondent to the remaining three weapons. The report also stated, however, that the agents had been unable to confirm or refute respondent's claim that he had found the guns in his car when he returned to it after visiting his son, a mail handler, at work. The stipulation into which the Assistant United States Attorney entered indicated that little additional information concerning the crimes was uncovered in the 17 months following the preparation of the Inspector's report.

To establish prejudice to the defense, respondent testified that he had lost the testimony of two material witnesses due to the delay. The first witness, Tom Stewart, died more than a year after the alleged crimes occurred. At the hearing respondent claimed that Stewart had been his source for two or three of the guns. The second witness, respondent's brother, died in April 1974, nine months after the crimes were completed. Respondent testified that his brother was present when respondent called Stewart to secure the guns, and witnessed all of respondent's sales. Respondent did not state how the witnesses would have aided the defense had they been willing to testify.

The Government made no systematic effort in the District Court to explain its long delay. The Assistant United States Attorney did expressly disagree, however,

---

[6]   It is quite likely, in fact, that the delay benefitted Doggett. At the time of his arrest, he had been living an apparently normal, law-abiding life for some five years—a point not lost on the District Court Judge, who, instead of imposing a prison term, sentenced him to three years' probation and a $1000 fine. Thus, the delay gave Doggett the opportunity to prove what most defendants can only promise: that he no longer posed a threat to society. There can be little doubt that, had he been tried immediately after his cocaine-importation activities, he would have received a harsher sentence.

with defense counsel's suggestion that the investigation had ended after the Postal Inspector's Report was prepared. The prosecutor also stated that it was the Government's theory that respondent's son, who had access to the mail at the railroad terminal from which the guns were "possibly stolen," was responsible for the thefts. Finally, the prosecutor elicited somewhat cryptic testimony from the Postal Inspector indicating that the case "as to these particular weapons involves other individuals"; that information had been presented to a grand jury "in regard to this case other than * * * [on] the day of the indictment itself"; and that he had spoken to the prosecutors about the case on four or five occasions.

Following the hearing, the District Court filed a brief opinion and order. The court found that by October 2, 1973, the date of the postal inspector's report, "The Government had all the information relating to defendant's alleged commission of the offense charged against him," and that the 17-month delay before the case was presented to the grand jury "had not been explained or justified" and was "unnecessary and unreasonable." The Court also found that "[a]s a result of the delay defendant has been prejudiced by reason of the death of Tom Stewart, a material witness on his behalf." Accordingly, the court dismissed the indictment.

The Government appealed to the United States Court of Appeals for the Eighth Circuit. In its brief the Government explained the months of inaction by stating:

> "[T]here was a legitimate Government interest in keeping the investigation open in the instant case. The defendant's son worked for the Terminal Railroad and had access to mail. It was the Government's position that the son was responsible for the theft and therefore further investigation to establish this fact was important.
>
> " * * * Although the investigation did not continue on a full time basis, there was contact between the United States Attorney's office and the Postal Inspector's office throughout * * * and certain matters were brought before a Federal Grand Jury prior to the determination that the case should be presented for indictment * * *."

The Court of Appeals accepted the Government's representation as to the motivation for the delay, but a majority of the court nevertheless affirmed the District Court's finding that the Government's actions were "unjustified, unnecessary, and unreasonable." The majority also found that respondent had established that his defense had been impaired by the loss of Stewart's testimony because it understood respondent to contend that "were Stewart's testimony available it would support [respondent's] claim that he did not know that the guns were stolen from the United States mails." * * *

We granted certiorari, and now reverse.

In *United States v. Marion*, 404 U.S. 307 (1971), this Court considered the significance, for constitutional purposes, of a lengthy preindictment delay. We held that as far as the Speedy Trial Clause of the Sixth Amendment is concerned, such delay is wholly irrelevant, since our analysis of the language, history, and purposes of the Clause persuaded us that only "a formal indictment or information or else the actual restraints imposed by arrest and holding to answer a criminal charge * * * engage the particular protections" of that provision. We went on to note that statutes of limitations, which provide predictable, legislatively enacted limits on prosecutorial delay, provide "the primary guarantee, against bringing overly stale criminal charges."[a] But we did acknowledge that the "statute of limitations does not fully define [defendants'] rights with respect to the events occurring prior to indictment," and that the Due Process Clause has a limited role to play in protecting against oppressive delay.[b]

Respondent seems to argue that due process bars prosecution whenever a defendant suffers prejudice as a result of preindictment delay. To support that proposition respondent relies on the concluding sentence of the Court's opinion in *Marion* where, in remanding the case, we stated that "[e]vents of the trial may demonstrate actual prejudice, but at the present time appellees' due process claims are speculative and premature." But the quoted sentence establishes only that proof of actual prejudice makes a due process claim concrete and ripe for adjudication, not that it makes the claim automatically valid. Indeed, two pages earlier in the opinion we expressly rejected the argument respondent advances here:

> "[W]e need not * * * determine when and in what circumstances actual prejudice resulting from preaccusation delay requires the dismissal of

---

[a]   The statute of limitations, in contrast to the speedy trial time limitations, runs from the date the offense is committed (or, in a few states, from the date the offense is discovered) to the date prosecution is commenced (in some states this means the date an indictment or information is filed, in others the date a warrant of arrest is issued). The typical statute specifies situations in which time is not counted against the period of limitation, such as when the defendant is out of the state or is away from his usual residence for the purpose of avoiding prosecution. "There are several reasons for the imposition of time limitations: First, and foremost, is the desirability that prosecutions be based upon reasonably fresh evidence. With the passage of time memories fade, witnesses die or leave the area, and physical evidence becomes more difficult to obtain, identify, or preserve. In short, possibility of erroneous conviction is minimized when prosecution is prompt. Second, if the actor long refrains from further criminal activity, the likelihood increases that he has reformed, diminishing the necessity for imposition of the criminal sanction. If he has repeated his criminal behavior, he can be prosecuted for recent offenses committed within the period of limitation. Hence, the need for protecting society against the perpetrator of a particular offense becomes less compelling as the years pass. Third, after a protracted period the retributive impulse which may have existed in the community is likely to yield to a sense of compassion aroused by the prosecution for an offense long forgotten. Fourth, it is desirable to reduce the possibility of blackmail based on a threat to prosecute or to disclose evidence to enforcement officials. Finally, statutes of limitations 'promote repose by giving security and stability to human affairs.'" *Model Penal Code* § 1.06, Comment (1985).

[b]   Regarding any *post-trial* right to "speedy" disposition, the Court in *Betterman v. Montana*, 136 S.Ct. 1609 (2016), held that "the Sixth Amendment's speedy trial guarantee * * * does not apply once a defendant has been found guilty at trial or has pled guilty to criminal charges," for "[a]s a measure protecting the presumptively innocent, the speedy trial right—like other similarly aimed measures—loses force upon conviction. * * *. That does not mean, however, that defendants lack any protection against undue delay at this stage. The primary safeguard comes from statutes and rules. The federal rule on point directs the court to 'impose sentence without unnecessary delay.' Fed. Rule Crim. Proc. 32(b)(1). Many States have provisions to the same effect, and some States prescribe numerical time limits. Further, as at the prearrest stage, due process serves as a backstop against exorbitant delay. After conviction, a defendant's due process right to liberty, while diminished, is still present. He retains an interest in a sentencing proceeding that is fundamentally fair. But because Betterman advanced no due process claim here, we express no opinion on how he might fare under that more pliable standard."

the prosecution. Actual prejudice to the defense of a criminal case may result from the shortest and most necessary delay; and no one suggests that every delay-caused detriment to a defendant's case should abort a criminal prosecution."

Thus *Marion* makes clear that proof of prejudice is generally a necessary but not sufficient element of a due process claim, and that the due process inquiry must consider the reasons for the delay as well as the prejudice to the accused.

The Court of Appeals found that the sole reason for the delay here was "a hope on the part of the Government that others might be discovered who may have participated in the theft * * *." It concluded that this hope did not justify the delay, and therefore affirmed the dismissal of the indictment. But the Due Process Clause does not permit courts to abort criminal prosecutions simply because they disagree with a prosecutor's judgment as to when to seek an indictment. Judges are not free, in defining "due process," to impose on law enforcement officials our "personal and private notions" of fairness and to "disregard the limits that bind judges in their judicial function." Our task is more circumscribed. We are to determine only whether the actions complained of—here, compelling respondent to stand trial after the Government delayed indictment to investigate further—violates those "fundamental conceptions of justice which lie at the base of our civil and political institutions," and which define "the community's sense of fair play and decency."

It requires no extended argument to establish that prosecutors do not deviate from "fundamental conceptions of justice" when they defer seeking indictments until they have probable cause to believe an accused is guilty; indeed it is unprofessional conduct for a prosecutor to recommend an indictment on less than probable cause. It should be equally obvious that prosecutors are under no duty to file charges as soon as probable cause exists but before they are satisfied they will be able to establish the suspect's guilt beyond a reasonable doubt. To impose such a duty "would have a deleterious effect both upon the rights of the accused and upon the ability of society to protect itself." From the perspective of potential defendants, requiring prosecutions to commence when probable cause is established is undesirable because it would increase the likelihood of unwarranted charges being filed, and would add to the time during which defendants stand accused but untried. * * * From the perspective of law enforcement officials, a requirement of immediate prosecution upon probable cause is equally unacceptable because it could make obtaining proof of guilt beyond a reasonable doubt impossible by causing potentially fruitful sources of information to evaporate before they are fully exploited. And from the standpoint of the courts, such a requirement is unwise because it would cause scarce resources to be consumed on cases that prove to be insubstantial, or that involve only some of the responsible parties or some of the criminal acts.[12] Thus, no one's interests would be well served by compelling prosecutors to initiate prosecutions as soon as they are legally entitled to do so.

---

[12] Defendants also would be adversely affected by trials involving less than all of the criminal acts for which they are responsible, since they likely would be subjected to multiple trials growing out of the same transaction or occurrence.

It might be argued that once the Government has assembled sufficient evidence to prove guilt beyond a reasonable doubt, it should be constitutionally required to file charges promptly, even if its investigation of the entire criminal transaction is not complete. Adopting such a rule, however, would have many of the same consequences as adopting a rule requiring immediate prosecution upon probable cause.

First, compelling a prosecutor to file public charges as soon as the requisite proof has been developed against one participant on one charge would cause numerous problems in those cases in which a criminal transaction involves more than one person or more than one illegal act. In some instances, an immediate arrest or indictment would impair the prosecutor's ability to continue his investigation, thereby preventing society from bringing lawbreakers to justice. In other cases, the prosecutor would be able to obtain additional indictments despite an early prosecution, but the necessary result would be multiple trials involving a single set of facts. Such trials place needless burdens on defendants, law enforcement officials, and courts.

Second, insisting on immediate prosecution once sufficient evidence is developed to obtain a conviction would pressure prosecutors into resolving doubtful cases in favor of early—and possibly unwarranted—prosecutions. The determination of when the evidence available to the prosecution is sufficient to obtain a conviction is seldom clear-cut, and reasonable persons often will reach conflicting conclusions. In the instant case, for example, since respondent admitted possessing at least five of the firearms, the primary factual issue in dispute was whether respondent knew the guns were stolen as required by 18 U.S.C. § 1708. Not surprisingly, the Postal Inspector's report contained no direct evidence bearing on this issue. The decision whether to prosecute, therefore, required a necessarily subjective evaluation of the strength of the circumstantial evidence available and the credibility of respondent's denial. Even if a prosecutor concluded that the case was weak and further investigation appropriate, he would have no assurance that a reviewing court would agree. To avoid the risk that a subsequent indictment would be dismissed for preindictment delay, the prosecutor might feel constrained to file premature charges with all the disadvantages that entails.[14]

Finally, requiring the Government to make charging decisions immediately upon assembling evidence sufficient to establish guilt would preclude the Government from giving full consideration to the desirability of not prosecuting in particular cases. The decision to file criminal charges, with the awesome consequences it entails, requires consideration of a wide range of factors in addition to the strength of the Government's case, in order to determine whether prosecution would be in the public interest. Prosecutors often need more information than proof of a suspect's guilt, therefore, before deciding whether to seek an indictment. Again the instant case provides a useful illustration. Although proof of the identity of the mail thieves was not necessary to convict respondent of

---

[14] In addition, if courts were required to decide in every case when the prosecution should have commenced, it would be necessary for them to trace the day-by-day progress of each investigation. Maintaining daily records would impose an administrative burden on prosecutors, and reviewing them would place an even greater burden on the courts.

the possessory crimes with which he was charged, it might have been crucial in assessing respondent's culpability, as distinguished from his legal guilt. If, for example, further investigation were to show that respondent had no role in or advance knowledge of the theft and simply agreed, out of paternal loyalty, to help his son dispose of the guns once respondent discovered his son had stolen them, the United States Attorney might have decided not to prosecute, especially since at the time of the crime respondent was over 60 years old and had no prior criminal record. Requiring prosecution once the evidence of guilt is clear, however, could prevent a prosecutor from awaiting the information necessary for such a decision.

We would be most reluctant to adopt a rule which would have these consequences absent a clear constitutional command to do so. We can find no such command in the Due Process Clause of the Fifth Amendment. In our view, investigative delay is fundamentally unlike delay undertaken by the Government solely "to gain tactical advantage over the accused," precisely because investigative delay is not so one-sided.[17] Rather than deviating from elementary standards of "fair play and decency," a prosecutor abides by them if he refuses to seek indictments until he is completely satisfied that he should prosecute and will be able promptly to establish guilt beyond a reasonable doubt. Penalizing prosecutors who defer action for these reasons would subordinate the goal of "orderly expedition" to that of "mere speed." This the Due Process Clause does not require. We therefore hold that to prosecute a defendant following investigative delay does not deprive him of due process, even if his defense might have been somewhat prejudiced by the lapse of time.

In the present case, the Court of Appeals stated that the only reason the Government postponed action was to await the results of additional investigation. Although there is, unfortunately, no evidence concerning the reasons for the delay in the record, the court's "finding" is supported by the prosecutor's implicit representation to the District Court, and explicit representation to the Court of Appeals, that the investigation continued during the time that the Government deferred taking action against respondent. The finding is, moreover, buttressed by the Government's repeated assertions in their Petition for Certiorari, their Brief, and their oral argument in this Court, "that the delay was caused by the Government's efforts to identify persons in addition to respondent who may have participated in the offenses." We must assume that these statements by counsel have been made in good faith. In light of this explanation, it follows that compelling respondent to stand trial would not be fundamentally unfair. The Court of Appeals therefore erred in affirming the District Court's decision dismissing the indictment.[c]

---

[17] In *Marion* we noted with approval that the Government conceded that a "tactical" delay would violate the Due Process Clause. The Government renews that concession here, and expands it somewhat by stating that "A due process violation might also be made out upon a showing of prosecutorial delay incurred in reckless disregard of circumstances, known to the prosecution, suggesting that there existed an appreciable risk that delay would impair the ability to mount an effective defense." As the Government notes, however, there is no evidence of recklessness here.

[c] Stevens, J., dissenting, agreed with the foregoing principles, but concluded the majority had erred in not deciding the case on the record made in the district court, wherein the government's delay was unexplained.

CHAPTER 13

THE DUTY TO DISCLOSE

■ ■ ■

In order to make the criminal trial "less a game of blindman's bluff and more a fair contest with the basic issues and facts disclosed to the fullest practical extent," *United States v. Procter & Gamble Co.*, 356 U.S. 677 (1958), the state and federal criminal justice systems, over the last few decades, have expanded dramatically the obligations of both prosecution and defense to disclose to the other side before trial the evidence that each intends to use at trial. This movement toward liberal pretrial "discovery" initially emphasized prosecution disclosure to the defense. The permissible scope of defense discovery varied,[a] but one constant objection to expanding such discovery was the absence of "reciprocity" in disclosure obligations—the failure to make discovery a "two-way street." This, in turn, led to expansion of the defense obligation to disclose its evidence to the prosecution. Most jurisdictions, however, concerned about possible constitutional objections to imposing such an obligation on the defense, initially provided the prosecution with very limited discovery. One of the earliest measures providing for prosecution discovery was the reciprocal alibi-notice statute. The first case in this chapter, *Williams v. Florida*, treats the constitutionality of such a statute. The ruling in *Williams* was seen by many as giving the states leeway constitutionally to grant the prosecution a fairly expansive right of discovery. It led to a variety of broadened reciprocal discovery requirements (e.g., requiring defense disclosure of the names of all of its intended witnesses), none of which have subsequently reached the Court.

While pretrial discovery requirements are designed primarily to avoid surprise and thereby allow a party ample time to build a case responsive to its opponent, the due process doctrine explored in *United States v. Bagley* actually requires the prosecution to assist the defense in building its case. In *Brady v. Maryland*, 373 U.S. 83 (1963), the Supreme Court established a constitutional duty of the prosecution to disclose to the defense exculpatory evidence that is material

---

[a] Some jurisdictions basically give the defense access to all of the evidence that the prosecution intends to use at trial, including not only a list of the prosecution's intended witnesses, but also any written summaries of statements those witnesses have made to the police or prosecutor. In other jurisdictions, discovery requirements are more limited out of concern that the defendant, if he knew who would be testifying for the prosecution and what they would say, would either develop perjured testimony to rebut their testimony or seek to intimidate those witnesses. Here disclosure is likely to be limited to documents, the reports of experts, and any recorded statements of defendant himself (usually given in response to police interrogation) that the prosecution intends to use at trial. What the states provide in the way of defense discovery is basically a matter of state choice. The Supreme Court had noted on several occasions that "there is no general constitutional right to discovery in a criminal case." *Weatherford v. Bursey*, 429 U.S. 545 (1977).

733

to the issues of either guilt or punishment.[b] *Bagley* explores the scope of this "*Brady* rule." *Pennsylvania v. Ritchie* raises the question of whether the prosecution's obligation to assist the defense in preparing its case goes beyond the *Brady* rule as a result of the defendant's Sixth Amendment rights to confront opposing witnesses and to present witnesses in his favor. Other aspects of those rights are considered in Chapter Eighteen.

WILLIAMS V. FLORIDA
399 U.S. 78, 90 S.Ct. 1893, 26 L.Ed.2d 446 (1970).

JUSTICE WHITE delivered the opinion of the Court.

Prior to his trial for robbery in the State of Florida, petitioner filed a "Motion for a Protective Order," seeking to be excused from the requirements of Rule 1.200 [now Rule 3.200] of the Florida Rules of Criminal Procedure. That rule requires a defendant, on written demand of the prosecuting attorney, to give notice in advance of trial if the defendant intends to claim an alibi, and to furnish the prosecuting attorney with information as to the place he claims to have been and with the names and addresses of the alibi witnesses he intends to use. In his motion petitioner openly declared his intent to claim an alibi, but objected to the further disclosure requirements on the ground that the Rule "compels the defendant in a criminal case to be a witness against himself" in violation of his Fifth and Fourteenth Amendment rights. The motion was denied. * * *

Florida's notice-of-alibi rule is in essence a requirement that a defendant submit to a limited form of pretrial discovery by the State whenever he intends to rely at trial on the defense of alibi. In exchange for the defendant's disclosure of the witnesses he proposes to use to establish that defense, the State in turn is required to notify the defendant of any witnesses it proposes to offer in rebuttal to that defense. Both sides are under a continuing duty promptly to disclose the names and addresses of additional witnesses bearing on the alibi as they become available. The threatened sanction for failure to comply is the exclusion at trial of the defendant's alibi evidence—except for his own testimony—or, in the case of the State, the exclusion of the State's evidence offered in rebuttal to the alibi.

In this case, following the denial of his Motion for a Protective Order, petitioner complied with the alibi rule and gave the State the name and address of one Mary Scotty. Mrs. Scotty was summoned to the office of the State Attorney on the morning of the trial, where she gave pretrial testimony. At the trial itself, Mrs. Scotty, petitioner and petitioner's wife all testified that the three of them had been in Mrs. Scotty's apartment during the time of the robbery. On two occasions during cross-examination of Mrs. Scotty, the prosecuting attorney confronted her with her earlier deposition in which she had given dates and times which in some respects did not correspond with the dates and times given at trial. Mrs. Scotty adhered to her trial story, insisting that she had been mistaken in her earlier testimony. The

---

[b]   The disclosure obligations discussed in *Bagley* and *Ritchie,* though often raised by a defendant's pretrial request for disclosure, flow from concerns relating to the fairness of the subsequent trial, and a nondisclosure therefore was rejected as a possible grounding for challenging a subsequent guilty plea in *United States v. Ruiz,* set forth at p. 773.

State also offered in rebuttal the testimony of one of the officers investigating the robbery who claimed that Mrs. Scotty had asked him for directions on the afternoon in question during the time when she claimed to have been in her apartment with petitioner and his wife.

We need not linger over the suggestion that the discovery permitted the State against petitioner in this case deprived him of "due process" or a "fair trial." Florida law provides for liberal discovery by the defendant against the State, and the notice-of-alibi rule is itself carefully hedged with reciprocal duties requiring state disclosure to the defendant.[a] Given the ease with which an alibi can be fabricated, the State's interest in protecting itself against an eleventh hour defense is both obvious and legitimate. Reflecting this interest, notice-of-alibi provisions, dating at least from 1927, are now in existence in a substantial number of States. The adversary system of trial is hardly an end to itself; it is not yet a poker game in which players enjoy an absolute right always to conceal their cards until played. We find ample room in that system, at least as far as "due process" is concerned, for the instant Florida rule, which is designed to enhance the search for truth in the criminal trial by insuring both the defendant and the State ample opportunity to investigate certain facts crucial to the determination of guilt or innocence.

Petitioner's major contention is that he was "compelled to be a witness against himself" contrary to the commands of the Fifth and Fourteenth Amendments because the notice-of-alibi rule required him to give the State the name and address of Mrs. Scotty in advance of trial and thus to furnish the State with information useful in convicting him. No pretrial statement of petitioner was introduced at trial; but armed with Mrs. Scotty's name and address and the knowledge that she was to be petitioner's alibi witness, the State was able to take her deposition in advance of trial and to find rebuttal testimony. Also, requiring him to reveal the elements of his defense is claimed to have interfered with his right to wait until after the State had presented its case to decide how to defend against it. We conclude, however, as has apparently every other court which has considered the issue, that the privilege against self-incrimination is not violated by a requirement that the defendant give notice of an alibi defense and disclose his alibi witnesses.

The defendant in a criminal trial is frequently forced to testify himself and to call other witnesses in an effort to reduce the risk of conviction. When he presents his witnesses, he must reveal their identity and submit them to cross-examination which in itself may prove incriminating or which may furnish the State with leads to incriminating rebuttal evidence. That the defendant faces such a dilemma demanding a choice between complete silence and presenting a defense has never been thought an invasion of the privilege against compelled self-incrimination. The pressures generated by the State's evidence may be severe but they do not vitiate the defendant's choice to present an alibi defense and witnesses to prove it, even

---

[a] The critical nature of this feature of the Florida alibi-discovery rule was later brought home in *Wardius v. Oregon*, 412 U.S. 470 (1973). Distinguishing *Williams*, the Court there held that an alibi-discovery rule which failed to provide reciprocal defense discovery violated due process. *Wardius* noted: "The State may not insist that trials be run as a 'search for the truth' so far as defense witnesses are concerned, while maintaining 'poker game secrecy' for its own witnesses."

though the attempted defense ends in catastrophe for the defendant. However "testimonial" and "incriminating" the alibi defense proves to be, it cannot be considered "compelled" within the meaning of the Fifth and Fourteenth Amendments.

Very similar constraints operate on the defendant when the State requires pretrial notice of alibi and the naming of alibi witnesses. Nothing in such a rule requires the defendant to rely on an alibi or prevents him from abandoning the defense; these matters are left to his unfettered choice. That choice must be made, but the pressures which bear on his pretrial decision are of the same nature as those which would induce him to call alibi witnesses at the trial: the force of historical fact beyond both his and the State's control and the strength of the State's case built on these facts. Response to that kind of pressure by offering evidence or testimony is not compelled self-incrimination transgressing the Fifth and Fourteenth Amendments.

In the case before us, the notice-of-alibi rule by itself in no way affected petitioner's crucial decision to call alibi witnesses or added to the legitimate pressures leading to that course of action. At most, the rule only compelled petitioner to accelerate the timing of his disclosure, forcing him to divulge at an earlier date information which the petitioner from the beginning planned to divulge at trial. Nothing in the Fifth Amendment privilege entitles a defendant as a matter of constitutional right to await the end of the State's case before announcing the nature of his defense, any more than it entitles him to await the jury's verdict on the State's case-in-chief before deciding whether or not to take the stand himself.

Petitioner concedes that absent the notice-of-alibi rule the Constitution would raise no bar to the court's granting the State a continuance at trial on the grounds of surprise as soon as the alibi witness is called. Nor would there be self-incrimination problems if, during that continuance, the State was permitted to do precisely what it did here prior to trial: to depose the witness and find rebuttal evidence. But if so utilizing a continuance is permissible under the Fifth and Fourteenth Amendments, then surely the same result may be accomplished through pretrial discovery, as it was here, avoiding the necessity of a disrupted trial.[17] We decline to hold that the privilege against compulsory self-incrimination guarantees the defendant the right to surprise the state with an alibi defense.

CHIEF JUSTICE BURGER, concurring.

I join fully in Mr. Justice White's opinion for the Court. I see an added benefit to the alibi notice rule in that it will serve important functions by way of disposing of cases without trial in appropriate circumstances—a matter of considerable importance when courts, prosecution offices and legal aid and defender agencies are vastly overworked. [The Chief Justice noted that a prosecutor receiving the names of alibi witnesses in advance of trial often would be able to determine whether an alibi defense was "reliable and unimpeachable" or "contrived and

---

[17] It might also be argued that the "testimonial" disclosures protected by the Fifth Amendment include only statements relating to the historical facts of the crime, not statements relating solely to what a defendant proposes to do at trial.

fabricated." The former determination "would very likely lead to dismissal of the charges," while the latter could lead to a defense decision to plead guilty. In either instance, the Chief Justice noted, "the ends of justice will have been served and the processes expedited."] * * *

JUSTICE BLACK, with whom JUSTICE DOUGLAS joins, dissenting.

* * * Although this case itself involves only a notice-of-alibi provision, it is clear that the decision means that a State can require a defendant to disclose in advance of trial any and all information he might possibly use to defend himself at trial. This decision, in my view, is a radical and dangerous departure from the historical and constitutionally guaranteed right of a defendant in a criminal case to remain completely silent, requiring the State to prove its case without any assistance of any kind from the defendant himself.

The core of the majority's decision is an assumption that compelling a defendant to give notice of an alibi defense before a trial is no different from requiring a defendant, after the State has produced the evidence against him at trial, to plead alibi before the jury retires to consider the case. * * * [But] when a defendant is required to indicate whether he might plead alibi in advance of trial, he faces a vastly different decision than that faced by one who can wait until the State has presented the case against him before making up his mind. Before trial the defendant knows only what the State's case *might* be. Before trial there is no such thing as the "strength of the State's case," there is only a range of possible cases. At that time there is no certainty as to what kind of case the State will ultimately be able to prove at trial. Therefore any appraisal of the desirability of pleading alibi will be beset with guesswork and gambling far greater than that accompanying the decision at the trial itself. * * * Clearly the pressures on defendants to plead an alibi created by this procedure are not only quite different than the pressures operating at the trial itself, but are in fact significantly greater. Contrary to the majority's assertion, the pretrial decision cannot be analyzed as simply a matter of "timing," influenced by the same factors operating at the trial itself.

The Court apparently also assumes that a defendant who has given the required notice can abandon his alibi without hurting himself. Such an assumption is implicit in and necessary for the majority's argument that the pretrial decision is no different than that at the trial itself. I, however, cannot so lightly assume that pretrial notice will have no adverse effects on a defendant who later decides to forego such a defense. Necessarily the defendant will have given the prosecutor the names of persons who may have some knowledge about the defendant himself or his activities. Necessarily the prosecutor will have every incentive to question these persons fully, and in doing so he may discover new leads or evidence. Undoubtedly there will be situations in which the State will seek to use such information—information it would probably never have obtained but for the defendant's coerced cooperation.

It is unnecessary for me, however, to engage in any such intellectual gymnastics concerning the practical effects of the notice-of-alibi procedure, because the Fifth Amendment itself clearly provides that "[n]o person * * * shall be compelled in any criminal case to be a witness against himself." If words are to be given their plain and obvious meaning, that provision, in my opinion, states that a criminal defendant cannot be required to give evidence, testimony, or any other assistance to the State to aid it in convicting him of crime. The Florida notice-of-alibi rule in my opinion is a patent violation of that constitutional provision because it requires a defendant to disclose information to the State so that the State can use that information to destroy him. * * *

It is no answer to this argument to suggest that the Fifth Amendment as so interpreted would give the defendant an unfair element of surprise, turning a trial into a "poker game" or "sporting contest," for that tactical advantage to the defendant is inherent in the type of trial required by our Bill of Rights. The Framers were well aware of the awesome investigative and prosecutorial powers of government and it was in order to limit those powers that they spelled out in detail in the Constitution the procedure to be followed in criminal trials. * * * The defendant, under our Constitution, need not do anything at all to defend himself, and certainly he cannot be required to help convict himself. Rather he has an absolute, unqualified right to compel the State to investigate its own case, find its own witnesses, prove its own facts, and convince the jury through its own resources. Throughout the process the defendant has a fundamental right to remain silent, in effect challenging the State at every point to "Prove it!" * * *

This constitutional right to remain absolutely silent cannot be avoided by superficially attractive analogies to any so-called "compulsion" inherent in the trial itself which may lead a defendant to put on evidence in his own defense. Obviously the Constitution contemplates that a defendant can be "compelled" to stand trial, and obviously there will be times when the trial process itself will require the defendant to do something in order to try to avoid a conviction. But nothing in the Constitution permits the State to add to the natural consequences of a trial and compel the defendant in advance of trial to participate in any way in the State's attempt to condemn him. * * *

On the surface this case involves only a notice-of-alibi provision, but in effect the decision opens the way for a profound change in one of the most important traditional safeguards of a criminal defendant. The rationale of today's decision is in no way limited to alibi defenses, or any other type or classification of evidence. The theory advanced goes at least so far as to permit the State to obtain under threat of sanction complete disclosure by the defendant in advance of trial of all evidence, testimony and tactics he plans to use at that trial. In each case the justification will be that the rule affects only the "timing" of the disclosure, and not the substantive decision itself. * * * [b]

---

[b] A footnote in the *Williams* opinion noted that the case there before the Court did not present the question of the "validity of the threatened sanction" (the exclusion of the testimony of unlisted witnesses) as "no such penalty was exacted here." In a later case, *Taylor v. Illinois*, 484 U.S. 400 (1988), the Court upheld the exclusion of the testimony of defense witness who had not been listed at discovery. In that case, as authorized by state law, the prosecution requested a pretrial listing of all defense witnesses after it had provided defense with a list of its witnesses. Defense counsel listed four witnesses, but during the midst of the trial, sought to add two additional witnesses. Counsel initially stated that he had just been informed about these persons and that they had probably seen the incident in question (a shooting). In response to the trial

UNITED STATES V. BAGLEY

473 U.S. 667, 105 S.Ct. 3375, 87 L.Ed.2d 481 (1985).

JUSTICE BLACKMUN announced the judgment of the Court and delivered an opinion of the Court except as to Part III.

In *Brady v. Maryland,* 373 U.S. 83 (1963), this Court held that "the suppression by the prosecution of evidence favorable to an accused upon request violates due process where the evidence is material either to guilt or punishment." The issue in the present case concerns the standard of materiality to be applied in determining whether a conviction should be reversed because the prosecutor failed to disclose requested evidence that could have been used to impeach Government witnesses.

I

[Respondent Bagley was indicted on 15 counts of violating federal narcotics and firearms statutes. The Government's two principal witnesses were O'Connor and Mitchell, private security guards who had assisted the Bureau of Alcohol, Tobacco and Firearms (ATF) in conducting an undercover investigation of respondent. Several weeks before trial, respondent filed a discovery motion that requested disclosure of a variety of matters, including "any deals, promises or inducements made to witnesses in exchange for their testimony." The Government's response to the discovery motion did not disclose that any "deals, promises or inducements" had been made to O'Connor or Mitchell. In apparent reply to another part of the discovery request, the Government produced a series of affidavits that O'Connor and Mitchell had signed while the undercover investigation was in progress. Those affidavits recounted in detail their undercover

---

judge's inquiry, counsel then acknowledged that the defendant had previously told him about one of the witnesses, but counsel stated that he had been unable until now to locate that witness. The trial court then questioned that witness and learned both that the witness had not actually seen the incident (although he claimed to have information that would be relevant to defendant's explanation of the shooting) and that counsel had met with the witness a week before trial. The trial court concluded that counsel's failure to give earlier notice of his intent to call the witness constituted a "blatant" and "willful" violation of the discovery rules that would require precluding the witness from testifying.

Sustaining the application of the preclusion sanction, the Supreme Court majority initially rejected the contention that the Sixth Amendment's compulsory process clause creates an absolute bar to the preclusion of the testimony of a surprise witness. It noted that the "adversary process could not function effectively without rules of procedure that govern the orderly presentation of facts and arguments to provide each party with a fair opportunity to assemble and submit evidence to contradict or explain the opponent's case," and that those rules served "the same high purpose" in "full and truthful disclosure of critical facts" as the compulsory process clause and other rights protected by the Sixth Amendment. Defendant argued that alternative and more appropriate sanctions than preclusion were available (e.g., allowing the state a continuance or disciplining the defense counsel), but the Court responded that, while "it may well be true that alternative sanctions are adequate and appropriate in most cases," a preclusion sanction could not be absolutely barred as it is "equally clear that [those alternative sanctions] would be less effective than the preclusion sanction and that there are instances in which they would perpetuate rather than limit the prejudice to the State and harm to the adversary process." As for the case before it, the Court concluded that circumstances clearly indicated that defense counsel was "deliberately seeking a tactical advantage," and "regardless of whether the prejudice to the prosecution could have been avoided," the case fit into "the category of willful misconduct in which the severest sanction is appropriate."

dealings with respondent. Each affidavit concluded with the statement, "I made this statement freely and voluntarily without any threats or rewards, or promises of reward having been made to me in return for it."]

[Respondent waived his right to a jury trial and was tried before the district court. At the trial, O'Connor and Mitchell testified about both the firearms and the narcotics charges. The court found respondent guilty on the narcotics charges, but not guilty on the firearms charges. Sometime later, respondent filed requests for information pursuant to the Freedom of Information Act. He received in response copies of ATF form contracts between ATF and O'Connor and Mitchell. The printed portion of the form stated that the informant would provide information to ATF and that "upon receipt of such information * * * and upon the accomplishment of the objective sought to be obtained by the use of such information to the satisfaction of (the ATF), the United States will pay to said vendor a sum commensurate with services and information rendered." The figure "$300.00" was handwritten in each form on a line entitled "Sum to Be Paid to Vendor." Because these contracts had not been disclosed in response to his pretrial discovery motion, respondent moved the district court to vacate his sentence. The Assistant United States Attorney who prosecuted respondent stated that he had not known that the contracts existed, and that he would have furnished them to respondent had he known of them, but the government also argued that there had been no constitutional error.]

[The motion came before the same district judge who had presided at respondent's bench trial. The district judge accepted the findings of a magistrate that the printed form contracts were blank when O'Connor and Mitchell signed them, that they were not signed by an ATF representative until after the trial, and that ATF made payments of $300 to both O'Connor and Mitchell at that time. Although the ATF case agent who dealt with O'Connor and Mitchell testified that the $300 payments simply reimbursed expenses, the district judge found that it was "probable" that O'Connor and Mitchell expected to receive compensation, in addition to their expenses. The judge concluded that "the United States did * * * withhold, during pretrial discovery, information as to any 'deals, promises or inducements' to these witnesses," but also found, beyond a reasonable doubt, that had the existence of the agreements been disclosed during trial, the disclosure would have had no effect upon his finding that the Government had proved its case on the narcotics charges. The United States Court of Appeals for the Ninth Circuit reversed, reasoning that the failure to disclose automatically required reversal of the conviction.]

II

The holding in *Brady v. Maryland*, 373 U.S. 83 (1963), requires disclosure only of evidence that is both favorable to the accused and "material either to guilt or punishment." The Court explained in *United States v. Agurs*, 427 U.S. 97 (1976): "A fair analysis of the holding in *Brady* indicates that implicit in the requirement of materiality is a concern that the suppressed evidence might have affected the outcome of the trial." The evidence suppressed in *Brady* would have been admissible only on the issue of punishment and not on the issue of guilt, and therefore could have affected only Brady's sentence and not his conviction.

Accordingly, the Court affirmed the lower court's restriction of Brady's new trial to the issue of punishment.[a]

The *Brady* rule is based on the requirement of due process. Its purpose is not to displace the adversary system as the primary means by which truth is uncovered, but to ensure that a miscarriage of justice does not occur.[6] Thus, the prosecutor is not required to deliver his entire file to defense counsel,[7] but only to disclose evidence favorable to the accused that, if suppressed, would deprive the defendant of a fair trial. * * * As *Agurs* noted: "For unless the omission deprived the defendant of a fair trial, there was no constitutional violation requiring that the verdict be set aside; and absent a constitutional violation, there was no breach of the prosecutor's constitutional duty to disclose. * * *" *United States v. Agurs*.

In *Brady* * * *, the prosecutor failed to disclose exculpatory evidence. In the present case, the prosecutor failed to disclose evidence that the defense might have used to impeach the Government's witnesses by showing bias or interest. Impeachment evidence, however, as well as exculpatory evidence, falls within the *Brady* rule. Such evidence is "evidence favorable to an accused," *Brady,* so that, if disclosed and used effectively, it may make the difference between conviction and acquittal. Cf. *Napue v. Illinois* [fn. 8 infra] ("The jury's estimate of the truthfulness and reliability of a given witness may well be determinative of guilt or innocence, and it is upon such subtle factors as the possible interest of the witness in testifying falsely that a defendant's life or liberty may depend"). * * *

III

It remains to determine the standard of materiality applicable to the nondisclosed evidence at issue in this case. Our starting point is the framework for evaluating the materiality of *Brady* evidence established in *United States v. Agurs*.

---

[a]   The defendant Brady and a companion, Boblit, had been found guilty of felony murder and sentenced to death. Prior to Brady's separate trial, his counsel had asked the prosecutor to allow him to examine all of the statements that Boblit had given to the police. Counsel was shown several of Boblit's statements, but for some unexplained reason failed to receive one statement in which Boblit admitted that he had done the actual killing. At trial, defendant admitted his participation in the crime, but claimed that he had not himself killed the victim. Defense counsel stressed this claim in his closing argument, asking the jury to show leniency and not impose the death penalty. Following defendant's conviction, defense counsel learned of the undisclosed statement and sought a new trial based on this newly discovered evidence. The Supreme Court affirmed a state court ruling granting a new trial as to the issue of punishment alone. Whether or not defendant himself killed the victim had no bearing on his liability for the homicide, and Boblit's statement therefore would not have been admissible in evidence on that issue. On the other hand, the statement could have been used to support defendant's plea for leniency as to punishment, and the prosecution's failure to disclose the statement had deprived Brady of a fair hearing on that issue.

[6]   By requiring the prosecutor to assist the defense in making its case, the *Brady* rule represents a limited departure from a pure adversary model. The Court has recognized, however, that the prosecutor's role transcends that of an adversary: he "is the representative not of an ordinary party to a controversy, but of a sovereignty * * * whose interest * * * in a criminal prosecution is not that it shall win a case, but that justice shall be done." *Berger v. United States,* 295 U.S. 78 (1935).

[7]   * * * An interpretation of *Brady* to create a broad, constitutionally required right of discovery "would entirely alter the character and balance of our present systems of criminal justice." *Giles v. Maryland,* 386 U.S. 66 (1967) (dissenting opinion). Furthermore, a rule that the prosecutor commits error by any failure to disclose evidence favorable to the accused, no matter how insignificant, would impose an impossible burden on the prosecutor and would undermine the interest in the finality of judgments.

The Court in *Agurs* distinguished three situations involving the discovery, after trial, of information favorable to the accused that had been known to the prosecution but unknown to the defense. The first situation was the prosecutor's knowing use of perjured testimony or, equivalently, the prosecutor's knowing failure to disclose that testimony used to convict the defendant was false. The Court noted the well-established rule that "a conviction obtained by the knowing use of perjured testimony is fundamentally unfair, and must be set aside if there is any reasonable likelihood that the false testimony could have affected the judgment of the jury." 427 U.S., at 103.[8] Although this rule is stated in terms that treat the knowing use of perjured testimony as error subject to harmless-error review, it may as easily be stated as a materiality standard under which the fact that testimony is perjured is considered material unless failure to disclose it would be harmless beyond a reasonable doubt. The Court in *Agurs* justified this standard of materiality on the ground that the knowing use of perjured testimony involves prosecutorial misconduct and, more importantly, involves "a corruption of the truth-seeking function of the trial process."

At the other extreme is the situation in *Agurs* itself, where the defendant does not make a *Brady* request and the prosecutor fails to disclose certain evidence favorable to the accused. The Court rejected a harmless-error rule in that situation, because under that rule every nondisclosure is treated as error, thus imposing on the prosecutor a constitutional duty to deliver his entire file to defense counsel. At the same time, the Court rejected a standard that would require the defendant to demonstrate that the evidence if disclosed probably would have resulted in acquittal.[b] The Court reasoned: "If the standard applied to the usual motion for a new trial based on newly discovered evidence were the same when the evidence was in the State's possession as when it was found in a neutral source, there would be no special significance to the prosecutor's obligation to serve the cause of justice." The standard of materiality applicable in the absence of a specific *Brady*

---

[8] In fact, the *Brady* rule has its roots in a series of cases dealing with convictions based on the prosecution's knowing use of perjured testimony. In *Mooney v. Holohan,* 294 U.S. 103 (1935), the Court established the rule that the knowing use by a state prosecutor of perjured testimony to obtain a conviction and the deliberate suppression of evidence that would have impeached and refuted the testimony constitutes a denial of due process. The Court reasoned that "a deliberate deception of court and jury by the presentation of testimony known to be perjured" is inconsistent with "the rudimentary demands of justice." The Court reaffirmed this principle in broader terms in *Napue v. Illinois,* 360 U.S. 264 (1959). In *Napue,* the principal witness for the prosecution falsely testified that he had been promised no consideration for his testimony. The Court held that the knowing use of false testimony to obtain a conviction violates due process regardless of whether the prosecutor solicited the false testimony or merely allowed it to go uncorrected when it appeared. The Court explained that the principle that a State may not knowingly use false testimony to obtain a conviction—even false testimony that goes only to the credibility of the witness—is "implicit in any concept of ordered liberty." Finally, the Court held that it was not bound by the state court's determination that the false testimony "could not in any reasonable likelihood have affected the judgment of the jury." The Court conducted its own independent examination of the record and concluded that the false testimony "may have had an effect on the outcome of the trial." Accordingly, the Court reversed the judgment of conviction.

[b] The reference here was to what *Agurs* described as the "Rule 33 Standard"—the test applied to a motion for a new trial based on evidence newly discovered by the defense. That standard typically requires that the defense establish (1) that its failure to learn of the evidence previously was due to no lack of diligence, (2) that the evidence is material, not merely "cumulative or impeaching," and (3) that the evidence "will probably produce an acquittal."

request is therefore stricter than the harmless-error standard but more lenient to the defense than the newly discovered evidence standard.

The third situation identified by the Court in *Agurs* is where the defense makes a specific request and the prosecutor fails to disclose responsive evidence. The Court did not define the standard of materiality applicable in this situation, but suggested that the standard might be more lenient to the defense than in the situation in which the defense makes no request or only a general request. The Court also noted: "When the prosecutor receives a specific and relevant request, the failure to make any response is seldom, if ever, excusable."

The Court has relied on and reformulated the *Agurs* standard for the materiality of undisclosed evidence in two subsequent cases arising outside the *Brady* context. In neither case did the Court's discussion of the *Agurs* standard distinguish among the three situations described in *Agurs*. In *United States v. Valenzuela-Bernal,* 458 U.S. 858 (1982), the Court held that due process is violated when testimony is made unavailable to the defense by Government deportation of witnesses "only if there is a reasonable likelihood that the testimony could have affected the judgment of the trier of fact." And in *Strickland v. Washington,* [p. 928], the Court held that a new trial must be granted when evidence is not introduced because of the incompetence of counsel only if "there is a reasonable probability that, but for counsel's unprofessional errors, the result of the proceeding would have been different." The *Strickland* Court defined a "reasonable probability" as "a probability sufficient to undermine confidence in the outcome."

We find the *Strickland* formulation of the *Agurs* test for materiality sufficiently flexible to cover the "no request," "general request," and "specific request" cases of prosecutorial failure to disclose evidence favorable to the accused: The evidence is material only if there is a reasonable probability that, had the evidence been disclosed to the defense, the result of the proceeding would have been different. A "reasonable probability" is a probability sufficient to undermine confidence in the outcome.[c]

---

[c] In *Kyles v. Whitley,* 514 U.S. 419 (1995), the Supreme Court further explored this standard. The Court noted that "four aspects of materiality under *Bagley* bear emphasis." First, "a showing of materiality does not require demonstration by a preponderance that disclosure of the suppressed evidence would have resulted ultimately in the defendant's acquittal * * *. *Bagley*'s touchstone of materiality is a 'reasonable probability' of a different result, and the adjective is important. The question is not whether the defendant would more likely than not have received a different verdict with the evidence, but whether in its absence he received a fair trial, understood as a trial resulting in a verdict worthy of confidence." Second, the "*Bagley* materiality [test] * * * is not a sufficiency of evidence test. A defendant need not demonstrate that after discounting the inculpatory evidence in light of the undisclosed evidence, there would not have been enough left to convict." Third, "once a reviewing court applying *Bagley* has found constitutional error there is no need for further harmless-error review." For if "a harmless error enquiry were to * * * [be undertaken], a *Bagley* error could not be treated as harmless, since 'a reasonable probability that had the evidence been disclosed to the defense, the result would have been different,' *Bagley,* necessarily entails the conclusion that the suppression must have had 'substantial and injurious effect or influence in determining the jury verdict,' *Brecht v. Abrahamson* [holding that an error having that impact is not harmless]." Fourth, "*Bagley* materiality" is to be judged by reference to the "suppressed evidence considered collectively, not item-by-item," with the focus on the "cumulative effect of suppression."

The Court in *Kyles* also refused to adopt "an even more lenient rule" where the "favorable evidence in issue * * * [was] known only to police investigators and not to the prosecutor." It noted:

The Government suggests that a materiality standard more favorable to the defendant reasonably might be adopted in specific request cases. The Government notes that an incomplete response to a specific request not only deprives the defense of certain evidence, but has the effect of representing to the defense that the evidence does not exist. In reliance on this misleading representation, the defense might abandon lines of independent investigation, defenses, or trial strategies that it otherwise would have pursued.

We agree that the prosecutor's failure to respond fully to a *Brady* request may impair the adversary process in this manner. And the more specifically the defense requests certain evidence, thus putting the prosecutor on notice of its value, the more reasonable it is for the defense to assume from the nondisclosure that the evidence does not exist, and to make pretrial and trial decisions on the basis of this assumption. This possibility of impairment does not necessitate a different standard of materiality, however, for under the *Strickland* formulation the reviewing court may consider directly any adverse effect that the prosecutor's failure to respond might have had on the preparation or presentation of the defendant's case. The reviewing court should assess the possibility that such effect might have occurred in light of the totality of the circumstances and with an awareness of the difficulty of reconstructing in a post-trial proceeding the course that the defense and the trial would have taken had the defense not been misled by the prosecutor's incomplete response.

In the present case, we think that there is a significant likelihood that the prosecutor's response to respondent's discovery motion misleadingly induced defense counsel to believe that O'Connor and Mitchell could not be impeached on the basis of bias or interest arising from inducements offered by the Government. Defense counsel asked the prosecutor to disclose any inducements that had been made to witnesses, and the prosecutor failed to disclose that the possibility of a reward had been held out to O'Connor and Mitchell if the information they supplied led to "the accomplishment of the objective sought to be obtained * * * to the satisfaction of [the Government]." This possibility of a reward gave O'Connor and Mitchell a direct, personal stake in respondent's conviction. The fact that the stake was not guaranteed through a promise or binding contract, but was expressly contingent on the Government's satisfaction with the end result, served only to strengthen any incentive to testify falsely in order to secure a conviction. Moreover, the prosecutor disclosed affidavits that stated that O'Connor and Mitchell received no promises of reward in return for providing information in the affidavits implicating respondent in criminal activity. In fact, O'Connor and Mitchell signed the last of these affidavits the very day after they signed the ATF contracts. While

---

"To accommodate the State in this manner would * * * amount to a serious change of course from the *Brady* line of cases. In the State's favor it may be said that no one doubts that police investigators sometimes fail to inform a prosecutor of all they know. But neither is there any serious doubt that 'procedures and regulations can be established to carry [the prosecutor's] burden and to insure communication of all relevant information on each case to every lawyer who deals with it.' * * * Since, then, the prosecutor has the means to discharge the government's *Brady* responsibility if he will, any argument for excusing a prosecutor from disclosing what he does not happen to know about boils down to a plea to substitute the police for the prosecutor, and even for the courts themselves, as the final arbiters of the government's obligation to ensure fair trials."

petitioner is technically correct that the blank contracts did not constitute a "promise of reward," the natural effect of these affidavits would be misleadingly to induce defense counsel to believe that O'Connor and Mitchell provided the information in the affidavits, and ultimately their testimony at trial recounting the same information, without any "inducements."

The District Court, nonetheless, found beyond a reasonable doubt that, had the information that the Government held out the possibility of reward to its witnesses been disclosed, the result of the criminal prosecution would not have been different. If this finding were sustained by the Court of Appeals, the information would be immaterial even under the standard of materiality applicable to the prosecutor's knowing use of perjured testimony. Although the express holding of the Court of Appeals was that the nondisclosure in this case required automatic reversal, the Court of Appeals also stated that it "disagreed" with the District Court's finding of harmless error. * * * Accordingly, we reverse the judgment of the Court of Appeals and remand the case to that court for a determination whether there is a reasonable probability that, had the inducement offered by the Government to O'Connor and Mitchell been disclosed to the defense, the result of the trial would have been different.

JUSTICE POWELL took no part in the decision of this case.

JUSTICE WHITE, with whom THE CHIEF JUSTICE and JUSTICE REHNQUIST join, concurring in part and concurring in the judgment.

I agree with the Court that respondent is not entitled to have his conviction overturned unless he can show that the evidence withheld by the Government was "material," and I therefore join Parts I and II of the Court's opinion. I also agree with Justice Blackmun that for purposes of this inquiry, "evidence is material only if there is a reasonable probability that, had the evidence been disclosed to the defense, the result of the proceeding would have been different." As the Justice correctly observes, this standard is "sufficiently flexible" to cover all instances of prosecutorial failure to disclose evidence favorable to the accused. Given the flexibility of the standard and the inherently fact-bound nature of the cases to which it will be applied, however, I see no reason to attempt to elaborate on the relevance to the inquiry of the specificity of the defense's request for disclosure, either generally or with respect to this case. I would hold simply that the proper standard is one of reasonable probability and that the Court of Appeals' failure to apply this standard necessitates reversal. I therefore concur in the judgment.

JUSTICE MARSHALL, with whom JUSTICE BRENNAN joins, dissenting.

The Court today chooses to reverse and remand the case for application of its newly stated standard to the facts of this case. While I believe that the evidence at issue here, which remained undisclosed despite a particular request, undoubtedly was material under the Court's standard, I also have serious doubts whether the Court's definition of the constitutional right at issue adequately takes account of the interests this Court sought to protect in its decision in *Brady v. Maryland.*

I begin from the fundamental premise, which hardly bears repeating, that "[t]he purpose of a trial is as much the acquittal of an innocent person as it is the conviction of a guilty one." When evidence favorable to the defendant is known to exist, disclosure only enhances the quest for truth; it takes no direct toll on that inquiry. Moreover, the existence of any small piece of evidence favorable to the defense may, in a particular case, create just the doubt that prevents the jury from returning a verdict of guilty. The private whys and wherefores of jury deliberations pose an impenetrable barrier to our ability to know just which piece of information might make, or might have made, a difference.

* * * We have long recognized that, within the limit of the State's ability to identify so-called exculpatory information, the State's concern for a fair verdict precludes it from withholding from the defense evidence favorable to the defendant's case in the prosecutor's files. * * * This recognition no doubt stems in part from the frequently considerable imbalance in resources between most criminal defendants and most prosecutors' offices. Many, perhaps most, criminal defendants in the United States are represented by appointed counsel, who often are paid minimal wages and operate on shoestring budgets. In addition, unlike police, defense counsel generally is not present at the scene of the crime, or at the time of arrest, but instead comes into the case late. Moreover, unlike the Government, defense counsel is not in the position to make deals with witnesses to gain evidence. Thus, an inexperienced, unskilled, or unaggressive attorney often is unable to amass the factual support necessary to a reasonable defense. When favorable evidence is in the hands of the prosecutor but not disclosed, the result may well be that the defendant is deprived of a fair chance before the trier of fact, and the trier of fact is deprived of the ingredients necessary to a fair decision. This grim reality, of course, poses a direct challenge to the traditional model of the adversary criminal process, and perhaps because this reality so directly questions the fairness of our longstanding processes, change has been cautious and halting. Thus, the Court has not gone the full road and expressly required that the State provide to the defendant access to the prosecutor's complete files, or investigators who will assure that the defendant has an opportunity to discover every existing piece of helpful evidence. Instead, in acknowledgment of the fact that important interests are served when potentially favorable evidence is disclosed, the Court has fashioned a compromise, requiring that the prosecution identify and disclose to the defendant favorable material that it possesses. This requirement is but a small, albeit important; step toward equality of justice.

Brady v. Maryland, of course, established this requirement of disclosure as a fundamental element of a fair trial by holding that a defendant was denied due process if he was not given access to favorable evidence that is material either to guilt or punishment. Since *Brady* was decided, this Court has struggled, in a series of decisions, to define how best to effectuate the right recognized. To my mind, the *Brady* decision, the reasoning that underlay it, and the fundamental interest in a fair trial, combine to give the criminal defendant the right to receive from the prosecutor, and the prosecutor the affirmative duty to turn over to the defendant, *all* information known to the government that might reasonably be considered favorable to the defendant's case. Formulation of this right, and imposition of this duty, are "the essence of due process of law. It is the State that tries a man, and it is the State that must insure that the trial is fair." * * * If that right is denied, or if that duty is shirked, however, I believe a reviewing court should not automatically reverse but instead should apply the harmless error test the Court has developed for instances of error affecting constitutional rights. See *Chapman v. California*, 386 U.S. 18 (1967).[d]

My view is based in significant part on the reality of criminal practice and on the consequently inadequate protection to the defendant that a different rule would offer. * * * At the trial level, the duty of the state to effectuate *Brady* devolves into the duty of the prosecutor; the dual role that the prosecutor must play poses a serious obstacle to implementing *Brady*. The prosecutor is by trade, if not necessity, a zealous advocate. He is a trained attorney who must aggressively seek convictions in court on behalf of a victimized public. At the same time, as a representative of the State, he must place foremost in his hierarchy of interests the determination of truth. Thus, for purposes of *Brady*, the prosecutor must abandon his role as an advocate and pore through his files, as objectively as possible, to identify the material that could undermine his case. Given this obviously unharmonious role, it is not surprising that these advocates oftentimes overlook or downplay potentially favorable evidence, often in cases in which there is no doubt that the failure to disclose was a result of absolute good faith. Indeed, one need only think of the Fourth Amendment's requirement of a neutral intermediary, who tests the strength of the policeman-advocate's facts, to recognize the curious status *Brady* imposes on a prosecutor. * * *

The prosecutor surely greets the moment at which he must turn over *Brady* material with little enthusiasm. In perusing his files, he must make the often difficult decision as to whether evidence is favorable, and must decide on which side to err when faced with doubt. In his role as advocate, the answers are clear. In his role as representative of the State, the answers should be equally clear, and often to the contrary. Evidence that is of doubtful worth in the eyes of the prosecutor could be of inestimable value to the defense, and might make the difference to the trier of fact.

Once the prosecutor suspects that certain information might have favorable implications for the defense, either because it is potentially exculpatory or relevant to credibility, I see no reason why he should not be required to disclose it. After all, favorable evidence indisputably enhances the truth-seeking process at trial. And it is the job of the defense, not the prosecution, to decide whether and in what way to use arguably favorable evidence. In addition, to require disclosure of all evidence that might reasonably be considered favorable to the defendant would have the precautionary effect of assuring that no information of potential consequence is mistakenly overlooked. By requiring full disclosure of favorable evidence in this way, courts could begin to assure that a possibly dispositive piece of information is not withheld from the trier of fact by a prosecutor who is torn between the two roles he must play. A clear rule of this kind, coupled with a presumption in favor of disclosure, also would facilitate the prosecutor's admittedly difficult task by removing a substantial amount of unguided discretion. * * *

---

[d] The *Chapman* standard is discussed in fn. d, p. 695, in the *Coleman* [pp. 698, 699] and *Hillery* [p. 706] cases set forth in Chapter 11, and in *Weaver* [pp. 961–963] in Chapter 17.

* * * The State's interest in nondisclosure at trial is minimal, and should therefore yield to the readily apparent benefit that full disclosure would convey to the search for truth. After trial, however, the benefits of disclosure may at times be tempered by the State's legitimate desire to avoid retrial when error has been harmless. However, in making the determination of harmlessness, I would apply our normal constitutional error test and reverse unless it is clear beyond a reasonable doubt that the withheld evidence would not have affected the outcome of the trial. See *Chapman v. California*.[6]

Any rule other than automatic reversal, of course, dilutes the *Brady* right to some extent and offers the prosecutor an incentive not to turn over all information. In practical effect, it might be argued, there is little difference between the rule I propose—that a prosecutor must disclose all favorable evidence in his files, subject to harmless error review—and the rule the Court adopts—that the prosecutor must disclose only the favorable information that might affect the outcome of the trial. According to this argument, if a constitutional right to all favorable evidence leads to reversal only when the withheld evidence might have affected the outcome of the trial, the result will be the same as with a constitutional right only to evidence that will affect the trial outcome. For several reasons, however, I disagree. First, I have faith that a prosecutor would treat a rule requiring disclosure of all information of a certain kind differently from a rule requiring disclosure only of some of that information. Second, persistent or egregious failure to comply with the constitutional duty could lead to disciplinary actions by the courts. Third, the standard of harmlessness I adopt is more protective of the defendant than that chosen by the Court, placing the burden on the prosecutor, rather than the defendant, to prove the harmlessness of his actions. It would be a foolish prosecutor who gambled too glibly with that standard of review. * * * [e]

PENNSYLVANIA V. RITCHIE

480 U.S. 39, 107 S.Ct. 989, 94 L.Ed.2d 40 (1987).

JUSTICE POWELL, announced the judgment of the Court and delivered the opinion of the Court with respect to Parts I, II, IIB, IIC, and IV, and an opinion with respect to Part IIA in which THE CHIEF JUSTICE, JUSTICE WHITE, and JUSTICE O'CONNOR join.

---

[6] In a case of deliberate prosecutorial misconduct, automatic reversal might well be proper. Certain kinds of constitutional error so infect the system of justice as to require reversal in all cases, such as discrimination in jury selection. A deliberate effort of the prosecutor to undermine the search for truth clearly is in the category of offenses anathema to our most basic vision of the role of the State in the criminal process.

[e] Justice Stevens' dissent is omitted. Justice Stevens argued that where there was a specific request for the disclosure of relevant evidence that was exculpatory, the standard applied in the perjured testimony cases should control in determining whether the failure to disclose required a reversal of a conviction. A standard more lenient to the prosecution had been established for non-request cases in *Agurs* because, "where there had been no specific defense request for the later-discovered evidence, there was no notice to the prosecution that the defense did not already have that evidence or that it considered the evidence to be of particular value." As *Agurs* had noted, "where the prosecutor receives a specific and relevant request, the failure to make any response is seldom, if ever, excusable."

I

[Respondent Ritchie's 13-year-old daughter reported to the police that she had been sexually assaulted by Ritchie two or three times per week over the previous four years. The matter was referred to Children and Youth Services (CYS), a state protective service agency charged with investigating the suspected mistreatment or neglect of children. Ritchie subsequently was charged with rape, involuntary deviate sexual intercourse, incest, and corruption of a minor. During pretrial discovery, Ritchie served CYS with a subpoena, seeking access to all of its records relating to the immediate charges, as well as to certain earlier records compiled when CYS investigated a separate report that Ritchie's children were being abused. CYS refused to comply with the subpoena. It cited a Pennsylvania statute providing that all CYS records must be kept confidential, subject to specified exceptions, including one authorizing disclosure to a "court of competent jurisdiction pursuant to a court order." At an in-chambers hearing, respondent Ritchie argued that he was entitled to the CYS file because it might contain the names of favorable witnesses, as well as other, unspecified exculpatory evidence. Ritchie also claimed that the file contained a medical report prepared in conjunction with the earlier investigation, but CYS asserted that there was no such report in the record. The trial judge, without examining the entire file, refused to order disclosure. At the subsequent trial, which resulted in respondent's conviction, the main witness against him was his daughter. She was cross-examined at length by defense counsel, who questioned her on all aspects of the reported incidents, including her reasons for not reporting them sooner.]

[On appeal, the Pennsylvania Superior Court held that the failure to disclose the CYS file resulted in a constitutional violation insofar as it denied defendant the opportunity to cross-examine his daughter with respect to recorded statements she made to the CYS counselor. It ordered that a new trial be held unless the trial judge determined that the failure to disclose those statements had constituted harmless error. On appeal by the prosecution, the Pennsylvania Supreme Court agreed that the conviction should be vacated and the case remanded to determine if a new trial was necessary. However, it issued a broader ruling then the Superior Court. It directed that Ritchie, through his lawyer, be entitled to review the entire file to search for any useful evidence. This ruling was based on both the Confrontation and Compulsory Process clauses of the Sixth Amendment.]

II

[In part II of his opinion, Justice Powell concluded that the decision below constituted a "final judgment or decree," as required for United States Supreme Court review.[a]]

III

The Pennsylvania Supreme Court held that Ritchie, through his lawyer, has the right to examine the full contents of the CYS records. The court found that this

---

[a] Justice Stevens' separate dissent on this point is omitted.

right of access is required by both the Confrontation Clause and the Compulsory Process Clause. We discuss these constitutional provisions in turn.

A

* * * Ritchie claims that by denying him access to the information necessary to prepare his defense, the trial court interfered with his right of cross-examination. Ritchie argues that he could not effectively question his daughter because, without the CYS material, he did not know which types of questions would best expose the weaknesses in her testimony. Had the files been disclosed, Ritchie argues that he might have been able to show that the daughter made statements to the CYS counselor that were inconsistent with her trial statements, or perhaps to reveal that the girl acted with an improper motive. * * * [R]itchie argues that the failure to disclose [such] information that might have made cross-examination more effective undermines the Confrontation Clause's purpose of increasing the accuracy of the truth-finding process at trial. The Pennsylvania Supreme Court accepted this argument, relying in part on our decision in *Davis v. Alaska* [p. 1045]. * * * The Pennsylvania Supreme Court apparently interpreted our decision in *Davis* to mean that a statutory privilege cannot be maintained when a defendant asserts a need, prior to trial, for the protected information that might be used at trial to impeach or otherwise undermine a witness' testimony.

If we were to accept this broad interpretation of *Davis,* the effect would be to transform the Confrontation Clause into a constitutionally-compelled rule of pretrial discovery. Nothing in the case law supports such a view. The opinions of this Court show that the right of confrontation is a *trial* right, designed to prevent improper restrictions on the types of questions that defense counsel may ask during cross-examination. * * * The ability to question adverse witnesses, however, does not include the power to require the pretrial disclosure of any and all information that might be useful in contradicting unfavorable testimony.[9] Normally the right to confront one's accusers is satisfied if defense counsel receives wide latitude at trial to question witnesses. *Delaware v. Fensterer*, 474 U.S. 15 (1985). In short, the Confrontation Clause only guarantees "an *opportunity* for effective cross-examination, not cross-examination that is effective in whatever way, and to whatever extent, the defense might wish." Id. * * *

The lower court's reliance on *Davis v. Alaska* therefore is misplaced. There the state court had prohibited defense counsel from questioning the witness about his criminal record, even though that evidence might have affected the witness' credibility. The constitutional error in that case was *not* that Alaska made this information confidential; it was that the defendant was denied the right "to expose to the jury the facts from which jurors * * * could appropriately draw inferences relating to the reliability of the witness." Similarly, in this case the Confrontation Clause was not violated by the withholding of the CYS file; it only would have been impermissible for the judge to have prevented Ritchie's lawyer from cross-

---

[9]   This is not to suggest, of course, that there are no protections for pretrial discovery in criminal cases. See discussion in Part III(B), infra. We simply hold that with respect to this issue, the Confrontation Clause only protects a defendant's trial rights, and does not compel the pretrial production of information that might be useful in preparing for trial. * * *

examining the daughter. Because defense counsel was able to cross-examine all of the trial witnesses fully, we find that the Pennsylvania Supreme Court erred in holding that the failure to disclose the CYS file violated the Confrontation Clause.

B

The Pennsylvania Supreme Court also suggested that the failure to disclose the CYS file violated the Sixth Amendment's guarantee of compulsory process. Ritchie asserts that the trial court's ruling prevented him from learning the names of the "witnesses in his favor," as well as other evidence that might be contained in the file. Although the basis for the Pennsylvania Supreme Court's ruling on this point is unclear, it apparently concluded that the right of compulsory process includes the right to have the State's assistance in uncovering arguably useful information, without regard to the existence of a state-created restriction—here, the confidentiality of the files. * * *

This Court has never squarely held that the Compulsory Process Clause guarantees the right to discover the *identity* of witnesses, or to require the Government to produce exculpatory evidence. * * * Instead, the Court traditionally has evaluated claims such as those raised by Ritchie under the broader protections of the Due Process Clause of the Fourteenth Amendment. See *United States v. Bagley* [p. 739]. Because the applicability of the Sixth Amendment to this type of case is unsettled, and because our Fourteenth Amendment precedents addressing the fundamental fairness of trials establish a clear framework for review, we adopt a due process analysis for purposes of this case. Although we conclude that compulsory process provides no *greater* protections in this area than those afforded by due process, we need not decide today whether and how the guarantees of the Compulsory Process Clause differ from those of the Fourteenth Amendment. It is enough to conclude that on these facts, Ritchie's claims more properly are considered by reference to due process.

It is well-settled that the Government has the obligation to turn over evidence in its possession that is both favorable to the accused and material to guilt or punishment. *Brady v. Maryland* [p. 740]. Although courts have used different terminologies to define "materiality," a majority of this Court has agreed, "[e]vidence is material only if there is a reasonable probability, that, had the evidence been disclosed to the defense, the result of the proceeding would have been different. A 'reasonable probability' is a probability sufficient to undermine confidence in the outcome." *United States v. Bagley,* supra (opinion of Blackmun, J.); see Id. (opinion of White, J.).

At this stage, of course, it is impossible to say whether any information in the CYS records may be relevant to Ritchie's claim of innocence, because neither the prosecution nor defense counsel has seen the information, and the trial judge acknowledged that he had not reviewed the full file. The Commonwealth, however, argues that no materiality inquiry is required, because a statute renders the contents of the file privileged. Requiring disclosure here, it is argued, would override the Commonwealth's compelling interest in confidentiality on the mere speculation that the file "might" have been useful to the defense.

Although we recognize that the public interest in protecting this type of sensitive information is strong, we do not agree that this interest necessarily prevents disclosure in all circumstances. This is not a case where a state statute grants CYS the absolute authority to shield its files from all eyes. Cf. 42 Pa.Cons.Stat. § 5945.1(b) (unqualified statutory privilege for communications between sexual assault counselors and victims).[14] Rather, the Pennsylvania law provides that the information shall be disclosed in certain circumstances, including when CYS is directed to do so by court order. Given that the Pennsylvania Legislature contemplated *some* use of CYS records in judicial proceedings, we cannot conclude that the statute prevents all disclosure in criminal prosecutions. In the absence of any apparent state policy to the contrary, we therefore have no reason to believe that relevant information would not be disclosed when a court of competent jurisdiction determines that the information is "material" to the defense of the accused. * * * Ritchie is entitled to have the CYS file reviewed by the trial court to determine whether it contains information that probably would have changed the outcome of his trial. * * *

C

This ruling does not end our analysis because the Pennsylvania Supreme Court did more than simply remand. It also held that defense counsel must be allowed to examine all of the confidential information, both relevant and irrelevant, and present arguments in favor of disclosure. The court apparently concluded that whenever a defendant alleges that protected evidence might be material, the appropriate method of assessing this claim is to grant full access to the disputed information, regardless of the State's interest in confidentiality. We cannot agree.

A defendant's right to discover exculpatory evidence does not include the unsupervised authority to search through the Commonwealth's files. Although the eye of an advocate may be helpful to a defendant in ferreting out information, this Court has never held—even in the absence of a statute restricting disclosure—that a defendant alone may make the determination as to the materiality of the information. Settled practice is to the contrary. * * *

We find that Ritchie's interest (as well as that of the Commonwealth) in ensuring a fair trial can be protected fully by requiring that the CYS files be submitted only to the trial court for *in camera* review. Although this rule denies Ritchie the benefits of an "advocate's eye," we note that the trial court's discretion is not unbounded. If a defendant is aware of specific information contained in the file (e.g., the medical report), he is free to request it directly from the court, and argue in favor of its materiality. * * *

To allow full disclosure to defense counsel in this type of case would sacrifice unnecessarily the Commonwealth's compelling interest in protecting its child abuse information. If the CYS records were made available to defendants, even through counsel, it could have a seriously adverse effect on Pennsylvania's efforts to uncover and treat abuse. Child abuse is one of the most difficult crimes to detect

---

[14] We express no opinion on whether the result in this case would have been different if the statute had protected the CYS files from disclosure to *anyone,* including law-enforcement and judicial personnel.

and prosecute, in large part because there often are no witnesses except the victim. A child's feelings of vulnerability and guilt, and his or her unwillingness to come forward are particularly acute when the abuser is a parent. It therefore is essential that the child have a state-designated person to whom he may turn, and to do so with the assurance of confidentiality. Relatives and neighbors who suspect abuse also will be more willing to come forward if they know that their identities will be protected. Recognizing this, the Commonwealth—like all other States—has made a commendable effort to assure victims and witnesses that they may speak to the CYS counselors without fear of general disclosure. The Commonwealth's purpose would be frustrated if this confidential material had to be disclosed upon demand to a defendant charged with criminal child abuse, simply because a trial court may not recognize exculpatory evidence. Neither precedent nor common sense requires such a result.

IV

We agree that Ritchie is entitled to know whether the CYS file contains information that may have changed the outcome of his trial had it been disclosed. Thus we agree that a remand is necessary. We disagree with the decision of the Pennsylvania Supreme Court to the extent that it allows defense counsel access to the CYS file. An *in camera* review by the trial court will serve Ritchie's interest without destroying the Commonwealth's need to protect the confidentiality of those involved in child-abuse investigations. The decision of the Pennsylvania Supreme Court is affirmed in part, reversed in part, and remanded for further proceedings not inconsistent with this opinion.

JUSTICE BLACKMUN, concurring in part and concurring in the judgment.

I join Parts I, II, IIB, IIC, and IV of the Court's opinion. I write separately, however, because I do not accept the plurality's conclusion, as expressed in Part IIA of Justice Powell's opinion, that the Confrontation Clause protects only a defendant's trial rights and has no relevance to pretrial discovery. * * * The plurality believes that [the Confrontation Clause] is satisfied so long as defense counsel can *question* a witness on any proper subject of cross-examination. For the plurality, the existence of a confrontation violation turns on whether counsel has the opportunity to conduct such questioning; the Court in effect dismisses—or, at best, downplays—any inquiry into the effectiveness of the cross-examination. * * * If I were to accept the plurality's effort to divorce confrontation analysis from any examination into the effectiveness of cross-examination, I believe that in some situations the confrontation right would become an empty formality. * * *

The similarities between *Davis* and this case are much greater than are any differences that may exist. * * * It is true that, in a technical sense, the situations of Davis and Ritchie are different. Davis' counsel had access to the juvenile record of the witness and could have used it but for the Alaska prohibition. Thus, the infringement upon Davis' confrontation right occurred at the trial stage when his counsel was unable to pursue an available line of inquiry. Respondent's attorney could not cross-examine his client's daughter with the help of the possible evidence in the CYS file because of the Pennsylvania prohibition that affected his pretrial preparations. I do not believe, however, that a State can avoid Confrontation

Clause problems simply by deciding to hinder the defendant's right to effective cross-examination, on the basis of a desire to protect the confidentiality interests of a particular class of individuals, at the pretrial, rather than at the trial, stage.

Despite my disagreement with the plurality's reading of the Confrontation Clause, I am able to concur in the Court's judgment because, in my view, the procedure the Court has set out for the lower court to follow on remand is adequate to address any confrontation problem. * * *

JUSTICE BRENNAN, with whom JUSTICE MARSHALL joins, dissenting.

* * * In this case, the trial court properly viewed Ritchie's vague speculations that the agency file might contain something useful as an insufficient basis for permitting general access to the file. However, in denying access to the prior statements of the victim the court deprived Ritchie of material crucial to any effort to impeach the victim at trial. I view this deprivation as a violation of the Confrontation Clause.

One way in which cross-examination may be restricted is through preclusion at trial itself of a line of inquiry that counsel seeks to pursue. The logic of our concern for restriction on the ability to engage in cross-examination does not suggest, however, that the Confrontation Clause prohibits *only* such limitation. A crucial avenue of cross-examination also may be foreclosed by the denial of access to material that would serve as the basis for this examination. Where denial of access is complete, counsel is in no position to formulate a line of inquiry potentially grounded on the material sought. Thus, he or she cannot point to a specific subject of inquiry that has been foreclosed, as can a counsel whose interrogation at trial has been limited by the trial judge. Nonetheless, there occurs as effective preclusion of a topic of cross-examination as if the judge at trial had ruled an entire area of questioning off limits.

* * * *Jencks v. United States,* 353 U.S. 657 (1957), held that the defendant was entitled to obtain the prior statements of persons to government agents when those persons testified against him at trial. * * * As I later noted in *Palermo v. United States,* 360 U.S. 343 (1959), *Jencks* was based on our supervisory authority rather than the Constitution, "but it would be idle to say that the commands of the Constitution were not close to the surface of the decision." * * *

The ability to obtain material information through reliance on a Due Process claim will not in all cases nullify the damage of the Court's overly restrictive reading of the Confrontation Clause. As the Court notes, evidence is regarded as material only if there is a reasonable probability that it might affect the outcome of the proceeding. Prior statements on their face may not appear to have such force, since their utility may lie in their more subtle potential for diminishing the credibility of a witness. The prospect that these statements will not be regarded as material is enhanced by the fact that due process analysis requires that information be evaluated by the trial judge, not defense counsel. By contrast, *Jencks,* informed by confrontation and cross-examination concerns, insisted that defense counsel, not the court, perform such an evaluation, "[b]ecause only the defense is adequately equipped to determine the effective use for the purpose of discrediting the Government's witness and thereby furthering the accused's defense." Therefore, while Confrontation Clause and due process analysis may in some cases be congruent, the Confrontation Clause has independent significance in protecting against infringements on the right to cross-examination.[b]

---

[b] In *Arizona v. Youngblood*, 488 U.S. 51 (1988), the Court adopted a different due process standard for cases involving governmental loss or destruction of evidence of potential use to the defendant. The defendant there had been convicted of child molestation, sexual assault, and kidnapping. Prior to his arrest, state agents had collected semen samples from the 10-year-old victim's body and clothing, but they had then inadvertently failed to preserve those samples in a condition that would permit blood substance testing that could be matched against the accused's blood group. The state court held that since defendant had claimed mistaken identity, the state's loss of the possibly useful evidence precluded a conviction consistent with due process. Rejecting that ruling, the Supreme Court majority reasoned: "The Due Process Clause of the Fourteenth Amendment, as interpreted in *Brady v. Maryland*, makes the good or bad faith of the State irrelevant when the State fails to disclose to the defendant material exculpatory evidence. But we think the Due Process Clause requires a different result when we deal with the failure of the State to preserve evidentiary material of which no more can be said than that it could have been subjected to tests, the results of which might have exonerated the defendant. Part of the reason for the difference in treatment is found in the observation made by the Court in [an earlier case] that '[w]henever potentially exculpatory evidence is permanently lost, courts face the treacherous task of divining the import of materials whose contents are unknown and, very often, disputed.' Part of it stems from our unwillingness to read the 'fundamental fairness' requirement of the Due Process Clause as imposing on the police an undifferentiated and absolute duty to retain and to preserve all material that might be of conceivable evidentiary significance in a particular prosecution. We think that requiring a defendant to show bad faith on the part of the police both limits the extent of the police's obligation to preserve evidence to reasonable bounds and confines it to that class of cases where the interests of justice most clearly require it, i.e., those cases in which the police themselves by their conduct indicate that the evidence could form a basis for exonerating the defendant. We therefore hold that unless a criminal defendant can show bad faith on the part of the police, failure to preserve potentially useful evidence does not constitute a denial of due process of law."

CHAPTER 14

GUILTY PLEAS

■ ■ ■

1. PLEA BARGAINING

All but a small percentage of criminal cases in the United States are disposed of by plea of guilty rather than by trial. The guilty plea is very often a negotiated plea, that is, a defendant's agreement to plead guilty to a criminal charge with the reasonable expectation of receiving some consideration from the government. Sometimes this plea is the result of nothing more than implicit plea bargaining; there is no actual bargaining between the defendant or his attorney and the prosecutor or judge, and the defendant enters his plea merely because it is generally known that this is the route to a lesser sentence. But more common is explicit bargaining in which the defendant enters a plea of guilty only after a commitment has been made that concessions will be granted (or at least sought) in his particular case.

One common form of plea negotiation known as a charge bargain consists of an arrangement whereby the defendant and prosecutor agree that the defendant should be permitted to plead guilty to a charge carrying less serious penalties or consequences than the charge supported by the evidence. A second form involves an agreement whereby the defendant pleads to the original charge in exchange for some kind of promise from the prosecutor concerning the sentence to be imposed (for example, that the prosecutor will recommend or not oppose a certain sentence, that the prosecutor will not seek specified sentence enhancements, or that the plea is contingent on the sentence not exceeding a certain amount). Still another kind of plea bargain—the one most likely to be illusory—is where the defendant pleads to the charged offense in exchange for the prosecutor's promise to drop or not file other charges.

Plea bargaining is a long time (though only recently highly visible) practice in the United States. There is considerable disagreement as to what caused this practice to develop and continue, though it seems likely a combination of factors is involved. One explanation is that plea bargaining is a response to crowded court dockets, but this is not inevitably the case, for negotiation practices have developed at times and places where there was no serious court congestion. Some have attributed plea bargaining to inadequate public defenders, the financial incentives of private attorneys, and the laziness of prosecutors and judges, but this is hardly an entirely accurate or complete explanation either. Other contributors may be more powerful leverage provided to prosecutors by mandatory minimum sentences and pretrial detention. Certainly there are at least some more favorable explanations, such as that there are today compared to the mid twentieth century fewer genuine disputes of fact to be resolved by trials because of the increased professionalism of police and prosecutors and the enhanced role of defense attorneys at the pretrial stages.

But whether the institution of plea bargaining is viewed favorably or unfavorably, there is no denying that this process of negotiation for and granting of concessions can give rise to difficult and important legal issues. Just how much pressure may the prosecutor put on the defendant in an effort to induce him to go the guilty plea route? What are the defendant's rights if notwithstanding his plea he does not receive the contemplated concessions? What constitutes ineffective assistance by defense counsel in a plea bargaining context? Is the prosecutor obligated in a guilty plea case to disclose to the defendant evidence favorable to the defense to the same extent as in a case going to trial? Those issues are explored in the Supreme Court decisions in this section.

BORDENKIRCHER V. HAYES

434 U.S. 357, 98 S.Ct. 663, 54 L.Ed.2d 604 (1978).

JUSTICE STEWART delivered the opinion of the Court. * * *

[Paul Hayes was indicted in Fayette County, Ky., on a charge of uttering a forged instrument in the amount of $88.30, punishable by two to 10 years in prison. Hayes and his retained counsel met with the prosecutor who offered to recommend a sentence of five years if Hayes would plead guilty and added that if Hayes did not plead guilty he would seek an indictment under the Kentucky Habitual Criminal Act, which would subject Hayes to a mandatory sentence of life imprisonment by reason of his two prior felony convictions. Hayes chose not to plead guilty, and the prosecutor did obtain such an indictment. A jury found Hayes guilty on the principal charge of uttering a forged instrument and, in a separate proceeding, further found that he had twice before been convicted of felonies. As required by the habitual offender statute, he was sentenced to a life term in the penitentiary. The Kentucky Court of Appeals rejected Hayes' constitutional objections to the enhanced sentence, and on Hayes' petition for a federal writ of habeas corpus the district court agreed that there had been no constitutional violation in the sentence or the indictment procedure. The Court of Appeals for the Sixth Circuit reversed on the ground that the prosecutor's conduct had violated the principles of *Blackledge v. Perry,* 417 U.S. 21 (1974), which "protect defendants from the vindictive exercise of a prosecutor's discretion."]

It may be helpful to clarify at the outset the nature of the issue in this case. While the prosecutor did not actually obtain the recidivist indictment until after the plea conferences had ended, his intention to do so was clearly put forth at the outset of the plea negotiations. Hayes was thus fully informed of the true terms of the offer when he made his decision to plead not guilty. This is not a situation, therefore, where the prosecutor without notice brought an additional and more serious charge after plea negotiations relating only to the original indictment had ended with the defendant's insistence on pleading not guilty. As a practical matter, in short, this case would be no different if the grand jury had indicted Hayes as a recidivist from the outset, and the prosecutor had offered to drop that charge as part of the plea bargain.

The Court of Appeals nonetheless drew a distinction between "concessions relating to prosecution under an existing indictment," and threats to bring more severe charges not contained in the original indictment—a line it thought necessary in order to establish a prophylactic rule to guard against the evil of prosecutorial vindictiveness. Quite apart from this chronological distinction, however, the Court of Appeals found that the prosecutor had acted vindictively in the present case since he had conceded that the indictment was influenced by his desire to induce a guilty plea. The ultimate conclusion of the Court of Appeals thus seems to have been that a prosecutor acts vindictively and in violation of due process of law whenever his charging decision is influenced by what he hopes to gain in the course of plea bargaining negotiations.

We have recently had occasion to observe that "[w]hatever might be the situation in an ideal world, the fact is that the guilty plea and the often concomitant plea bargain are important components of this country's criminal justice system. Properly administered, they can benefit all concerned." The open acknowledgment of this previously clandestine practice has led this Court to recognize the importance of counsel during plea negotiations, the need for a public record indicating that a plea was knowingly and voluntarily made, and the requirement that a prosecutor's plea bargaining promise must be kept. The decision of the Court of Appeals in the present case, however, did not deal with considerations such as these, but held that the substance of the plea offer itself violated the limitations imposed by the Due Process Clause of the Fourteenth Amendment. For the reasons that follow, we have concluded that the Court of Appeals was mistaken in so ruling.

This Court held in *North Carolina v. Pearce*, 395 U.S. 711 (1969), that the Due Process Clause of the Fourteenth Amendment "requires that vindictiveness against a defendant for having successfully attacked his first conviction must play no part in the sentence he receives after a new trial." The same principle was later applied to prohibit a prosecutor from reindicting a convicted misdemeanant on a felony charge after the defendant had invoked an appellate remedy, since in this situation there was also a "realistic likelihood of 'vindictiveness.'" *Blackledge v. Perry.*

In those cases the Court was dealing with the State's unilateral imposition of a penalty upon a defendant who had chosen to exercise a legal right to attack his original conviction—a situation "very different from the give-and-take negotiation common in plea bargaining between the prosecution and the defense, which arguably possess relatively equal bargaining power." The Court has emphasized that the due process violation in cases such as *Pearce* and *Perry* lay not in the possibility that a defendant might be deterred from the exercise of a legal right, but rather in the danger that the State might be retaliating against the accused for lawfully attacking his conviction.

To punish a person because he has done what the law plainly allows him to do is a due process violation of the most basic sort, and for an agent of the State to pursue a course of action whose objective is to penalize a person's reliance on his legal rights is "patently unconstitutional." But in the "give-and-take" of plea bargaining, there is no such element of punishment or retaliation so long as the accused is free to accept or reject the prosecution's offer.

Plea bargaining flows from "the mutuality of advantage" to defendants and prosecutors, each with his own reasons for wanting to avoid trial. *Brady v. United States*, 397 U.S. 742 (1970).ᵃ Defendants advised by competent counsel and protected by other procedural safeguards are presumptively capable of intelligent choice in response to prosecutorial persuasion, and unlikely to be driven to false self-condemnation. Indeed, acceptance of the basic legitimacy of plea bargaining necessarily implies rejection of any notion that a guilty plea is involuntary in a constitutional sense simply because it is the end result of the bargaining process. By hypothesis, the plea may have been induced by promises of a recommendation of a lenient sentence or a reduction of charges, and thus by fear of the possibility of a greater penalty upon conviction after a trial.

While confronting a defendant with the risk of more severe punishment clearly may have a "discouraging effect on the defendant's assertion of his trial rights, the imposition of these difficult choices [is] an inevitable"—and permissible—"attribute of any legitimate system which tolerates and encourages the negotiation of pleas." It follows that, by tolerating and encouraging the negotiation of pleas, this Court has necessarily accepted as constitutionally legitimate the simple reality that the prosecutor's interest at the bargaining table is to persuade the defendant to forego his right to plead not guilty.

It is not disputed here that Hayes was properly chargeable under the recidivist statute, since he had in fact been convicted of two previous felonies. In our system, so long as the prosecutor has probable cause to believe that the accused committed an offense defined by statute, the decision whether or not to prosecute, and what charge to file or bring before a grand jury, generally rests entirely in his discretion.[8] Within the limits set by the legislature's constitutionally valid

---

ᵃ   Although *Brady* did not involve a plea bargaining situation, the Court analogized the plea involved there to a plea obtained through plea bargaining, and then commented generally on the validity of a plea produced by the "mutuality of advantage" that flows from a negotiated plea: "We decline to hold * * * that a guilty plea is compelled and invalid under the Fifth Amendment whenever motivated by the defendant's desire to accept the certainty or probability of a lesser penalty rather than face a wider range of possibilities extending from acquittal to conviction and a higher penalty authorized by law for the crime charged. * * * [B]oth the state and the defendant often find it advantageous to preclude the possibility of the maximum penalty authorized by law. For a defendant who sees slight possibility of acquittal, the advantages of pleading guilty and limiting the probable penalty are obvious—his exposure is reduced, the correctional processes can begin immediately, and the practical burdens of a trial are eliminated. For the State there are also advantages—the more promptly imposed punishment after an admission of guilty may more effectively attain the objectives of punishment; and with the avoidance of trial, scarce judicial and prosecutorial resources are conserved for those cases in which there is a substantial issue of the defendant's guilt or in which there is substantial doubt that the State can sustain its burden of proof. It is this mutuality of advantage which perhaps explains the fact that at present well over three-fourths of the criminal convictions in this country rest on pleas of guilty, a great many of them no doubt motivated at least in part by the hope or assurance of a lesser penalty than might be imposed if there were a guilty verdict after a trial to judge or jury."

8   This case does not involve the constitutional implications of a prosecutor's offer during plea bargaining of adverse or lenient treatment for some person *other* than the accused, which might

definition of chargeable offenses, "the conscious exercise of some selectivity in enforcement is not in itself a federal constitutional violation" so long as "the selection was [not] deliberately based upon an unjustifiable standard such as race, religion, or other arbitrary classification." To hold that the prosecutor's desire to induce a guilty plea is an "unjustifiable standard," which, like race or religion, may play no part in his charging decision, would contradict the very premises that underlie the concept of plea bargaining itself. Moreover, a rigid constitutional rule that would prohibit a prosecutor from acting forthrightly in his dealings with the defense could only invite unhealthy subterfuge that would drive the practice of plea bargaining back into the shadows from which it has so recently emerged.

There is no doubt that the breadth of discretion that our country's legal system vests in prosecuting attorneys carries with it the potential for both individual and institutional abuse. And broad though that discretion may be, there are undoubtedly constitutional limits upon its exercise. We hold only that the course of conduct engaged in by the prosecutor in this case, which no more than openly presented the defendant with the unpleasant alternatives of foregoing trial or facing charges on which he was plainly subject to prosecution, did not violate the Due Process Clause of the Fourteenth Amendment.

Accordingly, the judgment of the Court of Appeals is reversed.

JUSTICE BLACKMUN, with whom JUSTICE BRENNAN and JUSTICE MARSHALL, join dissenting.

I feel that the Court, although purporting to rule narrowly (that is, on "the course of conduct engaged in by the prosecutor in this case"), is departing from, or at least restricting, the principles established in *North Carolina v. Pearce*, and in *Blackledge v. Perry*. * * *

In *Pearce*, as indeed the Court notes, it was held that "vindictiveness against a defendant for having successfully attacked his first conviction must play no part in the sentence he receives after a new trial." * * *

Then later, in *Perry*, the Court applied the same principle to prosecutorial conduct where there was a "realistic likelihood of 'vindictiveness.' " * * *

The Court now says, however, that this concern with vindictiveness is of no import in the present case, despite the difference between five years in prison and a life sentence, because we are here concerned with plea bargaining where there is give-and-take negotiation, and where, it is said, "there is no such element of punishment or retaliation so long as the accused is free to accept or reject the prosecution's offer." Yet in this case vindictiveness is present to the same extent as it was thought to be in *Pearce* and in *Perry:* the prosecutor here admitted that the sole reason for the new indictment was to discourage the respondent from exercising his right to a trial. Even had such an admission not been made, when plea negotiations, conducted in the face of the less serious charge under the first indictment, fail, charging by a second indictment a more serious crime for the same conduct creates "a strong inference" of vindictiveness. As then Judge McCree aptly

---

pose a greater danger of inducing a false guilty plea by skewing the assessment of the risks a defendant must consider.

observed, in writing for a unanimous panel of the Sixth Circuit, the prosecutor initially "makes a discretionary determination that the interests of the state are served by not seeking more serious charges." I therefore do not understand why, as in *Pearce*, due process does not require that the prosecution justify its action on some basis other than discouraging respondent from the exercise of his right to a trial.

Prosecutorial vindictiveness, it seems to me, in the present narrow context, is the fact against which the Due Process Clause ought to protect. I perceive little difference between vindictiveness after what the Court describes as the exercise of a "legal right to attack his original conviction," and vindictiveness in the "give-and-take negotiation common in plea bargaining." Prosecutorial vindictiveness in any context is still prosecutorial vindictiveness. The Due Process Clause should protect an accused against it, however it asserts itself. The Court of Appeals rightly so held, and I would affirm the judgment.

It might be argued that it really makes little difference how this case, now that it is here, is decided. The Court's holding gives plea bargaining full sway despite vindictiveness. A contrary result, however, merely would prompt the aggressive prosecutor to bring the greater charge initially in every case, and only thereafter to bargain. The consequences to the accused would still be adverse, for then he would bargain against a greater charge, face the likelihood of increased bail, and run the risk that the court would be less inclined to accept a bargain plea. Nonetheless, it is far preferable to hold the prosecution to the charge it was originally content to bring and to justify in the eyes of its public.[2]

---

[2] That prosecutors, without saying so, may sometimes bring charges more serious than they think appropriate for the ultimate disposition of a case, in order to gain bargaining leverage with a defendant, does not add support to today's decision, for this Court, in its approval of the advantages to be gained from plea negotiations, has never openly sanctioned such deliberate overcharging or taken such a cynical view of the bargaining process. Normally, of course, it is impossible to show that this is what the prosecutor is doing, and the courts necessarily have deferred to the prosecutor's exercise of discretion in initial charging decisions.

Even if overcharging is to be sanctioned, there are strong reasons of fairness why the charges should be presented at the beginning of the bargaining process, rather than as a filliped threat at the end. First, it means that a prosecutor is required to reach a charging decision without any knowledge of the particular defendant's willingness to plead guilty; hence the defendant who truly believes himself to be innocent, and wishes for that reason to go to trial, is not likely to be subject to quite such a devastating gamble since the prosecutor has fixed the incentives for the average case.

Second, it is healthful to keep charging practices visible to the general public, so that political bodies can judge whether the policy being followed is a fair one. Visibility is enhanced if the prosecutor is required to lay his cards on the table with an indictment of public record at the beginning of the bargaining process, rather than making use of unrecorded verbal warnings of more serious indictments yet to come.

Finally, I would question whether it is fair to pressure defendants to plead guilty by threat of reindictment on an enhanced charge for the same conduct when the defendant has no way of knowing whether the prosecutor would indeed be entitled to bring him to trial on the enhanced charge. Here, though there is no dispute that respondent met the then current definition of a habitual offender under Kentucky law, it is conceivable that a properly instructed Kentucky grand jury, in response to the same considerations that ultimately moved the Kentucky Legislature to amend the habitual offender statute, would have refused to subject respondent to such an onerous penalty for his forgery charge. There is no indication in the record that, once the new indictment was obtained, respondent was given another chance to plead guilty to the forged check charge in exchange for a five year sentence.

JUSTICE POWELL, dissenting.

Although I agree with much of the Court's opinion, I am not satisfied that the result in this case is just or that the conduct of the plea bargaining met the requirements of due process. * * *

The prosecutor's initial assessment of respondent's case led him to forego an indictment under the habitual criminal statute. The circumstances of respondent's prior convictions are relevant to this assessment and to my view of the case. Respondent was 17 years old when he committed his first offense. He was charged with rape but pled guilty to the lesser included offense of "detaining a female." One of the other participants in the incident was sentenced to life imprisonment. Respondent was sent not to prison but to a reformatory where he served five years. Respondent's second offense was robbery. This time he was found guilty by a jury and was sentenced to five years in prison, but he was placed on probation and served no time. Although respondent's prior convictions brought him within the terms of the Habitual Criminal Act, the offenses themselves did not result in imprisonment; yet the addition of a conviction on a charge involving $88.30 subjected respondent to a mandatory sentence of imprisonment for life. Persons convicted of rape and murder often are not punished so severely. * * *

It seems to me that the question to be asked under the circumstances is whether the prosecutor reasonably might have charged respondent under the Habitual Criminal Act in the first place. The deference that courts properly accord the exercise of a prosecutor's discretion perhaps would foreclose judicial criticism if the prosecutor originally had sought an indictment under that act, as unreasonable as it would have seemed.[2] But here the prosecutor evidently made a reasonable, responsible judgment not to subject an individual to a mandatory life sentence when his only new offense had societal implications as limited as those accompanying the uttering of a single $88 forged check and when the circumstances of his prior convictions confirmed the inappropriateness of applying the habitual criminal statute. I think it may be inferred that the prosecutor himself deemed it unreasonable and not in the public interest to put this defendant in jeopardy of a sentence of life imprisonment.

There may be situations in which a prosecutor would be fully justified in seeking a fresh indictment for a more serious offense. The most plausible justification might be that it would have been reasonable and in the public interest initially to have charged the defendant with the greater offense. In most cases a court could not know why the harsher indictment was sought, and an inquiry into the prosecutor's motive would neither be indicated nor likely to be fruitful. In those

---

[2] The majority suggests that this case cannot be distinguished from the case where the prosecutor initially obtains an indictment under an enhancement statute and later agrees to drop the enhancement charge in exchange for a guilty plea. I would agree that these two situations would be alike *only if* it were assumed that the hypothetical prosecutor's decision to charge under the enhancement statute was occasioned not by consideration of the public interest but by a strategy to discourage the defendant from exercising his constitutional rights. In theory, I would condemn both practices. In practice, the hypothetical situation is largely unreviewable. The majority's view confuses the propriety of a particular exercise of prosecutorial discretion with its unreviewability. In the instant case, however, we have no problem of proof.

cases, I would agree with the majority that the situation would not differ materially from one in which the higher charge was brought at the outset.

But this is not such a case. Here, any inquiry into the prosecutor's purpose is made unnecessary by his candid acknowledgement that he threatened to procure and in fact procured the habitual criminal indictment because of respondent's insistence on exercising his constitutional rights. [I]n *Brady v. United States,* we drew a distinction between the situation there approved and the "situation where the prosecutor or judge, or both, deliberately employ their charging and sentencing powers to induce a particular defendant to tender a plea of guilty."

The plea-bargaining process, as recognized by this Court, is essential to the functioning of the criminal-justice system. It normally affords genuine benefits to defendants as well as to society. And if the system is to work effectively, prosecutors must be accorded the widest discretion, within constitutional limits, in conducting bargaining. This is especially true when a defendant is represented by counsel and presumably is fully advised of his rights. Only in the most exceptional case should a court conclude that the scales of the bargaining are so unevenly balanced as to arouse suspicion. In this case, the prosecutor's actions denied respondent due process because their admitted purpose was to discourage and then to penalize with unique severity his exercise of constitutional rights. Implementation of a strategy calculated solely to deter the exercise of constitutional rights is not a constitutionally permissible exercise of discretion. I would affirm the opinion of the Court of Appeals on the facts of this case.

SANTOBELLO V. NEW YORK
404 U.S. 257, 92 S.Ct. 495, 30 L.Ed.2d 427 (1971).

CHIEF JUSTICE BURGER delivered the opinion of the Court.

[After negotiations with the prosecutor, petitioner withdrew his previous not-guilty plea to two felony counts and pleaded guilty to a lesser-included offense, the prosecutor having agreed to make no recommendation as to sentence. At petitioner's appearance for sentencing many months later a new prosecutor recommended the maximum sentence, which the judge (who stated that he was uninfluenced by that recommendation) imposed. Petitioner attempted unsuccessfully to withdraw his guilty plea, and his conviction was affirmed on appeal.]

* * * The disposition of criminal charges by agreement between the prosecutor and the accused, sometimes loosely called "plea bargaining," is an essential component of the administration of justice. Properly administered, it is to be encouraged. If every criminal charge were subjected to a full-scale trial, the States and the Federal Government would need to multiply by many times the number of judges and court facilities.

Disposition of charges after plea discussions is not only an essential part of the process but a highly desirable part for many reasons. It leads to prompt and largely final disposition of most criminal cases; it avoids much of the corrosive impact of enforced idleness during pretrial confinement for those who are denied release pending trial; it protects the public from those accused persons who are prone to continue criminal conduct even while on pretrial release; and, by shortening the time between charge and disposition, it enhances whatever may be the rehabilitative prospects of the guilty when they are ultimately imprisoned. * * *

This phase of the process of criminal justice, and the adjudicative element inherent in accepting a plea of guilty, must be attended by safeguards to insure the defendant what is reasonably due in the circumstances. Those circumstances will vary, but a constant factor is that when a plea rests in any significant degree on a promise or agreement of the prosecutor, so that it can be said to be part of the inducement or consideration, such promise must be fulfilled. * * *

We need not reach the question whether the sentencing judge would or would not have been influenced had he known all the details of the negotiations for the plea. He stated that the prosecutor's recommendation did not influence him and we have no reason to doubt that. Nevertheless, we conclude that the interests of justice and appropriate recognition of the duties of the prosecution in relation to promises made in the negotiation of pleas of guilty will be best served by remanding the case to the state courts for further consideration. The ultimate relief to which petitioner is entitled we leave to the discretion of the state court, which is in a better position to decide whether the circumstances of this case require only that there be specific performance of the agreement on the plea, in which case petitioner should be resentenced by a different judge, or whether, in the view of the state court, the circumstances require granting the relief sought by petitioner, i.e., the opportunity to withdraw his plea of guilty.[2] * * *

JUSTICE DOUGLAS, concurring. * * *

I join the opinion of the Court and favor a constitutional rule for this as well as for other pending or oncoming cases. Where the "plea bargain" is not kept by the prosecutor, the sentence must be vacated and the state court will decide in light of the circumstances of each case whether due process requires (a) that there be specific performance of the plea bargain or (b) that the defendant be given the option to go to trial on the original charges. One alternative may do justice in one case, and the other in a different case. In choosing a remedy, however, a court ought to accord a defendant's preference considerable, if not controlling, weight inasmuch as the fundamental rights flouted by a prosecutor's breach of a plea bargain are those of the defendant, not of the State.

JUSTICE MARSHALL, with whom JUSTICE BRENNAN and JUSTICE STEWART join, concurring in part and dissenting in part.

* * * When a prosecutor breaks the bargain, he undercuts the basis for the waiver of constitutional rights implicit in the plea. This, it seems to me, provides the defendant ample justification for rescinding the plea. Where a promise is "unfulfilled," *Brady v. United States* specifically denies that the plea "must stand." Of course, where the prosecutor has broken the plea agreement, it may be

---

[2] If the state court decides to allow withdrawal of the plea, the petitioner will, of course, plead anew to the original charge on two felony counts.

appropriate to permit the defendant to enforce the plea bargain. But that is not the remedy sought here.* Rather, it seems to me that a breach of the plea bargain provides ample reason to permit the plea to be vacated.

It is worth noting that in the ordinary case where a motion to vacate is made prior to sentencing, the government has taken no action in reliance on the previously entered guilty plea and would suffer no harm from the plea's withdrawal. More pointedly, here the State claims no such harm beyond disappointed expectations about the plea itself. At least where the government itself has broken the plea bargain, this disappointment cannot bar petitioner from withdrawing his guilty plea and reclaiming his right to a trial.

I would remand the case with instructions that the plea be vacated and petitioner given an opportunity to replead to the original charges in the indictment.

MISSOURI V. FRYE

566 U.S. 133, 132 S.Ct. 1399, 182 L.Ed.2d 379 (2012).

JUSTICE KENNEDY delivered the opinion of the Court.

[Frye was charged with driving with a revoked license after three prior convictions of that offense, a felony punishable by up to four years. In a letter to Frye's counsel, the prosecutor extended a choice of two plea bargains, the most lenient being reduction of the charge to a misdemeanor and recommendation of a 90-day sentence. Frye's attorney never advised him of the offers, and after their expiration (and after Frye had once again been arrested for the same offense) Frye pled guilty without any underlying plea agreement and was sentenced to three years in prison. At a later post-conviction hearing, Frye testified he would have entered a guilty plea to the misdemeanor had he known of the offer. On appeal, the state court held that Frye's counsel's performance was deficient and that Frye had been prejudiced.]

It is well settled that the right to the effective assistance of counsel applies to certain steps before trial. The "Sixth Amendment guarantees a defendant the right to have counsel present at all 'critical' stages of the criminal proceedings." Critical stages include arraignments, postindictment interrogations, postindictment lineups, and the entry of a guilty plea.

With respect to the right to effective counsel in plea negotiations, a proper beginning point is to discuss two cases from this Court considering the role of counsel in advising a client about a plea offer and an ensuing guilty plea: *Hill v. Lockhart*, 474 U.S. 53 (1958); and *Padilla v. Kentucky* [p. 777, fn. a].

---

*   Justice Douglas, although joining the Court's opinion (apparently because he thinks the remedy should be chosen by the state court), concludes that the state court "ought to accord a defendant's preference considerable, if not controlling, weight." Thus, a majority of the Court appears to believe that in cases like these, when the defendant seeks to vacate the plea, that relief should generally be granted. [**Editors' note:** there were two vacancies on the Court at the time.]

Hill established that claims of ineffective assistance of counsel in the plea bargain context are governed by the two-part test set forth in *Strickland* [see p. 932]. * * *

In *Hill*, the decision turned on the second part of the *Strickland* test. There, a defendant who had entered a guilty plea claimed his counsel had misinformed him of the amount of time he would have to serve before he became eligible for parole. But the defendant had not alleged that, even if adequate advice and assistance had been given, he would have elected to plead not guilty and proceed to trial. Thus, the Court found that no prejudice from the inadequate advice had been shown or alleged.

In *Padilla*, the Court again discussed the duties of counsel in advising a client with respect to a plea offer that leads to a guilty plea. * * * The Court made clear that "the negotiation of a plea bargain is a critical phase of litigation for purposes of the Sixth Amendment right to effective assistance of counsel."

In the case now before the Court the State, as petitioner, points out that the legal question presented is different from that in *Hill* and *Padilla*. In those cases the claim was that the prisoner's plea of guilty was invalid because counsel had provided incorrect advice pertinent to the plea. In the instant case, by contrast, the guilty plea that was accepted, and the plea proceedings concerning it in court, were all based on accurate advice and information from counsel. The challenge is not to the advice pertaining to the plea that was accepted but rather to the course of legal representation that preceded it with respect to other potential pleas and plea offers.

To give further support to its contention that the instant case is in a category different from what the Court considered in *Hill* and *Padilla*, the State urges that there is no right to a plea offer or a plea bargain in any event. See *Weatherford v. Bursey*, [p. 733, fn. a]. It claims Frye therefore was not deprived of any legal benefit to which he was entitled. Under this view, any wrongful or mistaken action of counsel with respect to earlier plea offers is beside the point.

The State is correct to point out that *Hill* and *Padilla* concerned whether there was ineffective assistance leading to acceptance of a plea offer, a process involving a formal court appearance with the defendant and all counsel present. Before a guilty plea is entered the defendant's understanding of the plea and its consequences can be established on the record. This affords the State substantial protection against later claims that the plea was the result of inadequate advice. At the plea entry proceedings the trial court and all counsel have the opportunity to establish on the record that the defendant understands the process that led to any offer, the advantages and disadvantages of accepting it, and the sentencing consequences or possibilities that will ensue once a conviction is entered based upon the plea. *Hill* and *Padilla* both illustrate that, nevertheless, there may be instances when claims of ineffective assistance can arise after the conviction is entered. Still, the State, and the trial court itself, have had a substantial opportunity to guard against this contingency by establishing at the plea entry proceeding that the defendant has been given proper advice or, if the advice received appears to have been inadequate, to remedy that deficiency before the plea is accepted and the conviction entered.

When a plea offer has lapsed or been rejected, however, no formal court proceedings are involved. This underscores that the plea-bargaining process is often in flux, with no clear standards or timelines and with no judicial supervision of the discussions between prosecution and defense. Indeed, discussions between client and defense counsel are privileged. So the prosecution has little or no notice if something may be amiss and perhaps no capacity to intervene in any event. And, as noted, the State insists there is no right to receive a plea offer. For all these reasons, the State contends, it is unfair to subject it to the consequences of defense counsel's inadequacies, especially when the opportunities for a full and fair trial, or, as here, for a later guilty plea albeit on less favorable terms, are preserved.

The State's contentions are neither illogical nor without some persuasive force, yet they do not suffice to overcome a simple reality. Ninety-seven percent of federal convictions and ninety-four percent of state convictions are the result of guilty pleas. The reality is that plea bargains have become so central to the administration of the criminal justice system that defense counsel have responsibilities in the plea bargain process, responsibilities that must be met to render the adequate assistance of counsel that the Sixth Amendment requires in the criminal process at critical stages. Because ours "is for the most part a system of pleas, not a system of trials," it is insufficient simply to point to the guarantee of a fair trial as a backstop that inoculates any errors in the pretrial process. * * * See also Barkow, *Separation of Powers and the Criminal Law,* 58 Stan. L.Rev. 989, 1034 (2006) ("[Defendants] who do take their case to trial and lose receive longer sentences than even Congress or the prosecutor might think appropriate, because the longer sentences exist on the books largely for bargaining purposes. This often results in individuals who accept a plea bargain receiving shorter sentences than other individuals who are less morally culpable but take a chance and go to trial"). In today's criminal justice system, therefore, the negotiation of a plea bargain, rather than the unfolding of a trial, is almost always the critical point for a defendant. * * *

The inquiry then becomes how to define the duty and responsibilities of defense counsel in the plea bargain process. This is a difficult question. "The art of negotiation is at least as nuanced as the art of trial advocacy and it presents questions farther removed from immediate judicial supervision." *Premo v. Moore,* 131 S.Ct. 733 (2011).[a] Bargaining is, by its nature, defined to a substantial degree

---

[a] In *Moore,* the Court rejected defendant's claim that he had been denied ineffective assistance of counsel because his counsel had not sought suppression of defendant's confession before advising him to plead no contest to felony murder in exchange for the minimum sentence for that offense:

"Whether before, during, or after trial, when the Sixth Amendment applies, the formulation of the standard is the same: reasonable competence in representing the accused. *Strickland.* In applying and defining this standard substantial deference must be accorded to counsel's judgment. But at different stages of the case that deference may be measured in different ways.

"In the case of an early plea, neither the prosecution nor the defense may know with much certainty what course the case may take. It follows that each side, of necessity, risks consequences that may arise from contingencies or circumstances yet unperceived. The absence of a developed or an extensive record and the circumstance that neither the prosecution nor the defense case has been well defined create a particular risk that an after-the-fact assessment will run counter to the deference that must be accorded counsel's judgment and perspective when the plea was negotiated, offered, and entered.

by personal style. The alternative courses and tactics in negotiation are so individual that it may be neither prudent nor practicable to try to elaborate or define detailed standards for the proper discharge of defense counsel's participation in the process.

This case presents neither the necessity nor the occasion to define the duties of defense counsel in those respects, however. Here the question is whether defense counsel has the duty to communicate the terms of a formal offer to accept a plea on terms and conditions that may result in a lesser sentence, a conviction on lesser charges, or both.

This Court now holds that, as a general rule, defense counsel has the duty to communicate formal offers from the prosecution to accept a plea on terms and conditions that may be favorable to the accused. Any exceptions to that rule need not be explored here, for the offer was a formal one with a fixed expiration date. When defense counsel allowed the offer to expire without advising the defendant or allowing him to consider it, defense counsel did not render the effective assistance the Constitution requires.

Though the standard for counsel's performance is not determined solely by reference to codified standards of professional practice, these standards can be important guides. The American Bar Association recommends defense counsel "promptly communicate and explain to the defendant all plea offers made by the prosecuting attorney," ABA Standards for Criminal Justice, Pleas of Guilty 14–3.2(a) (3d ed. 1999), and this standard has been adopted by numerous state and federal courts over the last 30 years. The standard for prompt communication and consultation is also set out in state bar professional standards for attorneys.

The prosecution and the trial courts may adopt some measures to help ensure against late, frivolous, or fabricated claims after a later, less advantageous plea offer has been accepted or after a trial leading to conviction with resulting harsh

---

"Prosecutors in the present case faced the cost of litigation and the risk of trying their case without Moore's confession to the police. Moore's counsel could reasonably believe that a swift plea bargain would allow Moore to take advantage of the State's aversion to these hazards. And whenever cases involve multiple defendants, there is a chance that prosecutors might convince one defendant to testify against another in exchange for a better deal. Moore's plea eliminated that possibility and ended an ongoing investigation. Delaying the plea for further proceedings would have given the State time to uncover additional incriminating evidence that could have formed the basis of a capital prosecution. It must be remembered, after all, that Moore's claim that it was an accident when he shot the victim through the temple might be disbelieved.

"It is not clear how the successful exclusion of the confession would have affected counsel's strategic calculus. The prosecution had at its disposal two witnesses able to relate another confession. True, Moore's brother and the girlfriend of his accomplice might have changed their accounts in a manner favorable to Moore. But the record before the state court reveals no reason to believe that either witness would violate the legal obligation to convey the content of Moore's confession. And to the extent that his accomplice's girlfriend had an ongoing interest in the matter, she might have been tempted to put more blame, not less, on Moore. Then, too, the accomplices themselves might have decided to implicate Moore to a greater extent than his own confession did, say by indicating that Moore shot the victim deliberately, not accidentally. All these possibilities are speculative. What counsel knew at the time was that the existence of the two witnesses to an additional confession posed a serious strategic concern.

"Moore's prospects at trial were thus anything but certain. Even now, he does not deny any involvement in the kidnaping and killing. In these circumstances, and with a potential capital charge lurking, Moore's counsel made a reasonable choice to opt for a quick plea bargain."

consequences. First, the fact of a formal offer means that its terms and its processing can be documented so that what took place in the negotiation process becomes more clear if some later inquiry turns on the conduct of earlier pretrial negotiations. Second, States may elect to follow rules that all offers must be in writing, again to ensure against later misunderstandings or fabricated charges. Third, formal offers can be made part of the record at any subsequent plea proceeding or before a trial on the merits, all to ensure that a defendant has been fully advised before those further proceedings commence. * * *

Here defense counsel did not communicate the formal offers to the defendant. As a result of that deficient performance, the offers lapsed. Under *Strickland*, the question then becomes what, if any, prejudice resulted from the breach of duty.

To show prejudice from ineffective assistance of counsel where a plea offer has lapsed or been rejected because of counsel's deficient performance, defendants must demonstrate a reasonable probability they would have accepted the earlier plea offer had they been afforded effective assistance of counsel. Defendants must also demonstrate a reasonable probability the plea would have been entered without the prosecution canceling it or the trial court refusing to accept it, if they had the authority to exercise that discretion under state law. To establish prejudice in this instance, it is necessary to show a reasonable probability that the end result of the criminal process would have been more favorable by reason of a plea to a lesser charge or a sentence of less prison time. * * *

In order to complete a showing of *Strickland* prejudice, defendants who have shown a reasonable probability they would have accepted the earlier plea offer must also show that, if the prosecution had the discretion to cancel it or if the trial court had the discretion to refuse to accept it, there is a reasonable probability neither the prosecution nor the trial court would have prevented the offer from being accepted or implemented. This further showing is of particular importance because a defendant has no right to be offered a plea, nor a federal right that the judge accept it. In at least some States, including Missouri, it appears the prosecution has some discretion to cancel a plea agreement to which the defendant has agreed. The Federal Rules, some state rules including in Missouri, and this Court's precedents give trial courts some leeway to accept or reject plea agreements. It can be assumed that in most jurisdictions prosecutors and judges are familiar with the boundaries of acceptable plea bargains and sentences. So in most instances it should not be difficult to make an objective assessment as to whether or not a particular fact or intervening circumstance would suffice, in the normal course, to cause prosecutorial withdrawal or judicial nonapproval of a plea bargain. The determination that there is or is not a reasonable probability that the outcome of the proceeding would have been different absent counsel's errors can be conducted within that framework. * * *

There appears to be a reasonable probability Frye would have accepted the prosecutor's original offer of a plea bargain if the offer had been communicated to him, because he pleaded guilty to a more serious charge, with no promise of a sentencing recommendation from the prosecutor. It may be that in some cases defendants must show more than just a guilty plea to a charge or sentence harsher than the original offer. For example, revelations between plea offers about the strength of the prosecution's case may make a late decision to plead guilty insufficient to demonstrate, without further evidence, that the defendant would have pleaded guilty to an earlier, more generous plea offer if his counsel had reported it to him. Here, however, that is not the case. * * *

The Court of Appeals failed, however, to require Frye to show that the first plea offer, if accepted by Frye, would have been adhered to by the prosecution and accepted by the trial court. Whether the prosecution and trial court are required to do so is a matter of state law, and it is not the place of this Court to settle those matters. * * *

We remand for the Missouri Court of Appeals to consider these state-law questions, because they bear on the federal question of *Strickland* prejudice. If, as the Missouri court stated here, the prosecutor could have canceled the plea agreement, and if Frye fails to show a reasonable probability the prosecutor would have adhered to the agreement, there is no *Strickland* prejudice. Likewise, if the trial court could have refused to accept the plea agreement, and if Frye fails to show a reasonable probability the trial court would have accepted the plea, there is no *Strickland* prejudice. In this case, given Frye's new offense for driving without a license on December 30, 2007, there is reason to doubt that the prosecution would have adhered to the agreement or that the trial court would have accepted it at the January 4, 2008, hearing, unless they were required by state law to do so. * * *b

JUSTICE SCALIA, with whom THE CHIEF JUSTICE, JUSTICE THOMAS, and JUSTICE ALITO join, dissenting. * * *

The Court announces its holding that "as a general rule, defense counsel has the duty to communicate formal offers from the prosecution" as though that resolves a disputed point; in reality, however, neither the State nor the Solicitor General argued that counsel's performance here was adequate. The only issue was whether the inadequacy deprived Frye of his constitutional right to a fair trial. In other cases, however, it will not be so clear that counsel's plea-bargaining skills, which must now meet a constitutional minimum, are adequate. "[H]ow to define the duty and responsibilities of defense counsel in the plea bargain process," the Court acknowledges, "is a difficult question," since "[b]argaining is, by its nature, defined to a substantial degree by personal style." Indeed. What if an attorney's "personal style" is to establish a reputation as a hard bargainer by, for example, advising clients to proceed to trial rather than accept anything but the most favorable plea offers? It seems inconceivable that a lawyer could compromise his client's constitutional rights so that he can secure better deals for other clients in the future; does a hard-bargaining "personal style" now violate the Sixth Amendment? The Court ignores such difficulties, however, since "[t]his case presents neither the necessity nor the occasion to define the duties of defense counsel in those respects." Perhaps not. But it does present the necessity of confronting the serious difficulties that will be created by constitutionalization of

---

b   For further discussion of the prejudice issue and the closely related question of what the proper remedy is, even assuming the *Strickland* test is otherwise satisfied, see the companion case of *Lafler v. Cooper*, p. 951.

the plea-bargaining process. It will not do simply to announce that they will be solved in the sweet by-and-by.

While the inadequacy of counsel's performance in this case is clear enough, whether it was prejudicial (in the sense that the Court's new version of *Strickland* requires) is not. The Court's description of how that question is to be answered on remand is alone enough to show how unwise it is to constitutionalize the plea-bargaining process. Prejudice is to be determined, the Court tells us, by a process of retrospective crystal-ball gazing posing as legal analysis. First of all, of course, we must estimate whether the defendant would have accepted the earlier plea bargain. Here that seems an easy question, but as the Court acknowledges, it will not always be. Next, since Missouri, like other States, permits accepted plea offers to be withdrawn by the prosecution (a reality which alone should suffice, one would think, to demonstrate that Frye had no entitlement to the plea bargain), we must estimate whether the prosecution would have withdrawn the plea offer. And finally, we must estimate whether the trial court would have approved the plea agreement. These last two estimations may seem easy in the present case, since Frye committed a new infraction before the hearing at which the agreement would have been presented; but they assuredly will not be easy in the mine run of cases.

The Court says "[i]t can be assumed that in most jurisdictions prosecutors and judges are familiar with the boundaries of acceptable plea bargains and sentences." Assuredly it can, just as it can be assumed that the sun rises in the west; but I know of no basis for the assumption. Virtually no cases deal with the standards for a prosecutor's withdrawal from a plea agreement beyond stating the general rule that a prosecutor may withdraw any time prior to, but not after, the entry of a guilty plea or other action constituting detrimental reliance on the defendant's part. And cases addressing trial courts' authority to accept or reject plea agreements almost universally observe that a trial court enjoys broad discretion in this regard. Of course after today's opinions there will be cases galore, so the Court's assumption would better be cast as an optimistic prediction of the certainty that will emerge, many years hence, from our newly created constitutional field of plea-bargaining law. Whatever the "boundaries" ultimately devised (if that were possible), a vast amount of discretion will still remain, and it is extraordinary to make a defendant's constitutional rights depend upon a series of retrospective mind-readings as to how that discretion, in prosecutors and trial judges, would have been exercised.

The plea-bargaining process is a subject worthy of regulation, since it is the means by which most criminal convictions are obtained. It happens not to be, however, a subject covered by the Sixth Amendment, which is concerned not with the fairness of bargaining but with the fairness of conviction. * * * A legislature could solve the problems presented by these cases in a much more precise and efficient manner. It might begin, for example, by penalizing the attorneys who made such grievous errors. That type of sub-constitutional remedy is not available to the Court, which is limited to penalizing (almost) everyone else by reversing valid convictions or sentences. Because that result is inconsistent with the Sixth Amendment and decades of our precedent, I respectfully dissent.

UNITED STATES V. RUIZ

536 U.S. 622, 122 S.Ct. 2450, 153 L.Ed.2d 586 (2002).

JUSTICE BREYER delivered the opinion of the Court.

In this case we primarily consider whether the Fifth and Sixth Amendments require federal prosecutors, before entering into a binding plea agreement with a criminal defendant, to disclose "impeachment information relating to any informants or other witnesses." We hold that the Constitution does not require that disclosure.

After immigration agents found 30 kilograms of marijuana in Angela Ruiz's luggage, federal prosecutors offered her what is known in the Southern District of California as a "fast track" plea bargain. That bargain—standard in that district—asks a defendant to waive indictment, trial, and an appeal. In return, the Government agrees to recommend to the sentencing judge a two-level departure downward from the otherwise applicable United States Sentencing Guidelines sentence. In Ruiz's case, a two-level departure downward would have shortened the ordinary Guidelines-specified 18- to 24-month sentencing range by 6 months, to 12 to 18 months.

The prosecutors' proposed plea agreement contains a set of detailed terms. Among other things, it specifies that "any [known] information establishing the factual innocence of the defendant" "has been turned over to the defendant," and it acknowledges the Government's "continuing duty to provide such information." At the same time it requires that the defendant "waiv[e] the right" to receive "impeachment information relating to any informants or other witnesses" as well as the right to receive information supporting any affirmative defense the defendant raises if the case goes to trial. Because Ruiz would not agree to this last-mentioned waiver, the prosecutors withdrew their bargaining offer. The Government then indicted Ruiz for unlawful drug possession. And despite the absence of any agreement, Ruiz ultimately pleaded guilty.

At sentencing, Ruiz asked the judge to grant her the same two-level downward departure that the Government would have recommended had she accepted the "fast track" agreement. The Government opposed her request, and the District Court denied it, imposing a standard Guideline sentence instead.

* * * Ruiz appealed her sentence to the United States Court of Appeals for the Ninth Circuit. The Ninth Circuit vacated the District Court's sentencing determination. The Ninth Circuit pointed out that the Constitution requires prosecutors to make certain impeachment information available to a defendant before trial. It decided that this obligation entitles defendants to receive that same information before they enter into a plea agreement. The Ninth Circuit also decided that the Constitution prohibits defendants from waiving their right to that information. And it held that the prosecutors' standard "fast track" plea agreement was unlawful because it insisted upon that waiver. * * *

The constitutional question concerns a federal criminal defendant's waiver of the right to receive from prosecutors exculpatory impeachment material—a right that the Constitution provides as part of its basic "fair trial" guarantee. See U.S.

Const., Amdts. 5, 6. See also *Brady v. Maryland,* [p. 740] (Due process requires prosecutors to "avoi[d] . . . an unfair trial" by making available "upon request" evidence "favorable to an accused . . . where the evidence is material either to guilt or to punishment"); *United States v. Agurs,* [p. 741] (defense request unnecessary); *Kyles v. Whitley,* [fn. c., p. 743] (exculpatory evidence is evidence the suppression of which would "undermin[e] confidence in the verdict"); *Giglio v. United States,* 405 U.S. 150 (1972) (exculpatory evidence includes "evidence affecting" witness "credibility," where the witness' "reliability" is likely "determinative of guilt or innocence").

When a defendant pleads guilty he or she, of course, forgoes not only a fair trial, but also other accompanying constitutional guarantees. *Boykin v. Alabama,* [p. 778] (pleading guilty implicates the Fifth Amendment privilege against self-incrimination, the Sixth Amendment right to confront one's accusers, and the Sixth Amendment right to trial by jury). Given the seriousness of the matter, the Constitution insists, among other things, that the defendant enter a guilty plea that is "voluntary" and that the defendant must make related waivers "knowing[ly], intelligent[ly], [and] with sufficient awareness of the relevant circumstances and likely consequences." *Brady v. United States* [fn. a, p. 760]; see also *Boykin, supra.*

In this case, the Ninth Circuit in effect held that a guilty plea is not "voluntary" (and that the defendant could not, by pleading guilty, waive his right to a fair trial) unless the prosecutors first made the same disclosure of material impeachment information that the prosecutors would have had to make had the defendant insisted upon a trial. We must decide whether the Constitution requires that preguilty plea disclosure of impeachment information. We conclude that it does not.

First, impeachment information is special in relation to the *fairness of a trial,* not in respect to whether a plea is *voluntary* ("knowing," "intelligent," and "sufficient[ly] aware"). Of course, the more information the defendant has, the more aware he is of the likely consequences of a plea, waiver, or decision, and the wiser that decision will likely be. But the Constitution does not require the prosecutor to share all useful information with the defendant. *Weatherford v. Bursey,* [fn. a, p. 733] ("There is no general constitutional right to discovery in a criminal case"). And the law ordinarily considers a waiver knowing, intelligent, and sufficiently aware if the defendant fully understands the nature of the right and how it would likely apply *in general* in the circumstances—even though the defendant may not know the *specific detailed* consequences of invoking it. A defendant, for example, may waive his right to remain silent, his right to a jury trial, or his right to counsel even if the defendant does not know the specific questions the authorities intend to ask, who will likely serve on the jury, or the particular lawyer the State might otherwise provide. Cf. *Colorado v. Spring,* [fn. a, p. 532] (Fifth Amendment privilege against self-incrimination waived when defendant received standard *Miranda* warnings regarding the nature of the right but not told the specific interrogation questions to be asked).

It is particularly difficult to characterize impeachment information as critical information of which the defendant must always be aware prior to pleading guilty given the random way in which such information may, or may not, help a particular defendant. The degree of help that impeachment information can provide will depend upon the defendant's own independent knowledge of the prosecution's potential case—a matter that the Constitution does not require prosecutors to disclose.

Second, we have found no legal authority embodied either in this Court's past cases or in cases from other circuits that provide significant support for the Ninth Circuit's decision. To the contrary, this Court has found that the Constitution, in respect to a defendant's awareness of relevant circumstances, does not require complete knowledge of the relevant circumstances, but permits a court to accept a guilty plea, with its accompanying waiver of various constitutional rights, despite various forms of misapprehension under which a defendant might labor. See *Brady v. United States* (defendant "misapprehended the quality of the State's case"); *ibid.* (defendant misapprehended "the likely penalties"); *ibid.* (defendant failed to "anticipate a change in the law regarding" relevant "punishments"); *McMann v. Richardson,* [p. 928] (counsel "misjudged the admissibility" of a "confession"); *United States v. Broce,* 488 U.S. 563 (1989) (counsel failed to point out a potential defense); *Tollett v. Henderson,* 411 U.S. 258 (1973) (counsel failed to find a potential constitutional infirmity in grand jury proceedings). It is difficult to distinguish, in terms of importance, (1) a defendant's ignorance of grounds for impeachment of potential witnesses at a possible future trial from (2) the varying forms of ignorance at issue in these cases.

Third, due process considerations, the very considerations that led this Court to find trial-related rights to exculpatory and impeachment information in *Brady* and *Giglio,* argue against the existence of the "right" that the Ninth Circuit found here. This Court has said that due process considerations include not only (1) the nature of the private interest at stake, but also (2) the value of the additional safeguard, and (3) the adverse impact of the requirement upon the Government's interests. *Ake v. Oklahoma,* [fn. a, p. 405]. Here, as we have just pointed out, the added value of the Ninth Circuit's "right" to a defendant is often limited, for it depends upon the defendant's independent awareness of the details of the Government's case. And in any case, as the proposed plea agreement at issue here specifies, the Government will provide "any information establishing the factual innocence of the defendant" regardless. That fact, along with other guilty-plea safeguards, see Fed. Rule Crim. Proc. 11, diminishes the force of Ruiz's concern that, in the absence of impeachment information, innocent individuals, accused of crimes, will plead guilty. Cf. *McCarthy v. United States,* 394 U.S. 459 (1969) (discussing Rule 11's role in protecting a defendant's constitutional rights).

At the same time, a constitutional obligation to provide impeachment information during plea bargaining, prior to entry of a guilty plea, could seriously interfere with the Government's interest in securing those guilty pleas that are factually justified, desired by defendants, and help to secure the efficient administration of justice. The Ninth Circuit's rule risks premature disclosure of Government witness information, which, the Government tells us, could "disrupt ongoing investigations" and expose prospective witnesses to serious harm. And the careful tailoring that characterizes most legal Government witness disclosure requirements suggests recognition by both Congress and the Federal Rules Committees that such concerns are valid. See, *e.g.*, 18 U.S.C. § 3432 (witness list disclosure required in capital cases three days before trial with exceptions); § 3500 (Government witness statements ordinarily subject to discovery only after testimony given); Fed. Rule Crim. Proc. 16(a)(2) (embodies limitations of 18 U.S.C. § 3500)

Consequently, the Ninth Circuit's requirement could force the Government to abandon its "general practice" of not "disclos[ing] to a defendant pleading guilty information that would reveal the identities of cooperating informants, undercover investigators, or other prospective witnesses." It could require the Government to devote substantially more resources to trial preparation prior to plea bargaining, thereby depriving the plea-bargaining process of its main resource-saving advantages. Or it could lead the Government instead to abandon its heavy reliance upon plea bargaining in a vast number—90% or more—of federal criminal cases. We cannot say that the Constitution's due process requirement demands so radical a change in the criminal justice process in order to achieve so comparatively small a constitutional benefit.

These considerations, taken together, lead us to conclude that the Constitution does not require the Government to disclose material impeachment evidence prior to entering a plea agreement with a criminal defendant.

In addition, we note that the "fast track" plea agreement requires a defendant to waive her right to receive information the Government has regarding any "affirmative defense" she raises at trial. We do not believe the Constitution here requires provision of this information to the defendant prior to plea bargaining— for most (though not all) of the reasons previously stated. That is to say, in the context of this agreement, the need for this information is more closely related to the *fairness* of a trial than to the *voluntariness* of the plea; the value in terms of the defendant's added awareness of relevant circumstances is ordinarily limited; yet the added burden imposed upon the Government by requiring its provision well in advance of trial (often before trial preparation begins) can be serious, thereby significantly interfering with the administration of the plea bargaining process. * * *

JUSTICE THOMAS, concurring in the judgment. * * * The Court * * * suggests that the constitutional analysis turns in some part on the "degree of help" such information would provide to the defendant at the plea stage, a distinction that is neither necessary nor accurate. * * * The principle supporting *Brady* was "avoidance of an unfair trial to the accused." That concern is not implicated at the plea stage regardless.

2. REQUISITES OF A VALID PLEA

At an earlier time, when the validity of plea bargaining was in doubt, the general practice was not to reveal in court at the time the guilty plea was received that a bargain had been struck. This is no longer the case. Moreover, there has been increased acceptance of the notion that the plea receiving process should be more cautious in other respects as well, so that today in most jurisdictions a court rule or statute imposes several responsibilities upon the judge in connection with receipt of defendant's guilty plea. Typical is Federal Rule of Criminal Procedure 11, which requires the judge to (i) inform the defendant and determine that he understands the nature of the charge and the possible penalty[a] and various rights

---

[a] It is typically said that the judge's obligation in this regard extends to those consequences that are "direct" but not those that are merely "collateral." A similar distinction had been drawn when the question, under the first prong of *Strickland v. Washington*, p. 928, is whether defense counsel has rendered ineffective assistance by failing to advise his client of certain consequences of pleading guilty. But in *Padilla v. Kentucky*, 559 U.S. 356 (2010), the Court declined to rely upon that distinction given "the unique nature of deportation." Instead, the Court stressed that under current immigration law "deportation is an integral part—indeed, sometimes the most important part—of the penalty that may be imposed on noncitizen defendants who plead guilty to specific crimes." The Court concluded (1) that counsel's representation in the instant case, erroneously telling defendant he could not be deported, "fell below an objective standard of reasonableness," given that "the terms of the relevant immigration statute are succinct, clear, and explicit in defining the removal consequence for Padilla's conviction"; (2) that "where the deportation consequence is truly clear, as it was in this case, the duty to give correct advice is equally clear," and (3) that in the "numerous situations in which the deportation consequences of a particular plea are unclear or uncertain" because "the law is not succinct and straightforward * * *, a criminal defense attorney need do no more than advise a noncitizen client that pending criminal charges may carry a risk of adverse immigration consequences." Regarding the Solicitor General's suggestion that the ruling be limited to "affirmative misadvice," the *Padilla* Court responded "that there is no relevant difference 'between an act of commission and an act of omission' in this context." (As for *Strickland*'s second prong, prejudice, the Court left that "to the Kentucky courts to consider in the first instance.")

The concurring opinion of Alito, J., joined by Roberts, C.J., concluded an "attorney must (1) refrain from unreasonably providing incorrect advice and (2) advise the defendant that a criminal conviction may have adverse immigration consequences and that, if the alien wants advice on this issue, the alien should consult an immigration attorney," and found the majority's approach "problematic" because, inter alia, (i) "it will not always be easy to tell whether a particular statutory provision is 'succinct, clear, and explicit,' " and (ii) "if defense counsel must provide advice regarding only one of the many collateral consequences of a criminal conviction, many defendants are likely to be misled." As for the majority's reliance upon "the seriousness of deportation as a consequence of a criminal plea," the concurrence countered that "criminal convictions can carry a wide variety of consequences other than conviction and sentencing" that are also serious, "but this Court has never held that a criminal defense attorney's Sixth Amendment duties extend to providing advice about such matters." Scalia, J., joined by Thomas, J, dissenting, did "not believe that affirmative misadvice about those consequences renders an attorney's assistance in defending against the prosecution constitutionally inadequate; or that the Sixth Amendment requires counsel to warn immigrant defendants that a conviction may render them removable. Statutory provisions can remedy these concerns in a more targeted fashion, and without producing permanent, and legislatively irreparable, overkill."

The Court later addressed the second *Strickland* prong, prejudice, in this context in *Lee v. United States*, 137 S.Ct. 1958 (2017). Lee, a noncitizen lawful permanent resident charged with possessing drugs with intent to distribute, opted to accept a plea offer carrying a lower sentence than he would have faced at trial after his counsel erroneously assured him he would not be deported. Lee later was not allowed to withdraw his guilty plea because of that ineffective assistance, on the ground he could not show prejudice. The Government asked the Supreme Court to "accept a *per se* rule that a defendant with no viable defense cannot show prejudice from the denial of his right to trial," a proposition the Court, per Roberts, C.J., deemed erroneous because (1) it utilizes a categorical rule when a "case-by-case examination" is called for; and (2) "more fundamentally, * * * the inquiry as presented in *Hill v. Lockhart* [see p. 952] "focuses on a defendant's decisionmaking, which may not turn solely on the likelihood of conviction after trial." But, the Court cautioned: "Courts should not upset a plea solely because of *post hoc* assertions from a defendant about how he would have pleaded but for his attorney's deficiencies. Judges should instead look to contemporaneous evidence to substantiate a defendant's expressed preferences." Given the "unusual circumstances of this case," the Court held Lee had "adequately

he is surrendering by pleading guilty; (ii) determine that the plea is voluntary; (iii) require disclosure of any plea agreement and accept or reject that agreement; and (iv) make sufficient inquiry to ensure there is a factual basis for the plea.[b]

As the cases in this section illustrate, constitutional considerations lie close to the surface of such provisions. *Boykin v. Alabama* deals with the waiver-of-rights aspect of a guilty plea, *Henderson v. Morgan* with the necessity that defendant understand the charge against him, and *North Carolina v. Alford* with the special circumstances in which a factual basis for the plea is constitutionally mandated.

BOYKIN V. ALABAMA
395 U.S. 238, 89 S.Ct. 1709, 23 L.Ed.2d 274 (1969).

JUSTICE DOUGLAS delivered the opinion of the Court.

In the spring of 1966, within the period of a fortnight, a series of armed robberies occurred in Mobile, Alabama. The victims, in each case, were local shopkeepers open at night who were forced by a gunman to hand over money. While robbing one grocery store, the assailant fired his gun once, sending a bullet through a door into the ceiling. A few days earlier in a drugstore, the robber had allowed his gun to discharge in such a way that the bullet, on ricochet from the floor, struck a customer in the leg. Shortly thereafter, a local grand jury returned five indictments against petitioner, a 27-year-old Negro, for common-law robbery—an offense punishable in Alabama by death.

Before the matter came to trial, the court determined that petitioner was indigent and appointed counsel to represent him. Three days later, at his arraignment, petitioner pleaded guilty to all five indictments. So far as the record shows, the judge asked no questions of petitioner concerning his plea, and petitioner did not address the court.

Trial strategy may of course make a plea of guilty seem the desirable course. But the record is wholly silent on that point and throws no light on it.

Alabama provides that when a defendant pleads guilty, "the court must cause the punishment to be determined by a jury" (except where it is required to be fixed by the court) and may "cause witnesses to be examined, to ascertain the character

---

demonstrated a reasonable probability that he would have rejected the plea had he known that it would lead to mandatory deportation," considering that (a) Lee repeatedly asked his attorney about whether there was any risk of deportation; (b) both Lee and his counsel testified he would have gone to trial had he know the true deportation consequences; (c) Lee's responses at his plea colloquy indicated the importance he placed on deportation; (d) Lee had strong connections with the U.S., where he had lived nearly 30 years, most of his life, and had no ties to South Korea; and (e) it would not be irrational for someone in Lee's situation to risk an additional few years of prison time in exchange for even a rather remote chance of acquittal.

[b] Rule 11 also declares that the "court must not participate in [plea] discussions." In *United States v. Davila*, 569 U.S. 597 (2013), the Court concluded that since this prohibition "was adopted as a prophylactic measure, not one impelled by the Due Process Clause or any other constitutional requirement," it follows that "pre-plea exhortations to admit guilt," just as with "[p]lea colloquy requirements [that] come into play *after* a defendant has agreed to plead guilty," are subject to that part of Rule 11 declaring that a "variance from the requirements of this rule is harmless error if it does not affect substantial rights."

of the offense." In the present case a trial of that dimension was held, the prosecution presenting its case largely through eyewitness testimony. Although counsel for petitioner engaged in cursory cross-examination, petitioner neither testified himself nor presented testimony concerning his character and background. There was nothing to indicate that he had a prior criminal record.

In instructing the jury, the judge stressed that petitioner had pleaded guilty in five cases of robbery, defined as "the felonious taking of money * * * from another against his will * * * by violence or by putting him in fear * * * [carrying] from ten years minimum in the penitentiary to the supreme penalty of death by electrocution." The jury, upon deliberation, found petitioner guilty and sentenced him severally to die on each of the five indictments. * * *

A plea of guilty is more than a confession which admits that the accused did various acts; it is itself a conviction; nothing remains but to give judgment and determine punishment. Admissibility of a confession must be based on a "reliable determination on the voluntariness issue which satisfies the constitutional rights of the defendant." The requirement that the prosecution spread on the record the prerequisites of a valid waiver is no constitutional innovation. In [dealing with a problem of waiver of the right to counsel we] held: "Presuming waiver from a silent record is impermissible. The record must show, or there must be an allegation and evidence which show, that an accused was offered counsel but intelligently and understandingly rejected the offer. Anything less is not waiver."

We think that the same standard must be applied to determining whether a guilty plea is voluntarily made. For, as we have said, a plea of guilty is more than an admission of conduct; it is a conviction. Ignorance, incomprehension, coercion, terror, inducements, subtle or blatant threats might be a perfect cover-up of unconstitutionality. The question of an effective waiver of a federal constitutional right in a proceeding is of course governed by federal standards.

Several federal constitutional rights are involved in a waiver that takes place when a plea of guilty is entered in a state criminal trial. First, is the privilege against compulsory self-incrimination guaranteed by the Fifth Amendment and applicable to the States by reason of the Fourteenth.[a] Second, is the right to trial by jury. Third, is the right to confront one's accusers. We cannot presume a waiver of these three important federal rights from a silent record.

What is at stake for an accused facing death or imprisonment demands the utmost solicitude of which courts are capable in canvassing the matter with the accused to make sure he has a full understanding of what the plea connotes and of its consequence. When the judge discharges that function, he leaves a record adequate for any review that may be later sought and forestalls the spin-off of collateral proceedings that seek to probe murky memories.

The three dissenting justices in the Alabama Supreme Court stated the law accurately when they concluded that there was reversible error "because the record

---

[a] As the Court later explained, the guilty plea is actually a waiver of a trial at which the privilege against self-incrimination would apply, and thus a guilty plea defendant may remain silent at the time of sentencing without an adverse inference being drawn from such silence. See *Mitchell v. United States*, p. 1159.

does not disclose that the defendant voluntarily and understandingly entered his pleas of guilty."

Reversed.

JUSTICE HARLAN, whom JUSTICE BLACK joins, dissenting. * * *

[T]he Court's disposition is plainly out of keeping with * * * *Halliday v. United States*, 394 U.S. 831 (1969), [where the Court] affirmed the conviction even though Halliday's guilty plea was accepted in 1954 without any explicit inquiry into whether it was knowingly and understandingly made * * * In justification, the Court noted that two lower courts had found in collateral proceedings that the plea was voluntary. * * *

It seems elementary that the Fifth Amendment due process to which petitioner Halliday was entitled must be at least as demanding as the Fourteenth Amendment process due petitioner Boykin. Yet petitioner Halliday's federal conviction has been affirmed as "constitutionally valid," despite the omission of any judicial inquiry of record at the time of his plea, because he initiated collateral proceedings which revealed that the plea was actually voluntary. Petitioner Boykin, on the other hand, today has his Alabama conviction reversed because of exactly the same omission, even though he too "may * * * resort to appropriate post-conviction remedies to attack his plea's voluntariness" and thus "is not without a remedy to correct constitutional defects in his conviction." In short, I find it utterly impossible to square today's holding with what the Court has so recently done. * * *

HENDERSON V. MORGAN
426 U.S. 637, 96 S.Ct. 2253, 49 L.Ed.2d 108 (1976).

[Respondent was indicted for first-degree murder, but by agreement with the prosecution and on counsel's advice respondent pleaded guilty to second-degree murder and was sentenced. Subsequently, after exhausting his state remedies in an unsuccessful attempt to have his conviction vacated on the ground that his guilty plea was involuntary, respondent filed a habeas corpus petition in Federal District Court, alleging that his guilty plea was involuntary because, *inter alia*, he was not aware that intent to cause death was an element of second-degree murder. The District Court ultimately heard the testimony of several witnesses, including respondent and his defense counsel in the original prosecution; and the transcript of the relevant state-court proceedings and certain psychological evaluations of respondent, who was substantially below average intelligence, were made part of the record. On the basis of the evidence thus developed the District Court found that respondent had not been advised by counsel or the state court that an intent to cause death was an essential element of second-degree murder, and, based on this finding, held that the guilty plea was involuntary and had to be set aside. The Court of Appeals affirmed.]

JUSTICE STEVENS delivered the opinion of the Court. * * *

Petitioner contends that the District Court applied an unrealistically rigid rule of law. Instead of testing the voluntariness of a plea by determining whether a ritualistic litany of the formal legal elements of an offense was read to the defendant, petitioner argues that the court should examine the totality of the circumstances and determine whether the substance of the charge, as opposed to its technical elements, was conveyed to the accused. We do not disagree with the thrust of petitioner's argument, but we are persuaded that even under the test which he espouses, this judgment finding respondent guilty of second-degree murder was defective.

We assume, as petitioner argues, that the prosecutor had overwhelming evidence of guilt available. We also accept petitioner's characterization of the competence of respondent's counsel and of the wisdom of their advice to plead guilty to a charge of second-degree murder. Nevertheless, such a plea cannot support a judgment of guilt unless it was voluntary in a constitutional sense.[13] And clearly the plea could not be voluntary in the sense that it constituted an intelligent admission that he committed the offense unless the defendant received "real notice of the true nature of the charge against him, the first and most universally recognized requirement of due process."

The charge of second-degree murder was never formally made. Had it been made, it necessarily would have included a charge that respondent's assault was "committed with a design to effect the death of the person killed." That element of the offense might have been proved by the objective evidence even if respondent's actual state of mind was consistent with innocence or manslaughter. But even if such a design to effect death would almost inevitably have been inferred from evidence that respondent repeatedly stabbed Mrs. Francisco, it is nevertheless also true that a jury would not have been required to draw that inference. The jury would have been entitled to accept defense counsel's appraisal of the incident as involving only manslaughter in the first degree. Therefore, an admission by respondent that he killed Mrs. Francisco does not necessarily also admit that he was guilty of second-degree murder.

There is nothing in this record that can serve as a substitute for either a finding after trial, or a voluntary admission, that respondent had the requisite intent. Defense counsel did not purport to stipulate to that fact; they did not explain to him that his plea would be an admission of that fact; and he made no factual statement or admission necessarily implying that he had such intent. In these circumstances it is impossible to conclude that his plea to the unexplained charge of second-degree murder was voluntary.

Petitioner argues that affirmance of the Court of Appeals will invite countless collateral attacks on judgments entered on pleas of guilty, since frequently the record will not contain a complete enumeration of the elements of the offense to

---

[13] A plea may be involuntary either because the accused does not understand the nature of the constitutional protections that he is waiving, or because he has such an incomplete understanding of the charge that his plea cannot stand as an intelligent admission of guilt. Without adequate notice of the nature of the charge against him, or proof that he in fact understood the charge, the plea cannot be voluntary in this latter sense.

which an accused person pleads guilty.[18] We think petitioner's fears are exaggerated.

Normally the record contains either an explanation of the charge by the trial judge, or at least a representation by defense counsel that the nature of the offense has been explained to the accused. Moreover, even without such an express representation, it may be appropriate to presume that in most cases defense counsel routinely explain the nature of the offense in sufficient detail to give the accused notice of what he is being asked to admit. This case is unique because the trial judge found as a fact that the element of intent was not explained to respondent. Moreover, respondent's unusually low mental capacity provides a reasonable explanation for counsel's oversight; it also forecloses the conclusion that the error was harmless beyond a reasonable doubt, for it lends at least a modicum of credibility to defense counsel's appraisal of the homicide as a manslaughter rather than a murder.

Since respondent did not receive adequate notice of the offense to which he pleaded guilty, his plea was involuntary and the judgment of conviction was entered without due process of law.

Affirmed.

JUSTICE WHITE, with whom JUSTICE STEWART, JUSTICE BLACKMUN, and JUSTICE POWELL join, concurring. * * *

The problem in this case is that the defendant's guilt has been established neither by a finding of guilt beyond a reasonable doubt after trial nor by the defendant's own admission that he is in fact guilty. The defendant did not expressly admit that he intended the victim's death (such intent being an element of the crime for which he stands convicted); and his plea of guilty cannot be construed as an implied admission that he intended her death because the District Court has found that he was not told and did not know that intent to kill was an element of the offense with which he was charged.[2] * * *

JUSTICE REHNQUIST, with whom THE CHIEF JUSTICE joins, dissenting.

Since it seems clear * * * that respondent's plea was "voluntarily made," and since it is undisputed that it was made with full understanding of its consequences, the only remaining issue is whether he was "properly advised." This inquiry, in turn, depends upon the sort of advice reasonably competent counsel would have been expected to give him. * * *

---

[18] There is no need in this case to decide whether notice of the true nature, or substance, of a charge always requires a description of every element of the offense; we assume it does not. Nevertheless, intent is such a critical element of the offense of second-degree murder that notice of that element is required.

[2] This case is unusual in that the offense to which the defendant pleaded was not charged in the indictment. The indictment charged first-degree murder. The defendant pleaded guilty to the included offense of second-degree murder, the elements of which were not set forth in any document which had been read to the defendant or to which he had access. In those cases in which the indictment is read to the defendant by the court at arraignment or at the time of his plea, his plea of guilty may well be deemed a factual admission that he did what he is charged with doing so that a judgment of conviction may validly be entered against him.

Respondent was originally indicted for the crime of first-degree murder, and that indictment charged that in April 1965, he had "willfully, feloniously and of malice aforethought, stabbed and cut Ada Francisco with a dangerous knife * * * and that thereafter * * * the said Ada Francisco died of said wounds and injuries, said killing being inexcusable and unjustifiable." Respondent's attorney at the habeas hearing testified that respondent had stabbed his victim "many times" which suggests that experienced counsel would not consider the "design to effect death" issue to be in serious dispute. * * *

I do not see how this Court, or any court, could conclude on this state of the record that respondent was not "properly advised" at the time he entered his plea of guilty to the charge of second-degree murder.

His attorneys were motivated by the eminently reasonable tactical judgment on their part that he should plead guilty to second-degree murder in order to avoid the possibility of conviction for first-degree murder with its more serious attendant penalties. Since the Court concedes both the competence of respondent's counsel and the wisdom of their advice, that should be the end of the matter.

There are intimations in the Court's opinion that the vice which it finds in the guilty plea is not that respondent was not *informed* of all the elements of the offense, but that instead he did not *admit* to all of those elements. But it is quite clear under our decision in *North Carolina v. Alford* that the latter fact, standing alone, is not sufficient to invalidate a guilty plea. * * *

NORTH CAROLINA V. ALFORD

400 U.S. 25, 91 S.Ct. 160, 27 L.Ed.2d 162 (1970).

JUSTICE WHITE delivered the opinion of the Court.

[Appellee was indicted for the capital crime of first-degree murder. At that time North Carolina law provided for the penalty of life imprisonment when a plea of guilty was accepted to a first-degree murder charge; for the death penalty following a jury verdict of guilty, unless the jury recommended life imprisonment; and for a penalty of from two to 30 years' imprisonment for second-degree murder. Appellee's attorney, in the face of strong evidence of guilt, recommended a guilty plea, but left the decision to appellee. The prosecutor agreed to accept a plea of guilty to second-degree murder. The trial court heard damaging evidence from certain witnesses before accepting a plea. Appellee pleaded guilty, although disclaiming guilt, because of the threat of the death penalty, and was sentenced to 30 years' imprisonment. The Court of Appeals, on an appeal from a denial of a writ of habeas corpus, found that appellee's guilty plea was involuntary because it was motivated principally by fear of the death penalty.]

We held in *Brady v. United States*, 397 U.S. 742 (1970), that a plea of guilty which would not have been entered except for the defendant's desire to avoid a possible death penalty and to limit the maximum penalty to life imprisonment or a term of years was not for that reason compelled within the meaning of the Fifth Amendment. * * * The standard was and remains whether the plea represents a voluntary and intelligent choice among the alternative courses of action open to the defendant. * * * That he would not have pleaded except for the opportunity to limit the possible penalty does not necessarily demonstrate that the plea of guilty was not the product of a free and rational choice, especially where the defendant was represented by competent counsel whose advice was that the plea would be to the defendant's advantage. The standard fashioned and applied by the Court of Appeals was therefore erroneous and we would, without more, vacate and remand the case for further proceedings with respect to any other claims of Alford which are properly before that court, if it were not for other circumstances appearing in the record which might seem to warrant an affirmance of the Court of Appeals.

As previously recounted after Alford's plea of guilty was offered and the State's case was placed before the judge, Alford denied that he had committed the murder but reaffirmed his desire to plead guilty to avoid a possible death sentence and to limit the penalty to the 30-year maximum provided for second-degree murder. Ordinarily, a judgment of conviction resting on a plea of guilty is justified by the defendant's admission that he committed the crime charged against him and his consent that judgment be entered without a trial of any kind. The plea usually subsumes both elements, and justifiably so, even though there is no separate, express admission by the defendant that he committed the particular acts claimed to constitute the crime charged in the indictment. Here Alford entered his plea but accompanied it with the statement that he had not shot the victim.

If Alford's statements were to be credited as sincere assertions of his innocence, there obviously existed a factual and legal dispute between him and the State. Without more, it might be argued that the conviction entered on his guilty plea was invalid, since his assertion of innocence negatived any admission of guilt, which, as we observed last Term in *Brady,* is normally "[c]entral to the plea and the foundation for entering judgment against the defendant * * *."

In addition to Alford's statement, however, the court had heard an account of the events on the night of the murder, including information from Alford's acquaintances that he had departed from his home with his gun stating his intention to kill and that he had later declared that he had carried out his intention. Nor had Alford wavered in his desire to have trial court determine his guilt without a jury trial. Although denying the charge against him, he nevertheless preferred the dispute between him and the State to be settled by the judge in the context of a guilty plea proceeding rather than by a formal trial. Thereupon, with the State's telling evidence and Alford's denial before it, the trial court proceeded to convict and sentence Alford for second-degree murder.

State and lower federal courts are divided upon whether a guilty plea can be accepted when it is accompanied by protestations of innocence and hence contains only a waiver of trial but no admission of guilt. Some courts, giving expression to the principle that "[o]ur law only authorizes a conviction where guilt is shown," require that trial judges reject such pleas. But others have concluded that they should not "force any defense on a defendant in a criminal case," particularly when advancement of the defense might "end in disaster * * *." They have argued that, since "guilt, or the degree of guilt, is at times uncertain and elusive," "[a]n accused, though believing in or entertaining doubts respecting his innocence, might reasonably conclude a jury would be convinced of his guilt and that he would fare better in the sentence by pleading guilty * * *."[7]

This Court has not confronted this precise issue, but prior decisions do yield relevant principles. In *Lynch v. Overholser,* 369 U.S. 705 (1962), Lynch, who had been charged in the Municipal Court of the District of Columbia with drawing and negotiating bad checks, a misdemeanor punishable by a maximum of one year in jail, sought to enter a plea of guilty, but the trial judge refused to accept the plea since a psychiatric report in the judge's possession indicated that Lynch had been suffering from "a manic depressive psychosis, at the time of the crime charged," and hence might have been not guilty by reason of insanity. Although at the subsequent trial Lynch did not rely on the insanity defense, he was found not guilty by reason of insanity and committed for an indeterminate period to a mental institution. On habeas corpus, the Court ordered his release, construing the congressional legislation seemingly authorizing the commitment as not reaching a case where the accused preferred a guilty plea to a plea of insanity. The Court expressly refused to rule that Lynch had an absolute right to have his guilty plea accepted, but implied that there would have been no constitutional error had his plea been accepted even though evidence before the judge indicated that there was a valid defense.

The issue in *Hudson v. United States,* 272 U.S. 451 (1926), was whether a federal court has power to impose a prison sentence after accepting a plea of *nolo contendere,* a plea by which a defendant does not expressly admit his guilt, but nonetheless waives his right to a trial and authorizes the court for purposes of the case to treat him as if he were guilty.[8] The Court held that a trial court does have such power, and except for the cases which were rejected in *Hudson,* the federal courts have uniformly followed this rule, even in cases involving moral turpitude. Implicit in the *nolo contendere* cases is a recognition that the Constitution does not bar imposition of a prison sentence upon an accused who is unwilling expressly to admit his guilt but who, faced with grim alternatives, is willing to waive his trial and accept the sentence.

These cases would be directly in point if Alford had simply insisted on his plea but refused to admit the crime. The fact that his plea was denominated a plea of guilty rather than a plea of *nolo contendere* is of no constitutional significance with respect to the issue now before us, for the Constitution is concerned with the practical consequences, not the formal categorizations, of state law. Thus, while

---

[7]　A third approach has been to decline to rule definitively that a trial judge must either accept or reject an otherwise valid plea containing a protestation of innocence, but to leave that decision to his sound discretion.

[8]　Courts have defined the plea of *nolo contendere* in a variety of different ways, describing it, on the one hand, as "in effect, a plea of guilty," and on the other, as a query directed to the court to determine the defendant's guilt. As a result, it is impossible to state precisely what a defendant does admit when he enters a *nolo* plea in a way that will consistently fit all the cases. * * *

Throughout its history, that is, the plea of *nolo contendere* has been viewed not as an express admission of guilt but as a consent by the defendant that he may be punished as if he were guilty and a prayer for leniency. Fed. Rule Crim.Proc. 11 preserves this distinction in its requirement that a court cannot accept a guilty plea "unless it is satisfied that there is a factual basis for the plea"; there is no similar requirement for pleas of *nolo contendere,* since it was thought desirable to permit defendants to plead *nolo* without making any inquiry into their actual guilt.

most pleas of guilty consist of both a waiver of trial and an express admission of guilt, the latter element is not a constitutional requisite to the imposition of criminal penalty. An individual accused of crime may voluntarily, knowingly, and understandingly consent to the imposition of a prison sentence even if he is unwilling or unable to admit his participation in the acts constituting the crime.

Nor can we perceive any material difference between a plea that refuses to admit commission of the criminal act and a plea containing a protestation of innocence when, as in the instant case, a defendant intelligently concludes that his interests require entry of a guilty plea and the record before the judge contains strong evidence of actual guilt. Here the State had a strong case of first-degree murder against Alford. Whether he realized or disbelieved his guilt, he insisted on his plea because in his view he had absolutely nothing to gain by a trial and much to gain by pleading. Because of the overwhelming evidence against him, a trial was precisely what neither Alford nor his attorney desired. Confronted with the choice between a trial for first-degree murder, on the one hand, and a plea of guilty to second-degree murder, on the other, Alford quite reasonably chose the latter and thereby limited the maximum penalty to a 30-year term. When his plea is viewed in light of the evidence against him, which substantially negated his claim of innocence and which further provided a means by which the judge could test whether the plea was being intelligently entered, its validity cannot be seriously questioned. In view of the strong factual basis for the plea demonstrated by the State and Alford's clearly expressed desire to enter it despite his professed belief in his innocence, we hold that the trial judge did not commit constitutional error in accepting it.[11] * * *

JUSTICE BLACK, * * * concurs in the judgment and in substantially all of the opinion in this case.

JUSTICE BRENNAN, with whom JUSTICE DOUGLAS and JUSTICE MARSHALL join, dissenting.

* * * [I]t is sufficient in my view to state that the facts set out in the majority opinion demonstrate that Alford was "so gripped by fear of the death penalty" that his decision to plead guilty was not voluntary but was "the product of duress as much so as choice reflecting physical constraint."

---

[11] Our holding does not mean that a trial judge must accept every constitutionally valid guilty plea merely because a defendant wishes so to plead. A criminal defendant does not have an absolute right under the Constitution to have his guilty plea accepted by the court, although the States may by statute or otherwise confer such a right. Likewise, the States may bar their courts from accepting guilty pleas from any defendants who assert their innocence. Cf. Fed.Rule Crim.Proc. 11, which gives a trial judge discretion to "refuse to accept a plea of guilty * * *." We need not now delineate the scope of that discretion.

3. THE EFFECT OF A GUILTY PLEA

CLASS V. UNITED STATES
583 U.S. ___, 138 S.Ct. 798, 200 L.Ed.2d 37 (2018).

JUSTICE BREYER delivered the opinion of the Court. * * *

[Rodney Class was indicted for violating federal law by possessing firearms in his vehicle while it was parked on the grounds of the U.S. Capitol. He unsuccessfully sought dismissal of the indictment, claiming (i) that the statute violated the Second Amendment and (ii) that in violation of due process he was denied fair notice weapons were banned in the parking lot. Class later pled guilty to the possession charge pursuant to a plea agreement listing five categories of rights he expressly agreed to waive and three categories he could raise on appeal, but which said nothing about the right to raise on direct appeal a claim that the statute of conviction was unconstitutional.]

The question is whether a guilty plea by itself bars a federal criminal defendant from challenging the constitutionality of the statute of conviction on direct appeal. We hold that it does not. Class did not relinquish his right to appeal the District Court's constitutional determinations simply by pleading guilty. As we shall explain, this holding flows directly from this Court's prior decisions.

Fifty years ago this Court directly addressed a similar claim (a claim that the statute of conviction was unconstitutional). And the Court stated that a defendant's "plea of guilty did not . . . waive his previous [constitutional] claim." *Haynes v. United States*, 390 U.S. 85 (1968). Though Justice Harlan's opinion for the Court in *Haynes* offered little explanation for this statement, subsequent decisions offered a rationale that applies here.

In *Blackledge v. Perry*, 417 U.S. 21 (1974), North Carolina indicted and convicted Jimmy Seth Perry on a misdemeanor assault charge. When Perry exercised his right under a North Carolina statute to a de novo trial in a higher court, the State reindicted him, but this time the State charged a felony, which carried a heavier penalty, for the same conduct. Perry pleaded guilty. He then sought habeas relief on the grounds that the reindictment amounted to an unconstitutional vindictive prosecution. The State argued that Perry's guilty plea barred him from raising his constitutional challenge. But this Court held that it did not.

The Court noted that a guilty plea bars appeal of many claims, including some " 'antecedent constitutional violations' " related to events (say, grand jury proceedings) that had " 'occurred prior to the entry of the guilty plea' "(quoting *Tollett v. Henderson*, 411 U.S. 258 (1973)). While *Tollett* claims were "of constitutional dimension," the Court explained that "the nature of the underlying constitutional infirmity is markedly different" from a claim of vindictive prosecution, which implicates "the very power of the State" to prosecute the defendant. Accordingly, the Court wrote that "the right" Perry "asserts and that we today accept is the right not to be haled into court at all upon the felony charge" since "[t]he very initiation of the proceedings" against Perry "operated to deprive him due process of law."

A year and a half later, in *Menna v. New York*, 423 U.S. 61 (1975), this Court repeated what it had said and held in *Blackledge*. After Menna served a 30-day jail term for refusing to testify before the grand jury on November 7, 1968, the State of New York charged him once again for (what Menna argued was) the same crime. Menna pleaded guilty, but subsequently appealed arguing that the new charge violated the Double Jeopardy Clause. U.S. Const., Amdt. 5. The lower courts held that Menna's constitutional claim had been "waived" by his guilty plea.

This Court reversed. Citing *Blackledge*, the Court held that "a plea of guilty to a charge does not waive a claim that—judged on its face—the charge is one which the State may not constitutionally prosecute." Menna's claim amounted to a claim that "the State may not convict" him "no matter how validly his factual guilt is established." Menna's "guilty plea, therefore, [did] not bar the claim." * * *

In more recent years, we have reaffirmed the *Menna-Blackledge* doctrine and refined its scope. In *United States v. Broce*, 488 U.S. 563 (1989), the defendants pleaded guilty to two separate indictments in a single proceeding which "on their face" described two separate bid-rigging conspiracies. They later sought to challenge their convictions on double jeopardy grounds, arguing that they had only admitted to one conspiracy. Citing *Blackledge* and *Menna*, this Court repeated that a guilty plea does not bar a claim on appeal "where on the face of the record the court had no power to enter the conviction or impose the sentence." However, because the defendants could not "prove their claim by relying on those indictments and the existing record" and "without contradicting those indictments," this Court held that their claims were "foreclosed by the admissions inherent in their guilty pleas."

Unlike the claims in *Broce*, Class' constitutional claims here, as we understand them, do not contradict the terms of the indictment or the written plea agreement. They are consistent with Class' knowing, voluntary, and intelligent admission that he did what the indictment alleged. Those claims can be "resolved without any need to venture beyond that record."

Nor do Class' claims focus upon case-related constitutional defects that " 'occurred prior to the entry of the guilty plea.' " *Blackledge*. They could not, for example, "have been 'cured' through a new indictment by a properly selected grand jury." Because the defendant has admitted the charges against him, a guilty plea makes the latter kind of constitutional claim "irrelevant to the constitutional validity of the conviction." *Haring v. Prosise*, 462 U.S. 306 (1983). But the cases to which we have referred make clear that a defendant's guilty plea does not make irrelevant the kind of constitutional claim Class seeks to make.

In sum, the claims at issue here do not fall within any of the categories of claims that Class' plea agreement forbids him to raise on direct appeal. They challenge the Government's power to criminalize Class' (admitted) conduct. They thereby call into question the Government's power to " 'constitutionally prosecute' " him. *Broce,* supra (quoting *Menna,* supra). A guilty plea does not bar a direct appeal in these circumstances. * * *

The Government and the dissent argue that [Fed.R.Crim.P.] 11(a)(2) means that "a defendant who pleads guilty cannot challenge his conviction on appeal on a forfeitable or waivable ground that he either failed to present to the district court or failed to reserve in writing."

The problem with this argument is that, by its own terms, the Rule itself does not say whether it sets forth the exclusive procedure for a defendant to preserve a constitutional claim following a guilty plea. At the same time, the drafters' notes acknowledge that the "Supreme Court has held that certain kinds of constitutional objections may be raised after a plea of guilty." The notes then specifically refer to the "*Menna-Blackledge* doctrine."

JUSTICE ALITO, with whom JUSTICE KENNEDY and JUSTICE THOMAS join, dissenting. * * *

I

There is no justification for the muddle left by today's decision. The question at issue is not conceptually complex. In determining whether a plea of guilty prevents a defendant in federal or state court from raising a particular issue on appeal, the first question is whether the Federal Constitution precludes waiver. If the Federal Constitution permits waiver, the next question is whether some other law nevertheless bars waiver. And if no law prevents waiver, the final question is whether the defendant knowingly and intelligently waived the right to raise the claim on appeal. * * *

Analyzing this case under the framework set out above, I think the Court of Appeals was clearly correct. First, the Federal Constitution does not prohibit the waiver of the rights Class asserts. We have held that most personal constitutional rights may be waived, and Class concedes that this is so with respect to the rights he is asserting.

Second, no federal statute or rule bars waiver. On the contrary, Rule 11 * * * makes it clear that, with one exception that I will discuss below, a defendant who enters an unconditional plea waives all nonjurisdictional claims. Although the Rule does not say this expressly, that is the unmistakable implication of subdivision (a)(2), which allows a defendant, "[w]ith the consent of the court and the government," to "enter a conditional plea of guilty or nolo contendere, reserving in writing the right to have an appellate court review an adverse determination of a specified pretrial motion." * * *

The Advisory Committee's Notes on Rule 11 make this clear, stating that an unconditional plea (with the previously mentioned exception) "constitutes a waiver of all nonjurisdictional defects." Advisory Committee's Notes on a federal rule of procedure "provide a reliable source of insight into the meaning of a rule, especially when, as here, the rule was enacted precisely as the Advisory Committee proposed." Subdivision (a)(2) was adopted against the backdrop of decisions of this Court holding that a guilty plea generally relinquishes all defenses to conviction, see, e.g., *Tollett v. Henderson,* 411 U.S. 258, 267 (1973), and Rule 11(a)(2) creates a limited exception to that general principle. Far from prohibiting the waiver of nonjurisdictional claims, Rule 11 actually bars the raising of such claims (once again, with the previously mentioned exception).

II

A

I now turn to the one exception mentioned in the Advisory Committee's Notes on Rule 11—what the Notes, rather grandly, term the *"Menna-Blackledge* doctrine." * * *

Because this doctrine is the only exception recognized in Rule 11 and because the doctrine figures prominently in the opinion of the Court, it is important to examine its foundation and meaning.

B

Blackledge and *Menna* represented marked departures from our prior decisions. Before they were handed down, our precedents were clear: When a defendant pleaded guilty to a crime, he relinquished his right to litigate all nonjurisdictional challenges to his conviction (except for the claim that his plea was not voluntary and intelligent), and the prosecution could assert this forfeiture to defeat a subsequent appeal. The theory was easy to understand. * * *

III

Blackledge and *Menna* diverged from these prior precedents, but neither case provided a clear or coherent explanation for the departure.

A

In *Blackledge*, the Court held that a defendant who pleaded guilty could nevertheless challenge his conviction on the ground that his right to due process was violated by a vindictive prosecution. The Court asserted that this right was "markedly different" from the equal protection and Fifth Amendment rights at stake in *Tollett* and the *Brady* trilogy because it "went to the very power of the State to bring the defendant into court to answer the charge brought against him." The meaning of this distinction, however, is hard to grasp.

The most natural way to understand *Blackledge*'s reference to "the very power of the State" would be to say that an argument survives a guilty plea if it attacks the court's jurisdiction. * * * But that cannot be what *Blackledge* meant.

First, the defendant in *Blackledge* had been tried in state court in North Carolina for a state-law offense, and the jurisdiction of state courts to entertain such prosecutions is purely a matter of state law * * *. Second, a rule that jurisdictional defects alone survive a guilty plea would not explain the result in *Blackledge* itself. Arguments attacking a court's subject-matter jurisdiction can neither be waived nor forfeited. But the due process right at issue in *Blackledge* was perfectly capable of being waived or forfeited—as is just about every other right that is personal to a criminal defendant.

So if the "very power to prosecute" theory does not refer to jurisdiction, what else might it mean? The only other possibility that comes to mind is that it might mean that a defendant can litigate a claim if it asserts a right not to be tried, as opposed to a right not to be convicted. But we have said that "virtually all rights of criminal defendants" are "merely . . . right[s] not to be convicted," as distinguished from "right[s] not to be tried." Even when a constitutional violation requires the dismissal of an indictment, that "does not mean that [the] defendant enjoy[ed] a 'right not to be tried' " on the charges.

The rule could hardly be otherwise. Most constitutional defenses (and plenty of statutory defenses), if successfully asserted in a pretrial motion, deprive the prosecution of the "power" to proceed to trial or secure a conviction. If that remedial consequence converted them all into rights not to be prosecuted, *Blackledge* would have no discernible limit. * * *

The upshot is that the supposed "right not to be prosecuted" has no intelligible meaning in this context. * * *

B

If the thinking behind *Blackledge* is hard to follow, *Menna* may be worse. In that case, the Court held that a defendant who pleaded guilty could challenge his conviction on double jeopardy grounds. The case was decided by a three-page per curiam opinion, its entire analysis confined to a single footnote[, where] the Court wrote:

> "[A] counseled plea of guilty is an admission of factual guilt so reliable that, where voluntary and intelligent, it quite validly removes the issue of factual guilt from the case. In most cases, factual guilt is a sufficient basis for the State's imposition of punishment. A guilty plea, therefore, simply renders irrelevant those constitutional violations not logically inconsistent with the valid establishment of factual guilt."

The wording of the final sentence is not easy to parse, but I interpret the Court's reasoning as follows: A defendant who pleads guilty does no more than admit that he committed the essential conduct charged in the indictment; therefore a guilty plea allows the litigation on appeal of any claim that is not inconsistent with the facts that the defendant necessarily admitted. * * * A holding of that scope is not what one expects to see in a footnote in a per curiam opinion, but if the Court meant less, its meaning is unclear.

C

When the Court returned to *Blackledge* and *Menna* in *United States v. Broce*, 488 U.S. 563 (1989), the Court essentially repudiated the theories offered in those earlier cases. * * * Like *Menna*, *Broce* involved a defendant (actually two defendants) who pleaded guilty but then sought to attack their convictions on double jeopardy grounds. This time, however, the Court held that their guilty pleas prevented them from litigating their claims.

The Court began by specifically disavowing *Menna*'s suggestion that a guilty plea admits only " 'factual guilt,' " meaning "the acts described in the indictments." Instead, the Court explained, an unconditional guilty plea admits "all of the factual and legal elements necessary to sustain a binding, final judgment of guilt and a lawful sentence." "By entering a plea of guilty, the accused is not simply stating that he did the discrete acts described in the indictment; he is admitting guilt of a substantive crime." * * * Thus, the Court concluded, a defendant's decision to plead guilty necessarily extinguishes whatever "potential defense[s]" he might have asserted in an effort to show that it would be unlawful to hold him liable for his conduct. So much for *Menna*.

As for *Blackledge*, by holding that the defendants' double jeopardy rights were extinguished by their pleas, *Broce* necessarily rejected the idea that a right not to be tried survives an unconditional guilty plea.

While *Broce* thus rejected the reasoning in *Blackledge* and *Menna*, the Court was content to distinguish those cases on the ground that they involved defendants who could succeed on appeal without going beyond "the existing record," whereas the defendants in *Broce* would have to present new evidence.

IV

A

This is where the *Menna-Blackledge* doctrine stood when we heard this case. Now, instead of clarifying the law, the Court sows new confusion by reiterating with seeming approval a string of catchphrases. The Court repeats the line that an argument survives if it "implicates 'the very power of the State' to prosecute the defendant," but this shibboleth is no more intelligible now than it was when first incanted in *Blackledge*. The Court also parrots the rule set out in the *Menna* footnote—that the only arguments waived by a guilty plea are those that contradict the facts alleged in the charging document, even though that rule is inconsistent with *Tollett*, the *Brady* trilogy, and *Broce*—and even though this reading would permit a defendant who pleads guilty to raise an uncertain assortment of claims never before thought to survive a guilty plea.

For example, would this rule permit a defendant to argue that his prosecution is barred by a statute of limitations or by the Speedy Trial Act? Presumably the answer is yes. By admitting commission of the acts alleged in an indictment or complaint, a defendant would not concede that the charge was timely. What about the argument that a defendant's alleged conduct does not violate the statute of conviction? Here again, the rule barring only those claims inconsistent with the facts alleged in the indictment or complaint would appear to permit the issue to be raised on appeal, but the Court says that a defendant who pleads guilty "has admitted the charges against him." What does this mean, exactly? * * *

Approaching the question from the opposite direction, the Court says that a guilty plea precludes a defendant from litigating "the constitutionality of case-related government conduct that takes place before the plea is entered." This category is most mysterious. I thought Class was arguing that the Government violated the Constitution at the moment when it initiated his prosecution. That sounds like he is trying to attack "the constitutionality of case-related government conduct that [took] place before the plea [was] entered." Yet the Court holds that he may proceed. Why?

Finally, the majority instructs that "a valid guilty plea relinquishes any claim that would contradict the 'admissions necessarily made upon entry of a voluntary plea of guilty' "(quoting *Broce*). I agree with that statement of the rule, but what the Court fails to acknowledge is that the scope of this rule depends on the law of the particular jurisdiction in question. If a defendant in federal court is told that under Rule 11 an unconditional guilty plea waives all nonjurisdictional claims (or as *Broce* put it, admits "all of the factual and legal elements necessary to sustain a binding, final judgment of guilt and a lawful sentence"), then that is the scope of the admissions implicit in the plea. * * *

In sum, the governing law in the present case is Rule 11 * * *. Under that Rule, an unconditional guilty plea waives all nonjurisdictional claims with the possible exception of the "*Menna-Blackledge* doctrine" created years ago by this Court. That doctrine is vacuous, has no sound foundation, and produces nothing but confusion. At a minimum, I would limit the doctrine to the particular types of claims involved in those cases. I certainly would not expand its reach. * * *

CHAPTER 15

TRIAL BY JURY; JUDICIAL IMPARTIALITY

■ ■ ■

1. RIGHT TO JURY TRIAL

The Sixth Amendment declares that in "all criminal prosecutions, the accused shall enjoy the right to a * * * trial, by an impartial jury of the State and district wherein the crime shall have been committed." *Duncan v. Louisiana* discusses why jury trial is so important in the American system of criminal justice and why, consequently, this Sixth Amendment right is also applicable to the states. *Blanton v. City of North Las Vegas* examines when an offense is "petty" and thus is not covered by the jury trial right. *Ramos v. Louisiana* addresses the Sixth Amendment's guarantee of a unanimous jury verdict, and raises questions about earlier decisions on jury size. The final case in this section, *Singer v. United States,* considers whether a defendant should have an unrestrained right to have his case tried by the judge alone.

DUNCAN V. LOUISIANA
[set forth at p. 35]

BLANTON V. CITY OF NORTH LAS VEGAS
489 U.S. 538, 109 S.Ct. 1289, 103 L.Ed.2d 550 (1989).

JUSTICE MARSHALL delivered the opinion of the Court.

The issue in this case is whether there is a constitutional right to a trial by jury for persons charged under Nevada law with driving under the influence of alcohol (DUI). We hold that there is not. * * *

It has long been settled "that there is a category of petty crimes or offenses which is not subject to the Sixth Amendment jury trial provision." *Duncan v. Louisiana.* In determining whether a particular offense should be categorized as "petty," our early decisions focused on the nature of the offense and on whether it was triable by a jury at common law. In recent years, however, we have sought more "objective indications of the seriousness with which society regards the offense." "[W]e have found the most relevant such criteria in the severity of the maximum authorized penalty." *Baldwin v. New York*, 399 U.S. 66, 68, 90 S.Ct. 1886, 1887, 26 L.Ed.2d 437 (1970). In fixing the maximum penalty for a crime, a legislature "include[s] within the definition of the crime itself a judgment about the seriousness of the offense." The judiciary should not substitute its judgment as to seriousness for that of a legislature, which is "far better equipped to perform the task, and [is] likewise more responsive to changes in attitude and more amenable to the recognition and correction of their misperceptions in this respect."

In using the word "penalty," we do not refer solely to the maximum prison term authorized for a particular offense. A legislature's view of the seriousness of an offense also is reflected in the other penalties that it attaches to the offense. * * *[6] Primary emphasis, however, must be placed on the maximum authorized period of incarceration. Penalties such as probation or a fine may engender "a significant infringement of personal freedom," but they cannot approximate in severity the loss of liberty that a prison term entails. Indeed, because incarceration is an "intrinsically different" form of punishment, it is the most powerful indication of whether an offense is "serious."

Following this approach, our decision in *Baldwin* established that a defendant is entitled to a jury trial whenever the offense for which he is charged carries a maximum authorized prison term of greater than six months. * * * As for a prison term of six months or less, we recognized that it will seldom be viewed by the defendant as "trivial or 'petty.'" But we found that the disadvantages of such a sentence, "onerous though they may be, may be outweighed by the benefits that result from speedy and inexpensive nonjury adjudications."

Although we did not hold in *Baldwin* that an offense carrying a maximum prison term of six months or less automatically qualifies as a "petty" offense, and decline to do so today, we do find it appropriate to presume for purposes of the Sixth Amendment that society views such an offense as "petty." A defendant is entitled to jury trial in such circumstances only if he can demonstrate that any additional statutory penalties, viewed in conjunction with the maximum authorized period of incarceration, are so severe that they clearly reflect a legislative determination that the offense in question is a "serious" one. This standard, albeit somewhat imprecise, should ensure the availability of a jury trial in the rare situation where a legislature packs an offense it deems "serious" with onerous penalties that nonetheless "do not puncture the 6-month incarceration line."[8]

Applying these principles here, it is apparent that petitioners are not entitled to a jury trial. The maximum authorized prison sentence for first-time DUI offenders does not exceed six months. A presumption therefore exists that the Nevada legislature views DUI as a "petty" offense for purposes of the Sixth Amendment.[a] Considering the additional statutory penalties as well, we do not

---

[6]   In criminal contempt prosecutions, "where no maximum penalty is authorized, the severity of the penalty actually imposed is the best indication of the seriousness of the particular offense."

[8]   In performing this analysis, only penalties resulting from state action, *e.g.*, those mandated by statute or regulation, should be considered. * * *

[a]   In *Lewis v. United States*, 518 U.S. 322 (1996), petitioner argued "that, where a defendant is charged with multiple petty offenses in a single prosecution, the Sixth Amendment requires that the aggregate potential penalty be the basis for determining whether a jury trial is required." The Court, per O'Connor, J., disagreed, noting that per *Blanton* "we determine whether an offense is serious by looking to the judgment of the legislature, primarily as expressed in the maximum authorized term of imprisonment. Here, by setting the maximum authorized prison term at six months, the legislature categorized the offense of obstructing the mail as petty. The fact that the petitioner was charged with two counts of a petty offense does not revise the legislative judgment

believe that the Nevada Legislature has clearly indicated that DUI is a "serious" offense.

In the first place, it is immaterial that a first-time DUI offender may face a minimum term of imprisonment. In settling on six months' imprisonment as the constitutional demarcation point, we have assumed that a defendant convicted of the offense in question would receive the *maximum* authorized prison sentence. It is not constitutionally determinative, therefore, that a particular defendant may be required to serve some amount of jail time *less* than six months. Likewise, it is of little moment that a defendant may receive the maximum prison term because of the prohibitions on plea bargaining and probation. As for the 90-day license suspension, it, too, will be irrelevant if it runs concurrently with the prison sentence, which we assume for present purposes to be the maximum of six months.[9]

We are also unpersuaded by the fact that, instead of a prison sentence, a DUI offender may be ordered to perform 48 hours of community service dressed in clothing identifying him as a DUI offender. Even assuming the outfit is the source of some embarrassment during the 48-hour period, such a penalty will be less embarrassing and less onerous than six months in jail. As for the possible $1,000 fine, it is well below the $5,000 level set by Congress in its most recent definition of a "petty" offense, 18 U.S.C. § 1, and petitioners do not suggest that this

---

as to the gravity of that particular offense, nor does it transform the petty offense into a serious one, to which the jury-trial right would apply." As for petitioner's reliance on *Codispoti v. Pennsylvania*, 418 U.S. 506 (1974), where the defendant was deemed entitled to jury trial because the aggregate penalties actually imposed exceeded six months, the Court distinguished that case on two grounds: (1) there "the legislature had not set a specific penalty for criminal contempt," in which case "courts use the severity of the penalty actually imposed as the measure of the character of the particular offense," and (2) the "benefit of a jury trial, 'as a protection against the arbitrary exercise of official power,' was deemed particularly important in [the criminal contempt] context."

Kennedy, J., joined by Breyer, J., concurring, concluded that the "right to jury trial extends as well to a defendant who is sentenced in one proceeding to more than six months' imprisonment." He reasoned that while a defendant has a right to jury trial as to a nonpetty offense, without regard to what sentence is actually imposed, because of the stigma which attaches because of the legislature's judgment that the offense is serious, "the Sixth Amendment also serves the different and more practical purpose of preventing a court from effecting a most serious deprivation of liberty—ordering a defendant to prison for a substantial period of time—without the Government's persuading a jury he belongs there. * * * If[, as in the instant case,] the trial court rules at the outset that no more than six months' imprisonment will be imposed for the combined petty offenses, however, the liberty the jury serves to protect will not be endangered, and there is no corresponding right to jury trial." Stevens, J., joined by Ginsburg, J., dissenting, agreed with Justice Kennedy except for that last point: "I see no basis for assuming that the dishonor associated with multiple convictions for petty offenses is less than the dishonor associated with conviction of a single serious crime. Because the right attaches at the moment of prosecution, a judge may not deprive a defendant of a jury trial by making a pretrial determination that the crimes charged will not warrant a sentence exceeding six months."

9   It is unclear whether the license suspension and prison sentence in fact run concurrently. But even if they do not, we cannot say that a 90-day license suspension is that significant as a Sixth Amendment matter, particularly when a restricted license may be obtained after only 45 days. Furthermore, the requirement that an offender attend an alcohol abuse education course can only be described as *de minimis*.

congressional figure is out of step with state practice for offenses carrying prison sentences of six months or less.[11] * * *

RAMOS V. LOUISIANA

590 U.S. ___, 140 S.Ct. 1390, 206 L.Ed.2d 583 (2020).

GORSUCH, J., announced the judgment of the Court, and delivered the opinion of the Court with respect to Parts I, II-A, III, and IV-B-1, in which GINSBURG, BREYER, SOTOMAYOR, and KAVANAUGH, JJ., joined, an opinion with respect to Parts II-B, IV-B-2, and V, in which GINSBURG, BREYER, and SOTOMAYOR, JJ., joined, and an opinion with respect to Part IV-A, in which GINSBURG and BREYER, JJ., joined.

Accused of a serious crime, Evangelisto Ramos insisted on his innocence and invoked his right to a jury trial. Eventually, 10 jurors found the evidence against him persuasive. But a pair of jurors believed that the State of Louisiana had failed to prove Mr. Ramos's guilt beyond reasonable doubt; they voted to acquit.

In 48 States and federal court, a single juror's vote to acquit is enough to prevent a conviction. But not in Louisiana. Along with Oregon, Louisiana has long punished people based on 10-to-2 verdicts like the one here. So instead of the mistrial he would have received almost anywhere else, Mr. Ramos was sentenced to life in prison without the possibility of parole.

Why do Louisiana and Oregon allow nonunanimous convictions? Though it's hard to say why these laws persist, their origins are clear. Louisiana first endorsed nonunanimous verdicts for serious crimes at a constitutional convention in 1898. According to one committee chairman, the avowed purpose of that convention was to "establish the supremacy of the white race," and the resulting document included many of the trappings of the Jim Crow era: a poll tax, a combined literacy and property ownership test, and a grandfather clause that in practice exempted white residents from the most onerous of these requirements.

Nor was it only the prospect of African-Americans voting that concerned the delegates. Just a week before the convention, the U.S. Senate passed a resolution calling for an investigation into whether Louisiana was systemically excluding African-Americans from juries. Seeking to avoid unwanted national attention, and aware that this Court would strike down any policy of overt discrimination against African-American jurors as a violation of the Fourteenth Amendment,[3] the delegates sought to undermine African-American participation on juries in another way. With a careful eye on racial demographics, the convention delegates sculpted a "facially race-neutral" rule permitting 10-to-2 verdicts in order "to ensure that African-American juror service would be meaningless."

Adopted in the 1930s, Oregon's rule permitting nonunanimous verdicts can be similarly traced to the rise of the Ku Klux Klan and efforts to dilute "the influence of racial, ethnic, and religious minorities on Oregon juries." In fact, no one before

---

[11] * * * We decline petitioners' invitation to survey the statutory penalties for drunken driving in other States. The question is not whether other States consider drunken driving a "serious" offense, but whether Nevada does.

[3] *Strauder* v. *West Virginia*, 100 U.S. 303, 310 (1880).

us contests any of this; courts in both Louisiana and Oregon have frankly acknowledged that race was a motivating factor in the adoption of their States' respective nonunanimity rules.

We took this case to decide whether the Sixth Amendment right to a jury trial—as incorporated against the States by way of the Fourteenth Amendment—requires a unanimous verdict to convict a defendant of a serious offense. Louisiana insists that this Court has never definitively passed on the question and urges us to find its practice consistent with the Sixth Amendment. By contrast, the dissent doesn't try to defend Louisiana's law on Sixth or Fourteenth Amendment grounds; tacitly, it seems to admit that the Constitution forbids States from using nonunanimous juries. Yet, unprompted by Louisiana, the dissent suggests our precedent requires us to rule for the State anyway. What explains all this? To answer the puzzle, it's necessary to say a bit more about the merits of the question presented, the relevant precedent, and, at last, the consequences that follow from saying what we know to be true.

I

The Sixth Amendment promises that "[i]n all criminal prosecutions, the accused shall enjoy the right to a speedy and public trial, by an impartial jury of the State and district wherein the crime shall have been committed, which district shall have been previously ascertained by law." The Amendment goes on to preserve other rights for criminal defendants but says nothing else about what a "trial by an impartial jury" entails.

Still, the promise of a jury trial surely meant *something*—otherwise, there would have been no reason to write it down. Nor would it have made any sense to spell out the places from which jurors should be drawn if their powers as jurors could be freely abridged by statute. Imagine a constitution that allowed a "jury trial" to mean nothing but a single person rubberstamping convictions without hearing any evidence—but simultaneously insisting that the lone juror come from a specific judicial district "previously ascertained by law." And if that's not enough, imagine a constitution that included the same hollow guarantee *twice*—not only in the Sixth Amendment, but also in Article III. No: The text and structure of the Constitution clearly suggest that the term "trial by an impartial jury" carried with it *some* meaning about the content and requirements of a jury trial.

One of these requirements was unanimity. Wherever we might look to determine what the term "trial by an impartial jury trial" meant at the time of the Sixth Amendment's adoption—whether it's the common law, state practices in the founding era, or opinions and treatises written soon afterward—the answer is unmistakable. A jury must reach a unanimous verdict in order to convict.

The requirement of juror unanimity emerged in 14th century England and was soon accepted as a vital right protected by the common law. As Blackstone explained, no person could be found guilty of a serious crime unless "the truth of every accusation . . . should . . . be confirmed by the unanimous suffrage of twelve of his equals and neighbors, indifferently chosen, and superior to all suspicion." A " 'verdict, taken from eleven, was no verdict' " at all.

This same rule applied in the young American States. * * *

It was against this backdrop that James Madison drafted and the States ratified the Sixth Amendment in 1791. By that time, unanimous verdicts had been required for about 400 years. If the term "trial by an impartial jury" carried any meaning at all, it surely included a requirement as long and widely accepted as unanimity.

Influential, postadoption treatises confirm this understanding. * * *

Nor is this a case where the original public meaning was lost to time and only recently recovered. This Court has, repeatedly and over many years, recognized that the Sixth Amendment requires unanimity. As early as 1898, the Court said that a defendant enjoys a "constitutional right to demand that his liberty should not be taken from him except by the joint action of the court and the unanimous verdict of a jury of twelve persons."[19] A few decades later, the Court elaborated that the Sixth Amendment affords a right to "a trial by jury as understood and applied at common law, . . . includ[ing] all the essential elements as they were recognized in this country and England when the Constitution was adopted."[20] And, the Court observed, this includes a requirement "that the verdict should be unanimous." In all, this Court has commented on the Sixth Amendment's unanimity requirement no fewer than 13 times over more than 120 years.

There can be no question either that the Sixth Amendment's unanimity requirement applies to state and federal criminal trials equally. This Court has long explained that the Sixth Amendment right to a jury trial is "fundamental to the American scheme of justice" and incorporated against the States under the Fourteenth Amendment.[23] This Court has long explained, too, that incorporated provisions of the Bill of Rights bear the same content when asserted against States as they do when asserted against the federal government.[24] So if the Sixth Amendment's right to a jury trial requires a unanimous verdict to support a conviction in federal court, it requires no less in state court.

II

A

How, despite these seemingly straightforward principles, have Louisiana's and Oregon's laws managed to hang on for so long? It turns out that the Sixth Amendment's otherwise simple story took a strange turn in 1972. That year, the Court confronted these States' unconventional schemes for the first time—in *Apodaca v. Oregon*[25] and a companion case, *Johnson v. Louisiana*.[26] Ultimately, the Court could do no more than issue a badly fractured set of opinions. Four dissenting Justices would not have hesitated to strike down the States' laws,

---

[19] *Thompson* v. *Utah*, 170 U.S. 343, 351 (1898). See also *Maxwell* v. *Dow*, 176 U.S. 581, 586 (1900).

[20] *Patton* v. *United States*, 281 U.S. 276, 288 (1930).

[23] *Duncan* v. *Louisiana*, 391 U.S. 145, 148–150 (1968).

[24] *Malloy* v. *Hogan*, 378 U.S. 1, 10–11 (1964).

[25] 406 U.S. 404 (plurality opinion).

[26] 406 U.S. 356.

recognizing that the Sixth Amendment requires unanimity and that this guarantee is fully applicable against the States under the Fourteenth Amendment. But a four-Justice plurality took a very different view of the Sixth Amendment. These Justices declared that the real question before them was whether unanimity serves an important "function" in "contemporary society." Then, having reframed the question, the plurality wasted few words before concluding that unanimity's costs outweigh its benefits in the modern era, so the Sixth Amendment should not stand in the way of Louisiana or Oregon.

The ninth Member of the Court adopted a position that was neither here nor there. On the one hand, Justice Powell agreed that, as a matter of "history and precedent, . . . the Sixth Amendment requires a unanimous jury verdict to convict." But, on the other hand, he argued that the Fourteenth Amendment does not render this guarantee against the federal government fully applicable against the States. In this way, Justice Powell doubled down on his belief in "dual-track" incorporation—the idea that a single right can mean two different things depending on whether it is being invoked against the federal or a state government.

Justice Powell acknowledged that his argument for dual-track incorporation came "late in the day." Late it was. The Court had already, nearly a decade earlier, "rejected the notion that the Fourteenth Amendment applies to the States only a 'watered-down, subjective version of the individual guarantees of the Bill of Rights.'" It's a point we've restated many times since, too, including as recently as last year.[32] Still, Justice Powell frankly explained, he was "unwillin[g]" to follow the Court's precedents. So he offered up the essential fifth vote to uphold Mr. Apodaca's conviction—if based only on a view of the Fourteenth Amendment that he knew was (and remains) foreclosed by precedent.

B

In the years following *Apodaca*, both Louisiana and Oregon chose to continue allowing nonunanimous verdicts. But their practices have always stood on shaky ground. After all, while Justice Powell's vote secured a favorable judgment for the States in *Apodaca*, it's never been clear what rationale could support a similar result in future cases. Only two possibilities exist: Either the Sixth Amendment allows nonunanimous verdicts, or the Sixth Amendment's guarantee of a jury trial applies with less force to the States under the Fourteenth Amendment. Yet, as we've seen, both bear their problems. In *Apodaca* itself, a majority of Justices—including Justice Powell—recognized that the Sixth Amendment demands unanimity, just as our cases have long said. And this Court's precedents, both then and now, prevent the Court from applying the Sixth Amendment to the States in some mutated and diminished form under the Fourteenth Amendment. So what could we possibly describe as the "holding" of *Apodaca*?

Really, no one has found a way to make sense of it. In later cases, this Court has labeled *Apodaca* an "exception," "unusual," and in any event "not an endorsement" of Justice Powell's view of incorporation. At the same time, we have

---

[32] See, *e.g.*, *Timbs* v. *Indiana*, 586 U.S. ___, ___ (2019) (slip op., at 3) (unanimously rejecting arguments for dual-track incorporation).

continued to recognize the historical need for unanimity. We've been studiously ambiguous, even inconsistent, about what *Apodaca* might mean. To its credit, Louisiana acknowledges the problem. The State expressly tells us it is not "asking the Court to accord Justice Powell's solo opinion in *Apodaca* precedential force." Instead, in an effort to win today's case, Louisiana embraces the idea that everything is up for grabs. It contends that this Court has never definitively ruled on the propriety of nonunanimous juries under the Sixth Amendment—and that we should use this case to hold for the first time that nonunanimous juries are permissible in state and federal courts alike.

III

Louisiana's approach may not be quite as tough as trying to defend Justice Powell's dual-track theory of incorporation, but it's pretty close. How does the State deal with the fact this Court has said 13 times over 120 years that the Sixth Amendment *does* require unanimity? Or the fact that five Justices in *Apodaca* said the same? The best the State can offer is to suggest that all these statements came in dicta. But even supposing (without granting) that Louisiana is right and it's dicta all the way down, why would the Court now walk away from many of its own statements about the Constitution's meaning? And what about the prior 400 years of English and American cases requiring unanimity—should we dismiss all those as dicta too?

Sensibly, Louisiana doesn't dispute that the common law required unanimity. Instead, it argues that the drafting history of the Sixth Amendment reveals an intent by the framers to leave this particular feature behind. The State points to the fact that Madison's proposal for the Sixth Amendment originally read: "The trial of all crimes . . . shall be by an impartial jury of freeholders of the vicinage, with the requisite of unanimity for conviction, of the right of challenge, and other accustomed requisites. . . ." Louisiana notes that the House of Representatives approved this text with minor modifications. Yet, the State stresses, the Senate replaced "impartial jury of freeholders of the vicinage" with "impartial jury of the State and district wherein the crime shall have been committed" and also removed the explicit references to unanimity, the right of challenge, and "other accustomed requisites." In light of these revisions, Louisiana would have us infer an intent to abandon the common law's traditional unanimity requirement.

But this snippet of drafting history could just as easily support the opposite inference. Maybe the Senate deleted the language about unanimity, the right of challenge, and "other accustomed prerequisites" because all this was so plainly included in the promise of a "trial by an impartial jury" that Senators considered the language surplusage. The truth is that we have little contemporaneous evidence shedding light on why the Senate acted as it did. So rather than dwelling on text left on the cutting room floor, we are much better served by interpreting the language Congress retained and the States ratified. And, as we've seen, at the time of the Amendment's adoption, the right to a jury trial *meant* a trial in which the jury renders a unanimous verdict.

Further undermining Louisiana's inference about the drafting history is the fact it proves too much. If the Senate's deletion of the word "unanimity" changed the meaning of the text that remains, then the same would seemingly have to follow for the other deleted words as well. So it's not just unanimity that died in the Senate, but all the "other accustomed requisites" associated with the common law jury trial right—*i.e.*, *everything* history might have taught us about what it means to have a jury trial. Taking the State's argument from drafting history to its logical conclusion would thus leave the right to a "trial by jury" devoid of meaning. A right mentioned twice in the Constitution would be reduced to an empty promise. That can't be right.

Faced with this hard fact, Louisiana's only remaining option is to invite us to distinguish between the historic features of common law jury trials that (we think) serve "important enough" functions to migrate silently into the Sixth Amendment and those that don't. And, on the State's account, we should conclude that unanimity isn't worthy enough to make the trip.

But to see the dangers of Louisiana's overwise approach, there's no need to look any further than *Apodaca* itself. There, four Justices, pursuing the functionalist approach Louisiana espouses, began by describing the " 'essential' " benefit of a jury trial as " 'the interposition . . . of the commonsense judgment of a group of laymen' " between the defendant and the possibility of an " 'overzealous prosecutor.' " And measured against that muddy yardstick, they quickly concluded that requiring 12 rather than 10 votes to convict offers no meaningful improvement. Meanwhile, these Justices argued, States have good and important reasons for dispensing with unanimity, such as seeking to reduce the rate of hung juries.

Who can profess confidence in a breezy cost-benefit analysis like that? Lost in the accounting are the racially discriminatory *reasons* that Louisiana and Oregon adopted their peculiar rules in the first place.[44] What's more, the plurality never explained why the promised benefit of abandoning unanimity—reducing the rate of hung juries—always scores as a credit, not a cost. But who can say whether any particular hung jury is a waste, rather than an example of a jury doing exactly what the plurality said it should—deliberating carefully and safeguarding against overzealous prosecutions? And what about the fact, too, that some studies suggest that the elimination of unanimity has only a small effect on the rate of hung juries? Or the fact that others profess to have found that requiring unanimity may provide other possible benefits, including more open-minded and more thorough deliberations? It seems the *Apodaca* plurality never even conceived of such possibilities.

---

[44] The dissent chides us for acknowledging the racist history of Louisiana's and Oregon's laws, and commends the *Apodaca* plurality's decision to disregard these facts. But if the Sixth Amendment calls on judges to assess the functional benefits of jury rules, as the *Apodaca* plurality suggested, how can that analysis proceed to ignore the very functions those rules were adopted to serve? The dissent answers that Louisiana and Oregon eventually recodified their nonunanimous jury laws in new proceedings untainted by racism. But that cannot explain *Apodaca*'s omission: The States' proceedings took place only *after* the Court's decision. Nor can our shared respect for "rational and civil discourse," supply an excuse for leaving an uncomfortable past unexamined. Still, the dissent is right about one thing—a jurisdiction adopting a nonunanimous jury rule even for benign reasons would still violate the Sixth Amendment.

Our real objection here isn't that the *Apodaca* plurality's cost-benefit analysis was too skimpy. The deeper problem is that the plurality subjected the ancient guarantee of a unanimous jury verdict to its own functionalist assessment in the first place. And Louisiana asks us to repeat the error today, just replacing *Apodaca*'s functionalist assessment with our own updated version. All this overlooks the fact that, at the time of the Sixth Amendment's adoption, the right to trial by jury *included* a right to a unanimous verdict. When the American people chose to enshrine that right in the Constitution, they weren't suggesting fruitful topics for future cost-benefit analyses. They were seeking to ensure that their children's children would enjoy the same hard-won liberty they enjoyed. As judges, it is not our role to reassess whether the right to a unanimous jury is "important enough" to retain. With humility, we must accept that this right may serve purposes evading our current notice. We are entrusted to preserve and protect that liberty, not balance it away aided by no more than social statistics.[47]

IV

A

* * * Justice Powell reached a different result only by relying on a dual-track theory of incorporation that a majority of the Court had already rejected (and continues to reject). And to accept *that* reasoning as precedential, we would have to embrace a new and dubious proposition: that a single Justice writing only for himself has the authority to bind this Court to propositions it has already rejected.

* * *

Apodaca's judgment line resolved that case for the parties in that case. It is binding in that sense. But stripped from any reasoning, its judgment alone cannot be read to repudiate this Court's repeated pre-existing teachings on the Sixth and Fourteenth Amendments.

B

1

* * * Even if we accepted the premise that *Apodaca* established a precedent, no one on the Court today is prepared to say it was rightly decided, and *stare decisis* isn't supposed to be the art of methodically ignoring what everyone knows to be true. Of course, the precedents of this Court warrant our deep respect as embodying the considered views of those who have come before. But *stare decisis* has never

---

[47] The dissent seems to suggest that we must abandon the Sixth Amendment's historical meaning in favor of *Apodaca*'s functionalism because a parade of horribles would follow otherwise. In particular, the dissent reminds us that, at points and places in our history, women were not permitted to sit on juries. But we hardly need *Apodaca*'s functionalism to avoid repeating that wrong. Unlike the rule of unanimity, rules about who qualified as a defendant's "peer" varied considerably at common law at the time of the Sixth Amendment's adoption. Reflecting that fact, the Judiciary Act of 1789—adopted by the same Congress that passed the Sixth Amendment— initially pegged the qualifications for federal jury service to the relevant state jury qualification requirements. 1 Stat. 88. As a result, for much of this Nation's early history the composition of federal juries varied both geographically and over time. Ultimately, however, the people themselves adopted further constitutional amendments that prohibit invidious discrimination. So today the Sixth Amendment's promise of a jury of one's peers means a jury selected from a representative cross-section of the entire community.

been treated as "an inexorable command." And the doctrine is "at its weakest when we interpret the Constitution" because a mistaken judicial interpretation of that supreme law is often "practically impossible" to correct through other means. To balance these considerations, when it revisits a precedent this Court has traditionally considered "the quality of the decision's reasoning; its consistency with related decisions; legal developments since the decision; and reliance on the decision." In this case, each factor points in the same direction.

Start with the quality of the reasoning. Whether we look to the plurality opinion or Justice Powell's separate concurrence, *Apodaca* was gravely mistaken; again, no Member of the Court today defends either as rightly decided. Without repeating what we've already explained in detail, it's just an implacable fact that the plurality spent almost no time grappling with the historical meaning of the Sixth Amendment's jury trial right, this Court's long-repeated statements that it demands unanimity, or the racist origins of Louisiana's and Oregon's laws. Instead, the plurality subjected the Constitution's jury trial right to an incomplete functionalist analysis of its own creation for which it spared one paragraph. And, of course, five Justices expressly rejected the plurality's conclusion that the Sixth Amendment does not require unanimity. Meanwhile, Justice Powell refused to follow this Court's incorporation precedents. Nine Justices (including Justice Powell) recognized this for what it was; eight called it an error.

* * *

[T]he only reliance interests that might be asserted here fall into two categories. The first concerns the fact Louisiana and Oregon may need to retry defendants convicted of felonies by nonunanimous verdicts whose cases are still pending on direct appeal. * * * Those States credibly claim that the number of nonunanimous felony convictions still on direct appeal are somewhere in the hundreds,[68] and retrying or plea bargaining these cases will surely impose a cost. But new rules of criminal procedures usually do, often affecting significant numbers of pending cases across the whole country. For example, after *Booker* v. *United States* held that the Federal Sentencing Guidelines must be advisory rather than mandatory, this Court vacated and remanded nearly 800 decisions to the courts of appeals. Similar consequences likely followed when *Crawford* v. *Washington* overturned prior interpretations of the Confrontation Clause or *Arizona* v. *Gant* changed the law for searches incident to arrests. Our decision here promises to cause less, and certainly nothing before us supports the dissent's surmise that it will cause wildly more, disruption than these other decisions.

2

* * * In light of our decision today, the dissent worries that defendants whose appeals are already complete might seek to challenge their nonunanimous convictions through collateral (*i.e.,* habeas) review. But again the worries outstrip the facts. Under *Teague* v. *Lane*, 489 U.S. 288 (1989) [see fn. a, p. 34], newly

---

68   * * * At most, Oregon says the number of cases remaining on direct appeal and affected by today's decision "easily may eclipse a thousand."

recognized rules of criminal procedure do not normally apply in collateral review. * * * Nor is the *Teague* question even before us. * * *

V

On what ground would anyone have us leave Mr. Ramos in prison for the rest of his life? Not a single Member of this Court is prepared to say Louisiana secured his conviction constitutionally under the Sixth Amendment. No one before us suggests that the error was harmless. Louisiana does not claim precedent commands an affirmance. In the end, the best anyone can seem to muster against Mr. Ramos is that, if we dared to admit in his case what we all know to be true about the Sixth Amendment, we might have to say the same in some others. But where is the justice in that? Every judge must learn to live with the fact he or she will make some mistakes; it comes with the territory. But it is something else entirely to perpetuate something we all know to be wrong only because we fear the consequences of being right. The judgment of the Court of Appeals is

Reversed.[a]

JUSTICE KAVANAUGH, concurring in part. * * * I agree with the Court that the time has come to overrule Apodaca. I therefore join the introduction and Parts I, II-A, III, and IV-B-1 of the Court's persuasive and important opinion. I write separately to explain my view of how stare decisis applies to this case. * * *

First, * * * the original meaning of the Sixth and Fourteenth Amendments and this Court's two lines of decisions—the Sixth Amendment jury cases and the Fourteenth Amendment incorporation cases—overwhelmingly demonstrate that *Apodaca*'s holding is egregiously wrong.[6] * * *

---

[a]   Justice Thomas filed an opinion concurring in the judgment. He argued that the basis for prohibiting a state from denying the Sixth Amendment right of unanimity is the Privileges and Immunities Clause of the Fourteenth Amendment, not the Due Process Clause. "As I have explained before, "[t]he notion that a constitutional provision that guarantees only 'process' before a person is deprived of life, liberty, or property could define the substance of those rights strains credulity for even the most casual user of words." The unreasonableness of this interpretation is underscored by the Court's struggle to find a "guiding principle to distinguish 'fundamental' rights that warrant protection from nonfundamental rights that do not," as well as its many incorrect decisions based on this theory. . . . I would simply hold that, because all of the opinions in *Apodaca* addressed the Due Process Clause, its Fourteenth Amendment ruling does not bind us because the proper question here is the scope of the Privileges or Immunities Clause." He added that "under my approach to *stare decisis*, there is no need to decide which reliance interests are important enough to save an incorrect precedent. I doubt that this question is susceptible of principled resolution in this case, or in any other case for that matter."

Justice Sotomayor's concurring opinion joined all but Part IV-A of Justice Gorsuch's opinion. In explaining why *Apodaca* required overruling, she emphasized that the reason that "*Apodaca*, was on shaky ground from the start" "was not because of the functionalist analysis of that Court's plurality: Reasonable minds have disagreed over time—and continue to disagree—about the best mode of constitutional interpretation. That the plurality in *Apodaca* used different interpretive tools from the majority here is not a reason on its own to discard precedent. What matters instead is that, as the majority rightly stresses, *Apodaca* is a universe of one—an opinion uniquely irreconcilable with not just one, but two, strands of constitutional precedent well established both before and after the decision."

[6]   Notwithstanding the splintered 4–1–4 decision in *Apodaca*, its bottom-line result carried precedential force. In the American system of *stare decisis*, the result and the reasoning each independently have precedential force, and courts are therefore bound to follow both the result and the reasoning of a prior decision. The result of *Apodaca* was that state criminal juries need

Second, *Apodaca* causes significant negative consequences. It is true that *Apodaca* is workable. But *Apodaca* sanctions the conviction at trial or by guilty plea of some defendants who might not be convicted under the proper constitutional rule (although exactly how many is of course unknowable). * * *

* * * Then and now, non-unanimous juries can silence the voices and negate the votes of black jurors, especially in cases with black defendants or black victims, and only one or two black jurors. The 10 jurors "can simply ignore the views of their fellow panel members of a different race or class." *Johnson v. Louisiana*, (Stewart, J., dissenting). That reality—and the resulting perception of unfairness and racial bias—can undermine confidence in and respect for the criminal justice system. The non-unanimous jury operates much the same as the unfettered peremptory challenge, a practice that for many decades likewise functioned as an engine of discrimination against black defendants, victims, and jurors. In effect, the non-unanimous jury allows backdoor and unreviewable peremptory strikes against up to 2 of the 12 jurors.

In its 1986 decision in *Batson* v. *Kentucky*, the Court recognized the pervasive racial discrimination woven into the traditional system of unfettered peremptory challenges. The Court therefore overruled a prior decision, *Swain*, that had allowed those challenges. In my view, *Apodaca* warrants the same fate as *Swain*. After all, the "requirements of unanimity and impartial selection thus complement each other in ensuring the fair performance of the vital functions of a criminal court jury." *Johnson*, (Stewart, J., dissenting). And as Justice Thurgood Marshall forcefully explained in dissent in *Apodaca*, to "fence out a dissenting juror fences out a voice from the community, and undermines the principle on which our whole notion of the jury now rests."

* * * [T]he Jim Crow origins and racially discriminatory effects (and the perception thereof) of non-unanimous juries in Louisiana and Oregon should matter and should count heavily in favor of overruling, in my respectful view. After all, the non-unanimous jury "is today the last of Louisiana's Jim Crow laws." And this Court has emphasized time and again the "imperative to purge racial prejudice from the administration of justice" generally and from the jury system in particular. *Peña-Rodriguez* v. *Colorado*, 580 U.S. ___, ___–___, 137 S.Ct. 855, 867, 197 L.Ed.2d 107 (2017) (collecting cases).* * *

Third, overruling *Apodaca* would not unduly upset reliance interests. * * * Except for the effects on that limited class of direct review cases, it will be relatively

---

not be unanimous. That precedential result has been followed by this Court and the other federal and state courts for the last 48 years. To be sure, *Apodaca* had no majority opinion. When the Court's decision is splintered, courts follow the result, and they also follow the reasoning or standards set forth in the opinion constituting the "narrowest grounds" of the Justices in the majority. See *Marks* v. *United States*, 430 U.S. 188, 193 (1977). That *Marks* rule is ordinarily commonsensical to apply and usually means that courts in essence heed the opinion that occupies the middle-ground position between (i) the broadest opinion among the Justices in the majority and (ii) the dissenting opinion. On very rare occasions, as in *Apodaca*, it can be difficult to discern which opinion's reasoning has precedential effect under *Marks*. But even when that happens, the *result* of the decision still constitutes a binding precedent for the federal and state courts, and for this Court, unless and until it is overruled by this Court. As I read the Court's various opinions today, six Justices treat the result in *Apodaca* as a precedent for purposes of *stare decisis* analysis. A different group of six Justices concludes that *Apodaca* should be and is overruled.

easy going forward for Louisiana and Oregon to transition to the unanimous jury rule that the other 48 States and the federal courts use. Indeed, in 2018, Louisiana amended its constitution to require jury unanimity in criminal trials for crimes committed on or after January 1, 2019 * * *. [A]ssuming that the Court faithfully applies *Teague,* today's decision will not apply retroactively on federal habeas corpus review and will not disturb convictions that are final. * * *

JUSTICE ALITO, with whom THE CHIEF JUSTICE joins, and with whom JUSTICE KAGAN joins as to all but Part III-D, dissenting.

* * * I would not overrule *Apodaca.* Whatever one may think about the correctness of the decision, it has elicited enormous and entirely reasonable reliance.

* * * [T]he origins of the Louisiana and Oregon rules have no bearing on the broad constitutional question that the Court decides. That history would be relevant if there were no legitimate reasons why anyone might think that allowing non-unanimous verdicts is good policy. But that is undeniably false. * * * If at some future time another State wanted to allow non-unanimous verdicts, today's decision would rule that out—even if all that State's lawmakers were angels.

* * *

III

* * *

B

* * * The majority's primary reason for overruling *Apodaca* is the supposedly poor "quality" of Justice White's plurality opinion and Justice Powell's separate opinion. * * *

* * * [I]t is hard to know what to make of the functionalist charge. One Member of the majority explicitly disavows this criticism, and it is most unlikely that all the Justices in the majority are ready to label all functionalist decisions as poorly reasoned. Most of the landmark criminal procedure decisions from roughly Apodaca's time fall into that category. *Mapp, Miranda, Gideon, Furman.* Are they all now up for grabs?

* * * No one questions that the Sixth Amendment incorporated *the core* of the common-law jury-trial right, but did it incorporate *every feature* of the right? Did it constitutionalize the requirement that there be 12 jurors even though nobody can say why 12 is the magic number? And did it incorporate features that we now find highly objectionable, such as the exclusion of women from jury service? At the time of the adoption of the Sixth Amendment (and for many years thereafter), women were not regarded as fit to serve as a defendant's peers. Unless one is willing to freeze in place late 18th-century practice, it is necessary to find a principle to distinguish between the features that were incorporated and those that were not. To do this, Justice White's opinion for the Court in *Williams* looked to the underlying purpose of the jury-trial right, which it identified as interposing a jury of the defendant's peers to protect against oppression by a " 'corrupt or overzealous prosecutor' " or a " 'compliant, biased, or eccentric judge.' "

The majority decries this "functionalist" approach but provides no alternative. It does not claim that the Sixth Amendment incorporated every feature of common-law practice, but it fails to identify any principle for identifying the features that were absorbed. On the question of jury service by women, the majority's only answer, buried in a footnote, is that the exclusion of women was outlawed by "further constitutional amendments," presumably the Fourteenth Amendment. Does that mean that the majority disagrees with the holding in *Taylor* v. *Louisiana*, 419 U.S. 522 (1975)—another opinion by Justice White—that the exclusion of women from jury service violates the Sixth Amendment?[26] * * *

The *Apodaca* plurality's reasoning was based on the same fundamental mode of analysis as that in *Williams*, 399 U.S. 78, which had held just two years earlier that the Sixth Amendment did not constitutionalize the common law's requirement that a jury have 12 members. Although only one State, Oregon, now permits non-unanimous verdicts, many more allow six-person juries.[29] Repudiating the reasoning of *Apodaca* will almost certainly prompt calls to overrule *Williams*.

* * *

C

* * * What convinces me that Apodaca should be retained are the enormous reliance interests of Louisiana and Oregon. * * *

* * * [T]he majority notes that we "vacated and remanded nearly 800 decisions" for resentencing after *United States v. Booker* held that the Federal Sentencing Guidelines are not mandatory. But the burden of resentencing cannot be compared with the burden of retrying cases. And while resentencing was possible in all the cases affected by *Booker*, there is no guarantee that all the cases affected by today's ruling can be retried. In some cases, key witnesses may not be available, and it remains to be seen whether the criminal justice systems of Oregon and Louisiana have the resources to handle the volume of cases in which convictions will be reversed.

* * * Two other Justices in the majority acknowledge that *Apodaca* was a precedent and thus would presumably regard today's decision as a "new rule," [not applicable on collateral review under *Teague*], but the question remains whether today's decision qualifies [for the *Teague* exception] as a "watershed rule." Justice Kavanaugh concludes that it does not * * * The remaining Justices in the majority, and those of us in dissent, express no view on this question, but the majority's depiction of the unanimity requirement as a hallowed right that Louisiana and Oregon flouted for ignominious reasons certainly provides fuel for the argument

---

[26] * * * Jury practice at the time of the founding differed from current practice in other important respects. Jurors were not selected at random. "[P]ublic officials called selectmen, supervisors, trustees, or 'sheriffs of the parish' exercised what Tocqueville called 'very extensive and very arbitrary' powers in summoning jurors." And "American trial judges . . . routinely summarized the evidence for jurors and often told jurors which witnesses they found most credible, and why." Any attempt to identify the aspects of late 18th-century practice that were incorporated into the Sixth Amendment should take the full picture into account and provide a principle for the distinction.

[29] See Ariz. Rev. Stat. Ann. § 21–102 (2013); Conn. Gen. Stat. § 54–82; Fla. Rule Crim. Proc. § 3.270 (2019); Ind. Code § 35–37–1–1(b)(2); Utah Code § 78B–1–104 (2019).

that the rule announced today meets the test. * * * Whatever the ultimate resolution of the retroactivity question, the reliance here is not only massive; it is concrete.[b]

* * *

SINGER V. UNITED STATES
380 U.S. 24, 85 S.Ct. 783, 13 L.Ed.2d 630 (1965).

CHIEF JUSTICE WARREN delivered the opinion of the Court.

Rule 23(a) of the Federal Rules of Criminal Procedure provides:

> "Cases required to be tried by jury shall be so tried unless the defendant waives a jury trial in writing with the approval of the court and the consent of the government."

Petitioner challenges the permissibility of this rule, arguing that the Constitution gives a defendant in a federal criminal case the right to waive a jury trial whenever he believes such action to be in his best interest, regardless of whether the prosecution and the court are willing to acquiesce in the waiver.

Petitioner was charged in a federal district court with 30 infractions of the mail fraud statute. * * * On the opening day of trial petitioner offered in writing to waive a trial by jury "[f]or the purpose of shortening the trial." The trial court was willing to approve the waiver, but the Government refused to give its consent. Petitioner was subsequently convicted by a jury on 29 of the 30 counts.

Petitioner's argument is that a defendant in a federal criminal case has not only an unconditional constitutional right, guaranteed by Art. III, § 2, and the Sixth Amendment, to a trial by jury, but also a correlative right to have his case decided by a judge alone if he considers such a trial to be to his advantage. * * *

We have examined petitioner's arguments and find them to be without merit. We can find no evidence that the common law recognized that defendants had the right to choose between court and jury trial. Although instances of waiver of jury trial can be found in certain of the colonies prior to the adoption of the Constitution, they were isolated instances occurring pursuant to colonial "constitutions" or statutes and were clear departures from the common law. There is no indication that the colonists considered the ability to waive a jury trial to be of equal importance to the right to demand one. Having found that the Constitution neither

---

[b] Part III.D of Justice Alito's dissent in *Ramos*, which Justice Kagan did not join, compared the reliance interests implicated in *Ramos* to those in prior cases.

In *Edwards v. Vannoy*, 141 S.Ct. 1547 (2021), the Court concluded that *Ramos* announced a new constitutional rule of procedure that does not apply retroactively on collateral review. See fn. a, p. 34. The Court in *Edwards* reasoned there was "no principled basis" for retroactively applying the jury-unanimity right when the Court had declined to give retroactive effect to three other "momentous and consequential" cases that "fundamentally reshaped criminal procedure throughout the United States:" (1) the right to a jury itself established in *Duncan v. Louisiana* [p. 35]; (2) the rule in *Crawford v. Washington* [p. 1022], which, like *Ramos*, was grounded in the original meaning of the Sixth Amendment; and (3) the rule in *Batson v. Kentucky* [p. 828], which, like *Ramos*, advances the goal of prohibiting racial discrimination in jury process.

confers nor recognizes a right of criminal defendants to have their cases tried before a judge alone, we also conclude that Rule 23(a) sets forth a reasonable procedure governing attempted waivers of jury trials.

English Common Law. * * * Not until 1827, long after the adoption of our Constitution, did England provide by statute for the trial of those who stood mute. Even this statute did not give the defendant the right to plead his case before a judge alone, but merely provided that he would be subject to jury trial without his formal consent.

Thus, as late as 1827 the English common law gave criminal defendants no option as to the mode of trial. * * *

The Colonial Experience. * * * The most that can be said for these examples [of jury waiver] is that they are evidence that the colonists believed it was possible to try criminal defendants without a jury. They in no way show that there was any general recognition of a defendant's right to be tried by the court instead of by a jury. Indeed, if there had been recognition of such a right, it would be difficult to understand why Article III and the Sixth Amendment were not drafted in terms which recognized an option.

The Constitution and Its Judicial Interpretation. The proceedings at the Constitutional Convention give little insight into what was meant by the direction in Art. III, § 2, that the "Trial of all Crimes * * * shall be by Jury." The clause was clearly intended to protect the accused from oppression by the Government, but, since the practice of permitting defendants a choice as to the mode of trial was not widespread, it is not surprising that some of the framers apparently believed that the Constitution designated trial by jury as the exclusive method of determining guilt. * * *

The issue whether a defendant could waive a jury trial in federal criminal cases was finally presented to this Court in *Patton v. United States,* 281 U.S. 276 (1930). * * * The Court examined Art. III, § 2, and the Sixth Amendment and concluded that a jury trial was a right which the accused might "forego at his election." The Court also spoke of jury trial as a "privilege," not an "imperative requirement," and remarked that jury trial was principally for the benefit of the accused. Nevertheless, the Court * * * concluded its opinion, with carefully chosen language that dispelled any notion that the defendant had an absolute right to demand trial before a judge sitting alone:

> "Not only must the right of the accused to a trial by a constitutional jury be jealously preserved, but the maintenance of the jury as a factfinding body in criminal cases is of such importance and has such a place in our traditions, that, before any waiver can become effective, the consent of government counsel and the sanction of the court must be had, in addition to the express and intelligent consent of the defendant. And the duty of the trial court in that regard is not to be discharged as a mere matter of rote, but with sound and advised discretion, with an eye to avoid unreasonable or undue departures from that mode of trial or from

any of the essential elements thereof, and with a caution increasing in degree as the offenses dealt with increase in gravity."

* * *

Thus, there is no federally recognized right to a criminal trial before a judge sitting alone, but a defendant can, as was held in *Patton,* in some instances waive his right to a trial by jury. The question remains whether the effectiveness of this waiver can be conditioned upon the consent of the prosecuting attorney and the trial judge.

The ability to waive a constitutional right does not ordinarily carry with it the right to insist upon the opposite of that right. For example, although a defendant can, under some circumstances, waive his constitutional right to a public trial, he has no absolute right to compel a private trial; although he can waive his right to be tried in the State and district where the crime was committed, he cannot in all cases compel transfer of the case to another district; and although he can waive his right to be confronted by the witnesses against him, it has never been seriously suggested that he can thereby compel the Government to try the case by stipulation. Moreover, it has long been accepted that the waiver of constitutional rights can be subjected to reasonable procedural regulations. * * *

Trial by jury has been established by the Constitution as the "normal and * * * preferable mode of disposing of issues of fact in criminal cases." As with any mode that might be devised to determine guilt, trial by jury has its weaknesses and the potential for misuse. However, the mode itself has been surrounded with safeguards to make it as fair as possible—for example, venue can be changed when there is a well-grounded fear of jury prejudice, and prospective jurors are subject to *voir dire* examination, to challenge for cause, and to peremptory challenge.

In light of the Constitution's emphasis on jury trial, we find it difficult to understand how the petitioner can submit the bald proposition that to compel a defendant in a criminal case to undergo a jury trial against his will is contrary to his right to a fair trial or to due process. A defendant's only constitutional right concerning the method of trial is to an impartial trial by jury. We find no constitutional impediment to conditioning a waiver of this right on the consent of the prosecuting attorney and the trial judge when, if either refuses to consent, the result is simply that the defendant is subject to an impartial trial by jury—the very thing that the Constitution guarantees him. The Constitution recognizes an adversary system as the proper method of determining guilt, and the Government, as a litigant, has a legitimate interest in seeing that cases in which it believes a conviction is warranted are tried before the tribunal which the Constitution regards as most likely to produce a fair result. * * *

We are aware that the States have adopted a variety of procedures relating to the waiver of jury trials in state criminal cases. Some have made waiver contingent on approval by the prosecutor. Others, while not giving the prosecutor a voice, have made court approval a prerequisite for waiver. Still others have provided that the question of waiver is a matter solely for the defendant's informed decision, however, the framers of the federal rules were aware of possible alternatives when they recommended the present rule to this Court; this Court promulgated the rule as recommended; and Congress can be deemed to have adopted it.

In upholding the validity of Rule 23(a), we reiterate that the government attorney in a criminal prosecution is not an ordinary party to a controversy, but a "servant of the law" with a "twofold aim * * * that guilt shall not escape or innocence suffer." It was in light of this concept of the role of prosecutor that Rule 23(a) was framed, and we are confident that it is in this light that it will continue to be invoked by government attorneys. Because of this confidence in the integrity of the federal prosecutor, Rule 23(a) does not require that the Government articulate its reasons for demanding a jury trial at the time it refuses to consent to a defendant's proffered waiver. Nor should we assume that federal prosecutors would demand a jury trial for an ignoble purpose. We need not determine in this case whether there might be some circumstances where a defendant's reasons for wanting to be tried by a judge alone are so compelling that the Government's insistence on trial by jury would result in the denial to a defendant of an impartial trial. Petitioner argues that there might arise situations where "passion, prejudice * * * public feeling" or some other factor may render impossible or unlikely an impartial trial by jury. However, since petitioner gave no reason for wanting to forgo jury trial other than to save time, this is not such a case, and petitioner does not claim that it is. * * *

2. JURY SELECTION

Although the procedures for selecting juries to serve in criminal cases are governed by statute in all jurisdictions, the operation of those procedures sometimes produces serious and difficult constitutional questions. In most states, lists of prospective jurors are prepared by random selection from those registered to vote. Certain other lists (e.g., drivers' licenses) are sometimes used in addition or instead. Some of those initially selected are thereafter stricken from the list because they are deemed lacking in qualifications for jury service. Others are excused by request, or on the assumption that they would find jury service especially burdensome. It is apparent that the manner in which these lists of prospective jurors are initially prepared and then reduced can have a significant effect upon the makeup of particular jury panels available for jury selection in particular cases. It is not surprising, therefore, that defendants sometimes challenge the above described procedures on constitutional grounds. The first case in this section, *Taylor v. Louisiana,* discusses the objection that the selection does not accord with the Sixth Amendment right to a jury drawn from a cross-section of the community.

A process called voir dire is used to select from the panel of prospective jurors those who will serve as jurors in a particular case. The prospective jurors are questioned by the attorneys or the judge in order to reveal facts relevant to the exercise of challenges for cause and peremptory challenges. Each side may challenge for cause any prospective juror for lack of impartiality, and in addition each side has a specified number of peremptory challenges, for which no reason ordinarily need be given. The last four cases in this section illustrate the kinds of problems of constitutional dimension which can arise from this voir dire process. *Turner v. Murray* concerns how far it is necessary to go to protect the defendant against biased jurors; *Lockhart v. McCree* involves, on the other hand, how much can be done to ensure against anti-prosecution bias without violating the defendant's rights; *Batson v. Kentucky* teaches that the litigant's manner of using peremptory challenges can run afoul of the Constitution, and *Peña-Rodriguez v. Colorado* addresses when the Sixth Amendment requires a court to consider juror affidavits reporting juror bias that voir dire failed to catch.

TAYLOR V. LOUISIANA
419 U.S. 522, 95 S.Ct. 692, 42 L.Ed.2d 690 (1975).

JUSTICE WHITE delivered the opinion of the Court.

When this case was tried, Art. VII, § 41, of the Louisiana Constitution, and Art. 402 of the Louisiana Code of Criminal Procedure provided that a woman should not be selected for jury service unless she had previously filed a written declaration of her desire to be subject to jury service. The constitutionality of these provisions is the issue in this case. * * *

The Louisiana jury selection system does not disqualify women from jury service, but in operation its conceded systematic impact is that only a very few women, grossly disproportionate to the number of eligible women in the community, are called for jury service.[a] In this case, no women were on the venire from which the petit jury was drawn. The issue we have, therefore, is whether a jury selection system which operates to exclude from jury service an identifiable class of citizens constituting 53% of eligible jurors in the community comports with the Sixth and Fourteenth Amendments.

The State first insists that Taylor, a male, has no standing to object to the exclusion of women from his jury. But Taylor's claim is that he was constitutionally entitled to a jury drawn from a venire constituting a fair cross section of the community and that the jury that tried him was not such a jury by reason of the exclusion of women. Taylor was not a member of the excluded class; but there is no rule that claims such as Taylor presents may be made only by those defendants who are members of the group excluded from jury service. * * * Taylor, in the case before us, was * * * entitled to tender and have adjudicated the claim that the exclusion of women from jury service deprived him of the kind of fact finder to which he was constitutionally entitled.

* * * Our inquiry is whether the presence of a fair cross section of the community on venires, panels or lists from which petit juries are drawn is essential to the fulfillment of the Sixth Amendment's guarantee of an impartial jury trial in criminal prosecutions. * * *

The unmistakable import of this Court's opinions, at least since 1941, and not repudiated by intervening decisions, is that the selection of a petit jury from a

---

[a]   It was stipulated that no more than 10% of the persons on the jury wheel were women, that only 12 females were among the 1,800 persons drawn to fill petit jury venires, and that this discrepancy was the result of the operation of the challenged provisions.

representative cross section of the community is an essential component of the Sixth Amendment right to a jury trial. * * *

We accept the fair cross section requirement as fundamental to the jury trial guaranteed by the Sixth Amendment and are convinced that the requirement has solid foundation. The purpose of a jury is to guard against the exercise of arbitrary power—to make available the common-sense judgment of the community as a hedge against the overzealous or mistaken prosecutor and in preference to the professional or perhaps overconditioned or biased response of a judge. This prophylactic vehicle is not provided if the jury pool is made up of only special segments of the populace or if large, distinctive groups are excluded from the pool. Community participation in the administration of the criminal law, moreover, is not only consistent with our democratic heritage but is also critical to public confidence in the fairness of the criminal justice system. Restricting jury service to only special groups or excluding identifiable segments playing major roles in the community cannot be squared with the constitutional concept of jury trial. * * *

We are also persuaded that the fair cross section requirement is violated by the systematic exclusion of women, who in the judicial district involved here amounted to 53% of the citizens eligible for jury service. This conclusion necessarily entails the judgment that women are sufficiently numerous and distinct from men that if they are systematically eliminated from jury panels, the Sixth Amendment's fair cross section requirement cannot be satisfied. This very matter was debated in *Ballard v. United States,* 329 U.S. 187 (1946). Positing the fair cross-section rule—there said to be a statutory one—the Court concluded that the systematic exclusion of women was unacceptable. The dissenting view that an all-male panel drawn from various groups in the community would be as truly representative as if women were included, was firmly rejected:

"The thought is that the factors which tend to influence the action of women are the same as those which influence the action of men—personality, background, economic status—and not sex. Yet it is not enough to say that women when sitting as jurors neither act nor tend to act as a class. Men likewise do not act as a class. But, if the shoe were on the other foot, who would claim that a jury was truly representative of the community if all men were intentionally and systematically excluded from the panel? The truth is that the two sexes are not fungible; a community made up exclusively of one is different from a community composed of both; the subtle interplay of influence one on the other is among the imponderables. To insulate the courtroom from either may not in a given case make an iota of difference. Yet a flavor, a distinct quality is lost if either sex is excluded. The exclusion of one may indeed make the jury less representative of the community than would be true if an economic or racial group were excluded."

In this respect, we agree with the Court in *Ballard:* If the fair cross-section rule is to govern the selection of juries, as we have concluded it must, women cannot be systematically excluded from jury panels from which petit juries are drawn. This conclusion is consistent with the current judgment of the country, now evidenced by legislative or constitutional provisions in every State and at the federal level qualifying women for jury service.

There remains the argument that women as a class serve a distinctive role in society and that jury service would so substantially interfere with that function that the State has ample justification for excluding women from service unless they volunteer, even though the result is that almost all jurors are men. It is true that *Hoyt v. Florida*, 368 U.S. 57 (1961), held that such a system did not deny due process of law or equal protection of the laws because there was a sufficiently rational basis for such an exemption. But *Hoyt* did not involve a defendant's Sixth Amendment right to a jury drawn from a fair cross section of the community and the prospect of depriving him of that right if women as a class are systematically excluded. The right to a proper jury cannot be overcome on merely rational grounds. There must be weightier reasons if a distinctive class representing 53% of the eligible jurors is for all practical purposes to be excluded from jury service. No such basis has been tendered here.

The States are free to grant exemptions from jury service to individuals in case of special hardship or incapacity and to those engaged in particular occupations the uninterrupted performance of which is critical to the community's welfare. It would not appear that such exemptions would pose substantial threats that the remaining pool of jurors would not be representative of the community. A system excluding all women, however, is a wholly different matter. It is untenable to suggest these days that it would be a special hardship for each and every woman to perform jury service or that society cannot spare *any* women from their present duties. This may be the case with many, and it may be burdensome to sort out those who should serve. But that task is performed in the case of men, and the administrative convenience in dealing with women as a class is insufficient justification for diluting the quality of community judgment represented by the jury in criminal trials. * * *

Our holding does not augur or authorize the fashioning of detailed jury selection codes by federal courts. The fair cross section principle must have much leeway in application. The States remain free to prescribe relevant qualifications for their jurors and to provide reasonable exemptions so long as it may be fairly said that the jury lists or panels are representative of the community. * * *

It should also be emphasized that in holding that petit juries must be drawn from a source fairly representative of the community we impose no requirement that petit juries actually chosen must mirror the community and reflect the various distinctive groups in the population. Defendants are not entitled to a jury of any particular composition; but the jury wheels, pools of names, panels or venires from which juries are drawn must not systematically exclude distinctive groups in the community and thereby fail to be reasonably representative thereof. * * *

Reversed and remanded.

CHIEF JUSTICE BURGER concurred in the result.

JUSTICE REHNQUIST, dissenting. * * *

I cannot conceive that today's decision is necessary to guard against oppressive or arbitrary law enforcement, or to prevent miscarriages of justice and to assure fair trials. Especially is this so when the criminal defendant involved makes no claims of prejudice or bias. The Court does accord some slight attention to justifying its ruling in terms of the basis on which the right to jury trial was read into the Fourteenth Amendment. It concludes that the jury is not effective, as a prophylaxis against arbitrary prosecutorial and judicial power, if the "jury pool is made up of only special segments of the populace or if large, distinctive groups are excluded from the pool." It fails, however, to provide any satisfactory explanation of the mechanism by which the Louisiana system undermines the prophylactic role of the jury, either in general or in this case. The best it can do is to posit "a flavor, a distinct quality," which allegedly is lost if either sex is excluded. However, this "flavor" is not of such importance that the Constitution is offended if any given petit jury is not so enriched. This smacks more of mysticism than of law. The Court does not even purport to practice its mysticism in a consistent fashion—presumably doctors, lawyers, and other groups, whose frequent exemption from jury service is endorsed by the majority, also offer qualities as distinct and important as those at issue here. * * *

TURNER V. MURRAY
476 U.S. 28, 106 S.Ct. 1683, 90 L.Ed.2d 27 (1986).

JUSTICE WHITE announced the judgment of the Court and delivered the opinion of the Court with respect to Parts I and III, and an opinion with respect to Parts II and IV, in which JUSTICE BLACKMUN, JUSTICE STEVENS, and JUSTICE O'CONNOR join.

[Petitioner, a black man, was indicted in Virginia on charges of capital murder for fatally shooting the white proprietor of a jewelry store in the course of a robbery. During *voir dire,* the state trial judge refused petitioner's request to question the prospective jurors on racial prejudice. The jury convicted petitioner, and, after a separate sentencing hearing, recommended that he be sentenced to death, a recommendation the trial judge accepted. The Virginia Supreme Court upheld the death sentence, rejecting petitioner's argument that the trial judge deprived him of a fair trial by refusing to question the prospective jurors on racial prejudice. Petitioner then sought habeas corpus relief in Federal District Court, which rejected the same argument and denied relief, and the Court of Appeals affirmed.]

II

The Fourth Circuit's opinion correctly states the analytical framework for evaluating petitioner's argument: "The broad inquiry in each case must be whether under all of the circumstances presented there was a constitutionally significant likelihood that, absent questioning about racial prejudice, the jurors would not be indifferent as they stand unsworn." The Fourth Circuit was correct, too, in holding that under *Ristaino* the mere fact that petitioner is black and his victim white does not constitute a "special circumstance" of constitutional proportions.[a] What sets this case apart from *Ristaino,* however, is that in addition to petitioner's being accused of a crime against a white victim, the crime charged was a capital offense.

In a capital sentencing proceeding before a jury, the jury is called upon to make a "highly subjective, 'unique, individualized judgment regarding the punishment that a particular person deserves.' " The Virginia statute under which petitioner was sentenced is instructive of the kinds of judgments a capital sentencing jury must make. First, in order to consider the death penalty, a Virginia jury must find either that the defendant is likely to commit future violent crimes or that his crime was "outrageously or wantonly vile, horrible or inhuman in that it involved torture, depravity of mind or an aggravated battery to the victim." Second, the jury must consider any mitigating evidence offered by the defendant. Mitigating evidence may include, but is not limited to, facts tending to show that the defendant acted under the influence of extreme emotional or mental disturbance, or that at the time of the crime the defendant's capacity "to appreciate the criminality of his conduct or to conform his conduct to the requirements of law was significantly impaired." Finally, even if the jury has found an aggravating factor, and irrespective of whether mitigating evidence has been offered, the jury has discretion not to recommend the death sentence, in which case it may not be imposed.

Virginia's death-penalty statute gives the jury greater discretion than other systems which we have upheld against constitutional challenge. However, our cases establish that every capital sentencer must be free to weigh relevant mitigating evidence before deciding whether to impose the death penalty, and that in the end it is the jury that must make the difficult, individualized judgment as to whether the defendant deserves the sentence of death.

Because of the range of discretion entrusted to a jury in a capital sentencing hearing, there is a unique opportunity for racial prejudice to operate but remain undetected. On the facts of this case, a juror who believes that blacks are violence-prone or morally inferior might well be influenced by that belief in deciding whether petitioner's crime involved the aggravating factors specified under Virginia law. Such a juror might also be less favorably inclined toward petitioner's evidence of mental disturbance as a mitigating circumstance. More subtle, less consciously held racial attitudes could also influence a juror's decision in this case.

---

[a]   The reference is to *Ristaino v. Ross,* 424 U.S. 589 (1976), where the Court elaborated upon *Ham v. South Carolina,* 409 U.S. 524 (1973). As the Court explained in fn. 3 of the instant case:

"In *Ham,* a young black man known in his small South Carolina hometown as a civil rights activist was arrested and charged with possession of marihuana. We held that the trial judge committed reversible error in refusing to honor Ham's request to question prospective jurors on racial prejudice. In *Ristaino,* supra, we specified the factors which mandated an inquiry into racial prejudice in *Ham:*

" 'Ham's defense was that he had been framed because of his civil rights activities. His prominence in the community as a civil rights activist, if not already known to veniremen, inevitably would have been revealed to the members of the jury in the course of his presentation of that defense. Racial issues therefore were inextricably bound up with the conduct of the trial. Further, Ham's reputation as a civil rights activist and the defense he interposed were likely to intensify any prejudice that individual members of the jury might harbor.' "

Fear of blacks, which could easily be stirred up by the violent facts of petitioner's crime, might incline a juror to favor the death penalty.[7]

The risk of racial prejudice infecting a capital sentencing proceeding is especially serious in light of the complete finality of the death sentence. "The Court, as well as the separate opinions of a majority of the individual Justices, has recognized that the qualitative difference of death from all other punishments requires a correspondingly greater degree of scrutiny of the capital sentencing determination." In the present case, we find the risk that racial prejudice may have infected petitioner's capital sentencing unacceptable in light of the ease with which that risk could have been minimized. By refusing to question prospective jurors on racial prejudice, the trial judge failed to adequately protect petitioner's constitutional right to an impartial jury.

III

We hold that a capital defendant accused of an interracial crime is entitled to have prospective jurors informed of the race of the victim and questioned on the issue of racial bias. The rule we propose is minimally intrusive; as in other cases involving "special circumstances," the trial judge retains discretion as to the form and number of questions on the subject, including the decision whether to question the venire individually or collectively. Also, a defendant cannot complain of a judge's failure to question the venire on racial prejudice unless the defendant has specifically requested such an inquiry.

IV

The inadequacy of *voir dire* in this case requires that petitioner's death sentence be vacated. It is not necessary, however, that he be retried on the issue of guilt. Our judgment in this case is that there was an unacceptable risk of racial prejudice infecting the *capital sentencing proceeding*. This judgment is based on a conjunction of three factors: the fact that the crime charged involved interracial violence, the broad discretion given the jury at the death-penalty hearing, and the special seriousness of the risk of improper sentencing in a "capital case." At the guilt phase of petitioner's trial, the jury had no greater discretion than it would have had if the crime charged had been noncapital murder. Thus, with respect to the guilt phase of petitioner's trial, we find this case to be indistinguishable from *Ristaino,* to which we continue to adhere.

THE CHIEF JUSTICE concurs in the judgment.

JUSTICE BRENNAN, concurring in part and dissenting in part. * * *

To sentence an individual to death on the basis of a proceeding tainted by racial bias would violate the most basic values of our criminal justice system. This

---

[7]   In referring to the facts of petitioner's crime, we do not retreat from our holding in *Ristaino*. The fact of interracial violence alone is not a "special circumstance" entitling the defendant to have prospective jurors questioned about racial prejudice. It should be clear, though, that our holding in *Ristaino* was not based on a blind belief that the facts presented in that case could not evoke racial prejudice. * * * *Ristaino* * * * simply leaves it to the trial judge's discretion to decide what measures to take in screening out racial prejudice, absent a showing of "significant likelihood that racial prejudice might infect [the] trial."

the Court understands. But what it seems not to comprehend is that to permit an individual to be *convicted* by a prejudiced jury violates those same values in precisely the same way. The incongruity of the Court's split judgment is made apparent after it is appreciated that the opportunity for bias to poison decisionmaking operates at a guilt trial in the same way as it does at a sentencing hearing and after one returns to the context of the case before us. Implicit in the Court's judgment is the acknowledgment that there was a likelihood that the jury that pronounced the death sentence acted, in part, on the basis of racial prejudice. But the exact same jury convicted Turner. Does the Court really mean to suggest that the constitutional entitlement to an impartial jury attaches only at the sentencing phase? Does the Court really believe that racial biases are turned on and off in the course of one criminal prosecution? * * *

JUSTICE MARSHALL, with whom JUSTICE BRENNAN joins, concurring in the judgment in part and dissenting in part.

* * * I believe that a criminal defendant is entitled to inquire on *voir dire* about the potential racial bias of jurors whenever the case involves a violent interracial crime. As the Court concedes, "it is plain that there is some risk of racial prejudice influencing a jury whenever there is a crime involving interracial violence." To my mind that risk plainly outweighs the slight cost of allowing the defendant to choose whether to make an inquiry concerning such possible prejudice. This Court did not identify in *Ristaino v. Ross,* nor does it identify today, any additional burdens that would accompany such a rule. I therefore cannot agree with the Court's continuing rejection of the simple prophylactic rule proposed in *Ristaino.* * * *

JUSTICE POWELL, with whom JUSTICE REHNQUIST joins, dissenting.

* * * In *Ristaino,* the Court expressly declined to adopt a *per se* rule requiring *voir dire* inquiry into racial bias in every trial for an interracial crime. Neither the Constitution nor sound policy considerations supported such a *per se* approach. But today the Court decides that the Constitution does require a *per se* rule in capital cases because the capital jury exercises discretion at the sentencing phase. The Court's reasoning ignores the many procedural and substantive safeguards, similar to those governing the jury's decision on guilt or innocence, that circumscribe the capital jury's sentencing decision.

Under Virginia law, murder is a capital offense only if it is "willful, deliberate and premeditated" and is committed while the perpetrator is engaged in another crime or under specified aggravating circumstances. As in any criminal prosecution, of course, the State carries the burden of proving all elements of the capital offense beyond a reasonable doubt. Following a sentencing hearing, the death sentence may not be imposed unless the State proves beyond a reasonable doubt statutorily defined aggravating factors. Virginia law recognizes only two aggravating factors: whether, based on the defendant's criminal record, there is a probability that he would commit future crimes of violence, and whether the defendant's crime was "outrageously or wantonly vile, horrible or inhuman, in that it involved torture, depravity of mind or aggravated battery to the victim." The jury also is required to consider any relevant mitigating evidence offered by the defendant.

The existence of these significant limitations on the jury's exercise of sentencing discretion illustrates why the Court's *per se* rule is wholly unfounded. Just as the trial judge's charge at the guilt phase instructs the jurors that they may consider only the evidence in the case and that they must determine if the prosecution has established each element of the crime beyond a reasonable doubt, the charge at the penalty phase directs the jurors to focus solely on considerations relevant to determination of appropriate punishment and to decide if the prosecution has established beyond a reasonable doubt factors warranting imposition of death. Accordingly, just as there is no reason to presume racial bias on the part of jurors who determine the guilt of a defendant who has committed a violent crime against a person of another race, there is no reason to constitutionalize such a presumption with respect to the jurors who sit to recommend the penalty in a capital case. * * *

LOCKHART V. MCCREE
476 U.S. 162, 106 S.Ct. 1758, 90 L.Ed.2d 137 (1986).

JUSTICE REHNQUIST delivered the opinion of the Court.

In this case we address the question left open by our decision nearly 18 years ago in *Witherspoon v. Illinois,* 391 U.S. 510 (1968)[a]: Does the Constitution prohibit

---

[a] In *Witherspoon* the Court held "that a sentence of death cannot be carried out if the jury that imposed or recommended it was chosen by excluding veniremen for cause simply because they voiced general objections to the death penalty or expressed conscientious or religious scruples against its infliction."

In *Gray v. Mississippi,* 481 U.S. 648 (1987), the Court declined to abandon the ruling in *Davis v. Georgia,* 429 U.S. 122 (1976), that even a single misapplication of *Witherspoon* invalidates a death sentence. One way of looking at the trial judge's granting of an invalid *Witherspoon* motion in the instant case was that it was intended to remedy an earlier erroneous denial of a *Witherspoon* motion regarding another prospective juror. As to this, the Court declined to "condone the 'correction' of one error by the commitment of another," especially where, as here, the first error was a violation of the prosecutor's statutory right and the second a violation of defendant's constitutional right. The Court next rejected the state court's reasoning "that a *Witherspoon* violation constitutes harmless error when the prosecutor has an unexercised peremptory challenge that he states he would have used to excuse the juror," stating:

> "The practical result of adoption of this unexercised peremptory argument would be to insulate jury-selection error from meaningful appellate review. By simply stating during *voir dire* that the State is prepared to exercise a peremptory challenge if the court denies its motion for cause, a prosecutor would ensure that a reviewing court would consider any erroneous exclusion harmless. A prosecutor, as a routine matter, would likely append a statement to this effect to his motion for cause."

Finally, as to the state's argument that a single *Witherspoon* error should be deemed harmless because it did not have any prejudicial effect, the Court found it "equally unavailing." Because courts do not generally review a prosecutor's exercise of peremptory challenges, which are often used (and in this case were used) to remove prospective jurors who express hesitation against the death penalty, "a court cannot say with confidence that an erroneous exclusion for cause of a scrupled, yet eligible, venire member is an isolated incident in that particular case."

In *Morgan v. Illinois,* 504 U.S. 719 (1992), the Court rejected the state court's conclusion that a trial judge need not, on defendant's request, ask a "reverse-*Witherspoon*" question on voir dire so as to identify and exclude any prospective juror who would vote for the death penalty in every capital case. "A juror who will automatically vote for the death penalty in every case will fail in good faith to consider the evidence of aggravating and mitigating circumstances as the instructions require him to do. Indeed, because such a juror has already formed an opinion on the merits, the presence or absence of either aggravating or mitigating circumstances is entirely irrelevant to such a juror. Therefore, based on the requirement of impartiality embodied in the Due Process Clause the removal for cause, prior to the guilt phase of a bifurcated capital trial, of prospective jurors whose opposition to the death penalty is so strong that it would prevent or substantially impair the performance of their duties as jurors at the sentencing phase of the trial? * * *

McCree was charged with capital felony murder. In accordance with Arkansas law, the trial judge at *voir dire* removed for cause, over McCree's objections, those prospective jurors who stated that they could not under any circumstances vote for the imposition of the death penalty. Eight prospective jurors were excluded for this reason. The jury convicted McCree of capital felony murder, but rejected the State's request for the death penalty, instead setting McCree's punishment at life imprisonment without parole. McCree's conviction was affirmed on direct appeal, and his petition for state post-conviction relief was denied.

McCree then filed a federal habeas corpus petition raising *inter alia* the claim that "death qualification," or the removal for cause of the so-called "*Witherspoon*-excludable" prospective jurors,[1] violated his right under the Sixth and Fourteenth Amendments to have his guilt or innocence determined by an impartial jury selected from a representative cross-section of the community. * * *

The District Court held a hearing on the "death qualification" issue in July 1981, receiving in evidence numerous social science studies concerning the attitudes and beliefs of "*Witherspoon*-excludables," along with the potential effects of excluding them from the jury prior to the guilt phase of a bifurcated capital trial. In August 1983, the court concluded, based on the social science evidence, that "death qualification" produced juries that "were more prone to convict" capital defendants than "non-death-qualified" juries. The court ruled that "death qualification" thus violated both the fair cross-section and impartiality requirements of the Sixth and Fourteenth Amendments, and granted McCree habeas relief.

The Eighth Circuit found "substantial evidentiary support" for the District Court's conclusion that the removal for cause of "*Witherspoon*-excludables" resulted in "conviction-prone" juries, and affirmed the grant of habeas relief on the ground that such removal for cause violated McCree's constitutional right to a jury selected from a fair cross-section of the community. * * *

Before turning to the legal issues in the case, we are constrained to point out what we believe to be several serious flaws in the evidence upon which the courts

---

of the Fourteenth Amendment, a capital defendant may challenge for cause any prospective juror who maintains such views. If even one such juror is empaneled and the death sentence is imposed, the State is disentitled to execute the sentence." As for the state's claim that the trial judge's "general fairness and 'follow the law' questions" sufficed, the Court answered that the state's "own request for questioning under *Witherspoon* * * * belies this argument."

[1]   [T]he proper constitutional standard is simply whether a prospective juror's views would " 'prevent or substantially impair the performance of his duties as a juror in accordance with his instructions and his oath.' " Thus, the term "*Witherspoon*-excludable" is something of a misnomer. Nevertheless, because the parties and the courts below have used the term "*Witherspoon*-excludables" to identify the group of prospective jurors at issue in this case, we will use the same term in this opinion.

below reached the conclusion that "death qualification" produces "conviction-prone" juries. * * *

Of the six studies introduced by McCree that at least purported to deal with the central issue in this case, namely, the potential effects on the determination of guilt or innocence of excluding "*Witherspoon*-excludables" from the jury, three were also before this Court when it decided *Witherspoon*. * * * It goes almost without saying that if these studies were "too tentative and fragmentary" to make out a claim of constitutional error in 1968, the same studies, unchanged but for having aged some eighteen years, are still insufficient to make out such a claim in this case.

Nor do the three post-*Witherspoon* studies introduced by McCree on the "death qualification" issue provide substantial support for the "*per se* constitutional rule" McCree asks this Court to adopt. All three of the "new" studies were based on the responses of individuals randomly selected from some segment of the population, but who were not actual jurors sworn under oath to apply the law to the facts of an actual case involving the fate of an actual capital defendant. We have serious doubts about the value of these studies in predicting the behavior of actual jurors. * * *

Having identified some of the more serious problems with McCree's studies, however, we will assume for purposes of this opinion that the studies are both methodologically valid and adequate to establish that "death qualification" in fact produces juries somewhat more "conviction-prone" than "non-death-qualified" juries. We hold, nonetheless, that the Constitution does not prohibit the States from "death qualifying" juries in capital cases.

The Eighth Circuit ruled that "death qualification" violated McCree's right under the Sixth Amendment, as applied to the States via incorporation through the Fourteenth Amendment, to a jury selected from a representative cross-section of the community. But we do not believe that the fair cross-section requirement can, or should, be applied as broadly as that court attempted to apply it. We have never invoked the fair cross-section principle to invalidate the use of either for-cause or peremptory challenges to prospective jurors, or to require petit juries, as opposed to jury panels or venires, to reflect the composition of the community at large. * * * The limited scope of the fair cross-section requirement is a direct and inevitable consequence of the practical impossibility of providing each criminal defendant with a truly "representative" petit jury. * * * We remain convinced that an extension of the fair cross-section requirement to petit juries would be unworkable and unsound, and we decline McCree's invitation to adopt such an extension.

But even if we were willing to extend the fair cross-section requirement to petit juries, we would still reject the Eighth Circuit's conclusion that "death qualification" violates that requirement. The essence of a "fair cross-section" claim is the systematic exclusion of "a 'distinctive' group in the community." In our view, groups defined solely in terms of shared attitudes that would prevent or substantially impair members of the group from performing one of their duties as jurors, such as the "*Witherspoon*-excludables" at issue here, are not "distinctive groups" for fair cross-section purposes.

We have never attempted to precisely define the term "distinctive group," and we do not undertake to do so today. But we think it obvious that the concept of "distinctiveness" must be linked to the purposes of the fair cross-section requirement. In *Taylor,* we identified those purposes as (1) "guard[ing] against the exercise of arbitrary power" and ensuring that the "commonsense judgment of the community" will act as "a hedge against the overzealous or mistaken prosecutor," (2) preserving "public confidence in the fairness of the criminal justice system," and (3) implementing our belief that "sharing in the administration of justice is a phase of civic responsibility."

Our prior jury-representativeness cases, whether based on the fair cross-section component of the Sixth Amendment or the Equal Protection Clause of the Fourteenth Amendment, have involved such groups as blacks, women, and Mexican-Americans. The wholesale exclusion of these large groups from jury service clearly contravened all three of the aforementioned purposes of the fair cross-section requirement. Because these groups were excluded for reasons completely unrelated to the ability of members of the group to serve as jurors in a particular case, the exclusion raised at least the possibility that the composition of juries would be arbitrarily skewed in such a way as to deny criminal defendants the benefit of the common-sense judgment of the community. In addition, the exclusion from jury service of large groups of individuals not on the basis of their inability to serve as jurors, but on the basis of some immutable characteristic such as race, gender, or ethnic background, undeniably gave rise to an "appearance of unfairness." Finally, such exclusion improperly deprived members of these often historically disadvantaged groups of their right as citizens to serve on juries in criminal cases.

The group of "*Witherspoon*-excludables" involved in the case at bar differs significantly from the groups we have previously recognized as "distinctive." "Death qualification," unlike the wholesale exclusion of blacks, women, or Mexican-Americans from jury service, is carefully designed to serve the State's concededly legitimate interest in obtaining a single jury that can properly and impartially apply the law to the facts of the case at both the guilt and sentencing phases of a capital trial. There is very little danger, therefore, and McCree does not even argue, that "death qualification" was instituted as a means for the State to arbitrarily skew the composition of capital-case juries.

Furthermore, unlike blacks, women, and Mexican-Americans, "*Witherspoon*-excludables" are singled out for exclusion in capital cases on the basis of an attribute that is within the individual's control. It is important to remember that not all who oppose the death penalty are subject to removal for cause in capital cases; those who firmly believe that the death penalty is unjust may nevertheless serve as jurors in capital cases so long as they state clearly that they are willing to temporarily set aside their own beliefs in deference to the rule of law. Because the group of "*Witherspoon*-excludables" includes only those who cannot and will not conscientiously obey the law with respect to one of the issues in a capital case,[b] "death qualification" hardly can be said to create an "appearance of unfairness."

Finally, the removal for cause of "*Witherspoon*-excludables" in capital cases does not prevent them from serving as jurors in other criminal cases, and thus leads to no substantial deprivation of their basic rights of citizenship. They are treated no differently than any juror who expresses the view that he would be unable to follow the law in a particular case. * * *

McCree argues that, even if we reject the Eighth Circuit's fair cross-section holding, we should affirm the judgment below on the alternative ground, adopted by the District Court, that "death qualification" violated his constitutional right to an impartial jury. * * * McCree argues that his jury lacked impartiality because the absence of "*Witherspoon*-excludables" "slanted" the jury in favor of conviction.

We do not agree. McCree's "impartiality" argument apparently is based on the theory that, because all individual jurors are to some extent predisposed towards one result or another, a constitutionally impartial *jury* can be constructed only by "balancing" the various predispositions of the individual *jurors*. Thus, according to McCree, when the State "tips the scales" by excluding prospective jurors with a particular viewpoint, an impermissibly partial jury results. We have consistently rejected this view of jury impartiality, including as recently as last Term when we squarely held that an impartial *jury* consists of nothing more than "*jurors* who will conscientiously apply the law and find the facts."

McCree argues, however, that this Court's decisions in *Witherspoon, supra,* and *Adams v. Texas,* 448 U.S. 38 (1980), [applying *Witherspoon,*] stand for the proposition that a State violates the Constitution whenever it "slants" the jury by excluding a group of individuals more likely than the population at large to favor the criminal defendant. We think McCree overlooks two fundamental differences between *Witherspoon* and *Adams* and the instant case, and therefore misconceives the import and scope of those two decisions.

First, the Court in *Witherspoon* viewed the Illinois system as having been deliberately slanted for the purpose of making the imposition of the death penalty more likely. * * *

Here, on the other hand, the removal for cause of "*Witherspoon*-excludables" serves the State's entirely proper interest in obtaining a single jury that could impartially decide all of the issues in McCree's case. Arkansas by legislative enactment and judicial decision provides for the use of a unitary jury in capital cases. * * *

---

[b]   The Court later described this standard as allowing the exclusion for cause of any "juror who is substantially impaired in his or her ability to impose the death penalty." *Uttecht v. Brown,* 551 U.S. 1 (2007). In *Uttecht,* the Court held that this standard allowed the removal of a juror for cause when state law authorized a sentence of life with no possibility of release and the trial judge had concluded that the juror would have had difficulty considering the death penalty unless there was a chance the defendant would be released. Dissenting, four justices maintained that the Court had misinterpreted the *Witherspoon* line of cases as allowing the removal of all but those jurors who "are willing to impose a death sentence in every situation in which a defendant is eligible for that sanction." This was "exactly the outcome we aimed to protect against in developing the standard," they argued.

The Arkansas Supreme Court recently explained the State's legislative choice to require unitary juries in capital cases:

> "It has always been the law in Arkansas, except when the punishment is mandatory, that the same jurors who have the responsibility for determining guilt or innocence must also shoulder the burden of fixing the punishment. That is as it should be, for the two questions are necessarily interwoven."

Another interest identified by the State in support of its system of unitary juries is the possibility that, in at least some capital cases, the defendant might benefit at the sentencing phase of the trial from the jury's "residual doubts" about the evidence presented at the guilt phase. * * * Finally, it seems obvious to us that in most, if not all, capital cases much of the evidence adduced at the guilt phase of the trial will also have a bearing on the penalty phase; if two different juries were to be required, such testimony would have to be presented twice, once to each jury. * * *

Second, and more importantly, both *Witherspoon* and *Adams* dealt with the special context of capital sentencing, where the range of jury discretion necessarily gave rise to far greater concern over the possible effects of an "imbalanced" jury. * * *

In the case at bar, by contrast, we deal not with capital sentencing, but with the jury's more traditional role of finding the facts and determining the guilt or innocence of a criminal defendant, where jury discretion is more channeled. We reject McCree's suggestion that *Witherspoon* and *Adams* have broad applicability outside the special context of capital sentencing, and conclude that those two decisions do not support the result reached by the Eighth Circuit here. * * *

JUSTICE BLACKMUN concurs in the result.

JUSTICE MARSHALL, with whom JUSTICE BRENNAN and JUSTICE STEVENS join, dissenting.

* * * The data strongly suggest that death qualification excludes a significantly large subset—at least 11% to 17%—of potential jurors who could be impartial during the guilt phase of trial. Among the members of this excludable class are a disproportionate number of blacks and women.

The perspectives on the criminal justice system of jurors who survive death qualification are systematically different from those of the excluded jurors. Death-qualified jurors are, for example, more likely to believe that a defendant's failure to testify is indicative of his guilt, more hostile to the insanity defense, more mistrustful of defense attorneys, and less concerned about the danger of erroneous convictions. This pro-prosecution bias is reflected in the greater readiness of death-qualified jurors to convict or to convict on more serious charges. And, finally, the very process of death qualification—which focuses attention on the death penalty before the trial has even begun—has been found to predispose the jurors that survive it to believe that the defendant is guilty.

The evidence thus confirms, and is itself corroborated by, the more intuitive judgments of scholars and of so many of the participants in capital trials—judges, defense attorneys, and prosecutors. * * *

Faced with the near unanimity of authority supporting respondent's claim that death qualification gives the prosecution a particular advantage in the guilt phase of capital trials, the majority here makes but a weak effort to contest that proposition. Instead, it merely assumes for the purposes of this opinion "that 'death-qualification' in fact produces juries somewhat more 'conviction-prone' than 'non-death-qualified' juries," and then holds that this result does not offend the Constitution. This disregard for the clear import of the evidence tragically misconstrues the settled constitutional principles that guarantee a defendant the right to a fair trial and an impartial jury whose composition is not biased toward the prosecution. * * *

As the *Witherspoon* Court recognized, "the State's interest in submitting the penalty issue to a jury capable of imposing capital punishment" may be accommodated without infringing a capital defendant's interest in a fair determination of his guilt if the State uses "one jury to decide guilt and another to fix punishment." Any exclusion of death-penalty opponents, the Court reasoned, could await the penalty phase of a trial. The question here is thus whether the State has *other* interests that require the use of a single jury and demand the subordination of a capital defendant's Sixth and Fourteenth Amendment rights.

The only two reasons that the Court invokes to justify the State's use of a single jury are efficient trial management and concern that a defendant at his sentencing proceedings may be able to profit from "residual doubts" troubling jurors who have sat through the guilt phase of his trial. The first of these purported justifications is merely unconvincing. The second is offensive. * * *

In a system using separate juries for guilt and penalty phases, time and resources would be saved every time a capital case did not require a penalty phase. The *voir dire* needed to identify nullifiers before the guilt phase is less extensive than the questioning that under the current scheme conducted before *every* capital trial. The State could, of course, choose to empanel a death-qualified jury at the start of every trial, to be used only if a penalty stage is required. However, if it opted for the cheaper alternative of empanelling a death-qualified jury only in the event that a defendant were convicted of capital charges, the State frequently would be able to avoid retrying the entire guilt phase for the benefit of the penalty jury. Stipulated summaries of prior evidence might, for example, save considerable time. Thus, it cannot fairly be said that the costs of accommodating a defendant's constitutional rights under these circumstances are prohibitive, or even significant.

Even less convincing is the Court's concern that a defendant be able to appeal at sentencing to the "residual doubts" of the jurors who found him guilty. Any suggestion that the current system of death qualification "may be in the defendant's best interests, seems specious unless the state is willing to grant the defendant the option to waive this paternalistic protection in exchange for better odds against conviction." Furthermore, this case will stand as one of the few times in which any legitimacy has been given to the power of a convicted capital defendant facing the possibility of a death sentence to argue as a mitigating factor the chance that he might be innocent. Where a defendant's sentence but not his conviction has been set aside on appeal, States have routinely empanelled juries whose only duty is to assess punishment, thereby depriving defendants of the chance to profit from the "residual doubts" that jurors who had already sat through a guilt phase might bring to the sentencing proceeding. * * *

But most importantly, it ill-behooves the majority to allude to a defendant's power to appeal to "residual doubts" at his sentencing when this Court has consistently refused to grant certiorari in state cases holding that these doubts cannot properly be considered during capital sentencing proceedings. * * *

BATSON V. KENTUCKY

476 U.S. 79, 106 S.Ct. 1712, 90 L.Ed.2d 69 (1986).

JUSTICE POWELL delivered the opinion of the Court.

This case requires us to reexamine that portion of *Swain v. Alabama*, 380 U.S. 202 (1965), concerning the evidentiary burden placed on a criminal defendant who claims that he has been denied equal protection through the State's use of peremptory challenges to exclude members of his race from the petit jury.[1]

Petitioner, a black man, was indicted in Kentucky on charges of second-degree burglary and receipt of stolen goods. On the first day of trial in Jefferson Circuit Court, the judge conducted *voir dire* examination of the venire, excused certain jurors for cause, and permitted the parties to exercise peremptory challenges. The prosecutor used his peremptory challenges to strike all four black persons on the venire, and a jury composed only of white persons was selected. Defense counsel moved to discharge the jury before it was sworn on the ground that the prosecutor's removal of the black veniremen violated petitioner's rights under the Sixth and Fourteenth Amendments to a jury drawn from a cross-section of the community, and under the Fourteenth Amendment to equal protection of the laws. Counsel requested a hearing on his motion. Without expressly ruling on the request for a hearing, the trial judge observed that the parties were entitled to use their peremptory challenges to "strike anybody they want to." The judge then denied petitioner's motion, reasoning that the cross-section requirement applies only to selection of the venire and not to selection of the petit jury itself.

The jury convicted petitioner on both counts. On appeal to the Supreme Court of Kentucky, petitioner pressed, among other claims, the argument concerning the prosecutor's use of peremptory challenges. Conceding that *Swain v. Alabama* apparently foreclosed an equal protection claim based solely on the prosecutor's conduct in this case, petitioner urged the court to follow decisions of other states, and to hold that such conduct violated his rights under the Sixth Amendment and

---

[1] Following the lead of a number of state courts construing their state's constitution, two federal Courts of Appeals recently have accepted the view that peremptory challenges used to strike black jurors in a particular case may violate the Sixth Amendment. Other Courts of Appeals have rejected that position * * *.

Section 11 of the Kentucky Constitution to a jury drawn from a cross-section of the community. Petitioner also contended that the facts showed that the prosecutor had engaged in a "pattern" of discriminatory challenges in this case and established an equal protection violation under *Swain*.

The Supreme Court of Kentucky affirmed. * * * We granted certiorari, and now reverse.

In *Swain v. Alabama,* this Court recognized that a "State's purposeful or deliberate denial to Negroes on account of race of participation as jurors in the administration of justice violates the Equal Protection Clause." This principle has been "consistently and repeatedly" reaffirmed, in numerous decisions of this Court both preceding and following *Swain*. We reaffirm the principle today.[4] * * *

Accordingly, the component of the jury selection process at issue here, the State's privilege to strike individual jurors through peremptory challenges, is subject to the commands of the Equal Protection Clause. Although a prosecutor ordinarily is entitled to exercise permitted peremptory challenges "for any reason at all, as long as that reason is related to his view concerning the outcome" of the case to be tried, the Equal Protection Clause forbids the prosecutor to challenge potential jurors solely on account of their race or on the assumption that black jurors as a group will be unable impartially to consider the State's case against a black defendant. * * *

Swain required the Court to decide, among other issues, whether a black defendant was denied equal protection by the State's exercise of peremptory challenges to exclude members of his race from the petit jury. The record in *Swain* showed that the prosecutor had used the State's peremptory challenges to strike the six black persons included on the petit jury venire. While rejecting the defendant's claim for failure to prove purposeful discrimination, the Court nonetheless indicated that the Equal Protection Clause placed some limits on the State's exercise of peremptory challenges.

The Court sought to accommodate the prosecutor's historical privilege of peremptory challenge free of judicial control, and the constitutional prohibition on exclusion of persons from jury service on account of race. While the Constitution does not confer a right to peremptory challenges, those challenges traditionally have been viewed as one means of assuring the selection of a qualified and

---

    [4] In this Court, petitioner has argued that the prosecutor's conduct violated his rights under the Sixth and Fourteenth Amendments to an impartial jury and to a jury drawn from a cross-section of the community. Petitioner has framed his argument in these terms in an apparent effort to avoid inviting the Court directly to reconsider one of its own precedents. On the other hand, the State has insisted that petitioner is claiming a denial of equal protection and that we must reconsider *Swain* to find a constitutional violation on this record. We agree with the State that resolution of petitioner's claim properly turns on application of equal protection principles and express no view on the merits of any of petitioner's Sixth Amendment arguments.

    [Editors' note: Later in *Holland v. Illinois*, 493 U.S. 474 (1990), the Court rejected, 5–4, "the thesis that a prosecutor's use of peremptory challenges to eliminate a distinctive group in the community deprives the defendant of a Sixth Amendment right to the 'fair possibility' of a representative jury. While statements in our prior cases have alluded to such a 'fair possibility' requirement, satisfying it has not been held to require anything beyond the inclusion of all cognizable groups in the venire, and the use of a jury numbering at least six persons."]

unbiased jury.[15] To preserve the peremptory nature of the prosecutor's challenge, the Court in *Swain* declined to scrutinize his actions in a particular case by relying on a presumption that he properly exercised the State's challenges.

The Court went on to observe, however, that a state may not exercise its challenges in contravention of the Equal Protection Clause. It was impermissible for a prosecutor to use his challenges to exclude blacks from the jury "for reasons wholly unrelated to the outcome of the particular case on trial" or to deny to blacks "the same right and opportunity to participate in the administration of justice enjoyed by the white population." Accordingly, a black defendant could make out a prima facie case of purposeful discrimination on proof that the peremptory challenge system was "being perverted" in that manner. For example, an inference of purposeful discrimination would be raised on evidence that a prosecutor, "in case after case, whatever the circumstances, whatever the crime and whoever the defendant or the victim may be, is responsible for the removal of Negroes who have been selected as qualified jurors by the jury commissioners and who have survived challenges for cause, with the result that no Negroes ever serve on petit juries." Evidence offered by the defendant in *Swain* did not meet that standard. While the defendant showed that prosecutors in the jurisdiction had exercised their strikes to exclude blacks from the jury, he offered no proof of the circumstances under which prosecutors were responsible for striking black jurors beyond the facts of his own case.

A number of lower courts following the teaching of *Swain* reasoned that proof of repeated striking of blacks over a number of cases was necessary to establish a violation of the Equal Protection Clause. Since this interpretation of *Swain* has placed on defendants a crippling burden of proof,[17] prosecutors' peremptory challenges are now largely immune from constitutional scrutiny. For reasons that follow, we reject this evidentiary formulation as inconsistent with standards that have been developed since *Swain* for assessing a prima facie case under the Equal Protection Clause.

[S]ince the decision in *Swain,* this Court has recognized that a defendant may make a prima facie showing of purposeful racial discrimination in selection of the venire by relying solely on the facts concerning its selection *in his case.* These decisions are in accordance with the proposition that "a consistent pattern of official racial discrimination" is not "a necessary predicate to a violation of the Equal Protection Clause. A single invidiously discriminatory governmental act" is not "immunized by the absence of such discrimination in the making of other comparable decisions." For evidentiary requirements to dictate that "several must

---

[15] In *Swain*, the Court reviewed the "very old credentials" of the peremptory challenge system and noted the "long and widely held belief that peremptory challenge is a necessary part of trial by jury."

[17] The lower courts have noted the practical difficulties of proving that the State systematically has exercised peremptory challenges to exclude blacks from the jury on account of race. [T]he defendant would have to investigate, over a number of cases, the race of persons tried in the particular jurisdiction, the racial composition of the venire and petit jury, and the manner in which both parties exercised their peremptory challenges. * * * In jurisdictions where court records do not reflect the jurors' race and where *voir dire* proceedings are not transcribed, the burden would be insurmountable.

suffer discrimination" before one could object, would be inconsistent with the promise of equal protection to all.

The standards for assessing a prima facie case in the context of discriminatory selection of the venire have been fully articulated since *Swain*. These principles support our conclusion that a defendant may establish a prima facie case of purposeful discrimination in selection of the petit jury solely on evidence concerning the prosecutor's exercise of peremptory challenges at the defendant's trial. To establish such a case, the defendant first must show that he is a member of a cognizable racial group, and that the prosecutor has exercised peremptory challenges to remove from the venire members of the defendant's race. Second, the defendant is entitled to rely on the fact, as to which there can be no dispute, that peremptory challenges constitute a jury selection practice that permits "those to discriminate who are of a mind to discriminate." Finally, the defendant must show that these facts and any other relevant circumstances raise an inference that the prosecutor used that practice to exclude the veniremen from the petit jury on account of their race. This combination of factors in the empanelling of the petit jury, as in the selection of the venire, raises the necessary inference of purposeful discrimination.

In deciding whether the defendant has made the requisite showing, the trial court should consider all relevant circumstances. For example, a "pattern" of strikes against black jurors included in the particular venire might give rise to an inference of discrimination. Similarly, the prosecutor's questions and statements during *voir dire* examination and in exercising his challenges may support or refute an inference of discriminatory purpose. These examples are merely illustrative. We have confidence that trial judges, experienced in supervising *voir dire,* will be able to decide if the circumstances concerning the prosecutor's use of peremptory challenges creates a prima facie case of discrimination against black jurors.

Once the defendant makes a prima facie showing, the burden shifts to the State to come forward with a neutral explanation for challenging black jurors. Though this requirement imposes a limitation in some cases on the full peremptory character of the historic challenge, we emphasize that the prosecutor's explanation need not rise to the level justifying exercise of a challenge for cause. But the prosecutor may not rebut the defendant's prima facie case of discrimination by stating merely that he challenged jurors of the defendant's race on the assumption—or his intuitive judgment—that they would be partial to the defendant because of their shared race. Just as the Equal Protection Clause forbids the States to exclude black persons from the venire on the assumption that blacks as a group are unqualified to serve as jurors, so it forbids the States to strike black veniremen on the assumption that they will be biased in a particular case simply because the defendant is black. The core guarantee of equal protection, ensuring citizens that their State will not discriminate on account of race, would be meaningless were we to approve the exclusion of jurors on the basis of such assumptions, which arise solely from the jurors' race. Nor may the prosecutor rebut the defendant's case merely by denying that he had a discriminatory motive or "affirming his good faith in individual selections." If these general assertions were accepted as rebutting a defendant's prima facie case, the Equal Protection Clause "would be but a vain and illusory requirement." The prosecutor therefore must articulate a neutral explanation related to the particular case to be tried. The trial court then will have the duty to determine if the defendant has established purposeful discrimination.

The State contends that our holding will eviscerate the fair trial values served by the peremptory challenge. Conceding that the Constitution does not guarantee a right to peremptory challenges and that *Swain* did state that their use ultimately is subject to the strictures of equal protection, the State argues that the privilege of unfettered exercise of the challenge is of vital importance to the criminal justice system.

While we recognize, of course, that the peremptory challenge occupies an important position in our trial procedures, we do not agree that our decision today will undermine the contribution the challenge generally makes to the administration of justice. The reality of practice, amply reflected in many state and federal court opinions, shows that the challenge may be, and unfortunately at times has been, used to discriminate against black jurors. By requiring trial courts to be sensitive to the racially discriminatory use of peremptory challenges, our decision enforces the mandate of equal protection and furthers the ends of justice.[22] In view of the heterogeneous population of our nation, public respect for our criminal justice system and the rule of law will be strengthened if we ensure that no citizen is disqualified from jury service because of his race.

Nor are we persuaded by the State's suggestion that our holding will create serious administrative difficulties. In those states applying a version of the evidentiary standard we recognize today, courts have not experienced serious administrative burdens, and the peremptory challenge system has survived. We decline, however, to formulate particular procedures to be followed upon a defendant's timely objection to a prosecutor's challenges.[24]

In this case, petitioner made a timely objection to the prosecutor's removal of all black persons on the venire. Because the trial court flatly rejected the objection without requiring the prosecutor to give an explanation for his action, we remand this case for further proceedings. If the trial court decides that the facts establish,

---

[22] While we respect the views expressed in Justice Marshall's concurring opinion, concerning prosecutorial and judicial enforcement of our holding today, we do not share them. The standard we adopt under the federal Constitution is designed to ensure that a State does not use peremptory challenges to strike any black juror because of his race. We have no reason to believe that prosecutors will not fulfill their duty to exercise their challenges only for legitimate purposes. Certainly, this Court may assume that trial judges, in supervising *voir dire* in light of our decision today, will be alert to identify a prima facie case of purposeful discrimination. Nor do we think that this historic trial practice, which long has served the selection of an impartial jury, should be abolished because of an apprehension that prosecutors and trial judges will not perform conscientiously their respective duties under the Constitution.

[24] In light of the variety of jury selection practices followed in our state and federal trial courts, we make no attempt to instruct these courts how best to implement our holding today. For the same reason, we express no view on whether it is more appropriate in a particular case, upon a finding of discrimination against black jurors, for the trial court to discharge the venire and select a new jury from a panel not previously associated with the case, or to disallow the discriminatory challenges and resume selection with the improperly challenged jurors reinstated on the venire.

prima facie, purposeful discrimination and the prosecutor does not come forward with a neutral explanation for his action, our precedents require that petitioner's conviction be reversed.

JUSTICE MARSHALL, concurring. * * *

I wholeheartedly concur in the Court's conclusion that use of the peremptory challenge to remove blacks from juries, on the basis of their race, violates the Equal Protection Clause. I would go further, however, in fashioning a remedy adequate to eliminate that discrimination. Merely allowing defendants the opportunity to challenge the racially discriminatory use of peremptory challenges in individual cases will not end the illegitimate use of the peremptory challenge.

Evidentiary analysis similar to that set out by the Court has been adopted as a matter of state law in States including Massachusetts and California. Cases from those jurisdictions illustrate the limitations of the approach. First, defendants cannot attack the discriminatory use of peremptory challenges at all unless the challenges are so flagrant as to establish a prima facie case. This means, in those States, that where only one or two black jurors survive the challenges for cause, the prosecutor need have no compunction about striking them from the jury because of their race. Prosecutors are left free to discriminate against blacks in jury selection provided that they hold that discrimination to an "acceptable" level.

Second, when a defendant can establish a prima facie case, trial courts face the difficult burden of assessing prosecutors' motives. Any prosecutor can easily assert facially neutral reasons for striking a juror, and trial courts are ill-equipped to second-guess those reasons. How is the court to treat a prosecutor's statement that he struck a juror because the juror had a son about the same age as defendant, or seemed "uncommunicative," or "never cracked a smile" and, therefore "did not possess the sensitivities necessary to realistically look at the issues and decide the facts in this case." If such easily generated explanations are sufficient to discharge the prosecutor's obligation to justify his strikes on nonracial grounds, then the protection erected by the Court today may be illusory.

Nor is outright prevarication by prosecutors the only danger here. "[I]t is even possible that an attorney may lie to himself in an effort to convince himself that his motives are legal." A prosecutor's own conscious or unconscious racism may lead him easily to the conclusion that a prospective black juror is "sullen," or "distant," a characterization that would not have come to his mind if a white juror had acted identically. A judge's own conscious or unconscious racism may lead him to accept such an explanation as well supported. * * *

The inherent potential of peremptory challenges to distort the jury process by permitting the exclusion of jurors on racial grounds should ideally lead the Court to ban them entirely from the criminal justice system. * * *

Some authors have suggested that the courts should ban prosecutors' peremptories entirely, but should zealously guard the defendant's peremptory as "essential to the fairness of trial by jury" and "one of the most important of the rights secured to the accused." I would not find that an acceptable solution. Our criminal justice system "requires not only freedom from any bias against the accused, but also from any prejudice against his prosecution. Between him and the state the scales are to be evenly held." We can maintain that balance, not by permitting both prosecutor and defendant to engage in racial discrimination in jury selection, but by banning the use of peremptory challenges by prosecutors and by allowing the States to eliminate the defendant's peremptory as well. * * *

CHIEF JUSTICE BURGER, joined by JUSTICE REHNQUIST, dissenting.

* * * The Court acknowledges, albeit in a footnote, the " 'very old credentials' " of the peremptory challenge and " 'the widely held belief that peremptory challenge is a necessary part of trial by jury.' " But proper resolution of this case requires more than a nodding reference to the purpose of the challenge. * * *

The Court's opinion, in addition to ignoring the teachings of history, also contrasts with *Swain* in its failure to even discuss the rationale of the peremptory challenge. *Swain* observed:

> "The function of the challenge is not only to eliminate extremes of partiality on both sides, but to assure the parties that the jurors before whom they try the case will decide on the basis of the evidence placed for them, and not otherwise. In this way the peremptory satisfies the rule that 'to perform its high function in the best way, justice must satisfy the appearance of justice.' "

Permitting unexplained peremptories has long been regarded as a means to strengthen our jury system in other ways as well. One commentator has recognized:

> "The peremptory, made without giving any reason, avoids trafficking in the core of truth in most common stereotypes. * * * Common human experience, common sense, psychosociological studies, and public opinion polls tell us that it is likely that certain classes of people statistically have predispositions that would make them inappropriate jurors for particular kinds of cases. But to allow this knowledge to be expressed in the evaluative terms necessary for challenges for cause would undercut our desire for a society in which all people are judged as individuals and in which each is held reasonable and open to compromise. * * * [For example,] [a]lthough experience reveals that black males as a class can be biased against young alienated blacks who have not tried to join the middle class, to enunciate this in the concrete expression required of a challenge for cause is societally divisive. Instead we have evolved in the peremptory challenge a system that allows the covert expression of what we dare not say but know is true more often than not."

For reasons such as these, this Court concluded in *Swain* that "the [peremptory] challenge is 'one of the most important of the rights' " in our justice system. For close to a century, then, it has been settled that "[t]he denial or impairment of the right is reversible error without a showing of prejudice."

[T]he Court also invokes general equal protection principles in support of its holding. But peremptory challenges are often lodged, of necessity, for reasons "normally thought irrelevant to legal proceedings or official action, namely, the race, religion, nationality, occupation or affiliations of people summoned for jury duty." *Swain*. Moreover, in making peremptory challenges, both the prosecutor and defense attorney necessarily act on only limited information or hunch. The process can not be indicted on the sole basis that such decisions are made on the basis of "assumption" or "intuitive judgment." As a result, unadulterated equal protection analysis is simply inapplicable to peremptory challenges exercised in any particular case. A clause that requires a minimum "rationality" in government actions has no application to " 'an arbitrary and capricious right' "; a constitutional principle that may invalidate state action on the basis of "stereotypic notions" does not explain the breadth of a procedure exercised on the " 'sudden impressions and unaccountable prejudices we are apt to conceive upon the bare looks and gestures of another.' "

That the Court is not applying conventional equal protection analysis is shown by its limitation of its new rule to allegations of impermissible challenge *on the basis of race;* the Court's opinion clearly contains such a limitation. * * * But if conventional equal protection principles apply, then presumably defendants could object to exclusions on the basis of not only race, but also sex, age, religious or political affiliation, mental capacity, number of children, living arrangements, and employment in a particular industry or profession.[4]

In short, it is quite probable that every peremptory challenge could be objected to on the basis that, because it excluded a venireman who had some characteristic not shared by the remaining members of the venire, it constituted a "classification" subject to equal protection scrutiny. Compounding the difficulties, under conventional equal protection principles some uses of peremptories would be reviewed under "strict scrutiny and * * * sustained only if * * * suitably tailored to serve a compelling state interest," others would be reviewed to determine if they were "substantially related to a sufficiently important government interest," and still others would be reviewed to determine whether they were "a rational means to serve a legitimate end."

The Court never applies this conventional equal protection framework to the claims at hand, perhaps to avoid acknowledging that the state interest involved here has historically been regarded by this Court as substantial, if not compelling. * * *

The Court also purports to express "no views on whether the Constitution imposes any limit on the exercise of peremptory challenges by *defense* counsel." But the clear and inescapable import of this novel holding will inevitably be to limit the use of this valuable tool to both prosecutors and defense attorneys alike. Once the Court has held that *prosecutors* are limited in their use of peremptory challenges, could we rationally hold that defendants are not?[6] * * *

---

[4] While all these distinctions might support a claim under conventional equal protection principles, a defendant would also have to establish standing to raise them before obtaining any relief.

[6] "[E]very jurisdiction which has spoken to the matter, and prohibited prosecution case-specific peremptory challenges on the basis of cognizable group affiliation, has held that the defense must likewise be so prohibited."

Confronted with the dilemma it created, the Court today attempts to decree a middle ground. To rebut a prima facie case, the Court requires a "neutral explanation" for the challenge, but is at pains to "emphasize" that the "explanation need not rise to the level justifying exercise of a challenge for cause." I am at a loss to discern the governing principles here. A "clear and reasonably specific" explanation of "legitimate reasons" for exercising the challenge will be difficult to distinguish from a challenge for cause. Anything short of a challenge for cause may well be seen as an "arbitrary and capricious" challenge, to use Blackstone's characterization of the peremptory. Apparently the Court envisions permissible challenges short of a challenge for cause that are just a little bit arbitrary—but not too much. While our trial judges are "experienced in supervising *voir dire*," they have no experience in administering rules like this.

An example will quickly demonstrate how today's holding, while purporting to "further the ends of justice," will not have that effect. Assume an Asian defendant, on trial for the capital murder of a white victim, asks prospective jury members, most of whom are white, whether they harbor racial prejudice against Asians. The basis for such a question is to flush out any "juror who believes that [Asians] are violence-prone or morally inferior." * * * Assume further that all white jurors deny harboring racial prejudice but that the defendant, on trial for his life, remains unconvinced by these protestations. Instead, he continues to harbor a hunch, an "assumption" or "intuitive judgment," that these white jurors will be prejudiced against him, presumably based in part on race. The time honored rule before today was that peremptory challenges could be exercised on such a basis. * * * The effect of the Court's decision, however, will be to force the defendant to come forward and "articulate a neutral explanation," for his peremptory challenge, a burden he probably cannot meet. This example demonstrates that today's holding will produce juries that the parties do not believe are truly impartial. This will surely do more than "disconcert" litigants; it will diminish confidence in the jury system. * * *

Today we mark the return of racial differentiation as the Court accepts a positive evil for a perceived one. Prosecutors and defense attorneys alike will build records in support of their claims that peremptory challenges have been exercised in a racially discriminatory fashion by asking jurors to state their racial background and national origin for the record, despite the fact that "such questions may be offensive to some jurors and thus are not ordinarily asked on voir dire." This process is sure to tax even the most capable counsel and judges since determining whether a prima facie case has been established will "require a continued monitoring and recording of the 'group' composition of the panel present and prospective. * * *" * * *

JUSTICE REHNQUIST with whom THE CHIEF JUSTICE joins, dissenting. * * *

I cannot subscribe to the Court's unprecedented use of the Equal Protection Clause to restrict the historic scope of the peremptory challenge, which has been described as "a necessary part of trial by jury." In my view, there is simply nothing "unequal" about the State using its peremptory challenges to strike blacks from the jury in cases involving black defendants, so long as such challenges are also used to exclude whites in cases involving white defendants, Hispanics in cases involving Hispanic defendants, Asians in cases involving Asian defendants, and so on. This case-specific use of peremptory challenges by the State does not single out blacks, or members of any other race for that matter, for discriminatory treatment. Such use of peremptories is at best based upon seat-of-the-pants instincts, which are undoubtedly crudely stereotypical and may in many cases be hopelessly mistaken. But as long as they are applied across the board to jurors of all races and nationalities, I do not see—and the Court most certainly has not explained—how their use violates the Equal Protection Clause.

Nor does such use of peremptory challenges by the State infringe upon any other constitutional interests. The Court does not suggest that exclusion of blacks from the jury through the State's use of peremptory challenges results in a violation of either the fair cross-section or impartiality component of the Sixth Amendment. And because the case-specific use of peremptory challenges by the State does not deny blacks the right to serve as jurors in cases involving non-black defendants, it harms neither the excluded jurors nor the remainder of the community.

The use of group affiliations, such as age, race, or occupation, as a "proxy" for potential juror partiality, based on the assumption or belief that members of one group are more likely to favor defendants who belong to the same group, has long been accepted as a legitimate basis for the State's exercise of peremptory challenges. Indeed, given the need for reasonable limitations on the time devoted to *voir dire,* the use of such "proxies" by both the State and the defendant may be extremely useful in eliminating from the jury persons who might be biased in one way or another. * * *

*Note: Post-*Batson *Developments*

In *Flowers v. Mississippi,* 139 S.Ct. 2228 (2019), the Court invalidated the defendant's conviction and death sentence after he had been tried for the sixth time. Of Mississippi's five earlier attempts to prosecute him, two had been reversed for prosecutorial misconduct, one for *Batson* error, and two ended in hung juries. In a fact-intensive decision applying the *Batson* framework, the Court found the trial judge clearly erred by concluding that the State's peremptory strike of a black prospective juror was not motivated in substantial part by discriminatory. The decision included the following summary the *Batson* doctrine:

* * * By taking steps to eradicate racial discrimination from the jury selection process, *Batson* sought to protect the rights of defendants and jurors, and to enhance public confidence in the fairness of the criminal justice system. *Batson* immediately revolutionized the jury selection process that takes place every day in federal and state criminal courtrooms throughout the United States.

In the decades since *Batson,* this Court's cases have vigorously enforced and reinforced the decision, and guarded against any backsliding. See *Foster v. Chatman,* 136 S.Ct. 1737 (2016); *Snyder v. Louisiana,* 552 U.S. 472 (2008); *Miller-El v. Dretke,* 545 U.S. 231 (2005). Moreover, the Court has extended *Batson* in certain ways. A defendant of any race may raise a *Batson* claim, and a defendant may raise a *Batson* claim even if the defendant and the excluded juror are of different races. See *Hernandez v. New York*, 500 U.S. 352 (1991); *Powers v. Ohio*, 499 U.S. 400 (1991). Moreover, *Batson* now applies to gender discrimination, to a criminal defendant's peremptory strikes, and to civil cases. See *J. E. B. v. Alabama ex rel. T. B.*, 511 U.S. 127 (1994); *Georgia v. McCollum*, 505 U.S. 42 (1992); *Edmonson v. Leesville Concrete Co.*, 500 U.S. 614 (1991).

Of particular relevance here, *Batson*'s holding raised several important evidentiary and procedural issues, three of which we underscore.

First, what factors does the trial judge consider in evaluating whether racial discrimination occurred? Our precedents allow criminal defendants raising *Batson* challenges to present a variety of evidence to support a claim that a prosecutor's peremptory strikes were made on the basis of race. For example, defendants may present:

- statistical evidence about the prosecutor's use of peremptory strikes against black prospective jurors as compared to white prospective jurors in the case;

- evidence of a prosecutor's disparate questioning and investigation of black and white prospective jurors in the case;

- side-by-side comparisons of black prospective jurors who were struck and white prospective jurors who were not struck in the case;

- a prosecutor's misrepresentations of the record when defending the strikes during the *Batson* hearing;

- relevant history of the State's peremptory strikes in past cases; or

- other relevant circumstances that bear upon the issue of racial discrimination.

Second, who enforces *Batson*? As the *Batson* Court itself recognized, the job of enforcing *Batson* rests first and foremost with trial judges. America's trial judges operate at the front lines of American justice. In criminal trials, trial judges possess the primary responsibility to enforce *Batson* and prevent racial discrimination from seeping into the jury selection process.

As the *Batson* Court explained and as the Court later reiterated, once a prima facie case of racial discrimination has been established, the prosecutor must provide race-neutral reasons for the strikes. The trial court must consider the prosecutor's race-neutral explanations in light of all of the relevant facts and circumstances, and in light of the arguments of the parties. The trial judge's assessment of the prosecutor's credibility is often important. The Court has explained that "the best evidence of discriminatory intent often will be the demeanor of the attorney who exercises the challenge "We have recognized that these determinations of credibility and demeanor lie peculiarly within a trial judge's province." The trial judge must determine whether the prosecutor's proffered reasons are the actual reasons, or whether the proffered reasons are pretextual and the prosecutor instead exercised peremptory strikes on the basis of race. The ultimate inquiry is whether the State was "motivated in substantial part by discriminatory intent."

Third, what is the role of appellate review? An appeals court looks at the same factors as the trial judge, but is necessarily doing so on a paper record. "Since the trial judge's findings in the context under consideration here largely will turn on evaluation of credibility, a reviewing court ordinarily should give those findings great deference." The Court has described the appellate standard of review of the trial court's factual determinations in a *Batson* hearing as "highly deferential." "On appeal, a trial court's ruling on the issue of discriminatory intent must be sustained unless it is clearly erroneous." * * *

PEÑA-RODRIGUEZ V. COLORADO
580 U.S. ___, 137 S.Ct. 855, 197 L.Ed.2d 107 (2017).

JUSTICE KENNEDY delivered the opinion of the Court.

The jury is a central foundation of our justice system and our democracy. Whatever its imperfections in a particular case, the jury is a necessary check on governmental power. The jury, over the centuries, has been an inspired, trusted, and effective instrument for resolving factual disputes and determining ultimate questions of guilt or innocence in criminal cases. Over the long course its judgments find acceptance in the community, an acceptance essential to respect for the rule of law. The jury is a tangible implementation of the principle that the law comes from the people.

In the era of our Nation's founding, the right to a jury trial already had existed and evolved for centuries, through and alongside the common law. The jury was considered a fundamental safeguard of individual liberty. See The Federalist No. 83, p. 451 (B. Warner ed. 1818) (A. Hamilton). The right to a jury trial in criminal cases was part of the Constitution as first drawn, and it was restated in the Sixth Amendment. Art. III, § 2, cl. 3; Amdt. 6. By operation of the Fourteenth Amendment, it is applicable to the States. *Duncan v. Louisiana,* 391 U.S. 145, 149–150, 88 S.Ct. 1444, 20 L.Ed.2d 491 (1968).

Like all human institutions, the jury system has its flaws, yet experience shows that fair and impartial verdicts can be reached if the jury follows the court's instructions and undertakes deliberations that are honest, candid, robust, and based on common sense. A general rule has evolved to give substantial protection to verdict finality and to assure jurors that, once their verdict has been entered, it will not later be called into question based on the comments or conclusions they expressed during deliberations. This principle, itself centuries old, is often referred to as the no-impeachment rule. The instant case presents the question whether there is an exception to the no-impeachment rule when, after the jury is discharged, a juror comes forward with compelling evidence that another juror made clear and explicit statements indicating that racial animus was a significant motivating factor in his or her vote to convict.

I

State prosecutors in Colorado brought criminal charges against petitioner, Miguel Angel Peña-Rodriguez, based on the following allegations. In 2007, in the bathroom of a Colorado horse-racing facility, a man sexually assaulted two teenage sisters. The girls told their father and identified the man as an employee of the racetrack. The police located and arrested petitioner. Each girl separately identified petitioner as the man who had assaulted her.

The State charged petitioner with harassment, unlawful sexual contact, and attempted sexual assault on a child. Before the jury was empaneled, members of the venire were repeatedly asked whether they believed that they could be fair and impartial in the case. A written questionnaire asked if there was "anything about you that you feel would make it difficult for you to be a fair juror." The court repeated the question to the panel of prospective jurors and encouraged jurors to speak in private with the court if they had any concerns about their impartiality. Defense counsel likewise asked whether anyone felt that "this is simply not a good case" for them to be a fair juror. None of the empaneled jurors expressed any reservations based on racial or any other bias. And none asked to speak with the trial judge.

After a 3-day trial, the jury found petitioner guilty of unlawful sexual contact and harassment, but it failed to reach a verdict on the attempted sexual assault charge. When the jury was discharged, the court gave them this instruction, as mandated by Colorado law:

"The question may arise whether you may now discuss this case with the lawyers, defendant, or other persons. For your guidance the court instructs you that whether you talk to anyone is entirely your own decision. . . . If any person persists in discussing the case over your objection, or becomes critical of your service either before or after any discussion has begun, please report it to me."

Following the discharge of the jury, petitioner's counsel entered the jury room to discuss the trial with the jurors. As the room was emptying, two jurors remained to speak with counsel in private. They stated that, during deliberations, another juror had expressed anti-Hispanic bias toward petitioner and petitioner's alibi witness. Petitioner's counsel reported this to the court and, with the court's supervision, obtained sworn affidavits from the two jurors.

The affidavits by the two jurors described a number of biased statements made by another juror, identified as Juror H.C. According to the two jurors, H.C. told the other jurors that he "believed the defendant was guilty because, in [H.C.'s] experience as an ex-law enforcement officer, Mexican men had a bravado that caused them to believe they could do whatever they wanted with women." The jurors reported that H.C. stated his belief that Mexican men are physically controlling of women because of their sense of entitlement, and further stated, " 'I think he did it because he's Mexican and Mexican men take whatever they want.' " According to the jurors, H.C. further explained that, in his experience, "nine times out of ten Mexican men were guilty of being aggressive toward women and young girls." Finally, the jurors recounted that Juror H.C. said that he did not find petitioner's alibi witness credible because, among other things, the witness was " 'an illegal.' " (In fact, the witness testified during trial that he was a legal resident of the United States.)

After reviewing the affidavits, the trial court acknowledged H.C.'s apparent bias. But the court denied petitioner's motion for a new trial, noting that "[t]he actual deliberations that occur among the jurors are protected from inquiry under [Colorado Rule of Evidence] 606(b)." Like its federal counterpart, Colorado's Rule 606(b) generally prohibits a juror from testifying as to any statement made during deliberations in a proceeding inquiring into the validity of the verdict. The Colorado Rule reads as follows:

"(b) Inquiry into validity of verdict or indictment. Upon an inquiry into the validity of a verdict or indictment, a juror may not testify as to any matter or statement occurring during the course of the jury's deliberations or to the effect of anything upon his or any other juror's mind or emotions as influencing him to assent to or dissent from the verdict or indictment or concerning his mental processes in connection therewith. But a juror may testify about (1) whether extraneous prejudicial information was improperly brought to the jurors' attention, (2) whether any outside influence was improperly brought to bear upon any juror, or (3) whether there was a mistake in entering the verdict onto the verdict form. A juror's affidavit or evidence of any statement by the juror may not be received on a matter about which the juror would be precluded from testifying." Colo. Rule Evid. 606(b) (2016).

The verdict deemed final, petitioner was sentenced to two years' probation and was required to register as a sex offender. A divided panel of the Colorado Court of Appeals affirmed petitioner's conviction, agreeing that H.C.'s alleged statements did not fall within an exception to Rule 606(b) and so were inadmissible to undermine the validity of the verdict.

The Colorado Supreme Court affirmed * * *. This Court granted certiorari to decide whether there is a constitutional exception to the no-impeachment rule for instances of racial bias.

Juror H.C.'s bias was based on petitioner's Hispanic identity, which the Court in prior cases has referred to as ethnicity, and that may be an instructive term here. Yet we have also used the language of race when discussing the relevant constitutional principles in cases involving Hispanic persons. Petitioner and respondent both refer to race, or to race and ethnicity, in this more expansive sense in their briefs to the Court. This opinion refers to the nature of the bias as racial in keeping with the primary terminology employed by the parties and used in our precedents.

II

A

At common law jurors were forbidden to impeach their verdict, either by affidavit or live testimony. This rule originated in *Vaise v. Delaval,* 1 T.R. 11, 99 Eng. Rep. 944 (K.B. 1785). There, Lord Mansfield excluded juror testimony that the jury had decided the case through a game of chance. The Mansfield rule, as it came to be known, prohibited jurors, after the verdict was entered, from testifying either about their subjective mental processes or about objective events that occurred during deliberations.

American courts adopted the Mansfield rule as a matter of common law, though not in every detail. Some jurisdictions adopted a different, more flexible version of the no-impeachment bar known as the "Iowa rule." Under that rule, jurors were prevented only from testifying about their own subjective beliefs, thoughts, or motives during deliberations. Jurors could, however, testify about objective facts and events occurring during deliberations, in part because other jurors could corroborate that testimony.

An alternative approach, later referred to as the federal approach, stayed closer to the original Mansfield rule. Under this version of the rule, the no-impeachment bar permitted an exception only for testimony about events extraneous to the deliberative process, such as reliance on outside evidence—newspapers, dictionaries, and the like—or personal investigation of the facts.

This Court's early decisions did not establish a clear preference for a particular version of the no-impeachment rule. * * * Later, however, the Court rejected the more lenient Iowa rule. In *McDonald v. Pless*, 238 U.S. 264 (1915), the Court affirmed the exclusion of juror testimony about objective events in the jury room. There, the jury allegedly had calculated a damages award by averaging the numerical submissions of each member. As the Court explained, admitting that evidence would have "dangerous consequences": "no verdict would be safe" and the practice would "open the door to the most pernicious arts and tampering with jurors." Yet the Court reiterated its admonition from *Reid,* again cautioning that the no-impeachment rule might recognize exceptions "in the gravest and most important cases" where exclusion of juror affidavits might well violate "the plainest principles of justice."

The common-law development of the no-impeachment rule reached a milestone in 1975, when Congress adopted the Federal Rules of Evidence, including Rule 606(b). Congress, like the *McDonald* Court, rejected the Iowa rule. Instead it endorsed a broad no-impeachment rule, with only limited exceptions.

The version of the rule that Congress adopted was "no accident." The Advisory Committee at first drafted a rule reflecting the Iowa approach, prohibiting admission of juror testimony only as it related to jurors' mental processes in reaching a verdict. The Department of Justice, however, expressed concern over the preliminary rule. The Advisory Committee then drafted the more stringent version now in effect, prohibiting all juror testimony, with exceptions only where the jury had considered prejudicial extraneous evidence or was subject to other outside influence. The Court adopted this second version and transmitted it to Congress.

The House favored the Iowa approach, but the Senate expressed concern that it did not sufficiently address the public policy interest in the finality of verdicts. Siding with the Senate, the Conference Committee adopted, Congress enacted, and the President signed the Court's proposed rule. The substance of the Rule has not changed since 1975, except for a 2006 modification permitting evidence of a clerical mistake on the verdict form.

The current version of Rule 606(b) states as follows:

"(1) *Prohibited Testimony or Other Evidence.* During an inquiry into the validity of a verdict or indictment, a juror may not testify about any statement made or incident that occurred during the jury's deliberations; the effect of anything on that juror's or another juror's vote; or any juror's mental processes concerning the verdict or indictment. The court may not receive a juror's affidavit or evidence of a juror's statement on these matters.

"(2) *Exceptions.* A juror may testify about whether:

"(A) extraneous prejudicial information was improperly brought to the jury's attention;

"(B) an outside influence was improperly brought to bear on any juror; or

"(C) a mistake was made in entering the verdict on the verdict form."

This version of the no-impeachment rule has substantial merit. It promotes full and vigorous discussion by providing jurors with considerable assurance that after being discharged they will not be summoned to recount their deliberations, and they will not otherwise be harassed or annoyed by litigants seeking to challenge the verdict. The rule gives stability and finality to verdicts.

* * *

C

In addressing the scope of the common-law no-impeachment rule before Rule 606(b)'s adoption, the [Court] noted the possibility of an exception to the rule in the "gravest and most important cases." *McDonald.* Yet since the enactment of Rule 606(b), the Court has addressed the precise question whether the Constitution mandates an exception to it in just two instances.

In its first case, *Tanner v. United States,* 483 U.S. 107 (1987), the Court rejected a Sixth Amendment exception for evidence that some jurors were under the influence of drugs and alcohol during the trial. Central to the Court's reasoning were the "long-recognized and very substantial concerns" supporting "the protection of jury deliberations from intrusive inquiry." The *Tanner* Court echoed *McDonald*'s concern that, if attorneys could use juror testimony to attack verdicts, jurors would be "harassed and beset by the defeated party," thus destroying "all frankness and freedom of discussion and conference." The Court was concerned, moreover, that attempts to impeach a verdict would "disrupt the finality of the process" and undermine both "jurors' willingness to return an unpopular verdict" and "the community's trust in a system that relies on the decisions of laypeople."

The *Tanner* Court outlined existing, significant safeguards for the defendant's right to an impartial and competent jury beyond post-trial juror testimony. At the outset of the trial process, *voir dire* provides an opportunity for the court and counsel to examine members of the venire for impartiality. As a trial proceeds, the court, counsel, and court personnel have some opportunity to learn of any juror misconduct. And, before the verdict, jurors themselves can report misconduct to the court. These procedures do not undermine the stability of a verdict once rendered. Even after the trial, evidence of misconduct other than juror testimony can be used to attempt to impeach the verdict. Balancing these interests and safeguards against the defendant's Sixth Amendment interest in that case, the Court affirmed the exclusion of affidavits pertaining to the jury's inebriated state. *Ibid.*

The second case to consider the general issue presented here was *Warger v. Shauers,* 574 U.S. ___, 135 S.Ct. 521 (2014). The Court again rejected the argument that, in the circumstances there, the jury trial right required an exception to the no-impeachment rule. *Warger* involved a civil case where, after the verdict was entered, the losing party sought to proffer evidence that the jury forewoman had failed to disclose prodefendant bias during *voir dire.* As in *Tanner,* the Court put substantial reliance on existing safeguards for a fair trial. The Court stated: "Even if jurors lie in *voir dire* in a way that conceals bias, juror impartiality is adequately assured by the parties' ability to bring to the court's attention any evidence of bias before the verdict is rendered, and to employ nonjuror evidence even after the verdict is rendered."

In *Warger,* however, the Court did reiterate that the no-impeachment rule may admit exceptions. As in *Reid* and *McDonald,* the Court warned of "juror bias so extreme that, almost by definition, the jury trial right has been abridged." "If and when such a case arises," the Court indicated it would "consider whether the usual safeguards are or are not sufficient to protect the integrity of the process."

The recognition in *Warger* that there may be extreme cases where the jury trial right requires an exception to the no-impeachment rule must be interpreted in context as a guarded, cautious statement. This caution is warranted to avoid formulating an exception that might undermine the jury dynamics and finality interests the no-impeachment rule seeks to protect. Today, however, the Court faces the question that *Reid, McDonald,* and *Warger* left open. The Court must decide whether the Constitution requires an exception to the no-impeachment rule when a juror's statements indicate that racial animus was a significant motivating factor in his or her finding of guilt.

III

It must become the heritage of our Nation to rise above racial classifications that are so inconsistent with our commitment to the equal dignity of all persons. This imperative to purge racial prejudice from the administration of justice was given new force and direction by the ratification of the Civil War Amendments.

"[T]he central purpose of the Fourteenth Amendment was to eliminate racial discrimination emanating from official sources in the States." *McLaughlin v. Florida,* 379 U.S. 184 (1964). In the years before and after the ratification of the Fourteenth Amendment, it became clear that racial discrimination in the jury system posed a particular threat both to the promise of the Amendment and to the integrity of the jury trial. "Almost immediately after the Civil War, the South began a practice that would continue for many decades: All-white juries punished black defendants particularly harshly, while simultaneously refusing to punish violence by whites, including Ku Klux Klan members, against blacks and Republicans." Forman, Juries and Race in the Nineteenth Century, 113 Yale L.J. 895, 909–910 (2004). To take one example, just in the years 1865 and 1866, all-white juries in Texas decided a total of 500 prosecutions of white defendants charged with killing African-Americans. All 500 were acquitted. The stark and unapologetic nature of race-motivated outcomes challenged the American belief that "the jury was a bulwark of liberty," and prompted Congress to pass legislation to integrate the jury system and to bar persons from eligibility for jury service if they had conspired to deny the civil rights of African-Americans. Members of Congress stressed that the legislation was necessary to preserve the right to a fair trial and to guarantee the equal protection of the laws.

The duty to confront racial animus in the justice system is not the legislature's alone. Time and again, this Court has been called upon to enforce the Constitution's guarantee against state-sponsored racial discrimination in the jury system. Beginning in 1880, the Court interpreted the Fourteenth Amendment to prohibit the exclusion of jurors on the basis of race. The Court has repeatedly struck down laws and practices that systematically exclude racial minorities from juries. To guard against discrimination in jury selection, the Court has ruled that no litigant may exclude a prospective juror on the basis of race. In an effort to ensure that individuals who sit on juries are free of racial bias, the Court has held that the Constitution at times demands that defendants be permitted to ask questions about racial bias during *voir dire*.

The unmistakable principle underlying these precedents is that discrimination on the basis of race, "odious in all aspects, is especially pernicious in the administration of justice." *Rose v. Mitchell,* 443 U.S. 545, 555 (1979). The jury is to be "a criminal defendant's fundamental 'protection of life and liberty against race or color prejudice.'" *McCleskey v. Kemp,* 481 U.S. 279, 310 (1987). Permitting racial prejudice in the jury system damages "both the fact and the perception" of the jury's role as "a vital check against the wrongful exercise of power by the State." *Powers v. Ohio,* 499 U.S. 400 (1991).

IV

A

This case lies at the intersection of the Court's decisions endorsing the no-impeachment rule and its decisions seeking to eliminate racial bias in the jury system. The two lines of precedent, however, need not conflict.

Racial bias of the kind alleged in this case differs in critical ways from the compromise verdict in *McDonald,* the drug and alcohol abuse in *Tanner,* or the pro-defendant bias in *Warger.* The behavior in those cases is troubling and unacceptable, but each involved anomalous behavior from a single jury—or juror—gone off course. Jurors are presumed to follow their oath, and neither history nor common experience show that the jury system is rife with mischief of these or similar kinds. To attempt to rid the jury of every irregularity of this sort would be to expose it to unrelenting scrutiny. "It is not at all clear . . . that the jury system could survive such efforts to perfect it." *Tanner*.

The same cannot be said about racial bias, a familiar and recurring evil that, if left unaddressed, would risk systemic injury to the administration of justice. This Court's decisions demonstrate that racial bias implicates unique historical, constitutional, and institutional concerns. An effort to address the most grave and serious statements of racial bias is not an effort to perfect the jury but to ensure that our legal system remains capable of coming ever closer to the promise of equal treatment under the law that is so central to a functioning democracy.

Racial bias is distinct in a pragmatic sense as well. In past cases this Court has relied on other safeguards to protect the right to an impartial jury. Some of those safeguards, to be sure, can disclose racial bias. *Voir dire* at the outset of trial, observation of juror demeanor and conduct during trial, juror reports before the verdict, and nonjuror evidence after trial are important mechanisms for discovering bias. Yet their operation may be compromised, or they may prove insufficient. For instance, this Court has noted the dilemma faced by trial court judges and counsel in deciding whether to explore potential racial bias at *voir dire*. Generic questions about juror impartiality may not expose specific attitudes or biases that can poison jury deliberations. Yet more pointed questions "could well exacerbate whatever prejudice might exist without substantially aiding in exposing it." *Rosales-Lopez v. United States*, 451 U.S. 182, 195 (1981) (Rehnquist, J., concurring in result).

The stigma that attends racial bias may make it difficult for a juror to report inappropriate statements during the course of juror deliberations. It is one thing to accuse a fellow juror of having a personal experience that improperly influences her consideration of the case, as would have been required in *Warger*. It is quite another to call her a bigot.

The recognition that certain of the *Tanner* safeguards may be less effective in rooting out racial bias than other kinds of bias is not dispositive. All forms of improper bias pose challenges to the trial process. But there is a sound basis to treat racial bias with added precaution. A constitutional rule that racial bias in the justice system must be addressed—including, in some instances, after the verdict has been entered—is necessary to prevent a systemic loss of confidence in jury verdicts, a confidence that is a central premise of the Sixth Amendment trial right.

B

For the reasons explained above, the Court now holds that where a juror makes a clear statement that indicates he or she relied on racial stereotypes or animus to convict a criminal defendant, the Sixth Amendment requires that the no-impeachment rule give way in order to permit the trial court to consider the evidence of the juror's statement and any resulting denial of the jury trial guarantee.

Not every offhand comment indicating racial bias or hostility will justify setting aside the no-impeachment bar to allow further judicial inquiry. For the inquiry to proceed, there must be a showing that one or more jurors made statements exhibiting overt racial bias that cast serious doubt on the fairness and impartiality of the jury's deliberations and resulting verdict. To qualify, the statement must tend to show that racial animus was a significant motivating factor in the juror's vote to convict. Whether that threshold showing has been satisfied is a matter committed to the substantial discretion of the trial court in light of all the circumstances, including the content and timing of the alleged statements and the reliability of the proffered evidence.

The practical mechanics of acquiring and presenting such evidence will no doubt be shaped and guided by state rules of professional ethics and local court rules, both of which often limit counsel's post-trial contact with jurors. These limits seek to provide jurors some protection when they return to their daily affairs after the verdict has been entered. But while a juror can always tell counsel they do not wish to discuss the case, jurors in some instances may come forward of their own accord.

That is what happened here. In this case the alleged statements by a juror were egregious and unmistakable in their reliance on racial bias. Not only did juror H.C. deploy a dangerous racial stereotype to conclude petitioner was guilty and his alibi witness should not be believed, but he also encouraged other jurors to join him in convicting on that basis.

Petitioner's counsel did not seek out the two jurors' allegations of racial bias. Pursuant to Colorado's mandatory jury instruction, the trial court had set limits on juror contact and encouraged jurors to inform the court if anyone harassed them about their role in the case. Similar limits on juror contact can be found in other jurisdictions that recognize a racial-bias exception.

With the understanding that they were under no obligation to speak out, the jurors approached petitioner's counsel, within a short time after the verdict, to relay their concerns about H.C.'s statements. * * * Pursuant to local court rules, petitioner's counsel then sought and received permission from the court to contact the two jurors and obtain affidavits limited to recounting the exact statements made by H.C. that exhibited racial bias.

While the trial court concluded that Colorado's Rule 606(b) did not permit it even to consider the resulting affidavits, the Court's holding today removes that bar. When jurors disclose an instance of racial bias as serious as the one involved in this case, the law must not wholly disregard its occurrence.

C

As the preceding discussion makes clear, the Court relies on the experiences of the 17 jurisdictions that have recognized a racial-bias exception to the no-impeachment rule—some for over half a century—with no signs of an increase in juror harassment or a loss of juror willingness to engage in searching and candid deliberations.

The experience of these jurisdictions, and the experience of the courts going forward, will inform the proper exercise of trial judge discretion in these and related matters. This case does not ask, and the Court need not address, what procedures a trial court must follow when confronted with a motion for a new trial based on juror testimony of racial bias. The Court also does not decide the appropriate standard for determining when evidence of racial bias is sufficient to require that the verdict be set aside and a new trial be granted. Compare, *Shillcutt*, 827 F.2d, at 1159 (inquiring whether racial bias "pervaded the jury room"), with, *e.g., Henley,* 238 F.3d, at 1120 ("One racist juror would be enough").

D

It is proper to observe as well that there are standard and existing processes designed to prevent racial bias in jury deliberations. The advantages of careful *voir dire* have already been noted. And other safeguards deserve mention.

Trial courts, often at the outset of the case and again in their final jury instructions, explain the jurors' duty to review the evidence and reach a verdict in a fair and impartial way, free from bias of any kind. Some instructions are framed by trial judges based on their own learning and experience. Model jury instructions likely take into account these continuing developments and are common across jurisdictions.

Probing and thoughtful deliberation improves the likelihood that other jurors can confront the flawed nature of reasoning that is prompted or influenced by improper biases, whether racial or otherwise. These dynamics can help ensure that the exception is limited to rare cases.

* * *

The Nation must continue to make strides to overcome race-based discrimination. The progress that has already been made underlies the Court's insistence that blatant racial prejudice is antithetical to the functioning of the jury system and must be confronted in egregious cases like this one despite the general bar of the no-impeachment rule. It is the mark of a maturing legal system that it seeks to understand and to implement the lessons of history. The Court now seeks to strengthen the broader principle that society can and must move forward by achieving the thoughtful, rational dialogue at the foundation of both the jury system and the free society that sustains our Constitution.

The judgment of the Supreme Court of Colorado is reversed, and the case is remanded for further proceedings not inconsistent with this opinion.

It is so ordered.

JUSTICE THOMAS, dissenting.

* * * I write separately to explain that the Court's holding also cannot be squared with the original understanding of the Sixth or Fourteenth Amendments. * * * At the time of the founding, the States took mixed approaches to this issue.* * * By the time the Fourteenth Amendment was ratified, Lord Mansfield's no-impeachment rule had become firmly entrenched in American law. * * * The vast majority of States adopted the no-impeachment rule as a matter of common law. * * * The Court today acknowledges that the States "adopted the Mansfield rule as a matter of common law," but ascribes no significance to that fact. I would hold that it is dispositive. Our common-law history does not establish that—in either 1791 (when the Sixth Amendment was ratified) or 1868 (when the Fourteenth Amendment was ratified)—a defendant had the right to impeach a verdict with juror testimony of juror misconduct. In fact, it strongly suggests that such evidence was prohibited. In the absence of a definitive common-law tradition permitting impeachment by juror testimony, we have no basis to invoke a constitutional provision that merely "follow[s] out the established course of the common law in all trials for crimes," 3 Story § 1785, at 662, to overturn Colorado's decision to preserve the no-impeachment rule.

* * *

Perhaps good reasons exist to curtail or abandon the no-impeachment rule. Some States have done so* * * and others have not. Ultimately, that question is not for us to decide. It should be left to the political process described by Justice ALITO. In its attempt to stimulate a "thoughtful, rational dialogue" on race relations, the Court today ends the political process and imposes a uniform, national rule. The Constitution does not require such a rule. Neither should we.

I respectfully dissent.

JUSTICE ALITO, with whom THE CHIEF JUSTICE and JUSTICE THOMAS join, dissenting.

* * * Juries occupy a unique place in our justice system. The other participants in a trial—the presiding judge, the attorneys, the witnesses—function in an arena governed by strict rules of law. Their every word is recorded and may be closely scrutinized for missteps.

When jurors retire to deliberate, however, they enter a space that is not regulated in the same way. Jurors are ordinary people. They are expected to speak, debate, argue, and make decisions the way ordinary people do in their daily lives. Our Constitution places great value on this way of thinking, speaking, and deciding. The jury trial right protects parties in court cases from being judged by a special class of trained professionals who do not speak the language of ordinary people and may not understand or appreciate the way ordinary people live their lives. To protect that right, the door to the jury room has been locked, and the confidentiality of jury deliberations has been closely guarded.

Today, with the admirable intention of providing justice for one criminal defendant, the Court not only pries open the door; it rules that respecting the privacy of the jury room, as our legal system has done for centuries, violates the Constitution. This is a startling development, and although the Court tries to limit the degree of intrusion, it is doubtful that there are principled grounds for preventing the expansion of today's holding.

The Court justifies its decision on the ground that the nature of the confidential communication at issue in this particular case—a clear expression of what the Court terms racial bias—is uniquely harmful to our criminal justice system. And the Court is surely correct that even a tincture of racial bias can inflict great damage on that system, which is dependent on the public's trust. But until today, the argument that the Court now finds convincing has not been thought to be sufficient to overcome confidentiality rules like the one at issue here.

Suppose that a prosecution witness gives devastating but false testimony against a defendant, and suppose that the witness's motivation is racial bias. Suppose that the witness admits this to his attorney, his spouse, and a member of the clergy. Suppose that the defendant, threatened with conviction for a serious crime and a lengthy term of imprisonment, seeks to compel the attorney, the spouse, or the member of the clergy to testify about the witness's admissions. Even though the constitutional rights of the defendant hang in the balance, the defendant's efforts to obtain the testimony would fail. The Court provides no good reason why the result in this case should not be the same.

I

* * * [T]he process that culminated in the adoption of Federal Rule of Evidence 606(b) was the epitome of reasoned democratic rulemaking. The "distinguished, Supreme Court-appointed" members of the Advisory Committee went through a 7-year drafting process, "produced two well-circulated drafts," and "considered numerous comments from persons involved in nearly every area of court-related law." Rothstein, The Proposed Amendments to the Federal Rules of Evidence, 62 Geo. L.J. 125 (1973). The work of the Committee was considered and approved by the experienced appellate and trial judges serving on the Judicial Conference and by our predecessors on this Court. After that, the matter went to Congress, which "specifically understood, considered, and rejected a version of [the rule] that would have allowed jurors to testify on juror conduct during deliberations." *Tanner*, 483 U.S., at 125. The judgment of all these participants in the process, which was informed by their assessment of an empirical issue, *i.e.*, the effect that the competing Iowa rule would have had on the jury system, is entitled to great respect. Colorado considered this same question, made the same judgment as the participants in the federal process, and adopted a very similar rule. In doing so, it joined the overwhelming majority of States. In the great majority of jurisdictions, strong no-impeachment rules continue to be "viewed as both promoting the finality of verdicts and insulating the jury from outside influences." *Warger*, 135 S.Ct., at 526.

II

A

Recognizing the importance of Rule 606(b), this Court has twice rebuffed efforts to create a Sixth Amendment exception—first in *Tanner* and then, just two Terms ago, in *Warger*.* * * Today, for the first time, the Court creates a constitutional exception to no-impeachment rules. Specifically, the Court holds that no-impeachment rules violate the Sixth Amendment to the extent that they preclude courts from considering evidence of a juror's racially biased comments. The Court attempts to distinguish *Tanner* and *Warger*, but its efforts fail.

Tanner and *Warger* rested on two basic propositions. First, no-impeachment rules advance crucial interests. Second, the right to trial by an impartial jury is adequately protected by mechanisms other than the use of juror testimony regarding jury deliberations. The first of these propositions applies regardless of the nature of the juror misconduct, and the Court does not argue otherwise. Instead, it contends that, in cases involving racially biased jurors, the *Tanner* safeguards are less effective and the defendant's Sixth Amendment interests are more profound. Neither argument is persuasive.

B

As noted above, *Tanner* identified four "aspects of the trial process" that protect a defendant's Sixth Amendment rights: (1) *voir dire*; (2) observation by the court, counsel, and court personnel; (3) pre-verdict reports by the jurors; and (4) non-juror evidence.[5] Although the Court insists that that these mechanisms "may be compromised" in cases involving allegations of racial bias, it addresses only two of them and fails to make a sustained argument about either.

1

First, the Court contends that the effectiveness of *voir dire* is questionable in cases involving racial bias because pointed questioning about racial attitudes may highlight racial issues and thereby exacerbate prejudice. *Ibid.* It is far from clear, however, that careful *voir dire* cannot surmount this problem. Lawyers may use questionnaires or individual questioning of prospective jurors in order to elicit frank answers that a juror might be reluctant to voice in the presence of other prospective jurors.[7] Moreover, practice guides are replete with advice on conducting effective *voir dire* on the subject of race. They outline a variety of subtle and nuanced approaches that avoid pointed questions. And of course, if an attorney is concerned that a juror is concealing bias, a peremptory strike may be used.[9]

The suggestion that *voir dire* is ineffective in unearthing bias runs counter to decisions of this Court holding that *voir dire* on the subject of race is constitutionally required in some cases, mandated as a matter of federal supervisory authority in others, and typically advisable in any case if a defendant requests it. If *voir dire* were not useful in identifying racial prejudice, those decisions would be pointless. Even the majority recognizes the "advantages of careful *voir dire* " as a "proces[s] designed to prevent racial bias in jury deliberations." And reported decisions substantiate that *voir dire* can be effective

---

[5] The majority opinion in this case identifies a fifth mechanism: jury instructions. It observes that, by explaining the jurors' responsibilities, appropriate jury instructions can promote "[p]robing and thoughtful deliberation," which in turn "improves the likelihood that other jurors can confront the flawed nature of reasoning that is prompted or influenced by improper biases." This mechanism, like those listed in Tanner, can help to prevent bias from infecting a verdict.

[7] See *People v. Harlan*, 8 P.3d 448, 500 (Colo.200) ("The trial court took precautions at the outset of the trial to foreclose the injection of improper racial considerations by including questions concerning racial issues in the jury questionnaire"); *Brewer v. Marshall*, 119 F.3d 993, 996 (C.A.1 1997) ("The judge asked each juror, out of the presence of other jurors, whether they had any bias or prejudice for or against black persons or persons of Hispanic origin"); 6 W. LaFave, J. Israel, N. King, & O. Kerr, Criminal Procedure § 22.3(a), p. 92 (4th ed.2015) (noting that "[j]udges commonly allow jurors to approach the bench and discuss sensitive matters there" and are also free to conduct "in chambers discussions").

[9] To the extent race does become salient during *voir dire,* there is social science research suggesting that this may actually combat rather than reinforce the jurors' biases.

in this regard. Thus, while *voir dire* is not a magic cure, there are good reasons to think that it is a valuable tool.

In any event, the critical point for present purposes is that the effectiveness of *voir dire* is a debatable empirical proposition. Its assessment should be addressed in the process of developing federal and state evidence rules. Federal and state rulemakers can try a variety of approaches, and they can make changes in response to the insights provided by experience and research. The approach taken by today's majority—imposing a federal constitutional rule on the entire country—prevents experimentation and makes change exceedingly hard.[10]

2

The majority also argues—even more cursorily—that "racial bias may make it difficult for a juror to report inappropriate statements during the course of juror deliberations." This is so, we are told, because it is difficult to "call [another juror] a bigot."

Since the Court's decision mandates the admission of the testimony of one juror about a statement made by another juror during deliberations, what the Court must mean in making this argument is that jurors are less willing to report biased comments by fellow jurors prior to the beginning of deliberations (while they are still sitting with the biased juror) than they are after the verdict is announced and the jurors have gone home. But this is also a questionable empirical assessment, and the Court's seat-of-the-pants judgment is no better than that of those with the responsibility of drafting and adopting federal and state evidence rules. There is no question that jurors *do* report biased comments made by fellow jurors prior to the beginning of deliberations. And the Court marshals no evidence that such pre-deliberation reporting is rarer than the post-verdict variety.

Even if there is something to the distinction that the Court makes between pre- and post-verdict reporting, it is debatable whether the difference is significant enough to merit different treatment. This is especially so because post-verdict reporting is both more disruptive and may be the result of extraneous influences. A juror who is initially in the minority but is ultimately persuaded by other jurors may have second thoughts after the verdict is announced and may be angry with others on the panel who pressed for unanimity. In addition, if a verdict is unpopular with a particular juror's family, friends, employer, co-workers, or neighbors, the juror may regret his or her vote and may feel pressured to rectify what the jury has done. * * *

III

A

The real thrust of the majority opinion is that the Constitution is less tolerant of racial bias than other forms of juror misconduct, but it is hard to square this

---

[10] It is worth noting that, even if *voir dire* were entirely ineffective at detecting racial bias (a proposition no one defends), that still would not suffice to distinguish this case from *Warger*. After all, the allegation in *Warger* was that the foreperson had entirely circumvented *voir dire* by lying in order to shield her bias. The Court, nevertheless, concluded that even where "jurors lie in *voir dire* in a way that conceals bias, juror impartiality is adequately assured" through other means.

argument with the nature of the Sixth Amendment right on which petitioner's argument and the Court's holding are based. What the Sixth Amendment protects is the right to an "impartial jury." Nothing in the text or history of the Amendment or in the inherent nature of the jury trial right suggests that the extent of the protection provided by the Amendment depends on the nature of a jury's partiality or bias. As the Colorado Supreme Court aptly put it, it is hard to "discern a dividing line between different *types* of juror bias or misconduct, whereby one form of partiality would implicate a party's.

Nor has the Court found any decision of this Court suggesting that the Sixth Amendment recognizes some sort of hierarchy of partiality or bias. The Court points to a line of cases holding that, in some narrow circumstances, the Constitution requires trial courts to conduct *voir dire* on the subject of race. Those decisions, however, were not based on a ranking of types of partiality but on the Court's conclusion that in certain cases racial bias was especially likely. Thus, this line of cases does not advance the majority's argument.

It is undoubtedly true that "racial bias implicates unique historical, constitutional, and institutional concerns." But it is hard to see what that has to do with the scope of an *individual criminal defendant's* Sixth Amendment right to be judged impartially. The Court's efforts to reconcile its decision with *McDonald, Tanner,* and *Warger* illustrate the problem. The Court writes that the misconduct in those cases, while "troubling and unacceptable," was "anomalous." By contrast, racial bias, the Court says, is a "familiar and recurring evil" that causes "systemic injury to the administration of justice."

Imagine two cellmates serving lengthy prison terms. Both were convicted for homicides committed in unrelated barroom fights. At the trial of the first prisoner, a juror, during deliberations, expressed animosity toward the defendant because of his race. At the trial of the second prisoner, a juror, during deliberations, expressed animosity toward the defendant because he was wearing the jersey of a hated football team. In both cases, jurors come forward after the trial and reveal what the biased juror said in the jury room. The Court would say to the first prisoner: "You are entitled to introduce the jurors' testimony, because racial bias is damaging to our society." To the second, the Court would say: "Even if you did not have an impartial jury, you must stay in prison because sports rivalries are not a major societal issue."

This disparate treatment is unsupportable under the Sixth Amendment. If the Sixth Amendment requires the admission of juror testimony about statements or conduct during deliberations that show one type of juror partiality, then statements or conduct showing any type of partiality should be treated the same way.

B

Recasting this as an equal protection case would not provide a ground for limiting the holding to cases involving racial bias. At a minimum, cases involving bias based on any suspect classification—such as national origin or religion—would merit equal treatment. So, I think, would bias based on sex, or the exercise of the

First Amendment right to freedom of expression or association. Indeed, convicting a defendant on the basis of any irrational classification would violate the Equal Protection Clause.

Attempting to limit the damage worked by its decision, the Court says that only "clear" expressions of bias must be admitted, but judging whether a statement is sufficiently "clear" will often not be easy. Suppose that the allegedly biased juror in this case never made reference to Peña-Rodriguez's race or national origin but said that he had a lot of experience with "this macho type" and knew that men of this kind felt that they could get their way with women. Suppose that other jurors testified that they were certain that "this macho type" was meant to refer to Mexican or Hispanic men. Many other similarly suggestive statements can easily be imagined, and under today's decision it will be difficult for judges to discern the dividing line between those that are "clear[ly]" based on racial or ethnic bias and those that are at least somewhat ambiguous.

IV

Today's decision—especially if it is expanded in the ways that seem likely—will invite the harms that no-impeachment rules were designed to prevent.

First, as the Court explained in *Tanner,* "postverdict scrutiny of juror conduct" will inhibit "full and frank discussion in the jury room." Or, as the Senate Report put it: "[C]ommon fairness requires that absolute privacy be preserved for jurors to engage in the full and free debate necessary to the attainment of just verdicts. Jurors will not be able to function effectively if their deliberations are to be scrutinized in post-trial litigation."

Today's ruling will also prompt losing parties and their friends, supporters, and attorneys to contact and seek to question jurors, and this pestering may erode citizens' willingness to serve on juries. Many jurisdictions now have rules that prohibit or restrict post-verdict contact with jurors, but whether those rules will survive today's decision is an open question—as is the effect of this decision on privilege rules such as those noted at the outset of this opinion.[15]

Where post-verdict approaches are permitted or occur, there is almost certain to be an increase in harassment, arm-twisting, and outright coercion. See S. Rep., at 14 (explaining that a laxer rule "would permit the harassment of former jurors by losing parties as well as the possible exploitation of disgruntled or otherwise badly-motivated ex-jurors").

---

[15] The majority's emphasis on the unique harms of racial bias will not succeed at cabining the novel exception to no-impeachment rules, but it may succeed at putting other kinds of rules under threat. For example, the majority approvingly refers to the widespread rules limiting attorneys' contact with jurors. *Ante,* at [847]. But under the reasoning of the majority opinion, it is not clear why such rules should be enforced when they come into conflict with a defendant's attempt to introduce evidence of racial bias. For instance, what will happen when a lawyer obtains clear evidence of racist statements by contacting jurors in violation of a local rule? (Something similar happened in Tanner, 483 U.S., at 126, 107 S.Ct. 2739.) It remains to be seen whether rules of this type—or other rules which exclude probative evidence, such as evidentiary privileges—will be allowed to stand in the way of the "imperative to purge racial prejudice from the administration of justice." *Ante,* at [844].

The majority's approach will also undermine the finality of verdicts. * * * accusations of juror bias—which may be "raised for the first time days, weeks, or months after the verdict"—can "seriously disrupt the finality of the process." This threatens to "degrad[e] the prominence of the trial itself" and to send the message that juror misconduct need not be dealt with promptly.

The Court itself acknowledges that strict no-impeachment rules "promot[e] full and vigorous discussion," protect jurors from "be[ing] harassed or annoyed by litigants seeking to challenge the verdict," and "giv[e] stability and finality to verdicts." By the majority's own logic, then, imposing exceptions on no-impeachment rules will tend to defeat full and vigorous discussion, expose jurors to harassment, and deprive verdicts of stability.

The Court's only response is that some jurisdictions already make an exception for racial bias, and the Court detects no signs of "a loss of juror willingness to engage in searching and candid deliberations." One wonders what sort of outward signs the Court would expect to see if jurors in these jurisdictions do not speak as freely in the jury room as their counterparts in jurisdictions with strict no-impeachment rules. Gathering and assessing evidence regarding the quality of jury deliberations in different jurisdictions would be a daunting enterprise, and the Court offers no indication that anybody has undertaken that task.

In short, the majority barely bothers to engage with the policy issues implicated by no-impeachment rules. But even if it had carefully grappled with those issues, it still would have no basis for exalting its own judgment over that of the many expert policymakers who have endorsed broad no-impeachment rules.

V

The Court's decision is well-intentioned. It seeks to remedy a flaw in the jury trial system, but as this Court said some years ago, it is questionable whether our system of trial by jury can endure this attempt to perfect it.

I respectfully dissent.

3. RIGHT TO IMPARTIAL JUDGE

Just as a defendant has a constitutional right to an "impartial" jury, he also has a constitutional right to an impartial judge. For example, recusal may be required in order to satisfy due process in a civil or criminal case if the judge has a financial interest in the outcome of the case (e.g., Tumey v. Ohio, 273 U.S. 510 (1927) (judge received the fees that he levied against violators). The *Williams* case below explains the Court's due process test, and applies it to a new context: post-conviction review.

WILLIAMS V. PENNSYLVANIA

579 U.S. ___, 136 S.Ct. 1899, 195 L.Ed.2d 132 (2016).

JUSTICE KENNEDY delivered the opinion of the Court.

In this case, the Supreme Court of Pennsylvania vacated the decision of a postconviction court, which had granted relief to a prisoner convicted of first-degree murder and sentenced to death. One of the justices on the State Supreme Court had been the district attorney who gave his official approval to seek the death penalty in the prisoner's case. The justice in question denied the prisoner's motion for recusal and participated in the decision to deny relief. The question presented is whether the justice's denial of the recusal motion and his subsequent judicial participation violated the Due Process Clause of the Fourteenth Amendment.

This Court's precedents set forth an objective standard that requires recusal when the likelihood of bias on the part of the judge " 'is too high to be constitutionally tolerable.' " *Caperton* v. *A. T. Massey Coal Co.*, 556 U.S. 868, 872 (2009) (quoting *Withrow* v. *Larkin*, 421 U.S. 35, 47 (1975)). Applying this standard, the Court concludes that due process compelled the justice's recusal.

I

[The state's evidence at trial indicated that Williams and a friend, Draper, killed the victim, Norwood. Draper testified and suggested the motive was robbery; Williams testified that he was not involved and did not know the victim. The jury sentenced Williams to death after finding two aggravating circumstances: that the murder was committed during the course of a robbery and that Williams had a significant history of violent felony convictions, including a previous conviction for murder.

The conviction and sentence were upheld on appeal, state postconviction review, and federal habeas review. Williams then filed another petition for state postconviction relief claiming new information, not mentioned at trial, that before trial Draper had informed the prosecutor that the real motive for the murder was not robbery, but Williams's sexual relationship with Norwood, and that the prosecutor had promised to write a letter to the state parole board on Draper's behalf in exchange for Draper's false testimony at Williams's trial. The state habeas court ("PCRA court") concluded that the state had violated Williams's rights under *Brady,* Ch. 13, stayed Williams's execution, and ordered a new sentencing hearing.

The state challenged this order in the Pennsylvania Supreme Court, where the Chief Justice was Ronald Castille. In the trial court, during the litigation of Williams's *Brady* claims, the state had disclosed a sentencing memorandum bearing a note written by Ronald Castille, then-District Attorney of Philadelphia, stating: "Approved to proceed on the death penalty." When the state sought review from the state Supreme Court, Williams filed a motion to recuse Chief Justice Castille from the case, which the Chief Justice denied. With Chief Justice Castille participating, the court then held Williams's *Brady* claims were time-barred and reinstated Williams's death sentence. Chief Justice Castille authored a concurrence denouncing both the trial court's decision and the "obstructionist anti-death penalty agenda" of Williams's attorneys from the Federal Community Defender Office.]

II

A

Williams contends that Chief Justice Castille's decision as district attorney to seek a death sentence against him barred the chief justice from later adjudicating Williams's petition to overturn that sentence. Chief Justice Castille, Williams argues, violated the Due Process Clause of the Fourteenth Amendment by acting as both accuser and judge in his case.

The Court's due process precedents do not set forth a specific test governing recusal when, as here, a judge had prior involvement in a case as a prosecutor. For the reasons explained below, however, the principles on which these precedents rest dictate the rule that must control in the circumstances here. The Court now holds that under the Due Process Clause there is an impermissible risk of actual bias when a judge earlier had significant, personal involvement as a prosecutor in a critical decision regarding the defendant's case.

Due process guarantees "an absence of actual bias" on the part of a judge. *In re Murchison*, 349 U.S. 133, 136 (1955). Bias is easy to attribute to others and difficult to discern in oneself. To establish an enforceable and workable framework, the Court's precedents apply an objective standard that, in the usual case, avoids having to determine whether actual bias is present. The Court asks not whether a judge harbors an actual, subjective bias, but instead whether, as an objective matter, "the average judge in his position is 'likely' to be neutral, or whether there is an unconstitutional 'potential for bias.' " *Caperton*. [In *Caperton*, the Court found such an unconstitutional "potential for bias" when one of the parties had donated $3 million to the judge's election campaign.] Of particular relevance to the instant case, the Court has determined that an unconstitutional potential for bias exists when the same person serves as both accuser and adjudicator in a case. This objective risk of bias is reflected in the due process maxim that "no man can be a judge in his own case and no man is permitted to try cases where he has an interest in the outcome."

The due process guarantee that "no man can be a judge in his own case" would have little substance if it did not disqualify a former prosecutor from sitting in judgment of a prosecution in which he or she had made a critical decision. This conclusion follows from the Court's analysis in *In re Murchison*. That case involved a "one-man judge-grand jury" proceeding, conducted pursuant to state law, in which the judge called witnesses to testify about suspected crimes. During the course of the examinations, the judge became convinced that two witnesses were obstructing the proceeding. He charged one witness with perjury and then, a few weeks later, tried and convicted him in open court. The judge charged the other witness with contempt and, a few days later, tried and convicted him as well. This Court overturned the convictions on the ground that the judge's dual position as accuser and decisionmaker in the contempt trials violated due process: "Having been a part of [the accusatory] process a judge cannot be, in the very nature of things, wholly disinterested in the conviction or acquittal of those accused."

No attorney is more integral to the accusatory process than a prosecutor who participates in a major adversary decision. When a judge has served as an advocate for the State in the very case the court is now asked to adjudicate, a serious question arises as to whether the judge, even with the most diligent effort, could set aside any personal interest in the outcome. There is, furthermore, a risk that the judge "would be so psychologically wedded" to his or her previous position as a prosecutor that the judge "would consciously or unconsciously avoid the appearance of having erred or changed position." *Withrow*. In addition, the judge's "own personal knowledge and impression" of the case, acquired through his or her role in the prosecution, may carry far more weight with the judge than the parties' arguments to the court. *Murchison*.

* * * The facts of *Murchison*, it should be acknowledged, differ in many respects from a case like this one. In *Murchison*, over the course of several weeks, a single official (the so-called judge-grand jury) conducted an investigation into suspected crimes; made the decision to charge witnesses for obstruction of that investigation; heard evidence on the charges he had lodged; issued judgments of conviction; and imposed sentence. By contrast, a judge who had an earlier involvement in a prosecution might have been just one of several prosecutors working on the case at each stage of the proceedings; the prosecutor's immediate role might have been limited to a particular aspect of the prosecution; and decades might have passed before the former prosecutor, now a judge, is called upon to adjudicate a claim in the case.

These factual differences notwithstanding, the constitutional principles explained in *Murchison* are fully applicable where a judge had a direct, personal role in the defendant's prosecution. The involvement of other actors and the passage of time are consequences of a complex criminal justice system, in which a single case may be litigated through multiple proceedings taking place over a period of years. This context only heightens the need for objective rules preventing the operation of bias that otherwise might be obscured. Within a large, impersonal system, an individual prosecutor might still have an influence that, while not so visible as the one-man grand jury in *Murchison*, is nevertheless significant. A prosecutor may bear responsibility for any number of critical decisions, including what charges to bring, whether to extend a plea bargain, and which witnesses to call. Even if decades intervene before the former prosecutor revisits the matter as a jurist, the case may implicate the effects and continuing force of his or her original decision. In these circumstances, there remains a serious risk that a judge would be influenced by an improper, if inadvertent, motive to validate and preserve the result obtained through the adversary process. The involvement of multiple actors and the passage of time do not relieve the former prosecutor of the duty to withdraw in order to ensure the neutrality of the judicial process in determining the consequences that his or her own earlier, critical decision may have set in motion.

B

This leads to the question whether Chief Justice Castille's authorization to seek the death penalty against Williams amounts to significant, personal involvement in a critical trial decision. The Court now concludes that it was a significant, personal involvement; and, as a result, Chief Justice Castille's failure to recuse from Williams's case presented an unconstitutional risk of bias.

As an initial matter, there can be no doubt that the decision to pursue the death penalty is a critical choice in the adversary process. Indeed, after a defendant is charged with a death-eligible crime, whether to ask a jury to end the defendant's life is one of the most serious discretionary decisions a prosecutor can be called upon to make.

Nor is there any doubt that Chief Justice Castille had a significant role in this decision. Without his express authorization, the Commonwealth would not have been able to pursue a death sentence against Williams. The importance of this decision and the profound consequences it carries make it evident that a responsible prosecutor would deem it to be a most significant exercise of his or her official discretion and professional judgment.

Pennsylvania nonetheless contends that Chief Justice Castille * * * was the head of a large district attorney's office in a city that saw many capital murder trials. * * * [H]is approval of the trial prosecutor's request to pursue capital punishment in Williams's case amounted to a brief administrative act limited to "the time it takes to read a one-and-a-half-page memo." In this Court's view, that characterization cannot be credited. The Court will not assume that then-District Attorney Castille treated so major a decision as a perfunctory task requiring little time, judgment, or reflection on his part.

Chief Justice Castille's own comments while running for judicial office refute the Commonwealth's claim that he played a mere ministerial role in capital sentencing decisions. During the chief justice's election campaign, multiple news outlets reported his statement that he "sent 45 people to death rows" as district attorney. Chief Justice Castille's willingness to take personal responsibility for the death sentences obtained during his tenure as district attorney indicate that, in his own view, he played a meaningful role in those sentencing decisions and considered his involvement to be an important duty of his office.

Although not necessary to the disposition of this case, the PCRA court's ruling underscores the risk of permitting a former prosecutor to be a judge in what had been his or her own case. The PCRA court determined that the trial prosecutor— Chief Justice Castille's former subordinate in the district attorney's office—had engaged in multiple, intentional *Brady* violations during Williams's prosecution. While there is no indication that Chief Justice Castille was aware of the alleged prosecutorial misconduct, it would be difficult for a judge in his position not to view the PCRA court's findings as a criticism of his former office and, to some extent, of his own leadership and supervision as district attorney.

The potential conflict of interest posed by the PCRA court's findings illustrates the utility of statutes and professional codes of conduct that "provide more protection than due process requires." *Caperton.* It is important to note that due process "demarks only the outer boundaries of judicial disqualifications." *Aetna Life Ins. Co. v. Lavoie,* 475 U.S. 813, 828 (1986). Most questions of recusal are addressed by more stringent and detailed ethical rules, which in many jurisdictions already require disqualification under the circumstances of this case. At the time Williams filed his recusal motion with the Pennsylvania Supreme Court, for example, Pennsylvania's Code of Judicial Conduct disqualified judges from any proceeding in which "they served as a lawyer in the matter in controversy, or a lawyer with whom they previously practiced law served during such association as a lawyer concerning the matter. . . ." The fact that most jurisdictions have these rules in place suggests that today's decision will not occasion a significant change in recusal practice.

Chief Justice Castille's significant, personal involvement in a critical decision in Williams's case gave rise to an unacceptable risk of actual bias. This risk so endangered the appearance of neutrality that his participation in the case "must be forbidden if the guarantee of due process is to be adequately implemented." *Withrow.*

III

Having determined that Chief Justice Castille's participation violated due process, the Court must resolve whether Williams is entitled to relief. In past cases, the Court has not had to decide the question whether a due process violation arising from a jurist's failure to recuse amounts to harmless error if the jurist is on a multimember court and the jurist's vote was not decisive. For the reasons discussed below, the Court holds that an unconstitutional failure to recuse constitutes structural error even if the judge in question did not cast a deciding vote.

The Court has little trouble concluding that a due process violation arising from the participation of an interested judge is a defect "not amenable" to harmless-error review, regardless of whether the judge's vote was dispositive. *Puckett* v. *United States,* 556 U.S. 129, 141 (2009). The deliberations of an appellate panel, as a general rule, are confidential. As a result, it is neither possible nor productive to inquire whether the jurist in question might have influenced the views of his or her colleagues during the decisionmaking process. Indeed, one purpose of judicial confidentiality is to assure jurists that they can reexamine old ideas and suggest new ones, while both seeking to persuade and being open to persuasion by their colleagues. As Justice Brennan wrote in his *Lavoie* concurrence,

"The description of an opinion as being 'for the court' connotes more than merely that the opinion has been joined by a majority of the participating judges. It reflects the fact that these judges have exchanged ideas and arguments in deciding the case. It reflects the collective process of deliberation which shapes the court's perceptions of which issues must be addressed and, more importantly, how they must be addressed. And, while the influence of any single participant in this process can never be measured with precision, experience teaches us that each member's involvement plays a part in shaping the court's ultimate disposition."

These considerations illustrate, moreover, that it does not matter whether the disqualified judge's vote was necessary to the disposition of the case. The fact that the interested judge's vote was not dispositive may mean only that the judge was successful in persuading most members of the court to accept his or her position. That outcome does not lessen the unfairness to the affected party.

A multimember court must not have its guarantee of neutrality undermined, for the appearance of bias demeans the reputation and integrity not just of one jurist, but of the larger institution of which he or she is a part. An insistence on the appearance of neutrality is not some artificial attempt to mask imperfection in the judicial process, but rather an essential means of ensuring the reality of a fair adjudication. Both the appearance and reality of impartial justice are necessary to the public legitimacy of judicial pronouncements and thus to the rule of law itself. When the objective risk of actual bias on the part of a judge rises to an unconstitutional level, the failure to recuse cannot be deemed harmless.

The Commonwealth points out that ordering a rehearing before the Pennsylvania Supreme Court may not provide complete relief to Williams because judges who were exposed to a disqualified judge may still be influenced by their colleague's views when they rehear the case. An inability to guarantee complete relief for a constitutional violation, however, does not justify withholding a remedy altogether. Allowing an appellate panel to reconsider a case without the participation of the interested member will permit judges to probe lines of analysis or engage in discussions they may have felt constrained to avoid in their first deliberations.

Chief Justice Castille's participation in Williams's case was an error that affected the State Supreme Court's whole adjudicatory framework below. Williams must be granted an opportunity to present his claims to a court unburdened by any "possible temptation . . . not to hold the balance nice, clear and true between the State and the accused." *Tumey.* * * *

Where a judge has had an earlier significant, personal involvement as a prosecutor in a critical decision in the defendant's case, the risk of actual bias in the judicial proceeding rises to an unconstitutional level. Due process entitles Terrance Williams to "a proceeding in which he may present his case with assurance" that no member of the court is "predisposed to find against him."

The judgment of the Supreme Court of Pennsylvania is vacated, and the case is remanded for further proceedings not inconsistent with this opinion.

CHIEF JUSTICE ROBERTS, with whom JUSTICE ALITO joins, dissenting.

* * * It is clear that a judge with "a direct, personal, substantial, pecuniary interest" in a case may not preside over that case. *Tumey* v. *Ohio*, 273 U.S. 510, 523 (1927). We have also held that a judge may not oversee a criminal contempt proceeding where the judge has previously served as grand juror in the same case, or where the party charged with contempt has conducted "an insulting attack upon the integrity of the judge carrying such potential for bias as to require disqualification." *Mayberry* v. *Pennsylvania*, 400 U.S. 455, 465–466 (1971). Prior to this Court's decision in *Caperton* v. *A. T. Massey Coal Co.*, 556 U.S. 868 (2009), we

had declined to require judicial recusal under the Due Process Clause beyond those defined situations. In *Caperton*, however, the Court adopted a new standard that requires recusal "when the probability of actual bias on the part of the judge or decisionmaker is too high to be constitutionally tolerable." The Court framed the inquiry as "whether, under a realistic appraisal of psychological tendencies and human weakness, the interest poses such a risk of actual bias or prejudgment that the practice must be forbidden if the guarantee of due process is to be adequately implemented."

* * * *Murchison* found a due process violation because the judge (sitting as grand jury) accused the witnesses of contempt, and then (sitting as judge) presided over their trial on that charge. As a result, the judge had made up his mind about the only issue in the case before the trial had even begun. * * * *Murchison* expressed concern that the judge's recollection of the testimony he had heard as grand juror was "likely to weigh far more heavily with him than any testimony given" at trial. * * * Neither of those due process concerns is present here. Chief Justice Castille was involved in the decision to seek the death penalty, and perhaps it would be reasonable under *Murchison* to require him to recuse himself from any challenge casting doubt on that recommendation. But that is not this case.

This case is about whether Williams may overcome the procedural bar on filing an untimely habeas petition, which required him to show that the government interfered with his ability to raise his habeas claim, and that "the information on which he relies could not have been obtained earlier with the exercise of due diligence." * * * The problem in *Murchison* was that the judge, having been "part of the accusatory process" regarding the guilt or innocence of the defendants, could not then be "wholly disinterested" when called upon to decide that very same issue. * * * In this case, in contrast, neither the procedural question nor Williams's merits claim in any way concerns the pretrial decision to seek the death penalty. * * * In sum, there was not such an "objective risk of actual bias," that it was fundamentally unfair for Chief Justice Castille to participate in the decision of an issue having nothing to do with his prior participation in the case. * * * Because the Due Process Clause does not mandate recusal in cases such as this, it is up to state authorities—not this Court—to determine whether recusal should be required.

JUSTICE THOMAS, dissenting.

* * * There has been * * * no "single case" in which Castille acted as both prosecutor and adjudicator. Castille was still serving in the district attorney's office when Williams' criminal proceedings ended and his sentence of death became final. Williams' filing of a petition for state postconviction relief did not continue (or resurrect) that already final criminal proceeding. A postconviction proceeding "is not part of the criminal proceeding itself " but "is in fact considered to be civil in nature," *Pennsylvania* v. *Finley*, 481 U.S. 551, 556–557 (1987), and brings with it fewer procedural protections. Williams' case therefore presents a much different question from that posited by the majority. It is more accurately characterized as whether a judge may review a petition for postconviction relief when that judge previously served as district attorney while the petitioner's criminal case was

pending. For the reasons that follow, that different question merits a different answer.

The "settled usages and modes of proceeding existing in the common and statute law of England before the emigration of our ancestors" are the touchstone of due process. *Tumey* v. *Ohio*, 273 U.S. 510, 523 (1927). What due process requires of the judicial proceedings in the Pennsylvania postconviction courts, therefore, is guided by the historical treatment of judicial disqualification. And here, neither historical practice nor this Court's case law constitutionalizing that practice requires a former prosecutor to recuse from a prisoner's postconviction proceedings. * * *

* * * Both *Tumey* and *Murchison* arguably reflect historical understandings of judicial disqualification. Traditionally, judges disqualified themselves when they had a direct and substantial pecuniary interest or when they served as counsel in the same case. Those same historical understandings of judicial disqualification resolve Williams' case. Castille did not serve as both prosecutor and judge in the case before us. Even assuming Castille's supervisory role as district attorney was tantamount to serving as "counsel" in Williams' criminal case, that case ended nearly five years before Castille joined the Supreme Court of Pennsylvania. Castille then participated in a separate proceeding by reviewing Williams' petition for postconviction relief * * * a new civil proceeding. Our case law bears out the many distinctions between the two proceedings. * * * [I]in postconviction proceedings, "the presumption of innocence [has] disappear[ed]." *Herrera* v. *Collins*, 506 U.S. 390, 399 (1993). The postconviction petitioner has no constitutional right to counsel. Nor has this Court ever held that he has a right to demand that his postconviction court consider a freestanding claim of actual innocence, or to demand the State to turn over exculpatory evidence. And, under the Court's precedents, his due process rights are "not parallel to a trial right, but rather must be analyzed in light of the fact that he has already been found guilty at a fair trial, and has only a limited interest in postconviction relief." *Osborne*. * * *

* * * This is not a case about the " 'accused.' " It is a case about the due process rights of the already convicted. Whatever those rights might be, they do not include policing alleged violations of state codes of judicial ethics in postconviction proceedings. * * *

CHAPTER 16

FAIR TRIAL/FREE PRESS

■ ■ ■

This chapter introduces a new participant in the criminal justice process—the media (or, if one prefers, the public that is the audience of the media). In many situations the interests of the media and the accused coincide; indeed, the accused's Sixth Amendment right to insist upon a public trial is premised on the significant value of public disclosure in ensuring that the trial is a fair one. *In re Oliver*, 333 U.S. 257 (1948).[a] But there are instances when potential conflicts arise between the media's right to report and the accused's right to a fair trial. In *Nebraska Press Association v. Stuart*, 427 U.S. 539 (1976), the Supreme Court reviewed what had long been its basic approach in responding to such conflicts.

The Court in *Nebraska Press* noted that "the authors of the Bill of Rights did not undertake to assign priorities as between First Amendment and Sixth Amendment rights [although] fully aware of the potential conflicts between them." This placed the Supreme Court in a similar position. It could not "rewrite the Constitution by undertaking what they [the framers] declined to do." Rather, it had sought to develop constitutional standards, responsive to the particular situation, that accommodated both the freedom of the press under the First Amendment and the constitutional rights of the accused. The cases in this chapter reflect several different aspects of the Court's efforts in this process of accommodation or "balancing."

Perhaps the most significant source of conflict between the media and the accused arises from the impact upon the jury selection process of extensive media coverage of a case prior to trial. That coverage often starts with the reporting on the commission of the crime and carries through to the eve of the trial, reporting not only matters of public record but also information developed by the media itself. It produces what the Court commonly describes as "pretrial publicity." Such publicity, often adverse to the accused and sometimes highly inflammatory, has the potential for influencing the attitudes of a large segment of the potential pool of jurors—both those who themselves read, saw, or listened to the coverage and others who have heard about it second-hand.

---

[a] *Oliver* noted that the public trial serves the defendant's interest in a fair trial in several ways: (i) the knowledge that the trial is "subject to contemporaneous review in the form of public opinion" serves as "an effective restraint on possible abuse of judicial power"; (ii) the presence of interested spectators assures testimonial trustworthiness by inducing a fear in witnesses that false testimony will be detected; and (iii) public disclosure may call the proceedings to the attention of key witnesses who might be unknown to the defense and who might respond by coming forward with critical testimony. As discussed in *Weaver v. Massachusetts*, p. 960, the Sixth Amendment right is subject to "exceptions," which permit closure, under special circumstances. See also the discussion of *Waller v. Georgia* at p. 908.

Nebraska Press presented a trial court's attempt to avoid the difficulties created by adverse pretrial publicity by precluding media publication. The trial court issued a pretrial order that barred the media from publishing reports that (1) described "any testimony given or evidence adduced in court" or (2) included "accounts of confessions or admissions made by the accused" to the police or third parties (other than reporters) or "other facts 'strongly implicative' of the accused." The Supreme Court found that the First Amendment absolutely barred an order retraining publication of what happened at an open judicial proceeding (here a preliminary hearing). Such an order violated the "settled principle" that, "once a public hearing has been held, what transpired there could not be subject to prior restraint." As to prohibiting the publication of information obtained from other sources, the First Amendment imposed rigorous prerequisites, including the clear inadequacy of measures within the criminal justice process that provide a shield against the potential impact of adverse pretrial publicity. While the Court was divided as to whether these First Amendment prerequisites could ever be met in practice, the *Nebraska Press* ruling was seen as basically closing the door to attempts to prevent adverse pretrial publicity by restricting media publications.[b] If adverse pretrial publicity was to be prevented, courts and legislatures would have to look to other measures. Moreover, here too, *Nebraska Press* indicated, the first line of response to the threat posed by adverse pretrial publicity would be to look to the measures that preserve the accused's right to an impartial jury without imposing upon First Amendment interests by restricting the information available to the media.

Nebraska Press offered the following listing of such measures: "(a) change of trial venue to a place less exposed to the intense publicity * * *; (b) postponement of the trial to allow public attention to subside; (c) searching questioning of prospective jurors * * * to screen out these with fixed opinion as to guilt or innocence; (d) the use of emphatic and clear instructions on the sworn duty of each juror to decide the issues only on evidence presented in open court." Of these four measures, the defense is least likely to look to the continuance. Where a defendant has failed to make bail (quite common in high profile cases), the defense will want

---

    [b] The Court in *Nebraska Press* noted that orders restraining publication had always been viewed as the "most serious and least tolerable infringements on First Amendment rights" and would be allowed only upon an extraordinary showing of justification. In the context of protecting the defendant's right to an impartial jury, this would require consideration of: "(a) the nature and extent of pretrial news coverage; (b) whether other measures would be likely to mitigate the effects of the unrestrained pretrial publicity; and (c) how effectively a restraining order would operate to prevent a threatened danger." Upon consideration of these factors, an order restraining publication would only be justified where " 'the gravity of the evil [to be avoided], discounted by its improbability, justifies such invasion of free speech as is necessary to avoid the danger.' " A concurring opinion for three Justices argued that this burden of justification could never be met, considering the "broad spectrum of [alternative] devices" judges have available for "ensuring that fundamental fairness is accorded the accused." Another concurring Justice agreed generally with that conclusion, leaving aside special situations (e.g., where the information to be published was obtained by illegal means or was patently false). Still another Justice expressed "grave doubt" that a restraining order could ever be justified, and yet another stressed the "unique burden" that would rest on a party who sought to establish the "necessity for a prior restraint on pretrial publicity." Thus, while the opinion for the Court noted that it was not "ruling out the possibility of [a defendant] showing the kind of threat to fair trial rights that would possess the requisite degree of certainty to justify restraint," the combination of opinions signaled, as a practical matter, a likely death knell for such restraining orders.

to pursue the right to a speedy trial. Also, while the publicity is likely to decrease over time, it is also likely to resume as the date of the delayed trial approaches. On the other side, the jury instruction noted in *Nebraska Press* is universally employed. Its value, however, is limited—as the Court implicitly recognized in holding that some prospective jurors exposed to adverse publicity must be excluded even though they state that they will follow such an instruction (setting aside any preconceived notion drawn from the publicity). See e.g., *Irvin v. Dowd* (discussed in *Skilling v. United States*, infra). Accordingly, the key protective measures tend to be the change of venue and the "searching questioning of prospective jurors" (typically *voir dire* questioning, but sometimes accompanied by juror questionnaires).

The effectiveness of a change of venue will depend on the distribution of the publicity and the jurisdiction involved. In small states, the publicity may be equally (or almost equally) intense throughout the state. As for the searching questioning, its effectiveness depends in part on the standard used in excluding jurors for cause. *Nebraska Press* spoke of excluding jurors with "fixed opinions," but courts have recognized that exclusion cannot be limited to prospective jurors who readily admit to a fixed opinion. Some jurors may deceive themselves and others may seek to deceive the court (a special problem in high profile cases, where some prospective jurors are likely to have a strong interest in being seated). The first case in this chapter, *Skilling v. United States*, presents the leading Supreme Court discussion of the constitutional requirements regarding; (1) the granting of a defense motion for change of venue; (2) the scope of the questioning of prospective jurors with respect to adverse publicity; and (3) the exclusion of prospective jurors. *Skilling* also adds an element only occasionally presented in high profile cases—the crime involved there had a widespread direct and indirect impact, which combined with extensive publicity in potentially tainting the jury pool.

Skilling addresses only constitutional requirements, and jurisdictions remain free to adopt less stringent requirements for a change of venue, to require more extensive questioning of prospective jurors, and to insist upon broader standards of exclusion. In light of the costs of such measures, as well as doubts about their effectiveness, it is not surprising that almost all jurisdictions have also adopted measures that seek to limit the range of potentially prejudicial pretrial publicity. In *Sheppard v. Maxwell* (discussed in *Skilling*, see p. 873), the Court suggested that this might be done by a trial court order which "proscribed extrajudicial statements by any lawyer, party, witness, or court official which divulged prejudicial matters." Responding to that suggestion, trial courts in high profile cases have issued such "gag orders," almost always directed to the attorneys and sometimes including other participants. The Supreme Court has not ruled on the constitutionality of "gag orders," but *Gentile v. State Bar of Nevada*, the second case in this chapter, considers the constitutionality of the legislative framework often incorporated in "gag orders" directed at lawyers.

Gentile considers the constitutionality of the application of a state rule of professional conduct restricting extrajudicial statements by attorneys. Almost all jurisdictions have adopted such prohibitions, and the vast majority, as in *Gentile*, have adopted a standard set forth in a version of the American Bar Association's

Model Rules of Professional Conduct. Very often, these standards are incorporated in the "gag orders" issued by judges in individual cases, and lower courts have held that any "gag order" must, at a minimum, meet the constitutional prerequisites announced in *Gentile*. However, the combination of rulings in *Gentile* has produced some confusion in identifying those standards. Note that the division of votes in this case is such that the initial opinion by Justice Kennedy does not set forth the majority position on the basic First Amendment standard defining the state's authority. That is provided by Parts I and II of Chief Justice Rehnquist's opinion. Also, because Justice O'Connor did not join either the Kennedy or Rehnquist discussion of the First Amendment standard as applied to the facts of this case, neither opinion reflects a majority position on that issue.

While *Nebraska Press* held that the press could not be banned from reporting on judicial proceedings open to the public, it left open the question of whether the First Amendment was implicated in the closing of a proceeding to the public (and thereby to the press). *Richmond Newspapers, Inc. v. Virginia*, 448 U.S. 555 (1980), marked the first time the Court was asked to decide "whether *a criminal trial itself* may be closed upon the unopposed request of a defendant, without any demonstration that closure is required to protect the defendant's superior right to a fair trial [or] some other overriding consideration." (Emphasis added.) No, answered the Court, holding that the right of the public and the press to attend criminal trials is implicit in the guarantees of the First Amendment. There was no opinion of the Court. In the lead opinion, Burger, C.J., joined by White and Stevens, JJ., observed that "the Bill of Rights was enacted against the backdrop of the long history of trials being presumptively open" and that "the First Amendment can be read as protecting the right of everyone to attend trials" "so as to give meaning" to the explicit guarantees of freedom of speech and press. Concurring Justice Brennan, joined by Marshall, J., emphasized that public access to trials is essential "to achieve the objective of maintaining public confidence in the administration of justice."

Richmond Newspapers left open the question whether the right of access to the criminal trial itself extended to *pretrial* proceedings. The Court suggested this possibility in *Press-Enterprise Co. v. Superior Court*, 464 U.S. 501 (1984) (*Press-Enterprise I*), when it held, without a dissent, that the First Amendment right of access applied to the *voir dire* examination of potential jurors. The Court emphasized the historical tradition of openness and the functional value of openness for the particular proceeding rather than any characterization of the jury selection process as a part of the trial itself. Two years later, in *Press-Enterprise II*, the third case in this chapter, the Court applied the public right of access to a proceeding that was clearly not part of the trial—the preliminary hearing.

The clash between the First Amendment interests of the media and the fair trial interests of the defendant can extend beyond the problems presented by pretrial publicity. The media coverage of the trial can raise concerns, even when the jury is sequestered, should the character of that coverage bear upon the ability of the trial participants (jurors, witnesses, lawyers, and judge) to carry out their respective responsibilities. Thus, *Sheppard v. Maxwell*, supra, characterized the disruptive activities of media representatives (both in the noise and confusion they created within the courtroom and in their behavior in photographing witnesses and jurors as they left the courtroom) as a key factor in contributing to the "carnival atmosphere" that pervaded the trial there and resulted in a denial of due process. *Estes v. Texas* (described at pp. 873, 916) concluded that the television coverage in that case had a similar impact. The last case in this chapter, *Chandler v. Florida*, addresses the contention that television coverage inherently has such a potentially pernicious impact. Although rejecting that contention, Chandler does not suggest that the media has a First Amendment right (stemming from *Richmond Newspapers*, supra) to insist upon televising trials. Lower courts uniformly have rejected that contention, and some jurisdictions (most notably the federal system) absolutely preclude televising trials, while others bar televising upon objection by the defendant.

SKILLING V. UNITED STATES

561 U.S. 358, 130 S.Ct. 2896, 177 L.Ed.2d 619 (2010).

JUSTICE GINSBURG delivered the opinion of the Court.[a]

In 2001, Enron Corporation, then the seventh highest-revenue-grossing company in America, crashed into bankruptcy. We consider in this opinion two questions arising from the prosecution of Jeffrey Skilling, a longtime Enron executive [and former president, COO and CEO], for crimes committed before the corporation's collapse. First, did pretrial publicity and community prejudice prevent Skilling from obtaining a fair trial? Second, did the jury improperly convict Skilling of conspiracy to commit "honest-services" wire fraud, 18 U.S.C. §§ 371, 1343, 1346?

Answering no to both questions, the Fifth Circuit affirmed Skilling's convictions. We conclude, in common with the Court of Appeals, that Skilling's fair-trial argument fails; Skilling, we hold, did not establish that a presumption of juror prejudice arose or that actual bias infected the jury that tried him. But we disagree with the Fifth Circuit's honest-services ruling. * * * Because Skilling's alleged misconduct entailed no bribe or kickback, it does not fall within § 1346's proscription. We therefore affirm in part and vacate in part [remanding for a determination as to how vacating the "honest services" conviction impacts Skilling's other convictions].

I.

The Government's investigation [of the Enron collapse] uncovered an elaborate conspiracy to prop up Enron's short-run stock prices by overstating the company's financial well-being. In the years following Enron's bankruptcy, the Government prosecuted dozens of Enron employees who participated in the scheme. In time, the Government worked its way up the corporation's chain of command: On July 7, 2004, a grand jury indicted Skilling, Donald Lay [Enron's

---

[a] Part I of this opinion was joined by Chief Justice Roberts and Justices Stevens, Scalia, Kennedy, Thomas, and Alito. Part II was joined by Chief Justice Roberts and Justices Scalia, Kennedy, and Thomas. Part III, dealing with the "honest services" charge, is omitted, as is Justice Scalia's separate opinion addressing that charge.

founder and former chairman], and Richard Causey, Enron's former chief accounting officer. Count 1 of the indictment charged Skilling with conspiracy to commit securities and wire fraud; in particular, it alleged that Skilling had sought to "depriv[e] Enron and its shareholders of the intangible right of [his] honest services." The indictment further charged Skilling with more than 25 substantive counts of securities fraud, wire fraud, making false representations to Enron's auditors, and insider trading. [The prosecution was brought in Houston, where Enron has been headquartered since its founding in 1985].

In November 2004, Skilling moved to transfer the trial to another venue; he contended that hostility toward him in Houston, coupled with extensive pretrial publicity, had poisoned potential jurors. To support this assertion, Skilling, aided by media experts, submitted hundreds of news reports detailing Enron's downfall; he also presented affidavits from the experts he engaged portraying community attitudes in Houston in comparison to other potential venues. * * * The U.S. District Court, in accord with rulings in two earlier instituted Enron-related prosecutions, denied the venue-transfer motion. Despite "isolated incidents of intemperate commentary," the court observed, media coverage "ha[d] [mostly] been objective and unemotional," and the facts of the case were "neither heinous nor sensational." Moreover, "courts ha[d] commonly" favored "effective voir dire . . . to ferret out any [juror] bias." * * *

In the months leading up to the trial, the District Court solicited from the parties questions the court might use to screen prospective jurors. Unable to agree on a questionnaire's format and content, Skilling and the Government submitted dueling documents. On venire members' sources of Enron-related news, for example, the Government proposed that they tick boxes from a checklist of generic labels such as "[t]elevision," "[n]ewspaper," and "[r]adio." Skilling proposed more probing questions asking venire members to list the specific names of their media sources and to report on "what st[ood] out in [their] mind[s]" of "all the things [they] ha[d] seen, heard or read about Enron." The District Court rejected the Government's sparer inquiries in favor of Skilling's submission. Skilling's questions "[we]re more helpful," the court said, "because [they] [we]re generally . . . open-ended and w[ould] allow the potential jurors to give us more meaningful information." The court converted Skilling's submission, with slight modifications, into a 77-question, 14-page document that asked prospective jurors about, *inter alia*, their sources of news and exposure to Enron-related publicity, beliefs concerning Enron and what caused its collapse, opinions regarding the defendants and their possible guilt or innocence, and relationships to the company and to anyone affected by its demise.

In November 2005, the District Court mailed the questionnaire to 400 prospective jurors and received responses from nearly all the addressees. The court granted hardship exemptions to approximately 90 individuals, and the parties, with the court's approval, further winnowed the pool by excusing another 119 for cause, hardship, or physical disability. The parties agreed to exclude, in particular, "each and every" prospective juror who said that a preexisting opinion about Enron or the defendants would prevent her from impartially considering the evidence at trial.

On December 28, 2005, three weeks before the date scheduled for the commencement of trial, Causey pleaded guilty. Skilling's attorneys immediately requested a continuance, and the District Court agreed to delay the proceedings until the end of January 2006. In the interim, Skilling renewed his change-of-venue motion, arguing that the juror questionnaires revealed pervasive bias and that news accounts of Causey's guilty plea further tainted the jury pool. If Houston remained the trial venue, Skilling urged that "jurors need to be questioned individually by both the Court *and* counsel" concerning their opinions of Enron and "publicity issues."

The District Court again declined to move the trial. Skilling, the court concluded, still had not "establish[ed] that pretrial publicity and/or community prejudice raise[d] a presumption of inherent jury prejudice." The questionnaires and *voir dire*, the court observed, provided safeguards adequate to ensure an impartial jury. * * * Denying Skilling's request for attorney-led *voir dire*, the court said that in 17 years on the bench: "I've found . . . I get more forthcoming responses from potential jurors than the lawyers on either side." * * * But the court promised to give counsel an opportunity to ask follow-up questions, and it agreed that venire members should be examined individually about pretrial publicity. The court also allotted the defendants jointly 14 peremptory challenges, 2 more than the standard number prescribed by Federal Rule of Criminal Procedure 24(b)(2) and (c)(4)(B).

Voir dire began on January 30, 2006. * * * After questioning the venire as a group, the District Court brought prospective jurors one by one to the bench for individual examination. Although the questions varied, the process generally tracked the following format: The court asked about exposure to Enron-related news and the content of any stories that stood out in the prospective juror's mind. Next, the court homed in on questionnaire answers that raised a red flag signaling possible bias. The court then permitted each side to pose follow-up questions. Finally, after the venire member stepped away, the court entertained and ruled on challenges for cause. In all, the court granted one of the Government's for-cause challenges and denied four; it granted three of the defendants' challenges and denied six. The parties agreed to excuse three additional jurors for cause and one for hardship.

By the end of the day, the court had qualified 38 prospective jurors, a number sufficient, allowing for peremptory challenges, to empanel 12 jurors and 4 alternates. Before the jury was sworn in, Skilling objected to the seating of six jurors. He did not contend that they were in fact biased; instead, he urged that he would have used peremptories to exclude them had he not exhausted his supply by striking several venire members after the court refused to excuse them for cause. The court overruled this objection.

* * * Following a 4-month trial and nearly five days of deliberation, the jury found Skilling guilty of 19 counts, including the honest-services-fraud conspiracy charge, and not guilty of 9 insider-trading counts. The District Court sentenced Skilling to 292 months' imprisonment, 3 years' supervised release, and $45 million in restitution.

On appeal, Skilling raised a host of challenges to his convictions, including the fair-trial and honest-services arguments he presses here. Regarding the former, the Fifth Circuit initially determined that the volume and negative tone of media coverage generated by Enron's collapse created a presumption of juror prejudice. The court also noted potential prejudice stemming from Causey's guilty plea and from the large number of victims in Houston—from the "[t]housands of Enron employees . . . [who] lost their jobs, and . . . saw their 401(k) accounts wiped out," to Houstonians who suffered spillover economic effects. * * * The Court of Appeals stated, however, that "the presumption [of prejudice] is rebuttable," and it therefore examined the *voir dire* to determine whether "the District Court empanelled an impartial jury." * * * [It found] the *voir dire* was * * * "proper and thorough," * * * that the Government had overcome the presumption of prejudice, and that Skilling had not "show[n] that any juror who actually sat was prejudiced against him." * * *

Skilling's fair-trial claim raises two distinct questions. First, did the District Court err by failing to move the trial to a different venue based on a presumption of prejudice? [11] Second, did actual prejudice contaminate Skilling's jury?

We begin our discussion by addressing the presumption of prejudice from which the Fifth Circuit's analysis in Skilling's case proceeded. The foundation precedent is *Rideau v. Louisiana*, 373 U.S. 723 (1963). Wilbert Rideau robbed a bank in a small Louisiana town, kidnapped three bank employees, and killed one of them. Police interrogated Rideau in jail without counsel present and obtained his confession. Without informing Rideau, no less seeking his consent, the police filmed the interrogation. On three separate occasions shortly before the trial, a local television station broadcast the film to audiences ranging from 24,000 to 53,000 individuals. Rideau moved for a change of venue, arguing that he could not receive a fair trial in the parish where the crime occurred, which had a population of approximately 150,000 people. The trial court denied the motion, and a jury eventually convicted Rideau. The Supreme Court of Louisiana upheld the conviction.

We reversed. "What the people [in the community] saw on their television sets," we observed, "was Rideau, in jail, flanked by the sheriff and two state troopers, admitting in detail the commission of the robbery, kidnapping, and murder." "[T]o the tens of thousands of people who saw and heard it," we explained, the interrogation "in a very real sense *was* Rideau's trial—at which he pleaded

---

[11] [transposed footnote] Venue transfer in federal court is governed by Federal Rule of Criminal Procedure 21, which instructs that a "court must transfer the proceeding . . . to another district if the court is satisfied that so great a prejudice against the defendant exists in the transferring district that the defendant cannot obtain a fair and impartial trial there." As the language of the Rule suggests, district-court calls on the necessity of transfer are granted a healthy measure of appellate-court respect. * * * Federal courts have invoked the Rule to move certain highly charged cases, for example, the prosecution arising from the bombing of the Alfred P. Murrah Federal Office Building in Oklahoma City. * * * They have also exercised discretion to deny venue-transfer requests in cases involving substantial pretrial publicity and community impact, for example, the prosecutions resulting from the 1993 World Trade Center bombing * * *. Skilling does not argue, distinct from his due process challenge, that the District Court abused its discretion under Rule 21 by declining to move his trial. We therefore review the District Court's venue-transfer decision only for compliance with the Constitution.

guilty." We therefore "d[id] not hesitate to hold, without pausing to examine a particularized transcript of the *voir dire*," that "[t]he kangaroo court proceedings" trailing the televised confession violated due process.

We followed *Rideau*'s lead in two later cases in which media coverage manifestly tainted a criminal prosecution. In *Estes v. Texas*, 381 U.S. 532 (1985), extensive publicity before trial swelled into excessive exposure during preliminary court proceedings as reporters and television crews overran the courtroom and "bombard[ed] . . . the community with the sights and sounds of" the pretrial hearing. The media's overzealous reporting efforts, we observed, "led to considerable disruption" and denied the "judicial serenity and calm to which [Billie Sol Estes] was entitled." Similarly, in *Sheppard v. Maxwell*, 384 U.S. 333 (1966), news reporters extensively covered the story of Sam Sheppard, who was accused of bludgeoning his pregnant wife to death. "[B]edlam reigned at the courthouse during the trial and newsmen took over practically the entire courtroom," thrusting jurors "into the role of celebrities." Pretrial media coverage, which we characterized as "months [of] virulent publicity about Sheppard and the murder," did not alone deny due process, we noted. But Sheppard's case involved more than heated reporting pretrial: We upset the murder conviction because a "carnival atmosphere" pervaded the trial.

In each of these cases, we overturned a "conviction obtained in a trial atmosphere that [was] utterly corrupted by press coverage"; our decisions, however, "cannot be made to stand for the proposition that juror exposure to . . . news accounts of the crime . . . alone presumptively deprives the defendant of due process." *Murphy v. Florida*, 421 U.S. 794 (1975).[12] See also, *e.g., Patton v. Yount*, 467 U.S. 1025 (1984).[13] Prominence does not necessarily produce prejudice, and juror *impartiality*, we have reiterated, does not require *ignorance. Irvin v. Dowd*, 366 U.S. 717, 722 (1961) (Jurors are not required to be "totally ignorant of the facts and issues involved"; "scarcely any of those best qualified to serve as jurors will not have formed some impression or opinion as to the merits of the case."). * * * A presumption of prejudice, our decisions indicate, attends only the extreme case.

---

[12] *Murphy* involved the robbery prosecution of the notorious Jack Murphy, a convicted murderer who helped mastermind the 1964 heist of the Star of India sapphire from New York's American Museum of Natural History. Pointing to "extensive press coverage" about him, Murphy moved to transfer venue. The trial court denied the motion and a jury convicted Murphy. We affirmed. Murphy's trial, we explained, was markedly different from the proceedings at issue in *Rideau v. Louisiana, Estes v. Texas*, and *Sheppard v. Maxwell*, * * * which "entirely lack[ed] . . . the solemnity and sobriety to which a defendant is entitled in a system that subscribes to any notion of fairness and rejects the verdict of a mob." *Voir dire* revealed no great hostility toward Murphy; "[s]ome of the jurors had a vague recollection of the robbery with which [he] was charged and each had some knowledge of [his] past crimes, but none betrayed any belief in the relevance of [his] past to the present case."

[13] In *Yount*, the media reported on Jon Yount's confession to a brutal murder and his prior conviction for the crime, which had been reversed due to a violation of *Miranda v. Arizona*. During *voir dire*, 77% of prospective jurors acknowledged they would carry an opinion into the jury box, and 8 of the 14 seated jurors and alternates admitted they had formed an opinion as to Yount's guilt. Nevertheless, we rejected Yount's presumption-of-prejudice claim. The adverse publicity and community outrage, we noted, were at their height prior to Yount's first trial, four years before the second prosecution; time had helped "sooth[e] and eras[e]" community prejudice.

Relying on *Rideau*, *Estes*, and *Sheppard*, Skilling asserts that we need not pause to examine the screening questionnaires or the *voir dire* before declaring his jury's verdict void. We are not persuaded. Important differences separate Skilling's prosecution from those in which we have presumed juror prejudice.[14]

First, we have emphasized in prior decisions the size and characteristics of the community in which the crime occurred. In *Rideau*, for example, we noted that the murder was committed in a parish of only 150,000 residents. Houston, in contrast, is the fourth most populous city in the Nation: At the time of Skilling's trial, more than 4.5 million individuals eligible for jury duty resided in the Houston area. Given this large, diverse pool of potential jurors, the suggestion that 12 impartial individuals could not be empaneled is hard to sustain. * * *

Second, although news stories about Skilling were not kind, they contained no confession or other blatantly prejudicial information of the type readers or viewers could not reasonably be expected to shut from sight. Rideau's dramatically staged admission of guilt, for instance, was likely imprinted indelibly in the mind of anyone who watched it. * * * Pretrial publicity about Skilling was less memorable and prejudicial. No evidence of the smoking-gun variety invited prejudgment of his culpability. * * *

Third, unlike cases in which trial swiftly followed a widely reported crime, *e.g.*, *Rideau*, over four years elapsed between Enron's bankruptcy and Skilling's trial. Although reporters covered Enron-related news throughout this period, the decibel level of media attention diminished somewhat in the years following Enron's collapse. *Yount* [supra fn. 13].

Finally, and of prime significance, Skilling's jury acquitted him of nine insider-trading counts. Similarly, earlier instituted Enron-related prosecutions yielded no overwhelming victory for the Government. In *Rideau*, *Estes*, and *Sheppard*, in marked contrast, the jury's verdict did not undermine in any way the supposition of juror bias. It would be odd for an appellate court to presume prejudice in a case in which jurors' actions run counter to that presumption. * * *

Skilling's trial, in short, shares little in common with those in which we approved a presumption of juror prejudice. The Fifth Circuit reached the opposite conclusion based primarily on the magnitude and negative tone of media attention directed at Enron. But "pretrial publicity—even pervasive, adverse publicity—does not inevitably lead to an unfair trial." * * * In this case, as just noted, news stories about Enron did not present the kind of vivid, unforgettable information we have recognized as particularly likely to produce prejudice, and Houston's size and diversity diluted the media's impact.[17] * * * Nor did Enron's "sheer number of victims" trigger a presumption of prejudice. Although the widespread community impact necessitated careful identification and inspection of prospective jurors'

---

[14] Skilling's reliance on *Estes* and *Sheppard* is particularly misplaced; those cases involved media interference with courtroom proceedings *during* trial. Skilling does not assert that news coverage reached and influenced his jury after it was empaneled.

[17] The Fifth Circuit, moreover, did not separate media attention aimed at Skilling from that devoted to Enron's downfall more generally. Data submitted by Skilling in support of his first motion for a venue transfer suggested that a slim percentage of Enron-related stories specifically named him.

connections to Enron, the extensive screening questionnaire and follow-up *voir dire* were well suited to that task. And hindsight shows the efficacy of these devices; as we discuss infra, jurors' links to Enron were either nonexistent or attenuated. * * * Finally, although Causey's "well-publicized decision to plead guilty" shortly before trial created a danger of juror prejudice, the District Court took appropriate steps to reduce that risk. The court delayed the proceedings by two weeks, lessening the immediacy of that development. And during *voir dire*, the court asked about prospective jurors' exposure to recent publicity, including news regarding Causey. Only two venire members recalled the plea; neither mentioned Causey by name, and neither ultimately served on Skilling's jury. Although publicity about a codefendant's guilty plea calls for inquiry to guard against actual prejudice, it does not ordinarily—and, we are satisfied, it did not here—warrant an automatic presumption of prejudice.

Persuaded that no presumption arose,[18] we conclude that the District Court, in declining to order a venue change, did not exceed constitutional limitations. We next consider whether actual prejudice infected Skilling's jury. *Voir dire*, Skilling asserts, did not adequately detect and defuse juror bias. "[T]he record ... affirmatively confirm[s]" prejudice, he maintains, because several seated jurors "prejudged his guilt." We disagree with Skilling's characterization of the *voir dire* and the jurors selected through it.

No hard-and-fast formula dictates the necessary depth or breadth of *voir dire*. Jury selection, we have repeatedly emphasized, is "particularly within the province of the trial judge." * * * When pretrial publicity is at issue, "primary reliance on the judgment of the trial court makes [especially] good sense" because the judge "sits in the locale where the publicity is said to have had its effect" and may base her evaluation on her "own perception of the depth and extent of news stories that might influence a juror." *Mu'Min* [fn. b infra]. Appellate courts making after-the-fact assessments of the media's impact on jurors should be mindful that their judgments lack the on-the-spot comprehension of the situation possessed by trial judges. * * * Reviewing courts are properly resistant to second-guessing the trial judge's estimation of a juror's impartiality, for that judge's appraisal is ordinarily influenced by a host of factors impossible to capture fully in the record—among them, the prospective juror's inflection, sincerity, demeanor, candor, body language, and apprehension of duty. In contrast to the cold transcript received by the appellate court, the in-the-moment *voir dire* affords the trial court a more intimate and immediate basis for assessing a venire member's fitness for jury service. We consider the adequacy of jury selection in Skilling's case, therefore, attentive to the respect due to district-court determinations of juror impartiality and of the measures necessary to ensure that impartiality.[20]

---

[18] The parties disagree about whether a presumption of prejudice can be rebutted, and, if it can, what standard of proof governs that issue. Compare Brief for Petitioner 25–35 with Brief for United States 24–32, 35–36. Because we hold that no presumption arose, we need not, and do not, reach these questions.

[20] The dissent recognizes "the 'wide discretion' owed to trial courts when it comes to jury-related issues", but its analysis of the District Court's *voir dire* sometimes fails to demonstrate that awareness. For example, the dissent faults the District Court for not questioning prospective jurors regarding their "knowledge of or feelings about" Causey's guilty plea. But the court could

Skilling deems the *voir dire* insufficient because, he argues, jury selection lasted "just five hours," "[m]ost of the court's questions were conclusory[,] high-level, and failed adequately to probe jurors' true feelings," and the court "consistently took prospective jurors at their word once they claimed they could be fair, no matter what other indications of bias were present." Our review of the record, however, yields a different appraisal.[21] The District Court initially screened venire members by eliciting their responses to a comprehensive questionnaire drafted in large part by Skilling. That survey helped to identify prospective jurors excusable for cause and served as a springboard for further questions put to remaining members of the array. *Voir dire* thus was, in the court's words, the "culmination of a lengthy process." * * * In other Enron-related prosecutions, we note, District Courts, after inspecting venire members' responses to questionnaires, completed the jury-selection process within one day.

The District Court conducted *voir dire*, moreover, aware of the greater-than-normal need, due to pretrial publicity, to ensure against jury bias. At Skilling's urging, the court examined each prospective juror individually, thus preventing the spread of any prejudicial information to other venire members. See *Mu'Min*.[b] To encourage candor, the court repeatedly admonished that there were "no right and wrong answers to th[e] questions." The court denied Skilling's request for attorney-led *voir dire* because, in its experience, potential jurors were "more forthcoming" when the court, rather than counsel, asked the question. The parties, however, were accorded an opportunity to ask follow-up questions of every prospective juror brought to the bench for colloquy. Skilling's counsel declined to

---

reasonably decline to ask direct questions involving Causey's plea to avoid tipping off until-that-moment uninformed venire members that the plea had occurred. * * * Nothing inhibited defense counsel from inquiring about venire members' knowledge of the plea; indeed, counsel posed such a question [citing the dissent's comment that one of the two venire members who recalled the plea did so "only after Skilling's counsel managed to squeeze in a follow-up as to whether he 'had read about any guilty pleas in this case over the last month or two'"]. From this Court's lofty and "panoramic" vantage point, lines of *voir dire* inquiry that "might be helpful in assessing whether a juror is impartial" are not hard to conceive. "To be constitutionally compelled, however, it is not enough that such questions might be helpful. Rather, the trial court's failure to ask these questions must render the defendant's trial fundamentally unfair." *Mu'Min.* * * *

[21] In addition to focusing on the adequacy of *voir dire*, our decisions have also "take[n] into account . . . other measures [that] were used to mitigate the adverse effects of publicity." *Nebraska Press Assn. v. Stuart* [fn. b, p. 866]. We have noted, for example, the prophylactic effect of "emphatic and clear instructions on the sworn duty of each juror to decide the issues only on evidence presented in open court." Here, the District Court's instructions were unequivocal; the jurors, the court emphasized, were duty bound "to reach a fair and impartial verdict in this case based solely on the evidence [they] hear[d] and read in th[e] courtroom." Peremptory challenges, too, "provid[e] protection against [prejudice]"; the District Court, as earlier noted, exercised its discretion to grant the defendants two extra peremptories.

[b] In *Mu'Min v. Virginia*, 500 U.S. 415 (1991), a divided Court rejected a defense challenge based on the trial judge's refusal to question each prospective jury separately, out of the presence of the other jurors, about the content of any "outside information" known to the juror. Writing for the majority, Chief Justice Rehnquist acknowledged that a "content inquiry" could be helpful, but stressed that the trial judge must be given "greater latitude" in shaping *voir dire* questions, especially since a content inquiry would require that prospective jurors be questioned in isolation (so other would not be exposed to the content each described), adding considerably to the length of the *voir dire*. In a separate concurring opinion, Justice O'Connor, who supplied the critical fifth vote, emphasized that the trial judge was aware of the content of the full range of publicity about the case and could appropriately conclude that even if the jurors were aware of that publicity, their assurances of impartiality were acceptable.

ask anything of more than half of the venire members questioned individually, including eight eventually selected for the jury, because, he explained, "the Court and other counsel have covered" everything he wanted to know.

Inspection of the questionnaires and *voir dire* of the individuals who actually served as jurors satisfies us that, notwithstanding the flaws Skilling lists, the selection process successfully secured jurors who were largely untouched by Enron's collapse.[24] Eleven of the seated jurors and alternates reported no connection at all to Enron, while all other jurors reported at most an insubstantial link. As for pretrial publicity, 14 jurors and alternates specifically stated that they had paid scant attention to Enron-related news.[26] * * * The remaining two jurors indicated that nothing in the news influenced their opinions about Skilling.

The questionnaires confirmed that, whatever community prejudice existed in Houston generally, Skilling's jurors were not under its sway. Although many expressed sympathy for victims of Enron's bankruptcy and speculated that greed contributed to the corporation's collapse, these sentiments did not translate into animus toward Skilling. When asked whether they "ha[d] an opinion about . . . Jeffrey Skilling," none of the seated jurors and alternates checked the "yes" box. And in response to the question whether "any opinion [they] may have formed regarding Enron or [Skilling] [would] prevent" their impartial consideration of the evidence at trial, every juror—despite options to mark "yes" or "unsure"—instead checked "no."

The District Court, Skilling asserts, should not have "accept[ed] *at face value* jurors' promises of fairness." In *Irvin v. Dowd*, 366 U.S., 717 (1961), Skilling points out, we found actual prejudice despite jurors' assurances that they could be impartial. Justice Sotomayor, in turn, repeatedly relies on *Irvin*, which she regards as closely analogous to this case. We disagree with that characterization of *Irvin*. The facts of *Irvin* are worlds apart from those presented here. Leslie Irvin stood accused of a brutal murder and robbery spree in a small rural community. In the months before Irvin's trial, "a barrage" of publicity was "unleashed against him," including reports of his confessions to the slayings and robberies. This Court's description of the media coverage in *Irvin* reveals why the dissent's "best case" is not an apt comparison. [The Court here quoted extensively from the *Irvin* opinion's

---

[24] In considering whether Skilling was tried before an impartial jury, the dissent relies extensively on venire members *not* selected for that jury [citing, inter alia, the dissent's comments on venire members 17, 29, 61, 74, and 101]. Statements by nonjurors do not themselves call into question the adequacy of the jury-selection process; elimination of these venire members is indeed one indicator that the process fulfilled its function. Critically, as discussed infra, the seated jurors showed little knowledge of or interest in, and were personally unaffected by, Enron's downfall.

[26] [The majority opinion cited excerpts from the statements of each of these 14 jurors/alternates that supported this description. Those excerpts included the following as to several of the jurors/alternates who were the subject of *voir dire* questioning characterized as insufficient by the dissent]: Juror 10 ("I haven't followed [Enron-related news] in detail of to any extreme at all.") Juror 11 (did not "get into the details of [the Enron case]" and "just kind of tune[d] [it] out"); Juror 20 ("I was out of [the] state when [Enron collapsed], and then personal circumstances kept me from paying much attention.") Juror 38 (recalled "nothing in particular" about media coverage); Juror 63 ("I don't really pay attention.") Juror 90 ("seldom" read the Houston Chronicle and did not watch any news programs); Juror 113 ("never really paid that much attention [to] it"); Juror 116 (had "rea[d] a number of different articles," but "since it hasn't affected me personally," could not "specifically recall" any of them).

description of the highly prejudicial content and wide circulation of the media coverage in that case.[c]]

Reviewing Irvin's fair-trial claim, this Court noted that "the pattern of deep and bitter prejudice" in the community "was clearly reflected in the sum total of the *voir dire*": "370 prospective jurors or almost 90% of those examined on the point . . . entertained some opinion as to guilt," and "[8] out of the 12 [jurors] thought [Irvin] was guilty." Although these jurors declared they could be impartial, we held that, "[w]ith his life at stake, it is not requiring too much that [Irvin] be tried in an atmosphere undisturbed by so huge a wave of public passion and by a jury other than one in which two-thirds of the members admit, before hearing any testimony, to possessing a belief in his guilt."

In this case, news stories about Enron contained nothing resembling the horrifying information rife in reports about Irvin's rampage of robberies and murders. Of key importance, Houston shares little in common with the rural community in which Irvin's trial proceeded, and circulation figures for Houston media sources were far lower than the 95% saturation level recorded in *Irvin*, see App. 15a ("The *Houston Chronicle* . . . reaches less than one-third of occupied households in Houston"). Skilling's seated jurors, moreover, exhibited nothing like the display of bias shown in *Irvin*. * * * In light of these large differences, the District Court had far less reason than did the trial court in *Irvin* to discredit jurors' promises of fairness.

The District Court, moreover, did not simply take venire members who proclaimed their impartiality at their word. As noted, all of Skilling's jurors had already affirmed on their questionnaires that they would have no trouble basing a verdict only on the evidence at trial. Nevertheless, the court followed up with each individually to uncover concealed bias. This face-to-face opportunity to gauge demeanor and credibility, coupled with information from the questionnaires regarding jurors' backgrounds, opinions, and sources of news, gave the court a sturdy foundation to assess fitness for jury service. * * * The jury's not-guilty verdict on nine insider-trading counts after nearly five days of deliberation,

---

[c]   As to the content of the publicity, the quoted excerpt noted: "Stories revealed the details of [Irvin's] background, including a reference to crimes committed when a juvenile, his convictions for arson almost 20 years previously, for burglary and by a court-martial on AWOL charges during the war." They also revealed that he confessed both to the six murders being investigated and a string of 24 robberies with similar modus operandi, and that he offered to plead guilty if promised a 99-year sentence, but the prosecutor was "determined to secure the death penalty." One story "dramatically relayed the promise of a sheriff to devote his life to securing [Irvin's] execution, while another characterized [Irvin] as remorseless and without conscience." Also "on the day before the trial the newspapers carried the story that Irvin had orally admitted [to] the murder of [one victim] as well as 'the robbery-murder of [a second individual]; the murder of [a third individual], and the slaughter of three members of [a different family].' "

As to the content of the publicity, the quoted excerpt noted: " '[N]ewspapers in which the[se] stories appeared were delivered regularly to 95% of the dwellings, in the county where the trial occurred, which had a population of only 30,000; radio and TV stations, which likewise blanketed that county, also carried extensive newscasts covering the same incidents.' "

meanwhile, suggests the court's assessments were accurate. Skilling, we conclude, failed to show that his *voir dire* fell short of constitutional requirements.[32]

Skilling also singles out several jurors in particular and contends they were openly biased. See *United States v. Martinez-Salazar*, 528 U.S. 304 (2000) ("[T]he seating of any juror who should have been dismissed for cause ... require[s] reversal."). In reviewing claims of this type, the deference due to district courts is at its pinnacle: "A trial court's findings of juror impartiality may be overturned only for manifest error." *Mu'Min*. Skilling, moreover, unsuccessfully challenged only one of the seated jurors for cause, "strong evidence that he was convinced the [other] jurors were not biased and had not formed any opinions as to his guilt." * * * With these considerations in mind, we turn to Skilling's specific allegations of juror partiality.

Skilling contends that Juror 11—the only seated juror he challenged for cause—"expressed the most obvious bias." Juror 11 stated that "greed on Enron's part" triggered the company's bankruptcy and that corporate executives, driven by avarice, "walk a line that stretches sometimes the legality of something." But, as the Fifth Circuit accurately summarized, Juror 11 "had 'no idea' whether Skilling had 'crossed that line,' and he 'didn't say that' every CEO is probably a crook. He also asserted that he could be fair and require the government to prove its case, that he did not believe everything he read in the paper, that he did not 'get into the details' of the Enron coverage, that he did not watch television, and that Enron was 'old news.' " * * * Despite his criticism of greed, Juror 11 remarked that Skilling "earned [his] salar[y]," and said he would have "no problem" telling his co-worker, who had lost 401(k) funds due to Enron's collapse, that the jury voted to acquit, if that scenario came to pass. The District Court, noting that it had "looked [Juror 11] in the eye and ... heard all his [answers]," found his assertions of impartiality credible. We agree with the Court of Appeals that "[t]he express finding that Juror 11 was fair is not reversible error."[33]

Skilling also objected at trial to the seating of six specific jurors whom, he said, he would have excluded had he not already exhausted his peremptory challenges. Juror 20, he observes, "said she was 'angry' about Enron's collapse and that she, too, had been 'forced to forfeit [her] own 401(k) funds to survive layoffs.' " But Juror 20 made clear during *voir dire* that she did not "personally blame" Skilling for the loss of her retirement account. Having not "pa[id] much attention" to Enron-related news, she "quite honestly" did not "have enough information to know" whether Skilling was probably guilty, and she "th[ought] [she] could be" fair and impartial.

---

[32] Skilling emphasizes that *voir dire* did not weed out every juror who suffered from Enron's collapse because the District Court failed to grant his for-cause challenge to Venire Member 29, whose retirement fund lost $50,000 due to ripple effects from the decline in the value of Enron stock. Critically, however, Venire Member 29 *did not sit on Skilling's jury*: Instead, Skilling struck her using a peremptory challenge. "[I]f [a] defendant elects to cure [a trial judge's erroneous for-cause ruling] by exercising a peremptory challenge, and is subsequently convicted by a jury on which no biased juror sat," we have held, "he has not been deprived of any ... constitutional right." *United States v. Martinez-Salazar*. Indeed, the "use [of] a peremptory challenge to effect an instantaneous cure of the error" exemplifies "a principal reason for peremptories: to help secure the constitutional guarantee of trial by an impartial jury."

[33] Skilling's trial counsel and jury consultants apparently did not regard Juror 11 as so "obvious[ly] bias[ed]," as to warrant exercise of a peremptory challenge.

In light of these answers, the District Court did not commit manifest error in finding Juror 20 fit for jury service.

The same is true of Juror 63, who, Skilling points out, wrote on her questionnaire "that [Skilling] 'probably knew [he] w[as] breaking the law.' " During *voir dire*, however, Juror 63 insisted that she did not "really have an opinion [about Skilling's guilt] either way," she did not "know what [she] was thinking" when she completed the questionnaire, but she "absolutely" presumed Skilling innocent and confirmed her understanding that the Government would "have to prove" his guilt. * * * "Jurors," we have recognized, "cannot be expected invariably to express themselves carefully or even consistently." *Yount*, [fn. 14 supra]. From where we sit, we cannot conclude that Juror 63 was biased. * * * The four remaining jurors Skilling said he would have excluded with extra peremptory strikes [Jurors 38, 67, 78, and 84] exhibited no sign of prejudice we can discern. * * *

In sum, Skilling failed to establish that a presumption of prejudice arose or that actual bias infected the jury that tried him. Jurors, the trial court correctly comprehended, need not enter the box with empty heads in order to determine the facts impartially. "It is sufficient if the juror[s] can lay aside [their] impression[s] or opinion[s] and render a verdict based on the evidence presented in court." *Irvin*. Taking account of the full record, rather than incomplete exchanges selectively culled from it, we find no cause to upset the lower courts' judgment that Skilling's jury met that measure. We therefore affirm the Fifth Circuit's ruling that Skilling received a fair trial.

JUSTICE ALITO, concurring in part and concurring in the judgment.

I write separately to address petitioner's jury-trial argument. * * * The Sixth Amendment guarantees criminal defendants a trial before "an impartial jury." In my view, this requirement is satisfied so long as no biased juror is actually seated at trial. Of course, evidence of pretrial media attention and widespread community hostility may play a role in the bias inquiry. Such evidence may be important in assessing the adequacy of *voir dire*, or in reviewing the denial of requests to dismiss particular jurors for cause. There are occasions in which such evidence weighs heavily in favor of a change of venue. In the end, however, if no biased jury is actually seated, there is no violation of the defendant's right to an impartial jury.

Petitioner advances a very different understanding of the jury-trial right. Where there is extraordinary pretrial publicity and community hostility, he contends, a court must presume juror prejudice and thus grant a change of venue. I disagree. Careful *voir dire* can often ensure the selection of impartial jurors even where pretrial media coverage has generated much hostile community sentiment. Moreover, once a jury has been selected, there are measures that a trial judge may take to insulate jurors from media coverage during the course of the trial. * * * The rule that petitioner advances departs from the text of the Sixth Amendment and is difficult to apply. It requires a trial judge to determine whether the adverse pretrial media coverage and community hostility in a particular case has reached a certain level of severity, but there is no clear way of demarcating that level or of determining whether it has been met. * * * Petitioner relies chiefly on three cases from the 1960s—*Sheppard v. Maxwell*, *Estes v. Texas*, and *Rideau v. Louisiana*. I do not read those cases as demanding petitioner's suggested approach. As the Court notes, *Sheppard* and *Estes* primarily "involved media interference with courtroom proceedings *during* trial." *Rideau* involved unique events in a small community.

I share some of Justice Sotomayor's concerns about the adequacy of the *voir dire* in this case and the trial judge's findings that certain jurors could be impartial. But those highly fact-specific issues are not within the question presented. Pet. for Cert. i. I also do not understand the opinion of the Court as reaching any question regarding a change of venue under Federal Rule of Criminal Procedure 21.

JUSTICE SOTOMAYOR, with whom JUSTICE STEVENS and JUSTICE BREYER join, concurring in part and dissenting in part.

I respectfully dissent, * * * from the Court's conclusion that Jeffrey Skilling received a fair trial before an impartial jury. Under our relevant precedents, the more intense the public's antipathy toward a defendant, the more careful a court must be to prevent that sentiment from tainting the jury. * * * The District Court's inquiry [here] lacked the necessary thoroughness and left serious doubts about whether the jury empaneled to decide Skilling's case was capable of rendering an impartial decision based solely on the evidence presented in the courtroom. Accordingly, I would grant Skilling relief on his fair-trial claim.

The majority understates the breadth and depth of community hostility toward Skilling and overlooks significant deficiencies in the District Court's jury selection process. The failure of Enron wounded Houston deeply. * * * Thousands of the company's employees lost their jobs and saw their retirement savings vanish. As the effects rippled through the local economy, thousands of additional jobs disappeared, businesses shuttered, and community groups that once benefited from Enron's largesse felt the loss of millions of dollars in contributions. * * * Enron's community ties were so extensive that the entire local U.S. Attorney's Office was forced to recuse itself from the Government's investigation into the company's fall.

With Enron's demise affecting the lives of so many Houstonians, local media coverage of the story saturated the community. According to a defense media expert, the Houston Chronicle—the area's leading newspaper—assigned as many as 12 reporters to work on the Enron story full time. The paper mentioned Enron in more than 4,000 articles during the 3-year period following the company's December 2001 bankruptcy filing. Hundreds of these articles discussed Skilling by name. Skilling's expert, a professional journalist and academic with 30 years' experience, could not "recall another instance where a local paper dedicated as many resources to a single topic over such an extended period of time as the Houston Chronicle . . . dedicated to Enron." Local television news coverage was similarly pervasive and, in terms of "editorial theme," "largely followed the Chronicle's lead." Between May 2002 and October 2004, local stations aired an estimated 19,000 news segments involving Enron, more than 1600 of which mentioned Skilling.

While many of the stories were straightforward news items, many others conveyed and amplified the community's outrage at the top executives perceived to be responsible for the company's bankruptcy. A Chronicle report on Skilling's 2002 testimony before Congress is typical of the coverage. It began, "Across Houston, Enron employees watched former chief executive Jeffrey Skilling's congressional testimony on television, turning incredulous, angry and then sarcastic by turns, as a man they knew as savvy and detail-oriented pleaded memory failure and ignorance about critical financial transactions at the now-collapsed energy giant." "'He is lying; he knew everything,' said [an employee], who said she had seen Skilling frequently over her 18 years with the firm, where Skilling was known for his intimate grasp of the inner doings at the company. 'I am getting sicker by the minute.'" * * * Articles deriding Enron's senior executives were juxtaposed with pieces expressing sympathy toward and solidarity with the company's many victims. Skilling's media expert counted nearly a hundred victim-related stories in the Chronicle, including a "multi-page layout entitled 'The Faces of Enron,'" which poignantly described the gut-wrenching experiences of former employees who lost vast sums of money, faced eviction from their homes, could not afford Christmas gifts for their children, and felt "scared," "hurt," "humiliat[ed]," "helpless," and "betrayed." The conventional wisdom that blame for Enron's devastating implosion and the ensuing human tragedy ultimately rested with Skilling and former Enron Chairman Kenneth Lay became so deeply ingrained in the popular imagination that references to their involvement even turned up on the sports pages: "If you believe the story about [Coach Bill Parcells] not having anything to do with the end of Emmitt Smith's Cowboys career, then you probably believe in other far-fetched concepts. Like Jeff Skilling having nothing to do with Enron's collapse." * * *

The Sixth Amendment right to an impartial jury and the due process right to a fundamentally fair trial guarantee to criminal defendants a trial in which jurors set aside preconceptions, disregard extrajudicial influences, and decide guilt or innocence "based on the evidence presented in court." *Irvin v. Dowd.* Community passions, often inflamed by adverse pretrial publicity, can call the integrity of a trial into doubt. In some instances, this Court has observed, the hostility of the community becomes so severe as to give rise to a "presumption of [juror] prejudice." *Patton v. Yount.* * * * The Court of Appeals incorporated the concept of presumptive prejudice into a burden-shifting framework: Once the defendant musters sufficient evidence of community hostility, the onus shifts to the Government to prove the impartiality of the jury. The majority similarly envisions a fixed point at which public passions become so intense that prejudice to a defendant's fair-trial rights must be presumed. The majority declines, however, to decide whether the presumption is rebuttable, as the Court of Appeals held.

This Court has never treated the notion of presumptive prejudice so formalistically. Our decisions instead merely convey the commonsense understanding that as the tide of public enmity rises, so too does the danger that the prejudices of the community will infiltrate the jury. The underlying question has always been this: Do we have confidence that the jury's verdict was "induced only by evidence and argument in open court, and not by any outside influence, whether of private talk or public print"? *Patterson v. Colorado ex rel. Attorney General of Colo.*, 205 U.S. 454 (1907). * * * This inquiry is necessarily case specific. * * * This Court's precedents illustrate the sort of steps required in different situations to safeguard a defendant's constitutional right to a fair trial before an impartial jury.

At one end of the spectrum, this Court has, on rare occasion, confronted such inherently prejudicial circumstances that it has reversed a defendant's conviction "without pausing to examine . . . the *voir dire* examination of the members of the jury." *Rideau v. Louisiana.* In *Rideau*, repeated television broadcasts of the defendant's confession to murder, robbery, and kidnapping so thoroughly poisoned local sentiment as to raise doubts that even the most careful *voir dire* could have secured an impartial jury. A change of venue, the Court determined, was thus the only way to assure a fair trial. * * * As the majority describes, this Court reached similar conclusions in *Estes v. Texas*, and *Sheppard v. Maxwell.* These cases involved not only massive pretrial publicity but also media disruption of the trial process itself. * * * *Estes* and *Sheppard* * * * applied *Rideau*'s insight that in particularly extreme circumstances even the most rigorous *voir dire* cannot suffice to dispel the reasonable likelihood of jury bias.

Apart from these exceptional cases, this Court has declined to discount *voir dire* entirely and has instead examined the particulars of the jury selection process to determine whether it sufficed to produce a jury untainted by pretrial publicity and community animus. The Court has recognized that when antipathy toward a defendant pervades the community there is a high risk that biased jurors will find their way onto the panel. The danger is not merely that some prospective jurors will deliberately hide their prejudices, but also that, as "part of a community deeply hostile to the accused," "they may unwittingly [be] influenced" by the fervor that surrounds them. *Murphy v. Florida.* To assure an impartial jury in such adverse circumstances, a trial court must carefully consider the knowledge and attitudes of prospective jurors and then closely scrutinize the reliability of their assurances of fairness.

Irvin v. Dowd offers an example of a case in which the trial court's *voir dire* did not suffice to counter the "wave of public passion" that had swept the community prior to the defendant's trial. * * * Despite the seated jurors' assurances of impartiality, this Court invalidated *Irvin*'s conviction for want of due process. * * * The Court did not "doubt [that] each juror was sincere when he said that he would be fair and impartial to [Irvin], but . . . [w]here so many, so many times, admitted prejudice, such a statement of impartiality can be given little weight."

The media coverage and community animosity in *Irvin* was particularly intense. In three subsequent cases, [*Murphy* v. *Florida, Patton v. Yount, and Mu'Min v. Virginia*], this Court recognized that high-profile cases may generate substantial publicity without stirring similar public passions. The jury selection process in such cases, the Court clarified, generally need not be as exhaustive as in a case such as *Irvin*. So long as the trial court conducts a reasonable inquiry into extrajudicial influences and the ability of prospective jurors to presume innocence and render a verdict based solely on the trial evidence, we would generally have no reason to doubt the jury's impartiality. * * *

It is necessary to determine how this case compares to our existing fair-trial precedents. Were the circumstances so inherently prejudicial that, as in *Rideau*, even the most scrupulous *voir dire* would have been "but a hollow formality" incapable of reliably producing an impartial jury? * * * Though the question is close, I agree with the Court that the prospect of seating an unbiased jury in Houston was not so remote as to compel the conclusion that the District Court acted unconstitutionally in denying Skilling's motion to change venue. * * * It is thus appropriate to examine the *voir dire* and determine whether it instills confidence in the impartiality of the jury actually selected. * * *

I am mindful of the "wide discretion" owed to trial courts when it comes to jury-related issues. Trial courts are uniquely positioned to assess public sentiment and the credibility of prospective jurors. Proximity to events, however, is not always a virtue. Persons in the midst of a tumult often lack a panoramic view. "[A]ppellate tribunals [thus] have the duty to make an independent evaluation of the circumstances." *Sheppard*. In particular, reviewing courts are well qualified to inquire into whether a trial court implemented procedures adequate to keep community prejudices from infecting the jury. If the jury selection process does not befit the circumstances of the case, the trial court's rulings on impartiality are necessarily called into doubt. * * *

As the Court of Appeals apprehended, the District Court gave short shrift to the mountainous evidence of public hostility. For Houstonians, Enron's collapse was an event of once-in-a-generation proportions. Not only was the volume of media coverage "immense" and frequently intemperate, but "the sheer number of victims" created a climate in which animosity toward Skilling ran deep and the desire for conviction was widely shared. * * * The level of public animus toward Skilling dwarfed that present in cases such as *Murphy* and *Mu'Min*. The much closer analogy is thus to *Irvin*, which similarly featured a "barrage" of media coverage and a "huge . . . wave of public passion," although even that case did not, as here, involve direct harm to entire segments of the community. * * * Attempting to distinguish *Irvin*, the majority suggests that Skilling's economic offenses were less incendiary than Irvin's violent crime spree and that "news stories about Enron contained nothing resembling the horrifying information rife in reports about Irvin's rampage of robberies and murders." * * * The majority also points to the four years that passed between Enron's declaration of bankruptcy and the start of Skilling's trial, that "the decibel level of media attention diminished somewhat" over this time. Neither of these arguments is persuasive.

First, while violent crimes may well provoke widespread community outrage more readily than crimes involving monetary loss, economic crimes are certainly capable of rousing public passions, particularly when thousands of unsuspecting people are robbed of their livelihoods and retirement savings. Indeed, the record in this case is replete with examples of visceral outrage toward Skilling and other Enron executives. Houstonians compared Skilling to, among other things, a rapist, an axe murderer, and an Al Qaeda terrorist. * * * The bad blood was so strong that Skilling and other top executives hired private security to protect themselves from persons inclined to take the law into their own hands.

Second, the passage of time did little to soften community sentiment. Contrary to the Court's suggestion, this case in no way resembles *Yount*, where, by the time of the defendant's retrial, "prejudicial publicity [had] greatly diminished" and community animus had significantly waned. * * * The Enron story was a continuing saga, and "publicity remained intense throughout." Not only did Enron's downfall generate wall-to-wall news coverage, but so too did a succession of subsequent Enron-related events. Of particular note is the highly publicized guilty plea of codefendant Causey just weeks before Skilling's trial. If anything, the time that elapsed between the bankruptcy and the trial made the task of seating an unbiased jury more difficult, not less. For many members of the jury pool, each highly publicized Enron-related guilty plea or conviction likely served to increase their certainty that Skilling too had engaged in—if not masterminded—criminal acts, particularly given that the media coverage reinforced this view.

Any doubt that the prevailing mindset in the Houston community remained overwhelmingly negative was dispelled by prospective jurors' responses to the written questionnaires. * * * More than one-third of the prospective jurors either knew victims of Enron's collapse or were victims themselves, and two-thirds gave responses suggesting an antidefendant bias. In many instances their contempt for Skilling was palpable. Only a small fraction of the prospective jurors raised no red flags in their responses. And this was *before* Causey's guilty plea and the flurry of news reports that accompanied the approach of trial. One of Skilling's experts, a political scientist who had studied pretrial publicity "for over 35 years" and consulted in more than 200 high-profile cases (in which he had recommended against venue changes more often than not), "c[a]me to the conclusion that the extent and depth of bias shown in these questionnaires is the highest or at least one of the very highest I have ever encountered."

Given the extent of the antipathy evident both in the community at large and in the responses to the written questionnaire, it was critical for the District Court to take "strong measures" to ensure the selection of "an impartial jury free from outside influences." As this Court has recognized, "[i]n a community where most veniremen will admit to a disqualifying prejudice, the reliability of the others' protestations may be drawn into question." *Murphy.* * * * Perhaps because it had underestimated the public's antipathy toward Skilling, the District Court's 5-hour *voir dire* was manifestly insufficient to identify and remove biased jurors.[13]

As an initial matter, important lines of inquiry were not pursued at all. The majority accepts, for instance, that "publicity about a codefendant's guilty plea calls for inquiry to guard against actual prejudice." Implying that the District Court undertook this inquiry, the majority states that "[o]nly two venire members recalled [Causey's] plea." In fact, the court asked very few prospective jurors any questions directed to their knowledge of or feelings about that event. Considering how much news the plea generated, many more than two venire members were

---

[13] * * * [I]n referencing the length of the *voir dire* in this case, I do not mean to suggest that length should be a principal measure of the adequacy of a jury selection process. Trial courts, including this one, should be commended for striving to be efficient, but they must always take care to ensure that their expeditiousness does not compromise a defendant's fair-trial right. I also express no view with respect to court-led versus attorney-led *voir dire*. Federal Rule of Criminal Procedure 24(a) gives district courts discretion to choose between these options, and I have no doubt that either is capable of producing an impartial jury even in high profile cases so long as the trial court assures that the scope of the *voir dire* is tailored to the circumstances.

likely aware of it. The lack of questioning, however, makes the prejudicial impact of the plea on those jurors impossible to assess.

The court also rarely asked prospective jurors to describe personal interactions they may have had about the case, or to consider whether they might have difficulty avoiding discussion of the case with family, friends, or colleagues during the course of the lengthy trial. The tidbits of information that trickled out on these subjects provided cause for concern. In response to general media-related questions, several prospective jurors volunteered that they had spoken with others about the case. Juror 74, for example, indicated that her husband was the "news person," that they had "talked about it," that she had also heard things "from work," and that what she heard was "all negative, of course." The court, however, did not seek elaboration about the substance of these interactions. Surely many prospective jurors had similar conversations, particularly once they learned upon receiving the written questionnaire that they might end up on Skilling's jury. * * * Prospective jurors' personal interactions, moreover, may well have left them with the sense that the community was counting on a conviction. Yet this too was a subject the District Court did not adequately explore. * * *

With respect to potential nonmedia sources of bias, the District Court's exchange with Juror 101 is particularly troubling. Although Juror 101 responded in the negative when asked whether she had "read anything in the newspaper that [stood] out in [her] mind," she volunteered that she "just heard that, between the two of them, [Skilling and Lay] had $43 million to contribute for their case and that there was an insurance policy that they could collect on, also." This information, she explained, "was just something I overheard today—other jurors talking." It seemed suspicious, she intimated, "to have an insurance policy ahead of time." The court advised her that "most corporations provide insurance for their officers and directors." The court, however, did not investigate the matter further, even though it had earlier instructed prospective jurors not to talk to each other about the case. It is thus not apparent whether other prospective jurors also overheard the information and whether they too believed that it reflected unfavorably on the defendants; nor is it apparent what other outside information may have been shared among the venire members. At the very least, Juror 101's statements indicate that the court's questions were failing to bring to light the extent of jurors' exposure to potentially prejudicial facts and that some prospective jurors were having difficulty following the court's directives.

The topics that the District Court did cover were addressed in cursory fashion. Most prospective jurors were asked just a few yes/no questions about their general exposure to media coverage and a handful of additional questions concerning any responses to the written questionnaire that suggested bias. In many instances, their answers were unenlightening. Yet the court rarely sought to draw them out with open-ended questions about their impressions of Enron or Skilling and showed limited patience for counsel's followup efforts.[17] When prospective jurors

---

[17] The majority's criticism of Skilling's counsel for failing to ask questions of many of the prospective jurors, is thus misplaced. Given the District Court's express warning early in the *voir dire* that it would not allow counsel "to ask individual questions if [they] abuse[d]" that right, counsel can hardly be blamed for declining to test the court's boundaries at every turn. Moreover,

were more forthcoming, their responses tended to highlight the ubiquity and negative tone of the local news coverage, thus underscoring the need to press the more guarded members of the venire for further information. Juror 17, for example, mentioned hearing a radio program that very morning in which a former Enron employee compared persons who did not think Skilling was guilty to Holocaust deniers. * * * Other jurors may well have encountered, and been influenced by, similarly incendiary rhetoric.

These deficiencies in the form and content of the *voir dire* questions contributed to a deeper problem: The District Court failed to make a sufficiently critical assessment of prospective jurors' assurances of impartiality. Although the Court insists otherwise, the *voir dire* transcript indicates that the District Court essentially took jurors at their word when they promised to be fair. Indeed, the court declined to dismiss for cause any prospective juror who ultimately gave a clear assurance of impartiality, no matter how much equivocation preceded it. Juror 29, for instance, wrote on her questionnaire that Skilling was "not an honest man." During questioning, she acknowledged having previously thought the defendants were guilty, and she disclosed that she lost $50,000–$60,000 in her 401(k) as a result of Enron's collapse. But she ultimately agreed that she would be able to presume innocence. Noting that she "blame[d] Enron for the loss of her money" and appeared to have "unshakeable bias," Skilling's counsel challenged her for cause. The court, however, declined to remove her, stating that "she answered candidly she's going to have an open mind now" and "agree[ing]" with the Government's assertion that "we have to take her at her word."[20]

Worse still, the District Court on a number of occasions accepted declarations of impartiality that were equivocal on their face. Prospective jurors who "hope[d]" they could presume innocence and did "not necessarily" think Skilling was guilty were permitted to remain in the pool. Juror 61, for instance, wrote of Lay on her questionnaire, "Shame on him." Asked by the court about this, she stated that, "innocent or guilty, he was at the helm" and "should have known what was going on at the company." * * * The court then asked, "can you presume, as you start this trial, that Mr. Lay is innocent?" She responded, "I hope so, but you know. I don't know. I can't honestly answer that one way or the other." See also App. 933a ("I bring in my past history. I bring in my biases. I would like to think I could rise above those, but I've never been in this situation before. So I don't know how I could honestly answer that question one way or the other. . . . I do have some concerns"). Eventually, however, Juror 61 answered "Yes" when the court asked if she would

---

the court's perfunctory exchanges with prospective jurors often gave counsel no clear avenue for further permissible inquiry.

   [20] The majority attempts to downplay the significance of Juror 29 by noting that she did not end up on the jury because Skilling used a peremptory challenge to remove her. See fn. 32. The majority makes a similar point with respect to other venire members who were not ultimately seated. See fn. 24. The comments of these venire members, however, are relevant in assessing the impartiality of the seated jurors, who were similarly "part of a community deeply hostile to the accused" and who may have been "unwittingly influenced by it." *Murphy v. Florida*. Moreover, the fact that the District Court failed to remove persons as dubiously qualified as Juror 29 goes directly to the adequacy of its *voir dire*. If Juror 29 made it through to the end of the selection process, it is difficult to have confidence in the impartiality of the jurors who sat, especially given how little is known about many of them.

be able to acquit if she had "a reasonable doubt that the defendants are guilty." Challenging her for cause, defense counsel insisted that they had not received "a clear and unequivocal answer" about her ability to be fair. The court denied the challenge, stating, "You know, she tried."

The majority takes solace in the fact that most of the persons actually seated as jurors and alternates "specifically stated that they had paid scant attention to Enron-related news." In context, however, these general declarations reveal little about the seated jurors' actual knowledge or views or the possible pressure they might have felt to convict, and thus cannot instill confidence that the jurors "were not under [the] sway" of the prevailing community sentiment. Juror 63, for instance, [as quoted by the majority] told the court that she "may have heard a little bit" about Enron-related litigation but had not "really pa[id] attention." Yet she was clearly aware of some specifics. On her questionnaire, despite stating that she had not followed Enron-related news, she wrote about "whistleblowers and Arthur Andersen lying about Enron's accounting," and she expressed the view that Skilling and Lay "probably knew they were breaking the law." During questioning, which lasted barely four minutes, the District Court obtained no meaningful information about the actual extent of Juror 63's familiarity with the case or the basis for her belief in Skilling's guilt. Yet it nevertheless accepted her assurance that she could "absolutely" presume innocence.

Indeed, the District Court's anemic questioning did little to dispel similar doubts about the impartiality of numerous other seated jurors and alternates. In my estimation, more than half of those seated made written and oral comments suggesting active antipathy toward the defendants. The majority thus misses the mark when it asserts that "Skilling's seated jurors . . . exhibited nothing like the display of bias shown in *Irvin*." Juror 10, for instance, reported on his written questionnaire that he knew several co-workers who owned Enron stock; that he personally may have owned Enron stock through a mutual fund; that he heard and read about the Enron cases from the "Houston Chronicle, all three Houston news channels, Fox news, talking with friends [and] co-workers, [and] Texas Lawyer Magazine"; that he believed Enron's collapse "was due to greed and mismanagement"; * * * and that the defendants were "suspect." During questioning, he said he "th[ought]" he could presume innocence and "believe[d]" he could put the Government to its proof, but he also acknowledged that he might have "some hesitancy" "in telling people the government didn't prove its case." Juror 11 wrote * * * [about various sources of "Enron-related news" and his belief "that 'greed on Enron's part'" caused the company's collapse]. During questioning, he stated that he would have "no problem" requiring the Government to prove its case, but he also told the court * * * that corporate executives are often "stretching the legal limits. . . . I'm not going to say that they're all crooks, but you know." Asked whether he would "start the case with sort of an inkling that because [Lay's] greedy he must have done something illegal," he offered an indeterminate "not necessarily."[23]

---

[23] Many other seated jurors and alternates expressed similarly troubling sentiments. (Juror 20) (obtained Enron-related news from the Chronicle and "local news stations"; blamed Enron's collapse on "[n]ot enough corporate controls or effective audit procedures to prevent

* * * In assessing the likelihood that bias lurked in the minds of at least some of these seated jurors, I find telling the way in which *voir dire* played out. When the District Court asked the prospective jurors as a group whether they had any reservations about their ability to presume innocence and put the Government to its proof, only two answered in the affirmative, and both were excused for cause. The District Court's individual questioning, though truncated, exposed disqualifying prejudices among numerous additional prospective jurors who had earlier expressed no concerns about their impartiality. It thus strikes me as highly likely that at least some of the seated jurors, despite stating that they could be fair, harbored similar biases that a more probing inquiry would likely have exposed. Cf. *Yount* (holding that the trial court's "particularly extensive" 10-day *voir dire* assured the jury's impartiality).[25]

The majority suggests, that the jury's decision to acquit Skilling on nine relatively minor insider trading charges confirms its impartiality. This argument, however, mistakes partiality with bad faith or blind vindictiveness. Jurors who act in good faith and sincerely believe in their own fairness may nevertheless harbor disqualifying prejudices. Such jurors may well acquit where evidence is wholly lacking, while subconsciously resolving closer calls against the defendant rather than giving him the benefit of the doubt. * * * In this regard, it is significant that the Government placed relatively little emphasis on the nine insider trading counts during its closing argument, declining to explain its theory on all but one of the counts in any detail whatsoever. The acquittals on those counts thus provide scant basis for inferring a lack of prejudice.

In sum, I cannot accept the majority's conclusion that *voir dire* gave the District Court "a sturdy foundation to assess fitness for jury service." Taken together, the District Court's failure to cover certain vital subjects, its superficial coverage of other topics, and its uncritical acceptance of assurances of impartiality leave me doubtful that Skilling's jury was indeed free from the deep-seated animosity that pervaded the community at large. "[R]egardless of the heinousness of the crime charged, the apparent guilt of the offender[,] or the station in life which

---

mismanagement of corporate assets"; and was "angry that so many people lost their jobs and their retirement savings"); (Juror 38) (followed Enron-related news from various sources, including the Chronicle; was "angry about what happened"; and "fe[lt] bad for those that worked hard and invested in the corp[oration] only to have it all taken away"); (Juror 90) (heard Enron-related news from his wife, co-workers, and television; wrote that "[i]t's not right for someone . . . to take" away the money that the "small average worker saves . . . for retirement all his life"; and described the Government's Enron investigation as "a good thing"); (Juror 113) (obtained information about Enron from a "co-worker [who] was in the jury pool for Mrs. Fastow's trial"; worked for an employer who lost money as a result of Enron's collapse; found it "sad" that the collapse had affected "such a huge number of people"; and thought "someone had to be doing something illegal"); (Juror 116) (knew a colleague who lost money in Enron's collapse; obtained Enron-related news from the "Houston Chronicle, Time Magazine, local TV news [and] radio, friends, family, [and] co-workers, [and] internet news sources"; and noted that what stood out was "[t]he employees and retirees that lost their savings").

[25] The majority suggests that the fact that Skilling "challenged only one of the seated jurors for cause" indicates that he did not believe the other jurors were biased. Our decisions, however, distinguish claims involving "the partiality of an individual juror" from antecedent claims directed at "the partiality of the trial jury as a whole." *Patton v. Yount*. If the jury selection process does not, as here, give a defendant a fair opportunity to identify biased jurors, the defendant can hardly be faulted for failing to make for-cause challenges.

he occupies," our system of justice demands trials that are fair in both appearance and fact. *Irvin.* Because I do not believe Skilling's trial met this standard, I would grant him relief.

GENTILE V. STATE BAR OF NEVADA
501 U.S. 1030, 111 S.Ct. 2720, 115 L.Ed.2d 888 (1991).

JUSTICE KENNEDY announced the judgment of the Court and delivered the opinion of the Court with respect to Parts III and VI, and an opinion with respect to Parts I, II, IV, and V in which JUSTICE MARSHALL, JUSTICE BLACKMUN and JUSTICE STEVENS joined.

[The Las Vegas Metropolitan Police Department (Metro) stored in a safety deposit box at Western Vault drugs and money used in an undercover operation. On February 2nd, 1987, the Las Vegas Sheriff announced in a press conference that large amounts of cocaine and travelers' checks were missing from that box. Announced as possible suspects were the police and Western Vault employees. Initial reports suggested that the primary suspects were two detectives (Schaub and Scholl) who had free access to the deposit box, but later reports suggested that the attention of investigators had turned to Grady Sanders, the owner of Western Vault. Media coverage continued over the next year with reports that: (1) others with deposit boxes at Western Vault had subsequently reported that items were missing from their boxes, and the police had opened still other deposit boxes in search of the missing items; (2) $264,900 had been found in a box listed as unrented, and that money had apparently been stored there by Tammy Markham, a person who had reported missing items, and who was facing drug charges in another jurisdiction; (3) another person who had reported missing items (Connick) was a "Columbian national" who was "not facing any drug related charges" and who had passed a lie detector test to substantiate her claim; (4) the initial police theory was that the theft from the Metro box was part of an effort to discredit the undercover police operation, and business records indicated a relationship between Sanders and the targets of that operation; (5) the subsequent police theory was that the thief had unwittingly stolen from the police; (6) the sheriff had expressed "complete faith and trust" in his officers, but the F.B.I. suspected that the officers were responsible for the theft and that had severely damaged relations between the F.B.I. and Metro; (7) the detectives Scholl and Schaub had been cleared by police investigators after passing lie detector tests; and (8) Sanders had refused to take a lie detector test.

[On February 4, 1988, Sanders was indicted on theft charges, and on February 5th, he was arraigned, with trial set for August 1988. The petitioner Gentile, the attorney representing Sanders, had advance notice of the indictment, and on the day of the arraignment held a press conference (his first in a long career as a defense attorney). At the press conference, Gentile issued a prepared statement in which he stated that: (1) the case was similar to those in other cities, but there the authorities had been "honest enough to indict the people who did it"—"the police department, crooked cops"; (2) when the case is tried the evidence will prove "not only [that] Sanders is an innocent person," but that Detective Scholl "was in the most direct position to have stolen the drugs and money"; (3) there is "far more evidence [that] Detective Scholl took the drugs [and] travelers' checks than any other living human being"; (4) "I feel [that] Sanders is being used as a scapegoat to cover up for what has to be obvious to [law enforcement authorities]"; and (5) with respect to the claimed thefts from other boxes, "the so-called victims" "are known drug dealers and convicted money launderers and drug dealers" and had accused Sanders in response to police pressure. In response to a question from a reporter, Gentile strongly implied that Detective Scholl could be observed in a videotape suffering from symptoms of cocaine use. In several instances, he refused to answer reporters' questions on specific details, noting that he could not elaborate "because ethics prohibit me from doing so." The two newspaper stories and two TV news broadcast that mentioned Gentile's press conference also mentioned a prosecution response and a police press conference in response. The prosecution characterized the indictment as legitimate, and the police stated that they remained satisfied that the two detectives were "above reproach."

[Some six months later, Sanders' criminal case was tried by a jury and he was acquitted on all counts. A state disciplinary board then brought proceedings against Gentile and concluded that he had violated Nevada Supreme Court Rule 177, set forth below.[a] That Rule was based on Rule 3.6 of the ABA Model Rules of

---

[a]   *Nevada Supreme Court Rule 177, "Trial Publicity*

"1.   A lawyer shall not make an extrajudicial statement that a reasonable person would expect to be disseminated by means of public communication if the lawyer knows or reasonably should know that it will have a substantial likelihood of materially prejudicing an adjudicative proceeding.

"2.   A statement referred to in subsection 1 ordinarily is likely to have such an effect when it refers to a civil matter triable to a jury, a criminal matter, or any other proceeding that could result in incarceration, and the statement relates to:

"(a)   the character, credibility, reputation or criminal record of a party, suspect in a criminal investigation or witness, or the identity of a witness, or the expected testimony of a party or witness;

"(b)   in a criminal case or proceeding that could result in incarceration, the possibility of a plea of guilty to the offense or the existence or contents of any confession, admission, or statement given by a defendant or suspect or that person's refusal or failure to make a statement;

"(c)   the performance or results of any examination or test or the refusal or failure of a person to submit to an examination or test, or the identity or nature of physical evidence expected to be presented;

"(d)   any opinion as to the guilt or innocence of a defendant or suspect in a criminal case or proceeding that could result in incarceration;

"(e)   information the lawyer knows or reasonably should know is likely to be inadmissible as evidence in a trial and would if disclosed create a substantial risk of prejudicing an impartial trial; or

"(f)   the fact that a defendant has been charged with a crime, unless there is included therein a statement explaining that the charge is merely an accusation and that the defendant is presumed innocent until and unless proven guilty.

"3.   Notwithstanding subsection 1 and 2(f), a lawyer involved in the investigation or litigation of a matter may state without elaboration:

"(a)   the general nature of the claim or defense;

"(b)   the information contained in a public record;

"(c)   that an investigation of the matter is in progress, including the general scope of the investigation, the offense or claim or defense involved and, except when prohibited by law, the identity of the persons involved;

Professional Conduct, and is an almost verbatim duplicate of ABA Rule 3.6. The disciplinary board recommended issuance of a private reprimand for violation of Rule 177. The state supreme court then affirmed that decision.]

I

* * * At issue here is the constitutionality of a ban on political speech critical of the government and its officials. Unlike other First Amendment cases * * * in which speech is not the direct target of the regulation or statute in question, this case involves punishment of pure speech in the political forum. Petitioner engaged not in solicitation of clients or advertising for his practice, as in our precedents from which some of our colleagues would discern a standard of diminished First Amendment protection. His words were directed at public officials and their conduct in office. * * *

The judicial system, and in particular our criminal justice courts, play a vital part in a democratic state, and the public has a legitimate interest in their operations. See, e.g., *Landmark Communications, Inc. v. Virginia*, 435 U.S. 829 (1978). "[I]t would be difficult to single out any aspect of government of higher concern and importance to the people than the manner in which criminal trials are conducted." *Richmond Newspapers, Inc. v. Virginia*, 448 U.S. 555 (1980). Public vigilance serves us well, for "[t]he knowledge that every criminal trial is subject to contemporaneous review in the forum of public opinion is an effective restraint on possible abuse of judicial power. . . . Without publicity, all other checks are insufficient; in comparison of publicity, all other checks are of small account." *In re Oliver*, 333 U.S. 257 (1948). * * *

Public awareness and criticism have even greater importance where, as here, they concern allegations of police corruption, see *Nebraska Press Assn. v. Stuart*, 427 U.S. 539 (1976) (Brennan, J., concurring in judgment) ("commentary on the fact that there is strong evidence implicating a government official in criminal activity goes to the very core of matters of public concern"), or where, as is also the present circumstance, the criticism questions the judgment of an elected public prosecutor. Our system grants prosecutors vast discretion at all stages of the criminal process. The public has an interest in its responsible exercise. * * *

We are not called upon to determine the constitutionality of the ABA Model Rule of Professional Conduct 3.6 (1981), but only Rule 177 as it has been

---

"(d)   the scheduling or result of any step in litigation;

"(e)   a request for assistance in obtaining evidence and information necessary thereto;

"(f)   a warning of danger concerning the behavior of a person involved, when there is reason to believe that there exists the likelihood of substantial harm to an individual or to the public interest; and

"(g)   in a criminal case:

"(i)   the identity, residence, occupation and family status of the accused;

"(ii)   if the accused has not been apprehended, information necessary to aid in apprehension of that person;

"(iii)   the fact, time and place of arrest; and

"(iv)   the identity of investigating and arresting officers or agencies and the length of the investigation."

interpreted and applied by the State of Nevada. Model Rule 3.6's requirement of substantial likelihood of material prejudice [duplicated in Rule 177(1)] is not necessarily flawed. Interpreted in a proper and narrow manner, for instance, to prevent an attorney of record from releasing information of grave prejudice on the eve of jury selection, the phrase substantial likelihood of material prejudice might punish only speech that creates a danger of imminent and substantial harm. A rule governing speech, even speech entitled to full constitutional protection, need not use the words "clear and present danger" in order to pass constitutional muster. * * * The drafters of Model Rule 3.6 apparently thought the substantial likelihood of material prejudice formulation approximated the clear and present danger test. See ABA Annotated Model Rules of Professional Conduct 243 (1984). * * *

The difference between the requirement of serious and imminent threat found in the disciplinary rules of some States and the more common formulation of substantial likelihood of material prejudice could prove mere semantics. Each standard requires an assessment of proximity and degree of harm. Each may be capable of valid application. Under those principles, nothing inherent in Nevada's formulation fails First Amendment review; but as this case demonstrates, Rule 177 has not been interpreted in conformance with those principles by the Nevada Supreme Court.

II

Even if one were to accept respondent's argument that lawyers participating in judicial proceedings may be subjected, consistent with the First Amendment, to speech restrictions that could not be imposed on the press or general public, the judgment should not be upheld. The record does not support the conclusion that petitioner knew or reasonably should have known his remarks created a substantial likelihood of material prejudice, if the Rule's terms are given any meaningful content.

We have held that "in cases raising First Amendment issues . . . an appellate court has an obligation to 'make an independent examination of the whole record' in order to make sure that 'the judgment does not constitute a forbidden intrusion on the field of free expression.' " *Bose Corp. v. Consumers Union of United States, Inc.*, 466 U.S. 485 (1984). Rather, this Court is

> "compelled to examine for [itself] the statements in issue and the circumstances under which they were made to see whether or not they do carry a threat of clear and present danger to the impartiality and good order of the courts or whether they are of a character which the principles of the First Amendment, as adopted by the Due Process Clause of the Fourteenth Amendment, protect." * * * *Landmark Communications, Inc. v. Virginia,* supra.

Whether one applies the standard set out in *Landmark Communications* or the lower standard our colleagues find permissible, an examination of the record reveals no basis for the Nevada court's conclusion that the speech presented a substantial likelihood of material prejudice. * * *

1. Petitioner's Motivation. As petitioner explained to the disciplinary board, his primary motivation was the concern that, unless some of the weaknesses in the State's case were made public, a potential jury venire would be poisoned by repetition in the press of information being released by the police and prosecutors, in particular the repeated press reports about polygraph tests and the fact that the two police officers were no longer suspects. Respondent distorts Rule 177 when it suggests this explanation admits a purpose to prejudice the venire and so proves a violation of the Rule. Rule 177 only prohibits the dissemination of information that one knows or reasonably should know has a "substantial likelihood of materially prejudicing an adjudicative proceeding." Petitioner did not indicate he thought he could sway the pool of potential jurors to form an opinion in advance of the trial, nor did he seek to discuss evidence that would be inadmissible at trial. He sought only to counter publicity already deemed prejudicial. The Southern Nevada Disciplinary Board so found. It said petitioner attempted

> "(i) to counter public opinion which he perceived as adverse to Mr. Sanders, (ii) . . . to refute certain matters regarding his client which had appeared in the media, (iii) to fight back against the perceived efforts of the prosecution to poison the prospective juror pool, and (iv) to publicly present Sanders' side of the case."

Far from an admission that he sought to "materially prejudic[e] an adjudicative proceeding," petitioner sought only to stop a wave of publicity he perceived as prejudicing potential jurors against his client and injuring his client's reputation in the community.

Petitioner gave a second reason for holding the press conference, which demonstrates the additional value of his speech. Petitioner acted in part because the investigation had taken a serious toll on his client. Sanders was "not a man in good health," having suffered multiple open-heart surgeries prior to these events. And prior to indictment, the mere suspicion of wrongdoing had caused the closure of Western Vault and the loss of Sanders' ground lease on an Atlantic City, New Jersey property.

An attorney's duties do not begin inside the courtroom door. He or she cannot ignore the practical implications of a legal proceeding for the client. Just as an attorney may recommend a plea bargain or civil settlement to avoid the adverse consequences of a possible loss after trial, so too an attorney may take reasonable steps to defend a client's reputation and reduce the adverse consequences of indictment, especially in the face of a prosecution deemed unjust or commenced with improper motives. A defense attorney may pursue lawful strategies to obtain dismissal of an indictment or reduction of charges, including an attempt to demonstrate in the court of public opinion that the client does not deserve to be tried.

2. Petitioner's Investigation of Rule 177. Rule 177 is phrased in terms of what an attorney "knows or reasonably should know." On the evening before the press conference, petitioner and two colleagues spent several hours researching the extent of an attorney's obligations under Rule 177. He decided, as we have held, see *Patton v. Yount,* 467 U.S. 1025 (1984), that the timing of a statement was crucial in the assessment of possible prejudice and the Rule's application, accord. * * * Petitioner knew, at the time of his statement, that a jury would not be empaneled for six months at the earliest, if ever. He recalled reported cases finding no prejudice resulting from juror exposure to "far worse" information two and four months before trial, and concluded that his proposed statement was not substantially likely to result in material prejudice.

A statement which reaches the attention of the venire on the eve of *voir dire* might require a continuance or cause difficulties in securing an impartial jury, and at the very least could complicate the jury selection process. * * * As turned out to be the case here, exposure to the same statement six months prior to trial would not result in prejudice, the content fading from memory long before the trial date.

In 1988, Clark County, Nevada had population in excess of 600,000 persons. Given the size of the community from which any potential jury venire would be drawn and the length of time before trial, only the most damaging of information could give rise to any likelihood of prejudice. The innocuous content of petitioner's statement reinforces my conclusion.

3. *The Content of Petitioner's Statement.* * * * Much of the information provided by petitioner had been published in one form or another, obviating any potential for prejudice. See ABA Annotated Model Rules of Professional Conduct 243 (1984) (extent to which information already circulated significant factor in determining likelihood of prejudice). The remainder, and details petitioner refused to provide, were available to any journalist willing to do a little bit of investigative work.

Petitioner's statement lacks any of the more obvious bases for a finding of prejudice. Unlike the police, he refused to comment on polygraph tests except to confirm earlier reports that Sanders had not submitted to the police polygraph; he mentioned no confessions, and no evidence from searches or test results; he refused to elaborate upon his charge that the other so-called victims were not credible, except to explain his general theory that they were pressured to testify in an attempt to avoid drug-related legal trouble, and that some of them may have asserted claims in an attempt to collect insurance money.

[4.] *Events Following the Press Conference.* Petitioner's judgment that no likelihood of material prejudice would result from his comments was vindicated by events at trial. While it is true that Rule 177's standard for controlling pretrial publicity must be judged at the time a statement is made, *ex post* evidence can have probative value in some cases. Here, where the Rule purports to demand, and the Constitution requires, consideration of the character of the harm and its heightened likelihood of occurrence, the record is altogether devoid of facts one would expect to follow upon any statement that created a real likelihood of material prejudice to a criminal jury trial.

The trial took place on schedule in August, 1988, with no request by either party for a venue change or continuance. The jury was empaneled with no apparent difficulty. The trial judge questioned the jury venire about publicity. Although many had vague recollections of reports that cocaine stored at Western Vault had been stolen from a police undercover operation, and, as petitioner had feared, one remembered that the police had been cleared of suspicion, not a single juror indicated any recollection of petitioner or his press conference.

At trial, all material information disseminated during petitioner's press conference was admitted in evidence before the jury, including information questioning the motives and credibility of supposed victims who testified against Sanders, and Detective Scholl's ingestion of drugs in the course of undercover operations (in order, he testified, to gain the confidence of suspects). The jury acquitted petitioner's client, and, as petitioner explained before the disciplinary board,

> "when the trial was over with and the man was acquitted the next week the foreman of the jury phoned me and said to me that if they would have had a verdict form before them with respect to the guilt of Steve Scholl they would have found the man proven guilty beyond a reasonable doubt."

There is no support for the conclusion that petitioner's statement created a likelihood of material prejudice, or indeed of any harm of sufficient magnitude or imminence to support a punishment for speech.

III

As interpreted by the Nevada Supreme Court, the Rule is void for vagueness, in any event, for its safe harbor provision, Rule 177(3), misled petitioner into thinking that he could give his press conference without fear of discipline. Rule 177(3)(a) provides that a lawyer "may state without elaboration . . . the general nature of the . . . defense." Statements under this provision are protected "[n]otwithstanding subsection 1 and 2(f)." By necessary operation of the word "notwithstanding," the Rule contemplates that a lawyer describing the "general nature of the . . . defense" "without elaboration" need fear no discipline, even if he comments on "[t]he character, credibility, reputation or criminal record of a . . . witness," and even if he "knows or reasonably should know that [the statement] will have a substantial likelihood of materially prejudicing an adjudicative proceeding."

Given this grammatical structure, and absent any clarifying interpretation by the state court, the Rule fails to provide " 'fair notice to those to whom [it] is directed.' " *Grayned v. City of Rockford,* 408 U.S. 104 (1972). A lawyer seeking to avail himself of Rule 177(3)'s protection must guess at its contours. The right to explain the "general" nature of the defense without "elaboration" provides insufficient guidance because "general" and "elaboration" are both classic terms of degree. In the context before us, these terms have no settled usage or tradition of interpretation in law. The lawyer has no principle for determining when his remarks pass from the safe harbor of the general to the forbidden sea of the elaborated.

Petitioner testified he thought his statements were protected by Rule 177(3), App. 59. A review of the press conference supports that claim. He gave only a brief opening statement, and on numerous occasions declined to answer reporters' questions seeking more detailed comments. * * * Nevertheless, the disciplinary board said only that petitioner's comments "went beyond the scope of the statements permitted by SCR 177(3)," and the Nevada Supreme Court's rejection of petitioner's defense based on Rule 177(3) was just as terse. The fact Gentile was found in violation of the Rules after studying them and making a conscious effort at compliance demonstrates that Rule 177 creates a trap for the wary as well as the unwary.

The prohibition against vague regulations of speech is based in part on the need to eliminate the impermissible risk of discriminatory enforcement, for history shows that speech is suppressed when either the speaker or the message is critical of those who enforce the law. The question is not whether discriminatory enforcement occurred here, and we assume it did not, but whether the Rule is so imprecise that discriminatory enforcement is a real possibility. The inquiry is of particular relevance when one of the classes most affected by the regulation is the criminal defense bar, which has the professional mission to challenge actions of the State. Petitioner, for instance, succeeded in preventing the conviction of his client, and the speech in issue involved criticism of the government.

IV

The analysis to this point resolves the case, and in the usual order of things the discussion should end here. Five members of the Court, however, endorse an extended discussion which concludes that Nevada may interpret its requirement of substantial likelihood of material prejudice under a standard more deferential than is the usual rule where speech is concerned. It appears necessary, therefore, to set forth my objections to that conclusion and to the reasoning which underlies it. * * *

Respondent would justify a substantial limitation on speech by attorneys because "lawyers have special access to information, including confidential statements from clients and information obtained through pretrial discovery or plea negotiations" and so lawyers' statements "are likely to be received as especially authoritative." Rule 177, however, does not reflect concern for the attorney's special access to client confidences, material gained through discovery, or other proprietary or confidential information. We have upheld restrictions upon the release of information gained "only by virtue of the trial court's discovery processes." *Seattle Times Co. v. Rhinehart,* 467 U.S. 20 (1984). And *Seattle Times* would prohibit release of discovery information by the attorney as well as the client. Similar rules require an attorney to maintain client confidences. See, *e.g.,* ABA Model Rule of Professional Conduct 1.6 (1981).

This case involves no speech subject to a restriction under the rationale of *Seattle Times.* Much of the information in petitioner's remarks was included by explicit reference or fair inference in earlier press reports. Petitioner could not have learned what he revealed at the press conference through the discovery process or other special access afforded to attorneys, for he spoke to the press on the day of indictment, at the outset of his formal participation in the criminal proceeding. We have before us no complaint from the prosecutors, police or presiding judge that petitioner misused information to which he had special access. And there is no claim that petitioner revealed client confidences, which may be waived in any event. Rule 177, on its face and as applied here, is neither limited to nor even directed at preventing release of information received through court proceedings or special access afforded attorneys.

Respondent [also] relies upon *obiter dicta* from *In re Sawyer,* 360 U.S. 622 (1959), *Sheppard v. Maxwell,* 384 U.S. 333 (1966), and *Nebraska Press Assn. v. Stuart,* 427 U.S. 539 (1976), for the proposition that an attorney's speech about ongoing proceedings must be subject to pervasive regulation in order to ensure the impartial adjudication of criminal proceedings. * * * Each case suggests restrictions upon information release, but none confronted their permitted scope. At the very least, our cases recognize that disciplinary rules governing the legal profession cannot punish activity protected by the First Amendment, and that First Amendment protection survives even when the attorney violates a disciplinary rule he swore to obey when admitted to the practice of law. * * * We have not in recent years accepted our colleagues' apparent theory that the practice of law brings with it comprehensive restrictions, or that we will defer to professional bodies when those restrictions impinge upon First Amendment freedoms. And none of the justifications put forward by respondent suffice to sanction abandonment of our normal First Amendment principles in the case of speech by an attorney regarding pending cases.

Even if respondent is correct, and as in *Seattle Times* we must balance "whether the 'practice in question [furthers] an important or substantial governmental interest unrelated to the suppression of expression' and whether 'the limitation of First Amendment freedoms [is] no greater than is necessary or essential to the protection of the particular governmental interest involved,' " *Seattle Times,* supra, the Rule as interpreted by Nevada fails the searching inquiry required by those precedents.

Only the occasional case presents a danger of prejudice from pretrial publicity. Empirical research suggests that in the few instances when jurors have been exposed to extensive and prejudicial publicity, they are able to disregard it and base their verdict upon the evidence presented in court. * * * *Voir dire* can play an important role in reminding jurors to set aside out-of-court information, and to decide the case upon the evidence presented at trial. All of these factors weigh in favor of affording an attorney's speech about ongoing proceedings our traditional First Amendment protections. Our colleagues' historical survey notwithstanding, respondent has not demonstrated any sufficient state interest in restricting the speech of attorneys to justify a lower standard of First Amendment scrutiny.

Still less justification exists for a lower standard of scrutiny here, as this speech involved not the prosecutor or police, but a criminal defense attorney. Respondent and its *amici* present not a single example where a defense attorney has managed by public statements to prejudice the prosecution of the state's case. Even discounting the obvious reason for a lack of appellate decisions on the topic— the difficulty of appealing a verdict of acquittal—the absence of anecdotal or survey evidence in a much-studied area of the law is remarkable.

The various bar association and advisory commission reports which resulted in promulgation of ABA Model Rule of Professional Conduct 3.6 (1981), and other regulations of attorney speech, and sources they cite, present no convincing case for restrictions upon the speech of defense attorneys. * * * The police, the prosecution, other government officials, and the community at large hold innumerable avenues for the dissemination of information adverse to a criminal defendant, many of which are not within the scope of Rule 177 or any other regulation. By contrast, a defendant cannot speak without fear of incriminating himself and prejudicing his defense, and most criminal defendants have insufficient means to retain a public relations team apart from defense counsel for the sole purpose of countering prosecution statements. These factors underscore my conclusion that blanket rules restricting speech of defense attorneys should not be accepted without careful First Amendment scrutiny.

Respondent uses the "officer of the court" label to imply that attorney contact with the press somehow is inimical to the attorney's proper role. Rule 177 posits no such inconsistency between an attorney's role and discussions with the press. It permits all comment to the press absent "a substantial likelihood of materially prejudicing an adjudicative proceeding." Respondent does not articulate the principle that contact with the press cannot be reconciled with the attorney's role or explain how this might be so.

Because attorneys participate in the criminal justice system and are trained in its complexities, they hold unique qualifications as a source of information about pending cases. "Since lawyers are considered credible in regard to pending litigation in which they are engaged and are in one of the most knowledgeable positions, they are a crucial source of information and opinion." *Chicago Council of Lawyers v. Bauer,* 522 F.2d 242, 250 (7th Cir.1975). To the extent the press and public rely upon attorneys for information because attorneys are well-informed, this may prove the value to the public of speech by members of the bar. If the dangers of their speech arise from its persuasiveness, from their ability to explain judicial proceedings, or from the likelihood the speech will be believed, these are not the sort of dangers that can validate restrictions. The First Amendment does not permit suppression of speech because of its power to command assent.

One may concede the proposition that an attorney's speech about pending cases may present dangers that could not arise from statements by a nonparticipant, and that an attorney's duty to cooperate in the judicial process may prevent him or her from taking actions with an intent to frustrate that process. The role of attorneys in the criminal justice system subjects them to fiduciary obligations to the court and the parties. An attorney's position may result in some added ability to obstruct the proceedings through well-timed statements to the press, though one can debate the extent of an attorney's ability to do so without violating other established duties. A court can require an attorney's cooperation to an extent not possible of nonparticipants. A proper weighing of dangers might consider the harm that occurs when speech about ongoing proceedings forces the court to take burdensome steps such as sequestration, continuance, or change of venue.

If as a regular matter speech by an attorney about pending cases raised real dangers of this kind then a substantial governmental interest might support additional regulation of speech. But this case involves the sanction of speech so innocuous, and an application of Rule 177(3)'s safe harbor provision so begrudging, that it is difficult to determine the force these arguments would carry in a different setting. The instant case is a poor vehicle for defining with precision the outer limits under the Constitution of a court's ability to regulate an attorney's statements about ongoing adjudicative proceedings. At the very least, however, we can say that the Rule which punished petitioner's statement represents a limitation of First Amendment freedoms greater than is necessary or essential to the protection of the particular governmental interest, and does not protect against a danger of the necessary gravity, imminence, or likelihood.

The vigorous advocacy we demand of the legal profession is accepted because it takes place under the neutral, dispassionate control of the judicial system. Though cost and delays undermine it in all too many cases, the American judicial trial remains one of the purest, most rational forums for the lawful determination of disputes. A profession which takes just pride in these traditions may consider them disserved if lawyers use their skills and insight to make untested allegations in the press instead of in the courtroom. But constraints of professional responsibility and societal disapproval will act as sufficient safeguards in most cases. And in some circumstances press comment is necessary to protect the rights of the client and prevent abuse of the courts. It cannot be said that petitioner's conduct demonstrated any real or specific threat to the legal process, and his statements have the full protection of the First Amendment. * * *

CHIEF JUSTICE REHNQUIST delivered the opinion of the Court with respect to parts I and II, and delivered a dissenting opinion with respect to part III in which JUSTICE WHITE, JUSTICE SCALIA, and JUSTICE SOUTER have joined. * * *

I

Petitioner's client was the subject of a highly publicized case, and in response to adverse publicity about his client, Gentile held a press conference on the day after Sanders was indicted. At the press conference, petitioner made, among others the following statements: * * * [that] "there is far more evidence that will establish that Detective Scholl took these drugs and American Express Travelers' checks than any other living being"; * * * [that] "the so-called other victims * * * are known drug dealers and convicted money launderers, three of whom didn't say a word about anything until after they were approached by Metro and after they were already in trouble and * * * trying to work themselves out of something"; * * * [that] "I know I represent an innocent man"; [and that] "we've got some video tapes that if you took a look at them, I'll tell you that [Scholl] either had a cold or he should have seen a better doctor."

The Southern Nevada Disciplinary Board found that petitioner knew the detective he accused of perpetrating the crime and abusing drugs would be a witness for the prosecution. It also found that petitioner believed others whom he characterized as money launderers and drug dealers would be called as prosecution witnesses. Petitioner's admitted purpose for calling the press conference was to counter public opinion which he perceived as adverse to his client, to fight back against the perceived efforts of the prosecution to poison the prospective juror pool, and to publicly present his client's side of the case. The Board found that in light of the statements, their timing, and petitioner's purpose, petitioner knew or should have known that there was a substantial likelihood that the statements would materially prejudice the Sanders trial.

The Nevada Supreme Court affirmed the Board's decision, finding by clear and convincing evidence that petitioner "knew or reasonably should have known that his comments had a substantial likelihood of materially prejudicing the adjudication of his client's case." The court noted that the case was "highly publicized"; that the press conference, held the day after the indictment and the same day as the arraignment, was "timed to have maximum impact"; and that petitioner's comments "related to the character, credibility, reputation or criminal record of the police detective and other potential witnesses." The court concluded that the "absence of actual prejudice does not establish that there was no substantial likelihood of material prejudice."

II

Gentile asserts that the same stringent standard applied in *Nebraska Press Assn. v. Stuart*, 427 U.S. 539 (1976), to restraints on press publication during the pendency of a criminal trial should be applied to speech by a lawyer whose client is a defendant in a criminal proceeding. * * * Respondent, on the other hand, relies on statements in cases such as *Sheppard v. Maxwell*, 384 U.S. 333 (1966), which sharply distinguished between restraints on the press and restraints on lawyers whose clients are parties to the proceeding:

> "Collaboration between counsel and the press as to information affecting the fairness of a criminal trial is not only subject to regulation, but is highly censurable and worthy of disciplinary measures."

To evaluate these opposing contentions, some references must be made to the history of the regulation of the practice of law by the courts.

In the United States, the courts have historically regulated admission to the practice of law before them, and exercised the authority to discipline and ultimately to disbar lawyers whose conduct departed from prescribed standards. * * * More than a century ago, the first official code of legal ethics promulgated in this country, the Alabama Code of 1887, warned attorneys to "Avoid Newspaper Discussion of Legal Matters," and stated that "[n]ewspaper publications by an attorney as to the merits of pending or anticipated litigation . . . tend to prevent a fair trial in the courts, and otherwise prejudice the due administration of justice." In 1908, the American Bar Association promulgated its own code, entitled "Canons of Professional Ethics," [which noted that]: "Newspaper publications by a lawyer as to pending or anticipated litigation may interfere with a fair trial * * * [G]enerally they are to be condemned. * * *"

In the last-quarter-century, the legal profession has reviewed its ethical limitations on extrajudicial statements by lawyers in the context of this Court's cases interpreting the First Amendment. ABA Model Rule of Professional

Responsibility 3.6 resulted from the recommendations of the Advisory Committee on Fair Trial and Free Press (Advisory Committee), created in 1964 upon the recommendation of the Warren Commission. The Warren Commission's report on the assassination of President Kennedy included the recommendation that

> "representatives of the bar, law enforcement associations, and the news media work together to establish ethical standards concerning the collection and presentation of information to the public so that there will be no interference with pending criminal investigations, court proceedings, or the right of individuals to a fair trial."

The Advisory Committee developed the ABA Standards Relating to Fair Trial and Free Press, comprehensive guidelines relating to disclosure of information concerning criminal proceedings, which were relied upon by the ABA in 1968 in formulating [the predecessor to] Rule 3.6. The need for and appropriateness of such a rule had been identified by this Court two years earlier in *Sheppard v. Maxwell.* * * * [Courts] proceeded to enact local rules incorporating these standards, and thus the "reasonable likelihood of prejudicing a fair trial" test was used by a majority of courts, state and federal, in the years following *Sheppard.* Ten years later, the ABA amended its guidelines, and the "reasonable likelihood" test was changed to a "clear and present danger" test.

When the Model Rules of Professional Conduct were drafted in the early 1980s, the drafters did not go as far as the revised Fair Trial-Free Press Standards in giving precedence to the lawyer's right to make extrajudicial statements when fair trial rights are implicated, and instead adopted the "substantial likelihood of material prejudice" test. Currently, 31 States in addition to Nevada have adopted— either verbatim or with insignificant variations—Rule 3.6 of the ABA's Model Rules. Eleven States have adopted Disciplinary Rule 7–107 of the ABA's Code of Professional Responsibility, which is less protective of lawyer speech than Model Rule 3.6, in that it applies a "reasonable likelihood of prejudice" standard. Only one State, Virginia, has explicitly adopted a clear and present danger standard, while four States and the District of Columbia have adopted standards that arguably approximate "clear and present danger."

Petitioner maintains, however, that the First Amendment to the United States Constitution requires a State, such as Nevada in this case, to demonstrate a "clear and present danger" of "actual prejudice or an imminent threat" before any discipline may be imposed on a lawyer who initiates a press conference such as occurred here. He relies on [cases in which] * * * we held that trial courts might not constitutionally punish, through use of the contempt power, newspapers and others for publishing editorials, cartoons, and other items critical of judges in particular cases. We held that such punishments could be imposed only if there were a clear and present danger of "some serious substantive evil which they are designed to avert." *Bridges v. California,* 314 U.S. 252 (1941). Petitioner also relies on *Wood v. Georgia,* 370 U.S. 375 (1962), which held that a court might not punish a sheriff for publicly criticizing a judge's charges to a grand jury. * * *

The question we must answer in this case is whether a lawyer who represents a defendant involved with the criminal justice system may insist on the same standard before he is disciplined for public pronouncements about the case, or whether the State instead may penalize that sort of speech upon a lesser showing. It is unquestionable that in the courtroom itself, during a judicial proceeding, whatever right to "free speech" an attorney has is extremely circumscribed. * * * Even outside the courtroom, a majority of the Court in two separate opinions in the case of *In re Sawyer,* 360 U.S. 622 (1959), observed that lawyers in pending cases were subject to ethical restrictions on speech to which an ordinary citizen would not be. * * * Likewise, in *Sheppard v. Maxwell,* where the defendant's conviction was overturned because extensive prejudicial pretrial publicity had denied the defendant a fair trial, we held that a new trial was a remedy for such publicity, but [we also] * * * expressly contemplated that the speech of *those participating before the courts* could be limited.[5] This distinction between participants in the litigation and strangers to it is brought into sharp relief by our holding in *Seattle Times Co. v. Rhinehart,* 467 U.S. 20 (1984). There, we unanimously held that a newspaper, which was itself a defendant in a libel action, could be restrained from publishing material about the plaintiffs and their supporters to which it had gained access through court-ordered discovery. In that case we said that "[a]lthough litigants do not 'surrender their First Amendment rights at the courthouse door,' those rights may be subordinated to other interests that arise in this setting," and noted that "on several occasions [we have] approved restriction on the communications of trial participants where necessary to ensure a fair trial for a criminal defendant." * * *

We think that the * * * statements from our opinions in *In re Sawyer* and *Sheppard v. Maxwell* rather plainly indicate that the speech of lawyers representing clients in pending cases may be regulated under a less demanding standard than that established for regulation of the press in *Nebraska Press Assn. v. Stuart.* Lawyers representing clients in pending cases are key participants in the criminal justice system, and the State may demand some adherence to the precepts of that system in regulating their speech as well as their conduct. As noted by Justice Brennan in his concurring opinion in *Nebraska Press,* which was joined by Justices Stewart and Marshall, "[a]s officers of the court, court personnel and attorneys have a fiduciary responsibility not to engage in public debate that will rebound to the detriment of the accused or that will obstruct the fair administration of justice." Because lawyers have special access to information through discovery and client communications, their extrajudicial statements pose a threat to the fairness of a pending proceeding since lawyers' statements are likely to be received as especially authoritative. See, *e.g., In re Hinds,* 90 N.J. 604, 627, 449 A.2d 483, 496 (1982) (statements by attorneys of record relating to the case

---

[5] The Nevada Supreme Court has consistently read all parts of Rule 177 as applying only to lawyers in pending cases, and not to other lawyers or nonlawyers. We express no opinion on the constitutionality of a rule regulating the statements of a lawyer who is not participating in the pending case about which the statements are made. We note that of all the cases petitioner cites as supporting the use of the clear and present danger standard, the only one that even arguably involved a non-third party was *Wood v. Georgia,* supra, where a county sheriff was held in contempt for publicly criticizing instructions given by a judge to a grand jury. Although the sheriff was technically an "officer of the court" by virtue of his position, the Court determined that his statements were made in his capacity as a private citizen, with no connection to his official duties. The same cannot be said about petitioner, whose statements were made in the course of and in furtherance of his role as defense counsel.

"are likely to be considered knowledgeable, reliable and true" because of attorneys' unique access to information); *In re Rachmiel,* 90 N.J. 646, 656, 449 A.2d 505, 511 (N.J.1982) (attorneys' role as advocates gives them "extraordinary power to undermine or destroy the efficacy of the criminal justice system"). We agree with the majority of the States that the "substantial likelihood of material prejudice" standard constitutes a constitutionally permissible balance between the First Amendment rights of attorneys in pending cases and the state's interest in fair trials.

When a state regulation implicates First Amendment rights, the Court must balance those interests against the State's legitimate interest in regulating the activity in question. The "substantial likelihood" test embodied in Rule 177 is constitutional under this analysis, for it is designed to protect the integrity and fairness of a state's judicial system, and it imposes only narrow and necessary limitations on lawyers' speech. The limitations are aimed at two principal evils: (1) comments that are likely to influence the actual outcome of the trial, and (2) comments that are likely to prejudice the jury venire, even if an untainted panel can ultimately be found. Few, if any, interests under the Constitution are more fundamental than the right to a fair trial by "impartial" jurors, and an outcome affected by extrajudicial statements would violate that fundamental right. * * * Even if a fair trial can ultimately be ensured through *voir dire,* change of venue, or some other device, these measures entail serious costs to the system. Extensive *voir dire* may not be able to filter out all of the effects of pretrial publicity, and with increasingly widespread media coverage of criminal trials, a change of venue may not suffice to undo the effects of statements such as those made by petitioner. The State has a substantial interest in preventing officers of the court, such as lawyers, from imposing such costs on the judicial system and on the litigants.

The restraint on speech is narrowly tailored to achieve those objectives. The regulation of attorneys' speech is limited—it applies only to speech that is substantially likely to have a materially prejudicial effect; it is neutral as to points of view, applying equally to all attorneys participating in a pending case; and it merely postpones the attorneys' comments until after the trial. While supported by the substantial state interest in preventing prejudice to an adjudicative proceeding by those who have a duty to protect its integrity, the rule is limited on its face to preventing only speech having a substantial likelihood of materially prejudicing that proceeding.

III

To assist a lawyer in deciding whether an extrajudicial statement is problematic, Rule 177 sets out statements that are likely to cause material prejudice. Contrary to petitioner's contention, these are not improper evidentiary presumptions. Model Rule 3.6, from which Rule 177 was derived, was specifically designed to avoid the categorical prohibitions of attorney speech contained in ABA Model Code of Professional Responsibility Disciplinary Rule 7–107 (1981). * * * The statements listed as likely to cause material prejudice closely track a similar list outlined by this Court in *Sheppard.* * * * [However,] Gentile claims that Rule 177 is overbroad, and thus unconstitutional on its face, because it applies to more speech than is necessary to serve the State's goals. The "overbreadth" doctrine applies if an enactment "prohibits constitutionally protected conduct." To be unconstitutional, overbreadth must be "substantial." Rule 177 is no broader than necessary to protect the State's interests. It applies only to lawyers involved in the pending case at issue, and even those lawyers involved in pending cases can make extrajudicial statements as long as such statements do not present a substantial risk of material prejudice to an adjudicative proceeding. The fact that Rule 177 applies to bench trials does not make it overbroad, for a substantial likelihood of prejudice is still required before the Rule is violated. That test will rarely be met where the judge is the trier of fact, since trial judges often have access to inadmissible and highly prejudicial information and are presumed to be able to discount or disregard it. For these reasons Rule 177 is constitutional on its face.

Gentile also argues that Rule 177 is void for vagueness because it did not provide adequate notice that his comments were subject to discipline. The void-for-vagueness doctrine is concerned with a defendant's right to fair notice and adequate warning that his conduct runs afoul of the law. Rule 177 was drafted with the intent to provide "an illustrative compilation that gives fair notice of conduct ordinarily posing unacceptable dangers to the fair administration of justice." Proposed Final Draft 143. The Rule provides sufficient notice of the nature of the prohibited conduct. Under the circumstances of his case, petitioner cannot complain about lack of notice, as he has admitted that his primary objective in holding the press conference was the violation of Rule 177's core prohibition—to prejudice the upcoming trial by influencing potential jurors. Petitioner was clearly given notice that such conduct was forbidden, and the list of conduct likely to cause prejudice, while only advisory, certainly gave notice that the statements made would violate the rule if they had the intended effect.

The majority agrees with petitioner that he was the victim of unconstitutional vagueness in the regulations because of the relationship between subsection 3 and subsections 1 and 2 of rule 177. Subsection 3 allows an attorney to state "the general nature of the claim or defense" notwithstanding the prohibition contained in subsection 1 and the examples contained in subsection 2. It is of course true, as the majority points out, that the word "general" and the word "elaboration" are both terms of degree. But combined as they are in the first sentence of subsection 3, they convey the very definite proposition that the authorized statements must not contain the sort of detailed allegations that petitioner made at his press conference. No sensible person could think that the following were "general" statements of a claim or defense made "without elaboration": "the person that was in the most direct position to have stolen the drugs and the money . . . is Detective Steve Scholl"; "there is far more evidence that will establish that Detective Scholl took these drugs and took these American Express travelers' checks than any other living human being"; "[Detective Scholl] either had a hell of a cold, or he should have seen a better doctor"; and "the so-called other victims . . . one, two—four of them are known drug dealers and convicted money launderers." Subsection 3, as an exception to the provisions of subsections 1 and 2, must be read in the light of the prohibitions and examples contained in the first two sections. It was obviously not intended to negate the prohibitions or the examples wholesale, but simply intended to provide a "safe harbor" where there might be doubt as to whether one of the examples covered proposed conduct. These provisions were not vague as to the conduct for which petitioner was disciplined; "[i]n determining the sufficiency of the notice a statute must of necessity be examined in the light of the conduct with which a defendant is charged." *United States v. National Dairy Products Corp.*, 372 U.S. 29, 33 (1963).

Petitioner's strongest arguments are that the statement was made well in advance of trial, and that the statements did not in fact taint the jury panel. But the Supreme Court of Nevada pointed out that petitioner's statements were not only highly inflammatory—they portrayed prospective government witnesses as drug users and dealers, and as money launderers—but the statements were timed to have maximum impact, when public interest in the case was at its height immediately after Sanders was indicted. Reviewing independently the entire record, we are convinced that petitioner's statements were "substantially likely to cause material prejudice" to the proceedings. While there is evidence pro and con on that point, we find it persuasive that, by his own admission, petitioner called the press conference for the express purpose of influencing the venire. It is difficult to believe that he went to such trouble, and took such a risk, if there was no substantial likelihood that he would succeed.

While in a case such as this we must review the record for ourselves, when the highest court of a state has reached a determination "we give most respectful attention to its reasoning and conclusion." The State Bar of Nevada, which made its own factual findings, and the Supreme Court of Nevada, which upheld those findings, were in a far better position than we are to appreciate the likely effect of petitioner's statements on potential members of a jury panel in a highly publicized case such as this. The Board and Nevada Supreme Court did not apply the list of statements likely to cause material prejudice as presumptions, but specifically found that petitioner had intended to prejudice the trial,[6] and that based upon the nature of the statements and their timing, they were in fact substantially likely to cause material prejudice. We cannot, upon our review of the record, conclude that they were mistaken.

Several amici argue that the First Amendment requires the state to show actual prejudice to a judicial proceeding before an attorney may be disciplined for extrajudicial statements, and since the Board and Nevada Supreme Court found

---

[6] Justice Kennedy appears to contend that there can be no material prejudice when the lawyer's publicity is in response to publicity favorable to the other side. Justice Kennedy would find that publicity designed to counter prejudicial publicity cannot be itself prejudicial, despite its likelihood of influencing potential jurors, unless it actually would go so far as to cause jurors to be affirmatively biased in favor of the lawyer's client. In the first place, such a test would be difficult, if not impossible, to apply. But more fundamentally, it misconceives the constitutional test for an impartial juror—whether the "juror can lay aside his impression or opinion and render a verdict on the evidence presented in Court." *Murphy v. Florida*, 421 U.S. 794 (1975). A juror who may have been initially swayed from open-mindedness by publicity favorable to the prosecution is not rendered fit for service by being bombarded by publicity favorable to the defendant. The basic premise of our legal system is that law suits should be tried in court, not in the media. A defendant may be protected from publicity by, or in favor of, the police and prosecution through voir dire, change of venue, jury instructions and, in extreme cases, reversal on due process grounds. The remedy for prosecutorial abuses that violate the rule lies not in self-help in the form of similarly prejudicial comments by defense counsel, but in disciplining the prosecutor.

no actual prejudice, petitioner should not have been disciplined. But this is simply another way of stating that the stringent standard of Nebraska Press should be applied to the speech of a lawyer in a pending case, and for the reasons heretofore given we decline to adopt it. An added objection to the stricter standard when applied to lawyer participants is that if it were adopted, even comments more flagrant than those made by petitioner could not serve as the basis for disciplinary action if, for wholly independent reasons, they had no effect on the proceedings. An attorney who made prejudicial comments would be insulated from discipline if the government, for reasons unrelated to the comments, decided to dismiss the charges, or if a plea bargain were reached. An equally culpable attorney whose client's case went to trial would be subject to discipline. The United States Constitution does not mandate such a fortuitous difference.

When petitioner was admitted to practice law before the Nevada courts, the oath which he took recited that "I will support, abide by and follow the Rules of Professional Conduct as are now or may hereafter be adopted by the Supreme Court . . . " Rule 73, Nevada Supreme Court Rules (1991). The First Amendment does not excuse him from that obligation, nor should it forbid the discipline imposed upon him by the Supreme Court of Nevada. I would affirm the decision of the Supreme Court of Nevada.

JUSTICE O'CONNOR, concurring.

I agree with much of The Chief Justice's opinion. In particular, I agree that a State may regulate speech by lawyers representing clients in pending cases more readily than it may regulate the press. Lawyers are officers of the court and, as such, may legitimately be subject to ethical precepts that keep them from engaging in what otherwise might be constitutionally protected speech. This does not mean, of course, that lawyers forfeit their First Amendment rights, only that a less demanding standard applies. I agree with The Chief Justice that the "substantial likelihood of material prejudice" standard articulated in Rule 177 passes constitutional muster. Accordingly, I join Parts I and II of The Chief Justice's opinion.

PRESS-ENTERPRISE CO. V. SUPERIOR COURT [PRESS-ENTERPRISE II]

478 U.S. 1, 106 S.Ct. 2735, 92 L.Ed.2d 1 (1986).

CHIEF JUSTICE BURGER delivered the opinion of the Court.

We granted certiorari to decide whether petitioner has a First Amendment right of access to transcripts of a preliminary hearing growing out of a criminal prosecution.

On December 23, 1981, the State of California filed a complaint in the Riverside County Municipal Court, charging Robert Diaz with 12 counts of murder and seeking the death penalty. The complaint alleged that Diaz, a nurse, murdered 12 patients by administering massive doses of the heart drug lidocaine. The preliminary hearing on the complaint commenced on July 6, 1982. Diaz moved to exclude the public from the proceedings under California Penal Code § 868, which requires such proceedings to be open unless "exclusion of the public is necessary in order to protect the defendant's right to a fair and impartial trial." The Magistrate granted the unopposed motion, finding that closure was necessary because the case had attracted national publicity and "only one side may get reported in the media."

The preliminary hearing continued for 41 days. Most of the testimony and the evidence presented by the State was medical and scientific; the remainder consisted of testimony by personnel who worked with Diaz on the shifts when the 12 patients died. Diaz did not introduce any evidence, but his counsel subjected most of the witnesses to vigorous cross-examination. Diaz was held to answer on all charges. At the conclusion of the hearing, petitioner Press-Enterprise Company asked that the transcript of the proceedings be released. The Magistrate refused and sealed the record.

On January 21, 1983, the State moved in Superior Court to have the transcripts of the preliminary hearing released to the public; petitioner later joined in support of the motion. Diaz opposed the motion, contending that release of the transcripts would result in prejudicial pretrial publicity. The Superior Court found that the information in the transcript was "as factual as it could be," and that the facts were neither "inflammatory" nor "exciting" but there was, nonetheless, "a reasonable likelihood that release of all or any part of the transcript might prejudice defendant's right to a fair and impartial trial."

Petitioner then filed a peremptory writ of mandate [seeking appellate review]. Meanwhile, Diaz waived his right to a jury trial and the Superior Court released the transcript. [The] California Supreme Court thereafter denied petitioner's peremptory writ of mandate, holding that there is no general First Amendment right of access to preliminary hearings. * * *

It is important to identify precisely what the California Supreme Court decided:

> "[W]e conclude that the magistrate shall close the preliminary hearing upon finding a reasonable likelihood of substantial prejudice which would impinge upon the right to a fair trial. Penal code section 868 makes clear that the primary right is the right to a fair trial and that the public's right of access must give way when there is conflict."

It is difficult to disagree in the abstract with that court's analysis balancing the defendant's right to a fair trial against the public right of access. It is also important to remember that these interests are not necessarily inconsistent. Plainly the defendant has a right to a fair trial but, as we have repeatedly recognized, one of the important means of assuring a fair trial is that the process be open to neutral observers.

The right to an open public trial is a shared right of the accused and the public, the common concern being the assurance of fairness. Only recently, in *Waller v. Georgia*, 467 U.S. 39 (1984), for example, we considered whether the defendant's Sixth Amendment right to an open trial prevented the closure of a suppression hearing over the defendant's objection. We noted that the First Amendment right of access would in most instances attach to such proceedings and that "the explicit

Sixth Amendment right of the accused is no less protective of a public trial than the implicit First Amendment right of the press and public." When the defendant objects to the closure of a suppression hearing, therefore, the hearing must be open unless the party seeking to close the hearing advances an overriding interest that is likely to be prejudiced.

Here, unlike *Waller,* the right asserted is not the defendant's Sixth Amendment right to a public trial since the defendant requested a *closed* preliminary hearing. Instead, the right asserted here is that of the public under the First Amendment. The California Supreme Court concluded that the First Amendment was not implicated because the proceeding was not a criminal trial, but a preliminary hearing. However, the First Amendment question cannot be resolved solely on the label we give the event, i.e., "trial" or otherwise, particularly where the preliminary hearing functions much like a full scale trial.

In cases dealing with the claim of a First Amendment right of access to criminal proceedings, our decisions have emphasized two complementary considerations. First, because a " 'tradition of accessibility implies the favorable judgment of experience,' " we have considered whether the place and process has historically been open to the press and general public. * * * Second, [the] Court has traditionally considered whether public access plays a significant positive role in the functioning of the particular process in question. Although many governmental processes operate best under public scrutiny, it takes little imagination to recognize that there are some kinds of government operations that would be totally frustrated if conducted openly. A classic example is that "the proper functioning of our grand jury system depends upon the secrecy of grand jury proceedings." Other proceedings plainly require public access. In *Press-Enterprise I,* we summarized the holdings of prior cases, noting that openness in criminal trials, including the selection of jurors, "enhances both the basic fairness of the criminal trial and the appearance of fairness so essential to public confidence in the system."

These considerations of experience and logic are, of course, related, for history and experience shape the functioning of governmental processes. If the particular proceeding in question passes these tests of experience and logic, a qualified First Amendment right of public access attaches. But even when a right of access attaches, it is not absolute. *Globe Newspaper Co. v. Superior Court* [infra note 2]. While open criminal proceedings give assurances of fairness to both the public and the accused, there are some limited circumstances in which the right of the accused to a fair trial might be undermined by publicity.[2] In such cases, the trial court must determine whether the situation is such that the rights of the accused override the qualified First Amendment right of access. In *Press-Enterprise I* we stated:

---

[2]　Similarly, the interests of those other than the accused may be implicated. The protection of victims of sex crimes from the trauma and embarrassment of public scrutiny may justify closing certain aspects of a criminal proceeding. See *Globe Newspaper Co. v. Superior Court,* 457 U.S. 596 (1982). [In *Globe Newspaper,* the Court struck down as overbroad a state statute that required the trial court, at rape and sex offense trials involving complainants under age 18, to exclude the press and general public. The Court agreed that a state interest in "safeguarding the physical and psychological well-being of a minor" was a "compelling" interest, but found that it "does not justify a *mandatory*-closure rule, for it is clear that the circumstances of the particular case may affect the significance of the interest."]

"the presumption may be overcome only by an overriding interest based on findings that closure is essential to preserve higher values and is narrowly tailored to serve that interest. The interest is to be articulated along with findings specific enough that a reviewing court can determine whether the closure order was properly entered."

The considerations that led the Court to apply the First Amendment right of access to criminal trials in *Richmond Newspapers* [and] the selection of jurors in *Press-Enterprise I* lead us to conclude that the right of access applies to preliminary hearings as conducted in California.

First, there has been a tradition of accessibility to preliminary hearings of the type conducted in California. Although grand jury proceedings have traditionally been closed to the public and the accused, preliminary hearings conducted before neutral and detached magistrates have been open to the public. Long ago in the celebrated trial of Aaron Burr for treason, for example, with Chief Justice Marshall sitting as trial judge, the probable cause hearing was held in the Hall of the House of Delegates in Virginia, the court room being too small to accommodate the crush of interested citizens. From *Burr* until the present day, the near uniform practice of state and federal courts has been to conduct preliminary hearings in open court. * * * Open preliminary hearings, therefore, have been accorded " 'the favorable judgment of experience.' "

The second question is whether public access to preliminary hearings as they are conducted in California plays a particularly significant positive role in the actual functioning of the process. We have already determined [that] public access to criminal trials and the selection of jurors is essential to the proper functioning of the criminal justice system. California preliminary hearings are sufficiently like a trial to justify the same conclusion. [The] accused has the right to personally appear at the hearing, to be represented by counsel, to cross-examine hostile witnesses, to present exculpatory evidence, and to exclude illegally obtained evidence. If the magistrate determines that probable cause exists, the accused is bound over for trial; such a finding leads to a guilty plea in the majority of cases.

It is true that unlike a criminal trial, the California preliminary hearing cannot result in the conviction of the accused and the adjudication is before a magistrate or other judicial officer without a jury. But these features, standing alone, do not make public access any less essential to the proper functioning of the proceedings in the overall criminal justice process. Because of its extensive scope, the preliminary hearing is often the final and most important step in the criminal proceeding. As the California Supreme Court stated, the preliminary hearing in many cases provides "the sole occasion for public observation of the criminal justice system."

Similarly, the absence of a jury, long recognized as "an inestimable safeguard against the corrupt or overzealous prosecutor and against the complaint, biased, or eccentric judge," makes the importance of public access to a preliminary hearing even more significant. "People in an open society do not demand infallibility from their institutions, but it is difficult for them to accept what they are prohibited from observing." *Richmond Newspapers.*

Denying the transcripts of a 41-day preliminary hearing would frustrate what we have characterized as the "community therapeutic value" of openness. Criminal acts, especially certain violent crimes, provoke public concern, outrage, and hostility. "When the public is aware that the law is being enforced and the criminal justice system is functioning, an outlet is provided for these understandable reactions and emotions." *Press-Enterprise I.* * * *

We therefore conclude that the qualified First Amendment right of access to criminal proceedings applies to preliminary hearings as they are conducted in California. Since [that right] attaches to preliminary hearings in California [the] proceedings cannot be closed unless specific, on the record findings are made demonstrating that "closure is essential to preserve higher values and is narrowly tailored to serve that interest." *Press-Enterprise I.* If the interest asserted is the right of the accused to a fair trial, the preliminary hearing shall be closed only if specific findings are made demonstrating that first, there is a substantial probability that the defendant's right to a fair trial will be prejudiced by publicity that closure would prevent and, second, reasonable alternatives to closure cannot adequately protect the defendant's free trial rights.

The California Supreme Court, interpreting its access statute, concluded "that the magistrate shall close the preliminary hearing upon finding a reasonable likelihood of substantial prejudice." As the court itself acknowledged, the "reasonable likelihood" test places a lesser burden on the defendant than the "substantial probability" test which we hold is called for by the First Amendment. Moreover, the court failed to consider whether alternatives short of complete closure would have protected the interests of the accused.

In *Gannett Co., Inc. v. DePasquale*, 443 U.S. 368 (1979) [involving the closure of a pretrial suppression hearing in which evidence was taken to determine the voluntariness of defendant's confession], we observed that:

> "Publicity concerning pretrial suppression hearings such as the one involved in the present case poses special risks of unfairness. The whole purpose of such hearings is to screen out unreliable or illegally obtained evidence and insure that this evidence does not become known to the jury. Publicity concerning the proceedings at a pretrial hearing, however, could influence public opinion against a defendant and inform potential jurors of inculpatory information wholly inadmissible at the actual trial."

But this risk of prejudice does not automatically justify refusing public access to hearings on every motion to suppress. Through *voir dire*, cumbersome as it is in some circumstances, a court can identify those jurors whose prior knowledge of the case would disable them from rendering an impartial verdict. And even if closure were justified for the hearings on a motion to suppress, closure of an entire 41-day proceeding would rarely be warranted. The First Amendment right of access cannot be overcome by the conclusory assertion that publicity might deprive the defendant of that right. And any limitation " 'must be narrowly tailored to serve that interest.' " *Press-Enterprise I.* * * *

JUSTICE STEVENS, with whom JUSTICE REHNQUIST joins as to Part II, dissenting.

The constitutional question presented by this case is whether members of the public have a First Amendment right to insist upon access to the transcript of a preliminary hearing during the period before the public trial, even though the accused, the prosecutor, and the trial judge have all agreed to the sealing of the transcript in order to assure a fair trial. * * *

I

Although perhaps obvious, it bears emphasis that the First Amendment right asserted by petitioner is not a right to publish or otherwise communicate information lawfully or unlawfully acquired. That right, which lies at the core of the First Amendment and which erased the legacy of restraints on publication against which the drafters of that Amendment rebelled, may be overcome only by a governmental objective of the highest order attainable in no less intrusive way. The First Amendment right asserted by petitioner in this case, in contrast, is not the right to publicize information in its possession, but the right to acquire access thereto.

I have long believed that a proper construction of the First Amendment embraces a right of access to information about the conduct of public affairs. * * * Neither our elected nor our appointed representatives may abridge the free flow of information simply to protect their own activities from public scrutiny. An official policy of secrecy must be supported by some legitimate justification that serves the interest of the public office. * * *

But it has always been apparent that the freedom to obtain information that the Government has a legitimate interest in not disclosing, is far narrower than the freedom to disseminate information, which is "virtually absolute" in most contexts, *Richmond Newspapers, Inc. v. Virginia* (Stevens, J., concurring). In this case, the risk of prejudice to the defendant's right to a fair trial is perfectly obvious. For me, that risk is far more significant than the countervailing interest in publishing the transcript of the preliminary hearing sooner rather than later. [The] interest in prompt publication—in my view—is no greater than the interest in prompt publication of grand jury transcripts. [W]e have always recognized the legitimacy of the governmental interest in the secrecy of grand jury proceedings, and I am unpersuaded that the difference between such proceedings and the rather elaborate procedure for determining probable cause that California has adopted strengthens the First Amendment claim to access asserted in this case.

II

[The Court] reaches the opposite conclusion by applying the "two complementary considerations," of "experience and logic." In my view neither the Court's reasoning nor the result it reaches is supported by our precedents.

The historical evidence proffered in this case is far less probative than the evidence adduced in prior cases granting public access to criminal proceedings. In those cases, a common law tradition of openness at the time the First Amendment was ratified suggested an intention and expectation on the part of the Framers and ratifiers that those proceedings would remain presumptively open. [In] this case, however, it is uncontroverted that a common law right of access did not inhere in preliminary proceedings at the time the First Amendment was adopted, and that the Framers and ratifiers of that provision could not have intended such proceedings to remain open.

[In] the final analysis, the Court's lengthy historical disquisition demonstrates only that in many States preliminary proceedings are generally open to the public. In other States, numbering California * * * among them, such proceedings have been closed. [That California's] particular approach has been adopted in few other States does not render [its] choice "unconstitutional." * * *

If the Court's historical evidence proves too little, the "value of openness," on which it relies proves too much, for this measure would open to public scrutiny far more than preliminary hearings "as they are conducted in California" (a comforting phrase invoked by the Court in one form or another more than 8 times in its opinion). In brief, the Court's rationale for opening the "California preliminary hearing" is that it "is often the final and most important step in the criminal proceeding"; that it provides " 'the sole occasion for public observation of the criminal justice system' "; that it lacks the protective presence of a jury; and that closure denies an outlet for community catharsis. The obvious defect in the Court's approach is that its reasoning applies to the traditionally secret grand jury with as much force as it applies to California preliminary hearings. A grand jury indictment is just as likely to be the "final step" in a criminal proceeding and the "sole occasion" for public scrutiny as is a preliminary hearing. Moreover, many critics of the grand jury maintain that the grand jury protects the accused less well than does a legally-knowledgeable judge who personally presides over a preliminary hearing. * * * Finally, closure of grand juries denies an outlet for community rage. When the Court's explanatory veneer is stripped away, what emerges is the reality that the California preliminary hearing is functionally identical to the traditional grand jury. [Yet] [t]his Court has previously described grand jury secrecy as "indispensable," and has remarked that "the proper functioning of our grand jury system depends upon the secrecy of grand jury proceedings."

In fact, the logic of the Court's access right extends even beyond the confines of the criminal justice system to encompass proceedings held on the civil side of the docket as well. * * * Despite the Court's valiant attempt to limit the logic of its holding, the *ratio decidendi* of today's decision knows no bounds. [The] presence of a legitimate reason for closure in this case requires an affirmance. The constitutionally-grounded fair trial interests of the accused if he is bound over for trial, and the reputational interests of the accused if he is not, provide a substantial reason for delaying access to the transcript for at least the short time before trial. * * *

CHANDLER V. FLORIDA

449 U.S. 560, 101 S.Ct. 802, 66 L.Ed.2d 740 (1981).

CHIEF JUSTICE BURGER delivered the opinion of the Court.

The question presented on this appeal is whether, consistent with constitutional guarantees, a state may provide for radio, television, and still photographic coverage of a criminal trial for public broadcast, notwithstanding the objection of the accused.

Background. Over the past 50 years, some criminal cases characterized as "sensational" have been subjected to extensive coverage by news media, sometimes seriously interfering with the conduct of the proceedings and creating a setting wholly inappropriate for the administration of justice. Judges, lawyers, and others soon became concerned, and in 1937, after study, the American Bar Association House of Delegates adopted Judicial Canon 35, declaring that all photographic and broadcast coverage of courtroom proceedings should be prohibited. In 1952, the House of Delegates amended Canon 35 to proscribe television coverage as well. [A] majority of the states, including Florida, adopted the substance of the ABA provision and its amendments. In Florida, the rule was embodied in Canon 3A(7) of the Florida Code of Judicial Conduct.

In February 1978, the American Bar Association Committee on Fair Trial-Free Press proposed revised standards. These included a provision permitting courtroom coverage by the electronic media under conditions to be established by local rule and under the control of the trial judge, but only if such coverage was carried out unobtrusively and without affecting the conduct of the trial. The revision was endorsed by the ABA's Standing Committee on Standards for Criminal Justice, [but] rejected by the House of Delegates on February 12, 1979.

[In] January 1975, while these developments were unfolding, the Post-Newsweek Stations of Florida petitioned the Supreme Court of Florida urging a change in Florida's Canon 3A(7). [The] Florida Supreme Court [eventually established a] 1-year pilot program during which the electronic media were permitted to cover all judicial proceedings in Florida without reference to the consent of participants, subject to detailed standards with respect to technology and the conduct of operators. * * * When the pilot program ended, the Florida Supreme Court received and reviewed briefs, reports, letters of comment, and studies. It conducted its own survey of attorneys, witnesses, jurors, and court personnel through the Office of the State Court Coordinator. A separate survey was taken of judges by the Florida Conference of Circuit Judges. The court also studied the experience of 6 States that had, by 1979, adopted rules relating to electronic coverage of trials, as well as that of the 10 other States that, like Florida, were experimenting with such coverage.

Following its review of this material, the Florida Supreme Court concluded "that on balance there [was] more to be gained than lost by permitting electronic media coverage of judicial proceedings subject to standards for such coverage." The Florida court was of the view that because of the significant effect of the courts on the day-to-day lives of the citizenry, it was essential that the people have confidence in the process. It felt that broadcast coverage of trials would contribute to wider public acceptance and understanding of decisions. Consequently, after revising the 1977 guidelines to reflect its evaluation of the pilot program, the Florida Supreme Court promulgated a revised Canon 3A(7). The Canon provides:

> "Subject at all times to the authority of the presiding judge to (i) control the conduct of proceedings before the court, (ii) ensure decorum and prevent distractions, and (iii) ensure the fair administration of justice in the pending cause, electronic media and still photography coverage of public judicial proceedings in the appellate and trial courts of this state shall be allowed in accordance with standards of conduct and technology promulgated by the Supreme Court of Florida." Ibid.

The implementing guidelines specify in detail the kind of electronic equipment to be used and the manner of its use. For example, no more than one television camera and only one camera technician are allowed. Existing recording systems used by court reporters are used by broadcasters for audio pickup. Where more than one broadcast news organization seeks to cover a trial, the media must pool coverage. No artificial lighting is allowed. The equipment is positioned in a fixed location, and it may not be moved during trial. Videotaping equipment must be remote from the courtroom. Film, videotape, and lenses may not be changed while the court is in session. No audio recording of conferences between lawyers, between parties and counsel, or at the bench is permitted. The judge has sole and plenary discretion to exclude coverage of certain witnesses, and the jury may not be filmed. The judge has discretionary power to forbid coverage whenever satisfied that coverage may have a deleterious effect on the paramount right of the defendant to a fair trial. * * *

In July 1977, appellants were charged with conspiracy to commit burglary, grand larceny, and possession of burglary tools. The counts covered breaking and entering a well-known Miami Beach restaurant.

The details of the alleged criminal conduct are not relevant to the issue before us, but several aspects of the case distinguish it from a routine burglary. At the time of their arrest, appellants were Miami Beach policemen. The State's principal witness was John Sion, an amateur radio operator who, by sheer chance, had overheard and recorded conversations between the appellants over their police walkie-talkie radios during the burglary. Not surprisingly, these novel factors attracted the attention of the media.

By pretrial motion, counsel for the appellants sought to have experimental Canon 3A(7) declared unconstitutional on its face and as applied. The trial court denied relief * * *. After several additional fruitless attempts by the appellants to prevent electronic coverage of the trial, the jury was selected. At *voir dire,* the appellants' counsel asked each prospective juror whether he or she would be able to be "fair and impartial" despite the presence of a television camera during some, or all, of the trial. Each juror selected responded that such coverage would not affect his or her consideration in any way. A television camera recorded the *voir dire.*

A defense motion to sequester the jury because of the television coverage was denied by the trial judge. However, the court instructed the jury not to watch or read anything about the case in the media and suggested that jurors "avoid the local news and watch only the national news on television." Subsequently, defense counsel requested that the witnesses be instructed not to watch any television accounts of testimony presented at trial. The trial court declined to give such an instruction, for "no witness' testimony was [being] reported or televised [on the evening news] in any way."

A television camera was in place for one entire afternoon, during which the State presented the testimony of Sion, its chief witness. No camera was present for the presentation of any part of the case for the defense. The camera returned to cover closing arguments. Only 2 minutes and 55 seconds of the trial below were broadcast—and those depicted only the prosecution's side of the case.

The jury returned a guilty verdict on all counts. Appellants moved for a new trial, claiming that because of the television coverage, they had been denied a fair and impartial trial. No evidence of specific prejudice was tendered.

[At] the outset, it is important to note that in promulgating the revised Canon 3A(7), the Florida Supreme Court pointedly rejected any state or federal constitutional right of access on the part of photographers or the broadcast media to televise or electronically record and thereafter disseminate court proceedings. [The] Florida court relied on our holding in *Nixon v. Warner Communications, Inc.*, 435 U.S. 589 (1978), where we said:

> "In the first place, [there] is no constitutional right to have [live witness] testimony recorded and broadcast. Second, while the guarantee of a public trial, in the words of Mr. Justice Black, is 'a safeguard against any attempt to employ our courts as instruments of persecution,' it confers no special benefit on the press. Nor does the Sixth Amendment require that the trial—or any part of it—be broadcast live or on tape to the public. The requirement of a public trial is satisfied by the opportunity of members of the public and the press to attend the trial and to report what they have observed."

The Florida Supreme Court predicated the revised Canon 3A(7) upon its supervisory authority over the Florida courts, and not upon any constitutional imperative. Hence, we have before us only the limited question of the Florida Supreme Court's authority to promulgate the Canon for the trial of cases in Florida courts. * * *

Appellants rely chiefly on *Estes v. Texas,* 381 U.S. 532 (1965), and Chief Justice Warren's separate concurring opinion in that case. They argue that the televising of criminal trials is inherently a denial of due process, and they read *Estes* as announcing a *per se* constitutional rule to that effect. Chief Justice Warren's concurring opinion, in which he was joined by Justices Douglas and Goldberg, indeed provides some support for the appellants' position. * * * [However], [t]he six separate opinions in *Estes* must be examined carefully to evaluate the claim that it represents a *per se* constitutional rule forbidding all electronic coverage.[a] Chief Justice Warren and Justices Douglas and Goldberg joined Justice Clark's opinion announcing the judgment, thereby creating only a plurality. Justice Harlan provided the fifth vote necessary in support of the judgment. In a separate opinion, he pointedly limited his concurrence:

> "I concur in the opinion of the Court, subject, however, to the reservations and only to the extent indicated in this opinion."

A careful analysis of Justice Harlan's opinion is therefore fundamental to an understanding of the ultimate holding of *Estes*.

Justice Harlan began by observing that the question of the constitutional permissibility of televised trials was one fraught with unusual difficulty:

> "Permitting television in the courtroom undeniably has mischievous potentialities for intruding upon the detached atmosphere which should always surround the judicial process. Forbidding this innovation, however, would doubtless impinge upon one of the valued attributes of our federalism by preventing the states from pursing a novel course of procedural experimentation. My conclusion is that there is no constitutional requirement that television be allowed in the courtroom, *and, at least as to a notorious criminal trial such as this one, the considerations against allowing television in the courtroom so far outweigh the countervailing factors advanced in its support as to require a holding that what was done in this case infringed the fundamental right to a fair trial* assured by the Due Process Clause of the Fourteenth Amendment." (emphasis added).

---

[a]   Justice Clark delivered an opinion in *Estes* that was titled the "opinion for the Court," although (as the *Chandler* opinion notes infra) Justice Harlan was listed as concurring only to the extent indicated in his separate opinion. Justice Clark's opinion reasoned: "The State * * * says that the use of television in the instant case was 'without injustice' to the person immediately concerned; basing its position on the fact that the petitioner has established no isolatable prejudice and that this must be shown in order to invalidate a conviction * * *. The State paints too broadly * * *, for this Court itself has found instances in which a showing of actual prejudice is not a prerequisite to reversal. This is such a case. [In *Rideau* and certain other cases, e.g., one in which two sheriffs deputies who were principle prosecution witnesses also had custody of the jurors], the Court did not stop to consider the actual effect of the practice, but struck down the conviction on the ground that prejudice was inherent. [T]he circumstances were held to be inherently suspect and therefore, such a showing [of actual prejudice] was not held to be a requisite to reversal. Likewise in this case the application of this principle is especially appropriate. Television in its present state and by its very nature, reaches into a variety of areas in which it may cause prejudice to an accused. Still one cannot put his finger on its specific mischief and prove with particularity wherein he was prejudiced. * * * Forty-eight of our states and the Federal Rules have deemed the use of television improper in the courtroom. This fact is most telling in buttressing our conclusion that any change in procedure which would permit its use would be inconsistent with our concepts of due process in this field."

Three members of the majority, speaking through Chief Justice Warren's concurring opinion stated that they "join[ed] the Court's opinion and agree[d] that televising of criminal trials is inherently a denial of due process," but wished to offer "additional views on why this is so." The concurring opinion of the fifth member of the majority, Justice Harlan, is discussed infra. In addition, there were three dissents (reflecting the views of four dissenters). The dissents argued against the adoption of a "per se rule" rendering the televising of trials constitutionally unacceptable without a showing that the risks of disruption, distraction, and juror viewing of the broadcasts actually had materialized in the particular case.

He then proceeded to catalog what he perceived as the inherent dangers of televised trials.

> "In the context of a trial of intense public interest, there is certainly a strong possibility that the timid or reluctant witness, for whom a court appearance even at its traditional best is a harrowing affair, will become more timid or reluctant when he finds he will also be appearing before a 'hidden audience' of unknown but large dimensions. There is certainly a strong possibility that the 'cocky' witness having a thirst for the limelight will become more 'cocky' under the influence of television. And who can say that the juror who is gratified by having been chosen for a front-line case, an ambitious prosecutor, a publicity-minded defense attorney, and even a conscientious judge will not stray, albeit unconsciously, from doing what 'comes naturally' into pluming themselves for a satisfactory television 'performance'?"

Justice Harlan faced squarely the reality that these possibilities carry "grave potentialities for distorting the integrity of the judicial process," and that, although such distortions may produce no telltale signs, "their effects may be far more pervasive and deleterious than the physical disruptions which all would concede would vitiate a conviction." The "countervailing factors" alluded to by Justice Harlan were, as here, the educational and informational value to the public.

[I]t is fair to say that Justice Harlan viewed the holding as limited to the proposition that "*what was done in this case* infringed the fundamental right to a fair trial assured by the Due Process Clause of the Fourteenth Amendment" (emphasis added). * * * Justice Harlan's opinion, upon which analysis of the constitutional holding of *Estes* turns, must be read as defining the scope of that holding; we conclude that *Estes* is not to be read as announcing a constitutional rule barring still photographic, radio, and television coverage in all cases and under all circumstances. [Since] we are satisfied that *Estes* did not announce a constitutional rule that all photographic or broadcast coverage of criminal trials is inherently a denial of due process, we turn to consideration, as a matter of first impression, of the appellants' suggestion that we now promulgate such a *per se* rule.

Any criminal case that generates a great deal of publicity presents some risks that the publicity may compromise the right of the defendant to a fair trial. Trial courts must be especially vigilant to guard against any impairment of the defendant's right to a verdict based solely upon the evidence and the relevant law. Over the years, courts have developed a range of curative devices to prevent publicity about a trial from infecting jury deliberations. See, e.g., *Nebraska Press Assn. v. Stuart.*

An absolute constitutional ban on broadcast coverage of trials cannot be justified simply because there is a danger that, in some cases, prejudicial broadcast accounts of pretrial and trial events may impair the ability of jurors to decide the issue of guilt or innocence uninfluenced by extraneous matter. The risk of juror prejudice in some cases does not justify an absolute ban on news coverage of trials by the printed media; so also the risk of such prejudice does not warrant an absolute constitutional ban on all broadcast coverage. A case attracts a high level of public attention because of its intrinsic interest to the public and the manner of reporting the event. The risk of juror prejudice is present in any publication of a trial, but the appropriate safeguard against such prejudice is the defendant's right to demonstrate that the media's coverage of his case—be it printed or broadcast—compromised the ability of the particular jury that heard the case to adjudicate fairly.

[T]he concurring opinions in *Estes* expressed concern that the very presence of media cameras and recording devices at a trial inescapably gives rise to an adverse psychological impact on the participants in the trial. This kind of general psychological prejudice, allegedly present whenever there is broadcast coverage of a trial, is different from the more particularized problem of prejudicial impact discussed earlier. If it could be demonstrated that the mere presence of photographic and recording equipment and the knowledge that the event would be broadcast invariably and uniformly affected the conduct of participants so as to impair fundamental fairness, our task would be simple; prohibition of broadcast coverage of trials would be required.

In confronting the difficult and sensitive question of the potential psychological prejudice associated with broadcast coverage of trials, we have been aided by *amici* briefs submitted by various state officers involved in law enforcement, the Conference of Chief Justices, and the Attorneys General of 17 States in support of continuing experimentation such as that embarked upon by Florida, and by the American College of Trial Lawyers, and various members of the defense bar representing essentially the views expressed by the concurring Justices in *Estes*.

Not unimportant to the position asserted by Florida and other states is the change in television technology since 1962, when Estes was tried. It is urged, and some empirical data are presented, that many of the negative factors found in *Estes*—cumbersome equipment, cables, distracting lighting, numerous camera technicians—are less substantial factors today than they were at that time.

It is also significant that safeguards have been built into the experimental programs in state courts, and into the Florida program, to avoid some of the most egregious problems envisioned by the six opinions in the *Estes* case. Florida admonishes its courts to take special pains to protect certain witnesses—for example, children, victims of sex crimes, some informants, and even the very timid witness or party—from the glare of publicity and the tensions of being "on camera."

The Florida guidelines place on trial judges positive obligations to be on guard to protect the fundamental right of the accused to a fair trial. The Florida Canon, being one of the few permitting broadcast coverage of criminal trials over the objection of the accused, raises problems not present in the rules of other states. Inherent in electronic coverage of a trial is the risk that the very awareness by the accused of the coverage and the contemplated broadcast may adversely affect the conduct of the participants and the fairness of the trial, yet leave no evidence of how the conduct or the trial's fairness was affected. Given this danger, it is significant that Florida requires that objections of the accused to coverage be heard and considered on the record by the trial court. In addition to providing a record for appellate review, a pre-trial hearing enables a defendant to advance the basis of his objection to broadcast coverage and allows the trial court to define the steps necessary to minimize or eliminate the risks of prejudice to the accused. Experiments such as the one presented here may well increase the number of appeals by adding a new basis for claims to reverse, but this is a risk Florida has chosen to take after preliminary experimentation. Here, the record does not indicate that appellants requested an evidentiary hearing to show adverse impact or injury. Nor does the record reveal anything more than generalized allegations of prejudice.

Nonetheless, it is clear that the general issue of the psychological impact of broadcast coverage upon the participants in a trial, and particularly upon the defendant, is still a subject of sharp debate—as the *amici* briefs of the American College of Trial Lawyers and others of the trial bar in opposition to Florida's experiment demonstrate. These *amici* state the view that the concerns expressed by the concurring opinions in *Estes,* have been borne out by actual experience. [Yet], [c]omprehensive empirical data are still not available—at least on some aspects of the problem. * * * Whatever may be the "mischievous potentialities [of broadcast coverage] for intruding upon the detached atmosphere which should always surround the judicial process," *Estes v. Texas,* at present no one has been able to present empirical data sufficient to establish that the mere presence of the broadcast media inherently has an adverse effect on that process. * * *

Where, as here, we cannot say that a denial of due process automatically results from activity authorized by a state, the admonition of Justice Brandeis, dissenting in *New State Ice Co. v. Liebmann,* 285 U.S. 262 (1932), is relevant:

> "To stay experimentation in things social and economic is a grave responsibility. Denial of the right to experiment may be fraught with serious consequences to the Nation. It is one of the happy incidents of the federal system that a single courageous State may, if its citizens choose, serve as a laboratory; and try novel social and economic experiments without risk to the rest of the country. This Court has the power to prevent an experiment. We may strike down the statute which embodies it on the ground that, in our opinion, the measure is arbitrary, capricious, or unreasonable. [But] in the exercise of this high power, we must be ever on our guard, lest we erect our prejudices into legal principles. If we would guide by the light of reason, we must let our minds be bold." (Footnote omitted.)

This concept of federalism, echoed by the states favoring Florida's experiment, must guide our decision.

Amici members of the defense bar vigorously contend that displaying the accused on television is in itself a denial of due process. This was a source of concern to Chief Justice Warren and Justice Harlan in *Estes:* that coverage of select cases "singles out certain defendants and subjects them to trials under prejudicial conditions not experienced by others." Selection of which trials, or parts of trials, to broadcast will inevitably be made not by judges but by the media, and will be governed by such factors as the nature of the crime and the status and position of the accused—or of the victim; the effect may be to titillate rather than to educate and inform. The unanswered question is whether electronic coverage will bring public humiliation upon the accused with such randomness that it will evoke due process concerns by being "unusual in the same way that being struck by lightning" is "unusual." *Furman v. Georgia,* 408 U.S. 238 (1972) (Stewart, J., concurring). Societies and political systems, that, from time to time, have put on "Yankee Stadium" "show trials" tell more about the power of the state than about its concern for the decent administration of justice—with every citizen receiving the same kind of justice.

The concurring opinion of Chief Justice Warren joined by Justices Douglas and Goldberg in *Estes* can fairly be read as viewing the very broadcast of some trials as potentially a form of punishment in itself—a punishment before guilt. This concern is far from trivial. But, whether coverage of a few trials will, in practice, be the equivalent of a "Yankee Stadium" setting—which Justice Harlan likened to the public pillory long abandoned as a barbaric perversion of decent justice—must also await the continuing experimentation.

To say that the appellants have not demonstrated that broadcast coverage is inherently a denial of due process is not to say that the appellants were in fact accorded all of the protections of due process in their trial. As noted earlier, a defendant has the right on review to show that the media's coverage of his case—printed or broadcast—compromised the ability of the jury to judge him fairly. Alternatively, a defendant might show that broadcast coverage of his particular case had an adverse impact on the trial participants sufficient to constitute a denial of due process. Neither showing was made in this case.

To demonstrate prejudice in a specific case a defendant must show something more than juror awareness that the trial is such as to attract the attention of broadcasters. *Murphy v. Florida* [fn. 12, p. 873]. No doubt the very presence of a camera in the courtroom made the jurors aware that the trial was thought to be of sufficient interest to the public to warrant coverage. Jurors, forbidden to watch all broadcasts, would have had no way of knowing that only fleeting seconds of the proceeding would be reproduced. But the appellants have not attempted to show with any specificity that the presence of cameras impaired the ability of the jurors to decide the case on only the evidence before them or that their trial was affected adversely by the impact on any of the participants of the presence of cameras and the prospect of broadcast.

Although not essential to our holding, we note that at *voir dire,* the jurors were asked if the presence of the camera would in any way compromise their ability to consider the case. Each answered that the camera would not prevent him or her from considering the case solely on the merits. The trial court instructed the jurors not to watch television accounts of the trial, and the appellants do not contend that any juror violated this instruction. The appellants have offered no evidence that any participant in this case was affected by the presence of cameras. In short, there is no showing that the trial was compromised by television coverage, as was the case in *Estes.*

[In] this setting, because this Court has no supervisory authority over state courts, our review is confined to whether there is a constitutional violation. We hold that the Constitution does not prohibit a state from experimenting with the program authorized by revised Canon 3A(7).

JUSTICE STEVENS took no part in the decision of this case.

JUSTICE STEWART, concurring in the result.

Although concurring in the judgment, I cannot join the opinion of the Court because I do not think the convictions in this case can be affirmed without overruling *Estes v. Texas*. I believe now, as I believed in dissent then, that *Estes* announced a *per se* rule that the Fourteenth Amendment "prohibits all television cameras from a state courtroom whenever a criminal trial is in progress." Accordingly, rather than join what seems to me a wholly unsuccessful effort to distinguish that decision, I would now flatly overrule it. * * *

JUSTICE WHITE, concurring in the judgment.

* * * Whether the decision in *Estes* is read broadly or narrowly, I agree with Justice Stewart that it should be overruled. I was in dissent in that case, and I remain unwilling to assume or conclude without more proof than has been marshaled to date that televising criminal trials is inherently prejudicial even when carried out under properly controlled conditions. * * * Although the Court's opinion today contends that it is consistent with *Estes*, I believe that it effectively eviscerates *Estes*. The Florida rule has no exception for the sensational or widely publicized case. Absent a showing of specific prejudice, *any* kind of case may be televised as long as the rule is otherwise complied with. Thus, even if the present case is precisely the kind of case referred to in Justice Harlan's concurrence in *Estes,* the Florida rule overrides the defendant's objections. The majority opinion does not find it necessary to deal with appellants' contention that because their case attracted substantial publicity, specific prejudice need not be shown. By affirming the judgment below, which sustained the rule, the majority indicates that not even the narrower reading of *Estes* will any longer be authoritative. * * *

CHAPTER 17

THE ROLE OF COUNSEL

■ ■ ■

1. INTRODUCTION

Chapter Five examined the constitutional right to representation by counsel at different stages in the criminal process, focusing, in particular, on whether there is a right to a lawyer provided by the state when the individual (suspect, accused, or convicted defendant) is indigent. That constitutional right, whether grounded in the Sixth Amendment or some other constitutional guarantee, assigns to counsel's representation a certain role—providing what the Sixth Amendment describes as the "assistance of counsel for his [the accused's] defense." That role, in turn, creates the grounding for constitutional challenges by the defendant as to: (1) representation by counsel that is so deficient as to result in a failure to provide the constitutionally guaranteed "assistance of counsel"; and (2) special settings of representation, such as conflicts of interest and governmental restrictions, that will prevent counsel from providing that constitutionally guaranteed level of assistance. This chapter considers, in addition to these two challenges, a third and fourth challenge also informed by the character of the assistance constitutionally guaranteed: (3) a defendant's assertion that counsel must consult and abide by the defendant's directions on a particular decision relating to the defense presentation; and (4) the exercise by the defendant of a claimed right to self-representation (thereby precluding the state from insisting that the defendant receive the constitutionally guaranteed "assistance of counsel").

This chapter is placed before the chapter on trials because all of these challenges may be presented (and resolved) prior to trial. Indeed the fourth challenge cited above ordinarily must be presented pretrial, as the right to self-representation is lost if not timely presented before trial. There is no similar timing requirement for the other three challenges, and here, the division in practice between raising the challenge pretrial and first raising it following trial (and conviction) varies with the character of the challenge.

As to some claims, both pretrial and after-conviction challenges are common. The claim that counsel cannot provide the constitutionally required assistance due to a conflict of interest falls in this category. That claim often will be raised pretrial through motions of the defendant (seeking the replacement of counsel)[a], the

---

[a]   In general, the defendant has no right to have appointed counsel replaced absent a showing that: (1) counsel faces an irreconcilable conflict of interests; (2) counsel refuses to abide by defendant's directive on a decision controlled by defendant's choice; or (3) there has been a "complete breakdown in communications between counsel and defendant" (not brought about by defendant's intentional misconduct). The defendant with retained counsel may automatically obtain the opportunity to replace counsel under the same three conditions, but even when those

defense counsel (seeking withdrawal), or the prosecution (seeking the disqualification of the conflicted defense counsel). However, absent such motions, unless the trial court directs the defendant's attention to the conflict and the dangers it presents, the defendant commonly will not be aware of the conflict, or if aware, appreciate its ramifications. Thus, the defendant ordinarily is not required to challenge pretrial his own counsel, even if aware of the conflict, and many defendants will raise a conflict challenge for the first time after conviction.

In the case of the challenge based on deficient performance, the objection is almost always first raised after conviction. Even where the allegedly deficient performance occurs pretrial and the defendant is aware of that deficiency, the defendant has no obligation to challenge his counsel pretrial, as the client-counsel relationship would be undermined by imposing such a requirement. Indeed, for most deficient-performance challenges, the defendant is not expected to raise the challenge even on appeal from the conviction. Deficient performance challenges commonly are first presented post-appeal in a postconviction collateral proceeding (see Ch. 1, step 18, p. 28).[b]

2. INEFFECTIVE ASSISTANCE OF COUNSEL

The four cases in this section—*Strickland v. Washington* (*Strickland*), *Harrington v. Richter* (*Richter*), *Lafler v. Cooper* (*Cooper*), and *Weaver v. Massachusetts* (*Weaver*)—present the most common challenge to defense counsel's representation—a claimed deficiency in counsel's performance (the first of the four challenges noted in the Introduction). Here the defendant is arguing that defense counsel's assistance was so inadequate as to constitutionally require that defendant's conviction be overturned. *Strickland*, the first case to fully explore such a challenge, described it as presenting a "claim of ineffective assistance of counsel" (a description today often shortened in commentary and judicial opinion to the "IAC claim"). Even before *Strickland*, the Court had established that the IAC claim could be used to challenge the performance of retained counsel as well as appointed counsel. As the Court noted: "The vital guarantee of the Sixth Amendment would stand for little if the often uninformed decision to retain a particular lawyer could

---

conditions do not apply, the defendant's constitutional right to "counsel of choice"(see fn. a, p. 936) will prevail if the replacement can be achieved without significantly interfering with "the public's interest in prompt and efficient administration of justice." See *Ungar v. Sarafite*, 376 U.S. 575 (1964) (constitutionally of denying replacement request based on timing considerations depends on case-by-case evaluation of the particular circumstances).

[b] A challenge to a conviction based on counsel's deficient performance often cannot be raised on appeal because: (1) the appellate counsel was the trial-court counsel, and a lawyer will not be allowed to create a conflict of interest by challenging his own competency; and (2) assessing the alleged deficiency in performance requires consideration of events and evidence outside of the trial-court record, and therefore not available to the appellate court. Accordingly, ineffective assistance challenges under the *Strickland* standards (discussed infra) are usually presented in a postconviction collateral challenge. Here, an evidentiary hearing is available to further develop the claim, and the conflict difficulty will be eliminated, as defendant is likely to have a different lawyer or will be forced to represent himself (there being no constitutional right to the assistance of appointed counsel beyond the first appeal, see *Ross v. Moffitt*, p. 401). Indeed, many jurisdictions prohibit raising a *Strickland* challenge on appeal even when the obstacles noted above are not present; they make the collateral proceedings the only available forum, as there all types of deficiencies can be considered in a single proceeding. But note, fn. a, p. 925.

reduce or forfeit the defendant's entitlement to constitutional protection. Since the State's conduct of a criminal trial itself implicates the State in the defendant's conviction, we see no basis for drawing a distinction between retained and appointed counsel that could deny equal justice to defendants who must choose their own lawyers." *Cuyler v. Sullivan*, 446 U.S. 335 (1980).

Strickland, Richter, Cooper and *Weaver* all involve challenges to the performance of trial-court counsel, but the IAC claim applies to all stages at which there is a constitutional right to counsel. The scope of that right, for these purposes, is determined by the right to appointed counsel for the indigent (as any broader right not to have the state preclude defendant's use of retained counsel in other proceedings would be based on a distinguishable, individual-liberty grounding). Thus, the IAC claim also applies to the representation by appellate counsel on a first appeal of right (see *Douglas v. California*, p. 397, establishing the constitutional right to appointed counsel in that proceeding); but it does not extend to the later stages at which the indigent defendant has no constitutional right to appointed counsel. Since the constitutional guarantee of effective assistance flows from the constitutional right to counsel's assistance, the existence of that right is a prerequisite for the IAC claim. See e.g., *Wainwright v. Torna*, 455 U.S. 586 (1982) (IAC claim not available where retained counsel failed to file a timely application for discretionary high court review, as there is no constitutional right to counsel at that stage); *Pennsylvania v. Finley*, 481 U.S. 551 (1987) (rejecting constitutional challenge based on the allegedly inappropriate withdrawal by a state-appointed counsel at a postconviction collateral proceeding as the state had no constitutional obligation to appoint counsel in that proceeding).[a]

Strickland is the seminal IAC ruling, setting forth the basic standards for determining whether counsel's performance resulted in a constitutional violation. The *Strickland* decision gave rise to an immense body of lower court precedent, and the Supreme Court itself has subsequently addressed IAC claims in over two dozen cases. *Richter* and *Cooper* are two of the latest rulings in that line of cases. Each has a special significance in the development of the post-*Strickland* caselaw.

---

[a] *Coleman v. Thompson*, 501 U.S. 722 (1991), left open the possibility of modifying this general rule as to collateral proceedings where, under state law, the collateral proceeding provides the first occasion to raise the claim that trial counsel had been ineffective (see fn. b, p. 924, as to such state requirements). The Court there noted that such an "initial review collateral proceeding" could be analogized to the first appeal of right, where the defendant does have a constitutional right to counsel and hence to effective representation by that counsel. *Martinez v. Ryan*, 566 U.S. 1 (2012), concluded that in the context of federal habeas corpus proceedings, where the issue left open in *Coleman* is most likely to be raised, there was no need to decide whether there was a constitutional right to effective assistance for such an initial review collateral proceeding. In a federal habeas proceeding, the procedural forfeiture of a constitutional claim under state law does not necessarily bar federal habeas review of that claim. Where state law limits the defense to first raising an IAC claim as to trial counsel in a collateral proceeding (thereby making it an "initial review" proceeding), and then procedurally defaults (i.e. forfeits) that IAC claim if it is not raised in that collateral proceeding, *Martinez* holds that "equitable considerations" allow the federal habeas court to ignore that default (and consider the IAC claim on the merits) if: (1) "the claim is substantial," and (2) either (i) the state "did not appoint counsel in the initial review proceeding for a claim of ineffective assistance at trial," or (ii) the defendant was represented by counsel in the initial review proceeding but that counsel was "ineffective under the standards of *Strickland*" with respect to the claim of trial-counsel ineffectiveness.

Richter is significant initially because of the procedural context in which the IAC claim there was raised.

Although several of the Supreme Court's post-*Strickland* IAC rulings have involved direct review of state high court decisions, the vast majority have presented the review of claims raised by state prisoners in federal habeas corpus petitions. That was true of *Strickland* itself, but when *Strickland* was decided, this special procedural context had no bearing on the standard of review applied to IAC claims. That changed in 1996, when Congress adopted the Antiterrorism and Effective Death Penalty Act (AEDPA). The AEDPA established a special review standard for federal habeas cases in which the state court had considered and rejected on the merits the constitutional claim that the state prisoner is now raising in his federal habeas petition. *Richter* presents the leading exposition of that review standard as applied to an IAC claim. That standard bears upon not only federal habeas cases, but also the reading of Supreme Court precedent decided under the AEDPA by the state courts applying *Strickland* under traditional appellate review standards.

The *Strickland* opinion established a two-prong test for assessing IAC claims. Most of the Court's post-*Strickland* decisions have focused on analyzing *Strickland*'s performance prong. In doing so, they have looked initially to the general directives on performance review announced in *Strickland*, and then, in applying those directives, often have further developed their content. Many of the most prominent of these rulings, however, have been limited to special settings (e.g., capital sentencing) and have produced opinions that appear to focus more on differences between the majority and dissent as to the appropriate reading of the record than advancing guidelines for reviewing performance even in those special settings. *Richter* in contrast, stands out as an almost unanimous ruling aimed at providing general directions to the lower courts in the assessment of common aspects of counsel's performance.

Cooper similarly stands out as a leading ruling on the prejudice prong of *Strickland*. Previous rulings applying the prejudice prong had concentrated on the bearing of counsel's incompetence upon the overall strength of the prosecution's evidence (as illustrated by the discussions of prejudice in *Strickland* and *Richter*). *Cooper*, in contrast, focuses on the basic function of the prejudice requirement, as it relates to a quire different type of prejudice, and produces a 5–4 split on that issue. Moreover, that split, unlike the division in *Lockhart v. Fretwell* [p. 953], is not tied to a highly unusual factual setting but to an everyday occurrence—the rejection of a plea offer. Combined with the rulings applying *Strickland* to cases in which defendants accepted negotiated pleas (e.g., *Missouri v. Frye*, p. 766, and *Padilla v. Kentucky*, fn. a, p. 777), *Cooper* establishes a foundation for the constitutional regulation of defense counsel's role in the plea bargaining process. Commentators have suggested that this line of cases has far greater potential for impacting the constitutional regulation of the criminal justice process than the cases applying the *Strickland* standards to trial presentations. In part that suggestion is based on the much higher rate of adjudications by guilty plea (as noted by the Court in both *Cooper* and *Frye*). But it also rests on the constitutional regulation of guilty plea adjudication (see Ch. 14) otherwise being far more limited than the constitutional regulation of trial adjudication, which is directly addressed in various constitutional guarantees (see e.g., Chapters 15, 18, & 19).

Weaver also addresses the prejudice prong of *Strickland*, but in a context that emphasizes a significant procedural role of the IAC claim, also recognized in *Richter*. As *Richter* stated [p. 945]: "[A]n ineffective-assistance claim can function as a way to escape rules of waiver and forfeiture and raise issues not presented at trial."[b] The IAC claim similarly can be characterized as the major exception to the general rule that a guilty plea waives any pre-existing procedural objection that could have been presented prior to the entry of the plea. Whether based on a trial or guilty plea adjudication, a conviction ordinarily cannot be challenged on the basis of an objection that counsel failed to raise, or failed to raise in a timely fashion, before the trial court. That objection can be taken into consideration, however, by arguing that counsel's failure constituted a *Strickland* violation. The rules of forfeiture or waiver generally hold the defendant to the actions and inactions of counsel, but that does not apply where that action or inaction reflected constitutionally deficient performance.[c] Here the court can consider the merits of the objection not raised and reverse the conviction if the prejudice standard of *Strickland* is met.[d] *Weaver* addresses (but does not fully answer) the question as to whether the *Strickland* prejudice prerequisite should automatically be met (and the forfeiture therefore excused) where the claim that the trial or appellate counsel incompetently failed to raise was a constitutional violation that would be classified as "structural" in another context (determining whether that violation, where

---

[b]   In referring separately to waiver and forfeiture, *Richter* was taking note of a distinction recognized in the leading rulings on "plain error" appellate review, discussed infra. A possible objection is "waived" when it is "intentionally relinquished." An objection is forfeited where the procedural rules, in the interest of furthering the orderly raising of claims, imposes the sanction of loss of the objection because it was not timely presented. In other contexts, the term "waiver" has been used to refer to both intentional waivers and forfeitures.

[c]   The IAC claim serves a similar function in escaping a major limitation attached to a motion for new trial based on newly discovered evidence. One of the prerequisites for that motion is that the newly discovered evidence could not have been discovered prior to trial with "due diligence." See fn. b., p. 742. Hence, where the new-evidence claim is based on previously unknown evidence that could have been uncovered with due diligence, the only avenue for relief may be a *Strickland* claim alleging deficient performance in failing to uncover that evidence. In *Herrera v. Collins*, discussed in fn. b., p. 50, the Court did leave open one possible alternative route. In recognizing the possibility of a new-evidence "actual innocence" claim in capital cases, the Court noted that the constitutional grounding of such a claim would override traditional state limitations on new-evidence motions.

[d]   This assumes that the IAC claim is itself timely raised, as that claim is not less subject to forfeiture rules than other claims. However, where the failure to raise the IAC claim occurs at a proceeding in which defendant had a constitutional right to counsel, that failure may constitute the grounding for a separate IAC claim, allowing for an escape from the forfeiture. Thus, should counsel at trial fail to raise an objection, and counsel on first appeal fail to advance an IAC claim based on trial counsel's failure, the defendant may later argue that the appellate counsel's failure violated the *Strickland* standards (e.g., that the trial counsel's failure constituted so obvious an IAC violation that no reasonable appellate counsel would have failed to include that claim). This escape route is not available, however, if the forfeiture of the IAC claim occurs at a later stage of the proceeding where there is no right to counsel (e.g., a failure to raise the claim on secondary, discretionary appellate review).

As discussed in fn. a supra, *Martinez v. Ryan* recognizes a federal habeas corpus route for escaping a state law forfeiture of a trial-counsel IAC claim where that forfeiture was based on the failure to raise that claim in an "initial-review" state collateral proceeding.

timely challenged, would require automatic appellate reversal of a conviction or be subject to harmless error analysis).

The significance of the IAC claim as a vehicle for avoiding the forfeiture of claims not timely raised varies from state to state, as all states recognize one or more other exceptions to forfeiture. Indeed, Supreme Court rulings establish another constitutional exception in the context of guilty pleas. Even though states generally are free to treat guilty pleas as forfeiting all constitutional claims not directly related to plea negotiation and acceptance, they must allow a postconviction defense challenge that rests on the defendant's "right not to be hailed into court at all," when the grounding of that claim is apparent on the record. Such claims remain open notwithstanding that counsel failed to raise them prior to the entry of the guilty plea (without regard to whether that failure reflects incompetency). See *Blackledge v. Perry*, 447 U.S. 21 (1974) (plea did not preclude collateral challenge based on vindictive prosecution); *Menna v. New York*, 423 U.S. 61 (1975) (collateral challenge based on double jeopardy bar prosecution). Compare *McMann v. Richardson*, 397 U.S. 759 (1970) (plea could not be challenged on the basis of an underlying coerced confession; only avenue to relief lies in the IAC claim that counsel was not reasonably competent in concluding that the confession should not be challenged and advising that plea should be entered).

The most prominent forfeiture exception under state law is the "plain error" rule, which allows an appellate court to consider an error that was not challenged before the trial court and/or not raised by appellate counsel. The error must be "plain," i.e., obvious on a trial record which is complete as to that violation (i.e., had the defense objected, the prosecution could not have introduced additional information which would establish that there was no violation). The error also must be prejudicial, and here the "structural errors" discussed in *Weaver* may or may not be viewed as per se prejudicial in the particular jurisdiction. In many jurisdictions (including the federal), the appellate court's authority to reverse a conviction on an otherwise forfeited error that is both plain and prejudicial is permissive, rather than mandatory, and appellate courts will exercise this authority only where the conviction constitutes "a miscarriage of justice." Where a plain error meets all these prerequisites, the appellate court has no need to consider whether counsel's failure to present the claim constituted ineffective assistance (an issue that may not be available on appeal, see fn. b, p. 924). However, as with other forfeiture exceptions, the stringent prerequisites of the plain error rule often made the IAC claim the only available avenue for gaining relief where counsel failed to timely challenge a trial court error.

STRICKLAND V. WASHINGTON
466 U.S. 668, 104 S.Ct. 2052, 80 L.Ed.2d 674 (1984).

JUSTICE O'CONNOR delivered the opinion of the Court.

This case requires us to consider the proper standards for judging a criminal defendant's contention that the Constitution requires a conviction or death sentence to be set aside because counsel's assistance at the trial or sentencing was ineffective.

During a 10-day period in September 1976, respondent planned and committed three groups of crimes, which included three brutal stabbing murders, torture, kidnaping, severe assaults, attempted murders, attempted extortion, and theft. After his two accomplices were arrested, respondent surrendered to police and voluntarily gave a lengthy statement confessing to the third of the criminal episodes. The State of Florida indicted respondent for kidnaping and murder and appointed an experienced criminal lawyer to represent him.

Counsel actively pursued pretrial motions and discovery. He cut his efforts short, however, and he experienced a sense of hopelessness about the case, when he learned that, against his specific advice, respondent had also confessed to the first two murders. By the date set for trial, respondent was subject to indictment for three counts of first-degree murder and multiple counts of robbery, kidnaping for ransom, breaking and entering and assault, attempted murder, and conspiracy to commit robbery. Respondent waived his right to a jury trial, again acting against counsel's advice, and pleaded guilty to all charges, including the three capital murder charges.

In the plea colloquy, respondent told the trial judge that, although he had committed a string of burglaries, he had no significant prior criminal record and that at the time of his criminal spree he was under extreme stress caused by his inability to support his family. He also stated, however, that he accepted responsibility for the crimes. The trial judge told respondent that he had "a great deal of respect for people who are willing to step forward and admit their responsibility" but that he was making no statement at all about his likely sentencing decision.

Counsel advised respondent to invoke his right under Florida law to an advisory jury at his capital sentencing hearing. Respondent rejected the advice and waived the right. He chose instead to be sentenced by the trial judge without a jury recommendation.

In preparing for the sentencing hearing, counsel spoke with respondent about his background. He also spoke on the telephone with respondent's wife and mother, though he did not follow up on the one unsuccessful effort to meet with them. He did not otherwise seek out character witnesses for respondent. Nor did he request a psychiatric examination, since his conversations with his client gave no indication that respondent had psychological problems.

Counsel decided not to present and hence not to look further for evidence concerning respondent's character and emotional state. That decision reflected trial counsel's sense of hopelessness about overcoming the evidentiary effect of respondent's confessions to the gruesome crimes. It also reflected the judgment that it was advisable to rely on the plea colloquy for evidence about respondent's background and about his claim of emotional stress: the plea colloquy communicated sufficient information about these subjects, and by forgoing the opportunity to present new evidence on these subjects, counsel prevented the State from cross-examining respondent on his claim and from putting on psychiatric evidence of its own.

Counsel also excluded from the sentencing hearing other evidence he thought was potentially damaging. He successfully moved to exclude respondent's "rap sheet." Because he judged that a presentence report might prove more detrimental than helpful, as it would have included respondent's criminal history and thereby would have undermined the claim of no significant history of criminal activity, he did not request that one be prepared.

At the sentencing hearing, counsel's strategy was based primarily on the trial judge's remarks at the plea colloquy as well as on his reputation as a sentencing judge who thought it important for a convicted defendant to own up to his crime. Counsel argued that respondent's remorse and acceptance of responsibility justified sparing him from the death penalty. Counsel also argued that respondent had no history of criminal activity and that respondent committed the crimes under extreme mental or emotional disturbance, thus coming within the statutory list of mitigating circumstances. He further argued that respondent should be spared death because he had surrendered, confessed, and offered to testify against a codefendant and because respondent was fundamentally a good person who had briefly gone badly wrong in extremely stressful circumstances. The State put on evidence and witnesses largely for the purpose of describing the details of the crimes. Counsel did not cross-examine the medical experts who testified about the manner of death of respondent's victims. * * *

[T]he trial judge found numerous aggravating circumstances and no (or a single comparatively insignificant) mitigating circumstance. With respect to each of the three convictions for capital murder, the trial judge concluded: "A careful consideration of all matters presented to the court impels the conclusion that there are insufficient mitigating circumstances * * * to outweigh the aggravating circumstances." He therefore sentenced respondent to death on each of the three counts of murder and to prison terms for the other crimes. The Florida Supreme Court upheld the convictions and sentences on direct appeal.

Respondent subsequently sought collateral relief in state court on numerous grounds, among them that counsel had rendered ineffective assistance at the sentencing proceeding. Respondent challenged counsel's assistance in six respects. He asserted that counsel was ineffective because he failed to move for a continuance to prepare for sentencing, to request a psychiatric report, to investigate and present character witnesses, to seek a presentence investigation report, to present meaningful arguments to the sentencing judge, and to investigate the medical examiner's reports or cross-examine the medical experts. In support of the claim, respondent submitted 14 affidavits from friends, neighbors, and relatives stating that they would have testified if asked to do so. He also submitted one psychiatric report and one psychological report stating that respondent, though not under the influence of extreme mental or emotional disturbance, was "chronically frustrated and depressed because of his economic dilemma" at the time of his crimes.

The trial court denied relief without an evidentiary hearing, finding that the record evidence conclusively showed that the ineffectiveness claim was meritless. * * * Applying the standard for ineffectiveness claims articulated by the Florida

Supreme Court * * *, the trial court concluded that respondent had not shown that counsel's assistance reflected any substantial and serious deficiency measurably below that of competent counsel that was likely to have affected the outcome of the sentencing proceeding. * * *

Respondent next filed a petition for a writ of habeas corpus in the United States District Court * * *. [After an evidentiary hearing,] the District Court disputed none of the state court factual findings concerning trial counsel's assistance and made findings of its own that are consistent with the state court findings. * * * [T]he District Court concluded that, although trial counsel made errors in judgment in failing to investigate nonstatutory mitigating evidence further than he did, no prejudice to respondent's sentence resulted from any such error in judgment. On appeal, * * * the Court of Appeals developed its own framework for analyzing ineffective assistance claims and reversed the judgment of the District Court and remanded the case for new factfinding under the newly announced standard. * * *

[P]utting guilty-plea cases to one side, [the Court of Appeals] attempted to classify cases presenting issues concerning the scope of the duty to investigate before proceeding to trial. If there is only one plausible line of defense, the court concluded, counsel must conduct a "reasonably substantial investigation" into that line of defense, since there can be no strategic choice that renders such an investigation unnecessary. * * * If there is more than one plausible line of defense, the court held, counsel should ideally investigate each line substantially before making a strategic choice about which lines to rely on at trial. * * * If counsel does not conduct a substantial investigation into each of several plausible lines of defense, assistance may nonetheless be effective. Counsel may not exclude certain lines of defense for other than strategic reasons. Limitations of time and money, however, may force early strategic choices, often based solely on conversations with the defendant and a review of the prosecution's evidence. * * * Among the factors relevant to deciding whether particular strategic choices are reasonable are the experience of the attorney, the inconsistency of unpursued and pursued lines of defense, and the potential for prejudice from taking an unpursued line of defense. * * * Petitioners, who are officials of the State of Florida, filed a petition for a writ of certiorari seeking review of the decision of the Court of Appeals. * * *

Because of the vital importance of counsel's assistance, this Court has held that, with certain exceptions, a person accused of a federal or state crime has the right to have counsel appointed if retained counsel cannot be obtained. See *Argersinger v. Hamlin* [p. 383]; *Gideon v. Wainwright* [p. 380]. That a person who happens to be a lawyer is present at trial alongside the accused, however, is not enough to satisfy the constitutional command. The Sixth Amendment recognizes the right to the assistance of counsel because it envisions counsel's playing a role that is critical to the ability of the adversarial system to produce just results. An accused is entitled to be assisted by an attorney, whether retained or appointed, who plays the role necessary to ensure that the trial is fair.

For that reason, the Court has recognized that "the right to counsel is the right to the effective assistance of counsel." *McMann v. Richardson,* 397 U.S. 759

(1970). Government violates the right to effective assistance when it interferes in certain ways with the ability of counsel to make independent decisions about how to conduct the defense. See, e.g., *Geders v. United States,* 425 U.S. 80 (1976) (bar on attorney-client consultation during overnight recess); *Herring v. New York,* 422 U.S. 853 (1975) (bar on summation at bench trial); *Brooks v. Tennessee,* 406 U.S. 605 (1972) (requirement that defendant be first defense witness); *Ferguson v. Georgia,* 365 U.S. 570 (1961) (bar on direct examination of defendant). Counsel, however, can also deprive a defendant of the right to effective assistance, simply by failing to render "adequate legal assistance," *Cuyler v. Sullivan,* 446 U.S. 335 (1980) (actual conflict of interest adversely affecting lawyer's performance renders assistance ineffective).

The Court has not elaborated on the meaning of the constitutional requirement of effective assistance in the latter class of cases—that is, those presenting claims of "actual ineffectiveness." In giving meaning to the requirement, however, we must take its purpose—to ensure a fair trial—as the guide. The benchmark for judging any claim of ineffectiveness must be whether counsel's conduct so undermined the proper functioning of the adversarial process that the trial cannot be relied on as having produced a just result.

The same principle applies to a capital sentencing proceeding such as that provided by Florida law. We need not consider the role of counsel in an ordinary sentencing, which may involve informal proceedings and standardless discretion in the sentencer, and hence may require a different approach to the definition of constitutionally effective assistance. A capital sentencing proceeding like the one involved in this case, however, is sufficiently like a trial in its adversarial format and in the existence of standards for decision, that counsel's role in the proceeding is comparable to counsel's role at trial—to ensure that the adversarial testing process works to produce a just result under the standards governing decision. For purposes of describing counsel's duties, therefore, Florida's capital sentencing proceeding need not be distinguished from an ordinary trial.

A convicted defendant's claim that counsel's assistance was so defective as to require reversal of a conviction or death sentence has two components. First, the defendant must show that counsel's performance was deficient. This requires showing that counsel made errors so serious that counsel was not functioning as the "counsel" guaranteed the defendant by the Sixth Amendment. Second, the defendant must show that the deficient performance prejudiced the defense. This requires showing that counsel's errors were so serious as to deprive the defendant of a fair trial, a trial whose result is reliable. Unless a defendant makes both showings, it cannot be said that the conviction or death sentence resulted from a breakdown in the adversary process that renders the result unreliable.

As all the Federal Courts of Appeals have now held, the proper standard for attorney performance is that of reasonably effective assistance. The Court indirectly recognized as much when it stated in *McMann v. Richardson* that a guilty plea cannot be attacked as based on inadequate legal advice unless counsel was not "a reasonably competent attorney" and the advice was not "within the range of competence demanded of attorneys in criminal cases." When a convicted defendant complains of the ineffectiveness of counsel's assistance, the defendant must show that counsel's representation fell below an objective standard of reasonableness.

More specific guidelines are not appropriate. The Sixth Amendment refers simply to "counsel," not specifying particular requirements of effective assistance. It relies instead on the legal profession's maintenance of standards sufficient to justify the law's presumption that counsel will fulfill the role in the adversary process that the Amendment envisions. The proper measure of attorney performance remains simply reasonableness under prevailing professional norms.

Representation of a criminal defendant entails certain basic duties. Counsel's function is to assist the defendant, and hence counsel owes the client a duty of loyalty, a duty to avoid conflicts of interest. From counsel's function as assistant to the defendant derive the overarching duty to advocate the defendant's cause and the more particular duties to consult with the defendant on important decisions and to keep the defendant informed of important developments in the course of the prosecution. Counsel also has a duty to bring to bear such skill and knowledge as will render the trial a reliable adversarial testing process.

These basic duties neither exhaustively define the obligations of counsel nor form a checklist for judicial evaluation of attorney performance. In any case presenting an ineffectiveness claim, the performance inquiry must be whether counsel's assistance was reasonable considering all the circumstances. Prevailing norms of practice as reflected in American Bar Association standards and the like are guides to determining what is reasonable, but they are only guides. No particular set of detailed rules for counsel's conduct can satisfactorily take account of the variety of circumstances faced by defense counsel or the range of legitimate decisions regarding how best to represent a criminal defendant. Any such set of rules would interfere with the constitutionally protected independence of counsel and restrict the wide latitude counsel must have in making tactical decisions. Indeed, the existence of detailed guidelines for representation could distract counsel from the overriding mission of vigorous advocacy of the defendant's cause. Moreover, the purpose of the effective assistance guarantee of the Sixth Amendment is not to improve the quality of legal representation, although that is a goal of considerable importance to the legal system. The purpose is simply to ensure that criminal defendants receive a fair trial.

Judicial scrutiny of counsel's performance must be highly deferential. It is all too tempting for a defendant to second-guess counsel's assistance after conviction or adverse sentence, and it is all too easy for a court, examining counsel's defense after it has proved unsuccessful, to conclude that a particular act or omission of counsel was unreasonable. A fair assessment of attorney performance requires that every effort be made to eliminate the distorting effects of hindsight, to reconstruct the circumstances of counsel's challenged conduct, and to evaluate the conduct from counsel's perspective at the time. Because of the difficulties inherent in making the evaluation, a court must indulge a strong presumption that counsel's conduct falls within the wide range of reasonable professional assistance; that is, the defendant must overcome the presumption that, under the circumstances, the challenged action "might be considered sound trial strategy." There are countless ways to provide effective assistance in any given case. Even the best criminal defense attorneys would not defend a particular client in the same way.

The availability of intrusive post-trial inquiry into attorney performance or of detailed guidelines for its evaluation would encourage the proliferation of ineffectiveness challenges. Criminal trials resolved unfavorably to the defendant would increasingly come to be followed by a second trial, this one of counsel's unsuccessful defense. Counsel's performance and even willingness to serve could be adversely affected. Intensive scrutiny of counsel and rigid requirements for acceptable assistance could dampen the ardor and impair the independence of defense counsel, discourage the acceptance of assigned cases, and undermine the trust between attorney and client.

Thus, a court deciding an actual ineffectiveness claim must judge the reasonableness of counsel's challenged conduct on the facts of the particular case, viewed as of the time of counsel's conduct. A convicted defendant making a claim of ineffective assistance must identify the acts or omissions of counsel that are alleged not to have been the result of reasonable professional judgment. The court must then determine whether, in light of all the circumstances, the identified acts or omissions were outside the wide range of professionally competent assistance. In making that determination, the court should keep in mind that counsel's function, as elaborated in prevailing professional norms, is to make the adversarial testing process work in the particular case. At the same time, the court should recognize that counsel is strongly presumed to have rendered adequate assistance and made all significant decisions in the exercise of reasonable professional judgment.

These standards require no special amplification in order to define counsel's duty to investigate, the duty at issue in this case. As the Court of Appeals concluded, strategic choices made after thorough investigation of law and facts relevant to plausible options are virtually unchallengeable; and strategic choices made after less than complete investigation are reasonable precisely to the extent that reasonable professional judgments support the limitations on investigation. In other words, counsel has a duty to make reasonable investigations or to make a reasonable decision that makes particular investigations unnecessary. In any ineffectiveness case, a particular decision not to investigate must be directly assessed for reasonableness in all the circumstances, applying a heavy measure of deference to counsel's judgments.

The reasonableness of counsel's actions may be determined or substantially influenced by the defendant's own statements or actions. Counsel's actions are usually based, quite properly, on informed strategic choices made by the defendant and on information supplied by the defendant. In particular, what investigation decisions are reasonable depends critically on such information. For example, when the facts that support a certain potential line of defense are generally known to counsel because of what the defendant has said, the need for further investigation may be considerably diminished or eliminated altogether. And when a defendant has given counsel reason to believe that pursuing certain investigations would be fruitless or even harmful, counsel's failure to pursue those investigations may not later be challenged as unreasonable. In short, inquiry into counsel's conversations with the defendant may be critical to a proper assessment of counsel's investigation decisions, just as it may be critical to a proper assessment of counsel's other litigation decisions.

An error by counsel, even if professionally unreasonable, does not warrant setting aside the judgment of a criminal proceeding if the error had no effect on the judgment. The purpose of the Sixth Amendment guarantee of counsel is to ensure that a defendant has the assistance necessary to justify reliance on the outcome of the proceeding. Accordingly, any deficiencies in counsel's performance must be prejudicial to the defense in order to constitute ineffective assistance under the Constitution.

In certain Sixth Amendment contexts, prejudice is presumed. Actual or constructive denial of the assistance of counsel altogether is legally presumed to result in prejudice. So are various kinds of state interference with counsel's assistance. See *United States v. Cronic*, [p. 969]. Prejudice in these circumstances is so likely that case-by-case inquiry into prejudice is not worth the cost. Moreover, such circumstances involve impairments of the Sixth Amendment right that are easy to identify and, for that reason and because the prosecution is directly responsible, easy for the government to prevent.

One type of actual ineffectiveness claim warrants a similar, though more limited, presumption of prejudice. In *Cuyler v. Sullivan*, 446 U.S. 335 (1980), the Court held that prejudice is presumed when counsel is burdened by an actual conflict of interest. In those circumstances, counsel breaches the duty of loyalty, perhaps the most basic of counsel's duties. Moreover, it is difficult to measure the precise effect on the defense of representation corrupted by conflicting interests. Given the obligation of counsel to avoid conflicts of interest and the ability of trial courts to make early inquiry in certain situations likely to give rise to conflicts, see, e.g., Fed.Rule Crim.Proc. 44(c), it is reasonable for the criminal justice system to maintain a fairly rigid rule of presumed prejudice for conflicts of interest. Even so, the rule is not quite the *per se* rule of prejudice that exists for the Sixth Amendment claims mentioned above. Prejudice is presumed only if the defendant demonstrates that counsel "actively represented conflicting interests" and that "an actual conflict of interest adversely affected his lawyer's performance." *Cuyler v. Sullivan*.

Conflict of interest claims aside, actual ineffectiveness claims alleging a deficiency in attorney performance are subject to a general requirement that the defendant affirmatively prove prejudice. The government is not responsible for, and hence not able to prevent, attorney errors that will result in reversal of a conviction or sentence. Attorney errors come in an infinite variety and are as likely to be utterly harmless in a particular case as they are to be prejudicial. They cannot be classified according to likelihood of causing prejudice. Nor can they be defined with sufficient precision to inform defense attorneys correctly just what conduct to avoid. Representation is an art, and an act or omission that is unprofessional in one case may be sound or even brilliant in another. Even if a defendant shows that particular errors of counsel were unreasonable, therefore, the defendant must show that they actually had an adverse effect on the defense.[a] * * *

It is not enough for the defendant to show that the errors had some conceivable effect on the outcome of the proceeding. Virtually every act or omission of counsel would meet that test, and not every error that conceivably could have influenced the outcome undermines the reliability of the result of the proceeding. * * * On the other hand, we believe that a defendant need not show that counsel's deficient conduct more likely than not altered the outcome in the case. This outcome-determinative standard has several strengths. It defines the relevant inquiry in a way familiar to courts, though the inquiry, as is inevitable, is anything but precise. The standard also reflects the profound importance of finality in criminal proceedings. * * * Nevertheless, the standard is not quite appropriate. * * * An ineffective assistance claim asserts the absence of one of the crucial assurances that the result of the proceeding is reliable, so finality concerns are somewhat weaker and the appropriate standard of prejudice should be somewhat lower. The result of a proceeding can be rendered unreliable, and hence the proceeding itself unfair, even if the errors of counsel cannot be shown by a preponderance of the evidence to have determined the outcome. [T]he appropriate test for prejudice finds its roots in the test for materiality of exculpatory information not disclosed to the defense by the prosecution, *United States v. Agurs,* 427 U.S. 97 (1976) and in the test for materiality of testimony made unavailable to the defense by Government deportation of a witness, *United States v. Valenzuela-Bernal,* 458 U.S. 858 (1982).[b] The defendant must show that there is a reasonable probability that, but for counsel's unprofessional errors, the result of the proceeding would have been different. A reasonable probability is a probability sufficient to undermine confidence in the outcome.

In making the determination whether the specified errors resulted in the required prejudice, a court should presume, absent challenge to the judgment on grounds of evidentiary insufficiency, that the judge or jury acted according to law. An assessment of the likelihood of a result more favorable to the defendant must exclude the possibility of arbitrariness, whimsy, caprice, "nullification," and the like. A defendant has no entitlement to the luck of a lawless decisionmaker, even if a lawless decision cannot be reviewed. The assessment of prejudice should

---

[a]   In *United States v. Gonzalez-Lopez,* 548 U.S. 140 (2006), the Court majority offered a further analysis of the grounding for this requirement. That case involved an erroneous denial of the defendant's representation by retained counsel of his own choosing [see *Wheat v. United States,* infra], and the Court rejected the government's contention that such a denial did not constitute a Sixth Amendment violation unless the defendant could also establish "prejudice" as defined in *Strickland.* The Court noted that "the Sixth Amendment right to counsel of choice * * * commands, not that a trial be fair, but that a particular guarantee of fairness be provided," and the constitutional violation therefore was "complete" with the denial of that guarantee. The requirement that counsel's assistance not be ineffective was distinguishable because that guarantee, initially based on the due process clause, was held to be a part of the Sixth Amendment as "a consequence of our perception that representation by counsel 'is critical to the ability of the adversarial system to produce just results' *Strickland.*" In contrast, the "right to select counsel of one's choice * * * has never been derived from the Sixth Amendment's purpose of ensuring a fair trial * * * [but is a part of] the root meaning of the constitutional guarantee." See also fn. a, p. 992.

[b]   The materiality standard applicable in these situations is further discussed in *Bagley,* Ch. 13, at pp. 741–744.

proceed on the assumption that the decisionmaker is reasonably, conscientiously, and impartially applying the standards that govern the decision. It should not depend on the idiosyncracies of the particular decisionmaker, such as unusual propensities toward harshness or leniency. Although these factors may actually have entered into counsel's selection of strategies and, to that limited extent, may thus affect the performance inquiry, they are irrelevant to the prejudice inquiry. Thus, evidence about the actual process of decision, if not part of the record of the proceeding under review, and evidence about, for example, a particular judge's sentencing practices, should not be considered in the prejudice determination.

The governing legal standard plays a critical role in defining the question to be asked in assessing the prejudice from counsel's errors. When a defendant challenges a conviction, the question is whether there is a reasonable probability that, absent the errors, the factfinder would have had a reasonable doubt respecting guilt. When a defendant challenges a death sentence such as the one at issue in this case, the question is whether there is a reasonable probability that, absent the errors, the sentencer—including an appellate court, to the extent it independently reweighs the evidence—would have concluded that the balance of aggravating and mitigating circumstances did not warrant death.

In making this determination, a court hearing an ineffectiveness claim must consider the totality of the evidence before the judge or jury. Some of the factual findings will have been unaffected by the errors, and factual findings that were affected will have been affected in different ways. Some errors will have had a pervasive effect on the inferences to be drawn from the evidence, altering the entire evidentiary picture, and some will have had an isolated, trivial effect. Moreover, a verdict or conclusion only weakly supported by the record is more likely to have been affected by errors than one with overwhelming record support. Taking the unaffected findings as a given, and taking due account of the effect of the errors on the remaining findings, a court making the prejudice inquiry must ask if the defendant has met the burden of showing that the decision reached would reasonably likely have been different absent the errors.

A number of practical considerations are important for the application of the standards we have outlined. Most important, in adjudicating a claim of actual ineffectiveness of counsel, a court should keep in mind that the principles we have stated do not establish mechanical rules. Although those principles should guide the process of decision, the ultimate focus of inquiry must be on the fundamental fairness of the proceeding whose result is being challenged. In every case the court should be concerned with whether, despite the strong presumption of reliability, the result of the particular proceeding is unreliable because of a breakdown in the adversarial process that our system counts on to produce just results. * * *

Although we have discussed the performance component of an ineffectiveness claim prior to the prejudice component, there is no reason for a court deciding an ineffective assistance claim to approach the inquiry in the same order or even to address both components of the inquiry if the defendant makes an insufficient showing on one. In particular, a court need not determine whether counsel's performance was deficient before examining the prejudice suffered by the defendant as a result of the alleged deficiencies. The object of an ineffectiveness claim is not to grade counsel's performance. If it is easier to dispose of an ineffectiveness claim on the ground of lack of sufficient prejudice, which we expect will often be so, that course should be followed. Courts should strive to ensure that ineffectiveness claims not become so burdensome to defense counsel that the entire criminal justice system suffers as a result. * * *

Having articulated general standards for judging ineffectiveness claims, we think it useful to apply those standards to the facts of this case in order to illustrate the meaning of the general principles. * * * The facts as described above make clear that the conduct of respondent's counsel at and before respondent's sentencing proceeding cannot be found unreasonable. They also make clear that, even assuming the challenged conduct of counsel was unreasonable, respondent suffered insufficient prejudice to warrant setting aside his death sentence.

With respect to the performance component, the record shows that respondent's counsel made a strategic choice to argue for the extreme emotional distress mitigating circumstance and to rely as fully as possible on respondent's acceptance of responsibility for his crimes. Although counsel understandably felt hopeless about respondent's prospects, nothing in the record indicates * * * that counsel's sense of hopelessness distorted his professional judgment. Counsel's strategy choice was well within the range of professionally reasonable judgments, and the decision not to seek more character or psychological evidence than was already in hand was likewise reasonable.

The trial judge's views on the importance of owning up to one's crimes were well known to counsel. The aggravating circumstances were utterly overwhelming. Trial counsel could reasonably surmise from his conversations with respondent that character and psychological evidence would be of little help. Respondent had already been able to mention at the plea colloquy the substance of what there was to know about his financial and emotional troubles. Restricting testimony on respondent's character to what had come in at the plea colloquy ensured that contrary character and psychological evidence and respondent's criminal history, which counsel had successfully moved to exclude, would not come in. On these facts, there can be little question, even without application of the presumption of adequate performance, that trial counsel's defense, though unsuccessful, was the result of reasonable professional judgment.

With respect to the prejudice component, the lack of merit of respondent's claim is even more stark. The evidence that respondent says his trial counsel should have offered at the sentencing hearing would barely have altered the sentencing profile presented to the sentencing judge. As the state courts and District Court found, at most this evidence shows that numerous people who knew respondent thought he was generally a good person and that a psychiatrist and a psychologist believed he was under considerable emotional stress that did not rise to the level of extreme disturbance. Given the overwhelming aggravating factors, there is no reasonable probability that the omitted evidence would have changed the conclusion that the aggravating circumstances outweighed the mitigating circumstances and, hence, the sentence imposed. Indeed, admission of the evidence respondent now offers might even have been harmful to his case: his "rap sheet" would probably have been admitted into evidence, and the psychological reports would have directly contradicted respondent's claim that the mitigating circumstance of extreme emotional disturbance applied to his case. * * *

Failure to make the required showing of either deficient performance or sufficient prejudice defeats the ineffectiveness claim. Here there is a double failure. More generally, respondent has made no showing that the justice of his sentence was rendered unreliable by a breakdown in the adversary process caused by deficiencies in counsel's assistance. Respondent's sentencing proceeding was not fundamentally unfair. We conclude, therefore, that the District Court properly declined to issue a writ of habeas corpus. The judgment of the Court of Appeals is accordingly reversed.

JUSTICE BRENNAN, concurring in part and dissenting in part.

I join the Court's opinion but dissent from its judgment.[c] * * *

I join the Court's opinion because I believe that the standards it sets out today will both provide helpful guidance to courts considering claims of actual ineffectiveness of counsel and also permit those courts to continue their efforts to achieve progressive development of this area of the law. * * *

[T]he standards announced today can and should be applied with concern for the special considerations that must attend review of counsel's performance in a capital sentencing proceeding. In contrast to a case in which a finding of ineffective assistance requires a new trial, a conclusion that counsel was ineffective with respect to only the penalty phase of a capital trial imposes on the state the far lesser burden of reconsideration of the sentence alone. On the other hand, the consequences to the defendant of incompetent assistance at a capital sentencing could not, of course, be greater. * * *

JUSTICE MARSHALL, dissenting. * * *

The opinion of the Court revolves around two holdings. First, the majority ties the constitutional minima of attorney performance to a simple "standard of reasonableness." Second, the majority holds that only an error of counsel that has sufficient impact on a trial to "undermine confidence in the outcome" is grounds for overturning a conviction. I disagree with both of these rulings.

My objection to the performance standard adopted by the Court is that it is so malleable that, in practice, it will either have no grip at all or will yield excessive variation in the manner in which the Sixth Amendment is interpreted and applied by different courts. To tell lawyers and the lower courts that counsel for a criminal defendant must behave "reasonably" and must act like "a reasonably competent attorney" is to tell them almost nothing. In essence, the majority has instructed judges called upon to assess claims of ineffective assistance of counsel to advert to their own intuitions regarding what constitutes "professional" representation, and

---

c   Adhering to his view that the death penalty is in all circumstances forbidden cruel and unusual punishment, Justice Brennan noted that he would vacate respondent's death sentence on that ground.

has discouraged them from trying to develop more detailed standards governing the performance of defense counsel. In my view, the Court has thereby not only abdicated its own responsibility to interpret the Constitution, but also impaired the ability of the lower courts to exercise theirs.

The debilitating ambiguity of an "objective standard of reasonableness" in this context is illustrated by the majority's failure to address important issues concerning the quality of representation mandated by the Constitution. It is an unfortunate but undeniable fact that a person of means, by selecting a lawyer and paying him enough to ensure he prepares thoroughly, usually can obtain better representation than that available to an indigent defendant, who must rely on appointed counsel, who, in turn, has limited time and resources to devote to a given case. Is a "reasonably competent attorney" a reasonably competent adequately paid retained lawyer or a reasonably competent appointed attorney? It is also a fact that the quality of representation available to ordinary defendants in different parts of the country varies significantly. Should the standard of performance mandated by the Sixth Amendment vary by locale? The majority offers no clues as to the proper responses to these questions.

* * * I agree that counsel must be afforded "wide latitude" when making "tactical decisions" regarding trial strategy, but many aspects of the job of a criminal defense attorney are more amenable to judicial oversight [than the majority indicates]. For example, much of the work involved in preparing for a trial, applying for bail, conferring with one's client, making timely objections to significant, arguably erroneous rulings of the trial judge, and filing a notice of appeal if there are colorable grounds therefor could profitably be made the subject of uniform standards. * * *

I object to the prejudice standard adopted by the Court for two independent reasons. First, it is often very difficult to tell whether a defendant convicted after a trial in which he was ineffectively represented would have fared better if his lawyer had been competent. Seemingly impregnable cases can sometimes be dismantled by good defense counsel. On the basis of a cold record, it may be impossible for a reviewing court confidently to ascertain how the government's evidence and arguments would have stood up against rebuttal and cross-examination by a shrewd, well prepared lawyer. The difficulties of estimating prejudice after the fact are exacerbated by the possibility that evidence of injury to the defendant may be missing from the record precisely because of the incompetence of defense counsel. In view of all these impediments to a fair evaluation of the probability that the outcome of a trial was affected by ineffectiveness of counsel, it seems to me senseless to impose on a defendant whose lawyer has been shown to have been incompetent the burden of demonstrating prejudice.

Second and more fundamentally, the assumption on which the Court's holding rests is that the only purpose of the constitutional guarantee of effective assistance of counsel is to reduce the chance that innocent persons will be convicted. In my view, the guarantee also functions to ensure that convictions are obtained only through fundamentally fair procedures. The majority contends that the Sixth

Amendment is not violated when a manifestly guilty defendant is convicted after a trial in which he was represented by a manifestly ineffective attorney. I cannot agree. Every defendant is entitled to a trial in which his interests are vigorously and conscientiously advocated by an able lawyer. A proceeding in which the defendant does not receive meaningful assistance in meeting the forces of the state does not, in my opinion, constitute due process. * * * I would thus hold that a showing that the performance of a defendant's lawyer departed from constitutionally prescribed standards requires a new trial regardless of whether the defendant suffered demonstrable prejudice thereby.

Even if I were inclined to join the majority's two central holdings, I could not abide the manner in which the majority elaborates upon its rulings. * * *

Experienced members of the death-penalty bar have long recognized the crucial importance of adducing evidence at a sentencing proceeding that establishes the defendant's social and familial connections. The State makes a colorable—though in my view not compelling—argument that defense counsel in this case might have made a reasonable "strategic" decision not to present such evidence at the sentencing hearing on the assumption that an unadorned acknowledgment of respondent's responsibility for his crimes would be more likely to appeal to the trial judge, who was reputed to respect persons who accepted responsibility for their actions. But however justifiable such a choice might have been after counsel had fairly assessed the potential strength of the mitigating evidence available to him, counsel's failure to make any significant effort to find out what evidence might be garnered from respondent's relatives and acquaintances surely cannot be described as "reasonable." Counsel's failure to investigate is particularly suspicious in light of his candid admission that respondent's confession and conduct in the course of the trial gave him a feeling of "hopelessness" regarding the possibility of saving respondent's life.

If counsel had investigated the availability of mitigating evidence, he might well have decided to present some such material at the hearing. If he had done so, there is a significant chance that respondent would have been given a life sentence. In my view, those possibilities, conjoined with the unreasonableness of counsel's failure to investigate, are more than sufficient to establish a violation of the Sixth Amendment and to entitle respondent to a new sentencing proceeding. * * *

HARRINGTON V. RICHTER

562 U.S. 86, 131 S.Ct. 770, 178 L.Ed.2d 624 (2011).

JUSTICE KENNEDY delivered the opinion of the Court.

* * * It is necessary to begin by discussing the details of a crime committed more than a decade and a half ago. * * * Sometime after midnight on December 20, 1994, sheriff's deputies in Sacramento County, California, arrived at the home of a drug dealer named Joshua Johnson. Hours before, Johnson had been smoking marijuana in the company of Richter and two other men, Christian Branscombe and Patrick Klein. When the deputies arrived, however, they found only Johnson and Klein. Johnson was hysterical and covered in blood. Klein was lying on a couch

in Johnson's living room, unconscious and bleeding. Klein and Johnson each had been shot twice. Johnson recovered; Klein died of his wounds.

Johnson gave investigators this account: After falling asleep, he awoke to find Richter and Branscombe in his bedroom, at which point Branscombe shot him. Johnson heard more gunfire in the living room and the sound of his assailants leaving. He got up, found Klein bleeding on the living room couch, and called 911. A gun safe, a pistol, and $6,000 cash, all of which had been in the bedroom, were missing. * * * Evidence at the scene corroborated Johnson's account. Investigators found spent shell casings in the bedroom (where Johnson said he had been shot) and in the living room (where Johnson indicated Klein had been shot). In the living room there were two casings, a .32 caliber and a .22 caliber. One of the bullets recovered from Klein's body was a .32 and the other was a .22. In the bedroom there were two more casings, both .32 caliber. In addition detectives found blood spatter near the living room couch and bloodstains in the bedroom. Pools of blood had collected in the kitchen and the doorway to Johnson's bedroom. Investigators took only a few blood samples from the crime scene. One was from a blood splash on the wall near the bedroom doorway, but no sample was taken from the doorway blood pool itself.

Investigators searched Richter's residence and found Johnson's gun safe, two boxes of .22-caliber ammunition, and a gun magazine loaded with cartridges of the same brand and type as the boxes. A ballistics expert later concluded the .22-caliber bullet that struck Klein and the .22-caliber shell found in the living room matched the ammunition found in Richter's home and bore markings consistent with the model of gun for which the magazine was designed.

Richter and Branscombe were arrested. At first Richter denied involvement. He would later admit taking Johnson's pistol and disposing of it and of the .32-caliber weapon Branscombe used to shoot Johnson and Klein. Richter's counsel produced Johnson's missing pistol, but neither of the guns used to shoot Johnson and Klein was found.

Branscombe and Richter were tried together on charges of murder, attempted murder, burglary, and robbery. Only Richter's case is presented here. * * * The prosecution built its case on Johnson's testimony and on circumstantial evidence. Its opening statement took note of the shell casings found at the crime scene and the ammunition and gun safe found at Richter's residence. Defense counsel offered explanations for the circumstantial evidence and derided Johnson as a drug dealer, a paranoid, and a trigger-happy gun fanatic who had drawn a pistol on Branscombe and Richter the last time he had seen them. And there were inconsistencies in Johnson's story. In his 911 call, for instance, Johnson first said there were four or five men who had broken into his house, not two; and in the call he did not identify Richter and Branscombe among the intruders.

Blood evidence does not appear to have been part of the prosecution's planned case prior to trial, and investigators had not analyzed the few blood samples taken from the crime scene. But the opening statement from the defense led the prosecution to alter its approach. Richter's attorney outlined the theory that Branscombe had fired on Johnson in self-defense and that Klein had been killed not on the living room couch but in the crossfire in the bedroom doorway. Defense counsel stressed deficiencies in the investigation, including the absence of forensic support for the prosecution's version of events.

The prosecution took steps to adjust to the counterattack now disclosed. Without advance notice and over the objection of Richter's attorney, one of the detectives who investigated the shootings testified for the prosecution as an expert in blood pattern evidence. He concluded it was unlikely Klein had been shot outside the living room and then moved to the couch, given the patterns of blood on Klein's face, as well as other evidence including "high velocity" blood spatter near the couch consistent with the location of a shooting. The prosecution also offered testimony from a serologist. She testified the blood sample taken near the pool by the bedroom door could be Johnson's but not Klein's.

Defense counsel's cross-examination probed weaknesses in the testimony of these two witnesses. The detective who testified on blood patterns acknowledged that his inferences were imprecise, that it was unlikely Klein had been lying down on the couch when shot, and that he could not say the blood in the living room was from either of Klein's wounds. Defense counsel elicited from the serologist a concession that she had not tested the bedroom blood sample for cross-contamination. She said that if the year-old sample had degraded, it would be difficult to tell whether blood of Klein's type was also present in the sample.

For the defense, Richter's attorney called seven witnesses. Prominent among these was Richter himself. Richter testified he and Branscombe returned to Johnson's house just before the shootings in order to deliver something to one of Johnson's roommates. By Richter's account, Branscombe entered the house alone while Richter waited in the driveway; but after hearing screams and gunshots, Richter followed inside. There he saw Klein lying not on the couch but in the bedroom doorway, with Johnson on the bed and Branscombe standing in the middle of the room. According to Richter, Branscombe said he shot at Johnson and Klein after they attacked him. Other defense witnesses provided some corroboration for Richter's story. His former girlfriend, for instance, said she saw the gun safe at Richter's house shortly before the shootings.

The jury returned a verdict of guilty on all charges. Richter was sentenced to life without parole. On appeal, his conviction was affirmed [by the California Court of Appeals]. * * * The California Supreme Court denied a petition for review, and Richter did not file a petition for certiorari with this Court. His conviction became final.

Richter later petitioned the California Supreme Court for a writ of habeas corpus. He asserted a number of grounds for relief, including ineffective assistance of counsel. As relevant here, he claimed his counsel was deficient for failing to present expert testimony on serology, pathology, and blood spatter patterns, testimony that, he argued, would disclose the source of the blood pool in the bedroom doorway. This, he contended, would bolster his theory that Johnson had moved Klein to the couch. * * * He offered affidavits from three types of forensic experts. First, he provided statements from two blood serologists who said there was a possibility Klein's blood was intermixed with blood of Johnson's type in the sample taken from near the pool in the bedroom doorway. Second, he provided a statement from a pathologist who said the blood pool was too large to have come from Johnson given the nature of his wounds and his own account of his actions while waiting for the police. Third, he provided a statement from an expert in bloodstain analysis who said the absence of "a large number of satellite droplets" in photographs of the area around the blood in the bedroom doorway was inconsistent with the blood pool coming from Johnson as he stood in the doorway. Richter argued this evidence established the possibility that the blood in the bedroom doorway came from Klein, not Johnson. If that were true, he argued, it would confirm his account, not Johnson's.

The California Supreme Court denied Richter's petition in a one-sentence summary order.[a] * * * Richter [then] filed a petition for habeas corpus in United States District Court. He reasserted the claims in his state petition. The District Court denied his petition, and a three-judge panel of the Court of Appeals for the Ninth Circuit affirmed. [However], the Court of Appeals granted rehearing en banc and reversed the District Court's decision. * * * As a preliminary matter, the Court of Appeals questioned whether 28 U.S.C. § 2254(d) [of the federal habeas statute] was applicable to Richter's petition, since the California Supreme Court issued only a summary denial when it rejected his *Strickland* claims; but it determined the California decision was unreasonable in any event and that Richter was entitled to relief. The court held Richter's trial counsel was deficient for failing to consult experts on blood evidence in determining and pursuing a trial strategy and in preparing to rebut expert evidence the prosecution might—and later did—offer. Four judges dissented from the en banc decision. * * *

The statutory authority of federal courts to issue habeas corpus relief for persons in state custody is provided by 28 U.S.C. § 2254, as amended by the Antiterrorism and Effective Death Penalty Act of 1996 (AEDPA). * * * Section 2254(d) bars relitigation of any claim "adjudicated on the merits" in state court, subject only to the exceptions in §§ 2254(d)(1) and (d)(2). * * * [Thus], federal habeas relief may not be granted for claims subject to § 2254(d) unless it is shown that the earlier state court's decision "was contrary to" federal law then clearly established in the holdings of this Court, § 2254(d)(1); or that it "involved an unreasonable application of" such law, § 2254(d)(1); or that it "was based on an unreasonable determination of the facts" in light of the record before the state court, § 2254(d)(2). The Court of Appeals relied on the second of these exceptions to § 2254(d)'s relitigation bar, the exception in § 2254(d)(1) permitting relitigation where the earlier state decision resulted from an "unreasonable application of" clearly established federal law. In the view of the Court of Appeals, the California

---

[a] California allows the state habeas petitioner to bypass lower courts and file directly with the California Supreme Court. The petition must state fully and particularly the facts establishing the grounds for relief, supported by "available documentary evidence * * * including trial transcripts and affidavits or declarations." If a prima facie case is established and the state's response establishes a factual dispute, an evidentiary hearing by a lower court will be ordered. If a prima facie case in not established (reading against the defendant all gaps, ambiguities, and inconsistencies in the alleged facts and accompanying documentary evidence), the petition is denied, typically in a summary ruling, issued without further argument and without opinion. That is what occurred in this case.

Supreme Court's decision on Richter's ineffective-assistance claim unreasonably applied the holding in *Strickland*. The Court of Appeals' lengthy opinion, however, discloses an improper understanding of § 2254(d)'s unreasonableness standard and of its operation in the context of a *Strickland* claim.

The pivotal question is whether the state court's application of the *Strickland* standard was unreasonable. This is different from asking whether defense counsel's performance fell below *Strickland's* standard. Were that the inquiry, the analysis would be no different than if, for example, this Court were adjudicating a *Strickland* claim on direct review of a criminal conviction in a United States district court. Under AEDPA, though, it is a necessary premise that the two questions are different. For purposes of § 2254(d)(1), "an *unreasonable* application of federal law is different from an *incorrect* application of federal law." * * * A state court must be granted a deference and latitude that are not in operation when the case involves review under the *Strickland* standard itself. * * * A state court's determination that a claim lacks merit precludes federal habeas relief so long as "fairminded jurists could disagree" on the correctness of the state court's decision. * * *. [Also,] as this Court has explained, "[E]valuating whether a rule application was unreasonable requires considering the rule's specificity. The more general the rule, the more leeway courts have in reaching outcomes in case-by-case determinations." "[I]t is not an unreasonable application of clearly established Federal law for a state court to decline to apply a specific legal rule that has not been squarely established by this Court." * * *

Here it is not apparent how the Court of Appeals' analysis would have been any different without AEDPA. The court explicitly conducted a *de novo* review; and after finding a *Strickland* violation, it declared, without further explanation, that the "state court's decision to the contrary constituted an unreasonable application of *Strickland*." AEDPA demands more. Under § 2254(d), a habeas court must determine what arguments or theories supported or, as here, could have supported, the state court's decision; and then it must ask whether it is possible fairminded jurists could disagree that those arguments or theories are inconsistent with the holding in a prior decision of this Court. The opinion of the Court of Appeals all but ignored * * * [this] question* * *. Because [it] had little doubt that Richter's *Strickland* claim had merit, the Court of Appeals concluded the state court must have been unreasonable in rejecting it. * * *

The conclusion of the Court of Appeals that Richter demonstrated an unreasonable application by the state court of the *Strickland* standard now must be discussed. * * * "Surmounting *Strickland's* high bar is never an easy task" * * *. An ineffective-assistance claim can function as a way to escape rules of waiver and forfeiture and raise issues not presented at trial, and so the *Strickland* standard must be applied with scrupulous care, lest "intrusive post-trial inquiry" threaten the integrity of the very adversary process the right to counsel is meant to serve. *Strickland*. Even under *de novo* review, the standard for judging counsel's representation is a most deferential one. Unlike a later reviewing court, the attorney observed the relevant proceedings, knew of materials outside the record, and interacted with the client, with opposing counsel, and with the judge. It is "all too tempting" to "second-guess counsel's assistance after conviction or adverse sentence." Ibid. * * *

Establishing that a state court's application of *Strickland* was unreasonable under § 2254(d) is all the more difficult. The standards created by *Strickland* and § 2254(d) are both "highly deferential," and when the two apply in tandem, review is "doubly" so. The *Strickland* standard is a general one, so the range of reasonable applications is substantial. Federal habeas courts must guard against the danger of equating unreasonableness under *Strickland* with unreasonableness under § 2254(d). When § 2254(d) applies, the question is not whether counsel's actions were reasonable. The question is whether there is any reasonable argument that counsel satisfied *Strickland*'s deferential standard. * * *

The Court of Appeals first held that Richter's attorney rendered constitutionally deficient service because he did not consult blood evidence experts in developing the basic strategy for Richter's defense or offer their testimony as part of the principal case for the defense. *Strickland*, however, permits counsel to "make a reasonable decision that makes particular investigations unnecessary." It was at least arguable that a reasonable attorney could decide to forgo inquiry into the blood evidence in the circumstances here.

Criminal cases will arise where the only reasonable and available defense strategy requires consultation with experts or introduction of expert evidence, whether pretrial, at trial, or both. There are, however, "countless ways to provide effective assistance in any given case. Even the best criminal defense attorneys would not defend a particular client in the same way." *Strickland*. Rare are the situations in which the "wide latitude counsel must have in making tactical decisions" will be limited to any one technique or approach. Ibid. It can be assumed that in some cases counsel would be deemed ineffective for failing to consult or rely on experts, but even that formulation is sufficiently general that state courts would have wide latitude in applying it. Here it would be well within the bounds of a reasonable judicial determination for the state court to conclude that defense counsel could follow a strategy that did not require the use of experts regarding the pool in the doorway to Johnson's bedroom.

From the perspective of Richter's defense counsel when he was preparing Richter's defense, there were any number of hypothetical experts—specialists in psychiatry, psychology, ballistics, fingerprints, tire treads, physiology, or numerous other disciplines and subdisciplines—whose insight might possibly have been useful. An attorney can avoid activities that appear "distractive from more important duties." *Bobby v. Van Hook*, 558 U.S. 4 (2009).[b] Counsel was entitled to

---

[b] In *Bobby v. Van Hook*, the Court, in a per curiam summary reversal of a Sixth Circuit ruling, concluded that a constitutionally satisfactory ruling did not require the absolute thoroughness of investigation seemingly demanded by the ABA's latest guidelines on capital representation. In addressing capital sentencing, counsel had presented considerable mitigating evidence, based on interviews with several relatives and expert witnesses. But counsel had not contacted still other sources who would have been familiar with his upbringing, as arguably required by those guidelines. The Court initially noted that the Sixth Circuit had erred in relying on ABA standards that had been adopted long after defendant's representation, and in failing to heed *Strickland*'s warning that professional guidelines were not to be treated as "inexorable commands." It then added: "Given all the evidence [counsel] unearthed from those closest to Van

formulate a strategy that was reasonable at the time and to balance limited resources in accord with effective trial tactics and strategies. * * *

In concluding otherwise the Court of Appeals failed to "reconstruct the circumstances of counsel's challenged conduct" and "evaluate the conduct from counsel's perspective at the time." *Strickland.* In its view Klein's location was "the single most critical issue in the case" given the differing theories of the prosecution and the defense, and the source of the blood in the doorway was therefore of central concern. But it was far from a necessary conclusion that this was evident at the time of the trial. There were many factual differences between prosecution and defense versions of the events on the night of the shootings. It is only because forensic evidence has emerged concerning the source of the blood pool that the issue could with any plausibility be said to stand apart. Reliance on "the harsh light of hindsight" to cast doubt on a trial that took place now more than 15 years ago is precisely what *Strickland* and AEDPA seek to prevent. * * *

Even if it had been apparent that expert blood testimony could support Richter's defense, it would be reasonable to conclude that a competent attorney might elect not to use it. The Court of Appeals opinion for the en banc majority rests in large part on a hypothesis that reasonably could have been rejected. The hypothesis is that without jeopardizing Richter's defense, an expert could have testified that the blood in Johnson's doorway could not have come from Johnson and could have come from Klein, thus suggesting that Richter's version of the shooting was correct and Johnson's a fabrication. This theory overlooks the fact that concentrating on the blood pool carried its own serious risks. If serological analysis or other forensic evidence demonstrated that the blood came from Johnson alone, Richter's story would be exposed as an invention. An attorney need not pursue an investigation that would be fruitless, much less one that might be harmful to the defense. Here Richter's attorney had reason to question the truth of his client's account, given, for instance, Richter's initial denial of involvement and the subsequent production of Johnson's missing pistol.

It would have been altogether reasonable to conclude that this concern justified the course Richter's counsel pursued. Indeed, the Court of Appeals recognized this risk insofar as it pertained to the suggestion that counsel should have had the blood evidence tested. * * * But the court failed to recognize that making a central issue out of blood evidence would have increased the likelihood of the prosecution's producing its own evidence on the blood pool's origins and composition; and once matters proceeded on this course, there was a serious risk that expert evidence could destroy Richter's case. Even apart from this danger, there was the possibility that expert testimony could shift attention to esoteric matters of forensic science, distract the jury from whether Johnson was telling the truth, or transform the case into a battle of the experts. * * * True, it appears that defense counsel's opening statement itself inspired the prosecution to introduce expert forensic evidence. But the prosecution's evidence may well have been weakened by the fact that it was assembled late in the process; and in any event

---

Hooks's upbringing and experts who reviewed his history, it was not unreasonable for counsel * * * [to conclude that they had reached] a point at which additional evidence can * * * reasonably be expected to be only cumulative and the search for it distractive from more important duties."

the prosecution's response shows merely that the defense strategy did not work out as well as counsel had hoped, not that counsel was incompetent.

To support a defense argument that the prosecution has not proved its case it sometimes is better to try to cast pervasive suspicion of doubt than to strive to prove a certainty that exonerates. All that happened here is that counsel pursued a course that conformed to the first option. If this case presented a *de novo* review of *Strickland*, the foregoing might well suffice to reject the claim of inadequate counsel, but that is an unnecessary step. The Court of Appeals must be reversed if there was a reasonable justification for the state court's decision. In light of the record here there was no basis to rule that the state court's determination was unreasonable.

The Court of Appeals erred in dismissing strategic considerations like these as an inaccurate account of counsel's actual thinking. Although courts may not indulge "*post hoc* rationalization" for counsel's decisionmaking that contradicts the available evidence of counsel's actions, *Wiggins v. Smith*, 539 U.S. 510 (2003),[c] neither may they insist counsel confirm every aspect of the strategic basis for his or her actions.[d] There is a "strong presumption" that counsel's attention to certain issues to the exclusion of others reflects trial tactics rather than "sheer neglect." *Yarborough v. Gentry*, 540 U.S. 1, 8 (2003).[e] After an adverse verdict at trial even

---

[c] In *Wiggins v. Smith*, the Court majority held that the state court rendered an "unreasonable application of Strickland" in rejecting the claim of ineffective assistance at a capital sentencing hearing where counsel failed to obtain a social history report. The state court had concluded that counsel made a reasonable strategic decision not to further investigate defendant's personal history, even though it was "standard practice" at the time to obtain a social history report and public defender funding had been available to obtain the report. The state court had reasoned that the two counsel, after examining sources providing "rudimentary knowledge" on defendant's background, decided (as they later testified) to focus their presentation entirely on defendant's lack of direct responsibility for the killing. Rejecting that analysis, the Supreme Court majority noted that the trial record strongly suggested that "counsels' failure to investigate thoroughly [defendant's personal history] resulted from inattention, not reasoned strategic judgment," as counsel had never abandoned the strategy of also presenting a mitigation defense. Thus, the state court's description of counsel's inaction as the product of "a reasoned strategic judgment" rested, improperly, on a "post hoc rationalization," rather than the actual strategy.

[d] The Ninth Circuit majority had concluded that the defense strategy posed by the Ninth Circuit dissenters (basically that set forth in the Supreme Court's opinion) was nothing more than a "post hoc rationalization," as evidenced by counsel's deposition (which was part of the record before the California Supreme Court, see fn. a supra). In that deposition, the Ninth Circuit majority noted: "Counsel was unable to provide any reasoned explanation for failing to consult forensic experts or to seek expert testimony in order to corroborate his client's testimony or prepare to rebut the prosecution's case," as counsel's explanation was simply that his strategy "was to pit his client's credibility against Johnson and to attack the evidentiary gaps in the police investigation of the crime scene." Indeed, the Ninth Circuit noted, "counsel acknowledged that he missed crucial information when conducting his cross-examination" and that with experts, "you don't make those mistakes like I made."

[e] *Yarborough v. Gentry* presented an IAC claim based upon claimed deficiencies in counsel's closing argument. Rejecting the Ninth Circuit's finding that counsel had been ineffective in calling the jury's attention to only some of the exculpatory aspects of the trial evidence, the Court noted: "When counsel focuses on some issues to the exclusion of others, there is a strong presumption that he did so for tactical reasons rather than through sheer neglect." The Court added that ineffectiveness might not be present even if counsel's omission had not been deliberate: "Moreover, even if an omission is inadvertent, relief is not automatic. The Sixth Amendment guarantees reasonable competence, not perfect advocacy judged with the benefit of hindsight. To recall the words of Justice (and former Solicitor General) Jackson: 'I made three arguments of every case. First came the one that I planned—as I thought, logical coherent, complete. Second, was the one

the most experienced counsel may find it difficult to resist asking whether a different strategy might have been better, and, in the course of that reflection, to magnify their own responsibility for an unfavorable outcome. *Strickland*, however, calls for an inquiry into the objective reasonableness of counsel's performance, not counsel's subjective state of mind.

The Court of Appeals also found that Richter's attorney was constitutionally deficient because he had not expected the prosecution to offer expert testimony and therefore was unable to offer expert testimony of his own in response. * * * The Court of Appeals erred in suggesting counsel had to be prepared for "any contingency." *Strickland* does not guarantee perfect representation, only a " 'reasonably competent attorney.' " * * * Representation is constitutionally ineffective only if it "so undermined the proper functioning of the adversarial process" that the defendant was denied a fair trial. *Strickland*. Just as there is no expectation that competent counsel will be a flawless strategist or tactician, an attorney may not be faulted for a reasonable miscalculation or lack of foresight or for failing to prepare for what appear to be remote possibilities.

Here, Richter's attorney was mistaken in thinking the prosecution would not present forensic testimony. But the prosecution itself did not expect to make that presentation and had made no preparations for doing so on the eve of trial. For this reason alone, it is at least debatable whether counsel's error was so fundamental as to call the fairness of the trial into doubt.

Even if counsel should have foreseen that the prosecution would offer expert evidence, Richter would still need to show it was indisputable that *Strickland* required his attorney to act upon that knowledge. Attempting to establish this, the Court of Appeals held that defense counsel should have offered expert testimony to rebut the evidence from the prosecution. But *Strickland* does not enact Newton's third law for the presentation of evidence, requiring for every prosecution expert an equal and opposite expert from the defense.

In many instances cross-examination will be sufficient to expose defects in an expert's presentation. When defense counsel does not have a solid case, the best strategy can be to say that there is too much doubt about the State's theory for a jury to convict. And while in some instances "even an isolated error" can support an ineffective-assistance claim if it is "sufficiently egregious and prejudicial," *Murray v. Carrier*, 477 U.S. 478 (1986), it is difficult to establish ineffective assistance when counsel's overall performance indicates active and capable advocacy. Here Richter's attorney represented him with vigor and conducted a skillful cross-examination. As noted, defense counsel elicited concessions from the State's experts and was able to draw attention to weaknesses in their conclusions stemming from the fact that their analyses were conducted long after investigators had left the crime scene. For all of these reasons, it would have been reasonable to find that Richter had not shown his attorney was deficient under Strickland.

---

actually presented—interrupted, incoherent, disjointed, disappointing. The third was the utterly devastating argument that I thought of after going to bed that night.' "

The Court of Appeals further concluded that Richter had established prejudice under *Strickland* given the expert evidence his attorney could have introduced. It held that the California Supreme Court would have been unreasonable in concluding otherwise. This too was error. * * * In assessing prejudice under *Strickland*, the question is not whether a court can be certain counsel's performance had no effect on the outcome or whether it is possible a reasonable doubt might have been established if counsel acted differently. * * * Instead, *Strickland* asks whether it is "reasonably likely" the result would have been different. This does not require a showing that counsel's actions "more likely than not altered the outcome," but the difference between *Strickland*'s prejudice standard and a more-probable-than-not standard is slight and matters "only in the rarest case." Id. The likelihood of a different result must be substantial, not just conceivable.

It would not have been unreasonable for the California Supreme Court to conclude Richter's evidence of prejudice fell short of this standard. His expert serology evidence established nothing more than a theoretical possibility that, in addition to blood of Johnson's type, Klein's blood may also have been present in a blood sample taken near the bedroom doorway pool. At trial, defense counsel extracted a concession along these lines from the prosecution's expert. The pathology expert's claim about the size of the blood pool could be taken to suggest only that the wounded and hysterical Johnson erred in his assessment of time or that he bled more profusely than estimated. And the analysis of the purported blood pattern expert indicated no more than that Johnson was not standing up when the blood pool formed.

It was also reasonable to find Richter had not established prejudice given that he offered no evidence directly challenging other conclusions reached by the prosecution's experts. For example, there was no dispute that the blood sample taken near the doorway pool matched Johnson's blood type. * * * Nor did Richter provide any direct refutation of the State's expert testimony describing how blood spatter near the couch suggested a shooting in the living room and how the blood patterns on Klein's face were inconsistent with Richter's theory that Klein had been killed in the bedroom doorway and moved to the couch.

There was, furthermore, sufficient conventional circumstantial evidence pointing to Richter's guilt. It included the gun safe and ammunition found at his home; his flight from the crime scene; his disposal of the .32-caliber gun and of Johnson's pistol; his shifting story concerning his involvement; the disappearance prior to the arrival of the law enforcement officers of the .22-caliber weapon that killed Klein; the improbability of Branscombe's not being wounded in the shootout that resulted in a combined four bullet wounds to Johnson and Klein; and the difficulties the intoxicated and twice-shot Johnson would have had in carrying the body of a dying man from bedroom doorway to living room couch, not to mention the lack of any obvious reason for him to do so. There was ample basis for the California Supreme Court to think any real possibility of Richter's being acquitted was eclipsed by the remaining evidence pointing to guilt. * * *

The California Supreme Court's decision on the merits of Richter's *Strickland* claim required more deference than it received. Richter was not entitled to the relief ordered by the Court of Appeals. The judgment is reversed, and the case is remanded for further proceedings consistent with this opinion.

JUSTICE KAGAN took no part in the consideration or decision of this case.

JUSTICE GINSBURG, concurring in the judgment.

In failing even to consult blood experts in preparation for the murder trial, Richter's counsel, I agree with the Court of Appeals, "was not functioning as the 'counsel' guaranteed the defendant by the Sixth Amendment." *Strickland v. Washington.* The strong force of the prosecution's case, however, was not significantly reduced by the affidavits offered in support of Richter's habeas petition. I would therefore not rank counsel's lapse "so serious as to deprive [Richter] of a fair trial, a trial whose result is reliable." Ibid. For that reason, I concur in the Court's judgment.

LAFLER V. COOPER
566 U.S. 156, 132 S.Ct. 1376, 182 L.Ed.2d 398 (2012).

JUSTICE KENNEDY delivered the opinion of the Court.

In this case, as in *Missouri v. Frye*, 566 U.S. 134 (2012) [p. 766], also decided today, a criminal defendant seeks a remedy when inadequate assistance of counsel caused nonacceptance of a plea offer and further proceedings led to a less favorable outcome. * * * Here, after the plea offer had been rejected, there was a full and fair trial before a jury. After a guilty verdict, the defendant received a sentence harsher than that offered in the rejected plea bargain. The instant case comes to the Court with the concession that counsel's advice with respect to the plea offer fell below the standard of adequate assistance of counsel guaranteed by the Sixth Amendment. * * *

[Respondent Cooper was charged in Michigan with assault with intent to murder and three related, lower level offenses. The prosecution offered to dismiss two of the charges and to recommend a 51- to 85-month sentence on the other two, in exchange for a guilty plea. In a communication with the court, respondent admitted his guilt and expressed a willingness to accept the offer. But he subsequently rejected the offer, allegedly after his attorney convinced him that the prosecution would be unable to establish intent to murder because the victim had been shot below the waist. At trial, respondent was convicted on all counts and received a mandatory minimum 185- to 360-month sentence. In a subsequent hearing, the state trial court rejected respondent's claim that his attorney's advice to reject the pleas constituted ineffective assistance. The Michigan Court of Appeals affirmed, rejecting the ineffective-assistance claim on the ground that the respondent acted knowingly and intelligently in turning down the plea offer and choosing to go to trial. Respondent renewed his claim in federal habeas. The federal district court granted the writ and ordered specific performance on the original plea offer. The Sixth Circuit then affirmed, and the Supreme Court granted review.]

* * * The question for this Court is how to apply *Strickland*'s prejudice test where ineffective assistance results in a rejection of the plea offer and the defendant is convicted at the ensuing trial. To establish *Strickland* prejudice a defendant must "show that there is a reasonable probability that, but for counsel's unprofessional errors, the result of the proceeding would have been different." In the context of pleas a defendant must show the outcome of the plea process would have been different with competent advice. * * * In *Hill v. Lockhart* [p. 766], when evaluating the petitioner's claim that ineffective assistance led to the improvident acceptance of a guilty plea, the Court required the petitioner to show "that there is a reasonable probability that, but for counsel's errors, [the defendant] would not have pleaded guilty and would have insisted on going to trial."

In contrast to *Hill*, here the ineffective advice led not to an offer's acceptance but to its rejection. Having to stand trial, not choosing to waive it, is the prejudice alleged. In these circumstances a defendant must show that but for the ineffective advice of counsel there is a reasonable probability that the plea offer would have been presented to the court (*i.e.*, that the defendant would have accepted the plea and the prosecution would not have withdrawn it in light of intervening circumstances), that the court would have accepted its terms, and that the conviction or sentence, or both, under the offer's terms would have been less severe than under the judgment and sentence that in fact were imposed. * * *

Petitioner and the Solicitor General propose a different, far more narrow, view of the Sixth Amendment. They contend there can be no finding of *Strickland* prejudice arising from plea bargaining if the defendant is later convicted at a fair trial. The three reasons petitioner and the Solicitor General offer for their approach are unpersuasive.

First, petitioner and the Solicitor General claim that the sole purpose of the Sixth Amendment is to protect the right to a fair trial. Errors before trial, they argue, are not cognizable under the Sixth Amendment unless they affect the fairness of the trial itself. * * * The Sixth Amendment, however, is not so narrow in its reach. The Sixth Amendment requires effective assistance of counsel at critical stages of a criminal proceeding. Its protections are not designed simply to protect the trial, even though "counsel's absence [in these stages] may derogate from the accused's right to a fair trial." *United States v. Wade*, 388 U.S. 218 (1967). The constitutional guarantee applies to pretrial critical stages that are part of the whole course of a criminal proceeding, a proceeding in which defendants cannot be presumed to make critical decisions without counsel's advice. This is consistent, too, with the rule that defendants have a right to effective assistance of counsel on appeal, even though that cannot in any way be characterized as part of the trial. * * * The precedents also establish that there exists a right to counsel during sentencing in both noncapital and capital cases. Even though sentencing does not concern the defendant's guilt or innocence, ineffective assistance of counsel during a sentencing hearing can result in *Strickland* prejudice because "any amount of [additional] jail time has Sixth Amendment significance." *Glover v. United States*, 531, U.S. 198 (2001). * * *

Second, petitioner claims this Court refined *Strickland*'s prejudice analysis in *Lockhart v. Fretwell*, 506 U.S. 364 (1993), to add an additional requirement that the defendant show that ineffective assistance of counsel led to his being denied a substantive or procedural right. The Court has rejected the argument that *Fretwell* modified *Strickland* before and does so again now. * * * [Defendant] Fretwell could not show *Strickland* prejudice resulting from his attorney's failure to object to the use of a sentencing factor the Eighth Circuit had erroneously (and temporarily) found to be impermissible. Because the objection upon which his ineffective-assistance-of-counsel claim was premised was meritless, Fretwell could not demonstrate an error entitling him to relief. The case presented the "unusual circumstance where the defendant attempts to demonstrate prejudice based on considerations that, as a matter of law, ought not inform the inquiry." Ibid. (O'Connor, J., concurring). See also ibid. (recognizing "[t]he determinative question—whether there is a reasonable probability that, but for counsel's unprofessional errors, the result of the proceeding would have been different—remains unchanged"). It is for this same reason a defendant cannot show prejudice based on counsel's refusal to present perjured testimony, even if such testimony might have affected the outcome of the case. See *Nix v. Whiteside*, 475 U.S. 157 (1986) (holding first that counsel's refusal to present perjured testimony breached no professional duty and second that it cannot establish prejudice under Strickland).

Both *Fretwell* and *Nix* are instructive in that they demonstrate "there are also situations in which it would be unjust to characterize the likelihood of a different outcome as legitimate 'prejudice,' " *Williams v. Taylor*, 529 U.S. 362 (2000), because defendants would receive a windfall as a result of the application of an incorrect legal principle or a defense strategy outside the law. Here, however, the injured client seeks relief from counsel's failure to meet a valid legal standard, not from counsel's refusal to violate it. He maintains that, absent ineffective counsel, he would have accepted a plea offer for a sentence the prosecution evidently deemed consistent with the sound administration of criminal justice. The favorable sentence that eluded the defendant in the criminal proceeding appears to be the sentence he or others in his position would have received in the ordinary course, absent the failings of counsel. If a plea bargain has been offered, a defendant has the right to effective assistance of counsel in considering whether to accept it. If that right is denied, prejudice can be shown if loss of the plea opportunity led to a trial resulting in a conviction on more serious charges or the imposition of a more severe sentence.

It is, of course, true that defendants have "no right to be offered a plea . . . nor a federal right that the judge accept it." *Frye*, supra. In the circumstances here, that is beside the point. If no plea offer is made, or a plea deal is accepted by the defendant but rejected by the judge, the issue raised here simply does not arise. Much the same reasoning guides cases that find criminal defendants have a right to effective assistance of counsel in direct appeals even though the Constitution does not require States to provide a system of appellate review at all. As in those cases, "[w]hen a State opts to act in a field where its action has significant discretionary elements, it must nonetheless act in accord with the dictates of the Constitution." * * *

Third, petitioner seeks to preserve the conviction obtained by the State by arguing that the purpose of the Sixth Amendment is to ensure "the reliability of [a] conviction following trial." This argument, too, fails to comprehend the full scope of the Sixth Amendment's protections; and it is refuted by precedent. *Strickland* recognized "[t]he benchmark for judging any claim of ineffectiveness must be whether counsel's conduct so undermined the proper functioning of the adversarial process that the trial cannot be relied on as having produced a just result." The goal of a just result is not divorced from the reliability of a conviction * * *; but here the question is not the fairness or reliability of the trial but the fairness and regularity of the processes that preceded it, which caused the defendant to lose benefits he would have received in the ordinary course but for counsel's ineffective assistance.

There are instances, furthermore, where a reliable trial does not foreclose relief when counsel has failed to assert rights that may have altered the outcome. In *Kimmelman v. Morrison*, 477 U.S. 365 (1986), the Court held that an attorney's failure to timely move to suppress evidence during trial could be grounds for federal habeas relief. The Court rejected the suggestion that the "failure to make a timely request for the exclusion of illegally seized evidence" could not be the basis for a Sixth Amendment violation because the evidence "is 'typically reliable and often the most probative information bearing on the guilt or innocence of the defendant.'" "The constitutional rights of criminal defendants," the Court observed, "are granted to the innocent and the guilty alike. Consequently, we decline to hold either that the guarantee of effective assistance of counsel belongs solely to the innocent or that it attaches only to matters affecting the determination of actual guilt." The same logic applies here. The fact that respondent is guilty does not mean he was not entitled by the Sixth Amendment to effective assistance or that he suffered no prejudice from his attorney's deficient performance during plea bargaining.

In the end, petitioner's three arguments amount to one general contention: A fair trial wipes clean any deficient performance by defense counsel during plea bargaining. That position ignores the reality that criminal justice today is for the most part a system of pleas, not a system of trials. Ninety-seven percent of federal convictions and ninety-four percent of state convictions are the result of guilty pleas. See *Frye*, supra. As explained in *Frye*, the right to adequate assistance of counsel cannot be defined or enforced without taking account of the central role plea bargaining plays in securing convictions and determining sentences.

* * * Even if a defendant shows ineffective assistance of counsel has caused the rejection of a plea leading to a trial and a more severe sentence, there is the question of what constitutes an appropriate remedy. That question must now be addressed. * * * Sixth Amendment remedies should be "tailored to the injury suffered from the constitutional violation and should not unnecessarily infringe on competing interests." * * *. Thus, a remedy must "neutralize the taint" of a constitutional violation, while at the same time not grant a windfall to the

defendant or needlessly squander the considerable resources the State properly invested in the criminal prosecution. * * *

The specific injury suffered by defendants who decline a plea offer as a result of ineffective assistance of counsel and then receive a greater sentence as a result of trial can come in at least one of two forms. In some cases, the sole advantage a defendant would have received under the plea is a lesser sentence. This is typically the case when the charges that would have been admitted as part of the plea bargain are the same as the charges the defendant was convicted of after trial. In this situation the court may conduct an evidentiary hearing to determine whether the defendant has shown a reasonable probability that but for counsel's errors he would have accepted the plea. If the showing is made, the court may exercise discretion in determining whether the defendant should receive the term of imprisonment the government offered in the plea, the sentence he received at trial, or something in between.

In some situations it may be that resentencing alone will not be full redress for the constitutional injury. If, for example, an offer was for a guilty plea to a count or counts less serious than the ones for which a defendant was convicted after trial, or if a mandatory sentence confines a judge's sentencing discretion after trial, a resentencing based on the conviction at trial may not suffice. In these circumstances, the proper exercise of discretion to remedy the constitutional injury may be to require the prosecution to reoffer the plea proposal. Once this has occurred, the judge can then exercise discretion in deciding whether to vacate the conviction from trial and accept the plea or leave the conviction undisturbed.

In implementing a remedy in both of these situations, the trial court must weigh various factors; and the boundaries of proper discretion need not be defined here. Principles elaborated over time in decisions of state and federal courts, and in statutes and rules, will serve to give more complete guidance as to the factors that should bear upon the exercise of the judge's discretion. At this point, however, it suffices to note two considerations that are of relevance.

First, a court may take account of a defendant's earlier expressed willingness, or unwillingness, to accept responsibility for his or her actions. Second, it is not necessary here to decide as a constitutional rule that a judge is required to prescind (that is to say disregard) any information concerning the crime that was discovered after the plea offer was made. The time continuum makes it difficult to restore the defendant and the prosecution to the precise positions they occupied prior to the rejection of the plea offer, but that baseline can be consulted in finding a remedy that does not require the prosecution to incur the expense of conducting a new trial. * * *

Respondent has satisfied *Strickland*'s two-part test. Regarding performance, perhaps it could be accepted that it is unclear whether respondent's counsel believed respondent could not be convicted for assault with intent to murder as a matter of law because the shots hit Mundy below the waist, or whether he simply thought this would be a persuasive argument to make to the jury to show lack of specific intent. And, as the Court of Appeals for the Sixth Circuit suggested, an erroneous strategic prediction about the outcome of a trial is not necessarily deficient performance. Here, however, the fact of deficient performance has been conceded by all parties. The case comes to us on that assumption, so there is no need to address this question.

As to prejudice, respondent has shown that but for counsel's deficient performance there is a reasonable probability he and the trial court would have accepted the guilty plea. In addition, as a result of not accepting the plea and being convicted at trial, respondent received a minimum sentence 3 1/2 times greater than he would have received under the plea. The standard for ineffective assistance under *Strickland* has thus been satisfied.

As a remedy, the District Court ordered specific performance of the original plea agreement. The correct remedy in these circumstances, however, is to order the State to reoffer the plea agreement. Presuming respondent accepts the offer, the state trial court can then exercise its discretion in determining whether to vacate the convictions and resentence respondent pursuant to the plea agreement, to vacate only some of the convictions and resentence respondent accordingly, or to leave the convictions and sentence from trial undisturbed. * * *

JUSTICE SCALIA, with whom JUSTICE THOMAS joins, and with whom The CHIEF JUSTICE joins as to all but Part IV, dissenting.

I.

This case and its companion, *Missouri v. Frye*, raise relatively straightforward questions about the scope of the right to effective assistance of counsel. Our case law originally derived that right from the Due Process Clause, and its guarantee of a fair trial, *United States v. Gonzalez-Lopez* [fn. a, p. 936], but the seminal case of *Strickland v. Washington* located the right within the Sixth Amendment. As the Court notes, the right to counsel does not begin at trial. It extends to "any stage of the prosecution, formal or informal, in court or out, where counsel's absence might derogate from the accused's right to a fair trial." * * * And it follows from this that acceptance of a plea offer is a critical stage. That, and nothing more, is the point of the Court's observation in *Padilla v. Kentucky* [fn. a, p. 777] that "the negotiation of a plea bargain is a critical phase of litigation for purposes of the Sixth Amendment right to effective assistance of counsel." The defendant in *Padilla* had accepted the plea bargain and pleaded guilty, abandoning his right to a fair trial; he was entitled to advice of competent counsel before he did so. The Court has never held that the rule articulated in [cases like] *Padilla* * * * extends to all aspects of plea negotiations, requiring not just advice of competent counsel before the defendant accepts a plea bargain and pleads guilty, but also the advice of competent counsel before the defendant rejects a plea bargain and stands on his constitutional right to a fair trial. The latter is a vast departure from our past cases, protecting not just the constitutionally prescribed right to a fair adjudication of guilt and punishment, but a judicially invented right to effective plea bargaining.

It is also apparent from *Strickland* that bad plea bargaining has nothing to do with ineffective assistance of counsel in the constitutional sense. *Strickland* explained that "[i]n giving meaning to the requirement [of effective assistance], . . . we must take its purpose—to ensure a fair trial—as the guide." Since "the right to the effective assistance of counsel is recognized not for its own sake, but because of the effect it has on the ability of the accused to receive a fair trial," *United States v. Cronic* [p. 969], the "benchmark" inquiry in evaluating any claim of ineffective assistance is whether counsel's performance "so undermined the proper functioning of the adversarial process" that it failed to produce a reliably "just result." *Strickland*. That is what *Strickland*'s requirement of "prejudice" consists of: Because the right to effective assistance has as its purpose the assurance of a fair trial, the right is not infringed unless counsel's mistakes call into question the basic justice of a defendant's conviction or sentence.

To be sure, *Strickland* stated a rule of thumb for measuring prejudice which, applied blindly and out of context, could support the Court's holding today: "The defendant must show that there is a reasonable probability that, but for counsel's unprofessional errors, the result of the proceeding would have been different." *Strickland* itself cautioned, however, that its test was not to be applied in a mechanical fashion, and that courts were not to divert their "ultimate focus" from "the fundamental fairness of the proceeding whose result is being challenged." And until today we have followed that course.

In *Lockhart v. Fretwell*, the deficient performance at issue was the failure of counsel for a defendant who had been sentenced to death to make an objection that would have produced a sentence of life imprisonment instead. The objection was fully supported by then-extant Circuit law, so that the sentencing court would have been compelled to sustain it, producing a life sentence that principles of double jeopardy would likely make final. * * * By the time Fretwell's claim came before us, however, the Circuit law had been overruled in light of one of our cases. We determined that a prejudice analysis "focusing solely on mere outcome determination, without attention to whether the result of the proceeding was fundamentally unfair or unreliable," would be defective. Because counsel's error did not "deprive the defendant of any substantive or procedural right to which the law entitles him," the defendant's sentencing proceeding was fair and its result was reliable, even though counsel's error may have affected its outcome.[2]

* * * As the Court itself observes, a criminal defendant has no right to a plea bargain. * * * Counsel's mistakes in this case thus did not "deprive the defendant of a substantive or procedural right to which the law entitles him." Far from being

---

[2]   *Kimmelman v. Morrison*, cited by the Court, does not contradict this principle. That case * * * considered whether our holding that Fourth Amendment claims fully litigated in state court cannot be raised in federal habeas [see *Stone v. Powell*, p. 86] "should be extended to Sixth Amendment claims of ineffective assistance of counsel where the principal allegation and manifestations of inadequate representation is counsel's failure to file a timely motion to suppress evidence allegedly obtained in violation of the Fourth Amendment." Our negative answer to that question had nothing to do with the issue here. The parties in *Kimmelman* had not raised the question "whether the admission of illegally seized but reliable evidence can ever constitute 'prejudice' under *Strickland*"—a question similar to the one presented her—and the Court therefore did not address it. Id. (Powell, J., concurring in judgment). Kimmelman made clear, however, how the answer to that question is to be determined: "The essence of an ineffective-assistance claim is that counsel's unprofessional errors so upset the adversarial balance between defense and prosecution *that the trial was rendered unfair and the verdict rendered suspect*," Id. (emphasis added). "Only those habeas petitioners who can prove under *Strickland that they have been denied a fair trial*—will be granted the writ, Id. (emphasis added). In short, *Kimmelman*'s only relevance is to prove the Court's opinion wrong.

"beside the point," *Ante* at [p. 953], that is critical to correct application of our precedents. Like *Fretwell*, this case "concerns the unusual circumstance where the defendant attempts to demonstrate prejudice based on considerations that, as a matter of law, ought not inform the inquiry." * * *

III.a

It is impossible to conclude discussion of today's extraordinary opinion without commenting upon the remedy it provides for the unconstitutional conviction. It is a remedy unheard-of in American jurisprudence—and, I would be willing to bet, in the jurisprudence of any other country.

The Court requires Michigan to "reoffer the plea agreement" that was rejected because of bad advice from counsel. That would indeed be a powerful remedy—but for the fact that Cooper's acceptance of that reoffered agreement is not conclusive. Astoundingly, "the state trial court can then exercise its discretion in determining whether to vacate the convictions and resentence respondent pursuant to the plea agreement, to vacate only some of the convictions and resentence respondent accordingly, *or to leave the convictions and sentence from trial undisturbed*." *Ante* at [p. 956] (emphasis added).

Why, one might ask, require a "reoffer" of the plea agreement, and its acceptance by the defendant? If the district court finds (as a necessary element, supposedly, of *Strickland* prejudice) that Cooper *would have accepted* the original offer, and would thereby have avoided trial and conviction, why not skip the reoffer-and-reacceptance minuet and simply leave it to the discretion of the state trial court what the remedy shall be? The answer, of course, is camouflage. Trial courts, after all, *regularly* accept or reject plea agreements, so there seems to be nothing extraordinary about their accepting or rejecting the new one mandated by today's decision. But the acceptance or rejection of a plea agreement that has no status whatever under the United States Constitution is worlds apart from what this is: "discretionary" specification of a remedy for an unconstitutional criminal conviction.

To be sure, the Court asserts that there are "factors" which bear upon (and presumably limit) exercise of this discretion—factors that it is not prepared to specify in full, much less assign some determinative weight. "Principles elaborated over time in decisions of state and federal courts, and in statutes and rules" will (in the Court's rosy view) sort all that out. I find it extraordinary that "statutes and rules" can specify the remedy for a criminal defendant's unconstitutional conviction. Or that the remedy for an unconstitutional conviction should *ever* be subject *at all* to a trial judge's discretion. Or, finally, that the remedy could *ever* include no remedy at all. * * *

---

a   In part II of the dissent, Justice Scalia addressed the question of whether § 2254(d)(1) barred relief in this federal habeas proceeding. The majority concluded that the § 2254(d)(1) standard, set forth in *Richter* [pp. 944–946] did not apply because the state court ruling has failed to apply *Strickland* in rejecting defendant's ineffective-assistance claim. The dissent disagreed, viewing the state court opinion as arguably rejecting the claim on the ground that no prejudice had been shown. That conclusion could not constitute an "unreasonable application of clearly established law" in light of the Court's prior rulings. "Novelty alone," the dissent noted "is the second, independent reason why the Court's decision is wrong."

IV.

In many—perhaps most—countries of the world, American-style plea bargaining is forbidden in cases as serious as this one, even for the purpose of obtaining testimony that enables conviction of a greater malefactor, much less for the purpose of sparing the expense of trial. In Europe, many countries adhere to what they aptly call the "legality principle" by requiring prosecutors to charge all prosecutable offenses, which is typically incompatible with the practice of charge-bargaining. * * * Such a system reflects an admirable belief that the law is the law, and those who break it should pay the penalty provided.

In the United States, we have plea bargaining a-plenty, but until today it has been regarded as a necessary evil. It presents grave risks of prosecutorial overcharging that effectively compels an innocent defendant to avoid massive risk by pleading guilty to a lesser offense; and for guilty defendants it often—perhaps usually—results in a sentence well below what the law prescribes for the actual crime. But even so, we accept plea bargaining because many believe that without it our long and expensive process of criminal trial could not sustain the burden imposed on it, and our system of criminal justice would grind to a halt.

Today, however, the Supreme Court of the United States elevates plea bargaining from a necessary evil to a constitutional entitlement. It is no longer a somewhat embarrassing adjunct to our criminal justice system; rather, as the Court announces in the companion case to this one, " 'it is the criminal justice system.' " *Frye.* * * * I am less saddened by the outcome of this case than I am by what it says about this Court's attitude toward criminal justice. The Court today embraces the sporting-chance theory of criminal law, in which the State functions like a conscientious casino-operator, giving each player a fair chance to beat the house, that is, to serve less time than the law says he deserves. And when a player is excluded from the tables, his *constitutional rights* have been violated. I do not subscribe to that theory. No one should, least of all the Justices of the Supreme Court.

JUSTICE ALITO dissenting.

For the reasons set out in Parts I and II of Justice Scalia's dissent, the Court's holding in this case misapplies our ineffective-assistance-of-counsel case law and violates the requirements of the Antiterrorism and Effective Death Penalty Act of 1996. Respondent received a trial that was free of any identified constitutional error, and, as a result, there is no basis for concluding that respondent suffered prejudice and certainly not for granting habeas relief.

The weakness in the Court's analysis is highlighted by its opaque discussion of the remedy that is appropriate when a plea offer is rejected due to defective legal representation. If a defendant's Sixth Amendment rights are violated when deficient legal advice about a favorable plea offer causes the opportunity for that bargain to be lost, the only logical remedy is to give the defendant the benefit of the favorable deal. But such a remedy would cause serious injustice in many instances, as I believe the Court tacitly recognizes. The Court therefore eschews the only logical remedy and relies on the lower courts to exercise sound discretion in determining what is to be done.

Time will tell how this works out. The Court, for its part, finds it unnecessary to define "the boundaries of proper discretion" in today's opinion. In my view, requiring the prosecution to renew an old plea offer would represent an abuse of discretion in at least two circumstances: first, when important new information about a defendant's culpability comes to light after the offer is rejected, and, second, when the rejection of the plea offer results in a substantial expenditure of scarce prosecutorial or judicial resources. * * *

WEAVER V. MASSACHUSETTS

582 U.S. ___, 137 S.Ct. 1899, 198 L.Ed.2d 420 (2017).

JUSTICE KENNEDY delivered the opinion of the Court. * * *

I

In 2003, a 15-year-old boy was shot and killed in Boston. A witness saw a young man fleeing the scene of the crime and saw him pull out a pistol. A baseball hat fell off of his head. The police recovered the hat, which featured a distinctive airbrushed Detroit Tigers logo on either side. The hat's distinctive markings linked it to 16-year-old Kentel Weaver. He is the petitioner here. DNA obtained from the hat matched petitioner's DNA. * * * Petitioner was [later] indicted in Massachusetts state court for first-degree murder and the unlicensed possession of a handgun. He pleaded not guilty and proceeded to trial.

The pool of potential jury members was large, some 60 to 100 people. The assigned courtroom could accommodate only 50 or 60 in the courtroom seating. As a result, the trial judge brought all potential jurors into the courtroom so that he could introduce the case and ask certain preliminary questions of the entire venire panel. Many of the potential jurors did not have seats and had to stand in the courtroom. After the preliminary questions, the potential jurors who had been standing were moved outside the courtroom to wait during the individual questioning of the other potential jurors. * * * As all of the seats in the courtroom were occupied by the venire panel, an officer of the court excluded from the courtroom any member of the public who was not a potential juror. So when petitioner's mother and her minister came to the courtroom to observe the two days of jury selection, they were turned away.

All this occurred before the Court's decision in *Presley v. Georgia*, 558 U.S. 209 (2010) (*per curiam*). *Presley* made it clear that the public-trial right extends to jury selection as well as to other portions of the trial. Before *Presley*, Massachusetts courts would often close courtrooms to the public during jury selection, in particular during murder trials. * * * In this case petitioner's mother told defense counsel about the closure at some point during jury selection. But counsel "believed that a courtroom closure for [jury selection] was constitutional." As a result, he "did not discuss the matter" with petitioner, or tell him "that his right to a public trial included the [jury *voir dire*]," or object to the closure.

During the ensuing trial, the government presented strong evidence of petitioner's guilt. Its case consisted of the incriminating details outlined above, including petitioner's confession to the police. The jury convicted petitioner on both counts. The court sentenced him to life in prison on the murder charge. * * * Five years later, petitioner filed a motion for a new trial in Massachusetts state court. As relevant here, he argued that his attorney had provided ineffective assistance by failing to object to the courtroom closure. After an evidentiary hearing, the trial court recognized a violation of the right to a public trial based on the following findings: The courtroom had been closed; the closure was neither *de minimis* nor trivial; the closure was unjustified; and the closure was full rather than partial (meaning that all members of the public, rather than only some of them, had been excluded from the courtroom). The trial court further determined that defense counsel failed to object because of "serious incompetency, inefficiency, or inattention." On the other hand, petitioner had not "offered any evidence or legal argument establishing prejudice." For that reason, the court held that petitioner was not entitled to relief.

Petitioner appealed the denial of the motion for a new trial to the Massachusetts Supreme Judicial Court. The court consolidated that appeal with petitioner's direct appeal. As noted, there had been no objection to the closure at trial; and the issue was not raised in the direct appeal. The Supreme Judicial Court then affirmed in relevant part. Although it recognized that "[a] violation of the Sixth Amendment right to a public trial constitutes structural error," the court stated that petitioner had "failed to show that trial counsel's conduct caused prejudice warranting a new trial." * * * There is disagreement among the Federal Courts of Appeals and some state courts of last resort about whether a defendant must demonstrate prejudice in a case like this one—in which a structural error is neither preserved nor raised on direct review but is raised later via a claim alleging ineffective assistance of counsel. * * * This Court granted certiorari to resolve that disagreement. The Court does so specifically and only in the context of trial counsel's failure to object to the closure of the courtroom during jury selection.

II

This case requires a discussion, and the proper application, of two doctrines: structural error and ineffective assistance of counsel. The two doctrines are intertwined; for the reasons an error is deemed structural may influence the proper standard used to evaluate an ineffective-assistance claim premised on the failure to object to that error.

The concept of structural error can be discussed first. In *Chapman v. California* (1967) [fn. d, p. 695], this Court "adopted the general rule that a constitutional error does not automatically require reversal of a conviction." If the government can show "beyond a reasonable doubt that the error complained of did not contribute to the verdict obtained," the Court held, then the error is deemed harmless and the defendant is not entitled to reversal. The Court recognized, however, that some errors should not be deemed harmless beyond a reasonable doubt. These errors came to be known as structural errors. The purpose of the structural error doctrine is to ensure insistence on certain basic, constitutional guarantees that should define the framework of any criminal trial. Thus, the defining feature of a structural error is that it "affect[s] the framework within which the trial proceeds," rather than being "simply an error in the trial process itself." For the same reason, a structural error "def[ies] analysis by harmless error standards." *Arizona v. Fulminante,* 499 U.S. 279 (1991). The precise reason why a particular error is not amenable to that kind of analysis—and thus the precise reason why the Court has deemed it structural—varies in a significant way from error to error. There appear to be at least three broad rationales.

First, an error has been deemed structural in some instances if the right at issue is not designed to protect the defendant from erroneous conviction but instead protects some other interest. This is true of the defendant's right to conduct his own defense, which, when exercised, "usually increases the likelihood of a trial outcome unfavorable to the defendant." *McKaskle v. Wiggins,* [fn. d, p. 1014]. That right is based on the fundamental legal principle that a defendant must be allowed to make his own choices about the proper way to protect his own liberty. See *Faretta v. California,* 422 U.S. 806 (1975). Because harm is irrelevant to the basis underlying the right, the Court has deemed a violation of that right structural error. See *United States v. Gonzalez-Lopez* [fn. a, p. 992].

Second, an error has been deemed structural if the effects of the error are simply too hard to measure. For example, when a defendant is denied the right to select his or her own attorney, the precise "effect of the violation cannot be ascertained." *Gonzalez-Lopez,* supra. Because the government will, as a result, find it almost impossible to show that the error was "harmless beyond a reasonable doubt," *Chapman,* at 24, the efficiency costs of letting the government try to make the showing are unjustified.

Third, an error has been deemed structural if the error always results in fundamental unfairness. For example, if an indigent defendant is denied an attorney or if the judge fails to give a reasonable-doubt instruction, the resulting trial is always a fundamentally unfair one. * * * It therefore would be futile for the government to try to show harmlessness.

These categories are not rigid. In a particular case, more than one of these rationales may be part of the explanation for why an error is deemed to be structural. For these purposes, however, one point is critical: An error can count as structural even if the error does not lead to fundamental unfairness in every case. See *Gonzalez-Lopez,* supra (rejecting as "inconsistent with the reasoning of our precedents" the idea that structural errors "always or necessarily render a trial fundamentally unfair and unreliable").

As noted above, a violation of the right to a public trial is a structural error. It is relevant to determine why that is so. In particular, the question is whether a public-trial violation counts as structural because it always leads to fundamental unfairness or for some other reason. * * * [*Waller v. Georgia* (p. 908) and *Pressley,* supra, address the scope of the public trial guarantee.] These opinions teach that courtroom closure is to be avoided, but that there are some circumstances when it is justified. The problems that may be encountered by trial courts in deciding whether some closures are necessary, or even in deciding which members of the public should be admitted when seats are scarce, are difficult ones. For example, there are often preliminary instructions that a judge may want to give to the venire as a whole, rather than repeating those instructions (perhaps with unintentional differences) to several groups of potential jurors. On the other hand, various constituencies of the public—the family of the accused, the family of the victim, members of the press, and other persons—all have their own interests in observing the selection of jurors. How best to manage these problems is not a topic discussed at length in any decision or commentary the Court has found.

So although the public-trial right is structural, it is subject to exceptions. * * * Though these cases [of justified closure] should be rare, a judge may deprive a defendant of his right to an open courtroom by making proper factual findings in support of the decision to do so. The fact that the public-trial right is subject to these exceptions suggests that not every public-trial violation results in fundamental unfairness.

A public-trial violation can occur, moreover, as it did in *Presley,* simply because the trial court omits to make the proper findings before closing the courtroom, even if those findings might have been fully supported by the evidence. It would be unconvincing to deem a trial fundamentally unfair just because a judge omitted to announce factual findings before making an otherwise valid decision to order the courtroom temporarily closed. As a result, it would be likewise unconvincing if the Court had said that a public-trial violation always leads to a fundamentally unfair trial. Indeed * * * in the two cases in which the Court has discussed the reasons for classifying a public-trial violation as structural error, the Court has said that a public-trial violation is structural for a different reason: because of the "difficulty of assessing the effect of the error." *Gonzalez-Lopez,* supra at n. 4; see also *Waller,* supra at n. 9.

The public-trial right also protects some interests that do not belong to the defendant. After all, the right to an open courtroom protects the rights of the public at large, and the press, as well as the rights of the accused. * * * *Press-Enterprise II* [p. 907]. So one other factor leading to the classification of structural error is that the public-trial right furthers interests other than protecting the defendant against unjust conviction. These precepts confirm the conclusion the Court now reaches that, while the public-trial right is important for fundamental reasons, in some cases an unlawful closure might take place and yet the trial still will be fundamentally fair from the defendant's standpoint.

III

The Court now turns to the proper remedy for addressing the violation of a structural right, and in particular the right to a public trial. Despite its name, the term "structural error" carries with it no talismanic significance as a doctrinal matter. It means only that the government is not entitled to deprive the defendant of a new trial by showing that the error was "harmless beyond a reasonable doubt." *Chapman.* Thus, in the case of a structural error where there is an objection at trial and the issue is raised on direct appeal, the defendant generally is entitled to "automatic reversal" regardless of the error's actual "effect on the outcome." *Neder v. United States,* 527 U.S. 1 (1999). * * * The question then becomes what showing is necessary when the defendant does not preserve a structural error on direct review but raises it later in the context of an ineffective-assistance-of-counsel claim. To obtain relief on the basis of ineffective assistance of counsel, the defendant as a general rule bears the burden to meet two standards: * * * deficient performance * * * [and] prejudice. *Strickland.*

The prejudice showing is in most cases a necessary part of a *Strickland* claim. * * * That said, the concept of prejudice is defined in different ways depending on the context in which it appears. In the ordinary *Strickland* case, prejudice means "a reasonable probability that, but for counsel's unprofessional errors, the result of the proceeding would have been different." But the *Strickland* Court cautioned that the prejudice inquiry is not meant to be applied in a "mechanical" fashion. *Strickland* at [p. 937]. For when a court is evaluating an ineffective-assistance claim, the ultimate inquiry must concentrate on "the fundamental fairness of the proceeding." Ibid. Petitioner therefore argues that under a proper interpretation of *Strickland,* even if there is no showing of a reasonable probability of a different outcome, relief still must be granted if the convicted person shows that attorney errors rendered the trial fundamentally unfair. For the analytical purposes of this case, the Court will assume that petitioner's interpretation of *Strickland* is the correct one. In light of the Court's ultimate holding, however, the Court need not decide that question here.

As explained above, not every public-trial violation will in fact lead to a fundamentally unfair trial. Nor can it be said that the failure to object to a public-trial violation always deprives the defendant of a reasonable probability of a different outcome. Thus, when a defendant raises a public-trial violation via an ineffective-assistance-of-counsel claim, *Strickland* prejudice is not shown automatically. Instead, the burden is on the defendant to show either a reasonable probability of a different outcome in his or her case or, as the Court has assumed for these purposes, to show that the particular public-trial violation was so serious as to render his or her trial fundamentally unfair.

Neither the reasoning nor the holding here calls into question the Court's precedents determining that certain errors are deemed structural and require reversal because they cause fundamental unfairness, either to the defendant in the specific case or by pervasive undermining of the systemic requirements of a fair and open judicial process. See Murray, A Contextual Approach to Harmless Error Review, 130 Harv. L.Rev. 1791, 1813, 1822 (2017) (noting that the "eclectic normative objectives of criminal procedure" go beyond protecting a defendant from erroneous conviction and include ensuring " 'that the administration of justice should reasonably appear to be disinterested' "). Those precedents include *Sullivan v. Louisiana,* 508 U.S. 275 (1993) (failure to give a reasonable-doubt instruction); *Tumey v. Ohio,* 273 U.S. 510 (1927) (biased judge); and *Vasquez v. Hillery,* 474 U.S. 254 (1986) (exclusion of grand jurors on the basis of race). This Court, in addition, has granted automatic relief to defendants who prevailed on claims alleging race or gender discrimination in the selection of the petit jury, see *Batson v. Kentucky* [p. 828], * * * though the Court has yet to label those errors structural in express terms. * * * The errors in those cases necessitated automatic reversal after they were preserved and then raised on direct appeal. And this opinion does not address whether the result should be any different if the errors were raised instead in an ineffective-assistance claim on collateral review.

The reason for placing the burden on the petitioner in this case, however, derives both from the nature of the error and the difference between a public-trial violation preserved and then raised on direct review and a public-trial violation raised as an ineffective-assistance-of-counsel claim. As explained above, when a defendant objects to a courtroom closure, the trial court can either order the courtroom opened or explain the reasons for keeping it closed. When a defendant first raises the closure in an ineffective-assistance claim, however, the trial court is deprived of the chance to cure the violation either by opening the courtroom or by explaining the reasons for closure.

Furthermore, when state or federal courts adjudicate errors objected to during trial and then raised on direct review, the systemic costs of remedying the error are diminished to some extent. That is because, if a new trial is ordered on direct review, there may be a reasonable chance that not too much time will have elapsed for witness memories still to be accurate and physical evidence not to be lost. There are also advantages of direct judicial supervision. Reviewing courts, in the regular course of the appellate process, can give instruction to the trial courts in a familiar context that allows for elaboration of the relevant principles based on review of an adequate record. For instance, in this case, the factors and circumstances that might justify a temporary closure are best considered in the regular appellate process and not in the context of a later proceeding, with its added time delays.

When an ineffective-assistance-of-counsel claim is raised in postconviction proceedings, the costs and uncertainties of a new trial are greater because more time will have elapsed in most cases. The finality interest is more at risk, see *Strickland* [p. 936] (noting the "profound importance of finality in criminal proceedings"), and direct review often has given at least one opportunity for an appellate review of trial proceedings. These differences justify a different standard for evaluating a structural error depending on whether it is raised on direct review or raised instead in a claim alleging ineffective assistance of counsel. * * * In sum, "[a]n ineffective-assistance claim can function as a way to escape rules of waiver and forfeiture and raise issues not presented at trial," thus undermining the finality of jury verdicts. *Harrington v. Richter* [p. 945]. For this reason, the rules governing ineffective assistance claims "must be applied with scrupulous care."

IV

The final inquiry concerns the ineffective-assistance claim in this case. Although the case comes on the assumption that petitioner has shown deficient performance by counsel, he has not shown prejudice in the ordinary sense, *i.e.*, a reasonable probability that the jury would not have convicted him if his attorney had objected to the closure. * * * It is of course possible that potential jurors might have behaved differently if petitioner's family had been present. And it is true that the presence of the public might have had some bearing on juror reaction. But here petitioner offered no "evidence or legal argument establishing prejudice" in the sense of a reasonable probability of a different outcome but for counsel's failure to object. * * * In other circumstances a different result might obtain. If, for instance, defense counsel errs in failing to object when the government's main witness testifies in secret, then the defendant might be able to show prejudice with little more detail. Even in those circumstances, however, the burden would remain on the defendant to make the prejudice showing, because a public-trial violation does not always lead to a fundamentally unfair trial.

In light of the above assumption that prejudice can be shown by a demonstration of fundamental unfairness, the remaining question is whether petitioner has shown that counsel's failure to object rendered the trial fundamentally unfair. The Court concludes that petitioner has not made the showing. Although petitioner's mother and her minister were indeed excluded from the courtroom for two days during jury selection, petitioner's trial was not conducted in secret or in a remote place. * * * The closure was limited to the jury *voir dire*; the courtroom remained open during the evidentiary phase of the trial; the closure decision apparently was made by court officers rather than the judge; there were many members of the venire who did not become jurors but who did observe the proceedings; and there was a record made of the proceedings that does not indicate any basis for concern, other than the closure itself.

There has been no showing, furthermore, that the potential harms flowing from a courtroom closure came to pass in this case. For example, there is no suggestion that any juror lied during *voir dire*; no suggestion of misbehavior by the prosecutor, judge, or any other party; and no suggestion that any of the participants failed to approach their duties with the neutrality and serious purpose that our system demands.

    * * *

In the criminal justice system, the constant, indeed unending, duty of the judiciary is to seek and to find the proper balance between the necessity for fair and just trials and the importance of finality of judgments. When a structural error is preserved and raised on direct review, the balance is in the defendant's favor, and a new trial generally will be granted as a matter of right. When a structural error is raised in the context of an ineffective-assistance claim, however, finality concerns are far more pronounced. For this reason, and in light of the other circumstances present in this case, petitioner must show prejudice in order to obtain a new trial.

JUSTICE THOMAS, with whom JUSTICE GORSUCH joins, concurring.

I write separately with two observations about the scope of the Court's holding. First, this case comes to us on the parties' "assumption[s]" that the closure of the courtroom during jury selection "was a Sixth Amendment violation" and that "defense counsel provided ineffective assistance" by "failing to object" to it. The Court previously held in a *per curiam* opinion—issued without the benefit of merits briefing or argument—that the Sixth Amendment right to a public trial extends to jury selection. See *Presley v. Georgia* (Thomas, J., dissenting). I have some doubts about whether that holding is consistent with the original understanding of the right to a public trial, and I would be open to reconsidering it in a case in which we are asked to do so.

Second, the Court "assume[s]," for the "analytical purposes of this case," that a defendant may establish prejudice under *Strickland* by demonstrating that his attorney's error led to a fundamentally unfair trial. * * * *Strickland* did not hold, as the Court assumes, that a defendant may establish prejudice by showing that his counsel's errors "rendered the trial fundamentally unfair." Because the Court concludes that the closure during petitioner's jury selection did not lead to fundamental unfairness in any event, no part of the discussion about fundamental unfairness is necessary to its result.

In light of these observations, I do not read the opinion of the Court to preclude the approach set forth in Justice Alito's opinion, which correctly applies our precedents.

JUSTICE ALITO, with whom JUSTICE GORSUCH joins, concurring in the judgment.

This case calls for a straightforward application of the familiar standard for evaluating ineffective assistance of counsel claims. *Strickland v. Washington.* * * * The [*Strickland*] prejudice requirement—which is the one at issue in this case— "arises from the very nature" of the right to effective representation: Counsel simply "cannot be 'ineffective' unless his mistakes have harmed the defense (or, at least, unless it is reasonably likely that they have)," *Gonzalez-Lopez.* In other words, "a violation of the Sixth Amendment right to *effective* representation is not 'complete' until the defendant is prejudiced." Ibid. * * *

Weaver makes much of the *Strickland* Court's statement that "the ultimate focus of inquiry must be on the fundamental fairness of the proceeding." *Strickland* [p. 937]. But the very next sentence clarifies what the Court had in mind, namely, the reliability of the proceeding. In that sentence, the Court explains that the proper concern—"[i]n every case"—is "whether, despite the strong presumption of reliability, the result of the particular proceeding is unreliable." Ibid. In other words, the focus on reliability is consistent throughout the *Strickland* opinion. * * * [T]here are two ways of meeting the *Strickland* prejudice requirement. A defendant must demonstrate either that the error at issue was prejudicial or that it belongs to the narrow class of attorney errors that are tantamount to a denial of counsel, for which an individualized showing of prejudice is unnecessary [*Cronic,* p. 969].

Weaver attempts to escape this framework by stressing that the deprivation of the right to a public trial has been described as a "structural" error, but this is irrelevant under *Strickland*. The concept of "structural error" comes into play when it is established that an error occurred at the trial level and it must be decided whether the error was harmless. * * * The prejudice prong of *Strickland* is entirely different. It does not ask whether an error was harmless but whether there was an error at all, for unless counsel's deficient performance prejudiced the defense, there was no Sixth Amendment violation in the first place. See *Gonzalez-Lopez* (even where an attorney's deficient performance "pervades the entire trial," "we do not allow reversal of a conviction for that reason without a showing of prejudice" because "the requirement of showing prejudice in ineffectiveness claims stems from the very definition of the right at issue"). Weaver's theory conflicts with *Strickland* because it implies that an attorney's error can be prejudicial even if it "had no effect," or only "some conceivable effect," on the outcome of his trial. That is precisely what *Strickland* rules out. * * *

JUSTICE BREYER, with whom JUSTICE KAGAN joins, dissenting.

The Court notes that *Strickland*'s "prejudice inquiry is not meant to be applied in a 'mechanical' fashion," and I agree. But, in my view, it follows from this principle that a defendant who shows that his attorney's constitutionally deficient performance produced a structural error should not face the additional—and often insurmountable—*Strickland* hurdle of demonstrating that the error changed the outcome of his proceeding. * * *

The Court has recognized that structural errors' distinctive attributes make them "defy analysis by 'harmless-error' standards." It has therefore *categorically* exempted structural errors from the case-by-case harmlessness review to which trial errors are subjected. Our precedent does not try to parse which structural errors are the truly egregious ones. It simply views *all* structural errors as "intrinsically harmful" and holds that *any* structural error warrants "automatic reversal" on direct appeal "without regard to [its] effect on the outcome" of a trial. *Neder v. United States.*

The majority here does not take this approach. It assumes that *some* structural errors—those that "lead to fundamental unfairness"—but not others, can warrant relief without a showing of actual prejudice under *Strickland.* While I agree that a showing of fundamental unfairness is sufficient to satisfy *Strickland,* I would not try to draw this distinction. * * * Even if some structural errors do not create fundamental unfairness, *all* structural errors nonetheless have features that make them "defy analysis by 'harmless-error' standards." *Fulminante.* This is why *all* structural errors—not just the "fundamental unfairness" ones—are exempt from harmlessness inquiry and warrant automatic reversal on direct review. Those same features mean that *all* structural errors defy an actual-prejudice analysis under *Strickland.*

For instance, the majority concludes that some errors—such as the public-trial error at issue in this case—have been labeled "structural" because they have effects that "are simply too hard to measure." * * * But how could any error whose effects are inherently indeterminate prove susceptible to actual-prejudice analysis under *Strickland?* Just as the "difficulty of assessing the effect" of such an error would turn harmless-error analysis into "a speculative inquiry into what might have occurred in an alternate universe," *Gonzalez-Lopez,* so too would it undermine a defendant's ability to make an actual-prejudice showing to establish an ineffective-assistance claim.

The problem is evident with regard to public-trial violations. This Court has recognized that "the benefits of a public trial are frequently intangible, difficult to prove, or a matter of chance." *Waller v. Georgia.* As a result, "a requirement that prejudice be shown 'would in most cases deprive [the defendant] of the [public-trial] guarantee, for it would be difficult to envisage a case in which he would have evidence available of specific injury.'" Ibid. In order to establish actual prejudice from an attorney's failure to object to a public-trial violation, a defendant would face the nearly impossible burden of establishing how his trial might have gone differently had it been open to the public.

I do not see how we can read *Strickland* as requiring defendants to prove what this Court has held cannot be proved. If courts do not presume prejudice when counsel's deficient performance leads to a structural error, then defendants may well be unable to obtain relief for incompetence that deprived them "of basic protections without which a criminal trial cannot reliably serve its function as a vehicle for determination n of guilt or innocence." *Neder*. This would be precisely the sort of "mechanical" application that *Strickland* tells us to avoid. * * *

3. COUNSEL CONFLICTS OF INTERESTS

As the *Strickland* Court notes, "in certain Sixth Amendment contexts, prejudice is presumed" [p. 935]. *United States v. Cronic*, 466 U.S. 648 (1984), cited in this connection, provides a more complete description of these instances of "*per se* Sixth Amendment violations.*" At issue in Cronic, which was decided the same day as *Strickland,* was a lower court ruling that found a Sixth Amendment violation without examining the actual performance of defense counsel. The lower court had held that a combination of circumstances required the inference that counsel would have been unable to provide the effective assistance required by the Sixth Amendment. Those circumstances were: (1) the limited time afforded counsel for investigation and preparation; (2) counsel's inexperience; (3) the gravity of the charge; (4) the complexity of possible defenses; and (5) the inaccessibility of witnesses to counsel. Rejecting the lower court's "inherent ineffectiveness" rationale, the *Cronic* Court stressed that the underlying function of the Sixth Amendment required an analysis of whether there had been an "actual breakdown of the adversary process" due to counsel's deficient performance. The five factors cited by the lower court, though of obvious relevance "in the evaluation of a lawyer's ineffectiveness in a particular case," were not sufficient to establish inherent ineffectiveness. The Court acknowledged that it had recognized in the past certain special settings in which a presumption of prejudicial defective performance had been adopted, but it refused to expand upon those situations.

In a discussion that was partially repeated in *Strickland* (see p. 935), *Cronic* identified three settings in which the Court previously has been willing to presume a breakdown in the adversary process. First, there was the situation in which "counsel was either totally absent or prevented from assisting the accused during a critical stage of the proceeding." Falling in this category were cases in which the trial court had unconstitutionally refused to appoint counsel or had restricted counsel's assistance.[a] The second situation was that on which counsel was physically present, but completely absent in effort. As the Court put it, "if counsel entirely fails to subject the prosecution's case to meaningful adversarial testing, then there has been a denial of Sixth Amendment rights that makes the adversary

---

[a] The cases in the latter category have been described as the "state interference cases." The leading interference cases, *Geders v. United States*, etc., are described in *Strickland* (see p. 932).

process itself presumptively unreliable."[b] Finally, there were "occasions when, although counsel is available to assist the accused during trial, the likelihood that any lawyer, even a fully competent one, could provide effective assistance is so small that a presumption of prejudice is appropriate without inquiry into the actual conduct of the trial." *Cronic* described *Powell v. Alabama* [p. 373] as such a case. The trial court there had ordered newly arrived out-of-state counsel to proceed immediately to trial, with whatever help the local bar (appointed *en masse*) might provide, even though that counsel had stated that he had no opportunity to prepare and was not familiar with local procedure.

Both *Strickland* and *Cronic* acknowledged still another line of cases that established an exception to Strickland, the conflict-of-interest cases. A potential conflict typically arises where defense counsel owes an obligation to a person other than the defendant that could favor action or inaction adverse to the interests of the defendant.[c] The possible application of what *Strickland* described as "more limited presumption of prejudice" [p. 935] arises on judicial review after conviction where the defense argues (often for the first time[d]) that defense counsel was subject to a conflict of interest. The first case in this section, *Mickens v. Taylor*, presents the leading Supreme Court discussion of this presumption. Mickens also includes the leading discussion of (1) the limited constitutional obligation of the trial court to inquire into the possibility of a conflict on its own initiative, and (2) the constitutionally required response of the trial court to a defense counsel's motion to withdraw which alleges a conflict of interest.

The second case in this section, *United States v. Wheat*, also relates to alleged conflicts of interest and the response of the trial court. Here, however, the issue before the Supreme Court is not what the trial constitutionally must do to protect

---

    b   *Bell v. Cone*, 535 U.S. 685 (2002), later held that this situation is presented only where counsel's "failure is complete," and not where the counsel simply failed to take particular steps (important though they might well be) in challenging the prosecution's case. Thus, the federal habeas court had erred in presuming prejudice as to a capital sentencing proceeding because counsel failed to introduce mitigating evidence and waived closing argument. Since counsel had challenged the state's case in other respects (including bringing out favorable evidence on cross-examination of the state's witness and calling the jury's attention in an opening statement to mitigating evidence that had been introduced as part of an insanity defense), the allegations as to not presenting mitigating evidence and waiving closing argument constituted no more than claims of "specific attorney error," which were "subject to *Strickland*'s [standards]."

    c   While conflicts most often arise from an obligation of loyalty owed to a past or current client of the defense counsel, a conflict can also exist because the attorney has a self-interest that could lead to action or inaction adverse to the client. That self-interest will often be economic (as where the attorney's fee is being paid by a person other than the defendant and that person's objectives may diverge from the defendant's interests), but it can also be personal (as where the defense counsel was involved in the same transaction as the defendant and has an interest in not revealing that participation).

    d   As noted in the § 1 Introduction, the conflict issue will sometimes have been raised prior to trial by a defendant's challenge to counsel, a defense counsel motion to withdraw, a prosecution motion to disqualify, or a court-initiated inquiry under a provision like Fed.R.Crim.P. 44 (discussed in *Mickens*). Here the appellate court will be reviewing what the defense characterizes as an inadequate pretrial response (the trial court having failed to disqualify counsel). More often, the issue will not have been raised before the trial court and will not be raised on appeal (either because the trial counsel is also the appellate counsel or because the character of the conflict and attorney's response thereto is not fully developed in the trial record). Here, as in the case of *Strickland* claims, the challenge typically will be brought in a postconviction collateral challenge. See fn. b, p. 924.

the defendant's Sixth Amendment right to effective assistance, but the limits on what the trial court may do. The pretrial objection to the conflict in *Wheat* is presented by the prosecution, and the defense opposes the relief proposed by the prosecution, disqualifying defendant's proposed counsel.[e] The constitutional issue here is whether that disqualification violated the defendant's Sixth Amendment right to counsel of his own choosing. That issue arises not only where the prosecution seeks disqualification, as in *Wheat*, but also when the trial court considers disqualification after conducting an inquiry on its own initiative, as discussed in *Mickens*.

MICKENS V. TAYLOR
535 U.S. 162, 122 S.Ct. 1237, 152 L.Ed.2d 291 (2002).

JUSTICE SCALIA delivered the opinion of the Court.

The question presented in this case is what a defendant must show in order to demonstrate a Sixth Amendment violation where the trial court fails to inquire into a potential conflict of interest about which it knew or reasonably should have known.

I

In 1993, a Virginia jury convicted petitioner Mickens of the premeditated murder of Timothy Hall during or following the commission of an attempted forcible sodomy. Finding the murder outrageously and wantonly vile, it sentenced petitioner to death. In June 1998, Mickens filed a petition for writ of habeas corpus, in the United States District Court * * * alleging, *inter alia,* that he was denied effective assistance of counsel because one of his court-appointed attorneys had a conflict of interest at trial. Federal habeas counsel had discovered that petitioner's lead trial attorney, Bryan Saunders, was representing Hall (the victim) on assault and concealed-weapons charges at the time of the murder. Saunders had been appointed to represent Hall, a juvenile, on March 20, 1992, and had met with him once for 15 to 30 minutes some time the following week. Hall's body was discovered on March 30, 1992, and four days later a juvenile court judge dismissed the charges against him, noting on the docket sheet that Hall was deceased. The one-page docket sheet also listed Saunders as Hall's counsel. On April 6, 1992, the same judge appointed Saunders to represent petitioner. Saunders did not disclose to the court, his co-counsel, or petitioner that he had previously represented Hall. Under Virginia law, juvenile case files are confidential and may not generally be disclosed without a court order, but petitioner learned about Saunders' prior representation when a clerk mistakenly produced Hall's file to federal habeas counsel.

The District Court held an evidentiary hearing and denied petitioner's habeas petition. A divided panel of the Court of Appeals for the Fourth Circuit reversed, and the Court of Appeals granted rehearing en banc. * * * [T]he 7–3 en banc majority assumed that the juvenile court judge had neglected a duty to inquire into

---

[e]   Where an actual conflict exists and the defendant requests replacement of counsel, state and federal law generally requires that the trial court discharge counsel. Replacement is also required under other circumstances, as discussed in fn. a, p. 923.

a potential conflict, but rejected petitioner's argument that this failure either mandated automatic reversal of his conviction or relieved him of the burden of showing that a conflict of interest adversely affected his representation. Relying on *Cuyler v. Sullivan,* 446 U.S. 335 (1980), the court held that a defendant must show "both an actual conflict of interest and an adverse effect even if the trial court failed to inquire into a potential conflict about which it reasonably should have known." Concluding that petitioner had not demonstrated adverse effect, it affirmed the District Court's denial of habeas relief.

II

* * * As a general matter, a defendant alleging a Sixth Amendment violation must demonstrate "a reasonable probability that, but for counsel's unprofessional errors, the result of the proceeding would have been different." *Strickland v. Washington.* There is an exception to this general rule. We have spared the defendant the need of showing probable effect upon the outcome, and have simply presumed such effect, where assistance of counsel has been denied entirely or during a critical stage of the proceeding. When that has occurred, the likelihood that the verdict is unreliable is so high that a case-by-case inquiry is unnecessary. See *United States v. Cronic.* But only in "circumstances of that magnitude" do we forgo individual inquiry into whether counsel's inadequate performance undermined the reliability of the verdict. *Cronic.*

We have held in several cases that "circumstances of that magnitude" may also arise when the defendant's attorney actively represented conflicting interests. The nub of the question before us is whether the principle established by these cases provides an exception to the general rule of *Strickland* under the circumstances of the present case. To answer that question, we must examine those cases in some detail.[1]

In *Holloway v. Arkansas,* 435 U.S. 475 (1978), defense counsel had objected that he could not adequately represent the divergent interests of three codefendants. Without inquiry, the trial court had denied counsel's motions for the appointment of separate counsel and had refused to allow counsel to cross-examine any of the defendants on behalf of the other two. The *Holloway* Court deferred to the judgment of counsel regarding the existence of a disabling conflict, recognizing

---

[1] Justice Breyer rejects [these cases], *Holloway v. Arkansas, Cuyler v. Sullivan,* and *Wood v. Georgia,* as a "a sensible [and] coherent framework for dealing with" this case, and proposes instead the "categorical rule" that when a "breakdown in the criminal justice system creates . . . the appearance that the proceeding will not reliably serve its function as a vehicle for determination of guilt and innocence, and the resulting criminal punishment will not be regarded as fundamentally fair," reversal must be decreed without proof of prejudice. This seems to us less a categorical rule of decision than a restatement of the issue to be decided. *Holloway, Sullivan,* and *Wood* establish the framework that they do precisely because that framework is thought to identify the situations in which the conviction will reasonably not be regarded as fundamentally fair. We believe it eminently performs that function in the case at hand, and that Justice Breyer is mistaken to think otherwise. But if he does think otherwise, a proper regard for the judicial function—and especially for the function of this Court, which must lay down rules that can be followed in the innumerable cases we are unable to review—would counsel that he propose some other "sensible and coherent framework," rather than merely saying that prior representation of the victim, plus the capital nature of the case, plus judicial appointment of the counsel, strikes him as producing a result that will not be regarded as fundamentally fair. This is not a rule of law but expression of an ad hoc "fairness" judgment (with which we disagree).

that a defense attorney is in the best position to determine when a conflict exists, that he has an ethical obligation to advise the court of any problem, and that his declarations to the court are "virtually made under oath." *Holloway* presumed, moreover, that the conflict, "which [the defendant] and his counsel tried to avoid by timely objections to the joint representation," undermined the adversarial process. The presumption was justified because joint representation of conflicting interests is inherently suspect, and because counsel's conflicting obligations to multiple defendants "effectively sea[l] his lips on crucial matters" and make it difficult to measure the precise harm arising from counsel's errors. *Holloway* thus creates an automatic reversal rule only where defense counsel is forced to represent codefendants over his timely objection, unless the trial court has determined that there is no conflict. * * *

In *Cuyler v. Sullivan*, supra, the respondent was one of three defendants accused of murder who were tried separately, represented by the same counsel. Neither counsel nor anyone else objected to the multiple representation, and counsel's opening argument at Sullivan's trial suggested that the interests of the defendants were aligned. We declined to extend Holloway's automatic reversal rule to this situation and held that, absent objection, a defendant must demonstrate that "a conflict of interest actually affected the adequacy of his representation." In addition to describing the defendant's burden of proof, *Sullivan* addressed separately a trial court's duty to inquire into the propriety of a multiple representation, construing *Holloway* to require inquiry only when "the trial court knows or reasonably should know that a particular conflict exists," *Sullivan*, fn. 2[2]—which is not to be confused with when the trial court is aware of a vague, unspecified possibility of conflict, such as that which "inheres in almost every instance of multiple representation." In *Sullivan,* no "special circumstances" triggered the trial court's duty to inquire.

Finally, in *Wood v. Georgia*, 450 U.S. 261 (1981), three indigent defendants convicted of distributing obscene materials had their probation revoked for failure to make the requisite $500 monthly payments on their $5,000 fines. We granted certiorari to consider whether this violated the Equal Protection Clause, but during the course of our consideration certain disturbing circumstances came to our attention: at the probation-revocation hearing (as at all times since their arrest) the defendants had been represented by the lawyer for their employer (the owner of the business that purveyed the obscenity), and their employer paid the attorney's fees. The employer had promised his employees he would pay their fines, and had generally kept that promise but had not done so in these defendants' case. This record suggested that the employer's interest in establishing a favorable equal-protection precedent (reducing the fines he would have to pay for his indigent

---

[2] In order to circumvent *Sullivan's* clear language, Justice Stevens suggests that a trial court must scrutinize representation by appointed counsel more closely than representation by retained counsel. But we have already rejected the notion that the Sixth Amendment draws such a distinction. "A proper respect for the Sixth Amendment disarms [the] contention that defendants who retain their own lawyers are entitled to less protection than defendants for whom the State appoints counsel. . . . The vital guarantee of the Sixth Amendment would stand for little if the often uninformed decision to retain a particular lawyer could reduce or forfeit the defendant's entitlement to constitutional protection." *Cuyler v. Sullivan.*

employees in the future) diverged from the defendants' interest in obtaining leniency or paying lesser fines to avoid imprisonment. Moreover, the possibility that counsel was actively representing the conflicting interests of employer and defendants "was sufficiently apparent at the time of the revocation hearing to impose upon the court a duty to inquire further." Because "[o]n the record before us, we [could not] be sure whether counsel was influenced in his basic strategic decisions by the interests of the employer who hired him," we remanded for the trial court "to determine whether the conflict of interest that this record strongly suggests actually existed."

Petitioner argues that the remand instruction in *Wood* established an "unambiguous rule" that where the trial judge neglects a duty to inquire into a potential conflict, the defendant, to obtain reversal of the judgment, need only show that his lawyer was subject to a conflict of interest, and need not show that the conflict adversely affected counsel's performance.[3] He relies upon the language in the remand instruction directing the trial court to grant a new revocation hearing if it determines that "an actual conflict of interest existed," without requiring a further determination that the conflict adversely affected counsel's performance. As used in the remand instruction, however, we think "an actual conflict of interest" meant precisely a conflict *that affected counsel's performance*—as opposed to a mere theoretical division of loyalties. It was shorthand for the statement in *Sullivan* that "a defendant who shows that a conflict of interest *actually affected the adequacy of his representation* need not demonstrate prejudice in order to obtain relief." (emphasis added). This is the only interpretation consistent with the *Wood* Court's earlier description of why it could not decide the case without a remand: "On the record before us, we cannot be sure whether counsel *was influenced in his basic strategic decisions* by the interests of the employer who hired him. *If this was the case*, the due process rights of petitioners were not respected. . . ." (emphasis added). The notion that *Wood* created a new rule *sub silentio*—and in a case where certiorari had been granted on an entirely different question, and the parties had neither briefed nor argued the conflict-of-interest issue—is implausible.

---

[3]   Petitioner no longer argues, as he did below and as Justice Souter does now, that the Sixth Amendment requires reversal of his conviction without further inquiry into whether the potential conflict that the judge should have investigated was real. * * *

Justice Souter labors to suggest that the *Wood* remand order is part of "a coherent scheme," in which automatic reversal is required when the trial judge fails to inquire into a potential conflict that was apparent before the proceeding was "held or completed," but a defendant must demonstrate adverse effect when the judge fails to inquire into a conflict that was not apparent before the end of the proceeding. The problem with this carefully concealed "coherent scheme" (no case has ever mentioned it) is that in *Wood* itself the court did not decree automatic reversal, even though it found that "the *possibility* of a conflict of interest was sufficiently apparent *at the time of* the revocation hearing to impose upon the court a duty to inquire further" (second emphasis added). Indeed, the State had actually notified the judge of a potential conflict of interest " '[d]uring the probation revocation hearing.' " Justice Souter's statement that "the signs that a conflict may have occurred were clear to the judge at the close of the probation revocation proceeding"—when it became apparent that counsel had neglected the "strategy more obviously in the defendants' interest, of requesting the court to reduce the fines or defer their collection"—would more accurately be phrased "the *effect of the conflict upon counsel's performance* was clear to the judge at the close of the probation revocation proceeding."

Petitioner's proposed rule of automatic reversal when there existed a conflict that did not affect counsel's performance, but the trial judge failed to make the *Sullivan*-mandated inquiry, makes little policy sense. As discussed, the rule applied when the trial judge is not aware of the conflict (and thus not obligated to inquire) is that prejudice will be presumed only if the conflict has significantly affected counsel's performance—thereby rendering the verdict unreliable, even though *Strickland* prejudice cannot be shown. The trial court's awareness of a potential conflict neither renders it more likely that counsel's performance was significantly affected nor in any other way renders the verdict unreliable. Nor does the trial judge's failure to make the *Sullivan*-mandated inquiry often make it harder for reviewing courts to determine conflict and effect, particularly since those courts may rely on evidence and testimony whose importance only becomes established at the trial.

Nor, finally, is automatic reversal simply an appropriate means of enforcing *Sullivan's* mandate of inquiry. Despite Justice Souter's belief that there must be a threat of sanction (to-wit, the risk of conferring a windfall upon the defendant) in order to induce "resolutely obdurate" trial judges to follow the law, we do not presume that judges are as careless or as partial as those police officers who need the incentive of the exclusionary rule, see *United States v. Leon* [p. 68]. And in any event, the *Sullivan* standard, which requires proof of effect upon representation but (once such effect is shown) presumes prejudice, already creates an "incentive" to inquire into a potential conflict. In those cases where the potential conflict is in fact an actual one, only inquiry will enable the judge to avoid all possibility of reversal by either seeking waiver or replacing a conflicted attorney. We doubt that the deterrence of "judicial dereliction" that would be achieved by an automatic reversal rule is significantly greater.

Since this was not a case in which (as in *Holloway*) counsel protested his inability simultaneously to represent multiple defendants; and since the trial court's failure to make the *Sullivan*-mandated inquiry does not reduce the petitioner's burden of proof; it was at least necessary, to void the conviction, for petitioner to establish that the conflict of interest adversely affected his counsel's performance. The Court of Appeals having found no such effect, the denial of habeas relief must be affirmed.

III

Lest today's holding be misconstrued, we note that the only question presented was the effect of a trial court's failure to inquire into a potential conflict upon the *Sullivan* rule that deficient performance of counsel must be shown. The case was presented and argued on the assumption that (absent some exception for failure to inquire) *Sullivan* would be applicable—requiring a showing of defective performance, but *not* requiring in addition (as *Strickland* does in other ineffectiveness-of-counsel cases), a showing of probable effect upon the outcome of trial.[a] That assumption was not unreasonable in light of the holdings of Courts of Appeals, which have applied *Sullivan* "unblinkingly" to "all kinds of alleged attorney ethical conflicts," *Beets v. Scott*, 65 F.3d 1258, 1266 (C.A.5 1995) (en banc).

---

[a]   The grounding for this exception to *Strickland* is discussed in *Strickland* at p. 935.

They have invoked the *Sullivan* standard not only when (as here) there is a conflict rooted in counsel's obligations to *former* clients, but even when representation of the defendant somehow implicates counsel's personal or financial interests, including a book deal, * * * a job with the prosecutor's office, * * * the teaching of classes to Internal Revenue Service agents, * * * a romantic "entanglement" with the prosecutor, * * * or fear of antagonizing the trial judge * * *.

It must be said, however, that the language of *Sullivan* itself does not clearly establish, or indeed even support, such expansive application. "[U]ntil," it said, "a defendant shows that his counsel *actively represented* conflicting interests, he has not established the constitutional predicate for his claim of ineffective assistance." (emphasis added). Both *Sullivan* itself and *Holloway* stressed the high probability of prejudice arising from multiple concurrent representation, and the difficulty of proving that prejudice. Not all attorney conflicts present comparable difficulties. Thus, the Federal Rules of Criminal Procedure treat concurrent representation and prior representation differently, requiring a trial court to inquire into the likelihood of conflict whenever jointly charged defendants are represented by a single attorney (Rule 44(c)), but not when counsel previously represented another defendant in a substantially related matter, even where the trial court is aware of the prior representation. See *Sullivan* (citing the Rule).

This is not to suggest that one ethical duty is more or less important than another. The purpose of our *Holloway* and *Sullivan* exceptions from the ordinary requirements of *Strickland,* however, is not to enforce the Canons of Legal Ethics, but to apply needed prophylaxis in situations where *Strickland* itself is evidently inadequate to assure vindication of the defendant's Sixth Amendment right to counsel. See *Nix v. Whiteside,* 475 U.S. 157 (1986) ("[B]reach of an ethical standard does not necessarily make out a denial of the Sixth Amendment guarantee of assistance of counsel"). In resolving this case on the grounds on which it was presented to us, we do not rule upon the need for the *Sullivan* prophylaxis in cases of successive representation. Whether *Sullivan* should be extended to such cases remains, as far as the jurisprudence of this Court is concerned, an open question. * * *

JUSTICE KENNEDY, with whom JUSTICE O'CONNOR joins, concurring.

In its comprehensive analysis the Court has said all that is necessary to address the issues raised by the question presented, and I join the opinion in full. The trial judge's failure to inquire into a suspected conflict is not the kind of error requiring a presumption of prejudice. We did not grant certiorari on a second question presented by petitioner: whether, if we rejected his proposed presumption, he had nonetheless established that a conflict of interest adversely affected his representation. I write separately to emphasize that the facts of this case well illustrate why a wooden rule requiring reversal is inappropriate for cases like this one.

At petitioner's request, the District Court conducted an evidentiary hearing on the conflict claim and issued a thorough opinion, which found that counsel's brief representation of the victim had no effect whatsoever on the course of petitioner's trial. The District Court's findings depend upon credibility judgments made after hearing the testimony of petitioner's counsel, Bryan Saunders, and other witnesses. As a reviewing court, our role is not to speculate about counsel's motives or about the plausibility of alternative litigation strategies. Our role is to defer to the District Court's factual findings unless we can conclude they are clearly erroneous. * * * The District Court found that Saunders did not believe he had any obligation to his former client, Timothy Hall, that would interfere with the litigation. * * * Although the District Court concluded that Saunders probably did learn some matters that were confidential, it found that nothing the attorney learned was relevant to the subsequent murder case. * * * Indeed, even if Saunders had learned relevant information, the District Court found that he labored under the impression he had no continuing duty at all to his deceased client. * * * While Saunders' belief may have been mistaken, it establishes that the prior representation did not influence the choices he made during the course of the trial. This conclusion is a good example of why a case-by-case inquiry is required, rather than simply adopting an automatic rule of reversal.

Petitioner's description of roads not taken would entail two degrees of speculation. We would be required to assume that Saunders believed he had a continuing duty to the victim, and we then would be required to consider whether in this hypothetical case, the counsel would have been blocked from pursuing an alternative defense strategy. The District Court concluded that the prosecution's case, coupled with the defendant's insistence on testifying, foreclosed the strategies suggested by petitioner after the fact. According to the District Court, there was no plausible argument that the victim consented to sexual relations with his murderer, given the bruises on the victim's neck, blood marks showing the victim was stabbed before or during sexual intercourse, and, most important, petitioner's insistence on testifying at trial that he had never met the victim. * * * The basic defense at the guilt phase was that petitioner was not at the scene; this is hardly consistent with the theory that there was a consensual encounter.

The District Court said the same for counsel's alleged dereliction at the sentencing phase. Saunders' failure to attack the character of the 17-year-old victim and his mother had nothing to do with the putative conflict of interest. This strategy was rejected as likely to backfire, not only by Saunders, but also by his co-counsel, who owed no duty to Hall. These facts, and others relied upon by the District Court, provide compelling evidence that a theoretical conflict does not establish a constitutional violation, even when the conflict is one about which the trial judge should have known.

The constitutional question must turn on whether trial counsel had a conflict of interest that hampered the representation, not on whether the trial judge should have been more assiduous in taking prophylactic measures. If it were otherwise, the judge's duty would not be limited to cases where the attorney is suspected of harboring a conflict of interest. The Sixth Amendment protects the defendant against an ineffective attorney, as well as a conflicted one. See *Strickland v. Washington*. It would be a major departure to say that the trial judge must step in every time defense counsel appears to be providing ineffective assistance, and indeed, there is no precedent to support this proposition. As the Sixth Amendment guarantees the defendant the assistance of counsel, the infringement of that right must depend on a deficiency of the lawyer, not of the trial judge. There is no reason to presume this guarantee unfulfilled when the purported conflict has had no effect on the representation.

JUSTICE STEVENS, dissenting.

This case raises three uniquely important questions about a fundamental component of our criminal justice system—the constitutional right of a person accused of a capital offense to have the effective assistance of counsel for his defense. The first is whether a capital defendant's attorney has a duty to disclose that he was representing the defendant's alleged victim at the time of the murder. Second, is whether, assuming disclosure of the prior representation, the capital defendant has a right to refuse the appointment of the conflicted attorney. Third, is whether the trial judge, who knows or should know of such prior representation, has a duty to obtain the defendant's consent before appointing that lawyer to represent him. Ultimately, the question presented by this case is whether, if these duties exist and if all of them are violated, there exist "circumstances that are so likely to prejudice the accused that the cost of litigating their effect in a particular case is unjustified." *United States v. Cronic.*

The first critical stage in the defense of a capital case is the series of pretrial meetings between the accused and his counsel when they decide how the case should be defended. A lawyer cannot possibly determine how best to represent a new client unless that client is willing to provide the lawyer with a truthful account of the relevant facts. When an indigent defendant first meets his newly appointed counsel, he will often falsely maintain his complete innocence. Truthful disclosures of embarrassing or incriminating facts are contingent on the development of the client's confidence in the undivided loyalty of the lawyer. Quite obviously, knowledge that the lawyer represented the victim would be a substantial obstacle to the development of such confidence. * * * It is equally true that a lawyer's decision to conceal such an important fact from his new client would have comparable ramifications. The suppression of communication and truncated investigation that would unavoidably follow from such a decision would also make it difficult, if not altogether impossible, to establish the necessary level of trust that should characterize the "delicacy of relation" between attorney and client.

In this very case, it is likely that Mickens misled his counsel, Bryan Saunders, given the fact that Mickens gave false testimony at his trial denying any involvement in the crime despite the overwhelming evidence that he had killed Timothy Hall after a sexual encounter. In retrospect, it seems obvious that the death penalty might have been avoided by acknowledging Mickens' involvement, but emphasizing the evidence suggesting that their sexual encounter was consensual. Mickens' habeas counsel garnered evidence suggesting that Hall was a male prostitute, that the area where Hall was killed was known for prostitution, and that there was no evidence that Hall was forced to the secluded area where he was ultimately murdered. An unconflicted attorney could have put forward a defense tending to show that Mickens killed Hall only after the two engaged in consensual sex, but Saunders offered no such defense. This was a crucial omission—a finding of forcible sodomy was an absolute prerequisite to Mickens' eligibility for the death penalty. Of course, since that strategy would have led to conviction of a noncapital offense, counsel would have been unable to persuade the defendant to divulge the information necessary to support such a defense and then ultimately to endorse the strategy unless he had earned the complete confidence of his client.

Saunders' concealment of essential information about his prior representation of the victim was a severe lapse in his professional duty. The lawyer's duty to disclose his representation of a client related to the instant charge is not only intuitively obvious, it is as old as the profession. * * * Mickens' lawyer's violation of this fundamental obligation of disclosure is indefensible. The relevance of Saunders' prior representation of Hall to the new appointment was far too important to be concealed.

If the defendant is found guilty of a capital offense, the ensuing proceedings that determine whether he will be put to death are critical in every sense of the word. At those proceedings, testimony about the impact of the crime on the victim, including testimony about the character of the victim, may have a critical effect on the jury's decision. Because a lawyer's fiduciary relationship with his deceased client survives the client's death, *Swidler & Berlin v. United States,* 524 U.S. 399 (1998), Saunders necessarily labored under conflicting obligations that were irreconcilable. He had a duty to protect the reputation and confidences of his deceased client, and a duty to impeach the impact evidence presented by the prosecutor. * * * Saunders' conflicting obligations to his deceased client, on the one hand, and to his living client, on the other, were unquestionably sufficient to give Mickens the right to insist on different representation. * * *

When an indigent defendant is unable to retain his own lawyer, the trial judge's appointment of counsel is itself a critical stage of a criminal trial. At that point in the proceeding, by definition, the defendant has no lawyer to protect his interests and must rely entirely on the judge. For that reason it is "the solemn duty of a . . . judge before whom a defendant appears without counsel to make a thorough inquiry and to take all steps necessary to insure the fullest protection of this constitutional right at every stage of the proceedings." *Von Moltke v. Gillies,* 332 U.S. 708, 722 (1948). This duty with respect to indigent defendants is far more imperative than the judge's duty to investigate the possibility of a conflict that arises when retained counsel represents either multiple or successive defendants. It is true that in a situation of retained counsel, "[u]nless the trial court knows or reasonably should know that a particular conflict exists, the court need not initiate an inquiry." *Cuyler v. Sullivan.*[8] But when, as was true in this case, the judge is

---

[8] Part III of the Court's opinion is a foray into an issue that is not implicated by the question presented. In dicta, the Court states that *Sullivan* may not even apply in the first place to *successive* representations. Most Courts of Appeals, however, have applied *Sullivan* to claims of successive representation as well as to some insidious conflicts arising from a lawyer's self-interest. * * * We have done the same. See *Wood v. Georgia* (applying *Sullivan* to a conflict stemming from a third-party payment arrangement). Neither we nor the Courts of Appeals have applied this standard "unblinkingly," as the Court accuses, but rather have relied upon principled reason. When a conflict of interest, whether multiple, successive, or otherwise, poses so substantial a risk that a lawyer's representation would be materially and adversely affected by diverging interests or loyalties and the trial court judge knows of this and yet fails to inquire, it is a "[c]ircumstanc[e] of [such] magnitude" that "the likelihood that any lawyer, even a fully competent

not merely reviewing the permissibility of the defendants' choice of counsel, but is responsible for making the choice herself, and when she knows or should know that a conflict does exist, the duty to make a thorough inquiry is manifest and unqualified. Indeed, under far less compelling circumstances, we squarely held that when a record discloses the "possibility of a conflict" between the interests of the defendants and the interests of the party paying their counsel's fees, the Constitution imposes a duty of inquiry on the state court judge even when no objection was made. *Wood v. Georgia.*

Mickens had a constitutional right to the services of an attorney devoted solely to his interests. That right was violated. The lawyer who did represent him had a duty to disclose his prior representation of the victim to Mickens and to the trial judge. That duty was violated. When Mickens had no counsel, the trial judge had a duty to "make a thorough inquiry and to take all steps necessary to insure the fullest protection of" his right to counsel. *Von Moltke.* Despite knowledge of the lawyer's prior representation, she violated that duty.

We will never know whether Mickens would have received the death penalty if those violations had not occurred nor precisely what effect they had on Saunders' representation of Mickens. We do know that he did not receive the kind of representation that the Constitution guarantees. If Mickens had been represented by an attorney-impostor who never passed a bar examination, we might also be unable to determine whether the impostor's educational shortcomings " 'actually affected the adequacy of his representation.' " (emphasis deleted). We would, however, surely set aside his conviction if the person who had represented him was not a real lawyer. Four compelling reasons make setting aside the conviction the proper remedy in this case.

First, it is the remedy dictated by our holdings in *Holloway v. Arkansas, Cuyler v. Sullivan,* and *Wood v. Georgia.* * * * Second, it is the only remedy that responds to the real possibility that Mickens would not have received the death penalty if he had been represented by conflict-free counsel during the critical stage of the proceeding in which he first met with his lawyer. We should presume that the lawyer for the victim of a brutal homicide is incapable of establishing the kind of relationship with the defendant that is essential to effective representation. * * * Third, it is the only remedy that is consistent with the legal profession's historic and universal condemnation of the representation of conflicting interests without the full disclosure and consent of all interested parties. The Court's novel and naïve assumption that a lawyer's divided loyalties are acceptable unless it can be proved that they actually affected counsel's performance is demeaning to the profession. * * * Finally, "justice must satisfy the appearance of justice." *Offutt v. United States,* 348 U.S. 11, 14 (1954). Setting aside Mickens' conviction is the only remedy that can maintain public confidence in the fairness of the procedures employed in capital cases. * * * A rule that allows the State to foist a murder victim's lawyer onto his accused is not only capricious; it poisons the integrity of our adversary system of justice. * * *

---

one, could provide effective assistance is so small that a presumption of prejudice is appropriate without inquiry into the actual conduct of the trial." *Cronic.*

JUSTICE SOUTER, dissenting.

* * * The District Judge reviewing the federal habeas petition in this case found that the state judge who appointed Bryan Saunders to represent petitioner Mickens on a capital murder charge knew or should have known that obligations stemming from Saunders's prior representation of the victim, Timothy Hall, potentially conflicted with duties entailed by defending Mickens. * * * The state judge was therefore obliged to look further into the extent of the risk and, if necessary, either secure Mickens's knowing and intelligent assumption of the risk or appoint a different lawyer. The state judge, however, did nothing to discharge her constitutional duty of care. In the one case in which we have devised a remedy for such judicial dereliction, we held that the ensuing judgment of conviction must be reversed and the defendant afforded a new trial. *Holloway.* * * * That should be the result here.

The Court today holds, instead, that Mickens should be denied this remedy because Saunders failed to employ a formal objection as a means of bringing home to the appointing judge the risk of conflict. Without an objection, the majority holds, Mickens should get no relief absent a showing that the risk turned into an actual conflict with adverse effect on the representation provided to Mickens at trial. But why should an objection matter when even without an objection the state judge knew or should have known of the risk and was therefore obliged to enquire further? What would an objection have added to the obligation the state judge failed to honor? The majority says that in circumstances like those now before us, we have already held such an objection necessary for reversal, absent proof of actual conflict with adverse effect, so that this case calls simply for the application of precedent, albeit precedent not very clearly stated.

The majority's position is error, resting on a mistaken reading of our cases. * * * *Holloway* * * * held that the motions [there] apprised the trial judge of a "risk" that continuing the joint representation would subject defense counsel in the pending trial to the impossible obligations of simultaneously furthering the conflicting interests of the several defendants, and we reversed the convictions on the basis of the judge's failure to respond to the prospective conflict, without any further showing of harm. In particular, we rejected the argument that a defendant tried subject to such a disclosed risk should have to show actual prejudice caused by subsequent conflict. * * *

Cuyler v. Sullivan held that multiple representation did not raise enough risk of impaired representation in a coming trial to trigger a trial court's duty to enquire further, in the absence of "special circumstances." The most obvious special circumstance would be an objection. Indeed, because multiple representation was not suspect *per se,* and because counsel was in the best position to anticipate a risk of conflict, the Court spoke at one point as though nothing but an objection would place a court on notice of a prospective conflict. * * * But the Court also explained that courts must rely on counsel in "large measure," that is, not exclusively, and it spoke in general terms of a duty to enquire that arises when "the trial court knows or reasonably should know that a particular conflict exists." * * * Accordingly, the Court did not rest the result simply on the failure of counsel to object, but said instead that "[n]othing in the circumstances of this case indicates that the trial court had a duty to inquire whether there was a conflict of interest." For that reason, it held respondent bound to show "that a conflict of interest actually affected the adequacy of his representation."

The different burdens on the *Holloway* and *Cuyler* defendants are consistent features of a coherent scheme for dealing with the problem of conflicted defense counsel; a prospective risk of conflict subject to judicial notice is treated differently from a retrospective claim that a completed proceeding was tainted by conflict, although the trial judge had not been derelict in any duty to guard against it. When the problem comes to the trial court's attention before any potential conflict has become actual, the court has a duty to act prospectively to assess the risk and, if the risk is not too remote, to eliminate it or to render it acceptable through a defendant's knowing and intelligent waiver. This duty is something more than the general responsibility to rule without committing legal error; it is an affirmative obligation to investigate a disclosed possibility that defense counsel will be unable to act with uncompromised loyalty to his client. It was the judge's failure to fulfill that duty of care to enquire further and do what might be necessary that the *Holloway* Court remedied by vacating the defendant's subsequent conviction. The error occurred when the judge failed to act, and the remedy restored the defendant to the position he would have occupied if the judge had taken reasonable steps to fulfill his obligation. But when the problem of conflict comes to judicial attention not prospectively, but only after the fact, the defendant must show an actual conflict with adverse consequence to him in order to get relief. Fairness requires nothing more, for no judge was at fault in allowing a trial to proceed even though fraught with hidden risk.

In light of what the majority holds today, it bears repeating that, in this coherent scheme established by *Holloway* and *Cuyler,* there is nothing legally crucial about an objection by defense counsel to tell a trial judge that conflicting interests may impair the adequacy of counsel's representation. * * * But in the majority's eyes, this conclusion takes insufficient account of *Wood,* whatever may have been the sensible scheme staked out by *Holloway* and *Cuyler,* with a defendant's burden turning on whether a court was apprised of a conflicts problem prospectively or retrospectively. The majority says that *Wood* holds that the distinction is between cases where counsel objected and all other cases, regardless of whether a trial court was put on notice prospectively in some way other than by an objection on the record. In *Wood,* according to the majority, the trial court had notice, there was no objection on the record, and the defendant was required to show actual conflict and adverse effect.

Wood is not easy to read, and I believe the majority misreads it. * * * Careful attention to *Wood* shows that the case did not involve prospective notice of risk unrealized, and that it held nothing about the general rule to govern in such circumstances. What *Wood* did decide was how to deal with a possible conflict of interests that becomes known to the trial court only at the conclusion of the trial proceeding at which it may have occurred, and becomes known not to a later habeas court but to the judge who handed down sentences at trial, set probation 19 months later after appeals were exhausted, and held a probation revocation proceeding 4 months after that. * * *

Treating the case as more like *Cuyler* and remanding was obviously the correct choice. *Wood* was not like *Holloway,* in which the judge was put on notice of a risk before trial, that is, a prospective possibility of conflict. It was, rather, much closer to *Cuyler,* since any notice to a court went only to a conflict, if there was one, that had pervaded a completed trial proceeding extending over two years. The only difference between *Wood* and *Cuyler* was that, in *Wood,* the signs that a conflict may have occurred were clear to the judge at the close of the probation revocation proceeding, whereas the claim of conflict in *Cuyler* was not raised until after judgment in a separate habeas proceeding. * * *

The disposition in *Wood* therefore raises no doubt about the consistency of the *Wood* Court. Contrary to the majority's conclusion (see n.2), there was no tension at all between acknowledging the rule of reversal to be applied when a judge fails to enquire into a known risk of prospective conflict, while at the same time sending the *Wood* case itself back for a determination about actual, past conflict. * * *

We should, therefore, follow the law settled until today, in vacating the conviction and affording Mickens a new trial. * * * Since the majority will not leave the law as it is, however, the question is whether there is any merit in the rule it now adopts, of treating breaches of a judge's duty to enquire into prospective conflicts differently depending on whether defense counsel explicitly objected. There is not. The distinction is irrational on its face, it creates a scheme of incentives to judicial vigilance that is weakest in those cases presenting the greatest risk of conflict and unfair trial, and it reduces the so-called judicial duty to enquire into so many empty words.

The most obvious reason to reject the majority's rule starts with the accepted view that a trial judge placed on notice of a risk of prospective conflict has an obligation then and there to do something about it. The majority does not expressly repudiate that duty, which is too clear for cavil. It should go without saying that the best time to deal with a known threat to the basic guarantee of fair trial is before the trial has proceeded to become unfair. * * * It would be absurd, after all, to suggest that a judge should sit quiescent in the face of an apparent risk that a lawyer's conflict will render representation illusory and the formal trial a waste of time, emotion, and a good deal of public money. And as if that were not bad enough, a failure to act early raises the specter, confronted by the *Holloway* Court, that failures on the part of conflicted counsel will elude demonstration after the fact, simply because they so often consist of what did not happen. While a defendant can fairly be saddled with the characteristically difficult burden of proving adverse effects of conflicted decisions after the fact when the judicial system was not to blame in tolerating the risk of conflict, the burden is indefensible when a judge was on notice of the risk but did nothing.

With so much at stake, why should it matter how a judge learns whatever it is that would point out the risk to anyone paying attention? Of course an objection from a conscientious lawyer suffices to put a court on notice, as it did in *Holloway;* and probably in the run of multiple-representation cases nothing short of objection will raise the specter of trouble. But sometimes a wide-awake judge will not need any formal objection to see a risk of conflict, as the federal habeas court's finding in this very case shows. Why, then, pretend contrary to fact that a judge can never perceive a risk unless a lawyer points it out? Why excuse a judge's breach of judicial duty just because a lawyer has fallen down in his own ethics or is short on competence? Transforming the factually sufficient trigger of a formal objection into a legal necessity for responding to any breach of judicial duty is irrational.

Nor is that irrationality mitigated by the Government's effort to analogize the majority's objection requirement to the general rule that in the absence of plain error litigants get no relief from error without objection. The Government as *amicus* argues for making a formal objection crucial because judges are not the only ones obliged to take care for the integrity of the system; defendants and their counsel need inducements to help the courts with timely warnings. The fallacy of the Government's argument, however, has been on the books since *Wood* was decided. * * * The objection requirement works elsewhere because the objecting lawyer believes that he sights an error being committed by the judge or opposing counsel. * * * That is hardly the motive to depend on when the risk of error, if there is one, is being created by the lawyer himself in acting subject to a risk of conflict. The law on conflicted counsel has to face the fact that one of our leading cases arose after a trial in which counsel may well have kept silent about conflicts not out of obtuseness or inattention, but for the sake of deliberately favoring a third party's interest over the clients, and this very case comes to us with reason to suspect that Saunders suppressed his conflicts for the sake of a second fee in a case getting public attention. While the perceptive and conscientious lawyer (as in *Holloway*) needs nothing more than ethical duty to induce an objection, the venal lawyer is not apt to be reformed by a general rule that says his client will have an easier time reversing a conviction down the road if the lawyer calls attention to his own venality.[10]

The irrationality of taxing defendants with a heavier burden for silent lawyers naturally produces an equally irrational scheme of incentives operating on the judges. The judge's duty independent of objection, as described in *Cuyler* and *Wood*, is made concrete by reversal for failure to honor it. The plain fact is that the specter of reversal for failure to enquire into risk is an incentive to trial judges to keep their eyes peeled for lawyers who wittingly or otherwise play loose with loyalty to their clients and the fundamental guarantee of a fair trial. * * * That incentive is

---

[10] The Government contends that not requiring a showing of adverse effect in no-objection cases would "provide the defense with a *dis*incentive to bring conflicts to the attention of the trial court, since remaining silent could afford a defendant with a reliable ground for reversal in the event of conviction." This argument, of course, has no force whatsoever in the case of the venal conflicted lawyer who remains silent out of personal self-interest or the obtuse lawyer who stays silent because he could not recognize a conflict if his own life depended on it. And these are precisely the lawyers presenting the danger in no-objection cases; the savvy and ethical lawyer would comply with his professional duty to disclose conflict concerns to the court. But even assuming the unlikely case of a savvy lawyer who recognizes a potential conflict and does not know for sure whether to object timely on that basis as a matter of professional ethics, an objection on the record is still the most reliable factually sufficient trigger of the judicial duty to enquire, dereliction of which would result in a reversal, and it is therefore beyond the realm of reasonable conjecture to suggest that such a lawyer would forgo an objection on the chance that a court in postconviction proceedings may find an alternative factual basis giving rise to a duty to enquire.

needed least when defense counsel points out the risk with a formal objection, and needed most with the lawyer who keeps risk to himself, quite possibly out of self-interest. Under the majority's rule, however, it is precisely in the latter situation that the judge's incentive to take care is at its ebb. With no objection on record, a convicted defendant can get no relief without showing adverse effect, minimizing the possibility of a later reversal and the consequent inducement to judicial care. This makes no sense. * * *

The Court's rule makes no sense unless, that is, the real point of this case is to eliminate the judge's constitutional duty entirely in no-objection cases, for that is certainly the practical consequence of today's holding. The defendant has the same burden to prove adverse effect (and the prospect of reversal is the same) whether the judge has no reason to know of any risk or every reason to know about it short of explicit objection. In that latter case, the duty explicitly described in *Cuyler* and *Wood* becomes just a matter of words, devoid of sanction; it ceases to be any duty at all. * * *

JUSTICE BREYER, with whom JUSTICE GINSBURG joins, dissenting.

The Commonwealth of Virginia seeks to put the petitioner, Walter Mickens, Jr., to death after having appointed to represent him as his counsel a lawyer who, at the time of the murder, was representing the very person Mickens was accused of killing. I believe that, in a case such as this one, a categorical approach is warranted and automatic reversal is required. To put the matter in language this Court has previously used: By appointing this lawyer to represent Mickens, the Commonwealth created a "structural defect affecting the framework within which the trial [and sentencing] proceeds, rather than simply an error in the trial process itself." *Arizona v. Fulminante*, 499 U.S. 279 (1991).

The parties spend a great deal of time disputing how this Court's precedents of *Holloway v. Arkansas, Cuyler v. Sullivan*, and *Wood v. Georgia* resolve the case. Those precedents involve the significance of a trial judge's "failure to inquire" if that judge "knew or should have known" of a "potential" conflict. The majority and dissenting opinions dispute the meaning of these cases as well. Although I express no view at this time about how our precedents should treat *most* ineffective-assistance-of-counsel claims involving an alleged conflict of interest (or, for that matter, whether *Holloway, Sullivan,* and *Wood* provide a sensible or coherent framework for dealing with those cases at all), I am convinced that *this* case is not governed by those precedents, for the following reasons.

First, this is the kind of representational incompatibility that is egregious on its face. Mickens was represented by the murder victim's lawyer; that lawyer had represented the victim on a criminal matter; and that lawyer's representation of the victim had continued until one business day before the lawyer was appointed to represent the defendant.

Second, the conflict is exacerbated by the fact that it occurred in a capital murder case. In a capital case, the evidence submitted by both sides regarding the victim's character may easily tip the scale of the jury's choice between life or death. Yet even with extensive investigation in post-trial proceedings, it will often prove difficult, if not impossible, to determine whether the prior representation affected defense counsel's decisions regarding, for example: which avenues to take when investigating the victim's background; which witnesses to call; what type of impeachment to undertake; which arguments to make to the jury; what language to use to characterize the victim; and, as a general matter, what basic strategy to adopt at the sentencing stage. Given the subtle forms that prejudice might take, the consequent difficulty of proving actual prejudice, and the significant likelihood that it will nonetheless occur when the same lawyer represents both accused killer and victim, the cost of litigating the existence of actual prejudice in a particular case cannot be easily justified. * * *

Third, the Commonwealth itself *created* the conflict in the first place. Indeed, it was the *same judge* who dismissed the case against the victim who then appointed the victim's lawyer to represent Mickens one business day later. In light of the judge's active role in bringing about the incompatible representation, I am not sure why the concept of a judge's "duty to inquire" is thought to be central to this case. No "inquiry" by the trial judge could have shed more light on the conflict than was obvious on the face of the matter, namely, that the lawyer who would represent Mickens today is the same lawyer who yesterday represented Mickens' alleged victim in a criminal case.

This kind of breakdown in the criminal justice system creates, at a minimum, the appearance that the proceeding will not " 'reliably serve its function as a vehicle for determination of guilt or innocence,' " and the resulting " 'criminal punishment' " will not " 'be regarded as fundamentally fair.' " *Fulminante*. This appearance, together with the likelihood of prejudice in the typical case, are serious enough to warrant a categorical rule—a rule that does not require proof of prejudice in the individual case.

The Commonwealth complains that this argument "relies heavily on the immediate visceral impact of learning that a lawyer previously represented the victim of his current client." And that is so. The "visceral impact," however, arises out of the obvious, unusual nature of the conflict. It arises from the fact that the Commonwealth seeks to execute a defendant, having provided that defendant with a lawyer who, only yesterday, represented the victim. In my view, to carry out a death sentence so obtained would invariably "diminis[h] faith" in the fairness and integrity of our criminal justice system. * * * That is to say, it would diminish that public confidence in the criminal justice system upon which the successful functioning of that system continues to depend.

WHEAT V. UNITED STATES
486 U.S. 153, 108 S.Ct. 1692, 100 L.Ed.2d 140 (1988).

[Petitioner, along with numerous codefendants, including Gomez-Barajas and Bravo, was charged with participating in a far-flung drug conspiracy. Both Gomez-Barajas and Bravo were represented by attorney Iredale. Gomez-Barajas was tried first and was acquitted on drug charges overlapping with those against petitioner. To avoid a second trial on still further charges, Gomez-Barajas offered to plead guilty to tax-evasion and illegal-importation offenses stemming from the conspiracy. However, at the commencement of petitioner's trial, that plea had not yet been accepted by the district court, so there remained the possibility that it could be rejected by the district court or withdrawn by Gomez-Barajas. Bravo pleaded guilty in a proceeding that occurred two days before defendant's scheduled trial.

[At the conclusion of Bravo's guilty plea proceeding, petitioner moved for the substitution of Iredale as his counsel. The government objected on the ground that Iredale's representation of the defendant as well as the two other codefendants created a multiple conflict of interest: (1) In the event that Gomez-Barajas's plea and negotiated sentencing arrangement were rejected by the court, or Gomez-Barajas withdrew his plea, petitioner was likely to be called as a witness for the prosecution at Gomez-Barajas's second trial, and Iredale would face a conflict in cross-examining him; (2) In the likely event that Bravo was called as a witness for the prosecution against petitioner, Iredale would face a conflict of interest in cross-examining Bravo. Iredale, in either situation, the government argued, would not be able to fully cross-examine the prosecution witness because of confidences received from previously representing him, and could not effectively represent the particular criminal defendant, petitioner or Gomez-Barajas, without having the capacity to fully cross-examine the witness.

[In response, to the government, petitioner emphasized his right to have counsel of his own choosing and his willingness, and the willingness of the other codefendants, to waive the right to conflict-free counsel. Moreover, maintained petitioner, the circumstances posited by the government that would create a conflict of interest were highly speculative and bore no connection to the true relationship among the co-conspirators. If called to testify against petitioner, Bravo would simply say that he did not know petitioner and had had no dealings with him. In the unlikely event that Gomez-Barajas went to trial, petitioner's lack of involvement in his alleged crimes made his appearance as a witness highly improbable. According to petitioner, the government was "manufacturing implausible conflicts" in an attempt to disqualify Iredale, who had already proved extremely effective in representing the other codefendants.

[The district court denied petitioner's request to substitute Iredale as his attorney, concluding, on the basis of the representation of the government, that it "really has no choice at this point other than to find that an irreconcilable conflict of interest exists." Petitioner proceeded to trial with his original counsel and was convicted of various drug offenses. The Court of Appeals for the Ninth Circuit affirmed.]

CHIEF JUSTICE REHNQUIST delivered the opinion of the Court.

* * * [W]hile the right to select and be represented by one's preferred attorney is comprehended by the Sixth Amendment, the essential aim of the Amendment is to guarantee an effective advocate for each criminal defendant rather than to ensure that a defendant will inexorably be represented by the lawyer whom he prefers.

The Sixth Amendment right to choose one's own counsel is circumscribed in several important respects. Regardless of his persuasive powers, an advocate who is not a member of the bar may not represent clients (other than himself) in court. Similarly, a defendant may not insist on representation by an attorney he cannot afford or who for other reasons declines to represent the defendant. Nor may a defendant insist on the counsel of an attorney who has a previous or ongoing relationship with an opposing party, even when the opposing party is the Government. The question raised in this case is the extent to which a criminal defendant's right under the Sixth Amendment to his chosen attorney is qualified by the fact that the attorney has represented other defendants charged in the same criminal conspiracy. * * *

Petitioner insists that the provision of waivers by all affected defendants cures any problems created by the multiple representation. But no such flat rule can be deduced from the Sixth Amendment presumption in favor of counsel of choice. Federal courts have an independent interest in ensuring that criminal trials are conducted within the ethical standards of the profession and that legal proceedings appear fair to all who observe them. Both the American Bar Association's Model Code of Professional Responsibility and its Model Rules of Professional Conduct, as well as the rules of the California Bar Association (which governed the attorneys in this case), impose limitations on multiple representation of clients. Not only the interest of a criminal defendant but the institutional interest in the rendition of just verdicts in criminal cases may be jeopardized by unregulated multiple representation.

For this reason, the Federal Rules of Criminal Procedure direct trial judges to investigate specially cases involving joint representation. In pertinent part, Rule 44(c) provides:

> "[T]he court shall promptly inquire with respect to such joint representation and shall personally advise each defendant of his right to the effective assistance of counsel, including separate representation. Unless it appears that there is good cause to believe no conflict of interest is likely to arise, the court shall take such measures as may be appropriate to protect each defendant's right to counsel."

Although Rule 44(c) does not specify what particular measures may be taken by a district court, one option suggested by the Notes of the Advisory Committee is an order by the court that the defendants be separately represented in subsequent proceedings in the case. This suggestion comports with our instructions in *Holloway* [p. 972], and in *Glasser v. United States*, 315 U.S. 60 (1942), that the trial courts, when alerted by objection from one of the parties, have an independent duty to ensure that criminal defendants receive a trial that is fair and does not contravene the Sixth Amendment.

To be sure, this need to investigate potential conflicts arises in part from the legitimate wish of District Courts that their judgments remain intact on appeal. As the Court of Appeals accurately pointed out, trial courts confronted with multiple representations face the prospect of being "whip-sawed" by assertions of error no matter which way they rule. If a district court agrees to the multiple representation, and the advocacy of counsel is thereafter impaired as a result, the defendant may well claim that he did not receive effective assistance. On the other hand, a district court's refusal to accede to the multiple representation may result in a challenge such as petitioner's in this case. Nor does a waiver by the defendant necessarily solve the problem, for we note, without passing judgment on, the apparent willingness of Courts of Appeals to entertain ineffective assistance claims from defendants who have specifically waived the right to conflict-free counsel.

Thus, where a court justifiably finds an actual conflict of interest, there can be no doubt that it may decline a proffer of waiver, and insist that defendants be separately represented.

Unfortunately for all concerned, a district court must pass on the issue of whether or not to allow a waiver of a conflict of interest by a criminal defendant not with the wisdom of hindsight after the trial has taken place, but the murkier pretrial context when relationships between parties are seen through a glass, darkly. The likelihood and dimensions of nascent conflicts of interest are notoriously hard to predict, even for those thoroughly familiar with criminal trials. It is a rare attorney who will be fortunate enough to learn the entire truth from his own client, much less be fully apprised before trial of what each of the Government's witnesses will say on the stand. A few bits of unforeseen testimony or a single previously unknown or unnoticed document may significantly shift the relationship between multiple defendants. These imponderables are difficult enough for a lawyer to assess, and even more difficult to convey by way of explanation to a criminal defendant untutored in the niceties of legal ethics. Nor is it amiss to observe that the willingness of an attorney to obtain such waivers from his clients may bear an inverse relation to the care with which he conveys all the necessary information to them.

For these reasons we think the District Court must be allowed substantial latitude in refusing waivers of conflicts of interest not only in those rare cases where an actual conflict may be demonstrated before trial, but in the more common cases where a potential for conflict exists which may or may not burgeon into an actual conflict as the trial progresses. In the circumstances of this case, with the motion for substitution of counsel made so close to the time of trial, the District Court relied on instinct and judgment based on experience in making its decision. We do not think it can be said that the court exceeded the broad latitude which must be accorded it in making this decision. Petitioner of course rightly points out that the government may seek to "manufacture" a conflict in order to prevent a defendant from having a particularly able defense counsel at his side; but trial courts are undoubtedly aware of this possibility, and must take it into consideration along with all of the other factors which inform this sort of a decision.

Here the District Court was confronted not simply with an attorney who wished to represent two coequal defendants in a straightforward criminal prosecution; rather, Iredale proposed to defend three conspirators of varying stature in a complex drug distribution scheme. The Government intended to call

Bravo as a witness for the prosecution at petitioner's trial.[4] The Government might readily have tied certain deliveries of marijuana by Bravo to petitioner, necessitating vigorous cross-examination of Bravo by petitioner's counsel. Iredale, because of his prior representation of Bravo, would have been unable ethically to provide that cross-examination.

Iredale had also represented Gomez-Barajas, one of the alleged kingpins of the distribution ring, and had succeeded in obtaining a verdict of acquittal for him. Gomez-Barajas had agreed with the Government to plead guilty to other charges, but the District Court had not yet accepted the plea arrangement. If the agreement were rejected, petitioner's probable testimony at the resulting trial of Gomez-Barajas would create an ethical dilemma for Iredale from which one or the other of his clients would likely suffer.

Viewing the situation as it did before trial, we hold that the District Court's refusal to permit the substitution of counsel in this case was within its discretion and did not violate petitioner's Sixth Amendment rights. Other district courts might have reached differing or opposite conclusions with equal justification, but that does not mean that one conclusion was "right" and the other "wrong." The District Court must recognize a presumption in favor of petitioner's counsel of choice, but that presumption may be overcome not only by a demonstration of actual conflict but by a showing of a serious potential for conflict. The evaluation of the facts and circumstances of each case under this standard must be left primarily to the informed judgment of the trial court. * * *

JUSTICE MARSHALL, with whom JUSTICE BRENNAN joins, dissenting.

* * * The right to counsel of choice, as the Court notes, is not absolute. When a defendant's selection of counsel, under the particular facts and circumstances of a case, gravely imperils the prospect of a fair trial, a trial court may justifiably refuse to accede to the choice. Thus, a trial court may in certain situations reject a defendant's choice of counsel on the ground of a potential conflict of interest, because a serious conflict may indeed destroy the integrity of the trial process. As the Court states, however, the trial court must recognize a presumption in favor of a defendant's counsel of choice. This presumption means that a trial court may not reject a defendant's chosen counsel on the ground of a potential conflict of interest absent a showing that both the likelihood and the dimensions of the feared conflict are substantial.[1] Unsupported or dubious speculation as to a conflict will not suffice. The Government must show a substantial potential for the kind of conflict that would undermine the fairness of the trial process. In these respects, I do not believe my position differs significantly, if at all, from that expressed in the opinion of the Court.

---

[4] Bravo was in fact called as a witness at petitioner's trial. His testimony was elicited to demonstrate the transportation of drugs that the prosecution hoped to link to petitioner.

[1] In stating this principle, I mean to address only cases in which all parties to the potential conflict have made a fully informed waiver of their right to conflict-free representation. It is undisputed in this case that petitioner, as well as Juvenal Gomez-Barajas and Javier Bravo, had agreed to waive this right.

I do disagree, however, with the Court's suggestion that the trial court's decision as to whether a potential conflict justifies rejection of a defendant's chosen counsel is entitled to some kind of special deference on appeal. The Court grants trial courts "broad latitude" over the decision to accept or reject a defendant's choice of counsel; although never explicitly endorsing a standard of appellate review, the Court appears to limit such review to determining whether an abuse of discretion has occurred. This approach, which the Court supports solely by noting the difficulty of evaluating the likelihood and magnitude of a conflict, accords neither with the nature of the trial court's decision nor with the importance of the interest at stake.

The trial court's decision as to whether the circumstances of a given case constitute grounds for rejecting a defendant's chosen counsel—that is, as to whether these circumstances present a substantial potential for a serious conflict of interest—is a mixed determination of law and fact. The decision is properly described in this way because it requires and results from the application of a legal standard to the established facts of a case. Appellate courts traditionally do not defer to such determinations. * * *

The inappropriateness of deferring to this determination becomes even more apparent when its constitutional significance is taken into account. * * * [The] interest at stake in this kind of decision is nothing less than a criminal defendant's Sixth Amendment right to counsel of his choice. The trial court simply does not have "broad latitude" to vitiate this right. In my view, a trial court that rejects a criminal defendant's chosen counsel on the ground of a potential conflict should make findings on the record to facilitate review, and an appellate court should scrutinize closely the basis for the trial court's decision. Only in this way can a criminal defendant's right to counsel of his choice be appropriately protected.

The Court's resolution of the instant case flows from its deferential approach to the District Court's denial of petitioner's motion to add or substitute counsel; absent deference, a decision upholding the District Court's ruling would be inconceivable. * * * At the time of petitioner's trial, Iredale's representation of Gomez-Barajas was effectively completed. * * * The only possible conflict this Court can divine from Iredale's representation of both petitioner and Gomez-Barajas rests on the premise that the trial court would reject the negotiated plea agreement and that Gomez-Barajas then would decide to go to trial. In this event, the Court tells us, "petitioner's probable testimony at the resulting trial of Gomez-Barajas would create an ethical dilemma for Iredale."

This argument rests on speculation of the most dubious kind. The Court offers no reason to think that the trial court would have rejected Gomez-Barajas's plea agreement; neither did the Government posit any such reason in its argument or brief before this Court. The most likely occurrence at the time petitioner moved to retain Iredale as his defense counsel was that the trial court would accept Gomez-Barajas's plea agreement, as the court in fact later did. Moreover, even if Gomez-Barajas had gone to trial, petitioner probably would not have testified. * * * The only alleged connection between petitioner and Gomez-Barajas sprang from the conspiracy to distribute marijuana, and a jury already had acquitted Gomez-

Barajas of that charge. It is therefore disingenuous to say that representation of both petitioner and Gomez-Barajas posed a serious potential for a conflict of interest.

   Similarly, Iredale's prior representation of Bravo was not a cause for concern. * * * [The facts] belie the claim that Bravo's anticipated testimony created a serious potential for conflict. Contrary to the Court's inference, Bravo could not have testified about petitioner's involvement in the alleged marijuana distribution scheme. As all parties were aware at the time, Bravo did not know and could not identify petitioner; indeed, prior to the commencement of legal proceedings, the two men never had heard of each other. Bravo's eventual testimony at petitioner's trial related to a shipment of marijuana in which petitioner was not involved; the testimony contained not a single reference to petitioner. Petitioner's counsel did not cross-examine Bravo, and neither petitioner's counsel nor the prosecutor mentioned Bravo's testimony in closing argument. All of these developments were predictable when the District Court ruled on petitioner's request that Iredale serve as trial counsel. * * * The District Court therefore had no authority to deny petitioner's Sixth Amendment right to retain counsel of his choice. * * *[a]

4. COUNSEL CONTROL VS. CLIENT CONTROL

   In *Faretta v. California* (p. 1007), in the course of recognizing a constitutional right to self-representation, the Court noted that only self-representation gives the defendant absolute control over his defense. For "when a defendant chooses to have a lawyer manage and present his case," he assumes some relinquishment of control, as "law and tradition may allocate to the counsel the power to make binding decisions of trial strategy in many areas" (p. 1009, 1st paragraph). *Jones v. Barnes*, 463 U.S. 745 (1983), was the first post-*Faretta* ruling to further explore the range of control relinquished by a defendant's choice to be represented by counsel.[a] *Jones v. Barnes* concluded that the range of "strategic" decisions within

---

  [a] In a separate dissent, Stevens, J., joined by Blackmun, J., noted agreement with "the Court's premise that district judges must be afforded wide latitude in passing on motions of this kind," but found it "abundantly clear" that the district judge here "abused his discretion."

  In *United States v. Gonzalez-Lopez*, 548 U.S. 140 (2006) (also discussed in fn. a, p. 936), the Court held that, although the right to counsel of choice is subject to various qualifications (as noted in *Wheat*), where that right has been violated, a subsequent conviction must be reversed. As in the case of a denial of the right to appointed counsel (see fn. d, p. 695), and the denial of the right to self-representation (see fn. d, p. 1014), the denial of the constitutional right to counsel of choice constitutes a "structural" constitutional error and therefore is not subject to the harmless error standard of *Chapman v. California* (see fn. d, p. 695). That denial qualifies as a structural error because its impact upon the proceedings leading to conviction is "necessarily unquantifiable and indeterminate." The Court majority rejected the dissent's contention that the defendant should be required to show "an identifiable difference in the quality of the representation between the disqualified counsel and the attorney who represents the defendant at trial."

  [a] As a practical matter, the extent of that relinquishment will differ as between appointed and retained counsel. Where counsel is appointed, the client's disagreement with counsel's choice as to a strategic decision within counsel's control does not allow defendant to insist upon substitution of new counsel, even when that substitution can be achieved without disrupting the trial schedule. Where counsel is retained, defendant may seek initially to employ a counsel willing to accept defendant's directions on all strategic decisions (allowable insofar as those directions do not require a breach of ethics). Where a disagreement on such a decision first arises after counsel has been retained, it can readily serve as a ground for gaining judicial permission to replace

counsel's ultimate control was not limited to trial strategy decisions (*Jones* concluded that appellate counsel had ultimate authority as to what contentions to include in an appeal) and was not limited to settings in which timing considerations precluded consultation with the defendant.[b] The Court also noted, however, that certain decisions were within the "ultimate authority" of the accused. Here, counsel had to consult and follow the direction of the accused. These decisions came to be characterized as "personal" or "fundamental rights" decisions (in contrast, to the category of "strategic" decisions, where counsel has ultimate authority). Personal decisions were not limited to waivers that required the personal, on-the-record participation of the defendant, such as the entry of a guilty plea or the waiver of a jury trial. Accordingly, whether a particular decision fell within defendant's control was an issue often presented through a post-conviction challenge, with the defendant claiming that he had never been informed that the decision was his to make and that he would have objected had he been so informed.[c] Post-*Jones*, in a series of rulings, primarily involving this procedural setting, the Court has addressed the proper characterization (within defendant's control or counsel's control) of a lengthy list of defense decisions. The latest in this line of rulings, *McCoy v. Louisiana*, both summarizes those earlier characterizations and addresses an area of decisionmaking that arguably reveals ambiguities in the analysis that controls the characterization.

---

counsel, although a disagreement of that type does not constitute an "irreconcilable conflict," which demands replacement in all settings. Where the replacement can be achieved without disrupting the trial schedule, defendant's right to counsel of choice typically demands that it be allowed. Where replacement requires granting a continuance, the trial court has considerable discretion, but even here, under some circumstances, the right to counsel of choice may so clearly outweigh competing considerations as to require granting the continuance and allowing the replacement. See W. LaFave, et al., 3 Criminal Procedure §§ 11.4(b), 11.4(c), 11.6(a) (2019 update).

   [b]   Dissenting in *Jones*, Justice Brennan, joined by Justice Marshall, rejected extending the attorney's control to decisions that were not subject to this limitation. The dissent noted: "A constitutional rule that encourages lawyers to disregard their clients wishes without compelling need can only exacerbate the clients' suspicion of their lawyers. * * * [U]ntil his conviction becomes final and he has had an opportunity to appeal, any restrictions on individual autonomy and dignity should be limited to the minimum necessary to vindicate the State's interest in speedy, effective prosecution. The role of the defense lawyer should be above all to function as the instrument and defender of the client's autonomy and dignity in all phases of the criminal process."

   [c]   Concurring in Gonzalez v. United States, 553 U.S. 242 (2008), Justice Scalia urged the Court to abandon distinguishing between "fundamental" and "strategic" decisions in this context— where there had been no objection by the client when the counsel implemented the now-challenged decision (typically counsel waiving by failing to object). In that setting, the Court should adopt "the rule that, as a constitutional matter, all waivable rights (except, of course, the right to counsel) can be waived by counsel." Justice Scalia described the "tactical-vs.-fundamental approach" as "vague and derived from nothing more substantial than this Court's say so." "Waiving *any* right can be a tactical decision" and "any right guaranteed by the Constitution would be fundamental." The "very notion of representative litigation [with counsel acting as the defendant's representative] suggests that the Constitution draws no distinction between one constitutional right (e.g., the right of confrontation, deemed "tactical" and within counsel's control) and another (e.g., the right to a jury trial, deemed "fundamental" and controlled only by the defendant). While distinctions might be drawn under procedural rules, absent a protest by the defendant withdrawing counsel's authority, there is "no basis for saying that the *Constitution* automatically invalidates *any* action not taken by the defendant personally, though taken by authorized counsel."

McCOY V. LOUISIANA

584 U.S. ___, 138 S.Ct. 1500, 200 L.Ed.2d 821 (2018).

JUSTICE GINSBURG delivered the opinion of the Court.

In *Florida* v. *Nixon*, 543 U.S. 175 (2004), this Court considered whether the Constitution bars defense counsel from conceding a capital defendant's guilt at trial "when [the] defendant, informed by counsel, neither consents nor objects." * * * We held that when counsel confers with the defendant and the defendant remains silent, neither approving nor protesting counsel's proposed concession strategy, "[no] blanket rule demand[s] the defendant's explicit consent" to implementation of that strategy.

In the case now before us, in contrast to *Nixon*, the defendant vociferously insisted that he did not engage in the charged acts and adamantly objected to any admission of guilt. App. 286–287, 505–506. Yet the trial court permitted counsel, at the guilt phase of a capital trial, to tell the jury the defendant "committed three murders. . . . [H]e's guilty." We hold that a defendant has the right to insist that counsel refrain from admitting guilt, even when counsel's experienced-based view is that confessing guilt offers the defendant the best chance to avoid the death penalty. Guaranteeing a defendant the right "to have the *Assistance* of Counsel for *his* defence," the Sixth Amendment so demands. With individual liberty—and, in capital cases, life—at stake, it is the defendant's prerogative, not counsel's, to decide on the objective of his defense: to admit guilt in the hope of gaining mercy at the sentencing stage, or to maintain his innocence, leaving it to the State to prove his guilt beyond a reasonable doubt. * * *

On May 5, 2008, Christine and Willie Young and Gregory Colston were shot and killed in the Youngs' home in Bossier City, Louisiana. The three victims were the mother, stepfather, and son of Robert McCoy's estranged wife, Yolanda. Several days later, police arrested McCoy in Idaho. Extradited to Louisiana, McCoy was appointed counsel from the public defender's office. A Bossier Parish grand jury indicted McCoy on three counts of first-degree murder, and the prosecutor gave notice of intent to seek the death penalty. McCoy pleaded not guilty. Throughout the proceedings, he insistently maintained he was out of State at the time of the killings and that corrupt police killed the victims when a drug deal went wrong. At defense counsel's request, a court-appointed sanity commission examined McCoy and found him competent to stand trial.

In December 2009 and January 2010, McCoy told the court his relationship with assigned counsel had broken down irretrievably. He sought and gained leave to represent himself until his parents engaged new counsel for him. In March 2010, Larry English, engaged by McCoy's parents, enrolled as McCoy's counsel. English eventually concluded that the evidence against McCoy was over-whelming and that, absent a concession at the guilt stage that McCoy was the killer, a death sentence would be impossible to avoid at the penalty phase.[1] McCoy, English

---

[1] Part of English's strategy was to concede that McCoy committed the murders and to argue that he should be convicted only of second-degree murder, because his "mental incapacity prevented him from forming the requisite specific intent to commit first degree murder." But the second-degree strategy would have encountered a shoal, for Louisiana does not permit introduction

reported, was "furious" when told, two weeks before trial was scheduled to begin, that English would concede McCoy's commission of the triple murders.[2] McCoy told English "not to make that concession," and English knew of McCoy's "complet[e] oppos[ition] to [English] telling the jury that [McCoy] was guilty of killing the three victims"; instead of any concession, McCoy pressed English to pursue acquittal.

At a July 26, 2011 hearing, McCoy sought to terminate English's representation, and English asked to be relieved if McCoy secured other counsel. With trial set to start two days later, the court refused to relieve English and directed that he remain as counsel of record. "[Y]ou are the attorney," the court told English when he expressed disagreement with McCoy's wish to put on a defense case, and "you have to make the trial decision of what you're going to proceed with."

At the beginning of his opening statement at the guilt phase of the trial, English told the jury there was "no way reasonably possible" that they could hear the prosecution's evidence and reach "any other conclusion than Robert McCoy was the cause of these individuals' death." McCoy protested; out of earshot of the jury, McCoy told the court that English was "selling [him] out" by maintaining that McCoy "murdered [his] family." The trial court reiterated that English was "representing" McCoy and told McCoy that the court would not permit "any other outbursts." Continuing his opening statement, English told the jury the evidence is "unambiguous," "my client committed three murders." McCoy testified in his own defense, maintaining his innocence and pressing an alibi difficult to fathom. In his closing argument, English reiterated that McCoy was the killer. On that issue, English told the jury that he "took [the] burden off of [the prosecutor]." The jury then returned a unanimous verdict of guilty of first-degree murder on all three counts. At the penalty phase, English again conceded "Robert McCoy committed these crimes," but urged mercy in view of McCoy's "serious mental and emotional issues." The jury returned three death verdicts.

Represented by new counsel, McCoy unsuccessfully moved for a new trial, arguing that the trial court violated his constitutional rights by allowing English to concede McCoy "committed three murders," over McCoy's objection. The Louisiana Supreme Court affirmed the trial court's ruling that defense counsel had authority so to concede guilt, despite the defendant's opposition to any admission of guilt. The concession was permissible, the court concluded, because counsel reasonably believed that admitting guilt afforded McCoy the best chance to avoid a death sentence.

We granted certiorari in view of a division of opinion among state courts of last resort on the question whether it is unconstitutional to allow defense counsel to concede guilt over the defendant's intransigent and unambiguous objection.

---

of evidence of a defendant's diminished capacity absent the entry of a plea of not guilty by reason of insanity.

[2] The dissent states that English told McCoy his proposed trial strategy eight months before trial. English did encourage McCoy, "[a] couple of months before the trial," to plead guilty rather than proceed to trial. But English declared under oath that "the first time [he] told [McCoy] that [he] intended to concede to the jury that [McCoy] was the killer" was July 12, 2011, two weeks before trial commenced. App. at 286. Encouraging a guilty plea pretrial, of course, is not equivalent to imparting to a defendant counsel's strategic determination to concede guilt should trial occur.

Compare with the instant case, *e.g., Cooke* v. *State*, 977 A. 2d 803, 842–846 (Del. 2009) (counsel's pursuit of a "guilty but mentally ill" verdict over defendant's "vociferous and repeated protestations" of innocence violated defendant's "constitutional right to make the fundamental decisions regarding his case"); *State* v. *Carter*, 270 Kan. 426, 440, 14 P. 3d 1138, 1148 (2000) (counsel's admission of client's involvement in murder when client adamantly maintained his innocence contravened Sixth Amendment right to counsel and due process right to a fair trial). * * *

The Sixth Amendment guarantees to each criminal defendant "the Assistance of Counsel for his defence." At common law, self-representation was the norm. * * * Even now, when most defendants choose to be represented by counsel, an accused may insist upon representing herself—however counterproductive that course may be, see *Faretta v. California*, [p. 1007]. As this Court explained, "[t]he right to defend is personal," and a defendant's choice in exercising that right "must be honored out of 'that respect for the individual which is the lifeblood of the law.' " *Ibid* [p. 1011].

The choice is not all or nothing: To gain assistance, a defendant need not surrender control entirely to counsel. For the Sixth Amendment, in "grant[ing] to the accused personally the right to make his defense," "speaks of the 'assistance' of counsel, and an assistant, however expert, is still an assistant." * * * Trial management is the lawyer's province: Counsel provides his or her assistance by making decisions such as "what arguments to pursue, what evidentiary objections to raise, and what agreements to conclude regarding the admission of evidence." *Gonzalez* v. *United States*, 553 U.S. 242, 248 (2008).[d] Some decisions, however, are reserved for the client—notably, whether to plead guilty, waive the right to a jury trial, testify in one's own behalf, and forgo an appeal. See *Jones* v. *Barnes*, 463 U.S. 745, 751 (1983).

Autonomy to decide that the objective of the defense is to assert innocence belongs in this latter category. Just as a defendant may steadfastly refuse to plead guilty in the face of overwhelming evidence against her, or reject the assistance of legal counsel despite the defendant's own inexperience and lack of professional qualifications, so may she insist on maintaining her innocence at the guilt phase of a capital trial. These are not strategic choices about how best to *achieve* a client's objectives; they are choices about what the client's objectives in fact *are*.

---

[d] In *Gonzalez*, the Court offered the following explanation of the defense attorney's full authority to manage the conduct of the trial (including, in this case, the authority to consent—apparently without previous client consultation—to having a magistrate, rather than the trial judge, conduct voir dire and jury selection): "Numerous choices affecting conduct of the trial, including the objections to make, the witnesses to call, and the arguments to advance, depend not only upon what is permissible under the rules of evidence and procedure but also upon tactical considerations of the moment and the larger strategic plan for the trial. These matters can be difficult to explain to a layperson; and to require in all instances that they be approved by the client could risk compromising the efficiencies and fairness that the trial process is designed to promote. In exercising professional judgment, moreover, the attorney draws upon the expertise and experience that members of the bar should bring to the trial process. In most instances the attorney will have a better understanding of the procedural choices than the client; or at least the laws should so assume."

Counsel may reasonably assess a concession of guilt as best suited to avoiding the death penalty, as English did in this case. But the client may not share that objective. He may wish to avoid, above all else, the opprobrium that comes with admitting he killed family members. Or he may hold life in prison not worth living and prefer to risk death for any hope, however small, of exoneration. When a client expressly asserts that the objective of "*his* defence" is to maintain innocence of the charged criminal acts, his lawyer must abide by that objective and may not override it by conceding guilt. U.S. Const., Amdt. 6 (emphasis added); see ABA Model Rule of Professional Conduct 1.2(a) (2016) (a "lawyer shall abide by a client's decisions concerning the objectives of the representation"). * * *

Preserving for the defendant the ability to decide whether to maintain his innocence should not displace counsel's, or the court's, respective trial management roles. See *Gonzalez* ("[n]umerous choices affecting conduct of the trial" do not require client consent, including "the objections to make, the witnesses to call, and the arguments to advance"). * * * In this case, the court had determined that McCoy was competent to stand trial, *i.e.*, that McCoy had "sufficient present ability to consult with his lawyer with a reasonable degree of rational understanding." *Godinez* v. *Moran*, [fn. c, p. 1006].[3] If, after consultations with English concerning the management of the defense, McCoy disagreed with English's proposal to concede McCoy committed three murders, it was not open to English to override McCoy's objection. English could not interfere with McCoy's telling the jury "I was not the murderer," although counsel could, if consistent with providing effective assistance, focus his own collaboration on urging that McCoy's mental state weighed against conviction.

Florida v. *Nixon* is not to the contrary. Nixon's attorney did not negate Nixon's autonomy by overriding Nixon's desired defense objective, for Nixon never asserted any such objective. Nixon "was generally unresponsive" during discussions of trial strategy, and "never verbally approved or protested" counsel's proposed approach. Nixon complained about the admission of his guilt only after trial.[e] McCoy, in contrast, opposed English's assertion of his guilt at every opportunity, before and during trial, both in conference with his lawyer and in open court. If a client declines to participate in his defense, then an attorney may permissibly guide the defense pursuant to the strategy she believes to be in the defendant's best interest.

---

[3]   Several times, English did express his view that McCoy was not, in fact, competent to stand trial.

[e]   The *Nixon* Court rejected the contention that counsel's concession was tantamount to a guilty plea, which requires automatic reversal absent defendant's participation. The lower court there had relied on *Brookhart v. Janis*, 384 U.S. 1 (1966). The *Brookhart* Court held that counsel unilaterally took action tantamount to entering a guilty plea by entering into an agreement "that all the state had to prove was a prima facie case, that he would not contest it, and that there would be no cross-examination of witnesses." Distinguishing *Brookhart*, the *Nixon* Court noted that counsel here did not accept a "truncated proceeding, shorn of the need * * * [to establish] guilt beyond a reasonable doubt." While acknowledging in his opening statement that defendant committed the murder, defense counsel: (1) did not thereby relieve the state of its obligation to present admissible evidence meeting the reasonable doubt standard; (2) retained the authority to object to the admission of prejudicial evidence and to cross-examine witnesses; and (3) did not preclude raising on appeal any "errors in the trial or jury instructions."

Presented with express statements of the client's will to maintain innocence, however, counsel may not steer the ship the other way. * * *

The Louisiana Supreme Court concluded that English's refusal to maintain McCoy's innocence was necessitated by Louisiana Rule of Professional Conduct 1.2(d) (2017), which provides that "[a] lawyer shall not counsel a client to engage, or assist a client, in conduct that the lawyer knows is criminal or fraudulent." Presenting McCoy's alibi defense, the court said, would put English in an "ethical conundrum," implicating English in perjury. 218 So.3d, at 565 (citing *Nix* v. *Whiteside*, [p. 953]). But McCoy's case does not resemble *Nix*, where the defendant told his lawyer that he intended to commit perjury. There was no such avowed perjury here. Cf. ABA Model Rule of Professional Conduct 3.3, Comment 8 ("The prohibition against offering false evidence only applies if the lawyer knows that the evidence is false."). English harbored no doubt that McCoy believed what he was saying; English simply disbelieved McCoy's account in view of the prosecution's evidence. English's express motivation for conceding guilt was not to avoid suborning perjury, but to try to build credibility with the jury, and thus obtain a sentence lesser than death. Louisiana's ethical rules might have stopped English from presenting McCoy's alibi evidence if English knew perjury was involved. But Louisiana has identified no ethical rule requiring English to admit McCoy's guilt over McCoy's objection. See 3 W. LaFave, J. Israel, N. King, & O. Kerr, Criminal Procedure § 11.6(c), p. 935 (4th ed. 2015) ("A lawyer is not placed in a professionally embarrassing position when he is reluctantly required . . . to go to trial in a weak case, since that decision is clearly attributed to his client.").

The dissent describes the conflict between English and McCoy as "rare" and "unlikely to recur." Yet the Louisiana Supreme Court parted ways with three other State Supreme Courts that have addressed this conflict in the past twenty years. * * * In each of the three cases, as here, the defendant repeatedly and adamantly insisted on maintaining his factual innocence despite counsel's preferred course: concession of the defendant's commission of criminal acts and pursuit of diminished capacity, mental illness, or lack of premeditation defenses. * * * These were not strategic disputes about whether to concede an element of a charged offense; they were intractable disagreements about the fundamental objective of the defendant's representation. For McCoy, that objective was to maintain "I did not kill the members of my family." In this stark scenario, we agree with the majority of state courts of last resort that counsel may not admit her client's guilt of a charged crime over the client's intransigent objection to that admission.

Because a client's autonomy, not counsel's competence, is in issue, we do not apply our ineffective-assistance-of-counsel jurisprudence, *Strickland* v. *Washington*, or *United States v. Cronic*, to McCoy's claim. To gain redress for attorney error, a defendant ordinarily must show prejudice. See *Strickland*. Here, however, the violation of McCoy's protected autonomy right was complete when the court allowed counsel to usurp control of an issue within McCoy's sole prerogative.

Violation of a defendant's Sixth Amendment-secured autonomy ranks as error of the kind our decisions have called "structural"; when present, such an error is not subject to harmless-error review. See, *e.g., McKaskle* [fn. d, p. 1014] (harmless-error analysis is inapplicable to deprivations of the self-representation right, because "[t]he right is either respected or denied; its deprivation cannot be harmless"); *United States v. Gonzalez-Lopez* [fn. a, p. 936] (choice of counsel is structural); *Waller* v. *Georgia*, [p. 962] (public trial is structural). Structural error "affect[s] the framework within which the trial proceeds," as distinguished from a lapse or flaw that is "simply an error in the trial process itself." *Arizona* v. *Fulminante*, 499 U.S. 279, 310 (1991). An error may be ranked structural, we have explained, "if the right at issue is not designed to protect the defendant from erroneous conviction but instead protects some other interest," such as "the fundamental legal principle that a defendant must be allowed to make his own choices about the proper way to protect his own liberty." *Weaver v. Massachusetts* [p. 960]. An error might also count as structural when its effects are too hard to measure, as is true of the right to counsel of choice, or where the error will inevitably signal fundamental unfairness, as we have said of a judge's failure to tell the jury that it may not convict unless it finds the defendant's guilt beyond a reasonable doubt. *Weaver.*

Under at least the first two rationales, counsel's admission of a client's guilt over the client's express objection is error structural in kind. Such an admission blocks the defendant's right to make the fundamental choices about his own defense. And the effects of the admission would be immeasurable, because a jury would almost certainly be swayed by a lawyer's concession of his client's guilt. McCoy must therefore be accorded a new trial without any need first to show prejudice.[4] * * *

JUSTICE ALITO, with whom JUSTICE THOMAS and JUSTICE GORSUCH join, dissenting.

The Constitution gives us the authority to decide real cases and controversies; we do not have the right to simplify or otherwise change the facts of a case in order to make our work easier or to achieve a desired result. But that is exactly what the Court does in this case. The Court overturns petitioner's convictions for three counts of first-degree murder by attributing to his trial attorney, Larry English, something that English never did. The Court holds that English violated petitioner's constitutional rights by "admit[ting] h[is] client's guilt of a charged crime over the client's intransigent objection." [p. 998].[1] But English did not admit

---

  [4]   The dissent suggests that a remand would be in order, so that the Louisiana Supreme Court, in the first instance, could consider the structural-error question. * * * "[W]e did not grant certiorari to review" that question. *Post* [p. 1004]. But McCoy raised his structural-error argument in his opening brief, and Louisiana explicitly chose not to grapple with it. In any event, "we have the authority to make our own assessment of the harmlessness of a constitutional error in the first instance." *Yates* v. *Evatt*, 500 U.S. 391, 407 (1991).

  [1]   When the Court expressly states its holding, it refers to a concession of guilt. See *ante* [p. 994]. ("We hold that a defendant has the right to insist that counsel refrain from admitting guilt, even when counsel's experienced-based view is that confessing guilt offers the defendant the best chance to avoid the death penalty"); *ante* [p. 998] ("counsel may not admit her client's guilt of a charged crime over the client's intransigent objection to that admission"). The opinion also contains many other references to the confession or admission of "guilt."). At a few points, however, the Court refers to the admission of criminal "acts." *Ante* [pp. 994, 997, 998]. A rule that a defense attorney may not admit the *actus reus* of an offense (or perhaps even any element of the *actus reus*) would be very different from the rule that the Court expressly adopts. I discuss some of the implications of such a broad rule in Part III of this opinion.

that petitioner was guilty of first-degree murder. Instead, faced with overwhelming evidence that petitioner shot and killed the three victims, English admitted that petitioner committed one element of that offense, *i.e.*, that he killed the victims. But English strenuously argued that petitioner was not guilty of first-degree murder because he lacked the intent (the *mens rea*) required for the offense. So the Court's newly discovered fundamental right simply does not apply to the real facts of this case.

I

The real case is far more complex. Indeed, the real situation English faced at the beginning of petitioner's trial was the result of a freakish confluence of factors that is unlikely to recur. * * * Retained by petitioner's family, English found himself in a predicament as the trial date approached. The evidence against his client was truly "overwhelming," as the Louisiana Supreme Court aptly noted. Among other things, the evidence showed the following. Before the killings took place, petitioner had abused and threatened to kill his wife, and she was therefore under police protection. On the night of the killings, petitioner's mother-in-law made a 911 call and was heard screaming petitioner's first name. She yelled: " 'She ain't here, Robert . . . I don't know where she is. The detectives have her. Talk to the detectives. She ain't in there, Robert.' " Moments later, a gunshot was heard, and the 911 call was disconnected.

Officers were dispatched to the scene, and on arrival, they found three dead or dying victims—petitioner's mother-in-law, her husband, and the teenage son of petitioner's wife. The officers saw a man who fit petitioner's description fleeing in petitioner's car. They chased the suspect, but he abandoned the car along with critical evidence linking him to the crime: the cordless phone petitioner's mother-in-law had used to call 911 and a receipt for the type of ammunition used to kill the victims. Petitioner was eventually arrested while hitchhiking in Idaho, and a loaded gun found in his possession was identified as the one used to shoot the victims. In addition to all this, a witness testified that petitioner had asked to borrow money to purchase bullets shortly before the shootings, and surveillance footage showed petitioner purchasing the ammunition on the day of the killings. And two of petitioner's friends testified that he confessed to killing at least one person.

Despite all this evidence, petitioner, who had been found competent to stand trial and had refused to plead guilty by reason of insanity, insisted that he did not kill the victims. He claimed that the victims were killed by the local police and that he had been framed by a far flung conspiracy of state and federal officials, reaching from Louisiana to Idaho. Petitioner believed that even his attorney and the trial judge had joined the plot. * * * Unwilling to go along with this incredible and uncorroborated defense, English told petitioner "some eight months" before trial that the only viable strategy was to admit the killings and to concentrate on attempting to avoid a sentence of death. 218 So. 3d, at 558. At that point—aware of English's strong views—petitioner could have discharged English and sought new counsel willing to pursue his conspiracy defense; under the Sixth Amendment, that was his right. See *United States* v. *Gonzalez-Lopez*, [fn. a, p. 992]. But petitioner stated "several different times" that he was "confident with Mr. English."

The weekend before trial, however, petitioner changed his mind. He asked the trial court to replace English, and English asked for permission to withdraw. Petitioner stated that he had secured substitute counsel, but he was unable to provide the name of this new counsel, and no new attorney ever appeared. The court refused these requests and also denied petitioner's last-minute request to represent himself. (Petitioner does not challenge these decisions here.) So petitioner and English were stuck with each other, and petitioner availed himself of his right to take the stand to tell his wild story. Under those circumstances, what was English supposed to do?

The Louisiana Supreme Court held that English could not have put on petitioner's desired defense without violating state ethics rules, but this Court effectively overrules the state court on this issue of state law. However, even if it is assumed that the Court is correct on this ethics issue, the result of mounting petitioner's conspiracy defense almost certainly would have been disastrous. That approach stood no chance of winning an acquittal and would have severely damaged English's credibility in the eyes of the jury, thus undermining his ability to argue effectively against the imposition of a death sentence at the penalty phase of the trial. * * * So, again, what was English supposed to do?

When pressed at oral argument before this Court, petitioner's current counsel eventually provided an answer: English was not required to take any affirmative steps to support petitioner's bizarre defense, but instead of conceding that petitioner shot the victims, English should have ignored that element entirely. Tr. of Oral Arg. 21–23. So the fundamental right supposedly violated in this case comes down to the difference between the two statements set out below.

Constitutional: "First-degree murder requires proof both that the accused killed the victim and that he acted with the intent to kill. I submit to you that my client did not have the intent required for conviction for that offense."

Unconstitutional: "First-degree murder requires proof both that the accused killed the victim and that he acted with the intent to kill. I admit that my client shot and killed the victims, but I submit to you that he did not have the intent required for conviction for that offense."

The practical difference between these two statements is negligible. If English had conspicuously refrained from endorsing petitioner's story and had based his defense solely on petitioner's dubious mental condition, the jury would surely have gotten the message that English was essentially conceding that petitioner killed the victims. But according to petitioner's current attorney, the difference is fundamental. The first formulation, he admits, is perfectly fine. The latter, on the other hand, is a violation so egregious that the defendant's conviction must be reversed even if there is no chance that the misstep caused any harm. It is no wonder that the Court declines to embrace this argument and instead turns to an issue that the case at hand does not actually present.

II

The constitutional right that the Court has now discovered—a criminal defendant's right to insist that his attorney contest his guilt with respect to all charged offenses—is like a rare plant that blooms every decade or so. Having made its first appearance today, the right is unlikely to figure in another case for many years to come. Why is this so?

First, it is hard to see how the right could come into play in any case other than a capital case in which the jury must decide both guilt and punishment. * * * Second, few rational defendants facing a possible death sentence are likely to insist on contesting guilt where there is no real chance of acquittal and where admitting guilt may improve the chances of avoiding execution. * * * Third, where a capital defendant and his retained attorney cannot agree on a basic trial strategy, the attorney and client will generally part ways unless, as in this case, the court is not apprised until the eve of trial. Fourth, if counsel is appointed, and unreasonably insists on admitting guilt over the defendant's objection, a capable trial judge will almost certainly grant a timely request to appoint substitute counsel. * * * Finally, even if all the above conditions are met, the right that the Court now discovers will not come into play unless the defendant expressly protests counsel's strategy of admitting guilt. Where the defendant is advised of the strategy and says nothing, or is equivocal, the right is deemed to have been waived. See *Nixon*. * * * In short, the right that the Court now discovers is likely to appear only rarely, and because the present case is so unique, it is hard to see how it meets our stated criteria for granting review. * * *

III

While the question that the Court decides is unlikely to make another appearance for quite some time, a related—and difficult—question may arise more frequently: When guilt is the sole issue for the jury, is it ever permissible for counsel to make the unilateral decision to concede an element of the offense charged? If today's decision were understood to address that question, it would have important implications.

Under current precedent, there are some decisions on which a criminal defendant has the final say. For example, a defendant cannot be forced to enter a plea against his wishes. See *Brookhart* v. *Janis*, [fn. e, p. 997]. Similarly, no matter what counsel thinks best, a defendant has the right to insist on a jury trial and to take the stand and testify in his own defense. See *Harris* v. *New York*, 401 U.S. 222, 225 (1971). And if, as in this case, a defendant and retained counsel do not see eye to eye, the client can always attempt to find another attorney who will accede to his wishes. See *Gonzalez-Lopez*. A defendant can also choose to dispense with counsel entirely and represent himself. *Faretta*.

While these fundamental decisions must be made by a criminal defendant, most of the decisions that arise in criminal cases are the prerogative of counsel. (Our adversarial system would break down if defense counsel were required to obtain the client's approval for every important move made during the course of the case.) Among the decisions that counsel is free to make unilaterally are the following: choosing the basic line of defense, moving to suppress evidence, delivering an opening statement and deciding what to say in the opening, objecting to the admission of evidence, cross-examining witnesses, offering evidence and calling defense witnesses, and deciding what to say in summation. See e.g., *New York v. Hill*, 528 U.S. 110 (2000) [listing such rulings and adding "scheduling matters," including deciding to waive the timing requirements of the Interstate Agreement on Detainees]. On which side of the line does conceding some but not all elements of the charged offense fall?

Some criminal offenses contain elements that the prosecution can easily prove beyond any shadow of a doubt. A prior felony conviction is a good example. Suppose that the prosecution is willing to stipulate that the defendant has a prior felony conviction but is prepared, if necessary, to offer certified judgments of conviction for multiple prior violent felonies. If the defendant insists on contesting the convictions on frivolous grounds, must counsel go along? Does the same rule apply to all elements? If there are elements that may not be admitted over the defendant's objection, must counsel go further and actually contest those elements? Or is it permissible if counsel refrains from expressly conceding those elements but essentially admits them by walking the fine line recommended at argument by petitioner's current attorney?

What about conceding that a defendant is guilty, not of the offense charged, but of a lesser included offense? That is what English did in this case. He admitted that petitioner was guilty of the noncapital offense of second-degree murder in an effort to prevent a death sentence.[4] Is admitting guilt of a lesser included offense over the defendant's objection always unconstitutional? Where the evidence strongly supports conviction for first-degree murder, is it unconstitutional for defense counsel to make the decision to admit guilt of any lesser included form of homicide—even manslaughter? What about simple assault?

These are not easy questions, and the fact that they have not come up in this Court for more than two centuries suggests that they will arise infrequently in the future. I would leave those questions for another day and limit our decision to the particular (and highly unusual) situation in the actual case before us. And given the situation in which English found himself when trial commenced, I would hold that he did not violate any fundamental right by expressly acknowledging that petitioner killed the victims instead of engaging in the barren exercise that petitioner's current counsel now recommends.

IV

Having discovered a new right not at issue in the real case before us, the Court compounds its error by summarily concluding that a violation of this right "ranks as error of the kind our decisions have called 'structural.' " * * * The Court concedes that the Louisiana Supreme Court did not decide the structural-error question and

---

[4]   The Court asserts that, under Louisiana law, English's "second-degree strategy would have encountered a shoal" and necessarily failed. *Ante*, n. 1 [p. 994]. But the final arbiter of Louisiana law—the Louisiana Supreme Court—disagreed. It held that "[t]he jury was left with several choices" after English's second-degree concession, "including returning a responsive verdict of second degree murder" and "not returning the death penalty."

that we " 'did not grant certiorari to review' that question." *Ante*, n. 4 [p. 999]. We have stated time and again that we are "a court of review, not of first view" and, for that reason, have refused to decide issues not addressed below. * * * Under comparable circumstances, we have refrained from taking the lead on the question of structural error. * * * There is no good reason to take a different approach in this case. * * *[f]

5.   THE RIGHT OF SELF-REPRESENTATION

Faretta v. California established the constitutional right to self-representation (i.e., the defendant's right to "proceed *pro se*"). Although later cases, as discussed below, have added refinements to the scope of that right, *Faretta* remains the primary source for defining that right in the context of a defendant who seeks to represent himself at trial.

Prior to *Faretta*, several state appellate courts recognized a broad discretion of trial courts to insist that defendant be represented by counsel. In reaching this result, they rejected the contention that either state law or the federal constitution law established a constitutional right to self-representation. These rulings arose in two quite distinct procedural settings. In some instances, a defendant, fully informed of his right to counsel (including appointed counsel if the defendant was indigent), expressed a desire to proceed *pro se* and the trial court responded that the defendant would not be allowed to do so if he went to trial (in contrast to entering a guilty plea without counsel, which would be acceptable with a proper waiver of the right to counsel). In others, the defendant did not initially seek to proceed *pro se*, but to replace his current counsel. However, after the trial court refused to allow replacement, he then asked to proceed *pro se*, with the trial court rejecting that request and insisting that the defendant continue with his current counsel. Here, the initial issue for the appellate court was whether the refusal to allow replacement was proper under governing standards (see fn. a, p. 923), but if the trial court had ruled correctly on that point, the appellate court then had to decide whether the trial court had the discretion to refuse to allow the alternative of self-representation.

Faretta presented a situation in which defendant initially sought self-representation, but the Sixth Amendment right it recognized would similarly be available to a defendant who preferred a different counsel, but clearly chose self-representation when replacement was denied. Indeed, a substantial portion of the

---

[f]   *Garza v. Idaho*, 139 S.Ct. 738 (2018), concluded that a presumption of prejudice also applies where counsel disregarded defendant's instruction to file an appeal, as the "bare decision whether to appeal is ultimately the defendant's, not counsel's, to make." Counsel's obligation and the presumption applied notwithstanding a plea agreement that included an appeal waiver, as "all jurisdictions treat at least some claims as unwaivable," including the "right to challenge whether the waiver itself is valid and enforceable." Where there was no directive, as counsel failed to consult with the defendant as to a possible appeal, the challenge to the lack of consultation is subject to *Strickland* analysis. As for the performance prong, incompetency is established by a showing either that (1) the circumstances of the case, were such that a "rational defendant would [have] wanted the appeal," or (2) the "particular defendant reasonably demonstrated to counsel that he was interested in appealing." As for the prejudice prong, that is met by a showing of a "reasonable probability that, but for counsel's deficient failure to consult with him about an appeal, he would have timely appealed," *Roe v. Flores Ortega*, 528 U.S. 470 (2000).

large body of lower court rulings interpreting *Faretta* have involved assertions of the right to self-representation after the defendant's request for replacing counsel was denied.

Challenges to convictions based on *Faretta* have come both from defendants who were denied self-representation and defendants who were granted self-representation. Those denied self-representation argue that the denial was not justified under *Faretta*. Those granted self-representation typically argue that they were not sufficiently informed of the dangers of self-representation, as required by *Faretta*, and therefore the waiver of the right to counsel was invalid. Although the leading Supreme Court case presenting a challenge by a defendant granted self-representation involved a claim that the actions of standby counsel undercut the defendant's *Faretta* right,[a] such claims have been far less common.

In three key post-*Faretta* rulings, the Supreme Court reexamined the grounding of *Faretta*, and concluded in each case that an aspect of *Faretta* should not be extended to a procedural setting held distinguishable from that presented in *Faretta*. In *Martinez v. Court of Appeal of California*, 528 U.S. 152 (2000), the Court distinguished *Faretta* as to history (see fn. b, p. 1010) and relevant constitutional structure (see fn. a, p. 1009) in holding that there was no constitutional right to self-representation in the appellate process, and the state judiciary therefore could insist that argument on appeal be presented by counsel. In *Iowa v. Tovar*, 541 U.S. 77 (2004), the Court rejected a lower court's extension of *Faretta*'s requirement that defendant "be made aware of the dangers and disadvantages of self-representation" [p. 1011]. Such a warning was not required constitutionally for a defendant's waiver of the right to be represented by counsel in the course of entering a guilty plea. The extent of the warnings required varied with the procedural setting, and as the Court had noted in a pretrial context, "less vigorous warnings" are satisfactory when "the full dangers and disadvantages of representation [are] less substantial and more obvious to the accused then they are at trial."[b]

Edwards v. Indiana, 554 U.S. 164 (2008), provides the most recent, and the arguably most significant, reexamination of *Faretta*. In *Martinez*, supra, two

---

[a] In *McKaskle v. Wiggins*, 465 U.S. 168 (1984), the standby counsel had gone beyond the traditional role of "steer[ing] defendant through the basic procedures of the trial," engaging in arguably unsolicited participation on various substantive matters. In part, this was due to confusion created by the defendant's frequently shifting position on the assistance he desired from counsel. While citing that factor, the Court also reasoned that unsolicited participation exceeding bypass counsel's appropriate role did not undercut defendant's *Faretta* right where: (1) it did not interfere with defendant's own actions in such a way as to deprive him of "actual control over the case he chose to present to the jury," and (2) it did not destroy the jury's perception that the defendant was representing himself.

[b] The *Tovar* Court offered the following description as to what was required in the context of a defendant seeking to proceed *pro se* in entering a guilty plea: "The constitutional requirement is satisfied when the trial court informs the accused of the nature of the charges against him, of his right to be counseled regarding his plea, and of the range of allowable punishments attendant upon the entry of a guilty plea. * * * [Our past decisions have not] prescribed any formula or script to be read to a defendant who states that he elects to proceed without counsel. The information a defendant must possess in order to make an intelligent election [will] depend on a range of case-specific factors, including the defendant's education or sophistication, the complex or easily grasped nature of the charge, and the stage of the proceedings."

concurring Justices viewed the majority opinion as "casting doubt upon the rationale of *Faretta*," and Justice Breyer's concurring opinion took note of lower court opinions that "expressed dismay about the practical consequences of *Faretta*." The *Edwards* Court, however, in an opinion by Justice Breyer, flatly rejected Indiana's request that the Court overrule *Faretta*. Justice Breyer's opinion acknowledged the concern that "*Faretta* has led to trials that are unfair," but noted that "recent empirical research suggests that such instances are not common." Moreover, those instances "may well be concentrated in the 20 percent or so of self-representation cases where the mental competence of the defendant is also at issue," and the Court's ruling in *Edwards*, Justice Breyer noted, would grant trial judges the "authority to deal appropriately" with such cases.

In *Edwards*, the majority rejected a lower court ruling which read *Faretta* and a later Supreme Court ruling as holding that, once a defendant is determined to be competent to stand trial, his mental illness becomes irrelevant and the only issue is whether he has the understanding of the disadvantages of proceeding *pro se* required by *Faretta*.[c] The Court held that the presence of mental illness distinguished *Faretta*, and that "the Constitution permits States to insist upon representation by counsel for those [defendants] competent enough to stand trial * * * but who still suffer severe mental illness to the point where they are not competent to conduct trial proceedings by themselves." The Court stressed the trial judge's capacity to make "fine-tuned mental capacity decisions tailored to the individualized circumstances of a particular defendant." It left open, however, the possible adoption in the future of a specific standard as to the "measure of a defendant's ability to conduct a trial," finding no need, at this point, to rule on the state's suggestion that would "deny a criminal defendant the right to represent himself at trial where the defendant cannot communicate coherently with the court or jury."[d]

---

[c]   The constitutional test for competency to stand trial, as summarized in *Edwards*, has two prongs: "(1) whether the defendant has a rational as well as factual understanding of the proceedings against him, and (2) whether the defendant has sufficient present ability *to consult with his lawyer* with a reasonable degree of rational understanding." (emphasis in *Edwards*). In *Godinez v. Moran*, 509 U.S. 389 (1993), the Court rejected the contention that a more rigorous competency standard was required when the defendant was proceeding *pro se*, whether entering a guilty plea or going to trial. While the competency standard was developed in the context of a defendant represented by counsel, that standard's required mental capacity encompassed a rational understanding of a variety of personal choices, and "there was no reason to believe that [the decision to waive counsel] * * * requires an appreciably higher level of mental functioning than the decision to waive other constitutional rights." The Court also warned, however, that the presence of competency did not relieve the trial court of the obligation to determine that the defendant has the necessary understanding for a waiver. The competency standard addresses only the potential "ability to understand the proceedings," not "whether the defendant *does* understand" (emphasis in *Godinez*). In *Edwards*, the trial court had found both that the defendant was competent to stand trial and that he had the understanding required by *Faretta*. The state appellate court held that, in light of those findings, under *Faretta* and *Godinez*, the trial court had lacked the authority to deny self-representation—which it had done on the ground that, with obvious continued schizophrenia, defendant was not "competent to defend himself."

[d]   Dissenting in *Edwards*, Justice Scalia, joined by Justice Thomas, contended that *Godinez*, fn. c supra, provided sufficient and controlling consideration of the issue of mental illness. In the end, the dissent argued, the Court was treating self-representation not as a constitutionally mandated right, but as a partially protected interest, subject to limitation by "a State's view of fairness." This flaw was compounded by the open-ended character of the Court's description of the

FARETTA V. CALIFORNIA
422 U.S. 806, 95 S.Ct. 2525, 45 L.Ed.2d 562 (1975).

JUSTICE STEWART delivered the opinion of the Court.

The Sixth and Fourteenth Amendments of our Constitution guarantee that a person brought to trial in any state or federal court must be afforded the right to the assistance of counsel before he can be validly convicted and punished by imprisonment. This clear constitutional rule has emerged from a series of cases decided here over the last 50 years. The question before us now is whether a defendant in a state criminal trial has a constitutional right to proceed *without* counsel when he voluntarily and intelligently elects to do so. Stated another way, the question is whether a State may constitutionally hale a person into its criminal courts and there force a lawyer upon him, even when he insists that he wants to conduct his own defense. It is not an easy question, but we have concluded that a State may not constitutionally do so.

Anthony Faretta was charged with grand theft in * * * the Superior Court of Los Angeles County, Cal. At the arraignment, the Superior Court Judge assigned to preside at the trial appointed the public defender to represent Faretta. Well before the date of trial, however, Faretta requested that he be permitted to represent himself. Questioning by the judge revealed that Faretta had once represented himself in a criminal prosecution, that he had a high school education, and that he did not want to be represented by the public defender because he believed that that office was "very loaded down with * * * a heavy case load." The judge responded that he believed Faretta was "making a mistake" and emphasized that in further proceedings Faretta would receive no special favors. Nevertheless, * * * the judge, in a "preliminary ruling," accepted Faretta's waiver of the assistance of counsel. The judge indicated, however, that he might reverse this ruling if it later appeared that Faretta was unable adequately to represent himself.

Several weeks thereafter, but still prior to trial, the judge *sua sponte* held a hearing to inquire into Faretta's ability to conduct his own defense, and questioned him specifically about both the hearsay rule and the state law governing the challenge of potential jurors. After consideration of Faretta's answers, and observation of his demeanor, the judge ruled that Faretta had not made an intelligent and knowing waiver of his right to the assistance of counsel, and also ruled that Faretta had no constitutional right to conduct his own defense. The judge, accordingly, reversed his earlier ruling permitting self-representation and again appointed the public defender to represent Faretta. Faretta's subsequent request for leave to act as cocounsel was rejected, as were his efforts to make certain motions on his own behalf. Throughout the subsequent trial, the judge required that Faretta's defense be conducted only through the appointed lawyer from the public defender's office. At the conclusion of the trial, the jury found Faretta guilty as charged, and the judge sentenced him to prison.

---

factors that justified denying self-representation, see fn. c, p. 1012, as those factors readily could be manipulated to serve the interests of the trial judges in "making their lives easier * * * by appointing knowledgeable and literate counsel.' "

The California Court of Appeal * * * affirmed the trial judge's ruling that Faretta had no federal or state constitutional right to represent himself, * * * and the California Supreme Court denied review.

In the federal courts, the right of self-representation has been protected by statute since the beginnings of our Nation. Section 35 of the Judiciary Act of 1789, 1 Stat. 73, 92, enacted by the First Congress and signed by President Washington one day before the Sixth Amendment was proposed, provided that "in all the courts of the United States, the parties may plead and manage their own causes personally or by the assistance of * * * counsel * * *." * * * With few exceptions, each of the several States also accords a defendant the right to represent himself in any criminal case. The Constitutions of 36 States explicitly confer that right. Moreover, many state courts have expressed the view that the right is also supported by the Constitution of the United States. This Court has more than once indicated the same view. * * * [And] the United States Courts of Appeals have repeatedly held that the right of self-representation is protected by the Bill of Rights.

This Court's past recognition of the right of self-representation, the federal-court authority holding the right to be of constitutional dimension, and the state constitutions pointing to the right's fundamental nature form a consensus not easily ignored. "[T]he mere fact that a path is a beaten one," Mr. Justice Jackson once observed, "is a persuasive reason for following it." We confront here a nearly universal conviction, on the part of our people as well as our courts, that forcing a lawyer upon an unwilling defendant is contrary to his basic right to defend himself if he truly wants to do so. This consensus is soundly premised. The right of self-representation finds support in the structure of the Sixth Amendment, as well as in the English and colonial jurisprudence from which the Amendment emerged.

The Sixth Amendment includes a compact statement of the rights necessary to a full defense. * * * The rights to notice, confrontation, and compulsory process, when taken together, guarantee that a criminal charge may be answered in a manner now considered fundamental to the fair administration of American justice—through the calling and interrogation of favorable witnesses, the cross-examination of adverse witnesses, and the orderly introduction of evidence. In short, the Amendment constitutionalizes the right in an adversary criminal trial to make a defense as we know it.

The Sixth Amendment does not provide merely that a defense shall be made for the accused; it grants to the accused personally the right to make his defense. It is the accused, not counsel, who must be "informed of the nature and cause of the accusation," who must be "confronted with the witnesses against him," and who must be accorded "compulsory process for obtaining witnesses in his favor." Although not stated in the Amendment in so many words, the right to self-representation—to make one's own defense personally—is thus necessarily implied by the structure of the Amendment.[15] The right to defend is given directly to the accused; for it is he who suffers the consequences if the defense fails.

---

[15] This Court has often recognized the constitutional stature of rights that, though not literally expressed in the document, are essential to due process of law in a fair adversary process.

The counsel provision supplements this design. It speaks of the "assistance" of counsel, and an assistant, however expert, is still an assistant. The language and spirit of the Sixth Amendment contemplate that counsel, like the other defense tools guaranteed by the Amendment, shall be an aid to a willing defendant—not an organ of the State interposed between an unwilling defendant and his right to defend himself personally. To thrust counsel upon the accused, against his considered wish, thus violates the logic of the Amendment. In such a case, counsel is not an assistant, but a master; and the right to make a defense is stripped of the personal character upon which the Amendment insists. It is true that when a defendant chooses to have a lawyer manage and present his case, law and tradition may allocate to the counsel the power to make binding decisions of trial strategy in many areas. This allocation can only be justified, however, by the defendant's consent, at the outset, to accept counsel as his representative. An unwanted counsel "represents" the defendant only through a tenuous and unacceptable legal fiction. Unless the accused has acquiesced in such representation, the defense presented is not the defense guaranteed him by the Constitution, for, in a very real sense, it is not *his* defense.

The Sixth Amendment, when naturally read, thus implies a right of self-representation.[a] This reading is reinforced by the Amendment's roots in English legal history. In the long history of British criminal jurisprudence, there was only one tribunal that ever adopted a practice of forcing counsel upon an unwilling

---

It is now accepted, for example, that an accused has a right to be present at all stages of the trial where his absence might frustrate the fairness of the proceedings, to testify on his own behalf, and to be convicted only if his guilt is proved beyond a reasonable doubt. * * *

The inference of rights is not, of course, a mechanical exercise. In *Singer v. United States* [p. 810], the Court held that an accused has no right to a bench trial, despite his capacity to waive his right to a jury trial. In so holding, the Court stated that "[t]he ability to waive a constitutional right does not ordinarily carry with it the right to insist upon the opposite of that right." But that statement was made only *after* the Court had concluded that the Constitution does not affirmatively protect any right to be tried by a judge. * * * We follow the approach of *Singer* here. Our concern is with an *independent* right of self-representation. We do not suggest that this right arises mechanically from a defendant's power to waive the right to the assistance of counsel. * * *

[a] In *Martinez v. Court of Appeal of California* [p. 1005], the Court distinguished *Faretta* as a ruling relying on the structure of the Sixth Amendment, a guarantee that did not apply to the appellate process. The constitutional right to the assistance of counsel on appeal was grounded in the due process clause, and any right to self-representation on appeal similarly would have to be based on due process. From the perspective afforded by due process, the Court was "entirely unpersuaded," in light of the "practices that prevail in the nation today," that the "risk of either disloyalty or suspicion of disloyalty [in representation] is of sufficient concern to conclude that a constitutional right of self-representation is a necessary component of a fair appellate proceeding." Also, with defendant's position having shifted from that of an "accused" to a convicted defendant, the "autonomy interests" presented at this point are "less compelling" than in *Faretta*.

Although concurring in the result, Justice Scalia questioned the significance of looking to due process rather than the Sixth Amendment. Indeed, he noted, "I might have rested the decision [in *Faretta*] upon Due Process rather than the Sixth Amendment." Surely, he added, "the Framers of our Constitution, who were suspicious enough of governmental power—including judicial power— that they insisted upon a citizen's right to be judged by an independent jury of private citizens, would not have found acceptable the compulsory assignment of counsel *by the government* to plead a criminal defendant's case." As for self-representation on appeal, the key was "the fact that there is no constitutional right to appeal": "Since a state could, as for the Constitution is concerned, subject its trial determinations to no review whatever, it could *a fortiori* subject them to review which consists of a nonadversarial reexamination of convictions by a panel of government experts. Adversarial review with counsel appointed by the State is even less questionable that that."

defendant in a criminal proceeding. The tribunal was the Star Chamber. That curious institution, which flourished in the late 16th and early 17th centuries, was of mixed executive and judicial character, and characteristically departed from common-law traditions. For those reasons, and because it specialized in trying "political" offenses, the Star Chamber has for centuries symbolized disregard of basic individual rights. * * *

In the American Colonies the insistence upon a right of self-representation was, if anything, more fervent than in England. The colonists brought with them an appreciation of the virtues of self-reliance and a traditional distrust of lawyers. When the Colonies were first settled, "the lawyer was synonymous with the cringing Attorneys-General and Solicitors-General of the Crown and the arbitrary Justices of the King's Court, all bent on the conviction of those who opposed the King's prerogatives, and twisting the law to secure convictions." This prejudice gained strength in the Colonies where "distrust of lawyers became an institution." * * *

This is not to say that the Colonies were slow to recognize the value of counsel in criminal cases. Colonial judges soon departed from ancient English practice and allowed accused felons the aid of counsel for their defense. At the same time, however, the basic right of self-representation was never questioned. We have found no instance where a colonial court required a defendant in a criminal case to accept as his representative an unwanted lawyer. Indeed, even where counsel was permitted, the general practice continued to be self-representation. * * * After the Declaration of Independence, the right of self-representation, along with other rights basic to the making of a defense, entered the new state constitutions in wholesale fashion. The right to counsel was clearly thought to supplement the primary right of the accused to defend himself, utilizing his personal rights to notice, confrontation, and compulsory process. * * * At the time James Madison drafted the Sixth Amendment, some state constitutions guaranteed an accused the right to be heard "by himself" and by counsel; others provided that an accused was to be "allowed" counsel. The various state proposals for the Bill of Rights had similar variations in terminology. In each case, however, the counsel provision was embedded in a package of defense rights granted personally to the accused. There is no indication that the differences in phrasing about "counsel" reflected any differences of principle about self-representation.[b] * * *

There can be no blinking the fact that the right of an accused to conduct his own defense seems to cut against the grain of this Court's decisions holding that the Constitution requires that no accused can be convicted and imprisoned unless he has been accorded the right to the assistance of counsel. See *Powell v. Alabama*; *Johnson v. Zerbst*; *Gideon v. Wainwright*; *Argersinger v. Hamlin* [all discussed in Ch. 5, § 1]. For it is surely true that the basic thesis of those decisions is that the

---

[b]   In *Martinez v. Court of Appeal of California* [p. 1005], the Court questioned the lessons drawn by *Faretta* from this history, as "it [the history] pertained to times when lawyers were scarce, often mistrusted, and not readily available to the average person accused of crime." In any event, "the scant historical evidence pertaining to the issue of self-representation on appeal * * * [was] even less helpful." At the time of the adoption of the Constitution, appellate review as of right did not exist and "appellate review of any sort was 'limited' and 'rarely allowed'."

help of a lawyer is essential to assure the defendant a fair trial. And a strong argument can surely be made that the whole thrust of those decisions must inevitably lead to the conclusion that a State may constitutionally impose a lawyer upon even an unwilling defendant.

But it is one thing to hold that every defendant, rich or poor, has the right to the assistance of counsel, and quite another to say that a State may compel a defendant to accept a lawyer he does not want. The value of state-appointed counsel was not unappreciated by the Founders, yet the notion of compulsory counsel was utterly foreign to them. And whatever else may be said of those who wrote the Bill of Rights, surely there can be no doubt that they understood the inestimable worth of free choice.

It is undeniable that in most criminal prosecutions defendants could better defend with counsel's guidance than by their own unskilled efforts. But where the defendant will not voluntarily accept representation by counsel, the potential advantage of a lawyer's training and experience can be realized, if at all, only imperfectly. To force a lawyer on a defendant can only lead him to believe that the law contrives against him. Moreover, it is not inconceivable that in some rare instances, the defendant might in fact present his case more effectively by conducting his own defense. Personal liberties are not rooted in the law of averages. The right to defend is personal. The defendant, and not his lawyer or the State, will bear the personal consequences of a conviction. It is the defendant, therefore, who must be free personally to decide whether in his particular case counsel is to his advantage. And although he may conduct his own defense ultimately to his own detriment, his choice must be honored out of "that respect for the individual which is the lifeblood of the law."[46]

When an accused manages his own defense, he relinquishes, as a purely factual matter, many of the traditional benefits associated with the right to counsel. For this reason, in order to represent himself, the accused must "knowingly and intelligently" forgo those relinquished benefits. Although a defendant need not himself have the skill and experience of a lawyer in order competently and intelligently to choose self-representation, he should be made aware of the dangers and disadvantages of self-representation, so that the record will establish that "he knows what he is doing and his choice is made with eyes open."

---

[46] We are told that many criminal defendants representing themselves may use the courtroom for deliberate disruption of their trials. But the right of self-representation has been recognized from our beginnings by federal law and by most of the States, and no such result has thereby occurred. Moreover, the trial judge may terminate self-representation by a defendant who deliberately engages in serious and obstructionist misconduct. See *Illinois v. Allen* [p. 1016]. Of course, a State may—even over objection by the accused—appoint a "standby counsel" to aid the accused if and when the accused requests help, and to be available to represent the accused in the event that termination of the defendant's self-representation is necessary.

The right of self-representation is not a license to abuse the dignity of the courtroom. Neither is it a license not to comply with relevant rules of procedural and substantive law. Thus, whatever else may or may not be open to him on appeal, a defendant who elects to represent himself cannot thereafter complain that the quality of his own defense amounted to a denial of "effective assistance of counsel."

Here, weeks before trial, Faretta clearly and unequivocally declared to the trial judge that he wanted to represent himself and did not want counsel. The record affirmatively shows that Faretta was literate, competent, and understanding, and that he was voluntarily exercising his informed free will.[c] The trial judge had warned Faretta that he thought it was a mistake not to accept the assistance of counsel, and that Faretta would be required to follow all the "ground rules" of trial procedure. We need make no assessment of how well or poorly Faretta had mastered the intricacies of the hearsay rule and the California code provisions that govern challenges of potential jurors on *voir dire*. For his technical legal knowledge, as such, was not relevant to an assessment of his knowing exercise of the right to defend himself.

In forcing Faretta, under these circumstances, to accept against his will a state-appointed public defender, the California courts deprived him of his constitutional right to conduct his own defense. * * *

CHIEF JUSTICE BURGER, with whom JUSTICE BLACKMUN and JUSTICE REHNQUIST join, dissenting. * * *

The most striking feature of the Court's opinion is that it devotes so little discussion to the matter which it concedes is the core of the decision, that is, discerning an independent basis in the Constitution for the supposed right to represent oneself in a criminal trial. Its ultimate assertion that such a right is tucked between the lines of the Sixth Amendment is contradicted by the Amendment's language and its consistent judicial interpretation.

[T]he conclusion that the rights guaranteed by the Sixth Amendment are "personal" to an accused reflects nothing more than the obvious fact that it is he who is on trial and therefore has need of a defense.[3] But neither that nearly trivial proposition nor the language of the Amendment, which speaks in uniformly mandatory terms, leads to the further conclusion that the right to counsel is merely supplementary and may be dispensed with at the whim of the accused. Rather, this Court's decisions have consistently included the right to counsel as an integral part of the bundle making up the larger "right to a defense as we know it." [The] reason for this hardly requires explanation. The fact of the matter is that in all but an

---

[c] In *Edwards v. Indiana* [p. 1005], the Court cited several factors as justifying a different treatment of self-representation where the defendant was competent, but mentally ill. These included: (1) the historical adoption of a competency limitation by some of the states that had recognized (pre-*Faretta*) a right of self-representation; (2) the character of mental illness is so varied as to preclude reliance solely upon the constitutional competency test; (3) a right of self-representation at trial "will not affirm the dignity of the defendant who lacks the mental capacity to conduct his defense," but instead could well produce "a spectacle * * * as likely to prove humiliating as enabling"; and (4) "proceedings must not only be fair, they must 'appear fair to all that observe them'." Justice Scalia's dissent criticized, in particular, the third and fourth factors. As to "dignity," he noted, the dignity protected by *Faretta* is being "the master of one's own fate" and "not a concern about the defendant making a fool of himself." As to the appearance of fairness, that factor had never been utilized to "deny the defendant a right."

[3] The Court's attempt to derive support for its position from the fact that the Sixth Amendment speaks in terms of the "Assistance of Counsel" requires little comment. It is most curious to suggest that an accused who exercises his right to "assistance" has thereby impliedly consented to subject himself to a "master." And counsel's responsibility to his client and role in the litigation do not vary depending upon whether the accused would have preferred to represent himself.

extraordinarily small number of cases an accused will lose whatever defense he may have if he undertakes to conduct the trial himself.

[Nor] is it accurate to suggest, as the Court seems to later in its opinion, that the quality of his representation at trial is a matter with which only the accused is legitimately concerned. Although we have adopted an adversary system of criminal justice, the prosecution is more than an ordinary litigant, and the trial judge is not simply an automaton who insures that technical rules are adhered to. Both are charged with the duty of insuring that justice, in the broadest sense of that term, is achieved in every criminal trial. That goal is ill-served, and the integrity of and public confidence in the system are undermined, when an easy conviction is obtained due to the defendant's ill-advised decision to waive counsel. The damage thus inflicted is not mitigated by the lame explanation that the defendant simply availed himself of the "freedom" "to go to jail under his own banner * * *." The system of criminal justice should not be available as an instrument of self-destruction.

* * * True freedom of choice and society's interest in seeing that justice is achieved can be vindicated only if the trial court retains discretion to reject any attempted waiver of counsel and insist that the accused be tried according to the Constitution. This discretion is as critical an element of basic fairness as a trial judge's discretion to decline to accept a plea of guilty. See *Santobello v. New York* [p. 764].

[The Court] attempts to use history to take it where legal analysis cannot. Piecing together shreds of English legal history and early state constitutional and statutory provisions, without a full elaboration of the context in which they occurred or any evidence that they were relied upon by the drafters of our Federal Constitution, creates more questions than it answers and hardly provides the firm foundation upon which the creation of new constitutional rights should rest. * * * In this case, * * * history ought to lead judges to conclude that the Constitution leaves to the judgment of legislatures, and the flexible process of statutory amendment, the question whether criminal defendants should be permitted to conduct their trials *pro se*. See *Betts v. Brady* [p. 376]. And the fact that we have not hinted at a contrary view for 185 years is surely entitled to some weight in the scales. * * *

Society has the right to expect that, when courts find new rights implied in the Constitution, their potential effect upon the resources of our criminal justice system will be considered. However, such considerations are conspicuously absent from the Court's opinion in this case. [The] Court blandly assumes that once an accused has elected to defend himself he will be bound by his choice and not be heard to complain of it later. n. 46. This assumption ignores the role of appellate review, for the reported cases are replete with instances of a convicted defendant being relieved of a deliberate decision even when made *with the advice of counsel*. It is totally unrealistic, therefore, to suggest that an accused will always be held to the consequences of a decision to conduct his own defense. Unless, as may be the case, most persons accused of crime have more wit than to insist upon the dubious benefit that the Court confers today, we can expect that many expensive and good-faith prosecutions will be nullified on appeal for reasons that trial courts are now deprived of the power to prevent.

JUSTICE BLACKMUN, with whom THE CHIEF JUSTICE and JUSTICE REHNQUIST join, dissenting.

* * * I fear that the right to self-representation constitutionalized today frequently will cause procedural confusion without advancing any significant strategic interest of the defendant. [Although] the Court indicates that a *pro se* defendant necessarily waives any claim he might otherwise make of ineffective assistance of counsel, n. 46, the opinion leaves open a host of other procedural questions. Must every defendant be advised of his right to proceed *pro se?* If so, when must that notice be given? Since the right to assistance of counsel and the right to self-representation are mutually exclusive, how is the waiver of each right to be measured? If a defendant has elected to exercise his right to proceed *pro se,* does he still have a constitutional right to assistance of standby counsel? How soon in the criminal proceeding must a defendant decide between proceeding by counsel or *pro se?* Must he be allowed to switch in midtrial? May a violation of the right to self-representation ever be harmless error? Must the trial court treat the *pro se* defendant differently than it would professional counsel? I assume that many of these questions will be answered with finality in due course. Many of them, however, such as the standards of waiver and the treatment of the *pro se* defendant, will haunt the trial of every defendant who elects to exercise his right to self-representation. The procedural problems spawned by an absolute right to self-representation will far outweigh whatever tactical advantage the defendant may feel he has gained by electing to represent himself.

If there is any truth to the old proverb that "one who is his own lawyer has a fool for a client," the Court by its opinion today now bestows a *constitutional* right on one to make a fool of himself.[d]

---

[d] The Supreme Court subsequently addressed only one of the issues raised by Justice Blackmun. Lower courts have been in general agreement in addressing the other issues.

The harmless error issue was addressed by the Supreme Court in *McKaskle v. Wiggins*, 465 U.S. 168 (1984), the standby counsel case discussed in fn. a, p. 1005. *McKaskle* concluded that denial of the right to self-representation should not be treated as harmless error even though the counsel who represented the defendant over his objection provided far better representation than the defendant could have given himself. The Court noted: "Since the right of representation is a right that when exercised usually increases the likelihood of a trial outcome unfavorable to the defendant, its denial is not amenable to 'harmless error' analysis." Lower courts speaking to other issues cited by Justice Blackmun have generally held that (1) the defendant need not be advised of a right to proceed *pro se* unless he or she expresses an interest in doing so; (2) the trial court has broad discretion to deny a request to proceed *pro se* on administrative grounds if the request is first presented after the trial has started; (3) *Faretta* does not demand that the defendant be given a standby counsel and does not require the court to allow a "hybrid representation"; and (4) *pro se* defendants will be treated on appeal no differently than defendants with counsel as to objections that were not properly raised at trial, as the trial court has no special obligation to bend rules relating to the presentation of evidence or the raising of objections (and, in the usual instance, defendant could have relied upon the assistance of standby counsel on those matters).

CHAPTER 18

THE TRIAL

■ ■ ■

As was noted in Chapter One, the trial has traditionally been viewed as the capstone of the criminal justice, the "crown jewel" that reflects most of the basic elements of the process. It is not surprising, therefore, that many of the Bill of Rights guarantees relating to the criminal justice process refer specifically to the trial. Materials in previous chapters explore the Supreme Court's interpretation of several of those guarantees—the rights to a speedy trial (Ch. 12), to a trial by an impartial jury (Ch. 15), to a public trial (discussed at various points in Ch. 16 in comparing the public's right of access), and to the assistance of counsel (Chs. 5 and 17). The cases in this chapter deal with still other trial guarantees.

1. PRESENCE OF THE DEFENDANT

Cases defining the defendant's constitutional "right of presence" tend to involve three different issues. First, the Sixth Amendment guarantees the defendant the right "to be confronted with the witnesses against him." This aspect of the right is treated in the *Bryant* case (see § 2).

Second, the constitutional right of presence, although "rooted to large extent in the confrontation clause of the Sixth Amendment," also has a due process component. *United States v. Gagnon,* 470 U.S. 522 (1985). Accordingly, the right is not restricted to those parts of the trial in which the defendant is "actually confronting witnesses or evidence against him," and the issue is presented as to what other aspects of the trial itself, or proceedings related to the trial, fall within the scope of the defendant's right. The critical question here is whether defendant's presence at the particular proceeding "has a relation, reasonably substantial to the fullness of his opportunity to defend against the charge." *Gagnon.* As to proceedings not directly a part of the trial, the Court tends to focus on the context of the particular case in answering that question. See e.g., *Kentucky v. Stincer,* 482 U.S. 730 (1987) (judge's in-chambers examination of two young victims of alleged sex offense, to determine solely whether they were competent to testify, did not constitutionally require defendant's presence where defense counsel participated and further questions concerning competency could be raised at trial with defendant present).

Another major issue presented in defining the defendant's right of presence is what conditions permissibly can be attached to that right, so that a defense failure to comply with those conditions results in a loss of the right. *Illinois v. Allen,* the single case in section one, deals with this issue. Prior to *Allen,* in *Taylor v. United States,* 414 U.S. 17 (1973), the Court had held that a defendant cannot complain if he voluntarily absents himself during trial and the court continues the trial through to verdict. The Court has not had occasion to rule on the state's authority to proceed to trial in defendant's absence where the defendant was not even present at the commencement of the trial.

ILLINOIS V. ALLEN
397 U.S. 337, 90 S.Ct. 1057, 25 L.Ed.2d 353 (1970).

JUSTICE BLACK delivered the opinion of the Court.

[Allen was convicted by an Illinois jury of armed robbery and was sentenced to a term of 10 to 30 years. Before trial, the judge acceded to Allen's wish to conduct his own defense, although court-appointed counsel would "sit in and protect the record." During the *voir dire* examination, Allen "started to argue with the judge in a most abusive and disrespectful manner" when the judge directed him to confine his questioning to matters relating to the prospective juror's qualifications. The judge then asked appointed counsel to proceed with the examination, upon which Allen continued to talk and concluded his remarks by saying to the judge, "When I go out for lunchtime, you're going to be a corpse here." The judge then warned Allen that he would be removed from the courtroom if there was another outbreak of that sort. Allen continued to talk back, saying, "There's not going to be no trial, either. I'm going to sit here and you're going to talk and you can bring your shackles out and straight jacket and put them on me and tape my mouth, but it will do no good because there's not going to be no trial." After more abusive remarks, the judge ordered the trial to proceed in Allen's absence. After a noon recess, the judge permitted Allen to return to the courtroom with the warning that he could remain only so long as he behaved himself. Shortly thereafter, Allen spoke out again, saying, "There is going to be no proceeding. I'm going to start talking all through the trial. There's not going to be no trial like this." The judge again ordered Allen removed, and he remained out of the courtroom during the presentation of the State's case-in-chief except when brought in for purposes of identification. Thereafter, Allen was permitted to return to the courtroom upon his promise to conduct himself properly, and he remained for the rest of the trial, principally his defense, which was conducted by his appointed counsel. Allen's conviction was affirmed by the Supreme Court of Illinois, and on federal habeas corpus the district court found no constitutional violation and declined to issue the writ. The court of appeals reversed.]

The Court of Appeals felt that the defendant's Sixth Amendment right to be present at his own trial was so "absolute" that, no matter how unruly or disruptive the defendant's conduct might be, he could never be held to have lost that right so long as he continued to insist upon it, as Allen clearly did. * * * We cannot agree that the Sixth Amendment, the cases upon which the Court of Appeals relied, or any other cases of this Court so handicap a trial judge in conducting a criminal trial. * * * We accept instead the statement of Justice Cardozo who, speaking for the Court in *Snyder v. Massachusetts,* 291 U.S. 97, 106 (1934), said: "No doubt the privilege [of personally confronting witnesses] may be lost by consent or at times even by misconduct." Although mindful that courts must indulge every reasonable presumption against the loss of constitutional rights, we explicitly hold today that a defendant can lose his right to be present at trial if, after he has been warned by the judge that he will be removed if he continues his disruptive behavior, he nevertheless insists on conducting himself in a manner so disorderly, disruptive, and disrespectful of the court that his trial cannot be carried on with him in the courtroom. Once lost, the right to be present can, of course, be reclaimed as soon as the defendant is willing to conduct himself consistently with the decorum and respect inherent in the concept of courts and judicial proceedings.

It is essential to the proper administration of criminal justice that dignity, order, and decorum be the hallmarks of all court proceedings in our country. The flagrant disregard in the courtroom of elementary standards of proper conduct should not and cannot be tolerated. We believe trial judges confronted with disruptive, contumacious, stubbornly defiant defendants must be given sufficient discretion to meet the circumstances of each case. No one formula for maintaining the appropriate courtroom atmosphere will be best in all situations. We think there are at least three constitutionally permissible ways for a trial judge to handle an obstreperous defendant like Allen: (1) bind and gag him, thereby keeping him present; (2) cite him for contempt; (3) take him out of the courtroom until he promises to conduct himself properly.

Trying a defendant for a crime while he sits bound and gagged before the judge and jury would to an extent comply with that part of the Sixth Amendment's purposes that accords the defendant an opportunity to confront the witnesses at the trial. But even to contemplate such a technique, much less see it, arouses a feeling that no person should be tried while shackled and gagged except as a last resort. Not only is it possible that the sight of shackles and gags might have a significant effect on the jury's feelings about the defendant, but the use of this technique is itself something of an affront to the very dignity and decorum of judicial proceedings that the judge is seeking to uphold. Moreover, one of the defendant's primary advantages of being present at the trial, his ability to communicate with his counsel, is greatly reduced when the defendant is in a condition of total physical restraint. It is in part because of these inherent disadvantages and limitations in this method of dealing with disorderly defendants that we decline to hold with the Court of Appeals that a defendant cannot under any possible circumstances be deprived of his right to be present at trial. However, in some situations which we need not attempt to foresee, binding and gagging might possibly be the fairest and most reasonable way to handle a defendant who acts as Allen did here.[a]

---

[a]   The Court addressed the permissible use of shackles to restrain defendants thirty five years later in *Deck v. Missouri*, 544 U.S. 622 (2005), where it held that "courts cannot routinely place defendants in shackles or other physical restraints visible to the jury during the penalty phase of a capital proceeding. The constitutional requirement, however, is not absolute. It permits a judge, in the exercise of his or her discretion, to take account of special circumstances, including security concerns, that may call for shackling. In so doing, it accommodates the important need to protect the courtroom and its occupants. But any such determination must be case specific; that is to say, it should reflect particular concerns, say special security needs or escape risks, related to the defendant on trial."

In a footnote the Court of Appeals suggested the possible availability of contempt of court as a remedy to make Allen behave in his robbery trial, and it is true that citing or threatening to cite a contumacious defendant for criminal contempt might in itself be sufficient to make a defendant stop interrupting a trial. If so, the problem would be solved easily, and the defendant could remain in the courtroom. Of course, if the defendant is determined to prevent *any* trial, then a court in attempting to try the defendant for contempt is still confronted with the identical dilemma that the Illinois court faced in this case. And criminal contempt has obvious limitations as a sanction when the defendant is charged with a crime so serious that a very severe sentence such as death or life imprisonment is likely to be imposed. In such a case the defendant might not be affected by a mere contempt sentence when he ultimately faces a far more serious sanction. Nevertheless, the contempt remedy should be borne in mind by a judge in the circumstances of this case.

Another aspect of the contempt remedy is the judge's power, when exercised consistently with state and federal law, to imprison an unruly defendant such as Allen for civil contempt and discontinue the trial until such time as the defendant promises to behave himself. This procedure is consistent with the defendant's right to be present at trial, and yet it avoids the serious shortcomings of the use of shackles and gags. It must be recognized, however, that a defendant might conceivably, as a matter of calculated strategy, elect to spend a prolonged period in confinement for contempt in the hope that adverse witnesses might be unavailable after a lapse of time. A court must guard against allowing a defendant to profit from his own wrong in this way.

The trial court in this case decided under the circumstances to remove the defendant from the courtroom and to continue his trial in his absence until and unless he promised to conduct himself in a manner befitting an American courtroom. As we said earlier, we find nothing unconstitutional about this procedure. Allen's behavior was clearly of such an extreme and aggravated nature as to justify either his removal from the courtroom or his total physical restraint. Prior to his removal he was repeatedly warned by the trial judge that he would be removed from the courtroom if he persisted in his unruly conduct, and, as Judge Hastings [of the Court of Appeals] observed in his dissenting opinion, the record demonstrates that Allen would not have been at all dissuaded by the trial judge's use of his criminal contempt powers. Allen was constantly informed that he could return to the trial when he would agree to conduct himself in an orderly manner. Under these circumstances we hold that Allen lost his right guaranteed by the Sixth and Fourteenth Amendments to be present throughout his trial. * * *

JUSTICE BRENNAN, concurring. * * *

I would add only that when a defendant is excluded from his trial, the court should make reasonable efforts to enable him to communicate with his attorney and, if possible, to keep apprised of the progress of his trial. Once the court has removed the contumacious defendant, it is not weakness to mitigate the disadvantages of his expulsion as far as technologically possible in the circumstances.

JUSTICE DOUGLAS. * * *

Our real problems of this type lie not with this case but with other kinds of trials. *First* are the political trials. They frequently recur in our history and insofar as they take place in federal courts we have broad supervisory powers over them. * * * In Anglo-American law, great injustices have at times been done to unpopular minorities by judges, as well as by prosecutors. I refer to London in 1670 when William Penn, the gentle Quaker, was tried for causing a riot when all that he did was to preach a sermon on Grace Church Street * * *. The panel of judges who tried William Penn were sincere, law-and-order men of their day. Though Penn was acquitted by the jury, he was jailed by the court for his contemptuous conduct [which consisted of repeatedly seeking to determine from the court "by what law it is you prosecute me, and upon what law you ground my indictment"]. Would we tolerate removal of a defendant from the courtroom during a trial because he was insisting on his constitutional rights, albeit vociferously, no matter how obnoxious his philosophy might have been to the bench that tried him? * * *

Second are trials used by minorities to destroy the existing constitutional system and bring on repressive measures. Radicals on the left historically have used those tactics to incite the extreme right with the calculated design of fostering a regime of repression from which the radicals on the left hope to emerge as the ultimate victor. The left in that role is the provocateur. The Constitution was not designed as an instrument for that form of rough-and-tumble contest. The social compact has room for tolerance, patience, and restraint, but not for sabotage and violence. Trials involving that spectacle strike at the very heart of constitutional government.

I would not try to provide in this case the guidelines for those two strikingly different types of cases. The case presented here is the classical criminal case without any political or subversive overtones. * * *

2. CONFRONTATION AND COMPULSORY PROCESS

The Supreme Court has characterized its cases dealing with the Sixth Amendment's confrontation clause as "fall[ing] into two broad, albeit not exclusive categories: 'cases involving the admission of out-of-court statements and cases involving restrictions imposed by law or by the trial court on the scope of cross-examination.'" *Kentucky v. Stincer,* 482 U.S. 730 (1987). The first two cases in this section fall within the first grouping while the third case falls within the second grouping.

The cases in the first grouping generally have involved the constitutionality of admitting into evidence "hearsay"—that is, a statement that was made out of court and is being offered in evidence to prove the truth of the facts asserted in that statement. Under the rules of evidence currently applied in the different states, as at common law, most hearsay testimony is not admissible in evidence, but there are exceptions. Certain types of out-of-court statements are classified as not truly hearsay (as measured by the primary functions of the hearsay ban) and others are viewed as within special exceptions to the ban that support their admissibility. Confrontation clause concerns obviously arise when a state, under one rationale or another, allows a prosecution witness to testify to a hearsay statement made by a third party; here only the witness is before the defendant and subject to cross-examination, not the third party (the hearsay declarant) whose statement is being used to prove the truth of its contents.

The first case in this section, *Michigan v. Bryant*, is one of a series of closely divided cases redefining the relationship of the Confrontation Clause to hearsay exceptions recognized under state law. The opinions here present the justices' ongoing disagreement about the scope of the Sixth Amendment's commands, and traces developments since the Court replaced its earlier approach, based upon the reliability of statements, with one based on whether the statements are "testimonial." *Richardson v. Marsh*, the second case, considers the question of the proper interpretation of the Confrontation Clause's bar against admissibility in the context of a joint trial, where the Confrontation Clause bars admission of a confession against one codefendant but not the other.

Davis v. Alaska, the third case, falls in the second grouping of Confrontation Clause cases—those cases concerned with the restriction of cross-examination opportunity by law or by trial court ruling. *Davis* should be read in light of *Pennsylvania v. Ritchie*, previously included in Chapter Thirteen on the duty to disclose. *Ritchie* not only discusses the scope of *Davis* but also speaks to the scope of the Sixth Amendment's guarantee of compulsory process. The Supreme Court has had very little to say about the Sixth Amendment's compulsory process clause. The leading case applying the clause, *Washington v. Texas*, 388 U.S. 14 (1967), struck down a state rule that the Court characterized as an "absurdity"—one that prohibited the defendant from introducing the testimony of an accomplice on his behalf but allowed the prosecution to put on the stand accomplices who would testify in its favor. See also *Holmes v. South Carolina*, infra § 4.

MICHIGAN V. BRYANT
562 U.S. 344, 131 S.Ct. 1143, 179 L.Ed.2d 93 (2011).

JUSTICE SOTOMAYOR delivered the opinion of the Court.

At respondent Richard Bryant's trial, the court admitted statements that the victim, Anthony Covington, made to police officers who discovered him mortally wounded in a gas station parking lot. A jury convicted Bryant of, *inter alia*, second-degree murder. On appeal, the Supreme Court of Michigan held that the Sixth Amendment's Confrontation Clause, as explained in our decisions in *Crawford v. Washington*, 541 U.S. 36 (2004), and *Davis v. Washington*, 547 U.S. 813 (2006), rendered Covington's statements inadmissible testimonial hearsay, and the court reversed Bryant's conviction. We granted the State's petition for a writ of certiorari to consider whether the Confrontation Clause barred the admission at trial of Covington's statements to the police. We hold that the circumstances of the interaction between Covington and the police objectively indicate that the "primary purpose of the interrogation" was "to enable police assistance to meet an ongoing emergency." Therefore, Covington's identification and description of the shooter and the location of the shooting were not testimonial statements, and their admission at Bryant's trial did not violate the Confrontation Clause. We vacate the judgment of the Supreme Court of Michigan and remand.

I

Around 3:25 a.m. on April 29, 2001, Detroit, Michigan police officers responded to a radio dispatch indicating that a man had been shot. At the scene, they found the victim, Anthony Covington, lying on the ground next to his car in a gas station parking lot. Covington had a gunshot wound to his abdomen, appeared to be in great pain, and spoke with difficulty.

The police asked him "what had happened, who had shot him, and where the shooting had occurred." Covington stated that "Rick" shot him at around 3 a.m. He also indicated that he had a conversation with Bryant, whom he recognized based on his voice, through the back door of Bryant's house. Covington explained that when he turned to leave, he was shot through the door and then drove to the gas station, where police found him.

Covington's conversation with the police ended within 5 to 10 minutes when emergency medical services arrived. Covington was transported to a hospital and died within hours. The police left the gas station after speaking with Covington, called for backup, and traveled to Bryant's house. They did not find Bryant there but did find blood and a bullet on the back porch and an apparent bullet hole in the back door. Police also found Covington's wallet and identification outside the house.

At trial, which occurred prior to our decisions in *Crawford* and *Davis*, the police officers who spoke with Covington at the gas station testified about what Covington had told them. The jury returned a guilty verdict on charges of second-degree murder, being a felon in possession of a firearm, and possession of a firearm during the commission of a felony.

Bryant appealed. * * * [T]he Supreme Court of Michigan held that the admission of Covington's statements constituted prejudicial plain error warranting reversal and ordered a new trial. * * *.[1]

* * *

II

The Confrontation Clause of the Sixth Amendment states: "In all criminal prosecutions, the accused shall enjoy the right . . . to be confronted with the witnesses against him." The Fourteenth Amendment renders the Clause binding on the States. In *Ohio v. Roberts,* 448 U.S. 56, 66 (1980), we explained that the confrontation right does not bar admission of statements of an unavailable witness if the statements "bea[r] adequate 'indicia of reliability.' " We held that reliability

---

[1]   * * * The trial court ruled that the statements were admissible as excited utterances and did not address their admissibility as dying declarations. This occurred prior to our 2004 decision in *Crawford,* where we first suggested that dying declarations, even if testimonial, might be admissible as a historical exception to the Confrontation Clause. * * * Because of the State's failure to preserve its argument with regard to dying declarations, we similarly need not decide that question here.

can be established if "the evidence falls within a firmly rooted hearsay exception," or if it does not fall within such an exception, then if it bears "particularized guarantees of trustworthiness."

Nearly a quarter century later, we decided *Crawford v. Washington*. Petitioner Michael Crawford was prosecuted for stabbing a man who had allegedly attempted to rape his wife, Sylvia. Sylvia witnessed the stabbing, and later that night, after she and her husband were both arrested, police interrogated her about the incident. At trial, Sylvia Crawford claimed spousal privilege and did not testify, but the State introduced a tape recording of Sylvia's statement to the police in an effort to prove that the stabbing was not in self-defense, as Michael Crawford claimed. The Washington Supreme Court affirmed Crawford's conviction because it found Sylvia's statement to be reliable, as required under *Ohio v. Roberts*. We reversed, overruling *Ohio v. Roberts*.

Crawford examined the common-law history of the confrontation right and explained that "the principal evil at which the Confrontation Clause was directed was the civil-law mode of criminal procedure, and particularly its use of *ex parte* examinations as evidence against the accused." We noted that in England, pretrial examinations of suspects and witnesses by government officials "were sometimes read in court in lieu of live testimony." In light of this history, we emphasized the word "witnesses" in the Sixth Amendment, defining it as "those who 'bear testimony.'" We defined "testimony" as "'[a] solemn declaration or affirmation made for the purpose of establishing or proving some fact.'" We noted that "[a]n accuser who makes a formal statement to government officers bears testimony in a sense that a person who makes a casual remark to an acquaintance does not." We therefore limited the Confrontation Clause's reach to testimonial statements and held that in order for testimonial evidence to be admissible, the Sixth Amendment "demands what the common law required: unavailability and a prior opportunity for cross-examination."[a] Although "leav[ing] for another day any effort to spell out a comprehensive definition of 'testimonial,'" *Crawford* noted that "at a minimum" it includes "prior testimony at a preliminary hearing, before a grand jury, or at a former trial; and . . . police interrogations."[b] Under this reasoning, we

---

[a]　Justice Scalia wrote for a majority in *Crawford*: "Where testimonial statements are involved, we do not think the Framers meant to leave the Sixth Amendment's protection to the vagaries of the rules of evidence, much less to amorphous notions of 'reliability.' Admitting statements deemed reliable by a judge is fundamentally at odds with the right of confrontation. * * * The Clause * * * reflects a judgment, not only about the desirability of reliable evidence * * * but about how reliability can best be determined."

[b]　In *Crawford*, Chief Justice Rehnquist, joined by Justice O'Connor, concurred in the judgment, but disagreed with the overruling of *Roberts*. Chief Justice Rehnquist reasoned: "The Court's distinction between testimonial and non-testimonial statements * * * is no better rooted in history than our current doctrine." While "testimonial statements such as accusatory statements to police officers likely would have been disapproved of in the 18th century, * * * [that] would not necessarily [be] because they resembled ex parte affidavits or depositions, as the Court reasons, but more likely than not, because they were not made under oath. * * * Thus, while I agree that * * * the Framers were mainly concerned about sworn affidavits and depositions, it does not follow that they were similarly concerned about the Court's broader category of testimonial statements." Moreover, "between 1700 and 1800 the rules regarding the admissibility of out-of-court statements were still being developed, * * * [with] exceptions [recognized] to the general rule of exclusion," so it was hardly "clear * * * that the Framers categorically wanted to eliminate further ones." As recognized in *Roberts*, "[e]xceptions to confrontation have been derived from the experience that

held that Sylvia Crawford's statements in the course of police questioning were testimonial and that their admission when Michael Crawford "had no opportunity to cross-examine her" due to spousal privilege was "sufficient to make out a violation of the Sixth Amendment."

In 2006, the Court in *Davis v. Washington* and *Hammon v. Indiana,* 547 U.S. 813, took a further step to "determine more precisely which police interrogations produce testimony" and therefore implicate a Confrontation Clause bar. We explained that when *Crawford* said that " 'interrogations by law enforcement officers fall squarely within [the] class' of testimonial hearsay, we had immediately in mind (for that was the case before us) interrogations solely directed at establishing the facts of a past crime, in order to identify (or provide evidence to convict) the perpetrator. The product of such interrogation, whether reduced to a writing signed by the declarant or embedded in the memory (and perhaps notes) of the interrogating officer, is testimonial." *Davis.*

We thus made clear in *Davis* that not all those questioned by the police are witnesses and not all "interrogations by law enforcement officers," are subject to the Confrontation Clause.[2]

Davis and *Hammon* were both domestic violence cases. In *Davis,* Michelle McCottry made the statements at issue to a 911 operator during a domestic disturbance with Adrian Davis, her former boyfriend. McCottry told the operator, " 'He's here jumpin' on me again,' " and, " 'He's usin' his fists.' " The operator then asked McCottry for Davis' first and last names and middle initial, and at that point in the conversation McCottry reported that Davis had fled in a car. McCottry did not appear at Davis' trial, and the State introduced the recording of her conversation with the 911 operator.

In *Hammon,* decided along with *Davis,* police responded to a domestic disturbance call at the home of Amy and Hershel Hammon, where they found Amy alone on the front porch. She appeared " 'somewhat frightened,' " but told them " 'nothing was the matter.' " She gave the police permission to enter the house, where they saw a gas heating unit with the glass front shattered on the floor. One officer remained in the kitchen with Hershel, while another officer talked to Amy in the living room about what had happened. Hershel tried several times to participate in Amy's conversation with the police and became angry when the police required him to stay separated from Amy. The police asked Amy to fill out and sign a battery affidavit. She wrote: " 'Broke our Furnace & shoved me down on the floor into the broken glass. Hit me in the chest and threw me down. Broke our lamps & phone. Tore up my van where I couldn't leave the house. Attacked my daughter.' " Amy did not appear at Hershel's trial, so the police officers who spoke

---

some out-of-court statements are just as reliable as cross-examined in-court testimony due to the circumstances under which they were made. * * * By creating an immutable category of excluded evidence, the Court adds little to a trial's truth-finding function and ignores this longstanding guidance."

    2   We noted in *Crawford* that "[w]e use the term 'interrogation' in its colloquial, rather than any technical legal, sense," and that "[j]ust as various definitions of 'testimonial' exist, one can imagine various definitions of 'interrogation,' and we need not select among them in this case."
* * *

with her testified as to her statements and authenticated the affidavit. The trial court admitted the affidavit as a present sense impression and admitted the oral statements as excited utterances under state hearsay rules. The Indiana Supreme Court affirmed Hammon's conviction, holding that Amy's oral statements were not testimonial and that the admission of the affidavit, although erroneous because the affidavit was testimonial, was harmless.

To address the facts of both cases, we expanded upon the meaning of "testimonial" that we first employed in *Crawford* and discussed the concept of an ongoing emergency. We explained:

> "Statements are nontestimonial when made in the course of police interrogation under circumstances objectively indicating that the primary purpose of the interrogation is to enable police assistance to meet an ongoing emergency. They are testimonial when the circumstances objectively indicate that there is no such ongoing emergency, and that the primary purpose of the interrogation is to establish or prove past events potentially relevant to later criminal prosecution." *Davis.*

Examining the *Davis* and *Hammon* statements in light of those definitions, we held that the statements at issue in *Davis* were nontestimonial and the statements in *Hammon* were testimonial. We distinguished the statements in *Davis* from the testimonial statements in *Crawford* on several grounds, including that the victim in *Davis* was "speaking about events *as they were actually happening,* rather than 'describ[ing] past events,'" that there was an ongoing emergency, that the "elicited statements were necessary to be able to *resolve* the present emergency," and that the statements were not formal. In *Hammon,* on the other hand, we held that, "[i]t is entirely clear from the circumstances that the interrogation was part of an investigation into possibly criminal past conduct." There was "no emergency in progress." The officer questioning Amy "was not seeking to determine . . . 'what is happening,' but rather 'what happened.'" It was "formal enough" that the police interrogated Amy in a room separate from her husband where, "some time after the events described were over," she "deliberately recounted, in response to police questioning, how potentially criminal past events began and progressed." Because her statements "were neither a cry for help nor the provision of information enabling officers immediately to end a threatening situation," we held that they were testimonial.

Davis did not "attemp[t] to produce an exhaustive classification of all conceivable statements—or even all conceivable statements in response to police interrogation—as either testimonial or nontestimonial."[3] The basic purpose of the Confrontation Clause was to "targe[t]" the sort of "abuses" exemplified at the notorious treason trial of Sir Walter Raleigh. *Crawford.* Thus, the most important

---

[3]   *Davis* explained that 911 operators "may at least be agents of law enforcement when they conduct interrogations of 911 callers," and therefore "consider[ed] their acts to be acts of the police" for purposes of the opinion. *Davis* explicitly reserved the question of "whether and when statements made to someone other than law enforcement personnel are 'testimonial.'" We have no need to decide that question in this case either because Covington's statements were made to police officers. * * *

instances in which the Clause restricts the introduction of out-of-court statements are those in which state actors are involved in a formal, out-of-court interrogation of a witness to obtain evidence for trial.[4] Even where such an interrogation is conducted with all good faith, introduction of the resulting statements at trial can be unfair to the accused if they are untested by cross-examination. Whether formal or informal, out-of-court statements can evade the basic objective of the Confrontation Clause, which is to prevent the accused from being deprived of the opportunity to cross-examine the declarant about statements taken for use at trial. When, as in *Davis,* the primary purpose of an interrogation is to respond to an "ongoing emergency," its purpose is not to create a record for trial and thus is not within the scope of the Clause. But there may be *other* circumstances, aside from ongoing emergencies, when a statement is not procured with a primary purpose of creating an out-of-court substitute for trial testimony. In making the primary purpose determination, standard rules of hearsay, designed to identify some statements as reliable, will be relevant. Where no such primary purpose exists, the admissibility of a statement is the concern of state and federal rules of evidence, not the Confrontation Clause.

Deciding this case also requires further explanation of the "ongoing emergency" circumstance addressed in *Davis.* Because *Davis* and *Hammon* arose in the domestic violence context, that was the situation "we had immediately in mind (for that was the case before us)." We now face a new context: a nondomestic dispute, involving a victim found in a public location, suffering from a fatal gunshot wound, and a perpetrator whose location was unknown at the time the police located the victim. Thus, we confront for the first time circumstances in which the "ongoing emergency" discussed in *Davis* extends beyond an initial victim to a potential threat to the responding police and the public at large. This new context requires us to provide additional clarification with regard to what *Davis* meant by "the primary purpose of the interrogation is to enable police assistance to meet an ongoing emergency."

III

To determine whether the "primary purpose" of an interrogation is "to enable police assistance to meet an ongoing emergency," *Davis,* which would render the resulting statements nontestimonial, we objectively evaluate the circumstances in which the encounter occurs and the statements and actions of the parties.

* * * The circumstances in which an encounter occurs—*e.g.,* at or near the scene of the crime versus at a police station, during an ongoing emergency or afterwards—are clearly matters of objective fact. The statements and actions of the

---

4　* * * For all of the reasons discussed in Justice Thomas' opinion concurring in the judgment, the situation presented in this case is nothing like the circumstances presented by Sir Walter Raleigh's trial. [**Editors' note:** In *Crawford,* Justice Scalia, writing for the Court, described that trial: "Lord Cobham, Raleigh's alleged accomplice, had implicated him in an examination before the Privy Council and in a letter. At Raleigh's trial, these were read to the jury. Raleigh argued that Cobham had lied to save himself * * * Suspecting that Cobham would recant, Raleigh demanded that the judges call him to appear, arguing that '[t]he Proof of the Common Law is by witness and jury: let Cobham be here, let him speak it. Call my accuser before my face. . . .' The judges refused, and, despite Raleigh's protestations that he was being tried 'by the Spanish Inquisition,' the jury convicted, and Raleigh was sentenced to death."]

parties must also be objectively evaluated. That is, the relevant inquiry is not the subjective or actual purpose of the individuals involved in a particular encounter, but rather the purpose that reasonable participants would have had, as ascertained from the individuals' statements and actions and the circumstances in which the encounter occurred. * * *

As our recent Confrontation Clause cases have explained, the existence of an "ongoing emergency" at the time of an encounter between an individual and the police is among the most important circumstances informing the "primary purpose" of an interrogation. The existence of an ongoing emergency is relevant to determining the primary purpose of the interrogation because an emergency focuses the participants on something other than "prov[ing] past events potentially relevant to later criminal prosecution."[8] Rather, it focuses them on "end[ing] a threatening situation." Implicit in *Davis* is the idea that because the prospect of fabrication in statements given for the primary purpose of resolving that emergency is presumably significantly diminished, the Confrontation Clause does not require such statements to be subject to the crucible of cross-examination.

This logic is not unlike that justifying the excited utterance exception in hearsay law. Statements "relating to a startling event or condition made while the declarant was under the stress of excitement caused by the event or condition," Fed. Rule Evid. 803(2) are considered reliable because the declarant, in the excitement, presumably cannot form a falsehood. An ongoing emergency has a similar effect of focusing an individual's attention on responding to the emergency. * * *

[W]hether an emergency exists and is ongoing is a highly context-dependent inquiry. * * * Because *Davis* and *Hammon* were domestic violence cases, we focused only on the threat to the victims and assessed the ongoing emergency from the perspective of whether there was a continuing threat *to them*. * * * An assessment of whether an emergency that threatens the police and public is ongoing cannot narrowly focus on whether the threat solely to the first victim has been neutralized because the threat to the first responders and public may continue.

The * * * duration and scope of an emergency may depend in part on the type of weapon employed. * * * Hershel Hammon was armed only with his fists when he attacked his wife, so removing Amy to a separate room was sufficient to end the emergency. If Hershel had been reported to be armed with a gun, however, separation by a single household wall might not have been sufficient to end the emergency.

* * * The medical condition of the victim is important to the primary purpose inquiry to the extent that it sheds light on the ability of the victim to have any purpose at all in responding to police questions and on the likelihood that any purpose formed would necessarily be a testimonial one. The victim's medical state

---

[8] The existence of an ongoing emergency must be objectively assessed from the perspective of the parties to the interrogation at the time, not with the benefit of hindsight. * * *

also provides important context for first responders to judge the existence and magnitude of a continuing threat to the victim, themselves, and the public.

* * * [N]one of this suggests that an emergency is ongoing in every place or even just surrounding the victim for the entire time that the perpetrator of a violent crime is on the loose. As we recognized in *Davis,* "a conversation which begins as an interrogation to determine the need for emergency assistance" can "evolve into testimonial statements." This evolution may occur if, for example, a declarant provides police with information that makes clear that what appeared to be an emergency is not or is no longer an emergency or that what appeared to be a public threat is actually a private dispute. It could also occur if a perpetrator is disarmed, surrenders, is apprehended, or, as in *Davis,* flees with little prospect of posing a threat to the public. Trial courts can determine in the first instance when any transition from nontestimonial to testimonial occurs, and exclude "the portions of any statement that have become testimonial, as they do, for example, with unduly prejudicial portions of otherwise admissible evidence."

* * * [W]hether an ongoing emergency exists is simply one factor—albeit an important factor—that informs the ultimate inquiry regarding the "primary purpose" of an interrogation.

Another factor the Michigan Supreme Court did not sufficiently account for is the importance of *informality* in an encounter between a victim and police. Formality is not the sole touchstone of our primary purpose inquiry because, although formality suggests the absence of an emergency and therefore an increased likelihood that the purpose of the interrogation is to "establish or prove past events potentially relevant to later criminal prosecution," informality does not necessarily indicate the presence of an emergency or the lack of testimonial intent. The court below, however, too readily dismissed the informality of the circumstances in this case in a single brief footnote and in fact seems to have suggested that the encounter in this case was formal. As we explain further below, the questioning in this case occurred in an exposed, public area, prior to the arrival of emergency medical services, and in a disorganized fashion. All of those facts make this case distinguishable from the formal station-house interrogation in *Crawford.* * * *

In addition to the circumstances in which an encounter occurs, the statements and actions of both the declarant and interrogators provide objective evidence of the primary purpose of the interrogation. See, *e.g., Davis* ("[T]he nature of what was *asked and answered* in *Davis,* again viewed objectively, was such that the elicited statements were necessary to be able to *resolve* the present emergency, rather than simply to learn (as in *Crawford*) what had happened in the past" (first emphasis added)). * * *

As the Michigan Supreme Court correctly recognized, *Davis* requires a combined inquiry that accounts for both the declarant and the interrogator. In many instances, the primary purpose of the interrogation will be most accurately ascertained by looking to the contents of both the questions and the answers. To give an extreme example, if the police say to a victim, "Tell us who did this to you so that we can arrest and prosecute them," the victim's response that "Rick did it," appears purely accusatory because by virtue of the phrasing of the question, the victim necessarily has prosecution in mind when she answers.

The combined approach also ameliorates problems that could arise from looking solely to one participant. Predominant among these is the problem of mixed motives on the part of both interrogators and declarants. Police officers in our society function as both first responders and criminal investigators. Their dual responsibilities may mean that they act with different motives simultaneously or in quick succession.

Victims are also likely to have mixed motives when they make statements to the police. During an ongoing emergency, a victim is most likely to want the threat to her and to other potential victims to end, but that does not necessarily mean that the victim wants or envisions prosecution of the assailant. A victim may want the attacker to be incapacitated temporarily or rehabilitated. Alternatively, a severely injured victim may have no purpose at all in answering questions posed; the answers may be simply reflexive. The victim's injuries could be so debilitating as to prevent her from thinking sufficiently clearly to understand whether her statements are for the purpose of addressing an ongoing emergency or for the purpose of future prosecution. Taking into account a victim's injuries does not transform this objective inquiry into a subjective one. The inquiry is still objective because it focuses on the understanding and purpose of a reasonable victim in the circumstances of the actual victim—circumstances that prominently include the victim's physical state.

The dissent suggests that we intend to give controlling weight to the "intentions of the police." That is a misreading of our opinion. At trial, the declarant's statements, not the interrogator's questions, will be introduced to "establis[h] the truth of the matter asserted," and must therefore pass the Sixth Amendment test. In determining whether a declarant's statements are testimonial, courts should look to all of the relevant circumstances. * * * [C]ourts making a "primary purpose" assessment should not be unjustifiably restrained from consulting all relevant information, including the statements and actions of interrogators. * * *

IV

As we suggested in *Davis,* when a court must determine whether the Confrontation Clause bars the admission of a statement at trial, it should determine the "primary purpose of the interrogation" by objectively evaluating the statements and actions of the parties to the encounter, in light of the circumstances in which the interrogation occurs. The existence of an emergency or the parties' perception that an emergency is ongoing is among the most important circumstances that courts must take into account in determining whether an interrogation is testimonial because statements made to assist police in addressing an ongoing emergency presumably lack the testimonial purpose that would subject them to the requirement of confrontation. As the context of this case brings into sharp relief, the existence and duration of an emergency depend on the type and scope of danger posed to the victim, the police, and the public.

* * *

We first examine the circumstances in which the interrogation occurred. The parties disagree over whether there was an emergency when the police arrived at the gas station. Bryant argues, and the Michigan Supreme Court accepted, that there was no ongoing emergency because "there . . . was no criminal conduct occurring. No shots were being fired, no one was seen in possession of a firearm, nor were any witnesses seen cowering in fear or running from the scene." Bryant, while conceding that "a serious or life-threatening injury creates a medical emergency for a victim," further argues that a declarant's medical emergency is not relevant to the ongoing emergency determination.

In contrast, Michigan and the Solicitor General explain that when the police responded to the call that a man had been shot and found Covington bleeding on the gas station parking lot, "they did not know who Covington was, whether the shooting had occurred at the gas station or at a different location, who the assailant was, or whether the assailant posed a continuing threat to Covington or others."

The Michigan Supreme Court stated that the police asked Covington, "what had happened, who had shot him, and where the shooting had occurred." * * * The officers basically agree on what information they learned from Covington, but not on the order in which they learned it or on whether Covington's statements were in response to general or detailed questions. They all agree that the first question was "what happened?" The answer was either "I was shot" or "Rick shot me."

As explained above, the scope of an emergency in terms of its threat to individuals other than the initial assailant and victim will often depend on the type of dispute involved. Nothing Covington said to the police indicated that the cause of the shooting was a purely private dispute or that the threat from the shooter had ended. The record reveals little about the motive for the shooting. The police officers who spoke with Covington at the gas station testified that Covington did not tell them what words Covington and Rick had exchanged prior to the shooting. What Covington did tell the officers was that he fled Bryant's back porch, indicating that he perceived an ongoing threat. The police did not know, and Covington did not tell them, whether the threat was limited to him. The potential scope of the dispute and therefore the emergency in this case thus stretches more broadly than those at issue in *Davis* and *Hammon* and encompasses a threat potentially to the police and the public.

This is also the first of our post-*Crawford* Confrontation Clause cases to involve a gun. The physical separation that was sufficient to end the emergency in *Hammon* was not necessarily sufficient to end the threat in this case; Covington was shot through the back door of Bryant's house. Bryant's argument that there was no ongoing emergency because "[n]o shots were being fired," surely construes ongoing emergency too narrowly. An emergency does not last only for the time between when the assailant pulls the trigger and the bullet hits the victim. If an out-of-sight sniper pauses between shots, no one would say that the emergency ceases during the pause. That is an extreme example and not the situation here, but it serves to highlight the implausibility, at least as to certain weapons, of construing the emergency to last only precisely as long as the violent act itself, as some have construed our opinion in *Davis*.

At no point during the questioning did either Covington or the police know the location of the shooter. In fact, Bryant was not at home by the time the police searched his house at approximately 5:30 a.m. At some point between 3 a.m. and 5:30 a.m., Bryant left his house. At bottom, there was an ongoing emergency here where an armed shooter, whose motive for and location after the shooting were unknown, had mortally wounded Covington within a few blocks and a few minutes of the location where the police found Covington.

This is not to suggest that the emergency continued until Bryant was arrested in California a year after the shooting. We need not decide precisely when the emergency ended because Covington's encounter with the police and all of the statements he made during that interaction occurred within the first few minutes of the police officers' arrival and well before they secured the scene of the shooting—the shooter's last known location.

We reiterate, moreover, that the existence *vel non* of an ongoing emergency is not the touchstone of the testimonial inquiry; rather, the ultimate inquiry is whether the "primary purpose of the interrogation [was] to enable police assistance to meet [the] ongoing emergency." *Davis,* We turn now to that inquiry, as informed by the circumstances of the ongoing emergency just described. The circumstances of the encounter provide important context for understanding Covington's statements to the police. When the police arrived at Covington's side, their first question to him was "What happened?"[18] Covington's response was either "Rick shot me" or "I was shot," followed very quickly by an identification of "Rick" as the shooter. In response to further questions, Covington explained that the shooting occurred through the back door of Bryant's house and provided a physical description of the shooter. When he made the statements, Covington was lying in a gas station parking lot bleeding from a mortal gunshot wound to his abdomen. His answers to the police officers' questions were punctuated with questions about when emergency medical services would arrive. He was obviously in considerable pain and had difficulty breathing and talking. From this description of his condition and report of his statements, we cannot say that a person in Covington's situation would have had a "primary purpose" "to establish or prove past events potentially relevant to later criminal prosecution." *Davis.*

For their part, the police responded to a call that a man had been shot. As discussed above, they did not know why, where, or when the shooting had occurred. Nor did they know the location of the shooter or anything else about the circumstances in which the crime occurred.[19] The questions they asked—"what had happened, who had shot him, and where the shooting occurred,"—were the exact

---

[18] Although the dissent claims otherwise, at least one officer asked Covington something akin to "how was he doing." * * *

[19] Contrary to the dissent's suggestion, and despite the fact that the record was developed prior to *Davis'* focus on the existence of an "ongoing emergency," the record contains some testimony to support the idea that the police officers were concerned about the location of the shooter when they arrived on the scene and thus to suggest that the purpose of the questioning of Covington was to determine the shooter's location. * * *

type of questions necessary to allow the police to " 'assess the situation, the threat to their own safety, and possible danger to the potential victim' " and to the public, including to allow them to ascertain "whether they would be encountering a violent felon," In other words, they solicited the information necessary to enable them "to meet an ongoing emergency."

Nothing in Covington's responses indicated to the police that, contrary to their expectation upon responding to a call reporting a shooting, there was no emergency or that a prior emergency had ended. Covington did indicate that he had been shot at another location about 25 minutes earlier, but he did not know the location of the shooter at the time the police arrived and, as far as we can tell from the record, he gave no indication that the shooter, having shot at him twice, would be satisfied that Covington was only wounded. In fact, Covington did not indicate any possible motive for the shooting, and thereby gave no reason to think that the shooter would not shoot again if he arrived on the scene. As we noted in *Davis,* "initial inquiries" may "*often* . . . produce nontestimonial statements." The initial inquiries in this case resulted in the type of nontestimonial statements we contemplated in *Davis.*

Finally, we consider the informality of the situation and the interrogation. This situation is more similar, though not identical, to the informal, harried 911 call in *Davis* than to the structured, station-house interview in *Crawford.* As the officers' trial testimony reflects, the situation was fluid and somewhat confused: the officers arrived at different times; apparently each, upon arrival, asked Covington "what happened?"; and, contrary to the dissent's portrayal, they did not conduct a structured interrogation. * * * The informality suggests that the interrogators' primary purpose was simply to address what they perceived to be an ongoing emergency, and the circumstances lacked any formality that would have alerted Covington to or focused him on the possible future prosecutorial use of his statements.

Because the circumstances of the encounter as well as the statements and actions of Covington and the police objectively indicate that the "primary purpose of the interrogation" was "to enable police assistance to meet an ongoing emergency," *Davis,* Covington's identification and description of the shooter and the location of the shooting were not testimonial hearsay. The Confrontation Clause did not bar their admission at Bryant's trial. * * * We leave for the Michigan courts to decide on remand whether the statements' admission was otherwise permitted by state hearsay rules. The judgment of the Supreme Court of Michigan is vacated, and the case is remanded for further proceedings not inconsistent with this opinion.[c]

JUSTICE KAGAN took no part in the consideration or decision of this case.

JUSTICE THOMAS, concurring in the judgment.

I agree with the Court that the admission of Covington's out-of-court statements did not violate the Confrontation Clause, but I reach this conclusion

---

[c] In 2015, the Court applied its "primary purpose" test to find non-testimonial a 3-year-old's statements concerning abuse, made to a teacher who was required by law to report those statements to law enforcement. *Ohio v. Clark,* 576 U.S. 237 (2015). Justice Thomas again applied his "indicia of solemnity" analysis to reach the same result.

because Covington's questioning by police lacked sufficient formality and solemnity for his statements to be considered "testimonial." See *Crawford*. * * * I have criticized the primary-purpose test as an "exercise in fiction" that is "disconnected from history" and "yields no predictable results" *Davis*. * * * Rather than attempting to reconstruct the "primary purpose" of the participants, I would consider the extent to which the interrogation resembles those historical practices that the Confrontational Clause addressed. * * * As the majority notes, Covington interacted with the police under highly informal circumstances, while he bled from a fatal gunshot wound. The police questioning was not "a formalized dialogue," did not result in "formalized testimonial materials" such as a deposition or affidavit, and bore no "indicia of solemnity." *Davis*. Nor is there any indication that the statements were offered at trial "in order to evade confrontation." *Davis* This interrogation bears little if any resemblance to the historical practices that the Confrontation Clause aimed to eliminate. Covington thus did not "bea[r] testimony" against Bryant, and the introduction of his statements at trial did not implicate the Confrontation Clause. I concur in the judgment.

JUSTICE SCALIA, dissenting.

Today's tale—a story of five officers conducting successive examinations of a dying man with the primary purpose, not of obtaining and preserving his testimony regarding his killer, but of protecting him, them, and others from a murderer somewhere on the loose—is so transparently false that professing to believe it demeans this institution. But reaching a patently incorrect conclusion on the facts is a relatively benign judicial mischief; it affects, after all, only the case at hand. In its vain attempt to make the incredible plausible, however—or perhaps as an intended second goal—today's opinion distorts our Confrontation Clause jurisprudence and leaves it in a shambles. Instead of clarifying the law, the Court makes itself the obfuscator of last resort. Because I continue to adhere to the Confrontation Clause that the People adopted, as described in *Crawford v. Washington*, I dissent.

I

* * * The Confrontation Clause of the Sixth Amendment, made binding on the States by the Fourteenth Amendment, provides that "[i]n all criminal prosecutions, the accused shall enjoy the right . . . to be confronted with the witnesses against him." In *Crawford,* we held that this provision guarantees a defendant his common-law right to confront those "who 'bear testimony' " against him. A witness must deliver his testimony against the defendant in person, or the prosecution must prove that the witness is unavailable to appear at trial and that the defendant has had a prior opportunity for cross-examination.

Not all hearsay falls within the Confrontation Clause's grasp. At trial a witness "bears testimony" by providing " '[a] solemn declaration or affirmation . . . for the purpose of establishing or proving some fact.' " *Id.* (quoting 2 N. Webster, An American Dictionary of the English Language (1828)). The Confrontation Clause protects defendants only from hearsay statements that do the same. In *Davis,* we explained how to identify testimonial hearsay prompted by police questioning in the field. A statement is testimonial "when the circumstances objectively indicate . . . that the primary purpose of the interrogation is to establish or prove past events potentially relevant to later criminal prosecution." When, however, the circumstances objectively indicate that the declarant's statements were "a cry for help [o]r the provision of information enabling officers immediately to end a threatening situation," they bear little resemblance to in-court testimony. "No 'witness' goes into court to proclaim an emergency and seek help."

Crawford and *Davis* did not address whose perspective matters—the declarant's, the interrogator's, or both—when assessing "the primary purpose of [an] interrogation." In those cases the statements were testimonial from any perspective. I think the same is true here, but because the Court picks a perspective so will I: The declarant's intent is what counts. In-court testimony is more than a narrative of past events; it is a solemn declaration made in the course of a criminal trial. For an out-of-court statement to qualify as testimonial, the declarant must intend the statement to be a solemn declaration rather than an unconsidered or offhand remark; and he must make the statement with the understanding that it may be used to invoke the coercive machinery of the State against the accused. * * *

A declarant-focused inquiry is also the only inquiry that would work in every fact pattern implicating the Confrontation Clause. The Clause applies to volunteered testimony as well as statements solicited through police interrogation. An inquiry into an officer's purposes would make no sense when a declarant blurts out "Rick shot me" as soon as the officer arrives on the scene. * * *

Looking to the declarant's purpose (as we should), this is an absurdly easy case. Roughly 25 minutes after Anthony Covington had been shot, Detroit police responded to a 911 call reporting that a gunshot victim had appeared at a neighborhood gas station. They quickly arrived at the scene, and in less than 10 minutes five different Detroit police officers questioned Covington about the shooting. Each asked him a similar battery of questions: "what happened" and when, "who shot the victim," and "where" did the shooting take place. After Covington would answer, they would ask follow-up questions, such as "how tall is" the shooter, "[h]ow much does he weigh," what is the exact address or physical description of the house where the shooting took place, and what chain of events led to the shooting. The battery relented when the paramedics arrived and began tending to Covington's wounds.

From Covington's perspective, his statements had little value except to ensure the arrest and eventual prosecution of Richard Bryant. He knew the "threatening situation," had ended six blocks away and 25 minutes earlier when he fled from Bryant's back porch. Bryant had not confronted him face-to-face before he was mortally wounded, instead shooting him through a door. Even if Bryant had pursued him (unlikely), and after seeing that Covington had ended up at the gas station was unable to confront him there before the police arrived (doubly unlikely), it was entirely beyond imagination that Bryant would again open fire while Covington was surrounded by five armed police officers. And Covington knew the shooting was the work of a drug dealer, not a spree killer who might randomly threaten others.

Covington's knowledge that he had nothing to fear differs significantly from Michelle McCottry's state of mind during her "frantic" statements to a 911 operator at issue in *Davis*. Her "call was plainly a call for help against a bona fide physical threat" describing "events *as they were actually happening*." She did not have the luxuries of police protection and of time and space separating her from immediate danger that Covington enjoyed when he made his statements.

Covington's pressing medical needs do not suggest that he was responding to an emergency, but to the contrary reinforce the testimonial character of his statements. He understood the police were focused on investigating a past crime, not his medical needs. None of the officers asked Covington how he was doing, attempted more than superficially to assess the severity of his wounds, or attempted to administer first aid. They instead primarily asked questions with little, if any, relevance to Covington's dire situation. Police, paramedics, and doctors do not need to know the address where a shooting took place, the name of the shooter, or the shooter's height and weight to provide proper medical care. Underscoring that Covington understood the officers' investigative role, he interrupted their interrogation to ask "when is EMS coming?" When, in other words, would the focus shift to his medical needs rather than Bryant's crime? * * *

Worse still for the repute of today's opinion, this is an absurdly easy case even if one (erroneously) takes the interrogating officers' purpose into account. The five officers interrogated Covington primarily to investigate past criminal events. None—absolutely none—of their actions indicated that they perceived an imminent threat. They did not draw their weapons, and indeed did not immediately search the gas station for potential shooters. To the contrary, all five testified that they questioned Covington *before conducting any investigation at the scene*. Would this have made any sense if they feared the presence of a shooter? Most tellingly, none of the officers started his interrogation by asking what would have been the obvious first question if any hint of such a fear existed: Where is the shooter?

But do not rely solely on my word about the officers' primary purpose. Listen to Sergeant Wenturine, who candidly admitted that he interrogated Covington because he "ha[d] a man here that [he] believe[d][was] dying [so he was] gonna find out who did this, period." In short, he needed to interrogate Covington to solve a crime. Wenturine never mentioned an interest in ending an ongoing emergency.

At the very least, the officers' intentions *turned* investigative during their 10-minute encounter with Covington, and the conversation "evolve[d] into testimonial statements." *Davis* * * * [T]he value of asking the same battery of questions a fifth time was to ensure that Covington told a consistent story and to see if any new details helpful to the investigation and eventual prosecution would emerge. Having the testimony of five officers to recount Covington's consistent story undoubtedly helped obtain Bryant's conviction. (Which came, I may note, after the first jury could not reach a verdict.)

D

A final word about the Court's active imagination. * * * Nothing suggests the five officers in this case shared the Court's dystopian view of Detroit, where drug dealers hunt their shooting victim down and fire into a crowd of police officers to finish him off, or where spree killers shoot through a door and then roam the streets leaving a trail of bodies behind. Because almost 90 percent of murders involve a single victim, it is much more likely—indeed, I think it certain—that the officers viewed their encounter with Covington for what it was: an investigation into a past crime with no ongoing or immediate consequences.

The Court's distorted view creates an expansive exception to the Confrontation Clause for violent crimes. Because Bryant posed a continuing threat to public safety in the Court's imagination, the emergency persisted for confrontation purposes at least until the police learned his "motive for and location after the shooting." It may have persisted in this case until the police "secured the scene of the shooting" two-and-a-half hours later. (The relevance of securing the scene is unclear so long as the killer is still at large—especially if, as the Court speculates, he may be a spree-killer.) This is a dangerous definition of emergency. Many individuals who testify against a defendant at trial first offer their accounts to police in the hours after a violent act. If the police can plausibly claim that a "potential threat to . . . the public" persisted through those first few hours, (and if the claim is plausible here it is always plausible) a defendant will have no constitutionally protected right to exclude the uncross-examined testimony of such witnesses. His conviction could rest (as perhaps it did here) solely on the officers' recollection at trial of the witnesses' accusations.

The Framers could not have envisioned such a hollow constitutional guarantee. No framing-era confrontation case that I know of, neither here nor in England, took such an enfeebled view of the right to confrontation. * * *

The Court's expansive definition of an "ongoing emergency" and its willingness to consider the perspective of the interrogator and the declarant cast a more favorable light on those trials than history or our past decisions suggest they deserve. Royal officials conducted many of the *ex parte* examinations introduced against Sir Walter Raleigh and Sir John Fenwick while investigating alleged treasonous conspiracies of unknown scope, aimed at killing or overthrowing the King. * * * Social stability in 16th- and 17th-century England depended mainly on the continuity of the ruling monarch, so such a conspiracy posed the most pressing emergency imaginable. Presumably, the royal officials investigating it would have understood the gravity of the situation and would have focused their interrogations primarily on ending the threat, not on generating testimony for trial. I therefore doubt that under the Court's test English officials acted improperly by denying Raleigh and Fenwick the opportunity to confront their accusers "face to face."

Under my approach, in contrast, those English trials remain unquestionably infamous. Lord Cobham did not speak with royal officials to end an ongoing emergency. He was a traitor! He spoke, as Raleigh correctly observed, to establish Raleigh's guilt and to save his own life. Cobham's statements, when assessed from his perspective, had only a testimonial purpose. The same is true of Covington's statements here.

II

* * * But today's decision is not only a gross distortion of the facts. It is a gross distortion of the law. * * * A statement during an ongoing emergency is sufficiently reliable, the Court says, "because the prospect of fabrication . . . is presumably significantly diminished," so it "does not [need] to be subject to the crucible of cross-examination."

Compare that with the holding of *Crawford:* "Where testimonial statements are at issue, the only indicium of reliability sufficient to satisfy constitutional demands is the one the Constitution actually prescribes: confrontation." * * *

The Court announces that in future cases it will look to "standard rules of hearsay, designed to identify some statements as reliable," when deciding whether a statement is testimonial. *Ohio v. Roberts* said something remarkably similar: An out-of-court statement is admissible if it "falls within a firmly rooted hearsay exception" or otherwise "bears adequate 'indicia of reliability.' " We tried that approach to the Confrontation Clause for nearly 25 years before *Crawford rejected* it as an unworkable standard unmoored from the text and the historical roots of the Confrontation Clause. The arguments in Raleigh's infamous 17th-century treason trial contained full debate about the reliability of Lord Cobham's *ex parte* accusations; that case remains the canonical example of a Confrontation Clause violation, not because Raleigh should have won the debate but because he should have been allowed cross-examination.

The Court attempts to fit its resurrected interest in reliability into the *Crawford* framework, but the result is incoherent. Reliability, the Court tells us, is a good indicator of whether "a statement is . . . an out-of-court substitute for trial testimony." That is patently false. Reliability tells us *nothing* about whether a statement is testimonial. Testimonial and nontestimonial statements alike come in varying degrees of reliability. An eyewitness's statements to the police after a fender-bender, for example, are both reliable and testimonial. Statements to the police from one driver attempting to blame the other would be similarly testimonial but rarely reliable.

The Court suggests otherwise because it "misunderstands the relationship" between qualification for one of the standard hearsay exceptions and exemption from the confrontation requirement. * * * Hearsay law exempts business records, for example, because businesses have a financial incentive to keep reliable records. See Fed. Rule Evid. 803(6). The Sixth Amendment also generally admits business records into evidence, but not because the records are reliable or because hearsay law says so. It admits them "because—having been created for the administration of an entity's affairs and not for the purpose of establishing or proving some fact at trial—they are not" weaker substitutes for live testimony. * * * Business records prepared specifically for use at a criminal trial are testimonial and require confrontation. * * *

The Court recedes from *Crawford* in a second significant way. It requires judges to conduct "open-ended balancing tests" and "amorphous, if not entirely subjective," inquiries into the totality of the circumstances bearing upon reliability.

Where the prosecution cries "emergency," the admissibility of a statement now turns on "a highly context-dependent inquiry," into the type of weapon the defendant wielded; the type of crime the defendant committed; the medical condition of the declarant; if the declarant is injured, whether paramedics have arrived on the scene; whether the encounter takes place in an "exposed public area"; whether the encounter appears disorganized; whether the declarant is capable of forming a purpose; whether the police have secured the scene of the crime; the formality of the statement; and finally, whether the statement strikes us as reliable. This is no better than the nine-factor balancing test we rejected in *Crawford.* I do not look forward to resolving conflicts in the future over whether knives and poison are more like guns or fists for Confrontation Clause purposes, or whether rape and armed robbery are more like murder or domestic violence. * * * [W]e did not disavow multifactor balancing for reliability in *Crawford* out of a preference for rules over standards. We did so because it "d[id] violence to" the Framers' design. It was judges' open-ended determination of what was reliable that violated the trial rights of Englishmen in the political trials of the 16th and 17th centuries. The Framers placed the Confrontation Clause in the Bill of Rights to ensure that those abuses (and the abuses by the Admiralty courts in colonial America) would not be repeated in this country. Not even the least dangerous branch can be trusted to assess the reliability of uncross-examined testimony in politically charged trials or trials implicating threats to national security. See *Crawford.*

* * *

For all I know, Bryant has received his just deserts. But he surely has not received them pursuant to the procedures that our Constitution requires. And what has been taken away from him has been taken away from us all.

JUSTICE GINSBURG, dissenting.

I agree with Justice Scalia that Covington's statements were testimonial and that "[t]he declarant's intent is what counts." * * * Today's decision, Justice Scalia rightly notes, "creates an expansive exception to the Confrontation Clause for violent crimes." In so doing, the decision confounds our recent Confrontation Clause jurisprudence, which made it plain that "[r]eliability tells us nothing about whether a statement is testimonial." * * *d

---

d   A narrow majority of the Court after Crawford concluded that "testimonial" statements included notarized lab reports in which analysts asserted a substance was cocaine, *Melendez-Diaz v. Massachusetts,* 557 U.S. 305 (2009) (concluding the defendant had a right to cross-examine the analysts who had authored such reports), and an analyst's lab report indicating a blood-alcohol concentration over the legal limit for drivers. *Bullcoming v. New Mexico,* 564 U.S. 647 (2011) (concluding that the Confrontation Clause prohibited the state from introducing that finding through the testimony of a person who worked at the laboratory but had not performed or observed the blood test or certified its results). But in *Williams v. Illinois,* 567 U.S. 50 (2012), the Court splintered over whether the Confrontation Clause was violated when an expert witness testified about a report of a DNA analysis that she did not conduct. No rationale for defining the application of the Confrontation clause to forensic and expert testimony commanded a majority in *Williams.* Four justices decided that the statements in the DNA analyst's report were not testimonial because they were not offered for their truth but were instead the basis for the opinion of the expert witness, because the report was "not inherently inculpatory," and because the report was "produced before any suspect was identified." All five other justices expressly rejected this reasoning. Four

RICHARDSON V. MARSH

481 U.S. 200, 107 S.Ct. 1702, 95 L.Ed.2d 176 (1987).

JUSTICE SCALIA delivered the opinion of the Court.

In *Bruton v. United States,* 391 U.S. 123 (1968), we held that a defendant is deprived of his rights under the Confrontation Clause when his nontestifying codefendant's confession naming him as a participant in the crime is introduced at their joint trial, even if the jury is instructed to consider that confession only against the codefendant. Today we consider whether *Bruton* requires the same result when the codefendant's confession is redacted to omit any reference to the defendant, but the defendant is nonetheless linked to the confession by evidence properly admitted against him at trial.

Respondent Clarissa Marsh, Benjamin Williams, and Kareem Martin were charged with assaulting Cynthia Knighton and murdering her 4-year-old son, Koran, and her aunt, Ollie Scott. Respondent and Williams were tried jointly, over her objection. (Martin was a fugitive at the time of trial). At the trial, Knighton testified as follows: On the evening of October 29, 1978, she and her son were at Scott's home when respondent and her boyfriend Martin visited. After a brief conversation in the living room, respondent announced that she had come to "pick up something" from Scott and rose from the couch. Martin then pulled out a gun, pointed it at Scott and the Knightons, and said that "someone had gotten killed and [Scott] knew something about it." Respondent immediately walked to the front door and peered out the peephole. The doorbell rang, respondent opened the door, and Williams walked in, carrying a gun. As Williams passed respondent, he asked, "Where's the money?" Martin forced Scott upstairs, and Williams went into the kitchen, leaving respondent alone with the Knightons. Knighton and her son attempted to flee, but respondent grabbed Knighton and held her until Williams returned. Williams ordered the Knightons to lie on the floor and then went upstairs to assist Martin. Respondent, again left alone with the Knightons, stood by the front door and occasionally peered out the peephole. A few minutes later, Martin, Williams, and Scott came down the stairs, and Martin handed a paper grocery bag to respondent. Martin and Williams then forced Scott and the Knightons into the basement, where Martin shot them. Only Cynthia Knighton survived.

In addition to Knighton's testimony, the State introduced (over respondent's objection) a confession given by Williams to the police shortly after his arrest. The

---

concluded that the case was indistinguishable from *Bullcoming* and would have found that introduction of the report through the expert witness denied the defendant his rights under the Confrontation Clause. Justice Thomas delivered a separate opinion that provided the fifth vote for rejecting the defendant's confrontation clause claim. Justice Thomas reasoned that the report was not testimonial because it lacked sufficient indicia of formality and solemnity. Justice Thomas reasoned that "the scope of the confrontation right is properly limited to extrajudicial statements similar in solemnity to the Marian examination practices that the Confrontation Clause was designed to prevent. * * * By certifying the truth of the analyst's representations, the unsworn *Bullcoming* report bore "a 'striking resemblance,' " to the Marian practice in which magistrates examined witnesses, typically on oath, and "certif[ied] the results to the court." And, in *Melendez-Diaz,* we observed that "certificates' are functionally identical to live, in-court testimony, doing precisely what a witness does on direct examination." Cellmark's report is marked by no such indicia of solemnity." Justice Thomas's Sixth Amendment test was also applied here in his separate opinion in *Bryant*; it was not joined by any other justice in either case.

confession was redacted to omit all reference to respondent—indeed, to omit all indication that *anyone* other than Martin and Williams participated in the crime.[1] The confession largely corroborated Knighton's account of the activities of persons other than respondent in the house. In addition, the confession described a conversation Williams had with Martin as they drove to the Scott home, during which, according to Williams, Martin said that he would have to kill the victims after the robbery. At the time the confession was admitted, the jury was admonished not to use it in any way against respondent. Williams did not testify.

After the State rested, respondent took the stand. She testified that on October 29, 1978, she had lost money that Martin intended to use to buy drugs. Martin was upset, and suggested to respondent that she borrow money from Scott, with whom she had worked in the past. Martin and respondent picked up Williams and drove to Scott's house. During the drive, respondent, who was sitting in the back seat, "knew that [Martin and Williams] were talking" but could not hear the conversation because "the radio was on and the speaker was right in [her] ear." Martin and respondent were admitted into the home, and respondent had a short conversation with Scott, during which she asked for a loan. Martin then pulled a gun, and respondent walked to the door to see where the car was. When she saw Williams, she opened the door for him. Respondent testified that during the robbery she did not feel free to leave and was too scared to flee. She said that she did not know why she prevented the Knightons from escaping. She admitted taking the bag from Martin, but said that after Martin and Williams took the victims into

---

[1]   The redacted confession in its entirety read:

"On Sunday evening, October the 29th, 1978, at about 6:30 p.m., I was over to my girlfriend's house at 237 Moss, Highland Park, when I received a phone call from a friend of mine named Kareem Martin. He said he had been looking for me and James Coleman, who I call Tom. He asked me if I wanted to go on a robbery with him. I said okay. Then he said he'd be by and pick me up. About 15 or 20 minutes later Kareem came by in his black Monte Carlo car. I got in the car and Kareem told me he was going to stick up this crib, told me the place was a numbers house. Kareem said there would be over $5,000 or $10,000 in the place. Kareem said he would have to take them out after the robbery. Kareem had a big silver gun. He gave me a long barrelled [sic] .22 revolver. We then drove over to this house and parked the car across the big street near the house. The plan was that I would wait in the car in front of the house and then I would move the car down across the big street because he didn't want anybody to see the car. Okay, Kareem went up to the house and went inside. A couple of minutes later I moved the car and went up to the house. As I entered, Kareem and this older lady were in the dining room, a little boy and another younger woman were sitting on the couch in the front room. I pulled my pistol and told the younger woman and the little boy to lay on the floor. Kareem took the older lady upstairs. He had a pistol, also. I stayed downstairs with the two people on the floor. After Kareem took the lady upstairs I went upstairs and the lady was laying on the bed in the room to the left as you get up the stairs. The lady had already given us two bags full of money before we ever got upstairs. Kareem had thought she had more money and that's why we had went upstairs. Me and Kareem started searching the rooms but I didn't find any money. I came downstairs and then Kareem came down with the lady. I said, 'Let's go, let's go.' Kareem said no. Kareem then took the two ladies and little boy down the basement and that's when I left to go to the car. I went to the car and got in the back seat. A couple of minutes later Kareem came to the car and said he thinks the girl was still living because she was still moving and he didn't have any more bullets. He asked me how come I didn't go down the basement and I said I wasn't doing no shit like that. He then dropped me back off at my girl's house in Highland Park and I was supposed to get together with him today, get my share of the robbery after he had counted the money. That's all."

the basement, she left the house without the bag. Respondent insisted that she had possessed no prior knowledge that Martin and Williams were armed, had heard no conversation about anyone's being harmed, and had not intended to rob or kill anyone.

During his closing argument, the prosecutor admonished the jury not to use Williams' confession against respondent. Later in his argument, however, he linked respondent to the portion of Williams' confession describing his conversation with Martin in the car.[2] (Respondent's attorney did not object to this.) After closing arguments, the judge again instructed the jury that Williams' confession was not to be considered against respondent. The jury convicted respondent of two counts of felony murder in the perpetration of an armed robbery and one count of assault with intent to commit murder. The Michigan Court of Appeals affirmed in an unpublished opinion, and the Michigan Supreme Court denied leave to appeal.

Respondent then filed a petition for a writ of habeas corpus pursuant to 28 U.S.C. § 2254. She alleged that * * * introduction of Williams' confession at the joint trial had violated her rights under the Confrontation Clause. The District Court denied the petition. The United States Court of Appeals * * * reversed. The Court of Appeals held that in determining whether *Bruton* bars the admission of a nontestifying codefendant's confession, a court must assess the confession's "inculpatory value" by examining not only the face of the confession, but also all of the evidence introduced at trial. Here, Williams' account of the conversation in the car was the only *direct* evidence that respondent knew before entering Scott's house that the victims would be robbed and killed. Respondent's own testimony placed her in that car. In light of the "paucity" of other evidence of malice and the prosecutor's linkage of respondent and the statement in the car during closing argument, admission of Williams' confession "was powerfully incriminating to [respondent] with respect to the critical element of intent." Thus, the Court of Appeals concluded, the Confrontation Clause was violated. We granted certiorari. * * *

The Confrontation Clause of the Sixth Amendment, extended against the States by the Fourteenth Amendment, guarantees the right of a criminal defendant "to be confronted with the witnesses against him." The right of confrontation includes the right to cross-examine witnesses. Therefore, where two defendants are tried jointly, the pretrial confession of one cannot be admitted against the other unless the confessing defendant takes the stand.

Ordinarily, a witness whose testimony is introduced at a joint trial is not considered to be a witness "against" a defendant if the jury is instructed to consider that testimony only against a codefendant. This accords with the almost invariable

---

[2]   The prosecutor said: "It's important in light of [respondent's] testimony when she says Kareem drives over to Benjamin Williams' home and picks him up to go over. What's the thing that she says? 'Well, I'm sitting in the back seat of the car.' 'Did you hear any conversation that was going on in the front seat between Kareem and Mr. Williams?' 'No, couldn't hear any conversation. The radio was too loud.' I asked [sic] you whether that is reasonable. Why did she say that? Why did she say she couldn't hear any conversation? She said, 'I know they were having conversation but I couldn't hear it because of the radio.' Because if she admits that she heard the conversation and she admits to the plan, she's guilty of at least armed robbery. So she can't tell you that."

assumption of the law that jurors follow their instructions, which we have applied in many varying contexts. For example, in *Harris v. New York,* 401 U.S. 222 (1971), we held that statements elicited from a defendant in violation of *Miranda v. Arizona* can be introduced to impeach that defendant's credibility, even though they are inadmissible as evidence of his guilt, so long as the jury is instructed accordingly. * * * In *Bruton,* however, we recognized a narrow exception to this principle: We held that a defendant is deprived of his Sixth Amendment right of confrontation when the facially incriminating confession of a nontestifying codefendant is introduced at their joint trial, even if the jury is instructed to consider the confession only against the codefendant. We said:

> "[T]here are some contexts in which the risk that the jury will not, or cannot, follow instructions is so great, and the consequences of failure so vital to the defendant, that the practical and human limitations of the jury system cannot be ignored. Such a context is presented here, where the powerfully incriminating extrajudicial statements of a codefendant, who stands accused side-by-side with the defendant, are deliberately spread before the jury in a joint trial * * *."

There is an important distinction between this case and *Bruton,* which causes it to fall outside the narrow exception we have created. In *Bruton,* the codefendant's confession "expressly implicat[ed]" the defendant as his accomplice. Thus, at the time that confession was introduced there was not the slightest doubt that it would prove "powerfully incriminating." By contrast, in this case the confession was not incriminating on its face, and became so only when linked with evidence introduced later at trial (the defendant's own testimony).

Where the necessity of such linkage is involved, it is a less valid generalization that the jury will not likely obey the instruction to disregard the evidence. Specific testimony that "the defendant helped me commit the crime" is more vivid than inferential incrimination, and hence more difficult to thrust out of mind. Moreover, with regard to such an explicit statement the only issue is, plain and simply, whether the jury can possibly be expected to forget it in assessing the defendant's guilt; whereas with regard to inferential incrimination the judge's instruction may well be successful in dissuading the jury from entering onto the path of inference in the first place, so that there is no incrimination to forget. In short, while it may not always be simple for the members of a jury to obey the instruction that they disregard an incriminating inference, there does not exist the overwhelming probability of their inability to do so that is the foundation of *Bruton*'s exception to the general rule.

Even more significantly, evidence requiring linkage differs from evidence incriminating on its face in the practical effects which application of the *Bruton* exception would produce. If limited to facially incriminating confessions, *Bruton* can be complied with by redaction—a possibility suggested in that opinion itself. If extended to confessions incriminating by connection, not only is that not possible, but it is not even possible to predict the admissibility of a confession in advance of trial. The "contextual implication" doctrine articulated by the Court of Appeals would presumably require the trial judge to assess at the end of each trial whether, in light of all of the evidence, a nontestifying codefendant's confession has been so "powerfully incriminating" that a new, separate trial is required for the defendant. This obviously lends itself to manipulation by the defense—and even without manipulation will result in numerous mistrials and appeals. It might be suggested that those consequences could be reduced by conducting a pretrial hearing at which prosecution and defense would reveal the evidence they plan to introduce, enabling the court to assess compliance with *Bruton ex ante* rather than *ex post*. If this approach is even feasible * * *, it would be time consuming and obviously far from foolproof.

One might say, of course, that a certain way of assuring compliance would be to try defendants separately whenever an incriminating statement of one of them is sought to be used. That is not as facile or as just a remedy as might seem. Joint trials play a vital role in the criminal justice system, accounting for almost one third of federal criminal trials in the past five years. Many joint trials—for example, those involving large conspiracies to import and distribute illegal drugs— involve a dozen or more codefendants. Confessions by one or more of the defendants are commonplace—and indeed the probability of confession increases with the number of participants, since each has reduced assurance that he will be protected by his own silence. It would impair both the efficiency and the fairness of the criminal justice system to require, in all these cases of joint crimes where incriminating statements exist, that prosecutors bring separate proceedings, presenting the same evidence again and again, requiring victims and witnesses to repeat the inconvenience (and sometimes trauma) of testifying, and randomly favoring the last-tried defendants who have the advantage of knowing the prosecution's case beforehand. Joint trials generally serve the interests of justice by avoiding inconsistent verdicts and enabling more accurate assessment of relative culpability—advantages which sometimes operate to the defendant's benefit. Even apart from these tactical considerations, joint trials generally serve the interests of justice by avoiding the scandal and inequity of inconsistent verdicts.[4] The other way of assuring compliance with an expansive *Bruton* rule would be to forgo use of codefendant confessions. That price also is too high, since confessions "are more than merely 'desirable'; they are essential to society's compelling interest in finding, convicting, and punishing those who violate the law." *Moran v. Burbine*, 475 U.S. 412 (1986).

The rule that juries are presumed to follow their instructions is a pragmatic one, rooted less in the absolute certitude that the presumption is true than in the belief that it represents a reasonable practical accommodation of the interests of the state and the defendant in the criminal justice process. On the precise facts of

---

4   The dissent notes that "all of the cases in this Court that involved joint trials conducted after *Bruton* was decided, in which compliance with the rule of that case was at issue, appear to have originated in a state court." It concludes from this that *"[f]ederal* prosecutors seem to have had little difficulty" in implementing *Bruton* as the dissent believes it must be implemented. Since the cases in question number only a handful, the fact that they happened to be state cases may signify nothing more than that there are many times more state prosecutions than federal. There is assuredly no basis to believe that federal prosecutors have been applying the dissent's interpretation of *Bruton*. Indeed the contrary proposition—as well as the harmfulness of that interpretation to federal law enforcement efforts—is suggested by the fact that the Solicitor General has appeared here as *amicus* to urge reversal for substantially the reasons we have given.

Bruton, involving a facially incriminating confession, we found that accommodation inadequate. As our discussion above shows, the calculus changes when confessions that do not name the defendant are at issue. While we continue to apply *Bruton* where we have found that its rationale validly applies, we decline to extend it further. We hold that the Confrontation Clause is not violated by the admission of a nontestifying codefendant's confession with a proper limiting instruction when, as here, the confession is redacted to eliminate not only the defendant's name, but any reference to her existence.[5]

In the present case, however, the prosecutor sought to undo the effect of the limiting instruction by urging the jury to use Williams' confession in evaluating respondent's case. See n. 2. On remand, the court should consider whether, in light of respondent's failure to object to the prosecutor's comments, the error can serve as the basis for granting a writ of habeas corpus.

JUSTICE STEVENS, with whom JUSTICE BRENNAN and JUSTICE MARSHALL join, dissenting.

The rationale of our decision in *Bruton v. United States,* applies without exception to all inadmissible confessions that are "powerfully incriminating." Today, however, the Court draws a distinction of constitutional magnitude between those confessions that directly identify the defendant and those that rely for their inculpatory effect on the factual and legal relationships of their contents to other evidence before the jury. Even if the jury's indirect inference of the defendant's guilt based on an inadmissible confession is much more devastating to the defendant's case than its inference from a direct reference in the codefendant's confession, the Court requires the exclusion of only the latter statement. This illogical result demeans the values protected by the Confrontation Clause. Moreover, neither reason nor experience supports the Court's argument that a consistent application of the rationale of the *Bruton* case would impose unacceptable burdens on the administration of justice. * * *

[T]he Court * * * draws a line between codefendant confessions that expressly name the defendant and those that do not. The Court relies on the presumption that in the latter category "it is a less valid generalization that the jury will not likely obey the instruction to disregard the evidence." I agree; but I do not read *Bruton* to require the exclusion of *all* codefendant confessions that do not mention the defendant. Some such confessions may not have any significant impact on the defendant's case. But others will. If we presume, as we must, that jurors give their full and vigorous attention to every witness and each item of evidence, the very

---

[5] We express no opinion on the admissibility of a confession in which the defendant's name has been replaced with a symbol or neutral pronoun.

[In *Gray v. Maryland,* 523 U.S. 185 (1998), the Court held that "*Bruton*'s protective rule" barred simply redacting the codefendant's confession "by substituting for the defendant's name a blank space or the word 'deleted' " where the confession (unlike that in *Richardson*) "refers directly to the 'existence of the nonconfessing defendant.' " In response to the question "who was in the group that beat [the victim]," the answer in the redacted confession had been read to the jury as: "Me, deleted, and a few other guys." The Court majority concluded that with such a redaction, "the jury will often realize that the confession refers directly to the defendant" and, indeed, "by encouraging the jury to speculate about the reference, the redaction may overemphasize the importance of the confession's accusation—once the jurors work out the reference."]

acts of listening and seeing will sometimes lead them down "the path of inference." Indeed, the Court tacitly acknowledges this point; while the Court speculates that the judge's instruction may dissuade the jury from making inferences at all, it also concedes the probability of their occurrence, arguing that there is no overwhelming probability that jurors will be unable to "disregard an incriminating inference." *Bruton* has always required trial judges to answer the question whether a particular confession is or is not "powerfully incriminating" on a case-by-case basis; they should follow the same analysis whether or not the defendant is actually named by his or her codefendant.

Instructing the jury that it was to consider Benjamin Williams' confession only against him, and not against Clarissa Marsh, failed to guarantee the level of certainty required by the Confrontation Clause. The uncertainty arose because the prosecution's case made it clear at the time Williams' statement was introduced that the statement would prove "powerfully incriminating" of the *petitioner* as well as of Williams himself. There can be absolutely no doubt that spreading Williams' carefully edited confession before the jury intolerably interfered with the jury's solemn duty to treat the statement as nothing more than meaningless sounds in its consideration of Marsh's guilt or innocence. * * *

The facts that joint trials conserve prosecutorial resources, diminish inconvenience to witnesses, and avoid delays in the administration of criminal justice have been well-known for a long time. It is equally well-known that joint trials create special risks of prejudice to one of the defendants, and that such risks often make it necessary to grant severances. See *Bruton*. The Government argues that the costs of requiring the prosecution to choose between severance and not offering the codefendant's confession at a joint trial outweigh the benefits to the defendant. Brief for United States as *Amicus Curiae*. On the scales of justice, however, considerations of fairness normally outweigh administrative concerns.

In the *Bruton* case the United States argued that the normal "benefits of joint proceedings should not have to be sacrificed by requiring separate trials in order to use the confession against the declarant." The Court endorsed the answer to this argument that Judge Lehman of the New York Court of Appeals had previously made:

> "We still adhere to the rule that an accused is entitled to confrontation of the witnesses against him and the right to cross-examine them. * * * We destroy the age-old rule which in the past has been regarded as a fundamental principle of our jurisprudence by a legalistic formula, required of the judge, that the jury may not consider any admissions against any party who did not join in them. We secure greater speed, economy and convenience in the administration of the law at the price of fundamental principles of constitutional liberty. That price is too high."

The concern about the cost of joint trials, even if valid, does not prevail over the interests of justice. Moreover, the Court's effort to revive this concern in a state criminal case rests on the use of irrelevant statistics. The Court makes the startling discovery that joint trials account for "almost one-third of federal criminal trials in the past five years." In the interest of greater precision, the Court might have stated that there were 10,904 federal criminal trials involving more than one defendant during that 5 year period. The Court might have added that the data base from which that figure was obtained does not contain any information at all to show the number of times that confessions were offered in evidence in those 10,904 federal cases. The relevance of this data is also difficult to discern because all of the cases in this Court that involved joint trials conducted after *Bruton* was decided, in which compliance with the rule of that case was at issue, appear to have originated in a state court. *Federal* prosecutors seem to have had little difficulty, in conducting the literally thousands of joint trials to which the Court points, in avoiding "the great harm to the criminal justice system" that the Court speculates will occur if *Bruton*'s reasoning is applied to this case. Presumably the options of granting immunity, making plea bargains, or simply waiting until after a confessing defendant has been tried separately before trying to use his admissions against an accomplice have enabled the Federal Government to enforce the criminal law without sacrificing the basic premise of the Confrontation Clause.

The Court also expresses concern that trial judges will be unable to determine whether a codefendant's confession that does not directly mention the defendant and is inadmissible against him will create a substantial risk of unfair prejudice. In most such cases the trial judge can comply with the dictates of *Bruton* by postponing his or her decision on the admissibility of the confession until the prosecution rests, at which time its potentially inculpatory effect can be evaluated in the light of the government's entire case. The Court expresses concern that such a rule would enable "manipulation by the defense," by which the Court presumably means the defense might tailor its evidence to make sure that a confession which does not directly mention the defendant is deemed powerfully incriminating when viewed in light of the prosecution's entire case. As a practical matter, I cannot believe that there are many defense lawyers who would deliberately pursue this high-risk strategy of "manipulating" their evidence in order to enhance the prejudicial impact of a codefendant's confession. Moreover, a great many experienced and competent trial judges throughout the Nation are fully capable of managing cases and supervising counsel in order to avoid the problems that seem insurmountable to appellate judges who are sometimes distracted by illogical distinctions and irrelevant statistics. I respectfully dissent.[8]

DAVIS V. ALASKA

415 U.S. 308, 94 S.Ct. 1105, 39 L.Ed.2d 347 (1974).

CHIEF JUSTICE BURGER delivered the opinion of the Court.

We granted certiorari in this case to consider whether the Confrontation Clause requires that a defendant in a criminal case be allowed to impeach the

---

[8] Except for Williams' confession, and the prosecutor's closing argument that will be separately considered on remand, there was a paucity of other evidence connecting respondent with the plan discussed in the car on the way to the victim's home. The Court of Appeals was thus unquestionably correct in concluding that the violation of the Confrontation Clause in this case was not harmless error.

credibility of a prosecution witness by cross-examination directed at possible bias deriving from the witness' probationary status as a juvenile delinquent when such an impeachment would conflict with a State's asserted interest in preserving the confidentiality of juvenile adjudications of delinquency.

When the Polar Bar in Anchorage closed in the early morning hours of February 16, 1970, well over a thousand dollars in cash and checks was in the bar's Mosler safe. About midday, February 16, it was discovered that the bar had been broken into and the safe, about two feet square and weighing several hundred pounds, had been removed from the premises. Later that afternoon the Alaska State Troopers received word that a safe had been discovered about 26 miles outside Anchorage near the home of Jess Straight * * *. The safe, which was subsequently determined to be the one stolen from the Polar Bar, had been pried open and the contents removed. Richard Green, Jess Straight's stepson, told investigating troopers on the scene that at about noon on February 16 he had seen and spoken with two Negro men standing alongside a late-model metallic blue Chevrolet sedan near where the safe was later discovered. The next day * * * Green was given six photographs of adult Negro males. After examining the photographs for 30 seconds to a minute, Green identified the photograph of petitioner as that of one of the men he had encountered the day before * * *. Petitioner was arrested the next day, February 18. On February 19, Green picked petitioner out of a lineup of seven Negro males.

At trial, evidence was introduced to the effect that paint chips found in the trunk of petitioner's rented blue Chevrolet could have originated from the surface of the stolen safe. Further, the trunk of the car contained particles which were identified as safe insulation characteristic of that found in Mosler safes. * * *

Richard Green was a crucial witness for the prosecution. He testified at trial that while on an errand for his mother he confronted two men standing beside a late-model metallic blue Chevrolet, parked on a road near his family's house. The man standing at the rear of the car spoke to Green asking if Green lived nearby and if his father was home. Green offered the men help, but his offer was rejected. On his return from the errand Green again passed the two men and he saw the man with whom he had had the conversation standing at the rear of the car with "something like a crowbar" in his hands. Green identified petitioner at the trial as the man with the "crowbar." The safe was discovered later that afternoon at the point, according to Green, where the Chevrolet had been parked.

Before testimony was taken at the trial of petitioner, the prosecutor moved for a protective order to prevent any reference to Green's juvenile record by the defense in the course of cross-examination. At the time of the trial and at the time of the events Green testified to, Green was on probation by order of a juvenile court after having been adjudicated a delinquent for burglarizing two cabins. Green was 16 years of age at the time of the Polar Bar burglary, but had turned 17 prior to trial.

In opposing the protective order, petitioner's counsel made it clear that he would not introduce Green's juvenile adjudication as a general impeachment of Green's character as a truthful person but, rather, to show specifically that at the same time Green was assisting the police in identifying petitioner he was on probation for burglary. From this petitioner would seek to show—or at least argue—that Green acted out of fear or concern of possible jeopardy to his probation. Not only might Green have made a hasty and faulty identification of petitioner to shift suspicion away from himself as one who robbed the Polar Bar, but Green might have been subject to undue pressure from the police and made his identifications under fear of possible probation revocation. Green's record would be revealed only as necessary to probe Green for bias and prejudice and not generally to call Green's good character into question.

The trial court granted the motion for a protective order, relying on Alaska Rule of Children's Procedure 23,[1] and Alaska Stat. § 47.10.080(g) (1971).[2]

Although prevented from revealing that Green had been on probation for the juvenile delinquency adjudication for burglary at the same time that he originally identified petitioner, counsel for petitioner did his best to expose Green's state of mind at the time Green discovered that a stolen safe had been discovered near his home. Green denied that he was upset or uncomfortable about the discovery of the safe. He claimed not to have been worried about any suspicions the police might have been expected to harbor against him, though Green did admit that it crossed his mind that the police might have thought he had something to do with the crime. * * * [After the defense counsel asked Green if he had "ever been questioned like that before by any law enforcement officers" and Green answered "No," the trial court cut off further questioning along this line on the prosecution's objection that such questioning was "a carry-on with rehash of the same thing"].

Since defense counsel was prohibited from making inquiry as to the witness' being on probation under a juvenile court adjudication, Green's protestations of unconcern over possible police suspicion that he might have had a part in the Polar Bar burglary and his categorical denial of ever having been the subject of any similar law-enforcement interrogation went unchallenged. The tension between the right of confrontation and the State's policy of protecting the witness with a juvenile record is particularly evident in the final answer given by the witness. Since it is probable that Green underwent some questioning by police when he was arrested for the burglaries on which his juvenile adjudication of delinquency rested, the answer can be regarded as highly suspect at the very least. The witness was in effect asserting, under protection of the trial court's ruling, a right to give a questionably truthful answer to a cross-examiner pursuing a relevant line of inquiry; it is doubtful whether the bold "No" answer would have been given by Green absent a belief that he was shielded from traditional cross-examination. It would be difficult to conceive of a situation more clearly illustrating the need for cross-examination. The remainder of the cross-examination was devoted to an attempt to prove that Green was making his identification at trial on the basis of

---

[1] Rule 23 provides: "No adjudication, order, or disposition of a juvenile case shall be admissible in a court not acting in the exercise of juvenile jurisdiction except for use in a presentencing procedure in a criminal case where the superior court, in its discretion, determines that such use is appropriate."

[2] Section 47.10.080(g) provides in pertinent part: "The commitment and placement of a child and evidence given in the court are not admissible as evidence against the minor in a subsequent case or proceedings in any other court. . . ."

what he remembered from his earlier identifications at the photographic display and lineup, and not on the basis of his February 16 confrontation with the two men on the road.

The Alaska Supreme Court affirmed petitioner's conviction, concluding that it did not have to resolve the potential conflict in this case between a defendant's right to a meaningful confrontation with adverse witnesses and the State's interest in protecting the anonymity of a juvenile offender since "our reading of the trial transcript convinces us that counsel for the defendant was able adequately to question the youth in considerable detail concerning the possibility of bias or motive." Although the court admitted that Green's denials of any sense of anxiety or apprehension upon the safe's being found close to his home were possibly self-serving, "the suggestion was nonetheless brought to the attention of the jury, and that body was afforded the opportunity to observe the demeanor of the youth and pass on his credibility." The court concluded that, in light of the indirect references permitted, there was no error.

Since we granted certiorari limited to the question of whether petitioner was denied his right under the Confrontation Clause to adequately cross-examine Green, the essential question turns on the correctness of the Alaska court's evaluation of the "adequacy" of the scope of cross-examination permitted. We disagree with that court's interpretation of the Confrontation Clause and we reverse.

The Sixth Amendment to the Constitution guarantees the right of an accused in a criminal prosecution "to be confronted with the witnesses against him." * * * Confrontation means more than being allowed to confront the witness physically. "Our cases construing the [confrontation] clause hold that a primary interest secured by it is the right of cross-examination." *Douglas v. Alabama,* 380 U.S. 415 (1965). * * *

Cross-examination is the principal means by which the believability of a witness and the truth of his testimony are tested. Subject always to the broad discretion of a trial judge to preclude repetitive and unduly harassing interrogation, the cross-examiner is not only permitted to delve into the witness' story to test the witness' perceptions and memory, but the cross-examiner has traditionally been allowed to impeach, i.e., discredit, the witness. One way of discrediting the witness is to introduce evidence of a prior criminal conviction of that witness. By so doing the cross-examiner intends to afford the jury a basis to infer that the witness' character is such that he would be less likely than the average trustworthy citizen to be truthful in his testimony. The introduction of evidence of a prior crime is thus a general attack on the credibility of the witness. A more particular attack on the witness' credibility is effected by means of cross-examination directed toward revealing possible biases, prejudices, or ulterior motives of the witness as they may relate directly to issues or personalities in the case at hand. * * * We have recognized that the exposure of a witness' motivation in testifying is a proper and important function of the constitutionally protected right of cross-examination. *Greene v. McElroy,* 360 U.S. 474 (1959).

In the instant case, defense counsel sought to show the existence of possible bias and prejudice of Green, causing him to make a faulty initial identification of petitioner, which in turn could have affected his later in-court identification of petitioner. We cannot speculate as to whether the jury, as sole judge of the credibility of a witness, would have accepted this line of reasoning had counsel been permitted to fully present it. But we do conclude that the jurors were entitled to have the benefit of the defense theory before them so that they could make an informed judgment as to the weight to place on Green's testimony which provided "a crucial link in the proof * * * of petitioner's act." *Douglas v. Alabama.* The accuracy and truthfulness of Green's testimony were key elements in the State's case against petitioner. The claim of bias which the defense sought to develop was admissible to afford a basis for an inference of undue pressure because of Green's vulnerable status as a probationer, as well as of Green's possible concern that he might be a suspect in the investigation.

We cannot accept the Alaska Supreme Court's conclusion that the cross-examination that was permitted defense counsel was adequate to develop the issue of bias properly to the jury. While counsel was permitted to ask Green *whether* he was biased, counsel was unable to make a record from which to argue *why* Green might have been biased or otherwise lacked that degree of impartiality expected of a witness at trial. On the basis of the limited cross-examination that was permitted, the jury might well have thought that defense counsel was engaged in a speculative and baseless line of attack on the credibility of an apparently blameless witness or, as the prosecutor's objection put it, a "rehash" of prior cross-examination. On these facts it seems clear to us that to make any such inquiry effective, defense counsel should have been permitted to expose to the jury the facts from which jurors, as the sole triers of fact and credibility, could appropriately draw inferences relating to the reliability of the witness. Petitioner was thus denied the right of effective cross-examination which "would be constitutional error of the first magnitude and no amount of showing of want of prejudice would cure it." *Smith v. Illinois,* 390 U.S. 129 (1968).

The claim is made that the State has an important interest in protecting the anonymity of juvenile offenders and that this interest outweighs any competing interest this petitioner might have in cross-examining Green about his being on probation. The State argues that exposure of a juvenile's record of delinquency would likely cause impairment of rehabilitative goals of the juvenile correctional procedures. This exposure, it is argued, might encourage the juvenile offender to commit further acts of delinquency, or cause the juvenile offender to lose employment opportunities or otherwise suffer unnecessarily for his youthful transgression.

We do not and need not challenge the State's interest as a matter of its own policy in the administration of criminal justice to seek to preserve the anonymity of a juvenile offender. Here, however, petitioner sought to introduce evidence of Green's probation for the purpose of suggesting that Green was biased and, therefore, that his testimony was either not to be believed in his identification of petitioner or at least very carefully considered in that light. Serious damage to the strength of the State's case would have been a real possibility had petitioner been allowed to pursue this line of inquiry. In this setting we conclude that the right of confrontation is paramount to the State's policy of protecting a juvenile offender. Whatever temporary embarrassment might result to Green or his family by disclosure of his juvenile record—if the prosecution insisted on using him to make its case—is outweighed by petitioner's right to probe into the influence of possible bias in the testimony of a crucial identification witness. * * *

The State's policy interest in protecting the confidentiality of a juvenile offender's record cannot require yielding of so vital a constitutional right as the effective cross-examination for bias of an adverse witness. The State could have protected Green from exposure of his juvenile adjudication in these circumstances by refraining from using him to make out its case; the State cannot, consistent with the right of confrontation, require the petitioner to bear the full burden of vindicating the State's interest in the secrecy of juvenile criminal records. The judgment affirming petitioner's convictions of burglary and grand larceny is reversed and the case is remanded for further proceedings not inconsistent with this opinion.

JUSTICE STEWART, concurring.

The Court holds that, in the circumstances of this case, the Sixth and Fourteenth Amendments conferred the right to cross-examine a particular prosecution witness about his delinquency adjudication for burglary and his status as a probationer. Such cross-examination was necessary in this case in order "to show the existence of possible bias and prejudice * * *." In joining the Court's opinion, I would emphasize that the Court neither holds nor suggests that the Constitution confers a right in every case to impeach the general credibility of a witness through cross-examination about his past delinquency adjudications or criminal convictions.

JUSTICE WHITE, with whom JUSTICE REHNQUIST joins, dissenting.

As I see it, there is no constitutional principle at stake here. This is nothing more than a typical instance of a trial court exercising its discretion to control or limit cross-examination, followed by a typical decision of a state appellate court refusing to disturb the judgment of the trial court and itself concluding that limiting cross-examination had done no substantial harm to the defense. Yet the Court insists on second-guessing the state courts and in effect inviting federal review of every ruling of a state trial judge who believes cross-examination has gone far enough. I would not undertake this task, if for no other reason than that I have little faith in our ability, in fact-bound cases and on a cold record, to improve on the judgment of trial judges and of the state appellate courts who agree with them. I would affirm the judgment.

3. THE RIGHT TO REMAIN SILENT—OR TESTIFY

The Fifth Amendment privilege against self-incrimination has been examined previously in the context of the investigatory process (see Chs. 6, 7, and 8) and pretrial disclosure (see Ch. 13). In its application to the defendant at trial, the privilege has special meaning, for it confers on defendant a right not simply to refuse to respond to questioning, but to refuse to be placed on the stand where he can be subjected to such questioning. This right not to be called to testify—commonly described as the defendant's "right of silence"—is a basic element of an accusatorial system of justice that requires the government to make its case through its own evidence and allows the accused "to remain inactive and secure, until the prosecution has taken up its burden and produced evidence and effected persuasion." *Taylor v. Kentucky,* 436 U.S. 478 (1978). *Griffin v. California,* the first case in this section, is the leading case on the reach of this right of silence. The Court there considers whether the Fifth Amendment requires that there be no adverse comment, by trial judge or prosecutor, on the defendant's exercise of that right.

The second case in this section, *Rock v. Arkansas,* marks the Court's recognition of a constitutional right of the defendant to take the stand and testify, a practice that was not allowed at the time of the adoption of the Constitution. *Rock* also considers the appropriate scope of state authority to impose evidentiary limitations that restrict the defendant's exercise of this right to testify.

GRIFFIN V. CALIFORNIA
380 U.S. 609, 85 S.Ct. 1229, 14 L.Ed.2d 106 (1965).

JUSTICE DOUGLAS delivered the opinion of the Court.

Petitioner was convicted of murder in the first degree after a jury trial in the California court. He did not testify at the trial on the issue of guilt, though he did testify at the separate trial on the issue of penalty. The trial court instructed the jury on the issue of guilt, stating that a defendant has a constitutional right not to testify. But it told the jury:[2]

> "As to any evidence or facts against him which the defendant can reasonably be expected to deny or explain because of facts within his knowledge, if he does not testify or if, though he does testify, he fails to deny or explain such evidence, the jury may take that failure into consideration as tending to indicate the truth of such evidence and as indicating that among the inferences that may be reasonably drawn therefrom those unfavorable to the defendant are the more probable."

It added, however, that no such inference could be drawn as to evidence respecting which he had no knowledge. It stated that failure of a defendant to deny or explain the evidence of which he had knowledge does not create a presumption of guilt nor by itself warrant an inference of guilt nor relieve the prosecution of any of its burden of proof.

---

[2] Article I, § 13, of the California Constitution provides in part: ". . . in any criminal case, whether the defendant testifies or not, his failure to explain or to deny by his testimony any evidence or facts in the case against him may be commented upon by the court and by counsel, and may be considered by the court or the jury."

Petitioner had been seen with the deceased the evening of her death, the evidence placing him with her in the alley where her body was found. The prosecutor made much of the failure of petitioner to testify:

> "The defendant certainly knows whether Essie Mae had this beat up appearance at the time he left her apartment and went down the alley with her.

> "What kind of a man is it that would want to have sex with a woman that beat up if she was beat up at the time he left?

> "He would know that. He would know how she got down the alley. He would know how the blood got on the bottom of the concrete steps. He would know how long he was with her in that box. He would know how her wig got off. He would know whether he beat her or mistreated her. He would know whether he walked away from that place cool as a cucumber when he saw Mr. Villasenor because he was conscious of his own guilt and wanted to get away from that damaged or injured woman.

> "These things he has not seen fit to take the stand and deny or explain.

> "And in the whole world, if anybody would know, this defendant would know.

> "Essie Mae is dead, she can't tell you her side of the story. The defendant won't."

The death penalty was imposed and the California Supreme Court affirmed. The case is here on a petition for a writ of certiorari which we granted to consider the single question whether comment on the failure to testify violated the Self-Incrimination Clause of the Fifth Amendment which we made applicable to the States * * *.

If this were a federal trial, reversible error would have been committed. *Wilson v. United States,* 149 U.S. 60 (1893) so holds. It is said, however, that the *Wilson* decision rested not on the Fifth Amendment, but on an Act of Congress. 18 U.S.C. § 3481. That indeed is the fact, as the opinion of the Court in the *Wilson* case states. * * * But that is the beginning, not the end of our inquiry. The question remains whether, statute or not, the comment rule, approved by California, violates the Fifth Amendment.

We think it does. It is in substance a rule of evidence that allows the State the privilege of tendering to the jury for its consideration the failure of the accused to testify. No formal offer of proof is made as in other situations; but the prosecutor's comment and the court's acquiescence are the equivalent of an offer of evidence and its acceptance. The Court in the *Wilson* case stated:

> " * * * the Act was framed with a due regard also to those who might prefer to rely upon the presumption of innocence which the law gives to every one, and not wish to be witnesses. It is not every one who can safely venture on the witness stand, though entirely innocent of the charge against him. Excessive timidity, nervousness when facing others and

attempting to explain transactions of a suspicious character, and offenses charged against him, will often confuse and embarrass him to such a degree as to increase rather than remove prejudices against him. It is not every one, however honest, who would therefore willingly be placed on the witness stand. The statute, in tenderness to the weakness of those who from the causes mentioned might refuse to ask to be witnesses, particularly when they may have been in some degree compromised by their association with others, declares that the failure of a defendant in a criminal action to request to be a witness shall not create any presumption against him."

If the words "Fifth Amendment" are substituted for "Act" and for "statute" the spirit of the Self-Incrimination Clause is reflected. For comment on the refusal to testify is a remnant of the "inquisitorial system of criminal justice" which the Fifth Amendment outlaws. It is a penalty imposed by courts for exercising a constitutional privilege. It cuts down on the privilege by making its assertion costly. It is said, however, that the inference of guilt for failure to testify as to facts peculiarly within the accused's knowledge is in any event natural and irresistible, and that comment on the failure does not magnify that inference into a penalty for asserting a constitutional privilege. What the jury may infer given no help from the court is one thing. What they may infer when the court solemnizes the silence of the accused into evidence against him is quite another. * * *

We * * * hold that the Fifth Amendment, in its direct application to the federal government and its bearing on the States by reason of the Fourteenth Amendment, forbids either comment by the prosecution on the accused's silence or instructions by the court that such silence is evidence of guilt.

Reversed.[a]

JUSTICE STEWART, with whom JUSTICE WHITE joins, dissenting. * * *

We must determine whether the petitioner has been "compelled to be a witness against himself." Compulsion is the focus of the inquiry. Certainly, if any compulsion be detected in the California procedure, it is of a dramatically different and less palpable nature than that involved in the procedures which historically gave rise to the Fifth Amendment guarantee. When a suspect was brought before the Court of High Commission or the Star Chamber, he was commanded to answer whatever was asked of him, and subjected to a far-reaching and deeply probing inquiry in an effort to ferret out some unknown and frequently unsuspected crime. He declined to answer on pain of incarceration, banishment, or mutilation. And if he spoke falsely, he was subject to further punishment. Faced with this formidable array of alternatives, his decision to speak was unquestionably coerced.

Those were the lurid realities which lay behind enactment of the Fifth Amendment, a far cry from the subject matter of the case before us. I think that the Court in this case stretches the concept of compulsion beyond all reasonable bounds, and that whatever compulsion may exist derives from the defendant's

---

[a]   The Chief Justice took no part in the decision of the case. Harlan, J., concurred "with great reluctance."

choice not to testify, not from any comment by court or counsel. In support of its conclusion that the California procedure does compel the accused to testify, the Court has only this to say: "It is a penalty imposed by courts for exercising a constitutional privilege. It cuts down on the privilege by making its assertion costly." Exactly what the penalty imposed consists of is not clear. It is not, as I understand the problem, that the jury becomes aware that the defendant has chosen not to testify in his own defense, for the jury will, of course, realize this quite evident fact, even though the choice goes unmentioned. Since comment by counsel and the court does not compel testimony by creating such an awareness, the Court must be saying that the California constitutional provision places some other compulsion upon the defendant to incriminate himself, some compulsion which the Court does not describe and which I cannot readily perceive.

* * * No doubt the prosecution's argument will seek to encourage the drawing of inferences unfavorable to the defendant. However, the defendant's counsel equally has an opportunity to explain the various other reasons why a defendant may not wish to take the stand, and thus rebut the natural if uneducated assumption that it is because the defendant cannot truthfully deny the accusations made. * * *

The California rule allowing comment by counsel and instruction by the judge on the defendant's failure to take the stand is hardly an idiosyncratic aberration. The Model Code of Evidence, and Uniform Rules of Evidence both sanction the use of such procedures. The practice had been endorsed by resolution of the American Bar Association and the American Law Institute, and has the support of the weight of scholarly opinion. * * *b

---

b   *United States v. Robinson*, 485 U.S. 25 (1988) recognized a "fair response" exception to the *Griffin* prohibition; where defense counsel argued that the government had never allowed defendant to tell his side of the story, the Fifth Amendment was not violated by the prosecutor's response that defendant could have "taken the stand." See also *Mitchell v. United States*, p. 1159, in which the majority extends *Griffin* to sentencing. Justice Scalia's dissent there not only opposes the extension but also questions the soundness of the *Griffin* ruling in an argument more extensive than the *Griffin* dissents.

   Carter v. Kentucky, 450 U.S. 288 (1981), held that the accused had a constitutional right to a requested instruction informing the jury that the defendant had a constitutional right not to testify and that "the fact that he does not [testify] cannot be used as an inference of guilt and should not prejudice him in any way." The Court reasoned that, while "no judge can prevent jurors from speculating about why a defendant stands mute in the face of a criminal accusation, * * * a judge can, and must, if requested to do so, use the unique power of the jury instruction to reduce speculation to a minimum." In *Lakeside v. Oregon*, 435 U.S. 333 (1978), the Court held that the trial court could insist upon giving a protective instruction even over objection of the defendant. Consider also the refusal to extend "the *Griffin* rationale" in *Portuondo v. Agard*, described in footnote a to *Rock v. Arkansas*, infra.

ROCK V. ARKANSAS

483 U.S. 44, 107 S.Ct. 2704, 97 L.Ed.2d 37 (1987).

JUSTICE BLACKMUN delivered the opinion of the Court.

The issue presented in this case is whether Arkansas' evidentiary rule prohibiting the admission of hypnotically refreshed testimony violated petitioner's constitutional right to testify on her own behalf as a defendant in a criminal case.

Petitioner Vickie Lorene Rock was charged with manslaughter in the death of her husband, Frank Rock, on July 2, 1983. A dispute had been simmering about Frank's wish to move from the couple's small apartment adjacent to Vickie's beauty parlor to a trailer she owned outside town. That night a fight erupted when Frank refused to let petitioner eat some pizza and prevented her from leaving the apartment to get something else to eat. When police arrived on the scene they found Frank on the floor with a bullet wound in his chest. Petitioner urged the officers to help her husband, and cried to a sergeant who took her in charge, "please save him" and "don't let him die." The police removed her from the building because she was upset and because she interfered with their investigation by her repeated attempts to use the telephone to call her husband's parents. According to the testimony of one of the investigating officers, petitioner told him that "she stood up to leave the room and [her husband] grabbed her by the throat and choked her and threw her against the wall and * * * at that time she walked over and picked up the weapon and pointed it toward the floor and he hit her again and she shot him."

Because petitioner could not remember the precise details of the shooting, her attorney suggested that she submit to hypnosis in order to refresh her memory. Petitioner was hypnotized twice by Doctor Betty Back, a licensed neuropsychologist with training in the field of hypnosis. Doctor Back interviewed petitioner for an hour prior to the first hypnosis session, taking notes on petitioner's general history and her recollections of the shooting. Both hypnosis sessions were recorded on tape. Petitioner did not relate any new information during either of the sessions, id., at 78, 83, but, after the hypnosis, she was able to remember that at the time of the incident she had her thumb on the hammer of the gun, but had not held her finger on the trigger. She also recalled that the gun had discharged when her husband grabbed her arm during the scuffle. As a result of the details that petitioner was able to remember about the shooting, her counsel arranged for a gun expert to examine the handgun, a single action Hawes .22 Deputy Marshal. That inspection revealed that the gun was defective and prone to fire, when hit or dropped, without the trigger's being pulled.

When the prosecutor learned of the hypnosis sessions, he filed a motion to exclude petitioner's testimony. The trial judge held a pretrial hearing on the motion and concluded that no hypnotically refreshed testimony would be admitted. The court issued an order limiting petitioner's testimony to "matters remembered and stated to the examiner prior to being placed under hypnosis." At trial, petitioner introduced testimony by the gun expert, but the court limited petitioner's own description of the events on the day of the shooting to a reiteration of the sketchy information in Doctor Back's notes. The jury convicted petitioner on the manslaughter charge and she was sentenced to 10 years imprisonment and a $10,000 fine.

On appeal, the Supreme Court of Arkansas rejected petitioner's claim that the limitations on her testimony violated her right to present her defense. The court concluded that "the dangers of admitting this kind of testimony outweigh whatever probative value it may have," and decided to follow the approach of States that have held hypnotically refreshed testimony of witnesses inadmissible *per se*. * * * [I]t ruled that the exclusion of petitioner's testimony did not violate her constitutional rights. Any "prejudice or deprivation" she suffered "was minimal and resulted from her own actions and not by any erroneous ruling of the court."

Petitioner's claim that her testimony was impermissibly excluded is bottomed on her constitutional right to testify in her own defense. At this point in the development of our adversary system, it cannot be doubted that a defendant in a criminal case has the right to take the witness stand and to testify in his or her own defense. This, of course, is a change from the historic common-law view, which was that all parties to litigation, including criminal defendants, were disqualified from testifying because of their interest in the outcome of the trial. The principal rationale for this rule was the possible untrustworthiness of a party's testimony. Under the common law, the practice did develop of permitting criminal defendants to tell their side of the story, but they were limited to making an unsworn statement that could not be elicited through direct examination by counsel and was not subject to cross-examination.

This Court in *Ferguson v. Georgia,* 365 U.S. 570 (1961), detailed the history of the transition from a rule of a defendant's incompetency to a rule of competency. As the Court there recounted, it came to be recognized that permitting a defendant to testify advances both the " 'detection of guilt' " and " 'the protection of innocence,' " and by the end of the second half of the 19th century, all States except Georgia had enacted statutes that declared criminal defendants competent to testify. * * *

The right to testify on one's own behalf at a criminal trial has sources in several provisions of the Constitution. It is one of the rights that "are essential to due process of law in a fair adversary process." *Faretta v. California*. [fn. 15, p. 1008]. The necessary ingredients of the Fourteenth Amendment's guarantee that no one shall be deprived of liberty without due process of law include a right to be heard and to offer testimony. * * *

The right to testify is also found in the Compulsory Process Clause of the Sixth Amendment, which grants a defendant the right to call "witnesses in his favor" * * *. Logically included in the accused's right to call witnesses whose testimony is "material and favorable to his defense," *United States v. Valenzuela-Bernal,* 458 U.S. 858 (1982), is a right to testify himself, should he decide it is in his favor to do so. In fact, the most important witness for the defense in many criminal cases is the defendant himself. There is no justification today for a rule that denies an accused the opportunity to offer his own testimony. Like the truthfulness of other witnesses, the defendant's veracity, which was the concern behind the original common-law rule, can be tested adequately by cross-examination.

Moreover, in *Faretta v. California,* the Court recognized that the Sixth Amendment "grants to the accused *personally* the right to make his defense." * * * Even more fundamental to a personal defense than the right of self-representation, which was found to be "necessarily implied by the structure of the Amendment," *Faretta,* is an accused's right to present his own version of events in his own words. A defendant's opportunity to conduct his own defense by calling witnesses is incomplete if he may not present himself as a witness.

The opportunity to testify is also a necessary corollary to the Fifth Amendment's guarantee against compelled testimony. In *Harris v. New York,* 401 U.S. 222 (1971), the Court stated: "Every criminal defendant is privileged to testify in his own defense, or to refuse to do so." Three of the dissenting Justices in that case agreed that the Fifth Amendment encompasses this right: "[The Fifth Amendment's privilege against self-incrimination] is fulfilled only when an accused is guaranteed the right 'to remain silent unless he chooses to speak in the unfettered exercise of his own will.' * * * The choice of whether to testify in one's own defense * * * is an exercise of the constitutional privilege." * * *

Of course, the right to present relevant testimony is not without limitation. The right "may, in appropriate cases, bow to accommodate other legitimate interests in the criminal trial process." *Chambers v. Mississippi* [see p. 1063]. But restrictions of a defendant's right to testify may not be arbitrary or disproportionate to the purposes they are designed to serve. In applying its evidentiary rules a State must evaluate whether the interests served by a rule justify the limitation imposed on the defendant's constitutional right to testify.

The Arkansas rule enunciated by the state courts does not allow a trial court to consider whether posthypnosis testimony may be admissible in a particular case; it is a *per se* rule prohibiting the admission at trial of any defendant's hypnotically refreshed testimony on the ground that such testimony is always unreliable. Thus, in Arkansas, an accused's testimony is limited to matters that he or she can prove were remembered *before* hypnosis. This rule operates to the detriment of any defendant who undergoes hypnosis, without regard to the reasons for it, the circumstances under which it took place, or any independent verification of the information it produced.

In this case, the application of that rule had a significant adverse effect on petitioner's ability to testify. It virtually prevented her from describing any of the events that occurred on the day of the shooting, despite corroboration of many of those events by other witnesses. Even more importantly, under the court's rule petitioner was not permitted to describe the actual shooting except in the words contained in Doctor Back's notes. The expert's description of the gun's tendency to misfire would have taken on greater significance if the jury had heard petitioner testify that she did not have her finger on the trigger and that the gun went off when her husband hit her arm.

In establishing its *per se* rule, the Arkansas Supreme Court simply followed the approach taken by a number of States that have decided that hypnotically enhanced testimony should be excluded at trial on the ground that it tends to be unreliable. Other States that have adopted an exclusionary rule, however, have done so for the testimony of *witnesses,* not for the testimony of a *defendant.* The Arkansas Supreme Court failed to perform the constitutional analysis that is necessary when a defendant's right to testify is at stake.

Although the Arkansas court concluded that any testimony that cannot be proved to be the product of prehypnosis memory is unreliable, many courts have eschewed a *per se* rule and permit the admission of hypnotically refreshed testimony. Hypnosis by trained physicians or psychologists has been recognized as a valid therapeutic technique since 1958, although there is no generally accepted theory to explain the phenomenon, or even a consensus on a single definition of hypnosis. The use of hypnosis in criminal investigations, however, is controversial, and the current medical and legal view of its appropriate role is unsettled.

Responses of individuals to hypnosis vary greatly. The popular belief that hypnosis guarantees the accuracy of recall is as yet without established foundation and, in fact, hypnosis often has no effect at all on memory. The most common response to hypnosis, however, appears to be an increase in both correct and incorrect recollections. Three general characteristics of hypnosis may lead to the introduction of inaccurate memories: the subject becomes "suggestible" and may try to please the hypnotist with answers the subject thinks will be met with approval; the subject is likely to "confabulate," that is, to fill in details from the imagination in order to make an answer more coherent and complete; and, the subject experiences "memory hardening," which gives him great confidence in both true and false memories, making effective cross-examination more difficult. See generally M. Orne, et al., Hypnotically Induced Testimony * * *. Despite the unreliability that hypnosis concededly may introduce, however, the procedure has been credited as instrumental in obtaining investigative leads or identifications that were later confirmed by independent evidence.

The inaccuracies the process introduces can be reduced, although perhaps not eliminated, by the use of procedural safeguards. One set of suggested guidelines calls for hypnosis to be performed only by a psychologist or psychiatrist with special training in its use and who is independent of the investigation. See Orne, The Use and Misuse of Hypnosis in Court * * *. These procedures reduce the possibility that biases will be communicated to the hypersuggestive subject by the hypnotist. Suggestion will be less likely also if the hypnosis is conducted in a neutral setting with no one present but the hypnotist and the subject. Tape or video recording of all interrogations, before, during, and after hypnosis, can help reveal if leading questions were asked. Such guidelines do not guarantee the accuracy of the testimony, because they cannot control the subject's own motivations or any tendency to confabulate, but they do provide a means of controlling overt suggestions.

The more traditional means of assessing accuracy of testimony also remain applicable in the case of a previously hypnotized defendant. Certain information recalled as a result of hypnosis may be verified as highly accurate by corroborating evidence. Cross-examination, even in the face of a confident defendant, is an effective tool for revealing inconsistencies. Moreover, a jury can be educated to the risks of hypnosis through expert testimony and cautionary instructions. Indeed, it is probably to a defendant's advantage to establish carefully the extent of his memory prior to hypnosis, in order to minimize the decrease in credibility the procedure might introduce.

We are not now prepared to endorse without qualifications the use of hypnosis as an investigative tool; scientific understanding of the phenomenon and of the means to control the effects of hypnosis is still in its infancy. Arkansas, however, has not justified the exclusion of *all* of a defendant's testimony that the defendant is unable to prove to be the product of prehypnosis memory. A State's legitimate interest in barring unreliable evidence does not extend to *per se* exclusions that may be reliable in an individual case. Wholesale inadmissibility of a defendant's testimony is an arbitrary restriction on the right to testify in the absence of clear evidence by the State repudiating the validity of all posthypnosis recollections. The State would be well within its powers if it established guidelines to aid trial courts in the evaluation of posthypnosis testimony and it may be able to show that testimony in a particular case is so unreliable that exclusion is justified. But it has not shown that hypnotically enhanced testimony is always so untrustworthy and so immune to the traditional means of evaluating credibility that it should disable a defendant from presenting her version of the events for which she is on trial.

In this case, the defective condition of the gun corroborated the details petitioner remembered about the shooting. The tape recordings provided some means to evaluate the hypnosis and the trial judge concluded that Doctor Back did not suggest responses with leading questions. Those circumstances present an argument for admissibility of petitioner's testimony in this particular case, an argument that must be considered by the trial court. Arkansas' *per se* rule excluding all posthypnosis testimony infringes impermissibly on the right of a defendant to testify on his or her own behalf.[20]

The judgment of the Supreme Court of Arkansas is vacated and the case is remanded to that court for further proceedings not inconsistent with this opinion.

CHIEF JUSTICE REHNQUIST, with whom JUSTICE WHITE, JUSTICE O'CONNOR, and JUSTICE SCALIA join, dissenting.

In deciding that petitioner Rock's testimony was properly limited at her trial, the Arkansas Supreme Court cited several factors that undermine the reliability of hypnotically induced testimony. Like the Court today, the Arkansas Supreme Court observed that a hypnotized individual becomes subject to suggestion, is likely to confabulate, and experiences artificially increased confidence in both true and false memories following hypnosis. No known set of procedures, both courts agree, can insure against the inherently unreliable nature of such testimony. Having acceded to the factual premises of the Arkansas Supreme Court, the Court nevertheless concludes that a state trial court must attempt to make its own

---

[20] This disposition makes it unnecessary to consider petitioner's claims that the trial court's order restricting her testimony was unconstitutionally broad and that the trial court's application of the order resulted in a denial of due process of law. We also need not reach petitioner's argument that Arkansas' restriction on her testimony interferes with her Sixth Amendment right to counsel. Petitioner concedes that there is a "substantial question" whether she raised this federal question on appeal to the Arkansas Supreme Court. Reply Brief for Petitioner 2.

scientific assessment of reliability in each case it is confronted with a request for the admission of hypnotically induced testimony. I find no justification in the Constitution for such a ruling.

In the Court's words, the decision today is "bottomed" on recognition of Rock's "constitutional right to testify in her own defense." While it is true that this Court, in dictum, has recognized the existence of such a right, the principles identified by the Court as underlying this right provide little support for invalidating the evidentiary rule applied by the Arkansas Supreme Court.

As a general matter, the Court first recites, a defendant's right to testify facilitates the truth-seeking function of a criminal trial by advancing both the " 'detection of guilt' " and " 'the protection of innocence.' " Quoting *Ferguson v. Georgia*. Such reasoning is hardly controlling here, where advancement of the truth-seeking function of Rock's trial was the sole motivation behind limiting her testimony. The Court also posits, however, that "a rule that denies an accused the opportunity to offer his own testimony" cannot be upheld because, "[l]ike the truthfulness of other witnesses, the defendant's veracity * * * can be tested adequately by cross-examination." But the Court candidly admits that the increased confidence inspired by hypnotism makes "cross-examination more difficult," thereby diminishing an adverse party's ability to test the truthfulness of defendants such as Rock. * * *

This Court has traditionally accorded the States "respect * * * in the establishment and implementation of their own criminal trial rules and procedures." *Chambers.* * * * One would think that this deference would be at its highest in an area such as this, where, as the Court concedes, "scientific understanding * * * is still in its infancy." * * * The Supreme Court of Arkansas' decision was an entirely permissible response to a novel and difficult question. M. Orne et al., Hypnotically Refreshed Testimony * * *. As an original proposition, the solution this Court imposes upon Arkansas may be equally sensible, though requiring the matter to be considered *res nova* by every single trial judge in every single case might seem to some to pose serious administrative difficulties. But until there is a much more general consensus on the use of hypnosis than there is now, the Constitution does not warrant this Court's mandating its own view of how to deal with the issue.[a]

---

[a] In *Portuondo v. Agard*, 529 U.S. 61 (2000), the prosecutor, in the course of a closing argument questioning the credibility of the defendant's testimony, pointed out that defendant, unlike other witnesses, had been present throughout the trial and was thus able to hear what other witnesses said before he testified. The Court rejected the contention that the "rationale of *Griffin*" should be extended to bar such comments as burdening the defendant's constitutional rights to be present at trial and to testify on his own behalf. It found *Griffin* to be a "poor analogue" for several reasons, including: (1) *Griffin* prohibited a prosecutor from urging a jury to do what it is not permitted to do, but it is "natural" and "appropriate" for a jury, "in evaluating the credibility of a witness who testifies last, to have in mind and weigh in the balance the fact that he heard the testimony of all those who preceded him"; and (2) "*Griffin* prohibited comments that suggest a defendant's silence is evidence of *guilt*," while the comment here challenges credibility, in accord with "the longstanding rule" that a defendant who takes the stand "may be impeached and his testimony assailed like that of any other witness."

4. DUE PROCESS REQUIREMENTS

The Supreme Court has long held that due process can be the source of trial rights not found in the more specific guarantees of the Sixth and Fifth Amendments. *Holmes v. South Carolina* examines constitutional protection for the defendant's opportunity to present a complete defense, protection rooted in the Due Process Clause as well as the Confrontation and Compulsory Process Clauses. Due process also imposes upon the state the obligation to establish guilt beyond a reasonable doubt. *In re Winship*, 397 U.S. 358 (1970). From that requirement flows a series of related constitutional prerequisites. *Taylor v. Kentucky* considers whether one of these is a jury instruction on the "presumption of innocence."

Constitutional challenges to alleged prosecutorial misconduct at trial also are raised under the "fundamental fairness" standard of due process. Building upon the prosecutor's role as a representative of the state "whose interest in criminal prosecution is not that it shall win the case, but that justice shall be done," *Berger v. United States,* 295 U.S. 78 (1935), the Court has recognized prosecutorial obligations to correct the material testimony of its witnesses known to be false and to disclose material exculpatory evidence within its control. See *United States v. Bagley,* Ch. 13. The second case in this section, *Darden v. Wainwright,* considers the application of the due process clause to the misconduct of the prosecutor in presenting the state's closing argument.

HOLMES v. SOUTH CAROLINA
547 U.S. 319, 126 S.Ct. 1727, 164 L.Ed.2d 503 (2006).

JUSTICE ALITO delivered the opinion of the Court.

This case presents the question whether a criminal defendant's federal constitutional rights are violated by an evidence rule under which the defendant may not introduce proof of third-party guilt if the prosecution has introduced forensic evidence that, if believed, strongly supports a guilty verdict.

On the morning of December 31, 1989, 86-year-old Mary Stewart was beaten, raped, and robbed in her home. She later died of complications stemming from her injuries. Petitioner was convicted by a South Carolina jury of murder, first-degree criminal sexual conduct, first-degree burglary, and robbery, and he was sentenced to death. The South Carolina Supreme Court affirmed his convictions and sentence, and this Court denied certiorari. Upon state postconviction review, however, petitioner was granted a new trial.

At the second trial, the prosecution relied heavily on the following forensic evidence:

> "(1) [Petitioner's] palm print was found just above the door knob on the interior side of the front door of the victim's house; (2) fibers consistent with a black sweatshirt owned by [petitioner] were found on the victim's bed sheets; (3) matching blue fibers were found on the victim's pink nightgown and on [petitioner's] blue jeans; (4) microscopically consistent fibers were found on the pink nightgown and

on [petitioner's] underwear; (5) [petitioner's] underwear contained a mixture of DNA from two individuals, and 99.99% of the population other than [petitioner] and the victim were excluded as contributors to that mixture; and (6) [petitioner's] tank top was found to contain a mixture of [petitioner's] blood and the victim's blood."

In addition, the prosecution introduced evidence that petitioner had been seen near Stewart's home within an hour of the time when, according to the prosecution's evidence, the attack took place.

As a major part of his defense, petitioner attempted to undermine the State's forensic evidence by suggesting that it had been contaminated and that certain law enforcement officers had engaged in a plot to frame him. Petitioner's expert witnesses criticized the procedures used by the police in handling the fiber and DNA evidence and in collecting the fingerprint evidence. Another defense expert provided testimony that petitioner cited as supporting his claim that the palm print had been planted by the police.

Petitioner also sought to introduce proof that another man, Jimmy McCaw White, had attacked Stewart. At a pretrial hearing, petitioner proffered several witnesses who placed White in the victim's neighborhood on the morning of the assault, as well as four other witnesses who testified that White had either acknowledged that petitioner was " 'innocent' " or had actually admitted to committing the crimes. One witness recounted that when he asked White about the "word . . . on the street" that White was responsible for Stewart's murder, White "put his head down and he raised his head back up and he said, well, you know I like older women." According to this witness, White added that "he did what they say he did" and that he had "no regrets about it at all." Another witness, who had been incarcerated with White, testified that White had admitted to assaulting Stewart, that a police officer had asked the witness to testify falsely against petitioner, and that employees of the prosecutor's office, while soliciting the witness' cooperation, had spoken of manufacturing evidence against petitioner. White testified at the pretrial hearing and denied making the incriminating statements. He also provided an alibi for the time of the crime, but another witness refuted his alibi.

The trial court excluded petitioner's third-party guilt evidence citing *State v. Gregory*, 198 S.C. 98, 16 S.E.2d 532 (1941), which held that such evidence is admissible if it " 'raise[s] a reasonable inference or presumption as to [the defendant's] own innocence' " but is not admissible if it merely " 'casts a bare suspicion upon another' " or " 'raises a conjectural inference as to the commission of the crime by another.' " On appeal, the South Carolina Supreme Court found no error in the exclusion of petitioner's third-party guilt evidence. * * * The State Supreme Court held that "where there is strong evidence of an appellant's guilt, especially where there is strong forensic evidence, the proffered evidence, about a third party's alleged guilt does not raise a reasonable inference as to the appellant's own innocence." Applying this standard, the court held that petitioner could not "overcome the forensic evidence against him to raise a reasonable inference of his own innocence." We granted certiorari.

"State and federal rulemakers have broad latitude under the Constitution to establish rules excluding evidence from criminal trials." *United States v. Scheffer*, 523 U.S. 303, 308 (1998); see also *Crane v. Kentucky*, 476 U.S. 683 (1986); *Chambers v. Mississippi*, 410 U.S. 284 (1973). This latitude, however, has limits. "Whether rooted directly in the Due Process Clause of the Fourteenth Amendment or in the Compulsory Process or Confrontation clauses of the Sixth Amendment, the Constitution guarantees criminal defendants 'a meaningful opportunity to present a complete defense.' " *Crane*, supra. This right is abridged by evidence rules that "infring[e] upon a weighty interest of the accused" and are " 'arbitrary' or 'disproportionate to the purposes they are designed to serve.' " *Scheffer*.

This Court's cases contain several illustrations of "arbitrary" rules, i.e., rules that excluded important defense evidence but that did not serve any legitimate interests. In *Washington v. Texas*, 388 U.S. 14 (1967), state statutes barred a person who had been charged as a participant in a crime from testifying in defense of another alleged participant unless the witness had been acquitted. As a result, when the defendant in Washington was tried for murder, he was precluded from calling as a witness a person who had been charged and previously convicted of committing the same murder. Holding that the defendant's right to put on a defense had been violated, we noted that the rule embodied in the *1732 statutes could not "even be defended on the ground that it rationally sets apart a group of persons who are particularly likely to commit perjury" since the rule allowed an alleged participant to testify if he or she had been acquitted or was called by the prosecution.

A similar constitutional violation occurred in *Chambers v. Mississippi*, supra. A murder defendant called as a witness a man named McDonald, who had previously confessed to the murder. When McDonald repudiated the confession on the stand, the defendant was denied permission to examine McDonald as an adverse witness based on the State's " 'voucher' rule," which barred parties from impeaching their own witnesses. Id., at 294. In addition, because the state hearsay rule did not include an exception for statements against penal interest, the defendant was not permitted to introduce evidence that McDonald had made self-incriminating statements to three other persons. Noting that the State had not even attempted to "defend" or "explain [the] underlying rationale" of the "voucher rule," id., at 297. This Court held that "the exclusion of [the evidence of McDonald's out-of-court statements], coupled with the State's refusal to permit [the defendant] to cross-examine McDonald, denied him a trial in accord with traditional and fundamental standards of due process."[a]

Another arbitrary rule was held unconstitutional in Crane v. Kentucky, supra. There, the defendant was prevented from attempting to show at trial that his confession was unreliable because of the circumstances under which it was

---

[a] The Court in *Fry v. Pliler*, 551 U.S. 112 (2007), declined to decide whether, in order to establish a violation of due process under *Chambers*, a defendant must show that the limitation on the presentation of his defense had some potential impact on the outcome of his trial. Other guarantees rooted in due process and protecting fundamental fairness at trial do require such a showing, including the protection against improper argument discussed in *Darden*, below, and the access-to-evidence standards discussed in Chapter 13.

obtained, and neither the State Supreme Court nor the prosecution "advanced any rational justification for the wholesale exclusion of this body of potentially exculpatory evidence."

In *Rock v. Arkansas* [p. 1055] this Court held that a rule prohibiting hypnotically refreshed testimony was unconstitutional because "[w]holesale inadmissibility of a defendant's testimony is an arbitrary restriction on the right to testify in the absence of clear evidence by the State repudiating the validity of all post-hypnotic recollections." By contrast, in *United States v. Scheffer*, supra, we held that a rule excluding all polygraph evidence did not abridge the right to present a defense because the rule "served several legitimate interests in the criminal trial process," was "neither arbitrary nor disproportionate in promoting these ends," and did not "implicate a sufficiently weighty interest of the defendant."

While the Constitution thus prohibits the exclusion of defense evidence under rules that serve no legitimate purpose or that are disproportionate to the ends that they are asserted to promote, well-established rules of evidence permit trial judges to exclude evidence if its probative value is outweighed by certain other factors such as unfair prejudice, confusion of the issues, or potential to mislead the jury. See, e.g., Fed. Rule Evid. 403. Plainly referring to rules of this type, we have stated that the Constitution permits judges "to exclude evidence that is 'repetitive . . . , only marginally relevant' or poses an undue risk of 'harassment, prejudice, [or] confusion of the issues.' " *Crane*.

A specific application of this principle is found in rules regulating the admission of evidence proffered by criminal defendants to show that someone else committed the crime with which they are charged. Such rules are widely accepted, and neither petitioner nor his amici challenge them here.

In *Gregory*, the South Carolina Supreme Court adopted and applied a rule apparently intended to be of this type, given the court's references to the "applicable rule" from Corpus Juris and American Jurisprudence:

> " 'Evidence offered by accused as to the commission of the crime by another person must be limited to such facts as are inconsistent with his own guilt, and to such facts as raise a reasonable inference or presumption as to his own innocence; evidence which can have (no) other effect than to cast a bare suspicion upon another, or to raise a conjectural inference as to the commission of the crime by another, is not admissible. . . . Before such testimony can be received, there must be such proof of connection with it, such a train of facts or circumstances, as tends clearly to point out such other person as the guilty party.' " 198 S.C., at 104–105, 16 S.E.2d, at 534–535 (quoting 16 C.J., Criminal Law § 1085, p. 560 (1918) and 20 Am.Jur., Evidence § 265, p. 254 (1939)). * * *

* * * [H]owever, the South Carolina Supreme Court radically changed and extended the rule. * * * [T]he State Supreme Court applied the rule that "where there is strong evidence of [a defendant's] guilt, especially where there is strong forensic evidence, the proffered evidence about a third party's alleged guilt" may (or perhaps must) be excluded.

Under this rule, the trial judge does not focus on the probative value or the potential adverse effects of admitting the defense evidence of third-party guilt. Instead, the critical inquiry concerns the strength of the prosecution's case: If the prosecution's case is strong enough, the evidence of third-party guilt is excluded even if that evidence, if viewed independently, would have great probative value and even if it would not pose an undue risk of harassment, prejudice, or confusion of the issues.

Furthermore, as applied in this case, the South Carolina Supreme Court's rule seems to call for little, if any, examination of the credibility of the prosecution's witnesses or the reliability of its evidence. Here, for example, the defense strenuously claimed that the prosecution's forensic evidence was so unreliable (due to mishandling and a deliberate plot to frame petitioner) that the evidence should not have even been admitted. The South Carolina Supreme Court responded that these challenges did not entirely "eviscerate" the forensic evidence and that the defense challenges went to the weight and not to the admissibility of that evidence. * * * Yet, in evaluating the prosecution's forensic evidence and deeming it to be "strong"—and thereby justifying exclusion of petitioner's third-party guilt evidence—the South Carolina Supreme Court made no mention of the defense challenges to the prosecution's evidence.

Interpreted in this way, the rule applied by the State Supreme Court does not rationally serve the end that the Gregory rule and its analogues in other jurisdictions were designed to promote, i.e., to focus the trial on the central issues by excluding evidence that has only a very weak logical connection to the central issues. The rule applied in this case appears to be based on the following logic: Where (1) it is clear that only one person was involved in the commission of a particular crime and (2) there is strong evidence that the defendant was the perpetrator, it follows that evidence of third-party guilt must be weak. But this logic depends on an accurate evaluation of the prosecution's proof, and the true strength of the prosecution's proof cannot be assessed without considering challenges to the reliability of the prosecution's evidence. Just because the prosecution's evidence, if credited, would provide strong support for a guilty verdict, it does not follow that evidence of third-party guilt has only a weak logical connection to the central issues in the case. And where the credibility of the prosecution's witnesses or the reliability of its evidence is not conceded, the strength of the prosecution's case cannot be assessed without making the sort of factual findings that have traditionally been reserved for the trier of fact and that the South Carolina courts did not purport to make in this case.

The rule applied in this case is no more logical than its converse would be, i.e., a rule barring the prosecution from introducing evidence of a defendant's guilt if the defendant is able to proffer, at a pretrial hearing, evidence that, if believed, strongly supports a verdict of not guilty. In the present case, for example, the petitioner proffered evidence that, if believed, squarely proved that White, not petitioner, was the perpetrator. It would make no sense, however, to hold that this proffer precluded the prosecution from introducing its evidence, including the forensic evidence that, if credited, provided strong proof of the petitioner's guilt.

The point is that, by evaluating the strength of only one party's evidence, no logical conclusion can be reached regarding the strength of contrary evidence offered by the other side to rebut or cast doubt. Because the rule applied by the State Supreme Court in this case did not heed this point, the rule is "arbitrary" in the sense that it does not rationally serve the end that the Gregory rule and other similar third-party guilt rules were designed to further. Nor has the State identified any other legitimate end that the rule serves. It follows that the rule applied in this case by the State Supreme Court violates a criminal defendant's right to have " 'a meaningful opportunity to present a complete defense.' " *Crane*, 476 U.S., at 690.

For these reasons, we vacate the judgment of the South Carolina Supreme Court and remand the case for further proceedings not inconsistent with this opinion. * * *

TAYLOR V. KENTUCKY
436 U.S. 478, 98 S.Ct. 1930, 56 L.Ed.2d 468 (1978).

JUSTICE POWELL delivered the opinion of the Court.

Only two Terms ago, this Court observed that the "presumption of innocence, although not articulated in the Constitution, is a basic component of a fair trial under our system of criminal justice." *Estelle v. Williams,* 425 U.S. 501 (1976). In this felony case, the trial court instructed the jury as to the prosecution's burden of proof beyond a reasonable doubt, but refused petitioner's timely request for instructions on the presumption of innocence and the indictment's lack of evidentiary value. We are asked to decide whether the Due Process Clause of the Fourteenth Amendment requires that either or both instructions be given upon timely defense motions.

Petitioner was tried for robbery in 1976, allegedly having forced his way into the home of James Maddox and stolen a house key and a billfold containing $10 to $15. During *voir dire* of the jury, defense counsel questioned the panel about their understanding of the presumption of innocence, the burden of proof beyond a reasonable doubt, and the fact that an indictment is not evidence. The prosecutor then read the indictment to the jury.

The Commonwealth's only witness was Maddox. He testified that he had known petitioner for several years and had entertained petitioner at his home on several occasions. According to Maddox, petitioner and a friend knocked on his door on the evening of February 16, 1976, asking to be admitted. Maddox refused, saying he had to go to bed. The two left, but returned 15 minutes later. They forced their way in, hit Maddox over the head, and fled with his billfold and house key, which were never recovered.

Petitioner then took the stand as the only witness for the defense. He admitted having been at Maddox's home on other occasions, but denied going there on February 16 or participating in the robbery. He stated that he had spent that night with two friends sitting in a parked car, watching a rainstorm and a power failure. Defense counsel requested the trial court to instruct the jury that "[t]he law presumes a defendant to be innocent of a crime," and that the indictment, previously read to the jury, was not evidence to be considered against the defendant. The court declined to give either instruction, and did not convey their substance in its charge to the jury. It did instruct the jury as to the Commonwealth's burden of proving petitioner's guilt beyond a reasonable doubt. Petitioner was found guilty and sentenced to five years of imprisonment. The Kentucky Court of Appeals affirmed * * *, the Supreme Court of Kentucky denied discretionary review, and we granted certiorari.

"The principle that there is a presumption of innocence in favor of the accused is the undoubted law, axiomatic and elementary, and its enforcement lies at the foundation of the administration of our criminal law." *Coffin v. United States*, 156 U.S. 432, 453 (1895). The *Coffin* Court traced the venerable history of the presumption from Deuteronomy through Roman law, English common law, and the common law of the United States. While *Coffin* held that the presumption of innocence and the equally fundamental principle that the prosecution bears the burden of proof beyond a reasonable doubt were logically separate and distinct, sharp scholarly criticism demonstrated the error of that view. Nevertheless, these same scholars advise against abandoning the instruction on the presumption of innocence, even when a complete explanation of the burden of proof beyond a reasonable doubt is provided. * * * This admonition derives from a perceived salutary effect upon lay jurors. While the legal scholar may understand that the presumption of innocence and the prosecution's burden of proof are logically similar, the ordinary citizen well may draw significant additional guidance from an instruction on the presumption of innocence. Wigmore described this effect as follows:

> "[I]n a criminal case the term [presumption of innocence] does convey a special and perhaps useful hint over and above the other form of the rule about the burden of proof, in that it cautions the jury to put away from their minds all the suspicion that arises from the arrest, the indictment, and the arraignment, and to reach their conclusion solely from the legal evidence adduced. In other words, the rule about burden of proof requires the prosecution by evidence to convince the jury of the accused's guilt; while the presumption of innocence, too, requires this, but conveys for the jury a special and additional caution (which is perhaps only an implied corollary to the other) to consider, in the material for their belief, *nothing but the evidence,* i.e., no surmises based on the present situation of the accused. This caution is indeed particularly needed in criminal cases."

This Court has declared that one accused of a crime is entitled to have his guilt or innocence determined solely on the basis of the evidence introduced at trial, and not on grounds of official suspicion, indictment, continued custody, or other circumstances not adduced as proof at trial. And it long has been recognized that an instruction on the presumption is one way of impressing upon the jury the importance of that right. * * *

Petitioner argues that in the circumstances of this case, the purging effect of an instruction on the presumption of innocence was essential to a fair trial. He points out that the trial court's instructions were themselves skeletal, placing little emphasis on the prosecution's duty to prove the case beyond a reasonable doubt and none at all on the jury's duty to judge petitioner only on the basis of the testimony heard at trial.

Against the background of the court's rather Spartan instructions, the prosecutor's closing argument ranged far and wide, asking the jury to draw inferences about petitioner's conduct from "facts" not in evidence, but propounded by the prosecutor. For example, he described the reasonable-doubt standard by declaring that petitioner, "*like every other defendant* who's ever been tried who's in the penitentiary or in the reformatory today, has this presumption of innocence until proved guilty beyond a reasonable doubt." (emphasis added). This statement linked petitioner to every defendant who turned out to be guilty and was sentenced to imprisonment. It could be viewed as an invitation to the jury to consider petitioner's status as a defendant as evidence tending to prove his guilt. Similarly, in responding to defense counsel's rhetorical query as to the whereabouts of the items stolen from Maddox, the prosecutor declared that "[o]ne of the first things *defendants do after they rip someone off,* they get rid of the evidence as fast and as quickly as they can." (emphasis added). This statement also implied that all defendants are guilty and invited the jury to consider that proposition in determining petitioner's guilt or innocence.[14]

Additionally, the prosecutor observed in his opening statement that Maddox "took out" a warrant against petitioner and that the grand jury had returned an indictment, which the prosecutor read to the jury. Thus, the jury not only was invited to consider the petitioner's status as a defendant, but also was permitted to draw inferences of guilt from the fact of arrest and indictment. The prosecutor's description of those events was not necessarily improper, but the combination of the skeletal instructions, the possible harmful inferences from the references to the indictment, and the repeated suggestions that petitioner's status as a defendant tended to establish his guilt created a genuine danger that the jury would convict petitioner on the basis of those extraneous considerations, rather than on the evidence introduced at trial. That risk was heightened because the trial essentially was a swearing contest between victim and accused.

Against the need for a presumption-of-innocence instruction, the Commonwealth argues first that such an instruction is not required where, as here, the jury is instructed as to the burden of proof beyond a reasonable doubt. The trial court's truncated discussion of reasonable doubt, however, was hardly a model of clarity. It defined reasonable doubt as "a substantial doubt, a real doubt." This definition, though perhaps not in itself reversible error, often has been criticized as confusing. See, e.g., *United States v. Muckenstrum,* 515 F.2d 568 (1975). And even if the instruction on reasonable doubt had been more clearly stated, the

---

[14] We do not suggest that such prosecutorial comments, standing alone, would rise to the level of reversible error, an issue not raised in this case. But they are relevant to the need for carefully framed instructions designed to assure that the accused be judged only on the evidence.

Commonwealth's argument ignores both the special purpose of a presumption-of-innocence instruction and the particular need for such an instruction in this case.

The Commonwealth also contends that no additional instructions were required, because defense counsel argued the presumption of innocence in both his opening and closing statements. But arguments of counsel cannot substitute for instructions by the court. Petitioner's right to have the jury deliberate solely on the basis of the evidence cannot be permitted to hinge upon a hope that defense counsel will be a more effective advocate for that proposition than the prosecutor will be in implying that extraneous circumstances may be considered. It was the duty of the court to safeguard petitioner's rights, a duty only it could have performed reliably. * * *

We hold that on the facts of this case the trial court's refusal to give petitioner's requested instruction on the presumption of innocence resulted in a violation of his right to a fair trial as guaranteed by the Due Process Clause of the Fourteenth Amendment. The judgment of conviction is reversed, and the case is remanded for further proceedings not inconsistent with this opinion.

JUSTICE BRENNAN, concurring.

I join the Court's opinion because in reversing petitioner's conviction it reaffirms that "the 'presumption of innocence, although not articulated in the Constitution, is a basic component of a fair trial under our system of criminal justice.'" It follows from this proposition, as is clear from the Court's opinion, that trial judges should instruct the jury on a criminal defendant's entitlement to a presumption of innocence in all cases where such an instruction is requested.

JUSTICE STEVENS, with whom JUSTICE REHNQUIST joins, dissenting.

In a federal court it is reversible error to refuse a request for a proper instruction on the presumption of innocence. *Coffin v. United States.* That is not, however, a sufficient reason for holding that such an instruction is constitutionally required in every criminal trial.

The function of the instruction is to make it clear that the burden of persuasion rests entirely on the prosecutor. The same function is performed by the instruction requiring proof beyond a reasonable doubt. One standard instruction adds emphasis to the other. Neither should be omitted, but an "omission, or an incomplete instruction, is less likely to be prejudicial than a misstatement of the law." *Henderson v. Kibbe,* 431 U.S. 145 (1977). In some cases the omission may be fatal, but the Court wisely avoids a holding that this is always so.

In this case the omission did not violate a specific constitutional guarantee, such as the privilege against compulsory self-incrimination. Nor did it deny the defendant his fundamental right to a fair trial. An instruction on reasonable doubt, admittedly brief, was given. The *voir dire* had made clear to each juror the defendant's right to be presumed innocent despite his indictment. The prosecutor's closing argument did not precipitate any objection from defense counsel who listened to it; it may not, therefore, provide the basis for a reversal. Although the Court's appraisal is not unreasonable, for this was by no means a perfect trial, I do not believe that constitutional error was committed. Accordingly, I respectfully dissent.[a]

DARDEN V. WAINWRIGHT
477 U.S. 168, 106 S.Ct. 2464, 91 L.Ed.2d 144 (1986).

JUSTICE POWELL delivered the opinion of the Court.

Petitioner was tried and found guilty of murder, robbery, and assault with intent to kill in the Circuit Court for Citrus County, Florida, in January 1974. Pursuant to Florida's capital sentencing statute, the same jury that convicted petitioner heard further testimony and argument in order to make a nonbinding recommendation as to whether a death sentence should be imposed. The jury recommended a death sentence, and the trial judge followed that recommendation. On direct appeal, the Florida Supreme Court affirmed the conviction and the sentence. Petitioner made several of the same arguments in that appeal that he makes here. With respect to the prosecutorial misconduct claim, the court disapproved of the closing argument, but reasoned that the law required a new trial "only in those cases in which it is reasonably evident that the remarks might have influenced the jury to reach a more severe verdict of guilt * * * or in which the comment is unfair." * * * It concluded that the comments had not rendered petitioner's trial unfair. * * *

Petitioner then sought federal habeas corpus relief, raising the same claims he raises here. * * * A divided panel of the Court of Appeals for the Eleventh Circuit affirmed. * * *

Because of the nature of petitioner's claims, the facts of this case will be stated in more detail than is normally necessary in this Court. On September 8, 1973, at about 5:30 p.m., a black adult male entered Carl's Furniture Store near Lakeland, Florida. The only other person in the store was the proprietor, Mrs. Turman, who lived with her husband in a house behind the store. Mr. Turman, who worked nights at a juvenile home, had awakened at about 5:00 p.m., had a cup of coffee at the store with his wife, and returned home to let their dogs out for a run. Mrs. Turman showed the man around the store. He stated that he was interested in purchasing about $600 worth of furniture for a rental unit, and asked to see several different items. He left the store briefly, stating that his wife would be back to look at some of the items.

---

[a] *Kentucky v. Whorton,* 441 U.S. 786 (1979), reversed on prosecution appeal a Kentucky Supreme Court ruling that read *Taylor* as requiring a presumption of innocence instruction "in all criminal trials." The Court stressed that the *Taylor* ruling "focused on the failure to give the instruction as it related to the overall fairness of the trial in its entirety" and that the *Taylor* majority specifically limited its holding to "the facts of this case." The Court remanded to the Kentucky Supreme Court for reconsideration in light of the "totality of the circumstances—including all instructions to the jury, the arguments of counsel, whether the weight of the evidence was overwhelming and other relevant factors." Three Justices dissented, arguing that an instruction on the presumption of innocence should be "constitutionally required in every case where a timely request has been made," although the failure to give the instruction could constitute harmless error.

The same man returned just a few minutes later asking to see some stoves, and inquiring about the price. When Mrs. Turman turned toward the adding machine, he grabbed her and pressed a gun to her back, saying "Do as I say and you won't get hurt." He took her to the rear of the store and told her to open the cash register. He took the money, then ordered her to the part of the store where some boxsprings and mattresses were stacked against the wall. At that time Mr. Turman appeared at the back door. Mrs. Turman screamed while the man reached across her right shoulder and shot Mr. Turman between the eyes. Mr. Turman fell backwards, with one foot partially in the building. Ordering Mrs. Turman not to move, the man tried to pull Mr. Turman into the building and close the door, but could not do so because one of Mr. Turman's feet was caught in the door. The man left Mr. Turman face-up in the rain, and told Mrs. Turman to get down on the floor approximately five feet from where her husband lay dying. While she begged to go to her husband, he told her to remove her false teeth. He unzipped his pants, unbuckled his belt, and demanded that Mrs. Turman perform oral sex on him. She began to cry "Lord, have mercy." He told her to get up and go towards the front of the store.

Meanwhile, a neighbor family, the Arnolds, became aware that something had happened to Mr. Turman. The mother sent her 16-year-old son Phillip, a part-time employee at the furniture store, to help. When Phillip reached the back door he saw Mr. Turman lying partially in the building. When Phillip opened the door to take Turman's body inside, Mrs. Turman shouted "Phillip, no, go back." Phillip did not know what she meant and asked the man to help get Turman inside. He replied, "Sure, buddy, I will help you." As Phillip looked up, the man was pointing a gun in his face. He pulled the trigger and the gun misfired; he pulled the trigger again and shot Phillip in the mouth. Phillip started to run away, and was shot in the neck. While he was still running, he was shot a third time in the side. Despite these wounds, Phillip managed to stumble to the home of a neighbor, Mrs. Edith Hill. She had her husband call an ambulance while she tried to stop Phillip's bleeding. While she was helping Phillip, she saw a late model green Chevrolet leave the store and head towards Tampa on state highway 92. Phillip survived the incident; Mr. Turman, who never regained consciousness, died later that night.

Minutes after the murder petitioner was driving towards Tampa on highway 92, just a few miles away from the furniture store. He was out on furlough from a Florida prison, and was driving a car borrowed from his girlfriend in Tampa. He was driving fast on a wet road. Petitioner testified that as he came up on a line of cars in his lane, he was unable to slow down. He attempted to pass, but was forced off the road to avoid a head-on collision with an oncoming car. Petitioner crashed into a telephone pole. The driver of the oncoming car, John Stone, stopped his car and went to petitioner to see if he could help. Stone testified that as he approached the car, petitioner was zipping up his pants and buckling his belt. Police at the crash site later identified petitioner's car as a 1969 Chevrolet Impala of greenish golden brown color. Petitioner paid a bystander to give him a ride to Tampa. Petitioner later returned with a wrecker, only to find that the car had been towed away by the police.

By the time the police arrived at the scene of the accident, petitioner had left. The fact that the car matched the description of the car leaving the scene of the murder, and that the accident had occurred within three and one-half miles of the furniture store and within minutes of the murder, led police to suspect that the car was driven by the murderer. They searched the area. An officer found a pistol—a revolver—about forty feet from the crash site. The arrangement of shells within the chambers exactly matched the pattern that should have been found in the murder weapon: one shot, one misfire, followed by three shots, with a live shell remaining in the next chamber to be fired. A specialist for the FBI examined the pistol and testified that it was a Smith & Wesson .38 special revolver. It had been manufactured as a standard .38; it later was sent to England to be rebored, making it a much rarer type of gun than the standard .38. An examination of the bullet that killed Mr. Turman revealed that it came from a .38 Smith & Wesson special.

On the day following the murder petitioner was arrested at his girlfriend's house in Tampa. A few days later Mrs. Turman identified him at a preliminary hearing as her husband's murderer. Phillip Arnold selected petitioner's picture out of a spread of six photographs as the man who had shot him.[1] * * *

Petitioner * * * contends that the prosecution's closing argument at the guilt-innocence stage of the trial rendered his conviction fundamentally unfair * * *. It is helpful as an initial matter to place these remarks in context. Closing argument came at the end of several days of trial. Because of a state procedural rule petitioner's counsel had the opportunity to present the initial summation as well as a rebuttal to the prosecutors' closing arguments. The prosecutors' comments must be evaluated in light of the defense argument that preceded it, which blamed the Polk County Sheriff's Office for a lack of evidence,[5] alluded to the death

---

[1]   There are some minor discrepancies in the eyewitness identification. Mrs. Turman first described her assailant immediately after the murder while her husband was being taken to the emergency room. She told the investigating officer that the attacker was a heavyset man. When asked if he was "neat in his appearance, clean-looking, clean-shaven," she responded "[a]s far as I can remember, yes, sir." Ibid. She also stated to the officer that she thought that the attacker was about her height, 5'6" tall, and that he was wearing a pullover shirt with a stripe around the neck. The first time she saw petitioner after the attack was when she identified him at the preliminary hearing. She had not read any newspaper accounts of the crime, nor had she seen any picture of petitioner. When she was asked if petitioner was the man who had committed the crimes, she said yes. She also repeatedly identified him at trial.

Phillip Arnold first identified petitioner in a photo line-up while in the hospital. He could not speak at the time, and in response to the written question whether petitioner had a mustache, Phillip wrote back "I don't think so." Phillip also testified at trial that the attacker was a heavyset man wearing a dull, light color knit shirt with a ring around the neck. He testified that the man was almost his height, about 6'2" tall.

A motorist who stopped at the scene of the accident testified that petitioner was wearing a white or off-grey button-down shirt and that he had a slight mustache. In fact, the witness stated that he "didn't know it was that [the mustache] or the raindrops on him or not. I couldn't really tell that much to it, it was real thin, that's all." Petitioner is about 5'10" tall, and at the time of trial testified that he weighed about 175 pounds.

[5]   "The Judge is going to tell you to consider the evidence or the lack of evidence. We have a lack of evidence, almost criminally negligent on the part of the Polk County Sheriff's Office in this case. You could go on and on about it." Record 728.

penalty,[6] characterized the perpetrator of the crimes as an "animal,"[7] and contained counsel's personal opinion of the strength of the state's evidence.[8]

The prosecutors then made their closing argument. That argument deserves the condemnation it has received from every court to review it, although no court has held that the argument rendered the trial unfair. Several comments attempted to place some of the blame for the crime on the Division of Corrections, because Darden was on weekend furlough from a prison sentence when the crime occurred.[9] Some comments implied that the death penalty would be the only guarantee against a future similar act.[10] Others incorporated the defense's use of the word "animal."[11] Prosecutor McDaniel made several offensive comments reflecting an emotional reaction to the case.[12] These comments undoubtedly were improper. But as both the District Court and the original panel of the Court of Appeals (whose opinion on this issue still stands) recognized, it "is not enough that the prosecutors' remarks were undesirable or even universally condemned." The relevant question is whether the prosecutors' comments "so infected the trial with unfairness as to make the resulting conviction a denial of due process." *Donnelly v. DeChristoforo*, 416 U.S. 637 (1974). Moreover, the appropriate standard of review for such a claim on writ of habeas corpus is "the narrow one of due process, and not the broad exercise of supervisory power." *DeChristoforo*.

---

[6] "They took a coincidence and magnified that into a capital case. And they are asking you to kill a man on coincidence." Record 730.

[7] "The first witness you saw was Mrs. Turman, who was a pathetic figure; who worked and struggled all of her life to build what little she had, the little furniture store; and a woman who was robbed, sexually assaulted, and then had her husband slaughtered before her eyes, by what would have to be a vicious animal." Record 717. "And this murderer ran after him, aimed again, and this poor kid with half his brains blown away. . . . It's the work of an animal, there's no doubt about it." Record 731–732.

[8] "So they come up here and ask Citrus County people to kill the man. You will be instructed on lesser included offenses. . . . The question is, do they have enough evidence to kill that man, enough evidence? And I honestly do not think they do." Record 736–737.

[9] "As far as I am concerned, there should be another Defendant in this courtroom, one more, and that is the division of corrections, the prisons. . . . Can we expect him to stay in a prison when they go there? Can we expect them to stay locked up once they go there? Do we know that they're going to be out on the public with guns, drinking?" Record 749–750. "Yes, there is another Defendant, but I regret that I know of no charges to place upon him, except the public condemnation of them, condemn them." Record 750–751.

[10] "I will ask you to advise the Court to give him death. That's the only way I know that he is not going to get out on the public. It's the only way I know. It's the only way I can be sure of it. It's the only way anybody can be sure of it now, because the people that turned him loose—" Record 753.

[11] "As far as I am concerned, and as Mr. Maloney said as he identified this man as an animal, this animal was on the public for one reason." Record 749.

[12] "He shouldn't be out of his cell unless he has a leash on him and a prison guard at the other end of that leash." Record 750. "I wish [Mr. Turman] had had a shotgun in his hand when he walked in the back door and blown his [Darden's] face off. I wish I could see him sitting here with no face, blown away by a shotgun." Record 758. "I wish someone had walked in the back door and blown his head off at that point." Record 759. "He fired in the boy's back, number five saving one. Didn't get a chance to use it. I wish he had used it on himself." Record 774. "I wish he had been killed in the accident, but he wasn't. Again, we are unlucky that time." Record 775. "Don't forget what he has done according to those witnesses, to make every attempt to change his appearance from September the 8th, 1973. The hair, the goatee, even the moustache and the weight. The only thing he hasn't done that I know of is cut his throat." Record 779. After this, the last in a series of such comments, defense counsel objected for the first time.

Under this standard of review, we agree with the reasoning of every court to consider these comments that they did not deprive petitioner of a fair trial. The prosecutors' argument did not manipulate or misstate the evidence, nor did it implicate other specific rights of the accused such as the right to counsel or the right to remain silent. Much of the objectionable content was invited by or was responsive to the opening summation of the defense. As we explained in *United States v. Young*, 470 U.S. 1 (1985), the idea of "invited response" is used not to excuse improper comments, but to determine their effect on the trial as a whole. The trial court instructed the jurors several times that their decision was to be made on the basis of the evidence alone, and that the arguments of counsel were not evidence. The weight of the evidence against petitioner was heavy; the "overwhelming eyewitness and circumstantial evidence to support a finding of guilt on all charges," 329 So.2d, at 291, reduced the likelihood that the jury's decision was influenced by argument. Finally, defense counsel made the tactical decision not to present any witness other than petitioner. This decision not only permitted them to give their summation prior to the prosecution's closing argument, but also gave them the opportunity to make a final rebuttal argument. Defense counsel were able to use the opportunity for rebuttal very effectively, turning much of the prosecutors' closing argument against them by placing many of the prosecutors' comments and actions in a light that was more likely to engender strong disapproval than result in inflamed passions against petitioner.[14] For these reasons, we agree with the District Court below that "Darden's trial was not perfect—few are—but neither was it fundamentally unfair." 513 F.Supp., at 958.

JUSTICE BLACKMUN, with whom JUSTICE BRENNAN, JUSTICE MARSHALL, and JUSTICE STEVENS join, dissenting. * * *

The Court's discussion of Darden's claim of prosecutorial misconduct is noteworthy for its omissions. Despite the fact that earlier this Term the Court relied heavily on standards governing the professional responsibility of defense counsel in ruling that an attorney's actions did not deprive his client of any constitutional right, see *Nix v. Whiteside* [Ch. 17], today it entirely ignores standards governing the professional responsibility of prosecutors in reaching the conclusion that the summations of Darden's prosecutors did not deprive him of a fair trial.

The prosecutors' remarks in this case reflect behavior as to which "virtually all the sources speak with one voice," *Nix v. Whiteside,* that is, a voice of strong condemnation. The following brief comparison of established standards of prosecutorial conduct with the prosecutors' behavior in this case merely illustrates, but hardly exhausts, the scope of the misconduct involved:

---

[14] "Mr. McDaniel made an impassioned plea . . . how many times did he repeat [it]? I wish you had been shot, I wish they had blown his face away. My God, I get the impression he would like to be the man that stands there and pulls the switch on him." Record 791.

One of Darden's counsel testified at the habeas corpus hearing that he made the tactical decision not to object to the improper comments. Based on his long experience with prosecutor McDaniel, he knew McDaniel would "get much more vehement in his remarks if you allowed him to go on." By not immediately objecting, he hoped to encourage the prosecution to commit reversible error. Supp.App. 46–47.

1. "A lawyer shall not . . . state a personal opinion as to . . . the credibility [of] a witness . . . or the guilt or innocence of an accused." Model Rules of Professional Conduct, Rule 3.4(e). * * * Yet one prosecutor, White, stated: "I am convinced, as convinced as I know I am standing before you today, that Willie Jasper Darden is a murderer, that he murdered Mr. Turman, that he robbed Mrs. Turman and that he shot to kill Phillip Arnold. I will be convinced of that the rest of my life." And the other prosecutor, McDaniel, stated, with respect to Darden's testimony: "Well, let me tell you something: If I am ever over in that chair over there, facing life or death, life imprisonment or death, I guarantee you I will lie until my teeth fall out."

2. "The prosecutor should refrain from argument which would divert the jury from its duty to decide the case on the evidence, by injecting issues broader than the guilt or innocence of the accused under the controlling law, or by making predictions of the consequences of the jury's verdict." ABA Standards, The Prosecution Function, § 3–5.8(d). * * * Yet McDaniel's argument was filled with references to Darden's status as a prisoner on furlough who "shouldn't be out of his cell unless he has a leash on him." Again and again, he sought to put on trial an absent "defendant," the State Department of Corrections that had furloughed Darden. He also implied that defense counsel would use improper tricks to deflect the jury from the real issue. Darden's status as a furloughed prisoner, the release policies of the Department of Corrections, and his counsel's anticipated tactics obviously had no legal relevance to the question the jury was being asked to decide: whether he had committed the robbery and murder at the Turmans' furniture store. Indeed, the State argued before this Court that McDaniel's remarks were harmless precisely *because* he "failed to discuss the issues, the weight of the evidence, or the credibility of the witnesses."

3. "The prosecutor should not use arguments calculated to inflame the passions or prejudices of the jury." ABA Standards, § 3–5.8(c). Yet McDaniel repeatedly expressed a wish "that I could see [Darden] sitting here with no face, blown away by a shotgun." Indeed, I do not think McDaniel's summation, taken as a whole, can accurately be described as anything but a relentless and single-minded attempt to inflame the jury. * * * Almost every page contains at least one offensive or improper statement; some pages contain little else. The misconduct here was not "slight or confined to a single instance, but . . . was pronounced and persistent, with a probable cumulative effect upon the jury which cannot be disregarded as inconsequential." *Berger v. United States.*

The Court presents what is, for me, an entirely unpersuasive one-page laundry list of reasons for ignoring this blatant misconduct. First, the Court says that the summations "did not manipulate or misstate the evidence [or] . . . implicate other specific rights of the accused such as the right to counsel or the right to remain silent." With all respect, that observation is quite beside the point. The "solemn purpose of endeavoring to ascertain the truth . . . is the *sine qua non* of a fair trial," and the summations cut to the very heart of the Due Process Clause by diverting the jury's attention "from the ultimate question of guilt or innocence that should be the central concern in a criminal proceeding."

Second, the Court says that "[m]uch of the objectionable content was invited by or was responsive to the opening summation of the defense." The Court identifies four portions of the defense summation that it thinks somehow "invited" McDaniel's sustained barrage. The State, however, did not object to any of these statements, and, to my mind, none of them is so objectionable that it would have justified a tactical decision to interrupt the defense summation and perhaps irritate the jury.

The Court begins by stating that defense counsel "blamed" the sheriff's office for a lack of evidence. The Court does not identify which, if any, of McDaniel's remarks represented a response to this statement. I cannot believe that the Court is suggesting, for example, that defense counsel's one mention of the "almost crimina[l] negligen[ce] on the part of the Polk County Sheriff's Office," justified McDaniel's express and repeated wish that he could try the Department of Corrections for murder.

Next, the Court notes that defense counsel "alluded" to the death penalty. While this allusion might have justified McDaniel's statement that "you are merely to determine his innocence or guilt, nothing else," it could hardly justify, for example, McDaniel's expressions of his personal wish that Darden be "blown away by a shotgun."

Moreover, the Court says, defense counsel twice referred to the perpetrator as an "animal." It is entirely unclear to me why this characterization called for any response from the prosecutor at all. Taken in context, defense counsel's statements did nothing more than tell the jury that, although everyone agreed that a heinous crime had been committed, the issue on which it should focus was whether *Darden* had committed it.

Finally, the Court finds that Darden brought upon himself McDaniel's tirade because defense counsel gave his "personal opinion of the strength of the State's evidence." Again, the Court gives no explanation of how the statement it quotes— a single, mild expression of defense counsel's overall assessment of the evidence— justified the "response" that followed, which consisted, to the extent it represented a comment on the evidence at all, of accusations of perjury, and personal disparagements of opposing counsel. In sum, McDaniel went so far beyond "respond[ing] substantially in order to 'right the scale,' " *Young*, that the reasoning in *Young* provides no basis at all for the Court's holding today.

The third reason the Court gives for discounting the effects of the improper summations is the supposed curative effect of the trial judge's instructions: the judge had instructed the jury that it was to decide the case on the evidence and that the arguments of counsel were not evidence. But the trial court overruled Darden's objection to McDaniel's repeated expressions of his wish that Darden had been killed, thus perhaps leaving the jury with the impression that McDaniel's comments were somehow relevant to the question before them. The trial judge's instruction that the attorneys were "trained in the law," and thus that their "analysis of the issues" could be "extremely helpful," might also have suggested to the jury that the substance of McDaniel's tirade was pertinent to their deliberations.

Fourth, the Court suggests that because Darden enjoyed the tactical advantage of having the last summation, he was able to "tur[n] much of the prosecutors' closing argument against them." But the issue before the jury was whether Darden was guilty, not whether McDaniel's summation was proper. And the question before this Court is not whether we agree with defense counsel's criticism of the summation but whether the jury was affected by it. Since Darden was ultimately convicted, it is hard to see what basis the Court has for its naked assertion that "[d]efense counsel were able to use the opportunity for rebuttal very effectively." * * *

Fifth, the Court finds, in essence, that any error was harmless: "The weight of the evidence against petitioner was heavy; the 'overwhelming eyewitness and circumstantial evidence to support a finding of guilt on all charges' reduced the likelihood that the jury's decision was influenced by argument." * * * I simply do not believe the evidence in this case was so overwhelming that this Court can conclude, on the basis of the written record before it, that the jury's verdict was not the product of the prosecutors' misconduct. The three most damaging pieces of evidence—the identifications of Darden by Phillip Arnold and Helen Turman and the ballistics evidence—are all sufficiently problematic that they leave me unconvinced that a jury not exposed to McDaniel's egregious summation would necessarily have convicted Darden.

Arnold first identified Darden in a photo array shown to him in the hospital. The trial court suppressed that out-of-court identification following a long argument concerning the reliability and constitutionality of the procedures by which it was obtained.

Mrs. Turman's initial identification was made under even more suggestive circumstances. She testified at trial that she was taken to a preliminary hearing at which Darden appeared in order "[t]o identify him." Instead of being asked to view Darden in a lineup, Mrs. Turman was brought into the courtroom, where Darden apparently was the only black man present. Over defense counsel's objection, after the prosecutor asked her whether "this man sitting here" was "the man that shot your husband," she identified Darden. * * * While the question whether the various in- and out-of-court identifications ought to have been suppressed is not now before the Court, my confidence in their reliability is nonetheless undermined by the suggestiveness of the procedures by which they were obtained, particularly in light of Mrs. Turman's earlier difficulties in describing the criminal.

Finally, the ballistics evidence is hardly overwhelming. The purported murder weapon was tied conclusively neither to the crime nor to Darden. Special Agent Cunningham of the FBI's Firearms Identification Unit testified that the bullets recovered at the scene of the crime "could have been fired" from the gun, but he was unwilling to say that they in fact had come from that weapon. He also testified, contrary to the Court's assertion, that rebored Smith & Wessons were fairly common. Deputy Sheriff Weatherford testified that the gun was discovered in a roadside ditch adjacent to where Darden had wrecked his car on the evening of the crime. But the gun was discovered the next day, and the ditch was also next to a bar's parking lot.

Darden testified at trial on his own behalf and denied any involvement in the robbery and murder. His account of his actions on the day of the crime was contradicted only by Mrs. Turman's and Arnold's identifications. Indeed, a number of the State's witnesses corroborated parts of Darden's account. The trial judge who had seen and heard Darden testify found that he "emotionally and with what appeared on its face to be sincerity, proclaimed his innocence." In setting sentence, he viewed the fact that Darden "repeatedly professed his complete innocence of the charges" as a mitigating factor.

Thus, at bottom, this case rests on the jury's determination of the credibility of three witnesses—Helen Turman and Phillip Arnold, on the one side, and Willie Darden, on the other. I cannot conclude that McDaniel's sustained assault on Darden's very humanity did not affect the jury's ability to judge the credibility question on the real evidence before it. Because I believe that he did not have a trial that was fair, I would reverse Darden's conviction; I would not allow him to go to his death until he has been convicted at a fair trial. * * *

CHAPTER 19

RETRIALS

■ ■ ■

Although it has some bearing on multiple punishments, the double jeopardy clause of the Fifth Amendment is concerned primarily with multiple trials. That concern extends to trials for both felonies and misdemeanors. The Court concluded, in its first major double jeopardy ruling, that the reference in the double jeopardy clause to "life and limb," when read against its common law background, was broad enough to encompass all criminal offenses without regard to the particular form of punishment that might be imposed. *Ex parte Lange*, 85 U.S. 163 (1873). The double jeopardy clause becomes applicable, however, only after the accused has been placed "in jeopardy", and that does not occur until (i) the jury is "empaneled and sworn" in a case involving a jury trial, or (ii) the first witness is sworn in a case involving a bench trial. *Crist v. Bretz*, 437 U.S. 28 (1978). Dismissals before jeopardy has attached, even where based on the ground that the prosecution's case is too weak to prevail, do not raise double jeopardy difficulties; since the defendant has not been placed in jeopardy at the point of dismissal, a reprosecution that results in a trial would not place him "twice" in jeopardy. Thus, double jeopardy does not bar returning a case to a grand jury after it has refused to indict, refiling charges and seeking a new preliminary hearing after the magistrate found a lack of probable cause at the first hearing, or refiling charges after a trial court dismissed the initial charges on some pretrial objection (e.g., an insufficiency of the pleading) that could be cured in a new indictment or information. So too, where a trial court dismisses charges before trial on grounds that would bar reprosecution (e.g., that the defendant had been denied his right to a speedy trial), no double jeopardy concerns are presented by allowing the state to appeal that dismissal and continue with the prosecution if it should win on appeal.

The principles described above are well established and fairly easy to apply. That is not true of all double jeopardy principles. Indeed, in *United States v. DiFrancesco*, 449 U.S. 117 (1980), Justice Blackmun's opinion for the Court, citing 21 double jeopardy cases decided by the Court over the previous decade, acknowledged that the application of the double jeopardy bar "has not proved to be facile or routine," as demonstrated by the various "changes in direction or in emphasis" found in the Court's rulings. The cases in this Chapter deal with the most significant of those double jeopardy principles that have proved troublesome in their definition or application.

1. THE "SAME OFFENSE" LIMITATION

The double jeopardy clause states that no person shall twice be put in jeopardy for the "same offence." It was well established at common law that prosecutions were not for the "same offense" where they involved the same statutory violation as to different victims, even when the violations occurred in the same incident. *Ashe v. Swenson,* the first case in this section, raises the question as to whether the double jeopardy bar places any limit on separate prosecutions in such situations. *Ashe,* through its adoption of the "collateral estoppel" doctrine, imposes such a limit, but it is restricted to instances in which the first prosecution results in an acquittal and that acquittal bears a special relationship to the offense charged in the second prosecution.

At common law, separate prosecutions involving the same incident and the same victim could be for "the same offense" even though alleging violations of different statutes. The second case in this section, *United States v. Dixon,* deals with the scope of the double jeopardy bar developed in this situation. Unlike the collateral estoppel doctrine of *Ashe,* the limitation imposed here does not depend upon the first prosecution having resulted in an acquittal. It should be kept in mind that state law may impose limitations beyond those mandated in *Ashe* and *Dixon.* Thus, some states require a single prosecution for all offenses arising from the same transaction, as urged by Justice Brennan in his concurring opinion in *Ashe,* and other states largely follow the standard of *Grady v. Corbin,* overruled in *Dixon.*

The third case in this section, *Gamble v. United States,* deals with the possible application of the double jeopardy bar to multiple prosecutions by different sovereigns. Multiple prosecutions for basically the same criminal activity by different jurisdictions (i.e., two states, or the federal government and a state) are most likely to arise between the federal government and a state, and here non-constitutional limitations restrict multiple prosecutions. The internal regulations of the Justice Department bar federal prosecution following a state prosecution "for substantially the same act" except upon the approval of an Assistant Attorney General, and many states have provisions that prohibit a state prosecution for any activity that has been the basis for a previous federal prosecution.

The last case in this section, *Hudson v. United States,* turns from the combination of separate prosecutions under different criminal statutes to the combination of a criminal prosecution and a proceeding designated as civil but which nonetheless may be seen as seeking to inflict "punishment" for the same violation as the criminal prosecution. The possible application of the double jeopardy bar to such a combination has great practical significance, as a wide range of criminal activity frequently leads not only to a criminal prosecution, but also to a "civil" proceeding brought by the government to gain a monetary or property award that is equal to (or exceeds) what may be obtained as part of the criminal sentence through a criminal fine or criminal forfeiture.

ASHE V. SWENSON

397 U.S. 436, 90 S.Ct. 1189, 25 L.Ed.2d 469 (1970).

JUSTICE STEWART delivered the opinion of the Court. * * *

Sometime in the early hours of the morning of January 10, 1960, six men were engaged in a poker game in the basement of the home of John Gladson at Lee's

Summit, Missouri. Suddenly three or four masked men, armed with a shotgun and pistols, broke into the basement and robbed each of the poker players of money and various articles of personal property. The robbers—and it has never been clear whether there were three or four of them—then fled in a car belonging to one of the victims of the robbery. Shortly thereafter the stolen car was discovered in a field, and later that morning three men were arrested by a state trooper while they were walking on a highway not far from where the abandoned car had been found. The petitioner was arrested by another officer some distance away.

The four were subsequently charged with seven separate offenses—the armed robbery of each of the six poker players and the theft of the car. In May 1960 the petitioner went to trial on the charge of robbing Donald Knight, one of the participants in the poker game. At the trial the State called Knight and three of his fellow poker players as prosecution witnesses. Each of them described the circumstances of the holdup and itemized his own individual losses. The proof that an armed robbery had occurred and that personal property had been taken from Knight as well as from each of the others was unassailable. The testimony of the four victims in this regard was consistent both internally and with that of the others. But the State's evidence that the petitioner had been one of the robbers was weak. Two of the witnesses thought that there had been only three robbers altogether, and could not identify the petitioner as one of them. Another of the victims, who was the petitioner's uncle by marriage, said that at the "patrol station" he had positively identified each of the other three men accused of the holdup, but could say only that the petitioner's voice "sounded very much like" that of one of the robbers. The fourth participant in the poker game did identify the petitioner, but only by his "size and height, and his actions."

The cross-examination of these witnesses was brief, and it was aimed primarily at exposing the weakness of their identification testimony. Defense counsel made no attempt to question their testimony regarding the holdup itself or their claims as to their losses. Knight testified without contradiction that the robbers had stolen from him his watch, $250 in cash, and about $500 in checks. His billfold, which had been found by the police in the possession of one of the three other men accused of the robbery, was admitted in evidence. The defense offered no testimony and waived final argument.

The trial judge instructed the jury that if it found that the petitioner was one of the participants in the armed robbery, the theft of "any money" from Knight would sustain a conviction. He also instructed the jury that if the petitioner was one of the robbers, he was guilty under the law even if he had not personally robbed Knight. The jury—though not instructed to elaborate upon its verdict—found the petitioner "not guilty due to insufficient evidence."

Six weeks later the petitioner was brought to trial again, this time for the robbery of another participant in the poker game, a man named Roberts. The petitioner filed a motion to dismiss, based on his previous acquittal. The motion was overruled, and the second trial began. The witnesses were for the most part the same, though this time their testimony was substantially stronger on the issue of the petitioner's identity. For example, two witnesses who at the first trial had been wholly unable to identify the petitioner as one of the robbers, now testified that his features, size, and mannerisms matched those of one of their assailants. Another witness who before had identified the petitioner only by his size and actions now also remembered him by the unusual sound of his voice. The State further refined its case at the second trial by declining to call one of the participants in the poker game whose identification testimony at the first trial had been conspicuously negative. The case went to the jury on instructions virtually identical to those given at the first trial. This time the jury found the petitioner guilty, and he was sentenced to a 35-year term in the state penitentiary. * * *

"Collateral estoppel" is an awkward phrase, but it stands for an extremely important principle in our adversary system of justice. It means simply that when an issue of ultimate fact has once been determined by a valid and final judgment, that issue cannot again be litigated between the same parties[a] in any future lawsuit. Although first developed in civil litigation, collateral estoppel has been an established rule of federal criminal law at least since this Court's decision more than 50 years ago in *United States v. Oppenheimer*, 242 U.S. 85 (1916). As Mr. Justice Holmes put the matter in that case, "It cannot be that the safeguards of the person, so often and so rightly mentioned with solemn reverence, are less than those that protect from a liability in debt." As a rule of federal law, therefore, "[i]t is much too late to suggest that this principle is not fully applicable to a former judgment in a criminal case, either because of lack of 'mutuality' or because the judgment may reflect only a belief that the Government had not met the higher burden of proof exacted in such cases for the Government's evidence as a whole although not necessarily as to every link in the chain."

The federal decisions have made clear that the rule of collateral estoppel in criminal cases is not to be applied with the hypertechnical and archaic approach of a 19th century pleading book, but with realism and rationality. Where a previous judgment of acquittal was based upon a general verdict, as is usually the case, this approach requires a court to "examine the record of a prior proceeding, taking into account the pleadings, evidence, charge, and other relevant matter, and conclude whether a rational jury could have grounded its verdict upon an issue other than that which the defendant seeks to foreclose from consideration." The inquiry "must be set in a practical frame, and viewed with an eye to all the circumstances of the proceedings." *Sealfon v. United States*, 332 U.S. 575 (1948). Any test more

---

[a] While this "same parties" limitation in *Ashe* means that a defendant may not base a collateral estoppel claim upon another case involving a different defendant, lower courts have sometimes granted relief in such circumstances on another basis, namely, that the use of inconsistent, irreconcilable theories to secure convictions against more than one defendant in prosecutions for the same crime violates the Due Process Clause. One such case reached the Supreme Court in *Bradshaw v. Stumpf*, 545 U.S. 175 (2005). Stumpf pleaded guilty to murder, and was then sentenced to death after the state argued to the sentencing jury that Stumpf had been the one who had shot the victim. At a later trial, Stumpf's accomplice Wesley was convicted of the same murder after the state introduced new evidence not available at the time of Stumpf's prosecution that Wesley had confessed to being the shooter. Stumpf then challenged his conviction and sentence. The Supreme Court upheld Stumpf's conviction, concluding that he had not explained how the state's post-plea use of an inconsistent argument had affected the knowing or voluntary nature of his guilty plea. The Court did remand Stumpf's death sentence to the Court of Appeals, however, for consideration of whether the inconsistent theories violated his due process rights.

technically restrictive would, of course, simply amount to a rejection of the rule of collateral estoppel in criminal proceedings, at least in every case where the first judgment was based upon a general verdict of acquittal.

Straightforward application of the federal rule to the present case can lead to but one conclusion. For the record is utterly devoid of any indication that the first jury could rationally have found that an armed robbery had not occurred, or that Knight had not been a victim of that robbery. The single rationally conceivable issue in dispute before the jury was whether the petitioner had been one of the robbers. And the jury by its verdict found that he had not. The federal rule of law, therefore, would make a second prosecution for the robbery of Roberts wholly impermissible.

The ultimate question to be determined, then * * * is whether this established rule of federal law is embodied in the Fifth Amendment guarantee against double jeopardy. We do not hesitate to hold that it is. For whatever else that constitutional guarantee may embrace, it surely protects a man who has been acquitted from having to "run the gantlet" a second time. *Green v. United States*, 355 U.S. 184 (1957).

The question is not whether Missouri could validly charge the petitioner with six separate offenses for the robbery of the six poker players. It is not whether he could have received a total of six punishments if he had been convicted in a single trial of robbing the six victims. It is simply whether, after a jury determined by its verdict that the petitioner was not one of the robbers, the State could constitutionally hale him before a new jury to litigate that issue again. * * *

In this case the State in its brief has frankly conceded that following the petitioner's acquittal, it treated the first trial as no more than a dry run for the second prosecution: "No doubt the prosecutor felt the state had a provable case on the first charge and, when he lost, he did what every good attorney would do—he refined his presentation in light of the turn of events at the first trial." But this is precisely what the constitutional guarantee forbids. * * *

Reversed and remanded.[b]

JUSTICE BRENNAN, whom JUSTICE DOUGLAS and JUSTICE MARSHALL join, concurring.

I agree that the Double Jeopardy Clause incorporates collateral estoppel as a constitutional requirement and therefore join the Court's opinion. However, even if the rule of collateral estoppel had been inapplicable to the facts of this case, it is my view that the Double Jeopardy Clause nevertheless bars the prosecution of petitioner a second time for armed robbery. The two prosecutions, the first for the robbery of Knight and the second for the robbery of Roberts, grew out of one criminal episode, and therefore I think it clear on the facts of this case that the Double Jeopardy Clause prohibited Missouri from prosecuting petitioner for each robbery at a different trial. * * *

---

[b]   Separate concurring opinions of Justices Harlan and Black are omitted.

The Double Jeopardy Clause is a guarantee "that the State with all its resources and power [shall] not be allowed to make repeated attempts to convict an individual for an alleged offense, thereby subjecting him to embarrassment, expense and ordeal and compelling him to live in a continuing state of anxiety and insecurity. . . ." *Green v. United States*, 355 U.S. 184 (1957). This guarantee is expressed as a prohibition against multiple prosecutions for the "same offence." Although the phrase "same offence" appeared in most of the early common-law articulations of the double-jeopardy principle, questions of its precise meaning rarely arose prior to the 18th century, and by the time the Bill of Rights was adopted it had not been authoritatively defined.

When the common law did finally attempt a definition, in *The King v. Vandercomb* (Crown 1796), it adopted the "same evidence" test, which provided little protection from multiple prosecution:

"[U]nless the first indictment were such as the prisoner might have been convicted upon by proof of the facts contained in the second indictment, an acquittal on the first indictment can be no bar to the second."

The "same evidence" test of "same offence" was soon followed by a majority of American jurisdictions, but its deficiencies are obvious. It does not enforce but virtually annuls the constitutional guarantee. For example, where a single criminal episode involves several victims, under the "same evidence" test a separate prosecution may be brought as to each. The "same evidence" test permits multiple prosecutions where a single transaction is divisible into chronologically discrete crimes. E.g., *Johnson v. Commonwealth*, 201 Ky. 314 (1923) (each of 75 poker hands a separate "offense"). Even a single criminal act may lead to multiple prosecutions if it is viewed from the perspectives of different statutes. Given the tendency of modern criminal legislation to divide the phases of a criminal transaction into numerous separate crimes, the opportunities for multiple prosecutions for an essentially unitary criminal episode are frightening. And given our tradition of virtually unreviewable prosecutorial discretion concerning the initiation and scope of a criminal prosecution, the potentialities for abuse inherent in the "same evidence" test are simply intolerable.

The "same evidence" test is not constitutionally required. It was first expounded *after* the adoption of the Fifth Amendment * * *. The "same evidence" test may once have been defensible at English common law, which, for reasons peculiar to English criminal procedure, severely restricted the power of prosecutors to combine several charges in a single trial. In vivid contrast, American criminal procedure generally allows a prosecutor freedom, subject to judicial control, to prosecute a person at one trial for all the crimes arising out of a single criminal transaction.

In my view, the Double Jeopardy Clause requires the prosecution, except in most limited circumstances, to join at one trial all the charges against a defendant that grow out of a single criminal act, occurrence, episode, or transaction. This "same transaction" test of "same offence" not only enforces the ancient prohibition against vexatious multiple prosecutions embodied in the Double Jeopardy Clause, but responds as well to the increasingly widespread recognition that the consolidation in one lawsuit of all issues arising out of a single transaction or occurrence best promotes justice, economy, and convenience. * * *

CHIEF JUSTICE BURGER, dissenting.

The Fifth Amendment to the constitution of the United States provides in part: "nor shall any person be subject for the same offence to be twice put in jeopardy of life or limb * * *." Nothing in the language or gloss previously placed on this provision of the Fifth Amendment remotely justifies the treatment that the Court today accords to the collateral-estoppel doctrine. Nothing in the purpose of the authors of the Constitution commands or even justifies what the Court decides today; this is truly a case of expanding a sound basic principle beyond the bounds— or needs—of its rational and legitimate objectives to preclude harassment of an accused. * * *

The concept of double jeopardy and our firm constitutional commitment is against repeated trials "for the *same offence*." This Court, like most American jurisdictions, has expanded that part of the Constitution into a "same evidence" test. *Blockburger v. United States*, 284 U.S. 299 (1932) * * *. Clearly and beyond dispute the charge against Ashe in the second trial required proof of a fact— robbery of Roberts—which the charge involving Knight did not. The Court, therefore, has had to reach out far beyond the accepted offense-defining rule to reach its decision in this case. What it has done is to superimpose on the same-evidence test a new and novel collateral-estoppel gloss. * * *

The collateral-estoppel concept—originally a product only of civil litigation— is a strange mutant as it is transformed to control this criminal case. In civil cases the doctrine was justified as conserving judicial resources as well as those of the parties to the actions and additionally as providing the finality needed to plan for the future. It ordinarily applies to parties on each side of the litigation who have the same interest as or who are identical with the parties in the initial litigation. Here the complainant in the second trial is not the same as in the first even though the State is a party in both cases. Very properly, in criminal cases, finality and conservation of private, public, and judicial resources are lesser values than in civil litigation. * * *

Some commentators have concluded that the harassment inherent in standing trial a second time is a sufficient reason for use of collateral estoppel in criminal trials. If the Court is today relying on a harassment concept to superimpose a new brand of collateral-estoppel gloss on the "same evidence" test, there is a short answer; this case does not remotely suggest harassment of an accused who robbed six victims and the harassment aspect does not rise to constitutional levels.

The essence of Justice Brennan's concurrence is that this was all one transaction, one episode, or, if I may so characterize it, one frolic, and, hence, only one crime. His approach, like that taken by the Court, totally overlooks the significance of there being *six entirely separate charges of robbery* against six individuals.

This "single transaction" concept is not a novel notion; it has been urged in various courts including this Court. One of the theses underlying the "single transaction" notion is that the criminal episode is "indivisible." The short answer to that is that to the victims, the criminal conduct is readily divisible and intensely personal; each offense is an offense against *a person*. For me it demeans the dignity of the human personality and individuality to talk of "a single transaction" in the context of six separate assaults on six individuals.

No court that elevates the individual rights and human dignity of the accused to a high place—as we should—ought to be so casual as to treat the victims as a single homogenized lump of human clay. I would grant the dignity of individual status to the victims as much as to those accused, not more but surely no less.

If it be suggested that multiple crimes can be separately punished but must be collectively tried, one can point to the firm trend in the law to allow severance of defendants and offenses into separate trials so as to avoid possible prejudice of one criminal act or of the conduct of one defendant to "spill over" on another.

What the Court holds today must be related to its impact on crimes more serious than ordinary housebreaking, followed by physical assault on six men and robbery of all of them. To understand its full impact we must view the holding in the context of four men who break and enter, rob, and then kill six victims. The concurrence tells us that unless all the crimes are joined in one trial the alleged killers cannot be tried for more than one of the killings even if the evidence is that they personally killed two, three, or more of the victims. Or alter the crime to four men breaking into a college dormitory and assaulting six girls. What the Court is holding is, in effect, that the second and third and fourth criminal acts are "free," unless the accused is tried for the multiple crimes in a single trial—something defendants frantically use every legal device to avoid, and often succeed in avoiding. This is the reality of what the Court holds today; it does not make good sense and it cannot make good law. * * *

UNITED STATES V. DIXON

509 U.S. 688, 113 S.Ct. 2849, 125 L.Ed.2d 556 (1993).

JUSTICE SCALIA announced the judgment of the Court and delivered the opinion of the Court with respect to Parts I, II, and IV, and an opinion with respect to Parts III and V, in which JUSTICE KENNEDY joins.

I

Respondent Alvin Dixon was arrested for second-degree murder and was released on bond. Consistent with the District of Columbia's bail law authorizing the judicial officer to impose any condition that "will reasonably assure the appearance of the person for trial or the safety of any other person or the community," Dixon's release form specified that he was not to commit "any criminal offense," and warned that any violation of the conditions of release would subject him "to revocation of release, an order of detention, and prosecution for contempt of court." See § 23–1329(a). While awaiting trial, Dixon was arrested and indicted for possession of cocaine with intent to distribute, in violation of D.C.Code Ann.

§ 33–541(a)(1). The court issued an order requiring Dixon to show cause why he should not be held in contempt or have the terms of his pretrial release modified. [Following] the show-cause hearing, * * * the court found Dixon guilty of criminal contempt under § 23–1329(c), [and sentenced him] to 180 days in jail. * * * He later moved to dismiss the cocaine indictment on double jeopardy grounds; the trial court granted the motion.

Respondent Michael Foster's route to this Court is similar. Based on Foster's alleged physical attacks upon her in the past, Foster's estranged wife Ana obtained a civil protection order (CPO) in Superior Court of the District of Columbia. * * * The order, to which Foster consented, required that he not " 'molest, assault, or in any manner threaten or physically abuse' " Ana Foster. * * * Over the course of eight months, Ana Foster filed three separate motions to have her husband held in contempt for numerous violations of the CPO. Of the 16 alleged episodes, the only charges relevant here are three separate instances of threats (on November 12, 1987, and March 26 and May 17, 1988) and two assaults (on November 6, 1987 and May 21, 1988). * * * After issuing a notice of hearing and ordering Foster to appear, the court held a 3-day bench trial. Counsel for Ana Foster and her mother prosecuted the action; the United States was not represented at trial, although the United States Attorney was apparently aware of the action, as was the court aware of a separate grand jury proceeding on some of the alleged criminal conduct. As to the assault charges, the court stated that Ana Foster would have "to prove as an element, first that there was a Civil Protection Order, and then [that] . . . the assault as defined by the criminal code, in fact occurred." [T]he court granted Foster's motion for acquittal on various counts, including the alleged threats on November 12 and May 17, [but] found Foster guilty beyond a reasonable doubt of four counts of criminal contempt (three violations of Ana Foster's CPO, and one violation of the CPO obtained by her mother), including the November 6, 1987 and May 21, 1988 assaults. He was sentenced to an aggregate 600 days' imprisonment. * * *

The United States Attorney's Office later obtained an indictment charging Foster with simple assault on or about November 6, 1987 (Count I, violation of § 22–504); threatening to injure another on or about November 12, 1987, and March 26 and May 17, 1988 (Counts II–IV, violation of § 22–2307); and assault with intent to kill on or about May 21, 1988 (Count V, violation of § 22–501). Ana Foster was the complainant in all counts; the first and last counts were based on the events for which Foster had been held in contempt, and the other three were based on the alleged events for which Foster was acquitted of contempt. Like Dixon, Foster filed a motion to dismiss, claiming a double jeopardy bar to all counts, and also collateral estoppel as to Counts II–IV. The trial court denied the double-jeopardy claim and did not rule on the collateral-estoppel assertion.

The Government appealed the double jeopardy ruling in Dixon, and Foster appealed the trial court's denial of his motion. The District of Columbia Court of Appeals consolidated the two cases, reheard them en banc, and, relying on our recent decision in *Grady v. Corbin,* 495 U.S. 508 (1990), ruled that both subsequent prosecutions were barred by the Double Jeopardy Clause. * * *

II

To place these cases in context, one must understand that they are the consequence of an historically anomalous use of the contempt power. In both Dixon and Foster, a court issued an order directing a particular individual not to commit criminal offenses. (In Dixon's case, the court incorporated the entire criminal code; in Foster's case, the criminal offense of simple assault.) That could not have occurred at common law, or in the 19th-century American judicial system, [which followed a long-held "tradition against judicial orders prohibiting violation of the law."] * * * It is not surprising, therefore, that the double jeopardy issue presented here—whether prosecution for criminal contempt based on violation of a criminal law incorporated into a court order bars a subsequent prosecution for the criminal offense—did not arise at common law, or even until quite recently in American cases. * * *

The Double Jeopardy Clause, whose application to this new context we are called upon to consider, provides that no person shall "be subject for the same offence to be twice put in jeopardy of life or limb." U.S. Const., Amdt. 5. This protection applies both to successive punishments and to successive prosecutions for the same criminal offense. See *North Carolina v. Pearce,* 395 U.S. 711 (1969). It is well established that criminal contempt, at least the sort enforced through nonsummary proceedings, is "a crime in the ordinary sense." *Bloom v. Illinois,* 391 U.S. 194 (1968). We have held that constitutional protections for criminal defendants other than the double jeopardy provision apply in nonsummary criminal contempt prosecutions just as they do in other criminal prosecutions. See, e.g., *Gompers v. Buck's Stove & Range Co.,* 221 U.S. 418 (1911) (presumption of innocence, proof beyond a reasonable doubt, and guarantee against self-incrimination); *Cooke v. United States,* 267 U.S. 517 (1925) (notice of charges, assistance of counsel, and right to present a defense); *In re Oliver,* 333 U.S. 257 (1948) (public trial). We think it obvious, and today hold, that the protection of the Double Jeopardy Clause likewise attaches.

In both the multiple punishment and multiple prosecution contexts, this Court has concluded that where the two offenses for which the defendant is punished or tried cannot survive the "same-elements" test, the double jeopardy bar applies. See, e.g., *Brown v. Ohio,* 432 U.S. 161 (1977); *Blockburger v. United States,* 284 U.S. 299 (1932) (multiple punishment); *Gavieres v. United States,* 220 U.S. 338 (1911) (successive prosecutions). The same-elements test, sometimes referred to as the "*Blockburger*" test, inquires whether each offense contains an element not contained in the other; if not, they are the "same offence" and double jeopardy bars additional punishment and successive prosecution. * * * We recently held in *Grady* that in addition to passing the *Blockburger* test, a subsequent prosecution must satisfy a "same-conduct" test to avoid the double jeopardy bar. The *Grady* test provides that, "if, to establish an essential element of an offense charged in that prosecution, the government will prove conduct that constitutes an offense for which the defendant has already been prosecuted," a second prosecution may not be had.[a]

III

The first question before us today is whether *Blockburger* analysis permits subsequent prosecution in this new criminal contempt context, where judicial order has prohibited criminal act. If it does, we must then proceed to consider whether *Grady* also permits it.

We begin with *Dixon*. The statute applicable in Dixon's contempt prosecution provides that "[a] person who has been conditionally released . . . and who has violated a condition of release shall be subject to . . . prosecution for contempt of court." § 23–1329(a). Obviously, Dixon could not commit an "offence" under this provision until an order setting out conditions was issued. The statute by itself imposes no legal obligation on anyone. Dixon's cocaine possession, although an offense under D.C.Code Ann. § 33–541(a), was not an offense under § 23–1329 until a judge incorporated the statutory drug offense into his release order.

In this situation, in which the contempt sanction is imposed for violating the order through commission of the incorporated drug offense, the later attempt to prosecute Dixon for the drug offense resembles the situation that produced our judgment of double jeopardy in *Harris v. Oklahoma,* 433 U.S. 682 (1977) (per curiam). There we held that a subsequent prosecution for robbery with a firearm was barred by the Double Jeopardy Clause, because the defendant had already been tried for felony-murder based on the same underlying felony. We have described our terse per curiam in *Harris* as standing for the proposition that, for double jeopardy purposes, "the crime generally described as felony murder" is not "a separate offense distinct from its various elements." *Illinois v. Vitale,* 447 U.S. 410 (1980). So too here, the "crime" of violating a condition of release cannot be abstracted from the "element" of the violated condition. The *Dixon* court order incorporated the entire governing criminal code in the same manner as the *Harris* felony-murder statute incorporated the several enumerated felonies. Here, as in Harris, the underlying substantive criminal offense is "a species of lesser-included offense."

* * * Both the Government and Justice Blackmun contend that the legal obligation in Dixon's case may serve "interests . . . fundamentally different" from the substantive criminal law, because it derives in part from the determination of a court rather than a determination of the legislature. That distinction seems questionable, since the court's power to establish conditions of release, and to punish their violation, was conferred by statute; the legislature was the ultimate

---

[a]   The defendant in *Grady* was charged initially with the offenses of driving while intoxicated and crossing the median, to which he pleaded guilty. He was then charged with criminally negligent homicide, with the prosecution in a bill of particulars listing the driving while intoxicated and the median crossing as two of the acts of negligence. Justice Brennan wrote for a 5–4 majority, joined by Justices White, Marshall, Blackmun, and Stevens. The *Blockburger* test did not bar the second prosecution because neither the median crossing nor the driving while intoxicated were necessary elements of the homicide offense, but the double jeopardy still applied, the majority concluded, because the same conduct for which the defendant had already been prosecuted in the traffic offenses was now being used to prove the element of negligence on the homicide charge.

source of both the criminal and the contempt prohibition. More importantly, however, the distinction is of no moment for purposes of the Double Jeopardy Clause, the text of which looks to whether the offenses are the same, not the interests that the offenses violate. And this Court stated long ago that criminal contempt, at least in its nonsummary form, "is a crime in every fundamental respect." *Bloom,* supra. Because Dixon's drug offense did not include any element not contained in his previous contempt offense, his subsequent prosecution violates the Double Jeopardy Clause.

The foregoing analysis obviously applies as well to Count I of the indictment against Foster, charging assault in violation of § 22–504, based on the same event that was the subject of his prior contempt conviction for violating the provision of the CPO forbidding him to commit simple assault under § 22–504. The subsequent prosecution for assault fails the *Blockburger* test, and is barred.[4]

* * * The remaining four counts in *Foster,* assault with intent to kill (Count V; § 22–501) and threats to injure or kidnap (Counts II–IV; § 22–2307), are not barred under *Blockburger.* As to Count V: Foster's conduct on May 21, 1988 was found to violate the Family Division's order that he not "molest, assault, or in any manner threaten or physically abuse" his wife. At the contempt hearing, the court stated that Ana Foster's attorney, who prosecuted the contempt, would have to prove first, knowledge of a CPO, and second, a willful violation of one of its conditions, here simple assault as defined by the criminal code. * * * On the basis of the same episode, Foster was then indicted for violation of § 22–501, which proscribes assault with intent to kill. Under governing law, that offense requires proof of specific intent to kill; simple assault does not. Similarly, the contempt offense required proof of knowledge of the CPO, which assault with intent to kill does not. Applying the *Blockburger* elements test, the result is clear: These crimes were different offenses and the subsequent prosecution did not violate the Double Jeopardy Clause. * * * Counts II, III, and IV of Foster's indictment are likewise not barred. These charged Foster under § 22–2307 (forbidding anyone to "threaten . . . to kidnap any person or to injure the person of another or physically damage the property of any person") for his alleged threats on three separate dates. Foster's contempt prosecution included charges that, on the same dates, he violated the CPO provision ordering that he not "in any manner threaten" Ana Foster. Conviction of the contempt required willful violation of the CPO—which conviction under § 22–2307 did not; and conviction under § 22–2307 required that the threat be a threat to kidnap, to inflict bodily injury, or to damage property—which conviction of the contempt (for violating the CPO provision that Foster not "in any manner threaten") did not. Each offense therefore contained a separate element, and the *Blockburger* test for double jeopardy was not met.

---

[4]   Justice White complains that this section of our opinion gives the arguments of the United States "short shrift," and treats them in "conclusory" fashion. * * * [A] part of Justice White's opinion that deals with this issue argues—by no means in conclusory fashion—that its practical consequences for law enforcement are not serious. He may be right. But we do not share his "pragmatic" view that the meaning of the Double Jeopardy Clause depends upon our approval of its consequences.

IV

Having found that at least some of the counts at issue here are not barred by the *Blockburger* test, we must consider whether they are barred by the new, additional double jeopardy test we announced three Terms ago in *Grady v. Corbin.* They undoubtedly are, since *Grady* prohibits "a subsequent prosecution if, to establish an essential element of an offense charged in that prosecution [here, assault as an element of assault with intent to kill, or threatening as an element of threatening bodily injury], the government will prove conduct that constitutes an offense for which the defendant has already been prosecuted [here, the assault and the threatening, which conduct constituted the offense of violating the CPO]."

We have concluded, however, that *Grady* must be overruled. Unlike *Blockburger* analysis, whose definition of what prevents two crimes from being the "same offence" has deep historical roots and has been accepted in numerous precedents of this Court, *Grady* lacks constitutional roots. The "same-conduct" rule it announced is wholly inconsistent with earlier Supreme Court precedent and with the clear common-law understanding of double jeopardy. We need not discuss the many proofs of these statements, which were set forth at length in the *Grady* dissent (Scalia, J., dissenting). We will respond, however, to the contrary contentions of today's pro-*Grady* dissents.

The centerpiece of Justice Souter's analysis is an appealing theory of a "successive prosecution" strand of the Double Jeopardy Clause that has a different meaning from its supposed "successive punishment" strand. We have often noted that the Clause serves the function of preventing both successive punishment and successive prosecution, see, e.g., *North Carolina v. Pearce,* 395 U.S. 711 (1969), but there is no authority, except *Grady,* for the proposition that it has different meanings in the two contexts. That is perhaps because it is embarrassing to assert that the single term "same offence" (the words of the Fifth Amendment at issue here) has two different meanings—that what is the same offense is yet not the same offense. Justice Souter provides no authority whatsoever (and we are aware of none) for the bald assertion that "we have long held that [the Government] must sometimes bring its prosecutions for [separate] offenses together." The collateral-estoppel effect attributed to the Double Jeopardy Clause, see *Ashe v. Swenson,* may bar a later prosecution for a separate offense where the Government has lost an earlier prosecution involving the same facts. But this does not establish that the Government "must . . . bring its prosecutions . . . together." It is entirely free to bring them separately, and can win convictions in both. Of course the collateral estoppel issue is not raised in this case.

Justice Souter relies upon four cases to establish the existence of some minimal antecedents to *Grady.* The fountainhead of the "same-conduct" rule, he asserts, is *In re Nielsen,* 131 U.S. 176 (1889). That is demonstrably wrong. *Nielsen* simply applies the common proposition, entirely in accord with *Blockburger,* that prosecution for a greater offense (cohabitation, defined to require proof of adultery) bars prosecution for a lesser included offense (adultery). * * * His second case comes almost a century later. *Brown v. Ohio,* 432 U.S. 161 (1977), contains no support for his position except a footnote that cites *Nielsen* for the proposition that "the *Blockburger* test is not the only standard for determining whether successive prosecutions impermissibly involve the same offense." *Brown,* at n. 6. Not only is this footnote the purest dictum, but it flatly contradicts the text of the opinion which, on the very next page, describes *Nielsen* as the first Supreme Court case to endorse the *Blockburger* rule. * * * The third case is *Harris,* which Justice Souter asserts was a reaffirmation of what he contends was the earlier holding in *Nielsen,* that the *Blockburger* test is "insufficient for determining when a successive prosecution [is] barred," and that conduct, and not merely elements of the offense must be the object of inquiry. Surely not. *Harris* never uses the word "conduct," and its entire discussion focuses on the elements of the two offenses. * * * Finally, [as to] *Vitale,* supra, * * * Justice Souter * * * elevates the statement in *Vitale* that, on certain hypothetical facts, the petitioner would have a "substantial" "claim" of double jeopardy on a *Grady*-type theory, into a holding that the petitioner would win on that theory. No Justice, the *Vitale* dissenters included, has ever construed this passage as answering, rather than simply raising, the question on which we later granted certiorari in *Grady.* * * * In contrast to the above-discussed dicta relied upon by Justice Souter, there are two pre-*Grady* (and post-*Nielsen*) cases that are directly on point. In both *Gavieres v. United States,* supra, and *Burton v. United States,* 202 U.S. 344 (1906), the Court upheld subsequent prosecutions after concluding that the *Blockburger* test (and only the *Blockburger* test) was satisfied. * * * Totally ignored by Justice Souter are the many early American cases construing the Double Jeopardy Clause, which support only an "elements" test. See *Grady* (Scalia, J., dissenting). * * *

But *Grady* was not only wrong in principle; it has already proved unstable in application. Less than two years after it came down, in *United States v. Felix,* 503 U.S. 378 (1992), we were forced to recognize a large exception to it. There we concluded that a subsequent prosecution for conspiracy to manufacture, possess, and distribute methamphetamine was not barred by a previous conviction for attempt to manufacture the same substance. We offered as a justification for avoiding a "literal" (i.e., faithful) reading of *Grady* "long-standing authority" to the effect that prosecution for conspiracy is not precluded by prior prosecution for the substantive offense. Of course the very existence of such a large and longstanding "exception" to the *Grady* rule gave cause for concern that the rule was not an accurate expression of the law. This "past practice" excuse is not available to support the ignoring of *Grady* in the present case, since there is no Supreme Court precedent even discussing this fairly new breed of successive prosecution (criminal contempt for violation of a court order prohibiting a crime, followed by prosecution for the crime itself).

A hypothetical based on the facts in *Harris* reinforces the conclusion that *Grady* is a continuing source of confusion and must be overruled. Suppose the State first tries the defendant for felony-murder, based on robbery, and then indicts the defendant for robbery with a firearm in the same incident. Absent *Grady,* our cases provide a clear answer to the double-jeopardy claim in this situation. Under *Blockburger,* the second prosecution is not barred—as it clearly was not barred at common law, as a famous case establishes. In *King v. Vandercomb,* 168 Eng.Rep. 455 (K.B.1796), the government abandoned, midtrial, prosecution of defendant for burglary by breaking and entering and stealing goods, because it turned out that no property had been removed on the date of the alleged burglary. The defendant was then prosecuted for burglary by breaking and entering with intent to steal. That second prosecution was allowed, because "these two offences are so distinct in their nature, that evidence of one of them will not support an indictment for the other."[15] * * *

Having encountered today yet another situation in which the pre-*Grady* understanding of the Double Jeopardy Clause allows a second trial, though the "same-conduct" test would not, we think it time to acknowledge what is now, three years after *Grady*, compellingly clear: the case was a mistake. We do not lightly reconsider a precedent, but, because *Grady* contradicted an "unbroken line of decisions," contained "less than accurate" historical analysis, and has produced "confusion," we do so here. *Solorio v. United States*, 483 U.S. 435 (1987). Although stare decisis is the "preferred course" in constitutional adjudication, "when governing decisions are unworkable or are badly reasoned, 'this Court has never felt constrained to follow precedent.' " *Payne v. Tennessee*, 501 U.S. 808 (1991). We would mock stare decisis and only add chaos to our double jeopardy jurisprudence by pretending that *Grady* survives when it does not. We therefore accept the Government's invitation to overrule *Grady*, and Counts II, III, IV, and V of Foster's subsequent prosecution are not barred.[17]

V

Dixon's subsequent prosecution, as well as Count I of Foster's subsequent prosecution, violate the Double Jeopardy Clause.[18] For the reasons set forth in Part IV, the other Counts of Foster's subsequent prosecution do not violate the Double Jeopardy Clause.[19] The judgment of the District of Columbia Court of Appeals is affirmed in part and reversed in part, and the case is remanded for proceedings not inconsistent with this opinion.

---

[15] Justice Souter dislikes this result because it violates "the principles behind the protection from successive prosecution included in the Fifth Amendment." The "principles behind" the Fifth Amendment are more likely to be honored by following longstanding practice than by following intuition. But in any case, Justice Souter's concern that prosecutors will bring separate prosecutions in order to perfect their case seems unjustified. They have little to gain and much to lose from such a strategy. Under *Ashe v. Swenson*, an acquittal in the first prosecution might well bar litigation of certain facts essential to the second one—though a conviction in the first prosecution would not excuse the Government from proving the same facts the second time. Surely, moreover, the Government must be deterred from abusive, repeated prosecutions of a single offender for similar offenses by the sheer press of other demands upon prosecutorial and judicial resources. Finally, even if Justice Souter's fear were well founded, no double-jeopardy bar short of a same-transaction analysis will eliminate this problem; but that interpretation of the Double Jeopardy Clause has been soundly rejected, and would require overruling numerous precedents. * * *

[17] We do not address the motion to dismiss the threat counts based on collateral estoppel, see *Ashe v. Swenson*, supra, because neither lower court ruled on that issue.

[18] Justices White, Stevens, and Souter concur in this portion of the judgment.

[19] Justice Blackmun concurs only in the judgment with respect to this portion.

CHIEF JUSTICE REHNQUIST, with whom JUSTICE O'CONNOR and JUSTICE THOMAS join, concurring in part and dissenting in part.

* * * I do not join Part III of Justice Scalia's opinion because I think that none of the criminal prosecutions in this case were barred under *Blockburger*. I must then confront the expanded version of double jeopardy embodied in *Grady*. For the reasons set forth in the *Grady* dissent, supra, (Scalia, J., dissenting), and in Part IV of the Court's opinion, I, too, think that *Grady* must be overruled. I therefore join Parts I, II, and IV of the Court's opinion * * *.

In my view, *Blockburger*'s same-elements test requires us to focus not on the terms of the particular court orders involved, but on the elements of contempt of court in the ordinary sense. Relying on *Harris v. Oklahoma,* a three-paragraph per curiam in an unargued case, Justice Scalia concludes otherwise today, and thus incorrectly finds in Part III of his opinion that the subsequent prosecutions of Dixon for drug distribution and of Foster for assault violated the Double Jeopardy Clause. In so doing, Justice Scalia rejects the traditional view—shared by every federal court of appeals and state supreme court that addressed the issue prior to *Grady*— that, as a general matter, double jeopardy does not bar a subsequent prosecution based on conduct for which a defendant has been held in criminal contempt. * * *

At the heart of this pre-*Grady* consensus lay the common belief that there was no double-jeopardy bar under *Blockburger*. There, we stated that two offenses are different for purposes of double jeopardy if "each provision requires proof of a fact which the other does not." Applying this test to the offenses at bar, it is clear that the elements of the governing contempt provision are entirely different from the elements of the substantive crimes. Contempt of court comprises two elements: (i) a court order made known to the defendant, followed by (ii) willful violation of that order. Neither of those elements is necessarily satisfied by proof that a defendant has committed the substantive offenses of assault or drug distribution. Likewise, no element of either of those substantive offenses is necessarily satisfied by proof that a defendant has been found guilty of contempt of court. * * * Our double jeopardy cases applying *Blockburger* have focused on the statutory elements of the offenses charged, not on the facts that must be proven under the particular indictment at issue—an indictment being the closest analogue to the court orders in this case. * * * By focusing on the facts needed to show a violation of the specific court orders involved in this case, and not on the generic elements of the crime of contempt of court, Justice Scalia's double-jeopardy analysis bears a striking resemblance to that found in *Grady*—not what one would expect in an opinion that overrules *Grady*. * * *

Close inspection of the crimes at issue in *Harris* reveals, moreover, that our decision in that case was not a departure from *Blockburger*'s focus on the statutory elements of the offenses charged. In *Harris*, we held that a conviction for felony murder based on a killing in the course of an armed robbery foreclosed a subsequent prosecution for robbery with a firearm. Though the felony-murder statute in *Harris* did not require proof of armed robbery, it did include as an element of proof that the defendant was engaged in the commission of some felony. We construed this generic reference to some felony as incorporating the statutory elements of the various felonies upon which a felony-murder conviction could rest. The criminal contempt provision involved here, by contrast, contains no such generic reference which by definition incorporates the statutory elements of assault or drug distribution.

Unless we are to accept the extraordinary view that the three-paragraph per curiam in *Harris* was intended to overrule sub silentio our previous decisions that looked to the statutory elements of the offenses charged in applying *Blockburger,* we are bound to conclude, as does Justice Scalia, that the ratio decidendi of our *Harris* decision was that the two crimes there were akin to greater and lesser included offenses. The crimes at issue here, however, cannot be viewed as greater and lesser included offenses, either intuitively or logically. A crime such as possession with intent to distribute cocaine is a serious felony that cannot easily be conceived of as a lesser included offense of criminal contempt, a relatively petty offense as applied to the conduct in this case. See D.C.Code Ann. § 33–541(a)(2)(A) (the maximum sentence for possession with intent to distribute cocaine is 15 years in prison). Indeed, to say that criminal contempt is an aggravated form of that offense defies common sense. * * *

JUSTICE WHITE with whom JUSTICE STEVENS joins, and with whom JUSTICE SOUTER joins as to Part I, concurring in the judgment in part and dissenting in part.

I

The chief issue before us is whether the Double Jeopardy Clause applies at all to cases such as these. Justice Scalia finds that it applies, but does so in conclusory fashion, without dealing adequately with * * * the Government's arguments or the practical consequences of today's decision. Both, in my view, are worthy of more.

The position of the United States is that, for the purpose of applying the Double Jeopardy Clause, a charge of criminal contempt for engaging in conduct that is proscribed by court order and that is in turn forbidden by the criminal code is an offense separate from the statutory crime. The United States begins by pointing to prior decisions of this Court to support its view. * * * [But its strongest] decisions concern the power to deal with acts interfering directly with the performance of legislative functions, a power to which not all constitutional restraints on the exercise of judiciary authority apply. * * * [W]hatever application * * * [they] might have in the context of judicial contempt is limited to cases of in-court contempts that constitute direct obstructions of the judicial process and for which summary proceedings remain acceptable. Neither *Dixon* nor *Foster* is such a case.

The United States' second, more powerful, argument is that contempt and the underlying substantive crime constitute two separate offenses for they involve injuries to two distinct interests, the one the interest of the court in preserving its authority, the other the public's interest in being protected from harmful conduct. This position finds support in Justice Blackmun's partial dissent, and is bolstered by reference to numerous decisions acknowledging the importance and role of the courts' contempt power. * * * The fact that two criminal prohibitions promote different interests may be indicative of legislative intent and, to that extent, important in deciding whether cumulative punishments imposed in a single prosecution violate the Double Jeopardy Clause. See *Missouri v. Hunter,* 459 U.S. 359 (1983). But the cases decided today involve instances of successive prosecutions in which the interests of the defendant are of paramount concern. To subject an individual to repeated prosecutions exposes him to "embarrassment, expense and ordeal," violates principles of finality, and increases the risk of a mistaken conviction. That one of the punishments is designed to protect the court rather than the public is, in this regard, of scant comfort to the defendant. * * *

Both the Government and amici submit that application of the Double Jeopardy Clause in this context carries grave practical consequences. * * * It would, it is argued, cripple the power to enforce court orders or, alternatively, allow individuals to escape serious punishment for statutory criminal offenses. The argument, an offshoot of the principle of necessity familiar to the law of contempt, is that, just as we have relaxed certain procedural requirements in contempt proceedings where time is of the essence and an immediate remedy is needed to "prevent a breakdown of the proceedings," so too should we exclude double jeopardy protections from this setting lest we do damage to the courts' authority. * * *

Adherence to double jeopardy principles in this context, however, will not seriously deter the courts from taking appropriate steps to ensure that their authority is not flouted. Courts remain free to hold transgressors in contempt and punish them as they see fit. The government counters that this possibility will prove to be either illusory—if the prosecuting authority declines to initiate proceedings out of fear that they could jeopardize more substantial punishment for the underlying crime—or too costly—if the prosecuting authority, the risk notwithstanding, chooses to go forward. But it is not fanciful to imagine that judges and prosecutors will select a third option, which is to ensure, where necessary or advisable, that the contempt and the substantive charge be tried at the same time, in which case the double jeopardy issue "would be limited to ensuring that the total punishment did not exceed that authorized by the legislature." *United States v. Halper,* 490 U.S. 435 (1989).

Against this backdrop, the appeal of the principle of necessity loses much of its force. Ultimately, the urgency of punishing such contempt violations is no less, but by the same token no more, than that of punishing violations of criminal laws of general application—in which case, we simply do not question the defendant's right to the "protections worked out carefully over the years and deemed fundamental to our system of justice," including the protection of the Double Jeopardy Clause. "Perhaps to some extent we sacrifice efficiency, expedition, and economy, but the choice . . . has been made, and retained, in the Constitution. We see no sound reason in logic or policy not to apply it in the area of criminal contempt." *Bloom v. Illinois.*

Dixon aptly illustrates these points. In that case, the motion requesting modification of the conditions of Dixon's release was filed by the government, the same entity responsible for prosecution of the drug offense. Indeed, in so doing it relied explicitly on the defendant's indictment on the cocaine charge. Logically, any problem of coordination or of advance notice of the impending prosecution for the substantive offense was at most minimal. Nor, aside from the legitimate desire to punish all offenders swiftly, does there appear to have been any real need to hold Dixon in contempt immediately, without waiting for the second trial. * * *

More difficult to deal with are the circumstances surrounding Foster's defiance of the court order. Realization of the scope of domestic violence—according to the American Medical Association (AMA), "the single largest cause of injury to women,"—has come with difficulty, and it has come late. There no doubt are time delays in the operation of the criminal justice system that are frustrating; they even can be perilous when an individual is left exposed to a defendant's potential violence. That is true in the domestic context; it is true elsewhere as well. Resort to more expedient methods therefore is appealing, and in many cases permissible. Under today's decision, for instance, police officers retain the power to arrest for violation of a civil protection order. Where the offense so warrants, judges can haul the assailant before the court, charge him with criminal contempt, and hold him without bail. See *United States v. Salerno* [p. 661]. Also, cooperation between the government and parties bringing contempt proceedings can be achieved. The various actors might not have thought such cooperation necessary in the past; after today's decision, I suspect they will. * * *

II

If, as the Court agrees, the Double Jeopardy Clause cannot be ignored in this context, my view is that the subsequent prosecutions in both *Dixon* and *Foster* were impermissible as to all counts. I reach this conclusion because the offenses at issue in the contempt proceedings were either identical to, or lesser included offenses of, those charged in the subsequent prosecutions. Justice Scalia's contrary conclusion as to some of Foster's counts, which he reaches by exclusive focus on the formal elements of the relevant crimes, is divorced from the purposes of the constitutional provision he purports to apply. Moreover, the results to which this approach would lead are indefensible.

* * * Because in a successive prosecution case the risk is that a person will have to defend himself more than once against the same charge, I would have put to the side the CPO (which, as it were, triggered the court's authority to punish the defendant for acts already punishable under the criminal laws) and compared the substantive offenses of which respondents stood accused in both prosecutions. * * * Under Justice Scalia's view, the double jeopardy barrier is * * * removed because each offense demands proof of an element the other does not: Foster's conviction for contempt requires proof of the existence and knowledge of a CPO, which conviction for assault with intent to kill does not; his conviction for assault with intent to kill requires proof of an intent to kill, which the contempt conviction did not. Finally, though he was acquitted in the contempt proceedings with respect to the alleged November 12, March 26, and May 17 threats, his conviction under the threat charge in the subsequent trial required the additional proof that the threat be to kidnap, to inflict bodily injury, or to damage property. As to these counts, and absent any collateral estoppel problem, Justice Scalia finds that the Constitution does not prohibit retrial.

The distinction drawn by Justice Scalia is predicated on a reading of the Double Jeopardy Clause that is abstracted from the purposes the constitutional provision is designed to promote. To focus on the statutory elements of a crime makes sense where cumulative punishment is at stake, for there the aim simply is to uncover legislative intent. The *Blockburger* inquiry, accordingly, serves as a means to determine this intent, as our cases have recognized. But, as Justice Souter shows, adherence to legislative will has very little to do with the important interests advanced by double jeopardy safeguards against successive prosecutions. The central purpose of the Double Jeopardy Clause being to protect against vexatious multiple prosecutions, these interests go well beyond the prevention of unauthorized punishment. The same-elements test is an inadequate safeguard, for it leaves the constitutional guarantee at the mercy of a legislature's decision to modify statutory definitions. * * * Take the example of Count V in *Foster:* For all intents and purposes, the offense for which he was convicted in the contempt proceeding was his assault against his wife. The majority, its eyes fixed on the rigid elements-test, would have his fate turn on whether his subsequent prosecution charges "simple assault" or "assault with intent to kill." Yet, because the crime of "simple assault" is included within the crime of "assault with intent to kill," the reasons that bar retrial under the first hypothesis are equally present under the second: These include principles of finality, protecting Foster from "embarrassment" and "expense," and preventing the government from gradually fine-tuning its strategy, thereby minimizing exposure to a mistaken conviction. * * *

To respond, as the majority appears to do, that concerns relating to the defendant's interests against repeat trials are "unjustified" because prosecutors "have little to gain and much to lose" from bringing successive prosecutions and because "the Government must be deterred from abusive, repeated prosecutions of a single offender for similar offenses by the sheer press of other demands upon prosecutorial and judicial resources," [n. 15 of Justice Scalia's opinion], is to get things exactly backwards. The majority's prophesies might be correct, and double jeopardy might be a problem that will simply take care of itself. Not so, however, according to the Constitution, whose firm prohibition against double jeopardy cannot be satisfied by wishful thinking. * * *

Once it is agreed that the Double Jeopardy Clause applies in this context, the Clause, properly construed, both governs this case and disposes of the distinction between Foster's charges upon which Justice Scalia relies. I therefore see little need to draw *Grady* into this dispute. * * * The majority nonetheless has chosen to consider *Grady* anew and to overrule it. I agree with Justice Blackmun and Justice Souter that such a course is both unwarranted and unwise. Hence, I dissent from the judgment overruling *Grady*.

JUSTICE BLACKMUN, concurring in the judgment in part and dissenting in part.

I agree with Justice Souter that "the *Blockburger* test is not the exclusive standard for determining whether the rule against successive prosecutions applies in a given case." I also share both his and Justice White's dismay that the Court so cavalierly has overruled a precedent that is barely three years old and that has proved neither unworkable nor unsound. * * * If this were a case involving successive prosecutions under the substantive criminal law (as was true in *Harris v. Oklahoma, Illinois v. Vitale,* and *Grady*), I would agree that the Double Jeopardy Clause could bar the subsequent prosecution. But we are concerned here with contempt of court, a special situation. * * * The purpose of contempt is not to punish an offense against the community at large but rather to punish the specific offense of disobeying a court order. This Court said nearly a century ago: "[A] court, enforcing obedience to its orders by proceedings for contempt, is not executing the criminal laws of the land, but only securing to suitors the rights which it has adjudged them entitled to." *In re Debs,* 158 U.S. 564 (1895). * * * This fact is poignantly stressed by the amici: "Contempt litigators and criminal prosecutors seek to further different interests. A battered woman seeks to enforce her private order to end the violence against her. In contrast, the criminal prosecutor is vindicating society's interest in enforcing its criminal law. The two interests are not the same, and to consider the contempt litigator and the criminal prosecutor as one and the same would be to adopt an absurd fiction" (emphasis in original). Brief for Ayuda et al. as Amici Curiae 20.

Finally, I cannot so easily distinguish between "summary" and "nonsummary" contempt proceedings, for the interests served in both are fundamentally similar. It is as much a "disruption of judicial process," to disobey a judge's conditional release order as it is to disturb a judge's courtroom. And the interests served in vindicating the authority of the court are fundamentally different from those served by the prosecution of violations of the substantive criminal law. Because I believe that neither Dixon nor Foster would be "subject for the same offence to be twice put in jeopardy of life or limb," U.S. Const., Amdt. 5, I would reverse the judgment of the District of Columbia Court of Appeals.

JUSTICE SOUTER, with whom JUSTICE STEVENS joins, concurring in the judgment in part and dissenting in part.

While I agree with the Court as far as it goes in holding that a citation for criminal contempt and an indictment for violating a substantive criminal statute may amount to charges of the "same offence" for purposes of the Double Jeopardy Clause, I cannot join the Court in restricting the Clause's reach and dismembering the protection against successive prosecution that the Constitution was meant to provide. The Court has read our precedents so narrowly as to leave them bereft of the principles animating that protection, and has chosen to overrule the most recent of the relevant cases, *Grady v. Corbin,* decided three years ago. Because I think that *Grady* was correctly decided, amounting merely to an expression of just those animating principles, and because, even if the decision had been wrong in the first instance, there is no warrant for overruling it now, I respectfully dissent. * * *

In providing that no person shall "be subject for the same offence to be twice put in jeopardy of life or limb," the Double Jeopardy Clause protects against two distinct types of abuses. It protects against being punished more than once for a single offense, or "multiple punishment." Where a person is being subjected to more than one sentence, the Double Jeopardy Clause ensures that he is not receiving for one offense more than the punishment authorized. The Clause also protects against being prosecuted for the same offense more than once, or "successive prosecution." * * * The Clause functions in different ways in the two contexts, and the analysis applied to claims of successive prosecution differs from that employed to analyze claims of multiple punishment.

In addressing multiple punishments, "the role of the constitutional guarantee is limited to assuring that the court does not exceed its legislative authorization by imposing multiple punishments for the same offense." *Brown v. Ohio*. Courts enforcing the federal guarantee against multiple punishment therefore must examine the various offenses for which a person is being punished to determine whether, as defined by the legislature, any two or more of them are the same offense. Over 60 years ago, this Court [in *Blockburger*] stated the test still used today to determine "whether two offenses are sufficiently distinguishable to permit the imposition of cumulative punishment." * * * The *Blockburger* test "emphasizes the elements of the two crimes." *Brown*. Indeed, the determination whether two statutes describe the "same offence" for multiple punishment purposes has been held to involve only a question of statutory construction. We ask what the elements of each offense are as a matter of statutory interpretation, to determine whether the legislature intended "to impose separate sanctions for multiple offenses arising in the course of a single act or transaction." * * * The Court has even gone so far as to say that the *Blockburger* test will not prevent multiple punishment where legislative intent to the contrary is clear, at least in the case of state law. * * * *Missouri v. Hunter*. * * *

The interests at stake in avoiding successive prosecutions are different from those at stake in the prohibition against multiple punishments, and our cases reflect this reality. The protection against successive prosecutions is the central protection provided by the Clause. * * * Consequently, while the government may punish a person separately for each conviction of at least as many different offenses as meet the *Blockburger* test, we have long held that it must sometimes bring its prosecutions for these offenses together. If a separate prosecution were permitted for every offense arising out of the same conduct, the government could manipulate the definitions of offenses, creating fine distinctions among them and permitting a zealous prosecutor to try a person again and again for essentially the same criminal conduct. While punishing different combinations of elements is consistent with the Double Jeopardy Clause in its limitation on the imposition of multiple punishments (a limitation rooted in concerns with legislative intent), permitting such repeated prosecutions would not be consistent with the principles underlying the Clause in its limitation on successive prosecution. The limitation on successive prosecution is thus a restriction on the government different in kind from that contained in the limitation on multiple punishments, and the government cannot get around the restriction on repeated prosecution of a single individual merely by precision in the way it defines its statutory offenses. Thus, "the *Blockburger* test is not the only standard for determining whether successive prosecutions impermissibly involve the same offense. Even if two offenses are sufficiently different to permit the imposition of consecutive sentences, successive prosecutions will be barred in some circumstances where the second prosecution requires the relitigation of factual issues already resolved by the first." *Brown* at n. 6.

An example will show why this should be so. Assume three crimes: robbery with a firearm, robbery in a dwelling and simple robbery. The elements of the three crimes are the same, except that robbery with a firearm has the element that a firearm be used in the commission of the robbery while the other two crimes do not, and robbery in a dwelling has the element that the robbery occur in a dwelling while the other two crimes do not.

If a person committed a robbery in a dwelling with a firearm and was prosecuted for simple robbery, all agree he could not be prosecuted subsequently for either of the greater offenses of robbery with a firearm or robbery in a dwelling. Under the lens of *Blockburger,* however, if that same person were prosecuted first for robbery with a firearm, he could be prosecuted subsequently for robbery in a dwelling, even though he could not subsequently be prosecuted on the basis of that same robbery for simple robbery.[3] This is true simply because neither of the crimes, robbery with a firearm and robbery in a dwelling, is either identical to or a lesser-included offense of the other. But since the purpose of the Double Jeopardy Clause's protection against successive prosecutions is to prevent repeated trials in which a defendant will be forced to defend against the same charge again and again, and in which the government may perfect its presentation with dress rehearsal after dress rehearsal, it should be irrelevant that the second prosecution would require the defendant to defend himself not only from the charge that he committed the robbery, but also from the charge of some additional fact, in this case, that the scene of the crime was a dwelling. If, instead, protection against successive prosecution were as limited as it would be by *Blockburger* alone, the doctrine would be as striking for its anomalies as for the limited protection it would provide. Thus, in the relatively few successive prosecution cases we have had over the years, we have not held that the *Blockburger* test is the only hurdle the government must clear (with one exception). * * *

The recognition that a *Blockburger* rule is insufficient protection against successive prosecution can be seen as long ago as *In re Nielsen,* 131 U.S. 176 (1889), where we held that conviction for one statutory offense precluded later prosecution for another, even though each required proof of a fact the other did not. * * * In the past 20 years the Court has addressed just this problem of successive prosecution on three occasions. In *Harris v. Oklahoma,* we held that prosecution for a robbery with firearms was barred by the Double Jeopardy Clause when the defendant had already been convicted of felony murder comprising the same robbery with firearms as the underlying felony. * * * Subsequently, in *Illinois v. Vitale,* the Court again indicated that a valid claim of double jeopardy would not necessarily be defeated by the fact that the two offenses are not the "same" under the *Blockburger* test. In that case, we were confronted with a prosecution for failure to reduce speed and a subsequent prosecution for involuntary manslaughter. The opinion of the Illinois Supreme Court below had not made it clear whether the

---

[3] Our cases have long made clear that the order in which one is prosecuted for two crimes alleged to be the same matters not in demonstrating a violation of double jeopardy. See *Brown v. Ohio* ("the sequence is immaterial").

elements of failure to slow were always necessarily included within the elements of involuntary manslaughter by automobile, and we remanded for clarification of this point, among other things. We held that "if, as a matter of Illinois law, a careless failure to slow is always a necessary element of manslaughter by automobile, then the two offenses are the 'same' under *Blockburger* and *Vitale*'s trial on the latter charge would constitute double jeopardy. . . ." Id., at 419–420. But that was not all. Writing for the Court, Justice White went on to say that, "in any event, it may be that to sustain its manslaughter case the State may find it necessary to prove a failure to slow or to rely on conduct necessarily involving such failure. . . . In that case, because Vitale has already been convicted for conduct that is a necessary element of the more serious crime for which he has been charged, his claim of double jeopardy would be substantial under *Brown* [*v. Ohio*] and our later decision in *Harris v. Oklahoma*."

Over a decade ago, then, we clearly understood *Harris* to stand for the proposition that when one has already been tried for a crime comprising certain conduct, a subsequent prosecution seeking to prove the same conduct is barred by the Double Jeopardy Clause.[7] * * * [But] even if this had not been clear since the time of *In re Nielsen,* any debate should have been settled by our decision three Terms ago in *Grady v. Corbin.* * * * As against this sequence of consistent reasoning from *Nielsen* to *Grady,* the Court's citation to two cases, *Gavieres v. United States,* and *Burton v. United States,* cannot validate its insistence that, prior to *Grady,* our exclusive standard for barring successive prosecutions under the Double Jeopardy Clause was the *Blockburger* test. * * * *Gavieres* is in fact the only case that may even be read to suggest that the Court ever treated a *Blockburger* analysis as the exclusive successive prosecution test under the Double Jeopardy Clause, and its precedential force is weak. * * * Whatever may have been the merits of the debate in *Grady,* the decision deserves more respect than it receives from the Court today. "Although adherence to precedent is not rigidly required in constitutional cases, any departure from the doctrine of stare decisis demands special justification." *Arizona v. Rumsey,* 467 U.S. 203 (1984).

GAMBLE V. UNITED STATES
587 U.S. ___, 139 S.Ct. 1960, 204 L.Ed.2d 322 (2019).

JUSTICE ALITO delivered the opinion of the Court.

We consider in this case whether to overrule a longstanding interpretation of the Double Jeopardy Clause of the Fifth Amendment. That Clause provides that no person may be "twice put in jeopardy" "for the same offence." Our double jeopardy case law is complex, but at its core, the Clause means that those acquitted or convicted of a particular "offence" cannot be tried a second time for the same "offence." But what does the Clause mean by an "offence"?

---

[7] In *Brown* we recognized that "[a]n exception may exist where the State is unable to proceed on the more serious charge at the outset because the additional facts necessary to sustain that charge have not occurred or have not been discovered despite the exercise of due diligence."

We have long held that a crime under one sovereign's laws is not "the same offence" as a crime under the laws of another sovereign. Under this "dual-sovereignty" doctrine, a State may prosecute a defendant under state law even if the Federal Government has prosecuted him for the same conduct under a federal statute.

Or the reverse may happen, as it did here. Terance Gamble, convicted by Alabama for possessing a firearm as a felon, now faces prosecution by the United States under its own felon-in-possession law. Attacking this second prosecution on double jeopardy grounds, Gamble asks us to overrule the dual-sovereignty doctrine. He contends that it departs from the founding-era understanding of the right enshrined by the Double Jeopardy Clause. But the historical evidence assembled by Gamble is feeble; pointing the other way are the Clause's text, other historical evidence, and 170 years of precedent. Today we affirm that precedent, and with it the decision below.

I

In November 2015, a local police officer in Mobile, Alabama, pulled Gamble over for a damaged headlight. Smelling marijuana, the officer searched Gamble's car, where he found a loaded 9-mm handgun. Since Gamble had been convicted of second-degree robbery, his possession of the handgun violated an Alabama law providing that no one convicted of "a crime of violence" "shall own a firearm or have one in his or her possession." After Gamble pleaded guilty to this state offense, federal prosecutors indicted him for the same instance of possession under a federal law—one forbidding those convicted of "a crime punishable by imprisonment for a term exceeding one year . . . to ship or transport in interstate or foreign commerce, or possess in or affecting commerce, any firearm or ammunition." 18 U.S.C. § 922(g)(1).

Gamble moved to dismiss on one ground: The federal indictment was for "the same offence" as the one at issue in his state conviction and thus exposed him to double jeopardy. But because this Court has long held that two offenses "are *not* the 'same offence'" for double jeopardy purposes if "prosecuted by different sovereigns," *Heath v. Alabama*, 474 U.S. 82, 92 (1985), the District Court denied Gamble's motion to dismiss. Gamble then pleaded guilty to the federal offense while preserving his right to challenge the denial of his motion to dismiss on double jeopardy grounds. But on appeal the Eleventh Circuit affirmed, citing the dual-sovereignty doctrine. We granted certiorari to determine whether to overturn that doctrine.[1]

II

Gamble contends that the Double Jeopardy Clause must forbid successive prosecutions by different sovereigns because that is what the founding-era common law did. But before turning to that historical claim, see Part III *infra*, we review the Clause's text and some of the cases Gamble asks us to overturn.

---

[1]   In addressing that question, we follow the parties' lead and assume, without deciding, that the state and federal offenses at issue here satisfy the other criteria for being the "same offence" under our double jeopardy precedent. See *Blockburger v. United States*, 284 U.S. 299 (1932).

A

We start with the text of the Fifth Amendment. Although the dual-sovereignty rule is often dubbed an "exception" to the double jeopardy right, it is not an exception at all. On the contrary, it follows from the text that defines that right in the first place. "[T]he language of the Clause . . . protects individuals from being twice put in jeopardy 'for the same *offence*,' not for the same *conduct* or *actions*," *Grady v. Corbin*, 495 U.S. 508, 529 (1990), as Justice Scalia wrote in a soon-vindicated dissent, see *United States v. Dixon*, 509 U.S. 688 (1993) (overruling *Grady*). And the term " '[o]ffence' was commonly understood in 1791 to mean 'transgression,' that is, 'the Violation or Breaking of a Law.' " As originally understood, then, an "offence" is defined by a law, and each law is defined by a sovereign. So where there are two sovereigns, there are two laws, and two "offences." * * *

Faced with this reading, Gamble falls back on an episode from the Double Jeopardy Clause's drafting history. The first Congress, working on an earlier draft that would have banned " 'more than one trial or one punishment for the same offence,' " voted down a proposal to add " 'by any law of the United States.' " 1 Annals of Cong. 753 (1789). In rejecting this addition, Gamble surmises, Congress must have intended to bar successive prosecutions regardless of the sovereign bringing the charge.

Even if that inference were justified—something that the Government disputes—it would count for little. The private intent behind a drafter's rejection of one version of a text is shoddy evidence of the public meaning of an altogether different text. * * * Besides, if we allowed conjectures about purpose to inform our reading of the text, the Government's conjecture would prevail. The Government notes that the Declaration of Independence denounced King George III for "protecting [British troops] by a mock Trial, from punishment for any Murders which they should commit on the Inhabitants of these States." The Declaration was alluding to "the so-called Murderers' Act, passed by Parliament after the Boston Massacre," Amar, Sixth Amendment First Principles, 84 Geo. L. J. 641, 687, n. 181 (1996), a law that allowed British officials indicted for murder in America to be " 'tried in England, beyond the control of local juries.' " "During the late colonial period, Americans strongly objected to . . . [t]his circumvention of the judgment of the victimized community." *Ibid.* Yet on Gamble's reading, the same Founders who quite literally *revolted* against the use of acquittals abroad to bar criminal prosecutions here would soon give us an Amendment allowing foreign acquittals to spare domestic criminals. We doubt it.

We see no reason to abandon the sovereign-specific reading of the phrase "same offence," from which the dual-sovereignty rule immediately follows.

B

Our cases reflect the same reading. A close look at them reveals how fidelity to the Double Jeopardy Clause's text does more than honor the formal difference between two distinct criminal codes. It honors the substantive differences between the interests that two sovereigns can have in punishing the same act.

The question of successive federal and state prosecutions arose in three antebellum cases implying and then spelling out the dual-sovereignty doctrine. The first, *Fox v. Ohio*, 5 How. 410 (1847), involved an Ohio prosecution for the passing of counterfeit coins. The defendant argued that since Congress can punish counterfeiting, the States must be barred from doing so, or else a person could face two trials for the same offense, contrary to the Fifth Amendment. We rejected the defendant's premise that under the Double Jeopardy Clause "offences falling within the competency of different authorities to restrain or punish them would not properly be subjected to the consequences which those authorities might ordain and affix to their perpetration." Indeed, we observed, the nature of the crime or its effects on "public safety" might well "deman[d]" separate prosecutions. Generalizing from this point, we declared in a second case that "the same act might, as to its character and tendencies, and the consequences it involved, constitute an offence against both the State and Federal governments, and might draw to its commission the penalties denounced by either, as appropriate to its character in reference to each." *United States v. Marigold*, 9 How. 560 (1850).

A third antebellum case, *Moore v. Illinois*, 14 How. 13, 55 U.S. 13, expanded on this concern for the different interests of separate sovereigns, after tracing it to the text in the manner set forth above. Recalling that the Fifth Amendment prohibits double jeopardy not "for the same ac[t]" but "for the same offence," and that "[a]n offence, in its legal signification, means the transgression of a law,", we drew the now-familiar inference: A single act "may be an offence or transgression of the laws of" two sovereigns, and hence punishable by both. Then we gave color to this abstract principle—and to the diverse interests it might vindicate—with an example. An assault on a United States marshal, we said, would offend against the Nation and a State: the first by "hindering" the "execution of legal process," and the second by "breach[ing]" the "peace of the State." That duality of harm explains how "one act" could constitute "two offences, for each of which [the offender] is justly punishable."

This principle comes into still sharper relief when we consider a prosecution in this country for crimes committed abroad. If, as Gamble suggests, only one sovereign may prosecute for a single act, no American court—state or federal—could prosecute conduct already tried in a foreign court. Imagine, for example, that a U.S. national has been murdered in another country. That country could rightfully seek to punish the killer for committing an act of violence within its territory. The foreign country's interest lies in protecting the peace in that territory rather than protecting the American specifically. But the United States looks at the same conduct and sees an act of violence against one of its nationals, a person under the particular protection of its laws. The murder of a U.S. national is an offense to the United States as much as it is to the country where the murder occurred and to which the victim is a stranger. That is why the killing of an American abroad is a federal offense that can be prosecuted in our courts, see 18 U.S.C. § 2332(a)(1), and why customary international law allows this exercise of jurisdiction.

There are other reasons not to offload all prosecutions for crimes involving Americans abroad. We may lack confidence in the competence or honesty of the other country's legal system. Less cynically, we may think that special protection for U.S. nationals serves key national interests related to security, trade, commerce, or scholarship. Such interests might also give us a stake in punishing crimes committed *by* U.S. nationals abroad—especially crimes that might do harm to our national security or foreign relations. See, *e.g.*, § 2332a(b) (bombings). These examples reinforce the foundation laid in our antebellum cases: that a crime against two sovereigns constitutes two offenses because each sovereign has an interest to vindicate.

We cemented that foundation 70 years after the last of those antebellum cases, in a decision upholding a federal prosecution that followed one by a State. See *United States v. Lanza*, 260 U.S. 377 (1922) ("[A]n act denounced as a crime by both national and state sovereignties is an offense against the peace and dignity of both and may be punished by each"). And for decades more, we applied our precedent without qualm or quibble. * * * When petitioners in 1959 asked us twice to reverse course, we twice refused, finding "[n]o consideration or persuasive reason not presented to the Court in the prior cases" for disturbing our "firmly established" doctrine. *Abbate v. United States*, 359 U.S. 187 (1959); see also *Bartkus v. Illinois*, 359 U.S. 121 (1959). And then we went on enforcing it, adding another six decades of cases to the doctrine's history. *See, e.g., Puerto Rico v. Sánchez Valle*, 579 U.S. ___, 136 S.Ct. 1863 (2016).[a]

C

We briefly address two objections to this analysis.

First, the dissents contend that our dual-sovereignty rule errs in treating the Federal and State *Governments* as two separate sovereigns when in fact sovereignty belongs to the people. This argument is based on a non sequitur. Yes, our Constitution rests on the principle that the people are sovereign, but that does not mean that they have conferred all the attributes of sovereignty on a single government. Instead, the people, by adopting the Constitution, " 'split the atom of sovereignty.' " As we explained last Term:

> "When the original States declared their independence, they claimed the powers inherent in sovereignty . . . . The Constitution limited but did not abolish the sovereign powers of the States, which retained 'a residuary and inviolable sovereignty.' The Federalist No. 39, p. 245 (C. Rossiter ed. 1961). Thus, both the Federal Government and the States wield sovereign powers, and that is why our system of government is said to be one of 'dual sovereignty.' "

It is true that the Republic is " 'ONE WHOLE,' " (opinion of GINSBURG, J.) (quoting The Federalist No. 82, p. 493 (C. Rossiter ed. 1961) (A. Hamilton)); accord,

---

[a] In *Sánchez Valle*, the Court explained that the dual-sovereignty rule focuses "not on the fact of self-rule, but on where it came from." Both States and tribes are treated as separate sovereigns because they possessed control over criminal law and local affairs "as an original matter, rather than deriving it from the Federal Government." A municipality is not a sovereign separate from a State under the rule because the State "is the furthest-back source of prosecutorial power." The Court held that because the authority of prosecutors in Puerto Rico "derived from, rather than pre-existed association with, the Federal Government," Puerto Rico is not a sovereign from the Federal Government under the Clause.

(opinion of GORSUCH, J.). But there is a difference between the whole and a single part, and that difference underlies decisions as foundational to our legal system as *McCulloch v. Maryland*, 4 Wheat. 316 (1819). There, in terms so directly relevant as to seem presciently tailored to answer this very objection, Chief Justice Marshall distinguished precisely between "the people of a State" and "[t]he people of all the States,"; between the "sovereignty which the people of a single state possess" and the sovereign powers "conferred by the people of the United States on the government of the Union,"; and thus between "the action of a part" and "the action of the whole,". In short, *McCulloch*'s famous holding that a State may not tax the national bank rested on a recognition that the States and the Nation have different "interests" and "right[s]." One strains to imagine a clearer statement of the premises of our dual-sovereignty rule, or a more authoritative source. The United States is a *federal* republic; it is not, contrary to Justice GORSUCH's suggestion, a unitary state like the United Kingdom.

Gamble and the dissents lodge a second objection to this line of reasoning. They suggest that because the division of federal and state power was meant to promote liberty, it cannot support a rule that exposes Gamble to a second sentence. See (opinion of GINSBURG, J.); (opinion of GORSUCH, J.). This argument fundamentally misunderstands the governmental structure established by our Constitution. Our federal system advances individual liberty in many ways. Among other things, it limits the powers of the Federal Government and protects certain basic liberties from infringement. But because the powers of the Federal Government and the States often overlap, allowing both to regulate often results in two layers of regulation. Taxation is an example that comes immediately to mind. It is also not at all uncommon for the Federal Government to permit activities that a State chooses to forbid or heavily restrict—for example, gambling and the sale of alcohol. And a State may choose to legalize an activity that federal law prohibits, such as the sale of marijuana. So while our system of federalism is fundamental to the protection of liberty, it does not always maximize individual liberty at the expense of other interests. And it is thus quite extraordinary to say that the venerable dual-sovereignty doctrine represents a " 'desecrat[ion]' " of federalism. (opinion of GORSUCH, J.).

III

Gamble claims that our precedent contradicts the common-law rights that the Double Jeopardy Clause was originally understood to engraft onto the Constitution—rights stemming from the "common-law pleas of *auterfoits acquit* [former acquittal] and *auterfoits convict* [former conviction]." These pleas were treated as "reason[s] why the prisoner ought not to answer [an indictment] at all, nor put himself upon his trial for the crime alleged." 4 W. Blackstone, Commentaries on the Laws of England 335 (1773). Gamble argues that those who ratified the Fifth Amendment understood these common-law principles (which the Amendment constitutionalized) to bar a domestic prosecution following one by a foreign nation. For support, he appeals to early English and American cases and treatises. We have highlighted one hurdle to Gamble's reading: the sovereign-specific original meaning of "offence." But the doctrine of *stare decisis* is another obstacle.

Stare decisis "promotes the evenhanded, predictable, and consistent development of legal principles, fosters reliance on judicial decisions, and contributes to the actual and perceived integrity of the judicial process." Of course, it is also important to be right, especially on constitutional matters, where Congress cannot override our errors by ordinary legislation. But even in constitutional cases, a departure from precedent "demands special justification." This means that something more than "ambiguous historical evidence" is required before we will "flatly overrule a number of major decisions of this Court." And the strength of the case for adhering to such decisions grows in proportion to their "antiquity." Here, as noted, Gamble's historical arguments must overcome *numerous* "major decisions of this Court" spanning *170 years*. In light of these factors, Gamble's historical evidence must, at a minimum, be better than middling.

And it is not. The English cases are a muddle. Treatises offer spotty support. And early state and federal cases are by turns equivocal and downright harmful to Gamble's position. All told, this evidence does not establish that those who ratified the Fifth Amendment took it to bar successive prosecutions under different sovereigns' laws—much less do so with enough force to break a chain of precedent linking dozens of cases over 170 years. * * *

IV

Besides appealing to the remote past, Gamble contends that recent changes— one doctrinal, one practical—blunt the force of *stare decisis* here. They do not.

A

If historical claims form the chorus of Gamble's argument, his refrain is "incorporation." In Gamble's telling, the recognition of the Double Jeopardy Clause's incorporation against the States washed away any theoretical foundation for the dual-sovereignty rule. But this incorporation-changes-everything argument trades on a false analogy.

The analogy Gamble draws is to the evolution of our doctrine on the Fourth Amendment right against unreasonable searches and seizures.[16] We have long enforced this right by barring courts from relying on evidence gathered in an illegal search. Thus, in *Weeks v. United States*, 232 U.S. 383 (1914), the Court held that federal prosecutors could not rely on the fruits of an unreasonable search undertaken by federal agents. But what if state or local police conducted a search that would have violated the Fourth Amendment if conducted by federal agents? Before incorporation, the state search would not have violated the Federal Constitution, so federal law would not have barred admission of the resulting evidence in a state prosecution. But by the very same token, under what was termed "the silver-platter doctrine," state authorities could hand such evidence over to *federal* prosecutors for use in a federal case.

Once the Fourth Amendment was held to apply to the States as well as the Federal Government, however, the silver-platter doctrine was scuttled. Now the

---

[16] He draws a similar analogy to the Fifth Amendment right against self-incrimination, but our response to his Fourth Amendment analogy would answer that argument as well.

fruits of unreasonable state searches are inadmissible in federal and state courts alike.

Gamble contends that the incorporation of the Double Jeopardy Clause should likewise end the dual-sovereignty rule, but his analogy fails. The silver-platter doctrine was based on the fact that the state searches to which it applied did not at that time violate federal law. Once the Fourth Amendment was incorporated against the States, the status of those state searches changed. Now they did violate federal law, so the basis for the silver-platter doctrine was gone. See *Elkins*, 364 U.S. at 213 ("The foundation upon which the admissibility of state-seized evidence in a federal trial originally rested—that unreasonable state searches did not violate the Federal Constitution—thus disappeared [with incorporation]").

By contrast, the premises of the dual-sovereignty doctrine have survived incorporation intact. Incorporation meant that the States were now required to abide by this Court's interpretation of the Double Jeopardy Clause. But that interpretation has long included the dual-sovereignty doctrine, and there is no logical reason why incorporation should change it. After all, the doctrine rests on the fact that only same-sovereign successive prosecutions are prosecutions for the "same offense," see Part II, *supra*—and that is just as true after incorporation as before.

B

If incorporation is the doctrinal shift that Gamble invokes to justify a departure from precedent, the practical change he cites is the proliferation of federal criminal law. Gamble says that the resulting overlap of federal and criminal codes heightens the risk of successive prosecutions under state and federal law for the same criminal conduct. Thus, Gamble contends, our precedent should yield to " 'far-reaching systemic and structural changes' " that make our "earlier error all the more egregious and harmful." But unlike Gamble's appeal to incorporation, this argument obviously assumes that the dual-sovereignty doctrine was legal error from the start. So the argument is only as strong as Gamble's argument about the original understanding of double jeopardy rights, an argument that we have found wanting.

Insofar as the expansion of the reach of federal criminal law has been questioned on constitutional rather than policy grounds, the argument has focused on whether Congress has overstepped its legislative powers under the Constitution. Eliminating the dual-sovereignty rule would do little to trim the reach of federal criminal law, and it would not even prevent many successive state and federal prosecutions for the same criminal conduct unless we also overruled the long-settled rule that an "offence" for double jeopardy purposes is defined by statutory elements, not by what might be described in a looser sense as a unit of criminal conduct. See *Blockburger*. Perhaps believing that two revolutionary assaults in the same case would be too much, Gamble has not asked us to overrule *Blockburger* along with the dual-sovereignty rule. * * *

The judgment of the Court of Appeals for the Eleventh Circuit is affirmed.

It is so ordered.

JUSTICE THOMAS, concurring.

I agree that the historical record does not bear out my initial skepticism of the dual-sovereignty doctrine. See *Puerto Rico v. Sánchez Valle* (GINSBURG, J., joined by THOMAS, J. concurring). The founding generation foresaw very limited potential for overlapping criminal prosecutions by the States and the Federal Government.[1] The Founders therefore had no reason to address the double jeopardy question that the Court resolves today. Given their understanding of Congress' limited criminal jurisdiction and the absence of an analogous dual-sovereign system in England, it is difficult to conclude that the People who ratified the Fifth Amendment understood it to prohibit prosecution by a State and the Federal Government for the same offense. And, of course, we are not entitled to interpret the Constitution to align it with our personal sensibilities about " 'unjust' " prosecutions. * * *

I write separately to address the proper role of the doctrine of *stare decisis*. In my view, the Court's typical formulation of the *stare decisis* standard does not comport with our judicial duty under Article III because it elevates demonstrably erroneous decisions—meaning decisions outside the realm of permissible interpretation—over the text of the Constitution and other duly enacted federal law. It is always "tempting for judges to confuse our own preferences with the requirements of the law," *Obergefell v. Hodges*, 135 S.Ct. 2584, 2612 (2015) (ROBERTS, C.J., dissenting), and the Court's *stare decisis* doctrine exacerbates that temptation by giving the veneer of respectability to our continued application of demonstrably incorrect precedents. By applying demonstrably erroneous precedent instead of the relevant law's text—as the Court is particularly prone to do when expanding federal power or crafting new individual rights—the Court exercises "force" and "will," two attributes the People did not give it. The Federalist No. 78.

We should restore our *stare decisis* jurisprudence to ensure that we exercise "mer[e] judgment," *ibid.*, which can be achieved through adherence to the correct, original meaning of the laws we are charged with applying. In my view, anything less invites arbitrariness into judging.

The Court currently views *stare decisis* as a " 'principle of policy' " that balances several factors to decide whether the scales tip in favor of overruling precedent. Among these factors are the "workability" of the standard, "the antiquity of the precedent, the reliance interests at stake, and of course whether the decision was well reasoned." The influence of this last factor tends to ebb and flow with the Court's desire to achieve a particular end, and the Court may cite additional, ad hoc factors to reinforce the result it chooses. But the shared theme

---

[1] As the Court suggests, Congress is responsible for the proliferation of duplicative prosecutions for the same offenses by the States and the Federal Government. By legislating beyond its limited powers, Congress has taken from the People authority that they never gave. U.S. Const., Art. I, § 8; The Federalist No. 22. And the Court has been complicit by blessing this questionable expansion of the Commerce Clause. See, *e.g.*, *Gonzales v. Raich*, 545 U.S. 1, 57–74 (2005) (THOMAS, J., dissenting). Indeed, it seems possible that much of Title 18, among other parts of the U.S. Code, is premised on the Court's incorrect interpretation of the Commerce Clause and is thus an incursion into the States' general criminal jurisdiction and an imposition on the People's liberty.

is the need for a "special reason over and above the belief that a prior case was wrongly decided" to overrule a precedent. The Court has advanced this view of *stare decisis* on the ground that "it promotes the evenhanded, predictable, and consistent development of legal principles" and "contributes to the actual and perceived integrity of the judicial process."

This approach to *stare decisis* might have made sense in a common-law legal system in which courts systematically developed the law through judicial decisions apart from written law. But our federal system is different. The Constitution tasks the political branches—not the Judiciary—with systematically developing the laws that govern our society. The Court's role, by contrast, is to exercise the "judicial Power," faithfully interpreting the Constitution and the laws enacted by those branches. Art. III, § 1.

* * *

Given that the primary role of federal courts today is to interpret legal texts with ascertainable meanings, precedent plays a different role in our exercise of the "judicial Power" than it did at common law. In my view, if the Court encounters a decision that is demonstrably erroneous—*i.e.*, one that is not a permissible interpretation of the text—the Court should correct the error, regardless of whether other factors support overruling the precedent. Federal courts may (but need not) adhere to an incorrect decision as precedent, but only when traditional tools of legal interpretation show that the earlier decision adopted a textually permissible interpretation of the law. A demonstrably incorrect judicial decision, by contrast, is tantamount to *making* law, and adhering to it both disregards the supremacy of the Constitution and perpetuates a usurpation of the legislative power.

When faced with a demonstrably erroneous precedent, my rule is simple: We should not follow it. * * * I am aware of no legitimate reason why a court may privilege a demonstrably erroneous interpretation of the Constitution over the Constitution itself. * * *

* * * Written laws "have a range of indeterminacy," and reasonable people may therefore arrive at different conclusions about the original meaning of a legal text after employing all relevant tools of interpretation. It is within that range of permissible interpretations that precedent is relevant. * * * The original meaning of legal texts "usually . . . is easy to discern and simple to apply." A. Scalia, Common Law Courts in a Civil-Law System, in A Matter of Interpretation: Federal Courts and the Law 45 (A. Gutmann ed. 1997). And even in difficult cases, that the original meaning is not obvious at first blush does not excuse the Court from diligently pursuing that meaning. * * * [A] legal text is not capable of multiple permissible interpretations merely because discerning its original meaning "requires a taxing inquiry."

This case is a good example. The historical record presents knotty issues about the original meaning of the Fifth Amendment, and Justice GORSUCH does an admirable job arguing against our longstanding interpretation of the Double Jeopardy Clause. Although Justice GORSUCH identifies support for his view in several postratification treatises, I do not find these treatises conclusive without a stronger showing that they reflected the understanding of the Fifth Amendment at the time of ratification. At that time, the common law certainly had not coalesced around this view, and petitioner has not pointed to contemporaneous judicial opinions or other evidence establishing that his view was widely shared. This lack of evidence, coupled with the unique two-sovereign federalist system created by our Constitution, leaves petitioner to rely on a general argument about "liberty." * * * Ultimately, I am not persuaded that our precedent is incorrect as an original matter, much less demonstrably erroneous.

         * * *

Our judicial duty to interpret the law requires adherence to the original meaning of the text. For that reason, we should not invoke *stare decisis* to uphold precedents that are demonstrably erroneous. Because petitioner and the dissenting opinions have not shown that the Court's dual-sovereignty doctrine is incorrect, much less demonstrably erroneous, I concur in the majority's opinion.

JUSTICE GINSBURG, dissenting.

Terance Martez Gamble pleaded guilty in Alabama state court to both possession of a firearm by a person convicted of "a crime of violence" and drug possession, and was sentenced to ten years' imprisonment, all but one year suspended. Apparently regarding Alabama's sentence as too lenient, federal prosecutors pursued a parallel charge, possession of a firearm by a convicted felon, in violation of federal law. Gamble again pleaded guilty and received nearly three more years in prison.

Had either the Federal Government or Alabama brought the successive prosecutions, the second would have violated Gamble's right not to be "twice put in jeopardy . . . for the same offence." Yet the Federal Government was able to multiply Gamble's time in prison because of the doctrine that, for double jeopardy purposes, identical criminal laws enacted by "separate sovereigns" are different "offence[s]."

I dissent from the Court's adherence to that misguided doctrine. Instead of "fritter[ing] away [Gamble's] libert[y] upon a metaphysical subtlety, two sovereignties," I would hold that the Double Jeopardy Clause bars "successive prosecutions [for the same offense] by parts of the whole USA." *Puerto Rico v. Sánchez Valle* (GINSBURG, J., concurring).

I

* * * The notion that the Federal Government and the States are separate sovereigns overlooks a basic tenet of our federal system. The doctrine treats *governments* as sovereign, with state power to prosecute carried over from years predating the Constitution. In the system established by the Federal Constitution, however, "ultimate sovereignty" resides in the *governed*. Insofar as a crime offends the "peace and dignity" of a sovereign, that "sovereign" is the people, the "original fountain of all legitimate authority," The Federalist No. 22. States may be separate, but their populations are part of the people composing the United States.

In our "compound republic," the division of authority between the United States and the States was meant to operate as "a double security [for] the rights of the people." The Federalist No. 51. The separate-sovereigns doctrine, however, scarcely shores up people's rights. Instead, it invokes federalism to withhold liberty.[1]

It is the doctrine's premise that each government has—and must be allowed to vindicate—a distinct interest in enforcing its own criminal laws. That is a peculiar way to look at the Double Jeopardy Clause, which by its terms safeguards the "person" and restrains the government. * * * "Looked at from the standpoint of the individual who is being prosecuted," the liberty-denying potential of successive prosecutions, when Federal and State Governments prosecute in tandem, is the same as it is when either prosecutes twice.

* * * In adopting and reaffirming the separate-sovereigns doctrine, the Court relied on dicta from 19th-century opinions. The persuasive force of those opinions is diminished by their dubious reasoning. While drawing upon dicta from prior opinions, the Court gave short shrift to contrary authority.

First, the Framers of the Bill of Rights voted down an amendment that would have permitted the Federal Government to reprosecute a defendant initially tried by a State. Nevermind that this amendment failed; the Court has attributed to the Clause the very meaning the First Congress refrained from adopting.[2]

Second, early American courts regarded with disfavor the prospect of successive prosecutions by the Federal and State Governments.* * * Most of the early state decisions cited by the parties regarded successive federal-state prosecutions as unacceptable. Only one court roundly endorsed a separate-sovereigns theory. The Court reads the state-court opinions as "distin[guishing] between believing successive prosecutions by separate sovereigns unjust and holding them unlawful." I would not read the Double Jeopardy Clause to tolerate "unjust" prosecutions and believe early American courts would have questioned the Court's distinction.

Finally, the Court has reasoned that the separate-sovereigns doctrine is necessary to prevent either the Federal Government or a State from encroaching on the other's law enforcement prerogatives. Without this doctrine, the Court has observed, the Federal Government, by prosecuting first, could bar a State from pursuing more serious charges for the same offense, and conversely, a State, by prosecuting first, could effectively nullify federal law. This concern envisions federal and state prosecutors working at cross purposes, but cooperation between authorities is the norm. And when federal-state tension exists, successive prosecutions for the federal and state offenses may escape double-jeopardy

---

[1]   The Court writes that federalism "advances individual liberty in many ways," but does not always do so. The analogy of the separate-sovereigns doctrine to dual regulation is inapt. The former erodes a constitutional safeguard against successive prosecutions, while the Constitution contains no guarantee against dual regulation.

[2]   The Court sees this history as poor evidence of congressional intent. On another day, the Court looked to the First Congress' rejection of proposed amendments as instructive. Moreover, a "compelling" principle of statutory interpretation is "the proposition that Congress does not intend *sub silentio* to enact statutory language that it has earlier discarded in favor of other language."

blockage under the test prescribed in *Blockburger*. Offenses are distinct, *Blockburger* held, if "each . . . requires proof of a fact which the other does not."

II

The separate-sovereigns doctrine, I acknowledge, has been embraced repeatedly by the Court. But "*[s]tare decisis* is not an inexorable command." Our adherence to precedent is weakest in cases "concerning procedural rules that implicate fundamental constitutional protections." Gamble's case fits that bill. I would lay the "separate-sovereigns" rationale to rest for the aforesaid reasons and those stated below.

A

* * * Before incorporation, the separate-sovereigns doctrine had a certain logic: Without a carve-out for successive prosecutions by separate sovereigns, the Double Jeopardy Clause would have barred the Federal Government from prosecuting a defendant previously tried by a State, but would not have prevented a State from prosecuting a defendant previously tried by the Federal Government. Incorporation changed this. Operative against the States since 1969, when the Court decided *Benton v. Maryland*, the double jeopardy proscription now applies to the Federal Government and the States alike. The remaining office of the separate-sovereigns doctrine, then, is to enable federal and state prosecutors, proceeding one after the other, to expose defendants to double jeopardy.

The separate-sovereigns doctrine's persistence contrasts with the fate of analogous dual-sovereignty doctrines following application of the rights at issue to the States. Prior to incorporation of the Fourth Amendment as a restraint on state action, federal prosecutors were free to use evidence obtained illegally by state or local officers, then served up to federal officers on a "silver platter." Once the Fourth Amendment applied to the States, abandonment of this "silver platter doctrine" was impelled by "principles of logic" and the reality that, from the perspective of the victim of an unreasonable search and seizure, it mattered not at all "whether his constitutional right ha[d] been invaded by a federal agent or by a state officer. As observed by Justice Harlan, *Elkins'* abandonment of a separate-sovereigns exception to the exclusionary rule was at odds with retention of the separate-sovereigns doctrine for double jeopardy purposes in *Abbate* and *Bartkus*.

Similarly, before incorporation of the Fifth Amendment privilege against self-incrimination, the Court held that the privilege did not prevent state authorities from compelling a defendant to provide testimony that could incriminate him or her in another jurisdiction. After application of the self-incrimination privilege to the States, the Court concluded that its prior position was incompatible with the "policies and purposes" of the privilege. No longer, the Court held, could a witness "be whipsawed into incriminating himself under both state and federal law *even though the constitutional privilege against self-incrimination is applicable to each.*"

The Court regards incorporation as immaterial because application of the Double Jeopardy Clause to the States did not affect comprehension of the word "offence" to mean the violation of one sovereign's law. But the Court attributed a separate-sovereigns meaning to "offence" at least in part because the Double

Jeopardy Clause did not apply to the States. Incorporation of the Clause should prompt the Court to consider the protection against double jeopardy from the defendant's perspective and to ask why each of two governments within the United States should be permitted to try a defendant once for the same offense when neither could try him or her twice.

B

The expansion of federal criminal law has exacerbated the problems created by the separate-sovereigns doctrine. Ill effects of the doctrine might once have been tempered by the limited overlap between federal and state criminal law. In the last half century, however, federal criminal law has been extended pervasively into areas once left to the States. This new "age of 'cooperative federalism,' [in which] the Federal and State Governments are waging a united front against many types of criminal activity," provides new opportunities for federal and state prosecutors to "join together to take a second bite at the apple." This situation might be less troublesome if successive prosecutions occurred only in "instances of peculiar enormity, or where the public safety demanded extraordinary rigor." The run-of-the-mill felon-in-possession charges Gamble encountered indicate that, in practice, successive prosecutions are not limited to exceptional circumstances.

C

Against all this, there is little to be said for keeping the separate-sovereigns doctrine. Gamble's case "do[es] not implicate the reliance interests of private parties." The closest thing to a reliance interest would be the interest Federal and State Governments have in avoiding avulsive changes that could complicate ongoing prosecutions. As the Court correctly explains, however, overruling the separate-sovereigns doctrine would not affect large numbers of cases. In prosecutions based on the same conduct, federal and state prosecutors will often charge offenses having different elements, charges that, under *Blockburger*, will not trigger double jeopardy protection.

Notably, the Federal Government has endeavored to reduce the incidence of "same offense" prosecutions. Under the *Petite* policy adopted by the Department of Justice,[5] the Department will pursue a federal prosecution "based on substantially the same act(s) or transaction(s)" previously prosecuted in state court only if the first prosecution left a "substantial federal interest . . . demonstrably unvindicated" and a Department senior official authorizes the prosecution.

At oral argument, the Government estimated that it authorizes only "about a hundred" *Petite* prosecutions per year. Some of these prosecutions will not implicate double jeopardy, as the *Petite* policy uses a same-conduct test that is broader than the *Blockburger* same-elements test. And more than half the States forbid successive prosecutions for all or some offenses previously resolved on the merits by a federal or state court. In short, it is safe to predict that eliminating the separate-sovereigns doctrine would spark no large disruption in practice.

---

[5]   Formally the "Dual and Successive Prosecution Policy," the policy is popularly known by the name of the case in which this Court first took note of it, *Petite* v. *United States*, 361 U.S. 529 (1960) (*per curiam*). The policy was adopted "in direct response to" *Bartkus* and *Abbate*.

* * *

The separate-sovereigns doctrine, especially since *Bartkus* and *Abbate*, has been subject to relentless criticism by members of the bench, bar, and academy. Nevertheless, the Court reaffirms the doctrine, thereby diminishing the individual rights shielded by the Double Jeopardy Clause. Different parts of the "WHOLE" United States should not be positioned to prosecute a defendant a second time for the same offense. I would reverse Gamble's federal conviction.

JUSTICE GORSUCH, dissenting.

A free society does not allow its government to try the same individual for the same crime until it's happy with the result. Unfortunately, the Court today endorses a colossal exception to this ancient rule against double jeopardy. My colleagues say that the federal government and each State are "separate sovereigns" entitled to try the same person for the same crime. So if all the might of one "sovereign" cannot succeed against the presumptively free individual, another may insist on the chance to try again. And if both manage to succeed, so much the better; they can add one punishment on top of the other. But this "separate sovereigns exception" to the bar against double jeopardy finds no meaningful support in the text of the Constitution, its original public meaning, structure, or history. Instead, the Constitution promises all Americans that they will never suffer double jeopardy. I would enforce that guarantee.

I

"Fear and abhorrence of governmental power to try people twice for the same conduct is one of the oldest ideas found in western civilization." Throughout history, people have worried about the vast disparity of power between governments and individuals, the capacity of the state to bring charges repeatedly until it wins the result it wants, and what little would be left of human liberty if that power remained unchecked. To address the problem, the law in ancient Athens held that "[a] man could not be tried twice for the same offense." The Roman Republic and Empire incorporated a form of double jeopardy protection in their laws. The Old Testament and later church teachings endorsed the bar against double jeopardy too. And from the earliest days of the common law, courts recognized that to "punish a man twice over for one offence" would be deeply unjust.

The rule against double jeopardy was firmly entrenched in both the American colonies and England at the time of our Revolution. And the Fifth Amendment, which prohibits placing a defendant "twice . . . in jeopardy of life or limb" for "the same offence" sought to carry the traditional common law rule into our Constitution. * * *

Given all this, it might seem that Mr. Gamble should win this case handily. Alabama prosecuted him for violating a state law that "prohibits a convicted felon from possessing a pistol" and sentenced him to a year in prison. But then the federal government, apparently displeased with the sentence, charged Mr. Gamble * * * with being a felon in possession of a firearm based on the same facts that gave rise to the state prosecution. * * * Most any ordinary speaker of English would say that Mr. Gamble was tried twice for "the same offence," precisely what the Fifth

Amendment prohibits. Tellingly, no one before us doubts that if either the federal government or Alabama had prosecuted Mr. Gamble twice on these facts and in this manner, it surely would have violated the Constitution.

* * * the Court supplies the following syllogism: "[A]n 'offence' is defined by a law, and each law is defined by a sovereign. So where there are two sovereigns, there are two laws, and two 'offences.' "

But the major premise of this argument—that "where there are two laws there are 'two offenses' "—is mistaken. We know that the Constitution is not so easily evaded and that two statutes *can* punish the same offense. The framers understood the term "offence" to mean a "transgression." And they understood that the same transgression might be punished by two pieces of positive law: After all, constitutional protections were not meant to be flimsy things but to embody "principles that are permanent, uniform, and universal." As this Court explained long ago in *Blockburger*, "where the same act or transaction constitutes a violation of two distinct statutory provisions, the test to be applied to determine whether there are two offenses or only one, is whether each provision requires proof of a fact which the other does not." So if two laws demand proof of the same facts to secure a conviction, they constitute a single offense under our Constitution and a second trial is forbidden. And by everyone's admission, that is exactly what we have here: The statute under which the federal government proceeded required it to prove no facts beyond those Alabama needed to prove under state law to win its conviction; the two prosecutions *were* for the same offense.

That leaves the government and the Court to rest on the fact that distinct governmental entities, federal and state, enacted these identical laws. This, we are told, is enough to transform what everyone agrees would otherwise be the same offense into two different offenses. But where is *that* distinction to be found in the Constitution's text or original public understanding? We know that the framers didn't conceive of the term "same offence" in some technical way as referring only to the same statute. And if double jeopardy prevents *one* government from prosecuting a defendant multiple times for the same offense under the banner of separate statutory labels, on what account can it make a difference when *many* governments collectively seek to do the same thing?

The government identifies no evidence suggesting that the framers understood the term "same offence" to bear such a lawyerly sovereign-specific meaning. * * * In 1786, a congressional committee endorsed federal control over import duties because otherwise "thirteen separate authorities" might "ordain various penalties for the same offence." In 1778, the Continental Congress passed a resolution declaring that a person should not be tried in state court "for the same offense, for which he had previous thereto been tried by a Court Martial." And in 1785, the Continental Congress considered an ordinance declaring that a defendant could "plead a formal Acquital on a Trial" in a maritime court "for the same supposed Offences, in a similar Court in one of the other United States." In all of these examples, early legislators—including many of the same people who would vote to add the Fifth Amendment to the Bill of Rights just a few years later—

recognized that transgressions of state and federal law could constitute the "same offence."

The history of the Double Jeopardy Clause itself supplies more evidence yet. The original draft prohibited "more than one trial or one punishment for the same offence." One representative then proposed adding the words "by any law of the United States" after "same offence." That proposal clearly would have codified the government's sovereign-specific view of the Clause's operation. Yet, Congress proceeded to reject it.

Viewed from the perspective of an ordinary reader of the Fifth Amendment, whether at the time of its adoption or in our own time, none of this can come as a surprise. Imagine trying to explain the Court's separate sovereigns rule to a criminal defendant, then or now. Yes, you were sentenced to state prison for being a felon in possession of a firearm. And don't worry—the State can't prosecute you again. But a federal prosecutor *can* send you to prison again for exactly the same thing. What's more, that federal prosecutor may work hand-in-hand with the same state prosecutor who already went after you. They can share evidence and discuss what worked and what didn't the first time around. And the federal prosecutor can pursue you even if you were *acquitted* in the state case. None of that offends the Constitution's plain words protecting a person from being placed "twice . . . in jeopardy of life or limb" for "the same offence." Really?

II

* * * The Court seems to assume that sovereignty in this country belongs to the state and federal governments, much as it once belonged to the King of England. But as Chief Justice Marshall explained, "[t]he government of the Union . . . is emphatically, and truly, a government of the people," and all sovereignty "emanates from them." Alexander Hamilton put the point this way: "[T]he national and State systems are to be regarded" not as different sovereigns foreign to one another but "as ONE WHOLE." Under our Constitution, the federal and state governments are but two expressions of a single and sovereign people.

This principle resonates throughout our history and law. State courts that refused to entertain federal causes of action found little sympathy when attempting the very separate sovereigns theory underlying today's decision. In time, too, it became clear that federal courts may decide state-law issues, and state courts may decide federal questions. Even in the criminal context, this Court has upheld removal of some state criminal actions to federal court. And any remaining doubt about whether the States and the federal government are truly separate sovereigns was ultimately "resolved by war."

From its mistaken premise, the Court continues to the flawed conclusion that the federal and state governments can successively prosecute the same person for the same offense. This turns the point of our federal experiment on its head. When the "ONE WHOLE" people of the United States assigned different aspects of their sovereign power to the federal and state governments, they sought not to *multiply* governmental power but to *limit* it. As this Court has explained, "[b]y denying any one government complete jurisdiction over all the concerns of public life, federalism protects the liberty of the individual from arbitrary power." Yet today's Court invokes federalism not to protect individual liberty but to threaten it, allowing two governments to achieve together an objective denied to each. * * * [t]he Court's examples—taxation, alcohol, and marijuana—involve areas that the federal and state governments each may regulate separately under the Constitution as interpreted by this Court. That is miles away from the separate sovereigns exception, which allows the federal and state governments to accomplish together what *neither* may do separately consistent with the Constitution's commands. As Justice Black understood, the Court's view today "misuse[s] and desecrat[es] . . . the concept" of federalism. For "it is just as much an affront to . . . human freedom for a man to be punished twice for the same offense" by two parts of the people's government "as it would be for one . . . to throw him in prison twice for the offense."

III

* * * 1791 when the Fifth Amendment was adopted, an array of common law authorities suggested that a prosecution in *any* court, so long as the court had jurisdiction over the offense, was enough to bar future reprosecution in another court. * * * Unable to summon any useful preratification common law sources of its own, the government is left to nitpick those that undermine its position. * * * What we know about the common law before the Fifth Amendment's ratification in 1791 finds further confirmation in how later legal thinkers in both England and America described the rule they had inherited.* * * This Court's early decisions reflected the same principle. * * * A number of early state cases followed the same rule. * * *

In the face of so much contrary authority, * * * the principal support the Court cites for its position is a state case that both (1) regarded transgressions of the laws of a State and a U.S. territory as the "same offence," and (2) expressed aversion at the thought of both jurisdictions punishing the defendant for that singular offense.

IV

With the text, principles of federalism, and history now arrayed against it, the government is left to suggest that we should retain the separate sovereigns exception under the doctrine of *stare decisis*. But if that's the real basis for today's result, let's at least acknowledge this: By all appearances, the Constitution as originally adopted and understood did *not* allow successive state and federal prosecutions for the same offense, yet the government wants this Court to tolerate the practice anyway.

Stare decisis has many virtues, but when it comes to enforcing the Constitution this Court must take (and always has taken) special care in the doctrine's application. After all, judges swear to protect and defend the Constitution, not to protect what it prohibits. And while we rightly pay heed to the considered views of those who have come before us, especially in close cases, *stare decisis* isn't supposed to be "the art of being methodically ignorant of what everyone knows." Indeed, blind obedience to *stare decisis* would leave this Court still abiding grotesque errors like *Dred Scott v. Sandford*, *Plessy v. Ferguson*, and *Korematsu v. United States*. As Justice Brandeis explained, "in cases involving the Federal Constitution, where correction through legislative action is practically impossible, this Court has often overruled its earlier decisions. The Court bows to the lessons of experience and the force of better reasoning, recognizing that the process of trial and error, so fruitful in the physical sciences, is appropriate also in the judicial function."

* * * In deciding whether one of our cases should be retained or overruled, this Court has traditionally considered "the quality of the decision's reasoning; its consistency with related decisions; legal developments since the decision; and reliance on the decision." Each of these factors, I believe, suggests we should reject the separate sovereigns exception.

Take the "quality of [the] reasoning." The first cases to suggest that successive prosecutions by state and federal authorities might be permissible did not seek to address the original meaning of the word "offence," the troubling federalism implications of the exception, or the relevant historical sources. * * *

Perhaps the first real roots of the separate sovereigns exception can be traced to this Court's 1852 decision in *Moore* v. *Illinois*. As it did five years later and more notoriously in *Dred Scott*, the Court in *Moore* did violence to the Constitution in the name of protecting slavery and slaveowners. In *Dred Scott* the Court held that the Due Process Clause prevented Congress from prohibiting slavery in the territories, though of course the Clause did nothing of the sort. And in *Moore* the Court upheld a state fugitive slave law that it judged important because the States supposedly needed "to protect themselves against the influx either of liberated or fugitive slaves, and to repel from their soil a population likely to become burdensome and injurious, either as paupers or criminals." The defendant, who had harbored a fugitive slave, objected that upholding the state law could potentially expose him to double prosecutions by the state and federal governments. The Court rejected that argument, reasoning simply that such double punishment could be consistent with the Constitution if the defendant had violated both state and federal law. Yet notably, even here, the Court did not actually approve a successive prosecution.

Nor did the trajectory of the separate sovereigns exception improve much from there. The first time the Court actually approved an "instance of double prosecution [and] failed to find some remedy . . . to avoid it" didn't arrive until 1922. In that case, *United States v. Lanza*, the federal government prosecuted the defendants for manufacturing, transporting, and possessing alcohol in violation of the National Prohibition Act. The defendants argued that they had already been prosecuted by the State of Washington for the same offense. But, notably, the defendants did not directly question the permissibility of successive prosecutions for the same offense under state and federal law. Instead, the defendants argued that both of the laws under which they were punished really derived from the "same sovereign:" the national government, by way of the Eighteenth Amendment that authorized Prohibition. After rejecting that argument as an "erroneous view of the matter," the Court proceeded on, perhaps unnecessarily, to offer its view that "an act denounced as a crime by both national and state sovereignties is an offense against the peace and dignity of both and may be punished by each." Given that the Court was not asked directly to consider the propriety of successive prosecutions under separate state and federal laws for the same offense, it is perhaps unsurprising the Court did not consult the original meaning of the Double Jeopardy Clause or consult virtually any of the relevant historical sources before offering its dictum.

It matters, too, that these cases "were decided by the narrowest of margins, over spirited dissents challenging the basic underpinnings of those decisions." In *Moore*, Justice McLean wrote that although "the Federal and State Governments emanate from different sovereignties," they "operate upon the same people, and should have the same end in view." He "deeply regret[ted] that our government should be an exception to a great principle of action, sanctioned by humanity and justice." *Bartkus* and *Abbate*, cases decided in the 1950s that more clearly approved the separate sovereigns exception, were decided only by 5-to-4 and 6-to-3 margins, and Justice Black's eloquent dissents in those cases have triggered an avalanche of persuasive academic support.

What is more, the "underpinnings" of the separate sovereigns exception have been "erode[d] by subsequent decisions of this Court." When this Court decided *Moore, Lanza, Bartkus*, and *Abbate*, the Double Jeopardy Clause applied only to the *federal* government under this Court's decision in *Palko v. Connecticut*. In those days, one might have thought, the separate sovereigns exception at least served to level the playing field between the federal government and the States: If a State could retry a defendant after a federal trial, then the federal government ought to be able to retry a defendant after a state trial. But in time the Court overruled *Palko* and held that the Double Jeopardy Clause *does* apply to the States—and, with that, a premise once thought important to the exception fell away.

Nor has only the law changed; the world has too. And when "far-reaching systemic and structural changes" make an "earlier error all the more egregious and harmful," *stare decisis* can lose its force. In the era when the separate sovereigns exception first emerged, the federal criminal code was new, thin, modest, and restrained. Today, it can make none of those of boasts. Some suggest that "the federal government has [now] duplicated virtually every major state crime." Others estimate that the U.S. Code contains more than 4,500 criminal statutes, not even counting the hundreds of thousands of federal regulations that can trigger criminal penalties. If long ago the Court could have thought "the benignant spirit" of prosecutors rather than unwavering enforcement of the Constitution sufficient protection against the threat of double prosecutions, it's unclear how we still might.

That leaves reliance. But the only people who have relied on the separate sovereigns exception are prosecutors who have sought to double-prosecute and double-punish. And this Court has long rejected the idea that "law enforcement reliance interests outweig[h] the interest in protecting individual constitutional rights so as to warrant fidelity to an unjustifiable rule." Instead, "[i]f it is clear that a practice is unlawful, individuals' interest in its discontinuance clearly outweighs any law enforcement 'entitlement' to its persistence." That is the case here.

The Court today disregards these lessons. It worries that overturning the separate sovereigns rule could undermine the reliance interests of prosecutors in transnational cases who might be prohibited from trying individuals already acquitted by a foreign court. Yet even on its own terms, this argument is unpersuasive. The government has not even attempted to quantify the scope of the alleged "problem," and perhaps for good reason. Domestic prosecutors regularly coordinate with their foreign counterparts when pursuing transnational criminals, so they can often choose the most favorable forum for their mutual efforts. And because *Blockburger* requires an identity of elements before the double jeopardy bar can take hold, domestic prosecutors, armed with their own abundant criminal codes, will often be able to find new offenses to charge if they are unsatisfied with outcomes elsewhere.

* * *

Enforcing the Constitution always bears its costs. But when the people adopted the Constitution and its Bill of Rights, they thought the liberties promised there worth the costs. It is not for this Court to reassess this judgment to make the prosecutor's job easier. Nor is there any doubt that the benefits the framers saw in prohibiting double prosecutions remain real, and maybe more vital than ever, today. When governments may unleash all their might in multiple prosecutions against an individual, exhausting themselves only when those who hold the reins of power are content with the result, it is "the poor and the weak," and the unpopular and controversial, who suffer first—and there is nothing to stop them from being the last. The separate sovereigns exception was wrong when it was invented, and it remains wrong today.

I respectfully dissent.

HUDSON V. UNITED STATES
522 U.S. 93, 118 S.Ct. 488, 139 L.Ed.2d 450 (1997).

CHIEF JUSTICE REHNQUIST delivered the opinion of the Court.

[Upon examination of two banks, the Office of the Comptroller of the Currency concluded several bank officers had used their positions to arrange loans to third parties in violation of federal banking statutes and regulations. The OCC took action to assess penalties against the bank officers, resulting in a consent order by which they would pay assessments of $16,500, $15,000, and $12,500, respectively, and agree not to "participate in any manner" in the affairs of any bank without OCC authorization. A few years later, they were indicted on several criminal charges because of the same lending transactions; the district court dismissed the charges on double jeopardy grounds; the court of appeals reversed.]

The Double Jeopardy Clause provides that no "person [shall] be subject for the same offence to be twice put in jeopardy of life or limb." We have long recognized that the Double Jeopardy Clause does not prohibit the imposition of any additional sanction that could, " 'in common parlance,' " be described as punishment. The Clause protects only against the imposition of multiple criminal punishments for the same offense, and then only when such occurs in successive proceedings.

Whether a particular punishment is criminal or civil is, at least initially, a matter of statutory construction. A court must first ask whether the legislature, "in establishing the penalizing mechanism, indicated either expressly or impliedly a preference for one label or the other." *United States v. Ward,* 448 U.S. 242 (1980). Even in those cases where the legislature "has indicated an intention to establish a civil penalty, we have inquired further whether the statutory scheme was so punitive either in purpose or effect, as to" transfor[m] what was clearly intended as a civil remedy into a criminal penalty. In making this latter determination, the factors listed in *Kennedy v. Mendoza-Martinez,* 372 U.S. 144 (1963), provide useful guideposts, including: (1) "[w]hether the sanction involves an affirmative disability or restraint"; (2) "whether it has historically been regarded as a punishment"; (3) "whether it comes into play only on a finding of scienter"; (4) "whether its operation will promote the traditional aims of punishment-retribution and deterrence"; (5) "whether the behavior to which it applies is already a crime"; (6) "whether an alternative purpose to which it may rationally be connected is assignable for it"; and (7) "whether it appears excessive in relation to the alternative purpose assigned." It is important to note, however, that "these factors must be considered in relation to the statute on its face," and "only the clearest proof" will suffice to override legislative intent and transform what has been denominated a civil remedy into a criminal penalty.

Our opinion in *United States v. Halper,* 490 U.S. 435 (1989), marked the first time we applied the Double Jeopardy Clause to a sanction without first determining that it was criminal in nature. In that case, Irwin Halper was convicted of, inter alia, violating the criminal false claims statute based on his submission of 65 inflated Medicare claims each of which overcharged the Government by $9. He was sentenced to two years' imprisonment and fined $5,000. The Government then brought an action against Halper under the civil False Claims Act. The remedial provisions of the False Claims Act provided that a violation of the Act rendered one "liable to the United States Government for a civil penalty of $2,000, an amount equal to 2 times the amount of damages the Government sustains because of the act of that person, and costs of the civil action." Given Halper's 65 separate violations of the Act, he appeared to be liable for a penalty of $130,000, despite the fact he actually defrauded the Government of less than $600. However, the District Court concluded that a penalty of this magnitude would violate the Double Jeopardy Clause in light of Halper's previous criminal conviction. While explicitly recognizing that the statutory damages provision of the Act "was not itself a criminal punishment," the District Court nonetheless concluded that application of the full penalty to Halper would constitute a second "punishment" in violation of the Double Jeopardy Clause.

On direct appeal, this Court affirmed. As the *Halper* Court saw it, the imposition of "punishment" of any kind was subject to double jeopardy constraints, and whether a sanction constituted "punishment" depended primarily on whether it served the traditional "goals of punishment," namely "retribution and deterrence." Any sanction that was so "overwhelmingly disproportionate" to the injury caused that it could not "fairly be said *solely* to serve [the] remedial purpose" of compensating the government for its loss, was thought to be explainable only as "serving either retributive or deterrent purposes." (emphasis added).

The analysis applied by the *Halper* Court deviated from our traditional double jeopardy doctrine in two key respects. First, the *Halper* Court bypassed the threshold question: whether the successive punishment at issue is a "criminal" punishment. Instead, it focused on whether the sanction, regardless of whether it was civil or criminal, was so grossly disproportionate to the harm caused as to constitute "punishment." In so doing, the Court elevated a single *Kennedy* factor— whether the sanction appeared excessive in relation to its nonpunitive purposes— to dispositive status. But as we emphasized in *Kennedy* itself, no one factor should be considered controlling as they "may often point in differing directions." The second significant departure in *Halper* was the Court's decision to "asses[s] the character of the actual sanctions imposed," rather than, as *Kennedy* demanded, evaluating the "statute on its face" to determine whether it provided for what amounted to a criminal sanction.

We believe that *Halper*'s deviation from longstanding double jeopardy principles was ill considered. As subsequent cases have demonstrated, *Halper*'s test for determining whether a particular sanction is "punitive," and thus subject to the strictures of the Double Jeopardy Clause, has proved unworkable. We have since recognized that all civil penalties have some deterrent effect. See *Department of Revenue of Mont. v. Kurth Ranch*, 511 U.S. 767 (1994); *United States v. Ursery*, 518 U.S. 267 (1996).[a] If a sanction must be "solely" remedial (i.e., entirely nondeterrent) to avoid implicating the Double Jeopardy Clause, then no civil penalties are beyond the scope of the Clause. Under *Halper*'s method of analysis, a court must also look at the "sanction actually imposed" to determine whether the Double Jeopardy Clause is implicated. Thus, it will not be possible to determine whether the Double Jeopardy Clause is violated until a defendant has proceeded through a trial to judgment. But in those cases where the civil proceeding follows the criminal proceeding, this approach flies in the face of the notion that the Double Jeopardy Clause forbids the government from even "attempting a second time to punish criminally."

Finally, it should be noted that some of the ills at which *Halper* was directed are addressed by other constitutional provisions. The Due Process and Equal Protection Clauses already protect individuals from sanctions which are downright irrational. The Eighth Amendment protects against excessive civil fines, including forfeitures. The additional protection afforded by extending double jeopardy

---

[a]   *Kurth Ranch* departed from the specific analysis of *Halper* in assessing whether a tax constituted punishment under the double jeopardy clause, although stating that the Court adhered to *Halper*'s underlying premise "that only 'the character of the actual sanctions' can substantiate a possible double jeopardy violation." The Court there held that a tax on marijuana was invalid under the double jeopardy clause where the taxpayer had already been convicted of owning the taxed marijuana. In determining that the tax was "so punitive as to constitute punishment," the Court stressed that the tax was conditioned on the commission of a crime, and was imposed only after the taxpayer had been arrested, thus limiting its applicability only to a person charged with a crime. Also, the tax applied even though the taxpayer did not own or possess the taxed marijuana at the time the tax was imposed.

Ursery held that forfeitures were to be judged by a two-part test established long before *Halper*. Initially, the Court asked whether Congress intended the forfeiture to be criminal or civil. Second, it asked whether the forfeiture was "so punitive in fact as to persuade us that the forfeiture proceedings may not legitimately be viewed as civil in nature." Here Congress clearly intended the forfeiture to be civil. On the second question, the evidence fell far short of the "clearest proof" needed to overcome Congress' civil designation. Though the forfeiture had punitive aspects, it also had nonpunitive goals (encouraging property owners to take care to avoid the use of their property for illegal purposes), was not tied to scienter, and was imposed *in rem* (rather than *in personam*).

protections to proceedings heretofore thought to be civil is more than offset by the confusion created by attempting to distinguish between "punitive" and "nonpunitive" penalties.

Applying traditional double jeopardy principles to the facts of this case, it is clear that the criminal prosecution of these petitioners would not violate the Double Jeopardy Clause. It is evident that Congress intended the OCC money penalties and debarment sanctions * * * to be civil in nature. As for the money penalties, [the statutes] which authorize the imposition of monetary penalties * * * expressly provide that such penalties are "civil." While the provision authorizing debarment contains no language explicitly denominating the sanction as civil, we think it significant that the authority to issue debarment orders is conferred upon the "appropriate Federal banking agenc[ies]." That such authority was conferred upon administrative agencies is prima facie evidence that Congress intended to provide for a civil sanction.

Turning to the second stage of the * * * test, we find that there is little evidence, much less the clearest proof that we require, suggesting that either OCC money penalties or debarment sanctions are "so punitive in form and effect as to render them criminal despite Congress' intent to the contrary." First, neither money penalties nor debarment have historically been viewed as punishment. We have long recognized that "revocation of a privilege voluntarily granted," such as a debarment, "is characteristically free of the punitive criminal element." Similarly, "the payment of fixed or variable sums of money [is a] sanction which ha[s] been recognized as enforcible by civil proceedings since the original revenue law of 1789."

Second, the sanctions imposed do not involve an "affirmative disability or restraint," as that term is normally understood. While petitioners have been prohibited from further participating in the banking industry, this is "certainly nothing approaching the 'infamous punishment' of imprisonment." Third, neither sanction comes into play "only" on a finding of scienter. The provisions under which the money penalties were imposed allow for the assessment of a penalty against any person "who violates" any of the underlying banking statutes, without regard to the violator's state of mind. "Good faith" is considered by OCC in determining the amount of the penalty to be imposed, but a penalty can be imposed even in the absence of bad faith. The fact that petitioners' "good faith" was considered in determining the amount of the penalty to be imposed in this case is irrelevant, as we look only to "the statute on its face" to determine whether a penalty is criminal in nature. Similarly, while debarment may be imposed for a "willful" disregard "for the safety or soundness of [an] insured depository institution," willfulness is not a prerequisite to debarment; it is sufficient that the disregard for the safety and soundness of the institution was "continuing."

Fourth, the conduct for which OCC sanctions are imposed may also be criminal (and in this case formed the basis for petitioners' indictments). This fact is insufficient to render the money penalties and debarment sanctions criminally punitive, particularly in the double jeopardy context.

Finally, we recognize that the imposition of both money penalties and debarment sanctions will deter others from emulating petitioners' conduct, a traditional goal of criminal punishment. But the mere presence of this purpose is insufficient to render a sanction criminal, as deterrence "may serve civil as well as criminal goals." *Ursery*. For example, the sanctions at issue here, while intended to deter future wrongdoing, also serve to promote the stability of the banking industry. To hold that the mere presence of a deterrent purpose renders such sanctions "criminal" for double jeopardy purposes would severely undermine the Government's ability to engage in effective regulation of institutions such as banks. * * *

JUSTICE SCALIA, with whom JUSTICE THOMAS joins, concurring.

I wholly agree with the Court's conclusion that *Halper*'s test for whether a sanction is "punitive" was ill-considered and unworkable. * * * [In *Kurth Ranch,* I concluded] that the Double Jeopardy Clause prohibits successive prosecution, not successive punishment, and that we should therefore "put the *Halper* genie back in the bottle." Today's opinion uses a somewhat different bottle than I would, returning the law to its state immediately prior to *Halper*—which acknowledged a constitutional prohibition of multiple punishments but required successive criminal prosecutions. So long as that requirement is maintained, our multiple punishments jurisprudence essentially duplicates what I believe to be the correct double-jeopardy law, and will be as harmless in the future as it was pre-*Halper*. Accordingly, I am pleased to concur.

JUSTICE STEVENS, concurring in the judgment.

The maxim that "hard cases make bad law" may also apply to easy cases. * * * [T]his case could easily be decided by the straightforward application of well-established precedent. Neither such a disposition, nor anything in the opinion of the Court of Appeals, would require a reexamination of the central holding in *United States v. Halper*, or of the language used in that unanimous opinion. * * * The two proceedings at issue here involved different offenses that were not even arguably the same under *Blockburger*. * * *

Despite my disagreement with the Court's decision to use this case as a rather lame excuse for writing a gratuitous essay about punishment, I do agree with its reaffirmation of the central holding of *Halper* and *Department of Revenue of Mont. v. Kurth Ranch*. Both of those cases held that sanctions imposed in civil proceedings constituted "punishment" barred by the Double Jeopardy Clause. Those holdings reconfirmed the settled proposition that the Government cannot use the "civil" label to escape entirely the Double Jeopardy Clause's command, as we have recognized for at least six decades. That proposition is extremely important because the States and the Federal Government have an enormous array of civil administrative sanctions at their disposal that are capable of being used to punish persons repeatedly for the same offense, violating the bedrock double jeopardy principle of finality. * * *

* * * However the Court chooses to recalibrate the meaning of punishment for double jeopardy purposes, our doctrine still limits multiple sanctions of the rare

sort contemplated by *Halper*. Today, as it did in *Halper* itself, the Court relies on the sort of multi-factor approach to the definition of punishment that we used in *Kennedy v. Mendoza-Martinez,* to identify situations in which a civil sanction is punitive. Whether the Court's reformulation of *Halper's* test will actually affect the outcome of any cases remains to be seen. Perhaps it will not, since the Court recommends consideration of whether a sanction's " 'operation will promote the traditional aims of punishment—retribution and deterrence,' " and " 'whether it appears excessive in relation to the alternative [non-punitive] purpose assigned.' " *Ante* (quoting *Kennedy*). Those factors look awfully similar to the reasoning in *Halper,* and while we are told that they are never by themselves dispositive, they should be capable of tipping the balance in extreme cases. The danger in changing approaches midstream, rather than refining our established approach on an incremental basis, is that the Government and lower courts may be unduly influenced by the Court's new attitude, rather than its specific prescribed test. * * *

JUSTICE SOUTER, concurring in the judgment.

I concur in the Court's judgment and with much of its opinion. * * * My acceptance of the *Kennedy-Ward* analytical scheme is subject to caveats, however. * * * While there are good and historically grounded reasons for using [the phrase "clearest proof"] to impose a substantial burden on anyone claiming that an apparently civil penalty is in truth criminal, what may be clear enough to be "clearest" is necessarily dependent on context * * *. I read the requisite "clearest proof" of criminal character, then, to be a function of the strength of the countervailing indications of civil nature (including the presumption of constitutionality enjoyed by an ostensibly civil statute making no provision for the safeguards guaranteed to criminal defendants). * * * I add further the caution to be wary of reading the "clearest proof" requirement as a guarantee that such a demonstration is as likely to be as rare in the future as it has been in the past. * * *

JUSTICE BREYER, with whom JUSTICE GINSBURG joins, concurring in the judgment. * * *

I agree with the majority and with Justice Souter that *United States v. Halper* does not provide proper guidance for distinguishing between criminal and non-criminal sanctions and proceedings. I also agree that *United States v. Ward* and *Kennedy v. Mendoza-Martinez* set forth the proper approach. * * * I do not join the Court's opinion, however, because I disagree with its reasoning in two respects. First, unlike the Court I would not say that " 'only the clearest proof' " will "transform" into a criminal punishment what a legislature calls a "civil remedy." I understand that the Court has taken this language from earlier cases. But the limitation that the language suggests is not consistent with what the Court has actually done. Rather, in fact if not in theory, the Court has simply applied factors of the *Kennedy* variety to the matter at hand. * * * The "clearest proof" language is consequently misleading, and I would consign it to the same legal limbo where *Halper* now rests.

Second, I would not decide now that a court should evaluate a statute only " 'on its face,' " rather than "assessing the character of the actual sanctions imposed." *Halper* involved an ordinary civil-fine statute that as normally applied would not have created any "double jeopardy" problem. It was not the statute itself, but rather the disproportionate relation between fine and conduct as the statute was applied in the individual case that led this Court, unanimously, to find that the "civil penalty" was, in those circumstances, a second "punishment" that constituted double jeopardy. Of course, the Court in *Halper* might have reached the same result through application of the constitutional prohibition of "excessive fines." But that is not what the Court there said. And nothing in the majority's opinion today explains why we should abandon this aspect of *Halper*'s holding. * * * It seems to me quite possible that a statute that provides for a punishment that normally is civil in nature could nonetheless amount to a criminal punishment as applied in special circumstances. And I would not now hold to the contrary.

That said, an analysis of the *Kennedy* factors still leads me to the conclusion that the statutory penalty in this case is not on its face a criminal penalty. Nor, in my view, does the application of the statute to the petitioners in this case amount to criminal punishment. I therefore concur in the result.

2. ABORTED PROCEEDINGS

The two cases in this section, *Arizona v. Washington* and *Oregon v. Kennedy,* set forth the basic double jeopardy standards applicable to reprosecutions following a mistrial. The mistrial should be distinguished from the mid-trial dismissal, which is discussed in the *Scott* case in the next section. In contrast to dismissals of the type involved in *Scott*, a court ordering a mistrial does not find some fatal flaw in the prosecution that would present an absolute bar to conviction on the offense charged. Rather, the trial court rules that it would be inappropriate or impossible to continue with the trial and orders its termination without ending the prosecution. The judge ordering a mistrial assumes that a reprosecution can be brought, but as *Washington* and *Kennedy* indicate, that is not always the case.[a]

ARIZONA V. WASHINGTON
434 U.S. 497, 98 S.Ct. 824, 54 L.Ed.2d 717 (1978).

JUSTICE STEVENS delivered the opinion of the Court.

In 1971 respondent was found guilty of murdering a hotel night clerk. In 1973, the Superior Court of Pima County, Ariz., ordered a new trial because the prosecutor had withheld exculpatory evidence from the defense. The Arizona Supreme Court affirmed the new trial order * * *.

Respondent's second trial began in January 1975. During the *voir dire* examination of prospective jurors, the prosecutor made reference to the fact that some of the witnesses whose testimony the jurors would hear had testified in proceedings four years earlier. Defense counsel told the prospective jurors "that

---

[a] Where the court grants during trial a motion to dismiss based on a legal defect that is curable (and therefore assumes reprosecution), the applicable standards are the same as used for mistrials. See *Lee v. United States*, 432 U.S. 23 (1977) (prosecution dismissed during trial on a defense motion citing a defect in the charging instrument; the double jeopardy standard for defense requested mistrials held to govern the state's authority to reprosecute).

there was evidence hidden from [respondent] at the last trial." In his opening statement, he made this point more forcefully:

> "You will hear testimony that notwithstanding the fact that we had a trial in May of 1971 in this matter, that the prosecutor hid those statements and didn't give those to the lawyer for George saying the man was Spanish speaking, didn't give those statements at all, hid them.

> "You will hear that that evidence was suppressed and hidden by the prosecutor in that case. You will hear that that evidence was purposely withheld. You will hear that because of the misconduct of the County Attorney at that time and because he withheld evidence, that the Supreme Court of Arizona granted a new trial in this case."

After opening statements were completed, the prosecutor moved for a mistrial. In colloquy during argument of the motion, the trial judge expressed the opinion that evidence concerning the reasons for the new trial, and specifically the ruling of the Arizona Supreme Court, was irrelevant to the issue of guilt or innocence and therefore inadmissible. Defense counsel asked for an opportunity "to find some law" that would support his belief that the Supreme Court opinion would be admissible. After further argument, the judge stated that he would withhold ruling on the admissibility of the evidence and denied the motion for mistrial. Two witnesses then testified.

The following morning the prosecutor renewed his mistrial motion. Fortified by an evening's research, he argued that there was no theory on which the basis for the new trial ruling could be brought to the attention of the jury, that the prejudice to the jury could not be repaired by any cautionary instructions, and that a mistrial was a "manifest necessity." Defense counsel * * * argued that his comment was invited by the prosecutor's reference to the witnesses' earlier testimony and that any prejudice could be avoided by curative instructions. * * * Ultimately the trial judge granted the motion, stating that his ruling was based upon defense counsel's remarks in his opening statement concerning the Arizona Supreme Court opinion. The trial judge did not expressly find that there was "manifest necessity" for a mistrial; nor did he expressly state that he had considered alternative solutions and concluded that none would be adequate. * * * [A federal district court, upon application for federal habeas corpus, granted the writ because of the absence in the record of such express findings. The Court of Appeals affirmed.]

* * * The constitutional protection against double jeopardy unequivocally prohibits a second trial following an acquittal. The public interest in the finality of criminal judgments is so strong that an acquitted defendant may not be retried even though "the acquittal was based upon an egregiously erroneous foundation." If the innocence of the accused has been confirmed by a final judgment, the Constitution conclusively presumes that a second trial would be unfair.

Because jeopardy attaches before the judgment becomes final, the constitutional protection also embraces the defendant's "valued right to have his trial completed by a particular tribunal." The reasons why this "valued right" merits constitutional protection are worthy of repetition. Even if the first trial is not completed, a second prosecution may be grossly unfair. It increases the financial and emotional burden on the accused, prolongs the period in which he is stigmatized by an unresolved accusation of wrongdoing, and may even enhance the risk that an innocent defendant may be convicted. The danger of such unfairness to the defendant exists whenever a trial is aborted before it is completed. Consequently, as a general rule, the prosecutor is entitled to one, and only one, opportunity to require an accused to stand trial.

Unlike the situation in which the trial has ended in an acquittal or conviction, retrial is not automatically barred when a criminal proceeding is terminated without finally resolving the merits of the charges against the accused. Because of the variety of circumstances that may make it necessary to discharge a jury before a trial is concluded, and because those circumstances do not invariably create unfairness to the accused, his valued right to have the trial concluded by a particular tribunal is sometimes subordinate to the public interest in affording the prosecutor one full and fair opportunity to present his evidence to an impartial jury. Yet in view of the importance of the right, and the fact that it is frustrated by any mistrial, the prosecutor must shoulder the burden of justifying the mistrial if he is to avoid the double jeopardy bar. His burden is a heavy one. The prosecutor must demonstrate "manifest necessity" for any mistrial declared over the objection of the defendant.

The words "manifest necessity" appropriately characterize the magnitude of the prosecutor's burden. For that reason Mr. Justice Story's classic formulation of the test has been quoted over and over again to provide guidance in the decision of a wide variety of cases. Nevertheless, those words do not describe a standard that can be applied mechanically or without attention to the particular problem confronting the trial judge. Indeed, it is manifest that the key word "necessity" cannot be interpreted literally; instead, contrary to the teaching of Webster, we assume that there are degrees of necessity and we require a "high degree" before concluding that a mistrial is appropriate.

The question whether that "high degree" has been reached is answered more easily in some kinds of cases than in others. At one extreme are cases in which a prosecutor requests a mistrial in order to buttress weaknesses in his evidence. Although there was a time when English judges served the Stuart monarchs by exercising a power to discharge a jury whenever it appeared that the Crown's evidence would be insufficient to convict, the prohibition against double jeopardy as it evolved in this country was plainly intended to condemn this "abhorrent" practice. * * * Thus, the strictest scrutiny is appropriate when the basis for the mistrial is the unavailability of critical prosecution evidence, or when there is reason to believe that the prosecutor is using the superior resources of the State to harass or to achieve a tactical advantage over the accused.

At the other extreme is the mistrial premised upon the trial judge's belief that the jury is unable to reach a verdict, long considered the classic basis for a proper mistrial. The argument that a jury's inability to agree establishes reasonable doubt as to the defendant's guilt, and therefore requires acquittal, has been uniformly rejected in this country. Instead, without exception, the courts have held that the trial judge may discharge a genuinely deadlocked jury and require the defendant to submit to a second trial. This rule accords recognition to society's interest in giving the prosecution one complete opportunity to convict those who have violated its laws.

Moreover, in this situation there are especially compelling reasons for allowing the trial judge to exercise broad discretion in deciding whether or not "manifest necessity" justifies a discharge of the jury. On the one hand, if he discharges the jury when further deliberations may produce a fair verdict, the defendant is deprived of his "valued right to have his trial completed by a particular tribunal." But if he fails to discharge a jury which is unable to reach a verdict after protracted and exhausting deliberations, there exists a significant risk that a verdict may result from pressures inherent in the situation rather than the considered judgment of all the jurors. If retrial of the defendant were barred whenever an appellate court views the "necessity" for a mistrial differently from the trial judge, there would be a danger that the latter, cognizant of the serious societal consequences of an erroneous ruling, would employ coercive means to break the apparent deadlock. Such a rule would frustrate the public interest in just judgments. The trial judge's decision to declare a mistrial when he considers the jury deadlocked is therefore accorded great deference by a reviewing court.

We are persuaded that, along the spectrum of trial problems which may warrant a mistrial and which vary in their amenability to appellate scrutiny, the difficulty which led to the mistrial in this case also falls in an area where the trial judge's determination is entitled to special respect.

In this case the trial judge ordered a mistrial because the defendant's lawyer made improper and prejudicial remarks during his opening statement to the jury. * * * We recognize that the extent of the possible bias cannot be measured, and that the [federal] District Court was quite correct in believing that some trial judges might have proceeded with the trial after giving the jury appropriate cautionary instructions. In a strict, literal sense, the mistrial was not "necessary." Nevertheless, the overriding interest in the evenhanded administration of justice requires that we accord the highest degree of respect to the trial judge's evaluation of the likelihood that the impartiality of one or more jurors may have been affected by the improper comment. * * * The consistent course of decision in this Court in cases involving possible juror bias supports this conclusion. * * *

An improper opening statement unquestionably tends to frustrate the public interest in having a just judgment reached by an impartial tribunal. * * * The trial judge, of course, may instruct the jury to disregard the improper comment. In extreme cases, he may discipline counsel, or even remove him from the trial as he did in *United States v. Dinitz,* 424 U.S. 600 (1976). Those actions, however, will not necessarily remove the risk of bias that may be created by improper argument. Unless unscrupulous defense counsel are to be allowed an unfair advantage, the trial judge must have the power to declare a mistrial in appropriate cases. The interest in orderly, impartial procedure would be impaired if he were deterred from exercising that power by a concern that any time a reviewing court disagreed with his assessment of the trial situation a retrial would automatically be barred. The adoption of a stringent standard of appellate review in this area, therefore, would seriously impede the trial judge in the proper performance of his "duty, in order to protect the integrity of the trial, to take prompt and affirmative action to stop * * * professional misconduct." *Dinitz.*

There are compelling institutional considerations militating in favor of appellate deference to the trial judge's evaluation of the significance of possible juror bias. He has seen and heard the jurors during their *voir dire* examination. He is the judge most familiar with the evidence and the background of the case on trial. He has listened to the tone of the argument as it was delivered and has observed the apparent reaction of the jurors. In short, he is far more "conversant with the factors relevant to the determination" than any reviewing court can possibly be.

Our conclusion that a trial judge's decision to declare a mistrial based on his assessment of the prejudicial impact of improper argument is entitled to great deference does not, of course, end the inquiry. As noted earlier, a constitutionally protected interest is inevitably affected by any mistrial decision. * * * In order to ensure that this interest is adequately protected, reviewing courts have an obligation to satisfy themselves that, in the words of Mr. Justice Story, the trial judge exercised "sound discretion" in declaring a mistrial. * * * [I]f a trial judge acts irrationally or irresponsibly, his action cannot be condoned. But our review of this record indicates that this was not such a case. * * *

One final matter requires consideration. The absence of an explicit finding of "manifest necessity" appears to have been determinative for the District Court and may have been so for the Court of Appeals. If those courts regarded that omission as critical, they required too much. Since the record provides sufficient justification for the state-court ruling, the failure to explain that ruling more completely does not render it constitutionally defective.

Review of any trial court decision is, of course, facilitated by findings and by an explanation of the reasons supporting the decision. No matter how desirable such procedural assistance may be, it is not constitutionally mandated in a case such as this. The basis for the trial judge's mistrial order is adequately disclosed by the record, which includes the extensive argument of counsel prior to the judge's ruling. The state trial judge's mistrial declaration is not subject to collateral attack in a federal court simply because he failed to find "manifest necessity" in those words or to articulate on the record all the factors which informed the deliberate exercise of his discretion. * * *

JUSTICE BLACKMUN concurs in the result.

JUSTICE WHITE, dissenting.

I cannot agree with the Court of Appeals that the failure of a state trial judge to express the legal standard under which he had declared a mistrial is, in itself and without further examination of the record, sufficient reason to infer constitutional error foreclosing a second trial. * * * I would not, however, undertake an examination of the record here in the first instance. Rather, I would vacate the judgment of the Court of Appeals and direct that court to remand the case to the District Court to make the initial judgment, under the correct legal standard, as to whether the writ should issue.

JUSTICE MARSHALL, with whom JUSTICE BRENNAN joins, dissenting.

My disagreement with the majority is a narrow one. * * * I agree that, where a mistrial is declared over a defendant's objections, a new trial is permissible only if the termination of the earlier trial was justified by a "manifest necessity" and that the prosecution must shoulder the "heavy" burden of demonstrating such a "high degree" of necessity. Nor do I quarrel with the proposition that reviewing courts must accord substantial deference to a trial judge's determination that the prejudicial impact of an improper opening statement is so great as to leave no alternative but a mistrial to secure the ends of public justice. * * * Where I part ways from the Court is in its assumption that an "assessment of the prejudicial impact of improper argument," sufficient to support the need for a mistrial, may be implied from this record. * * *

Defense counsel's improper remarks occupied only one page of a lengthy opening statement. Despite the fact that the prosecutor had vigorously interrupted the opening statement at numerous points to assert various objections, he made no objection to the remarks that formed the basis for the mistrial. If the argument of defense counsel had had a visibly obvious impact on the jurors when uttered, it is hard to believe that this prosecutor would have waited until after the opening statement was finished and the luncheon recess concluded before making his objection known.

Although from this distance and in the absence of express findings it is impossible to determine the precise extent to which defense counsel's remarks may have prejudiced the jury against the State, the circumstances set forth above suggest that any such prejudice may have been minimal and subject to cure through less drastic alternatives. For example, the jury could have been instructed to disregard any mention of prior legal rulings as irrelevant to the issues at hand, and to consider as evidence only the testimony and exhibits admitted through witnesses on the stand. Were there doubt whether such instructions alone would suffice to cure the taint, the jury could have been questioned about the extent of any prejudice. Given the anticipated length of the trial (almost two weeks), it is not unlikely that, had the jury been appropriately instructed when the court first found defense counsel to have erred in his opening statement, any prejudice would have dissipated before deliberations were to begin. For these reasons, it is impossible to conclude that a finding of necessity was implicit in the mere grant of the mistrial. * * *

I do not propose that the Constitution invariably requires a trial judge to make findings of necessity on the record to justify the declaration of a mistrial over a defendant's objections. * * * What the "manifest necessity" doctrine does require, in my view, is that the record make clear either that there were no meaningful and practical alternatives to a mistrial, or that the trial court scrupulously considered available alternatives and found all wanting but a termination of the proceedings. * * * The record here * * * does neither. * * *

Had the court here explored alternatives on the record, or made a finding of substantial and incurable prejudice or other "manifest necessity," this would be a different case and one in which I would agree with both the majority's reasoning and its result. On this ambiguous record, however, the absence of any such finding—and indeed of any express indication that the trial court applied the manifest-necessity doctrine—leaves open the substantial possibility that there was in fact no need to terminate the proceedings. * * *

OREGON V. KENNEDY

456 U.S. 667, 102 S.Ct. 2083, 72 L.Ed.2d 416 (1982).

JUSTICE REHNQUIST delivered the opinion of the Court.

* * * Respondent was charged with the theft of an oriental rug. During his first trial, the State called an expert witness on the subject of Middle Eastern rugs to testify as to the value and the identity of the rug in question. On cross-examination, respondent's attorney apparently attempted to establish bias on the part of the expert witness by asking him whether he had filed a criminal complaint against respondent. The witness eventually acknowledged this fact, but explained that no action had been taken on his complaint. On redirect examination, the prosecutor sought to elicit the reasons why the witness had filed a complaint against respondent, but the trial court sustained a series of objections to this line of inquiry.[1] The following colloquy then ensued:

"Prosecutor: Have you ever done business with the Kennedys?"

"Witness: No, I have not."

"Prosecutor: Is that because he is a crook?"

The trial court then granted respondent's motion for a mistrial.

When the State later sought to retry respondent, he moved to dismiss the charges because of double jeopardy. After a hearing at which the prosecutor testified, the trial court found as a fact that "it was not the intention of the prosecutor in this case to cause a mistrial." On the basis of this finding, the trial court held that double jeopardy principles did not bar retrial, and respondent was then tried and convicted.

Respondent then successfully appealed to the Oregon Court of Appeals, which sustained his double jeopardy claim. * * * The Court of Appeals accepted the trial court's finding that it was not the intent of the prosecutor to cause a mistrial. Nevertheless, the court held that retrial was barred because the prosecutor's conduct in this case constituted what it viewed as "overreaching." * * *

Where the trial is terminated over the objection of the defendant, the classical test for lifting the double jeopardy bar to a second trial is the "manifest necessity" standard first enunciated in Justice Story's opinion for the Court in *United States v. Perez* [22 U.S. 579 (1824)]. * * * The "manifest necessity" standard provides

---

[1] The Court of Appeals later explained that respondent's "objections were not well taken, and the judge's rulings were probably wrong." 49 Or.App. 415, 417, 619 P.2d 948, 949 (1980).

sufficient protection to the defendant's interests in having his case finally decided by the jury first selected while at the same time maintaining "the public's interest in fair trials designed to end in just judgments." But in the case of a mistrial declared at the behest of the defendant, quite different principles come into play. Here the defendant himself has elected to terminate the proceedings against him, and the "manifest necessity" standard has no place in the application of the Double Jeopardy Clause. *United States v. Dinitz,* [424 U.S. 600 (1976)]. * * *

Our cases, however, have indicated that even where the defendant moves for a mistrial, there is a narrow exception to the rule that the Double Jeopardy Clause is no bar to retrial. See, e.g., *United States v. Dinitz.* The circumstances under which respondent's first trial was terminated require us to delineate the bounds of that exception more fully than we have in previous cases.

Since one of the principal threads making up the protection embodied in the Double Jeopardy Clause is the right of the defendant to have his trial completed before the first jury empaneled to try him, it may be wondered as a matter of original inquiry why the defendant's election to terminate the first trial by his own motion should not be deemed a renunciation of that right for all purposes. We have recognized, however, that there would be great difficulty in applying such a rule where the prosecutor's actions giving rise to the motion for mistrial were done "in order to goad the [defendant] into requesting a mistrial." *United States v. Dinitz.* In such a case, the defendant's valued right to complete his trial before the first jury would be a hollow shell if the inevitable motion for mistrial were held to prevent a later invocation of the bar of double jeopardy in all circumstances. But the precise phrasing of the circumstances which *will* allow a defendant to interpose the defense of double jeopardy to a second prosecution where the first has terminated on his own motion for a mistrial have been stated with less than crystal clarity in our cases which deal with this area of the law. * * * The language [of *Dinitz* at points] would seem to broaden the test from one of *intent* to provoke a motion for a mistrial to a more generalized standard of "bad faith conduct" or "harassment" on the part of the judge or prosecutor. It was upon this language that the Oregon Court of Appeals apparently relied in concluding that the prosecutor's colloquy with the expert witness in this case amount to "overreaching."

The difficulty with the more general standards which would permit a broader exception than one merely based on intent is that they offer virtually no standards for their application. Every act on the part of a rational prosecutor during a trial is designed to "prejudice" the defendant by placing before the judge or jury evidence pleading to a finding of his guilt. Given the complexity of the rules of evidence, it will be a rare trial of any complexity in which some proffered evidence by the prosecutor or by the defendant's attorney will not be found objectionable by the trial court. Most such objections are undoubtedly curable by simply refusing to allow the proffered evidence to be admitted, or in the case of a particular line of inquiry taken by counsel with a witness, by an admonition to desist from a particular line of inquiry.

More serious infractions on the part of the prosecutor may provoke a motion for mistrial on the part of the defendant, and may in the view of the trial court warrant the granting of such a motion. The "overreaching" standard applied by the court below and urged today by Justice Stevens, however, would add another classification of prosecutorial error, one requiring dismissal of the indictment, but without supplying any standard by which to assess that error.[5]

By contrast, a standard that examines the intent of the prosecutor, though certainly not entirely free from practical difficulties, is a manageable standard to apply. It merely calls for the court to make a finding of fact. Inferring the existence or nonexistence of intent from objective facts and circumstances is a familiar process in our criminal justice system. When it is remembered that resolution of double jeopardy questions by state trial courts are reviewable not only within the state court system, but in the federal court system on habeas corpus as well, the desirability of an easily applied principle is apparent.

Prosecutorial conduct that might be viewed as harassment or overreaching, even if sufficient to justify a mistrial on defendant's motion, therefore, does not bar retrial absent intent on the part of the prosecutor to subvert the protections afforded by the Double Jeopardy Clause. A defendant's motion for a mistrial constitutes "a deliberate election on his part to forgo his valued right to have his guilt or innocence determined before the first trier of fact." *United States v. Scott* [§ 3 infra]. Where prosecutorial error even of a degree sufficient to warrant a mistrial has occurred, "[t]he important consideration, for purposes of the Double Jeopardy Clause, is that the defendant retain primary control over the course to be followed in the event of such error." *United States v. Dinitz*. Only where the governmental conduct in question is intended to "goad" the defendant into moving for a mistrial may a defendant raise the bar of double jeopardy to a second trial after having succeeded in aborting the first on his own motion.

Were we to embrace the broad and somewhat amorphous standard adopted by the Oregon Court of Appeals, we are not sure that criminal defendants as a class would be aided. Knowing that the granting of the defendant's motion for mistrial would all but inevitably bring with it an attempt to bar a second trial on grounds of double jeopardy, the judge presiding over the first trial might well be more loath to grant a defendant's motion for mistrial. If a mistrial were in fact warranted under the applicable law, of course, the defendant could in many instances successfully appeal a judgment of conviction on the same grounds that he urged a mistrial, and the Double Jeopardy Clause would present no bar to retrial. But some of the advantages secured to him by the Double Jeopardy Clause—the freedom from extended anxiety, and the necessity to confront the government's case only once—would be to a large extent lost in the process of trial to verdict, reversal on appeal, and subsequent retrial.

---

[5] If the Court were to hold, as would Justice Stevens, that such a determination requires an assessment of the facts and circumstances but without explaining how such an assessment ought to proceed, the Court would offer little guidance to the federal and state courts that must apply our decisions. Justice Stevens disagrees with this decision below because his reaction to a cold record is different from that of the Oregon Court of Appeals. The Court of Appeals found "overreaching"; Justice Stevens finds none. Neither articulates a basis for reaching their respective conclusions which can be applied to other factual situations. We are loath to adopt such an essentially standardless rule.

* * * We do not by this opinion lay down a flat rule that where a defendant in a criminal trial successfully moves for a mistrial, he may not thereafter invoke the bar of double jeopardy against a second trial. But we do hold that the circumstances under which such a defendant may invoke the bar of double jeopardy in a second effort to try him are limited to those cases in which the conduct giving rise to the successful motion for a mistrial was intended to provoke the defendant into moving for a mistrial. Since the Oregon trial court found, and the Oregon Court of Appeals accepted, that the prosecutorial conduct culminating in the termination of the first trial in this case was not so intended by the prosecutor, that is the end of the matter for purposes of the Double Jeopardy Clause of the Fifth Amendment to the United States Constitution. * * *

JUSTICE BRENNAN, with whom JUSTICE MARSHALL joins, concurring in the judgment.

I concur in the judgment and join in the opinion of Justice Stevens. However, it should be noted that nothing in the holding of the Court today prevents the state courts, on remand, from concluding that respondent's retrial would violate the provision of the Oregon Constitution that prohibits double jeopardy * * *.

JUSTICE POWELL, concurring.

I join the Court's opinion holding that the *intention* of a prosecutor determines whether his conduct, viewed by the defendant and the court as justifying a mistrial, bars a retrial of the defendant under the Double Jeopardy Clause. Because "subjective" intent often may be unknowable, I emphasize that a court—in considering a double jeopardy motion—should rely primarily upon the objective facts and circumstances of the particular case.

* * * [T]his would have been a close case for me if there had been substantial factual evidence of intent beyond the question itself. Here, however, other relevant facts and circumstances strongly support the view that prosecutorial intent to cause a mistrial was absent. First, there was no sequence of overreaching prior to the single prejudicial question. Moreover, it is evident from a colloquy between counsel and the court, out of the presence of the jury, that the prosecutor not only resisted, but also was surprised by, the defendant's motion for a mistrial. Finally, at the hearing on respondent's double jeopardy motion, the prosecutor testified— and the trial found as a fact and the appellate court agreed—that there was no " 'intention * * * to cause a mistrial.' " In view of these circumstances, the Double Jeopardy Clause provides no bar to retrial.

JUSTICE STEVENS, with whom JUSTICE BRENNAN, JUSTICE MARSHALL and JUSTICE BLACKMUN join, concurring in the judgment.

* * * The rationale for the exception to the general rule permitting retrial after a mistrial declared with the defendant's consent is illustrated by the situation in which the prosecutor commits prejudicial error with the intent to provoke a mistrial. * * * But the Court reaches out to limit the exception to that one situation, rejecting the previous recognition that prosecutorial overreaching or harassment is also within the exception.[22]

Even if I agreed that the balance of competing interests tipped in favor of a bar to reprosecution only in the situation in which the prosecutor intended to provoke a mistrial, I would not subscribe to a standard that conditioned such a bar on the determination that the prosecutor harbored such intent when he committed prejudicial error. It is almost inconceivable that a defendant could prove that the prosecutor's deliberate misconduct was motivated by an intent to provoke a mistrial instead of an intent simply to prejudice the defendant. The defendant must shoulder a strong burden to establish a bar to reprosecution when he has consented to the mistrial, but the Court's subjective intent standard would eviscerate the exception.

A broader objection to the Court's limitation of the exception is that the rationale for the exception extends beyond the situation in which the prosecutor intends to provoke a mistrial. There are other situations in which the defendant's double jeopardy interests outweigh society's interest in obtaining a judgment on the merits even though the defendant has moved for a mistrial. For example, a prosecutor may be interested in putting the defendant through the embarrassment, expense, and ordeal of criminal proceedings even if he cannot obtain a conviction. In such a case, with the purpose of harassing the defendant the prosecutor may commit repeated prejudicial errors and be indifferent between a mistrial or mistrials and an unsustainable conviction or convictions. Another example is when the prosecutor seeks to inject enough unfair prejudice into the trial to ensure a conviction but not so much as to cause a reversal of that conviction. This kind of overreaching would not be covered by the Court's standard because, by hypothesis, the prosecutor's intent is to obtain a conviction, not to provoke a mistrial. Yet the defendant's choice—to continue the tainted proceeding or to abort it and begin anew—can be just as "hollow" in this situation as when the prosecutor intends to provoke a mistrial.

To invoke the exception for overreaching, a court need not divine the exact motivation for the prosecutorial error. It is sufficient that the court is persuaded that egregious prosecutorial misconduct has rendered unmeaningful the defendant's choice to continue or to abort the proceeding. It is unnecessary and

---

[22] The Court offers two reasons for cutting back on the exception. First, the Court states that "[t]he difficulty with the more general standards which would permit a broader exception than one merely based on intent is that they offer virtually no standards for their application." As I indicate in the text, however, some generality in the formula is a virtue and, in any event, meaningful and principled standards can be developed on a case-by-case basis that will not inhibit legitimate prosecution practices. Moreover, the general standards could hardly be more difficult to apply than the Court's subjective intent standard. * * *

Second, the Court is "not sure that criminal defendants as a class would be aided" by a broader exception. If a mistrial will more frequently constitute a bar to reprosecution, the Court supposes that trial judges will tend to refuse the defendant's mistrial motion and permit the error to be corrected on appeal of the conviction, in which event there would be no bar to reprosecution. This reasoning is premised on the assumption that an appellate court that concluded not only that the defendant's mistrial motion should have been granted but also that the prosecutor intended to provoke a mistrial would not be obligated to bar reprosecution as well as reverse the conviction. The assumption is "irrational." *Commonwealth v. Potter*, 478 Pa. 251, 386 A.2d 918 (1978) (Roberts, J.) (Pomeroy, J.).

unwise to attempt to identify all the factors that might inform the court's judgment, but several considerations follow from the rationale for recognizing the exception. First, because the exception is justified by the intolerance of intentional manipulation of the defendant's double jeopardy interests, a finding of deliberate misconduct normally would be a prerequisite to a reprosecution bar. Second, because the defendant's option to abort the proceeding after prosecutorial misconduct would retain real meaning for the defendant in any case in which the trial was going badly for him, normally a required finding would be that the prosecutorial error virtually eliminated, or at least substantially reduced, the probability of acquittal in a proceeding that was going badly for the government. It should be apparent from these observations that only in a rare and compelling case will a mistrial declared at the request of the defendant or with his consent bar a retrial.

No one case, of course, is a proper vehicle for identifying the limits of the exception. The Court repeatedly has shunned inflexible standards in applying the comparable "manifest necessity" exception to the general rule that a defendant is entitled to go to final judgment before the initial tribunal. The value of the overreaching standard, like "[t]he value of the [manifest necessity standard], thus lies in [its] capacity for informed application under widely different circumstances without injury to defendants or to the public interest." *Wade v. Hunter,* 336 U.S. 684 [(1949)]. The inexactitude of the standard used to protect defendants in the exceptional case surely should not concern the Court any more than the equally ill-defined formula used to protect prosecutors in the exceptional case. * * *

* * * The isolated prosecutorial error [here] occurred early in the trial, too early to determine whether the case was going badly for the prosecution. If anyone was being harassed at that time, it was the prosecutor who was frustrated by improper defense objections in her attempt to rehabilitate her witness. The gist of the comment that the respondent was a "crook" could fairly have been elicited from the witness, since defense counsel injected the respondent's past alleged improprieties into the trial by questioning the witness about his bias towards the defendant. The comment therefore could not have injected the kind of prejudice that would render unmeaningful the defendant's option to proceed with the trial. Because the present case quite clearly does not come within the recognized exception, I join the Court's judgment.

3. REPROSECUTION POST-ACQUITTAL/CONVICTION

The double jeopardy clause was derived in large part from the common law pleas of *autrefois acquit* (formerly acquitted) and *autrefois convict* (formerly convicted), and the two bedrock elements of the clause are the prohibitions against reprosecution for the same offense following an acquittal or a conviction. It is here, however, more so than in any other area of double jeopardy jurisprudence, that the Court has found the need to reevaluate applicable standards. In both of the cases in this section, *United States v. Scott* and *Burks v. United States,* the Court found it necessary to reassess the assumptions of earlier rulings.

Scott raises the basic question of what type of ruling should be viewed as an "acquittal." In particular, should a trial court dismissal that bars reprosecution be viewed as an acquittal without regard to the grounding of that ruling? The fact that the ending of the case in *Scott* (through dismissal) came from the judge rather than the jury was not critical; the Court had long held that the acquittal rule applied to acquittals by judges as well as by juries, a position reaffirmed in a case decided the same day as *Scott, Sanabria v. United States,* 437 U.S. 54 (1978).

Burks considers the proper scope of the "*Ball* exception" to the prohibition against reprosecution following a conviction. By allowing a reprosecution whenever a conviction was successfully overturned on a defense challenge, the *Ball* exception had basically limited that prohibition to the situation in which the defendant was willing to abide by his conviction (i.e. bring no challenge), but the state desired to prosecute again in the hopes of either raising the charge or obtaining a higher sentence. *Burks* recognizes an exception to the *Ball* exception, whereby the prohibition can have a bearing, under limited circumstances, even where the defendant successfully challenges the conviction.

UNITED STATES V. SCOTT
437 U.S. 82, 98 S.Ct. 2187, 57 L.Ed.2d 65 (1978).

JUSTICE REHNQUIST delivered the opinion of the Court.

On March 5, 1975, respondent, a member of the police force in Muskegon, Mich., was charged * * * with distribution of various narcotics. Both before his trial in the United States District Court and twice during the trial, respondent moved to dismiss the two counts of the indictment which concerned transactions that took place during the preceding September, on the ground that his defense had been prejudiced by preindictment delay. At the close of all the evidence, the court granted respondent's motion. * * *

The Government sought to appeal the dismissals of the first two counts to the United States Court of Appeals for the Sixth Circuit. That court, relying on our opinion in *United States v. Jenkins,* 420 U.S. 358 (1975), concluded that any further prosecution of respondent was barred by the Double Jeopardy Clause of the Fifth Amendment, and therefore dismissed the appeal. * * * We granted certiorari to give further consideration to the applicability of the Double Jeopardy Clause to Government appeals from orders granting defense motions to terminate a trial before verdict. We now reverse. * * *

A detailed canvass of the history of the double jeopardy principles in *United States v. Wilson,* 420 U.S. 332 (1975), led us to conclude that the Double Jeopardy Clause was primarily "directed at the threat of multiple prosecutions," and posed no bar to Government appeals "where those appeals would not require a new trial." We accordingly held in *Jenkins,* that, whether or not a dismissal of an indictment after jeopardy had attached amounted to an acquittal on the merits, the Government had no right to appeal, because "further proceedings of some sort, devoted to the resolution of factual issues going to the elements of the offense charged, would have been required upon reversal and remand."[a]

If *Jenkins* is a correct statement of the law, the judgment of the Court of Appeals * * * would in all likelihood have to be affirmed. Yet, though our assessment of the history and meaning of the Double Jeopardy Clause in *Wilson, Jenkins,* and *Serfass v. United States,* 420 U.S. 377 (1975), occurred only three Terms ago, our vastly increased exposure to the various facets of the Double Jeopardy Clause has now convinced us that *Jenkins* was wrongly decided. It placed an unwarrantedly great emphasis on the defendant's right to have his guilt decided by the first jury empaneled to try him so as to include those cases where the defendant himself seeks to terminate the trial before verdict on grounds unrelated to factual guilt or innocence. We have therefore decided to overrule *Jenkins,* and thus to reverse the judgment of the Court of Appeals in this case.

* * * At the time the Fifth Amendment was adopted, its principles were easily applied, since most criminal prosecutions proceeded to final judgment, and neither the United States nor the defendant had any right to appeal an adverse verdict. The verdict in such a case was unquestionably final, and could be raised in bar against any further prosecution for the same offense.

* * * It was not until 1889 that Congress permitted criminal defendants to seek a writ of error in this Court, and then only in capital cases. Only then did it become necessary for this Court to deal with the issues presented by the challenge of verdicts on appeal. And, in the very first case presenting the issues, *Ball v. United States,* 163 U.S. 662 (1896), the Court established principles that have been adhered to ever since. Three persons had been tried together for murder; two were convicted, the other acquitted. This Court reversed the convictions, finding the indictment fatally defective, whereupon all three defendants were tried again. This time all three were convicted and they again sought review here. This Court held that the Double Jeopardy Clause precluded further prosecution of the defendant who had been *acquitted* at the original trial but that it posed no such bar to the prosecution of those defendants who had been *convicted* in the earlier proceeding.

* * * These then, at least, are two venerable principles of double jeopardy jurisprudence. The successful appeal of a judgment of conviction, on any ground other than the insufficiency of the evidence to support the verdict, *Burks v. United States* [p. 1145], poses no bar to further prosecution on the same charge. A judgment of acquittal, whether based on a jury verdict of not guilty or on a ruling by the court that the evidence is insufficient to convict, may not be appealed and

---

[a]   In *Wilson,* after the jury returned a verdict of guilty, the trial court reconsidered an earlier motion and dismissed the indictment on due process grounds. The Supreme Court concluded that no double jeopardy concerns were raised by an appeal of that ruling. An appellate court reversal of the dismissal would not require a new trial since the appellate court could simply reinstate the jury's verdict. In *Jenkins,* the dismissal was issued by the trial judge, sitting in a bench trial, before the judge reached a verdict. The trial judge's dismissal order was based on his interpretation of the substantive law, but the judge had not indicated what result he would have reached as the finder of fact if a contrary interpretation had been adopted. Thus, if the trial judge's order were reversed, further resolution of the facts relating to the elements of the offense would be required. The *Jenkins* opinion stressed this consequence of appellate reversal rather than the grounding of the trial court's ruling as a possible "acquittal."

terminates the prosecution when a second trial would be necessitated by a reversal. What may seem superficially to be a disparity in [these] rules governing a defendant's liability to be tried again is explainable by reference to the underlying purposes of the Double Jeopardy Clause. * * * [T]he law attaches particular significance to an acquittal. To permit a second trial after an acquittal, however mistaken the acquittal may have been, would present an unacceptably high risk that the Government, with its vastly superior resources, might wear down the defendant so that "even though innocent, he may be found guilty." *Green v. United States,* 355 U.S. 184 (1957). On the other hand, to require a criminal defendant to stand trial again after he has successfully invoked a statutory right of appeal to upset his first conviction is not an act of governmental oppression of the sort against which the Double Jeopardy Clause was intended to protect. * * *

Although the primary purpose of the Double Jeopardy Clause was to protect the integrity of a final judgment, this Court has also developed a body of law guarding the separate but related interest of a defendant in avoiding multiple prosecutions even where no final determination of guilt or innocence has been made. Such interests may be involved in two different situations: the first, in which the trial judge declares a mistrial; the second, in which the trial judge terminates the proceedings favorably to the defendant on a basis not related to factual guilt or innocence.

* * * In passing on the propriety of a declaration of mistrial granted at the behest of the prosecutor or on the court's own motion, this Court has [applied the *Perez* standard of manifest necessity]. * * * Where, on the other hand, a *defendant* successfully seeks to avoid his trial prior to its conclusion by a motion for mistrial, the Double Jeopardy Clause is not offended by a second prosecution. * * * Such a motion by the defendant is deemed to be a deliberate election on his part to forego his valued right to have his guilt or innocence determined before the first trier of fact. *United States v. Dinitz* [discussed in *Kennedy*, § 2 supra].

* * *

We turn now to the relationship between the Double Jeopardy Clause and reprosecution of a defendant who has successfully obtained not a mistrial, but a termination of the trial in his favor before any determination of factual guilt or innocence. Unlike the typical mistrial, the granting of a motion such as this obviously contemplates that the proceedings will terminate then and there in favor of the defendant. The prosecution, if it wishes to reinstate the proceedings in the face of such a ruling, ordinarily must seek reversal of the decision of the trial court. * * *

* * * It is quite true that the Government with all its resources and power should not be allowed to make repeated attempts to convict an individual for an alleged offense. This truth is expressed in the three common-law pleas of *autrefois acquit, autrefois convict,* and pardon, which lie at the core of the area protected by the Double Jeopardy Clause. As we have recognized in cases from *Ball* to *Sanabria v. United States,* 437 U.S. 54 (1978), a defendant once acquitted may not be again subjected to trial without violating the Double Jeopardy Clause.

But that situation is obviously a far cry from the present case, where the Government was quite willing to continue with its production of evidence to show the defendant guilty before the jury first empaneled to try him, but the defendant elected to seek termination of the trial on grounds unrelated to guilt or innocence. This is scarcely a picture of an all-powerful state relentlessly pursuing a defendant who had either been found not guilty or who had at least insisted on having the issue of guilt submitted to the first trier of fact. It is instead a picture of a defendant who chooses to avoid conviction and imprisonment, not because of his assertion that the Government has failed to make out a case against him, but because of a legal claim that the Government's case against him must fail even though it might satisfy the trier of fact that he was guilty beyond a reasonable doubt.

We have previously noted that "the trial judge's characterization of his own action cannot control the classification of the action." * * * [A] defendant is acquitted only when "the ruling of the judge, whatever its label, actually represents a resolution [in the defendant's favor], correct or not, of some or all of the factual elements of the offense charged." Where the court, before the jury returns a verdict, enters [an order entitled] a judgment of acquittal pursuant to Fed. Rule Crim.Proc. 29, appeal will be barred only when "it is plain that the District Court * * * evaluated the Government's evidence and determined that it was legally insufficient to support a conviction." *United States v. Martin Linen Supply Company*, 430 U.S. 564 (1977).

Our opinion in *Burks* [infra] necessarily holds that there has been a "failure of proof" requiring an acquittal when the Government does not submit sufficient evidence to rebut a defendant's essentially factual defense of insanity, though it may otherwise be entitled to have its case submitted to the jury. The defense of insanity, like the defense of entrapment, arises from "the notion that Congress could not have intended criminal punishment for a defendant who has committed all the elements of a proscribed offense," where other facts established to the satisfaction of the trier of fact provide a legally adequate justification for otherwise criminal acts. Such a factual finding *does* "necessarily establish the criminal defendant's lack of criminal culpability," post, (Brennan, J., dissenting), under the existing law; the fact that "the acquittal may result from erroneous evidentiary rulings or erroneous interpretations of governing legal principles," ibid., affects the accuracy of that determination, but it does not alter its essential character. By contrast, the dismissal of an indictment for preindictment delay represents a legal judgment that a defendant, although criminally culpable, may not be punished because of a supposed constitutional violation. * * *

[I]n the present case, [defendant] successfully avoided a submission of [a part] * * * of the indictment [to the jury] by persuading the trial court to dismiss it on a basis which did not depend on guilt or innocence. He was thus neither acquitted nor convicted, because he himself successfully undertook to persuade the trial court not to submit the issue of guilt or innocence to the jury which had been empaneled to try him. * * * [Defendant] has not been "deprived" of his valued right to go to the first jury; only the public has been deprived of its valued right to "one complete opportunity to convict those who have violated its laws." *Arizona v. Washington*. No interest protected by the Double Jeopardy Clause is invaded when the

Government is allowed to appeal and seek reversal of such a mid-trial termination of the proceedings in a manner favorable to the defendant. * * *

JUSTICE BRENNAN, with whom JUSTICE WHITE, JUSTICE MARSHALL, and JUSTICE STEVENS join, dissenting.

* * * While the Double Jeopardy Clause often has the effect of protecting the accused's interest in the finality of particular favorable determinations, this is not its objective. For the Clause often permits Government appeals from final judgments favorable to the accused. See *United States v. Wilson* (whether or not final judgment was an acquittal, Government may appeal if reversal would not necessitate a retrial). The purpose of the Clause, which the Court today fails sufficiently to appreciate, is to protect the accused against the agony and risks attendant upon undergoing more than one criminal trial for any single offense. * * * Society's "willingness to limit the Government to a single criminal proceeding to vindicate its very vital interest in enforcement of criminal laws" bespeaks society's recognition of the gross unfairness of requiring the accused to undergo the strain and agony of more than one trial for any single offense. *United States v. Jorn*, 400 U.S. 470 (1971). Accordingly, the policies of the Double Jeopardy Clause mandate that the Government be afforded but one complete opportunity to convict an accused and that when the first proceeding terminates in a final judgment favorable to the defendant any retrial be barred. The rule as to acquittals can only be understood as simply an application of this larger principle.

Judgments of acquittal normally result from jury or bench verdicts of not guilty. In such cases, the acquittal represents the factfinder's conclusion that, under the controlling legal principles, the evidence does not establish that the defendant can be convicted of the offense charged in the indictment. But the judgment does not necessarily establish the criminal defendant's lack of criminal culpability; the acquittal may result from erroneous evidentiary rulings or erroneous interpretations of governing legal principles induced by the defense. Yet the Double Jeopardy Clause bars a second trial. * * * The reason is not that the first trial established the defendant's factual innocence, but rather that the second trial would present all the untoward consequences the Clause was designed to prevent. Government would be allowed to seek to persuade a second trier of fact of the defendant's guilt, to strengthen any weaknesses in its first presentation, and to subject the defendant to the expense and anxiety of a second trial.

* * * The whole premise for today's * * * [decision] * * * is the Court's new theory that a criminal defendant who seeks to avoid conviction on a "ground unrelated to factual innocence" somehow stands on a different constitutional footing than a defendant whose participation in his criminal trial creates a situation in which a judgment of acquittal has to be entered. This premise is simply untenable. * * * [T]he reasons that bar a retrial following an acquittal are equally applicable to a final judgment entered on a ground "unrelated to factual innocence." The heavy personal strain of the second trial is the same in either case. So too is the risk that, though innocent, the defendant may be found guilty at a second trial. If the appeal is allowed in either situation, the Government will, following any reversal, not only obtain the benefit of the favorable appellate ruling but also be

permitted to shore up any other weak points of its case and obtain all the other advantages at the second trial that the Double Jeopardy Clause was designed to forbid.

Moreover, the Government's interest in retrying a defendant simply cannot vary depending on the ground of the final termination in the accused's favor. I reject as plainly erroneous the Court's suggestion that final judgments not based on innocence deprive the public of "its valued right to 'one complete opportunity to convict those who have violated its laws,' " quoting *Arizona v. Washington,* and therefore differ from "true acquittals." The Government has the same "complete opportunity" in either situation by virtue of its participation as an adversary at the criminal trial.

Equally significant, the distinction between the two is at best purely formal. Many acquittals are the consequence of rulings of law made on the accused's motion that are not related to the question of his factual guilt or innocence: e.g., a ruling on the law respecting the scope of the offense or excluding reliable evidence. * * *

* * * A critical feature of today's holding appears to be the Court's definition of acquittal as "a resolution [in the defendant's favor], correct or not, of some or all of the factual elements of the offense charged," * * *. The language quoted from *Martin Linen Supply Co.,* was tied to the particular issue in that case and was never intended to serve as an all encompassing definition of acquittal for all purposes. Rather, *Martin Linen Supply* referred generally to "acquittal" as "a legal determination on the basis of facts adduced at trial relating to the general issue of the case," and this is the accepted definition. This * * * traditional definition of "acquittal" obviously is responsive to the values protected by the Double Jeopardy Clause. * * *

BURKS V. UNITED STATES
437 U.S. 1, 98 S.Ct. 2141, 57 L.Ed.2d 1 (1978).

CHIEF JUSTICE BURGER delivered the opinion of the Court.

We granted certiorari to resolve the question of whether an accused may be subjected to a second trial when conviction in a prior trial was reversed by an appellate court solely for lack of sufficient evidence to sustain the jury's verdict.

Petitioner Burks was tried in the United States District Court for the crime of robbing a federally insured bank by use of a dangerous weapon * * *. Burks' principal defense was insanity. To prove this claim petitioner produced three expert witnesses who testified, albeit with differing diagnoses of his mental condition, that he suffered from a mental illness at the time of the robbery, which rendered him substantially incapable of conforming his conduct to the requirements of the law. In rebuttal the Government offered the testimony of two experts, one of whom testified that although petitioner possessed a character disorder, he was not mentally ill. The other prosecution witness acknowledged a character disorder in petitioner, but gave a rather ambiguous answer to the question of whether Burks had been capable of conforming his conduct to the law. Lay witnesses also testified for the Government, expressing their opinion that petitioner appeared to be capable of normal functioning and was sane at the time of the alleged offense.

Before the case was submitted to the jury, the court denied a motion for a judgment of acquittal. The jury found Burks guilty as charged. * * * On appeal petitioner narrowed the issues by admitting the affirmative factual elements of the charge against him, leaving only his claim concerning criminal responsibility to be resolved. With respect to this point, the Court of Appeals agreed with petitioner's claim that the evidence was insufficient to support the verdict and reversed his conviction. * * * [It concluded that] the prosecution's evidence with respect to Burks' mental condition, even when viewed in the light most favorable to the Government, did not "effectively rebu[t]" petitioner's proof with respect to insanity and criminal responsibility.

At this point, the Court of Appeals, rather than terminating the case against petitioner, remanded to the District Court "for a determination of whether a directed verdict of acquittal should be entered or a new trial ordered." * * * [It indicated] that the District Court should choose the appropriate course "from a balancing of the equities," * * *. The Court of Appeals assumed it had the power to order this "balancing" remedy by virtue of the fact that Burks had explicitly requested a new trial. As authority for this holding the court cited, *Bryan v. United States,* 338 U.S. 552 (1950). * * *

Petitioner's argument is straightforward. He contends that the Court of Appeals' holding was nothing more or less than a decision that the District Court had erred by not granting his motion for a judgment of acquittal. By implication, he argues, the appellate reversal was the operative equivalent of a district court's judgment of acquittal, entered either before or after verdict. Petitioner points out, however, that had the District Court found the evidence at the first trial inadequate, as the Court of Appeals said it should have done, a second trial would violate the Double Jeopardy Clause of the Fifth Amendment. Therefore, he maintains, it makes no difference that the determination of evidentiary insufficiency was made by a *reviewing* court since the double jeopardy considerations are the same, regardless of which court decides that a judgment of acquittal is in order.

The position advanced by petitioner has not been embraced by our prior holdings. Indeed, as the Court of Appeals here recognized, *Bryan v. United States,* would appear to be contrary. * * * [The Court here discussed *Bryan* at length and noted that *Bryan* and similar rulings had as their "common ancestor", *Ball v. United States,* 163 U.S. 662 (1896).]

* * * *Ball v. United States* * * * [therefore] provides a logical starting point for unraveling the conceptual confusion arising from *Bryan* and the cases which have followed in its wake. This is especially true since *Ball* appears to represent the first instance in which this Court considered in any detail the double jeopardy implications of an appellate reversal.

Ball came before the Court twice, the first occasion being on writ of error from federal convictions for murder. On this initial review, those defendants who had been found guilty obtained a reversal of their convictions due to a fatally defective indictment. On remand after appeal, the trial court dismissed the flawed indictment and proceeded to retry the defendants on a new indictment. They were again convicted and the defendants came once more to this Court, arguing that their second trial was barred because of former jeopardy. The Court rejected this plea in a brief statement:

> "[A] defendant, who procures a judgment against him upon an indictment to be set aside, may be tried anew upon the same indictment, or upon another indictment, for the same offence of which he had been convicted."

The reversal in *Ball* was therefore based not on insufficiency of evidence but rather on trial error, i.e., failure to dismiss a faulty indictment. Moreover, the cases cited as authority by *Ball* were ones involving trial errors.

We have no doubt that *Ball* was correct in allowing a new trial to rectify *trial error:*

> "The principle that [the Double Jeopardy Clause] does not preclude the Government's retrying a defendant whose conviction is set aside because of an *error in the proceedings* leading to conviction is a well-established part of our constitutional jurisprudence." *United States v. Tateo,* 377 U.S. 463 (1964) (emphasis supplied).

As we have seen * * *, the cases which have arisen since *Ball* generally do not distinguish between reversals due to trial error and those resulting from evidentiary insufficiency. We believe, however, that the failure to make this distinction has contributed substantially to the present state of conceptual confusion existing in this area of the law. Consequently, it is important to consider carefully the respective roles of these two types of reversals in double jeopardy analysis.

Various rationales have been advanced to support the policy of allowing retrial to correct trial error, but in our view the most reasonable justification is that advanced by *Tateo.*

> "It would be a high price indeed for society to pay were every accused granted immunity from punishment because of any defect sufficient to constitute reversible error in the proceedings leading to conviction."

In short, reversal for trial error, as distinguished from evidentiary insufficiency, does not constitute a decision to the effect that the government has failed to prove its case. As such, it implies nothing with respect to the guilt or innocence of the defendant. Rather, it is a determination that a defendant has been convicted through a judicial process which is defective in some fundamental respect, e.g., incorrect receipt or rejection of evidence, incorrect instructions, or prosecutorial misconduct. When this occurs, the accused has a strong interest in obtaining a fair readjudication of his guilt free from error, just as society maintains a valid concern for insuring that the guilty are punished.

The same cannot be said when a defendant's conviction has been overturned due to a failure of proof at trial, in which case the prosecution cannot complain of prejudice, for it has been given one fair opportunity to offer whatever proof it could assemble.[10] Moreover, such an appellate reversal means that the government's case was so lacking that it should not have even been *submitted* to the jury. Since we necessarily afford absolute finality to a jury's *verdict* of acquittal—no matter how erroneous its decision—it is difficult to conceive how society has any greater interest in retrying a defendant when, on review, it is decided as a matter of law that the jury could not properly have returned a verdict of guilty.

The importance of a reversal on grounds of evidentiary insufficiency for purposes of inquiry under the Double Jeopardy Clause is underscored by the fact that a federal court's role in deciding whether a case should be considered by the jury is quite limited. Even the trial court, which has heard the testimony of witnesses firsthand, is not to weigh the evidence or assess the credibility of witnesses when it judges the merits of a motion for acquittal. The prevailing rule has long been that a district judge is to submit a case to the jury if the evidence and inferences therefrom most favorable to the prosecution would warrant the jury's finding the defendant guilty beyond a reasonable doubt. Obviously a federal appellate court applies no higher a standard; rather, it must sustain the verdict if there is substantial evidence, viewed in the light most favorable to the Government, to uphold the jury's decision. While this is not the appropriate occasion to re-examine in detail the standards for appellate reversal on grounds of insufficient evidence, it is apparent that such a decision will be confined to cases where the prosecution's failure is clear. Given the requirements for entry of a judgment of acquittal, the purposes of the Clause would be negated were we to afford the government an opportunity for the proverbial "second bite at the apple."

In our view it makes no difference that a defendant has sought a new trial as one of his remedies, or even as the sole remedy. It cannot be meaningfully said that a person "waives" his right to a judgment of acquittal by moving for a new trial. * * * Since we hold today that the Double Jeopardy Clause precludes a second trial once the reviewing court has found the evidence legally insufficient, the only "just" remedy available for that court is the direction of a judgment of acquittal. To the extent that our prior decisions suggest that by moving for a new trial, a defendant

---

[10] In holding the evidence insufficient to sustain guilt, an appellate court determines that the prosecution has failed to prove guilt beyond a reasonable doubt. See *American Tobacco Co. v. United States*, 328 U.S. 781 (1946).

waives his right to a judgment of acquittal on the basis of evidentiary insufficiency, those cases are overruled. * * *

JUSTICE BLACKMUN took no part in the consideration or decision of this case.[a]

---

[a]   In *Lockhart v. Nelson*, 488 U.S. 33 (1988), the question presented was "whether the Double Jeopardy Clause allows retrial when a reviewing court determines that a defendant's conviction must be reversed because evidence was erroneously admitted against him, and also concludes that without the inadmissible evidence there was insufficient evidence to support a conviction." The Court concluded that the "logic of *Burks* requires the question to be answered in the affirmative." The Court reasoned that the situation presented here was "that * * * described in *Burks* as reversal for 'trial error'—the trial court erred in admitting a particular piece of evidence, and without it there was insufficient evidence to support a judgment of conviction. But clearly *with* that evidence, there was enough to support the sentence * * *. It is quite clear from our opinion in *Burks* that a reviewing court must consider all of the evidence admitted by the trial court in deciding whether retrial is permissible under the Double Jeopardy Clause * * *. The basis for the *Burks* exception to the general rule is that a reversal for insufficiency of the evidence should be treated no differently than a trial court's granting a judgment of acquittal at the close of all the evidence. A trial court in passing on such a motion considers all of the evidence it has admitted, and to make the analogy complete it must be this same quantum of evidence which is considered by the reviewing court."

CHAPTER 20

SENTENCING PROCEDURES

■ ■ ■

Sentencing procedures vary substantially from jurisdiction to jurisdiction. A state's sentencing procedures are determined in part by the structure of the state's sentencing system. That structure may vary both as to who has responsibility for sentencing and how much discretion is granted that sentencer. Apart from capital punishment (where jury sentencing is traditionally used), sentencing authority is usually vested in the judge. A small group of states, however, also employ jury sentencing for non-capital, felony sentencing. Such jury sentencing focuses largely on the nature of the crime. The jury imposes a sentence, within a maximum and minimum set by law, based on the evidence it has heard at trial. It does not have before it the information on the defendant's background that would be developed through the presentence report in a judicial sentencing system or through a sentencing hearing in a capital case. As with its decision on guilt, the jury announces its sentence without explaining its grounding. Moreover, in non-capital jury sentencing, ordinarily no attempt is made to guide the jury's exercise of discretion by offering illustrations of those factors that might justify the choice of one sentence or another within the range allowed by the legislature.

Judicial sentencing, like jury sentencing, starts with legislative direction as to the maximum and minimum sentences allowed. Under an indeterminate sentencing structure, where the sentence is to be incarceration, the legislature requires the court to impose a sentence consisting of both maximum and minimum periods of incarceration, with the parole board determining the actual length of the incarceration within those limits. In such jurisdictions, judges traditionally were given no direction as to choice of sentence within the legislatively prescribed limits, except that there must be a certain gap between the maximum and minimum sentence (e.g., the minimum can be no more than half of the maximum). The judge need not set forth any reason for selecting any particular maximum and minimum nor, where probation is a legislatively allowable alternative, for choosing incarceration over probation.

Judicial sentencing under an indeterminate sentencing structure traditionally was accompanied by limited procedural safeguards. The defense had the opportunity to present information that it believed to be relevant to sentencing and the defendant had a right to speak personally as to the sentence (a right of "allocution"). The defense did not necessarily know, however, what other information the judge was considering, or what factual assessments were being made by the judge in setting the sentence. That additional information came from a presentence report prepared by the probation department, and the defendant was given limited access, if any, to that report. Over the latter half of the twentieth century, however, a consensus gradually emerged that disclosure of the basic contents of the presentence report to the defense should be the norm.

Defense awareness of the factors considered by the judge in exercising sentencing discretion quite naturally led to due process challenges to both the factors considered by the judges and the evidentiary support for those factors. The first case in this chapter, *United States v. Grayson*, is a leading case considering the bearing of due process on such issues in the context of a traditional indeterminate sentencing structure.

The second case, *Mitchell v. United States*, like *Grayson*, relates to the exercise of a procedural right by the defendant. Here, however, the right exercised is the privilege against self-incrimination, and it is exercised in the context of an evidentiary hearing held as part of the sentencing process. The applicability of the privilege in this context is an issue not likely to be presented in a traditional indeterminate sentencing structure, as evidentiary hearings are not a standard procedural element of that structure. However, such hearings commonly are required where the legislature has prescribed mandatory minimum sentences (as in *Mitchell*) or has otherwise restricted or "channeled" discretion (as discussed below).

Since the 1970s, many jurisdictions have moved away from the traditional indeterminate sentencing structure to determinate sentences, eliminating discretionary release by a parole board and setting definite terms of incarceration (within the statutory maximums) that defendants must serve, subject to early release for "good time" credit acquired while incarcerated. Controls on judicial discretion have been even more popular, with nationwide adoption of at least some mandatory minimum sentences, and the implementation of judicial sentencing guidelines in about a third of the states and the federal system. Mandatory minimum sentences commonly are tied to the existence of particular circumstances (e.g., the offenders use of a weapon), and where the defendant contests the prosecution's request for sentencing under the mandatory minimum, the sentencing judge must make a determination of fact as to whether that condition was present. Under guideline sentencing, guidelines set by the legislature, the state court, or an administrative agency identify factors that should be considered by the sentencing court in setting a sentence within the statutory maximum. The guideline factors determine a presumed sentence in a binding guideline system, or a recommended sentence in an advisory system. Even in a binding guidelines system, the sentencing judge has limited discretion to depart from guidelines.

The third case in this chapter, *Blakely v. Washington*, considers if and when sentencing structures that base sentence length on factual determinations made by sentencing judge violate a defendant's right to a jury determination of every element of an offense. *Blakely* sustained that challenge in the context of the binding judicial sentencing guidelines used in Washington state, and, together with subsequent decisions, has prompted revision of sentencing structures in both state and federal courts.

The last set of cases in this chapter addresses two constitutional principles that continue to impact sentencing, particularly sentencing involving the death penalty, and life in prison with no parole. *McCleskey v. Kemp* considers a challenge under the Equal Protection Clause to the death penalty in Georgia, and *Graham v. Florida* addresses the bearing of the Eighth Amendment's Cruel and Unusual Punishment Clause on a state's ability sentence a juvenile offender to prison for the remainder of his life. Finally, the opinions from *Glossip v. Gross* illuminate the justices' views on the constitutionality of the death penalty and constitutional interpretation generally.

UNITED STATES V. GRAYSON

438 U.S. 41, 98 S.Ct. 2610, 57 L.Ed.2d 582 (1978).

CHIEF JUSTICE BURGER delivered the opinion of the Court.

We granted certiorari to review a holding of the Court of Appeals that it was improper for a sentencing judge, in fixing the sentence within the statutory limits, to give consideration to the defendant's false testimony observed by the judge during the trial.

In August 1975, respondent Grayson was confined in a federal prison camp under a conviction for distributing a controlled substance. In October, he escaped but was apprehended two days later by FBI agents in New York City. He was indicted for prison escape in violation of 18 U.S.C. § 751(a).

During its case in chief, the United States proved the essential elements of the crime, including his lawful confinement and the unlawful escape. In addition, it presented the testimony of the arresting FBI agents that Grayson, upon being apprehended, denied his true identity.

Grayson testified in his own defense. He admitted leaving the camp but asserted that he did so out of fear: "I had just been threatened with a large stick with a nail protruding through it by an inmate that was serving time at Allenwood, and I was scared, and I just ran." He testified that the threat was made in the presence of many inmates by prisoner Barnes who sought to enforce collection of a gambling debt and followed other threats and physical assaults made for the same purpose. Grayson called one inmate, who testified: "I heard [Barnes] talk to Grayson in a loud voice one day, but that's all. I never seen no harm, no hands or no shuffling whatsoever."

Grayson's version of the facts was contradicted by the Government's rebuttal evidence and by cross-examination on crucial aspects of his story. For example, Grayson stated that after crossing the prison fence he left his prison jacket by the side of the road. On recross, he stated that he also left his prison shirt but not his trousers. Government testimony showed that on the morning after the escape, a shirt marked with Grayson's number, a jacket, and a pair of prison trousers were found outside a hole in the prison fence.[1] Grayson also testified on cross-

---

[1] The testimony regarding the prison clothing was important for reasons in addition to the light it shed on quality of recollection. Grayson stated that after unpremeditatedly fleeing the prison with no possessions and crossing the fence, he hitchhiked to New York City—a difficult task for a man with no trousers. The United States suggested that by prearrangement Grayson met someone, possibly a woman friend, on the highway near the break in the fence and that this

examination: "I do believe that I phrased the rhetorical question to Captain Kurd, who was in charge of [the prison], and I think I said something if an inmate was being threatened by somebody, what would * * * he do? First of all he said he would want to know who it was." On further cross-examination, however, Grayson modified his description of the conversation. Captain Kurd testified that Grayson had never mentioned in any fashion threats from other inmates. Finally, the alleged assailant, Barnes, by then no longer an inmate, testified that Grayson had never owed him any money and that he had never threatened or physically assaulted Grayson.

The jury returned a guilty verdict, whereupon the District Judge ordered the United States Probation Office to prepare a presentence report. At the sentencing hearing, the judge stated:

> "I'm going to give my reasons for sentencing in this case with clarity, because one of the reasons may well be considered by a Court of Appeals to be impermissible; and although I could come into this Court Room and sentence this Defendant to a five-year prison term without any explanation at all, I think it is fair that I give the reasons so that if the Court of Appeals feels that one of the reasons which I am about to enunciate is an improper consideration for a trial judge, then the Court will be in a position to reverse this Court and send the case back for re-sentencing.

> "In my view a prison sentence is indicated, and the sentence that the Court is going to impose is to deter you, Mr. Grayson, and others who are similarly situated. Secondly, *it is my view that your defense was a complete fabrication without the slightest merit whatsoever. I feel it is proper for me to consider that fact in the sentencing, and I will do so."* (Emphasis added.)

He then sentenced Grayson to a term of two years' imprisonment, consecutive to his unexpired sentence.

On appeal, a divided panel of the Court of Appeals for the Third Circuit directed that Grayson's sentence be vacated and that he be resentenced by the District Court without consideration of false testimony. * * * We reverse.

In *Williams v. New York,* 337 U.S. 241 (1949), Mr. Justice Black observed that the "prevalent modern philosophy of penology [is] that the punishment should fit the offender and not merely the crime," and that, accordingly, sentences should be determined with an eye toward the "[r]eformation and rehabilitation of offenders." But it has not always been so. In the early days of the Republic, * * * the period of incarceration was generally prescribed with specificity by the legislature. Each crime had its defined punishment. * * *

Approximately a century ago, a reform movement asserting that the purpose of incarceration, and therefore the guiding consideration in sentencing, should be rehabilitation of the offender, dramatically altered the approach to sentencing. A

---

accomplice provided civilian clothes. It introduced evidence that the friend visited Grayson often at prison, including each of the three days immediately prior to his penultimate day in the camp.

fundamental proposal of this movement was a flexible sentencing system permitting judges and correctional personnel, particularly the latter, to set the release date of prisoners according to informed judgments concerning their potential for, or actual, rehabilitation and their likely recidivism. * * * Indeterminate sentencing under the rehabilitation model presented sentencing judges with a serious practical problem: how rationally to make the required predictions so as to avoid capricious and arbitrary sentences, which the newly conferred and broad discretion placed within the realm of possibility. An obvious, although only partial, solution was to provide the judge with as much information as reasonably practical concerning the defendant's "character and propensities[,] * * * his present purposes and tendencies," and, indeed, "every aspect of [his] life." *Williams v. New York.* Thus, most jurisdictions provided trained probation officers to conduct presentence investigations of the defendant's life and, on that basis, prepare a presentence report for the sentencing judge.

Constitutional challenges were leveled at judicial reliance on such information, however. In *Williams v. New York,* a jury convicted the defendant of murder but recommended a life sentence. The sentencing judge, partly on the basis of information not known to the jury but contained in a presentence report, imposed the death penalty. The defendant argued that this procedure deprived him of his federal constitutional right to confront and cross-examine those supplying information to the probation officer and, through him, to the sentencing judge. The Court rejected this argument. It noted that traditionally "a sentencing judge could exercise a wide discretion in the sources and types of evidence used to assist him in determining the kind and extent of punishment to be imposed within limits fixed by law." "And modern concepts individualizing punishment have made it all the more necessary that a sentencing judge not be denied an opportunity to obtain pertinent information," indeed, "[t]o deprive sentencing judges of this kind of information would undermine modern penological procedural policies that have been cautiously adopted throughout the nation after careful consideration and experimentation." Accordingly, the sentencing judge was held not to have acted unconstitutionally in considering either the defendant's participation in criminal conduct for which he had not been convicted or information secured by the probation investigator that the defendant was a "menace to society."

Of course, a sentencing judge is not limited to the often far-ranging material compiled in a presentence report. "[B]efore making [the sentencing] determination, a judge may appropriately conduct an inquiry broad in scope, largely unlimited either as to the kind of information he may consider, or the source from which it may come." *United States v. Tucker,* 404 U.S. 443 (1972). Congress recently reaffirmed this fundamental sentencing principle by enacting 18 U.S.C. § 3577:

> "No limitation shall be placed on the information concerning the background, character, and conduct of a person convicted of an offense which a court of the United States may receive and consider for the purpose of imposing an appropriate sentence."

Thus, we have acknowledged that a sentencing authority may legitimately consider the evidence heard during trial, as well as the demeanor of the accused.

Chaffin v. Stynchcombe, 412 U.S. 17 (1973). More to the point presented in this case, one serious study has concluded that the trial judge's "opportunity to observe the defendant, particularly if he chose to take the stand in his defense, can often provide useful insights into an appropriate disposition." ABA Sentencing Alternatives and Procedures § 5.1 (App.Draft 1968).

A defendant's truthfulness or mendacity while testifying on his own behalf, almost without exception, has been deemed probative of his attitudes toward society and prospects for rehabilitation and hence relevant to sentencing. Soon after *Williams* was decided, the Tenth Circuit concluded that "the attitude of a convicted defendant with respect to his willingness to commit a serious crime [perjury] * * * is a proper matter to consider in determining what sentence shall be imposed within the limitations fixed by statute." *Humes v. United States,* 186 F.2d 875 (1951). The Second, Fourth, Fifth, Sixth, Seventh, Eighth, and Ninth Circuits have since agreed. * * * Only one Circuit has directly rejected the probative value of the defendant's false testimony in his own defense. In *Scott v. United States,* 135 U.S.App.D.C. 377 (1969), the court argued that

> "the peculiar pressures placed upon a defendant threatened with jail and the stigma of conviction make his willingness to deny the crime an unpromising test of his prospects for rehabilitation if guilty. It is indeed unlikely that many men who commit serious offenses would balk on principle from lying in their own defense. The guilty man may quite sincerely repent his crime but yet, driven by the urge to remain free, may protest his innocence in a court of law."

The *Scott* rationale rests not only on the realism of the psychological pressures on a defendant in the dock—which we can grant—but also on a deterministic view of human conduct that is inconsistent with the underlying precepts of our criminal justice system. A "universal and persistent" foundation stone in our system of law, and particularly in our approach to punishment, sentencing, and incarceration, is the "belief in freedom of the human will and a consequent ability and duty of the normal individual to choose between good and evil." Given that long-accepted view of the "ability and duty of the normal individual to choose," we must conclude that the defendant's readiness to lie under oath—especially when, as here, the trial court finds the lie to be flagrant—may be deemed probative of his prospects for rehabilitation.

Against this background we evaluate Grayson's constitutional argument that the District Court's sentence constitutes punishment for the crime of perjury for which he has not been indicted, tried, or convicted by due process. A second argument is that permitting consideration of perjury will "chill" defendants from exercising their right to testify on their own behalf.

In his due process argument, Grayson does not contend directly that the District Court had an impermissible purpose in considering his perjury and selecting the sentence. Rather, he argues that this Court, in order to preserve due process rights, not only must prohibit the impermissible sentencing practice of incarcerating for the purpose of saving the Government the burden of bringing a separate and subsequent perjury prosecution but also must prohibit the otherwise *permissible* practice of considering a defendant's untruthfulness for the purpose of illuminating his need for rehabilitation and society's need for protection. He presents two interrelated reasons. The effect of both permissible and impermissible sentencing practices may be the same: additional time in prison. Further, it is virtually impossible, he contends, to identify and establish the impermissible practice. We find these reasons insufficient justification for prohibiting what the Court and the Congress have declared appropriate judicial conduct.

First, the evolutionary history of sentencing, set out [above] * * *, demonstrates that it is proper—indeed, even necessary for the rational exercise of discretion—to consider the defendant's whole person and personality, as manifested by his conduct at trial and his testimony under oath, for whatever light those may shed on the sentencing decision. * * * Second, in our view, *Williams* fully supports consideration of such conduct in sentencing. There the Court permitted the sentencing judge to consider the offender's history of prior antisocial conduct, including burglaries for which he had not been duly convicted.[a] * * * Third, the efficacy of Grayson's suggested "exclusionary rule" is open to serious doubt. No rule of law, even one garbed in constitutional terms, can prevent improper use of firsthand observations of perjury. The integrity of the judges, and their fidelity to their oaths of office, necessarily provide the only, and in our view adequate, assurance against that.

Grayson's argument that judicial consideration of his conduct at trial impermissibly "chills" a defendant's statutory right, 18 U.S.C. § 3481, and perhaps a constitutional right, to testify on his own behalf is without basis. The right guaranteed by law to a defendant is narrowly the right to testify truthfully in accordance with the oath—unless we are to say that the oath is mere ritual without meaning. This view of the right involved is confirmed by the unquestioned constitutionality of perjury statutes, which punish those who willfully give false

---

[a]　Should the defendant subsequently be prosecuted for other criminal conduct considered in sentencing the defendant for the offense in question, the separate sentence on that prosecution does not violate double jeopardy. This is so even under a determinate sentencing scheme that directs consideration of that other criminal conduct. In *Witte v. United States*, 515 U.S. 389 (1995), the defendant was initially charged with criminal liability for a planned 1991 shipment of marijuana. Under the federal sentencing guidelines for that offense, consideration was to be given to the total quantity of drugs involved in all conduct relevant to the charged offense, which encompassed all drug transactions "within the scope of the criminal activity that defendant jointly undertook" with others. Accordingly, in sentencing for the 1991 shipment, the sentencing judge added the quantity of narcotics to be shipped in a failed 1990 shipment that was part of the "same continuing conspiracy." This raised the defendant's offense-level score to 40, which produced a sentence of 144 months (within the statutory maximum of 40 years). When defendant was subsequently prosecuted for the conspiring to import narcotics in 1990, based on the failed shipment, he argued that double jeopardy barred that prosecution because he already had been punished for that activity. Rejecting that contention, the Supreme Court noted that a court's consideration of other criminal behavior in sentencing for a particular offense simply guided sentencing on the offense charged within the statutory maximum, but did not impose punishment for the other behavior. This was not altered by guidelines that directed the sentencing court to take account of specific related conduct in determining the severity of the offense within the statutory maximum. In *United States v. Watts*, 519 U.S. 148 (1997), the Court added that "relevant conduct" considered in federal guideline sentencing could include criminal conduct that had resulted in acquittal. The acquittal only establishes the presence of a reasonable doubt and consideration for sentencing purposes generally is satisfied by a preponderance of the evidence proof standard.

testimony. Further support for this is found in an important limitation on a defendant's right to the assistance of counsel: Counsel ethically cannot assist his client in presenting what the attorney has reason to believe is false testimony. Assuming, *arguendo,* that the sentencing judge's consideration of defendant's untruthfulness in testifying has any chilling effect on a defendant's decision to testify falsely, that effect is entirely permissible. There is no protected right to commit perjury.

Grayson's further argument that the sentencing practice challenged here will inhibit exercise of the right to testify truthfully is entirely frivolous. That argument misapprehends the nature and scope of the practice we find permissible. Nothing we say today requires a sentencing judge to enhance, in some wooden or reflex fashion, the sentences of all defendants whose testimony is deemed false. Rather, we are reaffirming the authority of a sentencing judge to evaluate carefully a defendant's testimony on the stand, determine—with a consciousness of the frailty of human judgment—whether that testimony contained willful and material falsehoods, and, if so, assess in light of all the other knowledge gained about the defendant the meaning of that conduct with respect to his prospects for rehabilitation and restoration to a useful place in society. Awareness of such a process realistically cannot be deemed to affect the decision of an accused but unconvicted defendant to testify truthfully in his own behalf. * * *

JUSTICE STEWART, with whom JUSTICE BRENNAN and JUSTICE MARSHALL join, dissenting.

The Court begins its consideration of this case with the assumption that the respondent gave false testimony at his trial. But there has been no determination that his testimony was false. This respondent was given a greater sentence than he would otherwise have received—how much greater we have no way of knowing—solely because a single judge *thought* that he had not testified truthfully.[1] In essence, the Court holds today that *whenever* a defendant testifies in his own behalf and is found guilty, he opens himself to the possibility of an enhanced sentence. Such a sentence is nothing more or less than a penalty imposed on the defendant's exercise of his constitutional and statutory rights to plead not guilty and to testify in his own behalf.

It does not change matters to say that the enhanced sentence merely reflects the defendant's "prospects for rehabilitation" rather than an additional punishment for testifying falsely. The fact remains that all defendants who choose to testify, and only those who do so, face the very real prospect of a greater sentence based upon the trial judge's unreviewable perception that the testimony was untruthful. The Court prescribes no limitations or safeguards to minimize a defendant's rational fear that his truthful testimony will be perceived as false. Indeed, encumbrance of the sentencing process with the collateral inquiries necessary to provide such assurance would be both pragmatically unworkable and

---

[1] We know this only because of the trial judge's laudable explication of his reasons for imposing the sentence in this case. In many cases it would be impossible to discern whether a sentencing judge had been influenced by his belief that the defendant had not testified truthfully, since there is no requirement that reasons be given. But that fact does not argue against correcting an erroneous sentencing policy that is apparent on the face of the record. * * *

theoretically inconsistent with the assumption that the trial judge is merely considering one more piece of information in his overall evaluation of the defendant's prospects for rehabilitation. But without such safeguards I fail to see how the Court can dismiss as "frivolous" the argument that this sentencing practice will "inhibit exercise of the right to testify truthfully." * * *

The minimal contribution that the defendant's possibly untruthful testimony might make to an overall assessment of his potential for rehabilitation, see n. 3, cannot justify imposing this additional burden on his right to testify in his own behalf. I do not believe that a sentencing judge's discretion to consider a wide range of information in arriving at an appropriate sentence, *Williams v. New York,* allows him to mete out additional punishment to the defendant simply because of his personal belief that the defendant did not testify truthfully at the trial. Accordingly, I would affirm the judgment of the Court of Appeals.[b]

MITCHELL V. UNITED STATES
526 U.S. 314, 119 S.Ct. 1307, 143 L.Ed.2d 424 (1999).

JUSTICE KENNEDY delivered the opinion of the Court.

Two questions relating to a criminal defendant's Fifth Amendment privilege against self-incrimination are presented to us. The first is whether, in the federal criminal system, a guilty plea waives the privilege in the sentencing phase of the case, either as a result of the colloquy preceding the plea or by operation of law when the plea is entered. We hold the plea is not a waiver of the privilege at sentencing. The second question is whether, in determining facts about the crime which bear upon the severity of the sentence, a trial court may draw an adverse inference from the defendant's silence. We hold a sentencing court may not draw the adverse inference.

Petitioner Amanda Mitchell and 22 other defendants were indicted for offenses arising from a conspiracy to distribute cocaine * * *. According to the indictment, the leader of the conspiracy, Harry Riddick, obtained large quantities of cocaine and resold the drug through couriers and street sellers, including

---

[b] In *United States v. Dunnigan,* 507 U.S. 87 (1993), the Court of Appeals had held unconstitutional a sentencing guideline for federal courts that treated a defendant's perjury at trial as conduct mandating enhancement of the guideline-specified sentence within the maximum provided for the offense of conviction. The Court of Appeals distinguished *Grayson* on the grounds that: (1) *Grayson* had relied on the perjury establishing a greater need for rehabilitation, but the federal sentencing guideline was aimed at punishment; and (2) the automatic character of the guideline enhancement constituted a "wooden or reflexive" response contrary to the admonition in *Grayson.* Reversing the Court of Appeals, a unanimous Supreme Court found *Grayson* controlling and neither of the above distinctions to be persuasive. While it was true that the rehabilitation was "no longer a goal of sentencing under the guidelines," the "lengthy discussion in *Grayson* of how a defendant's perjury was relevant to the potential for rehabilitation * * * was not meant to imply that rehabilitation was the only permissible justification for an increased sentence based on perjury." So too, the "cautionary remark" in *Grayson* regarding enhancement "in some 'wooden or reflexive fashion' did not invalidate the guideline." Under guideline procedures, where the enhancement is contested by the defendant, "the elements of perjury must be found by the district court [in independent factual findings] * * *, so the enhancement is far from automatic. And that the enhancement stems from a congressional mandate rather than from a court's discretionary judgment cannot be grounds, in these circumstances, for its invalidation."

petitioner. Petitioner was charged with one count of conspiring to distribute five or more kilograms of cocaine and with three counts of distributing cocaine within 1,000 feet of a school or playground. In 1995, without any plea agreement, petitioner pleaded guilty to all four counts. She reserved the right to contest the drug quantity attributable to her under the conspiracy count, and the District Court advised her the drug quantity would be determined at her sentencing hearing.

Before accepting the plea, the District Court made the inquiries required by Rule 11 of the Federal Rules of Criminal Procedure. Informing petitioner of the penalties for her offenses, the District Judge advised her, "the range of punishment here is very complex because we don't know how much cocaine the Government's going to be able to show you were involved in." * * * By pleading guilty, the District Court [also] explained, petitioner would waive various rights, including "the right at trial to remain silent under the Fifth Amendment." After the Government explained the factual basis for the charges, the judge, having put petitioner under oath, asked her, "Did you do that?" Petitioner answered, "Some of it." She indicated that, although present for one of the transactions charged as a substantive cocaine distribution count, she had not herself delivered the cocaine to the customer. The Government maintained she was liable nevertheless as an aider and abettor of the delivery by another courier. After discussion with her counsel, petitioner reaffirmed her intention to plead guilty to all the charges. * * *

In 1996, nine of petitioner's original 22 codefendants went to trial. Three other co-defendants had pleaded guilty and agreed to cooperate with the Government. They testified petitioner was a regular seller for ringleader Riddick. At petitioner's sentencing hearing, the three adopted their trial testimony, and one of them furnished additional information on the amount of cocaine petitioner sold. On cross-examination, the codefendant conceded he had not seen petitioner on a regular basis during the relevant period. * * * Petitioner put on no evidence at sentencing, nor did she testify to rebut the Government's evidence about drug quantity. Her counsel argued, however, that the three documented sales to Alvitta Mack [totaling two ounces] constituted the only evidence of sufficient reliability to be credited in determining the quantity of cocaine attributable to her for sentencing purposes.

After this testimony at the sentencing hearing the District Court ruled that, as a consequence of her guilty plea, petitioner had no right to remain silent with respect to the details of her crimes. The court found credible the testimony indicating petitioner had been a drug courier on a regular basis. Sales of 1 1/2 to 2 ounces twice a week for a year and a half put her over the 5-kilogram threshold, thus mandating a minimum sentence of 10 years. "One of the things" persuading the court to rely on the testimony of the codefendants was petitioner's "not testifying to the contrary." * * * The District Judge told petitioner: " 'I held it against you that you didn't come forward today and tell me that you really only did this a couple of times. . . . I'm taking the position that you should come forward and explain your side of this issue. Your counsel's taking the position that you have a Fifth Amendment right not to. . . . If he's—if it's determined by a higher Court that he's right in that regard, I would be willing to bring you back for resentencing. And

if you—if—and then I might take a closer look at the [codefendants'] testimony.' "
* * *

The District Court sentenced petitioner to the statutory minimum of 10 years of imprisonment, 6 years of supervised release, and a special assessment of $200. The Court of Appeals for the Third Circuit affirmed the sentence. According to the Court of Appeals, "By voluntarily and knowingly pleading guilty to the offense Mitchell waived her Fifth Amendment privilege." The court acknowledged other Circuits have held a witness can "claim the Fifth Amendment privilege if his or her testimony might be used to enhance his or her sentence," but it said this rule "does not withstand analysis." * * *

The Government maintains that petitioner's guilty plea was a waiver of the privilege against compelled self-incrimination with respect to all the crimes comprehended in the plea. We hold otherwise and rule that petitioner retained the privilege at her sentencing hearing. It is well established that a witness, in a single proceeding, may not testify voluntarily about a subject and then invoke the privilege against self-incrimination when questioned about the details. See *Rogers v. United States*, 340 U.S. 367, 373 (1951). The privilege is waived for the matters to which the witness testifies, and the scope of the "waiver is determined by the scope of relevant cross-examination," * * *. The justifications for the rule of waiver in the testimonial context are evident: A witness may not pick and choose what aspects of a particular subject to discuss without casting doubt on the trustworthiness of the statements and diminishing the integrity of the factual inquiry. As noted in *Rogers*, a contrary rule "would open the way to distortion of facts by permitting a witness to select any stopping place in the testimony." * * * The illogic of allowing a witness to offer only self-selected testimony should be obvious even to the witness, so there is no unfairness in allowing cross-examination when testimony is given without invoking the privilege.

We may assume for purposes of this opinion, then, that if petitioner had pleaded not guilty and, having taken the stand at a trial, testified she did "some of it," she could have been cross-examined on the frequency of her drug deliveries and the quantity of cocaine involved. The concerns which justify the cross-examination when the defendant testifies are absent at a plea colloquy, however. The purpose of a plea colloquy is to protect the defendant from an unintelligent or involuntary plea. The Government would turn this constitutional shield into a prosecutorial sword by having the defendant relinquish all rights against compelled self-incrimination upon entry of a guilty plea, including the right to remain silent at sentencing. * * * There is no convincing reason why the narrow inquiry at the plea colloquy should entail such an extensive waiver of the privilege. Unlike the defendant taking the stand, who "cannot reasonably claim that the Fifth Amendment gives him . . . an immunity from cross-examination on the matters he has himself put in dispute," * * * the defendant who pleads guilty puts nothing in dispute regarding the essentials of the offense. Rather, the defendant takes those matters out of dispute, often by making a joint statement with the prosecution or confirming the prosecution's version of the facts. Under these circumstances, there is little danger that the court will be misled by selective disclosure. In this respect a guilty plea is more like an offer to stipulate than a decision to take the stand.

Here, petitioner's statement that she had done "some of" the proffered conduct did not pose a threat to the integrity of factfinding proceedings, for the purpose of the District Court's inquiry was simply to ensure that petitioner understood the charges and that there was a factual basis for the Government's case.

Nor does Federal Rule of Criminal Procedure 11, which governs pleas, contemplate the broad waiver the Government envisions. * * * Of course, a court may discharge its duty of ensuring a factual basis for a plea by "question[ing] the defendant under oath, on the record, and in the presence of counsel about the offense to which the defendant has pleaded." Rule 11(c)(5). We do not question the authority of a district court to make whatever inquiry it deems necessary in its sound discretion to assure itself the defendant is not being pressured to offer a plea for which there is no factual basis. A defendant who withholds information by invoking the privilege against self-incrimination at a plea colloquy runs the risk the district court will find the factual basis inadequate. At least once the plea has been accepted, statements or admissions made during the preceding plea colloquy are later admissible against the defendant, as is the plea itself. A statement admissible against a defendant, however, is not necessarily a waiver of the privilege against self-incrimination. Rule 11 does not prevent the defendant from relying upon the privilege at sentencing.

Treating a guilty plea as a waiver of the privilege at sentencing would be a grave encroachment on the rights of defendants. At oral argument, we asked counsel for the United States whether, on the facts of this case, if the Government had no reliable evidence of the amount of drugs involved, the prosecutor "could say, well, we can't prove it, but we'd like to put her on the stand and cross-examine her and see if we can't get her to admit it." Counsel answered: "[T]he waiver analysis that we have put forward suggests that at least as to the facts surrounding the conspiracy to which she admitted, the Government could do that." Ibid. Over 90% of federal criminal defendants whose cases are not dismissed enter pleas of guilty or nolo contendere. * * * Were we to accept the Government's position, prosecutors could indict without specifying the quantity of drugs involved, obtain a guilty plea, and then put the defendant on the stand at sentencing to fill in the drug quantity. The result would be to enlist the defendant as an instrument in his or her own condemnation, undermining the long tradition and vital principle that criminal proceedings rely on accusations proved by the Government, not on inquisitions conducted to enhance its own prosecutorial power. * * *

The centerpiece of the Third Circuit's opinion is the idea that the entry of the guilty plea completes the incrimination of the defendant, thus extinguishing the privilege. Where a sentence has yet to be imposed, however, this Court has already rejected the proposition that "incrimination is complete once guilt has been adjudicated," *Estelle v. Smith*, 451 U.S. 454 (1981), and we reject it again today. * * * It is true, as a general rule, that where there can be no further incrimination, there is no basis for the assertion of the privilege. We conclude that principle applies to cases in which the sentence has been fixed and the judgment of conviction has become final. See, e.g., *Reina v. United States*, 364 U.S. 507 (1960). If no adverse consequences can be visited upon the convicted person by reason of further testimony, then there is no further incrimination to be feared.

Where the sentence has not yet been imposed a defendant may have a legitimate fear of adverse consequences from further testimony. As the Court stated in *Estelle*: "Any effort by the State to compel [the defendant] to testify against his will at the sentencing hearing clearly would contravene the Fifth Amendment." *Estelle* was a capital case, but we find no reason not to apply the principle to noncapital sentencing hearings as well. * * * The Government itself makes the implicit concession that the acceptance of a guilty plea does not eliminate the possibility of further incrimination. In its brief to the Court, the Government acknowledges that a defendant who awaits sentencing after having pleaded guilty may assert the privilege against self-incrimination if called as a witness in the trial of a codefendant, in part because of the danger of responding "to questions that might have an adverse impact on his sentence or on his prosecution for other crimes." * * *

The Government suggests in a footnote that even if petitioner retained an unwaived privilege against self-incrimination in the sentencing phase of her case, the District Court was entitled, based on her silence, to draw an adverse inference with regard to the amount of drugs attributable to her. The normal rule in a criminal case is that no negative inference from the defendant's failure to testify is permitted. *Griffin v. California* [p. 1051]. We decline to adopt an exception for the sentencing phase of a criminal case with regard to factual determinations respecting the circumstances and details of the crime.

This Court has recognized "the prevailing rule that the Fifth Amendment does not forbid adverse inferences against parties to civil actions when they refuse to testify in response to probative evidence offered against them," *Baxter v. Palmigiano*, 425 U.S. 308 (1976), at least where refusal to waive the privilege does not lead "automatically and without more to [the] imposition of sanctions." In ordinary civil cases, the party confronted with the invocation of the privilege by the opposing side has no capacity to avoid it, say, by offering immunity from prosecution. The rule allowing invocation of the privilege, though at the risk of suffering an adverse inference or even a default, accommodates the right not to be a witness against oneself while still permitting civil litigation to proceed. Another reason for treating civil and criminal cases differently is that "the stakes are higher" in criminal cases, where liberty or even life may be at stake, and where the Government's "sole interest is to convict." *Baxter*, supra.

Baxter itself involved state prison disciplinary proceedings which, as the Court noted, "are not criminal proceedings" and "involve the correctional process and important state interests other than conviction for crime." Cf. *Ohio Adult Parole Authority v. Woodard*, 523 U.S. 272 (1998) (adverse inference permissible from silence in clemency proceeding, a nonjudicial post-conviction process which is not part of the criminal case). Unlike a prison disciplinary proceeding, a sentencing hearing is part of the criminal case—the explicit concern of the self-incrimination privilege. In accordance with the text of the Fifth Amendment, we must accord the privilege the same protection in the sentencing phase of "any criminal case" as that which is due in the trial phase of the same case, see *Griffin*, supra.

The concerns which mandate the rule against negative inferences at a criminal trial apply with equal force at sentencing. Without question, the stakes are high: Here, the inference drawn by the District Court from petitioner's silence may have resulted in decades of added imprisonment. The Government often has a motive to demand a severe sentence, so the central purpose of the privilege—to protect a defendant from being the unwilling instrument of his or her own condemnation—remains of vital importance. * * *

The rule against adverse inferences from a defendant's silence in criminal proceedings, including sentencing, is of proven utility. Some years ago the Court expressed concern that "[t]oo many, even those who should be better advised, view this privilege as a shelter for wrongdoers. They too readily assume that those who invoke it are either guilty of crime or commit perjury in claiming the privilege." *Ullmann v. United States*, 350 U.S. 422 (1956). Later, it quoted with apparent approval Wigmore's observation that "[t]he layman's natural first suggestion would probably be that the resort to privilege in each instance is a clear confession of crime." * * * It is far from clear that citizens, and jurors, remain today so skeptical of the principle or are often willing to ignore the prohibition against adverse inferences from silence. Principles once unsettled can find general and wide acceptance in the legal culture, and there can be little doubt that the rule prohibiting an inference of guilt from a defendant's rightful silence has become an essential feature of our legal tradition. This process began even before *Griffin*. When *Griffin* was being considered by this Court, some 44 States did not allow a prosecutor to invite the jury to make an adverse inference from the defendant's refusal to testify at trial. * * * The rule against adverse inferences is a vital instrument for teaching that the question in a criminal case is not whether the defendant committed the acts of which he is accused. The question is whether the Government has carried its burden to prove its allegations while respecting the defendant's individual rights. The Government retains the burden of proving facts relevant to the crime at the sentencing phase and cannot enlist the defendant in this process at the expense of the self-incrimination privilege. Whether silence bears upon the determination of a lack of remorse, or upon acceptance of responsibility for purposes of the downward adjustment provided in § 3E1.1 of the United States Sentencing Guidelines (1998), is a separate question. It is not before us, and we express no view on it. * * * By holding petitioner's silence against her in determining the facts of the offense at the sentencing hearing, the District Court imposed an impermissible burden on the exercise of the constitutional right against compelled self-incrimination.[a]

---

[a] In a later case, the Court noted that "there are reasonable arguments that the logic of *Mitchell* does not apply" in a capital sentencing proceeding that follows a defendant's guilty plea in which he had admitted "every relevant fact on which [the state] bore the burden of proof." In such a case, the state "could not have shifted to respondent its 'burden of proving facts relevant to the crime.'" *White v. Woodall*, 572 U.S. 415 (2014). The Court also rejected the argument that the holdings of *Mitchell* and *Estelle v. Smith* necessarily require a blanket no-inference instruction (see *Carter v. Kentucky*, fn. b, p. 1054) during the penalty phase of a capital case, noting that *Mitchell* itself suggests that some inferences from silence regarding remorse might be permissible.

JUSTICE SCALIA, with whom THE CHIEF JUSTICE, JUSTICE O'CONNOR, and JUSTICE THOMAS join, dissenting.

I agree with the Court that Mitchell had the right to invoke her Fifth Amendment privilege during the sentencing phase of her criminal case. In my view, however, she did not have the right to have the sentencer abstain from making the adverse inferences that reasonably flow from her failure to testify. I therefore respectfully dissent.

The Fifth Amendment provides that "[n]o person . . . shall be compelled in any criminal case to be a witness against himself." As an original matter, it would seem to me that the threat of an adverse inference does not "compel" anyone to testify. It is one of the natural (and not governmentally imposed) consequences of failing to testify—as is the factfinder's increased readiness to believe the incriminating testimony that the defendant chooses not to contradict. Both of these consequences are assuredly cons rather than pros in the "to testify or not to testify" calculus, but they do not compel anyone to take the stand. Indeed, I imagine that in most instances, a guilty defendant would choose to remain silent despite the adverse inference, on the theory that it would do him less damage than his own cross-examined testimony.

Despite the text, we held in *Griffin v. California*, that it was impermissible for the prosecutor or judge to comment on a defendant's refusal to testify. We called it a "penalty" imposed on the defendant's exercise of the privilege. Ibid. And we did not stop there, holding in *Carter v. Kentucky*, that a judge must, if the defendant asks, instruct the jury that it may not sua sponte consider the defendant's silence as evidence of his guilt.

The majority muses that the no-adverse-inference rule has found "wide acceptance in the legal culture" and has even become "an essential feature of our legal tradition." Although the latter assertion strikes me as hyperbolic, the former may be true—which is adequate reason not to overrule these cases, a course I in no way propose. It is not adequate reason, however, to extend these cases into areas where they do not yet apply, since neither logic nor history can be marshaled in defense of them. The illogic of the *Griffin* line is plain, for it runs exactly counter to normal evidentiary inferences: If I ask my son whether he saw a movie I had forbidden him to watch, and he remains silent, the import of his silence is clear. Indeed, we have on other occasions recognized the significance of silence, saying that " '[f]ailure to contest an assertion . . . is considered evidence of acquiescence . . . if it would have been natural under the circumstances to object to the assertion in question.' " *Baxter v. Palmigiano*.

And as for history, *Griffin*'s pedigree is equally dubious. The question whether a factfinder may draw a logical inference from a criminal defendant's failure to offer formal testimony would not have arisen in 1791, because common-law evidentiary rules prevented a criminal defendant from testifying in his own behalf even if he wanted to do so. That is not to say, however, that a criminal defendant was not allowed to speak in his own behalf, and a tradition of expecting the defendant to do so, and of drawing an adverse inference when he did not, strongly suggests that *Griffin* is out of sync with the historical understanding of the Fifth

Amendment. Traditionally, defendants were expected to speak rather extensively at both the pretrial and trial stages of a criminal proceeding. The longstanding common-law principle, *nemo tenetur seipsum prodere*, was thought to ban only testimony forced by compulsory oath or physical torture, not voluntary, unsworn testimony.

Pretrial procedure in colonial America was governed (as it had been for centuries in England) by the Marian Committal Statute, which * * * [required the magistrate to "take the examination" of the arrested person not under oath and to record his response]. The justice of the peace [then] testified at trial as to the content of the defendant's statement; if the defendant refused to speak, this would also have been reported to the jury.

At trial, defendants were expected to speak directly to the jury. Sir James Stephen described 17th- and 18th-century English trials as follows: "[T]he prisoner in cases of felony could not be defended by counsel, and had therefore to speak for himself. He was thus unable to say . . . that his mouth was closed. On the contrary his mouth was not only open, but the evidence given against him operated as so much indirect questioning, and if he omitted to answer the questions it suggested he was very likely to be convicted." * * * Though it is clear that adverse inference from silence was permitted, I have been unable to find any case adverting to that inference in upholding a conviction—which suggests that defendants rarely thought it in their interest to remain silent.

No one, however, seemed to think this system inconsistent with the principle of *nemo tenetur seipsum prodere*. And there is no indication whatever that criminal procedure in America made an abrupt about-face when this principle was ratified as a fundamental right in the Fifth Amendment and its state-constitution analogues. Justices of the peace continued pretrial questioning of suspects, whose silence continued to be introduced against them at trial. * * * If any objection was raised to the pretrial procedure, it was on the purely statutory ground that the Marian Committal Statute had no force in the new republic. * * * And defendants continued to speak at their trials until the assistance of counsel became more common, which occurred gradually throughout the 19th century. * * *

The *Griffin* question did not arise until States began enacting statutes providing that criminal defendants were competent to testify under oath on their own behalf. Maine was first in 1864, and the rest of the States and Federal Government eventually followed. Although some of these statutes (including the federal statute, 18 U.S.C. § 3481) contained a clause cautioning that no negative inference should be drawn from the defendant's failure to testify, disagreement with this approach was sufficiently widespread that, as late as 1953, the Uniform Rules of Evidence drafted by the National Conference of Commissioners on Uniform State Laws provided that "[i]f an accused in a criminal action does not testify, counsel may comment upon [sic] accused's failure to testify, and the trier of fact may draw all reasonable inferences therefrom." Uniform Rule of Evidence 23(4). See also Model Code of Evidence Rule 201(3) (1942) (similar).

Whatever the merits of prohibiting adverse inferences as a legislative policy, the text and history of the Fifth Amendment give no indication that there is a federal constitutional prohibition on the use of the defendant's silence as demeanor evidence. Our hardy forebearers, who thought of compulsion in terms of the rack and oaths forced by the power of law, would not have viewed the drawing of a commonsensical inference as equivalent pressure. And it is implausible that the Americans of 1791, who were subject to adverse inferences for failing to give unsworn testimony, would have viewed an adverse inference for failing to give sworn testimony as a violation of the Fifth Amendment. Nor can it reasonably be argued that the new statutes somehow created a "revised" understanding of the Fifth Amendment that was incorporated into the Due Process Clause of the Fourteenth Amendment, since only nine States (and not the Federal Government) had enacted competency statutes when the Fourteenth Amendment was adopted, and three of them did not prohibit adverse inferences from failure to testify.

The Court's decision in *Griffin*, however, did not even pretend to be rooted in a historical understanding of the Fifth Amendment. Rather, in a breathtaking act of sorcery it simply transformed legislative policy into constitutional command, quoting a passage from an earlier opinion describing the benevolent purposes of 18 U.S.C. § 3481, and then decreeing, with literally nothing to support it: "If the words 'Fifth Amendment' are substituted for 'act' and for 'statute,' the spirit of the Self-Incrimination Clause is reflected." Imagine what a constitution we would have if this mode of exegesis were generally applied—if, for example, without any evidence to prove the point, the Court could simply say of all federal procedural statutes, "If the words 'Fifth Amendment' are substituted for 'act' and for 'statute,' the spirit of the Due Process Clause is reflected." To my mind, *Griffin* was a wrong turn—which is not cause enough to overrule it, but is cause enough to resist its extension.

The Court asserts that it will not "adopt an exception" to *Griffin* for the sentencing phase of a criminal case. That characterization of what we are asked to do is evidently demanded, in the Court's view, by the very text of the Fifth Amendment: The phrase "any criminal case" requires us to "accord the privilege the same protection in the sentencing phase . . . as that which is due in the trial phase of the same case." That is demonstrably not so.

Our case law has long recognized a natural dichotomy between the guilt and penalty phases. The jury-trial right contained in the Sixth Amendment—whose guarantees apply "[i]n all criminal prosecutions," a term indistinguishable for present purposes from the Fifth Amendment's "in any criminal case"—does not apply at sentencing. Nor does the Sixth Amendment's guarantee of the defendant's right "to be confronted with the witnesses against him." (The sentencing judge may consider, for example, reports of probation officers and psychiatrists without affording any cross-examination.) See *Williams v. New York*. Likewise inapplicable at sentencing is the requirement of the Due Process Clause that the prosecution prove the essential facts beyond a reasonable doubt. *McMillan v. Pennsylvania*, 477 U.S. 79, 92 (1986).

* * * Consistency with other areas of our jurisprudence points in the same direction. We have permitted adverse inferences to be drawn from silence where the consequence is a denial of clemency, and even deportation * * *. There is no reason why the increased punishment to which the defendant is exposed in the

sentencing phase of a completed criminal trial should be treated differently—unless it is the theory that the guilt and sentencing phases form one inseparable "criminal case," which I have refuted above. Nor, I might add—despite the broad dicta that it quotes from *Estelle*—does the majority really believe that the guilt and sentencing phases are a unified whole, else it would not leave open the possibility that the acceptance-of-responsibility sentencing guideline escapes the ban on negative inferences.

Which brings me to the greatest—the most bizarre—inconsistency of all: the combination of the rule that the Court adopts today with the balance of our jurisprudence relating to sentencing in particular. "[C]ourts in this country and in England," we have said, have "practiced a policy under which a sentencing judge [can] exercise a wide discretion in the sources and types of evidence used to assist him in determining the kind and extent of punishment to be imposed within limits fixed by law." *Williams v. New York*. "[A] sentencing judge 'may appropriately conduct an inquiry broad in scope, largely unlimited either as to the kind of information he may consider, or the source from which it may come.' " "Few facts available to a sentencing judge," we have observed, "are more relevant to 'the likelihood that [a defendant] will transgress no more, the hope that he may respond to rehabilitative efforts to assist with a lawful future career, [and] the degree to which he does or does not deem himself at war with his society' " than a defendant's willingness to cooperate. *Roberts v. United States*. Today's opinion states, in as inconspicuous a manner as possible at the very end of its analysis (one imagines that if the statement were delivered orally it would be spoken in a very low voice, and with the Court's hand over its mouth), that its holding applies only to inferences drawn from silence "in determining facts of the offense." "Whether silence bears upon the determination of a lack of remorse, or upon acceptance of responsibility for purposes of the downward adjustment provided in § 3E1.1 of the United States Sentencing Guidelines (1998) is a separate question" on which the majority expresses no view. Never mind that we have said before, albeit in dicta, that "[w]e doubt that a principled distinction may be drawn between 'enhancing' the punishment imposed upon the petitioner and denying him the 'leniency' he claims would be appropriate if he had cooperated." *Roberts*, supra.

Of course the clutter swept under the rug by limiting the opinion to "determining facts of the offense" is not merely application of today's opinion to § 3E1.1, but its application to all determinations of acceptance of responsibility, repentance, character, and future dangerousness, in both federal and state prosecutions—that is to say, to what is probably the bulk of what most sentencing is all about. If the Court ultimately decides—in the fullness of time and after a decent period of confusion in the lower courts—that the "no inference" rule is indeed limited to "determining facts of the offense," then we will have a system in which a state court can increase the sentence of a convicted drug possessor who refuses to say how many ounces he possessed—not because that suggests he possessed the larger amount (to make such an inference would be unconstitutional!) but because his refusal to cooperate suggests he is unrepentant. Apart from the fact that there is no logical basis for drawing such a line within the sentencing phase (whereas drawing a line between guilt and sentencing is entirely logical), the result produced provides new support for Mr. Bumble's renowned evaluation of the law. Its only sensible feature is that it will almost always be unenforceable, since it will ordinarily be impossible to tell whether the sentencer has used the silence for either purpose or for neither.

If, on the other hand, the Court ultimately decides—in the fullness of time and after a decent period of confusion in the lower courts—that the extension of *Griffin* announced today is not limited to "determining facts of the offense," then it will have created a system in which we give the sentencing judge access to all sorts of out-of-court evidence, including the most remote hearsay, concerning the character of the defendant, his prior misdeeds, his acceptance of responsibility and determination to mend his ways, but declare taboo the most obvious piece of first-hand evidence standing in front of the judge: the defendant's refusal to cooperate with the court. Such a rule orders the judge to avert his eyes from the elephant in the courtroom when it is the judge's job to size up the elephant. * * *

The Court asserts that the rule against adverse inferences from silence, even in sentencing proceedings, "is of proven utility." Significantly, however, the only utility it proceeds to describe—that it is a "vital instrument" for teaching jurors that "the question in a criminal case is not whether the defendant committed the acts of which he is accused," but rather "whether the Government has carried its burden to prove its allegations"—is a utility that has no bearing upon sentencing, or indeed even upon the usual sentencer, which is a judge rather than a jury. * * *

Though the Fifth Amendment protects Mitchell from being compelled to take the stand, and also protects her, as we have held, from adverse inferences drawn from her silence at the guilt phase of the trial, there is no reason why it must also shield her from the natural and appropriate consequences of her uncooperativeness at the sentencing stage. I respectfully dissent.

JUSTICE THOMAS, dissenting.

JUSTICE SCALIA's dissenting opinion persuasively demonstrates that this Court's decision in *Griffin v. California*, lacks foundation in the Constitution's text, history, or logic. * * * And, in my view, it also illustrates that Griffin and its progeny, including *Carter v. Kentucky*, should be reexamined. * * *

BLAKELY V. WASHINGTON
542 U.S. 296, 124 S.Ct. 2531, 159 L.Ed.2d 403 (2004).

JUSTICE SCALIA delivered the opinion of the Court.

Petitioner Ralph Howard Blakely, Jr., pleaded guilty to the kidnaping of his estranged wife. The facts admitted in his plea, standing alone, supported a maximum sentence of 53 months. Pursuant to state law, the court imposed an "exceptional" sentence of 90 months after making a judicial determination that he had acted with "deliberate cruelty." We consider whether this violated petitioner's Sixth Amendment right to trial by jury.

I

* * * In 1998, [petitioner abducted his wife Yolanda], binding her with duct tape and forcing her at knifepoint into a wooden box in the bed of his pickup truck. In the process, he implored her to dismiss [her] divorce suit and related trust proceedings. When the couple's 13-year-old son Ralphy returned home from school, petitioner ordered him to follow in another car, threatening to harm Yolanda with a shotgun if he did not do so. Ralphy escaped and sought help when they stopped at a gas station, but petitioner continued on with Yolanda to a friend's house in Montana. He was finally arrested after the friend called the police.

The State charged petitioner with first-degree kidnaping, Wash. Rev.Code Ann. § 9A.40.020(1). Upon reaching a plea agreement, however, it reduced the charge to second-degree kidnaping involving domestic violence and use of a firearm, see §§ 9A.40.030(1), 10.99.020(3)(p), 9.94A.125. Petitioner entered a guilty plea admitting the elements of second-degree kidnaping and the domestic-violence and firearm allegations, but no other relevant facts.

The case then proceeded to sentencing. In Washington, second-degree kidnaping is a class B felony. State law provides that "[n]o person convicted of a [class B] felony shall be punished by confinement exceeding . . . a term of ten years." Other provisions of state law, however, further limit the range of sentences a judge may impose. Washington's Sentencing Reform Act specifies, for petitioner's offense of second-degree kidnaping with a firearm, a "standard range" of 49 to 53 months. See § 9.94A.320 (seriousness level V for second-degree kidnaping); App. 27 (offender score 2 based on § 9.94A.360); § 9.94A.310(1), box 2-V (standard range of 13–17 months); § 9.94A.310(3)(b) (36-month firearm enhancement). A judge may impose a sentence above the standard range if he finds "substantial and compelling reasons justifying an exceptional sentence." § 9.94A.120(2). The Act lists aggravating factors that justify such a departure, which it recites to be illustrative rather than exhaustive. § 9.94A.390. Nevertheless, "[a] reason offered to justify an exceptional sentence can be considered only if it takes into account factors other than those which are used in computing the standard range sentence for the offense." *State v. Gore*, 143 Wash.2d 288, 315–316, 21 P.3d 262, 277 (2001). When a judge imposes an exceptional sentence, he must set forth findings of fact and conclusions of law supporting it. § 9.94A.120(3). A reviewing court will reverse the sentence if it finds that "under a clearly erroneous standard there is insufficient evidence in the record to support the reasons for imposing an exceptional sentence." *Gore*, supra.

Pursuant to the plea agreement, the State recommended a sentence within the standard range of 49 to 53 months. After hearing Yolanda's description of the kidnaping, however, the judge rejected the State's recommendation and imposed an exceptional sentence of 90 months—37 months beyond the standard maximum. He justified the sentence on the ground that petitioner had acted with "deliberate cruelty," a statutorily enumerated ground for departure in domestic-violence cases. § 9.94A.390(2)(h)(iii).

Faced with an unexpected increase of more than three years in his sentence, petitioner objected. The judge accordingly conducted a 3-day bench hearing featuring testimony from petitioner, Yolanda, Ralphy, a police officer, and medical experts. After the hearing, he issued 32 findings of fact, concluding: "The defendant's motivation to commit kidnapping was complex, contributed to by his mental condition and personality disorders, the pressures of the divorce litigation, the impending trust litigation trial and anger over his troubled interpersonal relationships with his spouse and children. While he misguidedly intended to forcefully reunite his family, his attempt to do so was subservient to his desire to terminate lawsuits and modify title ownerships to his benefit. * * * The defendant's methods were more homogeneous than his motive. He used stealth and surprise, and took advantage of the victim's isolation. He immediately employed physical violence, restrained the victim with tape, and threatened her with injury and death to herself and others. He immediately coerced the victim into providing information by the threatening application of a knife. He violated a subsisting restraining order."

The judge adhered to his initial determination of deliberate cruelty. Petitioner appealed, arguing that this sentencing procedure deprived him of his federal constitutional right to have a jury determine beyond a reasonable doubt all facts legally essential to his sentence. The State Court of Appeals affirmed * * *. The Washington Supreme Court denied discretionary review.

II

This case requires us to apply the rule we expressed in *Apprendi v. New Jersey*, 530 U.S. 466, 490 (2000): "Other than the fact of a prior conviction,[a] any fact that increases the penalty for a crime beyond the prescribed statutory maximum must be submitted to a jury, and proved beyond a reasonable doubt." This rule reflects two longstanding tenets of common-law criminal jurisprudence: that the "truth of every accusation" against a defendant "should afterwards be confirmed by the unanimous suffrage of twelve of his equals and neighbours," 4 W. Blackstone, *Commentaries on the Laws of England* 343 (1769), and that "an accusation which lacks any particular fact which the law makes essential to the

---

[a]　*Apprendi* recognized this "exception" based on the Court's earlier decision, *Almendarez-Torres v. United States*, 523 U.S. 224 (1998), which sustained an increase of defendant's sentence from two to twenty years based a judge's finding under a recidivist statute. The *Apprendi* Court noted in this regard: "Finally, * * * *Almendarez-Torres* represents at best an exceptional departure from the historic practice that we have described. * * * Because Almendarez-Torres had admitted the three earlier convictions for aggravated felonies—all of which had been entered pursuant to proceedings with substantial procedural safeguards of their own—no question concerning the right to a jury trial or the standard of proof that would apply to a contested issue of fact was before the Court. Although our conclusion in that case was based in part on our application of the criteria we had invoked in *McMillan* [described infra], the special question decided concerned the sufficiency of the indictment. More important, * * * our conclusion in *Almendarez-Torres* turned heavily upon the fact that the additional sentence to which the defendant was subject was 'the prior commission of a serious crime.' * * * Both the certainty that procedural safeguards attached to any 'fact' of prior conviction, and the reality that Almendarez-Torres did not challenge the accuracy of that 'fact' in his case, mitigated the due process and Sixth Amendment concerns otherwise implicated in allowing a judge to determine a 'fact' increasing punishment beyond the maximum of the statutory range. * * * Even though it is arguable that *Almendarez-Torres* was incorrectly decided, and that a logical application of our reasoning today should apply if the recidivist issue were contested, Apprendi does not contest the decision's validity and we need not revisit it for purposes of our decision today to treat the case as a narrow exception to the general rule we recalled at the outset."

punishment is . . . no accusation within the requirements of the common law, and it is no accusation in reason," 1 J. Bishop, *Criminal Procedure* § 87, p. 55 (2d ed. 1872). These principles have been acknowledged by courts and treatises since the earliest days of graduated sentencing; we compiled the relevant authorities in *Apprendi*, * * * and need not repeat them here.[6]

Apprendi involved a New Jersey hate-crime statute that authorized a 20-year sentence, despite the usual 10-year maximum, if the judge found the crime to have been committed " 'with a purpose to intimidate . . . because of race, color, gender, handicap, religion, sexual orientation or ethnicity.' " In *Ring v. Arizona*, 536 U.S. 584, 592–593 (2002), we applied *Apprendi* to an Arizona law that authorized the death penalty if the judge found one of ten aggravating factors. In each case, we concluded that the defendant's constitutional rights had been violated because the judge had imposed a sentence greater than the maximum he could have imposed under state law without the challenged factual finding.

In this case, petitioner was sentenced to more than three years above the 53-month statutory maximum of the standard range because he had acted with "deliberate cruelty." The facts supporting that finding were neither admitted by petitioner nor found by a jury. The State nevertheless contends that there was no *Apprendi* violation because the relevant "statutory maximum" is not 53 months, but the 10-year maximum for class B felonies. It observes that no exceptional sentence may exceed that limit. Our precedents make clear, however, that the "statutory maximum" for *Apprendi* purposes is the maximum sentence a judge may impose solely on the basis of the facts reflected in the jury verdict or admitted by the defendant. See *Ring*, supra * * *. In other words, the relevant "statutory maximum" is not the maximum sentence a judge may impose after finding additional facts, but the maximum he may impose without any additional findings. When a judge inflicts punishment that the jury's verdict alone does not allow, the jury has not found all the facts "which the law makes essential to the punishment," Bishop, supra, § 87, and the judge exceeds his proper authority.

The judge in this case could not have imposed the exceptional 90-month sentence solely on the basis of the facts admitted in the guilty plea. Those facts alone were insufficient because, as the Washington Supreme Court has explained, "[a] reason offered to justify an exceptional sentence can be considered only if it takes into account factors other than those which are used in computing the

---

[6]   As to Justice O'Connor's criticism of the quantity of historical support for the *Apprendi* rule * * *: It bears repeating that the issue between us is not *whether* the Constitution limits States' authority to reclassify elements as sentencing factors (we all agree that it does); it is only which line, ours or hers, the Constitution draws. Criticism of the quantity of evidence favoring our alternative would have some force if it were accompanied by *any* evidence favoring hers. Justice O'Connor does not even provide a coherent alternative meaning for the jury-trial guarantee, unless one considers "whatever the legislature chooses to leave to the jury, so long as it does not go too far" coherent.

[**Editors' note:** Later, in *Oregon v. Ice*, 555 U.S. 160 (2009), a different majority of the Court relied on historical practice and declined to extend the *Apprendi* rule to fact-finding required before judges can require multiple sentences to be served consecutively instead of concurrently. "[S]pecification of the regime for administering multiple sentences has long been considered the prerogative of state legislatures," concluded the Court, and the decision to impose sentences consecutively is "not within the traditional jury function."]

standard range sentence for the offense," *Gore,* supra, which in this case included the elements of second-degree kidnaping and the use of a firearm. Had the judge imposed the 90-month sentence solely on the basis of the plea, he would have been reversed. See § 9.94A.210(4). The "maximum sentence" is no more 10 years here than it was 20 years in *Apprendi* (because that is what the judge could have imposed upon finding a hate crime) or death in *Ring* (because that is what the judge could have imposed upon finding an aggravator).

The State defends the sentence by drawing an analogy to those we upheld in *McMillan v. Pennsylvania,* 477 U.S. 79 (1986), and *Williams v. New York,* 337 U.S. 241 (1949). Neither case is on point. *McMillan* involved a sentencing scheme that imposed a statutory minimum if a judge found a particular fact. We specifically noted that the statute "does not authorize a sentence in excess of that otherwise allowed for [the underlying] offense." Cf. *Harris v. United States,* 536 U.S. 545 (2002).[b] *Williams* involved an indeterminate-sentencing regime that allowed a judge (but did not compel him) to rely on facts outside the trial record in determining whether to sentence a defendant to death The judge could have "sentenced [the defendant] to death giving no reason at all." Thus, neither case involved a sentence greater than what state law authorized on the basis of the verdict alone.

Finally, the State tries to distinguish *Apprendi* and *Ring* by pointing out that the enumerated grounds for departure in its regime are illustrative rather than exhaustive. This distinction is immaterial. Whether the judge's authority to impose an enhanced sentence depends on finding a specified fact (as in *Apprendi*), one of

---

[b]   *Apprendi* was a 5–4 decision, and while Justice Stevens' opinion for the Court majority (Justices Stevens, Scalia, Souter, Thomas, and Ginsburg) distinguished *McMillan* as a case that "did not involve the imposition of a sentence more severe than the statutory maximum for the offense established by the jury's verdict," it also "reserve[d] for another day the question of whether stare decisis considerations preclude consideration of its narrower holding." The Court first reaffirmed *McMillan* in *Harris,* a 4:1:4 decision. Eleven years later, in *Alleyne v. United States,* 570 U.S. 99 (2013), the Court overruled both *Harris* and *McMillan.* "While *Harris* limited *Apprendi* to facts increasing the statutory maximum, the principle applied in *Apprendi* applies with equal force to facts increasing the mandatory minimum," Justice Thomas wrote for the Court in *Alleyne.* "[A] fact increasing either end of the range produces a new penalty and constitutes an ingredient of the offense," he reasoned. "Elevating the low-end of a sentencing range heightens the loss of liberty associated with the crime: the defendant's 'expected punishment has increased as a result of the narrowed range' and 'the prosecution is empowered, by invoking the mandatory minimum, to require the judge to impose a higher punishment than he might wish.' " "[T]he essential Sixth Amendment inquiry is whether a fact is an element of the crime. When a finding of fact alters the legally prescribed punishment so as to aggravate it, the fact necessarily forms a constituent part of a new offense and must be submitted to the jury."

Adding the fifth vote, Justice Breyer explained in a concurring opinion that it seemed "highly anomalous to read *Apprendi* as insisting that juries find sentencing facts that permit a judge to impose a higher sentence while not insisting that juries find sentencing facts that require a judge to impose a higher sentence." He stated that although he continued to disagree with *Apprendi,* he joined the majority because "the time ha[d] come to end this anomaly."

In dissent, Chief Justice Roberts, joined by Justices Scalia and Kennedy, noted the absence of historical evidence supporting the majority's ruling, and criticized the ruling as protecting judges from legislative attempts to guide sentencing discretion, not protecting the accused from judges, the intended purpose of the jury right. Justice Alito dissented separately, arguing that *Apprendi* should be overruled. He added that "if *Harris* is not entitled to stare decisis weight, then neither is the Court's opinion in this case. After all, only four Members of the Court think that the Court's holding is the correct reading of the Constitution."

several specified facts (as in *Ring*), or any aggravating fact (as here), it remains the case that the jury's verdict alone does not authorize the sentence. The judge acquires that authority only upon finding some additional fact.[8]

Because the State's sentencing procedure did not comply with the Sixth Amendment, petitioner's sentence is invalid.

III

Our commitment to *Apprendi* in this context reflects not just respect for longstanding precedent, but the need to give intelligible content to the right of jury trial. That right is no mere procedural formality, but a fundamental reservation of power in our constitutional structure. Just as suffrage ensures the people's ultimate control in the legislative and executive branches, jury trial is meant to ensure their control in the judiciary. See [citing, inter alia, the comments of John Adams and Thomas Jefferson]. *Apprendi* carries out this design by ensuring that the judge's authority to sentence derives wholly from the jury's verdict. Without that restriction, the jury would not exercise the control that the Framers intended.

Those who would reject *Apprendi* are resigned to one of two alternatives. The first is that the jury need only find whatever facts the legislature chooses to label elements of the crime, and that those it labels sentencing factors—no matter how much they may increase the punishment—may be found by the judge. This would mean, for example, that a judge could sentence a man for committing murder even if the jury convicted him only of illegally possessing the firearm used to commit it—or of making an illegal lane change while fleeing the death scene. Not even *Apprendi*'s critics would advocate this absurd result. Cf. *Apprendi*, at 552–53 (O'Connor, J., dissenting[c]). The jury could not function as circuitbreaker in the State's machinery of justice if it were relegated to making a determination that the defendant at some point did something wrong, a mere preliminary to a judicial inquisition into the facts of the crime the State actually seeks to punish.[10]

---

[8]   Nor does it matter that the judge must, after finding aggravating facts, make a judgment that they present a compelling ground for departure. He cannot make that judgment without finding some facts to support it beyond the bare elements of the offense. Whether the judicially determined facts *require* a sentence enhancement or merely *allow* it, the verdict alone does not authorize the sentence.

[c]   Justice O'Connor's dissent in *Apprendi* (joined by the Chief Justice and Justices Kennedy and Breyer) noted: "Because I do not believe the Court's 'increase in the maximum penalty' rule is required by the Constitution, I would evaluate New Jersey's sentence enhancement statute by analyzing the factors we have examined in past cases. * * * First, the New Jersey statute does not shift the burden of proof on an essential ingredient of the offense by presuming that ingredient upon proof of other elements of the offense. * * * Second, the magnitude of the New Jersey sentence enhancement, as applied in petitioner's case, is constitutionally permissible. Under New Jersey laws, the weapons possession offense to which petitioner pleaded guilty carries a sentence range of 5 to 10 years imprisonment. The fact that petitioner, in committing that offense, acted with a purpose to intimidate because of race exposed him to a higher sentence range of 10 to 20 years imprisonment. The 10-year increase in the maximum penalty to which petitioner was exposed falls well within the range we have found permissible. See *Almendarez-Torres* (approving 18-year enhancement). Third, the New Jersey statute gives no impression of having been enacted to evade the constitutional requirements that attach when a State makes a fact an element of the charged offense. For example, New Jersey did not take what had previously been an element of the weapons possession offense and transform it into a sentencing factor. See *McMillan*."

[10]   Justice O'Connor believes that "built-in political check" will prevent lawmakers from manipulating offense elements in this fashion. But the many immediate practical advantages of

The second alternative is that legislatures may establish legally essential sentencing factors *within limits*—limits crossed when, perhaps, the sentencing factor is a "tail which wags the dog of the substantive offense." *McMillan*, supra. What this means in operation is that the law must not go too far—it must not exceed the judicial estimation of the proper role of the judge. * * * The subjectivity of this standard is obvious. Petitioner argued below that second-degree kidnaping with deliberate cruelty was essentially the same as first-degree kidnaping, the very charge he had avoided by pleading to a lesser offense. The *Washington* court conceded this might be so but held it irrelevant. Petitioner's 90-month sentence exceeded the 53-month standard maximum by almost 70%; the Washington Supreme Court in other cases has upheld exceptional sentences 15 times the standard maximum. * * * Did the court go too far in any of these cases? There is no answer that legal analysis can provide. With too far as the yardstick, it is always possible to disagree with such judgments and never to refute them.[11]

Whether the Sixth Amendment incorporates this manipulable standard rather than *Apprendi*'s bright-line rule depends on the plausibility of the claim that the Framers would have left definition of the scope of jury power up to judges' intuitive sense of how far is too far. We think that claim not plausible at all, because the very reason the Framers put a jury-trial guarantee in the Constitution is that they were unwilling to trust government to mark out the role of the jury.

IV

By reversing the judgment below, we are not, as the State would have it, "find[ing] determinate sentencing schemes unconstitutional." This case is not about whether determinate sentencing is constitutional, only about how it can be implemented in a way that respects the Sixth Amendment. Several policies prompted Washington's adoption of determinate sentencing, including proportionality to the gravity of the offense and parity among defendants. Nothing we have said impugns those salutary objectives.

Justice O'Connor argues that, because determinate sentencing schemes involving judicial factfinding entail less judicial discretion than indeterminate schemes, the constitutionality of the latter implies the constitutionality of the former. This argument is flawed on a number of levels. First, the Sixth Amendment by its terms is not a limitation on judicial power, but a reservation of jury power. It limits judicial power only to the extent that the claimed judicial power infringes on the province of the jury. Indeterminate sentencing does not do so. It increases judicial discretion, to be sure, but not at the expense of the jury's traditional function of finding the facts essential to lawful imposition of the penalty. Of course indeterminate schemes involve judicial factfinding, in that a judge (like a parole

---

judicial factfinding, suggest that political forces would, if anything, pull in the opposite direction. In any case, the Framers' decision to entrench the jury-trial right in the Constitution shows that they did not trust government to make political decisions in this area.

[11]　Another example of conversion from separate crime to sentence enhancement that Justice O'Connor evidently does not consider going "too far" is the obstruction-of-justice enhancement, * * *. Why perjury during trial should be grounds for a judicial sentence enhancement on the underlying offense, rather than an entirely separate offense to be found by a jury beyond a reasonable doubt (as it has been for centuries, see 4 W. Blackstone, supra, 136–138), is unclear.

board) may implicitly rule on those facts he deems important to the exercise of his sentencing discretion. But the facts do not pertain to whether the defendant has a legal right to a lesser sentence—and that makes all the difference insofar as judicial impingement upon the traditional role of the jury is concerned. In a system that says the judge may punish burglary with 10 to 40 years, every burglar knows he is risking 40 years in jail. In a system that punishes burglary with a 10-year sentence, with another 30 added for use of a gun, the burglar who enters a home unarmed is entitled to no more than a 10-year sentence—and by reason of the Sixth Amendment the facts bearing upon that entitlement must be found by a jury.

But even assuming that restraint of judicial power unrelated to the jury's role is a Sixth Amendment objective, it is far from clear that *Apprendi* disserves that goal. Determinate judicial-factfinding schemes entail less judicial power than indeterminate schemes, but more judicial power than determinate jury-factfinding schemes. Whether *Apprendi* increases judicial power overall depends on what States with determinate judicial-factfinding schemes would do, given the choice between the two alternatives. Justice O'Connor simply assumes that the net effect will favor judges, but she has no empirical basis for that prediction. Indeed, what evidence we have points exactly the other way: When the Kansas Supreme Court found *Apprendi* infirmities in that State's determinate-sentencing regime * * *, the legislature responded not by reestablishing indeterminate sentencing but by applying *Apprendi*'s requirements to its current regime. The result was less, not more, judicial power.

Justice Breyer argues that *Apprendi* works to the detriment of criminal defendants who plead guilty by depriving them of the opportunity to argue sentencing factors to a judge. But nothing prevents a defendant from waiving his *Apprendi* rights. When a defendant pleads guilty, the State is free to seek judicial sentence enhancements so long as the defendant either stipulates to the relevant facts or consents to judicial factfinding. * * * If appropriate waivers are procured, States may continue to offer judicial factfinding as a matter of course to all defendants who plead guilty. Even a defendant who stands trial may consent to judicial factfinding as to sentence enhancements, which may well be in his interest if relevant evidence would prejudice him at trial. We do not understand how *Apprendi* can possibly work to the detriment of those who are free, if they think its costs outweigh its benefits, to render it inapplicable.[12]

Nor do we see any merit to Justice Breyer's contention that *Apprendi* is unfair to criminal defendants because, if States respond by enacting "17-element robbery crime[s]," prosecutors will have more elements with which to bargain. * * *

---

[12] Justice Breyer responds that States are not required to give defendants the option of waiving jury trial on some elements but not others. True enough. But why would the States that he asserts we are coercing into hard-heartedness—that is, States that want judge-pronounced determinate sentencing to be the norm but we won't let them—want to prevent a defendant from choosing that regime? Justice Breyer claims this alternative may prove "too expensive and unwieldy for States to provide," but there is no obvious reason why forcing defendants to choose between contesting all elements of his hypothetical 17-element robbery crime and contesting none of them is less expensive than also giving them the third option of pleading guilty to some elements and submitting the rest to judicial factfinding. Justice Breyer's argument rests entirely on a speculative prediction about the number of defendants likely to choose the first (rather than the second) option if denied the third.

Bargaining already exists with regard to sentencing factors because defendants can either stipulate or contest the facts that make them applicable. If there is any difference between bargaining over sentencing factors and bargaining over elements, the latter probably favors the defendant. Every new element that a prosecutor can threaten to charge is also an element that a defendant can threaten to contest at trial and make the prosecutor prove beyond a reasonable doubt. Moreover, given the sprawling scope of most criminal codes, and the power to affect sentences by making (even nonbinding) sentencing recommendations, there is already no shortage of in terrorem tools at prosecutors' disposal. * * *.

Any evaluation of *Apprendi*'s "fairness" to criminal defendants must compare it with the regime it replaced, in which a defendant, with no warning in either his indictment or plea, would routinely see his maximum potential sentence balloon from as little as five years to as much as life imprisonment, see 21 U.S.C. §§ 841(b)(1)(A), (D), based not on facts proved to his peers beyond a reasonable doubt, but on facts extracted after trial from a report compiled by a probation officer who the judge thinks more likely got it right than got it wrong. We can conceive of no measure of fairness that would find more fault in the utterly speculative bargaining effects Justice Breyer identifies than in the regime he champions. Suffice it to say that, if such a measure exists, it is not the one the Framers left us with. * * *

Justice Breyer also claims that *Apprendi* will attenuate the connection between "real criminal conduct and real punishment" by encouraging plea bargaining and by restricting alternatives to adversarial factfinding. The short answer to the former point (even assuming the questionable premise that *Apprendi* does encourage plea bargaining, but see * * * n. 12) is that the Sixth Amendment was not written for the benefit of those who choose to forgo its protection. It guarantees the right to jury trial. It does not guarantee that a particular number of jury trials will actually take place. That more defendants elect to waive that right (because, for example, government at the moment is not particularly oppressive) does not prove that a constitutional provision guaranteeing availability of that option is disserved. * * *

Ultimately, our decision cannot turn on whether or to what degree trial by jury impairs the efficiency or fairness of criminal justice. One can certainly argue that both these values would be better served by leaving justice entirely in the hands of professionals; many nations of the world, particularly those following civil-law traditions, take just that course There is not one shred of doubt, however, about the Framers' paradigm for criminal justice: not the civil-law ideal of administrative perfection, but the common-law ideal of limited state power accomplished by strict division of authority between judge and jury. As *Apprendi* held, every defendant has the right to insist that the prosecutor prove to a jury all facts legally essential to the punishment. Under the dissenters' alternative, he has no such right. That should be the end of the matter.

Petitioner was sentenced to prison for more than three years beyond what the law allowed for the crime to which he confessed, on the basis of a disputed finding that he had acted with "deliberate cruelty." The Framers would not have thought it too much to demand that, before depriving a man of three more years of his liberty, the State should suffer the modest inconvenience of submitting its accusation to "the unanimous suffrage of twelve of his equals and neighbours," 4 Blackstone, supra, at 343, rather than a lone employee of the State The judgment of the Washington Court of Appeals is reversed, and the case is remanded for further proceedings not inconsistent with this opinion.

JUSTICE O'CONNOR, with whom JUSTICE BREYER joins, and with whom THE CHIEF JUSTICE and JUSTICE KENNEDY join as to all but Part IB, dissenting. * * *

I

One need look no further than the history leading up to and following the enactment of Washington's guidelines scheme to appreciate the damage that today's decision will cause. Prior to 1981, Washington, like most other States and the Federal Government, employed an indeterminate sentencing scheme. Washington's criminal code separated all felonies into three broad categories: "class A," carrying a sentence of 20 years to life; "class B," carrying a sentence of 0 to 10 years; and "class C," carrying a sentence of 0 to 5 years. Sentencing judges, in conjunction with parole boards, had virtually unfettered discretion to sentence defendants to prison terms falling anywhere within the statutory range, including probation—i.e., no jail sentence at all. Boerner & Lieb, *Sentencing Reform in the Other Washington*, 28 Crime and Justice 71, 73 (M. Tonry ed.2001).

This system of unguided discretion inevitably resulted in severe disparities in sentences received and served by defendants committing the same offense and having similar criminal histories. Boerner & Lieb 126–127 * * *. Indeed, rather than reflect legally relevant criteria, these disparities too often were correlated with constitutionally suspect variables such as race. Boerner & Lieb 126–128. * * * To counteract these trends, the state legislature passed the Sentencing Reform Act of 1981. The Act had the laudable purposes of "mak[ing] the criminal justice system accountable to the public," and "[e]nsur[ing] that the punishment for a criminal offense is proportionate to the seriousness of the offense . . . [and] commensurate with the punishment imposed on others committing similar offenses." Wash. Rev.Code Ann. § 9.94A.010. The Act neither increased any of the statutory sentencing ranges for the three types of felonies (though it did eliminate the statutory mandatory minimum for class A felonies), nor reclassified any substantive offenses. It merely placed meaningful constraints on discretion to sentence offenders within the statutory ranges, and eliminated parole. There is thus no evidence that the legislature was attempting to manipulate the statutory elements of criminal offenses or to circumvent the procedural protections of the Bill of Rights. Rather, lawmakers were trying to bring some much-needed uniformity, transparency, and accountability to an otherwise " 'labyrinthine' sentencing and corrections system that 'lack[ed] any principle except unguided discretion.' " Boerner & Lieb 73 * * *.

II

Far from disregarding principles of due process and the jury trial right, as the majority today suggests, Washington's reform has served them. Before passage of the Act, a defendant charged with second degree kidnaping, like petitioner, had no idea whether he would receive a 10-year sentence or probation. The ultimate sentencing determination could turn as much on the idiosyncrasies of a particular judge as on the specifics of the defendant's crime or background. A defendant did not know what facts, if any, about his offense or his history would be considered relevant by the sentencing judge or by the parole board. After passage of the Act, a defendant charged with second degree kidnaping knows what his presumptive sentence will be; he has a good idea of the types of factors that a sentencing judge can and will consider when deciding whether to sentence him outside that range; he is guaranteed meaningful appellate review to protect against an arbitrary sentence. Boerner & Lieb 93 ("By consulting one sheet, practitioners could identify the applicable scoring rules for criminal history, the sentencing range, and the available sentencing options for each case"). Criminal defendants still face the same statutory maximum sentences, but they now at least know, much more than before, the real consequences of their actions.

Washington's move to a system of guided discretion has served equal protection principles as well. Over the past 20 years, there has been a substantial reduction in racial disparity in sentencing across the State. Id., at 126, 127 * * *. The reduction is directly traceable to the constraining effects of the guidelines— namely, its "presumptive range[s]" and limits on the imposition of "exceptional sentences" outside of those ranges. * * *

The majority does not, because it cannot, disagree that determinate sentencing schemes, like Washington's, serve important constitutional values. Thus, the majority says: "[t]his case is not about whether determinate sentencing is constitutional, only about how it can be implemented in a way that respects the Sixth Amendment." But extension of *Apprendi* to the present context will impose significant costs on a legislature's determination that a particular fact, not historically an element, warrants a higher sentence. While not a constitutional prohibition on guidelines schemes, the majority's decision today exacts a substantial constitutional tax.

The costs are substantial and real. Under the majority's approach, any fact that increases the upper bound on a judge's sentencing discretion is an element of the offense. Thus, facts that historically have been taken into account by sentencing judges to assess a sentence within a broad range—such as drug quantity, role in the offense, risk of bodily harm—all must now be charged in an indictment and submitted to a jury, simply because it is the legislature, rather than the judge, that constrains the extent to which such facts may be used to impose a sentence within a pre-existing statutory range.

While that alone is enough to threaten the continued use of sentencing guidelines schemes, there are additional costs. For example, a legislature might rightly think that some factors bearing on sentencing, such as prior bad acts or criminal history, should not be considered in a jury's determination of a defendant's guilt—such "character evidence" has traditionally been off limits during the guilt phase of criminal proceedings because of its tendency to inflame the passions of the jury. * * * If a legislature desires uniform consideration of such factors at sentencing, but does not want them to impact a jury's initial determination of guilt, the State may have to bear the additional expense of a separate, full-blown jury trial during the penalty phase proceeding.

Some facts that bear on sentencing either will not be discovered, or are not discoverable, prior to trial. For instance, a legislature might desire that defendants who act in an obstructive manner during trial or post-trial proceedings receive a greater sentence than defendants who do not. See, e.g., United States Sentencing Commission, Guidelines Manual, § 3C1.1 (Nov.2003) (hereinafter USSG) (2-point increase in offense level for obstruction of justice). In such cases, the violation arises too late for the State to provide notice to the defendant or to argue the facts to the jury. A State wanting to make such facts relevant at sentencing must now either vest sufficient discretion in the judge to account for them or bring a separate criminal prosecution for obstruction of justice or perjury. And, the latter option is available only to the extent that a defendant's obstructive behavior is so severe as to constitute an already-existing separate offense, unless the legislature is willing to undertake the unlikely expense of criminalizing relatively minor obstructive behavior.

Likewise, not all facts that historically have been relevant to sentencing always will be known prior to trial. For instance, trial or sentencing proceedings of a drug distribution defendant might reveal that he sold primarily to children. Under the majority's approach, a State wishing such a revelation to result in a higher sentence within a pre-existing statutory range either must vest judges with sufficient discretion to account for it (and trust that they exercise that discretion) or bring a separate criminal prosecution. Indeed, the latter choice might not be available—a separate prosecution, if it is for an aggravated offense, likely would be barred altogether by the Double Jeopardy Clause. * * *

The majority may be correct that States and the Federal Government will be willing to bear some of these costs. But simple economics dictate that they will not, and cannot, bear them all. To the extent that they do not, there will be an inevitable increase in judicial discretion with all of its attendant failings.[1]

III

Washington's Sentencing Reform Act did not alter the statutory maximum sentence to which petitioner was exposed. * * * Petitioner was informed in the charging document, his plea agreement, and during his plea hearing that he faced a potential statutory maximum of 10 years in prison. As discussed above, the guidelines served due process by providing notice to petitioner of the consequences of his acts; they vindicated his jury trial right by informing him of the stakes of risking trial; they served equal protection by ensuring petitioner that invidious characteristics such as race would not impact his sentence.

Given these observations, it is difficult for me to discern what principle besides doctrinaire formalism actually motivates today's decision. The majority

---

[1] The paucity of empirical evidence regarding the impact of extending *Apprendi v. New Jersey*, to guidelines schemes should come as no surprise to the majority. Prior to today, only one court had ever applied *Apprendi* to invalidate application of a guidelines scheme. * * * Thus, there is no map of the uncharted territory blazed by today's unprecedented holding.

chides the *Apprendi* dissenters for preferring a nuanced interpretation of the Due Process Clause and Sixth Amendment jury trial guarantee that would generally defer to legislative labels while acknowledging the existence of constitutional constraints—what the majority calls the "the law must not go too far" approach. If indeed the choice is between adopting a balanced case-by-case approach that takes into consideration the values underlying the Bill of Rights, as well as the history of a particular sentencing reform law, and adopting a rigid rule that destroys everything in its path, I will choose the former. * * * See *Apprendi*, 530 U.S., at 552–554 [described in fn. c supra] (O'Connor, J., dissenting) * * *.

* * * The pre-*Apprendi* rule of deference to the legislature retains a built-in political check to prevent lawmakers from shifting the prosecution for crimes to the penalty phase proceedings of lesser included and easier-to-prove offenses—e.g., the majority's hypothesized prosecution of murder in the guise of a traffic offense sentencing proceeding. There is no similar check, however, on application of the majority's " 'any fact that increases the upper bound of judicial discretion' " by courts.

The majority claims the mantle of history and original intent. But as I have explained elsewhere, a handful of state decisions in the mi19th century and a criminal procedure treatise have little if any persuasive value as evidence of what the Framers of the Federal Constitution intended in the late 18th century. See *Apprendi*, 530 U.S., at 525–528 (O'Connor, J., dissenting). Because broad judicial sentencing discretion was foreign to the Framers, id., at 478–479 * * *, they were never faced with the constitutional choice between submitting every fact that increases a sentence to the jury or vesting the sentencing judge with broad discretionary authority to account for differences in offenses and offenders.

IV

The consequences of today's decision will be as far reaching as they are disturbing. Washington's sentencing system is by no means unique. Numerous other States have enacted guidelines systems, as has the Federal Government. * * * Today's decision casts constitutional doubt over them all and, in so doing, threatens an untold number of criminal judgments. Every sentence imposed under such guidelines in cases currently pending on direct appeal is in jeopardy. And, despite the fact that we hold in *Schriro v. Summerlin,* 542 U.S. 348 (2004), that *Ring* (and a fortiori *Apprendi*) does not apply retroactively on habeas review, all criminal sentences imposed under the federal and state guidelines * * *. The practical consequences for trial courts, starting today, will be equally unsettling: How are courts to mete out guidelines sentences? Do courts apply the guidelines as to mitigating factors, but not as to aggravating factors? Do they jettison the guidelines altogether? The Court ignores the havoc it is about to wreak on trial courts across the country.[a] * * * I respectfully dissent.

---

[a]   The Court soon addressed whether sentences imposed under the federal guidelines suffered from the same constitutional infirmity that afflicted Blakely's sentence under the Washington State sentencing statutes. In *United States v. Booker,* 543 U.S. 220 (2005), the Court held in an opinion by Justice Stevens, "there is no distinction of constitutional significance between the Federal Sentencing Guidelines and the Washington procedures at issue in that case. * * * This conclusion rests on the premise, common to both systems, that the relevant sentencing rules are

JUSTICE KENNEDY, with whom JUSTICE BREYER joins, dissenting.

The majority opinion does considerable damage to our laws and to the administration of the criminal justice system for all the reasons well stated in Justice O'Connor's dissent, plus one more: The Court, in my respectful submission, disregards the fundamental principle under our constitutional system that different branches of government "converse with each other on matters of vital common interest." *Mistretta v. United States*, 488 U.S. 361 (1989). Constant, constructive discourse between our courts and our legislatures is an integral and admirable part of the constitutional design. * * * Sentencing guidelines are a prime example of this collaborative process. Dissatisfied with the wide disparity in sentencing, participants in the criminal justice system, including judges, pressed for legislative reforms. In response, legislators drew from these participants' shared experiences and enacted measures to correct the problems, which, as Justice O'Connor explains, could sometimes rise to the level of a constitutional injury. As *Mistretta* recognized, this interchange among different actors in the constitutional scheme is consistent with the Constitution's structural protections. * * * With no apparent sense of irony that the effect of today's decision is the destruction of a sentencing scheme devised by democratically elected legislators, the majority shuts down alternative, nonjudicial, sources of ideas and experience. It does so under a faintly disguised distrust of judges and their purported usurpation of the jury's function in criminal trials. It tells not only trial judges who have spent years studying the problem but also legislators who have devoted valuable time and resources "calling upon the accumulated wisdom and experience of the Judicial Branch on a matter uniquely within the ken of judges," *Mistretta*, supra, that their efforts and judgments were all for naught. * * * If the Constitution required this result, the majority's decision, while unfortunate, would at least be understandable and defensible. As Justice O'Connor's dissent demonstrates,

---

mandatory and impose binding requirements on all sentencing judges. If the Guidelines as currently written could be read as merely advisory provisions that recommended, rather than required, the selection of particular sentences in response to differing sets of facts, their use would not implicate the Sixth Amendment. We have never doubted the authority of a judge to exercise broad discretion in imposing a sentence within a statutory range. Indeed, everyone agrees that the constitutional issues presented by these cases would have been avoided entirely if congress had omitted from the [Act] the provisions that make the Guidelines binding on district judges * * *. For when a trial judge exercises his discretion to select a specific sentence within a defined range, the defendant has no right to a jury determination of the facts that the judge deems relevant. The Guidelines as written however, are not advisory; they are mandatory * * * [The Act] directs that the court 'shall impose a sentence of the kind, and within the range" established by the Guidelines, subject to departures in specific, limited cases. * * * Booker's case illustrates the mandatory nature of the Guidelines. The jury convicted him of possessing at least 50 grams of crack, in violation of 21 U.S.C.A. 841(b)(1)(A)(iii) based on evidence that he had 92.5 grams of crack in his duffel bag. Under these facts the Guidelines specified an offense level of 32, which, given the defendant's criminal history category, authorized a sentence of 210–262 months. Booker's is a run-of-the-mill drug case, and does not present any [basis for upward departure]. The sentencing judge would therefore have been reversed had he not imposed a sentence within the level 32 Guidelines range. Booker's actual sentence, however, was 360 months, almost 10 years longer than the Guidelines range supported by the jury verdict alone. To reach this sentence, the judge found facts beyond those found by the jury; namely, that Booker possessed 566 grams of crack in addition to the 92.5 grams in his duffel bag. The jury never heard any evidence of the additional drug quantity, and the judge found it true by a preponderance of the evidence. Thus, just as in Blakely, 'the jury's verdict alone does not authorize the sentence. The judge acquires that authority only upon finding some additional fact.' " The *Booker* decision is also discussed in fn. b, infra.

however, this is simply not the case. For that reason, and because the Constitution does not prohibit the dynamic and fruitful dialogue between the judicial and legislative branches of government that has marked sentencing reform on both the state and the federal levels for more than 20 years, I dissent.

JUSTICE BREYER, with whom JUSTICE O'CONNOR joins, dissenting.

* * *

I

The majority ignores the adverse consequences inherent in its conclusion. As a result of the majority's rule, sentencing must now take one of three forms, each of which risks either impracticality, unfairness, or harm to the jury trial right the majority purports to strengthen. This circumstance shows that the majority's Sixth Amendment interpretation cannot be right.

A first option for legislators is to create a simple, pure or nearly pure "charge offense" or "determinate" sentencing system. In such a system, an indictment would charge a few facts which, taken together, constitute a crime, such as robbery. Robbery would carry a single sentence, say, five years' imprisonment. And every person convicted of robbery would receive that sentence—just as, centuries ago, everyone convicted of almost any serious crime was sentenced to death. * * * Simple determinate sentencing has the virtue of treating like cases alike, but it simultaneously fails to treat different cases differently. Some commentators have leveled this charge at sentencing guideline systems themselves. * * * The charge is doubly applicable to simple "pure charge" systems that permit no departures from the prescribed sentences, even in extraordinary cases. * * *

A second option for legislators is to return to a system of indeterminate sentencing, such as California had before the recent sentencing reform movement. Under indeterminate systems, the length of the sentence is entirely or almost entirely within the discretion of the judge or of the parole board, which typically has broad power to decide when to release a prisoner. * * * When such systems were in vogue, they were criticized, and rightly so, for producing unfair disparities, including race-based disparities, in the punishment of similarly situated defendants. The length of time a person spent in prison appeared to depend on "what the judge ate for breakfast" on the day of sentencing, on which judge you got, or on other factors that should not have made a difference to the length of the sentence. * * * Returning to such a system would diminish the "reason" the majority claims it is trying to uphold. * * * It also would do little to "ensur[e] [the] control" of what the majority calls "the peopl[e,]" i.e., the jury, * * * since "the peopl[e]" would only decide the defendant's guilt, a finding with no effect on the duration of the sentence. While "the judge's authority to sentence" would formally derive from the jury's verdict, the jury would exercise little or no control over the sentence itself. * * *

A third option is that which the Court seems to believe legislators will in fact take. That is the option of retaining structured schemes that attempt to punish similar conduct similarly and different conduct differently, but modifying them to conform to *Apprendi*'s dictates. Judges would be able to depart downward from presumptive sentences upon finding that mitigating factors were present, but would not be able to depart upward unless the prosecutor charged the aggravating fact to a jury and proved it beyond a reasonable doubt. The majority argues, based on the single example of Kansas, that most legislatures will enact amendments along these lines in the face of the oncoming *Apprendi* train. * * * It is therefore worth exploring how this option could work in practice, as well as the assumption on which it depends

This option can be implemented in one of two ways. The first way would be for legislatures to subdivide each crime into a list of complex crimes, each of which would be defined to include commonly found sentencing factors such as drug quantity, type of victim, presence of violence, degree of injury, use of gun, and so on. A legislature, for example, might enact a robbery statute, modeled on robbery sentencing guidelines, that increases punishment depending upon (1) the nature of the institution robbed, (2) the (a) presence of, (b) brandishing of, (c) other use of, a firearm, (3) making of a death threat, (4) presence of (a) ordinary, (b) serious, (c) permanent or life threatening, bodily injury, (5) abduction, (6) physical restraint, (7) taking of a firearm, (8) taking of drugs, (9) value of property loss, etc. Cf. United States Sentencing Commission, Guidelines Manual § 2B3.1 (Nov.2003).

This possibility is, of course, merely a highly calibrated form of the "pure charge" system discussed [above] * * *. And it suffers from some of the same defects. The prosecutor, through control of the precise charge, controls the punishment, thereby marching the sentencing system directly away from, not toward, one important guideline goal: rough uniformity of punishment for those who engage in roughly the same real criminal conduct. The artificial (and consequently unfair) nature of the resulting sentence is aggravated by the fact that prosecutors must charge all relevant facts about the way the crime was committed before a presentence investigation examines the criminal conduct, perhaps before the trial itself, i.e., before many of the facts relevant to punishment are known. This "complex charge offense" system also prejudices defendants who seek trial, for it can put them in the untenable position of contesting material aggravating facts in the guilt phases of their trials. Consider a defendant who is charged, not with mere possession of cocaine, but with the specific offense of possession of more than 500 grams of cocaine. Or consider a defendant charged, not with murder, but with the new crime of murder using a machete. Or consider a defendant whom the prosecution wants to claim was a "supervisor," rather than an ordinary gang member. How can a Constitution that guarantees due process put these defendants, as a matter of course, in the position of arguing, "I did not sell drugs, and if I did, I did not sell more than 500 grams" or, "I did not kill him, and if I did, I did not use a machete," or "I did not engage in gang activity, and certainly not as a supervisor" to a single jury? * * *

The majority announces that there really is no problem here because "States may continue to offer judicial factfinding as a matter of course to all defendants who plead guilty" and defendants may "stipulat[e] to the relevant facts or consen[t] to judicial factfinding." The problem, of course, concerns defendants who do not want to plead guilty to those elements that, until recently, were commonly thought of as sentencing factors. As to those defendants, the fairness problem arises because States may very well decide that they will not permit defendants to carve subsets of facts out of the new, *Apprendi*-required 17-element robbery crime, seeking a judicial determination as to some of those facts and a jury determination as to others. Instead, States may simply require defendants to plead guilty to all 17 elements or proceed with a (likely prejudicial) trial on all 17 elements.

The majority does not deny that States may make this choice; it simply fails to understand why any State would want to exercise it. See [majority opinion] at n. 12. The answer is, as I shall explain in a moment, that the alternative may prove too expensive and unwieldy for States to provide. States that offer defendants the option of judicial factfinding as to some facts (i.e., sentencing facts), say, because of fairness concerns, will also have to offer the defendant a second sentencing jury— just as Kansas has done. I therefore turn to that alternative.

The second way to make sentencing guidelines *Apprendi*-compliant would be to require at least two juries for each defendant whenever aggravating facts are present: one jury to determine guilt of the crime charged, and an additional jury to try the disputed facts that, if found, would aggravate the sentence. Our experience with bifurcated trials in the capital punishment context suggests that requiring them for run-of-the-mill sentences would be costly, both in money and in judicial time and resources. * * * In the context of noncapital crimes, the potential need for a second indictment alleging aggravating facts, the likely need for formal evidentiary rules to prevent prejudice, and the increased difficulty of obtaining relevant sentencing information, all will mean greater complexity, added cost, and further delay. * * * The uncomfortable fact that could make [such a] system seem workable—even desirable in the minds of some, including defense attorneys—is called "plea bargaining." The Court can announce that the Constitution requires at least two jury trials for each criminal defendant—one for guilt, another for sentencing—but only because it knows full well that more than 90% of defendants will not go to trial even once, much less insist on two or more trials.

What will be the consequences of the Court's holding for the 90% of defendants who do not go to trial? The truthful answer is that we do not know. Some defendants may receive bargaining advantages if the increased cost of the "double jury trial" guarantee makes prosecutors more willing to cede certain sentencing issues to the defense. Other defendants may be hurt if a "single-jury-decides-all" approach makes them more reluctant to risk a trial—perhaps because they want to argue that they did not know what was in the cocaine bag, that it was a small amount regardless, that they were unaware a confederate had a gun, etc. * * *

At the least, the greater expense attached to trials and their greater complexity, taken together in the context of an overworked criminal justice system, will likely mean, other things being equal, fewer trials and a greater reliance upon plea bargaining—a system in which punishment is set not by judges or juries but by advocates acting under bargaining constraints. At the same time, the greater power of the prosecutor to control the punishment through the charge would likely weaken the relation between real conduct and real punishment as well. * * * Even if the Court's holding does not further embed plea-bargaining practices (as I fear it will), its success depends upon the existence of present practice. I do not understand how the Sixth Amendment could require a sentencing system that will work in practice only if no more than a handful of defendants exercise their right to a jury trial. The majority's only response is to state that "bargaining over elements . . . probably favors the defendant" * * *. But the basic problem is not one of "fairness" to defendants or, for that matter, "fairness" to prosecutors. Rather, it concerns the greater fairness of a sentencing system that a more uniform correspondence between real criminal conduct and real punishment helps to create. At a minimum, a two-jury system, by preventing a judge from taking account of an aggravating fact without the prosecutor's acquiescence, would undercut, if not nullify, legislative efforts to ensure through guidelines that punishments reflect a convicted offender's real criminal conduct, rather than that portion of the offender's conduct that a prosecutor decides to charge and prove. * * *

Is there a fourth option? Perhaps. Congress and state legislatures might, for example, rewrite their criminal codes, attaching astronomically high sentences to each crime, followed by long lists of mitigating facts, which, for the most part, would consist of the absence of aggravating facts. *Apprendi*, 530 U.S., at 541–542 (O'Connor, J., dissenting) (explaining how legislatures can evade the majority's rule by making yet another labeling choice). But political impediments to legislative action make such rewrites difficult to achieve; and it is difficult to see why the Sixth Amendment would require legislatures to undertake them. It may also prove possible to find combinations of, or variations upon, my first three options. But I am unaware of any variation that does not involve (a) the shift of power to the prosecutor (weakening the connection between real conduct and real punishment) inherent in any charge offense system, (b) the lack of uniformity inherent in any system of pure judicial discretion, or (c) the complexity, expense, and increased reliance on plea bargains involved in a "two-jury" system. The simple fact is that the design of any fair sentencing system must involve efforts to make practical compromises among competing goals. The majority's reading of the Sixth Amendment makes the effort to find those compromises—already difficult— virtually impossible.

II

The majority rests its conclusion in significant part upon a claimed historical (and therefore constitutional) imperative. * * * The historical sources upon which the majority relies, however, do not compel the result it reaches. That indictments historically had to charge all of the statutorily labeled elements of the offense is a proposition on which all can agree. * * * Neither Bishop nor any other historical treatise writer, however, disputes the proposition that judges historically had discretion to vary the sentence, within the range provided by the statute, based on facts not proved at the trial. The modern history of pre-guidelines sentencing likewise indicates that judges had broad discretion to set sentences within a statutory range based on uncharged conduct. * * * Modern structured sentencing schemes like Washington's do not change the statutorily fixed maximum penalty, nor do they purport to establish new elements for the crime. Instead, they undertake to structure the previously unfettered discretion of the sentencing judge, channeling and limiting his or her discretion even within the statutory range. * * * Historical treatises do not speak to such a practice because it was not done in the

19th century. * * * This make sense when one considers that prior to the 19th century, the prescribed penalty for felonies was very often death, which the judge had limited and sometimes no power to vary.

Given history's silence on the question of laws that structure a judge's discretion within the range provided by the legislatively labeled maximum term, it is not surprising that our modern, pre-*Apprendi* cases made clear that legislatures could, within broad limits, distinguish between "sentencing facts" and "elements of crimes." See *McMillan*, 477 U.S., at 85–88. By their choice of label, legislatures could indicate whether a judge or a jury must make the relevant factual determination. History does not preclude legislatures from making this decision. And, as I argued in Part I, supra, allowing legislatures to structure sentencing in this way has the dual effect of enhancing and giving meaning to the Sixth Amendment's jury trial right as to core crimes, while affording additional due process to defendants in the form of sentencing hearings before judges—hearings the majority's rule will eliminate for many. * * *

III

The majority also overlooks important institutional considerations. Congress and the States relied upon what they believed was their constitutional power to decide, within broad limits, whether to make a particular fact (a) a sentencing factor or (b) an element in a greater crime. They relied upon *McMillan* as guaranteeing the constitutional validity of that proposition. They created sentencing reform, an effort to change the criminal justice system so that it reflects systematically not simply upon guilt or innocence but also upon what should be done about this now-guilty offender. Those efforts have spanned a generation. * * * [B]ut I cannot believe the Constitution forbids the state legislatures and Congress to adopt such systems and to try to improve them over time. Nor can I believe that the Constitution hamstrings legislatures in the way that Justice O'Connor and I have discussed.

IV

* * * Why does the Sixth Amendment permit a jury trial right (in respect to a particular fact) to depend upon a legislative labeling decision, namely, the legislative decision to label the fact a sentencing fact, instead of an element of the crime? The answer is that the fairness and effectiveness of a sentencing system, and the related fairness and effectiveness of the criminal justice system itself, depends upon the legislature's possessing the constitutional authority (within due process limits) to make that labeling decision. To restrict radically the legislature's power in this respect, as the majority interprets the Sixth Amendment to do, prevents the legislature from seeking sentencing systems that are consistent with, and indeed may help to advance, the Constitution's greater fairness goals.

To say this is not simply to express concerns about fairness to defendants. It is also to express concerns about the serious practical (or impractical) changes that the Court's decision seems likely to impose upon the criminal process; about the tendency of the Court's decision to embed further plea bargaining processes that lack transparency and too often mean nonuniform, sometimes arbitrary, sentencing practices; about the obstacles the Court's decision poses to legislative efforts to bring about greater uniformity between real criminal conduct and real punishment; and ultimately about the limitations that the Court imposes upon legislatures' ability to make democratic legislative decisions. Whatever the faults of guidelines systems—and there are many—they are more likely to find their cure in legislation emerging from the experience of, and discussion among, all elements of the criminal justice community, than in a virtually unchangeable constitutional decision of this Court. * * *[b]

McCLESKEY V. KEMP

481 U.S. 279, 107 S.Ct. 1756, 95 L.Ed.2d 262 (1987).

JUSTICE POWELL delivered the opinion of the Court.

This case presents the question whether a complex statistical study that indicates a risk that racial considerations enter into capital sentencing determinations proves that petitioner McCleskey's capital sentence is unconstitutional under the Eighth or Fourteenth Amendment.

McCleskey, a black man, was convicted of two counts of armed robbery and one count of murder in the Superior Court of Fulton County, Georgia, on October 12, 1978. McCleskey's convictions arose out of the robbery of a furniture store and the killing of a white police officer during the course of the robbery. The evidence at trial indicated that McCleskey and three accomplices planned and carried out

---

[b] In *United States v. Booker*, 543 U.S. 220 (2005), Justice Breyer, speaking for the Court, adopted an alternative for coping with the effect of *Blakely* on the federal guidelines that resembled a legislative compromise. The *Booker* decision had two distinct holdings. In an opinion authored by Justice Stevens, described in note a. supra, the Court found that the Sixth Amendment prohibited certain sentences based on judicial findings of facts not admitted by the defendant or found by a jury. A different majority of the Court then addressed the question of remedy, which it framed as an issue of "severability." Writing this portion of the decision for the Court, Justice Breyer rejected the dissenters' view that the Sentencing Reform Act and guidelines could be applied constitutionally so long as any sentence beyond that provided by the base offense was imposed only after the fact permitting the higher sentence was admitted by the defendant or proven beyond a reasonable doubt to a jury. Such a system was not intended by Congress, he reasoned, would create too much complexity, and would undermine the statute's basic aim of allowing for more uniform sentences when prosecutors charge similar offenders with different offenses. Instead, he concluded that two provisions of the act that had the effect of making the Guidelines mandatory "must be invalidated in order to allow the statute to operate in a manner consistent with congressional intent." The Court "excised" the provision "that required courts to impose a sentence within the applicable Guidelines range (in the absence of circumstances that justify a departure), and the provision that sets forth standards of review on appeal." This modification "makes the Guidelines effectively advisory. It requires a sentencing court to consider Guidelines ranges, but it permits the court to tailor the sentence in light of other statutory concerns [listed in Section 3553(a)] as well." Under the remaining provisions of the statute, the Court continued, the courts of appeals will review sentences "to determine whether they are 'unreasonable' with regard to § 3553(a). * * * The district courts, while not bound to apply the Guidelines, must consult those Guidelines and take them into account when sentencing. The courts of appeals review sentencing decisions for unreasonableness. These features of the remaining system, while not the system Congress enacted, nonetheless continue to move sentencing in Congress' preferred direction, helping to avoid excessive sentencing disparities while maintaining flexibility sufficient to individualize sentences where necessary."

Stating "appellate 'reasonableness' review merely asks whether the trial court abused its discretion," the Court in *Rita v. United States*, 551 U.S. 338 (2007), upheld an appellate court's use of a presumption that within-Guidelines sentences are reasonable.

the robbery. * * * During the course of the robbery, a police officer, answering a silent alarm, entered the store through the front door. As he was walking down the center aisle of the store, two shots were fired. Both struck the officer. One hit him in the face and killed him. * * * At trial, the State introduced evidence that at least one of the bullets that struck the officer was fired from a .38 caliber Rossi revolver. This description matched the description of the gun that McCleskey had carried during the robbery. The State also introduced the testimony of two witnesses who had heard McCleskey admit to the shooting.

The jury convicted McCleskey of murder. At the penalty hearing, the jury heard arguments as to the appropriate sentence. Under Georgia law, the jury could not consider imposing the death penalty unless it found beyond a reasonable doubt that the murder was accompanied by one of the statutory aggravating circumstances. The jury in this case found two aggravating circumstances to exist beyond a reasonable doubt: the murder was committed during the course of an armed robbery, and the murder was committed upon a peace officer engaged in the performance of his duties, * * * The jury recommended that he be sentenced to death on the murder charge and to consecutive life sentences on the armed robbery charges. The court followed the jury's recommendation and sentenced McCleskey to death.

On appeal, the Supreme Court of Georgia affirmed the convictions and the sentences. This Court denied a petition for a writ of certiorari. The Superior Court of Fulton County denied McCleskey's extraordinary motion for a new trial. McCleskey then filed a petition for a writ of habeas corpus in the Superior Court of Butts County. After holding an evidentiary hearing, the Superior Court denied relief. The Supreme Court of Georgia denied McCleskey's application for a certificate of probable cause to appeal * * * and this Court again denied certiorari.

McCleskey next filed a petition for a writ of habeas corpus in the federal District Court for the Northern District of Georgia. His petition raised 18 claims, one of which was that the Georgia capital sentencing process is administered in a racially discriminatory manner in violation of the Eighth and Fourteenth Amendments to the United States Constitution. In support of his claim, McCleskey proffered a statistical study performed by Professors David C. Baldus, George Woodworth, and Charles Pulaski (the Baldus study) that purports to show a disparity in the imposition of the death sentence in Georgia based on the race of the murder victim and, to a lesser extent, the race of the defendant. The Baldus study is actually two sophisticated statistical studies that examine over 2,000 murder cases that occurred in Georgia during the 1970s. The raw numbers collected by Professor Baldus indicate that defendants charged with killing white persons received the death penalty in 11% of the cases, but defendants charged with killing blacks received the death penalty in only 1% of the cases. The raw numbers also indicate a reverse racial disparity according to the race of the defendant: 4% of the black defendants received the death penalty, as opposed to 7% of the white defendants.

Baldus also divided the cases according to the combination of the race of the defendant and the race of the victim. He found that the death penalty was assessed in 22% of the cases involving black defendants and white victims; 8% of the cases involving white defendants and white victims; 1% of the cases involving black defendants and black victims; and 3% of the cases involving white defendants and black victims. Similarly, Baldus found that prosecutors sought the death penalty in 70% of the cases involving black defendants and white victims; 32% of the cases involving white defendants and white victims; 15% of the cases involving black defendants and black victims; and 19% of the cases involving white defendants and black victims.

Baldus subjected his data to an extensive analysis, taking account of 230 variables that could have explained the disparities on nonracial grounds. One of his models concludes that, even after taking account of 39 nonracial variables, defendants charged with killing white victims were 4.3 times as likely to receive a death sentence as defendants charged with killing blacks. According to this model, black defendants were 1.1 times as likely to receive a death sentence as other defendants. Thus, the Baldus study indicates that black defendants, such as McCleskey, who kill white victims have the greatest likelihood of receiving the death penalty.

The District Court held an extensive evidentiary hearing on McCleskey's petition. * * * [That] court found that the methodology of the Baldus study was flawed in several respects.[6] * * * It dismissed the petition. The Court of Appeals for the Eleventh Circuit, sitting en banc, * * * assumed the validity of the study itself and addressed the merits of McCleskey's Eighth and Fourteenth Amendment claims. That is, the court assumed that the study "showed that systematic and substantial disparities existed in the penalties imposed upon homicide defendants in Georgia based on race of the homicide victim, that the disparities existed at a less substantial rate in death sentencing based on race of defendants, and that the factors of race of the victim and defendant were at work in Fulton County." Even assuming the study's validity, the Court of Appeals found the statistics "insufficient to demonstrate discriminatory intent or unconstitutional discrimination in the Fourteenth Amendment context, [and] insufficient to show

---

[6]   Baldus, among other experts, testified at the evidentiary hearing. The District Court "was impressed with the learning of all of the experts." Nevertheless, the District Court noted that in many respects the data were incomplete. In its view, the questionnaires used to obtain the data failed to capture the full degree of the aggravating or mitigating circumstances. The Court criticized the researcher's decisions regarding unknown variables. The researchers could not discover whether penalty trials were held in many of the cases, thus undercutting the value of the study's statistics as to prosecutorial decisions. In certain cases, the study lacked information on the race of the victim in cases involving multiple victims, on whether or not the prosecutor offered a plea bargain, and on credibility problems with witnesses. The court concluded that McCleskey had failed to establish by a preponderance of the evidence that the data was trustworthy. * * *

The District Court noted other problems with Baldus' methodology. First, the researchers assumed that all of the information available from the questionnaires was available to the juries and prosecutors when the case was tried. The court found this assumption "questionable." Second, the court noted the instability of the various models. Even with the 230-variable model, consideration of 20 further variables caused a significant drop in the statistical significance of race. In the court's view, this undermined the persuasiveness of the model that showed the greatest racial disparity, the 39-variable model. Third, the court found that the high correlation between race and many of the nonracial variables diminished the weight to which the study was entitled. * * * Finally, the District Court noted the inability of any of the models to predict the outcome of actual cases.

irrationality, arbitrariness and capriciousness under any kind of Eighth Amendment analysis." * * *

McCleskey's first claim is that the Georgia capital punishment statute violates the Equal Protection Clause of the Fourteenth Amendment.[7] He argues that race has infected the administration of Georgia's statute in two ways: persons who murder whites are more likely to be sentenced to death than persons who murder blacks, and black murderers are more likely to be sentenced to death than white murderers.[8] As a black defendant who killed a white victim, McCleskey claims that the Baldus study demonstrates that he was discriminated against because of his race and because of the race of his victim. In its broadest form, McCleskey's claim of discrimination extends to every actor in the Georgia capital sentencing process, from the prosecutor who sought the death penalty and the jury that imposed the sentence, to the State itself that enacted the capital punishment statute and allows it to remain in effect despite its allegedly discriminatory application. We agree with the Court of Appeals, and every other court that has considered such a challenge, that this claim must fail.

* * * [T]o prevail under the Equal Protection Clause, McCleskey must prove that the decisionmakers in *his* case acted with discriminatory purpose. He offers no evidence specific to his own case that would support an inference that racial considerations played a part in his sentence. Instead, he relies solely on the Baldus study. McCleskey argues that the Baldus study compels an inference that his sentence rests on purposeful discrimination. McCleskey's claim that these statistics are sufficient proof of discrimination, without regard to the facts of a particular case, would extend to all capital cases in Georgia, at least where the victim was white and the defendant is black.

The Court has accepted statistics as proof of intent to discriminate in certain limited contexts. First, this Court has accepted statistical disparities as proof of an equal protection violation in the selection of the jury venire in a particular district. * * * Second, this Court has accepted statistics in the form of multiple regression analysis to prove statutory violations under Title VII [employment discrimination].

---

[7]　Although the District Court rejected the findings of the Baldus study as flawed, the Court of Appeals assumed that the study is valid and reached the constitutional issues. Accordingly, those issues are before us. As did the Court of Appeals, we assume the study is valid statistically without reviewing the factual findings of the District Court. * * *

[8]　Although McCleskey has standing to claim that he suffers discrimination because of his own race, the State argues that he has no standing to contend that he was discriminated against on the basis of his victim's race. While it is true that we are reluctant to recognize "standing to assert the rights of third persons," this does not appear to be the nature of McCleskey's claim. He does not seek to assert some right of his victim, or the rights of black murder victims in general. Rather, McCleskey argues that application of the State's statute has created a classification that is "an irrational exercise of governmental power," because it is not "necessary to the accomplishment of some permissible state objective." *Loving v. Virginia,* 388 U.S. 1 (1967). See *McGowan v. Maryland,* 366 U.S. 420 (1961) (statutory classification cannot be "wholly irrelevant to the achievement of the State's objective"). It would violate the Equal Protection Clause for a State to base enforcement of its criminal laws on "an unjustifiable standard such as race, religion, or other arbitrary classification." *Oyler v. Boles,* 368 U.S. 448 (1962). Because McCleskey raises such a claim, he has standing.

But the nature of the capital sentencing decision, and the relationship of the statistics to that decision, are fundamentally different from the corresponding elements in the venire-selection or Title VII cases. Most importantly, each particular decision to impose the death penalty is made by a petit jury selected from a properly constituted venire. Each jury is unique in its composition, and the Constitution requires that its decision rest on consideration of innumerable factors that vary according to the characteristics of the individual defendant and the facts of the particular capital offense. Thus, the application of an inference drawn from the general statistics to a specific decision in a trial and sentencing simply is not comparable to the application of an inference drawn from general statistics to a specific venire-selection or Title VII case. In those cases, the statistics relate to fewer entities,[14] and fewer variables are relevant to the challenged decisions.[15]

Another important difference between the cases in which we have accepted statistics as proof of discriminatory intent and this case is that, in the venire-selection and Title VII contexts, the decisionmaker has an opportunity to explain the statistical disparity. Here, the State has no practical opportunity to rebut the Baldus study. "[C]ontrolling considerations of * * * public policy," dictate that jurors "cannot be called * * * to testify to the motives and influences that led to their verdict." Similarly, the policy considerations behind a prosecutor's traditionally "wide discretion" suggest the impropriety of our requiring prosecutors to defend their decisions to seek death penalties, "often years after they were made."[17] Moreover, absent far stronger proof, it is unnecessary to seek such a rebuttal, because a legitimate and unchallenged explanation for the decision is

---

[14] We refer here not to the number of entities involved in any particular decision, but to the number of entities whose decisions necessarily are reflected in a statistical display such as the Baldus study. The decisions of a jury commission or of an employer over time are fairly attributable to the commission or the employer. Therefore, an unexplained statistical discrepancy can be said to indicate a consistent policy of the decisionmaker. The Baldus study seeks to deduce a state "policy" by studying the combined effects of the decisions of hundreds of juries that are unique in their composition. It is incomparably more difficult to deduce a consistent policy by studying the decisions of these many unique entities. It is also questionable whether any consistent policy can be derived by studying the decisions of prosecutors. The District Attorney is elected by the voters in a particular county. Since decisions whether to prosecute and what to charge necessarily are individualized and involve infinite factual variations, coordination among DA offices across a State would be relatively meaningless. Thus, any inference from state-wide statistics to a prosecutorial "policy" is of doubtful relevance. Moreover, the statistics in Fulton County alone represent the disposition of far fewer cases than the state-wide statistics. Even assuming the statistical validity of the Baldus study as a whole, the weight to be given the results gleaned from this small sample is limited.

[15] In venire-selection cases, the factors that may be considered [i.e., the qualifications for jury service] are limited, usually by state statute. * * * These considerations are uniform for all potential jurors, and although some factors may be said to be subjective, they are limited and, to a great degree, objectively verifiable. While employment decisions may involve a number of relevant variables, these variables are to a great extent uniform for all employees because they must all have a reasonable relationship to the employee's qualifications to perform the particular job at issue. Identifiable qualifications for a single job provide a common standard by which to assess each employee. In contrast, a capital sentencing jury may consider *any* factor relevant to the defendant's background, character, and the offense. There is no common standard by which to evaluate all defendants who have or have not received the death penalty.

[17] Requiring a prosecutor to rebut a study that analyzes the past conduct of scores of prosecutors is quite different from requiring a prosecutor to rebut a contemporaneous challenge to his own acts. See *Batson v. Kentucky* [p. 828].

apparent from the record: McCleskey committed an act for which the United States Constitution and Georgia laws permit imposition of the death penalty.

Finally, McCleskey's statistical proffer must be viewed in the context of his challenge. McCleskey challenges decisions at the heart of the State's criminal justice system. "[O]ne of society's most basic tasks is that of protecting the lives of its citizens and one of the most basic ways in which it achieves the task is through criminal laws against murder." Implementation of these laws necessarily requires discretionary judgments. Because discretion is essential to the criminal justice process, we would demand exceptionally clear proof before we would infer that the discretion has been abused. The unique nature of the decisions at issue in this case also counsel against adopting such an inference from the disparities indicated by the Baldus study. Accordingly, we hold that the Baldus study is clearly insufficient to support an inference that any of the decisionmakers in McCleskey's case acted with discriminatory purpose.

McCleskey also suggests that the Baldus study proves that the State as a whole has acted with a discriminatory purpose. He appears to argue that the State has violated the Equal Protection Clause by adopting the capital punishment statute and allowing it to remain in force despite its allegedly discriminatory application. * * * For this claim to prevail, McCleskey would have to prove that the Georgia Legislature enacted or maintained the death penalty statute *because of* an anticipated racially discriminatory effect. In *Gregg v. Georgia*, 428 U.S. 153 (1976), this Court found that the Georgia capital sentencing system could operate in a fair and neutral manner. There was no evidence then, and there is none now, that the Georgia Legislature enacted the capital punishment statute to further a racially discriminatory purpose.[20]

Nor has McCleskey demonstrated that the legislature maintains the capital punishment statute because of the racially disproportionate impact suggested by the Baldus study. As legislatures necessarily have wide discretion in the choice of criminal laws and penalties, and as there were legitimate reasons for the Georgia Legislature to adopt and maintain capital punishment, see *Gregg v. Georgia*, we will not infer a discriminatory purpose on the part of the State of Georgia. Accordingly, we reject McCleskey's equal protection claims.

McCleskey also argues that the Baldus study demonstrates that the Georgia capital sentencing system violates the Eighth Amendment. We begin our analysis of this claim by reviewing the restrictions on death sentences established by our prior decisions under that Amendment. [The Court here described a series of earlier decisions, starting with *Furman v. Georgia*, 408 U.S. 238 (1972). *Furman* held unconstitutional a death penalty statute which prescribed no standards for the imposition of the penalty, simply leaving the choice of that penalty to the

---

[20] McCleskey relies on "historical evidence" to support his claim of purposeful discrimination by the State. This evidence focuses on Georgia laws in force during and just after the Civil War. Of course, the "historical background of the decision is one evidentiary source" for proof of intentional discrimination. *Arlington Heights v. Metropolitan Housing Dev. Corp.*, 429 U.S. 252 (1977). But unless historical evidence is reasonably contemporaneous with the challenged decision, it has little probative value. * * * Although the history of racial discrimination in this country is undeniable, we cannot accept official actions taken long ago as evidence of current intent.

unfettered discretion of the jury. In so ruling, the Court in *Furman* had "concluded that the death penalty was so irrationally imposed that any particular death sentence could be presumed excessive." In *Gregg v. Georgia,* 428 U.S. 153 (1976), the Court rejected the contention that the death penalty violated the Eighth Amendment "under all circumstances" and upheld the current Georgia statute, enacted after *Furman,* as having "met the concerns articulated in *Furman.*" That statute bifurcated guilt and sentencing proceedings, narrowed the class of murders subject to the death penalty to "cases in which the jury finds at least one statutory aggravating circumstance beyond a reasonable doubt," allowed the defense to introduce "any relevant mitigating evidence," required a "particularized inquiry into the circumstances of the offense together with the character and propensities of the offender," and provided for appellate review of the death sentence by the Georgia Supreme Court. Decisions after *Gregg* "imposed a number of requirements on the capital sentencing process to ensure that capital sentencing decisions rest on the individualized inquiry contemplated in *Gregg.*"] * * *

In sum, our decisions since *Furman* have identified a constitutionally permissible range of discretion in imposing the death penalty. First, there is a required threshold below which the death penalty cannot be imposed. In this context, the State must establish rational criteria that narrow the decisionmaker's judgment as to whether the circumstances of a particular defendant's case meet the threshold. * * * Second, States cannot limit the sentencer's consideration of any relevant circumstance that could cause it to decline to impose the penalty. In this respect, the State cannot channel the sentencer's discretion, but must allow it to consider any relevant information offered by the defendant.

In light of our precedents under the Eighth Amendment, McCleskey cannot argue successfully that his sentence is "disproportionate to the crime in the traditional sense." See *Pulley v. Harris,* 465 U.S. 37 (1984). He does not deny that he committed a murder in the course of a planned robbery, a crime for which this Court has determined that the death penalty constitutionally may be imposed. *Gregg v. Georgia.* His disproportionality claim "is of a different sort." McCleskey argues that the sentence in his case is disproportionate to the sentences in other murder cases.

On the one hand, he cannot base a constitutional claim on an argument that his case differs from other cases in which defendants *did* receive the death penalty. On automatic appeal, the Georgia Supreme Court found that McCleskey's death sentence was not disproportionate to other death sentences imposed in the State. * * * Moreover, where the statutory procedures adequately channel the sentencer's discretion, such proportionality review is not constitutionally required. *Pulley v. Harris.*

On the other hand, absent a showing that the Georgia capital punishment system operates in an arbitrary and capricious manner, McCleskey cannot prove a constitutional violation by demonstrating that other defendants who may be similarly situated did *not* receive the death penalty. In *Gregg,* the Court * * * [rejected] the argument that "the opportunities for discretionary action that are inherent in the processing of any murder case under Georgia law," specifically the opportunities for discretionary leniency, rendered the capital sentences imposed arbitrary and capricious. * * *

Although our decision in *Gregg* as to the facial validity of the Georgia capital punishment statute appears to foreclose McCleskey's disproportionality argument, he further contends that the Georgia capital punishment system is arbitrary and capricious in *application,* and therefore his sentence is excessive, because racial considerations may influence capital sentencing decisions in Georgia. We now address this claim.

To evaluate McCleskey's challenge, we must examine exactly what the Baldus study may show. Even Professor Baldus does not contend that his statistics *prove* that race enters into any capital sentencing decisions or that race was a factor in McCleskey's particular case. Statistics at most may show only a likelihood that a particular factor entered into some decisions. There is, of course, some risk of racial prejudice influencing a jury's decision in a criminal case. There are similar risks that other kinds of prejudice will influence other criminal trials. The question "is at what point that risk becomes constitutionally unacceptable," *Turner v. Murray* [p. 817]. McCleskey asks us to accept the likelihood allegedly shown by the Baldus study as the constitutional measure of an unacceptable risk of racial prejudice influencing capital sentencing decisions. This we decline to do.

Because of the risk that the factor of race may enter the criminal justice process, we have engaged in "unceasing efforts" to eradicate racial prejudice from our criminal justice system. *Batson v. Kentucky* [p. 828]. Our efforts have been guided by our recognition that "the inestimable privilege of trial by jury * * * is a vital principle, underlying the whole administration of criminal justice," *Ex parte Milligan,* 4 Wall. 2 (1866). Thus, it is the jury that is a criminal defendant's fundamental "protection of life and liberty against race or color prejudice." Specifically, a capital sentencing jury representative of a criminal defendant's community assures a " 'diffused impartiality,' " in the jury's task of "express[ing] the conscience of the community on the ultimate question of life or death."

Individual jurors bring to their deliberations "qualities of human nature and varieties of human experience, the range of which is unknown and perhaps unknowable." The capital sentencing decision requires the individual jurors to focus their collective judgment on the unique characteristics of a particular criminal defendant. It is not surprising that such collective judgments often are difficult to explain. But the inherent lack of predictability of jury decisions does not justify their condemnation. On the contrary, it is the jury's function to make the difficult and uniquely human judgments that defy codification and that "buil[d] discretion, equity, and flexibility into a legal system."

McCleskey's argument that the Constitution condemns the discretion allowed decisionmakers in the Georgia capital sentencing system is antithetical to the fundamental role of discretion in our criminal justice system. Discretion in the criminal justice system offers substantial benefits to the criminal defendant. Not only can a jury decline to impose the death sentence, it can decline to convict, or choose to convict of a lesser offense. Whereas decisions against a defendant's interest may be reversed by the trial judge or on appeal, these discretionary exercises of leniency are final and unreviewable. Similarly, the capacity of prosecutorial discretion to provide individualized justice is "firmly entrenched in American law." As we have noted, a prosecutor can decline to charge, offer a plea bargain, or decline to seek a death sentence in any particular case. Of course, "the power to be lenient [also] is the power to discriminate," but a capital-punishment system that did not allow for discretionary acts of leniency "would be totally alien to our notions of criminal justice." *Gregg v. Georgia.*

At most, the Baldus study indicates a discrepancy that appears to correlate with race. Apparent disparities in sentencing are an inevitable part of our criminal justice system. The discrepancy indicated by the Baldus study is "a far cry from the major systemic defects identified in *Furman,*" *Pulley v. Harris.* As this Court has recognized, any mode for determining guilt or punishment "has its weaknesses and the potential for misuse." Specifically, "there can be 'no perfect procedure for deciding in which cases governmental authority should be used to impose death.' " Despite these imperfections, our consistent rule has been that constitutional guarantees are met when "the mode [for determining guilt or punishment] itself has been surrounded with safeguards to make it as fair as possible." *Singer v. United States,* 380 U.S. 24 (1965). Where the discretion that is fundamental to our criminal process is involved, we decline to assume that what is unexplained is invidious. In light of the safeguards designed to minimize racial bias in the process, the fundamental value of jury trial in our criminal justice system, and the benefits that discretion provides to criminal defendants, we hold that the Baldus study does not demonstrate a constitutionally significant risk of racial bias affecting the Georgia capital-sentencing process.[37]

---

[37] Justice Brennan's eloquent dissent of course reflects his often repeated opposition to the death sentence. His views, that also are shared by Justice Marshall, are principled and entitled to respect. Nevertheless, since *Gregg* was decided in 1976, seven members of this Court consistently have upheld sentences of death under *Gregg*-type statutes providing for meticulous review of each sentence in both state and federal courts. The ultimate thrust of Justice Brennan's dissent is that *Gregg* and its progeny should be overruled. He does not, however, expressly call for the overruling of any prior decision. Rather, relying on the Baldus study, Justice Brennan, * * * questions the very heart of our criminal justice system: the traditional discretion that prosecutors and juries necessarily must have.

We have held that discretion in a capital punishment system is necessary to satisfy the Constitution. Yet, the dissent now claims that the "discretion afforded prosecutors and jurors in the Georgia capital sentencing system" violates the Constitution by creating "opportunities for racial considerations to influence criminal proceedings." The dissent contends that in Georgia "[n]o guidelines govern prosecutorial decisions * * *." Prosecutorial decisions necessarily involve both judgmental and factual decisions that vary from case to case. Thus, it is difficult to imagine guidelines that would produce the predictability sought by the dissent without sacrificing the discretion essential to a humane and fair system of criminal justice. Indeed, the dissent suggests no such guidelines for prosecutorial discretion. * * *

The dissent repeatedly emphasizes the need for "a uniquely high degree of rationality in imposing the death penalty." Again, no suggestion is made as to how greater "rationality" could be achieved under any type of statute that authorizes capital punishment. * * * Given the * * * safeguards already inherent in the imposition and review of capital sentences, the dissent's call for greater rationality is no less than a claim that a capital-punishment system cannot be administered in accord with the Constitution. As we reiterate, the requirement of heightened rationality in the imposition of capital punishment does not "plac[e] totally unrealistic conditions on its use." *Gregg.*

Two additional concerns inform our decision in this case. First, McCleskey's claim, taken to its logical conclusion, throws into serious question the principles that underlie our entire criminal justice system. The Eighth Amendment is not limited in application to capital punishment, but applies to all penalties. Thus, if we accepted McCleskey's claim that racial bias has impermissibly tainted the capital sentencing decision, we could soon be faced with similar claims as to other types of penalty.[38] Moreover, the claim that his sentence rests on the irrelevant factor of race easily could be extended to apply to claims based on unexplained discrepancies that correlate to membership in other minority groups,[39] and even to gender. Similarly, since McCleskey's claim relates to the race of his victim, other claims could apply with equally logical force to statistical disparities that correlate with the race or sex of other actors in the criminal justice system, such as defense attorneys, or judges. Also, there is no logical reason that such a claim need be limited to racial or sexual bias. If arbitrary and capricious punishment is the touchstone under the Eighth Amendment, such a claim could—at least in theory— be based upon any arbitrary variable, such as the defendant's facial characteristics, or the physical attractiveness of the defendant or the victim, that some statistical study indicates may be influential in jury decisionmaking. As these examples illustrate, there is no limiting principle to the type of challenge brought by McCleskey.[45] The Constitution does not require that a State eliminate any demonstrable disparity that correlates with a potentially irrelevant factor in order to operate a criminal justice system that includes capital punishment. As we have

---

[38] Studies already exist that allegedly demonstrate a racial disparity in the length of prison sentences. * * *

[39] In *Regents of the University of California v. Bakke,* 438 U.S. 265, 295 (1978) (opinion of Powell, J.), we recognized that the national "majority" "is composed of various minority groups, most of which can lay claim to a history of prior discrimination at the hands of the State and private individuals." * * *

[45] Justice Stevens, who would not overrule *Gregg,* suggests in his dissent that the infirmities alleged by McCleskey could be remedied by narrowing the class of death-eligible defendants to categories identified by the Baldus study where "prosecutors consistently seek, and juries consistently impose, the death penalty without regard to the race of the victim or the race of the offender." This proposed solution is unconvincing. First, "consistently" is a relative term, and narrowing the category of death-eligible defendants would simply shift the borderline between those defendants who received the death penalty and those who did not. A borderline area would continue to exist and vary in its boundaries. Moreover, because the discrepancy between borderline cases would be difficult to explain, the system would likely remain open to challenge on the basis that the lack of explanation rendered the sentencing decisions unconstitutionally arbitrary.

Second, even assuming that a category with theoretically consistent results could be identified, it is difficult to imagine how Justice Stevens' proposal would or could operate on a case-by-case basis. Whenever a victim is white and the defendant is a member of a different race, what steps would a prosecutor be required to take—in addition to weighing the customary prosecutorial considerations—before concluding in the particular case that he lawfully could prosecute? In the absence of a current, Baldus-type study focused particularly on the community in which the crime was committed, where would he find a standard? Would the prosecutor have to review the prior decisions of community prosecutors and determine the types of cases in which juries in his jurisdiction "consistently" had imposed the death penalty when the victim was white and the defendant was of a different race? And must he rely solely on statistics? Even if such a study were feasible, would it be unlawful for the prosecutor, in making his final decision in a particular case, to consider the evidence of guilt and the presence of aggravating and mitigating factors? However conscientiously a prosecutor might attempt to identify death-eligible defendants under the dissent's suggestion, it would be a wholly speculative task at best, likely to result in less rather than more fairness and consistency in the imposition of the death penalty.

stated specifically in the context of capital punishment, the Constitution does not "plac[e] totally unrealistic conditions on its use." *Gregg v. Georgia.*

Second, McCleskey's arguments are best presented to the legislative bodies. It is not the responsibility—or indeed even the right—of this Court to determine the appropriate punishment for particular crimes. It is the legislatures, the elected representatives of the people, that are "constituted to respond to the will and consequently the moral values of the people." *Furman v. Georgia* (Burger, C.J., dissenting). Legislatures also are better qualified to weigh and "evaluate the results of statistical studies in terms of their own local conditions and with a flexibility of approach that is not available to the courts," *Gregg v. Georgia.* Capital punishment is now the law in more than two thirds of our States. It is the ultimate duty of courts to determine on a case-by-case basis whether these laws are applied consistently with the Constitution. Despite McCleskey's wide ranging arguments that basically challenge the validity of capital punishment in our multi-racial society, the only question before us is whether in his case, the law of Georgia was properly applied. We agree with the District Court and the Court of Appeals for the Eleventh Circuit that this was carefully and correctly done in this case.

JUSTICE BRENNAN, with whom JUSTICE MARSHALL joins, and with whom JUSTICE BLACKMUN and JUSTICE STEVENS join in all but Part I, dissenting.

I.   Adhering to my view that the death penalty is in all circumstances cruel and unusual punishment forbidden by the Eighth and Fourteenth Amendments, I would vacate the decision below insofar as it left undisturbed the death sentence imposed in this case. * * * Even if I did not hold this position, however, I would reverse [for] petitioner McCleskey has clearly demonstrated that his death sentence was imposed in violation of the Eighth and Fourteenth Amendments. While I join [the parts] of Justice Blackmun's dissenting opinion discussing petitioner's Fourteenth Amendment claim, I write separately to emphasize how conclusively McCleskey has also demonstrated precisely the type of risk of irrationality in sentencing that we have consistently condemned in our Eighth Amendment jurisprudence.

II.   At some point in this case, Warren McCleskey doubtless asked his lawyer whether a jury was likely to sentence him to die. A candid reply to this question would have been disturbing. First, counsel would have to tell McCleskey that few of the details of the crime or of McCleskey's past criminal conduct were more important than the fact that his victim was white. Furthermore, counsel would feel bound to tell McCleskey that defendants charged with killing white victims in Georgia are 4.3 times as likely to be sentenced to death as defendants charged with killing blacks. In addition, frankness would compel the disclosure that it was more likely than not that the race of McCleskey's victim would determine whether he received a death sentence: 6 of every 11 defendants convicted of killing a white person would not have received the death penalty if their victims had been black, while, among defendants with aggravating and mitigating factors comparable to McCleskey, 20 of every 34 would not have been sentenced to die if their victims had been black. Finally, the assessment would not be complete without the information that cases involving black defendants and white victims are more likely to result in a death sentence than cases featuring any other racial combination of defendant and victim. The story could be told in a variety of ways, but McCleskey could not fail to grasp its essential narrative line: there was a significant chance that race would play a prominent role in determining if he lived or died.

The Court today holds that Warren McCleskey's sentence was constitutionally imposed. It finds no fault in a system in which lawyers must tell their clients that race casts a large shadow on the capital sentencing process. * * *

III. It is important to emphasize at the outset that the Court's observation that McCleskey cannot prove the influence of race on any particular sentencing decision is irrelevant in evaluating his Eighth Amendment claim. Since *Furman,* the Court has been concerned with the *risk* of the imposition of an arbitrary sentence, rather than the proven fact of one. * * * This emphasis on risk acknowledges the difficulty of divining the jury's motivation in an individual case. In addition, it reflects the fact that concern for arbitrariness focuses on the rationality of the system as a whole, and that a system that features a significant probability that sentencing decisions are influenced by impermissible considerations cannot be regarded as rational.[1] * * *

The statistical evidence in this case * * * relentlessly documents the risk that McCleskey's sentence was influenced by racial considerations. This evidence shows that there is a better than even chance in Georgia that race will influence the decision to impose the death penalty: a majority of defendants in white-victim crimes would not have been sentenced to die if their victims had been black. In determining whether this risk is acceptable, our judgment must be shaped by the awareness that "[t]he risk of racial prejudice infecting a capital sentencing proceeding is especially serious in light of the complete finality of the death sentence" [and] that "[i]t is of vital importance to the defendant and to the community that any decision to impose the death sentence be, and appear to be, based on reason rather than caprice or emotion." In determining the guilt of a defendant, a state must prove its case beyond a reasonable doubt. That is, we refuse to convict if the chance of error is simply less likely than not. Surely, we should not be willing to take a person's life if the chance that his death sentence was irrationally imposed is *more* likely than not. In light of the gravity of the interest at stake, petitioner's statistics on their face are a powerful demonstration of the type of risk that our Eighth Amendment jurisprudence has consistently condemned.

Evaluation of McCleskey's evidence cannot rest solely on the numbers themselves. We must also ask whether the conclusion suggested by those numbers is consonant with our understanding of history and human experience. Georgia's legacy of a race-conscious criminal justice system, as well as this Court's own recognition of the persistent danger that racial attitudes may affect criminal

---

[1] Once we can identify a pattern of arbitrary sentencing outcomes, we can say that a defendant runs a risk of being sentenced arbitrarily. It is thus immaterial whether the operation of an impermissible influence such as race is intentional. While the Equal Protection Clause forbids racial discrimination, and intent may be critical in a successful claim under that provision, the Eighth Amendment has its own distinct focus: whether punishment comports with social standards of rationality and decency. * * *

proceedings, indicate that McCleskey's claim is not a fanciful product of mere statistical artifice. * * *

[The dissent here noted that Georgia, at the time of the Civil War, had a "dual system" of criminal justice (distinguishing between crimes "committed by and against blacks and whites"). It noted further that Gunnar Myrdal's study of race relations in the United States (published in 1944) "mirrored McCleskey's evidence," that "the specter of race discrimination was acknowledged by the Court in striking down the Georgia death penalty statute in *Furman*," and that the Court in *Coker v. Georgia*, 433 U.S. 584 (1977), striking down the death penalty for rape, although "it did not explicitly mention race," had before it evidence "that black men who committed rape, particularly of white women, were considerably more likely to be sentenced to death."] * * * This historical review of Georgia criminal law is not intended as a bill of indictment calling the State to account for past transgressions. Citation of past practices does not justify the automatic condemnation of current ones. But it would be unrealistic to ignore the influence of history in assessing the plausible implications of McCleskey's evidence. * * *

* * * Our cases reflect a realization of the myriad of opportunities for racial considerations to influence criminal proceedings: in the exercise of peremptory challenges; in the selection of the grand jury; in the selection of the petit jury; in the exercise of prosecutorial discretion; in the conduct of argument; and in the conscious or unconscious bias of jurors. The discretion afforded prosecutors and jurors in the Georgia capital-sentencing system creates such opportunities. No guidelines govern prosecutorial decisions to seek the death penalty, and Georgia provides juries with no list of aggravating and mitigating factors, nor any standard for balancing them against one another. Once a jury identifies one aggravating factor, it has complete discretion in choosing life or death, and need not articulate its basis for selecting life imprisonment. The Georgia sentencing system therefore provides considerable opportunity for racial considerations, however subtle and unconscious, to influence charging and sentencing decisions.

IV. The Court cites four reasons for shrinking from the implications of McCleskey's evidence: the desirability of discretion for actors in the criminal-justice system, the existence of statutory safeguards against abuse of that discretion, the potential consequences for broader challenges to criminal sentencing, and an understanding of the contours of the judicial role. While these concerns underscore the need for sober deliberation, they do not justify rejecting evidence as convincing as McCleskey has presented.

The Court maintains that petitioner's claim "is antithetical to the fundamental role of discretion in our criminal justice system." It states that "[w]here the discretion that is fundamental to our criminal process is involved, we decline to assume that what is unexplained is invidious." Reliance on race in imposing capital punishment, however, is antithetical to the very rationale for granting sentencing discretion. Discretion is a means, not an end. * * *

The Court also declines to find McCleskey's evidence sufficient in view of "the safeguards designed to minimize racial bias in the [capital sentencing] process." * * * It is clear that *Gregg* bestowed no permanent approval on the Georgia system.

It simply held that the State's statutory safeguards were assumed sufficient to channel discretion without evidence otherwise. * * *

The Court next states that its unwillingness to regard the petitioner's evidence as sufficient is based in part on the fear that recognition of McCleskey's claim would open the door to widespread challenges to all aspects of criminal sentencing. Taken on its face, such a statement seems to suggest a fear of too much justice. Yet surely the majority would acknowledge that if striking evidence indicated that other minority groups, or women, or even persons with blond hair, were disproportionately sentenced to death, such a state of affairs would be repugnant to deeply rooted conceptions of fairness. The prospect that there may be more widespread abuse than McCleskey documents may be dismaying, but it does not justify complete abdication of our judicial role. * * *

In fairness, the Court's fear that McCleskey's claim is an invitation to descend a slippery slope also rests on the realization that any humanly imposed system of penalties will exhibit some imperfection. Yet to reject McCleskey's powerful evidence on this basis is to ignore both the qualitatively different character of the death penalty and the particular repugnance of racial discrimination, considerations which may properly be taken into account in determining whether various punishments are "cruel and unusual." Furthermore, it fails to take account of the unprecedented refinement and strength of the Baldus study. * * *

The Court also maintains that accepting McCleskey's claim would pose a threat to all sentencing because of the prospect that a correlation might be demonstrated between sentencing outcomes and other personal characteristics. Again, such a view is indifferent to the considerations that enter into a determination of whether punishment is "cruel and unusual." Race is a consideration whose influence is expressly constitutionally proscribed. We have expressed a moral commitment, as embodied in our fundamental law, that this specific characteristic should not be the basis for allotting burdens and benefits. * * *

Certainly, a factor that we would regard as morally irrelevant, such as hair color, at least theoretically could be associated with sentencing results to such an extent that we would regard as arbitrary a system in which that factor played a significant role. [However,] the evaluation of evidence suggesting such a correlation must be informed not merely by statistics, but by history and experience. One could hardly contend that this nation has on the basis of hair color inflicted upon persons deprivation comparable to that imposed on the basis of race. Recognition of this fact would necessarily influence the evaluation of data suggesting the influence of hair color on sentencing, and would require evidence of statistical correlation even more powerful than that presented by the Baldus study. * * *

Finally, the Court justifies its rejection of McCleskey's claim by cautioning against usurpation of the legislatures' role in devising and monitoring criminal punishment. The Court is, of course, correct to emphasize the gravity of constitutional intervention and the importance that it be sparingly employed. The fact that "[c]apital punishment is now the law in more than two thirds of our

States," however, does not diminish the fact that capital punishment is the most awesome act that a State can perform. The judiciary's role in this society counts for little if the use of governmental power to extinguish life does not elicit close scrutiny. [The Court] fulfills, rather than disrupts, the scheme of separation of powers by closely scrutinizing the imposition of the death penalty, for no decision of a society is more deserving of the "sober second thought." * * *

The Court's decision today will not change what attorneys in Georgia tell other Warren McCleskeys about their chances of execution. Nothing will soften the harsh message they must convey, nor alter the prospect that race undoubtedly will continue to be a topic of discussion. McCleskey's evidence will not have obtained judicial acceptance, but that will not affect what is said on death row. However many criticisms of today's decision may be rendered, these painful conversations will serve as the most eloquent dissents of all.

JUSTICE BLACKMUN, with whom JUSTICE MARSHALL and JUSTICE STEVENS join and with whom JUSTICE BRENNAN joins in all but Part IB,[a] dissenting. * * *

In analyzing an equal protection claim, a court must first determine the nature of the claim and the responsibilities of the state actors involved to determine what showing is required for the establishment of a prima facie case. The Court correctly points out: "In its broadest form, McCleskey's claim of discrimination extends to every actor in the Georgia capital sentencing process, from the prosecutor who sought the death penalty and the jury that imposed the sentence, to the State itself that enacted the capital punishment statute and allows it to remain in effect despite its allegedly discriminatory application." Having recognized the complexity of McCleskey's claim, however, the Court proceeds to ignore a significant element of that claim. The Court treats the case as if it is limited to challenges to the actions of two specific decisionmaking bodies—the petit jury and the state legislature. This self-imposed restriction enables the Court to distinguish this case from the venire-selection cases and Title VII cases in which it long has accepted statistical evidence and has provided an easily applicable framework for review.

Considering McCleskey's claim in its entirety, however, reveals that the claim fits easily within that same framework. A significant aspect of his claim is that racial factors impermissibly affected numerous steps in the Georgia capital-sentencing scheme between his indictment and the jury's vote to sentence him to death. The primary decisionmaker at each of the intervening steps of the process is the prosecutor, the quintessential state actor in a criminal proceeding. * * * [M]y analysis in this dissenting opinion * * * concentrate[s] on the decisions within the prosecutor's office through which the State decided to seek the death penalty and, in particular, the point at which the State proceeded to the penalty phase after conviction. This is a step at which the evidence of the effect of the racial factors was especially strong, but is ignored by the Court.

A criminal defendant alleging an equal protection violation must prove the existence of purposeful discrimination. He may establish a prima facie case of

---

[a]   The reference here is to the last paragraph of Justice Blackmun's dissent.

purposeful discrimination "by showing that the totality of the relevant facts gives rise to an inference of discriminatory purpose." *Batson v. Kentucky* [Ch. 15, § 2]. Once the defendant establishes a prima facie case, the burden shifts to the prosecution to rebut that case. * * *

Under *Batson v. Kentucky* and the framework established in [the jury selection cases], McCleskey must meet a three-factor standard. First, he must establish that he is a member of a group "that is a recognizable, distinct class, singled out for different treatment." Second, he must make a showing of a substantial degree of differential treatment. Third, he must establish that the allegedly discriminatory procedure is susceptible to abuse or is not racially neutral.

There can be no dispute that McCleskey has made the requisite showing under the first prong of the standard. The Baldus study demonstrates that black persons are a distinct group that are singled out for different treatment in the Georgia capital-sentencing system. The Court acknowledges, as it must, that the raw statistics included in the Baldus study and presented by petitioner indicate that it is much less likely that a death sentence will result from a murder of a black person than from a murder of a white person. * * * The raw figures also indicate that even within the group of defendants who are convicted of killing white persons and are thereby more likely to receive a death sentence, black defendants are more likely than white defendants to be sentenced to death.

With respect to the second prong, McCleskey must prove that there is a substantial likelihood that his death sentence is due to racial factors. * * * McCleskey demonstrated the degree to which his death sentence was affected by racial factors by introducing multiple-regression analyses that explain how much of the statistical distribution of the cases analyzed is attributable to the racial factors. * * * McCleskey produced evidence concerning the role of racial factors at the various steps in the decisionmaking process, focusing on the prosecutor's decision as to which cases merit the death sentence. McCleskey established that the race of the victim is an especially significant factor at the point where the defendant has been convicted of murder and the prosecutor must choose whether to proceed to the penalty phase of the trial and create the possibility that a death sentence may be imposed or to accept the imposition of a sentence of life imprisonment. McCleskey demonstrated this effect at both the statewide level, and in Fulton County where he was tried and sentenced. The statewide statistics indicated that black defendant/white victim cases advanced to the penalty trial at nearly five times the rate of the black defendant/black victim cases (70% vs. 15%), and over three times the rate of white defendant/black victim cases (70% vs. 19%). The multiple-regression analysis demonstrated that racial factors had a readily identifiable effect at a statistically significant level. The Fulton County statistics were consistent with this evidence although they involved fewer cases.

Individualized evidence relating to the disposition of the Fulton County cases that were most comparable to McCleskey's case was consistent with the evidence of the race-of-victim effect as well. Of the 17 defendants, including McCleskey, who were arrested and charged with homicide of a police officer in Fulton County during the 1973–1979 period, McCleskey, alone, was sentenced to death. The only other defendant whose case even proceeded to the penalty phase received a sentence of life imprisonment. That defendant had been convicted of killing a black police officer.

As to the final element of the prima facie case, McCleskey showed that the process by which the State decided to seek a death penalty in his case and to pursue that sentence throughout the prosecution was susceptible to abuse. Petitioner submitted the deposition of Lewis R. Slaton, who, as of the date of the deposition, had been the District Attorney for 18 years in the county in which McCleskey was tried and sentenced. As Mr. Slaton explained, the duties and responsibilities of that office are the prosecution of felony charges within the Atlanta Judicial Circuit that comprises Fulton County. He testified that during his years in the office, there were no guidelines informing the Assistant District Attorneys who handle the cases how they should proceed at any particular stage of the prosecution. There were no guidelines as to when they should seek an indictment for murder as opposed to lesser charges, when they should recommend acceptance of a guilty plea to murder, acceptance of a guilty plea to a lesser charge, reduction of charges, or dismissal of charges at the postindictment-preconviction stage, or when they should seek the death penalty. Slaton testified that these decisions were left to the discretion of the individual attorneys who then informed Slaton of their decisions as they saw fit.

Slaton's deposition proves that, at every stage of a prosecution, the Assistant District Attorney exercised much discretion. The only guidance given was "on-the-job training." * * * The sole effort to provide any consistency was Slaton's periodic pulling of files at random to check on the progress of cases. Slaton explained that as far as he knew, he was the only one aware of this checking. The files contained information only as to the evidence in the case, not any indication as to why an attorney made a particular decision. The attorneys were not required to record why they sought an indictment for murder as opposed to a lesser charge, or why they recommended a certain plea. The attorneys were not required to report to Slaton the cases in which they decided not to seek the death penalty, or the cases in which they did seek the death penalty * * *.

The above-described evidence, considered in conjunction with the other record evidence outlined by Justice Brennan, and discussed in opinions dissenting from the judgment of the Court of Appeals, gives rise to an inference of discriminatory purpose. * * * McCleskey's showing is of sufficient magnitude that, absent evidence to the contrary, one must conclude that racial factors entered into the decisionmaking process that yielded McCleskey's death sentence. The burden, therefore, shifts to the State to explain the racial selections. It must demonstrate that legitimate racially neutral criteria and procedures yielded this racially skewed result. * * *

The Court's explanations for its failure to apply this well-established equal protection analysis to this case are not persuasive. It first reasons that "each particular decision to impose the death penalty is made by a petit jury" and that the "application of an inference drawn from the general statistics to a specific decision in a trial and sentencing simply is not comparable to the application of an inference drawn from general statistics to a specific venire-selection or Title VII case." According to the Court, the statistical evidence is less relevant because, in the two latter situations, there are fewer variables relevant to the decision and the "statistics relate to fewer entities."

I disagree with the Court's assertion that there are fewer variables relevant to the decisions of jury commissioners or prosecutors in their selection of jurors, or to the decisions of employers in their selection, promotion, or discharge of employees. Such decisions involve a multitude of factors, some rational, some irrational. Second, I disagree with the comment that the venire-selection and employment decisions are "made by fewer entities." Certainly in the employment context, personnel decisions are often the product of several levels of decisionmaking within the business or government structure. The Court's statement that the decision to impose death is made by the petit jury also disregards the fact that the prosecutor screens the cases throughout the pretrial proceedings and decides to seek the death penalty and to pursue a capital case to the penalty phase where a death sentence can be imposed. McCleskey's claim in this regard lends itself to analysis under the framework we apply in assessing challenges to other prosecutorial actions. See *Batson v. Kentucky,* see also *Wayte v. United States* [p. 677].

The Court's other reason for treating this case differently from venire-selection and employment cases is that in these latter contexts, "the decisionmaker has an opportunity to explain the statistical disparity," but in the instant case the State had no practical opportunity to rebut the Baldus study. According to the Court, this is because jurors cannot be called to testify about their verdict and because policy considerations render it improper to require "prosecutors to defend their decisions to seek death penalties, 'often years after they were made.' "

I agree with the Court's observation as to the difficulty of examining the jury's decisionmaking process. * * * The Court's refusal to require that the prosecutor provide an explanation for his actions, however, is completely inconsistent with this Court's longstanding precedents. * * * Prosecutors undoubtedly need adequate discretion to allocate the resources of their offices and to fulfill their responsibilities to the public in deciding how best to enforce the law, but this does not place them beyond the constraints imposed on state action under the Fourteenth Amendment. Cf. *Ex parte Virginia,* 100 U.S. 339 (1880) (upholding validity of conviction of state judge for discriminating on the basis of race in his selection of jurors).

The Court attempts to distinguish the present case from *Batson v. Kentucky,* in which we recently reaffirmed the fact that prosecutors' actions are not unreviewable. I agree with the Court's observation that this case is "quite different" from the *Batson* case. The irony is that McCleskey presented proof in this case that would have satisfied the more burdensome standard of *Swain v. Alabama,* 380 U.S. 202 (1965), a standard that was described in *Batson* as having placed on defendants a "crippling burden of proof." As discussed above, McCleskey presented evidence of numerous decisions impermissibly affected by racial factors over a significant number of cases. The exhaustive evidence presented in this case certainly demands an inquiry into the prosecutor's actions. * * *

One of the final concerns discussed by the Court may be the most disturbing aspect of its opinion. Granting relief to McCleskey in this case, it is said, could lead to further constitutional challenges. That, of course, is no reason to deny *McCleskey* his rights under the Equal Protection Clause. If a grant of relief to him were to lead to a closer examination of the effects of racial considerations throughout the criminal-justice system, the system, and hence society, might benefit. Where no such factors come into play, the integrity of the system is enhanced. Where such considerations are shown to be significant, efforts can be made to eradicate their impermissible influence and to ensure an evenhanded application of criminal sanctions.

Like Justice Stevens, I do not believe acceptance of McCleskey's claim would eliminate capital punishment in Georgia. Justice Stevens points out that the evidence presented in this case indicates that in extremely aggravated murders the risk of discriminatory enforcement of the death penalty is minimized. I agree that narrowing the class of death-eligible defendants is not too high a price to pay for a death-penalty system that does not discriminate on the basis of race.[b] Moreover, the establishment of guidelines for Assistant District Attorneys as to the appropriate basis for exercising their discretion at the various steps in the prosecution of a case would provide at least a measure of consistency. The Court's emphasis on the procedural safeguards in the system ignores the fact that there are none whatsoever during the crucial process leading up to trial. As Justice White stated for the plurality in *Turner v. Murray,* I find "the risk that racial prejudice may have infected petitioner's capital sentencing unacceptable in light of the ease with which that risk could have been minimized." I dissent.

GRAHAM V. FLORIDA
560 U.S. 48, 130 S.Ct. 2011, 176 L.Ed.2d 825 (2010).

JUSTICE KENNEDY delivered the opinion of the Court.

The issue before the Court is whether the Constitution permits a juvenile offender to be sentenced to life in prison without parole for a nonhomicide crime. The sentence was imposed by the State of Florida. Petitioner challenges the sentence under the Eighth Amendment's Cruel and Unusual Punishments Clause,

---

[b] In a third dissenting opinion, Justice Stevens, joined by Blackmun, J., described the majority's evident fear "that the acceptance of McCleskey's claim would sound the death knell for capital punishment in Georgia" as "unfounded": "One of the lessons of the Baldus study is that there exist certain categories of extremely serious crimes for which prosecutors consistently seek, and juries consistently impose, the death penalty without regard to the race of the victim or the race of the offender. If Georgia were to narrow the class of death-eligible defendants to those categories, the danger of arbitrary and discriminatory imposition of the death penalty would be significantly decreased, if not eradicated."

Although Justice Stevens would reverse, he believed that further proceedings were needed to determine whether McCleskey's death sentence should be set aside: "First, the Court of Appeals must decide whether the Baldus study is valid. I am persuaded that it is, but orderly procedure requires that the Court of Appeals address this issue before we actually decide the question. Second, it is necessary for the District Court to determine whether the particular facts of McCleskey's crime and his background place this case within the range of cases that present an unacceptable risk that race played a decisive role in McCleskey's sentencing."

made applicable to the States by the Due Process Clause of the Fourteenth Amendment.

I

Petitioner is Terrance Jamar Graham. He was born on January 6, 1987. Graham's parents were addicted to crack cocaine, and their drug use persisted in his early years. Graham was diagnosed with attention deficit hyperactivity disorder in elementary school. He began drinking alcohol and using tobacco at age 9 and smoked marijuana at age 13.

In July 2003, when Graham was age 16, he and three other school-age youths attempted to rob a barbeque restaurant in Jacksonville, Florida. One youth, who worked at the restaurant, left the back door unlocked just before closing time. Graham and another youth, wearing masks, entered through the unlocked door. Graham's masked accomplice twice struck the restaurant manager in the back of the head with a metal bar. When the manager started yelling at the assailant and Graham, the two youths ran out and escaped in a car driven by the third accomplice. The restaurant manager required stitches for his head injury. No money was taken.

Graham was arrested for the robbery attempt. Under Florida law, it is within a prosecutor's discretion whether to charge 16- and 17-year-olds as adults or juveniles for most felony crimes. Graham's prosecutor elected to charge Graham as an adult. The charges against Graham were armed burglary with assault or battery, a first-degree felony carrying a maximum penalty of life imprisonment without the possibility of parole and attempted armed-robbery, a second-degree felony carrying a maximum penalty of 15 years' imprisonment.

On December 18, 2003, Graham pleaded guilty to both charges under a plea agreement. Graham wrote a letter to the trial court. After reciting "this is my first and last time getting in trouble," he continued "I've decided to turn my life around." Graham said "I made a promise to God and myself that if I get a second chance, I'm going to do whatever it takes to get to the [National Football League]."

The trial court accepted the plea agreement. The court withheld adjudication of guilt as to both charges and sentenced Graham to concurrent 3-year terms of probation. Graham was required to spend the first 12 months of his probation in the county jail, but he received credit for the time he had served awaiting trial, and was released on June 25, 2004.

Less than 6 months later, on the night of December 2, 2004, Graham again was arrested. The State's case was as follows: Earlier that evening, Graham participated in a home invasion robbery. His two accomplices were Meigo Bailey and Kirkland Lawrence, both 20-year-old men. According to the State, at 7 p.m. that night, Graham, Bailey, and Lawrence knocked on the door of the home where Carlos Rodriguez lived. Graham, followed by Bailey and Lawrence, forcibly entered the home and held a pistol to Rodriguez's chest. For the next 30 minutes, the three held Rodriguez and another man, a friend of Rodriguez, at gunpoint while they ransacked the home searching for money. Before leaving, Graham and his accomplices barricaded Rodriguez and his friend inside a closet.

The State further alleged that Graham, Bailey, and Lawrence, later the same evening, attempted a second robbery, during which Bailey was shot. Graham, who had borrowed his father's car, drove Bailey and Lawrence to the hospital and left them there. As Graham drove away, a police sergeant signaled him to stop. Graham continued at a high speed but crashed into a telephone pole. He tried to flee on foot but was apprehended. Three handguns were found in his car.

When detectives interviewed Graham, he denied involvement in the crimes. He said he encountered Bailey and Lawrence only after Bailey had been shot. One of the detectives told Graham that the victims of the home invasion had identified him. He asked Graham, "Aside from the two robberies tonight how many more were you involved in?" Graham responded, "Two to three before tonight." The night that Graham allegedly committed the robbery, he was 34 days short of his 18th birthday.

On December 13, 2004, Graham's probation officer filed with the trial court an affidavit asserting that Graham had violated the conditions of his probation by possessing a firearm, committing crimes, and associating with persons engaged in criminal activity. The trial court held hearings on Graham's violations about a year later, in December 2005 and January 2006. The judge who presided was not the same judge who had accepted Graham's guilty plea to the earlier offenses.

Graham maintained that he had no involvement in the home invasion robbery; but, even after the court underscored that the admission could expose him to a life sentence on the earlier charges, he admitted violating probation conditions by fleeing. The State presented evidence related to the home invasion, including testimony from the victims. The trial court noted that Graham, in admitting his attempt to avoid arrest, had acknowledged violating his probation. The court further found that Graham had violated his probation by committing a home invasion robbery, by possessing a firearm, and by associating with persons engaged in criminal activity.

The trial court held a sentencing hearing. Under Florida law the minimum sentence Graham could receive absent a downward departure by the judge was 5 years' imprisonment. The maximum was life imprisonment. Graham's attorney requested the minimum nondeparture sentence of 5 years. A presentence report prepared by the Florida Department of Corrections recommended that Graham receive an even lower sentence—at most 4 years' imprisonment. The State recommended that Graham receive 30 years on the armed burglary count and 15 years on the attempted armed robbery count.

After hearing Graham's testimony, the trial court explained the sentence it was about to pronounce:

"Mr. Graham, as I look back on your case, yours is really candidly a sad situation. You had, as far as I can tell, you have quite a family structure. You had a lot of people who wanted to try and help you get your life turned around including the court system, and you had a judge who took the step to try and give you direction through his probation order to give you a chance to get back onto track. And at the time you seemed through your letters that that is exactly what you wanted to do. And I don't know why it is that you threw your life away. I don't know why.

"But you did, and that is what is so sad about this today is that you have actually been given a chance to get through this, the original charge, which were very serious charges to begin with. . . . The attempted robbery with a weapon was a very serious charge.

. . .

"[I]n a very short period of time you were back before the Court on a violation of this probation, and then here you are two years later standing before me, literally the—facing a life sentence as to—up to life as to count 1 and up to 15 years as to count 2.

"And I don't understand why you would be given such a great opportunity to do something with your life and why you would throw it away. The only thing that I can rationalize is that you decided that this is how you were going to lead your life and that there is nothing that we can do for you. And as the state pointed out, that this is an escalating pattern of criminal conduct on your part and that we can't help you any further. We can't do anything to deter you. This is the way you are going to lead your life, and I don't know why you are going to. You've made that decision. I have no idea. But, evidently, that is what you decided to do.

"So then it becomes a focus, if I can't do anything to help you, if I can't do anything to get you back on the right path, then I have to start focusing on the community and trying to protect the community from your actions. And, unfortunately, that is where we are today is I don't see where I can do anything to help you any further. You've evidently decided this is the direction you're going to take in life, and it's unfortunate that you made that choice.

"I have reviewed the statute. I don't see where any further juvenile sanctions would be appropriate. I don't see where any youthful offender sanctions would be appropriate. Given your escalating pattern of criminal conduct, it is apparent to the Court that you have decided that this is the way you are going to live your life and that the only thing I can do now is to try and protect the community from your actions."

The trial court found Graham guilty of the earlier armed burglary and attempted armed robbery charges. It sentenced him to the maximum sentence authorized by law on each charge: life imprisonment for the armed burglary and 15 years for the attempted armed robbery. Because Florida has abolished its parole system, a life sentence gives a defendant no possibility of release unless he is granted executive clemency. [Graham's challenge to his sentence under the Eighth Amendment failed in the Florida courts]. We granted certiorari.

II

The Eighth Amendment states: "Excessive bail shall not be required, nor excessive fines imposed, nor cruel and unusual punishments inflicted." To determine whether a punishment is cruel and unusual, courts must look beyond historical conceptions to "'the evolving standards of decency that mark the progress of a maturing society.'" *Estelle v. Gamble,* 429 U.S. 97, 102 (1976) (quoting *Trop v. Dulles,* 356 U.S. 86, 101 (1958) (plurality opinion)). "This is because '[t]he standard of extreme cruelty is not merely descriptive, but necessarily embodies a moral judgment. The standard itself remains the same, but its applicability must change as the basic mores of society change.'" *Kennedy v. Louisiana,* 554 U.S. 407, 419 (2008) (quoting *Furman v. Georgia,* 408 U.S. 238, 382 (1972) (Burger, C.J., dissenting)).

The Cruel and Unusual Punishments Clause prohibits the imposition of inherently barbaric punishments under all circumstances. "[P]unishments of torture," for example, "are forbidden." *Wilkerson v. Utah,* 99 U.S. 130, 136 (1879). These cases underscore the essential principle that, under the Eighth Amendment, the State must respect the human attributes even of those who have committed serious crimes.

For the most part, however, the Court's precedents consider punishments challenged not as inherently barbaric but as disproportionate to the crime. The concept of proportionality is central to the Eighth Amendment. Embodied in the Constitution's ban on cruel and unusual punishments is the "precept of justice that punishment for crime should be graduated and proportioned to [the] offense." *Weems v. United States,* 217 U.S. 349, 367 (1910).

The Court's cases addressing the proportionality of sentences fall within two general classifications. The first involves challenges to the length of term-of-years sentences given all the circumstances in a particular case. The second comprises cases in which the Court implements the proportionality standard by certain categorical restrictions on the death penalty.

In the first classification the Court considers all of the circumstances of the case to determine whether the sentence is unconstitutionally excessive. Under this approach, the Court has held unconstitutional a life without parole sentence for the defendant's seventh nonviolent felony, the crime of passing a worthless check. *Solem v. Helm,* 463 U.S. 277 (1983). In other cases, however, it has been difficult for the challenger to establish a lack of proportionality. A leading case is *Harmelin v. Michigan,* 501 U.S. 957 (1991), in which the offender was sentenced under state law to life without parole for possessing a large quantity of cocaine. A closely divided Court upheld the sentence. The controlling opinion concluded that the Eighth Amendment contains a "narrow proportionality principle," that "does not require strict proportionality between crime and sentence" but rather "forbids only extreme sentences that are 'grossly disproportionate' to the crime." *Id.* (Kennedy, J., concurring in part and concurring in judgment). Again closely divided, the Court rejected a challenge to a sentence of 25 years to life for the theft of a few golf clubs under California's so-called three-strikes recidivist sentencing scheme. *Ewing v. California,* 538 U.S. 11 (2003); see also *Lockyer v. Andrade,* 538 U.S. 63 (2003). The

Court has also upheld a sentence of life with the possibility of parole for a defendant's third nonviolent felony, the crime of obtaining money by false pretenses, *Rummel v. Estelle*, 445 U.S. 263 (1980), and a sentence of 40 years for possession of marijuana with intent to distribute and distribution of marijuana, *Hutto v. Davis*, 454 U.S. 370 (1982) *(per curiam)*.

The controlling opinion in *Harmelin* explained its approach for determining whether a sentence for a term of years is grossly disproportionate for a particular defendant's crime. A court must begin by comparing the gravity of the offense and the severity of the sentence. "[I]n the rare case in which [this] threshold comparison . . . leads to an inference of gross disproportionality" the court should then compare the defendant's sentence with the sentences received by other offenders in the same jurisdiction and with the sentences imposed for the same crime in other jurisdictions. If this comparative analysis "validate[s] an initial judgment that [the] sentence is grossly disproportionate," the sentence is cruel and unusual.

The second classification of cases has used categorical rules to define Eighth Amendment standards. The previous cases in this classification involved the death penalty. The classification in turn consists of two subsets, one considering the nature of the offense, the other considering the characteristics of the offender. With respect to the nature of the offense, the Court has concluded that capital punishment is impermissible for nonhomicide crimes against individuals. *Kennedy.* [S]ee also *Enmund v. Florida*, 458 U.S. 782 (1982); *Coker v. Georgia*, 433 U.S. 584 (1977). In cases turning on the characteristics of the offender, the Court has adopted categorical rules prohibiting the death penalty for defendants who committed their crimes before the age of 18, *Roper v. Simmons*, 543 U.S. 551 (2005), or whose intellectual functioning is in a low range, *Atkins v. Virginia*, 536 U.S. 304 (2002).

In the cases adopting categorical rules the Court has taken the following approach. The Court first considers "objective indicia of society's standards, as expressed in legislative enactments and state practice" to determine whether there is a national consensus against the sentencing practice at issue. *Roper.* Next, guided by "the standards elaborated by controlling precedents and by the Court's own understanding and interpretation of the Eighth Amendment's text, history, meaning, and purpose," *Kennedy,* the Court must determine in the exercise of its own independent judgment whether the punishment in question violates the Constitution. *Roper.*

The present case involves an issue the Court has not considered previously: a categorical challenge to a term-of-years sentence. The approach in cases such as *Harmelin* and *Ewing* is suited for considering a gross proportionality challenge to a particular defendant's sentence, but here a sentencing practice itself is in question. This case implicates a particular type of sentence as it applies to an entire class of offenders who have committed a range of crimes. As a result, a threshold comparison between the severity of the penalty and the gravity of the crime does not advance the analysis. Here, in addressing the question presented, the appropriate analysis is the one used in cases that involved the categorical approach, specifically *Atkins, Roper,* and *Kennedy.*

III

A

The analysis begins with objective indicia of national consensus. "[T]he 'clearest and most reliable objective evidence of contemporary values is the legislation enacted by the country's legislatures.'" *Atkins*. Six jurisdictions do not allow life without parole sentences for any juvenile offenders. Seven jurisdictions permit life without parole for juvenile offenders, but only for homicide crimes. Thirty-seven States as well as the District of Columbia permit sentences of life without parole for a juvenile nonhomicide offender in some circumstances. Federal law also allows for the possibility of life without parole for offenders as young as 13. Relying on this metric, the State and its *amici* argue that there is no national consensus against the sentencing practice at issue.

This argument is incomplete and unavailing. "There are measures of consensus other than legislation." *Kennedy*. Actual sentencing practices are an important part of the Court's inquiry into consensus. Here, an examination of actual sentencing practices in jurisdictions where the sentence in question is permitted by statute discloses a consensus against its use. Although these statutory schemes contain no explicit prohibition on sentences of life without parole for juvenile nonhomicide offenders, those sentences are most infrequent. According to a recent study, nationwide there are only 109 juvenile offenders serving sentences of life without parole for nonhomicide offenses. See P. Annino, D. Rasmussen, & C. Rice, Juvenile Life without Parole for Non-Homicide Offenses: Florida Compared to Nation 2 (Sept. 14, 2009).

The State contends that this study's tally is inaccurate because it does not count juvenile offenders who were convicted of both a homicide and a nonhomicide offense, even when the offender received a life without parole sentence for the nonhomicide. This distinction is unpersuasive. Juvenile offenders who committed both homicide and nonhomicide crimes present a different situation for a sentencing judge than juvenile offenders who committed no homicide. * * * Florida further criticizes this study because the authors were unable to obtain complete information on some States and because the study was not peer reviewed. The State does not, however, provide any data of its own. Although in the first instance it is for the litigants to provide data to aid the Court, we have been able to supplement the study's findings. The study's authors were not able to obtain a definitive tally for Nevada, Utah, or Virginia. Our research shows that Nevada has five juvenile nonhomicide offenders serving life without parole sentences, Utah has none, and Virginia has eight. The study also did not note that there are six convicts in the federal prison system serving life without parole offenses for nonhomicide crimes.

Finally, since the study was completed, a defendant in Oklahoma has apparently been sentenced to life without parole for a rape and stabbing he committed at the age of 16. Thus, adding the individuals counted by the study to those we have been able to locate independently, there are 129 juvenile nonhomicide offenders serving life without parole sentences. A significant majority of those, 77 in total, are serving sentences imposed in Florida. The other 52 are imprisoned in just 10 States—California, Delaware, Iowa, Louisiana, Mississippi, Nebraska, Nevada, Oklahoma, South Carolina, and Virginia—and in the federal system. Thus, only 12 jurisdictions nationwide in fact impose life without parole sentences on juvenile nonhomicide offenders—and most of those impose the sentence quite rarely—while 26 States as well as the District of Columbia do not impose them despite apparent statutory authorization.

The numbers cited above reflect all current convicts in a jurisdiction's penal system, regardless of when they were convicted. It becomes all the more clear how rare these sentences are, even within the jurisdictions that do sometimes impose them, when one considers that a juvenile sentenced to life without parole is likely to live in prison for decades. Thus, these statistics likely reflect nearly all juvenile nonhomicide offenders who have received a life without parole sentence stretching back many years. It is not certain that this opinion has identified every juvenile nonhomicide offender nationwide serving a life without parole sentence, for the statistics are not precise. The available data, nonetheless, are sufficient to demonstrate how rarely these sentences are imposed even if there are isolated cases that have not been included in the presentations of the parties or the analysis of the Court.

It must be acknowledged that in terms of absolute numbers juvenile life without parole sentences for nonhomicides are more common than the sentencing practices at issue in some of this Court's other Eighth Amendment cases. See, *e.g.*, *Enmund* (only six executions of nontriggerman felony murderers between 1954 and 1982) *Atkins* (only five executions of mentally retarded defendants in 13-year period). This contrast can be instructive, however, if attention is first given to the base number of certain types of offenses. For example, in the year 2007 (the most recent year for which statistics are available), a total of 13,480 persons, adult and juvenile, were arrested for homicide crimes. That same year, 57,600 juveniles were arrested for aggravated assault; 3,580 for forcible rape; 34,500 for robbery; 81,900 for burglary; 195,700 for drug offenses; and 7,200 for arson. Although it is not certain how many of these numerous juvenile offenders were eligible for life without parole sentences, the comparison suggests that in proportion to the opportunities for its imposition, life without parole sentences for juveniles convicted of nonhomicide crimes is as rare as other sentencing practices found to be cruel and unusual.

The evidence of consensus is not undermined by the fact that many jurisdictions do not prohibit life without parole for juvenile nonhomicide offenders. The Court confronted a similar situation in *Thompson v. Oklahoma*, 487 U.S. 815 (1988), where a plurality concluded that the death penalty for offenders younger than 16 was unconstitutional. A number of States then allowed the juvenile death penalty if one considered the statutory scheme. As is the case here, those States authorized the transfer of some juvenile offenders to adult court; and at that point there was no statutory differentiation between adults and juveniles with respect to authorized penalties. The plurality concluded that the transfer laws show "that the States consider 15-year-olds to be old enough to be tried in criminal court for serious crimes (or too old to be dealt with effectively in juvenile court), *but tells us nothing about the judgment these States have made regarding the appropriate punishment for such youthful offenders.*" Justice O'Connor, concurring in the judgment, took a similar view. ("When a legislature provides for some 15-year-olds to be processed through the adult criminal justice system, and capital punishment is available for adults in that jurisdiction, the death penalty becomes at least theoretically applicable to such defendants. . . . [H]owever, it does not necessarily follow that the legislatures in those jurisdictions have deliberately concluded that it would be appropriate").

The same reasoning obtains here. Many States have chosen to move away from juvenile court systems and to allow juveniles to be transferred to, or charged directly in, adult court under certain circumstances. Once in adult court, a juvenile offender may receive the same sentence as would be given to an adult offender, including a life without parole sentence. But the fact that transfer and direct charging laws make life without parole possible for some juvenile nonhomicide offenders does not justify a judgment that many States intended to subject such offenders to life without parole sentences.

For example, under Florida law a child of any age can be prosecuted as an adult for certain crimes and can be sentenced to life without parole. The State acknowledged at oral argument that even a 5-year-old, theoretically, could receive such a sentence under the letter of the law. All would concede this to be unrealistic, but the example underscores that the statutory eligibility of a juvenile offender for life without parole does not indicate that the penalty has been endorsed through deliberate, express, and full legislative consideration. Similarly, the many States that allow life without parole for juvenile nonhomicide offenders but do not impose the punishment should not be treated as if they have expressed the view that the sentence is appropriate. The sentencing practice now under consideration is exceedingly rare. And "it is fair to say that a national consensus has developed against it." *Atkins.*

B

Community consensus, while "entitled to great weight," is not itself determinative of whether a punishment is cruel and unusual. *Kennedy.* In accordance with the constitutional design, "the task of interpreting the Eighth Amendment remains our responsibility." *Roper.* The judicial exercise of independent judgment requires consideration of the culpability of the offenders at issue in light of their crimes and characteristics, along with the severity of the punishment in question. In this inquiry the Court also considers whether the challenged sentencing practice serves legitimate penological goals.

Roper established that because juveniles have lessened culpability they are less deserving of the most severe punishments. As compared to adults, juveniles have a " 'lack of maturity and an underdeveloped sense of responsibility' "; they "are more vulnerable or susceptible to negative influences and outside pressures, including peer pressure"; and their characters are " not as well formed." *Id.* These salient characteristics mean that "[i]t is difficult even for expert psychologists to differentiate between the juvenile offender whose crime reflects unfortunate yet transient immaturity, and the rare juvenile offender whose crime reflects irreparable corruption." *Id.* Accordingly, "juvenile offenders cannot with reliability be classified among the worst offenders." *Id.* A juvenile is not absolved of responsibility for his actions, but his transgression "is not as morally reprehensible as that of an adult." *Thompson.*

No recent data provide reason to reconsider the Court's observations in *Roper* about the nature of juveniles. As petitioner's *amici* point out, developments in psychology and brain science continue to show fundamental differences between juvenile and adult minds. For example, parts of the brain involved in behavior control continue to mature through late adolescence. See Brief for American Medical Association et al. as *Amici Curiae*; Brief for American Psychological Association et al. as *Amici Curiae.* Juveniles are more capable of change than are adults, and their actions are less likely to be evidence of "irretrievably depraved character" than are the actions of adults. *Roper.* It remains true that "[f]rom a moral standpoint it would be misguided to equate the failings of a minor with those of an adult, for a greater possibility exists that a minor's character deficiencies will be reformed." *Ibid.* These matters relate to the status of the offenders in question; and it is relevant to consider next the nature of the offenses to which this harsh penalty might apply.

The Court has recognized that defendants who do not kill, intend to kill, or foresee that life will be taken are categorically less deserving of the most serious forms of punishment than are murderers. There is a line "between homicide and other serious violent offenses against the individual." *Kennedy.* Serious nonhomicide crimes "may be devastating in their harm . . . but 'in terms of moral depravity and of the injury to the person and to the public,' . . . they cannot be compared to murder in their 'severity and irrevocability.' " *Id.* This is because "[l]ife is over for the victim of the murderer," but for the victim of even a very serious nonhomicide crime, "life . . . is not over and normally is not beyond repair." *Ibid.* Although an offense like robbery or rape is "a serious crime deserving serious punishment," *Enmund,* those crimes differ from homicide crimes in a moral sense.

It follows that, when compared to an adult murderer, a juvenile offender who did not kill or intend to kill has a twice diminished moral culpability. The age of the offender and the nature of the crime each bear on the analysis.

As for the punishment, life without parole is "the second most severe penalty permitted by law." *Harmelin* (opinion of Kennedy, J.). It is true that a death sentence is "unique in its severity and irrevocability," *Gregg v. Georgia,* 428 U.S. 153, 187 (1976) (joint opinion of Stewart, Powell, and Stevens, JJ.); yet life without parole sentences share some characteristics with death sentences that are shared by no other sentences. The State does not execute the offender sentenced to life without parole, but the sentence alters the offender's life by a forfeiture that is irrevocable. It deprives the convict of the most basic liberties without giving hope of restoration, except perhaps by executive clemency—the remote possibility of which does not mitigate the harshness of the sentence. *Solem.* As one court observed in overturning a life without parole sentence for a juvenile defendant, this sentence "means denial of hope; it means that good behavior and character improvement are immaterial; it means that whatever the future might hold in store for the mind and spirit of [the convict], he will remain in prison for the rest of his days." *Naovarath v. State,* 105 Nev. 525, 526 (1989).

The Court has recognized the severity of sentences that deny convicts the possibility of parole. In *Rummel,* the Court rejected an Eighth Amendment challenge to a life sentence for a defendant's third nonviolent felony but stressed that the sentence gave the defendant the possibility of parole. Noting that "parole is an established variation on imprisonment of convicted criminals," it was evident that an analysis of the petitioner's sentence "could hardly ignore the possibility that he will not actually be imprisoned for the rest of his life." And in *Solem,* the only previous case striking down a sentence for a term of years as grossly disproportionate, the defendant's sentence was deemed "far more severe than the life sentence we considered in *Rummel,*" because it did not give the defendant the possibility of parole.

Life without parole is an especially harsh punishment for a juvenile. Under this sentence a juvenile offender will on average serve more years and a greater percentage of his life in prison than an adult offender. A 16-year-old and a 75-year-old each sentenced to life without parole receive the same punishment in name only. This reality cannot be ignored.

The penological justifications for the sentencing practice are also relevant to the analysis. Criminal punishment can have different goals, and choosing among them is within a legislature's discretion. It does not follow, however, that the purposes and effects of penal sanctions are irrelevant to the determination of Eighth Amendment restrictions. A sentence lacking any legitimate penological justification is by its nature disproportionate to the offense. With respect to life without parole for juvenile nonhomicide offenders, none of the goals of penal sanctions that have been recognized as legitimate—retribution, deterrence, incapacitation, and rehabilitation—provides an adequate justification.

Retribution is a legitimate reason to punish, but it cannot support the sentence at issue here. Society is entitled to impose severe sanctions on a juvenile nonhomicide offender to express its condemnation of the crime and to seek restoration of the moral imbalance caused by the offense. But "[t]he heart of the retribution rationale is that a criminal sentence must be directly related to the personal culpability of the criminal offender." *Tison.* And as *Roper* observed, "[w]hether viewed as an attempt to express the community's moral outrage or as an attempt to right the balance for the wrong to the victim, the case for retribution is not as strong with a minor as with an adult." The case becomes even weaker with respect to a juvenile who did not commit homicide. *Roper* found that "[r]etribution is not proportional if the law's most severe penalty is imposed" on the juvenile murderer. The considerations underlying that holding support as well the conclusion that retribution does not justify imposing the second most severe penalty on the less culpable juvenile nonhomicide offender.

Deterrence does not suffice to justify the sentence either. *Roper* noted that "the same characteristics that render juveniles less culpable than adults suggest . . . that juveniles will be less susceptible to deterrence." Because juveniles' "lack of maturity and underdeveloped sense of responsibility . . . often result in impetuous and ill-considered actions and decisions," *Johnson v. Texas,* 509 U.S. 350, 367 (1993), they are less likely to take a possible punishment into consideration when making decisions. This is particularly so when that punishment is rarely imposed. That the sentence deters in a few cases is perhaps plausible, but "[t]his argument does not overcome other objections." *Kennedy,* Even if the punishment has some connection to a valid penological goal, it must be shown that the punishment is not grossly disproportionate in light of the justification offered. Here, in light of juvenile nonhomicide offenders' diminished moral responsibility, any limited deterrent effect provided by life without parole is not enough to justify the sentence.

Incapacitation, a third legitimate reason for imprisonment, does not justify the life without parole sentence in question here. Recidivism is a serious risk to public safety, and so incapacitation is an important goal. See *Ewing* (plurality opinion) (statistics show 67 percent of former inmates released from state prisons are charged with at least one serious new crime within three years). But while incapacitation may be a legitimate penological goal sufficient to justify life without parole in other contexts, it is inadequate to justify that punishment for juveniles who did not commit homicide. To justify life without parole on the assumption that the juvenile offender forever will be a danger to society requires the sentencer to make a judgment that the juvenile is incorrigible. The characteristics of juveniles make that judgment questionable. "It is difficult even for expert psychologists to differentiate between the juvenile offender whose crime reflects unfortunate yet transient immaturity, and the rare juvenile offender whose crime reflects irreparable corruption." *Roper.* As one court concluded in a challenge to a life without parole sentence for a 14-year-old, "incorrigibility is inconsistent with youth." *Workman v. Commonwealth,* 429 S.W.2d 374, 378 (Ky.1968).

Here one cannot dispute that this defendant posed an immediate risk, for he had committed, we can assume, serious crimes early in his term of supervised release and despite his own assurances of reform. Graham deserved to be separated from society for some time in order to prevent what the trial court described as an "escalating pattern of criminal conduct," but it does not follow that he would be a risk to society for the rest of his life. Even if the State's judgment that Graham was incorrigible were later corroborated by prison misbehavior or failure to mature, the sentence was still disproportionate because that judgment was made at the outset. A life without parole sentence improperly denies the juvenile offender a chance to demonstrate growth and maturity. Incapacitation cannot override all other considerations, lest the Eighth Amendment's rule against disproportionate sentences be a nullity.

Finally there is rehabilitation, a penological goal that forms the basis of parole systems. The concept of rehabilitation is imprecise; and its utility and proper implementation are the subject of a substantial, dynamic field of inquiry and dialogue. It is for legislatures to determine what rehabilitative techniques are appropriate and effective.

A sentence of life imprisonment without parole, however, cannot be justified by the goal of rehabilitation. The penalty forswears altogether the rehabilitative ideal. By denying the defendant the right to reenter the community, the State makes an irrevocable judgment about that person's value and place in society. This judgment is not appropriate in light of a juvenile nonhomicide offender's capacity for change and limited moral culpability. A State's rejection of rehabilitation, moreover, goes beyond a mere expressive judgment. As one *amicus* notes, defendants serving life without parole sentences are often denied access to vocational training and other rehabilitative services that are available to other inmates. See Brief for Sentencing Project as *Amicus Curiae* 11–13. For juvenile offenders, who are most in need of and receptive to rehabilitation, see Brief for J. Lawrence Aber et al. as *Amici Curiae* 28–31 (hereinafter Aber Brief), the absence of rehabilitative opportunities or treatment makes the disproportionality of the sentence all the more evident.

In sum, penological theory is not adequate to justify life without parole for juvenile nonhomicide offenders. This determination; the limited culpability of juvenile nonhomicide offenders; and the severity of life without parole sentences all lead to the conclusion that the sentencing practice under consideration is cruel and unusual. This Court now holds that for a juvenile offender who did not commit homicide the Eighth Amendment forbids the sentence of life without parole. This clear line is necessary to prevent the possibility that life without parole sentences will be imposed on juvenile nonhomicide offenders who are not sufficiently culpable to merit that punishment. Because "[t]he age of 18 is the point where society draws the line for many purposes between childhood and adulthood," those who were below that age when the offense was committed may not be sentenced to life without parole for a nonhomicide crime. *Roper*.

A State is not required to guarantee eventual freedom to a juvenile offender convicted of a nonhomicide crime. What the State must do, however, is give defendants like Graham some meaningful opportunity to obtain release based on demonstrated maturity and rehabilitation. It is for the State, in the first instance, to explore the means and mechanisms for compliance. It bears emphasis, however, that while the Eighth Amendment forbids a State from imposing a life without parole sentence on a juvenile nonhomicide offender, it does not require the State to release that offender during his natural life. Those who commit truly horrifying crimes as juveniles may turn out to be irredeemable, and thus deserving of incarceration for the duration of their lives. The Eighth Amendment does not foreclose the possibility that persons convicted of nonhomicide crimes committed before adulthood will remain behind bars for life. It does forbid States from making the judgment at the outset that those offenders never will be fit to reenter society.

C

Categorical rules tend to be imperfect, but one is necessary here. Two alternative approaches are not adequate to address the relevant constitutional concerns. First, the State argues that the laws of Florida and other States governing criminal procedure take sufficient account of the age of a juvenile offender. Here, Florida notes that under its law prosecutors are required to charge 16- and 17-year-old offenders as adults only for certain serious felonies; that prosecutors have discretion to charge those offenders as adults for other felonies; and that prosecutors may not charge nonrecidivist 16- and 17-year-old offenders as adults for misdemeanors. The State also stresses that "in only the narrowest of circumstances" does Florida law impose no age limit whatsoever for prosecuting juveniles in adult court.

Florida is correct to say that state laws requiring consideration of a defendant's age in charging decisions are salutary. An offender's age is relevant to the Eighth Amendment, and criminal procedure laws that fail to take defendants' youthfulness into account at all would be flawed. Florida, like other States, has made substantial efforts to enact comprehensive rules governing the treatment of youthful offenders by its criminal justice system.

The provisions the State notes are, nonetheless, by themselves insufficient to address the constitutional concerns at issue. Nothing in Florida's laws prevents its courts from sentencing a juvenile nonhomicide offender to life without parole based on a subjective judgment that the defendant's crimes demonstrate an "irretrievably depraved character." *Roper*. This is inconsistent with the Eighth Amendment. Specific cases are illustrative. In Graham's case the sentencing judge decided to impose life without parole—a sentence greater than that requested by the prosecutor—for Graham's armed burglary conviction. The judge did so because he concluded that Graham was incorrigible: "[Y]ou decided that this is how you were going to lead your life and that there is nothing that we can do for you. . . . We can't do anything to deter you."

Another example comes from *Sullivan v. Florida,* No. 08–7621. *Sullivan* was argued the same day as this case, but the Court has now dismissed the writ of certiorari in *Sullivan* as improvidently granted. The facts, however, demonstrate the flaws of Florida's system. The petitioner, Joe Sullivan, was prosecuted as an adult for a sexual assault committed when he was 13 years old. Noting Sullivan's past encounters with the law, the sentencing judge concluded that, although Sullivan had been "given opportunity after opportunity to upright himself and take advantage of the second and third chances he's been given," he had demonstrated himself to be unwilling to follow the law and needed to be kept away from society for the duration of his life. The judge sentenced Sullivan to life without parole. As these examples make clear, existing state laws, allowing the imposition of these sentences based only on a discretionary, subjective judgment by a judge or jury that the offender is irredeemably depraved, are insufficient to prevent the possibility that the offender will receive a life without parole sentence for which he or she lacks the moral culpability.

Another possible approach would be to hold that the Eighth Amendment requires courts to take the offender's age into consideration as part of a case-specific gross disproportionality inquiry, weighing it against the seriousness of the crime. This approach would allow courts to account for factual differences between cases and to impose life without parole sentences for particularly heinous crimes. Few, perhaps no, judicial responsibilities are more difficult than sentencing. The task is usually undertaken by trial judges who seek with diligence and professionalism to take account of the human existence of the offender and the just demands of a wronged society.

The case-by-case approach to sentencing must, however, be confined by some boundaries. The dilemma of juvenile sentencing demonstrates this. For even if we were to assume that some juvenile nonhomicide offenders might have "sufficient psychological maturity, and at the same time demonstrat[e] sufficient depravity," *Roper*, to merit a life without parole sentence, it does not follow that courts taking a case-by-case proportionality approach could with sufficient accuracy distinguish the few incorrigible juvenile offenders from the many that have the capacity for change. *Roper* rejected the argument that the Eighth Amendment required only that juries be told they must consider the defendant's age as a mitigating factor in sentencing. The Court concluded that an "unacceptable likelihood exists that the brutality or cold-blooded nature of any particular crime would overpower mitigating arguments based on youth as a matter of course, even where the juvenile offender's objective immaturity, vulnerability, and lack of true depravity should require a sentence less severe than death." *Id.* Here, as with the death penalty, "[t]he differences between juvenile and adult offenders are too marked and well understood to risk allowing a youthful person to receive" a sentence of life without parole for a nonhomicide crime "despite insufficient culpability." *Id.*

Another problem with a case-by-case approach is that it does not take account of special difficulties encountered by counsel in juvenile representation. As some *amici* note, the features that distinguish juveniles from adults also put them at a significant disadvantage in criminal proceedings. Juveniles mistrust adults and have limited understandings of the criminal justice system and the roles of the institutional actors within it. They are less likely than adults to work effectively with their lawyers to aid in their defense. Difficulty in weighing long-term consequences; a corresponding impulsiveness; and reluctance to trust defense counsel seen as part of the adult world a rebellious youth rejects, all can lead to poor decisions by one charged with a juvenile offense. These factors are likely to impair the quality of a juvenile defendant's representation. A categorical rule avoids the risk that, as a result of these difficulties, a court or jury will erroneously conclude that a particular juvenile is sufficiently culpable to deserve life without parole for a nonhomicide.

Finally, a categorical rule gives all juvenile nonhomicide offenders a chance to demonstrate maturity and reform. The juvenile should not be deprived of the opportunity to achieve maturity of judgment and self-recognition of human worth and potential. In *Roper,* that deprivation resulted from an execution that brought life to its end. Here, though by a different dynamic, the same concerns apply. Life in prison without the possibility of parole gives no chance for fulfillment outside prison walls, no chance for reconciliation with society, no hope. Maturity can lead to that considered reflection which is the foundation for remorse, renewal, and rehabilitation. A young person who knows that he or she has no chance to leave prison before life's end has little incentive to become a responsible individual. In some prisons, moreover, the system itself becomes complicit in the lack of development. As noted above, it is the policy in some prisons to withhold counseling, education, and rehabilitation programs for those who are ineligible for parole consideration. A categorical rule against life without parole for juvenile nonhomicide offenders avoids the perverse consequence in which the lack of maturity that led to an offender's crime is reinforced by the prison term.

Terrance Graham's sentence guarantees he will die in prison without any meaningful opportunity to obtain release, no matter what he might do to demonstrate that the bad acts he committed as a teenager are not representative of his true character, even if he spends the next half century attempting to atone for his crimes and learn from his mistakes. The State has denied him any chance to later demonstrate that he is fit to rejoin society based solely on a nonhomicide crime that he committed while he was a child in the eyes of the law. This the Eighth Amendment does not permit.

D

There is support for our conclusion in the fact that, in continuing to impose life without parole sentences on juveniles who did not commit homicide, the United States adheres to a sentencing practice rejected the world over. This observation does not control our decision. The judgments of other nations and the international community are not dispositive as to the meaning of the Eighth Amendment. But " '[t]he climate of international opinion concerning the acceptability of a particular punishment' " is also " 'not irrelevant.' " *Enmund*. The Court has looked beyond our Nation's borders for support for its independent conclusion that a particular punishment is cruel and unusual. See, *e.g., Roper*; *Atkins*; *Thompson*; *Enmund*; *Coker*; *Trop*.

Today we continue that longstanding practice in noting the global consensus against the sentencing practice in question. A recent study concluded that only 11 nations authorize life without parole for juvenile offenders under any circumstances; and only 2 of them, the United States and Israel, ever impose the punishment in practice. * * * [A]ll of the seven Israeli prisoners whom commentators have identified as serving life sentences for juvenile crimes were convicted of homicide or attempted homicide.

Thus, as petitioner contends and respondent does not contest, the United States is the only Nation that imposes life without parole sentences on juvenile nonhomicide offenders. * * * Article 37(a) of the United Nations Convention on the Rights of the Child, Nov. 20, 1989, 1577 U.N.T.S. 3 (entered into force Sept. 2, 1990), ratified by every nation except the United States and Somalia, prohibits the imposition of "life imprisonment without possibility of release ... for offences committed by persons below eighteen years of age." As we concluded in *Roper* with respect to the juvenile death penalty, "the United States now stands alone in a world that has turned its face against" life without parole for juvenile nonhomicide offenders.

The State's *amici* stress that no international legal agreement that is binding on the United States prohibits life without parole for juvenile offenders and thus urge us to ignore the international consensus. These arguments miss the mark. The question before us is not whether international law prohibits the United States from imposing the sentence at issue in this case. The question is whether that punishment is cruel and unusual. In that inquiry, "the overwhelming weight of international opinion against" life without parole for nonhomicide offenses committed by juveniles "provide[s] respected and significant confirmation for our own conclusions." *Roper*.

The debate between petitioner's and respondent's *amici* over whether there is a binding *jus cogens* norm against this sentencing practice is likewise of no import. The Court has treated the laws and practices of other nations and international agreements as relevant to the Eighth Amendment not because those norms are binding or controlling but because the judgment of the world's nations that a particular sentencing practice is inconsistent with basic principles of decency demonstrates that the Court's rationale has respected reasoning to support it. * * *

The Constitution prohibits the imposition of a life without parole sentence on a juvenile offender who did not commit homicide. A State need not guarantee the offender eventual release, but if it imposes a sentence of life it must provide him or her with some realistic opportunity to obtain release before the end of that term. The judgment of the First District Court of Appeal of Florida affirming Graham's conviction is reversed, and the case is remanded for further proceedings not inconsistent with this opinion.

* * *

JUSTICE STEVENS, with whom JUSTICE GINSBURG and JUSTICE SOTOMAYOR join, concurring.

In his dissenting opinion, Justice Thomas argues that today's holding is not entirely consistent with the controlling opinions in *Lockyer, Ewing, Harmelin,* and *Rummel*. Given that "evolving standards of decency" have played a central role in our Eighth Amendment jurisprudence for at least a century, see *Weems*, this argument suggests the dissenting opinions in those cases more accurately describe the law today than does Justice Thomas' rigid interpretation of the Amendment. Society changes. Knowledge accumulates. We learn, sometimes, from our mistakes. Punishments that did not seem cruel and unusual at one time may, in the light of reason and experience, be found cruel and unusual at a later time; unless we are to abandon the moral commitment embodied in the Eighth Amendment, proportionality review must never become effectively obsolete. While Justice Thomas would apparently not rule out a death sentence for a $50 theft by a 7-year-old, see *post*, at n. 3, the Court wisely rejects his static approach to the law. Standards of decency have evolved since 1980. They will never stop doing so.

CHIEF JUSTICE ROBERTS, concurring in the judgment.

I agree with the Court that Terrance Graham's sentence of life without parole violates the Eighth Amendment's prohibition on "cruel and unusual punishments." Unlike the majority, however, I see no need to invent a new constitutional rule of dubious provenance in reaching that conclusion. Instead, my analysis is based on an application of this Court's precedents, in particular (1) our cases requiring "narrow proportionality" review of noncapital sentences and (2) our conclusion in *Roper*, that juvenile offenders are generally less culpable than adults who commit the same crimes.

These cases expressly allow courts addressing allegations that a noncapital sentence violates the Eighth Amendment to consider the particular defendant and particular crime at issue. The standards for relief under these precedents are rigorous, and should be. But here Graham's juvenile status—together with the nature of his criminal conduct and the extraordinarily severe punishment imposed—lead me to conclude that his sentence of life without parole is unconstitutional.

Our Court has struggled with whether and how to apply the Cruel and Unusual Punishments Clause to sentences for noncapital crimes. Some of my colleagues have raised serious and thoughtful questions about whether, as an original matter, the Constitution was understood to require any degree of proportionality between noncapital offenses and their corresponding punishments. Neither party here asks us to reexamine our precedents requiring such proportionality, however, and so I approach this case by trying to apply our past decisions to the facts at hand.

Graham's case arises at the intersection of two lines of Eighth Amendment precedent. The first consists of decisions holding that the Cruel and Unusual Punishments Clause embraces a "narrow proportionality principle" that we apply, on a case-by-case basis, when asked to review noncapital sentences. * * * we have explained that the Eighth Amendment " 'does not require strict proportionality between crime and sentence' "; rather, " 'it forbids only extreme sentences that are "grossly disproportionate" to the crime.' " *Ewing.*

Our cases indicate that courts conducting "narrow proportionality" review should begin with a threshold inquiry that compares "the gravity of the offense and the harshness of the penalty." *Solem.* This analysis can consider a particular offender's mental state and motive in committing the crime, the actual harm caused to his victim or to society by his conduct, and any prior criminal history. *Id.* (considering motive, past criminal conduct, alcoholism, and propensity for violence of the particular defendant). Only in "the rare case in which a threshold comparison of the crime committed and the sentence imposed leads to an inference of gross disproportionality," should courts proceed to an "intrajurisdictional" comparison of the sentence at issue with those imposed on other criminals in the same jurisdiction, and an "interjurisdictional" comparison with sentences imposed for the same crime in other jurisdictions. If these subsequent comparisons confirm the inference of gross disproportionality, courts should invalidate the sentence as a violation of the Eighth Amendment.

The second line of precedent relevant to assessing Graham's sentence consists of our cases acknowledging that juvenile offenders are *generally*—though not necessarily in every case—less morally culpable than adults who commit the same crimes. This insight animated our decision in *Thompson,* in which we invalidated a capital sentence imposed on a juvenile who had committed his crime under the age of 16. More recently, in *Roper,* we extended the prohibition on executions to those who committed their crimes before the age of 18.

Both *Thompson* and *Roper* arose in the unique context of the death penalty, a punishment that our Court has recognized "must be limited to those offenders who commit 'a narrow category of the most serious crimes' and whose extreme culpability makes them 'the most deserving of execution.' " *Roper*. *Roper's* prohibition on the juvenile death penalty followed from our conclusion that "[t]hree general differences between juveniles under 18 and adults demonstrate that juvenile offenders cannot with reliability be classified among the worst offenders." These differences are a lack of maturity and an underdeveloped sense of responsibility, a heightened susceptibility to negative influences and outside pressures, and the fact that the character of a juvenile is "more transitory" and "less fixed" than that of an adult. Together, these factors establish the "diminished culpability of juveniles," and "render suspect any conclusion" that juveniles are among "the worst offenders" for whom the death penalty is reserved.

Today, the Court views *Roper* as providing the basis for a new categorical rule that juveniles may never receive a sentence of life without parole for nonhomicide crimes. I disagree. In *Roper,* the Court tailored its analysis of juvenile characteristics to the specific question whether juvenile offenders could constitutionally be subject to capital punishment. Our answer that they could not be sentenced to death was based on the explicit conclusion that they "cannot with reliability be classified among the *worst* offenders." *Id.* (emphasis added).

This conclusion does not establish that juveniles can never be eligible for life without parole. A life sentence is of course far less severe than a death sentence, and we have never required that it be imposed only on the very worst offenders, as we have with capital punishment. Treating juvenile life sentences as analogous to capital punishment is at odds with our longstanding view that "the death penalty is different from other punishments in kind rather than degree." *Solem*. It is also at odds with *Roper* itself, which drew the line at capital punishment by blessing juvenile sentences that are "less severe than death" despite involving "forfeiture of some of the most basic liberties." *Roper* Indeed, *Roper* explicitly relied on the possible imposition of life without parole on some juvenile offenders.

But the fact that *Roper* does not support a categorical rule barring life sentences for all juveniles does not mean that a criminal defendant's age is irrelevant to those sentences. On the contrary, our cases establish that the "narrow proportionality" review applicable to noncapital cases itself takes the personal "culpability of the offender" into account in examining whether a given punishment is proportionate to the crime. *Solem*. There is no reason why an offender's juvenile status should be excluded from the analysis. Indeed, given *Roper's* conclusion that juveniles are typically less blameworthy than adults, an offender's juvenile status can play a central role in the inquiry.

Justice Thomas disagrees with even our limited reliance on *Roper* on the ground that the present case does not involve capital punishment. That distinction is important—indeed, it underlies our rejection of the categorical rule declared by the Court. But *Roper's* conclusion that juveniles are typically less culpable than adults has pertinence beyond capital cases, and rightly informs the case-specific inquiry I believe to be appropriate here.

In short, our existing precedent already provides a sufficient framework for assessing the concerns outlined by the majority. Not every juvenile receiving a life sentence will prevail under this approach. Not every juvenile should. But all will receive the protection that the Eighth Amendment requires.

Applying the "narrow proportionality" framework to the particular facts of this case, I conclude that Graham's sentence of life without parole violates the Eighth Amendment. * * * There is no question that the crime for which Graham received his life sentence—armed burglary of a nondomicil with an assault or battery—is "a serious crime deserving serious punishment." *Enmund.* So too is the home invasion robbery that was the basis of Graham's probation violation. But these crimes are certainly less serious than other crimes, such as murder or rape.

As for Graham's degree of personal culpability, he committed the relevant offenses when he was a juvenile—a stage at which, *Roper* emphasized, one's "culpability or blameworthiness is diminished, to a substantial degree, by reason of youth and immaturity." Graham's age places him in a significantly different category from the defendants in *Rummel, Harmelin,* and *Ewing,* all of whom committed their crimes as adults. Graham's youth made him relatively more likely to engage in reckless and dangerous criminal activity than an adult; it also likely enhanced his susceptibility to peer pressure. See, *e.g., Roper; Johnson; Eddings v. Oklahoma,* 455 U.S. 104, 115–117 (1982). There is no reason to believe that Graham should be denied the general presumption of diminished culpability that *Roper* indicates should apply to juvenile offenders. If anything, Graham's in-court statements—including his request for a second chance so that he could "do whatever it takes to get to the NFL"—underscore his immaturity.

The fact that Graham committed the crimes that he did proves that he was dangerous and deserved to be punished. But it does not establish that he was *particularly* dangerous—at least relative to the murderers and rapists for whom the sentence of life without parole is typically reserved. On the contrary, his lack of prior criminal convictions, his youth and immaturity, and the difficult circumstances of his upbringing noted by the majority, all suggest that he was markedly less culpable than a typical adult who commits the same offenses.

Despite these considerations, the trial court sentenced Graham to life in prison without the possibility of parole. This is the second-harshest sentence available under our precedents for *any* crime, and the most severe sanction available for a nonhomicide offense. See *Kennedy.* Indeed, as the majority notes, Graham's sentence far exceeded the punishment proposed by the Florida Department of Corrections (which suggested a sentence of four years), and the state prosecutors (who asked that he be sentenced to 30 years in prison for the armed burglary). No one in Graham's case other than the sentencing judge appears to have believed that Graham deserved to go to prison for life.

Based on the foregoing circumstances, I conclude that there is a strong inference that Graham's sentence of life imprisonment without parole was grossly disproportionate in violation of the Eighth Amendment. I therefore proceed to the next steps of the proportionality analysis. * * *

Both intrajurisdictional and interjurisdictional comparisons of Graham's sentence confirm the threshold inference of disproportionality.

Graham's sentence was far more severe than that imposed for similar violations of Florida law, even without taking juvenile status into account. For example, individuals who commit burglary or robbery offenses in Florida receive average sentences of less than 5 years and less than 10 years, respectively. Unsurprisingly, Florida's juvenile criminals receive similarly low sentences— typically less than five years for burglary and less than seven years for robbery. Graham's life without parole sentence was far more severe than the average sentence imposed on those convicted of murder or manslaughter, who typically receive under 25 years in prison. As the Court explained in *Solem*, "[i]f more serious crimes are subject to the same penalty, or to less serious penalties, that is some indication that the punishment at issue may be excessive."

Finally, the inference that Graham's sentence is disproportionate is further validated by comparison to the sentences imposed in other domestic jurisdictions. As the majority opinion explains, Florida is an outlier in its willingness to impose sentences of life without parole on juveniles convicted of nonhomicide crimes.

So much for Graham. But what about Milagro Cunningham, a 17-year-old who beat and raped an 8-year-old girl before leaving her to die under 197 pounds of rock in a recycling bin in a remote landfill? See Musgrave, Cruel or Necessary? Life Terms for Youths Spur National Debate, Palm Beach Post, Oct. 15, 2009, p. 1A. Or Nathan Walker and Jakaris Taylor, the Florida juveniles who together with their friends gang-raped a woman and forced her to perform oral sex on her 12-year-old son? See 3 Sentenced to Life for Gang Rape of Mother, Associated Press, Oct. 14, 2009. The fact that Graham cannot be sentenced to life without parole for his conduct says nothing whatever about these offenders, or others like them who commit nonhomicide crimes far more reprehensible than the conduct at issue here. The Court uses Graham's case as a vehicle to proclaim a new constitutional rule— applicable well beyond the particular facts of Graham's case—that a sentence of life without parole imposed on *any* juvenile for *any* nonhomicide offense is unconstitutional. This categorical conclusion is as unnecessary as it is unwise.

A holding this broad is unnecessary because the particular conduct and circumstances at issue in the case before us are not serious enough to justify Graham's sentence. In reaching this conclusion, there is no need for the Court to decide whether that same sentence would be constitutional if imposed for other more heinous nonhomicide crimes.

A more restrained approach is especially appropriate in light of the Court's apparent recognition that it is perfectly legitimate for a juvenile to receive a sentence of life without parole for committing murder. This means that there is nothing *inherently* unconstitutional about imposing sentences of life without parole on juvenile offenders; rather, the constitutionality of such sentences depends on the particular crimes for which they are imposed. But if the constitutionality of the sentence turns on the particular crime being punished, then the Court should limit its holding to the particular offenses that Graham committed here, and should decline to consider other hypothetical crimes not presented by this case.

In any event, the Court's categorical conclusion is also unwise. Most importantly, it ignores the fact that some nonhomicide crimes—like the ones committed by Milagro Cunningham, Nathan Walker, and Jakaris Taylor—are especially heinous or grotesque, and thus may be deserving of more severe punishment.

Those under 18 years old may as a general matter have "diminished" culpability relative to adults who commit the same crimes, *Roper*, but that does not mean that their culpability is always insufficient to justify a life sentence. See generally *Thompson* (O'Connor, J., concurring in judgment). It does not take a moral sense that is fully developed in every respect to know that beating and raping an 8-year-old girl and leaving her to die under 197 pounds of rocks is horribly wrong. The single fact of being 17 years old would not afford Cunningham protection against life without parole if the young girl had died—as Cunningham surely expected she would—so why should it do so when she miraculously survived his barbaric brutality?

The Court defends its categorical approach on the grounds that a "clear line is necessary to prevent the possibility that life without parole sentences will be imposed on juvenile nonhomicide offenders who are not sufficiently culpable to merit that punishment." It argues that a case-by-case approach to proportionality review is constitutionally insufficient because courts might not be able "with sufficient accuracy [to] distinguish the few incorrigible juvenile offenders from the many that have the capacity for change."

The Court is of course correct that judges will never have perfect foresight—or perfect wisdom—in making sentencing decisions. But this is true when they sentence adults no less than when they sentence juveniles. It is also true when they sentence juveniles who commit murder no less than when they sentence juveniles who commit other crimes.

Our system depends upon sentencing judges applying their reasoned judgment to each case that comes before them. As we explained in *Solem,* the whole enterprise of proportionality review is premised on the "justified" assumption that "courts are competent to judge the gravity of an offense, at least on a relative scale." * * *

In my view, Graham's age—together with the nature of his criminal activity and the unusual severity of his sentence—tips the constitutional balance. I thus concur in the Court's judgment that Graham's sentence of life without parole violated the Eighth Amendment. I would not, however, reach the same conclusion in every case involving a juvenile offender. Some crimes are so heinous, and some juvenile offenders so highly culpable, that a sentence of life without parole may be entirely justified under the Constitution. As we have said, "successful challenges" to noncapital sentences under the Eighth Amendment have been—and, in my view, should continue to be—"exceedingly rare." *Rummel* But Graham's sentence presents the exceptional case that our precedents have recognized will come along. * * *

JUSTICE THOMAS, with whom JUSTICE SCALIA joins, and with whom JUSTICE ALITO joins as to Parts I and III, dissenting.

The Court holds today that it is "grossly disproportionate" and hence unconstitutional for any judge or jury to impose a sentence of life without parole on an offender less than 18 years old, unless he has committed a homicide. Although the text of the Constitution is silent regarding the permissibility of this sentencing practice, and although it would not have offended the standards that prevailed at the founding, the Court insists that the standards of American society have evolved such that the Constitution now requires its prohibition.

The news of this evolution will, I think, come as a surprise to the American people. Congress, the District of Columbia, and 37 States allow judges and juries to consider this sentencing practice in juvenile nonhomicide cases, and those judges and juries have decided to use it in the very worst cases they have encountered.

The Court does not conclude that life without parole itself is a cruel and unusual punishment. It instead rejects the judgments of those legislatures, judges, and juries regarding what the Court describes as the "moral" question of whether this sentence can ever be "proportionat[e]" when applied to the category of offenders at issue here.

I am unwilling to assume that we, as members of this Court, are any more capable of making such moral judgments than our fellow citizens. Nothing in our training as judges qualifies us for that task, and nothing in Article III gives us that authority. * * *

II

The Eighth Amendment, which applies to the States through the Fourteenth, provides that "[e]xcessive bail shall not be required, nor excessive fines imposed, nor cruel and unusual punishments inflicted." It is by now well established that the Cruel and Unusual Punishments Clause was originally understood as prohibiting torturous " 'methods of punishment,' "—specifically methods akin to those that had been considered cruel and unusual at the time the Bill of Rights was adopted. With one arguable exception, see Weems; Harmelin (opinion of Scalia, J.) (discussing the scope and relevance of Weems' holding), this Court applied the Clause with that understanding for nearly 170 years after the Eighth Amendment's ratification.

More recently, however, the Court has held that the Clause authorizes it to proscribe not only methods of punishment that qualify as "cruel and unusual," but also any punishment that the Court deems "grossly disproportionate" to the crime committed. This latter interpretation is entirely the Court's creation. As has been described elsewhere at length, there is virtually no indication that the Cruel and Unusual Punishments Clause originally was understood to require proportionality in sentencing. See Harmelin (opinion of Scalia, J.). Here, it suffices to recall just two points. First, the Clause does not expressly refer to proportionality or invoke any synonym for that term, even though the Framers were familiar with the concept, as evidenced by several founding-era state constitutions that required (albeit without defining) proportional punishments. In addition, the penal statute adopted by the First Congress demonstrates that proportionality in sentencing was not considered a constitutional command. See *id.*; see also Preyer, Penal Measures in the American Colonies: An Overview, 26 Am. J. Legal Hist. 326, 348–349, 353 (1982) (explaining that crimes in the late 18th-century colonies generally were punished either by fines, whipping, or public "shaming," or by death, as intermediate sentencing options such as incarceration were not common).

* * *

The Court has nonetheless adopted categorical rules that shield entire classes of offenses and offenders from the death penalty on the theory that "evolving standards of decency" require this result. The Court has offered assurances that these standards can be reliably measured by " 'objective indicia' " of "national consensus," such as state and federal legislation, jury behavior, and (surprisingly, given that we are talking about "national" consensus) international opinion. Yet even assuming that is true, the Framers did not provide for the constitutionality of a particular type of punishment to turn on a "snapshot of American public opinion" taken at the moment a case is decided. By holding otherwise, the Court pretermits in all but one direction the evolution of the standards it describes, thus "calling a constitutional halt to what may well be a pendulum swing in social attitudes," and "stunt[ing] legislative consideration" of new questions of penal policy as they emerge.

But the Court is not content to rely on snapshots of community consensus in any event. Instead, it reserves the right to reject the evidence of consensus it finds whenever its own "independent judgment" points in a different direction. * * * The categorical proportionality review the Court employs in capital cases thus lacks a principled foundation. * * *

Until today, the Court has based its categorical proportionality rulings on the notion that the Constitution gives special protection to capital defendants because the death penalty is a uniquely severe punishment that must be reserved for only those who are "most deserving of execution." * * * "Death is different" no longer. The Court now claims not only the power categorically to reserve the "most severe punishment" for those the Court thinks are " 'the most deserving of execution,' " *but also* to declare that "less culpable" persons are categorically exempt from the "*second* most severe penalty." No reliable limiting principle remains to prevent the Court from immunizing any class of offenders from the law's third, fourth, fifth, or fiftieth most severe penalties as well. * * *

III

* * *

According to the Court, proper Eighth Amendment analysis "begins with objective indicia of national consensus,"[3] and "[t]he clearest and most reliable

---

[3]   The Court ignores entirely the threshold inquiry of whether subjecting juvenile offenders to adult penalties was one of the "modes or acts of punishment that had been considered cruel and unusual at the time that the Bill of Rights was adopted." As the Court has noted in the past, however, the evidence is clear that, at the time of the Founding, "the common law set a rebuttable presumption of incapacity to commit any felony at the age of 14, and theoretically permitted [even] capital punishment to be imposed on a person as young as age 7." It thus seems exceedingly

objective evidence of contemporary values is the legislation enacted by the country's legislatures." As such, the analysis should end quickly, because a national "consensus" in favor of the Court's result simply does not exist. * * * Only *five* States prohibit juvenile offenders from receiving a life-without-parole sentence that could be imposed on an adult convicted of the same crime.

No plausible claim of a consensus against this sentencing practice can be made in light of this overwhelming legislative evidence. The sole fact that federal law authorizes this practice singlehandedly refutes the claim that our Nation finds it morally repugnant. The additional reality that 37 out of 50 States (a supermajority of 74%) permit the practice makes the claim utterly implausible. Not only is there no consensus against this penalty, there is a clear legislative consensus *in favor* of its availability.

Undaunted, however, the Court brushes this evidence aside as "incomplete and unavailing," declaring that " '[t]here are measures of consensus other than legislation.' " This is nothing short of stunning. * * * [T]he Court has never banished into constitutional exile a sentencing practice that the laws of a majority, let alone a supermajority, of States expressly permit.[8]

Moreover, the consistency and direction of recent legislation—a factor the Court previously has relied upon when crafting categorical proportionality rules, underscores the consensus *against* the rule the Court announces here. * * * First, States over the past 20 years have consistently *increased* the severity of punishments for juvenile offenders. * * * Second, legislatures have moved away from parole over the same period. Congress abolished parole for federal offenders in 1984 * * * and several States have followed suit. In light of these developments, the argument that there is nationwide consensus that parole must be available to offenders less than 18 years old in *every* nonhomicide case simply fails.

The Court nonetheless dismisses existing legislation, pointing out that life-without-parole sentences are rarely imposed on juvenile nonhomicide offender129 times in recent memory by the Court's calculation, spread out across 11 States and the federal courts. Based on this rarity of use, the Court proclaims a consensus against the practice, implying that laws allowing it either reflect the consensus of a prior, less civilized time or are the work of legislatures tone-deaf to moral values of their constituents that this Court claims to have easily discerned from afar.

---

unlikely that the imposition of a life-without-parole sentence on a person of Graham's age would run afoul of those standards.

    [8]   *Kennedy* (prohibiting capital punishment for the rape of a child where only six States had enacted statutes authorizing the punishment [since *Furman*]); *Roper* (prohibiting capital punishment for offenders younger than 18 where 18 of 38 death-penalty States precluded imposition of the penalty on persons under 18 and the remaining 12 States did not permit capital punishment at all); *Atkins* (prohibiting capital punishment of mentally retarded persons where 18 of 38 death-penalty States precluded imposition of the penalty on such persons and the remaining States did not authorize capital punishment at all); *Thompson* (prohibiting capital punishment of offenders under 16 where 18 of 36 death-penalty States precluded imposition of the penalty on such persons and the remaining States did not permit capital punishment at all); *Enmund* (prohibiting capital punishment for felony murder without proof of intent to kill where eight States allowed the punishment without proof of that element); *Coker* (holding capital punishment for the rape of a woman unconstitutional where "[a]t no time in the last 50 years have a majority of the States authorized death as a punishment for rape").

This logic strains credulity. It has been rejected before. *Gregg* (joint opinion of Stewart, Powell, and Stevens, JJ.) ("[T]he relative infrequency of jury verdicts imposing the death sentence does not indicate rejection of capital punishment *per se*. Rather, [it] . . . may well reflect the humane feeling that this most irrevocable of sanctions should be reserved for a small number of extreme cases"). It should also be rejected here. That a punishment is rarely imposed demonstrates nothing more than a general consensus that it should be just that—rarely imposed. It is not proof that the punishment is one the Nation abhors. * * *

* * * The fact that the laws of a jurisdiction permit this sentencing practice demonstrates, at a minimum, that the citizens of that jurisdiction find tolerable the possibility that a jury of their peers could impose a life-without-parole sentence on a juvenile whose nonhomicide crime is sufficiently depraved.

The recent case of 16-year-old Keighton Budder illustrates this point. Just weeks before the release of this opinion, an Oklahoma jury sentenced Budder to life without parole after hearing evidence that he viciously attacked a 17-year-old girl who gave him a ride home from a party. Budder allegedly put the girl's head " 'into a headlock and sliced her throat,' " raped her, stabbed her about 20 times, beat her, and pounded her face into the rocks alongside a dirt road.

Budder's crime was rare in its brutality. The sentence the jury imposed was also rare. According to the study relied upon by this Court, Oklahoma had no such offender in its prison system before Budder's offense. Without his conviction, therefore, the Court would have counted Oklahoma's citizens as morally opposed to life-without-parole sentences for juveniles nonhomicide offenders.

Yet Oklahoma's experience proves the inescapable flaw in that reasoning: Oklahoma citizens have enacted laws that allow Oklahoma juries to consider life-without-parole sentences in juvenile nonhomicide cases. Oklahoma juries invoke those laws rarely—in the unusual cases that they find exceptionally depraved. I cannot agree with the Court that Oklahoma citizens should be constitutionally disabled from using this sentencing practice merely because they have not done so more frequently. If anything, the rarity of this penalty's use underscores just how judicious sentencing judges and juries across the country have been in invoking it.

* * * In sum, the Court's calculation that 129 juvenile nonhomicide life-without-parole sentences have been imposed nationwide in recent memory, even if accepted, hardly amounts to strong evidence that the sentencing practice offends our common sense of decency.[10]

---

[10] * * * [I]t seems odd that the Court counts only those juveniles sentenced to life without parole and excludes from its analysis all juveniles sentenced to lengthy term-of-years sentences (*e.g.*, 70 or 80 years' imprisonment). It is difficult to argue that a judge or jury imposing such a long sentence—which effectively denies the offender any material opportunity for parole—would express moral outrage at a life-without-parole sentence. * * * The only evidence submitted to this Court regarding the frequency of this sentence's imposition was a single study completed after this Court granted certiorari in this case. * * * The Court's questionable decision to "complete" the study on its own does not materially increase its reliability. For one thing, by finishing the study itself, the Court prohibits the parties from ever disputing its findings. Complicating matters further, the original study sometimes relied on third-party data rather than data from the States themselves; the study has never been peer reviewed; and specific data on all 129 offenders (age,

* * *

In the end, however, objective factors such as legislation and the frequency of a penalty's use are merely ornaments in the Court's analysis, window dressing that accompanies its judicial fiat.[11] By the Court's own decree, "[c]ommunity consensus . . . is not itself determinative." Only the independent moral judgment of this Court is sufficient to decide the question.

Lacking any plausible claim to consensus, the Court shifts to the heart of its argument: its "independent judgment" that this sentencing practice does not "serv[e] legitimate penological goals." The Court begins that analysis with the obligatory preamble that " '[t]he Eighth Amendment does not mandate adoption of any one penological theory,' " then promptly mandates the adoption of the theories the Court deems best.

First, the Court acknowledges that, at a minimum, the imposition of life-without-parole sentences on juvenile nonhomicide offenders serves two "legitimate" penological goals: incapacitation and deterrence. * * * Yet, the Court finds [incapacitation] *inadequate* to justify the life-without-parole sentences here. A similar fate befalls deterrence.

The Court looks more favorably on rehabilitation, but laments that life-without-parole sentences do little to promote this goal because they result in the offender's permanent incarceration. * * * Ultimately, however, the Court's "independent judgment" and the proportionality rule itself center on retribution— the notion that a criminal sentence should be proportioned to " 'the personal culpability of the criminal offender.' " The Court finds that retributive purposes are not served here for two reasons.

First, quoting *Roper,* the Court concludes that juveniles are less culpable than adults because, as compared to adults, they "have a ' "lack of maturity and an underdeveloped sense of responsibility," ' " and "their characters are 'not as well formed.' " As a general matter, this statement is entirely consistent with the evidence recounted above that judges and juries impose the sentence at issue quite infrequently, despite legislative authorization to do so in many more cases. See Part IIB, *supra.* Our society tends to treat the average juvenile as less culpable than the average adult. But the question here does not involve the average juvenile. The question, instead, is whether the Constitution prohibits judges and

---

date of conviction, crime of conviction, etc.), have not been collected, making verification of the Court's headcount impossible. * * *

    [11] I confine to a footnote the Court's discussion of foreign laws and sentencing practices because past opinions explain at length why such factors are irrelevant to the meaning of our Constitution or the Court's discernment of any longstanding tradition in *this* Nation. See *Atkins* (Rehnquist, C.J., dissenting). [**Editors' note:** In *Atkins,* Chief Justice Rehnquist wrote "if it is evidence of a *national* consensus for which we are looking, then the viewpoints of other countries simply are not relevant."] Here, two points suffice. First, despite the Court's attempt to count the actual number of juvenile nonhomicide offenders serving life-without-parole sentences in other nations (a task even more challenging than counting them within our borders), the *laws* of other countries permit juvenile life-without-parole sentences. Second, present legislation notwithstanding, democracies around the world remain free to adopt life-without-parole sentences for juvenile offenders tomorrow if they see fit. Starting today, ours can count itself among the few in which judicial decree prevents voters from making that choice.

juries from *ever* concluding that an offender under the age of 18 has demonstrated sufficient depravity and incorrigibility to warrant his permanent incarceration.

In holding that the Constitution imposes such a ban, the Court cites "developments in psychology and brain science" indicating that juvenile minds "continue to mature through late adolescence,", and that juveniles are "more likely [than adults] to engage in risky behaviors." But even if such generalizations from social science were relevant to constitutional rulemaking, the Court misstates the data on which it relies.

The Court equates the propensity of a fairly substantial number of youths to engage in "risky" or antisocial behaviors with the propensity of a much smaller group to commit violent crimes. But research relied upon by the *amici* cited in the Court's opinion differentiates between adolescents for whom antisocial behavior is a fleeting symptom and those for whom it is a lifelong pattern. That research further suggests that the pattern of behavior in the latter group often sets in before 18. And, notably, it suggests that violence itself is evidence that an adolescent offender's antisocial behavior is *not* transient. See Moffitt, A Review of Research on the Taxonomy of Life-Course Persistent Versus Adolescence-Limited Antisocial Behavior, in Taking Stock: The Status of Criminological Theory 277, 292–293 (F. Cullen, J. Wright, & K. Blevins eds.2006) (observing that "life-course persistent" males "tended to specialize in serious offenses (carrying a hidden weapon, assault, robbery, violating court orders), whereas adolescence-limited" ones "specialized in non-serious offenses (theft less than $5, public drunkenness, giving false information on application forms, pirating computer software, etc.)").

In sum, even if it were relevant, none of this psychological or sociological data is sufficient to support the Court's " 'moral' " conclusion that youth defeats culpability in *every* case.

The Court responds that a categorical rule is nonetheless necessary to prevent the " 'unacceptable likelihood' " that a judge or jury, unduly swayed by " '[the brutality or cold-blooded nature' " of a juvenile's nonhomicide crime, will sentence him to a life-without-parole sentence for which he possesses " 'insufficient culpability.' " I find that justification entirely insufficient. The integrity of our criminal justice system depends on the ability of citizens to stand between the defendant and an outraged public and dispassionately determine his guilt and the proper amount of punishment based on the evidence presented. That process necessarily admits of human error. But so does the process of judging in which we engage. As between the two, I find far more "unacceptable" that this Court, swayed by studies reflecting the general tendencies of youth, decree that the people of this country are not fit to decide for themselves when the rare case requires different treatment.

That is especially so because, in the end, the Court does not even believe its pronouncements about the juvenile mind. If it did, the categorical rule it announces today would be most peculiar because it leaves intact state and federal laws that permit life-without-parole sentences for juveniles who commit homicides. The Court thus acknowledges that there is nothing inherent in the psyche of a person less than 18 that prevents him from acquiring the moral agency necessary to warrant a life-without-parole sentence. Instead, the Court rejects overwhelming legislative consensus only on the question of which *acts* are sufficient to demonstrate that moral agency.

* * * Thus, the Court's conclusion that life-without-parole sentences are "grossly disproportionate" for juvenile nonhomicide offenders in fact has very little to do with its view of juveniles, and much more to do with its perception that "defendants who do not kill, intend to kill, or foresee that life will be taken are categorically less deserving of the most serious forms of punishment than are murderers."

That the Court is willing to impose such an exacting constraint on democratic sentencing choices based on such an untestable philosophical conclusion is remarkable. The question of what acts are "deserving" of what punishments is bound so tightly with questions of morality and social conditions as to make it, almost by definition, a question for legislative resolution. It is true that the Court previously has relied on the notion of proportionality in holding certain classes of offenses categorically exempt from capital punishment. But never before today has the Court relied on its own view of just deserts to impose a categorical limit on the imposition of a lesser punishment. Its willingness to cross that well-established boundary raises the question whether any democratic choice regarding appropriate punishment is safe from the Court's ever-expanding constitutional veto.

IV

Although the concurrence avoids the problems associated with expanding categorical proportionality review to noncapital cases, it employs noncapital proportionality analysis in a way that raises the same fundamental concern. * * *

Under the Court's precedents, I fail to see how an "inference" of gross disproportionality arises here. The concurrence notes several arguably mitigating facts—Graham's "lack of prior criminal convictions, his youth and immaturity, and the difficult circumstances of his upbringing." But the Court previously has upheld a life-without-parole sentence imposed on a first-time offender who committed a *nonviolent* drug crime. *Harmelin.* Graham's conviction for an actual violent felony is surely more severe than that offense. As for Graham's age, it is true that *Roper* held juveniles categorically ineligible for capital punishment, but as the concurrence explains, *Roper* was based on the "explicit conclusion that [juveniles] 'cannot with reliability be classified among the *worst* offenders'"; it did "not establish that juveniles can never be eligible for life without parole." In my view, *Roper*'s principles are thus not generally applicable outside the capital sentencing context.

By holding otherwise, the concurrence relies on the same type of subjective judgment as the Court, only it restrains itself to a case-by-case rather than a categorical ruling. The concurrence is quite ready to hand Graham "the general presumption of diminished culpability" for juveniles, apparently because it believes that Graham's armed burglary and home invasion crimes were "certainly less serious" than murder or rape. It recoils only from the prospect that the Court would extend the same presumption to a juvenile who commits a sex crime. I simply cannot accept that these subjective judgments of proportionality are ones the Eighth Amendment authorizes us to make.

The "objective" elements of the *Solem* test provide no additional support for the concurrence's conclusion. The concurrence compares Graham's sentence to "similar" sentences in Florida and concludes that Graham's sentence was "far more severe." But strangely, the concurrence uses average sentences for burglary or robbery offenses as examples of "similar" offenses, even though it seems that a run-of-the-mill burglary or robbery is not at all similar to Graham's criminal history, which includes a charge for armed burglary with assault, *and* a probation violation for invading a home at gunpoint.

And even if Graham's sentence is higher than ones he might have received for an armed burglary with assault in other jurisdictions, this hardly seems relevant if one takes seriously the principle that " '[a]bsent a constitutionally imposed uniformity inimical to traditional notions of federalism, some State will *always* bear the distinction of treating particular offenders more severely than any other State.' " *Harmelin* (opinion of Kennedy, J.). Applying *Solem*, the Court has upheld a 25-years-to-life sentence for theft under California's recidivist statute, despite the fact that the State and its *amici* could cite only "a single instance of a similar sentence imposed outside the context of California's three strikes law, out of a prison population [then] approaching two million individuals." *Ewing* (Breyer, J., dissenting). It has also upheld a life-without-parole sentence for a first-time drug offender in Michigan charged with possessing 672 grams of cocaine despite the fact that only one other State would have authorized such a stiff penalty for a first-time drug offense, and even that State required a far greater quantity of cocaine (10 kilograms) to trigger the penalty. See *Harmelin* (White, J., dissenting). Graham's sentence is certainly less rare than the sentences upheld in these cases, so his claim fails even under *Solem*.

* * *

Both the Court and the concurrence claim their decisions to be narrow ones, but both invite a host of line-drawing problems to which courts must seek answers beyond the strictures of the Constitution. The Court holds that "[a] State is not required to guarantee eventual freedom to a juvenile offender convicted of a nonhomicide crime," but must provide the offender with "some meaningful opportunity to obtain release based on demonstrated maturity and rehabilitation." But what, exactly, does such a "meaningful" opportunity entail? When must it occur? And what Eighth Amendment principles will govern review by the parole boards the Court now demands that States empanel? The Court provides no answers to these questions, which will no doubt embroil the courts for years. * * *

JUSTICE ALITO, dissenting.

I join Parts I and III of Justice Thomas's dissenting opinion. I write separately to make two points. * * * Nothing in the Court's opinion affects the imposition of a sentence to a term of years without the possibility of parole. * * * *Second*, the question whether petitioner's sentence violates the narrow, as-applied proportionality principle that applies to noncapital sentences is not properly before us in this case. * * * Because petitioner abandoned his as-applied claim, I would not reach that issue. * * * a

GLOSSIP ET AL. V. GROSS ET AL.

576 U.S. 863, 135 S.Ct. 2726, 192 L.Ed.2d 761 (2015).

[In *Baze* v. *Rees*, 553 U.S. 35 (2008), the Court held that the three-drug lethal injection protocol used by the state of Kentucky to implement the death penalty did not violate the Eighth Amendment's prohibition against cruel and unusual punishments. Anti-death-penalty advocates then pressured pharmaceutical companies to end the availability of the first of these drugs, sodium thiopental (and, later, another barbiturate called pentobarbital), for use in executions. Unable to obtain either drug, Oklahoma decided to use midazolam, a sedative, as the first drug in its three-drug protocol. Several death-row inmates sought to enjoin executions in Oklahoma, claiming that the use of midazolam violates the Eighth

---

a   The Court soon combined its reasoning concerning juvenile offenders in *Graham* and *Roper* with another line of Eighth Amendment cases barring mandatory death sentence statutes and requiring that capital defendants have the opportunity to present mitigating factors. In *Miller v. Alabama*, 567 U.S. 460 (2012), the Court relied on these decisions to hold that the Eighth Amendment prohibits mandatory life without parole for those under the age of 18 at the time of their crimes. Writing for the five-justice majority, Justice Kagan explained: "Mandatory life without parole for a juvenile precludes consideration of his chronological age and its hallmark features—among them, immaturity, impetuosity, and failure to appreciate risks and consequences. It prevents taking into account the family and home environment that surrounds him—and from which he cannot usually extricate himself—no matter how brutal or dysfunctional. It neglects the circumstances of the homicide offense, including the extent of his participation in the conduct and the way familial and peer pressures may have affected him. Indeed, it ignores that he might have been charged and convicted of a lesser offense if not for incompetencies associated with youth—for example, his inability to deal with police officers or prosecutors(including on a plea agreement) or his incapacity to assist his own attorneys. And finally, this mandatory punishment disregards the possibility of rehabilitation even when the circumstances most suggest it." Unlike the "flat ban" on life without parole sentences for juveniles who commit non-homicide offenses established in *Graham*, the Court in *Miller* set out a different rule—individualized sentencing—for homicide offenses. Under that rule, the Court stated, 'we think appropriate occasions for sentencing juveniles to this harshest possible penalty will be uncommon."

Chief Justice Roberts, who concurred with the judgment in *Graham*, dissented in *Miller*, joined by Justices Scalia, Thomas, and Alito (who also wrote separate dissenting opinions in *Miller*). He distinguished the question in *Graham*, and concluded that "neither the text of the Constitution nor our precedent prohibits legislatures from requiring that juvenile murderers be sentenced to life without parole." Unlike the sentence in *Graham*, he argued, this punishment was not "unusual"—more than 2000 juveniles were serving mandatory life without parole sentences for homicide compared to the 123 juveniles subjected to the punishment at issue in *Graham*. Nor could the large number of state statues authorizing the sentence be discounted as it was in *Graham*, he reasoned. In *Graham*, "the extreme rarity with which the sentence in question was imposed," combined with the preliminary step of transfer to adult court, "could suggest that legislatures did not really intend the inevitable result of the laws they passed." By contrast, "the widespread and recent imposition of [mandatory life without parole sentences for juvenile murderers] makes it implausible to characterize this sentencing practice as a collateral consequence of legislative ignorance." By abandoning the limitations of earlier rulings, he argued, the Court's reasoning could ultimately "bar all mandatory sentences for juveniles, or any juvenile sentence as harsh as what a similarly situated adult would receive."

The *Miller* majority later invalidated a state rule barring defendants with IQ scores of more than 70 from claiming ineligibility for the death penalty under *Atkins*, finding that such a rule disregards established medical practice and had been rejected by a "significant majority" of states. *Hall v. Florida*, 572 U.S. 701 (2014).

Amendment because it may not prevent torturous pain. Justice's Alito's opinion upholding the district court's rejection of that claim was joined by Chief Justice Roberts, and Justices Scalia, Kennedy, and Thomas. The majority agreed with the district court that the petitioners had failed to establish that any risk of harm was substantial when compared to a known and available alternative method of execution. Justice Sotomayor, joined by Justices Ginsburg, Breyer, and Kagan, filed a dissenting opinion contesting the district court's finding and concluding that the inmates should be allowed a stay of execution while they seek to prove midazolam's inadequacy. Because of the limited scope of the issue, neither of these opinions addressing the merits of the petitioners' basic claim are reproduced below.

Instead, included here in the order that they appear in the case are two other opinions addressing broader questions about the constitutionality of the death penalty: the concurring opinion of Justice Scalia (joined by Thomas, J.), and the dissenting opinion of Justice Breyer (joined by Ginsburg, J.). Together with the opinions in *Graham, supra*, these two opinions in *Glossip* aptly illustrate competing approaches to applying the Eighth Amendment, summarize the present state of the death penalty in the United States, highlight several issues that have made constitutional oversight of the death penalty so very challenging for the Supreme Court, and raise questions about methodology in constitutional analysis generally.

On that last point, it is important to note that in editing these opinions for length, other than the routine omission of case citations, redactions to Justice Breyer's opinion also deleted most of the citations to the dozens of empirical studies, reports, news stories, polls, and other statistical sources included in the opinion. That Justice Breyer's opinion relied so heavily on empirical studies is itself significant, as both the reliability of these studies and their relevance to constitutional analysis continues to be contested by some other justices.]

JUSTICE SCALIA, with whom JUSTICE THOMAS joins, concurring.[a]

I join the opinion of the Court, and write to respond to Justice Breyer's plea for judicial abolition of the death penalty.

Welcome to Groundhog Day. The scene is familiar: Petitioners, sentenced to die for the crimes they committed (including, in the case of one petitioner since put to death, raping and murdering an 11-month-old baby), come before this Court asking us to nullify their sentences as "cruel and unusual" under the Eighth

---

[a] Justice Thomas also filed a concurring opinion responding to Justice Breyer's dissent, joined by Justice Scalia. Justice Thomas reiterated his view that the Eighth Amendment "prohibits only those 'method[s] of execution' that are 'deliberately designed to inflict pain,'" and collected prior opinions in which various Justices had rejected other claims similar to those made by Justice Breyer. His opinion focused mainly on Justice Breyer's claim of arbitrariness, attacking the methodology of the studies Justice Breyer cited, and arguing that geographic differences were deliberately introduced by constitutional provisions that "place such decisions in the hands of jurors and trial courts located where 'the crime shall have been committed.'" He argued that the Court itself had contributed to the alleged arbitrariness, questioning its decision to mandatory death penalty schemes and maintaining that some of the "most 'egregious' cases have been those in which we have granted relief based on an unfounded Eighth Amendment claim," listing decisions barring execution for defendants who commit aggravated rape, defendants who are intellectually disabled, and defendants who are juveniles at the time of their offense.

Amendment. They rely on this provision because it is the only provision they *can* rely on. They were charged by a sovereign State with murder. They were afforded counsel and tried before a jury of their peers—tried twice, once to determine whether they were guilty and once to determine whether death was the appropriate sentence. They were duly convicted and sentenced. They were granted the right to appeal and to seek postconviction relief, first in state and then in federal court. And now, acknowledging that their convictions are unassailable, they ask us for clemency, as though clemency were ours to give.

The response is also familiar: A vocal minority of the Court, waving over their heads a ream of the most recent abolitionist studies (a superabundant genre) as though they have discovered the lost folios of Shakespeare, insist that *now*, at long last, the death penalty must be abolished for good. Mind you, not once in the history of the American Republic has this Court ever suggested the death penalty is categorically impermissible. The reason is obvious: It is impossible to hold unconstitutional that which the Constitution explicitly *contemplates*. The Fifth Amendment provides that "[n]o person shall be held to answer for a capital . . . crime, unless on a presentment or indictment of a Grand Jury," and that no person shall be "deprived of life . . . without due process of law." Nevertheless, today Justice Breyer takes on the role of the abolitionists in this long-running drama, arguing that the text of the Constitution and two centuries of history must yield to his "20 years of experience on this Court," and inviting full briefing on the continued permissibility of capital punishment.

Historically, the Eighth Amendment was understood to bar only those punishments that added " 'terror, pain, or disgrace' " to an otherwise permissible capital sentence. *Baze* v. *Rees*, 553 U.S. 35, 96 (2008) (Thomas, J., concurring in judgment). Rather than bother with this troubling detail, Justice Breyer elects to contort the constitutional text. Redefining "cruel" to mean "unreliable," "arbitrary," or causing "excessive delays," and "unusual" to include a "decline in use," he proceeds to offer up a white paper devoid of any meaningful legal argument.

Even accepting Justice Breyer's rewriting of the Eighth Amendment, his argument is full of internal contradictions and (it must be said) gobbledygook. He says that the death penalty is cruel because it is unreliable; but it is *convictions*, not *punishments*, that are unreliable. Moreover, the "pressure on police, prosecutors, and jurors to secure a conviction," which he claims increases the risk of wrongful convictions in capital cases, flows from the nature of the crime, not the punishment that follows its commission. Justice Breyer acknowledges as much: "[T]he crimes at issue in capital cases are typically horrendous murders, and thus accompanied by intense community pressure." That same pressure would exist, and the same risk of wrongful convictions, if horrendous death-penalty cases were converted into equally horrendous life-without-parole cases. The reality is that any innocent defendant is infinitely better off appealing a death sentence than a sentence of life imprisonment. (Which, again, Justice Breyer acknowledges: "[C]ourts (or State Governors) are 130 times more likely to exonerate a defendant where a death sentence is at issue.") The capital convict will obtain endless legal assistance from the abolition lobby (and legal favoritism from abolitionist judges), while the lifer languishes unnoticed behind bars.

Justice Breyer next says that the death penalty is cruel because it is arbitrary. To prove this point, he points to a study of 205 cases that "measured the 'egregiousness' of the murderer's conduct" with "a system of metrics," and then "compared the egregiousness of the conduct of the 9 defendants sentenced to death with the egregiousness of the conduct of defendants in the remaining 196 cases [who were not sentenced to death]." If only Aristotle, Aquinas, and Hume knew that moral philosophy could be so neatly distilled into a pocket-sized, *vade mecum* "system of metrics." Of course it cannot: Egregiousness is a moral judgment susceptible of few hard-and-fast rules. More importantly, egregiousness of the crime is only one of several factors that render a punishment condign—culpability, rehabilitative potential, and the need for deterrence also are relevant. That is why this Court has required an individualized consideration of all mitigating circumstances, rather than formulaic application of some egregiousness test.

It is because these questions are contextual and admit of no easy answers that we rely on juries to make judgments about the people and crimes before them. The fact that these judgments may vary across cases is an inevitable consequence of the jury trial, that cornerstone of Anglo-American judicial procedure. But when a punishment is authorized by law—if you kill you are subject to death—the fact that some defendants receive mercy from their jury no more renders the underlying punishment "cruel" than does the fact that some guilty individuals are never apprehended, are never tried, are acquitted, or are pardoned. Justice Breyer's third reason that the death penalty is cruel is that it entails delay, thereby (1) subjecting inmates to long periods on death row and (2) undermining the penological justifications of the death penalty. The first point is nonsense. Life without parole is an even lengthier period than the wait on death row; and if the objection is that death row is a more confining environment, the solution should be modifying the environment rather than abolishing the death penalty. As for the argument that delay undermines the penological rationales for the death penalty: In insisting that "the major alternative to capital punishment—namely, life in prison without possibility of parole—also incapacitates," Justice Breyer apparently forgets that one of the plaintiffs *in this very case* was already in prison when he committed the murder that landed him on death row. Justice Breyer further asserts that "whatever interest in retribution might be served by the death penalty as currently administered, that interest can be served almost as well by a sentence of life in prison without parole." My goodness. If he thinks the death penalty not much more harsh (and hence not much more retributive), why is he so keen to get rid of it? With all due respect, whether the death penalty and life imprisonment constitute more-or-less equivalent retribution is a question far above the judiciary's pay grade. Perhaps Justice Breyer is more forgiving—or more enlightened—than those who, like Kant, believe that death is the only just punishment for taking a life. I would not presume to tell parents whose life has been forever altered by the brutal murder of a child that life imprisonment is punishment enough.

And finally, Justice Breyer speculates that it does not "seem likely" that the death penalty has a "significant" deterrent effect. It seems very likely to me, and there are statistical studies that say so. * * * But we federal judges live in a world apart from the vast majority of Americans. After work, we retire to homes in placid suburbia or to high-rise co-ops with guards at the door. We are not confronted with the threat of violence that is ever present in many Americans' everyday lives. The suggestion that the incremental deterrent effect of capital punishment does not seem "significant" reflects, it seems to me, a let-them-eat-cake obliviousness to the needs of others. Let the People decide how much incremental deterrence is appropriate.

Of course, this delay is a problem of the Court's own making. As Justice Breyer concedes, for more than 160 years, capital sentences were carried out in an average of two years or less. But by 2014, he tells us, it took an average of 18 years to carry out a death sentence. What happened in the intervening years? Nothing other than the proliferation of labyrinthine restrictions on capital punishment, promulgated by this Court under an interpretation of the Eighth Amendment that empowered it to divine "the evolving standards of decency that mark the progress of a maturing society," *Trop* v. *Dulles*, 356 U.S. 86, 101 (1958) (plurality opinion)—a task for which we are eminently ill suited. Indeed, for the past two decades, Justice Breyer has been the Drum Major in this parade. His invocation of the resultant delay as grounds for abolishing the death penalty calls to mind the man sentenced to death for killing his parents, who pleads for mercy on the ground that he is an orphan. Amplifying the surrealism of his argument, Justice Breyer uses the fact that many States have abandoned capital punishment—have abandoned it *precisely because of* the costs those suspect decisions have imposed—to conclude that it is now "unusual." (A caution to the reader: Do not use the creative arithmetic that Justice Breyer employs in counting the number of States that use the death penalty when you prepare your next tax return; outside the world of our Eighth Amendment abolitionist-inspired jurisprudence, it will be regarded as more misrepresentation than math.)

If we were to travel down the path that Justice Breyer sets out for us and once again consider the constitutionality of the death penalty, I would ask that counsel also brief whether our cases that have abandoned the historical understanding of the Eighth Amendment, beginning with *Trop*, should be overruled. That case has caused more mischief to our jurisprudence, to our federal system, and to our society than any other that comes to mind. Justice Breyer's dissent is the living refutation of *Trop*'s assumption that this Court has the capacity to recognize "evolving standards of decency." Time and again, the People have voted to exact the death penalty as punishment for the most serious of crimes. Time and again, this Court has upheld that decision. And time and again, a vocal minority of this Court has insisted that things have "changed radically," and has sought to replace the judgments of the People with their own standards of decency.

Capital punishment presents moral questions that philosophers, theologians, and statesmen have grappled with for millennia. The Framers of our Constitution disagreed bitterly on the matter. For that reason, they handled it the same way they handled many other controversial issues: they left it to the People to decide. By arrogating to himself the power to overturn that decision, Justice Breyer does not just reject the death penalty, he rejects the Enlightenment.

JUSTICE BREYER, with whom JUSTICE GINSBURG joins, dissenting.

For the reasons stated in Justice Sotomayor's opinion, I dissent from the Court's holding. But rather than try to patch up the death penalty's legal wounds one at a time, I would ask for full briefing on a more basic question: whether the death penalty violates the Constitution.

The relevant legal standard is the standard set forth in the Eighth Amendment. The Constitution there forbids the "inflict[ion]" of "cruel and unusual punishments." Amdt. 8. The Court has recognized that a "claim that punishment is excessive is judged not by the standards that prevailed in 1685 when Lord Jeffreys presided over the 'Bloody Assizes' or when the Bill of Rights was adopted, but rather by those that currently prevail." * * *. Indeed, the Constitution prohibits various gruesome punishments that were common in Blackstone's day. See 4 W. Blackstone, Commentaries on the Laws of England 369–370 (1769) (listing mutilation and dismembering, among other punishments).

Nearly 40 years ago, this Court upheld the death penalty under statutes that, in the Court's view, contained safeguards sufficient to ensure that the penalty would be applied reliably and not arbitrarily. * * * The circumstances and the evidence of the death penalty's application have changed radically since then. Given those changes, I believe that it is now time to reopen the question.

In 1976, the Court thought that the constitutional infirmities in the death penalty could be healed; the Court in effect delegated significant responsibility to the States to develop procedures that would protect against those constitutional problems. Almost 40 years of studies, surveys, and experience strongly indicate, however, that this effort has failed. Today's administration of the death penalty involves three fundamental constitutional defects: (1) serious unreliability, (2) arbitrariness in application, and (3) unconscionably long delays that undermine the death penalty's penological purpose. Perhaps as a result, (4) most places within the United States have abandoned its use.

I shall describe each of these considerations, emphasizing changes that have occurred during the past four decades. For it is those changes, taken together with my own 20 years of experience on this Court, that lead me to believe that the death penalty, in and of itself, now likely constitutes a legally prohibited "cruel and unusual punishmen[t]." U.S. Const., Amdt. 8.

I

"Cruel"—Lack of Reliability

This Court has specified that the finality of death creates a "qualitative difference" between the death penalty and other punishments (including life in prison). That "qualitative difference" creates "a corresponding difference in the need for reliability in the determination that death is the appropriate punishment in a specific case." There is increasing evidence, however, that the death penalty as now applied lacks that requisite reliability. * * *

For one thing, despite the difficulty of investigating the circumstances surrounding an execution for a crime that took place long ago, researchers have found convincing evidence that, in the past three decades, innocent people have been executed. See, *e.g.,* Liebman, Fatal Injustice; Carlos DeLuna's Execution Shows That a Faster, Cheaper Death Penalty is a Dangerous Idea, L. A. Times, June 1, 2012, p. A19 (describing results of a 4-year investigation, later published as The Wrong Carlos: Anatomy of a Wrongful Execution (2014), that led its authors to conclude that Carlos DeLuna, sentenced to death and executed in 1989, six years after his arrest in Texas for stabbing a single mother to death in a convenience store, was innocent); Grann, Trial By Fire: Did Texas Execute An Innocent Man? The New Yorker, Sept. 7, 2009, p. 42 (describing evidence that Cameron Todd Willingham was convicted, and ultimately executed in 2004, for the apparently motiveless murder of his three children as the result of invalid scientific analysis of the scene of the house fire that killed his children). * * *

For another, the evidence that the death penalty has been wrongly *imposed* (whether or not it was carried out), is striking. As of 2002, this Court used the word "disturbing" to describe the number of instances in which individuals had been sentenced to death but later exonerated. At that time, there was evidence of approximately 60 exonerations in capital cases. * * *. (I use "exoneration" to refer to relief from *all* legal consequences of a capital conviction through a decision by a prosecutor, a Governor or a court, after new evidence of the defendant's innocence was discovered.) Since 2002, the number of exonerations in capital cases has risen to 115. * * * Last year, in 2014, six death row inmates were exonerated based on actual innocence. All had been imprisoned for more than 30 years (and one for almost 40 years) at the time of their exonerations. * * *.

Furthermore, exonerations occur far more frequently where capital convictions, rather than ordinary criminal convictions, are at issue. * * * Why is that so? To some degree, it must be because the law that governs capital cases is more complex. To some degree, it must reflect the fact that courts scrutinize capital cases more closely. But, to some degree, it likely also reflects a *greater likelihood of an initial wrongful conviction.* How could that be so? In the view of researchers who have conducted these studies, it could be so because the crimes at issue in capital cases are typically horrendous murders, and thus accompanied by intense community pressure on police, prosecutors, and jurors to secure a conviction. This pressure creates a greater likelihood of convicting the wrong person. * * *. in Glenn Ford's case, the prosecutor admitted that he was partly responsible for Ford's wrongful conviction, issuing a public apology to Ford and explaining that, at the time of Ford's conviction, he was "not as interested in justice as [he] was in winning."

Other factors may also play a role. One is the practice of death-qualification; no one can serve on a capital jury who is not willing to impose the death penalty * * * Another is the more general problem of flawed forensic testimony. * * * The Federal Bureau of Investigation (FBI), for example, recently found that flawed microscopic hair analysis was used in 33 of 35 capital cases under review * * * In light of these and other factors, researchers estimate that about 4% of those sentenced to death are actually innocent. * * *

Finally, if we expand our definition of "exoneration" (which we limited to errors suggesting the defendant was actually innocent) and thereby also categorize as "erroneous" instances in which courts failed to follow legally required procedures, the numbers soar. Between 1973 and 1995, courts identified prejudicial errors in 68% of the capital cases before them. * * *.

This research and these figures are likely controversial. Full briefing would allow us to scrutinize them with more care. But, at a minimum, they suggest a serious problem of reliability. They suggest that there are too many in- stances in which courts sentence defendants to death without complying with the necessary procedures; and they suggest that, in a significant number of cases, the death sentence is imposed on a person who did not commit the crime. * * * Unlike 40 years ago, we now have plausible *evidence* of unreliability that (perhaps due to DNA evidence) is stronger than the evidence we had before. In sum, there is significantly more research-based evidence today indicating that courts sentence to death individuals who may well be actually innocent or whose convictions (in the law's view) do not warrant the death penalty's application.

II

"Cruel"—Arbitrariness

The arbitrary imposition of punishment is the antithesis of the rule of law. For that reason, Justice Potter Stewart (who supplied critical votes for the holdings in *Furman* v. *Georgia*, 408 U.S. 238 (1972) (*per curiam*), and *Gregg* [v. *Georgia*, 428 U.S. 153 (1976)]) found the death penalty unconstitutional as administered in 1972:

> "These death sentences are cruel and unusual in the same way that being struck by lightning is cruel and unusual. For, of all the people convicted of [death-eligible crimes], many just as reprehensible as these, the[se] petitioners are among a capriciously selected random handful upon which the sentence of death has in fact been imposed." *Furman*, 408 U.S., at 309–310 (concurring opinion).

See also *id.*, at 310 ("[T]he Eighth and Fourteenth Amendments cannot tolerate the infliction of a sentence of death under legal systems that permit this unique penalty to be so wantonly and so freakishly imposed"); *id.*, at 313 (White, J., concurring) ("[T]he death penalty is exacted with great infrequency even for the most atrocious crimes and . . . there is no meaningful basis for distinguishing the few cases in which it is imposed from the many cases in which it is not").

When the death penalty was reinstated in 1976, this Court acknowledged that the death penalty is (and would be) unconstitutional if "inflicted in an arbitrary and capricious manner." *Gregg*, 428 U.S., at 188 (joint opinion of Stewart, Powell, and Stevens, JJ.); * * *

The Court has consequently sought to make the application of the death penalty less arbitrary by restricting its use to those whom Justice Souter called " 'the worst of the worst.' " *Kansas* v. *Marsh*, 548 U.S., at 206 (dissenting opinion); see also *Roper* v. *Simmons*, 543 U.S. 551, 568 (2005) ("Capital punishment must be limited to those offenders who commit a narrow category of the most serious crimes and whose extreme culpability makes them the most deserving of execution" (internal quotation marks omitted))* * *

Despite the *Gregg* Court's hope for fair administration of the death penalty, 40 years of further experience make it increasingly clear that the death penalty is imposed arbitrarily, *i.e.*, without the "reasonable consistency" legally necessary to reconcile its use with the Constitution's commands.

Thorough studies of death penalty sentences support this conclusion. A recent study, for example, examined all death penalty sentences imposed between 1973 and 2007 in Connecticut, a State that abolished the death penalty in 2012. * * * [It] compared the egregiousness of the conduct of the 9 defendants sentenced to death with the egregiousness of the conduct of defendants in the remaining 196 cases (those in which the defendant, though found guilty of a death-eligible offense, was ultimately not sentenced to death). Application of the studies' metrics made clear that only 1 of those 9 defendants was indeed the "worst of the worst" (or was, at least, within the 15% considered most "egregious"). The remaining eight were not. Their behavior was no worse than the behavior of at least 33 and as many as *170* other defendants (out of a total pool of 205) who had not been sentenced to death.

Such studies indicate that the factors that most clearly ought to affect application of the death penalty—namely, comparative egregiousness of the crime—often do not. Other studies show that circumstances that ought *not* to affect application of the death penalty, such as race, gender, or geography, often *do*.

Numerous studies, for example, have concluded that individuals accused of murdering white victims, as opposed to black or other minority victims, are more likely to receive the death penalty. * * * Fewer, but still many, studies have found that the gender of the defendant or the gender of the victim makes a not-otherwise-warranted difference.

Geography also plays an important role in determining who is sentenced to death. And that is not simply because some States permit the death penalty while others do not. Rather *within* a death penalty State, the imposition of the death penalty heavily depends on the county in which a defendant is tried. * * * Between 2004 and 2009, for example, just 29 counties (fewer than 1% of counties in the country) accounted for approximately half of all death sentences imposed nationwide. And in 2012, just 59 counties (fewer than 2% of counties in the country) accounted for *all* death sentences imposed nationwide. * * * What accounts for this county-by-county disparity? Some studies indicate that the disparity reflects the decision-making authority, the legal discretion, and ultimately the power of the local prosecutor. * * * Others suggest that the availability of resources for defense counsel (or the lack thereof) helps explain geo- graphical differences. * * * Still others indicate that the racial composition of and distribution within a county plays an important role. * * * Finally, some studies suggest that political pressures, including pressures on judges who must stand for election, can make a difference. See *Woodward v. Alabama,* 571 U.S. ___, ___ (2013) (Sotomayor, J., dissenting from denial of certiorari) (slip op., at 7) (noting that empirical evidence suggests that, when Alabama judges reverse jury recommendations, these "judges, who are elected in partisan proceedings, appear to have succumbed to electoral pressures"); *Harris* v. *Alabama*, 513 U.S. 504, 519 (1995) (Stevens, J., dissenting) (similar) * * *

Thus, whether one looks at research indicating that irrelevant or improper factors—such as race, gender, local geography, and resources—*do* significantly determine who receives the death penalty, or whether one looks at research indicating that proper factors—such as "egregious- ness"—do *not* determine who receives the death penalty, the legal conclusion must be the same: The research strongly suggests that the death penalty is imposed arbitrarily.

Justice Thomas catalogues the tragic details of various capital cases [see fn. a supra], but this misses my point. Every murder is tragic, but unless we return to the mandatory death penalty struck down in *Woodson* [v. *North Carolina*, 428 U.S. 280 (1976)], the constitutionality of capital punishment rests on its limited application to the worst of the worst. And this extensive body of evidence suggests that it is not so limited.

Four decades ago, the Court believed it possible to interpret the Eighth Amendment in ways that would significantly limit the arbitrary application of the death sentence. * * * But that no longer seems likely. * * *

The studies bear out my own view, reached after considering thousands of death penalty cases and last-minute petitions over the course of more than 20 years. I see discrepancies for which I can find no rational explanations. * * *

The question raised by these examples (and the many more I could give but do not), as well as by the research to which I have referred, is the same question Justice Stewart, Justice Powell, and others raised over the course of several decades: The imposition and implementation of the death penalty seems capricious, random, indeed, arbitrary. From a defendant's perspective, to receive that sentence, and certainly to find it implemented, is the equivalent of being struck by lightning. How then can we reconcile the death penalty with the demands of a Constitution that first and foremost insists upon a rule of law?

III

"Cruel"—Excessive Delays

The problems of reliability and unfairness almost inevitably lead to a third independent constitutional problem: excessively long periods of time that individuals typically spend on death row, alive but under sentence of death. That is to say, delay is in part a problem that the Constitution's own demands create. Given the special need for reliability and fairness in death penalty cases, the Eighth Amendment does, and must, apply to the death penalty "with special force." *Roper*, 543 U.S., at 568. Those who face "that most severe sanction must have a fair opportunity to show that the Constitution prohibits their execution." *Hall* v. *Florida*, 572 U.S. ___, ___ (2014) (slip op., at 22). At the same time, the Constitution insists that "every safeguard" be "observed" when "a defendant's life is at stake." * * * These procedural necessities take time to implement. And, unless we abandon the procedural requirements that assure fairness and reliability, we are forced to confront the problem of increasingly lengthy delays in capital cases. Ultimately, though these legal causes may help to explain, they do not mitigate the harms caused by delay itself. * * *

Consider first the statistics. In 2014, 35 individuals were executed. Those executions occurred, on average, nearly 18 years after a court initially pronounced its sentence of death. * * * Nearly half of the 3,000 inmates now on death row have been there for more than 15 years * * * These lengthy delays create two special constitutional difficulties. * * * First, a lengthy delay in and of itself is especially cruel because it "subjects death row inmates to decades of especially severe, dehumanizing conditions of confinement." * * * nearly all death penalty States keep death row inmates in isolation for 22 or more hours per day* * * The dehumanizing effect of solitary confinement is aggravated by uncertainty as to whether a death sentence will in fact be carried out * * *

The second constitutional difficulty resulting from lengthy delays is that those delays undermine the death penalty's penological rationale, perhaps irreparably so. The rationale for capital punishment, as for any punishment, classically rests upon society's need to secure deterrence, incapacitation, retribution, or rehabilitation. Capital punishment by definition does not rehabilitate. It does, of course, incapacitate the offender. But the major alternative to capital punishment—namely, life in prison without possibility of parole—also incapacitates. * * *

Thus, as the Court has recognized, the death penalty's penological rationale in fact rests almost exclusively upon a belief in its tendency to deter and upon its ability to satisfy a community's interest in retribution * * * Many studies have examined the death penalty's deterrent effect; some have found such an effect, whereas others have found a lack of evidence that it deters crime. * * * Recently, the National Research Council (whose members are drawn from the councils of the National Academy of Sciences, the National Academy of Engineering, and the Institute of Medicine) reviewed 30 years of empirical evidence and concluded that it was insufficient to establish a deterrent effect and thus should "not be used to inform" discussion about the deterrent value of the death penalty. National Research Council, Deterrence and the Death Penalty 2 (D. Nagin & J. Pepper eds. 2012) * * *

I recognize that a "lack of evidence" for a proposition does not prove the contrary. * * * But suppose that we add to these studies the fact that, today, very few of those sentenced to death are actually executed, and that even those executions occur, on average, after nearly two decades on death row. Then, does it still seem likely that the death penalty has a significant deterrent effect? * * * Of the 8,466 inmates under a death sentence at some point between 1973 and 2013, 16% were executed, 42% had their convictions or sentences overturned or commuted, and 6% died by other causes; the remainder (35%) are still on death row. * * * Thus an offender who is sentenced to death is two or three times more likely to find his sentence overturned or commuted than to be executed; and he has a good chance of dying from natural causes before any execution (or exoneration) can take place. In a word, executions are *rare*. And an individual contemplating a crime but evaluating the potential punishment would know that, in any event, he faces a potential sentence of life without parole.

These facts, when recurring, must have some offsetting effect on a potential perpetrator's fear of a death penalty. And, even if that effect is no more than slight, it makes it difficult to believe (given the studies of deterrence cited earlier) that such a rare event significantly deters horrendous crimes. * * *

But what about retribution? Retribution is a valid penological goal. I recognize that surviving relatives of victims of a horrendous crime, or perhaps the community itself, may find vindication in an execution. And a community that favors the death penalty has an understandable interest in representing their voices. * * * The relevant question here, however, is whether a "community's sense of retribution" can often find vindication in "a death that comes," if at all, "only several decades after the crime was committed." * * * By then the community is a different group of people. The offenders and the victims' families have grown far older. Feelings of outrage may have sub- sided. The offender may have found himself a changed human being. And sometimes repentance and even forgiveness can restore meaning to lives once ruined. At the same time, the community and victims' families will know that, even without a further death, the offender will serve decades in prison under a sentence of life without parole.

I recognize, of course, that this may not always be the case, and that sometimes the community believes that an execution could provide closure. Nevertheless, the delays and low probability of execution must play some role in any calculation that leads a community to insist on death as retribution. As I have already suggested, they may well attenuate the community's interest in retribution to the point where it cannot by itself amount to a significant justification for the death penalty. In any event, I believe that whatever interest in retribution might be served by the death penalty as currently administered, that interest can be served almost as well by a sentence of life in prison without parole (a sentence that every State now permits * * *).

Finally, the fact of lengthy delays undermines any effort to justify the death penalty in terms of its prevalence when the Founders wrote the Eighth Amendment. When the Founders wrote the Constitution, there were no 20- or 30-year delays. Execution took place soon after sentencing. * * * And, for reasons I shall describe we cannot return to the quick executions in the founding era.

The upshot is that lengthy delays both aggravate the cruelty of the death penalty and undermine its jurisprudential rationale. And this Court has said that, if the death penalty does not fulfill the goals of deterrence or retribution, "it is nothing more than the purposeless and needless imposition of pain and suffering and hence an unconstitutional punishment." *Atkins*, 536 U.S., at 319 (quoting *Enmund* v. *Florida*, 458 U.S. 782, 798 (1982)) * * *

Indeed, Justice Lewis Powell (who provided a crucial vote in *Gregg*) came to much the same conclusion, albeit after his retirement from this Court. Justice Powell had come to the Court convinced that the Federal Constitution did not outlaw the death penalty but rather left the matter up to individual States to determine. * * * Soon after Justice Powell's retirement, Chief Justice Rehnquist appointed him to chair a committee addressing concerns about delays in capital cases, the Ad Hoc Committee on Federal Habeas Corpus in Capital Cases (Committee). * * * Justice Powell, according to his official biographer, ultimately concluded that capital punishment:

> " 'serves no useful purpose.' The United States was 'unique among the industrialized nations of the West in maintaining the death penalty,' and it was enforced so rarely that it could not deter. More important, the haggling and delay and seemingly endless litigation in every capital case brought the law itself into disrepute." * * * In short, the problem of excessive delays led Justice Powell, at least in part, to conclude that the death penalty was unconstitutional.

As I have said, today delays are much worse. When Chief Justice Rehnquist appointed Justice Powell to the Committee, the average delay between sentencing and execution was 7 years and 11 months, compared with 17 years and 7 months today. * * *

C

One might ask, why can Congress or the States not deal directly with the delay problem? * * * The answer is that shortening delay is much more difficult than one might think. And that is in part because efforts to do so risk causing procedural harms that also undermine the death penalty's constitutionality. For one thing, delays have helped to make application of the death penalty more reliable. * * * In addition to those who are exonerated on the ground that they are innocent, there are other individuals whose sentences or convictions have been overturned for other reasons * * * In many of these cases, a court will have found that the individual did not merit the death penalty in a special sense—namely, he failed to receive all the procedural protections that the law requires for the death penalty's application. By eliminating some of these protections, one likely could reduce delay. But which protections should we eliminate? Should we eliminate the trial-related protections we have established for capital defendants: that they be able to present to the sentencing judge or jury all mitigating circumstances; that the State provide guidance adequate to reserve the application of the death penalty to particularly serious murders; that the State provide adequate counsel and, where warranted, adequate expert assistance; or that a jury must find the aggravating factors necessary to impose the death penalty? Should we no longer ensure that the State does not execute those who are seriously intellectually disabled? Should we eliminate the requirement that the manner of execution be constitutional, or the requirement that the inmate be mentally competent at the time of his execution? Or should we get rid of the criminal protections that all criminal defendants receive—for instance, that defendants claiming violation of constitutional guarantees (say "due process of law") may seek a writ of habeas corpus in federal courts? My answer to these questions is "surely not." But see *ante* (Scalia, J., concurring).

One might, of course, argue that courts, particularly federal courts providing additional layers of review, apply these and other requirements too strictly, and that causes delay. But, it is difficult for judges, as it would be difficult for anyone, *not* to apply legal requirements punctiliously when the consequence of failing to do so may well be death, particularly the death of an innocent person. * * * In my own view, our legal system's complexity, our federal system with its separate state and federal courts, our constitutional guarantees, our commitment to fair procedure, and, above all, a special need for reliability and fairness in capital cases, combine to make significant procedural "reform" unlikely in practice to reduce delays to an acceptable level.

And that fact creates a dilemma: A death penalty system that seeks procedural fairness and reliability brings with it delays that severely aggravate the cruelty of capital punishment and significantly undermine the rationale for imposing a sentence of death in the first place * * * But a death penalty system that minimizes delays would undermine the legal system's efforts to secure reliability and procedural fairness.

In this world, or at least in this Nation, we can have a death penalty that at least arguably serves legitimate penological purposes *or* we can have a procedural system that at least arguably seeks reliability and fairness in the death penalty's application. We cannot have both. And that simple fact, demonstrated convincingly over the past 40 years, strongly supports the claim that the death penalty violates the Eighth Amendment. A death penalty system that is unreliable or procedurally unfair would violate the Eighth Amendment. * * * And so would a system that, if reliable and fair in its application of the death penalty, would serve no legitimate penological purpose. * * *

IV

"Unusual"—Decline in Use of the Death Penalty[b]

The Eighth Amendment forbids punishments that are cruel and *unusual.* Last year, in 2014, only seven States carried out an execution. Perhaps more importantly, in the last two decades, the imposition and implementation of the death penalty have increasingly become unusual. I can illustrate the significant decline in the use of the death penalty in several ways.

* * * Between 1986 and 1999, 286 persons on average were sentenced to death each year. * * * Last year, just 73 persons were sentenced to death * * * That trend, a significant decline in the last 15 years, also holds true with respect to the number of annual executions. * * * Last year, that number was only 35.

* * * Often when deciding whether a punishment practice is, constitutionally speaking, "unusual," this Court has looked to the number of States engaging in that practice. * * * As of today, 19 States have abolished the death penalty (along with the District of Columbia), although some did so prospectively only. * * * In 11 other States that maintain the death penalty on the books, no execution has taken place for more than eight years. * * * In sum, if we look to States, in more than 60% there is effectively no death penalty, in an additional 18% an execution is rare and unusual, and 6%, *i.e.*, three States, account for 80% of all executions. If we look to

---

b   This section of the opinion referenced several maps and charts included as Appendices. The references and Appendices have been deleted.

population, about 66% of the Nation lives in a State that has not carried out an execution in the last three years. And if we look to counties, in 86% there is effectively no death penalty. It seems fair to say that it is now unusual to find capital punishment in the United States, at least when we consider the Nation as a whole.

* * * Moreover, we have said that it " 'is not so much the number of these States that is significant, but the consistency of the direction of change.' " * * * Judged in that way, capital punishment has indeed become unusual. Seven States have abolished the death penalty in the last decade, including (quite recently) Nebraska. * * * And several States have come within a single vote of eliminating the death penalty. [citing sources reporting on New Hampshire, Montana, and Delaware] * * * [T]he direction of change is consistent. In the past two decades, no State without a death penalty has passed legislation to reinstate the penalty. * * * Indeed, even in many States most associated with the death penalty, remarkable shifts have occurred. In Texas, the State that carries out the most executions, the number of executions fell from 40 in 2000 to 10 in 2014, and the number of death sentences fell from 48 in 1999 to 9 in 2013 (and 0 thus far in 2015. * * * These circumstances perhaps reflect the fact that a majority of Americans, when asked to choose between the death penalty and life in prison without parole, now choose the latter. * * *

I rely primarily upon domestic, not foreign events, in pointing to changes and circumstances that tend to justify the claim that the death penalty, constitutionally speaking, is "unusual." Those circumstances are sufficient to warrant our reconsideration of the death penalty's constitutionality. I note, however, that many nations—indeed, 95 of the 193 members of the United Nations—have formally abolished the death penalty and an additional 42 have abolished it in practice. * * *

V

I recognize a strong counterargument that favors constitutionality. We are a court. Why should we not leave the matter up to the people acting democratically through legislatures? The Constitution foresees a country that will make most important decisions democratically. Most nations that have abandoned the death penalty have done so through legislation, not judicial decision. And legislators, unlike judges, are free to take account of matters such as monetary costs, which I do not claim are relevant here. * * * The answer is that the matters I have discussed, such as lack of reliability, the arbitrary application of a serious and irreversible punishment, individual suffering caused by long delays, and lack of penological purpose are quintessentially judicial matters. They concern the infliction—indeed the unfair, cruel, and unusual infliction—of a serious punishment upon an individual. I recognize that in 1972 this Court, in a sense, turned to Congress and the state legislatures in its search for standards that would increase the fairness and reliability of imposing a death penalty. The legislatures responded. But, in the last four decades, considerable evidence has accumulated that those responses have not worked.

Thus we are left with a judicial responsibility. The Eighth Amendment sets forth the relevant law, and we must interpret that law * * * I believe it highly likely that the death penalty violates the Eighth Amendment. At the very least, the Court should call for full briefing on the basic question.

With respect, I dissent.

APPENDIX A

SELECTED PROVISIONS OF THE
UNITED STATES CONSTITUTION

■ ■ ■

ARTICLE I

Section 9. * * *

[2]   The privilege of the Writ of Habeas Corpus shall not be suspended, unless when in Cases of Rebellion or Invasion the public Safety may require it.

[3]   No Bill of Attainder or ex post facto Law shall be passed.

ARTICLE III

Section 1.The judicial Power of the United States, shall be vested in one supreme Court, and in such inferior Courts as the Congress may from time to time ordain and establish. The Judges, both of the supreme and inferior Courts, shall hold their Offices during good Behaviour, and shall, at stated Times, receive for their Services a Compensation, which shall not be diminished during their Continuance in Office.

Section 2.[1] The judicial Power shall extend to all Cases, in Law and Equity, arising under this Constitution, the Laws of the United States, and Treaties made, or which shall be made, under their Authority;—to all Cases affecting Ambassadors, other public Ministers and Consuls;—to all Cases of admiralty and maritime Jurisdiction;—to Controversies to which the United States shall be a Party;—to Controversies between two or more States;—between a State and Citizens of another State;—between Citizens of different States;—between Citizens of the same State claiming Lands under the Grants of different States, and between a State, or the Citizens thereof, and foreign States, Citizens or Subjects.

* * *

[3]   The trial of all Crimes, except in Cases of Impeachment, shall be by Jury; and such Trial shall be held in the State where the said Crimes shall have been committed; but when not committed within any State, the Trial shall be at such Place or Places as the Congress may by Law have directed.

Section 3.[1] Treason against the United States, shall consist only in levying War against them, or, in adhering to their Enemies, giving them Aid and Comfort. No Person shall be convicted of Treason unless on the Testimony of two Witnesses to the same overt Act, or on Confession in open Court.

[2]   The Congress shall have Power to declare the Punishment of Treason, but no Attainder of Treason shall work Corruption of Blood, or Forfeiture except during the Life of the Person attainted.

ARTICLE IV

Section 2. [1] The Citizens of each State shall be entitled to all Privileges and Immunities of Citizens in the several States.

[2]   A Person charged in any State with Treason, Felony, or other Crime, who shall flee from Justice, and be found in another State, shall on demand of the executive Authority of the State from which he fled, be delivered up, to be removed to the State having Jurisdiction of the Crime.

ARTICLE VI

[2]   This Constitution, and the Laws of the United States which shall be made in Pursuance thereof; and all Treaties made, or which shall be made, under the Authority of the United States, shall be the supreme Law.

AMENDMENT I [1791]

Congress shall make no law respecting an establishment of religion, or prohibiting the free exercise thereof; or abridging the freedom of speech, or of the press; or the right of the people peaceably to assemble, and to petition the Government for a redress of grievances.

AMENDMENT II [1791]

A well regulated Militia, being necessary to the security of a free State, the right of the people to keep and bear Arms, shall not be infringed.

AMENDMENT III [1791]

No Soldier shall, in time of peace be quartered in any house, without the consent of the Owner, nor in time of war, but in a manner to be prescribed by law.

AMENDMENT IV [1791]

The right of the people to be secure in their persons, houses, papers, and effects, against unreasonable searches and seizures, shall not be violated, and no Warrants shall issue, but upon probable cause, supported by Oath or affirmation, and particularly describing the place to be searched, and the persons or things to be seized.

AMENDMENT V [1791]

No person shall be held to answer for a capital, or otherwise infamous crime, unless on a presentment or indictment of a Grand Jury, except in cases arising in the land or naval forces, or in the Militia, when in actual service in time of War or public danger; nor shall any person be subject for the same offence to be twice put in jeopardy of life or limb; nor shall be compelled in any criminal case to be a witness against himself, nor be deprived of life, liberty, or property, without due process of law; nor shall private property be taken for public use, without just compensation.

AMENDMENT VI [1791]

In all criminal prosecutions, the accused shall enjoy the right to a speedy and public trial, by an impartial jury of the State and district wherein the crime shall have been committed, which district shall have been previously ascertained by law, and to be informed of the nature and cause of the accusation; to be confronted with the witnesses against him; to have compulsory process for obtaining witnesses in his favor, and to have the Assistance of Counsel for his defence.

AMENDMENT VII [1791]

In Suits at common law, where the value in controversy shall exceed twenty dollars, the right of trial by jury shall be preserved, and no fact tried by jury, shall be otherwise re-examined in any Court of the United States, than according to the rules of the common law.

AMENDMENT VIII [1791]

Excessive bail shall not be required, nor excessive fines imposed, nor cruel and unusual punishments inflicted.

AMENDMENT IX [1791]

The enumeration in the Constitution, of certain rights, shall not be construed to deny or disparage others retained by the people.

AMENDMENT X [1791]

The powers not delegated to the United States by the Constitution, nor prohibited by it to the States, are reserved to the States respectively, or to the people.

AMENDMENT XIII [1865]

Section 1. Neither slavery nor involuntary servitude, except as a punishment for crime whereof the party shall have been duly convicted, shall exist within the United States, or any place subject to their jurisdiction.

Section 2. Congress shall have power to enforce this article by appropriate legislation.

AMENDMENT XIV [1868]

Section 1. All persons born or naturalized in the United States, and subject to the jurisdiction thereof, are citizens of the United States and of the State wherein they reside. No State shall make or enforce any law which shall abridge the privileges or immunities of citizens of the United States; nor shall any State deprive any person of life, liberty, or property, without due process of law; nor deny to any person within its jurisdiction the equal protection of the laws.

Section 5. The Congress shall have the power to enforce, by appropriate legislation, the provisions of the article.

AMENDMENT XV [1870]

Section 1. The right of citizens of the United States to vote shall not be denied or abridged by the United States or by any State on account of race, color, or previous condition of servitude.

Section 2. The Congress shall have power to enforce this article by appropriate legislation.

APPENDIX B

JUSTICES OF THE SUPREME COURT

■ ■ ■

UNITED STATES SUPREME COURT
1940–1985

	1940	1945	1950	1955	1960	1965	1970	1975	1980	1985
Hughes 1930	Stone	Vinson			Warren			Burger		
Frankfurter 1939						Goldberg	Fortas	Blackmun		
Black 1937								Powell		
McReynolds 1914	Byrnes	Rutledge	Minton		Brennan					
Douglas 1939								Stevens		
Murphy 1940			Clark					Marshall		
Reed 1938					Whittaker	White				
Stone 1925	Jackson			Harlan			Rehnquist			Scalia
Roberts 1930		Burton			Stewart				O'Connor	

1985–PRESENT

	1985	1990	1995	2000	2005	2010	2015	2020			
Burger	Rehnquist				ROBERTS						
Blackmun			BREYER								
Powell	Kennedy							KAVANAUGH			
Brennan		Souter				SOTOMAYOR					
Stevens						KAGAN					
Marshall		THOMAS									
White		Ginsburg						BARRETT			
Scalia								GORSUCH			
O'Connor					ALITO						

The publishers wish to acknowledge that the above chart was developed from a suggestion by Dean Joe E. Covington of the University of Missouri Law School.